Comprehensive Commercial Law

2026 Statutory Supplement

Comprehensive Commercial Law

2026 Statutory Supplement

Pamela Foohey
Professor of Law
University of Minnesota Law School

Robert M. Lawless
Max L. Rowe Professor of Law
University of Illinois College of Law

Angela K. Littwin
Charles Sapp Chair in Banking, Financial, Commercial and Corporate Law
University of Texas School of Law

ASPEN
PUBLISHING

To contact Customer Service, e-mail customer.service@aspenpublishing.com, call 1-800-950-5259, or mail correspondence to:

Aspen Publishing
Attn: Order Department
1 Wall Street
Burlington, MA 01803

Printed in the United States of America.

1 2 3 4 5 6 7 8 9 0

ISBN 979-8-8996-3987-6

ABOUT ASPEN PUBLISHING

Aspen Publishing is a leading provider of legal education content and digital learning solutions in the United States and globally. Our innovative products and platforms—designed based on best practices in learning science—engage students and enhance outcomes. From textbooks and audiobooks authored by renowned experts to digital platforms and products like LEAF, Connected eBooks, Connected Quizzing, PracticePerfect, and JD-Next, we empower the next generation of legal professionals with innovative, trusted, and accessible resources.

The Aspen Casebook Series, affectionately known as the "red and black" casebooks among law faculty and students, includes hundreds of highly regarded textbooks across more than 80 disciplines. These range from foundational courses like Torts and Contracts to emerging electives such as Sustainability and the Law of Policing. Our study aids, including the popular *Examples & Explanations* series, help law students master complex topics with clarity and confidence.

Aspen's expertise extends to undergraduate education with our Paralegal, Criminal Justice, and Business Law series, offering the same hallmark quality to a broader audience. JD-Next, our groundbreaking online law school prep course and admissions test, provides a realistic preview of law school, equips students with essential skills for academic success, and evaluates their readiness for legal studies.

Aspen Publishing Is Proud to Be a UWorld Company

Since 2003, UWorld has been a global leader in developing high-quality learning tools for students preparing for high-stakes exams. With a commitment to excellence, UWorld has helped millions of students in undergraduate, graduate, and professional programs in fields such as medicine, nursing, finance, and law achieve their academic and career goals.

Founded by Chandra S. Pemmasani, M.D., during his medical residency, UWorld began focusing on medical education and has since expanded into various academic fields, including law. In 2020, UWorld launched its Legal vertical, starting with its comprehensive Multistate Bar Exam (MBE®) Question Bank, followed by the acquisition of Themis Bar Review, which integrated resources to provide a complete bar exam preparation experience. In 2024, UWorld expanded its offerings by acquiring Aspen Publishing, enhancing its suite of legal education products.

Today, UWorld offers an unparalleled range of study materials that blend active learning methods with expert content, ensuring students and educators can access the most effective resources. From bar preparation to law school success, UWorld is committed to supporting the next generation of legal professionals. Learn more at uworld.com.

Summary of Contents

Contents

Preface

This supplement provides the statutes and regulations students will need for most any course in bankruptcy or commercial law. Those courses include a broad survey course in commercial law as well as courses in sales, payment systems, commercial paper, and secured transactions. As such, the core of the supplement is the entirety of the Uniform Commercial Code (UCC), excluding the repealed Article 6, and the federal Bankruptcy Code. We also include relevant excerpts from federal statutes and their regulations, such as the Truth in Lending Act, the Electronic Funds Transfer Act, and the Fair Debt Collection Practices Act. Finally, the supplement includes materials from UNCITRAL private lawmaking groups such as the American Law Institute and the International Chamber of Commerce. All materials are current as of March 1, 2026.

This edition of the supplement brings a new set of authors who intend to support its publication for years to come. To keep the size and cost of the supplement down, we decided it was time to retire some old favorites. Twelve years after its renaming with some minor amendments, the Uniform Fraudulent Transfer Act now gives way to the Uniform Voidable Transactions Act. With its provisions largely enacted into chapter 15 of the Bankruptcy Code, we dropped the UNCITRAL Model Law on Cross-Border Insolvency. We also eliminated a few other scattered outdated materials.

Bankruptcy Code § 104 provides for administrative readjustment of certain dollar figures at three-year intervals beginning in 1998. In this supplement we have inserted the current dollar amounts, effective April 1, 2025. Those amounts will change again on April 1, 2028. Technically, the official version of the Bankruptcy Code lists the original amounts, but looking up the numbers is an unnecessary hurdle for the reader.

Throughout, we have done our best to reproduce the materials exactly as they were adopted. We do not correct or note what we think might be errors, even if they may seem apparent. In 2024, the Permanent Editorial Board of the UCC made comprehensive corrections to the cross-references and formatting of the official comments. This supplement now reflects those corrections exactly as adopted.

This supplement would not be possible without the hard work of our predecessors, Professors Ronald Mann, Elizabeth Warren, and Jay Westbrook. Professor Lynn LoPucki assisted for many years with keeping UCC Article 9 and the Bankruptcy Code updated. Their research assistants, many of whom are now in the legal academy, made invaluable contributions as now have our research assistants at our schools. The list of student research assistants who have worked on the supplement has grown too long to name them individually. We are so very grateful to everyone who has made possible the book you have in front of you. As its current stewards, we thank you for putting your trust in us and look forward to keeping it a reliable resource for years to come.

Pamela Foohey
Professor of Law
University of Minnesota

Robert M. Lawless
Max L. Rowe Professor of Law
University of Illinois

Angela K. Littwin
Charles Sapp Chair in Banking, Financial, Commercial and Corporate Law
University of Texas

April 2026

Comprehensive Commercial Law

2026 Statutory Supplement

PART I

THE UNIFORM COMMERCIAL CODE

Article 1—General Provisions

As adopted in 2001 and revised in: (i) 2002, in connection with revisions to the Official Comments to Article 9; (ii) 2003, in connection with the revision of Article 7; (iii) 2005, in connection with PEB amendments and corrections to the Official Comments; (iv) 2008, in connection with revision of § 1-301; (v) 2021, in connection with PEB Commentary No. 23; (vi) 2022, in connection with the 2022 Amendments to the Uniform Commercial Code; (vii) 2022, in connection with PEB Commentaries Nos. 25 and 27; and (viii) 2025 in connection with PEB Commentary No. 32.

PART 1. GENERAL PROVISIONS

Section

PART 2. GENERAL DEFINITIONS AND PRINCIPLES OF INTERPRETATION

PART 3. TERRITORIAL APPLICABILITY AND GENERAL RULES

PART 1. GENERAL PROVISIONS

Section 1-101. Short Titles

(a) This [Act] may be cited as the Uniform Commercial Code.

(b) This article may be cited as Uniform Commercial Code—General Provisions.

Official Comment

Source: Former Section 1-101.

Changes from Former Law: Subsection (b) is new. It is added in order to make the structure of Article 1 parallel with that of the other articles of the Uniform Commercial Code.

Each other article of the Uniform Commercial Code may also be cited by its own short title. See Sections 2-101, 2A-101, 3-101, 4-101, 4A-101, 5-101, 6-101, 7-101, 8-101, 9-101, 12-101, and A-101.

Section 1-102. Scope of Article

This article applies to a transaction to the extent that it is governed by another article of [the Uniform Commercial Code].

Official Comment

Source: New.

This section is intended to resolve confusion that has occasionally arisen as to the applicability of the substantive rules in this article. This section makes clear what has always been the case—the rules in Article 1 apply to transactions to the extent that those transactions are governed by one of the other articles of the Uniform Commercial Code. See also Comment 1 to Section 1-301.

Section 1-103. Construction Of [Uniform Commercial Code] to Promote Its Purposes and Policies; Applicability of Supplemental Principles of Law

(a) [The Uniform Commercial Code] must be liberally construed and applied to promote its underlying purposes and policies, which are:

(1) to simplify, clarify, and modernize the law governing commercial transactions;

(2) to permit the continued expansion of commercial practices through custom, usage, and agreement of the parties; and

(3) to make uniform the law among the various jurisdictions.

(b) Unless displaced by the particular provisions of [the Uniform Commercial Code], the principles of law and equity, including the law merchant and the law relative to capacity to contract, principal and agent, estoppel, fraud, misrepresentation, duress, coercion, mistake, bankruptcy, and other validating or invalidating cause supplement its provisions.

Official Comment

Source: Former Section 1-102(1), (2); Former Section 1-103.

Changes from Former Law: This section is derived from subsections (1) and (2) of former Section 1-102 and from former Section 1-103. Subsection (a) of this section combines subsections (1) and (2) of former Section 1-102. Except for changing the form of reference to the Uniform Commercial Code and minor stylistic changes, its language is the same as subsections (1) and (2) of former Section 1-102. Except for changing the form of reference to the Uniform Commercial Code and minor stylistic changes, subsection (b) of this section is identical to former Section 1-103. The provisions have been combined in this section to reflect the interrelationship between them.

1. The Uniform Commercial Code is drawn to provide flexibility so that, since it is intended to be a semi-permanent and infrequently-amended piece of legislation, it will provide its own machinery for expansion of commercial practices. It is intended to make it possible for the law embodied in the Uniform Commercial Code to be applied by the courts in the light of unforeseen and new circumstances and practices. The proper construction of the Uniform Commercial Code requires, of course, that its interpretation and application be limited to its reason.

Even prior to the enactment of the Uniform Commercial Code, courts were careful to keep broad acts from being hampered in their effects by later acts of limited scope. See *Pacific Wool Growers v. Draper & Co.*, 73 P.2d 1391 (Or. 1937), and compare Section 1-104. The courts have often recognized that the policies embodied in an act are applicable in reason to subject-matter that was not expressly included in the language of the act, *Commercial Nat. Bank of New Orleans v. Canal-Louisiana Bank & Trust Co.*, 239 U.S. 520 (1916) (bona fide purchase policy of Uniform Warehouse Receipts Act extended to case not covered but of equivalent nature), and did the same where reason and policy so required, even where the subject matter had been intentionally excluded from the act in general. *Agar v. Orda*, 190 N.E. 479 (N.Y. 1934) (Uniform Sales Act change in seller's remedies applied to contract for sale of choses in action even though the general coverage of that Act was intentionally limited to goods "other than things in action.") They implemented a statutory policy with liberal and useful remedies not provided in the statutory text. They disregarded a statutory limitation of remedy where the reason of the limitation did not apply. *Fiterman v. J. N. Johnson & Co.*, 194 N.W. 399 (Minn. 1923) (requirement of return of the goods as a condition to rescission for breach of warranty; also, partial rescission allowed). Nothing in the Uniform Commercial Code stands in the way of the continuance of such action by the courts.

The Uniform Commercial Code should be construed in accordance with its underlying purposes and policies. The text of each section should be read in the light of the purpose and policy of the rule or principle in question, as also of the Uniform Commercial Code as a whole, and the application of the language should be construed narrowly or broadly, as the case may be, in conformity with the purposes and policies involved.

2. Applicability of supplemental principles of law. Subsection (b) states the basic relationship of the Uniform Commercial Code to supplemental bodies of law. The Uniform Commercial Code was drafted against the backdrop of existing bodies of law, including the common law and equity, and relies on those bodies of law to supplement its provisions in many important ways. At the same time, the Uniform Commercial Code is the primary source of commercial law rules in areas that it governs, and its rules represent choices made by its drafters and the enacting legislatures about the appropriate policies to be furthered in the transactions it covers. Therefore, while principles of common law and equity may *supplement* provisions of the Uniform Commercial Code, they may not be used to *supplant* its provisions, or the purposes and policies those provisions reflect, unless a specific provision of the Uniform Commercial Code provides otherwise. In the absence of such a provision, the Uniform Commercial Code preempts principles of common law and equity that are inconsistent with either its provisions or its purposes and policies.

The language of subsection (b) is intended to reflect both the concept of supplementation and the concept of preemption. Some courts, however, had difficulty in applying the identical language of former Section 1-103 to determine when other law appropriately may be applied to supplement the Uniform Commercial Code, and when that law has been displaced by the Code. Some decisions applied other law in situations in which that application, while not inconsistent with the text of any particular provision of the Uniform Commercial Code, clearly was inconsistent with the underlying purposes and policies reflected in the relevant provisions of the Code. See, e.g., *Sheerbonnet, Ltd. v. American Express Bank, Ltd.*, 951 F. Supp. 403 (S.D.N.Y. 1995). In part, this difficulty arose from Comment 1 to former Section 1-103, which stated that "this section indicates the continued applicability to commercial contracts of all supplemental bodies of law except insofar as they are explicitly displaced by this Act." The "explicitly displaced" language of that Comment did not accurately reflect the proper scope of Uniform Commercial Code preemption, which extends to displacement of other law that is inconsistent with the purposes and policies of the Uniform Commercial Code, as well as with its text.

The supplemental principles of law and equity to which subsection (b) refers may evolve over time to take into account developments in technology. These developments may include, for example, developing case law on contract formation in an electronic environment and the use of automated transactions and arrangements that are sometimes referred to as "electronic agents" (which may or may not actually reflect or create agency relationships under the applicable law of agency). See generally Uniform Electronic Transactions Act (UETA); Restatement (Third) of Agency § 1.04, Reporter's Note to Comment *e* (2006) (discussing the relationship between "electronic agents" and the law of principal and agent). The supplementation recognized by subsection (b) should reflect this evolution.

3. Application of subsection (b) to statutes. The primary focus of Section 1-103 is on the relationship between the Uniform Commercial Code and principles of common law and equity as developed by the courts. State law, however, increasingly is statutory. Not only are there a growing number of state statutes addressing specific issues that come within the scope of the Uniform Commercial Code, but in some States many general principles of common law and equity have been codified. When the other law relating to a matter within the scope of the Uniform Commercial Code is a statute, the principles of subsection (b) remain relevant to the court's analysis of the relationship between that statute and the Uniform Commercial Code, but other principles of statutory interpretation that specifically address the interrelationship between statutes will be relevant as well. In some situations, the principles of subsection (b) still will be determinative. For example, the mere fact that an equitable principle is stated in statutory form rather than in judicial decisions should not change the court's analysis of whether the principle can be used to supplement the Uniform Commercial Code—under subsection (b), equitable principles may supplement provisions of the Uniform Commercial Code only if they are consistent with the purposes and policies of the Uniform Commercial Code as well as its text. In other situations, however, other interpretive principles addressing the interrelationship between statutes may lead the court to conclude that the other statute is controlling, even though it conflicts with the Uniform Commercial Code. This, for example, would be the result in a situation where the other statute was specifically intended to provide additional protection to a class of individuals engaging in transactions covered by the Uniform Commercial Code.

4. Listing not exclusive. The list of sources of supplemental law in subsection (b) is intended to be merely illustrative of the other law that may supplement the Uniform Commercial Code, and is not exclusive. No listing could be exhaustive. Further, the fact that a particular section of the Uniform Commercial Code makes express reference to other law is not intended to suggest the negation of the general application of the principles of subsection (b). Note also that the word "bankruptcy" in subsection (b), continuing the use of that word from former Section 1-103, should be understood not as a specific reference to federal bankruptcy law but, rather as a reference to general principles of insolvency, whether under federal or state law.

Section 1-104. Construction Against Implied Repeal

[The Uniform Commercial Code] being a general act intended as a unified coverage of its subject matter, no part of it shall be deemed to be impliedly repealed by subsequent legislation if such construction can reasonably be avoided.

Official Comment

Source: Former Section 1-104.

Changes from Former Law: Except for changing the form of reference to the Uniform Commercial Code, this section is identical to former Section 1-104.

This section embodies the policy that an act that bears evidence of carefully considered permanent regulative intention should not lightly be regarded as impliedly repealed by subsequent legislation. The Uniform Commercial Code, carefully integrated and intended as a uniform codification of permanent character covering an entire "field" of law, is to be regarded as particularly resistant to implied repeal.

Section 1-105. Severability

If any provision or clause of [the Uniform Commercial Code] or its application to any person or circumstance is held invalid, the invalidity does not affect other provisions or applications of [the Uniform Commercial Code] which can be given effect without the invalid provision or application, and to this end the provisions of [the Uniform Commercial Code] are severable.

Official Comment

Source: Former Section 1-108.

Changes from Former Law: Except for changing the form of reference to the Uniform Commercial Code, this section is identical to former Section 1-108.

This is the model severability section recommended by the National Conference of Commissioners on Uniform State Laws for inclusion in all acts of extensive scope.

Section 1-106. Use of Singular and Plural; Gender

In [the Uniform Commercial Code], unless the statutory context otherwise requires:

(1) words in the singular number include the plural, and those in the plural include the singular; and

(2) words of any gender also refer to any other gender.

Official Comment

Source: Former Section 1-102(5). See also 1 U.S.C. Section 1.

Changes from Former Law: Other than minor stylistic changes, this section is identical to former Section 1-102(5).

This section makes it clear that the use of singular or plural in the text of the Uniform Commercial Code is generally only a matter of drafting style—singular words may be applied in the plural, and plural words may be applied in the singular. Only when it is clear from the statutory context that the use of the singular or plural does not include the other is this rule inapplicable. See, e.g., Section 9-322.

Section 1-107. Section Captions

Section captions are part of [the Uniform Commercial Code].

Official Comment

Source: Former Section 1-109.

Changes from Former Law: None.

Section captions are a part of the text of the Uniform Commercial Code, and not mere surplusage. This is not the case, however, with respect to subsection headings appearing in Articles 9, 12, and A (Transitional Provisions). See Section 9-101, Comment 3 ("subsection headings are not a part of the official text itself and have not been approved by the sponsors."); Section 12-101, Comment; Section A-101, Comment.

Section 1-108. Relation to Electronic Signatures in Global and National Commerce Act

This [Act] modifies, limits, and supersedes the federal Electronic Signatures in Global and National Commerce Act (15 U.S.C. Section 7001 et seq.) but does not modify, limit, or supersede Section 101(c) of that act (15 U.S.C. Section 7001(c)) or authorize electronic delivery of any of the notices described in Section 103(b) of that act (15 U.S.C. Section 103(b)).

Official Comment

Source: New.

1. The federal Electronic Signatures in Global and National Commerce Act, 15 U.S.C. Section 7001 et seq., became effective in 2000. Section 102(a) of that Act provides that a State statute may modify, limit, or supersede the provisions of Section 101 of that Act with respect to state law if such statute, *inter alia*, specifies the alternative procedures or requirements for the use or acceptance (or both) of electronic records or electronic signatures to establish the legal effect, validity, or enforceability of contracts or other records, and (i) such alternative procedures or requirements are consistent with Titles I and II of that Act; (ii) such alternative procedures or requirements do not require, or accord greater legal status or effect to, the implementation or application of a specific technology or technical specification for performing the functions of creating, storing, generating, receiving, communicating, or authenticating electronic records or electronic signatures; and (iii) if enacted or adopted after the date of the enactment of that Act, makes specific reference to that Act. Article 1 fulfills the first two of those three criteria; this Section fulfills the third criterion listed above.

2. As stated in this section, however, Article 1 does not modify, limit, or supersede Section 101(c) of the Electronic Signatures in Global and National Commerce Act (requiring affirmative consent from a consumer to electronic delivery of transactional disclosures that are required by state law to be in writing); nor does it authorize electronic delivery of any of the notices described in Section 103(b) of that Act.

PART 2. GENERAL DEFINITIONS AND PRINCIPLES OF INTERPRETATION

Section 1-201. General Definitions

(a) Unless the context otherwise requires, words or phrases defined in this section, or in the additional definitions contained in other articles of [the Uniform Commercial Code] that apply to particular articles or parts thereof, have the meanings stated.

(b) Subject to definitions contained in other articles of [the Uniform Commercial Code] that apply to particular articles or parts thereof:

(1) "Action", in the sense of a judicial proceeding, includes recoupment, counterclaim, set-off, suit in equity, and any other proceeding in which rights are determined.

(2) "Aggrieved party" means a party entitled to pursue a remedy.

(3) "Agreement", as distinguished from "contract", means the bargain of the parties in fact, as found in their language or inferred from other circumstances, including course of performance, course of dealing, or usage of trade as provided in Section 1-303.

(4) "Bank" means a person engaged in the business of banking and includes a savings bank, savings and loan association, credit union, and trust company.

(5) "Bearer" means a person in possession of a negotiable instrument, document of title, or certificated security that is payable to bearer or indorsed in blank.

(6) "Bill of lading" means a document evidencing the receipt of goods for shipment issued by a person engaged in the business of transporting or forwarding goods.

(7) "Branch" includes a separately incorporated foreign branch of a bank.

(8) "Burden of establishing" a fact means the burden of persuading the trier of fact that the existence of the fact is more probable than its nonexistence.

(9) "Buyer in ordinary course of business" means a person that buys goods in good faith, without

knowledge that the sale violates the rights of another person in the goods, and in the ordinary course from a person, other than a pawnbroker, in the business of selling goods of that kind. A person buys goods in the ordinary course if the sale to the person comports with the usual or customary practices in the kind of business in which the seller is engaged or with the seller's own usual or customary practices. A person that sells oil, gas, or other minerals at the wellhead or minehead is a person in the business of selling goods of that kind. A buyer in ordinary course of business may buy for cash, by exchange of other property, or on secured or unsecured credit, and may acquire goods or documents of title under a preexisting contract for sale. Only a buyer that takes possession of the goods or has a right to recover the goods from the seller under Article 2 may be a buyer in ordinary course of business. "Buyer in ordinary course of business" does not include a person that acquires goods in a transfer in bulk or as security for or in total or partial satisfaction of a money debt.

(10) "Conspicuous", with reference to a term, means so written, displayed, or presented that, based on the totality of the circumstances, a reasonable person against which it is to operate ought to have noticed it. Whether a term is "conspicuous" or not is a decision for the court.

(11) "Consumer" means an individual who enters into a transaction primarily for personal, family, or household purposes.

(12) "Contract", as distinguished from "agreement", means the total legal obligation that results from the parties' agreement as determined by [the Uniform Commercial Code] as supplemented by any other applicable laws.

(13) "Creditor" includes a general creditor, a secured creditor, a lien creditor, and any representative of creditors, including an assignee for the benefit of creditors, a trustee in bankruptcy, a receiver in equity, and an executor or administrator of an insolvent debtor's or assignor's estate.

(14) "Defendant" includes a person in the position of defendant in a counterclaim, cross-claim, or third-party claim.

(15) "Delivery", with respect to an electronic document of title, means voluntary transfer of control and, with respect to an instrument, a tangible document of title, or an authoritative tangible copy of a record evidencing chattel paper, means voluntary transfer of possession.

(16) "Document of title" includes bill of lading, dock warrant, dock receipt, warehouse receipt or order for the delivery of goods, and also any other document which in the regular course of business or financing is treated as adequately evidencing that the person in possession of it is entitled to receive, hold, and dispose of the document and the goods it covers. To be a document of title, a document must purport to be issued by or addressed to a bailee and purport to cover goods in the bailee's possession which are either identified or are fungible portions of an identified mass.

(16A) "Electronic" means relating to technology having electrical, digital, magnetic, wireless, optical, electromagnetic, or similar capabilities.

(17) "Fault" means a default, breach, or wrongful act or omission.

(18) "Fungible goods" means:

(A) goods of which any unit, by nature or usage of trade, is the equivalent of any other like unit; or

(B) goods that by agreement are treated as equivalent.

(19) "Genuine" means free of forgery or counterfeiting.

(20) "Good faith," except as otherwise provided in Article 5, means honesty in fact and the observance of reasonable commercial standards of fair dealing.

(21) "Holder" means:

(A) the person in possession of a negotiable instrument that is payable either to bearer or to an identified person that is the person in possession; or

(B) the person in possession of a negotiable tangible document of title if the goods are deliverable either to bearer or to the order of the person in possession; or

(C) the person in control, other than pursuant to Section 7-106(g), of a negotiable electronic document of title.

(22) "Insolvency proceeding" includes an assignment for the benefit of creditors or other proceeding intended to liquidate or rehabilitate the estate of the person involved.

(23) "Insolvent" means:

(A) having generally ceased to pay debts in the ordinary course of business other than as a result of bona fide dispute;

(B) being unable to pay debts as they become due; or

(C) being insolvent within the meaning of federal bankruptcy law.

(24) "Money" means a medium of exchange that is currently authorized or adopted by a domestic or

foreign government. The term includes a monetary unit of account established by an intergovernmental organization, or pursuant to an agreement between two or more countries. The term does not include an electronic record that is a medium of exchange recorded and transferable in a system that existed and operated for the medium of exchange before the medium of exchange was authorized or adopted by the government.

(25) "Organization" means a person other than an individual.

(26) "Party", as distinguished from "third party", means a person that has engaged in a transaction or made an agreement subject to [the Uniform Commercial Code].

(27) "Person" means an individual, corporation, business trust, estate, trust, partnership, limited liability company, association, joint venture, government, governmental subdivision, agency, or instrumentality, or any other legal or commercial entity. The term includes a protected series, however denominated, of an entity if the protected series is established under law other than [the Uniform Commercial Code] that limits, or limits if conditions specified under the law are satisfied, the ability of a creditor of the entity or of any other protected series of the entity to satisfy a claim from assets of the protected series.

(28) "Present value" means the amount as of a date certain of one or more sums payable in the future, discounted to the date certain by use of either an interest rate specified by the parties if that rate is not manifestly unreasonable at the time the transaction is entered into or, if an interest rate is not so specified, a commercially reasonable rate that takes into account the facts and circumstances at the time the transaction is entered into.

(29) "Purchase" means taking by sale, lease, discount, negotiation, mortgage, pledge, lien, security interest, issue or reissue, gift, or any other voluntary transaction creating an interest in property.

(30) "Purchaser" means a person that takes by purchase.

(31) "Record" means information that is inscribed on a tangible medium or that is stored in an electronic or other medium and is retrievable in perceivable form.

(32) "Remedy" means any remedial right to which an aggrieved party is entitled with or without resort to a tribunal.

(33) "Representative" means a person empowered to act for another, including an agent, an officer of a corporation or association, and a trustee, executor, or administrator of an estate.

(34) "Right" includes remedy.

(35) "Security interest" means an interest in personal property or fixtures which secures payment or performance of an obligation. "Security interest" includes any interest of a consignor and a buyer of accounts, chattel paper, a payment intangible, or a promissory note in a transaction that is subject to Article 9. "Security interest" does not include the special property interest of a buyer of goods on identification of those goods to a contract for sale under Section 2-401, but a buyer may also acquire a "security interest" by complying with Article 9. Except as otherwise provided in Section 2-505, the right of a seller or lessor of goods under Article 2 or 2A to retain or acquire possession of the goods is not a "security interest", but a seller or lessor may also acquire a "security interest" by complying with Article 9. The retention or reservation of title by a seller of goods notwithstanding shipment or delivery to the buyer under Section 2-401 is limited in effect to a reservation of a "security interest." Whether a transaction in the form of a lease creates a "security interest" is determined pursuant to Section 1-203.

(36) "Send", in connection with a record, or notification, means:

(A) to deposit in the mail, deliver for transmission, or transmit by any other usual means of communication, with postage or cost of transmission provided for, addressed to any address reasonable under the circumstances; or

(B) to cause the record or notification to be received within the time it would have been received if properly sent under subparagraph (A).

(37) "Sign" means, with present intent to authenticate or adopt a record:

(A) execute or adopt a tangible symbol; or

(B) attach to or logically associate with the record an electronic symbol, sound, or process.

"Signed", "signing", and "signature" have corresponding meanings.

(38) "State" means a State of the United States, the District of Columbia, Puerto Rico, the United States Virgin Islands, or any territory or insular possession subject to the jurisdiction of the United States.

(39) "Surety" includes a guarantor or other secondary obligor.

(40) "Term" means a portion of an agreement that relates to a particular matter.

(41) "Unauthorized signature" means a signature made without actual, implied, or apparent authority. The term includes a forgery.

(42) "Warehouse receipt" means a receipt issued by a person engaged in the business of storing goods for hire.

(43) "Writing" includes printing, typewriting, or any other intentional reduction to tangible form. "Written" has a corresponding meaning.

Legislative Note: *A state should review and amend any statute or regulation that relies on or refers to the definition of "money" in subsection (b)(24) to account for the amendment to that definition.*

A state should enact the amendment to subsection (b)(27) whether the state has enacted the Uniform Protect Series Act (2017) or otherwise recognizes a protected series under its law. Because the amendment applies only under the enacting state's Uniform Commercial Code, inclusion of the amendment does not require the enacting state to recognize a limit on liability of a protected series organized under the law of another jurisdiction or a limit on liability of the entity that established the protected series. The amendment clarifies the status of a protected series as a "person" under the choice-of-law and substantive law rules of the enacting state's Uniform Commercial Code.

Official Comment

Source: Former Section 1-201.

Changes from Former Law: In order to make it clear that all definitions in the Uniform Commercial Code (not just those appearing in Article 1, as stated in former Section 1-201, but also those appearing in other Articles) do not apply if the context otherwise requires, a new subsection (a) to that effect has been added, and the definitions now appear in subsection (b). The reference in subsection (a) to the "context" is intended to refer to the context in which the defined term is used in the Uniform Commercial Code. In other words, the definition applies whenever the defined term is used unless the context in which the defined term is used in the statute indicates that the term was not used in its defined sense. Consider, for example, Sections 3-103(a)(12) (defining "promise," in relevant part, as "a written undertaking to pay money signed by the person undertaking to pay") and 3-303(a)(1) (indicating that an instrument is issued or transferred for value if "the instrument is issued or transferred for a promise of performance, to the extent that the promise has been performed"). It is clear from the statutory context of the use of the word "promise" in Section 3-303(a)(1) that the term was not used in the sense of its definition in Section 3-103(a)(12). Thus, the Section 3-103(a)(12) definition should not be used to give meaning to the word "promise" in Section 3-303(a).

Some definitions in former Section 1-201 have been reformulated as substantive provisions and have been moved to other sections. See Sections 1-202 (explicating concepts of notice and knowledge formerly addressed in Sections 1-201(25)-(27)), 1-204 (determining when a person gives value for rights, replacing the definition of "value" in former Section 1-201(44)), and 1-206 (addressing the meaning of presumptions, replacing the definitions of "presumption" and "presumed" in former Section 1-201(31)). Similarly, the portion of the definition of "security interest" in former Section 1-201(37) which explained the difference between a security interest and a lease has been relocated to Section 1-203.

Two definitions in former Section 1-201 have been deleted. The definition of "honor" in former Section 1-201(21) has been deleted but a definition of that term applicable to Article 5 remains in Section 5-102(a)(8). The definition of "telegram" in former Section 1-201(41) has been deleted because that word no longer appears in the definition of "conspicuous."

Other than minor stylistic changes and renumbering, the remaining definitions in this section are as in former Article 1 except as noted below.

1. "Action." Unchanged from former Section 1-201, which was derived from similar definitions in Section 191, Uniform Negotiable Instruments Law; Section 76, Uniform Sales Act; Section 58, Uniform Warehouse Receipts Act; Section 53, Uniform Bills of Lading Act.

2. "Aggrieved party." Unchanged from former Section 1-201.

3. "Agreement." Derived from former Section 1-201. As used in the Uniform Commercial Code the word is intended to include full recognition of usage of trade, course of dealing, course of performance and the surrounding circumstances as effective parts thereof, and of any agreement permitted under the provisions of the Uniform Commercial Code to displace a stated rule of law. Whether an agreement has legal consequences is determined by applicable provisions of the Uniform Commercial Code and, to the extent provided in Section 1-103, by the law of contracts. Concerning developments in technology, including, for example, contract formation in electronic environments, automated transactions, and electronic agents, see Section 1-103, Comment 2.

4. "Bank." Derived from Section 4A-105.

5. "Bearer." Unchanged from former Section 1-201, which was derived from Section 191, Uniform Negotiable Instruments Law.

6. "Bill of Lading." Derived from former Section 1-201. The reference to, and definition of, an "airbill" has been deleted as no longer necessary.

7. "Branch." Unchanged from former Section 1-201.

8. "Burden of establishing a fact." Unchanged from former Section 1-201.

9. "Buyer in ordinary course of business." Except for minor stylistic changes, identical to former Section 1-201 (as amended in conjunction with the 1999 revisions to Article 9). The major significance of the phrase lies in Section 2-403 and in the Article on Secured Transactions (Article 9).

The first sentence of paragraph (9) makes clear that a buyer from a pawnbroker cannot be a buyer in ordinary course of business. The second sentence explains what it means to buy "in the ordinary course." The penultimate sentence prevents a buyer that does not have the right to possession as against the seller from being a buyer in ordinary course of business. Concerning when a buyer obtains possessory rights, see Sections 2-502 and 2-716. However, the penultimate sentence is not intended to affect a buyer's status as a buyer in ordinary course of business in cases (such as a "drop shipment") involving delivery by the seller to a person buying from the buyer or a donee from the buyer. The requirement relates to whether as against the seller the buyer or one taking through the buyer has possessory rights. A buyer that does not have the right to recover the goods under Article 2 (Sections 2-502 and 2-716) does not qualify as a buyer in ordinary course of business unless the buyer has possession of the goods. A buyer does not have possession of goods for this purpose if the goods remain in the possession of the seller pursuant to an agreement that the seller holds the goods for the buyer's disposition. See PEB Commentary No. 32, dated February 27, 2025. The Commentary is available at https://www.ali.org/peb-ucc.

10. "Conspicuous." Derived from former Section 1-201(10). This definition states the general standard that to be conspicuous a term ought to be noticed by a reasonable person against which the term is to operate. Whether a term is conspicuous is an issue for the court. Whether the appearance and presentation of a particular term satisfy this standard is determined by reference to the totality of the circumstances and requires a case-by-case analysis.

Historically, contract terms were presented in writing, making the use of standards that relate to the size and appearance of type relevant to the determination of conspicuousness. Today terms in a record are frequently communicated electronically. New technologies have created opportunities for terms to be displayed or presented in novel ways, such as by the use of pop-up windows, text balloons, dynamically expanding or dynamically magnifying text, and non-visual elements such as vibrations, to name a few.

The definition has been revised in the Uniform Commercial Code Amendments (2022) (2022 Amendments) by deleting the statutory examples relating to the appearance of type and instead indicating in these comments a broader universe of factors that are applicable to both written and electronic presentations. This approach is intended to be both more protective of consumers and more useful to drafters by providing more clarity and flexibility in the methods that may be used to call attention to a term.

The attributes of a reasonable person against which a term is to operate can vary depending upon the nature of the transaction and the market in which the transaction occurs. For example, assume that a merchant of goods wishes to enter into a transaction for the sale or lease of goods which does not include an implied warranty of merchantability or fitness for particular purpose. Depending on the particular transaction, the person against which the term excluding implied warranties is to operate may be a large business buyer or lessee, a small business, or a consumer. Similarly, the determination of whether a term is conspicuous may, depending on the context, yield a different conclusion when the term is used in a standard form agreement than when terms of the agreement are the subject of negotiation or discussion.

Terms presented in an online record raise issues that differ in some respects from the issues associated with presenting the same terms in a writing. For example, how a term appears depends to some extent on the equipment and settings used by the person presented with the term.

The test of whether a term is conspicuous remains constant notwithstanding the different contexts referenced above. A term is conspicuous if its appearance and presentation are such that it ought to be noticed by a reasonable person against which the term is to operate. If the term is in a standard form intended for use in many agreements, the determination of whether the term is conspicuous may be made with reference to typical likely parties to the agreements, taking into account all aspects of the transaction, the range of likely equipment and settings used by such parties, and the education, sophistication, disabilities, and other attributes of such parties. If the term is not in a standard form, the determination of whether it is conspicuous should be made with reference to a reasonable person in the position of the actual person against which it is to operate.

Factors relevant to whether a term is conspicuous include, but are not limited to, the following:

(i) The use of headings and text that contrast with the surrounding text. For example, a term is likely to be conspicuous if it is introduced by a heading in uppercase letters equal to or greater in size than the surrounding text. Similarly, a term is likely to be conspicuous if set out in language in the body of a record or display in larger type than the surrounding text, or in contrasting type, font, or color to the surrounding text of the same size, or set off from surrounding text of the same size by symbols or other marks that call attention to the language. However, even with those characteristics, for a term to be conspicuous the overall statutory test must always be met. For example, even if in bold, uppercase letters, a term might not be conspicuous if placed among other terms also in bold, uppercase letters so there is no contrast with the surrounding text or if the application of other factors causes the term not to be provided such that a reasonable person against which it is to operate ought to have noticed it.

(ii) The placement of the term in the record. A term appearing at, or hyperlinked from, text at the beginning of a record, or near the place where the person against which the term is to operate must signify assent, is more likely to be conspicuous than a term in the middle of a lengthy record absent the use of a method reasonably designed to draw the person's attention to the term in middle of the record (for example, by providing separate reasonable notice of the term before presenting the record containing the term to the person for assent or forcing the person to stop on a screen highlighting the term during the presentation of the record for assent).

(iii) If terms are available only through the use of a hyperlink, in addition to the placement of the hyperlink as described above, factors to be considered include whether there is language drawing attention to the hyperlink and describing its function, and the size and color of the text used for the hyperlink and any related language.

(iv) The language of the heading, if any. A misleading heading – such as the heading "Warranty" for a paragraph that contains a disclaimer of warranties – might cause a reasonable person to fail to notice the language that would disclaim warranties, so that the term would not be conspicuous.

(v) The effort needed to access the term. The process and flow of the display and presentation is also relevant. For example, a term accessible only by triggering multiple hyperlinks is less likely to be conspicuous than a term accessible from a single hyperlink.

(vi) Whether the person against which the term is to operate must separately assent to or acknowledge the term. Obtaining separate assent or acknowledgment of a term is generally sufficient to make the term conspicuous.

As noted above, the evolution of technology has led to an evolution in the ways in which terms in an electronic record are displayed or presented. A term displayed or presented in a novel way utilizing emerging technologies is, of course, conspicuous if the effect of the display or presentation is that a reasonable person against which the term is to operate ought to have noticed it.

This definition deals only with requirements that a term be conspicuous (or noted conspicuously) that are stated in particular provisions of the Uniform Commercial Code. Other protective doctrines designed to assure that assent is meaningful that are found in law outside the UCC may also apply. See Section 1-103(b).

11. "Consumer." Derived from Section 9-102(a)(25).

12. "Contract." Except for minor stylistic changes, identical to former Section 1-201.

13. "Creditor." Unchanged from former Section 1-201.

14. "Defendant." Except for minor stylistic changes, identical to former Section 1-201, which was derived from Section 76, Uniform Sales Act.

15. "Delivery." Derived from former Section 1-201. The reference to certificated securities in a pre-2022 version was deleted in light of the more specific treatment of the matter in Section 8-301. The definition also was revised to accommodate electronic documents of title. Control of an electronic document of title is defined in Article 7 (Section 7-106). Another revision in the 2022 Amendments conformed the reference to chattel paper to the revised definition of that term and the revised methods of perfection. See Sections 9-102(a)(11) (defining "chattel paper"); 9-314 (perfection by possession and control of chattel paper).

16. "Document of title." Derived from former Section 1-201, which was derived from Section 76, Uniform Sales Act. This definition makes explicit that the obligation or designation of a third party as "bailee" is essential to a document of title and clearly rejects any such result as obtained in *Hixson v. Ward*, 254 Ill. App. 505 (1929), which treated a conditional sales contract as a document of title. Also the definition is left open so that new types of documents may be included, including documents which gain commercial recognition in the international arena. See UNCITRAL Draft Instrument on the Carriage of Goods by Sea. It is unforeseeable what documents may one day serve the essential purpose now filled by warehouse receipts and bills of lading. The definition is stated in terms of the function of the documents with the intention that any document which gains commercial recognition as accomplishing the desired result shall be included within its scope. Fungible goods are adequately identified within the language of the definition by identification of the mass of which they are a part.

Dock warrants were within the Sales Act definition of document of title apparently for the purpose of recognizing a valid tender by means of such paper. In current commercial practice a dock warrant or receipt is a kind of interim certificate issued by steamship companies upon delivery of the goods at the dock, entitling a designated person to have issued to him at the company's office a bill of lading. The receipt itself is invariably nonnegotiable in form although it may indicate that a negotiable bill is to be forthcoming. Such a document is not within the general compass of the definition, although trade usage may in some cases entitle such paper to be treated as a document of title. If the dock receipt actually represents a storage obligation undertaken by the shipping company, then it is a warehouse receipt within this section regardless of the name given to the instrument.

The goods must be "described," but the description may be by marks or labels and may be qualified in such a way as to disclaim personal knowledge of the issuer regarding contents or condition. However, baggage and parcel checks and similar "tokens" of storage which identify stored goods only as those received in exchange for the token are not covered by this Article.

The definition is broad enough to include an airway bill.

A document of title may be either tangible or electronic. Paper documents of title are "tangible documents of title." Electronic documents of title are documents that are stored in an electronic medium instead of in tangible form. "Electronic" is defined in paragraph 16A. As to reissuing a document of title in an alternative medium, see Article 7, Section 7-105. Control for electronic documents of title is defined in Article 7 (Section 7-106).

16A. "Electronic." The basic nature of most modern technologies and the need for a recognized, single term warrants the use of "electronic" as the defined term, even though not all technologies listed may be technically "electronic" in nature. The definition is intended to be applied broadly as new technologies develop. The term must be construed broadly in light of developing technologies in order to validate commercial transactions regardless of the medium used by the parties to document them. See generally Uniform Electronic Transactions Act, Section 2, Comment 4.

17. "Fault." Derived from former Section 1-201. "Default" has been added to the list of events constituting fault.

18. "Fungible goods." Derived from former Section 1-201. References to securities have been deleted because Article 8 no longer uses the term "fungible" to describe securities. Accordingly, this provision now defines the concept only in the context of goods.

19. "Genuine." Unchanged from former Section 1-201.

20. "Good faith." Former Section 1-201(19) defined "good faith" simply as honesty in fact; the definition contained no element of commercial reasonableness. Initially, that definition applied throughout the Code with only one exception. Former Section 2-103(1)(b) provided that in that article "'good faith' in the case of a merchant means honesty in fact and the observance of reasonable commercial standards of fair dealing in the trade." This alternative definition was limited in applicability though because it applied only to transactions within the scope of Article 2 and it applied only to merchants.

Over time, however, amendments to the Uniform Commercial Code brought the Article 2 merchant concept of good faith (subjective honesty and objective commercial standards of fair dealing) into other Articles. First, Article 2A explicitly incorporated the Article 2 standard. Then, other Articles broadened the applicability of that standard by adopting it for all parties rather than just for merchants. Finally, Articles 2 and 2A were amended to apply the standard to non-merchants as well as merchants. All of these definitions are comprised of two elements—honesty in fact *and* the observance of reasonable commercial standards of fair dealing. Only revised Article 5 continued to define "good faith" solely in terms of subjective honesty, and Article 6 (in the few states that have not chosen to delete the Article) is without a definition of "good faith." (It should be noted, though, that, while revised Article 6 did not define good faith, Comment 2 to revised Section 6-102 states that "this Article adopts the definition of 'good faith' in Article 1 in all cases, even when the buyer is a merchant.")

Thus, the definition of "good faith" in this section merely confirms what has been the case for a number of years as Articles of the UCC have been amended or revised—the obligation of "good faith," applicable in each Article, is to be interpreted in the context of all Articles except for Article 5 as including both the subjective element of honesty in fact and the objective element of the observance of reasonable commercial standards of fair dealing. As a result, both the subjective and objective elements are part of the standard of "good faith," whether that obligation is specifically referenced in another Article of the Code (other than Article 5) or is provided by this Article.

Of course, as noted in the statutory text, the definition of "good faith" in this section does not apply when the narrower definition of "good faith" in revised Article 5 is applicable.

As noted above, the definition of "good faith" in this section requires not only honesty in fact but also "observance of reasonable commercial standards of fair dealing." Although "fair dealing" is a broad term that must be defined in context, it is clear that it is concerned with the fairness of conduct rather than the care with which an act is performed. This is an entirely different concept than whether a party exercised ordinary care in conducting a transaction. Both concepts are to be determined in the light of reasonable commercial standards, but those standards in each case are directed to different aspects of commercial conduct. See, e.g., Sections 3-103(a)(9) and 4-104(c) and Comment 4 to Section 3-103.

21. "Holder." The definition has been reorganized for clarity and amended to provide for electronic negotiable documents of title. The definition excludes persons who have control of an electronic document of title pursuant to Section 7-106(g) through the acknowledgment by a person in control. This ensures that an issuer of a document can ascertain who is entitled to delivery from the document itself or from the system in which the document is recorded, without any obligation to look behind the document or the system to ascertain the identity of an undisclosed principal.

22. "Insolvency proceedings." Unchanged from former Section 1-201.

23. "Insolvent." Derived from former Section 1-201. The three tests of insolvency—"generally ceased to pay debts in the ordinary course of business other than as a result of a bona fide dispute as to them," "unable to pay debts as they become due," and "insolvent within the meaning of the federal bankruptcy law"—are expressly set up as alternative tests and must be approached from a commercial standpoint.

24. "Money." The definition of "money" applies to the term only as used in the Uniform Commercial Code. The definition does not determine whether an asset constitutes "money" for other purposes. Only something currently authorized or adopted as a medium of exchange by a government can be money. As further elaborated in the second sentence of the definition, adoption by a government may occur through establishment by an intergovernmental organization or pursuant to an agreement between governments. Coins and pager currency previously, but not currently, authorized or adopted as a medium of exchange by a government, and currently owned and traded only for their numismatic or historical value, are not money.

An electronic medium of exchange established pursuant to a country's law and that is recorded and transferable in a system that did not exist and did not operate for that medium of exchange before the electronic medium of exchange was authorized or adopted by the country's government also constitutes money. This is so even if ownership is established or maintained through a system not operated by the government. In contrast, an existing medium of exchange created or distributed by one or more private persons is not money solely because the government of one or more countries later authorizes or adopts the pre-existing medium of exchange.

Although the term "money" is used in several articles, the definition is particularly significant under Article 9. Under the pre-2022 version of this definition, money was generally understood to include only tangible coins, bills, notes, and the like, although the statutory text did not explicitly so limit the term. This worked well under Article 9, which provided that the only method of perfecting a security interest in money as original collateral was by taking possession of it. See pre-2022 Section 9-312(b)(3). The 2022 revised definition of money in Section 1-201(b)(24) is broader and includes both "tangible money" and "electronic money" (new defined types of collateral under the 2022 revisions to Article 9). As under the pre-2022 Article 9, a security interest in tangible money as original collateral may be perfected only by possession. Section 9-312(b)(3). A security interest in electronic money as original collateral may be perfected only by control. Section

9-102(a)(31A) (defining "electronic money"); 9- 312(b)(4) (perfection by control for electronic money). Note that the definition of "money" in Section 9-102(a)(54A) is narrower in two respects than the definition in this section—the Article 9 definition excludes deposit accounts and money in electronic form that cannot be subjected to control under Section 9-105A. See Section 9-102(a)(54A).

Examples: The following examples illustrate the definition of "money."

Example 1: Nation A enacts legislation authorizing or adopting an existing cryptocurrency (spitcoin), created on a private blockchain, as a medium of exchange. Because spitcoin was recorded and transferable in a system that existed and operated for that cryptocurrency before the electronic record was authorized or adopted by Nation A, spitcoin does not become "money" under this definition as a result of Nation A's legislation.

Example 2: Nation B creates a new cryptocurrency (beebuck) and authorizes or adopts it as a medium of exchange. Beebuck is "money." Beebuck is not recorded and transferable in a system that existed and operated for that cryptocurrency before the electronic record was authorized or adopted by Nation B.

Example 3: Nation C enacts legislation authorizing or adopting as a medium of exchange beebuck, the cryptocurrency previously adopted by Nation B in Example 2. Although beebuck is recorded and transferable in a system that existed and operated for beebuck before it was authorized or adopted by Nation C, beebuck was already money when authorized or adopted by Nation C. Consequently, beebuck is "money." Nation C's action had no relevance or effect on the characterization of beebuck as money.

25. "Organization." The former definition of this word has been replaced with the standard definition used in acts prepared by the National Conference of Commissioners on Uniform State Laws. A protected series formed under the Uniform Protected Series Act (2017) is a "person." See PEB Commentary No. 23, dated February 24, 2021. The Commentary is available at https://www.ali.org/peb-ucc.

26. "Party." Substantively identical to former Section 1-201. Mention of a party includes, of course, a person acting through an agent. However, where an agent comes into opposition or contrast to the principal, particular account is taken of that situation.

27. "Person." A previous definition of this term was replaced with the standard language used in acts prepared by the National Conference of Commissioners on Uniform State Laws. This definition recognizes the wide range of subjects that can enjoy legal rights and possess legal duties, including the catchall residual category of "any other legal or commercial entity." See, e.g., John Chipman Gray, The Nature and Sources of the Law 27 (Roland Gray rev., 2d ed., The MacMillan Co. 1931) ("a 'person' is a subject of legal rights and duties"). For additional authorities, see PEB Commentary No. 23, n.5. The reference to a "public corporation" in the pre-2022 text of the definition has been deleted as unnecessary and duplicative of other examples in the definition of entities that are persons.

The second sentence of the definition provides needed clarity as to the status of a protected series for purposes of the Uniform Commercial Code. See PEB Commentary No. 23. Several states have enacted statutes that provide for protected series within a limited liability company or other unincorporated organization. These statutes afford rights and impose duties upon a protected series and generally empower a protected series to conduct its own activities under its own name. The types of protected series that are included as persons under the definition include, but are not limited to, those established under the Uniform Protected Series Act.

Providing that a protected series is a "person" for purposes of the enacting state's Uniform Commercial Code will expressly permit a protected series, whether created under the law of the enacting state or of another jurisdiction, to be a "seller" or a "buyer" under Article 2, a "lessor" or a "lessee" under Article 2A, or an "organization." It also permits a protected series to be a "debtor" under Article 9, and, if the law under which the protected series is organized requires a public filing for the protected series to be recognized under that law, a "registered organization" under Article 9.

A protected series formed under the Uniform Protected Series Act (2017) is a "person." See PEB Commentary No. 23, dated February 24, 2021. The Commentary is available at https://www.ali.ord/peb-ucc.

28. "Present value." This definition was formerly contained within the definition of "security interest" in former Section 1-201(37).

29. "Purchase." Derived from former Section 1-201. The form of definition has been changed from "includes" to "means."

30. "Purchaser." Unchanged from former Section 1-201.

31. "Record." Derived from Section 9-102(a)(69).

32. "Remedy." Unchanged from former Section 1-201. The purpose is to make it clear that both remedy and right (as defined) include those remedial rights of "self help" which are among the most important bodies of rights under the Uniform Commercial Code, remedial rights being those to which an aggrieved party may resort on its own.

33. "Representative." Concerning developments in technology, including, for example, contract formation in electronic environments, automated transactions, and electronic agents, see Section 1-103, Comment 2.

34. "Right." Except for minor stylistic changes, identical to former Section 1-201.

35. "Security interest." The definition is the first paragraph of the definition of "security interest" in former Section 1-201, with minor stylistic changes. The remaining portion of that definition has been moved to Section 1-203. Note that, because of the scope of Article 9, the term includes the interest of certain outright buyers of certain kinds of property.

36. "Send." The definition of "send" adopts pre-2022 Section 9-102(a)(75). The explicit statement in the previous text of this definition on the appropriateness of sending to an agreed-upon address or to an "address reasonable under the circumstances" was limited to "the case of an instrument." The definition no longer includes that limitation relating to an instrument. Moreover, it is common for parties to rely on their agreement as to appropriate addresses for purposes of notifications and communications. Nothing in the definition or in the Uniform Commercial Code limits the effectiveness of sending a record or notification to an address that has been agreed upon by affected persons. See generally Sections 1-103 and 1-302.

37. "Sign." The definition of "sign" adopted in the 2022 Amendments is broad—it encompasses the authentication or adoption of all records, not just writings. The definition replaces the definition of "signed" in pre-2022 texts of this Article. This definition also makes it clear that, as the terms "sign," "signed," and "signature" are used in the Uniform Commercial Code, a complete signature is not necessary. A symbol may be printed, stamped, or written on, or electronically attached or associated with, a record. It may be by initials or by thumbprint or by electronic symbol, sound, or process. It may be on any part of a writing or other record and in appropriate cases may be found in a billhead or letterhead. No catalog of possible situations can be complete and the court must use common sense and commercial experience in passing upon these matters. The question always is whether the symbol, sound, or process was executed or adopted by the party with present intention to authenticate or adopt the record.

A "writing," which necessarily is in tangible form, must exist at the time it is signed and must be signed by the execution or adoption of a tangible symbol to qualify as a signed writing. A writing adopted only by use of an electronic symbol, sound, or process would not be a signed writing until and unless it results in a tangible symbol being on or affixed to the writing. Moreover, if an electronic record is electronically signed and subsequently printed in tangible form, the resulting writing would not constitute a signed writing unless and until some action is taken with "present intent to authenticate or adopt" the writing.

Concerning developments in technology, including, for example contract formation in electronic environments, automated transactions, and electronic agents, see also Section 1-103, Comment 2.

38. "State." This is the standard definition of the term used in acts prepared by the National Conference of Commissioners on Uniform State Laws.

39. "Surety." This definition makes it clear that "surety" includes all secondary obligors, not just those whose obligation refers to the person obligated as a surety. As to the nature of secondary obligations generally, see Restatement (Third), Suretyship and Guaranty Section 1 (1996).

40. "Term." Unchanged from former Section 1-201.

41. "Unauthorized signature." Unchanged from former Section 1-201.

42. "Warehouse receipt." Unchanged from former Section 1-201, which was derived from Section 76(1), Uniform Sales Act; Section 1, Uniform Warehouse Receipts Act. Receipts issued by a field warehouse are included, provided the warehouseman and the depositor of the goods are different persons.

43. "Written" or **"writing."** Several amendments to the Uniform Commercial Code over the years have replaced the terms "written" and "writing" with the term "record," defined in paragraph (31) and also in some other Articles. Pursuant to the 2022 Amendments, additional references to the terms "writing," "writings," and "written" have been replaced by "record." For example, the 2022 revisions to Articles 2 and 2A made these changes in provisions where an affected party may be assumed to have assented to the use of a record that is not a writing. Where references to those terms remain in Articles 2 and 2A, the use by parties of a record other than a writing may be given effect for purposes of those Articles under law other than the Uniform Commercial Code, such as the Electronic Signatures in Global and National Commerce Act, 15 U.S.C. Section 7001 et seq., and the Uniform Electronic Transactions Act. See Sections 2-207, Comment 8; 2A-102, Comment (g).

Section 1-202. Notice; Knowledge

(a) Subject to subsection (f), a person has "notice" of a fact if the person:

(1) has actual knowledge of it;

(2) has received a notice or notification of it; or

(3) from all the facts and circumstances known to the person at the time in question, has reason to know that it exists.

(b) "Knowledge" means actual knowledge. "Knows" has a corresponding meaning.

(c) "Discover", "learn", or words of similar import refer to knowledge rather than to reason to know.

(d) A person "notifies" or "gives" a notice or notification to another person by taking such steps as may be reasonably required to inform the other person in ordinary course, whether or not the other person actually comes to know of it.

(e) Subject to subsection (f), a person "receives" a notice or notification when:

(1) it comes to that person's attention; or

(2) it is duly delivered in a form reasonable under the circumstances at the place of business through which the contract was made or at another location held out by that person as the place for receipt of such communications.

(f) Notice, knowledge, or a notice or notification received by an organization is effective for a particular transaction from the time it is brought to the attention of the individual conducting that transaction and, in any event, from the time it would have been brought to the individual's attention if the organization had exercised due diligence. An organization exercises due diligence if it maintains reasonable routines for communicating significant information to the person conducting the transaction and there is reasonable compliance with the routines. Due diligence does not require an individual acting for the organization to communicate information unless the communication is part of the individual's regular duties or the individual has reason to know of the transaction and that the transaction would be materially affected by the information.

Official Comment

Source: Derived from former Section 1-201(25)-(27).

Changes from Former Law: These provisions are substantive rather than purely definitional. Accordingly, they have been relocated from Section 1-201 to this section. The reference to the "forgotten notice" doctrine has been deleted.

1. Under subsection (a), a person has notice of a fact when, *inter alia*, the person has received a notification of the fact in question.

2. As provided in subsection (d), the word "notifies" is used when the essential fact is the proper dispatch of the notice, not its receipt. Compare "Send." When the essential fact is the other party's receipt of the notice, that is stated. Subsection (e) states when a notification is received.

3. Subsection (f) makes clear that notice, knowledge, or a notification, although "received," for instance, by a clerk in Department A of an organization, is effective for a transaction conducted in Department B only from the time when it was or should have been communicated to the individual conducting that transaction.

Section 1-203. Lease Distinguished from Security Interest

(a) Whether a transaction in the form of a lease creates a lease or security interest is determined by the facts of each case.

(b) A transaction in the form of a lease creates a security interest if the consideration that the lessee is to pay the lessor for the right to possession and use of the goods is an obligation for the term of the lease and is not subject to termination by the lessee, and:

(1) the original term of the lease is equal to or greater than the remaining economic life of the goods;

(2) the lessee is bound to renew the lease for the remaining economic life of the goods or is bound to become the owner of the goods;

(3) the lessee has an option to renew the lease for the remaining economic life of the goods for no additional consideration or for nominal additional consideration upon compliance with the lease agreement; or

(4) the lessee has an option to become the owner of the goods for no additional consideration or for nominal additional consideration upon compliance with the lease agreement.

(c) A transaction in the form of a lease does not create a security interest merely because:

(1) the present value of the consideration the lessee is obligated to pay the lessor for the right to possession and use of the goods is substantially equal to or is greater than the fair market value of the goods at the time the lease is entered into;

(2) the lessee assumes risk of loss of the goods;

(3) the lessee agrees to pay, with respect to the goods, taxes, insurance, filing, recording, or registration fees, or service or maintenance costs;

(4) the lessee has an option to renew the lease or to become the owner of the goods;

(5) the lessee has an option to renew the lease for a fixed rent that is equal to or greater than the reasonably predictable fair market rent for the use of the goods for the term of the renewal at the time the option is to be performed; or

(6) the lessee has an option to become the owner of the goods for a fixed price that is equal to or greater than the reasonably predictable fair market value of the goods at the time the option is to be performed.

(d) Additional consideration is nominal if it is less than the lessee's reasonably predictable cost of performing under the lease agreement if the option is not exercised. Additional consideration is not nominal if:

(1) when the option to renew the lease is granted to the lessee, the rent is stated to be the fair market rent for the use of the goods for the term of the renewal determined at the time the option is to be performed; or

(2) when the option to become the owner of the goods is granted to the lessee, the price is stated to be the fair market value of the goods determined at the time the option is to be performed.

(e) The "remaining economic life of the goods" and "reasonably predictable" fair market rent, fair market value, or cost of performing under the lease agreement must be determined with reference to the facts and circumstances at the time the transaction is entered into.

Official Comment

Source: Former Section 1-201(37).

Changes from Former Law: This section is substantively identical to those portions of former Section 1-201(37) that distinguished "true" leases from security interests, except that the definition of "present value" formerly embedded in Section 1-201(37) has been placed in Section 1-201(b)(28).

1. An interest in personal property or fixtures which secures payment or performance of an obligation is a "security interest." See Section 1-201(b)(35). Security interests are sometimes created by transactions in the form of leases. Because it can be difficult to distinguish leases that create security interests from those that do not, this section provides rules that govern the determination of whether a transaction in the form of a lease creates a security interest.

2. One of the reasons it was decided to codify the law with respect to leases was to resolve an issue that created considerable confusion in the courts: what is a lease? The confusion existed, in part, due to the last two sentences of the definition of security interest in former Section 1-201(37), which prevailed until Article 2A was promulgated. The confusion was compounded by the rather considerable change in the federal, state and local tax laws and accounting rules as they relate to leases of goods. The answer is important because the definition of lease determines not only the rights and remedies of the parties to the lease but also those of third parties. If a transaction creates a lease and not a security interest, the lessee's interest in the goods is limited to its leasehold estate; the residual interest in the goods belongs to the lessor. This has significant implications to the lessee's creditors. "On common law theory, the lessor, since he has not parted with title, is entitled to full protection against the lessee's creditors and trustee in bankruptcy. . . ." 1 G. Gilmore, *Security Interests in Personal Property*, Section 3.6, at 76 (1965).

Under pre-UCC chattel security law there was generally no requirement that the lessor file the lease, a financing statement, or the like, to enforce the lease agreement against the lessee or any third party; the Article on Secured Transactions (Article 9) did not change the common law in that respect. Coogan, Leasing and the Uniform Commercial Code, in *Equipment Leasing—Leveraged Leasing* 681, 700 n.25, 729 n.80 (2d ed. 1980). The Article on Leases (Article 2A) did not change the law in that respect, except for leases of fixtures. Section 2A-309. An examination of the common law will not provide an adequate answer to the question of what is a lease. The definition of security interest previously in Section 1-201(37) provided that the Article on Secured Transactions (Article 9) governs security interests disguised as leases, i.e., leases intended as security; however, the definition became vague and outmoded.

Lease is defined in Article 2A as a transfer of the right to possession and use of goods for a term, in return for consideration. Section 2A-103(1)(j). The definition continues by stating that the retention or creation of a security interest is not a lease. Thus, the task of sharpening the line between true leases and security interests disguised as leases continues to be a function of this Article.

This section begins where Section 1-201(b)(35) leaves off. It draws a sharper line between leases and security interests disguised as leases to create greater certainty in commercial transactions.

Prior to enactment of the rules now codified in this section, Section 1-201(37) provided that whether a lease was intended as security (i.e., a security interest disguised as a lease) was to be determined from the facts of each case; however, (a) the inclusion of an option to purchase did not itself make the lease one intended for security, and (b) an agreement that upon compliance with the terms of the lease the lessee would become, or had the option to become, the owner of the property for no additional consideration, or for a nominal consideration, did make the lease one intended for security.

Reference to the intent of the parties to create a lease or security interest led to unfortunate results. In discovering intent, courts relied upon factors that were thought to be more consistent with sales or loans than leases. Most of these criteria, however, were as applicable to true leases as to security interests. Examples include the typical net lease provisions, a purported lessor's lack of storage facilities or its character as a financing party rather than a dealer in goods. Accordingly, this section contains no reference to the parties' intent.

Subsections (a) and (b) were originally taken from Section 1(2) of the Uniform Conditional Sales Act (act withdrawn 1943), modified to reflect current leasing practice. Thus, reference to the case law prior to the incorporation of those concepts in this article will provide a useful source of precedent. Grant Gilmore, *Security Law, Formalism and Article 9*, 47 Neb. L. Rev. 659, 671 (1968). Whether a transaction creates a lease or a security interest continues to be determined by the facts of each case. Subsection (b) further provides that a transaction creates a security interest if the lessee has an obligation to continue paying consideration for the term of the lease, if the obligation is not terminable by the lessee (thus correcting early statutory gloss, e.g., *In re Royer's Bakery, Inc.*, 1 U.C.C. Rep. Serv. (Callaghan) 342 (Bankr. E.D. Pa. 1963)) and if one of four additional tests is met. The first of these four tests, subparagraph (1), is that the original lease term is equal to or greater than the remaining economic life of the goods. The second of these tests, subparagraph (2), is that the lessee is either bound to renew the lease for the remaining economic life of the goods or to become the owner of the goods. *In re Gehrke Enters*, 1 B.R. 647, 651-52 (Bankr. W.D. Wis. 1979). The third of these tests, subparagraph (3), is whether the lessee has an option to renew the lease for the remaining economic life of the goods for no additional consideration or for nominal additional consideration, which is defined later in this section. *In re Celeryvale Transp.*, 44 B.R. 1007, 1014-15 (Bankr. E.D. Tenn. 1984). The fourth of these tests, subparagraph (4), is whether the lessee has an option to become the owner of the goods for no additional consideration or for nominal additional consideration. All of these tests focus on economics, not the intent of the parties. *In re Berge*, 32 B.R. 370, 371-73 (Bankr. W.D. Wis. 1983).

The focus on economics is reinforced by subsection (c). It states that a transaction does not create a security interest merely because the transaction has certain characteristics listed therein. Subparagraph (1) has no statutory derivative; it states that a full payout lease does not *per se* create a security interest. *Rushton v. Shea*, 419 F. Supp. 1349, 1365 (D. Del. 1976). Subparagraphs (2) and (3) provide the same regarding the provisions of the typical net lease. *Compare All-States Leasing Co. v. Ochs*, 600 P.2d 899 (Or. Ct. App. 1979), *with In re Tillery*, 571 F.2d 1361 (5th Cir. 1978). Subparagraph (4) restates and expands the provisions of former Section 1-201(37) to make clear that the option can be to buy or renew. Subparagraphs (5) and (6) treat fixed price options and provide that fair market value must be determined at the time the transaction is entered into. *Compare Arnold Mach. Co. v. Balls*, 624 P.2d 678 (Utah 1981), *with Aoki v. Shepherd Mach. Co.*, 665 F.2d 941 (9th Cir. 1982).

The relationship of subsection (b) to subsection (c) deserves to be explored. The fixed price purchase option provides a useful example. A fixed price purchase option in a lease does not of itself create a security interest. This is particularly true if the fixed price is equal to or greater than the reasonably predictable fair market value of the goods at the time the option is to be performed. A security interest is created only if the option price is nominal and the conditions stated in the introduction to the second paragraph of this subsection are met. There is a set of purchase options whose fixed price is less than fair market value but greater than nominal that must be determined on the facts of each case to ascertain whether the transaction in which the option is included creates a lease or a security interest.

It was possible to provide for various other permutations and combinations with respect to options to purchase and renew. For example, this section could have stated a rule to govern the facts of *In re Marhoefer Packing Co.*, 674 F.2d 1139 (7th Cir. 1982). This was not done because it would unnecessarily complicate the definition. Further development of this rule is left to the courts.

Subsections (d) and (e) provide definitions and rules of construction.

Section 1-204. Value

Except as otherwise provided in Articles 3, 4, 5, [6], and 12, a person gives value for rights if the person acquires them:

(1) in return for a binding commitment to extend credit or for the extension of immediately available credit, whether or not drawn upon and whether or not a charge-back is provided for in the event of difficulties in collection;

(2) as security for, or in total or partial satisfaction of, a preexisting claim;

(3) by accepting delivery under a preexisting contract for purchase; or

(4) in return for any consideration sufficient to support a simple contract.

Official Comment

Source: Former Section 1-201(44).

Changes from Former Law: Unchanged from former Section 1-201, which was derived from Sections 25, 26, 27, 191, Uniform Negotiable Instruments Law; Section 76, Uniform Sales Act; Section 53, Uniform Bills of Lading Act; Section 58, Uniform Warehouse Receipts Act; Section 22(1), Uniform Stock Transfer Act; Section 1, Uniform Trust Receipts Act. These provisions are substantive rather than purely definitional. Accordingly, they have been relocated from former Section 1-201 to this section.

1. Historically, most Uniform Acts in the commercial law field have carried definitions of "value." Those definitions provided that value was any consideration sufficient to support a simple contract, including the taking of property in satisfaction of or as security for a pre-existing claim. Subsections (1), (2), and (4) in substance continue the definitions of "value" in the earlier acts. Subsection (3) makes explicit that "value" is also given in a third situation: where a buyer by taking delivery under a pre-existing contract converts a contingent into a fixed obligation.

This definition is not applicable to Articles 3 and 4, but the express inclusion of immediately available credit as value follows the separate definitions in those Articles. See Sections 4-211, 4-214, 3-303. A bank or other financing agency which in good faith makes advances against property held as collateral becomes a bona fide purchaser of that property even though provision may be made for charge-back in case of trouble. Checking credit is "immediately available" within the meaning of this section if the bank would be subject to an action for slander of credit in case checks drawn against the credit were dishonored, and when a charge-back is not discretionary with the bank, but may only be made when difficulties in collection arise in connection with the specific transaction involved. Article 12 adopts the substance of the Article 3 definition. See Section 12-102(a)(4).

Section 1-205. Reasonable Time; Seasonableness

(a) Whether a time for taking an action required by [the Uniform Commercial Code] is reasonable depends on the nature, purpose, and circumstances of the action.

(b) An action is taken seasonably if it is taken at or within the time agreed or, if no time is agreed, at or within a reasonable time.

Official Comment

Source: Former Section 1-204(2)-(3).

Changes from Former Law: This section is derived from subsections (2) and (3) of former Section 1-204. Subsection (1) of that section is now incorporated in Section 1-302(b).

1. Subsection (a) makes it clear that requirements that actions be taken within a "reasonable" time are to be applied in the transactional context of the particular action.

2. Under subsection (b), the agreement that fixes the time need not be part of the main agreement, but may occur separately. Notice also that under the definition of "agreement" (Section 1-201) the circumstances of the transaction, including course of dealing or usages of trade or course of performance may be material. On the question what is a reasonable time these matters will often be important.

Section 1-206. Presumptions

Whenever [the Uniform Commercial Code] creates a "presumption" with respect to a fact, or provides that a fact is "presumed," the trier of fact must find the existence of the fact unless and until evidence is introduced that supports a finding of its nonexistence.

Legislative Note: *Former Section 1-206, a Statute of Frauds for sales of "kinds of personal property not otherwise covered," has been deleted. The other articles of the Uniform Commercial Code make individual determinations as to requirements for memorializing transactions within their scope, so that the primary effect of former Section 1-206 was to impose a writing requirement on sales transactions not otherwise governed by the UCC. Deletion of former Section 1-206 does not constitute a recommendation to legislatures as to whether such sales transactions should be covered by a Statute of Frauds; rather, it reflects a determination that there is no need for uniform commercial law to resolve that issue.*

Official Comment

Source: Former Section 1-201(31).

Changes from Former Law: None, other than stylistic changes.

Several sections of the Uniform Commercial Code state that there is a "presumption" as to a certain fact, or that the fact is "presumed." This section, derived from the definition appearing in former Section 1-201(31), indicates the effect of those provisions on the proof process.

PART 3. TERRITORIAL APPLICABILITY AND GENERAL RULES

Section 1-301. Territorial Applicability; Parties' Power to Choose Applicable Law

(a) Except as otherwise provided in this section, when a transaction bears a reasonable relation to this state and also to another state or nation the parties may agree that the law either of this state or of such other state or nation shall govern their rights and duties.

(b) In the absence of an agreement effective under subsection (a), and except as provided in subsection (c), [the Uniform Commercial Code] applies to transactions bearing an appropriate relation to this state.

(c) If one of the following provisions of [the Uniform Commercial Code] specifies the applicable law, that provision governs and a contrary agreement is effective only to the extent permitted by the law so specified:

(1) Section 2-402;
(2) Sections 2A-105 and 2A-106;
(3) Section 4-102;
(4) Section 4A-507;
(5) Section 5-116;
[(6) Section 6-103;]
(7) Section 8-110;
(8) Sections 9-301 through 9-307;
(9) Section 12-107.

Official Comment

Source: Former Section 1-105.

Changes from former law: This section is substantively identical to former Section 1-105. Changes in language are stylistic only.

1. Subsection (a) states affirmatively the right of the parties to a multi-state transaction or a transaction involving foreign trade to choose their own law. That right is subject to the firm rules stated in the sections listed in subsection (c), and is limited to jurisdictions to which the transaction bears a "reasonable relation." In general, the test of "reasonable relation" is similar to that laid down by the Supreme Court in *Seeman v. Philadelphia Warehouse Co.*, 274 U.S. 403 (1927). Ordinarily the law chosen must be that of a jurisdiction where a significant enough portion of the making or performance of the contract is to occur or occurs. But an agreement as to choice of law may sometimes take effect as a shorthand expression of the intent of the parties as to matters governed by their agreement, even though the transaction has no significant contact with the jurisdiction chosen.

2. Where there is no agreement as to the governing law, the Act is applicable to any transaction having an "appropriate" relation to any state which enacts it. Of course, the Act applies to any transaction which takes place in its entirety in a state which has enacted the Act. But the mere fact that suit is brought in a state does not make it appropriate to apply the substantive law of that state. Cases where a relation to the enacting state is not "appropriate" include, for example, those where the parties have clearly contracted on the basis of some other law, as where the law of the place of contracting and the law of the place of contemplated performance are the same and are contrary to the law under the Code.

3. Where a transaction has significant contacts with a state which has enacted the Act and also with other jurisdictions, the question what relation is "appropriate" is left to judicial decision. In deciding that question, the court is not strictly bound by precedents established in other contexts. Thus a conflict-of-laws decision refusing to apply a purely local statute or rule of law to a particular multi-state transaction may not be valid precedent for refusal to apply the Code in an analogous situation. Application of the Code in such circumstances may be justified by its comprehensiveness, by the policy of uniformity, and by the fact that it is in large part a reformulation and restatement of the law merchant and of the understanding of a business community which transcends state and even national boundaries. Compare *Global Commerce Corp. v. Clark-Babbitt Industries, Inc.*, 239 F.2d 716, 719 (2d Cir. 1956). In particular, where a transaction is governed in large part by the Code, application of another law to some detail of performance because of an accident of geography may violate the commercial understanding of the parties.

4. Subsection (c) spells out essential limitations on the parties' right to choose the applicable law. Especially in Article 9 parties taking a security interest or asked to extend credit which may be subject to a security interest must have sure ways to find out whether and where to file and where to look for possible existing filings.

5. Sections 9-301 through 9-307 should be consulted as to the rules for perfection of security interests and agricultural liens and the effect of perfection and nonperfection and priority. In transactions to which the Hague Securities Convention applies, the requirements for foreclosure and the like, the characterization of a transfer as being outright or by way of security, and certain other issues will generally be governed by the law specified in the account agreement. See PEB Commentary No. 19.

6. This section is subject to Section 1-102, which states the scope of Article 1. As that section indicates, the rules of Article 1, including this section, apply to a transaction to the extent that transaction is governed by one of the other Articles of the Uniform Commercial Code.

Section 1-302. Variation by Agreement

(a) Except as otherwise provided in subsection (b) or elsewhere in [the Uniform Commercial Code], the effect of provisions of [the Uniform Commercial Code] may be varied by agreement.

(b) The obligations of good faith, diligence, reasonableness, and care prescribed by [the Uniform Commercial Code] may not be disclaimed by agreement. The parties, by agreement, may determine the standards by which the performance of those obligations is to be measured if those standards are not manifestly unreasonable. Whenever [the Uniform Commercial Code] requires an action to be taken within a reasonable time, a time that is not manifestly unreasonable may be fixed by agreement.

(c) The presence in certain provisions of [the Uniform Commercial Code] of the phrase "unless otherwise agreed", or words of similar import, does not imply that the effect of other provisions may not be varied by agreement under this section.

Official Comment

Source: Former Sections 1-102(3)-(4) and 1-204(1).

Changes: This section combines the rules from subsections (3) and (4) of former Section 1-102 and subsection (1) of former Section 1-204. No substantive changes are made.

1. Subsection (a) states affirmatively at the outset that freedom of contract is a principle of the Uniform Commercial Code: "the effect" of its provisions may be varied by "agreement." The meaning of the statute itself must be found in its text, including its definitions, and in appropriate extrinsic aids; it cannot be varied by agreement. But the Uniform Commercial Code seeks to avoid the type of interference with evolutionary growth found in pre-Code cases such as *Manhattan Co. v. Morgan*, 150 N.E. 594 (N.Y. 1926). Thus, private parties cannot make an instrument negotiable within the meaning of Article 3 except as provided in Section 3-104; nor can they change the meaning of such terms as "bona fide purchaser," "holder in due course," or "due negotiation," as used in the Uniform Commercial Code. But an agreement can change the legal consequences that would otherwise flow from the provisions of the Uniform Commercial Code. "Agreement" here includes the effect given to course of dealing, usage of trade and course of performance by Sections 1-201 and 1-303; the effect of an agreement on the rights of third parties is left to specific provisions of the Uniform Commercial Code and to supplementary principles applicable under Section 1-103. The rights of third parties under Section 9-317 when a security interest is unperfected, for example, cannot be destroyed by a clause in the security agreement.

This principle of freedom of contract is subject to specific exceptions found elsewhere in the Uniform Commercial Code and to the general exception stated here. The specific exceptions vary in explicitness: the statute of frauds found in Section 2-201, for example, does not explicitly preclude oral waiver of the requirement of a writing, but a fair reading denies enforcement to such a waiver as part of the "contract" made unenforceable; Section 9-602, on the other hand, is a quite explicit limitation on freedom of contract. Under the exception for "the obligations of good faith, diligence, reasonableness and care prescribed by [the Uniform Commercial Code]," provisions of the Uniform Commercial Code prescribing such obligations are not to be disclaimed. However, the section also recognizes the prevailing practice of having agreements set forth standards by which due diligence is measured and explicitly provides that, in the absence of a showing that the standards manifestly are unreasonable, the agreement controls. In this connection, Section 1-303 incorporating into the agreement prior course of dealing and usages of trade is of particular importance.

Subsection (b) also recognizes that nothing is stronger evidence of a reasonable time than the fixing of such time by a fair agreement between the parties. However, provision is made for disregarding a clause which whether by inadvertence or overreaching fixes a time so unreasonable that it amounts to eliminating all remedy under the contract. The parties are not required to fix the most reasonable time but may fix any time which is not obviously unfair as judged by the time of contracting.

2. An agreement that varies the effect of provisions of the Uniform Commercial Code may do so by stating the rules that will govern in lieu of the provisions varied. Alternatively, the parties may vary the effect of such provisions by stating that their relationship will be governed by recognized bodies of rules or principles applicable to commercial transactions. Such bodies of rules or principles may include, for example, those that are promulgated by intergovernmental authorities such as

UNCITRAL or UNIDROIT (*see, e.g.*, UNIDROIT Principles of International Commercial Contracts), or non-legal codes such as trade codes.

3. Subsection (c) is intended to make it clear that, as a matter of drafting, phrases such as "unless otherwise agreed" have been used to avoid controversy as to whether the subject matter of a particular section does or does not fall within the exceptions to subsection (b), but absence of such words contains no negative implication since under subsection (b) the general and residual rule is that the effect of all provisions of the Uniform Commercial Code may be varied by agreement.

Section 1-303. Course of Performance, Course of Dealing, and Usage of Trade

(a) A "course of performance" is a sequence of conduct between the parties to a particular transaction that exists if:

(1) the agreement of the parties with respect to the transaction involves repeated occasions for performance by a party; and

(2) the other party, with knowledge of the nature of the performance and opportunity for objection to it, accepts the performance or acquiesces in it without objection.

(b) A "course of dealing" is a sequence of conduct concerning previous transactions between the parties to a particular transaction that is fairly to be regarded as establishing a common basis of understanding for interpreting their expressions and other conduct.

(c) A "usage of trade" is any practice or method of dealing having such regularity of observance in a place, vocation, or trade as to justify an expectation that it will be observed with respect to the transaction in question. The existence and scope of such a usage must be proved as facts. If it is established that such a usage is embodied in a trade code or similar record, the interpretation of the record is a question of law.

(d) A course of performance or course of dealing between the parties or usage of trade in the vocation or trade in which they are engaged or of which they are or should be aware is relevant in ascertaining the meaning of the parties' agreement, may give particular meaning to specific terms of the agreement, and may supplement or qualify the terms of the agreement. A usage of trade applicable in the place in which part of the performance under the agreement is to occur may be so utilized as to that part of the performance.

(e) Except as otherwise provided in subsection (f), the express terms of an agreement and any applicable course of performance, course of dealing, or usage of trade must be construed whenever reasonable as consistent with each other. If such a construction is unreasonable:

(1) express terms prevail over course of performance, course of dealing, and usage of trade;

(2) course of performance prevails over course of dealing and usage of trade; and

(3) course of dealing prevails over usage of trade.

(f) Subject to Section 2-209, a course of performance is relevant to show a waiver or modification of any term inconsistent with the course of performance.

(g) Evidence of a relevant usage of trade offered by one party is not admissible unless that party has given the other party notice that the court finds sufficient to prevent unfair surprise to the other party.

Official Comment

Source: Former Sections 1-205, 2-208, and Section 2A-207.

Changes from Former Law: This section integrates the "course of performance" concept from Articles 2 and 2A into the principles of former Section 1-205, which deals with course of dealing and usage of trade. In so doing, the section slightly modifies the articulation of the course of performance rules to fit more comfortably with the approach and structure of former Section 1-205. There are also slight modifications to be more consistent with the definition of "agreement" in former Section 1-201(3). It should be noted that a course of performance that might otherwise establish a defense to the obligation of a party to a negotiable instrument is not available as a defense against a holder in due course who took the instrument without notice of that course of performance.

1. The Uniform Commercial Code rejects both the "lay-dictionary" and the "conveyancer's" reading of a commercial agreement. Instead the meaning of the agreement of the parties is to be determined by the language used by them and by their action, read and interpreted in the light of commercial practices and other surrounding circumstances. The measure and background for interpretation are set by the commercial context, which may explain and supplement even the language of a formal or final writing.

2. "Course of dealing," as defined in subsection (b), is restricted, literally, to a sequence of conduct between the parties previous to the agreement. A sequence of conduct after or under the agreement, however, is a "course of performance." "Course of dealing" may enter the agreement either by explicit provisions of the agreement or by tacit recognition.

3. The Uniform Commercial Code deals with "usage of trade" as a factor in reaching the commercial meaning of the agreement that the parties have made. The language used is to be interpreted as meaning what it may fairly be expected to mean to parties involved in the particular commercial transaction in a given locality or in a given vocation or trade. By adopting in this context the term "usage of trade," the Uniform Commercial Code expresses its intent to reject those cases which see evidence of "custom" as representing an effort to displace or negate "established rules of law." A distinction is to be drawn between mandatory rules of law such as the Statute of

Frauds provisions of Article 2 on Sales whose very office is to control and restrict the actions of the parties, and which cannot be abrogated by agreement, or by a usage of trade, and those rules of law (such as those in Part 3 of Article 2 on Sales) which fill in points which the parties have not considered and in fact agreed upon. The latter rules hold "unless otherwise agreed" but yield to the contrary agreement of the parties. Part of the agreement of the parties to which such rules yield is to be sought for in the usages of trade which furnish the background and give particular meaning to the language used, and are the framework of common understanding controlling any general rules of law which hold only when there is no such understanding.

4. A usage of trade under subsection (c) must have the "regularity of observance" specified. The ancient English tests for "custom" are abandoned in this connection. Therefore, it is not required that a usage of trade be "ancient or immemorial," "universal," or the like. Under the requirement of subsection (c) full recognition is thus available for new usages and for usages currently observed by the great majority of decent dealers, even though dissidents ready to cut corners do not agree. There is room also for proper recognition of usage agreed upon by merchants in trade codes.

5. The policies of the Uniform Commercial Code controlling explicit unconscionable contracts and clauses (Sections 1-304, 2-302, 2A-108) apply to implicit clauses that rest on usage of trade and carry forward the policy underlying the ancient requirement that a custom or usage must be "reasonable." However, the emphasis is shifted. The very fact of commercial acceptance makes out a *prima facie* case that the usage is reasonable, and the burden is no longer on the usage to establish itself as being reasonable. But the anciently established policing of usage by the courts is continued to the extent necessary to cope with the situation arising if an unconscionable or dishonest practice should become standard.

6. Subsection (d), giving the prescribed effect to usages of which the parties "are or should be aware," reinforces the provision of subsection (c) requiring not universality but only the described "regularity of observance" of the practice or method. This subsection also reinforces the point of subsection (c) that such usages may be either general to trade or particular to a special branch of trade.

7. Although the definition of "agreement" in Section 1-201 includes the elements of course of performance, course of dealing, and usage of trade, the fact that express reference is made in some sections to those elements is not to be construed as carrying a contrary intent or implication elsewhere. Compare Section 1-302(c).

8. In cases of a well established line of usage varying from the general rules of the Uniform Commercial Code where the precise amount of the variation has not been worked out into a single standard, the party relying on the usage is entitled, in any event, to the minimum variation demonstrated. The whole is not to be disregarded because no particular line of detail has been established. In case a dominant pattern has been fairly evidenced, the party relying on the usage is entitled under this section to go to the trier of fact on the question of whether such dominant pattern has been incorporated into the agreement.

9. Subsection (g) is intended to insure that this Act's liberal recognition of the needs of commerce in regard to usage of trade shall not be made into an instrument of abuse.

Section 1-304. Obligation of Good Faith

Every contract or duty within [the Uniform Commercial Code] imposes an obligation of good faith in its performance and enforcement.

Official Comment

Source: Former Section 1-203.

Changes from Former Law: Except for changing the form of reference to the Uniform Commercial Code, this section is identical to former Section 1-203.

1. This section sets forth a basic principle running throughout the Uniform Commercial Code. The principle is that in commercial transactions good faith is required in the performance and enforcement of all agreements or duties. While this duty is explicitly stated in some provisions of the Uniform Commercial Code, the applicability of the duty is broader than merely these situations and applies generally, as stated in this section, to the performance or enforcement of every contract or duty within this Act. It is further implemented by Section 1-303 on course of dealing, course of performance, and usage of trade. This section does not support an independent cause of action for failure to perform or enforce in good faith. Rather, this section means that a failure to perform or enforce, in good faith, a specific duty or obligation under the contract, constitutes a breach of that contract or makes unavailable, under the particular circumstances, a remedial right or power. This distinction makes it clear that the doctrine of good faith merely directs a court towards interpreting contracts within the commercial context in which they are created, performed, and enforced, and does not create a separate duty of fairness and reasonableness which can be independently breached.

2. "Performance and enforcement" of contracts and duties within the Uniform Commercial Code include the exercise of rights created by the Uniform Commercial Code.

Section 1-305. Remedies To Be Liberally Administered

(a) The remedies provided by [the Uniform Commercial Code] must be liberally administered to the end that the aggrieved party may be put in as good a position as if the other party had fully performed but neither consequential or special damages nor penal damages may be had except as specifically provided in [the Uniform Commercial Code] or by other rule of law.

(b) Any right or obligation declared by [the Uniform Commercial Code] is enforceable by action unless the provision declaring it specifies a different and limited effect.

Official Comment

Source: Former Section 1-106.

Changes from Former Law: Other than changes in the form of reference to the Uniform Commercial Code, this section is identical to former Section 1-106.

1. Subsection (a) is intended to effect three propositions. The first is to negate the possibility of unduly narrow or technical interpretation of remedial provisions by providing that the remedies in the Uniform Commercial Code are to be liberally administered to the end stated in this section. The second is to make it clear that compensatory damages are limited to compensation. They do not include consequential or special damages, or penal damages; and the Uniform Commercial Code elsewhere makes it clear that damages must be minimized. Cf. Sections 1-304, 2-706(1), and 2-712(2). The third purpose of subsection (a) is to reject any doctrine that damages must be calculable with mathematical accuracy. Compensatory damages are often at best approximate: they have to be proved with whatever definiteness and accuracy the facts permit, but no more. Cf. Section 2-204(3).

2. Under subsection (b), any right or obligation described in the Uniform Commercial Code is enforceable by action, even though no remedy may be expressly provided other than in this section, unless a particular provision specifies a different and limited effect. Whether specific performance or other equitable relief is available in a particular case is determined not by this section but by specific provisions and by supplementary principles. Cf. Sections 1-103, 2-716, 9-625.

3. "Consequential" or "special" damages and "penal" damages are not defined in the Uniform Commercial Code; rather, these terms are used in the sense in which they are used outside the Uniform Commercial Code.

Section 1-306. Waiver or Renunciation of Claim or Right after Breach

A claim or right arising out of an alleged breach may be discharged in whole or in part without consideration by agreement of the aggrieved party in a signed record.

Official Comment

Source: Former Section 1-107.

Changes from Former Law: Former Section 1-107, requiring the "delivery" of a "written waiver or renunciation" merged the separate concepts of the aggrieved party's agreement to forego rights and the manifestation of that agreement. This section separates those concepts, and explicitly requires agreement of the aggrieved party.

1. This section makes consideration unnecessary to the effective renunciation or waiver of rights or claims arising out of an alleged breach of a contract where the agreement effecting such renunciation is memorialized in a record signed by the aggrieved party. Its provisions, however, must be read in conjunction with the section imposing an obligation of good faith. (Section 1-304.)

2. Consistent with the revised definition of "sign" in Section 1-201, the cognate term "signed" replaces the reference to "authenticated" in the pre-2022 text of this section.

Section 1-307. Prima Facie Evidence by Third-Party Documents

A document in due form purporting to be a bill of lading, policy or certificate of insurance, official weigher's or inspector's certificate, consular invoice, or any other document authorized or required by the contract to be issued by a third party is prima facie evidence of its own authenticity and genuineness and of the facts stated in the document by the third party.

Official Comment

Source: Former Section 1-202.

Changes from Former Law: Except for minor stylistic changes, this Section is identical to former Section 1-202.

1. This section supplies judicial recognition for documents that are relied upon as trustworthy by commercial parties.

2. This section is concerned only with documents that have been given a preferred status by the parties themselves who have required their procurement in the agreement, and for this reason the applicability of the section is limited to actions arising out of the contract that authorized or required the document. The list of documents is intended to be illustrative and not exclusive.

3. The provisions of this section go no further than establishing the documents in question as prima facie evidence and leave to the court the ultimate determination of the facts where the accuracy or authenticity of the documents is questioned. In this connection the section calls for a commercially reasonable interpretation.

4. Documents governed by this section need not be writings if records in another medium are generally relied upon in the context.

Section 1-308. Performance or Acceptance under Reservation of Rights

(a) A party that with explicit reservation of rights performs or promises performance or assents to performance in a manner demanded or offered by the other party does not thereby prejudice the rights reserved. Such words as "without prejudice," "under protest," or the like are sufficient.

(b) Subsection (a) does not apply to an accord and satisfaction.

Official Comment

Source: Former Section 1-207.

Changes from Former Law: This section is identical to former Section 1-207.

1. This section provides machinery for the continuation of performance along the lines contemplated by the contract despite a pending dispute, by adopting the mercantile device of going ahead with delivery, acceptance, or payment "without prejudice," "under protest," "under reserve," "with reservation of all our rights," and the like. All of these phrases completely reserve all rights within the meaning of this section. The section therefore contemplates that limited as well as general reservations and acceptance by a party may be made "subject to satisfaction of our purchaser," "subject to acceptance by our customers," or the like.

2. This section does not add any new requirement of language of reservation where not already required by law, but merely provides a specific measure on which a party can rely as that party makes or concurs in any interim adjustment in the course of performance. It does not affect or impair the provisions of this Act such as those under which the buyer's remedies for defect survive acceptance without being expressly claimed if notice of the defects is given within a reasonable time. Nor does it disturb the policy of those cases which restrict the effect of a waiver of a defect to reasonable limits under the circumstances, even though no such reservation is expressed.

The section is not addressed to the creation or loss of remedies in the ordinary course of performance but rather to a method of procedure where one party is claiming as of right something which the other believes to be unwarranted.

3. Subsection (b) states that this section does not apply to an accord and satisfaction. Section 3-311 governs if an accord and satisfaction is attempted by tender of a negotiable instrument as stated in that section. If Section 3-311 does not apply, the issue of whether an accord and satisfaction has been effected is determined by the law of contract. Whether or not Section 3-311 applies, this section has no application to an accord and satisfaction.

Section 1-309. Option to Accelerate at Will

A term providing that one party or that party's successor in interest may accelerate payment or performance or require collateral or additional collateral "at will" or when the party "deems itself insecure," or words of similar import, means that the party has power to do so only if that party in good faith believes that the prospect of payment or performance is impaired. The burden of establishing lack of good faith is on the party against which the power has been exercised.

Official Comment

Source: Former Section 1-208.

Changes from Former Law: Except for minor stylistic changes, this section is identical to former Section 1-208.

The common use of acceleration clauses in many transactions governed by the Uniform Commercial Code, including sales of goods on credit, notes payable at a definite time, and secured transactions, raises an issue as to the effect to be given to a clause that seemingly grants the power to accelerate at the whim and caprice of one party. This section is intended to make clear that despite language that might be so construed and which further might be held to make the agreement void as against public policy or to make the contract illusory or too indefinite for enforcement, the option is to be exercised only in the good faith belief that the prospect of payment or performance is impaired.

Obviously this section has no application to demand instruments or obligations whose very nature permits call at any time with or without reason. This section applies only to an obligation of payment or performance which in the first instance is due at a future date.

Section 1-310. Subordinated Obligations

An obligation may be issued as subordinated to performance of another obligation of the person obligated, or a creditor may subordinate its right to performance of an obligation by agreement with either the person obligated or another creditor of the person obligated. Subordination does not create a security interest as against either the common debtor or a subordinated creditor.

Official Comment

Source: Former Section 1-209.

Changes from Former Law: This section is substantively identical to former Section 1-209. The language in that section stating that it "shall be construed as declaring the law as it existed prior to the enactment of this section and not as modifying it" has been deleted.

1. Billions of dollars of subordinated debt are held by the public and by institutional investors. Commonly, the subordinated debt is subordinated on issue or acquisition and is evidenced by an investment security or by a negotiable or non-negotiable note. Debt is also sometimes subordinated after it arises, either by agreement between the subordinating creditor and the debtor, by agreement between two creditors of the same debtor, or by agreement of all three parties. The subordinated creditor may be a stockholder or other "insider" interested in the common debtor; the subordinated debt may consist of accounts or other rights to payment not evidenced by any instrument. All such cases are included in the terms "subordinated obligation," "subordination," and "subordinated creditor."

2. Subordination agreements are enforceable between the parties as contracts; and in the bankruptcy of the common debtor dividends otherwise payable to the subordinated creditor are turned over to the superior creditor. This "turn-over" practice has on occasion been explained in terms of "equitable lien," "equitable assignment," or "constructive trust," but whatever the label the practice is essentially an equitable remedy and does not mean that there is a transaction "that creates a security interest in personal property . . . by contract" or a "sale of accounts, chattel paper, payment intangibles, or promissory notes" within the meaning of Section 9-109. On the other hand, nothing in this section prevents one creditor from assigning his rights to another creditor of the same debtor in such a way as to create a security interest within Article 9, where the parties so intend.

3. The enforcement of subordination agreements is largely left to supplementary principles under Section 1-103. If the subordinated debt is evidenced by a certificated security, Section 8-202(a) authorizes enforcement against purchasers on terms stated or referred to on the security certificate. If the fact of subordination is noted on a negotiable instrument, a holder under Sections 3-302 and 3-306 is subject to the term because notice precludes him from taking free of the subordination. Sections 3-302(c)(i), 3-305(a)(2), and 8-112(a) severely limit the rights of levying creditors of a subordinated creditor in such cases.

Article 2—Sales

As adopted in 1962 and revised in: (i) 1966, in connection with a PEB Report; (ii) 1972, in connection with the revision of Article 9; (iii) 1989, in connection with the revision of Article 6; (iv) 1990, in connection with PEB Commentary No. 1; (v) 1994, to correct errata; (vi) 1995, in connection with the revision of Article 5; (vii) 1999, in connection with the revision of Article 9; (viii) 2001, in connection with the revision of Article 1; (ix) 2002, in connection with amendments to Article 9; (x) 2003, in connection with the revision of Article 7; (xi) 2004 and 2005, in connection with technical amendments; and (xii) 2022, in connection with the 2022 Amendments to the Uniform Commercial Code.

PART 1. SHORT TITLE, GENERAL CONSTRUCTION AND SUBJECT MATTER

Section

PART 2. FORM, FORMATION AND READJUSTMENT OF CONTRACT

PART 3. GENERAL OBLIGATION AND CONSTRUCTION OF CONTRACT

PART 4. TITLE, CREDITORS AND GOOD FAITH PURCHASERS

PART 5. PERFORMANCE

PART 6. BREACH, REPUDIATION AND EXCUSE

PART 7. REMEDIES

PART 1. SHORT TITLE, GENERAL CONSTRUCTION AND SUBJECT MATTER

Section 2-101. Short Title

This Article shall be known and may be cited as Uniform Commercial Code—Sales.

Official Comment

This Article is a complete revision and modernization of the Uniform Sales Act which was promulgated by the National Conference of Commissioners on Uniform State Laws in 1906 and has been adopted in 34 states and Alaska, the District of Columbia and Hawaii.

The coverage of the present Article is much more extensive than that of the old Sales Act and extends to the various bodies of case law which have been developed both outside of and under the latter.

The arrangement of the present Article is in terms of contract for sale and the various steps of its performance. The legal consequences are stated as following directly from the contract and action taken under it without resorting to the idea of when property or title passed or was to pass as being the determining factor. The purpose is to avoid making practical issues between practical men turn upon the location of an intangible something, the passing of which no man can prove by evidence and to substitute for such abstractions proof of words and actions of a tangible character.

Section 2-102. Scope; Certain Security and Other Transactions Excluded from This Article

(1) Unless the context otherwise requires, and except as provided in subsection (3), this Article applies to transactions in goods and, in the case of a hybrid transaction, it applies to the extent provided in subsection (2).

(2) In a hybrid transaction:

(a) If the sale-of-goods aspects do not predominate, only the provisions of this Article which relate primarily to the sale-of-goods aspects of the transaction apply, and the provisions that relate primarily to the transaction as a whole do not apply.

(b) If the sale-of-goods aspects predominate, this Article applies to the transaction but does not preclude application in appropriate circumstances of other law to aspects of the transaction which do not relate to the sale of goods.

(3) This Article does not:

(a) apply to a transaction that, even though in the form of an unconditional contract to sell or present sale, operates only to create a security interest; or

(b) impair or repeal any statute regulating sales to consumers, farmers or other specified classes of buyers.

Official Comment

Prior Uniform Statutory Provision: Section 75, Uniform Sales Act.

Changes: Section 75 has been rephrased.

Purposes:

1. Subsection (3) makes it clear that this Article does not govern aspects of a transaction that, although in the form of a sale or contract to sell, create a security interest. See Sections 1-201(b)(35); 9-109(a)(1). Of course, this Article does apply to any sales aspects of such a transaction.

2. Many ordinary transactions involve both a sale of goods and the provision of services, a lease of other goods, or a sale, lease, or license of property other than goods. In its original formulation, Article 2 provided no guidance on whether or to what extent the Article applied to such a hybrid transaction, although by defining a "sale" as "the passing of title [to goods] from the seller to the buyer for a price," Section 1-206 arguably regarded such transactions as sales. This section was substantially revised to address hybrid transactions pursuant to the Uniform Commercial Code Amendments (2022) (2022 Amendments). See Section 2-106(5) (defining "hybrid transaction").

In dealing with the issue of whether and to what extent, under the pre-2022 version of this section, Article 2 applied to hybrid transactions, most courts used some version of a "predominant purpose" test. Under those tests, Article 2 applied either in full or not at all, depending on whether the hybrid transaction, at its inception, was predominantly about the goods. In some cases, courts looked instead to the "gravamen of the claim," applying Article 2 to issues relating to the goods and applying other law to issues relating to other aspects of the transaction. Still other courts used what was sometimes referred to as the "bifurcation approach," under which Article 2 applied to the sale-of-goods aspect of a hybrid transaction and other law applied to the other aspects of the transaction. The bifurcation approach was similar to the gravamen of the claim, but instead of applying all of Article 2 to some, but not all, types of claims relating to a hybrid transaction, it distinguished the provisions in Article 2 that deal with the goods from those that deal with the transaction as a whole, and applied only the former in a hybrid transaction.

Subsection (2) codifies aspects of the predominant purpose test and the bifurcation approach, establishing a two-tiered test. If the sale-of-goods aspects of a hybrid transaction predominate, then Article 2 applies. If the other aspects of the hybrid transaction predominate, then the provisions of Article 2 which relate primarily to the sale of goods, as opposed to those that relate to the transaction as a whole, apply. This approach has the benefit, for example, of ensuring that a person acquiring ownership of goods in a transaction in which the sale-of-goods aspects do not predominate is a buyer that benefits from the warranty provisions of this Article and may have a right to recover the goods from the seller and thereby may qualify as a buyer in ordinary course of business under Section 1-201(b)(9).

3. It is important to note that, in contrast to the frequent reference (under prior case law in many states) to the predominant *purpose* of a hybrid transaction, subsection (2) focuses on which aspect of the transaction predominates without requiring a finding of the "purpose" of either or both parties (although that purpose, when evident, may be a relevant factor in deciding which aspect predominates). The determination of which aspect of a hybrid transaction predominates is left to the court, which should evaluate each transaction on a case-by-case basis without the necessity of applying any particular formula. Factors that may be relevant to that determination include, but are not limited to, the language of the agreement, the portion of the total price that is attributable to the sale of goods (as to which an agreed-upon allocation will ordinarily be binding on the parties), the purposes of the parties in entering into the transaction (when that is ascertainable), and the nature of the businesses of the parties (such as whether the seller is in the business of selling goods of that kind). Because the definition of "goods" expressly includes "specially manufactured goods," services involved in manufacturing goods are normally attributable to the sale-of-goods aspects of the transaction. Services in designing specially manufactured goods, however, would not normally be attributable to the sale-of-goods aspects of the transaction.

4. If the sale-of-goods aspects of a hybrid transaction predominate, then this Article applies to the transaction. However, the application of this Article to a hybrid transaction does not preclude the application of principles of law and equity to supplement the provisions of this Article, see Section 1-103(b), nor does it preclude, in appropriate circumstances, the application of other law to the non-sale-of-goods aspects of the transaction. Whether it is appropriate to apply such other law will depend in part on what purposes the other law is designed to achieve and whether application of the other law would be likely to interfere with the application of this Article.

Example 1. Owner hires Contractor to replace the roof on a structure. As part of the transaction, Contractor promises to remove the existing shingles and install new shingles, which Contractor is providing. The transaction is a hybrid transaction because it involves the passing of title to the new shingles and the provision of services. If the sale-of-goods aspects of the transaction predominate, this Article applies to the transaction.

Example 2. Same facts as in Example 1. Even if the sale-of-goods aspects of the transaction predominate, other law might apply to the services aspects of the transaction. For example, if applicable law regulates the provision of roofing services, such as by requiring the roofer to be licensed, requiring specified disclosures, requiring or implying a warranty with respect to the quality of services, or giving the property owner a brief period of time to cancel the contract, such other law might apply.

Example 3. In a single transaction, Seller agrees to sell a warehouse full of goods to Buyer. The transaction includes the goods contained in the warehouse, the warehouse itself, and the real property on which the warehouse is situated. Assume the goods aspects of the transaction predominate. The application of this Article to the transaction does not preclude the application of real property law to the real-property aspects of the transaction. Accordingly, whether the sale of the real property complies with the applicable requirements of real property law is determined by law other than this Article. Other law will also determine whether consummation of the sale of the real property is a condition to the parties' obligations to buy and sell the goods.

5. If the sale-of-goods aspects of a hybrid transaction do not predominate, under subsection (2), the provisions of this Article relating primarily to the sale of goods, as opposed to the transaction as a whole, apply. These provisions include those relating to warranties under Sections 2-312, 2-313, 2-314, 2-315, 2-316, 2-317, 2-318; tender of delivery and risk of loss under Sections 2-503, 2-504, 2-509, 2-510; acceptance, rejection, and cure under Sections 2-508, 2-601, 2-602, 2-603, 2-604, 2-605, 2-606; and remedies for non-delivery of the goods or for tender of nonconforming goods under Sections 2-711, 7-712, 7-713, 2-714, 2-715, 2-716. In contrast, the provisions of this Article dealing with the transaction as a whole do not apply. These provisions include those relating to: the requirement of a signed record, Section 2-201; contract formation, Sections 2-204 through 2-207; and whether consideration is needed to modify the agreement, Section 2-209.

Example 4. Owner sends a purchase order to Contractor offering to enter into a contract with Contractor to replace the roof on a structure. The proposed transaction involves Contractor removing the existing shingles and installing new shingles, which Contractor is to provide. Contractor responds with a confirmation purporting to accept but containing additional and different terms. The transaction is a hybrid transaction because it involves the passing of title to the new shingles and the provision of services. If the sale-of-goods aspects of the transaction do not predominate, this Article does not apply to determine whether a contract was formed. That issue is governed by other law.

Example 5. Under the facts of Example 1, assume that the sale-of-goods aspects of the transaction do not predominate. The agreement provides that the job will be completed by December 31. Due to unforeseen circumstances affecting the availability of supplies and labor, the job is not completed by the agreed-upon deadline. Whether Contractor's failure to perform on time is excused is determined by general contract law, rather than by this Article (Section 2-615).

Example 6. Under the facts of Example 1, assume that the sale-of-goods aspects of the transaction do not predominate. A dispute between the parties arises and during litigation one party seeks to admit evidence of usage of trade to supplement or explain the parties' written agreement. If the proffered evidence relates to the sale-of-goods aspects of the transaction, the parol evidence rule in this Article, Section 2-202 applies. If the proffered evidence relates to the other aspects of the transaction or to the transaction as a whole, other law will govern the admissibility of the evidence.

Example 7. Restaurateur hires Remodeler to remodel Restaurateur's kitchen. The transaction requires Remodeler to supply a new oven meeting detailed specifications, but the services aspects of the transaction predominate. The oven supplied does not meet a minor aspect of those specifications (but does substantially satisfy the specifications as a whole). Whether Restaurateur may reject the oven (or must retain it subject to price adjustment), whether Restaurateur has a right to cover by purchasing a substitute oven, and the measure of Restaurateur's damages for the oven's nonconformity to the specifications are determined by this Article.

Example 8. Restaurateur hires Remodeler to remodel Restaurateur's kitchen by a specified completion date. The transaction requires Remodeler to supply a new oven, but the services aspects of the transaction predominate. Remodeler breaches by failing to complete the project by the specified date. The measure of Restaurateur's damages for Remodeler's failure to timely complete the project is not determined by this Article.

6. The rules of subsections (1) and (2) are essentially gap fillers that apply when the parties' agreement is silent on what legal rules govern the different aspects of their transaction. In general, parties are free to preclude the application of this Article to the aspects of their transaction that are not about the sale of goods.

Example 9. Robotics Manufacturer contracts to design, build, and sell customized robotics to Car Maker. The transaction includes a sale of goods and the provision of services and is therefore a hybrid transaction. Assume that the sale-of-goods aspects predominate. The parties may, in their agreement, provide that Article 2 does not govern the services aspects of the transaction.

As Example 9 illustrates, parties may agree that Article 2 will not govern non-goods aspects of a hybrid transaction, even though the sale-of-goods aspects predominate. But, when sale-of-goods aspects predominate, the parties cannot agree that Article 2 does not govern matters that relate to the transaction as a whole, such as contract formation and enforceability. For example, in a situation such as Example 9, if the requirements of the Section 2-201 statute of frauds are not satisfied, it would make little sense to hold that the services aspects of the transaction are enforceable when the provision of services is clearly dependent on the existence of the sale-of- goods aspects. Of course, even when this Article applies, its provisions may be varied by agreement to the extent provided in section 1-302.

Cross Reference: Article 9

Definitional Cross References:

"Contract".	Section 1-201.
"Contract for sale".	Section 2-106.
"Goods".	Section 2-106.
"Present sale".	Section 2-106.
"Sale".	Section 2-106.

Section 2-103. Definitions and Index of Definitions

(1) In this Article unless the context otherwise requires

(a) "Buyer" means a person who buys or contracts to buy goods.

(b) [Reserved]

(c) "Receipt" of goods means taking physical possession of them.

(d) "Seller" means a person who sells or contracts to sell goods.

(2) Other definitions applying to this Article or to specified Parts thereof, and the sections in which they appear are:

"Acceptance".	Section 2-606.
"Banker's credit".	Section 2-325.
"Between merchants".	Section 2-104.
"Cancellation".	Section 2-106(4).
"Commercial unit".	Section 2-105.
"Confirmed credit".	Section 2-325.
"Conforming to contract".	Section 2-106.
"Contract for sale".	Section 2-106.
"Cover".	Section 2-712.
"Entrusting".	Section 2-403.
"Financing agency".	Section 2-104.
"Future goods".	Section 2-105.
"Goods".	Section 2-105.
"Identification".	Section 2-501.
"Installment contract".	Section 2-612.
"Letter of Credit".	Section 2-325.
"Lot".	Section 2-105.
"Merchant".	Section 2-104.
"Overseas".	Section 2-323.
"Person in position of seller".	Section 2-707.
"Present sale".	Section 2-106.
"Sale".	Section 2-106.
"Sale on approval".	Section 2-326.
"Sale or return".	Section 2-326.
"Termination".	Section 2-106.

(3) The following definitions in other Articles apply to this Article:

"Check".	Section 3-104.
"Consignee".	Section 7-102.
"Consignor".	Section 7-102.
"Consumer goods".	Section 9-102.
"Dishonor".	Section 3-502.
"Draft".	Section 3-104.

(4) In addition Article 1 contains general definitions and principles of construction and interpretation applicable throughout this Article.

As amended in 1994, 1999, and 2001.

Official Comment

Prior Uniform Statutory Provision: Subsection (1): Section 76, Uniform Sales Act.

Changes: The definitions of "buyer" and "seller" have been slightly rephrased, the reference in Section 76 of the prior Act to "any legal successor in interest of such person" being omitted. The definition of "receipt" is new.

Purposes of Changes and New Matter:

1. The phrase "any legal successor in interest of such person" has been eliminated since Section 2-210 of this Article, which limits some types of delegation of performance on assignment of a sales contract, makes it clear that not every such successor can be safely included in the definition. In every ordinary case, however, such successors are as of course included.

2. "Receipt" must be distinguished from delivery particularly in regard to the problems arising out of shipment of goods, whether or not the contract calls for making delivery by way of documents of title, since the seller may frequently fulfill his obligations to "deliver" even though the buyer may never "receive" the goods. Delivery with respect to documents of title is defined in Article 1 and requires transfer of physical delivery. Otherwise the many divergent incidents of delivery are handled incident by incident.

Cross References:

Point 1: See Section 2-210 and Comment thereon.

Point 2: Section 1-201.

Definitional Cross Reference:

"Person". Section 1-201.

Section 2-104. Definitions: "Merchant"; "Between Merchants"; "Financing Agency"

(1) "Merchant" means a person who deals in goods of the kind or otherwise by his occupation holds himself out as having knowledge or skill peculiar to the practices or goods involved in the transaction or to whom such knowledge or skill may be attributed by his employment of an agent or broker or other intermediary who by his occupation holds himself out as having such knowledge or skill.

(2) "Financing agency" means a bank, finance company or other person who in the ordinary course of business makes advances against goods or documents of title or who by arrangement with either the seller or the buyer intervenes in ordinary course to make or collect payment due or claimed under the contract for sale, as by purchasing or paying the seller's draft or making advances against it or by merely taking it for collection whether or not documents of title accompany the draft. "Financing agency" includes also a bank or other person who similarly intervenes between persons who are in the position of seller and buyer in respect to the goods (Section 2-707).

(3) "Between merchants" means in any transaction with respect to which both parties are chargeable with the knowledge or skill of merchants.

Official Comment

Prior Uniform Statutory Provision: None. But see Sections 15(2), (5), 16(c), 45(2) and 71, Uniform Sales Act, and Sections 35 and 37, Uniform Bills of Lading Act for examples of the policy expressly provided for in this Article.

Purposes:

1. This Article assumes that transactions between professionals in a given field require special and clear rules which may not apply to a casual or inexperienced seller or buyer. It thus adopts a policy of expressly stating rules applicable "between merchants" and "as against a merchant", wherever they are needed instead of making them depend upon the circumstances of each case as in the statutes cited above. This section lays the foundation of this policy by defining those who are to be regarded as professionals or "merchants" and by stating when a transaction is deemed to be "between merchants".

2. The term "merchant" as defined here roots in the "law merchant" concept of a professional in business. The professional status under the definition may be based upon specialized knowledge as to the goods, specialized knowledge as to business practices, or specialized knowledge as to both and which kind of specialized knowledge may be sufficient to establish the merchant status is indicated by the nature of the provisions.

The special provisions as to merchants appear only in this Article and they are of three kinds. Sections 2-201(2), 2-205, 2-207 and 2-209 dealing with the statute of frauds, firm offers, confirmatory memoranda and modification rest on normal business practices which are or ought to be typical of and familiar to any person in business. For purposes of these sections almost every person in business would, therefore, be deemed to be a "merchant" under the language "who . . . by his occupation holds himself out as having knowledge or skill peculiar to the practices . . . involved in the transaction . . ." since the practices involved in the transaction are non-specialized business practices such as answering mail. In this type of provision, banks or even universities, for example, well may be "merchants". But even these sections only apply to a merchant in his mercantile capacity; a lawyer or bank president buying fishing tackle for his own use is not a merchant.

On the other hand, in Section 2-314 on the warranty of merchantability, such warranty is implied only "if the seller is a merchant with respect to goods of that kind". Obviously this qualification restricts the implied warranty to a much smaller group than everyone who is engaged in business and requires a professional status as to particular kinds of goods. The exception in Section 2-402(2) for retention of possession by a merchant-seller falls in the same class; as does Section 2-403(2) on entrusting of possession to a merchant "who deals in goods of that kind".

A third group of sections includes 2-327(1)(c), 2-603 and 2-605, dealing with responsibilities of merchant buyers to follow seller's instructions, etc.; 2-509 on risk of loss, and 2-609 on adequate assurance of performance. This group of sections applies to persons who are merchants under either the "practices" or the "goods" aspect of the definition of merchant.

3. The "or to whom such knowledge or skill may be attributed by his employment of an agent or broker . . ." clause of the definition of merchant means that even persons such as universities, for example, can come within the definition of merchant if they have regular purchasing departments or business personnel who are familiar with business practices and who are equipped to take any action required.

Cross References:

Point 1: See Sections 1-102 and 1-304.

Point 2: See Sections 2-314, 2-315, 2-320 to 2-325, and Article 9.

Definitional Cross References:

"Bank".	Section 1-201.
"Buyer".	Section 2-103.
"Contract for sale".	Section 2-106.
"Document of title".	Section 1-201.
"Draft".	Section 3-104.
"Goods".	Section 2-105.
"Person".	Section 1-201.
"Purchase".	Section 1-201.
"Seller".	Section 2-103.

Section 2-105. Definitions: Transferability; "Goods"; "Future" Goods; "Lot"; "Commercial Unit"

(1) "Goods" means all things (including specially manufactured goods) which are movable at the time of identification to the contract for sale other than the money in which the price is to be paid, investment securities (Article 8) and things in action. "Goods" also includes the unborn young of animals and growing crops and other identified things attached to realty as described in the section on goods to be severed from realty (Section 2-107).

(2) Goods must be both existing and identified before any interest in them can pass. Goods which are not both existing and identified are "future" goods. A purported present sale of future goods or of any interest therein operates as a contract to sell.

(3) There may be a sale of a part interest in existing identified goods.

(4) An undivided share in an identified bulk of fungible goods is sufficiently identified to be sold although the quantity of the bulk is not determined. Any agreed proportion of such a bulk or any quantity thereof agreed upon by number, weight or other measure may to the extent of the seller's interest in the bulk be sold to the buyer who then becomes an owner in common.

(5) "Lot" means a parcel or a single article which is the subject matter of a separate sale or delivery, whether or not it is sufficient to perform the contract.

(6) "Commercial unit" means such a unit of goods as by commercial usage is a single whole for purposes of sale and division of which materially impairs its character or value on the market or in use. A commercial unit may be a single article (as a machine) or a set of articles (as a suite of furniture or an assortment of sizes) or a quantity (as a bale, gross, or carload) or any other unit treated in use or in the relevant market as a single whole.

Official Comment

Prior Uniform Statutory Provision: Subsections (1), (2), (3) and (4)—Sections 5, 6 and 76, Uniform Sales Act; Subsections (5) and (6)—none.

Changes: Rewritten.

Purposes of Changes and New Matter:

1. Subsection (1) on "goods": The phraseology of the prior uniform statutory provision has been changed so that:

The definition of goods is based on the concept of movability and the term "chattels personal" is not used. It is not intended to deal with things which are not fairly identifiable as movables before the contract is performed.

Growing crops are included within the definition of goods since they are frequently intended for sale. The concept of "industrial" growing crops has been abandoned, for under modern practices fruit, perennial hay, nursery stock and the like must be brought within the scope of this Article. The young of animals are also included expressly in this definition since they, too, are frequently intended for sale and may be contracted for before birth. The period of gestation of domestic animals is such that the provisions of the section on identification can apply as in the case of crops to be planted. The reason of this definition also leads to the inclusion of a wool crop or the like as "goods" subject to identification under this Article.

The exclusion of "money in which the price is to be paid" from the definition of goods does not mean that foreign currency which is included in the definition of money may not be the subject matter of a sales transaction. Goods is intended to cover the sale of money when money is being treated as a commodity but not to include it when money is the medium of payment.

As to contracts to sell timber, minerals, or structures to be removed from the land Section 2-107(1) (Goods to be severed from Realty: recording) controls.

The use of the word "fixtures" is avoided in view of the diversity of definitions of that term. This Article in including within its scope "things attached to realty" adds the further test that they must be capable of severance without material harm thereto. As between the parties any identified things which fall within that definition become "goods" upon the making of the contract for sale.

"Investment securities" are expressly excluded from the coverage of this Article. It is not intended by this exclusion, however, to prevent the application of a particular section of this Article by analogy to securities (as was done with the Original Sales Act in *Agar v. Orda,* 190 N.E. 479 (N.Y. 1934)) when the reason of that section makes such application sensible and the situation involved is not covered by the Article of this Act dealing specifically with such securities (Article 8).

2. References to the fact that a contract for sale can extend to future or contingent goods and that ownership in common follows the sale of a part interest have been omitted here as obvious without need for expression; hence no inference to negate these principles should be drawn from their omission.

3. Subsection (4) does not touch the question of how far an appropriation of a bulk of fungible goods may or may not satisfy the contract for sale.

4. Subsections (5) and (6) on "lot" and "commercial unit" are introduced to aid in the phrasing of later sections.

5. The question of when an identification of goods takes place is determined by the provisions of Section 2-501 and all that this section says is what kinds of goods may be the subject of a sale.

Cross References:

Point 1: Sections 2-107, 2-201, 2-501 and Article 8.

Point 5: Section 2-501.

See also Section 1-201.

Definitional Cross References:

"Buyer".	Section 2-103.
"Contract".	Section 1-201.
"Contract for sale".	Section 2-106.
"Fungible".	Section 1-201.
"Money".	Section 1-201.
"Present sale".	Section 2-106.
"Sale".	Section 2-106.
"Seller".	Section 2-103.

Section 2-106. Definitions: "Contract"; "Agreement"; "Contract for Sale"; "Sale"; "Present Sale"; "Conforming" to Contract; "Termination"; "Cancellation"

(1) In this Article unless the context otherwise requires "contract" and "agreement" are limited to those relating to the present or future sale of goods. "Contract for sale" includes both a present sale of goods and a contract to sell goods at a future time. A "sale" consists in the passing of title from the seller to the buyer for a price (Section 2-401). A "present sale" means a sale which is accomplished by the making of the contract.

(2) Goods or conduct including any part of a performance are "conforming" or conform to the contract when they are in accordance with the obligations under the contract.

(3) "Termination" occurs when either party pursuant to a power created by agreement or law puts an end to the contract otherwise than for its breach. On "termination" all obligations which are still executory on both sides are discharged but any right based on prior breach or performance survives.

(4) "Cancellation" occurs when either party puts an end to the contract for breach by the other and its effect is the same as that of "termination" except that the cancelling party also retains any remedy for breach of the whole contract or any unperformed balance.

(5) "Hybrid transaction" means a single transaction involving a sale of goods and:

(a) the provision of services;

(b) a lease of other goods; or

(c) a sale, lease, or license of property other than goods.

Official Comment

Prior Uniform Statutory Provision: Subsection (1)—Section 1(1) and (2), Uniform Sales Act; Subsection (2)—none, but subsection generally continues policy of Sections 11, 44 and 69, Uniform Sales Act; Subsections (3) and (4)—none.

Changes: Completely rewritten.

Purposes:

1. Subsection (1): "Contract for sale" is used as a general concept throughout this Article, but the rights of the parties do not vary according to whether the transaction is a present sale or a contract to sell unless the Article expressly so provides.

2. Subsection (2): It is in general intended to continue the policy of requiring exact performance by the seller of his obligations as a condition to his right to require acceptance. However, the seller is in part safeguarded against surprise as a result of sudden technicality on the buyer's part by the provisions of Section 2-508 on seller's cure of improper tender or delivery. Moreover usage of trade frequently permits commercial leeways in performance and the language of the agreement itself must be read in the light of such custom or usage and also, prior course of dealing, and in a long term contract, the course of performance.

3. Subsections (3) and (4): These subsections are intended to make clear the distinction carried forward throughout this Article between termination and cancellation.

4. In some transactions, the passing of title to goods from the seller to the buyer in return for a price is part of a larger transaction. The other aspects of the transaction might involve the seller providing services to the buyer, the seller leasing other goods to the buyer, or the seller transferring to the buyer rights to property other than goods. Such a transaction is a "hybrid transaction," as defined in subsection (5). Section 2-102 indicates the extent to which this Article applies to a hybrid transaction.

5. A hybrid transaction is a single transaction. If contracting parties enter into separate agreements at the same time, each agreement creating a separate transaction, each transaction must be evaluated separately to determine if it is a hybrid transaction.

> **Example 1.** To sell an ongoing business, Seller and Buyer enter into three separate written agreements: (i) a sale of goods used in the business; (ii) an agreement for Seller to provide consulting services to Buyer for a period of six months; and (iii) a sale of intangible assets associated with the business. Each agreement creates a separate transaction. None of those transactions involves both a sale of goods and the provision of services, the lease of other

goods, or the sale, lease, or license of property other than goods. Thus, none of the separate transactions constitutes a hybrid transaction.

Example 2. To sell an ongoing business, Seller and Buyer enter into two separate written agreements: (i) a sale of goods and intangible assets used in the business; and (ii) an agreement for Seller to provide consulting services to Buyer for a period of six months, and not to compete with Buyer for a period of one year. The agreement to sell goods and intangible assets creates a hybrid transaction. The agreement for consulting services, a separate transaction, is not a hybrid transaction.

Even when contracting parties enter into a single agreement involving both a sale of goods and a sale, lease, or license of other property or the provision of services, the elements of the single agreement may be so independent that they create separate transactions. In that case, no hybrid transaction would exist merely because the separate transactions arose out of the same agreement.

Example 3. Farmer A and Farmer B sign a written agreement pursuant to which Farmer A will sell a tractor to Farmer B and Farmer A will board and feed Farmer B's cattle until the cattle are sold. The agreement specifies a price for the tractor, which is due upon delivery, and specifies a mechanism for determining the price for Farmer A's services, which is to be paid when the cattle are sold. The parties would have entered into an agreement to buy and sell the tractor even if they had not entered into an agreement to board and feed the cattle, and vice versa. Two separate transactions arise from the single agreement, neither of which is a hybrid transaction. Article 2 applies to the sale of the tractor. Other law applies to the agreement to board and feed the cattle.

Example 4. In a single record, Landscaper agrees to sell plants to Homeowner and to install the plants on Homeowner's property. The agreement specifies a total price but provides no mechanism for determining what portion of the price is allocable to the sale of plants and what portion is allocable to the installation services. Because the terms of the agreement relating to the sale of goods and those relating to services are not severable, the transaction is a hybrid transaction.

Cross References: Point 2: Sections 1-303, 1-304 and 2-508.

Definitional Cross References:

"Agreement".	Section 1-201.
"Buyer".	Section 2-103.
"Contract".	Section 1-201.
"Goods".	Section 2-105.
"Party".	Section 1-201.
"Remedy".	Section 1-201.
"Right".	Section 1-201.
"Seller".	Section 2-103.

Section 2-107. Goods to Be Severed from Realty: Recording

(1) A contract for the sale of minerals or the like (including oil and gas) or a structure or its materials to be removed from realty is a contract for the sale of goods within this Article if they are to be severed by the seller but until severance a purported present sale thereof which is not effective as a transfer of an interest in land is effective only as a contract to sell.

(2) A contract for the sale apart from the land of growing crops or other things attached to realty and capable of severance without material harm thereto but not described in subsection (1) or of timber to be cut is a contract for the sale of goods within this Article whether the subject matter is to be severed by the buyer or by the seller even though it forms part of the realty at the time of contracting, and the parties can by identification effect a present sale before severance.

(3) The provisions of this section are subject to any third party rights provided by the law relating to realty records, and the contract for sale may be executed and recorded as a document transferring an interest in land and shall then constitute notice to third parties of the buyer's rights under the contract for sale.

As amended in 1972.

Official Comment

Prior Uniform Statutory Provision: See Section 76, Uniform Sales Act on prior policy; Section 7, Uniform Conditional Sales Act.

Purposes:

1. Subsection (1). Notice that this subsection applies only if the minerals or structures "are to be severed by the seller". If the buyer is to sever, such transactions are considered contracts affecting land and all problems of the Statute of Frauds and of the recording of land rights apply to them. Therefore, the Statute of Frauds section of this Article does not apply to such contracts though they must conform to the Statute of Frauds affecting the transfer of interests in land.

2. Subsection (2). "Things attached" to the realty which can be severed without material harm are goods within this Article regardless of who is to effect the severance. The word "fixtures" has been avoided because of the diverse definitions of this term, the test of "severance without material harm" being substituted.

The provision in subsection (3) for recording such contracts is within the purview of this Article since it is a means of preserving the buyer's rights under the contract of sale.

3. The security phases of things attached to or to become attached to realty are dealt with in the Article on Secured Transactions (Article 9) and it is to be noted that the definition of goods in that Article differs from the definition of goods in this Article.

However, both Articles treat as goods growing crops and also timber to be cut under a contract of severance.

Cross References:

Point 1:	Section 2-201.
Point 2:	Section 2-105.
Point 3:	Articles 9 and 9-105.

Definitional Cross References:

"Buyer".	Section 2-103.
"Contract".	Section 1-201.
"Contract for sale".	Section 2-106.
"Goods".	Section 2-105.
"Party".	Section 1-201.
"Present sale".	Section 2-106.
"Right".	Section 1-201.
"Seller".	Section 2-103.

PART 2. FORM, FORMATION AND READJUSTMENT OF CONTRACT

Section 2-201. Formal Requirements; Statute of Frauds

(1) Except as otherwise provided in this section a contract for the sale of goods for the price of $500 or more is not enforceable by way of action or defense unless there is a record sufficient to indicate that a contract for sale has been made between the parties and signed by the party against whom enforcement is sought or by the party's authorized agent or broker. A record is not insufficient because it omits or incorrectly states a term agreed upon but the contract is not enforceable under this subsection beyond the quantity of goods shown in the record.

(2) Between merchants if within a reasonable time a record in confirmation of the contract and sufficient against the sender is received and the party receiving it has reason to know its contents, it satisfies the requirements of subsection (1) against the party unless notice in a record of objection to its contents is given within 10 days after it is received.

(3) A contract which does not satisfy the requirements of subsection (1) but which is valid in other respects is enforceable

(a) if the goods are to be specially manufactured for the buyer and are not suitable for sale to others in the ordinary course of the seller's business and the seller, before notice of repudiation is received and under circumstances which reasonably indicate that the goods are for the buyer, has made either a substantial beginning of their manufacture or commitments for their procurement; or

(b) if the party against whom enforcement is sought admits in his pleading, testimony or otherwise in court that a contract for sale was made, but the contract is not enforceable under this provision beyond the quantity of goods admitted; or

(c) with respect to goods for which payment has been made and accepted or which have been received and accepted (Section 2-606).

Official Comment

Prior Uniform Statutory Provision: Section 4, Uniform Sales Act (which was based on Section 17 of the Statute of 29 Charles II).

Changes: Completely rephrased; restricted to sale of goods. See also Sections 2A-201, 5-104, and 9-203.

Purposes: This section is intended to make it clear that:

1. The required record need not contain all the material terms of the contract and such material terms as are stated need not be precisely stated. All that is required is that the record afford a basis for believing that the offered oral evidence rests on a real transaction. It may be written in lead pencil on a scratch pad or another medium. It need not indicate which party is the buyer and which the seller. The only term which must appear is the quantity term which need not be accurately stated but recovery is limited to the amount stated. The price, time and place of payment or delivery, the general quality of the goods, or any particular warranties may all be omitted.

Special emphasis must be placed on the permissibility of omitting the price term in view of the insistence of some courts on the express inclusion of this term even where the parties have contracted on the basis of a published price list. In many valid contracts for sale the parties do not mention the price in express terms, the buyer being bound to pay and the seller to accept a reasonable price which the trier of the fact may well be trusted to determine. Again, frequently the price is not mentioned since the parties have based their agreement on a price list or catalogue known to both of them and this list serves as an efficient safeguard against perjury. Finally, "market" prices and valuations that are current in the vicinity constitute a similar check. Thus if the price is not stated in the record evidencing the contract it can normally be supplied without danger of fraud. Of course if the "price" consists of goods rather than money the quantity of goods must be stated.

Only three definite and invariable requirements as to the record are made by this subsection. First, it must evidence a contract for the sale of goods; second, it must be "signed", a word which includes any authentication which identifies the party to be charged; and third, it must specify a quantity.

2. "Partial performance" as a substitute for the required memorandum can validate the contract only for the goods which have been accepted or for which payment has been made and accepted.

Receipt and acceptance either of goods or of the price constitutes an unambiguous overt admission by both parties that a contract actually exists. If the court can make a just apportionment, therefore, the agreed price of any goods actually delivered can be recovered without a writing or, if the price has been paid, the seller can be forced to deliver an apportionable part of the goods. The overt actions of the parties make admissible evidence of the other terms of the contract necessary to a just apportionment. This is true even though the actions of the parties are not in themselves inconsistent with a different transaction such as a consignment for resale or a mere loan of money.

Part performance by the buyer requires the delivery of something by him that is accepted by the seller as such performance. Thus, part payment may be made by money or check, accepted by the seller. If the agreed price consists of goods or services, then they must also have been delivered and accepted.

3. Between merchants, failure to answer a record confirming a contract within ten days of receipt is tantamount to a record under subsection (2) and is sufficient against both parties under subsection (1). The only effect, however, is to take away from the party who fails to answer the defense of the Statute of Frauds; the burden of persuading the trier of fact that a contract was in fact made orally prior to giving a record confirming a contract is unaffected. Compare the effect of a failure to reply under Section 2-207.

4. Failure to satisfy the requirements of this section does not render the contract void for all purposes, but merely prevents it from being judicially enforced in favor of a party to the contract. For example, a buyer who takes possession of goods as provided in an oral contract which the seller has not meanwhile repudiated, is not a trespasser. Nor would the Statute of Frauds provisions of this section be a defense to a third person who wrongfully induces a party to refuse to perform an oral contract, even though the injured party cannot maintain an action for damages against the party so refusing to perform.

5. The requirement of "signing" is discussed in Section 1-201, Comment 37.

6. For purposes of subsection (1), it is not necessary that the record be delivered to anybody. It need not be signed or authenticated by both parties but it is, of course, not sufficient against one who has not signed it. Prior to a dispute no one can determine which party's signing of the memorandum may be necessary but from the time of contracting each party should be aware that to him it is signing by the other which is important.

7. If the making of a contract is admitted in court, either in a written pleading, by stipulation or by oral statement before the court, no additional record is necessary for protection against fraud. Under this section it is no longer possible to admit the contract in court and still treat the Statute as a defense. However, the contract is not thus conclusively established. The admission so made by a party is itself evidential against him of the truth of the facts so admitted and of nothing more; as against the other party, it is not evidential at all.

8. In furtherance of medium neutrality, references to "writing" and "written" in the pre-2022 text of this section have been changed to refer to a "record."

Cross References: See Sections 1-201, 2-202, 2-207, 2-209 and 2-304.

Definitional Cross References:

"Action".	Section 1-201.
"Between merchants".	Section 2-104.
"Buyer".	Section 2-103.
"Contract".	Section 1-201.
"Contract for sale".	Section 2-106.
"Goods".	Section 2-105.
"Notice".	Section 1-202.
"Party".	Section 1-201.
"Reasonable time".	Section 1-205.
"Sale".	Section 2-106.
"Seller".	Section 2-103.

Section 2-202. Final Expression: Parol or Extrinsic Evidence

Terms with respect to which the confirmatory memoranda of the parties agree or which are otherwise set forth in a record intended by the parties as a final expression of their agreement with respect to such terms as are included therein may not be contradicted by evidence of any prior agreement or of a contemporaneous oral agreement but may be explained or supplemented:

(a) by course of performance, course of dealing, or usage of trade (Section 1-303); and

(b) by evidence of consistent additional terms unless the court finds the record to have been intended also as a complete and exclusive statement of the terms of the agreement.

Official Comment

Prior Uniform Statutory Provisions: None.

Purposes:

1. This section definitely rejects:

(a) Any assumption that because a record has been worked out which is final on some matters, it is to be taken as including all the matters agreed upon;

(b) The premise that the language used has the meaning attributable to such language by rules of construction existing in the law rather than the meaning which arises out of the commercial context in which it was used; and

(c) The requirement that a condition precedent to the admissibility of the type of evidence specified in paragraph (a) is an original determination by the court that the language used is ambiguous.

2. Paragraph (a) makes admissible evidence of course of dealing, usage of trade and course of performance to explain or supplement the terms of any record stating the agreement of the parties in order that the true understanding of the parties as to the agreement may be reached. Such records are to be read on the assumption that the course of prior dealings between the parties and the usages of trade were taken for granted when the document was phrased. Unless carefully negated they have become an element of the meaning of the words used. Similarly, the course of actual performance by the parties is considered the best indication of what they intended the record to mean.

3. Under paragraph (b) consistent additional terms, not reduced to a record, may be proved unless the court finds that the record was intended by both parties as a complete and exclusive statement of all the terms. If the additional terms are such that, if agreed upon, they would certainly have been included in the record in the view of the court, then evidence of their alleged making must be kept from the trier of fact.

4. In furtherance of medium neutrality, references to "writing" and "written" in the pre-2022 text of this section have been changed to refer to a "record."

Cross References: Point 3: Sections 1-303, 2-207, 2-302 and 2-316.

Definitional Cross References:

"Agreed" and "agreement".	Section 1-201.
"Course of dealing".	Section 1-303.
"Course of performance".	Section 1-303.
"Party".	Section 1-201.
"Term".	Section 1-201.
"Usage of trade".	Section 1-303.
"Written" and "writing".	Section 1-201.

Section 2-203. Seals Inoperative

The affixing of a seal to a record evidencing a contract for sale or an offer to buy or sell goods does not constitute the record a sealed instrument and the law with respect to sealed instruments does not apply to such a contract or offer.

Official Comment

Prior Uniform Statutory Provision: Section 3, Uniform Sales Act.

Changes: Portion pertaining to "seals" rewritten.

Purposes of Changes:

1. This section makes it clear that every effect of the seal which relates to "sealed instruments" as such is wiped out insofar as contracts for sale are concerned. However, the substantial effects of a seal, except extension of the period of limitations, may be had by appropriate drafting as in the case of firm offers (see Section 2-205).

2. This section leaves untouched any aspects of a seal which relate merely to signatures or to authentication of execution and the like. Thus, a statute providing that a purported signature gives prima facie evidence of its own authenticity or that a signature gives prima facie evidence of consideration is still applicable to sales transactions even though a seal may be held to be a signature within the meaning of such a statute. Similarly, the authorized affixing of a corporate seal bearing the corporate name to a contractual writing purporting to be made by the corporation may have effect as a signature without any reference to the law of sealed instruments.

3. In furtherance of medium neutrality, references to "writing" and "written" in the pre-2022 text of this section have been changed to refer to a "record."

Cross Reference: Point 1: Section 2-205.

Definitional Cross References:

"Contract for sale".	Section 2-106.
"Goods".	Section 2-105.
"Writing".	Section 1-201.

Section 2-204. Formation in General

(1) A contract for sale of goods may be made in any manner sufficient to show agreement, including conduct by both parties which recognizes the existence of such a contract.

(2) An agreement sufficient to constitute a contract for sale may be found even though the moment of its making is undetermined.

(3) Even though one or more terms are left open a contract for sale does not fail for indefiniteness if the parties have intended to make a contract and there is a reasonably certain basis for giving an appropriate remedy.

Official Comment

Prior Uniform Statutory Provision: Sections 1 and 3, Uniform Sales Act.

Changes: Completely rewritten by this and other sections of this Article.

Purposes of Changes:

Subsection (1) continues without change the basic policy of recognizing any manner of expression of agreement, oral, written or otherwise. The legal effect of such an agreement is, of course, qualified by other provisions of this Article.

Under subsection (1) appropriate conduct by the parties may be sufficient to establish an agreement. Subsection (2) is directed primarily to the situation where the interchanged correspondence does not disclose the exact point at which the deal was closed, but the actions of the parties indicate that a binding obligation has been undertaken.

Subsection (3) states the principle as to "open terms" underlying later sections of the Article. If the parties intend to enter into a binding agreement, this subsection recognizes that agreement as valid in law, despite missing terms, if there is any reasonably certain basis for granting a remedy. The test is not certainty as to what the parties were to do nor as to the exact amount of damages due the plaintiff. Nor is the fact that one or more terms are left to be agreed upon enough of itself to defeat an otherwise adequate agreement. Rather, commercial standards on the point of "indefiniteness" are intended to be applied, this Act making provision elsewhere for missing terms needed for performance, open price, remedies and the like.

The more terms the parties leave open, the less likely it is that they have intended to conclude a binding agreement, but their actions may be frequently conclusive on the matter despite the omissions.

Cross References:

Subsection (1):	Sections 1-103, 2-201 and 2-302.
Subsection (2):	Sections 2-205 through 2-209.
Subsection (3):	See Part 3.

Definitional Cross References:

"Agreement".	Section 1-201.
"Contract".	Section 1-201.
"Contract for sale".	Section 2-106.
"Goods".	Section 2-105.

"Party".	Section 1-201.
"Remedy".	Section 1-201.
"Term".	Section 1-201.

Section 2-205. Firm Offers

An offer by a merchant to buy or sell goods in a signed record which by its terms gives assurance that it will be held open is not revocable, for lack of consideration, during the time stated or if no time is stated for a reasonable time, but in no event may such period of irrevocability exceed three months; but any such term of assurance on a form supplied by the offeree must be separately signed by the offeror.

Official Comment

Prior Uniform Statutory Provision: Sections 1 and 3, Uniform Sales Act.

Changes: Completely rewritten by this and other sections of this Article.

Purposes:

1. This section is intended to modify the former rule which required that "firm offers" be sustained by consideration in order to bind, and to require instead that they must merely be characterized as such and expressed in signed records.

2. The primary purpose of this section is to give effect to the deliberate intention of a merchant to make a current firm offer binding. The deliberation is shown in the case of an individualized document by the merchant's signature to the offer, and in the case of an offer included on a form supplied by the other party to the transaction by the separate signing of the particular clause which contains the offer. "Signed" here also includes authentication but the reasonableness of the authentication herein allowed must be determined in the light of the purpose of the section. The circumstances surrounding the signing may justify something less than a formal signature or initialing but typically the kind of authentication involved here would consist of a minimum of initialing of the clause involved. A handwritten memorandum on the writer's letterhead purporting in its terms to "confirm" a firm offer already made would be enough to satisfy this section, although not subscribed, since under the circumstances it could not be considered a memorandum of mere negotiation and it would adequately show its own authenticity. Similarly, an authorized telegram will suffice, and this is true even though the original draft contained only a typewritten signature. See generally Section 1-201(b)(37) (defining "sign") and Comment 37. However, despite settled courses of dealing or usages of the trade whereby firm offers are made by oral communication and relied upon without more evidence, such offers remain revocable under this Article since authentication by a writing is the essence of this section.

3. This section is intended to apply to current "firm" offers and not to long term options, and an outside time limit of three months during which such offers remain irrevocable has been set. The three month period during which firm offers remain irrevocable under this section need not be stated by days or by date. If the offer states that it is "guaranteed" or "firm" until the happening of a contingency which will occur within the three month period, it will remain irrevocable until that event. A promise made for a longer period will operate under this section to bind the offeror only for the first three months of the period but may of course be renewed. If supported by consideration it may continue for as long as the parties specify. This section deals only with the offer which is not supported by consideration.

4. Protection is afforded against the inadvertent signing of a firm offer when contained in a form prepared by the offeree by requiring that such a clause be separately authenticated. If the offer clause is called to the offeror's attention and he separately authenticates it, he will be bound; Section 2-302 may operate, however, to prevent an unconscionable result which otherwise would flow from other terms appearing in the form.

5. Safeguards are provided to offer relief in the case of material mistake by virtue of the requirement of good faith and the general law of mistake.

6. In furtherance of medium neutrality, references to "writing" and "written" in the pre-2022 text of this section have been changed to refer to a "record."

Cross References:

Point 1:	Section 1-103.
Point 2:	Section 1-103.
Point 3:	Section 2-201.
Point 5:	Section 2-302.

Definitional Cross References:

"Goods".	Section 2-105.
"Merchant".	Section 2-104.
"Record".	Section 1-201.
"Signed".	Section 1-201.

Section 2-206. Offer and Acceptance in Formation of Contract

(1) Unless otherwise unambiguously indicated by the language or circumstances

(a) an offer to make a contract shall be construed as inviting acceptance in any manner and by any medium reasonable in the circumstances;

(b) an order or other offer to buy goods for prompt or current shipment shall be construed as inviting acceptance either by a prompt promise to ship or by the prompt or current shipment of conforming or non-conforming goods, but such a shipment of non-conforming goods does not constitute an acceptance if the seller seasonably notifies the buyer that the shipment is offered only as an accommodation to the buyer.

(2) Where the beginning of a requested performance is a reasonable mode of acceptance an offeror who is not notified of acceptance within a reasonable time may treat the offer as having lapsed before acceptance.

Official Comment

Prior Uniform Statutory Provision: Sections 1 and 3, Uniform Sales Act.

Changes: Completely rewritten in this and other sections of this Article.

Purposes of Changes: To make it clear that:

1. Any reasonable manner of acceptance is intended to be regarded as available unless the offeror has made quite clear that it will not be acceptable. Former technical rules as to acceptance, such as requiring that telegraphic offers be accepted by telegraphed acceptance, etc., are rejected and a criterion that the acceptance be "in any manner and by any medium reasonable under the circumstances", is substituted. This section is intended to remain flexible and its applicability to be enlarged as new media of communication develop or as the more time-saving present day media come into general use.

2. Either shipment or a prompt promise to ship is made a proper means of acceptance of an offer looking to current shipment. In accordance with ordinary commercial understanding the section interprets an order looking to current shipment as allowing acceptance either by actual shipment or by a prompt promise to ship and rejects the artificial theory that only a single mode of acceptance is normally envisaged by an offer. This is true even though the language of the offer happens to be "ship at once" or the like. "Shipment" is here used in the same sense as in Section 2-504; it does not include the beginning of delivery by the seller's own truck or by messenger. But loading on the seller's own truck might be a beginning of performance under subsection (2).

3. The beginning of performance by an offeree can be effective as acceptance so as to bind the offeror only if followed within a reasonable time by notice to the offeror. Such a beginning of performance must unambiguously express the offeree's intention to engage himself. For the protection of both parties it is essential that notice follow in due course to constitute acceptance. Nothing in this section however bars the possibility that under the common law performance begun may have an intermediate effect of temporarily barring revocation of the offer, or at the offeror's option, final effect in constituting acceptance.

4. Subsection (1)(b) deals with the situation where a shipment made following an order is shown by a notification of shipment to be referable to that order but has a defect. Such a non-conforming shipment is normally to be understood as intended to close the bargain, even though it proves to have been at the same time a breach. However, the seller by stating that the shipment is non-conforming and is offered only as an accommodation to the buyer keeps the shipment or notification from operating as an acceptance.

Definitional Cross References:

"Buyer".	Section 2-103.
"Conforming".	Section 2-106.
"Contract".	Section 1-201.
"Goods".	Section 2-105.
"Notifies".	Section 1-202.
"Reasonable time".	Section 1-205.

Section 2-207. Additional Terms in Acceptance or Confirmation

(1) A definite and seasonable expression of acceptance or a written confirmation which is sent within a reasonable time operates as an acceptance even though it states terms additional to or different from those offered or agreed upon, unless acceptance is expressly made conditional on assent to the additional or different terms.

(2) The additional terms are to be construed as proposals for addition to the contract. Between merchants such terms become part of the contract unless:

(a) the offer expressly limits acceptance to the terms of the offer;

(b) they materially alter it; or

(c) notification of objection to them has already been given or is given within a reasonable time after notice of them is received.

(3) Conduct by both parties which recognizes the existence of a contract is sufficient to establish a contract for sale although the writings of the parties do not otherwise establish a contract. In such case the terms of the particular contract consist of those terms on which the writings of the parties agree, together with any supplementary terms incorporated under any other provisions of this Act.

Official Comment

Prior Uniform Statutory Provision: Sections 1 and 3, Uniform Sales Act.

Changes: Completely rewritten by this and other sections of this Article.

Purposes of Changes:

1. This section is intended to deal with two typical situations. The one is the written confirmation, where an agreement has been reached either orally or by informal correspondence between the parties and is followed by one or both of the parties sending formal memoranda embodying the terms so far as agreed upon and adding terms not discussed. The other situation is offer and acceptance, in which a wire or letter expressed and intended as an acceptance or the closing of an agreement adds further minor suggestions or proposals such as "ship by Tuesday", "rush", "ship draft against bill of lading inspection allowed", or the like. A frequent example of the second situation is the exchange of printed purchase order and acceptance (sometimes called "acknowledgment") forms. Because the forms are oriented to the thinking of the respective drafting parties, the terms contained in them often do not correspond. Often the seller's form contains terms different from or additional to those set forth in the buyer's form. Nevertheless, the parties proceed with the transaction. [Comment 1 was amended in 1966.]

2. Under this Article a proposed deal which in commercial understanding has in fact been closed is recognized as a contract. Therefore, any additional matter contained in the confirmation or in the acceptance falls within subsection (2) and must be regarded as a proposal for an added term unless the acceptance is made conditional on the acceptance of the additional or different terms. [Comment 2 was amended in 1966.]

3. Whether or not additional or different terms will become part of the agreement depends upon the provisions of subsection (2). If they are such as materially to alter the original bargain, they will not be included unless expressly agreed to by the other party. If, however, they are terms which would not so change the bargain they will be incorporated unless notice of objection to them has already been given or is given within a reasonable time.

4. Examples of typical clauses which would normally "materially alter" the contract and so result in surprise or hardship if incorporated without express awareness by the other party are: a clause negating such standard warranties as that of merchantability or fitness for a particular purpose in circumstances in which either warranty normally attaches; a clause requiring a guaranty of 90% or 100% deliveries in a case such as a contract by cannery, where the usage of the trade allows greater quantity leeways; a clause reserving to the seller the power to cancel upon the buyer's failure to meet any invoice when due; a clause requiring that complaints be made in a time materially shorter than customary or reasonable.

5. Examples of clauses which involve no element of unreasonable surprise and which therefore are to be incorporated in the contract unless notice of objection is seasonably given are: a clause setting forth and perhaps enlarging slightly upon the seller's exemption due to supervening causes beyond his control, similar to those covered by the provision of this Article on merchant's excuse by failure of presupposed conditions or a clause fixing in advance any reasonable formula of proration under such circumstances; a clause fixing a reasonable time for complaints within customary limits, or in the case of a purchase for sub-sale, providing for inspection by the sub-purchaser; a clause providing for interest on overdue invoices or fixing the seller's standard credit terms where they are within the range of trade practice and do not limit any credit bargained for; a clause limiting the right of rejection for defects which fall within the customary trade tolerances for acceptance "with adjustment" or otherwise limiting remedy in a reasonable manner (see Sections 2-718 and 2-719).

6. If no answer is received within a reasonable time after additional terms are proposed, it is both fair and commercially sound to assume that their inclusion has been assented to. Where clauses on confirming forms sent by both parties conflict each party must be assumed to object to a clause of the other conflicting with one on the confirmation sent by himself. As a result the requirement that there be notice of objection which is found in subsection (2) is satisfied and the conflicting terms do not become a part of the contract. The contract then consists of the terms originally expressly agreed to, terms on which the confirmations agree, and terms supplied by this Act, including subsection (2). The written confirmation is also subject to Section 2-201. Under that section a failure to respond permits enforcement of a prior oral agreement; under this section a failure to respond permits additional terms to become part of the agreement. [Comment 6 was amended in 1966.]

7. In many cases, as where goods are shipped, accepted and paid for before any dispute arises, there is no question whether a contract has been made. In such cases, where the writings of the parties do not establish a contract, it is not necessary to determine which act or document constituted the offer and which the acceptance. See Section 2-204. The only question is what terms are included in the contract, and subsection (3) furnishes the governing rule. [Comment 7 was added in 1966.]

8. Pursuant to the 2022 Amendments, some references in this Article to the terms "writing," "writings," or "written" have been changed to refer to a "record." These changes are made in provisions where an affected party may be assumed to have assented to the use of a record that is not a writing. For example, Section 2-201 involves a record signed by an affected party and Section 2-202 refers to a record intended by parties to be a final expression of their agreement. However, in this section and some other sections in this Article references to these terms remain. Where such references remain in this Article, the use by parties of a record other than a writing may be given effect for purposes of this Article under law other than the Uniform Commercial Code, such as the Electronic Signatures in Global and National Commerce Act, 15 U.S.C. Section 7001, *et seq.*, and the Uniform Electronic Transactions Act.

Cross References:

See generally Section 2-302.

Point 5:	Sections 2-513, 2-602, 2-607, 2-609, 2-612, 2-614, 2-615, 2-616, 2-718 and 2-719.
Point 6:	Sections 1-103 and 2-104.

Definitional Cross References:

"Between merchants".	Section 2-104.
"Contract".	Section 1-201.
"Notification".	Section 1-202.
"Reasonable time".	Section 1-205.
"Seasonably".	Section 1-205.
"Send".	Section 1-201.
"Term".	Section 1-201.
"Written".	Section 1-201.

Editor's Note: Former UCC Section 2-208 was removed in connection with the revision of UCC Article 1. Its substance now appears in Revised UCC Section 1-303. That section formerly provided as follows:

(1) Where the contract for sale involves repeated occasions for performance by either party with knowledge of the nature of the performance and opportunity for objection to it by the other, any course of performance accepted or acquiesced in without objection shall be relevant to determine the meaning of the agreement.

(2) The express terms of the agreement and any such course of performance, as well as any course of dealing and usage of trade, shall be construed whenever reasonable as consistent with each other; but when such construction is unreasonable, express terms shall control course of performance and course of performance shall control both course of dealing and usage of trade (Section 1-205).

(3) Subject to the provisions of the next section on modification and waiver, such course of performance shall be relevant to show a waiver or modification of any term inconsistent with such course of performance.

Section 2-209. Modification, Rescission and Waiver

(1) An agreement modifying a contract within this Article needs no consideration to be binding.

(2) A signed agreement which excludes modification or rescission except by a signed writing or other record cannot be otherwise modified or rescinded, but except as between merchants such a requirement on a form supplied by the merchant must be separately signed by the other party.

(3) The requirements of the statute of frauds section of this Article (Section 2-201) must be satisfied if the contract as modified is within its provisions.

(4) Although an attempt at modification or rescission does not satisfy the requirements of subsection (2) or (3) it can operate as a waiver.

(5) A party who has made a waiver affecting an executory portion of the contract may retract the waiver by reasonable notification received by the other party that strict performance will be required of any term waived, unless the retraction would be unjust in view of a material change of position in reliance on the waiver.

Official Comment

Prior Uniform Statutory Provision: Subsection (1)—Compare Section 1, Uniform Written Obligations Act; Subsections (2) to (5)—none.

Purposes of Changes and New Matter:

1. This section seeks to protect and make effective all necessary and desirable modifications of sales contracts without regard to the technicalities which at present hamper such adjustments.

2. Subsection (1) provides that an agreement modifying a sales contract needs no consideration to be binding.

However, modifications made thereunder must meet the test of good faith imposed by this Act. The effective use of bad faith to escape performance on the original contract terms is barred, and the extortion of a "modification" without legitimate commercial reason is ineffective as a violation of the duty of good faith. Nor can a mere technical consideration support a modification made in bad faith.

The test of "good faith" includes "observance of reasonable commercial standards of fair dealing" (Section 1-201(b)(20)), and may in some situations require an objectively demonstrable reason for seeking a modification. But such matters as a market shift which makes performance come to involve a loss may provide such a reason even though there is no such unforeseen difficulty as would make out a legal excuse from performance under Sections 2-615 and 2-616.

3. Subsections (2) and (3) are intended to protect against false allegations of oral modifications. "Modification or rescission" includes abandonment or other change by mutual consent, contrary to the decision in *Green v. Doniger,* 90 N.E.2d 56 (N.Y. 1949); it does not include unilateral "termination" or "cancellation" as defined in Section 2-106.

The Statute of Frauds provisions of this Article are expressly applied to modifications by subsection (3). Under those provisions the "delivery and acceptance" test is limited to the goods which have been accepted, that is, to the past. "Modification" for the future cannot therefore be conjured up by oral testimony if the price involved is $500.00 or more since such modification must be shown at least by an authenticated memo. And since a memo is limited in its effect to the quantity of goods set forth in it there is safeguard against oral evidence.

Subsection (2) permits the parties in effect to make their own Statute of Frauds as regards any future modification of the contract by giving effect to a clause in a signed agreement which expressly requires any modification to be by signed writing or other signed record. But note that if a consumer is to be held to such a clause on a form supplied by a merchant it must be separately signed.

4. Subsection (4) is intended, despite the provisions of subsections (2) and (3), to prevent contractual provisions excluding modification except by a signed record from limiting in other respects the legal effect of the parties' actual later conduct. The effect of such conduct as a waiver is further regulated in subsection (5).

5. In furtherance of medium neutrality, references to "writing" and "written" in the pre-2022 text of this section have been changed to refer to a "record."

Cross References:

Point 1:	Section 1-304.
Point 2:	Sections 1-201, 1-304, 2-615 and 2-616.
Point 3:	Sections 2-106, 2-201 and 2-202.
Point 4:	Section 2-202.

Definitional Cross References:

"Agreement".	Section 1-201.
"Between merchants".	Section 2-104.
"Contract".	Section 1-201.
"Notification".	Section 1-202.
"Signed".	Section 1-201.
"Term".	Section 1-201.
"Writing".	Section 1-201.

Section 2-210. Delegation of Performance; Assignment of Rights

(1) A party may perform his duty through a delegate unless otherwise agreed or unless the other party has a substantial interest in having his original promisor perform or control the acts required by the contract. No delegation of performance relieves the party delegating of any duty to perform or any liability for breach.

(2) Except as otherwise provided in Section 9-406, unless otherwise agreed all rights of either seller or buyer can be assigned except where the assignment would materially change the duty of the other party, or increase materially the burden or risk imposed on him by his contract, or impair materially his chance of obtaining return performance. A right to damages for breach of the whole contract or a right arising out of the assignor's due performance of his entire obligation can be assigned despite agreement otherwise.

(3) The creation, attachment, perfection, or enforcement of a security interest in the seller's interest under a contract is not a transfer that materially changes the duty of or increases materially the burden or risk imposed on the buyer or impairs materially the buyer's chance of obtaining return performance within the purview of subsection (2) unless, and then only to the extent that, enforcement actually results in a delegation of material performance of the seller. Even in that event, the creation, attachment, perfection, and enforcement of the security interest remain effective, but (i) the seller is liable to the buyer for damages caused by the delegation to the extent that the damages could not reasonably be prevented by the buyer, and (ii) a court having jurisdiction may grant other appropriate relief, including cancellation of the contract for sale or an injunction against enforcement of the security interest or consummation of the enforcement.

(4) Unless the circumstances indicate the contrary a prohibition of assignment of "the contract" is to be construed as barring only the delegation to the assignee of the assignor's performance.

(5) An assignment of "the contract" or of "all my rights under the contract" or an assignment in similar general terms is an assignment of rights and unless the language or the circumstances (as in an assignment for security) indicate the contrary, it is a delegation of performance of the duties of the assignor and its acceptance by the assignee constitutes a promise by him to perform those duties. This promise is enforceable by either the assignor or the other party to the original contract.

(6) The other party may treat any assignment which delegates performance as creating reasonable grounds for insecurity and may without prejudice to his rights against the assignor demand assurances from the assignee (Section 2-609).

Official Comment

Prior Uniform Statutory Provision: None.

Purposes:

1. Generally, this section recognizes both delegation of performance and assignability as normal and permissible incidents of a contract for the sale of goods.

2. Delegation of performance, either in conjunction with an assignment or otherwise, is provided for by subsection (1) where no substantial reason can be shown as to why the delegated performance will not be as satisfactory as personal performance.

3. Under subsection (2) rights which are no longer executory such as a right to damages for breach may be assigned although the agreement prohibits assignment. In such cases no question of delegation of any performance is involved. Subsection (2) is subject to Section 9-406, which makes rights to payment for goods sold ("accounts"), whether or not earned, freely alienable notwithstanding a contrary agreement or rule of law.

4. The nature of the contract or the circumstances of the case, however, may bar assignment of the contract even where delegation of performance is not involved. This Article and this section are intended to clarify this problem, particularly in cases dealing with output requirement and exclusive dealing contracts. In the first place the section on requirements and exclusive dealing removes from the construction of the original contract most of the "personal discretion" element by substituting the reasonably objective standard of good faith operation of the plant or business to be supplied. Secondly, the section on insecurity and assurances, which is specifically referred to in subsection (5) of this section, frees the other party from the doubts and uncertainty which may afflict him under an assignment of the character in question by permitting him to demand adequate assurance of due performance without which he may suspend his own performance. Subsection (5) is not in any way intended to limit the effect of the section on insecurity and assurances and the word "performance" includes the giving of orders under a requirements contract. Of course, in any case where a material personal discretion is sought to be transferred, effective assignment is barred by subsection (2).

5. Subsection (4) lays down a general rule of construction distinguishing between a normal commercial assignment, which substitutes the assignee for the assignor both as to rights and duties, and a financing assignment in which only the assignor's rights are transferred.

This Article takes no position on the possibility of extending some recognition or power to the original parties to work out normal commercial readjustments of the contract in the case of financing assignments even after the original obligor has been notified of the assignment. This question is dealt with in the Article on Secured Transactions (Article 9).

6. Subsection (5) recognizes that the non-assigning original party has a stake in the reliability of the person with whom he has closed the original contract, and is, therefore, entitled to due assurance that any delegated performance will be properly forthcoming.

7. This section is not intended as a complete statement of the law of delegation and assignment but is limited to clarifying a few points doubtful under the case law. Particularly, neither this section nor this Article touches directly on such questions as the need or effect of notice of the assignment, the rights of successive assignees, or any question of the form of an assignment, either as between the parties or as against any third parties. Some of these questions are dealt with in Article 9.

Cross References:

Point 3: Articles 5 and 9.

Point 4: Sections 2-306 and 2-609.

Point 5: Article 9, Sections 9-402, 9-404, 9-405 and 9-406.

Point 7: Article 9.

Definitional Cross References:

"Agreement". Section 1-201.
"Buyer". Section 2-103.
"Contract". Section 1-201.
"Party". Section 1-201.
"Right". Section 1-201.
"Seller". Section 2-103.
"Term". Section 1-201.

PART 3. GENERAL OBLIGATION AND CONSTRUCTION OF CONTRACT

Section 2-301. General Obligations of Parties

The obligation of the seller is to transfer and deliver and that of the buyer is to accept and pay in accordance with the contract.

Official Comment

Prior Uniform Statutory Provision: Sections 11 and 41, Uniform Sales Act.

Changes: Rewritten.

Purposes of Changes: This section uses the term "obligation" in contrast to the term "duty" in order to provide for the "condition" aspects of delivery and payment insofar as they are not modified by other sections of this Article such as those on cure of tender. It thus replaces not only the general provisions of the Uniform Sales Act on the parties' duties, but also the general provisions of that Act on the effect of conditions. In order to determine what is "in accordance with the contract" under this Article usage of trade, course of dealing and performance, and the general background of circumstances must be given due consideration in conjunction with the lay meaning of the words used to define the scope of the conditions and duties.

Cross References: Section 1-305. See also Sections 1-303, 2-209, 2-508 and 2-612.

Definitional Cross References:

"Buyer". Section 2-103.
"Contract". Section 1-201.
"Party". Section 1-201.
"Seller". Section 2-103.

Section 2-302. Unconscionable Contract or Clause

(1) If the court as a matter of law finds the contract or any clause of the contract to have been unconscionable at the time it was made the court may refuse to enforce the contract, or it may enforce the remainder of the contract without the unconscionable clause, or it may so limit the application of any unconscionable clause as to avoid any unconscionable result.

(2) When it is claimed or appears to the court that the contract or any clause thereof may be unconscionable the parties shall be afforded a reasonable opportunity to present evidence as to its commercial setting, purpose and effect to aid the court in making the determination.

Official Comment

Prior Uniform Statutory Provision: None.

Purposes:

1. This section is intended to make it possible for the courts to police explicitly against the contracts or clauses which they find to be unconscionable. In the past such policing has been accomplished by adverse construction of language, by manipulation of the rules of offer and acceptance or by determinations that the clause is contrary to public policy or to the dominant purpose of the contract. This section is intended to allow the court to pass directly on the unconscionability of the contract or particular clause therein and to make a conclusion of law as to its unconscionability. The basic test is whether, in the light of the general commercial background and the commercial needs of the particular trade or case, the clauses involved are so one-sided as to be unconscionable under the circumstances existing at the time of the making of the contract. Subsection (2) makes it clear that it is proper for the court to hear evidence upon these questions. The principle is one of the prevention of oppression and unfair surprise (Cf. *Campbell Soup Co. v. Wentz,* 172 F.2d 80 (3d Cir. 1948)) and not of disturbance of allocation of risks because of superior bargaining power. The underlying basis of this section is illustrated by the results in cases such as the following:

Kansas City Wholesale Grocery Co. v. Weber Packing Corp., 73 P.2d 1272 (Utah 1937), where a clause limiting time for complaints was held inapplicable to latent defects in a shipment of catsup which could be discovered only by microscopic analysis; *Hardy v. General Motors Acceptance Corp.,* 144 S.E. 327 (Ga. Ct. App. 1928), holding that a disclaimer of warranty clause applied only to express warranties, thus letting in a fair implied warranty; *Andrews Bros. v. Singer & Co.* (1934 CA) 1 K.B. 17, holding that where a car with substantial mileage was delivered instead of a "new" car, a disclaimer of warranties, including those "implied", left unaffected an "express obligation" on the description, even though the Sale of Goods Act called such an implied warranty; *New Prague Flouring Mill Co. v. G. A. Spears,* 189 N.W. 815 (Iowa 1922), holding that a clause permitting the seller, upon the buyer's failure to supply shipping instructions, to cancel, ship, or allow delivery date to be indefinitely postponed 30 days at a time by the inaction, does not indefinitely postpone the date of measuring damages for the buyer's breach, to the seller's advantage; and *Kansas Flour Mills Co. v. Dirks,* 164 P. 273 (Kan. 1917), where under a similar clause in a rising market the court permitted the buyer to measure his damages for non-delivery at the end of only one 30 day postponement; *Green v. Arcos, Ltd.* (1931 CA) 47 T.L.R. 336, where a blanket clause prohibiting rejection of shipments by the buyer was restricted to apply to shipments where discrepancies represented merely mercantile variations; *Meyer v. Packard Cleveland Motor Co.,* 140 N.E. 118 (Ohio 1922), in which the court held that a "waiver" of all agreements not specified did not preclude implied warranty of fitness of a rebuilt dump truck for ordinary use as a dump truck; *Austin Co. v. J. H. Tillman Co.,* 209 P. 131 (Or. 1922), where a clause limiting the buyer's remedy to return was held to be applicable only if the seller had delivered a machine needed for a construction job which reasonably met the contract description; *Bekkevold v. Potts,* 216 N.W. 790 (Minn. 1927), refusing to allow warranty of fitness for purpose imposed by law to be negated by clause excluding all warranties "made" by the seller; *Robert A. Munroe & Co. v. Meyer* (1930) 2 K.B. 312, holding that the warranty of description overrides a clause reading "with all faults and defects" where adulterated meat not up to the contract description was delivered.

2. Under this section the court, in its discretion, may refuse to enforce the contract as a whole if it is permeated by the unconscionability, or it may strike any single clause or group of clauses which are so tainted or which are contrary to the essential purpose of the agreement, or it may simply limit unconscionable clauses so as to avoid unconscionable results.

3. The present section is addressed to the court, and the decision is to be made by it. The commercial evidence referred to in subsection (2) is for the court's consideration, not the jury's. Only the agreement which results from the court's action on these matters is to be submitted to the general triers of the facts.

Definitional Cross Reference: "Contract". Section 1-201.

Section 2-303. Allocation or Division of Risks

Where this Article allocates a risk or a burden as between the parties "unless otherwise agreed", the agreement may not only shift the allocation but may also divide the risk or burden.

Official Comment

Prior Uniform Statutory Provision: None.

Purposes:

1. This section is intended to make it clear that the parties may modify or allocate "unless otherwise agreed" risks or burdens imposed by this Article as they desire, always subject, of course, to the provisions on unconscionability.

Compare Section 1-302.

2. The risk or burden may be divided by the express terms of the agreement or by the attending circumstances, since under the definition of "agreement" in this Act the circumstances surrounding the transaction as well as the express language used by the parties enter into the meaning and substance of the agreement.

Cross References:

Point 1: Sections 1-302 and 2-302.

Point 2: Section 1-201.

Definitional Cross References:

"Party". Section 1-201.

"Agreement". Section 1-201.

Section 2-304. Price Payable in Money, Goods, Realty, or Otherwise

(1) The price can be made payable in money or otherwise. If it is payable in whole or in part in goods each party is a seller of the goods which he is to transfer.

(2) Even though all or part of the price is payable in an interest in realty the transfer of the goods and the seller's obligations with reference to them are subject to this Article, but not the transfer of the interest in realty or the transferor's obligations in connection therewith.

Official Comment

Prior Uniform Statutory Provision: Subsections (2) and (3) of Section 9, Uniform Sales Act.

Changes: Rewritten.

Purposes of Changes:

1. This section corrects the phrasing of the Uniform Sales Act so as to avoid misconstruction and produce greater accuracy in commercial result. While it continues the essential intent and purpose of the Uniform Sales Act it rejects any purely verbalistic construction in disregard of the underlying reason of the provisions.

2. Under subsection (1) the provisions of this Article are applicable to transactions where the "price" of goods is payable in something other than money. This does not mean, however, that this whole Article applies automatically and in its entirety simply because an agreed transfer of title to goods is not a gift. The basic purposes and reasons of the Article must always be considered in determining the applicability of any of its provisions.

3. Subsection (2) lays down the general principle that when goods are to be exchanged for realty, the provisions of this Article apply only to those aspects of the transaction which concern the transfer of title to goods but do not affect the transfer of the realty since the detailed regulation of various particular contracts which fall outside the scope of this Article is left to the courts and other legislation. However, the complexities of these situations may be such that each must be analyzed in the light of the underlying reasons in order to determine the applicable principles. Local statutes dealing with realty are not to be lightly disregarded or altered by language of this Article. In contrast, this Article declares definite policies in regard to certain matters legitimately within its scope though concerned with real property situations, and in those instances the provisions of this Article control.

Cross References:

Point 1: Section 1-103.

Point 3: Sections 1-103, 1-104 and 2-107.

Definitional Cross References:

"Goods". Section 2-105.

"Money". Section 1-201.

"Party". Section 1-201.

"Seller". Section 2-103.

Section 2-305. Open Price Term

(1) The parties if they so intend can conclude a contract for sale even though the price is not settled. In such a case the price is a reasonable price at the time for delivery if

(a) nothing is said as to price; or

(b) the price is left to be agreed by the parties and they fail to agree; or

(c) the price is to be fixed in terms of some agreed market or other standard as set or recorded by a third person or agency and it is not so set or recorded.

(2) A price to be fixed by the seller or by the buyer means a price for him to fix in good faith.

(3) When a price left to be fixed otherwise than by agreement of the parties fails to be fixed through fault of one party the other may at his option treat the contract as cancelled or himself fix a reasonable price.

(4) Where, however, the parties intend not to be bound unless the price be fixed or agreed and it is not fixed or agreed there is no contract. In such a case the buyer must return any goods already received or if unable so to do must pay their reasonable value at the time of delivery and the seller must return any portion of the price paid on account.

Official Comment

Prior Uniform Statutory Provision: Sections 9 and 10, Uniform Sales Act.

Changes: Completely rewritten.

Purposes of Changes:

1. This section applies when the price term is left open on the making of an agreement which is nevertheless intended by the parties to be a binding agreement. This Article rejects in these instances the formula that "an agreement to agree is unenforceable" if the case falls within subsection (1) of this section, and rejects also defeating such agreements on the ground of "indefiniteness". Instead this Article recognizes the dominant intention of the parties to have the deal continue to be binding upon both. As to future performance, since this Article recognizes remedies such as cover (Section 2-712), resale (Section 2-706) and specific performance (Section 2-716) which go beyond any mere arithmetic as between contract price and market price, there is usually a "reasonably certain basis for granting an appropriate remedy for breach" so that the contract need not fail for indefiniteness.

2. Under some circumstances the postponement of agreement on price will mean that no deal has really been concluded, and this is made express in the preamble of subsection (1) ("The parties *if they so intend*) and in subsection (4). Whether or not this is so is, in most cases, a question to be determined by the trier of fact.

3. Subsection (2), dealing with the situation where the price is to be fixed by one party rejects the uncommercial idea that an agreement that the seller may fix the price means that he may fix any price he may wish by the express qualification that the price so fixed must be fixed in good faith. Good faith includes observance of reasonable commercial standards of fair dealing. (Section 1-201(b)(20)). But in the normal case a "posted price" or a future seller's or buyer's "given price", "price in effect", "market price", or the like satisfies the good faith requirement.

4. The section recognizes that there may be cases in which a particular person's judgment is not chosen merely as a barometer or index of a fair price but is an essential condition to the parties' intent to make any contract at all. For example, the case where a known and trusted expert is to "value" a particular painting for which there is no market standard differs sharply from the situation where a named expert is to determine the grade of cotton, and the difference would support a finding that in the one the parties did not intend to make a binding agreement if that expert were unavailable whereas in the other they did so intend. Other circumstances would of course affect the validity of such a finding.

5. Under subsection (3), wrongful interference by one party with any agreed machinery for price fixing in the contract may be treated by the other party as a repudiation justifying cancellation, or merely as a failure to take cooperative action thus shifting to the aggrieved party the reasonable leeway in fixing the price.

6. Throughout the entire section, the purpose is to give effect to the agreement which has been made. That effect, however, is always conditioned by the requirement of good faith action which is made an inherent part of all contracts within this Act. (Section 1-304).

Cross References:

Point 1: Sections 2-204(3), 2-706, 2-712 and 2-716.

Point 3: Section 2-103.

Point 5: Sections 2-311 and 2-610.

Point 6: Section 1-304.

Definitional Cross References:

"Agreement". Section 1-201.

"Burden of establishing". Section 1-201.

"Buyer". Section 2-103.

"Cancellation". Section 2-106.

"Contract".	Section 1-201.
"Contract for sale".	Section 2-106.
"Fault".	Section 1-201.
"Goods".	Section 2-105.
"Party".	Section 1-201.
"Receipt of goods".	Section 2-103.
"Seller".	Section 2-103.
"Term".	Section 1-201.

Section 2-306. Output, Requirements and Exclusive Dealings

(1) A term which measures the quantity by the output of the seller or the requirements of the buyer means such actual output or requirements as may occur in good faith, except that no quantity unreasonably disproportionate to any stated estimate or in the absence of a stated estimate to any normal or otherwise comparable prior output or requirements may be tendered or demanded.

(2) A lawful agreement by either the seller or the buyer for exclusive dealing in the kind of goods concerned imposes unless otherwise agreed an obligation by the seller to use best efforts to supply the goods and by the buyer to use best efforts to promote their sale.

Official Comment

Prior Uniform Statutory Provision: None.

Purposes:

1. Subsection (1) of this section, in regard to output and requirements, applies to this specific problem the general approach of this Act which requires the reading of commercial background and intent into the language of any agreement and demands good faith in the performance of that agreement. It applies to such contracts of nonproducing establishments such as dealers or distributors as well as to manufacturing concerns.

2. Under this Article, a contract for output or requirements is not too indefinite since it is held to mean the actual good faith output or requirements of the particular party. Nor does such a contract lack mutuality of obligation since, under this section, the party who will determine quantity is required to operate his plant or conduct his business in good faith and according to commercial standards of fair dealing in the trade so that his output or requirements will approximate a reasonably foreseeable figure. Reasonable elasticity in the requirements is expressly envisaged by this section and good faith variations from prior requirements are permitted even when the variation may be such as to result in discontinuance. A shut-down by a requirements buyer for lack of orders might be permissible when a shut-down merely to curtail losses would not. The essential test is whether the party is acting in good faith. Similarly, a sudden expansion of the plant by which requirements are to be measured would not be included within the scope of the contract as made but normal expansion undertaken in good faith would be within the scope of this section. One of the factors in an expansion situation would be whether the market price had risen greatly in a case in which the requirements contract contained a fixed price. Reasonable variation of an extreme sort is exemplified in *Southwest Natural Gas Co. v. Oklahoma Portland Cement Co.*, 102 F.2d 630 (10th Cir. 1939). This Article takes no position as to whether a requirements contract is a provable claim in bankruptcy.

3. If an estimate of output or requirements is included in the agreement, no quantity unreasonably disproportionate to it may be tendered or demanded. Any minimum or maximum set by the agreement shows a clear limit on the intended elasticity. In similar fashion, the agreed estimate is to be regarded as a center around which the parties intend the variation to occur.

4. When an enterprise is sold, the question may arise whether the buyer is bound by an existing output or requirements contract. That question is outside the scope of this Article, and is to be determined on other principles of law. Assuming that the contract continues, the output or requirements in the hands of the new owner continue to be measured by the actual good faith output or requirements under the normal operation of the enterprise prior to sale. The sale itself is not grounds for sudden expansion or decrease.

5. Subsection (2), on exclusive dealing, makes explicit the commercial rule embodied in this Act under which the parties to such contracts are held to have impliedly, even when not expressly, bound themselves to use reasonable diligence as well as good faith in their performance of the contract. Under such contracts the exclusive agent is required, although no express commitment has been made, to use reasonable effort and due diligence in the expansion of the market or the promotion of the product, as the case may be. The principal is expected under such a contract to refrain from supplying any other dealer or agent within the exclusive territory. An exclusive dealing agreement brings into play all of the good faith aspects of the output and requirement problems of subsection (1). It also raises questions of insecurity and right to adequate assurance under this Article.

Cross References:

Point 4: Section 2-210.

Point 5: Sections 1-304 and 2-609.

Definitional Cross References:

"Agreement".	Section 1-201.
"Buyer".	Section 2-103.
"Contract for sale".	Section 2-106.
"Good faith".	Section 1-201.
"Goods".	Section 2-105.
"Party".	Section 1-201.
"Term".	Section 1-201.
"Seller".	Section 2-103.

Section 2-307. Delivery in Single Lot or Several Lots

Unless otherwise agreed all goods called for by a contract for sale must be tendered in a single delivery and payment is due only on such tender but where the circumstances give either party the right to make or demand delivery in lots the price if it can be apportioned may be demanded for each lot.

Official Comment

Prior Uniform Statutory Provision: Section 45(1), Uniform Sales Act.

Changes: Rewritten and expanded.

Purposes of Changes:

1. This section applies where the parties have not specifically agreed whether delivery and payment are to be by lots and generally continues the essential intent of original Act, Section 45(1) by assuming that the parties intended delivery to be in a single lot.

2. Where the actual agreement or the circumstances do not indicate otherwise, delivery in lots is not permitted under this section and the buyer is properly entitled to reject for a deficiency in the tender, subject to any privilege in the seller to cure the tender.

3. The "but" clause of this section goes to the case in which it is not commercially feasible to deliver or to receive the goods in a single lot as for example, where a contract calls for the shipment of ten carloads of coal and only three cars are available at a given time. Similarly, in a contract involving brick necessary to build a building the buyer's storage space may be limited so that it would be impossible to receive the entire amount of brick at once, or it may be necessary to assemble the goods as in the case of cattle on the range, or to mine them.

In such cases, a partial delivery is not subject to rejection for the defect in quantity alone, if the circumstances do not indicate a repudiation or default by the seller as to the expected balance or do not give the buyer ground for suspending his performance because of insecurity under the provisions of Section 2-609. However, in such cases the undelivered balance of goods under the contract must be forthcoming within a reasonable time and in a reasonable manner according to the policy of Section 2-503 on manner of tender of delivery. This is reinforced by the express provisions of Section 2-608 that if a lot has been accepted on the reasonable assumption that its nonconformity will be cured, the acceptance may be revoked if the cure does not seasonably occur. The section rejects the rule of *Kelly Construction Co. v. Hackensack Brick Co.*, 103 A. 417 (N.J. 1918) and approves the result in *Lynn M. Ranger, Inc. v. Gildersleeve*, 138 A. 142 (Conn. 1927) in which a contract was made for six carloads of coal then rolling from the mines and consigned to the seller but the seller agreed to divert the carloads to the buyer as soon as the car numbers became known to him. He arranged a diversion of two cars and then notified the buyer who then repudiated the contract. The seller was held to be entitled to his full remedy for the two cars diverted because simultaneous delivery of all of the cars was not contemplated by either party.

Where the circumstances indicate that a party has a right to delivery in lots, the price may be demanded for each lot if it is apportionable.

Cross References:

Point 1:	Section 1-201.
Point 2:	Sections 2-508 and 2-601.
Point 3:	Sections 2-503, 2-608 and 2-609.

Definitional Cross References:

"Contract for sale".	Section 2-106.
"Goods".	Section 2-105.
"Lot".	Section 2-105.
"Party".	Section 1-201.
"Right".	Section 1-201.

Section 2-308. Absence of Specified Place for Delivery

Unless otherwise agreed

(a) the place for delivery of goods is the seller's place of business or if he has none his residence; but

(b) in a contract for sale of identified goods which to the knowledge of the parties at the time of contracting are in some other place, that place is the place for their delivery; and

(c) documents of title may be delivered through customary banking channels.

Official Comment

Prior Uniform Statutory Provision: Paragraphs (a) and (b)—Section 43(1), Uniform Sales Act; Paragraph (c)—none.

Changes: Slight modification in language.

Purposes of Changes and New Matter:

1. Paragraphs (a) and (b) provide for those noncommercial sales and for those occasional commercial sales where no place or means of delivery has been agreed upon by the parties. Where delivery by carrier is "required or authorized by the agreement", the seller's duties as to delivery of the goods are governed not by this section but by Section 2-504.

2. Under paragraph (b) when the identified goods contracted for are known to both parties to be in some location other than the seller's place of business or residence, the parties are presumed to have intended that place to be the place of delivery. This paragraph also applies (unless, as would be normal, the circumstances show that delivery by way of documents is intended) to a bulk of goods in the possession of a bailee. In such a case, however, the seller has the additional obligation to procure the acknowledgment by the bailee of the buyer's right to possession.

3. Where "customary banking channels" call only for due notification by the banker that the documents are on hand, leaving the buyer himself to see to the physical receipt of the goods, tender at the buyer's address is not required under paragraph (c). But that paragraph merely eliminates the possibility of a default by the seller if "customary banking channels" have been properly used in giving notice to the buyer. Where the bank has purchased a draft accompanied by documents or has undertaken its collection on behalf of the seller, Part 5 of Article 4 spells out its duties and relations to its customer. Where the documents move forward under a letter of credit the Article on Letters of Credit spells out the duties and relations between the bank, the seller and the buyer.

4. The rules of this section apply only "unless otherwise agreed". The surrounding circumstances, usage of trade, course of dealing and course of performance, as well as the express language of the parties, may constitute an "otherwise agreement".

Cross References:

Point 1: Sections 2-504 and 2-505.
Point 2: Section 2-503.
Point 3: Section 2-512, Articles 4, Part 5 and 5.

Definitional Cross References:

"Contract for sale". Section 2-106.
"Delivery". Section 1-201.
"Document of title". Section 1-201.
"Goods". Section 2-105.
"Party". Section 1-201.
"Seller". Section 2-103.

Section 2-309. Absence of Specific Time Provisions; Notice of Termination

(1) The time for shipment or delivery or any other action under a contract if not provided in this Article or agreed upon shall be a reasonable time.

(2) Where the contract provides for successive performances but is indefinite in duration it is valid for a reasonable time but unless otherwise agreed may be terminated at any time by either party.

(3) Termination of a contract by one party except on the happening of an agreed event requires that reasonable notification be received by the other party and an agreement dispensing with notification is invalid if its operation would be unconscionable.

Official Comment

Prior Uniform Statutory Provision: Subsection (1): see Sections 43(2), 45(2), 47(1) and 48, Uniform Sales Act, for policy continued under this Article; Subsection (2): none; Subsection (3): none.

Changes: Completely different in scope.

Purposes of Changes and New Matter:

1. Subsection (1) requires that all actions taken under a sales contract must be taken within a reasonable time where no time has been agreed upon. The reasonable time under this provision turns on the criteria as to "reasonable time" and on good faith and commercial standards set forth in Sections 1-201(b)(20), 1-205 and 1-304. It thus depends upon what constitutes acceptable commercial conduct in view of the nature, purpose and circumstances of the action to be taken. Agreement as to a definite time, however, may be found in a term implied from the contractual circumstances, usage of trade or course of dealing or performance as well as in an express term. Such cases fall outside of this subsection since in them the time for action is "agreed" by usage.

2. The time for payment, where not agreed upon, is related to the time for delivery; the particular problems which arise in connection with determining the appropriate time of payment and the time for any inspection before payment which is both allowed by law and demanded by the buyer are covered in Section 2-513.

3. The facts in regard to shipment and delivery differ so widely as to make detailed provision for them in the text of this Article impracticable. The applicable principles, however, make it clear that surprise is to be avoided, good faith judgment is to be protected, and notice or negotiation to reduce the uncertainty to certainty is to be favored.

4. When the time for delivery is left open, unreasonably early offers of or demands for delivery are intended to be read under this Article as expressions of desire or intention, requesting the assent or acquiescence of the other party, not as final positions which may amount without more to breach or to create breach by the other side. See Sections 2-207 and 2-609.

5. The obligation of good faith under this Act requires reasonable notification before a contract may be treated as breached because a reasonable time for delivery or demand has expired. This operates both in the case of a contract originally indefinite as to time and of one subsequently made indefinite by waiver.

When both parties let an originally reasonable time go by in silence, the course of conduct under the contract may be viewed as enlarging the reasonable time for tender or demand of performance. The contract may be terminated by abandonment.

6. Parties to a contract are not required in giving reasonable notification to fix, at peril of breach, a time which is in fact reasonable in the unforeseeable judgment of a later trier of fact. Effective communication of a proposed time limit calls for a response, so that failure to reply will make out acquiescence. Where objection is made, however, or if the demand is merely for information as to when goods will be delivered or will be ordered out, demand for assurances on the ground of insecurity may be made under this Article pending further negotiations. Only when a party insists on undue delay or on rejection of the other party's reasonable proposal is there a question of flat breach under the present section.

7. Subsection (2) applies a commercially reasonable view to resolve the conflict which has arisen in the cases as to contracts of indefinite duration. The "reasonable time" of duration appropriate to a given arrangement is limited by the circumstances. When the arrangement has been carried on by the parties over the years, the "reasonable time" can continue indefinitely and the contract will not terminate until notice.

8. Subsection (3) recognizes that the application of principles of good faith and sound commercial practice normally call for such notification of the termination of a going contract relationship as will give the other party reasonable time to seek a substitute arrangement. An agreement dispensing with notification or limiting the time for the seeking of a substitute arrangement is, of course, valid under this subsection unless the results of putting it into operation would be the creation of an unconscionable state of affairs.

9. Justifiable cancellation for breach is a remedy for breach and is not the kind of termination covered by the present subsection.

10. The requirement of notification is dispensed with where the contract provides for termination on the happening of an "agreed event". "Event" is a term chosen here to contrast with "option" or the like.

Cross References:

Point 1: Sections 1-201(b)(20), 1-205 and 1-304.
Point 2: Sections 2-320, 2-321, 2-504, and 2-511 through 2-514.
Point 5: Section 1-304.
Point 6: Section 2-609.
Point 7: Section 2-204.
Point 9: Sections 2-106, 2-318, 2-610 and 2-703.

Definitional Cross References:

"Agreement". Section 1-201.
"Contract". Section 1-201.
"Notification". Section 1-202.
"Party". Section 1-201.
"Reasonable time". Section 1-205.
"Termination". Section 2-106.

Section 2-310. Open Time for Payment or Running of Credit; Authority to Ship Under Reservation

Unless otherwise agreed

(a) payment is due at the time and place at which the buyer is to receive the goods even though the place of shipment is the place of delivery; and

(b) if the seller is authorized to send the goods he may ship them under reservation, and may tender the documents of title, but the buyer may inspect the goods after their arrival before payment is due unless such inspection is inconsistent with the terms of the contract (Section 2-513); and

(c) if delivery is authorized and made by way of documents of title otherwise than by subsection (b) then payment is due at the time and place at which the buyer is to receive the documents regardless of where the goods are to be received; and

(d) where the seller is required or authorized to ship the goods on credit the credit period runs from the time of shipment but post-dating the invoice or delaying its dispatch will correspondingly delay the starting of the credit period.

Official Comment

Prior Uniform Statutory Provision: Sections 42 and 47(2), Uniform Sales Act.

Changes: Completely rewritten in this and other sections.

Purposes of Changes: This section is drawn to reflect modern business methods of dealing at a distance rather than face to face. Thus:

1. Paragraph (a) provides that payment is due at the time and place "the buyer is to receive the goods" rather than at the point of delivery except in documentary shipment cases (paragraph (c)). This grants an opportunity for the exercise by the buyer of his preliminary right to inspection before paying even though under the delivery term the risk of loss may have previously passed to him or the running of the credit period has already started.

2. Paragraph (b) while providing for inspection by the buyer before he pays, protects the seller. He is not required to give up possession of the goods until he has received payment, where no credit has been contemplated by the parties. The seller may collect through a bank by a sight draft against an order bill of lading "hold until arrival; inspection allowed". The obligations of the bank under such a provision are set forth in Part 5 of Article 4. In the absence of a credit term, the seller is permitted to ship under reservation and if he does payment is then due where and when the buyer is to receive the documents.

3. Unless otherwise agreed, the place for the receipt of the documents and payment is the buyer's city but the time for payment is only after arrival of the goods, since under paragraph (b), and Sections 2-512 and 2-513 the buyer is under no duty to pay prior to inspection.

4. Where the mode of shipment is such that goods must be unloaded immediately upon arrival, too rapidly to permit adequate inspection before receipt, the seller must be guided by the provisions of this Article on inspection which provide that if the seller wishes to demand payment before inspection, he must put an appropriate term into the contract. Even requiring payment against documents will not of itself have this desired result if the documents are to be held until the arrival of the goods. But under (b) and (c) if the terms are C.I.F., C.O.D., or cash against documents payment may be due before inspection.

5. Paragraph (d) states the common commercial understanding that an agreed credit period runs from the time of shipment or from that dating of the invoice which is commonly recognized as a representation of the time of shipment. The provision concerning any delay in sending forth the invoice is included because such conduct results in depriving the buyer of his full notice and warning as to when he must be prepared to pay.

Cross References:

Generally: Part 5.
Point 1: Section 2-509.
Point 2: Sections 2-505, 2-511, 2-512, 2-513 and Article 4.
Point 3: Sections 2-308(b), 2-512 and 2-513.
Point 4: Section 2-513(3)(b).

Definitional Cross References:

"Buyer". Section 2-103.
"Delivery". Section 1-201.
"Document of title". Section 1-201.
"Goods". Section 2-105.
"Receipt of goods". Section 2-103.
"Seller". Section 2-103.
"Send". Section 1-201.
"Term". Section 1-201.

Section 2-311. Options and Cooperation Respecting Performance

(1) An agreement for sale which is otherwise sufficiently definite (subsection (3) of Section 2-204)

to be a contract is not made invalid by the fact that it leaves particulars of performance to be specified by one of the parties. Any such specification must be made in good faith and within limits set by commercial reasonableness.

(2) Unless otherwise agreed specifications relating to assortment of the goods are at the buyer's option and except as otherwise provided in subsections (1)(c) and (3) of Section 2-319 specifications or arrangements relating to shipment are at the seller's option.

(3) Where such specification would materially affect the other party's performance but is not seasonably made or where one party's cooperation is necessary to the agreed performance of the other but is not seasonably forthcoming, the other party in addition to all other remedies

(a) is excused for any resulting delay in his own performance; and

(b) may also either proceed to perform in any reasonable manner or after the time for a material part of his own performance treat the failure to specify or to cooperate as a breach by failure to deliver or accept the goods.

Official Comment

Prior Uniform Statutory Provision: None.

Purposes:

1. Subsection (1) permits the parties to leave certain detailed particulars of performance to be filled in by either of them without running the risk of having the contract invalidated for indefiniteness. The party to whom the agreement gives power to specify the missing details is required to exercise good faith and to act in accordance with commercial standards so that there is no surprise and the range of permissible variation is limited by what is commercially reasonable. The "agreement" which permits one party so to specify may be found as well in a course of dealing, usage of trade, or implication from circumstances as in explicit language used by the parties.

2. Options as to assortment of goods or shipping arrangements are specifically reserved to the buyer and seller respectively under subsection (2) where no other arrangement has been made. This section rejects the test which mechanically and without regard to usage or the purpose of the option gave the option to the party "first under a duty to move" and applies instead a standard commercial interpretation to these circumstances. The "unless otherwise agreed" provision of this subsection covers not only express terms but the background and circumstances which enter into the agreement.

3. Subsection (3) applies when the exercise of an option or cooperation by one party is necessary to or materially affects the other party's performance, but it is not seasonably forthcoming; the subsection relieves the other party from the necessity for performance or excuses his delay in performance as the case may be. The contract-keeping party may at his option under this subsection proceed to perform in any commercially reasonable manner rather than wait. In addition to the special remedies provided, this subsection also reserves "all other remedies". The remedy of particular importance in this connection is that provided for insecurity. Request may also be made pursuant to the obligation of good faith for a reasonable indication of the time and manner of performance for which a party is to hold himself ready.

4. The remedy provided in subsection (3) is one which does not operate in the situation which falls within the scope of Section 2-614 on substituted performance. Where the failure to cooperate results from circumstances set forth in that Section, the other party is under a duty to proffer or demand (as the case may be) substitute performance as a condition to claiming rights against the non-cooperating party.

Cross References:

Point 1: Sections 1-201, 1-304 and 2-204.

Point 3: Sections 1-304 and 2-609.

Point 4: Section 2-614.

Definitional Cross References:

"Agreement".	Section 1-201.
"Buyer".	Section 2-103.
"Contract for sale".	Section 2-106.
"Goods".	Section 2-105.
"Party".	Section 1-201.
"Remedy".	Section 1-201.
"Seasonably".	Section 1-205.
"Seller".	Section 2-103.

Section 2-312. Warranty of Title and Against Infringement; Buyer's Obligation Against Infringement

(1) Subject to subsection (2) there is in a contract for sale a warranty by the seller that

(a) the title conveyed shall be good, and its transfer rightful; and

(b) the goods shall be delivered free from any security interest or other lien or encumbrance of which the buyer at the time of contracting has no knowledge.

(2) A warranty under subsection (1) will be excluded or modified only by specific language or by circumstances which give the buyer reason to know that the person selling does not claim title in himself or that he is purporting to sell only such right or title as he or a third person may have.

(3) Unless otherwise agreed a seller who is a merchant regularly dealing in goods of the kind warrants that the goods shall be delivered free of the rightful claim of any third person by way of infringement or the like but a buyer who furnishes specifications to the seller must hold the seller harmless against any such claim which arises out of compliance with the specifications.

Official Comment

Prior Uniform Statutory Provision: Section 13, Uniform Sales Act.

Changes: Completely rewritten, the provisions concerning infringement being new.

Purposes of Changes:

1. Subsection (1) makes provision for a buyer's basic needs in respect to a title which he in good faith expects to acquire by his purchase, namely, that he receive a good, clean title transferred to him also in a rightful manner so that he will not be exposed to a lawsuit in order to protect it.

The warranty extends to a buyer whether or not the seller was in possession of the goods at the time the sale or contract to sell was made.

The warranty of quiet possession is abolished. Disturbance of quiet possession, although not mentioned specifically, is one way, among many, in which the breach of the warranty of title may be established.

The "knowledge" referred to in subsection 1(b) is actual knowledge as distinct from notice.

2. The provisions of this Article requiring notification to the seller within a reasonable time after the buyer's discovery of a breach apply to notice of a breach of the warranty of title, where the seller's breach was innocent. However, if the seller's breach was in bad faith he cannot be permitted to claim that he has been misled or prejudiced by the delay in giving notice. In such case the "reasonable" time for notice should receive a very liberal interpretation. Whether the breach by the seller is in good or bad faith Section 2-725 provides that the cause of action accrues when the breach occurs. Under the provisions of that section the breach of the warranty of good title occurs when tender of delivery is made since the warranty is not one which extends to "future performance of the goods".

3. When the goods are part of the seller's normal stock and are sold in his normal course of business, it is his duty to see that no claim of infringement of a patent or trademark by a third party will mar the buyer's title. A sale by a person other than a dealer, however, raises no implication in its circumstances of such a warranty. Nor is there such an implication when the buyer orders goods to be assembled, prepared or manufactured on his own specifications. If, in such a case, the resulting product infringes a patent or trademark, the liability will run from buyer to seller. There is, under such circumstances, a tacit representation on the part of the buyer that the seller will be safe in manufacturing according to the specifications, and the buyer is under an obligation in good faith to indemnify him for any loss suffered.

4. This section rejects the cases which recognize the principle that infringements violate the warranty of title but deny the buyer a remedy unless he has been expressly prevented from using the goods. Under this Article "eviction" is not a necessary condition to the buyer's remedy since the buyer's remedy arises immediately upon receipt of notice of infringement; it is merely one way of establishing the fact of breach.

5. Subsection (2) recognizes that sales by sheriffs, executors, certain foreclosing lienors and persons similarly situated may be so out of the ordinary commercial course that their peculiar character is immediately apparent to the buyer and therefore no personal obligation is imposed upon the seller who is purporting to sell only an unknown or limited right. This subsection does not touch upon and leaves open all questions of restitution arising in such cases, when a unique article so sold is reclaimed by a third party as the rightful owner.

Foreclosure sales under Article 9 are another matter. Section 9-610 provides that a disposition of collateral under that section includes warranties such as those imposed by this section on a voluntary disposition of property of the kind involved. Consequently, unless properly excluded under subsection (2) or under the special provisions for exclusion in Section 9-610, a disposition under Section 9-610 of collateral consisting of goods includes the warranties imposed by subsection (1) and, if applicable, subsection (3).

6. The warranty of subsection (1) is not designated as an "implied" warranty, and hence is not subject to Section 2-316(3). Disclaimer of the warranty of title is governed instead by subsection (2), which requires either specific language or the described circumstances.

Cross References:

Point 1: Section 2-403.
Point 2: Sections 2-607 and 2-725.
Point 3: Section 1-304.
Point 4: Sections 2-609 and 2-725.
Point 6: Section 2-316.

Definitional Cross References:

"Buyer".	Section 2-103.
"Contract for sale".	Section 2-106.
"Goods".	Section 2-105.
"Person".	Section 1-201.
"Right".	Section 1-201.
"Seller".	Section 2-103.

Section 2-313. Express Warranties by Affirmation, Promise, Description, Sample

(1) Express warranties by the seller are created as follows:

(a) Any affirmation of fact or promise made by the seller to the buyer which relates to the goods and becomes part of the basis of the bargain creates an express warranty that the goods shall conform to the affirmation or promise.

(b) Any description of the goods which is made part of the basis of the bargain creates an express warranty that the goods shall conform to the description.

(c) Any sample or model which is made part of the basis of the bargain creates an express warranty that the whole of the goods shall conform to the sample or model.

(2) It is not necessary to the creation of an express warranty that the seller use formal words such as "warrant" or "guarantee" or that he have a specific intention

to make a warranty, but an affirmation merely of the value of the goods or a statement purporting to be merely the seller's opinion or commendation of the goods does not create a warranty.

Official Comment

Prior Uniform Statutory Provision: Sections 12, 14 and 16, Uniform Sales Act.

Changes: Rewritten.

Purposes of Changes: To consolidate and systematize basic principles with the result that:

1. "Express" warranties rest on "dickered" aspects of the individual bargain, and go so clearly to the essence of that bargain that words of disclaimer in a form are repugnant to the basic dickered terms. "Implied" warranties rest so clearly on a common factual situation or set of conditions that no particular language or action is necessary to evidence them and they will arise in such a situation unless unmistakably negated.

This section reverts to the older case law insofar as the warranties of description and sample are designated "express" rather than "implied".

2. Although this section is limited in its scope and direct purpose to warranties made by the seller to the buyer as part of a contract for sale, the warranty sections of this Article are not designed in any way to disturb those lines of case law growth which have recognized that warranties need not be confined either to sales contracts or to the direct parties to such a contract. They may arise in other appropriate circumstances such as in the case of bailments for hire, whether such bailment is itself the main contract or is merely a supplying of containers under a contract for the sale of their contents. The provisions of Section 2-318 on third party beneficiaries expressly recognize this case law development within one particular area. Beyond that, the matter is left to the case law with the intention that the policies of this Act may offer useful guidance in dealing with further cases as they arise.

3. The present section deals with affirmations of fact by the seller, descriptions of the goods or exhibitions of samples, exactly as any other part of a negotiation which ends in a contract is dealt with. No specific intention to make a warranty is necessary if any of these factors is made part of the basis of the bargain. In actual practice affirmations of fact made by the seller about the goods during a bargain are regarded as part of the description of those goods; hence no particular reliance on such statements need be shown in order to weave them into the fabric of the agreement. Rather, any fact which is to take such affirmations, once made, out of the agreement requires clear affirmative proof. The issue normally is one of fact.

4. In view of the principle that the whole purpose of the law of warranty is to determine what it is that the seller has in essence agreed to sell, the policy is adopted of those cases which refuse except in unusual circumstances to recognize a material deletion of the seller's obligation. Thus, a contract is normally a contract for a sale of something describable and described. A clause generally disclaiming "all warranties, express or implied" cannot reduce the seller's obligation with respect to such description and therefore cannot be given literal effect under Section 2-316.

This is not intended to mean that the parties, if they consciously desire, cannot make their own bargain as they wish. But in determining what they have agreed upon good faith is a factor and consideration should be given to the fact that the probability is small that a real price is intended to be exchanged for a pseudo-obligation.

5. Paragraph (1)(b) makes specific some of the principles set forth above when a description of the goods is given by the seller.

A description need not be by words. Technical specifications, blueprints and the like can afford more exact description than mere language and if made part of the basis of the bargain goods must conform with them. Past deliveries may set the description of quality, either expressly or impliedly by course of dealing. Of course, all descriptions by merchants must be read against the applicable trade usages with the general rules as to merchantability resolving any doubts.

6. The basic situation as to statements affecting the true essence of the bargain is no different when a sample or model is involved in the transaction. This section includes both a "sample" actually drawn from the bulk of goods which is the subject matter of the sale, and a "model" which is offered for inspection when the subject matter is not at hand and which has not been drawn from the bulk of the goods.

Although the underlying principles are unchanged, the facts are often ambiguous when something is shown as illustrative, rather than as a straight sample. In general, the presumption is that any sample or model just as any affirmation of fact is intended to become a basis of the bargain. But there is no escape from the question of fact. When the seller exhibits a sample purporting to be drawn from an existing bulk, good faith of course requires that the sample be fairly drawn. But in mercantile experience the mere exhibition of a "sample" does not of itself show whether it is merely intended to "suggest" or to "be" the character of the subject-matter of the contract. The question is whether the seller has so acted with reference to the sample as to make him responsible that the whole shall have at least the values shown by it. The circumstances aid in answering this question. If the sample has been drawn from an existing bulk, it must be regarded as describing values of the goods contracted for unless it is accompanied by an unmistakable denial of such responsibility. If, on the other hand, a model of merchandise not on hand is offered, the mercantile presumption that it has become a literal description of the subject matter is not so strong, and particularly so if modification on the buyer's initiative impairs any feature of the model.

7. The precise time when words of description or affirmation are made or samples are shown is not material. The sole question is whether the language or samples or models are fairly to be regarded as part of the contract. If language is used after the closing of the deal (as when the buyer when taking delivery asks and receives an additional assurance), the warranty becomes a modification, and need not be supported by consideration if it is otherwise reasonable and in order (Section 2-209).

8. Concerning affirmations of value or a seller's opinion or commendation under subsection (2), the basic question remains the same: What statements of the seller have in the circumstances and in objective judgment become part of the basis of the bargain? As indicated above, all of the statements of the seller do so unless good reason is shown to the contrary. The provisions of subsection (2) are included, however, since common experience discloses that some statements or predictions cannot fairly be viewed as entering into the bargain. Even as to false statements of value, however, the possibility is left open that a remedy may be provided by the law relating to fraud or misrepresentation.

Cross References:

Point 1:	Section 2-316.
Point 2:	Sections 1-302(b) and 2-318.
Point 3:	Section 2-316(2)(b).
Point 4:	Section 2-316.
Point 5:	Sections 1-303(e) and 2-314.
Point 6:	Section 2-316.
Point 7:	Section 2-209.
Point 8:	Section 1-103.

Definitional Cross References:

"Buyer".	Section 2-103.
"Conforming".	Section 2-106.
"Goods".	Section 2-105.
"Seller".	Section 2-103.

Section 2-314. Implied Warranty: Merchantability; Usage of Trade

(1) Unless excluded or modified (Section 2-316), a warranty that the goods shall be merchantable is implied in a contract for their sale if the seller is a merchant with respect to goods of that kind. Under this section the serving for value of food or drink to be consumed either on the premises or elsewhere is a sale.

(2) Goods to be merchantable must be at least such as

(a) pass without objection in the trade under the contract description; and

(b) in the case of fungible goods, are of fair average quality within the description; and

(c) are fit for the ordinary purposes for which such goods are used; and

(d) run, within the variations permitted by the agreement, of even kind, quality and quantity within each unit and among all units involved; and

(e) are adequately contained, packaged, and labeled as the agreement may require; and

(f) conform to the promises or affirmations of fact made on the container or label if any.

(3) Unless excluded or modified (Section 2-316) other implied warranties may arise from course of dealing or usage of trade.

Official Comment

Prior Uniform Statutory Provision: Section 15(2), Uniform Sales Act.

Changes: Completely rewritten.

Purposes of Changes: This section, drawn in view of the steadily developing case law on the subject, is intended to make it clear that:

1. The seller's obligation applies to present sales as well as to contracts to sell subject to the effects of any examination of specific goods. (Subsection (2) of Section 2-316). Also, the warranty of merchantability applies to sales for use as well as to sales for resale.

2. The question when the warranty is imposed turns basically on the meaning of the terms of the agreement as recognized in the trade. Goods delivered under an agreement made by a merchant in a given line of trade must be of a quality comparable to that generally acceptable in that line of trade under the description or other designation of the goods used in the agreement. The responsibility imposed rests on any merchant-seller, and the absence of the words "grower or manufacturer or not" which appeared in Section 15(2) of the Uniform Sales Act does not restrict the applicability of this section.

3. A specific designation of goods by the buyer does not exclude the seller's obligation that they be fit for the general purposes appropriate to such goods. A contract for the sale of second-hand goods, however, involves only such obligation as is appropriate to such goods for that is their contract description. A person making an isolated sale of goods is not a "merchant" within the meaning of the full scope of this section and, thus, no warranty of merchantability would apply. His knowledge of any defects not apparent on inspection would, however, without need for express agreement and in keeping with the underlying reason of the present section and the provisions on good faith, impose an obligation that known material but hidden defects be fully disclosed.

4. Although a seller may not be a "merchant" as to the goods in question, if he states generally that they are "guaranteed" the provisions of this section may furnish a guide to the content of the resulting express warranty. This has particular significance in the case of second-hand sales, and has further significance in limiting the effect of fine-print disclaimer clauses where their effect would be inconsistent with large-print assertions of "guarantee".

5. The second sentence of subsection (1) covers the warranty with respect to food and drink. Serving food or drink for value is a sale, whether to be consumed on the premises or elsewhere. Cases to the contrary are rejected. The principal warranty is that stated in subsections (1) and (2)(c) of this section.

6. Subsection (2) does not purport to exhaust the meaning of "merchantable" nor to negate any of its attributes not specifically mentioned in the text of the statute, but arising by usage of trade or through case law. The language used is "must be at least such as . . .", and the intention is to leave open other possible attributes of merchantability.

7. Paragraphs (a) and (b) of subsection (2) are to be read together. Both refer, as indicated above, to the standards of that line of the trade which fits the transaction and the seller's business. "Fair average" is a term directly appropriate to agricultural bulk products and means goods centering around the middle belt of quality, not the least or the worst that can be understood in the particular trade by the designation, but such as can pass "without objection". Of course a fair percentage of the least is permissible but the goods are not "fair average" if they are all of the least or worst quality possible under the description. In cases of doubt as to what quality is intended, the price at which a merchant closes a contract is an excellent index of the nature and scope of his obligation under the present section.

8. Fitness for the ordinary purposes for which goods of the type are used is a fundamental concept of the present section and is covered in paragraph (c). As stated above, merchantability is also a part of the obligation owing to the purchaser for use. Correspondingly, protection, under this aspect of the warranty, of the person buying for resale to the ultimate consumer is equally necessary, and merchantable goods must therefore be "honestly" resalable in the normal course of business because they are what they purport to be.

9. Paragraph (d) on evenness of kind, quality and quantity follows case law. But precautionary language has been added as a remainder of the frequent usages of trade which permit substantial variations both with and without an allowance or an obligation to replace the varying units.

10. Paragraph (e) applies only where the nature of the goods and of the transaction require a certain type of container, package or label. Paragraph (f) applies, on the other hand, wherever there is a label or container on which representations are made, even though the original contract, either by express terms or usage of trade, may not have required either the labelling or the representation. This follows from the general obligation of good faith which requires that a buyer should not be placed in the position of reselling or using goods delivered under false representations appearing on the package or container. No problem of extra consideration arises in this connection since, under this Article, an obligation is imposed by the original contract not to deliver mislabeled articles, and the obligation is imposed where mercantile good faith so requires and without reference to the doctrine of consideration.

11. Exclusion or modification of the warranty of merchantability, or of any part of it, is dealt with in the section to which the text of the present section makes explicit precautionary references. That section must be read with particular reference to its subsection (4) on limitation of remedies. The warranty of merchantability, wherever it is normal, is so commonly taken for granted that its exclusion from the contract is a matter threatening surprise and therefore requiring special precaution.

12. Subsection (3) is to make explicit that usage of trade and course of dealing can create warranties and that they are implied rather than express warranties and thus subject to exclusion or modification under Section 2-316. A typical instance would be the obligation to provide pedigree papers to evidence conformity of the animal to the contract in the case of a pedigreed dog or blooded bull.

13. In an action based on breach of warranty, it is of course necessary to show not only the existence of the warranty but the fact that the warranty was broken and that the breach of the warranty was the proximate cause of the loss sustained. In such an action an affirmative showing by the seller that the loss resulted from some action or event following his own delivery of the goods can operate as a defense. Equally, evidence indicating that the seller exercised care in the manufacture, processing or selection of the goods is relevant to the issue of whether the warranty was in fact broken. Action by the buyer following an examination of the goods which ought to have indicated the defect complained of can be shown as matter bearing on whether the breach itself was the cause of the injury.

Cross References:

Point 1:	Section 2-316.
Point 3:	Sections 1-304 and 2-104.
Point 5:	Section 2-315.
Point 11:	Section 2-316.
Point 12:	Sections 1-201, 1-303 and 2-316.

Definitional Cross References:

"Agreement".	Section 1-201.
"Contract".	Section 1-201.
"Contract for sale".	Section 2-106.
"Goods".	Section 2-105.
"Merchant".	Section 2-104.
"Seller".	Section 2-103.

Section 2-315. Implied Warranty: Fitness for Particular Purpose

Where the seller at the time of contracting has reason to know any particular purpose for which the goods are required and that the buyer is relying on the seller's skill or judgment to select or furnish suitable goods, there is unless excluded or modified under the next section an implied warranty that the goods shall be fit for such purpose.

Official Comment

Prior Uniform Statutory Provision: Section 15(1), (4), (5), Uniform Sales Act.

Changes: Rewritten.

Purposes of Changes:

1. Whether or not this warranty arises in any individual case is basically a question of fact to be determined by the circumstances of the contracting. Under this section the buyer need not bring home to the seller actual knowledge of the particular purpose for which the goods are intended or of his reliance on the seller's skill and judgment, if the circumstances are such that the seller has reason to realize the purpose intended or that the reliance exists. The buyer, of course, must actually be relying on the seller.

2. A "particular purpose" differs from the ordinary purpose for which the goods are used in that it envisages a specific use by the buyer which is peculiar to the nature of his business whereas the ordinary purposes for which goods are used are those envisaged in the concept of merchantability and go to uses which are customarily made of the goods in question. For example, shoes are generally used for the purpose of walking upon ordinary ground, but a seller may know that a particular pair was selected to be used for climbing mountains.

A contract may of course include both a warranty of merchantability and one of fitness for a particular purpose.

The provisions of this Article on the cumulation and conflict of express and implied warranties must be considered on the question of inconsistency between or among warranties. In such a case any question of fact as to which warranty was intended by the parties to apply must be resolved in favor of the warranty of fitness for particular purpose as against all other warranties except where the buyer has taken upon himself the responsibility of furnishing the technical specifications.

3. In connection with the warranty of fitness for a particular purpose the provisions of this Article on the allocation or division of risks are particularly applicable in any transaction in which the purpose for which the goods are to be used combines requirements both as to the quality of the goods themselves and compliance with certain laws or regulations. How the risks are divided is a question of fact to be determined, where not expressly contained in the agreement, from the circumstances of contracting, usage of trade, course of performance and the like, matters which may constitute the "otherwise agreement" of the parties by which they may divide the risk or burden.

4. The absence from this section of the language used in the Uniform Sales Act in referring to the seller, "whether he be the grower or manufacturer or not", is not intended to impose any requirement that the seller be a grower or manufacturer. Although normally the warranty will arise only where the seller is a merchant with the appropriate "skill or judgment", it can arise as to non-merchants where this is justified by the particular circumstances.

5. The elimination of the "patent or other trade name" exception constitutes the major extension of the warranty of fitness which has been made by the cases and continued in this Article. Under the present section the existence of a patent or other trade name and the designation of the article by that name, or indeed in any other definite manner, is only one of the facts to be considered on the question of whether the buyer actually relied on the seller, but it is not of itself decisive of the issue. If the buyer himself is insisting on a particular brand he is not relying on the seller's skill and judgment and so no warranty results. But the mere fact that the article purchased has a particular patent or trade name is not sufficient to indicate nonreliance if the article has been recommended by the seller as adequate for the buyer's purposes.

6. The specific reference forward in the present section to the following section on exclusion or modification of warranties is to call attention to the possibility of eliminating the warranty in any given case. However it must be noted that under the following section the warranty of fitness for a particular purpose must be excluded or modified by a conspicuous writing.

Cross References:

Point 2: Sections 2-314 and 2-317.
Point 3: Section 2-303.
Point 6: Section 2-316.

Definitional Cross References:

"Buyer". Section 2-103.
"Goods". Section 2-105.
"Seller". Section 2-103.

Section 2-316. Exclusion or Modification of Warranties

(1) Words or conduct relevant to the creation of an express warranty and words or conduct tending to negate or limit warranty shall be construed wherever reasonable as consistent with each other; but subject to the provisions of this Article on parol or extrinsic evidence (Section 2-202) negation or limitation is inoperative to the extent that such construction is unreasonable.

(2) Subject to subsection (3), to exclude or modify the implied warranty of merchantability or any part of it the language must mention merchantability and in case of a writing must be conspicuous, and to exclude or modify any implied warranty of fitness the exclusion must be by a writing and conspicuous. Language to exclude all implied warranties of fitness is sufficient if it states, for example, that "There are no warranties which extend beyond the description on the face hereof".

(3) Notwithstanding subsection (2)

(a) unless the circumstances indicate otherwise, all implied warranties are excluded by expressions like "as is", "with all faults" or other language which in common understanding calls the buyer's attention to the exclusion of warranties and makes plain that there is no implied warranty; and

(b) when the buyer before entering into the contract has examined the goods or the sample or model as fully as he desired or has refused to examine the goods there is no implied warranty with regard to defects which an examination ought in the circumstances to have revealed to him; and

(c) an implied warranty can also be excluded or modified by course of dealing or course of performance or usage of trade.

(4) Remedies for breach of warranty can be limited in accordance with the provisions of this Article on liquidation or limitation of damages and on contractual modification of remedy (Sections 2-718 and 2-719).

Official Comment

Prior Uniform Statutory Provision: None. See sections 15 and 71, Uniform Sales Act.

Purposes:

1. This section is designed principally to deal with those frequent clauses in sales contracts which seek to exclude "all warranties, express or implied". It seeks to protect a buyer from unexpected and unbargained language of disclaimer by denying effect to such language when inconsistent with language of express warranty and permitting the exclusion of implied warranties only by conspicuous language or other circumstances which protect the buyer from surprise.

2. The seller is protected under this Article against false allegations of oral warranties by its provisions on parol and extrinsic evidence and against unauthorized representations by the customary "lack of authority" clauses. This Article treats the limitation or avoidance of consequential damages as a matter of limiting remedies for breach, separate from the matter of creation of liability under a warranty. If no warranty exists, there is of course no problem of limiting remedies for breach of warranty. Under subsection (4) the question of limitation of remedy is governed by the sections referred to rather than by this section.

3. Disclaimer of the implied warranty of merchantability is permitted under subsection (2), but with the safeguard that such disclaimers must mention merchantability and in case of a writing must be conspicuous.

4. Unlike the implied warranty of merchantability, implied warranties of fitness for a particular purpose may be excluded by general language, but only if it is in writing and conspicuous.

5. Subsection (2) presupposes that the implied warranty in question exists unless excluded or modified. Whether or not language of disclaimer satisfies the requirements of this section, such language may be relevant under other sections to the question whether the warranty was ever in fact created. Thus, unless the provisions of this Article on parol and extrinsic evidence prevent, oral language of disclaimer may raise issues of fact as to whether reliance by the buyer occurred and whether the seller had "reason to know" under the section on implied warranty of fitness for a particular purpose.

6. The exceptions to the general rule set forth in paragraphs (a), (b) and (c) of subsection (3) are common factual situations in which the circumstances surrounding the transaction are in themselves sufficient to call the buyer's attention to the fact that no implied warranties are made or that a certain implied warranty is being excluded.

7. Paragraph (a) of subsection (3) deals with general terms such as "as is", "as they stand", "with all faults", and the like. Such terms in ordinary commercial usage are understood to mean that the buyer takes the entire risk as to the quality of the goods involved. The terms covered by paragraph (a) are in fact merely a particularization of paragraph (c) which provides for exclusion or modification of implied warranties by usage of trade.

8. Under paragraph (b) of subsection (3) warranties may be excluded or modified by the circumstances where the buyer examines the goods or a sample or model of them before entering into the contract. "Examination" as used in this paragraph is not synonymous with inspection before acceptance or at any other time after the contract has been made. It goes rather to the nature of the responsibility assumed by the seller at the time of the making of the contract. Of course if the buyer discovers the defect and uses the goods anyway, or if he unreasonably fails to examine the goods before he uses them, resulting injuries may be found to result from his own action rather than proximately from a breach of warranty. See Sections 2-314 and 2-715 and comments thereto.

In order to bring the transaction within the scope of "refused to examine" in paragraph (b), it is not sufficient that the goods are available for inspection. There must in addition be a demand by the seller that the buyer examine the goods fully. The seller by the demand puts the buyer on notice that he is assuming the risk of defects which the examination ought to reveal. The language "refused to examine" in this paragraph is intended to make clear the necessity for such demand.

Application of the doctrine of "caveat emptor" in all cases where the buyer examines the goods regardless of statements made by the seller is, however, rejected by this Article. Thus, if the offer of examination is accompanied by words as to their merchantability or specific attributes and the buyer indicates clearly that he is relying on those words rather than on his examination, they give rise to an "express" warranty. In such cases the question is one of fact as to whether a warranty of merchantability has been expressly incorporated in the agreement. Disclaimer of such an express warranty is governed by subsection (1) of the present section.

The particular buyer's skill and the normal method of examining goods in the circumstances determine what defects are excluded by the examination. A failure to notice defects which are obvious cannot excuse the buyer. However, an examination under circumstances which do not permit chemical or other testing of the goods would not exclude defects which could be ascertained only by such testing. Nor can latent defects be excluded by a simple examination. A professional buyer examining a product in his field will be held to have assumed the risk as to all defects which a professional in the field ought to observe, while a nonprofessional buyer will be held to have assumed the risk only for such defects as a layman might be expected to observe.

9. The situation in which the buyer gives precise and complete specifications to the seller is not explicitly covered in this section, but this is a frequent circumstance by which the implied warranties may be excluded. The warranty of fitness for a particular purpose would not normally arise since in such a situation there is usually no reliance on the seller by the buyer. The warranty of merchantability in such a transaction, however, must be considered in connection with the next section on the cumulation and conflict of warranties. Under paragraph (c) of that section in case of such an inconsistency the implied warranty of merchantability is displaced by the express warranty that the goods will comply with the specifications. Thus, where the buyer gives detailed specifications as to the goods, neither of the implied warranties as to quality will normally apply to the transaction unless consistent with the specifications.

10. As to the use of a record other than a writing and communications that are not written, see Section 2-207, Comment 8. Whether a term is conspicuous, including a term in a record other than a writing, is discussed in Section 1-201, Comment 10.

Cross References:

Point 2: Sections 2-202, 2-718 and 2-719.

Point 7: Sections 1-303.

Definitional Cross References:

"Agreement". Section 1-201.
"Buyer". Section 2-103.
"Contract". Section 1-201.
"Course of dealing". Section 1-303.
"Goods". Section 1-105.
"Remedy". Section 1-201.
"Seller". Section 2-103.
"Usage of trade". Section 1-303.

Section 2-317. Cumulation and Conflict of Warranties Express or Implied

Warranties whether express or implied shall be construed as consistent with each other and as cumulative, but if such construction is unreasonable the intention of the parties shall determine which warranty is dominant. In ascertaining that intention the following rules apply:

(a) Exact or technical specifications displace an inconsistent sample or model or general language of description.

(b) A sample from an existing bulk displaces inconsistent general language of description.

(c) Express warranties displace inconsistent implied warranties other than an implied warranty of fitness for a particular purpose.

Official Comment

Prior Uniform Statutory Provision: On cumulation of warranties see Sections 14, 15, and 16, Uniform Sales Act.

Changes: Completely rewritten into one section.

Purposes of Changes:

1. The present section rests on the basic policy of this Article that no warranty is created except by some conduct (either affirmative action or failure to disclose) on the part of the seller. Therefore, all warranties are made cumulative unless this construction of the contract is impossible or unreasonable.

This Article thus follows the general policy of the Uniform Sales Act except that in case of the sale of an article by its patent or trade name the elimination of the warranty of fitness depends solely on whether the buyer has relied on the seller's skill and judgment; the use of the patent or trade name is but one factor in making this determination.

2. The rules of this section are designed to aid in determining the intention of the parties as to which of inconsistent warranties which have arisen from the circumstances of their transaction shall prevail. These rules of intention are to be applied only where factors making for an equitable estoppel of the seller do not exist and where he has in perfect good faith made warranties which later turn out to be inconsistent. To the extent that the seller has led the buyer to believe that all of the warranties can be performed, he is estopped from setting up any essential inconsistency as a defense.

3. The rules in subsections (a), (b) and (c) are designed to ascertain the intention of the parties by reference to the factor which probably claimed the attention of the parties in the first instance. These rules are not absolute but may be changed by evidence showing that the conditions which existed at the time of contracting make the construction called for by the section inconsistent or unreasonable.

Cross Reference:

Point 1: Section 2-315.

Definitional Cross Reference:

"Party". Section 1-201.

Section 2-318. Third Party Beneficiaries of Warranties Express or Implied

Note: *If this Act is introduced in the Congress of the United States this section should be omitted. (States to select one alternative.)*

Alternative A. A seller's warranty whether express or implied extends to any natural person who is in the family or household of his buyer or who is a guest in his home if it is reasonable to expect that such person may use, consume or be affected by the goods and who is injured in person by breach of the warranty. A seller may not exclude or limit the operation of this section.

Alternative B. A seller's warranty whether express or implied extends to any natural person who may reasonably be expected to use, consume or be affected by the goods and who is injured in person by breach of the warranty. A seller may not exclude or limit the operation of this section.

Alternative C. A seller's warranty whether express or implied extends to any person who may reasonably be expected to use, consume or be affected by the goods and who is injured by breach of the warranty. A seller may not exclude or limit the operation of this section with respect to injury to the person of an individual to whom the warranty extends.

Official Comment

Prior Uniform Statutory Provision: None.

Purposes:

1. The last sentence of this section does not mean that a seller is precluded from excluding or disclaiming a warranty which might otherwise arise in connection with the sale provided such exclusion or modification is permitted by Section 2-316. Nor does that sentence preclude the seller from limiting the remedies of his own buyer and of any beneficiaries, in any manner provided in Sections 2-718 or 2-719. To the extent that the contract of sale contains provisions under which warranties are excluded or modified, or remedies for breach are limited, such provisions are equally operative against beneficiaries of warranties under this section. What this last sentence forbids is exclusion of liability by the seller to the persons to whom the warranties which he has made to his buyer would extend under this section.

2. The purpose of this section is to give certain beneficiaries the benefit of the same warranty which the buyer received in the contract of sale, thereby freeing any such beneficiaries from any technical rules as to "privity". It seeks to accomplish this purpose without any derogation of any right or remedy resting on negligence. It rests primarily upon the merchant-seller's warranty under this Article that the goods sold are merchantable and fit for the ordinary purposes for which such goods are used rather than the warranty of fitness for a particular purpose. Implicit in the section is that any beneficiary of a warranty may bring a direct action for breach of warranty against the seller whose warranty extends to him.

3. This section expressly includes as beneficiaries within its provisions the family, household, and guests of the purchaser. Beyond this, the section is neutral and is not intended to enlarge or restrict the developing case law on whether the seller's warranties, given to his buyer who resells, extend to other persons in the distributive chain. The second alternative is designed for states where the case law has already developed further and for those that desire to expand the class of beneficiaries. The third alternative goes further, following the trend of modern decisions as indicated by Restatement of Torts 2d § 402A (Tentative Draft No. 10, 1965) in extending the rule beyond injuries to the person.

Cross References:

Point 1: Sections 2-316, 2-718 and 2-719.

Point 2: Section 2-314.

Definitional Cross References:

"Buyer". Section 2-103.

"Goods". Section 2-105.

"Seller". Section 2-103.

Section 2-319. F.O.B. and F.A.S. Terms

(1) Unless otherwise agreed the term F.O.B. (which means "free on board") at a named place, even though used only in connection with the stated price, is a delivery term under which

(a) when the term is F.O.B. the place of shipment, the seller must at that place ship the goods in the manner provided in this Article (Section 2-504) and bear the expense and risk of putting them into the possession of the carrier; or

(b) when the term is F.O.B. the place of destination, the seller must at his own expense and risk transport the goods to that place and there tender delivery of them in the manner provided in this Article (Section 2-503);

(c) when under either (a) or (b) the term is also F.O.B. vessel, car or other vehicle, the seller must in addition at his own expense and risk load the goods on board. If the term is F.O.B. vessel the buyer must name the vessel and in an appropriate case the seller must comply with the provisions of this Article on the form of bill of lading (Section 2-323).

(2) Unless otherwise agreed the term F.A.S. vessel (which means "free alongside") at a named port, even though used only in connection with the stated price, is a delivery term under which the seller must

(a) at his own expense and risk deliver the goods alongside the vessel in the manner usual in that port or on a dock designated and provided by the buyer; and

(b) obtain and tender a receipt for the goods in exchange for which the carrier is under a duty to issue a bill of lading.

(3) Unless otherwise agreed in any case falling within subsection (1)(a) or (c) or subsection (2) the buyer must seasonably give any needed instructions for making delivery, including when the term is F.A.S. or F.O.B. the loading berth of the vessel and in an appropriate case its name and sailing date. The seller may treat the failure of needed instructions as a failure of cooperation under this Article (Section 2-311). He may also at his option move the goods in any reasonable manner preparatory to delivery or shipment.

(4) Under the term F.O.B. vessel or F.A.S. unless otherwise agreed the buyer must make payment against tender of the required documents and the seller may not tender nor the buyer demand delivery of the goods in substitution for the documents.

Official Comment

Prior Uniform Statutory Provision: None.

Purposes:

1. This section is intended to negate the uncommercial line of decision which treats an "F.O.B." term as "merely a price term". The distinctions taken in subsection (1) handle most of the issues which have on occasion led to the unfortunate judicial language just referred to. Other matters which have led to sound results being based on unhappy language in regard to F.O.B. clauses are dealt with in this Act by Section 2-311(2) (seller's option re arrangements relating to shipment) and Sections 2-614 and 615 (substituted performance and seller's excuse).

2. Subsection (1)(c) not only specifies the duties of a seller who engages to deliver "F.O.B. vessel", or the like, but ought to make clear that no agreement is soundly drawn when it looks to reshipment from San Francisco or New York, but speaks merely of "F.O.B." the place.

3. The buyer's obligations stated in subsection (1)(c) and subsection (3) are, as shown in the text, obligations of cooperation. The last sentence of subsection (3) expressly, though perhaps unnecessarily, authorizes the seller, pending instructions, to go ahead with such preparatory moves as shipment from the interior to the named point of delivery. The sentence presupposes the usual case in which instructions "fail"; a prior repudiation by the buyer, giving notice that breach was intended, would remove the reason for the sentence, and would normally bring into play, instead, the second sentence of Section 2-704, which duly calls for lessening damages.

4. The treatment of "F.O.B. vessel" in conjunction with F.A.S. fits, in regard to the need for payment against documents, with standard practice and case-law; but "F.O.B. vessel" is a term which by its very language makes express the need for an "on board" document. In this respect, that term is stricter than the ordinary overseas "shipment" contract (C.I.F., etc., Section 2-320).

Cross References:

Sections 2-311(3), 2-323, 2-503 and 2-504.

Definitional Cross References:

"Agreed".	Section 1-201.
"Bill of lading".	Section 1-201.
"Buyer".	Section 2-103.
"Goods".	Section 2-105.
"Seasonably".	Section 1-205.
"Seller".	Section 2-103.
"Term".	Section 1-201.

Section 2-320. C.I.F. and C. & F. Terms

(1) The term C.I.F. means that the price includes in a lump sum the cost of the goods and the insurance and freight to the named destination. The term C. & F. or C.F. means that the price so includes cost and freight to the named destination.

(2) Unless otherwise agreed and even though used only in connection with the stated price and destination, the term C.I.F. destination or its equivalent requires the seller at his own expense and risk to

(a) put the goods into the possession of a carrier at the port for shipment and obtain a negotiable bill or bills of lading covering the entire transportation to the named destination; and

(b) load the goods and obtain a receipt from the carrier (which may be contained in the bill of lading) showing that the freight has been paid or provided for; and

(c) obtain a policy or certificate of insurance, including any war risk insurance, of a kind and on terms then current at the port of shipment in the usual amount, in the currency of the contract, shown to cover the same goods covered by the bill of lading and providing for payment of loss to the order of the buyer or for the account of whom it may concern; but the seller may add to the price the amount of the premium for any such war risk insurance; and

(d) prepare an invoice of the goods and procure any other documents required to effect shipment or to comply with the contract; and

(e) forward and tender with commercial promptness all the documents in due form and with any indorsement necessary to perfect the buyer's rights.

(3) Unless otherwise agreed the term C. & F. or its equivalent has the same effect and imposes upon the seller the same obligations and risks as a C.I.F. term except the obligation as to insurance.

(4) Under the term C.I.F. or C. & F. unless otherwise agreed the buyer must make payment against tender of the required documents and the seller may not tender nor the buyer demand delivery of the goods in substitution for the documents.

Official Comment

Prior Uniform Statutory Provisions: None.

Purposes: To make it clear that:

1. The C.I.F. contract is not a destination but a shipment contract with risk of subsequent loss or damage to the goods passing to the buyer upon shipment if the seller has properly performed all his obligations with respect to the goods. Delivery to the carrier is delivery to the buyer for purposes of risk and "title". Delivery of possession of the goods is accomplished by delivery of the bill of lading, and upon tender of the required documents the buyer must pay the agreed price without awaiting the arrival of the goods and if they have been lost or damaged after proper shipment he must seek his remedy against the carrier or insurer. The buyer has no right of inspection prior to payment or acceptance of the documents.

2. The seller's obligations remain the same even though the C.I.F. term is "used only in connection with the stated price and destination".

3. The insurance stipulated by the C.I.F. term is for the buyer's benefit, to protect him against the risk of loss or damage to the goods in transit. A clause in a C.I.F. contract "insurance—for the account of sellers" should be viewed in its ordinary mercantile meaning that the sellers must pay for the insurance and not that it is intended to run to the seller's benefit.

4. A bill of lading covering the entire transportation from the port of shipment is explicitly required but the provision on this point must be read in the light of its reason to assure the buyer of as full protection as the conditions of shipment reasonably permit, remembering always that this type of contract is designed to move the goods in the channels commercially available. To enable the buyer to deal with the goods while they are afloat the bill of lading must be one that covers only the quantity of goods called for by the contract. The buyer is not required to accept his part of the goods without a bill of lading because the latter covers a larger quantity, nor is he required to accept a bill of lading for the whole quantity under a stipulation to hold the excess for the owner. Although the buyer is not compelled to accept either goods or documents under such circumstances he may of course claim his rights in any goods which have been identified to his contract.

5. The seller is given the option of paying or providing for the payment of freight. He has no option to ship "freight collect" unless the agreement so provides. The rule of the common law that the buyer need not pay the freight if the goods do not arrive is preserved.

Unless the shipment has been sent "freight collect" the buyer is entitled to receive documentary evidence that he is not obligated to pay the freight; the seller is therefore required to obtain a receipt "showing that the freight has been paid or provided for". The usual notation in the appropriate space on the bill of lading that the freight has been prepaid is a sufficient receipt, as at common law. The phrase "provided for" is intended to cover the frequent situation in which the carrier extends credit to a shipper for the freight on successive shipments and receives periodical payments of the accrued freight charges from him.

6. The requirement that unless otherwise agreed the seller must procure insurance "of a kind and on terms then current at the port for shipment in the usual amount, in the currency of the contract, sufficiently shown to cover the same goods covered by the bill of lading", applies to both marine and war risk insurance. As applied to marine insurance, it means such insurance as is usual or customary at the port for shipment with reference to the particular kind of goods involved, the character and equipment of the vessel, the route of the voyage, the port of destination and any other considerations that affect the risk. It is the substantial equivalent of the ordinary insurance in the particular trade and on the particular voyage and is subject to agreed specifications of type or extent of coverage. The language does not mean that the insurance must be adequate to cover all risks to which the goods may be subject in transit. There are some types of loss or damage that are not covered by the usual marine insurance and are excepted in bills of lading or in applicable statutes from the causes of loss or damage for which the carrier or the vessel is liable. Such risks must be borne by the buyer under this Article.

Insurance secured in compliance with a C.I.F. term must cover the entire transportation of the goods to the named destination.

7. An additional obligation is imposed upon the seller in requiring him to procure customary war risk insurance at the buyer's expense. This changes the common law on the point. The seller is not required to assume the risk of including in the C.I.F. price the cost of such insurance, since it often fluctuates rapidly, but is required to treat it simply as a necessary for the buyer's account. What war risk insurance is "current" or usual turns on the standard forms of policy or rider in common use.

8. The C.I.F. contract calls for insurance covering the value of the goods at the time and place of shipment and does not include any increase in market value during transit or any anticipated profit to the buyer on a sale by him.

The contract contemplates that before the goods arrive at their destination they may be sold again and again on C.I.F. terms and that the original policy of insurance and bill of lading will run with the interest in the goods by being transferred to each successive buyer. A buyer who becomes the seller in such an intermediate contract for sale does not thereby, if his sub-buyer knows the circumstances, undertake to insure the goods again at an increased price fixed in the new contract or to cover the increase in price by additional insurance, and his buyer may not reject the documents on the ground that the original policy does not cover such higher price. If such a sub-buyer desires additional insurance he must procure it for himself.

Where the seller exercises an option to ship "freight collect" and to credit the buyer with the freight against the C.I.F. price, the insurance need not cover the freight since the freight is not at the buyer's risk. On the other hand, where the seller prepays the freight upon shipping under a bill of lading requiring prepayment and providing that the freight shall be deemed earned and shall be retained by the carrier "ship and/or cargo lost or not lost", or using words of similar import, he must procure insurance that will cover the freight, because notwithstanding that the goods are lost in transit the buyer is bound to pay the freight as part of the C.I.F. price and will be unable to recover it back from the carrier.

9. Insurance "for the account of whom it may concern" is usual and sufficient. However, for a valid tender the policy of insurance must be one which can be disposed of together with the bill of lading and so must be "sufficiently shown to cover the same goods covered by the bill of lading". It must cover separately the quantity of goods called for by the buyer's contract and not merely insure his goods as part of a larger quantity in which others are interested, a case provided for in American mercantile practice by the use of negotiable certificates of insurance which are expressly authorized by this section. By usage these certificates are treated as the equivalent of separate policies and are good tender under C.I.F. contracts. The term "certificate of insurance", however, does not of itself include certificates or "cover notes" issued by the insurance broker and stating that the goods are covered by a policy. Their sufficiency as substitutes for policies will depend upon proof of an established usage or course of dealing. The present section rejects the English rule that not only brokers' certificates and "cover notes" but also certain forms of American insurance certificates are not the equivalent of policies and are not good tender under a C.I.F. contract.

The seller's failure to tender a proper insurance document is waived if the buyer refuses to make payment on other and untenable grounds at a time when proper insurance could have been obtained and tendered by the seller if timely objection had been made. Even a failure to insure on shipment may be cured by seasonable tender of a policy retroactive in effect; e.g., one insuring the goods "lost or not lost". The provisions of this Article on cure of improper tender and on waiver of buyer's objections by silence are applicable to insurance tenders under a C.I.F. term. Where there is no waiver by the buyer as described above, however, the fact that the goods arrive safely does not cure the seller's breach of his obligations to insure them and tender to the buyer a proper insurance document.

10. The seller's invoice of the goods shipped under a C.I.F. contract is regarded as a usual and necessary document upon which reliance may properly be placed. It is the document which evidences points of description, quality and the like which do not readily appear in other documents. This Article rejects those statements to the effect that the invoice is a usual but not a necessary document under a C.I.F. term.

11. The buyer needs all of the documents required under a C.I.F. contract, in due form and with necessary endorsements, so that before the goods arrive he may deal with them by negotiating the documents or may obtain prompt possession of the goods after their arrival. If the goods are lost or damaged in transit the documents are necessary to enable him promptly to assert his remedy against the carrier or insurer. The seller is therefore obligated to do what is mercantilely reasonable in the circumstances and should make every reasonable exertion to send forward the documents as soon as possible after the shipment. The requirement that the documents be forwarded with "commercial promptness" expresses a more urgent need for action than that suggested by the phrase "reasonable time".

12. Under a C.I.F. contract the buyer, as under the common law, must pay the price upon tender of the required documents without first inspecting the goods, but his payment in these circumstances does not constitute an acceptance of the goods nor does it impair his right of subsequent inspection or his options and remedies in the case of improper delivery. All remedies and rights for the seller's breach are reserved to him. The buyer must pay before inspection and assert his remedy against the seller afterward unless the nonconformity of the goods amounts to a real failure of consideration, since the purpose of choosing this form of contract is to give the seller protection against the buyer's unjustifiable rejection of the goods at a distant port of destination which would necessitate taking possession of the goods and suing the buyer there.

13. A valid C.I.F. contract may be made which requires part of the transportation to be made on land and part on the sea, as where the goods are to be brought by rail from an inland point to a seaport and thence transported by vessel to the named destination under a "through" or combination bill of lading issued by the railroad company. In such a case shipment by rail from the inland point within the contract period is a timely shipment notwithstanding that the loading of the goods on the vessel is delayed by causes beyond the seller's control.

14. Although subsection (2) stating the legal effects of the C.I.F. term is an "unless otherwise agreed" provision, the express language used in an agreement is frequently a precautionary, fuller statement of the normal C.I.F. terms and hence not intended as a departure or variation from them. Moreover, the dominant outlines of the C.I.F. term are so well understood commercially that any variation should, whenever reasonably possible, be read as falling within those dominant outlines rather than as destroying the whole meaning of a term which essentially indicates a contract for proper shipment rather than one for delivery at destination. Particularly careful consideration is necessary before a printed form or clause is construed to mean agreement otherwise and where a C.I.F. contract is prepared on a printed form designed for some other type of contract, the C.I.F. terms must prevail over printed clauses repugnant to them.

15. Under subsection (4) the fact that the seller knows at the time of the tender of the documents that the goods have been lost in transit does not affect his rights if he has performed his contractual obligations. Similarly, the seller cannot perform under a C.I.F. term by purchasing and tendering landed goods.

16. Under the C. & F. term, as under the C.I.F. term, title and risk of loss are intended to pass to the buyer on shipment. A stipulation in a C. & F. contract that the seller shall effect insurance on the goods and charge the buyer with the premium (in effect that he shall act as the buyer's agent for that purpose) is entirely in keeping with the pattern. On the other hand, it often happens that the buyer is in a more advantageous position than the seller to effect insurance on the goods or that he has in force an "open" or "floating" policy covering all shipments made by him or to him, in either of which events the C. & F. term is adequate without mention of insurance.

17. It is to be remembered that in a French contract the term "C.A.F." does not mean "Cost and Freight" but has exactly the same meaning as the term "C.I.F." since it is merely the French equivalent of that term. The "A" does not stand for "and" but for "assurance" which means insurance.

Cross References:

Point 4:	Section 2-323.
Point 6:	Section 2-509(1)(a).
Point 9:	Sections 2-508 and 2-605(1)(a).
Point 12:	Sections 2-321(3), 2-512 and 2-513(3) and Article 5.

Definitional Cross References:

"Bill of lading".	Section 1-201.
"Buyer".	Section 2-103.
"Contract".	Section 1-201.
"Goods".	Section 2-105.
"Right".	Section 1-201.
"Seller".	Section 2-103.
"Term".	Section 1-201.

Section 2-321. C.I.F. or C. & F.: "Net Landed Weights"; "Payment on Arrival"; Warranty of Condition on Arrival

Under a contract containing a term C.I.F. or C. & F.

(1) Where the price is based on or is to be adjusted according to "net landed weights", "delivered weights", "out turn" quantity or quality or the like, unless otherwise agreed the seller must reasonably estimate the price. The payment due on tender of the documents

called for by the contract is the amount so estimated, but after final adjustment of the price a settlement must be made with commercial promptness.

(2) An agreement described in subsection (1) or any warranty of quality or condition of the goods on arrival places upon the seller the risk of ordinary deterioration, shrinkage and the like in transportation but has no effect on the place or time of identification to the contract for sale or delivery or on the passing of the risk of loss.

(3) Unless otherwise agreed where the contract provides for payment on or after arrival of the goods the seller must before payment allow such preliminary inspection as is feasible; but if the goods are lost delivery of the documents and payment are due when the goods should have arrived.

Official Comment

Prior Uniform Statutory Provision: None.

Purposes: This section deals with two variations of the C.I.F. contract which have evolved in mercantile practice but are entirely consistent with the basic C.I.F. pattern. Subsections (1) and (2), which provide for a shift to the seller of the risk of quality and weight deterioration during shipment, are designed to conform the law to the best mercantile practice and usage without changing the legal consequences of the C.I.F. or C. & F. term as to the passing of marine risks to the buyer at the point of shipment. Subsection (3) provides that where under the contract documents are to be presented for payment after arrival of the goods, this amounts merely to a postponement of the payment under the C.I.F. contract and is not to be confused with the "no arrival, no sale" contract. If the goods are lost, delivery of the documents and payment against them are due when the goods should have arrived. The clause for payment on or after arrival is not to be construed as such a condition precedent to payment that if the goods are lost in transit the buyer need never pay and the seller must bear the loss.

Cross Reference: Section 2-324.

Definitional Cross References:

"Agreement". Section 1-201.
"Contract". Section 1-201.
"Delivery". Section 1-201.
"Goods". Section 2-105.
"Seller". Section 2-103.
"Term". Section 1-201.

Section 2-322. Delivery "Ex-Ship"

(1) Unless otherwise agreed a term for delivery of goods "ex-ship" (which means from the carrying vessel) or in equivalent language is not restricted to a particular ship and requires delivery from a ship which has reached a place at the named port of destination where goods of the kind are usually discharged.

(2) Under such a term unless otherwise agreed

(a) the seller must discharge all liens arising out of the carriage and furnish the buyer with a direction which puts the carrier under a duty to deliver the goods; and

(b) the risk of loss does not pass to the buyer until the goods leave the ship's tackle or are otherwise properly unloaded.

Official Comment

Prior Uniform Statutory Provision: None.

Purposes:

1. The delivery term, "ex-ship", as between seller and buyer, is the reverse of the f.a.s. term covered.

2. Delivery need not be made from any particular vessel under a clause calling for delivery "ex-ship", even though a vessel on which shipment is to be made originally is named in the contract, unless the agreement by appropriate language, restricts the clause to delivery from a named vessel.

3. The appropriate place and manner of unloading at the port of destination depend upon the nature of the goods and the facilities and usages of the port.

4. A contract fixing a price "ex-ship" with payment "cash against documents" calls only for such documents as are appropriate to the contract. Tender of a delivery order and of a receipt for the freight after the arrival of the carrying vessel is adequate. The seller is not required to tender a bill of lading as a document of title nor is he required to insure the goods for the buyer's benefit, as the goods are not at the buyer's risk during the voyage.

Cross Reference: Point 1: Section 2-319(2).

Definitional Cross References:

"Buyer". Section 2-103.
"Goods". Section 2-105.
"Seller". Section 2-103.
"Term". Section 1-201.

Section 2-323. Form of Bill of Lading Required in Overseas Shipment; "Overseas"

(1) Where the contract contemplates overseas shipment and contains a term C.I.F. or C. & F. or F.O.B. vessel, the seller unless otherwise agreed must obtain a negotiable bill of lading stating that the goods have been loaded in board or, in the case of a term C.I.F. or C. & F., received for shipment.

(2) Where in a case within subsection (1) a bill of lading has been issued in a set of parts, unless otherwise agreed if the documents are not to be sent from abroad the buyer may demand tender of the full set; otherwise only one part of the bill of lading need be tendered. Even if the agreement expressly requires a full set

(a) due tender of a single part is acceptable within the provisions of this Article on cure of improper delivery (subsection (1) of Section 2-508); and

(b) even though the full set is demanded, if the documents are sent from abroad the person tendering an incomplete set may nevertheless require payment upon furnishing an indemnity which the buyer in good faith deems adequate.

(3) A shipment by water or by air or a contract contemplating such shipment is "overseas" insofar as by usage of trade or agreement it is subject to the commercial, financing or shipping practices characteristic of international deep water commerce.

Official Comment

Prior Uniform Statutory Provision: None.

Purposes:

1. Subsection (1) follows the "American" rule that a regular bill of lading indicating delivery of the goods at the dock for shipment is sufficient, except under a term "F.O.B. vessel". See Section 2-319 and comment thereto.

2. Subsection (2) deals with the problem of bills of lading covering deep water shipments, issued not as a single bill of lading but in a set of parts, each part referring to the other parts and the entire set constituting in commercial practice and at law a single bill of lading. Commercial practice in international commerce is to accept and pay against presentation of the first part of a set if the part is sent from overseas even though the contract of the buyer requires presentation of a full set of bills of lading provided adequate indemnity for the missing parts is forthcoming.

This subsection codifies that practice as between buyer and seller. Banks presenting drafts under letters of credit may give indemnities against the missing parts, and this subsection means that the buyer must accept and act on such indemnities if he in good faith deems them adequate. But neither this subsection nor Article 5 decides whether a bank which has issued a letter of credit is similarly bound. The issuing bank's obligation under a letter of credit is independent and depends on its own terms. See Article 5.

Cross References: Section 2-508(2).

Definitional Cross References:

"Bill of lading".	Section 1-201.
"Buyer".	Section 2-103.
"Contract".	Section 1-201.
"Delivery".	Section 1-201.
"Financing agency".	Section 2-104.
"Person".	Section 1-201.
"Seller".	Section 2-103.
"Send".	Section 1-201.
"Term".	Section 1-201.

Section 2-324. "No Arrival, No Sale" Term

Under a term "no arrival, no sale" or terms of like meaning, unless otherwise agreed,

(a) the seller must properly ship conforming goods and if they arrive by any means he must tender them on arrival but he assumes no obligation that the goods will arrive unless he has caused the non-arrival; and

(b) where without fault of the seller the goods are in part lost or have so deteriorated as no longer to conform to the contract or arrive after the contract time, the buyer may proceed as if there had been casualty to identified goods (Section 2-613).

Official Comment

Prior Uniform Statutory Provision: None.

Purposes:

1. The "no arrival, no sale" term in a "destination" overseas contract leaves risk of loss on the seller but gives him an exemption from liability for non-delivery. Both the nature of the case and the duty of good faith require that the seller must not interfere with the arrival of the goods in any way. If the circumstances impose upon him the responsibility for making or arranging the shipment, he must have a shipment made despite the exemption clause. Further, the shipment made must be a conforming one, for the exemption under a "no arrival, no sale" term applies only to the hazards of transportation and the goods must be proper in all other respects.

The reason of this section is that where the seller is reselling goods bought by him as shipped by another and this fact is known to the buyer, so that the seller is not under any obligation to make the shipment himself, the seller is entitled under the "no arrival, no sale" clause to exemption from payment of damages for non-delivery if the goods do not arrive or if the goods which actually arrive are non-conforming. This does not extend to sellers who arrange shipment by their own agents, in which case the clause is limited to casualty due to marine hazards. But sellers who make known that they are contracting only with respect to what will be delivered to them by parties over whom they assume no control are entitled to the full quantum of the exemption.

2. The provisions of this Article on identification must be read together with the present section in order to bring the exemption into application. Until there is some designation of the goods in a particular shipment or on a particular ship as being those to which the contract refers there can be no application of an exemption for their non-arrival.

3. The seller's duty to tender the agreed or declared goods if they do arrive is not impaired because of their delay in arrival or by their arrival after transshipment.

4. The phrase "to arrive" is often employed in the same sense as "no arrival, no sale" and may then be given the same effect. But a "to arrive" term, added to a C.I.F. or C. & F. contract, does not have the full meaning given by this section to "no arrival, no sale". Such a "to arrive" term is usually intended to operate only to the extent that the risks are not covered by the agreed insurance and the loss or casualty is due to such uncovered hazards. In some instances the "to arrive" term may be regarded as a time of payment term, or, in the case of the reselling seller discussed in point 1 above, as negating responsibility for conformity of the goods, if they arrive, to any description which was based on his good faith belief of the quality. Whether this is the intention of the parties is a question of fact based on all the circumstances surrounding the resale and in case of ambiguity the rules of Sections 2-316 and 2-317 apply to preclude dishonor.

5. Paragraph (b) applies where goods arrive impaired by damage or partial loss during transportation and makes the policy of this Article on casualty to identified goods applicable to such a situation. For the term cannot be regarded as intending to give the seller an unforeseen profit through casualty; it is intended only to protect him from loss due to causes beyond his control.

Cross References:

Point 1:	Section 1-304.
Point 2:	Section 2-501(a) and (c).
Point 5:	Section 2-613.

Definitional Cross References:

"Buyer".	Section 2-103.
"Conforming".	Section 2-106.
"Contract".	Section 1-201.
"Fault".	Section 1-201.
"Goods".	Section 2-105.
"Sale".	Section 2-106.
"Seller".	Section 2-103.
"Term".	Section 1-201.

Section 2-325. "Letter of Credit" Term; "Confirmed Credit"

(1) Failure of the buyer seasonably to furnish an agreed letter of credit is a breach of the contract for sale.

(2) The delivery to seller of a proper letter of credit suspends the buyer's obligation to pay. If the letter of credit is dishonored, the seller may on seasonable notification to the buyer require payment directly from him.

(3) Unless otherwise agreed the term "letter of credit" or "banker's credit" in a contract for sale means an irrevocable credit issued by a financing agency of good repute and, where the shipment is overseas, of good international repute. The term "confirmed credit" means that the credit must also carry the direct obligation of such an agency which does business in the seller's financial market.

Official Comment

Prior Uniform Statutory Provision: None.

Purposes: To express the established commercial and banking understanding as to the meaning and effects of terms calling for "letters of credit" or "confirmed credit":

1. Subsection (2) follows the general policy of this Article and Article 3 (Section 3-310(b)) on conditional payment, under which payment by check or other short-term instrument is not ordinarily final as between the parties if the recipient duly presents the instrument and honor is refused. Thus the furnishing of a letter of credit does not substitute the financing agency's obligation for the buyer's, but the seller must first give the buyer reasonable notice of his intention to demand direct payment from him.

2. Subsection (2) requires that the credit be irrevocable and be a prime credit as determined by the standing of the issuer. It is not necessary, unless otherwise agreed, that the credit be a negotiation credit; the seller can finance himself by an assignment of the proceeds under Section 5-114.

3. The definition of "confirmed credit" is drawn on the supposition that the credit is issued by a bank which is not doing direct business in the seller's financial market; there is no intention to require the obligation of two banks both local to the seller.

Cross References:

Sections 2-403, 2-511(3) and 3-3110(b) and Article 5.

Definitional Cross References:

"Buyer".	Section 2-103.
"Contract for sale".	Section 2-106.
"Draft".	Section 3-104.
"Financing agency".	Section 2-104.
"Notifies".	Section 1-202.
"Overseas".	Section 2-323.
"Purchaser".	Section 1-201.
"Seasonably".	Section 1-205.
"Seller".	Section 2-103.
"Term".	Section 1-201.

Section 2-326. Sale on Approval and Sale or Return; Rights of Creditors

(1) Unless otherwise agreed, if delivered goods may be returned by the buyer even though they conform to the contract, the transaction is

(a) a "sale on approval" if the goods are delivered primarily for use, and

(b) a "sale or return" if the goods are delivered primarily for resale.

(2) Except as provided in subsection (3), goods held on approval are not subject to the claims of the buyer's creditors until acceptance; goods held on sale or return are subject to such claims while in the buyer's possession.

(3) Where goods are delivered to a person for sale and such person maintains a place of business at which he deals with goods of the kind involved, under a name other than the name of the person making delivery, then with respect to creditors of the person conducting the business the goods are deemed to be on sale or return. The provisions of this subsection are applicable even though an agreement purports to reserve title to the person making delivery until payment or resale or uses such words as "on consignment" or "on memorandum." However, this subsection is not applicable if the person making delivery

(a) complies with an applicable law providing for a consignor's interest or the like to be evidenced by a sign, or

(b) establishes that the person conducting the business is generally known by his creditors to be substantially engaged in selling the goods of others, or

(c) complies with the filing provisions of the Article on Secured Transactions (Article 9).

(3) Any "or return" term of a contract for sale is to be treated as a separate contract for sale within the statute of frauds section of this Article (Section 2-201) and as contradicting the sale aspect of the contract within the provisions of this Article on parol or extrinsic evidence (Section 2-202).

Official Comment

Prior Uniform Statutory Provision: Section 19(3), Uniform Sales Act.

Changes: Completely rewritten in this and the succeeding section.

Purposes of Changes: To make it clear that:

1. Both a "sale on approval" and a "sale or return" should be distinguished from other types of transactions with which they frequently have been confused. A "sale on approval", sometimes also called a sale "on trial" or "on satisfaction", deals with a contract under which the seller undertakes a risk in order to satisfy its prospective buyer with the appearance or performance of the goods that are sold. The goods are delivered to the proposed purchaser but they remain the property of the seller until the buyer accepts them. The price has already been agreed. The buyer's willingness to receive and test the goods is the consideration for the seller's engagement to deliver and sell. A "sale or return", on the other hand, is a sale to a merchant whose unwillingness to buy is overcome by the seller's engagement to take back the goods (or any commercial unit of goods) in lieu of payment if they fail to be resold. A sale or return is a present sale of goods which may be undone at the buyer's option. Accordingly, subsection (2) provides that goods delivered on approval are not subject to the prospective buyer's creditors until acceptance, and goods delivered in a sale or return are subject to the buyer's creditors while in the buyer's possession.

These two transactions are so strongly delineated in practice and in general understanding that every presumption runs against a delivery to a consumer being a "sale or return" and against a delivery to a merchant for resale being a "sale on approval".

2. The right to return the goods for failure to conform to the contract does not make the transaction a "sale on approval" or "sale or return" and has nothing to do with this section or Section 2-327. This section is not concerned with remedies for breach of contract. It deals instead with a power given by the contract to turn back the goods even though they are wholly as warranted. This section nevertheless presupposes that a contract for sale is contemplated by the parties although that contract may be of the peculiar character that this section addresses (i.e., a sale on approval or a sale or return).

If a buyer's obligation as a buyer is conditioned not on his personal approval but on the article's passing a described objective test, the risk of loss by casualty pending the test is properly the seller's and proper return is at his expense. On the point of "satisfaction" as meaning "reasonable satisfaction" when an industrial machine is involved, this Article takes no position.

3. Subsection (3) resolves a conflict in the pre-UCC case law by recognizing that an "or return" provision is so definitely at odds with any ordinary contract for sale of goods that if a written agreement is involved the "or return" term must be contained in a written memorandum. The "or return" aspect of a sales contract must be treated as a separate contract under the Statute of Frauds section and as contradicting the sale insofar as questions of parol or extrinsic evidence are concerned.

4. The transactions governed by this section are sales; the persons to whom the goods are delivered are buyers. This section has no application to transactions in which goods are delivered to a person who has neither bought the goods nor contracted to buy them. See PEB Commentary No. 20. Transactions in which a non-buyer takes delivery of goods for the purpose of selling them are bailments called consignments and are not "sale on approval" or "sale or return" transactions. Certain consignment transactions were dealt with in pre-1998 Sections 2-326(3) and 9-114. These provisions have been deleted and have been replaced by new provisions in Article 9. See, e.g., Sections 9-109(a)(4); 9-103(d) 9-319.

Cross References:

Point 2: Article 9.

Point 3: Sections 2-201 and 2-202.

Definitional Cross References:

"Between merchants".	Section 2-104.
"Buyer".	Section 2-103.
"Conform".	Section 2-106.
"Contract for sale".	Section 2-106.
"Creditor".	Section 1-201.
"Goods".	Section 2-105.
"Sale".	Section 2-106.
"Seller".	Section 2-103.

Section 2-327. Special Incidents of Sale on Approval and Sale or Return

(1) Under a sale on approval unless otherwise agreed

(a) although the goods are identified to the contract the risk of loss and the title do not pass to the buyer until acceptance; and

(b) use of the goods consistent with the purpose of trial is not acceptance but failure seasonably to notify the seller of election to return the goods is acceptance, and if the goods conform to the contract acceptance of any part is acceptance of the whole; and

(c) after due notification of election to return, the return is at the seller's risk and expense but a merchant buyer must follow any reasonable instructions.

(2) Under a sale or return unless otherwise agreed

(a) the option to return extends to the whole or any commercial unit of the goods while in substantially their original condition, but must be exercised seasonably; and

(b) the return is at the buyer's risk and expense.

Official Comment

Prior Uniform Statutory Provision: Section 19(3), Uniform Sales Act.

Changes: Completely rewritten in preceding and this section.

Purposes of Changes: To make it clear that:

1. In the case of a sale on approval, if all of the goods involved conform to the contract, the buyer's acceptance of part of the goods constitutes acceptance of the whole. Acceptance of part falls outside the normal intent of the parties in the "on approval" situation and the policy of this Article allowing partial acceptance of a defective delivery has no application here. A case where a buyer takes home two dresses to select one commonly involves two distinct contracts; if not, it is covered by the words "unless otherwise agreed".

2. In the case of a sale or return, the return of any unsold unit merely because it is unsold is the normal intent of the "sale or return" provision, and therefore the right to return for this reason alone is independent of any other action under the contract which would turn on wholly different considerations. On the other hand, where the return of goods is for breach, including return of items resold by the buyer and returned by the ultimate purchasers because of defects, the return procedure is governed not by the present section but by the provisions on the effects and revocation of acceptance.

3. In the case of a sale on approval the risk rests on the seller until acceptance of the goods by the buyer, while in a sale or return the risk remains throughout on the buyer.

4. Notice of election to return given by the buyer in a sale on approval is sufficient to relieve him of any further liability. Actual return by the buyer to the seller is required in the case of a sale or return contract. What constitutes due "giving" of notice, as required in "on approval" sales, is governed by the provisions on good faith and notice. "Seasonable" is used here as defined in Section 1-205. Nevertheless, the provisions of both this Article and of the contract on this point must be read with commercial reason and with full attention to good faith.

Cross References:

Point 1: Sections 2-501, 2-601 and 2-603.
Point 2: Sections 2-607 and 2-608.
Point 4: Sections 1-202 and 1-205.

Definitional Cross References:

"Agreement".	Section 1-201.
"Buyer".	Section 2-103.
"Commercial unit".	Section 2-105.
"Conform".	Section 2-106.
"Contract".	Section 1-201.
"Goods".	Section 2-105.
"Merchant".	Section 2-104.
"Notifies".	Section 1-202.
"Notification".	Section 1-202.
"Sale on approval".	Section 2-326.
"Sale or return".	Section 2-326.
"Seasonably".	Section 1-205.
"Seller".	Section 2-103.

Section 2-328. Sale by Auction

(1) In a sale by auction if goods are put up in lots each lot is the subject of a separate sale.

(2) A sale by auction is complete when the auctioneer so announces by the fall of the hammer or in other customary manner. Where a bid is made while the hammer is falling in acceptance of a prior bid the auctioneer may in his discretion reopen the bidding or declare the goods sold under the bid on which the hammer was falling.

(3) Such a sale is with reserve unless the goods are in explicit terms put up without reserve. In an auction with reserve the auctioneer may withdraw the goods at any time until he announces completion of the sale. In an auction without reserve, after the auctioneer calls for bids on an article or lot, that article or lot cannot be withdrawn unless no bid is made within a reasonable time. In either case a bidder may retract his bid until the auctioneer's announcement of completion of the sale, but a bidder's retraction does not revive any previous bid.

(4) If the auctioneer knowingly receives a bid on the seller's behalf or the seller makes or procures such a bid, and notice has not been given that liberty for such bidding is reserved, the buyer may at his option avoid the sale or take the goods at the price of the last good faith bid prior to the completion of the sale. This subsection shall not apply to any bid at a forced sale.

Official Comment

Prior Uniform Statutory Provision: Section 21, Uniform Sales Act.

Changes: Completely rewritten.

Purposes of Changes: To make it clear that:

1. The auctioneer may in his discretion either reopen the bidding or close the sale on the bid on which the hammer was falling when a bid is made at that moment. The recognition of a bid of this kind by the auctioneer in his discretion does not mean a closing in favor of such a bidder, but only that the bid has been accepted as a continuation of the bidding. If recognized, such a bid discharges the bid on which the hammer was falling when it was made.

2. An auction "with reserve" is the normal procedure. The crucial point, however, for determining the nature of an auction is the "putting up" of the goods. This Article accepts the view that the goods may be withdrawn before they are actually "put up", regardless of whether the auction is advertised as one without reserve, without liability on the part of the auction announcer to persons who are present. This is subject to any peculiar facts which might bring the case within the "firm offer" principle of this Article, but an offer to persons generally would require unmistakable language in order to fall within that section. The prior announcement of the nature of the auction either as with reserve or without reserve will, however, enter as an "explicit term" in the "putting up" of the goods and conduct thereafter must be governed accordingly. The present section continues the prior rule permitting withdrawal of bids in auctions both with and without reserve; and the rule is made explicit that the retraction of a bid does not revive a prior bid.

Cross Reference: Point 2: Section 2-205.

Definitional Cross References:

"Buyer".	Section 2-103.
"Good faith".	Section 1-201.
"Goods".	Section 2-105.
"Lot".	Section 2-105.
"Notice".	Section 1-202.
"Sale".	Section 2-106.
"Seller".	Section 2-103.

PART 4. TITLE, CREDITORS AND GOOD FAITH PURCHASERS

Section 2-401. Passing of Title; Reservation for Security; Limited Application of This Section

Each provision of this Article with regard to the rights, obligations and remedies of the seller, the buyer, purchasers or other third parties applies irrespective of title to the goods except where the provision refers to such title. Insofar as situations are not covered by the other provisions of this Article and matters concerning title become material the following rules apply:

(1) Title to goods cannot pass under a contract for sale prior to their identification to the contract (Section 2-501), and unless otherwise explicitly agreed the buyer acquires by their identification a special property as limited by this Act. Any retention or reservation by the seller of the title (property) in goods shipped or delivered to the buyer is limited in effect to a reservation of a security interest. Subject to these provisions and to the provisions of the Article on Secured Transactions (Article 9), title to goods passes from the seller to the buyer in any manner and on any conditions explicitly agreed on by the parties.

(2) Unless otherwise explicitly agreed title passes to the buyer at the time and place at which the seller completes his performance with reference to the physical delivery of the goods, despite any reservation of a security interest and even though a document of title is to be delivered at a different time or place; and in particular and despite any reservation of a security interest by the bill of lading

(a) if the contract requires or authorizes the seller to send the goods to the buyer but does not require him to deliver them at destination, title passes to the buyer at the time and place of shipment; but

(b) if the contract requires delivery at destination, title passes on tender there.

(3) Unless otherwise explicitly agreed where delivery is to be made without moving the goods,

(a) if the seller is to deliver a document of title, title passes at the time when and the place where he delivers such documents; or

(b) if the goods are at the time of contracting already identified and no documents are to be delivered, title passes at the time and place of contracting.

(4) A rejection or other refusal by the buyer to receive or retain the goods, whether or not justified, or a justified revocation of acceptance revests title to the goods in the seller. Such revesting occurs by operation of law and is not a "sale".

Official Comment

Prior Uniform Statutory Provision: See generally, Sections 17, 18, 19 and 20, Uniform Sales Act.

Purposes: To make it clear that:

1. This Article deals with the issues between seller and buyer in terms of step by step performance or non-performance under the contract for sale and not in terms of whether or not "title" to the goods has passed. That the rules of this section in no way alter the rights of either the buyer, seller or third parties declared elsewhere in the Article is made clear by the preamble of this section. This section, however, in no way intends to indicate which line of interpretation should be followed in cases where the applicability of "public" regulation depends upon a "sale" or upon location of "title" without further definition. The basic policy of this Article that known purpose and reason should govern interpretation cannot extend beyond the scope of its own provisions. It is therefore necessary to state what a "sale" is and when title passes under this Article in case the courts deem any public regulation to incorporate the defined term of the "private" law.

2. "Future" goods cannot be the subject of a present sale. Before title can pass the goods must be identified in the manner set forth in Section 2-501. The parties, however, have full liberty to arrange by specific terms for the passing of title to goods which are existing.

3. The "special property" of the buyer in goods identified to the contract is excluded from the definition of "security interest"; its incidents are defined in provisions of this Article such as those on the rights of the seller's creditors, on good faith purchase, on the buyer's right to goods on the seller's insolvency, and on the buyer's right to specific performance or replevin.

4. The factual situations in subsections (2) and (3) upon which passage of title turn actually base the test upon the time when the seller has finally committed himself in regard to specific goods. Thus in a "shipment" contract he commits himself by the act of making the shipment. If shipment is not contemplated subsection (3) turns on the seller's final commitment, i.e. the delivery of documents or the making of the contract.

Cross References:

Point 2: Sections 2-102, 2-501 and 2-502.

Point 3: Sections 1-201, 2-402, 2-403, 2-502 and 2-716.

Definitional Cross References:

"Agreement".	Section 1-201.
"Bill of lading".	Section 1-201.
"Buyer".	Section 2-103.
"Contract".	Section 1-201.
"Contract for sale".	Section 2-106.
"Delivery".	Section 1-201.
"Document of title".	Section 1-201.
"Good faith".	Section 1-201.
"Goods".	Section 2-105.
"Party".	Section 1-201.
"Purchaser".	Section 1-201.
"Receipt" of goods.	Section 2-103.
"Remedy".	Section 1-201.
"Right".	Section 1-201.
"Sale".	Section 2-106.
"Security interest".	Section 1-201.
"Seller".	Section 2-103.
"Send".	Section 1-201.

Section 2-402. Rights of Seller's Creditors Against Sold Goods

(1) Except as provided in subsections (2) and (3), rights of unsecured creditors of the seller with respect to goods which have been identified to a contract for sale are subject to the buyer's rights to recover the goods under this Article (Sections 2-502 and 2-716).

(2) A creditor of the seller may treat a sale or an identification of goods to a contract for sale as void if as against him a retention of possession by the seller is fraudulent under any rule of law of the state where the goods are situated, except that retention of possession in good faith and current course of trade by a merchant-seller for a commercially reasonable time after a sale or identification is not fraudulent.

(3) Nothing in this Article shall be deemed to impair the rights of creditors of the seller

(a) under the provisions of the Article on Secured Transactions (Article 9); or

(b) where identification to the contract or delivery is made not in current course of trade but in satisfaction of or as security for a pre-existing claim for money, security or the like and is made under circumstances which under any rule of law of the state where the goods are situated would apart from this Article constitute the transaction a fraudulent transfer or voidable preference.

Official Comment

Prior Uniform Statutory Provision: Subsection (2)—Section 26, Uniform Sales Act; Subsections (1) and (3)—none.

Changes: Rephrased.

Purposes of Changes and New Matter: To avoid confusion on ordinary issues between current sellers and buyers and issues in the field of preference and hindrance by making it clear that:

1. Local law on questions of hindrance of creditors by the seller's retention of possession of the goods are outside the scope of this Article, but retention of possession in the current course of trade is legitimate. Transactions which fall within the law's policy against improper preferences are reserved from the protection of this Article.

2. The retention of possession of the goods by a merchant seller for a commercially reasonable time after a sale or identification in current course is exempted from attack as fraudulent. Similarly, the provisions of subsection (3) have no application to identification or delivery made in the current course of trade, as measured against general commercial understanding of what a "current" transaction is.

Definitional Cross References:

"Contract for sale".	Section 2-106.
"Creditor".	Section 1-201.
"Good faith".	Section 1-201.
"Goods".	Section 2-105.
"Merchant".	Section 2-104.
"Money".	Section 1-201.
"Reasonable time".	Section 1-205.
"Right".	Section 1-201.
"Sale".	Section 2-106.
"Seller".	Section 2-103.

Section 2-403. Power to Transfer; Good Faith Purchase of Goods; "Entrusting"

(1) A purchaser of goods acquires all title which his transferor had or had power to transfer except that a purchaser of a limited interest acquires rights only to the extent of the interest purchased. A person with voidable title has power to transfer a good title to a good faith purchaser for value. When goods have been delivered under a transaction of purchase the purchaser has such power even though

(a) the transferor was deceived as to the identity of the purchaser, or

(b) the delivery was in exchange for a check which is later dishonored, or

(c) it was agreed that the transaction was to be a "cash sale", or

(d) the delivery was procured through fraud punishable as larcenous under the criminal law.

(2) Any entrusting of possession of goods to a merchant who deals in goods of that kind gives him power to transfer all rights of the entruster to a buyer in ordinary course of business.

(3) "Entrusting" includes any delivery and any acquiescence in retention of possession regardless of any condition expressed between the parties to the delivery or acquiescence and regardless of whether the procurement of the entrusting or the possessor's disposition of the goods have been such as to be larcenous under the criminal law.

[*Publisher's Editorial Note: If a state adopts the repealer of Article 6—Bulk Transfers (Alternative A), subsec. (4) should read as follows:*]

(4) The rights of other purchasers of goods and of lien creditors are governed by the Articles on Secured Transactions (Article 9) and Documents of Title (Article 7).

[Publisher's Editorial Note: If a state adopts Revised Article 6—Bulk Sales (Alternative B), subsec. (4) should read as follows:]

(4) The rights of other purchasers of goods and of lien creditors are governed by the Articles on Secured Transactions (Article 9), Bulk Sales (Article 6) and Documents of Title (Article 7).

As amended in 1988.

For material relating to the changes made in text in 1988, see section 3 of Alternative A (Repealer of Article 6—Bulk Transfers) and Conforming Amendment to Section 2-403 following end of Alternative B (Revised Article 6—Bulk Sales).

Official Comment

Prior Uniform Statutory Provision: Sections 20(4), 23, 24, 25, Uniform Sales Act; Section 9, especially 9(2), Uniform Trust Receipts Act; Section 9, Uniform Conditional Sales Act.

Changes: Consolidated and rewritten.

Purposes of Changes: To gather together a series of prior uniform statutory provisions and the case-law thereunder and to state a unified and simplified policy on good faith purchase of goods.

1. The basic policy of our law allowing transfer of such title as the transferor has is generally continued and expanded under subsection (1). In this respect the provisions of the section are applicable to a person taking by any form of "purchase" as defined by this Act. Moreover the policy of this Act expressly providing for the application of supplementary general principles of law to sales transactions wherever appropriate joins with the present section to continue unimpaired all rights acquired under the law of agency or of apparent agency or ownership or other estoppel, whether based on statutory provisions or on case law principles. The section also leaves unimpaired the powers given to selling factors under the earlier Factors Acts. In addition subsection (1) provides specifically for the protection of the good faith purchaser for value in a number of specific situations which have been troublesome under prior law.

On the other hand, the contract of purchase is of course limited by its own terms as in a case of pledge for a limited amount or of sale of a fractional interest in goods.

2. The many particular situations in which a buyer in ordinary course of business from a dealer has been protected against reservation of property or other hidden interest are gathered by subsections (2)-(4) into a single principle protecting persons who buy in ordinary course out of inventory. Consignors have no reason to complain, nor have lenders who hold a security interest in the inventory, since the very purpose of goods in inventory is to be turned into cash by sale.

The principle is extended in subsection (3) to fit with the abolition of the old law of "cash sale" by subsection (1) (c). It is also freed from any technicalities depending on the extended law of larceny; such extension of the concept of theft to include trick, particular types of fraud, and the like is for the purpose of helping conviction of the offender; it has no proper application to the long-standing policy of civil protection of buyers from persons guilty of such trick or fraud. Finally, the policy is extended, in the interest of simplicity and sense, to any entrusting by a bailor; this is in consonance with the explicit provisions of Section 7-205 on the powers of a warehouseman who is also in the business of buying and selling fungible goods of the kind he warehouses. As to entrusting by a secured party, subsection (2) is limited by the more specific provisions of Section 9-307(1), which deny protection to a person buying farm products from a person engaged in farming operations.

3. The definition of "buyer in ordinary course of business" (Section 1-201) applies here and preserves the essence of the healthy limitations engrafted by the case-law on the older statutes. The older loose concept of good faith and wide definition of value combined to create apparent good faith purchasers in many situations in which the result outraged common sense; the court's solution was to protect the original title especially by use of "cash sale" or of over-technical construction of the enabling clauses of the statutes. But such rulings then turned into limitations on the proper protection of buyers in the ordinary market. Section 1-201(b)(9) cuts down the category of buyer in ordinary course in such fashion as to take care of the results of the cases, but with no price either in confusion or in injustice to proper dealings in the normal market.

4. Except as provided in subsection (1), the rights of purchasers other than buyers in ordinary course are left to the Articles on Secured Transactions, Documents of Title, and, if not repealed, Bulk Sales.

Cross References:

Point 1:	Sections 1-103 and 1-201.
Point 2:	Sections 1-201, 2-402, 7-205, 9-203(c)(6) and 9-307(1).
Points 3 and 4:	Sections 1-201, 1-302, 2-104, 2-707 and Articles 7, 9 and, if not repealed, 6.

Definitional Cross References:

"Buyer in ordinary course of business".	Section 1-201.
"Good faith".	Sections 1-201 and 1-304.
"Goods".	Section 2-105.
"Person".	Section 1-201.
"Purchaser".	Section 1-201.
"Signed".	Section 1-201.
"Term".	Section 1-201.
"Value".	Section 1-204.

PART 5. PERFORMANCE

Section 2-501. Insurable Interest in Goods; Manner of Identification of Goods

(1) The buyer obtains a special property and an insurable interest in goods by identification of existing goods as goods to which the contract refers even though the goods so identified are non-conforming and he has an option to return or reject them. Such identification can be made at any time and in any manner explicitly agreed to by the parties. In the absence of explicit agreement identification occurs

(a) when the contract is made if it is for the sale of goods already existing and identified;

(b) if the contract is for the sale of future goods other than those described in paragraph (c), when goods are shipped, marked or otherwise designated by the seller as goods to which the contract refers;

(c) when the crops are planted or otherwise become growing crops or the young are conceived if the contract is for the sale of unborn young to be born within twelve months after contracting or for the sale of crops to be harvested within twelve months or the next normal harvest season after contracting whichever is longer.

(2) The seller retains an insurable interest in goods so long as title to or any security interest in the goods remains in him and where the identification is by the seller alone he may until default or insolvency or notification to the buyer that the identification is final substitute other goods for those identified.

(3) Nothing in this section impairs any insurable interest recognized under any other statute or rule of law.

Official Comment

Prior Uniform Statutory Provision: See Sections 17 and 19, Uniform Sales Act.

Purposes:

1. The present section deals with the manner of identifying goods to the contract so that an insurable interest in the buyer and the rights set forth in the next section will accrue. Generally speaking, identification may be made in any manner "explicitly agreed to" by the parties. The rules of paragraphs (a), (b) and (c) apply only in the absence of such "explicit agreement".

2. In the ordinary case identification of particular existing goods as goods to which the contract refers is unambiguous and may occur in one of many ways. It is possible, however, for the identification to be tentative or contingent. In view of the limited effect given to identification by this Article, the general policy is to resolve all doubts in favor of identification.

3. The provision of this section as to "explicit agreement" clarifies the present confusion in the law of sales which has arisen from the fact that under prior uniform legislation all rules of presumption with reference to the passing of title or to appropriation (which in turn depended upon identification) were regarded as subject to the contrary intention of the parties or of the party appropriating. Such uncertainty is reduced to a minimum under this section by requiring "explicit agreement" of the parties before the rules of paragraphs (a), (b) and (c) are displaced—as they would be by a term giving the buyer power to select the goods. An "explicit" agreement, however, need not necessarily be found in the terms used in the particular transaction. Thus, where a usage of the trade has previously been made explicit by reduction to a standard set of "rules and regulations" currently incorporated by reference into the contracts of the parties, a relevant provision of those "rules and regulations" is "explicit" within the meaning of this section.

4. In view of the limited function of identification there is no requirement in this section that the goods be in deliverable state or that all of the seller's duties with respect to the processing of the goods be completed in order that identification occur. For example, despite identification the risk of loss remains on the seller under the risk of loss provisions until completion of his duties as to the goods and all of his remedies remain dependent upon his not defaulting under the contract.

5. Undivided shares in an identified fungible bulk, such as grain in an elevator or oil in a storage tank, can be sold. The mere making of the contract with reference to an undivided share in an identified fungible bulk is enough under subsection (a) to effect an identification if there is no explicit agreement otherwise. The seller's duty, however, to segregate and deliver according to the contract is not affected by such an identification but is controlled by other provisions of this Article.

6. Identification of crops under paragraph (c) is made upon planting only if they are to be harvested within the year or within the next normal harvest season. The phrase "next normal harvest season" fairly includes nursery stock raised for normally quick "harvest", but plainly excludes a "timber" crop to which the concept of a harvest "season" is inapplicable.

Paragraph (c) is also applicable to a crop of wool or the young of animals to be born within twelve months after contracting. The product of a lumbering, mining or fishing operation, though seasonal, is not within the concept of "growing". Identification under a contract for all or part of the output of such an operation can be effected early in the operation.

Cross References:

Point 1: Section 2-502.

Point 4: Sections 2-509, 2-510 and 2-703.

Point 5: Sections 2-105, 2-308, 2-503 and 2-509.

Point 6: Sections 2-105(1), 2-107(1) and 2-402.

Definitional Cross References:

"Agreement". Section 1-201.
"Contract". Section 1-201.
"Contract for sale". Section 2-106.
"Future goods". Section 2-105.
"Goods". Section 2-105.
"Notification". Section 1-202.
"Party". Section 1-201.
"Sale". Section 2-106.
"Security interest". Section 1-201.
"Seller". Section 2-103.

Section 2-502. Buyer's Right to Goods on Seller's Repudiation, Failure to Deliver, or Insolvency

(1) Subject to subsections (2) and (3) and even though the goods have not been shipped a buyer who has paid a part or all of the price of goods in which he has a special property under the provisions of the immediately preceding section may on making and keeping good a tender of any unpaid portion of their price recover them from the seller if:

(a) in the case of goods bought for personal, family, or household purposes, the seller repudiates or fails to deliver as required by the contract; or

(b) in all cases, the seller becomes insolvent within ten days after receipt of the first installment on their price.

(2) The buyer's right to recover the goods under subsection (1)(a) vests upon acquisition of a special property, even if the seller had not then repudiated or failed to deliver.

(3) If the identification creating his special property has been made by the buyer he acquires the right to recover the goods only if they conform to the contract for sale.

Official Comment

Prior Uniform Statutory Provision: Compare Sections 17, 18 and 19, Uniform Sales Act.

Purposes:

1. This section gives an additional right to the buyer as a result of identification of the goods to the contract in the manner provided in Section 2-501. The buyer is given a right to recover the goods, conditioned upon making and keeping good a tender of any unpaid portion of the price, in two limited circumstances. First, the buyer may recover goods bought for personal, family, or household purposes if the seller repudiates the contract or fails to deliver the goods. Second, in any case, the buyer may recover the goods if the seller becomes insolvent within 10 days after the seller receives the first installment on their price. The buyer's right to recover the goods under this section is an exception to the usual rule, under which the disappointed buyer must resort to an action to recover damages.

2. The question of whether the buyer also acquires a security interest in identified goods and has rights to the goods when insolvency takes place after the ten-day period provided in this section depends upon compliance with the provisions of the Article on Secured Transactions (Article 9).

3. Under subsection (2), the buyer's right to recover consumer goods under subsection (1)(a) vests upon acquisition of a special property, which occurs upon identification of the goods to the contract. See Section 2-501. Inasmuch as a secured party normally acquires no greater rights in its collateral that its debtor had or had power to convey, see Section 2-403(1) (first sentence), a buyer who acquires a right to recover under this section will take free of a security interest created by the seller if it attaches to the goods after the goods have been identified to the contract. The buyer will take free, even if the buyer does not buy in ordinary course and even if the security interest is perfected. Of course, to the extent that the buyer pays the price after the security interest attaches, the payments will constitute proceeds of the security interest.

4. Subsection (3) is included to preclude the possibility of unjust enrichment, which would exist if the buyer were permitted to recover goods even though they were greatly superior in quality or quantity to that called for by the contract for sale.

Cross References:

Point 1: Sections 1-201 and 2-702.

Point 2: Article 9.

Definitional Cross References:

"Buyer". Section 2-103.
"Conform". Section 2-106.
"Contract for sale". Section 2-106.
"Goods". Section 2-105.
"Insolvent". Section 1-201.
"Right". Section 1-201.
"Seller". Section 2-103.

Section 2-503. Manner of Seller's Tender of Delivery

(1) Tender of delivery requires that the seller put and hold conforming goods at the buyer's disposition and give the buyer any notification reasonably necessary to

enable him to take delivery. The manner, time and place for tender are determined by the agreement and this Article, and in particular

(a) tender must be at a reasonable hour, and if it is of goods they must be kept available for the period reasonably necessary to enable the buyer to take possession; but

(b) unless otherwise agreed the buyer must furnish facilities reasonably suited to the receipt of the goods.

(2) Where the case is within the next section respecting shipment tender requires that the seller comply with its provisions.

(3) Where the seller is required to deliver at a particular destination tender requires that he comply with subsection (1) and also in any appropriate case tender documents as described in subsections (4) and (5) of this section.

(4) Where goods are in the possession of a bailee and are to be delivered without being moved

(a) tender requires that the seller either tender a negotiable document of title covering such goods or procure acknowledgment by the bailee of the buyer's right to possession of the goods; but

(b) tender to the buyer of a non-negotiable document of title or of a written direction to the bailee to deliver is sufficient tender unless the buyer seasonably objects, and receipt by the bailee of notification of the buyer's rights fixes those rights as against the bailee and all third persons; but risk of loss of the goods and of any failure by the bailee to honor the non-negotiable document of title or to obey the direction remains on the seller until the buyer has had a reasonable time to present the document or direction, and a refusal by the bailee to honor the document or to obey the direction defeats the tender.

(5) Where the contract requires the seller to deliver documents

(a) he must tender all such documents in correct form, except as provided in this Article with respect to bills of lading in a set (subsection (2) of Section 2-323); and

(b) tender through customary banking channels is sufficient and dishonor of a draft accompanying the documents constitutes non-acceptance or rejection.

Official Comment

Prior Uniform Statutory Provision: See Sections 11, 19, 20, 43(3) and (4), 46 and 51, Uniform Sales Act.

Changes: The general policy of the above sections is continued and supplemented but subsection (3) changes the rule of prior Section 19(5) as to what constitutes a "destination" contract and subsection (4) incorporates a minor correction as to tender of delivery of goods in the possession of a bailee.

Purposes of Changes:

1. The major general rules governing the manner of proper or due tender of delivery are gathered in this section. The term "tender" is used in this Article in two different senses. In one sense it refers to "due tender" which contemplates an offer coupled with a present ability to fulfill all the conditions resting on the tendering party and must be followed by actual performance if the other party shows himself ready to proceed. Unless the context unmistakably indicates otherwise this is the meaning of "tender" in this Article and the occasional addition of the word "due" is only for clarity and emphasis. At other times it is used to refer to an offer of goods or documents under a contract as if in fulfillment of its conditions even though there is a defect when measured against the contract obligation. Used in either sense, however, "tender" connotes such performance by the tendering party as puts the other party in default if he fails to proceed in some manner.

2. The seller's general duty to tender and deliver is laid down in Section 2-301 and more particularly in Section 2-507. The seller's right to a receipt if he demands one and receipts are customary is governed by Section 1-303. Subsection (1) of the present section proceeds to set forth two primary requirements of tender: first, that the seller "put and hold conforming goods at the buyer's disposition" and, second, that he "give the buyer any notice reasonably necessary to enable him to take delivery".

In cases in which payment is due and demanded upon delivery the "buyer's disposition" is qualified by the seller's right to retain control of the goods until payment by the provision of this Article on delivery on condition. However, where the seller is demanding payment on delivery he must first allow the buyer to inspect the goods in order to avoid impairing his tender unless the contract for sale is on C.I.F., C.O.D., cash against documents or similar terms negating the privilege of inspection before payment.

In the case of contracts involving documents the seller can "put and hold conforming goods at the buyer's disposition" under subsection (1) by tendering documents which give the buyer complete control of the goods under the provisions of Article 7 on due negotiation.

3. Under paragraph (a) of subsection (1) usage of the trade and the circumstances of the particular case determine what is a reasonable hour for tender and what constitutes a reasonable period of holding the goods available.

4. The buyer must furnish reasonable facilities for the receipt of the goods tendered by the seller under subsection (1), paragraph (b). This obligation of the buyer is no part of the seller's tender.

5. For the purposes of subsections (2) and (3) there is omitted from this Article the rule under prior uniform legislation that a term requiring the seller to pay the freight or cost of transportation to the buyer is equivalent to an agreement by the seller to deliver to the buyer or at an agreed destination. This omission is with the specific intention of negating the rule, for under this Article the "shipment" contract is regarded as the normal one and the "destination" contract as the variant type. The seller is not obligated to deliver at a named destination and bear the concurrent risk of loss until arrival, unless he has specifically agreed so to deliver or the commercial understanding of the terms used by the parties contemplates such delivery.

6. Paragraph (a) of subsection (4) continues the rule of the prior uniform legislation as to acknowledgment by the bailee. Paragraph (b) of subsection (4) adopts the rule that between the buyer and the seller the risk of loss remains on the seller during a period reasonable for securing acknowledgment of the transfer from the bailee, while as against all other parties the buyer's rights are fixed as of the time the bailee receives notice of the transfer.

7. Under subsection (5) documents are never "required" except where there is an express contract term or it is plainly implicit in the peculiar circumstances of the case or in a usage of trade. Documents may, of course, be "authorized" although not required, but such cases are not within the scope of this subsection. When documents are required, there are three main requirements of this subsection: (1) "All": each required document is essential to a proper tender; (2) "Such": the documents must be the ones actually required by the contract in terms of source and substance; (3) "Correct form": All documents must be in correct form.

When a prescribed document cannot be procured, a question of fact arises under the provision of this Article on substituted performance as to whether the agreed manner of delivery is actually commercially impracticable and whether the substitute is commercially reasonable.

Cross References:

Point 2:	Sections 1-303, 2-301, 2-310, 2-507 and 2-513 and Article 7.
Point 5:	Sections 2-308, 2-310 and 2-509.
Point 7:	Section 2-614(1).

Specific matters involving tender are covered in many additional sections of this Article. See Sections 1-303, 2-301, 2-306 to 2-319, 2-321(3), 2-504, 2-507(2), 2-511(1), 2-513, 2-612 and 2-614.

Definitional Cross References:

"Agreement".	Section 1-201.
"Bill of lading".	Section 1-201.
"Buyer".	Section 2-103.
"Conforming".	Section 2-106.
"Contract".	Section 1-201.
"Delivery".	Section 1-201.
"Dishonor".	Section 3-502.
"Document of title".	Section 1-201.
"Draft".	Section 3-104.
"Goods".	Section 2-105.
"Notification".	Section 1-202.
"Reasonable time".	Section 1-205.
"Receipt" of goods.	Section 2-103.
"Right".	Section 1-201.
"Seasonably".	Section 1-205.
"Seller".	Section 2-103.
"Written".	Section 1-201.

Section 2-504. Shipment by Seller.

Where the seller is required or authorized to send the goods to the buyer and the contract does not require him to deliver them at a particular destination, then unless otherwise agreed he must

(a) put the goods in the possession of such a carrier and make such a contract for their transportation as may be reasonable having regard to the nature of the goods and other circumstances of the case; and

(b) obtain and promptly deliver or tender in due form any document necessary to enable the buyer to obtain possession of the goods or otherwise required by the agreement or by usage of trade; and

(c) promptly notify the buyer of the shipment.

Failure to notify the buyer under paragraph (c) or to make a proper contract under paragraph (a) is a ground for rejection only if material delay or loss ensues.

Official Comment

Prior Uniform Statutory Provision: Section 46, Uniform Sales Act.

Changes: Rewritten.

Purposes of Changes: To continue the general policy of the prior uniform statutory provision while incorporating certain modifications with respect to the requirement that the contract with the carrier be made expressly on behalf of the buyer and as to the necessity of giving notice of the shipment to the buyer, so that:

1. The section is limited to "shipment" contracts as contrasted with "destination" contracts or contracts for delivery at the place where the goods are located. The general principles embodied in this section cover the special cases of F.O.B. point of shipment contracts and C.I.F. and C. & F. contracts. Under the preceding section on manner of tender of delivery, due tender by the seller requires that he comply with the requirements of this section in appropriate cases.

2. The contract to be made with the carrier under paragraph (a) must conform to all express terms of the agreement, subject to any substitution necessary because of failure of agreed facilities as provided in the later provision on substituted performance. However, under the policies of this Article on good faith and commercial standards and on buyer's rights on improper delivery, the requirements of explicit provisions must be read in terms of their commercial and not their literal meaning. This policy is made express with respect to bills of lading in a set in the provision of this Article on form of bills of lading required in overseas shipment.

3. In the absence of agreement, the provision of this Article on options and cooperation respecting performance gives the seller the choice of any reasonable carrier, routing and other arrangements. Whether or not the shipment is at the buyer's expense the seller must see to any arrangements, reasonable in the circumstances, such as refrigeration, watering of live stock, protection against cold, the sending along of any necessary help, selection of specialized cars and the like for paragraph (a) is intended to cover all necessary arrangements whether made by contract with the carrier or otherwise. There is, however, a proper relaxation of such requirements if the buyer is himself in a position to make the appropriate arrangements and the seller gives him reasonable notice of the need to do so. It is an improper contract under paragraph (a) for the seller to agree with the carrier to a limited valuation below the true value and thus cut off the buyer's opportunity to recover from the carrier in the event of loss, when the risk of shipment is placed on the buyer by his contract with the seller.

4. Both the language of paragraph (b) and the nature of the situation it concerns indicate that the requirement that the seller must obtain and deliver promptly to the buyer in due form any document necessary to enable him to obtain possession of the goods is intended to cumulate with the other duties of the seller such as those covered in paragraph (a).

In this connection, in the case of pool car shipments a delivery order furnished by the seller on the pool car consignee, or on the carrier for delivery out of a larger quantity, satisfies the requirements of paragraph (b) unless the contract requires some other form of document.

5. This Article, unlike the prior uniform statutory provision, makes it the seller's duty to notify the buyer of shipment in all cases. The consequences of his failure to do so, however, are limited in that the buyer may reject on this ground only where material delay or loss ensues.

A standard and acceptable manner of notification in open credit shipments is the sending of an invoice and in the case of documentary contracts is the prompt forwarding of the documents as under paragraph (b) of this section. It is also usual to send on a straight bill of lading but this is not necessary to the required notification. However, should such a document prove necessary or convenient to the buyer, as in the case of loss and claim against the carrier, good faith would require the seller to send it on request.

Frequently the agreement expressly requires prompt notification as by wire or cable. Such a term may be of the essence and the final clause of paragraph (c) does not prevent the parties from making this a particular ground for rejection. To have this vital and irreparable effect upon the seller's duties, such a term should be part of the "dickered" terms written in any "form", or should otherwise be called seasonably and sharply to the seller's attention.

6. Generally, under the final sentence of the section, rejection by the buyer is justified only when the seller's dereliction as to any of the requirements of this section in fact is followed by material delay or damage. It rests on the seller, so far as concerns matters not within the peculiar knowledge of the buyer, to establish that his error has not been followed by events which justify rejection.

Cross References:

Point 1: Sections 2-319, 2-320 and 2-503(2).
Point 2: Sections 1-204, 2-323(2), 2-601 and 2-614(1).
Point 3: Section 2-311(2).
Point 5: Section 1-304.

Definitional Cross References:

"Agreement".	Section 1-201.
"Buyer".	Section 2-103.
"Contract".	Section 1-201.
"Delivery".	Section 1-201.
"Goods".	Section 2-105.
"Notifies".	Section 1-202.
"Seller".	Section 2-103.
"Send".	Section 1-201.
"Usage of trade".	Section 1-303.

Section 2-505. Seller's Shipment Under Reservation

(1) Where the seller has identified goods to the contract by or before shipment:

(a) his procurement of a negotiable bill of lading to his own order or otherwise reserves in him a security interest in the goods. His procurement of the bill to the order of a financing agency or of the buyer indicates in addition only the seller's expectation of transferring that interest to the person named.

(b) a non-negotiable bill of lading to himself or his nominee reserves possession of the goods as security but except in a case of conditional delivery (subsection (2) of Section 2-507) a non-negotiable bill of lading naming the buyer as consignee reserves no security interest even though the seller retains possession of the bill of lading.

(2) When shipment by the seller with reservation of a security interest is in violation of the contract for sale it constitutes an improper contract for transportation within the preceding section but impairs neither the rights given to the buyer by shipment and identification of the goods to the contract nor the seller's powers as a holder of a negotiable document.

Official Comment

Prior Uniform Statutory Provision: Section 20(2), (3), (4), Uniform Sales Act.

Changes: Completely rephrased, the "powers" of the parties in cases of reservation being emphasized primarily rather than the "rightfulness" of reservation.

Purposes of Changes: To continue in general the policy of the prior uniform statutory provision with certain modifications of emphasis and language, so that:

1. The security interest reserved to the seller under subsection (1) is restricted to securing payment or performance by the buyer and the seller is strictly limited in his disposition and control of the goods as against the buyer and third parties. Under this Article, the provision as to the passing of interest expressly applies "despite any reservation of security title" and also provides that the "rights, obligations and remedies" of the parties are not altered by the incidence of title generally. The security interest, therefore, must be regarded as a means given to the seller to enforce his rights against the buyer which is unaffected by and in turn does not affect the location of title generally. The rules set forth in subsection (1) are not to be altered by any apparent "contrary intent" of the parties as to passing of title, since the rights and remedies of the parties to the contract of sale, as defined in this Article, rest on the contract and its performance or breach and not on stereotyped presumptions as to the location of title.

This Article does not attempt to regulate local procedure in regard to the effective maintenance of the seller's security interest when the action is in replevin by the buyer against the carrier.

2. Every shipment of identified goods under a negotiable bill of lading reserves a security interest in the seller under subsection (1) paragraph (a).

It is frequently convenient for the seller to make the bill of lading to the order of a nominee such as his agent at destination, the financing agency to which he expects to negotiate the document or the bank issuing a credit to him. In many instances, also, the buyer is made the order party. This Article does not deal directly with the question as to whether a bill of lading made out by the seller to the order of a nominee gives the carrier notice of any rights which the nominee may have so as to limit its freedom or obligation to honor the bill of lading in the hands of the seller as the original shipper if the expected negotiation fails. This is dealt with in the Article on Documents of Title (Article 7).

3. A non-negotiable bill of lading taken to a party other than the buyer under subsection (1) paragraph (b) reserves possession of the goods as security in the seller but if he seeks to withhold the goods improperly the buyer can tender payment and recover them.

4. In the case of a shipment by non-negotiable bill of lading taken to a buyer, the seller, under subsection (1) retains no security interest or possession as against the buyer and by the shipment he *de facto* loses control as against the carrier except where he rightfully and effectively stops delivery in transit. In cases in which the contract gives the seller the right to payment against delivery, the seller, by making an immediate demand for payment, can show that his delivery is conditional, but this does not prevent the buyer's power to transfer full title to a sub-buyer in ordinary course or other purchaser under Section 2-403.

5. Under subsection (2) an improper reservation by the seller which would constitute a breach in no way impairs such of the buyer's rights as result from identification of the goods. The security title reserved by the seller under subsection (1) does not protect his holding of the document or the goods for the purpose of exacting more than is due him under the contract.

Cross References:

Point 1:	Section 1-201.
Point 2:	Article 7.
Point 3:	Sections 2-501(2) and 2-504.
Point 4:	Sections 2-403, 2-507(2) and 2-705.
Point 5:	Sections 2-310, 2-319(4), 2-320(4), 2-501 and 2-502 and Article 7.

Definitional Cross References:

"Bill of lading".	Section 1-201.
"Buyer".	Section 2-103.
"Consignee".	Section 7-102.
"Contract".	Section 1-201.
"Contract for sale".	Section 2-106.
"Delivery".	Section 1-201.
"Financing agency".	Section 2-104.
"Goods".	Section 2-105.
"Holder".	Section 1-201.
"Person".	Section 1-201.
"Security interest".	Section 1-201.
"Seller".	Section 2-103.

Section 2-506. Rights of Financing Agency

(1) A financing agency by paying or purchasing for value a draft which relates to a shipment of goods acquires to the extent of the payment or purchase and in addition to its own rights under the draft and any document of title securing it any rights of the shipper in the goods including the right to stop delivery and the shipper's right to have the draft honored by the buyer.

(2) The right to reimbursement of a financing agency which has in good faith honored or purchased the draft under commitment to or authority from the buyer is not impaired by subsequent discovery of defects with reference to any relevant document which was apparently regular on its face.

Official Comment

Prior Uniform Statutory Provision: None.

Purposes:

1. "Financing agency" is broadly defined in this Article to cover every normal instance in which a party aids or intervenes in the financing of a sales transaction. The term as used in subsection (1) is not in any sense intended as a limitation and covers any other appropriate situation which may arise outside the scope of the definition.

2. "Paying" as used in subsection (1) is typified by the letter of credit, or "authority to pay" situation in which a banker, by arrangement with the buyer or other consignee, pays on his behalf a draft for the price of the goods. It is immaterial whether the draft is formally drawn on the party paying or his principal, whether it is a sight draft paid in cash or a time draft "paid" in the first instance by acceptance, or whether the payment is viewed as absolute or conditional. All of these cases constitute "payment" under this subsection. Similarly, "purchasing for value" is used to indicate the whole area of financing by the seller's banker, and the principle of subsection (1) is applicable without any niceties of distinction between "purchase", "discount", "advance against collection" or the like. But it is important to notice that the only right to have the draft honored that is acquired is that *against the buyer*; if any right against any one else is claimed it will have to be under some separate obligation of that other person. A letter of credit does not necessarily protect *purchasers* of drafts. See Article 5. And for the relations of the parties to documentary drafts see Part 5 of Article 4.

3. Subsection (1) is made applicable to payments or advances against a draft which "relates to" a shipment of goods and this has been chosen as a term of maximum breadth. In particular the term is intended to cover the case of a draft against an invoice or against a delivery order. Further, it is unnecessary that there be an explicit assignment of the invoice attached to the draft to bring the transaction within the reason of this subsection.

4. After shipment, "the rights of the shipper in the goods" are merely security rights and are subject to the buyer's right to force delivery upon tender of the price. The rights acquired by the financing agency are similarly limited and, moreover, if the agency fails to procure any outstanding negotiable document of title, it may find its exercise of these rights hampered or even defeated by the seller's disposition of the document to a third party. This section does not attempt to create any new rights in the financing agency against the carrier which would force the latter to honor a stop order from the agency, a stranger to the shipment, or any new rights against a holder to whom a document of title has been duly negotiated under Article 7.

Cross References:

Point 1: Section 2-104(2) and Article 4.
Point 2: Part 5 of Article 4, and Article 5.
Point 4: Sections 2-501 and 2-502(1) and Article 7.

Definitional Cross References:

"Buyer".	Section 2-103.
"Document of title".	Section 1-201.
"Draft".	Section 3-104.
"Financing agency".	Section 2-104.
"Good faith".	Section 1-201.
"Goods".	Section 2-105.
"Purchase".	Section 1-201.
"Right".	Section 1-201.
"Value".	Section 1-204.

Section 2-507. Effect of Seller's Tender; Delivery on Condition

(1) Tender of delivery is a condition to the buyer's duty to accept the goods and, unless otherwise agreed, to his duty to pay for them. Tender entitles the seller to acceptance of the goods and to payment according to the contract.

(2) Where payment is due and demanded on the delivery to the buyer of goods or documents of title, his right as against the seller to retain or dispose of them is conditional upon his making the payment due.

Official Comment

Prior Uniform Statutory Provision: See Sections 11, 41, 42 and 69, Uniform Sales Act.

Purposes:

1. Subsection (1) continues the policies of the prior uniform statutory provisions with respect to tender and delivery by the seller. Under this Article the same rules in these matters are applied to present sales and to contracts for sale. But the provisions of this subsection must be read within the framework of the other sections of this Article which bear upon the question of delivery and payment.

2. The "unless otherwise agreed" provision of subsection (1) is directed primarily to cases in which payment in advance has been promised or a letter of credit term has been included. Payment "according to the contract" contemplates immediate payment, payment at the end of an agreed credit term, payment by a time acceptance or the like. Under this Act, "contract" means the total obligation in law which results from the parties' agreement including the effect of this Article. In this context, therefore, there must be considered the effect in law of such provisions as those on means and manner of payment and on failure of agreed means and manner of payment.

3. Subsection (2) deals with the effect of a conditional delivery by the seller and in such a situation makes the buyer's "right as against the seller" conditional upon payment. These words are used as words of limitation to conform with the policy set forth in the bona fide purchase sections of this Article. Should the seller after making such a conditional delivery fail to follow up his rights, the condition is waived. This subsection (2) codifies the cash seller's right of reclamation which is in the nature of a lien. There is no specific time limit for a cash seller to exercise the right of reclamation. However, the right will be defeated by delay causing prejudice to the buyer, waiver, estoppel, or ratification of the buyer's right to retain possession. Common law rules and precedents governing such principles are applicable (Section 1-103). If third parties are involved, Section 2-403(1) protects good faith purchasers. See PEB Commentary No. 1.

Cross References:

Point 1: Sections 2-310, 2-503, 2-511, 2-601 and 2-711 to 2-713.
Point 2: Sections 1-201, 2-511 and 2-614.
Point 3: Sections 2-401, 2-403, and 2-702(1)(b).

Definitional Cross References:

"Buyer".	Section 2-103.
"Contract".	Section 1-201.
"Delivery".	Section 1-201.
"Document of title".	Section 1-201.
"Goods".	Section 2-105.
"Right".	Section 1-201.
"Seller".	Section 2-103.

Section 2-508. Cure by Seller of Improper Tender or Delivery; Replacement

(1) Where any tender or delivery by the seller is rejected because non-conforming and the time for performance has not yet expired, the seller may seasonably notify the buyer of his intention to cure and may then within the contract time make a conforming delivery.

(2) Where the buyer rejects a non-conforming tender which the seller had reasonable grounds to believe would be acceptable with or without money allowance the seller may if he seasonably notifies the buyer have a further reasonable time to substitute a conforming tender.

Official Comment

Prior Uniform Statutory Provision: None.

Purposes:

1. Subsection (1) permits a seller who has made a non-conforming tender in any case to make a conforming delivery within the contract time upon seasonable notification to the buyer. It applies even where the seller has taken back the non-conforming goods and refunded the purchase price. He may still make a good tender within the contract period. The closer, however, it is to the contract date, the greater is the necessity for extreme promptness on the seller's part in notifying of his intention to cure, if such notification is to be "seasonable" under this subsection.

The rule of this subsection, moreover, is qualified by its underlying reasons. Thus if, after contracting for June delivery, a buyer later makes known to the seller his need for shipment early in the month and the seller ships accordingly, the "contract time" has been cut down by the supervening modification and the time for cure of tender must be referred to this modified time term.

2. Subsection (2) seeks to avoid injustice to the seller by reason of a surprise rejection by the buyer. However, the seller is not protected unless he had "reasonable grounds to believe" that the tender would be acceptable. Such reasonable grounds can lie in prior course of dealing, course of performance or usage of trade as well as in the particular circumstances surrounding the making of the contract. The seller is charged with commercial knowledge of any factors in a particular sales situation which require him to comply strictly with his obligations under the contract as, for example, strict conformity of documents in an overseas shipment or the sale of precision parts or chemicals for use in manufacture. Further, if the buyer gives notice either implicitly, as by a prior course of dealing involving rigorous inspections, or expressly, as by the deliberate inclusion of a "no replacement" clause in the contract, the seller is to be held to rigid compliance. If the clause appears in a "form" contract evidence that it is out of line with trade usage or the prior course of dealing and was not called to the seller's attention may be sufficient to show that the seller had reasonable grounds to believe that the tender would be acceptable.

3. The words "a further reasonable time to substitute a conforming tender" are intended as words of limitation to protect the buyer. What is a "reasonable time" depends upon the attending circumstances. Compare Section 2-511 on the comparable case of a seller's surprise demand for legal tender.

4. Existing trade usages permitting variations without rejection but with price allowance enter into the agreement itself as contractual limitations of remedy and are not covered by this section.

Cross References:

Point 2: Section 2-302.
Point 3: Section 2-511.
Point 4: Sections 1-303 and 2-721.

Definitional Cross References:

"Buyer".	Section 2-103.
"Conforming".	Section 2-106.
"Contract".	Section 1-201.
"Money".	Section 1-201.
"Notifies".	Section 1-202.
"Reasonable time".	Section 1-205.
"Seasonably".	Section 1-205.
"Seller".	Section 2-103.

Section 2-509. Risk of Loss in the Absence of Breach

(1) Where the contract requires or authorizes the seller to ship the goods by carrier

(a) if it does not require him to deliver them at a particular destination, the risk of loss passes to the buyer when the goods are duly delivered to the carrier even though the shipment is under reservation (Section 2-505); but

(b) if it does require him to deliver them at a particular destination and the goods are there duly tendered while in the possession of the carrier, the risk of loss passes to the buyer when the goods are there duly so tendered as to enable the buyer to take delivery.

(2) Where the goods are held by a bailee to be delivered without being moved, the risk of loss passes to the buyer

(a) on his receipt of a negotiable document of title covering the goods; or

(b) on acknowledgment by the bailee of the buyer's right to possession of the goods; or

(c) after his receipt of a non-negotiable document of title or other written direction to deliver, as provided in subsection (4)(b) of Section 2-503.

(3) In any case not within subsection (1) or (2), the risk of loss passes to the buyer on his receipt of the goods if the seller is a merchant; otherwise the risk passes to the buyer on tender of delivery.

(4) The provisions of this section are subject to contrary agreement of the parties and to the provisions of this Article on sale on approval (Section 2-327) and on effect of breach on risk of loss (Section 2-510).

Official Comment

Prior Uniform Statutory Provision: Section 22, Uniform Sales Act.

Changes: Rewritten, subsection (3) of this section modifying prior law.

Purposes of Changes: To make it clear that:

1. The underlying theory of these sections on risk of loss is the adoption of the contractual approach rather than an arbitrary shifting of the risk with the "property" in the goods. The scope of the present section, therefore, is limited strictly to those cases where there has been no breach by the seller. Where for any reason his delivery or tender fails to conform to the contract, the present section does not apply and the situation is governed by the provisions on effect of breach on risk of loss.

2. The provisions of subsection (1) apply where the contract "requires or authorizes" shipment of the goods. This language is intended to be construed parallel to comparable language in the section on shipment by seller. In order that the goods be "duly delivered to the carrier" under paragraph (a) a contract must be entered into with the carrier which will satisfy the requirements of the section on shipment by the seller and the delivery must be made under circumstances which will enable the seller to take any further steps necessary to a due tender. The underlying reason of this subsection does not require that the shipment be made after contracting, but where, for example, the seller buys the goods afloat and later diverts the shipment to the buyer, he must identify the goods to the contract before the risk of loss can pass. To transfer the risk it is enough that a proper shipment and a proper identification come to apply to the same goods although, aside from special agreement, the risk will not pass retroactively to the time of shipment in such a case.

3. Whether the contract involves delivery at the seller's place of business or at the situs of the goods, a merchant seller cannot transfer risk of loss and it remains upon him until actual receipt by the buyer, even though full payment has been made and the buyer has been notified that the goods are at his disposal. Protection is afforded him, in the event of breach by the buyer, under the next section.

The underlying theory of this rule is that a merchant who is to make physical delivery at his own place continues meanwhile to control the goods and can be expected to insure his interest in them. The buyer, on the other hand, has no control of the goods and it is extremely unlikely that he will carry insurance on goods not yet in his possession.

4. Where the agreement provides for delivery of the goods as between the buyer and seller without removal from the physical possession of a bailee, the provisions on manner of tender of delivery apply on the point of transfer of risk. Due delivery of a negotiable document of title covering the goods or acknowledgment by the bailee that he holds for the buyer completes the "delivery" and passes the risk.

5. The provisions of this section are made subject by subsection (4) to the "contrary agreement" of the parties. This language is intended as the equivalent of the phrase "unless otherwise agreed" used more frequently throughout this Act. "Contrary" is in no way used as a word of limitation and the buyer and seller are left free to readjust their rights and risks as declared by this section in any manner agreeable to them. Contrary agreement can also be found in the circumstances of the case, a trade usage or practice, or a course of dealing or performance.

Cross References:

Point 1: Section 2-510(1).
Point 2: Sections 2-503 and 2-504.
Point 3: Sections 2-104, 2-503 and 2-510.
Point 4: Section 2-503(4).
Point 5: Section 1-201.

Definitional Cross References:

"Agreement".	Section 1-201.
"Buyer".	Section 2-103.
"Contract".	Section 1-201.
"Delivery".	Section 1-201.
"Document of title".	Section 1-201.
"Goods".	Section 2-105.
"Merchant".	Section 2-104.
"Party".	Section 1-201.
"Receipt" of goods.	Section 2-103.
"Sale on approval".	Section 2-326.
"Seller".	Section 2-103.

Section 2-510. Effect of Breach on Risk of Loss

(1) Where a tender or delivery of goods so fails to conform to the contract as to give a right of rejection the risk of their loss remains on the seller until cure or acceptance.

(2) Where the buyer rightfully revokes acceptance he may to the extent of any deficiency in his effective insurance coverage treat the risk of loss as having rested on the seller from the beginning.

(3) Where the buyer as to conforming goods already identified to the contract for sale repudiates or is otherwise in breach before risk of their loss has passed to him, the seller may to the extent of any deficiency in his effective insurance coverage treat the risk of loss as resting on the buyer for a commercially reasonable time.

Official Comment

Prior Uniform Statutory Provision: None.

Purposes: To make clear that:

1. Under subsection (1) the seller by his individual action cannot shift the risk of loss to the buyer unless his action conforms with all the conditions resting on him under the contract.

2. The "cure" of defective tenders contemplated by subsection (1) applies only to those situations in which the seller makes changes in goods already tendered, such as repair, partial substitution, sorting out from an improper mixture and the like since "cure" by repossession and new tender has no effect on the risk of loss of the goods originally tendered. The seller's privilege of cure does not shift the risk, however, until the cure is completed.

Where defective documents are involved a cure of the defect by the seller or a waiver of the defects by the buyer will operate to shift the risk under this section. However, if the goods have been destroyed prior to the cure or the buyer is unaware of their destruction at the time he waives the defect in the documents, the risk of the loss must still be borne by the seller, for the risk shifts only at the time of cure, waiver of documentary defects or acceptance of the goods.

3. In cases where there has been a breach of the contract, if the one in control of the goods is the aggrieved party, whatever loss or damage may prove to be uncovered by his insurance falls upon the contract breaker under subsections (2) and (3) rather than upon him. The word "effective" as applied to insurance coverage in those subsections is used to meet the case of supervening insolvency of the insurer. The "deficiency" referred to in the text means such deficiency in the insurance coverage as exists without subrogation. This section merely distributes the risk of loss as stated and is not intended to be disturbed by any subrogation of an insurer.

Cross Reference: Section 2-509.

Definitional Cross References:

"Buyer".	Section 2-103.
"Conform".	Section 2-106.
"Contract for sale".	Section 2-106.
"Goods".	Section 2-105.
"Seller".	Section 2-103.

Section 2-511. Tender of Payment by Buyer; Payment by Check

(1) Unless otherwise agreed tender of payment is a condition to the seller's duty to tender and complete any delivery.

(2) Tender of payment is sufficient when made by any means or in any manner current in the ordinary course of business unless the seller demands payment in legal tender and gives any extension of time reasonably necessary to procure it.

(3) Subject to the provisions of this Act on the effect of an instrument on an obligation (Section 3-310), payment by check is conditional and is defeated as between the parties by dishonor of the check on due presentment.

As amended in 1994.

Official Comment

Prior Uniform Statutory Provision: Section 42, Uniform Sales Act.

Changes: Rewritten by this section and Section 2-507.

Purposes of Changes:

1. The requirement of payment against delivery in subsection (1) is applicable to non-commercial sales generally and to ordinary sales at retail although it has no application to the great body of commercial contracts which carry credit terms. Subsection (1) applies also to documentary contracts in general and to contracts which look to shipment by the seller but contain no term on time and manner of payment, in which situations the payment may, in proper case, be demanded against delivery of appropriate documents.

In the case of specific transactions such as C.O.D. sales or agreements providing for payment against documents, the provisions of this subsection must be considered in conjunction with the special sections of the Article dealing with such terms. The provision that tender of payment is a condition to the seller's duty to tender and complete "any delivery" integrates this section with the language and policy of the section on delivery in several lots which call for separate payment. Finally, attention should be directed to the provision on right to adequate assurance of performance which recognizes, even before the time for tender, an obligation on the buyer not to impair the seller's expectation of receiving payment in due course.

2. Unless there is agreement otherwise the concurrence of the conditions as to tender of payment and tender of delivery requires their performance at a single place or time. This Article determines that place and time by determining in various other sections the place and time for tender of delivery under various circumstances and in particular types of transactions. The sections dealing with time and place of delivery together with the section on right to inspection of goods answer the subsidiary question as to when payment may be demanded before inspection by the buyer.

3. The essence of the principle involved in subsection (2) is avoidance of commercial surprise at the time of performance. The section on substituted performance covers the peculiar case in which legal tender is not available to the commercial community.

4. Subsection (3) is concerned with the rights and obligations as between the parties to a sales transaction when payment is made by check. This Article recognizes that the taking of a seemingly solvent party's check is commercially normal and proper and, if due diligence is exercised in collection, is not to be penalized in any way. The conditional character of the payment under this section refers only to the effect of the transaction "as between the parties" thereto and does not purport to cut into the law of "absolute" and "conditional" payment as applied to such other problems as the discharge of sureties or the responsibilities of a drawee bank which is at the same time an agent for collection.

The phrase "by check" includes not only the buyer's own but any check which does not effect a discharge under Article 3 (Section 3-310). Similarly the reason of this subsection should apply and the same result should be reached where the buyer "pays" by sight draft on a commercial firm which is financing him.

5. Under subsection (3) payment by check is defeated if it is not honored upon due presentment. This corresponds to the provisions of article on Commercial Paper. (Section 3-310). But if the seller procures certification of the check instead of cashing it, the buyer is discharged. (Sections 3-409 and 3-414(c)).

6. Where the instrument offered by the buyer is not a payment but a credit instrument such as a note or a check post-dated by even one day, the seller's acceptance of the instrument insofar as third parties are concerned, amounts to a delivery on credit and his remedies are set forth in the section on buyer's insolvency. As between the buyer and the seller, however, the matter turns on the present subsection and the section on conditional delivery and subsequent dishonor of the instrument gives the seller rights on it as well as for breach of the contract for sale.

Cross References:

Point 1: Sections 2-307, 2-310, 2-320, 2-325, 2-503, 2-513 and 2-609.

Point 2: Sections 2-307, 2-310, 2-319, 2-322, 2-503, 2-504 and 2-513.

Point 3: Section 2-614.

Point 4: Section 3-310.

Point 5: Article 3, esp. Sections 3-310, 3-409 and 3-414.

Point 6: Sections 2-507, 2-702, and Article 3.

Definitional Cross References:

"Buyer".	Section 2-103.
"Check".	Section 3-104.
"Dishonor".	Section 3-508.
"Party".	Section 1-201.
"Reasonable time".	Section 1-205.
"Seller".	Section 2-103.

Section 2-512. Payment by Buyer Before Inspection

(1) Where the contract requires payment before inspection non-conformity of the goods does not excuse the buyer from so making payment unless

(a) the non-conformity appears without inspection; or

(b) despite tender of the required documents the circumstances would justify injunction against honor under this Act (Section 5-109(b)).

(2) Payment pursuant to subsection (1) does not constitute an acceptance of goods or impair the buyer's right to inspect or any of his remedies.

As amended in 1995.

Official Comment

Prior Uniform Statutory Provision: None, but see Sections 47 and 49, Uniform Sales Act.

Purposes:

1. Subsection (1) of the present section recognizes that the essence of a contract providing for payment before inspection is the intention of the parties to shift to the buyer the risks which would usually rest upon the seller. The basic nature of the transaction is thus preserved and the buyer is in most cases required to pay first and litigate as to any defects later.

2. "Inspection" under this section is an inspection in a manner reasonable for detecting defects in goods whose surface appearance is satisfactory.

3. Clause (a) of this subsection states an exception to the general rule based on common sense and normal commercial practice. The apparent non-conformity referred to is one which is evident in the mere process of taking delivery.

4. Clause (b) is concerned with contracts for payment against documents and incorporates the general clarification and modification of the case law contained in the section on excuse of a financing agency. Section 5-109.

5. Subsection (2) makes explicit the general policy of the Uniform Sales Act that the payment required before inspection in no way impairs the buyer's remedies or rights in the event of a default by the seller. The remedies preserved to the buyer are all of his remedies, which include as a matter of reason the remedy for total non-delivery after payment in advance.

The provision on performance or acceptance under reservation of rights does not apply to the situations contemplated here in which payment is made in due course under the contract and the buyer need not pay "under protest" or the like in order to preserve his rights as to defects discovered upon inspection.

6. This section applies to cases in which the contract requires payment before inspection either by the express agreement of the parties or by reason of the effect in law of that contract. The present section must therefore be considered in conjunction with the provision on right to inspection of goods which sets forth the instances in which the buyer is not entitled to inspection before payment.

Cross References:

Point 4: Article 5.

Point 5: Section 1-308.

Point 6: Section 2-513(3).

Definitional Cross References:

"Buyer".	Section 2-103.
"Conform".	Section 2-106.
"Contract".	Section 1-201.
"Financing agency".	Section 2-104.
"Goods".	Section 2-105.
"Remedy".	Section 1-201.
"Right".	Section 1-201.

Section 2-513. Buyer's Right to Inspection of Goods

(1) Unless otherwise agreed and subject to subsection (3), where goods are tendered or delivered or identified to the contract for sale, the buyer has a right before payment or acceptance to inspect them at any reasonable place and time and in any reasonable manner. When the seller is required or authorized to send the goods to the buyer, the inspection may be after their arrival.

(2) Expenses of inspection must be borne by the buyer but may be recovered from the seller if the goods do not conform and are rejected.

(3) Unless otherwise agreed and subject to the provisions of this Article on C.I.F. contracts (subsection (3) of Section 2-321), the buyer is not entitled to inspect the goods before payment of the price when the contract provides

(a) for delivery "C.O.D." or on other like terms; or

(b) for payment against documents of title, except where such payment is due only after the goods are to become available for inspection.

(4) A place or method of inspection fixed by the parties is presumed to be exclusive but unless otherwise

expressly agreed it does not postpone identification or shift the place for delivery or for passing the risk of loss. If compliance becomes impossible, inspection shall be as provided in this section unless the place or method fixed was clearly intended as an indispensable condition failure of which avoids the contract.

Official Comment

Prior Uniform Statutory Provisions: Section 47(2), (3), Uniform Sales Act.

Changes: Rewritten, Subsections (2) and (3) being new.

Purposes of Changes and New Matter: To correspond in substance with the prior uniform statutory provision and to incorporate in addition some of the results of the better case law so that:

1. The buyer is entitled to inspect goods as provided in subsection (1) unless it has been otherwise agreed by the parties. The phrase "unless otherwise agreed" is intended principally to cover such situations as those outlined in subsections (3) and (4) and those in which the agreement of the parties negates inspection before tender of delivery. However, no agreement by the parties can displace the entire right of inspection except where the contract is simply for the sale of "this thing". Even in a sale of boxed goods "as is" inspection is a right of the buyer, since if the boxes prove to contain some other merchandise altogether the price can be recovered back; nor do the limitations of the provision on effect of acceptance apply in such a case.

2. The buyer's right of inspection is available to him upon tender, delivery or appropriation of the goods with notice to him. Since inspection is available to him on tender, where payment is due against delivery he may, unless otherwise agreed, make his inspection before payment of the price. It is also available to him after receipt of the goods and so may be postponed after receipt for a reasonable time. Failure to inspect before payment does not impair the right to inspect after receipt of the goods unless the case falls within subsection (4) on agreed and exclusive inspection provisions. The right to inspect goods which have been appropriated with notice to the buyer holds whether or not the sale was by sample.

3. The buyer may exercise his right of inspection at any reasonable time or place and in any reasonable manner. It is not necessary that he select the most appropriate time, place or manner to inspect or that his selection be the customary one in the trade or locality. Any reasonable time, place or manner is available to him and the reasonableness will be determined by trade usages, past practices between the parties and the other circumstances of the case.

The last sentence of subsection (1) makes it clear that the place of arrival of shipped goods is a reasonable place for their inspection.

4. Expenses of an inspection made to satisfy the buyer of the seller's performance must be assumed by the buyer in the first instance. Since the rule provides merely for an allocation of expense there is no policy to prevent the parties from providing otherwise in the agreement. Where the buyer would normally bear the expenses of the inspection but the goods are rightly rejected because of what the inspection reveals, demonstrable and reasonable costs of the inspection are part of his incidental damage caused by the seller's breach.

5. In the case of payment against documents, subsection (3) requires payment before inspection, since shipping documents against which payment is to be made will commonly arrive and be tendered while the goods are still in transit. This Article recognizes no exception in any peculiar case in which the goods happen to arrive before the documents. However, where by the agreement payment is to await the arrival of the goods, inspection before payment becomes proper since the goods are then "available for inspection".

Where by the agreement the documents are to be held until arrival the buyer is entitled to inspect before payment since the goods are then "available for inspection". Proof of usage is not necessary to establish this right, but if inspection before payment is disputed the contrary must be established by usage or by an explicit contract term to that effect.

For the same reason, that the goods are available for inspection, a term calling for payment against storage documents or a delivery order does not normally bar the buyer's right to inspection before payment under subsection (3)(b). This result is reinforced by the buyer's right under subsection (1) to inspect goods which have been appropriated with notice to him.

6. Under subsection (4) an agreed place or method of inspection is generally held to be intended as exclusive. However, where compliance with such an agreed inspection term becomes impossible, the question is basically one of intention. If the parties clearly intend that the method of inspection named is to be a necessary condition without which the entire deal is to fail, the contract is at an end if that method becomes impossible. On the other hand, if the parties merely seek to indicate a convenient and reliable method but do not intend to give up the deal in the event of its failure, any reasonable method of inspection may be substituted under this Article.

Since the purpose of an agreed place of inspection is only to make sure at that point whether or not the goods will be thrown back, the "exclusive" feature of the named place is satisfied under this Article if the buyer's failure to inspect there is held to be an acceptance with the knowledge of such defects as inspection would have revealed within the section on waiver of buyer's objections by failure to particularize. Revocation of the acceptance is limited to the situations stated in the section pertaining to that subject. The reasonable time within which to give notice of defects within the section on notice of breach begins to run from the point of the "acceptance".

7. Clauses on time of inspection are commonly clauses which limit the time in which the buyer must inspect and give notice of defects. Such clauses are therefore governed by the section of this Article which requires that such a time limitation must be reasonable.

8. Inspection under this Article is not to be regarded as a "condition precedent to the passing of title" so that risk until inspection remains on the seller. Under subsection (4) such an approach cannot be sustained. Issues between the buyer and seller are settled in this Article almost wholly by special provisions and not by the technical determination of the locus of the title. Thus "inspection as a condition to the passing of title" becomes a concept almost without meaning. However, in peculiar circumstances inspection may still have some of the consequences hitherto sought and obtained under that concept.

9. "Inspection" under this section has to do with the buyer's check-up on whether the seller's performance is in accordance with a contract previously made and is not to be confused with the "examination" of the goods or of a sample or model of them at the time of contracting which may affect the warranties involved in the contract.

Cross References:

Generally:	Sections 2-310(b), 2-321(3) and 2-606(1)(b).
Point 1:	Section 2-607.
Point 2:	Sections 2-501 and 2-502.
Point 4:	Section 2-715.
Point 5:	Section 2-321(3).
Point 6:	Sections 2-606 to 2-608.
Point 7:	Section 1-205.
Point 8:	Comment to Section 2-401.
Point 9:	Section 2-316(3)(b).

Definitional Cross References:

"Buyer".	Section 2-103.
"Conform".	Section 2-106.
"Contract".	Section 1-201.
"Contract for sale".	Section 2-106.
"Document of title".	Section 1-201.
"Goods".	Section 2-105.
"Party".	Section 1-201.
"Presumed".	Section 1-206.
"Reasonable time".	Section 1-205.
"Right".	Section 1-201.
"Seller".	Section 2-103.
"Send".	Section 1-201.
"Term".	Section 1-201.

Section 2-514. When Documents Deliverable on Acceptance; When on Payment

Unless otherwise agreed documents against which a draft is drawn are to be delivered to the drawee on acceptance of the draft if it is payable more than three days after presentment; otherwise, only on payment.

Official Comment

Prior Uniform Statutory Provision: Section 41, Uniform Bills of Lading Act.

Changes: Rewritten.

Purposes of Changes: To make the provision one of general application so that:

1. It covers any document against which a draft may be drawn, whatever may be the form of the document, and applies to interpret the action of a seller or consignor insofar as it may affect the rights and duties of any buyer, consignee or financing agency concerned with the paper. Supplementary or corresponding provisions are found in Sections 4-503 and 5-108.

2. An "arrival" draft is a sight draft within the purpose of this section.

Cross References: Point 1: See Sections 2-502, 2-505(2), 2-507(2), 2-512, 2-513, 2-607 concerning protection of rights of buyer and seller, and 4-503 and 5-108 on delivery of documents.

Definitional Cross References:

"Delivery".	Section 1-201.
"Draft".	Section 3-104.

Section 2-515. Preserving Evidence of Goods in Dispute

In furtherance of the adjustment of any claim or dispute

(a) either party on reasonable notification to the other and for the purpose of ascertaining the facts and preserving evidence has the right to inspect, test and sample the goods including such of them as may be in the possession or control of the other; and

(b) the parties may agree to a third party inspection or survey to determine the conformity or condition of the goods and may agree that the findings shall be binding upon them in any subsequent litigation or adjustment.

Official Comment

Prior Uniform Statutory Provision: None.

Purposes:

1. To meet certain serious problems which arise when there is a dispute as to the quality of the goods and thereby perhaps to aid the parties in reaching a settlement, and to further the use of devices which will promote certainty as to the condition of the goods, or at least aid in preserving evidence of their condition.

2. Under paragraph (a), to afford either party an opportunity for preserving evidence, whether or not agreement has been reached, and thereby to reduce uncertainty in any litigation and, in turn perhaps, to promote agreement.

Paragraph (a) does not conflict with the provisions on the seller's right to resell rejected goods or the buyer's similar right. Apparent conflict between these provisions which will be suggested in certain circumstances is to be resolved by requiring prompt action by the parties. Nor does paragraph (a) impair the effect of a term for payment before inspection. Short of such defects as amount to fraud or substantial failure of consideration, non-conformity is neither an excuse nor a defense to an action for non-acceptance of documents. Normally, therefore, until the buyer has made payment, inspected and rejected the goods, there is no occasion or use for the rights under paragraph (a).

3. Under paragraph (b), to provide for third party inspection upon the agreement of the parties, thereby opening the door to amicable adjustments based upon the findings of such third parties.

The use of the phrase "conformity or condition" makes it clear that the parties' agreement may range from a complete settlement of all aspects of the dispute by a third party to the use of a third party merely to determine and record the condition of the goods so that they can be resold or used to reduce the stake in controversy. "Conformity", at one end of the scale of possible issues, includes the whole question of interpretation of the agreement and its legal effect, the state of the goods in regard to quality and condition, whether any defects are due to factors which operate at the risk of the buyer, and the degree of non-conformity where that may be material. "Condition", at the other end of the scale, includes nothing but the degree of damage or deterioration which the goods show. Paragraph (b) is intended to reach any point in the gamut which the parties may agree upon.

The principle of the section on reservation of rights reinforces this paragraph in simplifying such adjustments as the parties wish to make in partial settlement while reserving their rights as to any further points. Paragraph (b) also suggests the use of arbitration, where desired, of any points left open, but nothing in this section is intended to repeal or amend any statute governing arbitration. Where any question arises as to the extent of the parties' agreement under the paragraph, the presumption should be that it was meant to extend only to the relation between the contract description and the goods as delivered, since that is what a craftsman in the trade would normally be expected to report upon. Finally, a written and authenticated report of inspection or tests by a third party, whether or not sampling has been practicable, is entitled to be admitted as evidence under this Act, for it is a third party document.

Cross References:

Point 2: Sections 2-513(3), 2-706 and 2-711(2) and Article 5.

Point 3: Sections 1-307 and 1-308.

Definitional Cross References:

"Conform".	Section 2-106.
"Goods".	Section 2-105.
"Notification".	Section 1-202.
"Party".	Section 1-201.

PART 6. BREACH, REPUDIATION AND EXCUSE

Section 2-601. Buyer's Rights on Improper Delivery

Subject to the provisions of this Article on breach in installment contracts (Section 2-612) and unless otherwise agreed under the sections on contractual limitations of remedy (Sections 2-718 and 2-719), if the goods or the tender of delivery fail in any respect to conform to the contract, the buyer may

(a) reject the whole; or

(b) accept the whole; or

(c) accept any commercial unit or units and reject the rest.

Official Comment

Prior Uniform Statutory Provision: No one general equivalent provision but numerous provisions, dealing with situations of non-conformity where buyer may accept or reject, including Sections 11, 44 and 69(1), Uniform Sales Act.

Changes: Partial acceptance in good faith is recognized and the buyer's remedies on the contract for breach of warranty and the like, where the buyer has returned the goods after transfer of title, are no longer barred.

Purposes of Changes: To make it clear that:

1. A buyer accepting a non-conforming tender is not penalized by the loss of any remedy otherwise open to him. This policy extends to cover and regulate the acceptance of a part of any lot improperly tendered in any case where the price can reasonably be apportioned. Partial acceptance is permitted whether the part of the goods accepted conforms or not. The only limitation on partial acceptance is that good faith and commercial reasonableness must be used to avoid undue impairment of the value of the remaining portion of the goods. This is the reason for the insistence on the "commercial unit" in paragraph (c). In this respect, the test is not only what unit has been the basis of contract, but whether the partial acceptance produces so materially adverse an effect on the remainder as to constitute bad faith.

2. Acceptance made with the knowledge of the other party is final. An original refusal to accept may be withdrawn by a later acceptance if the seller has indicated that he is holding the tender open. However, if the buyer attempts to accept, either in whole or in part, after his original rejection has caused the seller to arrange for other disposition of the goods, the buyer must answer for any ensuing damage since the next section provides that any exercise of ownership after rejection is wrongful as against the seller. Further, he is liable even though the seller may choose to treat his action as acceptance rather than conversion, since the damage flows from the misleading notice. Such arrangements for resale or other disposition of the goods by the seller must be viewed as within the normal contemplation of a buyer who has given notice of rejection. However, the buyer's attempts in good faith to dispose of defective goods where the seller has failed to give instructions within a reasonable time are not to be regarded as an acceptance.

Cross References:

Sections 2-602(2)(a), 2-612, 2-718 and 2-719.

Definitional Cross References:

"Buyer".	Section 2-103.
"Commercial unit".	Section 2-105.
"Conform".	Section 2-106.
"Contract".	Section 1-201.
"Goods".	Section 2-105.
"Installment contract".	Section 2-612.
"Right".	Section 1-201.

Section 2-602. Manner and Effect of Rightful Rejection

(1) Rejection of goods must be within a reasonable time after their delivery or tender. It is ineffective unless the buyer seasonably notifies the seller.

(2) Subject to the provisions of the two following sections on rejected goods (Sections 2-603 and 2-604),

(a) after rejection any exercise of ownership by the buyer with respect to any commercial unit is wrongful as against the seller; and

(b) if the buyer has before rejection taken physical possession of goods in which he does not have a security interest under the provisions of this Article (subsection (3) of Section 2-711), he is under a duty after rejection to hold them with reasonable care at the seller's disposition for a time sufficient to permit the seller to remove them; but

(c) the buyer has no further obligations with regard to goods rightfully rejected.

(3) The seller's rights with respect to goods wrongfully rejected are governed by the provisions of this Article on Seller's remedies in general (Section 2-703).

Official Comment

Prior Uniform Statutory Provision: Section 50, Uniform Sales Act.

Changes: Rewritten.

Purposes of Changes: To make it clear that:

1. A tender or delivery of goods made pursuant to a contract of sale, even though wholly non-conforming, requires affirmative action by the buyer to avoid acceptance. Under subsection (1), therefore, the buyer is given a reasonable time to notify the seller of his rejection, but without such seasonable notification his rejection is ineffective. The sections of this Article dealing with inspection of goods must be read in connection with the buyer's reasonable time for action under this subsection. Contract provisions limiting the time for rejection fall within the rule of the section on "Time" and are effective if the time set gives the buyer a reasonable time for discovery of defects. What constitutes a due "notifying" of rejection by the buyer to the seller is defined in Section 1-202.

2. Subsection (2) lays down the normal duties of the buyer upon rejection, which flow from the relationship of the parties. Beyond his duty to hold the goods with reasonable care for the buyer's [seller's] disposition, this section continues the policy of prior uniform legislation in generally relieving the buyer from any duties with respect to them, except when the circumstances impose the limited obligation of salvage upon him under the next section.

3. The present section applies only to rightful rejection by the buyer. If the seller has made a tender which in all respects conforms to the contract, the buyer has a positive duty to accept and his failure to do so constitutes a "wrongful rejection" which gives the seller immediate remedies for breach. Subsection (3) is included here to emphasize the sharp distinction between the rejection of an improper tender and the non-acceptance which is a breach by the buyer.

4. The provisions of this section are to be appropriately limited or modified when a negotiation is in process.

Cross References:

Point 1: Sections 1-202, 1-205, 1-302, 2-512(2), 2-513(1) and 2-606(1)(b).

Point 2: Section 2-603(1).

Point 3: Section 2-703.

Definitional Cross References:

"Buyer".	Section 2-103.
"Commercial unit".	Section 2-105.
"Goods".	Section 2-105.
"Merchant".	Section 2-104.
"Notifies".	Section 1-202.
"Reasonable time".	Section 1-205.
"Remedy".	Section 1-201.
"Right".	Section 1-201.
"Seasonably".	Section 1-205.
"Security interest".	Section 1-201.
"Seller".	Section 2-103.

Section 2-603. Merchant Buyer's Duties as to Rightfully Rejected Goods

(1) Subject to any security interest in the buyer (subsection (3) of Section 2-711), when the seller has no agent or place of business at the market of rejection a merchant buyer is under a duty after rejection of goods in his possession or control to follow any reasonable instructions received from the seller with respect to the goods and in the absence of such instructions to make reasonable efforts to sell them for the seller's account if they are perishable or threaten to decline in value speedily. Instructions are not reasonable if on demand indemnity for expenses is not forthcoming.

(2) When the buyer sells goods under subsection (1), he is entitled to reimbursement from the seller or out of the proceeds for reasonable expenses of caring for and selling them, and if the expenses include no selling commission then to such commission as is usual in the trade or if there is none to a reasonable sum not exceeding ten per cent on the gross proceeds.

(3) In complying with this section the buyer is held only to good faith and good faith conduct hereunder is neither acceptance nor conversion nor the basis of an action for damages.

Official Comment

Prior Uniform Statutory Provision: None.

Purposes:

1. This section recognizes the duty imposed upon the merchant buyer by good faith and commercial practice to follow any reasonable instructions of the seller as to reshipping, storing, delivery to a third party, reselling or the like. Subsection (1) goes further and extends the duty to include the making of reasonable efforts to effect a salvage sale where the value of the goods is threatened and the seller's instructions do not arrive in time to prevent serious loss.

2. The limitations on the buyer's duty to resell under subsection (1) are to be liberally construed. The buyer's duty to resell under this section arises from commercial necessity and thus is present only when the seller has "no agent or place of business at the market of rejection". A financing agency which is acting on behalf of the seller in handling the documents rejected by the buyer is sufficiently the seller's agent to lift the burden of salvage resale from the buyer. (See provisions of Sections 4-503 and 5-108(h) on a bank's duties with respect to rejected documents.) The buyer's duty to resell is extended only to goods in his "possession or control", but these are intended as words of wide, rather than narrow, import. In effect, the measure of the buyer's "control" is whether he can practicably effect control without undue commercial burden.

3. The explicit provisions for reimbursement and compensation to the buyer in subsection (2) are applicable and necessary only where he is not acting under instructions from the seller. As provided in subsection (1) the seller's instructions to be "reasonable" must on demand of the buyer include indemnity for expenses.

4. Since this section makes the resale of perishable goods an affirmative duty in contrast to a mere right to sell as under the case law, subsection (3) makes it clear that the buyer is liable only for the exercise of good faith in determining whether the value of the goods is sufficiently threatened to justify a quick resale or whether he has waited a sufficient length of time for instructions, or what a reasonable means and place of resale is.

5. A buyer who fails to make a salvage sale when his duty to do so under this section has arisen is subject to damages pursuant to the section on liberal administration of remedies.

Cross References:

Point 2: Sections 4-503 and 5-108.

Point 5: Section 1-305. Compare generally section 2-706.

Definitional Cross References:

"Buyer".	Section 2-103.
"Good faith".	Section 1-201.
"Goods".	Section 2-105.
"Merchant".	Section 2-104.
"Security interest".	Section 1-201.
"Seller".	Section 2-103.

Section 2-604. Buyer's Options As to Salvage of Rightfully Rejected Goods

Subject to the provisions of the immediately preceding section on perishables if the seller gives no instructions within a reasonable time after notification of rejection the buyer may store the rejected goods for the seller's account or reship them to him or resell them for the seller's account with reimbursement as provided in the preceding section. Such action is not acceptance or conversion.

Official Comment

Prior Uniform Statutory Provision: None.

Purposes: The basic purpose of this section is twofold: on the one hand it aims at reducing the stake in dispute and on the other at avoiding the pinning of a technical "acceptance" on a buyer who has taken steps towards realization on or preservation of the goods in good faith. This section is essentially a salvage section and the buyer's right to act under it is conditioned upon (1) non-conformity of the goods, (2) due notification of rejection to the seller under the section on manner of rejection, and (3) the absence of any instructions from the seller which the merchant-buyer has a duty to follow under the preceding section.

This section is designed to accord all reasonable leeway to a rightfully rejecting buyer acting in good faith. The listing of what the buyer may do in the absence of instructions from the seller is intended to be not exhaustive but merely illustrative. This is not a "merchant's" section and the options are pure options given to merchant and nonmerchant buyers alike. The merchant-buyer, however, may in some instances be under a duty rather than an option to resell under the provisions of the preceding section.

Cross References: Sections 2-602(1), and 2-603(1) and 2-706.

Definitional Cross References:

"Buyer".	Section 2-103.
"Notification".	Section 1-202.
"Reasonable time".	Section 1-205.
"Seller".	Section 2-103.

Section 2-605. Waiver of Buyer's Objections by Failure to Particularize

(1) The buyer's failure to state in connection with rejection a particular defect which is ascertainable by reasonable inspection precludes him from relying on the unstated defect to justify rejection or to establish breach

(a) where the seller could have cured it if stated seasonably; or

(b) between merchants when the seller has after rejection made a request in writing for a full and final written statement of all defects on which the buyer proposes to rely.

(2) Payment against documents made without reservation of rights precludes recovery of the payment for defects apparent on the face of the documents.

Official Comment

Prior Uniform Statutory Provision: None.

Purposes:

1. The present section rests upon a policy of permitting the buyer to give a quick and informal notice of defects in a tender without penalizing him for omissions in his statement, while at the same time protecting a seller who is reasonably misled by the buyer's failure to state curable defects.

2. Where the defect in a tender is one which could have been cured by the seller, a buyer who merely rejects the delivery without stating his objections to it is probably acting in commercial bad faith and seeking to get out of a deal which has become unprofitable. Subsection (1)(a), following the general policy of this Article which looks to preserving the deal wherever possible, therefore insists that the seller's right to correct his tender in such circumstances be protected.

3. When the time for cure is past, subsection (1)(b) makes it plain that a seller is entitled upon request to a final statement of objections upon which he can rely. What is needed is that he make clear to the buyer exactly what is being sought. A formal demand under paragraph (b) will be sufficient in the case of a merchant-buyer.

4. Subsection (2) applies to the particular case of documents the same principle which the section on effects of acceptance applies to the case of goods. The matter is dealt with in this section in terms of "waiver" of objections rather than of right to revoke acceptance, partly to avoid any confusion with the problems of acceptance of goods and partly because defects in documents which are not taken as grounds for rejection are generally minor ones. The only defects concerned in the present subsection are defects in the documents which are apparent on their face. Where payment is required against the documents they must be inspected before payment, and the payment then constitutes acceptance of the documents. Under the section dealing with this problem, such acceptance of the documents does not constitute an acceptance of the goods or impair any options or remedies of the buyer for their improper delivery. Where the documents are delivered without requiring such contemporary action as payment from the buyer, the reason of the next section on what constitutes acceptance of goods, applies. Their acceptance by non-objection is therefore postponed until after a reasonable time for their inspection. In either situation, however, the buyer "waives" only what is apparent on the face of the documents.

5. As to the use of a record other than a writing and communications that are not written, see Section 2-207, Comment 8.

Cross References:

Point 2: Section 2-508.

Point 4: Sections 2-512(2), 2-606(1)(b) and 2-607(2).

Definitional Cross References:

"Between merchants".	Section 2-104.
"Buyer".	Section 2-103.
"Seasonably".	Section 1-205.
"Seller".	Section 2-103.
"Writing" and "written".	Section 1-201.

Section 2-606. What Constitutes Acceptance of Goods

(1) Acceptance of goods occurs when the buyer

(a) after a reasonable opportunity to inspect the goods signifies to the seller that the goods are conforming or that he will take or retain them in spite of their non-conformity; or

(b) fails to make an effective rejection (subsection (1) of Section 2-602), but such acceptance does not occur until the buyer has had a reasonable opportunity to inspect them; or

(c) does any act inconsistent with the seller's ownership; but if such act is wrongful as against the seller it is an acceptance only if ratified by him.

(2) Acceptance of a part of any commercial unit is acceptance of that entire unit.

Official Comment

Prior Uniform Statutory Provision: Section 48, Uniform Sales Act.

Changes: Rewritten, the qualification in paragraph (c) and subsection (2) being new; otherwise the general policy of the prior legislation is continued.

Purposes of Changes and New Matter: To make it clear that:

1. Under this Article "acceptance" as applied to goods means that the buyer, pursuant to the contract, takes particular goods which have been appropriated to the contract as his own, whether or not he is obligated to do so, and whether he does so by words, action, or silence when it is time to speak. If the goods conform to the contract, acceptance amounts only to the performance by the buyer of one part of his legal obligation.

2. Under this Article acceptance of goods is always acceptance of identified goods which have been appropriated to the contract or are appropriated by the contract. There is no provision for "acceptance of title" apart from acceptance in general, since acceptance of title is not material under this Article to the detailed rights and duties of the parties. (See Section 2-401). The refinements of the older law between acceptance of goods and of title become unnecessary in view of the provisions of the sections on effect and revocation of acceptance, on effects of identification and on risk of loss, and those sections which free the seller's and buyer's remedies from the complications and confusions caused by the question of whether title has or has not passed to the buyer before breach.

3. Under paragraph (a), payment made after tender is always one circumstance tending to signify acceptance of the goods but in itself it can never be more than one circumstance and is not conclusive. Also, a conditional communication of acceptance always remains subject to its expressed conditions.

4. Under paragraph (c), any action taken by the buyer, which is inconsistent with his claim that he has rejected the goods, constitutes an acceptance. However, the provisions of paragraph (c) are subject to the sections dealing with rejection by the buyer which permit the buyer to take certain actions with respect to the goods pursuant to his options and duties imposed by those sections, without effecting an acceptance of the goods. The second clause of paragraph (c) modifies some of the prior case law and makes it clear that "acceptance" in law based on the wrongful act of the acceptor is acceptance only as against the wrongdoer and then only at the option of the party wronged.

In the same manner in which a buyer can bind himself, despite his insistence that he is rejecting or has rejected the goods, by an act inconsistent with the seller's ownership under paragraph (c), he can obligate himself by a communication of acceptance despite a prior rejection under paragraph (a). However, the sections on buyer's rights on improper delivery and on the effect of rightful rejection, make it clear that after he once rejects a tender, paragraph (a) does not operate in favor of the buyer unless the seller has re-tendered the goods or has taken affirmative action indicating that he is holding the tender open. See also Comment 2 to Section 2-601.

5. Subsection (2) supplements the policy of the section on buyer's rights on improper delivery, recognizing the validity of a partial acceptance but insisting that the buyer exercise this right only as to whole commercial units.

Cross References:

Point 2: Sections 2-401, 2-509, 2-510, 2-607, 2-608 and Part 7.

Point 4: Sections 2-601 through 2-604.

Point 5: Section 2-601.

Definitional Cross References:

"Buyer".	Section 2-103.
"Commercial unit".	Section 2-105.
"Goods".	Section 2-105.
"Seller".	Section 2-103.

Section 2-607. Effect of Acceptance; Notice of Breach; Burden of Establishing Breach after Acceptance; Notice of Claim or Litigation to Person Answerable Over

(1) The buyer must pay at the contract rate for any goods accepted.

(2) Acceptance of goods by the buyer precludes rejection of the goods accepted and if made with knowledge of a non-conformity cannot be revoked because of it unless the acceptance was on the reasonable assumption that the non-conformity would be seasonably cured but acceptance does not of itself impair any other remedy provided by this Article for non-conformity.

(3) Where a tender has been accepted

(a) the buyer must within a reasonable time after he discovers or should have discovered any breach notify the seller of breach or be barred from any remedy; and

(b) if the claim is one for infringement or the like (subsection (3) of Section 2-312) and the buyer is sued as a result of such a breach he must so notify the seller within a reasonable time after he receives notice of the litigation or be barred from any remedy over for liability established by the litigation.

(4) The burden is on the buyer to establish any breach with respect to the goods accepted.

(5) Where the buyer is sued for breach of a warranty or other obligation for which his seller is answerable over

(a) he may give his seller written notice of the litigation. If the notice states that the seller may come in and defend and that if the seller does not do so he will be bound in any action against him by his buyer by any determination of fact common to the two litigations, then unless the seller after seasonable receipt of the notice does come in and defend he is so bound.

(b) if the claim is one for infringement or the like (subsection (3) of Section 2-312) the original seller may demand in writing that his buyer turn over to him control of the litigation including settlement or else be barred from any remedy over and if he also agrees to bear all expense and to satisfy any adverse judgment, then unless the buyer after seasonable receipt of the demand does turn over control the buyer is so barred.

(6) The provisions of subsections (3), (4) and (5) apply to any obligation of a buyer to hold the seller harmless against infringement or the like (subsection (3) of Section 2-312).

Official Comment

Prior Uniform Statutory Provision: Subsection (1)—Section 41, Uniform Sales Act; Subsections (2) and (3)—Sections 49 and 69, Uniform Sales Act.

Changes: Rewritten.

Purposes of Changes: To continue the prior basic policies with respect to acceptance of goods while making a number of minor though material changes in the interest of simplicity and commercial convenience so that:

1. Under subsection (1), once the buyer accepts a tender the seller acquires a right to its price on the contract terms. In cases of partial acceptance, the price of any part accepted is, if possible, to be reasonably apportioned, using the type of apportionment familiar to the courts in quantum valebant cases, to be determined in terms of "the contract rate", which is the rate determined from the bargain in fact (the agreement) after the rules and policies of this Article have been brought to bear.

2. Under subsection (2) acceptance of goods precludes their subsequent rejection. Any return of the goods thereafter must be by way of revocation of acceptance under the next section. Revocation is unavailable for a non-conformity known to the buyer at the time of acceptance, except where the buyer has accepted on the reasonable assumption that the non-conformity would be seasonably cured.

3. All other remedies of the buyer remain unimpaired under subsection (2). This is intended to include the buyer's full rights with respect to future installments despite his acceptance of any earlier non-conforming installment.

4. The time of notification is to be determined by applying commercial standards to a merchant buyer. "A reasonable time" for notification from a retail consumer is to be judged by different standards so that in his case it will be extended, for the rule of requiring notification is designed to defeat commercial bad faith, not to deprive a good faith consumer of his remedy.

The content of the notification need merely be sufficient to let the seller know that the transaction is still troublesome and must be watched. There is no reason to require that the notification which saves the buyer's rights under this section must include a clear statement of all the objections that will be relied on by the buyer, as under the section covering statements of defects upon rejection (Section 2-605). Nor is there reason for requiring the notification to be a claim for damages or of any threatened litigation or other resort to a remedy. The notification which saves the buyer's rights under this Article need only be such as informs the seller that the transaction is claimed to involve a breach, and thus opens the way for normal settlement through negotiation.

5. Under this Article various beneficiaries are given rights for injuries sustained by them because of the seller's breach of warranty. Such a beneficiary does not fall within the reason of the present section in regard to discovery of defects and the giving of notice within a reasonable time after acceptance, since he has nothing to do with acceptance. However, the reason of this section does extend to requiring the beneficiary to notify the seller that an injury has occurred. What is said above, with regard to the extended time for reasonable notification from the lay consumer after the injury is also applicable here; but even a beneficiary can be properly held to the use of good faith in notifying, once he has had time to become aware of the legal situation.

6. Subsection (4) unambiguously places the burden of proof to establish breach on the buyer after acceptance. However, this rule becomes one purely of procedure when the tender accepted was non-conforming and the buyer has given the seller notice of breach under subsection (3). For subsection (2) makes it clear that acceptance leaves unimpaired the buyer's right to be made whole, and that right can be exercised by the buyer not only by way of cross-claim for damages, but also by way of recoupment in diminution or extinction of the price.

7. Subsections (3)(b) and (5)(b) give a warrantor against infringement an opportunity to defend or compromise third-party claims or be relieved of his liability. Subsection (5)(a) codifies for all warranties the practice of voucher to defend. Compare Section 3-119. Subsection (6) makes these provisions applicable to the buyer's liability for infringement under Section 2-312.

8. All of the provisions of the present section are subject to any explicit reservation of rights.

9. As to the use of a record other than a writing and communications that are not written, see Section 2-207, Comment 8.

Cross References:

Point 1: Section 1-201.
Point 2: Section 2-608.
Point 4: Sections 1-205 and 2-605.
Point 5: Section 2-318.
Point 6: Section 2-717.
Point 7: Sections 2-312 and 3-119.
Point 8: Section 1-308.

Definitional Cross References:

"Burden of establishing".	Section 1-201.
"Buyer".	Section 2-103.
"Conform".	Section 2-106.
"Contract".	Section 1-201.
"Goods".	Section 2-105.
"Notifies".	Section 1-202.
"Reasonable time".	Section 1-205.
"Remedy".	Section 1-201.
"Seasonably".	Section 1-205.

Section 2-608. Revocation of Acceptance in Whole or in Part

(1) The buyer may revoke his acceptance of a lot or commercial unit whose non-conformity substantially impairs its value to him if he has accepted it

(a) on the reasonable assumption that its non-conformity would be cured and it has not been seasonably cured; or

(b) without discovery of such non-conformity if his acceptance was reasonably induced either by the difficulty of discovery before acceptance or by the seller's assurances.

(2) Revocation of acceptance must occur within a reasonable time after the buyer discovers or should have discovered the ground for it and before any substantial change in condition of the goods which is not caused by their own defects. It is not effective until the buyer notifies the seller of it.

(3) A buyer who so revokes has the same rights and duties with regard to the goods involved as if he had rejected them.

Official Comment

Prior Uniform Statutory Provision: Section 69(1)(d), (3), (4) and (5), Uniform Sales Act.

Changes: Rewritten.

Purposes of Changes: To make it clear that:

1. Although the prior basic policy is continued, the buyer is no longer required to elect between revocation of acceptance and recovery of damages for breach. Both are now available to him. The non-alternative character of the two remedies is stressed by the terms used in the present section. The section no longer speaks of "rescission", a term capable of ambiguous application either to transfer of title to the goods or to the contract of sale and susceptible also of confusion with cancellation for cause of an executed or executory portion of the contract. The remedy under this section is instead referred to simply as "revocation of acceptance" of goods tendered under a contract for sale and involves no suggestion of "election" of any sort.

2. Revocation of acceptance is possible only where the non-conformity substantially impairs the value of the goods to the buyer. For this purpose the test is not what the seller had reason to know at the time of contracting; the question is whether the non-conformity is such as will in fact cause a substantial impairment of value to the buyer though the seller had no advance knowledge as to the buyer's particular circumstances.

3. "Assurances" by the seller under paragraph (b) of subsection (1) can rest as well in the circumstances or in the contract as in explicit language used at the time of delivery. The reason for recognizing such assurances is that they induce the buyer to delay discovery. These are the only assurances involved in paragraph (b). Explicit assurances may be made either in good faith or bad faith. In either case any remedy accorded by this Article is available to the buyer under the section on remedies for fraud.

4. Subsection (2) requires notification of revocation of acceptance within a reasonable time after discovery of the grounds for such revocation. Since this remedy will be generally resorted to only after attempts at adjustment have failed, the reasonable time period should extend in most cases beyond the time in which notification of breach must be given, beyond the time for discovery of non-conformity after acceptance and beyond the time for rejection after tender. The parties may by their agreement limit the time for notification under this section, but the same sanctions and considerations apply to such agreements as are discussed in the comment on manner and effect of rightful rejection.

5. The content of the notice under subsection (2) is to be determined in this case as in others by considerations of good faith, prevention of surprise, and reasonable adjustment. More will generally be necessary than the mere notification of breach required under the preceding section. On the other hand the requirements of the section on waiver of buyer's objections do not apply here. The fact that quick notification of trouble is desirable affords good ground for being slow to bind a buyer by his first statement. Following the general policy of this Article, the requirements of the content of notification are less stringent in the case of a non-merchant buyer.

6. Under subsection (2) the prior policy is continued of seeking substantial justice in regard to the condition of goods restored to the seller. Thus the buyer may not revoke his acceptance if the goods have materially deteriorated except by reason of their own defects. Worthless goods, however, need not be offered back and minor defects in the articles reoffered are to be disregarded.

7. The policy of the section allowing partial acceptance is carried over into the present section and the buyer may revoke his acceptance, in appropriate cases, as to the entire lot or any commercial unit thereof.

Cross References:

Point 3:	Section 2-721.
Point 4:	Sections 1-205, 2-602 and 2-607.
Point 5:	Sections 2-605 and 2-607.
Point 7:	Section 2-601.

Definitional Cross References:

"Buyer".	Section 2-103.
"Commercial unit".	Section 2-105.
"Conform".	Section 2-106.
"Goods".	Section 2-105.
"Lot".	Section 2-105.
"Notifies".	Section 1-202.
"Reasonable time".	Section 1-205.
"Right".	Section 1-201.
"Seasonably".	Section 1-205.
"Seller".	Section 2-103.

Section 2-609. Right to Adequate Assurance of Performance

(1) A contract for sale imposes an obligation on each party that the other's expectation of receiving due performance will not be impaired. When reasonable grounds for insecurity arise with respect to the performance of either party the other may in writing demand adequate assurance of due performance and until he receives such assurance may if commercially reasonable suspend any performance for which he has not already received the agreed return.

(2) Between merchants the reasonableness of grounds for insecurity and the adequacy of any assurance offered shall be determined according to commercial standards.

(3) Acceptance of any improper delivery or payment does not prejudice the aggrieved party's right to demand adequate assurance of future performance.

(4) After receipt of a justified demand failure to provide within a reasonable time not exceeding thirty days such assurance of due performance as is adequate under the circumstances of the particular case is a repudiation of the contract.

Official Comment

Prior Uniform Statutory Provision: See Sections 53, 54(1)(b), 55 and 63(2), Uniform Sales Act.

Purposes:

1. The section rests on the recognition of the fact that the essential purpose of a contract between commercial men is actual performance and they do not bargain merely for a promise, or for a promise plus the right to win a lawsuit and that a continuing sense of reliance and security that the promised performance will be forthcoming when due, is an important feature of the bargain. If either the willingness or the ability of a party to perform declines materially between the time of contracting and the time for performance, the other party is threatened with the loss of a substantial part of what he has bargained for. A seller needs protection not merely against having to deliver on credit to a shaky buyer, but also against having to procure and manufacture the goods, perhaps turning down other customers. Once he has been given reason to believe that the buyer's performance has become uncertain, it is an undue hardship to force him to continue his own performance. Similarly, a buyer who believes that the seller's deliveries have become uncertain cannot safely wait for the due date of performance when he has been buying to assure himself of materials for his current manufacturing or to replenish his stock of merchandise.

2. Three measures have been adopted to meet the needs of commercial men in such situations. First, the aggrieved party is permitted to suspend his own performance and any preparation therefor, with excuse for any resulting necessary delay, until the situation has been clarified. "Suspend performance" under this section means to hold up performance pending the outcome of the demand, and includes also the holding up of any preparatory action. This is the same principle which governs the ancient law of stoppage and seller's lien, and also of excuse of a buyer from prepayment if the seller's actions manifest that he cannot or will not perform. (Original Act, Section 63(2).)

Secondly, the aggrieved party is given the right to require adequate assurance that the other party's performance will be duly forthcoming. This principle is reflected in the familiar clauses permitting the seller to curtail deliveries if the buyer's credit becomes impaired, which when held within the limits of reasonableness and good faith actually express no more than the fair business meaning of any commercial contract.

Third, and finally, this section provides the means by which the aggrieved party may treat the contract as broken if his reasonable grounds for insecurity are not cleared up within a reasonable time. This is the principle underlying the law of anticipatory breach, whether by way of defective part performance or by repudiation. The present section merges these three principles of law and commercial practice into a single theory of general application to all sales agreements looking to future performance.

3. Subsection (2) of the present section requires that "reasonable" grounds and "adequate" assurance as used in subsection (1) be defined by commercial rather than legal standards. The express reference to commercial standards carries no connotation that the obligation of good faith is not equally applicable here.

Under commercial standards and in accord with commercial practice, a ground for insecurity need not arise from or be directly related to the contract in question. The law as to "dependence" or "independence" of promises within a single contract does not control the application of the present section.

Thus a buyer who falls behind in "his account" with the seller, even though the items involved have to do with separate and legally distinct contracts, impairs the seller's expectation of due performance. Again, under the same test, a buyer who requires precision parts which he intends to use immediately upon delivery, may have reasonable grounds for insecurity if he discovers that his seller is making defective deliveries of such parts to other buyers with similar needs. Thus, too, in a situation such as arose in *Jay Dreher Corp. v. Delco Appliance Corp.*, 93 F.2d 275 (2d Cir. 1937), where a manufacturer gave a dealer an exclusive franchise for the sale of his product but on two or three occasions breached the exclusive dealing clause, although there was no default in orders, deliveries or payments under the separate sales contract between the parties, the aggrieved dealer would be entitled to suspend his performance of the contract for sale under the present section and to demand assurance that the exclusive dealing contract would be lived up to. There is no need for an explicit clause tying the exclusive franchise into the contract for the sale of goods since the situation itself ties the agreements together.

The nature of the sales contract enters also into the question of reasonableness. For example, a report from an apparently trustworthy source that the seller had shipped defective goods or was planning to ship them would normally give the buyer reasonable grounds for insecurity. But when the buyer has assumed the risk of payment before inspection of the goods, as in a sales contract on C.I.F. or similar cash against documents terms, that risk is not to be evaded by a demand for assurance. Therefore no ground for insecurity would exist under this section unless the report went to a ground which would excuse payment by the buyer.

4. What constitutes "adequate" assurance of due performance is subject to the same test of factual conditions. For example, where the buyer can make use of a defective delivery, a mere promise by a seller of good repute that he is giving the matter his attention and that the defect will not be repeated, is normally sufficient. Under the same circumstances, however, a similar statement by a known corner-cutter might well be considered insufficient without the posting of a guaranty or, if so demanded by the buyer, a speedy replacement of the delivery involved. By the same token where a delivery has defects, even though easily curable, which interfere with easy use by the buyer, no verbal assurance can be deemed adequate which is not accompanied by replacement, repair, money-allowance, or other commercially reasonable cure.

A fact situation such as arose in *Corn Products Refining Co. v. Fasola,* 109 A. 505 (N.J. 1920) offers illustration both of reasonable grounds for insecurity and "adequate" assurance. In that case a contract for the sale of oils on 30 days' credit, 2% off for payment within 10 days, provided that credit was to be extended to the buyer only if his financial responsibility was satisfactory to the seller. The buyer had been in the habit of taking advantage of the discount but at the same time that he failed to make his customary 10 day payment, the seller heard rumors, in fact false, that the buyer's financial condition was shaky. Thereupon, the seller demanded cash before shipment or security satisfactory to him. The buyer sent a good credit report from his banker, expressed willingness to make payments when due on the 30 day terms and insisted on further deliveries under the contract. Under this Article the rumors, although false, were enough to make the buyer's financial condition "unsatisfactory" to the seller under the contract clause. Moreover, the buyer's practice of taking the cash discounts is enough, apart from the contract clause, to lay a commercial foundation for suspicion when the practice is suddenly stopped. These matters, however, go only to the justification of the seller's demand for security, or his "reasonable grounds for insecurity".

The adequacy of the assurance given is not measured as in the type of "satisfaction" situation affected with intangibles, such as in personal service cases, cases involving a third party's judgment as final, or cases in which the whole contract is dependent on one party's satisfaction, as in a sale on approval. Here, the seller must exercise good faith and observe commercial standards. This Article thus approves the statement of the court in *James B. Berry's Sons Co. of Illinois v. Monark Gasoline & Oil Co., Inc.,* 32 F.2d 74 (8th Cir. 1929), that the seller's satisfaction under such a clause must be based upon reason and must not be arbitrary or capricious; and rejects the purely personal "good faith" test of the *Corn Products Refining Co.* case, which held that in the seller's sole judgment, if for *any* reason he was dissatisfied, he was entitled to revoke the credit. In the absence of the buyer's failure to take the 2% discount as was his custom, the banker's report given in that case would have been "adequate" assurance under this Act, regardless of the language of the "satisfaction" clause. However, the seller is reasonably entitled to feel insecure at a sudden expansion of the buyer's use of a credit term, and should be entitled either to security or to a satisfactory explanation.

The entire foregoing discussion as to adequacy of assurance by way of explanation is subject to qualification when repeated occasions for the application of this section arise. This Act recognizes that repeated delinquencies must be viewed as cumulative. On the other hand, commercial sense also requires that if repeated claims for assurance are made under this section, the basis for these claims must be increasingly obvious.

5. A failure to provide adequate assurance of performance and thereby to re-establish the security of expectation, results in a breach only "by repudiation" under subsection (4). Therefore, the possibility is continued of retraction of the repudiation under the section dealing with that problem, unless the aggrieved party has acted on the breach in some manner.

The thirty day limit on the time to provide assurance is laid down to free the question of reasonable time from uncertainty in later litigation.

6. Clauses seeking to give the protected party exceedingly wide powers to cancel or readjust the contract when ground for insecurity arises must be read against the fact that good faith is a part of the obligation of the contract and not subject to modification by agreement and includes, in the case of a merchant, the reasonable observance of commercial standards of fair dealing in the trade. Such clauses can thus be effective to enlarge the protection given by the present section to a certain extent, to fix the reasonable time within which requested assurance must be given, or to define adequacy of the assurance in any commercially reasonable fashion. But any clause seeking to set up arbitrary standards for action is ineffective under this Article. Acceleration clauses are treated similarly in the Articles on Commercial Paper and Secured Transactions.

7. As to the use of a record other than a writing and communications that are not written, see Section 2-207, Comment 8.

Cross References:

Point 3: Section 1-304.
Point 5: Section 2-611.
Point 6: Sections 1-304 and 1-309 and Articles 3 and 9.

Definitional Cross References:

"Aggrieved party".	Section 1-201.
"Between merchants".	Section 2-104.
"Contract".	Section 1-201.
"Contract for sale".	Section 2-106.
"Party".	Section 1-201.
"Reasonable time".	Section 1-205.
"Right".	Section 1-201.
"Writing".	Section 1-201.

Section 2-610. Anticipatory Repudiation

When either party repudiates the contract with respect to a performance not yet due the loss of which will substantially impair the value of the contract to the other, the aggrieved party may

(a) for a commercially reasonable time await performance by the repudiating party; or

(b) resort to any remedy for breach (Section 2-703 or Section 2-711), even though he has notified the repudiating party that he would await the latter's performance and has urged retraction; and

(c) in either case suspend his own performance or proceed in accordance with the provisions of this Article on the seller's right to identify goods to the contract notwithstanding breach or to salvage unfinished goods (Section 2-704).

Official Comment

Prior Uniform Statutory Provision: See Sections 63(2) and 65, Uniform Sales Act.

Purposes: To make it clear that:

1. With the problem of insecurity taken care of by the preceding section and with provision being made in this Article as to the effect of a defective delivery under an installment contract, anticipatory repudiation centers upon an overt communication of intention or an action which renders performance impossible or demonstrates a clear determination not to continue with performance.

Under the present section when such a repudiation substantially impairs the value of the contract, the aggrieved party may at any time resort to his remedies for breach, or he may suspend his own performance while he negotiates with, or awaits performance by, the other party. But if he awaits performance beyond a commercially reasonable time he cannot recover resulting damages which he should have avoided.

2. It is not necessary for repudiation that performance be made literally and utterly impossible. Repudiation can result from action which reasonably indicates a rejection of the continuing obligation. And, a repudiation automatically results under the preceding section on insecurity when a party fails to provide adequate assurance of due future performance within thirty days after a justifiable demand therefor has been made. Under the language of this section, a demand by one or both parties for more than the contract calls for in the way of counter-performance is not in itself a repudiation nor does it invalidate a plain expression of desire for future performance. However, when under a fair reading it amounts to a statement of intention not to perform except on conditions which go beyond the contract, it becomes a repudiation.

3. The test chosen to justify an aggrieved party's action under this section is the same as that in the section on breach in installment contracts—namely the substantial value of the contract. The most useful test of substantial value is to determine whether material inconvenience or injustice will result if the aggrieved party is forced to wait and receive an ultimate tender minus the part or aspect repudiated.

4. After repudiation, the aggrieved party may immediately resort to any remedy he chooses provided he moves in good faith (see Section 1-304). Inaction and silence by the aggrieved party may leave the matter open but it cannot be regarded as misleading the repudiating party. Therefore the aggrieved party is left free to proceed at any time with his options under this section, unless he has taken some positive action which in good faith requires notification to the other party before the remedy is pursued.

Cross References:

Point 1: Sections 2-609 and 2-612.
Point 2: Section 2-609.
Point 3: Section 2-612.
Point 4: Section 1-304.

Definitional Cross References:

"Aggrieved party". Section 1-201.
"Contract". Section 1-201.
"Party". Section 1-201.
"Remedy". Section 1-201.

Section 2-611. Retraction of Anticipatory Repudiation

(1) Until the repudiating party's next performance is due he can retract his repudiation unless the aggrieved party has since the repudiation cancelled or materially changed his position or otherwise indicated that he considers the repudiation final.

(2) Retraction may be by any method which clearly indicates to the aggrieved party that the repudiating party intends to perform, but must include any assurance justifiably demanded under the provisions of this Article (Section 2-609).

(3) Retraction reinstates the repudiating party's rights under the contract with due excuse and allowance to the aggrieved party for any delay occasioned by the repudiation.

Official Comment

Prior Uniform Statutory Provision: None.

Purposes: To make it clear that:

1. The repudiating party's right to reinstate the contract is entirely dependent upon the action taken by the aggrieved party. If the latter has cancelled the contract or materially changed his position at any time after the repudiation, there can be no retraction under this section.

2. Under subsection (2) an effective retraction must be accompanied by any assurances demanded under the section dealing with right to adequate assurance. A repudiation is of course sufficient to give reasonable ground for insecurity and to warrant a request for assurance as an essential condition of the retraction. However, after a timely and unambiguous expression of retraction, a reasonable time for the assurance to be worked out should be allowed by the aggrieved party before cancellation.

Cross Reference: Point 2: Section 2-609.

Definitional Cross References:

"Aggrieved party". Section 1-201.
"Cancellation". Section 2-106.
"Contract". Section 1-201.
"Party". Section 1-201.
"Right". Section 1-201.

Section 2-612. "Installment Contract"; Breach

(1) An "installment contract" is one which requires or authorizes the delivery of goods in separate lots to be separately accepted, even though the contract contains a clause "each delivery is a separate contract" or its equivalent.

(2) The buyer may reject any installment which is non-conforming if the non-conformity substantially impairs the value of that installment and cannot be cured or if the non-conformity is a defect in the required documents; but if the non-conformity does not fall within subsection (3) and the seller gives adequate assurance of its cure the buyer must accept that installment.

(3) Whenever non-conformity or default with respect to one or more installments substantially impairs the value of the whole contract there is a breach of the whole. But the aggrieved party reinstates the contract if he accepts a non-conforming installment without seasonably notifying of cancellation or if he brings an action with respect only to past installments or demands performance as to future installments.

Official Comment

Prior Uniform Statutory Provision: Section 45(2), Uniform Sales Act.

Changes: Rewritten.

Purposes of Changes: To continue prior law but to make explicit the more mercantile interpretation of many of the rules involved, so that:

1. The definition of an installment contract is phrased more broadly in this Article so as to cover installment deliveries tacitly authorized by the circumstances or by the option of either party.

2. In regard to the apportionment of the price for separate payment this Article applies the more liberal test of what can be apportioned rather than the test of what is clearly apportioned by the agreement. This Article also recognizes approximate calculation or apportionment of price subject to subsequent adjustment. A provision for separate payment for each lot delivered ordinarily means that the price is at least roughly calculable by units of quantity, but such a provision is not essential to an "installment contract". If separate acceptance of separate deliveries is contemplated, no generalized contrast between wholly "entire" and wholly "divisible" contracts has any standing under this Article.

3. This Article rejects any approach which gives clauses such as "each delivery is a separate contract" their legalistically literal effect. Such contracts nonetheless call for installment deliveries. Even where a clause speaks of "a separate contract for all purposes", a commercial reading of the language under the section on good faith and commercial standards requires that the singleness of the document and the negotiation, together with the sense of the situation, prevail over any uncommercial and legalistic interpretation.

4. One of the requirements for rejection under subsection (2) is non-conformity substantially impairing the value of the installment in question. However, an installment agreement may require accurate conformity in quality as a condition to the right to acceptance if the need for such conformity is made clear either by express provision or by the circumstances. In such a case the effect of the agreement is to define explicitly what amounts to substantial impairment of value impossible to cure. A clause requiring accurate compliance as a condition to the right to acceptance must, however, have some basis in reason, must avoid imposing hardship by surprise and is subject to waiver or to displacement by practical construction.

Substantial impairment of the value of an installment can turn not only on the quality of the goods but also on such factors as time, quantity, assortment, and the like. It must be judged in terms of the normal or specifically known purposes of the contract. The defect in required documents refers to such matters as the absence of insurance documents under a C.I.F. contract, falsity of a bill of lading, or one failing to show shipment within the contract period or to the contract destination. Even in such cases, however, the provisions on cure of tender apply if appropriate documents are readily procurable.

5. Under subsection (2) an installment delivery must be accepted if the non-conformity is curable and the seller gives adequate assurance of cure. Cure of non-conformity of an installment in the first instance can usually be afforded by an allowance against the price, or in the case of reasonable discrepancies in quantity either by a further delivery or a partial rejection. This Article requires reasonable action by a buyer in regard to discrepant delivery and good faith requires that the buyer make any reasonable minor outlay of time or money necessary to cure an overshipment by severing out an acceptable percentage thereof. The seller must take over a cure which involves any material burden; the buyer's obligation reaches only to cooperation. Adequate assurance for purposes of subsection (2) is measured by the same standards as under the section on right to adequate assurance of performance.

6. Subsection (3) is designed to further the continuance of the contract in the absence of an overt cancellation. The question arising when an action is brought as to a single installment only is resolved by making such action waive the right of cancellation. This involves merely a defect in one or more installments, as contrasted with the situation where there is a true repudiation within the section on anticipatory repudiation. Whether the non-conformity in any given installment justifies cancellation as to the future depends, not on whether such non-conformity indicates an intent or likelihood that the future deliveries will also be defective, but whether the non-conformity substantially impairs the value of the whole contract. If only the seller's security in regard to future installments is impaired, he has the right to demand adequate assurances of proper future performance but has not an immediate right to cancel the entire contract. It is clear under this Article, however, that defects in prior installments are cumulative in effect, so that acceptance does not wash out the defect "waived". Prior policy is continued, putting the rule as to buyer's default on the same footing as that in regard to seller's default.

7. Under the requirement of seasonable notification of cancellation under subsection (3), a buyer who accepts a non-conforming installment which substantially impairs the value of the entire contract should properly be permitted to withhold his decision as to whether or not to cancel pending a response from the seller as to his claim for cure or adjustment. Similarly, a seller may withhold a delivery pending payment for prior ones, at the same time delaying his decision as to cancellation. A reasonable time for notifying of cancellation, judged by commercial standard under the section on good faith, extends of course to include the time covered by any reasonable negotiation in good faith. However, during this period the defaulting party is entitled, on request, to know whether the contract is still in effect, before he can be required to perform further.

Cross References:

Point 2: Sections 2-307 and 2-607.
Point 3: Section 1-304.
Point 5: Sections 2-609.
Point 6: Section 2-610.

Definitional Cross References:

"Action".	Section 1-201.
"Aggrieved party".	Section 1-201.
"Buyer".	Section 2-103.
"Cancellation".	Section 2-106.
"Conform".	Section 2-106.
"Contract".	Section 1-201.
"Lot".	Section 2-105.
"Notifies".	Section 1-202.
"Seasonably".	Section 1-205.
"Seller".	Section 2-103.

Section 2-613. Casualty to Identified Goods

Where the contract requires for its performance goods identified when the contract is made, and the goods suffer casualty without fault of either party before the risk of loss passes to the buyer, or in a proper case under a "no arrival, no sale" term (Section 2-324) then

(a) if the loss is total the contract is avoided; and

(b) if the loss is partial or the goods have so deteriorated as no longer to conform to the contract the buyer may nevertheless demand inspection and at his option either treat the contract as avoided or accept the goods with due allowance from the contract price for the deterioration or the deficiency in quantity but without further right against the seller.

Official Comment

Prior Uniform Statutory Provision: Sections 7 and 8, Uniform Sales Act.

Changes: Rewritten, the basic policy being continued but the test of a "divisible" or "indivisible" sale or contract being abandoned in favor of adjustment in business terms.

Purposes of Changes:

1. Where goods whose continued existence is presupposed by the agreement are destroyed without fault of either party, the buyer is relieved from his obligation but may at his option take the surviving goods at a fair adjustment. "Fault" is intended to include negligence and not merely wilful wrong. The buyer is expressly given the right to inspect the goods in order to determine whether he wishes to avoid the contract entirely or to take the goods with a price adjustment.

2. The section applies whether the goods were already destroyed at the time of contracting without the knowledge of either party or whether they are destroyed subsequently but before the risk of loss passes to the buyer. Where under the agreement, including of course usage of trade, the risk has passed to the buyer before the casualty, the section has no application. Beyond this, the essential question in determining whether the rules of this section are to be applied is whether the seller has or has not undertaken the responsibility for the continued existence of the goods in proper condition through the time of agreed or expected delivery.

3. The section on the term "no arrival, no sale" makes clear that delay in arrival, quite as much as physical change in the goods, gives the buyer the options set forth in this section.

Cross Reference: Point 3: Section 2-324.

Definitional Cross References:

"Buyer".	Section 2-103.
"Conform".	Section 2-106.
"Contract".	Section 1-201.
"Fault".	Section 1-201.
"Goods".	Section 2-105.
"Party".	Section 1-201.
"Right".	Section 1-201.
"Seller".	Section 2-103.

Section 2-614. Substituted Performance

(1) Where without fault of either party the agreed berthing, loading, or unloading facilities fail or an agreed type of carrier becomes unavailable or the agreed manner of delivery otherwise becomes commercially impracticable but a commercially reasonable substitute is available, such substitute performance must be tendered and accepted.

(2) If the agreed means or manner of payment fails because of domestic or foreign governmental regulation, the seller may withhold or stop delivery unless the buyer provides a means or manner of payment which is commercially a substantial equivalent. If delivery has already been taken, payment by the means or in the manner provided by the regulation discharges the buyer's obligation unless the regulation is discriminatory, oppressive or predatory.

Official Comment

Prior Uniform Statutory Provision: None.

Purposes:

1. Subsection (1) requires the tender of a commercially reasonable substituted performance where agreed to facilities have failed or become commercially impracticable. Under this Article, in the absence of specific agreement, the normal or usual facilities enter into the agreement either through the circumstances, usage of trade or prior course of dealing.

This section appears between Section 2-613 on casualty to identified goods and the next section on excuse by failure of presupposed conditions, both of which deal with excuse and complete avoidance of the contract where the occurrence or non-occurrence of a contingency which was a basic assumption of the contract makes the expected performance impossible. The distinction between the present section and those sections lies in whether the failure or impossibility of performance arises in connection with an incidental matter or goes to the very heart of the agreement. The differing lines of solution are contrasted in a comparison of *International Paper Co. v. Rockefeller,* 146 N.Y.S. 371 (App. Div. 1914) and *Meyer v. Sullivan*, 181 P. 847 (Cal. Ct. App. 1919). In the former case a contract for the sale of spruce to be cut from a particular tract of land was involved. When a fire destroyed the trees growing on that tract the seller was held excused since performance was impossible. In the latter case the contract called for delivery of wheat "f.o.b. Kosmos Steamer at Seattle". The war led to cancellation of that line's sailing schedule after space had been duly engaged and the buyer was held entitled to demand substituted delivery at the warehouse on the line's loading dock. Under this Article, of course, the seller would also be entitled, had the market gone the other way, to make a substituted tender in that manner.

There must, however, be a true commercial impracticability to excuse the agreed to performance and justify a substituted performance. When this is the case a reasonable substituted performance tendered by either party should excuse him from strict compliance with contract terms which do not go to the essence of the agreement.

2. The substitution provided in this section as between buyer and seller does not carry over into the obligation of a financing agency under a letter of credit, since such an agency is entitled to performance which is plainly adequate on its face and without need to look into commercial evidence outside of the documents. See Article 5, especially Sections 5-102, 5-108, and 5-109.

3. Under subsection (2) where the contract is still executory on both sides, the seller is permitted to withdraw unless the buyer can provide him with a commercially equivalent return despite the governmental regulation. Where, however, only the debt for the price remains, a larger leeway is permitted. The buyer may pay in the manner provided by the regulation even though this may not be commercially equivalent provided that the regulation is not "discriminatory, oppressive or predatory".

Cross Reference: Point 2: Article 5.

Definitional Cross References:

"Buyer". Section 2-103.
"Fault". Section 1-201.
"Party". Section 1-201.
"Seller". Section 2-103.

Section 2-615. Excuse by Failure of Presupposed Conditions

Except so far as a seller may have assumed a greater obligation and subject to the preceding section on substituted performance:

(a) Delay in delivery or non-delivery in whole or in part by a seller who complies with paragraphs (b) and (c) is not a breach of his duty under a contract for sale if performance as agreed has been made impracticable by the occurrence of a contingency the non-occurrence of which was a basic assumption on which the contract was made or by compliance in good faith with any applicable foreign or domestic governmental regulation or order whether or not it later proves to be invalid.

(b) Where the causes mentioned in paragraph (a) affect only a part of the seller's capacity to perform, he must allocate production and deliveries among his customers but may at his option include regular customers not then under contract as well as his own requirements for further manufacture. He may so allocate in any manner which is fair and reasonable.

(c) The seller must notify the buyer seasonably that there will be delay or non-delivery and, when allocation is required under paragraph (b), of the estimated quota thus made available for the buyer.

Official Comment

Prior Uniform Statutory Provision: None.

Purposes:

1. This section excuses a seller from timely delivery of goods contracted for, where his performance has become commercially impracticable because of unforeseen supervening circumstances not within the contemplation of the parties at the time of contracting. The destruction of specific goods and the problem of the use of substituted performance on points other than delay or quantity, treated elsewhere in this Article, must be distinguished from the matter covered by this section.

2. The present section deliberately refrains from any effort at an exhaustive expression of contingencies and is to be interpreted in all cases sought to be brought within its scope in terms of its underlying reason and purpose.

3. The first test for excuse under this Article in terms of basic assumption is a familiar one. The additional test of commercial impracticability (as contrasted with "impossibility", "frustration of performance" or "frustration of the venture") has been adopted in order to call attention to the commercial character of the criterion chosen by this Article.

4. Increased cost alone does not excuse performance unless the rise in cost is due to some unforeseen contingency which alters the essential nature of the performance. Neither is a rise or a collapse in the market in itself a justification, for that is exactly the type of business risk which business contracts made at fixed prices are intended to cover. But a severe shortage of raw materials or of supplies due to a contingency such as war, embargo, local crop failure, unforeseen shutdown of major sources of supply or the like, which either causes a marked increase in cost or altogether prevents the seller from securing supplies necessary to his performance, is within the contemplation of this section. See *Ford & Sons, Ltd., v. Henry Leetham & Sons, Ltd.,* 21 Com. Cas. 55 (1915, K.B.D.).

5. Where a particular source of supply is exclusive under the agreement and fails through casualty, the present section applies rather than the provision on destruction or deterioration of specific goods. The same holds true where a particular source of supply is shown by the circumstances to have been contemplated or assumed by the parties at the time of contracting. See *Davis Co. v. Hoffmann-LaRoche Chemical Works,* 166 N.Y.S. 179 (App. Div. 1917) and *International Paper Co. v. Rockefeller,* 146 N.Y.S. 371 (App. Div. 1914).) There is no excuse under this section, however, unless the seller has employed all due measures to assure himself that his source will not fail. See *Canadian Industrial Alcohol Co., Ltd., v. Dunbar Molasses Co.,* 179 N.E. 383 (N.Y. 1932) and *Washington Mfg. Co. v. Midland Lumber Co.,* 194 P. 777 (Wash. 1921).

In the case of failure of production by an agreed source for causes beyond the seller's control, the seller should, if possible, be excused since production by an agreed source is without more a basic assumption of the contract. Such excuse should not result in relieving the defaulting supplier from liability nor in dropping into the seller's lap an unearned bonus of damages over. The flexible adjustment machinery of this Article provides the solution under the provision on the obligation of good faith. A condition to his making good the claim of excuse is the turning over to the buyer of his rights against the defaulting source of supply to the extent of the buyer's contract in relation to which excuse is being claimed.

6. In situations in which neither sense nor justice is served by either answer when the issue is posed in flat terms of "excuse" or "no excuse", adjustment under the various provisions of this Article is necessary, especially the sections on good faith, on insecurity and assurance and on the reading of all provisions in the light of their purposes, and the general policy of this Act to use equitable principles in furtherance of commercial standards and good faith.

7. The failure of conditions which go to convenience or collateral values rather than to the commercial practicability of the main performance does not amount to a complete excuse. However, good faith and the reason of the present section and of the preceding one may properly be held to justify and even to require any needed delay involved in a good faith inquiry seeking a readjustment of the contract terms to meet the new conditions.

8. The provisions of this section are made subject to assumption of greater liability by agreement and such agreement is to be found not only in the expressed terms of the contract but in the circumstances surrounding the contracting, in trade usage and the like. Thus the exemptions of this section do not apply when the contingency in question is sufficiently foreshadowed at the time of contracting to be included among the business risks which are fairly to be regarded as part of the dickered terms, either consciously or as a matter of reasonable, commercial interpretation from the circumstances. See *Madeirense Do Brasil, S.A. v. Stulman-Emrick Lumber Co.,* 147 F.2d 399 (2d Cir. 1945). The exemption otherwise present through usage of trade under the present section may also be expressly negated by the language of the agreement. Generally, express agreements as to exemptions designed to enlarge upon or supplant the provisions of this section are to be read in the light of mercantile sense and reason, for this section itself sets up the commercial standard for normal and reasonable interpretation and provides a minimum beyond which agreement may not go.

Agreement can also be made in regard to the consequences of exemption as laid down in paragraphs (b) and (c) and the next section on procedure on notice claiming excuse.

9. The case of a farmer who has contracted to sell crops to be grown on designated land may be regarded as falling either within the section on casualty to identified goods or this section, and he may be excused, when there is a failure of the specific crop, either on the basis of the destruction of identified goods or because of the failure of a basic assumption of the contract.

Exemption of the buyer in the case of a "requirements" contract is covered by the "Output and Requirements" section both as to assumption and allocation of the relevant risks. But when a contract by a manufacturer to buy fuel or raw material makes no specific reference to a particular venture and no such reference may be drawn from the circumstances, commercial understanding views it as a general deal in the general market and not conditioned on any assumption of the continuing operation of the buyer's plant. Even when notice is given by the buyer that the supplies are needed to fill a specific contract of a normal commercial kind, commercial understanding does not see such a supply contract as conditioned on the continuance of the buyer's further contract for outlet. On the other hand, where the buyer's contract is in reasonable commercial understanding conditioned on a definite and specific venture or assumption as, for instance, a war procurement subcontract known to be based on a prime contract which is subject to termination, or a supply contract for a particular construction venture, the reason of the present section may well apply and entitle the buyer to the exemption.

10. Following its basic policy of using commercial practicability as a test for excuse, this section recognizes as of equal significance either a foreign or domestic regulation and disregards any technical distinctions between "law", "regulation", "order" and the like. Nor does it make the present action of the seller depend upon the eventual judicial determination of the legality of the particular governmental action. The seller's good faith belief in the validity of the regulation is the test under this Article and the best evidence of his good faith is the general commercial acceptance of the regulation. However, governmental interference cannot excuse unless it truly "supervenes" in such a manner as to be beyond the seller's assumption of risk. And any action by the party claiming excuse which causes or colludes in inducing the governmental action preventing his performance would be in breach of good faith and would destroy his exemption.

11. An excused seller must fulfill his contract to the extent which the supervening contingency permits, and if the situation is such that his customers are generally affected he must take account of all in supplying one. Subsections (a) and (b), therefore, explicitly permit in any proration a fair and reasonable attention to the needs of regular customers who are probably relying on spot orders for supplies. Customers at different stages of the manufacturing process may be fairly treated by including the seller's manufacturing requirements. A fortiori, the seller may also take account of contracts later in date than the one in question. The fact that such spot orders may be closed at an advanced price causes no difficulty, since any allocation which exceeds normal past requirements will not be reasonable. However, good faith requires, when prices have advanced, that the seller exercise real care in making his allocations, and in case of doubt his contract customers should be favored and supplies prorated evenly among them regardless of price. Save for the extra care thus required by changes in the market, this section seeks to leave every reasonable business leeway to the seller.

Cross References:

Point 1: Sections 2-613 and 2-614.
Point 2: Section 1-103.
Point 5: Sections 1-304 and 2-613.
Point 6: Sections 1-103, 1-304 and 2-609.
Point 7: Section 2-614.
Point 8: Sections 1-302, 2-302 and 2-616.
Point 9: Sections 1-103, 2-306 and 2-613.

Definitional Cross References:

"Between merchants".	Section 2-104.
"Buyer".	Section 2-103.
"Contract".	Section 1-201.
"Contract for sale".	Section 2-106.
"Good faith".	Section 1-201.
"Merchant".	Section 2-104.
"Notifies".	Section 1-202.
"Seasonably".	Section 1-205.
"Seller".	Section 2-103.

Section 2-616. Procedure on Notice Claiming Excuse

(1) Where the buyer receives notification of a material or indefinite delay or an allocation justified under the preceding section he may by written notification to the seller as to any delivery concerned, and where the prospective deficiency substantially impairs the value of the whole contract under the provisions of this Article relating to breach of installment contracts (Section 2-612), then also as to the whole,

(a) terminate and thereby discharge any unexecuted portion of the contract; or

(b) modify the contract by agreeing to take his available quota in substitution.

(2) If after receipt of such notification from the seller the buyer fails so to modify the contract within a reasonable time not exceeding thirty days the contract lapses with respect to any deliveries affected.

(3) The provisions of this section may not be negated by agreement except in so far as the seller has assumed a greater obligation under the preceding section.

Official Comment

Prior Uniform Statutory Provision: None.

Purposes:

1. This section seeks to establish simple and workable machinery for providing certainty as to when a supervening and excusing contingency "excuses" the delay, "discharges" the contract, or may result in a waiver of the delay by the buyer. When the seller notifies, in accordance with the preceding section, claiming excuse, the buyer may acquiesce, in which case the contract is so modified. No consideration is necessary in a case of this kind to support such a modification. If the buyer does not elect so to modify the contract, he may terminate it and under subsection (2) his silence after receiving the seller's claim of excuse operates as such a termination. Subsection (3) denies effect to any contract clause made in advance of trouble which would require the buyer to stand ready to take delivery whenever the seller is excused from delivery by unforeseen circumstances.

2. As to the use of a record other than a writing and communications that are not written, see Section 2-207, Comment 8.

Cross References: Point 1: Sections 2-209 and 2-615.

Definitional Cross References:

"Buyer".	Section 2-103.
"Contract".	Section 1-201.
"Installment contract".	Section 2-612.
"Notification".	Section 1-203.
"Reasonable time".	Section 1-205.
"Seller".	Section 2-103.
"Termination".	Section 2-106.
"Written".	Section 1-201.

PART 7. REMEDIES

Section 2-701. Remedies for Breach of Collateral Contracts Not Impaired

Remedies for breach of any obligation or promise collateral or ancillary to a contract for sale are not impaired by the provisions of this Article.

Official Comment

Prior Uniform Statutory Provision: None.

Purposes: Whether a claim for breach of an obligation collateral to the contract for sale requires separate trial to avoid confusion of issues is beyond the scope of this Article; but contractual arrangements which as a business matter enter vitally into the contract should be considered a part thereof in so far as cross-claims or defenses are concerned.

Definitional Cross References:

"Contract for sale".	Section 2-106.
"Remedy".	Section 1-201.

Section 2-702. Seller's Remedies on Discovery of Buyer's Insolvency

(1) Where the seller discovers the buyer to be insolvent he may refuse delivery except for cash including payment for all goods theretofore delivered under the contract, and stop delivery under this Article (Section 2-705).

(2) Where the seller discovers that the buyer has received goods on credit while insolvent he may reclaim the goods upon demand made within ten days after the receipt, but if misrepresentation of solvency has been made to the particular seller in writing within three months before delivery the ten day limitation does not apply. Except as provided in this subsection the seller may not base a right to reclaim goods on the buyer's fraudulent or innocent misrepresentation of solvency or of intent to pay.

(3) The seller's right to reclaim under subsection (2) is subject to the rights of a buyer in ordinary course or other good faith purchaser under this Article (Section 2-403). Successful reclamation of goods excludes all other remedies with respect to them.

As amended in 1966.

Official Comment

Prior Uniform Statutory Provision: Subsection (1): Sections 53(1)(b), 54(1)(c) and 57, Uniform Sales Act; Subsection (2) : none; Subsection (3) : Section 76(3), Uniform Sales Act.

Changes: Rewritten, the protection given to a seller who has sold on credit and has delivered goods to the buyer immediately preceding his insolvency being extended.

Purposes of Changes and New Matter: To make it clear that:

1. The seller's right to withhold the goods or to stop delivery except for cash when he discovers the buyer's insolvency is made explicit in subsection (1) regardless of the passage of title, and the concept of stoppage has been extended to include goods in the possession of any bailee who has not yet attorned to the buyer.

2. Subsection (2) takes as its base line the proposition that any receipt of goods on credit by an insolvent buyer amounts to a tacit business misrepresentation of solvency and therefore is fraudulent as against the particular seller. This Article makes discovery of the buyer's insolvency and demand within a ten day period a condition of the right to reclaim goods on this ground. The ten day limitation period operates from the time of receipt of the goods.

An exception to this time limitation is made when a written misrepresentation of solvency has been made to the particular seller within three months prior to the delivery. To fall within the exception the statement of solvency must be in writing, addressed to the particular seller and dated within three months of the delivery.

3. Because the right of the seller to reclaim goods under this section constitutes preferential treatment as against the buyer's other creditors, subsection (3) provides that such reclamation bars all his other remedies as to the goods involved.

4. As to the use of a record other than a writing and communications that are not written, see Section 2-207, Comment 8.

Cross References:

Point 1: Sections 2-401 and 2-705.

Compare Section 2-502.

Definitional Cross References:

"Buyer".	Section 2-103.
"Buyer in ordinary course of business".	Section 1-201.
"Contract".	Section 1-201.
"Good faith".	Section 1-201.
"Goods".	Section 2-105.
"Insolvent".	Section 1-201.
"Person".	Section 1-201.
"Purchaser".	Section 1-201.
"Receipt" of goods.	Section 2-103.
"Remedy".	Section 1-201.
"Right".	Section 1-201.
"Seller".	Section 2-103.
"Writing".	Section 1-201.

Section 2-703. Seller's Remedies in General

Where the buyer wrongfully rejects or revokes acceptance of goods or fails to make a payment due on or before delivery or repudiates with respect to a part or the whole, then with respect to any goods directly affected and, if the breach is of the whole contract (Section 2-612), then also with respect to the whole undelivered balance, the aggrieved seller may

(a) withhold delivery of such goods;

(b) stop delivery by any bailee as hereafter provided (Section 2-705);

(c) proceed under the next section respecting goods still unidentified to the contract;

(d) resell and recover damages as hereafter provided (Section 2-706);

(e) recover damages for non-acceptance (Section 2-708) or in a proper case the price (Section 2-709);

(f) cancel.

Official Comment

Prior Uniform Statutory Provision: No comparable index section. See Section 53, Uniform Sales Act.

Purposes:

1. This section is an index section which gathers together in one convenient place all of the various remedies open to a seller for any breach by the buyer. This Article rejects any doctrine of election of remedy as a fundamental policy and thus the remedies are essentially cumulative in nature and include all of the available remedies for breach. Whether the pursuit of one remedy bars another depends entirely on the facts of the individual case.

2. The buyer's breach which occasions the use of the remedies under this section may involve only one lot or delivery of goods, or may involve all of the goods which are the subject matter of the particular contract. The right of the seller to pursue a remedy as to all the goods when the breach is as to only one or more lots is covered by the section on breach in installment contracts. The present section deals only with the remedies available after the goods involved in the breach have been determined by that section.

3. In addition to the typical case of refusal to pay or default in payment, the language in the preamble, "fails to make a payment due", is intended to cover the dishonor of a check on due presentment, or the non-acceptance of a draft, and the failure to furnish an agreed letter of credit.

4. It should also be noted that this Act requires its remedies to be liberally administered and provides that any right or obligation which it declares is enforceable by action unless a different effect is specifically prescribed (Section 1-305).

Cross References:

Point 2: Section 2-612.

Point 3: Section 2-325.

Point 4: Section 1-305.

Definitional Cross References:

"Aggrieved party".	Section 1-201.
"Buyer".	Section 2-103.
"Cancellation".	Section 2-106.
"Contract".	Section 1-201.
"Goods".	Section 2-105.
"Remedy".	Section 1-201.
"Seller".	Section 2-103.

Section 2-704. Seller's Right to Identify Goods to the Contract Notwithstanding Breach or to Salvage Unfinished Goods

(1) An aggrieved seller under the preceding section may

(a) identify to the contract conforming goods not already identified if at the time he learned of the breach they are in his possession or control;

(b) treat as the subject of resale goods which have demonstrably been intended for the particular contract even though those goods are unfinished.

(2) Where the goods are unfinished an aggrieved seller may in the exercise of reasonable commercial judgment for the purposes of avoiding loss and of effective realization either complete the manufacture and wholly identify the goods to the contract or cease manufacture and resell for scrap or salvage value or proceed in any other reasonable manner.

Official Comment

Prior Uniform Statutory Provision: Sections 63(3) and 64(4), Uniform Sales Act.

Changes: Rewritten, the seller's rights being broadened.

Purposes of Changes:

1. This section gives an aggrieved seller the right at the time of breach to identify to the contract any conforming finished goods, regardless of their resalability, and to use reasonable judgment as to completing unfinished goods. It thus makes the goods available for resale under the resale section, the seller's primary remedy, and in the special case in which resale is not practicable, allows the action for the price which would then be necessary to give the seller the value of his contract.

2. Under this Article the seller is given express power to complete manufacture or procurement of goods for the contract unless the exercise of reasonable commercial judgment as to the facts as they appear at the time he learns of the breach makes it clear that such action will result in a material increase in damages. The burden is on the buyer to show the commercially unreasonable nature of the seller's action in completing manufacture.

Cross References: Sections 2-703 and 2-706.

Definitional Cross References:

"Aggrieved party".	Section 1-201.
"Conforming".	Section 2-106.
"Contract".	Section 1-201.
"Goods".	Section 2-105.
"Right".	Section 1-201.
"Seller".	Section 2-103.

Section 2-705. Seller's Stoppage of Delivery in Transit or Otherwise

(1) The seller may stop delivery of goods in the possession of a carrier or other bailee when he discovers the buyer to be insolvent (Section 2-702) and may stop delivery of carload, truckload, planeload or larger shipments of express or freight when the buyer repudiates or fails to make a payment due before delivery or if for any other reason the seller has a right to withhold or reclaim the goods.

(2) As against such buyer the seller may stop delivery until

(a) receipt of the goods by the buyer; or

(b) acknowledgment to the buyer by any bailee of the goods except a carrier that the bailee holds the goods for the buyer; or

(c) such acknowledgment to the buyer by a carrier by reshipment or as warehouseman; or

(d) negotiation to the buyer of any negotiable document of title covering the goods.

(3) (a) To stop delivery the seller must so notify as to enable the bailee by reasonable diligence to prevent delivery of the goods.

(b) After such notification the bailee must hold and deliver the goods according to the directions of the seller but the seller is liable to the bailee for any ensuing charges or damages.

(c) If a negotiable document of title has been issued for goods the bailee is not obliged to obey a notification to stop until surrender of the document.

(d) A carrier who has issued a non-negotiable bill of lading is not obliged to obey a notification to stop received from a person other than the consignor.

Official Comment

Prior Uniform Statutory Provision: Sections 57-59, Uniform Sales Act; see also Sections 12, 14 and 42, Uniform Bills of Lading Act and Sections 9, 11 and 49, Uniform Warehouse Receipts Act.

Changes: This section continues and develops the above sections of the Uniform Sales Act in the light of the other uniform statutory provisions noted.

Purposes: To make it clear that:

1. Subsection (1) applies the stoppage principle to other bailees as well as carriers.

It also expands the remedy to cover the situations, in addition to buyer's insolvency, specified in the subsection. But since stoppage is a burden in any case to carriers, and might be a very heavy burden to them if it covered all small shipments in all these situations, the right to stop for reasons other than insolvency is limited to carload, truckload, planeload or larger shipments. The seller shipping to a buyer of doubtful credit can protect himself by shipping C.O.D.

Where stoppage occurs for insecurity it is merely a suspension of performance, and if assurances are duly forthcoming from the buyer the seller is not entitled to resell or divert.

Improper stoppage is a breach by the seller if it effectively interferes with the buyer's right to due tender under the section on manner of tender of delivery. However, if the bailee obeys an unjustified order to stop he may also be liable to the buyer. The measure of his obligation is dependent on the provisions of the Documents of Title Article (Section 7-303). Subsection 3(b) therefore gives him a right of indemnity as against the seller in such a case.

2. "Receipt by the buyer" includes receipt by the buyer's designated representative, the sub-purchaser, when shipment is made direct to him and the buyer himself never receives the goods. It is entirely proper under this Article that the seller, by making such direct shipment to the sub-purchaser, be regarded as acquiescing in the latter's purchase and as thus barred from stoppage of the goods as against him.

As between the buyer and the seller, the latter's right to stop the goods at any time until they reach the place of final delivery is recognized by this section.

Under subsection (3)(c) and (d), the carrier is under no duty to recognize the stop order of a person who is a stranger to the carrier's contract. But the seller's right as against the buyer to stop delivery remains, whether or not the carrier is obligated to recognize the stop order. If the carrier does obey it, the buyer cannot complain merely because of that circumstance; and the seller becomes obligated under subsection (3) (b) to pay the carrier any ensuing damages or charges.

3. A diversion of a shipment is not a "reshipment" under subsection (2)(c) when it is merely an incident to the original contract of transportation. Nor is the procurement of "exchange bills" of lading which change only the name of the consignee to that of the buyer's local agent but do not alter the destination of a reshipment.

Acknowledgment by the carrier as a "warehouseman" within the meaning of this Article requires a contract of a truly different character from the original shipment, a contract not in extension of transit but as a warehouseman.

4. Subsection (3)(c) makes the bailee's obedience of a notification to stop conditional upon the surrender of any outstanding negotiable document.

5. Any charges or losses incurred by the carrier in following the seller's orders, whether or not he was obligated to do so, fall to the seller's charge.

6. After an effective stoppage under this section the seller's rights in the goods are the same as if he had never made a delivery.

Cross References:

Sections 2-702 and 2-703.

Point 1: Sections 2-503 and 2-609, and Article 7.

Point 2: Section 2-103 and Article 7.

Definitional Cross References:

"Buyer".	Section 2-103.
"Contract for sale".	Section 2-106.
"Document of title".	Section 1-201.
"Goods".	Section 2-105.
"Insolvent".	Section 1-201.
"Notification".	Section 1-202.
"Receipt" of goods.	Section 2-103.
"Right".	Section 1-201.
"Seller".	Section 2-103.

Section 2-706. Seller's Resale Including Contract for Resale

(1) Under the conditions stated in Section 2-703 on seller's remedies, the seller may resell the goods concerned or the undelivered balance thereof. Where the resale is made in good faith and in a commercially reasonable manner the seller may recover the difference between the resale price and the contract price together with any incidental damages allowed under the provisions of this Article (Section 2-710), but less expenses saved in consequence of the buyer's breach.

(2) Except as otherwise provided in subsection (3) or unless otherwise agreed resale may be at public or private sale including sale by way of one or more contracts to sell or of identification to an existing contract of the seller. Sale may be as a unit or in parcels and at any time and place and on any terms but every aspect of the sale including the method, manner, time, place and terms must be commercially reasonable. The resale must be reasonably identified as referring to the broken contract, but it is not necessary that the goods be in existence or that any or all of them have been identified to the contract before the breach.

(3) Where the resale is at private sale the seller must give the buyer reasonable notification of his intention to resell.

(4) Where the resale is at public sale

(a) only identified goods can be sold except where there is a recognized market for a public sale of futures in goods of the kind; and

(b) it must be made at a usual place or market for public sale if one is reasonably available and except in the case of goods which are perishable or threaten to decline in value speedily the seller must give the buyer reasonable notice of the time and place of the resale; and

(c) if the goods are not to be within the view of those attending the sale the notification of sale must state the place where the goods are located and provide for their reasonable inspection by prospective bidders; and

(d) the seller may buy.

(5) A purchaser who buys in good faith at a resale takes the goods free of any rights of the original buyer even though the seller fails to comply with one or more of the requirements of this section.

(6) The seller is not accountable to the buyer for any profit made on any resale. A person in the position of a seller (Section 2-707) or a buyer who has rightfully rejected or justifiably revoked acceptance must account for any excess over the amount of his security interest, as hereinafter defined (subsection (3) of Section 2-711).

Official Comment

Prior Uniform Statutory Provision: Section 60, Uniform Sales Act.

Changes: Rewritten.

Purposes of Changes: To simplify the prior statutory provision and to make it clear that:

1. The only condition precedent to the seller's right of resale under subsection (1) is a breach by the buyer within the section on the seller's remedies in general or insolvency. Other meticulous conditions and restrictions of the prior uniform statutory provision are disapproved by this Article and are replaced by standards of commercial reasonableness. Under this section the seller may resell the goods after any breach by the buyer. Thus, an anticipatory repudiation by the buyer gives rise to any of the seller's remedies for breach, and to the right of resale. This principle is supplemented by subsection (2) which authorizes a resale of goods which are not in existence or were not identified to the contract before the breach.

2. In order to recover the damages prescribed in subsection (1) the seller must act "in good faith and in a commercially reasonable manner" in making the resale. This standard is intended to be more comprehensive than that of "reasonable care and judgment" established by the prior uniform statutory provision. Failure to act properly under this section deprives the seller of the measure of damages here provided and relegates him to that provided in Section 2-708.

Under this Article the seller resells by authority of law, in his own behalf, for his own benefit and for the purpose of fixing his damages. The theory of a seller's agency is thus rejected.

3. If the seller complies with the prescribed standard of duty in making the resale, he may recover from the buyer the damages provided for in subsection (1). Evidence of market or current prices at any particular time or place is relevant only on the question of whether the seller acted in a commercially reasonable manner in making the resale.

The distinction drawn by some courts between cases where the title had not passed to the buyer and the seller had resold as owner, and cases where the title had passed and the seller had resold by virtue of his lien on the goods, is rejected.

4. Subsection (2) frees the remedy of resale from legalistic restrictions and enables the seller to resell in accordance with reasonable commercial practices so as to realize as high a price as possible in the circumstances. By "public" sale is meant a sale by auction. A "private" sale may be effected by solicitation and negotiation conducted either directly or through a broker. In choosing between a public and private sale the character of the goods must be considered and relevant trade practices and usages must be observed.

5. Subsection (2) merely clarifies the common law rule that the time for resale is a reasonable time after the buyer's breach, by using the language "commercially reasonable". What is such a reasonable time depends upon the nature of the goods, the condition of the market and the other circumstances of the case; its length cannot be measured by any legal yardstick or divided into degrees. Where a seller contemplating resale receives a demand from the buyer for inspection under the section of preserving evidence of goods in dispute, the time for resale may be appropriately lengthened.

On the question of the place for resale, subsection (2) goes to the ultimate test, the commercial reasonableness of the seller's choice as to the place for an advantageous resale. This Article rejects the theory that the seller is required to resell at the agreed place for delivery and that a resale elsewhere can be permitted only in exceptional cases.

6. The purpose of subsection (2) being to enable the seller to dispose of the goods to the best advantage, he is permitted in making the resale to depart from the terms and conditions of the original contract for sale to any extent "commercially reasonable" in the circumstances.

7. The provision of subsection (2) that the goods need not be in existence to be resold applies when the buyer is guilty of anticipatory repudiation of a contract for future goods, before the goods or some of them have come into existence. In such a case the seller may exercise the right of resale and fix his damages by "one or more contracts to sell" the quantity of conforming future goods affected by the repudiation. The companion provision of subsection (2) that resale may be made although the goods were not identified to the contract prior to the buyer's breach, likewise contemplates an anticipatory repudiation by the buyer but occurring after the goods are in existence. If the goods so identified conform to the contract, their resale will fix the seller's damages quite as satisfactorily as if they had been identified before the breach.

8. Where the resale is to be by private sale, subsection (3) requires that reasonable notification of the seller's intention to resell must be given to the buyer. The length of notification of a private sale depends upon the urgency of the matter. Notification of the time and place of this type of sale is not required.

Subsection (4)(b) requires that the seller give the buyer reasonable notice of the time and place of a public resale so that he may have an opportunity to bid or to secure the attendance of other bidders. An exception is made in the case of goods "which are perishable or threaten to decline speedily in value".

9. Since there would be no reasonable prospect of competitive bidding elsewhere, subsection (4) requires that a public resale "must be made at a usual place or market for public sale if one is reasonably available"; i.e., a place or market which prospective bidders may reasonably be expected to attend.

Such a market may still be "reasonably available" under this subsection, though at a considerable distance from the place where the goods are located. In such a case the expense of transporting the goods for resale is recoverable from the buyer as part of the seller's incidental damages under subsection (1). However, the question of availability is one of commercial reasonableness in the circumstances and if such "usual" place or market is not reasonably available, a duly advertised public resale may be held at another place if it is one which prospective bidders may reasonably be expected to attend, as distinguished from a place where there is no demand whatsoever for goods of the kind.

Paragraph (a) of subsection (4) qualifies the last sentence of subsection (2) with respect to resales of unidentified and future goods at public sale. If conforming goods are in existence the seller may identify them to the contract after the buyer's breach and then resell them at public sale. If the goods have not been identified, however, he may resell them at public sale only as "future" goods and only where there is a recognized market for public sale of futures in goods of the kind.

The provisions of paragraph (c) of subsection (4) are intended to permit intelligent bidding.

The provision of paragraph (d) of subsection (4) permitting the seller to bid and, of course, to become the purchaser, benefits the original buyer by tending to increase the resale price and thus decreasing the damages he will have to pay.

10. This Article departs in subsection (5) from the prior uniform statutory provision in permitting a good faith purchaser at resale to take a good title as against the buyer even though the seller fails to comply with the requirements of this section.

11. Under subsection (6), the seller retains profit, if any, without distinction based on whether or not he had a lien since this Article divorces the question of passage of title to the buyer from the seller's right of resale or the consequences of its exercise. On the other hand, where "a person in the position of a seller" or a buyer acting under the section on buyer's remedies, exercises his right of resale under the present section he does so only for the limited purpose of obtaining cash for his "security interest" in the goods. Once that purpose has been accomplished any excess in the resale price belongs to the seller to whom an accounting must be made as provided in the last sentence of subsection (6).

Cross References:

Point 1:	Sections 2-610, 2-702 and 2-703.
Point 2:	Section 1-201.
Point 3:	Sections 2-708 and 2-710.
Point 4:	Section 2-328.
Point 8:	Section 2-104.
Point 9:	Section 2-710.
Point 11:	Sections 2-401, 2-707 and 2-711(3).

Definitional Cross References:

"Buyer".	Section 2-103.
"Contract".	Section 1-201.
"Contract for sale".	Section 2-106.
"Good faith".	Section 1-102.
"Goods".	Section 2-105.
"Merchant".	Section 2-104.
"Notification".	Section 1-202.
"Person in position of seller".	Section 2-707.
"Purchase".	Section 1-201.
"Right".	Section 1-201.
"Sale".	Section 2-106.
"Security interest".	Section 1-201.
"Seller".	Section 2-103.

Section 2-707. "Person in the Position of a Seller"

(1) A "person in the position of a seller" includes as against a principal an agent who has paid or become responsible for the price of goods on behalf of his principal or anyone who otherwise holds a security interest or other right in goods similar to that of a seller.

(2) A person in the position of a seller may as provided in this Article withhold or stop delivery (Section 2-705) and resell (Section 2-706) and recover incidental damages (Section 2-710).

Official Comment

Prior Uniform Statutory Provision: Section 52(2), Uniform Sales Act.

Changes: Rewritten.

Purposes of Changes: To make it clear that: In addition to following in general the prior uniform statutory provision, the case of a financing agency which has acquired documents by honoring a letter of credit for the buyer or by discounting a draft for the seller has been included in the term "a person in the position of a seller".

Cross Reference: Article 5, Section 2-506.

Definitional Cross References:

"Consignee".	Section 7-102.
"Consignor".	Section 7-102.
"Goods".	Section 2-105.
"Security interest".	Section 1-201.
"Seller".	Section 2-103.

Section 2-708. Seller's Damages for Non-Acceptance or Repudiation

(1) Subject to subsection (2) and to the provisions of this Article with respect to proof of market price (Section 2-723), the measure of damages for non-acceptance or repudiation by the buyer is the difference between the market price at the time and place for tender and the unpaid contract price together with any incidental damages provided in this Article (Section 2-710), but less expenses saved in consequence of the buyer's breach.

(2) If the measure of damages provided in subsection (1) is inadequate to put the seller in as good a position as performance would have done then the measure of damages is the profit (including reasonable overhead) which the seller would have made from full performance

by the buyer, together with any incidental damages provided in this Article (Section 2-710), due allowance for costs reasonably incurred and due credit for payments or proceeds of resale.

Official Comment

Prior Uniform Statutory Provision: Section 64, Uniform Sales Act.

Changes: Rewritten.

Purposes of Changes: To make it clear that:

1. The prior uniform statutory provision is followed generally in setting the current market price at the time and place for tender as the standard by which damages for non-acceptance are to be determined. The time and place of tender is determined by reference to the section on manner of tender of delivery, and to the sections on the effect of such terms as FOB, FAS, CIF, C & F, Ex Ship and No Arrival, No Sale.

In the event that there is no evidence available of the current market price at the time and place of tender, proof of a substitute market may be made under the section on determination and proof of market price. Furthermore, the section on the admissibility of market quotations is intended to ease materially the problem of providing competent evidence.

2. The provision of this section permitting recovery of expected profit including reasonable overhead where the standard measure of damages is inadequate, together with the new requirement that price actions may be sustained only where resale is impractical, are designed to eliminate the unfair and economically wasteful results arising under the older law when fixed price articles were involved. This section permits the recovery of lost profits in all appropriate cases, which would include all standard priced goods. The normal measure there would be list price less cost to the dealer or list price less manufacturing cost to the manufacturer. It is not necessary to a recovery of "profit" to show a history of earnings, especially if a new venture is involved.

3. In all cases the seller may recover incidental damages.

Cross References:

Point 1: Sections 2-319 through 2-324, 2-503, 2-723 and 2-724.

Point 2: Section 2-709.

Point 3: Section 2-710.

Definitional Cross References:

"Buyer". Section 2-103.

"Contract". Section 1-201.

"Seller". Section 2-103.

Section 2-709. Action for the Price

(1) When the buyer fails to pay the price as it becomes due the seller may recover, together with any incidental damages under the next section, the price

(a) of goods accepted or of conforming goods lost or damaged within a commercially reasonable time after risk of their loss has passed to the buyer; and

(b) of goods identified to the contract if the seller is unable after reasonable effort to resell them at a reasonable price or the circumstances reasonably indicate that such effort will be unavailing.

(2) Where the seller sues for the price he must hold for the buyer any goods which have been identified to the contract and are still in his control except that if resale becomes possible he may resell them at any time prior to the collection of the judgment. The net proceeds of any such resale must be credited to the buyer and payment of the judgment entitles him to any goods not resold.

(3) After the buyer has wrongfully rejected or revoked acceptance of the goods or has failed to make a payment due or has repudiated (Section 2-610), a seller who is held not entitled to the price under this section shall nevertheless be awarded damages for non-acceptance under the preceding section.

Official Comment

Prior Uniform Statutory Provision: Section 63, Uniform Sales Act.

Changes: Rewritten, important commercially needed changes being incorporated.

Purposes of Changes: To make it clear that:

1. Neither the passing of title to the goods nor the appointment of a day certain for payment is now material to a price action.

2. The action for the price is now generally limited to those cases where resale of the goods is impracticable except where the buyer has accepted the goods or where they have been destroyed after risk of loss has passed to the buyer.

3. This section substitutes an objective test by action for the former "not readily resalable" standard. An action for the price under subsection (1)(b) can be sustained only after a "reasonable effort to resell" the goods "at reasonable price" has actually been made or where the circumstances "reasonably indicate" that such an effort will be unavailing.

4. If a buyer is in default not with respect to the price, but on an obligation to make an advance, the seller should recover not under this section for the price as such, but for the default in the collateral (though coincident) obligation to finance the seller. If the agreement between the parties contemplates that the buyer will acquire, on making the advance, a security interest in the goods, the buyer on making the advance has such an interest as soon as the seller has rights in the agreed collateral. See Section 9-204.

5. "Goods accepted" by the buyer under subsection (1)(a) include only goods as to which there has been no justified revocation of acceptance, for such a revocation means that there has been a default by the seller which bars his rights under this section. "Goods lost or damaged" are covered by the section on risk of loss. "Goods identified to the contract" under subsection (1)(b) are covered by the section on identification and the section on identification notwithstanding breach.

6. This section is intended to be exhaustive in its enumeration of cases where an action for the price lies.

7. If the action for the price fails, the seller may nonetheless have proved a case entitling him to damages for non-acceptance. In such a situation, subsection (3) permits recovery of those damages in the same action.

Cross References:

Point 4: Section 1-305.

Point 5: Sections 2-501, 2-509, 2-510 and 2-704.

Point 7: Section 2-708.

Definitional Cross References:

"Action".	Section 1-201.
"Buyer".	Section 2-103.
"Conforming".	Section 2-106.
"Contract".	Section 1-201.
"Goods".	Section 2-105.
"Seller".	Section 2-103.

Section 2-710. Seller's Incidental Damages

Incidental damages to an aggrieved seller include any commercially reasonable charges, expenses or commissions incurred in stopping delivery, in the transportation, care and custody of goods after the buyer's breach, in connection with return or resale of the goods or otherwise resulting from the breach.

Official Comment

Prior Uniform Statutory Provision: See Sections 64 and 70, Uniform Sales Act.

Purposes: To authorize reimbursement of the seller for expenses reasonably incurred by him as a result of the buyer's breach. The section sets forth the principal normal and necessary additional elements of damage flowing from the breach but intends to allow all commercially reasonable expenditures made by the seller.

Definitional Cross References:

"Aggrieved party".	Section 1-201.
"Buyer".	Section 2-103.
"Goods".	Section 2-105.
"Seller".	Section 2-103.

Section 2-711. Buyer's Remedies in General; Buyer's Security Interest in Rejected Goods

(1) Where the seller fails to make delivery or repudiates or the buyer rightfully rejects or justifiably revokes acceptance then with respect to any goods involved, and with respect to the whole if the breach goes to the whole contract (Section 2-612), the buyer may cancel and whether or not he has done so may in addition to recovering so much of the price as has been paid

(a) "cover" and have damages under the next section as to all the goods affected whether or not they have been identified to the contract; or

(b) recover damages for non-delivery as provided in this Article (Section 2-713).

(2) Where the seller fails to deliver or repudiates the buyer may also

(a) if the goods have been identified recover them as provided in this Article (Section 2-502); or

(b) in a proper case obtain specific performance or replevy the goods as provided in this Article (Section 2-716).

(3) On rightful rejection or justifiable revocation of acceptance a buyer has a security interest in goods in his possession or control for any payments made on their price and any expenses reasonably incurred in their inspection, receipt, transportation, care and custody and may hold such goods and resell them in like manner as an aggrieved seller (Section 2-706).

Official Comment

Prior Uniform Statutory Provision: No comparable index section; Subsection (3)—Section 69(5), Uniform Sales Act.

Changes: The prior uniform statutory provision is generally continued and expanded in Subsection (3).

Purposes of Changes and New Matter:

1. To index in this section the buyer's remedies, subsection (1) covering those remedies permitting the recovery of money damages, and subsection (2) covering those which permit reaching the goods themselves. The remedies listed here are those available to a buyer who has not accepted the goods or who has justifiably revoked his acceptance. The remedies available to a buyer with regard to goods finally accepted appear in the section dealing with breach in regard to accepted goods. The buyer's right to proceed as to all goods when the breach is as to only some of the goods is determined by the section on breach in installment contracts and by the section on partial acceptance.

Despite the seller's breach, proper retender of delivery under the section on cure of improper tender or replacement can effectively preclude the buyer's remedies under this section, except for any delay involved.

2. To make it clear in subsection (3) that the buyer may hold and resell rejected goods if he has paid a part of the price or incurred expenses of the type specified. "Paid" as used here includes acceptance of a draft or other time negotiable instrument or the signing of a negotiable note. His freedom of resale is coextensive with that of a seller under this Article except that the buyer may not keep any profit resulting from the resale and is limited to retaining only the amount of the price paid and the costs involved in the inspection and handling of the goods. The buyer's security interest in the goods is intended to be limited to the items listed in subsection (3), and the buyer is not permitted to retain such funds as he might believe adequate for his damages. The buyer's right to cover, or to have damages for non-delivery, is not impaired by his exercise of his right of resale.

3. It should also be noted that this Act requires its remedies to be liberally administered and provides that any right or obligation which it declares is enforceable by action unless a different effect is specifically prescribed (Section 1-305).

Cross References:

Point 1: Sections 2-508, 2-601(c), 2-608, 2-612 and 2-714.

Point 2: Section 2-706.

Point 3: Section 1-305.

Definitional Cross References:

"Aggrieved party".	Section 1-201.
"Buyer".	Section 2-103.
"Cancellation".	Section 2-106.
"Contract".	Section 1-201.
"Cover".	Section 2-712.
"Goods".	Section 2-105.
"Notifies".	Section 1-202.
"Receipt" of goods.	Section 2-103.
"Remedy".	Section 1-201.
"Security interest".	Section 1-201.
"Seller".	Section 2-103.

Section 2-712. "Cover"; Buyer's Procurement of Substitute Goods

(1) After a breach within the preceding section the buyer may "cover" by making in good faith and without unreasonable delay any reasonable purchase of or contract to purchase goods in substitution for those due from the seller.

(2) The buyer may recover from the seller as damages the difference between the cost of cover and the contract price together with any incidental or consequential damages as hereinafter defined (Section 2-715), but less expenses saved in consequence of the seller's breach.

(3) Failure of the buyer to effect cover within this section does not bar him from any other remedy.

Official Comment

Prior Uniform Statutory Provision: None.

Purposes:

1. This section provides the buyer with a remedy aimed at enabling him to obtain the goods he needs thus meeting his essential need. This remedy is the buyer's equivalent of the seller's right to resell.

2. The definition of "cover" under subsection (1) envisages a series of contracts or sales, as well as a single contract or sale; goods not identical with those involved but commercially usable as reasonable substitutes under the circumstances of the particular case; and contracts on credit or delivery terms differing from the contract in breach, but again reasonable under the circumstances. The test of proper cover is whether at the time and place the buyer acted in good faith and in a reasonable manner, and it is immaterial that hindsight may later prove that the method of cover used was not the cheapest or most effective.

The requirement that the buyer must cover "without unreasonable delay" is not intended to limit the time necessary for him to look around and decide as to how he may best effect cover. The test here is similar to that generally used in this Article as to reasonable time and seasonable action.

3. Subsection (3) expresses the policy that cover is not a mandatory remedy for the buyer. The buyer is always free to choose between cover and damages for non-delivery under the next section.

However, this subsection must be read in conjunction with the section which limits the recovery of consequential damages to such as could not have been obviated by cover. Moreover, the operation of the section on specific performance of contracts for "unique" goods must be considered in this connection for availability of the goods to the particular buyer for his particular needs is the test for that remedy and inability to cover is made an express condition to the right of the buyer to replevy the goods.

4. This section does not limit cover to merchants, in the first instance. It is the vital and important remedy for the consumer buyer as well. Both are free to use cover.

Cross References:

Point 1: Section 2-706.

Point 2: Section 1-205.

Point 3: Sections 2-713, 2-715 and 2-716.

Point 4: Section 1-304.

Definitional Cross References:

"Buyer".	Section 2-103.
"Contract".	Section 1-201.
"Good faith".	Section 1-201.
"Goods".	Section 2-105.
"Purchase".	Section 1-201.
"Remedy".	Section 1-201.
"Seller".	Section 2-103.

Section 2-713. Buyer's Damages for Non-Delivery or Repudiation

(1) Subject to the provisions of this Article with respect to proof of market price (Section 2-723), the measure of damages for non-delivery or repudiation by the seller is the difference between the market price at the time when the buyer learned of the breach and the contract price together with any incidental and consequential damages provided in this Article (Section 2-715), but less expenses saved in consequence of the seller's breach.

(2) Market price is to be determined as of the place for tender or, in cases of rejection after arrival or revocation of acceptance, as of the place of arrival.

Official Comment

Prior Uniform Statutory Provision: Section 67(3), Uniform Sales Act.

Changes: Rewritten.

Purposes of Changes: To clarify the former rule so that:

1. The general baseline adopted in this section uses as a yardstick the market in which the buyer would have obtained cover had he sought that relief. So the place for measuring damages is the place of tender (or the place of arrival if the goods are rejected or their acceptance is revoked after reaching their destination) and the crucial time is the time at which the buyer learns of the breach.

2. The market or current price to be used in comparison with the contract price under this section is the price for goods of the same kind and in the same branch of trade.

3. When the current market price under this section is difficult to prove the section on determination and proof of market price is available to permit a showing of a comparable market price or, where no market price is available, evidence of spot sale prices is proper. Where the unavailability of a market price is caused by a scarcity of goods of the type involved, a good case is normally made for specific performance under this Article. Such scarcity conditions, moreover, indicate that the price has risen and under the section providing for liberal administration of remedies, opinion evidence as to the value of the goods would be admissible in the absence of a market price and a liberal construction of allowable consequential damages should also result.

4. This section carries forward the standard rule that the buyer must deduct from his damages any expenses saved as a result of the breach.

5. The present section provides a remedy which is completely alternative to cover under the preceding section and applies only when and to the extent that the buyer has not covered.

Cross References:

Point 3: Sections 1-305, 2-716 and 2-723.

Point 5: Section 2-712.

Definitional Cross References:

"Buyer". Section 2-103.

"Contract". Section 1-201.

"Seller". Section 2-103.

Section 2-714. Buyer's Damages for Breach in Regard to Accepted Goods

(1) Where the buyer has accepted goods and given notification (subsection (3) of Section 2-607) he may recover as damages for any non-conformity of tender the loss resulting in the ordinary course of events from the seller's breach as determined in any manner which is reasonable.

(2) The measure of damages for breach of warranty is the difference at the time and place of acceptance between the value of the goods accepted and the value they would have had if they had been as warranted, unless special circumstances show proximate damages of a different amount.

(3) In a proper case any incidental and consequential damages under the next section may also be recovered.

Official Comment

Prior Uniform Statutory Provision: Section 69(6) and (7), Uniform Sales Act.

Changes: Rewritten.

Purposes of Changes:

1. This section deals with the remedies available to the buyer after the goods have been accepted and the time for revocation of acceptance has gone by. In general this section adopts the rule of the prior uniform statutory provision for measuring damages where there has been a breach of warranty as to goods accepted, but goes further to lay down an explicit provision as to the time and place for determining the loss.

The section on deduction of damages from price provides an additional remedy for a buyer who still owes part of the purchase price, and frequently the two remedies will be available concurrently. The buyer's failure to notify of his claim under the section on effects of acceptance, however, operates to bar his remedies under either that section or the present section.

2. The "non-conformity" referred to in subsection (1) includes not only breaches of warranties but also any failure of the seller to perform according to his obligations under the contract. In the case of such non-conformity, the buyer is permitted to recover for his loss "in any manner which is reasonable".

3. Subsection (2) describes the usual, standard and reasonable method of ascertaining damages in the case of breach of warranty but it is not intended as an exclusive measure. It departs from the measure of damages for non-delivery in utilizing the place of acceptance rather than the place of tender. In some cases the two may coincide, as where the buyer signifies his acceptance upon the tender. If, however, the non-conformity is such as would justify revocation of acceptance, the time and place of acceptance under this section is determined as of the buyer's decision not to revoke.

4. The incidental and consequential damages referred to in subsection (3), which will usually accompany an action brought under this section, are discussed in detail in the comment on the next section.

Cross References:

Point 1: Compare Section 2-711; Sections 2-607 and 2-717.

Point 2: Section 2-106.

Point 3: Sections 2-608 and 2-713.

Point 4: Section 2-715.

Definitional Cross References:

"Buyer". Section 2-103.

"Conform". Section 2-106.

"Goods". Section 2-105.

"Notification". Section 1-202.

"Seller". Section 2-103.

Section 2-715. Buyer's Incidental and Consequential Damages

(1) Incidental damages resulting from the seller's breach include expenses reasonably incurred in inspection, receipt, transportation and care and custody of

goods rightfully rejected, any commercially reasonable charges, expenses or commissions in connection with effecting cover and any other reasonable expense incident to the delay or other breach.

(2) Consequential damages resulting from the seller's breach include

(a) any loss resulting from general or particular requirements and needs of which the seller at the time of contracting had reason to know and which could not reasonably be prevented by cover or otherwise; and

(b) injury to person or property proximately resulting from any breach of warranty.

Official Comment

Prior Uniform Statutory Provisions: Subsection (2)(b)—Sections 69(7) and 70, Uniform Sales Act.

Changes: Rewritten.

Purposes of Changes and New Matter:

1. Subsection (1) is intended to provide reimbursement for the buyer who incurs reasonable expenses in connection with the handling of rightfully rejected goods or goods whose acceptance may be justifiably revoked, or in connection with effecting cover where the breach of the contract lies in non-conformity or non-delivery of the goods. The incidental damages listed are not intended to be exhaustive but are merely illustrative of the typical kinds of incidental damage.

2. Subsection (2) operates to allow the buyer, in an appropriate case, any consequential damages which are the result of the seller's breach. The "tacit agreement" test for the recovery of consequential damages is rejected. Although the older rule at common law which made the seller liable for all consequential damages of which he had "reason to know" in advance is followed, the liberality of that rule is modified by refusing to permit recovery unless the buyer could not reasonably have prevented the loss by cover or otherwise. Subparagraph (2) carries forward the provisions of the prior uniform statutory provision as to consequential damages resulting from breach of warranty, but modifies the rule by requiring first that the buyer attempt to minimize his damages in good faith, either by cover or otherwise.

3. In the absence of excuse under the section on merchant's excuse by failure of presupposed conditions, the seller is liable for consequential damages in all cases where he had reason to know of the buyer's general or particular requirements at the time of contracting. It is not necessary that there be a conscious acceptance of an insurer's liability on the seller's part, nor is his obligation for consequential damages limited to cases in which he fails to use due effort in good faith.

Particular needs of the buyer must generally be made known to the seller while general needs must rarely be made known to charge the seller with knowledge.

Any seller who does not wish to take the risk of consequential damages has available the section on contractual limitation of remedy.

4. The burden of proving the extent of loss incurred by way of consequential damage is on the buyer, but the section on liberal administration of remedies rejects any doctrine of certainty which requires almost mathematical precision in the proof of loss. Loss may be determined in any manner which is reasonable under the circumstances.

5. Subsection (2)(b) states the usual rule as to breach of warranty, allowing recovery for injuries "proximately" resulting from the breach. Where the injury involved follows the use of goods without discovery of the defect causing the damage, the question of "proximate" cause turns on whether it was reasonable for the buyer to use the goods without such inspection as would have revealed the defects. If it was not reasonable for him to do so, or if he did in fact discover the defect prior to his use, the injury would not proximately result from the breach of warranty.

6. In the case of sale of wares to one in the business of reselling them, resale is one of the requirements of which the seller has reason to know within the meaning of subsection (2)(a).

Cross References:

Point 1:	Section 2-608.
Point 3:	Sections 1-304, 2-615 and 2-719.
Point 4:	Section 1-305.

Definitional Cross References:

"Cover".	Section 2-712.
"Goods".	Section 1-205.
"Person".	Section 1-201.
"Receipt" of goods.	Section 2-103.
"Seller".	Section 2-103.

Section 2-716. Buyer's Right to Specific Performance or Replevin

(1) Specific performance may be decreed where the goods are unique or in other proper circumstances.

(2) The decree for specific performance may include such terms and conditions as to payment of the price, damages, or other relief as the court may deem just.

(3) The buyer has a right of replevin for goods identified to the contract if after reasonable effort he is unable to effect cover for such goods or the circumstances reasonably indicate that such effort will be unavailing or if the goods have been shipped under reservation and satisfaction of the security interest in them has been made or tendered. In the case of goods bought for personal, family, or household purposes, the buyer's right of replevin vests upon acquisition of a special property, even if the seller had not then repudiated or failed to deliver.

Official Comment

Prior Uniform Statutory Provision: Section 68, Uniform Sales Act.

Changes: Rephrased.

Purposes of Changes: To make it clear that:

1. The present section continues in general prior policy as to specific performance and injunction against breach. However, without intending to impair in any way the exercise of the court's sound discretion in the matter, this Article seeks to further a more liberal attitude than some courts have shown in connection with the specific performance of contracts of sale.

2. In view of this Article's emphasis on the commercial feasibility of replacement, a new concept of what are "unique" goods is introduced under this section. Specific performance is no longer limited to goods which are already specific or ascertained at the time of contracting. The test of uniqueness under this section must be made in terms of the total situation which characterizes the contract. Output and requirements contracts involving a particular or peculiarly available source or market present today the typical commercial specific performance situation, as contrasted with contracts for the sale of heirlooms or priceless works of art which were usually involved in the older cases. However, uniqueness is not the sole basis of the remedy under this section for the relief may also be granted "in other proper circumstances" and inability to cover is strong evidence of "other proper circumstances".

3. The legal remedy of replevin is given the buyer in cases in which cover is reasonably unavailable and goods have been identified to the contract. This is in addition to the buyer's right to recover identified goods under Section 2-502. For consumer goods, the buyer's right to replevin vests upon the buyer's acquisition of a special property, which occurs upon identification of the goods to the contract. See Section 2-501. Inasmuch as a secured party normally acquires no greater rights in its collateral than its debtor had or had power to convey, see Section 2-403(1) (first sentence), a buyer who acquires a right of replevin under subsection (3) will take free of a security interest created by the seller if it attaches to the goods after the goods have been identified to the contract. The buyer will take free, even if the buyer does not buy in ordinary course and even if the security interest is perfected. Of course, to the extent that the buyer pays the price after the security interest attaches, the payments will constitute proceeds of the security interest.

4. This section is intended to give the buyer rights to the goods comparable to the seller's rights to the price.

5. If a negotiable document of title is outstanding, the buyer's right of replevin relates of course to the document not directly to the goods. See Article 7, especially Section 7-602.

Cross References:

Point 3: Section 2-502.
Point 4: Section 2-709.
Point 5: Article 7.

Definitional Cross References:

"Buyer". Section 2-103.
"Goods". Section 1-205.
"Right". Section 1-201.

Section 2-717. Deduction of Damages from the Price

The buyer on notifying the seller of his intention to do so may deduct all or any part of the damages resulting from any breach of the contract from any part of the price still due under the same contract.

Official Comment

Prior Uniform Statutory Provision: See Section 69(1)(a), Uniform Sales Act.

Purposes:

1. This section permits the buyer to deduct from the price damages resulting from any breach by the seller and does not limit the relief to cases of breach of warranty as did the prior uniform statutory provision. To bring this provision into application the breach involved must be of the same contract under which the price in question is claimed to have been earned.

2. The buyer, however, must give notice of his intention to withhold all or part of the price if he wishes to avoid a default within the meaning of the section on insecurity and right to assurances. In conformity with the general policies of this Article, no formality of notice is required and any language which reasonably indicates the buyer's reason for holding up his payment is sufficient.

Cross Reference: Point 2: Section 2-609.

Definitional Cross References:

"Buyer". Section 2-103.
"Notifies". Section 1-202.

Section 2-718. Liquidation or Limitation of Damages; Deposits

(1) Damages for breach by either party may be liquidated in the agreement but only at an amount which is reasonable in the light of the anticipated or actual harm caused by the breach, the difficulties of proof of loss, and the inconvenience or nonfeasibility of otherwise obtaining an adequate remedy. A term fixing unreasonably large liquidated damages is void as a penalty.

(2) Where the seller justifiably withholds delivery of goods because of the buyer's breach, the buyer is entitled to restitution of any amount by which the sum of his payments exceeds

(a) the amount to which the seller is entitled by virtue of terms liquidating the seller's damages in accordance with subsection (1), or

(b) in the absence of such terms, twenty per cent of the value of the total performance for which the buyer is obligated under the contract or $500, whichever is smaller.

(3) The buyer's right to restitution under subsection (2) is subject to offset to the extent that the seller establishes

(a) a right to recover damages under the provisions of this Article other than subsection (1), and

(b) the amount or value of any benefits received by the buyer directly or indirectly by reason of the contract.

(4) Where a seller has received payment in goods their reasonable value or the proceeds of their resale shall be treated as payments for the purposes of subsection (2); but if the seller has notice of the buyer's breach before reselling goods received in part performance, his resale is subject to the conditions laid down in this Article on resale by an aggrieved seller (Section 2-706).

Official Comment

Prior Uniform Statutory Provision: None.

Purposes:

1. Under subsection (1) liquidated damage clauses are allowed where the amount involved is reasonable in the light of the circumstances of the case. The subsection sets forth explicitly the elements to be considered in determining the reasonableness of a liquidated damage clause. A term fixing unreasonably large liquidated damages is expressly made void as a penalty. An unreasonably small amount would be subject to similar criticism and might be stricken under the section on unconscionable contracts or clauses.

2. Subsection (2) refuses to recognize a forfeiture unless the amount of the payment so forfeited represents a reasonable liquidation of damages as determined under subsection (1). A special exception is made in the case of small amounts (20% of the price or $500, whichever is smaller) deposited as security. No distinction is made between cases in which the payment is to be applied on the price and those in which it is intended as security for performance. Subsection (2) is applicable to any deposit or down or part payment. In the case of a deposit or turn in of goods resold before the breach, the amount actually received on the resale is to be viewed as the deposit rather than the amount allowed the buyer for the trade in. However, if the seller knows of the breach prior to the resale of the goods turned in, he must make reasonable efforts to realize their true value, and this is assured by requiring him to comply with the conditions laid down in the section on resale by an aggrieved seller.

Cross References:

Point 1: Section 2-302.

Point 2: Section 2-706.

Definitional Cross References:

"Aggrieved party".	Section 1-201.
"Agreement".	Section 1-201.
"Buyer".	Section 2-103.
"Goods".	Section 2-105.
"Notice".	Section 1-202.
"Party".	Section 1-201.
"Remedy".	Section 1-201.
"Seller".	Section 2-103.
"Term".	Section 1-201.

Section 2-719. Contractual Modification or Limitation of Remedy

(1) Subject to the provisions of subsections (2) and (3) of this section and of the preceding section on liquidation and limitation of damages,

(a) the agreement may provide for remedies in addition to or in substitution for those provided in this Article and may limit or alter the measure of damages recoverable under this Article, as by limiting the buyer's remedies to return of the goods and repayment of the price or to repair and replacement of non-conforming goods or parts; and

(b) resort to a remedy as provided is optional unless the remedy is expressly agreed to be exclusive, in which case it is the sole remedy.

(2) Where circumstances cause an exclusive or limited remedy to fail of its essential purpose, remedy may be had as provided in this Act.

(3) Consequential damages may be limited or excluded unless the limitation or exclusion is unconscionable. Limitation of consequential damages for injury to the person in the case of consumer goods is prima facie unconscionable but limitation of damages where the loss is commercial is not.

Official Comment

Prior Uniform Statutory Provision: None.

Purposes:

1. Under this section parties are left free to shape their remedies to their particular requirements and reasonable agreements limiting or modifying remedies are to be given effect.

However, it is of the very essence of a sales contract that at least minimum adequate remedies be available. If the parties intend to conclude a contract for sale within this Article they must accept the legal consequence that there be at least a fair quantum of remedy for breach of the obligations or duties outlined in the contract. Thus any clause purporting to modify or limit the remedial provisions of this Article in an unconscionable manner is subject to deletion and in that event the remedies made available by this Article are applicable as if the stricken clause had never existed. Similarly, under subsection (2), where an apparently fair and reasonable clause because of circumstances fails in its purpose or operates to deprive either party of the substantial value of the bargain, it must give way to the general remedy provisions of this Article.

2. Subsection (1)(b) creates a presumption that clauses prescribing remedies are cumulative rather than exclusive. If the parties intend the term to describe the sole remedy under the contract, this must be clearly expressed.

3. Subsection (3) recognizes the validity of clauses limiting or excluding consequential damages but makes it clear that they may not operate in an unconscionable manner. Actually such terms are merely an allocation of unknown or undeterminable risks. The seller in all cases is free to disclaim warranties in the manner provided in Section 2-316.

Cross References:

Point 1: Section 2-302.

Point 3: Section 2-316.

Definitional Cross References:

"Agreement".	Section 1-201.
"Buyer".	Section 2-103.
"Conforming".	Section 2-106.
"Contract".	Section 1-201.
"Goods".	Section 2-105.
"Remedy".	Section 1-201.
"Seller".	Section 2-103.

Section 2-720. Effect of "Cancellation" or "Rescission" on Claims for Antecedent Breach

Unless the contrary intention clearly appears, expressions of "cancellation" or "rescission" of the contract or the like shall not be construed as a renunciation or discharge of any claim in damages for an antecedent breach.

Official Comment

Prior Uniform Statutory Provision: None.

Purpose: This section is designed to safeguard a person holding a right of action from any unintentional loss of rights by the ill-advised use of such terms as "cancellation", "rescission", or the like. Once a party's rights have accrued they are not to be lightly impaired by concessions made in business decency and without intention to forego them. Therefore, unless the cancellation of a contract expressly declares that it is "without reservation of rights", or the like, it cannot be considered to be a renunciation under this section.

Cross Reference: Section 1-306.

Definitional Cross References:

"Cancellation".	Section 2-106.
"Contract".	Section 1-201.

Section 2-721. Remedies for Fraud

Remedies for material misrepresentation or fraud include all remedies available under this Article for non-fraudulent breach. Neither rescission or a claim for rescission of the contract for sale nor rejection or return of the goods shall bar or be deemed inconsistent with a claim for damages or other remedy.

Official Comment

Prior Uniform Statutory Provision: None.

Purposes: To correct the situation by which remedies for fraud have been more circumscribed than the more modern and mercantile remedies for breach of warranty. Thus the remedies for fraud are extended by this section to coincide in scope with those for non-fraudulent breach. This section thus makes it clear that neither rescission of the contract for fraud nor rejection of the goods bars other remedies unless the circumstances of the case make the remedies incompatible.

Definitional Cross References:

"Contract for sale".	Section 2-106.
"Goods".	Section 1-105.
"Remedy".	Section 1-201.

Section 2-722. Who Can Sue Third Parties for Injury to Goods

Where a third party so deals with goods which have been identified to a contract for sale as to cause actionable injury to a party to that contract

(a) a right of action against the third party is in either party to the contract for sale who has title to or a security interest or a special property or an insurable interest in the goods; and if the goods have been destroyed or converted a right of action is also in the party who either bore the risk of loss under the contract for sale or has since the injury assumed that risk as against the other;

(b) if at the time of the injury the party plaintiff did not bear the risk of loss as against the other party to the contract for sale and there is no arrangement between them for disposition of the recovery, his suit or settlement is, subject to his own interest, as a fiduciary for the other party to the contract;

(c) either party may with the consent of the other sue for the benefit of whom it may concern.

Official Comment

Prior Uniform Statutory Provision: None.

Purposes: To adopt and extend somewhat the principle of the statutes which provide for suit by the real party in interest. The provisions of this section apply only after identification of the goods. Prior to that time only the seller has a right of action. During the period between identification and final acceptance (except in the case of revocation of acceptance) it is possible for both parties to have the right of action. Even after final acceptance both parties may have the right of action if the seller retains possession or otherwise retains an interest.

Definitional Cross References:

"Action".	Section 1-201.
"Buyer".	Section 2-103.
"Contract for sale".	Section 2-106.
"Goods".	Section 2-105.
"Party".	Section 1-201.
"Right".	Section 1-201.
"Security interest".	Section 1-201.

Section 2-723. Proof of Market Price: Time and Place

(1) If an action based on anticipatory repudiation comes to trial before the time for performance with respect to some or all of the goods, any damages based on market price (Section 2-708 or Section 2-713) shall be determined according to the price of such goods prevailing at the time when the aggrieved party learned of the repudiation.

(2) If evidence of a price prevailing at the times or places described in this Article is not readily available the price prevailing within any reasonable time before or after the time described or at any other place which

in commercial judgment or under usage of trade would serve as a reasonable substitute for the one described may be used, making any proper allowance for the cost of transporting the goods to or from such other place.

(3) Evidence of a relevant price prevailing at a time or place other than the one described in this Article offered by one party is not admissible unless and until he has given the other party such notice as the court finds sufficient to prevent unfair surprise.

Official Comment

Prior Uniform Statutory Provision: None.

Purposes: To eliminate the most obvious difficulties arising in connection with the determination of market price, when that is stipulated as a measure of damages by some provision of this Article. Where the appropriate market price is not readily available the court is here granted reasonable leeway in receiving evidence of prices current in other comparable markets or at other times comparable to the one in question. In accordance with the general principle of this Article against surprise, however, a party intending to offer evidence of such a substitute price must give suitable notice to the other party.

This section is not intended to exclude the use of any other reasonable method of determining market price or of measuring damages if the circumstances of the case make this necessary.

Definitional Cross References:

"Action".	Section 1-201.
"Aggrieved party".	Section 1-201.
"Goods".	Section 2-105.
"Notifies".	Section 1-202.
"Party".	Section 1-201.
"Reasonable time".	Section 1-205.
"Usage of trade".	Section 1-303.

Section 2-724. Admissibility of Market Quotations

Whenever the prevailing price or value of any goods regularly bought and sold in any established commodity market is in issue, reports in official publications or trade journals or in newspapers or periodicals of general circulation published as the reports of such market shall be admissible in evidence. The circumstances of the preparation of such a report may be shown to affect its weight but not its admissibility.

Official Comment

Prior Uniform Statutory Provision: None.

Purposes: To make market quotations admissible in evidence while providing for a challenge of the material by showing the circumstances of its preparation.

No explicit provision as to the weight to be given to market quotations is contained in this section, but such quotations, in the absence of compelling challenge, offer an adequate basis for a verdict.

Market quotations are made admissible when the price or value of goods traded "in any established market" is in issue. The reason of the section does not require that the market be closely organized in the manner of a produce exchange. It is sufficient if transactions in the commodity are frequent and open enough to make a market established by usage in which one price can be expected to affect another and in which an informed report of the range and trend of prices can be assumed to be reasonably accurate.

This section does not in any way intend to limit or negate the application of similar rules of admissibility to other material, whether by action of the courts or by statute. The purpose of the present section is to assure a minimum of mercantile administration in this important situation and not to limit any liberalizing trend in modern law.

Definitional Cross Reference:

"Goods". Section 2-105.

Section 2-725. Statute of Limitations in Contracts for Sale

(1) An action for breach of any contract for sale must be commenced within four years after the cause of action has accrued. By the original agreement the parties may reduce the period of limitation to not less than one year but may not extend it.

(2) A cause of action accrues when the breach occurs, regardless of the aggrieved party's lack of knowledge of the breach. A breach of warranty occurs when tender of delivery is made, except that where a warranty explicitly extends to future performance of the goods and discovery of the breach must await the time of such performance the cause of action accrues when the breach is or should have been discovered.

(3) Where an action commenced within the time limited by subsection (1) is so terminated as to leave available a remedy by another action for the same breach such other action may be commenced after the expiration of the time limited and within six months after the termination of the first action unless the termination resulted from voluntary discontinuance or from dismissal for failure or neglect to prosecute.

(4) This section does not alter the law on tolling of the statute of limitations nor does it apply to causes of action which have accrued before this Act becomes effective.

Official Comment

Prior Uniform Statutory Provision: None.

Purposes: To introduce a uniform statute of limitations for sales contracts, thus eliminating the jurisdictional variations and providing needed relief for concerns doing business on a nationwide scale whose contracts have heretofore been governed by several different periods of limitation depending upon the state in which the transaction occurred. This Article takes sales contracts out of the general laws limiting the time for commencing contractual actions and selects a four year period as the most appropriate to modern business practice. This is within the normal commercial record keeping period.

Subsection (1) permits the parties to reduce the period of limitation. The minimum period is set at one year. The parties may not, however, extend the statutory period.

Subsection (2), providing that the cause of action accrues when the breach occurs, states an exception where the warranty extends to future performance.

Subsection (3) states the saving provision included in many state statutes and permits an additional short period for bringing new actions, where suits begun within the four year period have been terminated so as to leave a remedy still available for the same breach.

Subsection (4) makes it clear that this Article does not purport to alter or modify in any respect the law on tolling of the Statute of Limitations as it now prevails in the various jurisdictions.

Definitional Cross References:

"Action".	Section 1-201.
"Aggrieved party".	Section 1-201.
"Agreement".	Section 1-201.
"Contract for sale".	Section 2-106.
"Goods".	Section 2-105.
"Party".	Section 1-201.
"Remedy".	Section 1-201.
"Term".	Section 1-201.
"Termination".	Section 2-106.

Article 2A — Leases

As adopted in 1987 and revised in: (i) 1990; (ii) 1994, to correct errata; (iii) 1999, in connection with the revision of Article 9; (iv) 2001, in connection with the revision of Article 1; (v) 2002, in connection with amendments to Article 9; (vi) 2003, in connection with the revision of Article 7; (vii) 2010, in connection with amendments to Article 9; and (viii) 2022, in connection with the 2022 Amendments to the Uniform Commercial Code.

B. DEFAULT BY LESSOR

C. DEFAULT BY LESSEE

PART 1. GENERAL PROVISIONS

Section 2A-101. Short Title

This Article shall be known and may be cited as the Uniform Commercial Code—Leases.

Official Comment

Rationale for Codification: There are several reasons for codifying the law with respect to leases of goods. An analysis of the case law as it applies to leases of goods suggests at least three significant issues to be resolved by codification. First, what is a lease? It is necessary to define lease to determine whether a transaction creates a lease or a security interest disguised as a lease. If the transaction creates a security interest disguised as a lease, the lessor will be required to file a financing statement or take other action to perfect its interest in the goods against third parties. There is no such requirement with respect to leases. Yet the distinction between a lease and a security interest disguised as a lease is not clear. Second, will the lessor be deemed to have made warranties to the lessee? If the transaction is a sale the express and implied warranties of Article 2 of the Uniform Commercial Code apply. However, the warranty law with respect to leases is uncertain. Third, what remedies are available to the lessor upon the lessee's default? If the transaction is a security interest disguised as a lease, the answer is stated in Part 5 of the Article on Secured Transactions (Article 9). There is no clear answer with respect to leases.

There are reasons to codify the law with respect to leases of goods in addition to those suggested by a review of the reported cases. The answer to this important question should not be limited to the issues raised in these cases. Is it not also proper to determine the remedies available to the lessee upon the lessor's default? It is, but that issue is not reached through a review of the reported cases. This is only one of the many issues presented in structuring, negotiating and documenting a lease of goods.

Statutory Analogue: After it was decided to proceed with the codification project, the drafting committee of the National Conference of Commissioners on Uniform State Laws looked for a statutory analogue, gradually narrowing the focus to the Article on Sales (Article 2) and the Article on Secured Transactions (Article 9). A review of the literature with respect to the sale of goods reveals that Article 2 is predicated upon certain assumptions: Parties to the sales transaction frequently are without counsel; the agreement of the parties often is oral or evidenced by scant writings; obligations between the parties are bilateral; applicable law is influenced by the need to preserve freedom of contract. A review of the literature with respect to personal property security law reveals that Article 9 is predicated upon very different assumptions: Parties to a secured transaction regularly are represented by counsel; the agreement of the parties frequently is reduced to a writing, extensive in scope; the obligations between the parties are essentially unilateral; and applicable law seriously limits freedom of contract.

The lease is closer in spirit and form to the sale of goods than to the creation of a security interest. While parties to a lease are sometimes represented by counsel and their agreement is often reduced to a writing, the obligations of the parties are bilateral and the common law of leasing is dominated by the need to preserve freedom of contract. Thus the drafting committee concluded that Article 2 was the appropriate statutory analogue.

Issues: The drafting committee then identified and resolved several issues critical to codification:

Scope: The scope of the Article was limited to leases (Section 2A-102). There was no need to include security interests in the form of leases, as they are adequately treated in Article 9. Further, even if security interests in the form of leases were included, the need to preserve the distinction would remain, as policy suggests treatment significantly different from that accorded leases.

Definition of Lease: Lease was defined to exclude security interests in the form of leases (Section 2A-103(1)(j)). Given the litigation to date a revised definition of security interest was suggested for inclusion in the Act. See pre-2001 Section 1-201(37). Section 1-203 now sharpens the distinction between leases and security interests disguised as leases.

Filing: Except to the extent necessary to ensure priority in fixtures (Section 2A-309), the lessor was not required to file a financing statement against the lessee or take any other action to protect the lessor's interest in the goods (Section 2A-301). The refined definition of security interest will more clearly signal the need to file to potential lessors of goods. Those lessors who are concerned will file a protective financing statement (Section 9-505).

Warranties: All of the express and implied warranties of the Article on Sales (Article 2) were included (Sections 2A-210 through 2A-216), revised to reflect differences in lease transactions. The lease of goods is sufficiently similar to the sale of goods to justify this decision. Further, many courts have reached the same decision.

Certificate of Title Laws: Many leasing transactions involve goods subject to certificate of title statutes. To avoid conflict with those statutes, this Article is subject to them (Section 2A-104(1)(a)).

Consumer Leases: Many leasing transactions involve parties subject to consumer protection statutes or decisions. To avoid conflict with those laws this Article is subject to them to the extent provided in Section 2A-104(1)(c) and (2). Further, certain consumer protections have been incorporated in the Article.

Finance Leases: Certain leasing transactions substitute the supplier of the goods for the lessor as the party responsible to the lessee with respect to warranties and the like. The definition of finance lease (Section 2A-103(1)(g)) was developed to describe these transactions. Various sections of the Article implement the substitution of the supplier for the lessor, including Sections 2A-209 and 2A-407. No attempt was made to fashion a special rule where the finance lessor is an affiliate of the supplier of goods; this is to be developed by the courts, case by case.

Sale and Leaseback: Sale and leaseback transactions are becoming increasingly common. A number of state statutes treat transactions where possession is retained by the seller as fraudulent *per se* or *prima facie* fraudulent. That position is not in accord with modern practice and thus is changed by the Article "if the buyer bought for value and in good faith" (Section 2A-308(3)).

Remedies: The Article has not only provided for lessor's remedies upon default by the lessee (Sections 2A-523 through 2A-532), but also for lessee's remedies upon default by the lessor (Sections 2A-508 through 2A-522). This is a significant departure from Article 9, which provides remedies only for the secured party upon default by the debtor. This difference is compelled by the bilateral nature of the obligations between the parties to a lease.

Damages: Many leasing transactions are predicated on the parties' ability to stipulate an appropriate measure of damages in the event of default. The rule with respect to sales of goods (Section 2-718) is not sufficiently flexible to accommodate this practice. Consistent with the common law emphasis upon freedom to contract, the Article has created a revised rule that allows greater flexibility with respect to leases of goods (Section 2A-504(1)).

History: This Article is a revision of the Uniform Personal Property Leasing Act, which was approved by the National Conference of Commissioners on Uniform State Laws in August, 1985. However, it was believed that the subject matter of the Uniform Personal Property Leasing Act would be better treated as an article of this Act. Thus, although the Conference promulgated the Uniform Personal Property Leasing Act as a Uniform Law, activity was held in abeyance to allow time to restate the Uniform Personal Property Leasing Act as Article 2A.

In August, 1986 the Conference approved and recommended this Article (including conforming amendments to Article 1 and Article 9) for promulgation as an amendment to this Act. In December, 1986 the Council of the American Law Institute approved and recommended this Article (including conforming amendments to Article 1 and Article 9), with official comments, for promulgation as an amendment to this Act. In March, 1987 the Permanent Editorial Board for the Uniform Commercial Code approved and recommended this Article (including conforming amendments to Article 1 and Article 9), with official comments, for promulgation as an amendment to this Act. In May, 1987 the American Law Institute approved and recommended this Article (including conforming amendments to Article 1 and Article 9), with official comments, for promulgation as an amendment to this Act. In August, 1987 the Conference confirmed its approval of the final text of this Article.

Upon its initial promulgation, Article 2A was rapidly enacted in several states, was introduced in a number of other states, and underwent bar association, law revision commission and legislative study in still further states. In that process debate emerged, principally sparked by the study of Article 2A by the California Bar Association, California's non-uniform amendments to Article 2A, and articles appearing in a symposium on Article 2A published after its promulgation in the Alabama Law Review. The debate chiefly centered on whether Article 2A had struck the proper balance or was clear enough concerning the ability of a lessor to grant a security interest in its leasehold interest and in the residual, priority between a secured party and the lessee, and the lessor's remedy structure under Article 2A.

This debate over issues on which reasonable minds could and did differ began to affect the enactment effort for Article 2A in a deleterious manner. Consequently, the Standby Committee for Article 2A, composed predominantly of the former members of the drafting committee, reviewed the legislative actions and studies in the various states, and opened a dialogue with the principal proponents of the non-uniform amendments. Negotiations were conducted in conjunction with, and were facilitated by, a study of the uniform Article and the non-uniform Amendments by the New York Law Revision Commission. Ultimately, a consensus was reached, which has been approved by the membership of the Conference, the Permanent Editorial Board, and the Council of the Institute. Rapid and uniform enactment of Article 2A is expected as a result of the completed amendments. The Article 2A experience reaffirms the essential viability of the procedures of the Conference and the Institute for creating and updating uniform state law in the commercial law area.

Relationship of Article 2A to Other Articles: The Article on Sales provided a useful point of reference for codifying the law of leases. Many of the provisions of that Article were carried over, changed to reflect differences in style, leasing terminology or leasing practices. Thus, the official comments to those sections of Article 2 whose provisions were carried over are incorporated by reference in Article 2A, as well; further, any case law interpreting those provisions should be viewed as persuasive but not binding on a court when deciding a similar issue with respect to leases. Any change in the sequence that has been made when carrying over a provision from Article 2 should be viewed as a matter of style, not substance. This is not to suggest that in other instances Article 2A did not also incorporate substantially revised provisions of Article 2, Article 9 or otherwise where the revision was driven by a concern over the substance; but for the lack of a mandate, the drafting committee might well have made the same or a similar change in the statutory analogue. Those sections in Article 2A include Sections 2A-104, 2A-105, 2A-106, 2A-108(2) and (4), 2A-109(2), 2A-208, 2A-214(2) and (3)(a), 2A-216, 2A-303, 2A-306, 2A-503, 2A-504(3)(b), 2A-506(2), and 2A-515. For lack of relevance or significance not all of the provisions of Article 2 were incorporated in Article 2A.

This codification was greatly influenced by the fundamental tenet of the common law as it has developed with respect to leases of goods: freedom of the parties to contract. Note that, like all other Articles of this Act, the principles of construction and interpretation contained in Article 1 are applicable throughout Article 2A (Section 2A-103(4)). These principles include the ability of the parties to vary the effect of the provisions of Article 2A, subject to certain limitations including those that relate to the obligations of good faith, diligence, reasonableness and care (Section 1-302(b)). Consistent with those principles no negative inference is to be drawn by the episodic use of the phrase "unless otherwise agreed" in certain provisions of Article 2A. Section 1-302(c). Indeed, the contrary is true, as the general rule in the Act, including this Article, is that the effect of the Act's provisions may be varied by agreement. Section 1-302(a). This conclusion follows even where the statutory analogue contains the phrase and the correlative provision in Article 2A does not.

Section 2A-102. Scope

(1) This Article applies to any transaction, regardless of form, that creates a lease and, in the case of a hybrid lease, it applies to the extent provided in subsection (2).

(2) In a hybrid lease:

(a) if the lease-of-goods aspects do not predominate:

(i) only the provisions of this Article which relate primarily to the lease-of-godds aspects of the transaction apply, and the provisions that relate primarily to the transaction as a whole do not apply;

(ii) Section 2A-209 applies if the lease is a finance lease; and

(iii) Section 2A-407 applies to the promises of the lessee in a finance lease to the extent the promises are consideration for the right to possession and use of the leased goods; and

(b) if the lease-of-goods aspects predominate, this Article applies to the transaction, but does not preclude application in appropriate circumstances of other law to aspects of the lease which do not relate to the lease of goods.

Official Comment

Uniform Statutory Source: Section 9-102(1). Throughout this Article, unless otherwise stated, references to "Section" are to other sections of this Act.

Changes: Substantially revised.

Purposes:

1. This Article governs transactions as diverse as the lease of a hand tool to an individual for a few hours and the leveraged lease of a complex line of industrial equipment to a multinational organization for a number of years.

To achieve that end it was necessary to provide that this Article applies to any transaction, regardless of form, that creates a lease. Since lease is defined as a transfer of the right to possession and use of goods (Section 2A-103(1)(j)) and goods is defined to include fixtures (Section 2A-103(1)(h)), application is limited to the extent the transaction relates to goods, including fixtures. Further, since the definition of lease does not include a sale (Section 2-106(1)) or retention or creation of a security interest (Section 1-201(b)(35)), application is further limited; sales and security interests are governed by other Articles of this Act.

2. In recognition of the diversity of the transactions to be governed, the sophistication of many of the parties to these transactions, and the common-law tradition as it applies to the bailment for hire or lease, freedom of contract has been preserved. Ronald DeKoven, Proceedings After Default by the Lessee

Under a True Lease of Equipment, in 1C Peter F. Coogan, William E. Hogan & Detlev F. Vagts, *Secured Transactions Under the Uniform Commercial Code*, § 29B.02[2] (1986). Thus, despite the extensive regulatory scheme established by this Article, the parties to a lease will be able to create private rules to govern their transaction. Sections 2A-103(4) and 1-302(a). However, there are special rules in this Article governing consumer leases, as well as other state and federal statutes, that may further limit freedom of contract with respect to consumer leases.

3. A court may apply this Article by analogy to any transaction, regardless of form, that creates a lease of personal property other than goods, taking into account the expressed intentions of the parties to the transaction and any differences between a lease of goods and a lease of other property. Such application has precedent as the provisions of the Article on Sales (Article 2) have been applied by analogy to leases of goods. E.g., William D. Hawkland, *The Impact of the Uniform Commercial Code on Equipment Leasing*, 1972 Ill.L.F. 446; Daniel E. Murray, *Under the Spreading Analogy of Article 2 of the Uniform Commercial Code*, 39 Fordham L.Rev. 447 (1971). Whether such application would be appropriate for other bailments of personal property, gratuitous or for hire, should be determined by the facts of each case. See *Mieske v. Bartell Drug Co.*, 593 P.2d 1308, 1312 (Wash. 1979).

Further, parties to a transaction creating a lease of personal property other than goods, or a bailment of personal property may provide by agreement that this Article applies. Upholding the parties' choice is consistent with the spirit of this Article.

4. If the lease-of-goods aspects of a hybrid lease do not predominate, under subsection (2)(a)(i) the provisions of this Article which relate primarily to the lease-of-goods aspects of the transaction apply and those that relate primarily to the transaction as a whole do not apply. Under subsection (2)(b), if the lease-of-goods aspects of a hybrid lease predominate, this Article applies to the transaction.

5. Relevant factors in determining whether the lease-of-goods aspects of a hybrid lease predominate include the language of the agreement and the portion of the total price that is attributable to the lease of goods, although neither is determinative. An agreed-upon allocation of a portion of the total price to the right to possession and use of the goods is ordinarily binding on the parties, as is an agreement that the transaction includes or does not include a finance lease.

6. A finance lease, defined in Section 2A-103(1)(g), may be included in a hybrid lease in which the lease-of-goods aspects of the transaction do not predominate. In such a situation, subsection (2)(a)(ii) makes Section 2A-209 applicable and subsection (2)(a)(iii) addresses the application of Section 2A-407 to the promises made by the lessee under the finance lease. That latter section applies to those promises that are consideration for the lessee's right to possession and use of the leased goods. Whether a promise of a lessee so qualifies is a question of fact but an agreed-upon allocation of a portion of the total price to the right to possession and use of the leased goods is ordinarily binding on the parties. The fact that subsection (2)(a)(ii) and (iii) expressly make Sections 2A-209 and 2A-407 applicable if the lease is a finance lease does not prevent application of other provisions of this Article relating to finance leases pursuant to subsection (2)(b).

Example 1. Lessor and Customer enter into a contract that provides for Lessor to: (i) lease equipment to Customer; and (ii) provide to Customer a variety of maintenance and consulting services. The services aspects of the transaction predominate. Lessor did not select, manufacture, or supply the goods; instead, the goods were selected by Customer, and Lessor acquired the goods from Supplier for the sole purpose of leasing the goods to Customer. Assume that the lease aspects of the transaction involve a finance lease under Section 2A-103(1)(g). Pursuant to subsection (3)(a), Sections 2A-212 and 2A-213 apply. Under those sections, because the lease aspect of the transaction is a finance lease, Lessor makes no implied warranty of merchantability or implied warranty of fitness for particular purpose. Pursuant to subsection (2)(a)(ii), Section 2A-209 applies. Under that section, all warranties made by Supplier to Lessor extend to Customer.

Example 2. Same facts as Example 1. As consideration for Lessor's obligations under the contract, Customer promises to pay a single monthly fee of a specified amount. The contract does not indicate what portion of the monthly fee is consideration for the services or what portion is consideration for possession and use of the equipment. Section 2A-407 applies to the lessee's promises that are consideration for the lessee's right to possession and use of the equipment. In an action involving the application of Section 2A-407, the determination of what portion of the monthly fee is for the right to possession and use of the equipment is a question of fact.

Example 3. Same facts as Example 1 except that the lease-of-goods aspects of the transaction predominate. Section 2A-407 applies to all of the lessee's promises under the transaction.

7. Even if the lease-of-goods aspects of a hybrid lease predominate and this Article applies to the transaction, the application of this Article to a hybrid lease does not preclude the application of principles of law and equity to supplement the provisions of this Article, see Section 1-103(b), nor does it preclude, in appropriate circumstances, the application of other law to the non-lease-of-goods aspects of the transaction. Whether it is appropriate to apply such other law will depend in part on what purposes the other law is designed to achieve and whether application of the other law would be likely to interfere with the application of this Article.

Example 4. Same facts as Example 3 (the lease-of-goods aspects of the transaction predominate) except that the lease is not a finance lease. This Article applies to the transaction. Nevertheless, because principles of law and equity also apply unless displaced by particular provisions the Uniform Commercial Code, see Section 1-103(b), and this Article does not displace other law relating to whether Lessor's performance of services conforms to the contract, other law determines whether the services conform to the contract.

8. The rules of subsections (2)(a) and (2)(b) are essentially gap fillers that apply when the parties' agreement is silent on what legal rules govern the different aspects of their transaction. In general, parties are free to preclude the application of this Article to the aspects of their transaction that are not about the lease of goods. See Section 2-102, Comment 6.

Cross References:

Sections 1-103(b), 1-302(a), 1-201(b)(35), 2-106(1), 2A-103(1)(g), (h), and (j), 2A-103(4), 2A-209, 2A-212, 2A-213, and 2A-407

Definitional Cross Reference:

"Finance lease". Section 2A-103(1)(g).
"Lease". Section 2A-103(1)(j).

Section 2A-103. Definitions and Index of Definitions

(1) In this Article unless the context otherwise requires:

(a) "Buyer in ordinary course of business" means a person who in good faith and without knowledge that the sale to him [or her] is in violation of the ownership rights or security interest or leasehold interest of a third party in the goods, buys in ordinary course from a person in the business of selling goods of that kind but does not include a pawnbroker. "Buying" may be for cash or by exchange of other property or on secured or unsecured credit and includes acquiring goods or documents of title under a pre-existing contract for sale but does not include a transfer in bulk or as security for or in total or partial satisfaction of a money debt.

(b) "Cancellation" occurs when either party puts an end to the lease contract for default by the other party.

(c) "Commercial unit" means such a unit of goods as by commercial usage is a single whole for purposes of lease and division of which materially impairs its character or value on the market or in use. A commercial unit may be a single article, as a machine, or a set of articles, as a suite of furniture or a line of machinery, or a quantity, as a gross or carload, or any other unit treated in use or in the relevant market as a single whole.

(d) "Conforming" goods or performance under a lease contract means goods or performance that are in accordance with the obligations under the lease contract.

(e) "Consumer lease" means a lease that a lessor regularly engaged in the business of leasing or selling makes to a lessee who is an individual and who takes under the lease primarily for a personal, family, or household purpose[, if the total payments to be made under the lease contract, excluding payments for options to renew or buy, do not exceed $________].

(f) "Fault" means wrongful act, omission, breach, or default.

(g) "Finance lease" means a lease with respect to which:

(i) the lessor does not select, manufacture, or supply the goods;

(ii) the lessor acquires the goods or the right to possession and use of the goods in connection with the lease; and

(iii) one of the following occurs:

(A) the lessee receives a copy of the contract by which the lessor acquired the goods or the right to possession and use of the goods before signing the lease contract;

(B) the lessee's approval of the contract by which the lessor acquired the goods or the right to possession and use of the goods is a condition to effectiveness of the lease contract;

(C) the lessee, before signing the lease contract, receives an accurate and complete statement designating the promises and warranties, and any disclaimers of warranties, limitations or modifications of remedies, or liquidated damages, including those of a third party, such as the manufacturer of the goods, provided to the lessor by the person supplying the goods in connection with or as part of the contract by which the lessor acquired the goods or the right to possession and use of the goods; or

(D) if the lease is not a consumer lease, the lessor, before the lessee signs the lease contract, informs the lessee in writing (a) of the identity of the person supplying the goods to the lessor, unless the lessee has selected that person and directed the lessor to acquire the goods or the right to possession and use of the goods from that person, (b) that the lessee is entitled under this Article to the promises and warranties, including those of any third party, provided to the lessor by the person supplying the goods in connection with or as part of the contract by which the lessor acquired the goods or the right to possession and use of the goods, and (c) that the lessee may communicate with the person supplying the goods to the lessor and receive an accurate and complete statement of those promises and warranties, including any disclaimers and limitations of them or of remedies.

(h) "Goods" means all things that are movable at the time of identification to the lease contract, or are fixtures (Section 2A-309), but the term does not include money, documents, instruments, accounts, chattel paper, general intangibles, or minerals or the like, including oil and gas, before extraction. The term also includes the unborn young of animals.

(h.1) "Hybrid lease" means a single transaction involving the lease of goods and:

(i) the provision of services;

(ii) a sale of other goods; or

(iii) a sale, lease, or license of property other than goods.

(i) "Installment lease contract" means a lease contract that authorizes or requires the delivery of goods in separate lots to be separately accepted, even though the lease contract contains a clause "each delivery is a separate lease" or its equivalent.

(j) "Lease" means a transfer of the right to possession and use of goods for a term in return for consideration, but a sale, including a sale on approval or a sale or return, or retention or creation of a security interest is not a lease. Unless the context clearly indicates otherwise, the term includes a sublease.

(k) "Lease agreement" means the bargain, with respect to the lease, of the lessor and the lessee in fact as found in their language or by implication from other circumstances including course of dealing or usage of trade or course of performance as provided in this Article. Unless the context clearly indicates otherwise, the term includes a sublease agreement.

(l) "Lease contract" means the total legal obligation that results from the lease agreement as affected by this Article and any other applicable rules of law. Unless the context clearly indicates otherwise, the term includes a sublease contract.

(m) "Leasehold interest" means the interest of the lessor or the lessee under a lease contract.

(n) "Lessee" means a person who acquires the right to possession and use of goods under a lease. Unless the context clearly indicates otherwise, the term includes a sublessee.

(o) "Lessee in ordinary course of business" means a person who in good faith and without knowledge that the lease to him [or her] is in violation of the ownership rights or security interest or leasehold interest of a third party in the goods, leases in ordinary course from a person in the business of selling or leasing goods of that kind but does not include a pawnbroker. "Leasing" may be for cash or by exchange of other property or on secured or unsecured credit and includes acquiring goods or documents of title under a pre-existing lease contract but does not include a transfer in bulk or as security for or in total or partial satisfaction of a money debt.

(p) "Lessor" means a person who transfers the right to possession and use of goods under a lease. Unless the context clearly indicates otherwise, the term includes a sublessor.

(q) "Lessor's residual interest" means the lessor's interest in the goods after expiration, termination, or cancellation of the lease contract.

(r) "Lien" means a charge against or interest in goods to secure payment of a debt or performance of an obligation, but the term does not include a security interest.

(s) "Lot" means a parcel or a single article that is the subject matter of a separate lease or delivery, whether or not it is sufficient to perform the lease contract.

(t) "Merchant lessee" means a lessee that is a merchant with respect to goods of the kind subject to the lease.

(u) [Deleted].

(v) "Purchase" includes taking by sale, lease, mortgage, security interest, pledge, gift, or any other voluntary transaction creating an interest in goods.

(w) "Sublease" means a lease of goods the right to possession and use of which was acquired by the lessor as a lessee under an existing lease.

(x) "Supplier" means a person from whom a lessor buys or leases goods to be leased under a finance lease.

(y) "Supply contract" means a contract under which a lessor buys or leases goods to be leased.

(z) "Termination" occurs when either party pursuant to a power created by agreement or law puts an end to the lease contract otherwise than for default.

(2) Other definitions applying to this Article and the sections in which they appear are:

"Accessions".	Section 2A-310(1).
"Construction mortgage".	Section 2A-309(1)(d).
"Encumbrance".	Section 2A-309(1)(e).
"Fixtures".	Section 2A-309(1)(a).
"Fixture filing".	Section 2A-309(1)(b).
"Purchase money lease".	Section 2A-309(1)(c).

(3) The following definitions in other Articles apply to this Article:

"Account".	Section 9-102(a)(2).
"Between merchants".	Section 2-104(3).
"Buyer".	Section 2-103(1)(a).
"Chattel paper".	Section 9-102(a)(11).
"Consumer goods".	Section 9-102(a)(23).
"Document".	Section 9-102(a)(30).
"Entrusting".	Section 2-403(3).
"General intangible".	Section 9-102(a)(42).
"Instrument".	Section 9-102(a)(47).
"Merchant".	Section 2-104(1).
"Mortgage".	Section 9-102(a)(55).
"Pursuant to commitment".	Section 9-102(a)(69).
"Receipt".	Section 2-103(1)(c).
"Sale".	Section 2-106(1).
"Sale on approval".	Section 2-326.
"Sale or return".	Section 2-326.
"Seller".	Section 2-103(1)(d).

(4) In addition Article 1 contains general definitions and principles of construction and interpretation applicable throughout this Article.

Official Comment

(a) "Buyer in ordinary course of business". Section 1-201(b)(9).

(b) "Cancellation". Section 2-106(4). The effect of a cancellation is provided in Section 2A-505(1).

(c) "Commercial unit". Section 2-105(6).

(d) "Conforming". Section 2-106(2).

(e) "Consumer lease". New. This Article includes a subset of rules that applies only to consumer leases. Sections 2A-106, 2A-108(2), 2A-108(4), 2A-109(2), 2A-221(b), 2A-309(5)(a), 2A-406(1)(b), 2A-407, 2A-504(3)(b), and 2A-516(3)(b).

For a transaction to qualify as a consumer lease it must first qualify as a lease. Section 2A-103(1)(j). Note that this Article regulates the transactional elements of a lease, including a consumer lease; consumer protection statutes, present and future, and existing consumer protection decisions are unaffected by this Article. Section 2A-104(1)(c) and (2). Of course, Article 2A as state law also is subject to federal consumer protection law.

This definition is modeled after the definition of consumer lease in the Consumer Leasing Act, 15 U.S.C. § 1667 (1982), and in the Unif. Consumer Credit Code § 1.301(14). However, this definition of consumer lease differs from its models in several respects: the lessor can be a person regularly engaged either in the business of leasing or of selling goods, the lease need not be for a term exceeding four months, a lease primarily for an agricultural purpose is not covered, and whether there should be a limitation by dollar amount and its amount is left up to the individual states.

This definition focuses on the parties as well as the transaction. If a lease is within this definition, the lessor must be regularly engaged in the business of leasing or selling, and the lessee must be an individual, not an organization; note that a lease to two or more individuals having a common interest through marriage or the like is not excluded as a lease to an organization under Section 1-201(b)(25). The lessee must take the interest primarily for a personal, family or household purpose. If required by the enacting state, total payments under the lease contract, excluding payments for options to renew or buy, cannot exceed the figure designated.

(f) "Fault". Section 1-201(b)(17).

(g) "Finance Lease". New. This Article includes a subset of rules that applies only to finance leases. Sections 2A-209, 2A-211(2), 2A-212(1), 2A-213, 2A-219(1), 2A-220(1)(a), 2A-221, 2A-405(c), 2A-407, 2A-516(2) and 2A-517(1)(a) and (2).

For a transaction to qualify as a finance lease it must first qualify as a lease. Section 2A-103(1)(j). Unless the lessor is comfortable that the transaction will qualify as a finance lease, the lease agreement should include provisions giving the lessor the benefits created by the subset of rules applicable to the transaction that qualifies as a finance lease under this Article.

A finance lease is the product of a three-party transaction. The supplier manufactures or supplies the goods pursuant to the lessee's specification, perhaps even pursuant to a purchase order, sales agreement or lease agreement between the supplier and the lessee. After the prospective finance lease is negotiated, a purchase order, sales agreement, or lease agreement is entered into by the lessor (as buyer or prime lessee) or an existing order, agreement or lease is assigned by the lessee to the lessor, and the lessor and the lessee then enter into a lease or sublease of the goods. Due to the limited function usually performed by the lessor, the lessee looks almost entirely to the supplier for representations, covenants and warranties. If a manufacturer's warranty carries through, the lessee may also look to that. Yet, this definition does not restrict the lessor's function solely to the supply of funds; if the lessor undertakes or performs other functions, express warranties, covenants and the common law will protect the lessee.

This definition focuses on the transaction, not the status of the parties; to avoid confusion it is important to note that in other contexts, e.g., tax and accounting, the term finance lease has been used to connote different types of lease transactions, including leases that are disguised secured transactions. Michael D. Rice, *Equipment Financing,* 62-71 (1981). A lessor who is a merchant with respect to goods of the kind subject to the lease may be a lessor under a finance lease. Many leases that are leases back to the seller of goods (Section 2A-308(3)) will be finance leases. This conclusion is easily demonstrated by a hypothetical. Assume that B has bought goods from C pursuant to a sales contract. After delivery to and acceptance of the goods by B, B negotiates to sell the goods to A and simultaneously to lease the goods back from A, on terms and conditions that, we assume, will qualify the transaction as a lease. Section 2A-103(1)(j). In documenting the sale and lease back, B assigns the original sales contract between B, as buyer, and C, as seller, to A. A review of these facts leads to the conclusion that the lease from A to B qualifies as a finance lease, as all three conditions of the definition are satisfied. Subparagraph (i) is satisfied as A, the lessor, had nothing to do with the selection, manufacture, or supply of the equipment. Subparagraph (ii) is satisfied as A, the lessor, bought the equipment at the same time that A leased the equipment to B, which certainly is in connection with the lease. Finally, subparagraph (iii)(A) is satisfied as A entered into the sales contract with B at the same time that A leased the equipment back to B. B, the lessee, will have received a copy of the sales contract in a timely fashion.

Subsection (i) requires the lessor to remain outside the selection, manufacture and supply of the goods; that is the rationale for releasing the lessor from most of its traditional liability. The lessor is not prohibited from possession, maintenance or operation of the goods, as policy does not require such prohibition. To insure the lessee's reliance on the supplier, and not on the lessor, subsection (ii) requires that the goods (where the lessor is the buyer of the goods) or that the right to possession and use of the goods (where the lessor is the prime lessee and the sublessor of the goods) be acquired in connection with the lease (or sublease) to qualify as a finance lease. The scope of the phrase "in connection with" is to be developed by the courts, case by case. Finally, as the lessee generally relies almost entirely upon the supplier for representations and covenants, and upon the supplier or a manufacturer, or both, for warranties with respect to the goods, subsection (iii) requires that one of the following occur: (A) the lessee receive a copy of the supply contract before signing the lease contract; (B) the lessee's approval of the supply contract is a condition to the effectiveness of the lease contract; (C) the lessee receive a statement describing the promises and warranties and any limitations relevant to the lessee before signing the lease contract; or (D) before signing the lease contract and except in a consumer lease, the lessee receive a writing identifying the supplier (unless the supplier was selected and required by the lessee) and the rights of the lessee under Section 2A-209, and advising the lessee a statement of promises and warranties is available from the supplier. Thus, even where oral supply orders or computer placed supply orders are compelled by custom and usage the transaction may still qualify as a finance lease if the lessee approves the supply contract before the lease contract is effective and such approval was a condition to the effectiveness of the lease contract. Moreover, where the lessor does not want the lessee to see the entire supply contract, including price information, the lessee may be provided with a separate statement of the terms of the supply contract relevant to the lessee; promises between the supplier and the lessor that do not affect the lessee need not be included. The statement can be a restatement of those terms or a copy of portions of the supply contract with the relevant terms clearly designated. Any implied warranties need not be designated, but a disclaimer or modification of remedy must be designated. A copy of any manufacturer's warranty is sufficient if that is the warranty provided. However, a copy of any Regulation M disclosure given pursuant to 12 C.F.R. § 213.4(g) concerning warranties in itself is not sufficient since those disclosures need only briefly identify express warranties and need not include any disclaimer of warranty.

If a transaction does not qualify as a finance lease, the parties may achieve the same result by agreement; no negative implications are to be drawn if the transaction does not qualify. Further, absent the application of special rules (fraud, duress, and the like), a lease that qualifies as a finance lease and is assigned by the lessor or the lessee to a third party does not lose its status as a finance lease under this Article. Finally, this Article creates no special rule where the lessor is an affiliate of the supplier; whether the transaction qualifies as a finance lease will be determined by the facts of each case.

Pursuant to the Uniform Commercial Code Amendments (2022), some references in this Article to the terms "writing," "writings," or "written" have been changed to refer to a "record." These changes are made in provisions where an affected party may be assumed to have assented to the use of a record that is not a writing. For example, Section 2A-201 involves a record signed by an affected party and Section 2A-202 refers to a record intended by parties to be a final expression of their agreement. Where such references remain in this Article, the use by parties of a record other than a writing may be given effect for purposes of this Article under law other than the Uniform Commercial Code, such as the Electronic Signatures in Global and National Commerce Act, 15 U.S.C. Section 7001 *et seq.*, and the Uniform Electronic Transactions Act.

(h) "Goods". Section 9-102(a)(44). See Section 2A-103(3) for reference to the definition of "Account", "Chattel paper", "Document", "General intangibles" and "Instrument". See Section 2A-217 for determination of the time and manner of identification.

(h.1) "Hybrid lease". In some transactions, the transfer of the right to possession and use of goods for a term in return for consideration (i.e., a lease), is part of a larger transaction. The other aspects of the transaction might involve the provision of services, a sale of other goods, or a transfer of rights to property other than goods. Such a transaction is a hybrid lease. Section 2A-102 indicates the extent to which this Article applies to a hybrid lease.

A hybrid lease is a single transaction. If contracting parties enter into separate agreements at the same time, each agreement must be evaluated separately to determine if it is a hybrid lease.

Example 1. Lessor and Customer A enter into a single agreement that provides for Lessor, in return for periodic payments from Customer A, to: (i) lease a photocopier to Customer A for twelve months; (ii) supply all the paper, staples, and toner needed to operate the copier during that period, and (iii) provide routine maintenance and repair services needed to keep the copier operating during that period. The transaction is a hybrid lease because it involves a lease of goods (the copier), a sale of goods (the paper, staples, and toner), and the provision of services.

Example 2. Lessor and Customer B enter into three separate written agreements at the same time: (i) a lease of a photocopier to Customer B for twelve months; (ii) a contract for Lessor to supply Customer B with all the paper, staples, and toner needed to operate the copier during that period, and (iii) a contract for Lessor to provide routine maintenance and repair services needed to keep the copier operating during that period. Because the parties executed three separate agreements, and the lease does not involve a sale, lease, or license of other property or the provision of services, the lease is not a hybrid lease.

Even when contracting parties enter into a single agreement involving both a lease of goods and a sale, lease, or license of other property or the provision of services, the agreement may involve separate transactions and not a single transaction. In that situation, the lease transaction would not be a hybrid lease if the lease of goods is unrelated to the other aspects of the agreement and the terms of the agreement relating to the lease of goods are readily severable from the terms of the agreement relating to the other transactions.

Example 3. Farmer A and Farmer B sign a written agreement pursuant to which Farmer A will lease a tractor to Farmer B for one year and Farmer B will board and feed Farmer A's cattle until the cattle are sold. The agreement specifies a rental payment for the tractor, which is due monthly, and a mechanism for determining the price for Farmer B's services, which is to be paid when the cattle are sold. The parties would have entered into an agreement to lease the tractor even if they had not entered into an agreement to board and feed the cattle, and vice versa. The transaction is not a hybrid lease. Article 2A applies to the lease of the tractor. Other law applies to the agreement to board and feed the cattle.

(i) "Installment lease contract". Section 2-612(1).

(j) "Lease". New. There are several reasons to codify the law with respect to leases of goods. An analysis of the case law as it applies to leases of goods suggests at least several significant issues to be resolved by codification. First and foremost is the definition of a lease. It is necessary to define lease to determine whether a transaction creates a lease or a security interest disguised as a lease. If the transaction creates a security interest disguised as a lease, the transaction will be governed by the Article on Secured Transactions (Article 9) and the lessor will be required to file a financing statement or take other action to perfect its interest in the goods against third parties. There is no such requirement with respect to leases under the common law and, except with respect to leases of fixtures (Section 2A-309), this Article imposes no such requirement. Yet the distinction between a lease and a security interest disguised as a lease is not clear from the case law at the time of the promulgation of this Article. Ronald DeKoven, *Leases of Equipment: Puritan Leasing Company v. August, A Dangerous Decision,* 12 U.S.F. L. Rev. 257 (1978).

At common law a lease of personal property is a bailment for hire. While there are several definitions of bailment for hire, all require a thing to be let and a price for the letting. Thus, in modern terms and as provided in this definition, a lease is created when the lessee agrees to furnish consideration for the right to the possession and use of goods over a specified period of time. Charles W. Mooney, *Personal Property Leasing: A Challenge,* 36 Bus. Law. 1605, 1607 (1981). Further, a lease is neither a sale (Section 2-106(1)) nor a retention or creation of a security interest (Section 1-201(b)(35) and 1-203). Due to extensive litigation to distinguish true leases from security interests, an amendment to former Section 1-201(37) (now codified as Section 1-203) was promulgated with this Article to create a sharper distinction.

This section as well as Section 1-203 must be examined to determine whether the transaction in question creates a lease or a security interest. The following hypotheticals indicate the parameters of the issue. Assume that A has purchased a number of copying machines, new, for $1,000 each; the machines have an estimated useful economic life of three years. A advertises that the machines are available to rent for a minimum of one month and that the monthly rental is $100.00. A intends to enter into leases where A provides all maintenance, without charge to the lessee. Further, the lessee will rent the machine, month to month, with no obligation to renew. At the end of the lease term the lessee will be obligated to return the machine to A's place of business. This transaction qualifies as a lease under the first clause of the definition, for the transaction includes a transfer by A to a prospective lessee of possession and use of the machine for a stated term, month to month. The machines are goods (Section 2A-103(1)(h)). The lessee is obligated to pay consideration in return, $100.00 for each month of the term.

However, the second half of the definition provides that a sale or a security interest is not a lease. Since there is no passing of title, there is no sale. Sections 2A-103(3) and 2-106(1). Under pre-Act security law this transaction would have created a bailment for hire or a true lease and not a conditional sale. *Da Rocha v. Macomber*, 116 N.E.2d 139, 142 (Mass. 1953). Under Section 1-203, the same result would follow. While the lessee is obligated to pay rent for the one-month term of the lease, one of the other four conditions of Section 1-203(b) must be met and none is. The term of the lease is one month and the economic life of the machine is 36 months; thus, Section 1-203(b)(1) is not now satisfied. Considering the amount of the monthly rent, absent economic duress or coercion, the lessee is not bound either to renew the lease for the remaining economic life of the goods or to become the owner. If the lessee did lease the machine for 36 months, the lessee would have paid the lessor $3,600 for a machine that could have been purchased for $1,000; thus, Section 1-203(b)(2) is not satisfied. Finally, there are no options; thus, subparagraphs (3) and (4) of Section 1-203(b) are not satisfied. This transaction creates a lease, not a security interest. However, with each renewal of the lease the facts and circumstances at the time of each renewal must be examined to determine if that conclusion remains accurate, as it is possible that a transaction that first creates a lease, later creates a security interest.

Assume that the facts are changed and that A requires each lessee to lease the goods for 36 months, with no right to terminate. Under pre-Act security law this transaction would have created a conditional sale, and not a bailment for hire or true lease. *Hervey v. Rhode Island Locomotive Works*, 93 U.S. 664, 672-73 (1876). Under this subsection, and Section 1-203, the same result would follow. The lessee's obligation for the term is not subject to termination by the lessee and the term is equal to the economic life of the machine.

Between these extremes there are many transactions that can be created. Some of the transactions were not properly categorized by the courts in applying the 1978 and earlier Official Texts of former Section 1-201(37). This subsection, together with Section 1-203, draws a brighter line, which should create a clearer signal to the professional lessor and lessee.

(k) "Lease agreement". This definition is derived from Section 1-201(b)(3). Because the definition of lease is broad enough to cover future transfers, lease agreement includes an agreement contemplating a current or subsequent transfer. Thus it was not necessary to make an express reference to an agreement for the future lease of goods (Section 2-106(1)). This concept is also incorporated in the definition of lease contract. Note that the definition of lease does not include transactions in ordinary building materials that are incorporated into an improvement on land. Section 2A-309(2).

The provisions of this Article, if applicable, determine whether a lease agreement has legal consequences; otherwise the law of bailments and other applicable law determine the same. Sections 2A-103(4) and 1-103.

(l) "Lease contract". This definition is derived from the definition of contract in Section 1-201(b)(12). Note that a lease contract may be for the future lease of goods, since this notion is included in the definition of lease.

(m) "Leasehold interest". New.

(n) "Lessee". New.

(o) "Lessee in ordinary course of business". Section 1-201(b)(9).

(p) "Lessor". New.

(q) "Lessor's residual interest". New.

(r) "Lien". New. This term is used in Section 2A-307 (Priority of Liens Arising by Attachment or Levy on, Security Interests in, and Other Claims to Goods).

(s) "Lot". Section 2-105(5).

(t) "Merchant lessee". New. This term is used in Section 2A-511 (Merchant Lessee's Duties as to Rightfully Rejected Goods). A person may satisfy the requirement of dealing in goods of the kind subject to the lease as lessor, lessee, seller, or buyer.

(u) "Present value" means the amount as of a date certain of one or more sums payable in the future, discounted to the date certain. The discount is determined by the interest rate specified by the parties if the rate was not manifestly unreasonable at the time the transaction was entered into; otherwise, the discount is determined by a commercially reasonable rate that takes into account the facts and circumstances of each case at the time the transaction was entered into.

(v) "Purchase". Section 1-201(b)(29). This definition omits the reference to lien contained in the definition of purchase in Article 1 (Section 1-201(b)(29)). This should not be construed to exclude consensual liens from the definition of purchase in this Article; the exclusion was mandated by the scope of the definition of lien in Section 2A-103(1)(r). Further, the definition of purchaser in this Article adds a reference to lease; as purchase is defined in Section 1-201(b)(29) to include any other voluntary transaction creating an interest in property, this addition is not substantive.

(w) "Sublease". New.

(x) "Supplier". New.

(y) "Supply contract". New.

(z) "Termination". Section 2-106(3). The effect of a termination is provided in Section 2A-505(2).

Section 2A-104. Leases Subject to Other Law

(1) A lease, although subject to this Article, is also subject to any applicable:

(a) certificate of title statute of this State: (list any certificate of title statutes covering automobiles, trailers, mobile homes, boats, farm tractors, and the like);

(b) certificate of title statute of another jurisdiction (Section 2A-105); or

(c) consumer protection statute of this State, or final consumer protection decision of a court of this State existing on the effective date of this Article.

(2) In case of conflict between this Article, other than Sections 2A-105, 2A-304(3), and 2A-305(3), and a statute or decision referred to in subsection (1), the statute or decision controls.

(3) Failure to comply with an applicable law has only the effect specified therein.

Official Comment

Uniform Statutory Source: Sections 9-203(4) and 9-302(3)(b) and (c).

Changes: Substantially revised.

Purposes:

1. This Article creates a comprehensive scheme for the regulation of transactions that create leases. Section 2A-102.

Thus, the Article supersedes all prior legislation dealing with leases, except to the extent set forth in this Section.

2. Subsection (1) states the general rule that a lease, although governed by the scheme of this Article, also may be governed by certain other applicable laws. This may occur in the case of a consumer lease. Section 2A-103(1)(e). Those laws may be state statutes existing prior to enactment of Article 2A or passed afterward. In this case, it is desirable for this Article to specify which statute controls. Or the law may be a pre-existing consumer protection decision. This Article preserves such decisions. Or the law may be a statute of the United States. Such a law controls without any statement in this Article under applicable principles of preemption.

An illustration of a statute of the United States that governs consumer leases is the Consumer Leasing Act, 15 U.S.C. §§ 1667-1667(e) (1982) and its implementing regulation, Regulation M, 12 C.F.R. § 213 (1986); the statute mandates disclosures of certain lease terms, delimits the liability of a lessee in leasing personal property, and regulates the advertising of lease terms. An illustration of a state statute that governs consumer leases and which if adopted in the enacting state prevails over this Article is the Uniform Consumer Credit Code, which includes many provisions similar to those of the Consumer Leasing Act, e.g., Unif. Consumer Credit Code §§ 3.202, 3.209, 3.401 (1974), as well as provisions in addition to those of the Consumer Leasing Act, e.g., Unif. Consumer Credit Code §§ 5.109-.111 (1974) (the right to cure a default). Such statutes may define consumer lease so as to govern transactions within and without the definition of consumer lease under this Article.

3. Under subsection (2), subject to certain limited exclusions, in case of conflict a statute or a decision described in subsection (1) prevails over this Article. For example, a provision like Unif. Consumer Credit Code § 5.112 (1974), limiting self-help repossession, prevails over Section 2A-525(3). A consumer protection decision rendered after the effective date of this Article may supplement its provisions. For example, in relation to Article 9 a court might conclude that an acceleration clause may not be enforced against an individual debtor after late payments have been accepted unless a prior notice of default is given. To the extent the decision establishes a general principle applicable to transactions other than secured transactions, it may supplement Section 2A-502.

4. Consumer protection in lease transactions is primarily left to other law. However, several provisions of this Article do contain special rules that may not be varied by agreement in the case of a consumer lease. E.g., Sections 2A-106, 2A-108(2), and 2A-109(2). Were that not so, the ability of the parties to govern their relationship by agreement together with the position of the lessor in a consumer lease too often could result in a one-sided lease agreement.

5. In construing this provision the reference to statute should be deemed to include applicable regulations. A consumer protection decision is "final" on the effective date of this Article if it is not subject to appeal on that date or, if subject to appeal, is not later reversed on appeal. Of course, such a decision can be overruled by a later decision or superseded by a later statute.

Cross References:

Sections 2A-103(1)(e), 2A-105, 2A-106, 2A-108(2), 2A-109(2), 2A-304(3), 2A-305(3), 2A-502, and 2A-525(3).

Definitional Cross Reference:

"Lease". Section 2A-103(1)(j).

Section 2A-105. Territorial Application of Article to Goods Covered by Certificate of Title

Subject to the provisions of Sections 2A-304(3) and 2A-305(3), with respect to goods covered by a certificate of title issued under a statute of this State or of another jurisdiction, compliance and the effect of compliance or noncompliance with a certificate of title statute are governed by the law (including the conflict of laws rules) of the jurisdiction issuing the certificate until the earlier of (a) surrender of the certificate, or (b) four months after the goods are removed from that jurisdiction and thereafter until a new certificate of title is issued by another jurisdiction.

Official Comment

Uniform Statutory Source: Section 9-103(2)(a) and (b).

Changes: Substantially revised. The provisions of the last sentence of Section 9-103(2)(b) have not been incorporated as it is superfluous in this context. The provisions of Section 9-103(2)(d) have not been incorporated because the problems dealt with are adequately addressed by this section and Sections 2A-304(3) and 2A-305(3).

Purposes: The new certificate referred to in (b) must be permanent, not temporary. Generally, the lessor or creditor whose interest is indicated on the most recently issued certificate of title will prevail over interests indicated on certificates issued previously by other jurisdictions. This provision reflects a policy that it is reasonable to require holders of interests in goods covered by a certificate of title to police the goods or risk losing their interests when a new certificate of title is issued by another jurisdiction.

Cross References:

Sections 2A-304(3), 2A-305(3), 9-303 and 9-316(d).

Definitional Cross Reference:

"Goods". Section 2A-103(1)(h).

Section 2A-106. Limitation on Power of Parties to Consumer Lease to Choose Applicable Law and Judicial Forum

(1) If the law chosen by the parties to a consumer lease is that of a jurisdiction other than a jurisdiction in which the lessee resides at the time the lease agreement becomes enforceable or within 30 days thereafter or in which the goods are to be used, the choice is not enforceable.

(2) If the judicial forum chosen by the parties to a consumer lease is a forum that would not otherwise have jurisdiction over the lessee, the choice is not enforceable.

Official Comment

Uniform Statutory Source: Unif. Consumer Credit Code § 1.201(8).

Changes: Substantially revised.

Purposes: There is a real danger that a lessor may induce a consumer lessee to agree that the applicable law will be a jurisdiction that has little effective consumer protection, or to agree that the applicable forum will be a forum that is inconvenient for the lessee in the event of litigation. As a result, this section invalidates these choice of law or forum clauses, except where the law chosen is that of the state of the consumer's residence or where the goods will be kept, or the forum chosen is one that otherwise would have jurisdiction over the lessee.

Subsection (1) limits potentially abusive choice of law clauses in consumer leases. The 30-day rule in subsection (1) was suggested by Section 9-103(1)(c). This section has no effect on choice of law clauses in leases that are not consumer leases. Such clauses would be governed by other law.

Subsection (2) prevents enforcement of potentially abusive jurisdictional consent clauses in consumer leases. By using the term judicial forum, this section does not limit selection of a nonjudicial forum, such as arbitration. This section has no effect on choice of forum clauses in leases that are not consumer leases; such clauses are, as a matter of current law, "prima facie valid". *The Bremen v. Zapata Off-Shore Co.*, 407 U.S. 1, 10 (1972). Such clauses would be governed by other law, including the Model Choice of Forum Act (1968).

Cross Reference:

Section 9-103(1)(c).

Definitional Cross References:

"Consumer lease".	Section 2A-103(1)(e).
"Lease agreement".	Section 2A-103(1)(k).
"Lessee".	Section 2A-103(1)(n).
"Goods".	Section 2A-103(1)(h).
"Party".s	Section 1-201(b)(26).

Section 2A-107. Waiver or Renunciation of Claim or Right After Default

Any claim or right arising out of an alleged default or breach of warranty may be discharged in whole or in part without consideration by a waiver or renunciation in a signed record delivered by the aggrieved party.

Official Comment

Uniform Statutory Source: Former Section 1-107.

Changes:

1. Revised to reflect leasing practices and terminology. The prior statement is used throughout the official comments to this Article to indicate the scope of change in the provisions of the Uniform Statutory Source included in the section; these changes range from one extreme, e.g., a significant difference in practice (a warranty as to merchantability is not implied in a finance lease (Section 2A-212)) to the other extreme, e.g., a modest difference in style or terminology (the transaction governed is a lease not a sale (Section 2A-103)).

2. In furtherance of medium neutrality, the reference to a signed "written" waiver or renunciation in the pre-2022 text of this section has been changed to refer to a waiver in a signed "record."

Cross References:

Sections 2A-103 and 2A-212.

Definitional Cross References:

"Aggrieved party".	Section 1-201(b)(2).
"Delivery".	Section 1-201(b)(15).
"Record".	Section 1-201(b)(31)
"Right".	Section 1-201(b)(34).
"Signed".	Section 1-201(b)(37).

Section 2A-108. Unconscionability

(1) If the court as a matter of law finds a lease contract or any clause of a lease contract to have been unconscionable at the time it was made the court may refuse to enforce the lease contract, or it may enforce the remainder of the lease contract without the unconscionable clause, or it may so limit the application of any unconscionable clause as to avoid any unconscionable result.

(2) With respect to a consumer lease, if the court as a matter of law finds that a lease contract or any clause of a lease contract has been induced by unconscionable conduct or that unconscionable conduct has occurred in the collection of a claim arising from a lease contract, the court may grant appropriate relief.

(3) Before making a finding of unconscionability under subsection (1) or (2), the court, on its own motion or that of a party, shall afford the parties a reasonable opportunity to present evidence as to the setting, purpose, and effect of the lease contract or clause thereof, or of the conduct.

(4) In an action in which the lessee claims unconscionability with respect to a consumer lease:

(a) If the court finds unconscionability under subsection (1) or (2), the court shall award reasonable attorney's fees to the lessee.

(b) If the court does not find unconscionability and the lessee claiming unconscionability has brought or maintained an action he [or she] knew to be groundless, the court shall award reasonable attorney's fees to the party against whom the claim is made.

(c) In determining attorney's fees, the amount of the recovery on behalf of the claimant under subsections (1) and (2) is not controlling.

Official Comment

Uniform Statutory Source: Section 2-302 and Unif. Consumer Credit Code § 5.108 (1974).

Changes: Subsection (1) is taken almost verbatim from the provisions of Section 2-302(1). Subsection (2) is suggested by the provisions of Unif. Consumer Credit Code § 5.108(1), (2) (1974). Subsection (3), taken from the provisions of Section 2-302(2), has been expanded to cover unconscionable conduct. Unif. Consumer Credit Code § 5.108(3) (1974). The provision for the award of attorney's fees to consumers, subsection (4), covers unconscionability under subsection (1) as well as (2). Subsection (4) is modeled on the provisions of Unif. Consumer Credit Code § 5.108(6) (1974).

Purposes: Subsections (1) and (3) of this section apply the concept of unconscionability reflected in the provisions of Section 2-302 to leases. See *Dillman & Assocs. v. Capitol Leasing Co.*, 442 N.E.2d 311, 316 (Ill. App. Ct. 1982). Subsection (3) omits the adjective "commercial" found in subsection 2-302(2) because subsection (3) is concerned with all leases and the relevant standard of conduct is determined by the context.

The balance of the section is modeled on the provisions of Unif. Consumer Credit Code § 5.108 (1974). Thus subsection (2) recognizes that a consumer lease or a clause in a consumer lease may not itself be unconscionable but that the agreement would never have been entered into if unconscionable means had not been employed to induce the consumer to agree. To make a statement to induce the consumer to lease the goods, in the expectation of invoking an integration clause in the lease to exclude the statement's admissibility in a subsequent dispute, may be unconscionable. Subsection (2) also provides a consumer remedy for unconscionable conduct, such as using or threatening to use force or violence, in the collection of a claim arising from a lease contract. These provisions are not exclusive. The remedies of this section are in addition to remedies otherwise available for the same conduct under other law, for example, an action in tort for abusive debt collection or under another statute of this State for such conduct. The reference to appropriate relief in subsection (2) is intended to foster liberal administration of this remedy. Sections 2A-103(4) and 1-305.

Subsection (4) authorizes an award of reasonable attorney's fees if the court finds unconscionability with respect to a consumer lease under subsection (1) or (2). Provision is also made for recovery by the party against whom the claim was made if the court does not find unconscionability and does find that the consumer knew the action to be groundless. Further, subsection (4)(b) is independent of, and thus will not override, a term in the lease agreement that provides for the payment of attorney's fees.

Cross References:

Sections 1-305, 2-302, and 2A-103(4).

Definitional Cross References:

"Action".	Section 1-201(b)(1).
"Consumer lease".	Section 2A-103(1)(e).
"Lease contract".	Section 2A-103(1)(*l*).
"Lessee".	Section 2A-103(1)(n).
"Party".	Section 1-201(b)(26).

Section 2A-109. Option to Accelerate at Will

(1) A term providing that one party or his [or her] successor in interest may accelerate payment or performance or require collateral or additional collateral "at will" or "when he [or she] deems himself [or herself] insecure" or in words of similar import must be construed to mean that he [or she] has power to do so only if he [or she] in good faith believes that the prospect of payment or performance is impaired.

(2) With respect to a consumer lease, the burden of establishing good faith under subsection (1) is on the party who exercised the power; otherwise the burden of establishing lack of good faith is on the party against whom the power has been exercised.

Official Comment

Uniform Statutory Source: Former Section 1-208 and Unif. Consumer Credit Code § 5.109(2) (1974).

Purposes: Subsection (1) reflects modest changes in style to the provisions of the first sentence of former Section 1-208.

Subsection (2), however, reflects a significant change in the provisions of the second sentence of former Section 1-208 by creating a new rule with respect to a consumer lease. A lease provision allowing acceleration at the will of the lessor or when the lessor deems itself insecure is of critical importance to the lessee. In a consumer lease it is a provision that is not usually agreed to by the parties but is usually mandated by the lessor. Therefore, where its invocation depends not on specific criteria but on the discretion of the lessor, its use should be regulated to prevent abuse. Subsection (1) imposes a duty of good faith upon its exercise. Subsection (2) shifts the burden of establishing good faith to the lessor in the case of a consumer lease, but not otherwise.

Cross Reference:

Former Section 1-208 (now codified as Section 1-309).

Definitional Cross References:

"Burden of establishing".	Section 1-201(b)(8).
"Consumer lease".	Section 2A-103(1)(e).
"Good faith".	Sections 1-201(b)(20).
"Party".	Section 1-201(b)(26).
"Term".	Section 1-201(b)(40).

PART 2. FORMATION AND CONSTRUCTION OF LEASE CONTRACT; ELECTRONIC CONTRACTING

Section 2A-201. Statute of Frauds

(1) A lease contract is not enforceable by way of action or defense unless:

(a) the total payments to be made under the lease contract, excluding payments for options to renew or buy, are less than $1,000; or

(b) there is a record, signed by the party against whom enforcement is sought or by that party's authorized agent, sufficient to indicate that a lease contract has been made between the parties and to describe the goods leased and the lease term.

(2) Any description of leased goods or of the lease term is sufficient and satisfies subsection (1)(b), whether or not it is specific, if it reasonably identifies what is described.

(3) A record is not insufficient because it omits or incorrectly states a term agreed upon, but the lease contract is not enforceable under subsection (1)(b) beyond the lease term and the quantity of goods shown in the record.

(4) A lease contract that does not satisfy the requirements of subsection (1), but which is valid in other respects, is enforceable:

(a) if the goods are to be specially manufactured or obtained for the lessee and are not suitable for lease or sale to others in the ordinary course of the lessor's business, and the lessor, before notice of repudiation is received and under circumstances that reasonably indicate that the goods are for the lessee, has made either a substantial beginning of their manufacture or commitments for their procurement;

(b) if the party against whom enforcement is sought admits in that party's pleading, testimony or otherwise in court that a lease contract was made, but the lease contract is not enforceable under this provision beyond the quantity of goods admitted; or

(c) with respect to goods that have been received and accepted by the lessee.

(5) The lease term under a lease contract referred to in subsection (4) is:

(a) if there is a record signed by the party against whom enforcement is sought or by that party's authorized agent specifying the lease term, the term so specified;

(b) if the party against whom enforcement is sought admits in that party's pleading, testimony, or otherwise in court a lease term, the term so admitted; or

(c) a reasonable lease term.

Official Comment

Uniform Statutory Source: Sections 2-201, 9-203(1) and 9-110.

Changes:

1. This section is modeled on Section 2-201, with changes to reflect the differences between a lease contract and a contract for the sale of goods. In particular, subsection (1)(b) adds a requirement that the writing "describe the goods leased and the lease term", borrowing that concept, with revisions, from the provisions of Section 9-203(1)(a). Subsection (2), relying on the statutory analogue in Section 9-110, sets forth the minimum criterion for satisfying that requirement.

2. In furtherance of medium neutrality, the references to a "writing" in the pre-2022 text of this section have been changed to refer to a "record."

Purposes: The changes in this section conform the provisions of Section 2-201 to custom and usage in lease transactions. Section 2-201(2), stating a special rule between merchants, was not included in this section as the number of such transactions involving leases, as opposed to sales, was thought to be modest. Subsection (4) creates no exception for transactions where payment has been made and accepted. This represents a departure from the analogue, Section 2-201(3)(c). The rationale for the departure is grounded in the distinction between sales and leases. Unlike a buyer in a sales transaction, the lessee does not tender payment in full for goods delivered, but only payment of rent for one or more months. It was decided that, as a matter of policy, this act of payment is not a sufficient substitute for the required memorandum. Subsection (5) was needed to establish the criteria for supplying the lease term if it is omitted, as the lease contract may still be enforceable under subsection (4).

Cross References:

Sections 2-201, 9-108, and 9-203(b)(3)(A).

Definitional Cross References:

"Action".	Section 1-201(b)(1).
"Agreement".	Section 1-201(b)(3).
"Buying".	Section 2A-103(1)(a).
"Goods".	Section 2A-103(1)(h).
"Lease".	Section 2A-103(1)(j).
"Lease contract".	Section 2A-103(1)(*l*).
"Lessee".	Section 2A-103(1)(n).
"Lessor".	Section 2A-103(1)(p).
"Notice".	Section 1-202(a).
"Party".	Section 1-201(b)(26).
"Record".	Section 1-201(b)(31)
"Sale".	Section 2-106(1).
"Signed".	Section 1-201(b)(37).
"Term".	Section 1-201(b)(40).

Section 2A-202. Final Expression: Parol or Extrinsic Evidence

Terms with respect to which the confirmatory memoranda of the parties agree or which are otherwise set forth in a record intended by the parties as a final expression of their agreement with respect to such terms as are included therein may not be contradicted by evidence of any prior agreement or of a contemporaneous oral agreement but may be explained or supplemented:

(a) by course of dealing or usage of trade or by course of performance; and

(b) by evidence of consistent additional terms unless the court finds the record to have been intended also as a complete and exclusive statement of the terms of the agreement.

Official Comment

Uniform Statutory Source: Section 2-202.

Changes: In furtherance of medium neutrality, the references to a "writing" have been changed to refer to a "record."

Definitional Cross References:

"Agreement".	Section 1-201(b)(3).
"Course of dealing".	Section 1-303(b).
"Party".	Section 1-201(b)(26).
"Record".	Section 1-201(b)(31).
"Term".	Section 1-201(b)(40).
"Usage of trade".	Section 1-303(c).

Section 2A-203. Seals Inoperative

The affixing of a seal to a record evidencing a lease contract or an offer to enter into a lease contract does not render the record a sealed instrument and the law with respect to sealed instruments does not apply to the lease contract or offer.

Official Comment

Uniform Statutory Source: Section 2-203.

Changes: Revised to reflect leasing practices and terminology. In furtherance of medium neutrality, the references to a "writing" have been changed to refer to a "record."

Definitional Cross References:

"Lease contract".	Section 2A-103(1)(*l*).
"Record".	Section 1-201(b)(31).

Section 2A-204. Formation in General

(1) A lease contract may be made in any manner sufficient to show agreement, including conduct by both parties which recognizes the existence of a lease contract.

(2) An agreement sufficient to constitute a lease contract may be found although the moment of its making is undetermined.

(3) Although one or more terms are left open, a lease contract does not fail for indefiniteness if the parties have intended to make a lease contract and there is a reasonably certain basis for giving an appropriate remedy.

Official Comment

Uniform Statutory Source: Section 2-204.

Changes: Revised to reflect leasing practices and terminology.

Definitional Cross References:

"Agreement".	Section 1-201(b)(3).
"Lease contract".	Section 2A-103(1)(*l*).
"Party".	Section 1-201(b)(26).
"Remedy".	Section 1-201(b)(32).
"Term".	Section 1-201(b)(40).

Section 2A-205. Firm Offers

An offer by a merchant to lease goods to or from another person in a signed record that by its terms gives assurance it will be held open is not revocable, for lack of consideration, during the time stated or, if no time is stated, for a reasonable time, but in no event may the period of irrevocability exceed 3 months. Any such term of assurance on a form supplied by the offeree must be separately signed by the offeror.

Official Comment

Uniform Statutory Source: Section 2-205.

Changes: Revised to reflect leasing practices and terminology. In furtherance of medium neutrality, the reference to a signed "writing" in the pre-2022 text of this section has been changed to refer to a signed "record."

Definitional Cross References:

"Goods".	Section 2A-103(1)(h).
"Lease".	Section 2A-103(1)(j).
"Merchant".	Section 2-104(1).
"Person".	Section 1-201(b)(27).
"Reasonable time".	Section 1-205(a).
"Record".	Section 1-201(b)(31).
"Signed".	Section 1-201(b)(37).
"Term".	Section 1-201(b)(40).

Section 2A-206. Offer and Acceptance in Formation of Lease Contract

(1) Unless otherwise unambiguously indicated by the language or circumstances, an offer to make a lease contract must be construed as inviting acceptance in any manner and by any medium reasonable in the circumstances.

(2) If the beginning of a requested performance is a reasonable mode of acceptance, an offeror who is not notified of acceptance within a reasonable time may treat the offer as having lapsed before acceptance.

Official Comment

Uniform Statutory Source: Section 2-206(1)(a) and (2).

Changes: Revised to reflect leasing practices and terminology.

Definitional Cross References:

"Lease contract".	Section 2A-103(1)(r).
"Notifies".	Section 1-202(d).
"Reasonable time".	Section 1-205(a).

Section 2A-207. [Deleted]

Section 2A-208. Modification, Rescission and Waiver

(1) An agreement modifying a lease contract needs no consideration to be binding.

(2) A signed lease agreement that excludes modification or rescission except by a signed record may not be otherwise modified or rescinded, but, except as between merchants, such a requirement on a form supplied by a merchant must be separately signed by the other party.

(3) Although an attempt at modification or rescission does not satisfy the requirements of subsection (2), it may operate as a waiver.

(4) A party who has made a waiver affecting an executory portion of a lease contract may retract the waiver by reasonable notification received by the other party that strict performance will be required of any term waived, unless the retraction would be unjust in view of a material change of position in reliance on the waiver.

Official Comment

Uniform Statutory Source: Section 2-209.

Changes:

1. Revised to reflect leasing practices and terminology, except that the provisions of subsection 2-209(3) were omitted.

2. In furtherance of medium neutrality, the reference to a signed "writing" in the pre-2022 text of this section has been changed to refer to a signed "record."

Purposes: Section 2-209(3) provides that "the requirements of the statute of frauds section of this Article (Section 2-201) must be satisfied if the contract as modified is within its provisions." This provision was not incorporated as it is unfair to allow an oral modification to make the entire lease contract unenforceable, e.g., if the modification takes it a few dollars over the dollar limit. At the same time, the problem could not be solved by providing that the lease contract would still be enforceable in its premodification state (if it then satisfied the statute of frauds) since in some cases that might be worse than no enforcement at all. Resolution of the issue is left to the courts based on the facts of each case.

Cross References:

Sections 2-201 and 2-209.

Definitional Cross References:

"Agreement".	Section 1-201(b)(3).
"Between merchants".	Section 2-104(3).
"Lease agreement".	Section 2A-103(1)(k).
"Lease contract".	Section 2A-103(1)(*l*).
"Merchant".	Section 2-104(1).
"Notification".	Section 1-202(d).
"Party".	Section 1-201(b)(26).
"Record".	Section 1-201(b)(31).
"Signed".	Section 1-201(b)(37).
"Term".	Section 1-201(b)(40).

Section 2A-209. Lessee Under Finance Lease as Beneficiary of Supply Contract

(1) The benefit of a supplier's promises to the lessor under the supply contract and of all warranties, whether express or implied, including those of any third party provided in connection with or as part of the supply contract, extends to the lessee to the extent of the lessee's leasehold interest under a finance lease related to the supply contract, but is subject to the terms of the warranty and of the supply contract and all defenses or claims arising therefrom.

(2) The extension of the benefit of a supplier's promises and of warranties to the lessee (Section 2A-209(1)) does not: (i) modify the rights and obligations of the parties to the supply contract, whether arising therefrom or otherwise, or (ii) impose any duty or liability under the supply contract on the lessee.

(3) Any modification or rescission of the supply contract by the supplier and the lessor is effective between the supplier and the lessee unless, before the modification or rescission, the supplier has received notice that the lessee has entered into a finance lease related to the supply contract. If the modification or rescission is effective between the supplier and the lessee, the lessor is deemed to have assumed, in addition to the obligations of the lessor to the lessee under the lease contract, promises of the supplier to the lessor and warranties that were so modified or rescinded as they existed and were available to the lessee before modification or rescission.

(4) In addition to the extension of the benefit of the supplier's promises and of warranties to the lessee under subsection (1), the lessee retains all rights that the lessee may have against the supplier which arise from an agreement between the lessee and the supplier or under other law.

Official Comment

Uniform Statutory Source: None.

Changes: This section is modeled on former Section 9-318 (now codified as Sections 9-404 through 9-406), the Restatement (Second) of Contracts §§ 302-315 (1981), and leasing practices. *See Earman Oil Co. v. Burroughs Corp.*, 625 F.2d 1291, 1296-97 (5th Cir. 1980).

Purposes:

1. The function performed by the lessor in a finance lease is extremely limited. Section 2A-103(1)(g). The lessee looks to the supplier of the goods for warranties and the like or, in some cases as to warranties, to the manufacturer if a warranty made by that person is passed on. That expectation is reflected in subsection (1), which is self-executing. As a matter of policy, the operation of this provision may not be excluded, modified or limited; however, an exclusion, modification, or limitation of any term of the supply contract or warranty, including any with respect to rights and remedies, and any defense or claim such as a statute of limitations, effective against the lessor as the acquiring party under the supply contract, is also effective against the lessee as the beneficiary designated under this provision. For example, the supplier is not precluded from excluding or modifying an express or implied warranty under a supply contract. Sections 2-312(2) and 2-316, or Section 2A-214. Further, the supplier is not precluded from limiting the rights and remedies of the lessor and from liquidating damages. Sections 2-718 and 2-719 or Sections 2A-503 and 2A-504. If the supply contract excludes or modifies warranties, limits remedies, or liquidates damages with respect to the lessor, such provisions are enforceable against the lessee as beneficiary. Thus, only selective discrimination against the beneficiaries designated under this section is precluded, i.e., exclusion of the supplier's liability to the lessee with respect to warranties made to the lessor. This section does not affect the development of other law with respect to products liability.

2. Enforcement of this benefit is by action. Sections 2A-103(4) and 1-305.

3. The benefit extended by these provisions is not without a price, as this Article also provides in the case of a finance lease that is not a consumer lease that the lessee's promises to the lessor under the lease contract become irrevocable and independent upon the lessee's acceptance of the goods. Section 2A-407.

4. Subsection (2) limits the effect of subsection (1) on the supplier and the lessor by preserving, notwithstanding the transfer of the benefits of the supply contract to the lessee, all of the supplier's and the lessor's rights and obligations with respect to each other and others; it further absolves the lessee of any duties with respect to the supply contract that might have been inferred from the extension of the benefits thereof.

5. Subsections (2) and (3) also deal with difficult issues related to modification or rescission of the supply contract. Subsection (2) states a rule that determines the impact of the statutory extension of benefit contained in subsection (1) upon the relationship of the parties to the supply contract and, in a limited respect, upon the lessee. This statutory extension of benefit, like that contained in Sections 2A-216 and 2-318, is not a modification of the supply contract by the parties. Thus, subsection (3) states the rules that apply to a modification or rescission of the supply contract by the parties. Subsection (3) provides that a modification or rescission is not effective between the supplier and the lessee if, before the modification or rescission occurs, the supplier received notice that the lessee has entered into the finance lease. On the other hand, if the modification or rescission is effective, then to the extent of the modification or rescission of the benefit or warranty, the lessor by statutory dictate assumes an obligation to provide to the lessee that which the lessee would otherwise lose. For example, assume a reduction in an express warranty from 4 years to 1 year. No prejudice to the lessee may occur if the goods perform as agreed. If, however, there is a breach of the express warranty after one year and before four years pass, the lessor is liable. A remedy for any prejudice to the lessee because of the bifurcation of the lessee's recourse resulting from the action of the supplier and the lessor is left to resolution by the courts based on the facts of each case.

6. Subsection (4) makes it clear that the rights granted to the lessee by this section do not displace any rights the lessee otherwise may have against the supplier.

Cross References:

Sections 1-305(b), 2-312(2), 2-316, 2-318, 2-718, 2-719, 2A-103(1)(g), 2A-103(4), 2A-214, 2A-216, 2A-407, 2A-503, 2A-504, 9-404, 9-405, and 9-406.

Definitional Cross References:

"Action".	Section 1-201(b)(1).
"Finance lease".	Section 2A-103(1)(g).
"Leasehold interest".	Section 2A-103(1)(m).
"Lessee".	Section 2A-103(1)(n).
"Lessor".	Section 2A-103(1)(p).
"Notice".	Section 1-202(a).
"Party".	Section 1-201(b)(26).
"Rights".	Section 1-201(b)(34).
"Supplier".	Section 2A-103(1)(x).
"Supply contract".	Section 2A-103(1)(y).
"Term".	Section 1-201(b)(40).

Section 2A-210. Express Warranties

(1) Express warranties by the lessor are created as follows:

(a) Any affirmation of fact or promise made by the lessor to the lessee which relates to the goods and becomes part of the basis of the bargain creates an express warranty that the goods will conform to the affirmation or promise.

(b) Any description of the goods which is made part of the basis of the bargain creates an express warranty that the goods will conform to the description.

(c) Any sample or model that is made part of the basis of the bargain creates an express warranty that the whole of the goods will conform to the sample or model.

(2) It is not necessary to the creation of an express warranty that the lessor use formal words, such as "warrant" or "guarantee," or that the lessor have a specific intention to make a warranty, but an affirmation merely of the value of the goods or a statement purporting to be merely the lessor's opinion or commendation of the goods does not create a warranty.

Official Comment

Uniform Statutory Source: Section 2-313.

Changes: Revised to reflect leasing practices and terminology.

Purposes: All of the express and implied warranties of the Article on Sales (Article 2) are included in this Article, revised to reflect the differences between a sale of goods and a lease of goods. Sections 2A-210 through 2A-216. The lease of goods is sufficiently similar to the sale of goods to justify this decision. William D. Hawkland, The Impact of the Uniform Commercial Code on Equipment Leasing, 1972 Ill.L.F. 446, 459-60. Many state and federal courts have reached the same conclusion.

Value of the goods, as used in subsection (2), includes rental value.

Cross References:

Sections 2-313 and 2A-210 through 2A-216.

Definitional Cross References:

"Conforming".	Section 2A-103(1)(d).
"Goods".	Section 2A-103(1)(h).
"Lessee".	Section 2A-103(1)(n).
"Lessor".	Section 2A-103(1)(p).
"Value".	Section 1-204.

Section 2A-211. Warranties Against Interference and Against Infringement; Lessee's Obligation Against Infringement

(1) There is in a lease contract a warranty that for the lease term no person holds a claim to or interest in the goods that arose from an act or omission of the lessor, other than a claim by way of infringement or the like, which will interfere with the lessee's enjoyment of its leasehold interest.

(2) Except in a finance lease there is in a lease contract by a lessor who is a merchant regularly dealing in goods of the kind a warranty that the goods are delivered free of the rightful claim of any person by way of infringement or the like.

(3) A lessee who furnishes specifications to a lessor or a supplier shall hold the lessor and the supplier harmless against any claim by way of infringement or the like that arises out of compliance with the specifications.

Official Comment

Uniform Statutory Source: Section 2-312.

Changes: This section is modeled on the provisions of Section 2-312, with modifications to reflect the limited interest transferred by a lease contract and the total interest transferred by a sale. Section 2-312(2), which is omitted here, is incorporated in Section 2A-214. The warranty of quiet possession was abolished with respect to sales of goods. Section 2-312 official Comment 1. Section 2A-211(1) reinstates the warranty of quiet possession with respect to leases. Inherent in the nature of the limited interest transferred by the lease—the right to possession and use of the goods—is the need of the lessee for protection greater than that afforded to the buyer. Since the scope of the protection is limited to claims or interests that arose from acts or omissions of the lessor, the lessor will be in position to evaluate the potential cost, certainly a far better position than that enjoyed by the lessee. Further, to the extent the market will allow, the lessor can attempt to pass on the anticipated additional cost to the lessee in the guise of higher rent.

Purposes: General language was chosen for subsection (1) that expresses the essence of the lessee's expectation: with an exception for infringement and the like, no person holding a claim or interest that arose from an act or omission of the lessor will be able to interfere with the lessee's use and enjoyment of the goods for the lease term. Subsection (2), like other similar provisions in later sections, excludes the finance lessor from extending this warranty; with few exceptions (Sections 2A-210 and 2A-211(1)), the lessee under a finance lease is to look to the supplier for warranties and the like or, in some cases as to warranties, to the manufacturer if a warranty made by that person is passed on. Subsections (2) and (3) are derived from Section 2-312(3). These subsections, as well as the analogue, should be construed so that applicable principles of law and equity supplement their provisions. Sections 2A-103(4) and 1-103(b).

Cross References:

Sections 1-103(b), 2-312, 2A-103(4), 2A-210 and 2A-214.

Definitional Cross References:

"Delivery".	Section 1-201(b)(15).
"Finance lease".	Section 2A-103(1)(g).
"Goods".	Section 2A-103(1)(h).
"Lease".	Section 2A-103(1)(j).
"Lease contract".	Section 2A-103(1)(*l*).
"Leasehold interest".	Section 2A-103(1)(m).
"Lessee".	Section 2A-103(1)(n).
"Lessor".	Section 2A-103(1)(p).
"Merchant".	Section 2-104(1).
"Person".	Section 1-201(b)(27).
"Supplier".	Section 2A-103(1)(x).

Section 2A-212. Implied Warranty of Merchantability

(1) Except in a finance lease, a warranty that the goods will be merchantable is implied in a lease contract

if the lessor is a merchant with respect to goods of that kind.

(2) Goods to be merchantable must be at least such as

(a) pass without objection in the trade under the description in the lease agreement;

(b) in the case of fungible goods, are of fair average quality within the description;

(c) are fit for the ordinary purposes for which goods of that type are used;

(d) run, within the variation permitted by the lease agreement, of even kind, quality, and quantity within each unit and among all units involved;

(e) are adequately contained, packaged, and labeled as the lease agreement may require; and

(f) conform to any promises or affirmations of fact made on the container or label.

(3) Other implied warranties may arise from course of dealing or usage of trade.

Official Comment

Uniform Statutory Source: Section 2-314.

Changes: Revised to reflect leasing practices and terminology. *E.g., Glenn Dick Equip. Co. v. Galey Constr., Inc.*, 541 P.2d 1184, 1193 (Idaho 1975) (implied warranty of merchantability (Article 2) extends to lease transactions).

Definitional Cross References:

"Conforming".	Section 2A-103(1)(d).
"Course of dealing".	Section 1-303(b).
"Finance lease".	Section 2A-103(1)(g).
"Fungible goods".	Section 1-201(b)(18).
"Goods".	Section 2A-103(1)(h).
"Lease agreement".	Section 2A-103(1)(k).
"Lease contract".	Section 2A-103(1)(*l*).
"Lessor".	Section 2A-103(1)(p).
"Merchant".	Section 2-104(1).
"Usage of trade".	Section 1-303(c).

Section 2A-213. Implied Warranty of Fitness for Particular Purpose

Except in a finance lease, if the lessor at the time the lease contract is made has reason to know of any particular purpose for which the goods are required and that the lessee is relying on the lessor's skill or judgment to select or furnish suitable goods, there is in the lease contract an implied warranty that the goods will be fit for that purpose.

Official Comment

Uniform Statutory Source: Section 2-315.

Changes: Revised to reflect leasing practices and terminology. E.g., *All-States Leasing Co. v. Bass*, 538 P.2d 1177, 1183 (Idaho 1975) (implied warranty of fitness for a particular purpose (Article 2) extends to lease transactions).

Definitional Cross References:

"Finance lease".	Section 2A-103(1)(l).
"Goods".	Section 2A-103(1)(n).
"Knows".	Section 1-202(b).
"Lease contract".	Section 2A-103(1)(r).
"Lessee".	Section 2A-103(1)(t).
"Lessor".	Section 2A-103(1)(v).

Section 2A-214. Exclusion or Modification of Warranties

(1) Words or conduct relevant to the creation of an express warranty and words or conduct tending to negate or limit a warranty must be construed wherever reasonable as consistent with each other; but, subject to the provisions of Section 2A-202 on parol or extrinsic evidence, negation or limitation is inoperative to the extent that the construction is unreasonable.

(2) Subject to subsection (3), to exclude or modify the implied warranty of merchantability or any part of it the language must mention "merchantability", be by a writing, and be conspicuous. Subject to subsection (3), to exclude or modify any implied warranty of fitness the exclusion must be by a writing and be conspicuous. Language to exclude all implied warranties of fitness is sufficient if it is in writing, is conspicuous and states, for example, "There is no warranty that the goods will be fit for a particular purpose".

(3) Notwithstanding subsection (2), but subject to subsection (4),

(a) unless the circumstances indicate otherwise, all implied warranties are excluded by expressions like "as is," or "with all faults," or by other language that in common understanding calls the lessee's attention to the exclusion of warranties and makes plain that there is no implied warranty, if in writing and conspicuous;

(b) if the lessee before entering into the lease contract has examined the goods or the sample or model as fully as desired or has refused to examine the goods, there is no implied warranty with regard to defects that an examination ought in the circumstances to have revealed; and

(c) an implied warranty may also be excluded or modified by course of dealing, course of performance, or usage of trade.

(4) To exclude or modify a warranty against interference or against infringement (Section 2A-211) or any part of it, the language must be specific, be by a writing, and be conspicuous, unless the circumstances, including

course of performance, course of dealing, or usage of trade, give the lessee reason to know that the goods are being leased subject to a claim or interest of any person.

Official Comment

Uniform Statutory Source: Sections 2-316 and 2-312(2).

Changes: Subsection (2) requires that a disclaimer of the warranty of merchantability be conspicuous and in writing as is the case for a disclaimer of the warranty of fitness; this is contrary to the rule stated in Section 2-316(2) with respect to the disclaimer of the warranty of merchantability. This section also provides that to exclude or modify the implied warranty of merchantability, fitness or against interference or infringement the language must be in writing and conspicuous. There are, however, exceptions to the rule. E.g., course of dealing, course of performance, or usage of trade may exclude or modify an implied warranty. Section 2A-214(3)(c). The analogue of Section 2-312(2) has been moved to subsection (4) of this section for a more unified treatment of disclaimers; there is no policy with respect to leases of goods that would justify continuing certain distinctions found in the Article on Sales (Article 2) regarding the treatment of the disclaimer of various warranties. Compare Sections 2-312(2) and 2-316(2). Finally, the example of a disclaimer of the implied warranty of fitness stated in subsection (2) differs from the analogue stated in Section 2-316(2); this example should promote a better understanding of the effect of the disclaimer.

Purposes:

1. These changes were made to reflect leasing practices. E.g., *FMC Finance Corp. v. Murphree,* 632 F.2d 413, 418 (5th Cir. 1980) (disclaimer of implied warranty under lease transactions must be conspicuous and in writing). The omission of the provisions of Section 2-316(4) was not substantive. Sections 2A-503 and 2A-504.

2. As to the use of a record other than a writing and communications that are not written, see Section 2A-103, Comment (g). Whether a term is conspicuous, including a term in a record other than a writing, is discussed in Section 1-201, Comment 10.

Cross References:

Sections 1-201(b)(10), 2-312(2), 2-316, 2A-202, 2A-211, 2A-503, and 2A-504.

Definitional Cross References:

"Conspicuous".	Section 1-201(b)(10).
"Course of dealing".	Section 1-303(b).
"Fault".	Section 2A-103(1)(f).
"Goods".	Section 2A-103(1)(h).
"Knows".	Section 1-202(b).
"Lease".	Section 2A-103(1)(j).
"Lease contract".	Section 2A-103(1)(*l*).
"Lessee".	Section 2A-103(1)(n).
"Person".	Section 1-201(b)(27).
"Usage of trade".	Section 1-303(c).
"Writing".	Section 1-201(b)(43).

Section 2A-215. Cumulation and Conflict of Warranties Express or Implied

Warranties, whether express or implied, must be construed as consistent with each other and as cumulative, but if that construction is unreasonable, the intention of the parties determines which warranty is dominant. In ascertaining that intention the following rules apply:

(a) Exact or technical specifications displace an inconsistent sample or model or general language of description.

(b) A sample from an existing bulk displaces inconsistent general language of description.

(c) Express warranties displace inconsistent implied warranties other than an implied warranty of fitness for a particular purpose.

Official Comment

Uniform Statutory Source: Section 2-317.

Definitional Cross Reference:

"Party". Section 1-201(b)(26).

Section 2A-216. Third-Party Beneficiaries of Express and Implied Warranties

ALTERNATIVE A

A warranty to or for the benefit of a lessee under this Article, whether express or implied, extends to any natural person who is in the family or household of the lessee or who is a guest in the lessee's home if it is reasonable to expect that such person may use, consume, or be affected by the goods and who is injured in person by breach of the warranty. This section does not displace principles of law and equity that extend a warranty to or for the benefit of a lessee to other persons. The operation of this section may not be excluded, modified, or limited, but an exclusion, modification, or limitation of the warranty, including any with respect to rights and remedies, effective against the lessee is also effective against any beneficiary designated under this section.

ALTERNATIVE B

A warranty to or for the benefit of a lessee under this Article, whether express or implied, extends to any natural person who may reasonably be expected to use, consume, or be affected by the goods and who is injured in person by breach of the warranty. This section does not displace principles of law and equity that extend a warranty to or for the benefit of a lessee to other persons. The operation of this section may not be excluded, modified, or limited, but an exclusion, modification, or limitation of the warranty, including any with respect to rights and remedies, effective against the lessee is also effective against the beneficiary designated under this section.

ALTERNATIVE C

A warranty to or for the benefit of a lessee under this Article, whether express or implied, extends to any person who may reasonably be expected to use, consume, or be affected by the goods and who is injured by breach of the warranty. The operation of this section may not be excluded, modified, or limited with respect to injury to the person of an individual to whom the warranty extends, but an exclusion, modification, or limitation of the warranty, including any with respect to rights and remedies, effective against the lessee is also effective against the beneficiary designated under this section.

Official Comment

Uniform Statutory Source: Section 2-318.

Changes: The provisions of Section 2-318 have been included in this section, modified in two respects: first, to reflect leasing practice, including the special practices of the lessor under a finance lease; second, to reflect and thus codify elements of the Official Comment to Section 2-318 with respect to the effect of disclaimers and limitations of remedies against third parties.

Purposes: Alternative A is based on the 1962 version of Section 2-318 and is least favorable to the injured person as the doctrine of privity imposed by other law is abrogated to only a limited extent. Alternatives B and C are based on later additions to Section 2-318 and are more favorable to the injured person. In determining which alternative to select, the state legislature should consider making its choice parallel to the choice it made with respect to Section 2-318, as interpreted by the courts.

The last sentence of each of Alternatives A, B and C does not preclude the lessor from excluding or modifying an express or implied warranty under a lease. Section 2A-214. Further, that sentence does not preclude the lessor from limiting the rights and remedies of the lessee and from liquidating damages. Sections 2A-503 and 2A-504. If the lease excludes or modifies warranties, limits remedies for breach, or liquidates damages with respect to the lessee, such provisions are enforceable against the beneficiaries designated under this section. However, this last sentence forbids selective discrimination against the beneficiaries designated under this section, i.e., exclusion of the lessor's liability to the beneficiaries with respect to warranties made by the lessor to the lessee.

Other law, including the Article on Sales (Article 2), may apply in determining the extent to which a warranty to or for the benefit of the lessor extends to the lessee and third parties. This is in part a function of whether the lessor has bought or leased the goods.

This Article does not purport to change the development of the relationship of the common law, with respect to products liability, including strict liability in tort (as restated in Restatement (Second) of Torts, § 402A (1965)), to the provisions of this Act. Compare *Cline v. Prowler Indus. of Maryland*, 418 A.2d 968 (Del.1980) and *Hawkins Constr. Co. v. Matthews Co.*, 209 N.W.2d 643 (Neb. 1973) with *Dippel v. Sciano*, 155 N.W.2d 55 (Wis. 1967).

Cross References:

Sections 2-318, 2A-214, 2A-503, and 2A-504.

Definitional Cross References:

"Goods".	Section 2A-103(1)(h).
"Lessee".	Section 2A-103(1)(n).
"Person".	Section 1-201(b)(27).
"Remedy".	Section 1-201(b)(32).
"Right".	Section 1-201(b)(34).

Section 2A-217. Identification

Identification of goods as goods to which a lease contract refers may be made at any time and in any manner explicitly agreed to by the parties. In the absence of explicit agreement, identification occurs:

(a) when the lease contract is made if the lease contract is for a lease of goods that are existing and identified;

(b) when the goods are shipped, marked, or otherwise designated by the lessor as goods to which the lease contract refers, if the lease contract is for a lease of goods that are not existing and identified; or

(c) when the young are conceived, if the lease contract is for a lease of unborn young of animals.

Official Comment

Uniform Statutory Source: Section 2-501.

Changes: This section, together with Section 2A-218, is derived from the provisions of Section 2-501, with changes to reflect lease terminology; however, this section omits as irrelevant to leasing practice the treatment of special property.

Purposes: With respect to subsection (b) there is a certain amount of ambiguity in the reference to when goods are designated, e.g., when the lessor is both selling and leasing goods to the same lessee/buyer and has marked goods for delivery but has not distinguished between those related to the lease contract and those related to the sales contract. As in Section 2-501(1)(b), this issue has been left to be resolved by the courts, case by case.

Cross References:

Sections 2-501 and 2A-218.

Definitional Cross References:

"Agreement".	Section 1-201(b)(3).
"Goods".	Section 2A-103(1)(h).
"Lease".	Section 2A-103(1)(j).

"Lease contract".	Section 2A-103(1)(*l*).
"Lessor".	Section 2A-103(1)(p).
"Party".	Section 1-201(b)(26).

Section 2A-218. Insurance and Proceeds

(1) A lessee obtains an insurable interest when existing goods are identified to the lease contract even though the goods identified are nonconforming and the lessee has an option to reject them.

(2) If a lessee has an insurable interest only by reason of the lessor's identification of the goods, the lessor, until default or insolvency or notification to the lessee that identification is final, may substitute other goods for those identified.

(3) Notwithstanding a lessee's insurable interest under subsections (1) and (2), the lessor retains an insurable interest until an option to buy has been exercised by the lessee and risk of loss has passed to the lessee.

(4) Nothing in this section impairs any insurable interest recognized under any other statute or rule of law.

(5) The parties by agreement may determine that one or more parties have an obligation to obtain and pay for insurance covering the goods and by agreement may determine the beneficiary of the proceeds of the insurance.

Official Comment

Uniform Statutory Source: Section 2-501.

Changes: This section, together with Section 2A-217, is derived from the provisions of Section 2-501, with changes and additions to reflect leasing practices and terminology.

Purposes: Subsection (2) states a rule allowing substitution of goods by the lessor under certain circumstances, until default or insolvency of the lessor, or until notification to the lessee that identification is final. Subsection (3) states a rule regarding the lessor's insurable interest that, by virtue of the difference between a sale and a lease, necessarily is different from the rule stated in Section 2-501(2) regarding the seller's insurable interest. For this purpose the option to buy shall be deemed to have been exercised by the lessee when the resulting sale is closed, not when the lessee gives notice to the lessor. Further, subsection (5) is new and reflects the common practice of shifting the responsibility and cost of insuring the goods between the parties to the lease transaction.

Cross References:

Sections 2-501 and 2A-217.

Definitional Cross References:

"Agreement".	Section 1-201(b)(3).
"Buying".	Section 2A-103(1)(a).
"Conforming".	Section 2A-103(1)(d).
"Goods".	Section 2A-103(1)(h).
"Insolvent".	Section 1-201(b)(23).
"Lease contract".	Section 2A-103(1)(*l*).
"Lessee".	Section 2A-103(1)(n).
"Lessor".	Section 2A-103(1)(p).
"Notification".	Section 1-202(d).
"Party".	Section 1-201(b)(26).

Section 2A-219. Risk of Loss

(1) Except in the case of a finance lease, risk of loss is retained by the lessor and does not pass to the lessee. In the case of a finance lease, risk of loss passes to the lessee.

(2) Subject to the provisions of this Article on the effect of default on risk of loss (Section 2A-220), if risk of loss is to pass to the lessee and the time of passage is not stated, the following rules apply:

(a) If the lease contract requires or authorizes the goods to be shipped by carrier

(i) and it does not require delivery at a particular destination, the risk of loss passes to the lessee when the goods are duly delivered to the carrier; but

(ii) if it does require delivery at a particular destination and the goods are there duly tendered while in the possession of the carrier, the risk of loss passes to the lessee when the goods are there duly so tendered as to enable the lessee to take delivery.

(b) If the goods are held by a bailee to be delivered without being moved, the risk of loss passes to the lessee on acknowledgment by the bailee of the lessee's right to possession of the goods.

(c) In any case not within subsection (a) or (b), the risk of loss passes to the lessee on the lessee's receipt of the goods if the lessor, or, in the case of a finance lease, the supplier, is a merchant; otherwise the risk passes to the lessee on tender of delivery.

Official Comment

Uniform Statutory Source: Section 2-509(1) through (3).

Changes: Subsection (1) is new. The introduction to subsection (2) is new, but subparagraph (a) incorporates the provisions of Section 2-509(1); subparagraph (b) incorporates the provisions of Section 2-509(2) only in part, reflecting current practice in lease transactions.

Purposes: Subsection (1) states rules related to retention or passage of risk of loss consistent with current practice in lease transactions. The provisions of subsection (4) of Section 2-509 are not incorporated as they are not necessary. This section does not deal with responsibility for loss caused by the wrongful act of either the lessor or the lessee.

Cross References:

Sections 2-509(1), 2-509(2), 2-509(4), and 2A-220.

Definitional Cross References:

"Delivery".	Section 1-201(b)(15).
"Finance lease".	Section 2A-103(1)(g).
"Goods".	Section 2A-103(1)(h).
"Lease contract".	Section 2A-103(1)(*l*).
"Lessee".	Section 2A-103(1)(n).
"Lessor".	Section 2A-103(1)(p).
"Merchant".	Section 2-104(1).
"Receipt".	Section 2-103(1)(c).
"Rights".	Section 1-201(b)(34).
"Supplier".	Section 2A-103(1)(x).

Section 2A-220. Effect of Default on Risk of Loss

(1) Where risk of loss is to pass to the lessee and the time of passage is not stated:

(a) If a tender or delivery of goods so fails to conform to the lease contract as to give a right of rejection, the risk of their loss remains with the lessor, or, in the case of a finance lease, the supplier, until cure or acceptance.

(b) If the lessee rightfully revokes acceptance, he [or she], to the extent of any deficiency in his [or her] effective insurance coverage, may treat the risk of loss as having remained with the lessor from the beginning.

(2) Whether or not risk of loss is to pass to the lessee, if the lessee as to conforming goods already identified to a lease contract repudiates or is otherwise in default under the lease contract, the lessor, or, in the case of a finance lease, the supplier, to the extent of any deficiency in his [or her] effective insurance coverage may treat the risk of loss as resting on the lessee for a commercially reasonable time.

Official Comment

Uniform Statutory Source: Section 2-510.

Changes: Revised to reflect leasing practices and terminology. The rule in Section (1)(b) does not allow the lessee under a finance lease to treat the risk of loss as having remained with the supplier from the beginning. This is appropriate given the limited circumstances under which the lessee under a finance lease is allowed to revoke acceptance. Section 2A-517 and Section 2A-516 Comment.

Cross References:

Sections 2A-516 and 2A-517.

Definitional Cross References:

"Conforming".	Section 2A-103(1)(d).
"Delivery".	Section 1-201(b)(15).
"Finance lease".	Section 2A-103(1)(g).
"Goods".	Section 2A-103(1)(h).
"Lease contract".	Section 2A-103(1)(*l*).
"Lessee".	Section 2A-103(1)(n).
"Lessor".	Section 2A-103(1)(p).
"Reasonable time".	Section 1-205(a).
"Rights".	Section 1-201(34).
"Supplier".	Section 2A-103(1)(x).

Section 2A-221. Casualty to Identified Goods

If a lease contract requires goods identified when the lease contract is made, and the goods suffer casualty without fault of the lessee, the lessor or the supplier before delivery, or the goods suffer casualty before risk of loss passes to the lessee pursuant to the lease agreement or Section 2A-219, then:

(a) if the loss is total, the lease contract is avoided; and

(b) if the loss is partial or the goods have so deteriorated as to no longer conform to the lease contract, the lessee may nevertheless demand inspection and at his [or her] option either treat the lease contract as avoided or, except in a finance lease that is not a consumer lease, accept the goods with due allowance from the rent payable for the balance of the lease term for the deterioration or the deficiency in quantity but without further right against the lessor.

Official Comment

Uniform Statutory Source: Section 2-613.

Changes: Revised to reflect leasing practices and terminology.

Purpose: Due to the vagaries of determining the amount of due allowance (Section 2-613(b)), no attempt was made in subsection (b) to treat a problem unique to lease contracts and installment sales contracts: determining how to recapture the allowance, e.g., application to the first or last rent payments or allocation, *pro rata*, to all rent payments.

Cross Reference:

Section 2-613.

Definitional Cross References:

"Conforming".	Section 2A-103(1)(d).
"Consumer lease".	Section 2A-103(1)(e).
"Delivery".	Section 1-201(b)(15).
"Fault".	Section 2A-103(1)(f).
"Finance lease".	Section 2A-103(1)(g).
"Goods".	Section 2A-103(1)(h).
"Lease".	Section 2A-103(1)(j).
"Lease agreement".	Section 2A-103(1)(k).
"Lease contract".	Section 2A-103(1)(*l*).
"Lessee".	Section 2A-103(1)(n).
"Lessor".	Section 2A-103(1)(p).
"Rights".	Section 1-201(34).
"Supplier".	Section 2A-103(1)(x).

PART 3. EFFECT OF LEASE CONTRACT

Section 2A-301. Enforceability of Lease Contract

Except as otherwise provided in this Article, a lease contract is effective and enforceable according to its terms between the parties, against purchasers of the goods and against creditors of the parties.

Official Comment

Uniform Statutory Source: Section 9-201.

Changes: The first sentence of Section 9-201 was incorporated, modified to reflect leasing terminology. The second sentence of Section 9-201 was eliminated as not relevant to leasing practices.

Purposes:

1. This section establishes a general rule regarding the validity and enforceability of a lease contract. The lease contract is effective and enforceable between the parties and against third parties. Exceptions to this general rule arise where there is a specific rule to the contrary in this Article. Enforceability is, thus, dependent upon the lease contract meeting the requirements of the Statute of Frauds provisions of Section 2A-201. Enforceability is also a function of the lease contract conforming to the principles of construction and interpretation contained in the Article on General Provisions (Article 1). Section 2A-103(4).

2. The effectiveness or enforceability of the lease contract is not dependent upon the lease contract or any financing statement or the like being filed or recorded; however, the priority of the interest of a lessor of fixtures with respect to the interests of certain third parties in such fixtures is subject to the provisions of the Article on Secured Transactions (Article 9). Section 2A-309. Prior to the adoption of this Article filing or recording was not required with respect to leases, only for nominal leases that created security interests. Section 1-203 now more clearly distinguishes leases from transactions that create security interests. Those lessors who are concerned about whether the transaction creates a lease or a security interest will continue to file a protective financing statement. Section 9-506.

3. Hypothetical:

(a) In construing this section it is important to recognize its relationship to other sections in this Article. This is best demonstrated by reference to a hypothetical. Assume that on February 1, A, a manufacturer of combines and other farm equipment, leased a fleet of six combines to B, a corporation engaged in the business of farming, for a 12-month term. Under the lease agreement between A and B, A agreed to defer B's payment of the first 2 months' rent to April 1. On March 1, B recognized that it would need only four combines and thus subleased two combines to C for an 11-month term.

(b) This hypothetical raises a number of issues that are answered by the sections contained in this part. Since lease is defined to include sublease (Section 2A-103(1)(j) and (w)), this section provides that the prime lease between A and B and the sublease between B and C are enforceable in accordance with their terms, except as otherwise provided in this Article; that exception, in this case, is one of considerable scope.

(c) The separation of ownership, which is in A, and possession, which is in B with respect to four combines and which is in C with respect to two combines, is not relevant. Section 2A-302. A's interest in the six combines cannot be challenged simply because A parted with possession to B, who in turn parted with possession of some of the combines to C. Yet it is important to note that by the terms of Section 2A-302 this conclusion is subject to change if otherwise provided in this Article.

(d) B's entering the sublease with C raises an issue that is treated by this part. In a dispute over the leased combines A may challenge B's right to sublease. The rule is permissive as to transfers of interests under a lease contract, including subleases. Section 2A-303(2). However, the rule has two significant qualifications. If the prime lease contract between A and B prohibits B from subleasing the combines, or makes such a sublease an event of default, Section 2A-303(2) applies; thus, while B's interest under the prime lease may be transferred under the sublease to C, A may have a remedy pursuant to Section 2A-303(5). Absent a prohibition or default provision in the prime lease contract A might be able to argue that the sublease to C materially increases A's risk; thus, while B's interest under the prime lease may be transferred under the sublease to C, A may have a remedy pursuant to Section 2A-303(5). Section 2A-303(5)(b)(ii).

(e) Resolution of this issue is also a function of the section dealing with the sublease of goods by a prime lessee (Section 2A-305). Subsection (1) of Section 2A-305, which is subject to the rules of Section 2A-303 stated above, provides that C takes subject to the interest of A under the prime lease between A and B. However, there are two exceptions. First, if B is a merchant (Sections 2A-103(3) and 2-104(1)) dealing in goods of that kind and C is a sublessee in the ordinary course of business (Sections 2A-103(1)(o) and 2A-103(1)(n)), C takes free of the prime lease between A and B. Second, if B has rejected the six combines under the prime lease with A, and B disposes of the goods by sublease to C, C takes free of the prime lease if C can establish good faith. Section 2A-511(4).

(f) If the facts of this hypothetical are expanded and we assume that the prime lease obligated B to maintain the combines, an additional issue may be presented. Prior to entering the sublease, B, in satisfaction of its maintenance covenant, brought the two combines that it desired to sublease to a local independent dealer of A's. The dealer did the requested work for B. C inspected the combines on the dealer's lot after the work was completed. C signed the sublease with B 2 days later. C, however, was prevented from taking delivery of the two combines as B refused to pay the dealer's invoice for the repairs. The dealer furnished the repair service to B in the ordinary course of the dealer's business. If under applicable law the dealer has a lien on repaired goods in the dealer's possession, the dealer's lien will take priority over B's and C's interests and also should take priority over A's interest, depending upon the terms of the lease contract and the applicable law. Section 2A-306.

(g) Now assume that C is in financial straits and one of C's creditors obtains a judgment against C. If the creditor levies on C's subleasehold interest in the two combines, who will prevail? Unless the levying creditor also holds a lien covered by Section 2A-306, discussed above, the judgment creditor will take its interest subject to B's rights under the sublease and A's rights under the prime lease. Section 2A-307(1). The hypothetical becomes more complicated if we assume that B is in financial straits and B's creditor holds the judgment. Here the judgment creditor takes subject to the sublease unless the lien attached to the two combines before the sublease contract became enforceable. Section 2A-307(2)(a). However, B's judgment creditor cannot prime A's interest in the goods because, with respect to A, the judgment creditor is a creditor of B in its capacity as lessee under the prime lease between A and B. Thus, here the judgment creditor's interest is subject to the lease between A and B. Section 2A-307(1).

(h) Finally, assume that on April 1, B is unable to pay A the deferred rent then due under the prime lease, but that C is current in its payments under the sublease from B. What effect will B's default under the prime lease between A and B have on C's rights under the sublease between B and C? Section 2A-301 provides that a lease contract is effective against the creditors of either party. Since a lease contract includes a sublease contract (Section 2A-103(1)(*l*)), the sublease contract between B and C arguably could be enforceable against A, a prime lessor who has extended unsecured credit to B, the prime lessee/sublessor, if the sublease contract meets the requirements of Section 2A-201. However, the rule stated in Section 2A-301 is subject to other provisions in this Article. Under Section 2A-305, C, as sublessee, would take subject to the prime lease contract in most cases. Thus, B's default under the prime lease will in most cases lead to A's recovery of the goods from C. Section 2A-523. A and C could provide otherwise by agreement. Section 2A-311. C's recourse will be to assert a claim for damages against B. Sections 2A-211(1) and 2A-508.

4. Relationship between sections:

(a) As the analysis of the hypothetical demonstrates, Part 3 of the Article focuses on issues that relate to the enforceability of the lease contract (Sections 2A-301, 2A-302 and 2A-303) and to the priority of various claims to the goods subject to the lease contract (Sections 2A-304, 2A-305, 2A-306, 2A-307, 2A-308, 2A-309, 2A-310 and 2A-311).

(b) This section states a general rule of enforceability, which is subject to specific rules to the contrary stated elsewhere in the Article. Section 2A-302 negates any notion that the separation of title and possession is fraudulent as a rule of law. Finally, Section 2A-303 states rules with respect to the transfer of the lessor's interest (as well as the residual interest in the goods) or the lessee's interest under the lease contract. Qualifications are imposed as a function of various issues, including whether the transfer is the creation or enforcement of a security interest or one that is material to the other party to the lease contract. In addition, a system of rules is created to deal with the rights and duties among assignor, assignee and the other party to the lease contract.

(c) Sections 2A-304 and 2A-305 are twins that deal with good-faith transferees of goods subject to the lease contract. Section 2A-304 creates a set of rules with respect to transfers by the lessor of goods subject to a lease contract; the transferee considered is a subsequent lessee of the goods. The priority dispute covered here is between the subsequent lessee and the original lessee of the goods (or persons claiming through the original lessee). Section 2A-305 creates a set of rules with respect to transfers by the lessee of goods subject to a lease contract; the transferees considered are buyers of the goods or sublessees of the goods. The priority dispute covered here is between the transferee and the lessor of the goods (or persons claiming through the lessor).

(d) Section 2A-306 creates a rule with respect to priority disputes between holders of liens for services or materials furnished with respect to goods subject to a lease contract and the lessor or the lessee under that contract. Section 2A-307 creates a rule with respect to priority disputes between the lessee and creditors of the lessor and priority disputes between the lessor and creditors of the lessee.

(e) Section 2A-308 creates a series of rules relating to allegedly fraudulent transfers and preferences. The most significant rule is that set forth in subsection (3) which validates sale-leaseback transactions if the buyer-lessor can establish that he or she bought for value and in good faith.

(f) Sections 2A-309 and 2A-310 create a series of rules with respect to priority disputes between various third parties and a lessor of fixtures or accessions, respectively, with respect thereto.

(g) Finally, Section 2A-311 allows parties to alter the statutory priorities by agreement.

Cross References:

Sections 1-203, 2-104(1), 2A-103(1(j), 2A-103(1)(*l*), 2A-103(1)(n), 2A-103(1)(*o*), 2A-103(3), 2A-103(4), 2A-201, 2A-211(1), 2A-301 through 2A-303, 2A-303(2), 2A-303(5), 2A-304 through 2A-307, 2A-307(1), 2A-307(2)(a), 2A-308 through 2A-311, 2A-508, 2A-511(4), 2A-523, 9-201, and 9-505.

Definitional Cross References:

"Creditor".	Section 1-201(b)(13).
"Goods".	Section 2A-103(1)(h).
"Lease contract".	Section 2A-103(1)(*l*).
"Party".	Section 1-201(b)(26).
"Purchaser".	Section 1-201(b)(30).
"Term".	Section 1-201(b)(40).

Section 2A-302. Title to and Possession of Goods

Except as otherwise provided in this Article, each provision of this Article applies whether the lessor or a third party has title to the goods, and whether the lessor, the lessee, or a third party has possession of the goods, notwithstanding any statute or rule of law that possession or the absence of possession is fraudulent.

Official Comment

Uniform Statutory Source: Section 9-202.

Changes: Section 9-202 was modified to reflect leasing terminology and to clarify the law of leases with respect to fraudulent conveyances or transfers.

Purposes: The separation of ownership and possession of goods between the lessor and the lessee (or a third party) has created problems under certain fraudulent conveyance statutes. *See, e.g., In re Ludlum Enters.*, 510 F.2d 996 (5th Cir. 1975); *Suburbia Fed. Sav. & Loan Ass'n v. Bel-Air Conditioning Co.*, 385 So. 2d 1151 (Fla. Dist. Ct. App. 1980). This section provides, among other things, that separation of ownership and possession *per se* does not affect the enforceability of the lease contract. Sections 2A-301 and 2A-308.

Cross References:

Sections 2A-301, 2A-308, and 9-202.

Definitional Cross References:

"Goods". Section 2A-103(1)(h).
"Lessee". Section 2A-103(1)(n).
"Lessor". Section 2A-103(1)(p).

Section 2A-303. Alienability of Party's Interest Under Lease Contract or of Lessor's Residual Interest in Goods; Delegation of Performance; Transfer of Rights

(1) As used in this section, "creation of a security interest" includes the sale of a lease contract that is subject to Article 9, Secured Transactions, by reason of Section 9-109(a)(3).

(2) Except as provided in subsection (3) and Section 9-407, a provision in a lease agreement which (i) prohibits the voluntary or involuntary transfer, including a transfer by sale, sublease, creation or enforcement of a security interest, or attachment, levy, or other judicial process, of an interest of a party under the lease contract or of the lessor's residual interest in the goods, or (ii) makes such a transfer an event of default, gives rise to the rights and remedies provided in subsection (4), but a transfer that is prohibited or is an event of default under the lease agreement is otherwise effective.

(3) A provision in a lease agreement which (i) prohibits a transfer of a right to damages for default with respect to the whole lease contract or of a right to payment arising out of the transferor's due performance of the transferor's entire obligation, or (ii) makes such a transfer an event of default, is not enforceable, and such a transfer is not a transfer that materially impairs the prospect of obtaining return performance by, materially changes the duty of, or materially increases the burden or risk imposed on, the other party to the lease contract within the purview of subsection (4).

(4) Subject to subsection (3) and Section 9-407:

(a) if a transfer is made which is made an event of default under a lease agreement, the party to the lease contract not making the transfer, unless that party waives the default or otherwise agrees, has the rights and remedies described in Section 2A-501(2);

(b) if paragraph (a) is not applicable and if a transfer is made that (i) is prohibited under a lease agreement or (ii) materially impairs the prospect of obtaining return performance by, materially changes the duty of, or materially increases the burden or risk imposed on, the other party to the lease contract, unless the party not making the transfer agrees at any time to the transfer in the lease contract or otherwise, then, except as limited by contract, (i) the transferor is liable to the party not making the transfer for damages caused by the transfer to the extent that the damages could not reasonably be prevented by the party not making the transfer and (ii) a court having jurisdiction may grant other appropriate relief, including cancellation of the lease contract or an injunction against the transfer.

(5) A transfer of "the lease" or of "all my rights under the lease", or a transfer in similar general terms, is a transfer of rights and, unless the language or the circumstances, as in a transfer for security, indicate the contrary, the transfer is a delegation of duties by the transferor to the transferee. Acceptance by the transferee constitutes a promise by the transferee to perform those duties. The promise is enforceable by either the transferor or the other party to the lease contract.

(6) Unless otherwise agreed by the lessor and the lessee, a delegation of performance does not relieve the transferor as against the other party of any duty to perform or of any liability for default.

(7) In a consumer lease, to prohibit the transfer of an interest of a party under the lease contract or to make a transfer an event of default, the language must be specific, by a writing, and conspicuous.

Official Comment

Uniform Statutory Source: Sections 2-210 and 9-311.

Changes: The provisions of Sections 2-210 and 9-311 were incorporated in this section, with substantial modifications to reflect leasing terminology and practice and to harmonize the principles of the respective provisions, i.e. limitations on delegation of performance on the one hand and alienability of rights on the other. In addition, unlike Section 2-210 which deals only with voluntary transfers, this section deals with involuntary as well as voluntary transfers. Moreover, the principle of Section 9-318(4) denying effectiveness to contractual terms prohibiting assignments of receivables due and to become due also is implemented.

Purposes:

1. Subsection (2) states a rule, consistent with Section 9-401(b), that voluntary and involuntary transfers of an interest of a party under the lease contract or of the lessor's residual interest, including by way of the creation or enforcement of a security interest, are effective, notwithstanding a provision in the lease agreement prohibiting the transfer or making the transfer an event of default. Although the transfers are effective, the provision in the lease agreement is nevertheless enforceable, but only as provided in subsection (4). Under subsection (4) the prejudiced party is limited to the remedies on "default under the lease contract" in this Article and, except as limited by this Article, as provided in the lease agreement, if the transfer has been made an event of default. Section 2A-501(2). Usually, there will be a specific provision to this effect or a general provision making a breach of a covenant an event of default. In those cases where the transfer is prohibited, but not made an event of default, the prejudiced party may recover damages; or, if the damage remedy would be ineffective adequately to protect that party, the court can order cancellation of the lease contract or enjoin the transfer. This rule that such provisions generally are enforceable is subject to subsection (3) and Section 9-407, which make such provisions unenforceable in certain instances.

2. Under Section 9-407, a provision in a lease agreement which prohibits the creation or enforcement of a security interest, including sales of lease contracts subject to Article 9 (Section 9-109(a)(3)), or makes it an event of default is generally not enforceable, reflecting the policy of Section 9-406 and former Section 9-318(4).

3. Subsection (3) is based upon Section 2-210(2) and Section 9-406. It makes unenforceable a prohibition against transfers of certain rights to payment or a provision making the transfer an event of default. It also provides that such transfers do not materially impair the prospect of obtaining return performance by, materially change the duty of, or materially increase the burden or risk imposed on, the other party to the lease contract so as to give rise to the rights and remedies stated in subsection (4). Accordingly, a transfer of a right to payment cannot be prohibited or made an event of default, or be one that materially impairs performance, changes duties or increases risk, if the right is already due or will become due without further performance being required by the party to receive payment. Thus, a lessor can transfer the right to future payments under the lease contract, including by way of a grant of a security interest, and the transfer will not give rise to the rights and remedies stated in subsection (4) if the lessor has no remaining performance under the lease contract. The mere fact that the lessor is obligated to allow the lessee to remain in possession and to use the goods as long as the lessee is not in default does not mean that there is remaining performance on the part of the lessor. Likewise, the fact that the lessor has potential liability under a "non-operating" lease contract for breaches of warranty does not mean that there is remaining performance. In contrast, the lessor would have remaining performance under a lease contract requiring the lessor to regularly maintain and service the goods or to provide "upgrades" of the equipment on a periodic basis in order to avoid obsolescence. The basic distinction is between a mere potential duty to respond which is not remaining performance, and an affirmative duty to render stipulated performance. Although the distinction may be difficult to draw in some cases, it is instructive to focus on the difference between "operating" and "non-operating" leases as generally understood in the marketplace. Even if there is remaining performance under a lease contract, a transfer for security of a right to payment that is made an event of default or that is in violation of a prohibition against transfer does not give rise to the rights and remedies under subsection (4) if it does not constitute an actual delegation of a material performance under Section 9-407.

4. The application of either the rule of Section 9-407 or the rule of subsection (3) to the grant by the lessor of a security interest in the lessor's right to future payment under the lease contract may produce the same result. Both provisions generally protect security transfers by the lessor in particular because the creation by the lessor of a security interest or the enforcement of that interest generally will not prejudice the lessee's rights if it does not result in a delegation of the lessor's duties. To the contrary, the receipt of loan proceeds or relief from the enforcement of an antecedent debt normally should enhance the lessor's ability to perform its duties under the lease contract. Nevertheless, there are circumstances where relief might be justified. For example, if ownership of the goods is transferred pursuant to enforcement of a security interest to a party whose ownership would prevent the lessee from continuing to possess the goods, relief might be warranted. See 49 U.S.C. § 1401(a) and (b) which places limitations on the operation of aircraft in the United States based on the citizenship or corporate qualification of the registrant.

5. Relief on the ground of material prejudice when the lease agreement does not prohibit the transfer or make it an event of default should be afforded only in extreme circumstances, considering the fact that the party asserting material prejudice did not insist upon a provision in the lease agreement that would protect against such a transfer.

6. Subsection (4) implements the rule of subsection (2). Subsection (2) provides that, even though a transfer is effective, a provision in the lease agreement prohibiting it or making it an event of default may be enforceable as provided in subsection (4). See *Brummund v. First Nat'l Bank of Clovis*, 656 P.2d 884 (N.M. 1983), stating the analogous rule for former Section 9-311 (now Section 9-401). If the transfer prohibited by the lease agreement is made an event of default, then, under subsection (4)(a), unless the default is waived or there is an agreement otherwise, the aggrieved party has the rights and remedies referred to in Section 2A-501(2), viz. those in this Article and, except as limited in the Article, those provided in the lease agreement. In the unlikely circumstance that the lease agreement prohibits the transfer without making a violation of the prohibition an event of default or, even if there is no prohibition against the transfer, and the transfer is one that materially impairs performance, changes duties, or increases risk (for example, a sublease or assignment to a party using the goods improperly or for an illegal purpose), then subsection (4)(b) is applicable. In that circumstance, unless the party aggrieved by the transfer has otherwise agreed in the lease contract, such as by assenting to a particular transfer or to transfers in general, or agrees in some other manner, the aggrieved party has the right to recover damages from the transferor and a court may, in appropriate circumstances, grant other relief, such as cancellation of the lease contract or an injunction against the transfer.

7. If a transfer gives rise to the rights and remedies provided in subsection (4), the transferee as an alternative may propose, and the other party may accept, adequate cure or compensation for past defaults and adequate assurance of future due performance under the lease contract. Subsection (4) does not preclude any other relief that may be available to a party to the lease contract aggrieved by a transfer subject to an enforceable prohibition, such as an action for interference with contractual relations.

8. Subsection (8) requires that a provision in a consumer lease prohibiting a transfer, or making it an event of default, must be specific, written and conspicuous. See Section 1-201(b)(10). This assists in protecting a consumer lessee against surprise assertions of default.

9. Subsection (6) is taken almost verbatim from the provisions of Section 2-210(5). The subsection states a rule of construction that distinguishes a commercial assignment, which substitutes the assignee for the assignor as to rights and duties, and an assignment for security or financing assignment, which substitutes the assignee for the assignor only as to rights. Note that the assignment for security or financing assignment is a subset of all security interests. Security interest is defined to include "any interest of a buyer of . . . chattel paper". Section 1-201(b)(35). Chattel paper is defined to include the right to payment arising under certain leases of specific goods. Section 9-102(a)(11). Thus, a buyer of the lessor's rights under such leases is the holder of a security interest in the leases. That conclusion should not influence this issue, as the policy is quite different. Whether a buyer of the lessor's right to payment under leases of goods is the holder of a commercial assignment, or an assignment for security or financing assignment should be determined by the language of the assignment or the circumstances of the assignment.

10. As to the use of a record other than a writing and communications that are not written, see Section 2A-103, Comment (g).

Cross References:

Sections 1-201(b)(10), 1-201(b)(35), 2-210, 2A-501(2), 9-102(a)(11), 9-109(a)(3), 9-401, 9-406, and 9-407.

Definitional Cross References:

"Agreement".	Section 1-201(b)(3).
"Conspicuous".	Section 1-201(b)(10).
"Consumer lease".	Section 2A-103(1)(e).
"Goods".	Section 2A-103(1)(h).
"Lease".	Section 2A-103(1)(j).
"Lease contract".	Section 2A-103(1)(*l*).
"Lessee".	Section 2A-103(1)(n).
"Lessor".	Section 2A-103(1)(p).
"Lessor's residual interest".	Section 2A-103(1)(q).
"Notice".	Section 1-202(a).
"Party".	Section 1-201(26).
"Person".	Section 1-201(27).
"Reasonable time".	Sections 1-205(a).
"Rights".	Section 1-201(34).
"Term".	Section 1-201(40).
"Writing".	Section 1-201(43).

Section 2A-304. Subsequent Lease of Goods by Lessor

(1) Subject to Section 2A-303, a subsequent lessee from a lessor of goods under an existing lease contract obtains, to the extent of the leasehold interest transferred, the leasehold interest in the goods that the lessor had or had power to transfer, and except as provided in subsection (2) and Section 2A-527(4), takes subject to the existing lease contract. A lessor with voidable title has power to transfer a good leasehold interest to a good faith subsequent lessee for value, but only to the extent set forth in the preceding sentence. If goods have been delivered under a transaction of purchase, the lessor has that power even though:

(a) the lessor's transferor was deceived as to the identity of the lessor;

(b) the delivery was in exchange for a check which is later dishonored;

(c) it was agreed that the transaction was to be a "cash sale"; or

(d) the delivery was procured through fraud punishable as larcenous under the criminal law.

(2) A subsequent lessee in the ordinary course of business from a lessor who is a merchant dealing in goods of that kind to whom the goods were entrusted by the existing lessee of that lessor before the interest of the subsequent lessee became enforceable against that lessor obtains, to the extent of the leasehold interest transferred, all of that lessor's and the existing lessee's rights to the goods, and takes free of the existing lease contract.

(3) A subsequent lessee from the lessor of goods that are subject to an existing lease contract and are covered by a certificate of title issued under a statute of this State or of another jurisdiction takes no greater rights than those provided both by this section and by the certificate of title statute.

Official Comment

Uniform Statutory Source: Section 2-403.

Changes: While Section 2-403 was used as a model for this section, the provisions of Section 2-403 were significantly revised to reflect leasing practices and to integrate this Article with certificate of title statutes.

Purposes:

1. This section must be read in conjunction with, as it is subject to, the provisions of Section 2A-303, which govern voluntary and involuntary transfers of rights and duties under a lease contract, including the lessor's residual interest in the goods.

2. This section must also be read in conjunction with Section 2-403. This section and Section 2A-305 are derived from Section 2-403, which states a unified policy on good faith purchases of goods. Given the scope of the definition of purchaser (Section 1-201(b)(30)), a person who bought goods to lease as well as a person who bought goods subject to an existing lease from a lessor will take pursuant to Section 2-403. Further, a person who leases such goods from the person who bought them should also be protected under Section 2-403, first because the lessee's rights are derivative and second because the definition of purchaser should be interpreted to include one who takes by lease; no negative implication should be drawn from the inclusion of lease in the definition of purchase in this Article. Section 2A-103(1)(v).

3. There are hypotheticals that relate to an entrustee's unauthorized lease of entrusted goods to a third party that are outside the provisions of Sections 2-403, 2A-304 and 2A-305. Consider a sale of goods by M, a merchant, to B, a buyer. After paying for the goods B allows M to retain possession of the goods as B is short of storage. Before B calls for the goods M leases the goods to L, a lessee. This transaction is not governed by Section 2-403(2) as L is not a buyer in the ordinary course of business. Section 1-201(b)(9). Further, this transaction is not governed by Section 2A-304(2) as B is not an existing lessee. Finally, this transaction is not governed by Section 2A-305(2) as B is not M's lessor. Section 2A-307(2) resolves the potential dispute between B, M and L. By virtue of B's entrustment of the goods to M and M's lease of the goods to L, B has a cause of action against M under the common law. Sections 2A-103(4) and 1-103. See, e.g., Restatement (Second) of Torts §§ 222A-243. Thus, B is a creditor of M. Sections 2A-103(4) and 1-201(b)(13). Section 2A-307(2) provides that B, as M's creditor, takes subject to M's lease to L. Thus, if L does not default under the lease, L's enjoyment and possession of the goods should be undisturbed. However, B is not without recourse. B's action should result in a judgment against M providing, among other things, a turnover of all proceeds arising from M's lease to L, as well as a transfer of all of M's right, title and interest as lessor under M's lease to L, including M's residual interest in the goods. Section 2A-103(1)(q).

4. Subsection (1) states a rule with respect to the leasehold interest obtained by a subsequent lessee from a lessor of goods under an existing lease contract. The interest will include such leasehold interest as the lessor has in the goods as well as the leasehold interest that the lessor had the power to transfer. Thus, the subsequent lessee obtains unimpaired all rights acquired under the law of agency, apparent agency, ownership or other estoppel, whether based upon statutory provisions or upon case law principles. Sections 2A-103(4) and 1-103. In general, the subsequent lessee takes subject to the existing lease contract, including the existing lessee's rights thereunder. Furthermore, the subsequent lease contract is, of course, limited by its own terms, and the subsequent lessee takes only to the extent of the leasehold interest transferred thereunder.

5. Subsection (1) further provides that a lessor with voidable title has power to transfer a good leasehold interest to a good faith subsequent lessee for value. In addition, subsections (1)(a) through (d) provide specifically for the protection of the good faith subsequent lessee for value in a number of specific situations which have been troublesome under prior law.

6. The position of an existing lessee who entrusts leased goods to its lessor is not distinguishable from the position of other entrusters. Thus, subsection (2) provides that the subsequent lessee in the ordinary course of business takes free of the existing lease contract between the lessor entrustee and the lessee entruster, if the lessor is a merchant dealing in goods of that kind. Further, the subsequent lessee obtains all of the lessor entrustee's and the lessee entruster's rights to the goods, but only to the extent of the leasehold interest transferred by the lessor entrustee. Thus, the lessor entrustee retains the residual interest in the goods. Section 2A-103(1)(q). However, entrustment by the existing lessee must have occurred before the interest of the subsequent lessee became enforceable against the lessor. Entrusting is defined in Section 2-403(3) and that definition applies here. Section 2A-103(3).

7. Subsection (3) states a rule with respect to a transfer of goods from a lessor to a subsequent lessee where the goods are subject to an existing lease and covered by a certificate of title. The subsequent lessee's rights are no greater than those provided by this section and the applicable certificate of title statute, including any applicable case law construing such statute. Where the relationship between the certificate of title statute and Section 2-403, the statutory analogue to this section, has been construed by a court, that construction is incorporated here. Sections 2A-103(4) and 1-103. The better rule is that the certificate of title statutes are in harmony with Section 2-403 and thus would be in harmony with this section. E.g., *Atwood Chevrolet-Olds v. Aberdeen Mun. School Dist.*, 431 So.2d 926, 928 (Miss. 1983); *Godfrey v. Gilsdorf*, 476 P.2d 3, 6 (Nev. 1970); *Martin v. Nager*, 469 A.2d 519, 523 (N.J. Super. Ct. Ch. Div. 1983). Where the certificate of title statute is silent on this issue of transfer, this section will control.

Cross References:

Sections 1-103, 1-201(b)(9), (13), (30), 2-403, 2A-103(1)(q), (v), 2A-103(3), (4), 2A-303, 2A-305, 2A-527(4), and 2A-307(2).

Definitional Cross References:

"Agreement".	Section 1-201(b)(3).
"Delivery".	Section 1-201(15).
"Entrusting".	Section 2-403(3).
"Good faith".	Sections 1-201(b)(20).
"Goods".	Section 2A-103(1)(h).
"Lease".	Section 2A-103(1)(j).
"Lease contract".	Section 2A-103(1)(*l*).

"Leasehold interest".	Section 2A-103(1)(m).
"Lessee".	Section 2A-103(1)(n).
"Lessee in the ordinary course of business".	Section 2A-103(1)(o).
"Lessor".	Section 2A-103(1)(p).
"Merchant".	Section 2-104(1).
"Purchase".	Section 2A-103(1)(v).
"Right".	Section 1-201(34).
"Value".	Section 1-204.

Section 2A-305. Sale or Sublease of Goods by Lessee

(1) Subject to the provisions of Section 2A-303, a buyer or sublessee from the lessee of goods under an existing lease contract obtains, to the extent of the interest transferred, the leasehold interest in the goods that the lessee had or had power to transfer, and except as provided in subsection (2) and Section 2A-511(4), takes subject to the existing lease contract. A lessee with a voidable leasehold interest has power to transfer a good leasehold interest to a good faith buyer for value or a good faith sublessee for value, but only to the extent set forth in the preceding sentence. When goods have been delivered under a transaction of lease the lessee has that power even though:

(a) the lessor was deceived as to the identity of the lessee;

(b) the delivery was in exchange for a check which is later dishonored; or

(c) the delivery was procured through fraud punishable as larcenous under the criminal law.

(2) A buyer in the ordinary course of business or a sublessee in the ordinary course of business from a lessee who is a merchant dealing in goods of that kind to whom the goods were entrusted by the lessor obtains, to the extent of the interest transferred, all of the lessor's and lessee's rights to the goods, and takes free of the existing lease contract.

(3) A buyer or sublessee from the lessee of goods that are subject to an existing lease contract and are covered by a certificate of title issued under a statute of this State or of another jurisdiction takes no greater rights than those provided both by this section and by the certificate of title statute.

Official Comment

Uniform Statutory Source: Section 2-403.

Changes: While Section 2-403 was used as a model for this section, the provisions of Section 2-403 were significantly revised to reflect leasing practice and to integrate this Article with certificate of title statutes.

Purposes: This section, a companion to Section 2A-304, states the rule with respect to the leasehold interest obtained by a buyer or sublessee from a lessee of goods under an existing lease contract. Cf. Section 2A-304 Comment. Note that this provision is consistent with existing case law, which prohibits the bailee's transfer of title to a good faith purchaser for value under Section 2-403(1). *Rohweder v. Aberdeen Prod. Credit Ass'n*, 765 F.2d 109 (8th Cir. 1985).

Subsection (2) is also consistent with existing case law. *American Standard Credit, Inc. v. National Cement Co.*, 643 F.2d 248, 269-70 (5th Cir. 1981); but cf. *Exxon Co., U.S.A. v. TLW Computer Indus.*, 37 U.C.C.Rep.Serv. (Callaghan) 1052, 1057-58 (D. Mass. 1983). Unlike Section 2A-304(2), this subsection does not contain any requirement with respect to the time that the goods were entrusted to the merchant. In Section 2A-304(2) the competition is between two customers of the merchant lessor; the time of entrusting was added as a criterion to create additional protection to the customer who was first in time: the existing lessee. In subsection (2) the equities between the competing interests were viewed as balanced.

There appears to be some overlap between Section 2-403(2) and Section 2A-305(2) with respect to a buyer in the ordinary course of business. However, an examination of this Article's definition of buyer in the ordinary course of business (Section 2A-103(1)(a)) makes clear that this reference was necessary to treat entrusting in the context of a lease.

Subsection (3) states a rule of construction with respect to a transfer of goods from a lessee to a buyer or sublessee, where the goods are subject to an existing lease and covered by a certificate of title. Cf. Section 2A-304 Comment.

Cross References:

Sections 2-403, 2A-103(1)(a), 2A-304, and 2A-511(4).

Definitional Cross References:

"Buyer".	Section 2-103(1)(a).
"Buyer in the ordinary course of business".	Section 2A-103(1)(a).
"Delivery".	Section 1-201(b)(15).
"Entrusting".	Section 2-403(3).
"Good faith".	Sections 1-201(b)(20).
"Goods".	Section 2A-103(1)(h).
"Lease".	Section 2A-103(1)(j).
"Lease contract".	Section 2A-103(1)(*l*).
"Leasehold interest."	Section 2A-103(1)(m).
"Lessee".	Section 2A-103(1)(n).
"Lessee in the ordinary course of business".	Section 2A-103(1)(o).
"Lessor".	Section 2A-103(1)(p).
"Merchant".	Section 2-104(1).
"Right".	Section 1-201(b)(34).
"Sale".	Section 2-106(1).
"Sublease".	Section 2A-103(1)(w).
"Value".	Section 1-204.

Section 2A-306. Priority of Certain Liens Arising by Operation of Law

If a person in the ordinary course of his [or her] business furnishes services or materials with respect to goods subject to a lease contract, a lien upon those goods in the possession of that person given by statute or rule of law for those materials or services takes priority over any interest of the lessor or lessee under the lease contract or this Article unless the lien is created by statute and the statute provides otherwise or unless the lien is created by rule of law and the rule of law provides otherwise.

Official Comment

Uniform Statutory Source: Section 9-310.

Changes: The approach reflected in the provisions of Section 9-310 was included, but revised to conform to leasing terminology and to expand the exception to the special priority granted to protected liens to cover liens created by rule of law as well as those created by statute.

Purposes: This section should be interpreted to allow a qualified lessor or a qualified lessee to be the competing lienholder if the statute or rule of law so provides. The reference to statute includes applicable regulations and cases; these sources must be reviewed in resolving a priority dispute under this section.

Cross Reference:

Section 9-310.

Definitional Cross References:

"Goods".	Section 2A-103(1)(h).
"Lease contract".	Section 2A-103(1)(*l*).
"Lessee".	Section 2A-103(1)(n).
"Lessor".	Section 2A-103(1)(p).
"Lien".	Section 2A-103(1)(r).
"Person".	Section 1-201(b)(27).

Section 2A-307. Priority of Liens Arising by Attachment or Levy on, Security Interests in, and Other Claims to Goods

(1) Except as otherwise provided in Section 2A-306, a creditor of a lessee takes subject to the lease contract.

(2) Except as otherwise provided in subsection (3) and in Sections 2A-306 and 2A-308, a creditor of a lessor takes subject to the lease contract unless the creditor holds a lien that attached to the goods before the lease contract became enforceable.

(3) Except as otherwise provided in Sections 9-317, 9-321, and 9-323, a lessee takes a leasehold interest subject to a security interest held by a creditor of the lessor.

Official Comment

Uniform Statutory Source: None for subsection (1). Subsection (2) is derived from Section 9-301, and subsections (3) and (4) are derived from Section 9-307(1) and (3), respectively.

Changes: The provisions of Sections 9-301 and 9-307(1) and (3) were incorporated, and modified to reflect leasing terminology and the basic concepts reflected in this Article.

Purposes:

1. Subsection (1) states a general rule of priority that a creditor of the lessee takes subject to the lease contract. The term lessee (Section 2A-103(1)(n)) includes sublessee. Therefore, this subsection not only covers disputes between the prime lessor and a creditor of the prime lessee but also disputes between the prime lessor, or the sublessor, and a creditor of the sublessee. Section 2A-301, Comment 3(g). Further, by using the term creditor (Section 1-201(b)(13)), this subsection will cover disputes with a general creditor, a secured creditor, a lien creditor and any representative of creditors. Section 2A-103(4).

2. Subsection (2) states a general rule of priority that a creditor of a lessor takes subject to the lease contract. Note the discussion above with regard to the scope of these rules. Section 2A-301 Comment 3(g). Thus, the section will not only cover disputes between the prime lessee and a creditor of the prime lessor but also disputes between the prime lessee, or the sublessee, and a creditor of the sublessor.

3. To take priority over the lease contract, and the interests derived therefrom, the creditor must come within the exception stated in subsection (2) or within one of the provisions of Article 9 mentioned in subsection (3). Subsection (2) provides that where the creditor holds a lien (Section 2A-103(1)(r)) that attached before the lease contract became enforceable (Section 2A-301), the creditor does not take subject to the lease. Subsection (3) provides that a lessee takes its leasehold interest subject to a security interest except as otherwise provided in Sections 9-317, 9-321, or 9-323.

4. The rules of this section operate in favor of whichever party to the lease contract may enforce it, even if one party perhaps may not, e.g., under Section 2A-201(1)(b).

Cross References:

Sections 1-201(b)(13), 2A-103(1)(n), 2A-103(1)(r), 2A-103(4), 2A-201(1)(b), 2A-306, 2-308,, 9-317, 9-321, and 9-323.

Definitional Cross References:

"Creditor".	Section 1-201(b)(13).
"Goods".	Section 2A-103(1)(h).
"Knowledge" and	Section 1-202(b).
"Lease".	Section 2A-103(1)(j).
"Lease contract".	Section 2A-103(1)(*l*).
"Leasehold interest".	Section 2A-103(1)(m).
"Lessee".	Section 2A-103(1)(n).
"Lessee in the ordinary course of business".	Section 2A-103(1)(o).
"Lessor".	Section 2A-103(1)(p).
"Lien".	Section 2A-103(1)(r).
"Party".	Section 1-201(b)(26).
"Pursuant to commitment".	Section 2A-103(3).
"Security interest".	Section 1-201(b)(35).

Section 2A-308. Special Rights of Creditors

(1) A creditor of a lessor in possession of goods subject to a lease contract may treat the lease contract

as void if as against the creditor retention of possession by the lessor is fraudulent under any statute or rule of law, but retention of possession in good faith and current course of trade by the lessor for a commercially reasonable time after the lease contract becomes enforceable is not fraudulent.

(2) Nothing in this Article impairs the rights of creditors of a lessor if the lease contract (a) becomes enforceable, not in current course of trade but in satisfaction of or as security for a pre-existing claim for money, security, or the like, and (b) is made under circumstances which under any statute or rule of law apart from this Article would constitute the transaction a fraudulent transfer or voidable preference.

(3) A creditor of a seller may treat a sale or an identification of goods to a contract for sale as void if as against the creditor retention of possession by the seller is fraudulent under any statute or rule of law, but retention of possession of the goods pursuant to a lease contract entered into by the seller as lessee and the buyer as lessor in connection with the sale or identification of the goods is not fraudulent if the buyer bought for value and in good faith.

Official Comment

Uniform Statutory Source: Section 2-402(2) and (3)(b).

Changes: Rephrased and new material added to conform to leasing terminology and practice.

Purposes: Subsection (1) states a general rule of avoidance where the lessor has retained possession of goods if such retention is fraudulent under any statute or rule of law. However, the subsection creates an exception under certain circumstances for retention of possession of goods for a commercially reasonable time after the lease contract becomes enforceable.

Subsection (2) also preserves the possibility of an attack on the lease by creditors of the lessor if the lease was made in satisfaction of or as security for a preexisting claim, and would constitute a fraudulent transfer or voidable preference under other law.

Finally, subsection (3) states a new rule with respect to sale-leaseback transactions, i.e., transactions where the seller sells goods to a buyer but possession of the goods is retained by the seller pursuant to a lease contract between the buyer as lessor and the seller as lessee. Notwithstanding any statute or rule of law that would treat such retention as fraud, whether *per se, prima facie,* or otherwise, the retention is not fraudulent if the buyer bought for value (Section 1-204) and in good faith (Section 1-201(b)(20)). Section 2A-103(3) and (4). This provision overrides Section 2-402(2) to the extent it would otherwise apply to a sale-leaseback transaction.

Cross References:

Sections 1-201(b)(20), 1-204, 2-402(2), 2-402(3)(b), and 2A-103(3) and (4).

Definitional Cross References:

"Buyer".	Section 2-103(1)(a).
"Contract".	Section 1-201(b)(12).
"Creditor".	Section 1-201(b)(13).
"Good faith".	Section 1-201(b)(20).
"Goods".	Section 2A-103(1)(h).
"Lease contract".	Section 2A-103(1)(*l*).
"Lessee".	Section 2A-103(1)(n).
"Lessor".	Section 2A-103(1)(p).
"Money".	Section 1-201(b)(24).
"Reasonable time".	Section 1-205(a).
"Rights".	Section 1-201(b)(34).
"Sale".	Section 2-106(1).
"Seller".	Section 2-103(1)(d).
"Value".	Section 1-204.

Section 2A-309. Lessor's and Lessee's Rights When Goods Become Fixtures

(1) In this section:

(a) goods are "fixtures" when they become so related to particular real estate that an interest in them arises under real estate law;

(b) a "fixture filing" is the filing, in the office where a record of a mortgage on the real estate would be filed or recorded, of a financing statement covering goods that are or are to become fixtures and conforming to the requirements of Section 9-502(a) and (b);

(c) a lease is a "purchase money lease" unless the lessee has possession or use of the goods or the right to possession or use of the goods before the lease agreement is enforceable;

(d) a mortgage is a "construction mortgage" to the extent it secures an obligation incurred for the construction of an improvement on land including the acquisition cost of the land, if the recorded writing so indicates; and

(e) "encumbrance" includes real estate mortgages and other liens on real estate and all other rights in real estate that are not ownership interests.

(2) Under this Article a lease may be of goods that are fixtures or may continue in goods that become fixtures, but no lease exists under this Article of ordinary building materials incorporated into an improvement on land.

(3) This Article does not prevent creation of a lease of fixtures pursuant to real estate law.

(4) The perfected interest of a lessor of fixtures has priority over a conflicting interest of an encumbrancer or owner of the real estate if:

(a) the lease is a purchase money lease, the conflicting interest of the encumbrancer or owner arises before the goods become fixtures, the interest of the lessor is perfected by a fixture filing before the goods become fixtures or within ten days thereafter, and the lessee has an interest of record in the real estate or is in possession of the real estate; or

(b) the interest of the lessor is perfected by a fixture filing before the interest of the encumbrancer or owner is of record, the lessor's interest has priority over any conflicting interest of a predecessor in title of the encumbrancer or owner, and the lessee has an interest of record in the real estate or is in possession of the real estate.

(5) The interest of a lessor of fixtures, whether or not perfected, has priority over the conflicting interest of an encumbrancer or owner of the real estate if:

(a) the fixtures are readily removable factory or office machines, readily removable equipment that is not primarily used or leased for use in the operation of the real estate, or readily removable replacements of domestic appliances that are goods subject to a consumer lease, and before the goods become fixtures the lease contract is enforceable; or

(b) the conflicting interest is a lien on the real estate obtained by legal or equitable proceedings after the lease contract is enforceable; or

(c) the encumbrancer or owner has consented in writing to the lease or has disclaimed an interest in the goods as fixtures; or

(d) the lessee has a right to remove the goods as against the encumbrancer or owner. If the lessee's right to remove terminates, the priority of the interest of the lessor continues for a reasonable time.

(6) Notwithstanding subsection (4)(a) but otherwise subject to subsections (4) and (5), the interest of a lessor of fixtures, including the lessor's residual interest, is subordinate to the conflicting interest of an encumbrancer of the real estate under a construction mortgage recorded before the goods become fixtures if the goods become fixtures before the completion of the construction. To the extent given to refinance a construction mortgage, the conflicting interest of an encumbrancer of the real estate under a mortgage has this priority to the same extent as the encumbrancer of the real estate under the construction mortgage.

(7) In cases not within the preceding subsections, priority between the interest of a lessor of fixtures, including the lessor's residual interest, and the conflicting interest of an encumbrancer or owner of the real estate who is not the lessee is determined by the priority rules governing conflicting interests in real estate.

(8) If the interest of a lessor of fixtures, including the lessor's residual interest, has priority over all conflicting interests of all owners and encumbrancers of the real estate, the lessor or the lessee may (i) on default, expiration, termination, or cancellation of the lease agreement but subject to the agreement and this Article, or (ii) if necessary to enforce other rights and remedies of the lessor or lessee under this Article, remove the goods from the real estate, free and clear of all conflicting interests of all owners and encumbrancers of the real estate, but the lessor or lessee must reimburse any encumbrancer or owner of the real estate who is not the lessee and who has not otherwise agreed for the cost of repair of any physical injury, but not for any diminution in value of the real estate caused by the absence of the goods removed or by any necessity of replacing them. A person entitled to reimbursement may refuse permission to remove until the party seeking removal gives adequate security for the performance of this obligation.

(9) Even though the lease agreement does not create a security interest, the interest of a lessor of fixtures, including the lessor's residual interest, is perfected by filing a financing statement as a fixture filing for leased goods that are or are to become fixtures in accordance with the relevant provisions of the Article on Secured Transactions (Article 9).

Official Comment

Uniform Statutory Source: Former Section 9-313 (now codified as Sections 9-334 and 9-604).

Changes: Revised to reflect leasing terminology and to add new material.

Purposes:

1. While former Section 9-313 (now codified as Sections 9-334 and 9-604) provided a model for this section, certain provisions were substantially revised.

2. Section 2A-309(1)(c), which is new, defines purchase money lease to exclude leases where the lessee had possession or use of the goods or the right thereof before the lease agreement became enforceable. This term is used in subsection (4)(a) as one of the conditions that must be satisfied to obtain priority over the conflicting interest of an encumbrancer or owner of the real estate.

3. Section 2A-309(4), which states one of several priority rules found in this section, deletes reference to office machines and the like (Section 9-313(4)(c)) as well as certain liens (Section 9-313(4)(d)). However, these items are included in subsection (5), another priority rule that is more permissive than the rule found in subsection (4) as it applies whether or not the interest of the lessor is perfected. In addition, subsection (5)(a) expands the scope of the provisions of Section 9-313(4)(c) to include readily removable equipment not primarily used or leased for use in the operation of real estate; the qualifier is intended to exclude from the expanded rule equipment integral to the operation of real estate, e.g., heating and air conditioning equipment.

4. The rule stated in subsection (7) is more liberal than the rule stated in Section 9-313(7) in that issues of priority not otherwise resolved in this subsection are left for resolution by the priority rules governing conflicting interests in real estate, as opposed to the Section 9-313(7) automatic subordination of the security interest in fixtures. Note that, for the purpose of this section, where the interest of an encumbrancer or owner of the real estate is paramount to the interest of the lessor, the latter term includes the residual interest of the lessor.

5. The rule stated in subsection (8) is more liberal than the rule stated in Section 9-313(8) in that the right of removal is extended to both the lessor and the lessee and the occasion for removal includes expiration, termination or cancellation of the lease agreement, and enforcement of rights and remedies under this Article, as well as default. The new language also provides that upon removal the goods are free and clear of conflicting interests of owners and encumbrancers of the real estate.

6. Subsection (9) provides a mechanism for the lessor of fixtures to perfect its interest by filing a financing statement under the provisions of the Article on Secured Transactions (Article 9), even though the lease agreement does not create a security interest. See Section 1-203. The relevant provisions of Article 9 must be interpreted permissively to give effect to this mechanism as it implicitly expands the scope of Article 9 so that its filing provisions apply to transactions that create a lease of fixtures, even though the lease agreement does not create a security interest.

7. As to the use of a record other than a writing and communications that are not written, see Section 2A-103, Comment (g).

Cross References:

Sections 2A-309(1)(c), 2A-309(4), 9-334, 9-502(a), and (b), 9-604 and 9-505.

Definitional Cross References:

"Agreement".	Section 1-201(b)(3).
"Cancellation".	Section 2A-103(1)(b).
"Conforming".	Section 2A-103(1)(d).
"Consumer lease".	Section 2A-103(1)(e).
"Goods".	Section 2A-103(1)(h).
"Lease".	Section 2A-103(1)(j).
"Lease agreement".	Section 2A-103(1)(k).
"Lease contract".	Section 2A-103(1)(*l*).
"Lessee".	Section 2A-103(1)(n).
"Lessor".	Section 2A-103(1)(p).
"Lien".	Section 2A-103(1)(r).
"Mortgage".	Section 9-102(a)(55).
"Party".	Section 1-201(b)(26).
"Person".	Section 1-201(b)(27).
"Reasonable time".	Section 1-205(a).
"Remedy".	Section 1-201(b)(32).
"Right".	Section 1-201(b)(34).
"Security interest".	Section 1-201(b)(35).
"Termination".	Section 2A-103(1)(z).
"Value".	Section 1-204.
"Writing".	Section 1-201(b)(43).

Section 2A-310. Lessor's and Lessee's Rights When Goods Become Accessions

(1) Goods are "accessions" when they are installed in or affixed to other goods.

(2) The interest of a lessor or a lessee under a lease contract entered into before the goods became accessions is superior to all interests in the whole except as stated in subsection (4).

(3) The interest of a lessor or a lessee under a lease contract entered into at the time or after the goods became accessions is superior to all subsequently acquired interests in the whole except as stated in subsection (4) but is subordinate to interests in the whole existing at the time the lease contract was made unless the holders of such interests in the whole have in writing consented to the lease or disclaimed an interest in the goods as part of the whole.

(4) The interest of a lessor or a lessee under a lease contract described in subsection (2) or (3) is subordinate to the interest of

(a) a buyer in the ordinary course of business or a lessee in the ordinary course of business of any interest in the whole acquired after the goods became accessions; or

(b) a creditor with a security interest in the whole perfected before the lease contract was made to the extent that the creditor makes subsequent advances without knowledge of the lease contract.

(5) When under subsections (2) or (3) and (4) a lessor or a lessee of accessions holds an interest that is superior to all interests in the whole, the lessor or the lessee may (a) on default, expiration, termination, or cancellation of the lease contract by the other party but subject to the provisions of the lease contract and this Article, or (b) if necessary to enforce his [or her] other rights and remedies under this Article, remove the goods from the whole, free and clear of all interests in the whole, but he [or she] must reimburse any holder of an interest in the whole who is not the lessee and who has not otherwise agreed for the cost of repair of any physical injury but not for any diminution in value of the whole caused by the absence of the goods removed or by any necessity for replacing them. A person entitled to reimbursement may refuse permission to remove until the party seeking removal gives adequate security for the performance of this obligation.

Official Comment

Uniform Statutory Source: Section 9-314.

Changes: Revised to reflect leasing terminology and to add new material.

Purposes: Subsections (1) and (2) restate the provisions of subsection (1) of Section 9-314 to clarify the definition of accession and to add leasing terminology to the priority rule that applies when the lease is entered into before the goods become accessions. Subsection (3) restates the provisions of subsection (2) of Section 9-314 to add leasing terminology to the priority rule that applies when the lease is entered into on or after the goods become accessions. Unlike the rule with respect to security interests, the lease is merely subordinate, not invalid.

Subsection (4) creates two exceptions to the priority rules stated in subsections (2) and (3). Subsection (4) deletes the special priority rule found in the provisions of Section 9-314(3)(b) as the interests of the lessor and lessee are entitled to greater protection.

Finally, subsection (5) is modeled on the provisions of Section 9-314(4) with respect to removal of accessions, restated to reflect the parallel changes in Section 2A-309(8).

Neither this section nor Section 9-314 governs where the accession to the goods is not subject to the interest of a lessor or a lessee under a lease contract and is not subject to the interest of a secured party under a security agreement. This issue is to be resolved by the courts, case by case.

As to the use of a record other than a writing and communications that are not written, see Section 2A-103, Comment (g).

Cross References:

Sections 2A-309(8), and 9-335.

Definitional Cross References:

"Agreement".	Section 1-201(b)(3).
"Buyer in the ordinary course of business".	Section 2A-103(1)(a).
"Cancellation".	Section 2A-103(1)(b).
"Creditor".	Section 1-201(b)(13).
"Goods".	Section 2A-103(1)(h).
"Holder".	Section 1-201(b)(21).
"Knowledge".	Section 1-202(b).
"Lease".	Section 2A-103(1)(j).
"Lease contract".	Section 2A-103(1)(*l*).
"Lessee".	Section 2A-103(1)(n).
"Lessee in the ordinary course of business".	Section 2A-103(1)(*o*).
"Lessor".	Section 2A-103(1)(p).
"Party".	Section 1-201(b)(26).
"Person".	Section 1-201(b)(27).
"Remedy".	Section 1-201(b)(32).
"Right".	Section 1-201(b)(34).
"Security interest".	Section 1-201(b)(35).
"Termination".	Section 2A-103(1)(z).
"Value".	Section 1-204.
"Writing".	Section 1-201(b)(43).

Section 2A-311. Priority Subject to Subordination

Nothing in this Article prevents subordination by agreement by any person entitled to priority.

Official Comment

Uniform Statutory Source: Section 9-316.

Purposes: The several preceding sections deal with questions of priority. This section is inserted to make it entirely clear that a person entitled to priority may effectively agree to subordinate the claim. Only the person entitled to priority may make such an agreement: The rights of such a person cannot be adversely affected by an agreement to which that person is not a party.

Cross References:

Sections 1-310.

Definitional Cross References:

"Agreement".	Section 1-201(b)(3).
"Person".	Section 1-201(b)(27).

PERFORMANCE OF LEASE CONTRACT: REPUDIATED, SUBSTITUTED AND EXCUSED

Section 2A-401. Insecurity: Adequate Assurance of Performance

(1) A lease contract imposes an obligation on each party that the other's expectation of receiving due performance will not be impaired.

(2) If reasonable grounds for insecurity arise with respect to the performance of either party, the insecure party may demand in writing adequate assurance of due performance. Until the insecure party receives that assurance, if commercially reasonable the insecure party may suspend any performance for which he [or she] has not already received the agreed return.

(3) A repudiation of the lease contract occurs if assurance of due performance adequate under the circumstances of the particular case is not provided to the insecure party within a reasonable time, not to exceed 30 days after receipt of a demand by the other party.

(4) Between merchants, the reasonableness of grounds for insecurity and the adequacy of any assurance offered must be determined according to commercial standards.

(5) Acceptance of any nonconforming delivery or payment does not prejudice the aggrieved party's right to demand adequate assurance of future performance.

Official Comment

Uniform Statutory Source: Section 2-609.

Changes: Revised to reflect leasing practices and terminology. Note that in the analogue to subsection (3) (Section 2-609(4)), the adjective "justified" modifies demand. The adjective was deleted here as unnecessary, implying no substantive change. As to the use of a record other than a writing and communications that are not written, see Section 2A-103, Comment (g).

Cross Reference:

Section 2-609(4).

Definitional Cross References:

"Aggrieved party".	Section 1-201(b)(2).
"Agreement".	Section 1-201(b)(3).
"Between merchants".	Section 2-104(3).
"Conforming".	Section 2A-103(1)(d).
"Delivery".	Section 1-201(b)(15).
"Lease contract".	Section 2A-103(1)(*l*).
"Party".	Section 1-201(b)(26).
"Reasonable time".	Section 1-205(a).
"Receipt".	Section 2-103(1)(c).
"Right".	Section 1-201(b)(34).
"Writing".	Section 1-201(b)(43).

Section 2A-402. Anticipatory Repudiation

If either party repudiates a lease contract with respect to a performance not yet due under the lease contract, the loss of which performance will substantially impair the value of the lease contract to the other, the aggrieved party may:

(a) for a commercially reasonable time, await retraction of repudiation and performance by the repudiating party;

(b) make demand pursuant to Section 2A-401 and await assurance of future performance adequate under the circumstances of the particular case; or

(c) resort to any right or remedy upon default under the lease contract or this Article, even though the aggrieved party has notified the repudiating party that the aggrieved party would await the repudiating party's performance and assurance and has urged retraction. In addition, whether or not the aggrieved party is pursuing one of the foregoing remedies, the aggrieved party may suspend performance or, if the aggrieved party is the lessor, proceed in accordance with the provisions of this Article on the lessor's right to identify goods to the lease contract notwithstanding default or to salvage unfinished goods (Section 2A-524).

Official Comment

Uniform Statutory Source: Section 2-610.

Changes: Revised to reflect leasing practices and terminology.

Cross References:

Sections 2A-401 and 2A-524.

Definitional Cross References:

"Aggrieved party".	Section 1-201(b)(2).
"Goods".	Section 2A-103(1)(h).
"Lease contract".	Section 2A-103(1)(*l*).
"Lessor".	Section 2A-103(1)(p).
"Notifies".	Section 1-202(d).
"Party".	Section 1-201(b)(26).
"Reasonable time".	Section 1-205(a).
"Remedy".	Section 1-201(b)(32).
"Right".	Section 1-201(b)(34).
"Value".	Section 1-204.

Section 2A-403. Retraction of Anticipatory Repudiation

(1) Until the repudiating party's next performance is due, the repudiating party can retract the repudiation unless, since the repudiation, the aggrieved party has cancelled the lease contract or materially changed the aggrieved party's position or otherwise indicated that the aggrieved party considers the repudiation final.

(2) Retraction may be by any method that clearly indicates to the aggrieved party that the repudiating party intends to perform under the lease contract and includes any assurance demanded under Section 2A-401.

(3) Retraction reinstates a repudiating party's rights under a lease contract with due excuse and allowance to the aggrieved party for any delay occasioned by the repudiation.

Official Comment

Uniform Statutory Source: Section 2-611.

Changes: Revised to reflect leasing practices and terminology. Note that in the analogue to subsection (2) (Section 2-611(2)) the adjective "justifiably" modifies demanded. The adjective was deleted here (as it was in Section 2A-401) as unnecessary, implying no substantive change.

Cross References:

Sections 2-611(2) and 2A-401.

Definitional Cross References:

"Aggrieved party".	Section 1-201(b)(2).
"Cancellation".	Section 2A-103(1)(b).
"Lease contract".	Section 2A-103(1)(*l*).
"Party".	Section 1-201(b)(26).
"Right".	Section 1-201(b)(34).

Section 2A-404. Substituted Performance

(1) If without fault of the lessee, the lessor and the supplier, the agreed berthing, loading, or unloading facilities fail or the agreed type of carrier becomes unavailable or the agreed manner of delivery otherwise becomes commercially impracticable, but a

commercially reasonable substitute is available, the substitute performance must be tendered and accepted.

(2) If the agreed means or manner of payment fails because of domestic or foreign governmental regulation:

(a) the lessor may withhold or stop delivery or cause the supplier to withhold or stop delivery unless the lessee provides a means or manner of payment that is commercially a substantial equivalent; and

(b) if delivery has already been taken, payment by the means or in the manner provided by the regulation discharges the lessee's obligation unless the regulation is discriminatory, oppressive, or predatory.

Official Comment

Uniform Statutory Source: Section 2-614.

Changes: Revised to reflect leasing practices and terminology.

Definitional Cross References:

"Agreement".	Section 1-201(b)(3).
"Delivery".	Section 1-201(b)(15).
"Fault".	Section 2A-103(1)(f).
"Lessee".	Section 2A-103(1)(n).
"Lessor".	Section 2A-103(1)(p).
"Supplier".	Section 2A-103(1)(x).

Section 2A-405. Excused Performance

Subject to Section 2A-404 on substituted performance, the following rules apply:

(a) Delay in delivery or nondelivery in whole or in part by a lessor or a supplier who complies with paragraphs (b) and (c) is not a default under the lease contract if performance as agreed has been made impracticable by the occurrence of a contingency the nonoccurrence of which was a basic assumption on which the lease contract was made or by compliance in good faith with any applicable foreign or domestic governmental regulation or order, whether or not the regulation or order later proves to be invalid.

(b) If the causes mentioned in paragraph (a) affect only part of the lessor's or the supplier's capacity to perform, he [or she] shall allocate production and deliveries among his [or her] customers but at his [or her] option may include regular customers not then under contract for sale or lease as well as his [or her] own requirements for further manufacture. He [or she] may so allocate in any manner that is fair and reasonable.

(c) The lessor seasonably shall notify the lessee and in the case of a finance lease the supplier seasonably shall notify the lessor and the lessee, if known, that there will be delay or nondelivery and, if allocation is required under paragraph (b), of the estimated quota thus made available for the lessee.

Official Comment

Uniform Statutory Source: Section 2-615.

Changes: Revised to reflect leasing practices and terminology.

Cross Reference:

Section 2A-404.

Definitional Cross References:

"Agreement".	Section 1-201(b)(3).
"Contract".	Section 1-201(b)(12).
"Delivery".	Section 1-201(b)(15).
"Finance lease".	Section 2A-103(1)(g).
"Good faith".	Sections 1-201(b)(20).
"Knows".	Section 1-202(b).
"Lease".	Section 2A-103(1)(j).
"Lease contract".	Section 2A-103(1)(*l*).
"Lessee".	Section 2A-103(1)(n).
"Lessor".	Section 2A-103(1)(p).
"Notifies".	Section 1-202(d).
"Sale".	Section 2-106(1).
"Seasonably".	Section 1-205(b).
"Supplier".	Section 2A-103(1)(x).

Section 2A-406. Procedure on Excused Performance

(1) If the lessee receives notification of a material or indefinite delay or an allocation justified under Section 2A-405, the lessee may by written notification to the lessor as to any goods involved, and with respect to all of the goods if under an installment lease contract the value of the whole lease contract is substantially impaired (Section 2A-510):

(a) terminate the lease contract (Section 2A-505(2)); or

(b) except in a finance lease that is not a consumer lease, modify the lease contract by accepting the available quota in substitution, with due allowance from the rent payable for the balance of the lease term for the deficiency but without further right against the lessor.

(2) If, after receipt of a notification from the lessor under Section 2A-405, the lessee fails so to modify the lease agreement within a reasonable time not exceeding 30 days, the lease contract lapses with respect to any deliveries affected.

Official Comment

Uniform Statutory Source: Section 2-616(1) and (2).

Changes:

1. Revised to reflect leasing practices and terminology. Note that subsection 1(a) allows the lessee under a lease, including a finance lease, the right to terminate the lease for excused performance (Sections 2A-404 and 2A-405). However, subsection 1(b), which allows the lessee the right to modify the lease for excused performance, excludes a finance lease that is not a consumer lease. This exclusion is compelled by the same policy that led to codification of provisions with respect to irrevocable promises. Section 2A-407.

2. As to the use of a record other than a writing and communications that are not written, see Section 2A-103, Comment (g).

Cross References:

Sections 2A-404, 2A-405, 2A-407.

Definitional Cross References:

"Consumer lease".	Section 2A-103(1)(e).
"Delivery".	Section 1-201(b)(15).
"Finance lease".	Section 2A-103(1)(g).
"Goods".	Section 2A-103(1)(h).
"Installment lease contract".	Section 2A-103(1)(i).
"Lease agreement".	Section 2A-103(1)(k).
"Lease contract".	Section 2A-103(1)(*l*).
"Lessee".	Section 2A-103(1)(n).
"Lessor".	Section 2A-103(1)(p).
"Notice".	Section 1-202(a).
"Reasonable time".	Section 1-205(a).
"Receipt".	Section 2-103(1)(c).
"Right".	Section 1-201(b)(34).
"Termination".	Section 2A-103(1)(z).
"Value".	Section 1-204.
"Written".	Section 1-201(b)(43).

Section 2A-407. Irrevocable Promises: Finance Leases

(1) In the case of a finance lease that is not a consumer lease the lessee's promises under the lease contract become irrevocable and independent upon the lessee's acceptance of the goods.

(2) A promise that has become irrevocable and independent under subsection (1):

(a) is effective and enforceable between the parties, and by or against third parties including assignees of the parties; and

(b) is not subject to cancellation, termination, modification, repudiation, excuse, or substitution without the consent of the party to whom the promise runs.

(3) This section does not affect the validity under any other law of a covenant in any lease contract making the lessee's promises irrevocable and independent upon the lessee's acceptance of the goods.

Official Comment

Uniform Statutory Source: None.

Purposes:

1. This section extends the benefits of the classic "hell or high water" clause to a finance lease that is not a consumer lease. This section is self-executing; no special provision need be added to the contract. This section makes covenants in a finance lease irrevocable and independent due to the function of the finance lessor in a three-party relationship: The lessee is looking to the supplier to perform the essential covenants and warranties. Section 2A-209. Thus, upon the lessee's acceptance of the goods the lessee's promises to the lessor under the lease contract become irrevocable and independent. The provisions of this section remain subject to the obligation of good faith (Sections 2A-103(4) and 1-304 [*sic*, should be 1-304]), and the lessee's revocation of acceptance (Section 2A-517).

2. The section requires the lessee to perform even if the lessor's performance after the lessee's acceptance is not in accordance with the lease contract; the lessee may, however, have and pursue a cause of action against the lessor, e.g., breach of certain limited warranties (Sections 2A-210 and 2A-211(1)). This is appropriate because the benefit of the supplier's promises and warranties to the lessor under the supply contract and, in some cases, the warranty of a manufacturer who is not the supplier, is extended to the lessee under the finance lease. Section 2A-209. Despite this balance, this section excludes a finance lease that is a consumer lease. That a consumer be obligated to pay notwithstanding defective goods or the like is a principle that is not tenable under case law (*Unico v. Owen*, 232 A.2d 405 (N.J. 1967)), state statute (Unif.Consumer Credit Code §§ 3.403-3.405, or federal statute (15 U.S.C. § 1666i (1982)).

3. The relationship of the three parties to a transaction that qualifies as a finance lease is best demonstrated by a hypothetical. A, the potential lessor, has been contacted by B, the potential lessee, to discuss the lease of an expensive line of equipment that B has recently placed an order for with C, the manufacturer of such goods. The negotiation is completed and A, as lessor, and B, as lessee, sign a lease of the line of equipment for a 60-month term. B, as buyer, assigns the purchase order with C to A. If this transaction creates a lease (Section 2A-103(1)(j)), this transaction should qualify as a finance lease. Section 2A-103(1)(g).

4. The line of equipment is delivered by C to B's place of business. After installation by C and testing by B, B accepts the goods by signing a certificate of delivery and acceptance, a copy of which is sent by B to A and C. One year later the line of equipment malfunctions and B falls behind in its manufacturing schedule.

5. Under this Article, because the lease is a finance lease, no warranty of fitness or merchantability is extended by A to B. Sections 2A-212(1) and 2A-213. Absent an express provision in the lease agreement, application of Section 2A-210 or Section 2A-211(1), or application of the principles of law and equity, including the law with respect to fraud, duress or the like (Sections 2A-103(4) and 1-103), B has no claim against

A. B's obligation to pay rent to A continues as the obligation became irrevocable and independent when B accepted the line of equipment (Section 2A-407(1)). B has no right of set-off with respect to any part of the rent still due under the lease. Section 2A-508(6). However, B may have another remedy. Despite the lack of privity between B and C (the purchase order with C having been assigned by B to A), B may have a claim against C. Section 2A-209(1).

6. This section does not address whether a "hell or high water" clause, i.e., a clause that is to the effect of this section, is enforceable if included in a finance lease that is a consumer lease or a lease that is not a finance lease. That issue will continue to be determined by the facts of each case and other law which this section does not affect. Sections 2A-104, 2A-103(4), 9-206 and 9-318. However, with respect to finance leases that are not consumer leases courts have enforced "hell or high water" clauses. *In re O.P.M. Leasing Servs.*, 21 B.R. 993, 1006 (Bankr. S.D.N.Y. 1982).

7. Subsection (2) further provides that a promise that has become irrevocable and independent under subsection (1) is enforceable not only between the parties but also against third parties. Thus, the finance lease can be transferred or assigned without disturbing enforceability. Further, subsection (2) also provides that the promise cannot, among other things, be cancelled or terminated without the consent of the lessor.

Cross References:

Sections 1-103, 1-304, 2A-103(1)(g), 2A-103(1)(j), 2A-103(4), 2A-209, 2A-210, 2A-211(1), 2A-212(1), 2A-213, 2A-407(1), 2A-508(6), 2A-517, 9-403, and 9-404.

Definitional Cross References:

"Cancellation".	Section 2A-103(1)(b).
"Consumer lease".	Section 2A-103(1)(e).
"Finance lease".	Section 2A-103(1)(g).
"Goods".	Section 2A-103(1)(h).
"Lease contract".	Section 2A-103(1)(*l*).
"Lessee".	Section 2A-103(1)(n).
"Party".	Section 1-201(b)(26).
"Termination".	Section 2A-103(1)(z).

DEFAULT

A. In General

Section 2A-501. Default: Procedure

(1) Whether the lessor or the lessee is in default under a lease contract is determined by the lease agreement and this Article.

(2) If the lessor or the lessee is in default under the lease contract, the party seeking enforcement has rights and remedies as provided in this Article and, except as limited by this Article, as provided in the lease agreement.

(3) If the lessor or the lessee is in default under the lease contract, the party seeking enforcement may reduce the party's claim to judgment, or otherwise enforce the lease contract by self-help or any available judicial procedure or nonjudicial procedure, including administrative proceeding, arbitration, or the like, in accordance with this Article.

(4) Except as otherwise provided in Section 1-106(1) or this Article or the lease agreement, the rights and remedies referred to in subsections (2) and (3) are cumulative.

(5) If the lease agreement covers both real property and goods, the party seeking enforcement may proceed under this Part as to the goods, or under other applicable law as to both the real property and the goods in accordance with that party's rights and remedies in respect of the real property, in which case this Part does not apply.

Official Comment

Uniform Statutory Source: Section 9-501.

Changes: Substantially revised.

Purposes:

1. Subsection (1) is new and represents a departure from the Article on Secured Transactions (Article 9) as the subsection makes clear that whether a party to the lease agreement is in default is determined by this Article as well as the agreement. Sections 2A-508 and 2A-523. It further departs from Article 9 in recognizing the potential default of either party, a function of the bilateral nature of the obligations between the parties to the lease contract.

2. Subsection (2) is a version of the first sentence of Section 9-501(1), revised to reflect leasing terminology.

3. Subsection (3), an expansive version of the second sentence of Section 9-501(1), lists the procedures that may be followed by the party seeking enforcement; in effect, the scope of the procedures listed in subsection (3) is consistent with the scope of the procedures available to the foreclosing secured party.

4. Subsection (4) establishes that the parties' rights and remedies are cumulative. Ronald M. DeKoven, *Leases of Equipment: Puritan Leasing Company v. August, A Dangerous Decision*, 12 U.S.F.L.Rev. 257, 276-80 (1978). Cumulation, and largely unrestricted selection, of remedies is allowed in furtherance of the general policy of the Commercial Code, stated in Section 1-106, that remedies be liberally administered to put the aggrieved party in as good a position as if the other party had fully performed. Therefore, cumulation of, or selection among, remedies is available to the extent necessary to put the aggrieved party in as good a position as it would have been in had there been full performance. However, cumulation of, or selection among, remedies is not available to the extent that the cumulation or selection would put the aggrieved party in a better position than it would have been in had there been full performance by the other party.

5. Section 9-501(3), which, among other things, states that certain rules, to the extent they give rights to the debtor and impose duties on the secured party, may not be waived or varied, was not incorporated in this Article. Given the significance of freedom of contract in the development of the common law as it applies to bailments for hire and the lessee's lack of an equity of redemption, there was no reason to impose that restraint.

Cross References:

Sections 1-305, 2A-508, 2A-523, 9-601, and 9-602.

Definitional Cross References:

"Goods".	Section 2A-103(1)(h).
"Lease agreement".	Section 2A-103(1)(k).
"Lease contract".	Section 2A-103(1)(*l*).
"Lessee".	Section 2A-103(1)(n).
"Lessor".	Section 2A-103(1)(p).
"Party".	Section 1-201(b)(26).
"Remedy".	Section 1-201(b)(32).
"Right".	Section 1-201(b)(34).

Section 2A-502. Notice after Default

Except as otherwise provided in this Article or the lease agreement, the lessor or lessee in default under the lease contract is not entitled to notice of default or notice of enforcement from the other party to the lease agreement.

Official Comment

Uniform Statutory Source: None.

Purposes: This section makes clear that absent agreement to the contrary or provision in this Article to the contrary, *e.g.*, Section 2A-516(3)(a), the party in default is not entitled to notice of default or enforcement. While a review of Part 5 of Article 9 leads to the same conclusion with respect to giving notice of default to the debtor, it is never stated. Although Article 9 requires notice of disposition and strict foreclosure, the different scheme of lessors' and lessees' rights and remedies developed under the common law, and codified by this Article, generally does not require notice of enforcement; furthermore, such notice is not mandated by due process requirements. However, certain Sections of this Article do require notice. *E.g.*, Section 2A-517(4).

Cross References:

Sections 2A-516(3)(a), 2A-517(4), and Article 9, Part 5.

Definitional Cross References:

"Lease agreement".	Section 2A-103(1)(k).
"Lease contract".	Section 2A-103(1)(*l*).
"Lessee".	Section 2A-103(1)(n).
"Lessor".	Section 2A-103(1)(p).
"Notice".	Section 1-202(a).
"Party".	Section 1-201(b)(26).

Section 2A-503. Modification or Impairment of Rights and Remedies

(1) Except as otherwise provided in this Article, the lease agreement may include rights and remedies for default in addition to or in substitution for those provided in this Article and may limit or alter the measure of damages recoverable under this Article.

(2) Resort to a remedy provided under this Article or in the lease agreement is optional unless the remedy is expressly agreed to be exclusive. If circumstances cause an exclusive or limited remedy to fail of its essential purpose, or provision for an exclusive remedy is unconscionable, remedy may be had as provided in this Article.

(3) Consequential damages may be liquidated under Section 2A-504, or may otherwise be limited, altered, or excluded unless the limitation, alteration, or exclusion is unconscionable. Limitation, alteration, or exclusion of consequential damages for injury to the person in the case of consumer goods is prima facie unconscionable but limitation, alteration, or exclusion of damages where the loss is commercial is not prima facie unconscionable.

(4) Rights and remedies on default by the lessor or the lessee with respect to any obligation or promise collateral or ancillary to the lease contract are not impaired by this Article.

Official Comment

Uniform Statutory Source: Sections 2-719 and 2-701.

Changes: Rewritten to reflect lease terminology and to clarify the relationship between this section and Section 2A-504.

Purposes:

1. A significant purpose of this Part is to provide rights and remedies for those parties to a lease who fail to provide them by agreement or whose rights and remedies fail of their essential purpose or are unenforceable. However, it is important to note that this implies no restriction on freedom to contract. Sections 2A-103(4) and 1-302(a). Thus, subsection (1), a revised version of the provisions of Section 2-719(1), allows the parties to the lease agreement freedom to provide for rights and remedies in addition to or in substitution for those provided in this Article and to alter or limit the measure of damages recoverable under this Article. Except to the extent otherwise provided in this Article (e.g., Sections 2A-105, 106 and 108(1) and (2)), this Part shall be construed neither to restrict the parties' ability to provide for rights and remedies or to limit or alter the measure of damages by agreement, nor to imply disapproval of rights and remedy schemes other than those set forth in this Part.

2. Subsection (2) makes explicit with respect to this Article what is implicit in Section 2-719 with respect to the Article on Sales (Article 2): if an exclusive remedy is held to be unconscionable, remedies under this Article are available. Section 2-719 Comment 1.

3. Subsection (3), a revision of Section 2-719(3), makes clear that consequential damages may also be liquidated. Section 2A-504(1).

4. Subsection (4) is a revision of the provisions of Section 2-701. This subsection leaves the treatment of default with respect to obligations or promises collateral or ancillary to the lease contract to other law. Sections 2A-103(4) and 1-103. An example of such an obligation would be that of the lessor to the secured creditor which has provided the funds to leverage the lessor's lease transaction; an example of such a promise would be that of the lessee, as seller, to the lessor, as buyer, in a sale-leaseback transaction.

Cross References:

Sections 1-103, 1-302(a), 2-701, 2-719, 2A-103(4), 2A-105, 2A-106, 2A-108(1), 2A-108(2), and 2A-504.

Definitional Cross References:

"Agreement".	Section 1-201(b)(3).
"Consumer goods".	Section 9-109(a)(23).
"Lease agreement".	Section 2A-103(1)(k).
"Lease contract".	Section 2A-103(1)(*l*).
"Lessee".	Section 2A-103(1)(n).
"Lessor".	Section 2A-103(1)(p).
"Person".	Section 1-201(b)(27).
"Remedy".	Section 1-201(b)(32).
"Right".	Section 1-201(b)(34).

Section 2A-504. Liquidation of Damages

(1) Damages payable by either party for default, or any other act or omission, including indemnity for loss or diminution of anticipated tax benefits or loss or damage to lessor's residual interest, may be liquidated in the lease agreement but only at an amount or by a formula that is reasonable in light of the then anticipated harm caused by the default or other act or omission.

(2) If the lease agreement provides for liquidation of damages, and such provision does not comply with subsection (1), or such provision is an exclusive or limited remedy that circumstances cause to fail of its essential purpose, remedy may be had as provided in this Article.

(3) If the lessor justifiably withholds or stops delivery of goods because of the lessee's default or insolvency (Section 2A-525 or 2A-526), the lessee is entitled to restitution of any amount by which the sum of his [or her] payments exceeds:

(a) the amount to which the lessor is entitled by virtue of terms liquidating the lessor's damages in accordance with subsection (1); or

(b) in the absence of those terms, 20 percent of the then present value of the total rent the lessee was obligated to pay for the balance of the lease term, or, in the case of a consumer lease, the lesser of such amount or $500.

(4) A lessee's right to restitution under subsection (3) is subject to offset to the extent the lessor establishes:

(a) a right to recover damages under the provisions of this Article other than subsection (1); and

(b) the amount or value of any benefits received by the lessee directly or indirectly by reason of the lease contract.

Official Comment

Uniform Statutory Source: Sections 2-718(1), (2), (3) and 2-719(2).

Changes: Substantially rewritten.

Purposes: Many leasing transactions are predicated on the parties' ability to agree to an appropriate amount of damages or formula for damages in the event of default or other act or omission. The rule with respect to sales of goods (Section 2-718) may not be sufficiently flexible to accommodate this practice. Thus, consistent with the common law emphasis upon freedom to contract with respect to bailments for hire, this section has created a revised rule that allows greater flexibility with respect to leases of goods.

Subsection (1), a significantly modified version of the provisions of Section 2-718(1), provides for liquidation of damages in the lease agreement at an amount or by a formula. Section 2-718(1) does not by its express terms include liquidation by a formula; this change was compelled by modern leasing practice. Subsection (1), in a further expansion of Section 2-718(1), provides for liquidation of damages for default as well as any other act or omission.

A liquidated damages formula that is common in leasing practice provides that the sum of lease payments past due, accelerated future lease payments, and the lessor's estimated residual interest, less the net proceeds of disposition (whether by sale or release) of the leased goods is the lessor's damages. Tax indemnities, costs, interest and attorney's fees are also added to determine the lessor's damages. Another common liquidated damages formula utilizes a periodic depreciation allocation as a credit to the aforesaid amount in mitigation of a lessor's damages. A third formula provides for a fixed number of periodic payments as a means of liquidating damages. Stipulated loss or stipulated damage schedules are also common. Whether these formulae are enforceable will be determined in the context of each case by applying a standard of reasonableness in light of the harm anticipated when the formula was agreed to. Whether the inclusion of these formulae will affect the classification of the transaction as a lease or a security interest is to be determined by the facts of each case. Section 1-203. E.g., *In re Noack*, 44 B.R. 172, 174-75 (Bankr. E.D. Wis. 1984).

This section does not incorporate two other tests that under sales law determine enforceability of liquidated damages, i.e., difficulties of proof of loss and inconvenience or nonfeasibility of otherwise obtaining an adequate remedy. The ability to liquidate damages is critical to modern leasing practice; given the parties' freedom to contract at common law, the policy behind retaining these two additional requirements here was thought to be outweighed. Further, given the expansion of subsection (1) to enable the parties to liquidate the amount payable with respect to an indemnity for loss or diminution of anticipated tax benefits resulted in another change: the last sentence of Section 2-718(1), providing that a term fixing unreasonably large liquidated damages is void as a penalty, was also not incorporated. The impact of local, state and federal tax laws on a leasing transaction can result in an amount payable with respect to the tax indemnity many times greater than the original purchase price of the goods. By deleting the reference to unreasonably large liquidated damages the parties are free to negotiate a formula, restrained by the rule of reasonableness in this section. These changes should invite the parties to liquidate damages. Ellen A. Peters, *Remedies for Breach of Contracts Relating to the Sale of Goods Under the Uniform Commercial Code: A Roadmap for Article Two*, 73 Yale L.J. 199, 278 (1963).

Subsection (2), a revised version of Section 2-719(2), provides that if the liquidated damages provision is not enforceable or fails of its essential purpose, remedy may be had as provided in this Article.

Subsection (3)(b) of this section differs from subsection (2)(b) of Section 2-718; in the absence of a valid liquidated damages amount or formula the lessor is permitted to retain 20 percent of the present value of the total rent payable under the lease. The alternative limitation of $500 contained in Section 2-718 is deleted as unrealistically low with respect to a lease other than a consumer lease.

Cross References:

Sections 1-203, 2-718, 2-719(2), 2A-525, and 2A-526.

Definitional Cross References:

"Consumer lease".	Section 2A-103(1)(e).
"Delivery".	Section 1-201(b)(15).
"Goods".	Section 2A-103(1)(h).
"Insolvent".	Section 1-201(b)(23).
"Lease agreement".	Section 2A-103(1)(k).
"Lease contract".	Section 2A-103(1)(*l*).
"Lessee".	Section 2A-103(1)(n).
"Lessor".	Section 2A-103(1)(p).
"Lessor's residual interest".	Section 2A-103(1)(q).
"Party".	Section 1-201(b)(26).
"Present value".	Section 1-201(b)(28).
"Remedy".	Section 1-201(32).
"Right".	Section 1-201(34).
"Term".	Section 1-201(40).
"Value".	Section 1-204.

Section 2A-505. Cancellation and Termination and Effect of Cancellation, Termination, Rescission, or Fraud on Rights and Remedies

(1) On cancellation of the lease contract, all obligations that are still executory on both sides are discharged, but any right based on prior default or performance survives, and the cancelling party also retains any remedy for default of the whole lease contract or any unperformed balance.

(2) On termination of the lease contract, all obligations that are still executory on both sides are discharged but any right based on prior default or performance survives.

(3) Unless the contrary intention clearly appears, expressions of "cancellation," "rescission," or the like of the lease contract may not be construed as a renunciation or discharge of any claim in damages for an antecedent default.

(4) Rights and remedies for material misrepresentation or fraud include all rights and remedies available under this Article for default.

(5) Neither rescission nor a claim for rescission of the lease contract nor rejection or return of the goods may bar or be deemed inconsistent with a claim for damages or other right or remedy.

Official Comment

Uniform Statutory Source: Sections 2-106(3) and (4), 2-720 and 2-721.

Changes: Revised to reflect leasing practices and terminology.

Definitional Cross References:

"Cancellation".	Section 2A-103(1)(b).
"Goods".	Section 2A-103(1)(h).
"Lease contract".	Section 2A-103(1)(*l*).
"Party".	Section 1-201(b)(26).
"Remedy".	Section 1-201(b)(32).
"Right".	Section 1-201(b)(34).
"Termination".	Section 2A-103(1)(z).

Section 2A-506. Statute of Limitations

(1) An action for default under a lease contract, including breach of warranty or indemnity, must be commenced within 4 years after the cause of action accrued. By the original lease contract the parties may reduce the period of limitation to not less than one year.

(2) A cause of action for default accrues when the act or omission on which the default or breach of warranty is based is or should have been discovered by the aggrieved party, or when the default occurs, whichever is later. A cause of action for indemnity accrues when the act or omission on which the claim for indemnity is based is or should have been discovered by the indemnified party, whichever is later.

(3) If an action commenced within the time limited by subsection (1) is so terminated as to leave available a remedy by another action for the same default or breach of warranty or indemnity, the other action may be commenced after the expiration of the time limited and within 6 months after the termination of the first action unless the termination resulted from voluntary

discontinuance or from dismissal for failure or neglect to prosecute.

(4) This section does not alter the law on tolling of the statute of limitations nor does it apply to causes of action that have accrued before this Article becomes effective.

Official Comment

Uniform Statutory Source: Section 2-725.

Changes: Substantially rewritten.

Purposes: Subsection (1) does not incorporate the limitation found in Section 2-725(1) prohibiting the parties from extending the period of limitation. Breach of warranty and indemnity claims often arise in a lease transaction; with the passage of time such claims often diminish or are eliminated. To encourage the parties to commence litigation under these circumstances makes little sense.

Subsection (2) states two rules for determining when a cause of action accrues. With respect to default, the rule of Section 2-725(2) is not incorporated in favor of a more liberal rule of the later of the date when the default occurs or when the act or omission on which it is based is or should have been discovered. With respect to indemnity, a similarly liberal rule is adopted.

Cross References:

Section 2-725(1) and (2).

Definitional Cross References:

"Action".	Section 1-201(b)(1).
"Aggrieved party".	Section 1-201(b)(2).
"Lease contract".	Section 2A-103(1)(*l*).
"Party".	Section 1-201(b)(26).
"Remedy".	Section 1-201(b)(32).
"Termination".	Section 2A-103(1)(z).

Section 2A-507. Proof of Market Rent: Time and Place

(1) Damages based on market rent (Section 2A-519 or 2A-528) are determined according to the rent for the use of the goods concerned for a lease term identical to the remaining lease term of the original lease agreement and prevailing at the times specified in Sections 2A-519 and 2A-528.

(2) If evidence of rent for the use of the goods concerned for a lease term identical to the remaining lease term of the original lease agreement and prevailing at the times or places described in this Article is not readily available, the rent prevailing within any reasonable time before or after the time described or at any other place or for a different lease term which in commercial judgment or under usage of trade would serve as a reasonable substitute for the one described may be used, making any proper allowance for the difference, including the cost of transporting the goods to or from the other place.

(3) Evidence of a relevant rent prevailing at a time or place or for a lease term other than the one described in this Article offered by one party is not admissible unless and until he [or she] has given the other party notice the court finds sufficient to prevent unfair surprise.

(4) If the prevailing rent or value of any goods regularly leased in any established market is in issue, reports in official publications or trade journals or in newspapers or periodicals of general circulation published as the reports of that market are admissible in evidence. The circumstances of the preparation of the report may be shown to affect its weight but not its admissibility.

Official Comment

Uniform Statutory Source: Sections 2-723 and 2-724.

Changes: Revised to reflect leasing practices and terminology. Sections 2A-519 and 2A-528 specify the times as of which market rent is to be determined.

Cross References:

Sections 2A-519 and 2A-528.

Definitional Cross References:

"Goods".	Section 2A-103(1)(h).
"Lease".	Section 2A-103(1)(j).
"Lease agreement".	Section 2A-103(1)(k).
"Notice".	Section 1-202(a).
"Party".	Section 1-201(b)(26).
"Reasonable time".	Sections 1-205(a).
"Usage of trade".	Section 1-303(c).
"Value".	Section 1-204.

B. Default by Lessor

Section 2A-508. Lessee's Remedies

(1) If a lessor fails to deliver the goods in conformity to the lease contract (Section 2A-509) or repudiates the lease contract (Section 2A-402), or a lessee rightfully rejects the goods (Section 2A-509) or justifiably revokes acceptance of the goods (Section 2A-517), then with respect to any goods involved, and with respect to all of the goods if under an installment lease contract the value of the whole lease contract is substantially impaired (Section 2A-510), the lessor is in default under the lease contract and the lessee may:

(a) cancel the lease contract (Section 2A-505(1));

(b) recover so much of the rent and security as has been paid and is just under the circumstances;

(c) cover and recover damages as to all goods affected whether or not they have been identified to the lease contract (Sections 2A-518 and 2A-520), or recover damages for nondelivery (Sections 2A-519 and 2A-520);

(d) exercise any other rights or pursue any other remedies provided in the lease contract.

(2) If a lessor fails to deliver the goods in conformity to the lease contract or repudiates the lease contract, the lessee may also:

(a) if the goods have been identified, recover them (Section 2A-522); or

(b) in a proper case, obtain specific performance or replevy the goods (Section 2A-521).

(3) If a lessor is otherwise in default under a lease contract, the lessee may exercise the rights and pursue the remedies provided in the lease contract, which may include a right to cancel the lease, and in Section 2A-519(3).

(4) If a lessor has breached a warranty, whether express or implied, the lessee may recover damages (Section 2A-519(4)).

(5) On rightful rejection or justifiable revocation of acceptance, a lessee has a security interest in goods in the lessee's possession or control for any rent and security that has been paid and any expenses reasonably incurred in their inspection, receipt, transportation, and care and custody and may hold those goods and dispose of them in good faith and in a commercially reasonable manner, subject to Section 2A-527(5).

(6) Subject to the provisions of Section 2A-407, a lessee, on notifying the lessor of the lessee's intention to do so, may deduct all or any part of the damages resulting from any default under the lease contract from any part of the rent still due under the same lease contract.

Official Comment

Uniform Statutory Source: Sections 2-711 and 2-717.
Changes: Substantially rewritten.
Purposes:

1. This section is an index to Sections 2A-509 through 522 which set out the lessee's rights and remedies after the lessor's default. The lessor and the lessee can agree to modify the rights and remedies available under this Article; they can, among other things, provide that for defaults other than those specified in subsection (1) the lessee can exercise the rights and remedies referred to in subsection (1); and they can create a new scheme of rights and remedies triggered by the occurrence of the default. Sections 2A-103(4) and 1-302(a).

2. Subsection (1), a substantially rewritten version of the provisions of Section 2-711(1), lists three cumulative remedies of the lessee where the lessor has failed to deliver conforming goods or has repudiated the contract, or the lessee has rightfully rejected or justifiably revoked. Sections 2A-501(2) and (4). Subsection (1) also allows the lessee to exercise any contractual remedy. This Article rejects any general doctrine of election of remedy. To determine if one remedy bars another in a particular case is a function of whether the lessee has been put in as good a position as if the lessor had fully performed the lease agreement. Use of multiple remedies is barred only if the effect is to put the lessee in a better position than it would have been in had the lessor fully performed under the lease. Sections 2A-103(4), 2A-501(4), and 1-305(a). Subsection (1)(b), in recognition that no bright line can be created that would operate fairly in all installment lease cases and in recognition of the fact that a lessee may be able to cancel the lease (revoke acceptance of the goods) after the goods have been in use for some period of time, does not require that all lease payments made by the lessee under the lease be returned upon cancellation. Rather, only such portion as is just of the rent and security payments made may be recovered. If a defect in the goods is discovered immediately upon tender to the lessee and the goods are rejected immediately, then the lessee should recover all payments made. If, however, for example, a 36-month equipment lease is terminated in the 12th month because the lessor has materially breached the contract by failing to perform its maintenance obligations, it may be just to return only a small part or none of the rental payments already made.

3. Subsection (2), a version of the provisions of Section 2-711(2) revised to reflect leasing terminology, lists two alternative remedies for the recovery of the goods by the lessee; however, each of these remedies is cumulative with respect to those listed in subsection (1).

4. Subsection (3) is new. It covers defaults which do not deprive the lessee of the goods and which are not so serious as to justify rejection or revocation of acceptance under subsection (1). It also covers defaults for which the lessee could have rejected or revoked acceptance of the goods but elects not to do so and retains the goods. In either case, a lessee which retains the goods is entitled to recover damages as stated in Section 2A-519(3). That measure of damages is "the loss resulting in the ordinary course of events from the lessor's default as determined in any manner that is reasonable together with incidental and consequential damages, less expenses saved in consequence of the lessor's breach."

5. Subsection (1)(d) and subsection (3) recognize that the lease agreement may provide rights and remedies in addition to or different from those which Article 2A provides. In particular, subsection (3) provides that the lease agreement may give the remedy of cancellation of the lease for defaults by the lessor that would not otherwise be material defaults which would justify cancellation under subsection (1). If there is a right to cancel, there is, of course, a right to reject or revoke acceptance of the goods.

6. Subsection (4) is new and merely adds to the completeness of the index by including a reference to the lessee's recovery of damages upon the lessor's breach of warranty; such breach may not rise to the level of a default by the lessor justifying revocation of acceptance. If the lessee properly rejects or revokes acceptance of the goods because of a breach of warranty, the rights and remedies are those provided in subsection (1) rather than those in Section 2A-519(4).

7. Subsection (5), a revised version of the provisions of Section 2-711(3), recognizes, on rightful rejection or justifiable revocation, the lessee's security interest in goods in its possession and control. Section 9-113, which recognized security interests arising under the Article on Sales (Article 2), was amended with the adoption of this Article to reflect the security interests arising under this Article. Pursuant to Section 2A-511(4), a purchaser who purchases goods from the lessee in good faith takes free of any rights of the lessor, or in the case of a finance lease, the supplier. Such goods, however, must have been rightfully rejected and disposed of pursuant to Section 2A-511 or 2A-512. However, Section 2A-517(5) provides that the lessee will have the same rights and duties with respect to goods where acceptance has been revoked as with respect to goods rejected. Thus, Section 2A-511(4) will apply to the lessee's disposition of such goods.

8. Pursuant to Section 2A-527(5), the lessee must account to the lessor for the excess proceeds of such disposition, after satisfaction of the claim secured by the lessee's security interest.

9. Subsection (6), a slightly revised version of the provisions of Section 2-717, sanctions a right of set-off by the lessee, subject to the rule of Section 2A-407 with respect to irrevocable promises in a finance lease that is not a consumer lease, and further subject to an enforceable "hell or high water" clause in the lease agreement. Section 2A-407 Comment. No attempt is made to state how the set-off should occur; this is to be determined by the facts of each case.

10. There is no special treatment of the finance lease in this section. Absent supplemental principles of law and equity to the contrary, in the case of most finance leases, following the lessee's acceptance of the goods, the lessee will have no rights or remedies against the lessor, because the lessor's obligations to the lessee are minimal. Sections 2A-210 and 2A-211(1). Since the lessee will look to the supplier for performance, this is appropriate. Section 2A-209.

Cross References:

Sections 1-302(a), 1-305(a), 2-711, 2-717, 2A-103(4), 2A-209, 2A-210, 2A-211(1), 2A-402, 2A-407, 2A-501(2), 2A-501(4), 2A-509 through 2A-522, 2A-527 and 9-110.

Definitional Cross References:

"Conforming".	Section 2A-103(1)(d).
"Consumer Lease".	Section 2A-103(1)(e).
"Delivery".	Section 1-201(b)(15).
"Good faith".	Sections 1-201(b)(20).
"Goods".	Section 2A-103(1)(h).
"Installment lease contract".	Section 2A-103(1)(i).
"Lease contract".	Section 2A-103(1)(*l*).
"Lessee".	Section 2A-103(1)(n).
"Lessor".	Section 2A-103(1)(p).
"Notifies".	Section 1-202(d).
"Receipt".	Section 2-103(1)(c).
"Remedy".	Section 1-201(b)(32).
"Right".	Section 1-201(b)(34).
"Security interest".	Section 1-201(b)(35).
"Value".	Section 1-204.

Section 2A-509. Lessee's Rights on Improper Delivery; Rightful Rejection

(1) Subject to the provisions of Section 2A-510 on default in installment lease contracts, if the goods or the tender or delivery fail in any respect to conform to the lease contract, the lessee may reject or accept the goods or accept any commercial unit or units and reject the rest of the goods.

(2) Rejection of goods is ineffective unless it is within a reasonable time after tender or delivery of the goods and the lessee seasonably notifies the lessor.

Official Comment

Uniform Statutory Source: Sections 2-601 and 2-602(1).

Changes: Revised to reflect leasing practices and terminology.

Definitional Cross References:

"Commercial unit".	Section 2A-103(1)(c).
"Conforming".	Section 2A-103(1)(d).
"Delivery".	Section 1-201(b)(15).
"Goods".	Section 2A-103(1)(h).
"Installment lease contract".	Section 2A-103(1)(i).
"Lease contract".	Section 2A-103(1)(*l*).
"Lessee".	Section 2A-103(1)(n).
"Lessor".	Section 2A-103(1)(p).
"Notifies".	Section 1-202(d).
"Reasonable time".	Section 1-205(a).
"Right".	Section 1-201(b)(34).
"Seasonably".	Section 1-205(b).

Section 2A-510. Installment Lease Contracts: Rejection and Default

(1) Under an installment lease contract a lessee may reject any delivery that is nonconforming if the nonconformity substantially impairs the value of that delivery and cannot be cured or the nonconformity is a defect in the required documents; but if the nonconformity does not fall within subsection (2) and the lessor or the supplier gives adequate assurance of its cure, the lessee must accept that delivery.

(2) Whenever nonconformity or default with respect to one or more deliveries substantially impairs the value of the installment lease contract as a whole there is a default with respect to the whole. But, the aggrieved party reinstates the installment lease contract as a whole if the aggrieved party accepts a nonconforming delivery without seasonably notifying of cancellation or brings an action with respect only to past deliveries or demands performance as to future deliveries.

Official Comment

Uniform Statutory Source: Section 2-612.

Changes: Revised to reflect leasing practices and terminology.

Definitional Cross References:

"Action".	Section 1-201(b)(1).
"Aggrieved party".	Section 1-201(b)(2).
"Cancellation".	Section 2A-103(1)(b).
"Conforming".	Section 2A-103(1)(d).
"Delivery".	Section 1-201(b)(15).
"Installment lease contract".	Section 2A-103(1)(i).
"Lessee".	Section 2A-103(1)(n).
"Lessor".	Section 2A-103(1)(p).
"Notifies".	Section 1-202(d).
"Seasonably".	Section 1-205(b).
"Supplier".	Section 2A-103(1)(x).
"Value".	Section 1-204.

Section 2A-511. Merchant Lessee's Duties as to Rightfully Rejected Goods

(1) Subject to any security interest of a lessee (Section 2A-508(5)), if a lessor or a supplier has no agent or place of business at the market of rejection, a merchant lessee, after rejection of goods in his [or her] possession or control, shall follow any reasonable instructions received from the lessor or the supplier with respect to the goods. In the absence of those instructions, a merchant lessee shall make reasonable efforts to sell, lease, or otherwise dispose of the goods for the lessor's account if they threaten to decline in value speedily. Instructions are not reasonable if on demand indemnity for expenses is not forthcoming.

(2) If a merchant lessee (subsection (1)) or any other lessee (Section 2A-512) disposes of goods, he [or she] is entitled to reimbursement either from the lessor or the supplier or out of the proceeds for reasonable expenses of caring for and disposing of the goods and, if the expenses include no disposition commission, to such commission as is usual in the trade, or if there is none, to a reasonable sum not exceeding 10 percent of the gross proceeds.

(3) In complying with this section or Section 2A-512, the lessee is held only to good faith. Good faith conduct hereunder is neither acceptance or conversion nor the basis of an action for damages.

(4) A purchaser who purchases in good faith from a lessee pursuant to this section or Section 2A-512 takes the goods free of any rights of the lessor and the supplier even though the lessee fails to comply with one or more of the requirements of this Article.

Official Comment

Uniform Statutory Source: Sections 2-603 and 2-706(5).

Changes: Revised to reflect leasing practices and terminology.

Cross References:

Sections 2A-508(5) and 2A-512.

Definitional Cross References:

"Action".	Section 1-201(b)(1).
"Good faith".	Sections 1-201(b)(20).
"Goods".	Section 2A-103(1)(h).
"Lease".	Section 2A-103(1)(j).
"Lessee".	Section 2A-103(1)(n).
"Lessor".	Section 2A-103(1)(p).
"Merchant lessee".	Section 2A-103(1)(t).
"Purchaser".	Section 1-201(b)(30).
"Right".	Section 1-201(b)(34).
"Security interest".	Section 1-201(b)(35).
"Supplier".	Section 2A-103(1)(x).
"Value".	Section 1-204.

Section 2A-512. Lessee's Duties as to Rightfully Rejected Goods

(1) Except as otherwise provided with respect to goods that threaten to decline in value speedily (Section 2A-511) and subject to any security interest of a lessee (Section 2A-508(5)):

(a) the lessee, after rejection of goods in the lessee's possession, shall hold them with reasonable care at the lessor's or the supplier's disposition for a reasonable time after the lessee's seasonable notification of rejection;

(b) if the lessor or the supplier gives no instructions within a reasonable time after notification of rejection, the lessee may store the rejected goods for the lessor's or the supplier's account or ship them to the lessor or the supplier or dispose of them for the lessor's or the supplier's account with reimbursement in the manner provided in Section 2A-511; but

(c) the lessee has no further obligations with regard to goods rightfully rejected.

(2) Action by the lessee pursuant to subsection (1) is not acceptance or conversion.

Official Comment

Uniform Statutory Source: Sections 2-602(2)(b) and (c) and 2-604.

Changes: Substantially rewritten.

Purposes: The introduction to subsection (1) references goods that threaten to decline in value speedily and not perishables, the reference in Section 2-604, the statutory analogue. This is a change in style, not substance, as the first phrase includes the second. Subparagraphs (a) and (c) are revised versions of the provisions of Section 2-602(2)(b) and (c).

Subparagraph (a) states the rule with respect to the lessee's treatment of goods in its possession following rejection; subparagraph (b) states the rule regarding such goods if the lessor or supplier then fails to give instructions to the lessee. If the lessee performs in a fashion consistent with subparagraphs (a) and (b), subparagraph (c) exonerates the lessee.

Cross References:

Sections 2-602(2)(b), 2-602(2)(c), 2-604, 2A-508(5), and 2A-511.

Definitional Cross References:

"Action".	Section 1-201(b)(1).
"Goods".	Section 2A-103(1)(h).
"Lessee".	Section 2A-103(1)(n).
"Lessor".	Section 2A-103(1)(p).
"Notification".	Section 1-202(d).
"Reasonable time".	Section 1-205(a).
"Seasonably".	Section 1-205(b).
"Security interest".	Section 1-201(b)(35).
"Supplier".	Section 2A-103(1)(x).
"Value".	Section 1-204.

Section 2A-513. Cure by Lessor of Improper Tender or Delivery; Replacement

(1) If any tender or delivery by the lessor or the supplier is rejected because nonconforming and the time for performance has not yet expired, the lessor or the supplier may seasonably notify the lessee of the lessor's or the supplier's intention to cure and may then make a conforming delivery within the time provided in the lease contract.

(2) If the lessee rejects a nonconforming tender that the lessor or the supplier had reasonable grounds to believe would be acceptable with or without money allowance, the lessor or the supplier may have a further reasonable time to substitute a conforming tender if he [or she] seasonably notifies the lessee.

Official Comment

Uniform Statutory Source: Section 2-508.

Changes: Revised to reflect leasing practices and terminology.

Definitional Cross References:

"Conforming".	Section 2A-103(1)(d).
"Delivery".	Section 1-201(b)(15).
"Lease contract".	Section 2A-103(1)(*l*).
"Lessee".	Section 2A-103(1)(n).
"Lessor".	Section 2A-103(1)(p).
"Money".	Section 1-201(24).
"Notifies".	Section 1-202(d).
"Reasonable time".	Sections 1-205(a).
"Seasonably".	Section 1-205(b).
"Supplier".	Section 2A-103(1)(x).

Section 2A-514. Waiver of Lessee's Objections

(1) In rejecting goods, a lessee's failure to state a particular defect that is ascertainable by reasonable inspection precludes the lessee from relying on the defect to justify rejection or to establish default:

(a) if, stated seasonably, the lessor or the supplier could have cured it (Section 2A-513); or

(b) between merchants if the lessor or the supplier after rejection has made a request in writing for a full and final written statement of all defects on which the lessee proposes to rely.

(2) A lessee's failure to reserve rights when paying rent or other consideration against documents precludes recovery of the payment for defects apparent on the face of the documents.

Official Comment

Uniform Statutory Source: Section 2-605.

Changes: Revised to reflect leasing practices and terminology.

Purposes:

1. The principles applicable to the commercial practice of payment against documents (subsection 2) are explained in Section 2-605 Comment 4, the statutory analogue to this section.

2. As to the use of a record other than a writing and communications that are not written, see Section 2A-103, Comment (g).

Cross Reference:

Section 2A-513.

Definitional Cross References:

"Between merchants".	Section 2-104(3).
"Goods".	Section 2A-103(1)(h).
"Lessee".	Section 2A-103(1)(n).
"Lessor".	Section 2A-103(1)(p).
"Right".	Section 1-201(b)(34).
"Seasonably".	Section 1-205(b).
"Supplier".	Section 2A-103(1)(x).
"Writing".	Section 1-201(b)(43).

Section 2A-515. Acceptance of Goods

(1) Acceptance of goods occurs after the lessee has had a reasonable opportunity to inspect the goods and

(a) the lessee signifies or acts with respect to the goods in a manner that signifies to the lessor or the supplier that the goods are conforming or that the lessee will take or retain them in spite of their nonconformity; or

(b) the lessee fails to make an effective rejection of the goods (Section 2A-509(2)).

(2) Acceptance of a part of any commercial unit is acceptance of that entire unit.

Official Comment

Uniform Statutory Source: Section 2-606.

Changes: The provisions of Section 2-606(1)(a) were substantially rewritten to provide that the lessee's conduct may signify acceptance. Further, the provisions of Section 2-606(1)(c) were not incorporated as irrelevant given the lessee's possession and use of the leased goods.

Cross References:

Sections 2-606(1)(a), 2-606(1)(c), and 2A-509(2).

Definitional Cross References:

"Commercial unit".	Section 2A-103(1)(c).
"Conforming".	Section 2A-103(1)(d).
"Goods".	Section 2A-103(1)(h).
"Lessee".	Section 2A-103(1)(n).
"Lessor".	Section 2A-103(1)(p).
"Supplier".	Section 2A-103(1)(x).

Section 2A-516. Effect of Acceptance of Goods; Notice of Default; Burden of Establishing Default after Acceptance; Notice of Claim or Litigation to Person Answerable Over

(1) A lessee must pay rent for any goods accepted in accordance with the lease contract, with due allowance for goods rightfully rejected or not delivered.

(2) A lessee's acceptance of goods precludes rejection of the goods accepted. In the case of a finance lease, if made with knowledge of a nonconformity, acceptance cannot be revoked because of it. In any other case, if made with knowledge of a nonconformity, acceptance cannot be revoked because of it unless the acceptance was on the reasonable assumption that the nonconformity would be seasonably cured. Acceptance does not of itself impair any other remedy provided by this Article or the lease agreement for nonconformity.

(3) If a tender has been accepted:

(a) within a reasonable time after the lessee discovers or should have discovered any default, the lessee shall notify the lessor and the supplier, if any, or be barred from any remedy against the party not notified;

(b) except in the case of a consumer lease, within a reasonable time after the lessee receives notice of litigation for infringement or the like (Section 2A-211) the lessee shall notify the lessor or be barred from any remedy over for liability established by the litigation; and

(c) the burden is on the lessee to establish any default.

(4) If a lessee is sued for breach of a warranty or other obligation for which a lessor or a supplier is answerable over the following apply:

(a) The lessee may give the lessor or the supplier, or both, written notice of the litigation. If the notice states that the person notified may come in and defend and that if the person notified does not do so that person will be bound in any action against that person by the lessee by any determination of fact common to the two litigations, then unless the person notified after seasonable receipt of the notice does come in and defend that person is so bound.

(b) The lessor or the supplier may demand in writing that the lessee turn over control of the litigation including settlement if the claim is one for infringement or the like (Section 2A-211) or else be barred from any remedy over. If the demand states that the lessor or the supplier agrees to bear all expense and to satisfy any adverse judgment, then unless the lessee after seasonable receipt of the demand does turn over control the lessee is so barred.

(5) Subsections (3) and (4) apply to any obligation of a lessee to hold the lessor or the supplier harmless against infringement or the like (Section 2A-211).

Official Comment

Uniform Statutory Source: Section 2-607.

Changes: Substantially revised.

Purposes:

1. Subsection (2) creates a special rule for finance leases, precluding revocation if acceptance is made with knowledge of nonconformity with respect to the lease agreement, as opposed to the supply agreement; this is not inequitable as the lessee has a direct claim against the supplier. Section 2A-209(1). Revocation of acceptance of a finance lease is permitted if the lessee's acceptance was without discovery of the nonconformity (with respect to the lease agreement, not the supply agreement) and was reasonably induced by the lessor's assurances. Section 2A-517(1)(b). Absent exclusion or modification, the lessor under a finance lease makes certain warranties to the lessee. Sections 2A-210 and 2A-211(1). Revocation of acceptance is not prohibited even after the lessee's promise has become irrevocable and independent. Section 2A-407 Comment. Where the finance lease creates a security interest, the rule may be to the contrary. *General Elec. Credit Corp. of Tennessee v. Ger-Beck Mach. Co.*, 806 F.2d 1207 (3d Cir. 1986).

2. Subsection (3)(a) requires the lessee to give notice of default, within a reasonable time after the lessee discovered or should have discovered the default. In a finance lease, notice may be given either to the supplier, the lessor, or both, but remedy is barred against the party not notified. In a finance lease, the lessor is usually not liable for defects in the goods and the essential notice is to the supplier. While notice to the finance lessor will often not give any additional rights to the lessee, it would be good practice to give the notice since the finance lessor has an interest in the goods. Subsection (3)(a) does not use the term finance lease, but the definition of supplier is a person from whom a lessor buys or leases goods to be leased under a finance lease. Section 2A-103(1)(x). Therefore, there can be a "supplier" only in a finance lease. Subsection (4) applies similar notice rules as to lessors and suppliers if a lessee is sued for a breach of warranty or other obligation for which a lessor or supplier is answerable over.

3. Subsection (3)(b) requires the lessee to give the lessor notice of litigation for infringement or the like. There is an exception created in the case of a consumer lease. While such an exception was considered for a finance lease, it was not created because it was not necessary—the lessor in a finance lease does not give a warranty against infringement. Section 2A-211(2). Even though not required under subsection (3)(b), the lessee who takes under a finance lease should consider giving notice of litigation for infringement or the like to the supplier, because the lessee obtains the benefit of the suppliers' promises subject to the suppliers' defenses or claims. Sections 2A-209(1) and 2-607(3)(b).

4. As to the use of a record other than a writing and communications that are not written, see Section 2A-103, Comment (g).

Cross References:

Sections 2-607(3)(b), 2A-103(1)(x), 2A-209(1), 2A-210, 2A-211(1), 2A-211(2), and 2A-517(1)(b).

Definitional Cross References:

"Action".	Section 1-201(b)(1).
"Agreement".	Section 1-201(b)(3).
"Burden of	Section 1-201(b)(8).
"Conforming".	Section 2A-103(1)(d).
"Consumer lease".	Section 2A-103(1)(e).
"Delivery".	Section 1-201(b)(15).
"Discover".	Section 1-202(c).
"Finance lease".	Section 2A-103(1)(g).
"Goods".	Section 2A-103(1)(h).
"Knowledge".	Section 1-202(b).
"Lease agreement".	Section 2A-103(1)(k).
"Lease contract".	Section 2A-103(1)(*l*).
"Lessee".	Section 2A-103(1)(n).
"Lessor".	Section 2A-103(1)(p).
"Notice".	Section 1-202(a).
"Notifies".	Section 1-202(d).
"Person".	Section 1-201(b)(27).
"Reasonable time".	Section 1-205(a).
"Receipt".	Section 2-103(1)(c).
"Remedy".	Section 1-201(b)(32).
"Seasonably".	Section 1-205(b).
"Supplier".	Section 2A-103(1)(x).
"Written".	Section 1-201(b)(43).

Section 2A-517. Revocation of Acceptance of Goods

(1) A lessee may revoke acceptance of a lot or commercial unit whose nonconformity substantially impairs its value to the lessee if the lessee has accepted it:

(a) except in the case of a finance lease, on the reasonable assumption that its nonconformity would be cured and it has not been seasonably cured; or

(b) without discovery of the nonconformity if the lessee's acceptance was reasonably induced either by the lessor's assurances or, except in the case of a finance lease, by the difficulty of discovery before acceptance.

(2) Except in the case of a finance lease that is not a consumer lease, a lessee may revoke acceptance of a lot or commercial unit if the lessor defaults under the lease contract and the default substantially impairs the value of that lot or commercial unit to the lessee.

(3) If the lease agreement so provides, the lessee may revoke acceptance of a lot or commercial unit because of other defaults by the lessor.

(4) Revocation of acceptance must occur within a reasonable time after the lessee discovers or should have discovered the ground for it and before any substantial change in condition of the goods which is not caused by the nonconformity. Revocation is not effective until the lessee notifies the lessor.

(5) A lessee who so revokes has the same rights and duties with regard to the goods involved as if the lessee had rejected them.

Official Comment

Uniform Statutory Source: Section 2-608.

Changes: Revised to reflect leasing practices and terminology. Note that in the case of a finance lease the lessee retains a limited right to revoke acceptance. Sections 2A-517(1)(b) and 2A-516 Comment. New subsections (2) and (3) added.

Purposes:

1. The section states the situations under which the lessee may return the goods to the lessor and cancel the lease. Subsection (2) recognizes that the lessor may have continuing obligations under the lease and that a default as to those obligations may be sufficiently material to justify revocation of acceptance of the leased items and cancellation of the lease by the lessee. For example, a failure by the lessor to fulfill its obligation to maintain leased equipment or to supply other goods which are necessary for the operation of the leased equipment may justify revocation of acceptance and cancellation of the lease.

2. Subsection (3) specifically provides that the lease agreement may provide that the lessee can revoke acceptance for defaults by the lessor which in the absence of such an agreement might not be considered sufficiently serious to justify revocation. That is, the parties are free to contract on the question of what defaults are so material that the lessee can cancel the lease.

Definitional Cross References:

"Commercial unit".	Section 2A-103(1)(c).
"Conforming".	Section 2A-103(1)(d).
"Consumer lease".	Section 2A-103(1)(e).
"Discover".	Section 1-202(c).
"Finance lease".	Section 2A-103(1)(g).
"Goods".	Section 2A-103(1)(h).
"Lessee".	Section 2A-103(1)(n).
"Lessor".	Section 2A-103(1)(p).

"Lot".	Section 2A-103(1)(s).
"Notifies".	Section 1-202(d).
"Reasonable time".	Sections 1-205(a).
"Right".	Section 1-201(b)(34).
"Seasonably".	Section 1-205(b).
"Value".	Section 1-204.

Section 2A-518. Cover; Substitute Goods

(1) After a default by a lessor under the lease contract of the type described in Section 2A-508(1), or, if agreed, after other default by the lessor, the lessee may cover by making any purchase or lease of or contract to purchase or lease goods in substitution for those due from the lessor.

(2) Except as otherwise provided with respect to damages liquidated in the lease agreement (Section 2A-504) or otherwise determined pursuant to agreement of the parties (Sections 1-102(3) and 2A-503), if a lessee's cover is by a lease agreement substantially similar to the original lease agreement and the new lease agreement is made in good faith and in a commercially reasonable manner, the lessee may recover from the lessor as damages (i) the present value, as of the date of the commencement of the term of the new lease agreement, of the rent under the new lease agreement applicable to that period of the new lease term which is comparable to the then remaining term of the original lease agreement minus the present value as of the same date of the total rent for the then remaining lease term of the original lease agreement, and (ii) any incidental or consequential damages, less expenses saved in consequence of the lessor's default.

(3) If a lessee's cover is by lease agreement that for any reason does not qualify for treatment under subsection (2), or is by purchase or otherwise, the lessee may recover from the lessor as if the lessee had elected not to cover and Section 2A-519 governs.

Official Comment

Uniform Statutory Source: Section 2-712.

Changes: Substantially revised.

Purposes:

1. Subsection (1) allows the lessee to take action to fix its damages after default by the lessor. Such action may consist of the lease of goods. The decision to cover is a function of commercial judgment, not a statutory mandate replete with sanctions for failure to comply. Cf. Section 9-507.

2. Subsection (2) states a rule for determining the amount of lessee's damages provided that there is no agreement to the contrary. The lessee's damages will be established using the new lease agreement as a measure if the following three criteria are met: (1) the lessee's cover is by lease agreement, (2) the lease agreement is substantially similar to the original lease agreement, and (3) such cover was effected in good faith, and in a commercially reasonable manner. Thus, the lessee will be entitled to recover from the lessor the present value, as of the date of commencement of the term of the new lease agreement, of the rent under the new lease agreement applicable to that period which is comparable to the then remaining term of the original lease agreement less the present value of the rent reserved for the remaining term under the original lease, together with incidental or consequential damages less expenses saved in consequence of the lessor's default. Consequential damages may include loss suffered by the lessee because of deprivation of the use of the goods during the period between the default and the acquisition of the goods under the new lease agreement. If the lessee's cover does not satisfy the criteria of subsection (2), Section 2A-519 governs.

3. Two of the three criteria to be met by the lessee are familiar, but the concept of the new lease agreement being substantially similar to the original lease agreement is not. Given the many variables facing a party who intends to lease goods and the rapidity of change in the market place, the policy decision was made not to draft with specificity. It was thought unwise to seek to establish certainty at the cost of fairness. Thus, the decision of whether the new lease agreement is substantially similar to the original will be determined case by case.

4. While the section does not draw a bright line, it is possible to describe some of the factors that should be considered in finding that a new lease agreement is substantially similar to the original. First, the goods subject to the new lease agreement should be examined. For example, in a lease of computer equipment the new lease might be for more modern equipment. However, it may be that at the time of the lessor's breach it was not possible to obtain the same type of goods in the marketplace. Because the lessee's remedy under Section 2A-519 is intended to place the lessee in essentially the same position as if he had covered, if goods similar to those to have been delivered under the original lease are not available, then the computer equipment in this hypothetical should qualify as a commercially reasonable substitute. See Section 2-712(1).

5. Second, the various elements of the new lease agreement should also be examined. Those elements include the presence or absence of options to purchase or release; the lessor's representations, warranties and covenants to the lessee, as well as those to be provided by the lessee to the lessor; and the services, if any, to be provided by the lessor or by the lessee. All of these factors allocate cost and risk between the lessor and the lessee and thus affect the amount of rent to be paid. If the differences between the original lease and the new lease can be easily valued, it would be appropriate for a court to adjust the difference in rental to take account of the difference between the two leases, find that the new lease is substantially similar to the old lease, and award cover damages under this section. If, for example, the new lease requires the lessor to insure the goods in the hands of the lessee, while the original lease required the lessee to insure, the usual cost of such insurance could be deducted from the rent due under the new lease before determining the difference in rental between the two leases.

6. Having examined the goods and the agreement, the test to be applied is whether, in light of these comparisons, the new lease agreement is substantially similar to the original lease agreement. These findings should not be made with scientific precision, as they are a function of economics, nor should they be made independently with respect to the goods and each element of the agreement, as it is important that a sense of commercial judgment pervade the finding. To establish the new lease as a proper measure of damage under subsection (2), these factors, taken as a whole, must result in a finding that the new lease agreement is substantially similar to the original.

7. A new lease can be substantially similar to the original lease even though its term extends beyond the remaining term of the original lease, so long as both (a) the lease terms are commercially comparable (e.g., it is highly unlikely that a 1-month rental and a 5-year lease would reflect similar commercial realities), and (b) the court can fairly apportion a part of the rental payments under the new lease to that part of the term of the new lease which is comparable to the remaining lease term under the original lease. Also, the lease term of the new lease may be comparable to the term of the original lease even though the beginning and ending dates of the two leases are not the same. For example, a 2-month lease of agricultural equipment for the months of August and September may be comparable to a 2-month lease running from the 15th of August to the 15th of October if in the particular location 2-month leases beginning on August 15th are basically interchangeable with 2-month leases beginning August 1st. Similarly, the term of a 1-year truck lease beginning on the 15th of January may be comparable to the term of a 1-year truck lease beginning January 2. If the lease terms are found to be comparable, the court may base cover damages on the entire difference between the costs under the two leases.

Cross References:

Sections 1-302, 2-712(1), 2A-503, 2A-504, 2A-508(1), 2A-519, 9-625, and 9-627.

Definitional Cross References:

"Agreement".	Section 1-201(b)(3).
"Contract".	Section 1-201(b)(12).
"Good faith".	Section 1-201(b)(20).
"Goods".	Section 2A-103(1)(h).
"Lease".	Section 2A-103(1)(j).
"Lease agreement".	Section 2A-103(1)(k).
"Lease contract".	Section 2A-103(1)(*l*).
"Lessee".	Section 2A-103(1)(n).
"Lessor".	Section 2A-103(1)(p).
"Party".	Section 1-201(b)(26).
"Present value".	Section 1-201(b)(28).
"Purchase".	Sections 1-201(b)(29) and 2A-103(1)(v).

Section 2A-519. Lessee's Damages for Non-delivery, Repudiation, Default, and Breach of Warranty in Regard to Accepted Goods

(1) Except as otherwise provided with respect to damages liquidated in the lease agreement (Section 2A-504) or otherwise determined pursuant to agreement of the parties (Sections 1-102(3) and 2A-503), if a lessee elects not to cover or a lessee elects to cover and the cover is by lease agreement that for any reason does not qualify for treatment under Section 2A-518(2), or is by purchase or otherwise, the measure of damages for non-delivery or repudiation by the lessor or for rejection or revocation of acceptance by the lessee is the present value, as of the date of the default, of the then market rent minus the present value as of the same date of the original rent, computed for the remaining lease term of the original lease agreement, together with incidental and consequential damages, less expenses saved in consequence of the lessor's default.

(2) Market rent is to be determined as of the place for tender or, in cases of rejection after arrival or revocation of acceptance, as of the place of arrival.

(3) Except as otherwise agreed, if the lessee has accepted goods and given notification (Section 2A-516(3)), the measure of damages for non-conforming tender or delivery or other default by a lessor is the loss resulting in the ordinary course of events from the lessor's default as determined in any manner that is reasonable together with incidental and consequential damages, less expenses saved in consequence of the lessor's default.

(4) Except as otherwise agreed, the measure of damages for breach of warranty is the present value at the time and place of acceptance of the difference between the value of the use of the goods accepted and the value if they had been as warranted for the lease term, unless special circumstances show proximate damages of a different amount, together with incidental and consequential damages, less expenses saved in consequence of the lessor's default or breach of warranty.

Official Comment

Uniform Statutory Source: Sections 2-713 and 2-714.

Changes: Substantially revised.

Purposes:

1. Subsection (1), a revised version of the provisions of Section 2-713(1), states the basic rule governing the measure of lessee's damages for nondelivery or repudiation by the lessor or for rightful rejection or revocation of acceptance by the lessee. This measure will apply, absent agreement to the contrary, if the lessee does not cover or if the cover does not qualify under Section 2A-518. There is no sanction for cover that does not qualify.

2. The measure of damage is the present value, as of the date of default, of the market rent for the remaining term of the lease less the present value of the original rent for the remaining term of the lease, plus incidental and consequential damages less expenses saved in consequence of the default. Note that the reference in Section 2A-519(1) is to the date of default not to the date of an event of default. An event of default under a lease agreement becomes a default under a lease agreement only after the expiration of any relevant period of grace and compliance with any notice requirements under this Article and the lease agreement. American Bar Foundation, *Commentaries on Indentures,* § 5-1, at 216-217 (1971). Section 2A-501(1). This conclusion is also a function of whether, as a matter of fact or law, the event of default has been waived, suspended or cured. Sections 2A-103(4) and 1-103.

3. Subsection (2), a revised version of the provisions of Section 2-713(2), states the rule with respect to determining market rent.

4. Subsection (3), a revised version of the provisions of Section 2-714(1) and (3), states the measure of damages where goods have been accepted and acceptance is not revoked. The subsection applies both to defaults which occur at the inception of the lease and to defaults which occur subsequently, such as failure to comply with an obligation to maintain the leased goods. The measure in essence is the loss, in the ordinary course of events, flowing from the default.

5. Subsection (4), a revised version of the provisions of Section 2-714(2), states the measure of damages for breach of warranty. The measure in essence is the present value of the difference between the value of the goods accepted and of the goods if they had been as warranted.

6. Subsections (1), (3) and (4) specifically state that the parties may by contract vary the damages rules stated in those subsections.

Cross References:

Sections 2-713(1), 2-713(2), 2-714, 2A-103(4), 2A-501(1), 2A-503, 2A-504, 2A-516(3), and 2A-518.

Definitional Cross References:

"Conforming".	Section 2A-103(1)(d).
"Delivery".	Section 1-201(b)(15).
"Goods".	Section 2A-103(1)(h).
"Lease".	Section 2A-103(1)(j).
"Lease agreement".	Section 2A-103(1)(k).
"Lessee".	Section 2A-103(1)(n).
"Lessor".	Section 2A-103(1)(p).
"Notification".	Section 1-202(d).
"Present value".	Section 1-201(b)(28).
"Value".	Section 1-204.

Section 2A-520. Lessee's Incidental and Consequential Damages

(1) Incidental damages resulting from a lessor's default include expenses reasonably incurred in inspection, receipt, transportation, and care and custody of goods rightfully rejected or goods the acceptance of which is justifiably revoked, any commercially reasonable charges, expenses or commissions in connection with effecting cover, and any other reasonable expense incident to the default.

(2) Consequential damages resulting from a lessor's default include:

(a) any loss resulting from general or particular requirements and needs of which the lessor at the time of contracting had reason to know and which could not reasonably be prevented by cover or otherwise; and

(b) injury to person or property proximately resulting from any breach of warranty.

Official Comment

Uniform Statutory Source: Section 2-715.

Changes: Revised to reflect leasing terminology and practices.

Purposes: Subsection (1), a revised version of the provisions of Section 2-715(1), lists some examples of incidental damages resulting from a lessor's default; the list is not exhaustive. Subsection (1) makes clear that it applies not only to rightful rejection, but also to justifiable revocation.

Subsection (2), a revised version of the provisions of Section 2-715(2), lists some examples of consequential damages resulting from a lessor's default; the list is not exhaustive.

Cross Reference:

Section 2-715.

Definitional Cross References:

"Goods".	Section 2A-103(1)(h).
"Knows".	Section 1-202(b).
"Lessee".	Section 2A-103(1)(n).
"Lessor".	Section 2A-103(1)(p).
"Person".	Section 1-201(b)(27).
"Receipt".	Section 2-103(1)(c).

Section 2A-521. Lessee's Right to Specific Performance or Replevin

(1) Specific performance may be decreed if the goods are unique or in other proper circumstances.

(2) A decree for specific performance may include any terms and conditions as to payment of the rent, damages, or other relief that the court deems just.

(3) A lessee has a right of replevin, detinue, sequestration, claim and delivery, or the like for goods identified to the lease contract if after reasonable effort the lessee is unable to effect cover for those goods or the circumstances reasonably indicate that the effort will be unavailing.

Official Comment

Uniform Statutory Source: Section 2-716.

Changes: Revised to reflect leasing practices and terminology, and to expand the reference to the right of replevin in subsection (3) to include other similar rights of the lessee.

Definitional Cross References:

"Delivery".	Section 1-201(b)(15).
"Goods".	Section 2A-103(1)(h).
"Lease contract".	Section 2A-103(1)(*l*).
"Lessee".	Section 2A-103(1)(n).
"Rights".	Section 1-201(b)(34).
"Term".	Section 1-201(b)(40).

Section 2A-522. Lessee's Right to Goods on Lessor's Insolvency

(1) Subject to subsection (2) and even though the goods have not been shipped, a lessee who has paid a part or all of the rent and security for goods identified to a lease contract (Section 2A-217) on making and keeping good a tender of any unpaid portion of the rent and security due under the lease contract may recover the goods identified from the lessor if the lessor becomes insolvent within 10 days after receipt of the first installment of rent and security.

(2) A lessee acquires the right to recover goods identified to a lease contract only if they conform to the lease contract.

Official Comment

Uniform Statutory Source: Section 2-502.

Changes: Revised to reflect leasing practices and terminology.

Cross Reference:

Section 2A-217.

Definitional Cross References:

"Conforming".	Section 2A-103(1)(d).
"Goods".	Section 2A-103(1)(h).
"Insolvent".	Section 1-201(b)(23).
"Lease contract".	Section 2A-103(1)(*l*).
"Lessee".	Section 2A-103(1)(n).
"Lessor".	Section 2A-103(1)(p).
"Receipt".	Section 2-103(1)(c).
"Right".	Section 1-201(b)(34).

C. Default by Lessee

Section 2A-523. Lessor's Remedies

(1) If a lessee wrongfully rejects or revokes acceptance of goods or fails to make a payment when due or repudiates with respect to a part or the whole, then, with respect to any goods involved, and with respect to all of the goods if under an installment lease contract the value of the whole lease contract is substantially impaired (Section 2A-510), the lessee is in default under the lease contract and the lessor may:

(a) cancel the lease contract (Section 2A-505(1));

(b) proceed respecting goods not identified to the lease contract (Section 2A-524);

(c) withhold delivery of the goods and take possession of goods previously delivered (Section 2A-525);

(d) stop delivery of the goods by any bailee (Section 2A-526);

(e) dispose of the goods and recover damages (Section 2A-527), or retain the goods and recover damages (Section 2A-528), or in a proper case recover rent (Section 2A-529);

(f) exercise any other rights or pursue any other remedies provided in the lease contract.

(2) If a lessor does not fully exercise a right or obtain a remedy to which the lessor is entitled under subsection (1), the lessor may recover the loss resulting in the ordinary course of events from the lessee's default as determined in any reasonable manner, together with incidental damages, less expenses saved in consequence of the lessee's default.

(3) If a lessee is otherwise in default under a lease contract, the lessor may exercise the rights and pursue the remedies provided in the lease contract, which may include a right to cancel the lease. In addition, unless otherwise provided in the lease contract:

(a) if the default substantially impairs the value of the lease contract to the lessor, the lessor may exercise the rights and pursue the remedies provided in subsections (1) or (2); or

(b) if the default does not substantially impair the value of the lease contract to the lessor, the lessor may recover as provided in subsection (2).

Official Comment

Uniform Statutory Source: Section 2-703.

Changes: Substantially revised.

Purposes:

1. Subsection (1) is an index to Sections 2A-524 through 2A-531 and states that the remedies provided in those sections are available for the defaults referred to in subsection (1): wrongful rejection or revocation of acceptance, failure to make a payment when due, or repudiation. In addition, remedies provided in the lease contract are available. Subsection (2) sets out a remedy if the lessor does not pursue to completion a right or actually obtain a remedy available under subsection (1), and subsection (3) sets out statutory remedies for defaults not specifically referred to in subsection (1). Subsection (3) provides that, if any default by the lessee other than those specifically referred to in subsection (1) is material, the lessor can exercise the remedies provided in subsection (1) or (2); otherwise the available remedy is as provided in subsection (3). A lessor who has brought an action seeking or has nonjudicially pursued one or more of the remedies available under subsection (1) may amend so as to claim or may nonjudicially pursue a remedy under subsection (2) unless the right or remedy first chosen has been pursued to an extent actually inconsistent with the new course of action. The intent of the provision is to reject the doctrine of election of remedies and to permit an alteration of course by the lessor unless such alteration would actually have an effect on the lessee that would be unreasonable under the circumstances. Further, the lessor may pursue remedies under both subsections (1) and (2) unless doing so would put the lessor in a better position than it would have been in had the lessee fully performed.

2. The lessor and the lessee can agree to modify the rights and remedies available under the Article; they can, among other things, provide that for defaults other than those specified in subsection (1) the lessor can exercise the rights and remedies referred to in subsection (1), whether or not the default would otherwise be held to substantially impair the value of the lease contract to the lessor; they can also create a new scheme of rights and remedies triggered by the occurrence of the default. Sections 2A-103(4) and 1-302(a).

3. Subsection (1), a substantially rewritten version of Section 2-703, lists various cumulative remedies of the lessor where the lessee wrongfully rejects or revokes acceptance, fails to make a payment when due, or repudiates. Section 2A-501(2) and (4). The subsection also allows the lessor to exercise any contractual remedy.

4. This Article rejects any general doctrine of election of remedy. Whether, in a particular case, one remedy bars another, is a function of whether lessor has been put in as good a position as if the lessee had fully performed the lease contract. Multiple remedies are barred only if the effect is to put the lessor in a better position than it would have been in had the lessee fully performed under the lease. Sections 2A-103(4), 2A-501(4), and 1-305(a).

5. Hypothetical: To better understand the application of subparagraphs (a) through (e), it is useful to review a hypothetical. Assume that A is a merchant in the business of selling and leasing new bicycles of various types. B is about to engage in the business of subleasing bicycles to summer residents of and visitors to an island resort. A, as lessor, has agreed to lease 60 bicycles to B. While there is one master lease, deliveries and terms are staggered. 20 bicycles are to be delivered by A to B's island location on June 1; the term of the lease of these bicycles is four months. 20 bicycles are to be delivered by A to B's island location on July 1; the term of the lease of these bicycles is three months. Finally, 20 bicycles are to be delivered by A to B's island location on August 1; the term of the lease of these bicycles is two months. B is obligated to pay rent to A on the 15th day of each month during the term for the lease. Rent is $50 per month, per bicycle. B has no option to purchase or release and must return the bicycles to A at the end of the term, in good condition, reasonable wear and tear excepted. Since the retail price of each bicycle is $400 and bicycles used in the retail rental business have a useful economic life of 36 months, this transaction creates a lease. Sections 2A-103(1)(j) and 1-203.

6. A's current inventory of bicycles is not large. Thus, upon signing the lease with B in February, A agreed to purchase 60 new bicycles from A's principal manufacturer, with special instructions to drop ship the bicycles to B's island location in accordance with the delivery schedule set forth in the lease.

7. The first shipment of 20 bicycles was received by B on May 21. B inspected the bicycles, accepted the same as conforming to the lease and signed a receipt of delivery and acceptance. However, due to poor weather that summer, business was terrible and B was unable to pay the rent due on June 15. Pursuant to the lease A sent B notice of default and proceeded to enforce his rights and remedies against B.

8. A's counsel first advised A that under Section 2A-510(2) and the terms of the lease B's failure to pay was a default with respect to the whole. Thus, to minimize A's continued exposure, A was advised to take possession of the bicycles. If A had possession of the goods A could refuse to deliver. Section 2A-525(1). However, the facts here are different. With respect to the bicycles in B's possession, A has the right to take possession of the bicycles, without breach of the peace. Section 2A-525(2). If B refuses to allow A access to the bicycles, A can proceed by action, including replevin or injunctive relief.

9. With respect to the 40 bicycles that have not been delivered, this Article provides various alternatives. First, assume that 20 of the remaining 40 bicycles have been manufactured and delivered by the manufacturer to a carrier for shipment to B. Given the size of the shipment, the carrier was using a small truck for the delivery and the truck had not yet reached the island ferry when the manufacturer (at the request of A) instructed the carrier to divert the shipment to A's place of business. A's right to stop delivery is recognized under these circumstances. Section 2A-526(1). Second, assume that the 20 remaining bicycles were in the process of manufacture when B defaulted. A retains the right (as between A as lessor and B as lessee) to exercise reasonable commercial judgment whether to complete manufacture or to dispose of the unfinished goods for scrap. Since A is not the manufacturer and A has a binding contract to buy the bicycles, A elected to allow the manufacturer to complete the manufacture of the bicycles, but instructed the manufacturer to deliver the completed bicycles to A's place of business. Section 2A-524(2).

10. Thus, so far A has elected to exercise the remedies referred to in subparagraphs (b) through (d) in subsection (1). None of these remedies bars any of the others because A's election and enforcement merely resulted in A's possession of the bicycles. Had B performed A would have recovered possession of the bicycles. Thus A is in the process of obtaining the benefit of his bargain. Note that A could exercise any other rights or pursue any other remedies provided in the lease contract (Section 2A-523(1)(f)), or elect to recover his loss due to the lessee's default under Section 2A-523(2).

11. A's counsel next would determine what action, if any, should be taken with respect to the goods. As stated in subparagraph (e) and as discussed fully in Section 2A-527(1) the lessor may, but has no obligation to, dispose of the goods by a substantially similar lease (indeed, the lessor has no obligation whatsoever to dispose of the goods at all) and recover damages based on that action, but lessor will not be able to recover damages which put it in a better position than performance would have done, nor will it be able to recover damages for losses which it could have reasonably avoided. In this case, since A is in the business of leasing and selling bicycles, A will probably inventory the 60 bicycles for its retail trade.

12. A's counsel then will determine which of the various means of ascertaining A's damages against B are available. Subparagraph (e) catalogues each relevant section. First, under Section 2A-527(2) the amount of A's claim is computed by comparing the original lease between A and B with any subsequent lease of the bicycles but only if the subsequent lease is substantially similar to the original lease contract. While the section does not define this term, the official comment does establish some parameters. If, however, A elects to lease the bicycles to his retail trade, it is unlikely that the resulting lease will be substantially similar to the original, as leases to retail customers are considerably different from leases to wholesale customers like B. If, however, the leases were substantially similar, the damage claim is for accrued and unpaid rent to the beginning of the new lease, plus the present value as of the same date, of the rent reserved under the original lease for the balance of its term less the present value as of the same date of the rent reserved under the replacement lease for a term comparable to the balance of the term of the original lease, together with incidental damages less expenses saved in consequence of the lessee's default.

13. If the new lease is not substantially similar or if A elects to sell the bicycles or to hold the bicycles, damages are computed under Section 2A-528 or 2A-529.

14. If A elects to pursue his claim under Section 2A-528(1) the damage rule is the same as that stated in Section 2A-528(2) except that damages are measured from default if the lessee never took possession of the goods or from the time when the lessor did or could have regained possession and that the standard of comparison is not the rent reserved under a substantially similar lease entered into by the lessor but a market rent, as defined in Section 2A-507. Further, if the facts of this hypothetical were more elaborate A may be able to establish that the measure of damage under subsection (1) is inadequate to put him in the same position that B's performance would have, in which case A can claim the present value of his lost profits.

15. Yet another alternative for computing A's damage claim against B which will be available in some situations is recovery of the present value, as of entry of judgment, of the rent for the then remaining lease term under Section 2A-529. However, this formulation is not available if the goods have been repossessed or tendered back to A. For the 20 bicycles repossessed and the remaining 40 bicycles, A will be able to recover the present value of the rent only if A is unable to dispose of them, or circumstances indicate the effort will be unavailing. If A has prevailed in an action for the rent, at any time up to collection of a judgment by A against B, A might dispose of the bicycles. In such case A's claim for damages against B is governed by Section 2A-527 or 2A-528. Section 2A-529(3). The resulting recalculation of claim should reduce the amount recoverable by A against B and the lessor is required to cause an appropriate credit to be entered against the earlier judgment. However, the nature of the post-judgment proceedings to resolve this issue, and the sanctions for a failure to comply, if any, will be determined by other law.

16. Finally, if the lease agreement had so provided pursuant to subparagraph (f), A's claim against B would not be determined under any of these statutory formulae, but pursuant to a liquidated damages clause. Section 2A-504(1).

17. These various methods of computing A's damage claim against B are alternatives subject to Section 2A-501(4). However, the pursuit of any one of these alternatives is not a bar to, nor has it been barred by, A's earlier action to obtain possession of the 60 bicycles. These formulae, which vary as a function of an overt or implied mitigation of damage theory, focus on allowing A a recovery of the benefit of his bargain with B. Had B performed, A would have received the rent as well as the return of the 60 bicycles at the end of the term.

18. Finally, A's counsel should also advise A of his right to cancel the lease contract under subparagraph (a). Section 2A-505(1). Cancellation will discharge all existing obligations but preserve A's rights and remedies.

19. Subsection (2) recognizes that a lessor who is entitled to exercise the rights or to obtain a remedy granted by subsection (1) may choose not to do so. In such cases, the lessor can recover damages as provided in subsection (2). For example, for non-payment of rent, the lessor may decide not to take possession of the goods and cancel the lease, but rather to merely sue for the unpaid rent as it comes due plus lost interest or other damages "determined in any reasonable manner." Subsection (2) also negates any loss of alternative rights and remedies by reason of having invoked or commenced the exercise or pursuit of any one or more rights or remedies.

20. Subsection (3) allows the lessor access to a remedy scheme provided in this Article as well as that contained in the lease contract if the lessee is in default for reasons other than those stated in subsection (1). Note that the reference to this Article includes supplementary principles of law and equity, e.g., fraud, misrepresentation and duress. Sections 2A-103(4) and 1-103(b).

21. There is no special treatment of the finance lease in this section. Absent supplementary principles of law to the contrary, in most cases the supplier will have no rights or remedies against the defaulting lessee. Section 2A-209(2)(ii). Given that the supplier will look to the lessor for payment, this is appropriate. However, there is a specific exception to this rule with respect to the right to identify goods to the lease contract. Section 2A-524(2). The parties are free to create a different result in a particular case. Sections 2A-103(4) and 1-302(a).

Cross References:

Sections 1-103(b), 1-203, 1-302(a), 1-305(a), 2-703, 2A-103(1)(j), 2A-103(4), 2A-209(2)(ii), 2A-501(2), 2A-501(4), 2A-504(1), 2A-505(1), 2A-507, 2A-510, and 2A-523(2) through 2A-531.

Definitional Cross References:

"Delivery".	Section 1-201(b)(15).
"Goods".	Section 2A-103(1)(h).
"Installment.	Section 2A-103(1)(i).
"Lease contract".	Section 2A-103(1)(*l*).
"Lessee".	Section 2A-103(1)(n).
"Lessor".	Section 2A-103(1)(p).
"Remedy".	Section 1-201(b)(32).

"Right".	Section 1-201(b)(34).
"Value".	Section 1-204.

Section 2A-524. Lessor's Right to Identify Goods to Lease Contract

(1) After default by the lessee under the lease contract of the type described in Section 2A-523(1) or 2A-523(3)(a) or, if agreed, after other default by the lessee, the lessor may:

(a) identify to the lease contract conforming goods not already identified if at the time the lessor learned of the default they were in the lessor's or the supplier's possession or control; and

(b) dispose of goods (Section 2A-527(1)) that demonstrably have been intended for the particular lease contract even though those goods are unfinished.

(2) If the goods are unfinished, in the exercise of reasonable commercial judgment for the purposes of avoiding loss and of effective realization, an aggrieved lessor or the supplier may either complete manufacture and wholly identify the goods to the lease contract or cease manufacture and lease, sell, or otherwise dispose of the goods for scrap or salvage value or proceed in any other reasonable manner.

Official Comment

Uniform Statutory Source: Section 2-704.

Changes: Revised to reflect leasing practices and terminology.

Purposes: The remedies provided by this section are available to the lessor (1) if there has been a default by the lessee which falls within Section 2A-523(1) or 2A-523(3)(a), or (2) if there has been any other default for which the lease contract gives the lessor the remedies provided by this section. Under "(2)", the lease contract may give the lessor the remedies of identification and disposition provided by this section in various ways. For example, a lease provision might specifically refer to the remedies of identification and disposition, or it might refer to this section by number (i.e., 2A-524), or it might do so by a more general reference such as "all rights and remedies provided by Article 2A for default by the lessee".

Cross References:

Sections 2A-523(1), 2A-523(3)(a), and 2A-527(1).

Definitional Cross References:

"Aggrieved party".	Section 1-201(b)(2).
"Conforming".	Section 2A-103(1)(d).
"Goods".	Section 2A-103(1)(h).
"Learn".	Section 1-202(c).
"Lease".	Section 2A-103(1)(j).
"Lease contract".	Section 2A-103(1)(*l*).
"Lessor".	Section 2A-103(1)(p).
"Right".	Section 1-201(b)(34).
"Supplier".	Section 2A-103(1)(x).
"Value".	Section 1-204.

Section 2A-525. Lessor's Right to Possession of Goods

(1) If a lessor discovers the lessee to be insolvent, the lessor may refuse to deliver the goods.

(2) After a default by the lessee under the lease contract of the type described in Section 2A-523(1) or 2A-523(3)(a) or, if agreed, after other default by the lessee, the lessor has the right to take possession of the goods. If the lease contract so provides, the lessor may require the lessee to assemble the goods and make them available to the lessor at a place to be designated by the lessor which is reasonably convenient to both parties. Without removal, the lessor may render unusable any goods employed in trade or business, and may dispose of goods on the lessee's premises (Section 2A-527).

(3) The lessor may proceed under subsection (2) without judicial process if it can be done without breach of the peace or the lessor may proceed by action.

Official Comment

Uniform Statutory Source: Sections 2-702(1) and 9-503.

Changes: Substantially revised.

Purposes:

1. Subsection (1), a revised version of the provisions of Section 2-702(1), allows the lessor to refuse to deliver goods if the lessee is insolvent. Note that the provisions of Section 2-702(2), granting the unpaid seller certain rights of reclamation, were not incorporated in this section. Subsection (2) made this unnecessary.

2. Subsection (2), a revised version of the provisions of Section 9-503, allows the lessor, on a Section 2A-523(1) or 2A-523(3)(a) default by the lessee, the right to take possession of or reclaim the goods. Also, the lessor can contract for the right to take possession of the goods for other defaults by the lessee. Therefore, since the lessee's insolvency is an event of default in a standard lease agreement, subsection (2) is the functional equivalent of Section 2-702(2). Further, subsection (2) sanctions the classic crate and delivery clause obligating the lessee to assemble the goods and to make them available to the lessor. Finally, the lessor may leave the goods in place, render them unusable (if they are goods employed in trade or business), and dispose of them on the lessee's premises.

3. Subsection (3), a revised version of the provisions of Section 9-503, allows the lessor to proceed under subsection (2) without judicial process, absent breach of the peace, or by action. Sections 2A-501(3), 2A-103(4) and 1-201(1) [*sic*, should be 1-201(b)(1)]. In the appropriate case action includes injunctive relief. *Clark Equip. Co. v. Armstrong Equip. Co.*, 431 F.2d 54 (5th Cir.1970), cert. denied, 402 U.S. 909 (1971). This section, as well as a number of other sections in this Part, are included in the Article to codify the lessor's common-law right to protect the lessor's reversionary interest in the goods. Section 2A-103(1)(q). These Sections are intended to supplement and not displace principles of law and equity with respect to the protection of such interest. Sections 2A-103(4) and 1-103. Such principles apply in many instances, e.g., loss or damage to goods if risk of loss passes to the lessee, failure of the lessee to return goods to the lessor in the condition stipulated in the lease, and refusal of the lessee to return goods to the lessor after termination or cancellation of the lease. See also Section 2A-532.

Cross References:

Sections 1-103, 1-201(b)(1), 2-702(1), 2-702(2), 2A-103(1)(q), 2A-103(4), 2A-501(3), 2A-523(1), 2A-523(3)(a), 2A-527, 2A-532, and 9-609.

Definitional Cross References:

"Action".	Section 1-201(b)(1).
"Delivery".	Section 1-201(b)(15).
"Discover".	Section 1-202(c).
"Goods".	Section 2A-103(1)(h).
"Insolvent".	Section 1-201(b)(23).
"Lease contract".	Section 2A-103(1)(*l*).
"Lessee".	Section 2A-103(1)(n).
"Lessor".	Section 2A-103(1)(p).
"Party".	Section 1-201(b)(26).
"Right".	Section 1-201(b)(34).

Section 2A-526. Lessor's Stoppage of Delivery in Transit or Otherwise

(1) A lessor may stop delivery of goods in the possession of a carrier or other bailee if the lessor discovers the lessee to be insolvent and may stop delivery of carload, truckload, planeload, or larger shipments of express or freight if the lessee repudiates or fails to make a payment due before delivery, whether for rent, security or otherwise under the lease contract, or for any other reason the lessor has a right to withhold or take possession of the goods.

(2) In pursuing its remedies under subsection (1), the lessor may stop delivery until

(a) receipt of the goods by the lessee;

(b) acknowledgment to the lessee by any bailee of the goods, except a carrier, that the bailee holds the goods for the lessee; or

(c) such an acknowledgment to the lessee by a carrier via reshipment or as warehouseman.

(3) (a) To stop delivery, a lessor shall so notify as to enable the bailee by reasonable diligence to prevent delivery of the goods.

(b) After notification, the bailee shall hold and deliver the goods according to the directions of the lessor, but the lessor is liable to the bailee for any ensuing charges or damages.

(c) A carrier who has issued a nonnegotiable bill of lading is not obliged to obey a notification to stop received from a person other than the consignor.

Official Comment

Uniform Statutory Source: Section 2-705.

Changes: Revised to reflect leasing practices and terminology.

Definitional Cross References:

"Bill of lading".	Section 1-201(b)(6).
"Delivery".	Section 1-201(b)(15).
"Discover".	Section 1-202(c).
"Goods".	Section 2A-103(1)(h).
"Insolvent".	Section 1-201(b)(23).
"Lease contract".	Section 2A-103(1)(*l*).
"Lessee".	Section 2A-103(1)(n).
"Lessor".	Section 2A-103(1)(p).
"Notifies" and	Section 1-202(d).
"Person".	Section 1-201(b)(27).
"Receipt".	Section 2-103(1)(c).
"Remedy".	Section 1-201(b)(32).
"Right".	Section 1-201(b)(34).

Section 2A-527. Lessor's Rights to Dispose of Goods

(1) After a default by a lessee under the lease contract of the type described in Section 2A-523(1) or 2A-523(3)(a) or after the lessor refuses to deliver or takes possession of goods (Section 2A-525 or 2A-526), or, if agreed, after other default by a lessee, the lessor may dispose of the goods concerned or the undelivered balance thereof by lease, sale, or otherwise.

(2) Except as otherwise provided with respect to damages liquidated in the lease agreement (Section 2A-504) or otherwise determined pursuant to agreement of the parties (Sections 1-302 and 2A-503), if the disposition is by lease agreement substantially similar to the original lease agreement and the new lease agreement is made in good faith and in a commercially reasonable manner, the lessor may recover from the lessee as damages (i) accrued and unpaid rent as of the date of the commencement of the term of the new lease agreement, (ii) the present value, as of the same date, of the total rent for the then remaining lease term of the original lease agreement minus the present value, as of the same date, of the rent under the new lease agreement applicable to that period of the new lease term which is comparable to the then remaining term of the original lease agreement, and (iii) any incidental damages allowed under Section 2A-530, less expenses saved in consequence of the lessee's default.

(3) If the lessor's disposition is by lease agreement that for any reason does not qualify for treatment under subsection (2), or is by sale or otherwise, the lessor may recover from the lessee as if the lessor had elected not to dispose of the goods and Section 2A-528 governs.

(4) A subsequent buyer or lessee who buys or leases from the lessor in good faith for value as a result of a disposition under this section takes the goods free of the original lease contract and any rights of the original lessee even though the lessor fails to comply with one or more of the requirements of this Article.

(5) The lessor is not accountable to the lessee for any profit made on any disposition. A lessee who has rightfully rejected or justifiably revoked acceptance shall account to the lessor for any excess over the amount of the lessee's security interest (Section 2A-508(5)).

Official Comment

Uniform Statutory Source: Section 2-706(1), (5) and (6).

Changes: Substantially revised.

Purposes:

1. Subsection (1), a revised version of the first sentence of subsection 2-706(1), allows the lessor the right to dispose of goods after a statutory or other material default by the lessee (even if the goods remain in the lessee's possession—Section 2A-525(2)), after the lessor refuses to deliver or takes possession of the goods, or, if agreed, after other contractual default. The lessor's decision to exercise this right is a function of a commercial judgment, not a statutory mandate replete with sanctions for failure to comply. Cf. Section 9-625. As the owner of the goods, in the case of a lessor, or as the prime lessee of the goods, in the case of a sublessor, compulsory disposition of the goods is inconsistent with the nature of the interest held by the lessor or the sublessor and is not necessary because the interest held by the lessee or the sublessee is not protected by a right of redemption under the common law or this Article. Subsection 2A-527(5).

2. The rule for determining the measure of damages recoverable by the lessor against the lessee is a function of several variables. If the lessor has elected to effect disposition under subsection (1) and such disposition is by lease that qualifies under subsection (2), the measure of damages set forth in subsection (2) will apply, absent agreement to the contrary. Sections 2A-504, 2A-103(4) and 1-302.

3. The lessor's damages will be established using the new lease agreement as a measure if the following three criteria are satisfied: (i) the lessor disposed of the goods by lease, (ii) the lease agreement is substantially similar to the original lease agreement, and (iii) such disposition was in good faith, and in a commercially reasonable manner. Thus, the lessor will be entitled to recover from the lessee the accrued and unpaid rent as of the date of commencement of the term of the new lease, and the present value, as of the same date, of the rent, under the original lease for the then remaining term less the present value as of the same date of the rent under the new lease agreement applicable to the period of the new lease comparable to the remaining term under the original lease, together with incidental damages less expenses saved in consequence of the lessee's default. If the lessor's disposition does not satisfy the criteria of subsection (2), the lessor may calculate its claim against the lessee pursuant to Section 2A-528. Section 2A-523(1)(e).

4. Two of the three criteria to be met by the lessor are familiar, but the concept of the new lease agreement that is substantially similar to the original lease agreement is not. Given the many variables facing a party who intends to lease goods and the rapidity of change in the market place, the policy decision was made not to draft with specificity. It was thought unwise to seek to establish certainty at the cost of fairness. The decision of whether the new lease agreement is substantially similar to the original will be determined case by case.

5. While the section does not draw a bright line, it is possible to describe some of the factors that should be considered in a finding that a new lease agreement is substantially similar to the original. The various elements of the new lease agreement should be examined. Those elements include the options to purchase or release; the lessor's representations, warranties and covenants to the lessee as well as those to be provided by the lessee to the lessor; and the services, if any, to be provided by the lessor or by the lessee. All of these factors allocate cost and risk between the lessor and the lessee and thus affect the amount of rent to be paid. These findings should not be made with scientific precision, as they are a function of economics, nor should they be made independently, as it is important that a sense of commercial judgment pervade the finding. See Section 2A-507(2). To establish the new lease as a proper measure of damage under subsection (2), these various factors, taken as a whole, must result in a finding that the new lease agreement is substantially similar to the original. If the differences between the original lease and the new lease can be easily valued, it would be appropriate for a court to find that the new lease is substantially similar to the old lease, adjust the difference in the rent between the two leases to take account of the differences, and award damages under this section. If, for example, the new lease requires the lessor to insure the goods in the hands of the lessee, while the original lease required the lessee to insure, the usual cost of such insurance could be deducted from rent due under the new lease before the difference in rental between the two leases is determined.

6. The following hypothetical illustrates the difficulty of providing a bright line. Assume that A buys a jumbo tractor for $1 million and then leases the tractor to B for a term of 36 months. The tractor is delivered to and is accepted by B on May 1. On June 1 B fails to pay the monthly rent to A. B returns the tractor to A, who immediately releases the tractor to C for a term identical to the term remaining under the lease between A and B. All terms and conditions under the lease between A and C are identical to those under the original lease between A and B, except that C does not provide any property damage or other insurance coverage, and B agreed to provide complete coverage. Coverage is expensive and difficult to obtain. It is a question of fact whether it is so difficult to adjust the recovery to take account of the difference between the two leases as to insurance that the second lease is not substantially similar to the original.

7. A new lease can be substantially similar to the original lease even though its term extends beyond the remaining term of the original lease, so long as both (a) the lease terms are commercially comparable (e.g., it is highly unlikely that a one-month rental and a five-year lease would reflect similar realities), and (b) the court can fairly apportion a part of the rental payments under the new lease to that part of the term of the new lease which is comparable to the remaining lease term under the original lease. Also, the lease term of the new lease may be comparable to the remaining term of the original lease even though the beginning and ending dates of the two leases are not the same. For example, a two-month lease of agricultural equipment for the months of August and September may be comparable to a two-month lease running from the 15th of August to the 15th of October if in the particular location two-month leases beginning on August 15th are basically interchangeable with two-month leases beginning August 1st. Similarly, the term of a one-year truck lease beginning on the 15th of January may be comparable to the term of a one-year truck lease beginning January 2d. If the lease terms are found to be comparable, the court may base cover damages on the entire difference between the costs under the two leases.

8. Subsection (3), which is new, provides that if the lessor's disposition is by lease that does not qualify under subsection (2), or is by sale or otherwise, Section 2A-528 governs.

9. Subsection (4), a revised version of subsection 2-706(5), applies to protect a subsequent buyer or lessee who buys or leases from the lessor in good faith and for value, pursuant to a disposition under this section. Note that by its terms, the rule in subsection 2A-304(1), which provides that the subsequent lessee takes subject to the original lease contract, is controlled by the rule stated in this subsection.

10. Subsection (5), a revised version of subsection 2-706(6), provides that the lessor is not accountable to the lessee for any profit made by the lessor on a disposition. This rule follows from the fundamental premise of the bailment for hire that the lessee under a lease of goods has no equity of redemption to protect.

Cross References:

Sections 1-302, 2-706(1), 2-706(5), 2-706(6), 2A-103(4), 2A-304(1), 2A-503, 2A-504, 2A-507(2), 2A-523(1), 2A-523(3)(a), 2A-525, 2A-526, 2A-527(5), 2A-528, 2A-530, 9-625, and 9-627.

Definitional Cross References:

"Buyer" and "Buying".	Section 2-103(1)(a).
"Delivery".	Section 1-201(b)(15).
"Good faith".	Section 1-201(b)(20).
"Goods".	Section 2A-103(1)(h).
"Lease".	Section 2A-103(1)(j).
"Lease contract".	Section 2A-103(1)(*l*).
"Lessee".	Section 2A-103(1)(n).
"Lessor".	Section 2A-103(1)(p).
"Present value".	Section 1-201(b)(28).
"Right".	Section 1-201(b)(34).
"Sale".	Section 2-106(1).
"Security interest".	Sections 1-201(b)(35) and 1-203.
"Value".	Section 1-204.

Section 2A-528. Lessor's Damages for Non-Acceptance, Failure to Pay, Repudiation, or Other Default

(1) Except as otherwise provided with respect to damages liquidated in the lease agreement (Section 2A-504) or otherwise determined pursuant to agreement of the parties (Sections 1-302 and 2A-503), if a lessor elects to retain the goods or a lessor elects to dispose of the goods and the disposition is by lease agreement that for any reason does not qualify for treatment under Section 2A-527(2), or is by sale or otherwise, the lessor may recover from the lessee as damages for a default of the type described in Section 2A-523(1) or 2A-523(3)(a), or, if agreed, for other default of the lessee, (i) accrued and unpaid rent as of the date of default if the lessee has never taken possession of the goods, or, if the lessee has taken possession of the goods, as of the date the lessor repossesses the goods or an earlier date on which the lessee makes a tender of the goods to the lessor, (ii) the present value as of the date determined under clause (i) of the total rent for the then remaining lease term of the original lease agreement minus the present value as of the same date of the market rent at the place where the goods are located computed for the same lease term, and (iii) any incidental damages allowed under Section 2A-530, less expenses saved in consequence of the lessee's default.

(2) If the measure of damages provided in subsection (1) is inadequate to put a lessor in as good a position as performance would have, the measure of damages is the present value of the profit, including reasonable overhead, the lessor would have made from full performance by the lessee, together with any incidental damages allowed under Section 2A-530, due allowance for costs reasonably incurred and due credit for payments or proceeds of disposition.

Official Comment

Uniform Statutory Source: Section 2-708.

Changes: Substantially revised.

Purposes:

1. Subsection (1), a substantially revised version of Section 2-708(1), states the basic rule governing the measure of lessor's damages for a default described in Section 2A-523(1) or (3)(a), and, if agreed, for a contractual default. This measure will apply if the lessor elects to retain the goods (whether undelivered, returned by the lessee, or repossessed by the lessor after acceptance and default by the lessee) or if the lessor's disposition does not qualify under subsection 2A-527(2). Section 2A-527(3). Note that under some of these conditions, the lessor may recover damages from the lessee pursuant to the rule set forth in Section 2A-529. There is no sanction for disposition that does not qualify under subsection 2A-527(2). Application of the rule set forth in this section is subject to agreement to the contrary. Sections 2A-504, 2A-103(4) and 1-302.

2. If the lessee has never taken possession of the goods, the measure of damage is the accrued and unpaid rent as of the date of default together with the present value, as of the date of default, of the original rent for the remaining term of the lease less the present value as of the same date of market rent, and incidental damages, less expenses saved in consequence of the default. Note that the reference in Section 2A-528(1)(i) and (ii) is to the date of default not to the date of an event of default. An event of default under a lease agreement becomes a default under a lease agreement only after the expiration of any relevant period of grace and compliance with any notice requirements under this Article and the lease agreement. American Bar Foundation, *Commentaries on Indentures*, § 5-1, at 216-17 (1971). Section 2A-501(1). This conclusion is also a function of whether, as a matter of fact or law, the event of default has been waived, suspended or cured. Sections 2A-103(4) and 1-103. If the lessee has taken possession of the goods, the measure of damages is the accrued and unpaid rent as of the earlier of the time the lessor repossesses the goods or the time the lessee tenders the goods to the lessor plus the difference between the present value, as of the same time, of the rent under the lease for the remaining lease term and the present value, as of the same time, of the market rent.

3. Market rent will be computed pursuant to Section 2A-507.

4. Subsection (2), a somewhat revised version of the provisions of subsection 2-708(2), states a measure of damages which applies if the measure of damages in subsection (1) is inadequate to put the lessor in as good a position as performance would have. The measure of damage is the lessor's profit, including overhead, together with incidental damages, with allowance for costs reasonably incurred and credit for payments or proceeds of disposition. In determining the amount of due credit with respect to proceeds of disposition a proper value should be attributed to the lessor's residual interest in the goods. Sections 2A-103(1)(q) and 2A-507(4).

5. In calculating profit, a court should include any expected appreciation of the goods, e.g. the foal of a leased brood mare. Because this subsection is intended to give the lessor the benefit of the bargain, a court should consider any reasonable benefit or profit expected by the lessor from the performance of the lease agreement. See *Honeywell, Inc. v. Lithonia Lighting, Inc.*, 317 F. Supp. 406, 413 (N.D. Ga. 1970); *Locks v. Wade*, 114 A.2d 875, 877 (N.J. Super. Ct. App. Div. 1955). Further, in calculating profit the concept of present value must be given effect. *Taylor v. Commercial Credit Equip. Corp.*, 316 S.E.2d 788 (Ga. Ct. App. 1984). *See generally* Section 2A-103(1)(u).

Cross References:

Sections 1-103, 1-302, 2-708, 2A-103(1)(q), 2A-103(1)(u), 2A-103(4), 2A-501(1), 2A-503, 2A-504, 2A-507, 2A-527(2), 2A-527(3), 2A-528(1), 2A-529, and 2A-530.

Definitional Cross References:

"Agreement".	Section 1-201(b)(3).
"Goods".	Section 2A-103(1)(h).
"Lease".	Section 2A-103(1)(j).
"Lease agreement".	Section 2A-103(1)(k).
"Lessee".	Section 2A-103(1)(n).
"Lessor".	Section 2A-103(1)(p).
"Party".	Section 1-201(b)(26).
"Present value".	Section 1-201(b)(28).
"Sale".	Section 2-106(1).

Section 2A-529. Lessor's Action for the Rent

(1) After default by the lessee under the lease contract of the type described in Section 2A-523(1) or 2A-523(3)(a) or, if agreed, after other default by the lessee, if the lessor complies with subsection (2), the lessor may recover from the lessee as damages:

(a) for goods accepted by the lessee and not repossessed by or tendered to the lessor, and for conforming goods lost or damaged within a commercially reasonable time after risk of loss passes to the lessee (Section 2A-219), (i) accrued and unpaid rent as of the date of entry of judgment in favor of the lessor, (ii) the present value as of the same date of the rent for the then remaining lease term of the lease agreement, and (iii) any incidental damages allowed under Section 2A-530, less expenses saved in consequence of the lessee's default; and

(b) for goods identified to the lease contract if the lessor is unable after reasonable effort to dispose of them at a reasonable price or the circumstances reasonably indicate that effort will be unavailing, (i) accrued and unpaid rent as of the date of entry of judgment in favor of the lessor, (ii) the present value as of the same date of the rent for the then remaining lease term of the lease agreement, and (iii) any incidental damages allowed under Section 2A-530, less expenses saved in consequence of the lessee's default.

(2) Except as provided in subsection (3), the lessor shall hold for the lessee for the remaining lease term of

the lease agreement any goods that have been identified to the lease contract and are in the lessor's control.

(3) The lessor may dispose of the goods at any time before collection of the judgment for damages obtained pursuant to subsection (1). If the disposition is before the end of the remaining lease term of the lease agreement, the lessor's recovery against the lessee for damages is governed by Section 2A-527 or Section 2A-528, and the lessor will cause an appropriate credit to be provided against a judgment for damages to the extent that the amount of the judgment exceeds the recovery available pursuant to Section 2A-527 or 2A-528.

(4) Payment of the judgment for damages obtained pursuant to subsection (1) entitles the lessee to the use and possession of the goods not then disposed of for the remaining lease term of and in accordance with the lease agreement.

(5) After default by the lessee under the lease contract of the type described in Section 2A-523(1) or Section 2A-523(3)(a) or, if agreed, after other default by the lessee, a lessor who is held not entitled to rent under this section must nevertheless be awarded damages for non-acceptance under Section 2A-527 or Section 2A-528.

Official Comment

Uniform Statutory Source: Section 2-709.

Changes: Substantially revised.

Purposes:

1. Absent a lease contract provision to the contrary, an action for the full unpaid rent (discounted to present value as of the time of entry of judgment as to rent due after that time) is available as to goods not lost or damaged only if the lessee retains possession of the goods or the lessor is or apparently will be unable to dispose of them at a reasonable price after reasonable effort. There is no general right in a lessor to recover the full rent from the lessee upon holding the goods for the lessee. If the lessee tenders goods back to the lessor, and the lessor refuses to accept the tender, the lessor will be limited to the damages it would have suffered had it taken back the goods. The rule in Article 2 that the seller can recover the price of accepted goods is rejected here. In a lease, the lessor always has a residual interest in the goods which the lessor usually realizes upon at the end of a lease term by either sale or a new lease. Therefore, it is not a substantial imposition on the lessor to require it to take back and dispose of the goods if the lessee chooses to tender them back before the end of the lease term: the lessor will merely do earlier what it would have done anyway, sell or relet the goods. Further, the lessee will frequently encounter substantial difficulties if the lessee attempts to sublet the goods for the remainder of the lease term. In contrast to the buyer who owns the entire interest in goods and can easily dispose of them, the lessee is selling only the right to use the goods under the terms of the lease and the sublessee must assume a relationship with the lessor. In that situation, it is usually more efficient to eliminate the original lessee as a middleman by allowing the lessee to return the goods to the lessor who can then redispose of them.

2. In some situations even where possession of the goods is reacquired, a lessor will be able to recover as damages the present value of the full rent due, not under this section, but under 2A-528(2) which allows a lost profit recovery if necessary to put the lessor in the position it would have been in had the lessee performed. Following is an example of such a case. A is a lessor of construction equipment and maintains a substantial inventory. B leases from A a backhoe for a period of two weeks at a rental of $1,000. After three days, B returns the backhoe and refuses to pay the rent. A has five backhoes in inventory, including the one returned by B. During the next 11 days after the return by B of the backhoe, A rents no more than three backhoes at any one time and, therefore, always has two on hand. If B had kept the backhoe for the full rental period, A would have earned the full rental on that backhoe, plus the rental on the other backhoes it actually did rent during that period. Getting this backhoe back before the end of the lease term did not enable A to make any leases it would not otherwise have made. The only way to put A in the position it would have been in had the lessee fully performed is to give the lessor the full rentals. A realized no savings at all because the backhoe was returned early and might even have incurred additional expense if it was paying for parking space for equipment in inventory. A has no obligation to relet the backhoe for the benefit of B rather than leasing that backhoe or any other in inventory for its own benefit. Further, it is probably not reasonable to expect A to dispose of the backhoe by sale when it is returned in an effort to reduce damages suffered by B. Ordinarily, the loss of a two-week rental would not require A to reduce the size of its backhoe inventory. Whether A would similarly be entitled to full rentals as lost profit in a one-year lease of a backhoe is a question of fact: in any event the lessor, subject to mitigation of damages rules, is entitled to be put in as good a position as it would have been had the lessee fully performed the lease contract.

3. Under subsection (2) a lessor who is able and elects to sue for the rent due under a lease must hold goods not lost or damaged for the lessee. Subsection (3) creates an exception to the subsection (2) requirement. If the lessor disposes of those goods prior to collection of the judgment (whether as a matter of law or agreement), the lessor's recovery is governed by the measure of damages in Section 2A-527 if the disposition is by lease that is substantially similar to the original lease, or otherwise by the measure of damages in Section 2A-528. Section 2A-523 Comment.

4. Subsection (4), which is new, further reinforces the requisites of Subsection (2). In the event the judgment for damages obtained by the lessor against the lessee pursuant to subsection (1) is satisfied, the lessee regains the right to use and possession of the remaining goods for the balance of the original lease term; a partial satisfaction of the judgment creates no right in the lessee to use and possession of the goods.

5. The relationship between subsections (2) and (4) is important to understand. Subsection (2) requires the lessor to hold for the lessee identified goods in the lessor's possession. Absent agreement to the contrary, whether in the lease or otherwise, under most circumstances the requirement that the lessor hold the goods for the lessee for the term will mean that the lessor is not allowed to use them. Sections 2A-103(4) and 1-304. Further, the lessor's use of the goods could be viewed as a disposition of the goods that would bar the lessor from recovery under this section, remitting the lessor to the two preceding sections for a determination of the lessor's claim for damages against the lessee.

6. Subsection (5), the analogue of subsection 2-709(3), further reinforces the thrust of subsection (3) by stating that a lessor who is held not entitled to rent under this section has not elected a remedy; the lessor must be awarded damages under Sections 2A-527 and 2A-528. This is a function of two significant policies of this Article—that resort to a remedy is optional, unless expressly agreed to be exclusive (Section 2A-503(2)) and that rights and remedies provided in this Article generally are cumulative. (Section 2A-501(2) and (4)).

Cross References:

Sections 1-304, 2-709(3), 2A-103(4), 2A-219, 2A-501(2), 2A-501(4), 2A-503(2), 2A-504, 2A-523(1), 2A-523(3)(a), 2A-525(2), 2A-527, and 2A-528.

Definitional Cross References:

"Action".	Section 1-201(b)(1).
"Conforming".	Section 2A-103(1)(d).
"Goods".	Section 2A-103(1)(h).
"Lease".	Section 2A-103(1)(j).
"Lease agreement".	Section 2A-103(1)(k).
"Lease contract".	Section 2A-103(1)(*l*).
"Lessee".	Section 2A-103(1)(n).
"Lessor".	Section 2A-103(1)(p).
"Present value".	Section 1-201(b)(28).
"Reasonable time".	Section 1-205(a).

Section 2A-530. Lessor's Incidental Damages

Incidental damages to an aggrieved lessor include any commercially reasonable charges, expenses, or commissions incurred in stopping delivery, in the transportation, care and custody of goods after the lessee's default, in connection with return or disposition of the goods, or otherwise resulting from the default.

Official Comment

Uniform Statutory Source: Section 2-710.

Changes: Revised to reflect leasing practices and terminology.

Definitional Cross References:

"Aggrieved party".	Section 1-201(b)(2).
"Delivery".	Section 1-201(b)(15).
"Goods".	Section 2A-103(1)(h).
"Lessee".	Section 2A-103(1)(n).
"Lessor".	Section 2A-103(1)(p).

Section 2A-531. Standing to Sue Third Parties for Injury to Goods

(1) If a third party so deals with goods that have been identified to a lease contract as to cause actionable injury to a party to the lease contract (a) the lessor has a right of action against the third party, and (b) the lessee also has a right of action against the third party if the lessee:

(i) has a security interest in the goods;

(ii) has an insurable interest in the goods; or

(iii) bears the risk of loss under the lease contract or has since the injury assumed that risk as against the lessor and the goods have been converted or destroyed.

(2) If at the time of the injury the party plaintiff did not bear the risk of loss as against the other party to the lease contract and there is no arrangement between them for disposition of the recovery, his [or her] suit or settlement, subject to his [or her] own interest, is as a fiduciary for the other party to the lease contract.

(3) Either party with the consent of the other may sue for the benefit of whom it may concern.

Official Comment

Uniform Statutory Source: Section 2-722.

Changes: Revised to reflect leasing practices and terminology.

Definitional Cross References:

"Action".	Section 1-201(b)(1).
"Goods".	Section 2A-103(1)(h).
"Lease contract".	Section 2A-103(1)(*l*).
"Lessee".	Section 2A-103(1)(n).
"Lessor".	Section 2A-103(1)(p).
"Party".	Section 1-201(b)(26).
"Right".	Section 1-201(b)(34).
"Security interest".	Section 1-201(b)(35).

Section 2A-532. Lessor's Rights to Residual Interest

In addition to any other recovery permitted by this Article or other law, the lessor may recover from the lessee an amount that will fully compensate the lessor for any loss of or damage to the lessor's residual interest in the goods caused by the default of the lessee.

Official Comment

Uniform Statutory Source: None.

Purposes: This section recognizes the right of the lessor to recover under this Article (as well as under other law) from the lessee for failure to comply with the lease obligations as to the condition of leased goods when returned to the lessor, for failure to return the goods at the end of the lease, or for any other default which causes loss or injury to the lessor's residual interest in the goods.

Article 3—Negotiable Instruments

As adopted in 1990 and revised in: (i) 1991, 1992, 1993 to correct errata; (ii) 1994 by PEB Commentary No. 11; (iii) 1994, in connection with the revision of Article 8; (iv) 2001, in connection with the revision of Article 1; (iv) [*sic*] 2002, 2003, 2005, and 2007, pursuant to minor amendments; and (v) [*sic*] 2022, in connection with the 2022 Amendments to the Uniform Commercial Code.

PART 1. GENERAL PROVISIONS AND DEFINITIONS

Section 3-101. Short Title

This Article may be cited as Uniform Commercial Code—Negotiable Instruments.

Section 3-102. Subject Matter

(a) This Article applies to negotiable instruments. It does not apply to money, to payment orders governed by Article 4A, or to securities governed by Article 8.

(b) If there is conflict between this Article and Article 4 or 9, Articles 4 and 9 govern.

(c) Regulations of the Board of Governors of the Federal Reserve System and operating circulars of the Federal Reserve Banks supersede any inconsistent provision of this Article to the extent of the inconsistency.

Official Comment

1. Former Article 3 had no provision affirmatively stating its scope. Former Section 3-103 was a limitation on scope. In revised Article 3, Section 3-102 states that Article 3 applies to "negotiable instruments," defined in Section 3-104. Section 3-104(b) also defines the term "instrument" as a synonym for "negotiable instrument." In most places Article 3 uses the shorter term "instrument." This follows the convention used in former Article 3.

2. The reference in former Section 3-103(1) to "documents of title" is omitted as superfluous because these documents contain no promise to pay money. The definition of "payment order" in Section 4A-103(a)(1)(iii) excludes drafts which are governed by Article 3. Section 3-102(a) makes clear that a payment order governed by Article 4A is not governed by Article 3. Thus, Article 3 and Article 4A are mutually exclusive.

Article 8 states in Section 8-103(d) that "A writing that is a security certificate is governed by this Article and not by Article 3, even though it also meets the requirements of that Article." Section 3-102(a) conforms to this provision. With respect to some promises or orders to pay money, there may be a question whether the promise or order is an instrument under Section 3-104(a) or a certificated security under Section 8-102(a)(4) and (15). Whether a writing is covered by Article 3 or Article 8 has important consequences. Among other things, under Section 8-207, the issuer of a certificated security may treat the registered owner as the owner for all purposes until the presentment for registration of a transfer. The issuer of a negotiable instrument, on the other hand, may discharge its obligation to pay the instrument only by paying a person entitled to enforce under Section 3-301. There are also important consequences to an indorser. An indorser of a security does not undertake the issuer's obligation or make any warranty that the issuer will honor the underlying obligation, while an indorser of a negotiable instrument becomes secondarily liable on the underlying obligation.

Ordinarily the distinction between instruments and certificated securities in non-bearer form should be relatively clear. A certificated security under Article 8 must be in registered form (Section 8-102(a)(13)) so that it can be registered on the issuer's records. By contrast, registration plays no part in Article 3. The distinction between an instrument and a certificated security in bearer form may be somewhat more difficult and will generally lie in the economic functions of the two writings. Ordinarily, negotiable instruments under Article 3 will be separate and distinct instruments, while certificated securities under Article 8 will be either one of a class or series or by their terms divisible into a class or series (Section 8-102(a)(15)(ii)). Thus, a promissory note in bearer form could come under either Article 3 if it were simply an individual note, or under Article 8 if it were one of a series of notes or divisible into a series. An additional distinction is whether the instrument is of the type commonly dealt in on securities exchanges or markets or commonly recognized as a medium for investment (Section 8-102(a)(15)(iii)). Thus, a check written in bearer form (i.e., a check made payable to "cash") would not be a certificated security within Article 8 of the Uniform Commercial Code.

Occasionally, a particular writing may fit the definition of both a negotiable instrument under Article 3 and of an investment security under Article 8. In such cases, the instrument is subject exclusively to the requirements of Article 8. Section 8-103(d) and Section 3-102(a).

3. Although the terms of Article 3 apply to transactions by Federal Reserve Banks, federal preemption would make ineffective any Article 3 provision that conflicts with federal law. The activities of the Federal Reserve Banks are governed by regulations of the Federal Reserve Board and by operating circulars issued by the Reserve Banks themselves. In some instances, the operating circulars are issued pursuant to a Federal Reserve Board regulation. In other cases, the Reserve Bank issues the operating circular under its own authority under the Federal Reserve Act, subject to review by the Federal Reserve Board. Section 3-102(c) states that Federal Reserve Board regulations and operating circulars of the Federal Reserve Banks supersede any inconsistent provision of Article 3 to the extent of the inconsistency. Federal Reserve Board regulations, being valid exercises of regulatory authority pursuant to a federal statute, take precedence over state law if there is an inconsistency. *Childs v. Federal Reserve Bank of Dallas,* 719 F.2d 812 (5th Cir. 1983), reh. den. 724 F.2d 127 (5th Cir. 1984). Section 3-102(c) treats operating circulars as having the same effect whether issued under the Reserve Bank's own authority or under a Federal Reserve Board regulation. Federal statutes may also preempt Article 3. For example, the Expedited Funds Availability Act, 12 U.S.C. § 4001 et seq., provides that the Act and the regulations issued pursuant to the Act supersede any inconsistent provisions of the UCC. 12 U.S.C. § 4007(b).

4. In *Clearfield Trust Co. v. United States,* 318 U.S. 363 (1943), the Court held that if the United States is a party to an instrument, its rights and duties are governed by federal common law in the absence of a specific federal statute or regulation. In *United States v. Kimbell Foods, Inc.,* 440 U.S. 715 (1979), the Court stated a three-pronged test to ascertain whether the federal common-law rule should follow the state rule. In most instances courts under the *Kimbell* test have shown a willingness to adopt UCC rules in formulating federal common law on the subject. In *Kimbell* the Court adopted the priorities rules of Article 9.

5. In 1989 the United Nations Commission on International Trade Law completed a Convention on International Bills of Exchange and International Promissory Notes. If the United States becomes a party to this Convention, the Convention will preempt state law with respect to international bills and notes governed by the Convention. Thus, an international bill of exchange or promissory note that meets the definition of instrument in Section 3-104 will not be governed by Article 3 if it is governed by the Convention. That Convention applies only to bills and notes that indicate on their face that they involve cross-border transactions. It does not apply at all to checks. Convention Articles 1(3), 2(1), 2(2). Moreover, because it applies only if the bill or note specifically calls for application of the Convention, Convention Article 1, there is little chance that the Convention will apply accidentally to a transaction that the parties intended to be governed by this Article.

Additional References:

3-104 Comment 2

4-102 Comment 1

Section 3-103. Definitions

(a) In this Article:

(1) "Acceptor" means a drawee who has accepted a draft.

(2) "Consumer account" means an account established by an individual primarily for personal, family, or household purposes.

(3) "Consumer transaction" means a transaction in which an individual incurs an obligation primarily for personal, family, or household purposes.

(4) "Drawee" means a person ordered in a draft to make payment.

(5) "Drawer" means a person who signs or is identified in a draft as a person ordering payment.

(6) "Good faith" means honesty in fact and the observance of reasonable commercial standards of fair dealing.

(7) "Maker" means a person who signs or is identified in a note as a person undertaking to pay.

(8) "Order" means a written instruction to pay money signed by the person giving the instruction. The instruction may be addressed to any person, including the person giving the instruction, or to one or more persons jointly or in the alternative but not in succession. An authorization to pay is not an order unless the person authorized to pay is also instructed to pay.

(9) "Ordinary care" in the case of a person engaged in business means observance of reasonable commercial standards, prevailing in the area in which the person is located, with respect to the business in which the person is engaged. In the case of a bank that takes an instrument for processing for collection or payment by automated means, reasonable commercial standards do not require the bank to examine the instrument if the failure to examine does not violate the bank's prescribed procedures and the bank's procedures do not vary unreasonably from general banking usage not disapproved by this Article or Article 4.

(10) "Party" means a party to an instrument.

(11) "Principal obligor," with respect to an instrument, means the accommodated party or any other party to the instrument against whom a secondary obligor has recourse under this Article.

(12) "Promise" means a written undertaking to pay money signed by the person undertaking to pay. An acknowledgment of an obligation by the obligor is not a promise unless the obligor also undertakes to pay the obligation.

(13) "Prove" with respect to a fact means to meet the burden of establishing the fact (Section 1-201(b)(8)).

(14) "Record" means information that is inscribed on a tangible medium or that is stored in an electronic or other medium and is retrievable in perceivable form.

(15) "Remitter" means a person who purchases an instrument from its issuer if the instrument is payable to an identified person other than the purchaser.

(16) "Remotely-created consumer item" means an item drawn on a consumer account, which is not created by the payor bank and does not bear a handwritten signature purporting to be the signature of the drawer.

(17) "Secondary obligor," with respect to an instrument, means (a) an indorser or an accommodation party, (b) a drawer having the obligation described in Section 3-414(d), or (c) any other party to the instrument that has recourse against another party to the instrument pursuant to Section 3-116(b).

(b) Other definitions applying to this Article and the sections in which they appear are:

"Acceptance".	Section 3-409
"Accommodated party".	Section 3-419
"Accommodation party".	Section 3-419
"Account".	Section 4-104
"Alteration".	Section 3-407
"Anomalous indorsement".	Section 3-205
"Blank indorsement".	Section 3-205
"Cashier's check".	Section 3-104
"Certificate of deposit".	Section 3-104
"Certified check".	Section 3-409
"Check".	Section 3-104
"Consideration".	Section 3-303
"Draft".	Section 3-104
"Holder in due course".	Section 3-302
"Incomplete instrument".	Section 3-115
"Indorsement".	Section 3-204
"Indorser".	Section 3-204
"Instrument".	Section 3-104
"Issue".	Section 3-105
"Issuer".	Section 3-105
"Negotiable instrument".	Section 3-104
"Negotiation".	Section 3-201
"Note".	Section 3-104
"Payable at a definite time".	Section 3-108
"Payable on demand".	Section 3-108
"Payable to bearer".	Section 3-109
"Payable to order".	Section 3-109
"Payment".	Section 3-602
"Person entitled to enforce".	Section 3-301
"Presentment".	Section 3-501
"Reacquisition".	Section 3-207
"Special indorsement".	Section 3-205
"Teller's check".	Section 3-104
"Transfer of instrument".	Section 3-203
"Traveler's check".	Section 3-104
"Value".	Section 3-303

(c) The following definitions in other Articles apply to this Article:

"Banking day".	Section 4-104
"Clearing house".	Section 4-104
"Collecting bank".	Section 4-105
"Depositary bank".	Section 4-105
"Documentary draft".	Section 4-104
"Intermediary bank".	Section 4-105
"Item".	Section 4-104
"Payor bank".	Section 4-105
"Suspends payments".	Section 4-104

(d) In addition, Article 1 contains general definitions and principles of construction and interpretation applicable throughout this Article.

Legislative Note: *A jurisdiction that enacts this statute that has not yet enacted the revised version of UCC Article 1 should add to Section 3-103 the definition of "good faith" that appears in the official version of Section 1-201(b)(20) and the definition of "record" that appears in the official version of Section 1-201(b)(31). Sections 3-103(a)(6) and (14) are reserved for that purpose. A jurisdiction that already has adopted or simultaneously adopts the revised Article 1 should not add those definitions, but should leave those numbers "reserved." If jurisdictions follow the numbering suggested here, the subsections will have the same numbering in all jurisdictions that have adopted these amendments (whether they have or have not adopted the revised version of UCC Article 1).*

Definitional Cross References:

"Acceptance".	Section 3-409(a)
"Bank".	Section 1-201(b)(4)
"Burden of Establishing".	Section 1-201(b)(8)
"Draft".	Section 3-104(e)
"Instrument".	Section 3-104(b)
"Issuer".	Section 3-105(c)
"Money"	Section 1-201(b)(24)
"Note".	Section 3-104(e)
"Payment".	Section 3-602(a)
"Person".	Section 1-201(b)(27)
"Purchase".	Section 1-201(b)(29)
"Purchaser".	Section 1-201(b)(30)
"Signed".	Section 1-201(b)(37)
"Written".	Section 1-201(b)(43)

Official Comment

1. Subsection (a) defines some common terms used throughout the Article that were not defined by former Article 3 and adds the definitions of "order" and "promise" found in former Section 3-102(1)(b) and (c).

2. The definition of "order" includes an instruction given by the signer to itself. The most common example of this kind of order is a cashier's check: a draft with respect to which the drawer and drawee are the same bank or branches of the same bank. Former Section 3-118(a) treated a cashier's check as a note. It stated "a draft drawn on the drawer is effective as a note." Although it is technically more correct to treat a cashier's check as a promise by the issuing bank to pay rather than an order to pay, a cashier's check is in the form of a check and it is normally referred to as a check. Thus, revised Article 3 follows banking practice in referring to a cashier's check as both a draft and a check rather than a note. Some insurance companies also follow the practice of issuing drafts in which the drawer draws on itself and makes the draft payable at or through a bank. These instruments are also treated as drafts. The obligation of the drawer of a cashier's check or other draft drawn on the drawer is stated in Section 3-412.

An order may be addressed to more than one person as drawee either jointly or in the alternative. The authorization of alternative drawees follows former Section 3-102(1)(b) and recognizes the practice of drawers, such as corporations issuing dividend checks, who for commercial convenience name a number of drawees, usually in different parts of the country. Section 3-501(b)(1) provides that presentment may be made to any one of multiple drawees. Drawees in succession are not permitted because the holder should not be required to make more than one presentment. Dishonor by any drawee named in the draft entitles the holder to rights of recourse against the drawer or indorsers.

3. The last sentence of subsection (a)(12) is intended to make it clear that an I.O.U. or other written acknowledgment of indebtedness is not a note unless there is also an undertaking to pay the obligation.

4. This Article now uses the broadened definition of good faith in revised Article 1. The definition requires not only honesty in fact but also "observance of reasonable commercial standards of fair dealing." Although fair dealing is a broad term that must be defined in context, it is clear that it is concerned with the fairness of conduct rather than the care with which an act is performed. Failure to exercise ordinary care in conducting a transaction is an entirely different concept than failure to deal fairly in conducting the transaction. Both fair dealing and ordinary care, which is defined in Section 3-103(a)(9), are to be judged in the light of reasonable commercial standards, but those standards in each case are directed to different aspects of commercial conduct.

5. Subsection (a)(9) is a definition of ordinary care which is applicable not only to Article 3 but to Article 4 as well. See Section 4-104(c). The general rule is stated in the first sentence of subsection (a)(9) and it applies both to banks and to persons engaged in businesses other than banking. Ordinary care means observance of reasonable commercial standards of the relevant businesses prevailing in the area in which the person is located. The second sentence of subsection (a)(9) is a particular rule limited to the duty of a bank to examine an instrument taken by a bank for processing for collection or payment by automated means. This particular rule applies primarily to Section 4-406 and it is discussed in Comment 4 to that section. Nothing in Section 3-103(a)(9) is intended to prevent a customer from proving that the procedures followed by a bank are unreasonable, arbitrary, or unfair.

6. The definition of consumer account includes a joint account established by more than one individual. See Section 1-106(1).

Additional References:

3-201 Comment 2
3-311 Comment 4
3-405 Comment 1
3-412 Comment 1
3-604 Comment 6
4-404 Comment 4
3-605 Comment 1, 2, 3
3-116 Comment 1
3-303 Comment 6

Section 3-104. Negotiable Instrument

(a) Except as provided in subsections (c) and (d), "negotiable instrument" means an unconditional promise or order to pay a fixed amount of money, with or without interest or other charges described in the promise or order, if it:

(1) is payable to bearer or to order at the time it is issued or first comes into possession of a holder;

(2) is payable on demand or at a definite time; and

(3) does not state any other undertaking or instruction by the person promising or ordering payment to do any act in addition to the payment of money, but the promise or order may contain (i) an undertaking or power to give, maintain, or protect collateral to secure payment, (ii) an authorization or power to the holder to confess judgment or realize on or dispose of collateral, (iii) a waiver of the benefit of any law intended for the advantage or protection of an obligor, (iv) a term that specifies the law that governs the promise or order, or (v) an undertaking to resolve in a specified forum a dispute concerning the promise or order.

(b) "Instrument" means a negotiable instrument.

(c) An order that meets all of the requirements of subsection (a), except paragraph (1), and otherwise falls within the definition of "check" in subsection (f) is a negotiable instrument and a check.

(d) A promise or order other than a check is not an instrument if, at the time it is issued or first comes into possession of a holder, it contains a conspicuous statement, however expressed, to the effect that the promise or order is not negotiable or is not an instrument governed by this Article.

(e) An instrument is a "note" if it is a promise and is a "draft" if it is an order. If an instrument falls within the definition of both "note" and "draft," a person entitled to enforce the instrument may treat it as either.

(f) "Check" means (i) a draft, other than a documentary draft, payable on demand and drawn on a bank or (ii) a cashier's check or teller's check. An instrument may be a check even though it is described on its face by another term, such as "money order."

(g) "Cashier's check" means a draft with respect to which the drawer and drawee are the same bank or branches of the same bank.

(h) "Teller's check" means a draft drawn by a bank (i) on another bank, or (ii) payable at or through a bank.

(i) "Traveler's check" means an instrument that (i) is payable on demand, (ii) is drawn on or payable at or through a bank, (iii) is designated by the term "traveler's check" or by a substantially similar term, and (iv) requires, as a condition to payment, a counter-signature by a person whose specimen signature appears on the instrument.

(j) "Certificate of deposit" means an instrument containing an acknowledgment by a bank that a sum of money has been received by the bank and a promise by the bank to repay the sum of money. A certificate of deposit is a note of the bank.

Definitional Cross References:

"Bank".	Section 1-201(b)(4)
"Branch".	Section 1-201(b)(7)
"Collateral".	Section 9-102(a)(12)
"Conspicuous".	Section 1-201(b)(10)
"Drawee".	Section 3-103(a)(4)
"Drawer".	Section 3-103(a)(5)
"Documentary Draft".	Section 4-104(a)(6)
"Holder".	Section 1-201(b)(21)
"Issue".	Section 3-105(a)
"Money".	Section 1-201(b)(24)
"Order".	Section 3-103(a)(8)
"Payable at or Through a Bank".	Section 4-106
"Payable on Demand or at a Definite Time".	Section 3-108
"Payable to Bearer or to Order".	Section 3-109
"Payment".	Section 3-602(a)
"Person".	Section 1-201(b)(27)
"Promise".	Section 3-103(a)(12)
"Unconditional Promise or Order".	Section 3-106

Official Comment

1. The definition of "negotiable instrument" defines the scope of Article 3 since Section 3-102 states: "This Article applies to negotiable instruments." The definition in Section 3-104(a) incorporates other definitions in Article 3. An instrument is either a "promise," defined in Section 3-103(a)(9), or "order," defined in Section 3-103(a)(6). A promise is a written undertaking to pay money signed by the person undertaking to pay. An order is a written instruction to pay money signed by the person giving the instruction. Thus, the term "negotiable instrument" is limited to a signed writing that orders or promises payment of money. "Money" is defined in Section 1-201(b)(24) and is not limited to United States dollars. It also includes a medium of exchange established by a foreign government or monetary units of account established by an inter-governmental organization or by agreement between two or more nations. Five other requirements are stated in Section 3-104(a): First, the promise or order must be "unconditional." The quoted term is explained in Section 3-106. Second, the amount of money must be "a fixed amount *** with or without interest or other charges described in the promise or order." Section 3-112(b) relates to "interest." Third, the promise or order must be "payable to bearer or to order." The quoted phrase is explained in Section 3-109. An exception to this requirement is stated in subsection (c). Fourth, the promise or order must be payable "on demand or at a definite time." The quoted phrase is explained in Section 3-108. Fifth, the promise or order may not state "any other undertaking or instruction by the person promising or ordering payment to do any act in addition to the payment of money" with five exceptions. The quoted phrase is based on the first sentence of N.I.L. Section 5 which is the precursor of "no other promise, order, obligation or power given by the maker or drawer" appearing in former Section 3-104(1)(b). The words "instruction" and "undertaking" are used instead of "order" and "promise" that are used in the N.I.L. formulation because the latter words are defined terms that include only orders or promises to pay money. The first three exceptions stated in Section 3-104(a)(3) are based on and are intended to have the same meaning as former Section 3-112(1)(b), (c), (d), and (e), as well as N.I.L. § 5(1), (2), and (3). The final two exceptions stated in Section 3-104(a)(3), added pursuant to the Uniform Commercial Code Amendments (2-022), deal with choice-of-law and choice-of-forum clauses. Subsection (b) states that "instrument" means a "negotiable instrument." This follows former Section 3-102(1)(e) which treated the two terms as synonymous.

2. Unless subsection (c) applies, the effect of subsection (a)(1) and Section 3-102(a) is to exclude from Article 3 any promise or order that is not payable to bearer or to order. There is no provision in revised Article 3 that is comparable to former Section 3-805. The comment to former Section 3-805 states that the typical example of a writing covered by that section is a check reading "Pay John Doe." Such a check was governed by former Article 3 but there could not be a holder in due course of the check. Under Section 3-104(c) such a check is governed by revised Article 3 and there can be a holder in due course of the check. But subsection (c) applies only to checks. The comment to former Section 3-805 does not state any example other than the check to illustrate that section. Subsection (c) is based on the belief that it is good policy to treat checks, which are payment instruments, as negotiable instruments whether or not they contain the words "to the order of". These words are almost always preprinted on the check form. Occasionally the drawer of a check may strike out these words before issuing the check. In the past some credit unions used check forms that did not contain the quoted words. Such check forms may still be in use but they are no longer common. Absence of the quoted words can easily be overlooked and should not affect the rights of holders who may pay money or give credit for a check without being aware that it is not in the conventional form.

Total exclusion from Article 3 of other promises or orders that are not payable to bearer or to order serves a useful purpose. It provides a simple device to clearly exclude a writing that does not fit the pattern of typical negotiable instruments and which is not intended to be a negotiable instrument. If a writing could be an instrument despite the absence of "to order" or "to bearer" language and a dispute arises with respect to the writing, it might be argued that the writing is a negotiable instrument because the other requirements of subsection (a) are somehow met. Even if the argument is eventually found to be without merit it can be used as a litigation ploy. Words making a promise or order payable to bearer or to order are the most distinguishing feature of a negotiable instrument and such words are frequently referred to as "words of negotiability." Article 3 is not meant to apply to contracts for the sale of goods or services or the sale or lease of real property or similar writings that may contain a promise to pay money. The use of words of negotiability in such contracts would be an aberration. Absence of the words precludes any argument that such contracts might be negotiable instruments.

An order or promise that is excluded from Article 3 because of the requirements of Section 3-104(a) may nevertheless be similar to a negotiable instrument in many respects. Although such a writing cannot be made a negotiable instrument within Article 3 by contract or conduct of its parties, nothing in Section 3-104 or in Section 3-102 is intended to mean that in a particular case involving such a writing a court could not arrive at a result similar to the result that would follow if the writing were a negotiable instrument. For example, a court might find that the obligor with respect to a promise that does not fall within Section 3-104(a) is precluded from asserting a defense against a bona fide purchaser. The preclusion could be based on estoppel or ordinary principles of contract. It does not depend upon the law of negotiable instruments. An example is stated in the paragraph following Case # 2 in Comment 4 to Section 3-302.

Moreover, consistent with the principle stated in Section 1-103(a)(2), the immediate parties to an order or promise that is not an instrument may provide by agreement that one or more of the provisions of Article 3 determine their rights and obligations under the writing. Upholding the parties' choice is not inconsistent with Article 3. Such an agreement may bind a transferee of the writing if the transferee has notice of it or the agreement arises from usage of trade and the agreement does not violate other law or public policy. An example of such an agreement is a provision that a transferee of the writing has the rights of a holder in due course stated in Article 3 if the transferee took rights under the writing in good faith, for value, and without notice of a claim or defense.

Even without an agreement of the parties to an order or promise that is not an instrument, it may be appropriate, consistent with the principles stated in Section 1-103(a), for a court to apply one or more provisions of Article 3 to the writing by analogy, taking into account the expectations of the parties and the differences between the writing and an instrument governed by Article 3. Whether such application is appropriate depends upon the facts of each case.

3. Subsection (d) allows exclusion from Article 3 of a writing that would otherwise be an instrument under subsection (a) by a statement to the effect that the writing is not negotiable or is not governed by Article 3. For example, a promissory note can be stamped with the legend NOT NEGOTIABLE. The effect under subsection (d) is not only to negate the possibility of a holder in due course, but to prevent the writing from being a negotiable instrument for any purpose. Subsection (d) does not, however, apply to a check. If a writing is excluded from Article 3 by subsection (d), a court could, nevertheless, apply Article 3 principles to it by analogy as stated in Comment 2.

4. Instruments are divided into two general categories: drafts and notes. A draft is an instrument that is an order. A note is an instrument that is a promise. Section 3-104(e). The term "bill of exchange" is not used in Article 3. It is generally understood to be a synonym for the term "draft." Subsections (f) through (j) define particular instruments that fall within the categories of draft and note. The term "draft," defined in subsection (e), includes a "check" which is defined in subsection (f). "Check" includes a share draft drawn on a credit union payable through a bank because the definition of bank (Section 4-105) includes credit unions. However, a draft drawn on an insurance company payable through a bank is not a check because it is not drawn on a bank. "Money orders" are sold both by banks and non-banks. They vary in form and their form determines how they are treated in Article 3. The most common form of money order sold by banks is that of an ordinary check drawn by the purchaser except that the amount is machine impressed. That kind of money order is a check under Article 3 and is subject to a stop order by the purchaser-drawer as in the case of ordinary checks. The seller bank is the drawee and has no obligation to a holder to pay the money order. If a money order falls within the definition of a teller's check, the rules applicable to teller's checks apply. Postal money orders are subject to federal law. "Teller's check" is separately defined in subsection (h). A teller's check is always drawn by a bank and is usually drawn on another bank. In some cases a teller's check is drawn on a nonbank but is made payable at or through a bank. Article 3 treats both types of teller's check identically, and both are included in the definition of "check." A cashier's check, defined in subsection (g), is also included in the definition of "check." Traveler's checks are issued both by banks and nonbanks and may be in the form of a note or draft. Subsection (i) states the essential characteristics of a traveler's check. The requirement that the instrument be "drawn on or payable at or through a bank" may be satisfied without words on the instrument that identify a bank as drawee or paying agent so long as the instrument bears an appropriate routing number that identifies a bank as paying agent.

The definitions in Regulation CC § 229.2 of the terms "check," "cashier's check," "teller's check," and "traveler's check" are different from the definitions of those terms in Article 3.

Certificates of deposit are treated in former Article 3 as a separate type of instrument. In revised Article 3, Section 3-104(j) treats them as notes.

5. There are some differences between the requirements of Article 3 and the requirements included in Article 3 of the Convention on International Bills of Exchange and International Promissory Notes. Most obviously, the Convention does not include the limitation on extraneous undertakings set forth in Section 3-104(a)(3), and does not permit documents payable to bearer that would be permissible under Section 3-104(a)(1) and Section 3-109. See Convention Article 3. In most respects, however, the requirements of Section 3-104 and Article 3 of the Convention are quite similar.

Additional References:

3-112 Comment 1, 2
3-412 Comment 1
3-303 Comment 6

Section 3-105. Issue of Instrument

(a) "Issue" means:

(1) the first delivery of an instrument by the maker or drawer, whether to a holder or non-holder, for the purpose of giving rights on the instrument to any person; or

(2) if agreed by the payee, the first transmission by the drawer to the payee of an image of an item and information derived from the item that enables the depositary bank to collect the item by transferring or presenting under federal law an electronic check.

(b) An unissued instrument, or an unissued incomplete instrument that is completed, is binding on the maker or drawer, but nonissuance is a defense. An instrument that is conditionally issued or is issued for a special purpose is binding on the maker or drawer, but failure of the condition or special purpose to be fulfilled is a defense.

(c) "Issuer" applies to issued and unissued instruments and means a maker or drawer of an instrument.

Definitional Cross References:

"Delivery".	Section 1-201(b)(15)
"Drawer".	Section 3-103(a)(5)
"Holder".	Section 1-201(b)(21)
"Incomplete Instrument".	Section 3-115
"Instrument".	Section 3-104(b)
"Maker".	Section 3-103(a)(7)
"Person".	Section 1-201(b)(27)

Official Comment

1. Under former Section 3-102(1)(a) "issue" was defined as the first delivery to a "holder or a remitter" but the term "remitter" was neither defined nor otherwise used. In revised Article 3, Section 3-105(a) defines "issue" more broadly to include the first delivery to anyone by the drawer or maker for the purpose of giving rights to anyone on the instrument. "Delivery" with respect to instruments is defined in Section 1-201(b)(15)] as meaning "voluntary transfer of possession." The reference in subsection (a)(2) to transmission of an image of an item and information derived from the item is derived from Section 4-110(a), dealing with electronic presentment.

Subsection (a) permits an instrument to be issued by an electronic transmission of an image of and information derived from the instrument by maker and drawer, rather than by delivery. Thus, for example, a drawer might, with the permission of the payee, write and sign a check, take a photograph of the check, send the photograph to the drawee for processing electronically, and destroy the original check. If the electronic image and the information derived from it can be processed as an "electronic check" under Regulation CC, see 12 C.F.R. § 229.2(ggg), the check is "issued" and hence can be enforced pursuant to this Article.

2. Subsection (b) continues the rule that nonissuance, conditional issuance or issuance for a special purpose is a defense of the maker or drawer of an instrument. Thus, the defense can be asserted against a person other than a holder in due course. The same rule applies to nonissuance of an incomplete instrument later completed.

3. Subsection (c) defines "issuer" to include the signer of an unissued instrument for convenience of reference in the statute.

Additional References:

3-201 Comment 2
3-305 Comment 2
3-412 Comment 2

Section 3-106. Unconditional Promise or Order

(a) Except as provided in this section, for the purposes of Section 3-104(a), a promise or order is unconditional unless it states (i) an express condition to payment, (ii) that the promise or order is subject to or governed by another record, or (iii) that rights or obligations with respect to the promise or order are stated in another record. A reference to another record does not of itself make the promise or order conditional.

(b) A promise or order is not made conditional (i) by a reference to another record for a statement of rights with respect to collateral, prepayment, or acceleration, or (ii) because payment is limited to resort to a particular fund or source.

(c) If a promise or order requires, as a condition to payment, a countersignature by a person whose specimen signature appears on the promise or order, the condition does not make the promise or order conditional for the purposes of Section 3-104(a). If the person whose specimen signature appears on an instrument fails to countersign the instrument, the failure to countersign is a defense to the obligation of the issuer, but the failure does not prevent a transferee of the instrument from becoming a holder of the instrument.

(d) If a promise or order at the time it is issued or first comes into possession of a holder contains a statement, required by applicable statutory or administrative law, to the effect that the rights of a holder or transferee are subject to claims or defenses that the issuer could assert against the original payee, the promise or order is not thereby made conditional for the purposes of Section 3-104(a); but if the promise or order is an instrument, there cannot be a holder in due course of the instrument.

Definitional Cross References:

"Collateral".	Section 9-102(a)(12)
"Holder".	Section 1-201(b)(21)
"Holder in Due Course".	Section 3-302
"Instrument".	Section 3-104(b)
"Issue".	Section 3-105(a)
"Issuer".	Section 3-105(c)
"Order".	Section 3-103(a)(8)
"Payment".	Section 3-602(a)
"Person".	Section 1-201(b)(27)
"Promise".	Section 3-103(a)(12)
"Record".	Section 3-103(a)(14)
"Signed".	Section 1-201(b)(37)
"Writing".	Section 1-201(b)(43)

Official Comment

1. This provision replaces former Section 3-105. Its purpose is to define when a promise or order fulfills the requirement in Section 3-104(a) that it be an "unconditional" promise or order to pay. Under Section 3-106(a) a promise or order is deemed to be unconditional unless one of the two tests of the subsection make the promise or order conditional. If the promise or order states an express condition to payment, the promise or order is not an instrument. For example, a promise states, "I promise to pay $100,000 to the order of John Doe if he conveys title to Blackacre to me." The promise is not an instrument because there is an express condition to payment. However, suppose a promise states, "In consideration of John Doe's promise to convey title to Blackacre I promise to pay $100,000 to the order of John Doe." That promise can be an instrument if Section 3-104 is otherwise satisfied. Although the recital of the executory promise of Doe to convey Blackacre might be read as an implied condition that the promise be performed, the condition is not an express condition as required by Section 3-106(a)(i). This result is consistent with former Section 3-105(1)(a) and (b). Former Section 3-105(1)(b) is not repeated in Section 3-106 because it is not necessary. It is an example of an implied condition. Former Section 3-105(1)(d), (e), and (f) and the first clause of former Section 3-105(1)(c) are other examples of implied conditions. They are not repeated in Section 3-106 because they are not necessary. The law is not changed.

Section 3-106(a)(ii) and (iii) carry forward the substance of former Section 3-105(2)(a). The only change is the use of "writing" instead of "agreement" and a broadening of the language that can result in conditionality. For example, a promissory note is not an instrument defined by Section 3-104 if it contains any of the following statements: 1. "This note is subject to a contract of sale dated April 1, 1990 between the payee and maker of this note." 2. "This note is subject to a loan and security agreement dated April 1, 1990 between the payee and maker of this note." 3. "Rights and obligations of the parties with respect to this note are stated in an agreement dated April 1, 1990 between the payee and maker of this note." It is not relevant whether any condition to payment is or is not stated in the writing to which reference is made. The rationale is that the holder of a negotiable instrument should not be required to examine another document to determine rights with respect to payment. But subsection (b)(i) permits reference to a separate writing for information with respect to collateral, prepayment, or acceleration.

Many notes issued in commercial transactions are secured by collateral, are subject to acceleration in the event of default, or are subject to prepayment. A statement of rights and obligations concerning collateral, prepayment, or acceleration does not prevent the note from being an instrument if the statement is in the note itself. See Section 3-104(a)(3) and Section 3-108(b). In some cases it may be convenient not to include a statement concerning collateral, prepayment, or acceleration in the note, but rather to refer to an accompanying loan agreement, security agreement or mortgage for that statement. Subsection (b)(i) allows a reference to the appropriate writing for a statement of these rights. For example, a note would not be made conditional by the following statement: "This note is secured by a security interest in collateral described in a security agreement dated April 1, 1990 between the payee and maker of this note. Rights and obligations with respect to the collateral are [stated in] [governed by] the security agreement." The bracketed words are alternatives, either of which complies.

Subsection (b)(ii) addresses the issues covered by former Section 3-105(1)(f), (g), and (h) and Section 3-105(2)(b). Under Section 3-106(a) a promise or order is not made conditional because payment is limited to payment from a particular source or fund. This reverses the result of former Section 3-105(2)(b). There is no cogent reason why the general credit of a legal entity must be pledged to have a negotiable instrument. Market forces determine the marketability of instruments of this kind. If potential buyers don't want promises or orders that are payable only from a particular source or fund, they won't take them, but Article 3 should apply.

2. Subsection (c) applies to traveler's checks or other instruments that may require a countersignature. Although the requirement of a countersignature is a condition to the obligation to pay, traveler's checks are treated in the commercial world as money substitutes and therefore should be governed by Article 3. The first sentence of subsection (c) allows a traveler's check to meet the definition of instrument by stating that the countersignature condition does not make it conditional for the purposes of Section 3-104. The second sentence states the effect of a failure to meet the condition. Suppose a thief steals a traveler's check and cashes it by skillfully imitating the specimen signature so that the countersignature appears to be authentic. The countersignature is for the purpose of identification of the owner of the instrument. It is not an indorsement. Subsection (c) provides that the failure of the owner to countersign does not prevent a transferee from becoming a holder. Thus, the merchant or bank that cashed the traveler's check becomes a holder when the traveler's check is taken. The forged countersignature is a defense to the obligation of the issuer to pay the instrument, and is included in defenses under Section 3-305(a)(2). These defenses may not be asserted against a holder in due course. Whether a holder has notice of the defense is a factual question. If the counter-signature is a very bad forgery, there may be notice. But if the merchant or bank cashed a traveler's check and the counter-signature appeared to be similar to the specimen signature, there might not be notice that the countersignature was forged. Thus, the merchant or bank could be a holder in due course.

3. Subsection (d) concerns the effect of a statement to the effect that the rights of a holder or transferee are subject to claims and defenses that the issuer could assert against the original payee. The subsection applies only if the statement is required by statutory or administrative law. The prime example is the Federal Trade Commission Rule (16 C.F.R. Part 433) preserving consumers' claims and defenses in consumer credit sales. The intent of the FTC rule is to make it impossible for there to be a holder in due course of a note bearing the FTC legend and undoubtedly that is the result. But, under former Article 3, the legend may also have had the unintended effect of making the note conditional, thus excluding the note from former Article 3 altogether. Subsection (d) is designed to make it possible to preclude the possibility of a holder in due course without excluding the instrument from Article 3. Most of the provisions of Article 3 are not affected by the holder-in-due-course doctrine and there is no reason why Article 3 should not apply to a note bearing the FTC legend if holder-in-due-course rights are not involved. Under subsection (d) the statement does not make the note conditional. If the note otherwise meets the requirements of Section 3-104(a) it is a negotiable instrument for all purposes except that there cannot be a holder in due course of the note. No particular form of legend or statement is required by subsection (d). The form of a particular legend or statement may be determined by the other statute or administrative law. For example, the FTC legend required in a note taken by the except that there cannot be a holder in due course of the note. No particular form of legend or statement is required by subsection (d). The form of a particular legend or statement may be determined by the other statute or administrative law. For example, the FTC legend required in a note taken by the seller in a consumer sale of goods or services is tailored to that particular transaction and therefore uses language that is somewhat different from that stated in subsection (d), but the difference in expression does not affect the essential similarity of the message conveyed. The effect of the FTC legend is to make the rights of a holder or transferee subject to claims or defenses that the issuer could assert against the original payee of the note.

Additional References:

3-204 Comment 1
3-302 Comment 7
3-305 Comment 2, 3, 6

Section 3-107. Instrument Payable in Foreign Money

Unless the instrument otherwise provides, an instrument that states the amount payable in foreign money may be paid in the foreign money or in an equivalent amount in dollars calculated by using the current bank-offered spot rate at the place of payment for the purchase of dollars on the day on which the instrument is paid.

Definitional Cross References:

"Bank".	Section 1-201(b)(4)
"Instrument".	Section 3-104(b)
"Money".	Section 1-201(b)(24)
"Payment".	Section 3-602(a)
"Purchase".	Section 1-201(b)(29)

Official Comment

The definition of instrument in Section 3-104 requires that the promise or order be payable in "money." That term is defined in Section 1-201(b)(24) and is not limited to United States dollars. Section 3-107 states than an instrument payable in foreign money may be paid in dollars if the instrument does not prohibit it. It also states a conversion rate which applies in the absence of a different conversion rate stated in the instrument. The reference in former Section 3-107(1) to instruments payable in "currency" or "current funds" has been dropped as superfluous.

Additional References:

4-214 Comment 7

Section 3-108. Payable on Demand or at Definite Time

(a) A promise or order is "payable on demand" if it (i) states that it is payable on demand or at sight, or otherwise indicates that it is payable at the will of the holder, or (ii) does not state any time of payment.

(b) A promise or order is "payable at a definite time" if it is payable on elapse of a definite period of time after sight or acceptance or at a fixed date or dates or at a time or times readily ascertainable at the time the promise or order is issued, subject to rights of (i) pre-payment, (ii) acceleration, (iii) extension at the option of the holder, or (iv) extension to a further definite time at the option of the maker or acceptor or automatically upon or after a specified act or event.

(c) If an instrument, payable at a fixed date, is also payable upon demand made before the fixed date, the instrument is payable on demand until the fixed date and, if demand for payment is not made before that date, becomes payable at a definite time on the fixed date.

Definitional Cross References:

"Acceptance".	Section 3-409(a)
"Acceptor".	Section 3-103(a)(1)
"Holder".	Section 1-201(b)(21)
"Instrument".	Section 3-104(b)
"Issue".	Section 3-105(a)
"Maker".	Section 3-103(a)(7)
"Order".	Section 3-103(a)(8)
"Payment".	Section 3-602(a)
"Promise".	Section 3-103(a)(12)

Official Comment

This section is a restatement of former Section 3-108 and Section 3-109. Subsection (b) broadens former Section 3-109 somewhat by providing that a definite time includes a time readily ascertainable at the time the promise or order is issued. Subsection (b)(iii) and (iv) restates former Section 3-109(1)(d). It adopts the generally accepted rule that a clause providing for extension at the option of the holder, even without a time limit, does not affect negotiability since the holder is given only a right which the holder would have without the clause. If the extension is to be at the option of the maker or acceptor or is to be automatic, a definite time limit must be stated or the time of payment remains uncertain and the order or promise is not a negotiable instrument. If a definite time limit is stated, the effect upon certainty of time of payment is the same as if the instrument were made payable at the ultimate date with a term providing for acceleration.

Section 3-109. Payable to Bearer or to Order

(a) A promise or order is payable to bearer if it:

(1) states that it is payable to bearer or to the order of bearer or otherwise indicates that the person in possession of the promise or order is entitled to payment;

(2) does not state a payee; or

(3) states that it is payable to or to the order of cash or otherwise indicates that it is not payable to an identified person.

(b) A promise or order that is not payable to bearer is payable to order if it is payable (i) to the order of an identified person or (ii) to an identified person or order. A promise or order that is payable to order is payable to the identified person.

(c) An instrument payable to bearer may become payable to an identified person if it is specially indorsed pursuant to Section 3-205(a). An instrument payable to an identified person may become payable to bearer if it is indorsed in blank pursuant to Section 3-205(b).

Definitional Cross References:

"Indorsed in Blank".	Section 3-205(b)
"Instrument".	Section 3-104(b)
"Order".	Section 3-103(a)(8)
"Payment".	Section 3-602(a)
"Person".	Section 1-201(b)(27)
"Promise".	Section 3-103(a)(12)

Official Comment

1. Under Section 3-104(a), a promise or order cannot be an instrument unless the instrument is payable to bearer or to order when it is issued or unless Section 3-104(c) applies. The terms "payable to bearer" and "payable to order" are defined in Section 3-109. The quoted terms are also relevant in determining how an instrument is negotiated. If the instrument is payable to bearer it can be negotiated by delivery alone. Section 3-201(b). An instrument that is payable to an identified person cannot be negotiated without the indorsement of the identified person. Section 3-201(b). An instrument payable to order is payable to an identified person. Section 3-109(b). Thus, an instrument payable to order requires the indorsement of the person to whose order the instrument is payable.

2. Subsection (a) states when an instrument is payable to bearer. An instrument is payable to bearer if it states that it is payable to bearer, but some instruments use ambiguous terms. For example, check forms usually have the words "to the order of" printed at the beginning of the line to be filled in for the name of the payee. If the drawer writes in the word "bearer" or "cash," the check reads "to the order of bearer" or "to the order of cash." In each case the check is payable to bearer. Sometimes the drawer will write the name of the payee "John Doe" but will add the words "or bearer." In that case the check is payable to bearer. Subsection (a). Under subsection (b), if an instrument is payable to bearer it can't be payable to order. This is different from former Section 3-110(3). An instrument that purports to be payable both to order and bearer states contradictory terms. A transferee of the instrument should be able to rely on the bearer term and acquire rights as a holder without obtaining the indorsement of the identified payee. An instrument is also payable to bearer if it does not state a payee. Instruments that do not state a payee are in most cases incomplete instruments. In some cases the drawer of a check may deliver or mail it to the person to be paid without filling in the line for the name of the payee. Under subsection (a) the check is payable to bearer when it is sent or delivered. It is also an incomplete instrument. This case is discussed in Comment 2 to Section 3-115. Subsection (a)(3) contains the words "otherwise indicates that it is not payable to an identified person." The quoted words are meant to cover uncommon cases in which an instrument indicates that it is not meant to be payable to a specific person. Such an instrument is treated like a check payable to "cash." The quoted words are not meant to apply to an instrument stating that it is payable to an identified person such as "ABC Corporation" if ABC Corporation is a nonexistent company. Although the holder of the check cannot be the nonexistent company, the instrument is not payable to bearer. Negotiation of such an instrument is governed by Section 3-404(b).

Additional References:

3-115 Comment 2

3-104 Comment 5

Section 3-110. Identification of Person to Whom Instrument Is Payable

(a) The person to whom an instrument is initially payable is determined by the intent of the person, whether or not authorized, signing as, or in the name or behalf of, the issuer of the instrument. The instrument is payable to the person intended by the signer even if that person is identified in the instrument by a name or other identification that is not that of the intended person. If more than one person signs in the name or behalf of the issuer of an instrument and all the signers do not intend the same person as payee, the instrument is payable to any person intended by one or more of the signers.

(b) If the signature of the issuer of an instrument is made by automated means, such as a check-writing machine, the payee of the instrument is determined by the intent of the person who supplied the name or identification of the payee, whether or not authorized to do so.

(c) A person to whom an instrument is payable may be identified in any way, including by name, identifying number, office, or account number. For the purpose of determining the holder of an instrument, the following rules apply:

(1) If an instrument is payable to an account and the account is identified only by number, the instrument is payable to the person to whom the account is payable. If an instrument is payable to an account identified by number and by the name of a person, the instrument is payable to the named person, whether or not that person is the owner of the account identified by number.

(2) If an instrument is payable to:

(i) a trust, an estate, or a person described as trustee or representative of a trust or estate, the instrument is payable to the trustee, the representative, or a successor of either, whether or not the beneficiary or estate is also named;

(ii) a person described as agent or similar representative of a named or identified person, the instrument is payable to the represented person, the representative, or a successor of the representative;

(iii) a fund or organization that is not a legal entity, the instrument is payable to a representative of the members of the fund or organization; or

(iv) an office or to a person described as holding an office, the instrument is payable to the named person, the incumbent of the office, or a successor to the incumbent.

(d) If an instrument is payable to two or more persons alternatively, it is payable to any of them and may be negotiated, discharged, or enforced by any or all of them in possession of the instrument. If an instrument is payable to two or more persons not alternatively, it is payable to all of them and may be negotiated, discharged, or enforced only by all of them. If an instrument payable to two or more persons is ambiguous as to whether it is payable to the persons alternatively, the instrument is payable to the persons alternatively.

Definitional Cross References:

"Account".	Section 4-104(a)(1)
"Instrument".	Section 3-104(b)
"Issuer".	Section 3-105(c)
"Discharge".	Section 3-601(a)
"Holder".	Section 1-201(b)(21)
"Negotiation".	Section 3-201(a)
"Organization".	Section 1-202(a) [*sic*, should be 1-201(b)(25)]
"Person".	Section 1-201(b)(27)
"Representative".	Section 1-201(b)(33)
"Signed".	Section 1-201(b)(37)

Official Comment

1. Section 3-110 states rules for determining the identity of the person to whom an instrument is initially payable if the instrument is payable to an identified person. This issue usually arises in a dispute over the validity of an indorsement in the name of the payee. Subsection (a) states the general rule that the person to whom an instrument is payable is determined by the intent of "the person, whether or not authorized, signing as, or in the name or behalf of, the issuer of the instrument." "Issuer" means the maker or drawer of the instrument. Section 3-105(c). If X signs a check as drawer of a check on X's account, the intent of X controls. If X, as President of Corporation, signs a check as President in behalf of Corporation as drawer, the intent of X controls. If X forges Y's signature as drawer of a check, the intent of X also controls. Under Section 3-103(a)(3), Y is referred to as the drawer of the check because the signing of Y's name identifies Y as the drawer. But since Y's signature was forged Y has no liability as drawer (Section 3-403(a)) unless some other provision of Article 3 or Article 4 makes Y liable. Since X, even though unauthorized, signed in the name of Y as issuer, the intent of X determines to whom the check is payable.

In the case of a check payable to "John Smith," since there are many people in the world named "John Smith" it is not possible to identify the payee of the check unless there is some further identification or the intention of the drawer is determined. Name alone is sufficient under subsection (a), but the intention of the drawer determines which John Smith is the person to whom the check is payable. The same issue is presented in cases of misdescriptions of the payee. The drawer intends to pay a person known to the drawer as John Smith. In fact that person's name is James Smith or John Jones or some other entirely different name. If the check identifies the payee as John Smith, it is nevertheless payable to the person intended by the drawer. That person may indorse the check in either the name John Smith or the person's correct name or in both names. Section 3-204(d). The intent of the drawer is also controlling in fictitious payee cases. Section 3-404(b). The last sentence of subsection (a) refers to rare cases in which the signature of an organization requires more than one signature and the persons signing on behalf of the organization do not all intend the same person as payee. Any person intended by a signer for the organization is the payee and an indorsement by that person is an effective indorsement.

Subsection (b) recognizes the fact that in a large number of cases there is no human signer of an instrument because the instrument, usually a check, is produced by automated means such as a check-writing machine. In that case, the relevant intent is that of the person who supplied the name of the payee. In most cases that person is an employee of the drawer, but in some cases the person could be an outsider who is committing a fraud by introducing names of payees of checks into the system that produces the checks. A check-writing machine is likely to be operated by means of a computer in which is stored information as to name and address of the payee and the amount of the check. Access to the computer may allow production of fraudulent checks without knowledge of the organization that is the issuer of the check. Section 3-404(b) is also concerned with this issue. See Case # 4 in Comment 2 to Section 3-404.

2. Subsection (c) allows the payee to be identified in any way including the various ways stated. Subsection (c)(1) relates to instruments payable to bank accounts. In some cases the account might be identified by name and number, and the name and number might refer to different persons. For example, a check is payable to "X Corporation Account No. 12345 in Bank of Podunk." Under the last sentence of subsection (c)(1), this check is payable to X Corporation and can be negotiated by X Corporation even if Account No. 12345 is some other person's account or the check is not deposited in that account. In other cases the payee is identified by an account number and the name of the owner of the account is not stated. For example, Debtor pays Creditor by issuing a check drawn on Payor Bank. The check is payable to a bank account owned by Creditor but identified only by number. Under the first sentence of subsection (c)(1) the check is payable to Creditor and, under Section 1-201(20), [*sic*, should be 1-201(b)(21)] Creditor becomes the holder when the check is delivered. Under Section 3-201(b), further negotiation of the check requires the indorsement of Creditor. But under Section 4-205(a), if the check is taken by a depositary bank for collection, the bank may become a holder without the indorsement. Under Section 3-102(b), provisions of Article 4 prevail over those of Article 3. The depositary bank warrants that the amount of the check was credited to the payee's account.

3. Subsection (c)(2) replaces former Section 3-117 and subsection (1)(e), (f), and (g) of former Section 3-110. This provision merely determines who can deal with an instrument as a holder. It does not determine ownership of the instrument or its proceeds. Subsection (c)(2)(i) covers trusts and estates. If the instrument is payable to the trust or estate or to the trustee or representative of the trust or estate, the instrument is payable to the trustee or representative or any successor. Under subsection (c)(2)(ii), if the instrument states that it is payable to Doe, President of X Corporation, either Doe or X Corporation can be holder of the instrument. Subsection (c)(2)(iii) concerns informal organizations that are not legal entities such as unincorporated clubs and the like. Any representative of the members of the organization can act as holder. Subsection (c)(2)(iv) applies principally to instruments payable to public offices such as a check payable to County Tax Collector.

4. Subsection (d) replaces former Section 3-116. An instrument payable to X or Y is governed by the first sentence of subsection (d). An instrument payable to X and Y is governed by the second sentence of subsection (d). If an instrument is payable to X or Y, either is the payee and if either is in possession that person is the holder and the person entitled to enforce the instrument. Section 3-301. If an instrument is payable to X and Y, neither X nor Y acting alone is the person to whom the instrument is payable. Neither person, acting alone, can be the holder of the instrument. The instrument is "payable to an identified person." The "identified person" is X and Y acting jointly. Section 3-109(b) and Section 1-106(1). Thus, under Section 1-201(b)(21) X or Y, acting alone, cannot be the holder or the person entitled to enforce or negotiate the instrument because neither, acting alone, is the identified person stated in the instrument.

The third sentence of subsection (d) is directed to cases in which it is not clear whether an instrument is payable to multiple payees alternatively. In the case of ambiguity persons dealing with the instrument should be able to rely on the indorsement of a single payee. For example, an instrument payable to X and/or Y is treated like an instrument payable to X or Y.

Additional References:
3-204 Comment 3
3-205 Comment 1
3-404 Comment 2
3-405 Comment 3
3-406 Comment 3
3-420 Comment 1, 2

Section 3-111. Place of Payment

Except as otherwise provided for items in Article 4, an instrument is payable at the place of payment stated in the instrument. If no place of payment is stated, an instrument is payable at the address of the drawee or maker stated in the instrument. If no address is stated, the place of payment is the place of business of the drawee or maker. If a drawee or maker has more than one place of business, the place of payment is any place of business of the drawee or maker chosen by the person entitled to enforce the instrument. If the drawee or maker has no place of business, the place of payment is the residence of the drawee or maker.

Definitional Cross References:

"Drawee".	Section 3-103(a)(4)
"Instrument".	Section 3-104(b)
"Item".	Section 4-104(a)(9)
"Maker".	Section 3-103(a)(7)
"Payment".	Section 3-602(a)
"Person Entitled to Enforce".	Section 3-301

Official Comment

If an instrument is payable at a bank in the United States, Section 3-501(b)(1) states that presentment must be made at the place of payment, i.e., the bank. The place of presentment of a check is governed by Regulation CC § 229.36.

Section 3-112. Interest

(a) Unless otherwise provided in the instrument, (i) an instrument is not payable with interest, and (ii) interest on an interest-bearing instrument is payable from the date of the instrument.

(b) Interest may be stated in an instrument as a fixed or variable amount of money or it may be expressed as a fixed or variable rate or rates. The amount or rate of interest may be stated or described in the instrument in any manner and may require reference to information not contained in the instrument. If an instrument provides for interest, but the amount of interest payable cannot be ascertained from the description, interest is payable at the judgment rate in effect at the place of payment of the instrument and at the time interest first accrues.

Definitional Cross References:

"Instrument".	Section 3-104(b)
"Money".	Section 1-201(b)(24)
"Payment".	Section 3-602(a)

Official Comment

1. Under Section 3-104(a) the requirement of a "fixed amount" applies only to principal. The amount of interest payable is that described in the instrument. If the description of interest in the instrument does not allow for the amount of interest to be ascertained, interest is payable at the judgment rate. Hence, if an instrument calls for interest, the amount of interest will always be determinable. If a variable rate of interest is prescribed, the amount of interest is ascertainable by reference to the formula or index described or referred to in the instrument. The last sentence of subsection (b) replaces subsection (d) of former Section 3-118.

2. The purpose of subsection (b) is to clarify the meaning of "interest" in the introductory clause of Section 3-104(a). It is not intended to validate a provision for interest in an instrument if that provision violates other law.

Section 3-113. Date of Instrument

(a) An instrument may be antedated or postdated. The date stated determines the time of payment if the instrument is payable at a fixed period after date. Except as provided in Section 4-401(c), an instrument payable on demand is not payable before the date of the instrument.

(b) If an instrument is undated, its date is the date of its issue or, in the case of an unissued instrument, the date it first comes into possession of a holder.

Definitional Cross References:

"Holder".	Section 1-201(b)(21)
"Instrument".	Section 3-104(b)
"Issue".	Section 3-105(a)
"Payable on Demand".	Section 3-108(a)

Official Comment

This section replaces former Section 3-114. Subsections (1) and (3) of former Section 3-114 are deleted as unnecessary. Section 3-113(a) is based in part on subsection (2) of former Section 3-114. The rule that a demand instrument is not payable before the date of the instrument is subject to Section 4-401(c) which allows the payor bank to pay a postdated check unless the drawer has notified the bank of the post-dating pursuant to a procedure prescribed in that subsection. With respect to an undated instrument, the date is the date of issue.

Section 3-114. Contradictory Terms of Instrument

If an instrument contains contradictory terms, typewritten terms prevail over printed terms, handwritten terms prevail over both, and words prevail over numbers.

Definitional Cross References:

"Instrument".	Section 3-104(b)

Official Comment

Section 3-114 replaces subsections (b) and (c) of former Section 3-118.

Section 3-115. Incomplete Instrument

(a) "Incomplete instrument" means a signed writing, whether or not issued by the signer, the contents of which show at the time of signing that it is incomplete but that the signer intended it to be completed by the addition of words or numbers.

(b) Subject to subsection (c), if an incomplete instrument is an instrument under Section 3-104, it may be enforced according to its terms if it is not completed, or according to its terms as augmented by completion. If an incomplete instrument is not an instrument under Section 3-104, but, after completion, the requirements of Section 3-104 are met, the instrument may be enforced according to its terms as augmented by completion.

(c) If words or numbers are added to an incomplete instrument without authority of the signer, there is an alteration of the incomplete instrument under Section 3-407.

(d) The burden of establishing that words or numbers were added to an incomplete instrument without authority of the signer is on the person asserting the lack of authority.

Definitional Cross References:

"Alteration".	Section 3-407
"Burden of Establishing".	Section 1-201(b)(8)
"Instrument".	Section 3-104(b)
"Issue".	Section 3-105(a)
"Person".	Section 1-201(b)(27)
"Signed".	Section 1-201(b)(37)
"Writing".	Section 1-201(b)(43)

Official Comment

1. This section generally carries forward the rules set out in former Section 3-115. The term "incomplete instrument" applies both to an "instrument," i.e. a writing meeting all the requirements of Section 3-104, and to a writing intended to be an instrument that is signed but lacks some element of an instrument. The test in both cases is whether the contents show that it is incomplete and that the signer intended that additional words or numbers be added.

2. If an incomplete instrument meets the requirements of Section 3-104 and is not completed it may be enforced in accordance with its terms. Suppose, in the following two cases, that a note delivered to the payee is incomplete solely because a space on the pre-printed note form for the due date is not filled in:

Case # 1. If the incomplete instrument is never completed, the note is payable on demand. Section 3-108(a)(ii). However, if the payee and the maker agreed to a due date, the maker may have a defense under Section 3-117 if demand for payment is made before the due date agreed to by the parties.

Case # 2. If the payee completes the note by filling in the due date agreed to by the parties, the note is payable on the due date stated. However, if the due date filled in was not the date agreed to by the parties there is an alteration of the note. Section 3-407 governs the case.

Suppose Debtor pays Creditor by giving Creditor a check on which the space for the name of the payee is left blank. The check is an instrument but it is incomplete. The check is enforceable in its incomplete form and it is payable to bearer because it does not state a payee. Section 3-109(a)(2). Thus, Creditor is a holder of the check. Normally in this kind of case Creditor would simply fill in the space with Creditor's name. When that occurs the check becomes payable to the Creditor.

3. In some cases the incomplete instrument does not meet the requirements of Section 3-104. An example is a check with the amount not filled in. The check cannot be enforced until the amount is filled in. If the payee fills in an amount authorized by the drawer the check meets the requirements of Section 3-104 and is enforceable as completed. If the payee fills in an unauthorized amount there is an alteration of the check and Section 3-407 applies.

4. Section 3-302(a)(1) also bears on the problem of incomplete instruments. Under that section a person cannot be a holder in due course of the instrument if it is so incomplete as to call into question its validity. Subsection (d) of Section 3-115 is based on the last clause of subsection (2) of former Section 3-115.

Additional References: 3-205 Comment 2

Section 3-116. Joint and Several Liability; Contribution

(a) Except as otherwise provided in the instrument, two or more persons who have the same liability on an instrument as makers, drawers, acceptors, indorsers who indorse as joint payees, or anomalous indorsers are jointly and severally liable in the capacity in which they sign.

(b) Except as provided in Section 3-419(f) or by agreement of the affected parties, a party having joint and several liability who pays the instrument is entitled to receive from any party having the same joint and several liability contribution in accordance with applicable law.

Definitional Cross References:

"Acceptor".	Section 3-103(a)(1)
"Agreement".	Section 1-201(b)(3)
"Anomalous Indorser".	Section 3-205(d)
"Drawer".	Section 3-103(a)(5)
"Indorsement".	Section 3-204(a)
"Instrument".	Section 3-104(b)
"Maker".	Section 3-103(a)(7)
"Party".	Section 3-103(a)(10)
"Person".	Section 1-201(b)(27)
"Signed".	Section 1-201(b)(37)

Official Comment

1. Subsection (a) replaces subsection (e) of former Section 3-118. Subsection (b) states contribution rights of parties with joint and several liability by referring to applicable law. But subsection (b) is subject to Section 3-419(f). If one of the parties with joint and several liability is an accommodation party and the other is the accommodated party, Section 3-419(f) applies. Because one of the joint and several obligors may have recourse against the other joint and several obligor under subsection (b), each party that is jointly and severally liable under subsection (a) is a secondary obligor in part and a principal obligor in part, as those terms are defined in Section 3-103(a). Accordingly, Section 3-605 determines the effect of a release, an extension of time, or a modification of the obligation of one of the joint and several obligors, as well as the effect of an impairment of collateral provided by one of those obligors.

2. Indorsers normally do not have joint and several liability. Rather, an earlier indorser has liability to a later indorser. But indorsers can have joint and several liability in two cases. If an instrument is payable to two payees jointly, both payees must indorse. The indorsement is a joint indorsement and the indorsers have joint and several liability and subsection (b) applies. The other case is that of two or more anomalous indorsers. The term is defined in Section 3-205(d). An anomalous indorsement normally indicates that the indorser signed as an accommodation party. If more than one accommodation party indorses a note as an accommodation to the maker, the indorsers have joint and several liability and subsection (b) applies.

Additional References:
3-415 Comment 5
3-605 Comment 3, 4

Section 3-117. Other Agreements Affecting Instrument

Subject to applicable law regarding exclusion of proof of contemporaneous or previous agreements, the obligation of a party to an instrument to pay the instrument may be modified, supplemented, or nullified by a separate agreement of the obligor and a person entitled to enforce the instrument, if the instrument is issued or the obligation is incurred in reliance on the agreement or as part of the same transaction giving rise to the agreement. To the extent an obligation is modified, supplemented, or nullified by an agreement under this section, the agreement is a defense to the obligation.

Definitional Cross References:

"Agreement".	Section 1-201(b)(3)
"Instrument".	Section 3-104(b)
"Issue".	Section 3-105(a)
"Party".	Section 3-103(a)(10)
"Person Entitled to Enforce".	Section 3-301

Official Comment

1. The separate agreement might be a security agreement or mortgage or it might be an agreement that contradicts the terms of the instrument. For example, a person may be induced to sign an instrument under an agreement that the signer will not be liable on the instrument unless certain conditions are met. Suppose X requested credit from Creditor who is willing to give the credit only if an acceptable accommodation party will sign the note of X as co-maker. Y agrees to sign as co-maker on the condition that Creditor also obtain the signature of Z as co-maker. Creditor agrees and Y signs as co-maker with X. Creditor fails to obtain the signature of Z on the note. Under Sections 3-412 and 3-419(b), Y is obliged to pay the note, but Section 3-117 applies. In this case, the agreement modifies the terms of the note by stating a condition to the obligation of Y to pay the note. This case is essentially similar to a case in which a maker of a note is induced to sign the note by fraud of the holder. Although the agreement that Y not be liable on the note unless Z also signs may not have been fraudulently made, a subsequent attempt by Creditor to require Y to pay the note in violation of the agreement is a bad faith act. Section 3-117, in treating the agreement as a defense, allows Y to assert the agreement against Creditor, but the defense would not be good against a subsequent holder in due course of the note that took it without notice of the agreement. If there cannot be a holder in due course because of Section 3-106(d), a subsequent holder that took the note in good faith, for value and without knowledge of the agreement would not be able to enforce the liability of Y. This result is consistent with the risk that a holder not in due course takes with respect to fraud in inducing issuance of an instrument.

2. The effect of merger or integration clauses to the effect that a writing is intended to be the complete and exclusive statement of the terms of the agreement or that the agreement is not subject to conditions is left to the supplementary law of the jurisdiction pursuant to Section 1-103. Thus, in the case discussed in Comment 1, whether Y is permitted to prove the condition to Y's obligation to pay the note is determined by that law. Moreover, nothing in this section is intended to validate an agreement which is fraudulent or void as against public policy, as in the case of a note given to deceive a bank examiner.

Additional References:

3-305 Comment 2

3-402 Comment 2

Section 3-118. Statute of Limitations

(a) Except as provided in subsection (e), an action to enforce the obligation of a party to pay a note payable at a definite time must be commenced within six years after the due date or dates stated in the note or, if a due date is accelerated, within six years after the accelerated due date.

(b) Except as provided in subsection (d) or (e), if demand for payment is made to the maker of a note payable on demand, an action to enforce the obligation of a party to pay the note must be commenced within six years after the demand. If no demand for payment is made to the maker, an action to enforce the note is barred if neither principal nor interest on the note has been paid for a continuous period of 10 years.

(c) Except as provided in subsection (d), an action to enforce the obligation of a party to an unaccepted draft to pay the draft must be commenced within three years after dishonor of the draft or 10 years after the date of the draft, whichever period expires first.

(d) An action to enforce the obligation of the acceptor of a certified check or the issuer of a teller's check, cashier's check, or traveler's check must be commenced within three years after demand for payment is made to the acceptor or issuer, as the case may be.

(e) An action to enforce the obligation of a party to a certificate of deposit to pay the instrument must be commenced within six years after demand for payment is made to the maker, but if the instrument states a due date and the maker is not required to pay before that date, the six-year period begins when a demand for payment is in effect and the due date has passed.

(f) An action to enforce the obligation of a party to pay an accepted draft, other than a certified check, must be commenced (i) within six years after the due date or dates stated in the draft or acceptance if the obligation of the acceptor is payable at a definite time, or (ii) within six years after the date of the acceptance if the obligation of the acceptor is payable on demand.

(g) Unless governed by other law regarding claims for indemnity or contribution, an action (i) for conversion of an instrument, for money had and received, or like action based on conversion, (ii) for breach of warranty, or (iii) to enforce an obligation, duty, or right arising under this Article and not governed by this section must be commenced within three years after the [cause of action] accrues.

Definitional Cross References:

"Acceptance".	Section 3-409(a)
"Acceptor".	Section 3-103(a)(1)
"Action".	Section 1-201(b)(1)
"Cashier's Check".	Section 3-104(g)

"Certificate of Deposit".	Section 3-104(j)
"Certified Check".	Section 3-409(d)
"Conversation".	Section 3-420
"Dishonor".	Section 3-502
"Draft".	Section 3-104(e)
"Instrument".	Section 3-104(b)
"Issuer".	Section 3-105(c)
"Maker".	Section 3-103(a)(7)
"Money".	Section 1-201(b)(24)
"Note".	Section 3-104(e)
"Party".	Section 3-103(a)(10)
"Payable at a Definite Time".	Section 3-108(b)
"Payable on Demand".	Section 3-108(a)
"Payment".	Section 3-602(a)
"Teller's Check".	Section 3-104(h)
"Traveler's Check".	Section 3-104(i)

Official Comment

1. Section 3-118 differs from former Section 3-122, which states when a cause of action accrues on an instrument. Section 3-118 does not define when a cause of action accrues. Accrual of a cause of action is stated in other sections of Article 3 such as those that state the various obligations of parties to an instrument. The only purpose of Section 3-118 is to define the time within which an action to enforce an obligation, duty, or right arising under Article 3 must be commenced. Section 3-118 does not attempt to state all rules with respect to a statute of limitations. For example, the circumstances under which the running of a limitations period may be tolled is left to other law pursuant to Section 1-103.

2. The first six subsections apply to actions to enforce an obligation of any party to an instrument to pay the instrument. This changes present law in that indorsers who may become liable on an instrument after issue are subject to a period of limitations running from the same date as that of the maker or drawer. Subsections (a) and (b) apply to notes. If the note is payable at a definite time, a six-year limitations period starts at the due date of the note, subject to prior acceleration. If the note is payable on demand, there are two limitations periods. Although a note payable on demand could theoretically be called a day after it was issued, the normal expectation of the parties is that the note will remain outstanding until there is some reason to call it. If the law provides that the limitations period does not start until demand is made, the cause of action to enforce it may never be barred. On the other hand, if the limitations period starts when demand for payment may be made, i.e. at any time after the note was issued, the payee of a note on which interest or portions of principal are being paid could lose the right to enforce the note even though it was treated as a continuing obligation by the parties. Some demand notes are not enforced because the payee has forgiven the debt. This is particularly true in family and other noncommercial transactions. A demand note found after the death of the payee may be presented for payment many years after it was issued. The maker may be a relative and it may be difficult to determine whether the note represents a real or a forgiven debt. Subsection (b) is designed to bar notes that no longer represent a claim to payment and to require reasonably prompt action to enforce notes on which there is default. If a demand for payment is made to the maker, a six-year limitations period starts to run when demand is made. The second sentence of subsection (b) bars an action to enforce a demand note if no demand has been made on the note and no payment of interest or principal has been made for a continuous period of 10 years. This covers the case of a note that does not bear interest or a case in which interest due on the note has not been paid. This kind of case is likely to be a family transaction in which a failure to demand payment may indicate that the holder did not intend to enforce the obligation but neglected to destroy the note. A limitations period that bars stale claims in this kind of case is appropriate if the period is relatively long.

3. Subsection (c) applies primarily to personal uncertified checks. Checks are payment instruments rather than credit instruments. The limitations period expires three years after the date of dishonor or 10 years after the date of the check, whichever is earlier. Teller's checks, cashier's checks, certified checks, and traveler's checks are treated differently under subsection (d) because they are commonly treated as cash equivalents. A great delay in presenting a cashier's check for payment in most cases will occur because the check was mislaid during that period. The person to whom traveler's checks are issued may hold them indefinitely as a safe form of cash for use in an emergency. There is no compelling reason for barring the claim of the owner of the cashier's check or traveler's check. Under subsection (d) the claim is never barred because the three-year limitations period does not start to run until demand for payment is made. The limitations period in subsection (d) in effect applies only to cases in which there is a dispute about the legitimacy of the claim of the person demanding payment.

4. Subsection (e) covers certificates of deposit. The limitations period of six years doesn't start to run until the depositor demands payment. Most certificates of deposit are payable on demand even if they state a due date. The effect of a demand for payment before maturity is usually that the bank will pay, but that a penalty will be assessed against the depositor in the form of a reduction in the amount of interest that is paid. Subsection (e) also provides for cases in which the bank has no obligation to pay until the due date. In that case the limitations period doesn't start to run until there is a demand for payment in effect and the due date has passed.

5. Subsection (f) applies to accepted drafts other than certified checks. When a draft is accepted it is in effect turned into a note of the acceptor. In almost all cases the acceptor will agree to pay at a definite time. Subsection (f) states that in that case the six-year limitations period starts to run on the due date. In the rare case in which the obligation of the acceptor is payable on demand, the six-year limitations period starts to run at the date of the acceptance.

6. Subsection (g) covers warranty and conversion cases and other actions to enforce obligations or rights arising under Article 3. A three-year period is stated and subsection (g) follows general law in stating that the period runs from the time the cause of action accrues. Since the traditional term "cause of action" may have been replaced in some states by "claim for relief" or some equivalent term, the words "cause of action" have been bracketed to indicate that the words may be replaced by an appropriate substitute to conform to local practice.

7. One of the most significant differences between this Article and the Convention on International Bills of Exchange and International Promissory Notes is that the statute of limitation under the Convention generally is only four years, rather than the six years provided by this section. See Convention Article 84.

Additional References: 4-111 Comment

Section 3-119. Notice of Right to Defend Action

In an action for breach of an obligation for which a third person is answerable over pursuant to this Article or Article 4, the defendant may give the third person notice of the litigation in a record, and the person notified may then give similar notice to any other person who is answerable over. If the notice states (i) that the person notified may come in and defend and (ii) that failure to do so will bind the person notified in an action later brought by the person giving the notice as to any deter-mination of fact common to the two litigations, the person notified is so bound unless after seasonable receipt of the notice the person notified does come in and defend.

Definitional Cross References:

"Action".	Section 1-201(b)(1)
"Defendant".	Section 1-201(b)(15) [*sic*, should be 1-201(b)(14)]
"Notifies".	Section 1-202(d)
"Person".	Section 1-201(b)(27)
"Record".	Section 3-103(a)(14)

Official Comment

This section is a restatement of former Section 3-803.

PART 2. NEGOTIATION, TRANSFER, AND INDORSEMENT

Section 3-201. Negotiation

(a) "Negotiation" means a transfer of possession, whether voluntary or involuntary, of an instrument by a person other than the issuer to a person who thereby becomes its holder.

(b) Except for negotiation by a remitter, if an instrument is payable to an identified person, negotiation requires transfer of possession of the instrument and its indorsement by the holder. If an instrument is payable to bearer, it may be negotiated by transfer of possession alone.

Definitional Cross References:

"Holder".	Section 1-201(b)(21)
"Indorsement".	Section 3-204(a)
"Instrument".	Section 3-104(b)
"Issuer".	Section 3-105(c)
"Payable to Bearer".	Section 3-109(a)
"Person".	Section 1-201(b)(27)
"Remitter".	Section 3-103(a)(15)

Official Comment

1. Subsections (a) and (b) are based in part on subsection (1) of former Section 3-202. A person can become holder of an instrument when the instrument is issued to that person, or the status of holder can arise as the result of an event that occurs after issuance. "Negotiation" is the term used in Article 3 to describe this post-issuance event. Normally, negotiation occurs as the result of a voluntary transfer of possession of an instrument by a holder to another person who becomes the holder as a result of the transfer. Negotiation always requires a change in possession of the instrument because nobody can be a holder without possessing the instrument, either directly or through an agent. But in some cases the transfer of possession is involuntary and in some cases the person transferring possession is not a holder. In defining "negotiation" former Section 3-202(1) used the word "transfer," an undefined term, and "delivery," defined in Section 1-201(b)(15) to mean voluntary change of possession. Instead, subsections (a) and (b) use the term "transfer of possession" and, subsection (a) states that negotiation can occur by an involuntary transfer of possession. For example, if an instrument is payable to bearer and it is stolen by Thief or is found by Finder, Thief or Finder becomes the holder of the instrument when possession is obtained. In this case there is an involuntary transfer of possession that results in negotiation to Thief or Finder.

2. In most cases negotiation occurs by a transfer of possession by a holder or remitter. Remitter transactions usually involve a cashier's or teller's check. For example, Buyer buys goods from Seller and pays for them with a cashier's check of Bank that Buyer buys from Bank. The check is issued by Bank when it is delivered to Buyer, regardless of whether the check is payable to Buyer or to Seller. Section 3-105(a). If the check is payable to Buyer, negotiation to Seller is done by delivery of the check to Seller after it is indorsed by Buyer. It is more common, however, that the check when issued will be payable to Seller. In that case Buyer is referred to as the "remitter." Section 3-103(a)(11). The remitter, although not a party to the check, is the owner of the check until ownership is transferred to Seller by delivery. This transfer is a negotiation because Seller becomes the holder of the check when Seller obtains possession. In some cases Seller may have acted fraudulently in obtaining possession of the check. In those cases Buyer may be entitled to rescind the transfer to Seller because of the fraud and assert a claim of ownership to the check under Section 3-306 against Seller or a subsequent transferee of the check. Section 3-202(b) provides for rescission of negotiation, and that provision applies to rescission by a remitter as well as by a holder.

3. Other sections of Article 3 may modify the rule stated in the first sentence of subsection (b). See for example, Sections 3-404, 3-405 and 3-406.

Additional References:

3-305 Comment 4
3-411 Comment 3
4-205 Comment
4-206 Comment

Section 3-202. Negotiation Subject to Rescission

(a) Negotiation is effective even if obtained (i) from an infant, a corporation exceeding its powers, or a person without capacity, (ii) by fraud, duress, or mistake, or (iii) in breach of duty or as part of an illegal transaction.

(b) To the extent permitted by other law, negotiation may be rescinded or may be subject to other remedies, but those remedies may not be asserted against a subsequent holder in due course or a person paying the instrument in good faith and without knowledge of facts that are a basis for rescission or other remedy.

Definitional Cross References:

"Good Faith".	Section 1-201(b)(20), Section 3-103(a)(6)
"Holder in Due Course".	Section 3-302
"Instrument".	Section 3-104(b)
"Negotiation".	Section 3-201(a)
"Person".	Section 1-201(b)(27)
"Remedy".	Section 1-201(b)(32)

Official Comment

1. This section is based on former Section 3-207. Subsection (2) of former Section 3-207 prohibited rescission of a negotiation against holders in due course. Subsection (b) of Section 3-202 extends this protection to payor banks.

2. Subsection (a) applies even though the lack of capacity or the illegality, is of a character which goes to the essence of the transaction and makes it entirely void. It is inherent in the character of negotiable instruments that any person in possession of an instrument which by its terms is payable to that person or to bearer is a holder and may be dealt with by anyone as a holder. The principle finds its most extreme application in the well settled rule that a holder in due course may take the instrument even from a thief and be protected against the claim of the rightful owner. The policy of subsection (a) is that any person to whom an instrument is negotiated is a holder until the instrument has been recovered from that person's possession. The remedy of a person with a claim to an instrument is to recover the instrument by replevin or otherwise; to impound it or to enjoin its enforcement, collection or negotiation; to recover its proceeds from the holder; or to intervene in any action brought by the holder against the obligor. As provided in Section 3-305(c), the claim of the claimant is not a defense to the obligor unless the claimant defends the action.

3. There can be no rescission or other remedy against a holder in due course or a person who pays in good faith and without notice, even though the prior negotiation may have been fraudulent or illegal in its essence and entirely void. As against any other party the claimant may have any remedy permitted by law. This section is not intended to specify what that remedy may be, or to prevent any court from imposing conditions or limitations such as prompt action or return of the consideration received. All such questions are left to the law of the particular jurisdiction. Section 3-202 gives no right that would not otherwise exist. The section is intended to mean that any remedies afforded by other law are cut off only by a holder in due course.

Additional References:

3-305 Comment 4
3-306 Comment
3-411 Comment 3

Section 3-203. Transfer of Instrument; Rights Acquired by Transfer

(a) An instrument is transferred when it is delivered by a person other than its issuer for the purpose of giving to the person receiving delivery the right to enforce the instrument.

(b) Transfer of an instrument, whether or not the transfer is a negotiation, vests in the transferee any right of the transferor to enforce the instrument, including any right as a holder in due course, but the transferee cannot acquire rights of a holder in due course by a transfer, directly or indirectly, from a holder in due course if the transferee engaged in fraud or illegality affecting the instrument.

(c) Unless otherwise agreed, if an instrument is transferred for value and the transferee does not become a holder because of lack of indorsement by the transferor, the transferee has a specifically enforceable right to the unqualified indorsement of the transferor, but negotiation of the instrument does not occur until the indorsement is made.

(d) If a transferor purports to transfer less than the entire instrument, negotiation of the instrument does not occur. The transferee obtains no rights under this Article and has only the rights of a partial assignee.

Definitional Cross References:

"Delivery".	Section 1-201(b)(15)
"Holder".	Section 1-201(b)(21)
"Holder in Due Course".	Section 3-302
"Indorsement".	Section 3-204(a)
"Instrument".	Section 3-104(b)
"Issuer".	Section 3-105(c)
"Negotiation".	Section 3-201(a)
"Person".	Section 1-201(b)(27)
"Value, Transferred for".	Section 3-303(a)

Official Comment

1. Section 3-203 is based on former Section 3-201 which stated that a transferee received such rights as the transferor had. The former section was confusing because some rights of the transferor are not vested in the transferee unless the transfer is a negotiation. For example, a transferee that did not become the holder could not negotiate the instrument, a right that the transferor had. Former Section 3-201 did not define "transfer." Subsection (a) defines transfer by limiting it to cases in which possession of the instrument is delivered for the purpose of giving to the person receiving delivery the right to enforce the instrument.

Although transfer of an instrument might mean in a particular case that title to the instrument passes to the transferee, that result does not follow in all cases. The right to enforce an instrument and ownership of the instrument are two different concepts. A thief who steals a check payable to bearer becomes the holder of the check and a person entitled to enforce it, but does not become the owner of the check. If the thief transfers the check to a purchaser the transferee obtains the right to enforce the check. If the purchaser is not a holder in due course, the owner's claim to the check may be asserted against the purchaser. Ownership rights in instruments may be determined by principles of the law of property, independent of Article 3, which do not depend upon whether the instrument was transferred under Section 3-203. Moreover, a person who has an ownership right in an instrument might not be a person entitled to enforce the instrument. For example, suppose X is the owner and holder of an instrument payable to X. X sells the instrument to Y but is unable to deliver immediate possession to Y. Instead, X signs a document conveying all of X's right, title, and interest in the instrument to Y. Although the document may be effective to give Y a claim to ownership of the instrument, Y is not a person entitled to enforce the instrument until Y obtains possession of the instrument. No transfer of the instrument occurs under Section 3-203(a) until it is delivered to Y.

An instrument is a reified right to payment. The right is represented by the instrument itself. The right to payment is transferred by delivery of possession of the instrument "by a person other than its issuer for the purpose of giving to the person receiving delivery the right to enforce the instrument." The quoted phrase excludes issue of an instrument, defined in Section 3-105, and cases in which a delivery of possession is for some purpose other than transfer of the right to enforce. For example, if a check is presented for payment by delivering the check to the drawee, no transfer of the check to the drawee occurs because there is no intent to give the drawee the right to enforce the check.

2. Subsection (b) states that transfer vests in the transferee any right of the transferor to enforce the instrument "including any right as a holder in due course." If the transferee is not a holder because the transferor did not indorse, the transferee is nevertheless a person entitled to enforce the instrument under Section 3-301 if the transferor was a holder at the time of transfer. Although the transferee is not a holder, under subsection (b) the transferee obtained the rights of the transferor as holder. Because the transferee's rights are derivative of the transferor's rights, those rights must be proved. Because the transferee is not a holder, there is no presumption under Section 3-308 that the transferee, by producing the instrument, is entitled to payment. The instrument, by its terms, is not payable to the transferee and the transferee must account for possession of the unindorsed instrument by proving the transaction through which the transferee acquired it. Proof of a transfer to the transferee by a holder is proof that the transferee has acquired the rights of a holder. At that point the transferee is entitled to the presumption under Section 3-308.

Under subsection (b) a holder in due course that transfers an instrument transfers those rights as a holder in due course to the purchaser. The policy is to assure the holder in due course a free market for the instrument. There is one exception to this rule stated in the concluding clause of subsection (b). A person who is party to fraud or illegality affecting the instrument is not permitted to wash the instrument clean by passing it into the hands of a holder in due course and then repurchasing it.

3. Subsection (c) applies only to a transfer for value. It applies only if the instrument is payable to order or specially indorsed to the transferor. The transferee acquires, in the absence of a contrary agreement, the specifically enforceable right to the indorsement of the transferor. Unless otherwise agreed, it is a right to the general indorsement of the transferor with full liability as indorser, rather than to an indorsement without recourse. The question may arise if the transferee has paid in advance and the indorsement is omitted fraudulently or through oversight. A transferor who is willing to indorse only without recourse or unwilling to indorse at all should make those intentions clear before transfer. The agreement of the transferee to take less than an unqualified indorsement need not be an express one, and the understanding may be implied from conduct, from past practice, or from the circumstances of the transaction. Subsection (c) provides that there is no negotiation of the instrument until the indorsement by the transferor is made. Until that time the transferee does not become a holder, and if earlier notice of a defense or claim is received, the transferee does not qualify as a holder in due course under Section 3-302.

4. The operation of Section 3-203 is illustrated by the following cases. In each case Payee, by fraud, induced Maker to issue a note to Payee. The fraud is a defense to the obligation of Maker to pay the note under Section 3-305(a)(2).

> *Case # 1.* Payee negotiated the note to X who took as a holder in due course. After the instrument became overdue X negotiated the note to Y who had notice of the fraud. Y succeeds to X's rights as a holder in due course and takes free of Maker's defense of fraud.
>
> *Case # 2.* Payee negotiated the note to X who took as a holder in due course. Payee then repurchased the note from X. Payee does not succeed to X's rights as a holder in due course and is subject to Maker's defense of fraud.

Case # 3. Payee negotiated the note to X who took as a holder in due course. X sold the note to Purchaser who received possession. The note, however, was indorsed to X and X failed to indorse it. Purchaser is a person entitled to enforce the instrument under Section 3-301 and succeeds to the rights of X as holder in due course. Purchaser is not a holder, however, and under Section 3-308 Purchaser will have to prove the transaction with X under which the rights of X as holder in due course were acquired.

Case # 4. Payee sold the note to Purchaser who took for value, in good faith and without notice of the defense of Maker. Purchaser received possession of the note but Payee neglected to indorse it. Purchaser became a person entitled to enforce the instrument but did not become the holder because of the missing indorsement. If Purchaser received notice of the defense of Maker before obtaining the indorsement of Payee, Purchaser cannot become a holder in due course because at the time notice was received the note had not been negotiated to Purchaser. If indorsement by Payee was made after Purchaser received notice, Purchaser had notice of the defense when it became the holder.

5. Subsection (d) restates former Section 3-202(3). The cause of action on an instrument cannot be split. Any indorsement which purports to convey to any party less than the entire amount of the instrument is not effective for negotiation. This is true of either "Pay A one-half," or "Pay A two-thirds and B one-third." Neither A nor B becomes a holder. On the other hand an indorsement reading merely "Pay A and B" is effective, since it transfers the entire cause of action to A and B as tenants in common. An indorsement purporting to convey less than the entire instrument does, however, operate as a partial assignment of the cause of action. Subsection (d) makes no attempt to state the legal effect of such an assignment, which is left to other law. A partial assignee of an instrument has rights only to the extent the applicable law gives rights, either at law or in equity, to a partial assignee.

6. The rules for transferring instruments set out in this section are similar to the rules in Article 13 of the Convention on International Bills of Exchange and International Promissory Notes.

Additional References:

3-204 Comment 2
3-308 Comment 2
3-416 Comment 2

Section 3-204. Indorsement

(a) "Indorsement" means a signature, other than that of a signer as maker, drawer, or acceptor, that alone or accompanied by other words is made on an instrument for the purpose of (i) negotiating the instrument, (ii) restricting payment of the instrument, or (iii) incurring indorser's liability on the instrument, but regardless of the intent of the signer, a signature and its accompanying words is an indorsement unless the accompanying words, terms of the instrument, place of the signature, or other circumstances unambiguously indicate that the signature was made for a purpose other than indorsement. For the purpose of determining whether a signature is made on an instrument, a paper affixed to the instrument is a part of the instrument.

(b) "Indorser" means a person who makes an indorsement.

(c) For the purpose of determining whether the transferee of an instrument is a holder, an indorsement that transfers a security interest in the instrument is effective as an unqualified indorsement of the instrument.

(d) If an instrument is payable to a holder under a name that is not the name of the holder, indorsement may be made by the holder in the name stated in the instrument or in the holder's name or both, but signature in both names may be required by a person paying or taking the instrument for value or collection.

Definitional Cross References:

"Acceptor".	Section 3-103(a)(1)
"Drawer".	Section 3-103(a)(5)
"Holder".	Section 1-201(b)(21)
"Instrument".	Section 3-104(b)
"Maker".	Section 3-103(a)(7)
"Negotiation".	Section 3-201(a)
"Payment".	Section 3-602(a)
"Person".	Section 1-201(b)(27)
"Security Interest".	Section 1-201(b)(35)
"Signed".	Section 1-201(b)(37)
"Value, Taken for".	Section 3-303(a)

Official Comment

1. Subsection (a) is a definition of "indorsement," a term which was not defined in former Article 3. Indorsement is defined in terms of the purpose of the signature. If a blank or special indorsement is made to give rights as a holder to a transferee the indorsement is made for the purpose of negotiating the instrument. Subsection (a)(i). If the holder of a check has an account in the drawee bank and wants to be sure that payment of the check will be made by credit to the holder's account, the holder can indorse the check by signing the holder's name with the accompanying words "for deposit only" before presenting the check for payment to the drawee bank. In that case the purpose of the quoted words is to restrict payment of the instrument. Subsection (a)(ii). If X wants to guarantee payment of a note signed by Y as maker, X can do so by signing X's name to the back of the note as an indorsement. This indorsement is known as an anomalous indorsement (Section 3-205(d)) and is made for the purpose of incurring indorser's liability on the note. Subsection (a)(iii). In some cases an indorsement may serve more than one purpose. For example, if the holder of a check deposits it to the holder's account in a depositary bank for collection and indorses the check by signing the holder's name with the accompanying words "for deposit only" the purpose of the indorsement is both to negotiate the check to the depositary bank and to restrict payment of the check.

The "but" clause of the first sentence of subsection (a) elaborates on former Section 3-402. In some cases it may not be clear whether a signature was meant to be that of an indorser, a party to the instrument in some other capacity such as drawer, maker or acceptor, or a person who was not signing as a party. The general rule is that a signature is an indorsement if the instrument does not indicate an unambiguous intent of the signer not to sign as an indorser. Intent may be determined by words accompanying the signature, the place of signature, or other circumstances. For example, suppose a depositary bank gives cash for a check properly indorsed by the payee. The bank requires the payee's employee to sign the back of the check as evidence that the employee received the cash. If the signature consists only of the initials of the employee it is not reasonable to assume that it was meant to be an indorsement. If there was a full signature but accompanying words indicated that it was meant as a receipt for the cash given for the check, it is not an indorsement. If the signature is not qualified in any way and appears in the place normally used for indorsements, it may be an indorsement even though the signer intended the signature to be a receipt. To take another example, suppose the drawee of a draft signs the draft on the back in the space usually used for indorsements. No words accompany the signature. Since the drawee has no reason to sign a draft unless the intent is to accept the draft, the signature is effective as an acceptance. Custom and usage may be used to determine intent. For example, by long-established custom and usage, a signature in the lower right hand corner of an instrument indicates an intent to sign as the maker of a note or the drawer of a draft. Any similar clear indication of an intent to sign in some other capacity or for some other purpose may establish that a signature is not an indorsement. For example, if the owner of a traveler's check countersigns the check in the process of negotiating it, the countersignature is not an indorsement. The countersignature is a condition to the issuer's obligation to pay and its purpose is to provide a means of verifying the identify of the person negotiating the traveler's check by allowing comparison of the specimen signature and the countersignature. The countersignature is not necessary for negotiation and the signer does not incur indorser's liability. See Comment 2 to Section 3-106.

The last sentence of subsection (a) is based on subsection (2) of former Section 3-202. An indorsement on an allonge is valid even though there is sufficient space on the instrument for an indorsement.

2. Assume that Payee indorses a note to Creditor as security for a debt. Under subsection (b) of Section 3-203 Creditor takes Payee's rights to enforce or transfer the instrument subject to the limitations imposed by Article 9. Subsection (c) of Section 3-204 makes clear that Payee's indorsement to Creditor, even though it mentions creation of a security interest, is an unqualified indorsement that gives to Creditor the right to enforce the note as its holder.

3. Subsection (d) is a restatement of former Section 3-203. Section 3-110(a) states that an instrument is payable to the person intended by the person signing as or in the name or behalf of the issuer even if that person is identified by a name that is not the true name of the person. In some cases the name used in the instrument is a misspelling of the correct name and in some cases the two names may be entirely different. The payee may indorse in the name used in the instrument, in the payee's correct name, or in both. In each case the indorsement is effective. But because an indorsement in a name different from that used in the instrument may raise a question about its validity and an indorsement in a name that is not the correct name of the payee may raise a problem of identifying the indorser, the accepted commercial practice is to indorse in both names. Subsection (d) allows a person paying or taking the instrument for value or collection to require indorsement in both names.

Additional References: 3-401 Comment 2

Section 3-205. Special Indorsement; Blank Indorsement; Anomalous Indorsement

(a) If an indorsement is made by the holder of an instrument, whether payable to an identified person or payable to bearer, and the indorsement identifies a person to whom it makes the instrument payable, it is a "special indorsement." When specially indorsed, an instrument becomes payable to the identified person and may be negotiated only by the indorsement of that person. The principles stated in Section 3-110 apply to special indorsements.

(b) If an indorsement is made by the holder of an instrument and it is not a special indorsement, it is a "blank indorsement." When indorsed in blank, an instrument becomes payable to bearer and may be negotiated by transfer of possession alone until specially indorsed.

(c) The holder may convert a blank indorsement that consists only of a signature into a special indorsement by writing, above the signature of the indorser, words identifying the person to whom the instrument is made payable.

(d) "Anomalous indorsement" means an indorsement made by a person who is not the holder of the instrument. An anomalous indorsement does not affect the manner in which the instrument may be negotiated.

Definitional Cross References:

"Holder".	Section 1-201(b)(21)
"Indorsement".	Section 3-204(a)
"Instrument".	Section 3-104(b)
"Negotiation".	Section 3-201(a)
"Payable to Bearer".	Section 3-109(a)
"Person".	Section 1-201(b)(27)
"Signed".	Section 1-201(b)(37)
"Writing".	Section 1-201(b)(43)

Official Comment

1. Subsection (a) is based on subsection (1) of former Section 3-204. It states the test of a special indorsement to be whether the indorsement identifies a person to whom the instrument is payable. Section 3-110 states rules for identifying the payee of an instrument. Section 3-205(a) incorporates the principles stated in Section 3-110 in identifying an indorsee. The language of Section 3-110 refers to language used by the issuer of the instrument. When that section is used with respect to an indorsement, Section 3-110 must be read as referring to the language used by the indorser.

2. Subsection (b) is based on subsection (2) of former Section 3-204. An indorsement made by the holder is either a special or blank indorsement. If the indorsement is made by a holder and is not a special indorsement, it is a blank indorsement. For example, the holder of an instrument, intending to make a special indorsement, writes the words "Pay to the order of" without completing the indorsement by writing the name of the indorsee. The holder's signature appears under the quoted words. The indorsement is not a special indorsement because it does not identify a person to whom it makes the instrument payable. Since it is not a special indorsement it is a blank indorsement and the instrument is payable to bearer. The result is analogous to that of a check in which the name of the payee is left blank by the drawer. In that case the check is payable to bearer. See the last paragraphs of Comment 2 to Section 3-115.

A blank indorsement is usually the signature of the indorser on the back of the instrument without other words. Subsection (c) is based on subsection (3) of former Section 3-204. A "restrictive indorsement" described in Section 3-206 can be either a blank indorsement or a special indorsement. "Pay to T, in trust for B" is a restrictive indorsement. It is also a special indorsement because it identifies T as the person to whom the instrument is payable. "For deposit only" followed by the signature of the payee of a check is a restrictive indorsement. It is also a blank indorsement because it does not identify the person to whom the instrument is payable.

3. The only effect of an "anomalous indorsement," defined in subsection (d), is to make the signer liable on the instrument as an indorser. Such an indorsement is normally made by an accommodation party. Section 3-419.

4. Articles 14 and 16 of the Convention on International Bills of Exchange and International Promissory Notes includes similar rules for blank and special indorsements.

Additional References:

3-116 Comment 2
3-204 Comment 1
3-414 Comment 3

Section 3-206. Restrictive Indorsement

(a) An indorsement limiting payment to a particular person or otherwise prohibiting further transfer or negotiation of the instrument is not effective to prevent further transfer or negotiation of the instrument.

(b) An indorsement stating a condition to the right of the indorsee to receive payment does not affect the right of the indorsee to enforce the instrument. A person paying the instrument or taking it for value or collection may disregard the condition, and the rights and liabilities of that person are not affected by whether the condition has been fulfilled.

(c) If an instrument bears an indorsement (i) described in Section 4-201(b), or (ii) in blank or to a particular bank using the words "for deposit," "for collection," or other words indicating a purpose of having the instrument collected by a bank for the indorser or for a particular account, the following rules apply:

(1) A person, other than a bank, who purchases the instrument when so indorsed converts the instrument unless the amount paid for the instrument is received by the indorser or applied consistently with the indorsement.

(2) A depositary bank that purchases the instrument or takes it for collection when so indorsed converts the instrument unless the amount paid by the bank with respect to the instrument is received by the indorser or applied consistently with the indorsement.

(3) A payor bank that is also the depositary bank or that takes the instrument for immediate payment over the counter from a person other than a collecting bank converts the instrument unless the proceeds of the instrument are received by the indorser or applied consistently with the indorsement.

(4) Except as otherwise provided in paragraph (3), a payor bank or intermediary bank may disregard the indorsement and is not liable if the proceeds of the instrument are not received by the indorser or applied consistently with the indorsement.

(d) Except for an indorsement covered by subsection (c), if an instrument bears an indorsement using words to the effect that payment is to be made to the indorsee as agent, trustee, or other fiduciary for the benefit of the indorser or another person, the following rules apply:

(1) Unless there is notice of breach of fiduciary duty as provided in Section 3-307, a person who purchases the instrument from the indorsee or takes the instrument from the indorsee for collection or payment may pay the proceeds of payment or the value given for the instrument to the indorsee without regard to whether the indorsee violates a fiduciary duty to the indorser.

(2) A subsequent transferee of the instrument or person who pays the instrument is neither given notice nor otherwise affected by the restriction in the

indorsement unless the transferee or payor knows that the fiduciary dealt with the instrument or its proceeds in breach of fiduciary duty.

(e) The presence on an instrument of an indorsement to which this section applies does not prevent a purchaser of the instrument from becoming a holder in due course of the instrument unless the purchaser is a converter under subsection (c) or has notice or knowledge of breach of fiduciary duty as stated in subsection (d).

(f) In an action to enforce the obligation of a party to pay the instrument, the obligor has a defense if payment would violate an indorsement to which this section applies and the payment is not permitted by this section.

Definitional Cross References:

"Account".	Section 4-104(a)(1)
"Action".	Section 1-201(b)(1)
"Bank".	Section 1-201(b)(4)
"Collecting Bank".	Section 4-105(5)
"Conversion".	Section 3-420
"Depositary Bank".	Section 4-105(2)
"Holder in Due Course".	Section 3-302
"Indorsement".	Section 3-204(a)
"Indorsement in Blank".	Section 3-205(b)
"Indorser".	Section 3-204(b)
"Instrument".	Section 3-104(b)
"Intermediary Bank".	Section 4-105(4)
"Negotiation".	Section 3-201(a)
"Party".	Section 3-103(a)(10)
"Payment".	Section 3-602(a)
"Payor Bank".	Section 4-105(3)
"Person".	Section 1-201(b)(27)
"Purchase".	Section 1-201(b)(29)
"Purchaser".	Section 1-201(b)(30)
"Transfer".	Section 3-203(a)
"Value, Taken for".	Section 3-303(a)

Official Comment

1. This section replaces former Sections 3-205 and 3-206 and clarifies the law of restrictive indorsements.

2. Subsection (a) provides that an indorsement that purports to limit further transfer or negotiation is ineffective to prevent further transfer or negotiation. If a payee indorses "Pay A only," A may negotiate the instrument to subsequent holders who may ignore the restriction on the indorsement. Subsection (b) provides that an indorsement that states a condition to the right of a holder to receive payment is ineffective to condition payment. Thus if a payee indorses "Pay A if A ships goods complying with our contract," the right of A to enforce the instrument is not affected by the condition. In the case of a note, the obligation of the maker to pay A is not affected by the indorsement. In the case of a check, the drawee can pay A without regard to the condition, and if the check is dishonored the drawer is liable to pay A. If the check was negotiated by the payee to A in return for a promise to perform a contract and the promise was not kept, the payee would have a defense or counterclaim against A if the check were dishonored and A sued the payee as indorser, but the payee would have that defense or counterclaim whether or not the condition to the right of A was expressed in the indorsement. Former Section 3-206 treated a conditional indorsement like indorsements for deposit or collection. In revised Article 3, Section 3-206(b) rejects that approach and makes the conditional indorsement ineffective with respect to parties other than the indorser and indorsee. Since the indorsements referred to in subsections (a) and (b) are not effective as restrictive indorsements, they are no longer described as restrictive indorsements.

3. The great majority of restrictive indorsements are those that fall within subsection (c) which continues previous law. The depositary bank or the payor bank, if it takes the check for immediate payment over the counter, must act consistently with the indorsement, but an intermediary bank or payor bank that takes the check from a collecting bank is not affected by the indorsement. Any other person is also bound by the indorsement. For example, suppose a check is payable to X, who indorses in blank but writes above the signature the words "For deposit only." The check is stolen and is cashed at a grocery store by the thief. The grocery store indorses the check and deposits it in Depositary Bank. The account of the grocery store is credited and the check is forwarded to Payor Bank which pays the check. Under subsection (c), the grocery store and Depositary Bank are converters of the check because X did not receive the amount paid for the check. Payor Bank and any intermediary bank in the collection process are not liable to X. This Article does not displace the law of waiver as it may apply to restrictive indorsements. The circumstances under which a restrictive indorsement may be waived by the person who made it is not determined by this Article.

4. Subsection (d) replaces subsection (4) of former Section 3-206. Suppose Payee indorses a check "Pay to T in trust for B." T indorses in blank and delivers it to (a) Holder for value; (b) Depositary Bank for collection; or (c) Payor Bank for payment. In each case these takers can safely pay T so long as they have no notice under Section 3-307 of any breach of fiduciary duty that T may be committing. For example, under subsection (b) of Section 3-307 these takers have notice of a breach of trust if the check was taken in any transaction known by the taker to be for T's personal benefit. Subsequent transferees of the check from Holder or Depositary Bank are not affected by the restriction unless they have knowledge that T dealt with the check in breach of trust.

5. Subsection (f) allows a restrictive indorsement to be used as a defense by a person obliged to pay the instrument if that person would be liable for paying in violation of the indorsement.

Additional References:

3-205 Comment 2

3-305 Comment 2

4-203 Comment

Section 3-207. Reacquisition

Reacquisition of an instrument occurs if it is transferred to a former holder, by negotiation or otherwise.

A former holder who reacquires the instrument may cancel indorsements made after the reacquirer first became a holder of the instrument. If the cancellation causes the instrument to be payable to the reacquirer or to bearer, the reacquirer may negotiate the instrument. An indorser whose indorsement is canceled is discharged, and the discharge is effective against any subsequent holder.

Definitional Cross References:

"Discharge".	Section 3-601(a)
"Holder".	Section 1-201(b)(21)
"Indorsement".	Section 3-204(a)
"Instrument".	Section 3-104(b)
"Negotiation".	Section 3-201(a)
"Transfer".	Section 3-203(a)

Official Comment

Section 3-207 restates former Section 3-208. Reacquisition refers to cases in which a former holder reacquires the instrument either by negotiation from the present holder or by a transfer other than negotiation. If the reacquisition is by negotiation, the former holder reacquires the status of holder. Although Section 3-207 allows the holder to cancel all indorsements made after the holder first acquired holder status, cancellation is not necessary. Status of holder is not affected whether or not cancellation is made. But if the reacquisition is not the result of negotiation the former holder can obtain holder status only by striking the former holder's indorsement and any subsequent indorsements. The latter case is an exception to the general rule that if an instrument is payable to an identified person, the indorsement of that person is necessary to allow a subsequent transferee to obtain the status of holder. Reacquisition without indorsement by the person to whom the instrument is payable is illustrated by two examples:

Case # 1. X, a former holder, buys the instrument from Y, the present holder. Y delivers the instrument to X but fails to indorse it. Negotiation does not occur because the transfer of possession did not result in X's becoming holder. Section 3-201(a). The instrument by its terms is payable to Y, not to X. But X can obtain the status of holder by striking X's indorsement and all subsequent indorsements. When these indorsements are struck, the instrument by its terms is payable either to X or to bearer, depending upon how X originally became holder. In either case X becomes holder. Section 1-201(b)(21).

Case # 2. X, the holder of an instrument payable to X, negotiates it to Y by special indorsement. The negotiation is part of an underlying transaction between X and Y. The underlying transaction is rescinded by agreement of X and Y, and Y returns the instrument without Y's indorsement. The analysis is the same as that in Case # 1. X can obtain holder status by cancelling X's indorsement to Y.

In Case # 1 and Case # 2, X acquired ownership of the instrument after reacquisition, but X's title was clouded because the instrument by its terms was not payable to X. Normally, X can remedy the problem by obtaining Y's indorsement, but in some cases X may not be able to conveniently obtain that indorsement. Section 3-207 is a rule of convenience which relieves X of the burden of obtaining an indorsement that serves no substantive purpose. The effect of cancellation of any indorsement under Section 3-207 is to nullify it. Thus, the person whose indorsement is canceled is relieved of indorser's liability. Since cancellation is notice of discharge, discharge is effective even with respect to the rights of a holder in due course. Sections 3-601 and 3-604.

Additional References: 4-201 Comment 7.

PART 3. ENFORCEMENT OF INSTRUMENTS

Section 3-301. Person Entitled to Enforce Instrument

"Person entitled to enforce" an instrument means (i) the holder of the instrument, (ii) a nonholder in possession of the instrument who has the rights of a holder, or (iii) a person not in possession of the instrument who is entitled to enforce the instrument pursuant to Section 3-309 or 3-418(d). A person may be a person entitled to enforce the instrument even though the person is not the owner of the instrument or is in wrongful possession of the instrument.

Definitional Cross References:

"Holder".	Section 1-201(b)(21)
"Instrument".	Section 3-104(b)
"Person".	Section 1-201(b)(27)

Official Comment

This section replaces former Section 3-301 that stated the rights of a holder. The rights stated in former Section 3-301 to transfer, negotiate, enforce, or discharge an instrument are stated in other sections of Article 3. In revised Article 3, Section 3-301 defines "person entitled to enforce" an instrument. The definition recognizes that enforcement is not limited to holders. The quoted phrase includes a person enforcing a lost or stolen instrument. Section 3-309. It also includes a person in possession of an instrument who is not a holder. A nonholder in possession of an instrument includes a person that acquired rights of a holder by subrogation or under Section 3-203(a). It also includes both a remitter that has received an instrument from the issuer but has not yet transferred or negotiated the instrument to another person and also any other person who under applicable law is a successor to the holder or otherwise acquires the holder's rights.

Additional References:

3-203 Comment 2
3-308 Comment 2
3-404 Comment 2
3-420 Comment 1

Section 3-302. Holder in Due Course

(a) Subject to subsection (c) and Section 3-106(d), "holder in due course" means the holder of an instrument if:

(1) the instrument when issued or negotiated to the holder does not bear such apparent evidence of forgery or alteration or is not otherwise so irregular or incomplete as to call into question its authenticity; and

(2) the holder took the instrument (i) for value, (ii) in good faith, (iii) without notice that the instrument is overdue or has been dishonored or that there is an uncured default with respect to payment of another instrument issued as part of the same series, (iv) without notice that the instrument contains an unauthorized signature or has been altered, (v) without notice of any claim to the instrument described in Section 3-306, and (vi) without notice that any party has a defense or claim in recoupment described in Section 3-305(a).

(b) Notice of discharge of a party, other than discharge in an insolvency proceeding, is not notice of a defense under subsection (a), but discharge is effective against a person who became a holder in due course with notice of the discharge. Public filing or recording of a document does not of itself constitute notice of a defense, claim in recoupment, or claim to the instrument.

(c) Except to the extent a transferor or predecessor in interest has rights as a holder in due course, a person does not acquire rights of a holder in due course of an instrument taken (i) by legal process or by purchase in an execution, bankruptcy, or creditor's sale or similar proceeding, (ii) by purchase as part of a bulk transaction not in ordinary course of business of the transferor, or (iii) as the successor in interest to an estate or other organization.

(d) If, under Section 3-303(a)(1), the promise of performance that is the consideration for an instrument has been partially performed, the holder may assert rights as a holder in due course of the instrument only to the fraction of the amount payable under the instrument equal to the value of the partial performance divided by the value of the promised performance.

(e) If (i) the person entitled to enforce an instrument has only a security interest in the instrument and (ii) the person obliged to pay the instrument has a defense, claim in recoupment, or claim to the instrument that may be asserted against the person who granted the security interest, the person entitled to enforce the instrument may assert rights as a holder in due course only to an amount payable under the instrument which, at the time of enforcement of the instrument, does not exceed the amount of the unpaid obligation secured.

(f) To be effective, notice must be received at a time and in a manner that gives a reasonable opportunity to act on it.

(g) This section is subject to any law limiting status as a holder in due course in particular classes of transactions.

Definitional Cross References:

"Alteration".	Section 3-407
"Creditor".	Section 1-201(b)(13)
"Discharge".	Section 3-601(a)
"Dishonor".	Section 3-502
"Good Faith".	Section 1-201(b)(20), Section 3-103(a)(6)
"Holder".	Section 1-201(b)(21)
"Incomplete Instrument".	Section 3-115
"Insolvency Proceeding".	Section 1-201(b)(22)
"Instrument".	Section 3-104(b)
"Issue".	Section 3-105(a)
"Negotiation".	Section 3-201(a)
"Notice".	Section 1-202(a)
"Overdue".	Section 3-304
"Party".	Section 3-103(a)(10)
"Payment".	Section 3-602(a)
"Person".	Section 1-201(b)(27)
"Person Entitled to Enforce".	Section 3-301
"Purchase".	Section 1-201(b)(29)
"Security Interest".	Section 1-201(b)(35)
"Signed".	Section 1-201(b)(37)
"Unauthorized Signature".	Section 1-201(b)(41)
"Value, Taken for".	Section 3-303(a)

Official Comment

1. Subsection (a)(1) is a return to the N.I.L. rule that the taker of an irregular or incomplete instrument is not a person the law should protect against defenses of the obligor or claims of prior owners. This reflects a policy choice against extending the holder in due course doctrine to an instrument that is so incomplete or irregular "as to call into question its authenticity." The term "authenticity" is used to make it clear that the irregularity or incompleteness must indicate that the instrument may not be what it purports to be. Persons who purchase or pay such instruments should do so at their own risk. Under subsection (1) of former Section 3-304, irregularity or incompleteness gave a purchaser notice of a claim or defense. But it was not clear from that provision whether the claim or defense had to be related to the irregularity or incomplete aspect of the instrument. This ambiguity is not present in subsection (a)(1).

2. Subsection (a)(2) restates subsection (1) of former Section 3-302. Section 3-305(a) makes a distinction between defenses to the obligation to pay an instrument and claims in recoupment by the maker or drawer that may be asserted to reduce the amount payable on the instrument. Because of this distinction, which was not made in former Article 3, the reference in subsection (a)(2)(vi) is to both a defense and a claim in recoupment. Notice of forgery or alteration is stated separately because forgery and alteration are not technically defenses under subsection (a) of Section 3-305.

3. Discharge is also separately treated in the first sentence of subsection (b). Except for discharge in an insolvency proceeding, which is specifically stated to be a real defense in Section 3-305(a)(1), discharge is not expressed in Article 3 as a defense and is not included in Section 3-305(a)(2). Discharge is effective against anybody except a person having rights of a holder in due course who took the instrument without notice of the discharge. Notice of discharge does not disqualify a person from becoming a holder in due course. For example, a check certified after it is negotiated by the payee may subsequently be negotiated to a holder. If the holder had notice that the certification occurred after negotiation by the payee, the holder necessarily had notice of the discharge of the payee as indorser. Section 3-415(d). Notice of that discharge does not prevent the holder from becoming a holder in due course, but the discharge is effective against the holder. Section 3-601(b). Notice of a defense under Section 3-305(a)(1) of a maker, drawer or acceptor based on a bankruptcy discharge is different. There is no reason to give holder in due course status to a person with notice of that defense. The second sentence of subsection (b) is from former Section 3-304(5).

4. Professor Britton in his treatise Bills and Notes 309 (1961) stated: "A substantial number of decisions before the [N.I.L.] indicates that at common law there was nothing in the position of the payee as such which made it impossible for him to be a holder in due course." The courts were divided, however, about whether the payee of an instrument could be a holder in due course under the N.I.L.. Some courts read N.I.L. § 52(4) to mean that a person could be a holder in due course only if the instrument was "negotiated" to that person. N.I.L. § 30 stated that "an instrument is negotiated when it is transferred from one person to another in such manner as to constitute the transferee the holder thereof." Normally, an instrument is "issued" to the payee; it is not transferred to the payee. N.I.L. § 191 defined "issue" as the "first delivery of the instrument *** to a person who takes it as a holder." Thus, some courts concluded that the payee never could be a holder in due course. Other courts concluded that there was no evidence that the N.I.L. was intended to change the common law rule that the payee could be a holder in due course. Professor Britton states on p. 318: "The typical situations which raise the [issue] are those where the defense of a maker is interposed because of fraud by a [maker who is] principal debtor *** against a surety co-maker, or where the defense of fraud by a purchasing remitter is interposed by the drawer of the instrument against the good faith purchasing payee."

Former Section 3-302(2) stated: "A payee may be a holder in due course." This provision was intended to resolve the split of authority under the N.I.L.. It made clear that there was no intent to change the common-law rule that allowed a payee to become a holder in due course. See Comment 2 to former Section 3-302. But there was no need to put subsection (2) in former Section 3-302 because the split in authority under the N.I.L. was caused by the particular wording of N.I.L. § 52(4). The troublesome language in that section was not repeated in former Article 3 nor is it repeated in revised Article 3. Former Section 3-302(2) has been omitted in revised Article 3 because it is surplusage and may be misleading. The payee of an instrument can be a holder in due course, but use of the holder-in-due-course doctrine by the payee of an instrument is not the normal situation.

The primary importance of the concept of holder in due course is with respect to assertion of defenses or claims in recoupment (Section 3-305) and of claims to the instrument (Section 3-306). The holder-in-due-course doctrine assumes the following case as typical. Obligor issues a note or check to Obligee. Obligor is the maker of the note or drawer of the check. Obligee is the payee. Obligor has some defense to Obligor's obligation to pay the instrument. For example, Obligor issued the instrument for goods that Obligee promised to deliver. Obligee never delivered the goods. The failure of Obligee to deliver the goods is a defense. Section 3-303(b). Although Obligor has a defense against Obligee, if the instrument is negotiated to Holder and the requirements of subsection (a) are met, Holder may enforce the instrument against Obligor free of the defense. Section 3-305(b). In the typical case the holder in due course is not the payee of the instrument. Rather, the holder in due course is an immediate or remote transferee of the payee. If Obligor in our example is the only obligor on the check or note, the holder-in-due-course doctrine is irrelevant in determining rights between Obligor and Obligee with respect to the instrument.

But in a small percentage of cases it is appropriate to allow the payee of an instrument to assert rights as a holder in due course. The cases are like those referred to in the quotation from Professor Britton referred to above, or other cases in which conduct of some third party is the basis of the defense of the issuer of the instrument. The following are examples:

> *Case # 1.* Buyer pays for goods bought from Seller by giving to Seller a cashier's check bought from Bank. Bank has a defense to its obligation to pay the check because Buyer bought the check from Bank with a check known to be drawn on an account with insufficient funds to cover the check. If Bank issued the check to Buyer as payee and Buyer indorsed it over to Seller, it is clear that Seller can be a holder in due course taking free of the defense if Seller had no notice of the defense. Seller is a transferee of the check. There is no good reason why Seller's position should be any different if Bank drew the check to the order of Seller as payee. In that case, when Buyer took delivery of the check from Bank, Buyer became the owner of the check even though Buyer was not the holder. Buyer was a remitter. Section 3-103(a)(11). At that point nobody was the holder. When Buyer delivered the check to Seller, ownership of the check was transferred to Seller who also became the holder. This is a negotiation. Section 3-201. The rights of Seller should not be affected by the fact that in one case the negotiation to Seller was by a holder and in the

other case the negotiation was by a remitter. Moreover, it should be irrelevant whether Bank delivered the check to Buyer and Buyer delivered it to Seller or whether Bank delivered it directly to Seller. In either case Seller can be a holder in due course that takes free of Bank's defense.

Case # 2. X fraudulently induces Y to join X in a spurious venture to purchase a business. The purchase is to be financed by a bank loan for part of the price. Bank lends money to X and Y by deposit in a joint account of X and Y who sign a note payable to Bank for the amount of the loan. X then withdraws the money from the joint account and absconds. Bank acted in good faith and without notice of the fraud of X against Y. Bank is payee of the note executed by Y, but its right to enforce the note against Y should not be affected by the fact that Y was induced to execute the note by the fraud of X. Bank can be a holder in due course that takes free of the defense of Y. Case # 2 is similar to Case # 1. In each case the payee of the instrument has given value to the person committing the fraud in exchange for the obligation of the person against whom the fraud was committed. In each case the payee was not party to the fraud and had no notice of it.

Suppose in Case # 2 that the note does not meet the requirements of Section 3-104(a) and thus is not a negotiable instrument covered by Article 3. In that case, Bank cannot be a holder in due course but the result should be the same. Bank's rights are determined by general principles of contract law. Restatement Second, Contracts § 164(2) governs the case. If Y is induced to enter into a contract with Bank by a fraudulent misrepresentation by X, the contract is voidable by Y unless Bank "in good faith and without reason to know of the misrepresentation either gives value or relies materially on the transaction." Comment e to § 164(2) states:

> "This is the same principle that protects an innocent person who purchases goods or commercial paper in good faith, without notice and for value from one who obtained them from the original owner by a misrepresentation. See Uniform Commercial Code §§ 2-403(1), 3-305. In the cases that fall within [§ 164(2)], however, the innocent person deals directly with the recipient of the misrepresentation, which is made by one not a party to the contract."

The same result follows in Case # 2 if Y had been induced to sign the note as an accommodation party (Section 3-419). If Y signs as co-maker of a note for the benefit of X, Y is a surety with respect to the obligation of X to pay the note but is liable as maker of the note to pay Bank. Section 3-419(b). If Bank is a holder in due course, the fraud of X cannot be asserted against Bank under Section 3-305(b). But the result is the same without resort to holder-in-due-course doctrine. If the note is not a negotiable instrument governed by Article 3, general rules of suretyship apply. Restatement, Security § 119 states that the surety (Y) cannot assert a defense against the creditor (Bank) based on the fraud of the principal (X) if the creditor "without knowledge of the fraud *** extended credit to the principal on the security of the surety's promise ***." The underlying principle of § 119 is the same as that of § 164(2) of Restatement Second, Contracts.

Case # 3. Corporation draws a check payable to Bank. The check is given to an officer of Corporation who is instructed to deliver it to Bank in payment of a debt owed by Corporation to Bank. Instead, the officer, intending to defraud Corporation, delivers the check to Bank in payment of the officer's personal debt, or the check is delivered to Bank for deposit to the officer's personal account. If Bank obtains payment of the check, Bank has received funds of Corporation which have been used for the personal benefit of the officer. Corporation in this case will assert a claim to the proceeds of the check against Bank. If Bank was a holder in due course of the check it took the check free of Corporation's claim. Section 3-306. The issue in this case is whether Bank had notice of the claim when it took the check. If Bank knew that the officer was a fiduciary with respect to the check, the issue is governed by Section 3-307.

Case # 4. Employer, who owed money to X, signed a blank check and delivered it to Secretary with instructions to complete the check by typing in X's name and the amount owed to X. Secretary fraudulently completed the check by typing in the name of Y, a creditor to whom Secretary owed money. Secretary then delivered the check to Y in payment of Secretary's debt. Y obtained payment of the check. This case is similar to Case # 3. Since Secretary was authorized to complete the check, Employer is bound by Secretary's act in making the check payable to Y. The drawee bank properly paid the check. Y received funds of Employer which were used for the personal benefit of Secretary. Employer asserts a claim to these funds against Y. If Y is a holder in due course, Y takes free of the claim. Whether Y is a holder in due course depends upon whether Y had notice of Employer's claim.

5. Subsection (c) is based on former Section 3-302(3). Like former Section 3-302(3), subsection (c) is intended to state existing case law. It covers a few situations in which the purchaser takes an instrument under unusual circumstances. The purchaser is treated as a successor in interest to the prior holder and can acquire no better rights. But if the prior holder was a holder in due course, the purchaser obtains rights of a holder in due course.

Subsection (c) applies to a purchaser in an execution sale or sale in bankruptcy. It applies equally to an attaching creditor or any other person who acquires the instrument by legal process or to a representative, such as an executor, administrator, receiver or assignee for the benefit of creditors, who takes the instrument as part of an estate. Subsection (c) applies to bulk purchases lying outside of the ordinary course of business of the seller. For example, it applies to the purchase by one bank of a substantial part of the paper held by another bank which is threatened with insolvency and seeking to liquidate its assets. Subsection (c) would also apply when a new partnership takes over for value all of the assets of an old one after a new member has entered the firm, or to a reorganized or consolidated corporation taking over the assets of a predecessor.

In the absence of controlling state law to the contrary, subsection (c) applies to a sale by a state bank commissioner of the assets of an insolvent bank. However, subsection (c) may be preempted by federal law if the Federal Deposit Insurance Corporation takes over an insolvent bank. Under the governing federal law, the FDIC and similar financial institution insurers are given holder in due course status and that status is also acquired by their assignees under the shelter doctrine.

6. Subsections (d) and (e) clarify two matters not specifically addressed by former Article 3:

> *Case # 5.* Payee negotiates a $1,000 note to Holder who agrees to pay $900 for it. After paying $500, Holder learns that Payee defrauded Maker in the transaction giving rise to the note. Under subsection (d) Holder may assert rights as a holder in due course to the extent of $555.55 ($500? $900 = .555? $1,000 = $555.55). This formula rewards Holder with a ratable portion of the bargained for profit.

> *Case # 6.* Payee negotiates a note of Maker for $1,000 to Holder as security for payment of Payee's debt to Holder of $600. Maker has a defense which is good against Payee but of which Holder has no notice. Subsection (e) applies. Holder may assert rights as a holder in due course only to the extent of $600. Payee does not get the benefit of the holder-in-due-course status of Holder. With respect to $400 of the note, Maker may assert any rights that Maker has against Payee. A different result follows if the payee of a note negotiated it to a person who took it as a holder in due course and that person pledged the note as security for a debt. Because the defense cannot be asserted against the pledgor, the pledgee can assert rights as a holder in due course for the full amount of the note for the benefit of both the pledgor and the pledgee.

7. There is a large body of state statutory and case law restricting the use of the holder in due course doctrine in consumer transactions as well as some business transactions that raise similar issues. Subsection (g) subordinates Article 3 to that law and any other similar law that may evolve in the future. Section 3-106(d) also relates to statutory or administrative law intended to restrict use of the holder-in-due-course doctrine. See Comment 3 to Section 3-106.

8. The status of holder in due course resembles the status of protected holder under Article 29 of the Convention on International Bills of Exchange and International Promissory Notes. The requirements for being a protected holder under Article 29 generally track those of Section 3-302.

Additional References:

3-115 Comment 4
3-203 Comment 3
3-304 Comment 1
3-305 Comment 2, 3
3-307 Comment 2
3-601 Comment
4-210 Comment 1

Section 3-303. Value and Consideration

(a) An instrument is issued or transferred for value if:

(1) the instrument is issued or transferred for a promise of performance, to the extent the promise has been performed;

(2) the transferee acquires a security interest or other lien in the instrument other than a lien obtained by judicial proceeding;

(3) the instrument is issued or transferred as payment of, or as security for, an antecedent claim against any person, whether or not the claim is due;

(4) the instrument is issued or transferred in exchange for a negotiable instrument; or

(5) the instrument is issued or transferred in exchange for the incurring of an irrevocable obligation to a third party by the person taking the instrument.

(b) "Consideration" means any consideration sufficient to support a simple contract. The drawer or maker of an instrument has a defense if the instrument is issued without consideration. If an instrument is issued for a promise of performance, the issuer has a defense to the extent performance of the promise is due and the promise has not been performed. If an instrument is issued for value as stated in subsection (a), the instrument is also issued for consideration.

Definitional Cross References:

"Contract".	Section 1-201(b)(12)
"Drawer".	Section 3-103(a)(5)
"Instrument".	Section 3-104(b)
"Issue".	Section 3-105(a)
"Maker".	Section 3-103(a)(7)
"Negotiable Instrument".	Section 3-104(a)
"Person".	Section 1-201(b)(27)
"Security Interest".	Section 1-201(b)(35)
"Transfer".	Section 3-203(a)

Official Comment

1. Subsection (a) is a restatement of former Section 3-303 and subsection (b) replaces former Section 3-408. The distinction between value and consideration in Article 3 is a very fine one. Whether an instrument is taken for value is relevant to the issue of whether a holder is a holder in due course. If an instrument is not issued for consideration the issuer has a defense to the obligation to pay the instrument. Consideration is defined in subsection (b) as "any consideration sufficient to support a simple contract." The definition of value in Section 1-204, which doesn't apply to Article 3, includes "any consideration sufficient to support a simple contract." Thus, outside Article 3, anything that is consideration is also value. A different rule applies in Article 3. Subsection (b) of Section 3-303 states that if an instrument is issued for value it is also issued for consideration.

Case # 1. X owes Y $1,000. The debt is not represented by a note. Later X issues a note to Y for the debt. Under subsection (a)(3) X's note is issued for value. Under subsection (b) the note is also issued for consideration whether or not, under contract law, Y is deemed to have given consideration for the note.

Case # 2. X issues a check to Y in consideration of Y's promise to perform services in the future. Although the executory promise is consideration for issuance of the check it is value only to the extent the promise is performed. Subsection (a)(1).

Case # 3. X issues a note to Y in consideration of Y's promise to perform services. If at the due date of the note Y's performance is not yet due, Y may enforce the note because it was issued for consideration. But if at the due date of the note, Y's performance is due and has not been performed, X has a defense. Subsection (b).

2. Subsection (a), which defines value, has primary importance in cases in which the issue is whether the holder of an instrument is a holder in due course and particularly to cases in which the issuer of the instrument has a defense to the instrument. Suppose Buyer and Seller signed a contract on April 1 for the sale of goods to be delivered on May 1. Payment of 50% of the price of the goods was due upon signing of the contract. On April 1 Buyer delivered to Seller a check in the amount due under the contract. The check was drawn by X to Buyer as payee and was indorsed to Seller. When the check was presented for payment to the drawee on April 2, it was dishonored because X had stopped payment. At that time Seller had not taken any action to perform the contract with Buyer. If X has a defense on the check, the defense can be asserted against Seller who is not a holder in due course because Seller did not give value for the check. Subsection (a)(1). The policy basis for subsection (a)(1) is that the holder who gives an executory promise of performance will not suffer an out-of-pocket loss to the extent the executory promise is unperformed at the time the holder learns of dishonor of the instrument. When Seller took delivery of the check on April 1, Buyer's obligation to pay 50% of the price on that date was suspended, but when the check was dishonored on April 2 the obligation revived. Section 3-310(b). If payment for goods is due at or before delivery and the buyer fails to make the payment, the seller is excused from performing the promise to deliver the goods. Section 2-703. Thus, Seller is protected from an out-of-pocket loss even if the check is not enforceable. Holder-in-due-course status is not necessary to protect Seller.

3. Subsection (a)(2) equates value with the obtaining of a security interest or a nonjudicial lien in the instrument. The term "security interest" covers Article 9 cases in which an instrument is taken as collateral as well as bank collection cases in which a bank acquires a security interest under Section 4-210. The acquisition of a common-law or statutory banker's lien is also value under subsection (a)(2). An attaching creditor or other person who acquires a lien by judicial proceedings does not give value for the purposes of subsection (a)(2).

4. Subsection (a)(3) follows former Section 3-303(b) in providing that the holder takes for value if the instrument is taken in payment of or as security for an antecedent claim, even though there is no extension of time or other concession, and whether or not the claim is due. Subsection (a)(3) applies to any claim against any person; there is no requirement that the claim arise out of contract. In particular the provision is intended to apply to an instrument given in payment of or as security for the debt of a third person, even though no concession is made in return.

5. Subsection (a)(4) and (5) restate former Section 3-303(c). They state generally recognized exceptions to the rule that an executory promise is not value. A negotiable instrument is value because it carries the possibility of negotiation to a holder in due course, after which the party who gives it is obliged to pay. The same reasoning applies to any irrevocable commitment to a third person, such as a letter of credit issued when an instrument is taken.

6. The term "promise" in paragraph (a)(1) is used in the phrase "promise of performance" and for that reason does not have the specialized meaning given that term in Section 3-103(a)(12). See Section 1-201 ("Changes from Former Law"). No inference should be drawn from the decision to use the phrase "promise of performance," although the phrase does include the word "promise," which has the specialized definition set forth in Section 3-103. Indeed, that is true even though "undertaking" is used instead of "promise" in Section 3-104(a)(3). See Section 3-104 Comment 1 (explaining the use of the term "undertaking" in Section 3-104 to avoid use of the defined term "promise").

Additional References:

3-305 Comment 2, 3
3-418 Comment 2
4-210 Comment 1
4-211 Comment

Section 3-304. Overdue Instrument

(a) An instrument payable on demand becomes overdue at the earliest of the following times:

(1) on the day after the day demand for payment is duly made;

(2) if the instrument is a check, 90 days after its date; or

(3) if the instrument is not a check, when the instrument has been outstanding for a period of time after its date which is unreasonably long under the circumstances of the particular case in light of the nature of the instrument and usage of the trade.

(b) With respect to an instrument payable at a definite time the following rules apply:

(1) If the principal is payable in installments and a due date has not been accelerated, the instrument becomes overdue upon default under the instrument for nonpayment of an installment, and

the instrument remains overdue until the default is cured.

(2) If the principal is not payable in installments and the due date has not been accelerated, the instrument becomes overdue on the day after the due date.

(3) If a due date with respect to principal has been accelerated, the instrument becomes overdue on the day after the accelerated due date.

(c) Unless the due date of principal has been accelerated, an instrument does not become overdue if there is default in payment of interest but no default in payment of principal.

Definitional Cross References:

"Check".	Section 1-201(b)(4) [*sic*, should be 3-104(f)]
"Instrument".	Section 3-104(b)
"Payable at a Definite Time".	Section 3-108(a)
"Payment".	Section 3-602(a)

Official Comment

1. To be a holder in due course, one must take without notice that an instrument is overdue. Section 3-302(a)(2)(iii). Section 3-304 replaces subsection (3) of former Section 3-304. For the sake of clarity it treats demand and time instruments separately. Subsection (a) applies to demand instruments. A check becomes stale after 90 days.

Under former Section 3-304(3)(c), a holder that took a demand note had notice that it was overdue if it was taken "more than a reasonable length of time after its issue." In substitution for this test, subsection (a)(3) requires the trier of fact to look at both the circumstances of the particular case and the nature of the instrument and trade usage. Whether a demand note is stale may vary a great deal depending on the facts of the particular case.

2. Subsections (b) and (c) cover time instruments. They follow the distinction made under former Article 3 between defaults in payment of principal and interest. In subsection (b) installment instruments and single payment instruments are treated separately. If an installment is late, the instrument is overdue until the default is cured.

Section 3-305. Defenses and Claims in Recoupment; Claims in Consumer Transactions

(a) Except as otherwise provided in this section, the right to enforce the obligation of a party to pay an instrument is subject to the following:

(1) a defense of the obligor based on (i) infancy of the obligor to the extent it is a defense to a simple contract, (ii) duress, lack of legal capacity, or illegality of the transaction which, under other law, nullifies the obligation of the obligor, (iii) fraud that induced the obligor to sign the instrument with neither knowledge nor reasonable opportunity to learn of its character or its essential terms, or (iv) discharge of the obligor in insolvency proceedings;

(2) a defense of the obligor stated in another section of this Article or a defense of the obligor that would be available if the person entitled to enforce the instrument were enforcing a right to payment under a simple contract; and

(3) a claim in recoupment of the obligor against the original payee of the instrument if the claim arose from the transaction that gave rise to the instrument; but the claim of the obligor may be asserted against a transferee of the instrument only to reduce the amount owing on the instrument at the time the action is brought.

(b) The right of a holder in due course to enforce the obligation of a party to pay the instrument is subject to defenses of the obligor stated in subsection (a)(1), but is not subject to defenses of the obligor stated in subsection (a)(2) or claims in recoupment stated in subsection (a)(3) against a person other than the holder.

(c) Except as stated in subsection (d), in an action to enforce the obligation of a party to pay the instrument, the obligor may not assert against the person entitled to enforce the instrument a defense, claim in recoupment, or claim to the instrument (Section 3-306) of another person, but the other person's claim to the instrument may be asserted by the obligor if the other person is joined in the action and personally asserts the claim against the person entitled to enforce the instrument. An obligor is not obliged to pay the instrument if the person seeking enforcement of the instrument does not have rights of a holder in due course and the obligor proves that the instrument is a lost or stolen instrument.

(d) In an action to enforce the obligation of an accommodation party to pay an instrument, the accommodation party may assert against the person entitled to enforce the instrument any defense or claim in recoupment under subsection (a) that the accommodated party could assert against the person entitled to enforce the instrument, except the defenses of discharge in insolvency proceedings, infancy, and lack of legal capacity.

(e) In a consumer transaction, if law other than this Article requires that an instrument include a statement to the effect that the rights of a holder or transferee are subject to a claim or defense that the issuer could assert against the original payee, and the instrument does not include such a statement:

(1) the instrument has the same effect as if the instrument included such a statement;

(2) the issuer may assert against the holder or transferee all claims and defenses that would have

been available if the instrument included such a statement; and

(3) the extent to which claims may be asserted against the holder or transferee is determined as if the instrument included such a statement.

(f) This section is subject to law other than this Article that establishes a different rule for consumer transactions.

Legislative Note: *If a consumer protection law in this state addresses the same issue as subsection (f), it should be examined for consistency with subsection (f) and, if inconsistent, should be amended.*

Definitional Cross References:

"Accommodation Party".	Section 3-419(a)
"Action".	Section 1-201(b)(1)
"Contract".	Section 1-201(b)(12)
"Consumer Transaction".	Section 3-103(a)(3)
"Discharge".	Section 3-601(a)
"Holder".	Section 1-201(b)(21)
"Holder in Due Course".	Section 3-302
"Insolvency Proceeding".	Section 1-201(b)(22)
"Instrument".	Section 3-104(b)
"Party".	Section 3-103(a)(10)
"Payment".	Section 3-602(a)
"Person".	Section 1-201(b)(27)
"Person Entitled to Enforce".	Section 3-301
"Prove".	Section 3-103(a)(13)

Official Comment

1. Subsection (a) states the defenses to the obligation of a party to pay the instrument. Subsection (a)(1) states the "real defenses" that may be asserted against any person entitled to enforce the instrument.

Subsection (a)(1)(i) allows assertion of the defense of infancy against a holder in due course, even though the effect of the defense is to render the instrument voidable but not void. The policy is one of protection of the infant even at the expense of occasional loss to an innocent purchaser. No attempt is made to state when infancy is available as a defense or the conditions under which it may be asserted. In some jurisdictions it is held that an infant cannot rescind the transaction or set up the defense unless the holder is restored to the position held before the instrument was taken which, in the case of a holder in due course, is normally impossible. In other states an infant who has misrepresented age may be estopped to assert infancy. Such questions are left to other law, as an integral part of the policy of each state as to the protection of infants.

Subsection (a)(1)(ii) covers mental incompetence, guardianship, ultra vires acts or lack of corporate capacity to do business, or any other incapacity apart from infancy. Such incapacity is largely statutory. Its existence and effect is left to the law of each state. If under the state law the effect is to render the obligation of the instrument entirely null and void, the defense may be asserted against a holder in due course. If the effect is merely to render the obligation voidable at the election of the obligor, the defense is cut off.

Duress, which is also covered by subsection (a)(ii), is a matter of degree. An instrument signed at the point of a gun is void, even in the hands of a holder in due course. One signed under threat to prosecute the son of the maker for theft may be merely voidable, so that the defense is cut off. Illegality is most frequently a matter of gambling or usury, but may arise in other forms under a variety of statutes. The statutes differ in their provisions and the interpretations given them. They are primarily a matter of local concern and local policy. All such matters are therefore left to the local law. If under that law the effect of the duress or the illegality is to make the obligation entirely null and void, the defense may be asserted against a holder in due course. Otherwise it is cut off.

Subsection (a)(1)(iii) refers to "real" or "essential" fraud, sometimes called fraud in the essence or fraud in the factum, as effective against a holder in due course. The common illustration is that of the maker who is tricked into signing a note in the belief that it is merely a receipt or some other document. The theory of the defense is that the signature on the instrument is ineffective because the signer did not intend to sign such an instrument at all. Under this provision the defense extends to an instrument signed with knowledge that it is a negotiable instrument, but without knowledge of its essential terms. The test of the defense is that of excusable ignorance of the contents of the writing signed. The party must not only have been in ignorance, but must also have had no reasonable opportunity to obtain knowledge. In determining what is a reasonable opportunity all relevant factors are to be taken into account, including the intelligence, education, business experience, and ability to read or understand English of the signer. Also relevant is the nature of the representations that were made, whether the signer had good reason to rely on the representations or to have confidence in the person making them, the presence or absence of any third person who might read or explain the instrument to the signer, or any other possibility of obtaining independent information, and the apparent necessity, or lack of it, for acting without delay. Unless the misrepresentation meets this test, the defense is cut off by a holder in due course.

Subsection (a)(1)(iv) states specifically that the defense of discharge in insolvency proceedings is not cut off when the instrument is purchased by a holder in due course. An "insolvency proceeding" is defined in Section 1-201(b)(22) and it includes bankruptcy whether or not the debtor is insolvent. Subsection (2)(e) of former Section 3-305 is omitted. The substance of that provision is stated in Section 3-601(b).

2. Subsection (a)(2) states other defenses that, pursuant to subsection (b), are cut off by a holder in due course. These defenses comprise those specifically stated in Article 3 and those based on common law contract principles. Article 3 defenses are nonissuance of the instrument, conditional issuance, and issuance for a special purpose (Section 3-105(b));

failure to countersign a traveler's check (Section 3-106(c)); modification of the obligation by a separate agreement (Section 3-117); payment that violates a restrictive indorsement (Section 3-206(f)); instruments issued without consideration or for which promised performance has not been given (Section 3-303(b)), and breach of warranty when a draft is accepted (Section 3-417(b)). The most prevalent common law defenses are fraud, misrepresentation or mistake in the issuance of the instrument. In most cases the holder in due course will be an immediate or remote transferee of the payee of the instrument. In most cases the holder-in-due-course doctrine is irrelevant if defenses are being asserted against the payee of the instrument, but in a small number of cases the payee of the instrument may be a holder in due course. Those cases are discussed in Comment 4 to Section 3-302.

Assume Buyer issues a note to Seller in payment of the price of goods that Seller fraudulently promises to deliver but which are never delivered. Seller negotiates the note to Holder who has no notice of the fraud. If Holder is a holder in due course, Holder is not subject to Buyer's defense of fraud. But in some cases an original party to the instrument is a holder in due course. For example, Buyer fraudulently induces Bank to issue a cashier's check to the order of Seller. The check is delivered by Bank to Seller, who has no notice of the fraud. Seller can be a holder in due course and can take the check free of Bank's defense of fraud. This case is discussed as Case # 1 in Comment 4 to Section 3-302. Former Section 3-305 stated that a holder in due course takes free of defenses of "any party to the instrument with whom the holder has not dealt." The meaning of this language was not at all clear and if read literally could have produced the wrong result. In the hypothetical case, it could be argued that Seller "dealt" with Bank because Bank delivered the check to Seller. But it is clear that Seller should take free of Bank's defense against Buyer regardless of whether Seller took delivery of the check from Buyer or from Bank. The quoted language is not included in Section 3-305. It is not necessary. If Buyer issues an instrument to Seller and Buyer has a defense against Seller, that defense can obviously be asserted. Buyer and Seller are the only people involved. The holder-in-due-course doctrine has no relevance. The doctrine applies only to cases in which more than two parties are involved. Its essence is that the holder in due course does not have to suffer the consequences of a defense of the obligor on the instrument that arose from an occurrence with a third party.

3. Subsection (a)(3) is concerned with claims in recoupment which can be illustrated by the following example. Buyer issues a note to the order of Seller in exchange for a promise of Seller to deliver specified equipment. If Seller fails to deliver the equipment or delivers equipment that is rightfully rejected, Buyer has a defense to the note because the performance that was the consideration for the note was not rendered. Section 3-303(b). This defense is included in Section 3-305(a)(2). That defense can always be asserted against Seller. This result is the same as that reached under former Section 3-408.

But suppose Seller delivered the promised equipment and it was accepted by Buyer. The equipment, however, was defective. Buyer retained the equipment and incurred expenses with respect to its repair. In this case, Buyer does not have a defense under Section 3-303(b). Seller delivered the equipment and the equipment was accepted. Under Article 2, Buyer is obliged to pay the price of the equipment which is represented by the note. But Buyer may have a claim against Seller for breach of warranty. If Buyer has a warranty claim, the claim may be asserted against Seller as a counterclaim or as a claim in recoupment to reduce the amount owing on the note. It is not relevant whether Seller is or is not a holder in due course of the note or whether Seller knew or had notice that Buyer had the warranty claim. It is obvious that holder-in-due-course doctrine cannot be used to allow Seller to cut off a warranty claim that Buyer has against Seller. Subsection (b) specifically covers this point by stating that a holder in due course is not subject to a "claim in recoupment *** against a person other than the holder."

Suppose Seller negotiates the note to Holder. If Holder had notice of Buyer's warranty claim at the time the note was negotiated to Holder, Holder is not a holder in due course (Section 3-302(a)(2)(iv)) and Buyer may assert the claim against Holder (Section 3-305(a)(3)) but only as a claim in recoupment, i.e. to reduce the amount owed on the note. If the warranty claim is $1,000 and the unpaid note is $10,000, Buyer owes $9,000 to Holder. If the warranty claim is more than the unpaid amount of the note, Buyer owes nothing to Holder, but Buyer cannot recover the unpaid amount of the warranty claim from Holder. If Buyer had already partially paid the note, Buyer is not entitled to recover the amounts paid. The claim can be used only as an offset to amounts owing on the note. If Holder had no notice of Buyer's claim and otherwise qualifies as a holder in due course, Buyer may not assert the claim against Holder. Section 3-305(b).

The result under Section 3-305 is consistent with the result reached under former Article 3, but the rules for reaching the result are stated differently. Under former Article 3 Buyer could assert rights against Holder only if Holder was not a holder in due course, and Holder's status depended upon whether Holder had notice of a defense by Buyer. Courts have held that Holder had that notice if Holder had notice of Buyer's warranty claim. The rationale under former Article 3 was "failure of consideration." This rationale does not distinguish between cases in which the seller fails to perform and those in which the buyer accepts the performance of seller but makes a claim against the seller because the performance is faulty. The term "failure of consideration" is subject to varying interpretations and is not used in Article 3. The use of the term "claim in recoupment" in Section 3-305(a)(3) is a more precise statement of the nature of Buyer's right against Holder. The use of the term does not change the law because the treatment of a defense under subsection (a)(2) and a claim in recoupment under subsection (a)(3) is essentially the same.

Under former Article 3, case law was divided on the issue of the extent to which an obligor on a note could assert against a transferee who is not a holder in due course a debt or other claim that the obligor had against the original payee of the instrument. Some courts limited claims to those that arose in the transaction that gave rise to the note. This is the approach taken in Section 3-305(a)(3). Other courts allowed the obligor on the note to use any debt or other claim, no matter how unrelated to the note, to offset the amount owed on the note. Under current judicial authority and non-UCC statutory law, there will be many cases in which a transferee of a note arising from a sale transaction will not qualify as a holder in due course. For example, applicable law may require the use of a note to which there cannot be a holder in due course. See Section 3-106(d) and Comment 3 to Section 3-106. It is reasonable to provide that the buyer should not be denied the right to assert claims arising out of the sale transaction. Subsection (a)(3) is based on the belief that it is not reasonable to require the transferee to bear the risk that wholly unrelated claims may also be asserted. The determination of whether a claim arose from the transaction that gave rise to the instrument is determined by law other than this Article and thus may vary as local law varies.

4. Subsection (c) concerns claims and defenses of a person other than the obligor on the instrument. It applies principally to cases in which an obligation is paid with the instrument of a third person. For example, Buyer buys goods from Seller and negotiates to Seller a cashier's check issued by Bank in payment of the price. Shortly after delivering the check to Seller, Buyer learns that Seller had defrauded Buyer in the sale transaction. Seller may enforce the check against Bank even though Seller is not a holder in due course. Bank has no defense to its obligation to pay the check and it may not assert defenses, claims in recoupment, or claims to the instrument of Buyer, except to the extent permitted by the "but" clause of the first sentence of subsection (c). Buyer may have a claim to the instrument under Section 3-306 based on a right to rescind the negotiation to Seller because of Seller's fraud. Section 3-202(b) and Comment 2 to Section 3-201. Bank cannot assert that claim unless Buyer is joined in the action in which Seller is trying to enforce payment of the check. In that case Bank may pay the amount of the check into court and the court will decide whether that amount belongs to Buyer or Seller. The last sentence of subsection (c) allows the issuer of an instrument such as a cashier's check to refuse payment in the rare case in which the issuer can prove that the instrument is a lost or stolen instrument and the person seeking enforcement does not have rights of a holder in due course.

5. Subsection (d) applies to instruments signed for accommodation (Section 3-419) and this subsection equates the obligation of the accommodation party to that of the accommodated party. The accommodation party can assert whatever defense or claim the accommodated party had against the person enforcing the instrument. The only exceptions are discharge in bankruptcy, infancy and lack of capacity. The same rule does not apply to an indorsement by a holder of the instrument in negotiating the instrument. The indorser, as transferor, makes a warranty to the indorsee, as transferee, that no defense or claim in recoupment is good against the indorser. Section 3-416(a)(4). Thus, if the indorsee sues the indorser because of dishonor of the instrument, the indorser may not assert the defense or claim in recoupment of the maker or drawer against the indorsee.

Section 3-305(d) must be read in conjunction with Section 3-605, which provides rules (usually referred to as suretyship defenses) for determining when the obligation of an accommodation party is discharged, in whole or in part, because of some act or omission of a person entitled to enforce the instrument. To the extent a rule stated in Section 3-605 is inconsistent with Section 3-305(d), the Section 3-605 rule governs. For example, Section 3-605(a) provides rules for determining when and to what extent a discharge of the accommodated party under Section 3-604 will discharge the accommodation party. As explained in Comment 2 to Section 3-605, discharge of the accommodated party is normally part of a settlement under which the holder of a note accepts partial payment from an accommodated party who is financially unable to pay the entire amount of the note. If the holder then brings an action against the accommodation party to recover the remaining unpaid amount of the note, the accommodation party cannot use Section 3-305(d) to nullify Section 3-605(a) by asserting the discharge of the accommodated party as a defense. On the other hand, suppose the accommodated party is a buyer of goods who issued the note to the seller who took the note for the buyer's obligation to pay for the goods. Suppose the buyer has a claim for breach of warranty with respect to the goods against the seller and the warranty claim may be asserted against the holder of the note. The warranty claim is a claim in recoupment. If the holder and the accommodated party reach a settlement under which the holder accepts payment less than the amount of the note in full satisfaction of the note and the warranty claim, the accommodation party could defend an action on the note by the holder by asserting the accord and satisfaction under Section 3-305(d). There is no conflict with Section 3-605(a) because that provision is not intended to apply to settlement of disputed claims.

6. Subsection (e) is added to clarify the treatment of an instrument that omits the notice currently required by the Federal Trade Commission Rule related to certain consumer credit sales and consumer purchase money loans (16 C.F.R. Part 433). This subsection adopts the view that the instrument should be treated as if the language required by the FTC Rule were present. It is based on the language describing that rule in Section 3-106(d) and the analogous provision in Section 9-404(d).

7. Subsection (f) is modeled on Sections 9-403(e) and 9-404(c). It ensures that Section 3-305 is interpreted to accommodate relevant consumer-protection laws. The absence of such a provision from other sections in Article 3 should not justify any inference about the meaning of those sections.

8. Articles 28 and 30 of the Convention on International Bills of Exchange and International Promissory Notes includes a similar dichotomy, with a narrower group of defenses available against a protected holder under Articles 28(1) and 30 than are available under Article 28(2) against a holder that is not a protected holder.

Additional References:
3-106 Comment 2
3-202 Comment 2
3-203 Comment 4
3-202 Comment 2, 3, 4
3-306 Comment
3-411 Comment 3
3-418 Comment 2
3-419 Comment 6
4-403 Comment 7

Editors' Note: 2002 amendments added in subsection (e) a provision (similar to Section 9-404(d)) indicating that a note for which the Federal Trade Commission requires a notice to be included will be treated as if the notice had been included.

Section 3-306. Claims to an Instrument.

A person taking an instrument, other than a person having rights of a holder in due course, is subject to a claim of a property or possessory right in the instrument or its proceeds, including a claim to rescind a negotiation and to recover the instrument or its proceeds. A person having rights of a holder in due course takes free of the claim to the instrument.

Definitional Cross References:

"Holder in Due Course".	Section 3-302
"Instrument".	Section 3-104(b)
"Negotiation".	Section 3-201(a)
"Person".	Section 1-201(b)(27)

Official Comment

This section expands on the reference to "claims to" the instrument mentioned in former Sections 3-305 and 3-306. Claims covered by the section include not only claims to ownership but also any other claim of a property or possessory right. It includes the claim to a lien or the claim of a person in rightful possession of an instrument who was wrongfully deprived of possession. Also included is a claim based on Section 3-202(b) for rescission of a negotiation of the instrument by the claimant. Claims to an instrument under Section 3-306 are different from claims in recoupment referred to in Section 3-305(a)(3). The rule of this section is similar to the rule of Article 30(2) of the Convention on International Bills of Exchange and International Promissory Notes.

Additional References:
3-302 Comment 4
3-305 Comment 4
3-307 Comment 2
3-306 Comment

Section 3-307. Notice of Breach of Fiduciary Duty.

(a) In this section:

(1) "Fiduciary" means an agent, trustee, partner, corporate officer or director, or other representative owing a fiduciary duty with respect to an instrument.

(2) "Represented person" means the principal, beneficiary, partnership, corporation, or other person to whom the duty stated in paragraph (1) is owed.

(b) If (i) an instrument is taken from a fiduciary for payment or collection or for value, (ii) the taker has knowledge of the fiduciary status of the fiduciary, and (iii) the represented person makes a claim to the instrument or its proceeds on the basis that the transaction of the fiduciary is a breach of fiduciary duty, the following rules apply:

(1) Notice of breach of fiduciary duty by the fiduciary is notice of the claim of the represented person.

(2) In the case of an instrument payable to the represented person or the fiduciary as such, the taker has notice of the breach of fiduciary duty if the instrument is (i) taken in payment of or as security for a debt known by the taker to be the personal debt of the fiduciary, (ii) taken in a transaction known by the taker to be for the personal benefit of the fiduciary, or (iii) deposited to an account other than an account of the fiduciary, as such, or an account of the represented person.

(3) If an instrument is issued by the represented person or the fiduciary as such, and made payable to the fiduciary personally, the taker does not have notice of the breach of fiduciary duty unless the taker knows of the breach of fiduciary duty.

(4) If an instrument is issued by the represented person or the fiduciary as such, to the taker as payee, the taker has notice of the breach of fiduciary duty if the instrument is (i) taken in payment of or as security for a debt known by the taker to be the personal debt of the fiduciary, (ii) taken in a transaction known by the taker to be for the personal benefit of the fiduciary, or (iii) deposited to an account other than an account of the fiduciary, as such, or an account of the represented person.

Definitional Cross References:

"Account".	Section 4-104(a)(1)
"Instrument".	Section 3-104(b)
"Issue".	Section 3-105(a)
"Knows".	Section 1-202(a)
"Knowledge".	Section 1-202(b)
"Notice".	Section 1-202(a)
"Payment".	Section 3-602(a)
"Person".	Section 1-201(b)(27)
"Representative".	Section 1-201(b)(33)
"Value, Taken for".	Section 3-303(a)

Official Comment

1. This section states rules for determining when a person who has taken an instrument from a fiduciary has notice of a breach of fiduciary duty that occurs as a result of the transaction with the fiduciary. Former Section 3-304(2) and (4)(e) related to this issue, but those provisions were unclear in their meaning. Section 3-307 is intended to clarify the law by stating rules that comprehensively cover the issue of when the taker of an instrument has notice of breach of a fiduciary duty and thus notice of a claim to the instrument or its proceeds.

2. Subsection (a) defines the terms "fiduciary" and "represented person" and the introductory paragraph of subsection (b) describes the transaction to which the section applies. The basic scenario is one in which the fiduciary in effect embezzles money of the represented person by applying the proceeds of an instrument that belongs to the represented person to the personal use of the fiduciary. The person dealing with the fiduciary may be a depositary bank that takes the instrument for collection or a bank or other person that pays value for the instrument. The section also covers a transaction in which an instrument is presented for payment to a payor bank that pays the instrument by giving value to the fiduciary. Subsections (b)(2), (3), and (4) state rules for determining when the person dealing with the fiduciary has notice of breach of fiduciary duty. Subsection (b)(1) states that notice of breach of fiduciary duty is notice of the represented person's claim to the instrument or its proceeds.

Under Section 3-306, a person taking an instrument is subject to a claim to the instrument or its proceeds, unless the taker has rights of a holder in due course. Under Section 3-302(a)(2)(v), the taker cannot be a holder in due course if the instrument was taken with notice of a claim under Section 3-306. Section 3-307 applies to cases in which a represented person is asserting a claim because a breach of fiduciary duty resulted in a misapplication of the proceeds of an instrument. The claim of the represented person is a claim described in Section 3-306. Section 3-307 states rules for determining when a person taking an instrument has notice of the claim which will prevent assertion of rights as a holder in due course. It also states rules for determining when a payor bank pays an instrument with notice of breach of fiduciary duty.

Section 3-307(b) applies only if the person dealing with the fiduciary "has knowledge of the fiduciary status of the fiduciary." Notice which does not amount to knowledge is not enough to cause Section 3-307 to apply. "Knowledge" is defined in Section 1-202(b). In most cases, the "taker" referred to in Section 3-307 will be a bank or other organization. Knowledge of an organization is determined by the rules stated in Section 1-202(f). In many cases, the individual who receives and processes an instrument on behalf of the organization that is the taker of the instrument "for payment or collection or for value" is a clerk who has no knowledge of any fiduciary status of the person from whom the instrument is received. In such cases, Section 3-307 doesn't apply because, under Section 1-202(f), knowledge of the organization is determined by the knowledge of the "individual conducting that transaction," i.e. the clerk who receives and processes the instrument. Furthermore, paragraphs (2) and (4) each require that the person acting for the organization have knowledge of facts that indicate a breach of fiduciary duty. In the case of an instrument taken for deposit to an account, the knowledge is found in the fact that the deposit is made to an account other than that of the represented person or a fiduciary account for benefit of that person. In other cases the person acting for the organization must know that the instrument is taken in payment or as security for a personal debt of the fiduciary or for the personal benefit of the fiduciary. For example, if the instrument is being used to buy goods or services, the person acting for the organization must know that the goods or services are for the personal benefit of the fiduciary. The requirement that the taker have knowledge rather than notice is meant to limit Section 3-307 to relatively uncommon cases in which the person who deals with the fiduciary knows all the relevant facts: the fiduciary status and that the proceeds of the instrument are being used for the personal debt or benefit of the fiduciary or are being paid to an account that is not an account of the represented person or of the fiduciary, as such. Mere notice of these facts is not enough to put the taker on notice of the breach of fiduciary duty and does not give rise to any duty of investigation by the taker.

3. Subsection (b)(2) applies to instruments payable to the represented person or the fiduciary as such. For example, a check payable to Corporation is indorsed in the name of Corporation by Doe as its President. Doe gives the check to Bank as partial repayment of a personal loan that Bank had made to Doe. The check was indorsed either in blank or to Bank. Bank collects the check and applies the proceeds to reduce the amount owed on Doe's loan. If the person acting for Bank in the transaction knows that Doe is a fiduciary and that the check is being used to pay a personal obligation of Doe, subsection (b)(2) applies. If Corporation has a claim to the proceeds of the check because the use of the check by Doe was a breach of fiduciary duty, Bank has notice of the claim and did not take the check as a holder in due course. The same result follows if Doe had indorsed the check to himself before giving it to Bank. Subsection (b)(2) follows Uniform Fiduciaries Act § 4 in providing that if the instrument is payable to the fiduciary, as such, or to the represented person, the taker has notice of a claim if the instrument is negotiated for the fiduciary's personal debt. If fiduciary funds are deposited to a personal account of the fiduciary or to an account that is not an account of the represented person or of the fiduciary, as such, there is a split of authority concerning whether the bank is on notice of a breach of fiduciary duty. Subsection (b)(2)(iii) states that the bank is given notice of breach of fiduciary duty because of the deposit. The Uniform Fiduciaries Act § 9 states that the bank is not on notice unless it has knowledge of facts that makes its receipt of the deposit an act of bad faith.

The rationale of subsection (b)(2) is that it is not normal for an instrument payable to the represented person or the fiduciary, as such, to be used for the personal benefit of the fiduciary. It is likely that such use reflects an unlawful use of the proceeds of the instrument. If the fiduciary is entitled to compensation from the represented person for services rendered or for expenses incurred by the fiduciary the normal mode of payment is by a check drawn on the fiduciary account to the order of the fiduciary.

4. Subsection (b)(3) is based on Uniform Fiduciaries Act § 6 and applies when the instrument is drawn by the represented person or the fiduciary as such to the fiduciary personally. The term "personally" is used as it is used in the Uniform Fiduciaries Act to mean that the instrument is payable to the payee as an individual and not as a fiduciary. For example, Doe as President of Corporation writes a check on Corporation's account to the order of Doe personally. The check is then indorsed over to Bank as in Comment 3. In this case there is no notice of breach of fiduciary duty because there is nothing unusual about the transaction. Corporation may have owed Doe money for salary, reimbursement for expenses incurred for the benefit of Corporation, or for any other reason. If Doe is authorized to write checks on behalf of Corporation to pay debts of Corporation, the check is a normal way of paying a debt owed to Doe. Bank may assume that Doe may use the instrument for his personal benefit.

5. Subsection (b)(4) can be illustrated by a hypothetical case. Corporation draws a check payable to an organization. X, an officer or employee of Corporation, delivers the check to a person acting for the organization. The person signing the check on behalf of Corporation is X or another person. If the person acting for the organization in the transaction knows that X is a fiduciary, the organization is on notice of a claim by Corporation if it takes the instrument under the same circumstances stated in subsection (b)(2). If the organization is a bank and the check is taken in repayment of a personal loan of the bank to X, the case is like the case discussed in Comment 3. It is unusual for Corporation, the represented person, to pay a personal debt of Doe by issuing a check to the bank. It is more likely that the use of the check by Doe reflects an unlawful use of the proceeds of the check. The same analysis applies if the check is made payable to an organization in payment of goods or services. If the person acting for the organization knew of the fiduciary status of X and that the goods or services were for X's personal benefit, the organization is on notice of a claim by Corporation to the proceeds of the check. See the discussion in the last paragraph of Comment 2.

Additional References:

3-206 Comment 4

3-405 Comment 3

Section 3-308. Proof of Signatures and Status As Holder in Due Course

(a) In an action with respect to an instrument, the authenticity of, and authority to make, each signature on the instrument is admitted unless specifically denied in the pleadings. If the validity of a signature is denied in the pleadings, the burden of establishing validity is on the person claiming validity, but the signature is presumed to be authentic and authorized unless the action is to enforce the liability of the purported signer and the signer is dead or incompetent at the time of trial of the issue of validity of the signature. If an action to enforce the instrument is brought against a person as the undisclosed principal of a person who signed the instrument as a party to the instrument, the plaintiff has the burden of establishing that the defendant is liable on the instrument as a represented person under Section 3-402(a).

(b) If the validity of signatures is admitted or proved and there is compliance with subsection (a), a plaintiff producing the instrument is entitled to payment if the plaintiff proves entitlement to enforce the instrument under Section 3-301, unless the defendant proves a defense or claim in recoupment. If a defense or claim in recoupment is proved, the right to payment of the plaintiff is subject to the defense or claim, except to the extent the plaintiff proves that the plaintiff has rights of a holder in due course which are not subject to the defense or claim.

Definitional Cross References:

"Action".	Section 1-201(b)(1)
"Burden of Establishing".	Section 1-201(b)(8)
"Defendant".	Section 1-201(b)(15) [*sic*, should be 1-201(b)(14)]
"Entitled to Enforce".	Section 3-301
"Holder in Due Course".	Section 3-302
"Instrument".	Section 3-104(b)
"Party".	Section 3-103(a)(10)
"Payment".	Section 3-602(a)
"Person".	Section 1-201(b)(27)
"Prove".	Section 3-103(a)(13)
"Signed".	Section 1-201(b)(37)

Official Comment

1. Section 3-308 is a modification of former Section 3-307. The first two sentences of subsection (a) are a restatement of former Section 3-307(1). The purpose of the requirement of a specific denial in the pleadings is to give the plaintiff notice of the defendant's claim of forgery or lack of authority as to the particular signature, and to afford the plaintiff an opportunity to investigate and obtain evidence. If local rules of pleading permit, the denial may be on information and belief, or it may be a denial of knowledge or information sufficient to form a belief. It need not be under oath unless the local statutes or rules require verification. In the absence of such specific denial the signature stands admitted, and is not in issue. Nothing in this section is intended, however, to prevent amendment of the pleading in a proper case.

The question of the burden of establishing the signature arises only when it has been put in issue by specific denial. "Burden of establishing" is defined in Section 1-201(b)(8). The burden is on the party claiming under the signature, but the signature is presumed to be authentic and authorized except as stated in the second sentence of subsection (a). Pursuant to Section 1-206, until some evidence is introduced which would support a finding that the signature is forged or unauthorized, the plaintiff is not required to prove that it is valid. The presumption rests upon the fact that in ordinary experience forged or unauthorized signatures are very uncommon, and normally any evidence is within the control of, or more accessible to, the defendant. The defendant is therefore required to make some sufficient showing of the grounds for the denial before the plaintiff is required to introduce evidence. The defendant's evidence need not be sufficient to require a directed verdict, but it must be enough to support the denial by permitting a finding in the defendant's favor. Until introduction of such evidence the presumption requires a finding for the plaintiff. Once such evidence is introduced the burden of establishing the signature by a preponderance of the total evidence is on the plaintiff. The presumption does not arise if the action is to enforce the obligation of a purported signer who has died or become incompetent before the evidence is required, and so is disabled from obtaining or introducing it. "Action" is defined in Section 1-201(b)(1) and includes a claim asserted against the estate of a deceased or an incompetent.

The last sentence of subsection (a) is a new provision that is necessary to take into account Section 3-402(a) that allows an undisclosed principal to be liable on an instrument signed by an authorized representative. In that case the person enforcing the instrument must prove that the undisclosed principal is liable.

2. Subsection (b) restates former Section 3-307(2) and (3). Once signatures are proved or admitted a holder, by mere production of the instrument, proves "entitlement to enforce the instrument" because under Section 3-301 a holder is a person entitled to enforce the instrument. Any other person in possession of an instrument may recover only if that person has the rights of a holder. Section 3-301. That person must prove a transfer giving that person such rights under Section 3-203(b) or that such rights were obtained by subrogation or succession.

If a plaintiff producing the instrument proves entitlement to enforce the instrument, either as a holder or a person with rights of a holder, the plaintiff is entitled to recovery unless the defendant proves a defense or claim in recoupment. Until proof of a defense or claim in recoupment is made, the issue as to whether the plaintiff has rights of a holder in due course does not arise. In the absence of a defense or claim in recoupment, any person entitled to enforce the instrument is entitled to recover. If a defense or claim in recoupment is proved, the plaintiff may seek to cut off the defense or claim in recoupment by proving that the plaintiff is a holder in due course or that the plaintiff has rights of a holder in due course under Section 3-203(b) or by subrogation or succession. All elements of Section 3-302(a) must be proved.

Nothing in this section is intended to say that the plaintiff must necessarily prove rights as a holder in due course. The plaintiff may elect to introduce no further evidence, in which case a verdict may be directed for the plaintiff or the defendant, or the issue of the defense or claim in recoupment may be left to the trier of fact, according to the weight and sufficiency of the defendant's evidence. The plaintiff may elect to rebut the defense or claim in recoupment by proof to the contrary, in which case a verdict may be directed for either party or the issue may be for the trier of fact. Subsection (b) means only that if the plaintiff claims the rights of a holder in due course against the defense or claim in recoupment, the plaintiff has the burden of proof on that issue.

Additional References: 3-203 Comment 2, 4

Section 3-309. Enforcement of Lost, Destroyed, or Stolen Instrument

(a) A person not in possession of an instrument is entitled to enforce the instrument if:

(1) the person seeking to enforce the instrument:

(A) was entitled to enforce the instrument when loss of possession occurred; or

(B) has directly or indirectly acquired ownership of the instrument from a person who was entitled to enforce the instrument when loss of possession occurred;

(2) the loss of possession was not the result of a transfer by the person or a lawful seizure; and

(3) the person cannot reasonably obtain possession of the instrument because the instrument was destroyed, its whereabouts cannot be determined, or it is in the wrongful possession of an unknown person or a person that cannot be found or is not amenable to service of process.

(b) A person seeking enforcement of an instrument under subsection (a) must prove the terms of the instrument and the person's right to enforce the instrument. If that proof is made, Section 3-308 applies to the case as if the person seeking enforcement had produced the instrument. The court may not enter judgment in favor of the person seeking enforcement unless it finds that the person required to pay the instrument is adequately protected against loss that might occur by reason of a claim by another person to enforce the instrument. Adequate protection may be provided by any reasonable means.

Definitional Cross References:

"Entitled to Enforce".	Section 3-301
"Instrument".	Section 3-104(b)
"Person".	Section 1-201(b)(27)
"Prove".	Section 3-103(a)(13)
"Transfer".	Section 3-203(a)

Official Comment

1. Section 3-309 is a modification of former Section 3-804. The rights stated are those of "a person entitled to enforce the instrument" at the time of loss rather than those of an "owner" as in former Section 3-804. Under subsection (b), judgment to enforce the instrument cannot be given unless the court finds that the defendant will be adequately protected against a claim to the instrument by a holder that may appear at some later time. The court is given discretion in determining how adequate protection is to be assured. Former Section 3-804 allowed the court to "require security indemnifying the defendant against loss." Under Section 3-309 adequate protection is a flexible concept. For example, there is substantial risk that a holder in due course may make a demand for payment if the instrument was payable to bearer when it was lost or stolen. On the other hand if the instrument was payable to the person who lost the instrument and that person did not indorse the instrument, no other person could be a holder of the instrument. In some cases there is risk of loss only if there is doubt about whether the facts alleged by the person who lost the instrument are true. Thus, the type of adequate protection that is reasonable in the circumstances may depend on the degree of certainty about the facts in the case.

2. Subsection (a) is intended to reject the result in *Dennis Joslin Co. v. Robinson Broadcasting Corp.*, 977 F. Supp. 491 (D.D.C. 1997). A transferee of a lost instrument need prove only that its transferor was entitled to enforce, not that the transferee was in possession at the time the instrument was lost. The protections of subsection (a) should also be available when instruments are lost during transit, because whatever the precise status of ownership at the point of loss, either the sender or the receiver ordinarily would have been entitled to enforce the instrument during the course of transit. The amendments to subsection (a) are not intended to alter in any way the rules that apply to the preservation of checks in connection with truncation or any other expedited method of check collection or processing.

3. A security interest may attach to the right of a person not in possession of an instrument to enforce the instrument. Although the secured party may not be the owner of the instrument, the secured party may nevertheless be entitled to exercise its debtor's right to enforce the instrument by resorting to its collection rights under the circumstances described in Section 9-607. This section does not address whether the person required to pay the instrument owes any duty to a secured party that is not itself the owner of the instrument.

4. The destruction of a check in connection with a truncation process in which information is extracted from the check and an image of the check is made, and then such information and image are transmitted for payment does not, by itself, prevent application of this section. See Section 3-604, Comment 2.

> **Example:** The payee of a check creates an image of the check, destroys the check, and transmits the image and information derived from the check for payment. Due to an error in transmission, the depositary bank never receives the transmission. The payee may be able to enforce the check if the payee can prove the terms of the check and otherwise satisfy the requirements of this section. The result would be different if there were no error in the transmission and the payor discharged its obligation on the check.

Additional References: 3-310 Comment 4

Editors' Note: Section 3-309 was amended in 2002 to make it clear that a party seeking to enforce a lost instrument need not have been in possession of the instrument at the time that it was lost. At least one case previously had held that the receiver of a failed bank could not enforce an instrument transferred to it in the portfolio of a failed bank if the instrument was lost before the transfer. The amendment rejects that result.

Section 3-310. Effect of Instrument on Obligation for Which Taken

(a) Unless otherwise agreed, if a certified check, cashier's check, or teller's check is taken for an obligation, the obligation is discharged to the same extent discharge would result if an amount of money equal to the amount of the instrument were taken in payment of the obligation. Discharge of the obligation does not affect any liability that the obligor may have as an indorser of the instrument.

(b) Unless otherwise agreed and except as provided in subsection (a), if a note or an uncertified check is taken for an obligation, the obligation is suspended to the same extent the obligation would be discharged if an amount of money equal to the amount of the instrument were taken, and the following rules apply:

(1) In the case of an uncertified check, suspension of the obligation continues until dishonor of the check or until it is paid or certified. Payment or certification of the check results in discharge of the obligation to the extent of the amount of the check.

(2) In the case of a note, suspension of the obligation continues until dishonor of the note or until it is paid. Payment of the note results in discharge of the obligation to the extent of the payment.

(3) Except as provided in paragraph (4), if the check or note is dishonored and the obligee of the obligation for which the instrument was taken is the person entitled to enforce the instrument, the obligee may enforce either the instrument or the obligation. In the case of an instrument of a third person which is negotiated to the obligee by the obligor, discharge of the obligor on the instrument also discharges the obligation.

(4) If the person entitled to enforce the instrument taken for an obligation is a person other than the obligee, the obligee may not enforce the obligation to the extent the obligation is suspended. If the obligee is the person entitled to enforce the instrument but no longer has possession of it because it was lost, stolen, or destroyed, the obligation may not be enforced to the extent of the amount payable on the instrument, and to that extent the obligee's

rights against the obligor are limited to enforcement of the instrument.

(c) If an instrument other than one described in subsection (a) or (b) is taken for an obligation, the effect is (i) that stated in subsection (a) if the instrument is one on which a bank is liable as maker or acceptor, or (ii) that stated in subsection (b) in any other case.

Definitional Cross References:

"Acceptor".	Section 3-103(a)(1)
"Bank".	Section 1-201(b)(4)
"Cashier's Check".	Section 3-104(g)
"Certified Check".	Section 3-409(d)
"Check".	Section 3-104(f)
"Discharge".	Section 3-601(a)
"Dishonor".	Section 3-502
"Indorser".	Section 3-204(b)
"Instrument".	Section 3-104(b)
"Maker".	Section 3-103(a)(7)
"Money".	Section 1-201(b)(24)
"Note".	Section 3-104(e)
"Payment".	Section 3-602(a)
"Person".	Section 1-201(b)(27)
"Person Entitled to Enforce".	Section 3-301
"Teller's Check".	Section 3-104(h)

Official Comment

1. Section 3-310 is a modification of former Section 3-802. As a practical matter, application of former Section 3-802 was limited to cases in which a check or a note was given for an obligation. Subsections (a) and (b) of Section 3-310 are therefore stated in terms of checks and notes in the interests of clarity. Subsection (c) covers the rare cases in which some other instrument is given to pay an obligation.

2. Subsection (a) deals with the case in which a certified check, cashier's check or teller's check is given in payment of an obligation. In that case the obligation is discharged unless there is an agreement to the contrary. Subsection (a) drops the exception in former Section 3-802 for cases in which there is a right of recourse on the instrument against the obligor. Under former Section 3-802(1)(a) the obligation was not discharged if there was a right of recourse on the instrument against the obligor. Subsection (a) changes this result. The underlying obligation is discharged, but any right of recourse on the instrument is preserved.

3. Subsection (b) concerns cases in which an uncertified check or a note is taken for an obligation. The typical case is that in which a buyer pays for goods or services by giving the seller the buyer's personal check, or in which the buyer signs a note for the purchase price. Subsection (b) also applies to the uncommon cases in which a check or note of a third person is given in payment of the obligation. Subsection (b) preserves the rule under former Section 3-802(1)(b) that the buyer's obligation to pay the price is suspended, but subsection (b) spells out the effect more precisely. If the check or note is dishonored, the seller may sue on either the dishonored instrument or the contract of sale if the seller has possession of the instrument and is the person entitled to enforce it. If the right to enforce the instrument is held by somebody other than the seller, the seller can't enforce the right to payment of the price under the sales contract because that right is represented by the instrument which is enforceable by somebody else. Thus, if the seller sold the note or the check to a holder and has not reacquired it after dishonor, the only right that survives is the right to enforce the instrument. What that means is that even though the suspension of the obligation may end upon dishonor under paragraph (b)(1), the obligation is not revived in the circumstances described in paragraph (b)(4).

The last sentence of subsection (b)(3) applies to cases in which an instrument of another person is indorsed over to the obligee in payment of the obligation. For example, Buyer delivers an uncertified personal check of X payable to the order of Buyer to Seller in payment of the price of goods. Buyer indorses the check over to Seller. Buyer is liable on the check as indorser. If Seller neglects to present the check for payment or to deposit it for collection within 30 days of the indorsement, Buyer's liability as indorser is discharged. Section 3-415(e). Under the last sentence of Section 3-310(b)(3) Buyer is also discharged on the obligation to pay for the goods.

4. There was uncertainty concerning the applicability of former Section 3-802 to the case in which the check given for the obligation was stolen from the payee, the payee's signature was forged, and the forger obtained payment. The last sentence of subsection (b)(4) addresses this issue. If the payor bank pays a holder, the drawer is discharged on the underlying obligation because the check was paid. Subsection (b)(1). If the payor bank pays a person not entitled to enforce the instrument, as in the hypothetical case, the suspension of the underlying obligation continues because the check has not been paid. Section 3-602(a). The payee's cause of action is against the depositary bank or payor bank in conversion under Section 3-420 or against the drawer under Section 3-309. In the latter case, the drawer's obligation under Section 3-414(b) is triggered by dishonor which occurs because the check is unpaid. Presentment for payment to the drawee is excused under Section 3-504(a)(i) and, under Section 3-502(e), dishonor occurs without presentment if the check is not paid. The payee cannot merely ignore the instrument and sue the drawer on the underlying contract. This would impose on the drawer the risk that the check when stolen was indorsed in blank or to bearer.

A similar analysis applies with respect to lost instruments that have not been paid. If a creditor takes a check of the debtor in payment of an obligation, the obligation is suspended under the introductory paragraph of subsection (b). If the creditor then loses the check, what are the creditor's rights? The creditor can request the debtor to issue a new check and in many cases, the debtor will issue a replacement check after stopping payment on the lost check. In that case both the debtor and creditor are protected. But the debtor is not obliged to issue a new check. If the debtor refuses to issue a replacement check, the last sentence of subsection (b)(4) applies. The creditor may not enforce the obligation of debtor for which the check was taken. The creditor may assert only rights on the check. The creditor can proceed under Section 3-309 to enforce the obligation of the debtor, as drawer, to pay the check.

5. Subsection (c) deals with rare cases in which other instruments are taken for obligations. If a bank is the obligor on the instrument, subsection (a) applies and the obligation is discharged. In any other case subsection (b) applies.

Additional References:

3-303 Comment 2

3-418 Comment 2

Section 3-311. Accord and Satisfaction by Use of Instrument

(a) If a person against whom a claim is asserted proves that (i) that person in good faith tendered an instrument to the claimant as full satisfaction of the claim, (ii) the amount of the claim was unliquidated or subject to a bona fide dispute, and (iii) the claimant obtained payment of the instrument, the following subsections apply.

(b) Unless subsection (c) applies, the claim is discharged if the person against whom the claim is asserted proves that the instrument or an accompanying written communication contained a conspicuous statement to the effect that the instrument was tendered as full satisfaction of the claim.

(c) Subject to subsection (d), a claim is not discharged under subsection (b) if either of the following applies:

(1) The claimant, if an organization, proves that (i) within a reasonable time before the tender, the claimant sent a conspicuous statement to the person against whom the claim is asserted that communications concerning disputed debts, including an instrument tendered as full satisfaction of a debt, are to be sent to a designated person, office, or place, and (ii) the instrument or accompanying communication was not received by that designated person, office, or place.

(2) The claimant, whether or not an organization, proves that within 90 days after payment of the instrument, the claimant tendered repayment of the amount of the instrument to the person against whom the claim is asserted. This paragraph does not apply if the claimant is an organization that sent a statement complying with paragraph (1)(i).

(d) A claim is discharged if the person against whom the claim is asserted proves that within a reasonable time before collection of the instrument was initiated, the claimant, or an agent of the claimant having direct responsibility with respect to the disputed obligation, knew that the instrument was tendered in full satisfaction of the claim.

Definitional Cross References:

"Conspicuous".	Section 1-201(b)(10)
"Discharge".	Section 3-601(a)
"Good Faith".	Section 1-201(b)(20), Section 3-103(a)(6)
"Instrument".	Section 3-104(b)
"Knows".	Section 1-202(a)
"Organization".	Section 1-202(a)
"Payment".	Section 3-602(a)
"Person".	Section 1-201(b)(27)
"Prove".	Section 3-103(a)(13)

Official Comment

1. This section deals with an informal method of dispute resolution carried out by use of a negotiable instrument. In the typical case there is a dispute concerning the amount that is owed on a claim.

> *Case # 1.* The claim is for the price of goods or services sold to a consumer who asserts that he or she is not obliged to pay the full price for which the consumer was billed because of a defect or breach of warranty with respect to the goods or services.

> *Case # 2.* A claim is made on an insurance policy. The insurance company alleges that it is not liable under the policy for the amount of the claim.

In either case the person against whom the claim is asserted may attempt an accord and satisfaction of the disputed claim by tendering a check to the claimant for some amount less than the full amount claimed by the claimant. A statement will be included on the check or in a communication accompanying the check to the effect that the check is offered as full payment or full satisfaction of the claim. Frequently, there is also a statement to the effect that obtaining payment of the check is an agreement by the claimant to a settlement of the dispute for the amount tendered. Before enactment of revised Article 3, the case law was in conflict over the question of whether obtaining payment of the check had the effect of an agreement to the settlement proposed by the debtor. This issue was governed by a common law rule, but some courts hold that the common law was modified by former Section 1-207 which they interpreted as applying to full settlement checks.

2. Comment d. to Restatement of Contracts, Section 281 discusses the full satisfaction check and the applicable common law rule. In a case like Case # 1, the buyer can propose a settlement of the disputed bill by a clear notation on the check indicating that the check is tendered as full satisfaction of the bill. Under the common law rule the seller, by obtaining payment of the check accepts the offer of compromise by the buyer. The result is the same if the seller adds a notation to the check indicating that the check is accepted under protest or in only partial satisfaction of the claim. Under the common law rule the seller can refuse the check or can accept it subject to the condition stated by the buyer, but the seller can't accept the check and refuse to be bound by the condition. The rule applies only to an unliquidated claim or a claim disputed in good faith by the buyer. The dispute in the courts was whether Section 1-207 changed the common law rule. The Restatement states that section "need not be read as changing this well-established rule."

3. As part of the revision of Article 3, Section 1-207 was amended to add subsection (2) stating that Section 1-207 "does not apply to an accord and satisfaction." That statement is now in Section 1-308(b). Because of that amendment and revised Article 3, Section 3-311 governs full satisfaction checks. Section 3-311 follows the common law rule with some minor variations to reflect modern business conditions. In cases covered by Section 3-311 there will often be an individual on one side of the dispute and a business organization on the other. This section is not designed to favor either the individual or the business organization. In Case # 1 the person seeking the accord and satisfaction is an individual. In Case # 2 the person seeking the accord and satisfaction is an insurance company. Section 3-311 is based on a belief that the common law rule produces a fair result and that informal dispute resolution by full satisfaction checks should be encouraged.

4. Subsection (a) states three requirements for application of Section 3-311. "Good faith" in subsection (a)(i) is defined in Section 3-103(a)(4) as not only honesty in fact, but the observance of reasonable commercial standards of fair dealing. The meaning of "fair dealing" will depend upon the facts in the particular case. For example, suppose an insurer tenders a check in settlement of a claim for personal injury in an accident clearly covered by the insurance policy. The claimant is necessitous and the amount of the check is very small in relationship to the extent of the injury and the amount recoverable under the policy. If the trier of fact determines that the insurer was taking unfair advantage of the claimant, an accord and satisfaction would not result from payment of the check because of the absence of good faith by the insurer in making the tender. Another example of lack of good faith is found in the practice of some business debtors in routinely printing full satisfaction language on their check stocks so that all or a large part of the debts of the debtor are paid by checks bearing the full satisfaction language, whether or not there is any dispute with the creditor. Under such a practice the claimant cannot be sure whether a tender in full satisfaction is or is not being made. Use of a check on which full satisfaction language was affixed routinely pursuant to such a business practice may prevent an accord and satisfaction on the ground that the check was not tendered in good faith under subsection (a)(i).

Section 3-311 does not apply to cases in which the debt is a liquidated amount and not subject to a bona fide dispute. Subsection (a)(ii). Other law applies to cases in which a debtor is seeking discharge of such a debt by paying less than the amount owed. For the purpose of subsection (a)(iii) obtaining acceptance of a check is considered to be obtaining payment of the check.

The person seeking the accord and satisfaction must prove that the requirements of subsection (a) are met. If that person also proves that the statement required by subsection (b) was given, the claim is discharged unless subsection (c) applies. Normally the statement required by subsection (b) is written on the check. Thus, the canceled check can be used to prove the statement as well as the fact that the claimant obtained payment of the check. Subsection (b) requires a "conspicuous" statement that the instrument was tendered in full satisfaction of the claim. "Conspicuous" is defined in Section 1-201(b)(10). If the claimant can reasonably be expected to examine the check, almost any statement on the check should be noticed and is therefore conspicuous. In cases in which the claimant is an individual the claimant will receive the check and will normally indorse it. Since the statement concerning tender in full satisfaction normally will appear above the space provided for the claimant's indorsement of the check, the claimant "ought to have noticed" the statement.

5. Subsection (c)(1) is a limitation on subsection (b) in cases in which the claimant is an organization. It is designed to protect the claimant against inadvertent accord and satisfaction. If the claimant is an organization payment of the check might be obtained without notice to the personnel of the organization concerned with the disputed claim. Some business organizations have claims against very large numbers of customers. Examples are department stores, public utilities and the like. These claims are normally paid by checks sent by customers to a designated office at which clerks employed by the claimant or a bank acting for the claimant process the checks and record the amounts paid. If the processing office is not designed to deal with communications extraneous to recording the amount of the check and the account number of the customer, payment of a full satisfaction check can easily be obtained without knowledge by the claimant of the existence of the full satisfaction statement. This is particularly true if the statement is written on the reverse side of the check in the area in which indorsements are usually written. Normally, the clerks of the claimant have no reason to look at the reverse side of checks. Indorsement by the claimant normally is done by mechanical means or there may be no indorsement at all. Section 4-205(a). Subsection (c)(1) allows the claimant to protect itself by advising customers by a conspicuous statement that communications regarding disputed debts must be sent to a particular person, office, or place. The statement must be given to the customer within a reasonable time before the tender is made. This requirement is designed to assure that the customer has reasonable notice that the full satisfaction check must be sent to a particular place. The reasonable time requirement could be satisfied by a notice on the billing statement sent to the customer. If the full satisfaction check is sent to the designated destination and the check is paid, the claim is discharged. If the claimant proves that the check was not received at the designated destination the claim is not discharged unless subsection (d) applies.

6. Subsection (c)(2) is also designed to prevent inadvertent accord and satisfaction. It can be used by a claimant other than an organization or by a claimant as an alternative to subsection (c)(1). Some organizations may be reluctant to use subsection (c)(1) because it may result in confusion of customers that causes checks to be routinely sent to the special designated person, office, or place. Thus, much of the benefit of rapid processing of checks may be lost. An organization that chooses not to send a notice complying with subsection (c)(1)(i) may prevent an inadvertent accord and satisfaction by complying with subsection (c)(2). If the claimant discovers that it has obtained payment of a full satisfaction check, it may prevent an accord and satisfaction if, within 90 days of the payment of the check, the claimant tenders repayment of the amount of the check to the person against whom the claim is asserted.

7. Subsection (c) is subject to subsection (d). If a person against whom a claim is asserted proves that the claimant obtained payment of a check known to have been tendered in full satisfaction of the claim by "the claimant or an agent of the claimant having direct responsibility with respect to the disputed obligation," the claim is discharged even if (i) the check was not sent to the person, office, or place required by a notice complying with subsection (c)(1), or (ii) the claimant tendered repayment of the amount of the check in compliance with subsection (c)(2).

A claimant knows that a check was tendered in full satisfaction of a claim when the claimant has "actual knowledge" of that fact. Section 1-202(b). Under Section 1-202(f), if the claimant is an organization, it has knowledge that a check was tendered in full satisfaction of the claim when that fact is

> "brought to the attention of the individual conducting that transaction, and in any event when it would have been brought to his attention if the organization had exercised due diligence. An organization exercises due diligence if it maintains reasonable routines for communicating significant information to the person conducting the transaction and there is reasonable compliance with the routines. Due diligence does not require an individual acting for the organization to communicate information unless such communication is part of his regular duties or unless he has reason to know of the transaction and that the transaction would be materially affected by the information."

With respect to an attempted accord and satisfaction the "individual conducting that transaction" is an employee or other agent of the organization having direct responsibility with respect to the dispute. For example, if the check and communication are received by a collection agency acting for the claimant to collect the disputed claim, obtaining payment of the check will result in an accord and satisfaction even if the claimant gave notice, pursuant to subsection (c)(1), that full satisfaction checks be sent to some other office. Similarly, if a customer asserting a claim for breach of warranty with respect to defective goods purchased in a retail outlet of a large chain store delivers the full satisfaction check to the manager of the retail outlet at which the goods were purchased, obtaining payment of the check will also result in an accord and satisfaction. On the other hand, if the check is mailed to the chief executive officer of the chain store subsection (d) would probably not be satisfied. The chief executive officer of a large corporation may have general responsibility for operations of the company, but does not normally have direct responsibility for resolving a small disputed bill to a customer. A check for a relatively small amount mailed to a high executive officer of a large organization is not likely to receive the executive's personal attention. Rather, the check would normally be routinely sent to the appropriate office for deposit and credit to the customer's account. If the check does receive the personal attention of the high executive officer and the officer is aware of the full-satisfaction language, collection of the check will result in an accord and satisfaction because subsection (d) applies. In this case the officer has assumed direct responsibility with respect to the disputed transaction.

If a full satisfaction check is sent to a lock box or other office processing checks sent to the claimant, it is irrelevant whether the clerk processing the check did or did not see the statement that the check was tendered as full satisfaction of the claim. Knowledge of the clerk is not imputed to the organization because the clerk has no responsibility with respect to an accord and satisfaction. Moreover, there is no failure of "due diligence" under Section 1-202(f) if the claimant does not require its clerks to look for full satisfaction statements on checks or accompanying communications. Nor is there any duty of the claimant to assign that duty to its clerks. Section 3-311(c) is intended to allow a claimant to avoid an inadvertent accord and satisfaction by complying with either subsection (c)(1) or (2) without burdening the check-processing operation with extraneous and wasteful additional duties.

8. In some cases the disputed claim may have been assigned to a finance company or bank as part of a financing arrangement with respect to accounts receivable. If the account debtor was notified of the assignment, the claimant is the assignee of the account receivable and the "agent of the claimant" in subsection (d) refers to an agent of the assignee.

Section 3-312. Lost, Destroyed, or Stolen Cashier's Check, Teller's Check, or Certified Check

(a) In this section:

(1) "Check" means a cashier's check, teller's check, or certified check.

(2) "Claimant" means a person who claims the right to receive the amount of a cashier's check, teller's check, or certified check that was lost, destroyed, or stolen.

(3) "Declaration of loss" means a statement, made in a record under penalty of perjury, to the effect that (i) the declarer lost possession of a check, (ii) the declarer is the drawer or payee of the check, in the case of a certified check, or the remitter or payee of the check, in the case of a cashier's check or teller's check, (iii) the loss of possession was not the result of a transfer by the declarer or a lawful

seizure, and (iv) the declarer cannot reasonably obtain possession of the check because the check was destroyed, its whereabouts cannot be determined, or it is in the wrongful possession of an unknown person or a person that cannot be found or is not amenable to service of process.

(4) "Obligated bank" means the issuer of a cashier's check or teller's check or the acceptor of a certified check.

(b) A claimant may assert a claim to the amount of a check by a communication to the obligated bank describing the check with reasonable certainty and requesting payment of the amount of the check, if (i) the claimant is the drawer or payee of a certified check or the remitter or payee of a cashier's check or teller's check, (ii) the communication contains or is accompanied by a declaration of loss of the claimant with respect to the check, (iii) the communication is received at a time and in a manner affording the bank a reasonable time to act on it before the check is paid, and (iv) the claimant provides reasonable identification if requested by the obligated bank. Delivery of a declaration of loss is a warranty of the truth of the statements made in the declaration. If a claim is asserted in compliance with this subsection, the following rules apply:

(1) The claim becomes enforceable at the later of (i) the time the claim is asserted, or (ii) the 90th day following the date of the check, in the case of a cashier's check or teller's check, or the 90th day following the date of the acceptance, in the case of a certified check.

(2) Until the claim becomes enforceable, it has no legal effect and the obligated bank may pay the check or, in the case of a teller's check, may permit the drawee to pay the check. Payment to a person entitled to enforce the check discharges all liability of the obligated bank with respect to the check.

(3) If the claim becomes enforceable before the check is presented for payment, the obligated bank is not obliged to pay the check.

(4) When the claim becomes enforceable, the obligated bank becomes obliged to pay the amount of the check to the claimant if payment of the check has not been made to a person entitled to enforce the check. Subject to Section 4-302(a)(1), payment to the claimant discharges all liability of the obligated bank with respect to the check.

(c) If the obligated bank pays the amount of a check to a claimant under subsection (b)(4) and the check is presented for payment by a person having rights of a holder in due course, the claimant is obliged to (i) refund the payment to the obligated bank if the check is paid, or (ii) pay the amount of the check to the person having rights of a holder in due course if the check is dishonored.

(d) If a claimant has the right to assert a claim under subsection (b) and is also a person entitled to enforce a cashier's check, teller's check, or certified check which is lost, destroyed, or stolen, the claimant may assert rights with respect to the check either under this section or Section 3-309.

Definitional Cross References:

"Acceptance".	Section 3-409(a)
"Acceptor".	Section 3-103(a)(1)
"Bank".	Section 1-201(b)(4)
"Cashier's Check".	Section 3-104(g)
"Certified Check".	Section 3-409(d)
"Check".	Section 3-104(f)
"Discharge".	Section 3-601(a)
"Dishonor".	Section 3-502
"Drawee".	Section 3-103(a)(4)
"Holder in Due Course".	Section 3-302
"Issuer".	Section 3-105(c)
"Payment".	Section 3-602(a)
"Person".	Section 1-201(b)(27)
"Person Entitled to Enforce".	Section 3-301
"Presentment".	Section 3-501(a)
"Record".	Section 3-103(a)(14)
"Remitter".	Section 3-103(a)(15)
"Teller's Check".	Section 3-104(h)
"Transfer".	Section 3-203(a)

Official Comment

1. This section applies to cases in which a cashier's check, teller's check, or certified check is lost, destroyed, or stolen. In one typical case a customer of a bank closes his or her account and takes a cashier's check or teller's check of the bank as payment of the amount of the account. The customer may be moving to a new area and the check is to be used to open a bank account in that area. In such a case the check will normally be payable to the customer. In another typical case a cashier's check or teller's check is bought from a bank for the purpose of paying some obligation of the buyer of the check. In such a case the check may be made payable to the customer and then negotiated to the creditor by indorsement. But often, the payee of the check is the creditor. In the latter case the customer is a remitter. The section covers loss of the check by either the remitter or the payee. The section also covers loss of a certified check by either the drawer or payee.

Under Section 3-309 a person seeking to enforce a lost, destroyed, or stolen cashier's check or teller's check may be required by the court to give adequate protection to the issuing bank against loss that might occur by reason of the claim by another person to enforce the check. This might require the posting of an expensive bond for the amount of the check. Moreover, Section 3-309 applies only to a person entitled to enforce the check. It does not apply to a remitter of a cashier's check or teller's check or to the drawer of a certified check. Section 3-312 applies to both. The purpose of Section 3-312 is to offer a person who loses such a check a means of getting refund of the amount of the check within a reasonable period of time without the expense of posting a bond and with full protection of the obligated bank.

2. A claim to the amount of a lost, destroyed, or stolen cashier's check, teller's check, or certified check may be made under subsection (b) if the following requirements of that subsection are met. First, a claim may be asserted only by the drawer or payee of a certified check or the remitter or payee of a cashier's check or teller's check. An indorsee of a check is not covered because the indorsee is not an original party to the check or a remitter. Limitation to an original party or remitter gives the obligated bank the ability to determine, at the time it becomes obligated on the check, the identity of the person or persons who can assert a claim with respect to the check. The bank is not faced with having to determine the rights of some person who was not a party to the check at that time or with whom the bank had not dealt. If a cashier's check is issued to the order of the person who purchased it from the bank and that person indorses it over to a third person who loses the check, the third person may assert rights to enforce the check under Section 3-309 but has no rights under Section 3-312.

Second, the claim must be asserted by a communication to the obligated bank describing the check with reasonable certainty and requesting payment of the amount of the check. "Obligated bank" is defined in subsection (a)(4). Third, the communication must be received in time to allow the obligated bank to act on the claim before the check is paid, and the claimant must provide reasonable identification if requested. Subsections (b)(iii) and (iv). Fourth, the communication must contain or be accompanied by a declaration of loss described in subsection (b). This declaration is an affidavit or other writing made under penalty of perjury alleging the loss, destruction, or theft of the check and stating that the declarer is a person entitled to assert a claim, i.e. the drawer or payee of a certified check or the remitter or payee of a cashier's check or teller's check.

A claimant who delivers a declaration of loss makes a warranty of the truth of the statements made in the declaration. The warranty is made to the obligated bank and anybody who has a right to enforce the check. If the declaration of loss falsely alleges loss of a cashier's check that did not in fact occur, a holder of the check who was unable to obtain payment because subsection (b)(3) and (4) caused the obligated bank to dishonor the check would have a cause of action against the declarer for breach of warranty.

The obligated bank may not impose additional requirements on the claimant to assert a claim under subsection (b). For example, the obligated bank may not require the posting of a bond or other form of security. Section 3-312(b) states the procedure for asserting claims covered by the section. Thus, procedures that may be stated in other law for stating claims to property do not apply and are displaced within the meaning of Section 1-103.

3. A claim asserted under subsection (b) does not have any legal effect, however, until the date it becomes enforceable, which cannot be earlier than 90 days after the date of a cashier's check or teller's check or 90 days after the date of acceptance of a certified check. Thus, if a lost check is presented for payment within the 90-day period, the bank may pay a person entitled to enforce the check without regard to the claim and is discharged of all liability with respect to the check. This ensures the continued utility of cashier's checks, teller's checks, and certified checks as cash equivalents. Virtually all such checks are presented for payment within 90 days.

If the claim becomes enforceable and payment has not been made to a person entitled to enforce the check, the bank becomes obligated to pay the amount of the check to the claimant. Subsection (b)(4). When the bank becomes obligated to pay the amount of the check to the claimant, the bank is relieved of its obligation to pay the check. Subsection (b)(3). Thus, any person entitled to enforce the check, including even a holder in due course, loses the right to enforce the check after a claim under subsection (b) becomes enforceable.

If the obligated bank pays the claimant under subsection (b)(4), the bank is discharged of all liability with respect to the check. The only exception is the unlikely case in which the obligated bank subsequently incurs liability under Section 4-302(a)(1) with respect to the check. For example, Obligated Bank is the issuer of a cashier's check and, after a claim becomes enforceable, it pays the claimant under subsection (b)(4). Later the check is presented to Obligated Bank for payment over the counter. Under subsection (b)(3), Obligated Bank is not obliged to pay the check and may dishonor the check by returning it to the person who presented it for payment. But the normal rules of check collection are not affected by Section 3-312. If Obligated Bank retains the check beyond midnight of the day of presentment without settling for it, it becomes accountable for the amount of the check under Section 4-302(a)(1) even though it had no obligation to pay the check.

An obligated bank that pays the amount of a check to a claimant under subsection (b)(4) is discharged of all liability on the check so long as the assertion of the claim meets the requirements of subsection (b) discussed in Comment 2. This is important in cases of fraudulent declarations of loss. For example, if the claimant falsely alleges a loss that in fact did not occur, the bank, subject to Section 1-304, may rely on the declaration of loss. On the other hand, a claim may be asserted only by a person described in subsection (b)(i). Thus, the bank is discharged under subsection (a)(4) only if it pays such a person. Although it is highly unlikely, it is possible that more than one person could assert a claim under subsection (b) to the amount of a check. Such a case could occur if one of the claimants makes a false declaration of loss. The obligated bank is not required to determine whether a claimant who complies with subsection (b) is acting wrongfully. The bank may utilize procedures outside this Article, such as interpleader, under which the conflicting claims may be adjudicated.

Although it is unlikely that a lost check would be presented for payment after the claimant was paid by the bank under subsection (b)(4), it is possible for it to happen. Suppose the declaration of loss by the claimant fraudulently alleged a loss that in fact did not occur. If the claimant negotiated the check, presentment for payment would occur shortly after negotiation in almost all cases. Thus, a fraudulent declaration of loss is not likely to occur unless the check is negotiated after the 90-day period has already expired or shortly before expiration. In such a case the holder of the check, who may not have noticed the date of the check, is not entitled to payment from the obligated bank if the check is presented for payment after the claim becomes enforceable. Subsection (b)(3). The remedy of the holder who is denied payment in that case is an action against the claimant under subsection (c) if the holder is a holder in due course, or for breach of warranty under subsection (b). The holder would also have common law remedies against the claimant under the law of restitution or fraud.

4. The following cases illustrate the operation of Section 3-312:

Case # 1. Obligated Bank (OB) certified a check drawn by its customer, Drawer (D), payable to Payee (P). Two days after the check was certified, D lost the check and then asserted a claim pursuant to subsection (b). The check had not been presented for payment when D's claim became enforceable 90 days after the check was certified. Under subsection (b)(4), at the time D's claim became enforceable OB became obliged to pay D the amount of the check. If the check is later presented for payment, OB may refuse to pay the check and has no obligation to anyone to pay the check. Any obligation owed by D to P, for which the check was intended as payment, is unaffected because the check was never delivered to P.

Case # 2. Obligated Bank (OB) issued a teller's check to Remitter (R) payable to Payee (P). R delivered the check to P in payment of an obligation. P lost the check and then asserted a claim pursuant to subsection (b). To carry out P's order, OB issued an order pursuant to Section 4-403(a) to the drawee of the teller's check to stop payment of the check effective on the 90th day after the date of the teller's check. The check was not presented for payment. On the 90th day after the date of the teller's check P's claim becomes enforceable and OB becomes obliged to pay P the amount of the check. As in Case # 1, OB has no further liability with respect to the check to anyone. When R delivered the check to P, R's underlying obligation to P was discharged under Section 3-310. Thus, R suffered no loss. Since P received the amount of the check, P also suffered no loss except with respect to the delay in receiving the amount of the check.

Case # 3. Obligated Bank (OB) issued a cashier's check to its customer, Payee (P). Two days after issue, the check was stolen from P who then asserted a claim pursuant to subsection (b). Ten days after issue, the check was deposited by X in an account in Depositary Bank (DB). X had found the check and forged the indorsement of P. DB promptly presented the check to OB and obtained payment on behalf of X. On the 90th day after the date of the check P's claim becomes enforceable and P is entitled to receive the amount of the check from OB. Subsection (b)(4). Although the check was presented for payment before P's claim becomes enforceable, OB is not discharged. Because of the forged indorsement X was not a holder and neither was DB. Thus, neither is a person entitled to enforce the check (Section 3-301) and OB is not discharged under Section 3-602(a). Thus, under subsection (b)(4), because OB did not pay a person entitled to enforce the check, OB must pay P. OB's remedy is against DB for breach of warranty under Section 4-208(a)(1). As an alternative to the remedy under Section 3-312, P could recover from DB for conversion under Section 3-420(a).

Case # 4. Obligated Bank (OB) issued a cashier's check to its customer, Payee (P). P made an unrestricted blank indorsement of the check and mailed the check to P's bank for deposit to P's account. The check was never received by P's bank. When P discovered the loss, P asserted a claim pursuant to subsection (b). X found the check and deposited it in X's account in Depositary Bank (DB) after indorsing the check. DB presented the check for payment before the end of the 90-day period after its date. OB paid the check. Because of the unrestricted blank indorsement by P, X became a holder of the check. DB also became a holder. Since the check was paid before P's claim became enforceable and payment was made to a person entitled to enforce the check, OB is discharged of all liability with respect to the check. Subsection (b)(2). Thus, P is not entitled to payment from OB. Subsection (b)(4) doesn't apply.

Case # 5. Obligated Bank (OB) issued a cashier's check to its customer, Payee (P). P made an unrestricted blank indorsement of the check and mailed the check to P's bank for deposit to P's account. The check was never received by P's bank. When P discovered the loss, P asserted a claim pursuant to subsection (b). At the end of the 90-day period after the date of the check, OB paid the amount of the check to P under subsection (b)(4). X then found the check and deposited it to X's account in Depositary Bank (DB). DB presented the check to OB for payment. OB is not obliged to pay the check. Subsection (b)(4). If OB dishonors the check, DB's remedy is to charge back X's account. Section 4-214(a). Although P, as an indorser, would normally have liability to DB under Section 3-415(a) because the check was dishonored, P is released from that liability under Section 3-415(e) because collection of the check was initiated more than 30 days after the indorsement. DB has a remedy only against X. A depositary bank that takes a cashier's check that cannot be presented for payment before expiration of the 90-day period after its date is on notice that the check might not be paid because of the possibility of a claim asserted under subsection (b) which would excuse the issuer of the check from paying the check. Thus, the depositary bank cannot safely release funds with respect to the check until it has assurance that the check has been paid. DB cannot be a holder in due course of the check because it took the check when the check was overdue. Section 3-304(a)(2). Thus, DB has no action against P under subsection (c).

Case # 6. Obligated Bank (OB) issued a cashier's check payable to bearer and delivered it to its customer, Remitter (R). R held the check for 90 days and then wrongfully asserted a claim to the amount of the check under subsection (b). The declaration of loss fraudulently stated that the check was lost. R received payment from OB under subsection (b)(4). R then negotiated the check to X for value. X presented the check to OB for payment. Although OB, under subsection (b)(2), was not obliged to pay the check, OB paid X by mistake. OB's teller did not notice that the check was more than 90 days old and was not aware that OB was not obliged to pay the check. If X took the check in good faith, OB may not recover from X. Section 3-418(c). OB's remedy is to recover from R for fraud or for breach of warranty in making a false declaration of loss. Subsection (b).

PART 4. LIABILITY OF PARTIES

Section 3-401. Signature

A person is not liable on an instrument unless (i) the person signed the instrument, or (ii) the person is represented by an agent or representative who signed the instrument and the signature is binding on the represented person under Section 3-402.

Definitional Cross References:

"Instrument".	Section 3-104(b)
"Person".	Section 1-201(b)(27)
"Representative".	Section 1-201(b)(33)
"Signed".	Section 1-201(b)(37)
"Writing".	Section 1-201(b)(43)

Official Comment

1. This section provides the fundamental rule that an obligation on an instrument depends on a signature that is binding on the obligor. The signature may be made by the obligor personally or by an agent or other representative authorized to act for the obligor. Signature by agents and other representatives is covered by Section 3-402. It is not necessary that the name of the obligor appear on the instrument, so long as there is a signature that binds the obligor. These obligations include those on an "order" (Section 3-103(a)(6)) and a "promise" (Section 3-103(a)(9)) and those of an "issuer," "maker," or "drawer" (Sections 3-103(a)(5) and (7), 3-105(c), 3-412, and 3-414), an "acceptor" (Sections 3-409 and 3-413), and an indorser (Sections 3-204(b) and 3-415).

2. Subsection (b) of the pre-2022 text of this section has been deleted as unnecessary in view of the 2022 revision of the definition of "sign." See Section 1-201(b)(37) and Comment 37. Although former subsection (b) had not proven to be problematic, its deletion eliminates any implication that the revised definition of "sign" is inadequate for purposes of this Article. For example, former subsection (b) provided examples of the means of making a signature with the present intention of authenticating a writing, such as by means of a device or machine, by the use of a trade name or assumed name, or by the use of a word, mark, or symbol. These means now are encompassed by the broad, general terms of the revised definition of "sign." A signature may appear in the body of the instrument, as in the case of "I, John Doe, promise to pay ***" without any other signature. It may be made in any name, including a name other than a designated payee. However, to be signed an instrument (a writing) must exist at the time it is signed by the execution or adoption of a tangible symbol on the instrument. The deletion of former subsection (b) effected no change in the law.

Section 3-402. Signature by Representative

(a) If a person acting, or purporting to act, as a representative signs an instrument by signing either the name of the represented person or the name of the signer, the represented person is bound by the signature to the same extent the represented person would be bound if the signature were on a simple contract. If the represented person is bound, the signature of the representative is the "authorized signature of the represented person" and the represented person is liable on the instrument, whether or not identified in the instrument.

(b) If a representative signs the name of the representative to an instrument and the signature is an authorized signature of the represented person, the following rules apply:

(1) If the form of the signature shows unambiguously that the signature is made on behalf of the represented person who is identified in the instrument, the representative is not liable on the instrument.

(2) Subject to subsection (c), if (i) the form of the signature does not show unambiguously that the signature is made in a representative capacity or (ii) the represented person is not identified in the instrument, the representative is liable on the instrument to a holder in due course that took the instrument without notice that the representative was not intended to be liable on the instrument. With respect to any other person, the representative is liable on the instrument unless the representative proves that the original parties did not intend the representative to be liable on the instrument.

(c) If a representative signs the name of the representative as drawer of a check without indication of the representative status and the check is payable from an account of the represented person who is identified on the check, the signer is not liable on the check if the signature is an authorized signature of the represented person.

Definitional Cross References:

"Account".	Section 4-104(a)(1)
"Check".	Section 3-104(f)
"Contract".	Section 1-201(b)(12)
"Drawer".	Section 3-103(a)(5)
"Holder in Due Course".	Section 3-302
"Instrument".	Section 3-104(b)
"Notice".	Section 1-202(a)
"Person".	Section 1-201(b)(27)
"Prove".	Section 3-103(a)(13)
"Representative".	Section 1-201(b)(33)
"Signed".	Section 1-201(b)(37)

Official Comment

1. Subsection (a) states when the represented person is bound on an instrument if the instrument is signed by a representative. If under the law of agency the represented person would be bound by the act of the representative in signing either the name of the represented person or that of the representative, the signature is the authorized signature of the represented person. Former Section 3-401(1) stated that "no person is liable on an instrument unless his signature appears thereon." This was interpreted as meaning that an undisclosed principal is not liable on an instrument. This interpretation provided an exception to ordinary agency law that binds an undisclosed principal on a simple contract.

It is questionable whether this exception was justified by the language of former Article 3 and there is no apparent policy justification for it. The exception is rejected by subsection (a) which returns to ordinary rules of agency. If P, the principal, authorized A, the agent, to borrow money on P's behalf and A signed A's name to a note without disclosing that the signature was on behalf of P, A is liable on the instrument. But if the person entitled to enforce the note can also prove that P authorized A to sign on P's behalf, why shouldn't P also be liable on the instrument? To recognize the liability of P takes nothing away from the utility of negotiable instruments. Furthermore, imposing liability on P has the merit of making it impossible to have an instrument on which nobody is liable even though it was authorized by P. That result could occur under former Section 3-401(1) if an authorized agent signed "as agent" but the note did not identify the principal. If the dispute was between the agent and the payee of the note, the agent could escape liability on the note by proving that the agent and the payee did not intend that the agent be liable on the note when the note was issued. Former Section 3-403(2)(b). Under the prevailing interpretation of former Section 3-401(1), the principal was not liable on the note under former 3-401(1) because the principal's name did not appear on the note. Thus, nobody was liable on the note even though all parties knew that the note was signed by the agent on behalf of the principal. Under Section 3-402(a) the principal would be liable on the note.

2. Subsection (b) concerns the question of when an agent who signs an instrument on behalf of a principal is bound on the instrument. The approach followed by former Section 3-403 was to specify the form of signature that imposed or avoided liability. This approach was unsatisfactory. There are many ways in which there can be ambiguity about a signature. It is better to state a general rule. Subsection (b)(1) states that if the form of the signature unambiguously shows that it is made on behalf of an identified represented person (for example, "P, by A, Treasurer") the agent is not liable. This is a workable standard for a court to apply. Subsection (b)(2) partly changes former Section 3-403(2). Subsection (b)(2) relates to cases in which the agent signs on behalf of a principal but the form of the signature does not fall within subsection (b)(1). The following cases are illustrative. In each case John Doe is the authorized agent of Richard Roe and John Doe signs a note on behalf of Richard Roe. In each case the intention of the original parties to the instrument is that Roe is to be liable on the instrument but Doe is not to be liable.

> *Case # 1.* Doe signs "John Doe" without indicating in the note that Doe is signing as agent. The note does not identify Richard Roe as the represented person.
>
> *Case # 2.* Doe signs "John Doe, Agent" but the note does not identify Richard Roe as the represented person.
>
> *Case # 3.* The name "Richard Roe" is written on the note and immediately below that name Doe signs "John Doe" without indicating that Doe signed as agent.

In each case Doe is liable on the instrument to a holder in due course without notice that Doe was not intended to be liable. In none of the cases does Doe's signature unambiguously show that Doe was signing as agent for an identified principal. A holder in due course should be able to resolve any ambiguity against Doe.

But the situation is different if a holder in due course is not involved. In each case Roe is liable on the note. Subsection (a). If the original parties to the note did not intend that Doe also be liable, imposing liability on Doe is a windfall to the person enforcing the note. Under subsection (b)(2) Doe is prima facie liable because his signature appears on the note and the form of the signature does not unambiguously refute personal liability. But Doe can escape liability by proving that the original parties did not intend that he be liable on the note. This is a change from former Section 3-403(2)(a).

A number of cases under former Article 3 involved situations in which an agent signed the agent's name to a note, without qualification and without naming the person represented, intending to bind the principal but not the agent. The agent attempted to prove that the other party had the same intention. Some of these cases involved mistake, and in some there was evidence that the agent may have been deceived into signing in that manner. In some of the cases the court refused to allow proof of the intention of the parties and imposed liability on the agent based on former Section 3-403(2)(a) even though both parties to the instrument may have intended that the agent not be liable. Subsection (b)(2) changes the result of those cases, and is consistent with Section 3-117 which allows oral or written agreements to modify or nullify apparent obligations on the instrument.

Former Section 3-403 spoke of the represented person being "named" in the instrument. Section 3-402 speaks of the represented person being "identified" in the instrument. This change in terminology is intended to reject decisions under former Section 3-403(2) requiring that the instrument state the legal name of the represented person.

3. Subsection (c) is directed at the check cases. It states that if the check identifies the represented person the agent who signs on the signature line does not have to indicate agency status. Virtually all checks used today are in personalized form which identify the person on whose account the check is drawn. In this case, nobody is deceived into thinking that the person signing the check is meant to be liable. This subsection is meant to overrule cases decided under former Article 3 such as *Griffin v. Ellinger,* 538 S.W.2d 97 (Tex. 1976).

Additional References:

3-308 Comment 1
3-401 Comment 1
3-405 Comment 3

Section 3-403. Unauthorized Signature

(a) Unless otherwise provided in this Article or Article 4, an unauthorized signature is ineffective except as the signature of the unauthorized signer in favor of a person who in good faith pays the instrument or takes it for value. An unauthorized signature may be ratified for all purposes of this Article.

(b) If the signature of more than one person is required to constitute the authorized signature of an organization, the signature of the organization is unauthorized if one of the required signatures is lacking.

(c) The civil or criminal liability of a person who makes an unauthorized signature is not affected by any provision of this Article which makes the unauthorized signature effective for the purposes of this Article.

Definitional Cross References:

"Good Faith".	Section 1-201(b)(20), Section 3-103(a)(6)
"Instrument".	Section 3-104(b)
"Organization".	Section 1-202(a)
"Payment".	Section 3-602(a)
"Person".	Section 1-201(b)(27)
"Signed".	Section 1-201(b)(37)
"Unauthorized Signature".	Section 1-201(b)(41)
"Value, Transferred for".	Section 3-303(a)

Official Comment

1. "Unauthorized signature" is defined in Section 1-201(b)(41) as one that includes a forgery as well as a signature made by one exceeding actual or apparent authority. Former Section 3-404(1) stated that an unauthorized signature was inoperative as the signature of the person whose name was signed unless that person "is precluded from denying it." Under former Section 3-406 if negligence by the person whose name was signed contributed to an unauthorized signature, that person "is precluded from asserting the . . . lack of authority." Both of these sections were applied to cases in which a forged signature appeared on an instrument and the person asserting rights on the instrument alleged that the negligence of the purported signer contributed to the forgery. Since the standards for liability between the two sections differ, the overlap between the sections caused confusion. Section 3-403(a) deals with the problem by removing the preclusion language that appeared in former Section 3-404.

2. The except clause of the first sentence of subsection (a) states the generally accepted rule that the unauthorized signature, while it is wholly inoperative as that of the person whose name is signed, is effective to impose liability upon the signer or to transfer any rights that the signer may have in the instrument. The signer's liability is not in damages for breach of warranty of authority, but is full liability on the instrument in the capacity in which the signer signed. It is, however, limited to parties who take or pay the instrument in good faith; and one who knows that the signature is unauthorized cannot recover from the signer on the instrument.

3. The last sentence of subsection (a) allows an unauthorized signature to be ratified. Ratification is a retroactive adoption of the unauthorized signature by the person whose name is signed and may be found from conduct as well as from express statements. For example, it may be found from the retention of benefits received in the transaction with knowledge of the unauthorized signature. Although the forger is not an agent, ratification is governed by the rules and principles applicable to ratification of unauthorized acts of an agent.

Ratification is effective for all purposes of this Article. The unauthorized signature becomes valid so far as its effect as a signature is concerned. Although the ratification may relieve the signer of liability on the instrument, it does not of itself relieve the signer of liability to the person whose name is signed. It does not in any way affect the criminal law. No policy of the criminal law prevents a person whose name is forged to assume liability to others on the instrument by ratifying the forgery, but the ratification cannot affect the rights of the state. While the ratification may be taken into account with other relevant facts in determining punishment, it does not relieve the signer of criminal liability.

4. Subsection (b) clarifies the meaning of "unauthorized" in cases in which an instrument contains less than all of the signatures that are required as authority to pay a check. Judicial authority was split on the issue whether the one-year notice period under former Section 4-406(4) (now Section 4-406(f)) barred a customer's suit against a payor bank that paid a check containing less than all of the signatures required by the customer to authorize payment of the check. Some cases took the view that if a customer required that a check contain the signatures of both A and B to authorize payment and only A signed, there was no unauthorized signature within the meaning of that term in former Section 4-406(4) because A's signature was neither unauthorized nor forged. The other cases correctly pointed out that it was the customer's signature at issue and not that of A; hence, the customer's signature was unauthorized if all signatures required to authorize payment of the check were not on the check. Subsection (b) follows the latter line of cases. The same analysis applies if A forged the signature of B. Because the forgery is not effective as a signature of B, the required signature of B is lacking.

Subsection (b) refers to "the authorized signature of an organization." The definition of "organization" in Section 1-201(b)(25) is very broad. It covers not only commercial entities but also "two or more persons having a joint or common interest." Hence subsection (b) would apply when a husband and wife are both required to sign an instrument.

Section 3-404. Impostors; Fictitious Payees

(a) If an impostor, by use of the mails or otherwise, induces the issuer of an instrument to issue the instrument to the impostor, or to a person acting in concert with the impostor, by impersonating the payee of the instrument or a person authorized to act for the payee, an indorsement of the instrument by any person in the name of the payee is effective as the indorsement of the payee in favor of a person who, in good faith, pays the instrument or takes it for value or for collection.

(b) If (i) a person whose intent determines to whom an instrument is payable (Section 3-110(a) or (b)) does not intend the person identified as payee to have any interest in the instrument, or (ii) the person identified as payee of an instrument is a fictitious person, the following rules apply until the instrument is negotiated by special indorsement:

(1) Any person in possession of the instrument is its holder.

(2) An indorsement by any person in the name of the payee stated in the instrument is effective as the indorsement of the payee in favor of a person who, in good faith, pays the instrument or takes it for value or for collection.

(c) Under subsection (a) or (b), an indorsement is made in the name of a payee if (i) it is made in a name substantially similar to that of the payee or (ii) the instrument, whether or not indorsed, is deposited in a depositary bank to an account in a name substantially similar to that of the payee.

(d) With respect to an instrument to which subsection (a) or (b) applies, if a person paying the instrument or taking it for value or for collection fails to exercise ordinary care in paying or taking the instrument and that failure substantially contributes to loss resulting from payment of the instrument, the person bearing the loss may recover from the person failing to exercise ordinary care to the extent the failure to exercise ordinary care contributed to the loss.

Definitional Cross References:

"Account".	Section 4-104(a)(1)
"Depositary Bank".	Section 4-105(2)
"Good Faith".	Section 1-201(b)(20), Section 3-103(a)(6)
"Holder".	Section 1-201(b)(21)
"Indorsement".	Section 3-204(a)
"Instrument".	Section 3-104(b)
"Issue".	Section 3-105(a)
"Issuer'.	Section 3-105(c)
"Ordinary Care".	Section 3-103(a)(9)
"Payment".	Section 3-602(a)
"Person".	Section 1-201(b)(27)
"Special Indorsement".	Section 3-205(a)
"Value, Taken for".	Section 3-303(a)

Official Comment

1. Under former Article 3, the impostor cases were governed by former Section 3-405(1)(a) and the fictitious payee cases were governed by Section 3-405(1)(b). Section 3-404 replaces former Section 3-405(1)(a) and (b) and modifies the previous law in some respects. Former Section 3-405 was read by some courts to require that the indorsement be in the exact name of the named payee. Revised Article 3 rejects this result. Section 3-404(c) requires only that the indorsement be made in a name "substantially similar" to that of the payee. Subsection (c) also recognizes the fact that checks may be deposited without indorsement. Section 4-205(a).

Subsection (a) changes the former law in a case in which the impostor is impersonating an agent. Under former Section 3-405(1)(a), if Impostor impersonated Smith and induced the drawer to draw a check to the order of Smith, Impostor could negotiate the check. If Impostor impersonated Smith, the president of Smith Corporation, and the check was payable to the order of Smith Corporation, the section did not apply. See the last paragraph of Comment 2 to former Section 3-405. In revised Article 3, Section 3-404(a) gives Impostor the power to negotiate the check in both cases.

2. Subsection (b) is based in part on former Section 3-405(1)(b) and in part on N.I.L. § 9(3). It covers cases in which an instrument is payable to a fictitious or nonexisting person and to cases in which the payee is a real person but the drawer or maker does not intend the payee to have any interest in the instrument. Subsection (b) applies to any instrument, but its primary importance is with respect to checks of corporations and other organizations. It also applies to forged check cases. The following cases illustrate subsection (b):

Case # 1. Treasurer is authorized to draw checks on behalf of Corporation. Treasurer fraudulently draws a check of Corporation payable to Supplier Co., a non-existent company. Subsection (b) applies because Supplier Co. is a fictitious person and because Treasurer did not intend Supplier Co. to have any interest in the check. Under subsection (b)(1) Treasurer, as the person in possession of the check, becomes the holder of the check. Treasurer indorses the check in the name "Supplier Co." and deposits it in Depositary Bank. Under subsection (b)(2) and (c)(i), the indorsement is effective to make Depositary Bank the holder and therefore a person entitled to enforce the instrument. Section 3-301.

Case # 2. Same facts as Case # 1 except that Supplier Co. is an actual company that does business with Corporation. If Treasurer intended to steal the check when the check was drawn, the result in Case # 2 is the same as the result in Case # 1. Subsection (b) applies because Treasurer did not intend Supplier Co. to have any interest in the check. It does not make any difference whether Supplier Co. was or was not a creditor of Corporation when the check was drawn. If Treasurer did not decide to steal the check until after the check was drawn, the case is covered by Section 3-405 rather than Section 3-404(b), but the result is the same. See Case # 6 in Comment 3 to Section 3-405.

Case # 3. Checks of Corporation must be signed by two officers. President and Treasurer both sign a check of Corporation payable to Supplier Co., a company that does business with Corporation from time to time but to which Corporation does not owe any money. Treasurer knows that no money is owed to Supplier Co. and does not intend that Supplier Co. have any interest in the check. President believes that money is owed to Supplier Co. Treasurer obtains possession of the check after it is signed. Subsection (b) applies because Treasurer is "a person whose intent determines to whom an instrument is payable" and Treasurer does not intend Supplier Co. to have any interest in the check. Treasurer becomes the holder of the check and may negotiate it by indorsing it in the name "Supplier Co."

Case # 4. Checks of Corporation are signed by a check-writing machine. Names of payees of checks produced by the machine are determined by information entered into the computer that operates the machine. Thief, a person who is not an employee or other agent of Corporation, obtains access to the computer and causes the check-writing machine to produce a check payable to Supplier Co., a non-existent company. Subsection (b)(ii) applies. Thief then obtains possession of the check. At that point Thief becomes the holder of the check because Thief is the person in possession of the instrument. Subsection (b)(1). Under Section 3-301 Thief, as holder, is the "person entitled to enforce the instrument" even though Thief does not have title to the check and is in wrongful possession of it. Thief indorses the check in the name "Supplier Co." and deposits it in an account in Depositary Bank which Thief opened in the name "Supplier Co." Depositary Bank takes the check in good faith and credits the "Supplier Co." account. Under subsection (b)(2) and (c)(i), the indorsement is effective. Depositary Bank becomes the holder and the person entitled to enforce the check. The check is presented to the drawee bank for payment and payment is made. Thief then withdraws the credit to the account. Although the check was issued without authority given by Corporation, the drawee bank is entitled to pay the check and charge Corporation's account if there was an agreement with Corporation allowing the bank to debit Corporation's account for payment of checks produced by the check-writing machine whether or not authorized. The indorsement is also effective if Supplier Co. is a real person. In that case subsection (b)(i) applies. Under Section 3-110(b) Thief is the person whose intent determines to whom the check is payable, and Thief did not intend Supplier Co. to have any interest in the check. When the drawee bank pays the check, there is no breach of warranty under Section 3-417(a)(1) or 4-208(a)(1) because Depositary Bank was a person entitled to enforce the check when it was forwarded for payment.

Case # 5. Thief, who is not an employee or agent of Corporation, steals check forms of Corporation. John Doe is president of Corporation and is authorized to sign checks on behalf of Corporation as drawer. Thief draws a check in the name of Corporation as drawer by forging the signature of Doe. Thief makes the check payable to the order of Supplier Co. with the intention of stealing it. Whether Supplier Co. is a fictitious person or a real person, Thief becomes the holder of the check and the person entitled to enforce it. The analysis is the same as that in Case # 4. Thief deposits the check in an account in Depositary Bank which Thief opened in the name "Supplier Co." Thief either indorses the check in a name other than "Supplier Co." or does not indorse the check at all. Under Section 4-205(a) a depositary bank may become holder of a check deposited to the account of a customer if the customer was a holder, whether or not the customer indorses. Subsection (c)(ii) treats deposit to an account in a name substantially similar to that of the payee as the equivalent of indorsement in the name of the payee. Thus, the deposit is an effective indorsement of the check. Depositary Bank becomes the holder of the check and the person entitled to enforce the check. If the check is paid by the drawee bank, there is no breach of warranty under Section 3-417(a)(1) or 4-208(a)(1) because Depositary Bank was a person entitled to enforce the check when it was forwarded for payment and, unless Depositary Bank knew about the forgery of Doe's signature, there is no breach of warranty under Section 3-417(a)(3) or 4-208(a)(3). Because the check was a forged check the drawee bank is not entitled to charge Corporation's account unless Section 3-406 or Section 4-406 applies.

3. In cases governed by subsection (a) the dispute will normally be between the drawer of the check that was obtained by the impostor and the drawee bank that paid it. The drawer is precluded from obtaining recredit of the drawer's account by arguing that the check was paid on a forged indorsement so long as the drawee bank acted in good faith in paying the check. Cases governed by subsection (b) are illustrated by Cases # 1 through # 5 in Comment 2. In Cases # 1, # 2, and # 3 there is no forgery of the check, thus the drawer of the check takes the loss if there is no lack of good faith by the banks involved. Cases # 4 and # 5 are forged check cases. Depositary Bank is entitled to retain the proceeds of the check if it didn't know about the forgery. Under Section 3-418 the drawee bank is not entitled to recover from Depositary Bank on the basis of payment by mistake because Depositary Bank took the check in good faith and gave value for the check when the credit given for the check was withdrawn. And there is no breach of warranty under Section 3-417(a)(1) or (3) or 4-208(a)(1) or (3). Unless Section 3-406 applies the loss is taken by the drawee bank if a forged check is paid, and that is the result in Case # 5. In Case # 4 the loss is taken by Corporation, the drawer, because an agreement between Corporation and the drawee bank allowed the bank to debit Corporation's account despite the unauthorized use of the check-writing machine.

If a check payable to an impostor, fictitious payee, or payee not intended to have an interest in the check is paid, the effect of subsections (a) and (b) is to place the loss on the drawer of the check rather than on the drawee or the depositary bank that took the check for collection. Cases governed by subsection (a) always involve fraud, and fraud is almost always involved in cases governed by subsection (b). The drawer is in the best position to avoid the fraud and thus should take the loss. This is true in Case # 1, Case # 2, and Case # 3. But in some cases the person taking the check might have detected the fraud and thus have prevented the loss by the exercise of ordinary care. In those cases, if that person failed to exercise ordinary care, it is reasonable that that person bear loss to the extent the failure contributed to the loss. Subsection (d) is intended to reach that result. It allows the person who suffers loss as a result of payment of the check to recover from the person who failed to exercise ordinary care. In Case # 1, Case # 2, and Case # 3, the person suffering the loss is Corporation, the drawer of the check. In each case the most likely defendant is the depositary bank that took the check and failed to exercise ordinary care. In those cases, the drawer has a cause of action against the offending bank to recover a portion of the loss. The amount of loss to be allocated to each party is left to the trier of fact. Ordinary care is defined in Section 3-103(a)(7). An example of the type of conduct by a depositary bank that could give rise to recovery under subsection (d) is discussed in Comment 4 to Section 3-405. That comment addresses the last sentence of Section 3-405(b) which is similar to Section 3-404(d).

In Case # 1, Case # 2, and Case # 3, there was no forgery of the drawer's signature. But cases involving checks payable to a fictitious payee or a payee not intended to have an interest in the check are often forged check cases as well. Examples are Case # 4 and Case # 5. Normally, the loss in forged check cases is on the drawee bank that paid the check. Case # 5 is an example. In Case # 4 the risk with respect to the forgery is shifted to the drawer because of the agreement between the drawer and the drawee bank. The doctrine that prevents a drawee bank from recovering payment with respect to a forged check if the payment was made to a person who took the check for value and in good faith is incorporated into Section 3-418 and Sections 3-417(a)(3) and 4-208(a)(3). This doctrine is based on the assumption that the depositary bank normally has no way of detecting the forgery because the drawer is not that bank's customer. On the other hand, the drawee bank, at least in some cases, may be able to detect the forgery by comparing the signature on the check with the specimen signature that the drawee has on file. But in some forged check cases the depositary bank is in a position to detect the fraud. Those cases typically involve a check payable to a fictitious payee or a payee not intended to have an interest in the check. Subsection (d) applies to those cases. If the depositary bank failed to exercise ordinary care and the failure substantially contributed to the loss, the drawer in Case # 4 or the drawee bank in Case # 5 has a cause of action against the depositary bank under subsection (d). Comment 4 to Section 3-405 can be used as a guide to the type of conduct that could give rise to recovery under Section 3-404(d).

Additional References:

3-110 Comment 1
3-405 Comment 2, 3, 4
3-417 Comment 6
4-406 Comment 4

Section 3-405. Employer's Responsibility for Fraudulent Indorsement by Employee

(a) In this section:

(1) "Employee" includes an independent contractor and employee of an independent contractor retained by the employer.

(2) "Fraudulent indorsement" means (i) in the case of an instrument payable to the employer, a forged indorsement purporting to be that of the employer, or (ii) in the case of an instrument with respect to which the employer is the issuer, a forged indorsement purporting to be that of the person identified as payee.

(3) "Responsibility" with respect to instruments means authority (i) to sign or indorse instruments on behalf of the employer, (ii) to process instruments received by the employer for bookkeeping purposes, for deposit to an account, or for other disposition, (iii) to prepare or process instruments for issue in the name of the employer, (iv) to supply information determining the names or addresses of payees of instruments to be issued in the name of the employer, (v) to control the disposition of instruments to be issued in the name of the employer, or (vi) to act otherwise with respect to instruments in a responsible capacity. "Responsibility" does not include authority that merely allows an employee to have access to instruments or blank or incomplete instrument forms that are being stored or transported or are part of incoming or outgoing mail, or similar access.

(b) For the purpose of determining the rights and liabilities of a person who, in good faith, pays an instrument or takes it for value or for collection, if an employer entrusted an employee with responsibility with respect to the instrument and the employee or a person acting in concert with the employee makes a fraudulent indorsement of the instrument, the indorsement is effective as the indorsement of the person to whom the instrument is payable if it is made in the name of that person. If the person paying the instrument or taking it for value or for collection fails to exercise ordinary care in paying or taking the instrument and that failure substantially contributes to loss resulting from the fraud, the person bearing the loss may recover from the person failing to exercise ordinary care to the extent the failure to exercise ordinary care contributed to the loss.

(c) Under subsection (b), an indorsement is made in the name of the person to whom an instrument is payable if (i) it is made in a name substantially similar to the name of that person or (ii) the instrument, whether or not indorsed, is deposited in a depositary bank to an account in a name substantially similar to the name of that person.

Definitional Cross References:

"Account".	Section 4-104(a)(1)
"Depositary Bank".	Section 4-105(2)
"Good Faith".	Section 1-201(b)(20), Section 3-103(a)(6)
"Indorsement".	Section 3-204(a)
"Instrument".	Section 3-104(b)
"Issue".	Section 3-105(a)
"Issuer".	Section 3-105(c)
"Ordinary Care".	Section 3-103(a)(9)
"Person".	Section 1-201(b)(27)
"Signed".	Section 1-201(b)(37)
"Value, Taken for".	Section 3-303(a)

Official Comment

1. Section 3-405 is addressed to fraudulent indorsements made by an employee with respect to instruments with respect to which the employer has given responsibility to the employee. It covers two categories of fraudulent indorsements: indorsements made in the name of the employer to instruments payable to the employer and indorsements made in the name of payees of instruments issued by the employer. This section applies to instruments generally but normally the instrument will be a check. Section 3-405 adopts the principle that the risk of loss for fraudulent indorsements by employees who are entrusted with responsibility with respect to checks should fall on the employer rather than the bank that takes the check or pays it, if the bank was not negligent in the transaction. Section 3-405 is based on the belief that the employer is in a far better position to avoid the loss by care in choosing employees, in supervising them, and in adopting other measures to prevent forged indorsements on instruments payable to the employer or fraud in the issuance of instruments in the name of the employer. If the bank failed to exercise ordinary care, subsection (b) allows the employer to shift loss to the bank to the extent the bank's failure to exercise ordinary care contributed to the loss. "Ordinary care" is defined in Section 3-103(a)(7). The provision applies regardless of whether the employer is negligent.

The first category of cases governed by Section 3-405 are those involving indorsements made in the name of payees of instruments issued by the employer. In this category, Section 3-405 includes cases that were covered by former Section 3-405(1)(c). The scope of Section 3-405 in revised Article 3 is, however, somewhat wider. It covers some cases not covered by former Section 3-405(1)(c) in which the entrusted employee makes a forged indorsement to a check drawn by the employer. An example is Case # 6 in Comment 3. Moreover, a larger group of employees is included in revised Section 3-405. The key provision is the definition of "responsibility" in subsection (a)(1) which identifies the kind of responsibility delegated to an employee which will cause the employer to take responsibility for the fraudulent acts of that employee. An employer can insure this risk by employee fidelity bonds.

The second category of cases governed by Section 3-405—fraudulent indorsements of the name of the employer to instruments payable to the employer—were covered in former Article 3 by Section 3-406. Under former Section 3-406, the employer took the loss only if negligence of the employer could be proved. Under revised Article 3, Section 3-406 need not be used with respect to forgeries of the employer's indorsement. Section 3-405 imposes the loss on the employer without proof of negligence.

2. With respect to cases governed by former Section 3-405(1)(c), Section 3-405 is more favorable to employers in one respect. The bank was entitled to the preclusion provided by former Section 3-405(1)(c) if it took the check in good faith. The fact that the bank acted negligently did not shift the loss to the bank so long as the bank acted in good faith. Under revised Section 3-405 the loss may be recovered from the bank to the extent the failure of the bank to exercise ordinary care contributed to the loss.

3. Section 3-404(b) and Section 3-405 both apply to cases of employee fraud. Section 3-404(b) is not limited to cases of employee fraud, but most of the cases to which it applies will be cases of employee fraud. The following cases illustrate the application of Section 3-405. In each case it is assumed that the bank that took the check acted in good faith and was not negligent.

Case # 1. Janitor, an employee of Employer, steals a check for a very large amount payable to Employer after finding it on a desk in one of Employer's offices. Janitor forges Employer's indorsement on the check and obtains payment. Since Janitor was not entrusted with "responsibility" with respect to the check, Section 3-405 does not apply. Section 3-406 might apply to this case. The issue would be whether Employer was negligent in safeguarding the check. If not, Employer could assert that the indorsement was forged and bring an action for conversion against the depositary or payor bank under Section 3-420.

Case # 2. X is Treasurer of Corporation and is authorized to write checks on behalf of Corporation by signing X's name as Treasurer. X draws a check in the name of Corporation and signs X's name as Treasurer. The check is made payable to X. X then indorses the check and obtains payment. Assume that Corporation did not owe any money to X and did not authorize X to write the check. Although the writing of the check was not authorized, Corporation is bound as drawer of the check because X had authority to sign checks on behalf of Corporation. This result follows from agency law and Section 3-402(a). Section 3-405 does not apply in this case because there is no forged indorsement. X was payee of the check so the indorsement is valid. Section 3-110(a).

Case # 3. The duties of Employee, a bookkeeper, include posting the amounts of checks payable to Employer to the accounts of the drawers of the checks. Employee steals a check payable to Employer which was entrusted to Employee and forges Employer's indorsement. The check is deposited by Employee to an account in Depositary Bank which Employee opened in the same name as Employer, and the check is honored by the drawee bank. The indorsement is effective as Employer's indorsement because Employee's duties include processing checks for bookkeeping purposes. Thus, Employee is entrusted with "responsibility" with respect to the check. Neither Depositary Bank nor the drawee bank is liable to Employer for conversion of the check. The same result follows if Employee deposited the check in the account in Depositary Bank without indorsement. Section 4-205(a). Under subsection (c) deposit in a depositary bank in an account in a name substantially similar to that of Employer is the equivalent of an indorsement in the name of Employer.

Case # 4. Employee's duties include stamping Employer's unrestricted blank indorsement on checks received by Employer and depositing them in Employer's bank account. After stamping Employer's unrestricted blank indorsement on a check, Employee steals the check and deposits it in Employee's personal bank account. Section 3-405 doesn't apply because there is no forged indorsement. Employee is authorized by Employer to indorse Employer's checks. The fraud by Employee is not the indorsement but rather the theft of the indorsed check. Whether Employer has a cause of action against the bank in which the check was deposited is determined by whether the bank had notice of the breach of fiduciary duty by Employee. The issue is determined under Section 3-307.

Case # 5. The computer that controls Employer's check-writing machine was programmed to cause a check to be issued to Supplier Co. to which money was owed by Employer. The address of Supplier Co. was included in the information in the computer. Employee is an accounts payable clerk whose duties include entering information into the computer. Employee fraudulently changed the address of Supplier Co. in the computer data bank to an address of Employee. The check was subsequently produced by the check-writing machine and mailed to the address that Employee had entered into the computer. Employee obtained possession of the check, indorsed it in the name of Supplier Co, and deposited it to an account in Depositary Bank which Employee opened in the name "Supplier Co." The check was honored by the drawee bank. The indorsement is effective under Section 3-405(b) because Employee's duties allowed Employee to supply information determining the address of the payee of the check. An employee that is entrusted with duties that enable the employee to determine the address to which a check is to be sent controls the disposition of the check and facilitates forgery of the indorsement. The employer is held responsible. The drawee may debit the account of Employer for the amount of the check. There is no breach of warranty by Depositary Bank under Section 3-417(a)(1) or 4-208(a)(1).

Case # 6. Treasurer is authorized to draw checks in behalf of Corporation. Treasurer draws a check of Corporation payable to Supplier Co., a company that sold goods to Corporation. The check was issued to pay the price of these goods. At the time the check was signed Treasurer had no intention of stealing the check. Later, Treasurer stole the check, indorsed it in the name "Supplier Co." and obtained payment by depositing it to an account in Depositary Bank which Treasurer opened in the name "Supplier Co.". The indorsement is effective under Section 3-405(b). Section 3-404(b) does not apply to this case.

Case # 7. Checks of Corporation are signed by Treasurer in behalf of Corporation as drawer. Clerk's duties include the preparation of checks for issue by Corporation. Clerk prepares a check payable to the order of Supplier Co. for Treasurer's signature. Clerk fraudulently informs Treasurer that the check is needed to pay a debt owed to Supplier Co, a company that does business with Corporation. No money is owed to Supplier Co. and Clerk intends to steal the check. Treasurer signs it and returns it to Clerk for mailing. Clerk does not indorse the check but deposits it to an account in Depositary Bank which Clerk opened in the name "Supplier Co.". The check is honored by the drawee bank. Section 3-404(b)(i) does not apply to this case because Clerk, under Section 3-110(a), is not the person whose intent determines to whom the check is payable. But Section 3-405 does apply and it treats the deposit by Clerk as an effective indorsement by Clerk because Clerk was entrusted with responsibility with respect to the check. If Supplier Co. is a fictitious person Section 3-404(b)(ii) applies. But the result is the same. Clerk's deposit is treated as an effective indorsement of the check whether Supplier Co. is a fictitious or a real person or whether money was or was not owing to Supplier Co. The drawee bank may debit the account of Corporation for the amount of the check and there is no breach of warranty by Depositary Bank under Section 3-417(1)(a).

4. The last sentence of subsection (b) is similar to subsection (d) of Section 3-404 which is discussed in Comment 3 to Section 3-404. In Case # 5, Case # 6, or Case # 7 the depositary bank may have failed to exercise ordinary care when it allowed the employee to open an account in the name "Supplier Co.," to deposit checks payable to "Supplier Co." in that account, or to withdraw funds from that account that were proceeds of checks payable to Supplier Co. Failure to exercise ordinary care is to be determined in the context of all the facts relating to the bank's conduct with respect to the bank's collection of the check. If the trier of fact finds that there was such a failure and that the failure substantially contributed to loss, it could find the depositary bank liable to the extent the failure contributed to the loss. The last sentence of subsection (b) can be illustrated by an example. Suppose in Case # 5 that the check is not payable to an obscure "Supplier Co." but rather to a well-known national corporation. In addition, the check is for a very large amount of money. Before depositing the check, Employee opens an account in Depositary Bank in the name of the corporation and states to the person conducting the transaction for the bank that Employee is manager of a new office being opened by the corporation. Depositary Bank opens the account without requiring Employee to produce any resolutions of the corporation's board of directors or other evidence of authorization of Employee to act for the corporation. A few days later, the check is deposited, the account is credited, and the check is presented for payment. After Depositary Bank receives payment, it allows Employee to withdraw the credit by a wire transfer to an account in a bank in a foreign country. The trier of fact could find that Depositary Bank did not exercise ordinary care and that the failure to exercise ordinary care contributed to the loss suffered by Employer. The trier of fact could allow recovery by Employer from Depositary Bank for all or part of the loss suffered by Employer.

Additional References:

3-404 Comment 2, 3
3-406 Comment 2, 4
3-417 Comment 6
4-406 Comment 4

Section 3-406. Negligence Contributing to Forged Signature or Alteration of Instrument

(a) A person whose failure to exercise ordinary care substantially contributes to an alteration of an instrument or to the making of a forged signature on an instrument is precluded from asserting the alteration or the forgery against a person who, in good faith, pays the instrument or takes it for value or for collection.

(b) Under subsection (a), if the person asserting the preclusion fails to exercise ordinary care in paying or taking the instrument and that failure substantially contributes to loss, the loss is allocated between the person precluded and the person asserting the preclusion according to the extent to which the failure of each to exercise ordinary care contributed to the loss.

(c) Under subsection (a), the burden of proving failure to exercise ordinary care is on the person asserting the preclusion. Under subsection (b), the burden of proving failure to exercise ordinary care is on the person precluded.

Definitional Cross References:

"Alteration".	Section 3-407
"Good Faith".	Section 1-201(b)(20), Section 3-103(a)(6)
"Instrument".	Section 3-104(b)
"Ordinary Care".	Section 3-103(a)(9)
"Person".	Section 1-201(b)(27)
"Signed".	Section 1-201(b)(37)
"Value, Taken for".	Section 3-303(a)

Official Comment

1. Section 3-406(a) is based on former Section 3-406. With respect to alteration, Section 3-406 adopts the doctrine of Young v. Grote, 4 Bing. 253 (1827), which held that a drawer who so negligently draws an instrument as to facilitate its material alteration is liable to a drawee who pays the altered instrument in good faith. Under Section 3-406 the doctrine is expanded to apply not only to drafts but to all instruments. It includes in the protected class any "person who, in good faith, pays the instrument or takes it for value or for collection." Section 3-406 rejects decisions holding that the maker of a note owes no duty of care to the holder because at the time the instrument is issued there is no contract between them. By issuing the instrument and "setting it afloat upon a sea of strangers" the maker or drawer voluntarily enters into a relation with later holders which justifies imposition of a duty of care. In this respect an instrument so negligently drawn as to facilitate alteration does not differ in principle from an instrument containing blanks which may be filled. Under Section 3-407 a person paying an altered instrument or taking it for value, in good faith and without notice of the alteration may enforce rights with respect to the instrument according to its original terms. If negligence of the obligor substantially contributes to an alteration, this section gives the holder or the payor the alternative right to treat the altered instrument as though it had been issued in the altered form.

No attempt is made to define particular conduct that will constitute "failure to exercise ordinary care [that] substantially contributes to an alteration." Rather, "ordinary care" is defined in Section 3-103(a)(7) in general terms. The question is left to the court or the jury for decision in the light of the circumstances in the particular case including reasonable commercial standards that may apply.

Section 3-406 does not make the negligent party liable in tort for damages resulting from the alteration. If the negligent party is estopped from asserting the alteration the person taking the instrument is fully protected because the taker can treat the instrument as having been issued in the altered form.

2. Section 3-406 applies equally to a failure to exercise ordinary care that substantially contributes to the making of a forged signature on an instrument. Section 3-406 refers to "forged signature" rather than "unauthorized signature" that appeared in former Section 3-406 because it more accurately describes the scope of the provision. Unauthorized signature is a broader concept that includes not only forgery but also the signature of an agent which does not bind the principal under the law of agency. The agency cases are resolved independently under agency law. Section 3-406 is not necessary in those cases.

The "substantially contributes" test of former Section 3-406 is continued in this section in preference to a "direct and proximate cause" test. The "substantially contributes" test is meant to be less stringent than a "direct and proximate cause" test. Under the less stringent test the preclusion should be easier to establish. Conduct "substantially contributes" to a material alteration or forged signature if it is a contributing cause of the alteration or signature and a substantial factor in bringing it about. The analysis of "substantially contributes" in former Section 3-406 by the court in *Thompson Maple Products v. Citizens Nat'l Bank of Corry,* 234 A.2d 32 (Pa. Super. Ct. 1967), states what is intended by the use of the same words in revised Section 3-406(b). Since Section 3-404(d) and Section 3-405(b) also use the words "substantially contributes" the analysis of these words also applies to those provisions.

3. The following cases illustrate the kind of conduct that can be the basis of a preclusion under Section 3-406(a):

Case # 1. Employer signs checks drawn on Employer's account by use of a rubber stamp of Employer's signature. Employer keeps the rubber stamp along with Employer's personalized blank check forms in an unlocked desk drawer. An unauthorized person fraudulently uses the check forms to write checks on Employer's account. The checks are signed by use of the rubber stamp. If Employer demands that Employer's account in the drawee bank be recredited because the forged check was not properly payable, the drawee bank may defend by asserting that Employer is precluded from asserting the forgery. The trier of fact could find that Employer failed to exercise ordinary care to safeguard the rubber stamp and the check forms and that the failure substantially contributed to the forgery of Employer's signature by the unauthorized use of the rubber stamp.

Case # 2. An insurance company draws a check to the order of Sarah Smith in payment of a claim of a policyholder, Sarah Smith, who lives in Alabama. The insurance company also has a policyholder with the same name who lives in Illinois. By mistake, the insurance company mails the check to the Illinois Sarah Smith who indorses the check and obtains payment. Because the payee of the check is the Alabama Sarah Smith, the indorsement by the Illinois Sarah Smith is a forged indorsement. Section 3-110(a). The trier of fact could find that the insurance company failed to exercise ordinary care when it mailed the check to the wrong person and that the failure substantially contributed to the making of the forged indorsement. In that event the insurance company could be precluded from asserting the forged indorsement against the drawee bank that honored the check.

Case # 3. A company writes a check for $10. The figure "10" and the word "ten" are typewritten in the appropriate spaces on the check form. A large blank space is left after the figure and the word. The payee of the check, using a typewriter with a typeface similar to that used on the check, writes the word "thousand" after the word "ten" and a comma and three zeros after the figure "10". The drawee bank in good faith pays $10,000 when the check is presented for payment and debits the account of the drawer in that amount. The trier of fact could find that the drawer failed to exercise ordinary care in writing the check and that the failure substantially contributed to the alteration. In that case the drawer is precluded from asserting the alteration against the drawee if the check was paid in good faith.

4. Subsection (b) differs from former Section 3-406 in that it adopts a concept of comparative negligence. If the person precluded under subsection (a) proves that the person asserting the preclusion failed to exercise ordinary care and that failure substantially contributed to the loss, the loss may be allocated between the two parties on a comparative negligence basis. In the case of a forged indorsement the litigation is usually between the payee of the check and the depositary bank that took the check for collection. An example is a case like Case # 1 of Comment 3 to Section 3-405. If the trier of fact finds that Employer failed to exercise ordinary care in safeguarding the check and that the failure substantially contributed to the making of the forged indorsement, subsection (a) of Section 3-406 applies. If Employer brings an action for conversion against the depositary bank that took the checks from the forger, the depositary bank could assert the preclusion under subsection (a). But suppose the forger opened an account in the depositary bank in a name identical to that of Employer, the payee of the check, and then deposited the check in the account. Subsection (b) may apply. There may be an issue whether the depositary bank should have been alerted to possible fraud when a new account was opened for a corporation shortly before a very large check payable to a payee with the same name is deposited. Circumstances surrounding the opening of the account may have suggested that the corporation to which the check was payable may not be the same as the corporation for which the account was opened. If the trier of fact finds that collecting the check under these circumstances was a failure to exercise ordinary care, it could allocate the loss between the depositary bank and Employer, the payee.

Additional References:

3-405 Comment 1
3-412 Comment 3
3-417 Comment 6
4-406 Comment 4, 5

Section 3-407. Alteration

(a) "Alteration" means (i) an unauthorized change in an instrument that purports to modify in any respect the obligation of a party, or (ii) an unauthorized addition of words or numbers or other change to an incomplete instrument relating to the obligation of a party.

(b) Except as provided in subsection (c), an alteration fraudulently made discharges a party whose obligation is affected by the alteration unless that party assents or is precluded from asserting the alteration. No other alteration discharges a party, and the instrument may be enforced according to its original terms.

(c) A payor bank or drawee paying a fraudulently altered instrument or a person taking it for value, in good faith and without notice of the alteration, may enforce rights with respect to the instrument (i) according to its original terms, or (ii) in the case of an incomplete instrument altered by unauthorized completion, according to its terms as completed.

Definitional Cross References:

"Discharge".	Section 3-601(a)
"Drawee".	Section 3-103(a)(4)
"Good Faith".	Section 1-201(b)(20), Section 3-103(a)(6)
"Incomplete Instrument".	Section 3-115
"Instrument".	Section 3-104(b)
"Notice".	Section 1-202(a)
"Party".	Section 3-103(a)(10)
"Payor Bank".	Section 4-105(3)
"Person".	Section 1-201(b)(27)
"Value, Taken for".	Section 3-303(a)

Official Comment

1. This provision restates former Section 3-407. Former Section 3-407 defined a "material" alteration as any alteration that changes the contract of the parties in any respect. Revised Section 3-407 refers to such a change as an alteration. As under subsection (2) of former Section 3-407, discharge because of alteration occurs only in the case of an alteration fraudulently made. There is no discharge if a blank is filled in the honest belief that it is authorized or if a change is made with a benevolent motive such as a desire to give the obligor the benefit of a lower interest rate. Changes favorable to the obligor are unlikely to be made with any fraudulent intent, but if such an intent is found the alteration may operate as a discharge.

Discharge is a personal defense of the party whose obligation is modified and anyone whose obligation is not affected is not discharged. But if an alteration discharges a party there is also discharge of any party having a right of recourse against the discharged party because the obligation of the party with the right of recourse is affected by the alteration. Assent to the alteration given before or after it is made will prevent the party from asserting the discharge. The phrase "or is precluded from asserting the alteration" in subsection (b) recognizes the possibility of an estoppel or other ground barring the defense which does not rest on assent.

2. Under subsection (c) a person paying a fraudulently altered instrument or taking it for value, in good faith and without notice of the alteration, is not affected by a discharge under subsection (b). The person paying or taking the instrument may assert rights with respect to the instrument according to its original terms or, in the case of an incomplete instrument that is altered by unauthorized completion, according to its terms as completed. If blanks are filled or an incomplete instrument is otherwise completed, subsection (c) places the loss upon the party who left the instrument incomplete by permitting enforcement in its completed form. This result is intended even though the instrument was stolen from the issuer and completed after the theft.

Additional References:

3-115 Comment 3

4-401 Comment 4

Section 3-408. Drawee Not Liable on Unaccepted Draft

A check or other draft does not of itself operate as an assignment of funds in the hands of the drawee available for its payment, and the drawee is not liable on the instrument until the drawee accepts it.

Definitional Cross References:

"Acceptance".	Section 3-409(a)
"Check".	Section 3-104(f)
"Draft".	Section 3-104(e)
"Drawee".	Section 3-103(a)(4)
"Instrument".	Section 3-104(b)

Official Comment

1. This section is a restatement of former Section 3-409(1). Subsection (2) of former Section 3-409 is deleted as misleading and superfluous. Comment 3 says of subsection (2): "It is intended to make it clear that this section does not in any way affect any liability which may arise apart from the instrument." In reality subsection (2) did not make anything clear and was a source of confusion. If all it meant was that a bank that has not certified a check may engage in other conduct that might make it liable to a holder, it stated the obvious and was superfluous. Section 1-103 is adequate to cover those cases.

2. Liability with respect to drafts may arise under other law. For example, Section 4-302 imposes liability on a payor bank for late return of an item.

Additional References:

3-409 Comment 4

3-414 Comment 4

Section 3-409. Acceptance of Draft; Certified Check

(a) "Acceptance" means the drawee's signed agreement to pay a draft as presented. It must be written on the draft and may consist of the drawee's signature alone. Acceptance may be made at any time and becomes effective when notification pursuant to instructions is given or the accepted draft is delivered for the purpose of giving rights on the acceptance to any person.

(b) A draft may be accepted although it has not been signed by the drawer, is otherwise incomplete, is overdue, or has been dishonored.

(c) If a draft is payable at a fixed period after sight and the acceptor fails to date the acceptance, the holder may complete the acceptance by supplying a date in good faith.

(d) "Certified check" means a check accepted by the bank on which it is drawn. Acceptance may be made as stated in subsection (a) or by a writing on the check which indicates that the check is certified. The drawee of a check has no obligation to certify the check, and refusal to certify is not dishonor of the check.

Definitional Cross References:

"Acceptor".	Section 3-103(a)(1)
"Agreement".	Section 1-201(b)(3)
"Bank".	Section 1-201(b)(4)
"Check".	Section 3-104(f)
"Delivery".	Section 1-201(b)(15)
"Dishonor".	Section 3-502
"Draft".	Section 3-104(e)
"Drawee".	Section 3-103(a)(4)
"Drawer".	Section 3-103(a)(5)
"Good Faith".	Section 1-201(b)(20), Section 3-103(a)(6)
"Holder".	Section 1-201(b)(21)
"Incomplete Instrument".	Section 3-115
"Notification, Gives".	Section 1-202(d)
"Overdue".	Section 3-304
"Payable at Sight".	Section 3-108(a)
"Person".	Section 1-201(b)(27)
"Presentment".	Section 3-501(a)
"Signed".	Section 1-201(b)(37)
"Writing".	Section 1-201(b)(43)

Official Comment

1. The first three subsections of Section 3-409 are a restatement of former Section 3-410. Subsection (d) adds a definition of certified check which is a type of accepted draft.

2. Subsection (a) states the generally recognized rule that the mere signature of the drawee on the instrument is a sufficient acceptance. Customarily the signature is written vertically across the face of the instrument, but since the drawee has no reason to sign for any other purpose a signature in any other place, even on the back of the instrument, is sufficient. It need not be accompanied by such words as "Accepted," "Certified," or "Good." It must not, however, bear any words indicating an intent to refuse to honor the draft. The last sentence of subsection (a) states the generally recognized rule that an acceptance written on the draft takes effect when the drawee notifies the holder or gives notice according to instructions.

3. The purpose of subsection (c) is to provide a definite date of payment if none appears on the instrument. An undated acceptance of a draft payable "thirty days after sight" is incomplete. Unless the acceptor writes in a different date the holder is authorized to complete the acceptance according to the terms of the draft by supplying a date of acceptance. Any date supplied by the holder is effective if made in good faith.

4. The last sentence of subsection (d) states the generally recognized rule that in the absence of agreement a bank is under no obligation to certify a check. A check is a demand instrument calling for payment rather than acceptance. The bank may be liable for breach of any agreement with the drawer, the holder, or any other person by which it undertakes to certify. Its liability is not on the instrument, since the drawee is not so liable until acceptance. Section 3-408. Any liability is for breach of the separate agreement.

Section 3-410. Acceptance Varying Draft

(a) If the terms of a drawee's acceptance vary from the terms of the draft as presented, the holder may refuse the acceptance and treat the draft as dishonored. In that case, the drawee may cancel the acceptance.

(b) The terms of a draft are not varied by an acceptance to pay at a particular bank or place in the United States, unless the acceptance states that the draft is to be paid only at that bank or place.

(c) If the holder assents to an acceptance varying the terms of a draft, the obligation of each drawer and indorser that does not expressly assent to the acceptance is discharged.

Definitional Cross References:

"Acceptance".	Section 3-409(a)
"Bank".	Section 1-201(b)(4)
"Discharge".	Section 3-601(a)
"Dishonor".	Section 3-502
"Draft".	Section 3-104(e)
"Drawee".	Section 3-103(a)(4)
"Drawer".	Section 3-103(a)(5)
"Holder".	Section 1-201(b)(21)
"Indorser".	Section 3-204(b)

Official Comment

1. This section is a restatement of former Section 3-412. It applies to conditional acceptances, acceptances for part of the amount, acceptances to pay at a different time from that required by the draft, or to the acceptance of less than all of the drawees. It applies to any other engagement changing the essential terms of the draft. If the drawee makes a varied acceptance the holder may either reject it or assent to it. The holder may reject by insisting on acceptance of the draft as presented. Refusal by the drawee to accept the draft as presented is dishonor. In that event the drawee is not bound by the varied acceptance and is entitled to have it canceled.

If the holder assents to the varied acceptance, the drawee's obligation as acceptor is according to the terms of the varied acceptance. Under subsection (c) the effect of the holder's assent is to discharge any drawer or indorser who does not also assent. The assent of the drawer or indorser must be affirmatively expressed. Mere failure to object within a reasonable time is not assent which will prevent the discharge.

2. Under subsection (b) an acceptance does not vary from the terms of the draft if it provides for payment at any particular bank or place in the United States unless the acceptance states that the draft is to be paid only at such bank or place. Section 3-501(b)(1) states that if an instrument is payable at a bank in the United States presentment must be made at the place of payment (Section 3-111) which in this case is at the designated bank.

Section 3-411. Refusal to Pay Cashier's Checks, Teller's Checks, and Certified Checks

(a) In this section, "obligated bank" means the acceptor of a certified check or the issuer of a cashier's check or teller's check bought from the issuer.

(b) If the obligated bank wrongfully (i) refuses to pay a cashier's check or certified check, (ii) stops payment of a teller's check, or (iii) refuses to pay a dishonored teller's check, the person asserting the right to enforce the check is entitled to compensation for expenses and loss of interest resulting from the nonpayment and may recover consequential damages if the obligated bank refuses to pay after receiving notice of particular circumstances giving rise to the damages.

(c) Expenses or consequential damages under subsection (b) are not recoverable if the refusal of the obligated bank to pay occurs because (i) the bank suspends payments, (ii) the obligated bank asserts a claim or defense of the bank that it has reasonable grounds to believe is available against the person entitled to enforce the instrument, (iii) the obligated bank has a reasonable doubt whether the person demanding payment is the person entitled to enforce the instrument, or (iv) payment is prohibited by law.

Definitional Cross References:

"Acceptor".	Section 3-103(a)(1)
"Bank".	Section 1-201(b)(4)
"Cashier's Check".	Section 3-104(g)
"Certified Check".	Section 3-409(d)
"Check".	Section 3-104(f)
"Dishonor".	Section 3-502
"Instrument".	Section 3-104(b)
"Issuer".	Section 3-105(c)
"Notice".	Section 1-202(a)
"Payment".	Section 3-602(a)
"Person".	Section 1-201(b)(27)
"Person Entitled to Enforce".	Section 3-301
"Stop Payment".	Section 4-403
"Suspends Payments".	Section 4-104(a)(12)
"Teller's Check".	Section 3-104(h)

Official Comment

1. In some cases a creditor may require that the debt be paid by an obligation of a bank. The debtor may comply by obtaining certification of the debtor's check, but more frequently the debtor buys from a bank a cashier's check or teller's check payable to the creditor. The check is taken by the creditor as a cash equivalent on the assumption that the bank will pay the check. Sometimes, the debtor wants to retract payment by inducing the obligated bank not to pay. The typical case involves a dispute between the parties to the transaction in which the check is given in payment. In the case of a certified check or cashier's check, the bank can safely pay the holder of the check despite notice that there may be an adverse claim to the check (Section 3-602). It is also clear that the bank that sells a teller's check has no duty to order the bank on which it is drawn not to pay it. A debtor using any of these types of checks has no right to stop payment. Nevertheless, some banks will refuse payment as an accommodation to a customer. Section 3-411 is designed to discourage this practice.

2. The term "obligated bank" refers to the issuer of the cashier's check or teller's check and the acceptor of the certified check. If the obligated bank wrongfully refuses to pay, it is liable to pay for expenses and loss of interest resulting from the refusal to pay. There is no express provision for attorney's fees, but attorney's fees are not meant to be necessarily excluded. They could be granted because they fit within the language "expenses . . . resulting from the nonpayment." In addition the bank may be liable to pay consequential damages if it has notice of the particular circumstances giving rise to the damages.

3. Subsection (c) provides that expenses or consequential damages are not recoverable if the refusal to pay is because of the reasons stated. The purpose is to limit that recovery to cases in which the bank refuses to pay even though its obligation to pay is clear and it is able to pay. Subsection (b) applies only if the refusal to honor the check is wrongful. If the bank is not obliged to pay there is no recovery. The bank may assert any claim or defense that it has, but normally the bank would not have a claim or defense. In the usual case it is a remitter that is asserting a claim to the check on the basis of a rescission of negotiation to the payee under Section 3-202. See Comment 2 to Section 3-201. The bank can assert that claim if there is compliance with Section 3-305(c), but the bank is not protected from damages under subsection (b) if the claim of the remitter is not upheld. In that case, the bank is insulated from damages only if payment is enjoined under Section 3-602(b)(1). Subsection (c)(iii) refers to cases in which the bank may have a reasonable doubt about the identity of the person demanding payment. For example, a cashier's check is payable to "Supplier Co." The person in possession of the check presents it for payment over the counter and claims to be an officer of Supplier Co. The bank may refuse payment until it has been given adequate proof that the presentment in fact is being made for Supplier Co., the person entitled to enforce the check.

Additional References:

3-602 Comment 1
4-403 Comment 4

Section 3-412. Obligation of Issuer of Note or Cashier's Check

The issuer of a note or cashier's check or other draft drawn on the drawer is obliged to pay the instrument (i) according to its terms at the time it was issued or, if not issued, at the time it first came into possession of a holder, or (ii) if the issuer signed an incomplete instrument, according to its terms when completed, to the extent stated in Sections 3-115 and 3-407. The obligation is owed to a person entitled to enforce the instrument or to an indorser who paid the instrument under Section 3-415.

Definitional Cross References:

"Cashier's Check".	Section 3-104(g)
"Draft".	Section 3-104(e)
"Drawer".	Section 3-103(a)(5)
"Holder".	Section 1-201(b)(21)
"Incomplete Instrument".	Section 3-115
"Indorser".	Section 3-204(b)
"Instrument".	Section 3-104(b)
"Issue".	Section 3-105(a)
"Issuer".	Section 3-105(c)
"Note".	Section 3-104(e)
"Person".	Section 1-201(b)(27)
"Person Entitled to Enforce".	Section 3-301
"Signed".	Section 1-201(b)(37)

Official Comment

1. The obligations of the maker, acceptor, drawer, and indorser are stated in four separate sections. Section 3-412 states the obligation of the maker of a note and is consistent with former Section 3-413(1). Section 3-412 also applies to the issuer of a cashier's check or other draft drawn on the drawer. Under former Section 3-118(a), since a cashier's check or other draft drawn on the drawer was "effective as a note," the drawer was liable under former Section 3-413(1) as a maker. Under Sections 3-103(a)(6) and 3-104(f) a cashier's check or other draft drawn on the drawer is treated as a draft to reflect common commercial usage, but the liability of the drawer is stated by Section 3-412 as being the same as that of the maker of a note rather than that of the drawer of a draft. Thus, Section 3-412 does not in substance change former law.

2. Under Section 3-105(b) nonissuance of either a complete or incomplete instrument is a defense by a maker or drawer against a person that is not a holder in due course.

3. The obligation of the maker may be modified in the case of alteration if, under Section 3-406, the maker is precluded from asserting the alteration.

4. The rule of this section is similar to the rule of Article 39 of the Convention on International Bills of Exchange and International Promissory Notes.

Additional References:

3-414 Comment 1

3-605 Comment 4

Section 3-413. Obligation of Acceptor

(a) The acceptor of a draft is obliged to pay the draft (i) according to its terms at the time it was accepted, even though the acceptance states that the draft is payable "as originally drawn" or equivalent terms, (ii) if the acceptance varies the terms of the draft, according to the terms of the draft as varied, or (iii) if the acceptance is of a draft that is an incomplete instrument, according to its terms when completed, to the extent stated in Sections 3-115 and 3-407. The obligation is owed to a person entitled to enforce the draft or to the drawer or an indorser who paid the draft under Section 3-414 or 3-415.

(b) If the certification of a check or other acceptance of a draft states the amount certified or accepted, the obligation of the acceptor is that amount. If (i) the certification or acceptance does not state an amount, (ii) the amount of the instrument is subsequently raised, and (iii) the instrument is then negotiated to a holder in due course, the obligation of the acceptor is the amount of the instrument at the time it was taken by the holder in due course.

Definitional Cross References:

"Acceptance".	Section 3-409(a)
"Acceptor".	Section 3-103(a)(1)
"Check".	Section 3-104(f)
"Draft".	Section 3-104(e)
"Drawer".	Section 3-103(a)(5)
"Holder in Due Course".	Section 3-302
"Incomplete Instrument".	Section 3-115
"Indorser".	Section 3-204(b)
"Instrument".	Section 3-104(b)
"Negotiation".	Section 3-201(a)
"Person Entitled to Enforce".	Section 3-301

Official Comment

Subsection (a) is consistent with former Section 3-413(1). Subsection (b) has primary importance with respect to certified checks. It protects the holder in due course of a certified check that was altered after certification and before negotiation to the holder in due course. A bank can avoid liability for the altered amount by stating on the check the amount the bank agrees to pay. The subsection applies to other accepted drafts as well. The rule of this section is similar to the rule of Article 41 of the Convention on International Bills of Exchange and International Promissory Notes. Articles 42 and 43 of the Convention include more detailed rules that in many respects do not have parallels in this Article.

Additional References:

3-414 Comment 4

4-404 Comment

3-605 Comment 4

Section 3-414. Obligation of Drawer.

(a) This section does not apply to cashier's checks or other drafts drawn on the drawer.

(b) If an unaccepted draft is dishonored, the drawer is obliged to pay the draft (i) according to its terms at the time it was issued or, if not issued, at the time it first came into possession of a holder, or (ii) if the drawer signed an incomplete instrument, according to its terms when completed, to the extent stated in Sections 3-115 and 3-407. The obligation is owed to a person entitled to enforce the draft or to an indorser who paid the draft under Section 3-415.

(c) If a draft is accepted by a bank, the drawer is discharged, regardless of when or by whom acceptance was obtained.

(d) If a draft is accepted and the acceptor is not a bank, the obligation of the drawer to pay the draft if the draft is dishonored by the acceptor is the same as the obligation of an indorser under Section 3-415(a) and (c).

(e) If a draft states that it is drawn "without recourse" or otherwise disclaims liability of the drawer to pay the draft, the drawer is not liable under subsection (b) to pay the draft if the draft is not a check. A disclaimer of the liability stated in subsection (b) is not effective if the draft is a check.

(f) If (i) a check is not presented for payment or given to a depositary bank for collection within 30 days after its date, (ii) the drawee suspends payments after expiration of the 30-day period without paying the check, and (iii) because of the suspension of payments, the drawer is deprived of funds maintained with the drawee to cover payment of the check, the drawer to the extent deprived of funds may discharge its obligation to pay the check by assigning to the person entitled to enforce the check the rights of the drawer against the drawee with respect to the funds.

Definitional Cross References:

"Acceptance".	Section 3-409(a)
"Acceptor".	Section 3-103(a)(1)
"Bank".	Section 1-201(b)(4)
"Cashier's Check".	Section 3-104(g)
"Check".	Section 3-104(f)
"Depositary Bank".	Section 4-105(2)
"Draft".	Section 3-104(e)
"Drawee".	Section 3-103(a)(4)
"Drawer".	Section 3-103(a)(5)
"Discharge".	Section 3-601(a)
"Dishonor".	Section 3-502
"Draft".	Section 3-104(e)
"Holder".	Section 1-201(b)(21)
"Incomplete Instrument".	Section 3-115
"Indorser".	Section 3-204(b)
"Issue".	Section 3-105(a)
"Payment".	Section 3-602(a)
"Person Entitled to Enforce".	Section 3-301
"Presentment".	Section 3-501(a)
"Signed".	Section 1-201(b)(37)
"Suspends Payments".	Section 4-104(a)(12)

Official Comment

1. Subsection (a) excludes cashier's checks because the obligation of the issuer of a cashier's check is stated in Section 3-412.

2. Subsection (b) states the obligation of the drawer on an unaccepted draft. It replaces former Section 3-413(2). The requirement under former Article 3 of notice of dishonor or protest has been eliminated. Under revised Article 3, notice of dishonor is necessary only with respect to indorser's liability. The liability of the drawer of an unaccepted draft is treated as a primary liability. Under former Section 3-102(1)(d) the term "secondary party" was used to refer to a drawer or indorser. The quoted term is not used in revised Article 3. The effect of a draft drawn without recourse is stated in subsection (e).

3. Under subsection (c) the drawer is discharged of liability on a draft accepted by a bank regardless of when acceptance was obtained. This changes former Section 3-411(1) which provided that the drawer is discharged only if the holder obtains acceptance. Holders that have a bank obligation do not normally rely on the drawer to guarantee the bank's solvency. A holder can obtain protection against the insolvency of a bank acceptor by a specific guaranty of payment by the drawer or by obtaining an indorsement by the drawer. Section 3-205(d).

4. Subsection (d) states the liability of the drawer if a draft is accepted by a drawee other than a bank and the acceptor dishonors. The drawer of an unaccepted draft is the only party liable on the instrument. The drawee has no liability on the draft. Section 3-408. When the draft is accepted, the obligations change. The drawee, as acceptor, becomes primarily liable and the drawer's liability is that of a person secondarily liable as a guarantor of payment. The drawer's liability is identical to that of an indorser, and subsection (d) states the drawer's liability that way. The drawer is liable to pay the person entitled to enforce the draft or any indorser that pays pursuant to Section 3-415. The drawer in this case is discharged if notice of dishonor is required by Section 3-503 and is not given in compliance with that section. A drawer that pays has a right of recourse against the acceptor. Section 3-413(a).

5. Subsection (e) does not permit the drawer of a check to avoid liability under subsection (b) by drawing the check without recourse. There is no legitimate purpose served by issuing a check on which nobody is liable. Drawing without recourse is effective to disclaim liability of the drawer if the draft is not a check. Suppose, in a documentary sale, Seller draws a draft on Buyer for the price of goods shipped to Buyer. The draft is payable upon delivery to the drawee of an order bill of lading covering the goods. Seller delivers the draft with the bill of lading to Finance Company that is named as payee of the draft. If Seller draws without recourse Finance Company takes the risk that Buyer will dishonor. If Buyer dishonors, Finance Company has no recourse against Seller but it can obtain reimbursement by selling the goods which it controls through the bill of lading.

6. Subsection (f) is derived from former Section 3-502(1)(b). It is designed to protect the drawer of a check against loss resulting from suspension of payments by the drawee bank when the holder of the check delays collection of the check. For example, X writes a check payable to Y for $1,000. The check is covered by funds in X's account in the drawee bank. Y delays initiation of collection of the check for more than 30 days after the date of the check. The drawee bank suspends payments after the 30-day period and before the check is presented for payment. If the $1,000 of funds in X's account have not been withdrawn, X has a claim for those funds against the drawee bank and, if subsection (e) were not in effect, X would be liable to Y on the check because the check was dishonored. Section 3-502(e). If the suspension of payments by the drawee bank will result in payment to X of less than the full amount of the $1,000 in the account or if there is a significant delay in payment to X, X will suffer a loss which would not have been suffered if Y had promptly initiated collection of the check. In most cases, X will not suffer any loss because of the existence of federal bank deposit insurance that covers accounts up to $100,000. Thus, subsection (e) has relatively little importance. There might be some cases, however, in which the account is not fully insured because it exceeds $100,000 or because the account doesn't qualify for deposit insurance. Subsection (f) retains the phrase "deprived of funds maintained with the drawee" appearing in former Section 3-502(1)(b). The quoted phrase applies if the suspension of payments by the drawee prevents the drawer from receiving the benefit of funds which would have paid the check if the holder had been timely in initiating collection. Thus, any significant delay in obtaining full payment of the funds is a deprivation of funds. The drawer can discharge drawer's liability by assigning rights against the drawee with respect to the funds to the holder.

7. The obligation of the drawer under this section is similar to the obligation of the drawer under Article 38 of the Convention on International Bills of Exchange and International Promissory Notes.

Additional References:

3-310 Comment 4
3-415 Comment 3
3-418 Comment 2
3-502 Comment 1
3-503 Comment 1
4-403 Comment 7
3-605 Comment 3, 4

Section 3-415. Obligation of Indorser

(a) Subject to subsections (b), (c), (d), (e) and to Section 3-419(d), if an instrument is dishonored, an indorser is obliged to pay the amount due on the instrument (i) according to the terms of the instrument at the time it was indorsed, or (ii) if the indorser indorsed an incomplete instrument, according to its terms when completed, to the extent stated in Sections 3-115 and 3-407. The obligation of the indorser is owed to a person entitled to enforce the instrument or to a subsequent indorser who paid the instrument under this section.

(b) If an indorsement states that it is made "without recourse" or otherwise disclaims liability of the indorser, the indorser is not liable under subsection (a) to pay the instrument.

(c) If notice of dishonor of an instrument is required by Section 3-503 and notice of dishonor complying with that section is not given to an indorser, the liability of the indorser under subsection (a) is discharged.

(d) If a draft is accepted by a bank after an indorsement is made, the liability of the indorser under subsection (a) is discharged.

(e) If an indorser of a check is liable under subsection (a) and the check is not presented for payment, or given to a depositary bank for collection, within 30 days after the day the indorsement was made, the liability of the indorser under subsection (a) is discharged.

Definitional Cross References:

"Bank".	Section 1-201(b)(4)
"Check".	Section 3-104(f)
"Depositary Bank".	Section 4-105(2)
"Discharge".	Section 3-601(a)
"Dishonor".	Section 3-502
"Draft".	Section 3-104(e)
"Incomplete Instrument".	Section 3-115
"Indorser".	Section 3-204(b)
"Instrument".	Section 3-104(b)
"Notice of Dishonor".	Section 3-503
"Payment".	Section 3-602(a)
"Person Entitled to Enforce".	Section 3-301
"Presentment".	Section 3-501(a)

Official Comment

1. Subsections (a) and (b) restate the substance of former Section 3-414(1). Subsection (2) of former Section 3-414 has been dropped because it is superfluous. Although notice of dishonor is not mentioned in subsection (a), it must be given in some cases to charge an indorser. It is covered in subsection (c). Regulation CC § 229.35(b) provides that a bank handling a check for collection or return is liable to a bank that subsequently handles the check to the extent the latter bank does not receive payment for the check. This liability applies whether or not the bank incurring the liability indorsed the check.

2. Section 3-503 states when notice of dishonor is required and how it must be given. If required notice of dishonor is not given in compliance with Section 3-503, subsection (c) of Section 3-415 states that the effect is to discharge the indorser's obligation.

3. Subsection (d) is similar in effect to Section 3-414(c) if the draft is accepted by a bank after the indorsement is made. See Comment 3 to Section 3-414. If a draft is accepted by a bank before the indorsement is made, the indorser incurs the obligation stated in subsection (a).

4. Subsection (e) modifies former Sections 3-503(2)(b) and 3-502(1)(a) by stating a 30-day rather than a seven-day period, and stating it as an absolute rather than a presumptive period.

5. As stated in subsection (a), the obligation of an indorser to pay the amount due on the instrument is generally owed not only to a person entitled to enforce the instrument but also to a subsequent indorser who paid the instrument. But if the prior indorser and the subsequent indorser are both anomalous indorsers, this rule does not apply. In that case, Section 3-116 applies. Under Section 3-116(a), the anomalous indorsers are jointly and severally liable and if either pays the instrument the indorser who pays has a right of contribution against the other. Section 3-116(b). The right to contribution in Section 3-116(b) is subject to "agreement of the affected parties." Suppose the subsequent indorser can prove an agreement with the prior indorser under which the prior indorser agreed to treat the subsequent indorser as a guarantor of the obligation of the prior indorser. Rights of the two indorsers between themselves would be governed by the agreement. Under suretyship law, the subsequent indorser under such an agreement is referred to as a subsurety. Under the agreement, if the subsequent indorser pays the instrument there is a right to reimbursement from the prior indorser; if the prior indorser pays the instrument, there is no right of recourse against the subsequent indorser. See PEB Commentary No. 11.

6. The rule of this section is similar to the rule of Article 44 of the Convention on International Bills of Exchange and International Promissory Notes.

Additional References:

3-302 Comment 3
3-310 Comment 3
3-419 Comment 4
3-502 Comment 1
3-605 Comment 3, 4

Section 3-416. Transfer Warranties

(a) A person who transfers an instrument for consideration warrants to the transferee and, if the transfer is by indorsement, to any subsequent transferee that:

(1) the warrantor is a person entitled to enforce the instrument;

(2) all signatures on the instrument are authentic and authorized;

(3) the instrument has not been altered;

(4) the instrument is not subject to a defense or claim in recoupment of any party which can be asserted against the warrantor;

(5) the warrantor has no knowledge of any insolvency proceeding commenced with respect to the maker or acceptor or, in the case of an unaccepted draft, the drawer; and

(6) with respect to a remotely-created consumer item, that the person on whose account the item is drawn authorized the issuance of the item in the amount for which the item is drawn.

(b) A person to whom the warranties under subsection (a) are made and who took the instrument in good faith may recover from the warrantor as damages for breach of warranty an amount equal to the loss suffered as a result of the breach, but not more than the amount of the instrument plus expenses and loss of interest incurred as a result of the breach.

(c) The warranties stated in subsection (a) cannot be disclaimed with respect to checks. Unless notice of a claim for breach of warranty is given to the warrantor within 30 days after the claimant has reason to know of the breach and the identity of the warrantor, the liability of the warrantor under subsection (b) is discharged to the extent of any loss caused by the delay in giving notice of the claim.

(d) A [cause of action] for breach of warranty under this section accrues when the claimant has reason to know of the breach.

Definitional Cross References:

"Acceptance".	Section 3-409(a)
"Acceptor".	Section 3-103(a)(1)
"Action".	Section 1-201(b)(1)
"Alteration".	Section 3-407
"Check".	Section 3-104(f)
"Discharge".	Section 3-601(a)
"Draft".	Section 3-104(e)
"Drawer".	Section 3-103(a)(5)
"Good Faith".	Section 1-201(b)(20), Section 3-103(a)(6)
"Indorsement".	Section 3-204(a)
"Insolvency Proceeding".	Section 1-201(b)(22)
"Instrument".	Section 3-104(b)
"Maker".	Section 3-1-039a)(7)
"Notice".	Section 1-202(a)
"Party".	Section 3-103(a)(10)
"Person".	Section 1-201(b)(27)
"Person Entitled to Enforce".	Section 3-301
"Remotely-created consumer item".	Section 3-103(a)(16)
"Signed".	Section 1-201(b)(37)
"Transfer".	Section 3-203(a)

Official Comment

1. Subsection (a) is taken from subsection (2) of former Section 3-417. Subsections (3) and (4) of former Section 3-417 are deleted. Warranties under subsection (a) in favor of the immediate transferee apply to all persons who transfer an instrument for consideration whether or not the transfer is accompanied by indorsement. Any consideration sufficient to support a simple contract will support those warranties. If there is an indorsement the warranty runs with the instrument and the remote holder may sue the indorser-warrantor directly and thus avoid a multiplicity of suits.

2. Since the purpose of transfer (Section 3-203(a)) is to give the transferee the right to enforce the instrument, subsection (a)(1) is a warranty that the transferor is a person entitled to enforce the instrument (Section 3-301). Under Section 3-203(b) transfer gives the transferee any right of the transferor to enforce the instrument. Subsection (a)(1) is in effect a warranty that there are no unauthorized or missing indorsements that prevent the transferor from making the transferee a person entitled to enforce the instrument.

3. The rationale of subsection (a)(4) is that the transferee does not undertake to buy an instrument that is not enforceable in whole or in part, unless there is a contrary agreement. Even if the transferee takes as a holder in due course who takes free of the defense or claim in recoupment, the warranty gives the transferee the option of proceeding against the transferor rather than litigating with the obligor on the instrument the issue of the holder-in-due-course status of the transferee. Subsection (3) of former Section 3-417 which limits this warranty is deleted. The rationale is that while the purpose of a "no recourse" indorsement is to avoid a guaranty of payment, the indorsement does not clearly indicate an intent to disclaim warranties.

4. Under subsection (a)(5) the transferor does not warrant against difficulties of collection, impairment of the credit of the obligor or even insolvency. The transferee is expected to determine such questions before taking the obligation. If an insolvency proceeding as defined in Section 1-201(b)(22) has been instituted against the party who is expected to pay and the transferor knows it, the concealment of that fact amounts to a fraud upon the transferee, and the warranty against knowledge of such proceedings is provided accordingly.

5. Transfer warranties may be disclaimed with respect to any instrument except a check. Between the immediate parties disclaimer may be made by agreement. In the case of an indorser, disclaimer of transferor's liability, to be effective, must appear in the indorsement with words such as "without warranties" or some other specific reference to warranties. But in the case of a check, subsection (c) of Section 3-416 provides that transfer warranties cannot be disclaimed at all. In the check collection process the banking system relies on these warranties.

6. Subsection (b) states the measure of damages for breach of warranty. There is no express provision for attorney's fees, but attorney's fees are not meant to be necessarily excluded. They could be granted because they fit within the phrase "expenses . . . incurred as a result of the breach." The intention is to leave to other state law the issue as to when attorney's fees are recoverable.

7. Since the traditional term "cause of action" may have been replaced in some states by "claim for relief" or some equivalent term, the words "cause of action" in subsection (d) have been bracketed to indicate that the words may be replaced by an appropriate substitute to conform to local practice.

8. Subsection (a)(6) is based on a number of nonuniform amendments designed to address concerns about certain kinds of check fraud. The provision implements a limited rejection of *Price v. Neal,* 97 Eng. Rep. 871 (K.B. 1762), so that in certain circumstances (those involving remotely-created consumer items) the payor bank can use a warranty claim to absolve itself of responsibility for honoring an unauthorized item. The provision rests on the premise that monitoring by depositary banks can control this type of fraud more effectively than any practices readily available to payor banks. The provision expressly includes both the case in which the consumer does not authorize the item at all and also the case in which the consumer authorizes the item but in an amount different from the amount in which the item is drawn. Similar provisions appear in Sections 3-417, 4-207, and 4-208.

The provision supplements applicable federal law, which requires telemarketers who submit instruments for payment to obtain the customer's "express verifiable authorization," which may be either in writing or tape recorded and must be made available upon request to the customer's bank. Federal Trade Commission's Telemarketing Sales Rule, 16 C.F.R. § 310.3(a)(3), implementing the Telemarketing and Consumer Fraud and Abuse Prevention Act, 15 U.S.C. §§ 6101-6108. Some states also have consumer-protection laws governing authorization of instruments in telemarketing transactions. See, e.g., 9 Vt. Stat. Ann. § 2464.

9. Article 45 of the Convention on International Bills of Exchange and International Promissory Notes includes warranties that are similar (except for the warranty in subsection (a)(6)).

Additional References:

3-305 Comment 5
3-417 Comment 4
4-207 Comment 1

Editors' Note: Responding to a variety of non-uniform amendments that dealt with responsibility for unauthorized telephone-generated checks, 2002 amendments to Sections 3-416, 3-417. 4-207, and 4-208 added transfer and presentment warranties that such items have been authorized in the amounts for which they are drawn. Subsequent similar revisions to Regulation CC have made those provisions nationally uniform.

Section 3-417. Presentment Warranties

(a) If an unaccepted draft is presented to the drawee for payment or acceptance and the drawee pays or accepts the draft, (i) the person obtaining payment or acceptance, at the time of presentment, and (ii) a previous transferor of the draft, at the time of transfer, warrant to the drawee making payment or accepting the draft in good faith that:

(1) the warrantor is, or was, at the time the warrantor transferred the draft, a person entitled to enforce the draft or authorized to obtain payment or acceptance of the draft on behalf of a person entitled to enforce the draft;

(2) the draft has not been altered;

(3) the warrantor has no knowledge that the signature of the drawer of the draft is unauthorized; and

(4) with respect to any remotely-created consumer item, that the person on whose account the item is drawn authorized the issuance of the item in the amount for which the item is drawn.

(b) A drawee making payment may recover from any warrantor damages for breach of warranty equal to the amount paid by the drawee less the amount the drawee received or is entitled to receive from the drawer because of the payment. In addition, the drawee is entitled to compensation for expenses and loss of interest resulting from the breach. The right of the drawee to recover damages under this subsection is not affected by any failure of the drawee to exercise ordinary care in making payment. If the drawee accepts the draft, breach of warranty is a defense to the obligation of the acceptor. If the acceptor makes payment with respect to the draft, the acceptor is entitled to recover from any warrantor for breach of warranty the amounts stated in this subsection.

(c) If a drawee asserts a claim for breach of warranty under subsection (a) based on an unauthorized indorsement of the draft or an alteration of the draft, the warrantor may defend by proving that the indorsement is effective under Section 3-404 or 3-405 or the drawer is precluded under Section 3-406 or 4-406 from asserting against the drawee the unauthorized indorsement or alteration.

(d) If (i) a dishonored draft is presented for payment to the drawer or an indorser or (ii) any other instrument is presented for payment to a party obliged to pay the instrument, and (iii) payment is received, the following rules apply:

(1) The person obtaining payment and a prior transferor of the instrument warrant to the person making payment in good faith that the warrantor is, or was, at the time the warrantor transferred the instrument, a person entitled to enforce the instrument or authorized to obtain payment on behalf of a person entitled to enforce the instrument.

(2) The person making payment may recover from any warrantor for breach of warranty an amount equal to the amount paid plus expenses and loss of interest resulting from the breach.

(e) The warranties stated in subsections (a) and (d) cannot be disclaimed with respect to checks. Unless notice of a claim for breach of warranty is given to the warrantor within 30 days after the claimant has reason to know of the breach and the identity of the warrantor, the liability of the warrantor under subsection (b) or (d) is discharged to the extent of any loss caused by the delay in giving notice of the claim.

(f) A [cause of action] for breach of warranty under this section accrues when the claimant has reason to know of the breach.

Definitional Cross References:

"Acceptance".	Section 3-409(a)
"Acceptor".	Section 3-103(a)(1)
"Action".	Section 1-201(b)(1)
"Alteration".	Section 3-407
"Check".	Section 3-104(f)
"Discharge".	Section 3-601(a)
"Dishonor".	Section 3-502
"Draft".	Section 3-104(e)
"Drawee".	Section 3-103(a)(4)
"Drawer".	Section 3-103(a)(5)
"Good Faith".	Section 1-201(b)(20), Section 3-103(a)(6)
"Indorsement".	Section 3-204(a)
"Indorser".	Section 3-204(b)
"Instrument".	Section 3-104(b)
"Knowledge".	Section 1-202(b)
"Notice".	Section 1-202(a)
"Ordinary Care".	Section 3-103(a)(9)
"Party".	Section 3-103(a)(10)
"Payment".	Section 3-602(a)
"Person".	Section 1-201(b)(27)
"Person Entitled to Enforce".	Section 3-301
"Presentment".	Section 3-501(a)
"Remotely-created consumer item".	Section 3-103(a)(16)
"Signed".	Section 1-201(b)(37)
"Transfer".	Section 3-203(a)

Official Comment

1. This section replaces subsection (1) of former Section 3-417. The former provision was difficult to understand because it purported to state in one subsection all warranties given to any person paying any instrument. The result was a provision replete with exceptions that could not be readily understood except after close scrutiny of the language. In revised Section 3-417, presentment warranties made to drawees of uncertified checks and other unaccepted drafts are stated in subsection (a). All other presentment warranties are stated in subsection (d).

2. Subsection (a) states three warranties. Subsection (a)(1) in effect is a warranty that there are no unauthorized or missing indorsements. "Person entitled to enforce" is defined in Section 3-301. Subsection (a)(2) is a warranty that there is no alteration. Subsection (a)(3) is a warranty of no knowledge that there is a forged drawer's signature. Subsection (a) states that the warranties are made to the drawee and subsections (b) and (c) identify the drawee as the person entitled to recover for breach of warranty. There is no warranty made to the drawer under subsection (a) when presentment is made to the drawee. Warranty to the drawer is governed by subsection (d) and that applies only when presentment for payment is made to the drawer with respect to a dishonored draft. In *Sun 'N Sand, Inc. v. United California Bank,* 582 P.2d 920 (Cal.1978), the court held that under former Section 3-417(1) a warranty was made to the drawer of a check when the check was presented to the drawee for payment. The result in that case is rejected.

3. Subsection (a)(1) retains the rule that the drawee does not admit the authenticity of indorsements and subsection (a)(3) retains the rule of *Price v. Neal,* 3 Burr. 1354 (1762), that the drawee takes the risk that the drawer's signature is unauthorized unless the person presenting the draft has knowledge that the drawer's signature is unauthorized. Under subsection (a)(3) the warranty of no knowledge that the drawer's signature is unauthorized is also given by prior transferors of the draft.

4. Subsection (d) applies to presentment for payment in all cases not covered by subsection (a). It applies to presentment of notes and accepted drafts to any party obliged to pay the instrument, including an indorser, and to presentment of dishonored drafts if made to the drawer or an indorser. In cases covered by subsection (d), there is only one warranty and it is the same as that stated in subsection (a)(1). There are no warranties comparable to subsections (a)(2) and (a)(3) because they are appropriate only in the case of presentment to the drawee of an unaccepted draft. With respect to presentment of an accepted draft to the acceptor, there is no warranty with respect to alteration or knowledge that the signature of the drawer is unauthorized. Those warranties were made to the drawee when the draft was presented for acceptance (Section 3-417(a)(2) and (3)) and breach of that warranty is a defense to the obligation of the drawee as acceptor to pay the draft. If the drawee pays the accepted draft the drawee may recover the payment from any warrantor who was in breach of warranty when the draft was accepted. Section 3-417(b). Thus, there is no necessity for these warranties to be repeated when the accepted draft is presented for payment. Former Section 3-417(1)(b)(iii) and (c)(iii) are not included in revised Section 3-417 because they are unnecessary. Former Section 3-417(1)(c)(iv) is not included because it is also unnecessary. The acceptor should know what the terms of the draft were at the time acceptance was made.

If presentment is made to the drawer or maker, there is no necessity for a warranty concerning the signature of that person or with respect to alteration. If presentment is made to an indorser, the indorser had itself warranted authenticity of signatures and that the instrument was not altered. Section 3-416(a)(2) and (3).

5. The measure of damages for breach of warranty under subsection (a) is stated in subsection (b). There is no express provision for attorney's fees, but attorney's fees are not meant to be necessarily excluded. They could be granted because they fit within the language "expenses . . . resulting from the breach." Subsection (b) provides that the right of the drawee to recover for breach of warranty is not affected by a failure of the drawee to exercise ordinary care in paying the draft. This provision follows the result reached under former Article 3 in *Hartford Accident & Indemnity Co. v. First Pennsylvania Bank,* 859 F.2d 295 (3d Cir. 1988).

6. Subsection (c) applies to checks and other unaccepted drafts. It gives to the warrantor the benefit of rights that the drawee has against the drawer under Section 3-404, 3-405, 3-406, or 4-406. If the drawer's conduct contributed to a loss from forgery or alteration, the drawee should not be allowed to shift the loss from the drawer to the warrantor.

7. The first sentence of subsection (e) recognizes that checks are normally paid by automated means and that payor banks rely on warranties in making payment. Thus, it is not appropriate to allow disclaimer or warranties appearing on checks that normally will not be examined by the payor bank. The second sentence requires a breach of warranty claim to be asserted within 30 days after the drawee learns of the breach and the identity of the warrantor.

8. Since the traditional term "cause of action" may have been replaced in some states by "claim for relief" or some equivalent term, the words "cause of action" in subsection (f) have been bracketed to indicate that the words may be replaced by an appropriate substitute to conform to local practice.

9. For discussion of subsection (a)(4), see Comment 8 to Section 3-416.

Additional References:
3-305 Comment 2
3-404 Comment 2, 3
3-405 Comment 3
3-420 Comment 1
4-208 Comment 1
3-416 Comment 8

Editors' Note: Responding to a variety of non-uniform amendments that dealt with responsibility for unauthorized telephone-generated checks, 2002 amendments to Sections 3-416, 3-417. 4-207, and 4-208 added transfer and presentment warranties that such items have been authorized in the amounts for which they are drawn. Subsequent similar revisions to Regulation CC have made those provisions nationally uniform.

Section 3-418. Payment or Acceptance by Mistake

(a) Except as provided in subsection (c), if the drawee of a draft pays or accepts the draft and the drawee acted on the mistaken belief that (i) payment of the draft had not been stopped pursuant to Section 4-403 or (ii) the signature of the drawer of the draft was authorized, the drawee may recover the amount of the draft from the person to whom or for whose benefit payment was made or, in the case of acceptance, may revoke the acceptance. Rights of the drawee under this subsection are not affected by failure of the drawee to exercise ordinary care in paying or accepting the draft.

(b) Except as provided in subsection (c), if an instrument has been paid or accepted by mistake and the case is not covered by subsection (a), the person paying or accepting may, to the extent permitted by the law governing mistake and restitution, (i) recover the payment from the person to whom or for whose benefit payment was made or (ii) in the case of acceptance, may revoke the acceptance.

(c) The remedies provided by subsection (a) or (b) may not be asserted against a person who took the instrument in good faith and for value or who in good faith changed position in reliance on the payment or acceptance. This subsection does not limit remedies provided by Section 3-417 or 4-407.

(d) Notwithstanding Section 4-215, if an instrument is paid or accepted by mistake and the payor or acceptor recovers payment or revokes acceptance under subsection (a) or (b), the instrument is deemed not to have been paid or accepted and is treated as dishonored, and the person from whom payment is recovered has rights as a person entitled to enforce the dishonored instrument.

Definitional Cross References:

"Acceptance".	Section 3-409(a)
"Acceptor".	Section 3-103(a)(1)
"Dishonor".	Section 3-502
"Draft".	Section 3-104(e)
"Drawee".	Section 3-103(a)(4)
"Drawer".	Section 3-103(a)(5)
"Good Faith".	Section 1-201(b)(20), Section 3-103(a)(6)
"Instrument".	Section 3-104(b)
"Ordinary Care".	Section 3-103(a)(9)
"Payment".	Section 3-602(a)
"Person".	Section 1-201(b)(27)
"Person Entitled to Enforce".	Section 3-301
"Signed".	Section 1-201(b)(37)
"Stop Payment".	Section 4-403
"Value, Taken for".	Section 3-303(a)

Official Comment

1. This section covers payment or acceptance by mistake and replaces former Section 3-418. Under former Article 3, the remedy of a drawee that paid or accepted a draft by mistake was based on the law of mistake and restitution, but that remedy was not specifically stated. It was provided by Section 1-103. Former Section 3-418 was simply a limitation on the unstated remedy under the law of mistake and restitution. Under revised Article 3, Section 3-418 specifically states the right of restitution in subsections (a) and (b). Subsection (a) allows restitution in the two most common cases in which the problem is presented: payment or acceptance of forged checks and checks on which the drawer has stopped payment. If the drawee acted under a mistaken belief that the check was not forged or had not been stopped, the drawee is entitled to recover the funds paid or to revoke the acceptance whether or not the drawee acted negligently. But in each case, by virtue of subsection (c), the drawee loses the remedy if the person receiving payment or acceptance was a person who took the check in good faith and for value or who in good faith changed position in reliance on the payment or acceptance. Subsections (a) and (c) are consistent with former Section 3-418 and the rule of *Price v. Neal.* The result in the two cases covered by subsection (a) is that the drawee in most cases will not have a remedy against the person paid because there is usually a person who took the check in good faith and for value or who in good faith changed position in reliance on the payment or acceptance.

2. If a check has been paid by mistake and the payee receiving payment did not give value for the check or did not change position in reliance on the payment, the drawee bank is entitled to recover the amount of the check under subsection (a) regardless of how the check was paid. The drawee bank normally pays a check by a credit to an account of the collecting bank that presents the check for payment. The payee of the check normally receives the payment by a credit to the payee's account in the depositary bank. But in some cases the payee of the check may have received payment directly from the drawee bank by presenting the check for payment over the counter. In those cases the payee is entitled to receive cash, but the payee may prefer another form of payment such as a cashier's check or teller's check issued by the drawee bank. Suppose Seller contracted to sell goods to Buyer. The contract provided for immediate payment by Buyer and delivery of the goods 20 days after payment. Buyer paid by mailing a check for $10,000 drawn on Bank payable to Seller. The next day Buyer gave a stop payment order to Bank with respect to the check Buyer had mailed to Seller. A few days later Seller presented Buyer's check to Bank for payment over the counter and requested a cashier's check as payment. Bank issued and delivered a cashier's check for $10,000 payable to Seller. The teller failed to discover Buyer's stop order. The next day Bank discovered the mistake and immediately advised Seller of the facts. Seller refused to return the cashier's check and did not deliver any goods to Buyer.

Under Section 4-215, Buyer's check was paid by Bank at the time it delivered its cashier's check to Seller. See Comment 3 to Section 4-215. Bank is obliged to pay the cashier's check and has no defense to that obligation. The cashier's check was issued for consideration because it was issued in payment of Buyer's check. Although Bank has no defense on its cashier's check it may have a right to recover $10,000, the amount of Buyer's check, from Seller under Section 3-418(a). Bank paid Buyer's check by mistake. Seller did not give value for Buyer's check because the promise to deliver goods to Buyer was never performed. Section 3-303(a)(1). And, on these facts, Seller did not change position in reliance on the payment of Buyer's check. Thus, the first sentence of Section 3-418(c) does not apply and Seller is obliged to return $10,000 to Bank. Bank is obliged to pay the cashier's check but it has a counterclaim against Seller based on its rights under Section 3-418(a). This claim can be asserted against Seller, but it cannot be asserted against some other person with rights of a holder in due course of the cashier's check. A person without rights of a holder in due course of the cashier's check would take subject to Bank's claim against Seller because it is a claim in recoupment. Section 3-305(a)(3).

If Bank recovers from Seller under Section 3-418(a), the payment of Buyer's check is treated as unpaid and dishonored.

Section 3-418(d). One consequence is that Seller may enforce Buyer's obligation as drawer to pay the check. Section 3-414. Another consequence is that Seller's rights against Buyer on the contract of sale are also preserved. Under Section 3-310(b) Buyer's obligation to pay for the goods was suspended when Seller took Buyer's check and remains suspended until the check is either dishonored or paid. Under Section 3-310(b)(1) the obligation is discharged when the check is paid. Since Section 3-418(d) treats Buyer's check as unpaid and dishonored, Buyer's obligation is not discharged and suspension of the obligation terminates. Under Section 3-310(b)(3), Seller may enforce either the contract of sale or the check subject to defenses and claims of Buyer.

If Seller had released the goods to Buyer before learning about the stop order, Bank would have no recovery against Seller under Section 3-418(a) because Seller in that case gave value for Buyer's check. Section 3-418(c). In this case Bank's sole remedy is under Section 4-407 by subrogation.

3. Subsection (b) covers cases of payment or acceptance by mistake that are not covered by subsection (a). It directs courts to deal with those cases under the law governing mistake and restitution. Perhaps the most important class of cases that falls under subsection (b), because it is not covered by subsection (a), is that of payment by the drawee bank of a check with respect to which the bank has no duty to the drawer to pay either because the drawer has no account with the bank or because available funds in the drawer's account are not sufficient to cover the amount of the check. With respect to such a case, under Restatement of Restitution § 29, if the bank paid because of a mistaken belief that there were available funds in the drawer's account sufficient to cover the amount of the check, the bank is entitled to restitution. But § 29 is subject to Restatement of Restitution § 33 which denies restitution if the holder of the check receiving payment paid value in good faith for the check and had no reason to know that the check was paid by mistake when payment was received.

The result in some cases is clear. For example, suppose Father gives Daughter a check for $10,000 as a birthday gift. The check is drawn on Bank in which both Father and Daughter have accounts. Daughter deposits the check in her account in Bank. An employee of Bank, acting under the belief that there were available funds in Father's account to cover the check, caused Daughter's account to be credited for $10,000. In fact, Father's account was overdrawn and Father did not have overdraft privileges. Since Daughter received the check gratuitously there is clear unjust enrichment if she is allowed to keep the $10,000 and Bank is unable to obtain reimbursement from Father. Thus, Bank should be permitted to reverse the credit to Daughter's account. But this case is not typical. In most cases the remedy of restitution will not be available because the person receiving payment of the check will have given value for it in good faith.

In some cases, however, it may not be clear whether a drawee bank should have a right of restitution. For example, a check-kiting scheme may involve a large number of checks drawn on a number of different banks in which the drawer's credit balances are based on uncollected funds represented by fraudulently drawn checks. No attempt is made in Section 3-418 to state rules for determining the conflicting claims of the various banks that may be victimized by such a scheme. Rather, such cases are better resolved on the basis of general principles of law and the particular facts presented in the litigation.

4. The right of the drawee to recover a payment or to revoke an acceptance under Section 3-418 is not affected by the rules under Article 4 that determine when an item is paid. Even though a payor bank may have paid an item under Section 4-215, it may have a right to recover the payment under Section 3-418. *Nat'l Savings & Trust Co. v. Park Corp.*, 722 F.2d 1303 (6th Cir. 1983), cert. denied, 466 U.S. 939 (1984), correctly states the law on the issue under former Article 3. Revised Article 3 does not change the previous law.

Additional References:

3-404 Comment 3
4-301 Comment 7
4-403 Comment 7

Section 3-419. Instruments Signed for Accommodation

(a) If an instrument is issued for value given for the benefit of a party to the instrument ("accommodated party") and another party to the instrument ("accommodation party") signs the instrument for the purpose of incurring liability on the instrument without being a direct beneficiary of the value given for the instrument, the instrument is signed by the accommodation party "for accommodation."

(b) An accommodation party may sign the instrument as maker, drawer, acceptor, or indorser and, subject to subsection (d), is obliged to pay the instrument in the capacity in which the accommodation party signs. The obligation of an accommodation party may be enforced notwithstanding any statute of frauds and whether or not the accommodation party receives consideration for the accommodation.

(c) A person signing an instrument is presumed to be an accommodation party and there is notice that the instrument is signed for accommodation if the signature is an anomalous indorsement or is accompanied by words indicating that the signer is acting as surety or guarantor with respect to the obligation of another party to the instrument. Except as provided in Section 3-605, the obligation of an accommodation party to pay the instrument is not affected by the fact that the person enforcing the obligation had notice when the instrument was taken by that person that the accommodation party signed the instrument for accommodation.

(d) If the signature of a party to an instrument is accompanied by words indicating unambiguously that the party is guaranteeing collection rather than payment of the obligation of another party to the instrument, the signer is obliged to pay the amount due on the instrument to a person entitled to enforce the instrument only if (i) execution of judgment against the other party has been returned unsatisfied, (ii) the other party is insolvent or in an insolvency proceeding, (iii) the other party cannot be served with process, or (iv) it is otherwise apparent that payment cannot be obtained from the other party.

(e) If the signature of a party to an instrument is accompanied by words indicating that the party guarantees payment or the signer signs the instrument as an accommodation party in some other manner that does not unambiguously indicate an intention to guarantee collection rather than payment, the signer is obliged to pay the amount due on the instrument to a person entitled to enforce the instrument in the same circumstances as the accommodated party would be obliged, without prior resort to the accommodated party by the person entitled to enforce the instrument.

(f) An accommodation party who pays the instrument is entitled to reimbursement from the accommodated party and is entitled to enforce the instrument against the accommodated party. In proper circumstances, an accommodation party may obtain relief that requires the accommodated party to perform its obligations on the instrument. An accommodated party that pays the instrument has no right of recourse against, and is not entitled to contribution from, an accommodation party.

Definitional Cross References:

"Acceptor".	Section 3-103(a)(1)
"Anomalous Indorsement".	Section 3-205(d)
"Drawer".	Section 3-103(a)(5)
"Indorser".	Section 3-204(b)
"Insolvency Proceeding".	Section 1-201(b)(22)
"Insolvent".	Section 1-201(b)(23)
"Instrument".	Section 3-104(b)
"Issue".	Section 3-105(a)
"Maker".	Section 3-103(a)(7)
"Notice".	Section 1-202(a)
"Party".	Section 3-103(a)(10)
"Payment".	Section 3-602(a)
"Person".	Section 1-201(b)(27)
"Person Entitled to Enforce".	Section 3-301
"Signed".	Section 1-201(b)(37)
"Surety".	Section 1-201(b)(39)
"Value, Issued for".	Section 3-303(a)

Official Comment

1. Section 3-419 replaces former Section 3-415 and 3-416. An accommodation party is a person who signs an instrument to benefit the accommodated party either by signing at the time value is obtained by the accommodated party or later, and who is not a direct beneficiary of the value obtained. An accommodation party will usually be a co-maker or anomalous indorser. Subsection (a) distinguishes between direct and indirect benefit. For example, if X cosigns a note of Corporation that is given for a loan to Corporation, X is an accommodation party if no part of the loan was paid to X or for X's direct benefit. This is true even though X may receive indirect benefit from the loan because X is employed by Corporation or is a stockholder of Corporation, or even if X is the sole stockholder so long as Corporation and X are recognized as separate entities.

2. It does not matter whether an accommodation party signs gratuitously either at the time the instrument is issued or after the instrument is in the possession of a holder. Subsection (b) of Section 3-419 takes the view stated in Comment 3 to former Section 3-415 that there need be no consideration running to the accommodation party: "The obligation of the accommodation party is supported by any consideration for which the instrument is taken before it is due. Subsection (2) is intended to change occasional decisions holding that there is no sufficient consideration where an accommodation party signs a note after it is in the hands of a holder who has given value. The [accommodation] party is liable to the holder in such a case even though there is no extension of time or other concession."

3. As stated in Comment 1, whether a person is an accommodation party is a question of fact. But it is almost always the case that a co-maker who signs with words of guaranty after the signature is an accommodation party. The same is true of an anomalous indorser. In either case a person taking the instrument is put on notice of the accommodation status of the co-maker or indorser. This is relevant to Section 3-605(e). But, under subsection (c), signing with words of guaranty or as an anomalous indorser also creates a presumption that the signer is an accommodation party. A party challenging accommodation party status would have to rebut this presumption by producing evidence that the signer was in fact a direct beneficiary of the value given for the instrument.

An accommodation party is always a surety. A surety who is not a party to the instrument, however, is not an accommodation party. For example, if M issues a note payable to the order of P, and S signs a separate contract in which S agrees to pay P the amount of the instrument if it is dishonored, S is a surety but is not an accommodation party. In such a case, S's rights and duties are determined under the general law of suretyship. In unusual cases two parties to an instrument may have a surety relationship that is not governed by Article 3 because the requirements of Section 3-419(a) are not met. In those cases the general law of suretyship applies to the relationship. See PEB Commentary No. 11.

4. Subsection (b) states that an accommodation party is liable on the instrument in the capacity in which the party signed the instrument. In most cases that capacity will be either that of a maker or indorser of a note. But subsection (d) provides a limitation on subsection (b). If the signature of the accommodation party is accompanied by words indicating unambiguously that the party is guaranteeing collection rather than payment of the instrument, liability is limited to that stated in subsection (d), which is based on former Section 3-416(2).

Former Article 3 was confusing because the obligation of a guarantor was covered both in Section 3-415 and in Section 3-416. The latter section suggested that a signature accompanied by words of guaranty created an obligation distinct from that of an accommodation party. Revised Article 3 eliminates that confusion by stating in Section 3-419 the obligation of a person who uses words of guaranty. Portions of former Section 3-416 are preserved. Former Section 3-416(2) is reflected in Section 3-419(d) and former Section 3-416(4) is reflected in Section 3-419(c). Words added to an anomalous indorsement indicating that payment of the instrument is guaranteed by the indorser do not change the liability of the indorser as stated in Section 3-415. This is a change from former Section 3-416(5). See PEB Commentary No. 11.

5. Subsection (f) like former Section 3-415(5), provides that an accommodation party that pays the instrument is entitled to enforce the instrument against the accommodated party. Since the accommodation party that pays the instrument is entitled to enforce the instrument against the accommodated party, the accommodation party also obtains rights to any security interest or other collateral that secures payment of the instrument. Subsection (f) also provides that an accommodation party that pays the instrument is entitled to reimbursement from the accommodated party. See PEB Commentary No. 11.

6. In occasional cases, the accommodation party might pay the instrument even though the accommodated party had a defense to its obligation that was available to the accommodation party under Section 3-305(d). In such cases, the accommodation party's right to reimbursement may conflict with the accommodated party's right to raise its defense. For example, suppose the accommodation party pays the instrument without being aware of the defense. In that case the accommodation party should be entitled to reimbursement. Suppose the accommodation party paid the instrument with knowledge of the defense. In that case, to the extent of the defense, reimbursement ordinarily would not be justified, but under some circumstances reimbursement may be justified depending upon the facts of the case. The resolution of this conflict is left to the general law of suretyship. Section 1-103. See PEB Commentary No. 11.

7. Section 3-419, along with Section 3-116(a) and (b), Section 3-305(d) and Section 3-605, provides rules governing the rights of accommodation parties. In addition, except to the extent that it is displaced by provisions of this Article, the general law of suretyship also applies to the rights of accommodation parties. Section 1-103. See PEB Commentary No. 11.

Additional References:

3-116 Comment 1
3-205 Comment 3
3-302 Comment 4
3-305 Comment 5
3-605 Comment 2, 4, 5, 8

Editors' Note: Detailed 2002 amendments to Sections 3-419 and 3-605 conformed those provisions to the Restatement of Suretyship and Guaranty.

Section 3-420. Conversion of Instrument

(a) The law applicable to conversion of personal property applies to instruments. An instrument is also converted if it is taken by transfer, other than a negotiation, from a person not entitled to enforce the instrument or a bank makes or obtains payment with respect to the instrument for a person not entitled to enforce the instrument or receive payment. An action for conversion of an instrument may not be brought by (i) the issuer or acceptor of the instrument or (ii) a payee or indorsee who did not receive delivery of the instrument either directly or through delivery to an agent or a co-payee.

(b) In an action under subsection (a), the measure of liability is presumed to be the amount payable on the instrument, but recovery may not exceed the amount of the plaintiff's interest in the instrument.

(c) A representative, other than a depositary bank, who has in good faith dealt with an instrument or its proceeds on behalf of one who was not the person entitled to enforce the instrument is not liable in conversion to that person beyond the amount of any proceeds that it has not paid out.

Definitional Cross References:

"Acceptor".	Section 3-103(a)(1)
"Action".	Section 1-201(b)(1)
"Bank".	Section 1-201(b)(4)
"Delivery".	Section 1-201(b)(15)
"Depositary Bank".	Section 4-105(2)
"Entitled to Enforce".	Section 3-301
"Good Faith".	Section 1-201(b)(20), Section 3-103(a)(6)
"Instrument".	Section 3-104(b)
"Issuer".	Section 3-105(c)
"Negotiation".	Section 3-201(a)
"Payment".	Section 3-602(a)
"Person".	Section 1-201(b)(27)
"Representative".	Section 1-201(b)(33)
"Transfer".	Section 3-203(a)

Official Comment

1. Section 3-420 is a modification of former Section 3-419. The first sentence of Section 3-420(a) states a general rule that the law of conversion applicable to personal property also applies to instruments. Paragraphs (a) and (b) of former Section 3-419(1) are deleted as inappropriate in cases of noncash items that may be delivered for acceptance or payment in collection letters that contain varying instructions as to what to do in the event of nonpayment on the day of delivery. It is better to allow such cases to be governed by the general law of conversion that would address the issue of when, under the circumstances prevailing, the presenter's right to possession has been denied. The second sentence of Section 3-420(a) states that an instrument is converted if it is taken by transfer other than a negotiation from a person not entitled to enforce the instrument or taken for collection or payment from a person not entitled to enforce the instrument or receive payment. This covers cases in which a depositary or payor bank takes an instrument bearing a forged indorsement. It also covers cases in which an instrument is payable to two persons and the two persons are not alternative payees, e.g. a check payable to John and Jane Doe. Under Section 3-110(d) the check can be negotiated or enforced only by both persons acting jointly. Thus, neither payee acting without the consent of the other, is a person entitled to enforce the instrument. If John indorses the check and Jane does not, the indorsement is not effective to allow negotiation of the check. If Depositary Bank takes the check for deposit to John's account, Depositary Bank is liable to Jane for conversion of the check if she did not consent to the transaction. John, acting alone, is not the person entitled to enforce the check because John is not the holder of the check. Section 3-110(d) and Comment 4 to Section 3-110. Depositary Bank does not get any greater rights under Section 4-205(1). If it acted for John as its customer, it did not become holder of the check under that provision because John, its customer, was not a holder.

Under former Article 3, the cases were divided on the issue of whether the drawer of a check with a forged indorsement can assert rights against a depositary bank that took the check. The last sentence of Section 3-420(a) resolves the conflict by following the rule stated in *Stone & Webster Eng'g Corp. v. First Nat'l Bank & Trust Co.*, 184 N.E.2d 358 (Mass. 1962). There is no reason why a drawer should have an action in conversion. The check represents an obligation of the drawer rather than property of the drawer. The drawer has an adequate remedy against the payor bank for recredit of the drawer's account for unauthorized payment of the check.

There was also a split of authority under former Article 3 on the issue of whether a payee who never received the instrument is a proper plaintiff in a conversion action. The typical case was one in which a check was stolen from the drawer or in which the check was mailed to an address different from that of the payee and was stolen after it arrived at that address. The thief forged the indorsement of the payee and obtained payment by depositing the check to an account in a depositary bank. The issue was whether the payee could bring an action in conversion against the depositary bank or the drawee bank. In revised Article 3, under the last sentence of Section 3-420(a), the payee has no conversion action because the check was never delivered to the payee. Until delivery, the payee does not have any interest in the check. The payee never became the holder of the check nor a person entitled to enforce the check. Section 3-301. Nor is the payee injured by the fraud. Normally the drawer of a check intends to pay an obligation owed to the payee. But if the check is never delivered to the payee, the obligation owed to the payee is not affected. If the check falls into the hands of a thief who obtains payment after forging the signature of the payee as an indorsement, the obligation owed to the payee continues to exist after the thief receives payment. Since the payee's right to enforce the underlying obligation is unaffected by the fraud of the thief, there is no reason to give any additional remedy to the payee. The drawer of the check has no conversion remedy, but the drawee is not entitled to charge the drawer's account when the drawee wrongfully honored the check. The remedy of the drawee is against the depositary bank for breach of warranty under Section 3-417(a)(1) or 4-208(a)(1). The loss will fall on the person who gave value to the thief for the check.

The situation is different if the check is delivered to the payee. If the check is taken for an obligation owed to the payee, the last sentence of Section 3-310(b)(4) provides that the obligation may not be enforced to the extent of the amount of the check. The payee's rights are restricted to enforcement of the payee's rights in the instrument. In this event the payee is injured by the theft and has a cause of action for conversion.

The payee receives delivery when the check comes into the payee's possession, as for example when it is put into the payee's mailbox. Delivery to an agent is delivery to the payee. If a check is payable to more than one payee, delivery to one of the payees is deemed to be delivery to all of the payees. Occasionally, the person asserting a conversion cause of action is an indorsee rather than the original payee. If the check is stolen before the check can be delivered to the indorsee and the indorsee's indorsement is forged, the analysis is similar. For example, a check is payable to the order of A. A indorses it to B and puts it into an envelope addressed to B. The envelope is never delivered to B. Rather, Thief steals the envelope, forges B's indorsement to the check and obtains payment. Because the check was never delivered to B, the indorsee, B has no cause of action for conversion, but A does have such an action. A is the owner of the check. B never obtained rights in the check. If A intended to negotiate the check to B in payment of an obligation, that obligation was not affected by the conduct of Thief. B can enforce that obligation. Thief stole A's property not B's.

2. Subsection (2) of former Section 3-419 is amended because it is not clear why the former law distinguished between the liability of the drawee and that of other converters. Why should there be a conclusive presumption that the liability is face amount if a drawee refuses to pay or return an instrument or makes payment on a forged indorsement, while the liability of a maker who does the same thing is only presumed to be the face amount? Moreover, it was not clear under former Section 3-419(2) what face amount meant. If a note for $10,000 is payable in a year at 10% interest, it is common to refer to $10,000 as the face amount, but if the note is converted the loss to the owner also includes the loss of interest. In revised Article 3, Section 3-420(b), by referring to "amount payable on the instrument," allows the full amount due under the instrument to be recovered.

The "but" clause in subsection (b) addresses the problem of conversion actions in multiple payee checks. Section 3-110(d) states that an instrument cannot be enforced unless all payees join in the action. But an action for conversion might be brought by a payee having no interest or a limited interest in the proceeds of the check. This clause prevents such a plaintiff from receiving a windfall. An example is a check payable to a building contractor and a supplier of building material. The check is not payable to the payees alternatively.

Section 3-110(d). The check is delivered to the contractor by the owner of the building. Suppose the contractor forges supplier's signature as an indorsement of the check and receives the entire proceeds of the check. The supplier should not, without qualification, be able to recover the entire amount of the check from the bank that converted the check. Depending upon the contract between the contractor and the supplier, the amount of the check may be due entirely to the contractor, in which case there should be no recovery, entirely to the supplier, in which case recovery should be for the entire amount, or part may be due to one and the rest to the other, in which case recovery should be limited to the amount due to the supplier.

3. Subsection (3) of former Section 3-419 drew criticism from the courts, that saw no reason why a depositary bank should have the defense stated in the subsection. See *Knesz v. Central Jersey Bank & Trust Co.*, 477 A.2d 806 (N.J. 1984). The depositary bank is ultimately liable in the case of a forged indorsement check because of its warranty to the payor bank under Section 4-208(a)(1) and it is usually the most convenient defendant in cases involving multiple checks drawn on different banks. There is no basis for requiring the owner of the check to bring multiple actions against the various payor banks and to require those banks to assert warranty rights against the depositary bank. In revised Article 3, the defense provided by Section 3-420(c) is limited to collecting banks other than the depositary bank. If suit is brought against both the payor bank and the depositary bank, the owner, of course, is entitled to but one recovery.

Additional References:

3-310 Comment 4

3-405 Comment 3

4-203 Comment

PART 5. DISHONOR

Section 3-501. Presentment

(a) "Presentment" means a demand made by or on behalf of a person entitled to enforce an instrument (i) to pay the instrument made to the drawee or a party obliged to pay the instrument or, in the case of a note or accepted draft payable at a bank, to the bank, or (ii) to accept a draft made to the drawee.

(b) The following rules are subject to Article 4, agreement of the parties, and clearing-house rules and the like:

(1) Presentment may be made at the place of payment of the instrument and must be made at the place of payment if the instrument is payable at a bank in the United States; may be made by any commercially reasonable means, including an oral, written, or electronic communication; is effective when the demand for payment or acceptance is received by the person to whom presentment is made; and is effective if made to any one of two or more makers, acceptors, drawees, or other payors.

(2) Upon demand of the person to whom presentment is made, the person making presentment must (i) exhibit the instrument, (ii) give reasonable identification and, if presentment is made on behalf of another person, reasonable evidence of authority to do so, and (iii) sign a receipt on the instrument for any payment made or surrender the instrument if full payment is made.

(3) Without dishonoring the instrument, the party to whom presentment is made may (i) return the instrument for lack of a necessary indorsement, or (ii) refuse payment or acceptance for failure of the presentment to comply with the terms of the instrument, an agreement of the parties, or other applicable law or rule.

(4) The party to whom presentment is made may treat presentment as occurring on the next business day after the day of presentment if the party to whom presentment is made has established a cut-off hour not earlier than 2 p.m. for the receipt and processing of instruments presented for payment or acceptance and presentment is made after the cut-off hour.

Definitional Cross References:

"Acceptance".	Section 3-409(a)
"Acceptor".	Section 3-103(a)(1)
"Agreement".	Section 1-201(b)(3)
"Bank".	Section 1-201(b)(4)
"Dishonor".	Section 3-502
"Draft".	Section 3-104(e)
"Drawee".	Section 3-103(a)(4)
"Indorsement".	Section 3-204(a)
"Instrument".	Section 3-104(b)
"Maker".	Section 3-103(a)(7)
"Note".	Section 3-104(e)
"Party".	Section 3-103(a)(10)
"Payment".	Section 3-602(a)
"Person".	Section 1-201(b)(27)
"Person Entitled to Enforce".	Section 3-301
"Written".	Section 1-201(b)(46)

Official Comment

Subsection (a) defines presentment. Subsection (b)(1) states the place and manner of presentment. Electronic presentment is authorized. The communication of the demand for payment or acceptance is effective when received. Subsection (b)(2) restates former Section 3-505. Subsection (b)(2)(i) allows the person to whom presentment is made to require exhibition of the instrument, unless the parties have agreed otherwise as in an electronic presentment agreement. Former Section 3-507(3) is the antecedent of subsection (b)(3)(i). Since a payor must decide whether to pay or accept on the day of presentment, subsection (b)(4) allows the payor to set a cut-off hour for receipt of instruments presented.

Additional References:

3-103 Comment 2
3-410 Comment 2
3-502 Comment 1
4-202 Comment 2
4-204 Comment 4
4-212 Comment 3

Section 3-502. Dishonor

(a) Dishonor of a note is governed by the following rules:

(1) If the note is payable on demand, the note is dishonored if presentment is duly made to the maker and the note is not paid on the day of presentment.

(2) If the note is not payable on demand and is payable at or through a bank or the terms of the note require presentment, the note is dishonored if presentment is duly made and the note is not paid on the day it becomes payable or the day of presentment, whichever is later.

(3) If the note is not payable on demand and paragraph (2) does not apply, the note is dishonored if it is not paid on the day it becomes payable.

(b) Dishonor of an unaccepted draft other than a documentary draft is governed by the following rules:

(1) If a check is duly presented for payment to the payor bank otherwise than for immediate payment over the counter, the check is dishonored if the payor bank makes timely return of the check or sends timely notice of dishonor or nonpayment under Section 4-301 or 4-302, or becomes accountable for the amount of the check under Section 4-302.

(2) If a draft is payable on demand and paragraph (1) does not apply, the draft is dishonored if presentment for payment is duly made to the drawee and the draft is not paid on the day of presentment.

(3) If a draft is payable on a date stated in the draft, the draft is dishonored if (i) presentment for payment is duly made to the drawee and payment is not made on the day the draft becomes payable or the day of presentment, whichever is later, or (ii) presentment for acceptance is duly made before the day the draft becomes payable and the draft is not accepted on the day of presentment.

(4) If a draft is payable on elapse of a period of time after sight or acceptance, the draft is dishonored if presentment for acceptance is duly made and the draft is not accepted on the day of presentment.

(c) Dishonor of an unaccepted documentary draft occurs according to the rules stated in subsection (b)(2), (3), and (4), except that payment or acceptance may be delayed without dishonor until no later than the close of the third business day of the drawee following the day on which payment or acceptance is required by those paragraphs.

(d) Dishonor of an accepted draft is governed by the following rules:

(1) If the draft is payable on demand, the draft is dishonored if presentment for payment is duly made to the acceptor and the draft is not paid on the day of presentment.

(2) If the draft is not payable on demand, the draft is dishonored if presentment for payment is duly made to the acceptor and payment is not made on the day it becomes payable or the day of presentment, whichever is later.

(e) In any case in which presentment is otherwise required for dishonor under this section and presentment is excused under Section 3-504, dishonor occurs without presentment if the instrument is not duly accepted or paid.

(f) If a draft is dishonored because timely acceptance of the draft was not made and the person entitled to demand acceptance consents to a late acceptance, from the time of acceptance the draft is treated as never having been dishonored.

Definitional Cross References:

"Acceptance".	Section 3-409(a)
"Acceptor".	Section 3-103(a)(1)
"Bank".	Section 1-201(b)(4)
"Check".	Section 3-104(f)
"Documentary Draft".	Section 4-104(a)(6)
"Draft".	Section 3-104(e)
"Drawee".	Section 3-103(a)(4)
"Instrument".	Section 3-104(b)
"Maker".	Section 3-103(a)(7)
"Note".	Section 3-104(e)
"Notice of Dishonor".	Section 3-503
"Payable at or Through a Bank".	Section 4-106
"Payable on Demand".	Section 3-108(a)
"Payment".	Section 3-602(a)
"Payor Bank".	Section 4-105(3)
"Person".	Section 1-201(b)(27)
"Presentment".	Section 3-501(a)
"Send".	Section 1-201(b)(36)

Official Comment

1. Section 3-415 provides that an indorser is obliged to pay an instrument if the instrument is dishonored and is discharged if the indorser is entitled to notice of dishonor and notice is not given. Under Section 3-414, the drawer is obliged to pay an unaccepted draft if it is dishonored. The drawer, however, is not entitled to notice of dishonor except to the extent required in a case governed by Section 3-414(d). Part 5 tells when an instrument is dishonored (Section 3-502) and what it means to give notice of dishonor (Section 3-503). Often dishonor does not occur until presentment (Section 3-501), and frequently presentment and notice of dishonor are excused (Section 3-504).

2. In the great majority of cases presentment and notice of dishonor are waived with respect to notes. In most cases a formal demand for payment to the maker of the note is not contemplated. Rather, the maker is expected to send payment to the holder of the note on the date or dates on which payment is due. If payment is not made when due, the holder usually makes a demand for payment, but in the normal case in which presentment is waived, demand is irrelevant and the holder can proceed against indorsers when payment is not received. Under former Article 3, in the small minority of cases in which presentment and dishonor were not waived with respect to notes, the indorser was discharged from liability (former Section 3-502(1)(a)) unless the holder made presentment to the maker on the exact day the note was due (former Section 3-503(1)(c)) and gave notice of dishonor to the indorser before midnight of the third business day after dishonor (former Section 3-508(2)). These provisions are omitted from Revised Article 3 as inconsistent with practice which seldom involves face-to-face dealings.

3. Subsection (a) applies to notes. Subsection (a)(1) applies to notes payable on demand. Dishonor requires presentment, and dishonor occurs if payment is not made on the day of presentment. There is no change from previous Article 3. Subsection (a)(2) applies to notes payable at a definite time if the note is payable at or through a bank or, by its terms, presentment is required. Dishonor requires presentment, and dishonor occurs if payment is not made on the due date or the day of presentment if presentment is made after the due date. Subsection (a)(3) applies to all other notes. If the note is not paid on its due date it is dishonored. This allows holders to collect notes in ways that make sense commercially without having to be concerned about a formal presentment on a given day.

4. Subsection (b) applies to unaccepted drafts other than documentary drafts. Subsection (b)(1) applies to checks. Except for checks presented for immediate payment over the counter, which are covered by subsection (b)(2), dishonor occurs according to rules stated in Article 4. Those rules contemplate four separate situations that warrant discussion. The first two situations arise in the normal course of affairs, in which the drawee bank makes settlement for the amount of the check to the presenting bank. In the first situation, the drawee bank under Section 4-301 recovers this settlement if it returns the check by its midnight deadline (Section 4-104). In that case the check is not paid and dishonor occurs under Section 3-502(b)(1). The second situation arises if the drawee bank has made such a settlement and does not return the check or give notice of dishonor or nonpayment within the midnight deadline. In that case, the settlement becomes final payment of the check under Section 4-215. Because the drawee bank already has paid such an item, it cannot be "accountable" for the item under the terms of Section 4-302(a)(1). Thus, no dishonor occurs regardless of whether the drawee bank retains the check indefinitely or for some reason returns the check after its midnight deadline.

The third and fourth situations arise less commonly, in cases in which the drawee bank does not settle for the check when it is received. Under Section 4-302 if the drawee bank is not also the depositary bank and retains the check without settling for it beyond midnight of the day it is presented for payment, the bank at that point becomes "accountable" for the amount of the check, i.e., it is obliged to pay the amount of the check. If the drawee bank is also the depositary bank, the bank becomes accountable for the amount of the check if the bank does not pay the check or return it or send notice of dishonor by its midnight deadline. Hence, if the drawee bank is also the depositary bank and does not either settle for the check when it is received (a settlement that would ripen into final payment if the drawee bank failed to take action to recover the settlement by its midnight deadline) or return the check or an appropriate notice by its midnight deadline, the drawee bank will become accountable for the amount of the check under Section 4-302. Thus, in all cases in which the drawee bank becomes accountable under Section 4-302, the check has not been paid (either by a settlement that became unrecoverable or otherwise) and thus, under Section 3-502(b)(1), the check is dishonored.

The fact that a bank that is accountable for the amount of the check under Section 4-302 is obliged to pay the check does not mean that the check has been paid. Indeed, because each of the paragraphs of Section 4-302(b) is limited by its terms to situations in which a bank has not paid the item, a drawee bank will be accountable under Section 4-302 only in situations in which it has not previously paid the check. Section 3-502(b)(1) reflects the view that a person presenting a check is entitled to payment, not just the ability to hold the drawee accountable under Section 4-302. If that payment is not made in a timely manner, the check is dishonored.

Regulation CC Section 229.36(d) provides that settlement between banks for the forward collection of checks is final. The relationship of that section to Articles 3 and 4 is discussed in the Commentary to that section.

Subsection (b)(2) applies to demand drafts other than those governed by subsection (b)(1). It covers checks presented for immediate payment over the counter and demand drafts other than checks. Dishonor occurs if presentment for payment is made and payment is not made on the day of presentment.

Subsection (b)(3) and (4) applies to time drafts. An unaccepted time draft differs from a time note. The maker of a note knows that the note has been issued, but the drawee of a draft may not know that a draft has been drawn on it. Thus, with respect to drafts, presentment for payment or acceptance is required. Subsection (b)(3) applies to drafts payable on a date stated in the draft. Dishonor occurs if presentment for payment is made and payment is not made on the day the draft becomes payable or the day of presentment if presentment is made after the due date. The holder of an unaccepted draft payable on a stated date has the option of presenting the draft for acceptance before the day the draft becomes payable to establish whether the drawee is willing to assume liability by accepting. Under subsection (b)(3)(ii) dishonor occurs when the draft is presented and not accepted. Subsection (b)(4) applies to unaccepted drafts payable on elapse of a period of time after sight or acceptance. If the draft is payable 30 days after sight, the draft must be presented for acceptance to start the running of the 30-day period. Dishonor occurs if it is not accepted. The rules in subsection (b)(3) and (4) follow former Section 3-501(1)(a).

5.. Subsection (c) gives drawees an extended period to pay documentary drafts because of the time that may be needed to examine the documents.

6. Subsection (d) governs accepted drafts. If the acceptor's obligation is to pay on demand the rule, stated in subsection (d)(1), is the same as for that of a demand note stated in subsection (a)(1). If the acceptor's obligation is to pay at a definite time the rule, stated in subsection (d)(2), is the same as that of a time note payable at a bank stated in subsection (b)(2).

7. Subsection (e) is a limitation on subsection (a)(1) and (2), subsection (b), subsection (c), and subsection (d). Each of those provisions states dishonor as occurring after presentment. If presentment is excused under Section 3-504, dishonor occurs under those provisions without presentment if the instrument is not duly accepted or paid.

8. Under subsection (b)(3)(ii) and (4) if a draft is presented for acceptance and the draft is not accepted on the day of presentment, there is dishonor. But after dishonor, the holder may consent to late acceptance. In that case, under subsection (f), the late acceptance cures the dishonor. The draft is treated as never having been dishonored. If the draft is subsequently presented for payment and payment is refused dishonor occurs at that time.

Additional References:

3-310 Comment 4
3-414 Comment 6

Section 3-503. Notice of Dishonor

(a) The obligation of an indorser stated in Section 3-415(a) and the obligation of a drawer stated in Section 3-414(d) may not be enforced unless (i) the indorser or drawer is given notice of dishonor of the instrument complying with this section or (ii) notice of dishonor is excused under Section 3-504(b).

(b) Notice of dishonor may be given by any person; may be given by any commercially reasonable means, including an oral, written, or electronic communication; and is sufficient if it reasonably identifies the instrument and indicates that the instrument has been dishonored or has not been paid or accepted. Return of an instrument given to a bank for collection is sufficient notice of dishonor.

(c) Subject to Section 3-504(c), with respect to an instrument taken for collection by a collecting bank, notice of dishonor must be given (i) by the bank before midnight of the next banking day following the banking day on which the bank receives notice of dishonor of the instrument, or (ii) by any other person within 30 days following the day on which the person receives notice of dishonor. With respect to any other instrument, notice of dishonor must be given within 30 days following the day on which dishonor occurs.

Definitional Cross References:

"Acceptance".	Section 3-409(a)
"Bank".	Section 1-201(b)(4)
"Banking Day".	Section 4-104(a)(3)
"Collecting Bank".	Section 4-105(5)
"Dishonor".	Section 3-502
"Drawer".	Section 3-103(a)(5)
"Indorser".	Section 3-204(b)
"Instrument".	Section 3-104(b)
"Person".	Section 1-201(b)(27)
"Written".	Section 1-201(b)(46)

Official Comment

1. Subsection (a) is consistent with former Section 3-501(2)(a), but notice of dishonor is no longer relevant to the liability of a drawer except for the case of a draft accepted by an acceptor other than a bank. Comments 2 and 4 to Section 3-414. There is no reason why drawers should be discharged on instruments they draw until payment or acceptance. They are entitled to have the instrument presented to the drawee and dishonored (Section 3-414(b)) before they are liable to pay, but no notice of dishonor need be made to them as a condition of liability. Subsection (b), which states how notice of dishonor is given, is based on former Section 3-508(3).

2. Subsection (c) replaces former Section 3-508(2). It differs from that section in that it provides a 30-day period for a person other than a collecting bank to give notice of dishonor rather than the three-day period allowed in former Article 3. Delay in giving notice of dishonor may be excused under Section 3-504(c).

Additional References:

3-414 Comment 4
3-415 Comment 2
3-502 Comment 1
4-301 Comment 5

Section 3-504. Excused Presentment and Notice of Dishonor

(a) Presentment for payment or acceptance of an instrument is excused if (i) the person entitled to present the instrument cannot with reasonable diligence make presentment, (ii) the maker or acceptor has repudiated an obligation to pay the instrument or is dead or in insolvency proceedings, (iii) by the terms of the instrument presentment is not necessary to enforce the obligation of indorsers or the drawer, (iv) the drawer or indorser whose obligation is being enforced has waived presentment or otherwise has no reason to expect or right to require that the instrument be paid or accepted, or (v) the drawer instructed the drawee not to pay or accept the draft or the drawee was not obligated to the drawer to pay the draft.

(b) Notice of dishonor is excused if (i) by the terms of the instrument notice of dishonor is not necessary to enforce the obligation of a party to pay the instrument, or (ii) the party whose obligation is being enforced waived notice of dishonor. A waiver of presentment is also a waiver of notice of dishonor.

(c) Delay in giving notice of dishonor is excused if the delay was caused by circumstances beyond the control of the person giving the notice and the person giving the notice exercised reasonable diligence after the cause of the delay ceased to operate.

Definitional Cross References:

"Acceptor".	Section 3-103(a)(1)
"Draft".	Section 3-104(e)
"Drawee".	Section 3-103(a)(4)
"Drawer".	Section 3-103(a)(5)
"Indorser".	Section 3-204(b)
"Insolvency Proceeding".	Section1-201(b)(22)
"Instrument".	Section 3-104(b)
"Maker".	Section 3-103(a)(7)
"Notice of Dishonor".	Section 3-503
"Party".	Section 3-103(a)(10)
"Payment".	Section 3-602(a)
"Person".	Section 1-201(b)(27)
"Presentment".	Section 3-501(a)

Official Comment

Section 3-504 is largely a restatement of former Section 3-511. Subsection (4) of former Section 3-511 is replaced by Section 3-502(f).

Additional References:

3-310 Comment 4
3-502 Comment 1, 7
3-503 Comment 3

Section 3-505. Evidence of Dishonor

(a) The following are admissible as evidence and create a presumption of dishonor and of any notice of dishonor stated:

(1) a document regular in form as provided in subsection (b) which purports to be a protest;

(2) a purported stamp or writing of the drawee, payor bank, or presenting bank on or accompanying the instrument stating that acceptance or payment has been refused unless reasons for the refusal are stated and the reasons are not consistent with dishonor;

(3) a book or record of the drawee, payor bank, or collecting bank, kept in the usual course of business which shows dishonor, even if there is no evidence of who made the entry.

(b) A protest is a certificate of dishonor made by a United States consul or vice consul, or a notary public or other person authorized to administer oaths by the law of the place where dishonor occurs. It may be made upon information satisfactory to that person. The protest must identify the instrument and certify either that presentment has been made or, if not made, the reason why it was not made, and that the instrument has been dishonored by nonacceptance or nonpayment. The protest may also certify that notice of dishonor has been given to some or all parties.

Definitional Cross References:

"Acceptance".	Section 3-409(a)
"Dishonor".	Section 3-502
"Drawee".	Section 3-103(a)(4)
"Instrument".	Section 3-104(b)
"Notice of Dishonor".	Section 3-503
"Payment".	Section 3-602(a)
"Payor Bank".	Section 4-105(3)
"Person".	Section 1-201(b)(27)
"Presenting Bank".	Section 4-105(6)
"Record".	Section 3-103(a)(14)
"Writing".	Section 1-201(b)(43)

Official Comment

Protest is no longer mandatory and must be requested by the holder. Even if requested, protest is not a condition to the liability of indorsers or drawers. Protest is a service provided by the banking system to establish that dishonor has occurred. Like other services provided by the banking system, it will be available if market incentives, interbank agreements, or governmental regulations require it, but liabilities of parties no longer rest on it. Protest may be a requirement for liability on international drafts governed by foreign law which this Article cannot affect.

PART 6. DISCHARGE AND PAYMENT

Section 3-601. Discharge and Effect of Discharge

(a) The obligation of a party to pay the instrument is discharged as stated in this Article or by an act or agreement with the party which would discharge an obligation to pay money under a simple contract.

(b) Discharge of the obligation of a party is not effective against a person acquiring rights of a holder in due course of the instrument without notice of the discharge.

Definitional Cross References:

"Agreement".	Section 1-201(b)(3)
"Contract".	Section 1-201(b)(12)

"Holder in Due Course".	Section 3-302
"Instrument".	Section 3-104(b)
"Money".	Section 1-201(b)(24)
"Notice".	Section 1-202(a)
"Party".	Section 3-103(a)(10)
"Person".	Section 1-201(b)(27)

Official Comment

Subsection (a) replaces subsections (1) and (2) of former Section 3-601. Subsection (b) restates former Section 3-602. Notice of discharge is not treated as notice of a defense that prevents holder in due course status. Section 3-302(b). Discharge is effective against a holder in due course only if the holder had notice of the discharge when holder in due course status was acquired. For example, if an instrument bearing a canceled indorsement is taken by a holder, the holder has notice that the indorser has been discharged. Thus, the discharge is effective against the holder even if the holder is a holder in due course.

Additional References: 3-302 Comment 3

Section 3-602. Payment

(a) Subject to subsection (e), an instrument is paid to the extent payment is made by or on behalf of a party obliged to pay the instrument, and to a person entitled to enforce the instrument.

(b) Subject to subsection (e), a note is paid to the extent payment is made by or on behalf of a party obliged to pay the note to a person that formerly was entitled to enforce the note only if at the time of the payment the party obliged to pay has not received adequate notification that the note has been transferred and that payment is to be made to the transferee. A notification is adequate only if it is signed by the transferor or the transferee; reasonably identifies the transferred note; and provides an address at which payments subsequently are to be made. Upon request, a transferee shall seasonably furnish reasonable proof that the note has been transferred. Unless the transferee complies with the request, a payment to the person that formerly was entitled to enforce the note is effective for purposes of subsection (c) even if the party obliged to pay the note has received a notification under this paragraph.

(c) Subject to subsection (e), to the extent of a payment under subsections (a) and (b), the obligation of the party obliged to pay the instrument is discharged even though payment is made with knowledge of a claim to the instrument under Section 3-306 by another person.

(d) Subject to subsection (e), a transferee, or any party that has acquired rights in the instrument directly or indirectly from a transferee, including any such party that has rights as a holder in due course, is deemed to have notice of any payment that is made under subsection (b) after the date that the note is transferred to the transferee but before the party obliged to pay the note receives adequate notification of the transfer.

(e) The obligation of a party to pay the instrument is not discharged under subsections (a) through (d) if:

(1) a claim to the instrument under Section 3-306 is enforceable against the party receiving payment and (i) payment is made with knowledge by the payor that payment is prohibited by injunction or similar process of a court of competent jurisdiction, or (ii) in the case of an instrument other than a cashier's check, teller's check, or certified check, the party making payment accepted, from the person having a claim to the instrument, indemnity against loss resulting from refusal to pay the person entitled to enforce the instrument; or

(2) the person making payment knows that the instrument is a stolen instrument and pays a person it knows is in wrongful possession of the instrument.

(f) As used in this section, "signed," with respect to a record that is not a writing, includes the attachment to or logical association with the record of an electronic symbol, sound, or process with the present intent to adopt or accept the record.

Definitional Cross References:

"Casher's Check".	Section 3-104(g)
"Certified Check".	Section 3-104(d)
"Discharge".	Section 3-601(a)
"Instrument".	Section 3-104(b)
"Knowledge".	Section 1-202(b)
"Party".	Section 3-103(a)(10)
"Person".	Section 1-201(b)(27)
"Person Entitled to Enforce".	Section 3-301
"Record".	Section 3-103(a)(14)
"Teller's Check".	Section 3-104(h)

Official Comment

1. This section replaces former Section 3-603(1). The phrase "claim to the instrument" in subsection (a) means, by reference to Section 3-306, a claim of ownership or possession and not a claim in recoupment. Subsection (e)(1)(ii) is added to conform to Section 3-411. Section 3-411 is intended to discourage an obligated bank from refusing payment of a cashier's check, certified check or dishonored teller's check at the request of a claimant to the check who provided the bank with indemnity against loss. See Comment 1 to Section 3-411. An obligated bank that refuses payment under those circumstances not only remains liable on the check but may also be liable to the holder of the check for consequential damages. Section 3-602(e)(1)(ii) and Section 3-411, read together, change the rule of former Section 3-603(1) with respect to the obligation of the obligated bank on the check. Payment to the holder of a cashier's check, teller's check, or certified check discharges the obligation of the obligated bank on the check to both the holder and the claimant even though indemnity has been given by the person asserting the claim. If the obligated bank pays the check in violation of an agreement with the claimant in connection with the indemnity agreement, any liability that the bank may have for violation of the agreement is not governed by Article 3, but is left to other law. This section continues the rule that the obligor is not discharged on the instrument if payment is made in violation of an injunction against payment. See Section 3-411(c)(iv).

2. Subsection (a) covers payments made in a traditional manner, to the person entitled to enforce the instrument. Subsection (b), which provides an alternative method of payment, deals with the situation in which a person entitled to enforce the instrument transfers the instrument without giving notice to parties obligated to pay the instrument. If that happens and one of those parties subsequently makes a payment to the transferor, the payment is effective even though it is not made to the person entitled to enforce the instrument. Unlike the earlier version of Section 3-602, this rule is consistent with Section 9-406(a), Restatement of Mortgages § 5.5, and Restatement of Contracts § 338(1).

3. Subsection (d) assures that the discharge provided by subsection (c) is effective against the transferee and those whose rights derive from the transferee. By deeming those persons to have notice of any payment made under subsection (b), subsection (d) gives those persons "notice of the discharge" within the meaning of Section 3-302(b). Accordingly, the discharge is effective against those persons, even if any of them has the rights of a holder in due course. Compare Section 3-601(b). The deemed notice provided by subsection (d) does not, however, prevent a person from becoming, or acquiring the rights of, a holder in due course. See Section 3-302(b). Thus, such a person does not become subject to other defenses described in Section 3-305(a)(2), claims in recoupment described in Section 3-305(a)(3), or claims to the instrument under Section 3-306. A transferee can prevent payment to the transferor from discharging the obligation on the note by assuring that each person who is obligated on the note receives adequate notification pursuant to subsection (b) prior to making a payment.

4. In determining the party to whom a payment is made for purposes of this section, courts should look to traditional rules of agency. Thus, if the original payee of a note transfers ownership of the note to a third party but continues to service the obligation, the law of agency might treat payments made to the original payee as payments made to the third party.

Additional References:

3-310 Comment 4

3-411 Comment 1, 3

4-403 Comment 2

Editors' Note: The 1990 version of Section 3-602 provided that payments made to a party that already had transferred a note were not effective. 2002 amendments to Section 3-602 (particularly in the subsections (b) & (d)) reject that rule and bring the UCC into conformity with the Restatement of Mortgages and the Restatement of Contracts.

Section 3-603. Tender of Payment

(a) If tender of payment of an obligation to pay an instrument is made to a person entitled to enforce the instrument, the effect of tender is governed by principles of law applicable to tender of payment under a simple contract.

(b) If tender of payment of an obligation to pay an instrument is made to a person entitled to enforce the instrument and the tender is refused, there is discharge, to the extent of the amount of the tender, of the obligation of an indorser or accommodation party having a right of recourse with respect to the obligation to which the tender relates.

(c) If tender of payment of an amount due on an instrument is made to a person entitled to enforce the instrument, the obligation of the obligor to pay interest after the due date on the amount tendered is discharged. If presentment is required with respect to an instrument and the obligor is able and ready to pay on the due date at every place of payment stated in the instrument, the obligor is deemed to have made tender of payment on the due date to the person entitled to enforce the instrument.

Definitional Cross References:

"Accommodation Party".	Section 3-419(a)
"Contract".	Section 1-201(b)(12)
"Discharge".	Section 3-601(a)
"Indorser".	Section 3-204(b)
"Instrument".	Section 3-104(b)
"Payment".	Section 3-602(a)
"Person Entitled to Enforce".	Section 3-301
"Presentment".	Section 3-501(a)

Official Comment

Section 3-603 replaces former Section 3-604. Subsection (a) generally incorporates the law of tender of payment applicable to simple contracts. Subsections (b) and (c) state particular rules. Subsection (b) replaces former Section 3-604(2). Under subsection (b) refusal of a tender of payment discharges any indorser or accommodation party having a right of recourse against the party making the tender. Subsection (c) replaces former Section 3-604(1) and (3).

Section 3-604. Discharge by Cancellation or Renunciation

(a) A person entitled to enforce an instrument, with or without consideration, may discharge the obligation of a party to pay the instrument (i) by an intentional voluntary act, such as surrender of the instrument to the party, destruction, mutilation, or cancellation of the instrument, cancellation or striking out of the party's signature, or the addition of words to the instrument indicating discharge, or (ii) by agreeing not to sue or otherwise renouncing rights against the party by a signed record. The obligation of a party to pay a check is not discharged solely by destruction of the check in connection with a process in which information is extracted from the check and an image of the check is made and, subsequently, the information and image are transmitted for payment.

(b) Cancellation or striking out of an indorsement pursuant to subsection (a) does not affect the status and rights of a party derived from the indorsement.

Definitional Cross References:

"Discharge".	Section 3-601(a)
"Indorsement".	Section 3-204(a)
"Instrument".	Section 3-104(b)
"Party".	Section 3-103(a)(10)
"Person Entitled to Enforce".	Section 3-301
"Record".	Section 3-103(a)(14)
"Signed".	Section 1-201(b)(37)
"Writing".	Section 1-201(b)(43)

Official Comment

1. Section 3-604 replaces former Section 3-605.

2. The destruction of a check in connection with a truncation process in which information is extracted from the check and an image of the check is made, and then such information and image are transmitted for payment is not within the scope of this section and does not by itself discharge the obligation of a party to pay the instrument. The destruction of the check also does not affect whether the check has been issued. See Section 3-105(a) and Comment 1.

3. Former subsection (c) has been deleted as unnecessary in view of the revised definition of "sign" in Section 1-201(b)(37).

Additional References: 3-305 Comment 5

Section 3-605. Discharge of Secondary Obligors

(a) If a person entitled to enforce an instrument releases the obligation of a principal obligor in whole or in part, and another party to the instrument is a secondary obligor with respect to the obligation of that principal obligor, the following rules apply:

(1) Any obligations of the principal obligor to the secondary obligor with respect to any previous payment by the secondary obligor are not affected. Unless the terms of the release preserve the secondary obligor's recourse, the principal obligor is discharged, to the extent of the release, from any other duties to the secondary obligor under this Article.

(2) Unless the terms of the release provide that the person entitled to enforce the instrument retains the right to enforce the instrument against the secondary obligor, the secondary obligor is discharged to the same extent as the principal obligor from any unperformed portion of its obligation on the instrument. If the instrument is a check and the obligation of the secondary obligor is based on an indorsement of the check, the secondary obligor is discharged without regard to the language or circumstances of the discharge or other release.

(3) If the secondary obligor is not discharged under paragraph (2), the secondary obligor is discharged to the extent of the value of the consideration for the release, and to the extent that the release would otherwise cause the secondary obligor a loss.

(b) If a person entitled to enforce an instrument grants a principal obligor an extension of the time at which one or more payments are due on the instrument and another party to the instrument is a secondary obligor with respect to the obligation of that principal obligor, the following rules apply:

(1) Any obligations of the principal obligor to the secondary obligor with respect to any previous payment by the secondary obligor are not affected. Unless the terms of the extension preserve the secondary obligor's recourse, the extension correspondingly extends the time for performance of any other duties owed to the secondary obligor by the principal obligor under this Article.

(2) The secondary obligor is discharged to the extent that the extension would otherwise cause the secondary obligor a loss.

(3) To the extent that the secondary obligor is not discharged under paragraph (2), the secondary obligor may perform its obligations to a person entitled to enforce the instrument as if the time for payment had not been extended or, unless the terms of the extension provide that the person entitled to enforce the instrument retains the right to enforce the instrument against the secondary obligor as if the time for payment had not been extended, treat the time for performance of its obligations as having been extended correspondingly.

(c) If a person entitled to enforce an instrument agrees, with or without consideration, to a modification of the obligation of a principal obligor other than a complete or partial release or an extension of the due date and another party to the instrument is a secondary obligor with respect to the obligation of that principal obligor, the following rules apply:

(1) Any obligations of the principal obligor to the secondary obligor with respect to any previous payment by the secondary obligor are not affected. The modification correspondingly modifies any

other duties owed to the secondary obligor by the principal obligor under this Article.

(2) The secondary obligor is discharged from any unperformed portion of its obligation to the extent that the modification would otherwise cause the secondary obligor a loss.

(3) To the extent that the secondary obligor is not discharged under paragraph (2), the secondary obligor may satisfy its obligation on the instrument as if the modification had not occurred, or treat its obligation on the instrument as having been modified correspondingly.

(d) If the obligation of a principal obligor is secured by an interest in collateral, another party to the instrument is a secondary obligor with respect to that obligation, and a person entitled to enforce the instrument impairs the value of the interest in collateral, the obligation of the secondary obligor is discharged to the extent of the impairment. The value of an interest in collateral is impaired to the extent the value of the interest is reduced to an amount less than the amount of the recourse of the secondary obligor, or the reduction in value of the interest causes an increase in the amount by which the amount of the recourse exceeds the value of the interest. For purposes of this subsection, impairing the value of an interest in collateral includes failure to obtain or maintain perfection or recordation of the interest in collateral, release of collateral without substitution of collateral of equal value or equivalent reduction of the underlying obligation, failure to perform a duty to preserve the value of collateral owed, under Article 9 or other law, to a debtor or other person secondarily liable, and failure to comply with applicable law in disposing of or otherwise enforcing the interest in collateral.

(e) A secondary obligor is not discharged under subsections (a)(3), (b), (c), or (d) unless the person entitled to enforce the instrument knows that the person is a secondary obligor or has notice under Section 3-419(c) that the instrument was signed for accommodation.

(f) A secondary obligor is not discharged under this section if the secondary obligor consents to the event or conduct that is the basis of the discharge, or the instrument or a separate agreement of the party provides for waiver of discharge under this section specifically or by general language indicating that parties waive defenses based on suretyship or impairment of collateral. Unless the circumstances indicate otherwise, consent by the principal obligor to an act that would lead to a discharge under this section constitutes consent to that act by the secondary obligor if the secondary obligor controls the principal obligor or deals with the person entitled to enforce the instrument on behalf of the principal obligor.

(g) A release or extension preserves a secondary obligor's recourse if the terms of the release or extension provide that:

(1) the person entitled to enforce the instrument retains the right to enforce the instrument against the secondary obligor; and

(2) the recourse of the secondary obligor continues as if the release or extension had not been granted.

(h) Except as otherwise provided in subsection (i), a secondary obligor asserting discharge under this section has the burden of persuasion both with respect to the occurrence of the acts alleged to harm the secondary obligor and loss or prejudice caused by those acts.

(i) If the secondary obligor demonstrates prejudice caused by an impairment of its recourse, and the circumstances of the case indicate that the amount of loss is not reasonably susceptible of calculation or requires proof of facts that are not ascertainable, it is presumed that the act impairing recourse caused a loss or impairment equal to the liability of the secondary obligor on the instrument. In that event, the burden of persuasion as to any lesser amount of the loss is on the person entitled to enforce the instrument.

Definitional Cross References:

"Agreement".	Section 1-201(b)(3)
"Discharge".	Section 3-601(a)
"Instrument".	Section 3-104(b)
"Knows".	Section 1-202(a)
"Notice".	Section 1-202(a)
"Party".	Section 3-103(a)(10)
"Person".	Section 1-201(b)(27)
"Person Entitled to Enforce".	Section 3-301
"Principal Obligor".	Section 3-103(a)(11)
"Signed".	Section 1-201(37)
"Surety".	Section 1-201(b)(39)

Official Comment

1. This section contains rules that are applicable when a secondary obligor (as defined in Section 3-103(a)(17)) is a party to an instrument. These rules essentially parallel modern interpretations of the law of suretyship and guaranty that apply when a secondary obligor is not a party to an instrument. See generally *Restatement of the Law, Third, Suretyship and Guaranty* (1996). Of course, the rules in this section do not resolve all possible issues concerning the rights and duties of the parties. In the event that a situation is presented that is not resolved by this section (or the other related sections of this Article), the resolution may be provided by the general law of suretyship because, pursuant to Section 1-103, that law is applicable unless displaced by provisions of this Act.

2. Like the law of suretyship and guaranty, Section 3-605 provides secondary obligors with defenses that are not available to other parties to instruments. The general operation of Section 3-605, and its relationship to the law of suretyship and guaranty, can be illustrated by an example. Bank agrees to lend $10,000 to Borrower, but only if Backer also is liable for repayment of the loan. The parties could consummate that transaction in three different ways. First, if Borrower and Backer incurred those obligations with contracts not governed by this Article (such as a note that is not an instrument for purposes of this Article), the general law of suretyship and guaranty would be applicable. Under modern nomenclature, Bank is the "obligee," Borrower is the "principal obligor," and Backer is the "secondary obligor." See *Restatement of Suretyship and Guaranty* § 1. Then assume that Bank and Borrower agree to a modification of their rights and obligations after the note is signed. For example, they might agree that Borrower may repay the loan at some date after the due date, or that Borrower may discharge its repayment obligation by paying Bank $3,000 rather than $10,000. Alternatively, suppose that Bank releases collateral that Borrower has given to secure the loan. Under the law of suretyship and guaranty, the secondary obligor may be discharged under certain circumstances if these modifications of the obligations between Bank (the obligee) and Borrower (the principal obligor) are made without the consent of Backer (the secondary obligor). The rights that the secondary obligor has to a discharge of its liability in such cases commonly are referred to as suretyship defenses. The extent of the discharge depends upon the particular circumstances. See *Restatement of Suretyship and Guaranty* §§ 37, 3944.

A second possibility is that the parties might decide to evidence the loan by a negotiable instrument. In that scenario, Borrower signs a note under which Borrower is obliged to pay $10,000 to the order of Bank on a due date stated in the note. Backer becomes liable for the repayment obligation by signing the note as a co-maker or indorser. In either case the note is signed for accommodation, Backer is an accommodation party, and Borrower is the accommodated party. See Section 3-419 (describing the obligations of accommodation parties). For purposes of Section 3-605, Backer is also a "secondary obligor" and Borrower is a "principal obligor," as those terms are defined in Section 3-103. Because Backer is a party to the instrument, its rights to a discharge based on any modification of obligations between Bank and Borrower are governed by Section 3-605 rather than by the general law of suretyship and guaranty. Within Section 3-605, subsection (a) describes the consequences of a release of Borrower, subsection (b) describes the consequences of an extension of time, and subsection (c) describes the consequences of other modifications.

The third possibility is that Borrower would use an instrument governed by this Article to evidence its repayment obligation, but Backer's obligation would be created in some way other than by becoming party to that instrument. In that case, Backer's rights are determined by suretyship and guaranty law rather than by this Article. See Comment 3 to Section 3-419.

A person also can acquire secondary liability without having been a secondary obligor at the time that the principal obligation was created. For example, a transferee of real or personal property that assumes the obligation of the transferor as maker of a note secured by the property becomes by operation of law a principal obligor, with the transferor becoming a secondary obligor. *Restatement of Suretyship and Guaranty* § 2(e); *Restatement of Mortgages* § 5.1. Article 3 does not determine the effect of the release of the transferee in that case because the assuming transferee is not a "party" to the instrument as defined in Section 3-103(a)(10). Section 3-605(a) does not apply then because the holder has not discharged the obligation of a "principal obligor," a term defined in Section 3-103(a)(11). Thus, the resolution of that question is governed by the law of suretyship. See *Restatement of Suretyship and Guaranty* § 39.

3. Section 3-605 is not, however, limited to the conventional situation of the accommodation party discussed in Comment 2. It also applies in four other situations. First, it applies to indorsers of notes who are not accommodation parties. Unless an indorser signs without recourse, the indorser's liability under Section 3-415(a) is functionally similar to that of a guarantor of payment. For example, if Bank in the second hypothetical discussed in Comment 2 indorsed the note and transferred it to Second Bank, Bank is liable to Second Bank in the event of dishonor of the note by Borrower. Section 3-415(a). Because of that secondary liability as indorser, Bank qualifies as a "secondary obligor" under Section 3-103(a)(17) and has the same rights under Section 3-605 as an accommodation party.

Second, a similar analysis applies to the drawer of a draft that is accepted by a party that is not a bank. Under Section 3-414(d), that drawer has liability on the same terms as an indorser under Section 3-415(a). Thus, the drawer in that case is a "secondary obligor" under Section 3-103(a)(17) and has rights under Section 3-605 to that extent.

Third, a similar principle justifies application of Section 3-605 to persons who indorse a check. Assume that Drawer draws a check to the order of Payee. Payee then indorses the check and transfers it to Transferee. If Transferee presents the check and it is dishonored, Transferee may recover from Drawer under Section 3-414 or Payee under Section 3-415. Because of that secondary liability as an indorser, Payee is a secondary obligor under Section 3-103(a)(17). Drawer is a "principal obligor" under Section 3-103(a)(11). As noted in Comment 4, below, however, Section 3-605(a)(3) will discharge indorsers of checks in some cases in which other secondary obligors will not be discharged by this section.

Fourth, this section also deals with the rights of co-makers of instruments, even when those co-makers do not qualify as accommodation parties. The co-makers' rights of contribution under Section 3-116 make each co-maker a secondary obligor to the extent of that right of contribution.

4. Subsection (a) is based on *Restatement of Suretyship and Guaranty* § 39. It addresses the effects of a release of the principal obligor by the person entitled to enforce the instrument. Paragraph (a)(1) governs the effect of that release on the principal obligor's duties to the secondary obligor; paragraphs (a)(2) and (a)(3) govern the effect of that release on the secondary obligor's duties to the person entitled to enforce the instrument.

With respect to the duties of the principal obligor, the release of course cannot affect obligations of the principal obligor with respect to payments that the secondary obligor already has made. But with respect to future payments by the secondary obligor, paragraph (a)(1) (based on *Restatement of Suretyship and Guaranty* § 39(a)) provides that the principal obligor is discharged, to the extent of the release, from any other duties to the secondary obligor. That rule is appropriate because otherwise the discharge granted to the principal obligor would be illusory: it would have obtained a release from a person entitled to enforce that instrument, but it would be directly liable for the same sum to the secondary obligor if the secondary obligor later complied with its secondary obligation to pay the instrument. This discharge does not occur, though, if the terms of the release effect a "preservation of recourse" as described in subsection (g). See Comment 10, below.

The discharge under paragraph (a)(1) of the principal obligor's duties to the secondary obligor is broad, applying to all duties under this Article. This includes not only the principal obligor's liability as a party to an instrument (as a maker, drawer or indorser under Sections 3-412 through 3-415) but also obligations under Sections 3-116 and 3-419.

Paragraph (a)(2) is based closely on *Restatement of Suretyship and Guaranty* § 39(b). It articulates a default rule that the release of a principal obligor also discharges the secondary obligor, to the extent of the release granted to the principal obligor, from any unperformed portion of its obligation on the instrument. The discharge of the secondary obligor under paragraph (a)(2) is phrased more narrowly than the discharge of the principal obligor is phrased under paragraph (a)(1) because, unlike principal obligors, the only obligations of secondary obligors in Article 3 are "on the instrument" as makers or indorsers.

The parties can opt out of that rule by including a contrary statement in the terms of the release. The provision does not contemplate that any "magic words" are necessary. Thus, discharge of the secondary obligor under paragraph (a)(2) is avoided not only if the terms of the release track the statutory language (e.g., the person entitled to enforce the instrument "retains the right to enforce the instrument" against the secondary obligor), or if the terms of the release effect a preservation of recourse under subsection (g), but also if the terms of the release include a simple statement that the parties intend to "release the principal obligor but not the secondary obligor" or that the person entitled to enforce the instrument "reserves its rights" against the secondary obligor. At the same time, because paragraph (a)(2) refers to the "terms of the release," extrinsic circumstances cannot be used to establish that the parties intended the secondary obligor to remain obligated. If a release of the principal obligor includes such a provision, the secondary obligor is, nonetheless, discharged to the extent of the consideration that is paid for the release; that consideration is treated as a payment in partial satisfaction of the instrument.

Notwithstanding language in the release that prevents discharge of the secondary obligor under paragraph (a)(2), paragraph (a)(3) discharges the secondary obligor from its obligation to a person entitled to enforce the instrument to the extent that the release otherwise would cause the secondary obligor a loss. The rationale for that provision is that a release of the principal obligor changes the economic risk for which the secondary obligor contracted. This risk may be increased in two ways. First, by releasing the principal obligor, the person entitled to enforce the instrument has eliminated the likelihood of future payments by the principal obligor that would lessen the obligation of the secondary obligor. Second, unless the release effects a preservation of the secondary obligor's recourse, the release eliminates the secondary obligor's claims against the principal obligor with respect to any future payment by the secondary obligor. The discharge provided by this paragraph prevents that increased risk from causing the secondary obligor a loss. Moreover, permitting releases to be negotiated between the principal obligor and the person entitled to enforce the instrument without regard to the consequences to the secondary obligor would create an undue risk of opportunistic behavior by the obligee and principal obligor. That concern is lessened, and the discharge is not provided by paragraph (a)(3), if the secondary obligor has consented to the release or is deemed to have consented to it under subsection (f) (which presumes consent by a secondary obligor to actions taken by a principal obligor if the secondary obligor controls the principal obligor or deals with the person entitled to enforce the instrument on behalf of the principal obligor). See Comment 9, below.

Subsection (a) (and Restatement Section 39(b), the concepts of which it follows quite closely) is designed to facilitate negotiated workouts between a creditor and a principal obligor, so long as they are not at the expense of a secondary obligor who has not consented to the arrangement (either specifically or by waiving its rights to discharge under this section). Thus, for example, the provision facilitates an arrangement in which the principal obligor pays some portion of a guaranteed obligation, the person entitled to enforce the instrument grants a release to the principal obligor in exchange for that payment, and the person entitled to enforce the instrument pursues the secondary obligor for the remainder of the obligation. Under paragraph (a)(2), the person entitled to enforce the instrument may pursue the secondary obligor despite the release of the principal obligor so long as the terms of the release provide for this result. Under paragraph (a)(3), though, the secondary obligor will be protected against any loss it might suffer by reason of that release (if the secondary obligor has not waived discharge under subsection (f)). It should be noted that the obligee may be able to minimize the risk of such loss (and, thus, of the secondary obligor's discharge) by giving the secondary obligor prompt notice of the release even though such notice is not required.

The foregoing principles are illustrated by the following cases:

Case 1. D borrows $1000 from C. The repayment obligation is evidenced by a note issued by D, payable to the order of C. S is an accommodation indorser of the note. As the due date of the note approaches, it becomes obvious that D cannot pay the full amount of the note and may soon be facing bankruptcy. C, in order to collect as much as possible from D and lessen the need to seek recovery from S, agrees to release D from its obligation under the note in exchange for $100 in cash. The agreement to release D is silent as to the effect of the release on S. Pursuant to Section 3-605(a)(2), the release of D discharges S from its obligations to C on the note.

Case 2. Same facts as Case 1, except that the terms of the release provide that C retains its rights to enforce the instrument against S. D is discharged from its obligations to S pursuant to Section 3-605(a)(1), but S is not discharged from its obligations to C pursuant to Section 3-605(a)(2). However, if S could have recovered from D any sum it paid to C (had D not been discharged from its obligation to S), S has been harmed by the release and is discharged pursuant to Section 3-605(a)(3) to the extent of that harm.

Case 3. Same facts as Case 1, except that the terms of the release provide that C retains its rights to enforce the instrument against S and that S retains its recourse against D. Under subsection (g), the release effects a preservation of recourse. Thus, S is not discharged from its obligations to C pursuant to Section 3-605(a)(2) and D is not discharged from its obligations to S pursuant to Section 3-605(a)(1). Because S's claims against D are preserved, S will not suffer the kind of loss described in Case 2. If no other loss is suffered by S as a result of the release, S is not discharged pursuant to this section.

Case 4. Same facts as Case 3, except that D had made arrangements to work at a second job in order to earn the money to fulfill its obligations on the note. When C released D, however, D canceled the plans for the second job. While S still retains its recourse against D, S may be discharged from its obligation under the instrument to the extent that D's decision to forgo the second job causes S a loss because forgoing the job renders D unable to fulfill its obligations to S under Section 3-419.

Subsection (a) reflects a change from former Section 3-605(b), which provided categorically that the release of a principal obligor by the person entitled to enforce the instrument did not discharge a secondary obligor's obligation on the instrument and assumed that the release also did not discharge the principal obligor's obligations to the secondary obligor under Section 3-419. The rule under subsection (a) is much closer to the policy of the *Restatement of Suretyship and Guaranty* than was former Section 3-605(b). The change, however, is likely to affect only a narrow category of cases. First, as discussed above, Section 3-605 applies only to transactions in which the payment obligation is represented by a negotiable instrument, and, within that set of transactions, only to those transactions in which the secondary obligation is incurred by indorsement or cosigning, not to transactions that involve a separate document of guaranty. See Comment 2, above. Second, as provided in subsection (f), secondary obligors cannot obtain a discharge under subsection (a) in any transaction in which they have consented to the challenged conduct. Thus, subsection (a) will not apply to any transaction that includes a provision waiving suretyship defenses (a provision that is almost universally included in commercial loan documentation) or to any transaction in which the creditor obtains the consent of the secondary obligor at the time of the release.

The principal way in which subsection (a) goes beyond the policy of *Restatement* § 39 is with respect to the liability of indorsers of checks. Specifically, the last sentence of paragraph (a)(2) provides that a release of a principal obligor grants a complete discharge to the indorser of a check, without requiring the indorser to prove harm. In that particular context, it seems likely that continuing responsibility for the indorser often would be so inconsistent with the expectations of the parties as to create a windfall for the creditor and an unfair surprise for the indorser. Thus, the statute implements a simple rule that grants a complete discharge. The creditor, of course, can avoid that rule by contracting with the secondary obligor for a different result at the time that the creditor grants the release to the principal obligor.

5. Subsection (b) is based on *Restatement of Suretyship and Guaranty* § 40 and relates to extensions of the due date of the instrument. An extension of time to pay a note is often beneficial to the secondary obligor because the additional time may enable the principal obligor to obtain the funds to pay the instrument. In some cases, however, the extension may cause loss to the secondary obligor, particularly if deterioration of the financial condition of the principal obligor reduces the amount that the secondary obligor is able to recover on its right of recourse when default occurs. For example, suppose that the instrument is an installment note and the principal debtor is temporarily short of funds to pay a monthly installment. The payee agrees to extend the due date of the installment for a month or two to allow the debtor to pay when funds are available. Paragraph (b)(2) provides that an extension of time results in a discharge of the secondary obligor, but only to the extent that the secondary obligor proves that the extension caused loss. See subsection (h) (discussing the burden of proof under Section 3-605). Thus, if the extension is for a long period, the secondary obligor might be able to prove that during the period of extension the principal obligor became insolvent, reducing the value of the right of recourse of the secondary obligor. In such a case, paragraph (b)(2) discharges the secondary obligor to the extent of that harm. Although not required to notify the secondary obligor of the extension, the payee can minimize the risk of loss by the secondary obligor by giving the secondary obligor prompt notice of the extension; prompt notice can enhance the likelihood that the secondary obligor's right of recourse can remain valuable, and thus can limit the likelihood that the secondary obligor will suffer a loss because of the extension. See *Restatement of Suretyship and Guaranty* § 38 Comment b.

If the secondary obligor is not discharged under paragraph (b)(2) (either because it would not suffer a loss by reason of the extension or because it has waived its right to discharge pursuant to subsection (f)), it is important to understand the effect of the extension on the rights and obligations of the secondary obligor. Consider the following cases:

Case 5. A borrows money from Lender and issues a note payable to the order of Lender that is due on April 1, 2002. B signs the note for accommodation at the request of Lender. B signed the note either as co-maker or as an anomalous indorser. In either case Lender subsequently makes an agreement with A extending the due date of A's obligation to pay the note to July 1, 2002. In either case B did not agree to the extension, and the extension did not address Lender's rights against B. Under paragraph (b)(1), A's obligations to B under this Article are also extended to July 1, 2002. Under paragraph (b)(3), if B is not discharged, B may treat its obligations to Lender as also extended, or may pay the instrument on the original due date.

Case 6. Same facts as Case 5, except that the extension agreement includes a statement that the Lender retains its right to enforce the note against B on its original terms. Under paragraph (b)(3), B is liable on the original due date, but under paragraph (b)(1), A's obligations to B under Section 3-419 are not due until July 1, 2002.

Case 7. Same facts as Case 5, except that the extension agreement includes a statement that the Lender retains its right to enforce the note against B on its original terms and B retains its recourse against A as though no extension had been granted. Under paragraph (b)(3), B is liable on the original due date. Under paragraph (b)(1), A's obligations to B under Section 3-419 are not extended.

Under section 3-605(b), the results in Case 5 and Case 7 are identical to the results that follow from the law of suretyship and guaranty. See *Restatement of Suretyship and Guaranty* § 40. The situation in Case 6 is not specifically addressed in the Restatement, but the resolution in this Section is consistent with the concepts of suretyship and guaranty law as reflected in the Restatement. If the secondary obligor is called upon to pay on the due date, it may be difficult to quantify the extent to which the extension has impaired the right of recourse of the secondary obligor at that time. Still, the secondary obligor does have a right to make a claim against the obligee at that time. As a practical matter a suit making such a claim should establish the facts relevant to the extent of the impairment. See *Restatement of Suretyship and Guaranty* § 37(4).

As a practical matter, an extension of the due date will normally occur only when the principal obligor is unable to pay on the due date. The interest of the secondary obligor normally is to acquiesce in the willingness of the person entitled to enforce the instrument to wait for payment from the principal obligor rather than to pay right away and rely on an action against the principal obligor that may have little or no value. But in unusual cases the secondary obligor may prefer to pay the holder on the original due date so as to avoid continuing accrual of interest. In such cases, the secondary obligor may do so. See paragraph (b)(3). If the terms of the extension provide that the person entitled to enforce the instrument retains its right to enforce the instrument against the secondary obligor on the original due date, though, those terms are effective and the secondary obligor may not delay payment until the extended due date. Unless the extension agreement effects a preservation of recourse, however, the secondary obligor may not proceed against the principal obligor under Section 3-419 until the extended due date. See paragraph (b)(1). To the extent that delay causes loss to the secondary obligor it is discharged under paragraph (b)(2).

Even in those cases in which a secondary obligor does not have a duty to pay the instrument on the original due date, it always has the right to pay the instrument on that date, and perhaps minimize its loss by doing so. The secondary obligor is not precluded, however, from asserting its rights to discharge under Section 3-605(b)(2) if it does not exercise that option. The critical issue is whether the extension caused the secondary obligor a loss by increasing the difference between its cost of performing its obligation on the instrument and the amount recoverable from the principal obligor under this Article. The decision by the secondary obligor not to exercise its option to pay on the original due date may, under the circumstances, be a factor to be considered in the determination of that issue, especially if the secondary obligor has been given prompt notice of the extension (as discussed above).

6. Subsection (c) is based on *Restatement of Suretyship and Guaranty* § 41. It is a residual provision, which applies to modifications of the obligation of the principal obligor that are not covered by subsections (a) and (b). Under subsection (c)(1), a modification of the obligation of the principal obligor on the instrument (other than a release covered by subsection (a) or an extension of the due date covered by subsection (b)), will correspondingly modify the duties of the principal obligor to the secondary obligor. Under subsection (c)(2), such a modification also will result in discharge of the secondary obligor to the extent the modification causes loss to the secondary obligor. To the extent that the secondary obligor is not discharged and the obligation changes the amount of money payable on the instrument, or the timing of such payment, subsection (c)(3) provides the secondary obligor with a choice: it may satisfy its obligation on the instrument as if the modification had not occurred, or it may treat its obligation to pay the instrument as having been modified in a manner corresponding to the modification of the principal obligor's obligation.

The following cases illustrate the application of subsection (c):

Case 8. Corporation borrows money from Lender and issues a note payable to Lender. X signs the note as an accommodation party for Corporation. The note refers to a loan agreement under which the note was issued, which states various events of default that allow Lender to accelerate the due date of the note. Among the events of default are breach of covenants not to incur debt beyond specified limits and not to engage in any line of business substantially different from that currently carried on by Corporation. Without consent of X, Lender agrees to modify the covenants to allow Corporation to enter into a new line of business that X considers to be risky, and to incur debt beyond the limits specified in the loan agreement to finance the new venture. This modification discharges X to the extent that the modification otherwise would cause X a loss.

Case 9. Corporation borrows money from Lender and issues a note payable to Lender in the amount of $100,000. X signs the note as an accommodation party for Corporation. The note calls for 60 equal monthly payments of interest and principal. Before the first payment is made, Corporation and Lender agree to modify the note by changing the repayment schedule to require four annual payments of interest only, followed by a fifth payment of interest and the entire $100,000 principal balance. To the extent that the modification does not discharge X, X has the option of fulfilling its obligation on the note in accordance with the original terms or the modified terms.

7. Subsection (d) is based on *Restatement of Suretyship and Guaranty* § 42 and deals with the discharge of secondary obligors by impairment of collateral. The last sentence of subsection (d) states four common examples of what is meant by impairment. Because it uses the term "includes," the provision allows a court to find impairment in other cases as well. There is extensive case law on impairment of collateral. The secondary obligor is discharged to the extent that the secondary obligor proves that impairment was caused by a person entitled to enforce the instrument. For example, assume that the payee of a secured note fails to perfect the security interest. The collateral is owned by the principal obligor who subsequently files in bankruptcy. As a result of the failure to perfect, the security interest is not enforceable in bankruptcy. If the payee were to obtain payment from the secondary obligor, the secondary obligor would be subrogated to the payee's security interest in the collateral under Section 3-419 and general principles of suretyship law. See *Restatement of Suretyship and Guaranty* § 28(1)(c). In this situation, though, the value of the security interest is impaired completely because the security interest is unenforceable. Thus, the secondary obligor is discharged from its obligation on the note to the extent of that impairment. If the value of the collateral impaired is as much or more than the amount of the note, and if there will be no recovery on the note as an unsecured claim, there is a complete discharge. Subsection (d) applies whether the collateral is personalty or realty, whenever the obligation in question is in the form of a negotiable instrument.

8. Subsection (e) is based on the former Section 3-605(h). The requirement of knowledge in the first clause is consistent with Section 9-628. The requirement of notice in the second clause is consistent with Section 3-419(c).

9. The importance of the suretyship defenses provided in Section 3-605 is greatly diminished by the fact that the right to discharge can be waived as provided in subsection (f). The waiver can be effectuated by a provision in the instrument or in a separate agreement. It is standard practice to include such a waiver of suretyship defenses in notes prepared by financial institutions or other commercial creditors. Thus, Section 3-605 will result in the discharge of an accommodation party on a note only in the occasional case in which the note does not include such a waiver clause and the person entitled to enforce the note nevertheless takes actions that would give rise to a discharge under this section without obtaining the consent of the secondary obligor.

Because subsection (f) by its terms applies only to a discharge "under this section," subsection (f) does not operate to waive a defense created by other law (such as the law governing enforcement of security interests under Article 9) that cannot be waived under that law. See, e.g., Section 9-602.

The last sentence of subsection (f) creates an inference of consent on the part of the secondary obligor whenever the secondary obligor controls the principal obligor or deals with the creditor on behalf of the principal obligor. That sentence is based on *Restatement of Suretyship and Guaranty* § 48(2).

10. Subsection (g) explains the criteria for determining whether the terms of a release or extension preserve the secondary obligor's recourse, a concept of importance in the application of subsections (a) and (b). First, the terms of the release or extension must provide that the person entitled to enforce the instrument retains the right to enforce the instrument against the secondary obligor. Second, the terms of the release or extension must provide that the recourse of the secondary obligor against the principal obligor continues as though the release or extension had not been granted. Those requirements are drawn from *Restatement of Suretyship and Guaranty* § 38.

11. Subsections (h) and (i) articulate rules for the burden of persuasion under Section 3-605. Those rules are based on *Restatement of Suretyship and Guaranty* § 49.

Additional References:

3-305 Comment 5

3-419 Comment 3

Editors' Note: Detailed revisions to Sections 3-419 and 3-605 conformed those provisions to the Restatement of Suretyship and Guaranty.

Article 4—Bank Deposit

As adopted in 1962 and revised in: (i) 1990, in connection with the revision of Article 3; (ii) 1991 to correct errata; (iii) 1994, in connection with the revision of Article 8; (iv) 1999, in connection with the revision of Article 9; (iv) 2001, in connection with the revision of Article 1; (v) 2002, in connection with amendments; (vi) 2003, in connection with the revision of Article 7; and (vii) 2022, in connection with the 2022 Amendments to the Uniform Commercial Code.

PREFATORY NOTE

PART 1. GENERAL PROVISIONS AND DEFINITIONS

Section

PART 2. COLLECTION OF ITEMS: DEPOSITARY AND COLLECTING BANKS

PART 3. COLLECTION OF ITEMS: PAYOR BANKS

PART 4. RELATIONSHIP BETWEEN PAYOR BANK AND ITS CUSTOMER

PART 5. COLLECTION OF DOCUMENTARY DRAFTS

PREFATORY NOTE

This project involves a small number of amendments to Articles 3 and 4 with respect to which there is a general consensus that the need for reform is plain and the opportunity for justifiable controversy small. The specific amendments cover the following topics.

1. Transferring Lost Instruments.—At least one case has held that the receiver of a failed bank cannot enforce an instrument transferred to it in the portfolio of a failed bank if the instrument was lost before the transfer. The result in that case poses a serious problem for the FDIC. An amendment to UCC § 3-309 calls for a contrary result, making it clear that the party seeking to enforce a lost instrument need not have been in possession of the instrument at the time that it was lost.

2. Payment and Discharge.—Amendments to UCC §§ 3-602 conform that provision to the rules for payment that appear in the *Restatement of Mortgages* and in the *Restatement of Contracts*.

3. Telephonically Generated Checks.—Several States have adopted non-uniform amendments dealing with the responsibility for unauthorized telephone-generated checks. The amendments include warranties that generally place the responsibility for such checks on depositary banks rather than payor banks. The warranties are limited to items that are drawn on a consumer account and do not bear a manual signature.

4. Suretyship.—Amendments to UCC §§ 3-419 and 3-605 generally conform those provisions to the rules in the *Restatement of Suretyship and Guaranty*.

5. Electronic Communications.—Amendments to various provisions of Articles 3 and 4 implement the policy of the Uniform Electronic Transactions Act to remove unnecessary obstacles to electronic communications.

6. Consumer Notes.—A provision analogous to UCC § 9-404(d) indicates that a note for which the Federal Trade Commission requires a notice to be included will be treated is if the notice had been included.

7. United Nations Convention on International Bills of Exchange and International Promissory Notes.—The draft includes several comments indicating similarities and differences between Article 3 and the United Nations Convention, designed to facilitate implementation of the Convention if the United States ratifies that convention in the coming years.

PART 1. GENERAL PROVISIONS AND DEFINITIONS

Section 4-101. Short Title

This Article may be cited as Uniform Commercial Code—Bank Deposits and Collections.

Official Comment

1. The great number of checks handled by banks and the country-wide nature of the bank collection process require uniformity in the law of bank collections. There is needed a uniform statement of the principal rules of the bank collection process with ample provision for flexibility to meet the needs of the large volume handled and the changing needs and conditions that are bound to come with the years. This Article meets that need.

2. In 1950 at the time Article 4 was drafted, 6.7 billion checks were written annually. By the time of the 1990 revision of Article 4 annual volume was estimated by the American Bankers Association to be about 50 billion checks. The banking system could not have coped with this increase in check volume had it not developed in the late 1950s and early 1960s an automated system for check collection based on encoding checks with machine-readable information by Magnetic Ink Character Recognition (MICR). An important goal of the 1990 revision of Article 4 is to promote the efficiency of the check collection process by making the provisions of Article 4 more compatible with the needs of an automated system and, by doing so, increase the speed and lower the cost of check collection for those who write and receive checks. An additional goal of the 1990 revision of Article 4 is to remove any statutory barriers in the Article to the ultimate adoption of programs allowing the presentment of checks to payor banks by electronic transmission of information captured from the MICR line on the checks. The potential of these programs for saving the time and expense of transporting the huge volume of checks from depositary to payor banks is evident.

3. Article 4 defines rights between parties with respect to bank deposits and collections. It is not a regulatory statute. It does not regulate the terms of the bank-customer agreement, nor does it prescribe what constraints different jurisdictions may wish to impose on that relationship in the interest of consumer protection. The revisions in Article 4 are intended to create a legal framework that accommodates automation and truncation for the benefit of all bank customers. This may raise consumer problems which enacting jurisdictions may wish to address in individual legislation. For example, with respect to Section 4-401(c), jurisdictions may wish to examine their unfair and deceptive practices laws to determine whether they are adequate to protect drawers who postdate checks from unscrupulous practices that may arise on the part of persons who induce drawers to issue postdated checks in the erroneous belief that the checks will not be immediately payable. Another example arises from the fact that under various truncation plans customers will no longer receive their cancelled checks and will no longer have the cancelled check to prove payment. Individual legislation might provide that a copy of a bank statement along with a copy of the check is prima facie evidence of payment.

Section 4-102. Applicability

(a) To the extent that items within this Article are also within Articles 3 and 8, they are subject to those

Articles. If there is conflict, this Article governs Article 3, but Article 8 governs this Article.

(b) The liability of a bank for action or non-action with respect to an item handled by it for purposes of presentment, payment, or collection is governed by the law of the place where the bank is located. In the case of action or non-action by or at a branch or separate office of a bank, its liability is governed by the law of the place where the branch or separate office is located.

Official Comment

1. The rules of Article 3 governing negotiable instruments, their transfer, and the contracts of the parties thereto apply to the items collected through banking channels wherever no specific provision is found in this Article. In the case of conflict, this Article governs. See Section 3-102(b).

Bonds and like instruments constituting investment securities under Article 8 may also be handled by banks for collection purposes. Various sections of Article 8 prescribe rules of transfer some of which (see Sections 8-108 and 8-304) may conflict with provisions of this Article (Sections 4-205, 4-207, and 4-208). In the case of conflict, Article 8 governs.

Section 4-210 deals specifically with overlapping problems and possible conflicts between this Article and Article 9. However, similar reconciling provisions are not necessary in the case of Articles 5 and 7. Sections 4-301 and 4-302 are consistent with Section 5-108. In the case of Article 7 documents of title frequently accompany items but they are not themselves items. See Section 4-104(a)(9).

In *Clearfield Trust Co. v. United States,* 318 U.S. 363 (1943), the Court held that if the United States is a party to an instrument, its rights and duties are governed by federal common law in the absence of a specific federal statute or regulation. In *United States v. Kimbell Foods, Inc.*, 440 U.S. 715 (1979), the Court stated a three-pronged test to ascertain whether the federal common-law rule should follow the state rule. In most instances courts under the *Kimbell* test have shown a willingness to adopt UCC rules in formulating federal common law on the subject. In *Kimbell* the Court adopted the priorities rules of Article 9.

In addition, applicable federal law may supersede provisions of this Article. One federal law that does so is the Expedited Funds Availability Act, 12 U.S.C. § 4001 et seq., and its implementing Regulation CC, 12 CFR Pt. 229. In some instances this law is alluded to in the statute, e.g., Section 4-215(e) and (f). In other instances, although not referred to in this Article, the provisions of the EFAA and Regulation CC control with respect to checks. For example, except between the depositary bank and its customer, all settlements are final and not provisional (Regulation CC, Section 229.36(d)), and the midnight deadline may be extended (Regulation CC, Section 229.30(c)). The comments to this Article suggest in most instances the relevant Regulation CC provisions.

2. Subsection (b) is designed to state a workable rule for the solution of otherwise vexatious problems of the conflicts of laws:

a. The routine and mechanical nature of bank collections makes it imperative that one law govern the activities of one office of a bank. The requirement found in some cases that to hold an indorser notice must be given in accordance with the law of the place of indorsement, since that method of notice became an implied term of the indorser's contract, is more theoretical than practical.

b. Adoption of what is in essence a tort theory of the conflict of laws is consistent with the general theory of this Article that the basic duty of a collecting bank is one of good faith and the exercise of ordinary care. Justification lies in the fact that, in using an ambulatory instrument, the drawer, payee, and indorsers must know that action will be taken with respect to it in other jurisdictions. This is especially pertinent with respect to the law of the place of payment.

c. The phrase "action or non-action with respect to any item handled by it for purposes of presentment, payment, or collection" is intended to make the conflicts rule of subsection (b) apply from the inception of the collection process of an item through all phases of deposit, forwarding, presentment, payment and remittance or credit of proceeds. Specifically the subsection applies to the initial act of a depositary bank in receiving an item and to the incidents of such receipt. The conflicts rule of *Weissman v. Banque De Bruxelles*, 173 N.E. 835 (N.Y. 1930), is rejected. The subsection applies to questions of possible vicarious liability of a bank for action or non-action of sub-agents (see Section 4-202(c)), and tests these questions by the law of the state of the location of the bank which uses the sub-agent. The conflicts rule of *St. Nicholas Bank of New York v. State Nat'l. Bank,* 27 N.E. 849 (N.Y. 1891), is rejected. The subsection applies to action or non-action of a payor bank in connection with handling an item (see Sections 4-215(a), 4-301, 4-302,4-303) as well as action or non-action of a collecting bank (Sections 4-201 through 4-216); to action or non-action of a bank which suspends payment or is affected by another bank suspending payment (Section 4-216); to action or non-action of a bank with respect to an item under the rule of Part 4 of Article 4.

d. In a case in which subsection (b) makes this Article applicable, Section 4-103(a) leaves open the possibility of an agreement with respect to applicable law. This freedom of agreement follows the general policy of Section 1-301.

Cross References:

Sections 1-301; 3-103(2) and Article 3; all sections of Article 4; 5-108; Article 7; 8-108 and 8-304; Article 9.

Definitional Cross References:

"Bank".	Section 1-201.
"Branch".	Section 1-201.
"Item".	Section 4-104.
"Payment".	Section 3-602.
"Presentment".	Section 3-501.

Section 4-103. Variation by Agreement; Measure of Damages; Action Constituting Ordinary Care

(a) The effect of the provisions of this Article may be varied by agreement, but the parties to the agreement cannot disclaim a bank's responsibility for its lack of good faith or failure to exercise ordinary care or limit the measure of damages for the lack or failure. However, the parties may determine by agreement the standards by which the bank's responsibility is to be measured if those standards are not manifestly unreasonable.

(b) Federal Reserve regulations and operating circulars, clearing-house rules, and the like have the effect of agreements under subsection (a), whether or not specifically assented to by all parties interested in items handled.

(c) Action or non-action approved by this Article or pursuant to Federal Reserve regulations or operating circulars is the exercise of ordinary care and, in the absence of special instructions, action or non-action consistent with clearing-house rules and the like or with a general banking usage not disapproved by this Article, is prima facie the exercise of ordinary care.

(d) The specification or approval of certain procedures by this Article is not disapproval of other procedures that may be reasonable under the circumstances.

(e) The measure of damages for failure to exercise ordinary care in handling an item is the amount of the item reduced by an amount that could not have been realized by the exercise of ordinary care. If there is also bad faith it includes any other damages the party suffered as a proximate consequence.

Official Comment

1. Section 1-302 states the general principles and rules for variation of the effect of this Act by agreement and the limitations to this power. Section 4-103 states the specific rules for variation of Article 4 by agreement and also certain standards of ordinary care. In view of the technical complexity of the field of bank collections, the enormous number of items handled by banks, the certainty that there will be variations from the normal in each day's work in each bank, the certainty of changing conditions and the possibility of developing improved methods of collection to speed the process, it would be unwise to freeze present methods of operation by mandatory statutory rules. This section, therefore, permits within wide limits variation of the effect of provisions of the Article by agreement.

2. Subsection (a) confers blanket power to vary all provisions of the Article by agreements of the ordinary kind. The agreements may not disclaim a bank's responsibility for its own lack of good faith or failure to exercise ordinary care and may not limit the measure of damages for the lack or failure, but this subsection like Section 1-302(b) approves the practice of parties determining by agreement the standards by which the responsibility is to be measured. In the absence of a showing that the standards manifestly are unreasonable, the agreement controls. Owners of items and other interested parties are not affected by agreements under this subsection unless they are parties to the agreement or are bound by adoption, ratification, estoppel or the like.

As here used "agreement" has the meaning given to it by Section 1-203(b)(3). The agreement may be direct, as between the owner and the depositary bank; or indirect, as in the case in which the owner authorizes a particular type of procedure and any bank in the collection chain acts pursuant to such authorization. It may be with respect to a single item; or to all items handled for a particular customer, e.g., a general agreement between the depositary bank and the customer at the time a deposit account is opened. Legends on deposit tickets, collection letters and acknowledgments of items, coupled with action by the affected party constituting acceptance, adoption, ratification, estoppel or the like, are agreements if they meet the tests of the definition of "agreement." See Section 1-201(b)(3). *First Nat'l Bank of Denver v. Federal Reserve Bank,* 6 F.2d 339 (8th Cir.1925) (deposit slip); *Jefferson County Bldg. Ass'n v. Southern Bank & Trust Co.,* 142 So. 66 (Ala. 1932) (signature card and deposit slip); *Semingson v. Stock Yards Nat'l Bank,* 203 N.W. 412 (Minn. 1925) (passbook); *Farmers State Bank v. Union Nat'l Bank,* 173 N.W. 789, 790 (N.D. 1919) (acknowledgment of receipt of item).

3. Subsection (a) (subject to its limitations with respect to good faith and ordinary care) goes far to meet the requirements of flexibility. However, it does not by itself confer fully effective flexibility. Since it is recognized that banks handle a great number of items every business day and that the parties interested in each item include the owner of the item, the drawer (if it is a check), all nonbank indorsers, the payor bank and from one to five or more collecting banks, it is obvious that it is impossible, practically, to obtain direct agreements from all of these parties on all items. In total, the interested parties constitute virtually every adult person and business organization in the United States. On the other hand they may become bound to agreements on the principle that collecting banks acting as agents have authority to make binding agreements with respect to items being handled. This conclusion was assumed but was not flatly decided in *Federal Reserve Bank of Richmond v. Malloy,* 264 U.S. 160, 167 (1924).

To meet this problem subsection (b) provides that official or quasi-official rules of collection, that is Federal Reserve regulations and operating circulars, clearing-house rules, and the like, have the effect of agreements under subsection (a), whether or not specifically assented to by all parties interested in items handled. Consequently, such official or quasi-official rules may, standing by themselves but subject to the good faith and ordinary care limitations, vary the effect of the provisions of Article 4.

Federal Reserve regulations. Various sections of the Federal Reserve Act (12 U.S.C. § 221 et seq.) authorize the Board of Governors of the Federal Reserve System to direct the Federal Reserve banks to exercise bank collection functions. For example, Section 16 (12 U.S.C. § 248(*o*)) authorizes the Board to require each Federal Reserve bank to exercise the functions of a clearing house for its members and Section 13 (12 U.S.C. § 342) authorizes each Federal Reserve bank to receive deposits from nonmember banks solely for the purposes of exchange or of collection. Under this statutory authorization the Board has issued Regulation J (Subpart A—Collection of Checks and Other Items). Under the supremacy clause of the Constitution, federal regulations prevail over state statutes. Moreover, the Expedited Funds Availability Act, 12 U.S.C. Section 4007(b) provides that the Act and Regulation CC, 12 CFR 229, supersede "any provision of the law of any State, including the Uniform Commercial Code as in effect in such State, which is inconsistent with this chapter or such regulations." See Comment 1 to Section 4-102.

Federal Reserve operating circulars. The regulations of the Federal Reserve Board authorize the Federal Reserve banks to promulgate operating circulars covering operating details. Regulation J, for example, provides that "Each Reserve Bank shall receive and handle items in accordance with this subpart, and shall issue operating circulars governing the details of its handling of items and other matters deemed appropriate by the Reserve Bank." This Article recognizes that "operating circulars" issued pursuant to the regulations and concerned with operating details as appropriate may, within their proper sphere, vary the effect of the Article.

Clearing-house rules. Local clearing houses have long issued rules governing the details of clearing; hours of clearing, media of remittance, time for return of mis-sent items and the like. The case law has recognized these rules, within their proper sphere, as binding on affected parties and as appropriate sources for the courts to look to in filling out details of bank collection law. Subsection (b) in recognizing clearing-house rules as a means of preserving flexibility continues the sensible approach indicated in the cases. Included in the term "clearing houses" are county and regional clearing houses as well as those within a single city or town. There is, of course, no intention of authorizing a local clearing house or a group of clearing houses to rewrite the basic law generally. The term "clearing-house rules" should be understood in the light of functions the clearing houses have exercised in the past.

And the like. This phrase is to be construed in the light of the foregoing. "Federal Reserve regulations and operating circulars" cover rules and regulations issued by public or quasi-public agencies under statutory authority. "Clearing-house rules" cover rules issued by a group of banks which have associated themselves to perform through a clearing house some of their collection, payment and clearing functions. Other agencies or associations of this kind may be established in the future whose rules and regulations could be appropriately looked on as constituting means of avoiding absolute statutory rigidity. The phrase "and the like" leaves open possibilities for future development. An agreement between a number of banks or even all the banks in an area simply because they are banks, would not of itself, by virtue of the phrase "and the like," meet the purposes and objectives of subsection (b).

4. Under this Article banks come under the general obligations of the use of good faith and the exercise of ordinary care. "Good faith" is defined in Section 1-201(b)(20). The term "ordinary care" is defined in Section 3-103(a)(9). These definitions are made to apply to Article 4 by Section 4-104(c). Section 4-202 states respects in which collecting banks must use ordinary care. Subsection (c) of Section 4-103 provides that action or non-action approved by the Article or pursuant to Federal Reserve regulations or operating circulars constitutes the exercise of ordinary care. Federal Reserve regulations and operating circulars constitute an affirmative standard of ordinary care equally with the provisions of Article 4 itself.

Subsection (c) further provides that, absent special instructions, action or non-action consistent with clearing-house rules and the like or with a general banking usage not disapproved by the Article, prima facie constitutes the exercise of ordinary care. Clearing-house rules and the phrase "and the like" have the significance set forth above in these Comments. The term "general banking usage" is not defined but should be taken to mean a general usage common to banks in the area concerned. See Section 1-303(c). In a case in which the adjective "general" is used, the intention is to require a usage broader than a mere practice between two or three banks but it is not intended to require a usage broader than a mere practice between two or three banks but it is not intended to require anything as broad as a country-wide usage. A usage followed generally throughout a state, a substantial portion of a state, a metropolitan area or the like would certainly be sufficient. Consistently with the principle of Section 1-303(c), action or non-action consistent with clearing-house rules or the like or with banking usages prima facie constitutes the exercise of ordinary care. However, the phrase "in the absence of special instructions" affords owners of items an opportunity to prescribe other standards and although there may be no direct supervision or control of clearing houses or banking usages by official supervisory authorities, the confirmation of ordinary care by compliance with these standards is prima facie only, thus conferring on the courts the ultimate power to determine ordinary care in any case in which it should appear desirable to do so. The prima facie rule does, however, impose on the party contesting the standards to establish that they are unreasonable, arbitrary or unfair as used by the particular bank.

5. Subsection (d), in line with the flexible approach required for the bank collection process is designed to make clear that a novel procedure adopted by a bank is not to be considered unreasonable merely because that procedure is not specifically contemplated by this Article or by agreement, or because it has not yet been generally accepted as a bank usage. Changing conditions constantly call for new procedures and someone has to use the new procedure first. If this procedure is found to be reasonable under the circumstances, provided, of course, that it is not inconsistent with any provision of the Article or other law or agreement, the bank which has followed the new procedure should not be found to have failed in the exercise of ordinary care.

6. Subsection (e) sets forth a rule for determining the measure of damages for failure to exercise ordinary care which, under subsection (a), cannot be limited by agreement. In the absence of bad faith the maximum recovery is the amount of the item concerned. The term "bad faith" is not defined; the connotation is the absence of good faith (Section 1-201(b)(20)). When it is established that some part or all of the item could not have been collected even by the use of ordinary care the recovery is reduced by the amount that would have been in any event uncollectible. This limitation on recovery follows the case law. Finally, if bad faith is established the rule opens to allow the recovery of other damages, whose "proximateness" is to be tested by the ordinary rules applied in comparable cases. Of course, it continues to be as necessary under subsection (e) as it has been under ordinary common law principles that, before the damage rule of the subsection becomes operative, liability of the bank and some loss to the customer or owner must be established.

Cross References:

Sections 1-201, 1-302, 1-303, 3-103, 4-102, 4-103, 4-104, 4-202.

Definitional Cross References:

"Bank".	Section 1-201.
"Good Faith".	Section 1-201.
"Item".	Section 4-104.
"Usage".	Section 1-303.

Section 4-104. Definitions and Index of Definitions

(a) In this Article, unless the context otherwise requires:

(1) "Account" means any deposit or credit account with a bank, including a demand, time, savings, passbook, share draft, or like account, other than an account evidenced by a certificate of deposit;

(2) "Afternoon" means the period of a day between noon and midnight;

(3) "Banking day" means the part of a day on which a bank is open to the public for carrying on substantially all of its banking functions;

(4) "Clearing house" means an association of banks or other payors regularly clearing items;

(5) "Customer" means a person having an account with a bank or for whom a bank has agreed to collect items, including a bank that maintains an account at another bank;

(6) "Documentary draft" means a draft to be presented for acceptance or payment if specified documents, certificated securities (Section 8-102) or instructions for uncertificated securities (Section 8-102), or other certificates, statements, or the like are to be received by the drawee or other payor before acceptance or payment of the draft;

(7) "Draft" means a draft as defined in Section 3-104 or an item, other than an instrument, that is an order;

(8) "Drawee" means a person ordered in a draft to make payment;

(9) "Item" means an instrument or a promise or order to pay money handled by a bank for collection or payment. The term does not include a payment order governed by Article 4A or a credit or debit card slip;

(10) "Midnight deadline" with respect to a bank is midnight on its next banking day following the banking day on which it receives the relevant item or notice or from which the time for taking action commences to run, whichever is later;

(11) "Settle" means to pay in cash, by clearing-house settlement, in a charge or credit or by remittance, or otherwise as agreed. A settlement may be either provisional or final;

(12) "Suspends payments" with respect to a bank means that it has been closed by order of the supervisory authorities, that a public officer has been appointed to take it over, or that it ceases or refuses to make payments in the ordinary course of business.

(b) Other definitions applying to this Article and the sections in which they appear are:

"Agreement for electronic presentment".	Section 4-110.
"Collecting bank".	Section 4-105.
"Depositary bank".	Section 4-105.
"Intermediary bank".	Section 4-105.
"Payor bank".	Section 4-105.
"Presenting bank".	Section 4-105.
"Presentment notice".	Section 4-110.

(c) "Control" as provided in Section 7-106 and the following definitions in other Articles apply to this Article:

"Acceptance".	Section 3-409.
"Alteration".	Section 3-407.
"Cashier's check".	Section 3-104.
"Certificate of deposit".	Section 3-104.
"Certified check".	Section 3-409.
"Check".	Section 3-104.
"Good faith".	Section 3-103.
"Holder in due course".	Section 3-302.
"Instrument".	Section 3-104.
"Notice of dishonor".	Section 3-503.
"Order".	Section 3-103.
"Ordinary care".	Section 3-103.
"Person entitled to enforce".	Section 3-301.

"Presentment".	Section 3-501.
"Promise".	Section 3-103.
"Prove".	Section 3-103.
"Record".	Section 3-103.
"Remotely created consumer item".	Section 3-103.
"Teller's check".	Section 3-104.
"Unauthorized signature".	Section 3-403.

(d) In addition, Article 1 contains general definitions and principles of construction and interpretation applicable throughout this Article.

Official Comment

1. Paragraph (a)(1): "Account" is defined to include both asset accounts in which a customer has deposited money and accounts from which a customer may draw on a line of credit. The limiting factor is that the account must be in a bank.

2. Paragraph (a)(3): "Banking day." Under this definition that part of a business day when a bank is open only for limited functions, e.g., to receive deposits and cash checks, but with loan, bookkeeping and other departments closed, is not part of a banking day.

3. Paragraph (a)(4): "Clearing house." Occasionally express companies, governmental agencies and other nonbanks deal directly with a clearing house; hence the definition does not limit the term to an association of banks.

4. Paragraph (a)(5): "Customer." It is to be noted that this term includes a bank carrying an account with another bank as well as the more typical nonbank customer or depositor.

5. Paragraph (a)(6): "Documentary draft" applies even though the documents do not accompany the draft but are to be received by the drawee or other payor before acceptance or payment of the draft. Documents may be either in electronic or tangible form. See Article 5, Section 5-102, Comment 2 and Article 1, Section 1-201(b)(16) (definition of "document of title").

6. Paragraph (a)(7): "Draft" is defined in Section 3-104 as a form of instrument. Since Article 4 applies to items that may not fall within the definition of instrument, the term is defined here to include an item that is a written order to pay money, even though the item may not qualify as an instrument. The term "order" is defined in Section 3-103.

7. Paragraph (a)(8): "Drawee" is defined in Section 3-103 in terms of an Article 3 draft which is a form of instrument. Here "drawee" is defined in terms of an Article 4 draft which includes items that may not be instruments.

8. Paragraph (a)(9): "Item" is defined broadly to include an instrument, as defined in Section 3-104, as well as promises or orders that may not be within the definition of "instrument." The terms "promise" and "order" are defined in Section 3-103. A promise is a written undertaking to pay money. An order is a written instruction to pay money. But see Section 4-110(c). Since bonds and other investment securities under Article 8 may be within the term "instrument" or "promise," they are items and when handled by banks for collection are subject to this Article. See Comment 1 to Section 4-102. The functional limitation on the meaning of this term is the willingness of the banking system to handle the instrument, undertaking or instruction for collection or payment.

9. Paragraph (a)(10): "Midnight deadline." The use of this phrase is an example of the more mechanical approach used in this Article. Midnight is selected as a termination point or time limit to obtain greater uniformity and definiteness than would be possible from other possible terminating points, such as the close of the banking day or business day.

10. Paragraph (a)(11): The term "settle" has substantial importance throughout Article 4. In the American Bankers Association Bank Collection Code, in deferred posting statutes, in Federal Reserve regulations and operating circulars, in clearing-house rules, in agreements between banks and customers and in legends on deposit tickets and collection letters, there is repeated reference to "conditional" or "provisional" credits or payments. Tied in with this concept of creditors or payments being in some way tentative, has been a related but somewhat different problem as to when an item is "paid" or "finally paid" either to determine the relative priority of the item as against attachments, stop-payment orders and the like or in insolvency situations. There has been extensive litigation in the various states on these problems. To a substantial extent the confusion, the litigation and even the resulting court decisions fail to take into account that in the collection process some debits or credits are provisional or tentative and others are final and that very many debits or credits are provisional or tentative for awhile but later become final. Similarly, some cases fail to recognize that within a single bank, particularly a payor bank, each item goes through a series of processes and that in a payor bank most of these processes are preliminary to the basic act of payment or "final payment."

The term "settle" is used as a convenient term to characterize a broad variety of conditional, provisional, tentative and also final payments of items. Such a comprehensive term is needed because it is frequently difficult or unnecessary to determine whether a particular action is tentative or final or when a particular credit shifts from the tentative class to the final class. Therefore, its use throughout the Article indicates that in that particular context it is unnecessary or unwise to determine whether the debit or the credit or the payment is tentative or final. However, if qualified by the adjective "provisional" its tentative nature is intended, and if qualified by the adjective "final" its permanent nature is intended.

Examples of the various types of settlement contemplated by the term include payments in cash; the efficient but somewhat complicated process of payment through the adjustment and offsetting of balances through clearing houses; debit or credit entries in accounts between banks; the forwarding of various types of remittance instruments, sometimes to cover a particular item but more frequently to cover an entire group of items received on a particular day.

11. Paragraph (a)(12): "Suspends payments." This term is designed to afford an objective test to determine when a bank is no longer operating as a part of the banking system.

Cross References:
Sections 3-502, 4-102, 4-208, 4-215, 4-403, 4-501.
Definitional Cross References:

"Bank".	Section 1-201.
"Documents".	Section 1-201.
"Money".	Section 1-201.
"Negotiable"	Section 3-104.
"Notice".	Section 1-202.
"Person".	Section 1-201.
"Securities".	Section 8-102.

Section 4-105. Definitions of Types of Banks

In this Article:

(1) "Bank" means a person engaged in the business of banking, including a savings bank, savings and loan association, credit union, or trust company;

(2) "Depositary bank" means the first bank to take an item even though it is also the payor bank, unless the item is presented for immediate payment over the counter;

(3) "Payor bank" means a bank that is the drawee of a draft;

(4) "Intermediary bank" means a bank to which an item is transferred in course of collection except the depositary or payor bank;

(5) "Collecting bank" means a bank handling an item for collection except the payor bank;

(6) "Presenting bank" means a bank presenting an item except a payor bank.

Legislative Note: *A jurisdiction that enacts this statute that has not yet enacted the revised version of UCC Article 1 should leave the definition of "Bank" in Section 4-105(1). Section 4-105(1) is reserved for that purpose. A jurisdiction that has adopted or simultaneously adopts the revised Article 1 should delete the definition of "Bank" from Section 4-105(1), but should leave those numbers "reserved." If jurisdictions follow the numbering suggested here, the subsections will have the same numbering in all jurisdictions that have adopted these amendments (whether they have or have not adopted the revised version of UCC Article 1). In either case, they should change the title of the section, as indicated in these revisions, so that all jurisdictions will have the same title for the section.*

Official Comment

1. The definitions in general exclude a bank to which an item is issued, as this bank does not take by transfer except in the particular case covered in which the item is issued to a payee for collection, as in the case in which a corporation is transferring balances from one account to another. Thus, the definition of "depositary bank" does not include the bank to which a check is made payable if a check is given in payment of a mortgage. This bank has the status of a payee under Article 3 on Negotiable Instruments and not that of a collecting bank.

2. Paragraph (1): "Bank" is defined in Section 1-201(b)(4) as meaning "a person engaged in the business of banking." The definition in paragraph (1) makes clear that "bank" includes savings banks, savings and loan associations, credit unions and trust companies, in addition to the commercial banks commonly denoted by use of the term "bank."

3. Paragraph (2): A bank that takes an "on us" item for collection, for application to a customer's loan, or first handles the item for other reasons is a depositary bank even though it is also the payor bank. However, if the holder presents the item for immediate payment over the counter, the payor bank is not a depositary bank.

4. Paragraph (3): The definition of "payor bank" is clarified by use of the term "drawee." That term is defined in Section 4-104 as meaning "a person ordered in a draft to make payment." An "order" is defined in Section 3-103 as meaning "a written instruction to pay money. . . . An authorization to pay is not an order unless the person authorized to pay is also instructed to pay." The definition of order is incorporated into Article 4 by Section 4-104(c). Thus a payor bank is one instructed to pay in the item. A bank does not become a payor bank by being merely authorized to pay or by being given an instruction to pay not contained in the item.

5. Paragraph (4): The term "intermediary bank" includes the last bank in the collection process if the drawee is not a bank. Usually the last bank is also a presenting bank.

Definitional Cross References:

"Bank".	Section 1-201.
"Customer".	Section 4-104.
"Drawee".	Section 4-104.
"Item".	Section 4-104.
"Order".	Section 3-103.

Section 4-106. Payable Through or Payable at Bank; Collecting Bank

(a) If an item states that it is "payable through" a bank identified in the item, (i) the item designates the bank as a collecting bank and does not by itself authorize the bank to pay the item, and (ii) the item may be presented for payment only by or through the bank.

ALTERNATIVE A

(b) If an item states that it is "payable at" a bank identified in the item, the item is equivalent to a draft drawn on the bank.

ALTERNATIVE B

(b) If an item states that it is "payable at" a bank identified in the item, (i) the item designates the bank as a collecting bank and does not by itself authorize the bank to pay the item, and (ii) the item may be presented for payment only by or through the bank.

(c) If a draft names a nonbank drawee and it is unclear whether a bank named in the draft is a co-drawee or a collecting bank, the bank is a collecting bank.

Official Comment

1. This section replaces former Sections 3-120 and 3-121. Some items are made "payable through" a particular bank. Subsection (a) states that such language makes the bank a collecting bank and not a payor bank. An item identifying a "payable through" bank can be presented for payment to the drawee only by the "payable through" bank. The item cannot be presented to the drawee over the counter for immediate payment or by a collecting bank other than the "payable through" bank.

2. Subsection (b) retains the alternative approach of the present law. Under Alternative A a note payable at a bank is the equivalent of a draft drawn on the bank and the midnight deadline provisions of Sections 4-301 and 4-302 apply. Under Alternative B a "payable at" bank is in the same position as a "payable through" bank under subsection (a).

3. Subsection (c) rejects the view of some cases that a bank named below the name of a drawee is itself a drawee. The commercial understanding is that this bank is a collecting bank and is not accountable under Section 4-302 for holding an item beyond its deadline. The liability of the bank is governed by Sections 4-202(a) and 4-103(e).

Cross References:

Section 4-403.

Definitional Cross References:

"Bank".	Section 1-201.
"Collecting bank".	Section 4-105.
"Draft".	Section 4-104.
"Drawee".	Section 4-104.
"Item".	Section 4-104.
"Presentment".	Section 3-501.

Section 4-107. Separate Office of Bank

A branch or separate office of a bank is a separate bank for the purpose of computing the time within which and determining the place at or to which action may be taken or notices or orders shall be given under this Article and under Article 3.

Official Comment

1. A rule with respect to the status of a branch or separate office of a bank as a part of any statute on bank collections is highly desirable if not absolutely necessary. However, practices in the operations of branches and separate offices vary substantially in the different states and it has not been possible to find any single rule that is logically correct, fair in all situations and workable under all different types of practices. The decision not to draft the section with greater specificity leaves to the courts the resolution of the issues arising under this section on the basis of the facts of each case.

2. In many states and for many purposes a branch or separate office of the bank should be treated as a separate bank. Many branches function as separate banks in the handling and payment of items and require time for doing so similar to that of a separate bank. This is particularly true if branch banking is permitted throughout a state or in different towns and cities. Similarly, if there is this separate functioning a particular branch or separate office is the only proper place for various types of action to be taken or orders or notices to be given. Examples include the drawing of a check on a particular branch by a customer whose account is carried at that branch; the presentment of that same check at that branch; the issuance of an order to the branch to stop payment on the check.

3. Section 1 of the American Bankers Association Bank Collection Code provided simply: "A branch or office of any such bank shall be deemed a bank." Although this rule appears to be brief and simple, as applied to particular sections of the ABA Code it produces illogical and, in some cases, unreasonable results. For example, under Section 11 of the ABA Code it seems anomalous for one branch of a bank to have charged an item to the account of the drawer and another branch to have the power to elect to treat the item as dishonored. Similar logical problems would flow from applying the same rule to Article 4. Warranties by one branch to another branch under Sections 4-207 and 4-208 (each considered a separate bank) do not make sense.

4. Assuming that it is not desirable to make each branch a separate bank for all purposes, this section provides that a branch or separate office is a separate bank for certain purposes. In so doing the single legal entity of the bank as a whole is preserved, thereby carrying with it the liability of the institution as a whole on such obligations as it may be under. On the other hand, in cases in which the Article provides a number of time limits for different types of action by banks, if a branch functions as a separate bank, it should have the time limits available to a separate bank. Similarly if in its relations to customers a branch functions as a separate bank, notices and orders with respect to accounts of customers of the branch should be given at the branch. For example, whether a branch has notice sufficient to affect its status as a holder in due course of an item taken by it should depend upon what notice that branch has received with respect to the item. Similarly the receipt of a stop-payment order at one branch should not be notice to another branch so as to impair the right of the second branch to be a holder in due course of the item, although in circumstances in which ordinary care requires the communication of a notice or order to the proper branch of a bank, the notice or order would be effective at the proper branch from the time it was or should have been received. See Section 1-202.

5. The bracketed language ("maintaining its own deposit ledger") in former Section 4-106 is deleted. Today banks keep records on customer accounts by electronic data storage. This has led most banks with branches to centralize to some degree their record keeping. The place where records are kept has little meaning if the information is electronically stored and is instantly retrievable at all branches of the bank. Hence, the inference to be drawn from the deletion of the bracketed language is that where record keeping is done is no longer an important factor in determining whether a branch is a separate bank.

Cross References:

Sections 1-202, 4-106, 4-207, 4-208.

Definitional Cross References:

"Bank".	Section 1-201.
"Branch".	Section 1-201.

Section 4-108. Time of Receipt of Items

(a) For the purpose of allowing time to process items, prove balances, and make the necessary entries on its books to determine its position for the day, a bank may fix an afternoon hour of 2 P.M. or later as a cutoff hour for the handling of money and items and the making of entries on its books.

(b) An item or deposit of money received on any day after a cutoff hour so fixed or after the close of the banking day may be treated as being received at the opening of the next banking day.

Official Comment

1. Each of the huge volume of checks processed each day must go through a series of accounting procedures that consume time. Many banks have found it necessary to establish a cutoff hour to allow time for these procedures to be completed within the time limits imposed by Article 4. Subsection (a) approves a cutoff hour of this type provided it is not earlier than 2 P.M. Subsection (b) provides that if such a cutoff hour is fixed, items received after the cutoff hour may be treated as being received at the opening of the next banking day. If the number of items received either through the mail or over the counter tends to taper off radically as the afternoon hours progress, a 2 P.M. cutoff hour does not involve a large portion of the items received but at the same time permits a bank using such a cutoff hour to leave its doors open later in the afternoon without forcing into the evening the completion of its settling and proving process.

2. The provision in subsection (b) that items or deposits received after the close of the banking day may be treated as received at the opening of the next banking day is important in cases in which a bank closes at twelve or one o'clock, e.g., on a Saturday, but continues to receive some items by mail or over the counter if, for example, it opens Saturday evening for the limited purpose of receiving deposits and cashing checks.

Cross References:

Sections 4-202, 4-303.

Definitional Cross References:

"Afternoon".	Section 4-104.
"Bank".	Section 1-201.
"Banking Day".	Section 4-104.
"Item".	Section 4-104.
"Money".	Section 1-201.

Section 4-109. Delays

(a) Unless otherwise instructed, a collecting bank in a good faith effort to secure payment of a specific item drawn on a payor other than a bank, and with or without the approval of any person involved, may waive, modify, or extend time limits imposed or permitted by this [Act] for a period not exceeding two additional banking days without discharge of drawers or indorsers or liability to its transferor or a prior party.

(b) Delay by a collecting bank or payor bank beyond time limits prescribed or permitted by this [Act] or by instructions is excused if (i) the delay is caused by interruption of communication or computer facilities, suspension of payments by another bank, war, emergency conditions, failure of equipment, or other circumstances beyond the control of the bank, and (ii) the bank exercises such diligence as the circumstances require.

Official Comment

1. Sections 4-202(b), 4-214, 4-301, and 4-302 prescribe various time limits for the handling of items. These are the limits of time within which a bank, in fulfillment of its obligation to exercise ordinary care, must handle items entrusted to it for collection or payment. Under Section 4-103 they may be varied by agreement or by Federal Reserve regulations or operating circular, clearing-house rules, or the like. Subsection (a) permits a very limited extension of these time limits. It authorizes a collecting bank to take additional time in attempting to collect drafts drawn on nonbank payors with or without the approval of any interested party. The right of a collecting bank to waive time limits under subsection (a) does not apply to checks. The two-day extension can only be granted in a good faith effort to secure payment and only with respect to specific items. It cannot be exercised if the customer instructs otherwise. Thus limited the escape provision should afford a limited degree of flexibility in special cases but should not interfere with the overall requirement and objective of speedy collections.

2. An extension granted under subsection (a) is without discharge of drawers or indorsers. It therefore extends the times for presentment or payment as specified in Article 3.

3. Subsection (b) is another escape clause from time limits. This clause operates not only with respect to time limits imposed by the Article itself but also time limits imposed by special instructions, by agreement or by Federal regulations or operating circulars, clearing-house rules or the like. The latter time limits are "permitted" by the Code. For example, a payor bank that fails to make timely return of a dishonored item may be accountable for the amount of the item. Subsection (b) excuses a bank from this liability when its failure to meet its midnight deadline resulted from, for example, a computer breakdown that was beyond the control of the bank, so long as the bank exercised the degree of diligence that the circumstances required. In *Port City State Bank v. American Nat'l Bank,* 486 F.2d 196 (10th Cir. 1973), the court held that a bank exercised sufficient diligence to be excused under this subsection. If delay is sought to be excused under this subsection, the bank has the burden of proof on the issue of whether it exercised "such diligence as the circumstances require." The subsection is consistent with Regulation CC, Section 229.38(e).

Cross References:

Sections 4-103, 4-202(b), 4-213, 4-214, 4-301, 4-302.

Definitional Cross References:

"Bank".	Section 1-201.
"Banking Day".	Section 4-104.
"Collecting bank".	Section 4-105.
"Drawer".	Section 3-103.
"Good Faith".	Section 1-201.
"Indorser".	Section 3-204.
"Item".	Section 4-104.
"Party".	Section 3-103.
"Payment".	Section 3-602.
"Payor Bank".	Section 4-105.
"Person".	Section 1-201.

Section 4-110. Electronic Presentment

(a) "Agreement for electronic presentment" means an agreement, clearing-house rule, or Federal Reserve regulation or operating circular, providing that presentment of an item may be made by transmission of an image of an item or information describing the item ("presentment notice") rather than delivery of the item itself. The agreement may provide for procedures governing retention, presentment, payment, dishonor, and other matters concerning items subject to the agreement.

(b) Presentment of an item pursuant to an agreement for presentment is made when the presentment notice is received.

(c) If presentment is made by presentment notice, a reference to "item" or "check" in this Article means the presentment notice unless the context otherwise indicates.

Official Comment

1. An "agreement for electronic presentment" refers to an agreement under which presentment may be made to a payor bank by a presentment notice rather than by presentment of the item. Under imaging technology now under development, the presentment notice might be an image of the item. The electronic presentment agreement may provide that the item may be retained by a depositary bank, other collecting bank, or even a customer of the depositary bank, or it may provide that the item will follow the presentment notice. The identifying characteristic of an electronic presentment agreement is that presentment occurs when the presentment notice is received. "An agreement for electronic presentment" does not refer to the common case of retention of items by payor banks because the item itself is presented to the payor bank in these cases. Payor bank check retention is a matter of agreement between payor banks and their customers. Provisions on payor bank check retention are found in Section 4-406(b).

2. The assumptions under which the electronic presentment amendments are based are as follows: No bank will participate in an electronic presentment program without an agreement. These agreements may be either bilateral (Section 4-103(a)), under which two banks that frequently do business with each other may agree to depositary bank check retention, or multilateral (Section 4-103(b)), in which large segments of the banking industry may participate in such a program. In the latter case, federal or other uniform regulatory standards would likely supply the substance of the electronic presentment agreement, the application of which could be triggered by the use of some form of identifier on the item. Regulation CC, Section 229.36(c) authorizes truncation agreements but forbids them from extending return times or otherwise varying requirements of the part of Regulation CC governing check collection without the agreement of all parties interested in the check. For instance, an extension of return time could damage a depositary bank which must make funds available to its customers under mandatory availability schedules. The Expedited Funds Availability Act, 12 U.S.C. Section 4008(b)(2), directs the Federal Reserve Board to consider requiring that banks provide for check truncation.

3. The parties affected by an agreement for electronic presentment, with the exception of the customer, can be expected to protect themselves. For example, the payor bank can probably be expected to limit its risk of loss from drawer forgery by limiting the dollar amount of eligible items (Federal Reserve program), by reconcilement agreements (ABA Safekeeping program), by insurance (credit union share draft program), or by other means. Because agreements will exist, only minimal amendments are needed to make clear that the UCC does not prohibit electronic presentment.

Cross References:

Sections 4-103, 4-406.

Definitional Cross References:

"Agreement".	Section 1-201.
"Check".	Section 3-104.
"Clearing House".	Section 4-104.
"Delivery".	Section 1-201.
"Dishonor".	Section 3-502.
"Item".	Section 4-104.
"Payment".	Section 3-602.
"Presentment".	Section 3-501.

Section 4-111. Statute of Limitations

An action to enforce an obligation, duty, or right arising under this Article must be commenced within three years after the [cause of action] accrues.

Definitional Cross References: "Action". Section 1-201(b)(1).

Official Comment

This section conforms to the period of limitations set by Section 3-118(g) for actions for breach of warranty and to enforce other obligations, duties or rights arising under Article 3. Bracketing "cause of action" recognizes that some states use a different term, such as "claim for relief."

Cross References:

Section 3-118.

PART 2. COLLECTION OF ITEMS: DEPOSITARY AND COLLECTING BANKS

Section 4-201. Status of Collecting Bank as Agent and Provisional Status of Credits; Applicability of Article; Item Indorsed "Pay Any Bank"

(a) Unless a contrary intent clearly appears and before the time that a settlement given by a collecting bank for an item is or becomes final, the bank, with respect to an item, is an agent or sub-agent of the owner of the item and any settlement given for the item is provisional. This provision applies regardless of the form of indorsement or lack of indorsement and even though credit given for the item is subject to immediate withdrawal as of right or is in fact withdrawn; but the continuance of ownership of an item by its owner and any rights of the owner to proceeds of the item are subject to rights of a collecting bank, such as those resulting from outstanding advances on the item and rights of recoupment or setoff. If an item is handled by banks for purposes of presentment, payment, collection, or return, the relevant provisions of this Article apply even though action of the parties clearly establishes that a particular bank has purchased the item and is the owner of it.

(b) After an item has been indorsed with the words "pay any bank" or the like, only a bank may acquire the rights of a holder until the item has been:

(1) returned to the customer initiating collection; or

(2) specially indorsed by a bank to a person who is not a bank.

Official Comment

1. This section states certain basic rules of the bank collection process. One basic rule, appearing in the last sentence of subsection (a), is that, to the extent applicable, the provisions of the Article govern without regard to whether a bank handling an item owns the item or is an agent for collection. Historically, much time has been spent and effort expended in determining or attempting to determine whether a bank was a purchaser of an item or merely an agent for collection. See discussion of this subject and cases cited in 11 A.L.R. 1043, 16 A.L.R. 1084, 42 A.L.R. 492, 68 A.L.R. 725, 99 A.L.R. 486. See also Section 4 of the American Bankers Association Bank Collection Code. The general approach of Article 4, similar to that of other articles, is to provide, within reasonable limits, rules or answers to major problems known to exist in the bank collection process without regard to questions of status and ownership but to keep general principles such as status and ownership available to cover residual areas not covered by specific rules. In line with this approach, the last sentence of subsection (a) says in effect that Article 4 applies to practically every item moving through banks for the purpose of presentment, payment or collection.

2. Within this general rule of broad coverage, the first two sentences of subsection (a) state a rule of agency status. "Unless a contrary intent clearly appears" the status of a collecting bank is that of an agent or sub-agent for the owner of the item. Although as indicated in Comment 1 it is much less important under Article 4 to determine status than has been the case heretofore, status may have importance in some residual areas not covered by specific rules. Further, since status has been considered so important in the past, to omit all reference to it might cause confusion. The status of agency "applies regardless of the form of indorsement or lack of indorsement and even though credit given for the item is subject to immediate withdrawal as of right or is in fact withdrawn." Thus questions heretofore litigated as to whether ordinary indorsements "for deposit," "for collection" or in blank have the effect of creating an agency status or a purchase, no longer have significance in varying the prima facie rule of agency. Similarly, the nature of the credit given for an item or whether it is subject to immediate withdrawal as of right or is in fact withdrawn, does not alter the agency status. See A.L.R. references supra in Comment 1.

A contrary intent can change agency status but this must be clear. An example of a clear contrary intent would be if collateral papers established or the item bore a legend stating that the item was sold absolutely to the depositary bank.

3. The prima facie agency status of collecting banks is consistent with prevailing law and practice today. Section 2 of the American Bankers Association Bank Collection Code so provided. Legends on deposit tickets, collection letters and acknowledgments of items and Federal Reserve operating circulars consistently so provide. The status is consistent with rights of charge-back (Section 4-214 and Section 11 of the ABA Code) and risk of loss in the event of insolvency (Section 4-216 and Section 13 of the ABA Code). The right of charge-back with respect to checks is limited by Regulation CC, Section 226.36(d).

4. Affirmative statement of a prima facie agency status for collecting banks requires certain limitations and qualifications. Under current practices substantially all bank collections sooner or later merge into bank credits, at least if collection is effected. Usually, this takes place within a few days of the initiation of collection. An intermediary bank receives final collection and evidences the result of its collection by a "credit" on its books to the depositary bank. The depositary bank evidences the results of its collection by a "credit" in the account of its customer. As used in these instances the term "credit" clearly indicates a debtor-creditor relationship. At some stage in the bank collection process the agency status of a collecting bank changes to that of debtor, a debtor of its customer. Usually at about the same time it also becomes a creditor for the amount of the item, a creditor of some intermediary, payor or other bank. Thus the collection is completed, all agency aspects are terminated and the identity of the item has become completely merged in bank accounts, that of the customer with the depositary bank and that of one bank with another.

Although Section 4-215(a) provides that an item is finally paid when the payor bank takes or fails to take certain action with respect to the item, the final payment of the item may or may not result in the simultaneous final settlement for the item in the case of all prior parties. If a series of provisional debits and credits for the item have been entered in accounts between banks, the final payment of the item by the payor bank may result in the automatic firming up of all these provisional debits and credits under Section 4-215(c), and the consequent receipt of final settlement for the item by each collecting bank and the customer of the depositary bank simultaneously with such action of the payor bank. However, if the payor bank or some intermediary bank accounts for the item with a remittance draft, the next prior bank usually does not receive final settlement for the item until the remittance draft finally clears. See Section 4-213(c). The first sentence of subsection (a) provides that the agency status of a collecting bank (whether intermediary or depositary) continues until the settlement given by it for the item is or becomes final. In the case of the series of provisional credits covered by Section 4-215(c), this could be simultaneously with the final payment of the item by the payor bank. In cases in which remittance drafts are used or in straight noncash collections, this would not be until the times specified in Sections 4-213(c) and 4-215(d). With respect to checks Regulation CC Sections 229.31(c), 229.32(b) and 229.36(d) provide that all settlements between banks are final in both the forward collection and return of checks.

Under Section 4-213(a) settlements for items may be made by any means agreed to by the parties. Since it is impossible to contemplate all the kinds of settlements that will be utilized, no attempt is made in Article 4 to provide when settlement is final in all cases. The guiding principle is that settlements should be final when the presenting person has received usable funds. Section 4-213(c) and (d) and Section 4-215(c) provide when final settlement occurs with respect to certain kinds of settlement, but these provisions are not intended to be exclusive.

A number of practical results flow from the rule continuing the agency status of a collecting bank until its settlement for the item is or becomes final, some of which are specifically set forth in this Article. One is that risk of loss continues in the owner of the item rather than the agent bank. See Section 4-214. Offsetting rights favorable to the owner are that pending such final settlement, the owner has the preference rights of Section 4-216 and the direct rights of Section 4-302 against the payor bank. It also follows from this rule that the dollar limitations of Federal Deposit Insurance are measured by the claim of the owner of the item rather than that of the collecting bank. With respect to checks, rights of the parties in insolvency are determined by Regulation CC Section 229.39 and the liability of a bank handling a check to a subsequent bank that does not receive payment because of suspension of payments by another bank is stated in Regulation CC Section 229.35(b).

5. In those cases in which some period of time elapses between the final payment of the item by the payor bank and the time that the settlement of the collecting bank is or becomes final, e.g., if the payor bank or an intermediary bank accounts for the item with a remittance draft or in straight noncash collections, the continuance of the agency status of the collecting bank necessarily carries with it the continuance of the owner's status as principal. The second sentence of subsection (a) provides that whatever rights the owner has to proceeds of the item are subject to the rights of collecting banks for outstanding advances on the item and other valid rights, if any. The rule provides a sound rule to govern cases of attempted attachment of proceeds of a non-cash item in the hands of the payor bank as property of the absent owner. If a collecting bank has made an advance on an item which is still outstanding, its right to obtain reimbursement for this advance should be superior to the rights of the owner to the proceeds or to the rights of a creditor of the owner. An intentional crediting of proceeds of an item to the account of a prior bank known to be insolvent, for the purpose of acquiring a right of setoff, would not produce a valid setoff. See *Zollman, Banks and Banking* (1936) Sec. 5443.

6. This section and Article 4 as a whole represent an intentional abandonment of the approach to bank collection problems appearing in Section 4 of the American Bankers Association Bank Collection Code. Because the tremendous volume of items handled makes impossible the examination by all banks of all indorsements on all items and thus in fact this examination is not made, except perhaps by depositary banks, it is unrealistic to base the rights and duties of all banks in the collection chain on variations in the form of indorsements. It is anomalous to provide throughout the ABA Code that the prima facie status of collecting banks is that of agent or sub-agent but in Section 4 to provide that subsequent holders (sub-agents) shall have the right to rely on the presumption that the bank of deposit (the primary agent) is the owner of the item. It is unrealistic, particularly in this background, to base rights and duties on status of agent or owner. Thus Section 4-201 makes the pertinent provisions of Article 4 applicable to substantially all items handled by banks for presentment, payment or collection, recognizes the prima facie status of most banks as agents, and then seeks to state appropriate limits and some attributes to the general rules so expressed.

7. Subsection (b) protects the ownership rights with respect to an item indorsed "pay any bank or banker" or in similar terms of a customer initiating collection or of any bank acquiring a security interest under Section 4-210, in the event the item is subsequently acquired under improper circumstances by a person who is not a bank and transferred by that person to another person, whether or not a bank. Upon return to the customer initiating collection of an item so indorsed, the indorsement may be cancelled (Section 3-207). A bank holding an item so indorsed may transfer the item out of banking channels by special indorsement; however, under Section 4-103(e), the bank would be liable to the owner of the item for any loss resulting therefrom if the transfer had been made in bad faith or with lack of ordinary care. If briefer and more simple forms of bank indorsements are developed under Section 4-206 (e.g., the use of bank transit numbers in lieu of present lengthy forms of bank indorsements), a depositary bank having the transit number "X100" could make subsection (b) operative by indorsements such as "Pay any bank—X100." Regulation CC Section 229.35(c) states the effect of an indorsement on a check by a bank.

Cross References:

Sections 3-207, 4-103, 4-201, 4-206, 4-210, 4-213, 4-214, 4-215, 4-216, 4-302.

Definitional Cross References:

"Bank".	Section 1-201.
"Collecting bank".	Section 4-105.
"Customer".	Section 4-104.
"Depository bank".	Section 4-105.
"Holder".	Section 1-201.
"Item"	Section 4-104.
"Indorsement".	Sections 3-204, 3-205 and 3-206.
"Person".	Section 1-201.
"Settle".	Section 4-104.

Section 4-202. Responsibility for Collection or Return; When Action Timely

(a) A collecting bank must exercise ordinary care in:

(1) presenting an item or sending it for presentment;

(2) sending notice of dishonor or nonpayment or returning an item other than a documentary draft to the bank's transferor after learning that the item has not been paid or accepted, as the case may be;

(3) settling for an item when the bank receives final settlement; and

(4) notifying its transferor of any loss or delay in transit within a reasonable time after discovery thereof.

(b) A collecting bank exercises ordinary care under subsection (a) by taking proper action before its midnight deadline following receipt of an item, notice, or settlement. Taking proper action within a reasonably longer time may constitute the exercise of ordinary care, but the bank has the burden of establishing timeliness.

(c) Subject to subsection (a)(1), a bank is not liable for the insolvency, neglect, misconduct, mistake, or default of another bank or person or for loss or destruction of an item in the possession of others or in transit.

Official Comment

1. Subsection (a) states the basic responsibilities of a collecting bank. Of course, under Section 1-304 a collecting bank is subject to the standard requirement of good faith. By subsection (a) it must also use ordinary care in the exercise of its basic collection tasks. By Section 4-103(a) neither requirement may be disclaimed.

2. If the bank makes presentment itself, subsection (a)(1) requires ordinary care with respect both to the time and manner of presentment. (Sections 3-501 and 4-212.) If it forwards the item to be presented the subsection requires ordinary care with respect to routing (Section 4-204), and also in the selection of intermediary banks or other agents.

3. Subsection (a) describes types of basic action with respect to which a collecting bank must use ordinary care. Subsection (b) deals with the time for taking action. It first prescribes the general standard for timely action, namely, for items received on Monday, proper action (such as forwarding or presenting) on Monday or Tuesday is timely. Although under current "production line" operations banks customarily move items along on regular schedules substantially briefer than two days, the subsection states an outside time within which a bank may know it has taken timely action. To provide flexibility from this standard norm, the subsection further states that action within a reasonably longer time may be timely but the bank has the burden of proof. In the case of time items, action after the midnight deadline, but sufficiently in advance of maturity for proper presentation, is a clear example of a "reasonably longer time" that is timely. The standard of requiring action not later than Tuesday in the case of Monday items is also subject to possibilities of variation under the general provisions of Section 4-103, or under the special provisions regarding time of receipt of items (Section 4-108), and regarding delays (Section 4-109). This subsection (b) deals only with collecting banks. The time limits applicable to payor banks appear in Sections 4-301 and 4-302.

4. At common law the so-called New York collection rule subjected the initial collecting bank to liability for the actions of subsequent banks in the collection chain; the so-called Massachusetts rule was that each bank, subject to the duty of selecting proper intermediaries, was liable only for its own negligence. Subsection (c) adopts the Massachusetts rule. But since this is stated to be subject to subsection (a)(1) a collecting bank remains responsible for using ordinary care in selecting properly qualified intermediary banks and agents and in giving proper instructions to them. Regulation CC Section 229.36(d) states the liability of a bank during the forward collection of checks.

Cross References:

Sections 1-304, 3-501, 4-103, 4-108, 4-109, 4-204, 4-212, 4-301, and 4-302.

Definitional Cross References:

"Collecting bank".	Section 4-105.
"Depository bank".	Section 4-105.
"Documentary draft".	Section 4-104.
"Item".	Section 4-104.
"Midnight deadline".	Section 4-104.
"Presentment".	Section 3-501.

Section 4-203. Effect of Instructions

Subject to Article 3 concerning conversion of instruments (Section 3-420) and restrictive indorsements (Section 3-206), only a collecting bank's transferor can give instructions that affect the bank or constitute notice to it, and a collecting bank is not liable to prior parties for any action taken pursuant to the instructions or in accordance with any agreement with its transferor.

Official Comment

This section adopts a "chain of command" theory which renders it unnecessary for an intermediary or collecting bank to determine whether its transferor is "authorized" to give the instructions. Equally the bank is not put on notice of any "revocation of authority" or "lack of authority" by notice received from any other person. The desirability of speed in the collection process and the fact that, by reason of advances made, the transferor may have the paramount interest in the item requires the rule.

The section is made subject to the provisions of Article 3 concerning conversion of instruments (Section 3-420) and restrictive indorsements (Section 3-206). Of course instructions from or an agreement with its transferor does not relieve a collecting bank of its general obligation to exercise good faith and ordinary care. See Section 4-103(a). If in any particular case a bank has exercised good faith and ordinary care and is relieved of responsibility by reason of instructions of or an agreement with its transferor, the owner of the item may still have a remedy for loss against the transferor (another bank) if such transferor has given wrongful instructions.

The rules of the section are applied only to collecting banks. Payor banks always have the problem of making proper payment of an item; whether such payment is proper should be based upon all of the rules of Articles 3 and 4 and all of the facts of any particular case, and should not be dependent exclusively upon instructions from or an agreement with a person presenting the item.

Cross References:

Sections 3-206, 3-420, 4-103(a).

Definitional Cross References:

"Collecting bank".	Section 4-105.
"Restrictive indorsement".	Section 3-206.

Section 4-204. Methods of Sending and Presenting; Sending Directly to Payor Bank

(a) A collecting bank shall send items by a reasonably prompt method, taking into consideration relevant instructions, the nature of the item, the number of those items on hand, the cost of collection involved, and the method generally used by it or others to present those items.

(b) A collecting bank may send:

(1) an item directly to the payor bank;

(2) an item to a nonbank payor if authorized by its transferor; and

(3) an item other than documentary drafts to a nonbank payor, if authorized by Federal Reserve regulation or operating circular, clearing-house rule, or the like.

(c) Presentment may be made by a presenting bank at a place where the payor bank or other payor has requested that presentment be made.

Official Comment

1. Subsection (a) prescribes the general standards applicable to proper sending or forwarding of items. Because of the many types of methods available and the desirability of preserving flexibility any attempt to prescribe limited or precise methods is avoided.

2. Subsection (b)(1) codifies the practice of direct mail, express, messenger or like presentment to payor banks. The practice is now country-wide and is justified by the need for speed, the general responsibility of banks, Federal Deposit Insurance protection and other reasons.

3. Full approval of the practice of direct sending is limited to cases in which a bank is a payor. Since nonbank drawees or payors may be of unknown responsibility, substantial risks may be attached to placing in their hands the instruments calling for payments from them. This is obviously so in the case of documentary drafts. However, in some cities practices have long existed under clearing-house procedures to forward certain types of items to certain nonbank payors. Examples include insurance loss drafts drawn by field agents on home offices. For the purpose of leaving the door open to legitimate practices of this kind, subsection (b)(3) affirmatively approves direct sending of any item other than documentary drafts to any nonbank payor, if authorized by Federal Reserve regulation or operating circular, clearing-house rule or the like.

On the other hand subsection (b)(2) approves sending any item directly to a nonbank payor if authorized by a collecting bank's transferor. This permits special instructions or agreements out of the norm and is consistent with the "chain of command" theory of Section 4-203. However, if a transferor other than the owner of the item, e.g., a prior collecting bank, authorizes a direct sending to a nonbank payor, such transferor assumes responsibility for the propriety or impropriety of such authorization.

4. Section 3-501(b) provides where presentment may be made. This provision is expressly subject to Article 4. Section 4-204(c) specifically approves presentment by a presenting bank at any place requested by the payor bank or other payor. The time when a check is received by a payor bank for presentment is governed by Regulation CC Section 229.36(b).

Cross References:

Sections 3-501, 4-203.

Definitional Cross References:

"Clearing house".	Section 4-104.
"Collecting bank".	Section 4-105.
"Documentary draft".	Section 4-104.
"Item".	Section 4-104.
"Payor bank".	Section 4-105.
"Presenting bank".	Section 4-105.
"Presentment".	Section 3-501.
"Send".	Section 1-201(b)(36).

Section 4-205. Depositary Bank Holder of Unindorsed Item

If a customer delivers an item to a depositary bank for collection:

(1) the depositary bank becomes a holder of the item at the time it receives the item for collection if the customer at the time of delivery was a holder of the item, whether or not the customer indorses the item, and, if the bank satisfies the other requirements of Section 3-302, it is a holder in due course; and

(2) the depositary bank warrants to collecting banks, the payor bank or other payor, and the drawer that the amount of the item was paid to the customer or deposited to the customer's account.

Official Comment

Section 3-201(b) provides that negotiation of an instrument payable to order requires indorsement by the holder. The rule of former Section 4-205(1) was that the depositary bank may supply a missing indorsement of its customer unless the item contains the words "payee's indorsement required" or the like. The cases have differed on the status of the depositary bank as a holder if it fails to supply its customer's indorsement. *Marine Midland Bank v. Price, Miller, Evans & Flowers,* 446 N.Y.S.2d 797 (N.Y. App. Div. 1981), *rev'd,* 455 N.Y.S.2d 565 (N.Y. 1982). It is common practice for depositary banks to receive unindorsed checks under so-called "lock-box" agreements from customers who receive a high volume of checks. No function would be served by requiring a depositary bank to run these items through a machine that would supply the customer's indorsement except to afford the drawer and the subsequent banks evidence that the proceeds of the item reached the customer's account. Paragraph (1) provides that the depositary bank becomes a holder when it takes the item for deposit if the depositor is a holder. Whether it supplies the customer's indorsement is immaterial. Paragraph (2) satisfies the need for a receipt of funds by the depositary bank by imposing on that bank a warranty that it paid the customer or deposited the item to the customer's account. This warranty runs not only to collecting banks and to the payor bank or nonbank drawee but also to the drawer, affording protection to these parties that the depositary bank received the item and applied it to the benefit of the holder.

Cross References:

Sections 3-201, 3-302.

Definitional Cross References:

"Account".	Section 4-104.
"Collecting bank".	Section 4-105.
"Customer".	Section 4-104.
"Depositary bank".	Section 4-105.
"Drawer".	Section 3-103.
"Holder".	Section 1-201.
"Holder in due course".	Section 3-302.
"Intermediary bank."	Section 4-105.
"Item".	Section 4-104.
"Payor bank".	Section 4-105.

Section 4-206. Transfer Between Banks

Any agreed method that identifies the transferor bank is sufficient for the item's further transfer to another bank.

Official Comment

This section is designed to permit the simplest possible form of transfer from one bank to another, once an item gets in the bank collection chain, provided only identity of the transferor bank is preserved. This is important for tracing purposes and if recourse is necessary. However, since the responsibilities of the various banks appear in the Article it becomes unnecessary to have liability or responsibility depend on more formal indorsements. Simplicity in the form of transfer is conducive to speed. If the transfer is between banks, this section takes the place of the more formal requirements of Section 3-201.

Cross References:

Section 3-201.

Definitional Cross References:

"Bank".	Section 1-201.
"Item".	Section 4-104.

Section 4-207. Transfer Warranties

(a) A customer or collecting bank that transfers an item and receives a settlement or other consideration warrants to the transferee and to any subsequent collecting bank that:

(1) the warrantor is a person entitled to enforce the item;

(2) all signatures on the item are authentic and authorized;

(3) the item has not been altered;

(4) the item is not subject to a defense or claim in recoupment (Section 3-305(a)) of any party that can be asserted against the warrantor;

(5) the warrantor has no knowledge of any insolvency proceeding commenced with respect to the maker or acceptor or, in the case of an unaccepted draft, the drawer; and

(6) with respect to any remotely-created consumer item, that the person on whose account the item is drawn authorized the issuance of the item in the amount for which the item is drawn.

(b) If an item is dishonored, a customer or collecting bank transferring the item and receiving settlement or other consideration is obliged to pay the amount due on the item (i) according to the terms of the item at the time it was transferred, or (ii) if the transfer was of an incomplete item, according to its terms when completed as stated in Sections 3-115 and 3-407. The obligation of a transferor is owed to the transferee and to any subsequent collecting bank that takes the item in good faith. A transferor cannot disclaim its obligation under this subsection by an indorsement stating that it is made "without recourse" or otherwise disclaiming liability.

(c) A person to whom the warranties under subsection (a) are made and who took the item in good faith may recover from the warrantor as damages for breach of warranty an amount equal to the loss suffered as a result of the breach, but not more than the amount of the item plus expenses and loss of interest incurred as a result of the breach.

(d) The warranties stated in subsection (a) cannot be disclaimed with respect to checks. Unless notice of a claim for breach of warranty is given to the warrantor within 30 days after the claimant has reason to know of the breach and the identity of the warrantor, the warrantor is discharged to the extent of any loss caused by the delay in giving notice of the claim.

(e) A cause of action for breach of warranty under this section accrues when the claimant has reason to know of the breach.

Official Comment

1. Except for subsection (b), this section conforms to Section 3-416 and extends its coverage to items. The substance of this section is discussed in the Comment to Section 3-416. Subsection (b) provides that customers or collecting banks that transfer items, whether by indorsement or not, undertake to pay the item if the item is dishonored. This obligation cannot be disclaimed by a "without recourse" indorsement or otherwise. With respect to checks, Regulation CC Section 229.34 states the warranties made by paying and returning banks.

2. For an explanation of subsection (a)(6), see comment 8 to Section 3-416.

3. The warranties provided for in this section and in Sections 4-208 and 4-209 are supplemented by warranties created under federal law. For example, under Section 4-209(b), a person who undertakes to retain an item in connection with an agreement for electronic presentment makes a warranty that retention and presentment comply with the agreement. Under federal law, a person might also make a warranty that no person will be asked to make payment based on a check already paid. See 12 C.F.R. § 229.34(a).

Cross References:

Sections 3-115, 3-305, 3-407, 3-416, 4-208, 4-209.

Definitional Cross References:

"Collecting bank".	Section 4-105.
"Customer".	Section 4-104.
"Draft".	Section 3-104.
"Genuine".	Section 1-201.
"Good faith".	Section 1-201.
"Holder".	Section 1-201.
"Holder in due course".	Section 3-302.
"Insolvency proceedings".	Section 1-201.
"Item".	Section 4-104.
"Party".	Section 1-201.
"Payor bank".	Section 4-105.
"Person".	Section 1-201.
"Presentment".	Section 3-504.
"Unauthorized signature".	Section 1-201.

Editors' Note: Responding to a variety of non- uniform amendments that dealt with responsibility for unauthorized telephone-generated checks, 2002 amendments to Sections 3-416, 3-417. 4-207, and 4-208 added transfer and presentment warranties that such items have been authorized in the amounts for which they are drawn. Subsequent similar revisions to Regulation CC have made those provisions nationally uniform.

Section 4-208. Presentment Warranties

(a) If an unaccepted draft is presented to the drawee for payment or acceptance and the drawee pays or accepts the draft, (i) the person obtaining payment or acceptance, at the time of presentment, and (ii) a previous transferor of the draft, at the time of transfer, warrant to the drawee that pays or accepts the draft in good faith that:

(1) the warrantor is, or was, at the time the warrantor transferred the draft, a person entitled to enforce the draft or authorized to obtain payment or acceptance of the draft on behalf of a person entitled to enforce the draft;

(2) the draft has not been altered; and

(3) the warrantor has no knowledge that the signature of the purported drawer of the draft is unauthorized; and

(4) with respect to any remotely-created consumer item, that the person on whose account the item is drawn authorized the issuance of the item in the amount for which the item is drawn.

(b) A drawee making payment may recover from a warrantor damages for breach of warranty equal to the amount paid by the drawee less the amount the drawee received or is entitled to receive from the drawer because of the payment. In addition, the drawee is entitled to compensation for expenses and loss of interest resulting from the breach. The right of the drawee to recover damages under this subsection is not affected by any failure of the drawee to exercise ordinary care in making payment. If the drawee accepts the draft (i) breach of warranty is a defense to the obligation of the acceptor, and (ii) if the acceptor makes payment with respect to the draft, the acceptor is entitled to recover from a warrantor for breach of warranty the amounts stated in this subsection.

(c) If a drawee asserts a claim for breach of warranty under subsection (a) based on an unauthorized indorsement of the draft or an alteration of the draft, the warrantor may defend by proving that the indorsement is effective under Section 3-404 or 3-405 or the drawer is precluded under Section 3-406 or 4-406 from asserting against the drawee the unauthorized indorsement or alteration.

(d) If (i) a dishonored draft is presented for payment to the drawer or an indorser or (ii) any other item is presented for payment to a party obliged to pay the item, and the item is paid, the person obtaining payment and a prior transferor of the item warrant to the person making payment in good faith that the warrantor is, or was, at the time the warrantor transferred the item, a person entitled to enforce the item or authorized to obtain payment on behalf of a person entitled to enforce the item. The person making payment may recover from any warrantor for breach of warranty an amount equal to the amount paid plus expenses and loss of interest resulting from the breach.

(e) The warranties stated in subsections (a) and (d) cannot be disclaimed with respect to checks. Unless notice of a claim for breach of warranty is given to the warrantor within 30 days after the claimant has reason to know of the breach and the identity of the warrantor, the warrantor is discharged to the extent of any loss caused by the delay in giving notice of the claim.

(f) A cause of action for breach of warranty under this section accrues when the claimant has reason to know of the breach.

Official Comment

1. This section conforms to Section 3-417 and extends its coverage to items. The substance of this section is discussed in the Comment to Section 3-417. "Draft" is defined in Section 4-104 as including an item that is an order to pay so as to make clear that the term "draft" in Article 4 may include items that are not instruments within Section 3-104.

2. For an explanation of subsection (a)(4), see comment 8 to Section 3-416.

Cross References:

Sections 3-104, 3-404, 3-405, 3-407, 3-416, 3-417.

Definitional Cross References:

"Acceptance".	Section 3-409.
"Acceptor".	Section 3-103.
"Action".	Section 1-201.
"Alteration".	Section 3-407.
"Check".	Section 3-104.
"Dishonor".	Section 3-502.
"Draft".	Section 4-104.
"Drawee".	Section 4-104.
"Drawer".	Section 3-103.
"Good faith".	Section 1-201.
"Indorsement".	Section 3-204.
"Item".	Section 4-104.
"Knowledge".	Section 1-202.
"Ordinary care".	Section 3-103.
"Party".	Section 1-201.
"Payment".	Section 3-602.
"Person".	Section 1-201.
"Person entitled to enforce".	Section 3-301.
"Presentment".	Section 3-504.
"Remotely-created consumer item".	Section 3-103.
"Transfer".	Section 3-203.

Editors' Note: Responding to a variety of non- uniform amendments that dealt with responsibility for unauthorized telephone-generated checks, 2002 amendments to Sections 3-416, 3-417. 4-207, and 4-208 added transfer and presentment warranties that such items have been authorized in the amounts for which they are drawn. Subsequent similar revisions to Regulation CC have made those provisions nationally uniform.

Section 4-209. Encoding and Retention Warranties

(a) A person who encodes information on or with respect to an item after issue warrants to any subsequent collecting bank and to the payor bank or other payor that the information is correctly encoded. If the customer of a depositary bank encodes, that bank also makes the warranty.

(b) A person who undertakes to retain an item pursuant to an agreement for electronic presentment warrants to any subsequent collecting bank and to the payor bank or other payor that retention and presentment of the item comply with the agreement. If a customer of a depositary bank undertakes to retain an item, that bank also makes this warranty.

(c) A person to whom warranties are made under this section and who took the item in good faith may recover from the warrantor as damages for breach of warranty an amount equal to the loss suffered as a result of the breach, plus expenses and loss of interest incurred as a result of the breach.

Official Comment

1. Encoding and retention warranties are included in Article 4 because they are unique to the bank collection process. These warranties are breached only by the person doing the encoding or retaining the item and not by subsequent banks handling the item. Encoding and check retention may be done by customers who are payees of a large volume of checks; hence, this section imposes warranties on customers as well as banks. If a customer encodes or retains, the depositary bank is also liable for any breach of this warranty.

2. A misencoding of the amount on the MICR line is not an alteration under Section 3-407(a) which defines alteration as changing the contract of the parties. If a drawer wrote a check for $2,500 and the depositary bank encoded $25,000 on the MICR line, the payor bank could debit the drawer's account for only $2,500. This subsection would allow the payor bank to hold the depositary bank liable for the amount paid out over $2,500 without first pursuing the person who received payment. Intervening collecting banks would not be liable to the payor bank for the depositary bank's error. If a drawer wrote a check for $25,000 and the depositary bank encoded $2,500, the payor bank becomes liable for the full amount of the check. The payor bank's rights against the depositary bank depend on whether the payor bank has suffered a loss. Since the payor bank can debit the drawer's account for $25,000, the payor bank has a loss only to the extent that the drawer's account is less than the full amount of the check. There is no requirement that the payor bank pursue collection against the drawer beyond the amount in the drawer's account as a condition to the payor bank's action against the depositary bank for breach of warranty. See *Georgia Railroad Bank & Trust Co. v. First Nat'l Bank & Trust,* 229 S.E.2d 482 (Ga. Ct. App. 1976), aff'd, 235 S.E.2d 1 (Ga. 1977), and *First Nat'l Bank of Boston v. Fidelity Bank,* 724 F. Supp. 1168 (E.D. Pa. 1989).

3. A person retaining items under an electronic presentment agreement (Section 4-110) warrants that it has complied with the terms of the agreement regarding its possession of the item and its sending a proper presentment notice. If the keeper is a customer, its depositary bank also makes this warranty.

Cross References:

Sections 3-407, 4-110.

Definitional Cross References:

"Agreement".	Section 1-201.
"Bank".	Section 1-201.
"Collecting bank".	Section 4-105.
"Customer".	Section 4-104.
"Depositary bank".	Section 4-105.
"Good faith".	Section 1-201.
"Issue".	Section 3-105.
"Item".	Section 4-104.
"Payor bank".	Section 4-105.
"Person".	Section 1-201.
"Presentment".	Section 3-501.

Section 4-210. Security Interest of Collecting Bank in Items, Accompanying Documents and Proceeds

(a) A collecting bank has a security interest in an item and any accompanying documents or the proceeds of either:

(1) in case of an item deposited in an account, to the extent to which credit given for the item has been withdrawn or applied;

(2) in case of an item for which it has given credit available for withdrawal as of right, to the extent of the credit given, whether or not the credit is drawn upon or there is a right of charge-back; or

(3) if it makes an advance on or against the item.

(b) If credit given for several items received at one time or pursuant to a single agreement is withdrawn or applied in part, the security interest remains upon all the items, any accompanying documents or the proceeds of either. For the purpose of this section, credits first given are first withdrawn.

(c) Receipt by a collecting bank of a final settlement for an item is a realization on its security interest in the item, accompanying documents, and proceeds. So long as the bank does not receive final settlement for the item or give up possession of the item or possession or control of the accompanying documents for purposes other than collection, the security interest continues to that extent and is subject to Article 9, but:

(1) no security agreement is necessary to make the security interest enforceable (Section 9-203(1)(a));

(2) no filing is required to perfect the security interest; and

(3) the security interest has priority over conflicting perfected security interests in the item, accompanying documents, or proceeds.

Official Comment

1. Subsection (a) states a rational rule for the interest of a bank in an item. The customer of the depositary bank is normally the owner of the item and the several collecting banks are agents of the customer (Section 4-201). A collecting agent may properly make advances on the security of paper held for collection, and acquires at common law a possessory lien for these advances. Subsection (a) applies an analogous principle to a bank in the collection chain which extends credit on items in the course of collection. The bank has a security interest to the extent stated in this section. To the extent of its security interest it is a holder for value (Sections 3-303, 4-211) and a holder in due course if it satisfies the other requirements for that status (Section 3-302). Subsection (a) does not derogate from the banker's general common law lien or right of setoff against indebtedness owing in deposit accounts. See Section 1-103(b). Rather subsection (a) specifically implements and extends the principle as a part of the bank collection process.

2. Subsection (b) spreads the security interest of the bank over all items in a single deposit or received under a single agreement and a single giving of credit. It also adopts the "first-in, first-out" rule.

3. Collection statistics establish that the vast majority of items handled for collection are in fact collected. The first sentence of subsection (c) reflects the fact that in the normal case the bank's security interest is self-liquidating. The remainder of the subsection correlates the security interest with the provisions of Article 9, particularly for use in the cases of noncollection in which the security interest may be important.

Cross References:

Sections 1-103, 3-302, 3-303, 4-211, 9-203(b)(3)(A).

Definitional Cross References:

"Account".	Section 4-104.
"Agreement".	Section 1-201.
"Bank".	Section 1-201.
"Charge-back".	Section 4-214.
"Collecting bank".	Section 4-105.
"Item".	Section 4-104.
"Security interest".	Section 1-201.
"Settle".	Section 4-104.

Section 4-211. When Bank Gives Value for Purposes of Holder in Due Course

For purposes of determining its status as a holder in due course, a bank has given value to the extent it has a security interest in an item, if the bank otherwise complies with the requirements of Section 3-302 on what constitutes a holder in due course.

Official Comment

The section completes the thought of the previous section and makes clear that a security interest in an item is "value" for the purpose of determining the holder's status as a holder in due course. The provision is in accord with the prior law (N.I.L. Section 27) and with Article 3 (Section 3-303). The section does not prescribe a security interest under Section 4-210 as a test of "value" generally because the meaning of "value" under other Articles is adequately defined in Section 1-204.

Cross References:

Sections 1-204, 3-302, 3-303, 4-210.

Definitional Cross References:

"Bank".	Section 1-201.
"Holder in due course".	Section 3-302.
"Item".	Section 4-104.
"Security interest".	Section 1-201.
"Value".	Section 1-204.

Section 4-212. Presentment by Notice of Item Not Payable by, Through, or at a Bank; Liability of Drawer or Indorser

(a) Unless otherwise instructed, a collecting bank may present an item not payable by, through, or at a bank by sending to the party to accept or pay a record providing notice that the bank holds the item for acceptance or payment. The notice must be sent in time to be received on or before the day when presentment is due and the bank must meet any requirement of the party to accept or pay under Section 3-501 by the close of the bank's next banking day after it knows of the requirement.

(b) If presentment is made by notice and payment, acceptance, or request for compliance with a requirement under Section 3-501 is not received by the close of business on the day after maturity or, in the case of demand items, by the close of business on the third banking day after notice was sent, the presenting bank may treat the item as dishonored and charge any drawer or indorser by sending it notice of the facts.

Official Comment

1. This section codifies a practice extensively followed in presentation of trade acceptances and documentary and other drafts drawn on nonbank payors. It imposes a duty on the payor to respond to the notice of the item if the item is not to be considered dishonored. Notice of such a dishonor charges drawers and indorsers. Presentment under this section is good presentment under Article 3. See Section 3-501.

2. A drawee not receiving notice is not, of course, liable to the drawer for wrongful dishonor.

3. A bank so presenting an instrument must be sufficiently close to the drawee to be able to exhibit the instrument on the day it is requested to do so or the next business day at the latest.

Cross References:

Section 3-501.

Definitional Cross References:

"Acceptance".	Section 3-409.
"Bank".	Section 1-201.
"Banking day".	Section 4-104.
"Collecting bank".	Section 4-105.
"Dishonor".	Section 3-502.
"Drawer".	Section 3-103.
"Indorser".	Section 3-204.
"Payable on demand".	Section 3-108.
"Item".	Section 4-104.
"Party".	Section 3-103.
"Payable at or through a bank".	Section 4-106.
"Payment".	Section 3-602.
"Presenting bank".	Section 4-105.
"Presentment".	Section 3-501.
"Record".	Section 3-103.
"Send".	Section 1-201(b)(36).

Section 4-213. Medium and Time of Settlement by Bank

(a) With respect to settlement by a bank, the medium and time of settlement may be prescribed by Federal Reserve regulations or circulars, clearing-house rules, and the like, or agreement. In the absence of such prescription:

(1) the medium of settlement is cash or credit to an account in a Federal Reserve bank of or specified by the person to receive settlement; and

(2) the time of settlement, is:

(i) with respect to tender of settlement by cash, a cashier's check, or teller's check, when the cash or check is sent or delivered;

(ii) with respect to tender of settlement by credit in an account in a Federal Reserve Bank, when the credit is made;

(iii) with respect to tender of settlement by a credit or debit to an account in a bank, when the credit or debit is made or, in the case of tender of settlement by authority to charge an account, when the authority is sent or delivered; or

(iv) with respect to tender of settlement by a funds transfer, when payment is made pursuant to Section 4A-406(a) to the person receiving settlement.

(b) If the tender of settlement is not by a medium authorized by subsection (a) or the time of settlement is not fixed by subsection (a), no settlement occurs until the tender of settlement is accepted by the person receiving settlement.

(c) If settlement for an item is made by cashier's check or teller's check and the person receiving settlement, before its midnight deadline:

(1) presents or forwards the check for collection, settlement is final when the check is finally paid; or

(2) fails to present or forward the check for collection, settlement is final at the midnight deadline of the person receiving settlement.

(d) If settlement for an item is made by giving authority to charge the account of the bank giving settlement in the bank receiving settlement, settlement is final when the charge is made by the bank receiving settlement if there are funds available in the account for the amount of the item.

Official Comment

1. Subsection (a) sets forth the medium of settlement that the person receiving settlement must accept. In nearly all cases the medium of settlement will be determined by agreement or by Federal Reserve regulations and circulars, clearing-house rules, and the like. In the absence of regulations, rules or agreement, the person receiving settlement may demand cash or credit in a Federal Reserve bank. If the person receiving settlement does not have an account in a Federal Reserve bank, it may specify the account of another bank in a Federal Reserve bank. In the unusual case in which there is no agreement on the medium of settlement and the bank making settlement tenders settlement other than cash or Federal Reserve bank credit, no settlement has occurred under subsection (b) unless the person receiving settlement accepts the settlement tendered. For example, if a payor bank, without agreement, tenders a teller's check, the bank receiving the settlement may reject the check and return it to the payor bank or it may accept the check as settlement.

2. In several provisions of Article 4 the time that a settlement occurs is relevant. Subsection (a) sets out a general rule that the time of settlement, like the means of settlement, may be prescribed by agreement. In the absence of agreement, the time of settlement for tender of the common agreed media of settlement is that set out in subsection (a)(2). The time of settlement by cash, cashier's or teller's check or authority to charge an account is the time the cash, check or authority is sent, unless presentment is over the counter in which case settlement occurs upon delivery to the presenter. If there is no agreement on the time of settlement and the tender of settlement is not made by one of the media set out in subsection (a), under subsection (b) the time of settlement is the time the settlement is accepted by the person receiving settlement.

3. Subsections (c) and (d) are special provisions for settlement by remittance drafts and authority to charge an account in the bank receiving settlement. The relationship between final settlement and final payment under Section 4-215 is addressed in subsection (b) of Section 4-215. With respect to settlement by cashier's checks or teller's checks, other than in response to over-the-counter presentment, the bank receiving settlement can keep the risk that the check will not be paid on the bank tendering the check in settlement by acting to initiate collection of the check within the midnight deadline of the bank receiving settlement. If the bank fails to initiate settlement before its midnight deadline, final settlement occurs at the midnight deadline, and the bank receiving settlement assumes the risk that the check will not be paid. If there is no agreement that permits the bank tendering settlement to tender a cashier's or teller's check, subsection (b) allows the bank receiving the check to reject it, and, if it does, no settlement occurs. However, if the bank accepts the check, settlement occurs and the time of final settlement is governed by subsection (c).

With respect to settlement by tender of authority to charge the account of the bank making settlement in the bank receiving settlement, subsection (d) provides that final settlement does not take place until the account charged has available funds to cover the amount of the item. If there is no agreement that permits the bank tendering settlement to tender an authority to charge an account as settlement, subsection (b) allows the bank receiving the tender to reject it. However, if the bank accepts the authority, settlement occurs and the time of final settlement is governed by subsection (d).

Cross References:

Section 4-215, 4A-406.

Definitional Cross References:

"Account".	Section 4-104.
"Bank".	Section 1-201.
"Clearing house".	Section 4-104.
"Collecting bank".	Section 4-105.
"Item".	Section 4-104.
"Midnight deadline".	Section 4-104.
"Money".	Section 1-201.
"Payor bank".	Section 4-105.
"Person".	Section 1-201.
"Settle".	Section 4-104.

Section 4-214. Right of Charge-Back or Refund; Liability of Collecting Bank; Return of Item

(a) If a collecting bank has made provisional settlement with its customer for an item and fails by reason of dishonor, suspension of payments by a bank, or otherwise to receive settlement for the item which is or becomes final, the bank may revoke the settlement given by it, charge back the amount of any credit given for the item to its customer's account, or obtain refund from its customer, whether or not it is able to return the item, if by its midnight deadline or within a longer reasonable time after it learns the facts it returns the item or sends notification of the facts. If the return or notice is delayed beyond the bank's midnight deadline or a longer reasonable time after it learns the facts, the bank may revoke the settlement, charge back the credit, or obtain refund from its customer, but it is liable for any loss resulting from the delay. These rights to revoke, charge back, and obtain refund terminate if and when a settlement for the item received by the bank is or becomes final.

(b) A collecting bank returns an item when it is sent or delivered to the bank's customer or transferor or pursuant to its instructions.

(c) A depositary bank that is also the payor may charge back the amount of an item to its customer's account or obtain refund in accordance with the section governing return of an item received by a payor bank for credit on its books (Section 4-301).

(d) The right to charge back is not affected by:

(1) previous use of a credit given for the item; or

(2) failure by any bank to exercise ordinary care with respect to the item, but a bank so failing remains liable.

(e) A failure to charge back or claim refund does not affect other rights of the bank against the customer or any other party.

(f) If credit is given in dollars as the equivalent of the value of an item payable in foreign money, the dollar amount of any charge-back or refund must be calculated on the basis of the bank-offered spot rate for the foreign money prevailing on the day when the person entitled to the charge-back or refund learns that it will not receive payment in ordinary course.

Official Comment

1. Under current bank practice, in a major portion of cases banks make provisional settlement for items when they are first received and then await subsequent determination of whether the item will be finally paid. This is the principal characteristic of what are referred to in banking parlance as "cash items." Statistically, this practice of settling provisionally first and then awaiting final payment is justified because the vast majority of such cash items are finally paid, with the result that in this great preponderance of cases it becomes unnecessary for the banks making the provisional settlements to make any further entries. In due course the provisional settlements become final simply with the lapse of time. However, in those cases in which the item being collected is not finally paid or if for various reasons the bank making the provisional settlement does not itself receive final payment, provision is made in subsection (a) for the reversal of the provisional settlements, charge-back of provisional credits and the right to obtain refund.

2. Various causes of a bank's not receiving final payment, with the resulting right of charge-back or refund, are stated or suggested in subsection (a). These include dishonor of the original item; dishonor of a remittance instrument given for it; reversal of a provisional credit for the item; suspension of payments by another bank. The causes stated are illustrative; the right of charge-back or refund is stated to exist whether the failure to receive final payment in ordinary course arises through one of them "or otherwise."

3. The right of charge-back or refund exists if a collecting bank has made a provisional settlement for an item with its customer but terminates if and when a settlement received by the bank for the item is or becomes final. If the bank fails to receive such a final settlement the right of charge-back or refund must be exercised promptly after the bank learns the facts. The right exists (if so promptly exercised) whether or not the bank is able to return the item. The second sentence of subsection (a) adopts the view of *Appliance Buyers Credit Corp. v. Prospect Nat'l Bank*, 708 F.2d 290 (7th Cir. 1983), that if the midnight deadline for returning an item or giving notice is not met, a collecting bank loses its rights only to the extent of damages for any loss resulting from the delay.

4. Subsection (b) states when an item is returned by a collecting bank. Regulation CC, Section 229.31 preempts this subsection with respect to checks by allowing direct return to the depositary bank. Because a returned check may follow a different path than in forward collection, settlement given for the check is final and not provisional except as between the depositary bank and its customer. Regulation CC Section

229.36(d). See also Regulation CC Sections 229.31(c) and 229.32(b). Thus owing to the federal preemption, this subsection applies only to noncheck items.

5. The rule of subsection (d) relating to charge-back (as distinguished from claim for refund) applies irrespective of the cause of the nonpayment, and of the person ultimately liable for nonpayment. Thus charge-back is permitted even if nonpayment results from the depositary bank's own negligence. Any other rule would result in litigation based upon a claim for wrongful dishonor of other checks of the customer, with potential damages far in excess of the amount of the item. Any other rule would require a bank to determine difficult questions of fact. The customer's protection is found in the general obligation of good faith (Sections 1-304 and 4-103). If bad faith is established the customer's recovery "includes other damages, if any, suffered by the party as a proximate consequence" (Section 4-103(e); see also Section 4-402).

6. It is clear that the charge-back does not relieve the bank from any liability for failure to exercise ordinary care in handling the item. The measure of damages for such failure is stated in Section 4-103(e).

7. Subsection (f) states a rule fixing the time for determining the rate of exchange if there is a charge-back or refund of a credit given in dollars for an item payable in a foreign currency. Compare Section 3-107. Fixing such a rule is desirable to avoid disputes. If in any case the parties wish to fix a different time for determining the rate of exchange, they may do so by agreement.

Cross References:

Sections 1-304, 3-107, 4-103, 4-301, 4-402.

Definitional Cross References:

"Account".	Section 4-104.
"Bank".	Section 1-201.
"Collecting bank".	Section 4-105.
"Customer".	Section 4-104.
"Depositary bank".	Section 4-105.
"Dishonor".	Section 3-502.
"Item".	Section 4-104.
"Midnight deadline".	Section 4-104.
"Money".	Section 1-201.
"Ordinary care".	Section 3-103.
"Party".	Section 3-103.
"Payor bank".	Section 4-105.
"Person".	Section 1-201.
"Return".	Section 4-301.
"Send".	Section 1-201(b)(36).
"Settle".	Section 4-104.
"Suspends payments".	Section 4-104.

Section 4-215. Final Payment of Item by Payor Bank; When Provisional Debits and Credits Become Final; When Certain Credits Become Available for Withdrawal

(a) An item is finally paid by a payor bank when the bank has first done any of the following:

(1) paid the item in cash;

(2) settled for the item without having a right to revoke the settlement under statute, clearing-house rule, or agreement; or

(3) made a provisional settlement for the item and failed to revoke the settlement in the time and manner permitted by statute, clearing-house rule, or agreement.

(b) If provisional settlement for an item does not become final, the item is not finally paid.

(c) If provisional settlement for an item between the presenting and payor banks is made through a clearing house or by debits or credits in an account between them, then to the extent that provisional debits or credits for the item are entered in accounts between the presenting and payor banks or between the presenting and successive prior collecting banks seriatim, they become final upon final payment of the item by the payor bank.

(d) If a collecting bank receives a settlement for an item which is or becomes final, the bank is accountable to its customer for the amount of the item and any provisional credit given for the item in an account with its customer becomes final.

(e) Subject to (i) applicable law stating a time for availability of funds and (ii) any right of the bank to apply the credit to an obligation of the customer, credit given by a bank for an item in a customer's account becomes available for withdrawal as of right:

(1) if the bank has received a provisional settlement for the item, when the settlement becomes final and the bank has had a reasonable time to receive return of the item and the item has not been received within that time;

(2) if the bank is both the depositary bank and the payor bank, and the item is finally paid, at the opening of the bank's second banking day following receipt of the item.

(f) Subject to applicable law stating a time for availability of funds and any right of a bank to apply a deposit to an obligation of the depositor, a deposit of money becomes available for withdrawal as of right at the opening of the bank's next banking day after receipt of the deposit.

Official Comment

1. By the definition and use of the term "settle" (Section 4-104(a)(11)) this Article recognizes that various debits or credits, remittances, settlements or payments given for an item may be either provisional or final, that settlements sometimes are provisional and sometimes are final and sometimes are provisional for awhile but later become final. Subsection (a) defines when settlement for an item constitutes final payment.

Final payment of an item is important for a number of reasons. It is one of several factors determining the relative priorities between items and notices, stop-payment orders, legal process and setoffs (Section 4-303). It is the "end of the line" in the collection process and the "turn around" point commencing the return flow of proceeds. It is the point at which many provisional settlements become final. See Section 4-215(c). Final payment of an item by the payor bank fixes preferential rights under Section 4-216.

2. If an item being collected moves through several states, e.g., is deposited for collection in California, moves through two or three California banks to the Federal Reserve Bank of San Francisco, to the Federal Reserve Bank of Boston, to a payor bank in Maine, the collection process involves the eastward journey of the item from California to Maine and the westward journey of the proceeds from Maine to California. Subsection (a) recognizes that final payment does not take place, in this hypothetical case, on the journey of the item eastward. It also adopts the view that neither does final payment occur on the journey westward because what in fact is journeying westward are *proceeds* of the item.

3. Traditionally and under various decisions payment in cash of an item by a payor bank has been considered final payment. Subsection (a)(1) recognizes and provides that payment of an item in cash by a payor bank is final payment.

4. Section 4-104(a)(11) defines "settle" as meaning "to pay in cash, by clearing-house settlement, in a charge or credit or by remittance, or otherwise as agreed. A settlement may be either provisional or final." Subsection (a)(2) of Section 4-215 provides that an item is finally paid by a payor bank when the bank has "settled for the item without having a right to revoke the settlement under statute, clearing-house rule or agreement." Former subsection (1)(b) is modified by subsection (a)(2) to make clear that a payor bank cannot make settlement provisional by unilaterally reserving a right to revoke the settlement. The right must come from a statute (e.g., Section 4-301), clearing-house rule or other agreement. Subsection (a)(2) provides in effect that if the payor bank finally settles for an item this constitutes final payment of the item. The subsection operates if nothing has occurred and no situation exists making the settlement provisional. If under statute, clearing-house rule or agreement, a right of revocation of the settlement exists, the settlement is provisional. Conversely, if there is an absence of a right to revoke under statute, clearing-house rule or agreement, the settlement is final and such final settlement constitutes final payment of the item.

A primary example of a statutory right on the part of the payor bank to revoke a settlement is the right to revoke conferred by Section 4-301. The underlying theory and reason for deferred posting statutes (Section 4-301) is to require a settlement on the date of receipt of an item but to keep that settlement provisional with the right to revoke prior to the midnight deadline. In any case in which Section 4-301 is applicable, any settlement by the payor bank is provisional solely by virtue of the statute, subsection (a)(2) of Section 4-215 does not operate, and such provisional settlement does not constitute final payment of the item. With respect to checks, Regulation CC Section 229.36(d) provides that settlement between banks for the forward collection of checks is final. The relationship of this provision to Article 4 is discussed in the Commentary to that section.

A second important example of a right to revoke a settlement is that arising under clearing-house rules. It is very common for clearing-house rules to provide that items exchanged and settled for in a clearing (e.g., before 10:00 a.m. on Monday) may be returned and the settlements revoked up to but not later than 2:00 p.m. on the same day (Monday) or under deferred posting at some hour on the next business day (e.g., 2:00 p.m. Tuesday). Under this type of rule the Monday morning settlement is provisional and being provisional does not constitute a final payment of the item.

An example of an agreement allowing the payor bank to revoke a settlement is a case in which the payor bank is also the depositary bank and has signed a receipt or duplicate deposit ticket or has made an entry in a passbook acknowledging receipt, for credit to the account of A, of a check drawn on it by B. If the receipt, deposit ticket, passbook or other agreement with A is to the effect that any credit so entered is provisional and may be revoked pending the time required by the payor bank to process the item to determine if it is in good form and there are funds to cover it, the agreement keeps the receipt or credit provisional and avoids its being either final settlement or final payment.

The most important application of subsection (a)(2) is that in which presentment of an item has been made over the counter for immediate payment. In this case Section 4-301(a) does not apply to make the settlement provisional, and final payment has occurred unless a rule or agreement provides otherwise.

5. Former Section 4-213(1)(c) provided that final payment occurred when the payor bank completed the "process of posting." The term was defined in former Section 4-109. In the present Article, Section 4-109 has been deleted and the process-of-posting test has been abandoned in Section 4-215(a) for determining when final payment is made. Difficulties in determining when the events described in former Section 4-109 take place make the process-of-posting test unsuitable for a system of automated check collection or electronic presentment.

6. The last sentence of former Section 4-213(1) is deleted as an unnecessary source of confusion. Initially the view that payor bank may be accountable for, that is, liable for the amount of, an item that it has already paid seems incongruous. This is particularly true in the light of the language formerly found in Section 4-302 stating that the payor bank can defend against liability for accountability by showing that it has already settled for the item. But, at least with respect to former Section 4-213(1)(c), such a provision was needed because under the process-of-posting test a payor bank may have paid an item without settling for it. Now that Article 4 has abandoned the process-of-posting test, the sentence is no longer needed. If the payor bank has neither paid the item nor returned it within its midnight deadline, the payor bank is accountable under Section 4-302.

7. Subsection (a)(3) covers the situation in which the payor bank makes a provisional settlement for an item, and this settlement becomes final at a later time by reason of the failure of the payor bank to revoke it in the time and manner permitted by statute, clearing-house rule or agreement. An example of this type of situation is the clearing-house settlement referred to in Comment 4. In the illustration there given if the time limit for the return of items received in the Monday morning clearing is 2:00 p.m. on Tuesday and the provisional settlement has not been revoked at that time in a manner permitted by the clearing-house rules, the provisional settlement made on Monday morning becomes final at 2:00 p.m. on Tuesday. Subsection (a)(3) provides specifically that in this situation the item is finally paid at 2:00 p.m. Tuesday. If on the other hand a payor bank receives an item in the mail on Monday and makes some provisional settlement for the item on Monday, it has until midnight on Tuesday to return the item or give notice and revoke any settlement under Section 4-301. In this situation subsection (a)(3) of Section 4-215 provides that if the provisional settlement made on Monday is not revoked before midnight on Tuesday as permitted by Section 4-301, the item is finally paid at midnight on Tuesday. With respect to checks, Regulation CC Section 229.30(c) allows an extension of the midnight deadline under certain circumstances. If a bank does not expeditiously return a check liability may accrue under Regulation CC Section 229.38. For the relationship of that liability to responsibility under this Article, see Regulation CC Sections 229.30 and 229.38.

8. Subsection (b) relates final settlement to final payment under Section 4-215. For example, if a payor bank makes provisional settlement for an item by sending a cashier's or teller's check and that settlement fails to become final under Section 4-213(c), subsection (b) provides that final payment has not occurred. If the item is not paid, the drawer remains liable, and under Section 4-302(a) the payor bank is accountable unless it has returned the item before its midnight deadline. In this regard, subsection (b) is an exception to subsection (a)(3). Even if the payor bank has not returned an item by its midnight deadline there is still no final payment if provisional settlement had been made and settlement failed to become final. However, if presentment of the item was over the counter for immediate payment, final payment has occurred under Section 4-215(a)(2). Subsection (b) does not apply because the settlement was not provisional. Section 4-301(a). In this case the presenting person, often the payee of the item, has the right to demand cash or the cash equivalent of federal reserve credit. If the presenting person accepts another medium of settlement such as a cashier's or teller's check, the presenting person takes the risk that the payor bank may fail to pay a cashier's check because of insolvency or that the drawee of a teller's check may dishonor it.

9. Subsection (c) states the country-wide usage that when the item is finally paid by the payor bank under subsection (a) this final payment automatically without further action "firms up" other provisional settlements made for it. However, the subsection makes clear that this "firming up" occurs only if the settlement between the presenting and payor banks was made either through a clearing house or by debits and credits in accounts between them. It does not take place if the payor bank remits for the item by sending some form of remittance instrument. Further, the "firming up" continues only to the extent that provisional debits and credits are entered seriatim in accounts between banks which are successive to the presenting bank. The automatic "firming up" is broken at any time that any collecting bank remits for the item by sending a remittance draft, because final payment to the remittee then usually depends upon final payment of the remittance draft.

10. Subsection (d) states the general rule that if a collecting bank receives settlement for an item which is or becomes final, the bank is accountable to its customer for the amount of the item. One means of accounting is to remit to its customer the amount it has received on the item. If previously it gave to its customer a provisional credit for the item in an account its receipt of final settlement for the item "firms up" this provisional credit and makes it final. When this credit given by it so becomes final, in the usual case its agency status terminates and it becomes a debtor to its customer for the amount of the item. See Section 4-201(a). If the accounting is by a remittance instrument or authorization to charge further time will usually be required to complete its accounting (Section 4-213).

11. Subsection (e) states when certain credits given by a bank to its customer become available for withdrawal as of right. Subsection (e)(1) deals with the situation in which a bank has given a credit (usually provisional) for an item to its customer and in turn has received a provisional settlement for the item from an intermediary or payor bank to which it has forwarded the item. In this situation before the provisional credit entered by the collecting bank in the account of its customer becomes available for withdrawal as of right, it is not only necessary that the provisional settlement received by the bank for the item becomes final but also that the collecting bank has a reasonable time to receive return of the item and the item has not been received within that time. How much time is "reasonable" for these purposes will of course depend on the distance the item has to travel and the number of banks through which it must pass (having in mind not only travel time by regular lines of transmission but also the successive midnight deadlines of the several banks) and other pertinent facts. Also, if the provisional settlement received is some form of a remittance instrument or authorization to charge, the "reasonable" time depends on the identity and location of the payor of the remittance instrument, the means for clearing such instrument, and other pertinent facts. With respect to checks Regulation CC Sections 229.10-229.13 or similar applicable state law (Section 229.20) control. This is also time for the situation described in Comment 12.

12. Subsection (e)(2) deals with the situation of a bank that is both a depositary bank and a payor bank. The subsection recognizes that if A and B are both customers of a depositary-payor bank and A deposits B's check on the depositary-payor in A's account on Monday, time must be allowed to permit the check under the deferred posting rules of Section 4-301 to reach the bookkeeper for B's account at some time on Tuesday, and, if there are insufficient funds in B's account, to reverse or charge back the provisional credit in A's account. Consequently this provisional credit in A's account does not become available for withdrawal as of right until the opening of business on Wednesday. If it is determined on Tuesday that there are insufficient funds in B's account to pay the check, the credit to A's account can be reversed on Tuesday. On the other hand if the item is in fact paid on Tuesday, the rule of subsection (e)(2) is desirable to avoid uncertainty and possible disputes between the bank and its customer as to exactly what hour within the day the credit is available.

Cross References:

Sections 4-104, 4-109, 4-201, 4-213, 4-215, 4-216, 4-301, 4-302, 4-303.

Definitional Cross References:

"Account".	Section 4-104.
"Agreement".	Section 1-201.
"Banking day".	Section 4-104.
"Clearing house".	Section 4-104.
"Collecting bank".	Section 4-105.
"Customer".	Section 4-104.
"Depositary bank".	Section 4-105.
"Item".	Section 4-104.
"Money".	Section 1-201.
"Notice"	Section 1-202.
"Payor bank".	Section 4-105.
"Presenting bank".	Section 4-105.
"Settle".	Section 4-104.

Section 4-216. Insolvency and Preference

(a) If an item is in or comes into the possession of a payor or collecting bank that suspends payment and the item has not been finally paid, the item must be returned by the receiver, trustee, or agent in charge of the closed bank to the presenting bank or the closed bank's customer.

(b) If a payor bank finally pays an item and suspends payments without making a settlement for the item with its customer or the presenting bank which settlement is or becomes final, the owner of the item has a preferred claim against the payor bank.

(c) If a payor bank gives or a collecting bank gives or receives a provisional settlement for an item and thereafter suspends payments, the suspension does not prevent or interfere with the settlement's becoming final if the finality occurs automatically upon the lapse of certain time or the happening of certain events.

(d) If a collecting bank receives from subsequent parties settlement for an item, which settlement is or becomes final and the bank suspends payments without making a settlement for the item with its customer which settlement is or becomes final, the owner of the item has a preferred claim against the collecting bank.

Official Comment

1. The underlying purpose of the provisions of this section is not to confer upon banks, holders of items or anyone else preferential positions in the event of bank failures over general depositors or any other creditors of the failed banks. The purpose is to fix as definitely as possible the cut-off point of time for the completion or cessation of the collection process in the case of items that happen to be in the process at the time a particular bank suspends payments. It must be remembered that in bank collections as a whole and in the handling of items by an individual bank, items go through a whole series of processes. It must also be remembered that at any particular point of time a particular bank (at least one of any size) is functioning as a depositary bank for some items, as an intermediary bank for others, as a presenting bank for still others and as a payor bank for still others, and that when it suspends payments it will have close to its normal load of items working through its various processes. For the convenience of receivers, owners of items, banks, and in fact substantially everyone concerned, it is recognized that at the particular moment of time that a bank suspends payment, a certain portion of the items being handled by it have progressed far enough in the bank collection process that it is preferable to permit them to continue the remaining distance, rather than to send them back and reverse the many entries that have been made or the steps that have been taken with respect to them. Therefore, having this background and these purposes in mind, the section states what items must be turned backward at the moment suspension intervenes and what items have progressed far enough that the collection process with respect to them continues, with the resulting necessary statement of rights of various parties flowing from this prescription of the cut-off time.

2. The rules stated are similar to those stated in the American Bankers Association Bank Collection Code, but with the abandonment of any theory of trust. On the other hand, some law previous to this Act may be relevant. See Note, Uniform Commercial Code: Stopping Payment of an Item Deposited with an Insolvent Depositary Bank, 40 Okla. L. Rev. 689 (1987). Although for practical purposes Federal Deposit Insurance affects materially the result of bank failures on holders of items and banks, no attempt is made to vary the rules of the section by reason of such insurance.

3. It is recognized that in view of *Jennings v. United States Fidelity & Guaranty Co.,* 294 U.S. 216 (1935), amendment of the National Bank Act would be necessary to have this section apply to national banks. But there is no reason why it should not apply to others. See Section 1-105.

Cross References:

Section 1-105.

Definitional Cross References:

"Collecting bank".	Section 4-105.
"Customer".	Section 4-104.
"Item".	Section 4-104.
"Payor bank".	Section 4-105.
"Presenting bank".	Section 4-105.
"Settle".	Section 4-104.
"Suspends payment".	Section 4-104.

PART 3: COLLECTION OF ITEMS: PAYOR BANKS

Section 4-301. Deferred Posting; Recovery of Payment by Return of Items; Time of Dishonor; Return of Items by Payor Bank

(a) If a payor bank settles for a demand item other than a documentary draft presented otherwise than for immediate payment over the counter before midnight of the banking day of receipt, the payor bank may revoke the settlement and recover the settlement if, before it has made final payment and before its midnight deadline, it

(1) returns the item;

(2) returns an image of the item, if the party to which the return is made has entered into an agreement to accept an image as a return of the item and the image is returned in accordance with that agreement; or

(3) sends a record providing notice of dishonor or nonpayment if the item is unavailable for return.

(b) If a demand item is received by a payor bank for credit on its books, it may return the item or send notice of dishonor and may revoke any credit given or recover the amount thereof withdrawn by its customer, if it acts within the time limit and in the manner specified in subsection (a).

(c) Unless previous notice of dishonor has been sent, an item is dishonored at the time when for purposes of dishonor it is returned or notice sent in accordance with this section.

(d) An item is returned:

(1) as to an item presented through a clearing house, when it is delivered to the presenting or last collecting bank or to the clearing house or is sent or delivered in accordance with clearing-house rules; or

(2) in all other cases, when it is sent or delivered to the bank's customer or transferor or pursuant to instructions.

Official Comment

1. The term "deferred posting" appears in the caption of Section 4-301. This refers to the practice permitted by statute in most of the states before the UCC under which a payor bank receives items on one day but does not post the items to the customer's account until the next day. Items dishonored were then returned after the posting on the day after receipt. Under Section 4-301 the concept of "deferred posting" merely allows a payor bank that has settled for an item on the day of receipt to return a dishonored item on the next day before its midnight deadline, without regard to when the item was actually posted. With respect to checks Regulation CC Section 229.30(c) extends the midnight deadline under the UCC under certain circumstances. See the Commentary to Regulation CC Section 229.38(d) on the relationship between the UCC and Regulation CC on settlement.

2. The function of this section is to provide the circumstances under which a payor bank that has made timely settlement for an item may return the item and revoke the settlement so that it may recover any settlement made. These circumstances are: (1) the item must be a demand item other than a documentary draft; (2) the item must be presented otherwise than for immediate payment over the counter; and (3) the payor bank must return the item (or give notice if the item is unavailable for return) before its midnight deadline and before it has paid the item. With respect to checks, see Regulation CC Section 229.31(f) on notice in lieu of return and Regulation CC Section 229.33 as to the different requirement of notice of nonpayment. An instance of when an item may be unavailable for return arises under a collecting bank check retention plan under which presentment is made by a presentment notice and the item is retained by the collecting bank. Section 4-215(a)(2) provides that final payment occurs if the payor bank has settled for an item without a right to revoke the settlement under statute, clearing-house rule or agreement. In any case in which Section 4-301(a) is applicable, the payor bank has a right to revoke the settlement by statute; therefore, Section 4-215(a)(2) is inoperable, and the settlement is provisional. Hence, if the settlement is not over the counter and the payor bank settles in a manner that does not constitute final payment, the payor bank can revoke the settlement by returning the item before its midnight deadline.

3. The relationship of Section 4-301(a) to final settlement and final payment under Section 4-215 is illustrated by the following case. Depositary Bank sends by mail an item to Payor Bank with instructions to settle by remitting a teller's check drawn on a bank in the city where Depositary Bank is located. Payor Bank sends the teller's check on the day the item was presented. Having made timely settlement, under the deferred posting provisions of Section 4-301(a), Payor Bank may revoke that settlement by returning the item before its midnight deadline. If it fails to return the item before its midnight deadline, it has finally paid the item if the bank on which the teller's check was drawn honors the check. But if the teller's check is dishonored there has been no final settlement under Section 4-213(c) and no final payment under Section 4-215(b). Since the Payor Bank has neither paid the item nor made timely return, it is accountable for the item under Section 4-302(a).

4. The time limits for action imposed by subsection (a) are adopted by subsection (b) for cases in which the payor bank is also the depositary bank, but in this case the requirement of a settlement on the day of receipt is omitted.

5. Subsection (c) fixes a base point from which to measure the time within which notice of dishonor must be given. See Section 3-503.

6. Subsection (d) leaves banks free to agree upon the manner of returning items but establishes a precise time when an item is "returned." For definition of "sent" as used in paragraphs (1) and (2) see Section 1-201(b)(36). Obviously the subsection assumes that the item has not been "finally paid" under Section 4-215(a). If it has been, this provision has no operation.

7. The fact that an item has been paid under proposed Section 4-215 does not preclude the payor bank from asserting rights of restitution or revocation under Section 3-418. *Nat'l Savings & Trust Co. v. Park Corp.*, 722 F.2d 1303 (6th Cir. 1983), cert. denied, 466 U.S. 939 (1984), is the correct interpretation of the present law on this issue.

8. Paragraph (a)(2) is designed to facilitate electronic check-processing by authorizing the payor bank to return an image of the item instead of the actual item. It applies only when the payor bank and the party to which the return has been made have agreed that the payor bank can make such a return and when the return complies with the agreement. The purpose of the paragraph is to prevent third parties (such as the depositor of the check) from contending that the payor bank missed its midnight deadline because it failed to return the actual item in a timely manner. If the payor bank missed its midnight deadline, payment would have become final under Section 4-215 and the depositary bank would have lost its right of chargeback under Section 4-214. Of course, the depositary bank might enter into an agreement with its depositor to resolve that problem, but it is not clear that agreements by banks with their customers can resolve all such issues. In any event, paragraph (a)(2) should eliminate the need for such agreements. The provision rests on the premise that it is inappropriate to penalize a payor bank simply because it returns the actual item a few business days after the midnight deadline if the payor bank sent notice before that deadline to a collecting bank that had agreed to accept such notices.

Nothing in paragraph (a)(2) authorizes the payor bank to destroy the check.

Cross References:

Sections 1-201, 3-418, 3-503, 4-213, 4-214, 4-215, 4-301, 4-302.

Definitional Cross References:

"Banking day".	Section 4-104.
"Clearing house".	Section 4-104.
"Collecting bank".	Section 4-105.
"Customer".	Section 4-104.
"Documentary draft".	Section 4-104.
"Item".	Section 4-104.
"Midnight deadline".	Section 4-104.
"Notice of dishonor".	Section 3-508.
"Payor bank".	Section 4-105.
"Presenting bank."	Section 4-105.
"Sent".	Section 1-201.
"Settlement".	Section 4-104.

Section 4-302. Payor Bank's Responsibility for Late Return of Item

(a) If an item is presented to and received by a payor bank, the bank is accountable for the amount of:

(1) a demand item, other than a documentary draft, whether properly payable or not, if the bank, in any case in which it is not also the depositary bank, retains the item beyond midnight of the banking day of receipt without settling for it or, whether or not it is also the depositary bank, does not pay or return the item or send notice of dishonor until after its midnight deadline; or

(2) any other properly payable item unless, within the time allowed for acceptance or payment of that item, the bank either accepts or pays the item or returns it and accompanying documents.

(b) The liability of a payor bank to pay an item pursuant to subsection (a) is subject to defenses based on breach of a presentment warranty (Section 4-208) or proof that the person seeking enforcement of the liability presented or transferred the item for the purpose of defrauding the payor bank.

Official Comment

1. Subsection (a)(1) continues the former law distinguishing between cases in which the payor bank is not also the depositary bank and those in which the payor bank is also the depositary bank ("on us" items). For "on us" items the payor bank is accountable if it retains the item beyond its midnight deadline without settling for it. If the payor bank is not the depositary bank it is accountable if it retains the item beyond midnight of the banking day of receipt without settling for it. It may avoid accountability either by settling for the item on the day of receipt and returning the item before its midnight deadline under Section 4-301 or by returning the item on the day of receipt. This rule is consistent with the deferred posting practice authorized by Section 4-301 which allows the payor bank to make provisional settlement for an item on the day of receipt and to revoke that settlement by returning the item on the next day. With respect to checks, Regulation CC Section 229.36(d) provides that settlements between banks for forward collection of checks are final when made. See the Commentary on that provision for its effect on the UCC.

2. If the settlement given by the payor bank does not become final, there has been no payment under Section 4-215(b), and the payor bank giving the failed settlement is accountable under subsection (a)(1) of Section 4-302. For instance, the payor bank makes provisional settlement by sending a teller's check that is dishonored. In such a case settlement is not final under Section 4-213(c) and no payment occurs under Section 4-215(b). Payor bank is accountable on the item. The general principle is that unless settlement provides the presenting bank with usable funds, settlement has failed and the payor bank is accountable for the amount of the item. On the other hand, if the payor bank makes a settlement for the item that becomes final under Section 4-215, the item has been paid and thus the payor bank is not accountable for the item under this Section.

3. Subsection (b) is an elaboration of the deleted introductory language of former Section 4-302: "In the absence of a valid defense such as breach of a presentment warranty (subsection (1) of Section 4-207), settlement effected or the like. . . ." A payor bank can defend an action against it based on accountability by showing that the item contained a forged indorsement or a fraudulent alteration. Subsection (b) drops the ambiguous "or the like" language and provides that the payor bank may also raise the defense of fraud. Decisions that hold an accountable bank's liability to be "absolute" are rejected. A payor bank that makes a late return of an item should not be liable to a defrauder operating a check kiting scheme. In *Bank of Leumi Trust Co. v. Bally's Park Place Inc.,* 528 F. Supp. 349 (S.D.N.Y. 1981), and *American Nat'l Bank v. Foodbasket,* 497 P.2d 546 (Wyo. 1972), banks that were accountable under Section 4-302 for missing their midnight deadline were successful in defending against parties who initiated collection knowing that the check would not be paid. The "settlement effected" language is deleted as unnecessary. If a payor bank is accountable for an item it is liable to pay it. If it has made final payment for an item, it is no longer accountable for the item.

Cross References:

Sections 4-207, 4-208, 4-213, 4-215, 4-301, 4-302.

Definitional Cross References:

"Acceptance".	Section 3-409.
"Bank".	Section 1-201.
"Banking day".	Section 4-104.
"Depositary bank".	Section 4-105.
"Documentary draft".	Section 4-104.
"Item".	Section 4-104.
"Midnight deadline".	Section 4-104.
"Payment".	Section 3-602.
"Payor bank".	Section 4-105.
"Person".	Section 1-201.
"Presentment".	Section 3-501.
"Properly payable".	Section 4-401.
"Return".	Section 4-301.
"Send".	Section 1-201(b)(36).
"Transfer".	Section 3-203.

Section 4-303. When Items Subject to Notice, Stop-Payment Order, Legal Process, or Setoff; Order in Which Items May Be Changed or Certified

(a) Any knowledge, notice, or stop-payment order received by, legal process served upon, or setoff exercised by a payor bank comes too late to terminate, suspend, or modify the bank's right or duty to pay an item or to charge its customer's account for the item if the knowledge, notice, stop-payment order, or legal process is received or served and a reasonable time for the bank to act thereon expires or the setoff is exercised after the earliest of the following:

(1) the bank accepts or certifies the item;

(2) the bank pays the item in cash;

(3) the bank settles for the item without having a right to revoke the settlement under statute, clearing-house rule, or agreement;

(4) the bank becomes accountable for the amount of the item under Section 4-302 dealing with the payor bank's responsibility for late return of items; or

(5) with respect to checks, a cutoff hour no earlier than one hour after the opening of the next banking day after the banking day on which the bank received the check and no later than the close of that next banking day or, if no cutoff hour is fixed, the close of the next banking day after the banking day on which the bank received the check.

(b) Subject to subsection (a), items may be accepted, paid, certified, or charged to the indicated account of its customer in any order.

Official Comment

1. While a payor bank is processing an item presented for payment, it may receive knowledge or a legal notice affecting the item, such as knowledge or a notice that the drawer has filed a petition in bankruptcy or made an assignment for the benefit of creditors; may receive an order of the drawer stopping payment on the item; may have served on it an attachment of the account of the drawer; or the bank itself may exercise a right of setoff against the drawer's account. Each of these events affects the account of the drawer and may eliminate or freeze all or part of whatever balance is available to pay the item. Subsection (a) states the rule for determining the relative priorities between these various legal events and the item.

2. The rule is that if any one of several things has been done to the item or if it has reached any one of several stages in its processing at the time the knowledge, notice, stop-payment order or legal process is received or served and a reasonable time for the bank to act thereon expires or the setoff is exercised, the knowledge, notice, stop-payment order, legal process or setoff comes too late, the item has priority and a charge to the customer's account may be made and is effective. With respect to the effect of the customer's bankruptcy, the bank's rights are governed by Bankruptcy Code Section 542(c) which codifies the result of *Bank of Marin v. England,* 385 U.S. 99 (1966). Section 4-405 applies to the death or incompetence of the customer.

3. Once a payor bank has accepted or certified an item or has paid the item in cash, the event has occurred that determines priorities between the item and the various legal events usually described as the "four legals." Paragraphs (1) and (2) of subsection (a) so provide. If a payor bank settles for an item presented over the counter for immediate payment by a cashier's check or teller's check which the presenting person agrees to accept, paragraph (3) of subsection (a) would control and the event determining priority has occurred. Because presentment was over the counter, Section 4-301(a) does not apply to give the payor bank the statutory right to revoke the settlement. Thus the requirements of paragraph (3) have been met unless a clearing-house rule or agreement of the parties provides otherwise.

4. In the usual case settlement for checks is by entries in bank accounts. Since the process-of-posting test has been abandoned as inappropriate for automated check collection, the determining event for priorities is a given hour on the day after the item is received. (Paragraph (5) of subsection (a).) The hour may be fixed by the bank no earlier than one hour after the opening on the next banking day after the bank received the check and no later than the close of that banking day. If an item is received after the payor bank's regular Section 4-108 cutoff hour, it is treated as received the next banking day. If a bank receives an item after its regular cutoff hour on Monday and an attachment is levied at noon on Tuesday, the attachment is prior to the item if the bank had not before that hour taken the action described in paragraphs (1), (2), and (3) of subsection (a). The Commentary to Regulation CC Section 229.36(d) explains that even though settlement by a paying bank for a check is final for Regulation CC purposes, the paying bank's right to return the check before its midnight deadline under the UCC is not affected.

5. Another event conferring priority for an item and a charge to the customer's account based upon the item is stated by the language "become accountable for the amount of the item under Section 4-302 dealing with the payor bank's responsibility for late return of items." Expiration of the deadline under Section 4-302 with resulting accountability by the payor bank for the amount of the item, establishes priority of the item over notices, stop-payment orders, legal process or setoff.

6. In the case of knowledge, notice, stop-payment orders and legal process the effective time for determining whether they were received too late to affect the payment of an item and a charge to the customer's account by reason of such payment, is receipt plus a reasonable time for the bank to act on any of these communications. Usually a relatively short time is required to communicate to the accounting department advice of one of these events but certainly some time is necessary. Compare Sections 1-202 and 4-403. In the case of setoff the effective time is when the setoff is actually made.

7. As between one item and another no priority rule is stated. This is justified because of the impossibility of stating a rule that would be fair in all cases, having in mind the almost infinite number of combinations of large and small checks in relation to the available balance on hand in the drawer's account; the possible methods of receipt; and other variables. Further, the drawer has drawn all the checks, the drawer should have funds available to meet all of them and has no basis for urging one should be paid before another; and the holders have no direct right against the payor bank in any event, unless of course, the bank has accepted, certified or finally paid a particular item, or has become liable for it under Section 4-302. Under subsection (b) the bank has the right to pay items for which it is itself liable ahead of those for which it is not.

Cross References:

Sections 1-202, 4-108, 4-301, 4-302, 4-403, 4-405.

Definitional Cross References:

"Accepted".	Section 3-410.
"Account".	Section 4-104.
"Agreement".	Section 1-201.
"Certified".	Section 3-411.
"Clearing house".	Section 4-104.
"Customer".	Section 4-104.
"Item".	Section 4-104.
"Notice".	Section 1-202.
"Payor bank".	Section 4-105.
"Settle".	Section 4-104.

PART 4. RELATIONSHIP BETWEEN PAYOR BANK AND ITS CUSTOMER

Section 4-401. When Bank May Charge Customer's Account

(a) A bank may charge against the account of a customer an item that is properly payable from the account even though the charge creates an overdraft. An item is properly payable if it is authorized by the customer and is in accordance with any agreement between the customer and bank.

(b) A customer is not liable for the amount of an overdraft if the customer neither signed the item nor benefited from the proceeds of the item.

(c) A bank may charge against the account of a customer a check that is otherwise properly payable from the account, even though payment was made before the date of the check, unless the customer has given notice to the bank of the postdating describing the check with reasonable certainty. The notice is effective for the period stated in Section 4-403(b) for stop-payment orders, and must be received at such time and in such manner as to afford the bank a reasonable opportunity to act on it before the bank takes any action with respect to the check described in Section 4-303. If a bank charges against the account of a customer a check before the date stated in the notice of postdating, the bank is liable for damages for the loss resulting from its act. The loss may include damages for dishonor of subsequent items under Section 4-402.

(d) A bank that in good faith makes payment to a holder may charge the indicated account of its customer according to:

(1) the original terms of the altered item; or

(2) the terms of the completed item, even though the bank knows the item has been completed unless the bank has notice that the completion was improper.

Official Comment

1. An item is properly payable from a customer's account if the customer has authorized the payment and the payment does not violate any agreement that may exist between the bank and its customer. For an example of a payment held to violate an agreement with a customer, see *Torrance Nat'l Bank v. Enesco Fed. Credit Union,* 285 P.2d 737 (Cal. Ct. App. 1955). An item drawn for more than the amount of a customer's account may be properly payable. Thus under subsection (a) a bank may charge the customer's account for an item even though payment results in an overdraft. An item containing a forged drawer's signature or forged indorsement is not properly payable. Concern has arisen whether a bank may require a customer to execute a stop-payment order when the customer notifies the bank of the loss of an unindorsed or specially indorsed check. Since such a check cannot be properly payable from the customer's account, it is inappropriate for a bank to require stop-payment order in such a case.

2. Subsection (b) adopts the view of case authority holding that if there is more than one customer who can draw on an account, the nonsigning customer is not liable for an overdraft unless that person benefits from the proceeds of the item.

3. Subsection (c) is added because the automated check collection system cannot accommodate postdated checks. A check is usually paid upon presentment without respect to the date of the check. Under the former law, if a payor bank paid a postdated check before its stated date, it could not charge the customer's account because the check was not "properly payable." Hence, the bank might have been liable for wrongfully dishonoring subsequent checks of the drawer that would have been paid had the postdated check not been prematurely paid. Under subsection (c) a customer wishing to postdate a check must notify the payor bank of its postdating in time to allow the bank to act on the customer's notice before the bank has to commit itself to pay the check. If the bank fails to act on the customer's timely notice, it may be liable for damages for the resulting loss which may include damages for dishonor of subsequent items. This Act does not regulate fees that banks charge their customers for a notice of postdating or other services covered by the Act, but under principles of law such as unconscionability or good faith and fair dealing, courts have reviewed fees and the bank's exercise of a discretion to set fees. *Perdue v. Crocker Nat'l Bank,* 702 P.2d 503 (Cal. 1985) (unconscionability); *Best v. United Bank of Oregon,* 739 P.2d 554, 562-566 (Or. 1987) (good faith and fair dealing). In addition, Section 1-304 provides that every contract or duty within this Act imposes an obligation of good faith in its performance or enforcement.

4. Section 3-407(c) states that a payor bank or drawee which pays a fraudulently altered instrument in good faith and without notice of the alteration may enforce rights with respect to the instrument according to its original terms or, in the case of an incomplete instrument altered by unauthorized completion, according to its terms as completed. Section 4-401(d) follows the rule stated in Section 3-407(c) by applying it to an altered item and allows the bank to enforce rights with respect to the altered item by charging the customer's account.

Cross References:

Sections 1-304, 3-407, 4-303, 4-402, 4-403.

Definitional Cross References:

"Account".	Section 4-104.
"Agreement".	Section 1-201.
"Alteration".	Section 3-407.
"Bank".	Section 1-201.
"Check".	Section 1-201.
"Customer".	Section 4-104.
"Dishonor".	Section 3-502.
"Good faith".	Section 1-201.
"Holder".	Section 1-201.
"Item".	Section 4-104.
"Notice".	Section 1-202.
"Payment".	Section 3-602.
"Signed".	Section 1-201.
"Term".	Section 1-201.

Section 4-402. Bank's Liability to Customer for Wrongful Dishonor; Time of Determining Insufficiency of Account

(a) Except as otherwise provided in this Article, a payor bank wrongfully dishonors an item if it dishonors an item that is properly payable, but a bank may dishonor an item that would create an overdraft unless it has agreed to pay the overdraft.

(b) A payor bank is liable to its customer for damages proximately caused by the wrongful dishonor of an item. Liability is limited to actual damages proved and may include damages for an arrest or prosecution of the customer or other consequential damages. Whether any consequential damages are proximately caused by the wrongful dishonor is a question of fact to be determined in each case.

(c) A payor bank's determination of the customer's account balance on which a decision to dishonor for insufficiency of available funds is based may be made at any time between the time the item is received by the payor bank and the time that the payor bank returns the item or gives notice in lieu of return, and no more than one determination need be made. If, at the election of the payor bank, a subsequent balance determination is made for the purpose of reevaluating the bank's decision to dishonor the item, the account balance at that time is determinative of whether a dishonor for insufficiency of available funds is wrongful.

Official Comment

1. Subsection (a) states positively what has been assumed under the original Article: that if a bank fails to honor a properly payable item it may be liable to its customer for wrongful dishonor. Under subsection (b) the payor bank's wrongful dishonor of an item gives rise to a statutory cause of action. Damages may include consequential damages. Confusion has resulted from the attempts of courts to reconcile the first and second sentences of former Section 4-402. The second sentence implied that the bank was liable for some form of damages other than those proximately caused by the dishonor if the dishonor was other than by mistake. But nothing in the section described what these noncompensatory damages might be. Some courts have held that in distinguishing between mistaken dishonors and nonmistaken dishonors, the so-called "trader" rule has been retained that allowed a "merchant or trader" to recover substantial damages for wrongful dishonor without proof of damages actually suffered. Comment 3 to former Section 4-402 indicated that this was not the intent of the drafters. White & Summers, Uniform Commercial Code, Section 18-4 (1988), states: "The negative implication is that when wrongful dishonors occur not 'through mistake' but willfully, the court may impose damages greater than 'actual damages'. . . . Certainly the reference to 'mistake' in the second sentence of 4-402 invites a court to adopt the relevant pre-Code distinction." Subsection (b) by deleting the reference to mistake in the second sentence precludes any inference that Section 4-402 retains the "trader" rule. Whether a bank is liable for noncompensatory damages, such as punitive damages, must be decided by Section 1-103 and Section 1-305 ("by other rule of law").

2. Wrongful dishonor is different from "failure to exercise ordinary care in handling an item," and the measure of damages is that stated in this section, not that stated in Section 4-103(e). By the same token, if a dishonor comes within this section, the measure of damages of this section applies and not another measure of damages. If the wrongful refusal of the beneficiary's bank to make funds available from a funds transfer causes the beneficiary's check to be dishonored, no specific guidance is given as to whether recovery is under this section or Article 4A. In each case this issue must be viewed in its factual context, and it was thought unwise to seek to establish certainty at the cost of fairness.

3. The second and third sentences of subsection (b) reject decisions holding that as a matter of law the dishonor of a check is not the "proximate cause" of the arrest and prosecution of the customer and leave to determination in each case as a question of fact whether the dishonor is or may be the "proximate cause."

4. Banks commonly determine whether there are sufficient funds in an account to pay an item after the close of banking hours on the day of presentment when they post debit and credit items to the account. The determination is made on the basis of credits available for withdrawal as of right or made available for withdrawal by the bank as an accommodation to its customer. When it is determined that payment of the item would overdraw the account, the item may be returned at any time before the bank's midnight deadline the following day. Before the item is returned new credits that are withdrawable as of right may have been added to the account. Subsection (c) eliminates uncertainty under Article 4 as to whether the failure to make a second determination before the item is returned on the day following presentment is a wrongful dishonor if new credits were added to the account on that day that would have covered the amount of the check.

5. Section 4-402 has been construed to preclude an action for wrongful dishonor by a plaintiff other than the bank's customer. *Loucks v. Albuquerque Nat'l Bank,* 418 P.2d 191 (N.M. 1966). Some courts have allowed a plaintiff other than the customer to sue when the customer is a business entity that is one and the same with the individual or individuals operating it. *Murdaugh Volkswagen, Inc. v. First Nat'l Bank,* 801 F.2d 719 (4th Cir. 1986) and *Karsh v. American City Bank,* 169 Cal. Rptr. 851 (Ct. App. 1980). However, where the wrongful dishonor impugns the reputation of an operator of the business, the issue is not merely, as the court in *Koger v. East First Nat'l Bank,* 443 So. 2d 141 (Fla. Ct. App. 1983), put it, one of a literal versus a liberal interpretation of Section 4-402. Rather the issue is whether the statutory cause of action in Section 4-402 displaces, in accordance with Section 1-103, any cause of action that existed at common law in a person who is not the customer whose reputation was damaged. See *Marcum v. Security Trust & Savings Co.,* 129 So. 74 (Ala. 1930). While Section 4-402 should not be interpreted to displace the latter cause of action, the section itself gives no cause of action to other than a "customer," however that definition is construed, and thus confers no cause of action on the holder of a dishonored item. *First American Nat'l Bank v. Commerce Union Bank,* 692 S.W.2d 642 (Tenn. Ct. App. 1985).

Cross References:

Sections 1-103, 1-305, 4-103, 4-402.

Definitional Cross References:

"Account".	Section 4-104.
"Bank".	Section 1-201.
"Customer".	Section 4-104.
"Dishonor".	Section 3-502.
"Item".	Section 4-104.
"Notice".	Section 1-202.
"Payor bank".	Section 4-105.
"Properly payable".	Section 4-401.
"Prove".	Section 3-103.
"Return".	Section 4-301.

Section 4-403. Customer's Right to Stop Payment; Burden of Proof of Loss

(a) A customer or any person authorized to draw on the account if there is more than one person may stop payment of any item drawn on the customer's account or close the account by an order to the bank describing the item or account with reasonable certainty received at a time and in a manner that affords the bank a reasonable opportunity to act on it before any action by the bank with respect to the item described in Section 4-303. If the signature of more than one person is required to draw on an account, any of these persons may stop payment or close the account.

(b) A stop-payment order is effective for six months, but it lapses after 14 calendar days if the original order was oral and was not confirmed in a record within that period. A stop-payment order may be renewed for additional six-month periods by a record given to the bank within a period during which the stop-payment order is effective.

(c) The burden of establishing the fact and amount of loss resulting from the payment of an item contrary to a stop-payment order or order to close an account is on the customer. The loss from payment of an item contrary to a stop-payment order may include damages for dishonor of subsequent items under Section 4-402.

Official Comment

1. The position taken by this section is that stopping payment or closing an account is a service which depositors expect and are entitled to receive from banks notwithstanding its difficulty, inconvenience and expense. The inevitable occasional losses through failure to stop or close should be borne by the banks as a cost of the business of banking.

2. Subsection (a) follows the decisions holding that a payee or indorsee has no right to stop payment. This is consistent with the provision governing payment or satisfaction. See Section 3-602. The sole exception to this rule is found in Section 4-405 on payment after notice of death, by which any person claiming an interest in the account can stop payment.

3. Payment is commonly stopped only on checks; but the right to stop payment is not limited to checks, and extends to any item payable by any bank. If the maker of a note payable at a bank is in a position analogous to that of a drawer (Section 4-106) the maker may stop payment of the note. By analogy the rule extends to drawees other than banks.

4. A cashier's check or teller's check purchased by a customer whose account is debited in payment for the check is not a check drawn on the customer's account within the meaning of subsection (a); hence, a customer purchasing a cashier's check or teller's check has no right to stop payment of such a check under subsection (a). If a bank issuing a cashier's check or teller's check refuses to pay the check as an accommodation to its customer or for other reasons, its liability on the check is governed by Section 3-411. There is no right to stop payment after certification of a check or other acceptance of a draft, and this is true no matter who procures the certification. See Sections 3-411 and 4-303. The acceptance is the drawee's own engagement to pay, and it is not required to impair its credit by refusing payment for the convenience of the drawer.

5. Subsection (a) makes clear that if there is more than one person authorized to draw on a customer's account any one of them can stop payment of any check drawn on the account or can order the account closed. Moreover, if there is a customer, such as a corporation, that requires its checks to bear the signatures of more than one person, any of these persons may stop payment on a check. In describing the item, the customer, in the absence of a contrary agreement, must meet the standard of what information allows the bank under the technology then existing to identify the item with reasonable certainty.

6. Under subsection (b), a stop-payment order is effective after the order, whether written or oral, is received by the bank and the bank has a reasonable opportunity to act on it. If the order is written it remains in effect for six months from that time. If the order is oral it lapses after 14 days unless there is written confirmation. If there is written confirmation within the 14-day period, the six-month period dates from the giving of the oral order. A stop-payment order may be renewed any number of times by written notice given during a six-month period while a stop order is in effect. A new stop-payment order may be given after a six-month period expires, but such a notice takes effect from the date given. When a stop-payment order expires it is as though the order had never been given, and the payor bank may pay the item in good faith under Section 4-404 even though a stop-payment order had once been given.

7. A payment in violation of an effective direction to stop payment is an improper payment, even though it is made by mistake or inadvertence. Any agreement to the contrary is invalid under Section 4-103(a) if in paying the item over the stop-payment order the bank has failed to exercise ordinary care. An agreement to the contrary which is imposed upon a customer as part of a standard form contract would have to be evaluated in the light of the general obligation of good faith. Sections 1-304 and 4-104(c). The drawee is, however, entitled to subrogation to prevent unjust enrichment (Section 4-407); retains common law defenses, e.g., that by conduct in recognizing the payment the customer has ratified the bank's action in paying over a stop-payment order (Section 1-103); and retains common law rights, e.g., to recover money paid under a mistake under Section 3-418. It has sometimes been said that payment cannot be stopped against a holder in due course, but the statement is inaccurate. The payment can be stopped but the drawer remains liable on the instrument to the holder in due course (Sections 3-305, 3-414) and the drawee, if it pays, becomes subrogated to the rights of the holder in due course against the drawer. Section 4-407. The relationship between Sections 4-403 and 4-407 is discussed in the comments to Section 4-407. Any defenses available against a holder in due course remain available to the drawer, but other defenses are cut off to the same extent as if the holder were bringing the action.

Cross References:

Sections 1-103, 1-304, 3-305, 3-411, 3-414, 3-418, 3-602, 4-103, 4-104, 4-106, 4-303, 4-402, 4-403, 4-405, 4-407.

Definitional Cross References:

"Account".	Section 4-104.
"Bank".	Section 1-201.
"Burden of establishing".	Section 1-201.
"Customer".	Section 4-104.
"Dishonor".	Section 3-502.
"Item".	Section 4-104.
"Person".	Section 1-201.
"Record".	Section 3-103.
"Writing".	Section 1-201.

Section 4-404. Bank Not Obliged to Pay Check More Than Six Months Old

A bank is under no obligation to a customer having a checking account to pay a check, other than a certified check, which is presented more than six months after its date, but it may charge its customer's account for a payment made thereafter in good faith.

Official Comment

This section incorporates a type of statute that had been adopted in 26 jurisdictions before the Code. The time limit is set at six months because banking and commercial practice regards a check outstanding for longer than that period as stale, and a bank will normally not pay such a check without consulting the depositor. It is therefore not required to do so, but is given the option to pay because it may be in a position to know, as in the case of dividend checks, that the drawer wants payment made.

Certified checks are excluded from the section because they are the primary obligation of the certifying bank (Sections 3-409 and 3-413). The obligation runs directly to the holder of the check. The customer's account was presumably charged when the check was certified.

Cross References:

Sections 3-409, 3-413.

Definitional Cross References:

"Account".	Section 4-104.
"Bank".	Section 1-201.
"Certified check".	Section 3-409.
"Check".	Section 1-201.
"Customer".	Section 4-104.
"Good faith".	Section 1-201.
"Payment".	Section 3-602.

Section 4-405. Death or Incompetence of Customer

(a) A payor or collecting bank's authority to accept, pay, or collect an item or to account for proceeds of its collection, if otherwise effective, is not rendered ineffective by incompetence of a customer of either bank existing at the time the item is issued or its collection is undertaken if the bank does not know of an adjudication of incompetence. Neither death nor incompetence of a customer revokes the authority to accept, pay, collect, or account until the bank knows of the fact of death or of an adjudication of incompetence and has reasonable opportunity to act on it.

(b) Even with knowledge, a bank may for 10 days after the date of death pay or certify checks drawn on or before that date unless ordered to stop payment by a person claiming an interest in the account.

Official Comment

1. Subsection (a) follows existing decisions holding that a drawee (payor) bank is not liable for the payment of a check before it has notice of the death or incompetence of the drawer. The justice and necessity of the rule are obvious. A check is an order to pay which the bank must obey under penalty of possible liability for dishonor. Further, with the tremendous volume of items handled any rule that required banks to verify the continued life and competency of drawers would be completely unworkable.

One or both of these same reasons apply to other phases of the bank collection and payment process and the rule is made wide enough to apply to these other phases. It applies to all kinds of "items"; to "customers" who own items as well as "customers" who draw or make them; to the function of collecting items as well as the function of accepting or paying them; to the carrying out of instructions to account for proceeds even though these may involve transfers to third parties; to depositary and intermediary banks as well as payor banks; and to incompetency existing at the time of the issuance of an item or the commencement of the collection or payment process as well as to incompetency occurring thereafter. Further, the requirement of actual knowledge makes inapplicable the rule of some cases that an adjudication of incompetency is constructive notice to all the world because obviously it is as impossible for banks to keep posted on such adjudications (in the absence of actual knowledge) as it is to keep posted as to death of immediate or remote customers.

2. Subsection (b) provides a limited period after death during which a bank may continue to pay checks (as distinguished from other items) even though it has notice. The purpose of the provision, as of the existing statutes, is to permit holders of checks drawn and issued shortly before death to cash them without the necessity of filing a claim in probate. The justification is that these checks normally are given in immediate payment of an obligation, that there is almost never any reason why they should not be paid, and that filing in probate is a useless formality, burdensome to the holder, the executor, the court and the bank.

This section does not prevent an executor or administrator from recovering the payment from the holder of the check. It is not intended to affect the validity of any gift causa mortis or other transfer in contemplation of death, but merely to relieve the bank of liability for the payment.

3. Any surviving relative, creditor or other person who claims an interest in the account may give a direction to the bank not to pay checks, or not to pay a particular check. Such notice has the same effect as a direction to stop payment. The bank has no responsibility to determine the validity of the claim or even whether it is "colorable." But obviously anyone who has an interest in the estate, including the person named as executor in a will, even if the will has not yet been admitted to probate, is entitled to claim an interest in the account.

Cross References:

Section 4-403.

Definitional Cross References:

"Account".	Section 4-104.
"Bank".	Section 1-201.
"Check".	Section 3-104.
"Collecting bank".	Section 4-105.
"Customer".	Section 4-104.
"Issue".	Section 3-105.
"Item".	Section 4-104.
"Knows".	Section 1-202.
"Person".	Section 1-201.

Section 4-406. Customer's Duty to Discover and Report Unauthorized Signature or Alteration

(a) A bank that sends or makes available to a customer a statement of account showing payment of items for the account shall either return or make available to the customer the items paid or provide information in the statement of account sufficient to allow the customer reasonably to identify the items paid. The statement of account provides sufficient information if the item is described by item number, amount, and date of payment.

(b) If the items are not returned to the customer, the person retaining the items shall either retain the items or, if the items are destroyed, maintain the capacity to furnish legible copies of the items until the expiration of seven years after receipt of the items. A customer may request an item from the bank that paid the item, and that bank must provide in a reasonable time either the item or, if the item has been destroyed or is not otherwise obtainable, a legible copy of the item.

(c) If a bank sends or makes available a statement of account or items pursuant to subsection (a), the customer must exercise reasonable promptness in examining the statement or the items to determine whether any payment was not authorized because of an alteration of an item or because a purported signature by or on behalf of the customer was not authorized. If, based on the statement or items provided, the customer should reasonably have discovered the unauthorized payment, the customer must promptly notify the bank of the relevant facts.

(d) If the bank proves that the customer failed, with respect to an item, to comply with the duties imposed on the customer by subsection (c), the customer is precluded from asserting against the bank:

(1) the customer's unauthorized signature or any alteration on the item, if the bank also proves that it suffered a loss by reason of the failure; and

(2) the customer's unauthorized signature or alteration by the same wrongdoer on any other item paid in good faith by the bank if the payment was made before the bank received notice from the customer of the unauthorized signature or alteration and after the customer had been afforded a reasonable period of time, not exceeding 30 days, in which to examine the item or statement of account and notify the bank.

(e) If subsection (d) applies and the customer proves that the bank failed to exercise ordinary care in paying the item and that the failure substantially contributed to loss, the loss is allocated between the customer precluded and the bank asserting the preclusion according to the extent to which the failure of the customer to comply with subsection (c) and the failure of the bank to exercise ordinary care contributed to the loss. If the customer proves that the bank did not pay the item in good faith, the preclusion under subsection (d) does not apply.

(f) Without regard to care or lack of care of either the customer or the bank, a customer who does not within one year after the statement or items are made available to the customer (subsection (a)) discover and report the customer's unauthorized signature on or any alteration on the item is precluded from asserting against the bank the unauthorized signature or alteration. If there is a preclusion under this subsection, the payor bank may not recover for breach of warranty under Section 4-208 with respect to the unauthorized signature or alteration to which the preclusion applies.

Official Comment

1. Under subsection (a), if a bank that has paid a check or other item for the account of a customer makes available to the customer a statement of account showing payment of the item, the bank must either return the item to the customer or provide a description of the item sufficient to allow the customer to identify it. Under subsection (c), the customer has a duty to exercise reasonable promptness in examining the statement or the returned item to discover any unauthorized signature of the customer or any alteration and to promptly notify the bank if the customer should reasonably have discovered the unauthorized signature or alteration.

The duty stated in subsection (c) becomes operative only if the "bank sends or makes available a statement of account or items pursuant to subsection (a)." A bank is not under a duty to send a statement of account or the paid items to the customer; but, if it does not do so, the customer does not have any duties under subsection (c).

Under subsection (a), a statement of account must provide information "sufficient to allow the customer reasonably to identify the items paid." If the bank supplies its customer with an image of the paid item, it complies with this standard. But a safe harbor rule is provided. The bank complies with the standard of providing "sufficient information" if "the item is described by item number, amount, and date of payment." This means that the customer's duties under subsection (c) are triggered if the bank sends a statement of account complying with the safe harbor rule without returning the paid items. A bank does not have to return the paid items unless it has agreed with the customer to do so. Whether there is such an agreement depends upon the particular circumstances. See Section 1-201(b)(3). If the bank elects to provide the minimum information that is "sufficient" under subsection (a) and, as a consequence, the customer could not "reasonably have discovered the unauthorized payment," there is no preclusion under subsection (d). If the customer made a record of the issued checks on the check stub or carbonized copies furnished by the bank in the checkbook, the customer should usually be able to verify the paid items shown on the statement of account and discover any unauthorized or altered checks. But there could be exceptional circumstances. For example, if a check is altered by changing the name of the payee, the customer could not normally detect the fraud unless the customer is given the paid check or the statement of account discloses the name of the payee of the altered check. If the customer could not "reasonably have discovered the unauthorized payment" under subsection (c) there would not be a preclusion under subsection (d).

The safe harbor provided by subsection (a) serves to permit a bank, based on the state of existing technology, to trigger the customer's duties under subsection (c) by providing a "statement of account showing payment of items" without having to return the paid items, in any case in which the bank has not agreed with the customer to return the paid items. The safe harbor does not, however, preclude a customer under subsection (d) from asserting its unauthorized signature or an alteration against a bank in those circumstances in which under subsection (c) the customer should not "reasonably have discovered the unauthorized payment." Whether the customer has failed to comply with its duties under subsection (c) is determined on a case-by-case basis.

The provision in subsection (a) that a statement of account contains "sufficient information if the item is described by item number, amount, and date of payment" is based upon the existing state of technology. This information was chosen because it can be obtained by the bank's computer from the check's MICR line without examination of the items involved. The other two items of information that the customer would normally want to know—the name of the payee and the date of the item—cannot currently be obtained from the MICR line. The safe harbor rule is important in determining the feasibility of payor or collecting bank check retention plans. A customer who keeps a record of checks written, e.g., on the check stubs or carbonized copies of the checks supplied by the bank in the checkbook, will usually have sufficient information to identify the items on the basis of item number, amount, and date of payment. But customers who do not utilize these record-keeping methods may not. The policy decision is that accommodating customers who do not keep adequate records is not as desirable as accommodating customers who keep more careful records. This policy results in less cost to the check collection system and thus to all customers of the system. It is expected that technological advances such as image processing may make it possible for banks to give customers more information in the future in a manner that is fully compatible with automation or truncation systems. At that time the Permanent Editorial Board may wish to make recommendations for an amendment revising the safe harbor requirements in the light of those advances.

2. Subsection (d) states the consequences of a failure by the customer to perform its duty under subsection (c) to report an alteration or the customer's unauthorized signature. Subsection (d)(1) applies to the unauthorized payment of the item to which the duty to report under subsection (c) applies. If the bank proves that the customer "should reasonably have discovered the unauthorized payment" (See Comment 1) and did not notify the bank, the customer is precluded from asserting against the bank the alteration or the customer's unauthorized signature if the bank proves that it suffered a loss as a result of the failure of the customer to perform its subsection (c) duty. Subsection (d)(2) applies to cases in which the customer fails to report an unauthorized signature or alteration with respect to an item in breach of the subsection (c) duty (See Comment 1) and the bank subsequently pays other items of the customer with respect to which there is an alteration or unauthorized signature of the customer and the same wrongdoer is involved. If the payment of the subsequent items occurred after the customer has had a reasonable time (not exceeding 30 days) to report with respect to the first item and before the bank received notice of the unauthorized signature or alteration of the first item, the customer is precluded from asserting the alteration or unauthorized signature with respect to the subsequent items.

If the customer is precluded in a single or multiple item unauthorized payment situation under subsection (d), but the customer proves that the bank failed to exercise ordinary care in paying the item or items and that the failure substantially contributed to the loss, subsection (e) provides a comparative negligence test for allocating loss between the customer and the bank. Subsection (e) also states that, if the customer proves that the bank did not pay the item in good faith, the preclusion under subsection (d) does not apply.

Subsection (d)(2) changes former subsection (2)(b) by adopting a 30-day period in place of a 14-day period. Although the 14-day period may have been sufficient when the original version of Article 4 was drafted in the 1950s, given the much greater volume of checks at the time of the revision, a longer period was viewed as more appropriate. The rule of subsection (d)(2) follows pre-Code case law that payment of an additional item or items bearing an unauthorized signature or alteration by the same wrongdoer is a loss suffered by the bank traceable to the customer's failure to exercise reasonable care (See Comment 1) in examining the statement and notifying the bank of objections to it. One of the most serious consequences of failure of the customer to comply with the requirements of subsection (c) is the opportunity presented to the wrongdoer to repeat the misdeeds. Conversely, one of the best ways to keep down losses in this type of situation is for the customer to promptly examine the statement and notify the bank of an unauthorized signature or alteration so that the bank will be alerted to stop paying further items. Hence, the rule of subsection (d)(2) is prescribed, and to avoid dispute a specific time limit, 30 days, is designated for cases to which the subsection applies. These considerations are not present if there are no losses resulting from the payment of additional items. In these circumstances, a reasonable period for the customer to comply with its duties under subsection (c) would depend on the circumstances (Section 1-205(a)) and the subsection (d)(2) time limit should not be imported by analogy into subsection (c).

3. Subsection (b) applies if the items are not returned to the customer. Check retention plans may include a simple payor bank check retention plan or the kind of check retention plan that would be authorized by a truncation agreement in which a collecting bank or the payee may retain the items. Even after agreeing to a check retention plan, a customer may need to see one or more checks for litigation or other purposes. The customer's request for the check may always be made to the payor bank. Under subsection (b) retaining banks may destroy items but must maintain the capacity to furnish legible copies for seven years. A legible copy may include an image of an item. This Act does not define the length of the reasonable period of time for a bank to provide the check or copy of the check. What is reasonable depends on the capacity of the bank and the needs of the customer. This Act does not specify sanctions for failure to retain or furnish the items or legible copies; this is left to other laws regulating banks. See Comment 3 to Section 4-101. Moreover, this Act does not regulate fees that banks charge their customers for furnishing items or copies or other services covered by the Act, but under principles of law such as unconscionability or good faith and fair dealing, courts have reviewed fees and the bank's exercise of a discretion to set fees. *Perdue v. Crocker Nat'l Bank,* 702 P.2d 503 (Cal. 1985) (unconscionability); *Best v. United Bank of Oregon,* 739 P.2d 554, 562-566 (Or. 1987) (good faith and fair dealing). In addition, Section 1-304 provides that every contract or duty within this Act imposes an obligation of good faith in its performance or enforcement.

4. Subsection (e) replaces former subsection (3) and poses a modified comparative negligence test for determining liability. See the discussion on this point in the Comments to Sections 3-404, 3-405, and 3-406. The term "good faith" is defined in Section 1-201(b)(20) as including "observance of reasonable commercial standards of fair dealing." The connotation of this standard is fairness and not absence of negligence.

The term "ordinary care" used in subsection (e) is defined in Section 3-103(a)(7), made applicable to Article 4 by Section 4-104(c), to provide that sight examination by a payor bank is not required if its procedure is reasonable and is commonly followed by other comparable banks in the area. The case law is divided on this issue. The definition of "ordinary care" in Section 3-103 rejects those authorities that hold, in effect, that failure to use sight examination is negligence as a matter of law. The effect of the definition of "ordinary care" on Section 4-406 is only to provide that in the small percentage of cases in which a customer's failure to examine its statement or returned items has led to loss under subsection (d) a bank should not have to share that loss solely because it has adopted an automated collection or payment procedure in order to deal with the great volume of items at a lower cost to all customers.

5. Several changes are made in former Section 4-406(5). First, former subsection (5) is deleted and its substance is made applicable only to the one-year notice preclusion in former subsection (4) (subsection (f)). Thus if a drawer has not notified the payor bank of an unauthorized check or material alteration within the one-year period, the payor bank may not choose to recredit the drawer's account and pass the loss to the collecting banks on the theory of breach of warranty. Second, the reference in former subsection (4) to unauthorized indorsements is deleted. Section 4-406 imposes no duties on the drawer to look for unauthorized indorsements. Section 4-111 sets out a statute of limitations allowing a customer a three-year period to seek a credit to an account improperly charged by payment of an item bearing an unauthorized indorsement. Third, subsection (c) is added to Section 4-208 to assure that if a depositary bank is sued for breach of a presentment warranty, it can defend by showing that the drawer is precluded by Section 3-406 or Section 4-406(c) and (d).

Cross References:

Sections 1-201, 1-205, 1-304, 3-103, 3-404, 3-405, 3-406, 4-104, 4-111, 4-208, 4-406.

Definitional Cross References:

"Alteration".	Section 3-407.
"Bank".	Section 1-201.
"Collecting bank".	Section 4-105.
"Customer".	Section 4-104.
"Good faith".	Section 1-201.
"Indorsement".	Section 3-204.
"Item".	Section 4-104.
"Ordinary care".	Section 3-103.
"Payor bank".	Section 4-105.
"Send".	Section 1-201.
"Unauthorized signature".	Section 1-201.

Section 4-407. Payor Bank's Right to Subrogation on Improper Payment

If a payor bank has paid an item over the order of the drawer or maker to stop payment, or after an account has been closed, or otherwise under circumstances giving a basis for objection by the drawer or maker, to prevent unjust enrichment and only to the extent necessary to prevent loss to the bank by reason of its payment of the item, the payor bank is subrogated to the rights

(1) of any holder in due course on the item against the drawer or maker;

(2) of the payee or any other holder of the item against the drawer or maker either on the item or under the transaction out of which the item arose; and

(3) of the drawer or maker against the payee or any other holder of the item with respect to the transaction out of which the item arose.

Official Comment

1. Section 4-403 states that a stop-payment order or an order to close an account is binding on a bank. If a bank pays an item over such an order it is prima facie liable, but under subsection (c) of Section 4-403 the burden of establishing the fact and amount of loss from such payment is on the customer. A defense frequently interposed by a bank in an action against it for wrongful payment over a stop-payment order is that the drawer or maker suffered no loss because it would have been liable to a holder in due course in any event. On this argument some cases have held that payment cannot be stopped against a holder in due course. Payment can be stopped, but if it is, the drawer or maker is liable and the sound rule is that the bank is subrogated to the rights of the holder in due course. The preamble and paragraph (1) of this section state this rule.

2. Paragraph (2) also subrogates the bank to the rights of the payee or other holder against the drawer or maker either on the item or under the transaction out of which it arose. It may well be that the payee is not a holder in due course but still has good rights against the drawer. These may be on the check but also may not be as, for example, where the drawer buys goods from the payee and the goods are partially defective so that the payee is not entitled to the full price, but the goods are still worth a portion of the contract price. If the drawer retains the goods it is obligated to pay a part of the agreed price. If the bank has paid the check it should be subrogated to this claim of the payee against the drawer.

3. Paragraph (3) subrogates the bank to the rights of the drawer or maker against the payee or other holder with respect to the transaction out of which the item arose. If, for example, the payee was a fraudulent salesman inducing the drawer to issue a check for defective securities, and the bank pays the check over a stop-payment order but reimburses the drawer for such payment, the bank should have a basis for getting the money back from the fraudulent salesman.

4. The limitations of the preamble prevent the bank itself from getting any double recovery or benefits out of its subrogation rights conferred by the section.

5. The spelling out of the affirmative rights of the bank in this section does not destroy other existing rights (Section 1-103). Among others these may include the defense of a payor bank that by conduct in recognizing the payment a customer has ratified the bank's action in paying in disregard of a stop-payment order or right to recover money paid under a mistake.

Cross References:

Sections 1-103, 4-403.

Definitional Cross References:

"Account".	Section 4-104.
"Bank".	Section 1-201.
"Drawer".	Section 3-103.
"Holder".	Section 1-201.
"Holder in due course".	Section 3-302.
"Item".	Section 4-104.
"Maker".	Section 3-103.
"Payment".	Section 3-602.
"Payor bank".	Section 4-105.
"Stop payment".	Section 4-403.

PART 5. COLLECTION OF DOCUMENTARY DRAFTS

Section 4-501. Handling of Documentary Drafts; Duty to Send for Presentment and to Notify Customer of Dishonor

A bank that takes a documentary draft for collection shall present or send the draft and accompanying documents for presentment and, upon learning that the draft has not been paid or accepted in due course, shall seasonably notify its customer of the fact even though it may have discounted or bought the draft or extended credit available for withdrawal as of right.

Official Comment

This section states the duty of a bank handling a documentary draft for a customer. "Documentary draft" is defined in Section 4-104. The duty stated exists even if the bank has bought the draft. This is because to the customer the draft normally represents an underlying commercial transaction, and if that is not going through as planned the customer should know it promptly. An electronic document of title may be presented through allowing access to the document or delivery of the document. Article 1, Section 1-201 (definition of "delivery").

Cross References:

Sections 1-201, 4-104.

Definitional Cross References:

"Acceptance".	Section 3-409.
"Bank".	Section 1-201.

"Customer".	Section 4-104.
"Documentary draft".	Section 4-104.
"Draft".	Section 4-104.
"Notifies".	Section 1-202.
"Presentment".	Section 3-501.
"Send".	Section 1-201(b)(36).

Section 4-502. Presentment of "On Arrival" Drafts

If a draft or the relevant instructions require presentment "on arrival", "when goods arrive" or the like, the collecting bank need not present until in its judgment a reasonable time for arrival of the goods has expired. Refusal to pay or accept because the goods have not arrived is not dishonor; the bank must notify its transferor of the refusal but need not present the draft again until it is instructed to do so or learns of the arrival of the goods.

Official Comment

The section is designed to establish a definite rule for "on arrival" drafts. The term includes not only drafts drawn payable "on arrival" but also drafts forwarded with instructions to present "on arrival." The term refers to the arrival of the relevant goods. Unless a bank has actual knowledge of the arrival of the goods, as for example, when it is the "notify" party on the bill of lading, the section only requires the exercise of such judgment in estimating time as a bank may be expected to have. Commonly the buyer-drawee will want the goods and will therefore call for the documents and take up the draft when they do arrive.

Definitional Cross References:

"Acceptance".	Section 3-409.
"Bank".	Section 1-201.
"Collecting bank".	Section 4-105.
"Dishonor".	Section 3-502.
"Draft".	Section 4-104.
"Goods".	Section 2-105.
"Notifies".	Section 1-202.
"Presentment".	Section 3-501.

Section 4-503. Responsibility of Presenting Bank for Documents and Goods; Report of Reasons for Dishonor; Referee in Case of Need

Unless otherwise instructed and except as provided in Article 5, a bank presenting a documentary draft:

(1) must deliver the documents to the drawee on acceptance of the draft if it is payable more than three days after presentment; otherwise, only on payment; and

(2) upon dishonor, either in the case of presentment for acceptance or presentment for payment, may seek and follow instructions from any referee in case of need designated in the draft or, if the presenting bank does not choose to utilize the referee's services, it must use diligence and good faith to ascertain the reason for dishonor, must notify its transferor of the dishonor and of the results of its effort to ascertain the reasons therefor, and must request instructions.

However, the presenting bank is under no obligation with respect to goods represented by the documents except to follow any reasonable instructions seasonably received; it has a right to reimbursement for any expense incurred in following instructions and to prepayment of or indemnity for those expenses.

Official Comment

1. This section states the rules governing, in the absence of instructions, the duty of the presenting bank in case either of honor or of dishonor of a documentary draft. The section should be read in connection with Section 2-514 on when documents are deliverable on acceptance, when on payment. In the case of a dishonor of the draft, the bank, subject to Section 4-504, must return possession or control of the documents to its principal.

2. If the draft is drawn under a letter of credit, Article 5 controls. See Sections 5-108 through 5-110.

Cross References:

Sections 2-514, 4-504, 5-108 through 5-110.

Definitional Cross References:

"Acceptance".	Section 3-409.
"Bank".	Section 1-201.
"Dishonor".	Section 3-502.
"Documentary draft".	Section 4-104.
"Draft".	Section 4-104.
"Drawee".	Section 4-104.
"Good faith".	Section 1-201.
"Goods".	Section 2-105.
"Payment".	Section 3-602.
"Presenting bank".	Section 4-105.
"Presentment".	Section 3-501.

Section 4-504. Privilege of Presenting Bank to Deal With Goods; Security Interest for Expenses

(a) A presenting bank that, following the dishonor of a documentary draft, has seasonably requested instructions but does not receive them within a reasonable time may store, sell, or otherwise deal with the goods in any reasonable manner.

(b) For its reasonable expenses incurred by action under subsection (a) the presenting bank has a lien upon the goods or their proceeds, which may be foreclosed in the same manner as an unpaid seller's lien.

Official Comment

The section gives the presenting bank, after dishonor, a privilege to deal with the goods in any commercially reasonable manner pending instructions from its transferor and, if still unable to communicate with its principal after a reasonable time, a right to realize its expenditures as if foreclosing on an unpaid seller's lien (Section 2-706). The provision includes situations in which storage of goods or other action becomes commercially necessary pending receipt of any requested instructions, even if the requested instructions are later received.

The "reasonable manner" referred to means one reasonable in the light of business factors and the judgment of a business man.

Cross References:

Section 2-706.

Definitional Cross References:

"Dishonor".	Section 3-502.
"Documentary draft".	Section 4-104.
"Goods".	Section 2-105.
"Presenting bank".	Section 4-105.
"Security interest".	Section 1-201.

Article 4A — Funds Transfers

As adopted in 1989 and revised in: (i) 1994, in connection with PEB Commentary No. 13; (ii) 2001, in connection with the revision of Article 1; (iii) 2012, in connection with an amendment to Section 4A-108; and (iv) 2022, in connection with the 2022 Amendments to the Uniform Commercial Code.

PREFATORY NOTE

The National Conference of Commissioners on Uniform State laws and The American Law Institute have approved a new Article 4A to the Uniform Commercial Code. Comments that follow each of the sections of the statute are intended as official comments. They explain in detail the purpose and meaning of the various sections and the policy considerations on which they are based.

Description of transaction covered by Article 4A. There are a number of mechanisms for making payments through the banking system. Most of these mechanisms are covered in whole or part by state or federal statutes. In terms of number of transactions, payments made by check or credit card are the most common payment methods. Payment by check is covered by Articles 3 and 4 of the UCC and some aspects of payment by credit card are covered by federal law. In recent years electronic funds transfers have been increasingly common in consumer transactions. For example, in some cases a retail customer can pay for purchases by use of an access or debit card inserted in a terminal at the retail store that allows the bank account of the customer to be instantly debited. Some aspects of these point-of-sale transactions and other consumer payments that are effected electronically are covered by a federal statute, the Electronic Fund Transfer Act (EFTA). If any part of a funds transfer is covered by EFTA, the entire funds transfer is excluded from Article 4A.

Another type of payment, commonly referred to as a wholesale wire transfer, is the primary focus of Article 4A. Payments that are covered by Article 4A are overwhelmingly between business or financial institutions. The dollar volume of payments made by wire transfer far exceeds the dollar volume of payments made by other means. The volume of payments by wire transfer over the two principal wire payment systems—the Federal Reserve wire transfer network (Fedwire) and the New York Clearing House Interbank Payments Systems (CHIPS)—exceeds one trillion dollars per day. Most payments carried out by use of automated clearing houses are consumer payments covered by EFTA and therefore not covered by Article 4A. There is, however, a significant volume of non-consumer ACH payments that closely resemble wholesale wire transfers. These payments are also covered by Article 4A.

There is some resemblance between payments made by wire transfer and payments made by other means such as paper-based checks and credit cards or electronically-based consumer payments, but there are also many differences. Article 4A excludes from its coverage these other payment mechanisms. Article 4A follows a policy of treating the transaction that it covers—a "funds transfer"—as a unique method of payment that is governed by unique principles of law that address the operational and policy issues presented by this kind of payment.

The funds transfer that is covered by Article 4A is not a complex transaction and can be illustrated by the following example which is used throughout the Prefatory Note as a basis for discussion. X, a debtor, wants to pay an obligation owed to Y. Instead of delivering to Y a negotiable instrument such as a check or some other writing such as a credit card slip that enables Y to obtain payment from a bank, X transmits an instruction to X's bank to credit a sum of money to the bank account of Y. In most cases X's bank and Y's bank are different banks. X's bank may carry out X's instruction by instructing Y's bank to credit Y's account in the amount that X requested. The instruction that X issues to its bank is a "payment order." X is the "sender" of the payment order and X's bank is the "receiving bank" with respect to X's order. Y is the "beneficiary" of X's order. When X's bank issues an instruction to Y's bank to carry out X's payment order, X's bank "executes" X's order. The instruction of X's bank to Y's bank is also a payment order. With respect to that order, X's bank is the sender, Y's bank is the receiving bank, and Y is the beneficiary. The entire series of transactions by which X pays Y is known as the "funds transfer." With respect to the funds transfer, X is the "originator," X's bank is the "originator's bank," Y is the "beneficiary" and Y's bank is the "beneficiary's bank." In more complex transactions there are one or more additional banks known as "intermediary banks" between X's bank and Y's bank. In the funds transfer the instruction contained in the payment order of X to its bank is carried out by a series of payment orders by each bank in the transmission chain to the next bank in the chain until Y's bank receives a payment order to make the credit to Y's account. In most cases, the payment order of each bank to the next bank in the chain is transmitted electronically, and often the payment order of X to its bank is also transmitted electronically, but the means of transmission does not have any legal significance. A payment order may be transmitted by any means, and in some cases the payment order is transmitted by a slow means such as first class mail. To reflect this fact, the broader term "funds transfer" rather than the narrower term "wire transfer" is used in Article 4A to describe the overall payment transaction.

Funds transfers are divided into two categories determined by whether the instruction to pay is given by the person making payment or the person receiving payment. If the instruction is given by the person making the payment, the transfer is commonly referred to as a "credit transfer." If the instruction is given by the person receiving payment, the transfer is commonly referred to as a "debit transfer." Article 4A governs credit transfers and excludes debit transfers.

<u>Why is Article 4A needed?</u> There is no comprehensive body of law that defines the rights and obligations that arise from wire transfers. Some aspects of wire transfers are governed by rules of the principal transfer systems. Transfers made by Fedwire are governed by Federal Reserve Regulation J and transfers over CHIPS are governed by the CHIPS rules. Transfers made by means of automated clearing houses are governed by uniform rules adopted by various associations of banks in various parts of the nation or by Federal Reserve rules or operating circulars. But the various funds transfer system rules apply to only limited aspects of wire transfer transactions. The resolution of the many issues that are not covered by funds transfer system rules depends on contracts of the parties, to the extent that they exist, or principles of law applicable to other payment mechanisms that might be applied by analogy. The result is a great deal of uncertainty. There is no consensus about the juridical nature of a wire transfer and consequently of the rights and obligations that are created. Article 4A is intended to provide the comprehensive body of law that we do not have today.

whether the electronic message has been authorized by its customer. To ensure that no unauthorized person is transmitting messages to the bank, the normal practice is to establish security procedures that usually involve the use of codes or identifying numbers or words. If the bank accepts a payment order that purports to be that of its customer after verifying its authenticity by complying with a security procedure agreed to by the customer and the bank, the customer is bound to pay the order even if it was not authorized. But there is an important limitation on this rule. The bank is entitled to payment in the case of an unauthorized order only if the court finds that the security procedure was a commercially reasonable method of providing security against unauthorized payment orders. The customer can also avoid liability if it can prove that the unauthorized order was not initiated by an employee or other agent of the customer having access to confidential security information or by a person who obtained that information from a source controlled by the customer. The policy issues are discussed in the comments following Section 4A-203. If the bank accepts an unauthorized payment order without verifying it in compliance with a security procedure, the loss falls on the bank.

Security procedures are also important in cases of error in the transmission of payment orders. There may be an error by the sender in the amount of the order, or a sender may transmit a payment order and then erroneously transmit a duplicate of the order. Normally, the sender is bound by the payment order even if it is issued by mistake. But in some cases an error of this kind can be detected by a security procedure. Although the receiving bank is not obliged to provide a security procedure for the detection of error, if such a procedure is agreed to by the bank Section 4A-205 provides that if the error is not detected because the receiving bank does not comply with the procedure, any resulting loss is borne by the bank failing to comply with the security procedure.

Insolvency losses. Some payment orders do not involve the granting of credit to the sender by the receiving bank. In those cases, the receiving bank accepts the sender's order at the same time the bank receives payment of the order. This is true of a transfer of funds by Fedwire or of cases in which the receiving bank can debit a funded account of the sender. But in some cases the granting of credit is the norm. This is true of a payment order over CHIPS. In a CHIPS transaction the receiving bank usually will accept the order before receiving payment from the sending bank. Payment is delayed until the end of the day when settlement is made through the Federal Reserve System. If the receiving bank is an intermediary bank, it will accept by issuing a payment order to another bank and the intermediary bank is obliged to pay that payment order. If the receiving bank is the beneficiary's bank, the bank usually will accept by releasing funds to the beneficiary before the bank has received payment. If a sending bank suspends payments before settling its liabilities at the end of the day, the financial stability of banks that are net creditors of the insolvent bank may also be put into jeopardy, because the dollar volume of funds transfers between the banks may be extremely large. With respect to two banks that are dealing with each other in a series of transactions in which each bank is sometimes a receiving bank and sometimes a sender, the risk of insolvency can be managed if amounts payable as a sender and amounts receivable as a receiving bank are roughly equal. But if these amounts are significantly out of balance, a net creditor bank may have a very significant credit risk during the day before settlement occurs. The Federal Reserve System and the banking community are greatly concerned with this risk, and various measures have been instituted to reduce this credit exposure. Article 4A also addresses this problem. A receiving bank can always avoid this risk by delaying acceptance of a payment order until after the bank has received payment. For example, if the beneficiary's bank credits the beneficiary's account it can avoid acceptance by not notifying the beneficiary of the receipt of the order or by notifying the beneficiary that the credit may not be withdrawn until the beneficiary's bank receives payment. But if the beneficiary's bank releases funds to the beneficiary before receiving settlement, the result in a funds transfer other than a transfer by means of an automated clearing house or similar provisional settlement system is that the beneficiary's bank may not recover the funds if it fails to receive settlement. This rule encourages the banking system to impose credit limitations on banks that issue payment orders. These limitations are already in effect. CHIPS has also proposed a loss-sharing plan to be adopted for implementation in the second half of 1990 under which CHIPS participants will be required to provide funds necessary to complete settlement of the obligations of one or more participants that are unable to meet settlement obligations. Under this plan, it will be a virtual certainty that there will be settlement on CHIPS in the event of failure by a single bank. Section 4A-403(b) and (c) are also addressed to reducing risks of insolvency. Under these provisions the amount owed by a failed bank with respect to payment orders it issued is the net amount owing after setting off amounts owed to the failed bank with respect to payment orders it received. This rule allows credit exposure to be managed by limitations on the net debit position of a bank.

International transfers. The major international legal document dealing with the subject of electronic funds transfers is the Model Law on International Credit Transfers adopted in 1992 by the United Nations Commission on International Trade Law. It covers basically the same type of transaction as does Article 4A, although it requires the funds transferred to have an international component. The Model Law and Article

4A basically live together in harmony, but to the extent there are differences they must be recognized and, to the extent possible, avoided or adjusted by agreement. See PEB Commentary No. 13.

PART 1. SUBJECT MATTER AND DEFINITIONS

Section 4A-101. Short Title

This Article may be cited as Uniform Commercial Code—Funds Transfers.

Section 4A-102. Subject Matter

Except as otherwise provided in Section 4A-108, this Article applies to funds transfers defined in Section 4A-104.

Official Comment

Article 4A governs a specialized method of payment referred to in the Article as a funds transfer but also commonly referred to in the commercial community as a wholesale wire transfer. A funds transfer is made by means of one or more payment orders. The scope of Article 4A is determined by the definitions of "payment order" and "funds transfer" found in Section 4A-103 and Section 4A-104.

The funds transfer governed by Article 4A is in large part a product of recent and developing technological changes. Before this Article was drafted there was no comprehensive body of law—statutory or judicial—that defined the juridical nature of a funds transfer or the rights and obligations flowing from payment orders. Judicial authority with respect to funds transfers is sparse, undeveloped and not uniform. Judges have had to resolve disputes by referring to general principles of common law or equity, or they have sought guidance in statutes such as Article 4 which are applicable to other payment methods. But attempts to define rights and obligations in funds transfers by general principles or by analogy to rights and obligations in negotiable instrument law or the law of check collection have not been satisfactory.

In the drafting of Article 4A, a deliberate decision was made to write on a clean slate and to treat a funds transfer as a unique method of payment to be governed by unique rules that address the particular issues raised by this method of payment. A deliberate decision was also made to use precise and detailed rules to assign responsibility, define behavioral norms, allocate risks and establish limits on liability, rather than to rely on broadly stated, flexible principles. In the drafting of these rules, a critical consideration was that the various parties to funds transfers need to be able to predict risk with certainty, to insure against risk, to adjust operational and security procedures, and to price funds transfer services appropriately. This consideration is particularly important given the very large amounts of money that are involved in funds transfers.

Funds transfers involve competing interests—those of the banks that provide funds transfer services and the commercial and financial organizations that use the services, as well as the public interest. These competing interests were represented in the drafting process and they were thoroughly considered. The rules that emerged represent a careful and delicate balancing of those interests and are intended to be the exclusive means of determining the rights, duties and liabilities of the affected parties in any situation covered by particular provisions of the Article. Consequently, resort to principles of law or equity outside of Article 4A is not appropriate to create rights, duties and liabilities inconsistent with those stated in this Article.

Section 4A-103. Payment Order—Definitions

(a) In this Article:

(1) "Payment order" means an instruction of a sender to a receiving bank, transmitted orally or in a record, to pay, or to cause another bank to pay, a fixed or determinable amount of money to a beneficiary if:

(i) the instruction does not state a condition to payment to the beneficiary other than time of payment,

(ii) the receiving bank is to be reimbursed by debiting an account of, or otherwise receiving payment from, the sender, and

(iii) the instruction is transmitted by the sender directly to the receiving bank or to an agent, funds-transfer system, or communication system for transmittal to the receiving bank.

(2) "Beneficiary" means the person to be paid by the beneficiary's bank.

(3) "Beneficiary's bank" means the bank identified in a payment order in which an account of the beneficiary is to be credited pursuant to the order or which otherwise is to make payment to the beneficiary if the order does not provide for payment to an account.

(4) "Receiving bank" means the bank to which the sender's instruction is addressed.

(5) "Sender" means the person giving the instruction to the receiving bank.

(b) If an instruction complying with subsection (a)(1) is to make more than one payment to a beneficiary, the instruction is a separate payment order with respect to each payment.

(c) A payment order is issued when it is sent to the receiving bank.

Official Comment

1. This section is discussed in the Comment following Section 4A-104.

2. Pursuant to the Uniform Commercial Code Amendments (2022) and in furtherance of medium neutrality, the reference to "electronically, or in writing" in the pre-2022 text of this section has been changed to refer to "in a record."

Section 4A-104. Funds Transfer—Definitions

In this Article:

(a) "Funds transfer" means the series of transactions, beginning with the originator's payment order, made for the purpose of making payment to the beneficiary of the order. The term includes any payment order issued by the originator's bank or an intermediary bank intended to carry out the originator's payment order. A funds transfer is completed by acceptance by the beneficiary's bank of a payment order for the benefit of the beneficiary of the originator's payment order.

(b) "Intermediary bank" means a receiving bank other than the originator's bank or the beneficiary's bank.

(c) "Originator" means the sender of the first payment order in a funds transfer.

(d) "Originator's bank" means (i) the receiving bank to which the payment order of the originator is issued if the originator is not a bank, or (ii) the originator if the originator is a bank.

Official Comment

1. Article 4A governs a method of payment in which the person making payment (the "originator") directly transmits an instruction to a bank either to make payment to the person receiving payment (the "beneficiary") or to instruct some other bank to make payment to the beneficiary. The payment from the originator to the beneficiary occurs when the bank that is to pay the beneficiary becomes obligated to pay the beneficiary. There are two basic definitions: "Payment order" stated in Section 4A-103 and "Funds transfer" stated in Section 4A-104. These definitions, other related definitions, and the scope of Article 4A can best be understood in the context of specific fact situations. Consider the following cases:

Case #1. X, which has an account in Bank A, instructs that bank to pay $1,000,000 to Y's account in Bank A. Bank A carries out X's instruction by making a credit of $1,000,000 to Y's account and notifying Y that the credit is available for immediate withdrawal. The instruction by X to Bank A is a "payment order" which was issued when it was sent to Bank A. Section 4A-103(a)(1) and (c). X is the "sender" of the payment order and Bank A is the "receiving bank." Section 4A-103(a)(5) and (a)(4). Y is the "beneficiary" of the payment order and Bank A is the "beneficiary's bank." Section 4A-103(a)(2) and (a)(3). When Bank A notified Y of receipt of the payment order, Bank A "accepted" the payment order. Section 4A-209(b)(1). When Bank A accepted the order it incurred an obligation to Y to pay the amount of the order. Section 4A-404(a). When Bank A accepted X's order, X incurred an obligation to pay Bank A the amount of the order. Section 4A-402(b). Payment from X to Bank A would normally be made by a debit to X's account in Bank A. Section 4A-403(a)(3). At the time Bank A incurred the obligation to pay Y, payment of $1,000,000 by X to Y was also made. Section 4A-406(a). Bank A paid Y when it gave notice to Y of a withdrawable credit of $1,000,000 to Y's account. Section 4A-405(a). The overall transaction, which comprises the acts of X and Bank A, in which the payment by X to Y is accomplished is referred to as the "funds transfer." Section 4A-104(a). In this case only one payment order was involved in the funds transfer. A one-payment-order funds transfer is usually referred to as a "book transfer" because the payment is accomplished by the receiving bank's debiting the account of the sender and crediting the account of the beneficiary in the same bank. X, in addition to being the sender of the payment order to Bank A, is the "originator" of the funds transfer. Section 4A-104(c). Bank A is the "originator's bank" in the funds transfer as well as the beneficiary's bank. Section 4A-104(d).

Case #2. Assume the same facts as in Case #1 except that X instructs Bank A to pay $1,000,000 to Y's account in Bank B. With respect to this payment order, X is the sender, Y is the beneficiary, and Bank A is the receiving bank. Bank A carries out X's order by instructing Bank B to pay $1,000,000 to Y's account. This instruction is a payment order in which Bank A is the sender, Bank B is the receiving bank, and Y is the beneficiary. When Bank A issued its payment order to Bank B, Bank A "executed" X's order. Section 4A-301(a). In the funds transfer, X is the originator, Bank A is the originator's bank, and Bank B is the beneficiary's bank. When Bank A executed X's order, X incurred an obligation to pay Bank A the amount of the order. Section 4A-402(c). When Bank B accepts the payment order issued to it by Bank A, Bank B incurs an obligation to Y to pay the amount of the order (Section 4A-404 (a)) and Bank A incurs an obligation to pay Bank B. Section 4A-402(b). Acceptance by Bank B also results in payment of $1,000,000 by X to Y. Section 4A-406(a). In this case two payment orders are involved in the funds transfer.

Case #3. Assume the same facts as in Case #2 except that Bank A does not execute X's payment order by issuing a payment order to Bank B. One bank will not normally act to carry out a funds transfer for another bank unless there is a preexisting arrangement between the banks for transmittal of payment orders and settlement of accounts. For example, if Bank B is a foreign bank with which Bank A has no relationship, Bank A can utilize a bank that is a correspondent of both Bank A and Bank B. Assume Bank A issues a payment order to Bank C to pay $1,000,000 to Y's account in Bank B. With respect to this order, Bank A is the sender, Bank C is the receiving bank, and Y is the beneficiary. Bank C will execute the payment order of Bank A by issuing a payment order to Bank B to pay $1,000,000 to Y's account in Bank B. With respect to Bank C's payment order, Bank C is the sender, Bank B is the receiving bank, and Y is the beneficiary. Payment of $1,000,000 by X to Y occurs when Bank B accepts the payment order issued to it by Bank C. In this case the funds transfer involves three payment orders. In the funds transfer, X is the originator, Bank A is the originator's bank, Bank B is the beneficiary's bank, and Bank C is an "intermediary bank." Section 4A-104 (b). In some cases there may be more than one intermediary bank, and in those cases each intermediary bank is treated like Bank C in Case #3.

As the three cases demonstrate, a payment under Article 4A involves an overall transaction, the funds transfer, in which the originator, X, is making payment to the beneficiary, Y, but the funds transfer may encompass a series of payment orders that are issued in order to effect the payment initiated by the originator's payment order.

In some cases the originator and the beneficiary may be the same person. This will occur, for example, when a corporation orders a bank to transfer funds from an account of the corporation in that bank to another account of the corporation in that bank or in some other bank. In some funds transfers the first bank to issue a payment order is a bank that is executing a payment order of a customer that is not a bank. In this case the customer is the originator. In other cases, the first bank to issue a payment order is not acting for a customer, but is making a payment for its own account. In that event the first bank to issue a payment order is the originator as well as the originator's bank.

2. "Payment order" is defined in Section 4A-103(a)(1) as an instruction to a bank to pay, or to cause another bank to pay, a fixed or determinable amount of money. The bank to which the instruction is addressed is known as the "receiving bank." Section 4A-103(a)(4). "Bank" is defined in Section 4A-105(a)(2). The effect of this definition is to limit Article 4A to payments made through the banking system. A transfer of funds made by an entity outside the banking system is excluded. A transfer of funds through an entity other than a bank is usually a consumer transaction involving relatively small amounts of money and a single contract carried out by transfers of cash or a cash equivalent such as a check. Typically, the transferor delivers cash or a check to the company making the transfer, which agrees to pay a like amount to a person designated by the transferor. Transactions covered by Article 4A typically involve very large amounts of money in which several transactions involving several banks may be necessary to carry out the payment. Payments are normally made by debits or credits to bank accounts. Originators and beneficiaries are almost always business organizations and the transfers are usually made to pay obligations. Moreover, these transactions are frequently done on the basis of very short-term credit granted by the receiving bank to the sender of the payment order. Wholesale wire transfers involve policy questions that are distinct from those involved in consumer-based transactions by nonbanks.

3. Further limitations on the scope of Article 4A are found in the three requirements found in subparagraphs (i), (ii), and (iii) of Section 4A-103(a)(1). Subparagraph (i) states that the instruction to pay is a payment order only if it "does not state a condition to payment to the beneficiary other than time of payment." An instruction to pay a beneficiary sometimes is subject to a requirement that the beneficiary perform some act such as delivery of documents.

Example: a New York bank may have issued a letter of credit in favor of X, a California seller of goods to be shipped to the New York bank's customer in New York. The terms of the letter of credit provide for payment to X if documents are presented to prove shipment of the goods. Instead of providing for presentment of the documents to the New York bank, the letter of credit states that they may be presented to a California bank that acts as an agent for payment. The New York bank sends an instruction to the California bank to pay X upon presentation of the required documents. The instruction is not covered by Article 4A because payment to the beneficiary is conditional upon receipt of shipping documents. The function of banks in a funds transfer under Article 4A is comparable to the role of banks in the collection and payment of checks in that it is essentially mechanical in nature. The low price and high speed that characterize funds transfers reflect this fact. Conditions to payment by the California bank other than time of payment impose responsibilities on that bank that go beyond those in Article 4A funds transfers. Although the payment by the New York bank to X under the letter of credit is not covered by Article 4A, if X is paid by the California bank, payment of the obligation of the New York bank to reimburse the California bank could be made by an Article 4A funds transfer. In such a case there is a distinction between the payment by the New York bank to X under the letter of credit and the payment by the New York bank to the California bank. For example, if the New York bank pays its reimbursement obligation to the California bank by a Fedwire naming the California bank as beneficiary (see Comment 1 to Section 4A-107), payment is made to the California bank rather than to X. That payment is governed by Article 4A and it could be made either before or after payment by the California bank to X. The payment by the New York bank to X under the letter of credit is not governed by Article 4A and it occurs when the California bank, as agent of the New York bank, pays X. No payment order was involved in that transaction. In this example, if the New York bank had erroneously sent an instruction to the California bank unconditionally instructing payment to X, the instruction would have been an Article 4A payment order. If the payment order was accepted (Section 4A-209(b)) by the California bank, a payment by the New York bank to X would have resulted (Section 4A-406(a)). But Article 4A would not prevent recovery of funds from X on the basis that X was not entitled to retain the funds under the law of mistake and restitution, letter of credit law or other applicable law.

An instruction to pay might be a component of a computer program or a transaction protocol intended to execute automatically under specified circumstances. The fact that the program or protocol itself is subject to a condition does not necessarily mean that an instruction to pay issued pursuant to that program or protocol "state[s] a condition to payment of the beneficiary" within the meaning of Section 4A-103(a)(1)(i). Whether the instruction does state such a condition depends on what the instruction says when it is received by the receiving bank. An instruction that neither grants discretion nor imposes a limitation on payment by the receiving bank does not state a condition to payment. What distinguishes the prior example is that the New York bank's instruction to the California bank did state a condition when the California bank received it.

Similarly, an instruction that is subject to a condition when received by Bank A, and which therefore does not constitute a payment order, does not become a payment order when the condition is satisfied. However, if, after the condition is satisfied, Bank A sends the instruction to Bank B without the stated condition, that second instruction could be a payment order if the instruction otherwise complies with Section 4A-103(a).

4. Transfers of funds made through the banking system are commonly referred to as either "credit" transfers or "debit" transfers. In a credit transfer the instruction to pay is given by the person making payment. In a debit transfer the instruction to pay is given by the person receiving payment. The purpose of subparagraph (ii) of subsection (a)(1) of Section 4A-103 is to include credit transfers in Article 4A and to exclude debit transfers. All of the instructions to pay in the three cases described in Comment 1 fall within subparagraph (ii). Take Case #2 as an example. With respect to X's instruction given to Bank A, Bank A will be reimbursed by debiting X's account or otherwise receiving payment from X. With respect to Bank A's instruction to Bank B, Bank B will be reimbursed by receiving payment from Bank A. In a debit transfer, a creditor, pursuant to authority from the debtor, is enabled to draw on the debtor's bank account by issuing an instruction to pay to the debtor's bank. If the debtor's bank pays, it will be reimbursed by the debtor rather than by the person giving the instruction. For example, the holder of an insurance policy may pay premiums by authorizing the insurance company to order the policyholder's bank to pay the insurance company. The order to pay may be in the form of a draft covered by Article 3, or it might be an instruction to pay that is not an instrument under that Article. The bank receives reimbursement by debiting the policyholder's account. Or, a subsidiary corporation may make payments to its parent by authorizing the parent to order the subsidiary's bank to pay the parent from the subsidiary's account. These transactions are not covered by Article 4A because subparagraph (2) is not satisfied. Article 4A is limited to transactions in which the account to be debited by the receiving bank is that of the person in whose name the instruction is given.

If the beneficiary of a funds transfer is the originator of the transfer, the transfer is governed by Article 4A if it is a credit transfer in form. If it is in the form of a debit transfer it is not governed by Article 4A. For example, Corporation has accounts in Bank A and Bank B. Corporation instructs Bank A to pay to Corporation's account in Bank B. The funds transfer is governed by Article 4A. Sometimes, Corporation will authorize Bank B to draw on Corporation's account in Bank A for the purpose of transferring funds into Corporation's account in Bank B. If Corporation also makes an agreement with Bank A under which Bank A is authorized to follow instructions of Bank B, as agent of Corporation, to transfer funds from Customer's account in Bank A, the instruction of Bank B is a payment order of Customer and is governed by Article 4A. This kind of transaction is known in the wire-transfer business as a "drawdown transfer." If Corporation does not make such an agreement with Bank A and Bank B instructs Bank A to make the transfer, the order is in form a debit transfer and is not governed by Article 4A. These debit transfers are normally ACH transactions in which Bank A relies on Bank B's warranties pursuant to ACH rules, including the warranty that the transfer is authorized.

5. The principal effect of subparagraph (iii) of subsection (a) of Section 4A-103 is to exclude from Article 4A payments made by check or credit card. In those cases the instruction of the debtor to the bank on which the check is drawn or to which the credit card slip is to be presented is contained in the check or credit card slip signed by the debtor. The instruction is not transmitted by the debtor directly to the debtor's bank. Rather, the instruction is delivered or otherwise transmitted by the debtor to the creditor who then presents it to the bank either directly or through bank collection channels. These payments are governed by Articles 3 and 4 and federal law. There are, however, limited instances in which the paper on which a check is printed can be used as the means of transmitting a payment order that is covered by Article 4A. Assume that Originator instructs Originator's Bank to pay $10,000 to the account of Beneficiary in Beneficiary's Bank. Since the amount of Originator's payment order is small, if Originator's Bank and Beneficiary's Bank do not have an account relationship, Originator's Bank may execute Originator's order by issuing a teller's check payable to Beneficiary's Bank for $10,000 along with instructions to credit Beneficiary's account in that amount. The instruction to Beneficiary's Bank to credit Beneficiary's account is a payment order. The check is the means by which Originator's Bank pays its obligation as sender of the payment order. The instruction of Originator's Bank to Beneficiary's Bank might be given in a letter accompanying the check or it may be written on the check itself. In either case the instruction to Beneficiary's Bank is a payment order but the check itself (which is an order to pay addressed to the drawee rather than to Beneficiary's Bank) is an instrument under Article 3 and is not a payment order. The check can be both the means by which Originator's Bank pays its obligation under § 4A-402(b) to Beneficiary's Bank and the means by which the instruction to Beneficiary's Bank is transmitted.

6. Most payments covered by Article 4A are commonly referred to as wire transfers and usually involve some kind of electronic transmission, but the applicability of Article 4A does not depend upon the means used to transmit the instruction of the sender. Transmission may be by letter or other written communication, oral communication or electronic communication. An oral communication is normally given by telephone. Frequently the message is recorded by the receiving bank to provide evidence of the transaction, but apart from problems of proof there is no need to record the oral instruction. Transmission of an instruction may be a direct communication between the sender and the receiving bank or through an intermediary such as an agent of the sender, a communication system such as international cable, or a funds transfer system such as CHIPS, SWIFT or an automated clearing house.

Section 4A-105. Other Definitions

(a) In this Article:

(1) "Authorized account" means a deposit account of a customer in a bank designated by the customer as a source of payment of payment orders issued by the customer to the bank. If a customer does not so designate an account, any account of the customer is an authorized account if payment of a payment order from that account is not inconsistent with a restriction on the use of that account.

(2) "Bank" means a person engaged in the business of banking and includes a savings bank, savings and loan association, credit union, and trust company. A branch or separate office of a bank is a separate bank for purposes of this Article.

(3) "Customer" means a person, including a bank, having an account with a bank or from whom a bank has agreed to receive payment orders.

(4) "Funds-transfer business day" of a receiving bank means the part of a day during which the receiving bank is open for the receipt, processing, and transmittal of payment orders and cancellations and amendments of payment orders.

(5) "Funds-transfer system" means a wire transfer network, automated clearing house, or other communication system of a clearing house or other association of banks through which a payment order by a bank may be transmitted to the bank to which the order is addressed.

(6) [Reserved]

(7) "Prove" with respect to a fact means to meet the burden of establishing the fact (Section 1-201(b)(8)).

(b) Other definitions applying to this Article and the sections in which they appear are:

"Acceptance"	Section 4A-209
"Beneficiary"	Section 4A-103
"Beneficiary's bank"	Section 4A-103
"Executed"	Section 4A-301
"Execution date"	Section 4A-301
"Funds transfer"	Section 4A-104
"Funds-transfer system rule"	Section 4A-501
"Intermediary bank"	Section 4A-104
"Originator"	Section 4A-104
"Originator's bank"	Section 4A-104
"Payment by beneficiary's bank to beneficiary"	Section 4A-405
"Payment by originator to beneficiary"	Section 4A-406
"Payment by sender to receiving bank"	Section 4A-403
"Payment date"	Section 4A-401
"Payment order"	Section 4A-103
"Receiving bank"	Section 4A-103
"Security procedure"	Section 4A-201
"Sender"	Section 4A-103

(c) The following definitions in Article 4 apply to this Article:

"Clearing house"	Section 4104
"Item"	Section 4104
"Suspends payments"	Section 4104

(d) In addition Article 1 contains general definitions and principles of construction and interpretation applicable throughout this Article.

Official Comment

1. The definition of "bank" in subsection (a)(2) includes some institutions that are not commercial banks. The definition reflects the fact that many financial institutions now perform functions previously restricted to commercial banks, including acting on behalf of customers in funds transfers. Since many funds transfers involve payment orders to or from foreign countries the definition also covers foreign banks. The definition also includes Federal Reserve Banks. Funds transfers carried out by Federal Reserve Banks are described in Comments 1 and 2 to Section 4A-107.

2. Funds transfer business is frequently transacted by banks outside of general banking hours. Thus, the definition of banking day in Section 4-104(a)(3) cannot be used to describe when a bank is open for funds transfer business. Subsection (a)(4) defines a new term, "funds transfer business day," which is applicable to Article 4A. The definition states, "is open for the receipt, processing, and transmittal of payment orders and cancellations and amendments of payment orders." In some cases it is possible to electronically transmit payment orders and other communications to a receiving bank at any time. If the receiving bank is not open for the processing of an order when it is received, the communication is stored in the receiving bank's computer for retrieval when the receiving bank is open for processing. The use of the conjunctive makes clear that the defined term is limited to the period during which all functions of the receiving bank can be performed, i.e., receipt, processing, and transmittal of payment orders, cancellations and amendments.

3. Subsection (a)(5) defines "funds transfer system." The term includes a system such as CHIPS which provides for transmission of a payment order as well as settlement of the obligation of the sender to pay the order. It also includes automated clearing houses, operated by a clearing house or other association of banks, which process and transmit payment orders of banks to other banks. In addition the term includes organizations that provide only transmission services such as SWIFT. The definition also includes the wire transfer network and automated clearing houses of Federal Reserve Banks. Systems of the Federal Reserve Banks, however, are treated differently from systems of other associations of banks. Funds transfer systems other than systems of the Federal Reserve Banks are treated in Article 4A as a means of communication of payment orders between participating banks. Section 4A-206. The Comment to that section and the Comment to Section 4A-107 explain how Federal Reserve Banks function under Article 4A. Funds transfer systems are also able to promulgate rules binding on participating banks that, under Section 4A-501, may supplement or in some cases may even override provisions of Article 4A.

4. Subsection (d) incorporates definitions stated in Article 1 as well as principles of construction and interpretation stated in that Article. Included is Section 1-103. The last paragraph of the Comment to Section 4A-102 is addressed to the issue of the extent to which general principles of law and equity should apply to situations covered by provisions of Article 4A.

Section 4A-106. Time Payment Order Is Received

(a) The time of receipt of a payment order or communication cancelling or amending a payment order is determined by the rules applicable to receipt of a notice stated in Section 1-202. A receiving bank may fix a cut-off time or times on a funds-transfer business day for the receipt and processing of payment orders and communications cancelling or amending payment orders. Different cut-off times may apply to payment orders, cancellations, or amendments, or to different categories of payment orders, cancellations, or amendments. A cut-off time may apply to senders generally or different cut-off times may apply to different senders or categories of payment orders. If a payment order or communication cancelling or amending a payment order is received after the close of a funds-transfer business day or after the appropriate cut-off time on a funds-transfer business day, the receiving bank may treat the payment order or communication as received at the opening of the next funds-transfer business day.

(b) If this Article refers to an execution date or payment date or states a day on which a receiving bank is required to take action, and the date or day does not fall on a funds-transfer business day, the next day that is a funds-transfer business day is treated as the date or day stated, unless the contrary is stated in this Article.

Official Comment

The time that a payment order is received by a receiving bank usually defines the payment date or the execution date of a payment order. Section 4A-401 and Section 4A-301. The time of receipt of a payment order, or communication cancelling or amending a payment order is defined in subsection (a) by reference to the rules stated in Section 1-202. Thus, time of receipt is determined by the same rules that determine when a notice is received. Time of receipt, however, may be altered by a cut-off time.

Section 4A-107. Federal Reserve Regulations and Operating Circulars

Regulations of the Board of Governors of the Federal Reserve System and operating circulars of the Federal Reserve Banks supersede any inconsistent provision of this Article to the extent of the inconsistency.

Official Comment

1. Funds transfers under Article 4A may be made, in whole or in part, by payment orders through a Federal Reserve Bank in what is usually referred to as a transfer by Fedwire. If Bank A, which has an account in Federal Reserve Bank X, wants to pay $1,000,000 to Bank B, which has an account in Federal Reserve Bank Y, Bank A can issue an instruction to Reserve Bank X requesting a debit of $1,000,000 to Bank A's Reserve account and an equal credit to Bank B's Reserve account. Reserve Bank X will debit Bank A's account and will credit the account of Reserve Bank Y. Reserve Bank X will issue an instruction to Reserve Bank Y requesting a debit of $1,000,000 to the account of Reserve Bank X and an equal credit to Bank B's account in Reserve Bank Y. Reserve Bank Y will make the requested debit and credit and will give Bank B an advice of credit. The definition of "bank" in Section 4A-105(a)(2) includes both Reserve Bank X and Reserve Bank Y. Bank A's instruction to Reserve Bank X to pay money to Bank B is a payment order under Section 4A-103(a)(1). Bank A is the sender and Reserve Bank X is the receiving bank. Bank B is the beneficiary of Bank A's order and of the funds transfer. Bank A is the originator of the funds transfer and is also the originator's bank. Section 4A-104(c) and (d). Reserve Bank X, an intermediary bank under Section 4A-104(b), executes Bank A's order by sending a payment order to Reserve Bank Y instructing that bank to credit the Federal Reserve account of Bank B. Reserve Bank Y is the beneficiary's bank.

Suppose the transfer of funds from Bank A to Bank B is part of a larger transaction in which Originator, a customer of Bank A, wants to pay Beneficiary, a customer of Bank B. Originator issues a payment order to Bank A to pay $1,000,000 to the account of Beneficiary in Bank B. Bank A may execute Originator's order by means of Fedwire which simultaneously transfers $1,000,000 from Bank A to Bank B and carries a message instructing Bank B to pay $1,000,000 to the account of Y. The Fedwire transfer is carried out as described in the previous paragraph, except that the beneficiary of the funds transfer is Beneficiary rather than Bank B. Reserve Bank X and Reserve Bank Y are intermediary banks. When Reserve Bank Y advises Bank B of the credit to its Federal Reserve account it will also instruct Bank B to pay to the account of Beneficiary. The instruction is a payment order to Bank B which is the beneficiary's bank. When Reserve Bank Y advises Bank B of the credit to its Federal Reserve account Bank B receives payment of the payment order issued to it by Reserve Bank Y. Section 4A-403(a)(1).

The payment order is automatically accepted by Bank B at the time it receives the payment order of Reserve Bank Y. Section 4A-209(b)(2). At the time of acceptance by Bank B payment by Originator to Beneficiary also occurs. Thus, in a Fedwire transfer, payment to the beneficiary's bank, acceptance by the beneficiary's bank and payment by the originator to the beneficiary all occur simultaneously by operation of law at the time the payment order to the beneficiary's bank is received.

If Originator orders payment to the account of Beneficiary in Bank C rather than Bank B, the analysis is somewhat modified. Bank A may not have any relationship with Bank C and may not be able to make payment directly to Bank C. In that case, Bank A could send a Fedwire instructing Bank B to instruct Bank C to pay Beneficiary. The analysis is the same as the previous case except that Bank B is an intermediary bank and Bank C is the beneficiary's bank.

2. A funds transfer can also be made through a Federal Reserve Bank in an automated clearing house transaction. In a typical case, Originator instructs Originator's Bank to pay to the account of Beneficiary in Beneficiary's Bank. Originator's instruction to pay a particular beneficiary is transmitted to Originator's Bank along with many other instructions for payment to other beneficiaries by many different beneficiary's banks. All of these instructions are contained in a magnetic tape or other electronic device. Transmission of instructions to the various beneficiary's banks requires that Originator's instructions be processed and repackaged with instructions of other originators so that all instructions to a particular beneficiary's bank are transmitted together to that bank. The repackaging is done in processing centers usually referred to as automated clearing houses. Automated clearing houses are operated either by Federal Reserve Banks or by other associations of banks. If Originator's Bank chooses to execute Originator's instructions by transmitting them to a Federal Reserve Bank for processing by the Federal Reserve Bank, the transmission to the Federal Reserve Bank results in the issuance of payment orders by Originator's Bank to the Federal Reserve Bank, which is an intermediary bank. Processing by the Federal Reserve Bank will result in the issuance of payment orders by the Federal Reserve Bank to Beneficiary's Bank as well as payment orders to other beneficiary's banks making payments to carry out Originator's instructions.

3. Although the terms of Article 4A apply to funds transfers involving Federal Reserve Banks, federal preemption would make ineffective any Article 4A provision that conflicts with federal law. The payments activities of the Federal Reserve Banks are governed by regulations of the Federal Reserve Board and by operating circulars issued by the Reserve Banks themselves. In some instances, the operating circulars are issued pursuant to a Federal Reserve Board regulation. In other cases, the Reserve Bank issues the operating circular under its own authority under the Federal Reserve Act, subject to review by the Federal Reserve Board. Section 4A-107 states that Federal Reserve Board regulations and operating circulars of the Federal Reserve Banks supersede any inconsistent provision of Article 4A to the extent of the inconsistency. Federal Reserve Board regulations, being valid exercises of regulatory authority pursuant to a federal statute, take precedence over state law if there is an inconsistency. *Childs v. Federal Reserve Bank of Dallas*, 719 F.2d 812 (5th Cir. 1983), reh. den. 724 F.2d 127 (5th Cir. 1984). Section 4A-107 treats operating circulars as having the same effect whether issued under the Reserve Bank's own authority or under a Federal Reserve Board regulation.

Section 4A-108. Exclusion of Consumer Transactions Governed by Federal Law

(a) Except as provided in subsection (b), this Article does not apply to a funds transfer any part of which is governed by the Electronic Fund Transfer Act of 1978 (Title XX, Public Law 95-630, 92 Stat. 3728, 15 U.S.C. § 1693 et seq.) as amended from time to time.

(b) This Article applies to a funds transfer that is a remittance transfer as defined in the Electronic Fund Transfer Act (15 U.S.C. Sec. 1693o-1) as amended from time to time, unless the remittance transfer is an electronic fund transfer as defined in the Electronic Fund Transfer Act (15 U.S.C. Sec. 1693a) as amended from time to time.

(c) In a funds transfer to which this Article applies, in the event of an inconsistency between an applicable provision of this Article and an applicable provision of the Electronic Fund Transfer Act, the provision of the Electronic Fund Transfer Act governs to the extent of the inconsistency.

Official Comment

1. The Electronic Fund Transfer Act (EFTA), implemented by Regulation E, 12 C.F.R. Part 1005, is a federal statute that covers a wide variety of electronic funds transfers involving consumers. EFTA also governs remittance transfers, defined in 15 U.S.C. Sec. 1693o-1, which involve transfers of funds through electronic means by consumers to recipients in another country through persons or financial institutions that provide such transfers in the normal course of their business. Not all "remittance transfers" as defined in EFTA, however, qualify as "electronic fund transfers" as defined under the EFTA, 15 U.S.C. Sec. 1693a(7). While Section 4A-108(a) broadly states that Article 4A does not apply to any funds transfer that is governed in any part by EFTA, subsection (b) provides an exception. While Section 4A-108(a) broadly states that Article 4A does not apply to any funds transfer that is governed in any part by EFTA, subsection (b) provides an exception.

The purpose of Section 4A-108(b) is to allow this Article to apply to a funds transfer as defined in Section 4A-104(a) (see Section 4A-102) that also is a remittance transfer as defined in EFTA, so long as that remittance transfer is not an electronic fund transfer as defined in EFTA. If the resulting application of this Article to an EFTA-defined "remittance transfer" that is not an EFTA-defined "electronic fund transfer" creates an inconsistency between an applicable provision of this Article and an applicable provision of EFTA, then, as a matter of federal supremacy, the provision of EFTA governs to the extent of the inconsistency. Section 4A-108(c). Of course, in the case of a funds transfer that also relates to another jurisdiction, the forum's conflict of laws principles determine whether it will apply the law in effect in this State (including this Article and EFTA) or the law of another jurisdiction to all or any part of the funds transfer. See Section 4A-507.

2. The following examples assume that choice of law principles or an enforceable choice of law provision will lead a court to examine the applicability of Article 4A to the funds transfer.

3. The following cases illustrate the relationship between EFTA and this Article pursuant to Section 4A-108.

Case # 1. A commercial customer of Bank A sends a payment order to Bank A, instructing Bank A to transfer funds from its account at Bank A to the account of a consumer at Bank B. The funds transfer is executed by a payment order from Bank A to an intermediary bank and is executed by the intermediary bank by means of an automated clearinghouse credit entry to the consumer's account at Bank B (the beneficiary's bank). The transfer into the consumer's account is an "electronic fund transfer" as defined in 15 U.S.C. Sec. 1693a(7). Pursuant to Section 4A-108(a), Article 4A does not apply to any part of the funds transfer because EFTA governs part of the funds transfer. The funds transfer is not a remittance transfer as defined in 15 U.S.C. Sec. 1693o-1 because the originator is not a consumer customer. Thus Section 4A-108(b) does not apply.

A court might, however, apply appropriate principles from Article 4A by analogy in analyzing any part of the funds transfer that is not subject to the provisions of EFTA or other law, such as the obligation of the intermediary bank to execute the payment order of the originator's bank (Section 4A-302) or whether the payment order of the commercial customer to Bank A is authorized or verified (Sections 4A-202 and 4A-203).

Case # 2. A consumer originates a payment order that is a remittance transfer as defined in 15 U.S.C. Sec. 1693o-1 and provides the remittance transfer provider (Bank A) with cash in the amount of the transfer plus any relevant fees. The funds transfer is routed through an intermediary bank for final credit to the designated recipient's account at Bank B. Bank A's payment order identifies the designated recipient by both name and account number in Bank B, but the name and number provided identify different persons. This funds transfer is not an "electronic fund transfer" as defined in 15 U.S.C. Sec. 1693a(7) because it is not initiated by electronic means and is not from a consumer's account, but does qualify as a "funds transfer" as defined in Section 4A-104. Both Article 4A and EFTA apply to the funds transfer. Sections 4A-102, 4A-108(a), (b). Article 4A's provision on mistakes in identifying the designated beneficiary, Section 4A-207, would apply as long as not inconsistent with the governing EFTA provisions. See 15 U.S.C. Sec. 1693o-1(d), Section 4A-108(c). See Comment 1 to this Section.

Case # 3. A consumer originates a payment order from the consumer's account at Bank A to the designated recipient's account at Bank B located outside the United States. Bank A uses the CHIPS system to execute that payment order. The funds transfer is a "remittance transfer" as defined in 15 U.S.C. Sec. 1693o-1. This transfer is not an "electronic fund transfer" as defined in 15 U.S.C. Sec. 1693a(7) because of the exclusion for transfers through systems such as CHIPS in 15 U.S.C. Sec. 1693a(7)(B), but qualifies as a "funds transfer" as defined in Section 4A-104. Under Sections 4A-102 and 4A-108(b), both Article 4A and EFTA apply to the funds transfer and EFTA. The EFTA will prevail to the extent of any inconsistency between EFTA and Article 4A. Section 4A-108(c). See Comment 1 to this Section. For example, if the consumer sub-sequently exercises a right under EFTA to cancel the remittance transfer and obtain a refund, Bank A would be required to comply with the EFTA rule even if Article 4A prevents Bank A from cancelling or reversing the payment order that Bank A sent to its receiving bank. Section 4A-211.

Case # 4. A person fraudulently originates an unauthorized payment order from a consumer's account through use of an online banking interface and the payment order is executed using a system that qualifies the transaction as an "electronic fund transfer" under EFTA. The funds transfer that results from execution of the unauthorized payment order is not governed by Article 4A. Section 4A-108(a). Whether the funds trans-fer also qualifies as a "remittance transfer" under EFTA has no bearing on the application of Article 4A.

Case # 5. A person fraudulently originates an unauthorized payment order from a consumer's account at Bank A through forging written documents that are provided in person to an employee of Bank A. This transaction is not an "electronic fund transfer" as defined in 15 U.S.C. Sec. 1693a(7) because it was not initiated by electronic means, but qualifies as a "funds transfer" as defined in Section 4A-104. Article 4A applies regardless of whether the funds transfer also qualifies as a "remittance transfer" under 15 U.S.C. Sec. 1693o-1. If the funds transfer is not a remittance transfer, the provisions of Section 4A-108 are not implicated because the funds transfer does not fall under EFTA, and the general scope provision of Article 4A governs. Section 4A-102. If the funds transfer is a remittance transfer, and thus governed by EFTA, Section 4A-108(b) pro-vides that Article 4A also applies. The provisions of Article 4A allocate the loss arising from the unauthorized payment order as long as those provisions are not inconsistent with the provisions of the EFTA applicable to remittance transfers. See 15 U.S.C. Sec. 1693o-1, Section 4A-108(c). See Comment 1 to this Section.

3. Regulation J, 12 C.F.R. Part 210, of the Federal Reserve Board addresses the application of that regulation and EFTA to fund transfers made through Fedwire. Fedwire transfers are further described in Official Comments 1 and 2 to Section 4A-107. In addition, funds transfer system rules may be applicable pursuant to Section 4A-501.

Legislative Note: *The reference to EFTA "as amended from time to time," means that the operation of this section at any particular time after enactment may depend on federal legislative action occurring after enactment. In states in which such an arrangement may constitute improper delegation, the language "as amended from time to time" may be deleted. In that case, however, the legislature should consider other mechanisms to assure that this section continues to operate harmoniously with EFTA as it may be subsequently amended.*

PART 2. ISSUE AND ACCEPTANCE OF PAYMENT ORDER

Section 4A-201. Security Procedure

"Security procedure" means a procedure established by agreement of a customer and a receiving bank for the purpose of (i) verifying that a payment order or communication amending or cancelling a payment order is that of the customer, or (ii) detecting error in the transmission or the content of the payment order or communication. A security procedure may impose an obligation on the receiving bank or the customer and may require the use of algorithms or other codes, identifying words, numbers, symbols, sounds, biometrics, encryption, callback procedures, or similar security devices. Comparison of a signature on a payment order or communication with an authorized specimen signature of the customer or requiring a payment order to be sent from a known email address, IP address, or telephone number is not by itself a security procedure.

Official Comment

1. A large percentage of payment orders and communications amending or cancelling payment orders are transmitted electronically and it is standard practice to use security procedures that are designed to assure the authenticity of the message through steps designed to assure the identity of the sender, the integrity of the message, or both. Security procedures can also be used to detect error in the content of messages or to detect payment orders that are transmitted by mistake as in the case of multiple transmission of the same payment order. Security procedures might also apply to communications that are transmitted by telephone or in a record. Section 4A-201 defines these security procedures. The second sentence of the definition provides several examples of a security procedure, but the list is not exhaustive. The inclusion of the phrase "or similar security devices" means that, as new technologies emerge, what can be a security procedure will evolve. The definition of security procedure limits the term to a procedure "established by agreement of a customer and a receiving bank." The term does not apply to procedures that the receiving bank may follow unilaterally in processing payment orders. The question of whether loss that may result from the transmission of a spurious or erroneous payment order will be borne by the receiving bank or the sender or purported sender is affected by whether a security procedure was or was not in effect and whether there was or was not compliance with the procedure. Security procedures are referred to in Sections 4A-202 and 4A-203, which deal with authorized and verified payment orders, and Section 4A-205, which deals with erroneous payment orders.

Requiring that a payment order be sent from a known email, IP address or phone number is not by itself a "security procedure" within the meaning of this section because it is possible to make a payment order with a different origin appear to have been sent from such an address or phone number. However, requiring that a payment order have such an apparent origin in combination with other security protocols might be a security procedure.

2. Several revisions to the pre-2022 text of this section were made in furtherance of medium neutrality. Other 2022 revisions were made for clarification.

Section 4A-202. Authorized and Verified Payment Orders

(a) A payment order received by the receiving bank is the authorized order of the person identified as sender if that person authorized the order or is otherwise bound by it under the law of agency.

(b) If a bank and its customer have agreed that the authenticity of payment orders issued to the bank in the name of the customer as sender will be verified pursuant to a security procedure, a payment order received by the receiving bank is effective as the order of the customer, whether or not authorized, if (i) the security procedure is a commercially reasonable method of providing security against unauthorized payment orders, and (ii) the bank proves that it accepted the payment order in good faith and in compliance with the bank's obligations under the security procedure and any agreement or instruction of the customer, evidenced by a record, restricting acceptance of payment orders issued in the name of the customer. The bank is not required to follow an instruction that violates an agreement with the customer, evidenced by a record, or notice of which is not received at a time and in a manner affording the bank a reasonable opportunity to act on it before the payment order is accepted.

(c) Commercial reasonableness of a security procedure is a question of law to be determined by considering the wishes of the customer expressed to the bank, the circumstances of the customer known to the bank, including the size, type, and frequency of payment orders normally issued by the customer to the bank, alternative security procedures offered to the customer, and security procedures in general use by customers and receiving banks similarly situated. A security procedure is deemed to be commercially reasonable if (i) the security procedure was chosen by the customer after the bank offered, and the customer refused, a security procedure that was commercially reasonable for that customer, and (ii) the customer expressly agreed in writing to be bound by any payment order, whether or not authorized, issued in its name and accepted by the bank in compliance with the bank's obligations under the security procedure chosen by the customer.

(d) The term "sender" in this Article includes the customer in whose name a payment order is issued if the order is the authorized order of the customer under subsection (a), or it is effective as the order of the customer under subsection (b).

(e) This section applies to amendments and cancellations of payment orders to the same extent it applies to payment orders.

(f) Except as provided in this section and in Section 4A-203(a)(1), rights and obligations arising under this section or Section 4A-203 may not be varied by agreement.

Official Comment

1. This section is discussed in the Comment following Section 4A-203.

2. In furtherance of medium neutrality, references to "written" and "writing" have been changed to refer to "evidenced by a record" and "a record." Other 2022 revisions were made for clarification.

Section 4A-203. Unenforceability of Certain Verified Payment Orders

(a) If an accepted payment order is not, under Section 4A-202(a), an authorized order of a customer identified as sender, but is effective as an order of the customer pursuant to Section 4A-202(b), the following rules apply:

(1) By express agreement evidenced by a record, the receiving bank may limit the extent to which it is entitled to enforce or retain payment of the payment order.

(2) The receiving bank is not entitled to enforce or retain payment of the payment order if the customer proves that the order was not caused, directly or indirectly, by a person (i) entrusted at any time with duties to act for the customer with respect to payment orders or the security procedure, or (ii) who obtained access to transmitting facilities of the customer or who obtained, from a source controlled by the customer and without authority of the receiving bank, information facilitating breach of the security procedure, regardless of how the information was obtained or whether the customer was at fault. Information includes any access device, computer software, or the like.

(b) This section applies to amendments of payment orders to the same extent it applies to payment orders.

Official Comment

1. Some person will always be identified as the sender of a payment order. Acceptance of the order by the receiving bank is based on a belief by the bank that the order was authorized by the person identified as the sender. If the receiving bank is the beneficiary's bank acceptance means that the receiving bank is obliged to pay the beneficiary. If the receiving bank is not the beneficiary's bank, acceptance means that the receiving bank has executed the sender's order and is obliged to pay the bank that accepted the order issued in execution of the sender's order. In either case the receiving bank may suffer a loss unless it is entitled to enforce payment of the payment order that it accepted. If the person identified as the sender of the order refuses to pay on the ground that the order was not authorized by that person, what are the rights of the receiving bank? In the absence of a statute or agreement that specifically addresses the issue, the question usually will be resolved by the law of agency. In some cases, the law of agency works well. For example, suppose the receiving bank executes a payment order given by means of a letter apparently written by a corporation that is a customer of the bank and apparently signed by an officer of the corporation. If the receiving bank acts solely on the basis of the letter, the corporation is not bound as the sender of the payment order unless the signature was that of the officer and the officer was authorized to act for the corporation in the issuance of payment orders, or some other agency doctrine such as apparent authority or estoppel causes the corporation to be bound. Estoppel can be illustrated by the following example. Suppose P is aware that A, who is unauthorized to act for P, has fraudulently misrepresented to T that A is authorized to act for P. T believes A and is about to rely on the misrepresentation. If P does not notify T of the true facts although P could easily do so, P may be estopped from denying A's lack of authority. A similar result could follow if the failure to notify T is the result of negligence rather than a deliberate decision. Restatement, Second, Agency § 8B. Other equitable principles such as subrogation or restitution might also allow a receiving bank to recover with respect to an unauthorized payment order that it accepted. In *Gatoil (U.S.A.), Inc. v. Forest Hill State Bank,* 1 U.C.C. Rep. Serv. 2d 171 (D. Md. 1986), a joint venturer not authorized to order payments from the account of the joint venture, ordered a funds transfer from the account. The transfer paid a bona fide debt of the joint venture. Although the transfer was unauthorized the court refused to require recredit of the account because the joint venture suffered no loss. The result can be rationalized on the basis of subrogation of the receiving bank to the right of the beneficiary of the funds transfer to receive the payment from the joint venture.

But in most cases these legal principles give the receiving bank very little protection in the case of an authorized payment order. Cases like those just discussed are not typical of the way that most payment orders are transmitted and accepted, and such cases are likely to become even less common. Given the large amount of the typical payment order, a prudent receiving bank will be unwilling to accept a payment order unless it has assurance that the order is what it purports to be. This assurance is normally provided by security procedures described in Section 4A-201.

In a very large percentage of cases covered by Article 4A, transmission of the payment order is made electronically. The receiving bank may be required to act on the basis of a message that appears on a computer screen. Common law concepts of authority of agent to bind principal are not helpful. There is no way of determining the identity or the authority of the person who caused the message to be sent. The receiving bank is not relying on the authority of any particular person to act for the purported sender. The case is not comparable to payment of a check by the drawee bank on the basis of a signature that is forged. Rather, the receiving bank relies on a security procedure pursuant to which the authenticity of the message can be "tested" by various devices which are designed to provide certainty that the message is that of the sender identified in the payment order. In the wire transfer business the concept of "authorized" is different from that found in agency law. In that business a payment order is treated as the order of the person in whose name it is issued if it is properly tested pursuant to a security procedure and the order passes the test.

Section 4A-202 reflects the reality of the wire transfer business. A person in whose name a payment order is issued is considered to be the sender of the order if the order is "authorized" as stated in subsection (a) or if the order is "verified" pursuant to a security procedure in compliance with subsection (b). If subsection (b) does not apply, the question of whether the customer is responsible for the order is determined by the law of agency. The issue is one of actual or apparent authority of the person who caused the order to be issued in the name of the customer. In some cases the law of agency might allow the customer to be bound by an unauthorized order if conduct of the customer can be used to find an estoppel against the customer to deny that the order was unauthorized. If the customer is bound by the order under any of these agency doctrines, subsection (a) treats the order as authorized and thus the customer is deemed to be the sender of the order. In most cases, however, subsection (b) will apply. In that event there is no need to make an agency law analysis to determine authority. Under Section 4A-202, the issue of liability of the purported sender of the payment order will be determined by agency law only if the receiving bank did not comply with subsection (b).

2. The scope of Section 4A-202 can be illustrated by the following cases. *Case #1.* A payment order purporting to be that of Customer is received by Receiving Bank but the order was fraudulently transmitted by a person who had no authority to act for Customer. *Case #2.* An authentic payment order was sent by Customer, but before the order was received by Receiving Bank the order was fraudulently altered by an unauthorized person to change the beneficiary. *Case #3.* An authentic payment order was received by Receiving Bank, but before the order was executed by Receiving Bank a person who had no authority to act for Customer fraudulently sent a communication purporting to amend the order by changing the beneficiary. In each case Receiving Bank acted on the fraudulent communication by accepting the payment order. These cases are all essentially similar and they are treated identically by Section 4A-202. In each case Receiving Bank acted on a communication that it thought was authorized by Customer when in fact the communication was fraudulent. No distinction is made between Case #1 in which Customer took no part at all in the transaction and Case #2 and Case #3 in which an authentic order was fraudulently altered or amended by an unauthorized person. If subsection (b) does not apply, each case is governed by subsection (a). If there are no additional facts on which an estoppel might be found, Customer is not responsible in Case #1 for the fraudulently issued payment order, in Case #2 for the fraudulent alteration or in Case #3 for the fraudulent amendment. Thus, in each case Customer is not liable to pay the order and Receiving Bank takes the loss. The only remedy of Receiving Bank is to seek recovery from the person who received payment as beneficiary of the fraudulent order. If there was verification in compliance with subsection (b), Customer will take the loss unless Section 4A-203 applies.

3. Subsection (b) of Section 4A-202 is based on the assumption that losses due to fraudulent payment orders can best be avoided by the use of commercially reasonable security procedures, and that the use of such procedures should be encouraged. The subsection is designed to protect both the customer and the receiving bank. A receiving bank needs to be able to rely on objective criteria to determine whether it can safely act on a payment order. Employees of the bank can be trained to "test" a payment order according to the various steps specified in the security procedure. The bank is responsible for the acts of these employees. Subsection (b)(ii) requires the bank to prove that it accepted the payment order in good faith and "in compliance with the bank's obligations under the security procedure." If the fraud was not detected because the bank's employee did not perform the acts required by the security procedure, the bank has not complied. Subsection (b)(ii) also requires the bank to prove that it complied with any agreement or instruction that restricts acceptance of payment orders issued in the name of the customer. If an agreement establishing a security procedure places obligations on both the sender and the receiving bank, the receiving bank need prove only that it complied with the obligations placed on the receiving bank. A customer may want to protect itself by imposing limitations on acceptance of payment orders by the bank. For example, the customer may prohibit the bank from accepting a payment order that is not payable from an authorized account, that exceeds the credit balance in specified accounts of the customer, or that exceeds some other amount. Another limitation may relate to the beneficiary. The customer may provide the bank with a list of authorized beneficiaries and prohibit acceptance of any payment order to a beneficiary not appearing on the list. Such limitations may be incorporated into the security procedure itself or they may be covered by a separate agreement or instruction. In either case, the bank must comply with the limitations if the conditions stated in subsection (b) are met. Normally limitations on acceptance would be incorporated into an agreement between the customer and the receiving bank, but in some cases the instruction might be unilaterally given by the customer. If standing instructions or an agreement state limitations on the ability of the receiving bank to act, provision must be made for later modification of the limitations. Normally this would be done by an agreement that specifies particular procedures to be followed. Thus, subsection (b) states that the receiving bank is not required to follow an instruction that violates an agreement evidenced by a record. The receiving bank is not bound by an instruction unless it has adequate notice of it. Section 1-202 applies.

Subsection (b)(i) assures that the interests of the customer will be protected by providing an incentive to a bank to make available to the customer a security procedure that is commercially reasonable. If a commercially reasonable security procedure is not made available to the customer, subsection (b) does not apply. The result is that subsection (a) applies and the bank acts at its peril in accepting a payment order that may be unauthorized. Prudent banking practice may require that security procedures be utilized in virtually all cases except for those in which personal contact between the customer and the bank eliminates the possibility of an unauthorized order. The burden of making available commercially reasonable security procedures is imposed on receiving banks because they generally determine what security procedures can be used and are in the best position to evaluate the efficacy of procedures offered to customers to combat fraud. The burden on the customer is to supervise its employees to assure compliance with the security procedure and to safeguard confidential security information and access to transmitting facilities so that the security procedure cannot be breached.

4. The principal issue that is likely to arise in litigation involving subsection (b) is whether the security procedure in effect when a fraudulent payment order was accepted was commercially reasonable. In considering this issue, a court will need to consider the totality of the security procedure, including each party's obligations under the procedure. The concept of what is commercially reasonable in a given case is flexible. Verification entails labor and equipment costs that can vary greatly depending upon the degree of security that is sought. A customer that transmits very large numbers of payment orders in very large amounts may desire and may reasonably expect to be provided with state-of-the-art procedures that provide maximum security. But the expense involved may make use of a state-of-the-art procedure infeasible for a customer that normally transmits payment orders infrequently or in relatively low amounts. Another variable is the type of receiving bank. It is reasonable to require large money center banks to make available state-of-the-art security procedures. On the other hand, the same requirement may not be reasonable for a small country bank. A receiving bank might have several security procedures that are designed to meet the varying needs of different customers. The type of payment order is another variable. For example, in a wholesale wire transfer, each payment order is normally transmitted electronically and individually. A testing procedure will be individually applied to each payment order. In funds transfers to be made by means of an automated clearing house many payment orders are incorporated into an electronic device such as a magnetic tape that is physically delivered. Testing of the individual payment orders is not feasible. Thus, a different kind of security procedure must be adopted to take into account the different mode of transmission.

The issue of whether a particular security procedure is commercially reasonable is a question of law. Whether the receiving bank complied with the procedure is a question of fact. It is appropriate to make the finding concerning commercial reasonability a matter of law because security procedures are likely to be standardized in the banking industry and a question of law standard leads to more predictability concerning the level of security that a bank must offer to its customers. The purpose of subsection (b) is to encourage banks to institute reasonable safeguards against fraud but not to make them insurers against fraud. A security procedure is not commercially unreasonable simply because another procedure might have been better or because the judge deciding the question would have opted for a more stringent procedure. For example, the use of a computer program to detect fraud is not commercially unreasonable merely because it does not detect all fraud or because another system or approach might be more successful at detecting fraud. The standard is not whether the security procedure is the best available. Rather it is whether the procedure is reasonable for the particular customer and the particular bank, which is a lower standard. What is reasonable for a particular customer requires the court to consider the circumstances of the customer known to the bank, including the size, type, and frequency of payment orders normally issued by the customer to the bank. Article 4A does not create an affirmative obligation on the receiving bank to obtain information about its customer. However, whatever knowledge the bank does have about the customer is relevant in determining the commercial reasonableness of the security procedure. A security procedure that fails to meet prevailing standards of good banking practice applicable to the particular bank should not be held to be commercially reasonable. Subsection (c) states factors to be considered by the judge in making the determination of commercial reasonableness. The reasonableness of a security procedure is to be determined at the time that a payment order is processed, not at the time the customer and the bank agree to the security procedure. Accordingly, a security procedure that was reasonable when agreed to might become unreasonable as technologies emerge, prevailing practices change, or the bank acquires knowledge about the customer. Sometimes an informed customer refuses a security procedure that is commercially reasonable and suitable for that customer and insists on using a higher-risk procedure because it is more convenient or cheaper. In that case, under the last sentence of subsection (c), the customer has voluntarily assumed the risk of failure of the procedure and cannot shift the loss to the bank. But this result follows only if the customer expressly agrees in writing to assume that risk. It is implicit in the last sentence of subsection (c) that a bank that accedes to the wishes of its customer in this regard is not acting in bad faith by so doing so long as the customer is made aware of the risk. In all cases, however, a receiving bank cannot get the benefit of subsection (b) unless it has made available to the customer a security procedure that is commercially reasonable and suitable for use by that customer. In most cases, the mutual interest of bank and customer to protect against fraud should lead to agreement to a security procedure which is commercially reasonable.

4A. Subsection (b) generally allows a receiving bank to treat a payment order as authorized by the customer if the bank accepts the payment order in good faith and in compliance with the bank's obligations under a commercially reasonable, agreed-upon security procedure. For this purpose, "good faith" requires the exercise of reasonable commercial standards of fair dealing, see Section 4A-105(a)(6), not the absence of negligence. Consequently, the bank has no duty, beyond that to which the bank has agreed, to investigate suspicious activity or to advise its customer of such activity. However, a bank that obtains knowledge that a customer's operations have been infiltrated or knowledge that the customer is the victim of identity fraud might not be acting in good faith if the bank, without receiving some assurance from the customer that the issue has been remediated, thereafter accepts a payment order.

5. The effect of Section 4A-202(b) is to place the risk of loss on the customer if an unauthorized payment order is accepted by the receiving bank after verification by the bank in compliance with a commercially reasonable security procedure. An exception to this result is provided by Section 4A-203(a)(2). The customer may avoid the loss resulting from such a payment order if the customer can prove that the fraud was not committed by a person described in that subsection. Breach of a commercially reasonable security procedure requires that the person committing the fraud have knowledge of how the procedure works and knowledge of codes, identifying devices, and the like. That person may also need access to transmitting facilities through an access device or other software in order to breach the security procedure. This confidential information must be obtained either from a source controlled by the customer or from a source controlled by the receiving bank. If the customer can prove that the person committing the fraud did not obtain the confidential information from an agent or former agent of the customer or from a source controlled by the customer, the loss is shifted to the bank. "Prove" is defined in Section 4A-105(a)(7). Because of bank regulation requirements, in this kind of case there will always be a criminal investigation as well as an internal investigation of the bank to determine the probable explanation for the breach of security. Because a funds transfer fraud usually will involve a very large amount of money, both the criminal investigation and the internal investigation are likely to be thorough. In some cases there may be an investigation by bank examiners as well. Frequently, these investigations will develop evidence of who is at fault and the cause of the loss. The customer will have access to evidence developed in these investigations and that evidence can be used by the customer in meeting its burden of proof.

6. The effect of Section 4A-202(b) may also be changed by an agreement meeting the requirements of Section 4A-203(a)(1). Some customers may be unwilling to take all or part of the risk of loss with respect to unauthorized payment orders even if all of the requirements of Section 4A-202(b) are met. By virtue of Section 4A-203(a)(1), a receiving bank may assume all of the risk of loss with respect to unauthorized payment orders or the customer and bank may agree that losses from unauthorized payment orders are to be divided as provided in the agreement.

7. In a large majority of cases the sender of a payment order is a bank. In many cases in which there is a bank sender, both the sender and the receiving bank will be members of a funds transfer system over which the payment order is transmitted. Since Section 4A-202(f) does not prohibit a funds transfer system rule from varying rights and obligations under Section 4A-202, a rule of the funds transfer system can determine how loss due to an unauthorized payment order from a participating bank to another participating bank is to be allocated. A funds transfer system rule, however, cannot change the rights of a customer that is not a participating bank. § 4A-501(b). Section 4A-202(f) also prevents variation by agreement except to the extent stated.

8. In furtherance of medium neutrality, the reference to "written" in the pre-2022 text of this section has been changed to refer to "evidenced by a record."

Section 4A-204. Refund of Payment and Duty of Customer to Report with Respect to Unauthorized Payment Order

(a) If a receiving bank accepts a payment order issued in the name of its customer as sender which is (i) not authorized and not effective as the order of the customer under Section 4A-202, or (ii) not enforceable, in whole or in part, against the customer under Section 4A-203, the bank shall refund any payment of the payment order received from the customer to the extent the bank is not entitled to enforce payment and shall pay interest on the refundable amount calculated from the date the bank received payment to the date of the refund. However, the customer is not entitled to interest from the bank on the amount to be refunded if the customer fails to exercise ordinary care to determine that the order was not authorized by the customer and to notify the bank of the relevant facts within a reasonable time not exceeding 90 days after the date the customer received notification from the bank that the order was accepted or that the customer's account was debited with respect to the order. The bank is not entitled to any recovery from the customer on account of a failure by the customer to give notification as stated in this section.

(b) Reasonable time under subsection (a) may be fixed by agreement as stated in Section 1302(b), but the obligation of a receiving bank to refund payment as stated in subsection (a) may not otherwise be varied by agreement.

Official Comment

1. With respect to unauthorized payment orders, in a very large percentage of cases a commercially reasonable security procedure will be in effect. Section 4A-204 applies only to cases in which (i) no commercially reasonable security procedure is in effect, (ii) the bank did not comply with a commercially reasonable security procedure that was in effect, (iii) the sender can prove, pursuant to Section 4A-203(a)(2), that the culprit did not obtain confidential security information controlled by the customer, or (iv) the bank, pursuant to Section 4A-203(a)(1) agreed to take all or part of the loss resulting from an unauthorized payment order. In each of these cases the bank takes the risk of loss with respect to an unauthorized payment order because the bank is not entitled to payment from the customer with respect to the order. The bank normally debits the customer's account or otherwise receives payment from the customer shortly after acceptance of the payment order. Subsection (a) of Section 4A-204 states that the bank must recredit the account or refund payment to the extent the bank is not entitled to enforce payment.

2. Section 4A-204 is designed to encourage a customer to promptly notify the receiving bank that it has accepted an unauthorized payment order. Since cases of unauthorized payment orders will almost always involve fraud, the bank's remedy is normally to recover from the beneficiary of the unauthorized order if the beneficiary was party to the fraud. This remedy may not be worth very much and it may not make any difference whether or not the bank promptly learns about the fraud. But in some cases prompt notification may make it easier for the bank to recover some part of its loss from the culprit. The customer will routinely be notified of the debit to its account with respect to an unauthorized order or will otherwise be notified of acceptance of the order. The customer has a duty to exercise ordinary care to determine that the order was unauthorized after it has received notification from the bank, and to advise the bank of the relevant facts within a reasonable time not exceeding 90 days after receipt of notification. Reasonable time is not defined and it may depend on the facts of the particular case. If a payment order for $1,000,000 is wholly unauthorized, the customer should normally discover it in far less than 90 days. If a $1,000,000 payment order was authorized but the name of the beneficiary was fraudulently changed, a much longer period may be necessary to discover the fraud. But in any event, if the customer delays more than 90 days the customer's duty has not been met. The only consequence of a failure of the customer to perform this duty is a loss of interest on the refund payable by the bank. A customer that acts promptly is entitled to interest from the time the customer's account was debited or the customer otherwise made payment. The rate of interest is stated in Section 4A-506. If the customer fails to perform the duty, no interest is recoverable for any part of the period before the bank learns that it accepted an unauthorized order. But the bank is not entitled to any recovery from the customer based on negligence for failure to inform the bank. Loss of interest is in the nature of a penalty on the customer designed to provide an incentive for the customer to police its account. There is no intention to impose a duty on the customer that might result in shifting loss from the unauthorized order to the customer.

Section 4A-205. Erroneous Payment Orders

(a) If an accepted payment order was transmitted pursuant to a security procedure for the detection of error and the payment order (i) erroneously instructed payment to a beneficiary not intended by the sender, (ii) erroneously instructed payment in an amount greater than the amount intended by the sender, or (iii) was an erroneously transmitted duplicate of a payment order previously sent by the sender, the following rules apply:

(1) If the sender proves that the sender or a person acting on behalf of the sender pursuant to Section 4A-206 complied with the security procedure and that the error would have been detected if the receiving bank had also complied, the sender is not obliged to pay the order to the extent stated in paragraphs (2) and (3).

(2) If the funds transfer is completed on the basis of an erroneous payment order described in clause (i) or (iii) of subsection (a), the sender is not obliged to pay the order and the receiving bank is entitled to recover from the beneficiary any amount paid to the beneficiary to the extent allowed by the law governing mistake and restitution.

(3) If the funds transfer is completed on the basis of a payment order described in clause (ii) of subsection (a), the sender is not obliged to pay the order to the extent the amount received by the beneficiary is greater than the amount intended by

the sender. In that case, the receiving bank is entitled to recover from the beneficiary the excess amount received to the extent allowed by the law governing mistake and restitution.

(b) If (i) the sender of an erroneous payment order described in subsection (a) is not obliged to pay all or part of the order, and (ii) the sender receives notification from the receiving bank that the order was accepted by the bank or that the sender's account was debited with respect to the order, the sender has a duty to exercise ordinary care, on the basis of information available to the sender, to discover the error with respect to the order and to advise the bank of the relevant facts within a reasonable time, not exceeding 90 days, after the bank's notification was received by the sender. If the bank proves that the sender failed to perform that duty, the sender is liable to the bank for the loss the bank proves it incurred as a result of the failure, but the liability of the sender may not exceed the amount of the sender's order.

(c) This section applies to amendments to payment orders to the same extent it applies to payment orders.

Official Comment

1. This section concerns error in the content or in the transmission of payment orders. It deals with three kinds of error. *Case #1.* The order identifies a beneficiary not intended by the sender. For example, Sender intends to wire funds to a beneficiary identified only by an account number. The wrong account number is stated in the order. *Case #2.* The error is in the amount of the order. For example, Sender intends to wire $1,000 to Beneficiary. Through error, the payment order instructs payment of $1,000,000. *Case #3.* A payment order is sent to the receiving bank and then, by mistake, the same payment order is sent to the receiving bank again. In Case #3, the receiving bank may have no way of knowing whether the second order is a duplicate of the first or is another order. Similarly, in Case #1 and Case #2, the receiving bank may have no way of knowing that the error exists. In each case, if this section does not apply and the funds transfer is completed, Sender is obliged to pay the order. Section 4A-402. Sender's remedy, based on payment by mistake, is to recover from the beneficiary that received payment.

Sometimes, however, transmission of payment orders of the sender to the receiving bank is made pursuant to a security procedure designed to detect one or more of the errors described above. Since "security procedure" is defined by Section 4A-201 as "a procedure established by agreement of a customer and a receiving bank for the purpose of * * * detecting error * * *," Section 4A-205 does not apply if the receiving bank and the customer did not agree to the establishment of a procedure for detecting error. A security procedure may be designed to detect an account number that is not one to which Sender normally makes payment. In that case, the security procedure may require a special verification that payment to the stated account number was intended. In the case of dollar amounts, the security procedure may require different codes for different dollar amounts. If a $1,000,000 payment order contains a code that is inappropriate for that amount, the error in amount should be detected. In the case of duplicate orders, the security procedure may require that each payment order be identified by a number or code that applies to no other order. If the number or code of each payment order received is registered in a computer base, the receiving bank can quickly identify a duplicate order. The three cases covered by this section are essentially similar. In each, if the error is not detected, some beneficiary will receive funds that the beneficiary was not intended to receive. If this section applies, the risk of loss with respect to the error of the sender is shifted to the bank which has the burden of recovering the funds from the beneficiary. The risk of loss is shifted to the bank only if the sender proves that the error would have been detected if there had been compliance with the procedure and that the sender (or an agent under Section 4A-206) complied. In the case of a duplicate order or a wrong beneficiary, the sender doesn't have to pay the order. In the case of an overpayment, the sender does not have to pay the order to the extent of the over-payment. If subsection (a)(1) applies, the position of the receiving bank is comparable to that of a receiving bank that erroneously executes a payment order as stated in Section 4A-303. However, failure of the sender to timely report the error is covered by Section 4A-205(b) rather than by Section 4A-304 which applies only to erroneous execution under Section 4A-303. A receiving bank to which the risk of loss is shifted by subsection (a)(1) or (2) is entitled to recover the amount erroneously paid to the beneficiary to the extent allowed by the law of mistake and restitution. Rights of the receiving bank against the beneficiary are similar to those of a receiving bank that erroneously executes a payment order as stated in Section 4A-303. Those rights are discussed in Comment 2 to Section 4A-303.

2. A security procedure established for the purpose of detecting error is not effective unless both sender and receiving bank comply with the procedure. Thus, the bank undertakes a duty of complying with the procedure for the benefit of the sender. This duty is recognized in subsection (a)(1). The loss with respect to the sender's error is shifted to the bank if the bank fails to comply with the procedure and the sender (or an agent under Section 4A-206) does comply. Although the customer may have been negligent in transmitting the erroneous payment order, the loss is put on the bank on a last-clear-chance theory. A similar analysis applies to subsection (b). If the loss with respect to an error is shifted to the receiving bank and the sender is notified by the bank that the erroneous payment order was accepted, the sender has a duty to exercise ordinary care to discover the error and notify the bank of the relevant facts within a reasonable time not exceeding 90 days. If the bank can prove that the sender failed in this duty it is entitled to compensation for the loss incurred as a result of the failure. Whether the bank is entitled to recover from the sender depends upon whether the failure to give timely notice would have made any difference. If the bank could not have recovered from the beneficiary that received payment under the erroneous payment order even if timely notice had been given, the sender's failure to notify did not cause any loss of the bank.

3. Section 4A-205 is subject to variation by agreement under Section 4A-501. Thus, if a receiving bank and its customer have agreed to a security procedure for detection of error, the liability of the receiving bank for failing to detect an error of the customer as provided in Section 4A-205 may be varied as provided in an agreement of the bank and the customer.

Section 4A-206. Transmission of Payment Order Through Funds-Transfer or Other Communication System

(a) If a payment order addressed to a receiving bank is transmitted to a funds-transfer system or other third-party communication system for transmittal to the bank, the system is deemed to be an agent of the sender for the purpose of transmitting the payment order to the bank. If there is a discrepancy between the terms of the payment order transmitted to the system and the terms of the payment order transmitted by the system to the bank, the terms of the payment order of the sender are those transmitted by the system. This section does not apply to a funds-transfer system of the Federal Reserve Banks.

(b) This section applies to cancellations and amendments of payment orders to the same extent it applies to payment orders.

Official Comment

1. A payment order may be issued to a receiving bank directly by delivery of a record or by an oral communication. If an agent of the sender is employed to transmit orders on behalf of the sender, the sender is bound by the order transmitted by the agent on the basis of agency law. Section 4A-206 is an application of that principle to cases in which a funds transfer or communication system acts as an intermediary in transmitting the sender's order to the receiving bank. The intermediary is deemed to be an agent of the sender for the purpose of transmitting payment orders and related messages for the sender. Section 4A-206 deals with error by the intermediary.

2. Transmission by an automated clearing house of an association of banks other than the Federal Reserve Banks is an example of a transaction covered by Section 4A-206. Suppose Originator orders Originator's Bank to cause a large number of payments to be made to many accounts in banks in various parts of the country. These payment orders are electronically transmitted to Originator's Bank and stored in an electronic device that is held by Originator's Bank. Or, transmission of the various payment orders is made by delivery to Originator's Bank of an electronic device containing the instruction to the bank. In either case the terms of the various payment orders by Originator are determined by the information contained in the electronic device. In order to execute the various orders, the information in the electronic device must be processed. For example, if some of the orders are for payments to accounts in Bank X and some to accounts in Bank Y, Originator's Bank will execute these orders of Originator by issuing a series of payment orders to Bank X covering all payments to accounts in that bank, and by issuing a series of payment orders to Bank Y covering all payments to accounts in that bank. The orders to Bank X may be transmitted together by means of an electronic device, and those to Bank Y may be included in another electronic device. Typically, this processing is done by an automated clearing house acting for a group of banks including Originator's Bank. The automated clearing house is a funds transfer system. Section 4A-105(a)(5). Originator's Bank delivers Originator's electronic device or transmits the information contained in the device to the funds transfer system for processing into payment orders of Originator's Bank to the appropriate beneficiary's banks. The processing may result in an erroneous payment order. Originator's Bank, by use of Originator's electronic device, may have given information to the funds transfer system instructing payment of $100,000 to an account in Bank X, but because of human error or an equipment malfunction the processing may have converted that instruction into an instruction to Bank X to make a payment of $1,000,000. Under Section 4A-206, Originator's Bank issued a payment order for $1,000,000 to Bank X when the erroneous information was sent to Bank X. Originator's Bank is responsible for the error of the automated clearing house. The liability of the funds transfer system that made the error is not governed by Article 4A. It is left to the law of contract, a funds transfer system rule, or other applicable law.

In the hypothetical case just discussed, if the automated clearing house is operated by a Federal Reserve Bank, the analysis is different. Section 4A-206 does not apply. Originator's Bank will execute Originator's payment orders by delivery or transmission of the electronic information to the Federal Reserve Bank for processing. The result is that Originator's Bank has issued payment orders to the Federal Reserve Bank which, in this case, is acting as an intermediary bank. When the Federal Reserve Bank has processed the information given to it by Originator's Bank it will issue payment orders to the various beneficiary's banks. If the processing results in an erroneous payment order, the Federal Reserve Bank has erroneously executed the payment order of Originator's Bank and the case is governed by Section 4A-303.

Section 4A-207. Misdescription of Beneficiary

(a) Subject to subsection (b), if, in a payment order received by the beneficiary's bank, the name, bank account number, or other identification of the beneficiary refers to a nonexistent or unidentifiable person or account, no person has rights as a beneficiary of the order and acceptance of the order cannot occur.

(b) If a payment order received by the beneficiary's bank identifies the beneficiary both by name and by an identifying or bank account number and the name and number identify different persons, the following rules apply:

(1) Except as otherwise provided in subsection (c), if the beneficiary's bank does not know that the name and number refer to different persons, it may rely on the number as the proper identification of the beneficiary of the order. The beneficiary's bank need not determine whether the name and number refer to the same person.

(2) If the beneficiary's bank pays the person identified by name or knows that the name and number identify different persons, no person has rights as beneficiary except the person paid by the beneficiary's bank if that person was entitled to receive payment from the originator of the funds transfer. If no person has rights as beneficiary, acceptance of the order cannot occur.

(c) If (i) a payment order described in subsection (b) is accepted, (ii) the originator's payment order described the beneficiary inconsistently by name and number, and (iii) the beneficiary's bank pays the person identified by number as permitted by subsection (b)(1), the following rules apply:

(1) If the originator is a bank, the originator is obliged to pay its order.

(2) If the originator is not a bank and proves that the person identified by number was not entitled to receive payment from the originator, the originator is not obliged to pay its order unless the originator's bank proves that the originator, before acceptance of the originator's order, had notice that payment of a payment order issued by the originator might be made by the beneficiary's bank on the basis of an identifying or bank account number even if it identifies a person different from the named beneficiary. Proof of notice may be made by any admissible evidence. The originator's bank satisfies the burden of proof if it proves that the originator, before the payment order was accepted, signed a record stating the information to which the notice relates.

(d) In a case governed by subsection (b)(1), if the beneficiary's bank rightfully pays the person identified by number and that person was not entitled to receive payment from the originator, the amount paid may be recovered from that person to the extent allowed by the law governing mistake and restitution as follows:

(1) If the originator is obliged to pay its payment order as stated in subsection (c), the originator has the right to recover.

(2) If the originator is not a bank and is not obliged to pay its payment order, the originator's bank has the right to recover.

Official Comment

1. Subsection (a) deals with the problem of payment orders issued to the beneficiary's bank for payment to nonexistent or unidentifiable persons or accounts. Since it is not possible in that case for the funds transfer to be completed, subsection (a) states that the order cannot be accepted. Under Section 4A-402(c), a sender of a payment order is not obliged to pay its order unless the beneficiary's bank accepts a payment order instructing payment to the beneficiary of that sender's order. Thus, if the beneficiary of a funds transfer is nonexistent or unidentifiable, each sender in the funds transfer that has paid its payment order is entitled to get its money back.

2. Subsection (b), which takes precedence over subsection (a), deals with the problem of payment orders in which the description of the beneficiary does not allow identification of the beneficiary because the beneficiary is described by name and by an identifying number or an account number and the name and number refer to different persons. A very large percentage of payment orders issued to the beneficiary's bank by another bank are processed by automated means using machines capable of reading orders on standard formats that identify the beneficiary by an identifying number or the number of a bank account. The processing of the order by the beneficiary's bank and the crediting of the beneficiary's account are done by use of the identifying or bank account number without human reading of the payment order itself. The process is comparable to that used in automated payment of checks. The standard format, however, may also allow the inclusion of the name of the beneficiary and other information which can be useful to the beneficiary's bank and the beneficiary but which plays no part in the process of payment. If the beneficiary's bank has both the account number and name of the beneficiary supplied by the originator of the funds transfer, it is possible for the beneficiary's bank to determine whether the name and number refer to the same person, but if a duty to make that determination is imposed on the beneficiary's bank the benefits of automated payment are lost. Manual handling of payment orders is both expensive and subject to human error. If payment orders can be handled on an automated basis there are substantial economies of operation and the possibility of clerical error is reduced. Subsection (b) allows banks to utilize automated processing by allowing banks to act on the basis of the number without regard to the name if the bank does not know that the name and number refer to different persons. "Knowledge" and "knows" are defined in Section 1-202(b) to mean actual knowledge, and Section 1-202(f states rules for determining when an organization has knowledge of information received by the organization. The time of payment is the pertinent time at which knowledge or lack of knowledge must be determined.

Although the clear trend is for beneficiary's banks to process payment orders by automated means, Section 4A-207 is not limited to cases in which processing is done by automated means. A bank that processes by semi-automated means or even manually may rely on number as stated in Section 4A-207.

In cases covered by subsection (b) the erroneous identification would in virtually all cases be the identifying or bank account number. In the typical case the error is made by the originator of the funds transfer. The originator should know the name of the person who is to receive payment and can further identify that person by an address that would normally be known to the originator. It is not unlikely, however, that the originator may not be sure whether the identifying or account number refers to the person the originator intends to pay. Subsection (b)(1) deals with the typical case in which the beneficiary's bank pays on the basis of the account number and is not aware at the time of payment that the named beneficiary is not the holder of the account which was paid. In some cases the false number will be the result of error by the originator. In other cases fraud is involved. For example, Doe is the holder of shares in Mutual Fund. Thief, impersonating Doe, requests redemption of the shares and directs Mutual Fund to wire the redemption proceeds to Doe's account #12345 in Beneficiary's Bank. Mutual Fund originates a funds transfer by issuing a payment order to Originator's Bank to make the payment to Doe's account #12345 in Beneficiary's Bank. Originator's Bank executes the order by issuing a conforming payment order to Beneficiary's Bank which makes payment to account #12345. That account is the account of Roe rather than Doe. Roe might be a person acting in concert with Thief or Roe might be an innocent third party. Assume that Roe is a gem merchant that agreed to sell gems to Thief who agreed to wire the purchase price to Roe's account in Beneficiary's Bank. Roe believed that the credit to Roe's account was a transfer of funds from Thief and released the gems to Thief in good faith in reliance on the payment. The case law is unclear on the responsibility of a beneficiary's bank in carrying out a payment order in which the identification of the beneficiary by name and number is conflicting. See *Securities Fund Services, Inc. v. American Nat'l Bank,* 542 F. Supp. 323 (N.D. Ill. 1982) and *Bradford Trust Co. v. Texas Am. Bank,* 790 F.2d 407 (5th Cir. 1986). Section 4A-207 resolves the issue.

If Beneficiary's Bank did not know about the conflict between the name and number, subsection (b)(1) applies. Beneficiary's Bank has no duty to determine whether there is a conflict and it may rely on the number as the proper identification of the beneficiary of the order. When it accepts the order, it is entitled to payment from Originator's Bank. Section 4A-402(b). On the other hand, if Beneficiary's Bank knew about the conflict between the name and number and nevertheless paid Roe, subsection (b)(2) applies. Under that provision, acceptance of the payment order of Originator's Bank did not occur because there is no beneficiary of that order. Since acceptance did not occur Originator's Bank is not obliged to pay Beneficiary's Bank. Section 4A-402(b). Similarly, Mutual Fund is excused from its obligation to pay Originator's Bank. Section 4A-402(c). Thus, Beneficiary's Bank takes the loss. Its only cause of action is against Thief. Roe is not obliged to return the payment to the beneficiary's bank because Roe received the payment in good faith and for value. Article 4A makes irrelevant the issue of whether Mutual Fund was or was not negligent in issuing its payment order.

3. Normally, subsection (b)(1) will apply to the hypothetical case discussed in Comment 2. Beneficiary's Bank will pay on the basis of the number without knowledge of the conflict. In that case subsection (c) places the loss on either Mutual Fund or Originator's Bank. It is not unfair to assign the loss to Mutual Fund because it is the person who dealt with the impostor and it supplied the wrong account number. It could have avoided the loss if it had not used an account number that it was not sure was that of Doe. Mutual Fund, however, may not have been aware of the risk involved in giving both name and number. Subsection (c) is designed to protect the originator, Mutual Fund, in this case. Under that subsection, the originator is responsible for the inconsistent description of the beneficiary if it had notice that the order might be paid by the beneficiary's bank on the basis of the number. If the originator is a bank, the originator always has that responsibility. The rationale is that any bank should know how payment orders are processed and paid. If the originator is not a bank, the originator's bank must prove that its customer, the originator, had notice. Notice can be proved by any admissible evidence, but the bank can always prove notice by providing the customer with a written statement of the required information and obtaining the customer's signature to the statement. That statement will then apply to any payment order accepted by the bank thereafter. The information need not be supplied more than once.

In the hypothetical case if Originator's Bank made the disclosure stated in the last sentence of subsection (c)(2), Mutual Fund must pay Originator's Bank. Under subsection (d)(1), Mutual Fund has an action to recover from Roe if recovery from Roe is permitted by the law governing mistake and restitution. Under the assumed facts Roe should be entitled to keep the money as a person who took it in good faith and for value since it was taken as payment for the gems. In that case, Mutual Fund's only remedy is against Thief. If Roe was not acting in good faith, Roe has to return the money to Mutual Fund. If Originator's Bank does not prove that Mutual Fund had notice as stated in subsection (c)(2), Mutual Fund is not required to pay Originator's Bank. Thus, the risk of loss falls on Originator's Bank whose remedy is against Roe or Thief as stated above. Subsection (d)(2).

4. In furtherance of medium neutrality, the reference to a "writing" in the pre-2022 text of this section has been changed to refer to a "record."

Section 4A-208. Misdescription of Intermediary Bank or Beneficiary's Bank

(a) This subsection applies to a payment order identifying an intermediary bank or the beneficiary's bank only by an identifying number.

(1) The receiving bank may rely on the number as the proper identification of the intermediary or beneficiary's bank and need not determine whether the number identifies a bank.

(2) The sender is obliged to compensate the receiving bank for any loss and expenses incurred by the receiving bank as a result of its reliance on the number in executing or attempting to execute the order.

(b) This subsection applies to a payment order identifying an intermediary bank or the beneficiary's bank both by name and an identifying number if the name and number identify different persons.

(1) If the sender is a bank, the receiving bank may rely on the number as the proper identification of the intermediary or beneficiary's bank if the receiving bank, when it executes the sender's order, does not know that the name and number identify different persons. The receiving bank need not determine whether the name and number refer to the same person or whether the number refers to a bank. The sender is obliged to compensate the receiving bank for any loss and expenses incurred by the receiving bank as a result of its reliance on the number in executing or attempting to execute the order.

(2) If the sender is not a bank and the receiving bank proves that the sender, before the payment order was accepted, had notice that the receiving bank might rely on the number as the proper identification of the intermediary or beneficiary's bank even if it identifies a person different from the bank identified by name, the rights and obligations of the sender and the receiving bank are governed by subsection (b)(1), as though the sender were a bank. Proof of notice may be made by any admissible evidence. The receiving bank satisfies the burden of proof if it proves that the sender, before the payment order was accepted, signed a record stating the information to which the notice relates.

(3) Regardless of whether the sender is a bank, the receiving bank may rely on the name as the proper identification of the intermediary or beneficiary's bank if the receiving bank, at the time it executes the sender's order, does not know that the name and number identify different persons. The receiving bank need not determine whether the name and number refer to the same person.

(4) If the receiving bank knows that the name and number identify different persons, reliance on either the name or the number in executing the sender's payment order is a breach of the obligation stated in Section 4A-302(a)(1).

Official Comment

1. This section addresses an issue similar to that addressed by Section 4A-207. Because of automation in the processing of payment orders, a payment order may identify the beneficiary's bank or an intermediary bank by an identifying number. The bank identified by number might or might not also be identified by name. The following two cases illustrate Section 4A-208(a) and (b):

Case #1. Originator's payment order to Originator's Bank identifies the beneficiary's bank as Bank A and instructs payment to Account #12345 in that bank. Originator's Bank executes Originator's order by issuing a payment order to Intermediary Bank. In the payment order of Originator's Bank the beneficiary's bank is identified as Bank A but is also identified by number, #67890. The identifying number refers to Bank B rather than Bank A. If processing by Intermediary Bank of the payment order of Originator's Bank is done by automated means, Intermediary Bank, in executing the order, will rely on the identifying number and will issue a payment order to Bank B rather than Bank A. If there is an Account #12345 in Bank B, the payment order of Intermediary Bank would normally be accepted and payment would be made to a person not intended by Originator. In this case, Section 4A-208(b)(1) puts the risk of loss on Originator's Bank. Intermediary Bank may rely on the number #67890 as the proper identification of the beneficiary's bank. Intermediary Bank has properly executed the payment order of Originator's Bank. By using the wrong number to describe the beneficiary's bank, Originator's Bank has improperly executed Originator's payment order because the payment order of Originator's Bank provides for payment to the wrong beneficiary, the holder of Account #12345 in Bank B rather than the holder of Account #12345 in Bank A. Section 4A-302(a) (1) and Section 4A-303(c). Originator's Bank is not entitled to payment from Originator but is required to pay Intermediary Bank. Section 4A-303(c) and Section 4A-402(c). Intermediary Bank is also entitled to compensation for any loss and expenses resulting from the error by Originator's Bank.

If there is no Account #12345 in Bank B, the result is that there is no beneficiary of the payment order issued by Originator's Bank and the funds transfer will not be completed. Originator's Bank is not entitled to payment from Originator and Intermediary Bank is not entitled to payment from Originator's Bank. Section 4A-402(c). Since Originator's Bank improperly executed Originator's payment order it may be liable for damages under Section 4A-305. As stated above, Intermediary Bank is entitled to compensation for loss and expenses resulting from the error by Originator's Bank.

Case #2. Suppose the same payment order by Originator to Originator's Bank as in Case #1. In executing the payment order Originator's Bank issues a payment order to Intermediary Bank in which the beneficiary's bank is identified only by number, #67890. That number does not refer to Bank A. Rather, it identifies a person that is not a bank. If processing by Intermediary Bank of the payment order of Originator's Bank is done by automated means, Intermediary Bank will rely on the number #67890 to identify the beneficiary's bank. Intermediary Bank has no duty to determine whether the number identifies a bank. The funds transfer cannot be completed in this case because no bank is identified as the beneficiary's bank. Subsection (a) puts the risk of loss on Originator's Bank. Originator's Bank is not entitled to payment from Originator. Section 4A-402(c). Originator's Bank has improperly executed Originator's payment order and may be liable for damages under Section 4A-305. Originator's Bank is obliged to compensate Intermediary Bank for loss and expenses resulting from the error by Originator's Bank.

Subsection (a) also applies if #67890 identifies a bank, but the bank is not Bank A. Intermediary Bank may rely on the number as the proper identification of the beneficiary's bank. If the bank to which Intermediary Bank sends its payment order accepts the order, Intermediary Bank is entitled to payment from Originator's Bank, but Originator's Bank is not entitled to payment from Originator. The analysis is similar to that in Case #1.

2. Subsection (b)(2) of Section 4A-208 addresses cases in which an erroneous identification of a beneficiary's bank or intermediary bank by name and number is made in a payment order of a sender that is not a bank. Suppose Originator issues a payment order to Originator's Bank that instructs that bank to use an intermediary bank identified as Bank A and by an identifying number, #67890. The identifying number refers to Bank B. Originator intended to identify Bank A as intermediary bank. If Originator's Bank relied on the number and issued a payment order to Bank B the rights of Originator's Bank depend upon whether the proof of notice stated in subsection (b)(2) is made by Originator's Bank. If proof is made, Originator's Bank's rights are governed by subsection (b)(1) of Section 4A-208. Originator's Bank is not liable for breach of Section 4A-302(a)(1) and is entitled to compensation from Originator for any loss and expenses resulting from Originator's error. If notice is not proved, Originator's Bank may not rely on the number in executing Originator's payment order. Since Originator's Bank does not get the benefit of subsection (b)(1) in that case, Originator's Bank improperly executed Originator's payment order and is in breach of the obligation stated in Section 4A-302(a)(1). If notice is not given, Originator's Bank can rely on the name if it is not aware of the conflict in name and number. Subsection (b)(3).

3. Although the principal purpose of Section 4A-208 is to accommodate automated processing of payment orders, Section 4A-208 applies regardless of whether processing is done by automation, semi-automated means or manually.

4. In furtherance of medium neutrality, the reference to a "writing" in the pre-2022 text of this section has been changed to refer to a "record."

Section 4A-209. Acceptance of Payment Order

(a) Subject to subsection (d), a receiving bank other than the beneficiary's bank accepts a payment order when it executes the order.

(b) Subject to subsections (c) and (d), a beneficiary's bank accepts a payment order at the earliest of the following times:

(1) when the bank (i) pays the beneficiary as stated in Section 4A-405(a) or 4A-405(b), or (ii) notifies the beneficiary of receipt of the order or that the account of the beneficiary has been credited with respect to the order unless the notice indicates that the bank is rejecting the order or that funds with respect to the order may not be withdrawn or used until receipt of payment from the sender of the order;

(2) when the bank receives payment of the entire amount of the sender's order pursuant to Section 4A-403(a)(1) or 4A-403(a)(2); or

(3) the opening of the next funds-transfer business day of the bank following the payment date of the order if, at that time, the amount of the sender's order is fully covered by a withdrawable credit balance in an authorized account of the sender or the bank has otherwise received full payment from the sender, unless the order was rejected before that time or is rejected within (i) one hour after that time, or (ii) one hour after the opening of the next business day of the sender following the payment date if that time is later. If notice of rejection is received by the sender after the payment date and the authorized account of the sender does not bear interest, the bank is obliged to pay interest to the sender on the amount of the order for the number of days elapsing after the payment date to the day the sender receives notice or learns that the order was not accepted, counting that day as an elapsed day. If the withdrawable credit balance during that period falls below the amount of the order, the amount of interest payable is reduced accordingly.

(c) Acceptance of a payment order cannot occur before the order is received by the receiving bank. Acceptance does not occur under subsection (b)(2) or (b)(3) if the beneficiary of the payment order does not have an account with the receiving bank, the account has been closed, or the receiving bank is not permitted by law to receive credits for the beneficiary's account.

(d) A payment order issued to the originator's bank cannot be accepted until the payment date if the bank is the beneficiary's bank, or the execution date if the bank is not the beneficiary's bank. If the originator's bank executes the originator's payment order before the execution date or pays the beneficiary of the originator's payment order before the payment date and the payment order is subsequently canceled pursuant to Section 4A-211(b), the bank may recover from the beneficiary any payment received to the extent allowed by the law governing mistake and restitution.

Official Comment

1. This section treats the sender's payment order as a request by the sender to the receiving bank to execute or pay the order and that request can be accepted or rejected by the receiving bank. Section 4A-209 defines when acceptance occurs. Section 4A-210 covers rejection. Acceptance of the payment order imposes an obligation on the receiving bank to the sender if the receiving bank is not the beneficiary's bank, or to the beneficiary if the receiving bank is the beneficiary's bank. These obligations are stated in Section 4A-302 and Section 4A-404.

2. Acceptance by a receiving bank other than the beneficiary's bank is defined in Section 4A-209(a). That subsection states the only way that a bank other than the beneficiary's bank can accept a payment order. A payment order to a bank other than the beneficiary's bank is, in effect, a request that the receiving bank execute the sender's order by issuing a payment order to the beneficiary's bank or to an intermediary bank. Normally, acceptance occurs at the time of execution, but there is an exception stated in subsection (d) and discussed in Comment 9. Execution occurs when the receiving bank "issues a payment order intended to carry out" the sender's order. Section 4A-301(a). In some cases the payment order issued by the receiving bank may not conform to the sender's order. For example, the receiving bank might make a mistake in the amount of its order, or the order might be issued to the wrong beneficiary's bank or for the benefit of the wrong beneficiary. In all of these cases there is acceptance of the sender's order by the bank when the receiving bank issues its order intended to carry out the sender's order, even though the bank's payment order does not in fact carry out the instruction of the sender. Improper execution of the sender's order may lead to liability to the sender for damages or it may mean that the sender is not obliged to pay its payment order. These matters are covered in Section 4A-303, Section 4A-305, and Section 4A-402.

3. A receiving bank has no duty to accept a payment order unless the bank makes an agreement, either before or after issuance of the payment order, to accept it, or acceptance is required by a funds transfer system rule. If the bank makes such an agreement it incurs a contractual obligation based on the agreement and may be held liable for breach of contract if a failure to execute violates the agreement. In many cases a bank will enter into an agreement with its customer to govern the rights and obligations of the parties with respect to payment orders issued to the bank by the customer or, in cases in which the sender is also a bank, there may be a funds transfer system rule that governs the obligations of a receiving bank with respect to payment orders transmitted over the system. Such agreements or rules can specify the circumstances under which a receiving bank is obliged to execute a payment order and can define the extent of liability of the receiving bank for breach of the agreement or rule. Section 4A-305(d) states the liability for breach of an agreement to execute a payment order.

4. In the case of a payment order issued to the beneficiary's bank, acceptance is defined in Section 4A-209(b). The function of a beneficiary's bank that receives a payment order is different from that of a receiving bank that receives a payment order for execution. In the typical case, the beneficiary's bank simply receives payment from the sender of the order, credits the account of the beneficiary and notifies the beneficiary of the credit. Acceptance by the beneficiary's bank does not create any obligation to the sender. Acceptance by the beneficiary's bank means that the bank is liable to the beneficiary for the amount of the order. Section 4A-404(a). There are three ways in which the beneficiary's bank can accept a payment order which are described in the following comments.

5. Under Section 4A-209(b)(1), the beneficiary's bank can accept a payment order by paying the beneficiary. In the normal case of crediting an account of the beneficiary, payment occurs when the beneficiary is given notice of the right to withdraw the credit, the credit is applied to a debt of the beneficiary, or "funds with respect to the order" are otherwise made available to the beneficiary. Section 4A-405(a). The quoted phrase covers cases in which funds are made available to the beneficiary as a result of receipt of a payment order for the benefit of the beneficiary but the release of funds is not expressed as payment of the order. For example, the beneficiary's bank might express a release of funds equal to the amount of the order as a "loan" that will be automatically repaid when the beneficiary's bank receives payment by the sender of the order. If the release of funds is designated as a loan pursuant to a routine practice of the bank, the release is conditional payment of the order rather than a loan, particularly if normal incidents of a loan such as the signing of a loan agreement or note and the payment of interest are not present. Such a release of funds is payment to the beneficiary under Section 4A-405(a). Under Section 4A-405(c) the bank cannot recover the money from the beneficiary if the bank does not receive payment from the sender of the payment order that it accepted. Exceptions to this rule are stated in § 4A-405(d) and (e). The beneficiary's bank may also accept by notifying the beneficiary that the order has been received. "Notifies" is defined in Section 1-202(d). In some cases a beneficiary's bank will receive a payment order during the day but settlement of the sender's obligation to pay the order will not occur until the end of the day. If the beneficiary's bank wants to defer incurring liability to the beneficiary until the beneficiary's bank receives payment, it can do so. The beneficiary's bank incurs no liability to the beneficiary with respect to a payment order that it receives until it accepts the order. If the bank does not accept pursuant to subsection (b)(1), acceptance does not occur until the end of the day when the beneficiary's bank receives settlement. If the sender settles, the payment order will be accepted under subsection (b)(2) and the funds will be released to the beneficiary the next morning. If the sender doesn't settle, no acceptance occurs. In either case the beneficiary's bank suffers no loss.

6. In most cases the beneficiary's bank will receive a payment order from another bank. If the sender is a bank and the beneficiary's bank receives payment from the sender by final settlement through the Federal Reserve System or a funds transfer system (Section 4A-403(a)(1)) or, less commonly, through credit to an account of the beneficiary's bank with the sender or another bank (Section 4A-403(a)(2)), acceptance by the beneficiary's bank occurs at the time payment is made. Section 4A-209(b)(2). A minor exception to this rule is stated in Section 4A-209(c). Section 4A-209(b)(2) results in automatic acceptance of payment orders issued to a beneficiary's bank by means of Fedwire because the Federal Reserve account of the beneficiary's bank is credited and final payment is made to that bank when the payment order is received.

Subsection (b)(2) would also apply to cases in which the beneficiary's bank mistakenly pays a person who is not the beneficiary of the payment order issued to the beneficiary's bank. For example, suppose the payment order provides for immediate payment to Account #12345. The beneficiary's bank erroneously credits Account #12346 and notifies the holder of that account of the credit. No acceptance occurs in this case under subsection (b)(1) because the beneficiary of the order has not been paid or notified. The holder of Account #12345 is the beneficiary of the order issued to the beneficiary's bank. But acceptance will normally occur if the beneficiary's bank takes no other action, because the bank will normally receive settlement with respect to the payment order. At that time the bank has accepted because the sender paid its payment order. The bank is liable to pay the holder of Account #12345. The bank has paid the holder of Account #12346 by mistake, and has a right to recover the payment if the credit is withdrawn, to the extent provided in the law governing mistake and restitution.

7. Subsection (b)(3) covers cases of inaction by the beneficiary's bank. It applies whether or not the sender is a bank and covers a case in which the sender and the beneficiary both have accounts with the receiving bank and payment will be made by debiting the account of the sender and crediting the account of the beneficiary. Subsection (b)(3) is similar to subsection (b)(2) in that it bases acceptance by the beneficiary's bank on payment by the sender. Payment by the sender is effected by a debit to the sender's account if the account balance is sufficient to cover the amount of the order. On the payment date (Section 4A-401) of the order the beneficiary's bank will normally credit the beneficiary's account and notify the beneficiary of receipt of the order if it is satisfied that the sender's account balance covers the order or is willing to give credit to the sender. In some cases, however, the bank may not be willing to give credit to the sender and it may not be possible for the bank to determine until the end of the day on the payment date whether there are sufficient good funds in the sender's account. There may be various transactions during the day involving funds going into and out of the account. Some of these transactions may occur late in the day or after the close of the banking day. To accommodate this situation, subsection (b)(3) provides that the status of the account is determined at the opening of the next funds transfer business day of the beneficiary's bank after the payment date of the order. If the sender's account balance is sufficient to cover the order, the beneficiary's bank has a source of payment and the result in almost all cases is that the bank accepts the order at that time if it did not previously accept under subsection (b)(1). In rare cases, a bank may want to avoid acceptance under subsection (b)(3) by rejecting the order as discussed in Comment 8.

8. Section 4A-209 is based on a general principle that a receiving bank is not obliged to accept a payment order unless it has agreed or is bound by a funds transfer system rule to do so. Thus, provision is made to allow the receiving bank to prevent acceptance of the order. This principle is consistently followed if the receiving bank is not the beneficiary's bank. If the receiving bank is not the beneficiary's bank, acceptance is in the control of the receiving bank because it occurs only if the order is executed. But in the case of the beneficiary's bank acceptance can occur by passive receipt of payment under subsection (b)(2) or (3). In the case of a payment made by Fedwire acceptance cannot be prevented. In other cases the beneficiary's bank can prevent acceptance by giving notice of rejection to the sender before payment occurs under Section 4A-403(a)(1) or (2). A minor exception to the ability of the beneficiary's bank to reject is stated in Section 4A-502(c)(3).

Under subsection (b)(3) acceptance occurs at the opening of the next funds transfer business day of the beneficiary's bank following the payment date unless the bank rejected the order before that time or it rejects within one hour after that time. In some cases the sender and the beneficiary's bank may not be in the same time zone or the beginning of the business day of the sender and the funds transfer business day of the beneficiary's bank may not coincide. For example, the sender may be located in California and the beneficiary's bank in New York. Since in most cases notice of rejection would be communicated electronically or by telephone, it might not be feasible for the bank to give notice before one hour after the opening of the funds transfer business day in New York because at that hour, the sender's business day may not have started in California. For that reason, there are alternative deadlines stated in subsection (b)(3). In the case stated, the bank acts in time if it gives notice within one hour after the opening of the business day of the sender. But if the notice of rejection is received by the sender after the payment date, the bank is obliged to pay interest to the sender if the sender's account does not bear interest. In that case the bank had the use of funds of the sender that the sender could reasonably assume would be used to pay the beneficiary. The rate of interest is stated in Section 4A-506. If the sender receives notice on the day after the payment date the sender is entitled to one day's interest. If receipt of notice is delayed for more than one day, the sender is entitled to interest for each additional day of delay.

9. Subsection (d) applies only to a payment order by the originator of a funds transfer to the originator's bank and it refers to the following situation. On April 1, Originator instructs Bank A to make a payment on April 15 to the account of Beneficiary in Bank B. By mistake, on April 1, Bank A executes Originator's payment order by issuing a payment order to Bank B instructing immediate payment to Beneficiary. Bank B credited Beneficiary's account and immediately released the funds to Beneficiary. Under subsection (d) no acceptance by Bank A occurred on April 1 when Originator's payment order was executed because acceptance cannot occur before the execution date which in this case would be April 15 or shortly before that date. Section 4A-301(b). Under Section 4A-402(c), Originator is not obliged to pay Bank A until the order is accepted and that can't occur until the execution date. But Bank A is required to pay Bank B when Bank B accepted Bank A's order on April 1. Unless Originator and Beneficiary are the same person, in almost all cases Originator is paying a debt owed to Beneficiary and early payment does not injure Originator because Originator does not have to pay Bank A until the execution date. Section 4A-402(c). Bank A takes the interest loss. But suppose that on April 3, Originator concludes that no debt was owed to Beneficiary or that the debt was less than the amount of the payment order. Under Section 4A-211(b) Originator can cancel its payment order if Bank A has not accepted. If early execution of Originator's payment order is acceptance, Originator can suffer a loss because cancellation after acceptance is not possible without the consent of Bank A and Bank B. Section 4A-211(c). If Originator has to pay Bank A, Originator would be required to seek recovery of the money from Beneficiary. Subsection (d) prevents this result and puts the risk of loss on Bank A by providing that the early execution does not result in acceptance until the execution date. Since on April 3 Originator's order was not yet accepted, Originator can cancel it under Section 4A-211(b). The result is that Bank A is not entitled to payment from Originator but is obliged to pay Bank B. Bank A has paid Beneficiary by mistake. If Originator's payment order is cancelled, Bank A becomes the originator of an erroneous funds transfer to Beneficiary. Bank A has the burden of recovering payment from Beneficiary on the basis of a payment by mistake. If Beneficiary received the money in good faith in payment of a debt owed to Beneficiary by Originator, the law of mistake and restitution may allow Beneficiary to keep all or part of the money received. If Originator owed money to Beneficiary, Bank A has paid Originator's debt and, under the law of restitution, which applies pursuant to Section 1103, Bank A is subrogated to Beneficiary's rights against Originator on the debt.

If Bank A is the Beneficiary's bank and Bank A credited Beneficiary's account and released the funds to Beneficiary on April 1, the analysis is similar. If Originator's order is cancelled, Bank A has paid Beneficiary by mistake. The right of Bank A to recover the payment from Beneficiary is similar to Bank A's rights in the preceding paragraph.

Section 4A-210. Rejection of Payment Order

(a) A payment order is rejected by the receiving bank by a notice of rejection transmitted to the sender orally or in a record. A notice of rejection need not use any particular words and is sufficient if it indicates that the receiving bank is rejecting the order or will not execute or pay the order. Rejection is effective when the notice is given if transmission is by a means that is reasonable in the circumstances. If notice of rejection is given by a means that is not reasonable, rejection is effective when the notice is received. If an agreement of the sender and receiving bank establishes the means to be used to reject a payment order, (i) any means complying with the agreement is reasonable and (ii) any means not complying is not reasonable unless no significant delay in receipt of the notice resulted from the use of the noncomplying means.

(b) This subsection applies if a receiving bank other than the beneficiary's bank fails to execute a payment order despite the existence on the execution date of a withdrawable credit balance in an authorized account of the sender sufficient to cover the order. If the sender does not receive notice of rejection of the order on the execution date and the authorized account of the sender does not bear interest, the bank is obliged to pay interest to the sender on the amount of the order for the number of days elapsing after the execution date to the earlier of the day the order is canceled pursuant to Section 4A-211(d) or the day the sender receives notice or learns that the order was not executed, counting the final day of the period as an elapsed day. If the withdrawable credit balance during that period falls below the amount of the order, the amount of interest is reduced accordingly.

(c) If a receiving bank suspends payments, all unaccepted payment orders issued to it are deemed rejected at the time the bank suspends payments.

(d) Acceptance of a payment order precludes a later rejection of the order. Rejection of a payment order precludes a later acceptance of the order.

Official Comment

1. With respect to payment orders issued to a receiving bank other than the beneficiary's bank, notice of rejection is not necessary to prevent acceptance of the order. Acceptance can occur only if the receiving bank executes the order. Section 4A-209(a). But notice of rejection will routinely be given by such a bank in cases in which the bank cannot or is not willing to execute the order for some reason. There are many reasons why a bank doesn't execute an order. The payment order may not clearly instruct the receiving bank because of some ambiguity in the order or an internal inconsistency. In some cases, the receiving bank may not be able to carry out the instruction because of equipment failure, credit limitations on the receiving bank, or some other factor which makes proper execution of the order infeasible. In those cases notice of rejection is a means of informing the sender of the facts so that a corrected payment order can be transmitted or the sender can seek alternate means of completing the funds transfer. The other major reason for not executing an order is that the sender's account is insufficient to cover the order and the receiving bank is not willing to give credit to the sender. If the sender's account is sufficient to cover the order and the receiving bank chooses not to execute the order, notice of rejection is necessary to prevent liability to pay interest to the sender if the case falls within Section 4A-210(b) which is discussed in Comment 3.

2. A payment order to the beneficiary's bank can be accepted by inaction of the bank. Section 4A-209(b)(2) and (3). To prevent acceptance under those provisions it is necessary for the receiving bank to send notice of rejection before acceptance occurs. Subsection (a) of Section 4A-210 states the rule that rejection is accomplished by giving notice of rejection. This incorporates the definitions in Section 1-202(d). Rejection is effective when notice is given if it is given by a means that is reasonable in the circumstances. Otherwise it is effective when the notice is received. The question of when rejection is effective is important only in the relatively few cases under subsection (b)(2) and (3) in which a notice of rejection is necessary to prevent acceptance. The question of whether a particular means is reasonable depends on the facts in a particular case. In a very large percentage of cases the sender and the receiving bank will be in direct electronic contact with each other and in those cases a notice of rejection can be transmitted instantaneously. Since time is of the essence in a large proportion of funds transfers, some quick means of transmission would usually be required, but this is not always the case. The parties may specify by agreement the means by which communication between the parties is to be made.

3. Subsection (b) deals with cases in which a sender does not learn until after the execution date that the sender's order has not been executed. It applies only to cases in which the receiving bank was assured of payment because the sender's account was sufficient to cover the order. Normally, the receiving bank will accept the sender's order if it is assured of payment, but there may be some cases in which the bank chooses to reject. Unless the receiving bank had obligated itself by agreement to accept, the failure to accept is not wrongful. There is no duty of the receiving bank to accept the payment order unless it is obliged to accept by express agreement. Section 4A-212. But even if the bank has not acted wrongfully, the receiving bank had the use of the sender's money that the sender could reasonably assume was to be the source of payment of the funds transfer. Until the sender learns that the order was not accepted the sender is denied the use of that money. Subsection (b) obliges the receiving bank to pay interest to the sender as restitution unless the sender receives notice of rejection on the execution date. The time of receipt of notice is determined pursuant to Section 1-202€ and (f)]. The rate of interest is stated in Section 4A-506. If the sender receives notice on the day after the execution date, the sender is entitled to one day's interest. If receipt of notice is delayed for more than one day, the sender is entitled to interest for each additional day of delay.

4. Subsection (d) treats acceptance and rejection as mutually exclusive. If a payment order has been accepted, rejection of that order becomes impossible. If a payment order has been rejected it cannot be accepted later by the receiving bank. Once notice of rejection has been given, the sender may have acted on the notice by making the payment through other channels. If the receiving bank wants to act on a payment order that it has rejected it has to obtain the consent of the sender. In that case the consent of the sender would amount to the giving of a second payment order that substitutes for the rejected first order. If the receiving bank suspends payments (Section 4104(1)(k)), subsection (c) provides that unaccepted payment orders are deemed rejected at the time suspension of payments occurs. This prevents acceptance by passage of time under Section 4A-209(b)(3).

5. In furtherance of medium neutrality, the reference to "electronically" in the pre-2022 text of this section has been deleted as unnecessary and the reference to a "writing" in the pre-2022 text has been changed to refer to a "record."

Section 4A-211. Cancellation and Amendment of Payment Order

(a) A communication of the sender of a payment order cancelling or amending the order may be transmitted to the receiving bank orally or in a record. If a security procedure is in effect between the sender and the receiving bank, the communication is not effective to cancel or amend the order unless the communication is verified pursuant to the security procedure or the bank agrees to the cancellation or amendment.

(b) Subject to subsection (a), a communication by the sender cancelling or amending a payment order is effective to cancel or amend the order if notice of the communication is received at a time and in a manner affording the receiving bank a reasonable opportunity to act on the communication before the bank accepts the payment order.

(c) After a payment order has been accepted, cancellation or amendment of the order is not effective unless the receiving bank agrees or a funds-transfer system rule allows cancellation or amendment without agreement of the bank.

(1) With respect to a payment order accepted by a receiving bank other than the beneficiary's bank, cancellation or amendment is not effective unless a conforming cancellation or amendment of the payment order issued by the receiving bank is also made.

(2) With respect to a payment order accepted by the beneficiary's bank, cancellation or amendment is not effective unless the order was issued in execution of an unauthorized payment order, or because of a mistake by a sender in the funds transfer which resulted in the issuance of a payment order (i) that is a duplicate of a payment order previously issued by the sender, (ii) that orders payment to a beneficiary not entitled to receive payment from the originator, or (iii) that orders payment in an amount greater than the amount the beneficiary was entitled

to receive from the originator. If the payment order is canceled or amended, the beneficiary's bank is entitled to recover from the beneficiary any amount paid to the beneficiary to the extent allowed by the law governing mistake and restitution.

(d) An unaccepted payment order is canceled by operation of law at the close of the fifth funds-transfer business day of the receiving bank after the execution date or payment date of the order.

(e) A canceled payment order cannot be accepted. If an accepted payment order is canceled, the acceptance is nullified and no person has any right or obligation based on the acceptance. Amendment of a payment order is deemed to be cancellation of the original order at the time of amendment and issue of a new payment order in the amended form at the same time.

(f) Unless otherwise provided in an agreement of the parties or in a funds-transfer system rule, if the receiving bank, after accepting a payment order, agrees to cancellation or amendment of the order by the sender or is bound by a funds-transfer system rule allowing cancellation or amendment without the bank's agreement, the sender, whether or not cancellation or amendment is effective, is liable to the bank for any loss and expenses, including reasonable attorney's fees, incurred by the bank as a result of the cancellation or amendment or attempted cancellation or amendment.

(g) A payment order is not revoked by the death or legal incapacity of the sender unless the receiving bank knows of the death or of an adjudication of incapacity by a court of competent jurisdiction and has reasonable opportunity to act before acceptance of the order.

(h) A funds-transfer system rule is not effective to the extent it conflicts with subsection (c)(2).

Official Comment

1. This section deals with cancellation and amendment of payment orders. It states the conditions under which cancellation or amendment is both effective and rightful. There is no concept of wrongful cancellation or amendment of a payment order. If the conditions stated in this section are not met the attempted cancellation or amendment is not effective. If the stated conditions are met the cancellation or amendment is effective and rightful. The sender of a payment order may want to withdraw or change the order because the sender has had a change of mind about the transaction or because the payment order was erroneously issued or for any other reason. One common situation is that of multiple transmission of the same order. The sender that mistakenly transmits the same order twice wants to correct the mistake by cancelling the duplicate order. Or, a sender may have intended to order a payment of $1,000,000 but mistakenly issued an order to pay $10,000,000. In this case the sender might try to correct the mistake by cancelling the order and issuing another order in the proper amount. Or, the mistake could be corrected by amending the order to change it to the proper amount. Whether the error is corrected by amendment or cancellation and reissue the net result is the same. This result is stated in the last sentence of subsection (e).

2. Subsection (a) allows a cancellation or amendment of a payment order to be communicated to the receiving bank "orally or in a record." The quoted phrase is consistent with the language of Section 4A-103(a) applicable to payment orders. Cancellations and amendments are normally subject to verification pursuant to security procedures to the same extent as payment orders. Subsection (a) recognizes this fact by providing that in cases in which there is a security procedure in effect between the sender and the receiving bank the bank is not bound by a communication cancelling or amending an order unless verification has been made. This is necessary to protect the bank because under subsection (b) a cancellation or amendment can be effective by unilateral action of the sender. Without verification the bank cannot be sure whether the communication was or was not effective to cancel or amend a previously verified payment order.

3. If the receiving bank has not yet accepted the order, there is no reason why the sender should not be able to cancel or amend the order unilaterally so long as the requirements of subsections (a) and (b) are met. If the receiving bank has accepted the order, it is possible to cancel or amend but only if the requirements of subsection (c) are met.

First consider the case of a receiving bank other than the beneficiary's bank. If the bank has not yet accepted the order, the sender can unilaterally cancel or amend. The communication amending or cancelling the payment order must be received in time to allow the bank to act on it before the bank issues its payment order in execution of the sender's order. The time that the sender's communication is received is governed by Section 4A-106. If a payment order does not specify a delayed payment date or execution date, the order will normally be executed shortly after receipt. Thus, as a practical matter, the sender will have very little time in which to instruct cancellation or amendment before acceptance. In addition, a receiving bank will normally have cut-off times for receipt of such communications, and the receiving bank is not obliged to act on communications received after the cut-off hour. Cancellation by the sender after execution of the order by the receiving bank requires the agreement of the bank unless a funds transfer rule otherwise provides. Subsection (c). Although execution of the sender's order by the receiving bank does not itself impose liability on the receiving bank (under Section 4A-402 no liability is incurred by the receiving bank to pay its order until it is accepted), it would commonly be the case that acceptance follows shortly after issuance. Thus, as a practical matter, a receiving bank that has executed a payment order will incur a liability to the next bank in the chain before it would be able to act on the cancellation request of its customer. It is unreasonable to impose on the receiving bank a risk of loss with respect to a cancellation request without the consent of the receiving bank.

The statute does not state how or when the agreement of the receiving bank must be obtained for cancellation after execution. The receiving bank's consent could be obtained at the time cancellation occurs or it could be based on a preexisting agreement. Or, a funds transfer system rule could provide that cancellation can be made unilaterally by the sender. By virtue of that rule any receiving bank covered by the rule is bound. Section 4A-501. If the receiving bank has already executed the sender's order, the bank would not consent to cancellation unless the bank to which the receiving bank has issued its payment order consents to cancellation of that order. It makes no sense to allow cancellation of a payment order unless all subsequent payment orders in the funds transfer that were issued because of the cancelled payment order are also cancelled. Under subsection (c)(1), if a receiving bank consents to cancellation of the payment order after it is executed, the cancellation is not effective unless the receiving bank also cancels the payment order issued by the bank.

4. With respect to a payment order issued to the beneficiary's bank, acceptance is particularly important because it creates liability to pay the beneficiary, it defines when the originator pays its obligation to the beneficiary, and it defines when any obligation for which the payment is made is discharged. Since acceptance affects the rights of the originator and the beneficiary it is not appropriate to allow the beneficiary's bank to agree to cancellation or amendment except in unusual cases. Except as provided in subsection (c)(2), cancellation or amendment after acceptance by the beneficiary's bank is not possible unless all parties affected by the order agree. Under subsection (c)(2), cancellation or amendment is possible only in the four cases stated. The following examples illustrate subsection (c)(2):

Case #1. Originator's Bank executed a payment order issued in the name of its customer as sender. The order was not authorized by the customer and was fraudulently issued. Beneficiary's Bank accepted the payment order issued by Originator's Bank. Under subsection (c)(2) Originator's Bank can cancel the order if Beneficiary's Bank consents. It doesn't make any difference whether the payment order that Originator's Bank accepted was or was not enforceable against the customer under Section 4A-202(b). Verification under that provision is important in determining whether Originator's Bank or the customer has the risk of loss, but it has no relevance under Section 4A-211(c)(2). Whether or not verified, the payment order was not authorized by the customer. Cancellation of the payment order to Beneficiary's Bank causes the acceptance of Beneficiary's Bank to be nullified. Subsection (e). Beneficiary's Bank is entitled to recover payment from the beneficiary to the extent allowed by the law of mistake and restitution. In this kind of case the beneficiary is usually a party to the fraud who has no right to receive or retain payment of the order.

Case #2. Originator owed Beneficiary $1,000,000 and ordered Bank A to pay that amount to the account of Beneficiary in Bank B. Bank A issued a complying order to Bank B, but by mistake issued a duplicate order as well. Bank B accepted both orders. Under subsection (c)(2)(i) cancellation of the duplicate order could be made by Bank A with the consent of Bank B. Beneficiary has no right to receive or retain payment of the duplicate payment order if only $1,000,000 was owed by Originator to Beneficiary. If Originator owed $2,000,000 to Beneficiary, the law of restitution might allow Beneficiary to retain the $1,000,000 paid by Bank B on the duplicate order. In that case Bank B is entitled to reimbursement from Bank A under subsection (f).

Case #3. Originator owed $1,000,000 to X. Intending to pay X, Originator ordered Bank A to pay $1,000,000 to Y's account in Bank B. Bank A issued a complying payment order to Bank B which Bank B accepted by releasing the $1,000,000 to Y. Under subsection (c)(2)(ii) Bank A can cancel its payment order to Bank B with the consent of Bank B if Y was not entitled to receive payment from Originator. Originator can also cancel its order to Bank A with Bank A's consent. Subsection (c) (1). Bank B may recover the $1,000,000 from Y unless the law of mistake and restitution allows Y to retain some or all of the amount paid. If no debt was owed to Y, Bank B should have a right of recovery.

Case #4. Originator owed Beneficiary $10,000. By mistake Originator ordered Bank A to pay $1,000,000 to the account of Beneficiary in Bank B. Bank A issued a complying order to Bank B which accepted by notifying Beneficiary of its right to withdraw $1,000,000. Cancellation is permitted in this case under subsection (c)(2)(iii). If Bank B paid Beneficiary it is entitled to recover the payment except to the extent the law of mistake and restitution allows Beneficiary to retain payment. In this case Beneficiary might be entitled to retain $10,000, the amount of the debt owed to Beneficiary. If Beneficiary may retain $10,000, Bank B would be entitled to $10,000 from Bank A pursuant to subsection (f). In this case Originator also cancelled its order. Thus Bank A would be entitled to $10,000 from Originator pursuant to subsection (f).

5. Unless constrained by a funds transfer system rule, a receiving bank may agree to cancellation or amendment of the payment order under subsection (c) but is not required to do so regardless of the circumstances. If the receiving bank has incurred liability as a result of its acceptance of the sender's order, there are substantial risks in agreeing to cancellation or amendment. This is particularly true for a beneficiary's bank. Cancellation or amendment after acceptance by the beneficiary's bank can be made only in the four cases stated and the beneficiary's bank may not have any way of knowing whether the requirements of subsection (c) have been met or whether it will be able to recover payment from the beneficiary that received payment. Even with indemnity the beneficiary's bank may be reluctant to alienate its customer, the beneficiary, by denying the customer the funds. Subsection (c) leaves the decision to the beneficiary's bank unless the consent of the beneficiary's bank is not required under a funds transfer system rule or other interbank agreement. If a receiving bank agrees to cancellation or amendment under subsection (c)(1) or (2), it is automatically entitled to indemnification from the sender under subsection (f). The indemnification provision recognizes that a sender has no right to cancel a payment order after it is accepted by the receiving bank. If the receiving bank agrees to cancellation, it is doing so as an accommodation to the sender and it should not incur a risk of loss in doing so.

6. Acceptance by the receiving bank of a payment order issued by the sender is comparable to acceptance of an offer under the law of contracts. Under that law the death or legal incapacity of an offeror terminates the offer even though the offeree has no notice of the death or incapacity. Restatement Second, Contracts § 48. Comment a. to that section states that the "rule seems to be a relic of the obsolete view that a contract requires a 'meeting of minds,' and it is out of harmony with the modern doctrine that a manifestation of assent is effective without regard to actual mental assent." Subsection (g), which reverses the Restatement rule in the case of a payment order, is similar to Section 4-405(a) which applies to checks. Subsection (g) does not address the effect of the bankruptcy of the sender of a payment order before the order is accepted, but the principle of subsection (g) has been recognized in *Bank of Marin v. England*, 385 U.S. 99 (1966). Although Bankruptcy Code Section 542(c) may not have been drafted with wire transfers in mind, its language can be read to allow the receiving bank to charge the sender's account for the amount of the payment order if the receiving bank executed it in ignorance of the bankruptcy.

7. Subsection (d) deals with stale payment orders. Payment orders normally are executed on the execution date or the day after. An order issued to the beneficiary's bank is normally accepted on the payment date or the day after. If a payment order is not accepted on its execution or payment date or shortly thereafter, it is probable that there was some problem with the terms of the order or the sender did not have sufficient funds or credit to cover the amount of the order. Delayed acceptance of such an order is normally not contemplated, but the order may not have been cancelled by the sender. Subsection (d) provides for cancellation by operation of law to prevent an unexpected delayed acceptance.

8. A funds transfer system rule can govern rights and obligations between banks that are parties to payment orders transmitted over the system even if the rule conflicts with Article 4A. In some cases, however, a rule governing a transaction between two banks can affect a third party in an unacceptable way. Subsection (h) deals with such a case. A funds transfer system rule cannot allow cancellation of a payment order accepted by the beneficiary's bank if the rule conflicts with subsection (c)(2). Because rights of the beneficiary and the originator are directly affected by acceptance, subsection (c)(2) severely limits cancellation. These limitations cannot be altered by funds transfer system rule.

9. In furtherance of medium neutrality, the reference to "electronically" in the pre-2022 text of this section has been deleted as unnecessary and the reference to a "writing" in the pre-2022 text has been changed to refer to a "record."

Section 4A-212. Liability and Duty of Receiving Bank Regarding Unaccepted Payment Order

If a receiving bank fails to accept a payment order that it is obliged by express agreement to accept, the bank is liable for breach of the agreement to the extent provided in the agreement or in this Article, but does not otherwise have any duty to accept a payment order or, before acceptance, to take any action, or refrain from taking action, with respect to the order except as provided in this Article or by express agreement. Liability based on acceptance arises only when acceptance occurs as stated in Section 4A-209, and liability is limited to that provided in this Article. A receiving bank is not the agent of the sender or beneficiary of the payment order it accepts, or of any other party to the funds transfer, and the bank owes no duty to any party to the funds transfer except as provided in this Article or by express agreement.

Official Comment

With limited exceptions stated in this Article, the duties and obligations of receiving banks that carry out a funds transfer arise only as a result of acceptance of payment orders or of agreements made by receiving banks. Exceptions are stated in Section 4A-209(b)(3) and Section 4A-210(b). A receiving bank is not like a collecting bank under Article 4. No receiving bank, whether it be an originator's bank, an intermediary bank or a beneficiary's bank, is an agent for any other party in the funds transfer.

PART 3. EXECUTION OF SENDER'S PAYMENT ORDER BY RECEIVING BANK

Section 4A-301. Execution and Execution Date

(a) A payment order is "executed" by the receiving bank when it issues a payment order intended to carry out the payment order received by the bank. A payment order received by the beneficiary's bank can be accepted but cannot be executed.

(b) "Execution date" of a payment order means the day on which the receiving bank may properly issue a payment order in execution of the sender's order. The execution date may be determined by instruction of the sender but cannot be earlier than the day the order is received and, unless otherwise determined, is the day the order is received. If the sender's instruction states a payment date, the execution date is the payment date or an earlier date on which execution is reasonably necessary to allow payment to the beneficiary on the payment date.

Official Comment

1. The terms "executed," "execution" and "execution date" are used only with respect to a payment order to a receiving bank other than the beneficiary's bank. The beneficiary's bank can accept the payment order that it receives, but it does not execute the order. Execution refers to the act of the receiving bank in issuing a payment order "intended to carry out" the payment order that the bank received. A receiving bank has executed an order even if the order issued by the bank does not carry out the order received by the bank. For example, the bank may have erroneously issued an order to the wrong beneficiary, or in the wrong amount or to the wrong beneficiary's bank. In each of these cases execution has occurred but the execution is erroneous. Erroneous execution is covered in Section 4A-303.

2. "Execution date" refers to the time a payment order should be executed rather than the day it is actually executed. Normally the sender will not specify an execution date, but most payment orders are meant to be executed immediately. Thus, the execution date is normally the day the order is received by the receiving bank. It is common for the sender to specify a "payment date" which is defined in Section 4A-401 as "the day on which the amount of the order is payable to the beneficiary by the beneficiary's bank." Except for automated clearing house transfers, if a funds transfer is entirely within the United States and the payment is to be carried out electronically, the execution date is the payment date unless the order is received after the payment date. If the payment is to be carried out through an automated clearing house, execution may occur before the payment date. In an ACH transfer the beneficiary is usually paid one or two days after issue of the originator's payment order. The execution date is determined by the stated payment date and is a date before the payment date on which execution is reasonably necessary to allow payment on the payment date. A funds transfer system rule could also determine the execution date of orders received by the receiving bank if both the sender and the receiving bank are participants in the funds transfer system. The execution date can be determined by the payment order itself or by separate instructions of the sender or an agreement of the sender and the receiving bank. The second sentence of subsection (b) must be read in the light of Section 4A-106 which states that if a payment order is received after the cut-off time of the receiving bank it may be treated by the bank as received at the opening of the next funds transfer business day.

3. Execution on the execution date is timely, but the order can be executed before or after the execution date. Section 4A-209(d) and Section 4A-402(c) state the consequences of early execution and Section 4A-305(a) states the consequences of late execution.

Section 4A-302. Obligations of Receiving Bank in Execution of Payment Order

(a) Except as provided in subsections (b) through (d), if the receiving bank accepts a payment order pursuant to Section 4A-209 (a), the bank has the following obligations in executing the order:

(1) The receiving bank is obliged to issue, on the execution date, a payment order complying with the sender's order and to follow the sender's instructions concerning (i) any intermediary bank or funds-transfer system to be used in carrying out the funds transfer, or (ii) the means by which payment orders are to be transmitted in the funds transfer. If the originator's bank issues a payment order to an intermediary bank, the originator's bank is obliged to instruct the intermediary bank according to the instruction of the originator. An intermediary bank in the funds transfer is similarly bound by an instruction given to it by the sender of the payment order it accepts.

(2) If the sender's instruction states that the funds transfer is to be carried out telephonically or by wire transfer or otherwise indicates that the funds transfer is to be carried out by the most expeditious means, the receiving bank is obliged to transmit its payment order by the most expeditious available means, and to instruct any intermediary bank accordingly. If a sender's instruction states a payment date, the receiving bank is obliged to transmit its payment order at a time and by means reasonably necessary to allow payment to the beneficiary on the payment date or as soon thereafter as is feasible.

(b) Unless otherwise instructed, a receiving bank executing a payment order may (i) use any funds-transfer system if use of that system is reasonable in the circumstances, and (ii) issue a payment order to the beneficiary's bank or to an intermediary bank through which a payment order conforming to the sender's order can expeditiously be issued to the beneficiary's bank if the receiving bank exercises ordinary care in the selection of the intermediary bank. A receiving bank is not required to follow an instruction of the sender designating a funds-transfer system to be used in carrying out the funds transfer if the receiving bank, in good faith, determines that it is not feasible to follow the instruction or that following the instruction would unduly delay completion of the funds transfer.

(c) Unless subsection (a)(2) applies or the receiving bank is otherwise instructed, the bank may execute a payment order by transmitting its payment order by first class mail or by any means reasonable in the circumstances. If the receiving bank is instructed to execute the sender's order by transmitting its payment order by a particular means, the receiving bank may issue its payment order by the means stated or by any means as expeditious as the means stated.

(d) Unless instructed by the sender, (i) the receiving bank may not obtain payment of its charges for services and expenses in connection with the execution of the sender's order by issuing a payment order in an amount equal to the amount of the sender's order less the amount of the charges, and (ii) may not instruct a subsequent receiving bank to obtain payment of its charges in the same manner.

Official Comment

1. In the absence of agreement, the receiving bank is not obliged to execute an order of the sender. Section 4A-212. Section 4A-302 states the manner in which the receiving bank may execute the sender's order if execution occurs. Subsection (a)(1) states the residual rule. The payment order issued by the receiving bank must comply with the sender's order and, unless some other rule is stated in the section, the receiving bank is obliged to follow any instruction of the sender concerning which funds transfer system is to be used, which intermediary banks are to be used, and what means of transmission is to be used. The instruction of the sender may be incorporated in the payment order itself or may be given separately. For example, there may be a master agreement between the sender and receiving bank containing instructions governing payment orders to be issued from time to time by the sender to the receiving bank. In most funds transfers, speed is a paramount consideration. A sender that wants assurance that the funds transfer will be expeditiously completed can specify the means to be used. The receiving bank can follow the instructions literally or it can use an equivalent means. For example, if the sender instructs the receiving bank to transmit by telex, the receiving bank could use a telephone instead. Subsection (c). In most cases the sender will not specify a particular means but will use a general term such as "by wire" or "wire transfer" or "as soon as possible." These words signify that the sender wants a same-day transfer. In these cases the receiving bank is required to use a telephonic or electronic communication to transmit its order and is also required to instruct any intermediary bank to which it issues its order to transmit by similar means. Subsection (a)(2). In other cases, such as an automated clearing house transfer, a same-day transfer is not contemplated. Normally the sender's instruction or the context in which the payment order is received makes clear the type of funds transfer that is appropriate. If the sender states a payment date with respect to the payment order, the receiving bank is obliged to execute the order at a time and in a manner to meet the payment date if that is feasible. Subsection (a)(2). This provision would apply to many ACH transfers made to pay recurring debts of the sender. In other cases, involving relatively small amounts, time may not be an important factor and cost may be a more important element. Fast means, such as telephone or electronic transmission, are more expensive than slow means such as mailing. Subsection (c) states that in the absence of instructions the receiving bank is given discretion to decide. It may issue its payment order by first class mail or by any means reasonable in the circumstances. Section 4A-305 states the liability of a receiving bank for breach of the obligations stated in Section 4A-302.

2. Subsection (b) concerns the choice of intermediary banks to be used in completing the funds transfer, and the funds transfer system to be used. If the receiving bank is not instructed about the matter, it can issue an order directly to the beneficiary's bank or can issue an order to an intermediary bank. The receiving bank also has discretion concerning use of a funds transfer system. In some cases it may be reasonable to use either an automated clearing house system or a wire transfer system such as Fedwire or CHIPS. Normally, the receiving bank will follow the instruction of the sender in these matters, but in some cases it may be prudent for the bank not to follow instructions. The sender may have designated a funds transfer system to be used in carrying out the funds transfer, but it may not be feasible to use the designated system because of some impediment such as a computer breakdown which prevents prompt execution of the order. The receiving bank is permitted to use an alternate means of transmittal in a good faith effort to execute the order expeditiously. The same leeway is not given to the receiving bank if the sender designates an intermediary bank through which the funds transfer is to be routed. The sender's designation of that intermediary bank may mean that the beneficiary's bank is expecting to obtain a credit from that intermediary bank and may have relied on that anticipated credit. If the receiving bank uses another intermediary bank the expectations of the beneficiary's bank may not be realized. The receiving bank could choose to route the transfer to another intermediary bank and then to the designated intermediary bank if there were some reason such as a lack of a correspondent-bank relationship or a bilateral credit limitation, but the designated intermediary bank cannot be circumvented. To do so violates the sender's instructions.

3. The normal rule, under subsection (a)(1), is that the receiving bank, in executing a payment order, is required to issue a payment order that complies as to amount with that of the sender's order. In most cases the receiving bank issues an order equal to the amount of the sender's order and makes a separate charge for services and expenses in executing the sender's order. In some cases, particularly if it is an intermediary bank that is executing an order, charges are collected by deducting them from the amount of the payment order issued by the executing bank. If that is done, the amount of the payment order accepted by the beneficiary's bank will be slightly less than the amount of the originator's payment order. For example, Originator, in order to pay an obligation of $1,000,000 owed to Beneficiary, issues a payment order to Originator's Bank to pay $1,000,000 to the account of Beneficiary in Beneficiary's Bank. Originator's Bank issues a payment order to Intermediary Bank for $1,000,000 and debits Originator's account for $1,000,010. The extra $10 is the fee of Originator's Bank. Intermediary Bank executes the payment order of Originator's Bank by issuing a payment order to Beneficiary's Bank for $999,990, but under § 4A-402(c) is entitled to receive $1,000,000 from Originator's Bank. The $10 difference is the fee of Intermediary Bank. Beneficiary's Bank credits Beneficiary's account for $999,990. When Beneficiary's Bank accepts the payment order of Intermediary Bank the result is a payment of $999,990 from Originator to Beneficiary. Section 4A-406(a). If that payment discharges the $1,000,000 debt, the effect is that Beneficiary has paid the charges of Intermediary Bank and Originator has paid the charges of Originator's Bank. Subsection (d) of Section 4A-302 allows Intermediary Bank to collect its charges by deducting them from the amount of the payment order, but only if instructed to do so by Originator's Bank. Originator's Bank is not authorized to give that instruction to Intermediary Bank unless Originator authorized the instruction. Thus, Originator can control how the charges of Originator's Bank and Intermediary Bank are to be paid. Subsection (d) does not apply to charges of Beneficiary's Bank to Beneficiary.

In the case discussed in the preceding paragraph the $10 charge is trivial in relation to the amount of the payment and it may not be important to Beneficiary how the charge is paid. But it may be very important if the $1,000,000 obligation represented the price of exercising a right such as an option favorable to Originator and unfavorable to Beneficiary. Beneficiary might well argue that it was entitled to receive $1,000,000. If the option was exercised shortly before its expiration date, the result could be loss of the option benefit because the required payment of $1,000,000 was not made before the option expired. Section 4A-406(c) allows Originator to preserve the option benefit. The amount received by Beneficiary is deemed to be $1,000,000 unless Beneficiary demands the $10 and Originator does not pay it.

Section 4A-303. Erroneous Execution of Payment Order

(a) A receiving bank that (i) executes the payment order of the sender by issuing a payment order in an amount greater than the amount of the sender's order, or (ii) issues a payment order in execution of the sender's order and then issues a duplicate order, is entitled to payment of the amount of the sender's order under Section 4A-402(c) if that subsection is otherwise satisfied. The bank is entitled to recover from the beneficiary of the erroneous order the excess payment received to the extent allowed by the law governing mistake and restitution.

(b) A receiving bank that executes the payment order of the sender by issuing a payment order in an amount less than the amount of the sender's order is entitled to payment of the amount of the sender's order under Section 4A-402(c) if (i) that subsection is otherwise satisfied and (ii) the bank corrects its mistake by issuing an additional payment order for the benefit of the beneficiary of the sender's order. If the error is not corrected, the issuer of the erroneous order is entitled to receive or retain payment from the sender of the order it accepted only to the extent of the amount of the erroneous order. This subsection does not apply if the receiving bank executes the sender's payment order by issuing a payment order in an amount less than the amount of the sender's order for the purpose of obtaining payment of its charges for services and expenses pursuant to instruction of the sender.

(c) If a receiving bank executes the payment order of the sender by issuing a payment order to a beneficiary different from the beneficiary of the sender's order and the funds transfer is completed on the basis of that error, the sender of the payment order that was erroneously executed and all previous senders in the funds transfer are not obliged to pay the payment orders they issued. The issuer of the erroneous order is entitled to recover from the beneficiary of the order the payment received to the extent allowed by the law governing mistake and restitution.

Official Comment

1. Section 4A-303 states the effect of erroneous execution of a payment order by the receiving bank. Under Section 4A-402(c) the sender of a payment order is obliged to pay the amount of the order to the receiving bank if the bank executes the order, but the obligation to pay is excused if the beneficiary's bank does not accept a payment order instructing payment to the beneficiary of the sender's order. If erroneous execution of the sender's order causes the wrong beneficiary to be paid, the sender is not required to pay. If erroneous execution causes the wrong amount to be paid the sender is not obliged to pay the receiving bank an amount in excess of the amount of the sender's order. Section 4A-303 takes precedence over Section 4A-402(c) and states the liability of the sender and the rights of the receiving bank in various cases of erroneous execution.

2. Subsections (a) and (b) deal with cases in which the receiving bank executes by issuing a payment order in the wrong amount. If Originator ordered Originator's Bank to pay $1,000,000 to the account of Beneficiary in Beneficiary's Bank, but Originator's Bank erroneously instructed Beneficiary's Bank to pay $2,000,000 to Beneficiary's account, subsection (a) applies. If Beneficiary's Bank accepts the order of Originator's Bank, Beneficiary's Bank is entitled to receive $2,000,000 from Originator's Bank, but Originator's Bank is entitled to receive only $1,000,000 from Originator. Originator's Bank is entitled to recover the overpayment from Beneficiary to the extent allowed by the law governing mistake and restitution. Originator's Bank would normally have a right to recover the overpayment from Beneficiary, but in unusual cases the law of restitution might allow Beneficiary to keep all or part of the overpayment. For example, if Originator owed $2,000,000 to Beneficiary and Beneficiary received the extra

$1,000,000 in good faith in discharge of the debt, Beneficiary may be allowed to keep it. In this case Originator's Bank has paid an obligation of Originator and under the law of restitution, which applies through Section 1103, Originator's Bank would be subrogated to Beneficiary's rights against Originator on the obligation paid by Originator's Bank.

If Originator's Bank erroneously executed Originator's order by instructing Beneficiary's Bank to pay less than $1,000,000, subsection (b) applies. If Originator's Bank corrects its error by issuing another payment order to Beneficiary's Bank that results in payment of $1,000,000 to Beneficiary, Originator's Bank is entitled to payment of $1,000,000 from Originator. If the mistake is not corrected, Originator's Bank is entitled to payment from Originator only in the amount of the order issued by Originator's Bank.

3. Subsection (a) also applies to duplicate payment orders. Assume Originator's Bank properly executes Originator's $1,000,000 payment order and then by mistake issues a second $1,000,000 payment order in execution of Originator's order. If Beneficiary's Bank accepts both orders issued by Originator's Bank, Beneficiary's Bank is entitled to receive $2,000,000 from Originator's Bank but Originator's Bank is entitled to receive only $1,000,000 from Originator. The remedy of Originator's Bank is the same as that of a receiving bank that executes by issuing an order in an amount greater than the sender's order. It may recover the overpayment from Beneficiary to the extent allowed by the law governing mistake and restitution and in a proper case as stated in Comment 2 may have subrogation rights if it is not entitled to recover from Beneficiary.

4. Suppose Originator instructs Originator's Bank to pay $1,000,000 to Account #12345 in Beneficiary's Bank. Originator's Bank erroneously instructs Beneficiary's Bank to pay $1,0000,000 to Account #12346 and Beneficiary's Bank accepted. Subsection (c) covers this case. Originator is not obliged to pay its payment order, but Originator's Bank is required to pay $1,000,000 to Beneficiary's Bank. The remedy of Originator's Bank is to recover $1,000,000 from the holder of Account #12346 that received payment by mistake. Recovery based on the law of mistake and restitution is described in Comment 2.

Section 4A-304. Duty of Sender to Report Erroneously Executed Payment Order

If the sender of a payment order that is erroneously executed as stated in Section 4A-303 receives notification from the receiving bank that the order was executed or that the sender's account was debited with respect to the order, the sender has a duty to exercise ordinary care to determine, on the basis of information available to the sender, that the order was erroneously executed and to notify the bank of the relevant facts within a reasonable time not exceeding 90 days after the notification from the bank was received by the sender. If the sender fails to perform that duty, the bank is not obliged to pay interest on any amount refundable to the sender under Section 4A-402(d) for the period before the bank learns of the execution error. The bank is not entitled to any recovery from the sender on account of a failure by the sender to perform the duty stated in this section.

Official Comment

This section is identical in effect to Section 4A-204 which applies to unauthorized orders issued in the name of a customer of the receiving bank. The rationale is stated in Comment 2 to Section 4A-204.

Section 4A-305. Liability for Late or Improper Execution or Failure to Execute Payment Order

(a) If a funds transfer is completed but execution of a payment order by the receiving bank in breach of Section 4A-302 results in delay in payment to the beneficiary, the bank is obliged to pay interest to either the originator or the beneficiary of the funds transfer for the period of delay caused by the improper execution. Except as provided in subsection (c), additional damages are not recoverable.

(b) If execution of a payment order by a receiving bank in breach of Section 4A-302 results in (i) noncompletion of the funds transfer, (ii) failure to use an intermediary bank designated by the originator, or (iii) issuance of a payment order that does not comply with the terms of the payment order of the originator, the bank is liable to the originator for its expenses in the funds transfer and for incidental expenses and interest losses, to the extent not covered by subsection (a), resulting from the improper execution. Except as provided in subsection (c), additional damages are not recoverable.

(c) In addition to the amounts payable under subsections (a) and (b), damages, including consequential damages, are recoverable to the extent provided in an express agreement of the receiving bank, evidenced by a record.

(d) If a receiving bank fails to execute a payment order it was obliged by express agreement to execute, the receiving bank is liable to the sender for its expenses in the transaction and for incidental expenses and interest losses resulting from the failure to execute. Additional damages, including consequential damages, are recoverable to the extent provided in an express agreement of the receiving bank, evidenced by a record, but are not otherwise recoverable.

(e) Reasonable attorney's fees are recoverable if demand for compensation under subsection (a) or (b) is made and refused before an action is brought on the claim. If a claim is made for breach of an agreement under subsection (d) and the agreement does not provide for damages, reasonable attorney's fees are recoverable if demand for compensation under subsection (d) is made and refused before an action is brought on the claim.

(f) Except as stated in this section, the liability of a receiving bank under subsections (a) and (b) may not be varied by agreement.

Official Comment

1. Subsection (a) covers cases of delay in completion of a funds transfer resulting from an execution by a receiving bank in breach of Section 4A-302(a). The receiving bank is obliged to pay interest on the amount of the order for the period of the delay. The rate of interest is stated in Section 4A-506. With respect to wire transfers (other than ACH transactions) within the United States, the expectation is that the funds transfer will be completed the same day. In those cases, the originator can reasonably expect that the originator's account will be debited on the same day as the beneficiary's account is credited. If the funds transfer is delayed, compensation can be paid either to the originator or to the beneficiary. The normal practice is to compensate the beneficiary's bank to allow that bank to compensate the beneficiary by back-valuing the payment by the number of days of delay. Thus, the beneficiary is in the same position that it would have been in if the funds transfer had been completed on the same day. Assume on Day 1, Originator's Bank issues its payment order to Intermediary Bank which is received on that day. Intermediary Bank does not execute that order until Day 2 when it issues an order to Beneficiary's Bank which is accepted on that day. Intermediary Bank complies with subsection (a) by paying one day's interest to Beneficiary's Bank for the account of Beneficiary.

2. Subsection (b) applies to cases of breach of Section 4A-302 involving more than mere delay. In those cases the bank is liable for damages for improper execution but they are limited to compensation for interest losses and incidental expenses of the sender resulting from the breach, the expenses of the sender in the funds transfer and attorney's fees. This subsection reflects the judgment that imposition of consequential damages on a bank for commission of an error is not justified.

The leading common law case on the subject of consequential damages is *Evra Corp. v. Swiss Bank Corp.*, 673 F.2d 951 (7th Cir. 1982), in which Swiss Bank, an intermediary bank, failed to execute a payment order. Because the beneficiary did not receive timely payment the originator lost a valuable ship charter. The lower court awarded the originator $2.1 million for lost profits even though the amount of the payment order was only $27,000. The Seventh Circuit reversed, in part on the basis of the common law rule of *Hadley v. Baxendale* that consequential damages may not be awarded unless the defendant is put on notice of the special circumstances giving rise to them. Swiss Bank may have known that the originator was paying the shipowner for the hire of a vessel but did not know that a favorable charter would be lost if the payment was delayed. "Electronic payments are not so unusual as to automatically place a bank on notice of extraordinary consequences if such a transfer goes awry. Swiss Bank did not have enough information to infer that if it lost a $27,000 payment order it would face liability in excess of $2 million." 673 F.2d at 956.

If *Evra* means that consequential damages can be imposed if the culpable bank has notice of particular circumstances giving rise to the damages, it does not provide an acceptable solution to the problem of bank liability for consequential damages. In the typical case transmission of the payment order is made electronically. Personnel of the receiving bank that process payment orders are not the appropriate people to evaluate the risk of liability for consequential damages in relation to the price charged for the wire transfer service. Even if notice is received by higher level management personnel who could make an appropriate decision whether the risk is justified by the price, liability based on notice would require evaluation of payment orders on an individual basis. This kind of evaluation is inconsistent with the high-speed, low-price, mechanical nature of the processing system that characterizes wire transfers. Moreover, in *Evra* the culpable bank was an intermediary bank with which the originator did not deal. Notice to the originator's bank would not bind the intermediary bank, and it seems impractical for the originator's bank to convey notice of this kind to intermediary banks in the funds transfer. The success of the wholesale wire transfer industry has largely been based on its ability to effect payment at low cost and great speed. Both of these essential aspects of the modern wire transfer system would be adversely affected by a rule that imposed on banks liability for consequential damages. A banking industry amicus brief in *Evra* stated: "Whether banks can continue to make EFT services available on a widespread basis, by charging reasonable rates, depends on whether they can do so without incurring unlimited consequential risks. Certainly, no bank would handle for $3.25 a transaction entailing potential liability in the millions of dollars."

As the court in *Evra* also noted, the originator of the funds transfer is in the best position to evaluate the risk that a funds transfer will not be made on time and to manage that risk by issuing a payment order in time to allow monitoring of the transaction. The originator, by asking the beneficiary, can quickly determine if the funds transfer has been completed. If the originator has sent the payment order at a time that allows a reasonable margin for correcting error, no loss is likely to result if the transaction is monitored. The other published cases on this issue reach the *Evra* result. *Central Coordinates, Inc. v. Morgan Guaranty Trust Co.*, 40 U.C.C. Rep. Serv. 1340 (N.Y. Sup. Ct. 1985), and *Gatoil (U.S.A.), Inc. v. Forest Hill State Bank*, 1 U.C.C. Rep. Serv. 2d 171 (D. Md. 1986).

Subsection (c) allows the measure of damages in subsection (b) to be increased by an express agreement of the receiving bank, evidenced by a record. An originator's bank might be willing to assume additional responsibilities and incur additional liability in exchange for a higher fee.

3. Subsection (d) governs cases in which a receiving bank has obligated itself by express agreement to accept payment orders of a sender. In the absence of such an agreement there is no obligation by a receiving bank to accept a payment order. Section 4A-212. The measure of damages for breach of an agreement to accept a payment order is the same as that stated in subsection (b). As in the case of subsection (b), additional damages, including consequential damages, may be recovered to the extent stated in an express agreement of the receiving bank, evidenced by a record.

4. Reasonable attorney's fees are recoverable only in cases in which damages are limited to statutory damages stated in subsection (a), (b) and (d). If additional damages are recoverable because provided for by an express agreement, evidenced by a record, attorney's fees are not recoverable. The rationale is that there is no need for statutory attorney's fees in the latter case, because the parties have agreed to a measure of damages which may or may not provide for attorney's fees.

5. The effect of subsection (f) is to prevent reduction of a receiving bank's liability under Section 4A-305.

6. In furtherance of medium neutrality, references to a "written" agreement have been changed to refer to an agreement "evidenced by a record."

PART 4. PAYMENT

Section 4A-401. Payment Date

"Payment date" of a payment order means the day on which the amount of the order is payable to the beneficiary by the beneficiary's bank. The payment date may be determined by instruction of the sender but cannot be earlier than the day the order is received by the beneficiary's bank and, unless otherwise determined, is the day the order is received by the beneficiary's bank.

Official Comment

"Payment date" refers to the day the beneficiary's bank is to pay the beneficiary. The payment date may be expressed in various ways so long as it indicates the day the beneficiary is to receive payment. For example, in ACH transfers the payment date is the equivalent of "settlement date" or "effective date." Payment date applies to the payment order issued to the beneficiary's bank, but a payment order issued to a receiving bank other than the beneficiary's bank may also state a date for payment to the beneficiary. In the latter case, the statement of a payment date is to instruct the receiving bank concerning time of execution of the sender's order. Section 4A-301(b).

Section 4A-402. Obligation of Sender to Pay Receiving Bank

(a) This section is subject to Sections 4A-205 and 4A-207.

(b) With respect to a payment order issued to the beneficiary's bank, acceptance of the order by the bank obliges the sender to pay the bank the amount of the order, but payment is not due until the payment date of the order.

(c) This subsection is subject to subsection (e) and to Section 4A-303. With respect to a payment order issued to a receiving bank other than the beneficiary's bank, acceptance of the order by the receiving bank obliges the sender to pay the bank the amount of the sender's order. Payment by the sender is not due until the execution date of the sender's order. The obligation of that sender to pay its payment order is excused if the funds transfer is not completed by acceptance by the beneficiary's bank of a payment order instructing payment to the beneficiary of that sender's payment order.

(d) If the sender of a payment order pays the order and was not obliged to pay all or part of the amount paid, the bank receiving payment is obliged to refund payment to the extent the sender was not obliged to pay. Except as provided in Sections 4A-204 and 4A-304, interest is payable on the refundable amount from the date of payment.

(e) If a funds transfer is not completed as stated in subsection (c) and an intermediary bank is obliged to refund payment as stated in subsection (d) but is unable to do so because not permitted by applicable law or because the bank suspends payments, a sender in the funds transfer that executed a payment order in compliance with an instruction, as stated in Section 4A-302(a)(1), to route the funds transfer through that intermediary bank is entitled to receive or retain payment from the sender of the payment order that it accepted. The first sender in the funds transfer that issued an instruction requiring routing through that intermediary bank is subrogated to the right of the bank that paid the intermediary bank to refund as stated in subsection (d).

(f) The right of the sender of a payment order to be excused from the obligation to pay the order as stated in subsection (c) or to receive refund under subsection (d) may not be varied by agreement.

Official Comment

1. Subsection (b) states that the sender of a payment order to the beneficiary's bank must pay the order when the beneficiary's bank accepts the order. At that point the beneficiary's bank is obliged to pay the beneficiary. Section 4A-404(a). The last clause of subsection (b) covers a case of premature acceptance by the beneficiary's bank. In some funds transfers, notably automated clearing house transfers, a beneficiary's bank may receive a payment order with a payment date after the day the order is received. The beneficiary's bank might accept the order before the payment date by notifying the beneficiary of receipt of the order. Although the acceptance obliges the beneficiary's bank to pay the beneficiary, payment is not due until the payment date. The last clause of subsection (b) is consistent with that result. The beneficiary's bank is also not entitled to payment from the sender until the payment date.

2. Assume that Originator instructs Bank A to order immediate payment to the account of Beneficiary in Bank B. Execution of Originator's payment order by Bank A is acceptance under Section 4A-209(a). Under the second sentence of Section 4A-402(c) the acceptance creates an obligation of Originator to pay Bank A the amount of the order. The last clause of that sentence deals with attempted funds transfers that are not completed. In that event the obligation of the sender to pay its payment order is excused. Originator makes payment to Beneficiary when Bank B, the beneficiary's bank, accepts a payment order for the benefit of Beneficiary. Section 4A-406(a). If that acceptance by Bank B does not occur, the funds transfer has miscarried because Originator has not paid Beneficiary. Originator doesn't have to pay its payment order, and if it has already paid it is entitled to refund of the payment with interest. The rate of interest is stated in Section 4A-506. This "money-back guarantee" is an important protection of Originator. Originator is assured that it will not lose its money if something goes wrong in the transfer. For example, risk of loss resulting from payment to the wrong beneficiary is borne by some bank, not by Originator. The most likely reason for noncompletion is a failure to execute or an erroneous execution of a payment order by Bank A or an intermediary bank. Bank A may have issued its payment order to the wrong bank or it may have identified the wrong beneficiary in its order. The money-back guarantee is particularly important to Originator if noncompletion of the funds transfer is due to the fault of an intermediary bank rather than Bank A. In that case Bank A must refund payment to Originator, and Bank A has the burden of obtaining refund from the intermediary bank that it paid.

Subsection (c) can result in loss if an intermediary bank suspends payments. Suppose Originator instructs Bank A to pay to Beneficiary's account in Bank B and to use Bank C as an intermediary bank. Bank A executes Originator's order by issuing a payment order to Bank C. Bank A pays Bank C. Bank C fails to execute the order of Bank A and suspends payments. Under subsections (c) and (d), Originator is not obliged to pay Bank A and is entitled to refund from Bank A of any payment that it may have made. Bank A is entitled to a refund from Bank C, but Bank C is insolvent. Subsection (e) deals with this case. Bank A was required to issue its payment order to Bank C because Bank C was designated as an intermediary bank by Originator. Section 4A-302(a)(1). In this case Originator takes the risk of insolvency of Bank C. Under subsection (e), Bank A is entitled to payment from Originator and Originator is subrogated to the right of Bank A under subsection (d) to refund of payment from Bank C.

3. A payment order is not like a negotiable instrument on which the drawer or maker has liability. Acceptance of the order by the receiving bank creates an obligation of the sender to pay the receiving bank the amount of the order. That is the extent of the sender's liability to the receiving bank and no other person has any rights against the sender with respect to the sender's order.

Section 4A-403. Payment by Sender to Receiving Bank

(a) Payment of the sender's obligation under Section 4A-402 to pay the receiving bank occurs as follows:

(1) If the sender is a bank, payment occurs when the receiving bank receives final settlement of the obligation through a Federal Reserve Bank or through a funds-transfer system.

(2) If the sender is a bank and the sender (i) credited an account of the receiving bank with the sender, or (ii) caused an account of the receiving bank in another bank to be credited, payment occurs when the credit is withdrawn or, if not withdrawn, at midnight of the day on which the credit is withdrawable and the receiving bank learns of that fact.

(3) If the receiving bank debits an account of the sender with the receiving bank, payment occurs when the debit is made to the extent the debit is covered by a withdrawable credit balance in the account.

(b) If the sender and receiving bank are members of a funds-transfer system that nets obligations multilaterally among participants, the receiving bank receives final settlement when settlement is complete in accordance with the rules of the system. The obligation of the sender to pay the amount of a payment order transmitted through the funds-transfer system may be satisfied, to the extent permitted by the rules of the system, by setting off and applying against the sender's obligation the right of the sender to receive payment from the receiving bank of the amount of any other payment order transmitted to the sender by the receiving bank through the funds-transfer system. The aggregate balance of obligations owed by each sender to each receiving bank in the funds-transfer system may be satisfied, to the extent permitted by the rules of the system, by setting off and applying against that balance the aggregate balance of obligations owed to the sender by other members of the system. The aggregate balance is determined after the right of setoff stated in the second sentence of this subsection has been exercised.

(c) If two banks transmit payment orders to each other under an agreement that settlement of the obligations of each bank to the other under Section 4A-402 will be made at the end of the day or other period, the total amount owed with respect to all orders transmitted by one bank shall be set off against the total amount owed with respect to all orders transmitted by the other bank. To the extent of the setoff, each bank has made payment to the other.

(d) In a case not covered by subsection (a), the time when payment of the sender's obligation under Section 4A-402(b) or 4A-402(c) occurs is governed by applicable principles of law that determine when an obligation is satisfied.

Official Comment

1. This section defines when a sender pays the obligation stated in Section 4A-402. If a group of two or more banks engage in funds transfers with each other, the participating banks will sometimes be senders and sometimes receiving banks. With respect to payment orders other than Fedwires, the amounts of the various payment orders may be credited and debited to accounts of one bank with another or to a clearing house account of each bank and amounts owed and amounts due are netted. Settlement is made through a Federal Reserve Bank by charges to the Federal Reserve accounts of the net debtor banks and credits to the Federal Reserve accounts of the net creditor banks. In the case of Fedwires the sender's obligation is settled by a debit to the Federal Reserve account of the sender and a credit to the Federal Reserve account of the receiving bank at the time the receiving bank receives the payment order. Both of these cases are covered by subsection (a)(1). When the Federal Reserve settlement becomes final the obligation of the sender under Section 4A-402 is paid.

2. In some cases a bank does not settle an obligation owed to another bank through a Federal Reserve Bank. This is the case if one of the banks is a foreign bank without access to the Federal Reserve payment system. In this kind of case, payment is usually made by credits or debits to accounts of the two banks with each other or to accounts of the two banks in a third bank. Suppose Bank B has an account in Bank A. Bank A advises Bank B that its account in Bank A has been credited $1,000,000 and that the credit is immediately withdrawable. Bank A also instructs Bank B to pay $1,000,000 to the account of Beneficiary in Bank B. This case is covered by subsection (a)(2). Bank B may want to immediately withdraw this credit. For example, it might do so by instructing Bank A to debit the account and pay some third party. Payment by Bank A to Bank B of Bank A's payment order occurs when the withdrawal is made. Suppose Bank B does not withdraw the credit. Since Bank B is the beneficiary's bank, one of the effects of receipt of payment by Bank B is that acceptance of Bank A's payment order automatically occurs at the time of payment. Section 4A-209(b)(2). Acceptance means that Bank B is obliged to pay $1,000,000 to Beneficiary. Section 4A-404(a). Subsection (a)(2) of Section 4A-403 states that payment does not occur until midnight if the credit is not withdrawn. This allows Bank B an opportunity to reject the order if it does not have time to withdraw the credit to its account and it is not willing to incur the liability to Beneficiary before it has use of the funds represented by the credit.

3. Subsection (a)(3) applies to a case in which the sender (bank or nonbank) has a funded account in the receiving bank. If Sender has an account in Bank and issues a payment order to Bank, Bank can obtain payment from Sender by debiting the account of Sender, which pays its Section 4A-402 obligation to Bank when the debit is made.

4. Subsection (b) deals with multilateral settlements made through a funds transfer system and is based on the CHIPS settlement system. In a funds transfer system such as CHIPS, which allows the various banks that transmit payment orders over the system to settle obligations at the end of each day, settlement is not based on individual payment orders. Each bank using the system engages in funds transfers with many other banks using the system. Settlement for any participant is based on the net credit or debit position of that participant with all other banks using the system. Subsection (b) is designed to make clear that the obligations of any sender are paid when the net position of that sender is settled in accordance with the rules of the funds transfer system. This provision is intended to invalidate any argument, based on common-law principles, that multilateral netting is not valid because mutuality of obligation is not present. Subsection (b) dispenses with any mutuality of obligation requirements. Subsection (c) applies to cases in which two banks send payment orders to each other during the day and settle with each other at the end of the day or at the end of some other period. It is similar to subsection (b) in that it recognizes that a sender's obligation to pay a payment order is satisfied by a setoff. The obligations of each bank as sender to the other as receiving bank are obligations of the bank itself and not as representative of customers. These two sections are important in the case of insolvency of a bank. They make clear that liability under Section 4A-402 is based on the net position of the insolvent bank after setoff.

5. Subsection (d) relates to the uncommon case in which the sender doesn't have an account relationship with the receiving bank and doesn't settle through a Federal Reserve Bank. An example would be a customer that pays over the counter for a payment order that the customer issues to the receiving bank. Payment would normally be by cash, check or bank obligation. When payment occurs is determined by law outside Article 4A.

Section 4A-404. Obligation of Beneficiary's Bank to Pay and Give Notice to Beneficiary

(a) Subject to Sections 4A-211(e), 4A-405(d), and 4A-405(e), if a beneficiary's bank accepts a payment order, the bank is obliged to pay the amount of the order to the beneficiary of the order. Payment is due on the payment date of the order, but if acceptance occurs on the payment date after the close of the funds-transfer business day of the bank, payment is due on the next funds-transfer business day. If the bank refuses to pay after demand by the beneficiary and receipt of notice of particular circumstances that will give rise to consequential damages as a result of nonpayment, the beneficiary may recover damages resulting from the refusal to pay to the extent the bank had notice of the damages, unless the bank proves that it did not pay because of a reasonable doubt concerning the right of the beneficiary to payment.

(b) If a payment order accepted by the beneficiary's bank instructs payment to an account of the beneficiary, the bank is obliged to notify the beneficiary of receipt of the order before midnight of the next funds-transfer business day following the payment date. If the payment order does not instruct payment to an account of the beneficiary, the bank is required to notify the beneficiary only if notice is required by the order. Notice may be given by first class mail or any other means reasonable in the circumstances. If the bank fails to give the required notice, the bank is obliged to pay interest to the beneficiary on the amount of the payment order from the day notice should have been given until the day the beneficiary learned of receipt of the payment order by the bank. No other damages are recoverable. Reasonable attorney's fees are also recoverable if demand for interest is made and refused before an action is brought on the claim.

(c) The right of a beneficiary to receive payment and damages as stated in subsection (a) may not be varied by agreement or a funds-transfer system rule. The right of a beneficiary to be notified as stated in subsection (b) may be varied by agreement of the beneficiary or by a funds-transfer system rule if the beneficiary is notified of the rule before initiation of the funds transfer.

Official Comment

1. The first sentence of subsection (a) states the time when the obligation of the beneficiary's bank arises. The second and third sentences state when the beneficiary's bank must make funds available to the beneficiary. They also state the measure of damages for failure, after demand, to comply. Since the Expedited Funds Availability Act, 12 U.S.C. 4001 et seq., also governs funds availability in a funds transfer, the second and third sentences of subsection (a) may be subject to preemption by that Act.

2. Subsection (a) provides that the beneficiary of an accepted payment order may recover consequential damages if the beneficiary's bank refuses to pay the order after demand by the beneficiary if the bank at that time had notice of the particular circumstances giving rise to the damages. Such damages are recoverable only to the extent the bank had "notice of the damages." The quoted phrase requires that the bank have notice of the general type or nature of the damages that will be suffered as a result of the refusal to pay and their general magnitude. There is no requirement that the bank have notice of the exact or even the approximate amount of the damages, but if the amount of damages is extraordinary the bank is entitled to notice of that fact. For example, in *Evra Corp. v. Swiss Bank Corp.*, 673 F.2d 951 (7th Cir. 1982), failure to complete a funds transfer of only $27,000 required to retain rights to a very favorable ship charter resulted in a claim for more than $2,000,000 of consequential damages. Since it is not reasonably foreseeable that a failure to make a relatively small payment will result in damages of this magnitude, notice is not sufficient if the beneficiary's bank has notice only that the $27,000 is necessary to retain rights on a ship charter. The bank is entitled to notice that an exceptional amount of damages will result as well. For example, there would be adequate notice if the bank had been made aware that damages of $1,000,000 or more might result.

3. Under the last clause of subsection (a) the beneficiary's bank is not liable for damages if its refusal to pay was "because of a reasonable doubt concerning the right of the beneficiary to payment." Normally there will not be any question about the right of the beneficiary to receive payment. Normally, the bank should be able to determine whether it has accepted the payment order and, if it has been accepted, the first sentence of subsection (a) states that the bank is obliged to pay. There may be uncommon cases, however, in which there is doubt whether acceptance occurred. For example, if acceptance is based on receipt of payment by the beneficiary's bank under Section 4A-403 (a)(1) or (2), there may be cases in which the bank is not certain that payment has been received. There may also be cases in which there is doubt about whether the person demanding payment is the person identified in the payment order as beneficiary of the order.

The last clause of subsection (a) does not apply to cases in which a funds transfer is being used to pay an obligation and a dispute arises between the originator and the beneficiary concerning whether the obligation is in fact owed. For example, the originator may try to prevent payment to the beneficiary by the beneficiary's bank by alleging that the beneficiary is not entitled to payment because of fraud against the originator or a breach of contract relating to the obligation. The fraud or breach of contract claim of the originator may be grounds for recovery by the originator from the beneficiary after the beneficiary is paid, but it does not affect the obligation of the beneficiary's bank to pay the beneficiary. Unless the payment order has been cancelled pursuant to Section 4A-211(c), there is no excuse for refusing to pay the beneficiary and, in a proper case, the refusal may result in consequential damages. Except in the case of a book transfer, in which the beneficiary's bank is also the originator's bank, the originator of a funds transfer cannot cancel a payment order to the beneficiary's bank, with or without the consent of that bank, because the originator is not the sender of that order. Thus, the beneficiary's bank may safely ignore any instruction by the originator to withhold payment to the beneficiary.

4. Subsection (b) states the duty of the beneficiary's bank to notify the beneficiary of receipt of the order. If acceptance occurs under Section 4A-209(b)(1) the beneficiary is normally notified. Thus, subsection (b) applies primarily to cases in which acceptance occurs under Section 4A-209(b)(2) or (3). Notice under subsection (b) is not required if the person entitled to the notice agrees or a funds transfer system rule provides that notice is not required and the beneficiary is given notice of the rule. In ACH transactions the normal practice is not to give notice to the beneficiary unless notice is requested by the beneficiary. This practice can be continued by adoption of a funds transfer system rule. Subsection (a) is not subject to variation by agreement or by a funds transfer system rule.

Section 4A-405. Payment by Beneficiary's Bank to Beneficiary

(a) If the beneficiary's bank credits an account of the beneficiary of a payment order, payment of the bank's obligation under Section 4A-404(a) occurs when and to the extent (i) the beneficiary is notified of the right to withdraw the credit, (ii) the bank lawfully applies the credit to a debt of the beneficiary, or (iii) funds with respect to the order are otherwise made available to the beneficiary by the bank.

(b) If the beneficiary's bank does not credit an account of the beneficiary of a payment order, the time when payment of the bank's obligation under Section 4A-404(a) occurs is governed by principles of law that determine when an obligation is satisfied.

(c) Except as stated in subsections (d) and (e), if the beneficiary's bank pays the beneficiary of a payment order under a condition to payment or agreement of the beneficiary giving the bank the right to recover payment from the beneficiary if the bank does not receive payment of the order, the condition to payment or agreement is not enforceable.

(d) A funds-transfer system rule may provide that payments made to beneficiaries of funds transfers made through the system are provisional until receipt of payment by the beneficiary's bank of the payment order it accepted. A beneficiary's bank that makes a payment that is provisional under the rule is entitled to refund from the beneficiary if (i) the rule requires that both the beneficiary and the originator be given notice of the provisional nature of the payment before the funds transfer is initiated, (ii) the beneficiary, the beneficiary's bank and the originator's bank agreed to be bound by the rule, and (iii) the beneficiary's bank did not receive payment of the payment order that it accepted. If the beneficiary is obliged to refund payment to the beneficiary's bank, acceptance of the payment order by the beneficiary's bank is nullified and no payment by the originator of the funds transfer to the beneficiary occurs under Section 4A-406.

(e) This subsection applies to a funds transfer that includes a payment order transmitted over a funds-transfer system that (i) nets obligations multilaterally among participants, and (ii) has in effect a loss-sharing agreement among participants for the purpose of providing funds necessary to complete settlement of the obligations of one or more participants that do not meet their settlement obligations. If the beneficiary's bank in the funds transfer accepts a payment order and the system fails to complete settlement pursuant to its rules with respect to any payment order in the funds transfer, (i) the acceptance by the beneficiary's bank is nullified and no person has any right or obligation based on the acceptance, (ii) the beneficiary's bank is entitled to recover payment from the beneficiary, (iii) no payment by the originator to the beneficiary occurs under Section 4A-406, and (iv) subject to Section 4A-402(e), each sender in the funds transfer is excused from its obligation to pay its payment order under Section 4A-402(c) because the funds transfer has not been completed.

Official Comment

1. This section defines when the beneficiary's bank pays the beneficiary and when the obligation of the beneficiary's bank under Section 4A-404 to pay the beneficiary is satisfied. In almost all cases the bank will credit an account of the beneficiary when it receives a payment order. In the typical case the beneficiary is paid when the beneficiary is given notice of the right to withdraw the credit. Subsection (a)(i). In some cases payment might be made to the beneficiary not by releasing funds to the beneficiary, but by applying the credit to a debt of the beneficiary. Subsection (a)(ii). In this case the beneficiary gets the benefit of the payment order because a debt of the beneficiary has been satisfied. The two principal cases in which payment will occur in this manner are setoff by the beneficiary's bank and payment of the proceeds of the payment order to a garnishing creditor of the beneficiary. These cases are discussed in Comment 2 to Section 4A-502.

2. If a beneficiary's bank releases funds to the beneficiary before it receives payment from the sender of the payment order, it assumes the risk that the sender may not pay the sender's order because of suspension of payments or other reason. Subsection (c). As stated in Comment 5 to Section 4A-209, the beneficiary's bank can protect itself against this risk by delaying acceptance. But if the bank accepts the order it is obliged to pay the beneficiary. If the beneficiary's bank has given the beneficiary notice of the right to withdraw a credit made to the beneficiary's account, the beneficiary has received payment from the bank. Once payment has been made to the beneficiary with respect to an obligation incurred by the bank under Section 4A-404(a), the payment cannot be recovered by the beneficiary's bank unless subsection (d) or (e) applies. Thus, a right to withdraw a credit cannot be revoked if the right to withdraw constituted payment of the bank's obligation. This principle applies even if funds were released as a "loan" (see Comment 5 to Section 4A-209), or were released subject to a condition that they would be repaid in the event the bank does not receive payment from the sender of the payment order, or the beneficiary agreed to return the payment if the bank did not receive payment from the sender.

3. Subsection (c) is subject to an exception stated in subsection (d) which is intended to apply to automated clearing house transfers. ACH transfers are made in batches. A beneficiary's bank will normally accept, at the same time and as part of a single batch, payment orders with respect to many different originator's banks. Comment 2 to Section 4A-206. The custom in ACH transactions is to release funds to the beneficiary early on the payment date even though settlement to the beneficiary's bank does not occur until later in the day. The understanding is that payments to beneficiaries are provisional until the beneficiary's bank receives settlement. This practice is similar to what happens when a depositary bank releases funds with respect to a check forwarded for collection. If the check is dishonored the bank is entitled to recover the funds from the customer. ACH transfers are widely perceived as check substitutes. Section 4A-405(d) allows the funds transfer system to adopt a rule making payments to beneficiaries provisional. If such a rule is adopted, a beneficiary's bank that releases funds to the beneficiary will be able to recover the payment if it doesn't receive payment of the payment order that it accepted. There are two requirements with respect to the funds transfer system rule. The beneficiary, the beneficiary's bank and the originator's bank must all agree to be bound by the rule and the rule must require that both the beneficiary and the originator be given notice of the provisional nature of the payment before the funds transfer is initiated. There is no requirement that the notice be given with respect to a particular funds transfer. Once notice of the provisional nature of the payment has been given, the notice is effective for all subsequent payments to or from the person to whom the notice was given. Subsection (d) provides only that the funds transfer system rule must require notice to the beneficiary and the originator. The beneficiary's bank will know what the rule requires, but it has no way of knowing whether the originator's bank complied with the rule. Subsection (d) does not require proof that the originator received notice. If the originator's bank failed to give the required notice and the originator suffered as a result, the appropriate remedy is an action by the originator against the originator's bank based on that failure. But the beneficiary's bank will not be able to get the benefit of subsection (d) unless the beneficiary had notice of the provisional nature of the payment because subsection (d) requires an agreement by the beneficiary to be bound by the rule. Implicit in an agreement to be bound by a rule that makes a payment provisional is a requirement that notice be given of what the rule provides. The notice can be part of the agreement or separately given. For example, notice can be given by providing a copy of the system's operating rules.

With respect to ACH transfers made through a Federal Reserve Bank acting as an intermediary bank, the Federal Reserve Bank is obliged under Section 4A-402(b) to pay a beneficiary's bank that accepts the payment order. Unlike Fedwire transfers, under current ACH practice a Federal Reserve Bank that processes a payment order does not obligate itself to pay if the originator's bank fails to pay the Federal Reserve Bank. It is assumed that the Federal Reserve will use its right of preemption which is recognized in Section 4A-107 to disclaim the Section 4A-402(b) obligation in ACH transactions if it decides to retain the provisional payment rule.

4. Subsection (e) is another exception to subsection (c). It refers to funds transfer systems having loss-sharing rules described in the subsection. CHIPS has proposed a rule that fits the description. Under the CHIPS loss-sharing rule the CHIPS banks will have agreed to contribute funds to allow the system to settle for payment orders sent over the system during the day in the event that one or more banks are unable to meet their settlement obligations. Subsection (e) applies only if CHIPS fails to settle despite the loss-sharing rule. Since funds under the loss-sharing rule will be instantly available to CHIPS and will be in an amount sufficient to cover any failure that can be reasonably anticipated, it is extremely unlikely that CHIPS would ever fail to settle. Thus, subsection (e) addresses an event that should never occur. If that event were to occur, all payment orders made over the system would be cancelled under the CHIPS rule. Thus, no bank would receive settlement, whether or not a failed bank was involved in a particular funds transfer. Subsection (e) provides that each funds transfer in which there is a payment order with respect to which there is a settlement failure is unwound. Acceptance by the beneficiary's bank in each funds transfer is nullified. The consequences of nullification are that the beneficiary has no right to receive or retain payment by the beneficiary's bank, no payment is made by the originator to the beneficiary and each sender in the funds transfer is, subject to Section 4A-402(e), not obliged to pay its payment order and is entitled to refund under Section 4A-402(d) if it has already paid.

Section 4A-406. Payment by Originator to Beneficiary; Discharge of Underlying Obligation

(a) Subject to Sections 4A-211(e), 4A-405(d), and 4A-405(e), the originator of a funds transfer pays the beneficiary of the originator's payment order (i) at the time a payment order for the benefit of the beneficiary is accepted by the beneficiary's bank in the funds transfer and (ii) in an amount equal to the amount of the order accepted by the beneficiary's bank, but not more than the amount of the originator's order.

(b) If payment under subsection (a) is made to satisfy an obligation, the obligation is discharged to the same extent discharge would result from payment to the beneficiary of the same amount in money, unless (i) the payment under subsection (a) was made by a means prohibited by the contract of the beneficiary with respect to the obligation, (ii) the beneficiary, within a reasonable time after receiving notice of receipt of the order by the beneficiary's bank, notified the originator of the beneficiary's refusal of the payment, (iii) funds with respect to the order were not withdrawn by the beneficiary or applied to a debt of the beneficiary, and (iv) the beneficiary would suffer a loss that could reasonably have been avoided if payment had been made by a means complying with the contract. If payment by the originator does not result in discharge under this section, the originator is subrogated to the rights of the beneficiary to receive payment from the beneficiary's bank under Section 4A-404(a).

(c) For the purpose of determining whether discharge of an obligation occurs under subsection (b), if the beneficiary's bank accepts a payment order in an amount equal to the amount of the originator's payment order less charges of one or more receiving banks in the funds transfer, payment to the beneficiary is deemed to be in the amount of the originator's order unless upon demand by the beneficiary the originator does not pay the beneficiary the amount of the deducted charges.

(d) Rights of the originator or of the beneficiary of a funds transfer under this section may be varied only by agreement of the originator and the beneficiary.

Official Comment

1. Subsection (a) states the fundamental rule of Article 4A that payment by the originator to the beneficiary is accomplished by providing to the beneficiary the obligation of the beneficiary's bank to pay. Since this obligation arises when the beneficiary's bank accepts a payment order, the originator pays the beneficiary at the time of acceptance and in the amount of the payment order accepted.

2. In a large percentage of funds transfers, the transfer is made to pay an obligation of the originator. Subsection (a) states that the beneficiary is paid by the originator when the beneficiary's bank accepts a payment order for the benefit of the beneficiary. When that happens the effect under subsection (b) is to substitute the obligation of the beneficiary's bank for the obligation of the originator. The effect is similar to that under Article 3 if a cashier's check payable to the beneficiary had been taken by the beneficiary. Normally, payment by funds transfer is sought by the beneficiary because it puts money into the hands of the beneficiary more quickly. As a practical matter the beneficiary and the originator will nearly always agree to the funds transfer in advance. Under subsection (b) acceptance by the beneficiary's bank will result in discharge of the obligation for which payment was made unless the beneficiary had made a contract with respect to the obligation which did not permit payment by the means used. Thus, if there is no contract of the beneficiary with respect to the means of payment of the obligation, acceptance by the beneficiary's bank of a payment order to the account of the beneficiary can result in discharge.

3. Suppose Beneficiary's contract stated that payment of an obligation owed by Originator was to be made by a cashier's check of Bank A. Instead, Originator paid by a funds transfer to Beneficiary's account in Bank B. Bank B accepted a payment order for the benefit of Beneficiary by immediately notifying Beneficiary that the funds were available for withdrawal. Before Beneficiary had a reasonable opportunity to withdraw the funds Bank B suspended payments. Under the unless clause of subsection (b) Beneficiary is not required to accept the payment as discharging the obligation owed by Originator to Beneficiary if Beneficiary's contract means that Beneficiary was not required to accept payment by wire transfer. Beneficiary could refuse the funds transfer as payment of the obligation and could resort to rights under the underlying contract to enforce the obligation. The rationale is that Originator cannot impose the risk of Bank B's insolvency on Beneficiary if Beneficiary had specified another means of payment that did not entail that risk. If Beneficiary is required to accept Originator's payment, Beneficiary would suffer a loss that would not have occurred if payment had been made by a cashier's check on Bank A, and Bank A has not suspended payments. In this case Originator will have to pay twice. It is obliged to pay the amount of its payment order to the bank that accepted it and has to pay the obligation it owes to Beneficiary which has not been discharged. Under the last sentence of subsection (b) Originator is subrogated to Beneficiary's right to receive payment from Bank B under Section 4A-404(a).

4. Suppose Beneficiary's contract called for payment by a Fedwire transfer to Bank B, but the payment order accepted by Bank B was not a Fedwire transfer. Before the funds were withdrawn by Beneficiary, Bank B suspended payments. The sender of the payment order to Bank B paid the amount of the order to Bank B. In this case the payment by Originator did not comply with Beneficiary's contract, but the noncompliance did not result in a loss to Beneficiary as required by subsection (b) (iv). A Fedwire transfer avoids the risk of insolvency of the sender of the payment order to Bank B, but it does not affect the risk that Bank B will suspend payments before withdrawal of the funds by Beneficiary. Thus, the unless clause of subsection (b) is not applicable and the obligation owed to Beneficiary is discharged.

5. Charges of receiving banks in a funds transfer normally are nominal in relationship to the amount being paid by the originator to the beneficiary. Wire transfers are normally agreed to in advance and the parties may agree concerning how these charges are to be divided between the parties. Subsection (c) states a rule that applies in the absence of agreement. In some funds transfers charges of banks that execute payment orders are collected by deducting the charges from the amount of the payment order issued by the bank, i.e. the bank issues a payment order that is slightly less than the amount of the payment order that is being executed. The process is described in Comment 3 to Section 4A-302. The result in such a case is that the payment order accepted by the beneficiary's bank will be slightly less than the amount of the originator's order. Subsection (c) recognizes the principle that a beneficiary is entitled to full payment of a debt paid by wire transfer as a condition to discharge. On the other hand, Subsection (c) prevents a beneficiary from denying the originator the benefit of the payment by asserting that discharge did not occur because deduction of bank charges resulted in less than full payment. The typical case is one in which the payment is made to exercise a valuable right such as an option which is unfavorable to the beneficiary. Subsection (c) allows discharge notwithstanding the deduction unless the originator fails to reimburse the beneficiary for the deducted charges after demand by the beneficiary.

PART 5. MISCELLANEOUS PROVISIONS

Section 4A-501. Variation by Agreement and Effect of Funds-Transfer System Rule

(a) Except as otherwise provided in this Article, the rights and obligations of a party to a funds transfer may be varied by agreement of the affected party.

(b) "Funds-transfer system rule" means a rule of an association of banks (i) governing transmission of payment orders by means of a funds-transfer system of the association or rights and obligations with respect to those orders, or (ii) to the extent the rule governs rights and obligations between banks that are parties to a funds transfer in which a Federal Reserve Bank, acting as an intermediary bank, sends a payment order to the beneficiary's bank. Except as otherwise provided in this Article, a funds-transfer system rule governing rights and obligations between participating banks using the system may be effective even if the rule conflicts with this Article and indirectly affects another party to the funds transfer who does not consent to the rule. A funds-transfer system rule may also govern rights and obligations of parties other than participating banks using the system to the extent stated in Sections 4A-404(c), 4A-405(d), and 4A-507(c).

Official Comment

1. This section is designed to give some flexibility to Article 4A. Funds transfer system rules govern rights and obligations between banks that use the system. They may cover a wide variety of matters such as form and content of payment orders, security procedures, cancellation rights and procedures, indemnity rights, compensation rules for delays in completion of a funds transfer, time and method of settlement, credit restrictions with respect to senders of payment orders and risk allocation with respect to suspension of payments by a participating bank. Funds transfer system rules can be very effective in supplementing the provisions of Article 4A and in filling gaps that may be present in Article 4A. To the extent they do not conflict with Article 4A there is no problem with respect to their effectiveness. In that case they merely supplement Article 4A. Section 4A-501 goes further. It states that unless the contrary is stated, funds transfer system rules can override provisions of Article 4A. Thus, rights and obligations of a sender bank and a receiving bank with respect to each other can be different from that stated in Article 4A to the extent a funds transfer system rule applies. Since funds transfer system rules are defined as those governing the relationship between participating banks, a rule can have a direct effect only on participating banks. But a rule that affects the conduct of a participating bank may indirectly affect the rights of nonparticipants such as the originator or beneficiary of a funds transfer, and such a rule can be effective even though it may affect nonparticipants without their consent. For example, a rule might prevent execution of a payment order or might allow cancellation of a payment order with the result that a funds transfer is not completed or is delayed. But a rule purporting to define rights and obligations of nonparticipants in the system would not be effective to alter Article 4A rights because the rule is not within the definition of funds transfer system rule. Rights and obligations arising under Article 4A may also be varied by agreement of the affected parties, except to the extent Article 4A otherwise provides. Rights and obligations arising under Article 4A can also be changed by Federal Reserve regulations and operating circulars of Federal Reserve Banks. Section 4A-107.

2. Subsection (b)(ii) refers to ACH transfers. Whether an ACH transfer is made through an automated clearing house of a Federal Reserve Bank or through an automated clearing house of another association of banks, the rights and obligations of the originator's bank and the beneficiary's bank are governed by uniform rules adopted by various associations of banks in various parts of the nation. With respect to transfers in which a Federal Reserve Bank acts as intermediary bank these rules may be incorporated, in whole or in part, in operating circulars of the Federal Reserve Bank. Even if not so incorporated these rules can still be binding on the association banks. If a transfer is made through a Federal Reserve Bank, the rules are effective under subsection (b)(ii). If the transfer is not made through a Federal Reserve Bank, the association rules are effective under subsection (b)(i).

Section 4A-502. Creditor Process Served on Receiving Bank; Setoff by Beneficiary's Bank

(a) As used in this section, "creditor process" means levy, attachment, garnishment, notice of lien, sequestration, or similar process issued by or on behalf of a creditor or other claimant with respect to an account.

(b) This subsection applies to creditor process with respect to an authorized account of the sender of a payment order if the creditor process is served on the receiving bank. For the purpose of determining rights with respect to the creditor process, if the receiving bank accepts the payment order the balance in the authorized account is deemed to be reduced by the amount of the payment order to the extent the bank did not otherwise receive payment of the order, unless the creditor process is served at a time and in a manner affording the bank a reasonable opportunity to act on it before the bank accepts the payment order.

(c) If a beneficiary's bank has received a payment order for payment to the beneficiary's account in the bank, the following rules apply:

(1) The bank may credit the beneficiary's account. The amount credited may be set off against an obligation owed by the beneficiary to the bank or may be applied to satisfy creditor process served on the bank with respect to the account.

(2) The bank may credit the beneficiary's account and allow withdrawal of the amount credited unless creditor process with respect to the account is served at a time and in a manner affording the bank a reasonable opportunity to act to prevent withdrawal.

(3) If creditor process with respect to the beneficiary's account has been served and the bank has had a reasonable opportunity to act on it, the bank may not reject the payment order except for a reason unrelated to the service of process.

(d) Creditor process with respect to a payment by the originator to the beneficiary pursuant to a funds transfer may be served only on the beneficiary's bank with respect to the debt owed by that bank to the beneficiary. Any other bank served with the creditor process is not obliged to act with respect to the process.

Official Comment

1. When a receiving bank accepts a payment order, the bank normally receives payment from the sender by debiting an authorized account of the sender. In accepting the sender's order the bank may be relying on a credit balance in the account. If creditor process is served on the bank with respect to the account before the bank accepts the order but the bank employee responsible for the acceptance was not aware of the creditor process at the time the acceptance occurred, it is unjust to the bank to allow the creditor process to take the credit balance on which the bank may have relied. Subsection (b) allows the bank to obtain payment from the sender's account in this case. Under that provision, the balance in the sender's account to which the creditor process applies is deemed to be reduced by the amount of the payment order unless there was sufficient time for notice of the service of creditor process to be received by personnel of the bank responsible for the acceptance.

2. Subsection (c) deals with payment orders issued to the beneficiary's bank. The bank may credit the beneficiary's account when the order is received, but under Section 4A-404(a) the bank incurs no obligation to pay the beneficiary until the order is accepted pursuant to Section 4A-209(b). Thus, before acceptance, the credit to the beneficiary's account is provisional. But under Section 4A-209(b) acceptance occurs if the beneficiary's bank pays the beneficiary pursuant to Section 4A-405(a). Under that provision, payment occurs if the credit to the beneficiary's account is applied to a debt of the beneficiary. Subsection (c)(1) allows the bank to credit the beneficiary's account with respect to a payment order and to accept the order by setting off the credit against an obligation owed to the bank or applying the credit to creditor process with respect to the account.

Suppose a beneficiary's bank receives a payment order for the benefit of a customer. Before the bank accepts the order, the bank learns that creditor process has been served on the bank with respect to the customer's account. Normally there is no reason for a beneficiary's bank to reject a payment order, but if the beneficiary's account is garnished, the bank may be faced with a difficult choice. If it rejects the order, the garnishing creditor's potential recovery of funds of the beneficiary is frustrated. It may be faced with a claim by the creditor that the rejection was a wrong to the creditor. If the bank accepts the order, the effect is to allow the creditor to seize funds of its customer, the beneficiary. Subsection (c)(3) gives the bank no choice in this case. It provides that it may not favor its customer over the creditor by rejecting the order. The beneficiary's bank may rightfully reject only if there is an independent basis for rejection.

3. Subsection (c)(2) is similar to subsection (b). Normally the beneficiary's bank will release funds to the beneficiary shortly after acceptance or it will accept by releasing funds. Since the bank is bound by a garnishment order served before funds are released to the beneficiary, the bank might suffer a loss if funds were released without knowledge that a garnishment order had been served. Subsection (c)(2) protects the bank if it did not have adequate notice of the garnishment when the funds were released.

4. A creditor may want to reach funds involved in a funds transfer. The creditor may try to do so by serving process on the originator's bank, an intermediary bank or the beneficiary's bank. The purpose of subsection (d) is to guide the creditor and the court as to the proper method of reaching the funds involved in a funds transfer. A creditor of the originator can levy on the account of the originator in the originator's bank before the funds transfer is initiated, but that levy is subject to the limitations stated in subsection (b). The creditor of the originator cannot reach any other funds because no property of the originator is being transferred. A creditor of the beneficiary cannot levy on property of the originator and until the funds transfer is completed by acceptance by the beneficiary's bank of a payment order for the benefit of the beneficiary, the beneficiary has no property interest in the funds transfer which the beneficiary's creditor can reach. A creditor of the beneficiary that wants to reach the funds to be received by the beneficiary must serve creditor process on the beneficiary's bank to reach the obligation of the beneficiary's bank to pay the beneficiary which arises upon acceptance by the beneficiary's bank under Section 4A-404(a).

5. "Creditor process" is defined in subsection (a) to cover a variety of devices by which a creditor of the holder of a bank account or a claimant to a bank account can seize the account. Procedure and nomenclature varies widely from state to state. The term used in Section 4A-502 is a generic term.

Section 4A-503. Injunction or Restraining Order with Respect to Funds Transfer

For proper cause and in compliance with applicable law, a court may restrain (i) a person from issuing a payment order to initiate a funds transfer, (ii) an originator's bank from executing the payment order of the originator, or (iii) the beneficiary's bank from releasing funds to the beneficiary or the beneficiary from withdrawing the funds. A court may not otherwise restrain a person from issuing a payment order, paying or receiving payment of a payment order, or otherwise acting with respect to a funds transfer.

Official Comment

This section is related to Section 4A-502(d) and to Comment 4 to Section 4A-502. It is designed to prevent interruption of a funds transfer after it has been set in motion. The initiation of a funds transfer can be prevented by enjoining the originator or the originator's bank from issuing a payment order. After the funds transfer is completed by acceptance of a payment order by the beneficiary's bank, that bank can be enjoined from releasing funds to the beneficiary or the beneficiary can be enjoined from withdrawing the funds. No other injunction is permitted. In particular, intermediary banks are protected, and injunctions against the originator and the originator's bank are limited to issuance of a payment order. Except for the beneficiary's bank, nobody can be enjoined from paying a payment order, and no receiving bank can be enjoined from receiving payment from the sender of the order that it accepted.

Section 4A-504. Order in Which Items and Payment Orders May Be Charged to Account; Order of Withdrawals from Account

(a) If a receiving bank has received more than one payment order of the sender or one or more payment orders and other items that are payable from the sender's account, the bank may charge the sender's account with respect to the various orders and items in any sequence.

(b) In determining whether a credit to an account has been withdrawn by the holder of the account or applied to a debt of the holder of the account, credits first made to the account are first withdrawn or applied.

Official Comment

Subsection (a) concerns priority among various obligations that are to be paid from the same account. A customer may have written checks on its account with the receiving bank and may have issued one or more payment orders payable from the same account. If the account balance is not sufficient to cover all of the checks and payment orders, some checks may be dishonored and some payment orders may not be accepted. Although there is no concept of wrongful dishonor of a payment order in Article 4A in the absence of an agreement to honor by the receiving bank, some rights and obligations may depend on the amount in the customer's account. Section 4A-209(b)(3) and Section 4A-210(b). Whether dishonor of a check is wrongful also may depend upon the balance in the customer's account. Under subsection (a), the bank is not required to consider the competing items and payment orders in any particular order. Rather it may charge the customer's account for the various items and orders in any order. Suppose there is $12,000 in the customer's account. If a check for $5,000 is presented for payment and the bank receives a $10,000 payment order from the customer, the bank could dishonor the check and accept the payment order. Dishonor of the check is not wrongful because the account balance was less than the amount of the check after the bank charged the account $10,000 on account of the payment order. Or, the bank could pay the check and not execute the payment order because the amount of the order is not covered by the balance in the account.

Section 4A-505. Preclusion of Objection to Debit of Customer's Account

If a receiving bank has received payment from its customer with respect to a payment order issued in the name of the customer as sender and accepted by the bank, and the customer received notification reasonably identifying the order, the customer is precluded from asserting that the bank is not entitled to retain the payment unless the customer notifies the bank of the customer's objection to the payment within one year after the notification was received by the customer.

Official Comment

This section is in the nature of a statute of repose for objecting to debits made to the customer's account. A receiving bank that executes payment orders of a customer may have received payment from the customer by debiting the customer's account with respect to a payment order that the customer was not required to pay. For example, the payment order may not have been authorized or verified pursuant to Section 4A-202 or the funds transfer may not have been completed. In either case the receiving bank is obliged to refund the payment to the customer and this obligation to refund payment cannot be varied by agreement. Section 4A-204 and Section 4A-402. Refund may also be required if the receiving bank is not entitled to payment from the customer because the bank erroneously executed a payment order. Section 4A-303. A similar analysis applies to that case. Section 4A-402(d) and (f) require refund and the obligation to refund may not be varied by agreement. Under 4A-505, however, the obligation to refund may not be asserted by the customer if the customer has not objected to the debiting of the account within one year after the customer received notification of the debit.

Section 4A-506. Rate of Interest

(a) If, under this Article, a receiving bank is obliged to pay interest with respect to a payment order issued to the bank, the amount payable may be determined (i) by agreement of the sender and receiving bank, or (ii) by a funds-transfer system rule if the payment order is transmitted through a funds-transfer system.

(b) If the amount of interest is not determined by an agreement or rule as stated in subsection (a), the amount is calculated by multiplying the applicable Federal Funds rate by the amount on which interest is payable, and then multiplying the product by the number of days for which interest is payable. The applicable Federal Funds rate is the average of the Federal Funds rates published by the Federal Reserve Bank of New York for each of the days for which interest is payable divided by 360. The Federal Funds rate for any day on which a published rate is not available is the same as the published rate for the next preceding day for which there is a published rate. If a receiving bank that accepted a payment order is required to refund payment to the sender of the order because the funds transfer was not completed, but the failure to complete was not due to any fault by the bank, the interest payable is reduced by a percentage equal to the reserve requirement on deposits of the receiving bank.

Official Comment

1. A receiving bank is required to pay interest on the amount of a payment order received by the bank in a number of situations. Sometimes the interest is payable to the sender and in other cases it is payable to either the originator or the beneficiary of the funds transfer. The relevant provisions are Section 4A-204(a), Section 4A-209(b) (3), Section 4A-210(b), Section 4A-305(a), Section 4A-402(d) and Section 4A-404(b). The rate of interest may be governed by a funds transfer system rule or by agreement as stated in subsection (a). If subsection (a) doesn't apply, the rate is determined under subsection (b). Subsection (b) is illustrated by the following example. A bank is obliged to pay interest on $1,000,000 for three days, July 3, July 4, and July 5. The published Fed Funds rate is .082 for July 3 and .081 for July 5. There is no published rate for July 4 because that day is not a banking day. The rate for July 3 applies to July 4. The applicable Fed Funds rate is .08167 (the average of .082, .082, and .081) divided by 360 which equals .0002268. The amount of interest payable is $1,000,000 × .0002268 × 3 = $680.40.

2. In some cases, interest is payable in spite of the fact that there is no fault by the receiving bank. The last sentence of subsection (b) applies to those cases. For example, a funds transfer might not be completed because the beneficiary's bank rejected the payment order issued to it by the originator's bank or an intermediary bank. Section 4A-402(c) provides that the originator is not obliged to pay its payment order and Section 4A-402(d) provides that the originator's bank must refund any payment received plus interest. The requirement to pay interest in this case is not based on fault by the originator's bank. Rather, it is based on restitution. Since the originator's bank had the use of the originator's money, it is required to pay the originator for the value of that use. The value of that use is not determined by multiplying the interest rate by the refundable amount because the originator's bank is required to deposit with the Federal Reserve a percentage of the bank's deposits as a reserve requirement. Since that deposit does not bear interest, the bank had use of the refundable amount reduced by a percentage equal to the reserve requirement. If the reserve requirement is 12%, the amount of interest payable by the bank under the formula stated in subsection (b) is reduced by 12%.

Section 4A-507. Choice of Law

(a) The following rules apply unless the affected parties otherwise agree or subsection (c) applies:

(1) The rights and obligations between the sender of a payment order and the receiving bank are governed by the law of the jurisdiction in which the receiving bank is located.

(2) The rights and obligations between the beneficiary's bank and the beneficiary are governed by the law of the jurisdiction in which the beneficiary's bank is located.

(3) The issue of when payment is made pursuant to a funds transfer by the originator to the beneficiary is governed by the law of the jurisdiction in which the beneficiary's bank is located.

(b) If the parties described in each paragraph of subsection (a) have made an agreement selecting the law of a particular jurisdiction to govern rights and obligations between each other, the law of that jurisdiction governs those rights and obligations, whether or not the payment order or the funds transfer bears a reasonable relation to that jurisdiction.

(c) A funds-transfer system rule may select the law of a particular jurisdiction to govern (i) rights and obligations between participating banks with respect to payment orders transmitted or processed through the system, or (ii) the rights and obligations of some or all parties to a funds transfer any part of which is carried out by means of the system. A choice of law made pursuant to clause (i) is binding on participating banks. A choice of law made pursuant to clause (ii) is binding on the originator, other sender, or a receiving bank having notice that the funds-transfer system might be used in the funds transfer and of the choice of law by the system when the originator, other sender, or receiving bank issued or accepted a payment order. The beneficiary of a funds transfer is bound by the choice of law if, when the funds transfer is initiated, the beneficiary has notice that the funds-transfer system might be used in the funds transfer and of the choice of law by the system. The law of a jurisdiction selected pursuant to this subsection may govern, whether or not that law bears a reasonable relation to the matter in issue.

(d) In the event of inconsistency between an agreement under subsection (b) and a choice-of-law rule under subsection (c), the agreement under subsection (b) prevails.

(e) If a funds transfer is made by use of more than one funds-transfer system and there is inconsistency between choice-of-law rules of the systems, the matter in issue is governed by the law of the selected jurisdiction that has the most significant relationship to the matter in issue.

Official Comment

1. Funds transfers are typically interstate or international in character. If part of a funds transfer is governed by Article 4A and another part is governed by other law, the rights and obligations of parties to the funds transfer may be unclear because there is no clear consensus in various jurisdictions concerning the juridical nature of the transaction. Unless all of a funds transfer is governed by a single law it may be very difficult to predict the result if something goes wrong in the transfer. Section 4A-507 deals with this problem. Subsection (b) allows parties to a funds transfer to make a choice-of-law agreement. Subsection (c) allows a funds transfer system to select the law of a particular jurisdiction to govern funds transfers carried out by means of the system. Subsection (a) states residual rules if no choice of law has occurred under subsection (b) or subsection (c).

2. Subsection (a) deals with three sets of relationships. Rights and obligations between the sender of a payment order and the receiving bank are governed by the law of the jurisdiction in which the receiving bank is located. If the receiving bank is the beneficiary's bank the rights and obligations of the beneficiary are also governed by the law of the jurisdiction in which the receiving bank is located. Suppose Originator, located in Canada, sends a payment order to Originator's Bank located in a state in which Article 4A has been enacted. The order is for payment to an account of Beneficiary in a bank in England. Under subsection (a)(1), the rights and obligations of Originator and Originator's Bank toward each other are governed by Article 4A if an action is brought in a court in the Article 4A state. If an action is brought in a Canadian court, the conflict of laws issue will be determined by Canadian law which might or might not apply the law of the state in which Originator's Bank is located. If that law is applied, the execution of Originator's order will be governed by Article 4A, but with respect to the payment order of Originator's Bank to the English bank, Article 4A may or may not be applied with respect to the rights and obligations between the two banks. The result may depend upon whether action is brought in a court in the state in which Originator's Bank is located or in an English court. Article 4A is binding only on a court in a state that enacts it. It can have extraterritorial effect only to the extent courts of another jurisdiction are willing to apply it. Subsection (c) also bears on the issues discussed in this Comment.

Under Section 4A-406 payment by the originator to the beneficiary of the funds transfer occurs when the beneficiary's bank accepts a payment order for the benefit of the beneficiary. A jurisdiction in which Article 4A is not in effect may follow a different rule or it may not have a clear rule. Under Section 4A-507(a)(3) the issue is governed by the law of the jurisdiction in which the beneficiary's bank is located. Since the payment to the beneficiary is made through the beneficiary's bank it is reasonable that the issue of when payment occurs be governed by the law of the jurisdiction in which the bank is located. Since it is difficult in many cases to determine where a beneficiary is located, the location of the beneficiary's bank provides a more certain rule.

3. Subsection (b) deals with choice-of-law agreements and it gives maximum freedom of choice. Since the law of funds transfers is not highly developed in the case law there may be a strong incentive to choose the law of a jurisdiction in which Article 4A is in effect because it provides a greater degree of certainly with respect to the rights of various parties. With respect to commercial transactions, it is often said that "[u]niformity and predictability based upon commercial convenience are the prime considerations in making the choice of governing law . . . . " R. Leflar, American Conflicts Law, § 185 (1977). Subsection (b) is derived in part from recently enacted choice-of-law rules in the States of New York and California. N.Y. Gen. Obligations Law 5-1401 (McKinney's 1989 Supp.) and California Civil Code § 1646.5. This broad endorsement of freedom of contract is an enhancement of the approach taken by Restatement (Second) of Conflict of Laws § 187(b) (1971). The Restatement recognizes the basic right of freedom of contract, but the freedom granted the parties may be more limited than the freedom granted here. Under the formulation of the Restatement, if there is no substantial relationship to the jurisdiction whose law is selected and there is no "other" reasonable basis for the parties' choice, then the selection of the parties need not be honored by a court. Further, if the choice is violative of a fundamental policy of a state which has a materially greater interest than the chosen state, the selection could be disregarded by a court. Those limitations are not found in subsection (b).

4. Subsection (c) may be the most important provision in regard to creating uniformity of law in funds transfers. Most rights stated in Article 4A regard parties who are in privity of contract such as originator and beneficiary, sender and receiving bank, and beneficiary's bank and beneficiary. Since they are in privity they can make a choice of law by agreement. But that is not always the case. For example, an intermediary bank that improperly executes a payment order is not in privity with either the originator or the beneficiary. The ability of a funds transfer system to make a choice of law by rule is a convenient way of dispensing with individual agreements and to cover cases in which agreements are not feasible. It is probable that funds transfer systems will adopt a governing law to increase the certainty of commercial transactions that are effected over such systems. A system rule might adopt the law of an Article 4A state to govern transfers on the system in order to provide a consistent, unitary, law governing all transfers made on the system. To the extent such system rules develop, individual choice-of-law agreements become unnecessary.

Subsection (c) has broad application. A system choice of law applies not only to rights and obligations between banks that use the system, but may also apply to other parties to the funds transfer so long as some part of the transfer was carried out over the system. The originator and any other sender or receiving bank in the funds transfer is bound if at the time it issues or accepts a payment order it had notice that the funds transfer involved use of the system and that the system chose the law of a particular jurisdiction. Under Section 4A-107, the Federal Reserve by regulation could make a similar choice of law to govern funds transfers carried out by use of Federal Reserve Banks. Subsection (d) is a limitation on subsection (c). If parties have made a choice-of-law agreement that conflicts with a choice of law made under subsection (c), the agreement prevails.

5. Subsection (e) addresses the case in which a funds transfer involves more than one funds transfer system and the systems adopt conflicting choice-of-law rules. The rule that has the most significant relationship to the matter at issue prevails. For example, each system should be able to make a choice of law governing payment orders transmitted over that system without regard to a choice of law made by another system.

Article 5—Letters of Credit

As adopted in 1995 and revised in: (i) 1999, in connection with the revision of Article 9; (ii) 2001, in connection with the revision of Article 1; (iii) 2002, to correct errata; (iv) 2003, in connection with the revision of Article 7; and (v) 2022, in connection with the 2022 Amendments to the Uniform Commercial Code.

PREFATORY NOTE

PREFATORY NOTE

Reason for Revision. When the original Article 5 was drafted 40 years ago, it was written for paper transactions and before many innovations in letters of credit. Now electronic and other media are used extensively. Since the 50's, standby letters of credit have developed and now nearly $500 billion standby letters of credit are issued annually worldwide, of which $250 billion are issued in the United States. The use of deferred payment letters of credit has also greatly increased. The customs and practices for letters of credit have evolved and are reflected in the Uniform Customs and Practice (UCP), usually incorporated into letters of credit, particularly international letters of credit, which have seen four revisions since the 1950's; the current version became effective in 1994 (UCP 500). Lastly, in a number of areas, court decisions have resulted in conflicting rules.

Prior to the appointment of a drafting committee, the ABA UCC Committee appointed a Task Force composed of knowledgeable practitioners and academics. The ABA Task Force studied the case law, evolving technologies and the changes in customs and practices. The Task Force identified a large number of issues which they discussed at some length, and made recommendations for revisions to Article 5. The Task Force stated in a foreword:

"As a result of these increases and changes in usage, practice, players, and pressure, it comes as no surprise that there has been a sizable increase in litigation. Indeed, the approximately 62 cases reported in the United States in 1987 constituted double the cumulative reported cases up to 1965. . . .

Moreover, almost forty years of hard use have revealed weaknesses, gaps and errors in the original statute which compromise its relevance. U.C.C. Article 5 was one of the few areas of the Uniform Commercial Code which did not benefit from prior codification and it should come as no surprise that it may require some revision. . . .

Measured in terms of these areas which are vital to any system of commercial law, the current combination of statute and case law is found wanting in major respects both as to predictability and certainty. What is at issue here are not matters of sophistry but important issues of substance which have not been resolved by the current case law/code method and which admit of little likelihood of such resolution." (45 Bus. Lawyer 1521, at 1532, 1535-6)*

The Drafting Committee began its deliberations with the Task Force Report in hand. The final work of the Drafting Committee varies from many of the suggestions of the Task Force.

Need for Uniformity. Letters of Credit are a major instrument in international trade, as well as domestic transactions. To facilitate its usefulness and competitiveness, it is essential that U.S. law be in harmony with international rules and practices, as well as flexible enough to accommodate changes in technology and practices that have, and are, evolving. Not only should the rules be consistent within the United States, but they need to be substantively and procedurally consistent with international practices.

Thus, the goals of the drafting effort were:

- conforming the Article 5 rules to current customs and practices;

---

* The Task Force members were: Professor James E. Byrne (George Mason University School of Law) Chair; Professor Boris Kozolchyk (University of Arizona College of Law); Michael Evan Avidon (Moses & Singer LLP); James G. Barnes (Baker & McKenzie LLP); Arthur G. Lloyd (Citibank N.A.); Janis S. Penton (Rosen, Wachtell & Gilbert); Richard F. Purcell (Connell, Rice & Sugar Co.); Alan L. Bloodgood (Morgan Guaranty Trust Co.); Charles del Busto (Manufacturers Hanover Trust Co.); Vincent Maulella (Manufacturers Hanover Trust Co.).

- accommodating new forms of Letters of Credit, changes in customs and practices, and evolving technology, particularly the use of electronic media;
- maintaining Letters of Credit as an inexpensive and efficient instrument facilitating trade; and
- resolving conflicts among reported decisions.

Process of Achieving Uniformity. The essence of uniform law revision is to obtain a sufficient consensus and balance among the interests of the various participants so that universal and uniform enactment by the various States may be achieved.

In part this is accomplished by extensive consultation on and broad circulation of the drafts from 1990, when the project began, until approval of the final draft by the American Law Institute (ALI) and the National Conference of Commissioners on Uniform State Laws (NCCUSL).

Hundreds of groups were invited to participate in the drafting process. Twenty Advisors were appointed, representing a cross-section of interested parties. In addition 20 Observers regularly attended drafting meetings and over 100 were on the mailing list to receive all drafts of the revision.

The Drafting Committee meetings were open and all those who attended were afforded full opportunity to express their views and participate in the dialogue. The Advisors and Observers were a balanced group with ten representatives of users (Beneficiaries and Applicants); five representatives of governmental agencies; five representatives of the U.S. Council on International Banking (USCIB); seven from major banks in letter of credit transactions; eight from regional banks; and seven law professors who teach and write on Letters of Credit.

Nine Drafting Committee meetings were held that began Friday morning and ended Sunday noon. In addition, the draft was twice debated in full by NCCUSL, once by the ALI Council, once considered by the ALI Consultative Group and once by an ad hoc Committee of the Council; and reviewed and discussed by the ABA Subcommittee on Letters of Credit semi-annually and by several state and city bar association committees.

The drafts were regularly reviewed and discussed in *The Business Lawyer*, *Letter of Credit Update*, and in other publications.

Section 5-101. Short Title

This Article may be cited as Uniform Commercial Code—Letters of Credit.

Official Comment

The Official Comment to the original Section 5-101 was a remarkably brief inaugural address. Noting that letters of credit had not been the subject of statutory enactment and that the law concerning them had been developed in the cases, the Comment stated that Article 5 was intended "within its limited scope" to set an independent theoretical frame for the further development of letters of credit. That statement addressed accurately conditions as they existed when the statement was made, nearly half a century ago. Since Article 5 was originally drafted, the use of letters of credit has expanded and developed, and the case law concerning these developments is, in some respects, discordant.

Revision of Article 5 therefore has required reappraisal both of the statutory goals and of the extent to which particular statutory provisions further or adversely affect achievement of those goals.

The statutory goal of Article 5 was originally stated to be: (1) to set a substantive theoretical frame that describes the function and legal nature of letters of credit; and (2) to preserve procedural flexibility in order to accommodate further development of the efficient use of letters of credit. A letter of credit is an idiosyncratic form of undertaking that supports performance of an obligation incurred in a separate financial, mercantile, or other transaction or arrangement. The objectives of the original and revised Article 5 are best achieved (1) by defining the peculiar characteristics of a letter of credit that distinguish it and the legal consequences of its use from other forms of assurance such as secondary guarantees, performance bonds, and insurance policies, and from ordinary contracts, fiduciary engagements, and escrow arrangements; and (2) by preserving flexibility through variation by agreement in order to respond to and accommodate developments in custom and usage that are not inconsistent with the essential definitions and substantive mandates of the statute. No statute can, however, prescribe the manner in which such substantive rights and duties are to be enforced or imposed without risking stultification of wholesome developments in the letter of credit mechanism. Letter of credit law should remain responsive to commercial reality and in particular to the customs and expectations of the international banking and mercantile community. Courts should read the terms of this Article in a manner consistent with these customs and expectations.

The subject matter in Article 5, letters of credit, may also be governed by an international convention that is now being drafted by UNCITRAL, the draft Convention on Independent Guarantees and Standby Letters of Credit. The Uniform Customs and Practice is an international body of trade practice that is commonly adopted by international and domestic letters of credit and as such is the "law of the transaction" by agreement of the parties. Article 5 is consistent with and was influenced by the rules in the existing version of the UCP. In addition to the UCP and the international convention, other bodies of law apply to letters of credit. For example, the federal bankruptcy law applies to letters of credit with respect to applicants and beneficiaries that are in bankruptcy; regulations of the Federal Reserve Board and the Comptroller of the Currency lay out requirements for banks that issue letters of credit and describe how letters of credit are to be treated for calculating asset risk and for the purpose of loan limitations. In addition there is an array of anti-boycott and other similar laws that may affect the issuance and performance of letters of credit. All of these laws are beyond the scope of Article 5, but in certain circumstances they will override Article 5.

Section 5-102. Definitions

(a) In this Article:

(1) "Adviser" means a person who, at the request of the issuer, a confirmer, or another adviser, notifies or requests another adviser to notify the beneficiary that a letter of credit has been issued, confirmed, or amended.

(2) "Applicant" means a person at whose request or for whose account a letter of credit is issued. The term includes a person who requests an issuer to issue a letter of credit on behalf of another if the person making the request undertakes an obligation to reimburse the issuer.

(3) "Beneficiary" means a person who under the terms of a letter of credit is entitled to have its complying presentation honored. The term includes a person to whom drawing rights have been transferred under a transferable letter of credit.

(4) "Confirmer" means a nominated person who undertakes, at the request or with the consent of the issuer, to honor a presentation under a letter of credit issued by another.

(5) "Dishonor" of a letter of credit means failure timely to honor or to take an interim action, such as acceptance of a draft, that may be required by the letter of credit.

(6) "Document" means a draft or other demand, document of title, investment security, certificate, invoice, or other record, statement, or representation of fact, law, right, or opinion (i) which is presented in a written or other medium permitted by the letter of credit or, unless prohibited by the letter of credit, by the standard practice referred to in Section 5-108(e) and (ii) which is capable of being examined for compliance with the terms and conditions of the letter of credit. A document may not be oral.

(7) "Good faith" means honesty in fact in the conduct or transaction concerned.

(8) "Honor" of a letter of credit means performance of the issuer's undertaking in the letter of credit to pay or deliver an item of value. Unless the letter of credit otherwise provides, "honor" occurs

(i) upon payment,

(ii) if the letter of credit provides for acceptance, upon acceptance of a draft and, at maturity, its payment, or

(iii) if the letter of credit provides for incurring a deferred obligation, upon incurring the obligation and, at maturity, its performance.

(9) "Issuer" means a bank or other person that issues a letter of credit, but does not include an individual who makes an engagement for personal, family, or household purposes.

(10) "Letter of credit" means a definite undertaking that satisfies the requirements of Section 5-104 by an issuer to a beneficiary at the request or for the account of an applicant or, in the case of a financial institution, to itself or for its own account, to honor a documentary presentation by payment or delivery of an item of value.

(11) "Nominated person" means a person whom the issuer (i) designates or authorizes to pay, accept, negotiate, or otherwise give value under a letter of credit and (ii) undertakes by agreement or custom and practice to reimburse.

(12) "Presentation" means delivery of a document to an issuer or nominated person for honor or giving of value under a letter of credit.

(13) "Presenter" means a person making a presentation as or on behalf of a beneficiary or nominated person.

(14) "Record" means information that is inscribed on a tangible medium, or that is stored in an electronic or other medium and is retrievable in perceivable form.

(15) "Successor of a beneficiary" means a person who succeeds to substantially all of the rights of a beneficiary by operation of law, including a corporation with or into which the beneficiary has been merged or consolidated, an administrator, executor, personal representative, trustee in bankruptcy, debtor in possession, liquidator, and receiver.

(b) Definitions in other Articles applying to this Article and the sections in which they appear are:

"Accept" or "Acceptance"	Section 3-409
"Value"	Sections 3-303, 4-211

(c) Article 1 contains certain additional general definitions and principles of construction and interpretation applicable throughout this Article.

Official Comment

1. Since no one can be a confirmer unless that person is a nominated person as defined in Section 5-102(a)(4) and (11), those who agree to "confirm" without the designation or authorization of the issuer are not confirmers under Article 5. Nonetheless, the undertakings to the beneficiary of such persons may be enforceable by the beneficiary as letters of credit issued by the "confirmer" for its own account or as guarantees or contracts outside of Article 5.

2. The definition of "document" contemplates and facilitates the growing recognition of electronic and other nonpaper media as "documents," however, for the time being, data in those media constitute documents only in certain circumstances. For example, a facsimile received by an issuer would be a document only if the letter of credit explicitly permitted it, if the standard practice authorized it and the letter did not prohibit it, or the agreement of the issuer and beneficiary permitted it. The fact that data transmitted in a nonpaper (unwritten) medium can be recorded on paper by a recipient's computer printer, facsimile machine, or the like does not under current practice render the data so transmitted a "document." A facsimile or S.W.I.F.T. message received directly by the issuer is in an electronic medium when it crosses the boundary of the issuer's place of business. One wishing to make a presentation by facsimile (an electronic medium) will have to procure the explicit agreement of the issuer (assuming that the standard practice does not authorize it). Article 5 contemplates that electronic documents may be presented under a letter of credit and the provisions of this Article should be read to apply to electronic documents as well as tangible documents. An electronic document of title is delivered through the voluntary transfer of control. Article 1, Section 1-201 (definition of "delivery"). See Article 7, Section 7-106 on control of an electronic document. Where electronic transmissions are authorized neither by the letter of credit nor by the practice, the beneficiary may transmit the data electronically to its agent who may be able to put it in written form and make a conforming presentation. Cf. Article 7, Section 7-105 on reissuing an electronic document in a tangible medium.

3. "Good faith" continues in revised Article 5 to be defined as "honesty in fact." "Observance of reasonable standards of fair dealing" has not been added to the definition. The narrower definition of "honesty in fact" reinforces the "independence principle" in the treatment of "fraud," "strict compliance," "preclusion," and other tests affecting the performance of obligations that are unique to letters of credit. This narrower definition — which does not include "fair dealing" — is appropriate to the decision to honor or dishonor a presentation of documents specified in a letter of credit. The narrower definition is also appropriate for other parts of revised Article 5 where greater certainty of obligations is necessary and is consistent with the goals of speed and low cost. It is important that U.S. letters of credit have continuing vitality and competitiveness in international transactions.

For example, it would be inconsistent with the "independence" principle if any of the following occurred: (i) the beneficiary's failure to adhere to the standard of "fair dealing" in the underlying transaction or otherwise in presenting documents were to provide applicants and issuers with an "unfairness" defense to dishonor even when the documents complied with the terms of the letter of credit; (ii) the issuer's obligation to honor in "strict compliance in accordance with standard practice" were changed to "reasonable compliance" by use of the "fair dealing" standard, or (iii) the preclusion against the issuer (Section 5-108(d)) were modified under the "fair dealing" standard to enable the issuer later to raise additional deficiencies in the presentation. The rights and obligations arising from presentation, honor, dishonor and reimbursement, are independent and strict, and thus "honesty in fact" is an appropriate standard.

The contract between the applicant and beneficiary is not governed by Article 5, but by applicable contract law, such as Article 2 or the general law of contracts. "Good faith" in that contract is defined by other law, such as Section 1-201(b)(20) or Restatement of Contracts 2d, § 205, which incorporate the principle of "fair dealing" in most cases, or a State's common law or other statutory provisions that may apply to that contract.

The contract between the applicant and the issuer (sometimes called the "reimbursement" agreement) is governed in part by this Article (e.g., Sections 5-108(i), 5-111(b), and 5-103(c)) and partly by other law (e.g., the general law of contracts). The definition of good faith in Section 5-102(a)(7) applies only to the extent that the reimbursement contract is governed by provisions in this Article; for other purposes good faith is defined by other law.

4. Payment and acceptance are familiar modes of honor. A third mode of honor, incurring an unconditional obligation, has legal effects similar to an acceptance of a time draft but does not technically constitute an acceptance. The practice of making letters of credit available by "deferred payment undertaking" as now provided in UCP 500 has grown up in other countries and spread to the United States. The definition of "honor" will accommodate that practice.

5. The exclusion of consumers from the definition of "issuer" is to keep creditors from using a letter of credit in consumer transactions in which the consumer might be made the issuer and the creditor would be the beneficiary. If that transaction were recognized under Article 5, the effect would be to leave the consumer without defenses against the creditor. That outcome would violate the policy behind the Federal Trade Commission Rule in 16 CFR Part 433. In a consumer transaction, an individual cannot be an issuer where that person would otherwise be either the principal debtor or a guarantor.

6. The label on a document is not conclusive; certain documents labelled "guarantees" in accordance with European (and occasionally, American) practice are letters of credit. On the other hand, even documents that are labelled "letter of credit" may not constitute letters of credit under the definition in Section 5-102(a). When a document labelled a letter of credit requires the issuer to pay not upon the presentation of documents, but upon the determination of an extrinsic fact such as applicant's failure to perform a construction contract, and where that condition appears on its face to be fundamental and would, if ignored, leave no obligation to the issuer under the document labelled letter of credit, the issuer's undertaking is not a letter of credit. It is probably some form of suretyship or other contractual arrangement and may be enforceable as such. See Sections 5-102(a)(10) and 5-103(d). Therefore, undertakings whose fundamental term requires an issuer to look beyond documents and beyond conventional reference to the clock, calendar, and practices concerning the form of various documents are not governed by Article 5. Although Comment 9 to Section 5-108(g) recognizes that certain nondocumentary conditions can be included in a letter of credit without denying the undertaking the status of letter of credit, that section does not apply to cases where the nondocumentary condition is fundamental to the issuer's obligation. The rules in Sections 5-102(a)(10), 5-103(d), and 5-108(g) approve the conclusion in *Wichita Eagle & Beacon Publishing Co. v. Pacific Nat'l Bank*, 493 F.2d 1285 (9th Cir. 1974).

The adjective "definite" is taken from the UCP. It approves cases that deny letter of credit status to documents that are unduly vague or incomplete. See, e.g., *Transparent Products Corp. v. Paysaver Credit Union*, 864 F.2d 60 (7th Cir. 1988). Note, however, that no particular phrase or label is necessary to establish a letter of credit. It is sufficient if the undertaking of the issuer shows that it is intended to be a letter of credit. In most cases the parties' intention will be indicated by a label on the undertaking itself indicating that it is a "letter of credit," but no such language is necessary.

A financial institution may be both the issuer and the applicant or the issuer and the beneficiary. Such letters are sometimes issued by a bank in support of the bank's own lease obligations or on behalf of one of its divisions as an applicant or to one of its divisions as beneficiary, such as an overseas branch. Because wide use of letters of credit in which the issuer and the applicant or the issuer and the beneficiary are the same would endanger the unique status of letters of credit, only financial institutions are authorized to issue them.

In almost all cases the ultimate performance of the issuer under a letter of credit is the payment of money. In rare cases the issuer's obligation is to deliver stock certificates or the like. The definition of letter of credit in Section 5-102(a)(10) contemplates those cases.

7. Under the UCP any bank is a nominated bank where the letter of credit is "freely negotiable." A letter of credit might also nominate by the following: "We hereby engage with the drawer, indorsers, and bona fide holders of drafts drawn under and in compliance with the terms of this credit that the same will be duly honored on due presentation" or "available with any bank by negotiation." A restricted negotiation credit might be "available with x bank by negotiation" or the like.

Several legal consequences may attach to the status of nominated person. First, when the issuer nominates a person, it is authorizing that person to pay or give value and is authorizing the beneficiary to make presentation to that person. Unless the letter of credit provides otherwise, the beneficiary need not present the documents to the issuer before the letter of credit expires; it need only present those documents to the nominated person. Secondly, a nominated person that gives value in good faith has a right to payment from the issuer despite fraud. Section 5-109(a)(1).

8. A "record" must be in or capable of being converted to a perceivable form. For example, an electronic message recorded in a computer memory that could be printed from that memory could constitute a record. Similarly, a tape recording of an oral conversation could be a record.

9. Absent a specific agreement to the contrary, documents of a beneficiary delivered to an issuer or nominated person are considered to be presented under the letter of credit to which they refer, and any payment or value given for them is considered to be made under that letter of credit. As the court held in *Alaska Textile Co. v. Chase Manhattan Bank, N.A.*, 982 F.2d 813, 820 (2d Cir. 1992), it takes a "significant showing" to make the presentation of a beneficiary's documents for "collection only" or otherwise outside letter of credit law and practice.

10. Although a successor of a beneficiary is one who succeeds "by operation of law," some of the successions contemplated by Section 5-102(a)(15) will have resulted from voluntary action of the beneficiary such as merger of a corporation. Any merger makes the successor corporation the "successor of a beneficiary" even though the transfer occurs partly by operation of law and partly by the voluntary action of the parties. The definition excludes certain transfers, where no part of the transfer is "by operation of law"—such as the sale of assets by one company to another.

11. "Draft" in Article 5 does not have the same meaning it has in Article 3. For example, a document may be a draft under Article 5 even though it would not be a negotiable instrument, and therefore would not qualify as a draft under Section 3-104(e).

Section 5-103. Scope

(a) This Article applies to letters of credit and to certain rights and obligations arising out of transactions involving letters of credit.

(b) The statement of a rule in this Article does not by itself require, imply, or negate application of the same or a different rule to a situation not provided for, or to a person not specified, in this Article.

(c) With the exception of this subsection, subsections (a) and (d), Sections 5-102(a)(9) and (10), 5-106(d), and 5-114(d), and except to the extent prohibited in Sections 1-302 and 5-117(d), the effect of this Article may be varied by agreement or by a provision stated or incorporated by reference in an undertaking. A term in an agreement or undertaking generally excusing liability or generally limiting remedies for failure to perform obligations is not sufficient to vary obligations prescribed by this Article.

(d) Rights and obligations of an issuer to a beneficiary or a nominated person under a letter of credit are independent of the existence, performance, or nonperformance of a contract or arrangement out of which the letter of credit arises or which underlies it, including contracts or arrangements between the issuer and the applicant and between the applicant and the beneficiary.

Official Comment

1. Sections 5-102(a)(10) and 5-103 are the principal limits on the scope of Article 5. Many undertakings in commerce and contract are similar, but not identical to the letter of credit. Principal among those are "secondary," "accessory," or "suretyship" guarantees. Although the word "guarantee" is sometimes used to describe an independent obligation like that of the issuer of a letter of credit (most often in the case of European bank undertakings but occasionally in the case of undertakings of American banks), in the United States the word "guarantee" is more typically used to describe a suretyship transaction in which the "guarantor" is only secondarily liable and has the right to assert the underlying debtor's defenses. This Article does not apply to secondary or accessory guarantees and it is important to recognize the distinction between letters of credit and those guarantees. It is often a defense to a secondary or accessory guarantor's liability that the underlying debt has been discharged or that the debtor has other defenses to the underlying liability. In letter of credit law, on the other hand, the independence principle recognized throughout Article 5 states that the issuer's liability is independent of the underlying obligation. That the beneficiary may have breached the underlying contract and thus have given a good defense on that contract to the applicant against the beneficiary is no defense for the issuer's refusal to honor. Only staunch recognition of this principle by the issuers and the courts will give letters of credit the continuing vitality that arises from the certainty and speed of payment under letters of credit. To that end, it is important that the law not carry into letter of credit transactions rules that properly apply only to secondary guarantees or to other forms of engagement.

2. Like all of the provisions of the Uniform Commercial Code, Article 5 is supplemented by Section 1-103 and, through it, by many rules of statutory and common law. Because this Article is quite short and has no rules on many issues that will affect liability with respect to a letter of credit transaction, law beyond Article 5 will often determine rights and liabilities in letter of credit transactions. Even within letter of credit law, the Article is far from comprehensive; it deals only with "certain" rights of the parties. Particularly with respect to the standards of performance that are set out in Section 5-108, it is appropriate for the parties and the courts to turn to customs and practice such as the Uniform Customs and Practice for Documentary Credits, currently published by the International Chamber of Commerce as I.C.C. Pub. No. 500 (hereafter UCP). Many letters of credit specifically adopt the UCP as applicable to the particular transaction. Where the UCP are adopted but conflict with Article 5 and except where variation is prohibited, the UCP terms are permissible contractual modifications under Sections 1-302 and 5-103(c). See Section 5-116(e). Normally Article 5 should not be considered to conflict with practice except when a rule explicitly stated in the UCP or other practice is different from a rule explicitly stated in Article 5.

Except by choosing the law of a jurisdiction that has not adopted the Uniform Commercial Code, it is not possible entirely to escape the Uniform Commercial Code. Since incorporation of the UCP avoids only "conflicting" Article 5 rules, parties who do not wish to be governed by the nonconflicting provisions of Article 5 must normally either adopt the law of a jurisdiction other than a State of the United States or state explicitly the rule that is to govern. When rules of custom and practice are incorporated by reference, they are considered to be explicit terms of the agreement or undertaking.

Neither the obligation of an issuer under Section 5-108 nor that of an adviser under Section 5-107 is an obligation of the kind that is invariable under Section 1-302(b). Section 5-103(c) and Comment 1 to Section 5-108 make it clear that the applicant and the issuer may agree to almost any provision establishing the obligations of the issuer to the applicant. The last sentence of subsection (c) limits the power of the issuer to achieve that result by a nonnegotiated disclaimer or limitation of remedy.

What the issuer could achieve by an explicit agreement with its applicant or by a term that explicitly defines its duty, it cannot accomplish by a general disclaimer. The restriction on disclaimers in the last sentence of subsection (c) is based more on procedural than on substantive unfairness. Where, for example, the reimbursement agreement provides explicitly that the issuer need not examine any documents, the applicant understands the risk it has undertaken. A term in a reimbursement agreement which states generally that an issuer will not be liable unless it has acted in "bad faith" or committed "gross negligence" is ineffective under Section 5-103(c). On the other hand, less general terms such as terms that permit issuer reliance on an oral or electronic message believed in good faith to have been received from the applicant or terms that entitle an issuer to reimbursement when it honors a "substantially" though not "strictly" complying presentation, are effective. In each case the question is whether the disclaimer or limitation is sufficiently clear and explicit in reallocating a liability or risk that is allocated differently under a variable Article 5 provision.

Of course, no term in a letter of credit, whether incorporated by reference to practice rules or stated specifically, can free an issuer from a conflicting contractual obligation to its applicant. If, for example, an issuer promised its applicant that it would pay only against an inspection certificate of a particular company but failed to require such a certificate in its letter of credit or made the requirement only a nondocumentary condition that had to be disregarded, the issuer might be obliged to pay the beneficiary even though its payment might violate its contract with its applicant.

3. Parties should generally avoid modifying the definitions in Section 5-102. The effect of such an agreement is almost inevitably unclear. To say that something is a "guarantee" in the typical domestic transaction is to say that the parties intend that particular legal rules apply to it. By acknowledging that something is a guarantee, but asserting that it is to be treated as a "letter of credit," the parties leave a court uncertain about where the rules on guarantees stop and those concerning letters of credit begin.

4. Section 5-102(2) and (3) of original Article 5 are omitted as unneeded; the omission does not change the law.

Section 5-104. Formal Requirements

A letter of credit, confirmation, advice, transfer, amendment, or cancellation may be issued in any form that is a signed record.

Official Comment

1. Neither Section 5-104 nor the definition of letter of credit in Section 5-102(a)(10) requires inclusion of all the terms that are normally contained in a letter of credit in order for an undertaking to be recognized as a letter of credit under Article 5. For example, a letter of credit will typically specify the amount available, the expiration date, the place where presentation should be made, and the documents that must be presented to entitle a person to honor. Undertakings that have the formalities required by Section 5-104 and meet the conditions specified in Section 5-102(a)(10) will be recognized as letters of credit even though they omit one or more of the items usually contained in a letter of credit.

2. This section was revised pursuant to the Uniform Commercial Code Amendments (2022). The reference in the pre-2022 text of this section to authentication by agreement of the parties or standard practice referred to in Section 5-108(e) is no longer necessary. Those forms of authentication are subsumed by the revised and expanded definition of "sign" in Section 1-201(b)(37), which is broad and flexible. The requirement that a record be signed as specified in this section is authentication or adoption only of the identity of the issuer, confirmer, or adviser.

3. Many banking transactions, including the issuance of many letters of credit, are now conducted mostly by electronic means. For example, S.W.I.F.T. is currently used to transmit letters of credit from issuing to advising banks. The letter of credit text so transmitted may be printed at the advising bank, stamped "original" and provided to the beneficiary in that form. The printed document may then be used as a way of controlling and recording payments and of recording and authorizing assignments of proceeds or transfers of rights under the letter of credit. Nothing in this section should be construed to conflict with that practice.

To be a record sufficient to serve as a letter of credit or other undertaking under this section, data must have a durability consistent with that function. Because consideration is not required for a binding letter of credit or similar undertaking (Section 5-105) yet those undertakings are to be strictly construed (Section 5-108), parties to a letter of credit transaction are especially dependent on the continued availability of the terms and conditions of the letter of credit or other undertaking. By declining to specify any particular medium in which the letter of credit must be established or communicated, Section 5-104 leaves room for future developments.

Section 5-105. Consideration

Consideration is not required to issue, amend, transfer, or cancel a letter of credit, advice, or confirmation.

Official Comment

It is not to be expected that any issuer will issue its letter of credit without some form of remuneration. But it is not expected that the beneficiary will know what the issuer's remuneration was or whether in fact there was any identifiable remuneration in a given case. And it might be difficult for the beneficiary to prove the issuer's remuneration. This section dispenses with this proof and is consistent with the position of Lord Mansfield in *Pillans v. Van Mierop*, 97 Eng. Rep. 1035 (K.B. 1765) in making consideration irrelevant.

Section 5-106. Issuance, Amendment, Cancellation, and Duration

(a) A letter of credit is issued and becomes enforceable according to its terms against the issuer when the issuer sends or otherwise transmits it to the person requested to advise or to the beneficiary. A letter of credit is revocable only if it so provides.

(b) After a letter of credit is issued, rights and obligations of a beneficiary, applicant, confirmer, and issuer are not affected by an amendment or cancellation to which that person has not consented except to the extent the letter of credit provides that it is revocable or that the issuer may amend or cancel the letter of credit without that consent.

(c) If there is no stated expiration date or other provision that determines its duration, a letter of credit expires one year after its stated date of issuance or, if none is stated, after the date on which it is issued.

(d) A letter of credit that states that it is perpetual expires five years after its stated date of issuance, or if none is stated, after the date on which it is issued.

Official Comment

1. This section adopts the position taken by several courts, namely that letters of credit that are silent as to revocability are irrevocable. See, e.g., *Weyerhaeuser Co. v. First Nat'l Bank*, 27 UCC Rep. Serv. 777 (S.D. Iowa 1979); *W. Va. Hous. Dev. Fund v. Sroka,* 415 F. Supp. 1107 (W.D. Pa. 1976). This is the position of the current UCP (500). Given the usual commercial understanding and purpose of letters of credit, revocable letters of credit offer unhappy possibilities for misleading the parties who deal with them.

2. A person can consent to an amendment by implication. For example, a beneficiary that tenders documents for honor that conform to an amended letter of credit but not to the original letter of credit has probably consented to the amendment. By the same token an applicant that has procured the issuance of a transferable letter of credit has consented to its transfer and to performance under the letter of credit by a person to whom the beneficiary's rights are duly transferred. If some, but not all of the persons involved in a letter of credit transaction consent to performance that does not strictly conform to the original letter of credit, those persons assume the risk that other nonconsenting persons may insist on strict compliance with the original letter of credit. Under subsection (b) those not consenting are not bound. For example, an issuer might agree to amend its letter of credit or honor documents presented after the expiration date in the belief that the applicant has consented or will consent to the amendment or will waive presentation after the original expiration date. If that belief is mistaken, the issuer is bound to the beneficiary by the terms of the letter of credit as amended or waived, even though it may be unable to recover from the applicant.

In general, the rights of a recognized transferee beneficiary cannot be altered without the transferee's consent, but the same is not true of the rights of assignees of proceeds from the beneficiary. When the beneficiary makes a complete transfer of its interest that is effective under the terms for transfer established by the issuer, adviser, or other party controlling transfers, the beneficiary no longer has an interest in the letter of credit, and the transferee steps into the shoes of the beneficiary as the one with rights under the letter of credit. Secion 5-102(a)(3). When there is a partial transfer, both the original beneficiary and the transferee beneficiary have an interest in performance of the letter of credit and each expects that its rights will not be altered by amendment unless it consents.

The assignee of proceeds under a letter of credit from the beneficiary enjoys no such expectation. Notwithstanding an assignee's notice to the issuer of the assignment of proceeds, the assignee is not a person protected by subsection (b). An assignee of proceeds should understand that its rights can be changed or completely extinguished by amendment or cancellation of the letter of credit. An assignee's claim is precarious, for it depends entirely upon the continued existence of the letter of credit and upon the beneficiary's preparation and presentation of documents that would entitle the beneficiary to honor under Section 5-108.

3. The issuer's right to cancel a revocable letter of credit does not free it from a duty to reimburse a nominated person who has honored, accepted, or undertaken a deferred obligation prior to receiving notice of the amendment or cancellation. Compare UCP Article 8.

4. Although all letters of credit should specify the date on which the issuer's engagement expires, the failure to specify an expiration date does not invalidate the letter of credit, or diminish or relieve the obligation of any party with respect to the letter of credit. A letter of credit that may be revoked or terminated at the discretion of the issuer by notice to the beneficiary is not "perpetual."

Section 5-107. Confirmer, Nominated Person, and Adviser

(a) A confirmer is directly obligated on a letter of credit and has the rights and obligations of an issuer to the extent of its confirmation. The confirmer also has rights against and obligations to the issuer as if the issuer were an applicant and the confirmer had issued the letter of credit at the request and for the account of the issuer.

(b) A nominated person who is not a confirmer is not obligated to honor or otherwise give value for a presentation.

(c) A person requested to advise may decline to act as an adviser. An adviser that is not a confirmer is not obligated to honor or give value for a presentation. An adviser undertakes to the issuer and to the beneficiary accurately to advise the terms of the letter of credit, confirmation, amendment, or advice received by that person and undertakes to the beneficiary to check the apparent authenticity of the request to advise. Even if the advice is inaccurate, the letter of credit, confirmation, or amendment is enforceable as issued.

(d) A person who notifies a transferee beneficiary of the terms of a letter of credit, confirmation, amendment, or advice has the rights and obligations of an adviser under subsection (c). The terms in the notice to the transferee beneficiary may differ from the terms in any notice to the transferor beneficiary to the extent permitted by the letter of credit, confirmation, amendment, or advice received by the person who so notifies.

Official Comment

1. A confirmer has the rights and obligations identified in Section 5-108. Accordingly, unless the context otherwise requires, the terms "confirmer" and "confirmation" should be read into this Article wherever the terms "issuer" and "letter of credit" appear.

A confirmer that has paid in accordance with the terms and conditions of the letter of credit is entitled to reimbursement by the issuer even if the beneficiary committed fraud (see Section 5-109(a)(1)(ii)) and, in that sense, has greater rights against the issuer than the beneficiary has. To be entitled to reimbursement from the issuer under the typical confirmed letter of credit, the confirmer must submit conforming documents, but the confirmer's presentation to the issuer need not be made before the expiration date of the letter of credit.

A letter of credit confirmation has been analogized to a guarantee of issuer performance, to a parallel letter of credit issued by the confirmer for the account of the issuer or the letter of credit applicant or both, and to a back-to-back letter of credit in which the confirmer is a kind of beneficiary of the original issuer's letter of credit. Like letter of credit undertakings, confirmations are both unique and flexible, so that no one of these analogies is perfect, but unless otherwise indicated in the letter of credit or confirmation, a confirmer should be viewed by the letter of credit issuer and the beneficiary as an issuer of a parallel letter of credit for the account of the original letter of credit issuer. Absent a direct agreement between the applicant and a confirmer, normally the obligations of a confirmer are to the issuer not the applicant, but the applicant might have a right to injunction against a confirmer under Section 5-109 or warranty claim under Section 5-110, and either might have claims against the other under Section 5-117.

2. No one has a duty to advise until that person agrees to be an adviser or undertakes to act in accordance with the instructions of the issuer. Except where there is a prior agreement to serve or where the silence of the adviser would be an acceptance of an offer to contract, a person's failure to respond to a request to advise a letter of credit does not in and of itself create any liability, nor does it establish a relationship of issuer and adviser between the two. Since there is no duty to advise a letter of credit in the absence of a prior agreement, there can be no duty to advise it timely or at any particular time. When the adviser manifests its agreement to advise by actually doing so (as is normally the case), the adviser cannot have violated any duty to advise in a timely way. This analysis is consistent with the result of *Sound of Market Street v. Continental Bank International*, 819 F.2d 384 (3d Cir. 1987) which held that there is no such duty. This section takes no position on the reasoning of that case, but does not overrule the result. By advising or agreeing to advise a letter of credit, the adviser assumes a duty to the issuer and to the beneficiary accurately to report what it has received from the issuer, but, beyond determining the apparent authenticity of the letter, an adviser has no duty to investigate the accuracy of the message it has received from the issuer. "Checking" the apparent authenticity of the request to advise means only that the prospective adviser must attempt to authenticate the message (e.g., by "testing" the telex that comes from the purported issuer), and if it is unable to authenticate the message must report that fact to the issuer and, if it chooses to advise the message, to the beneficiary. By proper agreement, an adviser may disclaim its obligation under this section.

3. An issuer may issue a letter of credit which the adviser may advise with different terms. The issuer may then believe that it has undertaken a certain engagement, yet the text in the hands of the beneficiary will contain different terms, and the beneficiary would not be entitled to honor if the documents it submitted did not comply with the terms of the letter of credit as originally issued. On the other hand, if the adviser also confirmed the letter of credit, then as a confirmer it will be independently liable on the letter of credit as advised and confirmed. If in that situation the beneficiary's ultimate presentation entitled it to honor under the terms of the confirmation but not under those in the original letter of credit, the confirmer would have to honor but might not be entitled to reimbursement from the issuer.

4. When the issuer nominates another person to "pay," "negotiate," or otherwise to take up the documents and give value, there can be confusion about the legal status of the nominated person. In rare cases the person might actually be an agent of the issuer and its act might be the act of the issuer itself. In most cases the nominated person is not an agent of the issuer and has no authority to act on the issuer's behalf. Its "nomination" allows the beneficiary to present to it and earns it certain rights to payment under Section 5-109 that others do not enjoy. For example, when an issuer issues a "freely negotiable credit," it contemplates that banks or others might take up documents under that credit and advance value against them, and it is agreeing to pay those persons but only if the presentation to the issuer made by the nominated person complies with the credit. Usually there will be no agreement to pay, negotiate, or to serve in any other capacity by the nominated person, therefore the nominated person will have the right to decline to take the documents. It may return them or agree merely to act as a forwarding agent for the documents but without giving value against them or taking any responsibility for their conformity to the letter of credit.

Section 5-108. Issuer's Rights and Obligations

(a) Except as otherwise provided in Section 5-109, an issuer shall honor a presentation that, as determined by the standard practice referred to in subsection (e), appears on its face strictly to comply with the terms and conditions of the letter of credit. Except as otherwise provided in Section 5-113 and unless otherwise agreed with the applicant, an issuer shall dishonor a presentation that does not appear so to comply.

(b) An issuer has a reasonable time after presentation, but not beyond the end of the seventh business day of the issuer after the day of its receipt of documents:

(1) to honor,

(2) if the letter of credit provides for honor to be completed more than seven business days after presentation, to accept a draft or incur a deferred obligation, or

(3) to give notice to the presenter of discrepancies in the presentation.

(c) Except as otherwise provided in subsection (d), an issuer is precluded from asserting as a basis for dishonor any discrepancy if timely notice is not given, or any discrepancy not stated in the notice if timely notice is given.

(d) Failure to give the notice specified in subsection (b) or to mention fraud, forgery, or expiration in the notice does not preclude the issuer from asserting as a basis for dishonor fraud or forgery as described in Section 5-109(a) or expiration of the letter of credit before presentation.

(e) An issuer shall observe standard practice of financial institutions that regularly issue letters of credit. Determination of the issuer's observance of the standard practice is a matter of interpretation for the court. The court shall offer the parties a reasonable opportunity to present evidence of the standard practice.

(f) An issuer is not responsible for:

(1) the performance or nonperformance of the underlying contract, arrangement, or transaction,

(2) an act or omission of others, or

(3) observance or knowledge of the usage of a particular trade other than the standard practice referred to in subsection (e).

(g) If an undertaking constituting a letter of credit under Section 5-102(a)(10) contains nondocumentary conditions, an issuer shall disregard the nondocumentary conditions and treat them as if they were not stated.

(h) An issuer that has dishonored a presentation shall return the documents or hold them at the disposal of, and send advice to that effect to, the presenter.

(i) An issuer that has honored a presentation as permitted or required by this Article:

(1) is entitled to be reimbursed by the applicant in immediately available funds not later than the date of its payment of funds;

(2) takes the documents free of claims of the beneficiary or presenter;

(3) is precluded from asserting a right of recourse on a draft under Sections 3-414 and 3-415;

(4) except as otherwise provided in Sections 5-110 and 5-117, is precluded from restitution of money paid or other value given by mistake to the extent the mistake concerns discrepancies in the documents or tender which are apparent on the face of the presentation; and

(5) is discharged to the extent of its performance under the letter of credit unless the issuer honored a presentation in which a required signature of a beneficiary was forged.

Official Comment

1. This section combines some of the duties previously included in Sections 5-114 and 5-109. Because a confirmer has the rights and duties of an issuer, this section applies equally to a confirmer and an issuer. See Section 5-107(a).

The standard of strict compliance governs the issuer's obligation to the beneficiary and to the applicant. By requiring that a "presentation" appear strictly to comply, the section requires not only that the documents themselves appear on their face strictly to comply, but also that the other terms of the letter of credit such as those dealing with the time and place of presentation are strictly complied with. Typically, a letter of credit will provide that presentation is timely if made to the issuer, confirmer, or any other nominated person prior to expiration of the letter of credit. Accordingly, a nominated person that has honored a demand or otherwise given value before expiration will have a right to reimbursement from the issuer even though presentation to the issuer is made after the expiration of the letter of credit. Conversely, where the beneficiary negotiates documents to one who is not a nominated person, the beneficiary or that person acting on behalf of the beneficiary must make presentation to a nominated person, confirmer, or issuer prior to the expiration date.

This section does not impose a bifurcated standard under which an issuer's right to reimbursement might be broader than a beneficiary's right to honor. However, the explicit deference to standard practice in Section 5-108(a) and (e) and elsewhere expands issuers' rights of reimbursement where that practice so provides. Also, issuers can and often do contract with their applicants for expanded rights of reimbursement. Where that is done, the beneficiary will have to meet a more stringent standard of compliance as to the issuer than the issuer will have to meet as to the applicant. Similarly, a nominated person may have reimbursement and other rights against the issuer based on this Article, the UCP, bank-to-bank reimbursement rules, or other agreement or undertaking of the issuer. These rights may allow the nominated person to recover from the issuer even when the nominated person would have no right to obtain honor under the letter of credit.

The section adopts strict compliance, rather than the standard that commentators have called "substantial compliance," the standard arguably applied in *Banco Español de Credito v. State Street Bank & Trust Co.*, 385 F.2d 230 (1st Cir. 1967) and *Flagship Cruises Ltd. v. New England Merchants Nat'l Bank*, 569 F.2d 699 (1st Cir. 1978). Strict compliance does not mean slavish conformity to the terms of the letter of credit. For example, standard practice (what issuers do) may recognize certain presentations as complying that an unschooled layman would regard as discrepant. By adopting standard practice as a way of measuring strict compliance, this Article indorses the conclusion of the court in *New Braunfels Nat'l Bank v. Odiorne*, 780 S.W.2d 313 (Tex. Ct. App. 1989) (beneficiary could collect when draft requested payment on "Letter of Credit No. 86-1225" and letter of credit specified "Letter of Credit No. 86-122S" holding strict compliance does not demand oppressive perfectionism). The section also indorses the result in *Tosco Corp. v. FDIC*, 723 F.2d 1242 (6th Cir. 1983). The letter of credit in that case called for "drafts Drawn under Bank of Clarksville Letter of Credit Number 105." The draft presented stated "drawn under Bank of Clarksville, Clarksville, Tennessee letter of Credit No. 105." The court correctly found that despite the change of upper case "L" to a lower case "l" and the use of the word "No." instead of "Number," and despite the addition of the words "Clarksville, Tennessee," the presentation conformed. Similarly a document addressed by a foreign person to General Motors as "Jeneral Motors" would strictly conform in the absence of other defects.

Identifying and determining compliance with standard practice are matters of interpretation for the court, not for the jury. As with similar rules in Sections 4A-202(c) and 2-302, it is hoped that there will be more consistency in the outcomes and speedier resolution of disputes if the responsibility for determining the nature and scope of standard practice is granted to the court, not to a jury. Granting the court authority to make these decisions will also encourage the salutary practice of courts' granting summary judgment in circumstances where there are no significant factual disputes. The statute encourages outcomes such as that in *American Coleman Co. v. Intrawest Bank*, 887 F.2d 1382 (10th Cir. 1989), where summary judgment was granted.

In some circumstances standards may be established between the issuer and the applicant by agreement or by custom that would free the issuer from liability that it might otherwise have. For example, an applicant might agree that the issuer would have no duty whatsoever to examine documents on certain presentations (e.g., those below a certain dollar amount). Where the transaction depended upon the issuer's payment in a very short time period (e.g., on the same day or within a few hours of presentation), the issuer and the applicant might agree to reduce the issuer's responsibility for failure to discover discrepancies. By the same token, an agreement between the applicant and the issuer might permit the issuer to examine documents exclusively by electronic or electro-optical means. Neither those agreements nor others like them explicitly made by issuers and applicants violate the terms of Section 5-108(a) or (b) or Section 5-103(c).

2. Section 5-108(a) balances the need of the issuer for time to examine the documents against the possibility that the examiner (at the urging of the applicant or for fear that it will not be reimbursed) will take excessive time to search for defects. What is a "reasonable time" is not extended to accommodate an issuer's procuring a waiver from the applicant. See Article 14c of the UCP.

Under both the UCC and the UCP the issuer has a reasonable time to honor or give notice. The outside limit of that time is measured in business days under the UCC and in banking days under the UCP, a difference that will rarely be significant. Neither business nor banking days are defined in Article 5, but a court may find useful analogies in Regulation CC, 12 CFR 229.2, in state law outside of the Uniform Commercial Code, and in Article 4.

Examiners must note that the seven-day period is not a safe harbor. The time within which the issuer must give notice is the lesser of a reasonable time or seven business days. Where there are few documents (as, for example, with the mine run standby letter of credit), the reasonable time would be less than seven days. If more than a reasonable time is consumed in examination, no timely notice is possible. What is a "reasonable time" is to be determined by examining the behavior of those in the business of examining documents, mostly banks. Absent prior agreement of the issuer, one could not expect a bank issuer to examine documents while the beneficiary waited in the lobby if the normal practice was to give the documents to a person who had the opportunity to examine those together with many others in an orderly process. That the applicant has not yet paid the issuer or that the applicant's account with the issuer is insufficient to cover the amount of the draft is not a basis for extension of the time period.

This section does not preclude the issuer from contacting the applicant during its examination; however, the decision to honor rests with the issuer, and it has no duty to seek a waiver from the applicant or to notify the applicant of receipt of the documents. If the issuer dishonors a conforming presentation, the beneficiary will be entitled to the remedies under Section 5-111, irrespective of the applicant's views.

Even though the person to whom presentation is made cannot conduct a reasonable examination of documents within the time after presentation and before the expiration date, presentation establishes the parties' rights. The beneficiary's right to honor or the issuer's right to dishonor arises upon presentation at the place provided in the letter of credit even though it might take the person to whom presentation has been made several days to determine whether honor or dishonor is the proper course. The issuer's time for honor or giving notice of dishonor may be extended or shortened by a term in the letter of credit. The time for the issuer's performance may be otherwise modified or waived in accordance with Section 5-106.

The issuer's time to inspect runs from the time of its "receipt of documents." Documents are considered to be received only when they are received at the place specified for presentation by the issuer or other party to whom presentation is made. "Receipt of documents" when documents of title are presented must be read in light of the definition of "delivery" in Article 1, Section 1-201 and the definition of "presentation" in Section 5-102(a)(12).

Failure of the issuer to act within the time permitted by subsection (b) constitutes dishonor. Because of the preclusion in subsection (c) and the liability that the issuer may incur under Section 5-111 for wrongful dishonor, the effect of such a silent dishonor may ultimately be the same as though the issuer had honored, i.e., it may owe damages in the amount drawn but unpaid under the letter of credit.

3. The requirement that the issuer send notice of the discrepancies or be precluded from asserting discrepancies is new to Article 5. It is taken from the similar provision in the UCP and is intended to promote certainty and finality.

The section thus substitutes a strict preclusion principle for the doctrines of waiver and estoppel that might otherwise apply under Section 1-103. It rejects the reasoning in *Flagship Cruises Ltd. v. New England Merchants' Nat'l Bank*, 569 F.2d 699 (1st Cir. 1978) and *Wing On Bank Ltd. v. American Nat'l Bank & Trust Co.*, 457 F.2d 328 (5th Cir. 1972) where the issuer was held to be estopped only if the beneficiary relied on the issuer's failure to give notice.

Assume, for example, that the beneficiary presented documents to the issuer shortly before the letter of credit expired, in circumstances in which the beneficiary could not have cured any discrepancy before expiration. Under the reasoning of *Flagship* and *Wing On*, the beneficiary's inability to cure, even if it had received notice, would absolve the issuer of its failure to give notice. The virtue of the preclusion obligation adopted in this section is that it forecloses litigation about reliance and detriment.

Even though issuers typically give notice of the discrepancy of tardy presentation when presentation is made after the expiration of a credit, they are not required to give that notice and the section permits them to raise late presentation as a defect despite their failure to give that notice.

4. To act within a reasonable time, the issuer must normally give notice without delay after the examining party makes its decision. If the examiner decides to dishonor on the first day, it would be obliged to notify the beneficiary shortly thereafter, perhaps on the same business day. This rule accepts the reasoning in cases such as *Datapoint Corp. v. M & I Bank*, 665 F. Supp. 722 (W.D. Wis. 1987) and *Esso Petroleum Canada, Div. of Imperial Oil, Ltd. v. Security Pacific Bank*, 710 F. Supp. 275 (D. Ore. 1989).

The section deprives the examining party of the right simply to sit on a presentation that is made within seven days of expiration. The section requires the examiner to examine the documents and make a decision and, having made a decision to dishonor, to communicate promptly with the presenter. Nevertheless, a beneficiary who presents documents shortly before the expiration of a letter of credit runs the risk that it will never have the opportunity to cure any discrepancies.

5. Confirmers, other nominated persons, and collecting banks acting for beneficiaries can be presenters and, when so, are entitled to the notice provided in subsection (b). Even nominated persons who have honored or given value against an earlier presentation of the beneficiary and are themselves seeking reimbursement or honor need notice of discrepancies in the hope that they may be able to procure complying documents. The issuer has the obligations imposed by this section whether the issuer's performance is characterized as "reimbursement" of a nominated person or as "honor."

6. In many cases a letter of credit authorizes presentation by the beneficiary to someone other than the issuer. Sometimes that person is identified as a "payor" or "paying bank," or as an "acceptor" or "accepting bank," in other cases as a "negotiating bank," and in other cases there will be no specific designation. The section does not impose any duties on a person other than the issuer or confirmer, however a nominated person or other person may have liability under this Article or at common law if it fails to perform an express or implied agreement with the beneficiary.

7. The issuer's obligation to honor runs not only to the beneficiary but also to the applicant. It is possible that an applicant who has made a favorable contract with the beneficiary will be injured by the issuer's wrongful dishonor. Except to the extent that the contract between the issuer and the applicant limits that liability, the issuer will have liability to the applicant for wrongful dishonor under Section 5-111 as a matter of contract law. A good faith extension of the time in Section 5-108(b) by agreement between the issuer and beneficiary binds the applicant even if the applicant is not consulted or does not consent to the extension.

The issuer's obligation to dishonor when there is no apparent compliance with the letter of credit runs only to the applicant. No other party to the transaction can complain if the applicant waives compliance with terms or conditions of the letter of credit or agrees to a less stringent standard for compliance than that supplied by this Article. Except as otherwise agreed with the applicant, an issuer may dishonor a noncomplying presentation despite an applicant's waiver.

Waiver of discrepancies by an issuer or an applicant in one or more presentations does not waive similar discrepancies in a future presentation. Neither the issuer nor the beneficiary can reasonably rely upon honor over past waivers as a basis for concluding that a future defective presentation will justify honor. The reasoning of *Courtaulds of N. Am. Inc. v. North Carolina Nat'l Bank*, 528 F.2d 802 (4th Cir. 1975) is accepted and that expressed in *Schweibish v. Pontchartrain State Bank*, 389 So. 2d 731 (La. Ct. App. 1980) and *Titanium Metals Corp. v. Space Metals, Inc.*, 529 P.2d 431 (Utah 1974) is rejected.

8. The standard practice referred to in subsection (e) includes (i) international practice set forth in or referenced by the Uniform Customs and Practice, (ii) other practice rules published by associations of financial institutions, and (iii) local and regional practice. It is possible that standard practice will vary from one place to another. Where there are conflicting practices, the parties should indicate which practice governs their rights. A practice may be overridden by agreement or course of dealing. See Section 1-303(e).

9. The responsibility of the issuer under a letter of credit is to examine documents and to make a prompt decision to honor or dishonor based upon that examination. Nondocumentary conditions have no place in this regime and are better accommodated under contract or suretyship law and practice. In requiring that nondocumentary conditions in letters of credit be ignored as surplusage, Article 5 remains aligned with the UCP (see UCP 500 Article 13c), approves cases like *Pringle-Associated Mortgage Corp. v. Southern Nat'l Bank*, 571 F.2d 871, 874 (5th Cir. 1978), and rejects the reasoning in cases such as *Sherwood & Roberts, Inc. v. First Security Bank*, 682 P.2d 149 (Mont. 1984).

Subsection (g) recognizes that letters of credit sometimes contain nondocumentary terms or conditions. Conditions such as a term prohibiting "shipment on vessels more than 15 years old," are to be disregarded and treated as surplusage. Similarly, a requirement that there be an award by a "duly appointed arbitrator" would not require the issuer to determine whether the arbitrator had been "duly appointed." Likewise a term in a standby letter of credit that provided for differing forms of certification depending upon the particular type of default does not oblige the issuer independently to determine which kind of default has occurred. These conditions must be disregarded by the issuer. Where the nondocumentary conditions are central and fundamental to the issuer's obligation (as for example a condition that would require the issuer to determine in fact whether the beneficiary had performed the underlying contract or whether the applicant had defaulted) their inclusion may remove the undertaking from the scope of Article 5 entirely. See Section 5-102(a)(10) and Comment 6 to Section 5-102.

Subsection (g) would not permit the beneficiary or the issuer to disregard terms in the letter of credit such as place, time, and mode of presentation. The rule in subsection (g) is intended to prevent an issuer from deciding or even investigating extrinsic facts, but not from consulting the clock, the calendar, the relevant law and practice, or its own general knowledge of documentation or transactions of the type underlying a particular letter of credit.

Even though nondocumentary conditions must be disregarded in determining compliance of a presentation (and thus in determining the issuer's duty to the beneficiary), an issuer that has promised its applicant that it will honor only on the occurrence of those nondocumentary conditions may have liability to its applicant for disregarding the conditions.

10. Subsection (f) condones an issuer's ignorance of "any usage of a particular trade"; that trade is the trade of the applicant, beneficiary, or others who may be involved in the underlying transaction. The issuer is expected to know usage that is commonly encountered in the course of document examination. For example, an issuer should know the common usage with respect to documents in the maritime shipping trade but would not be expected to understand synonyms used in a particular trade for product descriptions appearing in a letter of credit or an invoice.

11. Where the issuer's performance is the delivery of an item of value other than money, the applicant's reimbursement obligation would be to make the "item of value" available to the issuer.

12. An issuer is entitled to reimbursement from the applicant after honor of a forged or fraudulent drawing if honor was permitted under Section 5-109(a).

13. The last clause of Section 5-108(i)(5) deals with a special case in which the fraud is not committed by the beneficiary, but is committed by a stranger to the transaction who forges the beneficiary's signature. If the issuer pays against documents on which a required signature of the beneficiary is forged, it remains liable to the true beneficiary. This principle is applicable to both electronic and tangible documents.

Section 5-109. Fraud and Forgery

(a) If a presentation is made that appears on its face strictly to comply with the terms and conditions of the letter of credit, but a required document is forged or materially fraudulent, or honor of the presentation would facilitate a material fraud by the beneficiary on the issuer or applicant:

(1) the issuer shall honor the presentation, if honor is demanded by (i) a nominated person who has given value in good faith and without notice of forgery or material fraud, (ii) a confirmer who has honored its confirmation in good faith, (iii) a holder in due course of a draft drawn under the letter of credit which was taken after acceptance by the issuer or nominated person, or (iv) an assignee of the issuer's or nominated person's deferred obligation that was taken for value and without notice of forgery or material fraud after the obligation was incurred by the issuer or nominated person; and

(2) the issuer, acting in good faith, may honor or dishonor the presentation in any other case.

(b) If an applicant claims that a required document is forged or materially fraudulent or that honor of the presentation would facilitate a material fraud by the beneficiary on the issuer or applicant, a court of competent jurisdiction may temporarily or permanently enjoin the issuer from honoring a presentation or grant similar relief against the issuer or other persons only if the court finds that:

(1) the relief is not prohibited under the law applicable to an accepted draft or deferred obligation incurred by the issuer;

(2) a beneficiary, issuer, or nominated person who may be adversely affected is adequately protected against loss that it may suffer because the relief is granted;

(3) all of the conditions to entitle a person to the relief under the law of this State have been met; and

(4) on the basis of the information submitted to the court, the applicant is more likely than not to succeed under its claim of forgery or material fraud and the person demanding honor does not qualify for protection under subsection (a)(1).

Official Comment

1. This recodification makes clear that fraud must be found either in the documents or must have been committed by the beneficiary on the issuer or applicant. See *Cromwell v. Commerce & Energy Bank*, 464 So. 2d 721 (La. 1985).

Secondly, it makes clear that fraud must be "material." Necessarily courts must decide the breadth and width of "materiality." The use of the word requires that the fraudulent aspect of a document be material to a purchaser of that document or that the fraudulent act be significant to the participants in the underlying transaction. Assume, for example, that the beneficiary has a contract to deliver 1,000 barrels of salad oil. Knowing that it has delivered only 998, the beneficiary nevertheless submits an invoice showing 1,000 barrels. If two barrels in a 1,000 barrel shipment would be an insubstantial and immaterial breach of the underlying contract, the beneficiary's act, though possibly fraudulent, is not materially so and would not justify an injunction. Conversely, the knowing submission of those invoices upon delivery of only five barrels would be materially fraudulent. The courts must examine the underlying transaction when there is an allegation of material fraud, for only by examining that transaction can one determine whether a document is fraudulent or the beneficiary has committed fraud and, if so, whether the fraud was material.

Material fraud by the beneficiary occurs only when the beneficiary has no colorable right to expect honor and where there is no basis in fact to support such a right to honor. The section indorses articulations such as those stated in *Intraworld Indus. v. Girard Trust Bank*, 336 A.2d 316 (Pa. 1975), *Roman Ceramics Corp. v. People's Nat'l Bank*, 714 F.2d 1207 (3d Cir. 1983), and similar decisions and embraces certain decisions under Section 5-114 that relied upon the phrase "fraud in the transaction." Some of these decisions have been summarized as follows in *Ground Air Transfer v. Westate's Airlines*, 899 F.2d 1269, 127273 (1st Cir. 1990):

> We have said throughout that courts may not "*normally*" issue an injunction because of an important exception to the general "no injunction" rule. The exception, as we also explained in Itek, 730 F.2d at 2425, concerns "fraud" so serious as to make it obviously pointless and unjust to permit the beneficiary to obtain the money. Where the circumstances

"*plainly*" show that the underlying contract forbids the beneficiary to call a letter of credit, Itek, 730 F.2d at 24; where they show that the contract deprives the beneficiary of even a "*colorable*" right to do so, id., at 25; where the contract and circumstances reveal that the beneficiary's demand for payment has "absolutely no basis in fact," id.; see *Dynamics Corp. of America,* 356 F. Supp. at 999; where the beneficiary's conduct has "so vitiated the entire transaction that the legitimate purposes of the independence of the issuer's obligation would no longer be served," Itek, 730 F.2d at 25 (quoting *Roman Ceramics Corp. v. Peoples Nat'l Bank,* 714 F.2d 1207, 1212 n.12, 1215 (3d Cir. 1983) (quoting *Intraworld Indus.,* 336 A.2d at 32425)); *then* a court may enjoin payment.

2. Subsection (a)(2) makes clear that the issuer may honor in the face of the applicant's claim of fraud. The subsection also makes clear what was not stated in former Section 5-114, that the issuer may dishonor and defend that dishonor by showing fraud or forgery of the kind stated in subsection (a). Because issuers may be liable for wrongful dishonor if they are unable to prove forgery or material fraud, presumably most issuers will choose to honor despite applicant's claims of fraud or forgery unless the applicant procures an injunction. Merely because the issuer has a right to dishonor and to defend that dishonor by showing forgery or material fraud does not mean it has a duty to the applicant to dishonor. The applicant's normal recourse is to procure an injunction, if the applicant is unable to procure an injunction, it will have a claim against the issuer only in the rare case in which it can show that the issuer did not honor in good faith.

3. Whether a beneficiary can commit fraud by presenting a draft under a clean letter of credit (one calling only for a draft and no other documents) has been much debated. Under the current formulation it would be possible but difficult for there to be fraud in such a presentation. If the applicant were able to show that the beneficiary were committing material fraud on the applicant in the underlying transaction, then payment would facilitate a material fraud by the beneficiary on the applicant and honor could be enjoined. The courts should be skeptical of claims of fraud by one who has signed a "suicide" or clean credit and thus granted a beneficiary the right to draw by mere presentation of a draft.

4. The standard for injunctive relief is high, and the burden remains on the applicant to show, by evidence and not by mere allegation, that such relief is warranted. Some courts have enjoined payments on letters of credit on insufficient showing by the applicant. For example, in *Griffin Cos. v. First Nat'l Bank,* 374 N.W.2d 768 (Minn. Ct. App. 1985), the court enjoined payment under a standby letter of credit, basing its decision on plaintiff's allegation, rather than competent evidence, of fraud.

There are at least two ways to prohibit injunctions against honor under this section after acceptance of a draft by the issuer. First is to define honor (see Section 5-102(a)(8)) in the particular letter of credit to occur upon acceptance and without regard to later payment of the acceptance. Second is explicitly to agree that the applicant has no right to an injunction after acceptance—whether or not the acceptance constitutes honor.

5. Although the statute deals principally with injunctions against honor, it also cautions against granting "similar relief" and the same principles apply when the applicant or issuer attempts to achieve the same legal outcome by injunction against presentation (see *Ground Air Transfer Inc. v. Westates Airlines, Inc.*, 899 F.2d 1269 (1st Cir. 1990)), interpleader, declaratory judgment, or attachment. These attempts should face the same obstacles that face efforts to enjoin the issuer from paying. Expanded use of any of these devices could threaten the independence principle just as much as injunctions against honor. For that reason courts should have the same hostility to them and place the same restrictions on their use as would be applied to injunctions against honor. Courts should not allow the "sacred cow of equity to trample the tender vines of letter of credit law."

6. Section 5-109(a)(1) also protects specified third parties against the risk of fraud. By issuing a letter of credit that nominates a person to negotiate or pay, the issuer (ultimately the applicant) induces that nominated person to give value and thereby assumes the risk that a draft drawn under the letter of credit will be transferred to one with a status like that of a holder in due course who deserves to be protected against a fraud defense.

7. The "loss" to be protected against—by bond or otherwise under subsection (b)(2)—includes incidental damages. Among those are legal fees that might be incurred by the beneficiary or issuer in defending against an injunction action.

Section 5-110. Warranties

(a) If its presentation is honored, the beneficiary warrants:

(1) to the issuer, any other person to whom presentation is made, and the applicant that there is no fraud or forgery of the kind described in Section 5-109(a); and

(2) to the applicant that the drawing does not violate any agreement between the applicant and beneficiary or any other agreement intended by them to be augmented by the letter of credit.

(b) The warranties in subsection (a) are in addition to warranties arising under Article 3, 4, 7, and 8 because of the presentation or transfer of documents covered by any of those Articles.

Official Comment

1. Since the warranties in subsection (a) are not given unless a letter of credit has been honored, no breach of warranty under this subsection can be a defense to dishonor by the issuer. Any defense must be based on Section 5-108 or 5-109 and not on this section. Also, breach of the warranties by the beneficiary in subsection (a) cannot excuse the applicant's duty to reimburse.

2. The warranty in Section 5-110(a)(2) assumes that payment under the letter of credit is final. It does not run to the issuer, only to the applicant. In most cases the applicant will have a direct cause of action for breach of the underlying contract. This warranty has primary application in standby letters of credit or other circumstances where the applicant is not a party to an underlying contract with the beneficiary. It is not a warranty that the statements made on the presentation of the documents presented are truthful nor is it a warranty that the documents strictly comply under Section 5-108(a). It is a warranty that the beneficiary has performed all the acts expressly and implicitly necessary under any underlying agreement to entitle the beneficiary to honor. If, for example, an underlying sales contract authorized the beneficiary to draw only upon "due performance" and the beneficiary drew even though it had breached the underlying contract by delivering defective goods, honor of its draw would break the warranty. By the same token, if the underlying contract authorized the beneficiary to draw only upon actual default or upon its or a third party's determination of default by the applicant and if the beneficiary drew in violation of its authorization, then upon honor of its draw the warranty would be breached. In many cases, therefore, the documents presented to the issuer will contain inaccurate statements (concerning the goods delivered or concerning default or other matters), but the breach of warranty arises not because the statements are untrue but because the beneficiary's drawing violated its express or implied obligations in the underlying transaction.

3. The damages for breach of warranty are not specified in Section 5-111. Courts may find damage analogies in Section 2-714 in Article 2 and in warranty decisions under Articles 3 and 4.

Unlike wrongful dishonor cases—where the damages usually equal the amount of the draw—the damages for breach of warranty will often be much less than the amount of the draw, sometimes zero. Assume a seller entitled to draw only on proper performance of its sales contract. Assume it breaches the sales contract in a way that gives the buyer a right to damages but no right to reject. The applicant's damages for breach of the warranty in subsection (a)(2) are limited to the damages it could recover for breach of the contract of sale. Alternatively assume an underlying agreement that authorizes a beneficiary to draw only the "amount in default." Assume a default of $200,000 and a draw of $500,000. The damages for breach of warranty would be no more than $300,000.

Section 5-111. Remedies

(a) If an issuer wrongfully dishonors or repudiates its obligation to pay money under a letter of credit before presentation, the beneficiary, successor, or nominated person presenting on its own behalf may recover from the issuer the amount that is the subject of the dishonor or repudiation. If the issuer's obligation under the letter of credit is not for the payment of money, the claimant may obtain specific performance or, at the claimant's election, recover an amount equal to the value of performance from the issuer. In either case, the claimant may also recover incidental but not consequential damages. The claimant is not obligated to take action to avoid damages that might be due from the issuer under this subsection. If, although not obligated to do so, the claimant avoids damages, the claimant's recovery from the issuer must be reduced by the amount of damages avoided. The issuer has the burden of proving the amount of damages avoided. In the case of repudiation the claimant need not present any document.

(b) If an issuer wrongfully dishonors a draft or demand presented under a letter of credit or honors a draft or demand in breach of its obligation to the applicant, the applicant may recover damages resulting from the breach, including incidental but not consequential damages, less any amount saved as a result of the breach.

(c) If an adviser or nominated person other than a confirmer breaches an obligation under this Article or an issuer breaches an obligation not covered in subsection (a) or (b), a person to whom the obligation is owed may recover damages resulting from the breach, including incidental but not consequential damages, less any amount saved as a result of the breach. To the extent of the confirmation, a confirmer has the liability of an issuer specified in this subsection and subsections (a) and (b).

(d) An issuer, nominated person, or adviser who is found liable under subsection (a), (b), or (c) shall pay interest on the amount owed thereunder from the date of wrongful dishonor or other appropriate date.

(e) Reasonable attorney's fees and other expenses of litigation must be awarded to the prevailing party in an action in which a remedy is sought under this Article.

(f) Damages that would otherwise be payable by a party for breach of an obligation under this Article may be liquidated by agreement or undertaking, but only in an amount or by a formula that is reasonable in light of the harm anticipated.

Official Comment

1. The right to specific performance is new. The express limitation on the duty of the beneficiary to mitigate damages adopts the position of certain courts and commentators. Because the letter of credit depends upon speed and certainty of payment, it is important that the issuer not be given an incentive to dishonor. The issuer might have an incentive to dishonor if it could rely on the burden of mitigation falling on the beneficiary (e.g., to sell goods and sue only for the difference between the price of the goods sold and the amount due under the letter of credit). Under the scheme contemplated by Section 5-111(a), the beneficiary would present the documents to the issuer. If the issuer wrongfully dishonored, the beneficiary would have no further duty to the issuer with respect to the goods covered by documents that the issuer dishonored and returned. The issuer thus takes the risk that the beneficiary will let the goods rot or be destroyed. Of course the beneficiary may have a duty of mitigation to the applicant arising from the underlying agreement, but the issuer would not have the right to assert that duty by way of defense or setoff. See Section 5-117(d). If the beneficiary sells the goods covered by dishonored documents or if the beneficiary sells a draft after acceptance but before dishonor by the issuer, the net amount so gained should be subtracted from the amount of the beneficiary's damages—at least where the damage claim against the issuer equals or exceeds the damage suffered by the beneficiary. If, on the other hand, the beneficiary suffers damages in an underlying transaction in an amount that exceeds the amount of the wrongfully dishonored demand (e.g., where the letter of credit does not cover 100 percent of the underlying obligation), the damages avoided should not necessarily be deducted from the beneficiary's claim against the issuer. In such a case, the damages would be the lesser of (i) the amount recoverable in the absence of mitigation (that is, the amount that is subject to the dishonor or repudiation plus any incidental damages) and (ii) the damages remaining after deduction for the amount of damages actually avoided.

A beneficiary need not present documents as a condition of suit for anticipatory repudiation, but if a beneficiary could never have obtained documents necessary for a presentation conforming to the letter of credit, the beneficiary cannot recover for anticipatory repudiation of the letter of credit. *Doelger v. Battery Park Bank*, 194 N.Y.S. 582 (App. Div. 1922); *Decor by Nikkei Int'l, Inc. v. Federal Republic of Nigeria*, 497 F. Supp. 893 (S.D.N.Y. 1980), aff'd, 647 F.2d 300 (2d Cir. 1981), cert. denied, 454 U.S. 1148 (1982). The last sentence of subsection (c) does not expand the liability of a confirmer to persons to whom the confirmer would not otherwise be liable under Section 5-107.

Almost all letters of credit, including those that call for an acceptance, are "obligations to pay money" as that term is used in Section 5-111(a).

2. What damages "result" from improper honor is for the courts to decide. Even though an issuer pays a beneficiary in violation of Section 5-108(a) or of its contract with the applicant, it may have no liability to an applicant. If the underlying contract has been fully performed, the applicant may not have been damaged by the issuer's breach. Such a case would occur when *A* contracts for goods at $100 per ton, but, upon delivery, the market value of conforming goods has decreased to $25 per ton. If the issuer pays over discrepancies, there should be no recovery by *A* for the price differential if the issuer's breach did not alter the applicant's obligation under the underlying contract, i.e., to pay $100 per ton for goods now worth $25 per ton. On the other hand, if the applicant intends to resell the goods and must itself satisfy the strict compliance requirements under a second letter of credit in connection with its sale, the applicant may be damaged by the issuer's payment despite discrepancies because the applicant itself may then be unable to procure honor on the letter of credit where it is the beneficiary, and may be unable to mitigate its damages by enforcing its rights against others in the underlying transaction. Note that an issuer found liable to its applicant may have recourse under Section 5-117 by subrogation to the applicant's claim against the beneficiary or other persons.

One who inaccurately advises a letter of credit breaches its obligation to the beneficiary, but may cause no damage. If the beneficiary knows the terms of the letter of credit and understands the advice to be inaccurate, the beneficiary will have suffered no damage as a result of the adviser's breach.

3. Since the confirmer has the rights and duties of an issuer, in general it has an issuer's liability, see subsection (c). The confirmer is usually a confirming bank. A confirming bank often also plays the role of an adviser. If it breaks its obligation to the beneficiary, the confirming bank may have liability as an issuer or, depending upon the obligation that was broken, as an adviser. For example, a wrongful dishonor would give it liability as an issuer under Section 5-111(a). On the other hand a confirming bank that broke its obligation to advise the credit but did not commit wrongful dishonor would be treated under Section 5-111(c).

4. Consequential damages for breach of obligations under this Article are excluded in the belief that these damages can best be avoided by the beneficiary or the applicant and out of the fear that imposing consequential damages on issuers would raise the cost of the letter of credit to a level that might render it uneconomic. *A fortiori* punitive and exemplary damages are excluded, however, this section does not bar recovery of consequential or even punitive damages for breach of statutory or common law duties arising outside of this Article.

5. The section does not specify a rate of interest. It leaves the setting of the rate to the court. It would be appropriate for a court to use the rate that would normally apply in that court in other situations where interest is imposed by law.

6. The court must award attorney's fees to the prevailing party, whether that party is an applicant, a beneficiary, an issuer, a nominated person, or adviser. Since the issuer may be entitled to recover its legal fees and costs from the applicant under the reimbursement agreement, allowing the issuer to recover those fees from a losing beneficiary may also protect the applicant against undeserved losses. The party entitled to attorneys' fees has been described as the "prevailing party." Sometimes it will be unclear which party "prevailed," for example, where there are multiple issues and one party wins on some and the other party wins on others. Determining which is the prevailing party is in the discretion of the court. Subsection (e) authorizes attorney's fees in all actions where a remedy is sought "under this Article." It applies even when the remedy might be an injunction under Section 5-109 or when the claimed remedy is otherwise outside of Section 5-111. Neither an issuer nor a confirmer should be treated as a "losing" party when an injunction is granted to the applicant over the objection of the issuer or confirmer; accordingly neither should be liable for fees and expenses in that case.

"Expenses of litigation" is intended to be broader than "costs." For example, expense of litigation would include travel expenses of witnesses, fees for expert witnesses, and expenses associated with taking depositions.

7. For the purposes of Section 5-111(f) "harm anticipated" must be anticipated at the time when the agreement that includes the liquidated damage clause is executed or at the time when the undertaking that includes the clause is issued. See Section 2A-5504.

Section 5-112. Transfer of Letter of Credit

(a) Except as otherwise provided in Section 5-113, unless a letter of credit provides that it is transferable, the right of a beneficiary to draw or otherwise demand performance under a letter of credit may not be transferred.

(b) Even if a letter of credit provides that it is transferable, the issuer may refuse to recognize or carry out a transfer if:

(1) the transfer would violate applicable law; or

(2) the transferor or transferee has failed to comply with any requirement stated in the letter of credit or any other requirement relating to transfer imposed by the issuer which is within the standard practice referred to in Section 5-108(e) or is otherwise reasonable under the circumstances.

Official Comment

1. In order to protect the applicant's reliance on the designated beneficiary, letter of credit law traditionally has forbidden the beneficiary to convey to third parties its right to draw or demand payment under the letter of credit. Subsection (a) codifies that rule. The term "transfer" refers to the beneficiary's conveyance of that right. Absent incorporation of the UCP (which make elaborate provision for partial transfer of a commercial letter of credit) or similar trade practice and absent other express indication in the letter of credit that the term is used to mean something else, a term in the letter of credit indicating that the beneficiary has the right to transfer should be taken to mean that the beneficiary may convey to a third party its right to draw or demand payment. Even in that case, the issuer or other person controlling the transfer may make the beneficiary's right to transfer subject to conditions, such as timely notification, payment of a fee, delivery of the letter of credit to the issuer or other person controlling the transfer, or execution of appropriate forms to document the transfer. A nominated person who is not a confirmer has no obligation to recognize a transfer.

The power to establish "requirements" does not include the right absolutely to refuse to recognize transfers under a transferable letter of credit. An issuer who wishes to retain the right to deny all transfers should not issue transferable letters of credit or should incorporate the UCP. By stating its requirements in the letter of credit an issuer may impose any requirement without regard to its conformity to practice or reasonableness. Transfer requirements of issuers and nominated persons must be made known to potential transferors and transferees to enable those parties to comply with the requirements. A common method of making such requirements known is to use a form that indicates the information that must be provided and the instructions that must be given to enable the issuer or nominated person to comply with a request to transfer.

2. The issuance of a transferable letter of credit with the concurrence of the applicant is *ipso facto* an agreement by the issuer and applicant to permit a beneficiary to transfer its drawing right and permit a nominated person to recognize and carry out that transfer without further notice to them. In international commerce, transferable letters of credit are often issued under circumstances in which a nominated person or adviser is expected to facilitate the transfer from the original beneficiary to a transferee and to deal with that transferee. In those circumstances it is the responsibility of the nominated person or adviser to establish procedures satisfactory to protect itself against double presentation or dispute about the right to draw under the letter of credit. Commonly such a person will control the transfer by requiring that the original letter of credit be given to it or by causing a paper copy marked as an original to be issued where the original letter of credit was electronic. By keeping possession of the original letter of credit the nominated person or adviser can minimize or entirely exclude the possibility that the original beneficiary could properly procure payment from another bank. If the letter of credit requires presentation of the original letter of credit itself, no other payment could be procured. In addition to imposing whatever requirements it considers appropriate to protect itself against double payment the person that is facilitating the transfer has a right to charge an appropriate fee for its activity.

"Transfer" of a letter of credit should be distinguished from "assignment of proceeds." The former is analogous to a novation or a substitution of beneficiaries. It contemplates not merely payment to but also performance by the transferee. For example, under the typical terms of transfer for a commercial letter of credit, a transferee could comply with a letter of credit transferred to it by signing and presenting its own draft and invoice. An assignee of proceeds, on the other hand, is wholly dependent on the presentation of a draft and invoice signed by the beneficiary.

By agreeing to the issuance of a transferable letter of credit, which is not qualified or limited, the applicant may lose control over the identity of the person whose performance will earn payment under the letter of credit.

Section 5-113. Transfer by Operation of Law

(a) A successor of a beneficiary may consent to amendments, sign and present documents, and receive payment or other items of value in the name of the beneficiary without disclosing its status as a successor.

(b) A successor of a beneficiary may consent to amendments, sign and present documents, and receive payment or other items of value in its own name as the disclosed successor of the beneficiary. Except as otherwise provided in subsection (e), an issuer shall recognize a disclosed successor of a beneficiary as beneficiary in full substitution for its predecessor upon compliance with the requirements for recognition by the issuer of a transfer of drawing rights by operation of law under the standard practice referred to in Section 5-108(e) or, in the absence of such a practice, compliance with other reasonable procedures sufficient to protect the issuer.

(c) An issuer is not obliged to determine whether a purported successor is a successor of a beneficiary or whether the signature of a purported successor is genuine or authorized.

(d) Honor of a purported successor's apparently complying presentation under subsection (a) or (b) has the consequences specified in Section 5-108(i) even if the purported successor is not the successor of a beneficiary. Documents signed in the name of the beneficiary or of a disclosed successor by a person who is neither the beneficiary nor the successor of the beneficiary are forged documents for the purposes of Section 5-109.

(e) An issuer whose rights of reimbursement are not covered by subsection (d) or substantially similar law and any confirmer or nominated person may decline to recognize a presentation under subsection (b).

(f) A beneficiary whose name is changed after the issuance of a letter of credit has the same rights and obligations as a successor of a beneficiary under this section.

Official Comment

This section affirms the result in *Pastor v. Nat'l Republic Bank of Chicago*, 390 N.E.2d 894 (Ill. 1979) and *FDIC v. Bank of Boulder*, 911 F.2d 1466 (10th Cir. 1990). Both electronic and tangible documents may be signed.

An issuer's requirements for recognition of a successor's status might include presentation of a certificate of merger, a court order appointing a bankruptcy trustee or receiver, a certificate of appointment as bankruptcy trustee, or the like. The issuer is entitled to rely upon such documents which on their face demonstrate that presentation is made by a successor of a beneficiary. It is not obliged to make an independent investigation to determine the fact of succession.

Section 5-114. Assignment of Proceeds

(a) In this section, "proceeds of a letter of credit" means the cash, check, accepted draft, or other item of value paid or delivered upon honor or giving of value by the issuer or any nominated person under the letter of credit. The term does not include a beneficiary's drawing rights or documents presented by the beneficiary.

(b) A beneficiary may assign its right to part or all of the proceeds of a letter of credit. The beneficiary may do so before presentation as a present assignment of its right to receive proceeds contingent upon its compliance with the terms and conditions of the letter of credit.

(c) An issuer or nominated person need not recognize an assignment of proceeds of a letter of credit until it consents to the assignment.

(d) An issuer or nominated person has no obligation to give or withhold its consent to an assignment of proceeds of a letter of credit, but consent may not be unreasonably withheld if the assignee possesses and exhibits the letter of credit and presentation of the letter of credit is a condition to honor.

(e) Rights of a transferee beneficiary or nominated person are independent of the beneficiary's assignment of the proceeds of a letter of credit and are superior to the assignee's right to the proceeds.

(f) Neither the rights recognized by this section between an assignee and an issuer, transferee beneficiary, or nominated person nor the issuer's or nominated person's payment of proceeds to an assignee or a third person affect the rights between the assignee and any person other than the issuer, transferee beneficiary, or nominated person. The mode of creating and perfecting a security interest in or granting an assignment of a beneficiary's rights to proceeds is governed by Article 9 or other law. Against persons other than the issuer, transferee beneficiary, or nominated person, the rights and obligations arising upon the creation of a security interest or other assignment of a beneficiary's right to proceeds and its perfection are governed by Article 9 or other law.

Official Comment

1. Subsection (b) expressly validates the beneficiary's present assignment of letter of credit proceeds if made after the credit is established but before the proceeds are realized. This section adopts the prevailing usage—"assignment of proceeds"—to an assignee. That terminology carries with it no implication, however, that an assignee acquires no interest until the proceeds are paid by the issuer. For example, an "assignment of the right to proceeds" of a letter of credit for purposes of security that meets the requirements of Section 9-203(b) would constitute the present creation of a security interest in that right. This security interest can be perfected by control (Section 9-107). Although subsection (a) explains the meaning of " 'proceeds' of a letter of credit," it should be emphasized that those proceeds also may be Article 9 proceeds of other collateral. For example, if a seller of inventory receives a letter of credit to support the account that arises upon the sale, payments made under the letter of credit are Article 9 proceeds of the inventory, account, and any document of title covering the inventory. Thus, the secured party who had a perfected security interest in that inventory, account, or document has a perfected security interest in the proceeds collected under the letter of credit, so long as they are identifiable cash proceeds (Section 9-315(a), (d)). This perfection is continuous, regardless of whether the secured party perfected a security interest in the right to letter of credit proceeds.

2. An assignee's rights to enforce an assignment of proceeds against an issuer and the priority of the assignee's rights against a nominated person or transferee beneficiary are governed by Article 5. Those rights and that priority are stated in subsections (c), (d), and (e). Note also that Section 4-210 gives first priority to a collecting bank that has given value for a documentary draft.

3. By requiring that an issuer or nominated person consent to the assignment of proceeds of a letter of credit, subsections (c) and (d) follow more closely recognized national and international letter of credit practices than did prior law. In most circumstances, it has always been advisable for the assignee to obtain the consent of the issuer in order better to safeguard its right to the proceeds. When notice of an assignment has been received, issuers normally have required signatures on a consent form. This practice is reflected in the revision. By unconditionally consenting to such an assignment, the issuer or nominated person becomes bound, subject to the rights of the superior parties specified in subsection (e), to pay to the assignee the assigned letter of credit proceeds that the issuer or nominated person would otherwise pay to the beneficiary or another assignee.

Where the letter of credit must be presented as a condition to honor and the assignee holds and exhibits the letter of credit to the issuer or nominated person, the risk to the issuer or nominated person of having to pay twice is minimized. In such a situation, subsection (d) provides that the issuer or nominated person may not unreasonably withhold its consent to the assignment.

Section 5-115. Statute of Limitations

An action to enforce a right or obligation arising under this Article must be commenced within one year after the expiration date of the relevant letter of credit or one year after the [claim for relief] [cause of action] accrues, whichever occurs later. A [claim for relief] [cause of action] accrues when the breach occurs, regardless of the aggrieved party's lack of knowledge of the breach.

Official Comment

1. This section is based on Sections 4-111 and 2-725(2).

2. This section applies to all claims for which there are remedies under Section 5-111 and to other claims made under this Article, such as claims for breach of warranty under Section 5-110. Because it covers all claims under Section 5-111, the statute of limitations applies not only to wrongful dishonor claims against the issuer but also to claims between the issuer and the applicant arising from the reimbursement agreement. These might be for reimbursement (issuer v. applicant) or for breach of the reimbursement contract by wrongful honor (applicant v. issuer).

3. The statute of limitations, like the rest of the statute, applies only to a letter of credit issued on or after the effective date and only to transactions, events, obligations, or duties arising out of or associated with such a letter. If a letter of credit was issued before the effective date and an obligation on that letter of credit was breached after the effective date, the complaining party could bring its suit within the time that would have been permitted prior to the adoption of Section 5-115 and would not be limited by the terms of Section 5-115.

Section 5-116. Choice of Law and Forum

(a) The liability of an issuer, nominated person, or adviser for action or omission is governed by the law of the jurisdiction chosen by an agreement in the form of a record signed by the affected parties or by a provision in the person's letter of credit, confirmation, or other undertaking. The jurisdiction whose law is chosen need not bear any relation to the transaction.

(b) Unless subsection (a) applies, the liability of an issuer, nominated person, or adviser for action or omission is governed by the law of the jurisdiction in which the person is located. The person is considered to be located at the address indicated in the person's undertaking. If more than one address is indicated, the person is considered to be located at the address from which the person's undertaking was issued.

(c) For the purpose of jurisdiction, choice of law, and recognition of interbranch letters of credit, but not enforcement of a judgment, all branches of a bank are considered separate juridical entities and a bank is considered to be located at the place where its relevant branch is considered to be located under subsection (d).

(d) A branch of a bank is considered to be located at the address indicated in the branch's undertaking. If more than one address is indicated, the branch is considered to be located at the address from which the undertaking was issued.

(e) Except as otherwise provided in this subsection, the liability of an issuer, nominated person, or adviser is governed by any rules of custom or practice, such as the Uniform Customs and Practice for Documentary Credits, to which the letter of credit, confirmation, or other undertaking is expressly made subject. If (i) this Article would govern the liability of an issuer, nominated person, or adviser under subsection (a) or (b), (ii) the relevant undertaking incorporates rules of custom or practice, and (iii) there is conflict between this Article and those rules as applied to that undertaking, those rules govern except to the extent of any conflict with the nonvariable provisions specified in Section 5-103(c).

(f) If there is conflict between this Article and Article 3, 4, 4A, or 9, this Article governs.

(g) The forum for settling disputes arising out of an undertaking within this Article may be chosen in the manner and with the binding effect that governing law may be chosen in accordance with subsection (a).

Official Comment

1. Subsection (a) refers to a record signed by the affected parties. The reference in the pre-2022 text of subsection (a) to an authentication pursuant to an agreement of the parties or standard practice is no longer necessary in view of the 2022 revision of "sign" in Section 1-201. See Section 5-104, Comment 2.

Although it would be possible for the parties to agree otherwise, the law normally chosen by agreement under subsection (a) and that provided in the absence of agreement under subsection (b) is the substantive law of a particular jurisdiction not including the choice of law principles of that jurisdiction. Thus, two parties, an issuer and an applicant, both located in Oklahoma might choose the law of New York. Unless they agree otherwise, the section anticipates that they wish the substantive law of New York to apply to their transaction and they do not intend that a New York choice of law principle might direct a court to Oklahoma law. By the same token, the liability of an issuer located in New York is governed by New York substantive law—in the absence of agreement—even in circumstances in which choice of law principles found in the common law of New York might direct one to the law of another State. Subsection (b) states the relevant choice of law principles and it should not be subordinated to some other choice of law rule. Within the States of the United States *renvoi* will not be a problem once every jurisdiction has enacted Section 5-116 because every jurisdiction will then have the same choice of law rule and in a particular case all choice of law rules will point to the same substantive law.

Subsection (b) does not state a choice of law rule for the "liability of an applicant." However, subsection (b) does state a choice of law rule for the liability of an issuer, nominated person, or adviser, and since some of the issues in suits by applicants against those persons involve the "liability of an issuer, nominated person, or adviser," subsection (b) states the choice of law rule for those issues. Because an issuer may have liability to a confirmer both as an issuer (Section 5-108(a), Comment 5 to Section 5-108) and as an applicant (Section 5-107(a), Comment 1 to Section 5-107, Section 5-108(i)), subsection (b) may state the choice of law rule for some but not all of the issuer's liability in a suit by a confirmer.

1A. The last sentence of pre-2022 subsection (b) is now in a new subsection (c) and a new subsection (d) has been added. These revisions were necessary to eliminate a potential ambiguity arising from the first sentence of subsection (b). The first sentence has been construed incorrectly as meaning that the last sentence, which recognizes the separateness of bank branches for the specified purposes, is inapplicable when a governing law has been chosen pursuant to subsection (a). These revisions reject that construction and reject decisions such as *Zeeco, Inc. v. JPMorgan Chase Bank*, Case No. 17 - CV-384-JED-FHM, 2018 WL 1414119 (N.D. Okla. Mar. 21, 2018), *amending opinion dated March 20, 2018, both opinions vacated*, 2019 WL 3543081, 2019 U.S. Dist. LEXIS 133756 (Feb. 8, 2019).

2. Because the confirmer or other nominated person may choose different law from that chosen by the issuer or may be located in a different jurisdiction and fail to choose law, it is possible that a confirmer or nominated person may be obligated to pay (under their law) but will not be entitled to payment from the issuer (under its law). Similarly, the rights of an unreimbursed issuer, confirmer, or nominated person against a beneficiary under Section 5-109, 5-110, or 5-117, will not necessarily be governed by the same law that applies to the issuer's or confirmer's obligation upon presentation. Because the UCP and other practice are incorporated in most international letters of credit, disputes arising from different legal obligations to honor have not been frequent. Since Section 5-108 incorporates standard practice, these problems should be further minimized—at least to the extent that the same practice is and continues to be widely followed.

3. This section does not permit what is now authorized by the nonuniform Section 5-102(4) in New York. Under the current law in New York a letter of credit that incorporates the UCP is not governed in any respect by Article 5. Under revised Section 5-116 letters of credit that incorporate the UCP or similar practice will still be subject to Article 5 in certain respects. First, incorporation of the UCP or other practice does not override the nonvariable terms of Article 5. Second, where there is no conflict between Article 5 and the relevant provision of the UCP or other practice, both apply. Third, practice provisions incorporated in a letter of credit will not be effective if they fail to comply with Section 5-103(c). Assume, for example, that a practice provision purported to free a party from any liability unless it were "grossly negligent" or that the practice generally limited the remedies that one party might have against another. Depending upon the circumstances, that disclaimer or limitation of liability might be ineffective because of Section 5-103(c).

Even though Article 5 is generally consistent with UCP 500, it is not necessarily consistent with other rules or with versions of the UCP that may be adopted after Article 5's revision, or with other practices that may develop. The phrase in subsection 5-116(e), "rules of custom or practice, such as the Uniform Customs and Practice for Documentary Credits," includes the International Standby Practices and the Uniform Rules for Demand Guarantees, as well as the Supplement to the Uniform Customs and Practice for Documentary Credits for Electronic Presentation. Rules of practice incorporated in the letter of credit or other undertaking are those in effect when the letter of credit or other undertaking is issued. Except in the unusual cases discussed in the immediately preceding paragraph, practice adopted in a letter of credit will override the rules of Article 5 and the parties to letter of credit transactions must be familiar with practice that is explicitly adopted in letters of credit.

4. In several ways Article 5 conflicts with and overrides similar matters governed by Articles 3 and 4. For example, "draft" is more broadly defined in letter of credit practice than under Section 3-104. The time allowed for honor and the required notification of reasons for dishonor are different in letter of credit practice than in the handling of documentary and other drafts under Articles 3 and 4.

5. Subsection (g) must be read in conjunction with existing law governing subject matter jurisdiction. If the local law restricts a court to certain subject matter jurisdiction not including letter of credit disputes, subsection (g) does not authorize parties to choose that forum. For example, the parties' agreement under Section 5-116(g) would not confer jurisdiction on a probate court to decide a letter of credit case.

If the parties choose a forum under subsection (g) and if—because of other law—that forum will not take jurisdiction, the parties' agreement or undertaking should then be construed (for the purpose of forum selection) as though it did not contain a clause choosing a particular forum. That result is necessary to avoid sentencing the parties to eternal purgatory where neither the chosen State nor the State which would have jurisdiction but for the clause will take jurisdiction—the former in disregard of the clause and the latter in honor of the clause.

Section 5-117. Subrogation of Issuer, Applicant, and Nominated Person

(a) An issuer that honors a beneficiary's presentation is subrogated to the rights of the beneficiary to the same extent as if the issuer were a secondary obligor of the underlying obligation owed to the beneficiary and of the applicant to the same extent as if the issuer were the secondary obligor of the underlying obligation owed to the applicant.

(b) An applicant that reimburses an issuer is subrogated to the rights of the issuer against any beneficiary, presenter, or nominated person to the same extent as if the applicant were the secondary obligor of the obligations owed to the issuer and has the rights of subrogation of the issuer to the rights of the beneficiary stated in subsection (a).

(c) A nominated person who pays or gives value against a draft or demand presented under a letter of credit is subrogated to the rights of:

(1) the issuer against the applicant to the same extent as if the nominated person were a secondary obligor of the obligation owed to the issuer by the applicant;

(2) the beneficiary to the same extent as if the nominated person were a secondary obligor of the underlying obligation owed to the beneficiary; and

(3) the applicant to same extent as if the nominated person were a secondary obligor of the underlying obligation owed to the applicant.

(d) Notwithstanding any agreement or term to the contrary, the rights of subrogation stated in subsections (a) and (b) do not arise until the issuer honors the letter of credit or otherwise pays and the rights in subsection (c) do not arise until the nominated person pays or otherwise gives value. Until then, the issuer, nominated person, and the applicant do not derive under this section present or prospective rights forming the basis of a claim, defense, or excuse.

Official Comment

1. By itself this section does not grant any right of subrogation. It grants only the right that would exist if the person seeking subrogation "were a secondary obligor." (The term "secondary obligor" refers to a surety, guarantor, or other person against whom or whose property an obligee has recourse with respect to the obligation of a third party. See Restatement of the Law Third, Suretyship and Guaranty § 1 (1995).) If the secondary obligor would not have a right to subrogation in the circumstances in which one is claimed under this section, none is granted by this section. In effect, the section does no more than to remove an impediment that some courts have found to subrogation because they conclude that the issuer's or other claimant's rights are "independent" of the underlying obligation. If, for example, a secondary obligor would not have a subrogation right because its payment did not fully satisfy the underlying obligation, none would be available under this section. The section indorses the position of Judge Becker in *Tudor Dev. Group, Inc. v. United States Fidelity & Guaranty*, 968 F.2d 357 (3d Cir. 1991).

2. To preserve the independence of the letter of credit obligation and to insure that subrogation not be used as an offensive weapon by an issuer or others, the admonition in subsection (d) must be carefully observed. Only one who has completed its performance in a letter of credit transaction can have a right to subrogation. For example, an issuer may not dishonor and then defend its dishonor or assert a setoff on the ground that it is subrogated to another person's rights. Nor may the issuer complain after honor that its subrogation rights have been impaired by any good faith dealings between the beneficiary and the applicant or any other person. Assume, for example, that the beneficiary under a standby letter of credit is a mortgagee. If the mortgagee were obliged to issue a release of the mortgage upon payment of the underlying debt (by the issuer under the letter of credit), that release might impair the issuer's rights of subrogation, but the beneficiary would have no liability to the issuer for having granted that release.

Section 5-118. Security Interest of Issuer or Nominated Person

(a) An issuer or nominated person has a security interest in a document presented under a letter of credit to the extent that the issuer or nominated person honors or gives value for the presentation.

(b) So long as and to the extent that an issuer or nominated person has not been reimbursed or has not otherwise recovered the value given with respect to a security interest in a document under subsection (a), the security interest continues and is subject to Article 9, but:

(1) a security agreement is not necessary to make the security interest enforceable under Section 9-203(b)(3);

(2) if the document is presented in a medium other than a written or other tangible medium, the security interest is perfected; and

(3) if the document is resented in a written or other tangible medium and is not a certificated security, chattel paper, a document of title, an instrument, or a letter of credit, the security interest is perfected and has priority over a conflicting security interest in the document so long as the debtor does not have possession of the document.

Official Comment

1. This section gives the issuer of a letter of credit or a nominated person thereunder an automatic security interest in a "document" (as that term is defined in Section 5-102(a)(6)). The security interest arises only if the document is presented to the issuer or nominated person under the letter of credit and only to the extent of the value that is given. This security interest is analogous to that awarded to a collecting bank under Section 4-210. Subsection (b) contains special rules governing the security interest arising under this section. In all other resects, a security interest arising under this section is subject to Article 9. See Section 9-109. Thus, for example, a security interest arising under this section may give rise to a security interest in proceeds under Section 9-315.

2. Subsection (b)(1) makes a security agreement unnecessary to the creation of a security interest under this section. Under subsection (b)(2), a security interest arising under this section is perfected if the document is presented in a medium other than a written or tangible medium. Documents that are written and that are not an otherwise-defined type of collateral under Article 9 (e.g., an invoice or inspection certificate) may be goods, in which an issuer or nominated person could perfect its security interest by possession. Because the definition of document in Section 5-102(a)(6) includes records (e.g., electronic records) that may not be goods, subsection (b)(2) provides for automatic perfection (i.e., without filing or possession).

Under subsection (b)(3), if the document (i) is in a written or tangible medium, (ii) is not a certificated security, chattel paper, a document of title, an instrument, or a letter of credit and (iii) is not in the debtor's possession, the security interest is perfected and has priority over a conflicting security interest. If the document is a type of tangible collateral that subsection (b)(3) excludes from its perfection and priority rules, a security interest in the document arising under subsection (a) would be automatically perfected pursuant to Section 9-309(8) but subject to the applicable Article 9 priority rules. Documents to which subsection (b)(3) applies may be important to an issuer or nominated person. For example, a confirmer who pays the beneficiary must be assured that its rights to all documents are not impaired. It will find it necessary to present all of the required documents to the issuer in order to be reimbursed. Moreover, when a nominated person sends documents to an issuer in connection with the nominated person's reimbursement, that activity is not a collection, enforcement, or disposition of collateral under Article 9.

One purpose of this section is to protect an issuer or nominated person from claims of a beneficiary's creditors. It is a fallback provision inasmuch as issuers and nominated persons frequently may obtain and perfect security interests under the usual Article 9 rules, and, in many cases, the documents will be owned by the issuer, nominated person or applicant.

Article 7—Warehouse Receipts, Bills of Lading and Other Documents of Title

As adopted in 2003 and revised in: (i) 2004 to correct errata; and (ii) 2022, in connection with the 2022 Amendments to the Uniform Commercial Code.

PART 1. GENERAL

PART 2. WAREHOUSE RECEIPTS: SPECIAL PROVISIONS

PART 3. BILLS OF LADING: SPECIAL PROVISIONS

PART 4. WAREHOUSE RECEIPTS AND BILLS OF LADING: GENERAL OBLIGATIONS

PART 5. WAREHOUSE RECEIPTS AND BILLS OF LADING: NEGOTIATION AND TRANSFER

PART 6. WAREHOUSE RECEIPTS AND BILLS OF LADING: MISCELLANEOUS PROVISIONS

PART I. GENERAL

Section 7-101. Short Title

This Article may be cited as Uniform Commercial Code—Documents of Title.

Official Comment

Prior Uniform Statutory Provision: Former Section 7-101.

Changes: Revised for style only.

This Article is a revision of the 1962 Official Text with Comments as amended since 1962. The 1962 Official Text was a consolidation and revision of the Uniform Warehouse Receipts Act and the Uniform Bills of Lading Act, and embraced the provisions of the Uniform Sales Act relating to negotiation of documents of title.

This Article does not contain the substantive criminal provisions found in the Uniform Warehouse Receipts and Bills of Lading Acts. These criminal provisions are inappropriate to a Commercial Code, and for the most part duplicate portions of the ordinary criminal law relating to frauds. This revision deletes the former Section 7-105 that provided that courts could apply a rule from Parts 2 and 3 by analogy to a situation not explicitly covered in the provisions on warehouse receipts or bills of lading when it was appropriate. This is, of course, an unexceptional proposition and need not be stated explicitly in the statute. Thus former Section 7-105 has been deleted. Whether applying a rule by analogy to a situation is appropriate depends upon the facts of each case.

The Article does not attempt to define the tort liability of bailees, except to hold certain classes of bailees to a minimum standard of reasonable care. For important classes of bailees, liabilities in case of loss, damages or destruction, as well as other legal questions associated with particular documents of title, are governed by federal statutes, international treaties, and in some cases regulatory state laws, which supersede the provisions of this Article in case of inconsistency. See Section 7-103.

Section 7-102. Definitions and Index of Definitions

(a) In this Article, unless the context otherwise requires:

(1) "Bailee" means a person that by a warehouse receipt, bill of lading, or other document of title acknowledges possession of goods and contracts to deliver them.

(2) "Carrier" means a person that issues a bill of lading.

(3) "Consignee" means a person named in a bill of lading to which or to whose order the bill promises delivery.

(4) "Consignor" means a person named in a bill of lading as the person from which the goods have been received for shipment.

(5) "Delivery order" means a record that contains an order to deliver goods directed to a warehouse, carrier, or other person that in the ordinary course of business issues warehouse receipts or bills of lading.

(6) "Good faith" means honesty in fact and the observance of reasonable commercial standards of fair dealing.

(7) "Goods" means all things that are treated as movable for the purposes of a contract for storage or transportation.

(8) "Issuer" means a bailee that issues a document of title or, in the case of an unaccepted delivery order, the person that orders the possessor of goods to deliver. The term includes a person for which an agent or employee purports to act in issuing a document if the agent or employee has real or apparent authority to issue documents, even if the issuer did not receive any goods, the goods were misdescribed, or in any other respect the agent or employee violated the issuer's instructions.

(9) "Person entitled under the document" means the holder, in the case of a negotiable document of title, or the person to which delivery of the goods is to be made by the terms of, or pursuant to instructions in a record under, a nonnegotiable document of title.

(10) [Reserved]

(11) [Reserved]

(12) "Shipper" means a person that enters into a contract of transportation with a carrier.

(13) "Warehouse" means a person engaged in the business of storing goods for hire.

(b) Definitions in other Articles applying to this Article and the sections in which they appear are:

(1) "Contract for sale", Section 2-106.

(2) "Lessee in the ordinary course of business", Section 2A-103.

(3) "Receipt" of goods, Section 2-103.

(c) In addition, Article 1 contains general definitions and principles of construction and interpretation applicable throughout this Article.

Legislative Note: *If the state has enacted Revised Article 1, the definitions of "good faith" in subsection (a)(6) and "record" in (a)(10) need not be enacted in this section as they are contained in Article 1, Section 1-201. These* *subsections should be marked as "reserved" in order to provide for uniform numbering of subsections.*

Official Comment

Prior Uniform Statutory Provision: Former Section 7-102.

Changes: New definitions of "carrier", "good faith", "record", "sign" and "shipper". Other definitions revised to accommodate electronic mediums.

Purposes:

1. "Bailee" is used in this Article as a blanket term to designate carriers, warehousemen and others who normally issue documents of title on the basis of goods which they have received. The definition does not, however, require actual possession of the goods. If a bailee acknowledges possession when it does not have possession, the bailee is bound by sections of this Article which declare the "bailee's" obligations. (See definition of "Issuer" in this section and Sections 7-203 and 7-301 on liability in case of nonreceipt.) A "carrier" is one type of bailee and is defined as a person who issues a bill of lading. A "shipper" is a person who enters into the contract of transportation with the carrier. The definitions of "bailee", "consignee", "consignor", "goods" and "issuer" are unchanged in substance from prior law. "Document of title" is defined in Article 1, and may be in either tangible or electronic form.

2. The definition of "warehouse receipt" contained in the general definitions section of this Act (Section 1-201) does not require that the issuing warehouse be "lawfully engaged" in business or for profit. The warehouse's compliance with applicable state regulations such as the filing of a bond has no bearing on the substantive issues dealt with in this Article. Certainly the issuer's violations of law should not diminish its responsibility on documents the issuer has put in commercial circulation. But it is still essential that the business be storing goods "for hire" (Section 1-201 and this section). A person does not become a warehouse by storing its own goods.

3. When a delivery order has been accepted by the bailee it is for practical purposes indistinguishable from a warehouse receipt. Prior to such acceptance there is no basis for imposing obligations on the bailee other than the ordinary obligation of contract which the bailee may have assumed to the depositor of the goods. Delivery orders may be either electronic or tangible documents of title. See definition of "document of title" in Section 1-201(b)(16).

4. The obligation of good faith imposed by this Article and by Article 1, Section 1-304 includes the observance of reasonable commercial standards of fair dealing.

5. Pursuant to the Uniform Commercial Code Amendments (2022) (2022 Amendments), paragraphs (10) and (11) of subsection (a) have been deleted as unnecessary. Section 1-201 includes substantially equivalent definitions of "record" and "sign." The definitions of "record" and "sign" are included to facilitate electronic mediums. See Comment 9 to Section 9-102 discussing "record" and the Comment to amended Section 2-103 discussing "sign".

6. "Person entitled under the document" is moved from former Section 7-403.

In the case of a negotiable document of title, the person entitled is the holder. See Section 1-201(b)(21) (defining "holder"). For a nonnegotiable document of title, the person entitled is the person provided in the terms of the document or instructions under the document. A transferee of a nonnegotiable document to which the document has been delivered acquires the transferee's rights and rights that the transferor had actual authority to convey. Section 7-504(a). However, until but not after the bailee receives notice of a transfer, such a transferee's rights are subject to those of persons identified in Section 7-504(b), including "as against the bailee, by good faith dealings of the bailee with the transferor." Moreover, such a transferee is *not* a person entitled under the document unless so provided in the document or in instructions under the document.

Article 7 does not explain what constitutes an "instruction under" a nonnegotiable document, but instead leaves it to commercial practice, including usage of trade (Section 1-303(c)). In practice the term is generally understood to include a delivery order or other instruction to the bailee, by the person named in the document, to deliver the goods to a transferee of the document or to another person. A delivery order or other instruction under a nonnegotiable document should be distinguished from a mere "notice" or "notification" to the bailee of a transfer or security interest, as contemplated by Sections 7-504(b) and 9-312(d)(2). However, an instruction could, functionally, also constitute such a notice.

7. These definitions apply in this Article unless the context otherwise requires. The "context" is intended to refer to the context in which the defined term is used in the Uniform Commercial Code. The definition applies whenever the defined term is used unless the context in which the defined term is used in the statute indicates that the term was not used in its defined sense. See Comment to Section 1-201.

Cross References:

Point 1:	Sections 1-201, 7-203 and 7-301.
Point 2:	Sections 1-201 and 7-203.
Point 3:	Section 1-201.
Point 4:	Section 1-304.
Point 5:	Sections 9-102 and 2-103.

See general Comment to document of title in Section 1-201.

Definitional Cross References:

"Bill of lading".	Section 1-201.
"Contract".	Section 1-201.
"Contract for sale".	Section 2-106.
"Delivery".	Section 1-201.
"Document of title".	Section 1-201.
"Person".	Section 1-201.
"Purchase".	Section 1-201.
"Receipt of goods".	Section 2-103.
"Right".	Section 1-201.
"Warehouse receipt".	Section 1-201.

Section 7-103. Relation of Article to Treaty or Statute

(a) This Article is subject to any treaty or statute of the United States or regulatory statute of this state to the extent the treaty, statute, or regulatory statute is applicable.

(b) This Article does not modify or repeal any law prescribing the form or content of a document of title or the services or facilities to be afforded by a bailee, or otherwise regulating a bailee's business in respects not specifically treated in this Article. However, violation of such a law does not affect the status of a document of title that otherwise is within the definition of a document of title.

(c) This [act] modifies, limits, and supersedes the federal Electronic Signatures in Global and National Commerce Act (15 U.S.C. Section 7-001, et. seq.) but does not modify, limit, or supersede Section 101(c) of that act (15 U.S.C. Section 7-001(c)) or authorize electronic delivery of any of the notices described in Section 103(b) of that act (15 U.S.C. Section 7-003(b)).

(d) To the extent there is a conflict between [the Uniform Electronic Transactions Act] and this Article, this Article governs.

Legislative Note: *In states that have not enacted the Uniform Electronic Transactions Act in some form, states should consider their own state laws to determine whether there is a conflict between the provisions of this Article and those laws particularly as those other laws may affect electronic documents of title.*

Official Comment

Prior Uniform Statutory Provision: Former Sections 7-103 and 10-104.

Changes: Deletion of references to tariffs and classifications; incorporation of former Section 10-104 into subsection (b), provide for intersection with federal and state law governing electronic transactions.

Purposes:

1. To make clear what would of course be true without the section, that applicable Federal law is paramount.

2. To make clear also that regulatory state statutes (such as those fixing or authorizing a commission to fix rates and prescribe services, authorizing different charges for goods of different values, and limiting liability for loss to the declared value on which the charge was based) are not affected by the Article and are controlling on the matters which they cover unless preempted by federal law. The reference in former Section 7-103 to tariffs, classifications and regulations filed or issued pursuant to regulatory state statutes has been deleted as inappropriate in the modern era of diminished regulation of carriers and warehouses. If a regulatory scheme requires a carrier or warehouse to issue a tariff or classification, that tariff or classification would be given effect via the state regulatory scheme that this Article recognizes as controlling. Permissive tariffs or classifications would not displace the provisions of this Act, pursuant to this section, but may be given effect through the ability of parties to incorporate those terms by reference into their agreement.

3. The document of title provisions of this Act supplement the federal law and regulatory state law governing bailees. This Article focuses on the commercial importance and usage of documents of title. *State ex. rel Public Service Commission v. Gunkelman & Sons, Inc.*, 219 N.W.2d 853 (N.D. 1974).

4. Subsection (c) is included to make clear the interrelationship between the federal Electronic Signatures in Global and National Commerce Act and this Article and the conforming amendments to other Articles of the Uniform Commercial Code promulgated as part of the revision of this Article. Section 102 of the federal Act allows a state statute to modify, limit or supersede the provisions of Section 101 of the federal Act. See the Comments to Section 1-108.

5. Subsection (d) makes clear that once this Article is in effect, its provisions regarding electronic commerce and electronic documents of title control in the event there is a conflict with the provisions of the Uniform Electronic Transactions Act or other applicable state law governing electronic transactions.

Cross References:

Sections 1-108, 7-201, 7-202, 7-204, 7-206, 7-309, 7-401 and 7-403.

Definitional Cross Reference:

"Bill of lading". Section 1-201.

Section 7-104. Negotiable and Nonnegotiable Document of Title

(a) Except as otherwise provided in subsection (c), a document of title is negotiable if by its terms the goods are to be delivered to bearer or to the order of a named person.

(b) A document of title other than one described in subsection (a) is nonnegotiable. A bill of lading that states that the goods are consigned to a named person is not made negotiable by a provision that the goods are to be delivered only against an order in a record signed by the same or another named person.

(c) A document of title is nonnegotiable if, at the time it is issued, the document has a conspicuous legend, however expressed, that it is nonnegotiable.

Official Comment

Prior Uniform Statutory Provision: Former Section 7-104.

Changes: Subsection (a) is revised to reflect modern style and trade practice. Subsection (b) is revised for style and medium neutrality. Subsection (c) is new.

Purposes:

1. This Article deals with a class of commercial paper representing commodities in storage or transportation. This "commodity paper" is to be distinguished from what might be called "money paper" dealt with in the Article of this Act on Commercial Paper (Article 3) and "investment paper" dealt with in the Article of this Act on Investment Securities (Article 8). The class of "commodity paper" is designated "document of title" following the terminology of the Uniform Sales Act, Section 76. Section 1-201. The distinctions between negotiable and nonnegotiable documents in this section makes the most important subclassification employed in the Article, in that the holder of negotiable documents may acquire more rights than its transferor had (see Section 7-502). The former Section 7-104, which provided that a document of title was negotiable if it runs to a named person or assigns if such designation was recognized in overseas trade, has been deleted as not necessary in light of current commercial practice.

A document of title is negotiable only if it satisfies this section. "Deliverable on proper indorsement and surrender of this receipt" will not render a document negotiable. Bailees often include such provisions as a means of insuring return of nonnegotiable receipts for record purposes. Such language may be regarded as insistence by the bailee upon a particular kind of receipt in connection with delivery of the goods. Subsection (a) makes it clear that a document is not negotiable which provides for delivery to order or bearer only if written instructions to that effect are given by a named person. Either tangible or electronic documents of title may be negotiable if the document meets the requirement of this section.

2. Subsection (c) is derived from Section 3-104(d). Prior to issuance of the document of title, an issuer may stamp or otherwise provide by a notation on the document that it is nonnegotiable even if the document would otherwise comply with the requirement of subsection (a). Once issued as a negotiable document of title, the document cannot be changed from a negotiable document to a nonnegotiable document. A document of title that is nonnegotiable cannot be made negotiable by stamping or providing a notation that the document is negotiable. The only way to make a document of title negotiable is to comply with subsection (a). A negotiable document of title may fail to be duly negotiated if the negotiation does not comply with the requirements for "due negotiation" stated in Section 7-501.

Cross References:

Sections 7-501 and 7-502.

Definitional Cross References:

"Bearer".	Section 1-201.
"Bill of lading".	Section 1-201.
"Delivery".	Section 1-201.
"Document of title".	Section 1-201.
"Person".	Section 1-201.
"Sign".	Section 7-102
"Warehouse receipt".	Section 1-201.

Section 7-105. Reissuance in Alternative Medium

(a) Upon request of a person entitled under an electronic document of title, the issuer of the electronic document may issue a tangible document of title as a substitute for the electronic document if:

(1) the person entitled under the electronic document surrenders control of the document to the issuer; and

(2) the tangible document when issued contains a statement that it is issued in substitution for the electronic document.

(b) Upon issuance of a tangible document of title in substitution for an electronic document of title in accordance with subsection (a):

(1) the electronic document ceases to have any effect or validity; and

(2) the person that procured issuance of the tangible document warrants to all subsequent persons entitled under the tangible document that the warrantor was a person entitled under the electronic document when the warrantor surrendered control of the electronic document to the issuer.

(c) Upon request of a person entitled under a tangible document of title, the issuer of the tangible document may issue an electronic document of title as a substitute for the tangible document if:

(1) the person entitled under the tangible document surrenders possession of the document to the issuer; and

(2) the electronic document when issued contains a statement that it is issued in substitution for the tangible document.

(d) Upon issuance of an electronic document of title in substitution for a tangible document of title in accordance with subsection (c):

(1) the tangible document ceases to have any effect or validity; and

(2) the person that procured issuance of the electronic document warrants to all subsequent persons entitled under the electronic document that the warrantor was a person entitled under the tangible document when the warrantor surrendered possession of the tangible document to the issuer.

Official Comment

Prior Uniform Statutory Provisions: None.

Other Relevant Law: United Nations Convention on Contracts for the International Carriage of Goods Wholly or Partly by Sea (New York, 2008).

Purpose:

1. This section allows for documents of title issued in one medium to be reissued in another medium. This section applies to both negotiable and nonnegotiable documents. This section sets forth minimum requirements for giving the reissued document effect and validity. The issuer is not required to issue a document in an alternative medium and if the issuer chooses to do so, it may impose additional requirements. Because a document of title imposes obligations on the issuer of the document, it is imperative for the issuer to be the one who issues the substitute document in order for the substitute document to be effective and valid.

2. The request must be made to the issuer by the person entitled to enforce the document of title (Section 7-102(a)(9)) and that person must surrender possession or control of the original document to the issuer. The reissued document must have a notation that it has been issued as a substitute for the original document. These minimum requirements must be met in order to give the substitute document effect and validity. If these minimum requirements are not met for issuance of a substitute document of title, the original document of title continues to be effective and valid. Section 7-402. However, if the minimum requirements imposed by this section are met, in addition to any other requirements that the issuer may impose, the substitute document will be the document that is effective and valid.

3. To protect parties who subsequently take the substitute document of title, the person who procured issuance of the substitute document warrants that it was a person entitled under the original document at the time it surrendered possession or control of the original document to the issuer. This warranty is modeled after the warranty found in Section 4-209.

Cross References:

Sections 7-106, 7-402 and 7-601.

Definitional Cross Reference:

"Person entitled to enforce". Section 7-102.

Section 7-106. Control of Electronic Document of Title

(a) A person has control of an electronic document of title if a system employed for evidencing the transfer of interests in the electronic document reliably establishes that person as the person to which the electronic document was issued or transferred.

(b) A system satisfies subsection (a), and a person has control of an electronic document of title, if the document is created, stored, and transferred in a manner that:

(1) a single authoritative copy of the document exists which is unique, identifiable, and, except as otherwise provided in paragraphs (4), (5), and (6), unalterable;

(2) the authoritative copy identifies the person asserting control as:

(A) the person to which the document was issued; or

(B) if the authoritative copy indicates that the document has been transferred, the person to which the document was most recently transferred;

(3) the authoritative copy is communicated to and maintained by the person asserting control or its designated custodian;

(4) copies or amendments that add or change an identified transferee of the authoritative copy can be made only with the consent of the person asserting control;

(5) each copy of the authoritative copy and any copy of a copy is readily identifiable as a copy that is not the authoritative copy; and

(6) any amendment of the authoritative copy is readily identifiable as authorized or unauthorized.

(c) A system satisfies subsection (a), and a person has control of an electronic document of title, if an authoritative electronic copy of the document, a record attached to or logically associated with the electronic copy, or a system in which the electronic copy is recorded:

(1) enables the person readily to identify each electronic copy as either an authoritative copy or a nonauthoritative copy;

(2) enables the person readily to identify itself in any way, including by name, identifying number, cryptographic key, office, or account number, as the person to which each authoritative electronic copy was issued or transferred; and

(3) gives the person exclusive power, subject to subsection (d), to:

(A) prevent others from adding or changing the person to which each authoritative electronic copy has been issued or transferred; and

(B) transfer control of each authoritative electronic copy.

(d) Subject to subsection (e), a power is exclusive under subsection (c)(3)(A) and (B) even if:

(1) the authoritative electronic copy, a record attached to or logically associated with the authoritative electronic copy, or a system in which the authoritative electronic copy is recorded limits the use of the document of title or has a protocol that is programmed to cause a change, including a transfer or loss of control; or

(2) the power is shared with another person.

(e) A power of a person is not shared with another person under subsection (d)(2) and the person's power is not exclusive if:

(1) the person can exercise the power only if the power also is exercised by the other person; and

(2) the other person:

(A) can exercise the power without exercise of the power by the person; or

(B) is the transferor to the person of an interest in the document of title.

(f) If a person has the powers specified in subsection (c)(3)(A) and (B), the powers are presumed to be exclusive.

(g) A person has control of an electronic document of title if another person, other than the transferor to the person of an interest in the document:

(1) has control of the document and acknowledges that it has control on behalf of the person; or

(2) obtains control of the document after having acknowledged that it will obtain control of the document on behalf of the person.

(h) A person that has control under this section is not required to acknowledge that it has control on behalf of another person.

(i) If a person acknowledges that it has or will obtain control on behalf of another person, unless the person otherwise agrees or law other than this Article or Article 9 otherwise provides, the person does not owe any duty to the other person and is not required to confirm the acknowledgment to any other person.

Official Comment

Prior Uniform Statutory Provision: Uniform Electronic Transactions Act, Section 16.

Purpose:

1. The 2022 revision of this section on control of electronic documents of title preserves subsection (a), the general rule, and subsection (b), the "safe harbor" from the pre- 2022 section. The minor stylistic revisions are not substantive. The other revisions add a second "safe harbor" in subsection (c), explanatory provisions relating to exclusivity of powers in subsections (d) and (e), a presumption of exclusivity of powers in subsection (f), and a new subsection (g) on control through another person. The requirements for obtaining control under subsection (c) were inspired by Section 12-105 on control of controllable electronic records. See Section 12-105 and Comments.

This section defines "control" for electronic documents of title. Subsections (a) and (b) derive from the Uniform Electronic Transactions Act Section 16 on transferable records. Unlike under UETA Section 16, however, a document of title may be reissued in an alternative medium pursuant to Section 7-105. At any point in time in which a document of title is in electronic form, the control concept of this section is relevant. As under UETA Section 16, the control concept embodied in this section provides the legal framework for developing systems for electronic documents of title.

2. Control of an electronic document of title substitutes for the concept of indorsement (for negotiable documents) and possession (for tangible documents of title). See Section 7-501. A person with a tangible document of title delivers the document by voluntarily transferring possession and a person with an electronic document of title delivers the document by voluntarily transferring control. ("Delivery" is defined in Section 1-201(b)(15)).

3. Subsection (a) sets forth the general rule that the "system employed for evidencing the transfer of interests in the electronic document reliably establishes that person as the person to which the electronic document was issued or transferred". The key to having a system that satisfies this test is that identity of *the* person to which the document was issued or transferred must be reliably established. Of great importance to the functioning of the control concept under subsection (a), as well as under the safe harbors in subsections (b) and (c), is to be able to demonstrate and identify, at any point in time, *the person* entitled under the electronic document. For example, a carrier may issue an electronic bill of lading by having the required information in a database that is encrypted and accessible by virtue of a password. If the computer system in which the required information is maintained identifies the person as *the* person to which the electronic bill of lading was issued or transferred, that person has control of the electronic document of title. That identification may be by virtue of passwords or other encryption methods. Registry systems may satisfy this test. For example, see the electronic warehouse receipt system established pursuant to 7 C.F.R. Part 735. This Article leaves to the marketplace the development of sufficient technologies and business practices that will meet the test.

An electronic document of title is evidenced by a record consisting of information stored in an electronic medium. See Section 1-201(b)(16A) (defining "electronic") and (31) (defining "record"). For example, a record in a computer database could be an electronic document of title assuming that it otherwise meets the definition of document of title. To the extent that third parties wish to deal in paper mediums, Section 7-105 provides a mechanism for exiting the electronic environment by having the issuer reissue the document of title in a tangible medium. Thus if a person entitled to enforce an electronic document of title causes the information in the record to be printed onto paper without the issuer's involvement in issuing the document of title pursuant to Section 7-105, that paper is not a document of title.

4. Subsection (a) sets forth the general test for control. Subsections (b) and (c) set forth safe harbor tests that, if satisfied, result in control under the general test in subsection (a). The safe harbor in subsection (b) requires the existence of only one authoritative copy of the document but the safe harbor in sub section (c) allows for either a single authoritative copy or multiple authoritative copies.

Under subsection (b), at any point in time, a party should be able to identify the single authoritative copy which is unique and identifiable as the authoritative copy. This does not mean that once created the authoritative copy need be static and never moved or copied from its original location. To the extent that backup systems exist which result in multiple copies, the key to this idea is that at any point in time, the one authoritative copy needs to be unique and identifiable.

5. Article 7 has historically provided for rights under documents of title and rights of transferees of documents of title as those rights relate to the goods covered by the document. Third parties may possess or have control of documents of title. While misfeasance or negligence in failure to transfer or misdelivery of the document by those third parties may create serious issues, this Article has never dealt with those issues as it relates to tangible documents of title, preferring to leave those issues to the law of contracts, agency and tort law. In the electronic document of title regime, registry systems continue to evolve. To the extent that these systems evolve by use of the control concepts contained in this section, the law of contracts, agency and torts as it applies to the registry's misfeasance or negligence concerning the transfer of control of the electronic document will allocate the risks and liabilities of the parties as that other law now does so for third parties who hold tangible documents and fail to deliver the documents.

6. The subsection (c) "safe harbor" generally follows Section 12-105 for control of controllable electronic records as well as revised Section 9-105 on control of chattel paper evidenced by electronic records. See generally Sections 9-105 and 12-105 and Comments. It differs from subsection (b), which (as noted above) is based on a "single authoritative copy" of an electronic document of title and so is unavailable when the relevant record is maintained on a blockchain or another distributed ledger. The utility of distributed ledger technology depends on there being multiple authoritative copies of an electronic record. It is important to note that compliance with the conditions for control in subsection (c) also would satisfy the conditions provided in subsection (b). However, subsection (b) was retained out of an abundance of caution and to provide assurances that existing systems for control of electronic documents of title continue to be viable. The conditions for "control" in subsection (c) reflect the functions that possession serves with respect to writings, but in a more accurate and technologically flexible way than do the conditions in subsection (b).

7. Under subsection (c), to obtain control of an electronic document of title a person must be able to identify each electronic copy as authoritative or nonauthoritative and identify itself as the person to which each authoritative electronic copy has been issued or transferred. As to the means of identification, see Section 12-105, Comment 7. In addition, the person must have the exclusive powers, first, to prevent others from adding or changing an identified person to which each authoritative electronic copy has been issued or transferred and, second, to transfer control of each authoritative copy. However, once it is established that a person has received those powers, subsection (f) provides a presumption of exclusivity. Consequently, a person asserting control need not prove exclusivity in order to make out a *prima facie* case. Application of the presumption will be governed also by Section 1-206 (effects of a presumption under the UCC) and applicable non-UCC law (including rules of procedure and evidence). In addition, subsection (d) contains two qualifications of the term "exclusive" as used in subsection (c)(3). A power can be "exclusive" under subsection (c)(3) even if one or both of these qualifications apply.

Subsection (e) provides that in certain circumstances a power is not shared within the meaning of subsection (d)(2), the relaxation of the exclusivity requirement provided by subsection (d)(2) does not apply, and, consequently, a person's power is not exclusive. Subsection (e) provides that a person does not share an exclusive power with another person if the person can exercise the power only with the other person's cooperation (subsection (e)(1)) but the other person either (i) can exercise of the power without the person's cooperation (subsection (e)(2)(A)) or (ii) is the transferor to the person (transferee) of an interest in the document of title (subsection (e)(2)(B)). It follows that a person to which subsection (e) applies does not have control based on its exclusive powers (although it might have control through another person under subsection (g), discussed below, or if another person having control is acting as the person's agent). As to the rationale for disqualifying a transferee (which includes a secured party in a secured transaction) from the benefit of shared control under subsection (d)(2), as provided in subsection (e)(2)(B), and for examples of the operation of subsection (e) (in the context of the similar provision in Section 12-105), see Section 12-105, Comments 5 and 9.

8. Subsection (g) provides for a person to obtain control through the control of another person. It follows revisions to the corresponding provisions for control of a security entitlement (Section 8-106(d)(3)), control of deposit accounts (Section 9-104(a)(4)), control of authoritative electronic copies of records evidencing chattel paper (Section 9-105(g)), control of electronic money (Section 9-105A(e)), and control of controllable electronic records (Section 12-105(e)). For a brief discussion and background, see Section 12-105, Comment 8. Under subsection (g) for an acknowledgment by another person to be effective to confer control on a person, the other person making the acknowledgment must be one "other than the transferor of an interest in the electronic record" to the person. The rationale for this limitation is discussed in Section 12-105, Comment 9. Control based on an acknowledgment under subsection (g) by another person having control continues only while the other person retains control. This result necessarily follows because such control derives solely from the other person's continued control.

Subsections (h) and (i) derive from Section 9-313(f) and (g). Subsection (h) makes clear that a person that has control under this section has no duty to acknowledge that it has or will obtain control on behalf of another person. Arrangements for a person to acknowledge that it has or will obtain control on behalf of another person are not standardized. Accordingly, subsection (i) leaves to the agreement of the parties and to any other applicable law (other than this Article or Article 9) any duties of a person that does acknowledge that it has or will obtain control on behalf of another person and provides that a person making an acknowledgment is not required to confirm the acknowledgment to another person. For example, subsection (g) would apply to give control to a person, Alpha, when another person, Beta, has control of each authoritative electronic document of title and acknowledges that it has control on behalf of Alpha. However, under subsection (h), Beta is not required to so acknowledge. And under subsection (i), even if Beta does so acknowledge, Beta owes no duty to Alpha, unless Beta agrees or other law so provides, and Beta is not required to confirm its acknowledgment to any other person.

9. This section applies to both negotiable and nonnegotiable electronic documents of title. For negotiable electronic documents of title, "delivery" is a necessary condition for negotiation, and therefore for due negotiation, under Section 7-501(b). "Delivery" of an electronic document of title is defined in Section 1-201(b)(15) as the "voluntary transfer of control." The person in control of a negotiable document, other than pursuant to subsection (g), also is a "holder," as defined in Section 1-201(b)(21)(C). Of course, nonnegotiable documents cannot be negotiated.

A security interest in an electronic document of title, whether negotiable or nonnegotiable, may be perfected by control. Section 9-314(a). But perfection of a security interest by control in a nonnegotiable document does not perfect a security interest in goods covered by the document and does not confer on a secured party or other purchaser the status of a person entitled under the document. See Section 7-102(a)(9) (defining "person entitled under the document") and Comment 6. This distinction arises from the differing rights conferred by a negotiable document and a nonnegotiable document. Both types serve as a receipt for the goods delivered to the bailee and a contract of storage (in the case of a warehouse receipt) or contract of carriage (in the case of a bill of lading). However, a negotiable document is also a representation of the goods themselves, whereas a nonnegotiable document confers only the right to receive possession of the goods. (On perfection of security interests in negotiable documents of title and goods covered by negotiable and nonnegotiable documents of title, see generally Section 9-312(a), (c), and (g) and Comment 7.)

Cross References:

Sections 7-105 and 7-501.

Definitional Cross References:

"Delivery".	Section 1-201.
"Document of title".	Section 1-201.

PART 2. WAREHOUSE RECEIPTS: SPECIAL PROVISIONS

Section 7-201. Person That May Issue a Warehouse Receipt; Storage Under Bond

(a) A warehouse receipt may be issued by any warehouse.

(b) If goods, including distilled spirits and agricultural commodities, are stored under a statute requiring a bond against withdrawal or a license for the issuance of receipts in the nature of warehouse receipts, a receipt issued for the goods is deemed to be a warehouse receipt even if issued by a person that is the owner of the goods and is not a warehouse.

Official Comment

Prior Uniform Statutory Provision: Former Section 7-201.

Changes: Update for style only.

Purposes:

It is not intended by reenactment of subsection (a) to repeal any provisions of special licensing or other statutes regulating who may become a warehouse. Limitations on the transfer of the receipts and criminal sanctions for violation of such limitations are not impaired. Section 7-103. Compare Section 7-401(4) on the liability of the issuer in such cases. Subsection (b) covers receipts issued by the owner for whiskey or other goods stored in bonded warehouses under such statutes as 26 U.S.C. Chapter 51.

Cross References:

Sections 7-103 and 7-401.

Definitional Cross References:

"Warehouse".	Section 7-102.
"Warehouse receipt".	Section 1-201.

Section 7-202. Form of Warehouse Receipt; Effect of Omission

(a) A warehouse receipt need not be in any particular form.

(b) Unless a warehouse receipt provides for each of the following, the warehouse is liable for damages caused to a person injured by its omission:

(1) a statement of the location of the warehouse facility where the goods are stored;

(2) the date of issue of the receipt;

(3) the unique identification code of the receipt;

(4) a statement whether the goods received will be delivered to the bearer, to a named person, or to a named person or its order;

(5) the rate of storage and handling charges, unless goods are stored under a field warehousing arrangement, in which case a statement of that fact is sufficient on a nonnegotiable receipt;

(6) a description of the goods or the packages containing them;

(7) the signature of the warehouse or its agent;

(8) if the receipt is issued for goods that the warehouse owns, either solely, jointly, or in common with others, a statement of the fact of that ownership; and

(9) a statement of the amount of advances made and of liabilities incurred for which the warehouse claims a lien or security interest, unless the precise amount of advances made or liabilities incurred, at the time of the issue of the receipt, is unknown to the warehouse or to its agent that issued the receipt, in which case a statement of the fact that advances have been made or liabilities incurred and the purpose of the advances or liabilities is sufficient.

(c) A warehouse may insert in its receipt any terms that are not contrary to [the Uniform Commercial Code] and do not impair its obligation of delivery under Section

7-403 or its duty of care under Section 7-204. Any contrary provision is ineffective.

Official Comment

Prior Uniform Statutory Provision: Former Section 7-202.

Changes: Language is updated to accommodate electronic commerce and to reflect modern style.

Purposes:

1. This section does not displace any particular legislation that requires other terms in a warehouse receipt or that may require a particular form of a warehouse receipt. This section does not require that a warehouse receipt be issued. A warehouse receipt that is issued need not contain any of the terms listed in subsection (b) in order to qualify as a warehouse receipt as long as the receipt falls within the definition of "warehouse receipt" in Article 1. Thus the title has been changed to eliminate the phrase "essential terms" as provided in prior law. The only consequence of a warehouse receipt not containing any term listed in subsection (b) is that a person injured by a term's omission has a right as against the warehouse for harm caused by the omission. Cases such as *In re Celotex Corp.*, 134 B. R. 993 (Bankr.M.D.Fla. 1991), that held that in order to have a valid warehouse receipt all of the terms listed in this section must be contained in the receipt, are disapproved.

2. The unique identification code referred to in subsection (b)(3) can include any combination of letters, numbers, signs and/or symbols that provide a unique identification. Whether an electronic or tangible warehouse receipt contains a signature will be resolved with the definition of "sign" in Section 7-102.

Cross References:

Sections 7-103 and 7-401.

Definitional Cross References:

"Bearer".	Section 1-201.
"Delivery".	Section 1-201.
"Goods".	Section 7-102.
"Person".	Section 1-201.
"Security interest".	Section 1-201.
"Sign".	Section 7-102.
"Term".	Section 1-201.
"Warehouse".	Section 7-102.
"Warehouse receipt".	Section 1-201.

Section 7-203. Liability for Nonreceipt or Misdescription

A party to or purchaser for value in good faith of a document of title, other than a bill of lading, that relies upon the description of the goods in the document may recover from the issuer damages caused by the nonreceipt or misdescription of the goods, except to the extent that:

(1) the document conspicuously indicates that the issuer does not know whether all or part of the goods in fact were received or conform to the description, such as a case in which the description is in terms of marks or labels or kind, quantity, or condition, or the receipt or description is qualified by "contents, condition, and quality unknown", "said to contain", or words of similar import, if the indication is true; or

(2) the party or purchaser otherwise has notice of the nonreceipt or misdescription.

Official Comment

Prior Uniform Statutory Provision: Former Section 7-203.

Changes: Changes to this section are for style only.

Purpose:

This section is a simplified restatement of existing law as to the method by which a bailee may avoid responsibility for the accuracy of descriptions which are made by or in reliance upon information furnished by the depositor. The issuer is liable on documents issued by an agent, contrary to instructions of its principal, without receiving goods. No disclaimer of the latter liability is permitted.

Cross Reference:

Section 7-301.

Definitional Cross References:

"Conspicuous".	Section 1-201.
"Document of title".	Section 1-201.
"Good Faith".	Section 1-201. [7-102]
"Goods".	Section 7-102.
"Issuer".	Section 7-102.
"Notice".	Section 1-202.
"Party".	Section 1-201.
"Purchaser".	Section 1-201.
"Receipt of goods".	Section 2-103.
"Value".	Section 1-204.

Section 7-204. Duty of Care; Contractual Limitation of Warehouse Liability

(a) A warehouse is liable for damages for loss of or injury to the goods caused by its failure to exercise care with regard to the goods that a reasonably careful person would exercise under similar circumstances. Unless otherwise agreed, the warehouse is not liable for damages that could not have been avoided by the exercise of that care.

(b) Damages may be limited by a term in the warehouse receipt or storage agreement limiting the amount of liability in case of loss or damage beyond which the warehouse is not liable. Such a limitation is not effective with respect to the warehouse's liability for conversion to its own use. On request of the bailor in a record at the time of signing the storage agreement or within a reasonable time after receipt of the warehouse receipt, the warehouse's liability may be increased on part or all of the goods covered by the storage agreement or the warehouse receipt. In this event, increased rates may be charged based on an increased valuation of the goods.

(c) Reasonable provisions as to the time and manner of presenting claims and commencing actions based on the bailment may be included in the warehouse receipt or storage agreement.

[(d) This section does not modify or repeal [Insert reference to any statute that imposes a higher responsibility upon the warehouse or invalidates a contractual limitation that would be permissible under this Article].]

Legislative Note: *Insert in subsection (d) a reference to any statute which imposes a higher responsibility upon the warehouse or invalidates a contractual limitation that would be permissible under this Article. If no such statutes exist, this section should be deleted.*

Official Comment

Prior Uniform Statutory Provision: Former Section 7-204.

Changes: Updated to reflect modern, standard commercial practices.

Purposes of Changes:

1. Subsection (a) continues the rule without change from former Section 7-204 on the warehouse's obligation to exercise reasonable care.

2. Former Section 7-204(2) required that the term limiting damages do so by setting forth a specific liability per article or item or of a value per unit of weight. This requirement has been deleted as out of step with modern industry practice. Under subsection (b) a warehouse may limit its liability for damages for loss of or damage to the goods by a term in the warehouse receipt or storage agreement without the term constituting an impermissible disclaimer of the obligation of reasonable care. The parties cannot disclaim by contract the warehouse's obligation of care. Section 1-302. For example, limitations based upon per unit of weight, per package, per occurrence, or per receipt as well as limitations based upon a multiple of the storage rate may be commercially appropriate. As subsection (d) makes clear, the states or the federal government may supplement this section with more rigid standards of responsibility for some or all bailees.

3. Former Section 7-204(2) also provided that an increased rate cannot be charged if contrary to a tariff. That language has been deleted. If a tariff is required under state or federal law, pursuant to Section 7-103(a), the tariff would control over the rule of this section allowing an increased rate. The provisions of a non-mandatory tariff may be incorporated by reference in the parties' agreement. See Comment 2 to Section 7-103. Subsection (c) deletes the reference to tariffs for the same reason that the reference has been omitted in subsection (b).

4. As under former Section 7-204(2), subsection (b) provides that a limitation of damages is ineffective if the warehouse has converted the goods to its own use. A mere failure to redeliver the goods is not conversion to the warehouse's own use. See *Adams v. Ryan & Christie Storage, Inc.*, 563 F. Supp. 409 (E.D. Pa. 1983) *aff'd* 725 F.2d 666 (3d Cir.1983). Cases such as *I.C.C. Metals Inc. v. Municipal Warehouse Co.*, 409 N.E.2d 849 (N.Y. Ct. App. 1980) holding that mere failure to redeliver results in a presumption of conversion to the warehouse's own use are disapproved. "Conversion to its own use" is narrower than the idea of conversion generally. Cases such as *Lipman v. Peterson*, 575 P.2d 19 (Kan. 1978) holding to the contrary are disapproved.

5. Storage agreements commonly establish the contractual relationship between warehouses and depositors who have an on-going relationship. The storage agreement may allow for the movement of goods into and out of a warehouse without the necessity of issuing or amending a warehouse receipt upon each entry or exit of goods from the warehouse.

Cross References:

Sections 1-302, 7-103, 7-309 and 7-403.

Definitional Cross References:

"Goods".	Section 7-102.
"Reasonable time".	Section 1-205.
"Sign".	Section 7-102.
"Term".	Section 1-201.
"Value".	Section 1-204.
"Warehouse".	Section 7-102.
"Warehouse receipt".	Section 1-201.

Section 7-205. Title Under Warehouse Receipt Defeated in Certain Cases

A buyer in ordinary course of business of fungible goods sold and delivered by a warehouse that is also in the business of buying and selling such goods takes the goods free of any claim under a warehouse receipt even if the receipt is negotiable and has been duly negotiated.

Official Comment

Prior Uniform Statutory Provision: Former Section 7-205.

Changes: Changes for style only.

Purposes:

1. The typical case covered by this section is that of the warehouse-dealer in grain, and the substantive question at issue is whether in case the warehouse becomes insolvent the receipt holders shall be able to trace and recover grain shipped to farmers and other purchasers from the elevator. This was possible under the old Acts, although courts were eager to find estoppels to prevent it. The practical difficulty of tracing fungible grain means that the preservation of this theoretical right adds little to the commercial acceptability of negotiable grain receipts, which really circulate on the credit of the warehouse. Moreover, on default of the warehouse, the receipt holders at least share in what grain remains, whereas retaking the grain from a good-faith cash purchaser reduces the purchaser completely to the status of general creditor in a situation where there was very little the purchaser could do to guard against the loss. Compare 15 U.S.C. Section 714p enacted in 1955.

2. This provision applies to both negotiable and nonnegotiable warehouse receipts. The concept of due negotiation is provided for in Section 7-501. The definition of "buyer in ordinary course" is in Article 1 and provides, among other things, that a buyer must either have possession or a right to obtain the goods under Article 2 in order to be a buyer in ordinary course. This section requires actual delivery of the fungible goods to the buyer in ordinary course. Delivery requires voluntary transfer of possession of the fungible goods to the buyer. This section is not satisfied by the delivery of the document of title to the buyer in ordinary course.

Cross References:

Sections 2-403 and 9-320.

Definitional Cross References:

"Buyer in ordinary course of business".	Section 1-201.
"Delivery".	Section 1-201.
"Duly negotiate".	Section 7-501.
"Fungible goods".	Section 1-201.
"Goods".	Section 7-102.
"Value".	Section 1-204.
"Warehouse".	Section 7-102.
"Warehouse receipt".	Section 1-201.

Section 7-206. Termination of Storage at Warehouse's Option

(a) A warehouse, by giving notice to the person on whose account the goods are held and any other person known to claim an interest in the goods, may require payment of any charges and removal of the goods from the warehouse at the termination of the period of storage fixed by the document of title or, if a period is not fixed, within a stated period not less than 30 days after the warehouse gives notice. If the goods are not removed before the date specified in the notice, the warehouse may sell them pursuant to Section 7-210.

(b) If a warehouse in good faith believes that goods are about to deteriorate or decline in value to less than the amount of its lien within the time provided in subsection (a) and Section 7-210, the warehouse may specify in the notice given under subsection (a) any reasonable shorter time for removal of the goods and, if the goods are not removed, may sell them at public sale held not less than one week after a single advertisement or posting.

(c) If, as a result of a quality or condition of the goods of which the warehouse did not have notice at the time of deposit, the goods are a hazard to other property, the warehouse facilities, or other persons, the warehouse may sell the goods at public or private sale without advertisement or posting on reasonable notification to all persons known to claim an interest in the goods. If the warehouse, after a reasonable effort, is unable to sell the goods, it may dispose of them in any lawful manner and does not incur liability by reason of that disposition.

(d) A warehouse shall deliver the goods to any person entitled to them under this Article upon due demand made at any time before sale or other disposition under this section.

(e) A warehouse may satisfy its lien from the proceeds of any sale or disposition under this section but shall hold the balance for delivery on the demand of any person to which the warehouse would have been bound to deliver the goods.

Official Comment

Prior Uniform Statutory Provision: Former Section 7-206.

Changes: Changes for style.

Purposes:

1. This section provides for three situations in which the warehouse may terminate storage for reasons other than enforcement of its lien as permitted by Section 7-210. Most warehousing is for an indefinite term, the bailor being entitled to delivery on reasonable demand. It is necessary to define the warehouse's power to terminate the bailment, since it would be commercially intolerable to allow warehouses to order removal of the goods on short notice. The 30-day period provided where the document does not carry its own period of termination corresponds to commercial practice of computing rates on a monthly basis. The right to terminate under subsection (a) includes a right to require payment of "any charges", but does not depend on the existence of unpaid charges.

2. In permitting expeditious disposition of perishable and hazardous goods the pre-Code Uniform Warehouse Receipts Act, Section 34, made no distinction between cases where the warehouse knowingly undertook to store such goods and cases where the goods were discovered to be of that character subsequent to storage. The former situation presents no such emergency as justifies the summary power of removal and sale. Subsections (b) and (c) distinguish between the two situations. The reason of this section should apply if the goods become hazardous during the course of storage. The process for selling the goods described in Section 7-210 governs the sale of goods under this section except as provided in subsections (b) and (c) for the situations described in those subsections respectively.

3. Protection of its lien is the only interest which the warehouse has to justify summary sale of perishable goods which are not hazardous. This same interest must be recognized when the stored goods, although not perishable, decline in market value to a point which threatens the warehouse's security.

4. The right to order removal of stored goods is subject to provisions of the public warehousing laws of some states forbidding warehouses from discriminating among customers. Nor does the section relieve the warehouse of any obligation under the state laws to secure the approval of a public official before disposing of deteriorating goods. Such regulatory statutes and the regulations under them remain in force and operative. Section 7-103.

Cross References:

Sections 7-103 and 7-403.

Definitional Cross References:

"Delivery".	Section 1-201.
"Document of title".	Section 1-102. [*sic,* should be 1-201]
"Good faith".	Section 1-201 [7-102].
"Goods".	Section 7-102.
"Notice".	Section 1-202.
"Notification".	Section 1-202.
"Person".	Section 1-201.
"Reasonable time".	Section 1-205.
"Value".	Section 1-204.
"Warehouse".	Section 7-102.

Section 7-207. Goods Must Be Kept Separate; Fungible Goods

(a) Unless the warehouse receipt provides otherwise, a warehouse shall keep separate the goods covered by each receipt so as to permit at all times identification and delivery of those goods. However, different lots of fungible goods may be commingled.

(b) If different lots of fungible goods are commingled, the goods are owned in common by the persons entitled thereto and the warehouse is severally liable to each owner for that owner's share. If, because of overissue, a mass of fungible goods is insufficient to meet all the receipts the warehouse has issued against it, the persons entitled include all holders to which overissued receipts have been duly negotiated.

Official Comment

Prior Uniform Statutory Provision: Former Section 7-207.

Changes: Changes for style only.

Purposes:

No change of substance is made from former Section 7-207. Holders to whom overissued receipts have been duly negotiated shall share in a mass of fungible goods. Where individual ownership interests are merged into claims on a common fund, as is necessarily the case with fungible goods, there is no policy reason for discriminating between successive purchasers of similar claims.

Definitional Cross References:

"Delivery".	Section 1-201.
"Duly negotiate".	Section 7-501.
"Fungible goods".	Section 1-201.
"Goods".	Section 7-102.
"Holder".	Section 1-201.
"Person".	Section 1-201.
"Warehouse".	Section 7-102.
"Warehouse receipt".	Section 1-201.

Section 7-208. Altered Warehouse Receipts

If a blank in a negotiable tangible warehouse receipt has been filled in without authority, a good-faith purchaser for value and without notice of the lack of authority may treat the insertion as authorized. Any other unauthorized alteration leaves any tangible or electronic warehouse receipt enforceable against the issuer according to its original tenor.

Official Comment

Prior Uniform Statutory Provision: Former Section 7-208.

Changes: To accommodate electronic documents of title.

Purpose:

1. The execution of tangible warehouse receipts in blank is a dangerous practice. As between the issuer and an innocent purchaser the risks should clearly fall on the former. The purchaser must have purchased the tangible negotiable warehouse receipt in good faith and for value to be protected under the rule of the first sentence which is a limited exception to the general rule in the second sentence. Electronic document of title systems should have protection against unauthorized access and unauthorized changes. See Section 7-106. Thus the protection for good-faith purchasers found in the first sentence is not necessary in the context of electronic documents.

2. Under the second sentence of this section, an unauthorized alteration whether made with or without fraudulent intent does not relieve the issuer of its liability on the warehouse receipt as originally executed. The unauthorized alteration itself is of course ineffective against the warehouse. The rule stated in the second sentence applies to both tangible and electronic warehouse receipts.

Definitional Cross References:

"Good faith".	Section 1-201 [7-102].
"Issuer".	Section 7-102.
"Notice".	Section 1-202.
"Purchaser".	Section 1-201.
"Value".	Section 1-204.
"Warehouse receipt".	Section 1-201.

Section 7-209. Lien of Warehouse

(a) A warehouse has a lien against the bailor on the goods covered by a warehouse receipt or storage agreement or on the proceeds thereof in its possession for charges for storage or transportation, including demurrage and terminal charges, insurance, labor, or other charges, present or future, in relation to the goods, and for expenses necessary for preservation of the goods or reasonably incurred in their sale pursuant to law. If the person on whose account the goods are held is liable for similar charges or expenses in relation to other goods whenever deposited and it is stated in the warehouse receipt or storage agreement that a lien is claimed for charges and expenses in relation to other goods, the warehouse also has a lien against the goods covered by the warehouse receipt or storage agreement or on the proceeds thereof in its possession for those charges and expenses, whether or not the other goods have been delivered by the warehouse. However, as against a person to which a negotiable warehouse receipt is duly negotiated, a warehouse's lien is limited to charges in an amount or at a rate specified in the warehouse receipt or, if no charges are so specified, to a reasonable charge for storage of the specific goods covered by the receipt subsequent to the date of the receipt.

(b) A warehouse may also reserve a security interest against the bailor for the maximum amount specified on the receipt for charges other than those specified in subsection (a), such as for money advanced and interest. The security interest is governed by Article 9.

(c) A warehouse's lien for charges and expenses under subsection (a) or a security interest under subsection (b) is also effective against any person that so entrusted the bailor with possession of the goods that a pledge of them by the bailor to a good-faith purchaser for value would have been valid. However, the lien or security interest is not effective against a person that before issuance of a document of title had a legal interest or a perfected security interest in the goods and that did not:

(1) deliver or entrust the goods or any document of title covering the goods to the bailor or the bailor's nominee with:

(A) actual or apparent authority to ship, store, or sell;

(B) power to obtain delivery under Section 7-403; or

(C) power of disposition under Sections 2-403, 2A-304(2), 2A-305(2), 9-320, or 9-321(c) or other statute or rule of law; or

(2) acquiesce in the procurement by the bailor or its nominee of any document.

(d) A warehouse's lien on household goods for charges and expenses in relation to the goods under subsection (a) is also effective against all persons if the depositor was the legal possessor of the goods at the time of deposit. In this subsection, "household goods" means furniture, furnishings, or personal effects used by the depositor in a dwelling.

(e) A warehouse loses its lien on any goods that it voluntarily delivers or unjustifiably refuses to deliver.

Official Comment

Prior Uniform Statutory Provision: Former Sections 7-209 and 7-503.

Changes: Expanded to recognize warehouse lien when a warehouse receipt is not issued but goods are covered by a storage agreement.

Purposes:

1. Subsection (a) defines the warehouse's statutory lien. Other than allowing a warehouse to claim a lien under this section when there is a storage agreement and not a warehouse receipt, this section remains unchanged in substance from former Section 7-209(1). Under the first sentence, a specific lien attaches automatically without express notation on the receipt or storage agreement with regard to goods stored under the receipt or the storage agreement. That lien is limited to the usual charges arising out of a storage transaction.

> **Example 1:** Bailor stored goods with a warehouse and the warehouse issued a warehouse receipt. A lien against those goods arose as set forth in subsection (a), the first sentence, for the charges for storage and the other expenses of those goods. The warehouse may enforce its lien under Section 7-210 as against the bailor. Whether the warehouse receipt is negotiable or nonnegotiable is not important to the warehouse's rights as against the bailor.

Under the second sentence, by notation on the receipt or storage agreement, the lien can be made a general lien extending to like charges in relation to other goods. Both the specific lien and general lien are as to goods in the possession of the warehouse and extend to proceeds from the goods as long as the proceeds are in the possession of the warehouse. The same rules apply whether the receipt is negotiable or nonnegotiable.

> **Example 2:** Bailor stored goods (lot A) with a warehouse and the warehouse issued a warehouse receipt for those goods. In the warehouse receipt it is stated that the warehouse will also have a lien on goods covered by the warehouse receipt for storage charges and the other expenses for any other goods that are stored with the warehouse by the bailor. The statement about the lien on other goods does not specify an amount or a rate. Bailor then stored other goods (lot B) with the warehouse. Under subsection (a), first sentence, the warehouse has a lien on the specific goods (lot A) covered by the warehouse receipt. Under subsection (a), second sentence, the warehouse has a lien on the goods in lot A for the storage charges and the other expenses arising from the goods in lot B. That lien is enforceable as against the bailor regardless of whether the receipt is negotiable or nonnegotiable.

Under the third sentence, if the warehouse receipt is negotiable, the lien as against a holder of that receipt by due negotiation is limited to the amount or rate specified on the receipt for the specific lien or the general lien, or, if none is specified, to a reasonable charge for storage of the specific goods covered by the receipt for storage after the date of the receipt.

> **Example 3:** Same facts as Example 1 except that the warehouse receipt is negotiable and has been duly negotiated (Section 7-501) to a person other than the bailor. Under the last sentence of subsection (a), the warehouse

may enforce its lien against the bailor's goods stored in the warehouse as against the person to whom the negotiable warehouse receipt has been duly negotiated. Section 7-502. That lien is limited to the charges or rates specified in the receipt or a reasonable charge for storage as stated in the last sentence of subsection (a).

Example 4: Same facts as Example 2 except that the warehouse receipt is negotiable and has been duly negotiated (Section 7-501) to a person other than the bailor. Under the last sentence of subsection (a), the lien on lot A goods for the storage charges and the other expenses arising from storage of lot B goods is not enforceable as against the person to whom the receipt has been duly negotiated. Without a statement of a specified amount or rate for the general lien, the warehouse's general lien is not enforceable as against the person to whom the negotiable document has been duly negotiated. However, the warehouse lien for charges and expenses related to storage of lot A goods is still enforceable as against the person to whom the receipt was duly negotiated.

Example 5: Same facts as Examples 2 and 4 except the warehouse had stated on the negotiable warehouse receipt a specified amount or rate for the general lien on other goods (lot B). Under the last sentence of subsection (a), the general lien on lot A goods for the storage charges and the other expenses arising from storage of lot B goods is enforceable as against the person to whom the receipt has been duly negotiated.

2. Subsection (b) provides for a security interest based upon agreement. Such a security interest arises out of relations between the parties other than bailment for storage or transportation, as where the bailee assumes the role of financier or performs a manufacturing operation, extending credit in reliance upon the goods covered by the receipt. Such a security interest is not a statutory lien. Compare Sections 9-109 and 9-333. It is governed in all respects by Article 9, except that subsection (b) requires that the receipt specify a maximum amount and limits the security interest to the amount specified. A warehouse could also take a security interest to secure its charges for storage and the other expenses listed in subsection (a) to protect these claims upon the loss of the statutory possessory warehouse lien if the warehouse loses possession of the goods as provided in subsection (e).

Example 6: Bailor stores goods with a warehouse and the warehouse issues a warehouse receipt that states that the warehouse is taking a security interest in the bailed goods for charges of storage, expenses, for money advanced, for manufacturing services rendered, and all other obligations that the bailor may owe the warehouse. That is a security interest covered in all respects by Article 9. Subsection (b). As allowed by this section, a warehouse may rely upon its statutory possessory lien to protect its charges for storage and the other expenses related to storage. For those storage charges covered by the statutory possessory lien, the warehouse is not required to use a security interest under subsection (b).

3. Subsections (a) and (b) validate the lien and security interest "against the bailor". Under basic principles of derivative rights as provided in Section 7-504, the warehouse lien is also valid as against parties who obtain their rights from the bailor except as otherwise provided in subsection (a), third sentence, or subsection (c).

Example 7: Bailor stores goods with a warehouse and the warehouse issues a nonnegotiable warehouse receipt that also claims a general lien in other goods stored with the warehouse. A lien on the bailed goods for the charges for storage and the other expenses arises under subsection (a). Bailor notifies the warehouse that the goods have been sold to Buyer and the bailee acknowledges that fact to Buyer. Section 2-503. The warehouse lien for storage of those goods is effective against Buyer for both the specific lien and the general lien. Section 7-504.

Example 8: Bailor stores goods with a warehouse and the warehouse issues a nonnegotiable warehouse receipt. A lien on the bailed goods for the charges for storage and the other expenses arises under subsection (a). Bailor grants a security interest in the goods while the goods are in the warehouse's possession to Secured Party (SP) who properly perfects a security interest in the goods. See Revised 9312(d). The warehouse lien is superior in priority over SP's security interest. See Revised 9203(b)(2) (debtor can grant a security interest to the extent of debtor's rights in the collateral).

Example 9: Bailor stores goods with a warehouse and the warehouse issues a negotiable warehouse receipt. A lien on the bailed goods for the charges for storage and the other expenses arises under subsection (a). Bailor grants a security interest in the negotiable document to SP. SP properly perfects its interest in the negotiable document by taking possession through a "due negotiation". Revised 9312(c). SP's security interest is subordinate to the warehouse lien. Section 7-209(a), third sentence. Given that Bailor's rights are subject to the warehouse lien, Bailor cannot grant to SP greater rights than Bailor has under Section 9-203(b)(2), perfection of the security interest in the negotiable document and the goods covered by the document through SP's filing of a financing statement should not give a different result.

As against third parties who have interests in the goods prior to the storage with the warehouse, subsection (c) continues the rule under the Prior Uniform Statutory provision that to validate the lien or security interest of the warehouse, the owner must have entrusted the goods to the depositor, and that the circumstances must be such that a pledge by the depositor to a good-faith purchaser for value would have been valid. Thus the owner's interest will not be subjected to a lien or security interest arising out of a deposit of its goods by a thief. The warehouse may be protected because of the actual, implied or apparent authority of the depositor, because of a Factor's Act, or because of other circumstances which would protect a bona fide pledgee, unless those circumstances are denied effect under the second sentence of subsection (c). The language of Section 7-503 is brought into subsection (c) for purposes of clarity. The Comments to Section 7-503 are helpful in interpreting delivery, entrustment or acquiescence.

Where the third party is the holder of a security interest, obtained prior to the issuance of a negotiable warehouse receipt, the rights of the warehouse depend on the priority given to a hypothetical bona fide pledgee by Article 9, particularly Section 9-322. Thus the special priority granted to statutory liens by Section 9-333 does not apply to liens under subsection (a) of this section, since subsection (c), second sentence, "expressly provides otherwise" within the meaning of Section 9-333.

As to household goods, however, subsection (d) makes the warehouse's lien "for charges and expenses in relation to the goods" effective against all persons if the depositor was the legal possessor. The purpose of the exception is to permit the warehouse to accept household goods for storage in sole reliance on the value of the goods themselves, especially in situations of family emergency.

Example 10: Bailor grants a perfected security interest in the goods to SP prior to storage of the goods with the warehouse. Bailor then stores goods with the warehouse and the warehouse issues a warehouse receipt for the goods. A warehouse lien on the bailed goods for the charges for storage or other expenses arises under subsection (a). The warehouse lien is not effective as against SP unless SP entrusted the goods to Bailor with actual or apparent authority to ship, store or sell the goods or with power of disposition under subsection (c)(1) or acquiesced in Bailor's procurement of a document of title under subsection (c)(2). This result obtains whether the receipt is negotiable or nonnegotiable.

Example 11: Sheriff who had lawfully repossessed household goods in an eviction action stored the goods with a warehouse. A lien on the bailed goods arises under subsection (a). The lien is effective as against the owner of the goods. Subsection (d).

4. As under previous law, this section creates a statutory possessory lien in favor of the warehouse on the goods stored with the warehouse or on the proceeds of the goods. The warehouse loses its lien if it loses possession of the goods or the proceeds. Subsection (e).

5. Where goods have been stored under a nonnegotiable warehouse receipt and are sold by the person to whom the receipt has been issued, frequently the goods are not withdrawn by the new owner. The obligations of the seller of the goods in this situation are set forth in Section 2-503(4) on tender of delivery and include procurement of an acknowledgment by the bailee of the buyer's right to possession of the goods. If a new receipt is requested, such an acknowledgment can be withheld until storage charges have been paid or provided for. The statutory lien for charges on the goods sold, granted by the first sentence of subsection (a), continues valid unless the bailee gives it up. See Section 7-403. But once a new receipt is issued to the buyer, the buyer becomes "the person on whose account the goods are held" under the second sentence of subsection (a); unless the buyer undertakes liability for charges in relation to other goods stored by the seller, there is no general lien against the buyer for such charges. Of course, the bailee may preserve the general lien in such a case either by an arrangement by which the buyer "is liable for" such charges, or by reserving a security interest under subsection (b).

6. A possessory warehouse lien arises as provided under subsection (a) if the parties to the bailment have a storage agreement or a warehouse receipt is issued. In the modern warehouse, the bailor and the bailee may enter into a master contract governing the bailment with the bailee and bailor keeping track of the goods stored pursuant to the master contract by notation on their respective books and records and the parties send notification via electronic communication as to what goods are covered by the master contract. Warehouse receipts are not issued. See Comment 4 to Section 7-204. There is no particular form for a warehouse receipt and failure to contain any of the terms listed in Section 7-202 does not deprive the warehouse of its lien that arises under subsection (a). See the Comment to Section 7-202.

Cross References:

Point 1:	Sections 7-501 and 7-502.
Point 2:	Sections 9-109 and 9-333.
Point 3:	Sections 2-503, 7-503, 7-504, 9-203, 9-312 and 9-322.
Point 4:	Sections 2-503, 7-501, 7-502, 7-504, 9-312, 9-331, 9-333 and 9-401.
Point 5:	Sections 2-503 and 7-403.
Point 6:	Sections 7-202 and 7-204.

Definitional Cross References:

"Delivery".	Section 1-201.
"Document of title".	Section 1-201.
"Goods".	Section 7-102.
"Money".	Section 1-201.
"Person".	Section 1-201.
"Purchaser".	Section 1-201.
"Right".	Section 1-201.
"Security interest".	Section 1-201.
"Value".	Section 1-204.
"Warehouse".	Section 7-102.
"Warehouse receipt".	Section 1-201.

Section 7-210. Enforcement of Warehouse's Lien

(a) Except as otherwise provided in subsection (b), a warehouse's lien may be enforced by public or private sale of the goods, in bulk or in packages, at any time or place and on any terms that are commercially reasonable, after notifying all persons known to claim an interest in the goods. The notification must include a statement of the amount due, the nature of the proposed sale, and the time and place of any public sale. The fact that a better price could have been obtained by a sale at a different time or in a method different from that selected by the warehouse is not of itself sufficient to establish that the sale was not made in a commercially reasonable manner. The warehouse sells in a commercially reasonable manner if the warehouse sells the goods in the usual manner in any recognized market therefor, sells at the price current in that market at the time of the sale, or otherwise sells in conformity with commercially reasonable practices among dealers in the type of goods sold. A sale of more goods than apparently necessary to be offered to ensure satisfaction of the obligation is not commercially reasonable, except in cases covered by the preceding sentence.

(b) A warehouse may enforce its lien on goods, other than goods stored by a merchant in the course of its business, only if the following requirements are satisfied:

(1) All persons known to claim an interest in the goods must be notified.

(2) The notification must include an itemized statement of the claim, a description of the goods subject to the lien, a demand for payment within a specified time not less than 10 days after receipt of the notification, and a conspicuous statement that unless the claim is paid within that time the goods will be advertised for sale and sold by auction at a specified time and place.

(3) The sale must conform to the terms of the notification.

(4) The sale must be held at the nearest suitable place to where the goods are held or stored.

(5) After the expiration of the time given in the notification, an advertisement of the sale must be published once a week for two weeks consecutively in a newspaper of general circulation where the sale is to be held. The advertisement must include a description of the goods, the name of the person on whose account the goods are being held, and the time and place of the sale. The sale must take place at least 15 days after the first publication. If there is no newspaper of general circulation where the sale is to be held, the advertisement must be posted at least 10 days before the sale in not fewer than six conspicuous places in the neighborhood of the proposed sale.

(c) Before any sale pursuant to this section, any person claiming a right in the goods may pay the amount necessary to satisfy the lien and the reasonable expenses incurred in complying with this section. In that event, the goods may not be sold but must be retained by the warehouse subject to the terms of the receipt and this Article.

(d) A warehouse may buy at any public sale held pursuant to this section.

(e) A purchaser in good faith of goods sold to enforce a warehouse's lien takes the goods free of any rights of persons against which the lien was valid, despite the warehouse's noncompliance with this section.

(f) A warehouse may satisfy its lien from the proceeds of any sale pursuant to this section but shall hold the balance, if any, for delivery on demand to any person to which the warehouse would have been bound to deliver the goods.

(g) The rights provided by this section are in addition to all other rights allowed by law to a creditor against a debtor.

(h) If a lien is on goods stored by a merchant in the course of its business, the lien may be enforced in accordance with subsection (a) or (b).

(i) A warehouse is liable for damages caused by failure to comply with the requirements for sale under this section and, in case of willful violation, is liable for conversion.

Official Comment

Prior Uniform Statutory Provision: Former Section 7-210.

Changes: Update to accommodate electronic commerce and for style.

Purposes:

1. Subsection (a) makes "commercial reasonableness" the standard for foreclosure proceedings in all cases except noncommercial storage with a warehouse. The latter category embraces principally storage of household goods by private owners; and for such cases the detailed provisions as to notification, publication and public sale are retained in subsection (b) with one change. The requirement in former Section 7-210(2)(b) that the notification must be sent in person or by registered or certified mail has been deleted. Notification may be sent by any reasonable means as provided in Section 1-202. The swifter, more flexible procedure of subsection

(a) is appropriate to commercial storage. Compare Seller's power of resale on breach by Buyer under the provisions of the Article on Sales (Section 2-706). Commercial reasonableness is a flexible concept that allows for a wide variety of actions to satisfy the rule of this section, including electronic means of posting and sale.

2. The provisions of subsections (d) and (e) permitting the bailee to bid at public sales and confirming the title of purchasers at foreclosure sales are designed to secure more bidding and better prices and remain unchanged from former Section 7-210.

3. A warehouse may have recourse to an interpleader action in appropriate circumstances. See Section 7-603.

4. If a warehouse has both a warehouse lien and a security interest, the warehouse may enforce both the lien and the security interest simultaneously by using the procedures of Article 9. Section 7-210 adopts as its touchstone "commercial reasonableness" for the enforcement of a warehouse lien. Following the procedures of Article 9 satisfies "commercial reasonableness".

Cross References:

Sections 2-706, 7-403, 7-603 and Part 6 of Article 9.

Definitional Cross References:

"Bill of lading".	Section 1-201.
"Conspicuous".	Section 1-201.
"Creditor".	Section 1-201.
"Delivery".	Section 1-201.
"Document of title".	Section 1-201.
"Good faith".	Section 1-201 [7-102].
"Goods".	Section 7-102.
"Notification".	Section 1-202.
"Notifies".	Section 1-202.
"Person".	Section 1-201.
"Purchaser".	Section 1-201.
"Rights".	Section 1-201.
"Term".	Section 1-201.
"Warehouse".	Section 7-102.

PART 3. BILLS OF LADING: SPECIAL PROVISIONS

Section 7-301. Liability for Nonreceipt or Misdescription; "Said to Contain"; "Shipper's Weight, Load, and Count", Improper Handling

(a) A consignee of a nonnegotiable bill of lading which has given value in good faith, or a holder to which a negotiable bill has been duly negotiated, relying upon the description of the goods in the bill or upon the date shown in the bill, may recover from the issuer damages caused by the misdating of the bill or the nonreceipt or misdescription of the goods, except to the extent that the bill indicates that the issuer does not know whether any part or all of the goods in fact were received or conform to the description, such as in a case in which the description is in terms of marks or labels or kind, quantity, or condition or the receipt or description is qualified by "contents or condition of contents of packages unknown", "said to contain", "shipper's weight, load, and count," or words of similar import, if that indication is true.

(b) If goods are loaded by the issuer of a bill of lading;

(1) the issuer shall count the packages of goods if shipped in packages and ascertain the kind and quantity if shipped in bulk; and

(2) words such as "shipper's weight, load, and count," or words of similar import indicating that the description was made by the shipper are ineffective except as to goods concealed in packages.

(c) If bulk goods are loaded by a shipper that makes available to the issuer of a bill of lading adequate facilities for weighing those goods, the issuer shall ascertain the kind and quantity within a reasonable time after receiving the shipper's request in a record to do so. In that case, "shipper's weight" or words of similar import are ineffective.

(d) The issuer of a bill of lading, by including in the bill the words "shipper's weight, load, and count," or words of similar import, may indicate that the goods were loaded by the shipper, and, if that statement is true, the issuer is not liable for damages caused by the improper loading. However, omission of such words does not imply liability for damages caused by improper loading.

(e) A shipper guarantees to an issuer the accuracy at the time of shipment of the description, marks, labels, number, kind, quantity, condition, and weight, as furnished by the shipper, and the shipper shall indemnify the issuer against damage caused by inaccuracies in those particulars. This right of indemnity does not limit the issuer's responsibility or liability under the contract of carriage to any person other than the shipper.

Official Comment

Prior Uniform Statutory Provision: Former Section 7-301.

Changes: Changes for clarity, style and to recognize deregulation in the transportation industry.

Purposes:

1. This section continues the rules from former Section 7-301 with one substantive change. The obligations of the issuer of the bill of lading under former subsections (2) and (3) were limited to issuers who were common carriers. Subsections (b) and (c) apply the same rules to all issuers, not just common carriers. This section is compatible with the policies stated in the federal Bills of Lading Act, 49 U.S.C. § 80113 (2000).

2. The language of the pre-Code Uniform Bills of Lading Act suggested that a carrier is ordinarily liable for damage caused by improper loading, but may relieve itself of liability by disclosing on the bill that the shipper actually loaded. A more accurate statement of the law is that the carrier is not liable for losses caused by act or default of the shipper, which would include improper loading. *D. H. Overmyer Co. v. Nelson Brantley Glass Co.*, 168 S.E.2d 176 (Ga. Ct. App. 1969). There was some question whether under pre-Code law a carrier was liable even to a good-faith purchaser of a negotiable bill for such losses, if the shipper's faulty loading in fact caused the loss. Subsection (d) permits the carrier to bar, by disclosure of the shipper's loading, liability to a good-faith purchaser. There is no implication that decisions such as *Modern Tool Corp. v. Pennsylvania R. Co.*, 100 F. Supp. 595 (D.N.J. 1951), are disapproved.

3. This section is a restatement of existing law as to the method by which a bailee may avoid responsibility for the accuracy of descriptions which are made by or in reliance upon information furnished by the depositor or shipper. The wording in this section—"contents or condition of contents of packages unknown" or "shipper's weight, load and count"—to indicate that the shipper loaded the goods or that the carrier does not know the description, condition or contents of the loaded packages continues to be appropriate as commonly understood in the transportation industry. The reasons for this wording are as important in 2002 as when the prior section initially was approved. The issuer is liable on documents issued by an agent, contrary to instructions of his principal, without receiving goods. No disclaimer of this liability is permitted since it is not a matter either of the care of the goods or their description.

4. The shipper's erroneous report to the carrier concerning the goods may cause damage to the carrier. Subsection (e) therefore provides appropriate indemnity.

5. The word "freight" in the former Section 7-301 has been changed to "goods" to conform to international and domestic land transport usage in which "freight" means the price paid for carriage of the goods and not the goods themselves. Hence, changing the word "freight" to the word "goods" is a clarifying change that fits both international and domestic practice.

Cross References:

Sections 7-203, 7-309 and 7-501.

Definitional Cross References:

"Bill of lading".	Section 1-201.
"Consignee".	Section 7-102.
"Document of title".	Section 1-201.
"Duly negotiate".	Section 7-501.
"Good faith".	Section 1-201 [7-102].
"Goods".	Section 7-102.
"Holder".	Section 1-201.
"Issuer".	Section 7-102.
"Notice".	Section 1-202.
"Party".	Section 1-201.
"Purchaser."	Section 1-201.
"Receipt of goods".	Section 2-103.
"Value".	Section 1-204.

Section 7-302. Through Bills of Lading and Similar Documents of Titles

(a) The issuer of a through bill of lading, or other document of title embodying an undertaking to be performed in part by a person acting as its agent or by a performing carrier, is liable to any person entitled to recover on the bill or other document for any breach by the other person or the performing carrier of its obligation under the bill or other document. However, to the extent that the bill or other document covers an undertaking to be performed overseas or in territory not contiguous to the continental United States or an undertaking including matters other than transportation, this liability for breach by the other person or the performing carrier may be varied by agreement of the parties.

(b) If goods covered by a through bill of lading or other document of title embodying an undertaking to be performed in part by a person other than the issuer are received by that person, the person is subject, with respect to its own performance while the goods are in its possession, to the obligation of the issuer. The person's obligation is discharged by delivery of the goods to another person pursuant to the bill or other document and does not include liability for breach by any other person or by the issuer.

(c) The issuer of a through bill of lading or other document of title described in subsection (a) is entitled to recover from the performing carrier, or other person in possession of the goods when the breach of the obligation under the bill or other document occurred:

(1) the amount it may be required to pay to any person entitled to recover on the bill or other document for the breach, as may be evidenced by any receipt, judgment, or transcript of judgment; and

(2) the amount of any expense reasonably incurred by the issuer in defending any action commenced by any person entitled to recover on the bill or other document for the breach.

Official Comment

Prior Uniform Statutory Provision: Former Section 7-302.

Changes: To conform to current terminology and for style.

Purposes:

1. This section continues the rules from former Section 7-302 without substantive change. The term "performing carrier" is substituted for the term "connecting carrier" to conform the terminology of this section with terminology used in recent UNCITRAL and OAS proposals concerning transportation and through bills of lading. This change in terminology is not substantive. This section is compatible with liability on carriers under federal law. See 49 U.S.C. §§ 11706, 14706 and 15906.

The purpose of this section is to subject the initial carrier under a through bill to suit for breach of the contract of carriage by any performing carrier and to make it clear that any such performing carrier holds the goods on terms which are defined by the document of title even though such performing carrier did not issue the document. Since the performing carrier does hold the goods on the terms of the document, it must honor a proper demand for delivery or a diversion order just as the original bailee would have to. Similarly it has the benefits of the excuses for nondelivery and limitations of liability provided for the original bailee who issued the bill. Unlike the original bailee-issuer, the performing carrier's responsibility is limited to the period while the goods are in its possession. The section does not impose any obligation to issue through bills.

2. The reference to documents other than through bills looks to the possibility that multipurpose documents may come into use, e.g., combination warehouse receipts and bills of lading. As electronic documents of title come into common usage, storage documents (e.g., warehouse receipts) and transportation documents (e.g., bills of lading) may merge seamlessly into one electronic document that can serve both the storage and transportation segments of the movement of goods.

3. Under subsection (a) the issuer of a through bill of lading may become liable for the fault of another person. Subsection (c) gives the issuer appropriate rights of recourse.

4. Despite the broad language of subsection (a), Section 7-302 is subject to preemption by federal laws and treaties. Section 7-103. The precise scope of federal preemption in the transportation sector is a question determined under federal law.

Cross Reference:

Section 7-103.

Definitional Cross References:

"Agreement".	Section 1-201.
"Bailee".	Section 7-102.
"Bill of lading".	Section 1-201.
"Delivery".	Section 1-201.
"Document of title".	Section 1-201.
"Goods".	Section 7-102.
"Issuer".	Section 7-102.
"Party".	Section 1-201.
"Person".	Section 1-201.

Section 7-303. Diversion; Reconsignment; Change of Instructions

(a) Unless the bill of lading otherwise provides, a carrier may deliver the goods to a person or destination other than that stated in the bill or may otherwise dispose of the goods, without liability for misdelivery, on instructions from:

(1) the holder of a negotiable bill;

(2) the consignor on a nonnegotiable bill, even if the consignee has given contrary instructions;

(3) the consignee on a nonnegotiable bill in the absence of contrary instructions from the consignor, if the goods have arrived at the billed destination or if the consignee is in possession of the tangible bill or in control of the electronic bill; or

(4) the consignee on a nonnegotiable bill, if the consignee is entitled as against the consignor to dispose of the goods.

(b) Unless instructions described in subsection (a) are included in a negotiable bill of lading, a person to which the bill is duly negotiated may hold the bailee according to the original terms.

Official Comment

Prior Uniform Statutory Provision: Former Section 7-303.

Changes: To accommodate electronic documents and for style.

Purposes:

1. Diversion is a very common commercial practice which defeats delivery to the consignee originally named in a bill of lading. This section continues former Section 7-303's safe harbor rules for carriers in situations involving diversion and adapts those rules to electronic documents of title. This section works compatibly with Section 2-705. Carriers may as a business matter be willing to accept instructions from consignees in which case the carrier will be liable for misdelivery if the consignee was not the owner or otherwise empowered to dispose of the goods under subsection (a)(4). The section imposes no duty on carriers to undertake diversion. The carrier is of course subject to the provisions of mandatory filed tariffs as provided in Section 7-103.

2. It should be noted that the section provides only an immunity for carriers against liability for "misdelivery". It does not, for example, defeat the title to the goods which the consignee-buyer may have acquired from the consignor-seller upon delivery of the goods to the carrier under a nonnegotiable bill of lading. Thus if the carrier, upon instructions from the consignor, returns the goods to the consignor, the consignee may recover the goods from the consignor or the consignor's insolvent estate. However, under certain circumstances, the consignee's title may be defeated by diversion of the goods in transit to a different consignee. The rights that arise between the consignor-seller and the consignee-buyer out of a contract for the sale of goods are governed by Article 2.

Cross References:

Point 1:	Sections 2-705 and 7-103.
Point 2:	Article 2, Sections 7-403 and 7-504(3).

Definitional Cross References:

"Bailee".	Section 7-102.
"Bill of lading".	Section 1-201.
"Carrier".	Section 7-102.
"Consignee".	Section 7-102.
"Consignor".	Section 7-102.
"Delivery".	Section 1-201.
"Goods".	Section 7-102.
"Holder".	Section 1-201.
"Notice".	Section 1-202.
"Person".	Section 1-201.
"Purchaser".	Section 1-201.
"Term".	Section 1-201.

Section 7-304. Tangible Bills of Lading in a Set

(a) Except as customary in international transportation, a tangible bill of lading may not be issued in a set of parts. The issuer is liable for damages caused by violation of this subsection.

(b) If a tangible bill of lading is lawfully issued in a set of parts, each of which contains an identification code and is expressed to be valid only if the goods have not been delivered against any other part, the whole of the parts constitutes one bill.

(c) If a tangible negotiable bill of lading is lawfully issued in a set of parts and different parts are negotiated to different persons, the title of the holder to which the first due negotiation is made prevails as to both the document of title and the goods even if any later holder may have received the goods from the carrier in good faith and discharged the carrier's obligation by surrendering its part.

(d) A person that negotiates or transfers a single part of a tangible bill of lading issued in a set is liable to holders of that part as if it were the whole set.

(e) The bailee shall deliver in accordance with Part 4 against the first presented part of a tangible bill of lading lawfully issued in a set. Delivery in this manner discharges the bailee's obligation on the whole bill.

Official Comment

Prior Uniform Statutory Provision: Former Section 7-304.

Changes: To limit bills in a set to tangible bills of lading and to use terminology more consistent with modern usage.

Purposes:

1. Tangible bills of lading in a set are still used in some nations in international trade. Consequently, a tangible bill of lading part of a set could be at issue in a lawsuit that might come within Article 7. The statement of the legal effect of a lawfully issued set is in accord with existing commercial law relating to maritime and other international tangible bills of lading. This law has been codified in the Hague and Warsaw Conventions and in the Carriage of Goods by Sea Act, the provisions of which would ordinarily govern in situations where bills in a set are recognized by this Article. Tangible bills of lading in a set are prohibited in domestic trade.

2. Electronic bills of lading in domestic or international trade will not be issued in a set given the requirements of control necessary to deliver the bill to another person. An electronic bill of lading will be a single, authoritative copy. Section 7-106. Hence, this section differentiates between electronic bills of lading and tangible bills of lading. This section does not prohibit electronic data messages about goods in transit because these electronic data messages are not the issued bill of lading. Electronic data messages contain information for the carrier's management and handling of the cargo but this information for the carrier's use is not the issued bill of lading.

Cross References:

Sections 7-103, 7-303 and 7-106.

Definitional Cross References:

"Bailee".	Section 7-102.
"Bill of lading".	Section 1-201.
"Delivery".	Section 1-201.
"Document of title".	Section 1-201.
"Duly negotiate".	Section 7-501.
"Good faith".	Section 1-201 [7-102].
"Goods".	Section 7-102.
"Holder".	Section 1-201.
"Issuer".	Section 7-102.
"Person".	Section 1-201.
"Receipt of goods".	Section 2-103.

Section 7-305. Destination Bills

(a) Instead of issuing a bill of lading to the consignor at the place of shipment, a carrier, at the request of the consignor, may procure the bill to be issued at destination or at any other place designated in the request.

(b) Upon request of any person entitled as against a carrier to control the goods while in transit and on surrender of possession or control of any outstanding bill of lading or other receipt covering the goods, the issuer, subject to Section 7-105, may procure a substitute bill to be issued at any place designated in the request.

Official Comment

Prior Uniform Statutory Provision: Former Section 7-305.

Changes: To accommodate electronic bills of lading and for style.

Purposes:

1. Subsection (a) continues the rules of former Section 7-305(1) without substantive change. This proposal is designed to facilitate the use of order bills in connection with fast shipments. Use of order bills on high-speed shipments is impeded by the fact that the goods may arrive at destination before the documents, so that no one is ready to take delivery from the carrier. This is especially inconvenient for carriers by truck and air, who do not have terminal facilities where shipments can be held to await the consignee's appearance. Order bills would be useful

to take advantage of
C.O.D. shipment in
collecting and remi
this plan would be h
delivers the goods
bill in New York to
embodying this und
wires its New York
by Seller. Seller wi
New York bank ind
the draft. Normally
San Francisco, whi
airline's contract to
correspondent. This
no duty to issue suc
act as issuing agent

2. Subsection (b
305(2) with accomm
substitute bill chang
or vice versa, the is
with Section 7-105 t

Cross Referen
Section 7-105.

Definitional C
"Bill of lading"
"Consignor".
"Goods".
"Issuer".
"Receipt of goo

Section 7-306.

An unauthoriz
in a bill of lading
to its original teno

Prior Uniform S
Changes: Non
Purposes:

An unauthorized
made with or witho
issuer of its liability
This section applies
lading, applying the
The control concept
to the electronic doc
authorized or unauth
to Section 7-208 wh
thorized filling in of

Cross Referenc
Sections 7-106

Definitional Cr
"Bill of lading".
"Issuer".

Section 7-309. Duty of Care; Contractual Limitation of Carrier's Liability

(a) A carrier that issues a bill of lading, whether negotiable or nonnegotiable, shall exercise the degree of care in relation to the goods which a reasonably careful person would exercise under similar circumstances. This subsection does not affect any statute, regulation, or rule of law that imposes liability upon a common carrier for damages not caused by its negligence.

(b) Damages may be limited by a term in the bill of lading or in a transportation agreement that the carrier's liability may not exceed a value stated in the bill or transportation agreement if the carrier's rates are dependent upon value and the consignor is afforded an opportunity to declare a higher value and the consignor is advised of the opportunity. However, such a limitation is not effective with respect to the carrier's liability for conversion to its own use.

(c) Reasonable provisions as to the time and manner of presenting claims and commencing actions based on the shipment may be included in a bill of lading or a transportation agreement.

Official Comment

Prior Uniform Statutory Provision: Former Section 7-309.

Changes: References to tariffs eliminated because of deregulation, adding reference to transportation agreements, and for style.

Purposes:

1. A bill of lading may also serve as the contract between the carrier and the bailor. Parties in their contract should be able to limit the amount of damages for breach of that contract including breach of the duty to take reasonable care of the goods. The parties cannot disclaim by contract the carrier's obligation of care. Section 1-302.

Federal statutes and treaties for air, maritime and rail transport may alter the standard of care. These federal statutes and treaties preempt this section when applicable. Section 7-103. Subsection (a) does not impair any rule of law imposing the liability of an insurer on a common carrier in intrastate commerce. Subsection (b), however, applies to the common carrier's liability as an insurer as well as to liability based on negligence. Subsection (b) allows the term limiting damages to appear either in the bill of lading or in the parties' transportation agreement. Compare 7204(b). Subsection (c) allows the parties to agree to provisions regarding time and manner of presenting claims or commencing actions if the provisions are either in the bill of lading or the transportation agreement. Compare 7204(c). Transportation agreements are commonly used to establish agreed terms between carriers and shippers that have an on-going relationship.

2. References to public tariffs in former Section 7-309(2) and (3) have been deleted in light of the modern era of deregulation. See Comment 2 to Section 7-103. If a tariff is required under state or federal law, pursuant to Section 7-103(a), the tariff would control over the rule of this section. As governed by contract law, parties may incorporate by reference the limits on the amount of damages or the reasonable provisions as to the time and manner of presenting claims set forth in applicable tariffs, e.g., a maximum unit value beyond which goods are not taken or a disclaimer of responsibility for undeclared articles of extraordinary value.

3. As under former Section 7-309(2), subsection (b) provides that a limitation of damages is ineffective if the carrier has converted the goods to its own use. A mere failure to redeliver the goods is not conversion to the carrier's own use. "Conversion to its own use" is narrower than the idea of conversion generally. *Art Masters Associates, Ltd. v. United Parcel Serv.*, 567 N.E.2d 226 (N.Y. 1990); see *Kemper Ins. Co. v. Fed. Ex. Corp.*, 252 F.3d 509 (1st Cir.), *cert. denied* 534 U.S. 1020 (2001) (opinion interpreting federal law).

4. As used in this section, damages may include damages arising from delay in delivery. Delivery dates and times are often specified in the parties' contract. See Section 7-403.

Cross References:
Sections 1-302, 7-103, 7-204 and 7-403.

Definitional Cross References:

"Action".	Section 1-201.
"Bill of lading".	Section 1-201.
"Carrier".	Section 7-102.
"Consignor".	Section 7-102.
"Document of title".	Section 1-102 [*sic,* should be 1-201]
"Goods".	Section 7-102.
"Value".	Section 1-204.

PART 4. WAREHOUSE RECEIPTS AND BILLS OF LADING: GENERAL OBLIGATIONS

Section 7-401. Irregularities in Issue of Receipt or Bill or Conduct of Issuer

The obligations imposed by this Article on an issuer apply to a document of title even if:

(1) the document does not comply with the requirements of this Article or of any other statute, rule, or regulation regarding its issuance, form, or content;

(2) the issuer violated laws regulating the conduct of its business;

(3) the goods covered by the document were owned by the bailee when the document was issued; or

(4) the person issuing the document is not a warehouse but the document purports to be a warehouse receipt.

Official Comment

Prior Uniform Statutory Provision: Former Section 7-401.

Changes: Changes for style only.

Purposes:

The bailee's liability on its document despite nonreceipt or misdescription of the goods is affirmed in Sections 7-203 and 7-301. The purpose of this section is to make it clear that regardless of irregularities a document which falls within the definition of document of title imposes on the issuer the obligations stated in this Article. For example, a bailee will not be permitted to avoid its obligation to deliver the goods (Section 7-403) or its obligation of due care with respect to them (Sections 7-204 and 7-309) by taking the position that no valid "document" was issued because it failed to file a statutory bond or did not pay stamp taxes or did not disclose the place of storage in the document. *Tate v. Action Moving & Storage, Inc.*, 383 S.E.2d 229 (N.C. Ct. App. 1989), *rev. denied* 389 S.E.2d 104 (N.C. 1990). Sanctions against violations of statutory or administrative duties with respect to documents should be limited to revocation of license or other measures prescribed by the regulation imposing the duty. See Section 7-103.

Cross References:

Sections 7-103, 7-203, 7-204, 7-301 and 7-309.

Definitional Cross References:

"Bailee".	Section 7-102.
"Document of title".	Section 1-201.
"Goods".	Section 7-102.
"Issuer".	Section 7-102.
"Person".	Section 1-201.
"Warehouse".	Section 7-102.
"Warehouse receipt".	Section 1-201.

Section 7-402. Duplicate Document of Title; Overissue

A duplicate or any other document of title purporting to cover goods already represented by an outstanding document of the same issuer does not confer any right in the goods, except as provided in the case of tangible bills of lading in a set of parts, overissue of documents for fungible goods, substitutes for lost, stolen, or destroyed documents, or substitute documents issued pursuant to Section 7-105. The issuer is liable for damages caused by its overissue or failure to identify a duplicate document by a conspicuous notation.

Official Comment

Prior Uniform Statutory Provision: Former Section 7-402.

Changes: Changes to accommodate electronic documents.

Purposes:

1. This section treats a duplicate which is not properly identified as a duplicate like any other overissue of documents: A purchaser of such a document acquires no title but only a cause of action for damages against the person that made the deception possible, except in the cases noted in the section. But parts of a tangible bill lawfully issued in a set of parts are not "overissue" (Section 7-304). Of course, if the issuer has clearly indicated that a document is a duplicate so that no one can be deceived by it, and in fact the duplicate is a correct copy of the original, the issuer is not liable for preparing and delivering such a duplicate copy.

Section 7-105 allows documents of title to be reissued in another medium. Reissuance of a document in an alternative medium under Section 7-105 requires that the original document be surrendered to the issuer in order to make the substitute document the effective document. If the substitute document is not issued in compliance with Section 7-105, then the document should be treated as a duplicate under this section.

2. The section applies to nonnegotiable documents to the extent of providing an action for damages for one who acquires an unmarked duplicate from a transferor who knew the facts and would therefore have had no cause of action against the issuer of the duplicate. Ordinarily the transferee of a nonnegotiable document acquires only the rights of its transferor.

3. Overissue is defined so as to exclude the common situation where two valid documents of different issuers are outstanding for the same goods at the same time. Thus freight forwarders commonly issue bills of lading to their customers for small shipments to be combined into carload shipments for which the railroad will issue a bill of lading to the forwarder. So also a warehouse receipt may be outstanding against goods, and the holder of the receipt may issue delivery orders against the same goods. In these cases dealings with the subsequently issued documents may be effective to transfer title; e.g., negotiation of a delivery order will effectively transfer title in the ordinary case where no dishonesty has occurred and the goods are available to satisfy the orders. Section 7-503 provides for cases of conflict between documents of different issuers.

Cross References:

Point 1:	Sections 7-105, 7-207, 7-304 and 7-601.
Point 3:	Section 7-503.

Definitional Cross References:

"Bill of lading".	Section 1-201.
"Conspicuous".	Section 1-201.
"Document of title".	Section 1-201.
"Fungible goods."	Section 1-201.
"Goods".	Section 7-102.
"Issuer".	Section 7-102.
"Right".	Section 1-201.

Section 7-403. Obligation of Bailee to Deliver; Excuse

(a) A bailee shall deliver the goods to a person entitled under a document of title if the person complies with subsections (b) and (c), unless and to the extent that the bailee establishes any of the following:

(1) delivery of the goods to a person whose receipt was rightful as against the claimant;

(2) damage to or delay, loss, or destruction of the goods for which the bailee is not liable;

(3) previous sale or other disposition of the goods in lawful enforcement of a lien or on a warehouse's lawful termination of storage;

(4) the exercise by a seller of its right to stop delivery pursuant to Section 2-705 or by a lessor of its right to stop delivery pursuant to Section 2A-526;

(5) a diversion, reconsignment, or other disposition pursuant to Section 7-303;

(6) release, satisfaction, or any other personal defense against the claimant; or

(7) any other lawful excuse.

(b) A person claiming goods covered by a document of title shall satisfy the bailee's lien if the bailee so requests or if the bailee is prohibited by law from delivering the goods until the charges are paid.

(c) Unless a person claiming the goods is a person against which the document of title does not confer a right under Section 7-503(a):

(1) the person claiming under a document shall surrender possession or control of any outstanding negotiable document covering the goods for cancellation or indication of partial deliveries; and

(2) the bailee shall cancel the document or conspicuously indicate in the document the partial delivery or the bailee is liable to any person to which the document is duly negotiated.

Official Comment

Prior Uniform Statutory Provision: Former Section 7-403.

Changes: Definition in former Section 7-403(4) moved to Section 7-102; bracketed language in former Section 7-403(1)(b) deleted; added cross reference to Section 2A-526; changes for style.

Purposes:

1. The present section, following former Section 7-403, is constructed on the basis of stating what previous deliveries or other circumstances operate to excuse the bailee's normal obligation on the document. Accordingly, "justified" deliveries under the pre-Code uniform Acts now find their place as "excuse" under subsection (a).

2. The principal case covered by subsection (a)(1) is delivery to a person whose title is paramount to the rights represented by the document. For example, if a thief deposits stolen goods in a warehouse facility and takes a negotiable receipt, the warehouse is not liable on the receipt if it has surrendered the goods to the true owner, even though the receipt is held by a good-faith purchaser. See Section 7-503(a). However, if the owner entrusted the goods to a person with power of disposition, and that person deposited the goods and took a negotiable document, the owner receiving delivery would not be rightful as against a holder to whom the negotiable document was duly negotiated, and delivery to the owner would not give the bailee a defense against such a holder. See Sections 7-502(a)(2) and 7-503(a)(1).

3. Subsection (a)(2) amounts to a cross reference to all the tort law that determines the varying responsibilities and standards of care applicable to commercial bailees. A restatement of this tort law would be beyond the scope of this Act. Much of the applicable law as to responsibility of bailees for the preservation of the goods and limitation of liability in case of loss has been codified for particular classes of bailees in interstate and foreign commerce by federal legislation and treaty and for intrastate carriers and other bailees by the regulatory state laws preserved by Section 7-103. In the absence of governing legislation the common law will prevail subject to the minimum standard of reasonable care prescribed by Sections 7-204 and 7-309 of this Article.

The bracketed language found in former Section 7-403(1)(b) has been deleted thereby leaving the allocations of the burden of going forward with the evidence and the burden of proof to the procedural law of the various states.

Subsection (a)(4) contains a cross reference to both the seller's and the lessor's rights to stop delivery under Articles 2 and 2A, respectively.

4. As under former Section 7-403, there is no requirement that a request for delivery must be accompanied by a formal tender of the amount of the charges due. Rather, the bailee must request payment of the amount of its lien when asked to deliver, and only in case this request is refused is it justified in declining to deliver because of nonpayment of charges. Where delivery without payment is forbidden by law, the request is treated as implicit. Such a prohibition reflects a policy of uniformity to prevent discrimination by failure to request payment in particular cases. Subsection (b) must be read in conjunction with the priorities given to the warehouse lien and the carrier lien under Sections 7-209 and 7-307, respectively. If the parties are in dispute about whether the request for payment of the lien is legally proper, the bailee may have recourse to interpleader. See Section 7-603.

5. In addition to compliance with subsection (b), subsection (c) conditions the bailee's duty to deliver the goods to a person entitled under a negotiable document on the surrender of possession or control of the document for cancellation or indication of partial deliveries. It also states the obvious duty of a bailee to take up a negotiable document or note partial deliveries conspicuously thereon, and the result of failure in that duty. It is subject to only one exception, that stated in subsection (a)(1) of this section and in Section 7-503(a). Subsection (c) is limited to cases of delivery to a claimant; it has no application, for example, where goods held under a negotiable document are lawfully sold to enforce the bailee's lien.

Subsection (c) does not specify any conditions on the duty of the bailee to deliver the goods covered by a nonnegotiable document to a person entitled, other than the conditions inherent in the definition of "person entitled under the document." See Sections 7-102(a)(9) (defining "person entitled under the document") and Comment 6; 7-504. In addition, the document itself may specify that the person entitled must present the document to the bailee in order to obtain delivery of the goods.

6. When courts are considering subsection (a)(7), "any other lawful excuse", among others, refers to compliance with court orders under Sections 7-601, 7-602 and 7-603.

Cross References:

Point 2:	Sections 7-502 and 7-503.
Point 3:	Sections 2-705, 2A-526, 7-103, 7-204, 7-309 and 10-103.
Point 4:	Sections 7-209, 7-307 and 7-603.
Point 5:	Section 7-503(1).
Point 6:	Sections 7-601, 7-602 and 7-603.

Definitional Cross References:

"Bailee".	Section 7-102.
"Conspicuous".	Section 1-201.
"Delivery".	Section 1-201.
"Document of title".	Section 1-201.
"Duly negotiate".	Section 7-501.
"Goods".	Section 7-102.
"Lessor".	Section 2A-103.
"Person".	Section 1-201.
"Receipt of goods".	Section 2-103.
"Right".	Section 1-201.
"Term".	Section 1-201.
"Warehouse".	Section 7-102.

Section 7-404. No Liability for Good-Faith Delivery Pursuant to Document of Title

A bailee that in good faith has received goods and delivered or otherwise disposed of the goods according to the terms of a document of title or pursuant to this Article is not liable for the goods even if:

(1) the person from which the bailee received the goods did not have authority to procure the document or to dispose of the goods; or

(2) the person to which the bailee delivered the goods did not have authority to receive the goods.

Official Comment

Prior Uniform Statutory Provision: Former Section 7-404.

Changes: Changes reflect the definition of "good faith" in Section 1-201 [7-102] and for style.

Purposes:

This section uses the test of good faith, as defined in Section 1-201 [7-102], to continue the policy of former Section 7-404. Good faith now means "honesty in fact and the observance of reasonable commercial standards of fair dealing". The section states explicitly that the common-law rule of "innocent conversion" by unauthorized "intermeddling" with another's property is inapplicable to the operations of commercial carriers and warehousemen that in good faith perform obligations that they have assumed and that generally they are under a legal compulsion to assume. The section applies to delivery to a fraudulent holder of a valid document as well as to delivery to the holder of an invalid document. Of course, in appropriate circumstances, a bailee may use interpleader or other dispute resolution process. See Section 7-603.

Cross Reference:

Section 7-603.

Definitional Cross References:

"Bailee".	Section 7-102.
"Delivery".	Section 1-201.
"Document of title".	Section 1-201.
"Good faith".	Section 1-201 [7-102].
"Goods".	Section 7-102.
"Person".	Section 1-201.
"Receipt of goods".	Section 2-103.
"Term".	Section 1-201.

PART 5. WAREHOUSE RECEIPTS AND BILLS OF LADING: NEGOTIATION AND TRANSFER

Section 7-501. Form of Negotiation and Requirements of Due Negotiation

(a) The following rules apply to a negotiable tangible document of title:

(1) If the document's original terms run to the order of a named person, the document is negotiated by the named person's indorsement and delivery. After the named person's indorsement in blank or to bearer, any person may negotiate the document by delivery alone.

(2) If the document's original terms run to bearer, it is negotiated by delivery alone.

(3) If the document's original terms run to the order of a named person and it is delivered to the named person, the effect is the same as if the document had been negotiated.

(4) Negotiation of the document after it has been indorsed to a named person requires indorsement by the named person and delivery.

(5) A document is duly negotiated if it is negotiated in the manner stated in this subsection to a holder that purchases it in good faith, without notice of any defense against or claim to it on the part of any person, and for value, unless it is established that the negotiation is not in the regular course of business or financing or involves receiving the document in settlement or payment of a monetary obligation.

(b) The following rules apply to a negotiable electronic document of title:

(1) If the document's original terms run to the order of a named person or to bearer, the document is negotiated by delivery of the document to another person. Indorsement by the named person is not required to negotiate the document.

(2) If the document's original terms run to the order of a named person and the named person has control of the document, the effect is the same as if the document had been negotiated.

(3) A document is duly negotiated if it is negotiated in the manner stated in this subsection to a holder that purchases it in good faith, without notice of any defense against or claim to it on the part of any person, and for value, unless it is established that the negotiation is not in the regular course of business or financing or involves taking delivery of the document in settlement or payment of a monetary obligation.

(c) Indorsement of a nonnegotiable document of title neither makes it negotiable nor adds to the transferee's rights.

(d) The naming in a negotiable bill of lading of a person to be notified of the arrival of the goods does not limit the negotiability of the bill or constitute notice to a purchaser of the bill of any interest of that person in the goods.

Official Comment

Prior Uniform Statutory Provision: Former Section 7-501.

Changes: To accommodate negotiable electronic documents of title.

Purpose:

1. Subsection (a) has been limited to tangible negotiable documents of title but otherwise remains unchanged in substance from the rules in former Section 7-501. Subsection (b) is new and applies to negotiable electronic documents of title. Delivery of a negotiable electronic document is through voluntary transfer of control. Section 1-201 definition of "delivery". The control concept as applied to negotiable electronic documents of title is the substitute for both possession and indorsement as applied to negotiable tangible documents of title. Section 7-106.

Article 7 does not separately define the term "duly negotiated". However, the elements of "duly negotiated" are set forth in subsection (a)(5) for tangible documents and (b)(3) for electronic documents. As under former Section 7-501, in order to effect a "due negotiation" the negotiation must be in the "regular course of business or financing" in order to transfer greater rights than those held by the person negotiating. The foundation of the mercantile doctrine of good-faith purchase for value has always been, as shown by the case situations, the furtherance and protection of the regular course of trade. The reason for allowing a person, in bad faith or in error, to convey away rights which are not its own has from the beginning been to make possible the speedy handling of that great run of commercial transactions which are patently usual and normal.

There are two aspects to the usual and normal course of mercantile dealings, namely, the person making the transfer and the nature of the transaction itself. The first question which arises is: Is the transferor a person with whom it is reasonable to deal as having full powers? In regard to documents of title the only holder whose possession or control appears, commercially, to be in order is almost invariably a person in the trade. No commercial purpose is served by allowing a tramp or a professor to "duly negotiate" an order bill of lading for hides or cotton not their own, and since such a transfer is obviously not in the regular course of business, it is excluded from the scope of the protection of subsections (a)(5) or (b)(3).

The second question posed by the "regular course" qualification is: Is the transaction one which is normally proper to pass full rights without inquiry, even though the transferor itself may not have such rights to pass, and even though the transferor may be acting in breach of duty? In raising this question the "regular course" criterion has the further advantage of limiting, the effective wrongful disposition to transactions whose protection will really further trade. Obviously, the snapping up of goods for quick resale at a price suspiciously below the market deserves no protection as a matter of policy: It is also clearly outside the range of regular course.

Any notice on the document sufficient to put a merchant on inquiry as to the "regular course" quality of the transaction will frustrate a "due negotiation". Thus irregularity of the document or unexplained staleness of a bill of lading may appropriately be recognized as negating a negotiation in "regular" course.

A preexisting claim constitutes value, and "due negotiation" does not require "new value". A usual and ordinary transaction in which documents are received as security for credit previously extended may be in "regular" course, even though there is a demand for additional collateral because the creditor "deems himself insecure". But the matter has moved out of the regular course of financing if the debtor is thought to be insolvent, the credit previously extended is in effect cancelled, and the creditor snatches a plank in the shipwreck under the guise of a demand for additional collateral. Where a money debt is "paid" in commodity paper, any question of "regular" course disappears, as the case is explicitly excepted from "due negotiation".

2. Negotiation under this section may be made by any holder no matter how the holder acquired possession or control of the document.

3. Subsections (a)(3) and (b)(2) make explicit a matter upon which the intent of the pre-Code law was clear but the language somewhat obscure: A negotiation results from a delivery to a banker or buyer to whose order the document has been taken by the person making the bailment. There is no presumption of irregularity in such a negotiation; it may very well be in "regular course".

4. This Article does not contain any provision creating a presumption of due negotiation to, and full rights in, a holder of a document of title akin to that created by Uniform Commercial Code Article 3. But the reason of the provisions of this Act (Section 1-307) on the prima facie authenticity and accuracy of third-party documents, joins with the reason of the present section to work such a presumption in favor of any person who has power to make a due negotiation. It would not make sense for this Act to authorize a purchaser to indulge the presumption of regularity if the courts were not also called upon to do so. Allocations of the burden of going forward with the evidence and the burden of proof are left to the procedural law of the various states.

5. Subsections (c) and (d) are unchanged from prior law and apply to both tangible and electronic documents of title.

Cross References:

Sections 1-307, 7-502 and 7-503.

Definitional Cross References:

"Bearer".	Section 1-201.
"Control".	Section 7-106.
"Delivery".	Section 1-201.
"Document of title".	Section 1-201.
"Good faith".	Section 1-201 [7-102].
"Holder".	Section 1-201.
"Notice".	Section 1-202.
"Person".	Section 1-201.
"Purchase".	Section 1-201.
"Rights".	Section 1-201.
"Term".	Section 1-201.
"Value".	Section 1-204.

Section 7-502. Rights Acquired by Due Negotiation

(a) Subject to Sections 7-205 and 7-503, a holder to which a negotiable document of title has been duly negotiated acquires thereby:

(1) title to the document;

(2) title to the goods;

(3) all rights accruing under the law of agency or estoppel, including rights to goods delivered to the bailee after the document was issued; and

(4) the direct obligation of the issuer to hold or deliver the goods according to the terms of the document free of any defense or claim by the issuer except those arising under the terms of the document or under this Article, but in the case of a delivery order, the bailee's obligation accrues only upon the bailee's acceptance of the delivery order and the obligation acquired by the holder is that the issuer and any indorser will procure the acceptance of the bailee.

(b) Subject to Section 7-503, title and rights acquired by due negotiation are not defeated by any stoppage of the goods represented by the document of title or by surrender of the goods by the bailee and are not impaired even if:

(1) the due negotiation or any prior due negotiation constituted a breach of duty;

(2) any person has been deprived of possession of a negotiable tangible document or control of a negotiable electronic document by misrepresentation, fraud, accident, mistake, duress, loss, theft, or conversion; or

(3) a previous sale or other transfer of the goods or document has been made to a third person.

Official Comment

Prior Uniform Statutory Provision: Former Section 7-502.

Changes: To accommodate electronic documents of title and for style.

Purpose:

1. This section applies to both tangible and electronic documents of title. The elements of duly negotiated, which constitutes a due negotiation, are set forth in Section 7-501. The several necessary qualifications of the broad principle that the holder of a document acquired in a due negotiation is the owner of the document and the goods have been brought together in the next section (Section 7-503).

2. Subsection (a)(3) covers the case of "feeding" of a duly negotiated document by subsequent delivery to the bailee of such goods as the document falsely purported to cover; the bailee in such case is estopped as against the holder of the document.

3. The explicit statement in subsection (a)(4) of the bailee's direct obligation to the holder precludes the defense that the document in question was "spent" after the carrier had delivered the goods to a previous holder. But the holder is subject to such defenses as nonnegligent destruction even though not apparent on the document. The sentence on delivery orders applies only to delivery orders in negotiable form which have been duly negotiated. On delivery orders, see also Section 7-503(b) and Comment.

4. Subsection (b) continues the law which gave full effect to the issuance or due negotiation of a negotiable document. The subsection adds nothing to the effect of the rules stated in subsection (a), but it has been included since such explicit reference was provided under former Section 7-502 to preserve the right of a purchaser by due negotiation. The listing is not exhaustive. The language "any stoppage" is included lest an inference be drawn that a stoppage of the goods before or after transit might cut off or otherwise impair the purchaser's rights.

Cross References:

Sections 7-103, 7-205, 7-403, 7-501 and 7-503.

Definitional Cross References:

"Bailee".	Section 7-102.
"Control".	Section 7-106.
"Delivery".	Section 1-201.
"Delivery order".	Section 7-102.
"Document of title".	Section 1-201.
"Duly negotiate".	Section 7-501.

"Fungible".	Section 1-201.
"Goods".	Section 7-102.
"Holder".	Section 1-201.
"Issuer".	Section 7-102.
"Person".	Section 1-201.
"Rights".	Section 1-201.
"Term".	Section 1-201.
"Warehouse receipt".	Section 1-201.

Section 7-503. Document of Title to Goods Defeated in Certain Cases

(a) A document of title confers no right in goods against a person that before issuance of the document had a legal interest or a perfected security interest in the goods and that did not:

(1) deliver or entrust the goods or any document of title covering the goods to the bailor or the bailor's nominee with:

(A) actual or apparent authority to ship, store, or sell;

(B) power to obtain delivery under Section 7-403; or

(C) power of disposition under Section 2-403, 2A-304(2), 2A-305(2), 9-320, or 9-321(c) or other statute or rule of law; or

(2) acquiesce in the procurement by the bailor or its nominee of any document.

(b) Title to goods based upon an unaccepted delivery order is subject to the rights of any person to which a negotiable warehouse receipt or bill of lading covering the goods has been duly negotiated. That title may be defeated under Section 7-504 to the same extent as the rights of the issuer or a transferee from the issuer.

(c) Title to goods based upon a bill of lading issued to a freight forwarder is subject to the rights of any person to which a bill issued by the freight forwarder is duly negotiated. However, delivery by the carrier in accordance with Part 4 pursuant to its own bill of lading discharges the carrier's obligation to deliver.

Official Comment

Prior Uniform Statutory Provision: Former Section 7-503.

Changes: Changes to cross reference to Article 2A and for style.

Purposes:

1. In general it may be said that the title of a purchaser by due negotiation prevails over almost any interest in the goods which existed prior to the procurement of the document of title if the possession of the goods by the person obtaining the document derived from any action by the prior claimant which introduced the goods into the stream of commerce or carried them along that stream. A thief of the goods cannot indeed by shipping or storing them to the thief's own order acquire power to transfer them to a good-faith purchaser. Nor can a tenant or mortgagor defeat any rights of a landlord or mortgagee which have been perfected under the local law merely by wrongfully shipping or storing a portion of the crop or other goods. However, "acquiescence" by the landlord or mortgagee does not require active consent under subsection (a)(2) and knowledge of the likelihood of storage or shipment with no objection or effort to control it is sufficient to defeat the landlord's or the mortgagee's rights as against one who takes by due negotiation of a negotiable document. *In re Sharon Steel,* 176 B.R. 384 (Bankr. W.D. Pa. 1995); *In re R.V. Segars Co.,* 54 B.R. 170 (Bankr. S.C. 1985); *In re Jamestown Elevators, Inc.,* 49 B.R. 661 (Bankr. N.D. 1985).

On the other hand, where goods are delivered to a factor for sale, even though the factor has made no advances and is limited in its duty to sell for cash, the goods are "entrusted" to the factor "with actual . . . authority . . . to sell" under subsection (a)(1), and if the factor procures a negotiable document of title it can transfer the owner's interest to a purchaser by due negotiation. Further, where the factor is in the business of selling, goods entrusted to it simply for safekeeping or storage may be entrusted under circumstances which give the factor "apparent authority to ship, store or sell" under subsection (a)(1), or power of disposition under Sections 2-403, 2A-304(2), 2A-305(2), 7-205, 9-320 or 9-321(c) or under a statute such as the earlier Factors Acts, or under a rule of law giving effect to apparent ownership. See Section 1-103.

Persons having an interest in goods also frequently deliver or entrust them to agents or servants other than factors for the purpose of shipping or warehousing or under circumstances reasonably contemplating such action. This Act is clear that such persons assume full risk that the agent to whom the goods are so delivered may ship or store in breach of duty, take a document to the agent's own order and then proceed to misappropriate the negotiable document of title that embodies the goods. This Act makes no distinction between possession or mere custody in such situations and finds no exception in the case of larceny by a bailee or the like. The safeguard in such situations lies in the requirement that a due negotiation can occur only "in the regular course of business or financing" and that the purchase be in good faith and without notice. See Section 7-501. Documents of title have no market among the commercially inexperienced and the commercially experienced do not take them without inquiry from persons known to be truck drivers or petty clerks even though such persons purport to be operating in their own names.

Again, where the seller allows a buyer to receive goods under a contract for sale, though as a "conditional delivery" or under "cash sale" terms and on explicit agreement for immediate payment, the buyer thereby acquires power to defeat the seller's interest by transfer of the goods to certain good-faith purchasers. See Section 2-403. Both in policy and under the language of subsection (a)(1) that same power must be extended to accomplish the same result if the buyer procures a negotiable document of title to the goods and duly negotiates it.

This Comment should be considered in interpreting delivery, entrustment or acquiescence in application of Section 7-209(c)).

2. Under subsection (a) a delivery order issued by a person having no right in or power over the goods is ineffective unless the owner acts as provided in subsection (a)(1) or (2). Thus the rights of a transferee of a nonnegotiable warehouse receipt can be defeated by a delivery order subsequently issued by the transferor only if the transferee "delivers or entrusts" to the "person procuring" the delivery order or "acquiesces" in that person's procurement. Similarly, a second delivery order issued by the same issuer for the same goods will ordinarily be subject to the first, both under this section and under Section 7-402. After a delivery order is validly issued but before it is accepted, it may nevertheless be defeated under subsection (b) in much the same way that the rights of a transferee may be defeated under Section 7-504. For example, a buyer in ordinary course from the issuer may defeat the rights of the holder of a prior delivery order if the bailee receives notification of the buyer's rights before notification of the holder's rights. Section 7-504(b)(2). But an accepted delivery order has the same effect as a document issued by the bailee.

3. Under subsection (c) a bill of lading issued to a freight forwarder is subordinated to the freight forwarder's document of title, since the bill on its face gives notice of the fact that a freight forwarder is in the picture and the freight forwarder has in all probability issued a document of title. But the carrier is protected in following the terms of its own bill of lading.

Cross References:

Point 1: Sections 1-103, 2-403, 2A-304(2), 2A-305(2), 7-205, 7-209, 7-501, 9-320, 9-321(c) and 9-331.

Point 2: Sections 7-402 and 7-504.

Point 3: Sections 7-402, 7-403 and 7-404.

Definitional Cross References:

"Bill of lading".	Section 1-201.
"Contract for sale".	Section 2-106.
"Delivery".	Section 1-201.
"Delivery order".	Section 7-102.
"Document of title".	Section 1-201.
"Duly negotiate".	Section 7-501.
"Goods".	Section 7-102.
"Person".	Section 1-201.
"Right".	Section 1-201.
"Warehouse receipt".	Section 1-201.

Section 7-504. Rights Acquired in Absence of Due Negotiation; Effect of Diversion; Stoppage of Delivery

(a) A transferee of a document of title, whether negotiable or nonnegotiable, to which the document has been delivered but not duly negotiated, acquires the title and rights that its transferor had or had actual authority to convey.

(b) In the case of a transfer of a nonnegotiable document of title, until but not after the bailee receives notice of the transfer, the rights of the transferee may be defeated:

(1) by those creditors of the transferor which could treat the transfer as void under Section 2-402 or 2A308;

(2) by a buyer from the transferor in ordinary course of business if the bailee has delivered the goods to the buyer or received notification of the buyer's rights;

(3) by a lessee from the transferor in ordinary course of business if the bailee has delivered the goods to the lessee or received notification of the lessee's rights; or

(4) as against the bailee, by good-faith dealings of the bailee with the transferor.

(c) A diversion or other change of shipping instructions by the consignor in a nonnegotiable bill of lading which causes the bailee not to deliver the goods to the consignee defeats the consignee's title to the goods if the goods have been delivered to a buyer in ordinary course of business or a lessee in ordinary course of business and, in any event, defeats the consignee's rights against the bailee.

(d) Delivery of the goods pursuant to a nonnegotiable document of title may be stopped by a seller under Section 2-705 or a lessor under Section 2A-526, subject to the requirements of due notification in those sections. A bailee that honors the seller's or lessor's instructions is entitled to be indemnified by the seller or lessor against any resulting loss or expense.

Official Comment

Prior Uniform Statutory Provision: Former Section 7-504.

Changes: To include cross references to Article 2A and for style.

Purposes:

1. Under the general principles controlling negotiable documents, it is clear that in the absence of due negotiation a transferor cannot convey greater rights than the transferor has, even when the negotiation is formally perfect. This section recognizes the transferor's power to transfer rights which the transferor has or has "actual authority to convey". Thus, where a negotiable document of title is being transferred the operation of the principle of estoppel is not recognized, as contrasted with situations involving the transfer of the goods themselves. (Compare Section 2-403 on good-faith purchase of goods.) This section applies to both tangible and electronic documents of title.

A necessary part of the price for the protection of regular dealings with negotiable documents of title is an insistence that no dealing which is in any way irregular shall be recognized as a good-faith purchase of the document or of any rights pertaining to it. So, where the transfer of a negotiable document fails as a negotiation because a requisite indorsement is forged or otherwise missing, the purchaser in good faith and for value may be in the anomalous position of having less rights, in part, than if the purchaser had purchased the goods themselves. True, the purchaser's rights are not subject to defeat by attachment of the goods or surrender of them to the purchaser's transferor (contrast subsection (b)); but on the other hand, the purchaser cannot acquire enforceable rights to control or receive the goods over the bailee's objection merely by giving notice to the bailee. Similarly, a consignee who makes payment to its consignor against a straight bill of lading can thereby acquire the position of a good-faith purchaser of goods under provisions of the Article of this Act on Sales (Section 2-403), whereas the same payment made in good faith against an unendorsed order bill would not have such effect. The appropriate remedy of a purchaser in such a situation is to regularize its status by compelling indorsement of the document (see Section 7-506).

2. As in the case of transfer—as opposed to "due negotiation"—of negotiable documents, subsection (a) empowers the transferor of a nonnegotiable document to transfer only such rights as the transferor has or has "actual authority" to convey. In contrast to situations involving the goods themselves the operation of estoppel or agency principles is not here recognized to enable the transferor to convey greater rights than the transferor actually has. Subsection (b) makes it clear, however, that the transferee of a nonnegotiable document may acquire rights greater in some respects than those of his transferor by giving notice of the transfer to the bailee. Subsection (b)(3) provides for the rights of a lessee in the ordinary course.

Mere notice of a transfer of the document only prevents the persons identified in subsections (b)(1) through (4) from cutting off the rights of the transferee. For the transferee to become a "person entitled under the document," with a right to obtain delivery from the bailee under Section 7-403(a), either the document itself must provide for delivery to the transferee or the bailee must receive instructions in a record to deliver to the transferee. See Section 7-102(a)(9)(defining "person entitled under the document") and Comment 6.

Subsection (b)(2) and (3) requires delivery of the goods. Delivery of the goods means the voluntary transfer of physical possession of the goods.

3. Subsection (c) is in part a reiteration of the carrier's immunity from liability if it honors instructions of the consignor to divert, but there is added a provision protecting the title of the substituted consignee if the latter is a buyer in ordinary course of business. A typical situation would be where a manufacturer, having shipped a lot of standardized goods to A on nonnegotiable bill of lading, diverts the goods to customer B who pays for them. Under pre-Code passage-of-title-by-appropriation doctrine A might reclaim the goods from B. However, no consideration of commercial policy supports this involvement of an innocent third party in the default of the manufacturer on his contract to A; and the common commercial practice of diverting goods in transit suggests a trade understanding in accordance with this subsection. The same result should obtain if the substituted consignee is a lessee in ordinary course. The extent of the lessee's interest in the goods is less than a buyer's interest in the goods. However, as against the first consignee and the lessee in ordinary course as the substituted consignee, the lessee's rights in the goods as granted under the lease are superior to the first consignee's rights.

4. Subsection (d) gives the carrier an express right to indemnity where the carrier honors a seller's request to stop delivery.

5. Section 1-202 gives the bailee protection, if due diligence is exercised where the bailee's organization has not had time to act on a notification.

Cross References:

Point 1:	Sections 2-403 and 7-506.
Point 2:	Sections 2-403 and 2A-304.
Point 3:	Sections 7-303, 7-403(a)(5) and 7-404.
Point 4:	Sections 2-705 and 7-403(a)(4).
Point 5:	Section 1-202.

Definitional Cross References:

"Bailee".	Section 7-102.
"Bill of lading".	Section 1-201.
"Buyer in ordinary course of business".	Section 1-201.
"Consignee".	Section 7-102.
"Consignor".	Section 7-102.
"Creditor".	Section 1-201.
"Delivery".	Section 1-201.
"Document of title".	Section 1-201.
"Duly negotiate".	Section 7-501.
"Good faith".	Section 1-201 [7-102].
"Goods".	Section 7-102.
"Lessee in ordinary course".	Section 2A-103.
"Notification".	Section 1-202.
"Purchaser".	Section 1-201.
"Rights".	Section 1-201.

Section 7-505. Indorser Not Guarantor for Other Parties

The indorsement of a tangible document of title issued by a bailee does not make the indorser liable for any default by the bailee or previous indorsers.

Official Comment

Prior Uniform Statutory Provision: Former Section 7-505.

Changes: Limited to tangible documents of title.

Purposes:

This section is limited to tangible documents of title as the concept of indorsement is irrelevant to electronic documents of title. Electronic documents of title will be transferred by delivery of control. Section 7-106. The indorsement of a tangible document of title is generally understood to be directed toward perfecting the transferee's rights rather than toward assuming additional obligations. The language of the present section, however, does not preclude the one case in which an indorsement given for value guarantees future action, namely, that in which the bailee has not yet become liable upon the document at the time of the indorsement. Under such circumstances the indorser, of course, engages that appropriate honor of the document by the bailee will occur. See Section 7-502(a)(4) as to negotiable delivery orders. However, even in such a case, once the bailee attorns to the transferee, the indorser's obligation has been fulfilled and the policy of this section excludes any continuing obligation on the part of the indorser for the bailee's ultimate actual performance.

Cross References:

Sections 7-106 and 7-502.

Definitional Cross References:

"Bailee".	Section 7-102.
"Document of title".	Section 1-201.
"Party".	Section 1-201.

Section 7-506. Delivery Without Indorsement: Right to Compel Indorsement

The transferee of a negotiable tangible document of title has a specifically enforceable right to have its transferor supply any necessary indorsement, but the transfer becomes a negotiation only as of the time the indorsement is supplied.

Official Comment

Prior Uniform Statutory Provision: Former Section 7-506.

Changes: Limited to tangible documents of title.

Purposes:

1. This section is limited to tangible documents of title as the concept of indorsement is irrelevant to electronic documents of title. Electronic documents of title will be transferred by delivery of control. Section 7-106. From a commercial point of view the intention to transfer a tangible negotiable document of title which requires an indorsement for its transfer, is incompatible with an intention to withhold such indorsement and so defeat the effective use of the document. Further, the preceding section and the Comment thereto make it clear that an indorsement generally imposes no responsibility on the indorser.

2. Although this section provides that delivery of a tangible document of title without the necessary indorsement is effective as a transfer, the transferee, of course, has not regularized its position until such indorsement is supplied. Until this is done the transferee cannot claim rights under due negotiation within the requirements of this Article (Section 7-501(a)(5)) on "due negotiation". Similarly, despite the transfer to the transferee of the transferor's title, the transferee cannot demand the goods from the bailee until the negotiation has been completed and the document is in proper form for surrender. See Section 7-403(c).

Cross References:

Point 1:	Sections 7-106 and 7-505.
Point 2:	Sections 7-501(a)(5) and 7-403(c).

Definitional Cross References:

"Document of title".	Section 1-201.
"Rights".	Section 1-201.

Section 7-507. Warranties on Negotiation or Delivery of Document of Title

If a person negotiates or delivers a document of title for value, otherwise than as a mere intermediary under Section 7-508, unless otherwise agreed, the transferor, in addition to any warranty made in selling or leasing the goods, warrants to its immediate purchaser only that:

(1) the document is genuine;

(2) the transferor does not have knowledge of any fact that would impair the document's validity or worth; and

(3) the negotiation or delivery is rightful and fully effective with respect to the title to the document and the goods it represents.

Official Comment

Prior Uniform Statutory Provision: Former Section 7-507.

Changes: Substitution of the word "delivery" for the word "transfer", reference leasing transactions and style.

Purposes:

1. Delivery of goods by use of a document of title does not limit or displace the ordinary obligations of a seller or lessor as to any warranties regarding the goods that arises under other law. If the transfer of documents attends or follows the making of a contract for the sale or lease of goods, the general obligations on warranties as to the goods (Sections 2-312 through 2-318 and Sections 2A-210 through 2A-316) are brought to bear as well as the special warranties under this section.

2. The limited warranties of a delivering or collecting intermediary, including a collecting bank, are stated in Section 7-508.

Cross References:

Point 1:	Sections 2-312 through 2-318 and 2A-310 through 2A-316.
Point 2:	Section 7-508.

Definitional Cross References:

"Delivery".	Section 1-201.
"Document of title".	Section 1-201.
"Genuine".	Section 1-201.
"Goods".	Section 7-102.
"Person".	Section 1-201.
"Purchaser".	Section 1-201.
"Value".	Section 1-204.

Section 7-508. Warranties of Collecting Bank As to Documents of Title

A collecting bank or other intermediary known to be entrusted with documents of title on behalf of another or with collection of a draft or other claim against delivery of documents warrants by the delivery of the documents only its own good faith and authority even if the collecting bank or other intermediary has purchased or made advances against the claim or draft to be collected.

Official Comment

Prior Uniform Statutory Provision: Former Section 7-508.

Changes: Changes for style only.

Purposes:

1. To state the limited warranties given with respect to the documents accompanying a documentary draft.

2. In warranting its authority a collecting bank or other intermediary only warrants its authority from its transferor. See Section 4-203. It does not warrant the genuineness or effectiveness of the document. Compare Section 7-507.

3. Other duties and rights of banks handling documentary drafts for collection are stated in Article 4, Part 5. On the meaning of draft, see Section 4-104 and Section 5-102, Comment 11.

Cross References:

Sections 4-104, 4-203, 4-501 through 4-504, 5-102 and 7-507.

Definitional Cross References:

"Collecting bank".	Section 4-105.
"Delivery".	Section 1-201.
"Document of title".	Section 1-102 [*sic,* should be 1-201].
"Documentary draft".	Section 4-104.
"Intermediary bank".	Section 4-105.
"Good faith".	Section 1-201 [7-102].

Section 7-509. Adequate Compliance with Commercial Contract

Whether a document of title is adequate to fulfill the obligations of a contract for sale, a contract for lease, or the conditions of a letter of credit is determined by Article 2, 2A, or 5.

Official Comment

Prior Uniform Statutory Provision: Former Section 7-509.

Changes: To reference Article 2A.

Purposes:

To cross refer to the Articles of this Act which deal with the substantive issues of the type of document of title required under the contract entered into by the parties.

Cross References:

Articles 2, 2A and 5.

Definitional Cross References:

"Contract for sale".	Section 2-106.
"Document of title".	Section 1-201.
"Lease".	Section 2A-103.

PART 6. WAREHOUSE RECEIPTS AND BILLS OF LADING: MISCELLANEOUS PROVISIONS

Section 7-601. Lost, Stolen, or Destroyed Documents of Title

(a) If a document of title is lost, stolen, or destroyed, a court may order delivery of the goods or issuance of a substitute document and the bailee may without liability to any person comply with the order. If the document was negotiable, a court may not order delivery of the goods or issuance of a substitute document without the claimant's posting security unless it finds that any person that may suffer loss as a result of nonsurrender of possession or control of the document is adequately protected against the loss. If the document was nonnegotiable, the court may require security. The court may also order payment of the bailee's reasonable costs and attorney's fees in any action under this subsection.

(b) A bailee that, without a court order, delivers goods to a person claiming under a missing negotiable document of title is liable to any person injured thereby. If the delivery is not in good faith, the bailee is liable for conversion. Delivery in good faith is not conversion if the claimant posts security with the bailee in an amount at least double the value of the goods at the time of posting to indemnify any person injured by the delivery which files a notice of claim within one year after the delivery.

Official Comment

Prior Uniform Statutory Provision: Former Section 7-601.

Changes: To accommodate electronic documents; to provide flexibility to courts similar to the flexibility in Section 3-309; to update to the modern era of deregulation; and for style.

Purposes:

1. Subsection (a) authorizes courts to order compulsory delivery of the goods or compulsory issuance of a substitute document. Compare Section 7-402. Using language similar to that found in Section 3-309, courts are given discretion as to what is adequate protection when the lost, stolen or destroyed document was negotiable or whether security should be required when the lost, stolen or destroyed document was nonnegotiable. In determining whether a party is adequately protected against loss in the case of a negotiable document, the court should consider the likelihood that the party will suffer a loss. The court is also given discretion as to the bailee's costs and attorney fees. The rights and obligations of a bailee under this section depend upon whether the document of title is lost, stolen or destroyed and is in addition to the ability of the bailee to bring an action for interpleader. See Section 7-603.

2. Courts have the authority under this section to order a substitute document for either tangible or electronic documents. If the substitute document will be in a different medium than the original document, the court should fashion its order in light of the requirements of Section 7-105.

3. Subsection (b) follows prior Section 7-601 in recognizing the legality of the well established commercial practice of bailees making delivery in good faith when they are satisfied that the claimant is the person entitled under a missing (i.e., lost, stolen or destroyed) negotiable document. Acting without a court order, the bailee remains liable on the original negotiable document and, to avoid conversion liability, the bailee may insist that the claimant provide an indemnity bond. Cf. Section 7-403.

4. Claimants on nonnegotiable instruments are permitted to avail themselves of the subsection (a) procedure because straight (nonnegotiable) bills of lading sometimes contain provisions that the goods shall not be delivered except upon production of the bill. If the carrier should choose to insist upon production of the bill, the consignee should have some means of compelling delivery on satisfactory proof of entitlement. Without a court order, a bailee may deliver, subject to Section 7-403, to a person claiming goods under a nonnegotiable document that the same person claims is lost, stolen or destroyed.

5. The bailee's lien should be protected when a court orders delivery of the goods pursuant to this section.

Cross References:

Point 1:	Sections 3-309, 7-402 and 7-603.
Point 2:	Section 7-105.
Point 3:	Section 7-403.
Point 4:	Section 7-403.
Point 5:	Sections 7-209 and 7-307.

Definitional Cross References:

"Bailee".	Section 7-102.
"Delivery".	Section 1-201.
"Document of title".	Section 1-201.
"Good faith".	Section 1-201 [7-102].
"Goods".	Section 7-102.
"Person".	Section 1-201.

Section 7-602. Judicial Process Against Goods Covered by Negotiable Document of Title

Unless a document of title was originally issued upon delivery of the goods by a person that did not have power to dispose of them, a lien does not attach by virtue of any judicial process to goods in the possession of a bailee for which a negotiable document of title is outstanding unless possession or control of the document is first surrendered to the bailee or the document's negotiation is enjoined. The bailee may not be compelled to deliver the goods pursuant to process until possession or control of the document is surrendered to the bailee or to the court. A purchaser of the document for value without notice of the process or injunction takes free of the lien imposed by judicial process.

Official Comment

Prior Uniform Statutory Provisions: Former Section 7-602.

Changes: Changes to accommodate electronic documents of title and for style.

Purposes:

1. The purpose of the section is to protect the bailee from conflicting claims of the document of title holder and the judgment creditors of the person who deposited the goods. The rights of the former prevail unless, in effect, the judgment creditors immobilize the negotiable document of title through the surrender of possession of a tangible document or control of an electronic document. However, if the document of title was issued upon deposit of the goods by a person who had no power to dispose of the goods so that the document is ineffective to pass title, judgment liens are valid to the extent of the debtor's interest in the goods.

2. The last sentence covers the possibility that the holder of a document who has been enjoined from negotiating it will violate the injunction by negotiating to an innocent purchaser for value. In such case the lien will be defeated.

Cross References:

Sections 7-106 and 7-501 through 7-503.

Definitional Cross References:

"Bailee".	Section 7-102.
"Delivery".	Section 1-201.
"Document of title".	Section 1-201.
"Goods".	Section 7-102.
"Notice".	Section 1-202.
"Person".	Section 1-201.
"Purchase".	Section 1-201.
"Value".	Section 1-204.

Section 7-603. Conflicting Claims; Interpleader

If more than one person claims title to or possession of the goods, the bailee is excused from delivery until the bailee has a reasonable time to ascertain the validity of the adverse claims or to commence an action for interpleader. The bailee may assert an interpleader either in defending an action for nondelivery of the goods or by original action.

Official Comment

Prior Uniform Statutory Provisions: Former Section 7-603.

Changes: Changes for style only.

Purposes:

1. The section enables a bailee faced with conflicting claims to the goods to compel the claimants to litigate their claims with each other rather than with the bailee. The bailee is protected from legal liability when the bailee complies with court orders from the interpleader. See, e.g., *Northwestern Nat'l Sales, Inc. v. Commercial Cold Storage, Inc.*, 293 S.E.2d. 30 (Ga. Ct. App. 1982).

2. This section allows the bailee to bring an interpleader action but does not provide an exclusive basis for allowing interpleader. If either state or federal procedural rules allow an interpleader in other situations, the bailee may commence an interpleader under those rules. Even in an interpleader to which this section applies, the state or federal process of interpleader applies to the bailee's action for interpleader. For example, state or federal interpleader statutes or rules may permit a bailee to protect its lien or to seek attorney's fees and costs in the interpleader action.

Cross Reference:

Point 1: Section 7-403.

Definitional Cross References:

"Action".	Section 1-201.
"Bailee".	Section 7-102.
"Delivery".	Section 1-201.
"Goods".	Section 7-102.
"Person".	Section 1-201.
"Reasonable time".	Section 1-205.

Article 8—Investment Securities

PART 1. SHORT TITLE AND GENERAL MATTERS

Section 8-101. Short Title

This Article may be cited as Uniform Commercial Code—Investment Securities.

Section 8-102. Definitions

(a) In this Article:

(1) "Adverse claim" means a claim that a claimant has a property interest in a financial asset and that it is a violation of the rights of the claimant for another person to hold, transfer, or deal with the financial asset.

(2) "Bearer form," as applied to a certificated security, means a form in which the security is payable to the bearer of the security certificate according to its terms but not by reason of an indorsement.

(3) "Broker" means a person defined as a broker or dealer under the federal securities laws but without excluding a bank acting in that capacity.

(4) "Certificated security" means a security that is represented by a certificate.

(5) "Clearing corporation" means:

(i) a person that is registered as a "clearing agency" under the federal securities laws;

(ii) a federal reserve bank; or

(iii) any other person that provides clearance or settlement services with respect to financial assets that would require it to register as a clearing agency under the federal securities laws but for an exclusion or exemption from the registration requirement, if its activities as a clearing corporation, including promulgation of rules, are subject to regulation by a federal or state governmental authority.

(6) "Communicate" means to:

(i) send a signed record; or

(ii) transmit information by any mechanism agreed upon by the persons transmitting and receiving the information.

(7) "Entitlement holder" means a person identified in the records of a securities intermediary as the person having a security entitlement against the securities intermediary. If a person acquires a security entitlement by virtue of Section 8-501(b)(2) or (3), that person is the entitlement holder.

(8) "Entitlement order" means a notification communicated to a securities intermediary directing transfer or redemption of a financial asset to which the entitlement holder has a security entitlement.

(9) "Financial asset," except as otherwise provided in Section 8-103, means:

(i) a security;

(ii) an obligation of a person or a share, participation, or other interest in a person or in property or an enterprise of a person, which is, or is of a type, dealt in or traded on financial markets, or which is recognized in any area in which it is issued or dealt in as a medium for investment; or

(iii) any property that is held by a securities intermediary for another person in a securities account if the securities intermediary has expressly agreed with the other person that the property is to be treated as a financial asset under this Article.

As context requires, the term means either the interest itself or the means by which a person's claim to it is evidenced, including a certificated or uncertificated security, a security certificate, or a security entitlement.

(10) [Reserved]

(11) "Indorsement" means a signature that alone or accompanied by other words is made on a security certificate in registered form or on a separate document for the purpose of assigning, transferring, or redeeming the security or granting a power to assign, transfer, or redeem it.

(12) "Instruction" means a notification communicated to the issuer of an uncertificated security which directs that the transfer of the security be registered or that the security be redeemed.

(13) "Registered form," as applied to a certificated security, means a form in which:

(i) the security certificate specifies a person entitled to the security; and

(ii) a transfer of the security may be registered upon books maintained for that purpose by or on behalf of the issuer, or the security certificate so states.

(14) "Securities intermediary" means:

(i) a clearing corporation; or

(ii) a person, including a bank or broker, that in the ordinary course of its business maintains securities accounts for others and is acting in that capacity.

(15) "Security," except as otherwise provided in Section 8-103, means an obligation of an issuer or a share, participation, or other interest in an issuer or in property or an enterprise of an issuer:

(i) which is represented by a security certificate in bearer or registered form, or the transfer of which may be registered upon books maintained for that purpose by or on behalf of the issuer;

(ii) which is one of a class or series or by its terms is divisible into a class or series of shares, participations, interests, or obligations; and

(iii) which:

(A) is, or is of a type, dealt in or traded on securities exchanges or securities markets; or

(B) is a medium for investment and by its terms expressly provides that it is a security governed by this Article.

(16) "Security certificate" means a certificate representing a security.

(17) "Security entitlement" means the rights and property interest of an entitlement holder with respect to a financial asset specified in Part 5.

(18) "Uncertificated security" means a security that is not represented by a certificate.

(b) The following definitions in this Article and other Articles apply to this Article:

"Appropriate person"	Section 8-107
"Control"	Section 8-106
"Controllable account"	Section 9-102
"Controllable electronic record"	Section 12-102
"Controllable payment intangible"	Section 9-102
"Delivery"	Section 8-301
"Investment company security"	Section 8-103
"Issuer"	Section 8-201
"Overissue"	Section 8-210
"Protected purchaser"	Section 8-303
"Securities account"	Section 8-501

(c) In addition, Article 1 contains general definitions and principles of construction and interpretation applicable throughout this Article.

(d) The characterization of a person, business, or transaction for purposes of this Article does not determine the characterization of the person, business, or transaction for purposes of any other law, regulation, or rule.

Official Comment

1. "Adverse claim." The definition of the term "adverse claim" has two components. First, the term refers only to property interests. Second, the term means not merely that a person has a property interest in a financial asset but that it is a violation of the claimant's property interest for the other person to hold or transfer the security or other financial asset.

The term adverse claim is not, of course, limited to ownership rights, but extends to other property interests established by other law. A security interest, for example, would be an adverse claim with respect to a transferee from the debtor since any effort by the secured party to enforce the security interest against the property would be an interference with the transferee's interest.

The definition of adverse claim in the prior version of Article 8 might have been read to suggest that any wrongful action concerning a security, even a simple breach of contract, gave rise to an adverse claim. Insofar as such cases as *Fallon v. Wall Street Clearing Corp.*, 586 N.Y.S.2d 953 (App. Div. 1992), and *Pentech Intl. v. Wall St. Clearing Co.*, 983 F.2d 441 (2d Cir. 1993) were based on that view, they are rejected by the new definition which explicitly limits the term adverse claim to property interests. Suppose, for example, that A contracts to sell or deliver securities to B, but fails to do so and instead sells or pledges the securities to C. B, the promisee, has an action against A for breach of contract, but absent unusual circumstances the action for breach would not give rise to a property interest in the securities. Accordingly, B does not have an adverse claim. An adverse claim might, however, be based upon principles of equitable remedies that give rise to property claims. It would, for example, cover a right established by other law to rescind a transaction in which securities were transferred. Suppose, for example, that A holds securities and is induced by B's fraud to transfer them to B. Under the law of contract or restitution, A may have a right to rescind the transfer, which gives A a property claim to the securities. If so, A has an adverse claim to the securities in B's hands. By contrast, if B had committed no fraud, but had merely committed a breach of contract in connection with the transfer from A to B, A may have only a right to damages for breach, not a right to rescind. In that case, A would not have an adverse claim to the securities in B's hands.

2. "Bearer form." The definition of "bearer form" has remained substantially unchanged since the early drafts of the original version of Article 8. The requirement that the certificate be payable to bearer by its terms rather than by an indorsement has the effect of preventing instruments governed by other law, such as chattel paper or Article 3 negotiable instruments, from being inadvertently swept into the Article 8 definition of security merely by virtue of blank indorsements. Although the other elements of the definition of security in Section 8-102(a)(14) probably suffice for that purpose in any event, the language used in the prior version of Article 8 has been retained.

3. "Broker." Broker is defined by reference to the definitions of broker and dealer in the federal securities laws. The only difference is that banks, which are excluded from the federal securities law definition, are included in the Article 8 definition when they perform functions that would bring them within the federal securities law definition if it did not have the clause excluding banks. The definition covers both those who act as agents ("brokers" in securities parlance) and those who act as principals ("dealers" in securities parlance). Since the definition refers to persons "defined" as brokers or dealers under the federal securities law, rather than to persons required to "register" as brokers or dealers under the federal securities law, it covers not only registered brokers and dealers but also those exempt from the registration requirement, such as purely intrastate brokers. The only substantive rules that turn on the defined term broker are one provision of the section on warranties, Section 8-108(i), and the special perfection rule in Article 9 for security interests granted by brokers, Section 9-115(4)(c).

4. "Certificated security." The term "certificated security" means a security that is represented by a security certificate.

5. "Clearing corporation." The definition of clearing corporation limits its application to entities that are subject to a rigorous regulatory framework. Accordingly, the definition includes only federal reserve banks, persons who are registered as "clearing agencies" under the federal securities laws (which impose a comprehensive system of regulation of the activities and rules of clearing agencies), and other entities subject to a comparable system of regulatory oversight.

6. "Communicate." The term "communicate" assures that the Article 8 rules will be sufficiently flexible to adapt to changes in information technology. Sending a signed writing always suffices as a communication, but the parties can agree that a different means of transmitting information is to be used. Agreement is defined in Section 1-201(b)(3) as "the bargain of the parties in fact as found in their language or by implication from other circumstances including course of dealing or usage of trade or course of performance." Thus, use of an information transmission method might be found to be authorized by agreement, even though the parties have not explicitly so specified in a formal agreement. The term communicate is used in Sections 8-102(a)(7) (definition of entitlement order), 8-102(a)(11) (definition of instruction), and 8-403 (demand that issuer not register transfer). Also in furtherance of medium neutrality, pursuant to the Uniform Commercial Code Amendments (2022) (2022 Amendments) the reference in paragraph (6)(i) to a "signed writing" has been changed to refer to a "signed record."

7. "Entitlement holder." This term designates those who hold financial assets through intermediaries in the indirect holding system. Because many of the rules of Part 5 impose duties on securities intermediaries in favor of entitlement holders, the definition of entitlement holder is, in most cases, limited to the person specifically designated as such on the records of the intermediary. The last sentence of the definition covers the relatively unusual cases where a person may acquire a security entitlement under Section 8-501 even though the person may not be specifically designated as an entitlement holder on the records of the securities intermediary.

A person may have an interest in a security entitlement, and may even have the right to give entitlement orders to the securities intermediary with respect to it, even though the person is not the entitlement holder. For example, a person who holds securities through a securities account in its own name may have given discretionary trading authority to another person, such as an investment adviser. Similarly, the control provisions in Section 8-106 and the related provisions in Article 9 are designed to facilitate transactions in which a person who holds securities through a securities account uses them as collateral in an arrangement where the securities intermediary has agreed that if the secured party so directs the intermediary will dispose of the positions. In such arrangements, the debtor remains the entitlement holder but has agreed that the secured party can initiate entitlement orders. Moreover, an entitlement holder may be acting for another person as a nominee, agent, trustee, or in another capacity. Unless the entitlement holder is itself acting as a securities intermediary for the other person, in which case the other person would be an entitlement holder with respect to the securities entitlement, the relationship between an entitlement holder and another person for whose benefit the entitlement holder holds a securities entitlement is governed by other law.

8. "Entitlement order." This term is defined as a notification communicated to a securities intermediary directing transfer or redemption of the financial asset to which an entitlement holder has a security entitlement. The term is used in the rules for the indirect holding system in a fashion analogous to the use of the terms "indorsement" and "instruction" in the rules for the direct holding system. If a person directly holds a certificated security in registered form and wishes to transfer it, the means of transfer is an indorsement. If a person directly holds an uncertificated security and wishes to transfer it, the means of transfer is an instruction. If a person holds a security entitlement, the means of disposition is an entitlement order. An entitlement order includes a direction under Section 8-508 to the securities intermediary to transfer a financial asset to the account of the entitlement holder at another financial intermediary or to cause the financial asset to be transferred to the entitlement holder in the direct holding system (e.g., the delivery of a securities certificate registered in the name of the former entitlement holder). As noted in Comment 7, an entitlement order need not be initiated by the entitlement holder in order to be effective, so long as the entitlement holder has authorized the other party to initiate entitlement orders. See Section 8-107(b).

9. "Financial asset." The definition of "financial asset," in conjunction with the definition of "securities account" in Section 8-501, sets the scope of the indirect holding system rules of Part 5 of Revised Article 8. The Part 5 rules apply not only to securities held through intermediaries, but also to other financial assets held through intermediaries. The term financial asset is defined to include not only securities but also a broader category of obligations, shares, participations, and interests.

Having separate definitions of security and financial asset makes it possible to separate the question of the proper scope of the traditional Article 8 rules from the question of the proper scope of the new indirect holding system rules. Some forms of financial assets should be covered by the indirect holding system rules of Part 5, but not by the rules of Parts 2, 3, and 4. The term financial asset is used to cover such property. Because the term security entitlement is defined in terms of financial assets rather than securities, the rules concerning security entitlements set out in Part 5 of Article 8 and in Revised Article 9 apply to the broader class of financial assets.

It is not necessary for all of the Part 5 rules to be relevant to a particular financial asset for the relevant property to qualify as a "financial asset" credited to a securities account. Many of the duties set forth in Part 5 will often be relevant to a digital asset such as a "controllable electronic record" (Section 12-102), or a "controllable account" or "controllable payment intangible" (Section 9-102) evidenced by a controllable electronic record, treated as a financial asset credited to a securities account. These duties include the duty to exercise rights as directed by the entitlement holder, comply with the entitlement holder's entitlement orders, and change the position to another form of holding.

If the parties agree to treat a digital asset as a financial asset under Article 8 and the digital asset is in fact held in a securities account for an entitlement holder, the rules applicable to controllable electronic records under Article 12 would not apply to the entitlement holder's security entitlement related to the financial asset. If the financial asset itself is a controllable electronic record, however, then the rules in Article 12 could apply to the securities intermediary's rights with respect to the controllable electronic record if the intermediary holds the asset directly.

The fact that something does or could fall within the definition of financial asset does not, without more, trigger Article 8 coverage. The indirect holding system rules of Revised Article 8 apply only if the financial asset is in fact held in a securities account, so that the interest of the person who holds the financial asset through the securities account is a security entitlement. Thus, questions of the scope of the indirect holding system rules cannot be framed as "Is such-and-such a 'financial asset' under Article 8?" Rather, one must analyze whether the relationship between an institution and a person on whose behalf the institution holds an asset falls within the scope of the term securities account as defined in Section 8-501. That question turns in large measure on whether it makes sense to apply the Part 5 rules to the relationship.

The term financial asset is used to refer both to the underlying asset and the particular means by which ownership of that asset is evidenced. Thus, with respect to a certificated security, the term financial asset may, as context requires, refer either to the interest or obligation of the issuer or to the security certificate representing that interest or obligation. Similarly, if a person holds a security or other financial asset through a securities account, the term financial asset may, as context requires, refer either to the underlying asset or to the person's security entitlement.

10. "Good faith." Section 1-304 provides that "Every contract or duty within [the Uniform Commercial Code] imposes an obligation of good faith in its performance and enforcement." Section 1-201(b)(20) defines "good faith" as "honesty in fact and the observance of reasonable commercial standards of fair dealing." The reference to commercial standards makes clear that assessments of conduct are to be made in light of the commercial setting. The substantive rules of Article 8 have been drafted to take account of the commercial circumstances of the securities holding and processing system. For example, Section 8-115 provides that a securities intermediary acting on an effective entitlement order, or a broker or other agent acting as a conduit in a securities transaction, is not liable to an adverse claimant, unless the claimant obtained legal process or the intermediary acted in collusion with the wrongdoer. This and other similar provisions, see Sections 8-404 and 8-503(e) do not depend on notice of adverse claims, because it would impair rather than advance the interest of investors in having a sound and efficient securities clearance and settlement system to require intermediaries to investigate the propriety of the transactions they are processing. The good faith obligation does not supplant the standards of conduct established in provisions of this kind.

In Revised Article 8, the definition of good faith is not germane to the question whether a purchaser takes free from adverse claims. The rules on such questions as whether a purchaser who takes in suspicious circumstances is disqualified from protected purchaser status are treated not as an aspect of good faith but directly in the rules of Section 8-105 on notice of adverse claims.

11. "Indorsement" is defined as a signature made on a security certificate or separate document for purposes of transferring or redeeming the security. The definition is adapted from the language of Section 8-308(1) of the prior version and from the definition of indorsement in the Negotiable Instruments Article, see Section 3-204(a). The definition of indorsement does not include the requirement that the signature be made by an appropriate person or be authorized. Those questions are treated in the separate substantive provision on whether the indorsement is effective, rather than in the definition of indorsement. See Section 8-107.

12. "Instruction" is defined as a notification communicated to the issuer of an uncertificated security directing that transfer be registered or that the security be redeemed. Instructions are the analog for uncertificated securities of indorsements of certificated securities.

13. "Registered form." The definition of "registered form" is substantially the same as in the prior version of Article 8. Like the definition of bearer form, it serves primarily to distinguish Article 8 securities from instruments governed by other law, such as Article 3. Contrary to the holding in *Highland Capital Management LP v. Schneider*, 8 N.Y.3d 406 (2007), the registrability requirement in the definition of "registered form," and its parallel in the definition of "security," are satisfied only if books are maintained by or on behalf of the issuer for the purpose of registration of transfer, including the determination of rights under Section 8-207(a) (or if, in the case of a certificated security, the security certificate so states). It is not sufficient that the issuer records ownership, or records transfers thereof, for other purposes. Nor is it sufficient that the issuer, while not in fact maintaining books for the purpose of registration of transfer, could do so, for such is always the case.

Contrary to the holding in *Highland Cap. Mgmt. LP v. Schneider*, 834 N.Y.S. 2d 692 (N.Y. 2007), the registrability requirement in the definition of "registered form," and its parallel in the definition of "security," are satisfied only if books are maintained by or on behalf of the issuer for the purpose of registration of transfer, including the determination of rights under Section 8-207 (a) (or if, in the case of a certificated security, the security certificate so states). It is not sufficient that the issuer records ownership, or records transfers thereof, for other purposes. Nor is it sufficient that the issuer, while not in fact maintaining books for the purpose of registration of transfer, could do so, for such is always the case.

14. "Securities intermediary." A "securities intermediary" is a person that in the ordinary course of its business maintains securities accounts for others and is acting in that capacity. The most common examples of securities intermediaries would be clearing corporations holding securities for their participants, banks acting as securities custodians, and brokers holding securities on behalf of their customers. However, a person need not be such an entity in order to be a securities intermediary. Because a "securities account" is an account to which a financial asset is or may be credited under Section 8-501(a) and the definition of "financial asset" is not limited to securities, a person may be a "securities intermediary" even if that person does not credit "securities" (as defined in Article 8) to the account. Rather, the securities accounts that a securities intermediary maintains may consist exclusively of financial assets described in Section 8-102(a)(9)(ii) and (iii). For example, a cryptocurrency exchange that holds only cryptocurrencies (and not securities) for customers might be a securities intermediary.

Clearing corporations are listed separately as a category of securities intermediary in subparagraph (i) even though in most circumstances they would fall within the general definition in subparagraph (ii). The reason is to simplify the analysis of arrangements such as the NSCC-DTC system in which NSCC performs the comparison, clearance, and netting function, while DTC acts as the depository. Because NSCC is a registered clearing agency under the federal securities laws, it is a clearing corporation and hence a securities intermediary under Article 8, regardless of whether it is at any particular time or in any particular aspect of its operations holding securities on behalf of its participants.

The terms securities intermediary and broker have different meanings. Broker means a person engaged in the business of buying and selling securities, as agent for others or as principal. Securities intermediary means a person maintaining securities accounts for others. A stockbroker, in the colloquial sense, may or may not be acting as a securities intermediary.

The definition of securities intermediary includes the requirement that the person in question "in the ordinary course of its business maintain securities accounts for others". This "ordinary course" requirement does not have a fixed quantitative requirement and is determined by the facts of each case. Thus, a person need not necessarily satisfy a specified threshold of activity or necessarily have a minimum number of customers. Law other than the UCC may determine who may legally engage in such a business.

The definition of securities intermediary includes the requirement that the person in question is "acting in the capacity" of maintaining securities accounts for others. This is to take account of the fact that a particular entity, such as a bank, may act in many different capacities in securities transactions. A bank may act as a transfer agent for issuers, as a securities custodian for institutional investors and private investors, as a dealer in government securities, as a lender taking securities as collateral, and as a provider of general payment and collection services that might be used in connection with securities transactions. A bank that maintains securities accounts for its customers would be a securities intermediary with respect to those accounts; but if it takes a pledge of securities from a borrower to secure a loan, it is not thereby acting as a securities intermediary with respect to the pledged securities, since it holds them for its own account rather than for a customer. In other circumstances, those two functions might be combined. For example, if the bank is a government securities dealer it may maintain securities accounts for customers and also provide the customers with margin credit to purchase or carry the securities, in much the same way that brokers provide margin loans to their customers.

15. "Security." The definition of "security" has three components. First, there is the subparagraph (i) test that the interest or obligation be fully transferable, in the sense that the issuer either maintains transfer books or the obligation or interest is represented by a certificate in bearer or registered form. Second, there is the subparagraph (ii) test that the interest or obligation be divisible, that is, one of a class or series, as distinguished from individual obligations of the sort governed by ordinary contract law or by Article 3. Third, there is the subparagraph (iii) functional test, which generally turns on whether the interest or obligation is, or is of a type, dealt in or traded on securities markets or securities exchanges. There is, however, an "opt-in" provision in subparagraph (iii) which permits the issuer of any interest or obligation that is "a medium of investment" to specify that it is a security governed by Article 8.

The divisibility test of subparagraph (ii) applies to the security—that is, the underlying intangible interest—not the means by which that interest is evidenced. Thus, securities issued in book-entry only form meet the divisibility test because the underlying intangible interest is divisible via the mechanism of the indirect holding system. This is so even though the clearing corporation is the only eligible direct holder of the security.

The third component, the functional test in subparagraph (iii), provides flexibility while ensuring that the Article 8 rules do not apply to interests or obligations in circumstances so unconnected with the securities markets that parties are unlikely to have thought of the possibility that Article 8 might apply. Subparagraph (iii)(A) covers interests or obligations that either are dealt in or traded on securities exchanges or securities markets or are of a type dealt in or traded on securities exchanges or securities markets. The "is dealt in or traded on" phrase eliminates problems in the characterization of new forms of securities which are to be traded in the markets, even though no similar type has previously been dealt in or traded in the markets. Subparagraph (iii)(B) covers the broader category of media for investment, but it applies only if the terms of the interest or obligation specify that it is an Article 8 security.

This opt-in provision allows for deliberate expansion of the scope of Article 8.

Section 8-103 contains additional rules on the treatment of particular interests as securities or financial assets.

16. "Security certificate." The term "security" refers to the underlying asset, e.g., 1000 shares of common stock of Acme, Inc. The term "security certificate" refers to the paper certificates that have traditionally been used to embody the underlying intangible interest.

17. "Security entitlement" means the rights and property interest of a person who holds securities or other financial assets through a securities intermediary. A security entitlement is both a package of personal rights against the securities intermediary and an interest in the property held by the securities intermediary. A security entitlement is not, however, a specific property interest in any financial asset held by the securities intermediary or by the clearing corporation through which the securities intermediary holds the financial asset. See Sections 8-104(c) and 8-503. The formal definition of security entitlement set out in subsection (a)(17) of this section is a cross-reference to the rules of Part 5. In a sense, then, the entirety of Part 5 is the definition of security entitlement. The Part 5 rules specify the rights and property interest that comprise a security entitlement.

Rights and obligations relating to a security entitlement are enforceable by action. See Section 1-305(b) and PEB Commentary No. 25. The Commentary is available at https://www.ali.org/peb-ucc.

18. "Uncertificated security." The term "uncertificated security" means a security that is not represented by a security certificate—i.e., a paper certificate. This is so even if, for example, the organic documents related to the security refer to it as being "certificated" or refer to the electronic record evidencing the security as an "electronic certificate.. For uncertificated securities, there is no need to draw any distinction between the underlying asset and the means by which a direct holder's interest in that asset is evidenced. Compare "certificated security" and "security certificate."

As discussed above in Comment 9, a controllable electronic record may be a "financial asset." However, a controllable electronic record is not itself a "security," defined in part in Section 8-102(a)(15) as "an obligation of an issuer or a share, participation, or other interest in an issuer or in property or an enterprise of an issuer." It also is not "a share or similar equity interest," an "investment company security," or "an interest in a partnership or limited liability company." See Section 8-103(a), (b), and (c). Of course, a controllable electronic record might be involved in the issuance and distribution of something that is a security for other, non-Article 8 purposes, including the federal securities laws. For example, a controllable electronic record (perhaps labeled as a "token" or "coin") might provide a mechanism for facilitating investments in such securities. As Section 8-102(d) makes clear, however, characterization under Article 8 does not determine characterization for other purposes. The converse is also true—characterization for other purposes does not determine characterization under Article 8.

Although not itself an Article 8 security, a controllable electronic record might play a role in the facilitating transactions in Article 8 securities. The following examples address situations in which controllable electronic records may have such a role as well as situations in which investment property is not involved.

Example 1 (corporate shares: Article 8 uncertificated securities; token as instruction). A Delaware corporation (D Corp) issues shares of stock and maintains books and records evidencing the registered ownership of the shares. Because the shares are not represented by security certificates, they are uncertificated securities. Pursuant to the applicable law and the organic documentation of D Corp, D Corp creates, or causes to be created, controllable electronic records (CERs)—"tokens"—to facilitate transfers of the shares. Also pursuant to that law and documentation, the transfer of control of a token on the platform on which the token is recorded constitutes an instruction to D Corp, as issuer, for the transfer of registration of the share(s) represented by the token to the transferee of control. Following receipt of the instruction upon transfer of control of a token, D Corp transfers registration of the share(s) on its books and records. See Sections 8-102(a)(12) (defining "instruction"); 8-401 (duty of issuer to register transfer). Although Article 12 governs the tokens (as CERs) and the transfer of control thereof, other law, including Delaware corporate law and Delaware Article 8 (and Article 9 of the relevant jurisdiction, if applicable) governs rights in the uncertificated securities and the transfer of registration. See Sections 8-110(a); 12-104(f).

Example 2 (LLC membership interests: Article 8 uncertificated securities; token as instruction). A Delaware limited liability company (LLC) issues membership interests that are dealt in or traded on securities exchanges or in securities markets and which by their terms are securities governed by Article 8. See Section 8-103(c). LLC maintains books and records evidencing the registered ownership of the interests. Because the interests are not represented by security certificates, they are uncertificated securities. Pursuant to the applicable law and the organic documentation of LLC, LLC creates, or causes to be created, controllable electronic records (CERs)—"tokens"—to facilitate transfers of the interests. Also pursuant to that law and documentation, the transfer of control of a token on the platform on which the token is recorded constitutes an instruction to LLC, as issuer, for the transfer of registration of the interest(s) represented by the token to the transferee of control. Following receipt of the instruction upon transfer of control of a token, LLC transfers registration of the interest(s) on its books and records. See Sections 8-102(a)(12) (defining "instruction"); 8-401 (duty of issuer to register transfer). Although Article 12 governs the tokens (as CERs) and the transfer of control thereof, other law, including Delaware LLC law and Delaware Article 8 (and Article 9 of the relevant jurisdiction, if applicable), governs rights in the uncertificated securities and the transfer of registration. See Sections 8-110(a); 12-104(f).

Example 3 (LLC membership interests not covered by Article 8; interests are general intangibles). A Delaware limited liability company issues membership interests that are not securities governed by UCC Article 8 and, consequently, are not investment property. See Section 8-103(c). Instead, the membership interests are general intangibles. LLC maintains books and records evidencing ownership of the interests. Pursuant to the applicable law and the organic documentation of LLC, LLC creates, or causes to be created, controllable electronic records (CERs)—"tokens"—to facilitate transfers of the interests. Also pursuant to that law and documentation, the transfer of control of a token on the platform on which the token is recorded constitutes a request to LLC, as issuer, for the transfer of the interest(s) related to the token. Following receipt of the request upon transfer of control of a token, LLC transfers the interest(s) on its books and records. Although Article 12 governs the tokens (as CERs) and the transfer of control, other law (including Article 9 or the relevant jurisdiction, if applicable, but not Article 8) governs rights in the interests (general intangibles). See Section 12-104(f).

Examples 1 and 2 posit that controllable electronic records function as instructions to the issuers. For an analogous example in another context, see Section 4A-104, Comment 3 ("An instruction to pay might be a component of a computer program or a transaction protocol intended to execute automatically under specified circumstances."). The central point is that the roles of the controllable electronic records must comply with the organic corporate and LLC laws and documentation as well as the Article 8 regime for uncertificated securities. Although controllable electronic records might be structured to functionally "represent" the underlying uncertificated securities, Article 8 makes no provision for such a "representation" for uncertificated securities (unlike the role of security certificates for certificated securities). Whether it would be possible and feasible to expand the structure contemplated in Examples 1 and 2 so that transfer of control of a controllable electronic record would, *ipso facto*, constitute a transfer of registration on the issuer's books and records would depend on the terms of and compliance with both the underlying organic laws and documentation for the uncertificated securities, the requirements of Article 8, and, where applicable, other law.

If the securities issued by D Corp or LLC in Examples 1 and 2 were payment obligations of the issuers that met the definition of "security" in Section 8-102(a)(15)—i.e., debt securities—the same analysis discussed in those examples as to the applicability and scope of Articles 8 and 12 would apply. However, if the debt obligations were not Article 8 securities (as in Example 3) but were obligations of account debtors on controllable accounts or controllable payment intangibles, then the relevant provisions of Articles 9 and 12, and not those of Article 8, would apply. See, e.g., Sections 9-107A; 9-306B; 9-314; 12-104(a), (b), and (e) and Comments 6–10; Article 12, Prefatory Note 4.

Definitional Cross References:

"Agreement"	Section 1-201(b)(3)
"Bank"	Section 1-201(b)(4)
"Person"	Section 1-201(b)(27)
"Send"	Section 1-201(b)(36)
"Signed"	Section 1-201(b)(37)
"Writing"	Section 1-201(b)(43)

Section 8-103. Rules for Determining Whether Certain Obligations and Interests Are Securities or Financial Assets

(a) A share or similar equity interest issued by a corporation, business trust, joint stock company, or similar entity is a security.

(b) An "investment company security" is a security. "Investment company security" means a share or similar equity interest issued by an entity that is registered as an investment company under the federal investment company laws, an interest in a unit investment trust that is so registered, or a face-amount certificate issued by a face-amount certificate company that is so registered. Investment company security does not include an insurance policy or endowment policy or annuity contract issued by an insurance company.

(c) An interest in a partnership or limited liability company is not a security unless it is dealt in or traded on securities exchanges or in securities markets, its terms expressly provide that it is a security governed by this Article, or it is an investment company security. However, an interest in a partnership or limited liability company is a financial asset if it is held in a securities account.

(d) A writing that is a security certificate is governed by this Article and not by Article 3, even though it also meets the requirements of that Article. However, a negotiable instrument governed by Article 3 is a financial asset if it is held in a securities account.

(e) An option or similar obligation issued by a clearing corporation to its participants is not a security, but is a financial asset.

(f) A commodity contract, as defined in Section 9-102(a)(15), is not a security or a financial asset.

(g) A document of title is not a financial asset unless Section 8-102(a)(9)(iii) applies.

(h) A controllable account, controllable electronic record, or controllable payment is not a financial asset unless Section 8-102(a)(9)(iii) applies.

Official Comment

1. This section contains rules that supplement the definitions of "financial asset" and "security" in Section 8-102. The Section 8-102 definitions are worded in general terms because they must be sufficiently comprehensive and flexible to cover the wide variety of investment products that now exist or may develop. The rules in this section are intended to foreclose interpretive issues concerning the application of the general definitions to several specific investment products. No implication is made about the application of the Section 8-102 definitions to investment products not covered by this section.

2. Subsection (a) establishes an unconditional rule that ordinary corporate stock is a security. That is so whether or not the particular issue is dealt in or traded on securities exchanges or in securities markets. Thus, shares of closely held corporations are Article 8 securities.

3. Subsection (b) establishes that the Article 8 term "security" includes the various forms of the investment vehicles offered to the public by investment companies registered as such under the federal Investment Company Act of 1940, as amended. This clarification is prompted principally by the fact that the typical transaction in shares of open-end investment companies is an issuance or redemption, rather than a transfer of shares from one person to another as is the case with ordinary corporate stock. For similar reasons, the definitions of indorsement, instruction, and entitlement order in Section 8-102 refer to "redemptions" as well as "transfers," to ensure that the Article 8 rules on such matters as signature guaranties, Section 8-306, assurances, Sections 8-402 and 8-507, and effectiveness, Section 8-107, apply to directions to redeem mutual fund shares. The exclusion of insurance products is needed because some insurance company separate accounts are registered under the Investment Company Act of 1940, but these are not traded under the usual Article 8 mechanics.

4. Subsection (c) is designed to foreclose interpretive questions that might otherwise be raised by the application of the "of a type" language of Section 8-102(a)(15)(iii) to partnership interests. Subsection (c) establishes the general rule that partnership interests or shares of limited liability companies are not Article 8 securities unless they are in fact dealt in or traded on securities exchanges or in securities markets. The issuer, however, may explicitly "opt-in" by specifying that the interests or shares are securities governed by Article 8. Partnership interests or shares of limited liability companies are included in the broader term "financial asset." Thus, if they are held through a securities account, the indirect holding system rules of Part 5 apply, and the interest of a person who holds them through such an account is a security entitlement.

5. Subsection (d) deals with the line between Article 3 negotiable instruments and Article 8 investment securities. It continues the rule of the prior version of Article 8 that a writing that meets the Article 8 definition is covered by Article 8 rather than Article 3, even though it also meets the definition of negotiable instrument. However, subsection (d) provides that an Article 3 negotiable instrument is a "financial asset" so that the indirect holding system rules apply if the instrument is held through a securities intermediary. This facilitates making items such as money market instruments eligible for deposit in clearing corporations.

6. Subsection (e) is included to clarify the treatment of investment products such as traded stock options, which are treated as financial assets but not securities. Thus, the indirect holding system rules of Part 5 apply, but the direct holding system rules of Parts 2, 3, and 4 do not.

7. Subsection (f) excludes commodity contracts from all of Article 8. However, the Article 9 rules on security interests in investment property do apply to security interests in commodity positions. See Section 9-115 and Comment 8 thereto. "Commodity contract" is defined in Section 9-115.

8. Subsection (g) allows a document of title to be a financial asset and thus subject to the indirect holding system rules of Part 5 only to the extent that the intermediary and the person entitled under the document so agree pursuant to Section 8-102(a)(9)(iii). Subsection (h), added pursuant to the 2022 Amendments, adopts the same approach for a controllable account, controllable electronic record, or controllable payment intangible. This is to prevent the inadvertent application of the Part 5 rules to intermediaries who may hold electronic or tangible documents of title or controllable accounts, controllable electronic records, or controllable payment intangibles.

Definitional Cross References:

"Clearing corporation"	Section 8-102(a)(5)
"Commodity contract"	Section 9-115
"Financial asset"	Section 8-102(a)(9)
"Security"	Section 8-102(a)(15)
"Security certificate"	Section 8-102(a)(16)

Section 8-104. Acquisition of Security or Financial Asset or Interest Therein

(a) A person acquires a security or an interest therein, under this Article, if:

(1) the person is a purchaser to whom a security is delivered pursuant to Section 8-301; or

(2) the person acquires a security entitlement to the security pursuant to Section 8-501.

(b) A person acquires a financial asset, other than a security, or an interest therein, under this Article, if the person acquires a security entitlement to the financial asset.

(c) A person who acquires a security entitlement to a security or other financial asset has the rights specified in Part 5, but is a purchaser of any security, security entitlement, or other financial asset held by the securities intermediary only to the extent provided in Section 8-503.

(d) Unless the context shows that a different meaning is intended, a person who is required by other law, regulation, rule, or agreement to transfer, deliver, present, surrender, exchange, or otherwise put in the possession of another person a security or financial asset satisfies that requirement by causing the other person to acquire an interest in the security or financial asset pursuant to subsection (a) or (b).

Official Comment

1. This section lists the ways in which interests in securities and other financial assets are acquired under Article 8. In that sense, it describes the scope of Article 8. Subsection (a) describes the two ways that a person may acquire a security or interest therein under this Article: (1) by delivery (Section 8-301), and (2) by acquiring a security entitlement. Each of these methods is described in detail in the relevant substantive provisions of this Article. Part 3, beginning with the definition of "delivery" in Section 8-301, describes how interests in securities are acquired in the direct holding system. Part 5, beginning with the rules of Section 8-501 on how security entitlements are acquired, describes how interests in securities are acquired in the indirect holding system.

Subsection (b) specifies how a person may acquire an interest under Article 8 in a financial asset other than a security. This Article deals with financial assets other than securities only insofar as they are held in the indirect holding system. For example, a banker's acceptance falls within the definition of "financial asset," so if it is held through a securities account the entitlement holder's right to it is a security entitlement governed by Part 5. The banker's acceptance itself, however, is a negotiable instrument governed by Article 3, not by Article 8. Thus, the provisions of Parts 2, 3, and 4 of this Article that deal with the rights of direct holders of securities are not applicable. Article 3, not Article 8, specifies how one acquires a direct interest in a banker's acceptance. If a banker's acceptance is delivered to a clearing corporation to be held for the account of the clearing corporation's participants, the clearing corporation becomes the holder of the banker's acceptance under the Article 3 rules specifying how negotiable instruments are transferred. The rights of the clearing corporation's participants, however, are governed by Part 5 of this Article.

2. The distinction in usage in Article 8 between the term "security" (and its correlatives "security certificate" and "uncertificated security") on the one hand, and "security entitlement" on the other, corresponds to the distinction between the direct and indirect holding systems. For example, with respect to certificated securities that can be held either directly or through intermediaries, obtaining possession of a security certificate and acquiring a security entitlement are both means of holding the underlying security. For many other purposes, there is no need to draw a distinction between the means of holding. For purposes of commercial law analysis, however, the form of holding may make a difference. Where an item of property can be held in different ways, the rules on how one deals with it, including how one transfers it or how one grants a security interest in it, differ depending on the form of holding.

Although a security entitlement is means of holding the underlying security or other financial asset, a person who has a security entitlement does not have any direct claim to a specific asset in the possession of the securities intermediary. Subsection (c) provides explicitly that a person who acquires a security entitlement is a "purchaser" of any security, security entitlement, or other financial asset held by the securities intermediary only in the sense that under Section 8-503 a security entitlement is treated as a *sui generis* form of property interest.

3. Subsection (d) is designed to ensure that parties will retain their expected legal rights and duties under Revised Article 8. One of the major changes made by the revision is that the rules for the indirect holding system are stated in terms of the "security entitlements" held by investors, rather than speaking of them as holding direct interests in securities. Subsection (d) is designed as a translation rule to eliminate problems of coordination of terminology and facilitate the continued use of systems for the efficient handling of securities and financial assets through securities intermediaries and clearing corporations. The efficiencies of a securities intermediary or clearing corporation are, in part, dependent on the ability to transfer securities credited to securities accounts in the intermediary or clearing corporation to the account of an issuer, its agent, or other person by book entry in a manner that permits exchanges, redemptions, conversions, and other transactions (which may be governed by pre-existing or new agreements, constitutional documents, or other instruments) to occur and to avoid the need to withdraw from immobilization in an intermediary or clearing corporation physical securities in order to deliver them for such purposes. Existing corporate charters, indentures and like documents may require the "presentation," "surrender," "delivery," or "transfer" of securities or security certificates for purposes of exchange, redemption, conversion or other reason. Likewise, documents may use a wide variety of terminology to describe, in the context for example of a tender or exchange offer, the means of putting the offeror or the issuer or its agent in possession of the security. Subsection (d) takes the place of provisions of prior law which could be used to reach the legal conclusion that book-entry transfers are equivalent to physical delivery to the person to whose account the book entry is credited.

Definitional Cross References:

"Delivery"	Section 8-301
"Financial asset"	Section 8-102(a)(9)
"Person"	Section 1-201(b)(27)
"Purchaser"	Sections 1-201(b)(30) and 8-116
"Security"	Section 8-102(a)(15)
"Security entitlement"	Section 8-102(a)(17)

Section 8-105. Notice of Adverse Claim

(a) A person has notice of an adverse claim if:

(1) the person knows of the adverse claim;

(2) the person is aware of facts sufficient to indicate that there is a significant probability that the adverse claim exists and deliberately avoids information that would establish the existence of the adverse claim; or

(3) the person has a duty, imposed by statute or regulation, to investigate whether an adverse claim exists, and the investigation so required would establish the existence of the adverse claim.

(b) Having knowledge that a financial asset or interest therein is or has been transferred by a representative imposes no duty of inquiry into the rightfulness of a transaction and is not notice of an adverse claim. However, a person who knows that a representative has transferred a financial asset or interest therein in a transaction that is, or whose proceeds are being used, for the individual benefit of the representative or otherwise in breach of duty has notice of an adverse claim.

(c) An act or event that creates a right to immediate performance of the principal obligation represented by a security certificate or sets a date on or after which the certificate is to be presented or surrendered for redemption or exchange does not itself constitute notice of an adverse claim except in the case of a transfer more than:

(1) one year after a date set for presentment or surrender for redemption or exchange; or

(2) six months after a date set for payment of money against presentation or surrender of the certificate, if money was available for payment on that date.

(d) A purchaser of a certificated security has notice of an adverse claim if the security certificate:

(1) whether in bearer or registered form, has been indorsed "for collection" or "for surrender" or for some other purpose not involving transfer; or

(2) is in bearer form and has on it an unambiguous statement that it is the property of a person other than the transferor, but the mere writing of a name on the certificate is not such a statement.

(e) Filing of a financing statement under Article 9 is not notice of an adverse claim to a financial asset.

Official Comment

1. The rules specifying whether adverse claims can be asserted against persons who acquire securities or security entitlements, Sections 8-303, 8-502, and 8-510, provide that one is protected against an adverse claim only if one takes without notice of the claim. This section defines notice of an adverse claim.

Section 1-202(d), (e), and (f), on giving and receiving notice, does not apply to the interpretation of "notice of adverse claims." Section 1-202(d), (e), and (f) does, however, apply to giving and receiving notice under Article 8 in contexts other than notice of adverse claims.

2. This section must be interpreted in light of the definition of "adverse claim" in Section 8-102(a)(1). "Adverse claim" does not include all circumstances in which a third party has a property interest in securities, but only those situations where a security is transferred in violation of the claimant's property interest. Therefore, awareness that someone other than the transferor has a property interest is not notice of an adverse claim. The transferee must be aware that the transfer violates the other party's property interest. If A holds securities in which B has some form of property interest, and A transfers the securities to C, C may know that B has an interest but infer that A is acting in accordance with A's obligations to B. The mere fact that C knew that B had a property interest does not mean that C had notice of an adverse claim. Whether C had notice of an adverse claim depends on whether C had sufficient awareness that A was acting in violation of B's property rights. The rule in subsection (b) is a particularization of this general principle.

3. Paragraph (a)(1) provides that a person has notice of an adverse claim if the person has knowledge of the adverse claim. Knowledge is defined in Section 1-202(b) as actual knowledge.

4. Paragraph (a)(2) provides that a person has notice of an adverse claim if the person is aware of a significant probability that an adverse claim exists and deliberately avoids information that might establish the existence of the adverse claim. This is intended to codify the "willful blindness" test that has been applied in such cases. See *May v. Chapman*, 153 Eng. Rep. 1225 (1847); *Goodman v. Simonds*, 61 U.S. 343 (1857).

The first prong of the willful blindness test of paragraph (a)(2) turns on whether the person is aware facts sufficient to indicate that there is a significant probability that an adverse claim exists. The "awareness" aspect necessarily turns on the actor's state of mind. Whether facts known to a person make the person aware of a "significant probability" that an adverse claim exists turns on facts about the world and the conclusions that would be drawn from those facts, taking account of the experience and position of the person in question. A particular set of facts might indicate a significant probability of an adverse claim to a professional with considerable experience in the usual methods and procedures by which securities transactions are conducted, even though the same facts would not indicate a significant probability of an adverse claim to a non-professional.

The second prong of the willful blindness test of paragraph (a)(2) turns on whether the person "deliberately avoids information" that would establish the existence of the adverse claim. The test is the character of the person's response to the information the person has. The question is whether the person deliberately failed to seek further information because of concern that suspicions would be confirmed.

Application of the "deliberate avoidance" test to a transaction by an organization focuses on the knowledge and the actions of the individual or individuals conducting the transaction on behalf of the organization. Thus, an organization that purchases a security is not willfully blind to an adverse claim unless the officers or agents who conducted that purchase transaction are willfully blind to the adverse claim. Under the two prongs of the willful blindness test, the individual or individuals conducting a transaction must know of facts indicating a substantial probability that the adverse claim exists and deliberately fail to seek further information that might confirm or refute the indication. For this purpose, information known to individuals within an organization who are not conducting or aware of a transaction, but not forwarded to the individuals conducting the transaction, is not pertinent in determining whether the individuals conducting the transaction had knowledge of a substantial probability of the existence of the adverse claim. Cf. Section 1-202(f) (receipt of notice or knowledge by an organization). An organization may also "deliberately avoid information" if it acts to preclude or inhibit transmission of pertinent information to those individuals responsible for the conduct of purchase transactions.

5. Paragraph (a)(3) provides that a person has notice of an adverse claim if the person would have learned of the adverse claim by conducting an investigation that is required by other statute or regulation. This rule applies only if there is some other statute or regulation that explicitly requires persons dealing with securities to conduct some investigation. The federal securities laws require that brokers and banks, in certain specified circumstances, check with a stolen securities registry to determine whether securities offered for sale or pledge have been reported as stolen. If securities that were listed as stolen in the registry are taken by an institution that failed to comply with requirement to check the registry, the institution would be held to have notice of the fact that they were stolen under paragraph (a)(3). Accordingly, the institution could not qualify as a protected purchaser under Section 8-303. The same result has been reached under the prior version of Article 8. See *First Nat'l Bank of Cicero v. Lewco Securities*, 860 F.2d 1407 (7th Cir. 1988).

6. Subsection (b) provides explicitly for some situations involving purchase from one described or identifiable as a representative. Knowledge of the existence of the representative relation is not enough in itself to constitute "notice of an adverse claim" that would disqualify the purchaser from protected purchaser status. A purchaser may take a security on the inference that the representative is acting properly. Knowledge that a security is being transferred to an individual account of the representative or that the proceeds of the transaction will be paid into that account is not sufficient to constitute "notice of an adverse claim," but knowledge that the proceeds will be applied to the personal indebtedness of the representative is. See *State Bank of Binghamton v. Bache*, 293 N.Y.S. 667 (Sup. Ct. 1937).

7. Subsection (c) specifies whether a purchaser of a "stale" security is charged with notice of adverse claims, and therefore disqualified from protected purchaser status under Section 8-303. The fact of "staleness" is viewed as notice of certain defects after the lapse of stated periods, but the maturity of the security does not operate automatically to affect holders' rights. The periods of time here stated are shorter than those appearing in the provisions of this Article on staleness as notice of defects or defenses of an issuer (Section 8-203) since a purchaser who takes a security after funds or other securities are available for its redemption has more reason to suspect claims of ownership than issuer's defenses. An owner will normally turn in a security rather than transfer it at such a time. Of itself, a default never constitutes notice of a possible adverse claim. To provide otherwise would not tend to drive defaulted securities home and would serve only to disrupt current financial markets where many defaulted securities are actively traded. Unpaid or overdue coupons attached to a bond do not bring it within the operation of this subsection, though they may be relevant under the general test of notice of adverse claims in subsection (a).

8. Subsection (d) provides the owner of a certificated security with a means of protection while a security certificate is being sent in for redemption or exchange. The owner may endorse it "for collection" or "for surrender," and this constitutes notice of the owner's claims, under subsection (d).

Definitional Cross References:

"Adverse claim"	Section 8-102(a)(1)
"Bearer form"	Section 8-102(a)(2)
"Certificated security"	Section 8-102(a)(4)
"Financial asset"	Section 8-102(a)(9)
"Knowledge"	Section 1-202(b)
"Person"	Section 1-201(b)(27)
"Purchaser"	Sections 1-201(b)(30) and 8-116
"Registered form"	Section 8-102(a)(13)
"Representative"	Section 1-201(b)(33)
"Security certificate"	Section 8-102(a)(16)

Section 8-106. Control

(a) A purchaser has "control" of a certificated security in bearer form if the certificated security is delivered to the purchaser.

(b) A purchaser has "control" of a certificated security in registered form if the certificated security is delivered to the purchaser, and:

(1) the certificate is indorsed to the purchaser or in blank by an effective indorsement; or

(2) the certificate is registered in the name of the purchaser, upon original issue or registration of transfer by the issuer.

(c) A purchaser has "control" of an uncertificated security if:

(1) the uncertificated security is delivered to the purchaser; or

(2) the issuer has agreed that it will comply with instructions originated by the purchaser without further consent by the registered owner.

(d) A purchaser has "control" of a security entitlement if:

(1) the purchaser becomes the entitlement holder;

(2) the securities intermediary has agreed that it will comply with entitlement orders originated by the purchaser without further consent by the entitlement holder; or

(3) another person, other than the transferor to the purchaser of an interest in the security entitlement:

(A) has control of the security entitlement and acknowledges that it has control on behalf of the purchaser; or

(B) obtains control of the security entitlement after having acknowledged that it will obtain control of the security entitlement on behalf of the purchaser.

(e) If an interest in a security entitlement is granted by the entitlement holder to the entitlement holder's own securities intermediary, the securities intermediary has control.

(f) A purchaser who has satisfied the requirements of subsection (c) or (d) has control, even if the registered owner in the case of subsection (c) or the entitlement holder in the case of subsection (d) retains the right to make substitutions for the uncertificated security or security entitlement, to originate instructions or entitlement orders to the issuer or securities intermediary, or otherwise to deal with the uncertificated security or security entitlement.

(g) An issuer or a securities intermediary may not enter into an agreement of the kind described in subsection (c)(2) or (d)(2) without the consent of the registered owner or entitlement holder, but an issuer or a securities intermediary is not required to enter into such an agreement even though the registered owner or entitlement holder so directs. An issuer or securities intermediary that has entered into such an agreement is not required to confirm the existence of the agreement to another party unless requested to do so by the registered owner or entitlement holder.

(h) A person that has control under this section is not required to acknowledge that it has control on behalf of a purchaser.

(i) If a person acknowledges that is has or will obtain control on behalf of a purchaser, unless the person otherwise agrees or law other than this Article or Article 9 otherwise provides, the person does not owe any duty to the purchaser and is not required to confirm the acknowledgment to any other person.

Official Comment

1. The concept of "control" plays a key role in various provisions dealing with the rights of purchasers, including secured parties. See Sections 8-303 (protected purchasers); 8-503(e) (purchasers from securities intermediaries); 8-510 (purchasers of security entitlements from entitlement holders); 9-203(b)(3)(D) (attachment of security interests); 9-314 (perfection of security interests); 9-328 (priorities among conflicting security interests).

Obtaining "control" means that the purchaser has taken whatever steps are necessary, given the manner in which the securities or other financial assets are held, to place itself in a position where it can have the securities or other financial assets sold without further action by the owner, registered owner, entitlement holder, transferor, or other person with an interest in the securities or other financial assets.

2. Subsection (a) provides that a purchaser obtains "control" with respect to a certificated security in bearer form by taking "delivery," as defined in Section 8-301. Subsection (b) provides that a purchaser obtains "control" with respect to a certificated security in registered form by taking "delivery," as defined in Section 8-301, provided that the security certificate has been indorsed to the purchaser or in blank. Section 8-301 provides that delivery of a certificated security occurs when the purchaser obtains possession of the security certificate, or when an agent for the purchaser (other than a securities intermediary) either acquires possession or acknowledges that the agent holds for the purchaser.

3. Subsection (c) specifies the means by which a purchaser can obtain control over uncertificated securities which the transferor holds directly. Two mechanisms are possible.

Under subsection (c)(1), securities can be "delivered" to a purchaser. Section 8-301(b) provides that "delivery" of an uncertificated security occurs when the purchaser becomes the registered holder. So far as the issuer is concerned, the purchaser would then be entitled to exercise all rights of ownership. See Section 8-207. As between the parties to a purchase transaction, however, the rights of the purchaser are determined by their contract. Cf. Section 9-202. Arrangements covered by this paragraph are analogous to arrangements in which bearer certificates are delivered to a secured party—so far as the issuer or any other parties are concerned, the secured party appears to be the outright owner, although it is in fact holding as collateral property that belongs to the debtor.

Under subsection (c)(2), a purchaser has control if the issuer has agreed to act on the instructions of the purchaser, even though the owner remains listed as the registered owner. The issuer, of course, would be acting wrongfully against the registered owner if it entered into such an agreement without the consent of the registered owner. Subsection (g) makes this point explicit. The subsection (c)(2) provision makes it possible for issuers to offer a service akin to the registered pledge device of the 1978 version of Article 8, without mandating that all issuers offer that service.

4. Subsection (d) specifies the means by which a purchaser can obtain control of a security entitlement. Three mechanisms are possible, analogous to those provided in subsection (c) for uncertificated securities. Under subsection (d)(1), a purchaser has control if it is the entitlement holder. This subsection would apply whether the purchaser holds through the same intermediary that the debtor used, or has the securities position transferred to its own intermediary. Subsection (d)(2) provides that a purchaser has control if the securities intermediary has agreed to act on entitlement orders originated by the purchaser if no further consent by the entitlement holder is required. Under subsection (d)(2), control may be achieved even though the original entitlement holder remains as the entitlement holder. Finally, a purchaser may obtain control under subsection (d)(3) if another person has control and the person acknowledges that it has control on the purchaser's behalf. Control under subsection (d)(3) parallels the delivery of certificated securities and uncertificated securities under Section 8-301. See the discussion of subsection (d)(3) in Comment 4A, below.

Subsection (d) specifies only the minimum requirements that such an arrangement must meet to confer "control" of a security entitlement; the details of the arrangement can be specified by agreement. The arrangement might cover all of the positions in a particular account or subaccount, or only specified positions. There is no requirement that the control party's right to give entitlement orders be exclusive. The arrangement might provide, for example, that only the control party can give entitlement orders, that either the entitlement holder or the control party can give entitlement orders, that more than one person has unilateral control, or that two or more persons share control. The essential factor is whether a person may originate entitlement orders without further consent of the entitlement holder. See subsection (f).

The following examples Illustrate the application of subsection (d):

Example 1: Debtor grants Alpha Bank a security interest in a security entitlement that includes 1000 shares of XYZ Co. stock that Debtor holds through an account with Able & Co. Alpha Bank also has an account with Able. Debtor instructs Able to transfer the shares to Alpha Bank, and Able does so by crediting the shares to Alpha's account. Alpha has control of the 1000 shares under subsection (d)(1). Although Debtor may have become the beneficial owner of the new securities entitlement, as between Debtor and Alpha, Able has agreed to act on Alpha's entitlement orders because, as between Able and Alpha, Alpha has become the entitlement holder. See Section 8-506.

Example 2: Debtor grants Alpha Bank a security interest in a security entitlement that includes 1000 shares of XYZ Co. stock that Debtor holds through an account with Able & Co. Alpha does not have an account with Able. Alpha uses Beta Bank as its securities custodian. Debtor instructs Able to transfer the shares to Beta Bank, for the account of Alpha, and Able does so. Alpha has control of the 1000 shares under subsection (d)(1). As in Example 1, although Debtor may have become the beneficial owner of the new securities entitlement, as between Debtor and Alpha, Beta has agreed to act on Alpha's entitlement orders because, as between Beta and Alpha, Alpha has become the entitlement holder.

Example 3: Debtor grants Alpha Bank a security interest in a security entitlement that includes 1000 shares of XYZ Co. stock that Debtor holds through an account with Able & Co. Debtor, Able, and Alpha enter into an agreement under which Debtor will continue to receive dividends and distributions, and will continue to have the right to direct dispositions, but Alpha also has the right to direct dispositions. Alpha has control of the 1000 shares under subsection (d)(2).

Example 4: Able & Co., a securities dealer, grants Alpha Bank a security interest in a security entitlement that includes 1000 shares of XYZ Co. stock that Able holds through an account with Clearing Corporation. Able causes Clearing Corporation to transfer the shares into Alpha's account at Clearing Corporation. As in Example 1, Alpha has control of the 1000 shares under subsection (d)(1).

Example 5: Able & Co., a securities dealer, grants Alpha Bank a security interest in a security entitlement that includes 1000 shares of XYZ Co. stock that Able holds through an account with Clearing Corporation. Alpha does not have an account with Clearing Corporation. It holds its securities through Beta Bank, which does have an account with Clearing Corporation. Able causes Clearing Corporation to transfer the shares into Beta's account at Clearing Corporation. Beta credits the position to Alpha's account with Beta. As in Example 2, Alpha has control of the 1000 shares under subsection (d)(1).

Example 6: Able & Co. a securities dealer, grants Alpha Bank a security interest in a security entitlement that includes 1000 shares of XYZ Co. stock that Able holds through an account with Clearing Corporation. Able causes Clearing Corporation to transfer the shares into a pledge account, pursuant to an agreement under which Able will continue to receive dividends, distributions, and the like, but Alpha has the right to direct dispositions. As in Example 3, Alpha has control of the 1000 shares under subsection (d)(2).

Example 7: Able & Co. a securities dealer, grants Alpha Bank a security interest in a security entitlement that includes 1000 shares of XYZ Co. stock that Able holds through an account with Clearing Corporation. Able, Alpha, and Clearing Corporation enter into an agreement under which Clearing Corporation will act on instructions from Alpha with respect to the XYZ Co. stock carried in Able's account, but Able will continue to receive dividends, distributions, and the like, and will also have the right to direct dispositions. As in Example 3, Alpha has control of the 1000 shares under subsection (d)(2).

Example 8: Able & Co. a securities dealer, holds a wide range of securities through its account at Clearing

Corporation. Able enters into an arrangement with Alpha Bank pursuant to which Alpha provides financing to Able secured by securities identified as the collateral on lists provided by Able to Alpha on a daily or other periodic basis. Able, Alpha, and Clearing Corporation enter into an agreement under which Clearing Corporation agrees that if at any time Alpha directs Clearing Corporation to do so, Clearing Corporation will transfer any securities from Able's account at Alpha's instructions. Because Clearing Corporation has agreed to act on Alpha's instructions with respect to any securities carried in Able's account, at the moment that Alpha's security interest attaches to securities listed by Able, Alpha obtains control of those securities under subsection (d)(2). There is no requirement that Clearing Corporation be informed of which securities Able has pledged to Alpha.

Example 9: Debtor grants Alpha Bank a security interest in a security entitlement that includes 1000 shares of XYZ Co. stock that Debtor holds through an account with Able & Co. Beta Bank agrees with Alpha to act as Alpha's collateral agent with respect to the security entitlement. Debtor, Able, and Beta enter into an agreement under which Debtor will continue to receive dividends and distributions, and will continue to have the right to direct dispositions, but Beta also has the right to direct dispositions. Because Able has agreed that it will comply with entitlement orders originated by Beta without further consent by Debtor, Beta has control of the security entitlement (see Example 3). Because Beta has acknowledged that is has control on behalf of Alpha, Alpha also has control under subsection (d)(3). It is not necessary for Able to enter into an agreement directly with Alpha or for Able to be aware of Beta's agency relationship with Alpha.

4A. Pursuant to the 2022 Amendments, subsection (d)(3) was revised to conform the provision for control through another person to the corresponding provisions for control of other types of assets. *See* Section 12-105, Comment 8; see also Sections 7-106(g) (control of electronic document of title); 9-104(a)(4) (control of deposit account); 9-105(g) (control of authoritative electronic copy of a record evidencing chattel paper); 9-105A(e) (control of electronic money). Control based on an acknowledgment under subsection (d)(3) by another person having control continues only while the other person retains control. This result necessarily follows because such control derives solely from the other person's continued control. Under subsection (d)(3), for an acknowledgment to be effective to confer control, it must be made by a person "other than the transferor of an interest in the security entitlement." See Section 12-105, Comment 9 (discussing the rationale for this requirement). Subsections (h) and (i) derive from Section 9-313(f) and (g). Subsection (h) makes clear that a person that has control under this section has no duty to acknowledge that it has or will obtain control on behalf of a purchaser. Arrangements for a person to acknowledge that it has or will obtain control on behalf of another person are not standardized. Accordingly, subsection (i) leaves to the agreement of the parties and to any other applicable law (other than this Article or Article 9) any duties of a person that does acknowledge that it has or will obtain control on behalf of a purchaser and provides that a person making an acknowledgment is not required to confirm the acknowledgment to any other person.

5. For a purchaser to have "control" under subsection (c)(2) or (d)(2), it is essential that the issuer or securities intermediary, as the case may be, actually be a party to the agreement. If a debtor gives a secured party a power of attorney authorizing the secured party to act in the name of the debtor, but the issuer or securities intermediary does not specifically agree to this arrangement, the secured party does not have "control" within the meaning of subsection (c)(2) or (d)(2) because the issuer or securities intermediary is not a party to the agreement. The secured party does not have control under subsection (c)(1) or (d)(1) because, although the power of attorney might give the secured party authority to act on the debtor's behalf as an agent, the secured party has not actually become the registered owner or entitlement holder.

6. Subsection (e) provides that if an interest in a security entitlement is granted by an entitlement holder to the securities intermediary through which the security entitlement is maintained, the securities intermediary has control. A common transaction covered by this provision is a margin loan from a broker to its customer.

7. The term "control" is used in a particular defined sense. The requirements for obtaining control are set out in this section. The concept is not to be interpreted by reference to similar concepts in other bodies of law. In particular, the requirements for "possession" derived from the common law of pledge are not to be used as a basis for interpreting subsection (c)(2) or (d)(2). Those provisions are designed to supplant the concepts of "constructive possession" and the like. A principal purpose of the "control" concept is to eliminate the uncertainty and confusion that results from attempting to apply common law possession concepts to modern securities holding practices.

The key to the control concept is that the purchaser has the ability to have the securities sold or transferred without further action by the transferor. There is no requirement that the powers held by the purchaser be exclusive. For example, in a secured lending arrangement, if the secured party wishes, it can allow the debtor to retain the right to make substitutions, to direct the disposition of the uncertificated security or security entitlement, or otherwise to give instructions or entitlement orders. (As explained in Section 8-102, Comment 8, an entitlement order includes a direction under Section 8-508 to the securities intermediary to transfer a financial asset to the account of the entitlement holder at another financial intermediary or to cause the financial asset to be transferred to the entitlement holder in the direct holding system (e.g., by delivery of a securities certificate registered in the name of the former entitlement holder).) Subsection (f) is included to make clear the general point stated in subsections (c) and (d) that the test of control is whether the purchaser has obtained the requisite power, not whether the debtor has retained other powers. There is no implication that retention by the debtor of powers other than those mentioned in subsection (f) is inconsistent with the purchaser having control. Nor is there a requirement that the purchaser's powers be unconditional, provided that further consent of the entitlement holder is not a condition.

Example 10: Debtor grants to Alpha Bank and to Beta Bank a security interest in a security entitlement that includes 1000 shares of XYZ Co. stock that Debtor holds through an account with Able & Co. By agreement among the parties, Alpha's security interest is senior and Beta's is junior. Able agrees to act on the entitlement orders of either Alpha or Beta. Alpha and Beta each has control under subsection (d)(2). Moreover, Beta has control notwithstanding a term of Able's agreement to the effect that Able's obligation to act on Beta's entitlement orders is conditioned on Alpha's consent. The crucial distinction is that Able's agreement to act on Beta's entitlement orders is not conditioned on Debtor's further consent.

Example 11: Debtor grants to Alpha Bank a security interest in a security entitlement that includes 1000 shares of XYZ Co. stock that Debtor holds through an account with Able & Co. Able agrees to act on the entitlement orders of Alpha, but Alpha's right to give entitlement orders to the securities intermediary is conditioned on the Debtor's default. Alternatively, Alpha's right to give entitlement orders is conditioned upon Alpha's statement to Able that Debtor is in default. Because Able's agreement to act on Alpha's entitlement orders is not conditioned on Debtor's further consent, Alpha has control of the securities entitlement under either alternative.

In many situations, it will be better practice for both the securities intermediary and the purchaser to insist that any conditions relating in any way to the entitlement holder be effective only as between the purchaser and the entitlement holder. That practice would avoid the risk that the securities intermediary could be caught between conflicting assertions of the entitlement holder and the purchaser as to whether the conditions in fact have been met. Nonetheless, the existence of unfulfilled conditions effective against the intermediary would not preclude the purchaser from having control.

Definitional Cross References:

"Bearer form"	Section 8-102(a)(2)
"Certificated security"	Section 8-102(a)(4)
"Delivery"	Section 8-301
"Effective"	Section 8-107
"Entitlement holder"	Section 8-102(a)(7)
"Entitlement order"	Section 8-102(a)(8)
"Indorsement"	Section 8-102(a)(11)
"Instruction"	Section 8-102(a)(12)
"Purchaser"	Sections 1-201(b)(30) and 8-116
"Registered form"	Section 8-102(a)(13)
"Securities intermediary"	Section 8-102(a)(14)
"Security entitlement"	Section 8-102(a)(17)
"Uncertificated security"	Section 8-102(a)(18)

Section 8-107. Whether Indorsement, Instruction, or Entitlement Order Is Effective

(a) "Appropriate person" means:

(1) with respect to an indorsement, the person specified by a security certificate or by an effective special indorsement to be entitled to the security;

(2) with respect to an instruction, the registered owner of an uncertificated security;

(3) with respect to an entitlement order, the entitlement holder;

(4) if the person designated in paragraph (1), (2), or (3) is deceased, the designated person's successor taking under other law or the designated person's personal representative acting for the estate of the decedent; or

(5) if the person designated in paragraph (1), (2), or (3) lacks capacity, the designated person's guardian, conservator, or other similar representative who has power under other law to transfer the security or financial asset.

(b) An indorsement, instruction, or entitlement order is effective if:

(1) it is made by the appropriate person;

(2) it is made by a person who has power under the law of agency to transfer the security or financial asset on behalf of the appropriate person, including, in the case of an instruction or entitlement order, a person who has control under Section 8-106(c)(2) or (d)(2); or

(3) the appropriate person has ratified it or is otherwise precluded from asserting its ineffectiveness.

(c) An indorsement, instruction, or entitlement order made by a representative is effective even if:

(1) the representative has failed to comply with a controlling instrument or with the law of the State having jurisdiction of the representative relationship, including any law requiring the representative to obtain court approval of the transaction; or

(2) the representative's action in making the indorsement, instruction, or entitlement order or using the proceeds of the transaction is otherwise a breach of duty.

(d) If a security is registered in the name of or specially indorsed to a person described as a representative, or if a securities account is maintained in the name of a person described as a representative, an indorsement, instruction, or entitlement order made by the person is effective even though the person is no longer serving in the described capacity.

(e) Effectiveness of an indorsement, instruction, or entitlement order is determined as of the date the indorsement, instruction, or entitlement order is made, and an indorsement, instruction, or entitlement order does not become ineffective by reason of any later change of circumstances.

Official Comment

1. This section defines two concepts, "appropriate person" and "effective." Effectiveness is a broader concept than appropriate person. For example, if a security or securities account is registered in the name of Mary Roe, Mary Roe is the "appropriate person," but an indorsement, instruction, or entitlement order made by John Doe is "effective" if, under agency or other law, Mary Roe is precluded from denying Doe's authority. Treating these two concepts separately facilitates statement of the rules of Article 8 that state the legal effect of an indorsement, instruction, or entitlement order. For example, a securities intermediary is protected against liability if it acts on an effective entitlement order, but has a duty to comply with an entitlement order only if it is originated by an appropriate person. See Sections 8-115 and 8-507.

One important application of the "effectiveness" concept is in the direct holding system rules on the rights of purchasers. A purchaser of a certificated security in registered form can qualify as a protected purchaser who takes free from adverse claims under Section 8-303 only if the purchaser obtains "control." Section 8-106 provides that a purchaser of a certificated security in registered form obtains control if there has been an "effective" indorsement.

2. Subsection (a) provides that the term "appropriate person" covers two categories: (1) the person who is actually designated as the person entitled to the security or security entitlement, and (2) the successor or legal representative of that person if that person has died or otherwise lacks capacity. Other law determines who has power to transfer a security on behalf of a person who lacks capacity. For example, if securities are registered in the name of more than one person and one of the designated persons dies, whether the survivor is the appropriate person depends on the form of tenancy. If the two were registered joint tenants with right of survivorship, the survivor would have that power under other law and thus would be the "appropriate person." If securities are registered in the name of an individual and the individual dies, the law of decedents' estates determines who has power to transfer the decedent's securities. That would ordinarily be the executor or administrator, but if a "small estate statute" permits a widow to transfer a decedent's securities without administration proceedings, she would be the appropriate person. If the registration of a security or a securities account contains a designation of a death beneficiary under the Uniform Transfer on Death Security Registration Act or comparable legislation, the designated beneficiary would, under that law, have power to transfer upon the person's death and so would be the appropriate person. Article 8 does not contain a list of such representatives, because any list is likely to become outdated by developments in other law.

3. Subsection (b) sets out the general rule that an indorsement, instruction, or entitlement order is effective if it is made by the appropriate person or by a person who has power to transfer under agency law or if the appropriate person is precluded from denying its effectiveness. The control rules in Section 8-106 provide for arrangements where a person who holds securities through a securities intermediary, or holds uncertificated securities directly, enters into a control agreement giving the secured party the right to initiate entitlement orders of instructions. Paragraph 2 of subsection (b) states explicitly that an entitlement order or instruction initiated by a person who has obtained such a control agreement is "effective."

Subsections (c), (d), and (e) supplement the general rule of subsection (b) on effectiveness. The term "representative," used in subsections (c) and (d), is defined in Section 1-201(b)(33).

4. Subsection (c) provides that an indorsement, instruction, or entitlement order made by a representative is effective even though the representative's action is a violation of duties. The following example illustrates this subsection:

> **Example 1:** Certificated securities are registered in the name of John Doe. Doe dies and Mary Roe is appointed executor. Roe indorses the security certificate and transfers it to a purchaser in a transaction that is a violation of her duties as executor.

Roe's indorsement is effective, because Roe is the appropriate person under subsection (a)(4). This is so even though Roe's transfer violated her obligations as executor. The policies of free transferability of securities that underlie Article 8 dictate that neither a purchaser to whom Roe transfers the securities nor the issuer who registers transfer should be required to investigate the terms of the will to determine whether Roe is acting properly. Although Roe's indorsement is effective under this section, her breach of duty may be such that her beneficiary has an adverse claim to the securities that Roe transferred. The question whether that adverse claim can be asserted against purchasers is governed not by this section but by Section 8-303. Under Section 8-404, the issuer has no duties to an adverse claimant unless the claimant obtains legal process enjoining the issuer from registering transfer.

5. Subsection (d) deals with cases where a security or a securities account is registered in the name of a person specifically designated as a representative. The following example illustrates this subsection:

> **Example 2:** Certificated securities are registered in the name of "John Jones, trustee of the Smith Family Trust." John Jones is removed as trustee and Martha Moe is appointed successor trustee. The securities, however, are not reregistered, but remain registered in the name of "John Jones, trustee of the Smith Family Trust." Jones indorses the security certificate and transfers it to a purchaser.

Subsection (d) provides that an indorsement by John Jones as trustee is effective even though Jones is no longer serving in that capacity. Since the securities were registered in the name of "John Jones, trustee of the Smith Family Trust," a purchaser, or the issuer when called upon to register transfer, should be entitled to assume without further inquiry that Jones has the power to act as trustee for the Smith Family Trust.

Note that subsection (d) does not apply to a case where the security or securities account is registered in the name of principal rather than the representative as such. The following example illustrates this point:

> **Example 3:** Certificated securities are registered in the name of John Doe. John Doe dies and Mary Roe is appointed executor. The securities are not reregistered in the name of Mary Roe as executor. Later, Mary Roe is removed as executor and Martha Moe is appointed as her successor. After being removed, Mary Roe indorses the security certificate that is registered in the name of John Doe and transfers it to a purchaser.

Mary Roe's indorsement is not made effective by subsection (d), because the securities were not registered in the name of Mary Roe as representative. A purchaser or the issuer registering transfer should be required to determine whether Roe has power to act for John Doe. Purchasers and issuers can protect themselves in such cases by requiring signature guaranties. See Section 8-306.

6. Subsection (e) provides that the effectiveness of an indorsement, instruction, or entitlement order is determined as of the date it is made. The following example illustrates this subsection:

> **Example 4:** Certificated securities are registered in the name of John Doe. John Doe dies and Mary Roe is appointed executor. Mary Roe indorses the security certificate that is registered in the name of John Doe and transfers it to a purchaser. After the indorsement and transfer, but before the security certificate is presented to the issuer for registration of transfer, Mary Roe is removed as executor and Martha Moe is appointed as her successor.

Mary Roe's indorsement is effective, because at the time Roe indorsed she was the appropriate person under subsection (a)(4). Her later removal as executor does not render the indorsement ineffective. Accordingly, the issuer would not be liable for registering the transfer. See Section 8-404.

Definitional Cross References:

"Entitlement order"	Section 8-102(a)(8)
"Financial asset"	Section 8-102(a)(9)
"Indorsement"	Section 8-102(a)(11)
"Instruction"	Section 8-102(a)(12)
"Representative"	Section 1-201(b)(33)
"Securities account"	Section 8-501
"Security"	Section 8-102(a)(15)
"Security certificate"	Section 8-102(a)(16)
"Security entitlement"	Section 8-102(a)(17)
"Uncertificated security"	Section 8-102(a)(18)

Section 8-108. Warranties in Direct Holding

(a) A person who transfers a certificated security to a purchaser for value warrants to the purchaser, and an indorser, if the transfer is by indorsement, warrants to any subsequent purchaser, that:

(1) the certificate is genuine and has not been materially altered;

(2) the transferor or indorser does not know of any fact that might impair the validity of the security;

(3) there is no adverse claim to the security;

(4) the transfer does not violate any restriction on transfer;

(5) if the transfer is by indorsement, the indorsement is made by an appropriate person, or if the indorsement is by an agent, the agent has actual authority to act on behalf of the appropriate person; and

(6) the transfer is otherwise effective and rightful.

(b) A person who originates an instruction for registration of transfer of an uncertificated security to a purchaser for value warrants to the purchaser that:

(1) the instruction is made by an appropriate person, or if the instruction is by an agent, the agent has actual authority to act on behalf of the appropriate person;

(2) the security is valid;

(3) there is no adverse claim to the security; and

(4) at the time the instruction is presented to the issuer:

(i) the purchaser will be entitled to the registration of transfer;

(ii) the transfer will be registered by the issuer free from all liens, security interests, restrictions, and claims other than those specified in the instruction;

(iii) the transfer will not violate any restriction on transfer; and

(iv) the requested transfer will otherwise be effective and rightful.

(c) A person who transfers an uncertificated security to a purchaser for value and does not originate an instruction in connection with the transfer warrants that:

(1) the uncertificated security is valid;

(2) there is no adverse claim to the security;

(3) the transfer does not violate any restriction on transfer; and

(4) the transfer is otherwise effective and rightful.

(d) A person who indorses a security certificate warrants to the issuer that:

(1) there is no adverse claim to the security; and

(2) the indorsement is effective.

(e) A person who originates an instruction for registration of transfer of an uncertificated security warrants to the issuer that:

(1) the instruction is effective; and

(2) at the time the instruction is presented to the issuer the purchaser will be entitled to the registration of transfer.

(f) A person who presents a certificated security for registration of transfer or for payment or exchange warrants to the issuer that the person is entitled to the registration, payment, or exchange, but a purchaser for value and without notice of adverse claims to whom transfer is registered warrants only that the person has no knowledge of any unauthorized signature in a necessary indorsement.

(g) If a person acts as agent of another in delivering a certificated security to a purchaser, the identity of the principal was known to the person to whom the certificate was delivered, and the certificate delivered by the agent was received by the agent from the principal or received by the agent from another person at the direction of the principal, the person delivering the security certificate warrants only that the delivering person has authority to act for the principal and does not know of any adverse claim to the certificated security.

(h) A secured party who redelivers a security certificate received, or after payment and on order of the debtor delivers the security certificate to another person, makes only the warranties of an agent under subsection (g).

(i) Except as otherwise provided in subsection (g), a broker acting for a customer makes to the issuer and a purchaser the warranties provided in subsections (a) through (f). A broker that delivers a security certificate to its customer, or causes its customer to be registered as the owner of an uncertificated security, makes to the customer the warranties provided in subsection (a) or (b), and has the rights and privileges of a purchaser under this section. The warranties of and in favor of the broker acting as an agent are in addition to applicable warranties given by and in favor of the customer.

Official Comment

1. Subsections (a), (b), and (c) deal with warranties by security transferors to purchasers. Subsections (d) and (e) deal with warranties by security transferors to issuers. Subsection (f) deals with presentment warranties.

2. Subsection (a) specifies the warranties made by a person who transfers a certificated security to a purchaser for value. Paragraphs (3), (4), and (5) make explicit several key points that are implicit in the general warranty of paragraph (6) that the transfer is effective and rightful. Subsection (b) sets forth the warranties made to a purchaser for value by one who originates an instruction. These warranties are quite similar to those made by one transferring a certificated security, subsection (a), the principal difference being the absolute warranty of validity. If upon receipt of the instruction the issuer should dispute the validity of the security, the burden of proving validity is upon the transferor. Subsection (c) provides for the limited circumstances in which an uncertificated security could be transferred without an instruction, see Section 8-301(b)(2). Subsections (d) and (e) give the issuer the benefit of the warranties of an indorser or originator on those matters not within the issuer's knowledge.

3. Subsection (f) limits the warranties made by a purchaser for value without notice whose presentation of a security certificate is defective in some way but to whom the issuer does register transfer. The effect is to deny the issuer a remedy against such a person unless at the time of presentment the person had knowledge of an unauthorized signature in a necessary indorsement. The issuer can protect itself by refusing to make the transfer or, if it registers the transfer before it discovers the defect, by pursuing its remedy against a signature guarantor.

4. Subsection (g) eliminates all substantive warranties in the relatively unusual case of a delivery of certificated security by an agent of a disclosed principal where the agent delivers the exact certificate that it received from or for the principal. Subsection (h) limits the warranties given by a secured party who redelivers a certificate. Subsection (i) specifies the warranties of brokers in the more common scenarios.

5. Under Section 1-302(a) the warranty provisions apply "unless otherwise agreed" and the parties may enter into express agreements to allocate the risks of possible defects. Usual estoppel principles apply with respect to transfers of both certificated and uncertificated securities whenever the purchaser has knowledge of the defect, and these warranties will not be breached in such a case.

Definitional Cross References:

"Adverse claim"	Section 8-102(a)(1)
"Appropriate person"	Section 8-107
"Broker"	Section 8-102(a)(3)
"Certificated security"	Section 8-102(a)(4)
"Indorsement"	Section 8-102(a)(11)
"Instruction"	Section 8-102(a)(12)
"Issuer"	Section 8-201
"Person"	Section 1-201(b)(27)
"Purchaser"	Sections 1-201(b)(30) and 8-116
"Secured party"	Section 9-102(a)(73)
"Security"	Section 8-102(a)(15)
"Security certificate"	Section 8-102(a)(16)
"Uncertificated security"	Section 8-102(a)(18)
"Value"	Sections 1-204 and 8-116

Section 8-109. Warranties in Indirect Holding

(a) A person who originates an entitlement order to a securities intermediary warrants to the securities intermediary that:

(1) the entitlement order is made by an appropriate person, or if the entitlement order is by an agent, the agent has actual authority to act on behalf of the appropriate person; and

(2) there is no adverse claim to the security entitlement.

(b) A person who delivers a security certificate to a securities intermediary for credit to a securities account or originates an instruction with respect to an uncertificated security directing that the uncertificated security be credited to a securities account makes to the securities intermediary the warranties specified in Section 8-108(a) or (b).

(c) If a securities intermediary delivers a security certificate to its entitlement holder or causes its entitlement holder to be registered as the owner of an uncertificated security, the securities intermediary makes to the entitlement holder the warranties specified in Section 8-108(a) or (b).

Official Comment

1. Subsection (a) provides that a person who originates an entitlement order warrants to the securities intermediary that the order is authorized, and warrants the absence of adverse claims. Subsection (b) specifies the warranties that are given when a person who holds securities directly has the holding converted into indirect form. A person who delivers a certificate to a securities intermediary or originates an instruction for an uncertificated security gives to the securities intermediary the transfer warranties under Section 8-108. If the securities intermediary in turn delivers the certificate to a higher level securities intermediary, it gives the same warranties.

2. Subsection (c) states the warranties that a securities intermediary gives when a customer who has been holding securities in an account with the securities intermediary requests that certificates be delivered or that uncertificated securities be registered in the customer's name. The warranties are the same as those that brokers make with respect to securities that the brokers sell to or buy on behalf of the customers. See Section 8-108(i).

3. As with the Section 8-108 warranties, the warranties specified in this section may be modified by agreement under Section 1-302(a).

Definitional Cross References:

"Adverse claim"	Section 8-102(a)(1)
"Appropriate person"	Section 8-107
"Entitlement holder"	Section 8-102(a)(7)
"Entitlement order"	Section 8-102(a)(8)
"Instruction"	Section 8-102(a)(12)
"Person"	Section 1-201(b)(27)
"Securities account"	Section 8-501
"Securities intermediary"	Section 8-102(a)(14)
"Security certificate"	Section 8-102(a)(16)
"Uncertificated security"	Section 8-102(a)(18)

Section 8-110. Applicability; Choice of Law

(a) The local law of the issuer's jurisdiction, as specified in subsection (d), governs:

(1) the validity of a security;

(2) the rights and duties of the issuer with respect to registration of transfer;

(3) the effectiveness of registration of transfer by the issuer;

(4) whether the issuer owes any duties to an adverse claimant to a security; and

(5) whether an adverse claim can be asserted against a person to whom transfer of a certificated or uncertificated security is registered or a person who obtains control of an uncertificated security.

(b) The local law of the securities intermediary's jurisdiction, as specified in subsection (e), governs:

(1) acquisition of a security entitlement from the securities intermediary;

(2) the rights and duties of the securities intermediary and entitlement holder arising out of a security entitlement;

(3) whether the securities intermediary owes any duties to an adverse claimant to a security entitlement; and

(4) whether an adverse claim can be asserted against a person who acquires a security entitlement from the securities intermediary or a person who purchases a security entitlement or interest therein from an entitlement holder.

(c) The local law of the jurisdiction in which a security certificate is located at the time of delivery governs whether an adverse claim can be asserted against a person to whom the security certificate is delivered.

(d) "Issuer's jurisdiction" means the jurisdiction under which the issuer of the security is organized or, if permitted by the law of that jurisdiction, the law of another jurisdiction specified by the issuer. An issuer organized under the law of this State may specify the law of another jurisdiction as the law governing the matters specified in subsection (a)(2) through (5).

(e) The following rules determine a "securities intermediary's jurisdiction" for purposes of this section:

(1) If an agreement between the securities intermediary and its entitlement holder governing the securities account expressly provides that a particular jurisdiction is the securities intermediary's jurisdiction for purposes of this part, this article, or this [Act], that jurisdiction is the securities intermediary's jurisdiction.

(2) If paragraph (1) does not apply and an agreement between the securities intermediary and its entitlement holder governing the securities account expressly provides that the agreement is governed by the law of a particular jurisdiction, that jurisdiction is the securities intermediary's jurisdiction.

(3) If neither paragraph (1) nor paragraph (2) applies and an agreement between the securities intermediary and its entitlement holder governing the securities account expressly provides that the securities account is maintained at an office in a particular jurisdiction, that jurisdiction is the securities intermediary's jurisdiction.

(4) If none of the preceding paragraphs applies, the securities intermediary's jurisdiction is the jurisdiction in which the office identified in an account statement as the office serving the entitlement holder's account is located.

(5) If none of the preceding paragraphs applies, the securities intermediary's jurisdiction is the jurisdiction in which the chief executive office of the securities intermediary is located.

(f) A securities intermediary's jurisdiction is not determined by the physical location of certificates representing financial assets, or by the jurisdiction in which is organized the issuer of the financial asset with respect to which an entitlement holder has a security entitlement, or by the location of facilities for data processing or other record keeping concerning the account.

(g) The local law of the issuer's jurisdiction or the securities intermediary's jurisdiction governs a transaction specified in subsection (a) or (b) even if the matter or transaction does not bear any relation to the jurisdiction.

Official Comment

1. This section deals with applicability and choice of law issues concerning Article 8. The distinction between the direct and indirect holding systems plays a significant role in determining the governing law. An investor in the direct holding system is registered on the books of the issuer and/or has possession of a security certificate. Accordingly, the jurisdiction of incorporation of the issuer or location of the certificate determine the applicable law. By contrast, an investor in the indirect holding system has a security entitlement, which is a bundle of rights against the securities intermediary with respect to a security, rather than a direct interest in the underlying security. Accordingly, in the rules for the indirect holding system, the jurisdiction of incorporation of the issuer of the underlying security or the location of any certificates that might be held by the intermediary or a higher tier intermediary, do not determine the applicable law.

For securities in the indirect holding system, but not the direct holding system, this section's provisions are subject to the Convention on the Law Applicable to Certain Rights in Respect of Securities Held with an Intermediary (the "Convention" or "Hague Securities Convention"), to which the United States is a party. The Convention's primary rule is highly similar to this section, though there are potential differences as well. See Comments 3 and 5 through 7 below and PEB Commentary No. 19.

The Hague Securities Convention applies broadly to all instances "involving a choice between the laws of different [nations]", and can accordingly apply by reason of any of many elements, including without limitation a non-U.S. location of a party involved in the transaction, a non-U.S. party asserting an adverse claim, non-U.S. securities being credited to the securities account, or non-U.S. law being specified by the account agreement or other transaction document. Indeed one may wish to plan all indirect holding system transactions with the Hague Securities Convention as well as UCC Article 8 in mind, because even in transactions that appear wholly domestic, international factors may in fact be present (for example, if the securities intermediary holds securities for the entitlement holder through a non-U.S. intermediary) or may later become present (for example, if a non-U.S. party acquires an interest in or asserts an adverse claim to assets credited to the account).

In each of subsections (a), (b) and (c), the phrase "local law" refers to the law of a jurisdiction other than its conflict of laws rules. See Restatement (Second) of Conflict of Laws § 4.

2. Subsection (a) provides that the law of an issuer's jurisdiction governs certain issues where the substantive rules of Article 8 determine the issuer's rights and duties. Paragraph (1) of subsection (a) provides that the law of the issuer's jurisdiction governs the validity of the security. This ensures that a single body of law will govern the questions addressed in Part 2 of Article 8, concerning the circumstances in which an issuer can and cannot assert invalidity as a defense against purchasers. Similarly, paragraphs (2), (3), and (4) of subsection (a) ensure that the issuer will be able to look to a single body of law on the questions addressed in Part 4 of Article 8, concerning the issuer's duties and liabilities with respect to registration of transfer.

Paragraph (5) of subsection (a) applies the law of an issuer's jurisdiction to the question whether an adverse claim can be asserted against a purchaser to whom transfer has been registered, or who has obtained control over an uncertificated security. Although this issue deals with the rights of persons other than the issuer, the law of the issuer's jurisdiction applies because the purchasers to whom the provision applies are those whose protection against adverse claims depends on the fact that their interests have been recorded on the books of the issuer.

The principal policy reflected in the choice of law rules in subsection (a) is that an issuer and others should be able to look to a single body of law on the matters specified in subsection (a), rather than having to look to the law of all of the different jurisdictions in which security holders may reside. The choice of law policies reflected in this subsection do not require that the body of law governing all of the matters specified in subsection (a) be that of the jurisdiction in which the issuer is incorporated. Thus, subsection (d) provides that the term "issuer's jurisdiction" means the jurisdiction in which the issuer is organized, or, if permitted by that law, the law of another jurisdiction selected by the issuer. Subsection (d) also provides that issuers organized under the law of a State which adopts this Article may make such a selection, except as to the validity issue specified in paragraph (1). The question whether an issuer can assert the defense of invalidity may implicate significant policies of the issuer's jurisdiction of incorporation. See, e.g., Section 8-202 and Comments thereto.

Although subsection (a) provides that the issuer's rights and duties concerning registration of transfer are governed by the law of the issuer's jurisdiction, other matters related to registration of transfer, such as appointment of a guardian for a registered owner or the existence of agency relationships, might be governed by another jurisdiction's law. Neither this section nor Section 1-301 deals with what law governs the appointment of the administrator or executor; that question is determined under generally applicable choice of law rules.

3. Subsection (b) and, where the Hague Securities Convention applies, article 2(1) thereof provide that the law governing the issues concerning the indirect holding system that are dealt with in Article 8 are principally determined by the agreement between the securities intermediary and the entitlement holder governing the securities account.

Paragraphs (1) and (2) and Hague Securities Convention article 2(1)(a) cover the matters dealt with in the Article 8 rules defining the concept of security entitlement and specifying the duties of securities intermediaries. Paragraph (3) and Convention article 2(1)(e) cover whether the intermediary owes any duties to an adverse claimant. Paragraph (4) and Convention article 2(1)(a) and (d) cover whether adverse claims can be asserted against entitlement holders and others.

Subsection (e) and Hague Securities Convention article 4 provide that the account agreement may effectively determine the applicable law for the foregoing issues in either of two ways. Most directly and doubtless most frequently, under both subsection (e)(2) and article 4(1), the law chosen by the parties to govern the account agreement determines the applicable law. Alternatively, subsection (e)(1) and article 4(1) provide mutually comparable rules that require slightly different phrasing in the agreement. Under subsection (e)(1), if the account agreement expressly provides that a particular jurisdiction is the securities intermediary's jurisdiction for purposes of UCC Article 8, then that provision determines the applicable law, even if the agreement's overall governing law clause (if any) is different. Under Convention article 4(1)'s comparable rule, if the account agreement expressly provides that a particular jurisdiction's law is applicable to all the issues specified in article 2(1) of the Hague Securities Convention, then that provision determines the applicable law, even if the agreement's overall governing law clause (if any) is different. The policy is to ensure that a securities intermediary and all of its entitlement holders can look to a single, readily-identifiable body of law to determine their rights and duties.

Where the Hague Securities Convention applies, the foregoing provisions of an account agreement effectively determine the applicable law only if the intermediary, at the time of the agreement, had an office in the designated jurisdiction (which may be anywhere in the United States if the account agreement specifies a state of the United States) that is engaged in a regular activity of maintaining securities accounts (a "Qualifying Office"). However, because the policy of this section and the Convention is to enable parties to determine, in advance and with certainty, what law will apply to transactions governed by this Article, the validation of the parties' selection of governing law by agreement is not conditioned upon a determination that the jurisdiction whose law is chosen bear a "reasonable relation" to a matter or the transaction. Subsection (g) makes this explicit. See Comment 5A; see also Section 4A-507; compare Section 1-301(a). That is also true with respect to the similar provisions in subsection (d) of this section and in Section 9-305. The remaining paragraphs in subsection (e) and Convention article 5 contain additional default rules for determining the applicable law.

The Hague Securities Convention applies regardless of whether the law that it designates is that of a nation adhering thereto, though of course the Convention itself is the law only of adhering nations. The Convention applies to account agreements entered into before as well as after the Convention's effectiveness in the United States. However, for pre-Convention agreements that specify that a state of the United States is the securities intermediary's jurisdiction for purposes of UCC Article 8 and that do not expressly refer to the Convention, article 16(3) preserves the agreements' intended effect, by treating them as providing that the specified state's law is applicable to all the issues specified in article 2(1), if the Qualifying Office test is met. There is no doubt that the Convention, like UCC Article 8, applies to multiple tier holding arrangements, such as where the account holder holds through a broker which in turn holds through a clearing corporation.

Subsection (f) makes explicit a point that is implicit in the UCC Article 8 description of a security entitlement as a bundle of rights against the intermediary with respect to a security or other financial asset, rather than as a direct interest in the underlying security or other financial asset. The governing law for relationships in the indirect holding system is not determined by such matters as the jurisdiction of incorporation of the issuer of the securities held through the intermediary, or the location of any physical certificates held by the intermediary or a higher tier intermediary. Hague Securities Convention Article 6 is in accord.

4. Subsection (c) provides a choice of law rule for adverse claim issues that may arise in connection with delivery of security certificates in the direct holding system. It applies the law of the place of delivery. If a certificated security issued by an Idaho corporation is sold, and the sale is settled by physical delivery of the certificate from Seller to Buyer in New York, under subsection (c), New York law determines whether Buyer takes free from adverse claims. The domicile of Seller, Buyer, and any adverse claimant is irrelevant.

5. The following examples illustrate how a forum applying these rules would determine the governing law:

> **Example 1:** John Doe, a resident of Kansas, maintains a securities account with Able & Co. Able is incorporated in Delaware. Its chief executive offices are located in Illinois. The office where Doe transacts business with Able is located in Missouri. The agreement between Doe and Able provides that it is generally governed by the law of New York but also that Illinois is the securities intermediary's (Able's) jurisdiction for purposes of UCC Article 8 and that Illinois law is applicable to all the issues specified in article 2(1) of the Hague Securities Convention. Through the account, Doe holds securities of a Colorado corporation, which Able holds through Clearing Corporation. The rules of Clearing Corporation provide that the rights and duties of Clearing Corporation and its participants are governed by New York law. Subsection (a) specifies that a controversy concerning the rights and duties as between the issuer and Clearing Corporation is governed by Colorado law. Subsections (b) and (e) specify that a controversy concerning the rights and duties as between the Clearing Corporation and Able is governed by New York law, and that a controversy concerning the rights and duties as between Able and Doe is governed by Illinois law. Even if other facts cause the Hague Securities Convention to apply (see Comment 1), the Convention does not change the subsection (b) and (e) results, if at the time of the respective agreements Clearing Corporation and Able had offices in the United States engaged in a regular activity of maintaining securities accounts. The Convention does not apply to the subsection (a) result.

> **Example 2:** Same facts as to Doe and Able as in Example 1. Through the account, Doe holds securities of a Senegalese corporation, which Able holds through Clearing Corporation. Clearing Corporation's operations are located in Belgium, and its rules and agreements with its participants provide that they are governed by Belgian law. Clearing Corporation holds the securities through a custodial account at the Paris branch office of Global Bank, which is organized under English law. The agreement between Clearing Corporation and Global Bank provides that it is governed by French law. Subsection (a) specifies that a controversy concerning the rights and duties as between the issuer and Global Bank is governed by Senegalese law. Prior to United States implementation of the Hague Securities Convention, subsections (b) and (e) had the effect in a U.S. forum that a controversy concerning the rights and duties as between Global Bank and Clearing Corporation was governed by French law, that a controversy concerning the rights and duties as between Clearing Corporation and Able was governed by Belgian law, and that a controversy concerning the rights and duties as between Able and Doe was governed by Illinois law. Under the Convention, the subsection (b) and (e) results are unchanged, if at the time of the respective agreements Global Bank, Clearing Corporation and Able had offices in France, Belgium and the United States, respectively, engaged in a regular activity of maintaining securities accounts. The Convention does not apply to the subsection (a) result.

> **Example 3:** John Doe, a resident of Kansas, maintains a securities account with Able & Co. Able is organized in Switzerland and has its chief executive offices there. The agreement between Doe and Able provides that New York is the securities intermediary's jurisdiction for purposes of UCC Article 8. The agreement was entered into before the Hague Securities Convention's effectiveness in the United States, does not expressly provide that New York or any other law is applicable to all the issues specified in article 2(1) of the Hague Securities Convention, and does not otherwise expressly refer to the Convention. Through the account, Doe holds securities of a Japanese issuer. Roe, who lives in Japan, claims ownership of the securities and seeks to hold Able liable for not transferring the asset

to Roe. Because the agreement between Doe and Able was entered into before the Convention's effectiveness in the United States, Convention article 16(3) specifies that the controversy between Roe and Able is governed by the law of New York, but only if at the time of the agreement between Doe and Able, Able had an office in the United States engaged in a regular activity of maintaining securities accounts.

5A. Subsection (g) reflects what is stated in Comment 3—that the local law of the issuer's jurisdiction or securities intermediary's jurisdiction governs even if a matter or transaction bears no relation to that jurisdiction. This also is implicit in Section 1-301(c), which provides that the applicable law provided in this section (and other specified provisions) governs.

6. To the extent that this section or the Hague Securities Convention do not specify the governing law, general choice of law rules apply. For example, suppose that in Examples 1 or 2 in the preceding Comment [sic; should be Comment 5], Doe enters into an agreement with Roe in which Doe agrees to transfer all of his interests in the securities held through Able to Roe. Neither UCC Article 8 nor the Convention deals with whether such an agreement is enforceable or whether it gives Roe some interest in Doe's security entitlement. This section and the Convention specify what jurisdiction's law governs the issues that are dealt with in UCC Article 8 or listed in Convention article 2(1) respectively. UCC Article 8, however, does specify that securities intermediaries have only limited duties with respect to adverse claims. See Section 8-115. Subsection (b)(3) of this section and Convention article 2(1)(e) provide that Illinois law governs whether Able owes any duties to an adverse claimant. Thus, because Illinois has adopted Revised Article 8, Section 8-115 as enacted in Illinois determines whether Roe has any rights against Able.

7. The UCC choice of law provisions concerning security interests in securities and security entitlements are set out in Section 9-305, and within its scope the Hague Securities Convention also applies to such transactions.

Definitional Cross References:

"Adverse claim"	Section 8-102(a)(1)
"Agreement"	Section 1-201(b)(3)
"Certificated security"	Section 8-102(a)(4)
"Entitlement holder"	Section 8-102(a)(7)
"Financial asset"	Section 8-102(a)(9)
"Issuer"	Section 8-201
"Person"	Section 1-201(b)(27)
"Purchase"	Section 1-201(b)(29)
"Securities intermediary"	Section 8-102(a)(14)
"Security"	Section 8-102(a)(15)
"Security certificate"	Section 8-102(a)(16)
"Security entitlement"	Section 8-102(a)(17)
"Uncertificated security"	Section 8-102(a)(18)

Section 8-111. Clearing Corporation Rules

A rule adopted by a clearing corporation governing rights and obligations among the clearing corporation and its participants in the clearing corporation is effective even if the rule conflicts with this [Act] and affects another party who does not consent to the rule.

Official Comment

1. The experience of the past few decades shows that securities holding and settlement practices may develop rapidly, and in unforeseeable directions. Accordingly, it is desirable that the rules of Article 8 be adaptable both to ensure that commercial law can conform to changing practices and to ensure that commercial law does not operate as an obstacle to developments in securities practice. Even if practices were unchanging, it would not be possible in a general statute to specify in detail the rules needed to provide certainty in the operations of the clearance and settlement system.

The provisions of this Article and Article 1 on the effect of agreements provide considerable flexibility in the specification of the details of the rights and obligations of participants in the securities holding system by agreement. See Sections 8-504 through 8-509, and Section 1-302. Given the magnitude of the exposures involved in securities transactions, however, it may not be possible for the parties in developing practices to rely solely on private agreements, particularly with respect to matters that might affect others, such as creditors. For example, in order to be fully effective, rules of clearing corporations on the finality or reversibility of securities settlements must not only bind the participants in the clearing corporation but also be effective against their creditors. Section 8-111 provides that clearing corporation rules are effective even if they indirectly affect third parties, such as creditors of a participant. This provision does not, however, permit rules to be adopted that would govern the rights and obligations of third parties other than as a consequence of rules that specify the rights and obligations of the clearing corporation and its participants.

2. The definition of clearing corporation in Section 8-102 covers only federal reserve banks, entities registered as clearing agencies under the federal securities laws, and others subject to comparable regulation. The rules of registered clearing agencies are subject to regulatory oversight under the federal securities laws.

Definitional Cross Reference:

"Clearing corporation"	Section 8-102(a)(5)

Section 8-112. Creditor's Legal Process

(a) The interest of a debtor in a certificated security may be reached by a creditor only by actual seizure of the security certificate by the officer making the attachment or levy, except as otherwise provided in subsection (d). However, a certificated security for which the certificate has been surrendered to the issuer may be reached by a creditor by legal process upon the issuer.

(b) The interest of a debtor in an uncertificated security may be reached by a creditor only by legal process upon the issuer at its chief executive office in the United States, except as otherwise provided in subsection (d).

(c) The interest of a debtor in a security entitlement may be reached by a creditor only by legal process upon the securities intermediary with whom the debtor's securities account is maintained, except as otherwise provided in subsection (d).

(d) The interest of a debtor in a certificated security for which the certificate is in the possession of a secured party, or in an uncertificated security registered in the name of a secured party, or a security entitlement maintained in the name of a secured party, may be reached by a creditor by legal process upon the secured party.

(e) A creditor whose debtor is the owner of a certificated security, uncertificated security, or security entitlement is entitled to aid from a court of competent jurisdiction, by injunction or otherwise, in reaching the certificated security, uncertificated security, or security entitlement or in satisfying the claim by means allowed at law or in equity in regard to property that cannot readily be reached by other legal process.

Official Comment

1. In dealing with certificated securities the instrument itself is the vital thing, and therefore a valid levy cannot be made unless all possibility of the certificate's wrongfully finding its way into a transferee's hands has been removed. This can be accomplished only when the certificate is in the possession of a public officer, the issuer, or an independent third party. A debtor who has been enjoined can still transfer the security in contempt of court. See *Overlock v. Jerome-Portland Copper Mining Co.*, 243 P. 400 (Ariz. 1926). Therefore, although injunctive relief is provided in subsection (e) so that creditors may use this method to gain control of the certificated security, the security certificate itself must be reached to constitute a proper levy whenever the debtor has possession.

2. Subsection (b) provides that when the security is uncertificated and registered in the debtor's name, the debtor's interest can be reached only by legal process upon the issuer. The most logical place to serve the issuer would be the place where the transfer records are maintained, but that location might be difficult to identify, especially when the separate elements of a computer network might be situated in different places. The chief executive office is selected as the appropriate place by analogy to Section 9-307(b)(3). See Comment 2 to that section. This section indicates only how attachment is to be made, not when it is legally justified. For that reason there is no conflict between this section and *Shaffer v. Heitner*, 433 U.S. 186 (1977).

3. Subsection (c) provides that a security entitlement can be reached only by legal process upon the debtor's security intermediary. Process is effective only if directed to the debtor's own security intermediary. If Debtor holds securities through Broker, and Broker in turn holds through Clearing Corporation, Debtor's property interest is a security entitlement against Broker. Accordingly, Debtor's creditor cannot reach Debtor's interest by legal process directed to the Clearing Corporation. See also Section 8-115.

4. Subsection (d) provides that when a certificated security, an uncertificated security, or a security entitlement is controlled by a secured party, the debtor's interest can be reached by legal process upon the secured party. This section does not attempt to provide for rights as between the creditor and the secured party, as, for example, whether or when the secured party must liquidate the security.

Definitional Cross References:

"Certificated security"	Section 8-102(a)(4)
"Issuer"	Section 8-201
"Secured party"	Section 9-102(a)(73)
"Securities intermediary"	Section 8-102(a)(14)
"Security certificate"	Section 8-102(a)(16)
"Security entitlement"	Section 8-102(a)(17)
"Uncertificated security"	Section 8-102(a)(18)

Section 8-113. Statute of Frauds Inapplicable

A contract or modification of a contract for the sale or purchase of a security is enforceable whether or not there is a writing signed or record authenticated by a party against whom enforcement is sought, even if the contract or modification is not capable of performance within one year of its making.

Official Comment

This section provides that the statute of frauds does not apply to contracts for the sale of securities, reversing prior law which had a special statute of frauds in Section 8-319 (1978). With the increasing use of electronic means of communication, the statute of frauds is unsuited to the realities of the securities business. For securities transactions, whatever benefits a statute of frauds may play in filtering out fraudulent claims are outweighed by the obstacles it places in the development of modern commercial practices in the securities business.

Definitional Cross References:

"Action"	Section 1-201(b)(1)
"Contract"	Section 1-201(b)(11)
"Writing"	Section 1-201(b)(43)

Section 8-114. Evidentiary Rules Concerning Certificated Securities

The following rules apply in an action on a certificated security against the issuer:

(1) Unless specifically denied in the pleadings, each signature on a security certificate or in a necessary indorsement is admitted.

(2) If the effectiveness of a signature is put in issue, the burden of establishing effectiveness is on the party claiming under the signature, but the signature is presumed to be genuine or authorized.

(3) If signatures on a security certificate are admitted or established, production of the certificate entitles a holder to recover on it unless the defendant establishes a defense or a defect going to the validity of the security.

(4) If it is shown that a defense or defect exists, the plaintiff has the burden of establishing that the plaintiff or some person under whom the plaintiff claims is a person against whom the defense or defect cannot be asserted.

Official Comment

This section adapts the rules of negotiable instruments law concerning procedure in actions on instruments, see Section 3-308, to actions on certificated securities governed by this Article. An "action on a security" includes any action or proceeding brought against the issuer to enforce a right or interest that is part of the security, such as an action to collect principal or interest or a dividend, or to establish a right to vote or to receive a new security under an exchange offer or plan of reorganization. This section applies only to certificated securities; actions on uncertificated securities are governed by general evidentiary principles.

Definitional Cross References:

"Action"	Section 1-201(b)(1)
"Burden of establishing"	Section 1-201(b)(8)
"Certificated security"	Section 8-102(a)(4)
"Indorsement"	Section 8-102(a)(11)
"Issuer"	Section 8-201
"Presumed"	Section 1-206
"Security"	Section 8-102(a)(15)
"Security certificate"	Section 8-102(a)(16)

Section 8-115. Securities Intermediary and Others Not Liable to Adverse Claimant

A securities intermediary that has transferred a financial asset pursuant to an effective entitlement order, or a broker or other agent or bailee that has dealt with a financial asset at the direction of its customer or principal, is not liable to a person having an adverse claim to the financial asset, unless the securities intermediary, or broker or other agent or bailee:

(1) took the action after it had been served with an injunction, restraining order, or other legal process enjoining it from doing so, issued by a court of competent jurisdiction, and had a reasonable opportunity to act on the injunction, restraining order, or other legal process; or

(2) acted in collusion with the wrongdoer in violating the rights of the adverse claimant; or

(3) in the case of a security certificate that has been stolen, acted with notice of the adverse claim.

Official Comment

1. Other provisions of Article 8 protect certain purchasers against adverse claims, both for the direct holding system and the indirect holding system. See Sections 8-303 and 8-502. This section deals with the related question of the possible liability of a person who acted as the "conduit" for a securities transaction. It covers both securities intermediaries—the "conduits" in the indirect holding system—and brokers or other agents or bailees—the "conduits" in the direct holding system. The following examples illustrate its operation:

> **Example 1:** John Doe is a customer of the brokerage firm of Able & Co. Doe delivers to Able a certificate for 100 shares of XYZ Co. common stock, registered in Doe's name and properly indorsed, and asks the firm to sell it for him. Able does so. Later, John Doe's spouse Mary Doe brings an action against Able asserting that Able's action was wrongful against her because the XYZ Co. stock was marital property in which she had an interest, and John Doe was acting wrongfully against her in transferring the securities.

> **Example 2:** Mary Roe is a customer of the brokerage firm of Baker & Co. and holds her securities through a securities account with Baker. Roe instructs Baker to sell 100 shares of XYZ Co. common stock that she carried in her account. Baker does so. Later, Mary Roe's spouse John Roe brings an action against Baker asserting that Baker's action was wrongful against him because the XYZ Co. stock was marital property in which he had an interest, and Mary Roe was acting wrongfully against him in transferring the securities.

Under common law conversion principles, Mary Doe might be able to assert that Able & Co. is liable to her in Example 1 for exercising dominion over property inconsistent with her rights in it. On that or some similar theory John Roe might assert that Baker is liable to him in Example 2. Section 8-115 protects both Able and Baker from liability.

2. The policy of this section is similar to that of many other rules of law that protect agents and bailees from liability as innocent converters. If a thief steals property and ships it by mail, express service, or carrier, to another person, the recipient of the property does not obtain good title, even though the recipient may have given value to the thief and had no notice or knowledge that the property was stolen. Accordingly, the true owner can recover the property from the recipient or obtain damages in a conversion or similar action. An action against the postal service, express company, or carrier presents entirely different policy considerations. Accordingly, general tort law protects agents or bailees who act on the instructions of their principals or bailors. See Restatement (Second) of Torts § 235. See also UCC Section 7-404.

3. Except as provided in paragraph 3, this section applies even though the securities intermediary, or the broker or other agent or bailee, had notice or knowledge that another person asserts a claim to the securities. Consider the following examples:

> **Example 3:** Same facts as in Example 1, except that before John Doe brought the XYZ Co. security certificate to Able for sale, Mary Doe telephoned or wrote to the firm asserting that she had an interest in all of John Doe's securities and demanding that they not trade for him.

> **Example 4:** Same facts as in Example 2, except that before Mary Roe gave an entitlement order to Baker to sell the XYZ Co. securities from her account, John Roe telephoned or wrote to the firm asserting that he had an interest in all of Mary Roe's securities and demanding that they not trade for her.

Section 8-115 protects Able and Baker from liability. The protections of Section 8-115 do not depend on the presence or absence of notice of adverse claims. It is essential to the securities settlement system that brokers and securities intermediaries be able to act promptly on the directions of their customers. Even though a firm has notice that someone asserts a claim to a customer's securities or security entitlements, the firm should not be placed in the position of having to make a legal judgment about the validity of the claim at the risk of liability either to its customer or to the third party for guessing wrong. Under this section, the broker or securities intermediary is privileged to act on the instructions of its customer or entitlement holder, unless it has been served with a restraining order or other legal process enjoining it from doing so. This is already the law in many jurisdictions. For example a section of the New York Banking Law provides that banks need not recognize any adverse claim to funds or securities on deposit with them unless they have been served with legal process. N.Y. Banking Law § 134. Other sections of the UCC embody a similar policy. See Sections 3-602, 5-109(a)(2).

Paragraph (1) of this section refers only to a court order enjoining the securities intermediary or the broker or other agent or bailee from acting at the instructions of the customer. It does not apply to cases where the adverse claimant tells the intermediary or broker that the customer has been enjoined, or shows the intermediary or broker a copy of a court order binding the customer.

Paragraph (3) takes a different approach in one limited class of cases, those where a customer sells stolen certificated securities through a securities firm. Here the policies that lead to protection of securities firms against assertions of other sorts of claims must be weighed against the desirability of having securities firms guard against the disposition of stolen securities. Accordingly, paragraph (3) denies protection to a broker, custodian, or other agent or bailee who receives a stolen security certificate from its customer, if the broker, custodian, or other agent or bailee had notice of adverse claims. The circumstances that give notice of adverse claims are specified in Section 8-105. The result is that brokers, custodians, and other agents and bailees face the same liability for selling stolen certificated securities that purchasers face for buying them.

4. As applied to securities intermediaries, this section embodies one of the fundamental principles of the Article 8 indirect holding system rules—that a securities intermediary owes duties only to its own entitlement holders. The following examples illustrate the operation of this section in the multi-tiered indirect holding system:

> **Example 5:** Able & Co., a broker-dealer, holds 50,000 shares of XYZ Co. stock in its account at Clearing Corporation. Able acquired the XYZ shares from another firm, Baker & Co., in a transaction that Baker contends was tainted by fraud, giving Baker a right to rescind the transaction and recover the XYZ shares from Able. Baker sends notice to Clearing Corporation stating that Baker has a claim to the 50,000 shares of XYZ Co. in Able's account. Able then initiates an entitlement order directing Clearing Corporation to transfer the 50,000 shares of XYZ Co. to another firm in settlement of a trade. Under Section 8-115, Clearing Corporation is privileged to comply with Able's entitlement order, without fear of liability to Baker. This is so even though Clearing Corporation has notice of Baker's claim, unless Baker obtains a court order enjoining Clearing Corporation from acting on Able's entitlement order.

> **Example 6:** Able & Co., a broker-dealer, holds 50,000 shares of XYZ Co. stock in its account at Clearing Corporation. Able initiates an entitlement order directing Clearing Corporation to transfer the 50,000 shares of XYZ Co. to another firm in settlement of a trade. That trade was made by Able for its own account, and the proceeds were devoted to its own use. Able becomes insolvent, and it is discovered that Able has a shortfall in the shares of XYZ Co. stock that it should have been carrying for its customers. Able's customers bring an action against Clearing Corporation asserting that Clearing Corporation acted wrongfully in transferring the XYZ shares on Able's order because those were shares that should have been held by Able for its customers. Under Section 8-115, Clearing Corporation is not liable to Able's customers,

because Clearing Corporation acted on an effective entitlement order of its own entitlement holder, Able. Clearing Corporation's protection against liability does not depend on the presence or absence of notice or knowledge of the claim by Clearing Corporation.

5. If the conduct of a securities intermediary or a broker or other agent or bailee rises to a level of complicity in the wrongdoing of its customer or principal, the policies that favor protection against liability do not apply. Accordingly, paragraph (2) provides that the protections of this section do not apply if the securities intermediary or broker or other agent or bailee acted in collusion with the customer or principal in violating the rights of another person. The collusion test is intended to adopt a standard akin to the tort rules that determine whether a person is liable as an aider or abettor for the tortious conduct of a third party. See Restatement (Second) of Torts § 876.

Knowledge that the action of the customer is wrongful is a necessary but not sufficient condition of the collusion test. The aspect of the role of securities intermediaries and brokers that Article 8 deals with is the clerical or ministerial role of implementing and recording the securities transactions that their customers conduct. Faithful performance of this role consists of following the instructions of the customer. It is not the role of the record-keeper to police whether the transactions recorded are appropriate, so mere awareness that the customer may be acting wrongfully does not itself constitute collusion. That, of course, does not insulate an intermediary or broker from responsibility in egregious cases where its action goes beyond the ordinary standards of the business of implementing and recording transactions, and reaches a level of affirmative misconduct in assisting the customer in the commission of a wrong.

Definitional Cross References:

"Broker"	Section 8-102(a)(3)
"Effective"	Section 8-107
"Entitlement order"	Section 8-102(a)(8)
"Financial asset"	Section 8-102(a)(9)
"Securities intermediary"	Section 8-102(a)(14)
"Security certificate"	Section 8-102(a)(16)

Section 8-116. Securities Intermediary as Purchaser for Value

A securities intermediary that receives a financial asset and establishes a security entitlement to the financial asset in favor of an entitlement holder is a purchaser for value of the financial asset. A securities intermediary that acquires a security entitlement to a financial asset from another securities intermediary acquires the security entitlement for value if the securities intermediary acquiring the security entitlement establishes a security entitlement to the financial asset in favor of an entitlement holder.

Official Comment

1. This section is intended to make explicit two points that, while implicit in other provisions, are of sufficient importance to the operation of the indirect holding system that they warrant explicit statement. First, it makes clear that a securities intermediary that receives a financial asset and establishes a security entitlement in respect thereof in favor of an entitlement holder is a "purchaser" of the financial asset that the securities intermediary received. Second, it makes clear that by establishing a security entitlement in favor of an entitlement holder a securities intermediary gives value for any corresponding financial asset that the securities intermediary receives or acquires from another party, whether the intermediary holds directly or indirectly.

In many cases a securities intermediary that receives a financial asset will also be transferring value to the person from whom the financial asset was received. That, however, is not always the case. Payment may occur through a different system than settlement of the securities side of the transaction, or the securities might be transferred without a corresponding payment, as when a person moves an account from one securities intermediary to another. Even though the securities intermediary does not give value to the transferor, it does give value by incurring obligations to its own entitlement holder. Although the general definition of value in Section 1-204 should be interpreted to cover the point, this section is included to make this point explicit.

2. The following examples illustrate the effect of this section:

> **Example 1:** Buyer buys 1000 shares of XYZ Co. common stock through Buyer's broker Able & Co. to be held in Buyer's securities account. In settlement of the trade, the selling broker delivers to Able a security certificate in street name, indorsed in blank, for 1000 shares XYZ Co. stock, which Able holds in its vault. Able credits Buyer's account for securities in that amount. Section 8-116 specifies that Able is a purchaser of the XYZ Co. stock certificate, and gave value for it. Thus, Able can obtain the benefit of Section 8-303, which protects purchasers for value, if it satisfies the other requirements of that section.

> **Example 2:** Buyer buys 1000 shares XYZ Co. common stock through Buyer's broker Able & Co. to be held in Buyer's securities account. The trade is settled by crediting 1000 shares XYZ Co. stock to Able's account at Clearing Corporation. Able credits Buyer's account for securities in that amount. When Clearing Corporation credits Able's account, Able acquires a security entitlement under Section 8-501. Section 8-116 specifies that Able acquired this security entitlement for value. Thus, Able can obtain the benefit of Section 8-502, which protects persons who acquire security entitlements for value, if it satisfies the other requirements of that section.

Example 3: Thief steals a certificated bearer bond from Owner. Thief sends the certificate to his broker Able & Co. to be held in his securities account, and Able credits Thief's account for the bond. Section 8-116 specifies that Able is a purchaser of the bond and gave value for it. Thus, Able can obtain the benefit of Section 8-303, which protects purchasers for value, if it satisfies the other requirements of that section.

Definitional Cross References:

"Financial asset"	Section 8-102(a)(9)
"Securities intermediary"	Section 8-102(a)(14)
"Security entitlement"	Section 8-102(a)(17)
"Entitlement holder"	Section 8-102(a)(7)

PART 2. ISSUE AND ISSUER

Section 8-201. Issuer

(a) With respect to an obligation on or a defense to a security, an "issuer" includes a person that:

(1) places or authorizes the placing of its name on a security certificate, other than as authenticating trustee, registrar, transfer agent, or the like, to evidence a share, participation, or other interest in its property or in an enterprise, or to evidence its duty to perform an obligation represented by the certificate;

(2) creates a share, participation, or other interest in its property or in an enterprise, or undertakes an obligation, that is an uncertificated security;

(3) directly or indirectly creates a fractional interest in its rights or property, if the fractional interest is represented by a security certificate; or

(4) becomes responsible for, or in place of, another person described as an issuer in this section.

(b) With respect to an obligation on or defense to a security, a guarantor is an issuer to the extent of its guaranty, whether or not its obligation is noted on a security certificate.

(c) With respect to a registration of a transfer, issuer means a person on whose behalf transfer books are maintained.

Official Comment

1. The definition of "issuer" in this section functions primarily to describe the persons whose defenses may be cut off under the rules in Part 2. In large measure it simply tracks the language of the definition of security in Section 8-102(a)(15).

2. Subsection (b) distinguishes the obligations of a guarantor as issuer from those of the principal obligor. However, it does not exempt the guarantor from the impact of subsection (d) of Section 8-202. Whether or not the obligation of the guarantor is noted on the security is immaterial. Typically, guarantors are parent corporations, or stand in some similar relationship to the principal obligor. If that relationship existed at the time the security was originally issued the guaranty would probably have been noted on the security. However, if the relationship arose afterward, e.g., through a purchase of stock or properties, or through merger or consolidation, probably the notation would not have been made. Nonetheless, the holder of the security is entitled to the benefit of the obligation of the guarantor.

3. Subsection (c) narrows the definition of "issuer" for purposes of Part 4 of this Article (registration of transfer). It is supplemented by Section 8-407.

Definitional Cross References:

"Person"	Section 1-201(b)(27)
"Security"	Section 8-102(a)(15)
"Security certificate"	Section 8-102(a)(16)
"Uncertificated security"	Section 8-102(a)(18)

Section 8-202. Issuer's Responsibility and Defenses; Notice of Defect or Defense

(a) Even against a purchaser for value and without notice, the terms of a certificated security include terms stated on the certificate and terms made part of the security by reference on the certificate to another instrument, indenture, or document or to a constitution, statute, ordinance, rule, regulation, order, or the like, to the extent the terms referred to do not conflict with terms stated on the certificate. A reference under this subsection does not of itself charge a purchaser for value with notice of a defect going to the validity of the security, even if the certificate expressly states that a person accepting it admits notice. The terms of an uncertificated security include those stated in any instrument, indenture, or document or in a constitution, statute, ordinance, rule, regulation, order, or the like, pursuant to which the security is issued.

(b) The following rules apply if an issuer asserts that a security is not valid:

(1) A security other than one issued by a government or governmental subdivision, agency, or instrumentality, even though issued with a defect going to its validity, is valid in the hands of a purchaser for value and without notice of the particular defect unless the defect involves a violation of a constitutional provision. In that case, the security is valid in the hands of a purchaser for value and without notice of the defect, other than one who takes by original issue.

(2) Paragraph (1) applies to an issuer that is a government or governmental subdivision, agency, or instrumentality only if there has been substantial compliance with the legal requirements governing the issue or the issuer has received a substantial consideration for the issue as a whole or for the particular security and a stated purpose of the issue is one for which the issuer has power to borrow money or issue the security.

(c) Except as otherwise provided in Section 8-205, lack of genuineness of a certificated security is a complete defense, even against a purchaser for value and without notice.

(d) All other defenses of the issuer of a security, including nondelivery and conditional delivery of a certificated security, are ineffective against a purchaser for value who has taken the certificated security without notice of the particular defense.

(e) This section does not affect the right of a party to cancel a contract for a security "when, as and if issued" or "when distributed" in the event of a material change in the character of the security that is the subject of the contract or in the plan or arrangement pursuant to which the security is to be issued or distributed.

(f) If a security is held by a securities intermediary against whom an entitlement holder has a security entitlement with respect to the security, the issuer may not assert any defense that the issuer could not assert if the entitlement holder held the security directly.

Official Comment

1. In this Article the rights of the purchaser for value without notice are divided into two aspects, those against the issuer, and those against other claimants to the security. Part 2 of this Article, and especially this section, deal with rights against the issuer.

Subsection (a) states, in accordance with the prevailing case law, the right of the issuer (who prepares the text of the security) to include terms incorporated by adequate reference to an extrinsic source, so long as the terms so incorporated do not conflict with the stated terms. Thus, the standard practice of referring in a bond or debenture to the trust indenture under which it is issued without spelling out its necessarily complex and lengthy provisions is approved. Every stock certificate refers in some manner to the charter or articles of incorporation of the issuer. At least where there is more than one class of stock authorized applicable corporation codes specifically require a statement or summary as to preferences, voting powers and the like. References to constitutions, statutes, ordinances, rules, regulations or orders are not so common, except in the obligations of governments or governmental agencies or units; but where appropriate they fit into the rule here stated.

Courts have generally held that an issuer is estopped from denying representations made in the text of a security. *Delaware-New Jersey Ferry Co. v. Leeds*, 186 A. 913 (Del. Ch. Ct. 1936). Nor is a defect in form or the invalidity of a security normally available to the issuer as a defense. *Bonini v. Family Theatre Corp.*, 194 A. 498 (Pa. 1937); *First Nat'l Bank of Fairbanks v. Alaska Airmotive, Inc.*, 119 F.2d 267 (9th Cir. 1941).

2. The rule in subsection (a) requiring that the terms of a security be noted or referred to on the certificate is based on practices and expectations in the direct holding system for certificated securities. This rule does not express a general rule or policy that the terms of a security are effective only if they are communicated to beneficial owners in some particular fashion. Rather, subsection (a) is based on the principle that a purchaser who does obtain a certificate is entitled to assume that the terms of the security have been noted or referred to on the certificate. That policy does not come into play in a securities holding system in which purchasers do not take delivery of certificates.

The provisions of subsection (a) concerning notation of terms on security certificates are necessary only because paper certificates play such an important role for certificated securities that a purchaser should be protected against assertion of any defenses or rights that are not noted on the certificate. No similar problem exists with respect to uncertificated securities. The last sentence of subsection (a) is, strictly speaking, unnecessary, since it only recognizes the fact that the terms of an uncertificated security are determined by whatever other law or agreement governs the security. It is included only to preclude any inference that uncertificated securities are subject to any requirement analogous to the requirement of notation of terms on security certificates.

The rule of subsection (a) applies to the indirect holding system only in the sense that if a certificated security has been delivered to the clearing corporation or other securities intermediary, the terms of the security should be noted or referred to on the certificate. If the security is uncertificated, that principle does not apply even at the issuer-clearing corporation level. The beneficial owners who hold securities through the clearing corporation are bound by the terms of the security, even though they do not actually see the certificate. Since entitlement holders in an indirect holding system have not taken delivery of certificates, the policy of subsection (a) does not apply.

3. The penultimate sentence of subsection (a) and all of subsection (b) embody the concept that it is the duty of the issuer, not of the purchaser, to make sure that the security complies with the law governing its issue. The penultimate sentence of subsection (a) makes clear that the issuer cannot, by incorporating a reference to a statute or other document, charge the purchaser with notice of the security's invalidity. Subsection (b) gives to a purchaser for value without notice of the defect the right to enforce the security against the issuer despite the presence of a defect that otherwise would render the security invalid. There are three circumstances in which a purchaser does not gain such rights: first, if the defect involves a violation of constitutional provisions, these rights accrue only to a subsequent purchaser, that is, one who takes other than by original issue. This Article leaves to the law of each particular State the rights of a purchaser on original issue of a security with a constitutional defect. No negative implication is intended by the explicit grant of rights to a subsequent purchaser.

Second, governmental issuers are distinguished in subsection (b) from other issuers as a matter of public policy, and additional safeguards are imposed before governmental issues are validated. Governmental issuers are estopped from asserting defenses only if there has been substantial compliance with the legal requirements governing the issue or if substantial consideration has been received and a stated purpose of the issue is one for which the issuer has power to borrow money or issue the security. The purpose of the substantial compliance requirement is to make certain that a mere technicality as, e.g., in the manner of publishing election notices, shall not be a ground for depriving an innocent purchaser of rights in the security. The policy is here adopted of such cases as *Tommie v. City of Gadsden*, 158 So. 763 (Ala. 1935), in which minor discrepancies in the form of the election ballot used were overlooked and the bonds were declared valid since there had been substantial compliance with the statute.

A long and well established line of federal cases recognizes the principle of estoppel in favor of purchasers for value without notices where municipalities issue bonds containing recitals of compliance with governing constitutional and statutory provisions, made by the municipal authorities entrusted with determining such compliance. *Chaffee Cnty. v. Potter*, 142 U.S. 355 (1892); *Oregon v. Jennings*, 119 U.S. 74 (1886); *Gunnison Cnty. Comm'rs v. Rollins*, 173 U.S. 255 (1898). This rule has been qualified, however, by requiring that the municipality have power to issue the security. *Anthony v. County of Jasper*, 101 U.S. 693 (1879); *Town of South Ottawa v. Perkins*, 94 U.S. 260 (1876). This section follows the case law trend, simplifying the rule by setting up two conditions for an estoppel against a governmental issuer: (1) substantial consideration given, and (2) power in the issuer to borrow money or issue the security for the stated purpose. As a practical matter the problem of policing governmental issuers has been alleviated by the present practice of requiring legal opinions as to the validity of the issue. The bulk of the case law on this point is nearly 100 years old and it may be assumed that the question now seldom arises.

Section 8-210, regarding overissue, provides the third exception to the rule that an innocent purchase for value takes a valid security despite the presence of a defect that would otherwise give rise to invalidity. See that section and its Comment for further explanation.

4. Subsection (e) is included to make clear that this section does not affect the presently recognized right of either party to a "when, as and if" or "when distributed" contract to cancel the contract on substantial change.

5. Subsection (f) has been added because the introduction of the security entitlement concept requires some adaptation of the Part 2 rules, particularly those that distinguish between purchasers who take by original issue and subsequent purchasers. The basic concept of Part 2 is to apply to investment securities the principle of negotiable instruments law that an obligor is precluded from asserting most defenses against purchasers for value without notice. Section 8-202 describes in some detail which defenses issuers can raise against purchasers for value and subsequent purchasers for value. Because these rules were drafted with the direct holding system in mind, some interpretive problems might be presented in applying them to the indirect holding. For example, if a municipality issues a bond in book-entry only form, the only direct "purchaser" of that bond would be the clearing corporation. The policy of precluding the issuer from asserting defenses is, however, equally applicable. Subsection (f) is designed to ensure that the defense preclusion rules developed for the direct holding system will also apply to the indirect holding system.

Definitional Cross References:

"Certificated security"	Section 8-102(a)(4)
"Notice"	Section 1-202(a)
"Purchaser"	Sections 1-201(b)(30) and 8-116
"Security"	Section 8-102(a)(15)
"Uncertificated security"	Section 8-102(a)(18)
"Value"	Sections 1-204 and 8-116

Section 8-203. Staleness As Notice of Defect or Defense

After an act or event, other than a call that has been revoked, creating a right to immediate performance of the principal obligation represented by a certificated security or setting a date on or after which the security is to be presented or surrendered for redemption or exchange, a purchaser is charged with notice of any defect in its issue or defense of the issuer, if the act or event:

(1) requires the payment of money, the delivery of a certificated security, the registration of transfer of an uncertificated security, or any of them on presentation or surrender of the security certificate, the money or security is available on the date set for payment or exchange, and the purchaser takes the security more than one year after that date; or

(2) is not covered by paragraph (1) and the purchaser takes the security more than two years after the date set for surrender or presentation or the date on which performance became due.

Official Comment

1. The problem of matured or called securities is here dealt with in terms of the effect of such events in giving notice of the issuer's defenses and not in terms of "negotiability". The substance of this section applies only to certificated securities because certificates may be transferred to a purchaser by delivery after the security has matured, been called, or become redeemable or exchangeable. It is contemplated that uncertificated securities which have matured or been called will merely be canceled on the books of the issuer and the proceeds sent to the registered owner. Uncertificated securities which have become redeemable or exchangeable, at the option of the owner, may be transferred to a purchaser, but the transfer is effectuated only by registration of transfer, thus necessitating communication with the issuer. If defects or defenses in such securities exist, the issuer will necessarily have the opportunity to bring them to the attention of the purchaser.

2. The fact that a security certificate is in circulation long after it has been called for redemption or exchange must give rise to the question in a purchaser's mind as to why it has not been surrendered. After the lapse of a reasonable period of time a purchaser can no longer claim "no reason to know" of any defects or irregularities in its issue. Where funds are available for the redemption the security certificate is normally turned in more promptly and a shorter time is set as the "reasonable period" than is set where funds are not available.

Defaulted certificated securities may be traded on financial markets in the same manner as unmatured and undefaulted instruments and a purchaser might not be placed upon notice of irregularity by the mere fact of default. An issuer, however, should at some point be placed in a position to determine definitely its liability on an invalid or improper issue, and for this purpose a security under this section becomes "stale" two years after the default. A different rule applies when the question is notice not of issuer's defenses but of claims of ownership. Section 8-105 and Comment.

3. Nothing in this section is designed to extend the life of preferred stocks called for redemption as "shares of stock" beyond the redemption date. After such a call, the security represents only a right to the funds set aside for redemption.

Definitional Cross References:

"Certificated security"	Section 8-102(a)(4)
"Notice"	Section 1-202(a)
"Purchaser"	Sections 1-201(b)(30) and 8-116
"Security"	Section 8-102(a)(15)
"Security certificate"	Section 8-102(a)(16)
"Uncertificated security"	Section 8-102(a)(18)

Section 8-204. Effect of Issuer's Restriction on Transfer

A restriction on transfer of a security imposed by the issuer, even if otherwise lawful, is ineffective against a person without knowledge of the restriction unless:

(1) the security is certificated and the restriction is noted conspicuously on the security certificate; or

(2) the security is uncertificated and the registered owner has been notified of the restriction.

Official Comment

1. Restrictions on transfer of securities are imposed by issuers in a variety of circumstances and for a variety of purposes, such as to retain control of a close corporation or to ensure compliance with federal securities laws. Other law determines whether such restrictions are permissible. This section deals only with the consequences of failure to note the restriction on a security certificate.

This section imposes no bar to enforcement of a restriction on transfer against a person who has actual knowledge of it.

2. A restriction on transfer of a certificated security is ineffective against a person without knowledge of the restriction unless the restriction is noted conspicuously on the certificate. The word "noted" is used to make clear that the restriction need not be set forth in full text. Refusal by an issuer to register a transfer on the basis of an unnoted restriction would be a violation of the issuer's duty to register under Section 8-401.

3. The policy of this section is the same as in Section 8-202. A purchaser who takes delivery of a certificated security is entitled to rely on the terms stated on the certificate. That policy obviously does not apply to uncertificated securities. For uncertificated securities, this section requires only that the registered owner has been notified of the restriction. Suppose, for example, that A is the registered owner of an uncertificated security, and that the issuer has notified A of a restriction on transfer. A agrees to sell the security to B, in violation of the restriction. A completes a written instruction directing the issuer to register transfer to B, and B pays A for the security at the time A delivers the instruction to B. A does not inform B of the restriction, and B does not otherwise have notice or knowledge of it at the time B pays and receives the instruction. B presents the instruction to the issuer, but the issuer refuses to register the transfer on the grounds that it would violate the restriction. The issuer has complied with this section, because it did notify the registered owner A of the restriction. The issuer's refusal to register transfer is not wrongful. B has an action against A for breach of transfer warranty, see Section 8-108(b)(4)(iii). B's mistake was treating an uncertificated security transaction in the fashion appropriate only for a certificated security. The mechanism for transfer of uncertificated securities is registration of transfer on the books of the issuer; handing over an instruction only initiates the process. The purchaser should make arrangements to ensure that the price is not paid until it knows that the issuer has or will register transfer.

4. In the indirect holding system, investors neither take physical delivery of security certificates nor have uncertificated securities registered in their names. So long as the requirements of this section have been satisfied at the level of the relationship between the issuer and the securities intermediary that is a direct holder, this section does not preclude the issuer from enforcing a restriction on transfer. See Section 8-202(a) and Comment 2 thereto.

5. This section deals only with restrictions imposed by the issuer. Restrictions imposed by statute are not affected. See *Quiner v. Marblehead Social Co.*, 10 Mass. 476 (1813);

Madison Bank v. Price, 100 P. 280 (Kan. 1909); *Healey v. Steele Center Creamery Ass'n*, 133 N.W. 69 (Minn. 1911). Nor does it deal with private agreements between stockholders containing restrictive covenants as to the sale of the security.

Definitional Cross References:

"Certificated security"	Section 8-102(a)(4)
"Conspicuous"	Section 1-201(b)(10)
"Issuer"	Section 8-201
"Knowledge"	Section 1-202(b)
"Notifies"	Section 1-202(d)
"Purchaser"	Sections 1-201(b)(30) and 8-116
"Security"	Section 8-102(a)(15)
"Security certificate"	Section 8-102(a)(16)
"Uncertificated security"	Section 8-102(a)(18)

Section 8-205. Effect of Unauthorized Signature on Security Certificate

An unauthorized signature placed on a security certificate before or in the course of issue is ineffective, but the signature is effective in favor of a purchaser for value of the certificated security if the purchaser is without notice of the lack of authority and the signing has been done by:

(1) an authenticating trustee, registrar, transfer agent, or other person entrusted by the issuer with the signing of the security certificate or of similar security certificates, or the immediate preparation for signing of any of them; or

(2) an employee of the issuer, or of any of the persons listed in paragraph (1), entrusted with responsible handling of the security certificate.

Official Comment

1. The problem of forged or unauthorized signatures may arise where an employee of the issuer, transfer agent, or registrar has access to securities which the employee is required to prepare for issue by affixing the corporate seal or by adding a signature necessary for issue. This section is based upon the issuer's duty to avoid the negligent entrusting of securities to such persons. Issuers have long been held responsible for signatures placed upon securities by parties whom they have held out to the public as authorized to prepare such securities. See *Fifth Avenue Bank of New York v. The Forty-Second & Grand Street Ferry R.R.*, 33 N.E. 378 (N.Y. 1893); *Jarvis v. Manhattan Beach Co.*, 43 N.E. 68 (N.Y. 1896). The "apparent authority" concept of some of the case-law, however, is here extended and this section expressly rejects the technical distinction, made by courts reluctant to recognize forged signatures, between cases where forgers sign signatures they are authorized to sign under proper circumstances and those in which they sign signatures they are never authorized to sign. *Citizens' & Southern National Bank v. Trust Co. of Georgia*, 179 S.E. 278 (Ga. Ct. App. 1935). Normally the purchaser is not in a position to determine which signature a forger, entrusted with the preparation of securities, has "apparent authority" to sign. The issuer, on the other hand, can protect itself against such fraud by the careful selection and bonding of agents and employees, or by action over against transfer agents and registrars who in turn may bond their personnel.

2. The issuer cannot be held liable for the honesty of employees not entrusted, directly or indirectly, with the signing, preparation, or responsible handling of similar securities and whose possible commission of forgery it has no reason to anticipate. The result in such cases as *Hudson Trust Co. v. American Linseed Co.*, 134 N.E. 178 (N.Y. 1922), and *Dollar Savings Fund & Trust Co. v. Pittsburgh Plate Glass Co.*, 62 A. 916 (Pa. 1906), is here adopted.

3. This section is not concerned with forged or unauthorized indorsements, but only with unauthorized signatures of issuers, transfer agents, etc., placed upon security certificates during the course of their issue. The protection here stated is available to all purchasers for value without notice and not merely to subsequent purchasers.

Definitional Cross References:

"Certificated security"	Section 8-102(a)(4)
"Issuer"	Section 8-201
"Notice"	Section 1-202(a)
"Purchaser"	Sections 1-201(b)(30) and 8-116
"Security certificate"	Section 8-102(a)(14)
"Unauthorized signature"	Section 1-201(b)(41)

Section 8-206. Completion or Alteration of Security Certificate

(a) If a security certificate contains the signatures necessary to its issue or transfer but is incomplete in any other respect:

(1) any person may complete it by filling in the blanks as authorized; and

(2) even if the blanks are incorrectly filled in, the security certificate as completed is enforceable by a purchaser who took it for value and without notice of the incorrectness.

(b) A complete security certificate that has been improperly altered, even if fraudulently, remains enforceable, but only according to its original terms.

Official Comment

1. The problem of forged or unauthorized signatures necessary for the issue or transfer of a security is not involved here, and a person in possession of a blank certificate is not, by this section, given authority to fill in blanks with such signatures. Completion of blanks left in a transfer instruction is dealt with elsewhere (Section 8-305(a)).

2. Blanks left upon issue of a security certificate are the only ones dealt with here, and a purchaser for value without notice is protected. A purchaser is not in a good position to determine whether blanks were completed by the issuer or by some person not authorized to complete them. On the other hand the issuer can protect itself by not placing its signature on the writing until the blanks are completed or, if it does sign before all blanks are completed, by carefully selecting the agents and employees to whom it entrusts the writing after authentication. With respect to a security certificate that is completed by the issuer but later is altered, the issuer has done everything it can to protect the purchaser and thus is not charged with the terms as altered. However, it is charged according to the original terms, since it is not thereby prejudiced. If the completion or alteration is obviously irregular, the purchaser may not qualify as a purchaser who took without notice under this section.

3. Only the purchaser who physically takes the certificate is directly protected. However, a transferee may receive protection indirectly through Section 8-302(a).

4. The protection granted a purchaser for value without notice under this section is modified to the extent that an overissue may result where an incorrect amount is inserted into a blank (Section 8-210).

Definitional Cross References:

"Notice"	Section 1-202(a)
"Purchaser"	Sections 1-201(b)(30) and 8-116
"Security certificate"	Section 8-102(a)(16)
"Unauthorized signature"	Section 1-201(b)(41)
"Value"	Sections 1-204 and 8-116

Section 8-207. Rights and Duties of Issuer with Respect to Registered Owners

(a) Before due presentment for registration of transfer of a certificated security in registered form or of an instruction requesting registration of transfer of an uncertificated security, the issuer or indenture trustee may treat the registered owner as the person exclusively entitled to vote, receive notifications, and otherwise exercise all the rights and powers of an owner.

(b) This Article does not affect the liability of the registered owner of a security for a call, assessment, or the like.

Official Comment

1. Subsection (a) states the issuer's right to treat the registered owner of a security as the person entitled to exercise all the rights of an owner. This right of the issuer is limited by the provisions of Part 4 of this article. Once there has been due presentation for registration of transfer, the issuer has a duty to register ownership in the name of the transferee. Section 8-401. Thus its right to treat the old registered owner as exclusively entitled to the rights of ownership must cease.

The issuer may under this section make distributions of money or securities to the registered owners of securities without requiring further proof of ownership, provided that such distributions are distributable to the owners of all securities of the same issue and the terms of the security do not require surrender of a security certificate as a condition of payment or exchange. Any such distribution shall constitute a defense against a claim for the same distribution by a person, even if that person is in possession of the security certificate and is a protected purchaser of the security. See PEB Commentary No. 4.

2. Subsection (a) is permissive and does not require that the issuer deal exclusively with the registered owner. It is free to require proof of ownership before paying out dividends or the like if it chooses to. *Barbato v. Breeze Corp.*, 26 A.2d 53 (N.J. 1942).

3. This section does not operate to determine who is finally entitled to exercise voting and other rights or to receive payments and distributions. The parties are still free to incorporate their own arrangements as to these matters in seller-purchaser agreements which may be definitive as between them.

4. No change in existing state laws as to the liability of registered owners for calls and assessments is here intended; nor is anything in this section designed to estop record holders from denying ownership when assessments are levied if they are otherwise entitled to do so under state law. See *State ex rel. Squire v. Murfey, Blosson & Co.*, 2 N.E.2d 866 (Ohio 1936); *Willing v. Delaplaine*, 23 F. Supp. 579 (E.D. Pa. 1937).

5. No interference is intended with the common practice of closing the transfer books or taking a record date for dividend, voting, and other purposes, as provided for in by-laws, charters, and statutes.

Definitional Cross References:

"Certificated security"	Section 8-102(a)(4)
"Instruction"	Section 8-102(a)(12)
"Issuer"	Section 8-201
"Registered form"	Section 8-102(a)(13)
"Security"	Section 8-102(a)(15)
"Uncertificated security"	Section 8-102(a)(18)

Section 8-208. Effect of Signature of Authenticating Trustee, Registrar, or Transfer Agent

(a) A person signing a security certificate as authenticating trustee, registrar, transfer agent, or the like, warrants to a purchaser for value of the certificated security, if the purchaser is without notice of a particular defect, that:

(1) the certificate is genuine;

(2) the person's own participation in the issue of the security is within the person's capacity and within the scope of the authority received by the person from the issuer; and

(3) the person has reasonable grounds to believe that the certificated security is in the form and within the amount the issuer is authorized to issue.

(b) Unless otherwise agreed, a person signing under subsection (a) does not assume responsibility for the validity of the security in other respects.

Official Comment

1. The warranties here stated express the current understanding and prevailing case law as to the effect of the signatures of authenticating trustees, transfer agents, and registrars. See *Jarvis v. Manhattan Beach Co.*, 43 N.E. 68 (N.Y. 1896). Although it has generally been regarded as the particular obligation of the transfer agent to determine whether securities are in proper form as provided by the by-laws and Articles of Incorporation, neither a registrar nor an authenticating trustee should properly place a signature upon a certificate without determining whether it is at least regular on its face. The obligations of these parties in this respect have therefore been made explicit in terms of due care. See *Feldmeier v. Mortgage Securities, Inc.*, 93 P.2d 593 (Cal. Ct. App. 1939).

2. Those cases which hold that an authenticating trustee is not liable for any defect in the mortgage or property which secures the bond or for any fraudulent misrepresentations made by the issuer are not here affected since these matters do not involve the genuineness or proper form of the security. *Ainsa v. Mercantile Trust Co.*, 163 P. 898 (Cal. 1917); *Tschetinian v. City Trust Co.*, 79 N.E. 401 (N.Y. 1906); *Davidge v. Guardian Trust Co. of New York*, 96 N.E. 751 (N.Y. 1911).

3. The charter or an applicable statute may affect the capacity of a bank or other corporation undertaking to act as an authenticating trustee, registrar, or transfer agent. See, for example, the Federal Reserve Act (U.S.C.A., Title 12, Banks and Banking, Section 248) under which the Board of Governors of the Federal Reserve Bank is authorized to grant special permits to National Banks permitting them to act as trustees. Such corporations are therefore held to certify as to their legal capacity to act as well as to their authority.

4. Authenticating trustees, registrars, and transfer agents have normally been held liable for an issue in excess of the authorized amount. *Jarvis v. Manhattan Beach Co.*, supra; *Mullen v. Eastern Trust & Banking Co.*, 81 A. 948 (Me. 1911). In imposing upon these parties a duty of due care with respect to the amount they are authorized to help issue, this section does not necessarily validate the security, but merely holds persons responsible for the excess issue liable in damages for any loss suffered by the purchaser.

5. Aside from questions of genuineness and excess issue, these parties are not held to certify as to the validity of the security unless they specifically undertake to do so. The case law which has recognized a unique responsibility on the transfer agent's part to testify as to the validity of any security which it countersigns is rejected.

6. This provision does not prevent a transfer agent or issuer from agreeing with a registrar of stock to protect the registrar in respect of the genuineness and proper form of a security certificate signed by the issuer or the transfer agent or both. Nor does it interfere with proper indemnity arrangements between the issuer and trustees, transfer agents, registrars, and the like.

7. An unauthorized signature is a signature for purposes of this section if and only if it is made effective by Section 8-205.

Definitional Cross References:

"Certificated security"	Section 8-102(a)(4)
"Genuine"	Section 1-201(b)(19)
"Issuer"	Section 8-201
"Notice"	Section 1-202(a)
"Purchaser"	Sections 1-201(b)(30) and 8-116
"Security"	Section 8-102(a)(15)
"Security certificate"	Section 8-102(a)(16)
"Uncertificated security"	Section 8-102(a)(18)
"Value"	Sections 1-204 and 8-116

Section 8-209. Issuer's Lien

A lien in favor of an issuer upon a certificated security is valid against a purchaser only if the right of the issuer to the lien is noted conspicuously on the security certificate.

Official Comment

This section is similar to Sections 8-202 and 8-204 which require that the terms of a certificated security and any restriction on transfer imposed by the issuer be noted on the security certificate. This section differs from those two sections in that the purchaser's knowledge of the issuer's claim is irrelevant. "Noted" makes clear that the text of the lien provisions need not be set forth in full. However, this would not override a provision of an applicable corporation code requiring statement in haec verba. This section does not apply to uncertificated securities. It applies to the indirect holding system in the same fashion as Sections 8-202 and 8-204, see Comment 2 to Section 8-202.

Definitional Cross References:

"Certificated security"	Section 8-102(a)(4)
"Issuer"	Section 8-201
"Purchaser"	Sections 1-201(b)(30) and 8-116
"Security"	Section 8-102(a)(15)
"Security certificate"	Section 8-102(a)(16)

Section 8-210. Overissue

(a) In this section, "overissue" means the issue of securities in excess of the amount the issuer has corporate power to issue, but an overissue does not occur if appropriate action has cured the overissue.

(b) Except as otherwise provided in subsections (c) and (d), the provisions of this Article which validate a security or compel its issue or reissue do not apply to the extent that validation, issue, or reissue would result in overissue.

(c) If an identical security not constituting an overissue is reasonably available for purchase, a person entitled to issue or validation may compel the issuer to purchase the security and deliver it if certificated or register its transfer if uncertificated, against surrender of any security certificate the person holds.

(d) If a security is not reasonably available for purchase, a person entitled to issue or validation may recover from the issuer the price the person or the last purchaser for value paid for it with interest from the date of the person's demand.

Official Comment

1. Deeply embedded in corporation law is the conception that "corporate power" to issue securities stems from the statute, either general or special, under which the corporation is organized. Corporation codes universally require that the charter or articles of incorporation state, at least as to capital shares, maximum limits in terms of number of shares or total dollar capital. Historically, special incorporation statutes are similarly drawn and sometimes similarly limit the face amount of authorized debt securities. The theory is that issue of securities in excess of the authorized amounts is prohibited. See, for example, *McWilliams v. Geddes & Moss Undertaking Co.*, 169 So. 894 (La. 1936); *Crawford v. Twin City Oil Co.*, 113 So. 61 (Ala. 1927); *New York & New Haven R.R. v. Schuyler*, 34 N.Y. 30 (1865). This conception persists despite modern corporation codes under which, by action of directors and stockholders, additional shares can be authorized by charter amendment and thereafter issued. This section does not give a person entitled to validation, issue, or reissue of a security, the right to compel amendment of the charter to authorize additional shares. Therefore, in a case where issue of an additional security would require charter amendment, the plaintiff is limited to the two alternate remedies set forth in subsections (c) and (d). The last clause of subsection (a), which is added in Revised Article 8, does, however, recognize that under modern conditions, overissue may be a relatively minor technical problem that can be cured by appropriate action under governing corporate law.

2. Where an identical security is reasonably available for purchase, whether because traded on an organized market, or because one or more security owners may be willing to sell at a not unreasonable price, the issuer, although unable to issue additional shares, will be able to purchase them and may be compelled to follow that procedure. *West v. Tintic Standard Mining Co.*, 263 P. 490 (Utah 1928).

3. The right to recover damages from an issuer who has permitted an overissue to occur is well settled. *New York & New Haven R.R. v. Schuyler*, 34 N.Y. 30 (1865). The measure of such damages, however, has been open to question, some courts basing them upon the value of stock at the time registration is refused; some upon the value at the time of trial; and some upon the highest value between the time of refusal and the time of trial. *Allen v. South Boston Railroad*, 22 N.E. 917 (Mass. 1889); *Commercial Bank v. Kortright,* 22 Wend. (N.Y.) 348 (1839). The purchase price of the security to the last purchaser who gave value for it is here adopted as being the fairest means of reducing the possibility of speculation by the purchaser. Interest may be recovered as the best available measure of compensation for delay.

Definitional Cross References:

"Issuer"	Section 8-201
"Security"	Section 8-102(a)(15)
"Security certificate"	Section 8-102(a)(16)
"Uncertificated security"	Section 8-102(a)(18)

PART 3. TRANSFER OF CERTIFICATED AND UNCERTIFICATED SECURITIES

Section 8-301. Delivery

(a) Delivery of a certificated security to a purchaser occurs when:

(1) the purchaser acquires possession of the security certificate;

(2) another person, other than a securities intermediary, either acquires possession of the security certificate on behalf of the purchaser or, having previously acquired possession of the certificate, acknowledges that it holds for the purchaser; or

(3) a securities intermediary acting on behalf of the purchaser acquires possession of the security certificate, only if the certificate is in registered form and is (i) registered in the name of the purchaser, (ii) payable to the order of the purchaser, or (iii) specially indorsed to the purchaser by an effective indorsement and has not been indorsed to the securities intermediary or in blank.

(b) Delivery of an uncertificated security to a purchaser occurs when:

(1) the issuer registers the purchaser as the registered owner, upon original issue or registration of transfer; or

(2) another person, other than a securities intermediary, either becomes the registered owner of the uncertificated security on behalf of the purchaser or, having previously become the registered owner, acknowledges that it holds for the purchaser.

Official Comment

1. This section specifies the requirements for "delivery" of securities. Delivery is used in Article 8 to describe the formal steps necessary for a purchaser to acquire a direct interest in a security under this Article. The concept of delivery refers to the implementation of a transaction, not the legal categorization of the transaction which is consummated by delivery. Issuance and transfer are different kinds of transaction, though both may be implemented by delivery. Sale and pledge are different kinds of transfers, but both may be implemented by delivery.

2. Subsection (a) defines delivery with respect to certificated securities. Paragraph (1) deals with simple cases where purchasers themselves acquire physical possession of certificates. Paragraphs (2) and (3) of subsection (a) specify the circumstances in which delivery to a purchaser can occur although the certificate is in the possession of a person other than the purchaser. Paragraph (2) contains the general rule that a purchaser can take delivery through another person, so long as the other person is actually acting on behalf of the purchaser or acknowledges that it is holding on behalf of the purchaser. Paragraph (2) does not apply to acquisition of possession by a securities intermediary, because a person who holds securities through a securities account acquires a security entitlement, rather than having a direct interest. See Section 8-501. Subsection (a)(3) specifies the limited circumstances in which delivery of security certificates to a securities intermediary is treated as a delivery to the customer. Note that delivery is a method of perfecting a security interest in a certificated security. See Section 9-313(a), (e).

3. Subsection (b) defines delivery with respect to uncertificated securities. Use of the term "delivery" with respect to uncertificated securities, does, at least on first hearing, seem a bit solecistic. The word "delivery" is, however, routinely used in the securities business in a broader sense than manual tradition. For example, settlement by entries on the books of a clearing corporation is commonly called "delivery," as in the expression "delivery versus payment." The diction of this section has the advantage of using the same term for uncertificated securities as for certificated securities, for which "delivery" is conventional usage. Paragraph (1) of subsection (b) provides that delivery occurs when the purchaser becomes the registered owner of an uncertificated security, either upon original issue or registration of transfer. Paragraph (2) provides for delivery of an uncertificated security through a third person, in a fashion analogous to subsection (a)(2).

Definitional Cross References:

"Certificated security"	Section 8-102(a)(4)
"Effective"	Section 8-107
"Issuer"	Section 8-201
"Purchaser"	Sections 1-201(b)(30) and 8-116
"Registered form"	Section 8-102(a)(13)
"Securities intermediary"	Section 8-102(a)(14)
"Security certificate"	Section 8-102(a)(16)
"Special indorsement"	Section 8-304(a)
"Uncertificated security"	Section 8-102(a)(18)

Section 8-302. Rights of Purchaser

(a) Except as otherwise provided in subsections (b) and (c), a purchaser of a certificated or uncertificated security acquires all rights in the security that the transferor had or had power to transfer.

(b) A purchaser of a limited interest acquires rights only to the extent of the interest purchased.

(c) A purchaser of a certificated security who as a previous holder had notice of an adverse claim does not improve its position by taking from a protected purchaser.

Official Comment

1. Subsection (a) provides that a purchaser of a certificated or uncertificated security acquires all rights that the transferor had or had power to transfer. This statement of the familiar "shelter" principle is qualified by the exceptions that a purchaser of a limited interest acquires only that interest, subsection (b), and that a person who does not qualify as a protected purchaser cannot improve its position by taking from a subsequent protected purchaser, subsection (c).

2. Although this section provides that a purchaser acquires a property interest in a certificated or uncertificated security, it does not state that a person can acquire an interest in a security only by purchase. Article 8 also is not a comprehensive codification of all of the law governing the creation or transfer of interests in securities. For example, the grant of a security interest is a transfer of a property interest, but the formal steps necessary to effectuate such a transfer are governed by Article 9 not by Article 8. Under the Article 9 rules, a security interest in a certificated or uncertificated security can be created by execution of a security agreement under Section 9-203 and can be perfected by filing. A transfer of an Article 9 security interest can be implemented by an Article 8 delivery, but need not be.

Similarly, Article 8 does not determine whether a property interest in certificated or uncertificated security is acquired under other law, such as the law of gifts, trusts, or equitable remedies. Nor does Article 8 deal with transfers by operation of law. For example, transfers from decedent to administrator, from ward to guardian, and from bankrupt to trustee in bankruptcy are governed by other law as to both the time they occur and the substance of the transfer. The Article 8 rules do, however, determine whether the issuer is obligated to recognize the rights that a third party, such as a transferee, may acquire under other law. See Sections 8-207, 8-401, and 8-404.

Definitional Cross References:

"Certificated security"	Section 8-102(a)(4)
"Notice of adverse claim"	Section 8-105
"Protected purchaser"	Section 8-303
"Purchaser"	Sections 1-201(b)(30) and 8-116
"Uncertificated security"	Section 8-102(a)(18)
"Delivery"	Section 8-301

Section 8-303. Protected Purchaser

(a) "Protected purchaser" means a purchaser of a certificated or uncertificated security, or of an interest therein, who:

(1) gives value;

(2) does not have notice of any adverse claim to the security; and

(3) obtains control of the certificated or uncertificated security.

(b) A protected purchaser acquires its interest in the security free of any adverse claim.

Official Comment

1. Subsection (a) lists the requirements that a purchaser must meet to qualify as a "protected purchaser." Subsection (b) provides that a protected purchaser takes its interest free from adverse claims. "Purchaser" is defined broadly in Section 1-201. A secured party as well as an outright buyer can qualify as a protected purchaser. Also, "purchase" includes taking by issue, so a person to whom a security is originally issued can qualify as a protected purchaser.

2. To qualify as a protected purchaser under subsection (a), a purchaser must give value, take without notice of any adverse claim, and obtain control. Value is used in the broad sense defined in Section 1-204. See also Section 8-116 (securities intermediary as purchaser for value). Adverse claim is defined in Section 8-102(a)(1). Section 8-105 specifies whether a purchaser has notice of an adverse claim. Control is defined in Section 8-106. To qualify as a protected purchaser under subsection (b), there must be a time at which all of the requirements are satisfied. Thus if a purchaser obtains notice of an adverse claim before giving value or satisfying the requirements for control, the purchaser cannot be a protected purchaser. See also Section 8-304(d).

The requirement that a protected purchaser obtain control expresses the point that to qualify for the adverse claim cut-off rule a purchaser must take through a transaction that is implemented by the appropriate mechanism. By contrast, the rules in Part 2 provide that any purchaser for value of a security without notice of a defense may take free of the issuer's defense based on that defense. See Section 8-202.

The reference to the acquisition of the rights of a purchaser in the pre-2022 text of subsection (b) has been deleted. However, because a protected purchaser acquires the rights of a purchaser under Section 8-302, the revised text does not diminish a protected purchaser's rights. That revision aligned the text more closely to that of Section 12-104(e) on the rights of a qualifying purchaser of a controllable electronic record, controllable account, or controllable payment intangible.

3. The requirements for control differ depending on the form of the security. For securities represented by bearer certificates, a purchaser obtains control by delivery. See Sections 8-106(a) and 8-301(a). For securities represented by certificates in registered form, the requirements for control are: (1) delivery as defined in Section 8-301(b), plus (2) either an effective indorsement or registration of transfer by the issuer. See Section 8-106(b). Thus, a person who takes through a forged indorsement does not qualify as a protected purchaser by virtue of the delivery alone. If, however, the purchaser presents the certificate to the issuer for registration of transfer, and the issuer registers transfer over the forged indorsement, the purchaser can qualify as a protected purchaser of the new certificate. If the issuer registers transfer on a forged indorsement, the true owner will be able to recover from the issuer for wrongful registration, see Section 8-404, unless the owner's delay in notifying the issuer of a loss or theft of the certificate results in preclusion under Section 8-406.

For uncertificated securities, a purchaser can obtain control either by delivery, see Sections 8-106(c)(1) and 8-301(b), or by obtaining an agreement pursuant to which the issuer agrees to act on instructions from the purchaser without further consent from the registered owner, see Section 8-106(c)(2). The control agreement device of Section 8-106(c)(2) takes the place of the "registered pledge" concept of the 1978 version of Article 8. A secured lender who obtains a control agreement under Section 8-106(c)(2) can qualify as a protected purchaser of an uncertificated security.

4. This section states directly the rules determining whether one takes free from adverse claims without using the phrase "good faith." Whether a person who takes under suspicious circumstances is disqualified is determined by the rules of Section 8-105 on notice of adverse claims. The term "protected purchaser," which replaces the term "bona fide purchaser" used in the prior version of Article 8, is derived from the term "protected holder" used in the Convention on International Bills and Notes prepared by the United Nations Commission on International Trade Law ("UNCITRAL").

Definitional Cross References:

"Adverse claim"	Section 8-102(a)(1)
"Certificated security"	Section 8-102(a)(4)
"Control"	Section 8-106
"Notice of adverse claim"	Section 8-105
"Purchaser"	Sections 1-201(b)(30) and 8-116
"Uncertificated security"	Section 8-102(a)(18)
"Value"	Sections 1-204 and 8-116

Section 8-304. Indorsement

(a) An indorsement may be in blank or special. An indorsement in blank includes an indorsement to bearer. A special indorsement specifies to whom a security is to be transferred or who has power to transfer it. A holder may convert a blank indorsement to a special indorsement.

(b) An indorsement purporting to be only of part of a security certificate representing units intended by the issuer to be separately transferable is effective to the extent of the indorsement.

(c) An indorsement, whether special or in blank, does not constitute a transfer until delivery of the certificate on which it appears or, if the indorsement is on a separate document, until delivery of both the document and the certificate.

(d) If a security certificate in registered form has been delivered to a purchaser without a necessary indorsement, the purchaser may become a protected purchaser only when the indorsement is supplied. However, against a transferor, a transfer is complete upon delivery and the purchaser has a specifically enforceable right to have any necessary indorsement supplied.

(e) An indorsement of a security certificate in bearer form may give notice of an adverse claim to the certificate, but it does not otherwise affect a right to registration that the holder possesses.

(f) Unless otherwise agreed, a person making an indorsement assumes only the obligations provided in Section 8-108 and not an obligation that the security will be honored by the issuer.

Official Comment

1. By virtue of the definition of indorsement in Section 8-102 and the rules of this section, the simplified method of indorsing certificated securities previously set forth in the Uniform Stock Transfer Act is continued. Although more than one special indorsement on a given security certificate is possible, the desire for dividends or interest, as the case may be, should operate to bring the certificate home for registration of transfer within a reasonable period of time. The usual form of assignment which appears on the back of a stock certificate or in a separate "power" may be filled up either in the form of an assignment, a power of attorney to transfer, or both. If it is not filled up at all but merely signed, the indorsement is in blank. If filled up either as an assignment or as a power of attorney to transfer, the indorsement is special.

2. Subsection (b) recognizes the validity of a "partial" indorsement, e.g., as to fifty shares of the one hundred represented by a single certificate. The rights of a transferee under a partial indorsement to the status of a protected purchaser are left to the case law.

3. Subsection (c) deals with the effect of an indorsement without delivery. There must be a voluntary parting with control in order to effect a valid transfer of a certificated security as between the parties. *Levey v. Nason*, 181 N.E. 193 (Mass. 1932); *National Surety Co. v. Indemnity Ins. Co. of N. Am.*, 261 N.Y.S. 605 (App. Div. 1933). The provision in Section 10 of the Uniform Stock Transfer Act that an attempted transfer without delivery amounts to a promise to transfer is omitted. Even under that Act the effect of such a promise was left to the applicable law of contracts, and this Article by making no reference to such situations intends to achieve a similar result. With respect to delivery there is no counterpart to subsection (d) on right to compel indorsement, such as is envisaged in *Johnson v. Johnson*, 13 N.E.2d 788 (Mass. 1938), where the transferee under a written assignment was given the right to compel a transfer of the certificate.

4. Subsection (d) deals with the effect of delivery without indorsement. As between the parties the transfer is made complete upon delivery, but the transferee cannot become a protected purchaser until indorsement is made. The indorsement does not operate retroactively, and notice may intervene between delivery and indorsement so as to prevent the transferee from becoming a protected purchaser. Although a purchaser taking without a necessary indorsement may be subject to claims of ownership, any issuer's defense of which the purchaser had no notice at the time of delivery will be cut off, since the provisions of this Article protect all purchasers for value without notice (Section 8-202).

The transferee's right to compel an indorsement where a security certificate has been delivered with intent to transfer is recognized in the case law. See *Coats v. Guaranty Bank & Trust Co.*, 129 So. 513 (La. 1930). A proper indorsement is one of the requisites of transfer which a purchaser of a certificated security has a right to obtain (Section 8-307). A purchaser may not only compel an indorsement under that section but may also recover for any reasonable expense incurred by the transferor's failure to respond to the demand for an indorsement.

5. Subsection (e) deals with the significance of an indorsement on a security certificate in bearer form. The concept of indorsement applies only to registered securities. A purported indorsement of bearer paper is normally of no effect. An indorsement "for collection," "for surrender" or the like, charges a purchaser with notice of adverse claims (Section 8-105(d)) but does not operate beyond this to interfere with any right the holder may otherwise possess to have the security registered.

6. Subsection (f) makes clear that the indorser of a security certificate does not warrant that the issuer will honor the underlying obligation. In view of the nature of investment securities and the circumstances under which they are normally transferred, a transferor cannot be held to warrant as to the issuer's actions. As a transferor the indorser, of course, remains liable for breach of the warranties set forth in this Article (Section 8-108).

Definitional Cross References:

"Bearer form"	Section 8-102(a)(2)
"Certificated security"	Section 8-102(a)(4)
"Indorsement"	Section 8-102(a)(11)
"Purchaser"	Sections 1-201(b)(30) and 8-116
"Registered form"	Section 8-102(a)(13)
"Security certificate"	Section 8-102(a)(16)

Section 8-305. Instruction

(a) If an instruction has been originated by an appropriate person but is incomplete in any other respect, any person may complete it as authorized and the issuer may rely on it as completed, even though it has been completed incorrectly.

(b) Unless otherwise agreed, a person initiating an instruction assumes only the obligations imposed by Section 8-108 and not an obligation that the security will be honored by the issuer.

Official Comment

1. The term instruction is defined in Section 8-102(a)(12) as a notification communicated to the issuer of an uncertificated security directing that transfer be registered. Section 8-107 specifies who may initiate an effective instruction.

Functionally, presentation of an instruction is quite similar to the presentation of an indorsed certificate for reregistration.

Note that instruction is defined in terms of "communicate," see Section 8-102(a)(6). Thus, the instruction may be in the form of a writing signed by the registered owner or in any other form agreed upon by the issuer and the registered owner. Allowing nonwritten forms of instructions will permit the development and employment of means of transmitting instructions electronically.

When a person who originates an instruction leaves a blank and the blank later is completed, subsection (a) gives the issuer the same rights it would have had against the originating person had that person completed the blank. This is true regardless of whether the person completing the instruction had authority to complete it. Compare Section 8-206 and its Comment, dealing with blanks left upon issue.

2. Subsection (b) makes clear that the originator of an instruction, like the indorser of a security certificate, does not warrant that the issuer will honor the underlying obligation, but does make warranties as a transferor under Section 8-108.

Definitional Cross References:

"Appropriate person"	Section 8-107
"Instruction"	Section 8-102(a)(12)
"Issuer"	Section 8-201

Section 8-306. Effect of Guaranteeing Signature, Indorsement, or Instruction

(a) A person who guarantees a signature of an indorser of a security certificate warrants that at the time of signing:

(1) the signature was genuine;

(2) the signer was an appropriate person to indorse, or if the signature is by an agent, the agent had actual authority to act on behalf of the appropriate person; and

(3) the signer had legal capacity to sign.

(b) A person who guarantees a signature of the originator of an instruction warrants that at the time of signing:

(1) the signature was genuine;

(2) the signer was an appropriate person to originate the instruction, or if the signature is by an agent, the agent had actual authority to act on behalf of the appropriate person, if the person specified in the instruction as the registered owner was, in fact, the registered owner, as to which fact the signature guarantor does not make a warranty; and

(3) the signer had legal capacity to sign.

(c) A person who specially guarantees the signature of an originator of an instruction makes the warranties of a signature guarantor under subsection (b) and also warrants that at the time the instruction is presented to the issuer:

(1) the person specified in the instruction as the registered owner of the uncertificated security will be the registered owner; and

(2) the transfer of the uncertificated security requested in the instruction will be registered by the issuer free from all liens, security interests, restrictions, and claims other than those specified in the instruction.

(d) A guarantor under subsections (a) and (b) or a special guarantor under subsection (c) does not otherwise warrant the rightfulness of the transfer.

(e) A person who guarantees an indorsement of a security certificate makes the warranties of a signature guarantor under subsection (a) and also warrants the rightfulness of the transfer in all respects.

(f) A person who guarantees an instruction requesting the transfer of an uncertificated security makes the warranties of a special signature guarantor under subsection (c) and also warrants the rightfulness of the transfer in all respects.

(g) An issuer may not require a special guaranty of signature, a guaranty of indorsement, or a guaranty of instruction as a condition to registration of transfer.

(h) The warranties under this section are made to a person taking or dealing with the security in reliance on the guaranty, and the guarantor is liable to the person for loss resulting from their breach. An indorser or originator of an instruction whose signature, indorsement, or instruction has been guaranteed is liable to a guarantor for any loss suffered by the guarantor as a result of breach of the warranties of the guarantor.

Official Comment

1. Subsection (a) provides that a guarantor of the signature of the indorser of a security certificate warrants that the signature is genuine, that the signer is an appropriate person or has actual authority to indorse on behalf of the appropriate person, and that the signer has legal capacity. Subsection (b) provides similar, though not identical, warranties for the guarantor of a signature of the originator of an instruction for transfer of an uncertificated security.

Appropriate person is defined in Section 8-107(a) to include a successor or person who has power under other law to act for a person who is deceased or lacks capacity. Thus if a certificate registered in the name of Mary Roe is indorsed by Jane Doe as executor of Mary Roe, a guarantor of the signature of Jane Doe warrants that she has power to act as executor.

Although the definition of appropriate person in Section 8-107(a) does not itself include an agent, an indorsement by an agent is effective under Section 8-107(b) if the agent has authority to act for the appropriate person. Accordingly, this section provides an explicit warranty of authority for agents.

2. The rationale of the principle that a signature guarantor warrants the authority of the signer, rather than simply the genuineness of the signature, was explained in the leading case of *Jennie Clarkson Home for Children v. Missouri, K. & T. R.*

Co., 74 N.E. 571 (N.Y. 1905), which dealt with a guaranty of the signature of a person indorsing on behalf of a corporation. "If stock is held by an individual who is executing a power of attorney for its transfer, the member of the exchange who signs as a witness thereto guaranties not only the genuineness of the signature affixed to the power of attorney, but that the person signing is the individual in whose name the stock stands. With reference to stock standing in the name of a corporation, which can only sign a power of attorney through its authorized officers or agents, a different situation is presented. If the witnessing of the signature of the corporation is only that of the signature of a person who signs for the corporation, then the guaranty is of no value, and there is nothing to protect purchasers or the companies who are called upon to issue new stock in the place of that transferred from the frauds of persons who have signed the names of corporations without authority. If such is the only effect of the guaranty, purchasers and transfer agents must first go to the corporation in whose name the stock stands and ascertain whether the individual who signed the power of attorney had authority to so do. This will require time, and in many cases will necessitate the postponement of the completion of the purchase by the payment of the money until the facts can be ascertained. The broker who is acting for the owner has an opportunity to become acquainted with his customer, and may readily before sale ascertain, in case of a corporation, the name of the officer who is authorized to execute the power of attorney. It was therefore, we think, the purpose of the rule to cast upon the broker who witnesses the signature the duty of ascertaining whether the person signing the name of the corporation had authority to so do, and making the witness a guarantor that it is the signature of the corporation in whose name the stock stands."

3. Subsection (b) sets forth the warranties that can reasonably be expected from the guarantor of the signature of the originator of an instruction, who, though familiar with the signer, does not have any evidence that the purported owner is in fact the owner of the subject uncertificated security. This is in contrast to the position of the person guaranteeing a signature on a certificate who can see a certificate in the signer's possession in the name of or indorsed to the signer or in blank. Thus, the warranty in paragraph (2) of subsection (b) is expressly conditioned on the actual registration's conforming to that represented by the originator. If the signer purports to be the owner, the guarantor under paragraph (2), warrants only the identity of the signer. If, however, the signer is acting in a representative capacity, the guarantor warrants both the signer's identity and authority to act for the purported owner. The issuer needs no warranty as to the facts of registration because those facts can be ascertained from the issuer's own records.

4. Subsection (c) sets forth a "special guaranty of signature" under which the guarantor additionally warrants both registered ownership and freedom from undisclosed defects of record. The guarantor of the signature of an indorser of a security certificate effectively makes these warranties to a purchaser for value on the evidence of a clean certificate issued in the name of the indorser, indorsed to the indorser or indorsed in blank. By specially guaranteeing under subsection (c), the guarantor warrants that the instruction will, when presented to the issuer, result in the requested registration free from defects not specified.

5. Subsection (d) makes clear that the warranties of a signature guarantor are limited to those specified in this section and do not include a general warranty of rightfulness. On the other hand subsections (e) and (f) provide that a person guaranteeing an indorsement or an instruction does warrant that the transfer is rightful in all respects.

6. Subsection (g) makes clear what can be inferred from the combination of Sections 8-401 and 8-402, that the issuer may not require as a condition to transfer a guaranty of the indorsement or instruction nor may it require a special signature guaranty.

7. Subsection (h) specifies to whom the warranties in this section run, and also provides that a person who gives a guaranty under this section has an action against the indorser or originator for any loss suffered by the guarantor.

Definitional Cross References:

"Appropriate person"	Section 8-107
"Genuine"	Section 1-201(b)(19)
"Indorsement"	Section 8-102(a)(11)
"Instruction"	Section 8-102(a)(12)
"Issuer"	Section 8-201
"Security certificate"	Section 8-102(a)(16)
"Uncertificated security"	Section 8-102(a)(18)

Section 8-307. Purchaser's Right to Requisites for Registration of Transfer

Unless otherwise agreed, the transferor of a security on due demand shall supply the purchaser with proof of authority to transfer or with any other requisite necessary to obtain registration of the transfer of the security, but if the transfer is not for value, a transferor need not comply unless the purchaser pays the necessary expenses. If the transferor fails within a reasonable time to comply with the demand, the purchaser may reject or rescind the transfer.

Official Comment

1. Because registration of the transfer of a security is a matter of vital importance, a purchaser is here provided with the means of obtaining such formal requirements for registration as signature guaranties, proof of authority, transfer tax stamps and the like. The transferor is the one in a position to supply most conveniently whatever documentation may be requisite for registration of transfer, and the duty to do so upon demand within a reasonable time is here stated affirmatively. If an essential item is peculiarly within the province of the transferor so that the transferor is the only one who can obtain it, the purchaser may specifically enforce the right to obtain it. Compare Section 8-304(d). If a transfer is not for value the transferor need not pay expenses.

2. If the transferor's duty is not performed the transferee may reject or rescind the contract to transfer. The transferee is not bound to do so. An action for damages for breach of contract may be preferred.

Definitional Cross References:

"Purchaser"	Sections 1-201(b)(30) and 8-116
"Security"	Section 8-102(a)(15)
"Value"	Sections 1-204 and 8-116

PART 4. REGISTRATION

Section 8-401. Duty of Issuer to Register Transfer

(a) If a certificated security in registered form is presented to an issuer with a request to register transfer or an instruction is presented to an issuer with a request to register transfer of an uncertificated security, the issuer shall register the transfer as requested if:

(1) under the terms of the security the person seeking registration of transfer is eligible to have the security registered in its name;

(2) the indorsement or instruction is made by the appropriate person or by an agent who has actual authority to act on behalf of the appropriate person;

(3) reasonable assurance is given that the indorsement or instruction is genuine and authorized (Section 8-402);

(4) any applicable law relating to the collection of taxes has been complied with;

(5) the transfer does not violate any restriction on transfer imposed by the issuer in accordance with Section 8-204;

(6) a demand that the issuer not register transfer has not become effective under Section 8-403, or the issuer has complied with Section 8-403(b) but no legal process or indemnity bond is obtained as provided in Section 8-403(d); and

(7) the transfer is in fact rightful or is to a protected purchaser.

(b) If an issuer is under a duty to register a transfer of a security, the issuer is liable to a person presenting a certificated security or an instruction for registration or to the person's principal for loss resulting from unreasonable delay in registration or failure or refusal to register the transfer.

Official Comment

1. This section states the duty of the issuer to register transfers. A duty exists only if certain preconditions exist. If any of the preconditions do not exist, there is no duty to register transfer. If an indorsement on a security certificate is a forgery, there is no duty. If an instruction to transfer an uncertificated security is not originated by an appropriate person, there is no duty. If there has not been compliance with applicable tax laws, there is no duty. If a security certificate is properly indorsed but nevertheless the transfer is in fact wrongful, there is no duty unless the transfer is to a protected purchaser (and the other preconditions exist).

This section does not constitute a mandate that the issuer must establish that all preconditions are met before the issuer registers a transfer. The issuer may waive the reasonable assurances specified in paragraph (a)(3). If it has confidence in the responsibility of the persons requesting transfer, it may ignore questions of compliance with tax laws. Although an issuer has no duty if the transfer is wrongful, the issuer has no duty to inquire into adverse claims, see Section 8-404.

2. By subsection (b) the person entitled to registration may not only compel it but may hold the issuer liable in damages for unreasonable delay.

3. Section 8-201(c) provides that with respect to registration of transfer, "issuer" means the person on whose behalf transfer books are maintained. Transfer agents, registrars or the like within the scope of their respective functions have rights and duties under this Part similar to those of the issuer. See Section 8-407.

Definitional Cross References:

"Appropriate person"	Section 8-107
"Certificated security"	Section 8-102(a)(4)
"Genuine"	Section 1-201(b)(19)
"Indorsement"	Section 8-102(a)(11)
"Instruction"	Section 8-102(a)(12)
"Issuer"	Section 8-201
"Protected purchaser"	Section 8-303
"Registered form"	Section 8-102(a)(13)
"Uncertificated security"	Section 8-102(a)(18)

Section 8-402. Assurance That Indorsement or Instruction Is Effective

(a) An issuer may require the following assurance that each necessary indorsement or each instruction is genuine and authorized:

(1) in all cases, a guaranty of the signature of the person making an indorsement or originating an instruction including, in the case of an instruction, reasonable assurance of identity;

(2) if the indorsement is made or the instruction is originated by an agent, appropriate assurance of actual authority to sign;

(3) if the indorsement is made or the instruction is originated by a fiduciary pursuant to Section 8-107(a)(4) or (a)(5), appropriate evidence of appointment or incumbency;

(4) if there is more than one fiduciary, reasonable assurance that all who are required to sign have done so; and

(5) if the indorsement is made or the instruction is originated by a person not covered by another

provision of this subsection, assurance appropriate to the case corresponding as nearly as may be to the provisions of this subsection.

(b) An issuer may elect to require reasonable assurance beyond that specified in this section.

(c) In this section:

(1) "Guaranty of the signature" means a guaranty signed by or on behalf of a person reasonably believed by the issuer to be responsible. An issuer may adopt standards with respect to responsibility if they are not manifestly unreasonable.

(2) "Appropriate evidence of appointment or incumbency" means:

(i) in the case of a fiduciary appointed or qualified by a court, a certificate issued by or under the direction or supervision of the court or an officer thereof and dated within 60 days before the date of presentation for transfer; or

(ii) in any other case, a copy of a document showing the appointment or a certificate issued by or on behalf of a person reasonably believed by an issuer to be responsible or, in the absence of that document or certificate, other evidence the issuer reasonably considers appropriate.

Official Comment

1. An issuer is absolutely liable for wrongful registration of transfer if the indorsement or instruction is ineffective. See Section 8-404. Accordingly, an issuer is entitled to require such assurance as is reasonable under the circumstances that all necessary indorsements are effective, and thus to minimize its risk. This section establishes the requirements the issuer may make in terms of documentation which, except in the rarest of instances, should be easily furnished. Subsection (b) provides that an issuer may require additional assurances if that requirement is reasonable under the circumstances, but if the issuer demands more than reasonable assurance that the instruction or the necessary indorsements are genuine and authorized, the presenter may refuse the demand and sue for improper refusal to register. Section 8-401(b).

2. Under subsection (a)(1), the issuer may require in all cases a guaranty of signature. See Section 8-306. When an instruction is presented the issuer always may require reasonable assurance as to the identity of the originator. Subsection (c) allows the issuer to require that the person making these guaranties be one reasonably believed to be responsible, and the issuer may adopt standards of responsibility which are not manifestly unreasonable. Regulations under the federal securities laws, however, place limits on the requirements transfer agents may impose concerning the responsibility of eligible signature guarantors. See 17 CFR 240.17Ad-15.

3. This section, by paragraphs (2) through (5) of subsection (a), permits the issuer to seek confirmation that the indorsement or instruction is genuine and authorized. The permitted methods act as a double check on matters which are within the warranties of the signature guarantor. See Section 8-306. Thus, an agent may be required to submit a power of attorney, a corporation to submit a certified resolution evidencing the authority of its signing officer to sign, an executor or administrator to submit the usual "short-form certificate," etc. But failure of a fiduciary to obtain court approval of the transfer or to comply with other requirements does not make the fiduciary's signature ineffective. Section 8-107(c). Hence court orders and other controlling instruments are omitted from subsection (a).

Subsection (a)(3) authorizes the issuer to require "appropriate evidence" of appointment or incumbency, and subsection (c) indicates what evidence will be "appropriate." In the case of a fiduciary appointed or qualified by a court that evidence will be a court certificate dated within sixty days before the date of presentation, subsection (c)(2)(i). Where the fiduciary is not appointed or qualified by a court, as in the case of a successor trustee, subsection (c)(2)(ii) applies. In that case, the issuer may require a copy of a trust instrument or other document showing the appointment, or it may require the certificate of a responsible person. In the absence of such a document or certificate, it may require other appropriate evidence. If the security is registered in the name of the fiduciary as such, the person's signature is effective even though the person is no longer serving in that capacity, see Section 8-107(d), hence no evidence of incumbency is needed.

4. Circumstances may indicate that a necessary signature was unauthorized or was not that of an appropriate person. Such circumstances would be ignored at risk of absolute liability. To minimize that risk the issuer may properly exercise the option given by subsection (b) to require assurance beyond that specified in subsection (a). On the other hand, the facts at hand may reflect only on the rightfulness of the transfer. Such facts do not create a duty of inquiry, because the issuer is not liable to an adverse claimant unless the claimant obtains legal process. See Section 8-404.

Definitional Cross References:

"Appropriate person"	Section 8-107
"Genuine"	Section 1-201(b)(19)
"Indorsement"	Section 8-102(a)(11)
"Instruction"	Section 8-102(a)(12)
"Issuer"	Section 8-201

Section 8-403. Demand That Issuer Not Register Transfer

(a) A person who is an appropriate person to make an indorsement or originate an instruction may demand that the issuer not register transfer of a security by communicating to the issuer a notification that identifies the registered owner and the issue of which the security is a part and provides an address for communications directed to the person making the demand. The demand is effective only if it is received by the issuer at a time and in a manner affording the issuer reasonable opportunity to act on it.

(b) If a certificated security in registered form is presented to an issuer with a request to register transfer or an instruction is presented to an issuer with a request to register transfer of an uncertificated security after a demand that the issuer not register transfer has become effective, the issuer shall promptly communicate to (i) the person who initiated the demand at the address provided in the demand and (ii) the person who presented the security for registration of transfer or initiated the instruction requesting registration of transfer a notification stating that:

(1) the certificated security has been presented for registration of transfer or the instruction for registration of transfer of the uncertificated security has been received;

(2) a demand that the issuer not register transfer had previously been received; and

(3) the issuer will withhold registration of transfer for a period of time stated in the notification in order to provide the person who initiated the demand an opportunity to obtain legal process or an indemnity bond.

(c) The period described in subsection (b)(3) may not exceed 30 days after the date of communication of the notification. A shorter period may be specified by the issuer if it is not manifestly unreasonable.

(d) An issuer is not liable to a person who initiated a demand that the issuer not register transfer for any loss the person suffers as a result of registration of a transfer pursuant to an effective indorsement or instruction if the person who initiated the demand does not, within the time stated in the issuer's communication, either:

(1) obtain an appropriate restraining order, injunction, or other process from a court of competent jurisdiction enjoining the issuer from registering the transfer; or

(2) file with the issuer an indemnity bond, sufficient in the issuer's judgment to protect the issuer and any transfer agent, registrar, or other agent of the issuer involved from any loss it or they may suffer by refusing to register the transfer.

(e) This section does not relieve an issuer from liability for registering transfer pursuant to an indorsement or instruction that was not effective.

Official Comment

1. The general rule under this Article is that if there has been an effective indorsement or instruction, a person who contends that registration of the transfer would be wrongful should not be able to interfere with the registration process merely by sending notice of the assertion to the issuer. Rather, the claimant must obtain legal process. See Section 8-404. Section 8-403 is an exception to this general rule. It permits the registered owner—but not third parties—to demand that the issuer not register a transfer.

2. This section is intended to alleviate the problems faced by registered owners of certificated securities who lose or misplace their certificates. A registered owner who realizes that a certificate may have been lost or stolen should promptly report that fact to the issuer, lest the owner be precluded from asserting a claim for wrongful registration. See Section 8-406. The usual practice of issuers and transfer agents is that when a certificate is reported as lost, the owner is notified that a replacement can be obtained if the owner provides an indemnity bond. See Section 8-405. If the registered owner does not plan to transfer the securities, the owner might choose not to obtain a replacement, particularly if the owner suspects that the certificate has merely been misplaced.

Under this section, the owner's notification that the certificate has been lost would constitute a demand that the issuer not register transfer. No indemnity bond or legal process is necessary. If the original certificate is presented for registration of transfer, the issuer is required to notify the registered owner of that fact, and defer registration of transfer for a stated period. In order to prevent undue delay in the process of registration, the stated period may not exceed thirty days. This gives the registered owner an opportunity to either obtain legal process or post an indemnity bond and thereby prevent the issuer from registering transfer.

3. Subsection (e) makes clear that this section does not relieve an issuer from liability for registering a transfer pursuant to an ineffective indorsement. An issuer's liability for wrongful registration in such cases does not depend on the presence or absence of notice that the indorsement was ineffective. Registered owners who are confident that they neither indorsed the certificates, nor did anything that would preclude them from denying the effectiveness of another's indorsement, see Sections 8-107(b) and 8-406, might prefer to pursue their rights against the issuer for wrongful registration rather than take advantage of the opportunity to post a bond or seek a restraining order when notified by the issuer under this section that their lost certificates have been presented for registration in apparently good order.

Definitional Cross References:

"Appropriate person"	Section 8-107
"Certificated security"	Section 8-102(a)(4)
"Communicate"	Section 8-102(a)(6)
"Effective"	Section 8-107
"Indorsement"	Section 8-102(a)(11)
"Instruction"	Section 8-102(a)(12)
"Issuer"	Section 8-201
"Registered form"	Section 8-102(a)(13)
"Uncertificated security"	Section 8-102(a)(18)

Section 8-404. Wrongful Registration

(a) Except as otherwise provided in Section 8-406, an issuer is liable for wrongful registration of transfer if the issuer has registered a transfer of a security to a person not entitled to it, and the transfer was registered:

(1) pursuant to an ineffective indorsement or instruction;

(2) after a demand that the issuer not register transfer became effective under Section 8-403(a) and the issuer did not comply with Section 8-403(b);

(3) after the issuer had been served with an injunction, restraining order, or other legal process enjoining it from registering the transfer, issued by a court of competent jurisdiction, and the issuer had a reasonable opportunity to act on the injunction, restraining order, or other legal process; or

(4) by an issuer acting in collusion with the wrongdoer.

(b) An issuer that is liable for wrongful registration of transfer under subsection (a) on demand shall provide the person entitled to the security with a like certificated or uncertificated security, and any payments or distributions that the person did not receive as a result of the wrongful registration. If an overissue would result, the issuer's liability to provide the person with a like security is governed by Section 8-210.

(c) Except as otherwise provided in subsection (a) or in a law relating to the collection of taxes, an issuer is not liable to an owner or other person suffering loss as a result of the registration of a transfer of a security if registration was made pursuant to an effective indorsement or instruction.

Official Comment

1. Subsection (a)(1) provides that an issuer is liable if it registers transfer pursuant to an indorsement or instruction that was not effective. For example, an issuer that registers transfer on a forged indorsement is liable to the registered owner. The fact that the issuer had no reason to suspect that the indorsement was forged or that the issuer obtained the ordinary assurances under Section 8-402 does not relieve the issuer from liability. The reason that issuers obtain signature guaranties and other assurances is that they are liable for wrongful registration.

Subsection (b) specifies the remedy for wrongful registration. Pre-Code cases established the registered owner's right to receive a new security where the issuer had wrongfully registered a transfer, but some cases also allowed the registered owner to elect between an equitable action to compel issue of a new security and an action for damages. Cf. *Casper v. Kalt-Zimmers Mfg. Co.*, 149 N.W. 754 (Wis. 1914). Article 8 does not allow such election. The true owner of a certificated security is required to take a new security except where an overissue would result and a similar security is not reasonably available for purchase. See Section 8-210. The true owner of an uncertificated security is entitled and required to take restoration of the records to their proper state, with a similar exception for overissue.

2. Read together, subsections (c) and (a) have the effect of providing that an issuer has no duties to an adverse claimant unless the claimant serves legal process on the issuer to enjoin registration. Issuers, or their transfer agents, perform a record-keeping function for the direct holding system that is analogous to the functions performed by clearing corporations and securities intermediaries in the indirect holding system. This section applies to the record-keepers for the direct holding system the same standard that Section 8-115 applies to the record-keepers for the indirect holding system. Thus, issuers are not liable to adverse claimants merely on the basis of notice. As in the case of the analogous rules for the indirect holding system, the policy of this section is to protect the right of investors to have their securities transfers processed without the disruption or delay that might result if the record-keepers risked liability to third parties. It would be undesirable to apply different standards to the direct and indirect holding systems, since doing so might operate as a disincentive to the development of a book-entry direct holding system.

3. This section changes prior law under which an issuer could be held liable, even though it registered transfer on an effective indorsement or instruction, if the issuer had in some fashion been notified that the transfer might be wrongful against a third party, and the issuer did not appropriately discharge its duty to inquire into the adverse claim. See Section 8-403 (1978).

The rule of former Section 8-403 was anomalous inasmuch as Section 8-207 provides that the issuer is entitled to "treat the registered owner as the person exclusively entitled to vote, receive notifications, and otherwise exercise all the rights and powers of an owner." Under Section 8-207, the fact that a third person notifies the issuer of a claim does not preclude the issuer from treating the registered owner as the person entitled to the security. See *Kerrigan v. American Orthodontics Corp.*, 960 F.2d 43 (7th Cir. 1992). The change made in the present version of Section 8-404 ensures that the rights of registered owners and the duties of issuers with respect to registration of transfer will be protected against third-party interference in the same fashion as other rights of registered ownership.

Definitional Cross References:

"Certificated security"	Section 8-102(a)(4)
"Effective"	Section 8-107
"Indorsement"	Section 8-102(a)(11)
"Instruction"	Section 8-102(a)(12)
"Issuer"	Section 8-201
"Security"	Section 8-102(a)(15)
"Uncertificated security"	Section 8-102(a)(18)

Section 8-405. Replacement of Lost, Destroyed, or Wrongfully Taken Security Certificate

(a) If an owner of a certificated security, whether in registered or bearer form, claims that the certificate has been lost, destroyed, or wrongfully taken, the issuer shall issue a new certificate if the owner:

(1) so requests before the issuer has notice that the certificate has been acquired by a protected purchaser;

(2) files with the issuer a sufficient indemnity bond; and

(3) satisfies other reasonable requirements imposed by the issuer.

(b) If, after the issue of a new security certificate, a protected purchaser of the original certificate presents it for registration of transfer, the issuer shall register the transfer unless an overissue would result. In that case, the issuer's liability is governed by Section 8-210. In addition to any rights on the indemnity bond, an issuer may recover the new certificate from a person to whom it was issued or any person taking under that person, except a protected purchaser.

Official Comment

1. This section enables the owner to obtain a replacement of a lost, destroyed or stolen certificate, provided that reasonable requirements are satisfied and a sufficient indemnity bond supplied.

2. Where an "original" security certificate has reached the hands of a protected purchaser, the registered owner—who was in the best position to prevent the loss, destruction or theft of the security certificate—is now deprived of the new security certificate issued as a replacement. This changes the pre-UCC law under which the original certificate was ineffective after the issue of a replacement except insofar as it might represent an action for damages in the hands of a purchaser for value without notice. *Keller v. Eureka Brick Mach. Mfg. Co.*, 43 Mo. App. 84 (1890). Where both the original and the new certificate have reached protected purchasers the issuer is required to honor both certificates unless an overissue would result and the security is not reasonably available for purchase. See Section 8-210. In the latter case alone, the protected purchaser of the original certificate is relegated to an action for damages. In either case, the issuer itself may recover on the indemnity bond.

Definitional Cross References:

"Bearer form"	Section 8-102(a)(2)
"Certificated security"	Section 8-102(a)(4)
"Issuer"	Section 8-201
"Notice"	Section 1-202(a)
"Overissue"	Section 8-210
"Protected purchaser"	Section 8-303
"Registered form"	Section 8-102(a)(13)
"Security certificate"	Section 8-102(a)(16)

Section 8-406. Obligation to Notify Issuer of Lost, Destroyed, or Wrongfully Taken Security Certificate

If a security certificate has been lost, apparently destroyed, or wrongfully taken, and the owner fails to notify the issuer of that fact within a reasonable time after the owner has notice of it and the issuer registers a transfer of the security before receiving notification, the owner may not assert against the issuer a claim for registering the transfer under Section 8-404 or a claim to a new security certificate under Section 8-405.

Official Comment

An owner who fails to notify the issuer within a reasonable time after the owner knows or has reason to know of the loss or theft of a security certificate is estopped from asserting the ineffectiveness of a forged or unauthorized indorsement and the wrongfulness of the registration of the transfer. If the lost certificate was indorsed by the owner, then the registration of the transfer was not wrongful under Section 8-404, unless the owner made an effective demand that the issuer not register transfer under Section 8-403.

Definitional Cross References:

"Issuer"	Section 8-201
"Notifies"	Section 1-202(d)
"Security certificate"	Section 8-102(a)(16)

Section 8-407. Authenticating Trustee, Transfer Agent, and Registrar

A person acting as authenticating trustee, transfer agent, registrar, or other agent for an issuer in the registration of a transfer of its securities, in the issue of new security certificates or uncertificated securities, or in the cancellation of surrendered security certificates has the same obligation to the holder or owner of a certificated or uncertificated security with regard to the particular functions performed as the issuer has in regard to those functions.

Official Comment

1. Transfer agents, registrars, and the like are here expressly held liable both to the issuer and to the owner for wrongful refusal to register a transfer as well as for wrongful registration of a transfer in any case within the scope of their respective functions where the issuer would itself be liable. Those cases which have regarded these parties solely as agents of the issuer and have therefore refused to recognize their liability to the owner for mere non-feasance, i.e., refusal to register a transfer, are rejected. *Hulse v. Consolidated Quicksilver Mining Corp.*, 154 P.2d 149 (Idaho 1944); *Nicholson v. Morgan*, 196 N.Y.S. 147 (Mun. Ct. 1922); *Lewis v. Hargadine-McKittrick Dry Goods Co.*, 274 S.W. 1041 (Mo. 1924).

2. The practice frequently followed by authenticating trustees of issuing certificates of indebtedness rather than authenticating duplicate certificates where securities have been lost or stolen became obsolete in view of the provisions of Section 8-405, which makes express provision for the issue of substitute securities. It is not a breach of trust or lack of due diligence for trustees to authenticate new securities. Cf. *Switzerland Gen. Ins. Co. v. N.Y.C. & H.R.R. Co.*, 136 N.Y.S. 726 (App. Div. 1912).

Definitional Cross References:

"Certificated security"	Section 8-102(a)(4)
"Issuer"	Section 8-201
"Security"	Section 8-102(a)(15)
"Security certificate"	Section 8-102(a)(16)
"Uncertificated security"	Section 8-102(a)(18)

PART 5. SECURITY ENTITLEMENTS

Section 8-501. Securities Account; Acquisition of Security Entitlement from Securities Intermediary

(a) "Securities account" means an account to which a financial asset is or may be credited in accordance with an agreement under which the person maintaining the account undertakes to treat the person for whom the account is maintained as entitled to exercise the rights that comprise the financial asset.

(b) Except as otherwise provided in subsections (d) and (e), a person acquires a security entitlement if a securities intermediary:

(1) indicates by book entry that a financial asset has been credited to the person's securities account;

(2) receives a financial asset from the person or acquires a financial asset for the person and, in either case, accepts it for credit to the person's securities account; or

(3) becomes obligated under other law, regulation, or rule to credit a financial asset to the person's securities account.

(c) If a condition of subsection (b) has been met, a person has a security entitlement even though the securities intermediary does not itself hold the financial asset.

(d) If a securities intermediary holds a financial asset for another person, and the financial asset is registered in the name of, payable to the order of, or specially indorsed to the other person, and has not been indorsed to the securities intermediary or in blank, the other person is treated as holding the financial asset directly rather than as having a security entitlement with respect to the financial asset.

(e) Issuance of a security is not establishment of a security entitlement.

Official Comment

1. Part 5 rules apply to security entitlements, and Section 8-501(b) provides that a person has a security entitlement when a financial asset has been credited to a "securities account." Thus, the term "securities account" specifies the type of arrangements between intermediaries and their customers that are covered by Part 5. A securities account is a consensual arrangement in which the intermediary undertakes to treat the customer as entitled to exercise the rights that comprise the financial asset. The consensual aspect is covered by the requirement that the account be established pursuant to agreement. The term agreement is used in the broad sense defined in Section 1-201(b)(3). There is no requirement that a formal or written agreement be signed.

As the securities business is presently conducted, several significant relationships clearly fall within the definition of a securities account, including the relationship between a clearing corporation and its participants, a broker and customers who leave securities with the broker, and a bank acting as securities custodian and its custodial customers. Given the enormous variety of arrangements concerning securities that exist today, and the certainty that new arrangements will evolve in the future, it is not possible to specify all of the arrangements to which the term does and does not apply.

Whether an arrangement between an intermediary and another person concerning a security or other financial asset is a "securities account" under this Article depends on whether the firm has undertaken to treat the other person as entitled to exercise the rights that comprise the security or other financial asset. Section 1-103, however, states the fundamental principle of interpretation that the Code provisions should be construed and applied to promote their underlying purposes and policies. Thus, the question whether a given arrangement is a securities account should be decided not by dictionary analysis of the words of the definition taken out of context, but by considering whether it promotes the objectives of Article 8 to include the arrangement within the term securities account.

The effect of concluding that an arrangement is a securities account is that the rules of Part 5 apply. Accordingly, the definition of "securities account" must be interpreted in light of the substantive provisions in Part 5, which describe the core features of the type of relationship for which the commercial law rules of Revised Article 8 concerning security entitlements were designed. There are many arrangements between intermediaries and other persons concerning securities or other financial assets which do not fall within the definition of "securities account" because the intermediaries have not undertaken to treat the other persons as entitled to exercise the ordinary rights of an entitlement holder specified in the Part 5 rules. For example, the term securities account does not cover the relationship between a bank and its depositors or the relationship between a trustee and the beneficiary of an ordinary trust, because those are not relationships in which the holder of a financial asset has undertaken to treat the other as entitled to exercise the rights that comprise the financial asset in the fashion contemplated by the Part 5 rules.

In short, the primary factor in deciding whether an arrangement is a securities account is whether application of the Part 5 rules is consistent with the expectations of the parties to the relationship. Relationships not governed by Part 5 may be governed by other parts of Article 8 if the relationship gives rise to a new security, or may be governed by other law entirely.

2. Subsection (b) of this section specifies what circumstances give rise to security entitlements. Paragraph (1) of subsection (b) sets out the most important rule. It turns on the intermediary's conduct, reflecting a basic operating assumption of the indirect holding system that once a securities intermediary has acknowledged that it is carrying a position in a financial asset for its customer or participant, the intermediary is obligated to treat the customer or participant as entitled to the financial asset. Paragraph (1) does not attempt to specify exactly what accounting, record-keeping, or information transmission steps suffice to indicate that the intermediary has credited the account. That is left to agreement, trade practice, or rule in order to provide the flexibility necessary to accommodate varying or changing accounting and information processing systems. The point of paragraph (1) is that once an intermediary has acknowledged that it is carrying a position for the customer or participant, the customer or participant has a security entitlement. The precise form in which the intermediary manifests that acknowledgment is left to private ordering.

Paragraph (2) of subsection (b) sets out a different operational test, turning not on the intermediary's accounting system but on the facts that accounting systems are supposed to represent. Under paragraph (b)(2) a person has a security entitlement if the intermediary has received and accepted a financial asset for credit to the account of its customer or participant. For example, if a customer of a broker or bank custodian delivers a security certificate in proper form to the broker or bank to be held in the customer's account, the customer acquires a security entitlement. Paragraph (b)(2) also covers circumstances in which the intermediary receives a financial asset from a third person for credit to the account of the customer or participant. Paragraph (b)(2) is not limited to circumstances in which the intermediary receives security certificates or other financial assets in physical form. Paragraph (b)(2) also covers circumstances in which the intermediary acquires a security entitlement with respect to a financial asset which is to be credited to the account of the intermediary's own customer. For example, if a customer transfers her account from Broker A to Broker B, she acquires security entitlements against Broker B once the clearing corporation has credited the positions to Broker B's account. It should be noted, however, that paragraph (b)(2) provides that a person acquires a security entitlement when the intermediary not only receives but also accepts the financial asset for credit to the account. This limitation is included to take account of the fact that there may be circumstances in which an intermediary has received a financial asset but is not willing to undertake the obligations that flow from establishing a security entitlement. For example, a security certificate which is sent to an intermediary may not be in proper form, or may represent a type of financial asset which the intermediary is not willing to carry for others. It should be noted that in all but extremely unusual cases, the circumstances covered by paragraph (2) will also be covered by paragraph (1), because the intermediary will have credited the positions to the customer's account.

Paragraph (3) of subsection (b) sets out a residual test, to avoid any implication that the failure of an intermediary to make the appropriate entries to credit a position to a customer's securities account would prevent the customer from acquiring the rights of an entitlement holder under Part 5. As is the case with the paragraph (2) test, the paragraph (3) test would not be needed for the ordinary cases, since they are covered by paragraph (1).

3. In a sense, Section 8-501(b) is analogous to the rules set out in the provisions of Sections 8-313(1)(d) and 8-320 of the prior version of Article 8 that specified what acts by a securities intermediary or clearing corporation sufficed as a transfer of securities held in fungible bulk. Unlike the prior version of Article 8, however, this section is not based on the idea that an entitlement holder acquires rights only by virtue of a "transfer" from the securities intermediary to the entitlement holder. In the indirect holding system, the significant fact is that the securities intermediary has undertaken to treat the customer as entitled to the financial asset. It is up to the securities intermediary to take the necessary steps to ensure that it will be able to perform its undertaking. It is, for example, entirely possible that a securities intermediary might make entries in a customer's account reflecting that customer's acquisition of a certain security at a time when the securities intermediary did not itself happen to hold any units of that security. The person from whom the securities intermediary bought the security might have failed to deliver and it might have taken some time to clear up the problem, or there may have been an operational gap in time between the crediting of a customer's account and the receipt of securities from another securities intermediary. The entitlement holder's rights against the securities intermediary do not depend on whether or when the securities intermediary acquired its interests. Subsection (c) is intended to make this point clear. Subsection (c) does not mean that the intermediary is free to create security entitlements without itself holding sufficient financial assets to satisfy its entitlement holders. The duty of a securities intermediary to maintain sufficient assets is governed by Section 8-504 and regulatory law. Subsection (c) is included only to make it clear the question whether a person has acquired a security entitlement does not depend on whether the intermediary has complied with that duty.

4. Part 5 of Article 8 sets out a carefully designed system of rules for the indirect holding system. Persons who hold securities through brokers or custodians have security entitlements that are governed by Part 5, rather than being treated as the direct holders of securities. Subsection (d) specifies the limited circumstance in which a customer who leaves a financial asset with a broker or other securities intermediary has a direct interest in the financial asset, rather than a security entitlement.

The customer can be a direct holder only if the security certificate, or other financial asset, is registered in the name of, payable to the order of, or specially indorsed to the customer, and has not been indorsed by the customer to the securities intermediary or in blank. The distinction between those circumstances where the customer can be treated as direct owner and those where the customer has a security entitlement is essentially the same as the distinction drawn under the federal bankruptcy code between customer name securities and customer property. The distinction does not turn on any form of physical identification or segregation. A customer who delivers certificates to a broker with blank indorsements or stock powers is not a direct holder but has a security entitlement, even though the broker holds those certificates in some form of separate safe-keeping arrangement for that particular customer. The customer remains the direct holder only if there is no indorsement or stock power so that further action by the customer is required to place the certificates in a form where they can be transferred by the broker.

The rule of subsection (d) corresponds to the rule set out in Section 8-301(a)(3) specifying when acquisition of possession of a certificate by a securities intermediary counts as "delivery" to the customer.

Subsection (d) uses terminology applicable to conventional certificated securities (e.g., "indorsed") and contemplates the limited circumstances in which a securities intermediary (defined in Section 8-102(a)(14) to include only a clearing corporation or another person that in the ordinary course of its business maintains securities accounts for others and that is acting in that capacity) may hold a financial asset for a customer under a direct holding arrangement rather than as a security entitlement. However, assets such as controllable electronic records, controllable accounts, and controllable payment intangibles also might be associated with an intermediary as well as with its customer under a similar direct holding arrangement. For example, the intermediary and the customer might share control of the financial asset under an arrangement whereby the intermediary could exercise powers, such as the power to transfer control, only with the concurrent exercise of the powers by the customer. As with conventional certificated securities, whether an intermediary has created a security entitlement in favor of an entitlement holder or its customer is holding a financial asset directly depends on the nature of the relationship and the nature of the rights of the intermediary and the customer with respect to the financial asset. A securities intermediary and a customer wishing to establish the customer's direct holding status could avoid uncertainty by means of unambiguous contractual documentation of their relationship. Moreover, a person holding such an asset for the benefit of another may not be acting in the capacity of a securities intermediary at all, even if the person also regularly acts in that capacity. In such a case, subsection (d) would not apply and the relationship would be governed by the agreement of the parties and the application of law other than this Article.

5. Subsection (e) is intended to make clear that Part 5 does not apply to an arrangement in which a security is issued representing an interest in underlying assets, as distinguished from arrangements in which the underlying assets are carried in a securities account. A common mechanism by which new financial instruments are devised is that a financial institution that holds some security, financial instrument, or pool thereof, creates interests in that asset or pool which are sold to others. In many such cases, the interests so created will fall within the definition of "security" in Section 8-102(a)(15). If so, then by virtue of subsection (e) of Section 8-501, the relationship between the institution that creates the interests and the persons who hold them is not a security entitlement to which the Part 5 rules apply. Accordingly, an arrangement such as an American depositary receipt facility which creates freely transferable interests in underlying securities will be issuance of a security under Article 8 rather than establishment of a security entitlement to the underlying securities.

The subsection (e) rule can be regarded as an aspect of the definitional rules specifying the meaning of securities account and security entitlement. Among the key components of the definition of security in Section 8-102(a)(15) are the "transferability" and "divisibility" tests. Securities, in the Article 8 sense, are fungible interests or obligations that are intended to be tradable. The concept of security entitlement under Part 5 is quite different. A security entitlement is the package of rights that a person has against the person's own intermediary with respect to the positions carried in the person's securities account. That package of rights is not, as such, something that is traded. When a customer sells a security that she had held through a securities account, her security entitlement is terminated; when she buys a security that she will hold through her securities account, she acquires a security entitlement. In most cases, settlement of a securities trade will involve termination of one person's security entitlement and acquisition of a security entitlement by another person. That transaction, however, is not a "transfer" of the same entitlement from one person to another. That is not to say that an entitlement holder cannot transfer an interest in her security entitlement as such; granting a security interest in a security entitlement is such a transfer. On the other hand, the nature of a security entitlement is that the intermediary is undertaking duties only to the person identified as the entitlement holder.

6. Rights and obligations relating to a security entitlement are enforceable by action. See Section 1-305(b) and PEB Commentary No. 25.

Definitional Cross References:

"Financial asset"	Section 8-102(a)(9)
"Indorsement"	Section 8-102(a)(11)
"Securities intermediary"	Section 8-102(a)(14)
"Security"	Section 8-102(a)(15)
"Security entitlement"	Section 8-102(a)(17)

Section 8-502. Assertion of Adverse Claim Against Entitlement Holder

An action based on an adverse claim to a financial asset, whether framed in conversion, replevin, constructive trust, equitable lien, or other theory, may not be asserted against a person who acquires a security entitlement under Section 8-501 for value and without notice of the adverse claim.

Official Comment

1. The section provides investors in the indirect holding system with protection against adverse claims by specifying that no adverse claim can be asserted against a person who acquires a security entitlement under Section 8-501 for value and without notice of the adverse claim. It plays a role in the indirect holding system analogous to the rule of the direct holding system that protected purchasers take free from adverse claims (Section 8-303).

This section does not use the locution "takes free from adverse claims" because that could be confusing as applied to the indirect holding system. The nature of indirect holding system is that an entitlement holder has an interest in common with others who hold positions in the same financial asset through the same intermediary. Thus, a particular entitlement holder's interest in the financial assets held by its intermediary is necessarily "subject to" the interests of others. See Section 8-503. The rule stated in this section might have been expressed by saying that a person who acquires a security entitlement under Section 8-501 for value and without notice of adverse claims takes "that security entitlement" free from adverse claims. That formulation has not been used, however, for fear that it would be misinterpreted as suggesting that the person acquires a right to the underlying financial assets that could not be affected by the competing rights of others claiming through common or higher tier intermediaries. A security entitlement is a complex bundle of rights. This section does not deal with the question of what rights are in the bundle. Rather, this section provides that once a person has acquired the bundle, someone else cannot take it away on the basis of assertion that the transaction in which the security entitlement was created involved a violation of the claimant's rights.

2. Because securities trades are typically settled on a net basis by book-entry movements, it would ordinarily be impossible for anyone to trace the path of any particular security, no matter how the interest of parties who hold through intermediaries is described. Suppose, for example, that S has a 1000 share position in XYZ common stock through an account with a broker, Able & Co. S's identical twin impersonates S and directs Able to sell the securities. That same day, B places an order with Baker & Co., to buy 1000 shares of XYZ common stock. Later, S discovers the wrongful act and seeks to recover "her shares." Even if S can show that, at the stage of the trade, her sell order was matched with B's buy order, that would not suffice to show that "her shares" went to B. Settlement between Able and Baker occurs on a net basis for all trades in XYZ that day; indeed Able's net position may have been such that it received rather than delivered shares in XYZ through the settlement system.

In the unlikely event that this was the only trade in XYZ common stock executed in the market that day, one could follow the shares from S's account to B's account. The plaintiff in an action in conversion or similar legal action to enforce a property interest must show that the defendant has an item of property that belongs to the plaintiff. In this example, B's security entitlement is not the same item of property that formerly was held by S, it is a new package of rights that B acquired against Baker under Section 8-501. Principles of equitable remedies might, however, provide S with a basis for contending that if the position B received was the traceable product of the wrongful taking of S's property by S's twin, a constructive trust should be imposed on B's property in favor of S. See G. Palmer, The Law of Restitution § 2.14. Section 8-502 ensures that no such claims can be asserted against a person, such as B in this example, who acquires a security entitlement under Section 8-501 for value and without notice, regardless of what theory of law or equity is used to describe the basis of the assertion of the adverse claim.

In the above example, S would ordinarily have no reason to pursue B unless Able is insolvent and S's claim will not be satisfied in the insolvency proceedings. Because S did not give an entitlement order for the disposition of her security entitlement, Able must recredit her account for the 1000 shares of XYZ common stock. See Section 8-507(b).

3. The following examples illustrate the operation of Section 8-502.

> **Example 1:** Thief steals bearer bonds from Owner. Thief delivers the bonds to Broker for credit to Thief's securities account, thereby acquiring a security entitlement under Section 8-501(b). Under other law, Owner may have a claim to have a constructive trust imposed on the security entitlement as the traceable product of the bonds that Thief misappropriated. Because Thief was himself the wrongdoer, Thief obviously had notice of Owner's adverse claim. Accordingly, Section 8-502 does not preclude Owner from asserting an adverse claim against Thief.

> **Example 2:** Thief steals bearer bonds from Owner. Thief owes a personal debt to Creditor. Creditor has a securities account with Broker. Thief agrees to transfer the bonds to Creditor as security for or in satisfaction of his debt to Creditor. Thief does so by sending the bonds to Broker for credit to Creditor's securities account. Creditor thereby acquires a security entitlement under Section 8-501(b). Under other law, Owner may have a claim to have a constructive trust imposed on the security entitlement as the traceable product of the bonds that Thief misappropriated. Creditor acquired the security entitlement for value, since

Creditor acquired it as security for or in satisfaction of Thief's debt to Creditor. See Section 1-204. If Creditor did not have notice of Owner's claim, Section 8-502 precludes any action by Owner against Creditor, whether framed in constructive trust or other theory. Section 8-105 specifies what counts as notice of an adverse claim.

Example 3: Father, as trustee for Son, holds XYZ Co. shares in a securities account with Able & Co. In violation of his fiduciary duties, Father sells the XYZ Co. shares and uses the proceeds for personal purposes. Father dies, and his estate is insolvent. Assume—implausibly—that Son is able to trace the XYZ Co. shares and show that the "same shares" ended up in Buyer's securities account with Baker & Co. Section 8-502 precludes any action by Son against Buyer, whether framed in constructive trust or other theory, provided that Buyer acquired the security entitlement for value and without notice of adverse claims.

Example 4: Debtor holds XYZ Co. shares in a securities account with Able & Co. As collateral for a loan from Bank, Debtor grants Bank a security interest in the security entitlement to the XYZ Co. shares. Bank perfects by a method which leaves Debtor with the ability to dispose of the shares. See Section 9-312. In violation of the security agreement, Debtor sells the XYZ Co. shares and absconds with the proceeds. Assume—implausibly—that Bank is able to trace the XYZ Co. shares and show that the "same shares" ended up in Buyer's securities account with Baker & Co. Section 8-502 precludes any action by Bank against Buyer, whether framed in constructive trust or other theory, provided that Buyer acquired the security entitlement for value and without notice of adverse claims.

Example 5: Debtor owns controlling interests in various public companies, including Acme and Ajax. Acme owns 60% of the stock of another public company, Beta. Debtor causes the Beta stock to be pledged to Lending Bank as collateral for Ajax's debt. Acme holds the Beta stock through an account with a securities custodian, C Bank, which in turn holds through Clearing Corporation. Lending Bank is also a Clearing Corporation participant. The pledge of the Beta stock is implemented by Acme instructing C Bank to instruct Clearing Corporation to debit C Bank's account and credit Lending Bank's account. Acme and Ajax both become insolvent. The Beta stock is still valuable. Acme's liquidator asserts that the pledge of the Beta stock for Ajax's debt was wrongful as against Acme and seeks to recover the Beta stock from Lending Bank. Because the pledge was implemented by an outright transfer into Lending Bank's account at Clearing Corporation, Lending Bank acquired a security entitlement to the Beta stock under Section 8-501. Lending Bank acquired the security entitlement for value, since it acquired it as security for a debt. See Section 1-204. If Lending Bank did not have notice of Acme's claim, Section 8-502 will preclude any action by Acme against Lending Bank, whether framed in constructive trust or other theory.

Example 6: Debtor grants Alpha Co. a security interest in a security entitlement that includes 1000 shares of XYZ Co. stock that Debtor holds through an account with Able & Co. Alpha also has an account with Able. Debtor instructs Able to transfer the shares to Alpha, and Able does so by crediting the shares to Alpha's account. Alpha has control of the 1000 shares under Section 8-106(d). (The facts to this point are identical to those in Section 8-106, Comment 4, Example 1, except that Alpha Co. was Alpha Bank.) Alpha next grants Beta Co. a security interest in the 1000 shares included in Alpha's security entitlement. See Section 9-207(c)(3). Alpha instructs Able to transfer the shares to Gamma Co., Beta's custodian. Able does so, and Gamma credits the 1000 shares to Beta's account. Beta now has control under Section 8-106(d). By virtue of Debtor's explicit permission or by virtue of the permission inherent in Debtor's creation of a security interest in favor of Alpha and Alpha's resulting power to grant a security interest under Section 9-207, Debtor has no adverse claim to assert against Beta, assuming implausibly that Debtor could "trace" an interest to the Gamma account. Moreover, even if Debtor did hold an adverse claim, if Beta did not have notice of Debtor's claim, Section 8-502 will preclude any action by Debtor against Beta, whether framed in constructive trust or other theory.

4. Although this section protects entitlement holders against adverse claims, it does not protect them against the risk that their securities intermediary will not itself have sufficient financial assets to satisfy the claims of all of its entitlement holders. Suppose that Customer A holds 1000 shares of XYZ Co. stock in an account with her broker, Able & Co. Able in turn holds 1000 shares of XYZ Co. through its account with Clearing Corporation, but has no other positions in XYZ Co. shares, either for other customers or for its own proprietary account. Customer B places an order with Able for the purchase of 1000 shares of XYZ Co. stock, and pays the purchase price. Able credits B's account with a 1000 share position in XYZ Co. stock, but Able does not itself buy any additional XYZ Co. shares. Able fails, having only 1000 shares to satisfy the claims of A and B. Unless other insolvency law establishes a different distributional rule, A and B would share the 1000 shares held by Able pro rata, without regard to the time that their respective entitlements were established. See Section 8-503(b). Section 8-502 protects entitlement holders, such as A and B, against adverse claimants. In this case, however, the problem that A and B face is not that someone is trying to take away their entitlements, but that the entitlements are not worth what they thought. The only role that Section 8-502 plays in this case is to preclude any assertion that A has some form of claim against B by virtue of the fact that Able's establishment of an entitlement in favor of B diluted A's rights to the limited assets held by Able.

Definitional Cross References:

"Adverse claim"	Section 8-102(a)(1)
"Financial asset"	Section 8-102(a)(9)
"Notice of adverse claim"	Section 8-105
"Security entitlement"	Section 8-102(a)(17)
"Value"	Sections 1-204 and 8-116

Section 8-503. Property Interest of Entitlement Holder in Financial Asset Held by Securities Intermediary

(a) To the extent necessary for a securities intermediary to satisfy all security entitlements with respect to a particular financial asset, all interests in that financial asset held by the securities intermediary are held by the securities intermediary for the entitlement holders, are not property of the securities intermediary, and are not subject to claims of creditors of the securities intermediary, except as otherwise provided in Section 8-511.

(b) An entitlement holder's property interest with respect to a particular financial asset under subsection (a) is a pro rata property interest in all interests in that financial asset held by the securities intermediary, without regard to the time the entitlement holder acquired the security entitlement or the time the securities intermediary acquired the interest in that financial asset.

(c) An entitlement holder's property interest with respect to a particular financial asset under subsection (a) may be enforced against the securities intermediary only by exercise of the entitlement holder's rights under Sections 8-505 through 8-508.

(d) An entitlement holder's property interest with respect to a particular financial asset under subsection (a) may be enforced against a purchaser of the financial asset or interest therein only if:

(1) insolvency proceedings have been initiated by or against the securities intermediary;

(2) the securities intermediary does not have sufficient interests in the financial asset to satisfy the security entitlements of all of its entitlement holders to that financial asset;

(3) the securities intermediary violated its obligations under Section 8-504 by transferring the financial asset or interest therein to the purchaser; and

(4) the purchaser is not protected under subsection (e).

The trustee or other liquidator, acting on behalf of all entitlement holders having security entitlements with respect to a particular financial asset, may recover the financial asset, or interest therein, from the purchaser. If the trustee or other liquidator elects not to pursue that right, an entitlement holder whose security entitlement remains unsatisfied has the right to recover its interest in the financial asset from the purchaser.

(e) An action based on the entitlement holder's property interest with respect to a particular financial asset under subsection (a), whether framed in conversion, replevin, constructive trust, equitable lien, or other theory, may not be asserted against any purchaser of a financial asset or interest therein who gives value, obtains control, and does not act in collusion with the securities intermediary in violating the securities intermediary's obligations under Section 8-504.

Official Comment

1. This section specifies the sense in which a security entitlement is an interest in the property held by the securities intermediary. It expresses the ordinary understanding that securities that a firm holds for its customers are not general assets of the firm subject to the claims of creditors. Since securities intermediaries generally do not segregate securities in such fashion that one could identify particular securities as the ones held for customers, it would not be realistic for this section to state that "customers' securities" are not subject to creditors' claims. Rather subsection (a) provides that to the extent necessary to satisfy all customer claims, all units of that security held by the firm are held for the entitlement holders, are not property of the securities intermediary, and are not subject to creditors' claims, except as otherwise provided in Section 8-511.

An entitlement holder's property interest under this section is an interest with respect to a specific issue of securities or financial assets. For example, customers of a firm who have positions in XYZ common stock have security entitlements with respect to the XYZ common stock held by the intermediary, while other customers who have positions in ABC common stock have security entitlements with respect to the ABC common stock held by the intermediary.

Subsection (b) makes clear that the property interest described in subsection (a) is an interest held in common by all entitlement holders who have entitlements to a particular security or other financial asset. Temporal factors are irrelevant. One entitlement holder cannot claim that its rights to the assets held by the intermediary are superior to the rights of another entitlement holder by virtue of having acquired those rights before, or after, the other entitlement holder. Nor does it matter whether the intermediary had sufficient assets to satisfy all entitlement holders' claims at one point, but no longer does. Rather, all entitlement holders have a pro rata interest in whatever positions in that financial asset the intermediary holds.

Although this section describes the property interest of entitlement holders in the assets held by the intermediary, it does not necessarily determine how property held by a failed intermediary will be distributed in insolvency proceedings. If the intermediary fails and its affairs are being administered in an insolvency proceeding, the applicable insolvency law governs how the various parties having claims against the firm are treated. For example, the distributional rules for stockbroker liquidation proceedings under the Bankruptcy Code and Securities Investor Protection Act ("SIPA") provide that all customer property is distributed pro rata among all customers in proportion to the dollar value of their total positions, rather than dividing the property on an issue by issue basis. For intermediaries that are not subject to the Bankruptcy Code and SIPA, other insolvency law would determine what distributional rule is applied.

2. Although this section recognizes that the entitlement holders of a securities intermediary have a property interest in the financial assets held by the intermediary, the incidents of this property interest are established by the rules of Article 8, not by common law property concepts. The traditional Article 8 rules on certificated securities were based on the idea that a paper certificate could be regarded as a nearly complete reification of the underlying right. The rules on transfer and the consequences of wrongful transfer could then be written using the same basic concepts as the rules for physical chattels. A person's claim of ownership of a certificated security is a right to a specific identifiable physical object, and that right can be asserted against any person who ends up in possession of that physical certificate, unless cut off by the rules protecting purchasers for value without notice. Those concepts do not work for the indirect holding system. A security entitlement is not a claim to a specific identifiable thing; it is a package of rights and interests that a person has against the person's securities intermediary and the property held by the intermediary. The idea that discrete objects might be traced through the hands of different persons has no place in the Revised Article 8 rules for the indirect holding system. The fundamental principles of the indirect holding system rules are that an entitlement holder's own intermediary has the obligation to see to it that the entitlement holder receives all of the economic and corporate rights that comprise the financial asset, and that the entitlement holder can look only to that intermediary for performance of the obligations. The entitlement holder cannot assert rights directly against other persons, such as other intermediaries through whom the intermediary holds the positions, or third parties to whom the intermediary may have wrongfully transferred interests, except in extremely unusual circumstances where the third party was itself a participant in the wrongdoing. Subsections (c) through (e) reflect these fundamental principles.

Subsection (c) provides that an entitlement holder's property interest can be enforced against the intermediary only by exercise of the entitlement holder's rights under Sections 8-505 through 8-508. These are the provisions that set out the duty of an intermediary to see to it that the entitlement holder receives all of the economic and corporate rights that comprise the security. If the intermediary is in insolvency proceedings and can no longer perform in accordance with the ordinary Part 5 rules, the applicable insolvency law will determine how the intermediary's assets are to be distributed.

Subsections (d) and (e) specify the limited circumstances in which an entitlement holder's property interest can be asserted against a third person to whom the intermediary transferred a financial asset that was subject to the entitlement holder's claim when held by the intermediary. Subsection (d) provides that the property interest of entitlement holders cannot be asserted against any transferee except in the circumstances therein specified. So long as the intermediary is solvent, the entitlement holders must look to the intermediary to satisfy their claims. If the intermediary does not hold financial assets corresponding to the entitlement holders' claims, the intermediary has the duty to acquire them. See Section 8-504. Thus, paragraphs (1), (2), and (3) of subsection (d) specify that the only occasion in which the entitlement holders can pursue transferees is when the intermediary is unable to perform its obligation, and the transfer to the transferee was a violation of those obligations. Even in that case, a transferee who gave value and obtained control is protected by virtue of the rule in subsection (e), unless the transferee acted in collusion with the intermediary.

Subsections (d) and (e) have the effect of protecting transferees from an intermediary against adverse claims arising out of assertions by the intermediary's entitlement holders that the intermediary acted wrongfully in transferring the financial assets. These rules, however, operate in a slightly different fashion than traditional adverse claim cut-off rules. Rather than specifying that a certain class of transferee takes free from all claims, subsections (d) and (e) specify the circumstances in which this particular form of claim can be asserted against a transferee. Revised Article 8 also contains general adverse claim cut-off rules for the indirect holding system. See Sections 8-502 and 8-510. The rule of subsections (d) and (e) takes precedence over the general cut-off rules of those sections, because Section 8-503 itself defines and sets limits on the assertion of the property interest of entitlement holders. Thus, the question whether entitlement holders' property interest can be asserted as an adverse claim against a transferee from the intermediary is governed by the collusion test of Section 8-503(e), rather than by the "without notice" test of Sections 8-502 and 8-510.

3. The limitations that subsections (c) through (e) place on the ability of customers of a failed intermediary to recover securities or other financial assets from transferees are consistent with the fundamental policies of investor protection that underlie this Article and other bodies of law governing the securities business. The commercial law rules for the securities holding and transfer system must be assessed from the forward-looking perspective of their impact on the vast number of transactions in which no wrongful conduct occurred or will occur, rather than from the *post hoc* perspective of what rule might be most advantageous to a particular class of persons in litigation that might arise out of the occasional case in which someone has acted wrongfully. Although one can devise hypothetical scenarios where particular customers might find it advantageous to be able to assert rights against someone other than the customers' own intermediary, commercial law rules that permitted customers to do so would impair rather than promote the interest of investors and the safe and efficient operation of the clearance and settlement system. Suppose, for example, that Intermediary A transfers securities to B, that Intermediary A acted wrongfully as against its customers in so doing, and that after the transaction Intermediary A did not have sufficient securities to satisfy its obligations to its entitlement holders. Viewed solely from the standpoint of the customers of Intermediary A, it would seem that permitting the property to be recovered from B, would be good for investors. That, however, is not the case. B may itself be an intermediary with its own customers, or may be some other institution through which individuals invest, such as a pension fund or investment company. There is no reason to think that rules permitting customers of an intermediary to trace and recover securities that their intermediary wrongfully transferred work to the advantage of investors in general. To the contrary, application of such rules would often merely shift losses from one set of investors to another. The uncertainties that would result from rules permitting such recoveries would work to the disadvantage of all participants in the securities markets.

The use of the collusion test in Section 8-503(e) furthers the interests of investors generally in the sound and efficient operation of the securities holding and settlement system. The effect of the choice of this standard is that customers of a failed intermediary must show that the transferee from whom they seek to recover was affirmatively engaged in wrongful conduct, rather than casting on the transferee any burden of showing that the transferee had no awareness of wrongful conduct by the failed intermediary. The rule of Section 8-503(e) is based on the long-standing policy that it is undesirable to impose upon purchasers of securities any duty to investigate whether their sellers may be acting wrongfully.

Rather than imposing duties to investigate, the general policy of the commercial law of the securities holding and transfer system has been to eliminate legal rules that might induce participants to conduct investigations of the authority of persons transferring securities on behalf of others for fear that they might be held liable for participating in a wrongful transfer. The rules in Part 4 of Article 8 concerning transfers by fiduciaries provide a good example. Under *Lowry v. Commercial & Farmers' Bank*, 15 F. Cas. 1040 (Cir. Ct. Md. 1848), an issuer could be held liable for wrongful transfer if it registered transfer of securities by a fiduciary under circumstances where it had any reason to believe that the fiduciary may have been acting improperly. In one sense that seems to be advantageous for beneficiaries who might be harmed by wrongful conduct by fiduciaries. The consequence of the *Lowry* rule, however, was that in order to protect against risk of such liability, issuers developed the practice of requiring extensive documentation for fiduciary stock transfers, making such transfers cumbersome and time consuming. Accordingly, the rules in Part 4 of Article 8, and in the prior fiduciary transfer statutes, were designed to discourage transfer agents from conducting investigations into the rightfulness of transfers by fiduciaries.

The rules of Revised Article 8 implement for the indirect holding system the same policies that the rules on protected purchasers and registration of transfer adopt for the direct holding system. A securities intermediary is, by definition, a person who is holding securities on behalf of other persons. There is nothing unusual or suspicious about a transaction in which a securities intermediary sells securities that it was holding for its customers. That is exactly what securities intermediaries are in business to do. The interests of customers of securities intermediaries would not be served by a rule that required counterparties to transfers from securities intermediaries to investigate whether the intermediary was acting wrongfully against its customers. Quite the contrary, such a rule would impair the ability of securities intermediaries to perform the function that customers want.

The rules of Section 8-503(c) through (e) apply to transferees generally, including pledgees. The reasons for treating pledgees in the same fashion as other transferees are discussed in the Comments to Section 8-511. The statement in subsection (a) that an intermediary holds financial assets for customers and not as its own property does not, of course, mean that the intermediary lacks power to transfer the financial assets to others. For example, although Article 9 provides that for a security interest to attach the debtor must have "rights" in the collateral, see Section 9-203, the fact that an intermediary is holding a financial asset in a form that permits ready transfer means that it has such rights, even if the intermediary is acting wrongfully against its entitlement holders in granting the security interest. The question whether the secured party takes subject to the entitlement holder's claim in such a case is governed by Section 8-511, which is an application to secured transactions of the general principles expressed in subsections (d) and (e) of this section.

Definitional Cross References:

"Control"	Section 8-106
"Entitlement holder"	Section 8-102(a)(7)
"Financial asset"	Section 8-102(a)(9)
"Insolvency proceeding"	Section 1-201(b)(22)
"Purchaser"	Sections 1-201(b)(30) and 8-116

"Securities intermediary"	Section 8-102(a)(14)
"Security entitlement"	Section 8-102(a)(17)
"Value"	Sections 1-204 and 8-116

Section 8-504. Duty of Securities Intermediary to Maintain Financial Asset

(a) A securities intermediary shall promptly obtain and thereafter maintain a financial asset in a quantity corresponding to the aggregate of all security entitlements it has established in favor of its entitlement holders with respect to that financial asset. The securities intermediary may maintain those financial assets directly or through one or more other securities intermediaries.

(b) Except to the extent otherwise agreed by its entitlement holder, a securities intermediary may not grant any security interests in a financial asset it is obligated to maintain pursuant to subsection (a).

(c) A securities intermediary satisfies the duty in subsection (a) if:

(1) the securities intermediary acts with respect to the duty as agreed upon by the entitlement holder and the securities intermediary; or

(2) in the absence of agreement, the securities intermediary exercises due care in accordance with reasonable commercial standards to obtain and maintain the financial asset.

(d) This section does not apply to a clearing corporation that is itself the obligor of an option or similar obligation to which its entitlement holders have security entitlements.

Official Comment

1. This section expresses one of the core elements of the relationships for which the Part 5 rules were designed, to wit, that a securities intermediary undertakes to hold financial assets corresponding to the security entitlements of its entitlement holders. The locution "shall promptly obtain and shall thereafter maintain" is taken from the corresponding regulation under federal securities law, 17 C.F.R. § 240.15c3-3. This section recognizes the reality that as the securities business is conducted today, it is not possible to identify particular securities as belonging to customers as distinguished from other particular securities that are the firm's own property. Securities firms typically keep all securities in fungible form, and may maintain their inventory of a particular security in various locations and forms, including physical securities held in vaults or in transit to transfer agents, and book entry positions at one or more clearing corporations. Accordingly, this section states that a securities intermediary shall maintain a quantity of financial assets corresponding to the aggregate of all security entitlements it has established. The last sentence of subsection (a) provides explicitly that the securities intermediary may hold directly or indirectly. That point is implicit in the use of the term "financial asset," inasmuch as Section 8-102(a)(9) provides that the term "financial asset" may refer either to the underlying asset or the means by which it is held, including both security certificates and security entitlements.

2. Subsection (b) states explicitly a point that is implicit in the notion that a securities intermediary must maintain financial assets corresponding to the security entitlements of its entitlement holders, to wit, that it is wrongful for a securities intermediary to grant security interests in positions that it needs to satisfy customers' claims, except as authorized by the customers. This statement does not determine the rights of a secured party to whom a securities intermediary wrongfully grants a security interest; that issue is governed by Sections 8-503 and 8-511.

Margin accounts are common examples of arrangements in which an entitlement holder authorizes the securities intermediary to grant security interests in the positions held for the entitlement holder. Securities firms commonly obtain the funds needed to provide margin loans to their customers by "rehypothecating" the customers' securities. In order to facilitate rehypothecation, agreements between margin customers and their brokers commonly authorize the broker to commingle securities of all margin customers for rehypothecation to the lender who provides the financing. Brokers commonly rehypothecate customer securities having a value somewhat greater than the amount of the loan made to the customer, since the lenders who provide the necessary financing to the broker need some cushion of protection against the risk of decline in the value of the rehypothecated securities. The extent and manner in which a firm may rehypothecate customers' securities are determined by the agreement between the intermediary and the entitlement holder and by applicable regulatory law. Current regulations under the federal securities laws require that brokers obtain the explicit consent of customers before pledging customer securities or commingling different customers' securities for pledge. Federal regulations also limit the extent to which a broker may rehypothecate customer securities to 110% of the aggregate amount of the borrowings of all customers.

3. The statement in this section that an intermediary must obtain and maintain financial assets corresponding to the aggregate of all security entitlements it has established is intended only to capture the general point that one of the key elements that distinguishes securities accounts from other relationships, such as deposit accounts, is that the intermediary undertakes to maintain a direct correspondence between the positions it holds and the claims of its customers. This section is not intended as a detailed specification of precisely how the intermediary is to perform this duty, nor whether there may be special circumstances in which an intermediary's general duty is excused. Accordingly, the general statement of the duties of a securities intermediary in this and the following sections is supplemented by two other provisions. First, each of Sections 8-504 through 8-508 contains an "agreement/due care" provision. Second, Section 8-509 sets out general qualifications on the duties stated in these sections, including the important point that compliance with corresponding regulatory provisions constitutes compliance with the Article 8 duties.

4. The "agreement/due care" provision in subsection (c) of this section is necessary to provide sufficient flexibility to accommodate the general duty stated in subsection (a) to the wide variety of circumstances that may be encountered in the modern securities holding system. For the most common forms of publicly traded securities, the modern depository-based indirect holding system has made the likelihood of an actual loss of securities remote, though correctable errors in accounting or temporary interruptions of data processing facilities may occur. Indeed, one of the reasons for the evolution of book-entry systems is to eliminate the risk of loss or destruction of physical certificates. There are, however, some forms of securities and other financial assets which must still be held in physical certificated form, with the attendant risk of loss or destruction. Risk of loss or delay may be a more significant consideration in connection with foreign securities. An American securities intermediary may well be willing to hold a foreign security in a securities account for its customer, but the intermediary may have relatively little choice of or control over foreign intermediaries through which the security must in turn be held. Accordingly, it is common for American securities intermediaries to disclaim responsibility for custodial risk of holding through foreign intermediaries.

Subsection (c)(1) provides that a securities intermediary satisfies the duty stated in subsection (a) if the intermediary acts with respect to that duty in accordance with the agreement between the intermediary and the entitlement holder. Subsection (c)(2) provides that if there is no agreement on the matter, the intermediary satisfies the subsection (a) duty if the intermediary exercises due care in accordance with reasonable commercial standards to obtain and maintain the financial asset in question. This formulation does not state that the intermediary has a universally applicable statutory duty of due care. Section 1-302(b) provides that statutory duties of due care cannot be disclaimed by agreement, but the "agreement/due care" formula contemplates that there may be particular circumstances where the parties do not wish to create a specific duty of due care, for example, with respect to foreign securities. Under subsection (c)(1), compliance with the agreement constitutes satisfaction of the subsection (a) duty, whether or not the agreement provides that the intermediary will exercise due care.

In each of the sections where the "agreement/due care" formula is used, it provides that entering into an agreement and performing in accordance with that agreement is a method by which the securities intermediary may satisfy the statutory duty stated in that section. Accordingly, the general obligation of good faith performance of statutory and contract duties, see Sections 1-304 and 8-102(a)(10), would apply to such an agreement. It would not be consistent with the obligation of good faith performance for an agreement to purport to establish the usual sort of arrangement between an intermediary and entitlement holder, yet disclaim altogether one of the basic elements that define that relationship. For example, an agreement stating that an intermediary assumes no responsibilities whatsoever for the safekeeping any of the entitlement holder's securities positions would not be consistent with good faith performance of the intermediary's duty to obtain and maintain financial assets corresponding to the entitlement holder's security entitlements.

To the extent that no agreement under subsection (c)(1) has specified the details of the intermediary's performance of the subsection (a) duty, subsection (c)(2) provides that the intermediary satisfies that duty if it exercises due care in accordance with reasonable commercial standards. The duty of care includes both care in the intermediary's own operations and care in the selection of other intermediaries through whom the intermediary holds the assets in question. The statement of the obligation of due care is meant to incorporate the principles of the common law under which the specific actions or precautions necessary to meet the obligation of care are determined by such factors as the nature and value of the property, the customs and practices of the business, and the like.

5. This section necessarily states the duty of a securities intermediary to obtain and maintain financial assets only at the very general and abstract level. For the most part, these matters are specified in great detail by regulatory law. Broker-dealers registered under the federal securities laws are subject to detailed regulation concerning the safeguarding of customer securities. See 17 C.F.R. § 240.15c3-3. Section 8-509(a) provides explicitly that if a securities intermediary complies with such regulatory law, that constitutes compliance with Section 8-504. In certain circumstances, these rules permit a firm to be in a position where it temporarily lacks a sufficient quantity of financial assets to satisfy all customer claims. For example, if another firm has failed to make a delivery to the firm in settlement of a trade, the firm is permitted a certain period of time to clear up the problem before it is obligated to obtain the necessary securities from some other source.

6. Subsection (d) is intended to recognize that there are some circumstances, where the duty to maintain a sufficient quantity of financial assets does not apply because the intermediary is not holding anything on behalf of others. For example, the Options Clearing Corporation is treated as a "securities intermediary" under this Article, although it does not itself hold options on behalf of its participants. Rather, it becomes the issuer of the options, by virtue of guaranteeing the obligations of participants in the clearing corporation who have written or purchased the options cleared through it. See Section 8-103(e). Accordingly, the general duty of an intermediary under subsection (a) does not apply, nor would other provisions of Part 5 that depend upon the existence of a requirement that the securities intermediary hold financial assets, such as Sections 8-503 and 8-508.

Definitional Cross References:

"Agreement"	Section 1-201(b)(3)
"Clearing corporation"	Section 8-102(a)(5)
"Entitlement holder"	Section 8-102(a)(7)
"Financial asset"	Section 8-102(a)(9)
"Securities intermediary"	Section 8-102(a)(14)
"Security entitlement"	Section 8-102(a)(17)

Section 8-505. Duty of Securities Intermediary with Respect to Payments and Distributions

(a) A securities intermediary shall take action to obtain a payment or distribution made by the issuer of a financial asset. A securities intermediary satisfies the duty if:

(1) the securities intermediary acts with respect to the duty as agreed upon by the entitlement holder and the securities intermediary; or

(2) in the absence of agreement, the securities intermediary exercises due care in accordance with reasonable commercial standards to attempt to obtain the payment or distribution.

(b) A securities intermediary is obligated to its entitlement holder for a payment or distribution made by the issuer of a financial asset if the payment or distribution is received by the securities intermediary.

Official Comment

1. One of the core elements of the securities account relationships for which the Part 5 rules were designed is that the securities intermediary passes through to the entitlement holders the economic benefit of ownership of the financial asset, such as payments and distributions made by the issuer of the financial asset. Subsection (a) expresses the ordinary understanding that a securities intermediary will take appropriate action to see to it that any payments or distributions made by the issuer are received. One of the main reasons that investors make use of securities intermediaries is to obtain the services of a professional in performing the record-keeping and other functions necessary to ensure that payments and other distributions are received.

2. Subsection (a) incorporates the same "agreement/due care" formula as the other provisions of Part 5 dealing with the duties of a securities intermediary. See Comment 4 to Section 8-504. This formulation permits the parties to specify by agreement what action, if any, the intermediary is to take with respect to the duty to obtain payments and distributions. In the absence of specification by agreement, the intermediary satisfies the duty if the intermediary exercises due care in accordance with reasonable commercial standards. The provisions of Section 8-509 also apply to the Section 8-505 duty, so that compliance with applicable regulatory requirements constitutes compliance with the Section 8-505 duty.

3. Subsection (b) provides that a securities intermediary is obligated to its entitlement holder for those payments or distributions made by the issuer that are in fact received by the intermediary. It does not deal with the details of the time and manner of payment. Moreover, as with any other monetary obligation, the obligation to pay may be subject to other rights of the obligor, by way of set-off counterclaim or the like. Section 8-509(c) makes this point explicit.

4. This section applies to payments and distributions made by an issuer of a financial asset credited to a securities account. If a distribution is made to, or made available to, a securities intermediary on account of a financial asset as to which there is no issuer, the duties, if any, of the securities intermediary with respect to the distribution are subject to the agreement of the intermediary and the entitlement holder. However, in the absence of an agreement, this section may be applied by analogy in an appropriate case. If the securities intermediary is a secured party, Section 9-207(c) applies.

Definitional Cross References:

"Agreement"	Section 1-201(b)(3)
"Entitlement holder"	Section 8-102(a)(7)
"Financial asset"	Section 8-102(a)(9)
"Securities intermediary"	Section 8-102(a)(14)
"Security entitlement"	Section 8-102(a)(17)

Section 8-506. Duty of Securities Intermediary to Exercise Rights as Directed by Entitlement Holder

A securities intermediary shall exercise rights with respect to a financial asset if directed to do so by an entitlement holder. A securities intermediary satisfies the duty if:

(1) the securities intermediary acts with respect to the duty as agreed upon by the entitlement holder and the securities intermediary; or

(2) in the absence of agreement, the securities intermediary either places the entitlement holder in a position to exercise the rights directly or exercises due care in accordance with reasonable commercial standards to follow the direction of the entitlement holder.

Official Comment

1. Another of the core elements of the securities account relationships for which the Part 5 rules were designed is that although the intermediary may, by virtue of the structure of the indirect holding system, be the party who has the power to exercise the corporate and other rights that come from holding the security, the intermediary exercises these powers as representative of the entitlement holder rather than at its own discretion. This characteristic is one of the things that distinguishes a securities account from other arrangements where one person holds securities "on behalf of" another, such as the relationship between a mutual fund and its shareholders or a trustee and its beneficiary.

2. The fact that the intermediary exercises the rights of security holding as representative of the entitlement holder does not, of course, preclude the entitlement holder from conferring discretionary authority upon the intermediary. Arrangements are not uncommon in which investors do not wish to have their intermediaries forward proxy materials or other information. Thus, this section provides that the intermediary shall exercise corporate and other rights "if directed to do so" by the entitlement holder. Moreover, as with the other Part 5 duties, the "agreement/due care" formulation is used in stating how the intermediary is to perform this duty.

This section also provides that the intermediary satisfies the duty if it places the entitlement holder in a position to exercise the rights directly. This is to take account of the fact that some of the rights attendant upon ownership of the security, such as rights to bring derivative and other litigation, are far removed from the matters that intermediaries are expected to perform.

3. This section, and the two that follow, deal with the aspects of securities holding that are related to investment decisions. For example, one of the rights of holding a particular security that would fall within the purview of this section would be the right to exercise a conversion right for a convertible security. It is quite common for investors to confer discretionary authority upon another person, such as an investment adviser, with respect to these rights and other investment decisions. Because this section, and the other sections of Part 5, all specify that a securities intermediary satisfies the Part 5 duties if it acts in accordance with the entitlement holder's agreement, there is no inconsistency between the statement of duties of a securities intermediary and these common arrangements.

4. Section 8-509 also applies to the Section 8-506 duty, so that compliance with applicable regulatory requirements constitutes compliance with this duty. This is quite important in this context, since the federal securities laws establish a comprehensive system of regulation of the distribution of proxy materials and exercise of voting rights with respect to securities held through brokers and other intermediaries. By virtue of Section 8-509(a), compliance with such regulatory requirement constitutes compliance with the Section 8-506 duty.

Definitional Cross References:

"Agreement"	Section 1-201(b)(3)
"Entitlement holder"	Section 8-102(a)(7)
"Financial asset"	Section 8-102(a)(9)
"Securities intermediary"	Section 8-102(a)(14)
"Security entitlement"	Section 8-102(a)(17)

Section 8-507. Duty of Securities Intermediary to Comply with Entitlement Order

(a) A securities intermediary shall comply with an entitlement order if the entitlement order is originated by the appropriate person, the securities intermediary has had reasonable opportunity to assure itself that the entitlement order is genuine and authorized, and the securities intermediary has had reasonable opportunity to comply with the entitlement order. A securities intermediary satisfies the duty if:

(1) the securities intermediary acts with respect to the duty as agreed upon by the entitlement holder and the securities intermediary; or

(2) in the absence of agreement, the securities intermediary exercises due care in accordance with reasonable commercial standards to comply with the entitlement order.

(b) If a securities intermediary transfers a financial asset pursuant to an ineffective entitlement order, the securities intermediary shall reestablish a security entitlement in favor of the person entitled to it, and pay or credit any payments or distributions that the person did not receive as a result of the wrongful transfer. If the securities intermediary does not reestablish a security entitlement, the securities intermediary is liable to the entitlement holder for damages.

Official Comment

1. Subsection (a) of this section states another aspect of duties of securities intermediaries that make up security entitlements—the securities intermediary's duty to comply with entitlement orders. One of the main reasons for holding securities through securities intermediaries is to enable rapid transfer in settlement of trades. Thus the right to have one's orders for disposition of the security entitlement honored is an inherent part of the relationship. Subsection (b) states the correlative liability of a securities intermediary for transferring a financial asset from an entitlement holder's account pursuant to an entitlement order that was not effective.

2. The duty to comply with entitlement orders is subject to several qualifications. The intermediary has a duty only with respect to an entitlement order that is in fact originated by the appropriate person. Moreover, the intermediary has a duty only if it has had reasonable opportunity to assure itself that the order is genuine and authorized, and reasonable opportunity to comply with the order. The same "agreement/due care" formula is used in this section as in the other Part 5 sections on the duties of intermediaries, and the rules of Section 8-509 apply to the Section 8-507 duty.

3. Appropriate person is defined in Section 8-107. In the usual case, the appropriate person is the entitlement holder, see Section 8-107(a)(3). Entitlement holder is defined in Section 8-102(a)(7) as the person "identified in the records of a securities intermediary as the person having a security entitlement." Thus, the general rule is that an intermediary's duty with respect to entitlement orders runs only to the person with whom the intermediary has established a relationship. One of the basic principles of the indirect holding system is that securities intermediaries owe duties only to their own customers. See also Section 8-115. The only situation in which a securities intermediary has a duty to comply with entitlement orders originated by a person other than the person with whom the intermediary established a relationship is covered by Section 8-107(a)(4) and (a)(5), which provide that the term "appropriate person" includes the successor or personal representative of a decedent, or the custodian or guardian of a person who lacks capacity. If the entitlement holder is competent, another person does not fall within the defined term "appropriate person" merely by virtue of having power to act as an agent for the entitlement holder. Thus, an intermediary is not required to determine at its peril whether a person who purports to be authorized to act for an entitlement holder is in fact authorized to do so. If an entitlement holder wishes to be able to act through agents, the entitlement holder can establish appropriate arrangements in advance with the securities intermediary.

One important application of this principle is that if an entitlement holder grants a security interest in its security entitlements to a third-party lender, the intermediary owes no duties to the secured party, unless the intermediary has entered into a "control" agreement in which it agrees to act on entitlement orders originated by the secured party. See Section 8-106. Even though the security agreement or some other document may give the secured party authority to act as agent for the debtor, that would not make the secured party an "appropriate person" to whom the security intermediary owes duties. If the entitlement holder and securities intermediary have agreed to such a control arrangement, then the intermediary's action in following instructions from the secured party would satisfy the subsection (a) duty. Although an agent, such as the secured party in this example, is not an "appropriate person," an entitlement order is "effective" if originated by an authorized person. See Section 8-107(a) and (b). Moreover, Section 8-507(a) provides that the intermediary satisfies its duty if it acts in accordance with the entitlement holder's agreement.

4. Subsection (b) provides that an intermediary is liable for a wrongful transfer if the entitlement order was "ineffective." Section 8-107 specifies whether an entitlement order is effective. An "effective entitlement order" is different from an "entitlement order originated by an appropriate person." An entitlement order is effective under Section 8-107(b) if it is made by the appropriate person, or by a person who has power to act for the appropriate person under the law of agency, or if the appropriate person has ratified the entitlement order or is precluded from denying its effectiveness. Thus, although a securities intermediary does not have a duty to act on an entitlement order originated by the entitlement holder's agent, the intermediary is not liable for wrongful transfer if it does so.

Subsection (b), together with Section 8-107, has the effect of leaving to other law most of the questions of the sort dealt with by Article 4A for wire transfers of funds, such as allocation between the securities intermediary and the entitlement holder of the risk of fraudulent entitlement orders.

5. The term entitlement order does not cover all directions that a customer might give a broker concerning securities held through the broker. Article 8 is not a codification of all of the law of customers and stockbrokers. Article 8 deals with the settlement of securities trades, not the trades. The term entitlement order does not refer to instructions to a broker to make trades, that is, enter into contracts for the purchase or sale of securities. Rather, the entitlement order is the mechanism of transfer for securities held through intermediaries, just as indorsements and instructions are the mechanism for securities held directly. In the ordinary case the customer's direction to the broker to deliver the securities at settlement is implicit in the customer's instruction to the broker to sell. The distinction is, however, significant in that this section has no application to the relationship between the customer and broker with respect to the trade itself. For example, assertions by a customer that it was damaged by a broker's failure to execute a trading order sufficiently rapidly or in the proper manner are not governed by this Article.

Definitional Cross References:

"Agreement"	Section 1-201(b)(3)
"Appropriate person"	Section 8-107
"Effective"	Section 8-107
"Entitlement holder"	Section 8-102(a)(7)
"Entitlement order"	Section 8-102(a)(8)
"Financial asset"	Section 8-102(a)(9)
"Securities intermediary"	Section 8-102(a)(14)
"Security entitlement"	Section 8-102(a)(17)

Section 8-508. Duty of Securities Intermediary to Change Entitlement Holder's Position to Other Form of Security Holding

A securities intermediary shall act at the direction of an entitlement holder to change a security entitlement into another available form of holding for which the entitlement holder is eligible, or to cause the financial asset to be transferred to a securities account of the entitlement holder with another securities intermediary. A securities intermediary satisfies the duty if:

(1) the securities intermediary acts as agreed upon by the entitlement holder and the securities intermediary; or

(2) in the absence of agreement, the securities intermediary exercises due care in accordance with reasonable commercial standards to follow the direction of the entitlement holder.

Official Comment

1. This section states another aspect of the duties of securities intermediaries that make up security entitlements—the obligation of the securities intermediary to change an entitlement holder's position into any other form of holding for which the entitlement holder is eligible or to transfer the entitlement holder's position to an account at another intermediary. This section does not state unconditionally that the securities intermediary is obligated to turn over a certificate to the customer or to cause the customer to be registered on the books of the issuer, because the customer may not be eligible to hold the security directly. For example, municipal bonds are now commonly issued in "book-entry only" form, in which the only entity that the issuer will register on its own books is a depository.

If security certificates in registered form are issued for the security, and individuals are eligible to have the security registered in their own name, the entitlement holder can request that the intermediary deliver or cause to be delivered to the entitlement holder a certificate registered in the name of the entitlement holder or a certificate indorsed in blank or specially indorsed to the entitlement holder. If security certificates in bearer form are issued for the security, the entitlement holder can request that the intermediary deliver or cause to be delivered a certificate in bearer form. If the security can be held by individuals directly in uncertificated form, the entitlement holder can request that the security be registered in its name. The specification of this duty does not determine the pricing terms of the agreement in which the duty arises.

2. The same "agreement/due care" formula is used in this section as in the other Part 5 sections on the duties of intermediaries. So too, the rules of Section 8-509 apply to the Section 8-508 duty.

Definitional Cross References:

"Agreement"	Section 1-201(b)(3)
"Entitlement holder"	Section 8-102(a)(7)
"Financial asset"	Section 8-102(a)(9)
"Securities intermediary"	Section 8-102(a)(14)
"Security entitlement"	Section 8-102(a)(17)

Section 8-509. Specification of Duties of Securities Intermediary by Other Statute or Regulation; Manner of Performance of Duties of Securities Intermediary and Exercise of Rights of Entitlement Holder

(a) If the substance of a duty imposed upon a securities intermediary by Sections 8-504 through 8-508 is the subject of other statute, regulation, or rule, compliance with that statute, regulation, or rule satisfies the duty.

(b) To the extent that specific standards for the performance of the duties of a securities intermediary or the exercise of the rights of an entitlement holder are not specified by other statute, regulation, or rule or by agreement between the securities intermediary and entitlement holder, the securities intermediary shall perform its duties and the entitlement holder shall exercise its rights in a commercially reasonable manner.

(c) The obligation of a securities intermediary to perform the duties imposed by Sections 8-504 through 8-508 is subject to:

(1) rights of the securities intermediary arising out of a security interest under a security agreement with the entitlement holder or otherwise; and

(2) rights of the securities intermediary under other law, regulation, rule, or agreement to withhold performance of its duties as a result of unfulfilled obligations of the entitlement holder to the securities intermediary.

(d) Sections 8-504 through 8-508 do not require a securities intermediary to take any action that is prohibited by other statute, regulation, or rule.

Official Comment

This Article is not a comprehensive statement of the law governing the relationship between broker-dealers or other securities intermediaries and their customers. Most of the law governing that relationship is the common law of contract and agency, supplemented or supplanted by regulatory law. This Article deals only with the most basic commercial/property law principles governing the relationship. Although Sections 8-504 through 8-508 specify certain duties of securities intermediaries to entitlement holders, the point of these sections is to identify what it means to have a security entitlement, not to specify the details of performance of these duties.

For many intermediaries, regulatory law specifies in great detail the intermediary's obligations on such matters as safekeeping of customer property, distribution of proxy materials, and the like. To avoid any conflict between the general statement of duties in this Article and the specific statement of intermediaries' obligations in such regulatory schemes, subsection (a) provides that compliance with applicable regulation constitutes compliance with the duties specified in Sections 8-504 through 8-508.

Definitional Cross References:

"Agreement"	Section 1-201(b)(3)
"Entitlement holder"	Section 8-102(a)(7)
"Securities intermediary"	Section 8-102(a)(14)
"Security agreement"	Section 9-105(1)(l)
"Security interest"	Section 1-201(b)(35)

Section 8-510. Rights of Purchaser of Security Entitlement from Entitlement Holder

(a) In a case not covered by the priority rules in Article 9 or the rules stated in subsection (c), an action based on an adverse claim to a financial asset or security entitlement, whether framed in conversion, replevin, constructive trust, equitable lien, or other theory, may not be asserted against a person who purchases a security entitlement, or an interest therein, from an entitlement holder if the purchaser gives value, does not have notice of the adverse claim, and obtains control.

(b) If an adverse claim could not have been asserted against an entitlement holder under Section 8-502, the adverse claim cannot be asserted against a person who purchases a security entitlement, or an interest therein, from the entitlement holder.

(c) In a case not covered by the priority rules in Article 9, a purchaser for value of a security entitlement, or an interest therein, who obtains control has priority over a purchaser of a security entitlement, or an interest therein, who does not obtain control. Except as otherwise provided in subsection (d), purchasers who have control rank according to priority in time of:

(1) the purchaser's becoming the person for whom the securities account, in which the security entitlement is carried, is maintained, if the purchaser obtained control under Section 8-106(d)(1);

(2) the securities intermediary's agreement to comply with the purchaser's entitlement orders with

respect to security entitlements carried or to be carried in the securities account in which the security entitlement is carried, if the purchaser obtained control under Section 8-106(d)(2); or

(3) if the purchaser obtained control through another person under Section 8-106(d)(3), the time on which priority would be based under this subsection if the other person were the secured party.

(d) A securities intermediary as purchaser has priority over a conflicting purchaser who has control unless otherwise agreed by the securities intermediary.

Official Comment

1. This section specifies certain rules concerning the rights of persons who purchase interests in security entitlements from entitlement holders. The rules of this section are provided to take account of cases where the purchaser's rights are derivative from the rights of another person who is and continues to be the entitlement holder.

2. Subsection (a) provides that no adverse claim can be asserted against a purchaser of an interest in a security entitlement if the purchaser gives value, obtains control, and does not have notice of the adverse claim. The primary purpose of this rule is to give adverse claim protection to persons who take security interests in security entitlements and obtain control, but do not themselves become entitlement holders.

The following examples illustrate subsection (a):

Example 1: X steals a certificated bearer bond from Owner. X delivers the certificate to Able & Co. for credit to X's securities account. Later, X borrows from Bank and grants bank a security interest in the security entitlement. Bank obtains control under Section 8-106(d)(2) by virtue of an agreement in which Able agrees to comply with entitlement orders originated by Bank. X absconds.

Example 2: Same facts as in Example 1, except that Bank does not obtain a control agreement. Instead, Bank perfects by filing a financing statement.

In both of these examples, when X deposited the bonds X acquired a security entitlement under Section 8-501. Under other law, Owner may be able to have a constructive trust imposed on the security entitlement as the traceable product of the bonds that X misappropriated. X granted a security interest in that entitlement to Bank. Bank was a purchaser of an interest in the security entitlement from X. In Example 1, although Bank was not a person who acquired a security entitlement from the intermediary, Bank did obtain control. If Bank did not have notice of Owner's claim, Section 8-510(a) precludes Owner from asserting an adverse claim against Bank. In Example 2, Bank had a perfected security interest, but did not obtain control. Accordingly, Section 8-510(a) does not preclude Owner from asserting its adverse claim against Bank.

3. Subsection (b) applies to the indirect holding system a limited version of the "shelter principle." The following example illustrates the relatively limited class of cases for which it may be needed:

Example 3: Thief steals a certificated bearer bond from Owner. Thief delivers the certificate to Able & Co. for credit to Thief's securities account. Able forwards the certificate to a clearing corporation for credit to Able's account. Later Thief instructs Able to sell the positions in the bonds. Able sells to Baker & Co., acting as broker for Buyer. The trade is settled by book-entries in the accounts of Able and Baker at the clearing corporation, and in the accounts of Thief and Buyer at Able and Baker respectively. Owner may be able to reconstruct the trade records to show that settlement occurred in such fashion that the "same bonds" that were carried in Thief's account at Able are traceable into Buyer's account at Baker. Buyer later decides to donate the bonds to Alma Mater University and executes an assignment of its rights as entitlement holder to Alma Mater.

Buyer had a position in the bonds, which Buyer held in the form of a security entitlement against Baker. Buyer then made a gift of the position to Alma Mater. Although Alma Mater is a purchaser, Section 1-201(b)(30), it did not give value. Thus, Alma Mater is a person who purchased a security entitlement, or an interest therein, from an entitlement holder (Buyer). Buyer was protected against Owner's adverse claim by the Section 8-502 rule. Thus, by virtue of Section 8-510(b), Owner is also precluded from asserting an adverse claim against Alma Mater.

4. Subsection (c) specifies a priority rule for cases where an entitlement holder transfers conflicting interests in the same security entitlement to different purchasers. It follows the same principle as the Article 9 priority rule for investment property, that is, control trumps non-control. Indeed, the most significant category of conflicting "purchasers" may be secured parties. Priority questions for security interests, however, are governed by the rules in Article 9. Subsection (c) applies only to cases not covered by the Article 9 rules. It is intended primarily for disputes over conflicting claims arising out of repurchase agreement transactions that are not covered by the other rules set out in Articles 8 and 9.

The following example illustrates subsection (c):

Example 4: Dealer holds securities through an account at Alpha Bank. Alpha Bank in turns holds through a clearing corporation account. Dealer transfers securities to RP1 in a "hold in custody" repo transaction. Dealer then transfers the same securities to RP2 in another repo transaction. The repo to RP2 is implemented by transferring the securities from Dealer's regular account at Alpha Bank to a special account maintained by Alpha Bank for Dealer and RP2. The agreement among Dealer, RP2, and Alpha Bank provides that Dealer can make substitutions for the securities but RP2 can direct Alpha Bank to sell any securities held in the special account. Dealer becomes insolvent. RP1 claims a prior interest in the securities transferred to RP2.

In this example Dealer remained the entitlement holder but agreed that RP2 could initiate entitlement orders to Dealer's security intermediary, Alpha Bank. If RP2 had become the entitlement holder, the adverse claim rule of Section 8-502 would apply. Even if RP2 does not become the entitlement holder, the arrangement among Dealer, Alpha Bank, and RP2 does suffice to give RP2 control. Thus, under Section 8-510(c), RP2 has priority over RP1, because RP2 is a purchaser who obtained control, and RP1 is a purchaser who did not obtain control. The same result could be reached under Section 8-510(a) which provides that RP1's earlier in time interest cannot be asserted as an adverse claim against RP2. The same result would follow under the Article 9 priority rules if the interests of RP1 and RP2 are characterized as "security interests," see Section 9-328(1). The main point of the rules of Section 8-510(c) is to ensure that there will be clear rules to cover the conflicting claims of RP1 and RP2 without characterizing their interests as Article 9 security interests.

The priority rules in Article 9 for conflicting security interests also include a default temporal priority rule for cases where multiple secured parties have obtained control but omitted to specify their respective rights by agreement. See Section 9-328(2) and Comment 5 to Section 9-328. Because the purchaser priority rule in Section 8-510(c) is intended to track the Article 9 priority rules, it too has a temporal priority rule for cases where multiple non-secured party purchasers have obtained control but omitted to specify their respective rights by agreement. The rule is patterned on Section 9-328(2).

5. If a securities intermediary itself is a purchaser, subsection (d) provides that it has priority over the interest of another purchaser who has control. Article 9 contains a similar rule. See Section 9-328(3).

Definitional Cross References:

"Adverse claim"	Section 8-102(a)(1)
"Control"	Section 8-106
"Entitlement holder"	Section 8-102(a)(7)
"Notice of adverse claim"	Section 8-105
"Purchase"	Section 1-201(b)(29)
"Purchaser"	Sections 1-201(b)(30) and 8-116
"Securities intermediary"	Section 8-102(a)(14)
"Security entitlement"	Section 8-102(a)(17)
"Value"	Sections 1-204 and 8-116

Section 8-511. Priority among Security Interests and Entitlement Holders

(a) Except as otherwise provided in subsections (b) and (c), if a securities intermediary does not have sufficient interests in a particular financial asset to satisfy both its obligations to entitlement holders who have security entitlements to that financial asset and its obligation to a creditor of the securities intermediary who has a security interest in that financial asset, the claims of entitlement holders, other than the creditor, have priority over the claim of the creditor.

(b) A claim of a creditor of a securities intermediary who has a security interest in a financial asset held by a securities intermediary has priority over claims of the securities intermediary's entitlement holders who have security entitlements with respect to that financial asset if the creditor has control over the financial asset.

(c) If a clearing corporation does not have sufficient financial assets to satisfy both its obligations to entitlement holders who have security entitlements with respect to a financial asset and its obligation to a creditor of the clearing corporation who has a security interest in that financial asset, the claim of the creditor has priority over the claims of entitlement holders.

Official Comment

1. This section sets out priority rules for circumstances in which a securities intermediary fails leaving an insufficient quantity of securities or other financial assets to satisfy the claims of its entitlement holders and the claims of creditors to whom it has granted security interests in financial assets held by it. Subsection (a) provides that entitlement holders' claims have priority except as otherwise provided in subsection (b), and subsection (b) provides that the secured creditor's claim has priority if the secured creditor obtains control, as defined in Section 8-106. The following examples illustrate the operation of these rules.

Example 1: Able & Co., a broker, borrows from Alpha Bank and grants Alpha Bank a security interest pursuant to a written agreement which identifies certain securities that are to be collateral for the loan, either specifically or by category. Able holds these securities in a clearing corporation account. Able becomes insolvent and it is discovered that Able holds insufficient securities to satisfy the claims of customers who have paid for securities that they held in accounts with Able and the collateral claims of Alpha Bank. Alpha Bank's security interest in the security entitlements that Able holds through the clearing corporation account may be perfected under the automatic perfection rule of Section 9-115(4)(c), but Alpha Bank did not obtain control under Section 8-106. Thus, under Section 8-511(a) the entitlement holders' claims have priority over Alpha Bank's claim.

Example 2: Able & Co., a broker, borrows from Beta Bank and grants Beta Bank a security interest in securities that Able holds in a clearing corporation account. Pursuant to the security agreement, the securities are debited from Alpha's account and credited to Beta's account in the clearing corporation account. Able becomes insolvent and it is discovered that Able holds insufficient securities to satisfy the claims of customers who have paid for securities that they held in accounts with Able and the collateral claims of Alpha Bank. Although the transaction between Able and Beta took the form of an outright transfer on the clearing corporation's books, as between Able and Beta, Able remains the owner and Beta has a security interest. In that respect the situation is no different than if Able had delivered bearer bonds to Beta in pledge to secure a loan. Beta's security interest is perfected, and Beta obtained control. See Sections 8-106 and 9-115. Under Section 8-511(b), Beta Bank's security interest has priority over claims of Able's customers.

The result in Example 2 is an application to this particular setting of the general principle expressed in Section 8-503, and explained in the Comments thereto, that the entitlement holders of a securities intermediary cannot assert rights against third parties to whom the intermediary has wrongfully transferred interests, except in extremely unusual circumstances where the third party was itself a participant in the transferor's wrongdoing. Under subsection (b) the claim of a secured creditor of a securities intermediary has priority over the claims of entitlement holders if the secured creditor has obtained control. If, however, the secured creditor acted in collusion with the intermediary in violating the intermediary's obligation to its entitlement holders, then under Section 8-503(e), the entitlement holders, through their representative in insolvency proceedings, could recover the interest from the secured creditor, that is, set aside the security interest.

2. The risk that investors who hold through an intermediary will suffer a loss as a result of a wrongful pledge by the intermediary is no different than the risk that the intermediary might fail and not have the securities that it was supposed to be holding on behalf of its customers, either because the securities were never acquired by the intermediary or because the intermediary wrongfully sold securities that should have been kept to satisfy customers' claims. Investors are protected against that risk by the regulatory regimes under which securities intermediaries operate. Intermediaries are required to maintain custody, through clearing corporation accounts or in other approved locations, of their customers' securities and are prohibited from using customers' securities in their own business activities. Securities firms who are carrying both customer and proprietary positions are not permitted to grant blanket liens to lenders covering all securities which they hold, for their own account or for their customers. Rather, securities firms designate specifically which positions they are pledging. Under SEC Rules 8c-1 and 15c2-1, customers' securities can be pledged only to fund loans to customers, and only with the consent of the customers. Customers' securities cannot be pledged for loans for the firm's proprietary business; only proprietary positions can be pledged for proprietary loans. SEC Rule 15c3-3 implements these prohibitions in a fashion tailored to modern securities firm accounting systems by requiring brokers to maintain a sufficient inventory of securities, free from any liens, to satisfy the claims of all of their customers for fully paid and excess margin securities. Revised Article 8 mirrors that requirement, specifying in Section 8-504 that a securities intermediary must maintain a sufficient quantity of investment property to satisfy all security entitlements, and may not grant security interests in the positions it is required to hold for customers, except as authorized by the customers.

If a failed brokerage has violated the customer protection regulations and does not have sufficient securities to satisfy customers' claims, its customers are protected against loss from a shortfall by the Securities Investor Protection Act ("SIPA"). Securities firms required to register as brokers or dealers are also required to become members of the Securities Investor Protection Corporation ("SIPC"), which provides their customers with protection somewhat similar to that provided by FDIC and other deposit insurance programs for bank depositors. When a member firm fails, SIPC is authorized to initiate a liquidation proceeding under the provisions of SIPA. If the assets of the securities firm are insufficient to satisfy all customer claims, SIPA makes contributions to the estate from a fund financed by assessments on its members to protect customers against losses up to $500,000 for cash and securities held at member firms.

Article 8 is premised on the view that the important policy of protecting investors against the risk of wrongful conduct by their intermediaries is sufficiently treated by other law.

3. Subsection (c) sets out a special rule for secured financing provided to enable clearing corporations to complete settlement. The reasons that secured financing arrangements are needed in such circumstances are explained in Comment 7 to Section 9-115. In order to permit clearing corporations to establish liquidity facilities where necessary to ensure completion of settlement, subsection (c) provides a priority for secured lenders to such clearing corporations. Subsection (c) does not turn on control because the clearing corporation may be the top tier securities intermediary for the securities pledged, so that there may be no practicable method for conferring control on the lender.

Definitional Cross References:

"Clearing corporation"	Section 8-102(a)(5)
"Control"	Section 8-106
"Entitlement holder"	Section 8-102(a)(7)
"Financial asset"	Section 8-102(a)(9)
"Securities intermediary"	Section 8-102(a)(14)
"Security entitlement"	Section 8-102(a)(17)
"Security interest"	Section 1-201(b)(35)
"Value"	Sections 1-204 and 8-116

PART 6. TRANSITION PROVISIONS FOR REVISED ARTICLE 8

Section 8-601. Effective Date. This [Act] takes effect. . . .

Section 8-602. Repeals. This [Act] repeals. . . .

Official Comment

If the State has adopted the Uniform Act for the Simplification of Fiduciary Security Transfers, or similar legislation, it should be repealed.

Section 8-603. Savings Clause

(a) This [Act] does not affect an action or proceeding commenced before this [Act] takes effect.

(b) If a security interest in a security is perfected at the date this [Act] takes effect, and the action by which the security interest was perfected would suffice to perfect a security interest under this [Act], no further action is required to continue perfection. If a security interest in a security is perfected at the date this [Act] takes effect but the action by which the security interest was perfected would not suffice to perfect a security interest under this [Act], the security interest remains perfected for a period of four months after the effective date and continues perfected thereafter if appropriate action to perfect under this [Act] is taken within that period. If a security interest is perfected at the date this [Act] takes effect and the security interest can be perfected by filing under this [Act], a financing statement signed by the secured party instead of the debtor may be filed within that period to continue perfection or thereafter to perfect.

Official Comment

The revision of Article 8 should present few significant transition problems. Although the revision involves significant changes in terminology and analysis, the substantive rules are, in large measure, based upon the current practices and are consistent with results that could be reached, albeit at times with some struggle, by proper interpretation of the rules of present law. Thus, the new rules can be applied, without significant dislocations, to transactions and events that occurred prior to enactment.

The enacting provisions should not, whether by applicability, transition, or savings clause language, attempt to provide that old Article 8 continues to apply to "transactions," "events," "rights," "duties," "liabilities," or the like that occurred or accrued before the effective date and that new Article 8 applies to those that occur or accrue after the effective date. The reason for revising Article 8 and corresponding provisions of Article 9 is the concern that the provisions of old Article 8 could be interpreted or misinterpreted to yield results that impede the safe and efficient operation of the national system for the clearance and settlement of securities transactions. Accordingly, it is not the case that any effort should be made to preserve the applicability of old Article 8 to transactions and events that occurred before the effective date.

Only two circumstances seem to warrant continued application of rules of old Article 8. First, to avoid disruption in the conduct of litigation, it may make sense to provide for continued application of the old Article 8 rules to lawsuits pending before the effective date. Second, there are some limited circumstances in which prior law permitted perfection of security interests by methods that are not provided for in the revised version. Section 8-313(1)(h) (1978) permitted perfection of security interests in securities held through intermediaries by notice to the intermediary. Under Revised Articles 8 and 9, security interests can be perfected in such cases by control, which requires the agreement of the intermediary, or by filing. It is likely that secured parties who relied strongly on such collateral under prior law did not simply send notices but obtained agreements from the intermediaries that would suffice for control under the new rules. However, it seems appropriate to include a provision that gives a secured creditor some opportunity after the effective date to perfect in this or any other case in which there is doubt whether the method of perfection used under prior law would be sufficient under the new version.

Note on “Current” and “Revised” Article 1

[Editor’s Note: The Note in prior editions concerning cross-references to Article 1 from Article 9 has been omitted as no longer necessary. See Preface.]

UNIFORM COMMERCIAL CODE

Article 9 — Secured Transactions

As adopted in 1999 and revised in: (i) 1999 and 2000, to correct errata; (ii) 2003, in connection with the revision of Article 7; (iii) 2005, to make minor amendments; (iv) 2006, to correct errata; (v) 2010, to make amendments; (vi) 2012, in connection with PEB Commentary No. 17; (v) 2018, to make amendments; (vi) 2017, in connection with PEB Commentary No. 19; (vii) 2019, in connection with PEB Commentaries No. 20; (viii) 2020, in connection with PEB Commentary No. 21; (ix) 2021, in connection with PEB Commentary No. 23; (x) 2022, in connection with the 2022 Amendments to the Uniform Commercial Code; (xi) 2022, in connection with PEB Commentaries Nos. 24, 26, and 27; (xii) 2024, in connection with PEB Commentary No. 28; and (xii) 2025, in Connection with PEB Commentaries 29, 30, and 31.

PART 1. GENERAL PROVISIONS

[SUBPART 1. SHORT TITLE, DEFINITIONS, AND GENERAL CONCEPTS]

Section

[SUBPART 2. APPLICABILITY OF ARTICLE]

PART 2. EFFECTIVENESS OF SECURITY AGREEMENT; ATTACHMENT OF SECURITY INTEREST; RIGHTS OF PARTIES TO SECURITY AGREEMENT

[SUBPART 1. EFFECTIVENESS AND ATTACHMENT]

[SUBPART 2. RIGHTS AND DUTIES]

PART 3. PERFECTION AND PRIORITY

[SUBPART 1. LAW GOVERNING PERFECTION AND PRIORITY]

[SUBPART 2. PERFECTION]

[SUBPART 3. PRIORITY]

[SUBPART 4. RIGHTS OF BANK]

[SUBPART 2. NONCOMPLIANCE WITH ARTICLE]

PART 7. TRANSITION

PART 8. TRANSITION PROVISIONS FOR 2010 AMENDMENTS

APPENDICES

Collateral Index

GOODS

GOODS, GENERALLY

GOODS, CONSUMER GOODS

GOODS, EQUIPMENT

GOODS, FARM PRODUCTS

CHATTEL PAPER

COMMERCIAL TORT CLAIMS

DEPOSIT ACCOUNTS

DOCUMENTS

DOCUMENTS, GENERALLY

DOCUMENTS, ELECTRONIC

DOCUMENTS, NEGOTIABLE

GENERAL INTANGIBLES

GENERAL INTANGIBLES, GENERALLY

GENERAL INTANGIBLES, CONTROLLABLE ELECTRONIC RECORDS

GENERAL INTANGIBLES, PAYMENT INTANGIBLES

GENERAL INTANGIBLES, CONTROLLABLE PAYMENT INTANGIBLES

GENERAL INTANGIBLES, SOFTWARE

INSTRUMENTS

INSTRUMENTS, GENERALLY

INSTRUMENTS, PROMISSORY NOTES

9-406(d,e)	Terms Restricting Assignment Generally Ineffective
9-408	Restrictions on Assignment of Promissory Notes Ineffective
9-505	Filing and Compliance with Other Statutes and Treaties for Buyers of Promissory Notes
9-601(g)	No Duties Imposed by Part 6 on Buyers of Promissory Notes Except as Otherwise Provided in 9-607(c) and 9-608(b)
9-608(b)	No Surplus or Deficiency of Proceeds of Collection or Enforcement in Sales of Promissory Notes
9-615(e)	No Surplus or Deficiency of Proceeds of Disposition in Sales of Promissory Notes

INVESTMENT PROPERTY

INVESTMENT PROPERTY, GENERALLY

9-102(a)(49)	Definition
9-106	Control of Investment Property525
9-203(b)(3)(D)	Enforceability of Security Interests in Investment Property
9-203(c)	Subsection (b) Is Subject to 9-206 on Security Interests in Investment Property
9-206	Security Interest Arising in Purchase or Delivery of Financial Asset
9-207(c)	Rights and Duties when Secured Party is in Control
9-305	Law Governing Perfection and Priority of Security Interests in Investment Property
9-309(10)	Security Interest in Investment Property Created by a Broker or Securities Intermediary Perfects upon Attachment
9-310(b)(8)	Filing Not Necessary to Perfect a Security Interest in Investment Property under Certain Circumstances
9-312(a)	Perfection by Filing
9-314(a,c)	Perfection by Control
9-316(f)	Continued Perfection of Security Interest Following Change in Jurisdiction
9-317(d)	Certain Buyers of Investment Property Take Free of a Security Interest
9-322(d,e)	Conflicting Perfected Security Interests in Proceeds of Investment Property
9-328	Priority of Security Interests in Investment Property
9-601(b)	Rights of Secured Party are Provided in 9-207(c)

INVESTMENT PROPERTY, CERTIFICATED SECURITIES

8-102	Definition
9-106(a)	Control of Certificated Securities
9-203(b)(3)(C)	Enforceability of Security Interests in Certificated Securities
9-206(c)	Security Interest in Payment Against Delivery Transaction
9-305(a)(1)	Law Governing Perfection and Priority of Security Interests in Certificated Securities
9-310(b)(5,7)	Filing Not Necessary to Perfect a Security Interest in Certificated Securities Under Certain Circumstances
9-312(e,g)	Temporary Perfection of Certificated Securities
9-313(a,e)	Perfection by Delivery
9-314(c)(2)(A)	Perfection by Control
9-328(2)(A)	Priority of Security Interests in Securities
9-328(5)	Priority of Security Interests in Certificated Securities
9-331	Priority of Rights of Purchasers of Securities Under Other Articles

INVESTMENT PROPERTY, UNCERTIFICATED SECURITIES

8-102	Definition
9-106(a)	Control of Uncertificated Securities
9-305(a)(2)	Law Governing Perfection and Priority of Security Interests in Certificated Securities
9-314(c)(2)(B)	Perfection by Control
9-328(2)(A)	Priority of Security Interests in Securities
9-331	Priority of Rights of Purchasers of Securities Under Other Articles

INVESTMENT PROPERTY, SECURITY ENTITLEMENTS

8-102	Definition
9-106(a,c)	Control of Security Entitlements
9-108(d,e)	Sufficiency of Description
9-203(h)	Attachment of a Security Entitlement Carried in a Securities Account

INVESTMENT PROPERTY, SECURITIES ACCOUNTS

INVESTMENT PROPERTY, COMMODITY CONTRACTS

LETTER-OF-CREDIT RIGHTS

PART 1. GENERAL PROVISIONS

[Subpart 1. [Short Title, Definitions, And General Concepts]

Section 9-101. Short Title

This article may be cited as Uniform Commercial Code — Secured Transactions.

Official Comment

1. Source, Background, and History. In 1990, the Permanent Editorial Board for the UCC with the support of its sponsors, The American Law Institute and the National Conference of Commissioners on Uniform State Laws, established a committee to study Uniform Commercial Code (UCC) Article 9. The study committee issued its report as of December 1, 1992, recommending the creation of a drafting committee for the revision of Article 9 and also recommending numerous specific changes to Article 9. Organized in 1993, a drafting committee met fifteen times from 1993 to 1998. Extensive revisions of this Article were approved by its sponsors in 1998 (1998 Revisions). The Article was conformed to revised Article 1 in 2001 and to amendments to Article 7 in 2003. The sponsors approved amendments to selected sections of this Article in 2010.

The 1998 Revisions superseded former Article 9 (pre-1998 Article 9) and, as did their predecessor, provided a comprehensive scheme for the regulation of security interests in personal property and fixtures. For the most part the 1998 Article 9 followed the general approach and retains much of the terminology of pre-1998 Article 9. Comment 3 describes the material changes made by the 1998 Revisions. Pre-1998 Article 9 superseded the wide variety of pre- UCC security devices. Unlike the Comments to pre-1998 Article 9, however, these Comments dwell very little on the pre-UCC state of the law. For that reason, the Comments to pre-1998 Article 9 will remain of substantial historical value and interest. They also will remain useful in understanding the background and general conceptual approach of this Article.

Article 9 was again extensively revised in 2022 (2022 Article 9 Revisions) pursuant to the Uniform Commercial Code Amendments (2022) (2022 Amendments). In particular, the 2022 Article 9 Revisions conform and adapt Article 9 to Article 12, covering controllable electronic records and rights to payment that are tethered to controllable electronic records — controllable accounts and controllable payment intangibles. For a brief summary of the 2022 Article 9 Revisions, see Comment 4, below. Except as noted in Comments 3 and 4 below, the 1998 Article 9 remains substantially unchanged following the 2022 Article 9 Revisions.

Note also that citations to "Bankruptcy Code Section" in these Comments are to Title 11 of the United States Code as in effect on July 1, 2022.

2. 1998 Revisions: Reorganization and Renumbering; Captions; Style. The 1998 Revisions embraced a substantial reorganization of former Article 9 and renumbering of most sections of Article 9, including a new Part 4 dealing with several aspects of third-party rights and duties that are unrelated to perfection and priority. Some of these were covered by Part 3 of pre-1998 Article 9. Also added was Part 5, dealing with filing (formerly covered by pre-1998 Part 4), and Part 6, dealing with default and enforcement (formerly covered by pre-1998 Part 5. The 1998 Revisions also include headings for the subsections as an aid to readers. Unlike section captions, which are part of the UCC, see Section 1-107, subsection headings are not a part of the official text itself and have not been approved by the sponsors.

3. Summary of 1998 Revisions. Following is a brief summary of some of the more significant features of the 1998 Revisions of Article 9.

a. Scope of Article 9. The 1998 Revisions expanded the scope of Article 9 in several respects.

Deposit accounts. Section 9-109 includes within this Article's scope deposit accounts as original collateral, except in consumer transactions. Pre-1998 Article 9 dealt with deposit accounts only as proceeds of other collateral.

Sales of payment intangibles and promissory notes. Section 9-109 also includes within the scope of this Article most sales of "payment intangibles" (defined in Section 9-102 as general intangibles under which an account debtor's principal obligation is monetary) and "promissory notes" (also defined in Section 9-102). Pre-1998 Article 9 included sales of accounts and chattel paper, but not sales of payment intangibles or promissory notes. In its inclusion of sales of payment intangibles and promissory notes, this Article continues the drafting convention found in pre-1998 Article 9; the sale of accounts, chattel paper, payment intangibles, or promissory notes creates a "security interest." The definition of "account" in Section 9-102 also was expanded to include various rights to payment that were general intangibles under pre-1998 Article 9.

Health-care-insurance receivables. Section 9-109 narrows Article 9's exclusion of transfers of interests in insurance policies by carving out of the exclusion "health-care-insurance receivables" (defined in Section 9-102). A health-care-insurance receivable is included within the definition of "account" in Section 9-102.

Nonpossessory statutory agricultural liens. Section 9-109 also brings nonpossessory statutory agricultural liens within the scope of Article 9.

Consignments. Section 9-109 added "true" consignments—bailments for the purpose of sale by the bailee to the scope of Article 9, with certain exceptions. See Section 9-102 (defining "consignment"). Under the pre-1998 UCC, many consignments were subject to Article 9's filing requirements by operation of pre-1998 Section 2-326.

Supporting obligations and property securing rights to payment. The 1998 Revisions also addressed explicitly (i) obligations, such as guaranties and letters of credit, that support payment or performance of collateral such as accounts, chattel paper, and payment intangibles, and (ii) any property (including real property) that secures a right to payment or performance that is subject to an Article 9 security interest. See Sections 9-203, 9-308.

Commercial tort claims. Section 9-109 expands the scope of Article 9 to include the assignment of commercial tort claims by narrowing the exclusion of tort claims generally. However, Article 9 continues to exclude tort claims for bodily injury and other non-business tort claims of a natural person. See Section 9-102 (defining "commercial tort claim").

Transfers by States and governmental units of States. Section 9-109 narrows the exclusion of transfers by States and their governmental units by excluding only transfers covered by another statute (other than a statute generally applicable to security interests) to the extent the statute governs the creation, perfection, priority, or enforcement of security interests.

Nonassignable general intangibles, promissory notes, health-care-insurance receivables, and letter-of-credit rights. The 1998 Revisions enabled a security interest to attach to letter-of-credit rights, health-care-insurance receivables, promissory notes, and general intangibles, including contracts, permits, licenses, and franchises, notwithstanding a contractual or statutory prohibition against or limitation on assignment. The revised Article explicitly protects third parties against any adverse effect of the creation or attempted enforcement of the security interest. See Sections 9-408, 9-409.

Subject to Sections 9-408 and 9-409 and two other exceptions (Sections 9-406, concerning accounts, chattel paper, and payment intangibles, and 9-407, concerning interests in leased goods), Section 9-401 establishes a baseline rule that the inclusion of transactions and collateral within the scope of Article 9 has no effect on non-Article 9 law dealing with the alienability or inalienability of property. For example, if a commercial tort claim is nonassignable under other applicable law, the fact that a security interest in the claim is within the scope of Article 9 does not override the other applicable law's effective prohibition of assignment.

b. Duties of Secured Party. The 1998 Revisions provided for expanded duties of secured parties.

Release of control. Section 9-208 imposes upon a secured party having control of a deposit account, investment property, or a letter-of-credit right the duty to release control when there is no secured obligation and no commitment to give value. Section 9-209 contains analogous provisions when an account debtor has been notified to pay a secured party.

Information. Section 9-210 expands a secured party's duties to provide the debtor with information concerning collateral and the obligations that it secures.

Default and enforcement. Part 6 also includes some additional duties of secured parties in connection with default and enforcement. See, e.g., Section 9-616 (duty to explain calculation of deficiency or surplus in a consumer-goods transaction).

c. Choice of Law. The choice-of-law rules included in the 1998 Revisions for the law governing perfection, the effect of perfection or nonperfection, and priority are found in Part 3, Subpart 1 (Sections 9-301 through 9-307). See also Section 9-316.

Where to file: Location of debtor. The 1998 Revisions changed the choice-of-law rule governing perfection (i.e., where to file) for most collateral to the law of the jurisdiction where the debtor is located. See Section 9-301. Under pre-1998 Article 9, the jurisdiction of the debtor's location governed only perfection and priority of a security interest in accounts, general intangibles, mobile goods, and, for purposes of perfection by filing, chattel paper and investment property.

Determining debtor's location. As a baseline rule, Section 9-307 follows pre-1998 Section 9-103, under which the location of the debtor is the debtor's place of business (or chief executive office, if the debtor has more than one place of business). Section 9-307 contains three major exceptions. First, a "registered organization," such as a corporation or limited liability company, is located in the State under whose law the debtor is organized, e.g., a corporate debtor's State of incorporation. Second, an individual debtor is located at his or her principal residence. Third, there are special rules for determining the location of the United States and registered organizations organized under the law of the United States.

Location of non-U.S. debtors. If, applying the foregoing rules, a debtor is located in a jurisdiction whose law does not require public notice as a condition of perfection of a nonpossessory security interest, the entity is deemed located in the District of Columbia. See Section 9-307. Thus, to the extent that this Article applies to non-U.S. debtors, perfection could be accomplished in many cases by a domestic filing.

Priority. For tangible collateral such as goods and instruments, Section 9-301 provides that the law applicable to priority and the effect of perfection or nonperfection will remain the law of the jurisdiction where the collateral is located, as under pre-1998 Section 9-103 (but without the confusing "last event" test). For intangible collateral, such as accounts, the applicable law for priority is that of the jurisdiction in which the debtor is located.

Possessory security interests; agricultural liens. Perfection, the effect of perfection or nonperfection, and priority of a possessory security interest or an agricultural lien are governed by the law of the jurisdiction where the collateral subject to the security interest or lien is located. See Sections 9-301, 9-302.

Goods covered by certificates of title; deposit accounts; letter-of-credit rights; investment property. The 1998 Revisions to Article 9 included several refinements to the treatment of choice-of-law matters for goods covered by certificates of title. See Section 9-303. The revision also provided special choice-of-law rules, similar to those for investment property under current Articles 8 and 9, for deposit accounts (Section 9-304), investment property (Section 9-305), and letter-of-credit rights (Section 9-306).

Change in applicable law. Section 9-316 addresses perfection following a change in applicable law.

d. Perfection. The 1998 revised rules governing perfection of security interests and agricultural liens are found in Part 3, Subpart 2 (Sections 9-308 through 9-316).

Deposit accounts; letter-of-credit rights. With certain exceptions, the 1998 Revisions provided that a security interest in a deposit account or a letter-of-credit right may be perfected only by the secured party's acquiring "control" of the deposit account or letter-of-credit right. See Sections 9-312, 9-314. Under Section 9-104, a secured party has "control" of a deposit account when, with the consent of the debtor, the secured party obtains the depositary bank's agreement to act on the secured party's instructions (including when the secured party becomes the account holder) or when the secured party is itself the depositary bank. The control requirements are patterned on Section 8-106, which specifies the requirements for control of investment property. Under Section 9-107, "control" of a letter-of-credit right occurs when the issuer or nominated person consents to an assignment of proceeds under Section 5-114.

Electronic chattel paper and tangible chattel paper definitions deleted in 2022 Article 9 Revisions. Section 9-102 of the 1998 Revisions included new defined terms: "electronic chattel" and "tangible chattel paper." However, the 2022 Article 9 Revisions deleted those terms and modified the definition of "chattel paper" and the rules for chattel paper evidenced by electronic records, as discussed in Comment 4 and Section 9-102, Comment 5.b.

Investment property. The 1998 Revisions left the perfection requirements for "investment property" (defined in Section 9-102), including perfection by control under Section 9-106, substantially unchanged. However, a new provision in Section 9-314 is designed to ensure that a secured party retains control in "repledge" transactions that are typical in the securities markets.

Instruments and commercial tort claims. The 1998 Revisions expanded the types of collateral in which a security interest may be perfected by filing to include instruments. See Section 9-312. Under the revised Article security interests in commercial tort claims also are perfected by filing. See Sections 9-308, 9-310.

Sales of payment intangibles and promissory notes. Although pre-1998 Article 9 covered the outright sale of accounts and chattel paper, under the revised Article sales of most other types of receivables also are financing transactions to which Article 9 should apply. Accordingly, Section 9-102 expanded the definition of "account" to include many types of receivables (including "health-care-insurance receivables," defined in Section 9-102) that pre-1998 Article 9 classified as "general intangibles." It thereby subjects to Article 9's filing system sales of more types of receivables than did pre-1998 Article 9. Certain sales of payment intangibles—primarily bank loan participation transactions—should not be subject to the Article 9 filing rules. These transactions are placed in a residual category of collateral, "payment intangibles" (general intangibles under which the account debtor's principal obligation is monetary), the sale of which is exempt from the filing requirements of Article 9. See Sections 9-102, 9-109,

9-309 (perfection upon attachment). The perfection rules for sales of promissory notes are the same as those for sales of payment intangibles.

Possessory security interests. Several provisions of 1998 Article 9 address aspects of security interests involving a secured party or a third party who is in possession of collateral. In particular, Section 9-313 resolves a number of uncertainties under pre-1998 Section 9-305. It provides that a security interest in collateral in the possession of a third party is perfected when the third party acknowledges in an a signed record that it holds for the secured party's benefit. Section 9-313 also provides that a third party need not so acknowledge and that its acknowledgment does not impose any duties on it, unless it otherwise agrees. A special rule in Section 9-313 provides that if a secured party already is in possession of collateral, its security interest remains perfected by possession if it delivers the collateral to a third party and the collateral is accompanied by instructions to hold it for the secured party or to redeliver it to the secured party. Section 9-313 also clarifies the limited circumstances under which a security interest in goods covered by a certificate of title may be perfected by the secured party's taking possession.

Automatic perfection. The 1998 Revisions added Section 9-309, which lists various types of security interests as to which no public-notice step is required for perfection (e.g., purchase-money security interests in consumer goods other than automobiles). This automatic perfection also extends to a transfer of a health-care-insurance receivable to a health-care provider. Those transfers normally will be made by natural persons who receive health-care services; there is little value in requiring filing for perfection in that context. Automatic perfection also applies to security interests created by sales of payment intangibles and promissory notes. Section 9-308 provides that a perfected security interest in collateral supported by a "supporting obligation" (such as an account supported by a guaranty) also is a perfected security interest in the supporting obligation, and that a perfected security interest in an obligation secured by a security interest or lien on property (e.g., a real-property mortgage) also is a perfected security interest in the security interest or lien.

e. Priority; Special Rules for Banks and Deposit Accounts. The rules governing priority of security interests and agricultural liens under the 1998 Revisions are found in Part 3, Subpart 3 (Sections 9-317 through 9-342). The revised Article includes several new priority rules and some special rules relating to banks and deposit accounts (Sections 9-340 through 9-342).

Purchase-money security interests: General; consumer-goods transactions; inventory. Section 9-103 substantially rewrites the definition of purchase-money security interest (PMSI) (although the term is not formally "defined"). The substantive changes, however, apply only to non-consumer-goods transactions. (Consumer transactions and consumer-goods transactions are discussed below in Comment 4.j.) For non-consumer-goods transactions, Section 9-103 makes clear that a security interest in collateral may be (to some extent) both a PMSI as well as a non-PMSI, in accord with the "dual status" rule applied by some courts under pre-1998 Article 9 (thereby rejecting the "transformation" rule). The revised definition provides an even broader conception of a PMSI in inventory, yielding a result that accords with private agreements entered into in response to the uncertainty under pre-1998 Article 9. It also treats consignments as purchase-money security interests in inventory. Section 9-324 clarifies the PMSI priority rules, but for the most part without material change in substance. Section 9-324 also clarifies the priority rules for competing PMSIs in the same collateral.

Purchase-money security interests in livestock; agricultural liens. Section 9-324 provides a special PMSI priority, similar to the inventory PMSI priority rule, for livestock. Section 9-322 (the baseline first-to-file-or-perfect priority rule) also recognizes special non-Article 9 priority rules for agricultural liens, which can override the baseline first-in-time rule.

Purchase-money security interests in software. Section 9-324 contains a new priority rule for a software purchase-money security interest. (Section 9-102 includes a definition of "software.") Under Section 9-103, a software PMSI includes a PMSI in software that is used in goods that are also subject to a PMSI.

Investment property. The 1998 priority rules for investment property are substantially similar to the priority rules found in pre-1998 Section 9-115, which was added in conjunction with the 1994 revisions to UCC Article 8. Under Section 9-328, if a secured party has control of investment property (Sections 8-106, 9-106), its security interest is senior to a security interest perfected in another manner (e.g., by filing). Also under Section 9-328, security interests perfected by control generally rank according to the time that control is obtained or, in the case of a security entitlement or a commodity contract carried in a commodity account, the time when the control arrangement is entered into. That was a change from pre-1998 Section 9-115, under which the security interests ranked equally. However, as between a securities intermediary's security interest in a security entitlement that it maintains for the debtor and a security interest held by another secured party, the securities intermediary's security interest is senior.

Deposit accounts. The 1998 priority rules applicable to deposit accounts are found in Section 9-327 and are patterned on and similar to those for investment property in pre-1998 Section 9-115 and Section 9-328. Under Section 9-327, if a secured party has control of a deposit account, its security interest is senior to a security interest perfected in another manner (i.e., as cash proceeds). Also under Section 9-327, security interests perfected by control rank according to the time that control is obtained, but as between a depositary bank's security interest and one held by another secured party, the depositary bank's security interest is senior. A corresponding rule in Section 9-340 makes a depositary bank's right of set-off generally senior to a security interest held by another secured party. However, if the other secured party becomes the depositary bank's customer with respect to the deposit account, then its security interest is senior to the depositary bank's security interest and right of set-off. Sections 9-327, 9-340.

Letter-of-credit rights. The 1998 priority rules for security interests in letter-of-credit rights are set out in Section 9-329. They are somewhat analogous to those for deposit accounts. A security interest perfected by control has priority over one perfected in another manner (i.e., as a supporting obligation for the collateral in which a security interest is perfected). Security interests in a letter-of-credit right perfected by control rank according to the time that control is obtained. However, the rights of a transferee beneficiary or a nominated person are independent and superior to the extent provided in Section 5-114. See Section 9-109(c)(4).

Chattel paper and instruments. Section 9-330 is the 1998 successor to pre-1998 Section 9-308. As under pre-1998 Section 9-308, under the 1998 Revisions differing priority rules apply to purchasers of chattel paper who give new value and take possession (or, in the case of electronic chattel paper, obtain control) of the collateral—depending on whether a conflicting security interest in the collateral is claimed merely as proceeds. The principal change related to the role of knowledge and the effect of an indication of a previous assignment of the collateral. 1998 Section 9-330 also afforded priority to purchasers of instruments who take possession in good faith and without knowledge that the purchase violates the rights of the competing secured party. In addition, to qualify for priority, purchasers of chattel paper, but not of instruments, must purchase in the ordinary course of business. The 2022 Article 9 Revisions eliminated the defined terms "electronic chattel paper" and "tangible chattel paper," revised the definition of "chattel paper" in Section 9-102 and modified the Section 9-330 priority rule accordingly. See Comment 4.b. and Section 9-102, Comment 5.b.

Proceeds. 1998 Section 9-322 contains new priority rules that clarify when a special priority of a security interest in collateral continues or does not continue with respect to proceeds of the collateral. Other 1998 refinements to the priority rules for proceeds are included in Sections 9-324 (purchase-money security interest priority) and 9-330 (priority of certain purchasers of chattel paper and instruments).

Miscellaneous priority provisions. The 1998 Revisions to Article 9 also included (i) clarifications of selected good-faith-purchase and similar issues (Sections 9-317, 9-331); (ii) new priority rules to deal with the "double debtor" problem arising when a debtor creates a security interest in collateral acquired by the debtor subject to a security interest created by another person (Section 9-325); (iii) new priority rules to deal with the problems created when a change in corporate structure or the like results in a new entity that has become bound by the original debtor's after-acquired property agreement (Section 9-326); (iv) a provision enabling most transferees of funds from a deposit account or money to take free of a security interest (Section 9-332); (v) substantially rewritten and refined priority rules dealing with accessions and commingled goods (Sections 9-335, 9-336); (vi) revised priority rules for security interests in goods covered by a certificate of title (Section 9-337); and (vii) provisions designed to ensure that security interests in deposit accounts will not extend to most transferees of funds on deposit or payees from deposit accounts and will not otherwise "clog" the payments system (Sections 9-341, 9-342).

Model provisions relating to production-money security interests. Appendix II to the 1998 Revisions contained model definitions and priority rules relating to "production-money security interests" held by secured parties who give new value used in the production of crops. Because no consensus emerged on the wisdom of these provisions during the drafting process, the sponsors made no recommendation on whether these model provisions should be enacted.

f. Proceeds. Revised Section 9-102 provides an expanded definition of "proceeds" of collateral, which includes additional rights and property that arise out of collateral, such as distributions on account of collateral and claims arising out of the loss or nonconformity of, defects in, or damage to collateral. The revised definition of "proceeds" also includes collections on account of "supporting obligations," such as guarantees.

g. Part 4: Additional Provisions Relating to Third-Party Rights. The 1998 Revisions added a new Part 4 that includes several provisions relating to the relationships between certain third parties and the parties to secured transactions. Part 4 contains new Sections 9-401 (replacing pre-1998 Section 9-311) (alienability of debtor's rights), 9-402 (replacing pre-1998 Section 9-317) (secured party not obligated on debtor's contracts), 9-403 (replacing pre-1998 Section 9-206) (agreement not to assert defenses against assignee), 9-404, 9-405, and 9-406 (replacing pre-1998 Section 9-318) (rights acquired by assignee, modification of assigned contract, discharge of account debtor, restrictions on assignment of account, chattel paper, promissory note, or payment intangible ineffective), 9-407 (replacing some provisions of pre-1998 Section 2A-303) (restrictions on creation or enforcement of security interest in leasehold interest or lessor's residual interest ineffective). New Part 4 also added new Sections 9-408 (restrictions on assignment of promissory notes, health-care-insurance receivables ineffective, and certain general intangibles ineffective) and 9-409 (restrictions on assignment of letter-of-credit rights ineffective). See Comment 3.a.

h. Filing. New Part 5 (replacing pre-1998 Part 4) of Article 9 was substantially rewritten to simplify the statutory text and to deal with numerous problems of interpretation and implementation that have arisen over the years.

Medium-neutrality. Part 5 is "medium-neutral"; that is, it makes clear that parties may file and otherwise communicate with a filing office by means of records communicated and stored in media other than on paper.

Identity of person who files a record; authorization. Part 5 also is largely indifferent as to the person who effects a filing. Instead, it addresses whose authorization is necessary for a person to file a record with a filing office. The filing scheme does not contemplate that the identity of a "filer" will be a part of the searchable records. This approach is consistent with, and a necessary aspect of, eliminating signatures or other evidence of authorization from the system (except to the extent that filing offices may choose to employ authentication procedures in connection with electronic communications). As long as the appropriate person authorizes the filing, or, in the case of a termination statement, the debtor is entitled to the termination, it is largely insignificant whether the secured party or another person files any given record.

Section 9-509 collects in one place most of the rules that determine when a record may be filed. In general, the debtor's authorization is required for the filing of an initial financing statement or an amendment that adds collateral. With one further exception, a secured party of record's authorization is required for the filing of other amendments. The exception arises if a secured party has failed to provide a termination statement that is required because there is no outstanding secured obligation or commitment to give value. In that situation, a debtor is authorized to file a termination statement indicating that it has been filed by the debtor.

Financing statement formal requisites. The formal requisites for a financing statement under the 1998 Revisions are set out in Section 9-502. A financing statement must provide the name of the debtor and the secured party and an indication of the collateral that it covers. Sections 9-503 and 9-506 address the sufficiency of a name provided on a financing statement and clarify when a debtor's name is correct and when an incorrect name is insufficient. Section 9-504 addresses the indication of collateral covered. Under Section 9-504, a super-generic description (e.g., "all assets" or "all personal property") in a financing statement is a sufficient indication of the collateral. (Note, however, that a super-generic description is inadequate for purposes of a security agreement. See Sections 9-108, 9-203.) To facilitate electronic filing, this Article does not require that the debtor's signature or other authorization appear on a financing statement. Instead, it prohibits the filing of unauthorized financing statements and imposes liability upon those who violate the prohibition. See Sections 9-509, 9-626.

Filing-office operations. The 1998 Part 5 introduced several provisions governing filing operations. First, it prohibits the filing office from rejecting an initial financing statement or other record for a reason other than one of the few that are specified. See Sections 9-520, 9-516. Second, the filing office is obliged to link all subsequent records (e.g., assignments, continuation statements, etc.) to the initial financing statement to which they relate. See Section 9-519. Third, the filing office may delete a financing statement and related records from the files no earlier than one year after lapse (lapse normally is five years after the filing date), and then only if a continuation statement has not been filed. See Sections 9-515, 9-519, 9-522. Thus, a financing statement and related records would be discovered by a search of the files even after the filing of a termination statement. This approach helps eliminate filing-office discretion and also eases problems associated with multiple secured parties and multiple partial assignments. Fourth, Part 5 mandates performance standards for filing offices. See Sections 9-519, 9-520, 9-523. Fifth, it provides for the promulgation of filing-office rules to deal with details best left out of the statute and requires the filing office to submit periodic reports. See Sections 9-526, 9-527.

Defaulting or missing secured parties and fraudulent filings. In some areas of the country, serious problems had arisen from fraudulent financing statements filed against public officials and other persons. The 1998 Article addressed the fraud problem by providing the opportunity for a debtor to file a termination statement when a secured party wrongfully refuses or fails to provide a termination statement. See Section 9-509. This opportunity also addresses the problem of secured parties that simply disappear through mergers or liquidations. In addition, Section 9-518 provides a statutory method by which a debtor who believes that a filed record is inaccurate or was wrongfully filed may indicate that fact in the files, albeit without affecting the efficacy, if any, of the challenged record.

Extended period of effectiveness for certain financing statements. Section 9-515 contains an exception to the usual rule that financing statements are effective for five years unless a continuation statement is filed to continue the effectiveness for another five years. Under that section, an initial financing statement filed in connection with a "public-finance transaction" or a "manufactured-home transaction" (terms defined in Section 9-102) is effective for 30 years.

National form of financing statement and related forms. Section 9-521 provides for uniform, national written forms of financing statements and related written records that must be accepted by a filing office that accepts written records.

i. Default and Enforcement. Part 6 of the 1998 Revisions to Article 9 extensively revised and replaced pre-1998 Part 5. Provisions relating to enforcement of consumer-goods transactions and consumer transactions are discussed in Comment 4.j.

Debtor, secondary obligor; waiver. Section 9-602 clarifies the identity of persons who have rights and persons to whom a secured party owes specified duties under Part 6. Under that section, the rights and duties are enjoyed by and run to the "debtor," defined in Section 9-102 to mean any person with a non-lien property interest in collateral, and to any "obligor." However, with one exception (Section 9-616, as it relates to a consumer obligor), the rights and duties concerned affect non-debtor obligors only if they are "secondary obligors." "Secondary obligor" is defined in Section 9-102 to include one who is secondarily obligated on the secured obligation, e.g., a guarantor, or one who has a right of recourse against the debtor or another obligor with respect to an obligation secured by collateral. However, under Sections 9-605 and 9-628, the secured party is relieved from any duties and liabilities to any person unless the secured party knows that the person is a debtor or obligor. (The 2022 Article 9 Revisions have modified Sections 9-605 and 9-628. See 2022 Section 9-605, Comments 2 and 3.) Resolving an issue on which courts disagreed under pre-1998 Article 9, this revised Article 9 generally prohibits waiver by a secondary obligor of its rights and a secured party's duties under Part 6. See Section 9-602. However, Section 9-624 permits a secondary obligor or debtor to waive the right to notification of disposition of collateral and, in a non-consumer transaction, the right to redeem collateral, if the secondary obligor or debtor agrees to do so after default.

Rights of collection and enforcement of collateral. Section 9-607 explains in greater detail than pre-1998 Section 9-502 the rights of a secured party who seeks to collect or enforce collateral, including accounts, chattel paper, and payment intangibles. It also sets forth the enforcement rights of a depositary bank holding a security interest in a deposit account maintained with the depositary bank. Section 9-607 relates solely to the rights of a secured party vis-à-vis a debtor with respect to collections and enforcement. It does not affect the rights or duties of third parties, such as account debtors on collateral, which are addressed elsewhere (e.g., new Section 9-406). Section 9-608 clarifies the manner in which proceeds of collection or enforcement are to be applied.

Disposition of collateral: Warranties of title. Section 9-610 imposes on a secured party who disposes of collateral the warranties of title, quiet possession, and the like that are otherwise applicable under other law. It also provides rules for the exclusion or modification of those warranties.

Disposition of collateral: Notification, application of proceeds, surplus and deficiency, other effects. Section 9-611 requires a secured party to give notification of a disposition of collateral to other secured parties and lienholders who have filed financing statements against the debtor covering the collateral. (That duty was eliminated by the 1972 revisions to Article 9.) However, that section relieves the secured party from that duty when the secured party undertakes a search of the records and a report of the results is unreasonably delayed. Section 9-613, which applies only to non-consumer transactions, specifies the contents of a sufficient notification of disposition and provides that a notification sent 10 days or more before the earliest time for disposition is sent within a reasonable time. Section 9-615 addresses the application of proceeds of disposition, the entitlement of a debtor to any surplus, and the liability of an obligor for any deficiency. Section 9-619 clarifies the effects of a disposition by a secured party, including the rights of transferees of the collateral.

Rights and duties of secondary obligor. Section 9-618 provides that a secondary obligor obtains the rights and assumes the duties of a secured party if the secondary obligor receives an assignment of a secured obligation, agrees to assume the secured party's rights and duties upon a transfer to it of collateral, or becomes subrogated to the rights of the secured party with respect to the collateral. The assumption, transfer, or subrogation is not a disposition of collateral under Section 9-610, but it does relieve the former secured party of further duties. Pre-1998 Section 9-504(5) did not address whether a secured party was relieved of its duties in this situation.

Transfer of record or legal title. Section 9-619 contains a new provision making clear that a transfer of record or legal title to a secured party is not of itself a disposition under Part 6. This rule applies regardless of the circumstances under which the transfer of title occurs.

Strict foreclosure. Section 9-620, unlike pre-1998 Section 9-505, permits a secured party to accept collateral in partial satisfaction, as well as full satisfaction, of the obligations secured. This right of strict foreclosure extends to intangible as well as tangible property. Section 9-622 clarifies the effects of an acceptance of collateral on the rights of junior claimants. It rejects the approach taken by some courts—deeming a secured party to have constructively retained collateral in satisfaction of the secured obligations—in the case of a secured party's unreasonable delay in the disposition of collateral. Instead, unreasonable delay is relevant when determining whether a disposition under Section 9-610 is commercially reasonable.

Effect of noncompliance: "Rebuttable presumption" test. Section 9-626 adopts the "rebuttable presumption" test for the failure of a secured party to proceed in accordance with certain provisions of Part 6. (As discussed in Comment 4.j., the test does not necessarily apply to consumer transactions.) Under this approach, the deficiency claim of a noncomplying secured party is calculated by crediting the obligor with the greater of the actual net proceeds of a disposition and the amount of net proceeds that would have been realized if the disposition had been conducted in accordance with Part 6 (e.g., in a commercially reasonable manner). For non-consumer transactions, Section 9-626 rejects the "absolute bar" test that some courts have imposed; that approach bars a noncomplying secured party from recovering any deficiency, regardless of the loss (if any) the debtor suffered as a consequence of the noncompliance.

"Low-price" dispositions: Calculation of deficiency and surplus. Section 9-615(f) addresses the problem of procedurally regular dispositions that fetch a low price. Subsection (f) provides a special method for calculating a deficiency if the proceeds of a disposition of collateral to a secured party, a person related to the secured party, or a secondary obligor are "significantly below the range of proceeds that a complying disposition to a person other than the secured party, a person related to the secured party, or a secondary obligor would have brought." ("Person related to" is defined in Section 9-102.) In these situations there is reason to suspect that there may be inadequate incentives to obtain a better price. Consequently, instead of calculating a deficiency (or surplus) based on the actual net proceeds, the deficiency (or surplus) would be calculated based on the proceeds that would have been received in a disposition to a person other than the secured party, a person related to the secured party, or a secondary obligor.

j. Consumer Goods, Consumer-Goods Transactions, and Consumer Transactions. The 1998 Revisions (including the accompanying conforming revisions (see Appendix I)) included several special rules for "consumer goods," "consumer transactions," and "consumer-goods transactions." Each term is defined in Section 9-102.

(i) Revised Sections 2-502 and 2-716 provide a buyer of consumer goods with enhanced rights to possession of the goods, thereby accelerating and enhancing the opportunity to achieve "buyer in ordinary course of business" status under Section 1-201(b)(9).

(ii) Section 9-103(e) (allocation of payments for determining extent of purchase-money status), (f) (purchase-money status not affected by cross-collateralization, refinancing, restructuring, or the like), and (g) (secured party has burden of establishing extent of purchase-money status) do not apply to consumer-goods transactions. Section 9-103 also provides that the limitation of those provisions to transactions other than consumer-goods transactions leaves to the courts the proper rules for consumer-goods transactions and prohibits the courts from drawing inferences from that limitation.

(iii) Section 9-108 provides that in a consumer transaction a description of consumer goods, a security entitlement, securities account, or commodity account "only by [UCC-defined] type of collateral" is not a sufficient collateral description in a security agreement.

(iv) Sections 9-403 and 9-404 make effective the Federal Trade Commission's anti-holder-in-due-course rule (when applicable), 16 C.F.R. Part 433, even in the absence of the required legend.

(v) The 10-day safe-harbor for notification of a disposition provided by Section 9-612 does not apply in a consumer transaction.

(vi) Section 9-613 (contents and form of notice of disposition) does not apply to a consumer-goods transaction.

(vii) Section 9-614 contains special requirements for the contents of a notification of disposition and a safe-harbor, "plain English" form of notification, for consumer-goods transactions.

(viii) Section 9-616 requires a secured party in a consumer-goods transaction to provide a debtor with a notification of how it calculated a deficiency at the time it first undertakes to collect a deficiency.

(ix) Section 9-620 prohibits partial strict foreclosure with respect to consumer goods collateral and, unless the debtor agrees to waive the requirement in a signed record after default, in certain cases requires the secured party to dispose of consumer goods collateral that has been repossessed.

(x) Section 9-626 ("rebuttable presumption" rule) does not apply to a consumer transaction. Section 9-626 also provides that its limitation to transactions other than consumer transactions leaves to the courts the proper rules for consumer transactions and prohibits the courts from drawing inferences from that limitation.

k. Good Faith. The 1998 Revisions added in Section 9-102 a new definition of "good faith" that included not only "honesty in fact" but also "the observance of reasonable commercial standards of fair dealing." That definition was deleted by the conforming amendments to the 2001 revision of Article 1 as unnecessary, given the revised definition in Section 1-201(b)(20).

l. [Reserved.]

m. Conforming and Related Amendments to Other UCC Articles. Appendix I to the 1998 Revisions contained several proposed revisions to the provisions and Comments of other UCC articles. For the most part those revisions are explained in the Comments to the 1998 Revisions.

Article 1. Revised Section 1-201 provides revisions to the definitions of "buyer in ordinary course of business," "purchaser," and "security interest."

Articles 2 and 2A. Sections 2-210, 2-326, 2-502, 2-716, 2A-303, and 2A-307 are revised to address the intersection between Articles 2 and 2A and Article 9.

Article 5. New Section 5-118 is patterned on Section 4-210. It provides for a security interest in documents presented under a letter of credit in favor of the issuer and a nominated person on the letter of credit.

Article 8. Revisions to Section 8-106, which deals with "control" of securities and security entitlements, conform it to Section 8-302, which deals with "delivery." Revisions to Section 8-110, which deals with a "securities intermediary's jurisdiction," conform it to the revised treatment of a "commodity intermediary's jurisdiction" in Section 9-305. Sections 8-301 and 8-302 are revised for clarification. Section 8-510 is revised to conform it to the revised priority rules of Section 9-328. Several Comments in Article 8 also are revised.

4. Summary of 2022 Article 9 Revisions. Following is a brief summary of some of the more significant revisions that are included in the 2022 Article 9 Revisions. The 2022 amendments to Article 9 are extensive. Many of the amendments are necessary to conform Article 9 to new Article 12, which (along with its Comments) should be read along with the Article 9 amendments and Comments. Other material amendments include those relating to chattel paper and money, among other matters.

a. Article 12-Related Revisions. Article 12-related amendments to Article 9 include the addition of two new kinds of collateral under Article 9: controllable account (a subset of account) and controllable payment intangible (a subset of payment intangible, which is a subset of general intangible). A controllable account or controllable payment intangible is created when the account or payment intangible is evidenced by a controllable electronic record (defined in Section 12-102(a)(1), and a subset of general intangible), which results if the account debtor obligated on the account or payment intangible has agreed to pay the person in control of the controllable electronic record. Perfection of a security interest in a controllable electronic record, controllable account, or controllable payment intangible may be by control or by filing a financing statement. Control of a controllable electronic record is determined under Section 12-105. Control of a controllable account or controllable payment intangible is achieved by obtaining control of the controllable electronic record that evidences the account or payment intangible. Section 9- 107A(b). A security interest in a controllable account, controllable electronic record, or controllable payment intangible which is perfected by control has priority over a security interest held by a secured party that does not have control. Section 9-326A.

As is the case for secured parties protected by take-free rules under other articles, the rights of a secured party that takes free of competing property interests under Section 12-104(e) or that is protected from certain actions under Section 12-104(g), as a qualifying purchaser of a controllable account, controllable electronic record, or controllable payment intangible, are respected under Article 9. Section 9-331.

The law of the controllable electronic record's jurisdiction under Section 12-107 governs perfection by control and priority of a security interest in a controllable account, controllable electronic record, or controllable payment intangible. Section 9-306B(a). The law of the jurisdiction in which a debtor is located governs perfection by filing (but not priority) for such collateral. Section 9-306B(b).

The 2022 Article 9 Revisions also contains several other Article 12-related conforming amendments to Article 9.

b. Chattel Paper-Related Amendments. These amendments primarily address two issues that have arisen under the pre-2022 Article 9 with respect to transactions in chattel paper.

First, the definition of "chattel paper" created uncertainty in "bundled" or "hybrid" transactions in which monetary obligations exist not only under a lease of goods but also with respect to other property and services relating to the leased goods. Frequently, the value of the non-goods aspect of a transaction is substantially greater than the value of the lessee's rights under the lease of goods. Uncertainty existed among those who finance chattel paper and other rights to payment as to whether these transactions give rise to chattel paper. The revisions resolve this issue by treating only those transactions whose predominant purpose was to give the obligor (lessee) the right to possession and use of the goods as giving rise to "chattel paper." Some similar issues arise in connection with chattel paper that includes a security interest in specific goods. See Section 9-102, Comment 5.b.

Second, the pre-2022 statutory distinction between "tangible chattel paper" and "electronic chattel paper" caused practical problems. As to tangible chattel paper (i.e., evidenced by writings), problems arose in the case of multiple originals of writings and situations in which separate writings covered different components of chattel paper. Official comments issued in connection with the 1998 Revisions addressed, but did not entirely resolve, these issues. As to electronic chattel paper, the safe harbor for control was based on a "single authoritative copy" of the chattel paper. Moreover, in some situations tangible chattel paper is converted to electronic form and electronic chattel paper is converted to tangible form. Additional uncertainty existed when one or more records comprised one or more authoritative tangible copies of the records that evidenced the right to payment and rights in related property and one or more authoritative electronic copies of those records also existed.

The 2022 Article 9 Revisions provide a single rule, under Ih a security Interest In chattel paper can be perfected by taking possession of the authoritative tangible copies, if any, and obtaining control of the electronic authoritative copies, if any. This single rule addresses cases where some records evidencing chattel paper are electronic and some are tangible or where a record in one medium is replaced by a record in another.

The 2022 Article 9 Revisions also define chattel paper more accurately, as the right to payment of a monetary obligation that is secured by a security interest in specific goods or owed under a lease of specific goods, if the right to payment and interest in the goods are evidenced by a record.

Finally, the 2022 Article 9 Revisions provide a new choice-of-law rule for perfection and priority of security interests in chattel paper that is evidenced by authoritative electronic copies of records or by such electronic copies and authoritative tangible copies. For such chattel paper, Section 9-306A provides that perfection by control and possession of authoritative copies and priority are governed by the law of the "chattel paper's jurisdiction," based loosely on Sections 8-110 and 9-305. For chattel paper evidenced only by authoritative tangible copies, Section 9- 306A(d) provides that perfection by possession and priority are governed by the law of the location of the authoritative tangible copies. Perfection by filing continues to be governed by the law of the location of the debtor for all chattel paper.

c. Money-Related Amendments.

Section 1-201(b)(24) defines "money" as including "a medium of exchange currently authorized or adopted by a domestic or foreign government. . . ." There is no way of knowing how money in an intangible form might develop, but there are indications that some countries might authorize or adopt intangible tokens as a medium of exchange and others might authorize or adopt deposit accounts with a central bank as money. (These tokens or accounts sometimes are referred to as central bank digital currency or CBDC.) For many purposes, there is no need for the UCC to distinguish among types of money. For Article 9 purposes, however, distinctions must be drawn. Only tangible money is susceptible of perfection by possession. And the steps needed for perfection by control with respect to intangible tokens, such as controllable electronic records, will not work for deposit accounts with a central bank, and vice versa. For this reason, the revisions provide an Article 9 definition of "money" that is narrower than the Article 1 definition. The Article 9 definition expressly excludes deposit accounts (but not CBDC that is a token). Thus, "electronic money," defined in Section 9-102 as "money in an electronic form," would not include deposit accounts. The Article 9 definition of "money" also excludes money in an electronic form that cannot be subjected to control under Section 9-105A.

The Article 9 provisions governing "deposit accounts" would remain suitable for accounts with a central bank, even if a government has adopted these accounts as money. The revisions leave Article 9's treatment of deposit accounts largely unchanged. Under the revisions, a security interest in electronic money as original collateral can be perfected only by control. The requirements for obtaining control of electronic money under Section 9-105A are essentially the same as those for obtaining control of a controllable electronic record under Article 12.

The 2022 Article 9 Revisions also make changes to Section 9-332, the take-free rules for transferees of money, including the addition of a new rule applicable to electronic money, and transferees of funds from deposit accounts.

d. Transitional Rules. Article A to the 2022 Amendments provides important transitional rules. These rules are designed to protect the expectations of parties to transactions entered into before the effective date of a state's enactment of the revisions. They also provide for an adequate period of time for parties to pre-effective date transactions to make adjustments so as to preserve certain pre-effective date priorities.

Section 9-102. Definitions and Index of Definitions

(a) [Article 9 definitions.] In this article:

(1) "Accession" means goods that are physically united with other goods in such a manner that the identity of the original goods is not lost.

(2) "Account", except as used in "account for", "account statement", "account to", "commodity account" in paragraph (14), "customer's account", "deposit account" in paragraph (29), "on account of", and "statement of account", means a right to payment of a monetary obligation, whether or not earned by performance, (i) for property that has been or is to be sold, leased, licensed, assigned, or otherwise disposed of, (ii) for services rendered or to be rendered, (iii) for a policy of insurance issued or to be issued, (iv) for a secondary obligation incurred or to be incurred, (v) for energy provided or to be provided, (vi) for the use or hire of a vessel under a charter or other contract, (vii) arising out of the use of a credit or charge card or information contained on or for use with the card, or (viii) as winnings in a lottery or other game of chance operated or sponsored by a State, governmental unit of a State, or person licensed or authorized to operate the game by a State or governmental unit of a State. The term includes controllable accounts and health-care-insurance receivables. The term does not include (i) chattel paper, (ii) commercial tort claims, (iii) deposit accounts, (iv) investment property, (v) letter-of-credit rights or letters of credit, (vi) rights to payment for money or funds advanced or sold, other than rights arising out of the use of a credit or charge card or information contained on or for use with the card, or (vii) rights to payment evidenced by an instrument.

(3) "Account debtor" means a person obligated on an account, chattel paper, or general intangible. The term does not include persons obligated to pay a negotiable instrument, even if the negotiable instrument evidences chattel paper.

(4) "Accounting", except as used in "accounting for", means a record:

(A) signed by a secured party;

(B) indicating the aggregate unpaid secured obligations as of a date not more than 35 days earlier or 35 days later than the date of the record; and

(C) identifying the components of the obligations in reasonable detail.

(5) "Agricultural lien" means an interest in farm products:

(A) which secures payment or performance of an obligation for:

(i) goods or services furnished in connection with a debtor's farming operation; or

(ii) rent on real property leased by a debtor in connection with its farming operation;

(B) which is created by statute in favor of a person that:

(i) in the ordinary course of its business furnished goods or services to a debtor in connection with a debtor's farming operation; or

(ii) leased real property to a debtor in connection with the debtor's farming operation; and

(C) whose effectiveness does not depend on the person's possession of the personal property.

(6) "As-extracted collateral" means:

(A) oil, gas, or other minerals that are subject to a security interest that:

(i) is created by a debtor having an interest in the minerals before extraction; and

(ii) attaches to the minerals as extracted; or

(B) accounts arising out of the sale at the wellhead or minehead of oil, gas, or other minerals in which the debtor had an interest before extraction.

(7) [Reserved.]

(7A) "Assignee", except as used in "assignee for benefit of creditors", means a person (i) in whose favor a security interest that secures an obligation is created or provided for under a security agreement, whether or not the obligation is outstanding or (ii) to which an account, chattel paper, payment intangible, or promissory note has been sold. The term includes a person to which a security interest has been transferred by a secured party.

(7B) "Assignor" means a person that (i) under a security agreement creates or provides for a security interest that secures an obligation or (ii) sells an account, chattel paper, payment intangible, or promissory note. The term includes a secured party that has transferred a security interest to another person.

(8) "Bank" means an organization that is engaged in the business of banking. The term includes savings banks, savings and loan associations, credit unions, and trust companies.

(9) "Cash proceeds" means proceeds that are money, checks, deposit accounts, or the like.

(10) "Certificate of title" means a certificate of title with respect to which a statute provides for the security interest in question to be indicated on the certificate as a condition or result of the security interest's obtaining priority over the rights of a lien creditor with respect to the collateral. The term includes another record maintained as an alternative to a certificate of title by the governmental unit that issues certificates of title if a statute permits the security interest in question to be indicated on the record as a condition or result of the security interest's obtaining priority over the rights of a lien creditor with respect to the collateral.

(11) "Chattel paper" means:

(A) a right to payment of a monetary obligation secured by specific goods, if the right to payment and security agreement are evidenced by a record; or

(B) a right to payment of a monetary obligation owed by a lessee under a lease agreement with respect to specific goods and a monetary obligation owed by the lessee in connection with the transaction giving rise to the lease, if:

(i) the right to payment and lease agreement are evidenced by a record; and

(ii) the predominant purpose of the transaction giving rise to the lease was to give the lessee the right to possession and use of the goods.

The term does not include a right to payment arising out of a charter or other contract involving the use or hire of a vessel or a right to payment arising out of the use of a credit or charge card or information contained on or for use with the card.

(12) "Collateral" means the property subject to a security interest or agricultural lien. The term includes:

(A) proceeds to which a security interest attaches;

(B) accounts, chattel paper, payment intangibles, and promissory notes that have been sold; and

(C) goods that are the subject of a consignment.

(13) "Commercial tort claim" means a claim arising in tort with respect to which:

(A) the claimant is an organization; or

(B) the claimant is an individual and the claim:

(i) arose in the course of the claimant's business or profession; and

(ii) does not include damages arising out of personal injury to or the death of an individual.

(14) "Commodity account" means an account maintained by a commodity intermediary in which a commodity contract is carried for a commodity customer.

(15) "Commodity contract" means a commodity futures contract, an option on a commodity futures contract, a commodity option, or another contract if the contract or option is:

(A) traded on or subject to the rules of a board of trade that has been designated as a contract market for such a contract pursuant to federal commodities laws; or

(B) traded on a foreign commodity board of trade, exchange, or market, and is carried on the books of a commodity intermediary for a commodity customer.

(16) "Commodity customer" means a person for which a commodity intermediary carries a commodity contract on its books.

(17) "Commodity intermediary" means a person that:

(A) is registered as a futures commission merchant under federal commodities law; or

(B) in the ordinary course of its business provides clearance or settlement services for a board of trade that has been designated as a contract market pursuant to federal commodities law.

(18) "Communicate" means:

(A) to send a written or other tangible record;

(B) to transmit a record by any means agreed upon by the persons sending and receiving the record; or

(C) in the case of transmission of a record to or by a filing office, to transmit a record by any means prescribed by filing-office rule.

(19) "Consignee" means a merchant to which goods are delivered in a consignment.

(20) "Consignment" means a transaction, regardless of its form, in which a person delivers goods to a merchant for the purpose of sale and:

(A) the merchant:

(i) deals in goods of that kind under a name other than the name of the person making delivery;

(ii) is not an auctioneer; and

(iii) is not generally known by its creditors to be substantially engaged in selling the goods of others;

(B) with respect to each delivery, the aggregate value of the goods is $1,000 or more at the time of delivery;

(C) the goods are not consumer goods immediately before delivery; and

(D) the transaction does not create a security interest that secures an obligation.

(21) "Consignor" means a person that delivers goods to a consignee in a consignment.

(22) "Consumer debtor" means a debtor in a consumer transaction.

(23) "Consumer goods" means goods that are used or bought for use primarily for personal, family, or household purposes.

(24) "Consumer-goods transaction" means a consumer transaction in which:

(A) an individual incurs an obligation primarily for personal, family, or household purposes; and

(B) a security interest in consumer goods secures the obligation.

(25) "Consumer obligor" means an obligor who is an individual and who incurred the obligation as part of a transaction entered into primarily for personal, family, or household purposes.

(26) "Consumer transaction" means a transaction in which (i) an individual incurs an obligation primarily for personal, family, or household purposes, (ii) a security interest secures the obligation, and (iii) the collateral is held or acquired primarily for personal, family, or household purposes. The term includes consumer-goods transactions.

(27) "Continuation statement" means an amendment of a financing statement which:

(A) identifies, by its file number, the initial financing statement to which it relates; and

(B) indicates that it is a continuation statement for, or that it is filed to continue the effectiveness of, the identified financing statement.

(27A) "Controllable account" means an account evidenced by a controllable electronic record that provides that the account debtor undertakes to pay the person that has control under Section 12-105 of the controllable electronic record.

(27B) "Controllable payment intangible" means a payment intangible evidenced by a controllable electronic record that provides that the account debtor undertakes to pay the person that has control under Section 12-105 of the controllable electronic record.

(28) "Debtor" means:

(A) a person having an interest, other than a security interest or other lien, in the collateral, whether or not the person is an obligor;

(B) a seller of accounts, chattel paper, payment intangibles, or promissory notes; or

(C) a consignee.

(29) "Deposit account" means a demand, time, savings, passbook, or similar account maintained with a bank. The term does not include investment property or accounts evidenced by an instrument.

(30) "Document" means a document of title or a receipt of the type described in Section 7-201(b).

(31) [Reserved.]

(31A) "Electronic money" means money in an electronic form.

(32) "Encumbrance" means a right, other than an ownership interest, in real property. The term includes mortgages and other liens on real property.

(33) "Equipment" means goods other than inventory, farm products, or consumer goods.

(34) "Farm products" means goods, other than standing timber, with respect to which the debtor is engaged in a farming operation and which are:

(A) crops grown, growing, or to be grown, including:

(i) crops produced on trees, vines, and bushes; and

(ii) aquatic goods produced in aquacultural operations;

(B) livestock, born or unborn, including aquatic goods produced in aquacultural operations;

(C) supplies used or produced in a farming operation; or

(D) products of crops or livestock in their unmanufactured states.

(35) "Farming operation" means raising, cultivating, propagating, fattening, grazing, or any other farming, livestock, or aquacultural operation.

(36) "File number" means the number assigned to an initial financing statement pursuant to Section 9-519(a).

(37) "Filing office" means an office designated in Section 9-501 as the place to file a financing statement.

(38) "Filing-office rule" means a rule adopted pursuant to Section 9-526.

(39) "Financing statement" means a record or records composed of an initial financing statement

and any filed record relating to the initial financing statement.

(40) "Fixture filing" means the filing of a financing statement covering goods that are or are to become fixtures and satisfying Section 9-502(a) and (b). The term includes the filing of a financing statement covering goods of a transmitting utility which are or are to become fixtures.

(41) "Fixtures" means goods that have become so related to particular real property that an interest in them arises under real property law.

(42) "General intangible" means any personal property, including things in action, other than accounts, chattel paper, commercial tort claims, deposit accounts, documents, goods, instruments, investment property, letter-of-credit rights, letters of credit, money, and oil, gas, or other minerals before extraction. The term includes controllable electronic records, payment intangibles and software.

(43) [Reserved] ["Good faith" means honesty in fact and the observance of reasonably commercial standards of fair dealing.]

(44) "Goods" means all things that are movable when a security interest attaches. The term includes (i) fixtures, (ii) standing timber that is to be cut and removed under a conveyance or contract for sale, (iii) the unborn young of animals, (iv) crops grown, growing, or to be grown, even if the crops are produced on trees, vines, or bushes, and (v) manufactured homes. The term also includes a computer program embedded in goods and any supporting information provided in connection with a transaction relating to the program if (i) the program is associated with the goods in such a manner that it customarily is considered part of the goods, or (ii) by becoming the owner of the goods, a person acquires a right to use the program in connection with the goods. The term does not include a computer program embedded in goods that consist solely of the medium in which the program is embedded. The term also does not include accounts, chattel paper, commercial tort claims, deposit accounts, documents, general intangibles, instruments, investment property, letter-of-credit rights, letters of credit, money, or oil, gas, or other minerals before extraction.

(45) "Governmental unit" means a subdivision, agency, department, county, parish, municipality, or other unit of the government of the United States, a State, or a foreign country. The term includes an organization having a separate corporate existence if the organization is eligible to issue debt on which interest is exempt from income taxation under the laws of the United States.

(46) "Health-care-insurance receivable" means an interest in or claim under a policy of insurance which is a right to payment of a monetary obligation for health-care goods or services provided or to be provided.

(47) "Instrument" means a negotiable instrument or any other writing that evidences a right to the payment of a monetary obligation, is not itself a security agreement or lease, and is of a type that in ordinary course of business is transferred by delivery with any necessary indorsement or assignment. The term does not include (i) investment property, (ii) letters of credit, (iii) writings that evidence a right to payment arising out of the use of a credit or charge card or information contained on or for use with the card, or (iv) writings that evidence chattel paper.

(48) "Inventory" means goods, other than farm products, which:

(A) are leased by a person as lessor;

(B) are held by a person for sale or lease or to be furnished under a contract of service;

(C) are furnished by a person under a contract of service; or

(D) consist of raw materials, work in process, or materials used or consumed in a business.

(49) "Investment property" means a security, whether certificated or uncertificated, security entitlement, securities account, commodity contract, or commodity account.

(50) "Jurisdiction of organization", with respect to a registered organization, means the jurisdiction under whose law the organization is formed or organized.

(51) "Letter-of-credit right" means a right to payment or performance under a letter of credit, whether or not the beneficiary has demanded or is at the time entitled to demand payment or performance. The term does not include the right of a beneficiary to demand payment or performance under a letter of credit.

(52) "Lien creditor" means:

(A) a creditor that has acquired a lien on the property involved by attachment, levy, or the like;

(B) an assignee for benefit of creditors from the time of assignment;

(C) a trustee in bankruptcy from the date of the filing of the petition; or

(D) a receiver in equity from the time of appointment.

(53) "Manufactured home" means a structure, transportable in one or more sections, which, in the traveling mode, is eight body feet or more in width or 40 body feet or more in length, or, when erected on site, is 320 or more square feet, and which is built on a permanent chassis and designed to be used as a dwelling with or without a permanent foundation when connected to the required utilities, and includes the plumbing, heating, air-conditioning, and electrical systems contained therein. The term includes any structure that meets all of the requirements of this paragraph except the size requirements and with respect to which the manufacturer voluntarily files a certification required by the United States Secretary of Housing and Urban Development and complies with the standards established under Title 42 of the United States Code.

(54) "Manufactured-home transaction" means a secured transaction:

(A) that creates a purchase-money security interest in a manufactured home, other than a manufactured home held as inventory; or

(B) in which a manufactured home, other than a manufactured home held as inventory, is the primary collateral.

(54A) "Money" has the meaning in Section 1-201(b)(24), but does not include (i) a deposit account or (ii) money in an electronic form that cannot be subjected to control under Section 9-105A.

(55) "Mortgage" means a consensual interest in real property, including fixtures, which secures payment or performance of an obligation.

(56) "New debtor" means a person that becomes bound as debtor under Section 9-203(d) by a security agreement previously entered into by another person.

(57) "New value" means (i) money, (ii) money's worth in property, services, or new credit, or (iii) release by a transferee of an interest in property previously transferred to the transferee. The term does not include an obligation substituted for another obligation.

(58) "Noncash proceeds" means proceeds other than cash proceeds.

(59) "Obligor" means a person that, with respect to an obligation secured by a security interest in or an agricultural lien on the collateral, (i) owes payment or other performance of the obligation, (ii) has provided property other than the collateral to secure payment or other performance of the obligation, or (iii) is otherwise accountable in whole or in part for payment or other performance of the obligation. The term does not include issuers or nominated persons under a letter of credit.

(60) "Original debtor", except as used in Section 9-310(c), means a person that, as debtor, entered into a security agreement to which a new debtor has become bound under Section 9-203(d).

(61) "Payment intangible" means a general intangible under which the account debtor's principal obligation is a monetary obligation. The term includes a controllable payment intangible.

(62) "Person related to", with respect to an individual, means:

(A) the spouse of the individual;

(B) a brother, brother-in-law, sister, or sister-in-law of the individual;

(C) an ancestor or lineal descendant of the individual or the individual's spouse; or

(D) any other relative, by blood or marriage, of the individual or the individual's spouse who shares the same home with the individual.

(63) "Person related to", with respect to an organization, means:

(A) a person directly or indirectly controlling, controlled by, or under common control with the organization;

(B) an officer or director of, or a person performing similar functions with respect to, the organization;

(C) an officer or director of, or a person performing similar functions with respect to, a person described in subparagraph (A);

(D) the spouse of an individual described in subparagraph (A), (B), or (C); or

(E) an individual who is related by blood or marriage to an individual described in subparagraph (A), (B), (C), or (D) and shares the same home with the individual.

(64) "Proceeds", except as used in Section 9-609(b), means the following property:

(A) whatever is acquired upon the sale, lease, license, exchange, or other disposition of collateral;

(B) whatever is collected on, or distributed on account of, collateral;

(C) rights arising out of collateral;

(D) to the extent of the value of collateral, claims arising out of the loss, nonconformity, or interference with the use of, defects or infringement of rights in, or damage to, the collateral; or

(E) to the extent of the value of collateral and to the extent payable to the debtor or the secured party, insurance payable by reason of the loss or nonconformity of, defects or infringement of rights in, or damage to, the collateral.

(65) "Promissory note" means an instrument that evidences a promise to pay a monetary obligation, does not evidence an order to pay, and does not contain an acknowledgment by a bank that the bank has received for deposit a sum of money or funds.

(66) "Proposal" means a record signed by a secured party which includes the terms on which the secured party is willing to accept collateral in full or partial satisfaction of the obligation it secures pursuant to Sections 9-620, 9-621, and 9-622.

(67) "Public-finance transaction" means a secured transaction in connection with which:

(A) debt securities are issued;

(B) all or a portion of the securities issued have an initial stated maturity of at least 20 years; and

(C) the debtor, obligor, secured party, account debtor or other person obligated on collateral, assignor or assignee of a secured obligation, or assignor or assignee of a security interest is a State or a governmental unit of a State.

(68) "Public organic record" means a record that is available to the public for inspection and that is:

(A) a record consisting of the record initially filed with or issued by a State or the United States to form or organize an organization and any record filed with or issued by the State or the United States which amends or restates the initial record;

(B) an organic record of a business trust consisting of the record initially filed with a State and any record filed with the State which amends or restates the initial record, if a statute of the State governing business trusts requires that the record be filed with the State; or

(C) a record consisting of legislation enacted by the legislature of a State or the Congress of the United States which forms or organizes an organization, any record amending the legislation, and any record filed with or issued by the State or the United States which amends or restates the name of the organization.

(69) "Pursuant to commitment", with respect to an advance made or other value given by a secured party, means pursuant to the secured party's obligation, whether or not a subsequent event of default or other event not within the secured party's control has relieved or may relieve the secured party from its obligation.

(70) "Record", except as used in "for record", "of record", "record or legal title", and "record owner", means information that is inscribed on a tangible medium or which is stored in an electronic or other medium and is retrievable in perceivable form.

(71) "Registered organization" means an organization formed or organized solely under the law of a single State or the United States by the filing of a public organic record with, the issuance of a public organic record by, or the enactment of legislation by the State or the United States. The term includes a business trust that is formed or organized under the law of a single State if a statute of the State governing business trusts requires that the business trust's organic record be filed with the State.

(72) "Secondary obligor" means an obligor to the extent that:

(A) the obligor's obligation is secondary; or

(B) the obligor has a right of recourse with respect to an obligation secured by collateral against the debtor, another obligor, or property of either.

(73) "Secured party" means:

(A) a person in whose favor a security interest is created or provided for under a security agreement, whether or not any obligation to be secured is outstanding;

(B) a person that holds an agricultural lien;

(C) a consignor;

(D) a person to which accounts, chattel paper, payment intangibles, or promissory notes have been sold;

(E) a trustee, indenture trustee, agent, collateral agent, or other representative in whose favor a security interest or agricultural lien is created or provided for; or

(F) a person that holds a security interest arising under Section 2-401, 2-505, 2-711(3), 2A-508(5), 4-210, or 5-118.

(74) "Security agreement" means an agreement that creates or provides for a security interest.

(75) [Reserved.]

(76) "Software" means a computer program and any supporting information provided in connection with a transaction relating to the program. The term does not include a computer program that is included in the definition of goods.

(77) "State" means a State of the United States, the District of Columbia, Puerto Rico, the United States Virgin Islands, or any territory or insular possession subject to the jurisdiction of the United States.

(78) "Supporting obligation" means a letter-of-credit right or secondary obligation that supports the payment or performance of an account, chattel paper, a document, a general intangible, an instrument, or investment property.

(79) [Reserved.]

(79A) "Tangible money" means money in a tangible form.

(80) "Termination statement" means an amendment of a financing statement which:

(A) identifies, by its file number, the initial financing statement to which it relates; and

(B) indicates either that it is a termination statement or that the identified financing statement is no longer effective.

(81) "Transmitting utility" means a person primarily engaged in the business of:

(A) operating a railroad, subway, street railway, or trolley bus;

(B) transmitting communications electrically, electromagnetically, or by light;

(C) transmitting goods by pipeline or sewer; or

(D) transmitting or producing and transmitting electricity, steam, gas, or water.

(b) [Definitions in other articles.] "Control" as provided in Section 7-106 and the following definitions in other articles apply to this Article:

"Applicant"	Section 5-102
"Beneficiary"	Section 5-102
"Broker"	Section 8-102
"Certificated security"	Section 8-102
"Check"	Section 3-104
"Clearing corporation"	Section 8-102
"Contract for sale"	Section 2-106
"Controllable electronic record."	Section 12-102
"Customer"	Section 4-104
"Entitlement holder"	Section 8-102
"Financial asset"	Section 8-102
"Holder in due course"	Section 3-302
"Issuer" (with respect to a letter of credit or letter-of-credit right)	Section 5-102
"Issuer" (with respect to a security)	Section 8-201
"Issuer" (with respect to documents of title)	Section 7-102
"Lease"	Section 2A-103
"Lease agreement"	Section 2A-103
"Lease contract"	Section 2A-103
"Leasehold interest"	Section 2A-103
"Lessee"	Section 2A-103
"Lessee in ordinary course of business"	Section 2A-103
"Lessor"	Section 2A-103
"Lessor's residual interest"	Section 2A-103
"Letter of credit"	Section 5-102
"Merchant"	Section 2-104
"Negotiable instrument"	Section 3-104
"Nominated person"	Section 5-102
"Note"	Section 3-104
"Proceeds of a letter of credit"	Section 5-114
"Protected purchaser"	Section 8-303
"Prove"	Section 3-103
"Qualifying purchaser"	Section 12-102
"Sale"	Section 2-106
"Securities account"	Section 8-501
"Securities intermediary"	Section 8-102
"Security"	Section 8-102
"Security certificate"	Section 8-102
"Security entitlement"	Section 8-102
"Uncertificated security"	Section 8-102

(c) [Article 1 definitions and principles.] Article 1 contains general definitions and principles of construction and interpretation applicable throughout this article.

Legislative Note: *Replicate the formatting of the tabulated material in subsection (a)(11) exactly to ensure that the meaning of the material is preserved.*

The Definition of "good faith" in subsection (a)(43) was deleted from subsection (a) pursuant to a conforming amendment accompanying the 2001 amendments of Article 1. However, any jurisdiction that has not adopted the revised definition of "good faith" in Section 1-201(b)(20) should retain the definition of "good faith" in subsection (a)(43).

Official Comment

1. Source. All terms that are defined in Article 9 and used in more than one section are consolidated in this section. Note that the definition of "security interest" is found in Section 1-201, not in this Article. Many of the definitions in this section derive from those in pre-1998 Section 9-105. Other definition were added by the 1998 Revisions or modified or added by the 2022 Article 9 Revisions.

2. Parties to Secured Transactions.

a. "Debtor"; "Obligor"; "Secondary Obligor." Determining whether a person was a "debtor" under pre-1998 Section 9-105(1)(d) required a close examination of the context in which the term was used. To reduce the need for this examination, the 1998 Revisions redefined "debtor" and added new defined terms, "secondary obligor" and "obligor." In the context of Part 6 (default and enforcement), these definitions distinguish among three classes of persons: (i) those persons who may have a stake in the proper enforcement of a security interest by virtue of their non-lien property interest (typically, an ownership interest) in the collateral, (ii) those persons who may have a stake in the proper enforcement of the security interest because of their obligation to pay the secured debt, and (iii) those persons who have an obligation to pay the secured debt but have no stake in the proper enforcement of the security interest. Persons in the first class are debtors. Persons in the second class are secondary obligors if any portion of the obligation is secondary or if the obligor has a right of recourse against the debtor or another obligor with respect to an obligation secured by collateral. One must consult the law of suretyship to determine whether an obligation is secondary. The Restatement (3d), Suretyship and Guaranty Restatement (3d), Suretyship and Guaranty 1 (1996), contains a useful explanation of the concept. Obligors in the third class are neither debtors nor secondary obligors. With one exception (Section 9-616, as it relates to a consumer obligor), the rights and duties provided by Part 6 affect non-debtor obligors only if they are "secondary obligors."

By including in the definition of "debtor" all persons with a property interest (other than a security interest in or other lien on collateral), the definition includes transferees of collateral, whether or not the secured party knows of the transfer or the transferee's identity. Exculpatory provisions in Part 6 protect the secured party in that circumstance. See Sections 9-605 and 9-628. The definition renders unnecessary pre-1998 Section 9-112, which governed situations in which collateral was not owned by the debtor. The definition also includes a "consignee," as defined in this section, as well as a seller of accounts, chattel paper, payment intangibles, or promissory notes.

Secured parties and other lienholders are excluded from the definition of "debtor" because the interests of those parties normally derive from and encumber a debtor's interest. However, if in a separate secured transaction a secured party grants, as debtor, a security interest in its own interest (i.e., its security interest and any obligation that it secures), the secured party is a debtor in that transaction. This typically occurs when a secured party with a security interest in specific goods assigns chattel paper.

Consider the following examples:

Example 1: Behnfeldt borrows money and grants a security interest in her Miata to secure the debt. Behnfeldt is a debtor and an obligor.

Example 2: Behnfeldt borrows money and grants a security interest in her Miata to secure the debt. Bruno co-signs a negotiable note as maker. As before, Behnfeldt is the debtor and an obligor. As an accommodation party (see Section 3-419), Bruno is a secondary obligor. Bruno has this status even if the note states that her obligation is a primary obligation and that she waives all suretyship defenses.

Example 3: Behnfeldt borrows money on an unsecured basis. Bruno co-signs the note and grants a security interest in her Honda to secure her obligation. Inasmuch as Behnfeldt does not have a property interest in the Honda, Behnfeldt is not a debtor. Having granted the security interest, Bruno is the debtor. Because Behnfeldt is a principal obligor, she is not a secondary obligor. Whatever the outcome of enforcement of the security interest against the Honda or Bruno's secondary obligation, Bruno will look to Behnfeldt for her losses. The enforcement will not affect Behnfeldt's aggregate obligations.

When the principal obligor (borrower) and the secondary obligor (surety) each has granted a security interest in different collateral, the status of each is determined by the collateral involved.

Example 4: Behnfeldt borrows money and grants a security interest in her Miata to secure the debt. Bruno co-signs the note and grants a security interest in her Honda to secure her obligation. When the secured party enforces the security interest in Behnfeldt's Miata, Behnfeldt is the debtor, and Bruno is a secondary obligor. When the secured party enforces the security interest in the Honda, Bruno is the "debtor." As in Example 3, Behnfeldt is an obligor, but not a secondary obligor.

If a security interest is granted by a protected series of a limited liability company formed under the Uniform Protected Series Act (2017), the debtor is the protected series. See PEB Commentary No. 23. The 2022 definition of "person" in Section 1-201(b)(27) includes a protected series.

b. "Secured Party." The secured party is the person in whose favor the security interest has been created, as determined by reference to the security agreement. This definition controls, among other things, which person has the duties and potential liability that Part 6 imposes upon a secured party. The definition of "secured party" also includes a "consignor," a person to which accounts, chattel paper, payment intangibles, or promissory notes have been sold, and the holder of an agricultural lien.

The definition of "secured party" clarifies the status of various types of representatives. Consider, for example, a multi-bank facility under which Bank A, Bank B, and Bank C are lenders and Bank A serves as the collateral agent. If the security interest is granted to the banks, then they are the secured parties. If the security interest is granted to Bank A as collateral agent, then Bank A is the secured party.

b.1 "Assignee"; "Assignor." Instead of referring to a "debtor," "secured party," and "security interest," all of which are defined terms, several provisions of Article 9, including Part 4, refer to the "assignment" or the "transfer" of property interests and some refer to an "assignor," "assignee," or "assigned contract." None of those terms are defined in the UCC. Some courts have read the undefined terms in an unduly narrow way. In 2020, the Permanent Editorial Board for the UCC issued a Commentary clarifying the meanings of these terms and amended the official comments accordingly. PEB

Commentary No. 21. This Article generally follows common usage by using the terms "assignment" and "assign" to refer to transfers of rights to payment, claims, and liens and other security interests. It generally uses the term "transfer" to refer to other transfers of interests in property. Except when used in connection with a letter-of-credit transaction (see Section 9-107, Comment 4), no significance should be placed on the use of one term or the other. Depending on the substance of the transaction, each term as used in this Article refers to the assignment or transfer of an outright ownership interest or to the assignment or transfer of a limited interest, such as a security interest, or both.

The 2022 Article 9 Revisions added new definitions of "assignee" and "assignor." Paragraph 7A defines "assignee" as a person in whose favor a security interest securing an obligation is created or to which an account, chattel paper, a payment intangible, or a promissory note has been sold. Paragraph 7B defines "assignor" as a person creating a security interest securing an obligation or that sells an account, chattel paper, a payment intangible, or a promissory note. These definitions incorporate the essence of the 2020 PEB Commentary into the statutory text. The definitions also specify that an "assignor" includes a secured party that transfers a security interest to another person and an "assignee" includes a person to which a security interest has been transferred by a secured party. By their terms, the defined terms "assignee" and "assignor" contemplate assignments in particular contexts. However, several references in this article to "assigned," "assignment" and "assignee" include transfers in broader contexts than those addressed in the defined terms. See, e.g., subsection (a)(2) ("assigned," in definition of "account") and (a)(47) ("assignment," in definition of "instrument") and Sections 9-109, 9-408, 9-409, and 9-519.

Absent a contrary agreement, an assignee obtains the rights and powers of an assignor as against an account debtor on assigned collateral (e.g., under Section 9-406) and as between the assignee and the assignor (debtor) (e.g., under Section 9-607). See also Restatement (Second) of Contracts § 317(1) (1981) (emphasis added):

> An assignment of a right is a manifestation of the assignor's intention to transfer it *by virtue of which* the assignor's right to performance by the obligor is extinguished in whole or in part and *the assignee acquires a right to such performance.*

Several provisions of this Article and its official comments also refer to the "transfer" of property interests. Although that term and its cognates are not defined, depending on the context it may include an "assignment." Moreover, a transfer of property is not limited to transactions of "purchase" and may include the transfer of a limited interest. See also Section 9- 332, Comment 2A.

c. Other Parties. A "consumer obligor" is defined as the obligor in a consumer transaction. Definitions of "new debtor" and "original debtor" are used in the special rules found in Sections 9-326 and 9-508.

3. Definitions Relating to Creation of a Security Interest.

a. "Collateral." As under pre-1998 Section 9-105, "collateral" is the property subject to a security interest and includes accounts, chattel paper, payment intangibles, and promissory notes that have been sold. The 1998 Revisions expanded the term to include proceeds subject to a security interest and also broadened the scope of the Article to include as collateral property subject to an agricultural lien as well as payment intangibles and promissory notes that have been sold.

b. "Security Agreement." The definition of "security agreement" is substantially the same as under pre-1998 Section 9-105—an agreement that creates or provides for a security interest. However, the term frequently was used colloquially in pre-1998 Article 9 to refer to the document or writing that contained a debtor's security agreement. The 1998 Article 9 eliminated that usage, reserving the term for the more precise meaning specified in the definition.

Whether an agreement creates a security interest depends not on whether the parties intend that the law characterize the transaction as a security interest but rather on whether the transaction falls within the definition of "security interest" in Section 1-201(b)(35). Thus, an agreement that the parties characterize as a "lease" of goods may be a "security agreement," notwithstanding the parties' stated intention that the law treat the transaction as a lease and not as a secured transaction. See Section 1-203.

4. Goods-Related Definitions.

a. "Goods"; "Consumer Goods"; "Equipment"; "Farm Products"; "Farming Operation"; "Inventory." The definition of "goods" is substantially the same as the definition in pre-1998 Section 9-105. This Article also retains the four mutually-exclusive "types" of collateral that consist of goods: "consumer goods," "equipment," "farm products," and "inventory." The revisions are primarily for clarification.

The classes of goods are mutually exclusive. For example, the same property cannot simultaneously be both equipment and inventory. In borderline cases—a physician's car or a farmer's truck that might be either consumer goods or equipment—the principal use to which the property is put is determinative. Goods can fall into different classes at different times. For example, a radio may be inventory in the hands of a dealer and consumer goods in the hands of a consumer. As under pre-1998 Article 9, goods are "equipment" if they do not fall into another category.

The definition of "consumer goods" follows pre-1998 Section 9-109. The classification turns on whether the debtor uses or bought the goods for use "primarily for personal, family, or household purposes."

Goods are inventory if they are leased by a lessor or held by a person for sale or lease. The revised definition of "inventory" makes clear that the term includes goods leased by the debtor to others as well as goods held for lease. (The same result should have obtained under the pre-1998 definition.) Goods to be furnished or furnished under a service contract, raw materials, and work in process also are inventory. Implicit in the definition is the criterion that the sales or leases are or will be in the ordinary course of business. For example, machinery used in manufacturing is equipment, not inventory, even though it is the policy of the debtor to sell machinery when it becomes obsolete or worn. Inventory also includes goods that are consumed in a business (e.g., fuel used in operations). In general, goods used in a business are equipment if they are fixed assets or have, as identifiable units, a relatively long period of use, but are inventory, even though not held for sale or lease, if they are used up or consumed in a short period of time in producing a product or providing a service.

Goods are "farm products" if the debtor is engaged in farming operations with respect to the goods. Animals in a herd of livestock are covered whether the debtor acquires them by purchase or as a result of natural increase. Products of crops or livestock remain farm products as long as they have not been subjected to a manufacturing process. The terms "crops" and "livestock" are not defined. The new definition of "farming operations" is for clarification only.

Crops, livestock, and their products cease to be "farm products" when the debtor ceases to be engaged in farming operations with respect to them. If, for example, they come into the possession of a marketing agency for sale or distribution or of a manufacturer or processor as raw materials, they become inventory. Products of crops or livestock, even though they remain in the possession of a person engaged in farming operations, lose their status as farm products if they are subjected to a manufacturing process. What is and what is not a manufacturing process is not specified in this Article. At one end of the spectrum, some processes are so closely connected with farming—such as pasteurizing milk or boiling sap to produce maple syrup or sugar—that they would not constitute manufacturing. On the other hand an extensive canning operation would be manufacturing. Once farm products have been subjected to a manufacturing process, they normally become inventory.

The revised definition of "farm products" clarifies the distinction between crops and standing timber and makes clear that aquatic goods produced in aquacultural operations may be either crops or livestock. Although aquatic goods that are vegetable in nature often would be crops and those that are animal would be livestock, this Article leaves the courts free to classify the goods on a case-by-case basis. See Section 9-324, Comment 11.

The definitions of "goods" and "software" are also mutually exclusive. Computer programs usually constitute "software", and, as such, are not "goods" as this Article uses the terms. However, under the circumstances specified in the definition of "goods," computer programs embedded in goods are part of the "goods" and are not "software".

b. "Accession"; "Manufactured Home"; "Manufactured-Home Transaction." Other specialized definitions of goods include "accession" (see the special priority and enforcement rules in Section 9-335), and "manufactured home" (see Section 9-515, permitting a financing statement in a "manufactured-home transaction" to be effective for 30 years). The definition of "manufactured home" borrows from the federal Manufactured Housing Act, 42 U.S.C. §§ 5401 et seq., and is intended to have the same meaning.

c. "As-Extracted Collateral." Under this Article, oil, gas, and other minerals that have not been extracted from the ground are treated as real property, to which this Article does not apply. Upon extraction, minerals become personal property (goods) and eligible to be collateral under this Article. See the definition of "goods," which excludes "oil, gas, and other minerals before extraction." To take account of financing practices reflecting the shift from real to personal property, this Article contains special rules for perfecting security interests in minerals which attach upon extraction and in accounts resulting from the sale of minerals at the wellhead or minehead. See, e.g., Sections 9-301(4) (law governing perfection and priority); 9-501 (place of filing), 9-502 (contents of financing statement), 9-519 (indexing of records). The term "as-extracted collateral," added by the 1998 Revisions, refers to the minerals and related accounts to which the special rules apply. The term "at the wellhead" encompasses arrangements based on a sale of the product (goods) at the moment that it issues from the ground and is measured, without technical distinctions as to whether title passes at the "Christmas tree" of a well, the far side of a gathering tank, or at some other point. The term "at . . . the minehead" is comparable.

The following examples explain the operation of these provisions.

Example 5: Debtor owns an interest in oil that is to be extracted. To secure Debtor's obligations to Lender, Debtor enters into a signed agreement granting Lender an interest in the oil. Although Lender may acquire an interest in the oil under real-property law, Lender does not acquire a security interest under this Article until the oil becomes personal property, i.e., until is extracted and becomes "goods" to which this Article applies. Because Debtor had an interest in the oil before extraction and Lender's security interest attached to the oil as extracted, the oil is "as-extracted collateral."

Example 6: Debtor owns an interest in oil that is to be extracted and contracts to sell the oil to Buyer at the wellhead. In a signed agreement, Debtor agrees to sell to Lender the right to payment from Buyer. This right to payment is an account that constitutes "as-extracted collateral." If Lender then resells the account to Financer, Financer acquires a security interest. However, inasmuch as the debtor-seller in that transaction, Lender, had no interest in the oil before extraction, Financer's collateral (the account it owns) is not "as-extracted collateral."

Example 7: Under the facts of Example 6, before extraction, Buyer grants a security interest in the oil to Bank. Although Bank's security interest attaches when the oil is extracted, Bank's security interest is not in "as-extracted collateral," inasmuch as its debtor, Buyer, did not have an interest in the oil before extraction.

5. Receivables-Related Definitions.

a. "Account"; "Health-Care-Insurance Receivable"; "As-Extracted Collateral." The definition of "account" has been expanded and reformulated. It is no longer limited to rights to payment relating to goods or services. Many categories of rights to payment that were classified as general intangibles under pre-1998 Article 9 are accounts under this Article. Thus, if they are sold, a financing statement must be filed to perfect the buyer's interest in them. As used in the definition of "account," a right to payment "arising out of the use of a credit or charge card or information contained on or for use with the card" is the right of a card issuer to payment from its cardholder. A credit-card or charge-card transaction may give rise to other rights to payments; however, those other rights do not "arise out of the use" of the card or information contained on or for use with the card. Among the types of property that are expressly excluded from the definition of account is "a right to payment for money or funds advanced or sold." As used in the exclusion from the definition of "account," "funds" is a broader concept than money (although the term is not defined). For example, when a bank-lender credits a borrower's deposit account for the amount of a loan, the bank's advance of funds is not a transaction giving rise to an account. The 2022 Article 9 Revisions amended the definition of "money" in Section 1- 201(b)(24) and added a new, more narrow, definition of "money" in Section 9-102(a)(54A). See Comment 12A.

The definition of "health-care-insurance receivable" is new. It is a subset of the definition of "account." However, the rules generally applicable to account debtors on accounts do not apply to insurers obligated on health-care-insurance receivables. See Sections 9-404(e), 9-405(d), 9-406(i).

Note that certain accounts also are "as-extracted collateral." See Comment 4.c., Examples 6 and 7.

The 2022 Article 9 Revisions amended the definition of "account" to reflect the 2022 revised definition of "chattel paper," discussed in Comment 5.b. The revised definition of "account" also includes some additional exceptions that accommodate the use of the term "account" in other provisions. These new exceptions were implicit in the former definition. Moreover, the exceptions for the defined terms "commodity account" and "deposit account" implicitly apply to all uses of those terms in this Article.

b. "Chattel Paper." "Chattel paper" consists of a monetary obligation that is either secured by specific goods or arises in connection with a lease of specific goods, in each case if the obligation and security interest or lease is evidenced by a record. The monetary obligation itself need not be related to the goods. For example, a loan secured by specific goods and evidenced by one or more records creates chattel paper regardless of the purpose of the loan.

Rights to payment arising out of charters of vessels or the use of credit or charge cards are expressly excluded from the definition of chattel paper; they are accounts. The term "charter" as used in this section includes bareboat charters, time charters, successive voyage charters, contracts of affreightment, contracts of carriage, and all other arrangements for the use of vessels.

What distinguishes chattel paper from other rights to payment is the fact that creditor has an interest in specific goods to enforce the right to payment. For example, the fact that a secured party also has an interest in other property does not prevent the right to payment from being chattel paper, provided that the specific goods are the primary collateral.

> **Example 8.** To secure a loan, Borrower grants Lender a security interest in a specified item of equipment and a deposit account. The loan and the security interest are evidenced by one or more records. The right to payment is chattel paper, assuming the equipment is the primary collateral.

In Example 8, the inclusion of some incidental collateral, such as a deposit account, does not prevent characterization of the right to payment as chattel paper. Another typical example would be the inclusion of after-acquired replacement parts to be installed on the specific goods. On the other hand, to be chattel paper, a right to payment must be accompanied by a security interest in specific goods or a lease of specific goods. A right to payment secured by a security interest in rotating collateral is not chattel paper.

> **Example 9.** To secure a loan, Borrower grants Lender a security interest in all of Borrower's existing and after-acquired inventory. The loan and the security interest are evidenced by one or more records. The right to payment is not chattel paper.

> **Example 10.** To secure a loan, Borrower grants Lender a security interest in a specifically described item of equipment, which is not the primary collateral, and also in all of Borrower's existing and after-acquired equipment. The loan and the security interest are evidenced by one or more records. The right to payment is not chattel paper.

Example 9 is the easy case because no "specific goods" are identified. As to Example 10, it is true that the monetary obligation is secured by "specific goods" and the definition of chattel paper does not specify that the obligation must be secured only by specific goods. However, if the right to payment in Example 10 were to be characterized as chattel paper, it would be possible to convert virtually any monetary obligation evidenced by records and secured by any collateral into chattel paper merely by including as collateral a specific item of goods (whether inventory, equipment, consumer goods, or farm products). The special rules for chattel paper contemplate that specific goods are the primary collateral, even if some incidental property also might be included. If additional goods or other property are included and the specific goods are not the primary collateral, then classification as chattel paper would not be appropriate. Of course, there may be close cases. In those situations, parties should take appropriate precautions.

A right to payment arising from a lease of specific goods gives rise to chattel paper only if the predominant purpose of the transaction is to provide the lessee the right to possession and use of the goods. Therefore, under paragraph (11)(B)(ii), when a lease of specific goods is combined with an obligation to provide or right to receive other property or services, the resulting right to payment will be chattel paper only if the goods aspect of the transaction predominates.

Example 11. Customer and Car Dealer enter into a transaction, evidenced by one or more records, pursuant to which, in exchange for a payment of $2,000 per month: (i) Customer is entitled to possession of a specific vehicle for 36 months; (ii) Car Dealer will provide round-the-clock monitoring of the vehicle's location and condition, and alert authorities to provide road-side assistance in the event of a malfunction or accident; and (iii) Car Dealer will, from time to time, remotely update the vehicle's operating system. The value of the right to possess and use the vehicle is significantly greater than the value of the monitoring service and updates. Because the goods aspect of the transaction predominates, under paragraph (11)(B)(ii) Customer's monetary obligation, including the portion attributable to Car Dealer's obligation to provide monitoring and updates, constitutes chattel paper.

Example 12. Customer and Cableco enter into a transaction, evidenced by one or more records, pursuant to which, in exchange for a payment of $200 per month, Cableco will provide Customer with specified television programming and a device needed to access the programming (a "lease" of the device). If the components of the transaction were priced separately, the price for the programming would be substantially more than the price for possession and use of the device. Because the goods aspect of this transaction does not predominate, under paragraph (11)(B)(ii) Customer's monetary obligation does not constitute chattel paper.

The 2022 revision to the definition of chattel paper omits the references to "software used in the goods" and a "license of software used in the goods" as superfluous, inasmuch as there is no reason to single out software. Other types of property may secure an obligation or be included in a transaction involving a lease, as discussed above. See also Sections 2-102 (scope of Article 2); 2-106(5) (defining "hybrid transaction"); 2A-102 (scope of Article 2A); 2A-103(aa) (definition of "hybrid lease"). These references were omitted from the definition of chattel paper for clarification and did not result in any change in the scope of the definition.

The 2022 revision to the definition of "chattel paper" also changed the language from "a record or records that evidence a monetary obligation" to "a right to payment of a monetary obligation . . . evidenced by a record." This semantic change was for clarification purposes only; it does not imply a change in meaning. Chattel paper is and has always been a right to payment of a monetary obligation. Because the revised definition is based on the obligation, rather than the record, the definition no longer includes the following statement, which was included in the previous definition: "If a transaction is evidenced by records that include an instrument or series of instruments, the group of records taken together constitutes chattel paper." The omission of that statement also does not imply a change in meaning, except that writings evidencing chattel paper are excluded from the definition of "instrument" under Section 9-102(a)(47). Although the definition refers to "a record," chattel paper can be evidenced by one or more records because, under Section 1-106, unless the statutory context otherwise requires, words in the singular number include the plural.

Finally, the revised definition of "chattel paper" and the approach to perfection of a security interest by possession and control under Section 9-314A have eliminated the need to have separate definitions of "electronic chattel paper" and "tangible chattel paper" in Section 9-102. Consequently, those definitions have been deleted.

c. "Instrument"; "Promissory Note." The definition of "instrument" includes a negotiable instrument. As under pre-1998 Section 9-105, it also includes any other right to payment of a monetary obligation that is evidenced by a writing of a type that in ordinary course of business is transferred by delivery (and, if necessary, an indorsement or assignment). The 2022 revised definition of "instrument" explicitly excludes a writing that evidences a right to payment that is chattel paper. This revision clarifies and makes explicit the understanding before the revision that an obligation on an instrument that evidences chattel paper is to be treated (e.g., under Section 9-330) as an obligation on chattel paper and not on an instrument. With that exception, the fact that an instrument is secured by a security interest or encumbrance on property does not change the character of the instrument as such or convert the combination of the instrument and collateral into a separate classification of personal property. The definition also makes clear that rights to payment arising out of credit-card transactions are not instruments. The definition of "promissory note" added in the 1998 Revisions, was necessitated by the inclusion of sales of promissory notes within the scope of Article 9. It explicitly excludes obligations arising out of "orders" to pay (e.g., checks) as opposed to "promises" to pay. See Section 3-104. Under the 2022 Article 9 Revisions, Sections 9-406(d) and 9-408(g) adopt a modified meaning of "promissory note" as that term is used in Sections 9-406(d) and Sections 9-408(a) through (d). See Comment 5.h.; see also Sections 9-406, Comment 5; 9-408, Comment 11.

d. "General Intangible"; "Payment Intangible." "General intangible" is the residual category of personal property, including things in action, that is not included in the other defined types of collateral. Examples are various categories of intellectual property and the right to payment of a loan of funds that is not evidenced by chattel paper or an instrument. As used in the definition of "general intangible," "things in action" includes rights that arise under a license of intellectual property, including the right to exploit the intellectual property without liability for infringement. The definition was revised in 1998 to exclude commercial tort claims, deposit accounts, and letter-of-credit rights. Each of the three is a separate type of collateral. One important consequence of this exclusion is that tortfeasors (commercial tort claims), banks (deposit accounts), and persons obligated on letters of credit (letter-of-credit rights) are not "account debtors" having the rights and obligations set forth in Sections 9-404, 9-405, and 9-406. In particular, tortfeasors, banks, and persons obligated on letters of credit are not obligated to pay an assignee (secured party) upon receipt of the notification described in Section 9-404(a). See Comment 5.h. Another important consequence relates to the adequacy of the description in the security agreement. See Section 9-108.

"Payment intangible" is a subset of the definition of "general intangible." The sale of a payment intangible is subject to this Article. See Section 9-109(a)(3). Virtually any intangible right could give rise to a right to payment of money once one hypothesizes, for example, that the account debtor is in breach of its obligation. The term "payment intangible," however, embraces only those general intangibles "under which the account debtor's principal obligation is a monetary obligation." (Emphasis added.) A debtor's right to payment from another person of amounts received by the other person on the debtor's behalf, including the right of a merchant in a credit-card, debit-card, prepaid-card, or other payment-card transaction to payment of amounts received by its bank from the card system in settlement of the transaction, is a "payment intangible." (In contrast, the right of a credit-card issuer to payment arising out of the use of a credit card is an "account.") If a bank is the obligor on a monetary obligation not evidenced by an instrument or chattel paper, the obligation or the right to payment of the obligation may be a deposit account, an account, a payment intangible, or another type of collateral depending on the facts and circumstances. Of course, the classification of a monetary obligation or a right to payment of the obligation for purposes of this Article would not necessarily affect the application of laws regulating, for example, banking, securities, commodities, money transmission, and taxation.

In classifying intangible collateral, a court should begin by identifying the particular rights that have been assigned. The account debtor (promisor) under a particular contract may owe several types of monetary obligations as well as other, nonmonetary obligations. If the promisee's right to payment of money is assigned separately, the right is an account or payment intangible, depending on how the account debtor's obligation arose. When all the promisee's rights are assigned together, an account, a payment intangible, and a general intangible all may be involved, depending on the nature of the rights.

A right to the payment of money is frequently buttressed by ancillary rights, such as rights arising from covenants in a purchase agreement, note, or mortgage requiring insurance on the collateral or forbidding removal of the collateral, rights arising from covenants to preserve the creditworthiness of the promisor, and the lessor's rights with respect to leased goods that arise upon the lessee's default (see Section 2A-523). This Article does not treat these ancillary rights separately from the rights to payment to which they relate. For example, attachment and perfection of an assignment of a right to payment of a monetary obligation, whether it be an account or payment intangible, also carries these ancillary rights. Thus, an assignment of the lessor's right to payment under a lease also transfers the lessor's rights with respect to the leased goods under Section 2A-523. If, taken together, the lessor's rights to payment and with respect to the leased goods are evidenced by chattel paper, then, contrary to *In re Commercial Money Center, Inc.*, 350 B.R. 465 (Bankr. App. 9th Cir. 2006), an assignment of the lessor's right to payment constitutes an assignment of the chattel paper. Although an agreement excluding the lessor's rights with respect to the leased goods from an assignment of the lessor's right to payment may be effective between the parties, the agreement does not affect the characterization of the collateral to the prejudice of creditors of, and purchasers from, the assignor.

Every "payment intangible" is also a "general intangible." Likewise, "software" is a "general intangible" for purposes of this Article. See Comment 25. Accordingly, except as otherwise provided, statutory provisions applicable to general intangibles apply to payment intangibles and software.

d.1 "Controllable Account"; "Controllable Payment Intangible." Article 9 affords special treatment for security interests in controllable accounts and controllable payment intangibles, i.e., those accounts and payment intangibles that are evidenced by a controllable electronic record and as to which the account debtor (obligor) undertakes to pay the person having control of the controllable electronic record. Of course, a person would be an account debtor only if it were actually obligated on the account or payment intangible evidenced by the controllable electronic record. Although the definitions refer to a controllable electronic record that "provides" for an account debtor's undertaking, an account debtor's promise to pay normally would arise and be evidenced apart from the controllable electronic record itself. However, the definitions contemplate that a controllable electronic record evidencing an account or payment intangible (or an associated record) would indicate in some fashion an account debtor's obligation and that the controllable electronic record evidences the account or payment intangible. If a bank is the obligor on a monetary obligation payable to the person in control of a controllable electronic record, the obligation or the right to payment of the obligation may be a deposit account, a controllable account, a controllable payment intangible, or another type of collateral depending on the facts and circumstances. The classification of a monetary obligation or a right to payment of the obligation for purposes of this Article would not necessarily affect the application of laws regulating, for example, banking, securities, commodities, money transmission, and taxation.

An undertaking to pay the "person that has control" means an undertaking to pay the person that has control at the time payment is made. However, an undertaking to pay Smith, even though Smith happens to have control of the relevant controllable electronic record at the time the undertaking was made, is not an undertaking to pay the person that has control.

The special treatment for controllable accounts and controllable payment intangibles includes the following:

- Perfection of a security interest in a controllable account or controllable payment intangible can be achieved by filing a financing statement or by obtaining control of the controllable electronic record that evidences the controllable account or controllable payment intangible. Sections 9-312(a); 9-314(a); 9-107A(b).
- A security interest in a controllable electronic record, controllable account, or controllable payment intangible that is perfected by control has priority over a conflicting security interest that is perfected by another method. Section 9-326A.
- The benefit of the take-free and no-action rules for qualifying purchasers (including secured parties) of controllable electronic records also extends to qualifying purchasers of controllable accounts and controllable payment intangibles, whether or not the qualifying purchaser also purchases the related controllable electronic record. See Section 12-104(a) and Comments 5 through 8.

e. "Letter-of-Credit Right." The term "letter-of-credit right" embraces the rights to payment and performance under a letter of credit (defined in Section 5-102). However, it does not include a beneficiary's right to demand payment or performance. Transfer of those rights to a transferee beneficiary is governed by Article 5. See Sections 9-107, Comment 4, and 9-329, Comments 3 and 4.

f. "Supporting Obligation." This new term covers the most common types of credit enhancements—suretyship obligations (including guarantees) and letter-of-credit rights that support one of the types of collateral specified in the definition. As explained in Comment 2.a., suretyship law determines whether an obligation is "secondary" for purposes of this definition. Section 9-109 generally excludes from this Article transfers of interests in insurance policies. However, the regulation of a secondary obligation as an insurance product does not necessarily mean that it is a "policy of insurance" for purposes of the exclusion in Section 9-109. Thus, this Article may cover a secondary obligation (as a supporting obligation), even if the obligation is issued by a regulated insurance company and the obligation is subject to regulation as an "insurance" product.

This Article contains rules explicitly governing attachment, perfection, and priority of security interests in supporting obligations. See Sections 9-203, 9-308, 9-310, and 9-322. These provisions reflect the principle that a supporting obligation is an incident of the collateral it supports.

Collections of or other distributions under a supporting obligation are "proceeds" of the supported collateral as well as "proceeds" of the supporting obligation itself. See Section 9-102 (defining "proceeds") and Comment 13.b. As such, the collections and distributions are subject to the priority rules applicable to proceeds generally. See Section 9-322. However, under the special rule governing security interests in a letter-of-credit right, a secured party's failure to obtain control (Section 9-107) of a letter-of-credit right supporting collateral may leave its security interest exposed to a priming interest of a party who does take control. See Section 9-329 (security interest in a letter-of-credit right perfected by control has priority over a conflicting security interest).

g. "Commercial Tort Claim." A tort claim may serve as original collateral under this Article only if it is a "commercial tort claim." See Section 9-109(d). Although security interests in commercial tort claims are within its scope, this Article does not override other applicable law restricting the assignability of a tort claim. See Section 9-401. A security interest in a tort claim also may exist under this Article if the claim is proceeds of other collateral. See Section 9-204(b.1) and Comment 4A.

h. "Account Debtor." An "account debtor" is a person obligated on an account, chattel paper, or general intangible. The account debtor's obligation often is a monetary obligation; however, this is not always the case. For example, if a franchisee uses its rights under a franchise agreement (a general intangible) as collateral, then the franchisor is an "account debtor." As a general matter, Article 3, and not Article 9, governs obligations on negotiable instruments. Accordingly, the definition of "account debtor" excludes obligors on negotiable instruments constituting part of chattel paper. The principal effect of this change from the definition in pre-1998 Article 9 is that the rules in Sections 9-403, 9-404, 9-405, and 9-406, dealing with the rights of an assignee and duties of an account debtor, do not apply to an assignment of chattel paper in which the obligation to pay is evidenced by a negotiable instrument. (Section 9-406(d), however, does apply to a negotiable instrument that is a "promissory note", as that term is used in the 2022 revisions of subsection (d). See Comment 5.c.) Rather, the rights of an assignee of a negotiable instrument are governed by Article 3. Similarly, the duties of an obligor on a nonnegotiable instrument are governed by non-Article 9 law unless the nonnegotiable instrument is a part of chattel paper, in which case the obligor is an account debtor.

The definition of "account debtor" was revised in 2022 to add the modifier "negotiable" to the second reference to "instrument," making it clear that an obligor on a negotiable instrument is not an account debtor. This amendment (which is intended to clarify and not to change the meaning of the definition) is useful because the definition of "instrument" has been revised to exclude writings that evidence chattel paper. However, the definition of "negotiable instrument" in Section 3-104 continues to apply under Article 9. See Section 9- 102(a)(47) and (b); Comment 5.c. Of course, a record or records evidencing chattel paper must evidence either a security agreement or lease agreement in addition to a right to payment of a monetary obligation.

i. Receivables Under Government Entitlement Programs. This Article does not contain a defined term that encompasses specifically rights to payment or performance under the many and varied government entitlement programs. Depending on the nature of a right under a program, it could be an account, a payment intangible, a general intangible other than a payment intangible, or another type of collateral. The right also might be proceeds of collateral (e.g., crops).

6. Investment-Property-Related Definitions: "Commodity Account"; "Commodity Contract"; "Commodity Customer"; "Commodity Intermediary"; "Investment Property." These definitions are substantially the same as the corresponding definitions in pre-1998 Section 9-115. "Investment property" includes securities, both certificated and uncertificated, securities accounts, security entitlements, commodity accounts, and commodity contracts. The term investment property includes a "securities account" in order to facilitate transactions in which a debtor wishes to create a security interest in all of the investment positions held through a particular account rather than in particular positions carried in the account. Pre-1998 Section 9-115 was added in conjunction with Revised Article 8 and contained a variety of rules applicable to security interests in investment property. The 1998 Revisions relocated these rules to the appropriate sections of Article 9. See, e.g., Sections 9-203 (attachment), 9-314 (perfection by control), 9-328 (priority).

The terms "security," "security entitlement," and related terms are defined in Section 8-102, and the term "securities account" is defined in Section 8-501. The terms "commodity account," "commodity contract," "commodity customer," and "commodity intermediary" are defined in this section. Commodity contracts are not "securities" or "financial assets" under Article 8. See Section 8-103(f). Thus, the relationship between commodity intermediaries and commodity customers is not governed by the indirect-holding-system rules of Part 5 of Article 8. For securities, Article 9 contains rules on security interests, and Article 8 contains rules on the rights of transferees, including secured parties, on such matters as the rights of a transferee if the transfer was itself wrongful and gives rise to an adverse claim. For commodity contracts, Article 9 establishes rules on security interests, but questions relating to commodity contracts of the sort dealt with in Article 8 for securities are left to other law.

The indirect-holding-system rules of Article 8 are sufficiently flexible to be applied to new developments in the securities and financial markets, where that is appropriate. Accordingly, the definition of "commodity contract" is narrowly drafted to ensure that it does not operate as an obstacle to the application of the Article 8 indirect-holding-system rules to new products. The term "commodity contract" covers those contracts that are traded on or subject to the rules of a designated contract market and foreign commodity contracts that are carried on the books of American commodity intermediaries. The effect of this definition is that the category of commodity contracts that are excluded from Article 8 but governed by Article 9 is essentially the same as the category of contracts that fall within the exclusive regulatory jurisdiction of the federal Commodity Futures Trading Commission.

Commodity contracts are different from securities or other financial assets. A person who enters into a commodity futures contract is not buying an asset having a certain value and holding it in anticipation of increase in value. Rather the person is entering into a contract to buy or sell a commodity at set price for delivery at a future time. That contract may become advantageous or disadvantageous as the price of the commodity fluctuates during the term of the contract. The rules of the commodity exchanges require that the contracts be marked to market on a daily basis; that is, the customer pays or receives any increment attributable to that day's price change. Because commodity customers may incur obligations on their contracts, they are required to provide collateral at the outset, known as "original margin," and may be required to provide additional amounts, known as "variation margin," during the term of the contract.

The most likely setting in which a person would want to take a security interest in a commodity contract is where a lender who is advancing funds to finance an inventory of a physical commodity requires the borrower to enter into a commodity contract as a hedge against the risk of decline in the value of the commodity. The lender will want to take a security interest in both the commodity itself and the hedging commodity contract. Typically, such arrangements are structured as security interests in the entire commodity account in which the borrower carries the hedging contracts, rather than in individual contracts.

One important effect of including commodity contracts and commodity accounts in Article 9 is to provide a clearer legal structure for the analysis of the rights of commodity clearing organizations against their participants and futures commission merchants against their customers. The rules and agreements of commodity clearing organizations generally provide that the clearing organization has the right to liquidate any participant's positions in order to satisfy obligations of the participant to the clearing corporation. Similarly, agreements between futures commission merchants and their customers generally provide that the futures commission merchant has the right to liquidate a customer's positions in order to satisfy obligations of the customer to the futures commission merchant.

The main property that a commodity intermediary holds as collateral for the obligations that the commodity customer may incur under its commodity contracts is not other commodity contracts carried by the customer but the other property that the customer has posted as margin. Typically, this property will be securities. The commodity intermediary's security interest in such securities is governed by the rules of this Article on security interests in securities, not the rules on security interests in commodity contracts or commodity accounts.

Although there are significant analytic and regulatory differences between commodities and securities, the development of commodity contracts on financial products in the past few decades has resulted in a system in which the commodity markets and securities markets are closely linked. The rules on security interests in commodity contracts and commodity accounts provide a structure that may be essential in times of stress in the financial markets. Suppose, for example that a firm has a position in a securities market that is hedged by a position in a commodity market, so that payments that the firm is obligated to make with respect to the securities position will be covered by the receipt of funds from the commodity position. Depending upon the settlement cycles of the different markets, it is possible that the firm could find itself in a position where it is obligated to make the payment with respect to the securities position before it receives the matching funds from the commodity position. If cross-margining arrangements have not been developed between the two markets, the firm may need to borrow funds temporarily to make the earlier payment. The rules on security interests in investment property would facilitate the use of positions in one market as collateral for loans needed to cover obligations in the other market.

7. Consumer-Related Definitions: "Consumer Debtor"; "Consumer Goods"; "Consumer-Goods Transaction"; "Consumer Obligor"; "Consumer Transaction." The definition of "consumer goods" (discussed above) is substantially the same as the definition in pre-1998 Section 9-109. The 1998 Revisions added the definitions of "consumer debtor," "consumer obligor," "consumer-goods transaction," and "consumer transaction" in connection with various 1998 and pre-1998 consumer-related provisions and to designate certain provisions that are inapplicable in consumer transactions.

"Consumer-goods transaction" is a subset of "consumer transaction." Under each definition, both the obligation secured and the collateral must have a personal, family, or household purpose. However, "mixed" business and personal transactions also may be characterized as a consumer-goods transaction or consumer transaction. Subparagraph (A) of the definition of consumer-goods transactions and clause (i) of the definition of consumer transaction are primary purposes tests. Under these tests, it is necessary to determine the primary purpose of the obligation or obligations secured. Subparagraph (B) and clause (iii) of these definitions are satisfied if any of the collateral is consumer goods, in the case of a consumer-goods transaction, or "is held or acquired primarily for personal, family, or household purposes," in the case of a consumer transaction. The fact that some of the obligations secured or some of the collateral for the obligation does not satisfy the tests (e.g., some of the collateral is acquired for a business purpose) does not prevent a transaction from being a "consumer transaction" or "consumer-goods transaction."

8. Filing-Related Definitions: "Continuation Statement"; "File Number"; "Filing Office"; "Filing-Office Rule"; "Financing Statement"; "Fixture Filing"; "Manufactured-Home Transaction"; "New Debtor"; "Original Debtor"; "Public-Finance Transaction"; "Termination Statement"; "Transmitting Utility." These definitions are used exclusively or primarily in the filing-related provisions in Part 5. Most are self-explanatory and are discussed in the Comments to Part 5. A financing statement filed in a manufactured-home transaction or a public-finance transaction may remain effective for 30 years instead of the 5 years applicable to other financing statements. See Section 9-515(b). The definitions relating to medium neutrality also are significant for the filing provisions. See Comment 9.

The definition of "transmitting utility" embraces the business of transmitting communications generally to take account of new and future types of communications technology. The term designates a special class of debtors for whom separate filing rules are provided in Part 5, thereby obviating the many local fixture filings that would be necessary under the rules of Section 9-501 for a far-flung public-utility debtor. A transmitting utility will not necessarily be regulated by or operating as such in a jurisdiction where fixtures are located. For example, a utility might own transmission lines in a jurisdiction, although the utility generates no power and has no customers in the jurisdiction. Of course, the definition applies only for purposes of this Article and not for purposes of any other law, regulation, or rule.

9. Definitions Relating to Medium Neutrality.

a. "Record." In general the term "record" replaces the term "writing" and "written." A "record" includes information that is in intangible form (e.g., electronically stored) as well as tangible form (e.g., written on paper). Section 9-102(a)(70). Given the rapid development and commercial adoption of modern communication and storage technologies, requirements that documents or communications be "written," "in writing," or otherwise in tangible form do not necessarily reflect or aid commercial practices.

A "record" need not be permanent or indestructible, but the term does not include any oral or other communication that is not stored or preserved by any means. The information must be stored on paper or in some other medium. Information that has not been retained other than through human memory does not qualify as a record. Examples of current technologies commercially used to communicate or store information include, but are not limited to, magnetic media, optical discs, digital voice messaging systems, electronic mail, audio tapes, and photographic media, as well as paper. "Record" is an inclusive term that includes all of these methods of storing or communicating information. Any "writing" is a record. A record may be signed. See Comment 9.b. A record may be created without the knowledge or intent of a particular person.

Like the terms "written" or "in writing," the term "record" does not establish the purposes, permitted uses, or legal effect that a record may have under any particular provision of law. Whatever is filed in the Article 9 filing system, including financing statements, continuation statements, and termination statements, whether transmitted in tangible or intangible form, would fall within the definition. However, in some instances, statutes or filing-office rules may require that a paper record be filed. In such cases, even if this Article permits the filing of an electronic record, compliance with those statutes or rules is necessary. Similarly, a filer must comply with a statute or rule that requires a particular type of encoding or formatting for an electronic record.

This Article sometimes uses the terms "for record," "of record," "record or legal title," and "record owner." Some of these are terms traditionally used in real-property law. The definition of "record" in this Article now explicitly excepts these usages from the defined term. Also, this Article refers to a record that is filed or recorded in real-property recording systems to record a mortgage as a "record of a mortgage." This usage recognizes that the defined term "mortgage" means an interest in real property; it does not mean the record that evidences, or is filed or recorded with respect to, the mortgage.

b. "Sign"; "Communicate"; "Send." The defined term "authenticate" has been deleted in the 2022 Article 9 Revisions. That term and "authenticated" were generally used in Article 9 instead of "sign" and "signed." However, the 2022 revised definition of "sign" in Section 1-201(b)(37), encompasses authentication of all records, not just writings. Accordingly, "sign" and "signed" are now used in Article 9. (References to signing of, e.g., an agreement, demand, or notification mean, of course, signing of a record containing an agreement, demand, or notification.) The terms "communicate" and "send" also contemplate the possibility of communication by nonwritten media. These definitions include the act of transmitting both tangible and intangible records. The 2022 Amendments deleted the definition of "send" in this section and modified the corresponding definition in Section 1-201(b)(36), replacing the pre-2022 definition in that section.

10. Scope-Related Definitions.

a. Expanded Scope of Article: "Agricultural Lien"; "Consignment"; "Payment Intangible"; "Promissory Note." These definitions reflect the expanded scope of 1998 Article 9, as provided in Section 9-109(a).

b. Reduced Scope of Exclusions: "Governmental Unit"; "Health-Care-Insurance Receivable"; "Commercial Tort Claims." These definitions reflect the reduced scope of the 1998 exclusions, provided in Section 9-109(c) and (d), of transfers by governmental debtors and assignments of interests in insurance policies and commercial tort claims.

11. Choice-of-Law-Related Definitions: "Certificate of Title"; "Governmental Unit"; "Jurisdiction of Organization"; "Public Organic Record"; "Registered Organization"; "State." These definitions reflect the changes in the law governing perfection and priority of security interests and agricultural liens provided in Part 3, Subpart 1 of the 1998 Revisions.

Statutes often require applicants for a certificate of title to identify all security interests on the application and require the issuing agency to indicate the identified security interests on the certificate. Some of these statutes provide that priority over the rights of a lien creditor (i.e., perfection of a security interest) in goods covered by the certificate occurs upon indication of the security interest on the certificate; that is, they provide for the indication of the security interest on the certificate as a "condition" of perfection. Other statutes contemplate that perfection is achieved upon the occurrence of another act, e.g., delivery of the application to the issuing agency, that "results" in the indication of the security interest on the certificate. A certificate governed by either type of statute can qualify as a "certificate of title" under this Article. The statute providing for the indication of a security interest need not expressly state the connection between the indication and perfection. For example, a certificate issued pursuant to a statute that requires applicants to identify security interests, requires the issuing agency to indicate the identified security interests on the certificate, but is silent concerning the legal consequences of the indication would be a "certificate of title" if, under a judicial interpretation of the statute, perfection of a security interest is a legal consequence of the indication. Likewise, a certificate would be a "certificate of title" if another statute provides, expressly or as interpreted, the requisite connection between the indication and perfection.

The first sentence of the definition of "certificate of title" includes certificates consisting of tangible records, of electronic records, and of combinations of tangible and electronic records.

In many States, a certificate of title covering goods that are encumbered by a security interest is delivered to the secured party by the issuing authority. To eliminate the need for the issuance of a paper certificate under these circumstances, several States have revised their certificate-of-title statutes to permit or require a State agency to maintain an electronic record that evidences ownership of the goods and in which a security interest in the goods may be noted. The second sentence of the definition provides that such a record is a "certificate of title" if it is in fact maintained as an alternative to the issuance of a paper certificate of title, regardless of whether the certificate-of-title statute provides that the record is a certificate of title and even if the statute does not expressly state that the record is maintained instead of issuing a paper certificate.

Not every organization that may provide information about itself in the public records is a "registered organization." For example, a general partnership is not a "registered organization," even if it files a statement of partnership authority under Section 303 of the Uniform Partnership Act (1994) or an assumed name ("dba") certificate. This is because such a partnership is not formed or organized by the filing of a record with, or the issuance of a record by, a State or the United States. Likewise, a limited liability partnership, which is a form of general partnership under the Uniform Partnership Act (1997), is not a "registered organization" even if it has filed a record that is a statement of qualification under Section 1-001 of the Uniform Partnership Act (1997). The filing of the record does not form or organize the partnership. The filing only provides the partners in the general partnership with a limited liability shield and evidences that the general partnership has limited liability partnership status. See PEB Commentary No. 17. As discussed in PEB Commentary No. 17, the same conclusion would apply to a limited liability partnership formed under the law of state that has not adopted the Uniform Partnership Act (1997) but has adopted for limited liability partnerships similar legislation having the material attributes of that Act. Also as discussed in PEB Commentary No. 17, the same conclusion would apply whether before or after giving effect to the 2010 amendments to this Article. In contrast, corporations, limited liability companies, and limited partnerships ordinarily are "registered organizations."

Not every record concerning a registered organization that is filed with, or issued by, a State or the United States is a "public organic record." For example, a certificate of good standing issued with respect to a corporation or a published index of domestic corporations would not be a "public organic record" because its issuance or publication does not form or organize the corporations named.

When collateral is held in a trust, one must look to non-UCC law to determine whether the trust is a "registered organization." Non-UCC law typically distinguishes between statutory trusts and common-law trusts. A statutory trust is formed by the filing of a record, commonly referred to as a certificate of trust, in a public office pursuant to a statute. See, e.g., Uniform Statutory Trust Entity Act § 201 (2009); Delaware Statutory Trust Act, Del. Code Ann. tit. 12, § 3-801 et seq. A statutory trust is a juridical entity, separate from its trustee and beneficial owners, that may sue and be sued, own property, and transact business in its own name. Inasmuch as a statutory trust is a "legal or commercial entity," it qualifies as a "person other than an individual," and therefore as an "organization," under Section 1-201(b)(25). A statutory trust that is formed by the filing of a record in a public office is a "registered organization," and the filed record is a "public organic record" of the statutory trust, if the filed record is available to the public for inspection. (The requirement that a record be "available to the public for inspection" is satisfied if a copy of the relevant record is available for public inspection.)

Unlike a statutory trust, a common-law trust—whether its purpose is donative or commercial—arises from private action without the filing of a record in a public office. See Uniform Trust Code § 401 (2000); Restatement (Third) of Trusts § 10 (2003). Moreover, under traditional law, a common-law trust is not itself a juridical entity and therefore must sue and be sued, own property, and transact business in the name of the trustee acting in the capacity of trustee. A common-law trust that is a "business trust," i.e., that has a business or commercial purpose, is an "organization" under Section 1-201(b)(25). However, such a trust would not be a "registered organization" if, as is typically the case, the filing of a public record is not needed to form it.

In some states, however, the trustee of a common-law trust that has a commercial or business purpose is required by statute to file a record in a public office following the trust's formation. See, e.g., Mass. Gen. Laws Ch. 182, § 2; Fla. Stat. Ann. § 609.02. A business trust that is required to file its organic record in a public office is a "registered organization" under the second sentence of the definition if the filed record is available to the public for inspection. Any organic record required to be filed, and filed, with respect to a common-law business trust after the trust is formed is a "public organic record" of the trust. Some statutes require a trust or other organization to file, after formation or organization, a record other than an organic record. See, e.g., N.Y. Gen Assn's Law § 18 (requiring associations doing business within New York to file a certificate designating the secretary of state as an agent upon whom process may be served). This requirement does not render the organization a "registered organization" under the second sentence of the definition, and the record is not a "public organic record."

12. Deposit-Account-Related Definitions: "Deposit Account"; "Bank." The 1998 revised definition of "deposit account" incorporates the definition of "bank," which is new. The new definition derives from the definitions of "bank" in Sections 4-105(1) and 4A-105(a)(2), which focus on whether the organization is "engaged in the business of banking."

Deposit accounts evidenced by Article 9 "instruments" are excluded from the term "deposit account." In contrast, pre-1998 Section 9-105 excluded from the former definition "an account evidenced by a certificate of deposit." The revised definition clarifies the proper treatment of nonnegotiable or uncertificated certificates of deposit. Under the definition, an uncertificated certificate of deposit would be a deposit account (assuming there is no writing evidencing the bank's obligation to pay) whereas a nonnegotiable certificate of deposit would be a deposit account only if it is not an "instrument" as defined in this section (a question that turns on whether the nonnegotiable certificate of deposit is "of a type that in ordinary course of business is transferred by delivery with any necessary indorsement or assignment").

A deposit account evidenced by an instrument is subject to the rules applicable to instruments generally. As a consequence, a security interest in such an instrument cannot be perfected by "control" (see Section 9-104), and the special priority rules applicable to deposit accounts (see Sections 9-327 and 9-340) do not apply. If a bank is the obligor on a monetary obligation not evidenced by an instrument or chattel paper, the obligation or the right to payment of the obligation may be a deposit account, an account, a payment intangible, or another type of collateral depending on the facts and circumstances. Of course, the classification of a monetary obligation or a right to payment of the obligation for purposes of this Article would not necessarily affect the application of laws regulating, for example, banking, securities, commodities, money transmission, and taxation.

The term "deposit account" does not include "investment property," such as securities and security entitlements. Thus, the term also does not include shares in a money-market mutual fund, even if the shares are redeemable by check.

12A. Money-Related Definitions and Terms: "Money"; "Electronic Money"; "Tangible Money"; "Funds"; "Monetary Obligation." The Article 9 definition of "money" in subsection (a)(54A), added by the 2022 Article 9 Revisions, is a subset of the definition of "money" as defined in Section 1-201(b)(24). It follows that cryptocurrencies, such as bitcoin, that are not "money" as defined in Section 1-201(b)(24) because they were in existence and used before adoption by a government, also are not Article 9 money. An obligation to pay in such cryptocurrencies would not be an account, chattel paper, or a payment intangible or an obligation on an instrument because the obligation would not be a "monetary obligation" or an obligation to pay money. One purpose of the Article 9 definition is to ensure that even if some deposit accounts were to become "money" as defined in Article 1, the provisions relating to perfection and priority for security interests in deposit accounts, and not those for money, will apply to that collateral. Some countries may authorize or adopt deposit accounts with a central bank as a form of "money." See Section 9-101, Comment 4.c. However, the Article 9 provisions governing "deposit accounts" would remain suitable for such accounts with a central bank, even if a government has adopted these accounts as money. The 2022 Article 9 Revisions leave Article 9's treatment of deposit accounts largely unchanged. However, for purposes of Article 9 and in the interest of clarity, the definition of "money" in Section 9-102(a)(31A) excludes deposit accounts. Under this definition, deposit accounts would not be money for Article 9 purposes even if they were to become money under the Article 1 definition. Another purpose of the Article 9 definition of "money" is to exclude from that definition money (as defined in Section 1- 201(b)(24)) in an electronic form that cannot be subjected to control under Section 9-105A. Such property would be a general intangible, governed by the perfection and priority rules for that type of collateral.

Some countries may authorize or adopt intangible tokens as a medium of exchange that would be "money" as defined in both Article 1 and Article 9. See Section 9-101, Comment 4.c. Such intangible tokens would be "electronic money," as defined in Section 9-102(a)(31A). A security interest in electronic money as original collateral can be perfected only by control. Sections 9-312(b)(4); 9-314; 9-105A. The requirements for obtaining control of electronic money are essentially the same as those for obtaining control of a controllable electronic record under Article 12. Sections 9-105A; 12-105. The definition of "tangible money" in Section 9- 102(a)(79A) uses the word "tangible" with its normal meaning (as something that has physical or corporeal existence, such as goods).

"Monetary obligation" as used in the Uniform Commercial Code (including in Article 9) is not a defined term. The term contemplates an obligation to pay "money" as defined in Section 1-201(b)(24). Consequently, for example, a right to payment of money in an electronic form that cannot be subjected to control, excluded from the Article 9 definition of "money" in subsection (a)(54A), would be a monetary obligation. It follows that such a right to payment could be an account, chattel paper, a payment intangible, or an instrument—including a negotiable instrument, which is defined to include a promise to pay "money" as the term is defined in Section 1-201(b)(24). See Section 3-104(a) (defining "negotiable instrument"). Also, the term "funds" (like "monetary obligation," an undefined term), as used in the Uniform Commercial Code includes a right to payment of money as defined in Section 1-201(b)(24). As mentioned above, because cryptocurrencies such as bitcoin are not "money" as defined in Section 1-201(b)(24) (unless they were not in existence and used before adoption by a government), a cryptocurrency or an obligation to pay in cryptocurrency would not be a "monetary obligation" or "funds."

13. Proceeds-Related Definitions: "Cash Proceeds"; "Noncash Proceeds"; "Proceeds." The revised definition of "proceeds" expanded the definition beyond that contained in pre-1998 Section 9-306 and resolves ambiguities in the former definition. Article 9's references to personal property as "proceeds" is a description of the origin of the property and not an identification of the property as a separate type of property. The fact that a particular item of personal property is also a type of collateral does not preclude that personal property from constituting "proceeds" of other personal property. See PEB Commentary No. 31, dated February 27, 2025. The Commentary is available at https://www.ali.org/peb-ucc.

a. Distributions on Account of Collateral. The phrase "whatever is collected on, or distributed on account of, collateral," in subparagraph (B), is broad enough to cover cash or stock dividends distributed on account of securities or other investment property that is original collateral. Compare pre-1998 Section 9-306 ("Any payments or distributions made with respect to investment property collateral are proceeds."). This section rejects the holding of *Hastie v. FDIC,* 2 F.3d 1042 (10th Cir. 1993) (postpetition cash dividends on stock subject to a prepetition pledge are not "proceeds" under Bankruptcy Code Section 552(b)), to the extent the holding relies on the Article 9 definition of "proceeds."

b. Distributions on Account of Supporting Obligations. Under subparagraph (B), collections on and distributions on account of collateral consisting of various credit-support arrangements ("supporting obligations," as defined in Section 9-102) also are proceeds. Consequently, they are afforded treatment identical to proceeds collected from or distributed by the obligor on the underlying (supported) right to payment or other collateral. Proceeds of supporting obligations also are proceeds of the underlying rights to payment or other collateral.

c. Proceeds of Proceeds. The definition of "proceeds" no longer provides that proceeds of proceeds are themselves proceeds. That idea is expressed in the revised definition of "collateral" in Section 9-102. No change in meaning is intended.

d. Proceeds Received by Person Who Did Not Create Security Interest. When collateral is sold subject to a security interest and the buyer then resells the collateral, a question arose under pre-1998 Article 9 concerning whether the "debtor" had "received" what the buyer received on resale and, therefore, whether those receipts were "proceeds" under pre-1998 Section 9-306(2). This Article contains no requirement that property be "received" by the debtor for the property to qualify as proceeds. It is necessary only that the property be traceable, directly or indirectly, to the original collateral.

e. Cash Proceeds and Noncash Proceeds. The definition of "cash proceeds" is substantially the same as the corresponding definition in pre-1998 Section 9-306. The phrase "and the like" covers property that is functionally equivalent to "money, checks, or deposit accounts," such as some money-market accounts that are securities or part of securities entitlements. Proceeds other than cash proceeds are noncash proceeds.

f. Forks and Airdrops for Controllable Electronic Records. Sometimes there occurs a change in the software (code) of a system (sometimes referred to as a "protocol" or "platform") in which a controllable electronic record is recorded. When such a change occurs in a blockchain platform, the blockchain may remain intact, no new blockchain may result, and the change sometimes is colloquially referred to as a "soft fork." If, instead, such a change results in a new, separate blockchain that exists alongside the original blockchain and a new controllable electronic record is created, the change is sometimes referred to as a "hard fork." But the terms "fork," "soft fork," and "hard fork" are ambiguous and not used consistently. Even in a hard fork situation the pre-fork controllable electronic record typically would remain intact (although its value might be affected). A person in control of the original record may not automatically obtain control of a new record. Additional steps may be required for the person in control of the original record to obtain control of the new record.

Depending on the nature and structure of the fork, a new controllable electronic record arising under a hard fork may be property "distributed on account of" the original record or "rights arising out of" the original record, thereby constituting proceeds of the original record under subparagraph (B) or (C), or both, of the definition of "proceeds." If the new record is identifiable "proceeds," then the rules on attachment, perfection, priority under Sections 9- 203(f), 9-315, and 9-322 would apply. If a security interest in the original record is perfected by control, the creation of the new record in connection with a hard fork typically results in the secured party obtaining control (or having the opportunity to obtain control) of the new record. If that is not the case and perfection of the security interest in the original record is only by control, however, then perfection would continue in the new record only until the 21st day after the security interest attaches to the new record, unless one of the exceptions under subsection (d) applies. Section 9-315(c), (d). For this reason, a secured party may wish also to perfect its security interest by filing so that the perfection would continue thereafter in any proceeds under Section 9-315(d)(1). A secured party that does so may, to ensure the priority of its perfected security interest, also wish to consider obtaining a release or subordination from any earlier filed secured party whose financing statement covers the same type of property. Even if that is achieved, a security interest in the record that is perfected by control (even if control is later obtained) would have priority over a security interest perfected only by filing. Section 9-326A.

New controllable electronic records also may be provided to persons in control of existing records by way of an "airdrop" that does not involve a fork in an existing blockchain. Depending on the circumstances, these new records may or may not be proceeds of the existing, original record.

If the original record were a financial asset credited to a securities account, the new record might become proceeds of a security entitlement for the reasons described above. Concerning the duties, if any, of a securities intermediary with respect to such a distribution, see Section 8-505, Comment 4.

This discussion focuses on forks and airdrops related to controllable electronic records in the context of blockchain technology, the prevailing relevant technology in 2022. In determining whether property may be proceeds of collateral in the contexts of other and future technologies, the principles and policies reflected in this discussion should be considered.

14. Consignment-Related Definitions: "Consignee"; "Consignment"; "Consignor." The definition of "consignment," added by the 1998, excludes, in subparagraphs (B) and (C), transactions for which filing would be inappropriate or of insufficient benefit to justify the costs. A consignment excluded from the application of this Article by one of those subparagraphs may still be a true consignment; however, it is governed by non-Article 9 law. The definition also excludes, in subparagraph (D), what have been called "consignments intended for security." These "consignments" are not bailments but secured transactions. Accordingly, all of Article 9 applies to them. See Sections 1-201(b)(35), 9-109(a)(1). The "consignor" is the person who delivers goods to the "consignee" in a consignment.

The definition of "consignment" requires that the goods be delivered "to a merchant for the purpose of sale." If the goods are delivered for another purpose as well, such as milling or processing, the transaction is a consignment nonetheless because a purpose of the delivery is "sale." On the other hand, if a merchant-processor-bailee will not be selling the goods itself but will be delivering to buyers to which the owner-bailor agreed to sell the goods, the transaction would not be a consignment.

Under clause (iii) of subparagraph (A), a transaction is not an Article 9 "consignment" if the consignee is "generally known by its creditors to be substantially engaged in selling the goods of others." Clause (iii) does not apply solely because a particular competing claimant knows that the goods are held on consignment. See PEB Commentary No. 20.

15. "Accounting." This definition describes the record and information that a debtor is entitled to request under Section 9-210. Consistent with the revised definition of "sign" in Section 1-201(b)(37), the cognate term "signed" replaces the reference to "authenticated" in the pre- 2022 text of this definition.

16. "Document." The definition of "document" incorporates both tangible and electronic documents of title. See Section 1-201(b)(16) and Comment 16.

Legislative Note: *Former Article 1 defined document of title in Section 1-201(15) and accompanying Comment 15. Revised Article 1 defines document of title in Section 1-201(b)(16) and accompanying Comment 16. Cross references should be adapted depending upon which version of Article 1 is in force in the jurisdiction.*

17. "Encumbrance"; "Mortgage." The definitions of "encumbrance" and "mortgage" are unchanged in substance from the corresponding definitions in pre-1998 Section 9-105. They are used primarily in the special real-property-related priority and other provisions relating to crops, fixtures, and accessions.

18. "Fixtures." This definition is unchanged in substance from the corresponding definition in pre-1998 Section 9-313. See Section 9-334 (priority of security interests in fixtures and crops).

19. "Good Faith." The definition of "good faith" added by the 1998 Revisions, which incorporated the concept of "reasonable commercial standards of fair dealing," was deleted by the conforming amendments to the 2001 revision of Article 1. The definition is unnecessary given the revised definition in Section 1-201(b)(20).

20. "Lien Creditor." This definition is unchanged in substance from the corresponding definition in pre-1998 Section 9-301.

21. "New Value." The 1998 Revisions deleted pre-1998 Section 9-108. Its broad formulation of new value, which embraced the taking of after-acquired collateral for a pre-existing claim, was unnecessary, counterintuitive, and ineffective for its original purpose of sheltering after-acquired collateral from attack as a voidable preference in bankruptcy. The new definition of "new value" derives from Bankruptcy Code Section 547(a). The term is used with respect to temporary perfection of security interests in instruments, certificated securities, or negotiable documents under Section 9-312(e) and with respect to chattel paper priority in Section 9-330.

22. "Person Related To." Section 9-615 provides a special method for calculating a deficiency or surplus when "the secured party, a person related to the secured party, or a secondary obligor" acquires the collateral at a foreclosure disposition. Separate definitions of the term are provided with respect to an individual secured party and with respect to a secured party that is an organization. The definitions are patterned on the corresponding definition in Section 1.301(32) of the Uniform Consumer Credit Code (1974).

23. "Proposal." This definition describes a record that is sufficient to propose to retain collateral in full or partial satisfaction of a secured obligation. See Sections 9-620, 9-621, 9-622. Consistent with the revised definition of "sign" in Section 1-201(b)(37), the 2022 revision of the definition adopts the cognate term "signed" to replace the term "authenticated" used in the pre- 2022 text.

24. "Pursuant to Commitment." This definition is unchanged in substance from the corresponding definition in pre-1998 Section 9-105. It is used in connection with special priority rules applicable to future advances. See Section 9-323.

25. "Software." The definition of "software" is used in connection with the priority rules applicable to purchase-money security interests. See Sections 9-103, 9-324. Software, like a payment intangible, is a type of general intangible for purposes of this Article. See Comment 4.a., above, regarding the distinction between "goods" and "software."

Section 9-103. Purchase-Money Security Interest; Application of Payments; Burden of Establishing

(a) [Definitions.] In this section:

(1) "purchase-money collateral" means goods or software that secures a purchase-money obligation incurred with respect to that collateral; and

(2) "purchase-money obligation" means an obligation of an obligor incurred as all or part of the price of the collateral or for value given to enable the debtor to acquire rights in or the use of the collateral if the value is in fact so used.

(b) [Purchase-money security interest in goods.] A security interest in goods is a purchase-money security interest:

(1) to the extent that the goods are purchase-money collateral with respect to that security interest;

(2) if the security interest is in inventory that is or was purchase-money collateral, also to the extent that the security interest secures a purchase-money obligation incurred with respect to other inventory in which the secured party holds or held a purchase-money security interest; and

(3) also to the extent that the security interest secures a purchase-money obligation incurred with respect to software in which the secured party holds or held a purchase-money security interest.

(c) [Purchase-money security interest in software.] A security interest in software is a purchase-money security interest to the extent that the security interest also secures a purchase-money obligation incurred with respect to goods in which the secured party holds or held a purchase-money security interest if:

(1) the debtor acquired its interest in the software in an integrated transaction in which it acquired an interest in the goods; and

(2) the debtor acquired its interest in the software for the principal purpose of using the software in the goods.

(d) [Consignor's inventory purchase-money security interest.] The security interest of a consignor in goods that are the subject of a consignment is a purchase-money security interest in inventory.

(e) [Application of payment in non-consumer-goods transaction.] In a transaction other than a consumer-goods transaction, if the extent to which a security interest is a purchase-money security interest depends on the application of a payment to a particular obligation, the payment must be applied:

(1) in accordance with any reasonable method of application to which the parties agree;

(2) in the absence of the parties' agreement to a reasonable method, in accordance with any intention of the obligor manifested at or before the time of payment; or

(3) in the absence of an agreement to a reasonable method and a timely manifestation of the obligor's intention, in the following order:

(A) to obligations that are not secured; and

(B) if more than one obligation is secured, to obligations secured by purchase-money security interests in the order in which those obligations were incurred.

(f) [No loss of status of purchase-money security interest in non-consumer-goods transaction.] In a transaction other than a consumer-goods transaction, a purchase-money security interest does not lose its status as such, even if:

(1) the purchase-money collateral also secures an obligation that is not a purchase-money obligation;

(2) collateral that is not purchase-money collateral also secures the purchase-money obligation; or

(3) the purchase-money obligation has been renewed, refinanced, consolidated, or restructured.

(g) [Burden of proof in non-consumer-goods transaction.] In a transaction other than a consumer-goods transaction, a secured party claiming a purchase-money security interest has the burden of establishing the extent to which the security interest is a purchase-money security interest.

(h) [Non-consumer-goods transactions; no inference.] The limitation of the rules in subsections (e), (f), and (g) to transactions other than consumer-goods transactions is intended to leave to the court the determination of the proper rules in consumer-goods transactions. The court may not infer from that limitation the nature of the proper rule in consumer-goods transactions and may continue to apply established approaches.

Definitional Cross References:

Agreement	Section 1-201(b)(3)
Burden of establishing	Section 1-201(b)(8)
Collateral	Section 9-102(a)(12)
Consignment	Section 9-102(a)(20)
Consignor	Section 9-102(a)(21)
Consumer-goods transaction	Section 9-102(a)(24)
Debtor	Section 9-102(a)(28)
Goods	Section 9-102(a)(44)
Inventory	Section 9-102(a)(48)
Obligor	Section 9-102(a)(59)
Right	Section 1-201(b)(34)
Secured party	Section 9-102(a)(73)
Security interest	Section 1-201(b)(35)
Software	Section 9-102(a)(76)
Value	Section 1-204

Comment References: 9-109 C6

Official Comment

1. Source. Former Section 9-107.

2. Scope of This Section. Under Section 9-309(1), a purchase-money security interest in consumer goods is perfected when it attaches. Sections 9-317 and 9-324 provide special priority rules for purchase-money security interests in a variety of contexts. This section explains when a security interest enjoys purchase-money status.

3. "Purchase-Money Collateral"; "Purchase-Money Obligation"; "Purchase-Money Security Interest." Subsection (a) defines "purchase-money collateral" and "purchase-money obligation." These terms are essential to the description of what constitutes a purchase-money security interest under subsection (b). As used in subsection (a)(2), the definition of "purchase-money obligation," the "price" of collateral or the "value given to enable" includes obligations for expenses incurred in connection with acquiring rights in the collateral, sales taxes, duties, finance charges, interest, freight charges, costs of storage in transit, demurrage, administrative charges, expenses of collection and enforcement, attorney's fees, and other similar obligations.

The concept of "purchase-money security interest" requires a close nexus between the acquisition of collateral and the secured obligation. Thus, a security interest does not qualify as a purchase-money security interest if a debtor acquires property on unsecured credit and subsequently creates the security interest to secure the purchase price.

4. Cross-Collateralization of Purchase-Money Security Interests in Inventory. Subsection (b)(2) deals with the problem of cross-collateralized purchase-money security interests in inventory. Consider a simple example:

> **Example:** Seller (S) sells an item of inventory (Item-1) to Debtor (D), retaining a security interest in Item-1 to secure Item-1's price and all other obligations, existing and future, of D to S. S then sells another item of inventory to D (Item-2), again retaining a security interest in Item-2 to secure Item-2's price as well as all other obligations of D to S. D then pays to S Item-1's price. D then sells Item-2 to a buyer in ordinary course of business, who takes Item-2 free of S's security interest.
>
> Under subsection (b)(2), S's security interest in *Item-1* securing *Item-2's unpaid* price would be a purchase-money security interest. This is so because S has a purchase-money security interest in Item-1, Item-1 secures the price of (a "purchase-money obligation incurred with respect to") Item-2 ("other inventory"), and Item-2 itself was subject to a purchase-money security interest. Note that, to the extent Item-1 secures the price of Item-2, S's security interest in Item-1 would not be a purchase-money security interest under subsection (b)(1). The security interest in Item-1 is a purchase-money security interest under subsection (b)(1) only to the extent that Item-1 is "purchase-money collateral," i.e., only to the extent that Item-1 "secures a purchase-money obligation incurred with respect to that collateral" (i.e., Item-1). See subsection (a)(1).

5. Purchase-Money Security Interests in Goods and Software. Subsections (b) and (c) limit purchase-money security interests to security interests in goods, including fixtures, and software. Otherwise, no change in meaning from former

Section 9-107 is intended. The second sentence of former Section 9-115(5)(f) made the purchase-money priority rule (former Section 9-312(4)) inapplicable to investment property. This section's limitation makes that provision unnecessary.

Subsection (c) describes the limited circumstances under which a security interest in goods may be accompanied by a purchase-money security interest in software. The software must be acquired by the debtor in a transaction integrated with the transaction in which the debtor acquired the goods, and the debtor must acquire the software for the principal purpose of using the software in the goods. "Software" is defined in Section 9-102.

6. Consignments. Under former Section 9-114, the priority of the consignor's interest is similar to that of a purchase-money security interest. Subsection (d) achieves this result more directly, by defining the interest of a "consignor," defined in Section 9-102, to be a purchase-money security interest in inventory for purposes of this Article. This drafting convention obviates any need to set forth special priority rules applicable to the interest of a consignor. Rather, the priority of the consignor's interest as against the rights of lien creditors of the consignee, competing secured parties, and purchasers of the goods from the consignee can be determined by reference to the priority rules generally applicable to inventory, such as Sections 9-317, 9-320, 9-322, and 9-324. For other purposes, including the rights and duties of the consignor and consignee as between themselves, the consignor would remain the owner of goods under a bailment arrangement with the consignee. See Section 9-319.

7. Provisions Applicable Only to Non-consumer-goods Transactions.

a. "Dual-Status" Rule. For transactions other than consumer-goods transactions, this Article approves what some cases have called the "dual-status" rule, under which a security interest may be a purchase-money security interest to some extent and a non-purchase-money security interest to some extent. (Concerning consumer-goods transactions, see subsection (h) and Comment 8.) Some courts have found this rule to be explicit or implicit in the words "to the extent," found in former Section 9-107 and continued in subsections (b)(1) and (b)(2). The rule is made explicit in subsection (e). For non-consumer-goods transactions, this Article rejects the "transformation" rule adopted by some cases, under which any cross-collateralization, refinancing, or the like destroys the purchase-money status entirely.

Consider, for example, what happens when a $10,000 loan secured by a purchase-money security interest is refinanced by the original lender, and, as part of the transaction, the debtor borrows an additional $2,000 secured by the collateral. Subsection (f) resolves any doubt that the security interest remains a purchase-money security interest. Under subsection (b), however, it enjoys purchase-money status only to the extent of $10,000.

b. Allocation of Payments. Continuing with the example, if the debtor makes a $1,000 payment on the $12,000 obligation, then one must determine the extent to which the security interest remains a purchase-money security interest—$9,000 or $10,000. Subsection (e)(1) expresses the overriding principle, applicable in cases other than consumer-goods transactions, for determining the extent to which a security interest is a purchase-money security interest under these circumstances: freedom of contract, as limited by principle of reasonableness. An unconscionable method of application, for example, is not a reasonable one and so would not be given effect under subsection (e)(1). In the absence of agreement, subsection (e)(2) permits the obligor to determine how payments should be allocated. If the obligor fails to manifest its intention, obligations that are not secured will be paid first. (As used in this Article, the concept of "obligations that are not secured" means obligations for which the debtor has not created a security interest. This concept is different from and should not be confused with the concept of an "unsecured claim" as it appears in Bankruptcy Code Section 506(a).) The obligor may prefer this approach, because unsecured debt is likely to carry a higher interest rate than secured debt. A creditor who would prefer to be secured rather than unsecured also would prefer this approach.

After the unsecured debt is paid, payments are to be applied first toward the obligations secured by purchase-money security interests. In the event that there is more than one such obligation, payments first received are to be applied to obligations first incurred. See subsection (e)(3). Once these obligations are paid, there are no purchase-money security interests and no additional allocation rules are needed.

Subsection (f) buttresses the dual-status rule by making it clear that (in a transaction other than a consumer-goods transaction) cross-collateralization and renewals, refinancings, and restructurings do not cause a purchase-money security interest to lose its status as such. The statutory terms "renewed," "refinanced," and "restructured" are not defined. Whether the terms encompass a particular transaction depends upon whether, under the particular facts, the purchase-money character of the security interest fairly can be said to survive. Each term contemplates that an identifiable portion of the purchase-money obligation could be traced to the new obligation resulting from a renewal, refinancing, or restructuring.

c. Burden of Proof. As is the case when the extent of a security interest is in issue, under subsection (g) the secured party claiming a purchase-money security interest in a transaction other than a consumer-goods transaction has the burden of establishing whether the security interest retains its purchase-money status. This is so whether the determination is to be made following a renewal, refinancing, or restructuring or otherwise.

8. Consumer-Goods Transactions; Characterization Under Other Law. Under subsection (h), the limitation of subsections (e), (f), and (g) to transactions other than consumer-goods transactions leaves to the court the determination of the proper rules in consumer-goods transactions. Subsection (h) also instructs the court not to draw any inference from this limitation as to the proper rules for consumer-goods transactions and leaves the court free to continue to apply established approaches to those transactions.

This section addresses only whether a security interest is a "purchase-money security interest" under this Article, primarily for purposes of perfection and priority. See, e.g., Sections 9-317, 9-324. In particular, its adoption of the dual-status rule, allocation of payments rules, and burden of proof standards for non-consumer-goods transactions is not intended to affect or influence characterizations under other statutes. Whether a security interest is a "purchase-money security interest" under other law is determined by that law. For example, decisions under Bankruptcy Code Section 522(f) have applied both the dual-status and the transformation rules. The Bankruptcy Code does not expressly adopt the state law definition of "purchase-money security interest." Where federal law does not defer to this Article, this Article does not, and could not, determine a question of federal law.

Section 9-104. Control of Deposit Account

(a) [Requirements for control.] A secured party has control of a deposit account if:

(1) the secured party is the bank with which the deposit account is maintained;

(2) the debtor, secured party, and bank have agreed in a signed record that the bank will comply with instructions originated by the secured party directing disposition of the funds in the deposit account without further consent by the debtor; or

(3) the secured party becomes the bank's customer with respect to the deposit account; or

(4) another person, other than the debtor:

(A) has control of the deposit account and acknowledges that it has control on behalf of the secured party; or

(B) obtains control of the deposit account after having acknowledged that it will obtain control of the deposit account on behalf of the secured party.

(b) [Debtor's right to direct disposition.] A secured party that has satisfied subsection (a) has control, even if the debtor retains the right to direct the disposition of funds from the deposit account.

Definitional Cross References:

Account	Section 9-102(a)(2)
Bank	Section 9-102(a)(8)
Customer	Section 4-104(a)(5)
Debtor	Section 9-102(a)(28)
Deposit account	Section 9-102(a)(29)
Person	Section 1-201(b)(27)
Record	Section 9-102(a)(70)
Secured party	Section 9-102(a)(73)
Sign	Section 1-201(b)(37)

Comment References: 9-105 C4

Official Comment

1. Source. Derived Section 8-106.

2. Why "Control" Matters. This section explains the concept of "control" of a deposit account. "Control" under this section may serve two functions. First, "control . . . pursuant to the debtor's security agreement" may substitute for a signed security agreement as an element of attachment. See Section 9-203(b)(3)(D). Second, when a deposit account is taken as original collateral, the only method of perfection is obtaining control under this section. See Section 9-312(b)(1).

3. Requirements for "Control: In General." This section derives from Section 8-106 of Revised Article 8, which defines "control" of securities and certain other investment property. Under subsection (a)(1), the bank with which the deposit account is maintained has control. The effect of this provision is to afford the bank automatic perfection. No other form of public notice is necessary; all actual and potential creditors of the debtor are always on notice that the bank with which the debtor's deposit account is maintained may assert a claim against the deposit account.

> **Example**: D maintains a deposit account with Bank A. To secure a loan from Banks X, Y, and Z, D creates a security interest in the deposit account in favor of Bank A, as agent for Banks X, Y, and Z. Because Bank A is a "secured party" as defined in Section 9-102, the security interest is perfected by control under subsection (a)(1).

Under subsection (a)(2), a secured party may obtain control by obtaining the bank's signed agreement that it will comply with the secured party's instructions without further consent by the debtor. The analogous provision in Section 8-106 does not require that the agreement be signed. An agreement to comply with the secured party's instructions suffices for "control" of a deposit account under this section even if the bank's agreement is subject to specified conditions, e.g., that the secured party's instructions are accompanied by a certification that the debtor is in default. (Of course, if the condition is the debtor's further consent, the statute explicitly provides that the agreement would not confer control.) See Section 8-106, Comment 7.

Under subsection (a)(3), a secured party may obtain control by becoming the bank's "customer," as defined in Section 4-104. As the customer, the secured party would enjoy the right (but not necessarily the exclusive right) to withdraw funds from, or close, the deposit account. See Sections 4-401(a), 4-403(a).

As is the case with possession under Section 9-313, in determining whether a particular person has control under subsection (a), the principles of agency apply. See Section 1-103(b) and Restatement (3d), Agency § 8.12, Comment *b.*

Although the arrangements giving rise to control may themselves prevent, or may enable the secured party at its discretion to prevent, the debtor from reaching the funds on deposit, subsection (b) makes clear that the debtor's ability to reach the funds is not inconsistent with "control."

Perfection by control is not available for bank accounts evidenced by an instrument (e.g., certain certificates of deposit), which by definition are "instruments" and not "deposit accounts." See Section 9-102 (defining "deposit account" and "instrument").

4. Control on behalf of another person. Subsection (a)(4) provides for a secured party to obtain control of a deposit account by virtue of the acknowledgment by another person, other than the debtor, in control of the deposit account. It generally follows revisions to the corresponding provisions for control of electronic documents of title (Section 7-106(g)), control of a security entitlement (8-106(d)), control of an electronic copy of a record evidencing chattel paper (Section 9-105(g)), control of electronic money (Section 9-105A(e)), and control of controllable electronic records (Section 12-105(e)). For a brief discussion, see Section 12-105, Comments 8 and 9.

An acknowledgment by a person in control under subsection (a)(4) would not impose any duties on the bank with which the deposit account is maintained. Indeed, the bank may have no knowledge or involvement whatsoever with a control person's acknowledgment under that subsection. On the other hand, subsection (a)(4) should not be construed to permit the bank with which the deposit account is maintained to short-circuit subsection (a)(2), which provides for control through a control agreement among the debtor, the bank, and the control person. However, it would be possible for the bank, acting in a capacity other than as the depositary bank (for example, as a secured party) to acknowledge that it has control on behalf of another purchaser under subsection (a)(4).

Section 9-107B(a) makes clear that a person that has control under this section has no duty to acknowledge that it has or will obtain control on behalf of another person. Arrangements for a person to acknowledge that it has or will obtain control on behalf of another person are not standardized. Accordingly, Section 9-107B(b) leaves to the agreement of the parties and to any other applicable law any duties of a person that does acknowledge that it has or will obtain control on behalf of another person and provides that a person making an acknowledgment is not required to confirm the acknowledgment to another person.

Section 9-105. Control of Electronic Copy of Record Evidencing Chattel Paper

(a) [General rule: control of electronic copy of record evidencing chattel paper.] A purchaser has control of an authoritative electronic copy of a record evidencing chattel paper if a system employed for evidencing the assignment of interests in the chattel paper reliably establishes the purchaser as the person to which the authoritative electronic copy was assigned.

(b) [Single authoritative copy.] A system satisfies subsection (a) if the record or records evidencing the chattel paper are created, stored, and assigned in a manner that:

(1) a single authoritative copy of the record or records exists which is unique, identifiable, and, except as otherwise provided in paragraphs (4), (5), and (6), unalterable;

(2) the authoritative copy identifies the purchaser as the assignee of the record or records;

(3) the authoritative copy is communicated to and maintained by the purchaser or its designated custodian;

(4) copies or amendments that add or change an identified assignee of the authoritative copy can be made only with the consent of the purchaser;

(5) each copy of the authoritative copy and any copy of a copy is readily identifiable as a copy that is not the authoritative copy; and

(6) any amendment of the authoritative copy is readily identifiable as authorized or unauthorized.

(c) [One or more authoritative copies.] A system satisfies subsection (a), and a purchaser has control of an authoritative electronic copy of a record evidencing chattel paper, if the electronic copy, a record attached to or logically associated with the electronic copy, or a system in which the electronic copy is recorded:

(1) enables the purchaser readily to identify each electronic copy as either an authoritative copy or a nonauthoritative copy;

(2) enables the purchaser readily to identify itself in any way, including by name, identifying number, cryptographic key, office, or account number, as the assignee of the authoritative electronic copy; and

(3) gives the purchaser exclusive power, subject to subsection (d), to:

(A) prevent others from adding or changing an identified assignee of the authoritative electronic copy; and

(B) transfer control of the authoritative electronic copy.

(d) [Meaning of exclusive.] Subject to subsection (e), a power is exclusive under subsection (c)(3)(A) and (B) even if:

(1) the authoritative electronic copy, a record attached to or logically associated with the authoritative electronic copy, or a system in which the authoritative electronic copy is recorded limits the use of the authoritative electronic copy or has a protocol programmed to cause a change, including a transfer or loss of control; or

(2) the power is shared with another person.

(e) [When power not shared with another person.] A power of a purchaser is not shared with another person under subsection (d)(2) and the purchaser's power is not exclusive if:

(1) the purchaser can exercise the power only if the power also is exercised by the other person; and

(2) the other person:

(A) can exercise the power without exercise of the power by the purchaser; or

(B) is the transferor to the purchaser of an interest in the chattel paper.

(f) [Presumption of exclusivity of certain powers.] If a purchaser has the powers specified in subsection (c)(3)(A) and (B), the powers are presumed to be exclusive.

(g) [Obtaining control through another person.] A purchaser has control of an authoritative electronic copy of a record evidencing chattel paper if another person, other than the transferor to the purchaser of an interest in the chattel paper:

(1) has control of the authoritative electronic copy and acknowledges that it has control on behalf of the purchaser; or

(2) obtains control of the authoritative electronic copy after having acknowledged that it will obtain control of the electronic copy on behalf of the purchaser.

Definitional Cross References:

Account	Section 9-102(a)(2)
Assignee	Section 9-102(a)(7A)
Chattel paper	Section 9-102(a)(11)
Communicate	Section 9-102(a)(18)
Electronic	Section 1-201(b)(16A)
Person	Section 1-201(b)(27)
Purchaser	Section 1-201(b)(30)
Record	Section 9-102(a)(70)
Secured party	Section 9-102(a)(73)

Official Comment

1. The Functions of Control. A secured party can perfect a security interest in chattel paper by filing. See Section 9-312(a). Alternatively, a secured party can perfect a security interest in chattel paper by taking possession of all authoritative tangible copies of the record evidencing the chattel paper and obtaining control of all authoritative electronic copies of the record evidencing chattel paper. Section 9-314A. Possession and control also are conditions for achieving priority under Section 9-330(a), (b), and (c). A secured party's possession or control of chattel paper also may substitute for a signed security agreement for purposes of attachment under Section 9-203. Subsection (e) provides that in certain circumstances a power is not shared within the meaning of subsection (d)(2), the relaxation of the exclusivity requirement provided by subsection (d)(2) does not apply, and, consequently, a purchaser's power is not exclusive.

2. Conditions for Obtaining Control: In General. This section provides the requirements for obtaining control of chattel paper. As explained in the comment to the definition of "chattel paper," the definitions of "electronic chattel paper" and "tangible chattel paper" have been deleted as unnecessary. See Section 9-102, Comment 5.b.

Subsections (a) and (b) are substantially unchanged under the 2022 Article 9 Revisions. Subsection (a), which derives from Section 16 of the Uniform Electronic Transactions Act, sets forth the general test for control. (The amendments to subsection (a) primarily reflect the changes to the definition of chattel paper in Section 9-102.) Subsections (b) and (c) set forth safe harbor tests that, if satisfied, establish control under the general test in subsection (a). It is important to note that compliance with the conditions for control in subsection (c) would satisfy the conditions provided in subsection (b). However, subsection (b) has been retained out of an abundance of caution and to provide assurances of the continuing viability of pre-2022 systems for control of chattel paper evidenced by electronic records.

3. Development of Control Systems and Application of Subsection (b). This Article leaves to the marketplace the development of systems and procedures, through a combination of suitable technologies and business practices, for dealing with control of chattel paper in a commercial context. As under UETA and under the general standard for control under subsection (a), for control under subsection (b), as supplemented by subsection (g), a system must be shown to reliably establish that the secured party is the assignee of the chattel paper. Reliability is a high standard and encompasses the general principle of identifiability of an assignee of an authoritative copy as found in subsection (b), but without setting forth specific guidelines as to how compliance with this principle must be achieved. Under subsection (b), at any point in time, a party should be able to identify the single authoritative copy of the record or records evidencing the chattel paper which is unique and identifiable as the authoritative copy. This does not mean that once created the authoritative copy need be static and never moved or copied from its original location. To the extent that backup systems exist which result in multiple copies, the key to this idea is that at any point in time, the one authoritative copy needs to be unique and identifiable. However, the standards applied to determine whether a party is in control of chattel paper should not be more stringent than the pre-2022 standards applied to determine whether a party is in possession of tangible chattel paper. For example, just as a secured party does not lose possession of tangible chattel paper merely by virtue of the possibility that a person acting on its behalf could wrongfully redeliver the chattel paper to the debtor, so control of chattel paper evidenced by an electronic copy of a record or records would not be defeated by the possibility that the secured party's control could be subverted by the wrongful conduct of a person (such as a custodian) acting on its behalf.

4. Subsection (c) Safe Harbor: In General. The subsection (c) "safe harbor" generally follows Section 12-105 for control of controllable electronic records. See generally Section 12-105 and Comments. It differs from subsection (b), which (as explained above) is based on a "single authoritative copy" of an electronic record or records. Subsection (b) would be inapplicable when the relevant record is maintained on a blockchain or another distributed ledger. The utility of distributed ledger technology depends on there being multiple authoritative copies of a record. However, as with subsection (b), control under subsection (c) also meets the high standard of reliability under subsection (a) as to the identifiability of an assignee of authoritative copies. The conditions for "control" in subsection (c) are meant to reflect the functions that possession serves with respect to writings, but in a more accurate and technologically flexible way than does the definition in subsection (b).

Subsection (c), as supplemented by subsections (d) through (g), sets forth the requirements for a purchaser to have "control of an authoritative electronic copy of a record evidencing chattel paper." However, for purposes of perfection of a security interest in the chattel paper under Section 9-314A and qualification for non-temporal priority under Section 9-330, the purchaser must obtain control of each authoritative electronic copy (i.e., all of the copies) of a record evidencing the chattel paper and take possession of each tangible copy (if any) of the record evidencing the chattel paper.

5. Control of Electronic Copy of Record Evidencing Chattel Paper under Subsection (c). Under subsection (c), to obtain control of an electronic copy of a record evidencing chattel paper a purchaser must be able to identify each electronic copy as authoritative or nonauthoritative and identify itself as the assignee of the authoritative copy. As to the means of identification, see Section 12-105, Comment 7. In addition, the purchaser must have the exclusive power to prevent others from adding or changing an identified assignee and to transfer control of the authoritative copy. However, once it is established that a person has received those powers, subsection (f) provides a presumption of exclusivity. Consequently, a person asserting control need not prove exclusivity in order to make out a prima facie case. Application of the presumption will be governed also by Section 1-206 (effects of a presumption under the UCC) and applicable non-UCC law (including rules of procedure and evidence). See generally Section 12-105, Comment 5. Subsection (d) contains two qualifications of the term "exclusive" as used in subsection (c)(3). A power can be "exclusive" under subsection (c)(3) even if one or both of these qualifications apply.

Subsection (e) provides that a purchaser does not share an exclusive power with another person if the purchaser can exercise the power only with the other person's cooperation (subsection (e)(1)) but the other person either (i) can exercise the power without the purchaser's cooperation (subsection (e)(2)(A)) or (ii) is the transferor to the purchaser of an interest in the chattel paper (subsection (e)(2)(B)). It follows that a purchaser to which subsection (e) applies does not have control based on its exclusive powers (although it might have control through another person under subsection (g), discussed below, or if another person having control is acting as the person's agent). As to the rationale for disqualifying a purchaser (which includes a secured party in a secured transaction) from sharing powers with a transferor to the purchaser, as provided in subsection (e)(2)(B), and from the benefit of shared control under subsection (d)(2), and for examples of the operation of subsection (e) (in the context of the similar provision in Section 12- 105), see Section 12-105, Comments 5 and 9.

6. Control Through Another Person. Subsection (g) provides for a purchaser to obtain control of an electronic copy by virtue of the acknowledgment by another person in control of the electronic copy. It follows revisions to the corresponding provisions for control of electronic documents of title (Section 7-106(g)), control of a security entitlement (Section 8- 106(d)(3)), control of deposit accounts (Section 9-104(a)(4)), control of electronic money (Section 9-105A(e)), and control of controllable electronic records (Section 12-105(e)). For a brief discussion, see Section 12-105, Comment 8. For an acknowledgment by another person to be effective to confer control on a purchaser under subsection (g), the other person making the acknowledgment must be one "other than the transferor to the purchaser of an interest in the chattel paper." The rationale for this limitation is discussed in Section 12-105, Comment 9.

Section 9-107B(a) makes clear that a person that has control under this section has no duty to acknowledge that it has or will obtain control on behalf of another person. Arrangements for a person to acknowledge that it has or will obtain control on behalf of another person are not standardized. Accordingly, Section 9-107B(b) leaves to the agreement of the parties and to any other applicable law any duties of a person that does acknowledge that it has or will obtain control on behalf of another person and provides that a person making an acknowledgment is not required to confirm the acknowledgment to another person. For example, subsection (g) would apply to give control to a person, Alpha, when another person, Beta, has control of each authoritative electronic copy of a record evidencing chattel paper and acknowledges that it has control on behalf of Alpha. However, under Section 9-107B(a), Beta is not required to so acknowledge. And under Section 9-107B(b), even if Beta does so acknowledge, Beta owes no duty to Alpha unless Beta agrees or other law so provides and Beta is not required to confirm its acknowledgment to any other person.

7. References to "Secured Party" Changed to "Purchaser." References to a "secured party" in the pre-2022 text of this section have been changed to refer to a "purchaser." This change aligns the text with the priority rules of Section 9-330(a), (b), and (c).

Section 9-105A. Control of Electronic Money

(a) [General rule: control of electronic money.] A person has control of electronic money if:

(1) the electronic money, a record attached to or logically associated with the electronic money, or a system in which the electronic money is recorded gives the person:

(A) power to avail itself of substantially all the benefit from the electronic money; and

(B) exclusive power, subject to subsection (b), to:

(i) prevent others from availing themselves of substantially all the benefit from the electronic money; and

(ii) transfer control of the electronic money to another person or cause another person to obtain control of other electronic money as a result of the transfer of the electronic money; and

(2) the electronic money, a record attached to or logically associated with the electronic money, or a system in which the electronic money is recorded enables the person readily to identify itself in any way, including by name, identifying number, cryptographic key, office, or account number, as having the powers under paragraph (1).

(b) [Meaning of exclusive.] Subject to subsection (c), a power is exclusive under subsection (a)(1)(B)(i) and (ii) even if:

(1) the electronic a record attached to or logically associated with the electronic money, or a system in which the electronic money is recorded limits the use of the electronic money or has a protocol programmed to cause a change, including a transfer or loss of control; or

(2) the power is shared with another person.

(c) [When power not shared with another person.] A power of a person is not shared with another person under subsection (b)(2) and the person's power is not exclusive if:

(1) the person can exercise the power only if the power also is exercised by the other person; and

(2) the other person:

(A) can exercise the power without exercise of the power by the person; or

(B) is the transferor to the person of an interest in the electronic money.

(d) [Presumption of exclusivity of certain powers.] If a person has the powers specified in subsection (a)(1)(B)(i) and (ii), the powers are presumed to be exclusive.

(e) [Control through another person.] A person has control of electronic money if another person, other than the transferor to the person of an interest in the electronic money:

(1) has control of the electronic money and acknowledges that it has control on behalf of the person; or

(2) obtains control of the electronic money after having acknowledged that it will obtain control of the electronic money on behalf of the person.

Definitional Cross References:

Account	Section 9-102(a)(2)
Electronic	Section 1-201(b)(16A)
Electronic money	Section 9-102(a)(31A)
Money	Section 9-102(a)(54A)
Person	Section 1-201(b)(27)
Record	Section 9-102(a)(70)

Official Comment

1. "Control of Electronic Money: In General. A security interest in electronic money as original collateral may be perfected only by control pursuant to this section. Section 9- 312(b)(4). These requirements for obtaining control generally track those in Section 12-105 for controllable electronic records. See generally Section 12-105, Comments.

2. Control on Behalf of Another Person. Subsection (e) provides for a person to obtain control of electronic money by virtue of the acknowledgment by another person in control of the electronic money. It follows revisions to the corresponding provisions for control of electronic documents of title (Section 7-106(g)), control of a security entitlement (Section 8- 106(d)(3)), control of deposit accounts (Section 9-104(a)(4)), control of an electronic copy of a record evidencing chattel paper (Section 9-105(g)), and control of controllable electronic records (Section 12-105(e)). For a brief discussion, see Section 12-105, Comment 8.

Section 9-107B(a) makes clear that a person that has control under this section has no duty to acknowledge that it has or will obtain control on behalf of another person. Arrangements for a person to acknowledge that it has or will obtain control on behalf of another person are not standardized. Accordingly, Section 9-107B(b) leaves to the agreement of the parties and to any other applicable law any duties of a person that does acknowledge that it has or will obtain control on behalf of another person and provides that a person making an acknowledgment is not required to confirm the acknowledgment to another person.

Section 9-106. Control of Investment Property

(a) [Control under Section 8-106.] A person has control of a certificated security, uncertificated security, or security entitlement as provided in Section 8-106.

(b) [Control of commodity contract.] A secured party has control of a commodity contract if:

(1) the secured party is the commodity intermediary with which the commodity contract is carried; or

(2) the commodity customer, secured party, and commodity intermediary have agreed that the commodity intermediary will apply any value distributed

on account of the commodity contract as directed by the secured party without further consent by the commodity customer.

(c) [Effect of control of securities account or commodity account.] A secured party having control of all security entitlements or commodity contracts carried in a securities account or commodity account has control over the securities account or commodity account.

Definitional Cross References:

Certificated security	Section 8-102(a)(4)
Commodity account	Section 9-102(a)(14)
Commodity contract	Section 9-102(a)(15)
Commodity customer	Section 9-102(a)(16)
Commodity intermediary	Section 9-102(a)(17)
Control	Section 8-106
Investment property	Section 9-102(a)(49)
Person	Section 1-201(b)(27)
Secured party	Section 9-102(a)(73)
Securities account	Section 8-501(a)
Security entitlement	Section 8-102(a)(17)
Uncertificated security	Section 8-102(a)(18)
Value	Section 1-204
Comment References:	9-105 C4

Comment References: 9-105 C4

Official Comment

1. Source. Former Section 9-115(e).

2. "Control" Under Article 8. For an explanation of "control" of securities and certain other investment property, see Section 8-106, Comments 4 and 7.

3. "Control" of Commodity Contracts. This section, as did former Section 9-115(1)(e), contains provisions relating to control of commodity contracts which are analogous to those in Section 8-106 for other types of investment property.

4. Securities Accounts and Commodity Accounts. For drafting convenience, control with respect to a securities account or commodity account is defined in terms of obtaining control over the security entitlements or commodity contracts. Of course, an agreement that provides that (without further consent of the debtor) the securities intermediary or commodity intermediary will honor instructions from the secured party concerning a securities account or commodity account described as such is sufficient. Such an agreement necessarily implies that the intermediary will honor instructions concerning all security entitlements or commodity contracts carried in the account and thus affords the secured party control of all the security entitlements or commodity contracts.

Section 9-107. Control Of Letter-of-Credit Right

A secured party has control of a letter-of-credit right to the extent of any right to payment or performance by the issuer or any nominated person if the issuer or nominated person has consented to an assignment of proceeds of the letter of credit under Section 5-114(c) or otherwise applicable law or practice.

Definitional Cross References:

Issuer (letter of credit/ letter-of-credit right)	Section 5-102(a)(9)
Letter of credit	Section 5-102(a)(10)
Letter-of-credit right	Section 9-102(a)(51)
Nominated person	Section 5-102(a)(11)
Proceeds	Section 9-102(a)(64)
Secured party	Section 9-102(a)(73)

Comment References: 9-105 C4

Official Comment

1. Source. New.

2. "Control" of Letter-of-Credit Right. Whether a secured party has control of a letter-of-credit right may determine the secured party's priority as against competing secured parties. See Section 9-329. This section provides that a secured party acquires control of a letter-of-credit right by receiving an assignment if the secured party obtains the consent of the issuer or any nominated person, such as a confirmer or negotiating bank, under Section 5-114 or other applicable law or practice. Because both issuers and nominated persons may give or be obligated to give value under a letter of credit, this section contemplates that a secured party obtains control of a letter-of-credit right with respect to the issuer or a particular nominated person only to the extent that the issuer or that nominated person consents to the assignment. For example, if a secured party obtains control to the extent of an issuer's obligation but fails to obtain the consent of a nominated person, the secured party does not have control to the extent that the nominated person gives value. In many cases the person or persons who will give value under a letter of credit will be clear from its terms. In other cases, prudence may suggest obtaining consent from more than one person. The details of the consenting issuer's or nominated person's duties to pay or otherwise render performance to the secured party are left to the agreement of the parties.

3. "Proceeds of a Letter of Credit." Section 5-114 follows traditional banking terminology by referring to a letter of credit beneficiary's assignment of its right to receive payment thereunder as an assignment of the "proceeds of a letter of credit." However, as the seller of goods can assign its right to receive payment (an "account") before it has been earned by delivering the goods to the buyer, so the beneficiary of a letter of credit can assign its contingent right to payment before the letter of credit has been honored. See Section 5-114(b). If the assignment creates a security interest, the security interest can be perfected at the time it is created. An assignment of, including the creation of a security interest in, a letter-of-credit right is an assignment of a present interest.

4. "Transfer" vs. "Assignment." Letter-of-credit law and practice distinguish the "transfer" of a letter of credit from an "assignment." Under a transfer, the transferee itself becomes the beneficiary and acquires the right to draw. Whether a new, substitute credit is issued or the issuer advises the transferee of its status as such, the transfer constitutes a novation under which the transferee is the new, substituted beneficiary (but only to the extent of the transfer, in the case of a partial transfer).

Section 5-114(e) provides that the rights of a transferee beneficiary or nominated person are independent of the beneficiary's assignment of the proceeds of a letter of credit and are superior to the assignee's right to the proceeds. For this reason, transfer does not appear in this Article as a means of control or perfection. Section 9-109(c)(4) recognizes the independent and superior rights of a transferee beneficiary under Section 5-114(e); this Article does not apply to the rights of a transferee beneficiary or nominated person to the extent that those rights are independent and superior under Section 5-114.

5. Supporting Obligation: Automatic Attachment and Perfection. A letter-of-credit right is a type of "supporting obligation," as defined in Section 9-102. Under Sections 9-203 and 9-308, a security interest in a letter-of-credit right automatically attaches and is automatically perfected if the security interest in the supported obligation is a perfected security interest. However, unless the secured party has control of the letter-of-credit right or itself becomes a transferee beneficiary, it cannot obtain any rights against the issuer or a nominated person under Article 5. Consequently, as a practical matter, the secured party's rights would be limited to its ability to locate and identify proceeds distributed by the issuer or nominated person under the letter of credit.

Section 9-107A. Control of Controllable Electronic Record, Controllable Account, or Controllable Payment Intangible

(a) [Control under Section 12-105.] A secured party has control of a controllable electronic record as provided in Section 12-105.

(b) [Control of controllable account and controllable payment intangible.] A secured party has control of a controllable account or controllable payment intangible if the secured party has control of the controllable electronic record that evidences the controllable account or controllable payment intangible.

Definitional Cross References:

Control	Section 12-105
Controllable account	Section 9-102(a)(27A)
Controllable electronic record	Section 12-102(a)(1)
Controllable payment intangible	Section 9-102(a)(27B)
Secured party	Section 9-102(a)(73)

Official Comment

1. Perfection by Control or Filing for Controllable Electronic Records. Perfection by filing and perfection by control are alternative methods of perfection for a controllable electronic record. See Sections 9-312, 9-314. Under this section, a secured party has control of a controllable electronic record as provided in Section 12-105. Under Section 9- 326A, a security interest in a controllable electronic record that is perfected by control has priority over a security interest perfected by another method.

2. Perfection by Control or Filing and Priority for Controllable Account or Controllable Payment Intangible. Perfection by filing and perfection by control also are alternative methods of perfection for a controllable account or controllable payment intangible. See Sections 9-312, 9-314. Under this section, a secured party would obtain control of a controllable account or controllable payment intangible by obtaining control of the controllable electronic record that evidences the controllable account or controllable payment intangible. Under Section 9-326A, a security interest in a controllable account or controllable payment intangible that is perfected by control has priority over a security interest perfected by another method.

By definition, a controllable account would be an Article 9 "account," and a controllable payment intangible would be an Article 9 "payment intangible." Section 9-102. The fact that an account or payment intangible is a controllable account or controllable payment intangible does not affect a secured party's alternative of perfection by filing. Moreover, that fact does not affect the applicability of other provisions of Article 9, including the provisions governing an account debtor's agreement not to assert defenses (Section 9-403) and the statutory overrides of legal and contractual restrictions on the assignability of accounts and payment intangibles (Sections 9-406 and 9-408).

Section 9-107B. No Requirement to Acknowledge or Confirm; No Duties

(a) [No requirement to acknowledge.] A person that has control under Section 9-104, 9-105, or 9-105A is not required to acknowledge that it has control on behalf of another person.

(b) [No duties or confirmation.] If a person acknowledges that it has or will obtain control on behalf of another person, unless the person otherwise agrees or law other than this article otherwise provides, the person does not owe any duty to the other person and is not required to confirm the acknowledgment to any other person.

Definitional Cross References:

Person	Section 1-201(b)(27)
Control	Sections 9-104, 9-105, 9-105A

Official Comment

1. Source. Section 9-107B derives from Sections 8-106(g) and 9-313(f) and (g).

2. Purpose. Subsection (a) makes clear that a person that has control under the specified sections has no duty to acknowledge that it has or will obtain control on behalf of another person. Arrangements for a person to acknowledge that it has control on behalf of another person are not standardized. Accordingly, subsection (b) leaves to the agreement of the parties and to any other applicable law any duties of a person that does acknowledge that it has or will obtain control on behalf of any other person.

Section 9-108. Sufficiency of Description

(a) [Sufficiency of description.] Except as otherwise provided in subsections (c), (d), and (e), a description of personal or real property is sufficient, whether or not it is specific, if it reasonably identifies what is described.

(b) [Examples of reasonable identification.] Except as otherwise provided in subsection (d), a description of collateral reasonably identifies the collateral if it identifies the collateral by:

(1) specific listing;

(2) category;

(3) except as otherwise provided in subsection (e), a type of collateral defined in [the Uniform Commercial Code];

(4) quantity;

(5) computational or allocational formula or procedure; or

(6) except as otherwise provided in subsection (c), any other method, if the identity of the collateral is objectively determinable.

(c) [Supergeneric description not sufficient.] A description of collateral as "all the debtor's assets" or "all the debtor's personal property" or using words of similar import does not reasonably identify the collateral.

(d) [Investment property.] Except as otherwise provided in subsection (e), a description of a security entitlement, securities account, or commodity account is sufficient if it describes:

(1) the collateral by those terms or as investment property; or

(2) the underlying financial asset or commodity contract.

(e) [When description by type insufficient.] A description only by type of collateral defined in [the Uniform Commercial Code] is an insufficient description of:

(1) a commercial tort claim; or

(2) in a consumer transaction, consumer goods, a security entitlement, a securities account, or a commodity account.

Definitional Cross References:

Collateral	Section 9-102(a)(12)
Commercial tort claim	Section 9-102(a)(13)
Commodity account	Section 9-102(a)(14)
Commodity contract	Section 9-102(a)(15)
Consumer goods	Section 9-102(a)(23)
Consumer transaction	Section 9-102(a)(26)
Debtor	Section 9-102(a)(28)
Financial asset	Section 8-102(a)(9)
Investment property	Section 9-102(a)(49)
Securities account	Section 8-501(a)
Security entitlement	Section 8-102(a)(17)

Comment References: 9-203 C5

Official Comment

1. Source. Former Sections 9-110, 9-115(3).

2. General Rules. Subsection (a) retains substantially the same formulation as former Section 9-110. Subsection (b) expands upon subsection (a) by indicating a variety of ways in which a description might reasonably identify collateral. Whereas a provision similar to subsection (b) was applicable only to investment property under former Section 9-115(3), subsection (b) applies to all types of collateral, subject to the limitation in subsection (d). Subsection (b) is subject to subsection (c), which follows prevailing case law and adopts the view that an "all assets" or "all personal property" description for purposes of a security agreement is not sufficient. Note, however, that under Section 9-504, a financing statement sufficiently indicates the collateral if it "covers all assets or all personal property."

The purpose of requiring a description of collateral in a security agreement under Section 9-203 is evidentiary. The test of sufficiency of a description under this section, as under former Section 9-110, is that the description does the job assigned to it: make possible the identification of the collateral described. This section rejects any requirement that a description is insufficient unless it is exact and detailed (the so-called "serial number" test).

3. After-Acquired Collateral. Much litigation has arisen over whether a description in a security agreement is sufficient to include after-acquired collateral if the agreement does not explicitly so provide. This question is one of contract interpretation and is not susceptible to a statutory rule (other than a rule to the effect that it is a question of contract interpretation). Accordingly, this section contains no reference to descriptions of after-acquired collateral.

4. Investment Property. Under subsection (d)(2), the use of the wrong Article 8 or commodities terminology does not render a description invalid (e.g., a security agreement intended to cover a debtor's "security entitlements" is sufficient if it refers to the debtor's "securities"); nor does subsection (d) require the use of the terms "security entitlement," "securities account," "commodity account," or "investment property" if the collateral description is otherwise sufficient under subsection (a). See PEB Commentary No. 28, dated January 16, 2024. The Commentary is available at https://www.ali.org/peb-ucc. Note also that given the broad definition of "securities account" in Section 8-501, a security interest in a securities account also includes all other rights of the debtor against the securities intermediary arising out of the securities account. For example, a security interest in a securities account would include credit balances due to the debtor from the securities intermediary, whether or not they are proceeds of a security entitlement. Moreover, describing collateral as a securities account is a simple way of describing all of the security entitlements carried in the account.

5. Consumer Investment Property; Commercial Tort Claims. Subsection (e) requires greater specificity of description in order to prevent debtors from inadvertently encumbering certain property. Subsection (e) provides that a description by defined "type" of collateral alone of a commercial tort claim or, in a consumer transaction, of a security entitlement, securities account, or commodity account, is not sufficient. For example, "all existing and after-acquired investment property" or "all existing and after-acquired security entitlements," without more, would be insufficient in a consumer transaction to describe a security entitlement, securities account, or commodity account. The reference to "only by type" in subsection (e) means that a description is sufficient if it satisfies subsection (a) and contains a descriptive component beyond the "type" alone. For example, a description such as "all goods now or hereafter sold by secured party to debtor" would suffice, but note that Section 9-204(b)(1) would apply except in the case of a purchase-money security interest. See Section 9- 204, Comment 3. Moreover, if the collateral consists of a securities account or commodity account, a description of the account is sufficient to cover all existing and future security entitlements or commodity contracts carried in the account. See Section 9-203(h), (i).

Under Section 9-204, an after-acquired collateral clause in a security agreement will not reach future commercial tort claims. It follows that when an effective security agreement (or amendment) covering a commercial tort claim as original collateral is entered into the claim already will exist. Subsection (e) does not require a description to be specific, so long as it extends beyond the "type." For example, a description such as "all tort claims arising out of the explosion of debtor's factory" would suffice, even if the exact amount of the claim, the theory on which it may be based, and the identity of the tortfeasor(s) are not described. (Indeed, those facts may not be known at the time.)

The enhanced specificity (beyond the "type") that subsection (e) requires does not apply to the attachment of security interests in commercial tort claims or collateral in consumer transactions that are identifiable proceeds of other collateral. A security interest automatically attaches to such property under Sections 9-203(f) and 9-315(a)(2). This point is confirmed by Section 9-204(b.1).

[SUBPART 2. APPLICABILITY OF ARTICLE]

Section 9-109. Scope

(a) [General scope of article.] Except as otherwise provided in subsections (c) and (d), this article applies to:

(1) a transaction, regardless of its form, that creates a security interest in personal property or fixtures by contract;

(2) an agricultural lien;

(3) a sale of accounts, chattel paper, payment intangibles, or promissory notes;

(4) a consignment;

(5) a security interest arising under Section 2-401, 2-505, 2-711(3), or 2A-508(5), as provided in Section 9-110; and

(6) a security interest arising under Section 4-210 or 5-118.

(b) [Security interest in secured obligation.] The application of this article to a security interest in a secured obligation is not affected by the fact that the obligation is itself secured by a transaction or interest to which this article does not apply.

(c) [Extent to which article does not apply.] This article does not apply to the extent that:

(1) a statute, regulation, or treaty of the United States preempts this article;

(2) another statute of this State expressly governs the creation, perfection, priority, or enforcement of a security interest created by this State or a governmental unit of this State;

(3) a statute of another State, a foreign country, or a governmental unit of another State or a foreign country, other than a statute generally applicable to security interests, expressly governs creation, perfection, priority, or enforcement of a security interest created by the State, country, or governmental unit; or

(4) the rights of a transferee beneficiary or nominated person under a letter of credit are independent and superior under Section 5-114.

(d) [Inapplicability of article.] This article does not apply to:

(1) a landlord's lien, other than an agricultural lien;

(2) a lien, other than an agricultural lien, given by statute or other rule of law for services or materials, but Section 9-333 applies with respect to priority of the lien;

(3) an assignment of a claim for wages, salary, or other compensation of an employee;

(4) a sale of accounts, chattel paper, payment intangibles, or promissory notes as part of a sale of the business out of which they arose;

(5) an assignment of accounts, chattel paper, payment intangibles, or promissory notes which is for the purpose of collection only;

(6) an assignment of a right to payment under a contract to an assignee that is also obligated to perform under the contract;

(7) an assignment of a single account, payment intangible, or promissory note to an assignee in full or partial satisfaction of a preexisting indebtedness;

(8) a transfer of an interest in or an assignment of a claim under a policy of insurance, other than an assignment by or to a health-care provider of a health-care-insurance receivable and any subsequent assignment of the right to payment, but Sections

9-315 and 9-322 apply with respect to proceeds and priorities in proceeds;

(9) an assignment of a right represented by a judgment, other than a judgment taken on a right to payment that was collateral;

(10) a right of recoupment or set-off, but:

(A) Section 9-340 applies with respect to the effectiveness of rights of recoupment or set-off against deposit accounts; and

(B) Section 9-404 applies with respect to defenses or claims of an account debtor;

(11) the creation or transfer of an interest in or lien on real property, including a lease or rents thereunder, except to the extent that provision is made for:

(A) liens on real property in Sections 9-203 and 9-308;

(B) fixtures in Section 9-334;

(C) fixture filings in Sections 9-501, 9-502, 9-512, 9-516, and 9-519; and

(D) security agreements covering personal and real property in Section 9-604;

(12) an assignment of a claim arising in tort, other than a commercial tort claim, but Sections 9-315 and 9-322 apply with respect to proceeds and priorities in proceeds; or

(13) an assignment of a deposit account in a consumer transaction, but Sections 9-315 and 9-322 apply with respect to proceeds and priorities in proceeds.

Definitional Cross References:

Account	Section 9-102(a)(2)
Account debtor	Section 9-102(a)(3)
Agricultural lien	Section 9-102(a)(5)
Beneficiary	Section 5-102(a)(3)
Chattel paper	Section 9-102(a)(11)
Collateral	Section 9-102(a)(12)
Commercial tort claim	Section 9-102(a)(13)
Consignment	Section 9-102(a)(20)
Consumer transaction	Section 9-102(a)(26)
Contract	Section 1-201(b)(12)
Deposit account	Section 9-102(a)(29)
Fixture filing	Section 9-102(a)(40)
Fixtures	Section 9-102(a)(41)
Governmental unit	Section 9-102(a)(45)
Health-care-insurance receivable	Section 9-102(a)(46)
Lease	Section 2A-103(1)(j)
Letter of credit	Section 5-102(a)(10)
Nominated person	Section 5-102(a)(11)
Payment intangible	Section 9-102(a)(61)
Proceeds	Section 9-102(a)(64)
Promissory note	Section 9-102(a)(65)
Right	Section 1-201(b)(34)
Sale	Section 2-106(1)
Security agreement	Section 9-102(a)(74)
Security interest	Section 1-201(b)(35)
State	Section 9-102(a)(77)

Official Comment

1. Source. Former Sections 9-102, 9-104.

2. Basic Scope Provision. Subsection (a)(1) derives from former Section 9-102(1) and (2). These subsections have been combined and shortened. No change in meaning is intended. Under subsection (a)(1), all consensual security interests in personal property and fixtures are covered by this Article, except for transactions excluded by subsections (c) and (d). As to which transactions give rise to a "security interest," the definition of that term in Section 1-201(b)(35) must be consulted. When a security interest is created, this Article applies regardless of the form of the transaction or the name that parties have given to it. Likewise, the subjective intention of the parties with respect to the legal characterization of their transaction is irrelevant to whether this Article applies, as it was to the application of former Article 9 under the proper interpretation of former Section 9-102.

3. Agricultural Liens. Subsection (a)(2) is new. It expands the scope of this Article to cover agricultural liens, as defined in Section 9-102.

4. Sales of Accounts, Chattel Paper, Payment Intangibles, Promissory Notes, and Other Receivables. Under subsection (a)(3), as under former Section 9-102, this Article applies to sales of accounts and chattel paper. This approach generally has been successful in avoiding difficult problems of distinguishing between transactions in which a receivable secures an obligation and those in which the receivable has been sold outright. In many commercial financing transactions the distinction is blurred.

Subsection (a)(3) added by the 1998 Revisions, expanded the scope of this Article by including the sale of a "payment intangible" (defined in Section 9-102 as "a general intangible under which the account debtor's principal obligation is a monetary obligation") and a "promissory note" (also defined in Section 9-102). To a considerable extent, this Article affords these transactions treatment identical to that given sales of accounts and chattel paper. In some respects, however, sales of payment intangibles and promissory notes are treated differently from sales of other receivables. See, e.g., Sections 9-309 (automatic perfection upon attachment), 9-408 (effect of restrictions on assignment). By virtue of the 1998 expanded definition of "account" (defined in Section 9-102), this Article covers sales of (and other security interests in) "health-care-insurance receivables" (also defined in Section 9-102). Although this Article occasionally distinguishes between outright sales of receivables and sales that secure an obligation, neither this Article nor the definition of "security interest" (Section 1-201(b)(35)) delineates how a particular transaction is to be classified. That issue is left to the courts.

5. Transfer of Ownership in Sales of Receivables. A "sale" of an account, chattel paper, a promissory note, or a payment intangible includes a sale of a right in the receivable, such as a sale of a participation interest. The term also includes the sale of an enforcement right. For example, a "[p]erson entitled to enforce" a negotiable promissory note (Section 3-301) may sell its ownership rights in the instrument. See Section 3-203, Comment 1 ("Ownership rights in instruments may be determined by principles of the law of property, independent of Article 3, which do not depend upon whether the instrument was transferred under Section 3-203."). Also, the right under Section 3-309 to enforce a lost, destroyed, or stolen negotiable promissory note may be sold to a purchaser who could enforce that right by causing the seller to provide the proof required under that section. This Article rejects decisions reaching a contrary result, e.g., *Dennis Joslin Co. v. Robinson Broadcasting*, 977 F. Supp. 491 (D.D.C. 1997).

Nothing in this section or any other provision of Article 9 prevents the transfer of full and complete ownership of an account, chattel paper, an instrument, or a payment intangible in a transaction of sale. However, as mentioned in Comment 4, neither this Article nor the definition of "security interest" in Section 1-201(b)(35) provides rules for distinguishing sales transactions from those that create a security interest securing an obligation. This Article applies to both types of transactions. The principal effect of this coverage is to apply this Article's perfection and priority rules to these sales transactions. Use of terminology such as "security interest," "debtor," and "collateral" is merely a drafting convention adopted to reach this end, and its use has no relevance to distinguishing sales from other transactions. See PEB Commentary No. 14.

Following a debtor's outright sale and transfer of ownership of a receivable, the debtor-seller retains no legal or equitable rights in the receivable that has been sold. See Section 9-318(a). This is so whether or not the buyer's security interest is perfected. (A security interest arising from the sale of a promissory note or payment intangible is perfected upon attachment without further action. See Section 9-309.) However, if the buyer's interest in accounts or chattel paper is unperfected, a subsequent lien creditor, perfected secured party, or qualified buyer can reach the sold receivable and achieve priority over (or take free of) the buyer's unperfected security interest under Section 9-317. This is so not because the seller of a receivable retains rights in the property sold; it does not. Nor is this so because the seller of a receivable is a "debtor" and the buyer of a receivable is a "secured party" under this Article (they are). It is so for the simple reason that Sections 9-318(b), 9-317, and 9-322 make it so, as did former Sections 9-301 and 9-312. Because the buyer's security interest is unperfected, for purposes of determining the rights of creditors of and purchasers for value from the debtor-seller, under Section 9-318(b) the debtor-seller is deemed to have the rights and title it sold. Section 9-317 subjects the buyer's unperfected interest in accounts and chattel paper to that of the debtor-seller's lien creditor and other persons who qualify under that section.

6. Consignments. Subsection (a)(4) was added by the 1998 Revisions. This Article applies to every "consignment." The term, defined in Section 9-102, includes many but not all "true" consignments (i.e., bailments for the purpose of sale). If a transaction is a "sale or return," as defined in revised Section 2-326, it is not a "consignment." In a "sale or return" transaction, the buyer becomes the owner of the goods, and the seller may obtain an enforceable security interest in the goods only by satisfying the requirements of Section 9-203.

Under common law, creditors of a bailee were unable to reach the interest of the bailor (in the case of a consignment, the consignor-owner). Like former Section 2-326 and former Article 9, this Article changes the common-law result; however, it does so in a different manner. For purposes of determining the rights and interests of third-party creditors of, and purchasers of the goods from, the consignee, but not for other purposes, such as remedies of the consignor, the consignee is deemed to acquire under this Article whatever rights and title the consignor had or had power to transfer. See Section 9-319. The interest of a consignor is defined to be a security interest under revised Section 1-201(b)(35), more specifically, a purchase-money security interest in the consignee's inventory. See Section 9-103(d). Thus, the rules pertaining to lien creditors, buyers, and attachment, perfection, and priority of competing security interests apply to consigned goods. The relationship between the consignor and consignee is left to other law. Consignors also have no duties under Part 6. See Section 9-601(g).

Sometimes parties characterize transactions that secure an obligation (other than the bailee's obligation to returned bailed goods) as "consignments." These transactions are not "consignments" as contemplated by Section 9-109(a)(4). See Section 9-102. This Article applies also to these transactions, by virtue of Section 9-109(a)(1). They create a security interest within the meaning of the first sentence of Section 1-201(b)(35).

This Article does not apply to a bailment for sale that falls outside the definition of "consignment" in Section 9-102. See PEB Commentary No. 20, dated January 24, 2019.

7. Security Interest in Obligation Secured by Non-Article 9 Transaction. Subsection (b) is unchanged in substance from former Section 9-102(3). The following example provides an illustration.

> **Example 1:** O borrows $10,000 from M and secures its repayment obligation, evidenced by a promissory note, by granting to M a mortgage on O's land. This Article does not apply to the creation of the real-property mortgage. However, if M sells the promissory note to X or gives a security interest in the note to secure M's own obligation to X, this Article applies to the security interest thereby created in favor of X. The security interest in the promissory note is covered by this Article even though the note is secured by a real-property mortgage. Also, X's security interest in the note gives X an attached security interest in the mortgage lien that secures the note and, if the security interest in the note is perfected, the security interest in the mortgage lien likewise is perfected. See Sections 9-203, 9-308.

It also follows from subsection (b) that an attempt to obtain or perfect a security interest in a secured obligation by complying with non-Article 9 law, as by an assignment of record of a real-property mortgage, would be ineffective. Finally, it is implicit from subsection (b) that one cannot obtain a security interest in a lien, such as a mortgage on real property, that is not also coupled with an equally effective security interest in the secured obligation. This Article rejects cases such as *In re Maryville Savings & Loan Corp.*, 743 F.2d 413 (6th Cir. 1984), clarified on reconsideration, 760 F.2d 119 (1985).

8. Federal Preemption. Former Section 9-104(a) excluded from Article 9 "a security interest subject to any statute of the United States, to the extent that such statute governs the rights of parties to and third parties affected by transactions in particular types of property." Some (erroneously) read the former section to suggest that Article 9 sometimes deferred to federal law even when federal law did not preempt Article 9. Subsection (c)(1) recognizes explicitly that this Article defers to federal law only when and to the extent that it must—i.e., when federal law preempts it.

9. Governmental Debtors. Former Section 9-104(e) excluded transfers by governmental debtors. It has been revised and replaced by the exclusions in new paragraphs (2) and (3) of subsection (c). These paragraphs reflect the view that Article 9 should apply to security interests created by a State, foreign country, or a "governmental unit" (defined in Section 9-102) of either except to the extent that another statute governs the issue in question. Under paragraph (2), this Article defers to all statutes of the forum State. (A forum cannot determine whether it should consult the choice-of-law rules in the forum's UCC unless it first determines that its UCC applies to the transaction before it.) Paragraph (3) defers to statutes of another State or a foreign country only to the extent that those statutes contain rules applicable specifically to security interests created by the governmental unit in question.

Example 2: A New Jersey state commission creates a security interest in favor of a New York bank. The validity of the security interest is litigated in New York. The relevant security agreement provides that it is governed by New York law. To the extent that a New Jersey statute contains rules peculiar to creation of security interests by governmental units generally, to creation of security interests by state commissions, or to creation of security interests by this particular state commission, then that law will govern. On the other hand, to the extent that New Jersey law provides that security interests created by governmental units, state commissions, or this state commission are governed by the law generally applicable to secured transactions (i.e., New Jersey's Article 9), then New York's Article 9 will govern.

Example 3: An airline that is an instrumentality of a foreign country creates a security interest in favor of a New York bank. The analysis used in the previous example would apply here. That is, if the matter is litigated in New York, New York law would govern except to the extent that the foreign country enacted a statute applicable to security interests created by governmental units generally or by the airline specifically.

The fact that New York law applies does not necessarily mean that perfection is accomplished by filing in New York. Rather, it means that the court should apply New York's Article 9, including its choice-of-law provisions. Under New York's Section 9-301, perfection is governed by the law of the jurisdiction in which the debtor is located. Section 9-307 determines the debtor's location for choice-of-law purposes.

If a transaction does not bear an appropriate relation to the forum State, then that State's Article 9 will not apply, regardless of whether the transaction would be excluded by paragraph (3).

Example 4: A Belgian governmental unit grants a security interest in its equipment to a Swiss secured party. The equipment is located in Belgium. A dispute arises and, for some reason, an action is brought in a New Mexico state court. Inasmuch as the transaction bears no "appropriate relation" to New Mexico, New Mexico's UCC, including its Article 9, is inapplicable. See Section 1-301(b). New Mexico's Section 9-109(c) on excluded transactions should not come into play. Even if the parties agreed that New Mexico law would govern, the parties' agreement would not be effective because the transaction does not bear a "reasonable relation" to New Mexico. See Section 1-301(a).

Conversely, Article 9 will come into play only if the litigation arises in a UCC jurisdiction or if a foreign choice-of-law rule leads a foreign court to apply the law of a UCC jurisdiction. For example, if issues concerning a security interest granted by a foreign airline to a New York bank are litigated overseas, the court may be bound to apply the law of the debtor's jurisdiction and not New York's Article 9.

10. Certain Statutory and Common-Law Liens; Interests in Real Property. With few exceptions (nonconsensual agricultural liens being one), this Article applies only to consensual security interests in personal property. Following former Section 9-104(b) and (j), paragraphs (1) and (11) of subsection (d) exclude landlord's liens and leases and most other interests in or liens on real property. These exclusions generally reiterate the limitations on coverage (i.e., "by contract," "in personal property and fixtures") made explicit in subsection (a)(1). Similarly, most jurisdictions provide special liens to suppliers of many types of services and materials, either by statute or by common law. With the exception of agricultural liens, it is not necessary for this Article to provide general codification of this lien structure, which is determined in large part by local conditions and which is far removed from ordinary commercial financing. As under former Section 9-104(c), subsection (d)(2) excludes these suppliers' liens (other than agricultural liens) from this Article. However, Section 9-333 provides a rule for determining priorities between certain possessory suppliers' liens and security interests covered by this Article.

11. Wage and Similar Claims. As under former Section 9-104(d), subsection (d)(3) excludes assignments of claims for wages and the like from this Article. These assignments present important social issues that other law addresses. The

Federal Trade Commission has ruled that, with some exceptions, the taking of an assignment of wages or other earnings is an unfair act or practice under the Federal Trade Commission Act. See 16 C.F.R. Part 444. State statutes also may regulate such assignments.

12. Certain Sales and Assignments of Receivables; Judgments. In general this Article covers security interests in (including sales of) accounts, chattel paper, payment intangibles, and promissory notes. Paragraphs (4), (5), (6), and (7) of subsection (d) exclude from the Article certain sales and assignments of receivables that, by their nature, do not concern commercial financing transactions. These paragraphs add to the exclusions in former Section 9-104(f) analogous sales and assignments of payment intangibles and promissory notes. For similar reasons, subsection (d)(9) retains the exclusion of assignments of judgments under former Section 9-104(h) (other than judgments taken on a right to payment that itself was collateral under this Article).

13. Insurance. Subsection (d)(8) narrows somewhat the broad exclusion of interests in insurance policies under former Section 9-104(g). This Article now covers assignments by or to a health-care provider of "health-care-insurance receivables" (defined in Section 9-102).

14. Set-Off. Subsection (d)(10) adds two exceptions to the general exclusion of set-off rights from Article 9 under former Section 9-104(i). The first takes account of new Section 9-340, which regulates the effectiveness of a set-off against a deposit account that stands as collateral. The second recognizes Section 9-404, which affords the obligor on an account, chattel paper, or general intangible the right to raise claims and defenses against an assignee (secured party).

15. Tort Claims. Subsection (d)(12) narrows somewhat the broad exclusion of transfers of tort claims under former Section 9-104(k). This Article now applies to assignments of "commercial tort claims" (defined in Section 9-102) as well as to security interests in tort claims that constitute proceeds of other collateral (e.g., a right to payment for negligent destruction of the debtor's inventory). Note that once a claim arising in tort has been settled and reduced to a contractual obligation to pay, the right to payment becomes a payment intangible and ceases to be a claim arising in tort.

This Article contains two special rules governing creation of a security interest in tort claims. First, a description of collateral in a security agreement as "all tort claims" is insufficient to meet the requirement for attachment. See Section 9-108(e). Second, no security interest attaches under an after-acquired property clause to a tort claim. See Section 9-204(b). In addition, this Article does not determine whom the tortfeasor must pay to discharge its obligation. Inasmuch as a tortfeasor is not an "account debtor," the rules governing waiver of defenses and discharge of an obligation by an obligor (Sections 9-403, 9-404, 9-405, and 9-406) are inapplicable to tort-claim collateral.

16. Deposit Accounts. Except in consumer transactions, deposit accounts may be taken as original collateral under this Article. Under former Section 9-104(*l*), deposit accounts were excluded as original collateral, leaving security interests in deposit accounts to be governed by the common law. The common law is nonuniform, often difficult to discover and comprehend, and frequently costly to implement. As a consequence, debtors who wished to use deposit accounts as collateral sometimes were precluded from doing so as a practical matter. By excluding deposit accounts from the Article's scope as original collateral in consumer transactions, subsection (d)(13) leaves those transactions to law other than this Article. However, in both consumer and non-consumer transactions, Sections 9-315 and 9-322 apply to deposit accounts as proceeds and with respect to priorities in proceeds.

This Article contains several safeguards to protect debtors against inadvertently encumbering deposit accounts and to reduce the likelihood that a secured party will realize a windfall from a debtor's deposit accounts. For example, because "deposit account" is a separate type of collateral, a security agreement covering general intangibles will not adequately describe deposit accounts. Rather, a security agreement must reasonably identify the deposit accounts that are the subject of a security interest, e.g., by using the term "deposit accounts." See Section 9-108.

To perfect a security interest in a deposit account as original collateral, a secured party (other than the bank with which the deposit account is maintained) must obtain "control" of the account either by obtaining the bank's signed agreement or by becoming the bank's customer with respect to the deposit account. See Sections 9-312(b)(1), 9-104. Either of these steps requires the debtor's consent.

This Article also contains new rules that determine which State's law governs perfection and priority of a security interest in a deposit account (Section 9-304), priority of conflicting security interests in and set-off rights against a deposit account (Sections 9-327, 9-340), the rights of transferees of funds from an encumbered deposit account (Section 9-332), the obligations of the bank (Section 9-341), enforcement of security interests in a deposit account (Section 9-607(c)), and the duty of a secured party to terminate control of a deposit account (Section 9-208(b)).

Section 9-110. Security Interests Arising under Article 2 or 2A

A security interest arising under Section 2-401, 2-505, 2-711(3), or 2A-508(5) is subject to this article. However, until the debtor obtains possession of the goods:

(1) the security interest is enforceable, even if Section 9-203(b)(3) has not been satisfied;

(2) filing is not required to perfect the security interest;

(3) the rights of the secured party after default by the debtor are governed by Article 2 or 2A; and

(4) the security interest has priority over a conflicting security interest created by the debtor.

Definitional Cross References:

Debtor	Section 9-102(a)(28)
Goods	Section 9-102(a)(44)
Right	Section 1-201(b)(34)
Secured party	Section 9-102(a)(73)
Security interest	Section 1-201(b)(35)

Official Comments

1. Source. Former Section 9-113.

2. Background. Former Section 9-113, from which this section derives, referred generally to security interests "arising solely under the Article on Sales (Article 2) or the Article on Leases (Article 2A)." Views differed as to the precise scope of that section. In contrast, Section 9-110 specifies the security interests to which it applies.

3. Security Interests Under Articles 2 and 2A. Section 2-505 explains how a seller of goods may reserve a security interest in them. Section 2-401 indicates that a reservation of title by the seller of goods, despite delivery to the buyer, is limited to reservation of a security interest. As did former Article 9, this Article governs a security interest arising solely under one of those sections; however, until the buyer obtains possession of the goods, the security interest is enforceable even in the absence of a security agreement, filing is not necessary to perfect the security interest, and the seller-secured party's rights on the buyer's default are governed by Article 2.

Sections 2-711(3) and 2A-508(5) create a security interest in favor of a buyer or lessee in possession of goods that were rightfully rejected or as to which acceptance was justifiably revoked. As did former Article 9, this Article governs a security interest arising solely under one of those sections; however, until the seller or lessor obtains possession of the goods, the security interest is enforceable even in the absence of a security agreement, filing is not necessary to perfect the security interest, and the secured party's (buyer's or lessee's) rights on the debtor's (seller's or lessor's) default are governed by Article 2 or 2A, as the case may be.

4. Priority. This section adds to former Section 9-113 a priority rule. Until the debtor obtains possession of the goods, a security interest arising under one of the specified sections of Article 2 or 2A has priority over conflicting security interests created by the debtor. Thus, a security interest arising under Section 2-401 or 2-505 has priority over a conflicting security interest in the buyer's after-acquired goods, even if the goods in question are inventory. Arguably, the same result would obtain under Section 9-322, but even if it would not, a purchase-money-like priority is appropriate. Similarly, a security interest under Section 2-711(3) or 2A-508(5) has priority over security interests claimed by the seller's or lessor's secured lender. This result is appropriate, inasmuch as the payments giving rise to the debt secured by the Article 2 or 2A security interest are likely to be included among the lender's proceeds.

Example: Seller owns equipment subject to a security interest created by Seller in favor of Lender. Buyer pays for the equipment, accepts the goods, and then justifiably revokes acceptance. As long as Seller does not recover possession of the equipment, Buyer's security interest under Section 2-711(3) is senior to that of Lender.

In the event that a security interest referred to in this section conflicts with a security interest that is created by a person other than the debtor, Section 9-325 applies. Thus, if Lender's security interest in the example was created not by Seller but by the person from whom Seller acquired the goods, Section 9-325 would govern.

5. Relationship to Other Rights and Remedies Under Articles 2 and 2A. This Article does not specifically address the conflict between (i) a security interest created by a buyer or lessee and (ii) the seller's or lessor's right to withhold delivery under Section 2-702(1), 2-703(a), or 2A-525, the seller's or lessor's right to stop delivery under Section 2-705 or 2A-526, or the seller's right to reclaim under Section 2-507(2) or 2-702(2). These conflicts are governed by the first sentence of Section 2-403(1), under which the buyer's secured party obtains no greater rights in the goods than the buyer had or had power to convey, or Section 2A-307(1), under which creditors of the lessee take subject to the lease contract.

PART 2. EFFECTIVENESS OF SECURITY AGREEMENT; ATTACHMENT OF SECURITY INTEREST; RIGHTS OF PARTIES TO SECURITY AGREEMENT

[SUBPART 1. EFFECTIVENESS AND ATTACHMENT]

Section 9-201. General Effectiveness of Security Agreement

(a) [General effectiveness.] Except as otherwise provided in [the Uniform Commercial Code], a security agreement is effective according to its terms between the parties, against purchasers of the collateral, and against creditors.

(b) [Applicable consumer laws and other law.] A transaction subject to this article is subject to any applicable rule of law which establishes a different rule for consumers and [insert reference to (i) any other statute or regulation that regulates the rates, charges, agreements, and practices for loans, credit sales, or other extensions of credit and (ii) any consumer-protection statute or regulation].

(c) [Other applicable law controls.] In case of conflict between this article and a rule of law, statute, or regulation described in subsection (b), the rule of law, statute, or regulation controls. Failure to comply with a statute or regulation described in subsection (b) has only the effect the statute or regulation specifies.

(d) [Further deference to other applicable law.] This article does not:

(1) validate any rate, charge, agreement, or practice that violates a rule of law, statute, or regulation described in subsection (b); or

(2) extend the application of the rule of law, statute, or regulation to a transaction not otherwise subject to it.

Definitional Cross References:

Agreement	Section 1-201(b)(3)
Collateral	Section 9-102(a)(12)
Creditor	Section 1-201(b)(13)
Purchaser	Section 1-201(b)(30)
Sale	Section 2-106(1)
Security agreement	Section 9-102(a)(74)
Term	Section 1-201(b)(40)

Official Comment

1. Source. Former Sections 9-201, 9-203(4).

2. Effectiveness of Security Agreement. Subsection (a) provides that a security agreement is generally effective. With certain exceptions, a security agreement is effective between the debtor and secured party and is likewise effective against third parties. Note that "security agreement" is used here (and elsewhere in this Article) as it is defined in Section 9-102: "an agreement that creates or provides for a security interest." It follows that subsection (a) does not provide that every term or provision contained in a record that contains a security agreement or that is so labeled is effective. Properly read, former Section 9-201 was to the same effect. Exceptions to the general rule of subsection (a) arise where there is an overriding provision in this Article or any other Article of the UCC. For example, Section 9-317 subordinates unperfected security interests to lien creditors and certain buyers, and several provisions in Part 3 subordinate some security interests to other security interests and interests of purchasers.

3. Law, Statutes, and Regulations Applicable to Certain Transactions. Subsection (b) makes clear that certain transactions, although subject to this Article, also are subject to other applicable laws relating to consumers or specified in that subsection. Subsection (c) provides that the other law is controlling in the event of a conflict, and that a violation of other law does not *ipso facto* constitute a violation of this Article. Subsection (d) provides that this Article does not validate violations under or extend the application of the other applicable laws.

Section 9-202. Title to Collateral Immaterial

Except as otherwise provided with respect to consignments or sales of accounts, chattel paper, payment intangibles, or promissory notes, the provisions of this article with regard to rights and obligations apply whether title to collateral is in the secured party or the debtor.

Definitional Cross References:

Account	Section 9-102(a)(2)
Chattel paper	Section 9-102(a)(11)
Collateral	Section 9-102(a)(12)
Consignment	Section 9-102(a)(20)
Debtor	Section 9-102(a)(28)
Payment intangible	Section 9-102(a)(61)
Promissory note	Section 9-102(a)(65)
Right	Section 1-201(b)(34)
Sale	Section 2-106(1)
Secured party	Section 9-102(a)(73)

Official Comment

1. Source. Former Section 9-202.

2. Title Immaterial. The rights and duties of parties to a secured transaction and affected third parties are provided in this Article without reference to the location of "title" to the collateral. For example, the characteristics of a security interest that secures the purchase price of goods are the same whether the secured party appears to have retained title or the debtor appears to have obtained title and then conveyed title or a lien to the secured party.

3. When Title Matters.

a. Under This Article. This section explicitly acknowledges two circumstances in which the effect of certain Article 9 provisions turns on ownership (title). First, in some respects sales of accounts, chattel paper, payment intangibles, and promissory notes receive special treatment. See, e.g., Sections 9-207(a), 9-210(b), 9-615(e). Buyers of receivables under former Article 9 were treated specially, as well. See, e.g., former Section 9-502(2). Second, the remedies of a consignor under a true consignment and, for the most part, the remedies of a buyer of accounts, chattel paper, payment intangibles, or promissory notes are determined by other law and not by Part 6. See Section 9-601(g).

b. Under Other Law. This Article does not determine which line of interpretation (e.g., title theory or lien theory, retained title or conveyed title) should be followed in cases in which the applicability of another rule of law depends upon who has title. If, for example, a revenue law imposes a tax on the "legal" owner of goods or if a corporation law makes a vote of the stockholders prerequisite to a corporation "giving" a security interest but not if it acquires property "subject" to a security interest, this Article does not attempt to define whether the secured party is a "legal" owner or whether the transaction "gives" a security interest for the purpose of such laws. Other rules of law or the agreement of the parties determines the location and source of title for those purposes.

Section 9-203. Attachment and Enforceability of Security Interest; Proceeds; Supporting Obligations; Formal Requisites

(a) [Attachment.] A security interest attaches to collateral when it becomes enforceable against the debtor with respect to the collateral, unless an agreement expressly postpones the time of attachment.

(b) [Enforceability.] Except as otherwise provided in subsections (c) through (i), a security interest is enforceable against the debtor and third parties with respect to the collateral only if:

(1) value has been given;

(2) the debtor has rights in the collateral or the power to transfer rights in the collateral to a secured party; and

(3) one of the following conditions is met:

(A) the debtor has signed a security agreement that provides a description of the collateral and, if the security interest covers timber to be cut, a description of the land concerned;

(B) the collateral is not a certificated security and is in the possession of the secured party under Section 9-313 pursuant to the debtor's security agreement;

(C) the collateral is a certificated security in registered form and the security certificate has been delivered to the secured party under Section 8-301 pursuant to the debtor's security agreement;

(D) the collateral is controllable accounts, controllable electronic records, controllable payment intangibles, deposit accounts, electronic documents, electronic money, investment property, or letter-of-credit rights, and the secured party has control under Sections 7-106, 9-104, 9-105A, 9-106, 9-107, or 9-107A pursuant to the debtor's security agreement.

(E) the collateral is chattel paper and the secured party has possession and control under Section 9-314A pursuant to the debtor's security agreement.

(c) [Other UCC provisions.] Subsection (b) is subject to Section 4-210 on the security interest of a collecting bank, Section 5-118 on the security interest of a letter-of-credit issuer or nominated person, Section 9-110 on a security interest arising under Article 2 or 2A, and Section 9-206 on security interests in investment property.

(d) [When person becomes bound by another person's security agreement.] A person becomes bound as debtor by a security agreement entered into by another person if, by operation of law other than this article or by contract:

(1) the security agreement becomes effective to create a security interest in the person's property; or

(2) the person becomes generally obligated for the obligations of the other person, including the obligation secured under the security agreement, and acquires or succeeds to all or substantially all of the assets of the other person.

(e) [Effect of new debtor becoming bound.] If a new debtor becomes bound as debtor by a security agreement entered into by another person:

(1) the agreement satisfies subsection (b)(3) with respect to existing or after-acquired property of the new debtor to the extent the property is described in the agreement; and

(2) another agreement is not necessary to make a security interest in the property enforceable.

(f) [Proceeds and supporting obligations.] The attachment of a security interest in collateral gives the secured party the rights to proceeds provided by Section 9-315 and is also attachment of a security interest in a supporting obligation for the collateral.

(g) [Lien securing right to payment.] The attachment of a security interest in a right to payment or performance secured by a security interest or other lien on personal or real property is also attachment of a security interest in the security interest, mortgage, or other lien.

(h) [Security entitlement carried in securities account.] The attachment of a security interest in a securities account is also attachment of a security interest in the security entitlements carried in the securities account.

(i) [Commodity contracts carried in commodity account.] The attachment of a security interest in a commodity account is also attachment of a security interest in the commodity contracts carried in the commodity account.

Definitional Cross References:

Agreement	Section 1-201(b)(3)
Bank	Section 9-102(a)(8)
Certificated security	Section 8-102(a)(4)
Chattel paper	Section 9-102(a)(11)
Collateral	Section 9-102(a)(12)
Commodity account	Section 9-102(a)(14)
Commodity contract	Section 9-102(a)(15)
Contract	Section 1-201(b)(12)
Controllable account	Section 9-102(a)(27A)
Controllable electronic record	Section 12-102(a)(1)
Controllable payment intangible	Section 9-102(a)(27B)

Debtor	Section 9-102(a)(28)
Deposit account	Section 9-102(a)(29)
Document	Section 9-102(a)(30)
Electronic	Section 1-201(b)(16A)
Electronic money	Section 9-102(a)(31A)
Investment property	Section 9-102(a)(49)
Issuer (letter of credit/ letter-of-credit right)	Section 5-102(a)(9)
Letter-of-credit right	Section 9-102(a)(51)
Money	Section 9-102(a)(54A)
Mortgage	Section 9-102(a)(55)
New debtor	Section 9-102(a)(56)
Nominated person	Section 5-102(a)(11)
Proceeds	Section 9-102(a)(64)
Right	Section 1-201(b)(34)
Secured party	Section 9-102(a)(73)
Securities account	Section 8-501(a)
Security agreement	Section 9-102(a)(74)
Security certificate	Section 8-102(a)(16)
Security entitlement	Section 8-102(a)(17)
Security interest	Section 1-201(b)(35)
Sign	Section 1-201(b)(37)
Supporting obligation	Section 9-102(a)(78)
Value	Section 1-204

Comment References:
9-107 C5
9-108 C5
9-206 C4
9-322 C6

Official Comment

1. Source. Former Sections 9-203, 9-115(2), (6).

2. Creation, Attachment, and Enforceability. Subsection (a) states the general rule that a security interest attaches to collateral only when it becomes enforceable against the debtor. Subsection (b) specifies the circumstances under which a security interest becomes enforceable. Subsection (b) states three basic prerequisites to the existence of a security interest: value (paragraph (1)), rights or power to transfer rights in collateral (paragraph (2)), and agreement plus satisfaction of an evidentiary requirement (paragraph (3)). When all of these elements exist, a security interest becomes enforceable between the parties and attaches under subsection (a). Subsection (c) identifies certain exceptions to the general rule of subsection (b).

3. Security Agreement; Signed. Under subsection (b)(3), enforceability requires the debtor's security agreement and compliance with an evidentiary requirement in the nature of a Statute of Frauds. Paragraph (3)(A) represents the most basic of the evidentiary alternatives, under which the debtor must sign a security agreement that provides a description of the collateral. Under Section 9-102, a "security agreement" is "an agreement that creates or provides for a security interest." Neither that definition nor the requirement of paragraph (3)(A) rejects the deeply rooted doctrine that a bill of sale, although absolute in form, may be shown in fact to have been given as security. Under this Article, as under prior law, a debtor may show by parol evidence that a transfer purporting to be absolute was in fact for security. Similarly, a self-styled "lease" may serve as a security agreement if the agreement creates a security interest. See Section 1-203 (distinguishing security interest from lease). Consistent with the revised definition of "sign" in Section 1-201(b)(37), the cognate terms "signed" and "signing" replace the references to "authenticated" and "authentication" in the pre-2022 text of this Section.

4. Possession, Delivery, or Control Pursuant to Security Agreement. The other alternatives in subsection (b)(3) dispense with the requirement of a signed security agreement and provide alternative evidentiary tests. Under paragraph (3)(B), the secured party's possession substitutes for the debtor's signed security agreement under paragraph (3)(A) if the secured party's possession is "pursuant to the debtor's security agreement." That phrase refers to the debtor's agreement to the secured party's possession in connection with the creation of a security interest. The phrase should not be confused with the phrase "debtor has signed a security agreement," used in paragraph (3)(A), which contemplates the debtor's signing of a record. In the unlikely event that possession is obtained without the debtor's agreement, possession would not suffice as a substitute for a signed security agreement. However, once the security interest has become enforceable and has attached, it is not impaired by the fact that the secured party's possession is maintained without the agreement of a subsequent debtor (e.g., a transferee). Possession as contemplated by Section 9-313 is possession for purposes of subsection (b)(3)(B), even though it may not constitute possession "pursuant to the debtor's agreement" and consequently might not serve as a substitute for a signed security agreement under subsection (b)(3)(A). Subsection (b)(3)(C) provides that delivery of a certificated security to the secured party under Section 8-301 pursuant to the debtor's security agreement is sufficient as a substitute for a signed security agreement. Similarly, under subsection (b)(3)(D), control of controllable accounts, controllable electronic records, controllable payment intangibles, deposit accounts, electronic documents, electronic money, investment property, or letter-of-credit rights satisfies the evidentiary test if control is pursuant to the debtor's security agreement, and under subsection (b)(3)(E), possession and control of chattel paper under Section 9-314A satisfies the evidentiary test if pursuant to the debtor's security agreement.

5. Collateral Covered by Other Statute or Treaty. One evidentiary purpose of the formal requisites stated in subsection (b) is to minimize the possibility of future disputes as to the terms of a security agreement (e.g., as to the property that stands as collateral for the obligation secured). One should distinguish the evidentiary functions of the formal requisites of attachment and enforceability (such as the requirement that a security agreement contain a description of the collateral) from the more limited goals of "notice filing" for financing statements under Part 5, explained in Section 9-502, Comment 2. When perfection is achieved by compliance with the requirements of a statute or treaty described in Section 9-311(a), such as a federal recording act or a certificate-of-title statute, the manner of describing the collateral in a registry imposed by the statute or treaty may or may not be adequate for purposes of this section and Section 9-108. However, the description contained in the security agreement, not the description in a public registry or on a certificate of title, controls for purposes of this section.

6. Debtor's Rights; Debtor's Power to Transfer Rights. Subsection (b)(2) conditions attachment on the debtor's having "rights in the collateral or the power to transfer rights in the collateral to a secured party." A debtor's limited rights in collateral, short of full ownership, are sufficient for a security interest to attach. However, in accordance with basic personal property conveyancing principles, the baseline rule is that a security interest attaches only to whatever rights a debtor may have, broad or limited as those rights may be.

Certain exceptions to the baseline rule enable a debtor to transfer, and a security interest to attach to, greater rights than the debtor has. See Part 3, Subpart 3 (priority rules). The phrase, "or the power to transfer rights in the collateral to a secured party," accommodates those exceptions. Thus, when a debtor engages in two transactions and each transaction, if considered separately from the other, would create an enforceable security interest in the same item of property, the effect of each transaction on the other is determined by the priority rules in Sections 9-322 et seq. and the rights of the secured party in the second transaction are not limited solely because, as a result of the first transaction, the rights of the debtor in the collateral were diminished.

> **Example 1**: On February 1, A files a financing statement covering a certain item of Debtor's equipment. At that time, Debtor has not granted to A a security interest in the equipment. On March 1, B makes a loan to Debtor secured by a security interest in the same equipment and files a financing statement covering the equipment. On April 1, A makes a loan to Debtor and Debtor signs a security agreement granting A a security interest in the item of equipment. A's security interest is enforceable and has attached and, under the priority rules of Section 9-322, has priority over that of B. This is the case even though, after March 1, Debtor's rights in the equipment were diminished by the security interest granted to B. The reason is that Debtor had "the power to transfer" greater rights in the equipment than Debtor had.

> **Example 2**: On February 1, A files a financing statement covering certain of Debtor's accounts. At that time, Debtor has not granted to A a security interest in the accounts. On March 1, Debtor sells the accounts to B (creating a security interest in them) and B files a financing statement covering the accounts. On April 1, A makes a loan to Debtor and Debtor signs a security agreement granting A a security interest in the accounts. A's security interest is enforceable and has attached and, under the priority rules of Section 9-322, has priority over that of B. This is the case even though, after March 1, Debtor no longer had rights in the accounts (see Section 9-318), because Debtor had "the power to transfer" greater rights in the accounts than Debtor had.

See PEB Commentary No. 29, dated February 27, 2025. The Commentary is available at https://www.ali.org/peb-ucc.

In some cases, a debtor may have power to transfer another person's rights only to a class of transferees that excludes secured parties. See, e.g., Section 2-403(2) (giving certain merchants power to transfer an entruster's rights to a buyer in ordinary course of business). Under those circumstances, the debtor would not have the power to create a security interest in the other person's rights, and the condition in subsection (b)(2) would not be satisfied.

7. New Debtors. Subsection (e) makes clear that the enforceability requirements of subsection (b)(3) are met when a new debtor becomes bound under an original debtor's security agreement. If a new debtor becomes bound as debtor by a security agreement entered into by another person, the security agreement satisfies the requirement of subsection (b)(3) as to the existing and after-acquired property of the new debtor to the extent the property is described in the agreement.

Subsection (d) explains when a new debtor becomes bound. Persons who become bound under paragraph (2) are limited to those who both become primarily liable for the original debtor's obligations and succeed to (or acquire) its assets. Thus, the paragraph excludes sureties and other secondary obligors as well as persons who become obligated through veil piercing and other non-successorship doctrines. In many cases, paragraph (2) will exclude successors to the assets and liabilities of a division of a debtor. See also Section 9-508, Comment 3.

8. Proceeds and Supporting Obligations. Under subsection (f), attachment of a security interest in original collateral also is attachment of a security interest in identifiable proceeds as provided in Section 9-315(a)(2). It is not necessary for a security agreement to mention "proceeds" or otherwise to describe collateral consisting of proceeds. See also Section 9-108, Comment 5. Also under subsection (f), a security interest in a "supporting obligation" (defined in Section 9-102) automatically follows from a security interest in the underlying, supported collateral. This result was implicit under pre-1998 Article 9. Implicit in subsection (f) is the principle that the secured party's interest in a supporting obligation extends to the supporting obligation only to the extent that it supports the collateral in which the secured party has a security interest. Complex issues may arise, however, if a supporting obligation supports many separate obligations of a particular account debtor and if the supported obligations are separately assigned as security to several secured parties. The problems may be exacerbated if a supporting obligation is limited to an aggregate amount that is less than the aggregate amount of the obligations it supports. This Article does not contain provisions dealing with competing claims to a limited supporting obligation. As under pre-1998 Article 9, the law of suretyship and the agreements of the parties will control.

9. Collateral Follows Right to Payment or Performance. Subsection (g) codifies the common-law rule that a transfer of an obligation secured by a security interest or other lien on personal or real property also transfers the security interest or lien. See Restatement (3d), Property (Mortgages) rule that a transfer of an obligation secured by a security interest or other lien on personal or real property also transfers the security interest or lien. See Restatement (3d), Property (Mortgages) § 5.4(a) (1997). See also Section 9-308(e) (analogous rule for perfection).

10. Investment Property. Subsections (h) and (i) make clear that attachment of a security interest in a securities account or commodity account is also attachment in security entitlements or commodity contracts carried in the accounts.

Section 9-204. After-acquired Property; Future Advances

(a) [After-Acquired Collateral.] Except as otherwise provided in subsection (b), a security agreement may create or provide for a security interest in after-acquired collateral.

(b) [When after-acquired property clause not effective.] Subject to subsection (b.1), a security interest does not attach under a term constituting an after-acquired property clause to:

(1) consumer goods, other than an accession when given as additional security, unless the debtor acquires rights in them within 10 days after the secured party gives value; or

(2) a commercial tort claim.

(b.1) [Limitation on subsection (b).] Subsection (b) does not prevent a security interest from attaching:

(1) to consumer goods as proceeds under Section 9-315(a) or commingled goods under Section 9-336(c);

(2) to a commercial tort claim as proceeds under Section 9-315(a); or

(3) under an after-acquired property clause to property that is proceeds of consumer goods or a commercial tort claim.

(c) [Future advances and other value.] A security agreement may provide that collateral secures, or that accounts, chattel paper, payment intangibles, or promissory notes are sold in connection with, future advances or other value, whether or not the advances or value are given pursuant to commitment.

Definitional Cross References:

Accession	Section 9-102(a)(1)
Account	Section 9-102(a)(2)
Chattel paper	Section 9-102(a)(11)
Collateral	Section 9-102(a)(12)
Commercial tort claim	Section 9-102(a)(13)
Consumer goods	Section 9-102(a)(23)
Debtor	Section 9-102(a)(28)
Goods	Section 9-102(a)(44)
Payment intangible	Section 9-102(a)(61)
Proceeds	Section 9-102(a)(64)
Promissory note	Section 9-102(a)(65)
Pursuant to commitment	Section 9-102(a)(69)
Right	Section 1-201(b)(34)
Secured party	Section 9-102(a)(73)
Security agreement	Section 9-102(a)(74)
Security interest	Section 1-201(b)(35)
Term	Section 1-201(b)(40)
Value	Section 1-204

Comment References:
9-108 C5
9-109 C15

Official Comment

1. Source. Former Section 9-204.

2. After-Acquired Property; Continuing General Lien. Subsection (a) makes clear that a security interest arising by virtue of an after-acquired property clause is no less valid than a security interest in collateral in which the debtor has rights at the time value is given. A security interest in after-acquired property is not merely an "equitable" interest; no further action by the secured party — such as a supplemental agreement covering the new collateral — is required. This section adopts the principle of a "continuing general lien" or "floating lien." It validates a security interest in the debtor's existing and (upon acquisition) future assets, even though the debtor has liberty to use or dispose of collateral without being required to account for proceeds or substitute new collateral. See Section 9-205. Subsection (a), together with subsection (c), also validates "cross-collateral" clauses under which collateral acquired at any time secures advances whenever made.

3. After-Acquired Consumer Goods. Subsection (b)(1) makes ineffective an after-acquired property clause covering consumer goods (defined in Section 9-102(a)(23)), except as accessions (see Section 9-335), acquired more than 10 days after the secured party gives value. Subsection (b)(1) is unchanged in substance from the corresponding provision in pre-1998 Section 9-204(2). However, a term granting a security interest in consumer goods that will be purchase-money collateral in the transaction is not "a term constituting an after-acquired property clause." Consequently, subsection (b)(1) does not prevent the security interest from attaching to the purchase-money collateral even if the collateral is not an accession and the debtor acquires rights in the collateral more than 10 days after the secured party gives value.

4. Commercial Tort Claims. Subsection (b)(2) provides that an after-acquired property clause in a security agreement does not reach future commercial tort claims. In order for a security interest in a tort claim as original collateral to attach, the claim must be in existence when the security agreement is signed. In addition, the security agreement must describe the tort claim with greater specificity than simply "all tort claims." See Section 9-108(e).

4A. Proceeds and Commingled Goods. Subsection (b.1) clarifies and makes explicit what is implicit in the pre-2022 text of subsection (b). Subsection (b) does not prevent a security interest from attaching to consumer goods as proceeds or as commingled goods, to commercial tort claims as proceeds, or under an after-acquired property clause to proceeds of consumer goods or commercial tort claims. This clarification corrects and rejects the erroneous holdings of several cases addressing commercial tort claims that are proceeds. As to proceeds, this result also follows from Section 9-203(f).

5. Future Advances; Obligations Secured. Under subsection (c) collateral may secure future as well as past or present advances if the security agreement so provides. This is in line with the policy of this Article toward security interests in after-acquired property under subsection (a). Indeed, the parties are free to agree that a security interest secures any obligation whatsoever. Determining the obligations secured by collateral is solely a matter of construing the parties' agreement under applicable law. This Article rejects the holdings of cases decided under former Article 9 that applied other tests, such as whether a future advance or other subsequently incurred obligation was of the same or a similar type or class as earlier advances and obligations secured by the collateral.

6. Sales of Receivables. Subsections (a) and (c) expressly validate after-acquired property and future advance clauses not only when the transaction is for security purposes but also when the transaction is the sale of accounts, chattel paper, payment intangibles, or promissory notes. This result was implicit under former Article 9.

7. Financing Statements. The effect of after-acquired property and future advance clauses as components of a security agreement should not be confused with the requirements applicable to financing statements under this Article's system of perfection by notice filing. The references to after-acquired property clauses and future advance clauses in this section are limited to security agreements. There is no need to refer to after-acquired property or future advances or other obligations secured in a financing statement. See Section 9-502, Comment 2.

Section 9-205. Use or Disposition of Collateral Permissible

(a) [When security interest not invalid or fraudulent.] A security interest is not invalid or fraudulent against creditors solely because:

(1) the debtor has the right or ability to:

(A) use, commingle, or dispose of all or part of the collateral, including returned or repossessed goods;

(B) collect, compromise, enforce, or otherwise deal with collateral;

(C) accept the return of collateral or make repossessions; or

(D) use, commingle, or dispose of proceeds; or

(2) the secured party fails to require the debtor to account for proceeds or replace collateral.

(b) [Requirements of possession not relaxed.] This section does not relax the requirements of possession if attachment, perfection, or enforcement of a security interest depends upon possession of the collateral by the secured party.

Definitional Cross References:

Collateral	Section 9-102(a)(12)
Creditor	Section 1-201(b)(12)
Debtor	Section 9-102(a)(28)
Goods	Section 9-102(a)(44)
Proceeds	Section 9-102(a)(64)
Security interest	Section 1-201(b)(35)
Secured party	Section 9-102(a)(73)
Security agreement	Section 9-102(a)(74)

Official Comment

1. Source. Former Section 9-205.

2. Validity of Unrestricted "Floating Lien." This Article expressly validates the "floating lien" on shifting collateral. See Sections 9-201, 9-204 and Comment 2. This section provides that a security interest is not invalid or fraudulent by reason of the debtor's liberty to dispose of the collateral without being required to account to the secured party for proceeds or substitute new collateral. As did former Section 9-205, this section repeals the rule of *Benedict v. Ratner,* 268 U.S. 353 (1925), and other cases which held such arrangements void as a matter of law because the debtor was given unfettered dominion or control over collateral. The *Benedict* rule did not effectively discourage or eliminate security transactions in inventory and receivables. Instead, it forced financing arrangements to be self-liquidating. Although this section repeals *Benedict,* the filing and other perfection requirements (see Part 3, Subpart 2, and Part 5) provide for public notice that overcomes any potential misleading effects of a debtor's use and control of collateral. Moreover, nothing in this section prevents the debtor and secured party from agreeing to procedures by which the secured party polices or monitors collateral or to restrictions on the debtor's dominion. However, this Article leaves these matters to agreement based on business considerations, not on legal requirements.

3. Possessory Security Interests. Subsection (b) makes clear that this section does not relax the requirements for perfection by possession under Section 9-313. If a secured party allows the debtor access to and control over collateral its security interest may be or become unperfected.

4. Permissible Freedom for Debtor to Enforce Collateral. Former Section 9-205 referred to a debtor's "liberty . . . to collect or compromise accounts or chattel paper." This section recognizes the broader rights of a debtor to "enforce," as well as to "collect" and "compromise" collateral. This section's reference to collecting, compromising, and enforcing "collateral" instead of "accounts or chattel paper" contemplates the many other types of collateral that a debtor may wish to "collect, compromise, or enforce": e.g., deposit accounts, documents, general intangibles, instruments, investment property, and letter-of-credit rights.

Section 9-206. Security Interest Arising in Purchase or Delivery of Financial Asset

(a) [Security interest when person buys through securities intermediary.] A security interest in favor of a securities intermediary attaches to a person's security entitlement if:

(1) the person buys a financial asset through the securities intermediary in a transaction in which the person is obligated to pay the purchase price to the securities intermediary at the time of the purchase; and

(2) the securities intermediary credits the financial asset to the buyer's securities account before the buyer pays the securities intermediary.

(b) [Security interest secures obligation to pay for financial asset.] The security interest described in subsection (a) secures the person's obligation to pay for the financial asset.

(c) [Security interest in payment against delivery transaction.] A security interest in favor of a person that delivers a certificated security or other financial asset represented by a writing attaches to the security or other financial asset if:

(1) the security or other financial asset:

(A) in the ordinary course of business is transferred by delivery with any necessary indorsement or assignment; and

(B) is delivered under an agreement between persons in the business of dealing with such securities or financial assets; and

(2) the agreement calls for delivery against payment.

(d) [Security interest secures obligation to pay for delivery.] The security interest described in subsection (c) secures the obligation to make payment for the delivery.

Definitional Cross References:

Agreement	Section 1-201(b)(3)
Certificated security	Section 8-102(a)(4)
Delivery	Section 1-201(b)(15)
Financial asset	Section 8-102(a)(9)
Purchase	Section 1-201(b)(29)
Securities account	Section 8-501(a)
Securities intermediary	Section 8-102(a)(14)
Security entitlement	Section 8-102(a)(17)
Security interest	Section 1-201(b)(35)
Security	Section 8-102(a)(15)
Writing	Section 1-201(b)(43)

Official Comment

1. Source. Former 9-116.

2. Codification of "Broker's Lien." Depending upon a securities intermediary's arrangements with its entitlement holders, the securities intermediary may treat the entitlement holder as entitled to financial assets before the entitlement holder has actually made payment for them. For example, many brokers permit retail customers to pay for financial assets by check. The broker may not receive final payment of the check until several days after the broker has credited the customer's securities account for the financial assets. Thus, the customer will have acquired a security entitlement prior to payment. Subsection (a) provides that, in such circumstances, the securities intermediary has a security interest in the entitlement holder's security entitlement. Under subsection (b) the security interest secures the customer's obligation to pay for the financial asset in question. Subsections (a) and (b) codify and adapt to the indirect holding system the so-called "broker's lien," which has long been recognized. See Restatement, Security § 12.

3. Financial Assets Delivered Against Payment. Subsection (c) creates a security interest in favor of persons who deliver certificated securities or other financial assets in physical form, such as money market instruments, if the agreed payment is not received. In some arrangements for settlement of transactions in physical financial assets, the seller's securities custodian will deliver physical certificates to the buyer's securities custodian and receive a time-stamped delivery receipt. The buyer's securities custodian will examine the certificate to ensure that it is in good order, and that the delivery matches a trade in which the buyer has instructed the seller to deliver to that custodian. If all is in order, the receiving custodian will settle with the delivering custodian through whatever funds settlement system has been agreed upon or is used by custom and usage in that market. The understanding of the trade, however, is that the delivery is conditioned upon payment, so that if payment is not made for any reason, the security will be returned to the deliverer. Subsection (c) clarifies the rights of persons making deliveries in such circumstances. It provides the person making delivery with a security interest in the securities or other financial assets; under subsection (d), the security interest secures the seller's right to receive payment for the delivery. Section 8-301 specifies when delivery of a certificated security occurs; that section should be applied as well to other financial assets as well for purposes of this section.

4. Automatic Attachment and Perfection. Subsections (a) and (c) refer to attachment of a security interest. Attachment under this section has the same incidents (enforceability, right to proceeds, etc.) as attachment under Section 9-203. This section overrides the general attachment rules in Section 9-203. See Section 9-203(c). A securities intermediary's security interest under subsection (a) is perfected by control without further action. See Section 8-106 (control); 9-314 (perfection). Security interests arising under subsection (b) are automatically perfected. See Section 9-309(9).

[SUBPART 2. RIGHTS AND DUTIES]

Section 9-207. Rights and Duties of Secured Party Having Possession or Control of Collateral

(a) [Duty of care when secured party in possession.] Except as otherwise provided in subsection (d), a secured party shall use reasonable care in the custody and preservation of collateral in the secured party's possession. In the case of chattel paper or an instrument, reasonable care includes taking necessary steps to preserve rights against prior parties unless otherwise agreed.

(b) [Expenses, risks, duties, and rights when secured party in possession.] Except as otherwise provided in subsection (d), if a secured party has possession of collateral:

(1) reasonable expenses, including the cost of insurance and payment of taxes or other charges, incurred in the custody, preservation, use, or operation of the collateral are chargeable to the debtor and are secured by the collateral;

(2) the risk of accidental loss or damage is on the debtor to the extent of a deficiency in any effective insurance coverage;

(3) the secured party shall keep the collateral identifiable, but fungible collateral may be commingled; and

(4) the secured party may use or operate the collateral:

(A) for the purpose of preserving the collateral or its value;

(B) as permitted by an order of a court having competent jurisdiction; or

(C) except in the case of consumer goods, in the manner and to the extent agreed by the debtor.

(c) [Duties and rights when secured party in possession or control.] Except as otherwise provided in subsection (d), a secured party having possession of collateral or control of collateral under Sections 7-106, 9-104, 9-105, 9-105A, 9-106, 9-107, or 9-107A:

(1) may hold as additional security any proceeds, except money or funds, received from the collateral;

(2) shall apply money or funds received from the collateral to reduce the secured obligation, unless remitted to the debtor; and

(3) may create a security interest in the collateral.

(d) [Buyer of certain rights to payment.] If the secured party is a buyer of accounts, chattel paper, payment intangibles, or promissory notes or a consignor:

(1) subsection (a) does not apply unless the secured party is entitled under an agreement:

(A) to charge back uncollected collateral; or

(B) otherwise to full or limited recourse against the debtor or a secondary obligor based on the nonpayment or other default of an account debtor or other obligor on the collateral; and

(2) subsections (b) and (c) do not apply.

Definitional Cross References:

Account	Section 9-102(a)(2)
Account debtor	Section 9-102(a)(3)
Agreement	Section 1-201(b)(3)
Chattel paper	Section 9-102(a)(11)
Collateral	Section 9-102(a)(12)
Consignor	Section 9-102(a)(21)
Consumer goods	Section 9-102(a)(23)
Debtor	Section 9-102(a)(28)
Fungible goods	Section 1-201(b)(18)
Instrument	Section 9-102(a)(47)
Money	Section 1-201(b)(24)
Obligor	Section 9-102(a)(59)
Payment intangible	Section 9-102(a)(61)
Proceeds	Section 9-102(a)(64)
Promissory note	Section 9-102(a)(65)
Right	Section 1-201(b)(34)
Secondary obligor	Section 9-102(a)(72)
Secured party	Section 9-102(a)(73)
Security interest	Section 1-201(b)(35)
Security	Section 8-102(a)(15)
Value	Section 1-204

Comment References: 9-208 C4

Official Comment

1. Source. Former Section 9-207.

2. Duty of Care for Collateral in Secured Party's Possession. Like former section 9-207, subsection (a) imposes a duty of care, similar to that imposed on a pledgee at common law, on a secured party in possession of collateral. See Restatement, Security §§ 17, 18. In many cases a secured party in possession of collateral may satisfy this duty by notifying the debtor of action that should be taken and allowing the debtor to take the action itself. If the secured party itself takes action, its reasonable expenses may be added to the secured obligation. The revised definitions of "collateral," "debtor," and "secured party" in Section 9-102 make this section applicable to collateral subject to an agricultural lien if the collateral is in the lienholder's possession. Under Section 1-302(b) the duty to exercise reasonable care may not be disclaimed by agreement, although under that section the parties remain free to determine by agreement standards that are not manifestly unreasonable as to what constitutes reasonable care. Unless otherwise agreed, for a secured party in possession of chattel paper or an instrument, reasonable care includes the preservation of rights against prior parties. The secured party's right to have instruments or documents indorsed or transferred to it or its order is dealt with in the relevant sections of Articles 3, 7, and 8. See Sections 3-203(c), 7-506, 8-304(d).

3. Specific Rules When Secured Party in Possession or Control of Collateral. Subsections (b) and (c) provide rules following common-law precedents which apply unless the parties otherwise agree. The rules in subsection (b) apply to typical issues that may arise while a secured party is in possession of collateral, including expenses, insurance, and taxes, risk of loss or damage, identifiable and fungible collateral, and use or operation of collateral. Subsection (c) contains rules that apply in certain circumstances that may arise when a secured party is in either possession or control of collateral. These circumstances include the secured party's receiving proceeds from the collateral and the secured party's creation of a security interest in the collateral.

4. Applicability Following Default. This section applies when the secured party has possession of collateral either before or after default. See Sections 9-601(b), 9-609. Subsection (b)(4)(C) limits agreements concerning the use or operation of collateral to collateral other than consumer goods. Under Section 9-602(1), a debtor cannot waive or vary that limitation.

5. "Repledges" and Right of Redemption. Subsection (c)(3) eliminates the qualification in former Section 9-207 to the effect that the terms of a "repledge" may not "impair" a debtor's "right to redeem" collateral. The change is primarily for clarification. There is no basis on which to draw from subsection (c)(3) any inference concerning the debtor's right to redeem the collateral. The debtor enjoys that right under Section 9-623; this section need not address it. For example, if the collateral is a negotiable note that the secured party (SP-1) repledges to SP-2, nothing in this section suggests that the debtor (D) does not retain the right to redeem the note upon payment to SP-1 of all obligations secured by the note. But, as explained below, the debtor's unimpaired right to redeem as against the debtor's original secured party nevertheless may not be enforceable as against the new secured party.

In resolving questions that arise from the creation of a security interest by SP-1, one must take care to distinguish D's rights against SP-1 from D's rights against SP-2. Once D discharges the secured obligation, D becomes entitled to the note; SP-1 has no legal basis upon which to withhold it. If, as a practical matter, SP-1 is unable to return the note because SP-2 holds it as collateral for SP-1's unpaid debt, then SP-1 is liable to D under the law of conversion.

Whether SP-2 would be liable to D depends on the relative priority of SP-2's security interest and D's interest. By permitting SP-1 to create a security interest in the collateral (repledge), subsection (c)(3) provides a statutory power for SP-1 to give SP-2 a security interest (subject, of course, to any agreement by SP-1 not to give a security interest). In the vast majority of cases where repledge rights are significant, the security interest of the second secured party, SP-2 in the example, will be senior to the debtor's interest. By virtue of the debtor's consent or applicable legal rules, SP-2 typically would cut off D's rights in investment property or be immune from D's claims. See Sections 9-331, 3-306 (holder in due course), 8-303 (protected purchaser), 8-502 (acquisition of a security entitlement), 8-503(e) (action by entitlement holder), 12-104 (qualifying purchaser). Moreover, the expectations and business practices in some markets, such as the securities markets, are such that D's consent to SP-2's taking free of D's rights inheres in D's creation of SP-1's security interest which gives rise to SP-1's power under this section. In these situations, D would have no right to recover the collateral or recover damages from SP-2. Nevertheless, D would have a damage claim against SP-1 if SP-1 had given a security interest to SP-2 in breach of its agreement with D. Moreover, if SP-2's security interest secures an amount that is less than the amount secured by SP-1's security interest (granted by D), then D's exercise of its right to redeem would provide value sufficient to discharge SP-1's obligations to SP-2.

For the most part this section does not change the law under former Section 9-207, although eliminating the reference to the debtor's right of redemption may alter the secured party's right to repledge in one respect. Former Section 9-207 could have been read to limit the secured party's statutory right to repledge collateral to repledge transactions in which the collateral did not secure a greater obligation than that of the original debtor. Inasmuch as this is a matter normally dealt with by agreement between the debtor and secured party, any change would appear to have little practical effect.

6. "Repledges" of Investment Property. The following example will aid the discussion of "repledges" of investment property.

> **Example:** Debtor grants Alpha Bank a security interest in a security entitlement that includes 1000 shares of XYZ Co. stock that Debtor holds through an account with Able & Co. Alpha does not have an account with Able. Alpha uses Beta Bank as its securities custodian. Debtor instructs Able to transfer the shares to Beta, for the account of Alpha, and Able does so. Beta then credits Alpha's account. Alpha has control of the security entitlement for the 1000 shares under Section 8-106(d). (These are the facts of Example 2, Section 8-106, Comment 4.) Although, as between Debtor and Alpha, Debtor may have become the beneficial owner of the new securities entitlement with Beta, Beta has agreed to act on Alpha's entitlement orders because, as between Beta and Alpha, Alpha has become the entitlement holder.
>
> Next, Alpha grants Gamma Bank a security interest in the security entitlement with Beta that includes the 1000 shares of XYZ Co. stock. In order to afford Gamma control of the entitlement, Alpha instructs Beta to transfer the stock to Gamma's custodian, Delta Bank, which credits Gamma's account for 1000 shares. At this point Gamma holds its securities entitlement for its benefit as well as that of its debtor, Alpha. Alpha's derivative rights also are for the benefit of Debtor.
>
> In many, probably most, situations and at any particular point in time, it will be impossible for Debtor or Alpha to "trace" Alpha's "repledge" to any particular securities entitlement or financial asset of Gamma or anyone else.

Debtor would retain, of course, a right to redeem the collateral from Alpha upon satisfaction of the secured obligation. However, in the absence of a traceable interest, Debtor would retain only a personal claim against Alpha in the event Alpha failed to restore the security entitlement to Debtor. Moreover, even in the unlikely event that Debtor could trace a property interest, in the context of the financial markets, normally the operation of this section, Debtor's explicit agreement to permit Alpha to create a senior security interest, or legal rules permitting Gamma to cut off Debtor's rights or become immune from Debtor's claims would effectively subordinate Debtor's interest to the holder of a security interest created by Alpha. And, under the shelter principle, all subsequent transferees would obtain interests to which Debtor's interest also would be subordinate.

7. Buyers of Chattel Paper and Other Receivables; Consignors. This section has been revised to reflect the fact that a seller of accounts, chattel paper, payment intangibles, or promissory notes retains no interest in the collateral and so is not disadvantaged by the secured party's noncompliance with the requirements of this section. Accordingly, subsection (d) provides that subsection (a) applies only to security interests that secure an obligation and to sales of receivables in which the buyer has recourse against the debtor. (Of course, a buyer of accounts or payment intangibles could not have "possession" of original collateral, but might have possession of proceeds, such as promissory notes or checks.) The meaning of "recourse" in this respect is limited to recourse arising out of the account debtor's failure to pay or other default.

Subsection (d) makes subsections (b) and (c) inapplicable to buyers of accounts, chattel paper, payment intangibles, or promissory notes and consignors. Of course, there is no reason to believe that a buyer of receivables or a consignor could not, for example, create a security interest or otherwise transfer an interest in the collateral, regardless of who has possession of the collateral. However, this section leaves the rights of those owners to law other than Article 9.

Section 9-208. Additional Duties of Secured Party Having Control of Collateral

(a) [Applicability of section.] This section applies to cases in which there is no outstanding secured obligation and the secured party is not committed to make advances, incur obligations, or otherwise give value.

(b) [Duties of secured party after receiving demand from debtor.] Within 10 days after receiving a signed demand by the debtor:

(1) a secured party having control of a deposit account under Section 9-104(a)(2) shall send to the bank with which the deposit account is maintained a signed record that releases the bank from any further obligation to comply with instructions originated by the secured party;

(2) a secured party having control of a deposit account under Section 9-104(a)(3) shall:

(A) pay the debtor the balance on deposit in the deposit account; or

(B) transfer the balance on deposit into a deposit account in the debtor's name;

(3) a secured party, other than a buyer, having control under Section 9-105 of an authoritative electronic copy of a record evidencing chattel paper shall transfer control of the electronic copy to the debtor or a person designated by the debtor;

(4) a secured party having control of investment property under Section 8-106(d)(2) or 9-106(b) shall send to the securities intermediary or commodity intermediary with which the security entitlement or commodity contract is maintained a signed record that releases the securities intermediary or commodity intermediary from any further obligation to comply with entitlement orders or directions originated by the secured party;

(5) a secured party having control of a letter-of-credit right under Section 9-107 shall send to each person having an unfulfilled obligation to pay or deliver proceeds of the letter of credit to the secured party a signed release from any further obligation to pay or deliver proceeds of the letter of credit to the secured party;

(6) a secured party having control under Section 7-106 of an authoritative electronic copy of an electronic document shall transfer control of the electronic copy to the debtor or a person designated by the debtor;

(7) a secured party having control under Section 9-105A of electronic money shall transfer control of the electronic money to the debtor or a person designated by the debtor; and

(8) a secured party having control under Section 12-105 of a controllable electronic record, other than a buyer of a controllable account or controllable payment intangible evidenced by the controllable electronic record, shall transfer control of the controllable electronic record to the debtor or a person designated by the debtor.

Definitional Cross References:

Action	Section 1-201(b)(1)
Bank	Section 9-102(a)(8)
Chattel paper	Section 9-102(a)(11)
Collateral	Section 9-102(a)(12)
Commodity contract	Section 9-102(a)(15)
Commodity intermediary	Section 9-102(a)(17)
Communicate	Section 9-102(a)(18)
Controllable account	Section 9-102(a)(27A)
Controllable electronic record	Section 12-102(a)(1)

Controllable payment intangible	Section 9-102(a)(27B)
Debtor	Section 9-102(a)(28)
Deposit account	Section 9-102(a)(29)
Document	Section 9-102(a)(30)
Electronic	Section 1-201(b)(16A)
Electronic money	Section 9-102(a)(31A)
Investment property	Section 9-102(a)(49)
Letter of credit	Section 5-102(a)(10)
Letter-of-credit right	Section 9-102(a)(51)
Person	Section 1-201(b)(27)
Proceeds	Section 9-102(a)(64)
Record	Section 9-102(a)(70)
Secured party	Section 9-102(a)(73)
Securities intermediary	Section 8-102(a)(14)
Security entitlement	Section 8-102(a)(17)
Send	Section 1-201(b)(36)
Sign	Section 1-201(b)(37)
Value	Section 1-204

Official Comment

1. Source. New.

2. Scope and Purpose. This section imposes duties on a secured party who has control of a deposit account, an electronic copy of a record evidencing chattel paper, investment property, a letter-of-credit right, an electronic document of title, electronic money, or a controllable electronic record. The duty to terminate the secured party's control is analogous to the duty to file a termination statement, imposed by Section 9-513. Under subsection (a), it applies only when there is no outstanding secured obligation and the secured party is not committed to give value. The requirements of this section can be varied by agreement under Section 1-302(a). For example, a debtor could by contract agree that the secured party may comply with subsection (b) by releasing control more than 10 days after demand. Also, duties under this section should not be read to conflict with the terms of the collateral itself. For example, if the collateral is a time deposit account, subsection (b)(2) should not require a secured party with control to make an early withdrawal of the funds (assuming that were possible) in order to pay them over to the debtor or put them in an account in the debtor's name.

Note that subsection (b)(8) addresses secured parties that have control of a controllable electronic record. That control may have been obtained for the purpose of perfecting a security interest in a controllable account or controllable payment intangible evidenced by the controllable electronic record, even if the secured party did not have a security interest in the controllable electronic record itself.

This section does not explicitly impose duties on a secured party whose control is based on the acknowledgment under Section 7-106(g), 9-104(a)(4), or 9-105A(e) or under 9-107A and 12-105(e) by another person having control. Such a secured party would have control only while the other, acknowledging person retains control. This result necessarily follows because such a secured party's control derives solely from the other person's continued control. See, e.g., Section 9-314, Comment 2. Upon compliance with this section by an acknowledging person having control, the control of a person having control through such person's acknowledgment would cease.

3. Remedy for Failure to Relinquish Control. If a secured party fails to comply with the requirements of subsection (b), the debtor has the remedy set forth in Section 9-625(e). This remedy is identical to that applicable to failure to provide or file a termination statement under Section 9-513.

4. Duty to Relinquish Possession. Although Section 9-207 addresses directly the duties of a secured party in possession of collateral, that section does not require the secured party to relinquish possession when the secured party ceases to hold a security interest. Under common law, absent agreement to the contrary, the failure to relinquish possession of collateral upon satisfaction of the secured obligation would constitute a conversion. Inasmuch as problems apparently have not surfaced in the absence of statutory duties under former Article 9 and the common-law duty appears to have been sufficient, this Article does not impose a statutory duty to relinquish possession.

5. "Signed Replaces "Authenticated." Consistent with the revised definition of "sign" in Section 1-201(b)(37), the cognate term "signed" replaces references to "authenticated" in the pre-2022 text of this section.

Section 9-209. Duties of Secured Party If Account Debtor Has Been Notified of Assignment

(a) [Applicability of section.] Except as otherwise provided in subsection (c), this section applies if:

(1) there is no outstanding secured obligation; and

(2) the secured party is not committed to make advances, incur obligations, or otherwise give value.

(b) [Duties of secured party after receiving demand from debtor.] Within 10 days after receiving a signed demand by the debtor, a secured party shall send to an account debtor that has received notification under Section 9-406(a) or 12-106(b) of an assignment to the secured party as assignee a signed record that releases the account debtor from any further obligation to the secured party.

(c) [Inapplicability to sales.] This section does not apply to an assignment constituting the sale of an account, chattel paper, or payment intangible.

Definitional Cross References:

Account	Section 9-102(a)(2)
Account debtor	Section 9-102(a)(3)
Chattel paper	Section 9-102(a)(11)
Debtor	Section 9-102(a)(28)
Payment intangible	Section 9-102(a)(61)
Record	Section 9-102(a)(70)

Sale	Section 2-106(1)
Secured party	Section 9-102(a)(73)
Send	Section 1-201(b)(36)
Sign	Section 1-201(b)(37)
Value	Section 1-204

Official Comment

1. Source. New.

2. Scope and Purpose. Like Sections 9-208 and 9-513, which require a secured party to relinquish control of collateral and to file or provide a termination statement for a financing statement, this section requires a secured party to free up collateral when there no longer is any outstanding secured obligation or any commitment to give value in the future. This section addresses the case in which account debtors have been notified to pay a secured party to whom the receivables have been assigned. It requires the secured party (assignee) to inform the account debtors that they no longer are obligated to make payment to the secured party. See subsection (b). It does not apply to account debtors whose obligations on an account, chattel paper, or payment intangible have been sold. See subsection (c).

3. "Signed" Replaces "Authenticated." Consistent with the revised definition of "sign" in Section 1-201(b)(37), the cognate term "signed" replaces references to "authenticated" in the pre-2022 text of this section.

Section 9-210. Request for Accounting; Request Regarding List of Collateral or Statement of Account

(a) [Definitions.] In this section:

(1) "Request" means a record of a type described in paragraph (2), (3), or (4).

(2) "Request for an accounting" means a record signed by a debtor requesting that the recipient provide an accounting of the unpaid obligations secured by collateral and reasonably identifying the transaction or relationship that is the subject of the request.

(3) "Request regarding a list of collateral" means a record signed by a debtor requesting that the recipient approve or correct a list of what the debtor believes to be the collateral securing an obligation and reasonably identifying the transaction or relationship that is the subject of the request.

(4) "Request regarding a statement of account" means a record signed by a debtor requesting that the recipient approve or correct a statement indicating what the debtor believes to be the aggregate amount of unpaid obligations secured by collateral as of a specified date and reasonably identifying the transaction or relationship that is the subject of the request.

(b) [Duty to respond to requests.] Subject to subsections (c), (d), (e), and (f), a secured party, other than a buyer of accounts, chattel paper, payment intangibles, or promissory notes or a consignor, shall comply with a request within 14 days after receipt:

(1) in the case of a request for an accounting, by signing and sending to the debtor an accounting; and

(2) in the case of a request regarding a list of collateral or a request regarding a statement of account, by signing and sending to the debtor an approval or correction.

(c) [Request regarding list of collateral; statement concerning type of collateral.] A secured party that claims a security interest in all of a particular type of collateral owned by the debtor may comply with a request regarding a list of collateral by sending to the debtor a signed record including a statement to that effect within 14 days after receipt.

(d) [Request regarding list of collateral; no interest claimed.] A person that receives a request regarding a list of collateral, claims no interest in the collateral when it receives the request, and claimed an interest in the collateral at an earlier time shall comply with the request within 14 days after receipt by sending to the debtor a signed record:

(1) disclaiming any interest in the collateral; and

(2) if known to the recipient, providing the name and mailing address of any assignee of or successor to the recipient's interest in the collateral.

(e) [Request for accounting or regarding statement of account; no interest in obligation claimed.] A person that receives a request for an accounting or a request regarding a statement of account, claims no interest in the obligations when it receives the request, and claimed an interest in the obligations at an earlier time shall comply with the request within 14 days after receipt by sending to the debtor a signed record:

(1) disclaiming any interest in the obligations; and

(2) if known to the recipient, providing the name and mailing address of any assignee of or successor to the recipient's interest in the obligations.

(f) [Charges for responses.] A debtor is entitled without charge to one response to a request under this section during any six-month period. The secured party may require payment of a charge not exceeding $25 for each additional response.

Definitional Cross References:

Account	Section 9-102(a)(2)
Accounting	Section 9-102(a)(4)
Chattel paper	Section 9-102(a)(11)
Collateral	Section 9-102(a)(12)
Consignor	Section 9-102(a)(21)
Debtor	Section 9-102(a)(28)
Payment intangible	Section 9-102(a)(61)

Promissory note	Section 9-102(a)(65)
Record	Section 9-102(a)(70)
Secured party	Section 9-102(a)(73)
Security interest	Section 1-201(b)(35)
Send	Section 9-102(a)(75)
Sign	Section 1-201(b)(37)

Official Comment

1. Source. Former Section 9-208.

2. Scope and Purpose. This section provides a procedure whereby a debtor may obtain from a secured party information about the secured obligation and the collateral in which the secured party may claim a security interest. It clarifies and resolves some of the issues that arose under former Section 9-208 and makes information concerning the secured indebtedness readily available to debtors, both before and after default. It applies to agricultural lien transactions (see the definitions of "debtor," secured party," and "collateral" in Section 9-102), but generally not to sales of receivables. See subsection (b).

3. Requests by Debtors Only. A financing statement filed under Part 5 may disclose only that a secured party may have a security interest in specified types of collateral. In most cases the financing statement will contain no indication of the obligation (if any) secured, whether any security interest actually exists, or the particular property subject to a security interest. Because creditors of and prospective purchasers from a debtor may have legitimate needs for more detailed information, it is necessary to provide a procedure under which the secured party will be required to provide information. On the other hand, the secured party should not be under a duty to disclose any details of the debtor's financial affairs to any casual inquirer or competitor who may inquire. For this reason, this section gives the right to request information to the debtor only. The debtor may submit a request in connection with negotiations with subsequent creditors and purchasers, as well as for the purpose of determining the status of its credit relationship or demonstrating which of its assets are free of a security interest.

4. Permitted Types of Requests for Information. Subsection (a) contemplates that a debtor may request three types of information by submitting three types of "requests" to the secured party. First, the debtor may request the secured party to prepare and send an "accounting" (defined in Section 9-102). Second, the debtor may submit to the secured party a list of collateral for the secured party's approval or correction. Third, the debtor may submit to the secured party for its approval or correction a statement of the aggregate amount of unpaid secured obligations. Inasmuch as a secured party may have numerous transactions and relationships with a debtor, each request must identify the relevant transactions or relationships. Subsections (b) and (c) require the secured party to respond to a request within 14 days following receipt of the request.

5. Recipients Claiming No Interest in the Transaction. A debtor may be unaware that a creditor with whom it has dealt has assigned its security interest or the secured obligation. Subsections (d) and (e) impose upon recipients of requests under this section the duty to inform the debtor that they claim no interest in the collateral or secured obligation, respectively, and to inform the debtor of the name and mailing address of any known assignee or successor. As under subsections (b) and (c), a response to a request under subsection (d) or (e) is due 14 days following receipt.

6. Waiver; Remedy for Failure to Comply. The debtor's rights under this section may not be waived or varied. See Section 9-602(2). Section 9-625 sets forth the remedies for noncompliance with the requirements of this section.

7. Limitation on Free Responses to Requests. Under subsection (f), during a six-month period a debtor is entitled to receive from the secured party one free response to a request. The debtor is not entitled to a free response to each type of request (i.e., three free responses) during a six-month period.

8. "Signed" and "Signing" Replaces "Authenticated" and "Authenticating." Consistent with the revised definition of "sign" in Section 1-201(b)(37), the cognate terms "signed" and "signing" replaces references to "authenticated" and "authenticating" in the pre-2022 text of this section.

PART 3. PERFECTION AND PRIORITY

[Subpart 1. Law Governing Perfection and Priority]

Section 9-301. Law Governing Perfection and Priority of Security Interests

Except as otherwise provided in Sections 9-303 through 9-306B, the following rules determine the law governing perfection, the effect of perfection or nonperfection, and the priority of a security interest in collateral:

(1) Except as otherwise provided in this section, while a debtor is located in a jurisdiction, the local law of that jurisdiction governs perfection, the effect of perfection or nonperfection, and the priority of a security interest in collateral.

(2) While collateral is located in a jurisdiction, the local law of that jurisdiction governs perfection, the effect of perfection or nonperfection, and the priority of a possessory security interest in that collateral.

(3) Except as otherwise provided in paragraph (4), while negotiable tangible documents, goods, instruments, or tangible money is located in a jurisdiction, the local law of that jurisdiction governs:

(A) perfection of a security interest in the goods by filing a fixture filing;

(B) perfection of a security interest in timber to be cut; and

(C) the effect of perfection or nonperfection and the priority of a nonpossessory security interest in the collateral.

(4) The local law of the jurisdiction in which the wellhead or minehead is located governs perfection, the effect of perfection or nonperfection, and the priority of a security interest in as-extracted collateral.

Definitional Cross References:

As-extracted collateral	Section 9-102(a)(6)
Collateral	Section 9-102(a)(12)
Debtor	Section 9-102(a)(28)
Document	Section 9-102(a)(30)
Fixture filing	Section 9-102(a)(40)
Goods	Section 9-102(a)(44)
Instrument	Section 9-102(a)(47)
Money	Section 9-102(a)(54A)
Security interest	Section 1-201(b)(35)
Tangible money	Section 9-102(a)(79A)

Official Comment

1. Source. Former Sections 9-103(1)(a), (b), 9-103(3)(a), (b), 9-103(5), substantially modified.

2. Scope of This Subpart. Part 3, Subpart 1 (Sections 9-301 through 9-307) contains choice-of-law rules similar to those of former Section 9-103. Former Section 9-103 generally addresses which State's law governs "perfection and the effect of perfection or non-perfection of" security interests. See, e.g., former Section 9-103(1)(b). This Article follows the broader and more precise formulation in former Section 9-103(6)(b), which was revised in connection with the promulgation of Revised Article 8 in 1994: "perfection, the effect of perfection or non-perfection, and the priority of" security interests. Priority, in this context, subsumes all of the rules in Part 3, including "cut off" or "take free" rules such as Sections 9-317(b), (c), and (d), 9-320(a), (b), and (d), and 9-332. The Hague Securities Convention may sometimes modify certain of this subpart's choice-of-law rules, as well as applying them to the requirements for foreclosure and the like, the characterization of a transfer as being outright or by way of security as it affects rights of third parties, and certain other issues. See Commentary No. 19, dated April 11, 2017. The Commentary is available at https://www.ali.org/peb-ucc.

This subpart does not address choice of law for other purposes. For example, the law applicable to issues such as attachment, validity, characterization of a transaction (e.g., true lease or security interest) as it affects rights between the parties to the transaction, and enforcement is governed by the rules in Section 1-301(a) and (b); that governing law typically is specified in the same agreement that contains the security agreement. And, another jurisdiction's law may govern other third-party matters addressed in this Article. See Section 9-401, Comment 3. As to the law applicable to characterization, see PEB Commentary No. 24, dated August 12, 2022. The Commentary is available at https://www.ali.org/peb-ucc.

3. Scope of Referral. In designating the jurisdiction whose law governs, this Article directs the court to apply only the substantive ("local") law of a particular jurisdiction and not its choice-of-law rules.

Example 1: Litigation over the priority of a security interest in accounts arises in State X. State X has adopted the official text of this Article, which provides that priority is determined by the local law of the jurisdiction in which the debtor is located. See Section 9-301(1). The debtor is located in State Y. Even if State Y has retained former Article 9 or enacted a nonuniform choice-of-law rule (e.g., one that provides that perfection is governed by the law of State Z), a State X court should look only to the substantive law of State Y and disregard State Y's choice-of-law rule. State Y's substantive law (e.g., its Section 9-501) provides that financing statements should be filed in a filing office in State Y. Note, however, that if the identical perfection issue were to be litigated in State Y, the court would look to State Y's former Section 9-103 or nonuniform 9-301 and conclude that a filing in State Y is ineffective.

Example 2: In the preceding Example, assume that State X has adopted the official text of this Article, and State Y has adopted a nonuniform Section 9-301(1) under which perfection is governed by the whole law of State X, including its choice-of-law rules. If litigation occurs in State X, the court should look to the substantive law of State Y, which provides that financing statements are to be filed in a filing office in State Y. If litigation occurs in State Y, the court should look to the law of State X, whose choice-of-law rule requires that the court apply the substantive law of State Y. Thus, regardless of the jurisdiction in which the litigation arises, the financing statement should be filed in State Y.

4. Law Governing Perfection: General Rule. Paragraph (1) contains the general rule: the law governing perfection of security interests in both tangible and intangible collateral, whether perfected by filing or automatically, is the law of the jurisdiction of the debtor's location, as determined under Section 9-307.

Paragraph (1) substantially simplifies the choice-of-law rules. Former Section 9-103 contained different choice-of-law rules for different types of collateral. Under Section 9-301(1), the law of a single jurisdiction governs perfection with respect to most types of collateral, both tangible and intangible. Paragraph (1) eliminates the need for former Section 9-103(1)(c), which concerned purchase-money security interests in tangible collateral that is intended to move from one jurisdiction to the other. It is likely to reduce the frequency of cases in which the governing law changes after a financing statement is properly filed. (Presumably, debtors change their own location less frequently than they change the location of their collateral.) The approach taken in paragraph (1) also eliminates some difficult priority issues and the need to distinguish between "mobile" and "ordinary" goods, and it reduces the number of filing offices in which secured parties must file or search when collateral is located in several jurisdictions.

5. Law Governing Perfection: Exceptions. The general rule is subject to several exceptions. It does not apply to goods covered by a certificate of title (see Section 9-303), deposit accounts (see Section 9-304), investment property (see Section 9-305), letter-of-credit rights (see Section 9-306), chattel paper (see Section 9-306A), or controllable accounts, controllable electronic records, or controllable payment intangibles (see Section 9-306B). Nor does it apply to possessory security interests, i.e., security interests that the secured party has perfected by taking possession of the collateral (see paragraph (2)), security interests perfected by filing a fixture filing (see paragraph (4)), security interests in timber to be cut (paragraph (5)), or security interests in as-extracted collateral (see paragraph (6)). No exception is made for electronic money and the general rule applies (unless preempted by federal law).

a. Possessory Security Interests. Paragraph (2) applies to possessory security interests and provides that perfection and priority is governed by the local law of the jurisdiction in which the collateral is located. This is the rule of pre-1998 Section 9-103(1)(b), except paragraph (2) eliminates the troublesome "last event" test of former law.

The distinction between nonpossessory and possessory security interests creates the potential for the same jurisdiction to apply two different choice-of-law rules to determine perfection in the same collateral. For example, were a secured party in possession of an instrument or a tangible document to relinquish possession in reliance on temporary perfection, the applicable law immediately would change from that of the location of the collateral to that of the location of the debtor. The applicability of two different choice-of-law rules for perfection is unlikely to lead to any material practical problems. The perfection rules of one Article 9 jurisdiction are likely to be identical to those of another. Moreover, under paragraph (3), the relative priority of competing security interests in tangible collateral is resolved by reference to the law of the jurisdiction in which the collateral is located, regardless of how the security interests are perfected.

b. Fixtures Filings. Under the general rule in paragraph (1), a security interest in fixtures may be perfected by filing in the office specified by Section 9-501(a) as enacted in the jurisdiction in which the debtor is located. However, application of this rule to perfection of a security interest by filing a fixture filing could yield strange results. For example, perfection of a security interest in fixtures located in Arizona and owned by a Delaware corporation would be governed by the law of Delaware. Although Delaware law would send one to a filing office in Arizona for the place to file a financing statement as a fixture filing, see Section 9-501, Delaware law would not take account of local, nonuniform, real-property filing and recording requirements that Arizona law might impose. For this reason, paragraph (3)(A) contains a special rule for security interests perfected by a fixture filing; the law of the jurisdiction in which the fixtures are located governs perfection, including the formal requisites of a fixture filing. Under paragraph (3)(C), the same law governs priority. Fixtures are "goods" as defined in Section 9-102.

The filing of a financing statement to perfect a security interest in collateral of a transmitting utility constitutes a fixture filing with respect to goods that are or become fixtures. See Section 9-501(b). Accordingly, to perfect a security interest in goods of this kind by a fixture filing, a financing statement must be filed in the office specified by Section 9-501(b) as enacted in the jurisdiction in which the goods are located. If the fixtures collateral is located in more than one State, filing in all of those States will be necessary to perfect a security interest in all the fixtures collateral by a fixture filing. Of course, a security interest in nearly all types of collateral (including fixtures) of a transmitting utility may be perfected by filing in the office specified by Section 9-501(b) as enacted in the jurisdiction in which the transmitting utility is located. However, such a filing will not be effective as a fixture filing except with respect to goods that are located in that jurisdiction.

c. Timber to Be Cut. Application of the general rule in paragraph (1) to perfection of a security interest in timber to be cut would yield undesirable results analogous to those described with respect to fixtures. Paragraph (3)(B) adopts a similar solution: perfection is governed by the law of the jurisdiction in which the timber is located. As with fixtures, under paragraph (3)(C), the same law governs priority. Timber to be cut also is "goods" as defined in Section 9-102.

Paragraph (3)(B) applies only to "timber to be cut," not to timber that has been cut. Consequently, once the timber is cut, the general choice-of-law rule in paragraph (1) becomes applicable. To ensure continued perfection, a secured party should file in both the jurisdiction in which the timber to be cut is located and in the state where the debtor is located. The former filing would be with the office in which a real property mortgage would be filed, and the latter would be a central filing. See Section 9-501.

d. As-Extracted Collateral. Paragraph (4) adopts the rule of former Section 9-103(5) with respect to certain security interests in minerals and related accounts. Like security interests in fixtures perfected by filing a fixture filing, security interests in minerals that are as-extracted collateral are perfected by filing in the office designated for the filing or recording of a mortgage on the real property. For the same reasons, the law governing perfection and priority is the law of the jurisdiction in which the wellhead or minehead is located.

6. Change in Law Governing Perfection. When the debtor changes its location to another jurisdiction, the jurisdiction whose law governs perfection under paragraph (1) changes, as well. Similarly, the law governing perfection of a possessory security interest in collateral under paragraph (2) changes when the collateral is removed to another jurisdiction. Nevertheless, these changes will not result in an immediate loss of perfection. See Section 9-316(a), (b).

7. Law Governing Effect of Perfection and Priority: Goods, Documents, Instruments, Money, Negotiable Documents, and Tangible Chattel Paper. Under former Section 9-103, the law of a single jurisdiction governed both questions of perfection and those of priority. This Article generally adopts that approach. See paragraph (1). But the approach may create problems if the debtor and collateral are located in different jurisdictions. For example, assume a security interest in equipment located in Pennsylvania is perfected by filing in Illinois, where the debtor is located. If the law of the jurisdiction in which the debtor is located were to govern priority, then the priority of an execution lien on goods located in Pennsylvania would be governed by rules enacted by the Illinois legislature.

To address this problem, paragraph (3)(C) divorces questions of perfection from questions of "the effect of perfection or nonperfection and the priority of a security interest." Under paragraph (3)(C), the rights of competing claimants to tangible collateral are resolved by reference to the law of the jurisdiction in which the collateral is located. A similar bifurcation applied to security interests in investment property under former Section 9-103(6). See Section 9-305.

Paragraph (3)(C) applies the law of the situs to determine priority only with respect to goods (including fixtures), instruments, money, negotiable tangible documents, and tangible chattel paper. Compare former Section 9-103(1), which applied the law of the location of the collateral to documents, instruments, and "ordinary" (as opposed to "mobile") goods. This Article does not distinguish among types of goods. The ordinary/mobile goods distinction appears to address concerns about where to file and search, rather than concerns about priority. There is no reason to preserve this distinction under the bifurcated approach.

Particularly serious confusion may arise when the choice-of-law rules of a given jurisdiction result in each of two competing security interests in the same collateral being governed by a different priority rule. The potential for this confusion existed under former Section 9-103(4) with respect to chattel paper: Perfection by possession was governed by the law of the location of the paper, whereas perfection by filing was governed by the law of the location of the debtor. Consider the mess that would have been created if the language or interpretation of former Section 9-308 were to differ in the two relevant States, or if one of the relevant jurisdictions (e.g., a foreign country) had not adopted Article 9. The potential for confusion could have been exacerbated when a secured party perfected both by taking possession in the State where the collateral is located (State A) and by filing in the State where the debtor is located (State B)—a common practice for some chattel paper financers. By providing that the law of the jurisdiction in which the collateral is located governs priority, paragraph (3) substantially diminishes this problem.

8. Non-U.S. Debtors. This Article applies the same choice-of-law rules to all debtors, foreign and domestic. For example, it adopts the bifurcated approach for determining the law applicable to security interests in goods and other tangible collateral. See Comment 5.a., above. The Article contains a new rule specifying the location of non-U.S. debtors for purposes of this Part. The rule appears in Section 9-307 and is explained in the Comments to that section. Pre-1998 Section 9-103(3)(c), which contained a special choice-of-law rule governing security interests created by debtors located in a non-U.S. jurisdiction, proved unsatisfactory and was deleted.

Section 9-302. Law Governing Perfection and Priority of Agricultural Liens

While farm products are located in a jurisdiction, the local law of that jurisdiction governs perfection, the effect of perfection or nonperfection, and the priority of an agricultural lien on the farm products.

Definitional Cross References:

Agricultural lien	Section 9-102(a)(5)
Farm products	Section 9-102(a)(34)

Official Comment

1. Source. New.

2. Agricultural Liens. This section provides choice-of-law rules for agricultural liens on farm products. Perfection, the effect of perfection or nonperfection, and priority all are governed by the law of the jurisdiction in which the farm products are located. Other choice-of-law rules, including Section 1-301, determine which jurisdiction's law governs other matters, such as the secured party's rights on default. See Section 9-301, Comment 2. Inasmuch as no agricultural lien on proceeds arises under this Article, this section does not expressly apply to proceeds of agricultural liens. However, if another statute creates an agricultural lien on proceeds, it may be appropriate for courts to apply the choice-of-law rule in this section to determine priority in the proceeds.

Section 9-303. Law Governing Perfection and Priority of Security Interests in Goods Covered by a Certificate of Title

(a) [Applicability of section.] This section applies to goods covered by a certificate of title, even if there is no other relationship between the jurisdiction under whose certificate of title the goods are covered and the goods or the debtor.

(b) [When goods covered by certificate of title.] Goods become covered by a certificate of title when a valid application for the certificate of title and the applicable fee are delivered to the appropriate authority. Goods cease to be covered by a certificate of title at the earlier of the time the certificate of title ceases to be effective under the law of the issuing jurisdiction or the time the goods become covered subsequently by a certificate of title issued by another jurisdiction.

(c) [Applicable law.] The local law of the jurisdiction under whose certificate of title the goods are covered governs perfection, the effect of perfection or nonperfection, and the priority of a security interest in goods covered by a certificate of title from the time the goods become covered by the certificate of title until the goods cease to be covered by the certificate of title.

Definitional Cross References:

Certificate of title	Section 9-102(a)(10)
Debtor	Section 9-102(a)(28)
Goods	Section 9-102(a)(44)
Security interest	Section 1-201(b)(35)

Official Comment

1. Source. Former Section 9-103(2)(a), (b), substantially revised.

2. Scope of This Section. This section applies to "goods covered by a certificate of title." The new definition of "certificate of title" in Section 9-102 makes clear that this section applies not only to certificate-of-title statutes under which perfection occurs upon notation of the security interest on the certificate but also to those that contemplate notation but provide that perfection is achieved by another method, e.g., delivery of designated documents to an official. Subsection (a), which is new, makes clear that this section applies to certificates of a jurisdiction having no other contacts with the goods or the debtor. This result comports with most of the reported cases on the subject and with contemporary business practices in the trucking industry.

3. Law Governing Perfection and Priority. Subsection (c) is the basic choice-of-law rule for goods covered by a certificate of title. Perfection and priority of a security interest are governed by the law of the jurisdiction under whose certificate of title the goods are covered from the time the goods become covered by the certificate of title until the goods cease to be covered by the certificate of title.

Normally, under the law of the relevant jurisdiction, the perfection step would consist of compliance with that jurisdiction's certificate-of-title statute and a resulting notation of the security interest on the certificate of title. See Section 9-311(b). In the typical case of an automobile or over-the-road truck, a person who wishes to take a security interest in the vehicle can ascertain whether it is subject to any security interests by looking at the certificate of title. But certificates of title cover certain types of goods in some States but not in others. A secured party who does not realize this may extend credit and attempt to perfect by filing in the jurisdiction in which the debtor is located. If the goods had been titled in another jurisdiction, the lender would be unperfected.

Subsection (b) explains when goods become covered by a certificate of title and when they cease to be covered. Goods may become covered by a certificate of title, even though no certificate of title has issued. Former Section 9-103(2)(b) provided that the law of the jurisdiction issuing the certificate ceases to apply upon "surrender" of the certificate. This Article eliminates the concept of "surrender." However, if the certificate is surrendered in conjunction with an appropriate application for a certificate to be issued by another jurisdiction, the law of the original jurisdiction ceases to apply because the goods became covered subsequently by a certificate of title from another jurisdiction. Alternatively, the law of the original jurisdiction ceases to apply when the certificate "ceases to be effective" under the law of that jurisdiction. Given the diversity in certificate-of-title statutes, the term "effective" is not defined.

4. Continued Perfection. The fact that the law of one State ceases to apply under subsection (b) does not mean that a security interest perfected under that law becomes unperfected automatically. In most cases, the security interest will remain perfected. See Section 9-316(d), (e). Moreover, a perfected security interest may be subject to defeat by certain buyers and secured parties. See Section 9-337.

5. Inventory. Compliance with a certificate-of-title statute generally is not the method of perfecting security interests in inventory. Section 9-311(d) provides that a security interest created in inventory held by a person in the business of selling goods of that kind is subject to the normal filing rules; compliance with a certificate-of-title statute is not necessary or effective to perfect the security interest. Most certificate-of-title statutes are in accord.

The following example explains the subtle relationship between this rule and the choice-of-law rules in Section 9-303 and former Section 9-103(2):

> **Example:** Goods are located in State A and covered by a certificate of title issued under the law of State A. The State A certificate of title is "clean"; it does not reflect a security interest. Owner takes the goods to State B and sells (trades in) the goods to Dealer, who is in the business of selling goods of that kind and is located (within the meaning of Section 9-307) in State B. As is customary, Dealer retains the duly assigned State A certificate of title pending resale of the goods. Dealer's inventory financer, SP, obtains a security interest in the goods under its after-acquired property clause.
>
> Under Section 9-311(d) of both State A and State B, Dealer's inventory financer, SP, must perfect by filing instead of complying with a certificate-of-title statute. If Section 9-303 were read to provide that the law applicable to perfection of SP's security interest is that of State A, because the goods are covered by a State A certificate, then SP would be required to file in State A under State A's Section 9-501. That result would be anomalous, to say the least, since the principle underlying Section 9-311(d) is that the inventory should be treated as ordinary goods.
>
> Section 9-303 (and former Section 9-103(2)) should be read as providing that the law of State B, not State A, applies. A court looking to the forum's Section 9-303(a) would find that Section 9-303 applies only if two conditions are met: (i) the goods are covered by the certificate as explained in Section 9-303(b), i.e., application had been made for a State (here, State A) to issue a certificate of title covering the goods and (ii) the certificate is a "certificate of title" as defined in Section 9-102, i.e., "a statute provides for the security interest in question to be indicated on the certificate as a condition or result of the security interest's

obtaining priority over the rights of a lien creditor." Stated otherwise, Section 9-303 applies only when compliance with a certificate-of-title statute, and not filing, is the appropriate method of perfection. Under the law of State A, *for purposes of perfecting SP's security interest in the dealer's inventory,* the proper method of perfection is filing—not compliance with State A's certificate-of-title statute. For that reason, the goods are not covered by a "certificate of title," and the second condition is not met. Thus, Section 9-303 does not apply to the goods. Instead, Section 9-301 applies, and the applicable law is that of State B, where the debtor (dealer) is located.

6. External Constraints on This Section. The need to coordinate Article 9 with a variety of nonuniform certificate-of-title statutes, the need to provide rules to take account of situations in which multiple certificates of title are outstanding with respect to particular goods, and the need to govern the transition from perfection by filing in one jurisdiction to perfection by notation in another all create pressure for a detailed and complex set of rules. In an effort to minimize complexity, this Article does not attempt to coordinate Article 9 with the entire array of certificate-of-title statutes. In particular, Sections 9-303, 9-311, and 9-316(d) and (e) assume that the certificate-of-title statutes to which they apply do not have relation-back provisions (i.e., provisions under which perfection is deemed to occur at a time earlier than when the perfection steps actually are taken). A Legislative Note to Section 9-311 recommends the elimination of relation-back provisions in certificate-of-title statutes affecting perfection of security interests.

Ideally, at any given time, only one certificate of title is outstanding with respect to particular goods. In fact, however, sometimes more than one jurisdiction issues more than one certificate of title with respect to the same goods. This situation results from defects in certificate-of-title laws and the interstate coordination of those laws, not from deficiencies in this Article. As long as the possibility of multiple certificates of title remains, the potential for innocent parties to suffer losses will continue. At best, this Article can identify clearly which innocent parties will bear the losses in familiar fact patterns.

Section 9-304. Law Governing Perfection and Priority of Security Interests in Deposit Accounts

(a) [Law of bank's jurisdiction governs.] The local law of a bank's jurisdiction governs perfection, the effect of perfection or nonperfection, and the priority of a security interest in a deposit account maintained with that bank even if the transaction does not bear any relation to the bank's jurisdiction.

(b) [Bank's jurisdiction.] The following rules determine a bank's jurisdiction for purposes of this part:

(1) If an agreement between the bank and its customer governing the deposit account expressly provides that a particular jurisdiction is the bank's jurisdiction for purposes of this part, this article, or [the Uniform Commercial Code], that jurisdiction is the bank's jurisdiction.

(2) If paragraph (1) does not apply and an agreement between the bank and its customer governing the deposit account expressly provides that the agreement is governed by the law of a particular jurisdiction, that jurisdiction is the bank's jurisdiction.

(3) If neither paragraph (1) nor paragraph (2) applies and an agreement between the bank and its customer governing the deposit account expressly provides that the deposit account is maintained at an office in a particular jurisdiction, that jurisdiction is the bank's jurisdiction.

(4) If none of the preceding paragraphs applies, the bank's jurisdiction is the jurisdiction in which the office identified in an account statement as the office serving the customer's account is located.

(5) If none of the preceding paragraphs applies, the bank's jurisdiction is the jurisdiction in which the chief executive office of the bank is located.

Definitional Cross References:

Account	Section 9-102(a)(2)
Agreement	Section 1-201(b)(3)
Bank	Section 9-102(a)(8)
Customer	Section 4-104(a)(5)
Debtor	Section 9-102(a)(28)
Deposit account	Section 9-102(a)(29)
Security interest	Section 1-201(b)(35)

Official Comment

1. Source. New; derived from Section 8-110(e) and former Section 9-103(6).

2. Deposit Accounts. Under this section, the law of the "bank's jurisdiction" governs perfection and priority of a security interest in deposit accounts. Subsection (b) contains rules for determining the "bank's jurisdiction." The substance of these rules is substantially similar to that of the rules determining the "security intermediary's jurisdiction" under former Section 8-110(e), except that subsection (b)(1) provides more flexibility than the analogous provision in former Section 8-110(e)(1). Subsection (b)(1) permits the parties to choose the law of one jurisdiction to govern perfection and priority of security interests and a different governing law for other purposes. The parties' choice is effective, even if the jurisdiction whose law is chosen bears no relationship to the parties or the transaction. Section 8-110(e)(1) has been conformed to subsection (b)(1) of this section, and Section 9-305(b)(1), concerning a commodity intermediary's jurisdiction, makes a similar departure from former Section 9-103(6)(e)(i).

3. Change in Law Governing Perfection. When the bank's jurisdiction changes, the jurisdiction whose law governs perfection under subsection (a) changes, as well. Nevertheless, the change will not result in an immediate loss of perfection. See Section 9-316(f), (g).

4. No relation to Bank's Jurisdiction Required. As to the final clause of subsection (a), see Section 8-110, Comment 5A.

Section 9-305. Law Governing Perfection and Priority of Security Interests in Investment Property

(a) [Governing law: general rules.] Except as otherwise provided in subsection (c), the following rules apply:

(1) While a security certificate is located in a jurisdiction, the local law of that jurisdiction governs perfection, the effect of perfection or nonperfection, and the priority of a security interest in the certificated security represented thereby.

(2) The local law of the issuer's jurisdiction as specified in Section 8-110(d) governs perfection, the effect of perfection or nonperfection, and the priority of a security interest in an uncertificated security.

(3) The local law of the securities intermediary's jurisdiction as specified in Section 8-110(e) governs perfection, the effect of perfection or nonperfection, and the priority of a security interest in a security entitlement or securities account.

(4) The local law of the commodity intermediary's jurisdiction governs perfection, the effect of perfection or nonperfection, and the priority of a security interest in a commodity contract or commodity account.

(5) Paragraphs (2), (3), and (4) apply even if the transaction does not bear any relation to the jurisdiction.

(b) [Commodity intermediary's jurisdiction.] The following rules determine a commodity intermediary's jurisdiction for purposes of this part:

(1) If an agreement between the commodity intermediary and commodity customer governing the commodity account expressly provides that a particular jurisdiction is the commodity intermediary's jurisdiction for purposes of this part, this article, or [the Uniform Commercial Code], that jurisdiction is the commodity intermediary's jurisdiction.

(2) If paragraph (1) does not apply and an agreement between the commodity intermediary and commodity customer governing the commodity account expressly provides that the agreement is governed by the law of a particular jurisdiction, that jurisdiction is the commodity intermediary's jurisdiction.

(3) If neither paragraph (1) nor paragraph (2) applies and an agreement between the commodity intermediary and commodity customer governing the commodity account expressly provides that the commodity account is maintained at an office in a particular jurisdiction, that jurisdiction is the commodity intermediary's jurisdiction.

(4) If none of the preceding paragraphs applies, the commodity intermediary's jurisdiction is the jurisdiction in which the office identified in an account statement as the office serving the commodity customer's account is located.

(5) If none of the preceding paragraphs applies, the commodity intermediary's jurisdiction is the jurisdiction in which the chief executive office of the commodity intermediary is located.

(c) [When perfection governed by law of jurisdiction where debtor located.] The local law of the jurisdiction in which the debtor is located governs:

(1) perfection of a security interest in investment property by filing;

(2) automatic perfection of a security interest in investment property created by a broker or securities intermediary; and

(3) automatic perfection of a security interest in a commodity contract or commodity account created by a commodity intermediary.

Definitional Cross References:

Account	Section 9-102(a)(2)
Agreement	Section 1-201(b)(3)
Broker	Section 8-102(a)(3)
Certificated security	Section 8-102(a)(4)
Commodity account	Section 9-102(a)(14)
Commodity contract	Section 9-102(a)(15)
Commodity customer	Section 9-102(a)(16)
Commodity intermediary	Section 9-102(a)(17)
Debtor	Section 9-102(a)(28)
Investment property	Section 9-102(a)(49)
Issuer (security)	Section 8-201(a)
Securities account	Section 8-501(a)
Securities intermediary	Section 8-102(a)(14)
Security certificate	Section 8-102(a)(16)
Security entitlement	Section 8-102(a)(17)
Security interest	Section 1-201(b)(35)
Uncertificated security	Section 8-102(a)(18)

Official Comment

1. Source. Former Section 9-103(6).

2. Investment Property: General Rules. This section specifies choice-of-law rules for perfection and priority of security interests in investment property. Subsection (a)(1) covers security interests in certificated securities. Subsection (a)(2) covers security interests in uncertificated securities. Subsection (a)(3) covers security interests in security entitlements and securities accounts, and where the Hague Securities Convention applies it may in occasional instances modify subsection (a)(3)'s results as discussed in Comments 3, 5 and 6 to Section 8-110. Subsection (a)(4) covers security interests in commodity contracts and commodity accounts. The approach of each of these paragraphs is essentially the same. They identify the jurisdiction's law that governs questions of perfection and priority by using the same principles that Article 8 uses to determine other questions concerning that form of investment property. Thus, for certificated securities, the law of the jurisdiction in which the certificate is located governs. Cf. Section 8-110(c). For uncertificated securities, the law of the issuer's jurisdiction governs. Cf. Section 8-110(a). For security entitlements and securities accounts, the law designated by the agreement between the securities intermediary and the entitlement holder governing the securities account generally governs. Cf. Section 8-110(b), (e)(1) and (2) and Convention article 4(1).

For commodity contracts and commodity accounts, the law of the commodity intermediary's jurisdiction governs, though if particular assets of this type qualify as securities held with an intermediary within the meaning of the Convention, the Convention would also apply. Commodity contracts and commodity accounts are not governed by Article 8, and for this reason subsection (b) contains rules that specify the commodity intermediary's jurisdiction that are analogous to the rules in Section 8-110(e) specifying a securities intermediary's jurisdiction. Subsection (b)(1) affords the parties greater flexibility than did former Section 9-103(6)(3). See also Section 9-304(b) (bank's jurisdiction); Revised Section 8-110(e)(1) and (2) (securities intermediary's jurisdiction).

3. Investment Property: Exceptions. Subsection (c) establishes an exception to the general rules discussed in the preceding Comment. It provides that perfection of a security interest by filing, automatic perfection of a security interest in investment property created by a debtor who is a broker or securities intermediary (see Section 9-309(10)), and automatic perfection of a security interest in a commodity contract or commodity account of a debtor who is a commodity intermediary (see Section 9-309(11)) are governed by the law of the jurisdiction in which the debtor is located, as determined under Section 9-307.

The Hague Securities Convention generally preserves these rules for perfection by filing. However, if the debtor is located in a non-U.S. jurisdiction, or if the account agreement designates the law of a non-U.S. jurisdiction, then filing may be appropriate only in a different jurisdiction or altogether unavailable. See Convention articles 12(2)(b) and 4(1), respectively, and PEB Commentary No. 19, particularly footnote 25.

4. Examples: The following examples illustrate the rules in this section:

Example 1: A customer residing in New Jersey maintains a securities account with Able & Co. The agreement between the customer and Able specifies that it is governed by Pennsylvania law but expressly provides that California is Able's jurisdiction for purposes of the Uniform Commercial Code. Through the account the customer holds securities of a Massachusetts corporation, which Able holds through a clearing corporation located in New York. The customer obtains a margin loan from Able. Subsection (a)(3) provides that California law—the law of the securities intermediary's jurisdiction—governs perfection and priority of the security interest, even if California has no other relationship to the parties or the transaction. Even if other facts cause the Hague Securities Convention to apply (see Comment 1 to Section 8-110), the Convention does not change this result, provided that the account agreement either was entered into before the Convention's effectiveness in the United States or expressly specifies that the law of California is applicable to all issues specified in Convention article 2(1), and also provided that at the time of the agreement Able had an office in the United States engaged in a regular activity of maintaining securities accounts.

Example 2: A customer residing in New Jersey maintains a securities account with Able & Co. The agreement between the customer and Able specifies that it is governed by Pennsylvania law. Through the account the customer holds securities of a Massachusetts corporation, which Able holds through a clearing corporation located in New York. The customer obtains a loan from a lender located in Illinois. The lender takes a security interest and perfects by obtaining an agreement among the debtor, itself, and Able, which satisfies the requirement of Section 8-106(d)(2) to give the lender control. Subsection (a)(3) provides that Pennsylvania law—the law of the securities intermediary's jurisdiction—governs perfection and priority of the security interest, even if Pennsylvania has no other relationship to the parties or the transaction. Even if other facts cause the Hague Securities Convention to apply, the Convention does not change this result, provided that, at the time of the agreement between the customer and Able, Able had an office in the United States engaged in a regular activity of maintaining securities accounts.

Example 3: A customer residing in New Jersey maintains a securities account with Able & Co. The agreement between the customer and Able specifies that it is governed by Pennsylvania law. Through the account, the customer holds securities of a Massachusetts corporation, which Able holds through a clearing corporation located in New York. The customer borrows from SP-1, and SP-1 files a financing statement in New Jersey. Later, the customer obtains a loan from SP-2. SP-2 takes a security interest and perfects by obtaining an agreement among the debtor, itself, and Able, which satisfies the requirement of Section 8-106(d)(2) to give SP-2 control. Subsection (c)(1) provides that perfection of SP-1's security interest by filing is governed by the location of the debtor, so the filing in New Jersey was appropriate. Even if other facts cause the

Hague Securities Convention to apply, Convention article 12(2)(b) preserves this result. Subsection (a)(3), however, provides that Pennsylvania law—the law designated by the agreement between the customer and Able—governs all other questions of perfection and priority, and the Convention preserves this result, provided that at the time of the agreement between the customer and Able, Able had an office in the United States engaged in a regular activity of maintaining securities accounts. Thus, Pennsylvania law governs perfection of SP-2's security interest, and Pennsylvania law also governs the priority of the security interests of SP-1 and SP-2.

Example 4: A customer maintains a securities account with Able & Co. The customer is an Ontario, Canada corporation with its chief executive office in Toronto. The agreement between the customer and Able specifies that it is governed by New York law, and at the time of the agreement Able had an office in the United States engaged in a regular activity of maintaining securities accounts. The customer obtains a loan secured by the securities account, and the lender wishes to perfect by filing. Subsection (c)(1) provides that perfection of the security interest by filing is generally governed by the law of the location of the debtor (in this case Ontario), assuming that it has a filing system described by Section 9-307(c)); however, Convention article 12(2)(b) recognizes Article 9's place-of-filing rules only when they designate a U.S. jurisdiction for the filing. As a result, subsection (c)(1) does not govern filing for this transaction, and perfection of the security interest is governed by the substantive law of the jurisdiction designated by the account agreement (in this case New York).

Example 5: A customer maintains a securities account with Able & Co. The customer is a Texas corporation. The agreement between the customer and Able specifies that it is governed by English law, and at the time of the agreement Able had an office in England engaged in a regular activity of maintaining securities accounts. The customer obtains a loan secured by the securities account, and the lender wishes to perfect by filing. Subsection (c)(1), if it applied, would provide that perfection of the security interest by filing is governed by the law of the location of the debtor (in this case Texas); however, under Convention article 4(1), perfection of the security interest is governed by the law of the jurisdiction designated by the account agreement (in this case England), rather than by the law of any UCC jurisdiction.

5. Change in Law Governing Perfection. When the issuer's jurisdiction, the securities intermediary's jurisdiction, or commodity intermediary's jurisdiction changes, the jurisdiction whose law governs perfection under subsection (a) changes, as well. Similarly, the law governing perfection of a possessory security interest in a certificated security changes when the collateral is removed to another jurisdiction, see subsection (a)(1), and the law governing perfection by filing changes when the debtor changes its location. See subsection (c). Nevertheless, under the UCC these changes will not result in an immediate loss of perfection. See Section 9-316. Along generally similar lines in cases to which the Hague Securities Convention applies, article 7 provides that when the account agreement is amended to designate a new jurisdiction's law under article 4(1), the new law governs perfection, except that the old law continues to govern the perfection of security or other property interests that arose before the amendment and a limited number of other issues affecting such interests, without limitation as to time.

6. No Relation of Transaction to Issuer's, Securities intermediary's, or Commodity Intermediary Jurisdiction Required. As to subsection (a)(5), see Section 8-110, Comment 5A.

Section 9-306. Law Governing Perfection and Priority of Security Interests in Letter-Of-Credit Rights

(a) [Governing law: issuer's or nominated person's jurisdiction.] Subject to subsection (c), the local law of the issuer's jurisdiction or a nominated person's jurisdiction governs perfection, the effect of perfection or nonperfection, and the priority of a security interest in a letter-of-credit right if the issuer's jurisdiction or nominated person's jurisdiction is a State.

(b) [Issuer's or nominated person's jurisdiction.] For purposes of this part, an issuer's jurisdiction or nominated person's jurisdiction is the jurisdiction whose law governs the liability of the issuer or nominated person with respect to the letter-of-credit right as provided in Section 5-116.

(c) [When section not applicable.] This section does not apply to a security interest that is perfected only under Section 9-308(d).

Definitional Cross References:

Issuer (letter of credit/ letter-of-credit right)	Section 5-102(a)(9)
Letter-of-credit right	Section 9-102(a)(51)
Nominated person	Section 5-102(a)(11)
Security interest	Section 1-201(b)(35)
State	Section 9-102(a)(77)

Official Comment

1. Source. New; derived in part from Section 8-110(e) and former Section 9-103(6).

2. *Sui Generis* Treatment. This section governs the applicable law for perfection and priority of security interests in letter-of-credit rights, other than a security interest perfected only under Section 9-308(d) (i.e., as a supporting obligation). The treatment differs substantially from that provided in Section 9-304 for deposit accounts. The basic rule is that the law of the issuer's or nominated person's (e.g., confirmer's) jurisdiction, derived from the terms of the letter of credit itself, controls perfection and priority, but only if the issuer's or nominated person's jurisdiction is a State, as defined in Section 9-102. If the issuer's or nominated person's jurisdiction is not a State, the baseline rule of Section 9-301 applies—perfection and priority are governed by the law of the debtor's location, determined under Section 9-307. Export transactions typically involve a foreign issuer and a domestic nominated person, such as a confirmer, located in a State. The principal goal of this section is to reduce the likelihood that perfection and priority would be governed by the law of a foreign jurisdiction in a transaction that is essentially domestic from the standpoint of the debtor-beneficiary, its creditors, and a domestic nominated person.

3. Issuer's or Nominated Person's Jurisdiction. Subsection (b) defers to the rules established under Section 5-116 for determination of an issuer's or nominated person's jurisdiction.

Example: An Italian bank issues a letter of credit that is confirmed by a New York bank. The beneficiary is a Connecticut corporation. The letter of credit provides that the issuer's liability is governed by Italian law, and the confirmation provides that the confirmer's liability is governed by the law of New York. Under Sections 9-306(b) and 5-116(a), Italy is the issuer's jurisdiction and New York is the confirmer's (nominated person's) jurisdiction. Because the confirmer's jurisdiction is a State, the law of New York governs perfection and priority of a security interest in the beneficiary's letter-of-credit right against the confirmer. See Section 9-306(a). However, because the issuer's jurisdiction is not a State, the law of that jurisdiction does not govern. See Section 9-306(a). Rather, the choice-of-law rule in Section 9-301(1) applies to perfection and priority of a security interest in the beneficiary's letter-of-credit right against the issuer. Under that section, perfection and priority are governed by the law of the jurisdiction in which the debtor (beneficiary) is located. That jurisdiction is Connecticut. See Section 9-307.

4. Scope of This Section. This section specifies only the law governing perfection, the effect of perfection or nonperfection, and priority of security interests. Section 5-116 specifies the law governing the liability of, and Article 5 (or other applicable law) deals with the rights and duties of, an issuer or nominated person. Perfection, nonperfection, and priority have no effect on those rights and duties.

5. Change in Law Governing Perfection. When the issuer's jurisdiction, or nominated person's jurisdiction changes, the jurisdiction whose law governs perfection under subsection (a) changes, as well. Nevertheless, this change will not result in an immediate loss of perfection. See Section 9-316(f), (g).

Section 9-306A. Law Governing Perfection and Priority of Security Interests in Chattel Paper

(a) [Chattel paper evidenced by authoritative electronic copy.] Except as provided in subsection (d), if chattel paper is evidenced only by an authoritative electronic copy of the chattel paper or is evidenced by an authoritative electronic copy and an authoritative tangible copy, the local law of the chattel paper's jurisdiction governs perfection, the effect of perfection or nonperfection, and the priority of a security interest in the chattel paper, even if the transaction does not bear any relation to the chattel paper's jurisdiction.

(b) [Chattel paper's jurisdiction.] The following rules determine the chattel paper's jurisdiction under this section:

(1) If the authoritative electronic copy of the record evidencing chattel paper, or a record attached to or logically associated with the electronic copy and readily available for review, expressly provides that a particular jurisdiction is the chattel paper's jurisdiction for purposes of this part, this article, or [the Uniform Commercial Code], that jurisdiction is the chattel paper's jurisdiction.

(2) If paragraph (1) does not apply and the rules of the system in which the authoritative electronic copy is recorded are readily available for review and expressly provide that a particular jurisdiction is the chattel paper's jurisdiction for purposes of this part, this article, or [the Uniform Commercial Code], that jurisdiction is the chattel paper's jurisdiction.

(3) If paragraphs (1) and (2) do not apply and the authoritative electronic copy, or a record attached to or logically associated with the electronic copy and readily available for review, expressly provides that the chattel paper is governed by the law of a particular jurisdiction, that jurisdiction is the chattel paper's jurisdiction.

(4) If paragraphs (1), (2), and (3) do not apply and the rules of the system in which the authoritative electronic copy is recorded are readily available for review and expressly provide that the chattel paper or the system is governed by the law of a particular jurisdiction, that jurisdiction is the chattel paper's jurisdiction.

(5) If paragraphs (1) through (4) do not apply, the chattel paper's jurisdiction is the jurisdiction in which the debtor is located.

(c) [Chattel paper evidenced by authoritative tangible copy.] If an authoritative tangible copy of a record evidences chattel paper and the chattel paper is not evidenced by an authoritative electronic copy, while the authoritative tangible copy of the record evidencing chattel paper is located in a jurisdiction, the local law of that jurisdiction governs:

(1) perfection of a security interest in the chattel paper by possession under Section 9-314A; and

(2) the effect of perfection or nonperfection and the priority of a security interest in the chattel paper.

(d) [When perfection governed by law of jurisdiction where debtor located.] The local law of the jurisdiction in which the debtor is located governs perfection of a security interest in chattel paper by filing.

Definitional Cross References:

Chattel paper	Section 9-102(a)(11)
Debtor	Section 9-102(a)(28)
Electronic	Section 1-201(b)(16A)
Security interest	Section 1-201(b)(35)
Record	Section 9-102(a)(70)

Official Comment

1. Source. Section 9-306A(a) and (b) derive from Sections 8-110(e) and 9-305 on law governing perfection and priority of security interests in investment property (as do Sections 9-306B and 12-107).

2. Applicability of this Section. This section determines the law governing perfection and priority of security interests in chattel paper. Subsections (a) and (b) apply to chattel paper that is evidenced only by an authoritative electronic copy of the chattel paper or by an authoritative electronic copy and an authoritative tangible copy. Subsection (c) applies to chattel paper that is evidenced by an authoritative tangible copy but not evidenced by an authoritative electronic copy. Subsection (d) applies to perfection by filing for all chattel paper.

3. Authoritative Electronic Copy: Chattel Paper's Jurisdiction. Subsection (a) specifies the law governing perfection and priority of security interests in chattel paper evidenced by an authoritative electronic copy of the chattel paper, even if it is also evidenced by an authoritative tangible copy. Subject to subsection (d) on perfection by filing, the law governing perfection and priority is the local law of the chattel paper's jurisdiction. Drawing on Sections 8-110 and 9-305, it is the authoritative electronic copy itself, records attached thereto or associated therewith, or the system in which the authoritative electronic copy is recorded that determines the chattel paper's jurisdiction and, therefore, the governing law. Subsection (b) provides a "waterfall" of rules based on provisions that identify a particular jurisdiction as the chattel paper's jurisdiction or alternatively that provide the governing law of the chattel paper or of the system in which the electronic copy is recorded. When no such identification or provision is made, it is the debtor's location, determined under Section 9-307, that is the chattel paper's jurisdiction. As to the final clause of subsection (a), see Section 8-110, Comment 5A.

4. Rationale for Subsection (a). A buyer of, or secured lender against, chattel paper may arrange for authoritative electronic copies of chattel paper that it wishes to have assigned to it to be originated in or submitted into a system for the control and assignment of the chattel paper. The secured parties and lessors that will be assigning the chattel paper may be located in many different jurisdictions. As to assignments of the chattel paper by these secured parties and lessors (assignor-debtors), but for this section perfection and priority would be governed by the law of each assignor-debtor's location under Section 9-301(1). Under this section, however, the law of a single jurisdiction—the chattel paper's jurisdiction—could govern perfection and priority with respect to all of the assignments. By avoiding the application of the laws of multiple jurisdictions to perfection and priority, this rule could substantially reduce transaction costs.

5. Authoritative tangible copy. Subsection (c) ties the choice-of-law rules to the location of the authoritative tangible copy when no authoritative electronic copy exists. In that circumstance, the local law of the jurisdiction where the authoritative tangible copy is physically located governs perfection of a security interest in the chattel paper by possession, under Section 9-314A, and priority. Like its predecessor, subsection (c) assumes that all the authoritative tangible copies are located in the same jurisdiction. However, assuming the secured party is in possession of all the tangible copies, even if the copies are located in more than one jurisdiction the situation is unlikely to be problematic.

6. Perfection by filing. Subsection (d) provides that the local law of the jurisdiction where the debtor is located governs perfection by filing for all chattel paper.

Section 9-306B. Law Governing Perfection and Priority of Security Interests in Controllable Accounts, Controllable Electronic Records, and Controllable Payment Intangibles

(a) [Governing law: general rules.] Except as provided in subsection (b), the local law of the controllable electronic record's jurisdiction specified in Section 12-107(c) and (d) governs perfection, the effect of perfection or nonperfection, and the priority of a security interest in a controllable electronic record and a security interest in a controllable account or controllable payment intangible evidenced by the controllable electronic record.

(b) [When perfection governed by law of jurisdiction where debtor located.] The local law of the jurisdiction in which the debtor is located governs:

(1) perfection of a security interest in a controllable account, controllable electronic record, or controllable payment intangible by filing; and

(2) automatic perfection of a security interest in a controllable payment intangible created by a sale of the controllable payment intangible.

Definitional Cross References:

Controllable account	Section 9-102(a)(27A)
Controllable electronic record	Section 12-102(a)(1)
Controllable payment intangible	Section 9-102(a)(27B)
Debtor	Section 9-102(a)(28)
Sale	Section 2-106(1)
Security interest	Section 1-201(b)(35)

Official Comment

1. Perfection by control and priority. Subsection (a) deals with perfection of a security interest in a controllable account, controllable electronic record, or controllable payment intangible other than by filing—i.e., perfection by control under Section 12-105—and priority. For these purposes the governing law is that of the controllable electronic record's jurisdiction under Section 12-107(c) and (d).

2. Perfection by filing. Under subsection (b) the local law of the jurisdiction of the debtor's location governs perfection of a security interest in a controllable account, controllable electronic record, or controllable payment intangible by filing (but not priority, as to which subsection (a) would apply). Because controllable electronic records are general intangibles and controllable accounts and controllable payment intangibles are subsets of accounts and payment intangibles, this provision does not change prior law.

Section 9-307. Location of Debtor

(a) ["Place of business."] In this section, "place of business" means a place where a debtor conducts its affairs.

(b) [Debtor's location: general rules.] Except as otherwise provided in this section, the following rules determine a debtor's location:

(1) A debtor who is an individual is located at the individual's principal residence.

(2) A debtor that is an organization and has only one place of business is located at its place of business.

(3) A debtor that is an organization and has more than one place of business is located at its chief executive office.

(c) [Limitation of applicability of subsection (b).] Subsection (b) applies only if a debtor's residence, place of business, or chief executive office, as applicable, is located in a jurisdiction whose law generally requires information concerning the existence of a nonpossessory security interest to be made generally available in a filing, recording, or registration system as a condition or result of the security interest's obtaining priority over the rights of a lien creditor with respect to the collateral. If subsection (b) does not apply, the debtor is located in the District of Columbia.

(d) [Continuation of location: cessation of existence, etc.] A person that ceases to exist, have a residence, or have a place of business continues to be located in the jurisdiction specified by subsections (b) and (c).

(e) [Location of registered organization organized under State law.] A registered organization that is organized under the law of a State is located in that State.

(f) [Location of registered organization organized under federal law; bank branches and agencies.] Except as otherwise provided in subsection (i), a registered organization that is organized under the law of the United States and a branch or agency of a bank that is not organized under the law of the United States or a State are located:

(1) in the State that the law of the United States designates, if the law designates a State of location;

(2) in the State that the registered organization, branch, or agency designates, if the law of the United States authorizes the registered organization, branch, or agency to designate its State of location, including by designating its main office, home office, or other comparable office; or

(3) in the District of Columbia, if neither paragraph (1) nor paragraph (2) applies.

(g) [Continuation of location: change in status of registered organization.] A registered organization continues to be located in the jurisdiction specified by subsection (e) or (f) notwithstanding:

(1) the suspension, revocation, forfeiture, or lapse of the registered organization's status as such in its jurisdiction of organization; or

(2) the dissolution, winding up, or cancellation of the existence of the registered organization.

(h) [Location of United States.] The United States is located in the District of Columbia.

(i) [Location of foreign bank branch or agency if licensed in only one state.] A branch or agency of a bank that is not organized under the law of the United States or a State is located in the State in which the branch or agency is licensed, if all branches and agencies of the bank are licensed in only one State.

(j) [Location of foreign air carrier.] A foreign air carrier under the Federal Aviation Act of 1958, as amended, is located at the designated office of the agent upon which service of process may be made on behalf of the carrier.

(k) [Section applies only to this part.] This section applies only for purposes of this part.

Definitional Cross References:

Bank	Section 9-102(a)(8)
Branch	Section 1-201(b)(7)
Collateral	Section 9-102(a)(12)
Debtor	Section 9-102(a)(28)
Jurisdiction of organization	Section 9-102(a)(50)
Lien creditor	Section 9-102(a)(52)
Organization	Section 1-201(b)(25)
Registered organization	Section 9-102(a)(71)
Right	Section 1-201(b)(34)
Security interest	Section 1-201(b)(35)
State	Section 9-102(a)(77)

Official Comment

1. Source. Former Section 9-103(3)(d), substantially revised.

2. General Rules. As a general matter, the location of the debtor determines the jurisdiction whose law governs perfection of a security interest. See Sections 9-301(1), 9-305(c). It also governs priority of a security interest in certain types of intangible collateral, such as accounts, electronic chattel paper, and general intangibles. This section determines the location of the debtor for choice-of-law purposes, but not for other purposes. See subsection (k).

Subsection (b) states the general rules: An individual debtor is deemed to be located at the individual's principal residence with respect to both personal and business assets. Any other debtor is deemed to be located at its place of business if it has only one, or at its chief executive office if it has more than one place of business.

As used in this section, a "place of business" means a place where the debtor conducts its affairs. See subsection (a). Thus, every organization, even eleemosynary institutions and other organizations that do not conduct "for profit" business activities, has a "place of business." Under subsection (d), a person who ceases to exist, have a residence, or have a place of business continues to be located in the jurisdiction determined by subsection (b).

The term "chief executive office" is not defined in this Section or elsewhere in the Uniform Commercial Code. "Chief executive office" means the place from which the debtor manages the main part of its business operations or other affairs. This is the place where persons dealing with the debtor would normally look for credit information, and is the appropriate place for filing. With respect to most multi-state debtors, it will be simple to determine which of the debtor's offices is the "chief executive office." Even when a doubt arises, it would be rare that there could be more than two possibilities. A secured party in such a case may protect itself by perfecting under the law of each possible jurisdiction.

Similarly, the term "principal residence" is not defined. If the security interest in question is a purchase-money security interest in consumer goods which is perfected upon attachment, see Section 9-309(1), the choice of law may make no difference. In other cases, when a doubt arises, prudence may dictate perfecting under the law of each jurisdiction that might be the debtor's "principal residence."

Questions sometimes arise about the location of the debtor with respect to collateral held in a common-law trust. A typical common-law trust is not itself a juridical entity capable of owning property and so would not be a "debtor" as defined in Section 9-102. Rather, the debtor with respect to property held in a common-law trust typically is the trustee of the trust acting in the capacity of trustee. (The beneficiary would be a "debtor" with respect to its beneficial interest in the trust, but not with respect to the property held in the trust.) If a common-law trust has multiple trustees located in different jurisdictions, a secured party who perfects by filing would be well advised to file a financing statement in each jurisdiction in which a trustee is located, as determined under Section 9-307. Filing in all relevant jurisdictions would insure perfection and minimize any priority complications that otherwise might arise.

The general rules are subject to several exceptions, each of which is discussed below.

3. Non-U.S. Debtors. Under the general rules of this section, a non-U.S. debtor normally would be located in a foreign jurisdiction and, as a consequence, foreign law would govern perfection. When foreign law affords no public notice of security interests, the general rule yields unacceptable results.

Accordingly, subsection (c) provides that the normal rules for determining the location of a debtor (i.e., the rules in subsection (b)) apply only if they yield a location that is "a jurisdiction whose law generally requires information concerning the existence of a nonpossessory security interest to be made generally available in a filing, recording, or registration system as a condition or result of the security interest's obtaining priority over the rights of a lien creditor with respect to the collateral." The phrase "generally requires" is meant to include legal regimes that generally require notice in a filing or recording system as a condition of perfecting nonpossessory security interests, but which permit perfection by another method (e.g., control, automatic perfection, temporary perfection) in limited circumstances. A jurisdiction that has adopted this Article or an earlier version of this Article is such a jurisdiction. If the rules in subsection (b) yield a jurisdiction whose law does not generally require notice in a filing or registration system and none of the special rules in subsections (e), (f), (i), and (j) applies, the debtor is located in the District of Columbia.

[Ed. Note. The remainder of this comment was deleted from the Official Text, probably inadvertently.]

> **Example 1:** Debtor is an English corporation with 7 offices in the United States and its chief executive office in London, England. Debtor creates a security interest in its accounts. Under subsection (b)(3), Debtor would be located in England. However, subsection (c) provides that subsection (b) applies only if English law generally conditions perfection on giving public notice in a filing, recording, or registration system. Otherwise, Debtor is located in the District of Columbia. Under Section 9-301(1), perfection, the effect of perfection, and priority are governed by the law of the jurisdiction of the debtor's location — here, England or the District of Columbia (depending on the content of English law).

> **Example 2:** Debtor is an English corporation with 7 offices in the United States and its chief executive office in London, England. Debtor creates a security interest in equipment located in London. Under subsection (b)(3) Debtor would be located in England. However, subsection (c) provides that subsection (b) applies only if English law generally conditions perfection on giving public notice in a filing, recording, or registration system. Otherwise, Debtor is located in the District of Columbia. Under Section 9-301(1), perfection is governed by the law of the

jurisdiction of the debtor's location, whereas, under Section 9-301(3), the law of the jurisdiction in which the collateral is located—here, England—governs priority.

The foregoing discussion assumes that each transaction bears an appropriate relation to the forum State. In the absence of an appropriate relation, the forum State's entire UCC, including the choice-of-law provisions in Article 9 (Sections 9-301 through 9-307), will not apply. See Section 9-109, Comment 9.

4. Registered Organizations Organized Under Law of a State. Under subsection (e), a "registered organization" (defined in Section 9-102 so as to ordinarily include corporations, limited partnerships, limited liability companies, and statutory trusts) organized under the law of a "State" (defined in Section 9-102) is located in its State of organization. The term "registered organization" includes a business trust described in the second sentence of the term's definition. See Section 9-102. The trust's public organic record, typically the trust agreement, usually will indicate the jurisdiction under whose law the trust is organized. A protected series formed under the Uniform Protected Series Act (2017) is a registered organization. See PEB Commentary No. 23, dated February 24, 2021. The Commentary is available at https://www.ali.org/peb-ucc.

Subsection (g) makes clear that events affecting the status of a registered organization, such as the dissolution of a corporation or revocation of its charter, do not affect its location for purposes of subsection (e). However, certain of these events may result in, or be accompanied by, a transfer of collateral from the registered organization to another debtor. This section does not determine whether a transfer occurs, nor does it determine the legal consequences of any transfer.

Determining the registered organization-debtor's location by reference to the jurisdiction of organization could provide some important side benefits for the filing systems. A jurisdiction could structure its filing system so that it would be impossible to make a mistake in a registered organization-debtor's name on a financing statement. For example, a filer would be informed if a filed record designated an incorrect corporate name for the debtor. Linking filing to the jurisdiction of organization also could reduce pressure on the system imposed by transactions in which registered organizations cease to exist—as a consequence of merger or consolidation, for example. The jurisdiction of organization might prohibit such transactions unless steps were taken to ensure that existing filings were refiled against a successor or terminated by the secured party.

5. Registered Organizations Organized Under Law of United States; Branches and Agencies of Banks Not Organized Under Law of United States. Subsection (f) specifies the location of a debtor that is a registered organization organized under the law of the United States. It defers to the law of the United States, to the extent that that law determines, or authorizes the debtor to determine, the debtor's location. Thus, if the law of the United States designates a particular State as the debtor's location, that State is the debtor's location for purposes of this Article's choice-of-law rules. Similarly, if the law of the United States authorizes the registered organization to designate its State of location, the State that the registered organization designates is the State in which it is located for purposes of this Article's choice-of-law rules. In other cases, the debtor is located in the District of Columbia.

In some cases, the law of the United States authorizes the registered organization to designate a main office, home office, or other comparable office. See, e.g., 12 U.S.C. Sections 22 and 1464(a); 12 C.F.R. Section 552.3. Designation of such an office constitutes the designation of the State of location for purposes of Section 9-307(f)(2).

Subsection (f) also specifies the location of a branch or agency in the United States of a foreign bank that has one or more branches or agencies in the United States. The law of the United States authorizes a foreign bank (or, on behalf of the bank, a federal agency) to designate a single home state for all of the foreign bank's branches and agencies in the United States. See 12 U.S.C. Section 3-103(c) and 12 C.F.R. Section 211.22. As authorized, the designation constitutes the State of location for the branch or agency for purposes of Section 9-307(f), unless all of a foreign bank's branches or agencies that are in the United States are licensed in only one State, in which case the branches and agencies are located in that State. See subsection (i).

In cases not governed by subsection (f) or (i), the location of a foreign bank is determined by subsections (b) and (c).

6. United States. To the extent that Article 9 governs (see Sections 1-301, 9-109(c)), the United States is located in the District of Columbia for purposes of this Article's choice-of-law rules. See subsection (h).

7. Foreign Air Carriers. Subsection (j) follows former Section 9-103(3)(d). To the extent that it is applicable, the Convention on the International Recognition of Rights in Aircraft (Geneva Convention) supersedes state legislation on this subject, as set forth in Section 9-311(b), but some nations are not parties to that Convention.

[SUBPART 2. PERFECTION]

Section 9-308. When Security Interest or Agricultural Lien Is Perfected; Continuity of Perfection

(a) [Perfection of security interest.] Except as otherwise provided in this section and Section 9-309, a security interest is perfected if it has attached and all of the applicable requirements for perfection in Sections 9-310 through 9-316 have been satisfied. A security interest is perfected when it attaches if the applicable requirements are satisfied before the security interest attaches.

(b) [Perfection of agricultural lien.] An agricultural lien is perfected if it has become effective and all of the applicable requirements for perfection in Section 9-310 have been satisfied. An agricultural lien is perfected when it becomes effective if the applicable requirements are satisfied before the agricultural lien becomes effective.

(c) [Continuous perfection; perfection by different methods.] A security interest or agricultural lien is perfected continuously if it is originally perfected by one method under this article and is later perfected by another method under this article, without an intermediate period when it was unperfected.

(d) [Supporting obligation.] Perfection of a security interest in collateral also perfects a security interest in a supporting obligation for the collateral.

(e) [Lien securing right to payment.] Perfection of a security interest in a right to payment or performance also perfects a security interest in a security interest, mortgage, or other lien on personal or real property securing the right.

(f) [Security entitlement carried in securities account.] Perfection of a security interest in a securities account also perfects a security interest in the security entitlements carried in the securities account.

(g) [Commodity contract carried in commodity account.] Perfection of a security interest in a commodity account also perfects a security interest in the commodity contracts carried in the commodity account.

Legislative Note: *Any statute conflicting with subsection (e) must be made expressly subject to that subsection.*

Definitional Cross References:

Agricultural lien	Section 9-102(a)(5)
Collateral	Section 9-102(a)(12)
Commodity account	Section 9-102(a)(14)
Commodity contract	Section 9-102(a)(15)
Mortgage	Section 9-102(a)(55)
Securities account	Section 8-501(a)
Security entitlement	Section 8-102(a)(17)
Security interest	Section 1-201(b)(35)
Supporting obligation	Section 9-102(a)(78)

Comment References:

9-107 C5
9-322 C6

Official Comment

1. Source. Former Sections 9-303, 9-115(2).

2. General Rule. This Article uses the term "attach" to describe the point at which property becomes subject to a security interest. The requisites for attachment are stated in Section 9-203. When it attaches, a security interest may be either perfected or unperfected. "Perfected" means that the security interest has attached and the secured party has taken all the steps required by this Article as specified in Sections 9-310 through 9-316. A perfected security interest may still be or become subordinate to other interests. See, e.g., Sections 9-320, 9-322. However, in general, after perfection the secured party is protected against creditors and transferees of the debtor and, in particular, against any representative of creditors in insolvency proceedings instituted by or against the debtor. See, e.g., Section 9-317.

Subsection (a) explains that the time of perfection is when the security interest has attached and any necessary steps for perfection, such as taking possession or filing, have been taken. The "except" clause refers to the perfection-upon-attachment rules appearing in Section 9-309. It also reflects that other subsections of this section, e.g., subsection (d), contain automatic-perfection rules. If the steps for perfection have been taken in advance, as when the secured party files a financing statement before giving value or before the debtor acquires rights in the collateral, then the security interest is perfected when it attaches.

3. Agricultural Liens. Subsection (b) is new. It describes the elements of perfection of an agricultural lien.

4. Continuous Perfection. The following example illustrates the operation of subsection (c):

> **Example 1:** Debtor, an importer, creates a security interest in goods that it imports and the documents of title that cover the goods. The secured party, Bank, takes possession of a negotiable tangible bill of lading covering certain imported goods and thereby perfects its security interest in the bill of lading and the goods. See Sections 9-313(a), 9-312(c)(1). Bank releases the bill of lading to the debtor for the purpose of procuring the goods from the carrier and selling them. Under Section 9-312(f), Bank continues to have a perfected security interest in the document and goods for 20 days. Bank files a financing statement covering the collateral before the expiration of the 20-day period. Its security interest now continues perfected for as long as the filing is good.
>
> If the successive stages of Bank's security interest succeed each other without an intervening gap, the security interest is "perfected continuously," and the date of perfection is when the security interest first became perfected (i.e., when Bank received possession of the tangible bill of lading). If, however, there is a gap between stages—for example, if Bank does not file until after the expiration of the 20-day period specified in Section 9-312(f) and leaves the collateral in the debtor's possession—then, the chain being broken, the perfection is no longer continuous. The date of perfection would now be the date of filing (after expiration of the 20-day period). Bank's security interest would be vulnerable to any interests arising during the gap period which under Section 9-317 take priority over an unperfected security interest.

5. Supporting Obligations. Subsection (d) is new. It provides for automatic perfection of a security interest in a supporting obligation for collateral if the security interest in the collateral is perfected. This is unlikely to effect any change in the law prior to adoption of this Article.

> **Example 2:** Buyer is obligated to pay Debtor for goods sold. Buyer's president guarantees the obligation. Debtor creates a security interest in the right to payment (account) in favor of Lender. Under Section 9-203(f), the security interest attaches to Debtor's rights under the guarantee (supporting obligation). Under subsection (d), perfection of the security interest in the account constitutes perfection of the security interest in Debtor's rights under the guarantee.

6. Rights to Payment Secured by Lien. Subsection (e) is new. It deals with the situation in which a security interest is created in a right to payment that is secured by a security interest, mortgage, or other lien.

> **Example 3:** Owner gives to Mortgagee a mortgage on Blackacre to secure a loan. Owner's obligation to pay is evidenced by a promissory note. In need of working capital, Mortgagee borrows from Financer and creates a security interest in the note in favor of Financer. Section 9-203(g) adopts the traditional view that the mortgage follows the note; i.e., the transferee of the note acquires the mortgage, as well. This subsection adopts a similar principle: perfection of a security interest in the right to payment constitutes perfection of a security interest in the mortgage securing it.

> An important consequence of the rules in Section 9-203(g) and subsection (e) is that, by acquiring a perfected security interest in a mortgage (or other secured) note, the secured party acquires a security interest in the mortgage (or other lien) that is senior to the rights of a person who becomes a lien creditor of the mortgagee (Article 9 debtor). See Section 9-317(a)(2). This result helps prevent the separation of the mortgage (or other lien) from the note.

> Under this Article, attachment and perfection of a security interest in a secured right to payment do not of themselves affect the obligation to pay. For example, if the obligation is evidenced by a negotiable note, then Article 3 dictates the person whom the maker must pay to discharge the note and any lien securing it. See Section 3-602. If the right to payment is a payment intangible, then Section 9-406 determines whom the account debtor must pay.

> Similarly, this Article does not determine who has the power to release a mortgage of record. That issue is determined by real-property law.

7. Investment Property. Subsections (f) and (g) follow former Section 9-115(2).

Section 9-309. Security Interest Perfected upon Attachment

The following security interests are perfected when they attach:

(1) a purchase-money security interest in consumer goods, except as otherwise provided in Section 9-311(b) with respect to consumer goods that are subject to a statute or treaty described in Section 9-311(a);

(2) an assignment of accounts or payment intangibles which does not by itself or in conjunction with other assignments to the same assignee transfer a significant part of the assignor's outstanding accounts or payment intangibles;

(3) a sale of a payment intangible;

(4) a sale of a promissory note;

(5) a security interest created by the assignment of a health-care-insurance receivable to the provider of the health-care goods or services;

(6) a security interest arising under Section 2-401, 2-505, 2-711(3), or 2A-508(5), until the debtor obtains possession of the collateral;

(7) a security interest of a collecting bank arising under Section 4-210;

(8) a security interest of an issuer or nominated person arising under Section 5-118;

(9) a security interest arising in the delivery of a financial asset under Section 9-206(c);

(10) a security interest in investment property created by a broker or securities intermediary;

(11) a security interest in a commodity contract or a commodity account created by a commodity intermediary;

(12) an assignment for the benefit of all creditors of the transferor and subsequent transfers by the assignee thereunder;

(13) a security interest created by an assignment of a beneficial interest in a decedent's estate; and

(14) a sale by an individual of an account that is a right to payment of winnings in a lottery or other game of chance.

Definitional Cross References:

Account	Section 9-102(a)(2)
Bank	Section 9-102(a)(8)
Broker	Section 8-102(a)(3)
Collateral	Section 9-102(a)(12)
Commodity account	Section 9-102(a)(14)
Commodity contract	Section 9-102(a)(15)
Commodity intermediary	Section 9-102(a)(17)
Consumer goods	Section 9-102(a)(23)
Creditor	Section 1-201(b)(13)
Debtor	Section 9-102(a)(28)
Delivery	Section 1-201(b)(15)
Financial asset	Section 8-102(a)(9)
Goods	Section 9-102(a)(44)
Investment property	Section 9-102(a)(49)
Issuer (letter of credit/ letter-of-credit right)	Section 5-102(a)(9)
Nominated person	Section 5-102(a)(11)
Payment intangible	Section 9-102(a)(61)

Promissory note	Section 9-102(a)(65)
Purchase Money Security Interest	Section 9-103
Sale	Section 2-106(1)
Securities intermediary	Section 8-102(a)(14)
Security interest	Section 1-201(b)(35)

Comment References: 9-323 C3

Official Comment

1. Source. Derived from former Sections 9-302(1), 9-115(4)(c), (d), 9-116.

2. Automatic Perfection. This section contains the perfection-upon-attachment rules previously located in former Sections 9-302(1), 9-115(4)(c), (d), and 9-116. Rather than continue to state the rule by indirection, this section explicitly provides for perfection upon attachment.

3. Purchase-Money Security Interest in Consumer Goods. Former Section 9-302(1)(d) has been revised and appears here as paragraph (1). No filing or other step is required to perfect a purchase-money security interest in consumer goods, other than goods, such as automobiles, that are subject to a statute or treaty described in Section 9-311(a). However, filing is required to perfect a non-purchase-money security interest in consumer goods and is necessary to prevent a buyer of consumer goods from taking free of a security interest under Section 9-320(b). A fixture filing is required for priority over conflicting interests in fixtures to the extent provided in Section 9-334.

4. Rights to Payment. Paragraph (2) expands upon former Section 9-302(1)(e) by affording automatic perfection to certain assignments of payment intangibles as well as accounts. The purpose of paragraph (2) is to save from ex post facto invalidation casual or isolated assignments—assignments which no one would think of filing. Any person who regularly takes assignments of any debtor's accounts or payment intangibles should file. In this connection Section 9-109(d)(4) through (7), which excludes certain transfers of accounts, chattel paper, payment intangibles, and promissory notes from this Article, should be consulted.

Paragraphs (3) and (4), which are new, afford automatic perfection to sales of payment intangibles and promissory notes, respectively. They reflect the practice under former Article 9. Under that Article, filing a financing statement did not affect the rights of a buyer of payment intangibles or promissory notes, inasmuch as the former Article did not cover those sales. To the extent that the exception in paragraph (2) covers outright sales of payment intangibles, which automatically are perfected under paragraph (3), the exception is redundant.

Paragraph (14), which is new, affords automatic perfection to sales by individuals of an "account" (as defined in Section 9-102) consisting of the right to winnings in a lottery or other game of chance. Payments on these accounts typically extend for periods of twenty years or more. It would be unduly burdensome for the secured party, who would have no other reason to maintain contact with the seller, to monitor the seller's whereabouts for such a length of time. This paragraph was added in 2001. It applies to a sale of an account described in it, even if the sale was entered into before the effective date of the paragraph. However, if the relative priorities of conflicting claims to the account were established before the paragraph took effect, Article 9 as in effect immediately prior to the date the paragraph took effect determines priority.

5. Health-Care-Insurance Receivables. Paragraph (5) extends automatic perfection to assignments of health-care-insurance receivables if the assignment is made to the health-care provider that provided the health-care goods or services. The primary effect is that, when an individual assigns a right to payment under an insurance policy to the person who provided health-care goods or services, the provider has no need to file a financing statement against the individual. The normal filing requirements apply to other assignments of health-care-insurance receivables covered by this Article, e.g., assignments from the health-care provider to a financer.

6. Investment Property. Paragraph (9) replaces the last clause of former Section 9-116(2), concerning security interests that arise in the delivery of a financial asset.

Paragraphs (10) and (11) replace former Section 9-115(4)(c) and (d), concerning secured financing of securities and commodity firms and clearing corporations. The former sections indicated that, with respect to certain security interests created by a securities intermediary or commodity intermediary, "[t]he filing of a financing statement . . . has no effect for purposes of perfection or priority with respect to that security interest." No change in meaning is intended by the deletion of the quoted phrase.

Secured financing arrangements for securities firms are currently implemented in various ways. In some circumstances, lenders may require that the transactions be structured as "hard pledges," where the securities are transferred on the books of a clearing corporation from the debtor's account to the lender's account or to a special pledge account for the lender where they cannot be disposed of without the specific consent of the lender. In other circumstances, lenders are content with so-called "agreement to pledge" or "agreement to deliver" arrangements, where the debtor retains the positions in its own account, but reflects on its books that the positions have been hypothecated and promises that the securities will be transferred to the secured party's account on demand.

The perfection and priority rules of this Article are designed to facilitate current secured financing arrangements for securities firms as well as to provide sufficient flexibility to accommodate new arrangements that develop in the future. Hard pledge arrangements are covered by the concept of control. See Sections 9-314, 9-106, 8-106. Non-control secured financing arrangements for securities firms are covered by the automatic perfection rule of paragraph (10). Before the 1994 revision of Articles 8 and 9, agreement to pledge arrangements could be implemented under a provision that a security interest in securities given for new value under a written security agreement was perfected without filing or possession for a period of 21 days. Although the security interests were temporary in legal theory, the financing arrangements could, in practice, be continued indefinitely by rolling over the loans at least every 21 days. Accordingly, a knowledgeable creditor of a securities firm realizes that the firm's securities may be subject to security interests that are not discoverable from any public records. The automatic-perfection rule of paragraph (10) makes it unnecessary to engage in the purely formal practice of rolling over these arrangements every 21 days.

In some circumstances, a clearing corporation may be the debtor in a secured financing arrangement. For example, a clearing corporation that settles delivery-versus-payment transactions among its participants on a net, same-day basis relies on timely payments from all participants with net obligations due to the system. If a participant that is a net debtor were to default on its payment obligation, the clearing corporation would not receive some of the funds needed to settle with participants that are net creditors to the system. To complete end-of-day settlement after a payment default by a participant, a clearing corporation that settles on a net, same-day basis may need to draw on credit lines and pledge securities of the defaulting participant or other securities pledged by participants in the clearing corporation to secure such drawings. The clearing corporation may be the top-tier securities intermediary for the securities pledged, so that it would not be practical for the lender to obtain control. Even where the clearing corporation holds some types of securities through other intermediaries, however, the clearing corporation is unlikely to be able to complete the arrangements necessary to convey "control" over the securities to be pledged in time to complete settlement in a timely manner. However, the term "securities intermediary" is defined in Section 8-102(a)(14) to include clearing corporations. Thus, the perfection rule of paragraph (10) applies to security interests in investment property granted by clearing corporations.

7. Beneficial Interests in Trusts. Under former Section 9-302(1)(c), filing was not required to perfect a security interest created by an assignment of a beneficial interest in a trust. Because beneficial interests in trusts are now used as collateral with greater frequency in commercial transactions, under this Article filing is required to perfect a security interest in a beneficial interest.

8. Assignments for Benefit of Creditors. No filing or other action is required to perfect an assignment for the benefit of creditors. These assignments are not financing transactions, and the debtor ordinarily will not be engaging in further credit transactions.

9. Not Exclusive. This section does not provide the exclusive method by which the security interests that it covers may be perfected. Compare, e.g., Sections 9-311(b) and 9-312(b), which declare exclusive certain methods of perfection for certain types of collateral. In some circumstances, a secured party whose security interest is or will be perfected without filing under this section may wish to perfect by another method as well. For example, a buyer of a payment intangible or promissory note may wish to file a financing statement before buying the item in order to establish an earlier priority date under the "first to file or perfect" rule of Section 9-322(a)(1):

Example: At time T, SP-1 with proper authorization files a financing statement against Debtor covering payment intangibles. Debtor does not grant SP-1 an interest in any payment intangible. At time T+1, Debtor signs an agreement that grants to SP-2, for value, a security interest in a particular payment intangible owned by Debtor ("payment intangible X"), which security interest secures an obligation. SP-2 files a financing statement against Debtor covering payment intangible X. At time T+2, Debtor signs an agreement that sells payment intangible X to SP-1, for value. SP-1's ownership interest in payment intangible X is a security interest as defined in Section 1-201(b)(35), and paragraph (3) of this section provides that the security interest is perfected upon attachment. Priority between the perfected security interests of SP-1 and SP-2 is resolved by the "first to file or perfect" rule of Section 9-322(a)(1). Under that rule, SP-1's security interest has priority over SP-2's security interest because of SP-1's filing at time T. If SP-1 had not filed a financing statement at time T but instead had relied solely upon perfection under this section, SP-2's security interest would have priority over SP-1's security interest under Section 9-322(a)(1). In that event, SP-1 would own X subject to SP-2's security interest.

See PEB Commentary No. 30, dated February 27, 2025. The Commentary is available at https://www.ali .org/peb-ucc.

Section 9-310. When Filing Required to Perfect Security Interest or Agricultural Lien; Security Interests and Agricultural Liens to Which Filing Provisions Do Not Apply

(a) [General rule: perfection by filing.] Except as otherwise provided in subsection (b) and Section 9-312(b), a financing statement must be filed to perfect all security interests and agricultural liens.

(b) [Exceptions: filing not necessary.] The filing of a financing statement is not necessary to perfect a security interest:

(1) that is perfected under Section 9-308(d), (e), (f), or (g);

(2) that is perfected under Section 9-309 when it attaches;

(3) in property subject to a statute, regulation, or treaty described in Section 9-311(a);

(4) in goods in possession of a bailee which is perfected under Section 9-312(d)(1) or (2);

(5) in certificated securities, documents, goods, or instruments which is perfected without filing, control, or possession under Section 9-312(e), (f), or (g);

(6) in collateral in the secured party's possession under Section 9-313;

(7) in a certificated security which is perfected by delivery of the security certificate to the secured party under Section 9-313;

(8) in controllable accounts, controllable electronic records, controllable payment intangibles, deposit accounts, electronic documents, investment property, or letter-of-credit rights which is perfected by control under Section 9-314;

(8.1) in chattel paper which is perfect by possession and control under Section 9-314A;

(9) in proceeds which is perfected under Section 9-315; or

(10) that is perfected under Section 9-316.

(c) [Assignment of perfected security interest.] If a secured party assigns a perfected security interest or agricultural lien, a filing under this article is not required to continue the perfected status of the security interest against creditors of and transferees from the original debtor.

Definitional Cross References:

Agricultural lien	Section 9-102(a)(5)
Certificated security	Section 8-102(a)(4)
Chattel paper	Section 9-102(a)(11)
Collateral	Section 9-102(a)(12)
Controllable account	Section 9-102(a)(27A)
Controllable electronic record	Section 12-102(a)(1)
Controllable payment intangible	Section 9-102(a)(27B)
Creditor	Section 1-201(b)(13)
Delivery	Section 1-201(b)(15)
Deposit account	Section 9-102(a)(29)
Document	Section 9-102(a)(30)
Electronic	Section 1-201(b)(16A)
Financing statement	Section 9-102(a)(39)
Goods	Section 9-102(a)(44)
Instrument	Section 9-102(a)(47)
Investment property	Section 9-102(a)(49)
Letter-of-credit right	Section 9-102(a)(51)
Original debtor	Section 9-102(a)(60)
Proceeds	Section 9-102(a)(64)
Secured party	Section 9-102(a)(73)
Security certificate	Section 8-102(a)(16)
Security interest	Section 1-201(b)(35)

Official Comment

1. Source. Former Section 9-302(1), (2).

2. General Rule. Subsection (a) establishes a central Article 9 principle: Filing a financing statement is necessary for perfection of security interests and agricultural liens. However, filing is not necessary to perfect a security interest that is perfected by another permissible method, see subsection (b), nor does filing ordinarily perfect a security interest in a deposit account, letter-of-credit right, or money. See Section 9-312(b). Part 5 of the Article deals with the office in which to file, mechanics of filing, and operations of the filing office.

3. Exemptions from Filing. Subsection (b) lists the security interests for which filing is not required as a condition of perfection, because they are perfected automatically upon attachment (subsections (b)(2) and (b)(9)) or upon the occurrence of another event (subsections (b)(1), (b)(5), and (b)(9)), because they are perfected under the law of another jurisdiction (subsection (b)(10)), or because they are perfected by another method, such as by the secured party's taking possession or control (subsections (b)(3), (b)(4), (b)(5), (b)(6), (b)(7), (b)(8), and (b)(8.1)).

4. Assignments of Perfected Security Interests. Subsection (c) concerns assignment of a perfected security interest or agricultural lien. It provides that no filing is necessary in connection with an assignment by a secured party to an assignee in order to maintain perfection as against creditors of and transferees from the original debtor.

> **Example 1:** Buyer buys goods from Seller, who retains a security interest in them. After Seller perfects the security interest by filing, Seller assigns the perfected security interest to X. The security interest, in X's hands and without further steps on X's part, continues perfected against *Buyer's* transferees and creditors.

> **Example 2:** Dealer creates a security interest in specific equipment in favor of Lender. After Lender perfects the security interest in the equipment by filing, Lender assigns the chattel paper (which includes the perfected security interest in Dealer's equipment) to X. The security interest in the equipment, in X's hands and without further steps on X's part, continues perfected against Dealer's transferees and creditors. However, regardless of whether Lender made the assignment to secure Lender's obligation to X or whether the assignment was an outright sale of the chattel paper, the assignment creates a security interest in the chattel paper in favor of X. Accordingly, X must take whatever steps may be required for perfection in order to be protected against Lender's transferees and creditors with respect to the chattel paper.

Subsection (c) applies not only to an assignment of a security interest perfected by filing but also to an assignment of a security interest perfected by a method other than by filing, such as by control or by possession. Although subsection (c) addresses explicitly only the absence of an additional filing requirement, the same result normally will follow in the case of an assignment of a security interest perfected by a method other than by filing. For example, as long as possession of collateral is maintained by an assignee or by the assignor or another person on behalf of the assignee, no further perfection steps need be taken on account of the assignment to continue perfection as against creditors and transferees of the original debtor. Of course, additional action may be required for perfection of the assignee's interest as against creditors and transferees of the *assignor*.

Similarly, subsection (c) applies to the assignment of a security interest perfected by compliance with a statute, regulation, or treaty under Section 9-311(b), such as a certificate-of-title statute. Unless the statute expressly provides to the contrary, the security interest will remain perfected against creditors of and transferees from the original debtor, even if the assignee takes no action to cause the certificate of title to reflect the assignment or to cause its name to appear on the certificate of title. See PEB Commentary No. 12, which discusses this issue under former Section 9-302(3). Compliance with the statute is "equivalent to filing" under Section 9-311(b).

Section 9-311. Perfection of Security Interests in Property Subject to Certain Statutes, Regulations, and Treaties

(a) [Security interest subject to other law.] Except as otherwise provided in subsection (d), the filing of a financing statement is not necessary or effective to perfect a security interest in property subject to:

(1) a statute, regulation, or treaty of the United States whose requirements for a security interest's obtaining priority over the rights of a lien creditor with respect to the property preempt Section 9-310(a);

(2) [list any statute covering automobiles, trailers, mobile homes, boats, farm tractors, or the like, which provides for a security interest to be indicated on a certificate of title as a condition or result of perfection, and any non-Uniform Commercial Code central filing statute]; or

(3) a statute of another jurisdiction which provides for a security interest to be indicated on a certificate of title as a condition or result of the security interest's obtaining priority over the rights of a lien creditor with respect to the property.

(b) [Compliance with other law.] Compliance with the requirements of a statute, regulation, or treaty described in subsection (a) for obtaining priority over the rights of a lien creditor is equivalent to the filing of a financing statement under this article. Except as otherwise provided in subsection (d) and Sections 9-313 and 9-316(d) and (e) for goods covered by a certificate of title, a security interest in property subject to a statute, regulation, or treaty described in subsection (a) may be perfected only by compliance with those requirements, and a security interest so perfected remains perfected notwithstanding a change in the use or transfer of possession of the collateral.

(c) [Duration and renewal of perfection.] Except as otherwise provided in subsection (d) and Section 9-316(d) and (e), duration and renewal of perfection of a security interest perfected by compliance with the requirements prescribed by a statute, regulation, or treaty described in subsection (a) are governed by the statute, regulation, or treaty. In other respects, the security interest is subject to this article.

(d) [Inapplicability to certain inventory.] During any period in which collateral subject to a statute specified in subsection (a)(2) is inventory held for sale or lease by a person or leased by that person as lessor and that person is in the business of selling goods of that kind, this section does not apply to a security interest in that collateral created by that person.

Legislative Note: *This Article contemplates that perfection of a security interest in goods covered by a certificate of title occurs upon receipt by appropriate State officials of a properly tendered application for a certificate of title on which the security interest is to be indicated, without a relation back to an earlier time. States whose certificate-of-title statutes provide for perfection at a different time or contain a relation-back provision should amend the statutes accordingly.*

Definitional Cross References:

Certificate of title	Section 9-102(a)(10)
Collateral	Section 9-102(a)(12)
Debtor	Section 9-102(a)(28)
Financing statement	Section 9-102(a)(39)
Goods	Section 9-102(a)(44)
Inventory	Section 9-102(a)(48)
Lease	Section 2A-103(1)(j)
Lessor	Section 2A-103(1)(p)
Lien creditor	Section 9-102(a)(52)
Right	Section 1-201(b)(34)
Sale	Section 2-106(1)
Security interest	Section 1-201(b)(35)
State	Section 9-102(a)(77)

Comment References:

9-203 C5
9-303 C5
9-303 C6

Official Comment

1. Source. Former Section 9-302(3), (4).

2. Federal Statutes, Regulations, and Treaties. Subsection (a)(1) exempts from the filing provisions of this Article transactions as to which a system of filing—state or federal—has been established under federal law. Subsection (b) makes clear that when such a system exists, perfection of a relevant security interest can be achieved only through compliance with that system (i.e., filing under this Article is not a permissible alternative).

An example of the type of federal statute referred to in subsection (a)(1) is 49 U.S.C. §§ 44107–44111, for civil aircraft of the United States. The Assignment of Claims Act of 1940, as amended, provides for notice to contracting and disbursing officers and to sureties on bonds but does not establish a national filing system and therefore is not within the scope of subsection (a)(1). An assignee of a claim against the United

States may benefit from compliance with the Assignment of Claims Act. But regardless of whether the assignee complies with that Act, the assignee must file under this Article in order to perfect its security interest against creditors and transferees of its assignor.

Subsection (a)(1) provides explicitly that the filing requirement of this Article defers only to federal statutes, regulations, or treaties whose requirements for a security interest's obtaining priority over the rights of a lien creditor preempt Section 9-310(a). The provision eschews reference to the term "perfection," inasmuch as Section 9-308 specifies the meaning of that term and a preemptive rule may use other terminology.

3. State Statutes. Subsections (a)(2) and (3) exempt from the filing requirements of this Article transactions covered by State certificate-of-title statutes covering motor vehicles and the like. The description of certificate-of-title statutes in subsections (a)(2) and (a)(3) tracks the language of the definition of "certificate of title" in Section 9-102. For a discussion of the operation of state certificate-of-title statutes in interstate contexts, see the Comments to Section 9-303.

Some states have enacted central filing statutes with respect to secured transactions in kinds of property that are of special importance in the local economy. Subsection (a)(2) defers to these statutes with respect to filing for that property.

4. Inventory Covered by Certificate of Title. Under subsection (d), perfection of a security interest in the inventory of a person in the business of selling goods of that kind is governed by the normal perfection rules, even if the inventory is subject to a certificate-of-title statute. Compliance with a certificate-of-title statute is both unnecessary and ineffective to perfect a security interest in inventory to which this subsection applies. Thus, a secured party who finances an automobile dealer that is in the business of selling and leasing its inventory of automobiles can perfect a security interest in all the automobiles by filing a financing statement but not by compliance with a certificate-of-title statute.

Subsection (d), and thus the filing and other perfection provisions of this Article, does not apply to inventory that is subject to a certificate-of-title statute and is of a kind that the debtor is not in the business of selling. For example, if goods are subject to a certificate-of-title statute and the debtor is in the business of leasing but not of selling, goods of that kind, the other subsections of this section govern perfection of a security interest in the goods. The fact that the debtor eventually sells the goods does not, of itself, mean that the debtor "is in the business of selling goods of that kind."

The filing and other perfection provisions of this Article apply to goods subject to a certificate-of-title statute only "during any period in which collateral is inventory held for sale or lease or leased." If the debtor takes goods of this kind out of inventory and uses them, say, as equipment, a filed financing statement would not remain effective to perfect a security interest.

5. Compliance with Perfection Requirements of Other Statute. Subsection (b) makes clear that compliance with the perfection requirements (i.e., the requirements for obtaining priority over a lien creditor), but not other requirements, of a statute, regulation, or treaty described in subsection (a) is sufficient for perfection under this Article. Perfection of a security interest under such a statute, regulation, or treaty has all the consequences of perfection under this Article.

The interplay of this section with certain certificate-of-title statutes may create confusion and uncertainty. For example, statutes under which perfection does not occur until a certificate of title is issued will create a gap between the time that the goods are covered by the certificate under Section 9-303 and the time of perfection. If the gap is long enough, it may result in turning some unobjectionable transactions into avoidable preferences under Bankruptcy Code Section 547. (The preference risk arises if more than 30 days passes between the time a security interest attaches (or the debtor receives possession of the collateral, in the case of a purchase-money security interest) and the time it is perfected.) Accordingly, the Legislative Note to this section instructs the legislature to amend the applicable certificate-of-title statute to provide that perfection occurs upon receipt by the appropriate State official of a properly tendered application for a certificate of title on which the security interest is to be indicated.

Under some certificate-of-title statutes, including the Uniform Motor Vehicle Certificate of Title and Anti-Theft Act, perfection generally occurs upon delivery of specified documents to a state official but may, under certain circumstances, relate back to the time of attachment. This relation-back feature can create great difficulties for the application of the rules in Sections 9-303 and 9-311(b). Accordingly, the Legislative Note also recommends to legislatures that they remove any relation-back provisions from certificate-of-title statutes affecting security interests.

6. Compliance with Perfection Requirements of Other Statute as Equivalent to Filing. Under Subsection (b), compliance with the perfection requirements (i.e., the requirements for obtaining priority over a lien creditor) of a statute, regulation, or treaty described in subsection (a) "is equivalent to the filing of a financing statement."

The quoted phrase appeared in former Section 9-302(3). Its meaning was unclear, and many questions arose concerning the extent to which and manner in which Article 9 rules referring to "filing" were applicable to perfection by compliance with a certificate-of-title statute. This Article takes a variety of approaches for applying Article 9's filing rules to compliance with other statutes and treaties. First, as discussed above in Comment 5, it leaves the determination of some rules, such as the rule establishing time of perfection (Section 9-516(a)), to the other statutes themselves. Second, this Article explicitly applies some Article 9 filing rules to perfection under other statutes or treaties. See, e.g., Section 9-505. Third, this Article makes other Article 9 rules applicable to security interests perfected by compliance with another statute through the "equivalent to . . . " provision in the first sentence of Section 9-311(b). The third approach is reflected for the most part in occasional Comments explaining how particular rules apply when perfection is accomplished under Section 9-311(b). See, e.g., Section 9-310, Comment 4; Section 9-315, Comment 6; Section 9-317, Comment 8. The absence of a Comment indicating that a particular filing provision applies to perfection pursuant to Section 9-311(b) does not mean the provision is inapplicable.

7. Perfection by Possession of Goods Covered by Certificate-of-Title Statute. A secured party who holds a security interest perfected under the law of State A in goods that subsequently are covered by a State B certificate of title may face a predicament. Ordinarily, the secured party will have four months under State B's Section 9-316(c) and (d) in which to (re)perfect as against a purchaser of the goods by having its security interest noted on a State B certificate. This procedure is likely to require the cooperation of the debtor and any competing secured party whose security interest has been noted on the certificate. Comment 4(e) to former Section 9-103 observed that "that cooperation is not likely to be forthcoming from an owner who wrongfully procured the issuance of a new certificate not showing the out-of-state security interest, or from a local secured party finding himself in a priority contest with the out-of-state secured party." According to that Comment, "[t]he only solution for the out-of-state secured party under present certificate of title statutes seems to be to reperfect by possession, i.e., by repossessing the goods." But the "solution" may not have worked: Former Section 9-302(4) provided that a security interest in property subject to a certificate-of-title statute "can be perfected only by compliance therewith."

Sections 9-316(d) and (e), 9-311(c), and 9-313(b) of this Article resolve the conflict by providing that a security interest that remains perfected solely by virtue of Section 9-316(e) can be (re)perfected by the secured party's taking possession of the collateral. These sections contemplate only that taking possession of goods covered by a certificate of title will work as a method of perfection. None of these sections creates a right to take possession. Section 9-609 and the agreement of the parties define the secured party's right to take possession.

Section 9-312. Perfection of Security Interests in Chattel Paper, Controllable Accounts, Controllable Electronic Records, Controllable Payment Intangibles, Deposit Accounts, Negotiable Documents, Goods Covered by Documents, Instruments, Investment Property, Letter-Of-Credit Rights, and Money; Perfection by Permissive Filing; Temporary Perfection Without Filing or Transfer of Possession

(a) [Perfection by filing permitted.] A security interest in chattel paper, controllable accounts, controllable electronic records, controllable payment intangibles, instruments, investment property, or negotiable documents may be perfected by filing.

(b) [Control or possession of certain collateral.] Except as otherwise provided in Section 9-315(c) and (d) for proceeds:

(1) a security interest in a deposit account may be perfected only by control under Section 9-314;

(2) and except as otherwise provided in Section 9-308(d), a security interest in a letter-of-credit right may be perfected only by control under Section 9-314;

(3) a security interest in tangible money may be perfected only by the secured party's taking possession under Section 9-313; and

(4) a security interest in electronic money may be perfected only by control under Section 9-314.

(c) [Goods covered by negotiable document.] While goods are in the possession of a bailee that has issued a negotiable document covering the goods:

(1) a security interest in the goods may be perfected by perfecting a security interest in the document; and

(2) a security interest perfected in the document has priority over any security interest that becomes perfected in the goods by another method during that time.

(d) [Goods covered by nonnegotiable document.] While goods are in the possession of a bailee that has issued a nonnegotiable document covering the goods, a security interest in the goods may be perfected by:

(1) issuance of a document in the name of the secured party;

(2) the bailee's receipt of notification of the secured party's interest; or

(3) filing as to the goods.

(e) [Temporary perfection: new value.] A security interest in certificated securities, negotiable documents, or instruments is perfected without filing or the taking of possession or control for a period of 20 days from the time it attaches to the extent that it arises for new value given under a signed security agreement.

(f) [Temporary perfection: goods or documents made available to debtor.] A perfected security interest in a negotiable document or goods in possession of a bailee, other than one that has issued a negotiable document for the goods, remains perfected for 20 days without filing if the secured party makes available to the debtor the goods or documents representing the goods for the purpose of:

(1) ultimate sale or exchange; or

(2) loading, unloading, storing, shipping, transshipping, manufacturing, processing, or otherwise

dealing with them in a manner preliminary to their sale or exchange.

(g) [Temporary perfection: delivery of security certificate or instrument to debtor.] A perfected security interest in a certificated security or instrument remains perfected for 20 days without filing if the secured party delivers the security certificate or instrument to the debtor for the purpose of:

(1) ultimate sale or exchange; or

(2) presentation, collection, enforcement, renewal, or registration of transfer.

(h) [Expiration of temporary perfection.] After the 20-day period specified in subsection (e), (f), or (g) expires, perfection depends upon compliance with this article.

Definitional Cross References:

Certificated security	Section 8-102(a)(4)
Chattel paper	Section 9-102(a)(11)
Collateral	Section 9-102(a)(12)
Controllable account	Section 9-102(a)(27A)
Controllable electronic Record	Section 12-102(a)(1)
Controllable payment intangible	Section 9-102(a)(27B)
Debtor	Section 9-102(a)(28)
Delivery	Section 1-201(b)(15)
Deposit account	Section 9-102(a)(29)
Document	Section 9-102(a)(30)
Electronic money	Section 9-102(a)(31A)
Goods	Section 9-102(a)(44)
Instrument	Section 9-102(a)(47)
Investment property	Section 9-102(a)(49)
Letter-of-credit right	Section 9-102(a)(51)
Money	Section 9-102(a)(54A)
New value	Section 9-102(a)(57)
Proceeds	Section 9-102(a)(64)
Sale	Section 2-106(1)
Secured party	Section 9-102(a)(73)
Security agreement	Section 9-102(a)(74)
Security certificate	Section 8-102(a)(16)
Security interest	Section 1-201(b)(35)
Sign	Section 1-201(b)(37)
Tangible money	Section 9-102(a)(79A)

Comment References: 9-323 C3

Official Comment

1. Source. Former Section 9-304, with additions and some changes.

2. Instruments. Under subsection (a), a security interest in instruments may be perfected by filing. This rule represents an important change from former Article 9, under which the secured party's taking possession of an instrument was the only method of achieving long-term perfection. The rule is likely to be particularly useful in transactions involving a large number of notes that a debtor uses as collateral but continues to collect from the makers. A security interest perfected by filing is subject to defeat by certain subsequent purchasers (including secured parties). Under Section 9-330(d), purchasers for value who take possession of an instrument without knowledge that the purchase violates the rights of the secured party generally would achieve priority over a security interest in the instrument perfected by filing. In addition, Section 9-331 provides that filing a financing statement does not constitute notice that would preclude a subsequent purchaser from becoming a holder in due course and taking free of all claims under Section 3-306.

3. Chattel Paper; Negotiable Documents. Subsection (a) further provides that filing is available as a method of perfection for security interests in chattel paper and negotiable documents. Tangible chattel paper is sometimes delivered to the assignee, and sometimes left in the hands of the assignor for collection. Subsection (a) allows the assignee to perfect its security interest by filing in the latter case. Alternatively, the assignee may perfect by taking possession. See Section 9-313(a). An assignee of electronic chattel paper may perfect by taking control. See Sections 9-314(a), 9-105. The security interest of an assignee who takes possession or control may qualify for priority over a competing security interest perfected by filing. See Section 9-330.

Negotiable documents may be, and usually are, delivered to the secured party. See Article 1, Section 1-201(b)(15) (definition of "delivery"). The secured party's taking possession of a tangible document or control of an electronic document will suffice as a perfection step. See Sections 9-313(a), 9-314 and 7-106. However, as is the case with chattel paper, a security interest in a negotiable document may be perfected by filing.

4. Investment Property. A security interest in investment property, including certificated securities, uncertificated securities, security entitlements, and securities accounts, may be perfected by filing. However, security interests created by brokers, securities intermediaries, or commodity intermediaries are automatically perfected; filing is of no effect. See Section 9-309(10), (11). A security interest in all kinds of investment property also may be perfected by control, see Sections 9-314, 9-106, and a security interest in a certificated security also may be perfected by the secured party's taking delivery under Section 8-301. See Section 9-313(a). A security interest perfected only by filing is subordinate to a conflicting security interest perfected by control or delivery. See Section 9-328(1), (5). Thus, although filing is a permissible method of perfection, a secured party who perfects by filing takes the risk that the debtor has granted or will grant a security interest in the same collateral to another party who obtains control. Also, perfection by filing would not give the secured party protection against other types of adverse claims, since the Article 8 adverse claim cut-off rules require control. See Section 8-510.

4A. Controllable Accounts, Controllable Electronic Records, and Controllable Payment Intangibles. Consistent with the treatment of chattel paper, instruments, investment property, and negotiable documents, under subsection (a) a security interest in controllable accounts, controllable electronic records, and controllable payment intangibles may be perfected by filing. A security interest in that collateral also may be perfected by control. Section 9-314.

5. Deposit Accounts. Under new subsection (b)(1), the only method of perfecting a security interest in a deposit account as original collateral is by control. Filing is ineffective, except as provided in Section 9-315 with respect to proceeds. As explained in Section 9-104, "control" can arise as a result of an agreement among the secured party, debtor, and bank, whereby the bank agrees to comply with instructions of the secured party with respect to disposition of the funds on deposit, even though the debtor retains the right to direct disposition of the funds. Thus, subsection (b)(1) takes an intermediate position between certain non-UCC law, which conditions the effectiveness of a security interest on the secured party's enjoyment of such dominion and control over the deposit account that the debtor is unable to dispose of the funds, and the approach this Article takes to securities accounts, under which a secured party who is unable to reach the collateral without resort to judicial process may perfect by filing. By conditioning perfection on "control," rather than requiring the secured party to enjoy absolute dominion to the exclusion of the debtor, subsection (b)(1) permits perfection in a wide variety of transactions, including those in which the secured party actually relies on the deposit account in extending credit and maintains some meaningful dominion over it, but does not wish to deprive the debtor of access to the funds altogether.

6. Letter-of-Credit Rights. Letter-of-credit rights commonly are "supporting obligations," as defined in Section 9-102. Perfection as to the related account, chattel paper, document, general intangible, instrument, or investment property will perfect as to the letter-of-credit rights. See Section 9-308(d). Subsection (b)(2) provides that, in other cases, a security interest in a letter-of-credit right may be perfected only by control. "Control," for these purposes, is explained in Section 9-107.

6A. Money. Under subsection (b)(3), a security interest in tangible money may be perfected only by possession under Section 9-313. Similarly, under subsection (b)(4), a security interest in electronic money may be perfected only by control under Section 9-314.

7. Goods Covered by Document of Title. Subsection (c) applies to goods in the possession of a bailee who has issued a negotiable document covering the goods. Subsection (d) applies to goods in the possession of a bailee who has issued a nonnegotiable document of title, including a document of title that is "non-negotiable" under Section 7-104. Section 9-313 governs perfection of a security interest in goods in the possession of a bailee who has not issued a document of title.

Subsection (c) clarifies the perfection and priority rules in former Section 9-304(2). Consistently with the provisions of Article 7, subsection (c) takes the position that, as long as a negotiable document covering goods is outstanding, title to the goods is, so to say, locked up in the document. Accordingly, a security interest in goods covered by a negotiable document may be perfected by perfecting a security interest in the document. The security interest also may be perfected by another method, e.g., by filing. The priority rule in subsection (c) governs only priority between (i) a security interest in goods which is perfected by perfecting in the document and (ii) a security interest in the goods which becomes perfected by another method while the goods are covered by the document.

> **Example 1:** While wheat is in a grain elevator and covered by a negotiable warehouse receipt, Debtor creates a security interest in the wheat in favor of SP-1 and SP-2. SP-1 perfects by filing a financing statement covering "wheat." Thereafter, SP-2 perfects by filing a financing statement describing the warehouse receipt. Subsection (c)(1) provides that SP-2's security interest is perfected. Subsection (c)(2) provides that SP-2's security interest is senior to SP-1's.

> **Example 2:** The facts are as in Example 1, but SP-1's security interest attached and was perfected before the goods were delivered to the grain elevator. Subsection (c)(2) does not apply, because SP-1's security interest did not become perfected during the time that the wheat was in the possession of a bailee. Rather, the first-to-file-or-perfect priority rule applies. See Sections 7-503 and 9-322.

A secured party may become "a holder to whom a negotiable document of title has been duly negotiated" under Section 7-501. If so, the secured party acquires the rights specified by Article 7. Article 9 does not limit those rights, which may include the right to priority over an earlier-perfected security interest. See Section 9-331(a).

Subsection (d) takes a different approach to the problem of goods covered by a nonnegotiable document. Here, title to the goods is not looked on as being locked up in the document. For example, a transferee that takes delivery of a nonnegotiable document receives, under Section 7-504(a), "the title and rights" of the transferor, but the transferee would not thereby become a "person entitled under the document" with a right to receive delivery of the goods from the bailee. The secured party may perfect its security interest directly in the goods by filing as to them. The subsection provides two other methods of perfection: issuance of the document in the secured party's name (as consignee of a straight bill of lading or the person to whom delivery would be made under a non-negotiable warehouse receipt) and receipt of notification of the secured party's interest by the bailee. Issuance (or reissuance) of the nonnegotiable document in the secured party's name would allow the secured party to become a "person entitled under the document." However, the bailee's receipt of notification would not confer on the secured party the status of a person entitled unless the notification resulted from an instruction under the document. See Section 7-102(a)(9) (defining "person entitled under the document") and Comment 6. Perfection under subsection (d) occurs when the bailee receives notification of the secured party's interest in the goods, regardless of who sends the notification. Receipt of notification is effective to perfect, regardless of whether the bailee responds. Unlike pre-1998 Section 9-304(3), from which it derives, subsection (d) does not apply to goods in the possession of a bailee who has not issued a document of title. Section 9-313(c) covers that case and provides that perfection by possession as to goods not covered by a document requires the bailee's acknowledgment.

Subsection (a) makes clear that a security interest in negotiable documents (and other collateral mentioned there) may be perfected by filing, but it makes no mention of nonnegotiable documents. However, under the general rule of Section 9-310, a security interest in a nonnegotiable document can be perfected by filing. A security interest in an electronic document, negotiable or nonnegotiable, can be perfected by control under Section 7-106. Section 9-314(a). But a security interest in a nonnegotiable tangible document cannot be perfected by possession. Section 9-313(a). Although a perfected security interest in a nonnegotiable document might provide useful benefits for the secured party, it would not perfect a security interest in the goods. And by perfecting a security interest in the nonnegotiable document the secured party would not thereby become a "person entitled under the document." Indeed, unless the secured party also took delivery of the document (i.e., possession or control under Section 1- 201(b)(15)), it would not obtain the rights of a transferee under Section 7-504(a).

8. Temporary Perfection Without Having First Otherwise Perfected. Subsection (e) follows pre-1998 Section 9-304(4) in giving perfected status to security interests in certificated securities, instruments, and negotiable documents for a short period (reduced from 21 to 20 days, which is the time period generally applicable in this Article), although there has been no filing and the collateral is in the debtor's possession or control. The 20-day temporary perfection runs from the date of attachment. There is no limitation on the purpose for which the debtor is in possession, but the secured party must have given "new value" (defined in Section 9-102) under a signed security agreement.

9. Maintaining Perfection After Surrendering Possession. There are a variety of legitimate reasons—many of them are described in subsections (f) and (g)—why certain types of collateral must be released temporarily to a debtor. No useful purpose would be served by cluttering the files with records of such exceedingly short term transactions.

Subsection (f) affords the possibility of 20-day perfection in negotiable documents and goods in the possession of a bailee but not covered by a negotiable document. Subsection (g) provides for 20-day perfection in certificated securities and instruments. These subsections derive from former Section 9-305(5). However, the period of temporary perfection has been reduced from 21 to 20 days, which is the time period generally applicable in this Article, and "enforcement" has been added in subsection (g) as one of the special and limited purposes for which a secured party can release an instrument or certificated security to the debtor and still remain perfected. The period of temporary perfection runs from the date a secured party who already has a perfected security interest turns over the collateral to the debtor. There is no new value requirement, but the turnover must be for one or more of the purposes stated in subsection (f) or (g). The 20-day period may be extended by perfecting as to the collateral by another method before the period expires. However, if the security interest is not perfected by another method until after the 20-day period expires, there will be a gap during which the security interest is unperfected.

Temporary perfection extends only to the negotiable document or goods under subsection (f) and only to the certificated security or instrument under subsection (g). It does not extend to proceeds. If the collateral is sold, the security interest will continue in the proceeds for the period specified in Section 9-315.

Subsections (f) and (g) deal only with perfection. Other sections of this Article govern the priority of a security interest in goods after surrender of possession or control of the document covering them. In the case of a purchase-money security interest in inventory, priority may be conditioned upon giving notification to a prior inventory financer. See Section 9-324.

10. "Signed" Replaces "Authenticated." Consistent with the revised definition of "sign" in Section 1-201(b)(37), the cognate term "signed" replaces the reference to "authenticated" in the pre-2022 text of this section.

Section 9-313. When Possession by or Delivery to Secured Party Perfects Security Interest Without Filing

(a) [Perfection by possession or delivery.] Except as otherwise provided in subsection (b), a secured party may perfect a security interest in goods, instruments, negotiable tangible documents, or tangible money by taking possession of the collateral. A secured party may perfect a security interest in certificated securities by taking delivery of the certificated securities under Section 8-301.

(b) [Goods covered by certificate of title.] With respect to goods covered by a certificate of title issued by this State, a secured party may perfect a security interest in the goods by taking possession of the goods only in the circumstances described in Section 9-316(d).

(c) [Collateral in possession of person other than debtor.] With respect to collateral other than certificated securities and goods covered by a document, a secured party takes possession of collateral in the possession of a person other than the debtor, the secured party, or a lessee of the collateral from the debtor in the ordinary course of the debtor's business, when:

(1) the person in possession signs a record acknowledging that it holds possession of the collateral for the secured party's benefit; or

(2) the person takes possession of the collateral after having signed a record acknowledging that it will hold possession of the collateral for the secured party's benefit.

(d) [Time of perfection by possession; continuation of perfection.] If perfection of a security interest depends upon possession of the collateral by a secured party, perfection occurs not earlier than the time the secured party takes possession and continues only while the secured party retains possession.

(e) [Time of perfection by delivery; continuation of perfection.] A security interest in a certificated security in registered form is perfected by delivery when delivery of the certificated security occurs under Section 8-301 and remains perfected by delivery until the debtor obtains possession of the security certificate.

(f) [Acknowledgment not required.] A person in possession of collateral is not required to acknowledge that it holds possession for a secured party's benefit.

(g) [Effectiveness of acknowledgment; no duties or confirmation.] If a person acknowledges that it holds possession for the secured party's benefit:

(1) the acknowledgment is effective under subsection (c) or Section 8-301(a), even if the acknowledgment violates the rights of a debtor; and

(2) unless the person otherwise agrees or law other than this article otherwise provides, the person does not owe any duty to the secured party and is not required to confirm the acknowledgment to another person.

(h) [Secured party's delivery to person other than debtor.] A secured party having possession of collateral does not relinquish possession by delivering the collateral to a person other than the debtor or a lessee of the collateral from the debtor in the ordinary course of the debtor's business if the person was instructed before the delivery or is instructed contemporaneously with the delivery:

(1) to hold possession of the collateral for the secured party's benefit; or

(2) to redeliver the collateral to the secured party.

(i) [Effect of delivery under subsection (h); no duties or confirmation.] A secured party does not relinquish possession, even if a delivery under subsection (h) violates the rights of a debtor. A person to which collateral is delivered under subsection (h) does not owe any duty to the secured party and is not required to confirm the delivery to another person unless the person otherwise agrees or law other than this article otherwise provides.

Definitional Cross References:

Certificate of title	Section 9-102(a)(10)
Certificated security	Section 8-102(a)(4)
Collateral	Section 9-102(a)(12)
Debtor	Section 9-102(a)(28)
Delivery	Section 1-201(b)(15)
Document	Section 9-102(a)(30)
Goods	Section 9-102(a)(44)
Instrument	Section 9-102(a)(47)
Lessee	Section 2A-103(1)(n)
Money	Section 9-102(a)(54A)
Person	Section 1-201(b)(27)
Record	Section 9-102(a)(70)
Right	Section 1-201(b)(34)
Secured party	Section 9-102(a)(73)
Security certificate	Section 8-102(a)(16)
Security interest	Section 1-201(b)(35)
Sign	Section 1-201(b)(37)
State	Section 9-102(a)(77)
Tangible money	Section 9-102(a)(79A)

Comment References: 9-203 C4

Official Comment

1. Source. Former Sections 9-305, 9-115(6).

2. Perfection by Possession. As under the common law of pledge, no filing is required by this Article to perfect a security interest if the secured party takes possession of the collateral. See Section 9-310(b)(6).

This section permits a security interest to be perfected by the taking of possession only when the collateral is goods, instruments, negotiable tangible documents, or tangible money. Accounts, commercial tort claims, deposit accounts, investment property, letter-of-credit rights, letters of credit, and oil, gas, or other minerals before extraction are excluded. (But see Comment 6, below, regarding certificated securities.) A security interest in accounts and payment intangibles—property not ordinarily represented by any writing whose delivery operates to transfer the right to payment—may under this Article be perfected only by filing. This rule would not be affected by the fact that a security agreement or other record described the assignment of such collateral as a "pledge." Section 9-309(2) exempts from filing certain assignments of accounts or payment intangibles which are out of the ordinary course of financing. These exempted assignments are perfected when they attach. Similarly, under Section 9-309(3), sales of payment intangibles are automatically perfected.

Perfection by possession of chattel paper evidenced by an authoritative tangible record (formerly defined as "tangible chattel paper") has been removed from this section. Instead, perfection by possession and control of chattel paper is governed by Section 9-314A.

3. "Possession." This section does not define "possession." It adopts the general concept as it developed under former Article 9. As under former Article 9, in determining whether a particular person has possession, the principles of agency apply. For example, if the collateral is in possession of an agent of the secured party for the purposes of possessing on behalf of the secured party, and if the agent is not also an agent of the debtor, the secured party has taken actual possession, and subsection (c) does not apply. Sometimes a person holds collateral both as an agent of the secured party and as an agent of the debtor. The fact of dual agency is not of itself inconsistent with the secured party's having taken possession (and thereby having rendered subsection (c) inapplicable). The debtor cannot qualify as an agent for the secured party for purposes of the secured party's taking possession. And, under appropriate circumstances, a court may determine that a person in possession is so closely connected to or controlled by the debtor that the debtor has retained effective possession, even though the person may have agreed to take possession on behalf of the secured party. If so, the person's taking possession would not constitute the secured party's taking possession and would not be sufficient for perfection. See also Section 9-205(b). In a typical escrow arrangement, where the escrowee has possession of collateral as agent for both the secured party and the debtor, the debtor's relationship to the escrowee is not such as to constitute retention of possession by the debtor.

4. Goods in Possession of Third Party: Perfection. Former Section 9-305 permitted perfection of a security interest by notification to a bailee in possession of collateral. This Article distinguishes between goods in the possession of a bailee who has issued a document of title covering the goods and goods in the possession of a third party who has not issued a document. Section 9-312(c) or (d) applies to the former, depending on whether the document is negotiable. Section 9-313(c) applies to the latter. It provides a method of perfection by possession when the collateral is possessed by a third person who is not the secured party's agent.

Notification of a third person does not suffice to perfect under Section 9-313(c). Rather, perfection does not occur unless the third person signs an acknowledgment that it holds possession of the collateral for the secured party's benefit. Compare Section 9-312(d), under which receipt of notification of the security party's interest by a bailee holding goods covered by a nonnegotiable document is sufficient to perfect, even if the bailee does not acknowledge receipt of the notification. A third person may acknowledge that it will hold for the secured party's benefit goods to be received in the future. Under these circumstances, perfection by possession occurs when the third person obtains possession of the goods.

Under subsection (c), acknowledgment of notification by a "lessee . . . in . . . ordinary course of . . . business" (defined in Section 2A-103) does not suffice for possession. The section thus rejects the reasoning of *In re Atlantic Systems, Inc.*, 135 B.R. 463 (Bankr. S.D.N.Y. 1992) (holding that notification to debtor-lessor's lessee sufficed to perfect security interest in leased goods). See Steven O. Weise, *Perfection by Possession: The Need for an Objective Test,* 29 Idaho Law Rev. 705 (1992-93) (arguing that lessee's possession in ordinary course of debtor-lessor's business does not provide adequate public notice of possible security interest in leased goods). Inclusion of a per se rule concerning lessees is not meant to preclude a court, under appropriate circumstances, from determining that a third person is so closely connected to or controlled by the debtor that the debtor has retained effective possession. If so, the third person's acknowledgment would not be sufficient for perfection.

In some cases, it may be uncertain whether a person who has possession of collateral is an agent of the secured party or a non-agent bailee. Under those circumstances, prudence might suggest that the secured party obtain the person's acknowledgment to avoid litigation and ensure perfection by possession regardless of how the relationship between the secured party and the person is characterized.

5. No Relation Back; time of perfection and continuation of perfection. Former Section 9-305 provided that a security interest is perfected by possession from the time possession is taken "without a relation back." As the Comment to pre-1998 Section 9-305 observed, the relation-back theory, under which the taking of possession was deemed to relate back to the date of the original security agreement, has had little vitality since the 1938 revision of the Federal Bankruptcy Act. The theory is inconsistent with pre-1998 Article 9 and with this Article. See Section 9-313(d). Accordingly, this Article deletes the quoted phrase as unnecessary. Under Subsection (d), where a pledge (perfection by possession) transaction is contemplated, perfection dates only from the time possession is taken. The only exceptions to this rule are the short, 20-day periods of perfection provided in Section 9-312(e), (f), and (g), during which a debtor may have possession of specified collateral in which there is a perfected security interest. Also under subsection (d), perfection continues only while the secured party retains possession. However, if a secured party's possession is based on an acknowledgment under Section 9-313(c) by another person in possession, the secured party remains perfected by possession only while the other person retains possession. This result necessarily follows because such a secured party's possession derives solely from the other person's continued possession.

6. Certificated Securities. The second sentence of subsection (a) reflects the traditional rule for perfection of a security interest in certificated securities. Compare Section 9-115(6) (1994 Official Text); Sections 8-321, 8-313(1)(a) (1978 Official Text); Section 9-305 (1972 Official Text). It has been modified to refer to "delivery" under Section 8-301. Corresponding changes appear in Section 9-203(b).

Subsection (e), which is new, applies to a secured party in possession of security certificates or another person who has taken delivery of security certificates and holds them for the secured party's benefit under Section 8-301. See Comment 8.

Under subsection (e), a possessory security interest in a certificated security remains perfected until the debtor obtains possession of the security certificate. This rule is analogous to that of Section 9-314(c), which deals with perfection of security interests in investment property by control. See Section 9-314, Comment 3.

7. Goods Covered by Certificate of Title. Subsection (b) is necessary to effect changes to the choice-of-law rules governing goods covered by a certificate of title. These changes are described in the Comments to Section 9-311. Subsection (b), like subsection (a), does not create a right to take possession. Rather, it indicates the circumstances under which the secured party's taking possession of goods covered by a certificate of title is effective to perfect a security interest in the goods: the goods become covered by a certificate of title issued by this State at a time when the security interest is perfected by any method under the law of another jurisdiction.

8. Goods in Possession of Third Party: No Duty to Acknowledge; Consequences of Acknowledgment. Subsections (f) and (g) are new and address matters as to which former Article 9 was silent. They derive in part from Section 8-106(g). Subsection (f) provides that a person in possession of collateral is not required to acknowledge that it holds for a secured party. Subsection (g)(1) provides that an acknowledgment is effective even if wrongful as to the debtor. Subsection (g)(2) makes clear that an acknowledgment does not give rise to any duties or responsibilities under this Article. Arrangements involving the possession of goods are hardly standardized. They include bailments for services to be performed on the goods (such as repair or processing), for use (leases), as security (pledges), for carriage, and for storage. This Article leaves to the agreement of the parties and to any other applicable law the imposition of duties and responsibilities upon a person who acknowledges under subsection (c). For example, by acknowledging, a third party does not become obliged to act on the secured party's direction or to remain in possession of the collateral unless it agrees to do so or other law so provides.

9. Delivery to Third Party by Secured Party. Subsections (h) and (i) address the practice of mortgage warehouse lenders. These lenders typically send mortgage notes to prospective purchasers under cover of letters advising the prospective purchasers that the lenders hold security interests in the notes. These lenders relied on notification to maintain perfection under pre-1998 Section 9-305. Requiring them to obtain signed acknowledgments from each prospective purchaser under subsection (c) could be unduly burdensome and disruptive of established practices. Under subsection (h), when a secured party in possession itself delivers the collateral to a third party, instructions to the third party would be sufficient to maintain perfection by possession; an acknowledgment would not be necessary. Under subsection (i), the secured party does not relinquish possession by making a delivery under subsection (h), even if the delivery violates the rights of the debtor. That subsection also makes clear that a person to whom collateral is delivered under subsection (h) does not owe any duty to the secured party and is not required to confirm the delivery to another person unless the person otherwise agrees or law other than this Article provides otherwise.

10. "Signs" and "Signed" Replaces "Authenticates" and "Authenticated." Consistent with the revised definition of "sign" in Section 1-201(b)(37), the cognate terms "signs" and "signed" replace the references to "authenticates" and "authenticated" in the pre-2022 text of this section.

Section 9-314. Perfection by Control

(a) [Perfection by control.] A security interest in controllable accounts, controllable electronic records, controllable payment intangibles, deposit accounts, electronic documents, electronic money, investment property, or letter-of-credit rights may be perfected by control of the collateral under Sections 7-106, 9-104, 9-105A, 9-106, 9-107, or 9-107A.

(b) [Specified collateral: time of perfection by control; continuation of perfection.] A security interest in controllable accounts, controllable electronic records, controllable payment intangibles, deposit accounts, electronic documents, electronic money, or letter-of-credit rights is perfected by control under Sections 7-106, 9-104, 9-105A, 9-107, or 9-107A not earlier than the time the secured party obtains control and remains perfected by control only while the secured party retains control.

(c) [Investment property: time of perfection by control; continuation of perfection.] A security interest in investment property is perfected by control under Section 9-106 not earlier than the time the secured party obtains control and remains perfected by control until:

(1) the secured party does not have control; and

(2) one of the following occurs:

(A) if the collateral is a certificated security, the debtor has or acquires possession of the security certificate;

(B) if the collateral is an uncertificated security, the issuer has registered or registers the debtor as the registered owner; or

(C) if the collateral is a security entitlement, the debtor is or becomes the entitlement holder.

Definitional Cross References:

Certificated security	Section 8-102(a)(4)
Collateral	Section 9-102(a)(12)
Controllable account	Section 9-102(a)(27A)
Controllable electronic Record	Section 12-102(a)(1)
Controllable payment intangible	Section 9-102(a)(27B)
Debtor	Section 9-102(a)(28)
Deposit account	Section 9-102(a)(29)
Document	Section 9-102(a)(30)
Electronic	Section 1-201(b)(16A)
Electronic money	Section 9-102(a)(31A)
Entitlement holder	Section 8-102(a)(7)
Investment property	Section 9-102(a)(49)
Issuer (security)	Section 8-201(a)
Letter-of-credit right	Section 9-102(a)(51)
Secured party	Section 9-102(a)(73)
Security certificate	Section 8-102(a)(16)
Security entitlement	Section 8-102(a)(17)
Security interest	Section 1-201(b)(35)
Uncertificated security	Section 8-102(a)(18)

Official Comment

1. Source. Substantially new; derived in part from former Section 9-115(4).

2. Control. This section provides for perfection by control with respect to controllable accounts, controllable electronic records, controllable payment intangibles, deposit accounts, electronic documents, electronic money, investment property, and letter-of-credit rights. Concerning how a secured party takes control of these types of collateral, see Sections 7-106, 9-104, 9-105A, 9-107, and 9-107A, and Comments. Subsection (b) explains when a security interest is perfected by control and how long a security interest remains perfected by control. Like Section 9-313(d) and for the same reasons, subsection (b) makes no reference to the doctrine of "relation back." See Section 9-313, Comment 5. As to an electronic document that is reissued in a tangible medium, (see Section 7-105), a secured party that is perfected by control in the electronic document should file as to the document before relinquishing control in order to maintain continuous perfection in the document. See Section 9-308. If a secured party's control is based on an acknowledgment under Section 7-106(g), 9- 104(a)(4), or 9-105A(e) or under 9-107A and 12-105(e) by another person having control, the secured party remains perfected by control only while the other person retains control. This result necessarily follows because such a secured party's control derives solely from the other person's continued control.

Perfection by control of chattel paper evidenced by an authoritative electronic record (formerly defined as "electronic chattel paper") has been removed from this section. Instead, perfection by possession and control of chattel paper is governed by Section 9-314A.

3. Investment Property. Subsection (c) provides a special rule for investment property. Once a secured party has control, its security interest remains perfected by control until the secured party ceases to have control and the debtor receives possession of collateral that is a certificated security, becomes the registered owner of collateral that is an uncertificated security, or becomes the entitlement holder of collateral that is a security entitlement. The result is particularly important in the "repledge" context. See Section 9-207, Comment 5.

In a transaction in which a secured party who has control grants a security interest in investment property or sells outright the investment property, by virtue of the debtor's consent or applicable legal rules, a purchaser from the secured party typically will cut off the debtor's rights in the investment property or be immune from the debtor's claims. See Section 9-207, Comments 5 and 6. If the investment property is a security, the debtor normally would retain no interest in the security following the purchase from the secured party, and a claim of the debtor against the secured party for redemption (Section 9-623) or otherwise with respect to the security would be a purely personal claim. If the investment property transferred by the secured party is a financial asset in which the debtor had a security entitlement credited to a securities account maintained with the secured party as a securities intermediary, the debtor's claim against the secured party could arise as a part of its securities account notwithstanding its personal nature. (This claim would be analogous to a "credit balance" in the securities account, which is a component of the securities account even though it is a personal claim against the intermediary.) In the case in which the debtor may retain an interest in investment property notwithstanding a repledge or sale by the secured party, subsection (c) makes clear that the security interest will remain perfected by control. Notwithstanding subsection (c), if a secured party's control is based on an acknowledgment under Section 8-106(d)(3) by another person having control, the secured party remains perfected by control only while the other person retains control. This result necessarily follows because such a secured party's control derives solely from the other person's continued control. Although Section 8-106(d)(3) was amended by the 2022 Article 9 Revisions, this result also applied to a secured party in control under pre-2022 subsection (d)(3).

3A. Shared control between debtor and secured party (and other transferor and transferee) and control through another person. Sections 7-106 (control of electronic documents), 9-105 (control of authoritative electronic records evidencing chattel paper), 9-105A (control of electronic money), and 12-105 (control of controllable electronic records, on which control of controllable accounts and controllable payment intangibles under Section 9-107A depends) contemplate the possibility that both a debtor and a secured party may have control of the relevant collateral by sharing an exclusive power. Such shared control between a debtor and secured party does not necessarily impair perfection of a security interest under this section or Section 9-314A. On shared exclusive powers, see generally Section 12-105, Comment 5. However, if a secured party can exercise a power only if the power is exercised also by the debtor, the power would not be shared and, consequently, the secured party would not have control based on the exclusive power. This result follows from Section 12-105(c) and corresponding subsections in the other provisions on control cited above. Under Section 12- 105(c), because a debtor would be a "transferor of an interest" in a controllable electronic record or a controllable account or payment intangible evidenced by the record, the debtor's "blocking power" (i.e., the secured party can exercise the power only if the debtor also exercises the power) with respect to the secured party's exercise of the power would disqualify the secured party from sharing (and, consequently, enjoying) the exclusive power and perfection by control based on exclusive powers. Similarly, a purchaser in that situation would be disqualified from having control and thereby from enjoying the status and benefits of a qualifying purchaser (Section 12- 102(a)(2)) under Section 12-104(e) and (g) if the purchaser takes from a transferor of an interest and the transferor has such a blocking power (whether or not the transferor is a debtor).

Section 12-105(e) contains a similar limitation in connection with control through another person. An acknowledging person must be one "other than the transferor of an interest in the electronic record." The same or a similar limitation is found in the other provisions relating to control through another person. See Sections 7-106(g) (control of electronic document of title); 8-106(d)(3) (control of a security entitlement); 9-104(a)(4) (control of deposit accounts); 9-105(g) (control of authoritative electronic copy of record evidencing chattel paper); 9-105A)(e) (control of electronic money).

For a discussion of the rationale for these limitations on sharing exclusive control and control through another person, see Section 12-105, Comment 9.

Section 9-314A. Perfection by Possession and Control of Chattel Paper

(a) [Perfection by possession and control.] A secured party may perfect a security interest in chattel paper by taking possession of each authoritative tangible copy of the record evidencing the chattel paper and obtaining control of each authoritative electronic copy of the electronic record evidencing the chattel paper.

(b) [Time of perfection; continuation of perfection.] A security interest is perfected under subsection (a) not earlier than the time the secured party takes possession and obtains control and remains perfected under subsection (a) only while the secured party retains possession and control.

(c) [Application of Section 9-313 to perfection by possession of chattel paper.] Section 9-313(c) and (f) through (i) applies to perfection by possession of an authoritative tangible copy of a record evidencing chattel paper.

Definitional Cross References:

Chattel paper	Section 9-102(a)(11)
Electronic	Section 1-201(b)(16A)
Record	Section 9-102(a)(70)
Secured party	Section 9-102(a)(73)
Security interest	Section 1-201(b)(35)

Official Comment

1. "Authoritative copy." To perfect a security interest in chattel paper other than by filing, this section provides that a secured party must obtain control of all authoritative electronic copies and take possession of all authoritative tangible copies.

Like the pre-2022 text, Section 9-105(b) distinguishes between authoritative and nonauthoritative copies of electronic chattel paper and refers to copies that are "authoritative." And, like its predecessor, Section 9-105(b) does not define the term "authoritative." However, it also applies this concept to tangible records that evidence chattel paper.

To show that it has possession of all authoritative tangible copies of a record evidencing chattel paper and all authoritative electronic copies of a record evidencing chattel paper, a purchaser can produce the tangible copies in its possession and prove control of the electronic copies and provide evidence that these are authoritative copies. The purchaser need not prove a negative—i.e., that no other tangible or electronic authoritative copies exist—to make a prima facie case. The purchaser's possession of the authoritative tangible copies and control of the authoritative electronic copies gives the purchaser the power to prevent others from taking possession or control of the copies and the power to transfer possession and control of the copies.

Perfection of a security interest in chattel paper by taking possession of the collateral generally has been understood to mean taking possession of the wet-ink "original." Experience has shown that the concept of an original breaks down when one allows for the possibility of the same monetary obligation being evidenced by different media over time, such as where electronic records evidencing the chattel paper are "papered out" (replaced with tangible records evidencing the same chattel paper) or tangible records are "converted" to electronic records.

Whether an electronic or tangible copy of a record evidencing chattel paper is authoritative depends on the facts and circumstances. The determination should turn on whether the copy provides reasonable notice to third parties that it is one that must be subject to control or possession for purposes of perfection and priority. To accommodate current practices and future technology, parties are allowed considerable flexibility in determining the method used to establish whether a particular copy is authoritative, provided that third parties are able to reasonably identify the authoritative copies that must be possessed or controlled to achieve perfection. For example, the parties could develop a system or protocol where each tangible or electronic copy is "watermarked" as authoritative or nonauthoritative or where the terms of the records themselves describe how to determine which copies are authoritative and which are not.

2. Time of perfection; continuation of perfection. Subsection (b) is modeled on Sections 9-313(d) and 9-314(b). If a secured party's possession or control is based on the acknowledgment under Section 9-313(c) or 9-105(g) by another person in possession or control, the secured party remains perfected by possession or control only while the other person retains possession or control. This result necessarily follows because such a secured party's possession or control derives solely from the other person's continued possession or control.

3. Applicability of Section 9-313. Subsection (c) makes specified subsections of Section 9-313 applicable to possession of authoritative tangible copies of records evidencing chattel paper.

4. Shared control. As to the sharing of powers over an authoritative electronic copy of a record evidencing chattel paper (see Section 9-105(c)(2)) by a debtor and a secured party (or by another transferor and transferee) and control through another person (see Section 9-105(g)), see Sections 9-314, Comment 3A; 12-105, Comment 9.

Section 9-315. Secured Party's Rights on Disposition of Collateral and in Proceeds

(a) [Disposition of collateral: continuation of security interest or agricultural lien; proceeds.] Except as otherwise provided in this article and in Section 2-403(2):

(1) a security interest or agricultural lien continues in collateral notwithstanding sale, lease, license, exchange, or other disposition thereof unless the secured party authorized the disposition free of the security interest or agricultural lien; and

(2) a security interest attaches to any identifiable proceeds of collateral.

(b) [When commingled proceeds identifiable.] Proceeds that are commingled with other property are identifiable proceeds:

(1) if the proceeds are goods, to the extent provided by Section 9-336; and

(2) if the proceeds are not goods, to the extent that the secured party identifies the proceeds by a method of tracing, including application of equitable principles, that is permitted under law other than this article with respect to commingled property of the type involved.

(c) [Perfection of security interest in proceeds.] A security interest in proceeds is a perfected security interest if the security interest in the original collateral was perfected.

(d) [Continuation of perfection.] A perfected security interest in proceeds becomes unperfected on the 21st day after the security interest attaches to the proceeds unless:

(1) the following conditions are satisfied:

(A) a filed financing statement covers the original collateral;

(B) the proceeds are collateral in which a security interest may be perfected by filing in the office in which the financing statement has been filed; and

(C) the proceeds are not acquired with cash proceeds;

(2) the proceeds are identifiable cash proceeds; or

(3) the security interest in the proceeds is perfected other than under subsection (c) when the security interest attaches to the proceeds or within 20 days thereafter.

(e) [When perfected security interest in proceeds becomes unperfected.] If a filed financing statement covers the original collateral, a security interest in proceeds which remains perfected under subsection (d)(1) becomes unperfected at the later of:

(1) when the effectiveness of the filed financing statement lapses under Section 9-515 or is terminated under Section 9-513; or

(2) the 21st day after the security interest attaches to the proceeds.

Definitional Cross References:

Agricultural lien	Section 9-102(a)(5)
Cash proceeds	Section 9-102(a)(9)
Collateral	Section 9-102(a)(12)
Financing statement	Section 9-102(a)(39)
Goods	Section 9-102(a)(44)
Lease	Section 2A-103(1)(j)
Proceeds	Section 9-102(a)(64)
Right	Section 1-201(b)(34)
Sale	Section 2-106(1)
Secured party	Section 9-102(a)(73)
Security interest	Section 1-201(b)(35)

Comment References: 9-109 C16, 9-205 C3

Official Comment

1. Source. Former Section 9-306.

2. Continuation of Security Interest or Agricultural Lien Following Disposition of Collateral. Subsection (a)(1), which derives from former Section 9-306(2), contains the general rule that a security interest survives disposition of the collateral. In these cases, the secured party may repossess the collateral from the transferee or, in an appropriate case, maintain an action for conversion. The secured party may claim both any proceeds and the original collateral but, of course, may have only one satisfaction.

In many cases, a purchaser or other transferee of collateral will take free of a security interest, and the secured party's only right will be to proceeds. For example, the general rule does not apply, and a security interest does not continue in collateral, if the secured party authorized the disposition, in the agreement that contains the security agreement or otherwise. Subsection (a)(1) adopts the view of PEB Commentary No. 3 and makes explicit that the authorized disposition to which it refers is an authorized disposition "free of" the security interest or agricultural lien. The secured party's right to proceeds under this section or under the express terms of an agreement does not in itself constitute an authorization of disposition. The change in language from former Section 9-306(2) is not intended to address the frequently litigated situation in which the effectiveness of the secured party's consent to a disposition is conditioned upon the secured party's receipt of the proceeds. In that situation, subsection (a) leaves the determination of authorization to the courts, as under former Article 9.

This Article contains several provisions under which a transferee takes free of a security interest or agricultural lien. For example, Section 9-317 states when transferees take free of unperfected security interests; Sections 9-320 and 9-321 on goods, 9-321 on general intangibles, 9-330 on chattel paper and instruments, and 9-331 on negotiable instruments, negotiable documents, and securities state when purchasers of such collateral take free of a security interest, even though perfected and even though the disposition was not authorized. Section 9-332 enables most transferees (including non-purchasers) of funds from a deposit account and most transferees of money to take free of a perfected security interest in the deposit account or money.

Likewise, the general rule that a security interest survives disposition does not apply if the secured party entrusts goods collateral to a merchant who deals in goods of that kind and the merchant sells the collateral to a buyer in ordinary course of business. Section 2-403(2) gives the merchant the power to transfer all the secured party's rights to the buyer, even if the sale is wrongful as against the secured party. Thus, under subsection (a)(1), an entrusting secured party runs the same risk as any other entruster.

3. Secured Party's Right to Identifiable Proceeds. Under subsection (a)(2), which derives from former Section 9-306(2), a security interest attaches to any identifiable "proceeds," as defined in Section 9-102. See also Section 9-203(f). Subsection (b) is new. It indicates when proceeds commingled with other property are identifiable proceeds and permits the use of whatever methods of tracing other law permits with respect to the type of property involved. Among the "equitable principles" whose use other law may permit is the "lowest intermediate balance rule." See Restatement (2d), Trusts § 202.

4. Automatic Perfection in Proceeds: General Rule. Under subsection (c), a security interest in proceeds is a perfected security interest if the security interest in the original collateral was perfected. This Article extends the period of automatic perfection in proceeds from 10 days to 20 days. Generally, a security interest in proceeds becomes unperfected on the 21st day after the security interest attaches to the proceeds. See subsection (d). The loss of perfected status under subsection (d) is prospective only. Compare, e.g., Section 9-515(c) (deeming security interest unperfected retroactively).

5. Automatic Perfection in Proceeds: Proceeds Acquired with Cash Proceeds. Subsection (d)(1) derives from former Section 9-306(3)(a). It carries forward the basic rule that a security interest in proceeds remains perfected beyond the period of automatic perfection if a filed financing statement covers the original collateral (e.g., inventory) and the proceeds are collateral in which a security interest may be perfected by filing in the office where the financing statement has been filed (e.g., equipment). A different rule applies if the proceeds are acquired with cash proceeds, as is the case if the original collateral (inventory) is sold for cash (cash proceeds) that is used to purchase equipment (proceeds). Under these circumstances, the security interest in the equipment proceeds remains perfected only if the description in the filed financing indicates the type of property constituting the proceeds (e.g., "equipment").

This section reaches the same result but takes a different approach. It recognizes that the treatment of proceeds acquired with cash proceeds under former Section 9-306(3)(a) essentially was superfluous. In the example, had the filing covered "equipment" as well as "inventory," the security interest in the proceeds would have been perfected under the usual rules governing after-acquired equipment (see former Sections 9-302, 9-303); paragraph (3)(a) added only an exception to the general rule. Subsection (d)(1)(C) of this section takes a more direct approach. It makes the general rule of continued perfection inapplicable to proceeds acquired with cash proceeds, leaving perfection of a security interest in those proceeds to the generally applicable perfection rules under subsection (d)(3).

Example 1: Lender perfects a security interest in Debtor's inventory by filing a financing statement covering "inventory." Debtor sells the inventory and deposits the buyer's check into a deposit account. Debtor draws a check on the deposit account and uses it to pay for equipment. Under the "lowest intermediate balance rule," which is a permitted method of tracing in the relevant jurisdiction, see Comment 3, the funds used to pay for the equipment were identifiable proceeds of the inventory. Because the proceeds (equipment) were acquired with cash proceeds (deposit account), subsection (d)(1) does not extend perfection beyond the 20-day automatic period.

Example 2: Lender perfects a security interest in Debtor's inventory by filing a financing statement covering "all debtor's property." As in Example 1, Debtor sells the inventory, deposits the buyer's check into a deposit account, draws a check on the deposit account, and uses the check to pay for equipment. Under the "lowest intermediate balance rule," which is a permitted method of tracing in the relevant jurisdiction, see Comment 3, the funds used to pay for the equipment were identifiable proceeds of the inventory. Because the proceeds (equipment) were acquired with cash proceeds (deposit account), subsection (d)(1) does not extend perfection beyond the 20-day automatic period. However, because the financing statement is sufficient to perfect a security interest in debtor's equipment, under subsection (d)(3) the security interest in the equipment proceeds remains perfected beyond the 20-day period.

6. Automatic Perfection in Proceeds: Lapse or Termination of Financing Statement During 20-Day Period; Perfection under Other Statute or Treaty. Subsection (e) provides that a security interest in proceeds perfected under subsection (d)(1) ceases to be perfected when the financing statement covering the original collateral lapses or is terminated. If the lapse or termination occurs before the 21st day after the security interest attaches, however, the security interest in the proceeds remains perfected until the 21st day. Section 9-311(b) provides that compliance with the perfection requirements of a statute or treaty described in Section 9-311(a) "is equivalent to the filing of a financing statement." It follows that collateral subject to a security interest perfected by such compliance under Section 9-311(b) is covered by a "filed financing statement" within the meaning of Section 9-315(d) and (e).

Automatic Perfection in Proceeds: Continuation of Perfection in Cash Proceeds. Former Section 9-306(3)(b) provided that if a filed financing statement covered original collateral, a security interest in identifiable cash proceeds of the collateral remained perfected beyond the ten-day period of automatic perfection. Former Section 9-306(3)(c) contained a similar rule with respect to identifiable cash proceeds of investment property. Subsection (d)(2) extends the benefits of former Sections 9-306(3)(b) and (3)(c) to identifiable cash proceeds of all types of original collateral in which a security interest is perfected by any method. Under subsection (d)(2), if the security interest in the original collateral was perfected, a security interest in identifiable cash proceeds will remain perfected indefinitely, regardless of whether the security interest in the original collateral remains perfected. In many cases, however, a purchaser or other transferee of the cash proceeds will take free of the perfected security interest. See, e.g., Sections 9-330(d) (purchaser of check), 9-331 (holder in due course of check), 9-332 (transferee of money or funds from a deposit account).

8. Insolvency Proceedings; Returned and Repossessed Goods. This Article deletes former Section 9-306(4), which dealt with proceeds in insolvency proceedings. Except as otherwise provided by the Bankruptcy Code, the debtor's entering into bankruptcy does not affect a secured party's right to proceeds.

This Article also deletes former Section 9-306(5), which dealt with returned and repossessed goods. Section 9-330, Comments 9 to 11 explain and clarify the application of priority rules to returned and repossessed goods as proceeds of chattel paper.

9. Proceeds of Collateral Subject to Agricultural Lien. This Article does not determine whether a lien extends to proceeds of farm products encumbered by an agricultural lien. If, however, the proceeds are themselves farm products on which an "agricultural lien" (defined in Section 9-102) arises under other law, then the agricultural-lien provisions of this Article apply to the agricultural lien on the proceeds in the same way in which they would apply had the farm products not been proceeds.

Section 9-316. Effect of Change in Governing Law

(a) [General rule: effect on perfection of change in governing law.] A security interest perfected pursuant to the law of the jurisdiction designated in Section 9-301(1), 9-305(c), 9-306A(d), or 9-306B(b) remains perfected until the earliest of:

(1) the time perfection would have ceased under the law of that jurisdiction;

(2) the expiration of four months after a change of the debtor's location to another jurisdiction; or

(3) the expiration of one year after a transfer of collateral to a person that thereby becomes a debtor and is located in another jurisdiction.

(b) [Security interest perfected or unperfected under law of new jurisdiction.] If a security interest described in subsection (a) becomes perfected under the law of the other jurisdiction before the earliest time or event described in that subsection, it remains perfected thereafter. If the security interest does not become perfected under the law of the other jurisdiction before the earliest time or event, it becomes unperfected and is deemed never to have been perfected as against a purchaser of the collateral for value.

(c) [Possessory security interest in collateral moved to new jurisdiction.] A possessory security interest in collateral, other than goods covered by a certificate of title and as-extracted collateral consisting of goods, remains continuously perfected if:

(1) the collateral is located in one jurisdiction and subject to a security interest perfected under the law of that jurisdiction;

(2) thereafter the collateral is brought into another jurisdiction; and

(3) upon entry into the other jurisdiction, the security interest is perfected under the law of the other jurisdiction.

(d) [Goods covered by certificate of title from this state.] Except as otherwise provided in subsection (e), a security interest in goods covered by a certificate of title which is perfected by any method under the law of another jurisdiction when the goods become covered by a certificate of title from this State remains perfected until the security interest would have become unperfected under the law of the other jurisdiction had the goods not become so covered.

(e) [When subsection (d) security interest becomes unperfected against purchasers.] A security interest described in subsection (d) becomes unperfected as against a purchaser of the goods for value and is deemed never to have been perfected as against a purchaser of the goods for value if the applicable requirements for perfection under Section 9-311(b) or 9-313 are not satisfied before the earlier of:

(1) the time the security interest would have become unperfected under the law of the other jurisdiction had the goods not become covered by a certificate of title from this State; or

(2) the expiration of four months after the goods had become so covered.

(f) [Change in jurisdiction of chattel paper, controllable electronic record, bank, issuer, nominated person, securities intermediary, or commodity intermediary.] A security interest in chattel paper, controllable accounts, controllable electronic records, controllable payment intangibles, deposit accounts, letter-of-credit rights, or investment property which is perfected under the law of the chattel paper's jurisdiction, the controllable electronic record's jurisdiction, the bank's jurisdiction, the issuer's jurisdiction, a nominated person's jurisdiction, the securities intermediary's jurisdiction, or the commodity intermediary's jurisdiction, as applicable, remains perfected until the earlier of:

(1) the time the security interest would have become unperfected under the law of that jurisdiction; or

(2) the expiration of four months after a change of the applicable jurisdiction to another jurisdiction.

(g) [Subsection (f) security interest perfected or unperfected under law of new jurisdiction.] If a security interest described in subsection (f) becomes perfected under the law of the other jurisdiction before the earlier of the time or the end of the period described in that subsection, it remains perfected thereafter. If the security interest does not become perfected under the law of the other jurisdiction before the earlier of that time or the end of that period, it becomes unperfected and is deemed never to have been perfected as against a purchaser of the collateral for value.

(h) [Effect on filed financing statement of change in governing law.] The following rules apply to collateral to which a security interest attaches within four months after the debtor changes its location to another jurisdiction:

(1) A financing statement filed before the change pursuant to the law of the jurisdiction designated in Section 9-301(1) or 9-305(c) is effective to perfect a security interest in the collateral if the financing statement would have been effective to perfect a security interest in the collateral had the debtor not changed its location.

(2) If a security interest perfected by a financing statement that is effective under paragraph (1) becomes perfected under the law of the other jurisdiction before the earlier of the time the financing statement would have become ineffective under the law of the jurisdiction designated in Section 9-301(1) or 9-305(c) or the expiration of the four-month period, it remains perfected thereafter. If the security interest does not become perfected under the law of the other jurisdiction before the earlier time or event, it becomes unperfected and is deemed never to have been perfected as against a purchaser of the collateral for value.

(i) [Effect of change in governing law on financing statement filed against original debtor.] If a financing statement naming an original debtor is filed pursuant to the law of the jurisdiction designated in Section 9-301(1) or 9-305(c) and the new debtor is located in another jurisdiction, the following rules apply:

(1) The financing statement is effective to perfect a security interest in collateral acquired by the new debtor before, and within four months after, the new debtor becomes bound under Section 9-203(d), if the financing statement would have been effective to perfect a security interest in the collateral had the collateral been acquired by the original debtor.

(2) A security interest perfected by the financing statement and which becomes perfected under the law of the other jurisdiction before the earlier of the time the financing statement would have become ineffective under the law of the jurisdiction designated in Section 9-301(1) or 9-305(c) or the expiration of the four-month period remains perfected thereafter. A security interest that is perfected by the financing statement but which does not become perfected under the law of the other jurisdiction before the earlier time or event becomes unperfected and is deemed never to have been perfected as against a purchaser of the collateral for value.

Definitional Cross References:

As-extracted collateral	Section 9-102(a)(6)
Bank	Section 9-102(a)(8)
Certificate of title	Section 9-102(a)(10)
Chattel paper	Section 9-102(a)(11)
Collateral	Section 9-102(a)(12)
Commodity intermediary	Section 9-102(a)(17)
Controllable account	Section 9-102(a)(27A)
Controllable electronic Record	Section 12-102(a)(1)
Controllable payment intangible	Section 9-102(a)(27B)
Debtor	Section 9-102(a)(28)
Deposit account	Section 9-102(a)(29)
Financing Statement	Section 9-102(a)(39)
Goods	Section 9-102(a)(44)
Investment property	Section 9-102(a)(49)
Issuer (letter of credit/ letter-of-credit right)	Section 5-102(a)(9)
Letter-of-credit right	Section 9-102(a)(51)
Nominated person	Section 5-102(a)(11)
Original debtor	Section 9-102(a)(60)
Person	Section 1-201(b)(27)
Purchaser	Section 1-201(b)(30)
Securities intermediary	Section 8-102(a)(14)
Security interest	Section 1-201(b)(35)
State	Section 9-102(a)(77)
Value	Section 1-204

Comment References: 9-303 C6

Official Comment

1. Source. Former Section 9-103(1)(d), (2)(b), (3)(e), as modified.

2. Continued Perfection. Subsections (a) through (g) deal with continued perfection of security interests that have been perfected under the law of another jurisdiction. The fact that the law of a particular jurisdiction ceases to govern perfection under Sections 9-301 through 9-307 does not necessarily mean that a security interest perfected under that law automatically becomes unperfected. To the contrary: This section generally provides that a security interest perfected under the law of one jurisdiction remains perfected for a fixed period of time (four months or one year, depending on the circumstances), even though the jurisdiction whose law governs perfection changes. However, cessation of perfection under the law of the original jurisdiction cuts short the fixed period. The four-month and one-year periods are long enough for a secured party to discover in most cases that the law of a different jurisdiction governs perfection and to reperfect (typically by filing) under the law of that jurisdiction. If a secured party properly reperfects a security interest before it becomes unperfected under subsection (a), then the security interest remains perfected continuously thereafter. See subsection (b).

Example 1: Debtor is a general partnership whose chief executive office is in Pennsylvania. Lender perfects a security interest in Debtor's equipment by filing in Pennsylvania on May 15, 2002. On April 1, 2005, without Lender's knowledge, Debtor moves its chief executive office to New Jersey. Lender's security interest remains perfected for four months after the move. See subsection (a)(2).

Example 2: Debtor is a general partnership whose chief executive office is in Pennsylvania. Lender perfects a security interest in Debtor's equipment by filing in Pennsylvania on May 15, 2002. On April 1, 2007, without Lender's knowledge, Debtor moves its chief executive office to New Jersey. Lender's security interest remains perfected only through May 14, 2007, when the effectiveness of the filed financing statement lapses. See subsection (a)(1). Although, under these facts, Lender would have only a short period of time to discover that Debtor had relocated and to reperfect under New Jersey law, Lender could have protected itself by filing a continuation statement in Pennsylvania before Debtor relocated. By doing so, Lender would have prevented lapse and allowed itself the full four months to discover Debtor's new location and refile there or, if Debtor is in default, to perfect by taking possession of the equipment.

Example 3: Under the facts of Example 2, Lender files a financing statement in New Jersey before the effectiveness of the Pennsylvania financing statement lapses. Under subsection (b), Lender's security interest is continuously perfected beyond May 14, 2007, for a period determined by New Jersey's Article 9.

Subsection (a)(3) allows a one-year period in which to reperfect. The longer period is necessary, because, even with the exercise of due diligence, the secured party may be unable to discover that the collateral has been transferred to a person located in another jurisdiction. In any event, the period is cut short if the financing statement becomes ineffective under the law of the jurisdiction in which it is filed.

Example 4: Debtor is a Pennsylvania corporation. On January 1, Lender perfects a security interest in Debtor's equipment by filing in Pennsylvania. Debtor's shareholders decide to "reincorporate" in Delaware. On March 1, they form a Delaware corporation (Newcorp) into which they merge Debtor. The merger effectuates a transfer of the collateral from Debtor to Newcorp, which thereby becomes a debtor and is located in another jurisdiction. Under subsection (a)(3), the security interest remains perfected for one year after the merger. If a financing statement is filed in Delaware against Newcorp within the year following the merger, then the security interest remains perfected thereafter for a period determined by Delaware's Article 9.

Note that although Newcorp is a "new debtor" as defined in Section 9-102, the application of subsection (a)(3) is not limited to transferees who are new debtors. Note also that, under Section 9-507, the financing statement naming Debtor remains effective even though Newcorp has become the debtor.

Subsection (a) addresses security interests that are perfected (i.e., that have attached and as to which any required perfection step has been taken) before the debtor changes its location. Subsection (h) applies to security interests that have not attached before the location changes. See Comment 7.

3. Retroactive Unperfection. Subsection (b) sets forth the consequences of the failure to reperfect before perfection ceases under subsection (a): the security interest becomes unperfected prospectively and, as against purchasers for value, including buyers and secured parties, but not as against donees or lien creditors, retroactively. The rule applies to agricultural liens, as well. See also Section 9-515 (taking the same approach with respect to lapse). Although this approach creates the potential for circular priorities, the alternative—retroactive unperfection against lien creditors—would create substantial and unjustifiable preference risks.

Example 5: Under the facts of Example 4, six months after the merger, Buyer bought from Newcorp some equipment formerly owned by Debtor. At the time of the purchase, Buyer took subject to Lender's perfected security interest, of which Buyer was unaware. See Section 9-315(a)(1). However, subsection (b) provides that if Lender fails to reperfect in Delaware within a year after the merger, its security interest becomes unperfected and is deemed never to have been perfected against Buyer. Having given value and received delivery of the equipment without knowledge of the security interest and before it was perfected, Buyer would take free of the security interest. See Section 9-317(b).

Example 6: Under the facts of Example 4, one month before the merger, Debtor created a security interest in certain equipment in favor of Financer, who perfected by filing in Pennsylvania. At that time, Financer's security interest is subordinate to Lender's. See Section 9-322(a)(1). Financer reperfects by filing in Delaware within a year after the merger, but Lender fails to do so. Under subsection (b), Lender's security interest is deemed never to have been perfected against Financer, a purchaser for value. Consequently, under Section 9-322(a)(2), Financer's security interest is now senior.

Of course, the expiration of the time period specified in subsection (a) does not of itself prevent the secured party from later reperfecting under the law of the new jurisdiction. If the secured party does so, however, there will be a gap in perfection, and the secured party may lose priority as a result. Thus, in Example 6, if Lender perfects by filing in Delaware more than one year under the merger, it will have a new date of filing and perfection for purposes of Section 9-322(a)(1).

Financer's security interest, whose perfection dates back to the filing in Pennsylvania under subsection (b), will remain senior.

4. Possessory Security Interests. Subsection (c) deals with continued perfection of possessory security interests. It applies not only to security interests perfected solely by the secured party's having taken possession of the collateral. It also applies to security interests perfected by a method that includes as an element of perfection the secured party's having taken possession, such as perfection by taking delivery of a certificated security in registered form, see Section 9-313(a), perfection by obtaining control over a certificated security, see Section 9-314(a), and perfection by taking possession of and control over authoritative copies of records evidencing chattel paper, see Section 9-314A(a).

5. Goods Covered by Certificate of Title. Subsections (d) and (e) address continued perfection of a security interest in goods covered by a certificate of title. The following examples explain the operation of those subsections.

> **Example 7:** Debtor's automobile is covered by a certificate of title issued by Illinois. Lender perfects a security interest in the automobile by complying with Illinois' certificate-of-title statute. Thereafter, Debtor applies for a certificate of title in Indiana. Six months thereafter, Creditor acquires a judicial lien on the automobile. Under Section 9-303(b), Illinois law ceases to govern perfection; rather, once Debtor delivers the application and applicable fee to the appropriate Indiana authority, Indiana law governs. Nevertheless, under Indiana's Section 9-316(d), Lender's security interest remains perfected until it would become unperfected under Illinois law had no certificate of title been issued by Indiana. (For example, Illinois' certificate-of-title statute may provide that the surrender of an Illinois certificate of title in connection with the issuance of a certificate of title by another jurisdiction causes a security interest noted thereon to become unperfected.) If Lender's security interest remains perfected, it is senior to Creditor's judicial lien.

> **Example 8:** Under the facts in Example 8, five months after Debtor applies for an Indiana certificate of title, Debtor sells the automobile to Buyer. Under subsection (e)(2), because Lender did not reperfect within the four months after the goods became covered by the Indiana certificate of title, Lender's security interest is deemed never to have been perfected against Buyer. Under Section 9-317(b), Buyer is likely to take free of the security interest. Lender could have protected itself by perfecting its security interest either under Indiana's certificate-of-title statute, see Section 9-311, or, if it had a right to do so under an agreement or Section 9-609, by taking possession of the automobile. See Section 9-313(b).

The results in Examples 8 and 9 do not depend on the fact that the original perfection was achieved by notation on a certificate of title. Subsection (d) applies regardless of the method by which a security interest is perfected under the law of another jurisdiction when the goods became covered by a certificate of title from this State.

Section 9-337 affords protection to a limited class of persons buying or acquiring a security interest in the goods while a security interest is perfected under the law of another jurisdiction but after this State has issued a clean certificate of title.

6. Controllable Accounts, Controllable Electronic Records, Controllable Payment Intangibles, Chattel Paper, Deposit Accounts, Letter-of-Credit Rights, and Investment Property. Subsections (f) and (g) address changes in the jurisdiction of a bank, controllable electronic record, chattel paper, issuer of an uncertificated security, issuer of or nominated person under a letter of credit, securities intermediary, and commodity intermediary. The provisions are analogous to those of subsections (a) and (b).

7. Security Interests That Attach After Debtor Changes Location. In contrast to subsections (a) and (b), which address security interests that are perfected (i.e., that have attached and as to which any required perfection step has been taken) before the debtor changes its location, subsection (h) addresses security interests that attach within four months after the debtor changes its location. Under subsection (h), a filed financing statement that would have been effective to perfect a security interest in the collateral if the debtor had not changed its location is effective to perfect a security interest in collateral acquired within four months after the relocation.

> **Example 9:** Debtor, an individual whose principal residence is in Pennsylvania, grants to Lender a security interest in Debtor's existing and after-acquired inventory. Lender perfects the security interest by filing a proper financing statement in Pennsylvania on January 2, 2014. On March 31, 2014, Debtor's principal residence is relocated to New Jersey. Upon the relocation, New Jersey law governs perfection of a security interest in Debtor's inventory. See Sections 9-301, 9-307. Under New Jersey's Section 9-316(a), Lender's security interest in Debtor's inventory on hand at the time of the relocation remains perfected for four months thereafter. Had Debtor not relocated, the financing statement filed in Pennsylvania would have been effective to perfect Lender's security interest in inventory acquired by Debtor after March 31, 2014. Accordingly, under subsection (h), the financing statement is effective to perfect Lender's security interest in inventory that Debtor acquires within the four months after Debtor's location changed.

In Example 9, Lender's security interest in the inventory acquired within the four months after Debtor's relocation will be perfected when it attaches. It will remain perfected if, before the expiration of the four-month period, the security interest is perfected under the law of New Jersey. Otherwise, the security interest will become unperfected at the end of the four-month period and will be deemed never to have been perfected as against a purchaser for value. See subsection (h)(2).

8. Collateral Acquired by New Debtor. Subsection (i) is similar to subsection (h). Whereas subsection (h) addresses security interests that attach within four months after a debtor changes its location, subsection (i) addresses security interests that attach within four months after a new debtor becomes bound as debtor by a security agreement entered into by another person. Subsection (i) also addresses collateral acquired by the new debtor before it becomes bound.

Example 10: Debtor, a Pennsylvania corporation, grants to Lender a security interest in Debtor's existing and after-acquired inventory. Lender perfects the security interest by filing a proper financing statement in Pennsylvania on January 2, 2014. On March 31, 2014, Debtor merges into Survivor, a Delaware corporation. Because Survivor is located in Delaware, Delaware law governs perfection of a security interest in Survivor's inventory. See Sections 9-301, 9-307. Under Delaware's Section 9-316(a), Lender's security interest in the inventory that Survivor acquired from Debtor remains perfected for one year after the transfer. See Comment 2. By virtue of the merger, Survivor becomes bound as debtor by Debtor's security agreement. See Section 9-203(d). As a consequence, Lender's security interest attaches to all of Survivor's inventory under Section 9-203, and Lender's collateral now includes inventory in which Debtor never had an interest. The financing statement filed in Pennsylvania against Debtor is effective under Delaware's Section 9-316(i) to perfect Lender's security interest in inventory that Survivor acquired before, and within the four months after, becoming bound as debtor by Debtor's security agreement. This is because the financing statement filed in Pennsylvania would have been effective to perfect Lender's security interest in this collateral had Debtor, rather than Survivor, acquired it.

If the financing statement is effective, Lender's security interest in the collateral that Survivor acquired before, and within four months after, Survivor became bound as debtor will be perfected upon attachment. It will remain perfected if, before the expiration of the four-month period, the security interest is perfected under Delaware law. Otherwise, the security interest will become unperfected at the end of the four-month period and will be deemed never to have been perfected as against a purchaser for value.

Section 9-325 contains special rules governing the priority of competing security interests in collateral that is transferred, by merger or otherwise, to a new debtor or other person who becomes a debtor with respect to the collateral. Section 9-326 contains special rules governing the priority of competing security interests in collateral acquired by a new debtor other than by transfer from the original debtor.

9. Agricultural Liens. This section does not apply to agricultural liens.

Example 11: Supplier holds an agricultural lien on corn. The lien arises under an Iowa statute. Supplier perfects by filing a financing statement in Iowa, where the corn is located. See Section 9-302. Debtor stores the corn in Missouri. Assume the Iowa agricultural lien survives or an agricultural lien arises under Missouri law (matters that this Article does not govern). Once the corn is located in Missouri, Missouri becomes the jurisdiction whose law governs perfection. See Section 9-302. Thus, the agricultural lien will not be perfected unless Supplier files a financing statement in Missouri.

[SUBPART 3. PRIORITY]

Section 9-317. Interests That Take Priority over or Take Free of Security Interest or Agricultural Lien

(a) [Conflicting security interests and rights of lien creditors.] A security interest or agricultural lien is subordinate to the rights of:

(1) a person entitled to priority under Section 9-322; and

(2) except as otherwise provided in subsection (e), a person that becomes a lien creditor before the earlier of the time

(A) the security interest or agricultural lien is perfected; or

(B) one of the conditions specified in Section 9-203(b)(3) is met and a financing statement covering the collateral is filed.

(b) [Buyers that receive delivery.] Except as otherwise provided in subsection (e), a buyer, other than a secured party, of goods, instruments, tangible documents, or a certificated security takes free of a security interest or agricultural lien if the buyer gives value and receives delivery of the collateral without knowledge of the security interest or agricultural lien and before it is perfected.

(c) [Lessees that receive delivery.] Except as otherwise provided in subsection (e), a lessee of goods takes free of a security interest or agricultural lien if the lessee gives value and receives delivery of the collateral without knowledge of the security interest or agricultural lien and before it is perfected.

(d) [Licensees and buyers of certain collateral.] Subject to subsection (f) through (i), a licensee of a general intangible or a buyer, other than a secured party, of collateral other than electronic money, goods, instruments, tangible documents, or a certificated security takes free of a security interest if the licensee or buyer gives value without knowledge of the security interest and before it is perfected.

(e) [Purchase-money security interest.] Except as otherwise provided in Sections 9-320 and 9-321, if a person files a financing statement with respect to a purchase-money security interest before or within 20 days after the debtor receives delivery of the collateral, the security interest takes priority over the rights of a buyer, lessee, or lien creditor which arise between the time the security interest attaches and the time of filing.

(f) [Buyers of chattel paper.] A buyer, other than a secured party, of chattel paper takes free of a security interest if, without knowledge of the security interest and before it is perfected, the buyer gives value and:

(1) receives delivery of each authoritative tangible copy of the record evidencing the chattel paper; and

(2) if each authoritative electronic copy of the record evidencing the chattel paper can be subjected to control under Section 9-105, obtains control of each authoritative electronic copy.

(g) [Buyers of electronic documents.] A buyer of an electronic document takes free of a security interest if, without knowledge of the security interest and before it is perfected, the buyer gives value and, if each authoritative electronic copy of the document can be subjected to control under Section 7-106, obtains control of each authoritative electronic copy.

(h) [Buyers of controllable electronic records.] A buyer of a controllable electronic record takes free of a security interest if, without knowledge of the security interest and before it is perfected, the buyer gives value and obtains control of the controllable electronic record.

(i) [Buyers of controllable accounts and controllable payment intangibles.] A buyer, other than a secured party, of a controllable account or a controllable payment intangible takes free of a security interest if, without knowledge of the security interest and before it is perfected, the buyer gives value and obtains control of the controllable account or controllable payment intangible.

Definitional Cross References:

Account	Section 9-102(a)(2)
Agricultural lien	Section 9-102(a)(5)
Certificated security	Section 8-102(a)(4)
Chattel paper	Section 9-102(a)(11)
Collateral	Section 9-102(a)(12)
Controllable account	Section 9-102(a)(27A)
Controllable electronic record	Section 12-102(a)(1)
Controllable payment intangible	Section 9-102(a)(27B)
Debtor	Section 9-102(a)(28)
Delivery	Section 1-201(b)(15)
Document	Section 9-102(a)(30)
Electronic	Section 1-201(b)(16A)
Electronic money	Section 9-102(a)(31A)
Financing statement	Section 9-102(a)(39)
General intangible	Section 9-102(a)(42)
Goods	Section 9-102(a)(44)
Instrument	Section 9-102(a)(47)
Investment property	Section 9-102(a)(49)
Lessee	Section 2A-103(1)(n)
Lien creditor	Section 9-102(a)(52)
Person	Section 1-201(b)(27)
Purchase-money security interest	Section 9-103
Record	Section 9-102(a)(70)
Right	Section 1-201(b)(34)
Secured party	Section 9-102(a)(73)
Security certificate	Section 8-102(a)(16)
Security interest	Section 1-201(b)(35)
Value	Section 1-204

Comment References:
9-109 C5
9-323 C4

Official Comment

1. Source. Former Sections 9-301, 2A-307(2).

2. Scope of This Section. As did former Section 9-301, this section lists the classes of persons who take priority over, or take free of, an unperfected security interest. Section 9-308 explains when a security interest or agricultural lien is "perfected." A security interest that has attached (see Section 9-203) but as to which a required perfection step has not been taken is "unperfected." Certain provisions have been moved from former Section 9-301. The definition of "lien creditor" now appears in Section 9-102, and the rules governing priority in future advances are found in Section 9-323.

3. Competing Security Interests. Section 9-322 states general rules for determining priority among conflicting security interests and refers to other sections that state special rules of priority in a variety of situations. The security interests given priority under Section 9-322 and the other sections to which it refers take priority in general even over a perfected security interest. *A fortiori* they take priority over an unperfected security interest.

4. Filed But Unattached Security Interest vs. Lien Creditor. Under former Section 9-301(1)(b), a lien creditor's rights had priority over an unperfected security interest. Perfection required attachment (former Section 9-303) and attachment required the giving of value (former Section 9-203). It followed that, if a secured party had filed a financing statement, but the debtor had not entered into a security agreement and value had not yet been given, an intervening lien creditor whose lien arose after filing but before attachment of the security interest acquired rights that are senior to those of the secured party who later gives value. This result comported with the *nemo dat* concept: When the security interest attached, the collateral was already subject to the judicial lien.

On the other hand, this approach treated the first secured advance differently from all other advances, even in circumstances in which a security agreement covering the collateral had been entered into before the judicial lien attached. The special rule for future advances in former Section 9-301(4) (substantially reproduced in Section 9-323(b)) afforded priority to a discretionary advance made by a secured party within 45 days after the lien creditor's rights arose as long as the secured party was "perfected" when the lien creditor's lien arose—i.e., as long as the advance was not the first one and an earlier advance had been made.

Subsection (a)(2)(b) revises former Section 9-301(1)(b) and, in appropriate cases, treats the first advance the same as subsequent advances. More specifically, a judicial lien that arises after the security-agreement condition of Section 9-203(b)(3) is satisfied and a financing statement is filed but before the security interest attaches and becomes perfected is subordinate to all advances secured by the security interest, even the first advance, except as otherwise provided in Section 9-323(b). However, if the security interest becomes unperfected (e.g., because the effectiveness of the filed financing statement lapses) before the judicial lien arises, the security interest is subordinate. If a financing statement is filed but a security interest does not attach, then no priority contest arises. The lien creditor has the only enforceable claim to the property.

5. Security Interest of Consignor or Receivables Buyer vs. Lien Creditor. Section 1-201(b)(35) defines "security interest" to include the interest of most true consignors of goods and the interest of most buyers of certain receivables (including accounts, chattel paper, payment intangibles, and promissory notes). A consignee of goods or a seller of accounts or chattel paper each is deemed to have rights in the collateral which a lien creditor may reach, as long as the competing security interest of the consignor or buyer is unperfected. This is so even though, as between the consignor and the debtor-consignee, the latter has only limited rights, and, as between the buyer and debtor-seller, the latter does not have any rights in the collateral. See Sections 9-318 (seller), 9-319 (consignee). Security interests arising from sales of payment intangibles and promissory notes are automatically perfected. See Section 9-309. Accordingly, a subsequent judicial lien always would be subordinate to the rights of a buyer of those types of receivables.

6. Purchasers Other Than Secured Parties. Subsections (b), (c), (d), and (f) through (i) afford priority over an unperfected security interest to certain buyers (other than secured parties) of collateral. They derive in part from pre-1998 Sections 9-301(1)(c), 2A-307(2), and 9-301(d). Pre-1998 Section 9-301(1)(c) and (1)(d) provided that unperfected security interests are "subordinate" to the rights of certain purchasers. But, as pre-1998 Comment 9 suggested, the practical effect of subordination in this context is that the purchaser takes free of the security interest. To avoid any possible misinterpretation, these subsections now use the phrase "takes free."

Subsection (b) governs goods, as well as intangibles of the type whose transfer is effected by physical delivery of the representative piece of paper (tangible documents, instruments, and security certificates). To obtain priority, a buyer must both give value and receive delivery of the collateral without knowledge of the existing security interest and before perfection. Even if the buyer gave value without knowledge and before perfection, the buyer would take subject to the security interest if perfection occurred before physical delivery of the collateral to the buyer. Subsection (c) contains a similar rule with respect to lessees of goods. Note that a lessee of goods in ordinary course of business takes free of all security interests created by the lessor, even if perfected. See Section 9-321.

Normally, there will be no question when a buyer of tangible chattel paper, tangible documents, instruments, or security certificates "receives delivery" of the property. See Section 1-201 (defining "delivery"). However, sometimes a buyer or lessee of goods, such as complex machinery, takes delivery of the goods in stages and completes assembly at its own location. Under those circumstances, the buyer or lessee "receives delivery" within the meaning of subsections (b) and (c) when, after an inspection of the portion of the goods remaining with the seller or lessor, it would be apparent to a potential lender to the seller or lessor that another person might have an interest in the goods.

Subsection (b) no longer applies to chattel paper. The take-free rule in subsection (f) for buyers of chattel paper reflects the corresponding 2022 changes in the definition of chattel paper and in the methods of perfection. See Sections 9-102(a)(11) (defining "chattel paper"); 9-314A (perfection by possession and control). Note that subsection (f) applies only to a buyer of chattel paper "other than a secured party" and most buyers of chattel paper are secured parties. See Sections 9-102(a)(73) (defining "secured party" as including a person to which chattel paper has been sold); 9-109(a)(3) (Article 9 applies to a sale of chattel paper); 1-201(b)(35) (defining "security interest" to include the interest of a buyer of chattel paper). However, Article 9 does not apply to "a sale of . . . chattel paper . . . as part of a sale of the business out of which . . . [the chattel paper] arose" and, accordingly, subsection (f) could apply to a buyer of chattel paper in such a sale-of-business transaction. Subsection (f) provides that such a buyer of chattel paper takes free of a security interest if, without knowledge of the security interest and before it is perfected, the buyer gives value and receives delivery of each authoritative tangible copy of the record evidencing the chattel paper and, if the chattel paper can be subjected to control, the buyer obtains control of each authoritative electronic copy.

Although chattel paper has been removed from subsection (b), the phrase "other than a secured party" has been retained because buyers of instruments that are promissory notes, but not buyers of other instruments, are secured parties. See Sections 9-109(a)(3) (Article 9 applies to a sale of a promissory note); 1-201(b)(35) (defining "security interest" to include the interest of a buyer of a promissory note).

The rule of subsection (b) obviously is not appropriate where the collateral consists of intangibles and there is no representative piece of paper whose physical delivery is the only or the customary method of transfer or no means of taking control of the collateral as a functional equivalent of a delivery. Therefore, with respect to such intangibles (including accounts other than controllable accounts, electronic documents not subject to control, general intangibles other than controllable payment intangibles, and investment property other than certificated securities), subsection (d) gives priority to any buyer who gives value without knowledge, and before perfection, of the security interest. Buyers of electronic money also are excluded from the application of subsection (d) because transferees of electronic money which obtain control take free of security interests under Section 9-332(c), which provides a standard more generous to transferees than subsection (d). A licensee of a general intangible takes free of an unperfected security interest in the general intangible under the same circumstances. Note that a licensee of a general intangible in ordinary course of business takes rights under a nonexclusive license free of security interests created by the licensor, even if perfected. See Section 9-321.

Unless Section 9-109 excludes the transaction from this Article, a buyer of accounts, payment intangibles, or promissory notes is a "secured party" (defined in Section 9-102), and subsection (d) does not determine priority of the security interest created by the sale. Rather, the priority rules generally applicable to competing security interests apply. See, e.g., Section 9-322.

6A. [Buyers of Electronic Documents, Controllable Electronic Records, Controllable Accounts, and Controllable Payment Intangibles.] Subsection (g) provides a take-free rule for electronic documents, subsection (h) so provides for controllable electronic records, and subsection (i) so provides for controllable accounts and controllable payment intangibles. Subsection (g) conditions the take-free rule on the buyer obtaining control of authoritative electronic copies of the document only if the authoritative electronic copies can be subjected to control. Subsection (h) conditions the take-free rule for a buyer of a controllable electronic record on the buyer's obtaining control of the electronic record. Similarly, under subsection (i), the take-free rule for a buyer, other than a secured party, of a controllable account or controllable payment intangible is conditioned on the buyer's obtaining control of the account or payment intangible. Although in general a buyer of an account or a payment intangible is a secured party, there are limited exceptions. See Sections 1-201(b)(35) ("security interest" includes interest of buyer of accounts or payment intangibles); 9-109(d)(4) (inapplicability of Article 9 to sale of accounts or payment intangibles as a part of the sale of a business).

7. Agricultural Liens. Subsections (a), (b), and (c) subordinate unperfected agricultural liens in the same manner in which they subordinate unperfected security interests.

8. Purchase-Money Security Interests. Subsection (e) derives from former Section 9-301(2). It provides that, if a purchase-money security interest is perfected by filing no later than 20 days after the debtor receives delivery of the collateral, the security interest takes priority over the rights of buyers, lessees, or lien creditors which arise between the time the security interest attaches and the time of filing. Subsection (e) differs from former Section 9-301(2) in two significant respects. First, subsection (e) protects a purchase-money security interest against all buyers and lessees, not just against transferees in bulk. Second, subsection (e) conditions this protection on filing within 20, as opposed to ten, days after delivery.

Section 9-311(b) provides that compliance with the perfection requirements of a statute or treaty described in Section 9-311(a) "is equivalent to the filing of a financing statement." It follows that a person who perfects a security interest in goods covered by a certificate of title by complying with the perfection requirements of an applicable certificate-of-title statute "files a financing statement" within the meaning of subsection (e).

Section 9-318. No Interest Retained in Right to Payment That Is Sold; Rights and Title of Seller of Account or Chattel Paper with Respect to Creditors and Purchasers

(a) [Seller retains no interest.] A debtor that has sold an account, chattel paper, payment intangible, or promissory note does not retain a legal or equitable interest in the collateral sold.

(b) [Deemed rights of debtor if buyer's security interest unperfected.] For purposes of determining the rights of creditors of, and purchasers for value of an account or chattel paper from, a debtor that has sold an account or chattel paper, while the buyer's security interest is unperfected, the debtor is deemed to have rights and title to the account or chattel paper identical to those the debtor sold.

Definitional Cross References:

Account	Section 9-102(a)(2)
Chattel paper	Section 9-102(a)(11)
Collateral	Section 9-102(a)(12)
Creditor	Section 1-201(b)(13)
Debtor	Section 9-102(a)(28)
Payment intangible	Section 9-102(a)(61)
Promissory note	Section 9-102(a)(65)
Purchaser	Section 1-201(b)(30)
Right	Section 1-201(b)(34)
Security interest	Section 1-201(b)(35)
Value	Section 1-204

Comment References: 9-109 C5

Official Comment

1. Source. New.

2. Sellers of Accounts, Chattel Paper, Payment Intangibles, and Promissory Notes. Section 1-201(b)(35) defines "security interest" to include the interest of a buyer of accounts, chattel paper, payment intangibles, or promissory notes. See also Section 9-109(a) and Comment 5. Subsection (a) makes explicit what was implicit, but perfectly obvious, under former Article 9: The fact that a sale of an account or chattel paper gives rise to a "security interest" does not imply that the seller retains an interest in the property that has been sold. To the contrary, a seller of an account or chattel paper retains no interest whatsoever in the property to the extent that it has been sold. Subsection (a) also applies to sales of payment intangibles and promissory notes, transactions that were not covered by former Article 9. Neither this Article nor the definition of "security interest" in Section 1-201(b)(35) provides rules for distinguishing sales transactions from those that create a security interest securing an obligation.

3. Buyers of Accounts and Chattel Paper. Another aspect of sales of accounts and chattel paper also was implicit, and equally obvious, under former Article 9: If the buyer's security interest is unperfected, then for purposes of determining the rights of certain third parties, the seller (debtor) is deemed to have all rights and title that the seller sold. The seller is deemed to have these rights even though, as between the parties, it has sold all its rights to the buyer. Subsection (b) makes this explicit. As a consequence of subsection (b), if the buyer's security interest is unperfected, the seller can transfer, and the creditors of the seller can reach, the account or chattel paper as if it had not been sold.

Example: Debtor sells accounts or chattel paper to Buyer-1 and retains no interest in them. Buyer-1 does not file a financing statement. Debtor then sells the same receivables to Buyer-2. Buyer-2 files a proper financing statement. Having sold the receivables to Buyer-1, Debtor would not have any rights in the collateral so as to permit Buyer-2's security (ownership) interest to attach. Nevertheless, under this section, for purposes of determining the rights of purchasers for value from Debtor, Debtor is deemed to have the rights that Debtor sold. Accordingly, Buyer-2's security interest attaches, is perfected by the filing, and, under Section 9-322, is senior to Buyer-1's interest.

4. Effect of Perfection. If the security interest of a buyer of accounts or chattel paper is perfected, ordinarily transferees from and creditors of the seller cannot later acquire an interest in an item so sold because, after the security interest is perfected, the seller no longer has a legal or equitable interest in the item. This does not always mean, however, that the seller cannot thereafter create a security interest in the item. A debtor may create a security in an item of property if it has either "rights in the collateral" or "the power to transfer rights in the collateral. See Section 9-203(b)(2). One example of a situation in which a debtor has the power to transfer rights in an account or an item of chattel paper—and, thus, to create a security interest in it—even after the account or chattel paper has been sold and the buyer has perfected its security interest is provided in Section 9-203, Comment 6, Example 2 (describing a transaction in which the post-sale security interest was perfected by a financing statement filed before the sale). See PEB Commentary No. 29, dated February 27, 2025. The Commentary is available at https://www.ali.org/peb-ucc.

Section 9-319. Rights and Title of Consignee with Respect to Creditors and Purchasers

(a) [Consignee has consignor's rights.] Except as otherwise provided in subsection (b), for purposes of determining the rights of creditors of, and purchasers for value of goods from, a consignee, while the goods are in the possession of the consignee, the consignee is deemed to have rights and title to the goods identical to those the consignor had or had power to transfer.

(b) [Applicability of other law.] For purposes of determining the rights of a creditor of a consignee, law other than this article determines the rights and title of a consignee while goods are in the consignee's possession if, under this part, a perfected security interest held by the consignor would have priority over the rights of the creditor.

Definitional Cross References:

Consignee	Section 9-102(a)(19)
Consignor	Section 9-102(a)(21)
Creditor	Section 1-201(b)(13)
Goods	Section 9-102(a)(44)
Purchaser	Section 1-201(b)(30)
Right	Section 1-201(b)(34)
Security interest	Section 1-201(b)(35)
Value	Section 1-204

Comment References: 9-109 C6

Official Comment

1. Source. New.

2. Consignments. This section takes an approach to consignments similar to that taken by Section 9-318 with respect to buyers of accounts and chattel paper. Revised Section 1-201(b)(35) defines "security interest" to include the interest of a consignor of goods under many true consignments. Section 9-319(a) provides that, for purposes of determining the rights of certain third parties, the consignee is deemed to acquire all rights and title that the consignor had, if the consignor's security interest is unperfected. The consignee acquires these rights even though, as between the parties, it purchases a limited interest in the goods (as would be the case in a true consignment, under which the consignee acquires only the interest of a bailee). As a consequence of this section, creditors of the consignee can acquire judicial liens and security interests in the goods while the goods are in the possession of the consignee.

The termination of a consignment does not ipso facto cause the consignee to lose its status as such with respect to the consignee's creditors whose claims to the goods arose before termination. Return of the goods to the consignor causes the consignee to lose its deemed rights and title, but it does not discharge a security interest or judicial lien that attached while the consignee was in possession. See PEB Commentary No. 20, dated January 24, 2019.

Insofar as creditors of the consignee are concerned, this Article to a considerable extent reformulates the former law, which appeared in former Sections 2-326 and 9-114, without changing the results. However, neither Article 2 nor former Article 9 specifically addresses the rights of non-ordinary course buyers from the consignee. Former Section 9-114 contained priority rules applicable to security interests in consigned goods. Under this Article, the priority rules for purchase-money security interests in inventory apply to consignments. See Section 9-103(d). Accordingly, a special section containing priority rules for consignments no longer is needed. Section 9-317 determines whether the rights of a judicial lien creditor are senior to the interest of the consignor, Sections 9-322 and 9-324 govern competing security interests in consigned goods, and Sections 9-317, 9-315, and 9-320 determine whether a buyer takes free of the consignor's interest.

The following example explains the operation of this section:

Example 1: SP-1 delivers goods to Debtor in a transaction constituting a "consignment" as defined in Section 9-102. SP-1 does not file a financing statement. Debtor then grants a security interest in the goods to SP-2. SP-2 files a proper financing statement. Assuming Debtor is a mere bailee, as in a "true" consignment, Debtor would not have any rights in the collateral (beyond those of a bailee) so as to permit SP-2's security interest to attach to any greater rights. Nevertheless, under this section, for purposes of determining the rights of Debtor's creditors, Debtor is deemed to acquire SP-1's rights. Accordingly, SP-2's security interest attaches, is perfected by the filing, and, under Section 9-322, is senior to SP-1's interest.

3. Effect of Perfection. Subsection (b) contains a special rule with respect to consignments that are perfected. If application of this Article would result in the consignor having priority over a competing creditor, then other law determines the rights and title of the consignee.

Example 2: SP-1 delivers goods to Debtor in a transaction constituting a "consignment" as defined in Section 9-102. SP-1 files a proper financing statement. Debtor then grants a security interest in the goods to SP-2. Under Section 9-322, SP-1's security interest is senior to SP-2's. Subsection (b) indicates that, for purposes of determining SP-2's rights, other law determines the rights and title of the consignee. If, for example, a consignee obtains only the special property of a bailee, then SP-2's security interest would attach only to that special property.

Example 3: SP-1 obtains a security interest in all Debtor's existing and after-acquired inventory. SP-1 perfects its security interest with a proper filing. Then SP-2 delivers goods to Debtor in a transaction constituting a "consignment" as defined in Section 9-102. SP-2 files a proper financing statement but does not send notification to SP-1 under Section 9-324(b). Accordingly, SP-2's security interest is junior to SP-1's under Section 9-322(a). Under Section 9-319(a), Debtor is deemed to have the consignor's rights and title, so that SP-1's security interest attaches to SP-2's ownership interest in the goods. Thereafter, Debtor grants a security interest in the goods to SP-3, and SP-3 perfects by filing. Because SP-2's perfected security interest is senior to SP-3's under Section 9-322(a), Section 9-319(b) applies: Other law determines Debtor's rights and title to the goods insofar as SP-3 is concerned, and SP-3's security interest attaches to those rights.

Section 9-320. Buyer of Goods

(a) [Buyer in ordinary course of business.] Except as otherwise provided in subsection (e), a buyer in ordinary course of business, other than a person buying farm products from a person engaged in farming operations, takes free of a security interest created by the buyer's seller, even if the security interest is perfected and the buyer knows of its existence.

(b) [Buyer of consumer goods.] Except as otherwise provided in subsection (e), a buyer of goods from a person who used or bought the goods for use primarily for personal, family, or household purposes takes free of a security interest, even if perfected, if the buyer buys:

(1) without knowledge of the security interest;

(2) for value;

(3) primarily for the buyer's personal, family, or household purposes; and

(4) before the filing of a financing statement covering the goods.

(c) [Effectiveness of filing for subsection (b).] To the extent that it affects the priority of a security interest over a buyer of goods under subsection (b), the period of effectiveness of a filing made in the jurisdiction in which the seller is located is governed by Section 9-316(a) and (b).

(d) [Buyer in ordinary course of business at wellhead or minehead.] A buyer in ordinary course of business buying oil, gas, or other minerals at the wellhead or minehead or after extraction takes free of an interest arising out of an encumbrance.

(e) [Possessory security interest not affected.] Subsections (a) and (b) do not affect a security interest in goods in the possession of the secured party under Section 9-313.

Definitional Cross References:

Buyer in ordinary course of business	Section 1-201(b)(9)
Consumer goods	Section 9-102(a)(23)
Encumbrance	Section 9-102(a)(32)
Farm products	Section 9-102(a)(34)
Farming operation	Section 9-102(a)(35)
Financing statement	Section 9-102(a)(39)
Goods	Section 9-102(a)(44)
Person	Section 1-201(b)(27)
Secured party	Section 9-102(a)(73)
Security interest	Section 1-201(b)(35)
Value	Section 1-204

Comment References: 9-323 C6

Official Comment

1. Source. Former Section 9-307.

2. Scope of This Section. This section states when buyers of goods take free of a security interest even though perfected. Of course, a buyer who takes free of a perfected security interest takes free of an unperfected one. Section 9-317 should be consulted to determine what purchasers, in addition to the buyers covered in this section, take free of an unperfected security interest. Article 2 states general rules on purchase of goods from a seller with defective or voidable title (Section 2-403).

3. Buyers in Ordinary Course. Subsection (a) derives from former Section 9-307(1). The definition of "buyer in ordinary course of business" in Section 1-201(b)(9) restricts its application to buyers "from a person, other than a pawnbroker, in the business of selling goods of that kind." Thus subsection (a) applies primarily to inventory collateral. The subsection further excludes from its operation buyers of "farm products" (defined in Section 9-102) from a person engaged in farming operations. The buyer in ordinary course of business is defined as one who buys goods "in good faith, without knowledge that the sale violates the rights of another person and in the ordinary course." Subsection (a) provides that such a buyer takes free of a security interest, even though perfected, and even though the buyer knows the security interest exists. Reading the definition together with the rule of law results in the buyer's taking free if the buyer merely knows that a security interest covers the goods but taking subject if the buyer knows, in addition, that the sale violates a term in an agreement with the secured party.

As did former Section 9-307(1), subsection (a) applies only to security interests created by the seller of the goods to the buyer in ordinary course. However, under certain circumstances a buyer in ordinary course who buys goods that were encumbered with a security interest created by a person other than the seller may take free of the security interest, as Example 2 explains. See also Comment 6, below.

Example 1: Manufacturer, who is in the business of manufacturing appliances, owns manufacturing equipment subject to a perfected security interest in favor of Lender. Manufacturer sells the equipment to Dealer, who is in the business of buying and selling used equipment. Buyer buys the equipment from Dealer. Even if Buyer qualifies as a buyer in the ordinary course of business, Buyer does not take free of Lender's security interest under subsection (a), because Dealer did not create the security interest; Manufacturer did.

Example 2: Manufacturer, who is in the business of manufacturing appliances, owns manufacturing equipment subject to a perfected security interest in favor of Lender. Manufacturer sells the equipment to Dealer, who is in the business of buying and selling used equipment. Lender learns of the sale but does nothing to assert its security interest. Buyer buys the equipment from Dealer. Inasmuch as Lender's acquiescence constitutes an "entrusting" of the goods to Dealer within the meaning of Section 2-403(3) Buyer takes free of Lender's security interest under Section 2-403(2) if Buyer qualifies as a buyer in ordinary course of business.

4. Buyers of Farm Products. This section does not enable a buyer of farm products to take free of a security interest created by the seller, even if the buyer is a buyer in ordinary course of business. However, a buyer of farm products may take free of a security interest under Section 1324 of the Food Security Act of 1985, 7 U.S.C. § 1631.

5. Buyers of Consumer Goods. Subsection (b), which derives from former Section 9-307(2), deals with buyers of collateral that the debtor-seller holds as "consumer goods" (defined in Section 9-102). Under Section 9-309(1), a purchase-money interest in consumer goods, except goods that are subject to a statute or treaty described in Section 9-311(a) (such as automobiles that are subject to a certificate-of-title statute), is perfected automatically upon attachment. There is no need to file to perfect. Under subsection (b) a buyer of consumer goods takes free of a security interest, even though perfected, if the buyer buys (1) without knowledge of the security interest, (2) for value, (3) primarily for the buyer's own personal, family, or household purposes, and (4) before a financing statement is filed.

As to purchase-money security interests which are perfected without filing under Section 9-309(1): A secured party may file a financing statement, although filing is not required for perfection. If the secured party does file, all buyers take subject to the security interest. If the secured party does not file, a buyer who meets the qualifications stated in the preceding paragraph takes free of the security interest.

As to security interests for which a perfection step is required: This category includes all non-purchase-money security interests, and all security interests, whether or not purchase-money, in goods subject to a statute or treaty described in Section 9-311(a), such as automobiles covered by a certificate-of-title statute. As long as the required perfection step has not been taken and the security interest remains unperfected, not only the buyers described in subsection (b) but also the purchasers described in Section 9-317 will take free of the security interest. After a financing statement has been filed or the perfection requirements of the applicable certificate-of-title statute have been complied with (compliance is the equivalent of filing a financing statement; see Section 9-311(b)), all subsequent buyers, under the rule of subsection (b), are subject to the security interest.

The rights of a buyer under subsection (b) turn on whether a financing statement has been filed against consumer goods. Occasionally, a debtor changes his or her location after a filing is made. Subsection (c), which derives from former Section 9-103(1)(d)(iii), deals with the continued effectiveness of the filing under those circumstances. It adopts the rules of Sections 9-316(a) and (b). These rules are explained in the Comments to that section.

6. Authorized Dispositions. The limitations that subsections (a) and (b) impose on the persons who may take free of a security interest apply of course only to unauthorized sales by the debtor. If the secured party authorized the sale in an express agreement or otherwise, the buyer takes free under Section 9-315(a) without regard to the limitations of this section. (That section also states the right of a secured party to the proceeds of a sale, authorized or unauthorized.) Moreover, the buyer also takes free if the secured party waived or otherwise is precluded from asserting its security interest against the buyer. See Section 1-103(b).

7. Oil, Gas, and Other Minerals. Under subsection (d), a buyer in ordinary course of business of minerals at the wellhead or minehead or after extraction takes free of a security interest created by the seller. Specifically, it provides that qualified buyers take free not only of Article 9 security interests but also of interests "arising out of an encumbrance." As defined in Section 9-102, the term "encumbrance" means "a right, other than an ownership interest, in real property." Thus, to the extent that a mortgage encumbers minerals not only before but also after extraction, subsection (d) enables a buyer in ordinary course of the minerals to take free of the mortgage. This subsection does not, however, enable these buyers to take free of interests arising out of ownership interests in the real property. This issue is significant only in a minority of states. Several of them have adopted special statutes and nonuniform amendments to Article 9 to provide special protections to mineral owners, whose interests often are highly fractionalized in the case of oil and gas. See Terry I. Cross, *Oil and Gas Product Liens—Statutory Security Interests for Producers and Royalty Owners Under the Statutes of Kansas, New Mexico, Oklahoma, Texas and Wyoming,* 50 Consumer Fin. L. Q. Rep. 418 (1996). Inasmuch as a complete resolution of the issue would require the addition of complex provisions to this Article, and there are good reasons to believe that a uniform solution would not be feasible, this Article leaves its resolution to other legislation.

8. Possessory Security Interests. Subsection (e) is new. It rejects the holding of *Tanbro Fabrics Corp. v. Deering Milliken, Inc.,* 350 N.E.2d 590 (N.Y. 1976) and, together with Section 9-317(b), prevents a buyer of goods collateral from taking free of a security interest if the collateral is in the possession of the secured party. "The secured party" referred in subsection (e) is the holder of the security interest referred to in subsection (a) or (b). Section 9-313 determines whether a secured party is in possession for purposes of this section. Under some circumstances, Section 9-313 provides that a secured party is in possession of collateral even if the collateral is in the physical possession of a third party.

Section 9-321. Licensee of General Intangible and Lessee of Goods in Ordinary Course of Business

(a) ["Licensee in ordinary course of business."] In this section, "licensee in ordinary course of business" means a person that becomes a licensee of a general intangible in good faith, without knowledge that the license violates the rights of another person in the general intangible, and in the ordinary course from a person in the business of licensing general intangibles of that kind. A person becomes a licensee in the ordinary course if the license to the person comports with the usual or customary practices in the kind of business in which the licensor is engaged or with the licensor's own usual or customary practices.

(b) [Rights of licensee in ordinary course of business.] A licensee in ordinary course of business takes its rights under a nonexclusive license free of a security interest in the general intangible created by the licensor, even if the security interest is perfected and the licensee knows of its existence.

(c) [Rights of lessee in ordinary course of business.] A lessee in ordinary course of business takes its leasehold interest free of a security interest in the goods created by the lessor, even if the security interest is perfected and the lessee knows of its existence.

Definitional Cross References:

General intangible	Section 9-102(a)(42)
Good faith	Section 1-201(b)(20)
Goods	Section 9-102(a)(44)
Leasehold interest	Section 2A-103(1)(m)
Lessee in ordinary course of business	Section 2A-103(1)(o)
Lessee	Section 2A-103(1)(n)
Lessor	Section 2A-103(1)(p)
Person	Section 1-201(b)(27)
Right	Section 1-201(b)(34)
Security interest	Section 1-201(b)(35)

Comment References: 9-323 C6

Official Comment

1. Source. Derived from Sections 2A-103(1)(o), 2A-307(3).

2. Licensee in Ordinary Course. Like the analogous rules in Section 9-320(a) with respect to buyers in ordinary course and subsection (c) with respect to lessees in ordinary course, the new rule in subsection (b) reflects the expectations of the parties and the marketplace: a licensee under a nonexclusive license takes subject to a security interest unless the secured party authorizes the license free of the security interest or other, controlling law such as that of this section (protecting ordinary-course licensees) dictates a contrary result. See Sections 9-201, 9-315. The definition of "licensee in ordinary course of business" in subsection (a) is modeled upon that of "buyer in ordinary course of business."

3. Lessee in Ordinary Course. Subsection (c) contains the rule formerly found in Section 2A-307(3). The rule works in the same way as that of Section 9-320(a).

Section 9-322. Priorities among Conflicting Security Interests in and Agricultural Liens on Same Collateral

(a) [General priority rules.] Except as otherwise provided in this section, priority among conflicting security interests and agricultural liens in the same collateral is determined according to the following rules:

(1) Conflicting perfected security interests and agricultural liens rank according to priority in time of filing or perfection. Priority dates from the earlier of the time a filing covering the collateral is first made or the security interest or agricultural lien is

first perfected, if there is no period thereafter when there is neither filing nor perfection.

(2) A perfected security interest or agricultural lien has priority over a conflicting unperfected security interest or agricultural lien.

(3) The first security interest or agricultural lien to attach or become effective has priority if conflicting security interests and agricultural liens are unperfected.

(b) [Time of perfection: proceeds and supporting obligations.] For the purposes of subsection (a)(1):

(1) the time of filing or perfection as to a security interest in collateral is also the time of filing or perfection as to a security interest in proceeds; and

(2) the time of filing or perfection as to a security interest in collateral supported by a supporting obligation is also the time of filing or perfection as to a security interest in the supporting obligation.

(c) [Special priority rules: proceeds and supporting obligations.] Except as otherwise provided in subsection (f), a security interest in collateral which qualifies for priority over a conflicting security interest under Section 9-327, 9-328, 9-329, 9-330, or 9-331 also has priority over a conflicting security interest in:

(1) any supporting obligation for the collateral; and

(2) proceeds of the collateral if:

(A) the security interest in proceeds is perfected;

(B) the proceeds are cash proceeds or of the same type as the collateral; and

(C) in the case of proceeds that are proceeds of proceeds, all intervening proceeds are cash proceeds, proceeds of the same type as the collateral, or an account relating to the collateral.

(d) [First-to-file priority rule for certain collateral.] Subject to subsection (e) and except as otherwise provided in subsection (f), if a security interest in chattel paper, deposit accounts, negotiable documents, instruments, investment property, or letter-of-credit rights is perfected by a method other than filing, conflicting perfected security interests in proceeds of the collateral rank according to priority in time of filing.

(e) [Applicability of subsection (d).] Subsection (d) applies only if the proceeds of the collateral are not cash proceeds, chattel paper, negotiable documents, instruments, investment property, or letter-of-credit rights.

(f) [Limitations on subsections (a) through (e).] Subsections (a) through (e) are subject to:

(1) subsection (g) and the other provisions of this part;

(2) Section 4-210 with respect to a security interest of a collecting bank;

(3) Section 5-118 with respect to a security interest of an issuer or nominated person; and

(4) Section 9-110 with respect to a security interest arising under Article 2 or 2A.

(g) [Priority under agricultural lien statute.] A perfected agricultural lien on collateral has priority over a conflicting security interest in or agricultural lien on the same collateral if the statute creating the agricultural lien so provides.

Definitional Cross References:

Account	Section 9-102(a)(2)
Agricultural lien	Section 9-102(a)(5)
Bank	Section 9-102(a)(8)
Cash proceeds	Section 9-102(a)(9)
Chattel paper	Section 9-102(a)(11)
Collateral	Section 9-102(a)(12)
Deposit account	Section 9-102(a)(29)
Document	Section 9-102(a)(30)
Instrument	Section 9-102(a)(47)
Investment property	Section 9-102(a)(49)
Issuer (letter of credit/ letter-of-credit right)	Section 5-102(a)(9)
Letter-of-credit right	Section 9-102(a)(51)
Nominated person	Section 5-102(a)(11)
Proceeds	Section 9-102(a)(64)
Security interest	Section 1-201(b)(35)
Supporting obligation	Section 9-102(a)(78)

Comment References:

9-109 C16

9-110 C4

9-323 C3

Official Comment

1. Source. Former Section 9-312(5), (6).

2. Scope of This Section. In a variety of situations, two or more people may claim a security interest in the same collateral. This section states general rules of priority among conflicting security interests. As subsection (f) provides, the general rules in subsections (a) through (e) are subject to the rule in subsection (g) governing perfected agricultural liens and to the other rules in this Part of this Article. Rules that override this section include those applicable to purchase-money security interests (Section 9-324) and those qualifying for special priority in particular types of collateral. See, e.g., Section 9-327 (deposit accounts); Section 9-328 (investment property); Section 9-329 (letter-of-credit rights); Section 9-330 (chattel paper and instruments); Section 9-334 (fixtures). In addition, the general rules of sections (a) through (e) are subject to priority rules governing security interests arising under Articles 2, 2A, 4, and 5.

3. General Rules. Subsection (a) contains three general rules. Subsection (a)(1) governs the priority of competing perfected security interests. Subsection (a)(2) governs the priority of competing security interests if one is perfected and the other is not. Subsection (a)(3) governs the priority of competing unperfected security interests. The rules may be regarded as adaptations of the idea, deeply rooted at common law, of a race of diligence among creditors. The first two rules are based on precedence in the time as of which the competing secured parties either filed their financing statements or obtained perfected security interests. Under subsection (a)(1), the first secured party who files or perfects has priority. Under subsection (a)(2), which is new, a perfected security interest has priority over an unperfected one. Under subsection (a)(3), if both security interests are unperfected, the first to attach has priority. Note that Section 9-709(b) may affect the application of subsection (a) to a filing that occurred before the effective date of this Article and which would be ineffective to perfect a security interest under former Article 9 but effective under this Article.

4. Competing Perfected Security Interests. When there is more than one perfected security interest, the security interests rank according to priority in time of filing or perfection. "Filing," of course, refers to the filing of an effective financing statement. "Perfection" refers to the acquisition of a perfected security interest, i.e., one that has attached and as to which any required perfection step has been taken. See Sections 9-308 and 9-309.

Example 1: On February 1, A files a financing statement covering a certain item of Debtor's equipment. On March 1, B files a financing statement covering the same equipment. On April 1, B makes a loan to Debtor and obtains a security interest in the equipment. On May 1, A makes a loan to Debtor and obtains a security interest in the same collateral. A has priority even though B's loan was made earlier and was perfected when made. It makes no difference whether A knew of B's security interest when A made its advance.

The problem stated in Example 1 is peculiar to a notice-filing system under which filing may occur before the security interest attaches (see Section 9-502). The justification for determining priority by order of filing lies in the necessity of protecting the filing system — that is, of allowing the first secured party who has filed to make subsequent advances without each time having to check for subsequent filings as a condition of protection. Note, however, that this first-to-file protection is not absolute. For example, Section 9-324 affords priority to certain purchase-money security interests, even if a competing secured party was the first to file or perfect.

Under a notice-filing system, a filed financing statement indicates to third parties that a person may have a security interest in the collateral indicated. With further inquiry, they may discover the complete state of affairs. When a financing statement that is ineffective when filed becomes effective thereafter, the policy underlying the notice-filing system determines the "time of filing" for purposes of subsection (a)(1). For example, the unauthorized filing of an otherwise sufficient initial financing statement becomes authorized, and the financing statement becomes effective, upon the debtor's post-filing authorization or ratification of the filing. See Section 9-509, Comment 3. Because the notice value of the financing statement is independent of the timing of authorization or ratification, the time of the unauthorized filing is the "time of filing" for purposes of subsection (a)(1). The same policy applies to the other priority rules in this part.

Example 2: A and B make non-purchase-money advances secured by the same collateral. The collateral is in Debtor's possession, and neither security interest is perfected when the second advance is made. Whichever secured party first perfects its security interest (by taking possession of the collateral or by filing) takes priority. It makes no difference whether that secured party knows of the other security interest at the time it perfects its own.

The rule of subsection (a)(1), affording priority to the first to file or perfect, applies to security interests that are perfected by any method, including temporarily (Section 9-312) or upon attachment (Section 9-309), even though there may be no notice to creditors or subsequent purchasers and notwithstanding any common-law rule to the contrary. The form of the claim to priority, i.e., filing or perfection, may shift from time to time, and the rank will be based on the first filing or perfection as long as there is no intervening period without filing or perfection. See Section 9-308(c).

Example 3: On October 1, A acquires a temporarily perfected (20-day) security interest, unfiled, in a negotiable tangible document in the debtor's possession under Section 9-312(e). On October 5, B files and thereby perfects a security interest that previously had attached to the same document. On October 10, A files. A has priority, even after the 20-day period expires, regardless of whether A knows of B's security interest when A files. A was the first to perfect and maintained continuous perfection or filing since the start of the 20-day period. However, the perfection of A's security interest extends only "to the extent it arises for new value given." To the extent A's security interest secures advances made by A beyond the 20-day period, its security interest would be subordinate to B's, inasmuch as B was the first to file.

In general, the rule in subsection (a)(1) does not distinguish among various advances made by a secured party. The priority of every advance dates from the earlier of filing or perfection. However, in rare instances, the priority of an advance dates from the time the advance is made. See Example 3 and Section 9-323.

5. Priority in After-Acquired Property. The application of the priority rules to after-acquired property must be considered separately for each item of collateral. Priority does not depend only on time of perfection but may also be based on priority in filing before perfection.

Example 4: On February 1, A makes advances to Debtor under a security agreement covering "all Debtor's machinery, both existing and after-acquired." A promptly files a financing statement. On April 1, B takes a security interest in all Debtor's machinery, existing and after-acquired, to secure an outstanding loan. The following day, B files a financing statement. On May 1, Debtor acquires a new machine. When Debtor acquires rights in the new machine, both A and B acquire security interests in the machine simultaneously. Both security interests are perfected simultaneously. However, A has priority because A filed before B.

When after-acquired collateral is encumbered by more than one security interest, one of the security interests often is a purchase-money security interest that is entitled to special priority under Section 9-324.

6. Priority in Proceeds: General Rule. Subsection (b)(1) follows former Section 9-312(6). It provides that the baseline rules of subsection (a) apply generally to priority conflicts in proceeds except where otherwise provided (e.g., as in subsections (c) through (e)). Under Section 9-203, attachment cannot occur (and therefore, under Section 9-308, perfection cannot occur) as to particular collateral until the collateral itself comes into existence and the debtor has rights in it. Thus, a security interest in proceeds of original collateral does not attach and is not perfected until the proceeds come into existence and the debtor acquires rights in them.

Example 5: On April 1, Debtor signs a security agreement granting to A a security interest in all Debtor's existing and after-acquired inventory. The same day, A files a financing statement covering inventory. On May 1, Debtor signs a security agreement granting B a security interest in all Debtor's existing and future accounts. On June 1, Debtor sells inventory to a customer on 30-day unsecured credit. When Debtor acquires the account, B's security interest attaches to it and is perfected by B's financing statement. At the very same time, A's security interest attaches to the account as proceeds of the inventory and is automatically perfected. See Section 9-315. Under subsection (b) of this section, for purposes of determining A's priority in the account, the time of filing as to the original collateral (April 1, as to inventory) is also the time of filing as to proceeds (account). Accordingly, A's security interest in the account has priority over B's. Of course, had B filed its financing statement before A filed (e.g., on March 1), then B would have priority in the accounts.

Section 9-324 governs the extent to which a special purchase-money priority in goods or software carries over into the proceeds of the original collateral.

7. Priority in Proceeds: Special Rules. Subsections (c), (d), and (e), which are new, provide additional priority rules for proceeds of collateral in situations where the temporal (first-in-time) rules of subsection (a)(1) are not appropriate. These new provisions distinguish what these Comments refer to as "non-filing collateral" from what they call "filing collateral." As used in these Comments, non-filing collateral is collateral of a type for which perfection may be achieved by a method other than filing (possession or control, mainly) and for which secured parties who so perfect generally do not expect or need to conduct a filing search. More specifically, non-filing collateral is chattel paper, deposit accounts, negotiable documents, instruments, investment property, and letter-of-credit rights. Other collateral—accounts, commercial tort claims, general intangibles, goods, nonnegotiable documents, and payment intangibles—is filing collateral.

8. Proceeds of Non-Filing Collateral: Non-Temporal Priority. Subsection (c)(2) provides a baseline priority rule for proceeds of non-filing collateral which applies if the secured party has taken the steps required for non-temporal priority over a conflicting security interest in non-filing collateral (e.g., control, in the case of deposit accounts, letter-of-credit rights, investment property, and in some cases, electronic negotiable documents, Section 9-331). This rule determines priority in proceeds of non-filing collateral whether or not there exists an actual conflicting security interest in the original non-filing collateral. Under subsection (c)(2), the priority in the original collateral continues in proceeds if the security interest in proceeds is perfected and the proceeds are cash proceeds or non-filing proceeds "of the same type" as the original collateral. As used in subsection (c)(2), "type" means a type of collateral defined in the Uniform Commercial Code and should be read broadly. For example, a security is "of the same type" as a security entitlement (i.e., investment property), and a promissory note is "of the same type" as a draft (i.e., an instrument).

Example 6: SP-1 perfects its security interest in investment property by filing. SP-2 perfects subsequently by taking control of a certificated security. Debtor receives cash proceeds of the security (e.g., dividends deposited into Debtor's deposit account). If the first-to-file-or-perfect rule of subsection (a)(1) were applied, SP-1's security interest in the cash proceeds would be senior, although SP-2's security interest continues perfected under Section 9-315 beyond the 20-day period of automatic perfection. This was the result under former Article 9. Under subsection (c), however, SP-2's security interest is senior.

Note that a different result would obtain in Example 6 (i.e., SP-1's security interest would be senior) if SP-1 were to obtain control of the deposit-account proceeds. This is so because subsection (c) is subject to subsection (f), which in turn provides that the priority rules under subsections (a) through (e) are subject to "the other provisions of this part." One of those "other provisions" is Section 9-327, which affords priority to a security interest perfected by control. See Section 9-327(1).

Example 7: SP-1 perfects its security interest in investment property by filing. SP-2 perfects subsequently by taking control of a certificated security. Debtor receives proceeds of the security consisting of a new certificated security issued as a stock dividend on the original collateral. Although the new security is of the same type as the original collateral (i.e., investment property), once the 20-day period of automatic perfection expires (see Section 9-315(d)), SP-2's security interest is unperfected. (SP-2 has not filed or taken delivery or control, and no temporary-perfection rule applies.) Consequently, once the 20-day period expires, subsection (c) does not confer priority, and, under subsection (a)(2), SP-1's security interest in the security is senior. This was the result under former Article 9.

Example 8: SP-1 perfects its security interest in investment property by filing. SP-2 perfects subsequently by taking control of a certificated security and also by filing against investment property. Debtor receives proceeds of the security consisting of a new certificated security issued as a stock dividend of the collateral. Because the new security is of the same type as the original collateral (i.e., investment property) and (unlike Example 7) SP-2's security interest is perfected by filing, SP-2's security interest is senior under subsection (c). If the new security were redeemed by the issuer upon surrender and yet another security were received by Debtor, SP-2's security interest would continue to enjoy priority under subsection (c). The new security would be proceeds of proceeds.

Example 9: SP-1 perfects its security interest in instruments by filing. SP-2 subsequently perfects its security interest in investment property by taking control of a certificated security and also by filing against investment property. Debtor receives proceeds of the security consisting of a dividend check that it deposits to a deposit account. Because the check and the deposit account are cash proceeds, SP-1's and SP-2's security interests in the cash proceeds are perfected under Section 9-315 beyond the 20-day period of automatic perfection. However, SP-2's security interest is senior under subsection (c).

Example 10: SP-1 perfects its security interest in investment property by filing. SP-2 perfects subsequently by taking control of a certificated security and also by filing against investment property. Debtor receives an instrument as proceeds of the security. (Assume that the instrument is not cash proceeds.) Because the instrument is not of the same type as the original collateral (i.e., investment property), SP-2's security interest, although perfected by filing, does not achieve priority under subsection (c). Under the first-to-file-or-perfect rule of subsection (a)(1), SP-1's security interest in the proceeds is senior.

The proceeds of proceeds are themselves proceeds. See Section 9-102 (defining "proceeds" and "collateral"). Sometimes competing security interests arise in proceeds that are several generations removed from the original collateral. As the following example explains, the applicability of subsection (c) may turn on the nature of the intervening proceeds.

Example 11: SP-1 perfects its security interest in Debtor's deposit account by obtaining control. Thereafter, SP-2 files against inventory, (presumably) searches, finds no indication of a conflicting security interest, and advances against Debtor's existing and after-acquired inventory. Debtor uses funds from the deposit account to purchase inventory, which SP-1 can trace as identifiable proceeds of its security interest in Debtor's deposit account, and which SP-2 claims as original collateral. The inventory is sold and the proceeds deposited into another deposit account, as to which SP-1 has not obtained control. Subsection (c) does not govern priority in this other deposit account. This deposit account is cash proceeds and is also the same type of collateral as SP-1's original collateral, as required by subsections (c)(2)(A) and (B). However, SP-1's security interest does not satisfy subsection (c)(2)(C) because the inventory proceeds, which intervened between the original deposit account and the deposit account constituting the proceeds at issue, are not cash proceeds, proceeds of the same type as the collateral (original deposit account), or an account relating to the collateral. Stated otherwise, once proceeds other than cash proceeds, proceeds of the same type as the original collateral, or an account relating to the original collateral intervene in the chain of proceeds, priority under subsection (c) is thereafter unavailable. The special priority rule in subsection (d) also is inapplicable to this case. See Comment 9, Example 13, below. Instead, the general first-to-file-or-perfect rule of subsections (a) and (b) apply. Under that rule, SP-1 has priority unless its security interest in the inventory proceeds became unperfected under Section 9-315(d). Had SP-2 filed against inventory before SP-1 obtained control of the original deposit account, then SP-2 would have had priority even if SP-1's security interest in the inventory proceeds remained perfected.

If two security interests in the same original collateral are entitled to priority in an item of proceeds under subsection (c)(2), the security interest having priority in the original collateral has priority in the proceeds.

9. Proceeds of Non-Filing Collateral: Special Temporal Priority. Under subsections (d) and (e), if a security interest in non-filing collateral is perfected by a method other than filing (e.g., control or possession), it does not retain its priority over a conflicting security interest in proceeds that are filing collateral. Moreover, it is not entitled to priority in proceeds under the first-to-file-or-perfect rule of subsections (a)(1) and (b). Instead, under subsection (d), priority is determined by a new first-to-file rule.

Example 12: SP-1 perfects its security interest in Debtor's deposit account by obtaining control. Thereafter, SP-2 files against equipment, (presumably) searches, finds no indication of a conflicting security interest, and advances against Debtor's equipment. SP-1 then files against Debtor's equipment. Debtor uses funds from the deposit account to purchase equipment, which SP-1 can trace as proceeds of its security interest in Debtor's deposit account. If the first-to-file-or-perfect rule were applied, SP-1's security interest would be senior under subsections (a)(1) and (b), because it was the first to perfect in the original collateral and there was no period during which its security interest was unperfected. Under subsection (d), however, SP-2's security interest would be senior because it filed first. This corresponds with the likely expectations of the parties.

Note that under subsection (e), the first-to-file rule of subsection (d) applies only if the proceeds in question are other than non-filing collateral (i.e., if the proceeds are filing collateral). If the proceeds are non-filing collateral, either the first-to-file-or-perfect rule under subsections (a) and (b) or the non-temporal priority rule in subsection (c) would apply, depending on the facts.

Example 13: SP-1 perfects its security interest in Debtor's deposit account by obtaining control. Thereafter, SP-2 files against inventory, (presumably) searches, finds no indication of a conflicting security interest, and advances against Debtor's existing and after-acquired inventory. Debtor uses funds from the deposit account to purchase inventory, which SP-1 can trace as identifiable proceeds of its security interest in Debtor's deposit account, and which SP-2 claims as original collateral. The inventory is sold and the proceeds deposited into another deposit account, as to which SP-1 has not obtained control. As discussed above in Comment 8, Example 11, subsection (c) does not govern priority in this deposit account. Subsection (d) also does not govern, because the proceeds at issue (the deposit account) are cash proceeds. See subsection (e). Rather, the general rules of subsections (a) and (b) govern.

10. Priority in Supporting Obligations. Under subsections (b)(2) and (c)(1), a security interest having priority in collateral also has priority in a supporting obligation for that collateral. However, the rules in these subsections are subject to the special rule in Section 9-329 governing the priority of security interests in a letter-of-credit right. See subsection (f). Under Section 9-329, a secured party's failure to obtain control (Section 9-107) of a letter-of-credit right that serves as supporting collateral leaves its security interest exposed to a priming interest of a party who does take control.

11. Unperfected Security Interests. Under subsection (a)(3), if conflicting security interests are unperfected, the first to attach has priority. This rule may be of merely theoretical interest, inasmuch as it is hard to imagine a situation where the case would come into litigation without either secured party's having perfected its security interest. If neither security interest had been perfected at the time of the filing of a petition in bankruptcy, ordinarily neither would be good against the trustee in bankruptcy under the Bankruptcy Code.

12. Agricultural Liens. Statutes other than this Article may purport to grant priority to an agricultural lien as against a conflicting security interest or agricultural lien. Under subsection (g), if another statute grants priority to an agricultural lien, the agricultural lien has priority only if the same statute creates the agricultural lien and the agricultural lien is perfected. Otherwise, subsection (a) applies the same priority rules to an agricultural lien as to a security interest, regardless of whether the agricultural lien conflicts with another agricultural lien or with a security interest.

Inasmuch as no agricultural lien on proceeds arises under this Article, subsections (b) through (e) do not apply to proceeds of agricultural liens. However, if an agricultural lien has priority under subsection (g) and the statute creating the agricultural lien gives the secured party a lien on proceeds of the collateral subject to the lien, a court should apply the principle of subsection (g) and award priority in the proceeds to the holder of the perfected agricultural lien.

Section 9-323. Future Advances

(a) [When priority based on time of advance.] Except as otherwise provided in subsection (c), for purposes of determining the priority of a perfected security interest under Section 9-322(a)(1), perfection of the security interest dates from the time an advance is made to the extent that the security interest secures an advance that:

(1) is made while the security interest is perfected only:

(A) under Section 9-309 when it attaches; or

(B) temporarily under Section 9-312(e), (f), or (g); and

(2) is not made pursuant to a commitment entered into before or while the security interest is perfected by a method other than under Section 9-309 or 9-312(e), (f), or (g).

(b) [Lien creditor.] Except as otherwise provided in subsection (c), a security interest is subordinate to the rights of a person that becomes a lien creditor to the extent that the security interest secures an advance made more than 45 days after the person becomes a lien creditor unless the advance is made:

(1) without knowledge of the lien; or

(2) pursuant to a commitment entered into without knowledge of the lien.

(c) [Buyer of receivables.] Subsections (a) and (b) do not apply to a security interest held by a secured party that is a buyer of accounts, chattel paper, payment intangibles, or promissory notes or a consignor.

(d) [Buyer of goods.] Except as otherwise provided in subsection (e), a buyer of goods takes free of a security interest to the extent that it secures advances made after the earlier of:

(1) the time the secured party acquires knowledge of the buyer's purchase; or

(2) 45 days after the purchase.

(e) [Advances made pursuant to commitment: priority of buyer of goods.] Subsection (d) does not apply if the advance is made pursuant to a commitment entered into without knowledge of the buyer's purchase and before the expiration of the 45-day period.

(f) [Lessee of goods.] Except as otherwise provided in subsection (g), a lessee of goods, takes the leasehold interest free of a security interest to the extent that it secures advances made after the earlier of:

(1) the time the secured party acquires knowledge of the lease; or

(2) 45 days after the lease contract becomes enforceable.

(g) [Advances made pursuant to commitment: priority of lessee of goods.] Subsection (f) does not apply if the advance is made pursuant to a commitment entered into without knowledge of the lease and before the expiration of the 45-day period.

Definitional Cross References:

Account	Section 9-102(a)(2)
Buyer in ordinary course of business	Section 1-201(b)(9)
Chattel paper	Section 9-102(a)(11)
Consignor	Section 9-102(a)(21)
Goods	Section 9-102(a)(44)
Lease contract	Section 2A-103(1)(l)
Lease	Section 2A-103(1)(j)
Leasehold interest	Section 2A-103(1)(m)
Lessee	Section 2A-103(1)(n)
Lessee in ordinary course of business	Section 2A-103(1)(o)
Lien creditor	Section 9-102(a)(52)
Payment intangible	Section 9-102(a)(61)
Person	Section 1-201(b)(27)
Promissory note	Section 9-102(a)(65)
Purchase	Section 1-201(b)(29)
Pursuant to commitment	Section 9-102(a)(69)
Right	Section 1-201(b)(34)
Secured party	Section 9-102(a)(73)
Security interest	Section 1-201(b)(35)

Comment References:

9-317 C4

9-322 C4

Official Comment

1. Source. Former Sections 9-312(7), 9-301(4), 9-307(3), 2A-307(4).

2. Scope of This Section. A security agreement may provide that collateral secures future advances. See Section 9-204(c). This section collects all of the special rules dealing with the priority of advances made by a secured party after a third party acquires an interest in the collateral. Subsection (a) applies when the third party is a competing secured party. It replaces and clarifies former Section 9-312(7). Subsection (b) deals with lien creditors and replaces former Section 9-301(4). Subsections (d) and (e) deal with buyers and replace former Section 9-307(3). Subsections (f) and (g) deal with lessees and replace former Section 2A-307(4).

3. Competing Security Interests. Under a proper reading of the first-to-file-or-perfect rule of Section 9-322(a)(1) (and former Section 9-312(5)), it is abundantly clear that the time when an advance is made plays no role in determining priorities among conflicting security interests except when a financing statement was not filed and the advance is the giving of value as the last step for attachment and perfection. Thus, a secured party takes subject to all advances secured by a competing security interest having priority under Section 9-322(a)(1). This result generally obtains regardless of how the competing security interest is perfected and regardless of whether the advances are made "pursuant to commitment" (Section 9-102). Subsection (a) of this section states the only other instance when the time of an advance figures in the priority scheme in Section 9-322: when the security interest is perfected only automatically under Section 9-309 or temporarily under Section 9-312(e), (f), or (g), and the advance is not made pursuant to a commitment entered into while the security interest was perfected by another method. Thus, an advance has priority from the date it is made only in the rare case in which it is made without commitment and while the security interest is perfected only temporarily under Section 9-312.

The new formulation in subsection (a) clarifies the result when the initial advance is paid and a new ("future") advance is made subsequently. Under former Section 9-312(7), the priority of the new advance turned on whether it was "made while a security interest is perfected." This section resolves any ambiguity by omitting the quoted phrase.

Example 1: On February 1, A makes an advance secured by machinery in the debtor's possession and files a financing statement. On March 1, B makes an advance secured by the same machinery and files a financing statement. On April 1, A makes a further advance, under the original security agreement, against the same machinery. A was the first to file and so, under the first-to-file-or-perfect rule of Section 9-322(a)(1), A's security interest has priority over B's, both as to the February 1 and as to the April 1 advance. It makes no difference whether A knows of B's intervening advance when A makes the second advance. Note that, as long as A was the first to file or perfect, A would have priority with respect to both advances if either A or B had perfected by taking possession of the collateral. Likewise, A would have priority if A's April 1 advance was not made under the original agreement with the debtor, but was under a new agreement.

Example 2: On October 1, A acquires a temporarily perfected (20-day) security interest, unfiled, in a negotiable tangible document in the debtor's possession under Section 9-312(e) or (f). The security interest secures an advance made on that day as well as future advances. On October 5, B files and thereby perfects a security interest that previously had attached to the same document. On October 8, A makes an additional advance. On October 10, A files. Under Section 9-322(a)(1), because A was the first to perfect and maintained continuous perfection or filing since the start of the 20-day period, A has priority, even after the 20-day period expires. See Section 9-322, Comment 4, Example 3. However, under this section, for purposes of Section 9-322(a)(1), to the extent A's security interest secures the October 8 advance, the security interest was perfected on October 8. Inasmuch as B perfected on October 5, B has priority over the October 8 advance.

The rule in subsection (a) is more liberal toward the priority of future advances than the corresponding rules applicable to intervening lien creditors (subsection (b)), buyers (subsections (d) and (e)), and lessees (subsections (f) and (g)).

4. Competing Lien Creditors. Subsection (b) replaces former Section 9-301(4) and addresses the rights of a "lien creditor," as defined in Section 9-102. Under Section 9-317(a)(2), a security interest is senior to the rights of a person who becomes a lien creditor, unless the person becomes a lien creditor before the security interest is perfected and before a financing statement covering the collateral is filed and Section 9-203(b)(3) is satisfied. Subsection (b) of this section provides that a security interest is subordinate to those rights to the extent that the specified circumstances occur. Subsection (b) does not elevate the priority of a security interest that is subordinate to the rights of a lien creditor under Section 9-317(a)(2); it only subordinates.

As under former Section 9-301(4), a secured party's knowledge does not cut short the 45-day period during which future advances can achieve priority over an intervening lien creditor's interest. Rather, because of the impact of the rule in subsection (b) on the question whether the security interest for future advances is "protected" under Section 6323(c)(2) and (d) of the Internal Revenue Code as amended by the Federal Tax Lien Act of 1966, the priority of the security interest for future advances over a lien creditor is made absolute for 45 days regardless of knowledge of the secured party concerning the lien. If, however, the advance is made after the 45 days, the advance will not have priority unless it was made or committed without knowledge of the lien.

5. Sales of Receivables; Consignments. Subsections (a) and (b) do not apply to outright sales of accounts, chattel paper, payment intangibles, or promissory notes, nor do they apply to consignments.

6. Competing Buyers and Lessees. Under subsections (d) and (e), a buyer will not take subject to a security interest to the extent it secures advances made after the secured party has knowledge that the buyer has purchased the collateral or more than 45 days after the purchase unless the advances were made pursuant to a commitment entered into before the expiration of the 45-day period and without knowledge of the purchase. Subsections (f) and (g) provide an analogous rule for lessees. Subsections (d) and (e) replace pre-1998 Section 9-307(3), and subsections (f) and (g) replace pre-1998 Section 2A-307(4). No change in meaning is intended.

Of course, a buyer in ordinary course who takes free of the security interest under Section 9-320 and a lessee in ordinary course who takes free under Section 9-321 are not subject to any future advances. However, the exceptions for a buyer in ordinary course of business and a lessee in ordinary course of business in the 1998 text of subsections (d) and (f) have been deleted. Even if such a buyer or lessee does not meet the requirements under Section 9-320 or 9-321 to take free of a security interest, it should be entitled to the benefits of those subsections, which apply to buyers generally. This change is consistent with the intended result under the 1998 text.

Section 9-324. Priority of Purchase-Money Security Interests

(a) [General rule: purchase-money priority.] Except as otherwise provided in subsection (g), a perfected purchase-money security interest in goods other than inventory or livestock has priority over a conflicting security interest in the same goods, and, except as otherwise provided in Section 9-327, a perfected security interest in its identifiable proceeds also has priority, if the purchase-money security interest is perfected when the debtor receives possession of the collateral or within 20 days thereafter.

(b) [Inventory purchase-money priority.] Subject to subsection (c) and except as otherwise provided in subsection (g), a perfected purchase-money security interest in inventory has priority over a conflicting security interest in the same inventory, has priority over a conflicting security interest in chattel paper or an instrument constituting proceeds of the inventory and in proceeds of the chattel paper, if so provided in Section 9-330, and, except as otherwise provided in Section 9-327, also has priority in identifiable cash proceeds of the inventory to the extent the identifiable cash proceeds are received on or before the delivery of the inventory to a buyer, if:

(1) the purchase-money security interest is perfected when the debtor receives possession of the inventory;

(2) the purchase-money secured party sends a signed notification to the holder of the conflicting security interest;

(3) the holder of the conflicting security interest receives the notification within five years before the debtor receives possession of the inventory; and

(4) the notification states that the person sending the notification has or expects to acquire a purchase-money security interest in inventory of the debtor and describes the inventory.

(c) [Holders of conflicting inventory security interests to be notified.] Subsections (b)(2) through (4) apply only if the holder of the conflicting security interest had filed a financing statement covering the same types of inventory:

(1) if the purchase-money security interest is perfected by filing, before the date of the filing; or

(2) if the purchase-money security interest is temporarily perfected without filing or possession under Section 9-312(f), before the beginning of the 20-day period thereunder.

(d) [Livestock purchase-money priority.] Subject to subsection (e) and except as otherwise provided in subsection (g), a perfected purchase-money security interest in livestock that are farm products has priority over a conflicting security interest in the same livestock, and, except as otherwise provided in Section 9-327, a perfected security interest in their identifiable proceeds and identifiable products in their unmanufactured states also has priority, if:

(1) the purchase-money security interest is perfected when the debtor receives possession of the livestock;

(2) the purchase-money secured party sends a signed notification to the holder of the conflicting security interest;

(3) the holder of the conflicting security interest receives the notification within six months before the debtor receives possession of the livestock; and

(4) the notification states that the person sending the notification has or expects to acquire a purchase-money security interest in livestock of the debtor and describes the livestock.

(e) [Holders of conflicting livestock security interests to be notified.] Subsections (d)(2) through (4) apply only if the holder of the conflicting security interest had filed a financing statement covering the same types of livestock:

(1) if the purchase-money security interest is perfected by filing, before the date of the filing; or

(2) if the purchase-money security interest is temporarily perfected without filing or possession under Section 9-312(f), before the beginning of the 20-day period thereunder.

(f) [Software purchase-money priority.] Except as otherwise provided in subsection (g), a perfected purchase-money security interest in software has priority over a conflicting security interest in the same collateral, and, except as otherwise provided in Section 9-327, a perfected security interest in its identifiable proceeds also has priority, to the extent that the purchase-money security interest in the goods in which the software was acquired for use has priority in the goods and proceeds of the goods under this section.

(g) [Conflicting purchase-money security interests.] If more than one security interest qualifies for priority in the same collateral under subsection (a), (b), (d), or (f):

(1) a security interest securing an obligation incurred as all or part of the price of the collateral has priority over a security interest securing an obligation incurred for value given to enable the debtor to acquire rights in or the use of collateral; and

(2) in all other cases, Section 9-322(a) applies to the qualifying security interests.

Definitional Cross References:

Cash proceeds	Section 9-102(a)(9)
Chattel paper	Section 9-102(a)(11)
Collateral	Section 9-102(a)(12)
Debtor	Section 9-102(a)(28)
Delivery	Section 1-201(b)(15)
Farm products	Section 9-102(a)(34)
Financing statement	Section 9-102(a)(39)
Goods	Section 9-102(a)(44)
Holder	Section 1-201(b)(21)
Instrument	Section 9-102(a)(47)
Inventory	Section 9-102(a)(48)
Person	Section 1-201(b)(27)
Proceeds	Section 9-102(a)(64)
Right	Section 1-201(b)(34)
Secured party	Section 9-102(a)(73)
Security interest	Section 1-201(b)(35)
Send	Section 1-201(b)(36)
Sign	Section 1-201(b)(37)
Software	Section 9-102(a)(76)
Value	Section 1-204

Official Comment

1. Source. Former Section 9-312(3), (4).

2. Priority of Purchase-Money Security Interests. This section contains the priority rules applicable to purchase-money security interests, as defined in Section 9-103. It affords a special, non-temporal priority to those purchase-money security interests that satisfy the statutory conditions. In most cases, priority will be over a security interest asserted under an after-acquired property clause. See Section 9-204 on the extent to which security interests in after-acquired property are validated.

A purchase-money security interest can be created only in goods and software. See Section 9-103. Section 9-324(a), which follows former Section 9-312(4), contains the general rule for purchase-money security interests in goods. It is subject to subsections (b) and (c), which derive from former Section 9-312(3) and apply to purchase-money security interests in inventory, and subsections (d) and (e), which apply to purchase-money security interests in livestock that are farm products. Subsection (f) applies to purchase-money security interests in software. Subsection (g) deals with the relatively unusual case in which a debtor creates two purchase-money security interests in the same collateral and both security interests qualify for special priority under one of the other subsections.

Former Section 9-312(2) contained a rule affording special priority to those who provided secured credit that enabled a debtor to produce crops. This rule proved unworkable and has been eliminated from this Article. Instead, model Section 9-324A contains a revised production-money priority rule. That section is a model, not uniform, provision. The sponsors of the UCC have taken no position as to whether it should be enacted, instead leaving the matter for state legislatures to consider if they are so inclined.

3. Purchase-Money Priority in Goods Other Than Inventory and Livestock. Subsection (a) states a general rule applicable to all types of goods except inventory and farm-products livestock: the purchase-money interest takes priority if it is perfected when the debtor receives possession of the collateral or within 20 days thereafter. (As to the 20-day "grace period," compare Section 9-317(e). Former Sections 9-312(4) and 9-301(2) contained a 10-day grace period.) The perfection requirement means that the purchase-money secured party either has filed a financing statement before that time or has a temporarily perfected security interest in goods covered by documents under Section 9-312(e) and (f) which is continued in a perfected status by filing before the expiration of the 20-day period specified in that section. A purchase-money security interest qualifies for priority under subsection (a), even if the purchase-money secured party knows that a conflicting security interest has been created and/or that the holder of the conflicting interest has filed a financing statement covering the collateral.

Normally, there will be no question when "the debtor receives possession of the collateral" for purposes of subsection (a). However, sometimes a debtor buys goods and takes possession of them in stages, and then assembly and testing are completed (by the seller or debtor-buyer) at the debtor's location. Under those circumstances, the buyer "takes possession" within the meaning of subsection (a) when, after an inspection of the portion of the goods in the debtor's possession, it would be apparent to a potential lender to the debtor that the debtor has acquired an interest in the goods taken as a whole.

A similar issue concerning the time when "the debtor receives possession" arises when a person acquires possession of goods under a transaction that is not governed by this Article and then later agrees to buy the goods on secured credit. For example, a person may take possession of goods as lessee under a lease contract and then exercise an option to purchase the goods from the lessor on secured credit. Under Section 2A-307(1), creditors of the lessee generally take subject to the lease contract; filing a financing statement against the lessee is unnecessary to protect the lessor's leasehold or residual interest. Once the lease is converted to a security interest, filing a financing statement is necessary to protect the seller's (former lessor's) security interest. Accordingly, the 20-day period in subsection (a) does not commence until the goods become "collateral" (defined in Section 9-102), i.e., until they are subject to a security interest.

4. Purchase-Money Security Interests in Inventory. Subsections (b) and (c) afford a means by which a purchase-money security interest in inventory can achieve priority over an earlier-filed security interest in the same collateral. To achieve priority, the purchase-money security interest must be perfected when the debtor receives possession of the inventory. For a discussion of when "the debtor receives possession," see Comment 3, above. The 20-day grace period of subsection (a) does not apply.

The arrangement between an inventory secured party and its debtor typically requires the secured party to make periodic advances against incoming inventory or periodic releases of old inventory as new inventory is received. A fraudulent debtor may apply to the secured party for advances even though it has already given a purchase-money security interest in the inventory to another secured party. For this reason, subsections (b)(2) through (4) and (c) impose a second condition for the purchase-money security interest's achieving priority: the purchase-money secured party must give notification to the holder of a conflicting security interest who filed against the same item or type of inventory before the purchase-money secured party filed or its security interest became perfected temporarily under Section 9-312(e) or (f). The notification requirement protects the non-purchase-money inventory secured party in such a situation: if the inventory secured party has received notification, it presumably will not make an advance; if it has not received notification (or if the other security interest does not qualify as purchase-money), any advance the inventory secured party may make ordinarily will have priority under Section 9-322. Inasmuch as an arrangement for periodic advances against incoming goods is unusual outside the inventory field, subsection (a) does not contain a notification requirement.

5. Notification to Conflicting Inventory Secured Party: Timing. Under subsection (b)(3), the perfected purchase-money security interest achieves priority over a conflicting security interest only if the holder of the conflicting security interest receives a notification within five years before the debtor receives possession of the purchase-money collateral. If the debtor never receives possession, the five-year period never begins, and the purchase-money security interest has priority, even if notification is not given. However, where the purchase-money inventory financing began by the purchase-money secured party's possession of a negotiable document of title, to retain priority the secured party must give the notification required by subsection (b) at or before the usual time, i.e., when the debtor gets possession of the inventory, even though the security interest remains perfected for 20 days under Section 9-312(e) or (f).

Some people have mistakenly read former Section 9-312(3)(b) to require, as a condition of purchase-money priority in inventory, that the purchase-money secured party give the notification before it files a financing statement. Read correctly, the "before" clauses compare (i) the time when the holder of the conflicting security interest filed a financing statement with (ii) the time when the purchase-money security interest becomes perfected by filing or automatically perfected temporarily. Only if (i) occurs before (ii) must notification be given to the holder of the conflicting security interest. Subsection (c) has been rewritten to clarify this point.

6. Notification to Conflicting Inventory Secured Party: Address. Inasmuch as the address provided as that of the secured party on a filed financing statement is an "address that is reasonable under the circumstances," the holder of a purchase-money security interest may satisfy the requirement to "send" notification to the holder of a conflicting security interest in inventory by sending a notification to that address, even if the address is or becomes incorrect. See Section 9-102 (definition of "send"). Similarly, because the address is "held out by [the holder of the conflicting security interest] as the place for receipt of such communications [i.e., communications relating to security interests]," the holder is deemed to have "received" a notification delivered to that address. See Section 1-202(e).

7. Consignments. Subsections (b) and (c) also determine the priority of a consignor's interest in consigned goods as against a security interest in the goods created by the consignee. Inasmuch as a consignment subject to this Article is defined to be a purchase-money security interest, see Section 9-103(d), no inference concerning the nature of the transaction should be drawn from the fact that a consignor uses the term "security interest" in its notice under subsection (b)(4). Similarly, a notice stating that the consignor has delivered or expects to deliver goods, properly described, "on consignment" meets the requirements of subsection (b)(4), even if it does not contain the term "security interest," and even if the transaction subsequently is determined to be a security interest. Cf. Section 9-505 (use of "consignor" and "consignee" in financing statement).

8. Priority in Proceeds: General. When the purchase-money secured party has priority over another secured party, the question arises whether this priority extends to the proceeds of the original collateral. Subsections (a), (d), and (f) give an affirmative answer, but only as to proceeds in which the security interest is perfected (see Section 9-315). Although this qualification did not appear in former Section 9-312(4), it was implicit in that provision.

In the case of inventory collateral under subsection (b), where financing frequently is based on the resulting accounts, chattel paper, or other proceeds, the special priority of the purchase-money secured interest carries over into only certain types of proceeds. As under former Section 9-312(3), the purchase-money priority in inventory under subsection (b) carries over into identifiable cash proceeds (defined in Section 9-102) received on or before the delivery of the inventory to a buyer.

As a general matter, also like former Section 9-312(3), the purchase-money priority in inventory does not carry over into proceeds consisting of accounts or chattel paper. Many parties financing inventory are quite content to protect their first-priority security interest in the inventory itself. They realize that when the inventory is sold, someone else will be financing the resulting receivables (accounts or chattel paper), and the priority for inventory will not run forward to the receivables constituting the proceeds. Indeed, the cash supplied by the receivables financer often will be used to pay the inventory financing. In some situations, the party financing the inventory on a purchase-money basis makes contractual arrangements that the proceeds of receivables financing by another be devoted to paying off the inventory security interest.

However, the purchase-money priority in inventory does carry over to proceeds consisting of chattel paper and its proceeds (and also to instruments) to the extent provided in Section 9-330. Under Section 9-330(e), the holder of a purchase-money security interest in inventory is deemed to give new value for proceeds consisting of chattel paper. Taken together, Sections 9-324(b) and 9-330(e) enable a purchase-money inventory secured party to obtain priority in chattel paper constituting proceeds of the inventory, even if the secured party does not actually give new value for the chattel paper, provided the purchase-money secured party satisfies the other conditions for achieving priority.

When the proceeds of original collateral (goods or software) consist of a deposit account, Section 9-327 governs priority to the extent it conflicts with the priority rules of this section.

9. Priority in Accounts Constituting Proceeds of Inventory. The application of the priority rules in subsection (b) is shown by the following examples:

> **Example 1:** Debtor creates a security interest in its existing and after-acquired inventory in favor of SP-1, who files a financing statement covering inventory. SP-2 subsequently takes a purchase-money security interest in certain inventory and, under subsection (b), achieves priority in this inventory over SP-1. This inventory is then sold, producing accounts. Accounts are not cash proceeds, and so the special purchase-money priority in the inventory does not control the priority in the accounts. Rather, the first-to-file-or-perfect rule of Section 9-322(a)(1) applies. The time of SP-1's filing as to the inventory is also the time of filing as to the accounts under Section 9-322(b). Assuming that each security interest in the accounts proceeds remains perfected under Section 9-315, SP-1 has priority as to the accounts.

> **Example 2:** In Example 1, if SP-2 had filed directly against accounts, the date of that filing as to accounts would be compared with the date of SP-1's filing as to the inventory. The first filed would prevail under Section 9-322(a)(1).

> **Example 3:** If SP-3 had filed against accounts in Example 1 before either SP-1 or SP-2 filed against inventory, SP-3's filing against accounts would have priority over the filings of SP-1 and SP-2. This result obtains even though the filings against inventory are effective to continue the perfected status of SP-1's and SP-2's security interest in the accounts beyond the 20-day period of automatic perfection. See Section 9-315. SP-1's and SP-2's

position as to the inventory does not give them a claim to accounts (as proceeds of the inventory) which is senior to someone who has filed earlier against accounts. If, on the other hand, either SP-1's or SP-2's filing against the inventory preceded SP-3's filing against accounts, SP-1 or SP-2 would outrank SP-3 as to the accounts.

10. Purchase-Money Security Interests in Livestock. New subsections (d) and (e) provide a purchase-money priority rule for farm-products livestock. They are patterned on the purchase-money priority rule for inventory found in subsections (b) and (c) and include a requirement that the purchase-money secured party notify earlier-filed parties. Two differences between subsections (b) and (d) are noteworthy. First, unlike the purchase-money inventory lender, the purchase-money livestock lender enjoys priority in all proceeds of the collateral. Thus, under subsection (d), the purchase-money secured party takes priority in accounts over an earlier-filed accounts financer. Second, subsection (d) affords priority in certain products of the collateral as well as proceeds.

11. Purchase-Money Security Interests in Aquatic Farm Products. Aquatic goods produced in aquacultural operations (e.g., catfish raised on a catfish farm) are farm products. See Section 9-102 (definition of "farm products"). The definition does not indicate whether aquatic goods are "crops," as to which the model production money security interest priority in Section 9-324A applies, or "livestock," as to which the purchase-money priority in subsection (d) of this section applies. This Article leaves courts free to determine the classification of particular aquatic goods on a case-by-case basis, applying whichever priority rule makes more sense in the overall context of the debtor's business.

12. Purchase-Money Security Interests in Software. Subsection (f) governs the priority of purchase-money security interests in software. Under Section 9-103(c), a purchase-money security interest arises in software only if the debtor acquires its interest in the software for the principal purpose of using the software in goods subject to a purchase-money security interest. Under subsection (f), a purchase-money security interest in software has the same priority as the purchase-money security interest in the goods in which the software was acquired for use. This priority is determined under subsections (b) and (c) (for inventory) or (a) (for other goods).

13. Multiple Purchase-Money Security Interests. New subsection (g) governs priority among multiple purchase-money security interests in the same collateral. It grants priority to purchase-money security interests securing the price of collateral (i.e., created in favor of the seller) over purchase-money security interests that secure enabling loans. Section 7.2(c) of the Restatement (3d) of the Law of Property (Mortgages) (1997) adopts this rule with respect to real property mortgages. As Comment *d* to that section explains:

> the equities favor the vendor. Not only does the vendor part with specific real estate rather than money, but the vendor would never relinquish it at all except on the understanding that the vendor will be able to use it to satisfy the obligation to pay the price. This is the case even though the vendor may know that the mortgagor is going to finance the transaction in part by borrowing from a third party and giving a mortgage to secure that obligation. In the final analysis, the law is more sympathetic to the vendor's hazard of losing real estate previously owned than to the third party lender's risk of being unable to collect from an interest in real estate that never previously belonged to it.

The first-to-file-or-perfect rule of Section 9-322 applies to multiple purchase-money security interests securing enabling loans.

14. "Signed Replaces "Authenticated." Consistent with the revised definition of "sign" in Section 1-201(b)(37), the cognate term "signed" replaces the references to authenticated in the pre-2022 text of this section.

Section 9-325. Priority of Security Interests in Transferred Collateral

(a) [Subordination of security interest in transferred collateral.] Except as otherwise provided in subsection (b), a security interest created by a debtor is subordinate to a security interest in the same collateral created by another person if:

(1) the debtor acquired the collateral subject to the security interest created by the other person;

(2) the security interest created by the other person was perfected when the debtor acquired the collateral; and

(3) there is no period thereafter when the security interest is unperfected.

(b) [Limitation of subsection (a) subordination.] Subsection (a) subordinates a security interest only if the security interest:

(1) otherwise would have priority solely under Section 9-322(a) or 9-324; or

(2) arose solely under Section 2-711(3) or 2A-508(5).

Definitional Cross References:

Collateral	Section 9-102(a)(12)
Debtor	Section 9-102(a)(28)
Person	Section 1-201(b)(27)
Security interest	Section 1-201(b)(35)

Comment References: 9-110 C4

Official Comment

1. Source. New.

2. "Double Debtor Problem." This section addresses the "double debtor" problem, which arises when a debtor acquires property that is subject to a security interest created by another debtor.

3. Taking Subject to Perfected Security Interest. Consider the following scenario:

> **Example 1:** A owns an item of equipment subject to a perfected security interest in favor of SP-A. A sells the equipment to B, not in the ordinary course of business.

B acquires its interest subject to SP-A's security interest. See Sections 9-201, 9-315(a)(1). Under this section, if B creates a security interest in the equipment in favor of SP-B, SP-B's security interest is subordinate to SP-A's security interest, even if SP-B filed against B before SP-A filed against A, and even if SP-B took a purchase-money security interest. Normally, SP-B could have investigated the source of the equipment and discovered SP-A's filing before making an advance against the equipment, whereas SP-A had no reason to search the filings against someone other than its debtor, A.

4. Taking Subject to Unperfected Security Interest. This section applies only if the security interest in the transferred collateral was perfected when the transferee acquired the collateral. See subsection (a)(2). If this condition is not met, then the normal priority rules apply.

Example 2: A owns an item of equipment subject to an unperfected security interest in favor of SP-A. A sells the equipment to B, who gives value and takes delivery of the equipment without knowledge of the security interest. B takes free of the security interest. See Section 9-317(b). If B then creates a security interest in favor of SP-B, no priority issue arises; SP-B has the only security interest in the equipment.

Example 3: The facts are as in Example 2, except that B knows of SP-A's security interest and therefore takes the equipment subject to it. If B creates a security interest in the equipment in favor of SP-B, this section does not determine the relative priority of the security interests. Rather, the normal priority rules govern. If SP-B perfects its security interest, then, under Section 9-322(a)(2), SP-A's unperfected security interest will be junior to SP-B's perfected security interest. The award of priority to SP-B is premised on the belief that SP-A's failure to file could have misled SP-B.

5. Taking Subject to Perfected Security Interest That Becomes Unperfected. This section applies only if the security interest in the transferred collateral did not become unperfected at any time after the transferee acquired the collateral. See subsection (a)(3). If this condition is not met, then the normal priority rules apply.

Example 4: As in Example 1, A owns an item of equipment subject to a perfected security interest in favor of SP-A. A sells the equipment to B, not in the ordinary course of business. B acquires its interest subject to SP-A's security interest. See Sections 9-201, 9-315(a)(1). B creates a security interest in favor of SP-B, and SP-B perfects its security interest. This section provides that SP-A's security interest is senior to SP-B's. However, if SP-A's financing statement lapses while SP-B's security interest is perfected, then the normal priority rules would apply, and SP-B's security interest would become senior to SP-A's security interest. See Sections 9-322(a)(2), 9-515(c).

6. Unusual Situations. The appropriateness of the rule of subsection (a) is most apparent when it works to subordinate security interests having priority under the basic priority rules of Section 9-322(a) or the purchase-money priority rules of Section 9-324. The rule also works properly when applied to the security interest of a buyer under Section 2-711(3) or a lessee under Section 2A-508(5). However, subsection (a) may provide an inappropriate resolution of the "double debtor" problem in some of the wide variety of other contexts in which the problem may arise. Although subsection (b) limits the application of subsection (a) to those cases in which subordination is known to be appropriate, courts should apply the rule in other settings, if necessary to promote the underlying purposes and policies of the Uniform Commercial Code. See Section 1-103(a).

Section 9-326. Priority of Security Interests Created by New Debtor

(a) [Subordination of security interest created by new debtor.] Subject to subsection (b), a security interest that is created by a new debtor in collateral in which the new debtor has or acquires rights and is perfected solely by a filed financing statement that would be ineffective to perfect the security interest but for the application of Section 9-316(i)(1) or 9-508 is subordinate to a security interest in the same collateral which is perfected other than by such a filed financing statement.

(b) [Priority under other provisions; multiple original debtors.] The other provisions of this part determine the priority among conflicting security interests in the same collateral perfected by filed financing statements described in subsection (a). However, if the security agreements to which a new debtor became bound as debtor were not entered into by the same original debtor, the conflicting security interests rank according to priority in time of the new debtor's having become bound.

Definitional Cross References:

Collateral	Section 9-102(a)(12)
Debtor	Section 9-102(a)(28)
Financing statement	Section 9-102(a)(39)
New debtor	Section 9-102(a)(56)
Original debtor	Section 9-102(a)(60)
Right	Section 1-201(b)(34)
Security agreement	Section 9-102(a)(74)
Security interest	Section 1-201(b)(35)

Official Comment

1. Source. New.

2. Subordination of Security Interests Created by New Debtor. This section addresses the priority contests that may arise when a new debtor becomes bound by the security agreement of an *original debtor* and each debtor has a secured creditor.

Subsection (a) subordinates the original debtor's secured party's security interest perfected against the new debtor by a filed financing statement that would be ineffective to perfect the security interest but for Section 9-508 or, if the original debtor and new debtor are located in different jurisdictions, Section 9-316(i)(1). The security interest is subordinated to security interests in the same collateral perfected by another method, e.g., by filing against the new debtor. This section does not subordinate a security interest perfected by a new initial financing statement providing the name of the new debtor, even if the initial financing statement is filed to maintain the effectiveness of a financing statement under the circumstances described in Section 9-508(b). Nor does it subordinate a security interest perfected by a financing statement filed against the original debtor which remains effective against collateral transferred by the original debtor to the new debtor. See Section 9-508(c). Concerning priority contests involving transferred collateral, see Sections 9-325 and 9-507.

Example 1: SP-X holds a perfected-by-filing security interest in X Corp's existing and after-acquired inventory, and SP-Z holds a perfected-by-possession security interest in an item of Z Corp's inventory. Both X Corp and Z Corp are located in the same jurisdiction under Section 9-307. Z Corp becomes bound as debtor by X Corp's security agreement (e.g., Z Corp buys X Corp's assets and assumes its security agreement). See Section 9-203(d). But for Section 9-508, SP-X's financing statement would be ineffective to perfect a security interest in the item of inventory in which Z Corp has rights. However, subsection (a) provides that SP-X's perfected security interest is subordinate to SP-Z's, regardless of whether SP-X's financing statement was filed before SP-Z perfected its security interest.

Example 2: SP-X holds a perfected-by-filing security interest in X Corp's existing and after-acquired inventory, and SP-Z holds a perfected-by-filing security interest in Z Corp's existing and after-acquired inventory. Both X Corp and Z Corp are located in the same jurisdiction under Section 9-307. Z Corp becomes bound as debtor by X Corp's security agreement. Immediately thereafter, and before the effectiveness of SP-X's financing statement lapses, Z Corp acquires a new item of inventory. But for Section 9-508, SP-X's financing statement would be ineffective to perfect a security interest in the new item of inventory in which Z Corp has rights. However, because SP-Z's security interest was perfected by a filing whose effectiveness does not depend on Section 9-316(i)(1) or 9-508, subsection (a) subordinates SP-X's perfected security interest to SP-Z's. This would be the case even if SP-Z filed after Z Corp became bound by X Corp's security agreement, and regardless of which financing statement was filed first.

The same result would obtain if X Corp and Z Corp were located in different jurisdictions. SP- X's security interest would be perfected by a financing statement that would be ineffective but for Section 9-316(i)(1), whereas the effectiveness of SP-Z's filing does not depend on Section 9-316(i)(1) or 9-508.

3. Other Priority Rules. Subsection (b) addresses the priority among security interests created by the original debtor (X Corp). By invoking the other priority rules of this subpart, as applicable, subsection (b) preserves the relative priority of security interests created by the original debtor.

Example 3: Under the facts of Example 2, SP-Y also holds a perfected-by-filing security interest in X Corp's existing and after-acquired inventory. SP-Y filed after SP-X. Inasmuch as both SP-X's and SP-Y's security interests in inventory acquired by Z Corp after it became bound would be unperfected but for the application of Section 9-508, the normal priority rules determine their relative priorities. Under the "first-to-file-or-perfect" rule of Section 9-322(a)(1), SP-X has priority over SP-Y.

Example 4: Under the facts of Example 3, after Z Corp became bound by X Corp's security agreement, SP-Y promptly filed a new initial financing statement against Z Corp. SP-X's security interest remains perfected only by virtue of its original filing against X Corp which "would be ineffective to perfect the security interest but for the application of Section 9-508." Because SP-Y's security interest is perfected by the filing of a financing statement whose effectiveness does not depend on Section 9-508 or 9-316(i)(1), subsection (a) subordinates SP-X's security interest to SP-Y's. If both SP-X and SP-Y file a new initial financing statement against Z Corp, then the "first-to-file-or-perfect" rule of Section 9-322(a)(1) governs their priority inter se as well as their priority against SP-Z.

The second sentence of subsection (b) effectively limits the applicability of the first sentence to situations in which a new debtor has become bound by more than one security agreement entered into by the same original debtor. When the new debtor has become bound by security agreements entered into by different original debtors, the second sentence provides that priority is based on priority in time of the new debtor's becoming bound.

Example 5: Under the facts of Example 2, SP-W holds a perfected-by-filing security interest in W Corp's existing and after-acquired inventory. After Z Corp became bound by X Corp's security agreement in favor of SP-X, Z Corp became bound by W Corp's security agreement. Under subsection (b), SP-W's security interest in inventory acquired by Z Corp is subordinate to that of SP-X, because Z Corp became bound under SP-X's security agreement before it became bound under SP-W's security agreement. This is the result regardless of which financing statement (SP-X's or SP-W's) was filed first.

The second sentence of subsection (b) reflects the generally accepted view that priority based on the first-to-file rule is inappropriate for resolving priority disputes when the filings were made against different debtors. Like subsection (a) and the first sentence of subsection (b), however, the second sentence of subsection (b) relates only to priority conflicts among security interests that would be unperfected but for the application of Section 9-316(i)(1) or 9-508.

Example 6: Under the facts of Example 5, after Z Corp became bound by W Corp's security agreement,

SP-W promptly filed a new initial financing statement against Z Corp. At that time, SP-X's security interest was perfected only pursuant to its original filing against X Corp which "would be ineffective to perfect the security interest but for the application of Section 9-508." Because SP-W's security interest is perfected by the filing of a financing statement whose effectiveness does not depend on Section 9-316(i)(1) or 9-508, subsection (a) subordinates SP-X's security interest to SP-W's. If both SP-X and SP-W file a new initial financing statement against Z Corp, then the "first-to-file-or-perfect" rule of Section 9-322(a)(1) governs their priority inter se as well as their priority against SP-Z.

Section 9-326A. Priority of Security Interest in Controllable Account, Controllable Electronic Record, and Controllable Payment Intangible

A security interest in a controllable account, controllable electronic record, or controllable payment intangible held by a secured party having control of the account, electronic record, or payment intangible has priority over a conflicting security interest held by a secured party that does not have control.

Definitional Cross References:

Account	Section 9-102(a)(2)
Controllable account	Section 9-102(a)(27A)
Controllable electronic record	Section 12-102(a)(1)
Controllable payment intangible	Section 9-102(a)(27B)
Electronic	Section 1-201(b)(16A)
Payment intangible	Section 9-102(a)(61)
Record	Section 9-102(a)(70)
Secured party	Section 9-102(a)(73)
Security interest	Section 1-201(b)(35)

Official Comment

1. [Control priority.] This section adopts an approach to priority in controllable accounts, controllable electronic records, and controllable payment intangibles that is similar to the approach of Sections 9-327 (deposit accounts) and 9-328 (investment property): A security interest perfected by control has priority over conflicting security interests that are not perfected by control.

2. [Multiple persons having control.] This section does not apply if more than one secured party has control of a controllable account, controllable electronic record, or controllable payment intangible, which may occur through shared control or a person in control acknowledging that it has control on behalf of another person. See Section 12-105(b)(2) (shared control), (e) (control through another person). In those situations, the residual first-to-file-or- perfect rule of Section 9-322(a)(1) would apply. However, affected persons may believe that the application of that first-in-time rule is not appropriate in some circumstances.

> **Example:** A person (A) has a security interest in a controllable electronic record perfected by control (other than through an acknowledgment by another person under Section 12—105(e)) and A acknowledges that it has control on behalf of another person (B). B has a security interest perfected by a financing statement filed before A obtained control. Under Section 9-322(a) (the first-to-file-or-perfect rule), by obtaining control through A's acknowledgment B's security interest would have priority over A's previously senior security interest. To avoid that result, A might insist on B's subordination as a condition to A's acknowledgment. See Section 9-339 (subordination by agreement). In cases of multiple persons having control, it will be important for interested persons to adjust priorities by agreement, when appropriate. See also Section 12-105, Comment 5.

A secured party that relies on perfection by control resulting from the acknowledgment of another person under Section 12-105(e) need not prove a formal agency relationship with the acknowledging person. This is a principal rationale underlying the various provisions in Articles 7, 8, 9, and 12 which provide for a person to obtain control through another person's control and acknowledgment. However, a person obtaining control through an acknowledgment necessarily must rely on the integrity of the acknowledging person. In the case of perfection by control in the Example, the acknowledging person presumably also has control for the benefit of the debtor. The secured party's (B 's) control, and perfection, depends on the acknowledging person's (A's) continued control. The secured party's (B's) perfection would be lost if the acknowledging person (A) were to lose or give up control, as by transferring control to the debtor or any other person. See, e.g., Section 9-314, Comment 2.

An acknowledging person also might serially acknowledge over time that it holds for the benefit of multiple purchasers (secured parties or buyers). Putting aside perfection by filing as in the Example, secured parties so perfected would have priority based on priority of timing of control under Section 9-322(a). However, a transfer of control by the acknowledging person to a qualifying purchaser, or an acknowledgment by that the person that it has control on behalf of a buyer or secured party that is a qualifying purchaser, would allow the qualifying purchaser to take free of (or have priority over) earlier security interests or other interests. It follows that a first-to-control priority rule for security interests would not protect a secured party having control through another person's acknowledgment from having its interest cut off or subordinated by a later-in-time qualifying purchaser. Such a "first-to-control" priority rule would be illusory inasmuch as purchasers relying on control through another person's acknowledgment would have no reliable method of determining priority over subsequent transferees other than reliance on the acknowledging person's integrity.

Section 9-327. Priority of Security Interests in Deposit Account

The following rules govern priority among conflicting security interests in the same deposit account:

(1) A security interest held by a secured party having control of the deposit account under Section 9-104 has priority over a conflicting security interest held by a secured party that does not have control.

(2) Except as otherwise provided in paragraphs (3) and (4), security interests perfected by control under Section 9-314 rank according to priority in time of obtaining control.

(3) Except as otherwise provided in paragraph (4), a security interest held by the bank with which the deposit account is maintained has priority over a conflicting security interest held by another secured party.

(4) A security interest perfected by control under Section 9-104(a)(3) has priority over a security interest held by the bank with which the deposit account is maintained.

Definitional Cross References:

Bank	Section 9-102(a)(8)
Deposit account	Section 9-102(a)(29)
Secured party	Section 9-102(a)(73)
Security interest	Section 1-201(b)(35)

Comment References: 9-322 C8

Official Comment

1. Source. New; derived from former Section 9-115(5).

2. Scope of This Section. This section contains the rules governing the priority of conflicting security interests in deposit accounts. It overrides conflicting priority rules. See Sections 9-322(f)(1), 9-324(a), (b), (d), (f). This section does not apply to accounts evidenced by an instrument (e.g., certain certificates of deposit), which by definition are not "deposit accounts."

3. Control. Under paragraph (1), security interests perfected by control (Sections 9-314, 9-104) take priority over those perfected otherwise, e.g., as identifiable cash proceeds under Section 9-315. Secured parties for whom the deposit account is an integral part of the credit decision will, at a minimum, insist upon the right to immediate access to the deposit account upon the debtor's default (i.e., control). Those secured parties for whom the deposit account is less essential will not take control, thereby running the risk that the debtor will dispose of funds on deposit (either outright or for collateral purposes) after default but before the account can be frozen by court order or the secured party can obtain control.

Paragraph (2) governs the case (expected to be very rare) in which a bank enters into a Section 9-104(a)(2) control agreement with more than one secured party. It provides that the security interests rank according to time of obtaining control. If the bank is solvent and the control agreements are well drafted, the bank will be liable to each secured party, and the priority rule will have no practical effect.

4. Priority of Bank. Under paragraph (3), the security interest of the bank with which the deposit account is maintained normally takes priority over all other conflicting security interests in the deposit account, regardless of whether the deposit account constitutes the competing secured party's original collateral or its proceeds. A rule of this kind enables banks to extend credit to their depositors without the need to examine either the public record or their own records to determine whether another party might have a security interest in the deposit account.

A secured party who takes a security interest in the deposit account as original collateral can protect itself against the results of this rule in one of two ways. It can take control of the deposit account by becoming the bank's customer. Under paragraph (4), this arrangement operates to subordinate the bank's security interest. Alternatively, the secured party can obtain a subordination agreement from the bank. See Section 9-339.

A secured party who claims the deposit account as proceeds of other collateral can reduce the risk of becoming junior by obtaining the debtor's agreement to deposit proceeds into a specific cash-collateral account and obtaining the agreement of that bank to subordinate all its claims to those of the secured party. But if the debtor violates its agreement and deposits funds into a deposit account other than the cash-collateral account, the secured party risks being subordinated.

5. Priority in Proceeds of, and Funds Transferred from, Deposit Account. The priority afforded by this section does not extend to proceeds of a deposit account. Rather, Section 9-322(c) through (e) and the provisions referred to in Section 9-322(f) govern priorities in proceeds of a deposit account. Section 9-315(d) addresses continuation of perfection in proceeds of deposit accounts. As to funds transferred from a deposit account that serves as collateral, see Section 9-332.

Section 9-328. Priority of Security Interests in Investment Property

The following rules govern priority among conflicting security interests in the same investment property:

(1) A security interest held by a secured party having control of investment property under Section 9-106 has priority over a security interest held by a secured party that does not have control of the investment property.

(2) Except as otherwise provided in paragraphs (3) and (4), conflicting security interests held by secured parties each of which has control under Section 9-106 rank according to priority in time of:

(A) if the collateral is a security, obtaining control;

(B) if the collateral is a security entitlement carried in a securities account and:

(i) if the secured party obtained control under Section 8-106(d)(1), the secured party's becoming the person for which the securities account is maintained;

(ii) if the secured party obtained control under Section 8-106(d)(2), the securities intermediary's agreement to comply with the secured party's entitlement orders with respect to security entitlements carried or to be carried in the securities account; or

(iii) if the secured party obtained control through another person under Section 8-106(d)(3), the time on which priority would be based under this paragraph if the other person were the secured party; or

(C) if the collateral is a commodity contract carried with a commodity intermediary, the satisfaction of the requirement for control specified in Section 9-106(b)(2) with respect to commodity contracts carried or to be carried with the commodity intermediary.

(3) A security interest held by a securities intermediary in a security entitlement or a securities account maintained with the securities intermediary has priority over a conflicting security interest held by another secured party.

(4) A security interest held by a commodity intermediary in a commodity contract or a commodity account maintained with the commodity intermediary has priority over a conflicting security interest held by another secured party.

(5) A security interest in a certificated security in registered form which is perfected by taking delivery under Section 9-313(a) and not by control under Section 9-314 has priority over a conflicting security interest perfected by a method other than control.

(6) Conflicting security interests created by a broker, securities intermediary, or commodity intermediary which are perfected without control under Section 9-106 rank equally.

(7) In all other cases, priority among conflicting security interests in investment property is governed by Sections 9-322 and 9-323.

Definitional Cross References:

Agreement	Section 1-201(b)(3)
Broker	Section 8-102(a)(3)
Certificated security	Section 8-102(a)(4)
Collateral	Section 9-102(a)(12)
Commodity account	Section 9-102(a)(14)
Commodity contract	Section 9-102(a)(15)
Commodity intermediary	Section 9-102(a)(17)
Delivery	Section 1-201(b)(15)
Investment property	Section 9-102(a)(49)
Person	Section 1-201(b)(27)
Secured party	Section 9-102(a)(73)
Securities account	Section 8-501(a)
Securities intermediary	Section 8-102(a)(14)
Security entitlement	Section 8-102(a)(17)
Security interest	Section 1-201(b)(35)
Security	Section 8-102(a)(15)

Official Comment

1. Source. Former Section 9-115(5).

2. Scope of This Section. This section contains the rules governing the priority of conflicting security interests in investment property. Paragraph (1) states the most important general rule—that a secured party who obtains control has priority over a secured party who does not obtain control. Paragraphs (2) through (4) deal with conflicting security interests each of which is perfected by control. Paragraph (5) addresses the priority of a security interest in a certificated security which is perfected by delivery but not control. Paragraph (6) deals with the relatively unusual circumstance in which a broker, securities intermediary, or commodity intermediary has created conflicting security interests none of which is perfected by control. Paragraph (7) provides that the general priority rules of Sections 9-322 and 9-323 apply to cases not covered by the specific rules in this section. The principal application of this residual rule is that the usual first in time of filing rule applies to conflicting security interests that are perfected only by filing. Because the control priority rule of paragraph (1) provides for the ordinary cases in which persons purchase securities on margin credit from their brokers, there is no need for special rules for purchase-money security interests. See also Section 9-103 (limiting purchase-money collateral to goods and software).

3. General Rule: Priority of Security Interest Perfected by Control. Under paragraph (1), a secured party who obtains control has priority over a secured party who does not obtain control. The control priority rule does not turn on either temporal sequence or awareness of conflicting security interests. Rather, it is a structural rule, based on the principle that a lender should be able to rely on the collateral without question if the lender has taken the necessary steps to assure itself that it is in a position where it can foreclose on the collateral without further action by the debtor. The control priority rule is necessary because the perfection rules provide considerable flexibility in structuring secured financing arrangements. For example, at the "retail" level, a secured lender to an investor who wants the full measure of protection can obtain control, but the creditor may be willing to accept the greater measure of risk that follows from perfection by filing. Similarly, at the "wholesale" level, a lender to securities firms can leave the collateral with the debtor and obtain a perfected security interest under the automatic perfection rule of Section 9-309(a)(10), but a lender who wants to be entirely sure of its position will want to obtain control. The control priority rule of paragraph

(1) is an essential part of this system of flexibility. It is feasible to provide more than one method of perfecting security interests only if the rules ensure that those who take the necessary steps to obtain the full measure of protection do not run the risk of subordination to those who have not taken such steps. A secured party who is unwilling to run the risk that the debtor has granted or will grant a conflicting control security interest should not make a loan without obtaining control of the collateral.

As applied to the retail level, the control priority rule means that a secured party who obtains control has priority over a conflicting security interest perfected by filing without regard to inquiry into whether the control secured party was aware of the filed security interest. Prior to the 1994 revisions to Articles 8 and 9, Article 9 did not permit perfection of security interests in securities by filing. Accordingly, parties who deal in securities never developed a practice of searching the UCC files before conducting securities transactions. Although filing is now a permissible method of perfection, in order to avoid disruption of existing practices in this business it is necessary to give perfection by filing a different and more limited effect for securities than for some other forms of collateral. The priority rules are not based on the assumption that parties who perfect by the usual method of obtaining control will search the files. Quite the contrary, the control priority rule is intended to ensure that, with respect to investment property, secured parties who do obtain control are entirely unaffected by filings. To state the point another way, perfection by filing is intended to affect only general creditors or other secured creditors who rely on filing. The rule that a security interest perfected by filing can be primed by a control security interest, without regard to awareness, is a consequence of the system of perfection and priority rules for investment property. These rules are designed to take account of the circumstances of the securities markets, where filing is not given the same effect as for some other forms of property. No implication is made about the effect of filing with respect to security interests in other forms of property, nor about other Article 9 rules, e.g., Section 9-330, which govern the circumstances in which security interests in other forms of property perfected by filing can be primed by subsequent perfected security interests.

The following examples illustrate the application of the priority rule in paragraph (1):

Example 1: Debtor borrows from Alpha and grants Alpha a security interest in a variety of collateral, including all of Debtor's investment property. At that time Debtor owns 1000 shares of XYZ Co. stock for which Debtor has a certificate. Alpha perfects by filing. Later, Debtor borrows from Beta and grants Beta a security interest in the 1000 shares of XYZ Co. stock. Debtor delivers the certificate, properly indorsed, to Beta. Alpha and Beta both have perfected security interests in the XYZ Co. stock. Beta has control, see Section 8-106(b)(1), and hence has priority over Alpha.

Example 2: Debtor borrows from Alpha and grants Alpha a security interest in a variety of collateral, including all of Debtor's investment property. At that time Debtor owns 1000 shares of XYZ Co. stock, held through a securities account with Able & Co. Alpha perfects by filing. Later, Debtor borrows from Beta and grants Beta a security interest in the 1000 shares of XYZ Co. stock. Debtor instructs Able to have the 1000 shares transferred through the clearing corporation to Custodian Bank, to be credited to Beta's account with Custodian Bank. Alpha and Beta both have perfected security interests in the XYZ Co. stock. Beta has control, see Section 8-106(d)(1), and hence has priority over Alpha.

Example 3: Debtor borrows from Alpha and grants Alpha a security interest in a variety of collateral, including all of Debtor's investment property. At that time Debtor owns 1000 shares of XYZ Co. stock, which is held through a securities account with Able & Co. Alpha perfects by filing. Later, Debtor borrows from Beta and grants Beta a security interest in the 1000 shares of XYZ Co. stock. Debtor, Able, and Beta enter into an agreement under which Debtor will continue to receive dividends and distributions, and will continue to have the right to direct dispositions, but Beta will also have the right to direct dispositions and receive the proceeds. Alpha and Beta both have perfected security interests in the XYZ Co. stock (more precisely, in the Debtor's security entitlement to the financial asset consisting of the XYZ Co. stock). Beta has control, see Section 8-106(d)(2), and hence has priority over Alpha.

Example 4: Debtor borrows from Alpha and grants Alpha a security interest in a variety of collateral, including all of Debtor's investment property. At that time Debtor owns 1000 shares of XYZ Co. stock, held through a securities account with Able & Co. Alpha perfects by filing. Debtor's agreement with Able & Co. provides that Able has a security interest in all securities carried in the account as security for any obligations of Debtor to Able. Debtor incurs obligations to Able and later defaults on the obligations to Alpha and Able. Able has control by virtue of the rule of Section 8-106(e) that if a customer grants a security interest to its own intermediary, the intermediary has control. Since Alpha does not have control, Able has priority over Alpha under the general control priority rule of paragraph (1).

4. Conflicting Security Interests Perfected by Control: Priority of Securities Intermediary or Commodity Intermediary. Paragraphs (2) through (4) govern the priority of conflicting security interests each of which is perfected by control. The following example explains the application of the rules in paragraphs (3) and (4):

Example 5: Debtor holds securities through a securities account with Able & Co. Debtor's agreement with Able & Co. provides that Able has a security interest in all securities carried in the account as security for any obligations of Debtor to Able. Debtor borrows from Beta and grants Beta a security interest in 1000 shares of XYZ Co. stock carried in the account. Debtor, Able, and Beta enter into an agreement under which Debtor will continue to receive dividends and distributions and will continue to have the right to direct dispositions, but Beta will also have the right to direct dispositions and receive the proceeds. Debtor incurs obligations to Able and later defaults on the obligations to Beta and Able. Both Beta and Able have control, so the general control priority rule of paragraph (1) does not apply. Compare Example 4. Paragraph (3) provides that a security interest held by a securities intermediary in positions of its own customer has priority over a conflicting security interest of an external lender, so Able has priority over Beta. (Paragraph (4) contains a parallel rule for commodity intermediaries.) The agreement among Able, Beta, and Debtor could, of course, determine the relative priority of the security interests of Able and Beta, see Section 9-339, but the fact that the intermediary has agreed to act on the instructions of a secured party such as Beta does not itself imply any agreement by the intermediary to subordinate.

5. Conflicting Security Interests Perfected by Control: Temporal Priority. Former Section 9-115 introduced into Article 9 the concept of conflicting security interests that rank equally. Paragraph (2) of this section governs priority in those circumstances in which more than one secured party (other than a broker, securities intermediary, or commodity intermediary) has control. It replaces the equal-priority rule for conflicting security interests in investment property with a temporal rule. For securities, both certificated and uncertificated, under paragraph (2)(A) priority is based on the time that control is obtained. For security entitlements carried in securities accounts, the treatment is more complex. Paragraph (2)(B) bases priority on the timing of the steps taken to achieve control. The following example illustrates the application of paragraph (2).

Example 6: Debtor borrows from Alpha and grants Alpha a security interest in a variety of collateral, including all of Debtor's investment property. At that time Debtor owns a security entitlement that includes 1000 shares of XYZ Co. stock that Debtor holds through a securities account with Able & Co. Debtor, Able, and Alpha enter into an agreement under which Debtor will continue to receive dividends and distributions, and will continue to have the right to direct dispositions, but Alpha will also have the right to direct dispositions and receive the proceeds. Later, Debtor borrows from Beta and grants Beta a security interest in all its investment property, existing and after-acquired. Debtor, Able, and Beta enter into an agreement under which Debtor will continue to receive dividends and distributions, and will continue to have the right to direct dispositions, but Beta will also have the right to direct dispositions and receive the proceeds. Alpha and Beta both have perfected-by-control security interests in the security entitlement to the XYZ Co. stock by virtue of their agreements with Able. See Sections 9-314(a), 9-106(a), 8-106(d)(2). Under paragraph (2)(B)(ii), the priority of each security interest dates from the time of the secured party's agreement with Able. Because Alpha's agreement was first in time, Alpha has priority. This priority applies equally to security entitlements to financial assets credited to the account after the agreement was entered into.

The priority rule is analogous to "first-to-file" priority under Section 9-322 with respect to after-acquired collateral. Paragraphs (2)(B)(i) and (2)(B)(iii) provide similar rules for security entitlements as to which control is obtained by other methods, and paragraph (2)(C) provides a similar rule for commodity contracts carried in a commodity account. Section 8-510 also has been revised to provide a temporal priority conforming to paragraph (2)(B).

6. Certificated Securities. A long-standing practice has developed whereby secured parties whose collateral consists of a security evidenced by a security certificate take possession of the security certificate. If the security certificate is in bearer form, the secured party's acquisition of possession constitutes "delivery" under Section 8-301(a)(1), and the delivery constitutes "control" under Section 8-106(a). Comment 5 discusses the priority of security interests perfected by control of investment property.

If the security certificate is in registered form, the secured party will not achieve control over the security unless the security certificate contains an appropriate indorsement or is (re)registered in the secured party's name. See Section 8-106(b). However, the secured party's acquisition of possession constitutes "delivery" of the security certificate under Section 8-301 and serves to perfect the security interest under Section 9-313(a), even if the security certificate has not been appropriately indorsed and has not been (re)registered in the secured party's name. A security interest perfected by this method has priority over a security interest perfected other than by control (e.g., by filing). See paragraph (5).

The priority rule stated in paragraph (5) may seem anomalous, in that it can afford less favorable treatment to purchasers who buy collateral outright that to those who take a security interest in it. For example, a buyer of a security certificate would cut off a security interest perfected by filing only if the buyer achieves the status of a protected purchaser under Section 8-303. The buyer would not be a protected purchaser, for example, if it does not obtain "control" under Section 8-106 (e.g., if it fails to obtain a proper indorsement of the certificate) or if it had notice of an adverse claim under Section 8-105. The apparent anomaly disappears, however, when one understands the priority rule not as one intended to protect careless or guilty parties, but as one that eliminates the need to conduct a search of the public records only insofar as necessary to serve the needs of the securities markets.

7. Secured Financing of Securities Firms. Priority questions concerning security interests granted by brokers and securities intermediaries are governed by the general control-beats-non-control priority rule of paragraph (1), as supplemented by the special rules set out in paragraphs (2) (temporal priority—first to control), (3) (special priority for securities intermediary), and (6) (equal priority for non-control). The following examples illustrate the priority rules as applied to this setting. (In all cases it is assumed that the debtor retains sufficient other securities to satisfy all customers' claims. This section deals with the relative rights of secured lenders to a securities firm. Disputes between a secured lender and the firm's own customers are governed by Section 8-511.)

Example 7: Able & Co., a securities dealer, enters into financing arrangements with two lenders, Alpha Bank and Beta Bank. In each case the agreements provide that the lender will have a security interest in the securities identified on lists provided to the lender on a daily basis, that the debtor will deliver the securities to the lender on demand, and that the debtor will not list as collateral any securities which the debtor has pledged to any other lender. Upon Able's insolvency it is discovered that Able has listed the same securities on the collateral lists provided to both Alpha and Beta. Alpha and Beta both have perfected security interests under the automatic-perfection rule of Section 9-309(10). Neither Alpha nor Beta has control. Paragraph (6) provides that the security interests of Alpha and Beta rank equally, because each of them has a non-control security interest granted by a securities firm. They share pro-rata.

Example 8: Able enters into financing arrangements, with Alpha Bank and Beta Bank as in Example 7. At some point, however, Beta decides that it is unwilling to continue to provide financing on a non-control basis. Able directs the clearing corporation where it holds its principal inventory of securities to move specified securities into Beta's account. Upon Able's insolvency it is discovered that a list of collateral provided to Alpha includes securities that had been moved to Beta's account. Both Alpha and Beta have perfected security interests; Alpha under the automatic-perfection rule of Section 9-309(10), and Beta under that rule and also the perfection-by-control rule in Section 9-314(a). Beta has control but Alpha does not. Beta has priority over Alpha under paragraph (1).

Example 9: Able & Co. carries its principal inventory of securities through Clearing Corporation, which offers a "shared control" facility whereby a participant securities firm can enter into an arrangement with a lender under which the securities firm will retain the power to trade and otherwise direct dispositions of securities carried in its account, but Clearing Corporation agrees that, at any time the lender so directs, Clearing Corporation will transfer any securities from the firm's account to the lender's account or otherwise dispose of them as directed by the lender. Able enters into financing arrangements with two lenders, Alpha and Beta, each of which obtains such a control agreement from Clearing Corporation. The agreement with each lender provides that Able will designate specific securities as collateral on lists provided to the lender on a daily or other periodic basis, and that it will not pledge the same securities to different lenders. Upon Able's insolvency, it is discovered that Able has listed the same securities on the collateral lists provided to both Alpha and Beta. Both Alpha and Beta have control over the disputed securities. Paragraph (2) awards priority to whichever secured party first entered into the agreement with Clearing Corporation.

8. Relation to Other Law. Section 1-103(b) provides that "unless displaced by particular provisions of [the Uniform Commercial Code], the principles of law and equity . . . supplement its provision." There may be circumstances in which a secured party's action in acquiring a security interest that has priority under this section constitutes conduct that is wrongful under other law. Though the possibility of such resort to other law may provide an appropriate "escape valve" for cases of egregious conduct, care must be taken to ensure that this does not impair the certainty and predictability of the priority rules. Whether a court may appropriately look to other law to impose liability upon or estop a secured party from asserting its Article 9 priority depends on an assessment of the secured party's conduct under the standards established by such other law as well as a determination of whether the particular application of such other law is displaced by the UCC.

Some circumstances in which other law is clearly displaced by the UCC rules are readily identifiable. Common law "first in time, first in right" principles, or correlative tort liability rules such as common law conversion principles under which a purchaser may incur liability to a person with a prior property interest without regard to awareness of that claim, are necessarily displaced by the priority rules set out in this section since these rules determine the relative ranking of security interests in investment property. So too, Article 8 provides protections against adverse claims to certain purchasers of interests in investment property. In circumstances where a secured party not only has priority under Section 9-328, but also qualifies for protection against adverse claims under Section 8-303, 8-502, or 8-510, resort to other law would be precluded.

In determining whether it is appropriate in a particular case to look to other law, account must also be taken of the policies that underlie the commercial law rules on securities markets and security interests in securities. A principal objective of the 1994 revision of Article 8 and the provisions of Article 9 governing investment property was to ensure that secured financing transactions can be implemented on a simple, timely, and certain basis. One of the circumstances that led to the revision was the concern that uncertainty in the application of the rules on secured transactions involving securities and other financial assets could contribute to systemic risk by impairing the ability of financial institutions to provide liquidity to the markets in times of stress. The control priority rule is designed to provide a clear and certain rule to ensure that lenders who have taken the necessary steps to establish control do not face a risk of subordination to other lenders who have not done so.

The control priority rule does not turn on an inquiry into the state of a secured party's awareness of potential conflicting claims because a rule under which a person's rights depended on that sort of after-the-fact inquiry could introduce an unacceptable measure of uncertainty. If an inquiry into awareness could provide a complete and satisfactory resolution of the problem in all cases, the priority rules of this section would have incorporated that test. The fact that they do not necessarily means that resort to other law based solely on that factor is precluded, though the question whether a control secured party induced or encouraged its financing arrangement with actual knowledge that the debtor would be violating the rights of another secured party may, in some circumstances, appropriately be treated as a factor in determining whether the control party's action is the kind of egregious conduct for which resort to other law is appropriate.

Section 9-329. Priority of Security Interests in Letter-Of-Credit Right

The following rules govern priority among conflicting security interests in the same letter-of-credit right:

(1) A security interest held by a secured party having control of the letter-of-credit right under Section 9-107 has priority to the extent of its control over a conflicting security interest held by a secured party that does not have control.

(2) Security interests perfected by control under Section 9-314 rank according to priority in time of obtaining control.

Definitional Cross References:

Letter-of-credit right	Section 9-102(a)(51)
Secured party	Section 9-102(a)(73)
Security interest	Section 1-201(b)(35)

Comment References: 9-322 C10

Official Comment

1. Source. New; loosely modeled after former Section 9-115(5).

2. General Rule. Paragraph (1) awards priority to a secured party who perfects a security interest directly in letter-of-credit rights (i.e., one that takes an assignment of proceeds and obtains consent of the issuer or any nominated person under Section 5-114(c)) over another conflicting security interest (i.e., one that is perfected automatically in the letter-of-credit rights as supporting obligations under Section 9-308(d)). This is consistent with international letter-of-credit practice and provides finality to payments made to recognized assignees of letter-of-credit proceeds. If an issuer or nominated person recognizes multiple security interests in a letter-of-credit right, resulting in multiple parties having control (Section 9-107), under paragraph (2) the security interests rank according to the time of obtaining control.

3. Drawing Rights; Transferee Beneficiaries. Drawing under a letter of credit is personal to the beneficiary and requires the beneficiary to perform the conditions for drawing under the letter of credit. Accordingly, a beneficiary's grant of a security interest in a letter of credit includes the beneficiary's "letter-of-credit right" as defined in Section 9-102 and the right to "proceeds of [the] letter of credit" as defined in Section 5-114(a), but does not include the right to demand payment under the letter of credit.

Section 5-114(e) provides that the "[r]ights of a transferee beneficiary or nominated person are independent of the beneficiary's assignment of the proceeds of a letter of credit and are superior to the assignee's right to the proceeds." To the extent the rights of a transferee beneficiary or nominated person are independent and superior, this Article does not apply. See Section 9-109(c).

Under Article 5, there is in effect a novation upon the transfer with the issuer becoming bound on a new, independent obligation to the transferee. The rights of nominated persons and transferee beneficiaries under a letter of credit include the right to demand payment from the issuer. Under Section 5-114(e), their rights to payment are independent of their obligations to the beneficiary (or original beneficiary) and superior to the rights of assignees of letter of credit proceeds (Section 5-114(c)) and others claiming a security interest in the beneficiary's (or original beneficiary's) letter of credit rights.

A transfer of drawing rights under a transferable letter of credit establishes independent Article 5 rights in the transferee and does not create or perfect an Article 9 security interest in the transferred drawing rights. The definition of "letter-of-credit right" in Section 9-102 excludes a beneficiary's drawing rights. The exercise of drawing rights by a transferee beneficiary may breach a contractual obligation of the transferee to the original beneficiary concerning when and how much the transferee may draw or how it may use the funds received under the letter of credit. If, for example, drawing rights are transferred to support a sale or loan from the transferee to the original beneficiary, then the transferee would be obligated to the original beneficiary under the sale or loan agreement to account for any drawing and for the use of any funds received. The transferee's obligation would be governed by the applicable law of contracts or restitution.

4. Secured Party-Transferee Beneficiaries. As described in Comment 3, drawing rights under letters of credit are transferred in many commercial contexts in which the transferee is not a secured party claiming a security interest in an underlying receivable supported by the letter of credit. Consequently, a transfer of a letter of credit is not a method of "perfection" of a security interest. The transferee's independent right to draw under the letter of credit and to receive and retain the value thereunder (in effect, priority) is not based on Article 9 but on letter-of-credit law and the terms of the letter of credit. Assume, however, that a secured party does hold a security interest in a receivable that is owned by a beneficiary-debtor and supported by a transferable letter of credit. Assume further that the beneficiary-debtor causes the letter of credit to be transferred to the secured party, the secured party draws under the letter of credit, and, upon the issuer's payment to the secured party-transferee, the underlying account debtor's obligation to the original beneficiary-debtor is satisfied. In this situation, the payment to the secured party-transferee is proceeds of the receivable collected by the secured party-transferee. Consequently, the secured party-transferee would have certain duties to the debtor and third parties under Article 9. For example, it would be obliged to collect under the letter of credit in a commercially reasonable manner and to remit any surplus pursuant to Sections 9-607 and 9-608.

This scenario is problematic under letter-of-credit law and practice, inasmuch as a transferee beneficiary collects in its own right arising from its own performance. Accordingly, under Section 5-114, the independent and superior rights of a transferee control over any inconsistent duties under Article 9. A transferee beneficiary may take a transfer of drawing rights to avoid reliance on the original beneficiary's credit and collateral, and it may consider any Article 9 rights superseded by its Article 5 rights. Moreover, it will not always be clear (i) whether a transferee beneficiary has a security interest in the underlying collateral, (ii) whether any security interest is senior to the rights of others, or (iii) whether the transferee beneficiary is aware that it holds a security interest. There will be clear cases in which the role of a transferee beneficiary as such is merely incidental to a conventional secured financing. There also will be cases in which the existence of a security interest may have little to do with the position of a transferee beneficiary as such. In dealing with these cases and less clear cases involving the possible application of Article 9 to a nominated person or a transferee beneficiary, the right to demand payment under a letter of credit should be distinguished from letter-of-credit rights. The courts also should give appropriate consideration to the policies and provisions of Article 5 and letter-of-credit practice as well as Article 9.

Section 9-330. Priority of Purchaser of Chattel Paper or Instrument

(a) [Purchaser's priority: security interest claimed merely as proceeds.] A purchaser of chattel paper has priority over a security interest in the chattel paper which is claimed merely as proceeds of inventory subject to a security interest if:

(1) in good faith and in the ordinary course of the purchaser's business, the purchaser gives new value, takes possession of each authoritative tangible copy of the record evidencing the chattel paper, and obtains control under Section 9-105 of each authoritative electronic copy of the record evidencing the chattel paper; and

(2) the authoritative copies of the record evidencing the chattel paper do not indicate that the chattel paper has been assigned to an identified assignee other than the purchaser.

(b) [Purchaser's priority: other security interests.] A purchaser of chattel paper has priority over a security interest in the chattel paper which is claimed other than merely as proceeds of inventory subject to a security interest if the purchaser gives new value, takes possession of each authoritative tangible copy of the record evidencing the chattel paper, and obtains control under Section 9-105 of each authoritative electronic copy of the record evidencing the chattel paper in good faith, in the ordinary course of the purchaser's business, and without knowledge that the purchase violates the rights of the secured party.

(c) [Chattel paper purchaser's priority in proceeds.] Except as otherwise provided in Section 9-327, a purchaser having priority in chattel paper under subsection (a) or (b) also has priority in proceeds of the chattel paper to the extent that:

(1) Section 9-322 provides for priority in the proceeds; or

(2) the proceeds consist of the specific goods covered by the chattel paper or cash proceeds of the specific goods, even if the purchaser's security interest in the proceeds is unperfected.

(d) [Instrument purchaser's priority.] Except as otherwise provided in Section 9-331(a), a purchaser of an instrument has priority over a security interest in the instrument perfected by a method other than possession if the purchaser gives value and takes possession of the instrument in good faith and without knowledge that the purchase violates the rights of the secured party.

(e) [Holder of purchase-money security interest gives new value.] For purposes of subsections (a) and (b), the holder of a purchase-money security interest in inventory gives new value for chattel paper constituting proceeds of the inventory.

(f) [Indication of assignment gives knowledge.] For purposes of subsections (b) and (d), if the authoritative copies of the record evidencing chattel paper or an instrument indicate that the chattel paper or instrument has been assigned to an identified secured party other than the purchaser, a purchaser of the chattel paper or instrument has knowledge that the purchase violates the rights of the secured party.

Definitional Cross References:

Assignee	Section 9-102(a)(7A)
Cash proceeds	Section 9-102(a)(9)
Chattel paper	Section 9-102(a)(11)
Electronic	Section 1-201(b)(16A)
Good faith	Section 1-201(b)(20)
Goods	Section 9-102(a)(44)
Holder	Section 1-201(b)(21)
Instrument	Section 9-102(a)(47)
Inventory	Section 9-102(a)(48)
New value	Section 9-102(a)(57)
Proceeds	Section 9-102(a)(64)

Purchase	Section 1-201(b)(29)
Purchase-money security interest	Section 9-103
Purchaser	Section 1-201(b)(30)
Record	Section 9-102(a)(70)
Right	Section 1-201(b)(34)
Secured party	Section 9-102(a)(72)
Security interest	Section 1-201(b)(35)
Value	Section 1-204

Comment References: 9-324C8.

Official Comment

1. Source. Former Section 9-308.

2. Non-Temporal Priority. This Article permits a security interest to be perfected in chattel paper either by filing or by the secured party's possession and control under Section 9-314A and in instruments either by filing or by the secured party's taking possession under Sections 9-312 and 9-313. This section enables secured parties and other purchasers of chattel paper (evidenced by either or both authoritative electronic and tangible records) and instruments to obtain priority over earlier-perfected security interests, thereby promoting the negotiability of these types of receivables.

3. Chattel Paper. Subsections (a) and (b) follow former Section 9-308 in distinguishing between earlier-perfected security interests in chattel paper that is claimed merely as proceeds of inventory subject to a security interest and chattel paper that is claimed other than merely as proceeds. Like former Section 9-308, this section does not elaborate upon the phrase "merely as proceeds." For an elaboration, see PEB Commentary No. 8.

This section makes explicit the "good faith" requirement and retains the pre-1998 requirements of "the ordinary course of the purchaser's business" and the giving of "new value" as conditions for priority. Concerning the last, this Article deletes pre-1998 Section 9-108 and adds to Section 9-102 a completely different definition of the term "new value." See Section 9-102, Comment 21 (discussing "new value"). Under subsection (e), the holder of a purchase-money security interest in inventory is deemed to give "new value" for chattel paper constituting the proceeds of the inventory. Accordingly, the purchase-money secured party may qualify for priority in the chattel paper under subsection (a) or (b), whichever is applicable, even if it does not make an additional advance against the chattel paper.

If a security interest in chattel paper that is perfected by possession and control under Section 9-314A does not qualify for priority under this section, it may be subordinate to a perfected-by-filing security interest under Section 9-322(a)(1).

4. Possession and Control. To qualify for priority under subsection (a) or (b), a purchaser must "take[] possession of each authoritative tangible copy of the record evidencing the chattel paper obtain[] control under Section 9-105 of each authoritative electronic copy of the record evidencing the chattel paper." Note that possession and control are methods of perfection under Section 9-314A. In determining which of several related records constitutes chattel paper and thus is relevant to possession or control, the form of the records is irrelevant. Rather, the possession-and-control requirement is based on the premise that it affords public notice. For example, because possession or control of an amendment extending the term of a lease would not afford the contemplated public notice, the amendment would not constitute a record evidencing chattel paper regardless of whether the amendment is in tangible form and the lease is in electronic form, the amendment is electronic and the lease is tangible, the amendment and lease are both tangible, or the amendment and lease are both electronic.

Two common practices have raised particular concerns with respect to the possession requirement. First, in some cases the parties create more than one copy or counterpart of chattel paper evidencing a single secured obligation or lease. This practice raises questions as to which counterpart is the "original" and whether it is necessary for a purchaser to take possession of all counterparts in order to "take possession" of the chattel paper. Second, parties sometimes enter into a single "master" agreement. The master agreement contemplates that the parties will enter into separate "schedules" from time to time, each evidencing chattel paper. Must a purchaser of an obligation or lease evidenced by a single schedule also take possession of the record evidencing the master agreement as well as the record evidencing the schedule in order to "take possession" of each authoritative tangible copy of the record evidencing the chattel paper?

The problem raised by the first practice is easily solved. The parties may in the terms of their agreement and by designation on the chattel paper identify only one counterpart as the original, authoritative tangible copy of the chattel paper for purposes of the possession requirement. Concerns about the second practice also are easily solved by careful drafting. Each schedule should provide that it incorporates the terms of the master agreement, not the other way around. This will make it clear that each schedule is a "stand alone" document.

A secured party may wish to convert chattel paper evidenced by authoritative tangible copies to chattel paper evidenced by electronic copies and vice versa. The priority of a security interest in chattel paper under subsection (a) or (b) may be preserved, even if the form of the chattel paper changes. The principle implied in the preceding paragraph, i.e., that not every copy of chattel paper is relevant, applies to "control" as well as to "possession." When there are multiple copies of chattel paper, a secured party may take "possession" or obtain "control" of the chattel paper if it acts with respect to the copy or copies that are reliably identified as the authoritative copy or copies. Concerning the identification of copies as authoritative or nonauthoritative, see Section 9-105(c) and Comment 3.

5. Chattel Paper Claimed Merely as Proceeds. Under subsection (a), purchaser who meets the possession-and-control, good faith, ordinary course, and new value requirements takes priority over a competing security interest claimed merely as proceeds of inventory unless the authoritative copies of the record evidencing the chattel paper indicate that it has been assigned to an identified assignee other than the purchaser. Thus subsection (a) recognizes the common practice of placing a "legend" on chattel paper to indicate that it has been assigned. This approach, under which the chattel paper purchaser who gives new value in ordinary course can rely on possession and control of unlegended, chattel paper without any concern for other facts that it may know, comports with the expectations of both inventory and chattel paper financers.

6. Chattel Paper Claimed Other Than Merely as Proceeds. Under subsection (b), a purchaser who meets the possession-and-control, good faith, ordinary course, and new value requirements takes priority over a competing security interest claimed other than merely as proceeds of inventory if it takes "without knowledge that the purchase violates the rights of the secured party." This standard derives from the definition of "buyer in ordinary course of business" in Section 1-201(b)(9). The source of the purchaser's knowledge is irrelevant. Note, however, that "knowledge" means "actual knowledge." Section 1-202(b).

In contrast to a junior secured party in accounts, who may be required in some special circumstances to undertake a search under the "good faith" requirement, see Comment 5 to Section 9-331, a purchaser of chattel paper under this section is not required as a matter of good faith to make a search in order to determine the existence of prior security interests. There may be circumstances where the purchaser undertakes a search nevertheless, either on its own volition or because other considerations make it advisable to do so, e.g., where the purchaser also is purchasing accounts. Without more, a purchaser of chattel paper who has seen a financing statement covering the chattel paper or who knows that the chattel paper is encumbered with a security interest, does not have knowledge that its purchase violates the secured party's rights. However, if a purchaser sees a statement in a financing statement to the effect that a purchase of chattel paper from the debtor would violate the rights of the filed secured party, the purchaser would have such knowledge. Likewise, under subsection (f), if the authoritative copies of the chattel paper indicate that it had been assigned to an identified secured party other than the purchaser, the purchaser would have wrongful knowledge for purposes of subsection (b), thereby preventing the purchaser from qualifying for priority under that subsection, even if the purchaser did not have actual knowledge. In the case of authoritative tangible copies of a record evidencing chattel paper, the indication normally would consist of a written legend on the copies. In the case of authoritative electronic copies of the record evidencing chattel paper, this Article leaves to developing market and technological practices the manner in which the copies would indicate an assignment.

Subsections (a) and (f) each refer to the possibility that authoritative copies of records evidencing chattel paper may indicate that the chattel paper has been assigned to an identified assignee. Those subsections should be read and interpreted in a manner consistent with Section 9-105 on control of authoritative electronic copies of records evidencing chattel paper. Accordingly, references in subsections (a) and (f) to an indication in a record evidencing chattel paper also embrace, for authoritative electronic copies of such records, records attached to or logically associated with the authoritative electronic copies and systems in which the authoritative electronic copies are recorded. See Section 9-105(c) and (d)(1).

7. Instruments. Subsection (d) contains a special priority rule for instruments. Under this subsection, a purchaser of an instrument has priority over a security interest perfected by a method other than possession (e.g., by filing, temporarily under Section 9-312(e) or (g), as proceeds under Section 9-315(d), or automatically upon attachment under Section 9-309(4) if the security interest arises out of a sale of the instrument) if the purchaser gives value and takes possession of the instrument in good faith and without knowledge that the purchase violates the rights of the secured party. Generally, to the extent subsection (d) conflicts with Section 3-306, subsection (d) governs. See Section 3-102(b). For example, notice of a conflicting security interest precludes a purchaser from becoming a holder in due course under Section 3-302 and thereby taking free of all claims to the instrument under Section 3-306. However, a purchaser who takes even with knowledge of the security interest qualifies for priority under subsection (d) if it takes without knowledge that the purchase violates the rights of the holder of the security interest. Likewise, a purchaser qualifies for priority under subsection (d) if it takes for "value" as defined in Section 1-204, even if it does not take for "value" as defined in Section 3-303.

Subsection (d) is subject to Section 9-331(a), which provides that Article 9 does not limit the rights of a holder in due course under Article 3. Thus, in the rare case in which the purchaser of an instrument qualifies for priority under subsection (d), but another person has the rights of a holder in due course of the instrument, the other person takes free of the purchaser's claim. See Section 3-306.

The rule in subsection (d) is similar to the rules in subsections (a) and (b), which govern priority in chattel paper. The observations in Comment 6 concerning the requirement of good faith and the phrase "without knowledge that the purchase violates the rights of the secured party," including the operation of subsection (f) if an instrument indicates that it has been assigned to an identified secured party, apply equally to purchasers of instruments. However, unlike a purchaser of chattel paper, to qualify for priority under subsection (d) a purchaser of an instrument need only give "value" as defined in Section 1-204; it need not give "new value." Also, the purchaser need not purchase the instrument in the ordinary course of its business.

Subsection (d) applies to checks as well as notes. For example, to collect and retain checks that are proceeds (collections) of accounts free of a senior secured party's claim to the same checks, a junior secured party must satisfy the good-faith requirement (honesty in fact and the observance of reasonable commercial standards of fair dealing) of this subsection. This is the same good-faith requirement applicable to holders in due course. See Section 9-331, Comment 5.

8. Priority in Proceeds of Chattel Paper. Subsection (c) sets forth the two circumstances under which the priority afforded to a purchaser of chattel paper under subsection (a) or (b) extends also to proceeds of the chattel paper. The first is if the purchaser would have priority under the normal priority rules applicable to proceeds. The second, which the following Comments discuss in greater detail, is if the proceeds consist of the specific goods covered by the chattel paper. Former Article 9 generally was silent as to the priority of a security interest in proceeds when a purchaser qualifies for priority under Section 9-308 (but see former Section 9-306(5)(b), concerning returned and repossessed goods).

9. Priority in Returned and Repossessed Goods. Returned and repossessed goods may constitute proceeds of chattel paper. The following Comments explain the treatment of returned and repossessed goods as proceeds of chattel paper. The analysis is consistent with that of PEB Commentary No. 5, which these Comments replace, and is based upon the following example:

> **Example:** SP-1 has a security interest in all the inventory of a dealer in goods (Dealer); SP-1's security interest is perfected by filing. Dealer sells some of its inventory to a buyer in the ordinary course of business (BIOCOB) pursuant to a conditional sales contract (chattel paper) that does not indicate that it has been assigned to SP-1. SP-2 purchases the chattel paper from Dealer and takes possession of the paper in good faith, in the ordinary course of business, and without knowledge that the purchase violates the rights of SP-1. Subsequently, BIOCOB returns the goods to Dealer because they are defective. Alternatively, Dealer acquires possession of the goods following BIOCOB's default.

10. Assignment of Non-Lease Chattel Paper.

a. Loan by SP-2 to Dealer Secured by Chattel Paper (or Functional Equivalent Pursuant to Recourse Arrangement).

(1) Returned Goods. If BIOCOB returns the goods to Dealer for repairs, Dealer is merely a bailee and acquires thereby no meaningful rights in the goods to which SP-1's security interest could attach. (Although SP-1's security interest could attach to Dealer's interest as a bailee, that interest is not likely to be of any particular value to SP-1.) Dealer is the owner of the chattel paper (i.e., the owner of a right to payment secured by a security interest in the goods); SP-2 has a security interest in the chattel paper, as does SP-1 (as proceeds of the goods under Section 9-315). Under Section 9-330, SP-2's security interest in the chattel paper is senior to that of SP-1. SP-2 enjoys this priority regardless of whether, or when, SP-2 filed a financing statement covering the chattel paper. Because chattel paper and goods represent different types of collateral, Dealer does not have any meaningful interest in goods to which either SP-1's or SP-2's security interest could attach in order to secure Dealer's obligations to either creditor. See Section 9-102 (defining "chattel paper" and "goods").

Now assume that BIOCOB returns the goods to Dealer under circumstances whereby Dealer once again becomes the owner of the goods. This would be the case, for example, if the goods were defective and BIOCOB was entitled to reject or revoke acceptance of the goods. See Sections 2-602 (rejection), 2-608 (revocation of acceptance). Unless BIOCOB has waived its defenses as against assignees of the chattel paper, SP-1's and SP-2's rights against BIOCOB would be subject to BIOCOB's claims and defenses. See Sections 9-403, 9-404. SP-1's security interest would attach again because the returned goods would be proceeds of the chattel paper. Dealer's acquisition of the goods easily can be characterized as "proceeds" consisting of an "in kind" collection on or distribution on account of the chattel paper. See Section 9-102 (definition of "proceeds"). Assuming that SP-1's security interest is perfected by filing against the goods and that the filing is made in the same office where a filing would be made against the chattel paper, SP-1's security interest in the goods would remain perfected beyond the 20-day period of automatic perfection. See Section 9-315(d).

Because Dealer's newly reacquired interest in the goods is proceeds of the chattel paper, SP-2's security interest also would attach in the goods as proceeds. If SP-2 had perfected its security interest in the chattel paper by filing (again, assuming that filing against the chattel paper was made in the same office where a filing would be made against the goods), SP-2's security interest in the reacquired goods would be perfected beyond 20 days. See Section 9-315(d). However, if SP-2 had relied only on its possession of the chattel paper for perfection and had not filed against the chattel paper or the goods, SP-2's security interest would be unperfected after the 20-day period. See Section 9-315(d). Nevertheless, SP-2's unperfected security interest in the goods would be senior to SP-1's security interest under Section 9-330(c). The result in this priority contest is not affected by SP-2's acquiescence or non-acquiescence in the return of the goods to Dealer.

(2) Repossessed Goods. As explained above, Dealer owns the chattel paper covering the goods, subject to security interests in favor of SP-1 and SP-2. In Article 9 parlance, Dealer has an interest in chattel paper, not goods. If Dealer, SP-1, or SP-2 repossesses the goods upon BIOCOB's default, whether the repossession is rightful or wrongful as among Dealer, SP-1, or SP-2, Dealer's interest will not change. The location of goods and the party who possesses them does not affect the fact that Dealer's interest is in chattel paper, not goods. The goods continue to be owned by BIOCOB. SP-1's security interest in the goods does not attach until such time as Dealer reacquires an interest (other than a bare possessory interest) in the goods. For example, Dealer might buy the goods at a foreclosure sale from SP-2 (whose security interest in the chattel paper is senior to that of SP-1); that disposition would cut off BIOCOB's rights in the goods. Section 9-617.

In many cases the matter would end upon sale of the goods to Dealer at a foreclosure sale and there would be no priority contest between SP-1 and SP-2; Dealer would be unlikely to buy the goods under circumstances whereby SP-2 would retain its security interest. There can be exceptions, however. For example, Dealer may be obliged to purchase the goods from SP-2 and SP-2 may be obliged to convey the goods to Dealer, but Dealer may fail to pay SP-2. Or, one could imagine that SP-2, like SP-1, has a general security interest in the inventory of Dealer. In the latter case, SP-2 should not receive the benefit of any special priority rule, since its interest in no way derives from priority under Section 9-330. In the former case, SP-2's security interest in the goods reacquired by Dealer is senior to SP-1's security interest under Section 9-330.

b. Dealer's Outright Sale of Chattel Paper to SP-2. Article 9 also applies to a transaction whereby SP-2 buys the chattel paper in an outright sale transaction without recourse against Dealer. Sections 1-201(b)(35), 9-109(a). Although Dealer does not, in such a transaction, retain any residual ownership interest in the chattel paper, the chattel paper constitutes proceeds of the goods to which SP-1's security interest will attach and continue following the sale of the goods. Section 9-315(a). Even though Dealer has not retained any interest in the chattel paper, as discussed above BIOCOB subsequently may return the goods to Dealer under circumstances whereby Dealer reacquires an interest in the goods. The priority contest between SP-1 and SP-2 will be resolved as discussed above; Section 9-330 makes no distinction among purchasers of chattel paper on the basis of whether the purchaser is an outright buyer of chattel paper or one whose security interest secures an obligation of Dealer.

11. Assignment of Lease Chattel Paper. As defined in Section 9-102, "chattel paper" includes not only rights to payment secured by specific goods but also rights to payment owed by a lessee under a true lease of goods.

The analysis with respect to lease chattel paper is similar to that set forth above with respect to non-lease chattel paper. It is complicated, however, by the fact that, unlike the case of chattel paper arising out of a sale, Dealer retains a residual interest in the *goods*. See Section 2A-103(1)(q) (defining "lessor's residual interest"); *In re Leasing Consultants, Inc.*, 486 F.2d 367 (2d Cir. 1973) (lessor's residual interest under true lease is an interest in goods and is a separate type of collateral from lessor's interest in the lease). If Dealer leases goods to a "lessee in ordinary course of business" (LIOCOB), then LIOCOB takes its interest under the lease (i.e., its "leasehold interest") free of the security interest of SP-1. See Sections 2A-307(3), 2A-103(1)(m) (defining "leasehold interest"), (1)(o) (defining "lessee in ordinary course of business"). SP-1 would, however, retain its security interest in the residual interest. In addition, SP-1 would acquire an interest in the lease chattel paper as proceeds. If Dealer then assigns the lease chattel paper to SP-2, Section 9-330 gives SP-2 priority over SP-1 with respect to the chattel paper, *but not* with respect to the residual interest in the *goods*. Consequently, assignees of lease chattel paper typically take a security interest in and file against the lessor's residual interest in goods, expecting their priority in the goods to be governed by the first-to-file-or-perfect rule of Section 9-322.

If the goods are returned to Dealer, other than upon expiration of the lease term, then the security interests of both SP-1 and SP-2 normally would attach to the goods as proceeds of the chattel paper. (If the goods are returned to Dealer at the expiration of the lease term and the lessee has made all payments due under the lease, however, then Dealer no longer has any rights under the chattel paper. Dealer's interest in the goods consists solely of its residual interest, as to which SP-2 has no claim.) This would be the case, for example, when the lessee rescinds the lease or when the lessor recovers possession in the exercise of its remedies under Article 2A. See, e.g., Section 2A-525. If SP-2 enjoyed priority in the chattel paper under Section 9-330, then SP-2 likewise would enjoy priority in the returned goods as proceeds. This does not mean that SP-2 necessarily is entitled to the entire value of the returned goods. The value of the goods represents the sum of the present value of (i) the value of their use for the term of the lease and (ii) the value of the residual interest. SP-2 has priority in the former, but SP-1 ordinarily would have priority in the latter. Thus, an allocation of a portion of the value of the goods to each component may be necessary. Where, as here, one secured party has a security interest in the lessor's residual interest and another has a priority security interest in the chattel paper, it may be advisable for the conflicting secured parties to establish a method for making such an allocation and otherwise to determine their relative rights in returned goods by agreement.

Section 9-331. Priority of Rights of Purchasers of Controllable Accounts, Controllable Electronic Records, Controllable Payment Intangibles, Documents, Instruments, and Securities under Other Articles; Priority of Interests in Financial Assets and Security Entitlements and Protection Against Assertion of Claim under Articles 8 and 12

(a) [Rights under Articles 3, 7, 8, and 12 not limited.] This article does not limit the rights of a holder in due course of a negotiable instrument, a holder to which a negotiable document of title has been duly negotiated, a protected purchaser of a security, or a qualifying purchaser of a controllable account, controllable electronic record, or controllable payment intangible. These holders or purchasers take priority over an earlier security interest, even if perfected, to the extent provided in Articles 3, 7, 8, and 12.

(b) [Protection under Articles 8 and 12.] This article does not limit the rights of or impose liability on a person to the extent that the person is protected against the assertion of a claim under Article 8 or 12.

(c) [Filing not notice.] Filing under this article does not constitute notice of a claim or defense to the holders, or purchasers, or persons described in subsections (a) and (b).

Definitional Cross References:

Controllable account	Section 9-102(a)(27A)
Controllable electronic record	Section 12-102(a)(1)
Controllable payment intangible	Section 9-102(a)(27B)
Document	Section 9-102(a)(30)

Document of title	Section 1-201(b)(16)
Financial asset	Section 8-102(a)(9)
Holder	Section 1-201(b)(21)
Holder in due course	Section 3-302(a)
Instrument	Section 9-102(a)(47)
Negotiable instrument	Section 3-104(a)
Notice	Section 1-202(a)
Person	Section 1-201(b)(27)
Protected purchaser	Section 8-303(a)
Purchaser	Section 1-201(b)(30)
Qualifying purchaser	Section 12-102(a)(2)
Right	Section 1-201(b)(34)
Security	Section 8-102(a)(15)
Security entitlement	Section 8-102(a)(17)
Security interest	Section 1-201(b)(35)

Official Comment

1. Source. Former Section 9-309.

2. "Priority." In some provisions, this Article distinguishes between claimants that take collateral free of a security interest (in the sense that the security interest no longer encumbers the collateral) and those that take an interest in the collateral that is senior to a surviving security interest. See, e.g., Section 9-317. Whether a holder or purchaser referred to in this section takes free or is senior to a security interest depends on whether the purchaser is a buyer of the collateral or takes a security interest in it. The term "priority" is meant to encompass both scenarios, as it does in Section 9-330.

3. Rights Acquired by Purchasers. The rights to which this section refers are set forth in Sections 3-305 and 3-306 (holder in due course), 7-502 (holder to whom a negotiable document of title has been duly negotiated), and 8-303 (protected purchaser). The holders and purchasers referred to in this section do not always take priority over a security interest. See, e.g., Section 7-503 (affording paramount rights to certain owners and secured parties as against holder to whom a negotiable document of title has been duly negotiated). Accordingly, this section adds the clause, "to the extent provided in Articles 3, 7, and 8" to former Section 9-309.

The state-law Uniform Electronic Transactions Act (UETA) and the federal Electronic Signature in Global and National Commerce Act, 15 U.S.C. §§ 7001 et seq. (E-SIGN), provide certain rules for records referred to and defined as "transferable records." See UETA Section 16 and E-SIGN, 15 U.S.C. § 7021. When certain conditions have been met, those acts confer on a person the status of a "holder" (as defined in 1-201(b)(21)) of an "equivalent record" under pre-1998 Section 9-308 (now, in part, Section 9-330) and the rights and defenses of a "purchaser" under that section, among other effects. E-SIGN also refers to the rights and defenses of a purchaser under Section 9-330. As a matter of the application of the Uniform Commercial Code, those are not the only sections of the Uniform Commercial Code that would logically be affected by UETA and E-SIGN. For example, the rights of a holder in due course under Section 9-331(a) would also be covered by the application of those acts, when the conditions for applicability have been satisfied.

4. Financial Assets and Security Entitlements. New subsection (b) provides explicit protection for those who deal with financial assets and security entitlements and who are immunized from liability under Article 8. See, e.g., Sections 8-502, 8-503(e), 8-510, 8-511. The new subsection makes explicit in Article 9 what is implicit in former Article 9 and explicit in several provisions of Article 8. It does not change the law.

5. Collections by Junior Secured Party. Under this section, a secured party with a junior security interest in receivables (accounts, chattel paper, promissory notes, or payment intangibles) may collect and retain the proceeds of those receivables free of the claim of a senior secured party to the same receivables, if the junior secured party is a holder in due course of the proceeds. In order to qualify as a holder in due course, the junior must satisfy the requirements of Section 3-302, which include taking in "good faith." This means that the junior not only must act "honestly" but also must observe "reasonable commercial standards of fair dealing" under the particular circumstances. See Section 9-102(a). Although "good faith" does not impose a general duty of inquiry, e.g., a search of the records in filing offices, there may be circumstances in which "reasonable commercial standards of fair dealing" would require such a search.

Consider, for example, a junior secured party in the business of financing or buying accounts who fails to undertake a search to determine the existence of prior security interests. Because a search, under the usages of trade of that business, would enable it to know or learn upon reasonable inquiry that collecting the accounts violated the rights of a senior secured party, the junior may fail to meet the good-faith standard. See *Utility Contractors Financial Services, Inc. v. Amsouth Bank*, 985 F.2d 1554 (11th Cir. 1993). Likewise, a junior secured party who collects accounts when it knows or should know under the particular circumstances that doing so would violate the rights of a senior secured party, because the debtor had agreed not to grant a junior security interest in, or sell, the accounts, may not meet the good-faith test. Thus, if a junior secured party conducted or should have conducted a search and a financing statement filed on behalf of the senior secured party states such a restriction, the junior's collection would not meet the good-faith standard. On the other hand, if there was a course of performance between the senior secured party and the debtor which placed no such restrictions on the debtor and allowed the debtor to collect and use the proceeds without any restrictions, the junior secured party may then satisfy the requirements for being a holder in due course. This would be more likely in those circumstances where the junior secured party was providing additional financing to the debtor on an on-going basis by lending against or buying the accounts and had no notice of any restrictions against doing so. Generally, the senior secured party would not be prejudiced because the practical effect of such payment to the junior secured party is little different than if the debtor itself had made the collections and subsequently paid the secured party from the debtor's general funds. Absent collusion, the junior secured party would take the funds free of the senior security interests. See Section 9-332. In contrast, the senior secured party is likely to be prejudiced if the debtor is going out of business and the junior secured party collects the accounts by notifying the account debtors to make payments directly to the junior. Those collections may not be consistent with "reasonable commercial standards of fair dealing."

Whether the junior secured party qualifies as a holder in due course is fact-sensitive and should be decided on a case-by-case basis in the light of those circumstances. Decisions such as *Financial Mgmt. Servs. Inc. v. Familian,* 905 P.2d 506 (Ariz. App. Div. 1995) (finding holder in due course status) could be determined differently under this application of the good- faith requirement.

The concepts addressed in this Comment are also applicable to junior secured parties as purchasers of instruments under Section 9-330(d). See Section 9-330, Comment 7.

Section 9-332. Transfer of Money; Transfer of Funds from Deposit Account

(a) [Transferee of tangible money.] A transferee of tangible money takes the money free of a security interest if the transferee receives possession of the money without acting in collusion with the debtor in violating the rights of the secured party.

(b) [Transferee of funds from deposit account.] A transferee of funds from a deposit account takes the funds free of a security interest in the deposit account if the transferee receives the funds without acting in collusion with the debtor in violating the rights of the secured party.

(c) [Transferee of electronic money.] A transferee of electronic money takes the money free of a security interest if the transferee obtains control of the money without acting in collusion with the debtor in violating the rights of the secured party.

Definitional Cross References:

Debtor	Section 9-102(a)(28)
Deposit account	Section 9-102(a)(29)
Electronic money	Section 9-102(a)(31A)
Money	Section 9-102(a)(54A)
Right	Section 1-201(b)(34)
Secured party	Section 9-102(a)(73)
Security interest	Section 1-201(b)(35)
Tangible money	Section 9-102(a)(79A)

Official Comment

1. Source. New.

2. Scope of This Section. This section affords broad protection for transferees of money and of funds from a deposit account to take free of a security interest.

2A. Meaning of "Transfer." The term "transferee" is not defined; however, the debtor itself is not a transferee. Thus this section does not cover the case in which a debtor withdraws money (currency) from its deposit account or the case in which a bank debits an encumbered account and credits another account it maintains for the debtor.

A "transfer" of property occurs when the transferee has obtained a property interest in the relevant property. See Section 9-102, Comment 2.b.1 ("Several provisions of this Article and its official comments also refer to the 'transfer' of property interests." (emphasis added)). Other law determines when the transferee has acquired a property interest. See Section 9-408, Comment 3 ("Other law determines whether a debtor has a property interest ('rights in the collateral') and the nature of that interest."). Although the terms "transfer" and "transferee" are not defined in the UCC, the term "transfer" is broader in scope than "purchase," which requires taking in a "voluntary transaction creating an interest in property." Section 1-201(b)(29). For example, "transfer" includes an involuntary transfer such as the acquisition of a judicial lien by a lien creditor. See Section 9-102(a)(52) (defining "lien creditor"). However, many references to a "transfer" in the UCC and official comments relate to a voluntary transfer to a purchaser, as indicated by the context.

2B. Transferees of Tangible Money. Subsection (a) conditions the take-free rule on the transferee's receipt of possession of tangible money. This reflects what had always been assumed under the pre-2022 text—that a transfer of an interest in tangible money which is not accompanied by a physical transfer of possession would not impair the rights of third parties.

2C. Transferees of Funds from Deposit Account. Subsection (b) reflects the corresponding change for a transfer of funds from a deposit account. To qualify for the take-free protection under subsection (b), the transferee must "receive[] the funds without acting in collusion. . ." The amendments to subsections (a) and (b) clarify what was implicit under the original text. Although "funds" is not defined in the UCC, if deposit accounts with a central bank or another bank were to become money, as defined in Section 1-201(b)(24), transfers from such deposit accounts would be covered by subsection (b) and not subsection (c) (discussed in Comment 2.D.). See Section 9-102(a)(54A) (defining "money," for purposes of Article 9, to exclude deposit accounts).

A transfer of funds from a deposit account, to which subsection (b) applies, normally will be made by check, by funds transfer, or by debiting the debtor's deposit account and crediting another depositor's account.

Example 1: Debtor maintains a deposit account with Bank A. The deposit account is subject to a perfected security interest in favor of Lender. Debtor draws a check on the account, payable to Payee. Inasmuch as the check is not the proceeds of the deposit account (it is an order to pay funds from the deposit account), Lender's security interest in the deposit account does not give rise to a security interest in the check. Payee deposits the check into its own deposit account, and Bank A pays it. Unless Payee acted in collusion with Debtor in violating Lender's rights, Payee takes the funds (the credits running in favor of Payee) free of Lender's security interest. This is true regardless of whether Payee is a holder in due course of the check and even if Payee gave no value for the check.

Example 2: Debtor maintains a deposit account with Bank A. The deposit account is subject to a perfected security interest in favor of Lender. At Bank B's suggestion, Debtor moves the funds from the account at Bank A to Debtor's deposit account with Bank B. Unless Bank B acted in collusion with Debtor in violating Lender's rights, Bank B takes the funds (the credits running in favor of Bank B) free from Lender's security interest. See subsection (b). However, inasmuch as the deposit account maintained with Bank B constitutes the proceeds of the deposit account at Bank A, Lender's security interest would attach to that account as proceeds. See Section 9-315.

Subsection (b) also would apply if, in these examples, Bank A debited Debtor's deposit account in exchange for the issuance of Bank A's cashier's check. Lender's security interest would attach to the cashier's check as proceeds of the deposit account, and the rules applicable to instruments would govern any competing claims to the cashier's check. See, e.g., Sections 3-306, 9-322, 9-330, 9-331.

If Debtor withdraws funds from an encumbered deposit account, receives the funds in the form of tangible money, and transfers the money to a third party, then subsection (a), to the extent not displaced by federal law relating to money, applies to the transfer. It contains substantially the same rule as subsection (b).

Subsection (b) applies to transfers of funds from a deposit account; it does not apply to transfers of the deposit account itself or of an interest therein. Because a deposit account is a monetary obligation (debt) of the depositary bank to its depositor, a transfer of the deposit account itself does not transfer the funds credited to the deposit account. For example, this section does not apply to the creation of a security interest in a deposit account. Competing claims to the deposit account itself are dealt with by other Article 9 priority rules. See Sections 9-317(a), 9-327, 9-340, 9-341. Similarly, a corporate merger normally would not result in a transfer of funds from a deposit account. Rather, it might result in a transfer of the deposit account itself. If so, the normal rules applicable to transferred collateral would apply; this section would not.

The depositor's creditors (whether secured parties or lien creditors) do not have any interest in any funds (or any other assets of the depositary bank) as a result of having an interest in the deposit account (the right to payment of the bank's obligation). Consequently, a transferee of funds that takes free of a security interest under subsection (b) does so whether the security interest in the deposit account from which the funds were transferred arises as original collateral or as proceeds.

A transferee of an interest in the deposit account, such as a garnishing lien creditor, does not take free of a security interest in a deposit account under subsection (b). A transferee takes free under subsection (b) only upon the actual receipt of funds from the deposit account. The proper construction of subsection (b) rejects cases that treat garnishment of a deposit account as an immediate transfer of funds or an interest in funds credited to the deposit account.

The last event that provides a recovery for a creditor in a garnishment action virtually always would be a transfer of funds from a deposit account. However, this does not mean that a perfected security interest will always be cut off by a garnishing creditor. By intervening in the garnishment proceeding to assert its senior security interest before funds are disbursed, the secured party might assert and retain its priority. However, the relevant procedural law may not provide the secured party with adequate advance notice. In some cases, a control agreement that perfects a security interest in the deposit account may require the garnished bank to provide prompt notice to the secured party. But not all control agreements will so provide. Moreover, the secured party's priority is not absolute. See, e.g., Section 9-401, Comment 6 (explaining that the equitable doctrine of marshaling may be appropriate in the case of a lien creditor's interest in collateral when a senior secured party is oversecured).

2D. Transferees of Electronic Money. Because "electronic money" is new, no pattern of past practices or understandings exists. However, subsection (c) provides a take-free rule for electronic money that complements subsection (a) by conditioning the take-free rule on the transferee's obtaining control.

2E. Temporal Aspect of Collusion Test. For a transferee to take free of a security interest under this section the transferee must receive delivery of tangible money, receive funds from a deposit account, or obtain control of electronic money without acting in collusion. Whether the transferee is acting without collusion is determined as of the time of delivery to the transferee or receipt of funds or obtaining control by the transferee.

3. Policy. Broad protection for transferees helps to ensure that security interests in deposit accounts do not impair the free flow of funds. It also minimizes the likelihood that a secured party will enjoy a claim to whatever the transferee purchases with the funds. Rules concerning recovery of payments traditionally have placed a high value on finality. The opportunity to upset a completed transaction, or even to place a completed transaction in jeopardy by bringing suit against the transferee of funds, should be severely limited. Although the giving of value usually is a prerequisite for receiving the ability to take free from third-party claims, where payments are concerned the law is even more protective. Thus, Section 3-418(c) provides that, even where the law of restitution otherwise would permit recovery of funds paid by mistake, no recovery may be had from a person "who in good faith changed position in reliance on the payment." Rather than adopt this standard, this section eliminates all reliance requirements whatsoever.

Payments made by mistake are relatively rare, but payments of funds from encumbered deposit accounts (e.g., deposit accounts containing collections from accounts receivable) occur with great regularity. In most cases, unlike payment by mistake, no one would object to these payments. In the vast proportion of cases, the transferee probably would be able to show a change of position in reliance on the payment. This section does not put the transferee to the burden of having to make this proof.

4. "Bad Actors." To deal with the question of the "bad actor," this section borrows "collusion" language from Article 8. See, e.g., Sections 8-115, 8-503(e). This is the most protective (i.e., least stringent) of the various standards now found in the UCC. Compare, e.g., Section 1-201(b)(9) ("without knowledge that the sale violates the rights of another person," in the definition of "buyer in ordinary course of business"); Section 1-201(b)(20) (defining "good faith" as "honesty in fact and the observance of reasonable commercial standards of fair dealing"); Section 3-302(a)(2)(v) ("without notice of any claim").

5. Transferee Who Does Not Take Free. This section sets forth the circumstances under which certain transferees of money or funds take free of security interests. It does not determine the rights of a transferee who does not take free of a security interest.

> **Example 3:** The facts are as in Example 2, but, in wrongfully moving the funds from the deposit account at Bank A to Debtor's deposit account with Bank B, Debtor acts in collusion with Bank B. Bank B does not take the funds free of Lender's security interest under this section. If Debtor grants a security interest to Bank B, Section 9-327 governs the relative priorities of Lender and Bank B. Under Section 9-327(3), Bank B's security interest in the Bank B deposit account is senior to Lender's security interest in the deposit account as proceeds. However, Bank B's senior security interest does not protect Bank B against any liability to Lender that might arise from Bank B's wrongful conduct.

Section 9-333. Priority of Certain Liens Arising by Operation of Law

(a) ["Possessory lien."] In this section, "possessory lien" means an interest, other than a security interest or an agricultural lien:

(1) which secures payment or performance of an obligation for services or materials furnished with respect to goods by a person in the ordinary course of the person's business;

(2) which is created by statute or rule of law in favor of the person; and

(3) whose effectiveness depends on the person's possession of the goods.

(b) [Priority of possessory lien.] A possessory lien on goods has priority over a security interest in the goods unless the lien is created by a statute that expressly provides otherwise.

Definitional Cross References:

Agricultural lien	Section 9-102(a)(5)
Goods	Section 9-102(a)(44)
Person	Section 1-201(b)(27)
Security interest	Section 1-201(b)(35)

Official Comment

1. Source. Former Section 9-310.

2. "Possessory Liens." This section governs the relative priority of security interests arising under this Article and "possessory liens," i.e., common-law and statutory liens whose effectiveness depends on the lienor's possession of goods with respect to which the lienor provided services or furnished materials in the ordinary course of its business. As under former Section 9-310, the possessory lien has priority over a security interest unless the possessory lien is created by a statute that expressly provides otherwise. If the statute creating the possessory lien is silent as to its priority relative to a security interest, this section provides a rule of interpretation that the possessory lien takes priority, even if the statute has been construed judicially to make the possessory lien subordinate.

Section 9-334. Priority of Security Interests in Fixtures and Crops

(a) [Security interest in fixtures under this article.] A security interest under this article may be created in goods that are fixtures or may continue in goods that become fixtures. A security interest does not exist under this article in ordinary building materials incorporated into an improvement on land.

(b) [Security interest in fixtures under real-property law.] This article does not prevent creation of an encumbrance upon fixtures under real property law.

(c) [General rule: subordination of security interest in fixtures.] In cases not governed by subsections (d) through (h), a security interest in fixtures is subordinate to a conflicting interest of an encumbrancer or owner of the related real property other than the debtor.

(d) [Fixtures purchase-money priority.] Except as otherwise provided in subsection (h), a perfected security interest in fixtures has priority over a conflicting interest of an encumbrancer or owner of the real property if the debtor has an interest of record in or is in possession of the real property and:

(1) the security interest is a purchase-money security interest;

(2) the interest of the encumbrancer or owner arises before the goods become fixtures; and

(3) the security interest is perfected by a fixture filing before the goods become fixtures or within 20 days thereafter.

(e) [Priority of security interest in fixtures over interests in real property.] A perfected security interest in fixtures has priority over a conflicting interest of an encumbrancer or owner of the real property if:

(1) the debtor has an interest of record in the real property or is in possession of the real property and the security interest:

(A) is perfected by a fixture filing before the interest of the encumbrancer or owner is of record; and

(B) has priority over any conflicting interest of a predecessor in title of the encumbrancer or owner;

(2) before the goods become fixtures, the security interest is perfected by any method permitted by this article and the fixtures are readily removable:

(A) factory or office machines;

(B) equipment that is not primarily used or leased for use in the operation of the real property; or

(C) replacements of domestic appliances that are consumer goods;

(3) the conflicting interest is a lien on the real property obtained by legal or equitable proceedings after the security interest was perfected by any method permitted by this article; or

(4) the security interest is:

(A) created in a manufactured home in a manufactured-home transaction; and

(B) perfected pursuant to a statute described in Section 9-311(a)(2).

(f) [Priority based on consent, disclaimer, or right to remove.] A security interest in fixtures, whether or not perfected, has priority over a conflicting interest of an encumbrancer or owner of the real property if:

(1) the encumbrancer or owner has, in a signed record, consented to the security interest or disclaimed an interest in the goods as fixtures; or

(2) the debtor has a right to remove the goods as against the encumbrancer or owner.

(g) [Continuation of paragraph (f)(2) priority.] The priority of the security interest under paragraph (f)(2) continues for a reasonable time if the debtor's right to remove the goods as against the encumbrancer or owner terminates.

(h) [Priority of construction mortgage.] A mortgage is a construction mortgage to the extent that it secures an obligation incurred for the construction of an improvement on land, including the acquisition cost of the land, if a recorded record of the mortgage so indicates. Except as otherwise provided in subsections (e) and (f), a security interest in fixtures is subordinate to a construction mortgage if a record of the mortgage is recorded before the goods become fixtures and the goods become fixtures before the completion of the construction. A mortgage has this priority to the same extent as a construction mortgage to the extent that it is given to refinance a construction mortgage.

(i) [Priority of security interest in crops.] A perfected security interest in crops growing on real property has priority over a conflicting interest of an encumbrancer or owner of the real property if the debtor has an interest of record in or is in possession of the real property.

(j) [Subsection (i) prevails.] Subsection (i) prevails over any inconsistent provisions of the following statutes:

[List here any statutes containing provisions inconsistent with subsection (i).]

Legislative Note: *States that amend statutes to remove provisions inconsistent with subsection (i) need not enact subsection (j).*

Definitional Cross References:

Consumer goods	Section 9-102(a)(23)
Debtor	Section 9-102(a)(28)
Encumbrance	Section 9-102(a)(32)
Equipment	Section 9-102(a)(33)
Fixture filing	Section 9-102(a)(40)
Fixtures	Section 9-102(a)(41)
Goods	Section 9-102(a)(44)
Lease	Section 2A-103(1)(j)
Manufactured home	Section 9-102(a)(53)
Manufactured-home transaction	Section 9-102(a)(54)
Mortgage	Section 9-102(a)(55)
Purchase-money security interest	Section 9-103
Record	Section 9-102(a)(70)
Security interest	Section 1-201(b)(35)
Sign	Section 1-201(b)(37)
State	Section 9-102(a)(77)

Official Comment

1. Source. Former Section 9-313.

2. Scope of This Section. This section contains rules governing the priority of security interests in fixtures and crops as against persons who claim an interest in real property. Priority contests with other Article 9 security interests are governed by the other priority rules of this Article. The provisions with respect to fixtures follow those of former Section 9-313. However, they have been rewritten to conform to Section 2A-309 and to prevailing style conventions. Subsections (i) and (j), which apply to crops, are new.

3. Security Interests in Fixtures. Certain goods that are the subject of personal-property (chattel) financing become so affixed or otherwise so related to real property that they become part of the real property. These goods are called "fixtures." See Section 9-102 (definition of "fixtures"). Some fixtures retain their personal-property nature: a security interest under this Article may be created in fixtures and may continue in goods that become fixtures. See subsection (a). However, if the goods are ordinary building materials incorporated into an improvement on land, no security interest in them exists. Rather, the priority of claims to the building materials are determined by the law governing claims to real property. (Of course, the fact that no security interest exists in ordinary building materials incorporated into an improvement on land does not prejudice any rights the secured party may have against the debtor or any other person who violated the secured party's rights by wrongfully incorporating the goods into real property.)

Thus, this section recognizes three categories of goods: (1) those that retain their chattel character entirely and are not part of the real property; (2) ordinary building materials that have become an integral part of the real property and cannot retain their chattel character for purposes of finance; and (3) an intermediate class that has become real property for certain purposes, but as to which chattel financing may be preserved.

To achieve priority under certain provisions of this section, a security interest must be perfected by making a "fixture filing" (defined in Section 9-102) in the real-property records. Because the question whether goods have become fixtures often is a difficult one under applicable real-property law, a secured party may make a fixture filing as a precaution. Courts should not infer from a fixture filing that the secured party concedes that the goods are or will become fixtures.

4. Priority in Fixtures: General. In considering priority problems under this section, one must first determine whether real-property claimants per se have an interest in the crops or fixtures as part of real property. If not, it is immaterial, so far as concerns real property parties as such, whether a security interest arising under this Article is perfected or unperfected. In no event does a real-property claimant (e.g., owner or mortgagee) acquire an interest in a "pure" chattel just because a security interest therein is unperfected. If on the other hand real-property law gives real-property parties an interest in the goods, a conflict arises and this section states the priorities.

5. Priority in Fixtures: Residual Rule. Subsection (c) states the residual priority rule, which applies only if one of the other rules does not: A security interest in fixtures is subordinate to a conflicting interest of an encumbrancer or owner of the related real property other than the debtor.

6. Priority in Fixtures: First to File or Record. Subsection (e)(1), which follows former Section 9-313(4)(b), contains the usual priority rule of conveyancing, that is, the first to file or record prevails. In order to achieve priority under this rule, however, the security interest must be perfected by a "fixture filing" (defined in Section 9-102), i.e., a filing for record in the real property records and indexed therein, so that it will be found in a real-property search. The condition in subsection (e)(1)(B), that the security interest must have had priority over any conflicting interest of a predecessor in title of the conflicting encumbrancer or owner, appears to limit to the first-in-time principle. However, this apparent limitation is nothing other than an expression of the usual rule that a person must be entitled to transfer what he has. Thus, if the fixture security interest is subordinate to a mortgage, it is subordinate to an interest of an assignee of the mortgage, even though the assignment is a later recorded instrument. Similarly if the fixture security interest is subordinate to the rights of an owner, it is subordinate to a subsequent grantee of the owner and likewise subordinate to a subsequent mortgagee of the owner.

7. Priority in Fixtures: Purchase-Money Security Interests. Subsection (d), which follows former Section 9-313(4)(a), contains the principal exception to the first-to-file-or-record rule of subsection (e)(1). It affords priority to purchase-money security interests in fixtures as against prior recorded real-property interests, provided that the purchase-money security interest is filed as a fixture filing in the real-property records before the goods become fixtures or within 20 days thereafter. This priority corresponds to the purchase-money priority under Section 9-324(a). (Like other 10-day periods in former Article 9, the 10-day period in this section has been changed to 20 days.)

It should be emphasized that this purchase-money priority with the 20-day grace period for filing is limited to rights against real-property interests that arise before the goods become fixtures. There is no such priority with the 20-day grace period as against real-property interests that arise subsequently. The fixture security interest can defeat subsequent real-property interests only if it is filed first and prevails under the usual conveyancing rule in subsection (e)(1) or one of the other rules in this section.

8. Priority in Fixtures: Readily Removable Goods. Subsection (e)(2), which derives from Section 2A-309 and former Section 9-313(4)(d), contains another exception to the usual first-to-file-or-perfect rule. It affords priority to the holders of security interests in certain types of readily removable goods—factory and office machines, equipment that is not primarily used or leased for use in the operation of the real property, and (as discussed below) certain replacements of domestic appliances. This rule is made necessary by the confusion in the law as to whether certain machinery, equipment, and appliances become fixtures. It protects a secured party who, perhaps in the mistaken belief that the readily removable goods will not become fixtures, makes a UCC filing (or otherwise perfects under this Article) rather than making a fixture filing.

Frequently, under applicable law, goods of the type described in subsection (e)(2) will not be considered to have become part of the real property. In those cases, the fixture security interest does not conflict with a real-property interest, and resort to this section is unnecessary. However, if the goods have become part of the real property, subsection (e)(2) enables a fixture secured party to take priority over a conflicting real-property interest if the fixture security interest is perfected by a fixture filing or by any other method permitted by this Article. If perfection is by fixture filing, the fixture security interest would have priority over subsequently recorded real-property interests under subsection (e)(1) and, if the fixture security interest is a purchase-money security interest (a likely scenario), it would also have priority over most real property interests under the purchase-money priority of subsection (d). Note, however, that unlike the purchase-money priority rule in subsection (d), the priority rules in subsection (e) override the priority given to a construction mortgage under subsection (h).

The rule in subsection (e)(2) is limited to readily removable replacements of domestic appliances. It does not apply to original installations. Moreover, it is limited to appliances that are "consumer goods" (defined in Section 9-102) in the hands of the debtor. The principal effect of the rule is to make clear that a secured party financing occasional replacements of domestic appliances in noncommercial, owner-occupied contexts need not concern itself with real-property descriptions or records; indeed, for a purchase-money replacement of consumer goods, perfection without any filing will be possible. See Section 9-309(1).

9. Priority in Fixtures: Judicial Liens. Subsection (e)(3), which follows former Section 9-313(4)(d), adopts a first-in-time rule applicable to conflicts between a fixture security interest and a lien on the real property obtained by legal or equitable proceedings. Such a lien is subordinate to an earlier-perfected security interest, regardless of the method by which the security interest was perfected. Judgment creditors generally are not reliance creditors who search real-property records. Accordingly, a perfected fixture security interest takes priority over a subsequent judgment lien or other lien obtained by legal or equitable proceedings, even if no evidence of the security interest appears in the relevant real-property records. Subsection (e)(3) thus protects a perfected fixture security interest from avoidance by a trustee in bankruptcy under Bankruptcy Code Section 544(a), regardless of the method of perfection.

10. Priority in Fixtures: Manufactured Homes. A manufactured home may become a fixture. New subsection (e)(4) contains a special rule granting priority to certain security interests created in a "manufactured home" as part of a "manufactured-home transaction" (both defined in Section 9-102). Under this rule, a security interest in a manufactured home that becomes a fixture has priority over a conflicting interest of an encumbrancer or owner of the real property if the security interest is perfected under a certificate-of-title statute (see Section 9-311). Subsection (e)(4) is only one of the priority rules applicable to security interests in a manufactured home that becomes a fixture. Thus, a security interest in a manufactured home which does not qualify for priority under this subsection may qualify under another.

11. Priority in Fixtures: Construction Mortgages. The purchase-money priority presents a difficult problem in relation to construction mortgages. The latter ordinarily will have been recorded even before the commencement of delivery of materials to the job, and therefore would take priority over fixture security interests were it not for the purchase-money priority. However, having recorded first, the holder of a construction mortgage reasonably expects to have first priority in the improvement built using the mortgagee's advances. Subsection (g) [sic — should be (h)] expressly gives priority to the construction mortgage recorded before the filing of the purchase-money security interest in fixtures. A refinancing of a construction mortgage has the same priority as the construction mortgage itself. The phrase "an obligation incurred for the construction of an improvement" covers both optional advances and advances pursuant to commitment. Both types of advances have the same priority under subsection (g) [sic — should be (h)].

The priority under this subsection applies only to goods that become fixtures during the construction period leading to the completion of the improvement. The construction priority will not apply to additions to the building made long after completion of the improvement, even if the additions are financed by the real-property mortgagee under an open-end clause of the construction mortgage. In such case, subsections (d), (e), and (f) govern.

Although this subsection affords a construction mortgage priority over a purchase-money security interest that otherwise would have priority under subsection (d), the subsection is subject to the priority rules in subsections (e) and (f). Thus, a construction mortgage may be junior to a fixture security interest perfected by a fixture filing before the construction mortgage was recorded. See subsection (e)(1).

12. Crops. Growing crops are "goods" in which a security interest may be created and perfected under this Article. In some jurisdictions, a mortgage of real property may cover crops, as well. In the event that crops are encumbered by both a mortgage and an Article 9 security interest, subsection (i) provides that the security interest has priority. States whose real-property law provides otherwise should either amend that law directly or override it by enacting subsection (j).

13. "Signed" Replaces "Authenticated." Consistent with the revised definition of "sign" in Section 1-201(b)(37), the cognate term "signed" replaces the reference to "authenticated" in the pre-2022 text of this section.

Section 9-335. Accessions

(a) [Creation of security interest in accession.] A security interest may be created in an accession and continues in collateral that becomes an accession.

(b) [Perfection of security interest.] If a security interest is perfected when the collateral becomes an accession, the security interest remains perfected in the collateral.

(c) [Priority of security interest.] Except as otherwise provided in subsection (d), the other provisions of this part determine the priority of a security interest in an accession.

(d) [Compliance with certificate-of-title statute.] A security interest in an accession is subordinate to a security interest in the whole which is perfected by compliance with the requirements of a certificate-of-title statute under Section 9-311(b).

(e) [Removal of accession after default.] After default, subject to Part 6, a secured party may remove an accession from other goods if the security interest in the accession has priority over the claims of every person having an interest in the whole.

(f) [Reimbursement following removal.] A secured party that removes an accession from other goods under subsection (e) shall promptly reimburse any holder of a security interest or other lien on, or owner of, the whole or of the other goods, other than the debtor, for the cost of repair of any physical injury to the whole or the other goods. The secured party need not reimburse the holder or owner for any diminution in value of the whole or the other goods caused by the absence of the accession removed or by any necessity for replacing it. A person entitled to reimbursement may refuse permission to remove until the secured party gives adequate assurance for the performance of the obligation to reimburse.

Definitional Cross References:

Accession	Section 9-102(a)(1)
Collateral	Section 9-102(a)(12)
Debtor	Section 9-102(a)(28)
Goods	Section 9-102(a)(44)
Holder	Section 1-201(b)(21)
Person	Section 1-201(b)(27)
Secured party	Section 9-102(a)(73)
Security interest	Section 1-201(b)(35)
Value	Section 1-204

Official Comment

1. Source. Former Section 9-314.

2. "Accession." This section applies to an "accession," as defined in Section 9-102, regardless of the cost or difficulty of removing the accession from the other goods, and regardless of whether the original goods have come to form an integral part of the other goods. This section does not apply to goods whose identity has been lost. Goods of that kind are "commingled goods" governed by Section 9-336. Neither this section nor the following one addresses the case of collateral that changes form without the addition of other goods.

3. "Accession" vs. "Other Goods." This section distinguishes among the "accession," the "other goods," and the "whole." The last term refers to the combination of the "accession" and the "other goods." If one person's collateral becomes physically united with another person's collateral, each is an "accession."

> **Example 1:** SP-1 holds a security interest in the debtor's tractors (which are not subject to a certificate-of-title statute), and SP-2 holds a security interest in a particular tractor engine. The engine is installed in a tractor. From the perspective of SP-1, the tractor becomes an "accession" and the engine is the "other goods." From the perspective of SP-2, the engine is the "accession" and the tractor is the "other goods." The completed tractor—tractor cum engine—constitutes the "whole."

4. Scope. This section governs only a few issues concerning accessions. Subsection (a) contains rules governing continuation of a security interest in an accession. Subsection (b) contains a rule governing continued perfection of a security interest in goods that become an accession. Subsection (d) contains a special priority rule governing accessions that become part of a whole covered by a certificate of title. Subsections (e) and (f) govern enforcement of a security interest in an accession.

5. Matters Left to Other Provisions of This Article: Attachment and Perfection. Other provisions of this Article often govern accession-related issues. For example, this section does not address whether a secured party acquires a security interest in the whole if its collateral becomes an accession. Normally this will turn on the description of the collateral in the security agreement.

> **Example 2:** Debtor owns a computer subject to a perfected security interest in favor of SP-1. Debtor acquires memory and installs it in the computer. Whether SP-1's security interest attaches to the memory depends on whether the security agreement covers it.

Similarly, this section does not determine whether perfection against collateral that becomes an accession is effective to perfect a security interest in the whole. Other provisions of this Article, including the requirements for indicating the collateral covered by a financing statement, resolve that question.

6. Matters Left to Other Provisions of This Article: Priority. With one exception, concerning goods covered by a certificate of title (see subsection (d)), the other provisions of this Part, including the rules governing purchase-money security interests, determine the priority of most security interests in an accession, including the relative priority of a security interest in an accession and a security interest in the whole. See subsection (c).

> **Example 3:** Debtor owns an office computer subject to a security interest in favor of SP-1. Debtor acquires memory and grants a perfected security interest in the memory to SP-2. Debtor installs the memory in the computer, at which time (one assumes) SP-1's security interest attaches to the memory. The first-to-file-or-perfect rule of Section 9-322 governs priority in the memory. If, however, SP-2's security interest is a purchase-money security interest, Section 9-324(a) would afford priority in the memory to SP-2, regardless of which security interest was perfected first.

7. Goods Covered by Certificate of Title. This section does govern the priority of a security interest in an accession that is or becomes part of a whole that is subject to a security interest perfected by compliance with a certificate-of-title statute. Subsection (d) provides that a security interest in the whole, perfected by compliance with a certificate-of-title statute, takes priority over a security interest in the accession. It enables a secured party to rely upon a certificate of title without having to check the UCC files to determine whether any components of the collateral may be encumbered. The subsection imposes a corresponding risk upon those who finance goods that may become part of goods covered by a certificate of title. In doing so, it reverses the priority that appeared reasonable to most pre-UCC courts.

Example 4: Debtor owns an automobile subject to a security interest in favor of SP-1. The security interest is perfected by notation on the certificate of title. Debtor buys tires subject to a perfected-by-filing purchase-money security interest in favor of SP-2 and mounts the tires on the automobile's wheels. If the security interest in the automobile attaches to the tires, then SP-1 acquires priority over SP-2. The same result would obtain if SP-1's security interest attached to the automobile and was perfected after the tires had been mounted on the wheels.

Section 9-336. Commingled Goods

(a) ["Commingled goods."] In this section, "commingled goods" means goods that are physically united with other goods in such a manner that their identity is lost in a product or mass.

(b) [No security interest in commingled goods as such.] A security interest does not exist in commingled goods as such. However, a security interest may attach to a product or mass that results when goods become commingled goods.

(c) [Attachment of security interest to product or mass.] If collateral becomes commingled goods, a security interest attaches to the product or mass.

(d) [Perfection of security interest.] If a security interest in collateral is perfected before the collateral becomes commingled goods, the security interest that attaches to the product or mass under subsection (c) is perfected.

(e) [Priority of security interest.] Except as otherwise provided in subsection (f), the other provisions of this part determine the priority of a security interest that attaches to the product or mass under subsection (c).

(f) [Conflicting security interests in product or mass] If more than one security interest attaches to the product or mass under subsection (c), the following rules determine priority:

(1) A security interest that is perfected under subsection (d) has priority over a security interest that is unperfected at the time the collateral becomes commingled goods.

(2) If more than one security interest is perfected under subsection (d), the security interests rank equally in proportion to value of the collateral at the time it became commingled goods.

Definitional Cross References:

Collateral	Section 9-102(a)(12)
Goods	Section 9-102(a)(44)
Security interest	Section 1-201(b)(35)
Value	Section 1-204

Official Comment

1. Source. Former Section 9-315.

2. "Commingled Goods." Subsection (a) defines "commingled goods." It is meant to include not only goods whose identity is lost through manufacturing or production (e.g., flour that has become part of baked goods) but also goods whose identity is lost by commingling with other goods from which they cannot be distinguished (e.g., ball bearings).

3. Consequences of Becoming "Commingled Goods." By definition, the identity of the original collateral cannot be determined once the original collateral becomes commingled goods. Consequently, the security interest in the specific original collateral alone is lost once the collateral becomes commingled goods, and no security interest in the original collateral can be created thereafter except as a part of the resulting product or mass. See subsection (b).

Once collateral becomes commingled goods, the secured party's security interest is transferred from the original collateral to the product or mass. See subsection (c). If the security interest in the original collateral was perfected, the security interest in the product or mass is a perfected security interest. See subsection (d). This perfection continues until lapse.

4. Priority of Perfected Security Interests That Attach Under This Section. This section governs the priority of competing security interests in a product or mass only when both security interests arise under this section. In that case, if both security interests are perfected by operation of this section (see subsections (c) and (d)), then the security interests rank equally, in proportion to the value of the collateral at the time it became commingled goods. See subsection (f)(2).

Example 1: SP-1 has a perfected security interest in Debtor's eggs, which have a value of $300 and secure a debt of $400, and SP-2 has a perfected security interest in Debtor's flour, which has a value of $500 and secures a debt of $700. Debtor uses the flour and eggs to make cakes, which have a value of $1000. The two security interests rank equally and share in the ratio of 3:5. Applying this ratio to the entire value of the product, SP-1 would be entitled to $375 (i.e., 3/8 $1000), and SP-2 would be entitled to $625 (i.e., 5/8 $1000).

Example 2: Assume the facts of Example 1, except that SP-1's collateral, worth $300, secures a debt of $200. Recall that, if the cake is worth $1000, then applying the ratio of 3:5 would entitle SP-1 to $375 and SP-2 to $625. However, SP-1 is not entitled to collect from the product more than it is owed. Accordingly, SP-1's share would be only $200, SP-2 would receive the remaining value, up to the amount it is owed ($700).

Example 3: Assume that the cakes in the previous examples have a value of only $600. Again, the parties share in the ratio of 3:5. If, as in Example 1, SP-1 is owed $400, then SP-1 is entitled to $225 (i.e., 3/8 $600), and SP-2 is entitled to $375 (i.e., 5/8 $600). Debtor receives nothing. If, however, as in Example 2, SP-1 is owed only $200, then SP-2 receives $400.

The results in the foregoing examples remain the same, regardless of whether SP-1 or SP-2 (or each) has a purchase-money security interest.

5. Perfection: Unperfected Security Interests. The rule explained in the preceding Comment applies only when both security interests in original collateral are perfected when the goods become commingled goods. If a security interest in original collateral is unperfected at the time the collateral becomes commingled goods, subsection (f)(1) applies.

Example 4: SP-1 has a perfected security interest in the debtor's eggs, and SP-2 has an unperfected security interest in the debtor's flour. Debtor uses the flour and eggs to make cakes. Under subsection (c), both security interests attach to the cakes. But since SP-1's security interest was perfected at the time of commingling and SP-2's was not, only SP-1's security interest in the cakes is perfected. See subsection (d). Under subsection (f)(1) and Section 9-322(a)(2), SP-1's perfected security interest has priority over SP-2's unperfected security interest.

If both security interests are unperfected, the rule of Section 9-322(a)(3) would apply.

6. Multiple Security Interests. On occasion, a single input may be encumbered by more than one security interest. In those cases, the multiple secured parties should be treated like a single secured party for purposes of determining their collective share under subsection (f)(2). The normal priority rules would determine how that share would be allocated between them. Consider the following example, which is a variation on Example 1 above:

Example 5: SP-1A has a perfected, first-priority security interest in Debtor's eggs. SP-1B has a perfected, second-priority security interest in the same collateral. The eggs have a value of $300. Debtor owes $200 to SP-1A and $200 to SP-1B. SP-2 has a perfected security interest in Debtor's flour, which has a value of $500 and secures a debt of $600. Debtor uses the flour and eggs to make cakes, which have a value of $1000.

For purposes of subsection (f)(2), SP-1A and SP-1B should be treated like a single secured party. The collective security interest would rank equally with that of SP-2. Thus, the secured parties would share in the ratio of 3 (for SP-1A and SP-1B combined) to 5 (for SP-2). Applying this ratio to the entire value of the product, SP-1A and SP-1B in the aggregate would be entitled to $375 (i.e., 3/8 $1000), and SP-2 would be entitled to $625 (i.e., 5/8 $1000).

SP-1A and SP-1B would share the $375 in accordance with their priority, as established under other rules. Inasmuch as SP-1A has first priority, it would receive $200, and SP-1B would receive $175.

7. Priority of Security Interests That Attach Other Than by Operation of This Section. Under subsection (e), the normal priority rules determine the priority of a security interest that attaches to the product or mass other than by operation of this section. For example, assume that SP-1 has a perfected security interest in Debtor's existing and after-acquired baked goods, and SP-2 has a perfected security interest in Debtor's flour. When the flour is processed into cakes, subsections (c) and (d) provide that SP-2 acquires a perfected security interest in the cakes. If SP-1 filed against the baked goods before SP-2 filed against the flour, then SP-1 will enjoy priority in the cakes. See Section 9-322 (first-to-file-or perfect). But if SP-2 filed against the flour before SP-1 filed against the baked goods, then SP-2 will enjoy priority in the cakes to the extent of its security interest.

Section 9-337. Priority of Security Interests in Goods Covered by Certificate of Title

If, while a security interest in goods is perfected by any method under the law of another jurisdiction, this State issues a certificate of title that does not show that the goods are subject to the security interest or contain a statement that they may be subject to security interests not shown on the certificate:

(1) a buyer of the goods, other than a person in the business of selling goods of that kind, takes free of the security interest if the buyer gives value and receives delivery of the goods after issuance of the certificate and without knowledge of the security interest; and

(2) the security interest is subordinate to a conflicting security interest in the goods that attaches, and is perfected under Section 9-311(b), after issuance of the certificate and without the conflicting secured party's knowledge of the security interest.

Official Comment

1. Source. Derived from former Section 9-103(2)(d).

2. Protection for Buyers and Secured Parties. This section affords protection to certain good-faith purchasers for value who are likely to have relied on a "clean" certificate of title, i.e., one that neither shows that the goods are subject to a particular security interest nor contains a statement that they may be subject to security interests not shown on the certificate. Under this section, a buyer can take free of, and the holder of a conflicting security interest can acquire priority over, a security interest that is perfected by any method under the law of another jurisdiction. The fact that the security interest has been reperfected by possession under Section 9-313 does not of itself disqualify the holder of a conflicting security interest from protection under paragraph (2).

Definitional Cross References:

Certificate of title	Section 9-102(a)(10)
Delivery	Section 1-201(b)(15)
Goods	Section 9-102(a)(44)
Person	Section 1-201(b)(27)
Secured party	Section 9-102(a)(73)
Security interest	Section 1-201(b)(35)
State	Section 9-102(a)(77)
Value	Section 1-204

Section 9-338. Priority of Security Interest or Agricultural Lien Perfected by Filed Financing Statement Providing Certain Incorrect Information

If a security interest or agricultural lien is perfected by a filed financing statement providing information described in Section 9-516(b)(5) which is incorrect at the time the financing statement is filed:

(1) the security interest or agricultural lien is subordinate to a conflicting perfected security interest in the collateral to the extent that the holder of the conflicting security interest gives value in reasonable reliance upon the incorrect information; and

(2) a purchaser, other than a secured party, of the collateral takes free of the security interest or agricultural lien to the extent that, in reasonable reliance upon the incorrect information, the purchaser gives value and, in the case of tangible chattel paper, tangible documents, goods, instruments, or a security certificate, receives delivery of the collateral.

Definitional Cross References:

Agricultural lien	Section 9-102(a)(5)
Chattel paper	Section 9-102(a)(11)
Collateral	Section 9-102(a)(12)
Delivery	Section 1-201(b)(15)
Document	Section 9-102(a)(30)
Financing statement	Section 9-102(a)(39)
Goods	Section 9-102(a)(44)
Holder	Section 1-201(b)(21)
Instrument	Section 9-102(a)(47)
Purchaser	Section 1-201(b)(30)
Secured party	Section 9-102(a)(73)
Security certificate	Section 8-102(a)(16)
Security interest	Section 1-201(b)(35)
Value	Section 1-204

Official Comment

1. Source. New.

2. Effect of Incorrect Information in Financing Statement. Section 9-520(a) requires the filing office to reject financing statements that do not contain information concerning the debtor as specified in Section 9-516(b)(5). An error in this information does not render the financing statement ineffective. On rare occasions, a subsequent purchaser of the collateral (i.e., a buyer or secured party) may rely on the misinformation to its detriment. This section subordinates a security interest or agricultural lien perfected by an effective, but flawed, financing statement to the rights of a buyer or holder of a perfected security interest to the extent that, in reasonable reliance on the incorrect information, the purchaser gives value and, in the case of tangible collateral, receives delivery of the collateral. A purchaser who has not made itself aware of the information in the filing office with respect to the debtor cannot act in "reasonable reliance" upon incorrect information.

3. Relationship to Section 9-507. This section applies to financing statements that contain information that is incorrect at the time of filing and imposes a small risk of subordination on the filer. In contrast, Section 9-507 deals with financing statements containing information that is correct at the time of filing but which becomes incorrect later. Except as provided in Section 9-507 with respect to changes in the name that is sufficient as the name of the debtor under Section 9-503(a), an otherwise effective financing statement does not become ineffective if the information contained in it becomes inaccurate.

Section 9-339. Priority Subject to Subordination

This article does not preclude subordination by agreement by a person entitled to priority.

Definitional Cross References:

Agreement	Section 1-201(b)(3)
Person	Section 1-201(b)(27)

Official Comment

1. Source. Former Section 9-316.

2. Subordination by Agreement. The preceding sections deal elaborately with questions of priority. This section makes it entirely clear that a person entitled to priority may effectively agree to subordinate its claim. Only the person entitled to priority may make such an agreement: a person's rights cannot be adversely affected by an agreement to which the person is not a party.

[SUBPART 4. RIGHTS OF BANK]

Section 9-340. Effectiveness of Right of Recoupment or Set-Off against Deposit Account

(a) [Exercise of recoupment or set-off.] Except as otherwise provided in subsection (c), a bank with which a deposit account is maintained may exercise any right of recoupment or set-off against a secured party that holds a security interest in the deposit account.

(b) [Recoupment or set-off not affected by security interest.] Except as otherwise provided in subsection (c), the application of this article to a security interest in a deposit account does not affect a right of recoupment or set-off of the secured party as to a deposit account maintained with the secured party.

(c) [When set-off ineffective.] The exercise by a bank of a set-off against a deposit account is ineffective against a secured party that holds a security interest in the deposit account which is perfected by control under Section 9-104(a)(3), if the set-off is based on a claim against the debtor.

Definitional Cross References:

Bank	Section 9-102(a)(8)
Debtor	Section 9-102(a)(28)
Deposit account	Section 9-102(a)(29)
Secured party	Section 9-102(a)(73)
Security interest	Section 1-201(b)(35)

Official Comment

1. Source. New; subsection (b) is based on a nonuniform Illinois amendment.

2. Set-Off vs. Security Interest. This section resolves the conflict between a security interest in a deposit account and the bank's rights of recoupment and set-off.

Subsection (a) states the general rule and provides that the bank may effectively exercise rights of recoupment and set-off against the secured party. Subsection (c) contains an exception: if the secured party has control under Section 9-104(a)(3) (i.e., if it has become the bank's customer), then any set-off exercised by the bank against a debt owed by the debtor (as opposed to a debt owed to the bank by the secured party) is ineffective. The bank may, however, exercise its recoupment rights effectively. This result is consistent with the priority rule in Section 9-327(4), under which the security interest of a bank in a deposit account is subordinate to that of a secured party who has control under Section 9-104(a)(3).

This section deals with rights of set-off and recoupment that a bank may have under other law. It does not create a right of set-off or recoupment, nor is it intended to override any limitations or restrictions that other law imposes on the exercise of those rights.

3. Preservation of Set-Off Right. Subsection (b) makes clear that a bank may hold both a right of set-off against, and an Article 9 security interest in, the same deposit account. By holding a security interest in a deposit account, a bank does not impair any right of set-off it would otherwise enjoy. This subsection does not pertain to accounts evidenced by an instrument (e.g., certain certificates of deposit), which are excluded from the definition of "deposit accounts."

Section 9-341. Bank's Rights and Duties with Respect to Deposit Account

Except as otherwise provided in Section 9-340(c), and unless the bank otherwise agrees in a signed record, a bank's rights and duties with respect to a deposit account maintained with the bank are not terminated, suspended, or modified by:

(1) the creation, attachment, or perfection of a security interest in the deposit account;

(2) the bank's knowledge of the security interest; or

(3) the bank's receipt of instructions from the secured party.

Definitional Cross References:

Bank	Section 9-102(a)(8)
Deposit account	Section 9-102(a)(29)
Record	Section 9-102(a)(70)
Right	Section 1-201(b)(34)
Secured party	Section 9-102(a)(73)
Security interest	Section 1-201(b)(35)
Sign	Section 1-201(b)(37)

Official Comment

1. Source. New.

2. Free Flow of Funds. This section is designed to prevent security interests in deposit accounts from impeding the free flow of funds through the payment system. Subject to two exceptions, it leaves the bank's rights and duties with respect to the deposit account and the funds on deposit unaffected by the creation or perfection of a security interest or by the bank's knowledge of the security interest. In addition, the section permits the bank to ignore the instructions of the secured party unless it had agreed to honor them or unless other law provides to the contrary. A secured party who wishes to deprive the debtor of access to funds on deposit or to appropriate those funds for itself needs to obtain the agreement of the bank, utilize the judicial process, or comply with procedures set forth in other law. Section 4-303(a), concerning the effect of notice on a bank's right and duty to pay items, is not to the contrary. That section addresses only whether an otherwise effective notice comes too late; it does not determine whether a timely notice is otherwise effective.

3. Operation of Rule. The general rule of this section is subject to Section 9-340(c), under which a bank's right of set-off may not be exercised against a deposit account in the secured party's name if the right is based on a claim against the debtor. This result reflects current law in many jurisdictions and does not appear to have unduly disrupted banking practices or the payments system. The more important function of this section, which is not impaired by Section 9-340, is the bank's right to follow the debtor's (customer's) instructions (e.g., by honoring checks, permitting withdrawals, etc.) until such time as the depository institution is served with judicial process or receives instructions with respect to the funds on deposit from a secured party who has control over the deposit account.

4. Liability of Bank. This Article does not determine whether a bank that pays out funds from an encumbered deposit is liable to the holder of a security interest. Although the fact that a secured party has control over the deposit account and the manner by which control was achieved may be relevant to the imposition of liability, whatever rule applies generally when a bank pays out funds in which a third party has an interest would determine liability to a secured party. Often, this rule is found in a non-UCC adverse claim statute.

5. Certificates of Deposit. This section does not address the obligations of banks that issue instruments evidencing deposits (e.g., certain certificates of deposit).

6. "Signed" Replaces "Authenticated." Consistent with the revised definition of "sign" in Section 1-201(b)(37), the cognate term "signed" replaces the reference to "authenticated" in the pre-2022 text of this section.

Section 9-342. Bank's Right to Refuse to Enter into or Disclose Existence of Control Agreement

This article does not require a bank to enter into an agreement of the kind described in Section 9-104(a)(2), even if its customer so requests or directs. A bank that has entered into such an agreement is not required to confirm the existence of the agreement to another person unless requested to do so by its customer.

Definitional Cross References:

Agreement	Section 1-201(b)(3)
Bank	Section 9-102(a)(8)
Customer	Section 4-104(a)(5)
Person	Section 1-201(b)(27)

Official Comment

1. Source. New; derived from Section 8-106(g).

2. Protection for Bank. This section protects banks from the need to enter into agreements against their will and from the need to respond to inquiries from persons other than their customers.

PART 4. RIGHTS OF THIRD PARTIES

Section 9-401. Alienability of Debtor's Rights

(a) [Other law governs alienability; exceptions.] Except as otherwise provided in subsection (b) and Sections 9-406, 9-407, 9-408, and 9-409, whether a debtor's rights in collateral may be voluntarily or involuntarily transferred is governed by law other than this article.

(b) [Agreement does not prevent transfer.] An agreement between the debtor and secured party which prohibits a transfer of the debtor's rights in collateral or makes the transfer a default does not prevent the transfer from taking effect.

Definitional Cross References:

Agreement	Section 1-201(b)(3)
Collateral	Section 9-102(a)(12)
Debtor	Section 9-102(a)(28)
Right	Section 1-201(b)(34)
Secured party	Section 9-102(a)(73)

Official Comment

1. Source. Former Section 9-311.

2. Scope of This Part. This Part deals with several issues affecting third parties (i.e., parties other than the debtor and the secured party). These issues are not addressed in Part 3, Subpart 3, which deals with priorities. This Part primarily addresses the rights and duties of account debtors and other persons obligated on collateral who are not, themselves, parties to a secured transaction.

3. Governing Law. There was some uncertainty under former Article 9 as to which jurisdiction's law (usually, which jurisdiction's version of Article 9) applied to the matters that this Part addresses. Part 3, Subpart 1, does not determine the law governing these matters because they do not relate to perfection, the effect of perfection or nonperfection, or priority. However, it might be inappropriate for a designation of applicable law by a debtor and secured party under Section 1-301 to control the law applicable to an independent transaction or relationship between the debtor and an account debtor.

Consider an example under Section 9-408.

> **Example 1:** State X has adopted this Article; former Article 9 is the law of State Y. A general intangible (e.g., a franchise agreement) between a debtor-franchisee, D, and an account debtor-franchisor, AD, is governed by the law of State Y. D grants to SP a security interest in its rights under the franchise agreement. The franchise agreement contains a term prohibiting D's assignment of its rights under the agreement. D and SP agree that their secured transaction is governed by the law of State X. Under State X's Section 9-408, the restriction on D's assignment is ineffective to prevent the creation, attachment, or perfection of SP's security interest. State Y's former Section 9-318(4), however, does not address restrictions on the creation of security interests in general intangibles other than general intangibles for money due or to become due. Accordingly, it does not address restrictions on the assignment to SP of D's rights under the franchise agreement. The non-Article-9 law of State Y, which does address restrictions, provides that the prohibition on assignment is effective.
>
> This Article does not provide a specific answer to the question of which State's law applies to the restriction on assignment in the example. However, assuming that under non-UCC choice-of-law principles the effectiveness of the restriction would be governed by the law of State Y, which governs the franchise agreement, the fact that State X's Article 9 governs the secured transaction between SP and D would not override the otherwise applicable law governing the agreement. Of course, to the extent that jurisdictions eventually adopt identical versions of this Article and courts interpret it consistently, the inability to identify the applicable law in circumstances such as those in the example may be inconsequential.

4. Inalienability Under Other Law. Subsection (a) addresses the question whether property necessarily is transferable by virtue of its inclusion (i.e., its eligibility as collateral) within the scope of Article 9. It gives a negative answer, subject to the identified exceptions. The substance of subsection (a) was implicit under former Article 9.

5. Negative Pledge Covenant. Subsection (b) is an exception to the general rule in subsection (a). It makes clear that in secured transactions under this Article the debtor has rights in collateral (whether legal title or equitable) which it can transfer and which its creditors can reach. It is best explained with an example.

> **Example 2:** A debtor, D, grants to SP a security interest to secure a debt in excess of the value of the collateral. D agrees with SP that it will not create a subsequent security interest in the collateral and that any security interest purportedly granted in violation of the agreement will be void. Subsequently, in violation of its agreement with SP, D purports to grant a security interest in the same collateral to another secured party.
>
> Subsection (b) validates D's creation of the subsequent (prohibited) security interest, which might even achieve priority over the earlier security interest. See Comment 7. However, unlike some other provisions of this Part, such as Section 9-406, subsection (b) does not provide that the agreement restricting assignment itself is "ineffective." Consequently, the debtor's breach may create a default.

6. Rights of Lien Creditors. Difficult problems may arise with respect to attachment, levy, and other judicial procedures under which a debtor's creditors may reach collateral subject to a security interest. For example, an obligation may be secured by collateral worth many times the amount of the obligation. If a lien creditor has caused all or a portion of the collateral to be seized under judicial process, it may be difficult to determine the amount of the debtor's "equity" in the collateral that has been seized. The section leaves resolution of this problem to the courts. The doctrine of marshaling may be appropriate.

7. Sale of Receivables. If a debtor sells an account, chattel paper, payment intangible, or promissory note outright, as against the buyer the debtor has no remaining rights to transfer. If, however, the buyer fails to perfect its interest, then solely insofar as the rights of certain third parties are concerned, the debtor is deemed to retain its rights and title. See Section 9-318. The debtor has the power to convey these rights to a subsequent purchaser. If the subsequent purchaser (buyer or secured lender) perfects its interest, it will achieve priority over the earlier, unperfected purchaser. See Section 9-322(a)(1).

8. Use of the Term "Assignment." The term "assignment," as used in this Article, refers to both an outright transfer of ownership and a transfer of an interest to secure an obligation. See Section 9-102, Comment 2.b.1; PEB Commentary No. 21.

Section 9-402. Secured Party Not Obligated on Contract of Debtor or in Tort

The existence of a security interest, agricultural lien, or authority given to a debtor to dispose of or use collateral, without more, does not subject a secured party to liability in contract or tort for the debtor's acts or omissions.

Definitional Cross References:

Agricultural lien	Section 9-102(a)(5)
Collateral	Section 9-102(a)(12)
Contract	Section 1-201(b)(12)
Debtor	Section 9-102(a)(28)
Secured party	Section 9-102(a)(73)
Security interest	Section 1-201(b)(35)

Official Comment

1. Source. Former Section 9-317.

2. Nonliability of Secured Party. This section, like former Section 9-317, rejects theories on which a secured party might be held liable on a debtor's contracts or in tort merely because a security interest exists or because the debtor is entitled to dispose of or use collateral. This section expands former Section 9-317 to cover agricultural liens.

Section 9-403. Agreement Not to Assert Defenses against Assignee

(a) ["Value."] In this section, "value" has the meaning provided in Section 3-303(a).

(b) [Agreement not to assert claim or defense.] Except as otherwise provided in this section, an agreement between an account debtor and an assignor not to assert against an assignee any claim or defense that the account debtor may have against the assignor is enforceable by an assignee that takes an assignment:

(1) for value;

(2) in good faith;

(3) without notice of a claim of a property or possessory right to the property assigned; and

(4) without notice of a defense or claim in recoupment of the type that may be asserted against a person entitled to enforce a negotiable instrument under Section 3-305(a).

(c) [When subsection (b) not applicable.] Subsection (b) does not apply to defenses of a type that may be asserted against a holder in due course of a negotiable instrument under Section 3-305(b).

(d) [Omission of required statement in consumer transaction.] In a consumer transaction, if a record evidences the account debtor's obligation, law other than this article requires that the record include a statement to the effect that the rights of an assignee are subject to claims or defenses that the account debtor could assert against the original obligee, and the record does not include such a statement:

(1) the record has the same effect as if the record included such a statement; and

(2) the account debtor may assert against an assignee those claims and defenses that would have been available if the record included such a statement.

(e) [Rule for individual under other law.] This section is subject to law other than this article which establishes a different rule for an account debtor who is an individual and who incurred the obligation primarily for personal, family, or household purposes.

(f) [Other law not displaced.] Except as otherwise provided in subsection (d), this section does not displace law other than this article which gives effect to an agreement by an account debtor not to assert a claim or defense against an assignee.

Definitional Cross References:

Account debtor	Section 9-102(a)(3)
Agreement	Section 1-201(b)(3)
Assignee	Section 9-102(a)(7A)
Assignor	Section 9-102(a)(7B)
Consumer transaction	Section 9-102(a)(26)
Good faith	Section 1-201(b)(20)
Holder in due course	Section 3-302(a)
Negotiable instrument	Section 3-104(a)
Notice	Section 1-202(a)
Person	Section 1-201(b)(27)
Record	Section 9-102(a)(70)
Right	Section 1-201(b)(34)
Value	Section 3-303(a)

Comment References: 9-109 C15

Official Comment

1. Source. Former Section 9-206.

2. Scope and Purpose. Subsection (b), like former Section 9-206, generally validates an agreement between an account debtor and an assignor that the account debtor will not assert against an assignee claims and defenses that it may have against the assignor. These agreements are typical in installment sale agreements and leases. However, this section expands former Section 9-206 to apply to all account debtors; it is not limited to account debtors that have bought or leased goods. This section applies only to the obligations of an "account debtor," as defined in Section 9-102. Thus, it does not determine the circumstances under which and the extent to which a person who is obligated on a negotiable instrument is disabled from asserting claims and defenses. Rather, Article 3 must be consulted. See, e.g., Sections 3-305, 3-306. Article 3 governs even when the negotiable instrument constitutes part of chattel paper. See Section 9-102 (an obligor on a negotiable instrument constituting part of chattel paper is not an "account debtor").

3. Conditions of Validation; Relationship to Article 3. Subsection (b) validates an account debtor's agreement only if the assignee takes an assignment for value, in good faith, and without notice of conflicting claims to the property assigned or of certain claims or defenses of the account debtor. Like pre-1998 Section 9-206, this section is designed to put the assignee in a position that is no better and no worse than that of a holder in due course of a negotiable instrument under Article 3. However, pre-1998 Section 9-206 left open certain issues, e.g., whether the section incorporated the special Article 3 definition of "value" in Section 3-303 or the generally applicable definition in Article 1 (Section 1-204). Subsection (a) addresses this question; it provides that "value" has the meaning specified in Section 3-303(a). Similarly, subsection (c) provides that subsection (b) does not validate an agreement with respect to defenses that could be asserted against a holder in due course under Section 3-305(b) (the so-called "real" defenses). In 1990, the definition of "holder in due course" (Section 3-302) and the articulation of the rights of a holder in due course (Sections 3-305 and 3-306) were revised substantially. This section tracks more closely the rules of Sections 3-302, 3-305, and 3-306.

4. Relationship to Terms of Assigned Property. Former Section 9-206(2), concerning warranties accompanying the sale of goods, has been deleted as unnecessary. This Article does not regulate the terms of the account, chattel paper, or general intangible that is assigned, except insofar as the account, chattel paper, or general intangible itself creates a security interest (as often is the case with chattel paper). Thus, Article 2, and not this Article, determines whether a seller of goods makes or effectively disclaims warranties, even if the sale is secured. Similarly, other law, and not this Article, determines the effectiveness of an account debtor's undertaking to pay notwithstanding, and not to assert, any defenses or claims against an assignor—e.g., a "hell-or-high-water" provision in the underlying agreement that is assigned. If other law gives effect to this undertaking, then, under principles of nemo dat, the undertaking would be enforceable by the assignee (secured party). If other law prevents the assignor from enforcing the undertaking, this section nevertheless might permit the assignee to do so. The right of the assignee to enforce would depend upon whether, under the particular facts, the account debtor's undertaking fairly could be construed as an agreement that falls within the scope of this section and whether the assignee meets the requirements of this section.

5. Relationship to Federal Trade Commission Rule. Subsection (d) is new. It applies to rights evidenced by a record that is required to contain, but does not contain, the notice set forth in Federal Trade Commission Rule 433, 16 C.F.R. Part 433 (the "Holder-in-Due-Course Regulations"). Under this subsection, an assignee of such a record takes subject to the consumer account debtor's claims and defenses to the same extent as it would have if the writing had contained the required notice. Thus, subsection (d) effectively renders waiver-of-defense clauses ineffective in the transactions with consumers to which it applies.

6. Relationship to Other Law. Like former Section 9-206(1), this section takes no position on the enforceability of waivers of claims and defenses by consumer account debtors, leaving that question to other law. However, the reference to "law other than this article" in subsection (e) encompasses administrative rules and regulations; the reference in former Section 9-206(1) that it replaces ("statute or decision") arguably did not.

This section does not displace other law that gives effect to a non-consumer account debtor's agreement not to assert defenses against an assignee, even if the agreement would not qualify under subsection (b). See subsection (f). It validates, but does not invalidate, agreements made by a non-consumer account debtor. This section also does not displace other law to the extent that the other law permits an assignee, who takes an assignment with notice of a claim of a property or possessory right, a defense, or a claim in recoupment, to enforce an account debtor's agreement not to assert claims and defenses against the assignor (e.g., a "hell-or-high-water" agreement). See Comment 4. It also does not displace an assignee's right to assert that an account debtor is estopped from asserting a claim or defense. Nor does this section displace other law with respect to waivers of potential future claims and defenses that are the subject of an agreement between the account debtor and the assignee. Finally, it does not displace Section 1-306, concerning waiver of a breach that allegedly already has occurred.

Section 9-404. Rights Acquired by Assignee; Claims and Defenses against Assignee

(a) [Assignee's rights subject to terms, claims, and defenses; exceptions.] Unless an account debtor has made an enforceable agreement not to assert defenses or claims, and subject to subsections (b) through (e), the rights of an assignee are subject to:

(1) all terms of the agreement between the account debtor and assignor and any defense or claim in recoupment arising from the transaction that gave rise to the contract; and

(2) any other defense or claim of the account debtor against the assignor which accrues before the account debtor receives a notification of the assignment signed by the assignor or the assignee.

(b) [Account debtor's claim reduces amount owed to assignee.] Subject to subsection (c) and except as otherwise provided in subsection (d), the claim of an account debtor against an assignor may be asserted against an assignee under subsection (a) only to reduce the amount the account debtor owes.

(c) [Rule for individual under other law.] This section is subject to law other than this article which establishes a different rule for an account debtor who is an individual and who incurred the obligation primarily for personal, family, or household purposes.

(d) [Omission of required statement in consumer transaction.] In a consumer transaction, if a record evidences the account debtor's obligation, law other than this article requires that the record include a statement to the effect that the account debtor's recovery against an assignee with respect to claims and defenses against the assignor may not exceed amounts paid by the account debtor under the record, and the record does not include such a statement, the extent to which a claim of an account debtor against the assignor may be asserted against an assignee is determined as if the record included such a statement.

(e) [Inapplicability to health-care-insurance receivable.] This section does not apply to an assignment of a health-care-insurance receivable.

Definitional Cross References:

Account debtor	Section 9-102(a)(3)
Agreement	Section 1-201(b)(3)
Assignee	Section 9-102(a)(7A)
Assignor	Section 9-102(a)(7B)
Consumer transaction	Section 9-102(a)(26)
Contract	Section 1-201(b)(12)
Health-care-insurance receivable	Section 9-102(a)(46)
Record	Section 9-102(a)(70)
Right	Section 1-201(b)(34)
Sign	Section 1-201(b)(37)
Term	Section 1-201(b)(40)

Comment References: 9-109 C15

Official Comment

1. Source. Former Section 9-318(1).

2. Purpose; Rights of Assignee in General. Subsection (a), like former Section 9-318(1), provides that an assignee generally takes an assignment subject to defenses and claims of an account debtor. Under subsection (a)(1), if the account debtor's defenses on an assigned claim arise from the transaction that gave rise to the contract with the assignor, it makes no difference whether the defense or claim accrues before or after the account debtor is notified of the assignment. Under subsection (a)(2), the assignee takes subject to other defenses or claims only if they accrue before the account debtor has been notified of the assignment. Of course, an account debtor may waive its right to assert defenses or claims against an assignee under Section 9-403 or other applicable law. Subsection (a) tracks Section 3-305(a)(3) more closely than its predecessor.

3. Limitation on Affirmative Claims. Subsection (b) is new. It limits the claim that the account debtor may assert against an assignee. Borrowing from Section 3-305(a)(3) and cases construing former Section 9-318, subsection (b) generally does not afford the account debtor the right to an affirmative recovery from an assignee.

4. Consumer Account Debtors; Relationship to Federal Trade Commission Rule. Subsections (c) and (d) also are new. Subsection (c) makes clear that the rules of this section are subject to other law establishing special rules for consumer account debtors. An "account debtor who is an individual" as used in subsection (c) includes individuals who are jointly or jointly and severally obligated. Subsection (d) applies to rights evidenced by a record that is required to contain, but does not contain, the notice set forth in Federal Trade Commission Rule 433, 16 C.F.R. Part 433 (the "Holder-in-Due-Course Regulations"). Under subsection (d), a consumer account debtor has the same right to an affirmative recovery from an assignee of such a record as the consumer would have had against the assignee had the record contained the required notice.

5. Scope; Application to "Account Debtor." This section deals only with the rights and duties of "account debtors"—and for the most part only with account debtors on accounts, chattel paper, and payment intangibles. Subsection (e) provides that the obligation of an insurer with respect to a health-care-insurance receivable is governed by other law. References in this section to an "account debtor" include account debtors on collateral that is proceeds. Neither this section nor any other provision of this Article, including Sections 9-408 and 9-409, provides analogous regulation of the rights and duties of other obligors on collateral, such as the maker of a negotiable instrument (governed by Article 3), the issuer of or nominated person under a letter of credit (governed by Article 5), or the issuer of a security (governed by Article 8). Article 9 leaves those rights and duties untouched; however, Section 9-409 deals with the special case of letters of credit. When chattel paper is composed in part of a negotiable instrument, the obligor on the instrument is not an "account debtor," and Article 3 governs the rights of the assignee of the chattel paper with respect to the issues that this section addresses. See, e.g., Section 3-601 (dealing with discharge of an obligation to pay a negotiable instrument).

6. "Signed" Replaces "Authenticated." Consistent with the revised definition of "sign" in Section 1-201(b)(37), the cognate term "signed" replaces the reference to "authenticated" in the pre-2022 text of this section.

Section 9-405. Modification of Assigned Contract

(a) [Effect of modification on assignee.] A modification of or substitution for an assigned contract is effective against an assignee if made in good faith. The assignee acquires corresponding rights under the modified or substituted contract. The assignment may provide that the modification or substitution is a breach of contract by the assignor. This subsection is subject to subsections (b) through (d).

(b) [Applicability of subsection (a).] Subsection (a) applies to the extent that:

(1) the right to payment or a part thereof under an assigned contract has not been fully earned by performance; or

(2) the right to payment or a part thereof has been fully earned by performance and the account debtor has not received notification of the assignment under Section 9-406(a).

(c) [Rule for individual under other law.] This section is subject to law other than this article which establishes a different rule for an account debtor who is an individual and who incurred the obligation primarily for personal, family, or household purposes.

(d) [Inapplicability to health-care-insurance receivable.] This section does not apply to an assignment of a health-care-insurance receivable.

Definitional Cross References:

Account debtor	Section 9-102(a)(3)
Contract	Section 1-201(b)(12)
Good faith	Section 1-201(b)(20)
Health-care-insurance receivable	Section 9-102(a)(46)
Right	Section 1-201(b)(34)

Comment References: 9-109 C15

Official Comment

1. Source. Former Section 9-318(2).

2. Modification of Assigned Contract. The ability of account debtors and assignors to modify assigned contracts can be important, especially in the case of government contracts and complex contractual arrangements (e.g., construction contracts) with respect to which modifications are customary. Subsections (a) and (b) provide that good-faith modifications of assigned contracts are binding against an assignee to the extent that (i) the right to payment has not been fully earned or (ii) the right to payment has been earned and notification of the assignment has not been given to the account debtor. Former Section 9-318(2) did not validate modifications of fully-performed contracts under any circumstances, whether or not notification of the assignment had been given to the account debtor. Subsection (a) protects the interests of assignees by (i) limiting the effectiveness of modifications to those made in good faith, (ii) affording the assignee with corresponding rights under the contract as modified, and (iii) recognizing that the modification may be a breach of the assignor's agreement with the assignee.

3. Consumer Account Debtors. Subsection (c) is new. It makes clear that the rules of this section are subject to other law establishing special rules for consumer account debtors.

4. Account Debtors on Health-Care-Insurance Receivables. Subsection (d) also is new. It provides that this section does not apply to an assignment of a heath-care-insurance receivable. The obligation of an insurer with respect to a health-care-insurance receivable is governed by other law.

Section 9-406. Discharge of Account Debtor; Notification of Assignment; Identification and Proof of Assignment; Restrictions on Assignment of Accounts, Chattel Paper, Payment Intangibles, and Promissory Notes Ineffective

(a) [Discharge of account debtor; effect of notification.] Subject to subsections (b) through (i) and (l), an account debtor on an account, chattel paper, or a payment intangible may discharge its obligation by paying the assignor until, but not after, the account debtor receives a notification, signed by the assignor or the assignee, that the amount due or to become due has been assigned and that payment is to be made to the assignee. After receipt of the notification, the account debtor may discharge its obligation by paying the assignee and may not discharge the obligation by paying the assignor.

(b) [When notification ineffective.] Subject to subsections (h) and (l), notification is ineffective under subsection (a):

(1) if it does not reasonably identify the rights assigned;

(2) to the extent that an agreement between an account debtor and a seller of a payment intangible limits the account debtor's duty to pay a person other than the seller and the limitation is effective under law other than this article; or

(3) at the option of an account debtor, if the notification notifies the account debtor to make less than the full amount of any installment or other periodic payment to the assignee, even if:

(A) only a portion of the account, chattel paper, or payment intangible has been assigned to that assignee;

(B) a portion has been assigned to another assignee; or

(C) the account debtor knows that the assignment to that assignee is limited.

(c) [Proof of assignment.] Subject to subsections (h) and (l), if requested by the account debtor, an assignee shall seasonably furnish reasonable proof that the assignment has been made. Unless the assignee complies, the account debtor may discharge its obligation by paying the assignor, even if the account debtor has received a notification under subsection (a).

(d) [Term restricting assignment generally ineffective.] In this subsection, "promissory note" includes a negotiable instrument that evidences chattel paper. Except as otherwise provided in subsections (e) and (k) and Sections 2A-303 and 9-407, and subject to subsection (h), a term in an agreement between an account debtor and an assignor or in a promissory note is ineffective to the extent that it:

(1) prohibits, restricts, or requires the consent of the account debtor or person obligated on the promissory note to the assignment or transfer of, or the creation, attachment, perfection, or enforcement of a security interest in, the account, chattel paper, payment intangible, or promissory note; or

(2) provides that the assignment or transfer or the creation, attachment, perfection, or enforcement of the security interest may give rise to a default, breach, right of recoupment, claim, defense, termination, right of termination, or remedy under the account, chattel paper, payment intangible, or promissory note.

(e) [Inapplicability of subsection (d) to certain sales.] Subsection (d) does not apply to the sale of a payment intangible or promissory note, other than a sale pursuant to a disposition under Section 9-610 or an acceptance of collateral under Section 9-620.

(f) [Legal restrictions on assignment generally ineffective.] Except as otherwise provided in subsection (k) and Sections 2A-303 and 9-407 and subject to subsections (h) and (i), a rule of law, statute, or regulation that prohibits, restricts, or requires the consent of a government, governmental body or official, or account debtor to the assignment or transfer of, or creation of a security interest in, an account or chattel paper is ineffective to the extent that the rule of law, statute, or regulation:

(1) prohibits, restricts, or requires the consent of the government, governmental body or official, or account debtor to the assignment or transfer of, or the creation, attachment, perfection, or enforcement of a security interest in the account or chattel paper; or

(2) provides that the assignment or transfer or the creation, attachment, perfection, or enforcement of the security interest may give rise to a default, breach, right of recoupment, claim, defense, termination, right of termination, or remedy under the account or chattel paper.

(g) [Subsection (b)(3) not waivable.] Subject to subsections (h) and (l), an account debtor may not waive or vary its option under subsection (b)(3).

(h) [Rule for individual under other law.] This section is subject to law other than this article which establishes a different rule for an account debtor who is an individual and who incurred the obligation primarily for personal, family, or household purposes.

(i) [Inapplicability to health-care-insurance receivable.] This section does not apply to an assignment of a health-care-insurance receivable.

(j) [Section prevails over specified inconsistent law.] This section prevails over any inconsistent provisions of the following statutes, rules, and regulations:

[List here any statutes, rules, and regulations containing provisions inconsistent with this section.]

(k) [Inapplicability to interests in certain entities.] Subsections (d), (f), and (j) do not apply to a security interest in an ownership interest in a general partnership, limited partnership, or limited liability company.

(l) [Inapplicability of certain subsections.] Subsections (a), (b), (c), and (g) do not apply to a controllable account or controllable payment intangible.

Legislative Note: *In 2018, a new subsection (k) was added to Section 9-406. A state that has not previously enacted that subsection should consider doing so in connection with the enactment of the 2022 Amendments.*

States that amend statutes, rules, and regulations to remove provisions inconsistent with this section need not enact subsection (j).

Definitional Cross References:

Account	Section 9-102(a)(2)
Account debtor	Section 9-102(a)(3)
Agreement	Section 1-201(b)(3)
Assignee	Section 9-102(a)(7A)
Assignor	Section 9-102(a)(7B)
Chattel paper	Section 9-102(a)(11)
Collateral	Section 9-102(a)(12)
Controllable account	Section 9-102(a)(27A)
Controllable payment intangible	Section 9-102(a)(27B)
Health-care-insurance receivable	Section 9-102(a)(46)
Negotiable instrument	Section 3-104(a)
Payment intangible	Section 9-102(a)(61)
Person	Section 1-201(b)(27)
Promissory note	Section 9-102(a)(65)
Remedy	Section 1-201(b)(32)
Right	Section 1-201(b)(34)
Sale	Section 2-106(1)
Security interest	Section 1-201(b)(35)
Sign	Section 1-201(b)(37)
State	Section 9-102(a)(77)
Term	Section 1-201(b)(40)

Comment References: 9-109 C15

Official Comment

1. Source. Former Section 9-318(3), (4).

2. Account Debtor's Right to Pay Assignor Until Notification. Subsection (a) provides the general rule concerning an account debtor's right to pay the assignor until the account debtor receives appropriate notification. The revision makes clear that once the account debtor receives the notification, the account debtor cannot discharge its obligation by paying the assignor. It also makes explicit that payment to the assignor before notification, or payment to the assignee after notification, discharges the obligation. No change in meaning from pre-1998 Section 9-318 is intended. Nothing in this section conditions the effectiveness of a notification on the identity of the person who gives it. An account debtor that doubts whether the right to payment has been assigned may avail itself of the procedures in subsection (c). See Comment 4. As to the rights and powers of an assignee generally, see Section 9-102(a)(7A) (defining "assignee"), (7B) (defining "assignor"), and Comment 2.b.1.

An effective notification under subsection (a) must be signed. This requirement normally could be satisfied by sending notification on the notifying person's letterhead or on a form on which the notifying person's name appears. In each case the printed name would be a symbol adopted by the notifying person for the purpose of identifying the person and adopting the notification. See Section 1-201(b)(37) (defining "sign").

Subsection (a) applies only to account debtors on accounts, chattel paper, and payment intangibles. (Section 9-102 defines the term "account debtor" more broadly, to include those obligated on all general intangibles.) Although subsection (a) is more precise than its predecessor, it probably does not change the rule that applied under former Article 9. Former Section 9-318(3) referred to the account debtor's obligation to "pay," indicating that the subsection was limited to account debtors on accounts, chattel paper, and other payment obligations.

3. Limitations on Effectiveness of Notification. Subsection (b) contains some special rules concerning the effectiveness of a notification under subsection (a).

Subsection (b)(1) tracks former Section 9-318(3) by making ineffective a notification that does not reasonably identify the rights assigned. A reasonable identification need not identify the right to payment with specificity, but what is reasonable also is not left to the arbitrary decision of the account debtor. If an account debtor has doubt as to the adequacy of a notification, it may not be safe in disregarding the notification unless it notifies the assignee with reasonable promptness as to the respects in which the account debtor considers the notification defective.

Subsection (b)(2), which is new, applies only to sales of payment intangibles. It makes a notification ineffective to the extent that other law gives effect to an agreement between an account debtor and a seller of a payment intangible that limits the account debtor's duty to pay a person other than the seller. Payment intangibles are substantially less fungible than accounts and chattel paper. In some (e.g., commercial bank loans), account debtors customarily and legitimately expect that they will not be required to pay any person other than the financial institution that has advanced funds.

It has become common in financing transactions to assign interests in a single obligation to more than one assignee.

Requiring an account debtor that owes a single obligation to make multiple payments to multiple assignees would be unnecessarily burdensome. Thus, under subsection (b)(3), an account debtor that is notified to pay an assignee less than the full amount of any installment or other periodic payment has the option to treat the notification as ineffective, ignore the notice, and discharge the assigned obligation by paying the assignor. Some account debtors may not realize that the law affords them the right to ignore certain notices of assignment with impunity. By making the notification ineffective at the account debtor's option, subsection (b)(3) permits an account debtor to pay the assignee in accordance with the notice and thereby to satisfy its obligation *pro tanto*. Under subsection (g), the rights and duties created by subsection (b)(3) cannot be waived or varied.

4. Proof of Assignment. Subsection (c) links payment with discharge, as in subsection (a). It follows former Section 9-318(3) in referring to the right of the account debtor to pay the assignor if the requested proof of assignment is not seasonably forthcoming. Even if the proof is not forthcoming, the notification of assignment would remain effective, so that, in the absence of reasonable proof of the assignment, the account debtor could discharge the obligation by paying either the assignee or the assignor. Of course, if the assignee did not in fact receive an assignment, the account debtor cannot discharge its obligation by paying a putative assignee who is a stranger. The observations in Comment 3 concerning the reasonableness of an identification of a right to payment also apply here. An account debtor that questions the adequacy of proof submitted by an assignee would be well advised to promptly inform the assignee of the defects.

An account debtor may face another problem if its obligation becomes due while the account debtor is awaiting reasonable proof of the assignment that it has requested from the assignee. This section does not excuse the account debtor from timely compliance with its obligations. Consequently, an account debtor that has received a notification of assignment and who has requested reasonable proof of the assignment may discharge its obligation by paying the assignor at the time (or even earlier if reasonably necessary to avoid risk of default) when a payment is due, even if the account debtor has not yet received a response to its request for proof. On the other hand, after requesting reasonable proof of the assignment, an account debtor may not discharge its obligation by paying the assignor substantially in advance of the time that the payment is due unless the assignee has failed to provide the proof seasonably.

5. Contractual Restrictions on Assignment. Pre-1998 Section 9-318(4) rendered ineffective an agreement between an account debtor and an assignor which prohibited assignment of an account (whether outright or to secure an obligation) or prohibited a security assignment of a general intangible for the payment of money due or to become due. Subsection (d) essentially follows pre-1998 Section 9-318(4), but expands the rule of free assignability to chattel paper (subject to Sections 2A-303 and 9-407) and promissory notes and explicitly overrides both restrictions and prohibitions of assignment. The policies underlying the ineffectiveness of contractual restrictions under this section build on common-law developments that essentially have eliminated legal restrictions on assignments of rights to payment as security and other assignments of rights to payment such as accounts and chattel paper. Any that might linger for accounts and chattel paper are addressed by subsection (f). See Comment 6.

The first sentence of subsection (d) ensures that the subsection applies to a negotiable instrument that would be a promissory note but for (i) the exclusion of writings that evidence chattel paper from the definition of "instrument" (Section 9-102(a)(47), as revised in 2022) and (ii) the definition of "promissory note" (Section 9-102(a)(65)) as a subset of "instrument." That sentence also ensures that subsection (d) applies to an obligor on such a negotiable instrument, even though the obligor is not an "account debtor" (Section 9-102(a)(3)). The sentence restores the scope of subsection (d) to apply to all obligations and obligors on chattel paper, as was the case prior to the revision of the definition of "instrument".

Former Section 9-318(4) did not apply to a sale of a payment intangible (as described in the former provision, "a general intangible for money due or to become due") but did apply to an assignment of a payment intangible for security. Subsection (e) continues this approach and also makes subsection (d) inapplicable to sales of promissory notes. Section 9-408 addresses anti-assignment clauses with respect to sales of payment intangibles and promissory notes.

Like former Section 9-318(4), subsection (d) provides that anti-assignment clauses are "ineffective." The quoted term means that the clause is of no effect whatsoever; the clause does not prevent the assignment from taking effect between the parties and the prohibited assignment does not constitute a default under the agreement between the account debtor and assignor. However, subsection (d) does not override terms that do not directly prohibit, restrict, or require consent to an assignment but which might, nonetheless, present a practical impairment of the assignment. Properly read, however, subsection (d) reaches only covenants that prohibit, restrict, or require consents to assignments; it does not override all terms that might "impair" an assignment in fact.

> **Example:** Buyer enters into an agreement with Seller to buy equipment that Seller is to manufacture according to Buyer's specifications. Buyer agrees to make a series of prepayments during the construction process. In return, Seller agrees to set aside the prepaid funds in a special account and to use the funds solely for the manufacture of the designated equipment. Seller also agrees that it will not assign any of its rights under the sale agreement with Buyer. Nevertheless, Seller grants to Secured Party a security interest in its accounts. Seller's anti-assignment agreement is ineffective under subsection (d); its agreement concerning the use of prepaid funds, which is not a restriction or prohibition on assignment, is not. However, if Secured Party notifies Buyer to make all future payments directly to Secured Party, Buyer will be obliged to do so under subsection (a) if it wishes the payments to discharge

its obligation. Unless Secured Party releases the funds to Seller so that Seller can comply with its use-of-funds covenant, Seller will be in breach of that covenant.

In the example, there appears to be a plausible business purpose for the use-of-funds covenant. However, a court may conclude that a covenant with no business purpose other than imposing an impediment to an assignment actually is a direct restriction that is rendered ineffective by subsection (d).

6. Legal Restrictions on Assignment. Former Section 9-318(4), like subsection (d) of this section, addressed only contractual restrictions on assignment. The former section was grounded on the reality that legal, as opposed to contractual, restrictions on assignments of rights to payment had largely disappeared. New subsection (f) codifies this principle of free assignability for accounts and chattel paper. For the most part the discussion of contractual restrictions in Comment 5 applies as well to legal restrictions rendered ineffective under subsection (f).

7. Multiple Assignments. This section, like former Section 9-318, is not a complete codification of the law of assignments of rights to payment. In particular, it is silent concerning many of the ramifications for an account debtor in cases of multiple assignments of the same right. For example, an assignor might assign the same receivable to multiple assignees (which assignments could be either inadvertent or wrongful). Or, the assignor could assign the receivable to assignee-1, which then might reassign it to assignee-2, and so forth. The rights and duties of an account debtor in the face of multiple assignments and in other circumstances not resolved in the statutory text are left to the common-law rules. See, e.g., Restatement (2d), Contracts §§ 338(3), 339. The failure of former Article 9 to codify these rules does not appear to have caused problems.

8. Consumer Account Debtors. Subsection (h) is new. It makes clear that the rules of this section are subject to other law establishing special rules for consumer account debtors.

9. Account Debtors on Health-Care-Insurance Receivables. Subsection (i) also is new. The obligation of an insurer with respect to a health-care-insurance receivable is governed by other law. Section 9-408 addresses contractual and legal restrictions on the assignment of a health-care-insurance receivable.

10. Inapplicability to Certain Ownership Interests. Subsection (k) provides that subsections (d), (f), and (j) do not apply to a security interest in an ownership interest in a limited liability company, limited partnership, or general partnership, regardless of the name of the interest and whether the interest: (i) pertains to economic rights, governance rights, or both; (ii) arises under: (a) an operating agreement, the applicable limited liability company act, or both; or (b) a partnership agreement, the applicable partnership act, or both; or (iii) is owned by: (a) a member of a company or transferee or assignee of a member; or (b) a partner or a transferee or assignee of a partner; or (iv) comprises contractual, property, other rights, or some combination thereof. Ownership interests referred to in subsection (k) include interests in a series of a limited liability company, limited partnership, or general partnership, if the series is a "person" (Section 1-201(b)(27)).

11. Controllable Accounts and Controllable payment intangibles. For controllable accounts and controllable payment intangibles, subsection (l) recognizes that subsections (a), (b), (c) and (g) are replaced by analogous provisions in Section 12-106.

12. "Signed" Replaces "Authenticated." Consistent with the revised definition of "sign" in Section 1-201(b)(37), the cognate term "signed" replaces the reference to "authenticated" in the pre-2022 text of this section.

Section 9-407. Restrictions on Creation or Enforcement of Security Interest in Leasehold Interest or in Lessor's Residual Interest

(a) [Term restricting assignment generally ineffective.] Except as otherwise provided in subsection (b), a term in a lease agreement is ineffective to the extent that it:

(1) prohibits, restricts, or requires the consent of a party to the lease to the assignment or transfer of, or the creation, attachment, perfection, or enforcement of a security interest in an interest of a party under the lease contract or in the lessor's residual interest in the goods; or

(2) provides that the assignment or transfer or the creation, attachment, perfection, or enforcement of the security interest may give rise to a default, breach, right of recoupment, claim, defense, termination, right of termination, or remedy under the lease.

(b) [Effectiveness of certain terms.] Except as otherwise provided in Section 2A-303(7), a term described in subsection (a)(2) is effective to the extent that there is:

(1) a transfer by the lessee of the lessee's right of possession or use of the goods in violation of the term; or

(2) a delegation of a material performance of either party to the lease contract in violation of the term.

(c) [Security interest not material impairment.] The creation, attachment, perfection, or enforcement of a security interest in the lessor's interest under the lease contract or the lessor's residual interest in the goods is not a transfer that materially impairs the lessee's prospect of obtaining return performance or materially changes the duty of or materially increases the burden or risk imposed on the lessee within the purview of Section 2A-303(4) unless, and then only to the extent that, enforcement actually results in a delegation of material performance of the lessor.

Definitional Cross References:

Goods	Section 9-102(a)(44)
Lease	Section 2A-103(1)(j)
Lease agreement	Section 2A-103(1)(k)
Lease contract	Section 2A-103(1)(l)
Leasehold interest	Section 2A-103(1)(m)
Lessee	Section 2A-103(1)(n)
Lessor	Section 2A-103(1)(p)
Lessor's residual interest	Section 2A-103(1)(q)
Party	Section 1-201(b)(26)
Remedy	Section 1-201(b)(32)
Security interest	Section 1-201(b)(35)
Term	Section 1-201(b)(40)

Official Comment

1. Source. Section 2A-303.

2. Restrictions on Assignment Generally Ineffective. Under subsection (a), as under former Section 2A-303(3), a term in a lease agreement which prohibits or restricts the creation of a security interest generally is ineffective. This reflects the general policy of Section 9-406(d) and former Section 9-318(4). This section has been conformed in several respects to analogous provisions in Sections 9-406, 9-408, and 9-409, including the substitution of "ineffective" for "not enforceable" and the substitution of "assignment or transfer of, or the creation, attachment, perfection, or enforcement of a security interest" for "creation or enforcement of a security interest."

3. Exceptions for Certain Transfers and Delegations. Subsection (b) provides exceptions to the general ineffectiveness of restrictions under subsection (a). A term that otherwise is ineffective under subsection (a)(2) is effective to the extent that a lessee transfers its right to possession and use of goods or if either party delegates material performance of the lease contract in violation of the term. However, under subsection (c), as under former Section 2A-303(3), a lessor's creation of a security interest in its interest in a lease contract or its residual interest in the leased goods is not a material impairment under Section 2A-303(4) (former Section 2A-303(5)), absent an actual delegation of the lessor's material performance. The terms of the lease contract determine whether the lessor, in fact, has any remaining obligations to perform. If it does, it is then necessary to determine whether there has been an actual delegation of "material performance." See Section 2A-303, Comments 3 and 4.

Section 9-408. Restrictions on Assignment of Promissory Notes, Health-Care-Insurance Receivables, and Certain General Intangibles Ineffective

(a) [Term restricting assignment generally ineffective.] Except as otherwise provided in subsections (b) and (f), a term in a promissory note or in an agreement between an account debtor and a debtor which relates to a health-care-insurance receivable or a general intangible, including a contract, permit, license, or franchise, and which term prohibits, restricts, or requires the consent of the person obligated on the promissory note or the account debtor to, the assignment or transfer of, or creation, attachment, or perfection of a security interest in, the promissory note, health-care-insurance receivable, or general intangible, is ineffective to the extent that the term:

(1) would impair the creation, attachment, or perfection of a security interest; or

(2) provides that the assignment or the transfer or the creation, attachment, or perfection of the security interest may give rise to a default, breach, right of recoupment, claim, defense, termination, right of termination, or remedy under the promissory note, health-care-insurance receivable, or general intangible.

(b) [Applicability of subsection (a) to sales of certain rights to payment.] Subsection (a) applies to a security interest in a payment intangible or promissory note only if the security interest arises out of a sale of the payment intangible or promissory note, other than a sale pursuant to a disposition under Section 9-610 or an acceptance of collateral under Section 9-620.

(c) [Legal restrictions on assignment generally ineffective.] Except as otherwise provided in subsection (f), a rule of law, statute, or regulation that prohibits, restricts, or requires the consent of a government, governmental body or official, person obligated on a promissory note, or account debtor to the assignment or transfer of, or creation of a security interest in, a promissory note, health-care-insurance receivable, or general intangible, including a contract, permit, license, or franchise between an account debtor and a debtor, is ineffective to the extent that the rule of law, statute, or regulation:

(1) would impair the creation, attachment, or perfection of a security interest; or

(2) provides that the assignment or the transfer or the creation, attachment, or perfection of the security interest may give rise to a default, breach, right of recoupment, claim, defense, termination, right of termination, or remedy under the promissory note, health-care-insurance receivable, or general intangible.

(d) [Limitation on ineffectiveness under subsections (a) and (c).] To the extent that a term in a promissory note or in an agreement between an account debtor and a debtor which relates to a health-care-insurance receivable or general intangible or a rule of law, statute, or regulation described in subsection (c) would be effective under law other than this article but is ineffective under subsection (a) or (c), the creation, attachment, or perfection of a security interest in the promissory note, health-care-insurance receivable, or general intangible:

(1) is not enforceable against the person obligated on the promissory note or the account debtor;

(2) does not impose a duty or obligation on the person obligated on the promissory note or the account debtor;

(3) does not require the person obligated on the promissory note or the account debtor to recognize the security interest, pay or render performance to the secured party, or accept payment or performance from the secured party;

(4) does not entitle the secured party to use or assign the debtor's rights under the promissory note, health-care-insurance receivable, or general intangible, including any related information or materials furnished to the debtor in the transaction giving rise to the promissory note, health-care-insurance receivable, or general intangible;

(5) does not entitle the secured party to use, assign, possess, or have access to any trade secrets or confidential information of the person obligated on the promissory note or the account debtor; and

(6) does not entitle the secured party to enforce the security interest in the promissory note, health-care-insurance receivable, or general intangible.

(e) [Section prevails over specified inconsistent law.] This section prevails over any inconsistent provisions of the following statutes, rules, and regulations:

[List here any statutes, rules, and regulations containing provisions inconsistent with this section.]

(f) [Inapplicability to interests in certain entities.] This section does not apply to a security interest in an ownership interest in a general partnership, limited partnership, or limited liability company.

(g) ["Promissory note."] In this section, "promissory note" includes a negotiable instrument that evidences chattel paper.

Legislative Note: *States that amend statutes, rules, and regulations to remove provisions inconsistent with this section need not enact subsection (e).*

In 2018, a new subsection (f) was added to Section 9-408. A state that has not previously enacted that subsection should consider doing so in connection with the enactment of the 2022 Amendments.

Definitional Cross References:

Account debtor	Section 9-102(a)(3)
Agreement	Section 1-201(b)(3)
Chattel paper	Section 9-102(a)(11)
Contract	Section 1-201(b)(12)
Collateral	Section 9-102(a)(12)
Debtor	Section 9-102(a)(28)
General intangible	Section 9-102(a)(42)
Health-care-insurance receivable	Section 9-102(a)(46)
Negotiable instrument	Section 3-104(a)
Payment intangible	Section 9-102(a)(61)
Person	Section 1-201(b)(27)
Promissory note	Section 9-102(a)(65)
Remedy	Section 1-201(b)(32)
Right	Section 1-201(b)(34)
Sale	Section 2-106(1)
Secured party	Section 9-102(a)(73)
Security interest	Section 1-201(b)(35)
State	Section 9-102(a)(77)
Term	Section 1-201(b)(40)

Official Comment

1. Source. New.

2. Free Assignability. This section makes ineffective any attempt to restrict the assignment of a general intangible, health-care-insurance receivable, or promissory note, whether the restriction appears in the terms of a promissory note or the agreement between an account debtor and a debtor (subsection (a)) or in a rule of law, including a statute or governmental rule or regulation (subsection (c)). This result allows the creation, attachment, and perfection of a security interest in a general intangible, such as an agreement for the nonexclusive license of software, as well as sales of certain receivables, such as a health-care-insurance receivable (which is an "account"), payment intangible, or promissory note, without giving rise to a default or breach by the assignor or from triggering a remedy of the account debtor or person obligated on a promissory note. This enhances the ability of certain debtors to obtain credit. On the other hand, subsection (d) protects the other party—the "account debtor" on a general intangible or the person obligated on a promissory note—from adverse effects arising from the security interest. It leaves the account debtor's or obligated person's rights and obligations unaffected in all material respects if a restriction rendered ineffective by subsection (a) or (c) would be effective under law other than Article 9.

Example 1: A term of an agreement for the nonexclusive license of computer software prohibits the licensee from assigning any of its rights as licensee with respect to the software. The agreement also provides that an attempt to assign rights in violation of the restriction is a default entitling the licensor to terminate the license agreement. The licensee, as debtor, grants to a secured party a security interest in its rights under the license and in the computers in which it is installed. Under this section, the term prohibiting assignment and providing for a default upon an attempted assignment is ineffective to prevent the creation, attachment, or perfection of the security interest or entitle the licensor to terminate the license agreement. However, under subsection (d), the secured party (absent the licensor's agreement) is not entitled to enforce the license or to use, assign, or otherwise enjoy the benefits of the licensed software, and the licensor need not recognize (or pay any attention to) the secured party. Even if the secured party takes possession of the computers on the debtor's default, the debtor would remain free to remove the software from the computer, load it on another computer, and continue to use it, if the license so permits. If the debtor does not remove the software, other law may require the secured party to remove it before disposing of the computer. Disposition of the software with the computer could violate an effective pro\hibition on enforcement of the security interest. See subsection (d).

3. Nature of Debtor's Interest. Neither this section nor any other provision of this Article determines whether a debtor has a property interest. The definition of the term "security interest" provides that it is an "interest in personal property." See Section 1-201(b)(35). Ordinarily, a debtor can create a security interest in collateral only if it has "rights in the collateral." See Section 9-203(b). Other law determines whether a debtor has a property interest ("rights in the collateral") and the nature of that interest. For example, the nonexclusive license addressed in Example 1 may not create any property interest whatsoever in the intellectual property (e.g., copyright) that underlies the license and that effectively enables the licensor to grant the license. The debtor's property interest may be confined solely to its interest in the promises made by the licensor in the license agreement (e.g., a promise not to sue the debtor for its use of the software).

4. Scope: Sales of Payment Intangibles and Other General Intangibles; Assignments Unaffected by This Section. Subsections (a) and (c) render ineffective restrictions on assignments only "to the extent" that the assignments restrict the "creation, attachment, or perfection of a security interest," including sales of payment intangibles and promissory notes. This section does not render ineffective a restriction on an assignment that does not create a security interest. For example, if the debtor in Comment 2, Example 1 purported to assign the license to another entity that would use the computer software itself, other law would govern the effectiveness of the anti-assignment provisions.

Subsection (a) applies to a security interest in payment intangibles only if the security interest arises out of sale of the payment intangibles. Contractual restrictions directed to security interests in payment intangibles which secure an obligation are subject to Section 9-406(d). Subsection (a) also deals with sales of promissory notes which also create security interests. See Section 9-109(a). Subsection (c) deals with all security interests in payment intangibles or promissory notes, whether or not arising out of a sale.

Subsection (a) does not render ineffective any term, and subsection (c) does not render ineffective any law, statute or regulation, that restricts outright sales of general intangibles other than payment intangibles. They deal only with restrictions on security interests. The only sales of general intangibles that create security interests are sales of payment intangibles.

5. Terminology: "Account Debtor"; "Person Obligated on a Promissory Note." This section uses the term "account debtor" as it is defined in Section 9-102. The term refers to the party, other than the debtor, to a general intangible, including a permit, license, franchise, or the like, and the person obligated on a health-care-insurance receivable, which is a type of account. The definition of "account debtor" does not limit the term to persons who are obligated to pay under a general intangible. Rather, the term includes all persons who are obligated on a general intangible, including those who are obligated to render performance in exchange for payment. In some cases, e.g., the creation of a security interest in a franchisee's rights under a franchise agreement, the principal payment obligation may be owed by the debtor (franchisee) to the account debtor (franchisor). This section also refers to a "person obligated on a promissory note," inasmuch as those persons do not fall within the definition of "account debtor."

Example 2: A licensor and licensee enter into an agreement for the nonexclusive license of computer software. The licensee's interest in the license agreement is a general intangible. If the licensee grants to a secured party a security interest in its rights under the license agreement, the licensee is the debtor and the licensor is the account debtor. On the other hand, if the licensor grants to a secured party a security interest in its right to payment (an account) under the license agreement, the licensor is the debtor and the licensee is the account debtor. (This section applies to the security interest in the general intangible but not to the security interest in the account, which is not a health-care-insurance receivable.)

6. Effects on Account Debtors and Persons Obligated on Promissory Notes. Subsections (a) and (c) affect two classes of persons. These subsections affect account debtors on general intangibles and health-care-insurance receivables and persons obligated on promissory notes. Subsection (c) also affects governmental entities that enact or determine rules of law. *However, subsection (d) ensures that these affected persons are not affected adversely.* That provision removes any burdens or adverse effects on these persons for which any rational basis could exist to restrict the effectiveness of an assignment or to exercise any remedies. For this reason, the effects of subsections (a) and (c) are immaterial insofar as those persons are concerned.

Subsection (a) does not override terms that do not directly prohibit, restrict, or require consent to an assignment but which might, nonetheless, present a practical impairment of the assignment. Properly read, however, this section, like Section 9-406(d), reaches only covenants that prohibit, restrict, or require consents to assignments; it does not override all terms that might "impair" an assignment in fact.

Example 3: A licensor and licensee enter into an agreement for the nonexclusive license of valuable business software. The license agreement includes terms (i) prohibiting the licensee from assigning its rights under the license, (ii) prohibiting the licensee from disclosing to anyone certain information relating to the software and the licensor, and (iii) deeming prohibited assignments and prohibited disclosures to be defaults. The licensee wishes to obtain financing and, in exchange, is willing to grant a security interest in its rights under the license agreement. The secured party, reasonably, refuses to extend credit unless the licensee discloses the information that it is prohibited from disclosing under the license agreement. The secured party cannot determine the value of the proposed collateral in the absence of this information. Under this section, the terms of the license prohibiting the assignment (grant of the security interest) and making the assignment a default are ineffective. However, the nondisclosure covenant is not a term that prohibits the assignment or creation of a security interest in the license. Consequently, the nondisclosure term is enforceable even though the practical effect is to restrict the licensee's ability to use its rights under the license agreement as collateral.

The nondisclosure term also would be effective in the factual setting of Comment 2, Example 1. If the secured party's possession of the computers loaded with software would put it in a position to discover confidential information that the debtor was prohibited from disclosing, the licensor should be entitled to enforce its rights against the secured party. Moreover, the licensor could have required the debtor to obtain the secured party's agreement that (i) it would immediately return all copies of software loaded on the computers and that (ii) it would not examine or otherwise acquire any information contained in the software. This section does not prevent an account debtor from protecting by agreement its independent interests that are unrelated to the "creation, attachment, or perfection" of a security interest. In Example 1, moreover, the secured party is not in possession of copies of software by virtue of its security interest or in connection with enforcing its security interest in the debtor's license of the software. Its possession is incidental to its possession of the computers, in which it has a security interest. Enforcing against the secured party a restriction relating to the software in no way interferes with its security interest in the computers.

7. Effect in Assignor's Bankruptcy. This section could have a substantial effect if the assignor enters bankruptcy. Roughly speaking, Bankruptcy Code Section 552 invalidates security interests in property acquired after a bankruptcy petition is filed, except to the extent that the postpetition property constitutes proceeds of prepetition collateral.

Example 4: A debtor is the owner of a cable television franchise that, under applicable law, cannot be assigned without the consent of the municipal franchisor. A lender wishes to extend credit to the debtor, provided that the credit is secured by the debtor's "going business" value. To secure the loan, the debtor grants a security interest in all its existing and after-acquired property. The franchise represents the principal value of the business. The municipality refuses to consent to any assignment for collateral purposes. If other law were given effect, the security interest in the franchise would not attach; and if the debtor were to enter bankruptcy and sell the business, the secured party would receive but a fraction of the business's value. Under this section, however, the security interest would attach to the franchise. As a result, the security interest would attach to the proceeds of any sale of the franchise while a bankruptcy is pending. However, this section would protect the interests of the municipality by preventing the secured party from enforcing its security interest to the detriment of the municipality.

8. Effect Outside of Bankruptcy. The principal effects of this section will take place outside of bankruptcy. Compared to the relatively few debtors that enter bankruptcy, there are many more that do not. By making available previously unavailable property as collateral, this section should enable debtors to obtain additional credit. For purposes of determining whether to extend credit, under some circumstances a secured party may ascribe value to the collateral to which its security interest has attached, even if this section precludes the secured party from enforcing the security interest without the agreement of the account debtor or person obligated on the promissory note. This may be the case where the secured party sees a likelihood of obtaining that agreement in the future. This may also be the case where the secured party anticipates that the collateral will give rise to a type of proceeds as to which this section would not apply.

Example 5: Under the facts of Example 4, the debtor does not enter bankruptcy. Perhaps in exchange for a fee, the municipality agrees that the debtor may transfer the franchise to a buyer. As consideration for the transfer, the debtor receives from the buyer its check for part of the purchase price and its promissory note for the balance. The security interest attaches to the check and promissory note as proceeds. See Section 9-315(a)(2). This section does not apply to the security interest in the check, which is not a promissory note, health-care-insurance receivable, or general intangible. Nor does it apply to the security interest in the promissory note, inasmuch as it was not sold to the secured party.

9. Contrary Federal Law. This section does not override federal law to the contrary. However, it does reflect an important policy judgment that should provide a template for future federal law reforms.

10. Inapplicability to Certain Ownership Interests. This section does not apply to an ownership interest in a limited liability company, limited partnership, or general partnership, regardless of the name of the interest and whether the interest: (i) pertains to economic rights, governance rights, or both; (ii) arises under: (a) an operating agreement, the applicable limited liability company act, or both; or (b) a partnership agreement, the applicable partnership act, or both; or (iii) is owned by: (a) a member of a company or transferee or assignee of a member; or (b) a partner or a transferee or assignee of a partner; or (iv) comprises contractual, property, other rights, or some combination thereof.

11. Applicability to Promissory Notes. Subsection (g) ensures that this section applies to a negotiable instrument that would be a promissory note but for (i) the exclusion of writings that evidence chattel paper from the definition of "instrument" (Section 9-102(a)(47), as revised in 2022) and (ii) the definition of "promissory note" (Section 9-102(a)(65)) as a subset of "instrument." See Section 9-406, Comment 5.

Section 9-409. Restrictions on Assignment of Letter-Of-Credit Rights Ineffective

(a) [Term or law restricting assignment generally ineffective.] A term in a letter of credit or a rule of law, statute, regulation, custom, or practice applicable to the letter of credit which prohibits, restricts, or requires the consent of an applicant, issuer, or nominated person to a beneficiary's assignment of or creation of a security interest in a letter-of-credit right is ineffective to the extent that the term or rule of law, statute, regulation, custom, or practice:

(1) would impair the creation, attachment, or perfection of a security interest in the letter-of-credit right; or

(2) provides that the assignment or the creation, attachment, or perfection of the security interest may give rise to a default, breach, right of recoupment, claim, defense, termination, right of termination, or remedy under the letter-of-credit right.

(b) [Limitation on ineffectiveness under subsection (a).] To the extent that a term in a letter of credit is ineffective under subsection (a) but would be effective under law other than this article or a custom or practice applicable to the letter of credit, to the transfer of a right to draw or otherwise demand performance under the letter of credit, or to the assignment of a right to proceeds of the letter of credit, the creation, attachment, or perfection of a security interest in the letter-of-credit right:

(1) is not enforceable against the applicant, issuer, nominated person, or transferee beneficiary;

(2) imposes no duties or obligations on the applicant, issuer, nominated person, or transferee beneficiary; and

(3) does not require the applicant, issuer, nominated person, or transferee beneficiary to recognize the security interest, pay or render performance to the secured party, or accept payment or other performance from the secured party.

Definitional Cross References:

Applicant	Section 5-102(a)(2)
Beneficiary	Section 5-102(a)(3)
Issuer (letter of credit/ letter-of-credit right)	Section 5-102(a)(9)
Letter of credit	Section 5-102(a)(10)
Letter-of-credit right	Section 9-102(a)(51)
Nominated person	Section 5-102(a)(11)
Proceeds	Section 9-102(a)(64)
Remedy	Section 1-201(b)(32)
Secured party	Section 9-102(a)(73)
Security interest	Section 1-201(b)(35)
Term	Section 1-201(b)(40)

Official Comment

1. Source. New.

2. Purpose and Relevance. This section, patterned on Section 9-408, limits the effectiveness of attempts to restrict the creation, attachment, or perfection of a security interest in letter-of-credit rights, whether the restriction appears in the letter of credit or a rule of law, custom, or practice applicable to the letter of credit. It protects the creation, attachment, and perfection of a security interest while preventing these events from giving rise to a default or breach by the assignor or from triggering a remedy or defense of the issuer or other person obligated on a letter of credit. Letter-of-credit rights are a type of supporting obligation. See Section 9-102. Under Sections 9-203 and 9-308, a security interest in a supporting obligation attaches and is perfected automatically if the security interest in the supported obligation attaches and is perfected. See Section 9-107, Comment 5. The automatic attachment and perfection under Article 9 would be anomalous or misleading if, under other law (e.g., Article 5), a restriction on transfer or assignment were effective to block attachment and perfection.

3. Relationship to Letter-of-Credit Law. Although restrictions on an assignment of a letter of credit are ineffective to prevent creation, attachment, and perfection of a security interest, subsection (b) protects the issuer and other parties from any adverse effects of the security interest by preserving letter-of-credit law and practice that limits the right of a beneficiary to transfer its right to draw or otherwise demand performance (Section 5-112) and limits the obligation of an issuer or nominated person to recognize a beneficiary's assignment of letter-of-credit proceeds (Section 5-114). Thus, this section's treatment of letter-of-credit rights differs from this Article's treatment of instruments and investment property. Moreover, under Section 9-109(c)(4), this Article does not apply to the extent that the rights of a transferee beneficiary or nominated person are independent and superior under Section 5-114, thereby preserving the "independence principle" of letter-of-credit law.

PART 5. FILING

[Subpart 1. Filing Office; Contents and Effectiveness Of Financing Statement]

Section 9-501. Filing Office

(a) Except as otherwise provided in subsection (b), if the local law of this State governs perfection of a security interest or agricultural lien, the office in which to file a financing statement to perfect the security interest or agricultural lien is:

(1) the office designated for the filing or recording of a record of a mortgage on the related real property, if:

(A) the collateral is as-extracted collateral or timber to be cut; or

(B) the financing statement is filed as a fixture filing and the collateral is goods that are or are to become fixtures; or

(2) the office of [] [or any office duly authorized by []], in all other cases, including a case in which the collateral is goods that are or are to become fixtures and the financing statement is not filed as a fixture filing.

(b) The office in which to file a financing statement to perfect a security interest in collateral, including fixtures, of a transmitting utility is the office of []. The financing statement also constitutes a fixture filing as to the collateral indicated in the financing statement which is or to become fixtures.

Legislative Note: *The State should designate the filing office where the brackets appear. The filing office may be that of a governmental official (e.g., the Secretary of State) or a private party that maintains the State's filing system.*

Definitional Cross References:

Agricultural lien	Section 9-102(a)(5)
As-extracted collateral	Section 9-102(a)(6)
Collateral	Section 9-102(a)(12)
Filing office	Section 9-102(a)(37)
Financing statement	Section 9-102(a)(39)
Fixture filing	Section 9-102(a)(40)
Fixtures	Section 9-102(a)(41)
Goods	Section 9-102(a)(44)
Mortgage	Section 9-102(a)(55)
Party	Section 1-201(b)(26)
Record	Section 9-102(a)(70)
Security interest	Section 1-201(b)(35)
State	Section 9-102(a)(77)
Transmitting utility	Section 9-102(a)(81)

Official Comment

1. Source. Derived from former Section 9-401.

2. Where to File. Subsection (a) indicates where in a given State a financing statement is to be filed. Former Article 9 afforded each State three alternative approaches, depending on the extent to which the State desires central filing (usually with the Secretary of State), local filing (usually with a county office), or both. As Comment 1 to former Section 9-401 observed, "The principal advantage of state-wide filing is ease of access to the credit information which the files exist to provide. Consider for example the national distributor who wishes to have current information about the credit standing of the thousands of persons he sells to on credit. The more completely the files are centralized on a state-wide basis, the easier and cheaper it becomes to procure credit information; the more the files are scattered in local filing units, the more burdensome and costly." Local filing increases the net costs of secured transactions also by increasing uncertainty and the number of required filings. Any benefit that local filing may have had in the 1950's is now insubstantial. Accordingly, this Article dictates central filing for most situations, while retaining local filing for real-estate-related collateral and special filing provisions for transmitting utilities.

3. Minerals and Timber. Under subsection (a)(1), a filing in the office where a record of a mortgage on the related real property would be filed will perfect a security interest in as-extracted collateral. Inasmuch as the security interest does not attach until extraction, the filing continues to be effective after extraction. A different result occurs with respect to timber to be cut, however. Unlike as-extracted collateral, standing timber may be goods before it is cut. See Section 9-102 (defining "goods"). Once cut, however, it is no longer timber to be cut, and the filing in the real-property-mortgage office ceases to be effective. The timber then becomes ordinary goods, and filing in the office specified in subsection (a)(2) is necessary for perfection. Note also that after the timber is cut the law of the debtor's location, not the location of the timber, governs perfection under Section 9-301.

4. Fixtures. There are two ways in which a secured party may file a financing statement to perfect a security interest in goods that are or are to become fixtures. It may file in the Article 9 records, as with most other goods. See subsection (a)(2). Or it may file the financing statement as a "fixture filing," defined in Section 9-102, in the office in which a record of a mortgage on the related real property would be filed. See subsection (a)(1)(B).

5. Transmitting Utilities. The usual filing rules do not apply well for a transmitting utility (defined in Section 9-102). Many pre-UCC statutes provided special filing rules for railroads and in some cases for other public utilities, to avoid the requirements for filing with legal descriptions in every county in which such debtors had property. Former Section 9-401(5) recreated and broadened these provisions, and subsection (b) follows this approach. The nature of the debtor will inform persons searching the record as to where to make a search.

A given State's subsection (b) applies only if the local law of that State governs perfection. As to most collateral, perfection by filing is governed by the law of the jurisdiction in which the debtor is located. See Section 9-301(1). However, the law of the jurisdiction in which goods that are or become fixtures are located governs perfection by filing a fixture filing. See Section 9-301(3)(A). As a consequence, filing in the filing office of more than one State may be necessary to perfect a security interest in fixtures collateral of a transmitting utility by filing a fixture filing. See Section 9-301, Comment 5.b.

Section 9-502. Contents of Financing Statement; Record of Mortgage as Financing Statement; Time of Filing Financing Statement

(a) [Sufficiency of financing statement.] Subject to subsection (b), a financing statement is sufficient only if it:

(1) provides the name of the debtor;

(2) provides the name of the secured party or a representative of the secured party; and

(3) indicates the collateral covered by the financing statement.

(b) [Real-property-related financing statements.] Except as otherwise provided in Section 9-501(b), to be sufficient, a financing statement that covers as-extracted collateral or timber to be cut, or which is filed as a fixture filing and covers goods that are or are to become fixtures, must satisfy subsection (a) and also:

(1) indicate that it covers this type of collateral;

(2) indicate that it is to be filed [for record] in the real property records;

(3) provide a description of the real property to which the collateral is related [sufficient to give constructive notice of a mortgage under the law of this State if the description were contained in a record of the mortgage of the real property]; and

(4) if the debtor does not have an interest of record in the real property, provide the name of a record owner.

(c) [Record of mortgage as financing statement.] A record of a mortgage is effective, from the date of recording, as a financing statement filed as a fixture filing or as a financing statement covering as-extracted collateral or timber to be cut only if:

(1) the record indicates the goods or accounts that it covers;

(2) the goods are or are to become fixtures related to the real property described in the record or the collateral is related to the real property described in the record and is as-extracted collateral or timber to be cut;

(3) the record satisfies the requirements for a financing statement in this section, but:

(A) the record need not indicate that it is to be filed in the real property records; and

(B) the record sufficiently provides the name of a debtor who is an individual if it provides the individual name of the debtor or the surname and first personal name of the debtor, even if the debtor is an individual to whom Section 9-503(a)(4) applies; and

(4) the record is [duly] recorded.

(d) [Filing before security agreement or attachment.] A financing statement may be filed before a security agreement is made or a security interest otherwise attaches.

Legislative Note: *Language in brackets is optional. Where the State has any special recording system for real property other than the usual grantor-grantee index (as, for instance, a tract system or a title registration or Torrens system) local adaptations of subsection (b) and Section 9-519(d) and (e) may be necessary. See, e.g., Mass. Gen. Laws Chapter 106, Section 9-410. A State should enact the 2010 amendments to Section 9-502 only if the State enacts Alternative A of the 2010 amendments to Section 9-503.*

Definitional Cross References:

Account	Section 9-102(a)(2)
As-extracted collateral	Section 9-102(a)(6)
Collateral	Section 9-102(a)(12)
Debtor	Section 9-102(a)(28)
Financing statement	Section 9-102(a)(39)
Fixture filing	Section 9-102(a)(40)
Fixtures	Section 9-102(a)(41)
Goods	Section 9-102(a)(44)
Mortgage	Section 9-102(a)(55)
Notice	Section 1-202(a)
Record	Section 9-102(a)(70)
Representative	Section 1-201(b)(33)
Secured party	Section 9-102(a)(73)
Security agreement	Section 9-102(a)(74)
Security interest	Section 1-201(b)(35)
State	Section 9-102(a)(77)

Official Comment

1. Source. Former Section 9-402(1), (5), (6).

2. "Notice Filing." This section adopts the system of "notice filing." What is required to be filed is not, as under pre-UCC chattel mortgage and conditional sales acts, the security agreement itself, but only a simple record providing a limited amount of information (financing statement). The financing statement may be filed before the security interest attaches or thereafter. See subsection (d). See also Section 9-308(a) (contemplating situations in which a financing statement is filed before a security interest attaches).

The notice itself indicates merely that a person may have a security interest in the collateral indicated. Further inquiry from the parties concerned will be necessary to disclose the complete state of affairs. Section 9-210 provides a statutory procedure under which the secured party, at the debtor's request, may be required to make disclosure. However, in many cases, information may be forthcoming without the need to resort to the formalities of that section.

Notice filing has proved to be of great use in financing transactions involving inventory, accounts, and chattel paper, because it obviates the necessity of refiling on each of a series of transactions in a continuing arrangement under which the collateral changes from day to day. However, even in the case of filings that do not necessarily involve a series of transactions (e.g., a loan secured by a single item of equipment), a financing statement is effective to encompass transactions under a security agreement not in existence and not contemplated at the time the notice was filed, if the indication of collateral in the financing statement is sufficient to cover the collateral concerned. Similarly, a financing statement is effective to cover after-acquired property of the type indicated and to perfect with respect to future advances under security agreements, regardless of whether after-acquired property or future advances are mentioned in the financing statement and even if not in the contemplation of the parties at the time the financing statement was authorized to be filed.

3. Debtor's Signature; Required Authorization. Subsection (a) sets forth the simple formal requirements for an effective financing statement. These requirements are: (1) the debtor's name; (2) the name of a secured party or representative of the secured party; and (3) an indication of the collateral.

Whereas former Section 9-402(1) required the debtor's signature to appear on a financing statement, this Article contains no signature requirement. The elimination of the signature requirement facilitates paperless filing. (However, as PEB Commentary No. 15 indicates, a paperless financing statement was sufficient under former Article 9.) Elimination of the signature requirement also makes the exceptions provided by former Section 9-402(2) unnecessary.

The fact that this Article does not require that an authenticating symbol be contained in the public record does not mean that all filings are authorized. Rather, Section 9-509(a) entitles a person to file an initial financing statement, an amendment that adds collateral, or an amendment that adds a debtor only if the debtor authorizes the filing, and Section 9-509(d) entitles a person other than the debtor to file a termination statement only if the secured party of record authorizes the filing. Of course, a filing has legal effect only to the extent it is authorized. See Section 9-510.

Law other than this Article, including the law with respect to ratification of past acts, generally determines whether a person has the requisite authority to file a record under this Article. See Sections 1-103 and 9-509, Comment 3. However, under Section 9-509(b), the debtor's signing of (or becoming bound by) a security agreement *ipso facto* constitutes the debtor's authorization of the filing of a financing statement covering the collateral described in the security agreement. The secured party need not obtain a separate authorization.

Section 9-625 provides a remedy for unauthorized filings. Making an unauthorized filing also may give rise to civil or criminal liability under other law. In addition, this Article contains provisions that assist in the discovery of unauthorized filings and the amelioration of their practical effect. For example, Section 9-518 provides a procedure whereby a person may add to the public record a statement to the effect that a financing statement indexed under the person's name was wrongfully filed, and Section 9-509(d) entitles any person to file a termination statement if the secured party of record fails to comply with its obligation to file or send one to the debtor, the debtor authorizes the filing, and the termination statement so indicates. However, the filing office is neither obligated nor permitted to inquire into issues of authorization. See Section 9-520(a).

4. Certain Other Requirements. Subsection (a) deletes other provisions of former Section 9-402(1) because they seems unwise (real-property description for financing statements covering crops), unnecessary (adequacy of copies of financing statements), or both (copy of security agreement as financing statement). In addition, the filing office must reject a financing statement lacking certain other information formerly required as a condition of perfection (e.g., an address for the debtor or secured party). See Sections 9-516(b), 9-520(a). However, if the filing office accepts the record, it is effective nevertheless. See Section 9-520(c).

5. Real-Property-Related Filings. Subsection (b) contains the requirements for financing statements filed as fixture filings and financing statements covering timber to be cut or minerals and minerals-related accounts constituting as-extracted collateral. A description of the related real property must be sufficient to reasonably identify it. See Section 9-108. This formulation rejects the view that the real property description must be by metes and bounds, or otherwise conforming to traditional real-property practice in conveyancing, but, of course, the incorporation of such a description by reference to the recording data of a deed, mortgage or other instrument containing the description should suffice under the most stringent standards. The proper test is that a description of real property must be sufficient so that the financing statement will fit into the real-property search system and be found by a real-property searcher. Under the optional language in subsection (b)(3), the test of adequacy of the description is whether it would be adequate in a record of a mortgage of the real property. As suggested in the Legislative Note, more detail may be required if there is a tract indexing system or a land registration system.

If the debtor does not have an interest of record in the real property, a real-property-related financing statement must show the name of a record owner, and Section 9-519(d) requires the financing statement to be indexed in the name of that owner. This requirement also enables financing statements covering as-extracted collateral or timber to be cut and financing statements filed as fixture filings to fit into the real-property search system.

6. Record of Mortgage Effective as Financing Statement. Subsection (c) explains when a record of a mortgage is effective as a financing statement filed as a fixture filing or to cover timber to be cut or as-extracted collateral. Use of the term "record of a mortgage" recognizes that in some systems the record actually filed is not the record pursuant to which a mortgage is created. Moreover, "mortgage" is defined in Section 9-102 as an "interest in real property," not as the record that creates or evidences the mortgage or the record that is filed in the public recording systems. A record creating a mortgage may also create a security interest with respect to fixtures (or other goods) in conformity with this Article. A single agreement creating a mortgage on real property and a security interest in chattels is common and useful for certain purposes. Under subsection (c), the recording of the record evidencing a mortgage (if it satisfies the requirements for a financing statement) constitutes the filing of a financing statement as to the fixtures (but not, of course, as to other goods). Section 9-515(g) makes the usual five-year maximum life for financing statements inapplicable to mortgages that operate as fixture filings under Section 9-502(c). Such mortgages are effective for the duration of the real-property recording.

Of course, if a combined mortgage covers chattels that are not fixtures, a regular financing statement filing is necessary with respect to the chattels, and subsection (c) is inapplicable. Likewise, a financing statement filed as a "fixture filing" is not effective to perfect a security interest in personal property other than fixtures.

In some cases it may be difficult to determine whether goods are or will become fixtures. Nothing in this Part prohibits the filing of a "precautionary" fixture filing, which would provide protection in the event goods are determined to be fixtures. The fact of filing should not be a factor in the determining whether goods are fixtures. Cf. Section 9-505(b).

Section 9-503. Name of Debtor and Secured Party

(a) [Sufficiency of debtor's name.] A financing statement sufficiently provides the name of the debtor:

(1) except as otherwise provided in paragraph (3), if the debtor is a registered organization or the collateral is held in a trust that is a registered organization, only if the financing statement provides the name that is stated to be the registered organization's name on the public organic record most recently filed with or issued or enacted by the registered organization's jurisdiction of organization which purports to state, amend, or restate the registered organization's name;

(2) subject to subsection (f), if the collateral is being administered by the personal representative of a decedent, only if the financing statement provides, as the name of the debtor, the name of the decedent and, in a separate part of the financing statement, indicates that the collateral is being administered by a personal representative;

(3) if the collateral is held in a trust that is not a registered organization, only if the financing statement:

(A) provides, as the name of the debtor:

(i) if the organic record of the trust specifies a name for the trust, the name specified; or

(ii) if the organic record of the trust does not specify a name for the trust, the name of the settlor or testator; and

(B) in a separate part of the financing statement:

(i) if the name is provided in accordance with subparagraph (A)(i), indicates that the collateral is held in a trust; or

(ii) if the name is provided in accordance with subparagraph (A)(ii), provides additional information sufficient to distinguish the trust from other trusts having one or more of the same settlors or the same testator and indicates that the collateral is held in a trust, unless the additional information so indicates;

ALTERNATIVE A

(4) subject to subsection (g), if the debtor is an individual to whom this State has issued a [driver's license] that has not expired, only if the financing statement provides the name of the individual which is indicated on the [driver's license];

(5) if the debtor is an individual to whom paragraph (4) does not apply, only if the financing statement provides the individual name of the debtor or the surname and first personal name of the debtor; and

(6) in other cases:

(A) if the debtor has a name, only if the financing statement provides the organizational name of the debtor; and

(B) if the debtor does not have a name, only if it provides the names of the partners, members, associates, or other persons comprising the debtor, in a manner that each name provided would be sufficient if the person named were the debtor.

(b) [Additional debtor-related information.] A financing statement that provides the name of the debtor in accordance with subsection (a) is not rendered ineffective by the absence of:

(1) a trade name or other name of the debtor; or

(2) unless required under subsection (a)(6)(B), names of partners, members, associates, or other persons comprising the debtor.

ALTERNATIVE B

(4) if the debtor is an individual, only if the financing statement:

(A) provides the individual name of the debtor;

(B) provides the surname and first personal name of the debtor; or

(C) subject to subsection (g), provides the name of the individual which is indicated on a [driver's license] that this State has issued to the individual and which has not expired; and

(5) in other cases:

(A) if the debtor has a name, only if the financing statement provides the organizational name of the debtor; and

(B) if the debtor does not have a name, only if the financing statement provides the names of the partners, members, associates, or other persons comprising the debtor, in a manner that each name provided would be sufficient if the person named were the debtor.

(b) [Additional debtor-related information.] A financing statement that provides the name of the debtor in accordance with subsection (a) is not rendered ineffective by the absence of:

(1) a trade name or other name of the debtor; or

(2) unless required under subsection (a)(5)(B), names of partners, members, associates, or other persons comprising the debtor.

END OF ALTERNATIVES

(c) [Debtor's trade name insufficient.] A financing statement that provides only the debtor's trade name does not sufficiently provide the name of the debtor.

(d) [Representative capacity.] Failure to indicate the representative capacity of a secured party or representative of a secured party does not affect the sufficiency of a financing statement.

(e) [Multiple debtors and secured parties.] A financing statement may provide the name of more than one debtor and the name of more than one secured party.

(f) [Name of decedent.] The name of the decedent indicated on the order appointing the personal representative of the decedent issued by the court having jurisdiction over the collateral is sufficient as the "name of the decedent" under subsection (a)(2).

ALTERNATIVE A

(g) [Multiple driver's licenses.] If this State has issued to an individual more than one [driver's license] of a kind described in subsection (a)(4), the one that was issued most recently is the one to which subsection (a)(4) refers.

ALTERNATIVE B

(g) [Multiple driver's licenses.] If this State has issued to an individual more than one [driver's license] of a kind described in subsection (a)(4)(C), the one that was issued most recently is the one to which subsection (a)(4)(C) refers.

END OF ALTERNATIVES

(h) [Definition.] In this section, the "name of the settlor or testator" means:

(1) if the settlor is a registered organization, the name that is stated to be the settlor's name on the public organic record most recently filed with or issued or enacted by the settlor's jurisdiction of organization which purports to state, amend, or restate the settlor's name; or

(2) in other cases, the name of the settlor or testator indicated in the trust's organic record.

Legislative Note:

1. *This Act contains two alternative sets of amendments relating to the names of individual debtors. A State should enact the same Alternative, A or B, for both subsections (a) and (i) of Section 9-503. A State that enacts Alternative A of the amendments to this section should also enact the amendments to Section 9-502.*

2. *Both Alternatives refer, in part, to the name as shown on a debtor's driver's license. The Legislature should be aware that, in some States, certain characters that may be used by the State's department of motor vehicles (or similar agency) in the name on a driver's license may not be accepted by the State's central or local UCC filing offices under current regulations or internal protocols. This may occur because of technological limitations of the filing offices or merely as a result of inconsistent procedures. Similar issues may exist for field sizes as well. In these situations, perfection of a security interest granted by a debtor with such a driver's license may be impossible under Alternative A of the amendments and the utility of Alternative B, under which the name on the driver's license is one of the names that is sufficient, may be reduced. Accordingly, the State may wish to determine if one or more of these issues exist and, if so, to make certain that such issues have been resolved. A successful resolution might be accomplished by statute, agency regulation, or technological change effectuated before or as part of the enactment of this Act.*

3. *Regardless of which Alternative is enacted, in States in which a single agency issues driver's licenses*

and non-driver identification cards as an alternative to a driver's license, such that at any given time an individual may hold either a driver's license or an identification card but not both, the State should replace each use of the term "driver's license" with a phrase meaning "driver's license or identification card" but containing the analogous terms used in the enacting State. In other States, the State should replace the term "driver's license" with the analogous term used in the enacting State.

Definitional Cross References:

Debtor	Section 9-102(a)(28)
Document	Section 9-102(a)(30)
Financing statement	Section 9-102(a)(39)
Jurisdiction of organization	Section 9-102(a)(50)
Organization	Section 1-201(b)(25)
Person	Section 1-201(b)(27)
Public organic record	Section 9-102(a)(68)
Record	Section 9-102(a)(70)
Registered organization	Section 9-102(a)(71)
Representative	Section 1-201(b)(33)
Secured party	Section 9-102(a)(73)

Official Comment

1. Source. Subsections (a)(4)(A), (b), and (c) derive from former Section 9-402(7); otherwise, new.

2. Debtor's Name. The requirement that a financing statement provide the debtor's name is particularly important. Financing statements are indexed under the name of the debtor, and those who wish to find financing statements search for them under the debtor's name. Subsection (a) explains what the debtor's name is for purposes of a financing statement.

a. Registered Organizations. As a general matter, if the debtor is a "registered organization" (defined in Section 9-102 so as to ordinarily include corporations, limited partnerships, limited liability companies, and statutory trusts), then the debtor's name is the name shown on the public organic record" of the debtor's "jurisdiction of organization" (both also defined in Section 9-102).

b. Collateral Held in a Trust. When a financing statement covers collateral that is held in a trust that is a registered organization, subsection (a)(1) governs the name of the debtor. If, however, the collateral is held in a trust that is not a registered organization, subsection (a)(3) applies. (As used in this Article, collateral "held in a trust" includes collateral as to which the trust is the debtor as well as collateral as to which the trustee is the debtor.) This subsection adopts a convention that generally results in the name of the trust or the name of the trust's settlor being provided as the name of the debtor on the financing statement, even if, as typically is the case with common-law trusts, the "debtor" (defined in Section 9-102) is a trustee acting with respect to the collateral. This convention provides more accurate information and eases the burden for searchers, who otherwise would have difficulty with respect to debtor trustees that are large financial institutions.

More specifically, if a trust's organic record specifies a name for the trust, subsection (a)(3) requires the financing statement to provide, as the name of the debtor, the name for the trust specified in the organic record. In addition, the financing statement must indicate, in a separate part of the financing statement, that the collateral is held in a trust.

If the organic record of the trust does not specify a name for the trust, the name required for the financing statement is the name of the settlor or, in the case of a testamentary trust, the testator, in each case as determined under subsection (h). In addition, the financing statement must provide sufficient additional information to distinguish the trust from other trusts having one or more of the same settlors or the same testator. In many cases an indication of the date on which the trust was settled will satisfy this requirement. If neither the name nor the additional information indicates that the collateral is held in a trust, the financing statement must indicate that fact, but not as part of the debtor's name.

Neither the indication that the collateral is held in a trust nor the additional information that distinguishes the trust from other trusts having one or more of the same settlors or the same testator is part of the debtor's name. Nevertheless, a financing statement that fails to provide, in a separate part of the financing statement, any required indication or additional information does not sufficiently provide the name of the debtor under Sections 9-502(a) and 9-503(a)(3), does not "substantially satisfy[] the requirements" of Part 5 within the meaning of Section 9-506(a), and so is ineffective.

c. Collateral Administered by a Personal Representative. Subsection (a)(2) deals with collateral that is being administered by an executor, administrator, or other personal representative of a decedent. Even if, as often is the case, the representative is the "debtor" (defined in Section 9-102), the financing statement must provide the name of the decedent as the name of the debtor. Subsection (f) provides a safe harbor, under which the name of the decedent indicated on the order appointing the personal representative issued by the court having jurisdiction over the collateral is sufficient as the name of the decedent. If the order indicates more than one name for the decedent, the first name in the list qualifies under subsection (f); however, other names in the list also may qualify as the "name of the decedent" within the meaning of subsection (a)(2). In addition to providing the name of the decedent, the financing statement must indicate, in a separate part of the financing statement, that the collateral is being administered by a personal representative. Although the indication is not part of the debtor's name, a financing statement that fails to provide the indication does not sufficiently provide the name of the debtor under Sections 9-502(a) and 9-503(a)(2), does not "substantially satisfy[] the requirements" of Part 5 within the meaning of Section 9-506(a), and so is ineffective.

d. Individuals. This Article provides alternative approaches towards the requirement for providing the name of a debtor who is an individual.

Alternative A. Alternative A distinguishes between two groups of individual debtors. For debtors holding an unexpired driver's license issued by the State where the financing statement is filed (ordinarily the State where the debtor maintains the debtor's principal residence), Alternative A requires that a financing statement provide the name indicated on the license. When a debtor does not hold an unexpired driver's license issued by the relevant State, the requirement can be satisfied in either of two ways. A financing statement is sufficient if it provides the "individual name" of the debtor. Alternatively, a financing statement is sufficient if it provides the debtor's surname (i.e., family name) and first personal name (i.e., first name other than the surname).

Alternative B. Alternative B provides three ways in which a financing statement may sufficiently provide the name of an individual who is a debtor. The "individual name" of the debtor is sufficient, as is the debtor's surname and first personal name. If the individual holds an unexpired driver's license issued by the State where the financing statement is filed (ordinarily the State of the debtor's principal residence), the name indicated on the driver's license also is sufficient.

Name indicated on the driver's license. A financing statement does not "provide the name of the individual which is indicated" on the debtor's driver's license unless the name it provides is the same as the name indicated on the license. This is the case even if the name indicated on the debtor's driver's license contains an error.

> **Example 1**: Debtor, an individual whose principal residence is in Illinois, grants a security interest to SP in certain business equipment. SP files a financing statement with the Illinois filing office. The financing statement provides the name appearing on Debtor's Illinois driver's license, "Joseph Allan Jones." Regardless of which Alternative is in effect in Illinois, this filing would be sufficient under Illinois' Section 9-503(a), even if Debtor's correct middle name is Alan, not Allan.

A filing against "Joseph A. Jones" or "Joseph Jones" would not "provide the name of the individual which is indicated" on the debtor's driver's license. However, these filings might be sufficient if Alternative A is in effect in Illinois and Jones has no current (i.e., unexpired) Illinois driver's license, or if Illinois has enacted Alternative B.

Determining the name that should be provided on the financing statement must not be done mechanically. The order in which the components of an individual's name appear on a driver's license differs among the States. Had the debtor in Example 1 obtained a driver's license from a different State, the license might have indicated the name as "Jones Joseph Allan." Regardless of the order on the driver's license, the debtor's surname must be provided in the part of the financing statement designated for the surname.

Alternatives A and B both refer to a license issued by "this State." Perfection of a security interest by filing ordinarily is determined by the law of the jurisdiction in which the debtor is located. See Section 9-301(1). (Exceptions to the general rule are found in Section 9-301(3) and (4), concerning fixture filings, timber to be cut, and as-extracted collateral.) A debtor who is an individual ordinarily is located at the individual's principal residence. See Section 9-307(b). (An exception appears in Section 9-307(c).) Thus, a given State's Section 9-503 ordinarily will apply during any period when the debtor's principal residence is located in that State, even if during that time the debtor holds or acquires a driver's license from another State.

When a debtor's principal residence changes, the location of the debtor under Section 9-307 also changes and perfection by filing ordinarily will be governed by the law of the debtor's new location. As a consequence of the application of that jurisdiction's Section 9-316, a security interest that is perfected by filing under the law of the debtor's former location will remain perfected for four months after the relocation, and thereafter if the secured party perfects under the law of the debtor's new location. Likewise, a financing statement filed in the former location may be effective to perfect a security interest that attaches after the debtor relocates. See Section 9-316(h).

Individual name of the debtor. Article 9 does not determine the "individual name" of a debtor. Nor does it determine which element or elements in a debtor's name constitute the surname. In some cases, determining the "individual name" of a debtor may be difficult, as may determining the debtor's surname. This is because in the case of individuals, unlike registered organizations, there is no public organic record to which reference can be made and from which the name and its components can be definitively determined.

Names can take many forms in the United States. For example, whereas a surname is often colloquially referred to as a "last name," the sequence in which the elements of a name are presented is not determinative. In some cultures, the surname appears first, while in others it may appear in a location that is neither first nor last. In addition, some surnames are composed of multiple elements that, taken together, constitute a single surname. These elements may or may not be separated by a space or connected by a hyphen, "i," or "y." In other instances, some or all of the same elements may not be part of the surname. In some cases, a debtor's entire name might be composed of only a single element, which should be provided in the part of the financing statement designated for the surname.

In disputes as to whether a financing statement sufficiently provides the "individual name" of a debtor, a court should refer to any non-UCC law concerning names. However, case law about names may have developed in contexts that implicate policies different from those of Article 9. A court considering an individual's name for purposes of determining the sufficiency of a financing statement is not necessarily bound by cases that were decided in other contexts and for other purposes.

Individuals are asked to provide their names on official documents such as tax returns and bankruptcy petitions. An individual may provide a particular name on an official document in response to instructions relating to the document rather than because the name is actually the individual's name. Accordingly, a court should not assume that the name an individual provides on an official document necessarily constitutes the "individual name" for purposes of the sufficiency of the debtor's name on a financing statement. Likewise, a court should not assume that the name as presented on an individual's birth certificate is necessarily the individual's current name.

In applying non-UCC law for purposes of determining the sufficiency of a debtor's name on a financing statement, a court should give effect to the instruction in Section 1-103(a)(1) that the UCC "must be liberally construed and applied to promote its underlying purposes and policies," which include simplifying and clarifying the law governing commercial transactions. Thus, determination of a debtor's name in the context of the Article 9 filing system must take into account the needs of both filers and searchers. Filers need a simple and predictable system in which they can have a reasonable degree of confidence that, without undue burden, they can determine a name that will be sufficient so as to permit their financing statements to be effective. Likewise, searchers need a simple and predictable system in which they can have a reasonable degree of confidence that, without undue burden, they will discover all financing statements pertaining to the debtor in question. The court also should take into account the purpose of the UCC to make the law uniform among the various jurisdictions. See Section 1-103(a)(3).

Of course, once an individual debtor's name has been determined to be sufficient for purposes of Section 9-503, a financing statement that provides a variation of that name, such as a "nickname" that does not constitute the debtor's name, does not sufficiently provide the name of the debtor under this section. Cf. Section 9-503(c) (a financing statement providing only a debtor's trade name is not sufficient).

If there is any doubt about an individual debtor's name, a secured party may choose to file one or more financing statements that provide a number of possible names for the debtor and a searcher may similarly choose to search under a number of possible names.

Note that, even if the name provided in an initial financing statement is correct, the filing office nevertheless must reject the financing statement if it does not identify an individual debtor's surname (e.g., if it is not clear whether the debtor's surname is Perry or Mason). See Section 9-516(b)(3)(C).

3. Secured Party's Name. New subsection (d) makes clear that when the secured party is a representative, a financing statement is sufficient if it names the secured party, whether or not it indicates any representative capacity. Similarly, a financing statement that names a representative of the secured party is sufficient, even if it does not indicate the representative capacity.

> **Example 2:** Debtor creates a security interest in favor of Bank X, Bank Y, and Bank Z, but not to their representative, the collateral agent (Bank A). The collateral agent is not itself a secured party. See Section 9-102. Under Sections 9-502(a) and 9-503(d), however, a financing statement is effective if it names as secured party Bank A and not the actual secured parties, even if it omits Bank A's representative capacity.

Each person whose name is provided in an initial financing statement as the name of the secured party or representative of the secured party is a secured party of record. See Section 9-511.

4. Multiple Names. Subsection (e) makes explicit what is implicit under former Article 9: a financing statement may provide the name of more than one debtor and secured party. See Section 1-106 (words in the singular include the plural). With respect to records relating to more than one debtor, see Section 9-520(d). With respect to financing statements providing the name of more than one secured party, see Sections 9-509(e) and 9-510(b).

Section 9-504. Indication of Collateral

A financing statement sufficiently indicates the collateral that it covers if the financing statement provides:

(1) a description of the collateral pursuant to Section 9-108; or

(2) an indication that the financing statement covers all assets or all personal property.

Definitional Cross References:

Collateral	Section 9-102(a)(12)
Financing statement	Section 9-102(a)(39)

Official Comment

1. Source. Former Section 9-402(1).

2. Indication of Collateral. To comply with Section 9-502(a), a financing statement must "indicate" the collateral it covers. A financing statement sufficiently indicates collateral claimed to be covered by the financing statement if it satisfies the purpose of conditioning perfection on the filing of a financing statement, i.e., if it provides notice that a person may have a security interest in the collateral claimed. See Section 9-502, Comment 2. In particular, an indication of collateral that would have satisfied the requirements of former Section 9-402(1) (i.e., a "statement indicating the types, or describing the items, of collateral") suffices under Section 9-502(a). An indication may satisfy the requirements of Section 9-502(a), even if it would not have satisfied the requirements of former Section 9-402(1). A financing statement (including any attachments) that does not itself supply information satisfying Section(a)(3) or Section 9-504(a), but, rather, refers solely to a record not attached to the financing statement for information seeking to satisfy those provisions, does not satisfy the sufficiency requirement of Section 9-502(a)(3) that the financing statement indicate the collateral that it covers. See PEB Commentary No. 26, dated August 12, 2022. The Commentary is available at https://www.ali.org/peb-ucc.

This section provides two safe harbors. Under paragraph (1), a "description" of the collateral (as the term is explained in Section 9-108) suffices as an indication for purposes of the sufficiency of a financing statement.

Debtors sometimes create a security interest in all, or substantially all, of their assets. To accommodate this practice, paragraph (2) expands the class of sufficient collateral references to embrace "an indication that the financing statement covers all assets or all personal property." If the property in question belongs to the debtor and is personal property, any searcher will know that the property is covered by the financing statement. Of course, regardless of its breadth, a financing statement has no effect with respect to property indicated but to which a security interest has not attached. Note that a broad statement of this kind (e.g., "all debtor's personal property") would not be a sufficient "description" for purposes of a security agreement. See Sections 9-203(b)(3)(A), 9-108. It follows that a somewhat narrower description than "all assets," e.g., "all assets other than automobiles," is sufficient for purposes of this section, even if it does not suffice for purposes of a security agreement.

Section 9-505. Filing and Compliance with Other Statutes and Treaties for Consignments, Leases, Other Bailments, and Other Transactions

(a) [Use of terms other than "debtor" and "secured party."] A consignor, lessor, or other bailor of goods, a licensor, or a buyer of a payment intangible or promissory note may file a financing statement, or may comply with a statute or treaty described in Section 9-311(a), using the terms "consignor", "consignee", "lessor", "lessee", "bailor", "bailee", "licensor", "licensee", "owner", "registered owner", "buyer", "seller", or words of similar import, instead of the terms "secured party" and "debtor".

(b) [Effect of financing statement under subsection (a).] This part applies to the filing of a financing statement under subsection (a) and, as appropriate, to compliance that is equivalent to filing a financing statement under Section 9-311(b), but the filing or compliance is not of itself a factor in determining whether the collateral secures an obligation. If it is determined for another reason that the collateral secures an obligation, a security interest held by the consignor, lessor, bailor, licensor, owner, or buyer which attaches to the collateral is perfected by the filing or compliance.

Definitional Cross References:

Collateral	Section 9-102(a)(12)
Consignee	Section 9-102(a)(19)
Consignment	Section 9-102(a)(20)
Consignor	Section 9-102(a)(21)
Debtor	Section 9-102(a)(28)
Financing statement	Section 9-102(a)(39)
Goods	Section 9-102(a)(44)
Lease	Section 2A-103(1)(j)
Lessee	Section 2A-103(1)(n)
Lessor	Section 2A-103(1)(p)
Payment intangible	Section 9-102(a)(61)
Promissory note	Section 9-102(a)(65)
Secured party	Section 9-102(a)(73)
Security interest	Section 1-201(b)(35)
Term	Section 1-201(b)(40)

Official Comment

1. Source. Former Section 9-408.

2. Precautionary Filing. Occasionally, doubts arise concerning whether a transaction creates a relationship to which this Article or its filing provisions apply. For example, questions may arise over whether a "lease" of equipment in fact creates a security interest or whether the "sale" of payment intangibles in fact secures an obligation, thereby requiring action to perfect the security interest. This section, which derives from former Section 9-408, affords the option of filing of a financing statement with appropriate changes of terminology but without affecting the substantive question of classification of the transaction.

3. Changes from Former Section 9-408. This section expands the rule of former Section 9-408 to embrace more generally other bailments and transactions, as well as sales transactions, primarily sales of payment intangibles and promissory notes. It provides the same benefits for compliance with a statute or treaty described in Section 9-311(a) that former Section 9-408 provided for filing, in connection with the use of terms such as "lessor," consignor," etc. The references to "owner" and "registered owner" are intended to address, for example, the situation where a putative lessor is the registered owner of an automobile covered by a certificate of title and the transaction is determined to create a security interest. Although this section provides that the security interest is perfected, the relevant certificate-of-title statute may expressly provide to the contrary or may be ambiguous. If so, it may be necessary or advisable to amend the certificate-of-title statute to ensure that perfection of the security interest will be achieved.

As did former Section 1-201, pre-1998 Article 9 referred to transactions, including leases and consignments, "intended as security." This misleading phrase created the erroneous impression that the parties to a transaction can dictate how the law will classify it (e.g., as a bailment or as a security interest) and thus affect the rights of third parties. This Article deletes the phrase wherever it appears. Subsection (b) expresses the principle more precisely by referring to a security interest that "secures an obligation."

4. Consignments. Although a "true" consignment is a bailment, the filing and priority provisions of former Article 9 applied to "true" consignments. See former Sections 2-326(3), 9-114. A consignment "intended as security" created a security interest that was in all respects subject to former Article 9. This Article subsumes most true consignments under the rubric of "security interest." See Sections 9-102 (definition of "consignment"), 9-109(a)(4), 1-201(b)(35) (definition of "security interest"). Nevertheless, it maintains the distinction between a (true) "consignment," as to which only certain aspects of Article 9 apply, and a so-called consignment that actually "secures an obligation," to which Article 9 applies in full. The revisions to this section reflect the change in terminology.

Section 9-506. Effect of Errors or Omissions

(a) [Minor errors and omissions.] A financing statement substantially satisfying the requirements of this part is effective, even if it has minor errors or omissions, unless the errors or omissions make the financing statement seriously misleading.

(b) [Financing statement seriously misleading.] Except as otherwise provided in subsection (c), a financing statement that fails sufficiently to provide the name of the debtor in accordance with Section 9-503(a) is seriously misleading.

(c) [Financing statement not seriously misleading.] If a search of the records of the filing office under the debtor's correct name, using the filing office's standard search logic, if any, would disclose a financing statement that fails sufficiently to provide the name of the debtor in accordance with Section 9-503(a), the name provided does not make the financing statement seriously misleading.

(d) ["Debtor's correct name."] For purposes of Section 9-508(b), the "debtor's correct name" in subsection (c) means the correct name of the new debtor.

Definitional Cross References:

Debtor	Section 9-102(a)(28)
Filing office	Section 9-102(a)(37)
Financing statement	Section 9-102(a)(39)
New debtor	Section 9-102(a)(56)
Record	Section 9-102(a)(70)

Official Comment

1. Source. Former Section 9-402(8).

2. Errors and Omissions. Like former Section 9-402(8), subsection (a) is in line with the policy of this Article to simplify formal requisites and filing requirements. It is designed to discourage the fanatical and impossibly refined reading of statutory requirements in which courts occasionally have indulged themselves. Subsection (a) provides the standard applicable to indications of collateral. Subsections (b) and (c), which are new, concern the effectiveness of financing statements in which the debtor's name is incorrect. Subsection (b) contains the general rule: a financing statement that fails sufficiently to provide the debtor's name in accordance with Section 9-503(a) is seriously misleading as a matter of law. Subsection (c) provides an exception: If the financing statement nevertheless would be discovered in a search under the debtor's correct name, using the filing office's standard search logic, if any, then as a matter of law the incorrect name does not make the financing statement seriously misleading. A financing statement that is seriously misleading under this section is ineffective even if it is disclosed by (i) using a search logic other than that of the filing office to search the official records, or (ii) using the filing office's standard search logic to search a data base other than that of the filing office. For purposes of subsection (c), any name that satisfies Section 9-503(a) at the time of the search is a "correct name."

This section and Section 9-503 balance the interests of filers and searchers. Searchers are not expected to ascertain nicknames, trade names, and the like by which the debtor may be known and then search under each of them. Rather, it is the secured party's responsibility to provide the name of the debtor sufficiently in a filed financing statement. Subsection (c) sets forth the only situation in which a financing statement that fails sufficiently to provide the name of the debtor is not seriously misleading. As stated in subsection (b), if the name of the debtor provided on a financing statement is insufficient and subsection (c) is not satisfied, the financing statement is seriously misleading. Such a financing statement is ineffective even if the debtor is known in some contexts by the name provided on the financing statement and even if searchers know or have reason to know that the name provided on the financing statement refers to the debtor. Any suggestion to the contrary in a judicial opinion is incorrect.

To satisfy the requirements of Section 9-503(a)(2), a financing statement must indicate that the collateral is being administered by a personal representative. To satisfy the requirements of Section 9-503(a)(3), a financing statement must indicate that the collateral is held in a trust and provide additional information that distinguishes the trust from certain other trusts. The indications and additional information are not part of the debtor's name. Nevertheless, a financing statement that fails to provide an indication or the additional information when required does not sufficiently provide the name of the debtor under Sections 9-502(a) and 9-503(a), does not "substantially satisfy[] the requirements" of Part 5 within the meaning of this section and so is ineffective.

In addition to requiring the debtor's name and an indication of the collateral, Section 9-502(a) requires a financing statement to provide the name of the secured party or a representative of the secured party. Inasmuch as searches are not conducted under the secured party's name, and no filing is needed to continue the perfected status of security interest after it is assigned, an error in the name of the secured party or its representative will not be seriously misleading. However, in an appropriate case, an error of this kind may give rise to an estoppel in favor of a particular holder of a conflicting claim to the collateral. See Section 1-103(b).

3. New Debtors. Subsection (d) provides that, in determining the extent to which a financing statement naming an original debtor is effective against a new debtor, the sufficiency of the financing statement should be tested against the name of the new debtor.

Section 9-507. Effect of Certain Events on Effectiveness of Financing Statement

(a) [Disposition.] A filed financing statement remains effective with respect to collateral that is sold, exchanged, leased, licensed, or otherwise disposed of and in which a security interest or agricultural lien continues, even if the secured party knows of or consents to the disposition.

(b) [Information becoming seriously misleading.] Except as otherwise provided in subsection (c) and Section 9-508, a financing statement is not rendered ineffective if, after the financing statement is filed, the information provided in the financing statement becomes seriously misleading under Section 9-506.

(c) [Change in debtor's name.] If the name that a filed financing statement provides for a debtor becomes insufficient as the name of the debtor under Section 9-503(a) so that the financing statement becomes seriously misleading under Section 9-506:

(1) the financing statement is effective to perfect a security interest in collateral acquired by the debtor before, or within four months after, the filed financing statement becomes seriously misleading; and

(2) the financing statement is not effective to perfect a security interest in collateral acquired by the debtor more than four months after the filed financing statement becomes seriously misleading, unless an amendment to the financing statement which renders the financing statement not seriously misleading is filed within four months after the filed financing statement becomes seriously misleading.

Definitional Cross References:

Agricultural lien	Section 9-102(a)(5)
Collateral	Section 9-102(a)(12)
Debtor	Section 9-102(a)(28)
Financing statement	Section 9-102(a)(39)
Secured party	Section 9-102(a)(73)
Security interest	Section 1-201(b)(35)

Official Comment

1. Source. Former Section 9-402(7).

2. Scope of Section. This section deals with situations in which the information in a proper financing statement becomes inaccurate after the financing statement is filed. Compare Section 9-338, which deals with situations in which a financing statement contains a particular kind of information concerning the debtor (i.e., the information described in Section 9-516(b)(5)) that is incorrect at the time it is filed.

3. Post-Filing Disposition of Collateral. Under subsection (a), a financing statement remains effective even if the collateral is sold or otherwise disposed of. This subsection clarifies the third sentence of former Section 9-402(7) by providing that a financing statement remains effective following the disposition of collateral only when the security interest or agricultural lien continues in that collateral. This result is consistent with the conclusion of PEB Commentary No. 3. Normally, a security interest does continue after disposition of the collateral. See Section 9-315(a). Law other than this Article determines whether an agricultural lien survives disposition of the collateral.

As a consequence of the disposition, the collateral may be owned by a person other than the debtor against whom the financing statement was filed. Under subsection (a), the secured party remains perfected even if it does not correct the public record. For this reason, any person seeking to determine whether a debtor owns collateral free of security interests must inquire as to the debtor's source of title and, if circumstances seem to require it, search in the name of a former owner. Subsection (a) addresses only the sufficiency of the information contained in the financing statement. A disposition of collateral may result in loss of perfection for other reasons. See Section 9-316.

Example 1: Dee Corp. is an Illinois corporation. It creates a security interest in its equipment in favor of Secured Party. Secured Party files a proper financing statement in Illinois. Dee Corp. sells an item of equipment to Bee Corp., a Pennsylvania corporation, subject to the security interest. The security interest continues, see Section 9-315(a), and remains perfected, see Section 9-507(a), notwithstanding that the financing statement is filed under "D" (for Dee Corp.) and not under "B." However, because Bee Corp. is located in Pennsylvania and not Illinois, see Section 9-307, unless Secured Party perfects under Pennsylvania law within one year after the transfer, its security interest will become unperfected and will be deemed to have been unperfected against purchasers of the collateral. See Section 9-316.

4. Other Post-Filing Changes. Subsection (b) provides that, as a general matter, post-filing changes that render a financing statement seriously misleading have no effect on a financing statement. The financing statement remains effective. It is subject to two exceptions: Section 9-508 and Section 9-507(c). Section 9-508 addresses the effectiveness of a financing statement filed against an original debtor when a new debtor becomes bound by the original debtor's security agreement. It is discussed in the Comments to that section. Section 9-507(c) addresses cases in which a filed financing statement provides a name that, at the time of filing, satisfies the requirements of Section 9-503(a) with respect to the named debtor but, at a later time, no longer does so.

Example 2: Debtor, an individual whose principal residence is in California, grants a security interest to SP in certain business equipment. SP files a financing statement with the California filing office. Alternative A is in effect in California. The financing statement provides the name appearing on Debtor's California driver's license, "James McGinty." Debtor obtains a court order changing his name to "Roger McGuinn" but does not change his driver's license. Even after the court order issues, the name provided for the debtor in the financing statement is sufficient under Section 9-503(a). Accordingly, Section 9-507(c) does not apply.

The same result would follow if Alternative B is in effect in California.

Under Section 9-503(a)(4) (Alternative A), if the debtor holds a current (i.e., unexpired) driver's license issued by the State where the financing statement is filed, the name required for the financing statement is the name indicated on the license that was issued most recently by that State. If the debtor does not have a current driver's license issued by that State, then the debtor's name is determined under subsection (a)(5). It follows that a debtor's name may change, and a financing statement providing the name on the debtor's then-current driver's license may become seriously misleading, if the license expires and the debtor's name under subsection (a)(5) is different. The same consequences may follow if a debtor's driver's license is renewed and the names on the licenses differ.

Example 3: The facts are as in Example 2. Debtor's driver's license expires one year after the entry of the court order changing Debtor's name. Debtor does not renew the license. Upon expiration of the license, the name required for sufficiency by Section 9-503(a) is the individual name of the debtor or the debtor's surname and first personal name. The name "James McGinty" has become insufficient.

Example 4: The facts are as in Example 2. Before the license expires, Debtor renews the license. The name indicated on the new license is "Roger McGuinn." Upon issuance of the new license, "James McGinty" becomes insufficient as the debtor's name under Section 9-503(a).

The same results would follow if Alternative B is in effect in California (assuming that, following the issuance of the court order, "James McGinty" is neither the individual name of the debtor nor the debtor's surname and first personal name).

Even if the name provided as the name of the debtor becomes insufficient under Section 9-503(a), the filed financing statement does not become seriously misleading, and Section 9-507(c) does not apply, if the financing statement can be found by searching under the debtor's "correct" name, using the filing office's standard search logic. See Section 9-506. Any name that satisfies Section 9-503(a) at the time of the search is a "correct name" for these purposes. Thus, assuming that a search of the records of the California filing office under "Roger McGuinn," using the filing office's standard search logic, would not disclose a financing statement naming "James McGinty," the financing statement in Examples 3 and 4 has become seriously misleading and Section 9-507(c) applies.

If a filed financing statement becomes seriously misleading because the name it provides for a debtor becomes insufficient, the financing statement, unless amended to provide a sufficient name for the debtor, is effective only to perfect a security interest in collateral acquired by the debtor before, or within four months after, the change. If an amendment that provides a sufficient name is filed within four months after the change, the financing statement as amended would be effective also with respect to collateral acquired more than four months after the change. If an amendment that provides a sufficient name is filed more than four months after the change, the financing statement as amended would be effective also with respect to collateral acquired more than four months after the change, but only from the time of the filing of the amendment.

Section 9-508. Effectiveness of Financing Statement If New Debtor Becomes Bound by Security Agreement

(a) [Financing statement naming original debtor.] Except as otherwise provided in this section, a filed financing statement naming an original debtor is effective to perfect a security interest in collateral in which a new debtor has or acquires rights to the extent that the financing statement would have been effective had the original debtor acquired rights in the collateral.

(b) [Financing statement becoming seriously misleading.] If the difference between the name of the original debtor and that of the new debtor causes a filed financing statement that is effective under subsection (a) to be seriously misleading under Section 9-506:

(1) the financing statement is effective to perfect a security interest in collateral acquired by the new debtor before, and within four months after, the new debtor becomes bound under Section 9-203(d); and

(2) the financing statement is not effective to perfect a security interest in collateral acquired by the new debtor more than four months after the new debtor becomes bound under Section 9-203(d) unless an initial financing statement providing the name of the new debtor is filed before the expiration of that time.

(c) [When section not applicable.] This section does not apply to collateral as to which a filed financing statement remains effective against the new debtor under Section 9-507(a).

Definitional Cross References:

Collateral	Section 9-102(a)(12)
Financing statement	Section 9-102(a)(39)
New debtor	Section 9-102(a)(56)
Original debtor	Section 9-102(a)(60)
Right	Section 1-201(b)(34)
Security agreement	Section 9-102(a)(74)
Security interest	Section 1-201(b)(35)

Official Comment

1. Source. New.

2. The Problem. Section 9-203(d) and (e) and this section deal with situations where one party (the "new debtor") becomes bound as debtor by a security agreement entered into by another person (the "original debtor"). These situations often arise as a consequence of changes in business structure. For example, the original debtor may be an individual debtor who operates a business as a sole proprietorship and then incorporates it. Or, the original debtor may be a corporation that is merged into another corporation. Under both former Article 9 and this Article, collateral that is transferred in the course of the incorporation or merger normally would remain subject to a perfected security interest. See Sections 9-315(a), 9-507(a). Former Article 9 was less clear with respect to whether an after-acquired property clause in a security agreement signed by the original debtor would be effective to create a security interest in property acquired by the new corporation or the merger survivor and, if so, whether a financing statement filed against the original debtor would be effective to perfect the security interest. This section and Sections 9-203(d) and (e) are a clarification.

3. How New Debtor Becomes Bound. Normally, a security interest is unenforceable unless the debtor has signed a security agreement describing the collateral. See Section 9-203(b). Section 9-203(e) creates an exception, under which a security agreement entered into by one person is effective with respect to the property of another. This exception comes into play if a "new debtor" becomes bound as debtor by a security agreement entered into by another person (the "original debtor"). (The quoted terms are defined in Section 9-102.) If a new debtor does become bound, then the security agreement entered into by the original debtor satisfies the security-agreement requirement of Section 9-203(b)(3) as to existing or after-acquired property of the new debtor to the extent the property is described in the security agreement. In that case, no other agreement is necessary to make a security interest enforceable in that property. See Section 9-203(e).

Section 9-203(d) explains when a new debtor becomes bound by an original debtor's security agreement. Under Section 9-203(d)(1), a new debtor becomes bound as debtor if, by contract or operation of other law, the security agreement becomes effective to create a security interest in the new debtor's property. For example, if the applicable corporate law of mergers provides that when A Corp merges into B Corp, B Corp becomes a debtor under A Corp's security agreement, then B Corp would become bound as debtor following such a merger. Similarly, B Corp would become bound as debtor if B Corp contractually assumes A's obligations under the security agreement.

Under certain circumstances, a new debtor becomes bound for purposes of this Article even though it would not be bound under other law. Under Section 9-203(d)(2), a new debtor becomes bound when, by contract or operation of other law, it (i) becomes obligated not only for the secured obligation but also generally for the obligations of the original debtor and (ii) acquires or succeeds to substantially all the assets of the original debtor. For example, some corporate laws provide that, when two corporations merge, the surviving corporation succeeds to the assets of its merger partner and "has all liabilities" of both corporations. In the case where, for example, A Corp merges into B Corp (and A Corp ceases to exist), some people have questioned whether A Corp's grant of a security interest in its existing and after-acquired property becomes a "liability" of B Corp, such that B Corp's existing and after-acquired property becomes subject to a security interest in favor of A Corp's lender. Even if corporate law were to give a negative answer, under Section 9-203(d)(2), B Corp would become bound for purposes of Section 9-203(e) and this section. The "substantially all of the assets" requirement of Section 9-203(d)(2) excludes sureties and other secondary obligors as well as persons who become obligated through veil piercing and other non-successorship doctrines. In most cases, it will exclude successors to the assets and liabilities of a division of a debtor.

4. When Financing Statement Effective Against New Debtor. Subsection (a) provides that a filing against the original debtor generally is effective to perfect a security interest in collateral that a new debtor has at the time it becomes bound by the original debtor's security agreement and collateral that it acquires after the new debtor becomes bound. Under subsection (b), however, if the filing against the original debtor is seriously misleading as to the new debtor's name, the filing is effective as to collateral acquired by the new debtor more than four months after the new debtor becomes bound only if a person files during the four-month period an initial financing statement providing the name of the new debtor. Compare Section 9-507(c) (four-month period of effectiveness with respect to collateral acquired by a debtor after the name provided for the debtor becomes insufficient as the name of the debtor). As to the meaning of "initial financing statement" in this context, see Section 9-512, Comment 5.

5. Transferred Collateral. This section does not apply to collateral transferred by the original debtor to a new debtor. See subsection (c). Under those circumstances, the filing against the original debtor continues to be effective until it lapses or perfection is lost for another reason. See Sections 9-316, 9-507(a).

6. Priority. Section 9-326 governs the priority contest between a secured creditor of the original debtor and a secured creditor of the new debtor.

Section 9-509. Persons Entitled to File a Record

(a) [Person entitled to file record.] A person may file an initial financing statement, amendment that adds collateral covered by a financing statement, or amendment that adds a debtor to a financing statement only if:

(1) the debtor authorizes the filing in a signed record or pursuant to subsection (b) or (c); or

(2) the person holds an agricultural lien that has become effective at the time of filing and the financing statement covers only collateral in which the person holds an agricultural lien.

(b) [Security agreement as authorization.] By signing or becoming bound as debtor by a security agreement, a debtor or new debtor authorizes the filing of an initial financing statement, and an amendment, covering:

(1) the collateral described in the security agreement; and

(2) property that becomes collateral under Section 9-315(a)(2), whether or not the security agreement expressly covers proceeds.

(c) [Acquisition of collateral as authorization.] By acquiring collateral in which a security interest or agricultural lien continues under Section 9-315(a)(1), a debtor authorizes the filing of an initial financing statement, and an amendment, covering the collateral and property that becomes collateral under Section 9-315(a)(2).

(d) [Person entitled to file certain amendments.] A person may file an amendment other than an amendment that adds collateral covered by a financing statement or an amendment that adds a debtor to a financing statement only if:

(1) the secured party of record authorizes the filing; or

(2) the amendment is a termination statement for a financing statement as to which the secured party of record has failed to file or send a termination statement as required by Section 9-513(a) or (c), the debtor authorizes the filing, and the termination statement indicates that the debtor authorized it to be filed.

(e) [Multiple secured parties of record.] If there is more than one secured party of record for a financing statement, each secured party of record may authorize the filing of an amendment under subsection (d).

Definitional Cross References:

Agricultural lien	Section 9-102(a)(5)
Collateral	Section 9-102(a)(12)
Debtor	Section 9-102(a)(28)
Financing statement	Section 9-102(a)(39)
New debtor	Section 9-102(a)(56)
Person	Section 1-201(b)(27)
Proceeds	Section 9-102(a)(64)
Record	Section 9-102(a)(70)
Secured party	Section 9-102(a)(73)
Security agreement	Section 9-102(a)(74)
Security interest	Section 1-201(b)(35)
Send	Section 1-201(b)(36)
Sign	Section 1-201(b)(37)
Termination statement	Section 9-102(a)(80)

Official Comment

1. Source. New.

2. Scope and Approach of This Section. This section collects in one place most of the rules determining whether a record may be filed. Section 9-510 explains the extent to which a filed record is effective. Under these sections, the identity of the person who effects a filing is immaterial. The filing scheme contemplated by this Part does not contemplate that the identity of a "filer" will be a part of the searchable records. This is consistent with, and a necessary aspect of, eliminating signatures or other evidence of authorization from the system. (Note that the 1972 amendments to this Article eliminated the requirement that a financing statement contain the signature of the secured party.) As long as the appropriate person authorizes the filing, or, in the case of a termination statement, the debtor is entitled to the termination, it is insignificant whether the secured party or another person files any given record. The question of authorization is one for the court, not the filing office. However, a filing office may choose to employ authentication procedures in connection with electronic communications, e.g., to verify the identity of a filer who seeks to charge the filing fee.

3. Unauthorized Filings. Records filed in the filing office do not require signatures for their effectiveness. Subsection (a)(1) substitutes for the debtor's signature on a financing statement the requirement that the debtor authorize in a signed record the filing of an initial financing statement or an amendment that adds collateral. Also, under subsection (a)(1), if an amendment adds a debtor, the debtor who is added must authorize the amendment. A person who files an unauthorized record in violation of subsection (a)(1) is liable under Section 9-625(a) and (e) for actual and statutory damages. Of course, a filed financing statement is ineffective to perfect a security interest if the filing is not authorized. See Section 9-510(a). Law other than this Article, including the law with respect to ratification of past acts, generally determines whether a person has the requisite authority to file a record under this section. See Sections 1-103, 9-502, Comment 3. This Article applies to other issues, such as the priority of a security interest perfected by the filing of a financing statement. See Section 9-322, Comment 4.

4. *Ipso Facto* Authorization. Under subsection (b), the signing of a security agreement *ipso facto* constitutes the debtor's authorization of the filing of a financing statement covering the collateral described in the security agreement. The secured party need not obtain a separate authorization. Similarly, a new debtor's becoming bound by a security agreement *ipso facto* constitutes the new debtor's authorization of the filing of a financing statement covering the collateral described in the security agreement by which the new debtor has become bound. And, under subsection (c), the acquisition of collateral in which a security interest continues after disposition under Section 9-315(a)(1) *ipso facto* constitutes an authorization to file an initial financing statement against the person who acquired the collateral. The authorization to file an initial financing statement also constitutes an authorization to file a record covering actual proceeds of the original collateral, even if the security agreement is silent as to proceeds.

Example 1: Debtor signs a security agreement creating a security interest in Debtor's inventory in favor of Secured Party. Secured Party files a financing statement covering inventory and accounts. The financing statement is authorized insofar as it covers inventory and unauthorized insofar as it covers accounts. (Note, however, that the financing statement will be effective to perfect a security interest in accounts constituting proceeds of the inventory to the same extent as a financing statement covering only inventory.)

Example 2: Debtor signs a security agreement creating a security interest in Debtor's inventory in favor of Secured Party. Secured Party files a financing statement covering inventory. Debtor sells some inventory, deposits the buyer's payment into a deposit account, and withdraws the funds to purchase equipment. As long as the equipment can be traced to the inventory, the security interest continues in the equipment. See Section 9-315(a)(2). However, because the equipment was acquired with cash proceeds, the financing statement becomes ineffective to perfect the security interest in the equipment on the 21st day after the security interest attaches to the equipment unless Secured Party continues perfection beyond the 20-day period by filing a financing statement against the equipment or amending the filed financing statement to cover equipment. See Section 9-315(d). Debtor's signing of the security agreement authorizes the filing of an initial financing statement or amendment covering the equipment, which is "property that becomes collateral under Section 9-315(a)(2)." See Section 9-509(b)(2).

5. Agricultural Liens. Under subsection (a)(2), the holder of an agricultural lien may file a financing statement covering collateral subject to the lien without obtaining the debtor's authorization. Because the lien arises as matter of law, the debtor's consent is not required. A person who files an unauthorized record in violation of this subsection is liable under Section 9-625(e) for a statutory penalty and damages.

6. Amendments; Termination Statements Authorized by Debtor. Most amendments may not be filed unless the secured party of record, as determined under Section 9-511, authorizes the filing. See subsection (d)(1). However, under subsection (d)(2), the authorization of the secured party of record is not required for the filing of a termination statement if the secured party of record failed to send or file a termination statement as required by Section 9-513, the debtor authorizes it to be filed, and the termination statement so indicates. An authorization to file a record under subsection (d) is effective even if the authorization is not in a signed record. Compare subsection (a)(1). However, both the person filing the record and the person giving the authorization may wish to obtain and retain a record indicating that the filing was authorized.

7. Multiple Secured Parties of Record. Subsection (e) deals with multiple secured parties of record. It permits each secured party of record to authorize the filing of amendments. However, Section 9-510(b) protects the rights and powers of one secured party of record from the effects of filings made by another secured party of record. See Section 9-510, Comment 3.

8. Successor to Secured Party of Record. A person may succeed to the powers of the secured party of record by operation of other law, e.g., the law of corporate mergers. In that case, the successor has the power to authorize filings within the meaning of this section.

9. "Signed" and "Signing" Replace "Authenticated" and "Authenticating." Consistent with the revised definition of "sign" in Section 1-201(b)(37), the cognate terms "signed" and "signing" replace the references to "authenticated" and "authenticating" in the pre-2022 text of this section.

Section 9-510. Effectiveness of Filed Record

(a) [Filed record effective if authorized.] A filed record is effective only to the extent that it was filed by a person that may file it under Section 9-509.

(b) [Authorization by one secured party of record.] A record authorized by one secured party of record does not affect the financing statement with respect to another secured party of record.

(c) [Continuation statement not timely filed.] A continuation statement that is not filed within the six-month period prescribed by Section 9-515(d) is ineffective.

Definitional Cross References:

Continuation statement	Section 9-102(a)(27)
Financing statement	Section 9-102(a)(39)
Person	Section 1-201(b)(27)
Record	Section 9-102(a)(70)
Secured party	Section 9-102(a)(73)

Official Comment

1. Source. New.

2. Ineffectiveness of Unauthorized or Overbroad Filings. Subsection (a) provides that a filed financing statement is effective only to the extent it was filed by a person entitled to file it.

Example 1: Debtor authorizes the filing of a financing statement covering inventory. Under Section 9-509, the secured party may file a financing statement covering only inventory; it may not file a financing statement covering other collateral. The secured party files a financing statement covering inventory and equipment. This section provides that the financing statement is effective only to the extent the secured party may file it. Thus, the financing statement is effective to perfect a security interest in inventory but ineffective to perfect a security interest in equipment.

3. Multiple Secured Parties of Record. Section 9-509(e) permits any secured party of record to authorize the filing of most amendments. Subsection (b) of this section prevents a filing authorized by one secured party of record from affecting the rights and powers of another secured party of record without the latter's consent.

Example 2: Debtor creates a security interest in favor of A and B. The filed financing statement names A and B as the secured parties. An amendment deleting some collateral covered by the financing statement is filed pursuant to B's authorization. Although B's security interest in the deleted collateral becomes unperfected, A's security interest remains perfected in all the collateral.

Example 3: Debtor creates a security interest in favor of A and B. The financing statement names A and B as the secured parties. A termination statement is filed pursuant to B's authorization. Although the effectiveness of the financing statement terminates with respect to B's security interest, A's rights are unaffected. That is, the financing statement continues to be effective to perfect A's security interest.

4. Continuation Statements. A continuation statement may be filed only within the six months immediately before lapse. See Section 9-515(d). The filing office is obligated to reject a continuation statement that is filed outside the six-month period. See Sections 9-520(a), 9-516(b)(7). Subsection (c) provides that if the filing office fails to reject a continuation statement that is not filed in a timely manner, the continuation statement is ineffective nevertheless.

Section 9-511. Secured Party of Record

(a) [Secured party of record.] A secured party of record with respect to a financing statement is a person whose name is provided as the name of the secured party or a representative of the secured party in an initial financing statement that has been filed. If an initial financing statement is filed under Section 9-514(a), the assignee named in the initial financing statement is the secured party of record with respect to the financing statement.

(b) [Amendment naming secured party of record.] If an amendment of a financing statement which provides the name of a person as a secured party or a representative of a secured party is filed, the person named in the amendment is a secured party of record. If an amendment is filed under Section 9-514(b), the assignee named in the amendment is a secured party of record.

(c) [Amendment deleting secured party of record.] A person remains a secured party of record until the filing of an amendment of the financing statement which deletes the person.

Definitional Cross References:

Financing statement	Section 9-102(a)(39)
Person	Section 1-201(b)(27)
Representative	Section 1-201(b)(33)
Secured party	Section 9-102(a)(73)

Official Comment

1. Source. New.

2. Secured Party of Record. This new section explains how the secured party of record is to be determined. If SP-1 is named as the secured party in an initial financing statement, it is the secured party of record. Similarly, if an initial financing statement reflects a total assignment from SP-0 to SP-1, then SP-1 is the secured party of record. See subsection (a). If, subsequently, an amendment is filed assigning SP-1's status to SP-2, then SP-2 becomes the secured party of record in place of SP-1. The same result obtains if a subsequent amendment deletes the reference to SP-1 and substitutes therefor a reference to SP-2. If, however, a subsequent amendment adds SP-2 as a secured party but does not purport to remove SP-1 as a secured party, then SP-2 and SP-1 each is a secured party of record. See subsection (b). An amendment purporting to remove the only secured party of record without providing a successor is ineffective. See Section 9-512(e). At any point in time, all effective records that comprise a financing statement must be examined to determine the person or persons that have the status of secured party of record.

3. Successor to Secured Party of Record. Application of other law may result in a person succeeding to the powers of a secured party of record. For example, if the secured party of record (A) merges into another corporation (B) and the other corporation (B) survives, other law may provide that B has all of A's powers. In that case, B is authorized to take all actions under this Part that A would have been authorized to take. Similarly, acts taken by a person who is authorized under generally applicable principles of agency to act on behalf of the secured party of record are effective under this Part.

Section 9-512. Amendment of Financing Statement

ALTERNATIVE A

(a) [Amendment of information in financing statement.] Subject to Section 9-509, a person may add or delete collateral covered by, continue or terminate the effectiveness of, or, subject to subsection (e), otherwise amend the information provided in, a financing statement by filing an amendment that:

(1) identifies, by its file number, the initial financing statement to which the amendment relates; and

(2) if the amendment relates to an initial financing statement filed [or recorded] in a filing office described in Section 9-501(a)(1), provides the information specified in Section 9-502(b).

ALTERNATIVE B

(a) [Amendment of information in financing statement.] Subject to Section 9-509, a person may add or delete collateral covered by, continue or terminate the effectiveness of, or, subject to subsection (e), otherwise amend the information provided in, a financing statement by filing an amendment that:

(1) identifies, by its file number, the initial financing statement to which the amendment relates; and

(2) if the amendment relates to an initial financing statement filed [or recorded] in a filing office described in Section 9-501(a)(1), provides the date [and time] that the initial financing statement was filed [or recorded] and the information specified in Section 9-502(b).

END OF ALTERNATIVES

(b) [Period of effectiveness not affected.] Except as otherwise provided in Section 9-515, the filing of an amendment does not extend the period of effectiveness of the financing statement.

(c) [Effectiveness of amendment adding collateral.] A financing statement that is amended by an amendment that adds collateral is effective as to the added collateral only from the date of the filing of the amendment.

(d) [Effectiveness of amendment adding debtor.] A financing statement that is amended by an amendment that adds a debtor is effective as to the added debtor only from the date of the filing of the amendment.

(e) [Certain amendments ineffective.] An amendment is ineffective to the extent it:

(1) purports to delete all debtors and fails to provide the name of a debtor to be covered by the financing statement; or

(2) purports to delete all secured parties of record and fails to provide the name of a new secured party of record.

Legislative Note: *States whose real-estate filing offices require additional information in amendments and cannot search their records by both the name of the debtor and the file number should enact Alternative B to Sections 9-512(a), 9-518(b), 9-518(d), 9-519(f), and 9-522(a).*

Definitional Cross References:

Collateral	Section 9-102(a)(12)
Debtor	Section 9-102(a)(28)
File number	Section 9-102(a)(36)
Filing office	Section 9-102(a)(37)
Financing statement	Section 9-102(a)(39)
Person	Section 1-201(b)(27)
Record	Section 9-102(a)(70)
State	Section 9-102(a)(77)

Official Comment

1. Source. Former 9-402(4).

2. Changes to Financing Statements. This section addresses changes to financing statements, including addition and deletion of collateral. Although termination statements, assignments, and continuation statements are types of amendment, this Article follows former Article 9 and contains separate sections containing additional provisions applicable to particular types of amendments. See Section 9-513 (termination statements); 9-514 (assignments); 9-515 (continuation statements). One should not infer from this separate treatment that this Article requires a separate amendment to accomplish each change. Rather, a single amendment would be legally sufficient to, e.g., add collateral and continue the effectiveness of the financing statement.

3. Amendments. An amendment under this Article may identify only the information contained in a financing statement that is to be changed; alternatively, it may take the form of an amended and restated financing statement. The latter would state, for example, that the financing statement "is amended and restated to read as follows:" References in this Part to an "amended financing statement" are to a financing statement as amended by an amendment using either technique.

This section revises former Section 9-402(4) to permit secured parties of record to make changes in the public record without the need to obtain the debtor's signature. However, the filing of an amendment that adds collateral or adds a debtor must be authorized by the debtor or it will not be effective. See Sections 9-509(a), 9-510(a).

4. Amendment Adding Debtor. An amendment that adds a debtor is effective, provided that the added debtor authorizes the filing. See Section 9-509(a). However, filing an amendment adding a debtor to a previously filed financing statement affords no advantage over filing an initial financing statement against that debtor and may be disadvantageous. With respect to the added debtor, for purposes of determining the priority of the security interest, the time of filing is the time of the filing of the amendment, not the time of the filing of the initial financing statement. See subsection (d). However, the effectiveness of the financing statement lapses with respect to added debtor at the time it lapses with respect to the original debtor. See subsection (b).

5. Amendment Adding Debtor Name. Many states have enacted statutes governing the "conversion" of one organization organized under the law of that state, e.g., a corporation, into another such organization, e.g., a limited liability company. This Article defers to those statutes to determine whether the resulting organization is the same legal person as the initial, converting organization (albeit with a different name) or whether the resulting organization is a different legal person. When the governing statute does not clearly resolve the question, a secured party whose debtor is the converting organization may wish to proceed as if the statute provides for both results. In these circumstances, an amendment adding to the initial financing statement the name of the resulting organization may be preferable to an amendment substituting that name for the name of the debtor provided on the initial financing statement. In the event the governing statute is construed as providing that the resulting organization is the same legal person as the converting organization, but with a different name, the timely filing of such an amendment would satisfy the requirement of Section 9-507(c)(2). If, however, the governing statute is construed as providing that the resulting organization is a different legal person, the financing statement (which continues to provide the name of the original debtor) would be effective as to collateral acquired by the resulting organization ("new debtor") before, and within four months after, the conversion. See Section 9-508(b)(1). Inasmuch as it is the first financing statement filed against the resulting organization by the secured party, the record adding the name of the resulting organization as a debtor would constitute "an initial financing statement providing the name of the new debtor" under Section 9-508(b)(2). The secured party also may wish to file another financing statement naming the resulting organization as debtor. See Comment 4.

6. Deletion of All Debtors or Secured Parties of Record. Subsection (e) assures that there will be a debtor and secured party of record for every financing statement.

Example: A filed financing statement names A and B as secured parties of record and covers inventory and equipment. An amendment deletes equipment and purports to delete A and B as secured parties of record without adding a substitute secured party. The amendment is ineffective to the extent it purports to delete the secured parties of record but effective with respect to the deletion of collateral. As a consequence, the financing statement, as amended, covers only inventory, but A and B remain as secured parties of record.

Section 9-513. Termination Statement

(a) [Consumer goods.] A secured party shall cause the secured party of record for a financing statement to file a termination statement for the financing statement if the financing statement covers consumer goods and:

(1) there is no obligation secured by the collateral covered by the financing statement and no commitment to make an advance, incur an obligation, or otherwise give value; or

(2) the debtor did not authorize the filing of the initial financing statement.

(b) [Time for compliance with subsection (a).] To comply with subsection (a), a secured party shall cause the secured party of record to file the termination statement:

(1) within one month after there is no obligation secured by the collateral covered by the financing statement and no commitment to make an advance, incur an obligation, or otherwise give value; or

(2) if earlier, within 20 days after the secured party receives a signed demand from a debtor.

(c) [Other collateral.] In cases not governed by subsection (a), within 20 days after a secured party receives a signed demand from a debtor, the secured party shall cause the secured party of record for a financing statement to send to the debtor a termination statement for the financing statement or file the termination statement in the filing office if:

(1) except in the case of a financing statement covering accounts or chattel paper that has been sold or goods that are the subject of a consignment, there is no obligation secured by the collateral covered by the financing statement and no commitment to make an advance, incur an obligation, or otherwise give value;

(2) the financing statement covers accounts or chattel paper that has been sold but as to which the account debtor or other person obligated has discharged its obligation;

(3) the financing statement covers goods that were the subject of a consignment to the debtor but are not in the debtor's possession; or

(4) the debtor did not authorize the filing of the initial financing statement.

(d) [Effect of filing termination statement.] Except as otherwise provided in Section 9-510, upon the filing of a termination statement with the filing office, the financing statement to which the termination statement relates ceases to be effective. Except as otherwise provided in Section 9-510, for purposes of Sections 9-519(g), 9-522(a), and 9-523(c), the filing with the filing office of a termination statement relating to a financing statement that indicates that the debtor is a transmitting utility also causes the effectiveness of the financing statement to lapse.

Definitional Cross References:

Account	Section 9-102(a)(2)
Account debtor	Section 9-102(a)(3)
Chattel paper	Section 9-102(a)(11)
Collateral	Section 9-102(a)(12)
Consignment	Section 9-102(a)(20)
Consumer goods	Section 9-102(a)(23)
Debtor	Section 9-102(a)(28)
Filing office	Section 9-102(a)(37)
Financing statement	Section 9-102(a)(39)
Goods	Section 9-102(a)(44)
Secured party	Section 9-102(a)(73)
Send	Section 1-201(b)(36)
Sign	Section 1-201(b)(37)
Termination statement	Section 9-102(a)(80)
Value	Section 1-204

Official Comment

1. Source. Former Section 9-404.

2. Duty to File or Send. This section specifies when a secured party must cause the secured party of record to file or send to the debtor a termination statement for a financing statement. Because most financing statements expire in five years unless a continuation statement is filed (Section 9-515), no compulsion is placed on the secured party to file a termination statement unless demanded by the debtor, except in the case of consumer goods. Because many consumers will not realize the importance to them of clearing the public record, an affirmative duty is put on the secured party in that case. But many purchase-money security interests in consumer goods will not be filed, except for motor vehicles. See Section 9-309(1). Under Section 9-311(b), compliance with a certificate-of-title statute is "equivalent to the filing of a financing statement under this article." Thus, this section applies to a certificate of title unless the section is superseded by a certificate-of-title statute that contains a specific rule addressing a secured party's duty to cause a notation of a security interest to be removed from a certificate of title. In the context of a certificate of title, however, the secured party could comply with this section by causing the removal itself or providing the debtor with documentation sufficient to enable the debtor to effect the removal.

Subsections (a) and (b) apply to a financing statement covering consumer goods. Subsection (c) applies to other financing statements. Subsection (a) and (c) each makes explicit what was implicit under former Article 9: If the debtor did not authorize the filing of a financing statement in the first place, the secured party of record should file or send a termination statement. The liability imposed upon a secured party that fails to comply with subsection (a) or (c) is identical to that imposed for the filing of an unauthorized financing statement or amendment. See Section 9-625(e).

References to a "termination statement" in this section and in Part 5 generally should be interpreted functionally, based on the purposes of the termination. A termination statement includes any amendment that meets the definition of that term by containing an indication that the amendment "is a termination statement" or that the identified financing statement "is no longer effective." Section 9-102(a)(80). The amendment may terminate the effectiveness of a financing statement in whole or in part. For example, if a person did not authorize the filing of a financing statement against it as debtor, under subsection (a)(2) and (c)(4) the person may demand that the financing statement be terminated as to that person, even if the financing statement remains of record and effective as to one or more other persons named as debtors in the financing statement. Such a termination statement may take the form of an amendment that deletes the person as a debtor. Similarly, if a person authorized the filing of a financing statement as to some collateral but not as to other property identified as collateral on the financing statement, the person may demand that the financing statement be terminated as to the unauthorized identified collateral, even if the financing statement remains of record and effective as to other identified collateral. Such a termination statement may take the form of an amendment that deletes the unauthorized identified collateral from coverage of the financing statement. Even if such amendments do not indicate explicitly that they are termination statements, they would nonetheless indicate that the financing statement "is no longer effective" to the extent specified and fall within the definition of "termination statement."

3. "Bogus" Filings. A secured party's duty to send a termination statement arises when the secured party "receives" a signed demand from the debtor. In the case of an unauthorized financing statement, the person named as debtor in the financing statement may have no relationship with the named secured party and no reason to know the secured party's address. Inasmuch as the address in the financing statement is "held out by [the person named as secured party in the financing statement] as the place for receipt of such communications [i.e., communications relating to security interests]," the putative secured party is deemed to have "received" a notification delivered to that address. See Section 1-202(e). If a termination statement is not forthcoming, the person named as debtor itself may authorize the filing of a termination statement, which will be effective if it indicates that the person authorized it to be filed. See Sections 9-509(d)(2), 9-510(a).

4. Buyers of Receivables. Applied literally, former Section 9-404(1) would have required many buyers of receivables to file a termination statement immediately upon filing a financing statement because "there is no outstanding secured obligation and no commitment to make advances, incur obligations, or otherwise give value." Subsections (c)(1) and (2) remedy this problem. While the security interest of a buyer of accounts or chattel paper (B-1) is perfected, the debtor is not deemed to retain an interest in the sold receivables and thus could transfer no interest in them to another buyer (B-2) or to a lien creditor (LC). However, for purposes of determining the rights of the debtor's creditors and certain purchasers of accounts or chattel paper from the debtor, while B-1's security interest is unperfected, the debtor-seller is deemed to have rights in the sold receivables, and a competing security interest or judicial lien may attach to those rights. See Sections 9-318, 9-109, Comment 5. Suppose that B-1's security interest in certain accounts and chattel paper is perfected by filing, but the effectiveness of the financing statement lapses. Both before and after lapse, B-1 collects some of the receivables. After lapse, LC acquires a lien on the accounts and chattel paper. B-1's unperfected security interest in the accounts and chattel paper is subordinate to LC's rights. See Section 9-317(a)(2). But collections on accounts and chattel paper are not "accounts" or "chattel paper." Even if B-1's security interest in the accounts and chattel paper is or becomes unperfected, neither the debtor nor LC acquires rights to the collections that B-1 collects (and owns) before LC acquires a lien.

5. Effect of Filing. Subsection (d) states the effect of filing a termination statement: the related financing statement ceases to be effective. If one of several secured parties of record files a termination statement, subsection (d) applies only with respect to the rights of the person who authorized the filing of the termination statement. See Section 9-510(b). The financing statement remains effective with respect to the rights of the others. However, even if a financing statement is terminated (and thus no longer is effective) with respect to all secured parties of record, the financing statement, including the termination statement, will remain of record until at least one year after it lapses with respect to all secured parties of record. See Section 9-519(g).

6. "Signed" Replaces "Authenticated." Consistent with the revised definition of "sign" in Section 1-201(b)(37), the cognate term "signed" replaces the references to "authenticated" in the pre-2022 text of this section.

Section 9-514. Assignment of Powers of Secured Party of Record

(a) [Assignment reflected on initial financing statement.] Except as otherwise provided in subsection (c), an initial financing statement may reflect an assignment of all of the secured party's power to authorize an amendment to the financing statement by providing the name and mailing address of the assignee as the name and address of the secured party.

(b) [Assignment of filed financing statement.] Except as otherwise provided in subsection (c), a secured party of record may assign of record all or part of its power to authorize an amendment to a financing statement by filing in the filing office an amendment of the financing statement which:

(1) identifies, by its file number, the initial financing statement to which it relates;

(2) provides the name of the assignor; and

(3) provides the name and mailing address of the assignee.

(c) [Assignment of record of mortgage.] An assignment of record of a security interest in a fixture covered by a record of a mortgage which is effective as a financing statement filed as a fixture filing under Section 9-502(c) may be made only by an assignment of record of the mortgage in the manner provided by law of this State other than [the Uniform Commercial Code].

Definitional Cross References:

File number	Section 9-102(a)(36)
Filing office	Section 9-102(a)(37)
Financing statement	Section 9-102(a)(39)
Fixture filing	Section 9-102(a)(40)
Fixtures	Section 9-102(a)(41)
Mortgage	Section 9-102(a)(55)
Secured party	Section 9-102(a)(73)
Security interest	Section 1-201(b)(35)
State	Section 9-102(a)(77)

Official Comment

1. Source. Former Section 9-405.

2. Assignments. This section provides a permissive device whereby a secured party of record may effectuate an assignment of its power to affect a financing statement. It may also be useful for a secured party who has assigned all or part of its security interest or agricultural lien and wishes to have the fact noted of record, so that inquiries concerning the transaction would be addressed to the assignee. See Section 9-502, Comment 2. Upon the filing of an assignment, the assignee becomes the "secured party of record" and may authorize the filing of a continuation statement, termination statement, or other amendment. Note that under Section 9-310(c) no filing of an assignment is required as a condition of continuing the perfected status of the security interest against creditors and transferees of the original debtor. However, if an assignment is not filed, the assignor remains the secured party of record, with the power (even if not the right) to authorize the filing of effective amendments. See Sections 9-511(c), 9-509(d).

Where a record of a mortgage is effective as a financing statement filed as a fixture filing (Section 9-502(c)), then an assignment of record of the security interest may be made only in the manner in which an assignment of record of the mortgage may be made under local real-property law.

3. Comparison to Prior Law. Most of the changes reflected in this section are for clarification or to embrace medium-neutral drafting. As a general matter, this section preserves the opportunity given by former Section 9-405 to assign a security interest of record in one of two different ways. Under subsection (a), a secured party may assign all of its power to affect a financing statement by naming an assignee in the initial financing statement. The secured party of record may accomplish the same result under subsection (b) by making a subsequent filing. Subsection (b) also may be used for an assignment of only some of the secured party of record's power to affect a financing statement, e.g., the power to affect the financing statement as it relates to particular items of collateral or as it relates to an undivided interest in a security interest in all the collateral. An initial financing statement may not be used to change the secured party of record under these circumstances. However, an amendment adding the assignee as a secured party of record may be used.

Section 9-515. Duration and Effectiveness of Financing Statement; Effect of Lapsed Financing Statement

(a) [Five-year effectiveness.] Except as otherwise provided in subsections (b), (e), (f), and (g), a filed financing statement is effective for a period of five years after the date of filing.

(b) [Public-finance or manufactured-home transaction.] Except as otherwise provided in subsections (e), (f), and (g), an initial financing statement filed in connection with a public-finance transaction or manufactured-home transaction is effective for a period of 30 years after the date of filing if it indicates that it is filed in connection with a public-finance transaction or manufactured-home transaction.

(c) [Lapse and continuation of financing statement.] The effectiveness of a filed financing statement lapses on the expiration of the period of its effectiveness unless before the lapse a continuation statement is filed pursuant to subsection (d). Upon lapse, a financing statement ceases to be effective and any security interest or agricultural lien that was perfected by the financing statement becomes unperfected, unless the security interest is perfected otherwise. If the security interest or agricultural lien becomes unperfected upon lapse, it is deemed never to have been perfected as against a purchaser of the collateral for value.

(d) [When continuation statement may be filed.] A continuation statement may be filed only within six months before the expiration of the five-year period specified in subsection (a) or the 30-year period specified in subsection (b), whichever is applicable.

(e) [Effect of filing continuation statement.] Except as otherwise provided in Section 9-510, upon timely filing of a continuation statement, the effectiveness of the initial financing statement continues for a period of five years commencing on the day on which the financing statement would have become ineffective in the absence of the filing. Upon the expiration of the five-year period, the financing statement lapses in the same manner as provided in subsection (c), unless, before the lapse, another continuation statement is filed pursuant to subsection (d). Succeeding continuation statements may be filed in the same manner to continue the effectiveness of the initial financing statement.

(f) [Transmitting utility financing statement.] If a debtor is a transmitting utility and a filed initial financing statement so indicates, the financing statement is effective until a termination statement is filed.

(g) [Record of mortgage as financing statement.] A record of a mortgage that is effective as a financing statement filed as a fixture filing under Section 9-502(c) remains effective as a financing statement filed as a fixture filing until the mortgage is released or satisfied of record or its effectiveness otherwise terminates as to the real property.

Definitional Cross References:

Agricultural lien	Section 9-102(a)(5)
Collateral	Section 9-102(a)(12)
Continuation statement	Section 9-102(a)(27)
Debtor	Section 9-102(a)(28)
Financing statement	Section 9-102(a)(39)
Fixture filing	Section 9-102(a)(40)
Manufactured-home transaction	Section 9-102(a)(54)
Mortgage	Section 9-102(a)(55)
Public-finance transaction	Section 9-102(a)(67)
Purchaser	Section 1-201(b)(30)
Record	Section 9-102(a)(70)
Security interest	Section 1-201(b)(35)
Termination statement	Section 9-102(a)(80)
Transmitting utility	Section 9-102(a)(81)
Value	Section 1-204

Official Comment

1. Source. Former Section 9-403(2), (3), (6).

2. Period of Financing Statement's Effectiveness. Subsection (a) states the general rule: a financing statement is effective for a five-year period unless its effectiveness is continued under this section or terminated under Section 9-513. Subsection (b) provides that if the financing statement relates to a public-finance transaction or a manufactured-home transaction and so indicates, the financing statement is effective for 30 years. These financings typically extend well beyond the standard, five-year period. Under subsection (f), a financing statement filed against a transmitting utility remains effective indefinitely, until a termination statement is filed. Likewise, under subsection (g), a mortgage effective as a fixture filing remains effective until its effectiveness terminates under real-property law.

3. Lapse. When the period of effectiveness under subsection (a) or (b) expires, the effectiveness of the financing statement lapses. The last sentence of subsection (c) addresses the effect of lapse. The deemed retroactive unperfection applies only with respect to purchasers for value; unlike former Section 9-403(2), it does not apply with respect to lien creditors.

Example 1: SP-1 and SP-2 both hold security interests in the same collateral. Both security interests are perfected by filing. SP-1 filed first and has priority under Section 9-322(a)(1). The effectiveness of SP-1's filing lapses. As long as SP-2's security interest remains perfected thereafter, SP-2 is entitled to priority over SP-1's security interest, which is deemed never to have been perfected as against a purchaser for value (SP-2). See Section 9-322(a)(2).

Example 2: SP holds a security interest perfected by filing. On July 1, LC acquires a judicial lien on the collateral. Two weeks later, the effectiveness of the financing statement lapses. Although the security interest becomes unperfected upon lapse, it was perfected when LC acquired its lien. Accordingly, notwithstanding the lapse, the perfected security interest has priority over the rights of LC, who is not a purchaser. See Section 9-317(a)(2).

4. Effect of Debtor's Bankruptcy. Under former Section 9-403(2), lapse was tolled if the debtor entered bankruptcy or another insolvency proceeding. Nevertheless, being unaware that insolvency proceedings had been commenced, filing offices routinely removed records from the files as if lapse had not been tolled. Subsection (c) deletes the former tolling provision and thereby imposes a new burden on the secured party: to be sure that a financing statement does not lapse during the debtor's bankruptcy. The secured party can prevent lapse by filing a continuation statement, even without first obtaining relief from the automatic stay. See Bankruptcy Code Section 362(b)(3). Of course, if the debtor enters bankruptcy before lapse, the provisions of this Article with respect to lapse would be of no effect to the extent that federal bankruptcy law dictates a contrary result (e.g., to the extent that the Bankruptcy Code determines rights as of the date of the filing of the bankruptcy petition).

5. Continuation Statements. Subsection (d) explains when a continuation statement may be filed. A continuation statement filed at a time other than that prescribed by subsection (d) is ineffective, see Section 9-510(c), and the filing office may not accept it. See Sections 9-520(a), 9-516(b). Subsection (e) specifies the effect of a continuation statement and provides for successive continuation statements.

Section 9-516. What Constitutes Filing; Effectiveness of Filing

(a) [What constitutes filing.] Except as otherwise provided in subsection (b), communication of a record to a filing office and tender of the filing fee or acceptance of the record by the filing office constitutes filing.

(b) [Refusal to accept record; filing does not occur.] Filing does not occur with respect to a record that a filing office refuses to accept because:

(1) the record is not communicated by a method or medium of communication authorized by the filing office;

(2) an amount equal to or greater than the applicable filing fee is not tendered;

(3) the filing office is unable to index the record because:

(A) in the case of an initial financing statement, the record does not provide a name for the debtor;

(B) in the case of an amendment or information statement, the record:

(i) does not identify the initial financing statement as required by Section 9-512 or 9-518, as applicable; or

(ii) identifies an initial financing statement whose effectiveness has lapsed under Section 9-515;

(C) in the case of an initial financing statement that provides the name of a debtor identified as an individual or an amendment that provides a name of a debtor identified as an individual which was not previously provided in the financing statement to which the record relates, the record does not identify the debtor's surname; or

(D) in the case of a record filed [or recorded] in the filing office described in Section 9-501(a)(1), the record does not provide a sufficient description of the real property to which it relates;

(4) in the case of an initial financing statement or an amendment that adds a secured party of record, the record does not provide a name and mailing address for the secured party of record;

(5) in the case of an initial financing statement or an amendment that provides a name of a debtor which was not previously provided in the financing statement to which the amendment relates, the record does not:

(A) provide a mailing address for the debtor; or

(B) indicate whether the name provided as the name of the debtor is the name of an individual or an organization;

(6) in the case of an assignment reflected in an initial financing statement under Section 9-514(a) or an amendment filed under Section 9-514(b), the record does not provide a name and mailing address for the assignee; or

(7) in the case of a continuation statement, the record is not filed within the six-month period prescribed by Section 9-515(d).

(c) [Rules applicable to subsection (b).] For purposes of subsection (b):

(1) a record does not provide information if the filing office is unable to read or decipher the information; and

(2) a record that does not indicate that it is an amendment or identify an initial financing statement to which it relates, as required by Section 9-512, 9-514, or 9-518, is an initial financing statement.

(d) [Refusal to accept record; record effective as filed record.] A record that is communicated to the filing office with tender of the filing fee, but which the filing office refuses to accept for a reason other than one set forth in subsection (b), is effective as a filed record except as against a purchaser of the collateral which gives value in reasonable reliance upon the absence of the record from the files.

Definitional Cross References:

Collateral	Section 9-102(a)(12)
Communicate	Section 9-102(a)(18)
Continuation statement	Section 9-102(a)(27)
Debtor	Section 9-102(a)(28)
Filing office	Section 9-102(a)(37)
Financing statement	Section 9-102(a)(39)
Jurisdiction of organization	Section 9-102(a)(50)
Organization	Section 1-201(b)(25)
Purchaser	Section 1-201(b)(30)
Record	Section 9-102(a)(70)
Secured party	Section 9-102(a)(73)
Value	Section 1-204

Official Comment

1. Source. Subsection (a): former Section 9-403(1); the remainder is new.

2. What Constitutes Filing. Subsection (a) deals generically with what constitutes filing of a record, including an initial financing statement and amendments of all kinds (e.g., assignments, termination statements, and continuation statements). It follows former Section 9-403(1), under which either acceptance of a record by the filing office or presentation of the record and tender of the filing fee constitutes filing.

3. Effectiveness of Rejected Record. Subsection (b) provides an exclusive list of grounds upon which the filing office may reject a record. See Section 9-520(a). Although some of these grounds would also be grounds for rendering a filed record ineffective (e.g., an initial financing statement does not provide a name for the debtor), many others would not be (e.g., an initial financing statement does not provide a mailing address for the debtor or secured party of record). Neither this section nor Section 9-520 requires or authorizes the filing office to determine, or even consider, the accuracy of information provided in a record.

A financing statement or other record that is communicated to the filing office but which the filing office refuses to accept provides no public notice, regardless of the reason for the rejection. However, this section distinguishes between records that the filing office rightfully rejects and those that it wrongfully rejects. A filer is able to prevent a rightful rejection by complying with the requirements of subsection (b). No purpose is served by giving effect to records that justifiably never find their way into the system, and subsection (b) so provides.

Subsection (d) deals with the filing office's unjustified refusal to accept a record. Here, the filer is in no position to prevent the rejection and as a general matter should not be prejudiced by it. Although wrongfully rejected records generally are effective, subsection (d) contains a special rule to protect a third-party purchaser of the collateral (e.g., a buyer or competing secured party) who gives value in reliance upon the apparent absence of the record from the files. As against a person who searches the public record and reasonably relies on what the public record shows, subsection (d) imposes upon the filer the risk that a record failed to make its way into the filing system because of the filing office's wrongful rejection of it. (Compare Section 9-517, under which a mis-indexed financing statement is fully effective.) This risk is likely to be small, particularly when a record is presented electronically, and the filer can guard against this risk by conducting a post-filing search of the records. Moreover, Section 9-520(b) requires the filing office to give prompt notice of its refusal to accept a record for filing.

4. Method or Medium of Communication. Rejection pursuant to subsection (b)(1) for failure to communicate a record properly should be understood to mean noncompliance with procedures relating to security, signing, or other communication-related requirements that the filing office may impose. Subsection (b)(1) does not authorize a filing office to impose additional substantive requirements. See Section 9-520, Comment 2.

5. Address for Secured Party of Record. Under subsection (b)(4) and Section 9-520(a), the lack of a mailing address for the secured party of record requires the filing office to reject an initial financing statement. The failure to include an address for the secured party of record no longer renders a financing statement ineffective. See Section 9-502(a). The function of the address is not to identify the secured party of record but rather to provide an address to which others can send required notifications, e.g., of a purchase-money security interest in inventory or of the disposition of collateral. Inasmuch as the address shown on a filed financing statement is an "address that is reasonable under the circumstances," a person required to send a notification to the secured party may satisfy the requirement by sending a notification to that address, even if the address is or becomes incorrect. See Section 9-102 (definition of "send"). Similarly, because the address is "held out by [the secured party] as the place for receipt of such communications [i.e., communications relating to security interests]," the secured party is deemed to have received a notification delivered to that address. See Section 1-202(e).

6. Uncertainty Concerning Individual Debtor's Surname. Subsection (b)(3)(C) requires the filing office to reject an initial financing statement or amendment adding an individual debtor if the office cannot index the record because it does not identify the debtor's surname (e.g., it is unclear whether the debtor's surname is Elton or John).

7. Inability of Filing Office to Read or Decipher Information. Under subsection (c)(1), if the filing office cannot read or decipher information, the information is not provided by a record for purposes of subsection (b).

8. Classification of Records. For purposes of subsection (b), a record that does not indicate it is an amendment or identify an initial financing statement to which it relates is deemed to be an initial financing statement. See subsection (c)(2).

9. Effectiveness of Rejectable But Unrejected Record. Section 9-520(a) requires the filing office to refuse to accept an initial financing statement for a reason set forth in subsection (b). However, if the filing office accepts such a financing statement nevertheless, the financing statement generally is effective if it complies with the requirements of Section 9-502(a) and (b). See Section 9-520(c). Similarly, an otherwise effective financing statement generally remains so even though the information in the financing statement becomes incorrect. See Section 9-507(b). (Note that if the information required by subsection (b)(5) is incorrect when the financing statement is filed, Section 9-338 applies.)

Section 9-517. Effect of Indexing Errors

The failure of the filing office to index a record correctly does not affect the effectiveness of the filed record.

Definitional Cross References:

Filing office	Section 9-102(a)(37)
Record	Section 9-102(a)(70)

Official Comment

1. Source. New.

2. Effectiveness of Mis-Indexed Records. This section provides that the filing office's error in mis-indexing a record does not render ineffective an otherwise effective record. As did former Section 9-401, this section imposes the risk of filing-office error on those who search the files rather than on those who file.

Section 9-518. Claim Concerning Inaccurate or Wrongfully Filed Record

(a) [Statement with respect to record indexed under person's name.] A person may file in the filing office an information statement with respect to a record indexed there under the person's name if the person believes that the record is inaccurate or was wrongfully filed.

ALTERNATIVE A

(b) [Contents of statement under subsection (a).] An information statement under subsection (a) must:

(1) identify the record to which it relates by the file number assigned to the initial financing statement to which the record relates;

(2) indicate that it is an information statement; and

(3) provide the basis for the person's belief that the record is inaccurate and indicate the manner in which the person believes the record should be amended to cure any inaccuracy or provide the basis for the person's belief that the record was wrongfully filed.

ALTERNATIVE B

(b) [Contents of statement under subsection (a).] An information statement under subsection (a) must:

(1) identify the record to which it relates by:

(A) the file number assigned to the initial financing statement to which the record relates; and

(B) if the information statement relates to a record filed [or recorded] in a filing office described in Section 9-501(a)(1), the date [and time] that the initial financing statement was filed [or recorded] and the information specified in Section 9-502(b);

(2) indicate that it is an information statement; and

(3) provide the basis for the person's belief that the record is inaccurate and indicate the manner in which the person believes the record should be amended to cure any inaccuracy or provide the basis for the person's belief that the record was wrongfully filed.

END OF ALTERNATIVES

(c) [Statement by secured party of record.] A person may file in the filing office an information statement with respect to a record filed there if the person is a secured party of record with respect to the financing statement to which the record relates and believes that the person that filed the record was not entitled to do so under Section 9-509(d).

ALTERNATIVE A

(d) [Contents of statement under subsection (c).] An information statement under subsection (c) must:

(1) identify the record to which it relates by the file number assigned to the initial financing statement to which the record relates;

(2) indicate that it is an information statement; and

(3) provide the basis for the person's belief that the person that filed the record was not entitled to do so under Section 9-509(d).

ALTERNATIVE B

(d) [Contents of statement under subsection (c).] An information statement under subsection (c) must:

(1) identify the record to which it relates by:

(A) the file number assigned to the initial financing statement to which the record relates; and

(B) if the information statement relates to a record filed [or recorded] in a filing office described in Section 9-501(a)(1), the date [and time] that the initial financing statement was filed [or recorded] and the information specified in Section 9-502(b);

(2) indicate that it is an information statement; and

(3) provide the basis for the person's belief that the person that filed the record was not entitled to do so under Section 9-509(d).

END OF ALTERNATIVES

(e) [Record not affected by information statement.] The filing of a correction statement does not affect the effectiveness of an initial financing statement or other filed record.

Legislative Note: *States whose real-estate filing offices require additional information in amendments and cannot search their records by both the name of the debtor and the file number should enact Alternative B to Sections 9-512(a), 9-518(b), 9-518(d), 9-519(f), and 9-522(a).*

Definitional Cross References:

Debtor	Section 9-102(a)(28)
File number	Section 9-102(a)(36)
Filing office	Section 9-102(a)(37)
Financing statement	Section 9-102(a)(39)
Person	Section 1-201(b)(27)
Record	Section 9-102(a)(70)
State	Section 9-102(a)(77)

Official Comment

1. Source. New.

2. Information Statements. Former Article 9 did not afford a nonjudicial means for a debtor to indicate that financing statement or other record was inaccurate or wrongfully filed. Subsection (a) affords the debtor the right to file an information statement. Among other requirements, the information statement must provide the basis for the debtor's belief that the public record should be corrected. See subsection (b). These provisions, which resemble the analogous remedy in the Fair Credit Reporting Act, 15 U.S.C. § 1681i, afford an aggrieved person the opportunity to state its position on the public record. They do not permit an aggrieved person to change the legal effect of the public record. Thus, although a filed information statement becomes part of the "financing statement," as defined in Section 9-102, the filing does not affect the effectiveness of the initial financing statement or any other filed record. See subsection (e).

Sometimes a person files a termination statement or other record relating to a filed financing statement without being entitled to do so. A secured party of record with respect to the financing statement who believes that such a record has been filed may, but need not, file an information statement indicating that the person that filed the record was not entitled to do so. See subsection (c). An information statement has no legal effect. Its sole purpose is to provide some limited public notice that the efficacy of a filed record is disputed. If the person that filed the record was not entitled to do so, the filed record is ineffective, regardless of whether the secured party of record files an information statement. Likewise, if the person that filed the record was entitled to do so, the filed record is effective, even if the secured party of record files an information statement. See Section 9-510(a), 9-518(e). Because an information statement filed under subsection (c) has no legal effect, a secured party of record—even one who is aware of the unauthorized filing of a record—has no duty to file one. Just as searchers bear the burden of determining whether the filing of initial financing statement was authorized, searchers bear the burden of determining whether the filing of every subsequent record was authorized.

Inasmuch as the filing of an information statement has no legal effect, this section does not provide a mechanism by which a secured party can correct an error that it discovers in its own financing statement.

This section does not displace other provisions of this Article that impose liability for making unauthorized filings or failing to file or send a termination statement (see Section 9-625(e)), nor does it displace any available judicial remedies.

3. Resort to Other Law. This Article cannot provide a satisfactory or complete solution to problems caused by misuse of the public records. The problem of "bogus" filings is not limited to the UCC filing system but extends to the real-property records, as well. A summary judicial procedure for correcting the public record and criminal penalties for those who misuse the filing and recording systems are likely to be more effective and put less strain on the filing system than provisions authorizing or requiring action by filing and recording offices.

[Subpart 2. Duties and Operation of Filing Office]

Section 9-519. Numbering, Maintaining, and Indexing Records; Communicating Information Provided in Records

(a) [Filing office duties.] For each record filed in a filing office, the filing office shall:

(1) assign a unique number to the filed record;

(2) create a record that bears the number assigned to the filed record and the date and time of filing;

(3) maintain the filed record for public inspection; and

(4) index the filed record in accordance with subsections (c), (d), and (e).

(b) [File number.] A file number [assigned after January 1, 2002,] must include a digit that:

(1) is mathematically derived from or related to the other digits of the file number; and

(2) aids the filing office in determining whether a number communicated as the file number includes a single-digit or transpositional error.

(c) [Indexing: general.] Except as otherwise provided in subsections (d) and (e), the filing office shall:

(1) index an initial financing statement according to the name of the debtor and index all filed

records relating to the initial financing statement in a manner that associates with one another an initial financing statement and all filed records relating to the initial financing statement; and

(2) index a record that provides a name of a debtor which was not previously provided in the financing statement to which the record relates also according to the name that was not previously provided.

(d) [Indexing: real-property-related financing statement.] If a financing statement is filed as a fixture filing or covers as-extracted collateral or timber to be cut, [it must be filed for record and] the filing office shall index it:

(1) under the names of the debtor and of each owner of record shown on the financing statement as if they were the mortgagors under a mortgage of the real property described; and

(2) to the extent that the law of this State provides for indexing of records of mortgages under the name of the mortgagee, under the name of the secured party as if the secured party were the mortgagee thereunder, or, if indexing is by description, as if the financing statement were a record of a mortgage of the real property described.

(e) [Indexing: real-property-related assignment.] If a financing statement is filed as a fixture filing or covers as-extracted collateral or timber to be cut, the filing office shall index an assignment filed under Section 9-514(a) or an amendment filed under Section 9-514(b):

(1) under the name of the assignor as grantor; and

(2) to the extent that the law of this State provides for indexing a record of the assignment of a mortgage under the name of the assignee, under the name of the assignee.

ALTERNATIVE A

(f) [Retrieval and association capability.] The filing office shall maintain a capability:

(1) to retrieve a record by the name of the debtor and by the file number assigned to the initial financing statement to which the record relates; and

(2) to associate and retrieve with one another an initial financing statement and each filed record relating to the initial financing statement.

ALTERNATIVE B

(f) [Retrieval and association capability.] The filing office shall maintain a capability:

(1) to retrieve a record by the name of the debtor and:

(A) if the filing office is described in Section 9-501(a)(1), by the file number assigned to the initial financing statement to which the record relates and the date [and time] that the record was filed [or recorded]; or

(B) if the filing office is described in Section 9-501(a)(2), by the file number assigned to the initial financing statement to which the record relates; and

(2) to associate and retrieve with one another an initial financing statement and each filed record relating to the initial financing statement.

END OF ALTERNATIVES

(g) [Removal of debtor's name.] The filing office may not remove a debtor's name from the index until one year after the effectiveness of a financing statement naming the debtor lapses under Section 9-515 with respect to all secured parties of record.

(h) [Timeliness of filing office performance.] The filing office shall perform the acts required by subsections (a) through (e) at the time and in the manner prescribed by filing-office rule, but not later than two business days after the filing office receives the record in question.

[(i) [Inapplicability to real-property-related filing office.] Subsection[s] [(b)] [and] [(h)] do[es] not apply to a filing office described in Section 9-501(a)(1).]

Legislative Notes:

1. *States whose filing offices currently assign file numbers that include a verification number, commonly known as a "check digit," or can implement this requirement before the effective date of this Article should omit the bracketed language in subsection (b).*

2. *In States in which writings will not appear in the real property records and indices unless actually recorded the bracketed language in subsection (d) should be used.*

3. *States whose real-estate filing offices require additional information in amendments and cannot*

search their records by both the name of the debtor and the file number should enact Alternative B to Sections 9-512(a), 9-518(b), 9-518(d), 9-519(f), and 9-522(a).

4. A State that elects not to require real-estate filing offices to comply with either or both of subsections (b) and (h) may adopt an applicable variation of subsection (i) and add "Except as otherwise provided in subsection (i)," to the appropriate subsection or subsections.

Definitional Cross References:

As-extracted collateral	Section 9-102(a)(6)
Communicate	Section 9-102(a)(18)
Debtor	Section 9-102(a)(28)
File number	Section 9-102(a)(36)
Filing office	Section 9-102(a)(37)
Filing-office rule	Section 9-102(a)(38)
Financing statement	Section 9-102(a)(39)
Fixture filing	Section 9-102(a)(40)
Mortgage	Section 9-102(a)(55)
Record	Section 9-102(a)(70)
Secured party	Section 9-102(a)(73)
State	Section 9-102(a)(77)
Writing	Section 1-201(b)(43)

Official Comment

1. Source. Former Sections 9-403(4), (7), 9-405(2).

2. Filing Office's Duties. Subsections (a) through (e) set forth the duties of the filing office with respect to filed records. Subsection (h), which is new, imposes a minimum standard of performance for those duties. Prompt indexing is crucial to the effectiveness of any filing system. An accepted but unindexed record affords no public notice. Subsection (f) requires the filing office to maintain appropriate storage and retrieval facilities, and subsection (g) contains minimum requirements for the retention of records.

3. File Number. Subsection (a)(1) requires the filing office to assign a unique number to each filed record. That number is the "file number" only if the record is an initial financing statement. See Section 9-102.

4. Time of Filing. Subsection (a)(2) and Section 9-523 refer to the "date and time" of filing. The statutory text does not contain any instructions to a filing office as to how the time of filing is to be determined. The method of determining or assigning a time of filing is an appropriate matter for filing-office rules to address.

5. Related Records. Subsections (c) and (f) are designed to ensure that an initial financing statement and all filed records relating to it are associated with one another, indexed under the name of the debtor, and retrieved together. To comply with subsection (f), a filing office (other than a real-property recording office in a State that enacts subsection (f), Alternative B) must be capable of retrieving records in each of two ways: by the name of the debtor and by the file number of the initial financing statement to which the record relates.

6. Prohibition on Deleting Names from Index. This Article contemplates that the filing office will not delete the name of a debtor from the index until at least one year passes after the effectiveness of the financing statement lapses as to all secured parties of record. See subsection (g). This rule applies even if the filing office accepts an amendment purporting to delete or modify the name of a debtor or terminate the effectiveness of the financing statement. If an amendment provides a modified name for a debtor, the amended name should be added to the index, see subsection (c)(2), but the pre-amendment name should remain in the index.

Compared to former Article 9, the rule in subsection (g) increases the amount of information available to those who search the public records. The rule also contemplates that searchers—not the filing office—will determine the significance and effectiveness of filed records.

Section 9-520. Acceptance and Refusal to Accept Record

(a) [Mandatory refusal to accept record.] A filing office shall refuse to accept a record for filing for a reason set forth in Section 9-516(b) and may refuse to accept a record for filing only for a reason set forth in Section 9-516(b).

(b) [Communication concerning refusal.] If a filing office refuses to accept a record for filing, it shall communicate to the person that presented the record the fact of and reason for the refusal and the date and time the record would have been filed had the filing office accepted it. The communication must be made at the time and in the manner prescribed by filing-office rule but [, in the case of a filing office described in Section 9-501(a)(2),] in no event more than two business days after the filing office receives the record.

(c) [When filed financing statement effective.] A filed financing statement satisfying Section 9-502(a) and (b) is effective, even if the filing office is required to refuse to accept it for filing under subsection (a). However, Section 9-338 applies to a filed financing statement providing information described in Section 9-516(b)(5) which is incorrect at the time the financing statement is filed.

(d) [Separate application to multiple debtors.] If a record communicated to a filing office provides information that relates to more than one debtor, this part applies as to each debtor separately.

Legislative Note: *A State that elects not to require real-property filing offices to comply with subsection (b) should include the bracketed language.*

Definitional Cross References:

Communicate	Section 9-102(a)(18)
Debtor	Section 9-102(a)(28)
Filing office	Section 9-102(a)(37)
Filing-office rule	Section 9-102(a)(38)
Financing statement	Section 9-102(a)(39)
Person	Section 1-201(b)(27)
Record	Section 9-102(a)(70)
State	Section 9-102(a)(77)

Official Comment

1. Source. New.

2. Refusal to Accept Record for Filing. In some States, filing offices considered themselves obligated by former Article 9 to review the form and content of a financing statement and to refuse to accept those that they determine are legally insufficient. Some filing offices imposed requirements for or conditions to filing that do not appear in the statute. Under this section, the filing office is not expected to make legal judgments and is not permitted to impose additional conditions or requirements.

Subsection (a) both prescribes and limits the bases upon which the filing office must and may reject records by reference to the reasons set forth in Section 9-516(b). For the most part, the bases for rejection are limited to those that prevent the filing office from dealing with a record that it receives—because some of the requisite information (e.g., the debtor's name) is missing or cannot be deciphered, because the record is not communicated by a method (e.g., it is MIME- rather than UU-encoded) or medium (e.g., it is written rather than electronic) that the filing office accepts, or because the filer fails to tender an amount equal to or greater than the filing fee.

3. Consequences of Accepting Rejectable Record. Section 9-516(b) includes among the reasons for rejecting an initial financing statement the failure to give certain information that is not required as a condition of effectiveness. In conjunction with Section 9-516(b)(5), this section requires the filing office to refuse to accept a financing statement that is legally sufficient to perfect a security interest under Section 9-502 but does not contain a mailing address for the debtor or disclose whether the debtor is an individual or an organization. The information required by Section 9-516(b)(5) assists searchers in weeding out "false positives," i.e., records that a search reveals but which do not pertain to the debtor in question. It assists filers by helping to ensure that the debtor's name is correct and that the financing statement is filed in the proper jurisdiction.

If the filing office accepts a financing statement that does not give this information at all, the filing is fully effective. Section 9-520(c). The financing statement also generally is effective if the information is given but is incorrect; however, Section 9-338 affords protection to buyers and holders of perfected security interests who give value in reasonable reliance upon the incorrect information.

4. Filing Office's Duties with Respect to Rejected Record. Subsection (b) requires the filing office to communicate the fact of rejection and the reason therefor within a fixed period of time. Inasmuch as a rightfully rejected record is ineffective and a wrongfully rejected record is not fully effective, prompt communication concerning any rejection is important.

5. Partial Effectiveness of Record. Under subsection (d), the provisions of this Part apply to each debtor separately. Thus, a filing office may reject an initial financing statement or other record as to one named debtor but accept it as to the other.

> **Example:** An initial financing statement is communicated to the filing office. The financing statement names two debtors, John Smith and Jane Smith. It contains all of the information described in Section 9-516(b)(5) with respect to John but lacks some of the information with respect to Jane. The filing office must accept the financing statement with respect to John, reject it with respect to Jane, and notify the filer of the rejection.

Section 9-521. Uniform Form of Written Financing Statement and Amendment

(a) [Initial financing statement form.] A filing office that accepts written records may not refuse to accept a written initial financing statement in the following form and format except for a reason set forth in Section 9-516(b):

[redacted]

UCC FINANCING STATEMENT

FOLLOW INSTRUCTIONS

A. NAME & PHONE OF CONTACT AT FILER (optional)

B. E-MAIL CONTACT AT FILER (optional)

C. SEND ACKNOWLEDGMENT TO: (Name and Address)

THE ABOVE SPACE IS FOR FILING OFFICE USE ONLY

1. DEBTOR'S NAME: Provide only one Debtor name (1a or 1b) (use exact, full name; do not omit, modify, or abbreviate any part of the Debtor's name); if any part of the Individual Debtor's name will not fit in line 1b, leave all of item 1 blank, check here ☐ and provide the Individual Debtor information in item 10 of the Financing Statement Addendum (Form UCC1Ad)

	1a. ORGANIZATION'S NAME				
OR	1b. INDIVIDUAL'S SURNAME	FIRST PERSONAL NAME	ADDITIONAL NAME(S)/INITIAL(S)		SUFFIX
1c.	MAILING ADDRESS	CITY	STATE	POSTAL CODE	COUNTRY

2. DEBTOR'S NAME: Provide only one Debtor name (2a or 2b) (use exact, full name; do not omit, modify, or abbreviate any part of the Debtor's name); if any part of the Individual Debtor's name will not fit in line 2b, leave all of item 2 blank, check here ☐ and provide the Individual Debtor information in item 10 of the Financing Statement Addendum (Form UCC1Ad)

	2a. ORGANIZATION'S NAME				
OR	2b. INDIVIDUAL'S SURNAME	FIRST PERSONAL NAME	ADDITIONAL NAME(S)/INITIAL(S)		SUFFIX
2c.	MAILING ADDRESS	CITY	STATE	POSTAL CODE	COUNTRY

3. SECURED PARTY'S NAME (or NAME of ASSIGNEE of ASSIGNOR SECURED PARTY): Provide only one Secured Party name (3a or 3b)

	3a. ORGANIZATION'S NAME				
OR	3b. INDIVIDUAL'S SURNAME	FIRST PERSONAL NAME	ADDITIONAL NAME(S)/INITIAL(S)		SUFFIX
3c.	MAILING ADDRESS	CITY	STATE	POSTAL CODE	COUNTRY

4. COLLATERAL: This financing statement covers the following collateral:

5. Check only if applicable and check only one box: Collateral is ☐ held in a Trust (see UCC1Ad, item 17 and Instructions) ☐ being administered by a Decedent's Personal Representative

6a. Check only if applicable and check only one box: ☐ Public-Finance Transaction ☐ Manufactured-Home Transaction ☐ A Debtor is a Transmitting Utility

6b. Check only if applicable and check only one box: ☐ Agricultural Lien ☐ Non-UCC Filing

7. ALTERNATIVE DESIGNATION (if applicable): ☐ Lessee/Lessor ☐ Consignee/Consignor ☐ Seller/Buyer ☐ Bailee/Bailor ☐ Licensee/Licensor

8. OPTIONAL FILER REFERENCE DATA:

UCC FINANCING STATEMENT (Form UCC1) (Rev. 04/20/11)

UCC FINANCING STATEMENT ADDENDUM

FOLLOW INSTRUCTIONS

9. NAME OF FIRST DEBTOR: Same as line 1a or 1b on Financing Statement; if line 1b was left blank because Individual Debtor name did not fit, check here ☐

9a. ORGANIZATION'S NAME	
OR 9b. INDIVIDUAL'S SURNAME	
FIRST PERSONAL NAME	
ADDITIONAL NAME(S)/INITIAL(S)	SUFFIX

THE ABOVE SPACE IS FOR FILING OFFICE USE ONLY

10. DEBTOR'S NAME: Provide (10a or 10b) only one additional Debtor name or Debtor name that did not fit in line 1b or 2b of the Financing Statement (Form UCC1) (use exact, full name; do not omit, modify, or abbreviate any part of the Debtor's name) and enter the mailing address in line 10c

10a. ORGANIZATION'S NAME				
OR 10b. INDIVIDUAL'S SURNAME				
INDIVIDUAL'S FIRST PERSONAL NAME				
INDIVIDUAL'S ADDITIONAL NAME(S)/INITIAL(S)				SUFFIX
10c. MAILING ADDRESS	CITY	STATE	POSTAL CODE	COUNTRY

11. ☐ ADDITIONAL SECURED PARTY'S NAME or ☐ ASSIGNOR SECURED PARTY'S NAME: Provide only one name (11a or 11b)

11a. ORGANIZATION'S NAME				
OR 11b. INDIVIDUAL'S SURNAME	FIRST PERSONAL NAME	ADDITIONAL NAME(S)/INITIAL(S)		SUFFIX
11c. MAILING ADDRESS	CITY	STATE	POSTAL CODE	COUNTRY

12. ADDITIONAL SPACE FOR ITEM 4 (Collateral):

13. ☐ This FINANCING STATEMENT is to be filed [for record] (or recorded) in the REAL ESTATE RECORDS (if applicable)	14. This FINANCING STATEMENT: ☐ covers timber to be cut ☐ covers as-extracted collateral ☐ is filed as a fixture filing
15. Name and address of a RECORD OWNER of real estate described in item 16 (if Debtor does not have a record interest):	16. Description of real estate:

17. MISCELLANEOUS:

UCC FINANCING STATEMENT ADDENDUM (Form UCC1Ad) (Rev. 04/20/11)

(b) [Amendment form.] A filing office that accepts written records may not refuse to accept a written record in the following form and format except for a reason set forth in Section 9-516(b):

UCC FINANCING STATEMENT AMENDMENT

FOLLOW INSTRUCTIONS

A. NAME & PHONE OF CONTACT AT FILER (optional)

B. E-MAIL CONTACT AT FILER (optional)

C. SEND ACKNOWLEDGMENT TO: (Name and Address)

THE ABOVE SPACE IS FOR FILING OFFICE USE ONLY

1a. INITIAL FINANCING STATEMENT FILE NUMBER

1b. ☐ This FINANCING STATEMENT AMENDMENT is to be filed [for record] (or recorded) in the REAL ESTATE RECORDS
Filer: attach Amendment Addendum (Form UCC3Ad) and provide Debtor's name in item 13

2. ☐ TERMINATION: Effectiveness of the Financing Statement identified above is terminated with respect to the security interest(s) of Secured Party authorizing this Termination Statement

3. ☐ ASSIGNMENT (full or partial): Provide name of Assignee in item 7a or 7b, and address of Assignee in item 7c and name of Assignor in item 9
For partial assignment, complete items 7 and 9 and also indicate affected collateral in item 8

4. ☐ CONTINUATION: Effectiveness of the Financing Statement identified above with respect to the security interest(s) of Secured Party authorizing this Continuation Statement is continued for the additional period provided by applicable law

5. ☐ PARTY INFORMATION CHANGE:
Check one of these two boxes:
This Change affects ☐ Debtor or ☐ Secured Party of record
AND Check one of these three boxes to:
☐ CHANGE name and/or address: Complete item 6a or 6b; and item 7a or 7b and item 7c
☐ ADD name: Complete item 7a or 7b, and item 7c
☐ DELETE name: Give record name to be deleted in item 6a or 6b

6. CURRENT RECORD INFORMATION: Complete for Party Information Change - provide only one name (6a or 6b)

6a. ORGANIZATION'S NAME

OR

6b. INDIVIDUAL'S SURNAME	FIRST PERSONAL NAME	ADDITIONAL NAME(S)/INITIAL(S)	SUFFIX

7. CHANGED OR ADDED INFORMATION: Complete for Assignment or Party Information Change - provide only one name (7a or 7b) (use exact, full name; do not omit, modify, or abbreviate any part of the Debtor's name)

7a. ORGANIZATION'S NAME

OR

7b. INDIVIDUAL'S SURNAME

INDIVIDUAL'S FIRST PERSONAL NAME

INDIVIDUAL'S ADDITIONAL NAME(S)/INITIAL(S) | SUFFIX

7c. MAILING ADDRESS	CITY	STATE	POSTAL CODE	COUNTRY

8. ☐ COLLATERAL CHANGE: Also check one of these four boxes: ☐ ADD collateral ☐ DELETE collateral ☐ RESTATE covered collateral ☐ ASSIGN collateral
Indicate collateral:

9. NAME OF SECURED PARTY OF RECORD AUTHORIZING THIS AMENDMENT: Provide only one name (9a or 9b) (name of Assignor, if this is an Assignment)
If this is an Amendment authorized by a DEBTOR, check here ☐ and provide name of authorizing Debtor

9a. ORGANIZATION'S NAME

OR

9b. INDIVIDUAL'S SURNAME	FIRST PERSONAL NAME	ADDITIONAL NAME(S)/INITIAL(S)	SUFFIX

10. OPTIONAL FILER REFERENCE DATA:

UCC FINANCING STATEMENT AMENDMENT (Form UCC3) (Rev. 04/20/11)

UCC FINANCING STATEMENT AMENDMENT ADDENDUM

FOLLOW INSTRUCTIONS

11. INITIAL FINANCING STATEMENT FILE NUMBER: Same as item 1a on Amendment form

12. NAME OF PARTY AUTHORIZING THIS AMENDMENT: Same as item 9 on Amendment form

12a. ORGANIZATION'S NAME

OR 12b. INDIVIDUAL'S SURNAME

FIRST PERSONAL NAME

ADDITIONAL NAME(S)/INITIAL(S) | SUFFIX

THE ABOVE SPACE IS FOR FILING OFFICE USE ONLY

13. Name of DEBTOR on related financing statement (Name of a current Debtor of record required for indexing purposes only in some filing offices - see Instruction item 13): Provide only one Debtor name (13a or 13b) (use exact, full name; do not omit, modify, or abbreviate any part of the Debtor's name); see Instructions if name does not fit

13a. ORGANIZATION'S NAME

OR 13b. INDIVIDUAL'S SURNAME	FIRST PERSONAL NAME	ADDITIONAL NAME(S)/INITIAL(S)	SUFFIX

14. ADDITIONAL SPACE FOR ITEM 8 (Collateral):

15. This FINANCING STATEMENT AMENDMENT:

☐ covers timber to be cut ☐ covers as-extracted collateral ☐ is filed as a fixture filing

16. Name and address of a RECORD OWNER of real estate described in item 17 (if Debtor does not have a record interest):

17. Description of real estate:

18. MISCELLANEOUS:

UCC FINANCING STATEMENT AMENDMENT ADDENDUM (Form UCC3Ad) (Rev. 04/20/11)

Definitional Cross References:

Filing office	Section 9-102(a)(37)
Financing statement	Section 9-102(a)(39)
Record	Section 9-102(a)(70)
Writing	Section 1-201(b)(43)

Official Comment

1. Source. New.

2. "Safe Harbor" Written Forms. Although Section 9-520 limits the bases upon which the filing office can refuse to accept records, this section provides sample written forms that must be accepted in every filing office in the country, as long as the filing office's rules permit it to accept written communications. By completing one of the forms in this section, a secured party can be certain that the filing office is obligated to accept it.

The forms in this section are based upon national financing statement forms that were in use under former Article 9. Those forms were developed over an extended period and reflect the comments and suggestions of filing officers, secured parties and their counsel, and service companies. The formatting of those forms and of the ones in this section has been designed to reduce error by both filers and filing offices.

A filing office that accepts written communications may not reject, on grounds of form or format, a filing using these forms. Although filers are not required to use the forms, they are encouraged and can be expected to do so, inasmuch as the forms are well designed and avoid the risk of rejection on the basis of form or format. As their use expands, the forms will rapidly become familiar to both filers and filing-office personnel. Filing offices may and should encourage the use of these forms by declaring them to be the "standard" (but not exclusive) forms for each jurisdiction, albeit without in any way suggesting that alternative forms are unacceptable.

The multi-purpose form in subsection (b) covers changes with respect to the debtor, the secured party, the collateral, and the status of the financing statement (termination and continuation). A single form may be used for several different types of amendments at once (e.g., both to change a debtor's name and continue the effectiveness of the financing statement).

Section 9-522. Maintenance and Destruction of Records

ALTERNATIVE A

(a) [Post-lapse maintenance and retrieval of information.] The filing office shall maintain a record of the information provided in a filed financing statement for at least one year after the effectiveness of the financing statement has lapsed under Section 9-515 with respect to all secured parties of record. The record must be retrievable by using the name of the debtor and by using the file number assigned to the initial financing statement to which the record relates.

ALTERNATIVE B

(a) [Post-lapse maintenance and retrieval of information.] The filing office shall maintain a record of the information provided in a filed financing statement for at least one year after the effectiveness of the financing statement has lapsed under Section 9-515 with respect to all secured parties of record. The record must be retrievable by using the name of the debtor and:

(1) if the record was filed [or recorded] in the filing office described in Section 9-501(a)(1), by using the file number assigned to the initial financing statement to which the record relates and the date [and time] that the record was filed [or recorded]; or

(2) if the record was filed in the filing office described in Section 9-501(a)(2), by using the file number assigned to the initial financing statement to which the record relates.

END OF ALTERNATIVES

(b) [Destruction of written records.] Except to the extent that a statute governing disposition of public records provides otherwise, the filing office immediately may destroy any written record evidencing a financing statement. However, if the filing office destroys a written record, it shall maintain another record of the financing statement which complies with subsection (a).

Legislative Note: *States whose real-estate filing offices require additional information in amendments and cannot search their records by both the name of the debtor and the file number should enact Alternative B to Sections 9-512(a), 9-518(b), 9-518(d), 9-519(f), and 9-522(a).*

Definitional Cross References:

Debtor	Section 9-102(a)(28)
File number	Section 9-102(a)(36)
Filing office	Section 9-102(a)(37)
Financing statement	Section 9-102(a)(39)
Record	Section 9-102(a)(70)
State	Section 9-102(a)(77)
Writing	Section 1-201(b)(43)

Official Comment

1. Source. Former Section 9-403(3), revised substantially.

2. Maintenance of Records. Section 9-523 requires the filing office to provide information concerning certain lapsed financing statements. Accordingly, subsection (a) requires the filing office to maintain a record of the information in a financing statement for at least one year after lapse. During that time, the filing office may not delete any information with respect to a filed financing statement; it may only add information. This approach relieves the filing office from any duty to determine whether to substitute or delete information upon receipt of an amendment. It also assures searchers that they will receive all information with respect to financing statements filed against a debtor and thereby be able themselves to determine the state of the public record.

The filing office may maintain this information in any medium. Subsection (b) permits the filing office immediately to destroy written records evidencing a financing statement, provided that the filing office maintains another record of the information contained in the financing statement as required by subsection (a).

Section 9-523. Information from Filing Office; Sale or License of Records

(a) [Acknowledgment of filing written record.] If a person that files a written record requests an acknowledgment of the filing, the filing office shall send to the person an image of the record showing the number assigned to the record pursuant to Section 9-519(a)(1) and the date and time of the filing of the record. However, if the person furnishes a copy of the record to the filing office, the filing office may instead:

(1) note upon the copy the number assigned to the record pursuant to Section 9-519(a)(1) and the date and time of the filing of the record; and

(2) send the copy to the person.

(b) [Acknowledgment of filing other record.] If a person files a record other than a written record, the filing office shall communicate to the person an acknowledgment that provides:

(1) the information in the record;

(2) the number assigned to the record pursuant to Section 9-519(a)(1); and

(3) the date and time of the filing of the record.

(c) [Communication of requested information.] The filing office shall communicate or otherwise make available in a record the following information to any person that requests it:

(1) whether there is on file on a date and time specified by the filing office, but not a date earlier than three business days before the filing office receives the request, any financing statement that:

(A) designates a particular debtor [or, if the request so states, designates a particular debtor at the address specified in the request];

(B) has not lapsed under Section 9-515 with respect to all secured parties of record; and

(C) if the request so states, has lapsed under Section 9-515 and a record of which is maintained by the filing office under Section 9-522(a);

(2) the date and time of filing of each financing statement; and

(3) the information provided in each financing statement.

(d) [Medium for communicating information.] In complying with its duty under subsection (c), the filing office may communicate information in any medium. However, if requested, the filing office shall communicate information by issuing [its written certificate] [a record that can be admitted into evidence in the courts of this State without extrinsic evidence of its authenticity].

(e) [Timeliness of filing office performance.] The filing office shall perform the acts required by subsections (a) through (d) at the time and in the manner prescribed by filing-office rule, but not later than two business days after the filing office receives the request.

(f) [Public availability of records.] At least weekly, the [insert appropriate official or governmental agency] [filing office] shall offer to sell or license to the public on a nonexclusive basis, in bulk, copies of all records filed in it under this part, in every medium from time to time available to the filing office.

Legislative Notes:

1. *States whose filing office does not offer the additional service of responding to search requests limited to a particular address should omit the bracketed language in subsection (c)(1)(A).*

2. *A State that elects not to require real-estate filing offices to comply with either or both of subsections (e) and (f) should specify in the appropriate subsection(s) only the filing office described in Section 9-501(a)(2).*

Definitional Cross References:

Communicate	Section 9-102(a)(18)
Debtor	Section 9-102(a)(28)
Filing office	Section 9-102(a)(37)
Filing-office rule	Section 9-102(a)(38)
Financing statement	Section 9-102(a)(39)
Person	Section 1-201(b)(27)
Record	Section 9-102(a)(70)
Sale	Section 2-106(1)
Send	Section 1-201(b)(36)
State	Section 9-102(a)(77)
Writing	Section 1-201(b)(43)

Official Comment

1. Source. Former Section 9-407; subsections (d) and (e) are new.

2. Filing Office's Duty to Provide Information. Former Section 9-407, dealing with obtaining information from the filing office, was bracketed to suggest to legislatures that its enactment was optional. Experience has shown that the method by which interested persons can obtain information concerning the public records should be uniform. Accordingly, the analogous provisions of this Article are not in brackets.

Most of the other changes from former Section 9-407 are for clarification, to embrace medium-neutral drafting, or to impose standards of performance on the filing office.

3. Acknowledgments of Filing. Subsections (a) and (b) require the filing office to acknowledge the filing of a record. Under subsection (a), the filing office is required to acknowledge the filing of a written record only upon request of the filer. Subsection (b) requires the filing office to acknowledge the filing of a non-written record even in the absence of a request from the filer.

4. Response to Search Request. Subsection (c)(3) requires the filing office to provide "the information contained in each financing statement" to a person who requests it. This requirement can be satisfied by providing copies, images, or reports. The requirement does not in any manner inhibit the filing office from also offering to provide less than all of the information (presumably for a lower fee) to a person who asks for less. Thus, subsection (c) accommodates the practice of providing only the type of record (e.g., initial financing statement, continuation statement), number assigned to the record, date and time of filing, and names and addresses of the debtor and secured party when a requesting person asks for no more (i.e., when the person does not ask for copies of financing statements). In contrast, the filing office's obligation under subsection (b) to provide an acknowledgment containing "the information contained in the record" is not defined by a customer's request. Thus unless the filer stipulates otherwise, to comply with subsection (b) the filing office's acknowledgment must contain all of the information in a record.

Subsection (c) assures that a minimum amount of information about filed records will be available to the public. It does not preclude a filing office from offering additional services.

5. Lapsed and Terminated Financing Statements. This section reflects the policy that terminated financing statements will remain part of the filing office's data base. The filing office may remove from the data base only lapsed financing statements, and then only when at least a year has passed after lapse. See Section 9-519(g). Subsection (c)(1)(C) requires a filing office to conduct a search and report as to lapsed financing statements that have not been removed from the data base, when requested.

6. Search by Debtor's Address. Subsection (c)(1)(A) contemplates that, by making a single request, a searcher will receive the results of a search of the entire public record maintained by any given filing office. Addition of the bracketed language in subsection (c)(1)(A) would permit a search report limited to financing statements showing a particular address for the debtor, but only if the search request is so limited. With or without the bracketed language, this subsection does not permit the filing office to compel a searcher to limit a request by address.

7. Medium of Communication; Certificates. Former Article 9 provided that the filing office respond to a request for information by providing a certificate. The principle of medium-neutrality would suggest that the statute not require a written certificate. Subsection (d) follows this principle by permitting the filing office to respond by communicating "in any medium." By permitting communication "in any medium," subsection (d) is not inconsistent with a system in which persons other than filing office staff conduct searches of the filing office's (computer) records.

Some searchers find it necessary to introduce the results of their search into evidence. Because official written certificates might be introduced into evidence more easily than official communications in another medium, subsection (d) affords States the option of requiring the filing office to issue written certificates upon request. The alternative bracketed language in subsection (d) recognizes that some States may prefer to permit the filing office to respond in another medium, as long as the response can be admitted into evidence in the courts of that State without extrinsic evidence of its authenticity.

8. Performance Standard. The utility of the filing system depends on the ability of searchers to get current information quickly. Accordingly, subsection (e) requires that the filing office respond to a request for information no later than two business days after it receives the request. The information contained in the response must be current as of a date no earlier than three business days before the filing office receives the request. See subsection (c)(1). The failure of the filing office to comply with performance standards, such as subsection (e), has no effect on the private rights of persons affected by the filing of records.

9. Sales of Records in Bulk. Subsection (f), which is new, mandates that the appropriate official or the filing office sell or license the filing records to the public in bulk, on a nonexclusive basis, in every medium available to the filing office. The details of implementation are left to filing-office rules

.Section 9-524. Delay by Filing Office

Delay by the filing office beyond a time limit prescribed by this part is excused if:

(1) the delay is caused by interruption of communication or computer facilities, war, emergency conditions, failure of equipment, or other circumstances beyond control of the filing office; and

(2) the filing office exercises reasonable diligence under the circumstances.

Definitional Cross References:

Equipment	Section 9-102(a)(33)
Filing office	Section 9-102(a)(37)

Official Comment

Source. New; derived from Section 4-109.

Section 9-525. Fees

(a) [Initial financing statement or other record: general rule.] Except as otherwise provided in subsection (e), the fee for filing and indexing a record under this part, other than an initial financing statement of the kind described in subsection (b), is [the amount specified in subsection (c), if applicable, plus]:

(1) $ [X] if the record is communicated in writing and consists of one or two pages;

(2) $ [2X] if the record is communicated in writing and consists of more than two pages; a

(3) $ [1/2X] if the record is communicated by another medium authorized by filing-office rule.

(b) [Initial financing statement: public-finance and manufactured-housing transactions.] Except as otherwise provided in subsection (e), the fee for filing and indexing an initial financing statement of the following kind is [the amount specified in subsection (c), if applicable, plus]:

(1) $ if the financing statement indicates that it is filed in connection with a public-finance transaction;

(2) $ if the financing statement indicates that it is filed in connection with a manufactured-home transaction.

ALTERNATIVE A

(c) [Number of names.] The number of names required to be indexed does not affect the amount of the fee in subsections (a) and (b).

ALTERNATIVE B

(c) [Number of names.] Except as otherwise provided in subsection (e), if a record is communicated in writing, the fee for each name more than two required to be indexed is $.

END OF ALTERNATIVES

(d) [Response to information request.] The fee for responding to a request for information from the filing office, including for [issuing a certificate showing] [communicating] whether there is on file any financing statement naming a particular debtor, is:

(1) $ if the request is communicated in writing; and

(2) $ if the request is communicated by another medium authorized by filing-office rule.

(e) [Record of mortgage.] This section does not require a fee with respect to a record of a mortgage which is effective as a financing statement filed as a fixture filing or as a financing statement covering as-extracted collateral or timber to be cut under Section 9-502(c). However, the recording and satisfaction fees that otherwise would be applicable to the record of the mortgage apply.

Legislative Notes:

1. *To preserve uniformity, a State that places the provisions of this section together with statutes setting fees for other services should do so without modification.*

2. *A State should enact subsection (c), Alternative A, and omit the bracketed language in subsections (a) and (b) unless its indexing system entails a substantial additional cost when indexing additional names.*

Definitional Cross References:

As-extracted collateral	Section 9-102(a)(6)
Communicate	Section 9-102(a)(18)
Debtor	Section 9-102(a)(28)
Filing office	Section 9-102(a)(37)
Financing statement	Section 9-102(a)(39)
Fixture filing	Section 9-102(a)(40)
Mortgage	Section 9-102(a)(55)
Public-finance transaction	Section 9-102(a)(67)
Record	Section 9-102(a)(70)
State	Section 9-102(a)(77)
Writing	Section 1-201(b)(43)

Official Comment

1. Source. Various sections of former Part 4.

2. Fees. This section contains all fee requirements for filing, indexing, and responding to requests for information. Uniformity in the fee structure (but not necessarily in the amount of fees) makes this Article easier for secured parties to use and reduces the likelihood that a filed record will be rejected for failure to pay at least the correct amount of the fee. See Section 9-516(b)(2).

The costs of processing electronic records are less than those with respect to written records. Accordingly, this section mandates a lower fee as an incentive to file electronically and imposes the additional charge (if any) for multiple debtors only with respect to written records. When written records are used, this Article encourages the use of the uniform forms in Section 9-521. The fee for filing these forms should be no greater than the fee for other written records.

To make the relevant information included in a filed record more accessible once the record is found, this section mandates a higher fee for longer written records than for shorter ones. Finally, recognizing that financing statements naming more than one debtor are most often filed against a husband and wife, any additional charge for multiple debtors applies to records filed with respect to more than two debtors, rather than with respect to more than one.

Section 9-526. Filing-Office Rules

(a) [Adoption of filing-office rules.] The [insert appropriate governmental official or agency] shall adopt and publish rules to implement this article. The filing-office rules must be:

(1) consistent with this article; and

(2) adopted and published in accordance with the [insert any applicable state administrative procedure act].

(b) [Harmonization of rules.] To keep the filing-office rules and practices of the filing office in harmony with the rules and practices of filing offices in other jurisdictions that enact substantially this part, and to keep the technology used by the filing office compatible with the technology used by filing offices in other jurisdictions that enact substantially this part, the [insert appropriate governmental official or agency], so far as is consistent with the purposes, policies, and provisions of this article, in adopting, amending, and repealing filing-office rules, shall:

(1) consult with filing offices in other jurisdictions that enact substantially this part; and

(2) consult the most recent version of the Model Rules promulgated by the International Association of Corporate Administrators or any successor organization; and

(3) take into consideration the rules and practices of, and the technology used by, filing offices in other jurisdictions that enact substantially this part.

Definitional Cross References:

Filing office	Section 9-102(a)(37)
Filing-office rule	Section 9-102(a)(38)
Organization	Section 1-201(b)(25)
State	Section 9-102(a)(77)

Official Comment

1. Source. New; subsection (b) derives in part from the Uniform Consumer Credit Code (1974).

2. Rules Required. Operating a filing office is a complicated business, requiring many more rules and procedures than this Article can usefully provide. Subsection (a) requires the adoption of rules to carry out the provisions of Article 9. The filing-office rules must be consistent with the provisions of the statute and adopted in accordance with local procedures. The publication requirement informs secured parties about filing-office practices, aids secured parties in evaluating filing-related risks and costs, and promotes regularity of application within the filing office.

3. Importance of Uniformity. In today's national economy, uniformity of the policies and practices of the filing offices will reduce the costs of secured transactions substantially. The International Association of Corporate Administrators (IACA), referred to in subsection (b), is an organization whose membership includes filing officers from every State. These individuals are responsible for the proper functioning of the Article 9 filing system and have worked diligently to develop model filing-office rules, with a view toward efficiency and uniformity.

Although uniformity is an important desideratum, subsection (a) affords considerable flexibility in the adoption of filing-office rules. Each State may adopt a version of subsection (a) that reflects the desired relationship between the statewide filing office described in Section 9-501(a)(2) and the local filing offices described in Section 9-501(a)(1) and that takes into account the practices of its filing offices. Subsection (a) need not designate a single official or agency to adopt rules applicable to all filing offices, and the rules applicable to the statewide filing office need not be identical to those applicable to the local filing office. For example, subsection (a) might provide for the statewide filing office to adopt filing-office rules, and, if not prohibited by other law, the filing office might adopt one set of rules for itself and another for local offices. Or, subsection (a) might designate one official or agency to adopt rules for the statewide filing office and another to adopt rules for local filing offices.

Section 9-527. Duty to Report

The [insert appropriate governmental official or agency] shall report [annually on or before] to the [Governor and Legislature] on the operation of the filing office. The report must contain a statement of the extent to which:

(1) the filing-office rules are not in harmony with the rules of filing offices in other jurisdictions that enact substantially this part and the reasons for these variations; and

(2) the filing-office rules are not in harmony with the most recent version of the Model Rules promulgated by the International Association of Corporate Administrators, or any successor organization, and the reasons for these variations.

Definitional Cross References:

Filing office	Section 9-102(a)(37)
Filing-office rule	Section 9-102(a)(38)
Organization	Section 1-201(b)(25)

Official Comment

1. Source. New; derived in part from the Uniform Consumer Credit Code (1974).

2. Duty to Report. This section is designed to promote compliance with the standards of performance imposed upon the filing office and with the requirement that the filing office's policies, practices, and technology be consistent and compatible with the policies, practices, and technology of other filing offices.

PART 6. DEFAULT

[Subpart 1. Default and Enforcement of Security Interest]

Section 9-601. Rights after Default; Judicial Enforcement; Consignor or Buyer of Accounts, Chattel Paper, Payment Intangibles, or Promissory Notes

(a) [Rights of secured party after default.] After default, a secured party has the rights provided in this part and, except as otherwise provided in Section 9-602, those provided by agreement of the parties. A secured party:

(1) may reduce a claim to judgment, foreclose, or otherwise enforce the claim, security interest, or agricultural lien by any available judicial procedure; and

(2) if the collateral is documents, may proceed either as to the documents or as to the goods they cover.

(b) [Rights and duties of secured party in possession or control.] A secured party in possession of collateral or control of collateral under Sections 7-106, 9-104, 9-105, 9-105A, 9-106, 9-107, or 9-107A has the rights and duties provided in Section 9-207.

(c) [Rights cumulative; simultaneous exercise.] The rights under subsections (a) and (b) are cumulative and may be exercised simultaneously.

(d) [Rights of debtor and obligor.] Except as otherwise provided in subsection (g) and Section 9-605, after default, a debtor and an obligor have the rights provided in this part and by agreement of the parties.

(e) [Lien of levy after judgment.] If a secured party has reduced its claim to judgment, the lien of any levy that may be made upon the collateral by virtue of an execution based upon the judgment relates back to the earliest of:

(1) the date of perfection of the security interest or agricultural lien in the collateral;

(2) the date of filing a financing statement covering the collateral; or

(3) any date specified in a statute under which the agricultural lien was created.

(f) [Execution sale.] A sale pursuant to an execution is a foreclosure of the security interest or agricultural lien by judicial procedure within the meaning of this section. A secured party may purchase at the sale and thereafter hold the collateral free of any other requirements of this article.

(g) [Consignor or buyer of certain rights to payment.] Except as otherwise provided in Section 9-607(c), this part imposes no duties upon a secured party that is a consignor or is a buyer of accounts, chattel paper, payment intangibles, or promissory notes.

Definitional Cross References:

Account	Section 9-102(a)(2)
Agreement	Section 1-201(b)(3)
Agricultural lien	Section 9-102(a)(5)
Chattel paper	Section 9-102(a)(11)
Collateral	Section 9-102(a)(12)
Consignor	Section 9-102(a)(21)
Debtor	Section 9-102(a)(28)
Document	Section 9-102(a)(30)
Financing statement	Section 9-102(a)(39)
Goods	Section 9-102(a)(44)
Obligor	Section 9-102(a)(59)
Payment intangible	Section 9-102(a)(61)
Promissory note	Section 9-102(a)(65)
Purchase	Section 1-201(b)(29)
Right	Section 1-201(b)(34)
Sale	Section 2-106(1)
Secured party	Section 9-102(a)(73)
Security interest	Section 1-201(b)(35)

Comment References: 9-109 C6

Official Comment

1. Source. Former Section 9-501(1), (2), (5).

2. Enforcement: In General. The rights of a secured party to enforce its security interest in collateral after the debtor's default are an important feature of a secured transaction. (Note that the term "right," as defined in Section 1-201(b)(34), includes a "remedy.") This Part provides those rights as well as certain limitations on their exercise for the protection of the defaulting debtor, other creditors, and other affected persons. However, subsections (a) and (d) make clear that the rights provided in this Part do not exclude other rights provided by agreement.

3. When Remedies Arise. Under subsection (a) the secured party's rights arise "[a]fter default." As did former Section 9-501, this Article leaves to the agreement of the parties the circumstances giving rise to a default. This Article does not determine whether a secured party's post-default conduct can constitute a waiver of default in the face of an agreement stating that such conduct shall not constitute a waiver. Rather, it continues to leave to the parties' agreement, as supplemented by law other than this Article, the determination whether a default has occurred or has been waived. See Section 1-103(b).

4. Possession of Collateral; Section 9-207. After a secured party takes possession of collateral following a default, there is no longer any distinction between a security interest that before default was nonpossessory and a security interest that was possessory before default, as under a common-law pledge. This Part generally does not distinguish between the rights of a secured party with a nonpossessory security interest and those of a secured party with a possessory security interest. However, Section 9-207 addresses rights and duties with respect to collateral in a secured party's possession. Under subsection (b) of this section, Section 9-207 applies not only to possession before default but also to possession after default. Subsection (b) also has been conformed to Section 9-207, which, unlike former Section 9-207, applies to secured parties having control of collateral.

5. Cumulative Remedies. Former Section 9-501(1) provided that the secured party's remedies were cumulative, but it did not explicitly provide whether the remedies could be exercised simultaneously. Subsection (c) permits the simultaneous exercise of remedies if the secured party acts in good faith. The liability scheme of Subpart 2 affords redress to an aggrieved debtor or obligor. Moreover, permitting the simultaneous exercise of remedies under subsection (c) does not override any non-UCC law, including the law of tort and statutes regulating collection of debts, under which the simultaneous exercise of remedies in a particular case constitutes abusive behavior or harassment giving rise to liability.

6. Judicial Enforcement. Under subsection (a) a secured party may reduce its claim to judgment or foreclose its interest by any available procedure outside this Article under applicable law. Subsection (e) generally follows former Section 9-501(5). It makes clear that any judicial lien that the secured party may acquire against the collateral effectively is a continuation of the original security interest (if perfected) and not the acquisition of a new interest or a transfer of property on account of a preexisting obligation. Under former Section 9-501(5), the judicial lien was stated to relate back to the date of perfection of the security interest. Subsection (e), however, provides that the lien relates back to the earlier of the date of filing or the date of perfection. This provides a secured party who enforces a security interest by judicial process with the benefit of the "first-to-file-or-perfect" priority rule of Section 9-322(a)(1).

7. Agricultural Liens. Part 6 provides parallel treatment for the enforcement of agricultural liens and security interests. Because agricultural liens are statutory rather than consensual, this Article does draw a few distinctions between these liens and security interests. Under subsection (e), the statute creating an agricultural lien would govern whether and the date to which an execution lien relates back. Section 9-606 explains when a "default" occurs in the agricultural lien context.

8. Execution Sales. Subsection (f) also follows former Section 9-501(5). It makes clear that an execution sale is an appropriate method of foreclosure contemplated by this Part. However, the sale is governed by other law and not by this Article, and the limitations under Section 9-610 on the right of a secured party to purchase collateral do not apply.

9. Sales of Receivables; Consignments. Subsection (g) provides that, except as provided in Section 9-607(c), the duties imposed on secured parties do not apply to buyers of accounts, chattel paper, payment intangibles, or promissory notes. Although denominated "secured parties," these buyers own the entire interest in the property sold and so may enforce their rights without regard to the seller ("debtor") or the seller's creditors. Likewise, a true consignor may enforce its ownership interest under other law without regard to the duties that this Part imposes on secured parties. Note, however, that Section 9-615 governs cases in which a consignee's secured party (other than a consignor) is enforcing a security interest that is senior to the security interest (i.e., ownership interest) of a true consignor.

Section 9-602. Waiver and Variance of Rights and Duties

Except as otherwise provided in Section 9-624, to the extent that they give rights to a debtor or obligor and impose duties on a secured party, the debtor or obligor may not waive or vary the rules stated in the following listed sections:

(1) Section 9-207(b)(4)(C), which deals with use and operation of the collateral by the secured party;

(2) Section 9-210, which deals with requests for an accounting and requests concerning a list of collateral and statement of account;

(3) Section 9-607(c), which deals with collection and enforcement of collateral;

(4) Sections 9-608(a) and 9-615(c) to the extent that they deal with application or payment of noncash proceeds of collection, enforcement, or disposition;

(5) Sections 9-608(a) and 9-615(d) to the extent that they require accounting for or payment of surplus proceeds of collateral;

(6) Section 9-609 to the extent that it imposes upon a secured party that takes possession of collateral without judicial process the duty to do so without breach of the peace;

(7) Sections 9-610(b), 9-611, 9-613, and 9-614, which deal with disposition of collateral;

(8) Section 9-615(f), which deals with calculation of a deficiency or surplus when a disposition is made to the secured party, a person related to the secured party, or a secondary obligor;

(9) Section 9-616, which deals with explanation of the calculation of a surplus or deficiency;

(10) Sections 9-620, 9-621, and 9-622, which deal with acceptance of collateral in satisfaction of obligation;

(11) Section 9-623, which deals with redemption of collateral;

(12) Section 9-624, which deals with permissible waivers; and

(13) Sections 9-625 and 9-626, which deal with the secured party's liability for failure to comply with this article.

Definitional Cross References:

Account	Section 9-102(a)(2)
Accounting	Section 9-102(a)(4)
Collateral	Section 9-102(a)(12)
Debtor	Section 9-102(a)(28)
Noncash proceeds	Section 9-102(a)(58)
Obligor	Section 9-102(a)(59)
Person related to individual	Section 9-102(a)(62)
Person related to organization	Section 9-102(a)(63)
Proceeds	Section 9-102(a)(64)
Right	Section 1-201(b)(34)
Secondary obligor	Section 9-102(a)(72)
Secured party	Section 9-102(a)(73)

Official Comment

1. Source. Former Section 9-501(3).

2. Waiver: In General. Section 1-302 addresses which provisions of the UCC are mandatory and which may be varied by agreement. With exceptions relating to good faith, diligence, reasonableness, and care, immediate parties, as between themselves, may vary its provisions by agreement. However, in the context of rights and duties after default, our legal system traditionally has looked with suspicion on agreements that limit the debtor's rights and free the secured party of its duties. As stated in former Section 9-501, Comment 4, "no mortgage clause has ever been allowed to clog the equity of redemption." The context of default offers great opportunity for overreaching. The suspicious attitudes of the courts have been grounded in common sense. This section, like former Section 9-501(3), codifies this long-standing and deeply rooted attitude. The specified rights of the debtor and duties of the secured party may not be waived or varied except as stated. Provisions that are not specified in this section are subject to the general rules in Section 1-302(a).

3. Nonwaivable Rights and Duties. This section revises former Section 9-501(3) by restricting the ability to waive or modify additional specified rights and duties: (i) duties under Section 9-207(b)(4)(C), which deals with the use and operation of consumer goods, (ii) the right to a response to a request for an accounting, concerning a list of collateral, or concerning a statement of account (Section 9-210), (iii) the duty to collect collateral in a commercially reasonable manner (Section 9-607), (iv) the implicit duty to refrain from a breach of the peace in taking possession of collateral under Section 9-609, (v) the duty to apply noncash proceeds of collection or disposition in a commercially reasonable manner (Sections 9-608 and 9-615), (vi) the right to a special method of calculating a surplus or deficiency in certain dispositions to a secured party, a person related to secured party, or a secondary obligor (Section 9-615), (vii) the duty to give an explanation of the calculation of a surplus or deficiency (Section 9-616), (viii) the right to limitations on the effectiveness of certain waivers (Section 9-624), and (ix) the right to hold a secured party liable for failure to comply with this Article (Sections 9-625 and 9-626). For clarity and consistency, this Article uses the term "waive or vary" instead of "renounc[e] or modify[]," which appeared in former Section 9-504(3).

This section provides generally that the specified rights and duties "may not be waived or varied." However, it does not restrict the ability of parties to agree to settle, compromise, or renounce claims for past conduct that may have constituted a violation or breach of those rights and duties, even if the settlement involves an express "waiver."

Section 9-610(c) limits the circumstances under which a secured party may purchase at its own private disposition. Transactions of this kind are equivalent to "strict foreclosures" and are governed by Sections 9-620, 9-621, and 9-622. The provisions of these sections can be waived only to the extent provided in Section 9-624(b). See Section 9-602.

4. Waiver by Debtors and Obligors. The restrictions on waiver contained in this section apply to obligors as well as debtors. This resolves a question under former Article 9 as to whether secondary obligors, assuming that they were "debtors" for purposes of former Part 5, were permitted to waive, under the law of suretyship, rights and duties under that Part.

5. Certain Post-Default Waivers. Section 9-624 permits post-default waivers in limited circumstances. These waivers must be made in agreements that are signed. Under Section 1-201(b)(3), an " 'agreement' means "the bargain of the parties in fact." In considering waivers under Section 9-624 and analogous agreements in other contexts, courts should carefully scrutinize putative agreements that appear in records that also address many additional or unrelated matters.

Section 9-603. Agreement on Standards Concerning Rights and Duties

(a) [Agreed standards.] The parties may determine by agreement the standards measuring the fulfillment of the rights of a debtor or obligor and the duties of a secured party under a rule stated in Section 9-602 if the standards are not manifestly unreasonable.

(b) [Agreed standards inapplicable to breach of peace.] Subsection (a) does not apply to the duty under Section 9-609 to refrain from breaching the peace.

Definitional Cross References:

Agreement	Section 1-201(b)(3)
Debtor	Section 9-102(a)(28)
Obligor	Section 9-102(a)(59)
Right	Section 1-201(b)(34)
Secured party	Section 9-102(a)(73)

Official Comment

1. Source. Former Section 9-501(3).

2. Limitation on Ability to Set Standards. Subsection (a), like former Section 9-501(3), permits the parties to set standards for compliance with the rights and duties under this

Part if the standards are not "manifestly unreasonable." Under subsection (b), the parties are not permitted to set standards measuring fulfillment of the secured party's duty to take collateral without breaching the peace.

Section 9-604. Procedure If Security Agreement Covers Real Property or Fixtures

(a) [Enforcement: personal and real property.] If a security agreement covers both personal and real property, a secured party may proceed:

(1) under this part as to the personal property without prejudicing any rights with respect to the real property; or

(2) as to both the personal property and the real property in accordance with the rights with respect to the real property, in which case the other provisions of this part do not apply.

(b) [Enforcement: fixtures.] Subject to subsection (c), if a security agreement covers goods that are or become fixtures, a secured party may proceed:

(1) under this part; or

(2) in accordance with the rights with respect to real property, in which case the other provisions of this part do not apply.

(c) [Removal of fixtures.] Subject to the other provisions of this part, if a secured party holding a security interest in fixtures has priority over all owners and encumbrancers of the real property, the secured party, after default, may remove the collateral from the real property.

(d) [Injury caused by removal.] A secured party that removes collateral shall promptly reimburse any encumbrancer or owner of the real property, other than the debtor, for the cost of repair of any physical injury caused by the removal. The secured party need not reimburse the encumbrancer or owner for any diminution in value of the real property caused by the absence of the goods removed or by any necessity of replacing them. A person entitled to reimbursement may refuse permission to remove until the secured party gives adequate assurance for the performance of the obligation to reimburse.

Definitional Cross References:

Collateral	Section 9-102(a)(12)
Debtor	Section 9-102(a)(28)
Fixtures	Section 9-102(a)(41)
Goods	Section 9-102(a)(44)
Person	Section 1-201(b)(27)
Right	Section 1-201(b)(34)
Secured party	Section 9-102(a)(73)
Security agreement	Section 9-102(a)(74)
Security interest	Section 1-201(b)(35)
Value	Section 1-204

Official Comment

1. Source. Former Sections 9-501(4), 9-313(8).

2. Real-Property-Related Collateral. The collateral in many transactions consists of both real and personal property. In the interest of simplicity, speed, and economy, subsection (a), like former Section 9-501(4), permits (but does not require) the secured party to proceed as to both real and personal property in accordance with its rights and remedies with respect to the real property. Subsection (a) also makes clear that a secured party who exercises rights under Part 6 with respect to personal property does not prejudice any rights under real-property law.

This Article does not address certain other real-property-related problems. In a number of States, the exercise of remedies by a creditor who is secured by both real property and non-real property collateral is governed by special legal rules. For example, under some anti-deficiency laws, creditors risk loss of rights against personal property collateral if they err in enforcing their rights against the real property. Under a "one-form-of-action" rule (or rule against splitting a cause of action), a creditor who judicially enforces a real property mortgage and does not proceed in the same action to enforce a security interest in personalty may (among other consequences) lose the right to proceed against the personalty. Although statutes of this kind create impediments to enforcement of security interests, this Article does not override these limitations under other law.

3. Fixtures. Subsection (b) is new. It makes clear that a security interest in fixtures may be enforced either under real-property law or under any of the applicable provisions of Part 6, including sale or other disposition either before or after removal of the fixtures (see subsection (c)). Subsection (b) also serves to overrule cases holding that a secured party's only remedy after default is the removal of the fixtures from the real property. See, e.g., *Maplewood Bank & Trust v. Sears, Roebuck & Co.,* 625 A.2d 537 (N.J. Super. Ct. App. Div. 1993).

Subsection (c) generally follows former Section 9-313(8). It gives the secured party the right to remove fixtures under certain circumstances. A secured party whose security interest in fixtures has priority over owners and encumbrancers of the real property may remove the collateral from the real property. However, subsection (d) requires the secured party to reimburse any owner (other than the debtor) or encumbrancer for the cost of repairing any physical injury caused by the removal. This right to reimbursement is implemented by the last sentence of subsection (d), which gives the owner or encumbrancer a right to security or indemnity as a condition for giving permission to remove.

Section 9-605. Unknown Debtor or Secondary Obligor

(a) [In general: No duty owed by secured party.] Except as provided in subsection (b), a secured party does not owe a duty based on its status as secured party:

(1) to a person that is a debtor or obligor, unless the secured party knows:

(A) that the person is a debtor or obligor;

(B) the identity of the person; and

(C) how to communicate with the person; or

(2) to a secured party or lienholder that has filed a financing statement against a person, unless the secured party knows:

(A) that the person is a debtor; and

(B) the identity of the person.

(b) [Exception: Secured party owes duty to debtor or obligor.] A secured party owes a duty based on its status as a secured party to a person if, at the time the secured party obtains control of collateral that is a controllable account, controllable electronic record, or controllable payment intangible or at the time the security interest attaches to the collateral, whichever is later:

(1) the person is a debtor or obligor; and

(2) the secured party knows that the information in subsection (a)(1)(A), (B), or (C) relating to the person is not provided by the collateral, a record attached to or logically associated with the collateral, or the system in which the collateral is recorded.

Definitional Cross References:

Collateral	Section 9-102(a)(12)
Communicate	Section 9-102(a)(18)
Controllable account	Section 9-102(a)(27A)
Controllable electronic record	Section 12-102(a)(1)
Controllable payment intangible	Section 9-102(a)(27B)
Debtor	Section 9-102(a)(28)
Financing statement	Section 9-102(a)(39)
Obligor	Section 9-102(a)(59)
Person	Section 1-201(b)(27)
Record	Section 9-102(a)(70)
Secondary obligor	Section 9-102(a)(72)
Secured party	Section 9-102(a)(73)
Security interest	Section 1-201(b)(35)

Official Comment

1. Source. New.

2. Duties to Unknown Persons and Limitation of Liability. This section relieves a secured party from duties owed to a debtor or obligor, if the secured party does not know about the debtor or obligor. Similarly, it relieves a secured party from duties owed to a secured party or lienholder who has filed a financing statement against the debtor, if the secured party does not know about the debtor. Section 9-628(a) and (b) provide analogous limitations of liability. For example, a secured party may be unaware that the original debtor has sold the collateral subject to the security interest and that the new owner has become the debtor. If so, the secured party owes no duty to the new owner (debtor) or to a secured party who has filed a financing statement against the new owner. Note that it relieves a secured party not only from duties arising under this Article but also from duties arising under other law by virtue of the secured party's status as such under this Article, unless the other law otherwise provides.

This section should be read in conjunction with the limitations on liability contained in the exculpatory provisions in subsections (a), (b), and (c) of Section 9-628. Without this group of provisions, a secured party could incur liability to unknown persons and under circumstances that would not allow the secured party to protect itself. The broadened definition of the term "debtor" underscores the need for these provisions. For example, as noted above, a debtor may dispose of collateral subject to a security interest, resulting in the transferee becoming a debtor, but the secured party may have no knowledge of the disposition or that the transferee has become a debtor. In that situation the secured party will have no means of giving notice to or accounting to the transferee debtor. Sections 9-605 and 9-628 contemplate such situations by relieving the secured party of its duties to the debtor and limiting the secured party's liability to the debtor.

3. Exceptions to Relief from Duties and Limitation of Liability. In some cases, lenders may extend secured credit without knowing, or having the ability to discover, the identity of their borrowers. Pre-2022 Sections 9-605(a) and 9-628(a) and (b) would excuse these secured parties from having duties to their debtors and obligors, including, for example, the duty to notify the debtor or secondary obligor before disposing of the collateral and the duty to account to the debtor for any surplus arising from a disposition, and would limit the secured parties' liability to their debtors and obligors. In many cases these debtors and obligors may be aware that their identities are unknown to their secured parties. By failing to make their identities and contact information known, these debtors and obligors may be impairing the ability of their secured parties to comply with their duties under Article 9. However, such debtor complicity notwithstanding, if secured parties were relieved of their duties in these circumstances, it would conflict with the policy of Section 9-602, which prohibits a waiver or variance of many rights of debtors and obligors and duties of secured parties.

Sections 9-605(b) and 9-628(f) reflect the policy that a secured party should not be free to avoid statutory duties or absolve itself from liability to a debtor or obligor when the secured party knows that the collateral, records attached to or logically associated with the collateral, and the system in which the collateral is recorded do not provide the secured party with the information necessary to fulfill its statutory duties. As discussed in the following paragraph, the secured party's knowledge that it may not be able to comply with its duties enables the secured party to protect itself from being in breach of these duties. (A person has knowledge of or knows a fact if it has "actual knowledge." Section 1-202(b).) The exceptions from the exculpatory protections otherwise afforded to secured parties are determined by the secured party's knowledge at the later of the time the secured party obtains control of a controllable account, controllable electronic record, or controllable payment intangible or the time that the security interest attaches to the collateral.

Obtaining control or attachment of the security interest serves as a rough proxy for the context in which a secured party may know that it may be unable to comply with its duties, usually because the transferor is pseudonymous. The carve-out from the exculpatory protection is limited to duties owed to and liability to a debtor—the transferor of a controllable account, controllable electronic record, or controllable payment intangible over which the secured party obtains control—or obligor. The secured party in such situations could protect itself by choosing not to enter into a transaction in which it might be unable to comply with its statutory duties or by conditioning its participation on disclosure of the debtor's or obligor's identity and contact information. Ideally, systems providing for the transfer of controllable electronic records would provide mechanisms that would permit compliance with such duties (such as methods of communication and making payments that would preserve a debtor's or obligor's pseudonymity, where that is desired). The amendments to Sections 9-605 and 9-628 provide incentives for system design that would allow for compliance with Article 9 duties.

Secured parties that enter into transactions with knowledge that they may not be able to comply with their Article 9 duties do so at their own peril. Of course, if a secured party possesses, or can obtain, the information necessary to comply with its duties, there is no need for the exculpation from those duties. Note, however, that the limitation on a secured party's relief from duties and liability relates only to secured transactions involving controllable accounts, controllable electronic records, or controllable payment intangibles. Designing systems for these assets that would afford secured parties with opportunities to comply with their Article 9 duties, as suggested above, could eliminate the risks to secured parties and also provide for the protection of debtors' and obligors' rights.

Section 9-606. Time of Default for Agricultural Lien

For purposes of this part, a default occurs in connection with an agricultural lien at the time the secured party becomes entitled to enforce the lien in accordance with the statute under which it was created.

Definitional Cross References:

Agricultural lien	Section 9-102(a)(5)
Secured party	Section 9-102(a)(73)

Official Comment

1. Source. New.

2. Time of Default. Remedies under this Part become available upon the debtor's "default." See Section 9-601. This section explains when "default" occurs in the agricultural-lien context. It requires one to consult the enabling statute to determine when the lienholder is entitled to enforce the lien.

Section 9-607. Collection and Enforcement by Secured Party

(a) [Collection and enforcement generally.] If so agreed, and in any event after default, a secured party:

(1) may notify an account debtor or other person obligated on collateral to make payment or otherwise render performance to or for the benefit of the secured party;

(2) may take any proceeds to which the secured party is entitled under Section 9-315;

(3) may enforce the obligations of an account debtor or other person obligated on collateral and exercise the rights of the debtor with respect to the obligation of the account debtor or other person obligated on collateral to make payment or otherwise render performance to the debtor, and with respect to any property that secures the obligations of the account debtor or other person obligated on the collateral;

(4) if it holds a security interest in a deposit account perfected by control under Section 9-104(a)(1), may apply the balance of the deposit account to the obligation secured by the deposit account; and

(5) if it holds a security interest in a deposit account perfected by control under Section 9-104(a)(2) or (3), may instruct the bank to pay the balance of the deposit account to or for the benefit of the secured party.

(b) [Nonjudicial enforcement of mortgage.] If necessary to enable a secured party to exercise under subsection (a)(3) the right of a debtor to enforce a mortgage nonjudicially, the secured party may record in the office in which a record of the mortgage is recorded:

(1) a copy of the security agreement that creates or provides for a security interest in the obligation secured by the mortgage; and

(2) the secured party's sworn affidavit in recordable form stating that:

(A) a default has occurred with respect to the obligation secured by the mortgage; and

(B) the secured party is entitled to enforce the mortgage nonjudicially.

(c) [Commercially reasonable collection and enforcement.] A secured party shall proceed in a commercially reasonable manner if the secured party:

(1) undertakes to collect from or enforce an obligation of an account debtor or other person obligated on collateral; and

(2) is entitled to charge back uncollected collateral or otherwise to full or limited recourse against the debtor or a secondary obligor.

(d) [Expenses of collection and enforcement.] A secured party may deduct from the collections made pursuant to subsection (c) reasonable expenses of collection and enforcement, including reasonable attorney's fees and legal expenses incurred by the secured party.

(e) [Duties to secured party not affected.] This section does not determine whether an account debtor, bank, or other person obligated on collateral owes a duty to a secured party.

Definitional Cross References:

Account debtor	Section 9-102(a)(3)
Bank	Section 9-102(a)(8)
Collateral	Section 9-102(a)(12)
Debtor	Section 9-102(a)(28)
Deposit account	Section 9-102(a)(29)
Mortgage	Section 9-102(a)(55)
Notify	Section 1-202(d)
Proceeds	Section 9-102(a)(64)
Right	Section 1-201(b)(34)
Secondary obligor	Section 9-102(a)(72)
Secured party	Section 9-102(a)(73)
Security agreement	Section 9-102(a)(74)
Security interest	Section 1-201(b)(35)

Official Comment

1. Source. Former Section 9-502; subsections (b), (d), and (e) are new.

2. Collections: In General. Collateral consisting of rights to payment is not only the most liquid asset of a typical debtor's business but also is property that may be collected without any interruption of the debtor's business. This situation is far different from that in which collateral is inventory or equipment, whose removal may bring the business to a halt. Furthermore, problems of valuation and identification, present with collateral that is tangible personal property, frequently are not as serious in the case of rights to payment and other intangible collateral. Consequently, this section, like former Section 9-502, recognizes that financing through assignments of intangibles lacks many of the complexities that arise after default in other types of financing. This section allows the assignee to liquidate collateral by collecting whatever may become due on the collateral, whether or not the method of collection contemplated by the security arrangement before default was direct (i.e., payment by the account debtor to the assignee, "notification" financing) or indirect (i.e., payment by the account debtor to the assignor, "nonnotification" financing).

3. Scope. The scope of this section is broader than that of former Section 9-502. It applies not only to collections from account debtors and obligors on instruments but also to enforcement more generally against all persons obligated on collateral. It explicitly provides for the secured party's enforcement of the debtor's rights in respect of the account debtor's (and other third parties') obligations and for the secured party's enforcement of supporting obligations with respect to those obligations. (Supporting obligations are components of the collateral under Section 9-203(f).) The rights of a secured party under subsection (a) include the right to enforce claims that the debtor may enjoy against others. For example, the claims might include a breach-of-warranty claim arising out of a defect in equipment that is collateral or a secured party's action for an injunction against infringement of a patent that is collateral. Those claims typically would be proceeds of original collateral under Section 9-315.

4. Collection and Enforcement Before Default. Like Part 6 generally, this section deals with the rights and duties of secured parties following default. However, as did former Section 9-502 with respect to collection rights, this section also applies to the collection and enforcement rights of secured parties even if a default has not occurred, as long as the debtor has so agreed. It is not unusual for debtors to agree that secured parties are entitled to collect and enforce rights against account debtors prior to default.

5. Collections by Junior Secured Party. A secured party who holds a security interest in a right to payment may exercise the right to collect and enforce under this section, even if the security interest is subordinate to a conflicting security interest in the same right to payment. Whether the junior secured party has priority in the collected proceeds depends on whether the junior secured party qualifies for priority as a purchaser of an instrument (e.g., the account debtor's check) under Section 9-330(d), as a holder in due course of an instrument under Sections 3-305 and 9-331(a), or as a transferee of money under Section 9-332(a) or (c). See Sections 9-330, Comment 7; 9-331, Comment 5; and 9-332.

6. Relationship to Rights and Duties of Persons Obligated on Collateral. This section permits a secured party to collect and enforce obligations included in collateral in its capacity as a secured party. It is not necessary for a secured party first to become the owner of the collateral pursuant to a disposition or acceptance. However, the secured party's rights, as between it and the debtor, to collect from and enforce collateral against account debtors and others obligated on collateral under subsection (a) are subject to Section 9-341, Part 4, and other applicable law. Neither this section nor former Section 9-502 should be understood to regulate the duties of an account debtor or other person obligated on collateral. Subsection (e) makes this explicit. For example, the secured party may be unable to exercise the debtor's rights under an instrument if the debtor is in possession of the instrument, or under a non-transferable letter of credit if the debtor is the beneficiary. Unless a secured party has control over a letter-of-credit right and is entitled to receive payment or performance from the issuer or a nominated person under Article 5, its remedies with respect to the letter-of-credit right may be limited to the recovery of any identifiable proceeds from the debtor. This section establishes only the baseline rights of the secured party vis-à-vis the debtor — the secured party is entitled to enforce and collect after default or earlier if so agreed.

7. Deposit Account Collateral. Subsections (a)(4) and (5) set forth the self-help remedy for a secured party whose collateral is a deposit account. Subsection (a)(4) addresses the rights of a secured party that is the bank with which the deposit account is maintained. That secured party automatically has control of the deposit account under Section 9-104(a)(1). After default, and otherwise if so agreed, the bank/secured party may apply the funds on deposit to the secured obligation.

If a security interest of a third party is perfected by control (Section 9-104(a)(2) or (a)(3)), then after default, and otherwise if so agreed, the secured party may instruct the bank to pay out the funds in the account. If the third party has control under Section 9-104(a)(3), the depositary institution is obliged to obey the instruction because the secured party is its customer. See Section 4-401. If the third party has control under Section 9-104(a)(2), the control agreement determines the depositary institution's obligation to obey.

If a security interest in a deposit account is unperfected, or is perfected by filing by virtue of the proceeds rules of Section 9-315, the depositary institution ordinarily owes no obligation to obey the secured party's instructions. See Section 9-341. To reach the funds without the debtor's cooperation, the secured party must use an available judicial procedure.

8. Rights Against Mortgagor of Real Property. Subsection (b) addresses the situation in which the collateral consists of a mortgage note (or other obligation secured by a mortgage on real property). After the debtor's (mortgagee's) default, the secured party (assignee) may wish to proceed with a nonjudicial foreclosure of the mortgage securing the note but may be unable to do so because it has not become the assignee of record. The assignee/secured party may not have taken a recordable assignment at the commencement of the transaction (perhaps the mortgage note in question was one of hundreds assigned to the secured party as collateral). Having defaulted, the mortgagee may be unwilling to sign a recordable assignment. This section enables the secured party (assignee) to become the assignee of record by recording in the applicable real-property records the security agreement and an affidavit certifying default. Of course, the secured party's rights derive from those of its debtor. Subsection (b) would not entitle the secured party to proceed with a foreclosure unless the mortgagor also were in default or the debtor (mortgagee) otherwise enjoyed the right to foreclose.

9. Commercial Reasonableness. Subsection (c) provides that the secured party's collection and enforcement rights under subsection (a) must be exercised in a commercially reasonable manner. These rights include the right to settle and compromise claims against the account debtor. The secured party's failure to observe the standard of commercial reasonableness could render it liable to an aggrieved person under Section 9-625, and the secured party's recovery of a deficiency would be subject to Section 9-626. Subsection (c) does not apply if, as is characteristic of most sales of accounts, chattel paper, payment intangibles, and promissory notes, the secured party (buyer) has no right of recourse against the debtor (seller) or a secondary obligor. However, if the secured party does have a right of recourse, the commercial-reasonableness standard applies to collection and enforcement even though the assignment to the secured party was a "true" sale. The obligation to proceed in a commercially reasonable manner arises because the collection process affects the extent of the seller's recourse liability, not because the seller retains an interest in the sold collateral (the seller does not). Concerning classification of a transaction, see Section 9-109, Comment 4.

10. Attorney's Fees and Legal Expenses. The phrase "reasonable attorney's fees and legal expenses," which appears in subsection (d), includes only those fees and expenses incurred in proceeding against account debtors or other third parties. The secured party's right to recover these expenses from the collections arises automatically under this section. The secured party also may incur other attorney's fees and legal expenses in proceeding against the debtor or obligor. Whether the secured party has a right to recover those fees and expenses depends on whether the debtor or obligor has agreed to pay them, as is the case with respect to attorney's fees and legal expenses under Sections 9-608(a)(1)(A) and 9-615(a)(1). The parties also may agree to allocate a portion of the secured party's overhead to collection and enforcement under subsection (d) or Section 9-608(a).

Section 9-608. Application of Proceeds of Collection or Enforcement; Liability for Deficiency and Rights to Surplus

(a) [Application of proceeds, surplus, and deficiency if obligation secured.] If a security interest or agricultural lien secures payment or performance of an obligation, the following rules apply:

(1) A secured party shall apply or pay over for application the cash proceeds of collection or enforcement under Section 9-607 in the following order to:

(A) the reasonable expenses of collection and enforcement and, to the extent provided for by agreement and not prohibited by law, reasonable attorney's fees and legal expenses incurred by the secured party;

(B) the satisfaction of obligations secured by the security interest or agricultural lien under which the collection or enforcement is made; and

(C) the satisfaction of obligations secured by any subordinate security interest in or other lien on the collateral subject to the security interest or agricultural lien under which the collection or enforcement is made if the secured party receives a signed demand for proceeds before distribution of the proceeds is completed.

(2) If requested by a secured party, a holder of a subordinate security interest or other lien shall furnish reasonable proof of the interest or lien within

a reasonable time. Unless the holder complies, the secured party need not comply with the holder's demand under paragraph (1)(C).

(3) A secured party need not apply or pay over for application noncash proceeds of collection and enforcement under Section 9-607 unless the failure to do so would be commercially unreasonable. A secured party that applies or pays over for application noncash proceeds shall do so in a commercially reasonable manner.

(4) A secured party shall account to and pay a debtor for any surplus, and the obligor is liable for any deficiency.

(b) [No surplus or deficiency in sales of certain rights to payment.] If the underlying transaction is a sale of accounts, chattel paper, payment intangibles, or promissory notes, the debtor is not entitled to any surplus, and the obligor is not liable for any deficiency.

Definitional Cross References:

Account	Section 9-102(a)(2)
Agreement	Section 1-201(b)(3)
Agricultural lien	Section 9-102(a)(5)
Chattel paper	Section 9-102(a)(11)
Collateral	Section 9-102(a)(12)
Debtor	Section 9-102(a)(28)
Holder	Section 1-201(b)(21)
Noncash proceeds	Section 9-102(a)(58)
Obligor	Section 9-102(a)(59)
Payment intangible	Section 9-102(a)(61)
Proceeds	Section 9-102(a)(64)
Promissory note	Section 9-102(a)(65)
Right	Section 1-201(b)(34)
Sale	Section 2-106(1)
Secured party	Section 9-102(a)(73)
Security interest	Section 1-201(b)(35)
Sign	Section 1-201(b)(37)

Official Comment

1. Source. Subsection (a) is new; subsection (b) derives from former Section 9-502(2).

2. Modifications of Prior Law. Subsections (a) and (b) modify former Section 9-502(2) by explicitly providing for the application of proceeds recovered by the secured party in substantially the same manner as provided in Section 9-615(a) and (e) for dispositions of collateral.

3. Surplus and Deficiency. Subsections (a)(4) and (b) omit, as unnecessary, the references contained in former Section 9-502(2) to agreements varying the baseline rules on surplus and deficiency. The parties are always free to agree that an obligor will not be liable for a deficiency, even if the collateral secures an obligation, and that an obligor is liable for a deficiency, even if the transaction is a sale of receivables. For parallel provisions, see Section 9-615(d) and (e).

4. Noncash Proceeds. Subsection (a)(3) addresses the situation in which an enforcing secured party receives noncash proceeds.

> **Example:** An enforcing secured party receives a promissory note from an account debtor who is unable to pay an account when it is due. The secured party accepts the note in exchange for extending the date on which the account debtor's obligation is due. The secured party may wish to credit its debtor (the assignor) with the principal amount of the note upon receipt of the note, but probably will prefer to credit the debtor only as and when the note is paid.

Under subsection (a)(3), the secured party is under no duty to apply the note or its value to the outstanding obligation unless its failure to do so would be commercially unreasonable. If the secured party does apply the note to the outstanding obligation, however, it must do so in a commercially reasonable manner. The parties may provide for the method of application of noncash proceeds by agreement, if the method is not manifestly unreasonable. See Section 9-603. This section does not explain when the failure to apply noncash proceeds would be commercially unreasonable; it leaves that determination to case-by-case adjudication. In the example, the secured party appears to have accepted the account debtor's note in order to increase the likelihood of payment and decrease the likelihood that the account debtor would dispute its obligation. Under these circumstances, it may well be commercially reasonable for the secured party to credit its debtor's obligations only as and when cash proceeds are collected from the account debtor, especially given the uncertainty that attends the account debtor's eventual payment. For an example of a secured party's receipt of noncash proceeds in which it may well be commercially unreasonable for the secured party to delay crediting its debtor's obligations with the value of noncash proceeds, see Section 9-615, Comment 3.

When the secured party is not required to "apply or pay over for application noncash proceeds," the proceeds nonetheless remain collateral subject to this Article. If the secured party were to dispose of them, for example, appropriate notification would be required (see Section 9-611), and the disposition would be subject to the standards provided in this Part (see Section 9-610). Moreover, a secured party in possession of the noncash proceeds would have the duties specified in Section 9-207.

5. No Effect on Priority of Senior Security Interest. The application of proceeds required by subsection (a) does not affect the priority of a security interest in collateral which is senior to the interest of the secured party who is collecting or enforcing collateral under Section 9-607. Although subsection (a) imposes a duty to apply proceeds to the enforcing secured party's expenses and to the satisfaction of the secured obligations owed to it and to subordinate secured parties, that duty applies only among the enforcing secured party and those persons. Concerning the priority of a junior secured party who collects and enforces collateral, see Section 9-607, Comment 5.

6. "Signed" Replaces "Authenticated." Consistent with the revised definition of "sign" in Section 1-201(b)(37), the cognate term "signed" replaces the reference to "authenticated" in the pre-2022 text of this section.

Section 9-609. Secured Party's Right to Take Possession after Default

(a) [Possession; rendering equipment unusable; disposition on debtor's premises.] After default, a secured party:

(1) may take possession of the collateral; and

(2) without removal, may render equipment unusable and dispose of collateral on a debtor's premises under Section 9-610.

(b) [Judicial and nonjudicial process.] A secured party may proceed under subsection (a):

(1) pursuant to judicial process; or

(2) without judicial process, if it proceeds without breach of the peace.

(c) [Assembly of collateral.] If so agreed, and in any event after default, a secured party may require the debtor to assemble the collateral and make it available to the secured party at a place to be designated by the secured party which is reasonably convenient to both parties.

Definitional Cross References:

Collateral	Section 9-102(a)(12)
Debtor	Section 9-102(a)(28)
Equipment	Section 9-102(a)(33)
Proceeds	Section 9-102(a)(64)
Secured party	Section 9-102(a)(73)

Official Comment

1. Source. Former Section 9-503.

2. Secured Party's Right to Possession. This section follows former Section 9-503 and earlier uniform legislation. It provides that the secured party is entitled to take possession of collateral after default.

3. Judicial Process; Breach of Peace. Subsection (b) permits a secured party to proceed under this section without judicial process if it does so "without breach of the peace." Although former Section 9-503 placed the same condition on a secured party's right to take possession of collateral, subsection (b) extends the condition to the right provided in subsection (a)(2) as well. Like former Section 9-503, this section does not define or explain the conduct that will constitute a breach of the peace, leaving that matter for continuing development by the courts. In considering whether a secured party has engaged in a breach of the peace, however, courts should hold the secured party responsible for the actions of others taken on the secured party's behalf, including independent contractors engaged by the secured party to take possession of collateral.

This section does not authorize a secured party who repossesses without judicial process to utilize the assistance of a law-enforcement officer. A number of cases have held that a repossessing secured party's use of a law-enforcement officer without benefit of judicial process constituted a failure to comply with former Section 9-503.

4. Damages for Breach of Peace. Concerning damages that may be recovered based on a secured party's breach of the peace in connection with taking possession of collateral, see Section 9-625, Comment 3.

5. Multiple Secured Parties. More than one secured party may be entitled to take possession of collateral under this section. Conflicting rights to possession among secured parties are resolved by the priority rules of this Article. Thus, a senior secured party is entitled to possession as against a junior claimant. Non-UCC law governs whether a junior secured party in possession of collateral is liable to the senior in conversion. Normally, a junior who refuses to relinquish possession of collateral upon the demand of a secured party having a superior possessory right to the collateral would be liable in conversion.

6. Secured Party's Right to Disable and Dispose of Equipment on Debtor's Premises. In the case of some collateral, such as heavy equipment, the physical removal from the debtor's plant and the storage of the collateral pending disposition may be impractical or unduly expensive. This section follows former Section 9-503 by providing that, in lieu of removal, the secured party may render equipment unusable or may dispose of collateral on the debtor's premises. Unlike former Section 9-503, however, this section explicitly conditions these rights on the debtor's default. Of course, this section does not validate unreasonable action by a secured party. Under Section 9-610, all aspects of a disposition must be commercially reasonable.

7. Debtor's Agreement to Assemble Collateral. This section follows former Section 9-503 also by validating a debtor's agreement to assemble collateral and make it available to a secured party at a place that the secured party designates. Similar to the treatment of agreements to permit collection prior to default under Section 9-607 and former 9-502, however, this section validates these agreements whether or not they are conditioned on the debtor's default. For example, a debtor might agree to make available to a secured party, from time to time, any instruments or negotiable documents that the debtor receives on account of collateral. A court should not infer from this section's validation that a debtor's agreement to assemble and make available collateral would not be enforceable under other applicable law.

8. Agreed Standards. Subject to the limitation imposed by Section 9-603(b), this section's provisions concerning agreements to assemble and make available collateral and a secured party's right to disable equipment and dispose of collateral on a debtor's premises are likely topics for agreement on standards as contemplated by Section 9-603.

Section 9-610. Disposition of Collateral after Default

(a) [Disposition after default.] After default, a secured party may sell, lease, license, or otherwise dispose of any or all of the collateral in its present condition or following any commercially reasonable preparation or processing.

(b) [Commercially reasonable disposition.] Every aspect of a disposition of collateral, including the method, manner, time, place, and other terms, must be commercially reasonable. If commercially reasonable, a secured party may dispose of collateral by public or private proceedings, by one or more contracts, as a unit or in parcels, and at any time and place and on any terms.

(c) [Purchase by secured party.] A secured party may purchase collateral:

(1) at a public disposition; or

(2) at a private disposition only if the collateral is of a kind that is customarily sold on a recognized market or the subject of widely distributed standard price quotations.

(d) [Warranties on disposition.] A contract for sale, lease, license, or other disposition includes the warranties relating to title, possession, quiet enjoyment, and the like which by operation of law accompany a voluntary disposition of property of the kind subject to the contract.

(e) [Disclaimer of warranties.] A secured party may disclaim or modify warranties under subsection (d):

(1) in a manner that would be effective to disclaim or modify the warranties in a voluntary disposition of property of the kind subject to the contract of disposition; or

(2) by communicating to the purchaser a record evidencing the contract for disposition and including an express disclaimer or modification of the warranties.

(f) [Record sufficient to disclaim warranties.] A record is sufficient to disclaim warranties under subsection (e) if it indicates "There is no warranty relating to title, possession, quiet enjoyment, or the like in this disposition" or uses words of similar import.

Definitional Cross References:

Collateral	Section 9-102(a)(12)
Contract	Section 1-201(b)(12)
Contract for sale	Section 2-106(1)
Lease	Section 2A-103(1)(j)
Purchase	Section 1-201(b)(29)
Purchaser	Section 1-201(b)(30)
Record	Section 9-102(a)(70)
Secured party	Section 9-102(a)(73)
Term	Section 1-201(b)(40)

Official Comment

1. Source. Former Section 9-504(1), (3).

2. Commercially Reasonable Dispositions. Subsection (a) follows former Section 9-504 by permitting a secured party to dispose of collateral in a commercially reasonable manner following a default. Although subsection (b) permits both public and private dispositions, including public and private dispositions conducted over the Internet, "every aspect of a disposition . . . must be commercially reasonable." This section encourages private dispositions on the assumption that they frequently will result in higher realization on collateral for the benefit of all concerned. Subsection (a) does not restrict dispositions to sales; collateral may be sold, leased, licensed, or otherwise disposed. Section 9-627 provides guidance for determining the circumstances under which a disposition is "commercially reasonable."

3. Time of Disposition. This Article does not specify a period within which a secured party must dispose of collateral. This is consistent with this Article's policy to encourage private dispositions through regular commercial channels. It may, for example, be prudent not to dispose of goods when the market has collapsed. Or, it might be more appropriate to sell a large inventory in parcels over a period of time instead of in bulk. Of course, under subsection (b) every aspect of a disposition of collateral must be commercially reasonable. This requirement explicitly includes the "method, manner, time, place and other terms." For example, if a secured party does not proceed under Section 9-620 and holds collateral for a long period of time without disposing of it, and if there is no good reason for not making a prompt disposition, the secured party may be determined not to have acted in a "commercially reasonable" manner. See also Section 1-304 (general obligation of good faith).

4. Pre-Disposition Preparation and Processing. Former Section 9-504(1) appeared to give the secured party the choice of disposing of collateral either "in its then condition or following any commercially reasonable preparation or processing." Some courts held that the "commercially reasonable" standard of former Section 9-504(3) nevertheless could impose an affirmative duty on the secured party to process or prepare the collateral prior to disposition. Subsection (a) retains the substance of the quoted language. Although courts should not be quick to impose a duty of preparation or processing on the secured party, subsection (a) does not grant the secured party the right to dispose of the collateral "in its then condition" under all circumstances. A secured party may not dispose of collateral "in its then condition" when, taking into account the costs and probable benefits of preparation or processing and the fact that the secured party would be advancing the costs at its risk, it would be commercially unreasonable to dispose of the collateral in that condition.

5. Disposition by Junior Secured Party. Disposition rights under subsection (a) are not limited to first-priority security interests. Rather, any secured party as to whom there has been a default enjoys the right to dispose of collateral under this subsection. The exercise of this right by a secured party whose security interest is subordinate to that of another secured party does not of itself constitute a conversion or otherwise give rise to liability in favor of the holder of the senior security interest. Section 9-615 addresses application of the proceeds of a disposition by a junior secured party. Under Section 9-615(a), a junior secured party owes no obligation to apply the proceeds of disposition to the satisfaction of obligations secured by a senior security interest. Section 9-615(g) builds on this general rule by protecting certain juniors from claims of a senior concerning cash proceeds of the disposition. Even if a senior were to have a non-Article 9 claim to proceeds of a junior's disposition, Section 9-615(g) would protect a junior that acts in good faith and without knowledge that its actions violate the rights of a senior party. Because the disposition by a junior would not cut off a senior's security interest or other lien (see Section 9-617), in many (probably most) cases the junior's receipt of the cash proceeds would not violate the rights of the senior.

The holder of a senior security interest is entitled, by virtue of its priority, to take possession of collateral from the junior secured party and conduct its own disposition, provided that the senior enjoys the right to take possession of the collateral from the debtor. See Section 9-609. The holder of a junior security interest normally must notify the senior secured party of an impending disposition. See Section 9-611. Regardless of whether the senior receives a notification from the junior, the junior's disposition does not of itself discharge the senior's security interest. See Section 9-617. Unless the senior secured party has authorized the disposition free and clear of its security interest, the senior's security interest ordinarily will survive the disposition by the junior and continue under Section 9-315(a). If the senior enjoys the right to repossess the collateral from the debtor, the senior likewise may recover the collateral from the transferee.

When a secured party's collateral is encumbered by another security interest or other lien, one of the claimants may seek to invoke the equitable doctrine of marshaling. As explained by the Supreme Court, that doctrine "rests upon the principle that a creditor having two funds to satisfy his debt, may not by his application of them to his demand, defeat another creditor, who may resort to only one of the funds." *Meyer v. United States,* 375 U.S. 233, 236 (1963), quoting *Sowell v. Federal Reserve Bank,* 268 U.S. 449, 456-57 (1925). The purpose of the doctrine is "to prevent the arbitrary action of a senior lienor from destroying the rights of a junior lienor or a creditor having less security." Id. at 237. Because it is an equitable doctrine, marshaling "is applied only when it can be equitably fashioned as to all of the parties" having an interest in the property. Id. This Article leaves courts free to determine whether marshaling is appropriate in any given case. See Section 1-103(b).

6. Security Interests of Equal Rank. Sometimes two security interests enjoy the same priority. This situation may arise by contract, e.g., pursuant to "equal and ratable" provisions in indentures, or by operation of law. See Section 9-328(6). This Article treats a security interest having equal priority like a senior security interest in many respects. Assume, for example, that SP-X and SP-Y enjoy equal priority, SP-W is senior to them, and SP-Z is junior. If SP-X disposes of the collateral under this section, then (i) SP-W's and SP-Y's security interests survive the disposition but SP-Z's does not, see Section 9-617, and (ii) neither SP-W nor SP-Y is entitled to receive a distribution of proceeds, but SP-Z is. See Section 9-615(a)(3).

When one considers the ability to obtain possession of the collateral, a secured party with equal priority is unlike a senior secured party. As the senior secured party, SP-W should enjoy the right to possession as against SP-X. See Section 9-609, Comment 5. If SP-W takes possession and disposes of the collateral under this section, it is entitled to apply the proceeds to satisfy its secured claim. SP-Y, however, should not have such a right to take possession from SP-X; otherwise, once SP-Y took possession from SP-X, SP-X would have the right to get possession from SP-Y, which would be obligated to redeliver possession to SP-X, and so on. Resolution of this problem is left to the parties and, if necessary, the courts.

7. Public vs. Private Dispositions. This Part maintains two distinctions between "public" and other dispositions: (i) the secured party may buy at the former, but normally not at the latter (Section 9-610(c)), and (ii) the debtor is entitled to notification of "the time and place of a public disposition" and notification of "the time after which" a private disposition or other intended disposition is to be made (Section 9-613(a) (1)(E)). It does not retain the distinction under former Section 9-504(4), under which transferees in a noncomplying public disposition could lose protection more easily than transferees in other noncomplying dispositions. Instead, Section 9-617(b) adopts a unitary standard. Although the term is not defined, as used in this Article, a "public disposition" is one at which the price is determined after the public has had a meaningful opportunity for competitive bidding. "Meaningful opportunity" is meant to imply that some form of advertisement or public notice must precede the sale (or other disposition) and that the public must have access to the sale (disposition).

A secured party's purchase of collateral at its own private disposition is equivalent to a "strict foreclosure" and is governed by Sections 9-620, 9-621, and 9-622. The provisions of these sections can be waived only to the extent provided in Section 9-624(b). See Section 9-602.

8. Investment Property. Dispositions of investment property may be regulated by the federal securities laws. Although a "public" disposition of securities under this Article may implicate the registration requirements of the Securities Act of 1933, it need not do so. A disposition that qualifies for a "private placement" exemption under the Securities Act of 1933 nevertheless may constitute a "public" disposition within the meaning of this section. Moreover, the "commercially reasonable" requirements of subsection (b) need not prevent a secured party from conducting a foreclosure sale without the issuer's compliance with federal registration requirements.

9. "Recognized Market." A "recognized market," as used in subsection (c)(2), Section 9-611(d), and Section 9-627(b)(1) and (2), is one in which the items sold are fungible and which generally produces market prices that are not lower than those that would be expected to result from, as applicable, (i) commercially reasonable dispositions to persons other than the secured party, (ii) commercially reasonable dispositions made with otherwise required notifications to the debtor or other affected persons, or (iii) dispositions otherwise made in a commercially reasonable manner. (As used here, "fungible" items are those that are considered interchangeable in the relevant market and not only items that are strictly "identical" to the other items.) The intended goals of the recognized market exceptions are to ensure that neither the debtor nor other affected parties would be disadvantaged by the special treatment given to recognized markets and to facilitate the efficiencies and cost savings that the special treatment may provide. The purpose of including in subsection (c)(2) collateral that is "the subject of widely distributed standard price quotations" and the criteria for determining whether price quotations meet this standard in subsection (c)(2) are the same as for a recognized market, although the availability of such standard price quotations may be based on, but distributed independently of, a "market" in which acquisitions and dispositions are made. Although a recognized market need not be subject to direct or indirect (e.g., self-regulatory) regulation or supervision, the existence of regulatory requirements or guidelines that are designed to arrive at prices consistent with those contemplated by subsection (c)(2) may provide useful guidance for applying the regulated market standard.

Traditionally, it has been understood that a market in which prices are individually negotiated is not a recognized market, even if the items are the subject of widely disseminated price guides (such as the Kelly Blue Book for automobiles) or are disposed of through specialized auctions (such as those conducted for dealers in livestock and automobiles). However, this does not suggest that, for example, dispositions at prices reflected in such guides or of livestock or automobiles at such auctions could not be commercially reasonable.

The New York Stock Exchange, NASDAQ, the Chicago Mercantile Exchange, and ICE Futures U.S., Inc. are examples of recognized markets. Such exchanges match buy and sell orders submitted by or on behalf of buyers and sellers that are not typically known to each other and do not involve individual negotiations. Other parties, such as inter-dealer brokers in the on- the-run U.S. Treasury market and broker-dealers in the equities market, often operate similar trading facilities that would likewise not involve known buyers or sellers or individual negotiations and may constitute recognized markets. These markets provide for robust trading with active bidding on fungible assets. There is no reason to believe that prices obtained on these markets would be less favorable to debtors, other obligors, and other interested persons than if collateral were disposed of in an off-market public or private disposition.

Trading environments generally referred to as "over-the-counter" or "OTC" markets, however, typically have involved prospective buyers and sellers that can know each other and have direct communication in order to make trades. Unlike typical exchanges, OTC markets normally do involve the individual negotiation of a price. See Carl S. Bjerre, *Investment Securities*, 71 Bus. Law. 1311, 1316-17 (2016) (contrasting exchanges and typical OTC markets for equity securities and explaining that OTC markets have tended to feature thinner markets with less liquidity and more variability of pricing).

In considering the recognized market exceptions, it is important to appreciate that recognized markets and other systems that produce equivalent "widely distributed standard price quotations" are not limited to traditional exchanges, such as those mentioned above. In particular, the exchange-OTC dichotomy no longer offers such a reliable, bright-line test for determining status as a recognized market or as a source of widely distributed standard price quotations. To be sure, some OTC markets do not qualify for the exceptions. However, recent years have witnessed a variety of new trading platforms, the use of new technologies, and new sources of providing and consuming information. There now exist markets, in particular for debt securities (including United States Treasury securities), that might be classified as OTC markets under the traditional taxonomy, but which qualify for the exceptions as recognized markets or as sources of data for widely distributed standard price quotations. Market participants rely on prices provided by these markets to the same extent and for the same purposes (including in connection with default and enforcement of security interests) as they rely on prices generated by traditional securities and commodities exchanges. These prices are widely available from business publications and online sources as well as from private subscription-based service providers. It can safely be assumed that these financial markets and the data that they provide to the public will continue to evolve. The touchstone for determining whether a market structure is a recognized market or one that produces equivalent price quotations is a functional one. It is not based on the "type" of market (e.g., "exchange," "OTC," or other classification). It is based on whether the market or distribution of price quotations provides reliable and trusted data on prices consistent with the purposes of subsection (c)(2) and the corresponding provisions of Sections 9- 611 and 9-627.

10. Relevance of Price. While not itself sufficient to establish a violation of this Part, a low price suggests that a court should scrutinize carefully all aspects of a disposition to ensure that each aspect was commercially reasonable. Note also that even if the disposition is commercially reasonable, Section 9-615(f) provides a special method for calculating a deficiency or surplus if (i) the transferee in the disposition is the secured party, a person related to the secured party, or a secondary obligor, and (ii) the amount of proceeds of the disposition is significantly below the range of proceeds that a complying disposition to a person other than the secured party, a person related to the secured party, or a secondary obligor would have brought.

11. Warranties. Subsection (d) affords the transferee in a disposition under this section the benefit of any title, possession, quiet enjoyment, and similar warranties that would have accompanied the disposition by operation of non-Article 9 law had the disposition been conducted under other circumstances. For example, the Article 2 warranty of title would apply to a sale of goods, the analogous warranties of Article 2A would apply to a lease of goods, and any common-law warranties of title would apply to dispositions of other types of collateral. See, e.g., Restatement (2d), Contracts § 333, the analogous warranties of Article 2A would apply to a lease of goods, and any common-law warranties of title would apply to dispositions of other types of collateral.

Subsection (e) explicitly provides that these warranties can be disclaimed either under other applicable law or by communicating a record containing an express disclaimer. The record need not be written, but an oral communication would not be sufficient. See Section 9-102 (definition of "record"). Subsection (f) provides a sample of wording that will effectively exclude the warranties in a disposition under this section, whether or not the exclusion would be effective under non-Article 9 law.

The warranties incorporated by subsection (d) are those relating to "title, possession, quiet enjoyment, and the like." Depending on the circumstances, a disposition under this section also may give rise to other statutory or implied warranties, e.g., warranties of quality or fitness for purpose. Law other than this Article determines whether such other warranties apply to a disposition under this section. Other law also determines issues relating to disclaimer of such warranties. For example, a foreclosure sale of a car by a car dealer could give rise to an implied warranty of merchantability (Section 2-314) unless effectively disclaimed or modified (Section 2-316).

This section's approach to these warranties conflicts with the former Comment to Section 2-312. This Article rejects the baseline assumption that commercially reasonable dispositions under this section are out of the ordinary commercial course or peculiar. The Comment to Section 2-312 has been revised accordingly.

Section 9-611. Notification before Disposition of Collateral

(a) ["Notification date."] In this section, "notification date" means the earlier of the date on which:

(1) a secured party sends to the debtor and any secondary obligor a signed notification of disposition; or

(2) the debtor and any secondary obligor waive the right to notification.

(b) [Notification of disposition required.] Except as otherwise provided in subsection (d), a secured party that disposes of collateral under Section 9-610 shall send to the persons specified in subsection (c) a reasonable signed notification of disposition.

(c) [Persons to be notified.] To comply with subsection (b), the secured party shall send a signed notification of disposition to:

(1) the debtor;

(2) any secondary obligor; and

(3) if the collateral is other than consumer goods:

(A) any other person from which the secured party has received, before the notification date, a signed notification of a claim of an interest in the collateral;

(B) any other secured party or lienholder that, 10 days before the notification date, held a security interest in or other lien on the collateral perfected by the filing of a financing statement that:

(i) identified the collateral;

(ii) was indexed under the debtor's name as of that date; and

(iii) was filed in the office in which to file a financing statement against the debtor covering the collateral as of that date; and

(C) any other secured party that, 10 days before the notification date, held a security interest in the collateral perfected by compliance with a statute, regulation, or treaty described in Section 9-311(a).

(d) [Subsection (b) inapplicable: perishable collateral; recognized market.] Subsection (b) does not apply if the collateral is perishable or threatens to decline speedily in value or is of a type customarily sold on a recognized market.

(e) [Compliance with subsection (c)(3)(B).] A secured party complies with the requirement for notification prescribed by subsection (c)(3)(B) if:

(1) not later than 20 days or earlier than 30 days before the notification date, the secured party requests, in a commercially reasonable manner, information concerning financing statements indexed under the debtor's name in the office indicated in subsection (c)(3)(B); and

(2) before the notification date, the secured party:

(A) did not receive a response to the request for information; or

(B) received a response to the request for information and sent a signed notification of disposition to each secured party or other lienholder named in that response whose financing statement covered the collateral.

Definitional Cross References:

Collateral	Section 9-102(a)(12)
Consumer goods	Section 9-102(a)(23)
Debtor	Section 9-102(a)(28)
Financing statement	Section 9-102(a)(39)
Person	Section 1-201(b)(27)
Secondary obligor	Section 9-102(a)(72)
Secured party	Section 9-102(a)(73)
Security interest	Section 1-201(b)(35)
Send	Section 1-201(b)(36)
Sign	Section 1-201(b)(37)
Value	Section 1-204

Official Comment

1. Source. Former Section 9-504(3).

2. Reasonable Notification. This section requires a secured party who wishes to dispose of collateral under Section 9-610 to send "a reasonable signed notification of disposition" to specified interested persons, subject to certain exceptions. The notification must be reasonable as to the manner in which it is sent, its timeliness (i.e., a reasonable time before the disposition is to take place), and its content. See Sections 9-612 (timeliness of notification), 9-613 (contents of notification generally), 9-614 (contents of notification in consumer-goods transactions).

3. Notification to Debtors and Secondary Obligors. This section imposes a duty to send notification of a disposition not only to the debtor but also to any secondary obligor. Subsections (b) and (c) resolve an uncertainty under former Article 9 by providing that secondary obligors (sureties) are entitled to receive notification of an intended disposition of collateral, regardless of who created the security interest in the collateral. If the surety created the security interest, it would be the debtor. If it did not, it would be a secondary obligor. (This Article also resolves the question of the secondary obligor's ability to waive, pre-default, the right to notification — waiver generally is not permitted. See Section 9-602.) Section 9-605 relieves a secured party from any duty to send notification to a debtor or secondary obligor unknown to the secured party.

Under subsection (b), the principal obligor (borrower) is not always entitled to notification of disposition.

> **Example:** Behnfeldt borrows on an unsecured basis, and Bruno grants a security interest in her car to secure the debt. Behnfeldt is a primary obligor, not a secondary obligor. As such, she is not entitled to notification of disposition under this section.

4. Notification to Other Secured Parties. Prior to the 1972 amendments to Article 9, former Section 9-504(3) required the enforcing secured party to send reasonable notification of the disposition:

> except in the case of consumer goods to any other person who has a security interest in the collateral and who has duly filed a financing statement indexed in the name of the debtor in this State or who is known by the secured party to have a security interest in the collateral.

The 1972 amendments eliminated the duty to give notice to secured parties other than those from whom the foreclosing secured party had received written notice of a claim of an interest in the collateral.

Many of the problems arising from dispositions of collateral encumbered by multiple security interests can be ameliorated or solved by informing all secured parties of an intended disposition and affording them the opportunity to work with one another. To this end, subsection (c)(3)(B) expands the duties of the foreclosing secured party to include the duty to notify (and the corresponding burden of searching the files to discover) certain competing secured parties. The subsection imposes a search burden that in some cases may be greater than the pre-1972 burden on foreclosing secured parties but certainly is more modest than that faced by a new secured lender.

To determine who is entitled to notification, the foreclosing secured party must determine the proper office for filing a financing statement as of a particular date, measured by reference to the "notification date," as defined in subsection (a). This determination requires reference to the choice-of-law provisions of Part 3. The secured party must ascertain whether any financing statements covering the collateral and indexed under the debtor's name, as the name existed as of that date, in fact were filed in that office. The foreclosing secured party generally need not notify secured parties whose effective financing statements have become more difficult to locate because of changes in the location of the debtor, proceeds rules, or changes in the name that is sufficient as the name of the debtor under Section 9-503(a).

Under subsection (c)(3)(C), the secured party also must notify a secured party who has perfected a security interest by complying with a statute or treaty described in Section 9-311(a), such as a certificate-of-title statute.

Subsection (e) provides a "safe harbor" that takes into account the delays that may be attendant to receiving information from the public filing offices. It provides, generally, that the secured party will be deemed to have satisfied its notification duty under subsection (c)(3)(B) if it requests a search from the proper office at least 20 but not more than 30 days before sending notification to the debtor and if it also sends a notification to all secured parties (and other lienholders) reflected on the search report. The secured party's duty under subsection (c)(3)(B) also will be satisfied if the secured party requests but does not receive a search report before the notification is sent to the debtor. Thus, if subsection (e) applies, a secured party who is entitled to notification under subsection (c)(3)(B) has no remedy against a foreclosing secured party who does not send the notification. The foreclosing secured party has complied with the notification requirement. Subsection (e) has no effect on the requirements of the other paragraphs of subsection (c). For example, if the foreclosing secured party received a notification from the holder of a conflicting security interest in accordance with subsection (c)(3)(A) but failed to send to the holder a notification of the disposition, the holder of the conflicting security interest would have the right to recover any loss under Section 9-625(b).

5. Signature Requirement. Subsections (b), (c), and (e) explicitly provide that notifications must be "signed." Some cases read pre-1998 Section 9-504(3) as validating oral notification. Consistent with the revised definition of "sign" in Section 1-201(b)(37), the cognate term "signed" replaces the references to "authenticated" in the pre-2022 text of this section.

6. Second Try. This Article leaves to judicial resolution, based upon the facts of each case, the question whether the requirement of "reasonable notification" requires a "second try," i.e., whether a secured party who sends notification and learns that the debtor did not receive it must attempt to locate the debtor and send another notification.

7. Recognized Market; Perishable Collateral. Subsection (d) makes it clear that there is no obligation to give notification of a disposition in the case of perishable collateral or collateral customarily sold on a recognized market (e.g., marketable securities). As to what constitutes a recognized market, see Section 9-610, Comment 9.

8. Failure to Conduct Notified Disposition. Nothing in this Article prevents a secured party from electing not to conduct a disposition after sending a notification. Nor does this Article prevent a secured party from electing to send a revised notification if its plans for disposition change. This assumes, however, that the secured party acts in good faith, the revised notification is reasonable, and the revised plan for disposition and any attendant delay are commercially reasonable.

9. Waiver. A debtor or secondary obligor may waive the right to notification under this section only by a post-default signed agreement. See Section 9-624(a).

10. Other Law. Other State or federal law may contain requirements concerning notification of a disposition of property by a secured party. For example, federal law imposes notification requirements with respect to the enforcement of mortgages on federally documented vessels. Principles of statutory interpretation and, in the context of federal law, supremacy and preemption determine whether and to what extent law other than this Article supplements, displaces, or is displaced by this Article. See Sections 1-103, 1-104, 9-109(c)(1).

Section 9-612. Timeliness of Notification before Disposition of Collateral

(a) [Reasonable time is question of fact.] Except as otherwise provided in subsection (b), whether a notification is sent within a reasonable time is a question of fact.

(b) [10-day period sufficient in non-consumer transaction.] In a transaction other than a consumer transaction, a notification of disposition sent after default and 10 days or more before the earliest time of disposition set forth in the notification is sent within a reasonable time before the disposition.

Definitional Cross References:

Collateral	Section 9-102(a)(12)
Consumer transaction	Section 9-102(a)(26)

Official Comment

1. Source. New.

2. Reasonable Notification. Section 9-611(b) requires the secured party to send a "reasonable signed notification." Under that section, as under pre-1998 Section 9-504(3), one aspect of a reasonable notification is its timeliness. This generally means that the notification must be sent at a reasonable time in advance of the date of a public disposition or the date after which a private disposition is to be made. A notification that is sent so near to the disposition date that a notified person could not be expected to act on or take account of the notification would be unreasonable.

3. Timeliness of Notification: Safe Harbor. The 10-day notice period in subsection (b) is intended to be a "safe harbor" and not a minimum requirement. To qualify for the "safe harbor" the notification must be sent after default. A notification also must be sent in a commercially reasonable manner. See Section 9-611(b) ("reasonable signed notification"). These requirements prevent a secured party from taking advantage of the "safe harbor" by, for example, giving the debtor a notification at the time of the original extension of credit or sending the notice by surface mail to a debtor overseas.

Section 9-613. Contents and Form of Notification before Disposition of Collateral: General

(a) [Contents and form of notification] Except in a consumer-goods transaction, the following rules apply:

(1) The contents of a notification of disposition are sufficient if the notification:

(A) describes the debtor and the secured party;

(B) describes the collateral that is the subject of the intended disposition;

(C) states the method of intended disposition;

(D) states that the debtor is entitled to an accounting of the unpaid indebtedness and states the charge, if any, for an accounting; and

(E) states the time and place of a public disposition or the time after which any other disposition is to be made.

(2) Whether the contents of a notification that lacks any of the information specified in paragraph (1) are nevertheless sufficient is a question of fact.

(3) The contents of a notification providing substantially the information specified in paragraph (1) are sufficient, even if the notification includes:

(A) information not specified by that paragraph; or

(B) minor errors that are not seriously misleading.

(4) A particular phrasing of the notification is not required.

(5) The following form of notification and the form appearing in Section 9-614(a)(3), when completed in accordance with the instructions in subsection (b) and Section 9-614(b), each provides sufficient information:

NOTIFICATION OF DISPOSITION OF COLLATERAL

To: (*Name of debtor, obligor, or other person to which the notification is sent*)

From: (*Name, address, and telephone number of secured party*)

{1} Name of any debtor that is not an addressee: (*Name of each debtor*)

{2} We will sell (*describe collateral*) (to the highest qualified bidder) at public sale. A sale could include a lease or license. The sale will be held as follows:

(Date) ____________________

(Time) ____________________

(Place) ____________________

{3} We will sell (*describe collateral*) at private sale sometime after (*date*). A sale could include a lease or license.

{4} You are entitled to an accounting of the unpaid indebtedness secured by the property that we intend to sell or, as applicable, lease or license.

{5} If you request an accounting you must pay a charge of $ (*amount*).

{6} You may request an accounting by calling us at (*telephone number*).

[End of Form]

(b) [Instructions for form of notification.] The following instructions apply to the form of notification in subsection (a)(5):

(1) The instructions in this subsection refer to the numbers in braces before items in the form of notification in subsection (a)(5). Do not include the numbers or braces in the notification. The numbers and braces are used only for the purpose of these instructions.

(2) Include and complete item {1} only if there is a debtor that is not an addressee of the notification and list the name or names.

(3) Include and complete either item {2}, if the notification relates to a public disposition of the collateral, or item {3}, if the notification relates to a private disposition of the collateral. If item {2} is included, include the words "to the highest qualified bidder" only if applicable.

(4) Include and complete items {4} and {6}

(5) Include and complete item {5} only if the sender will charge the recipient for an accounting.

Definitional Cross References:

Accounting	Section 9-102(a)(4)
Collateral	Section 9-102(a)(12)
Consumer-goods transaction	Section 9-102(a)(24)
Debtor	Section 9-102(a)(28)
Lease	Section 2A-103(1)(j)
Obligor	Section 9-102(a)(59)
Sale	Section 2-106(1)
Secured party	Section 9-102(a)(73)

Official Comment

1. Source. New.

2. Contents of Notification. To comply with the "reasonable signed notification" requirement of Section 9-611(b), the contents of a notification must be reasonable. Except in a consumer-goods transaction, the contents of a notification that includes the information set forth in paragraph (a)(1) are sufficient as a matter of law, unless the parties agree otherwise. (The reference to "time" of disposition means here, as it did in former Section 9-504(3), not only the hour of the day but also the date.) Although a secured party may choose to include additional information concerning the transaction or the debtor's rights and obligations, no additional information is required unless the parties agree otherwise. A notification that lacks some of the information set forth in paragraph (a)(1) nevertheless may be sufficient if found to be reasonable by the trier of fact, under paragraph (a)(2). A properly completed sample form of notification in paragraph (a)(5) or in Section 9-614(a)(3) is an example of a notification that would contain the information set forth in paragraph (a)(1). Under paragraph (a)(4), however, no particular phrasing of the notification is required.

This section applies to a notification of a public disposition conducted electronically. A notification of an electronic disposition satisfies subparagraph (a)(1)(E) if it states the time when the disposition is scheduled to begin and states the electronic location. For example, under the technology current in 2010, the Uniform Resource Locator (URL) or other Internet address where the site of the public disposition can be accessed suffices as an electronic location.

3. Style Changes in Safe-Harbor Form and Medium Netrality No change in substance is intended by the changes in style to the form provided in paragraph (5) of the pre-2022 text of this section. However, the presentation and explanation of how to use the form has been simplified and clarified.

Section 9-614. Contents and Form of Notification before Disposition of Collateral: Consumer-goods Transaction

(a) [Contents and form of notification] In a consumer-goods transaction, the following rules apply:

(1) A notification of disposition must provide the following information:

(A) the information specified in Section 9-613(a)(1);

(B) a description of any liability for a deficiency of the person to which the notification is sent;

(C) a telephone number from which the amount that must be paid to the secured party to redeem the collateral under Section 9-623 is available; and

(D) a telephone number or mailing address from which additional information concerning the disposition and the obligation secured is available.

(2) A particular phrasing of the notification is not required.

(3) The following form of notification, when completed in accordance with the instructions in subsection (b), provides sufficient information:

(*Name and address of secured party*)

(*Date*)

NOTICE OF OUR PLAN TO SELL PROPERTY

(*Name and address of any obligor who is also a debtor*)

Subject: (*Identify Transaction*)

We have your (*describe collateral*), because you broke promises in our agreement.

{1} We will sell (*describe collateral*) at public sale. A sale could include a lease or license. The sale will be held as follows:

(Date) ____________________

(Time) ____________________

(Place) ____________________

You may attend the sale and bring bidders if you want.

{2} We will sell (*describe collateral*) at private sale sometime after (date). A sale could include a lease or license.

{3} The money that we get from the sale, after paying our costs, will reduce the amount you owe. If we get less money than you owe, you (*will or will not, as applicable*) still owe us the difference. If we get more money than you owe, you will get the extra money, unless we must pay it to someone else.

{4} You can get the property back at any time before we sell it by paying us the full amount you owe, not just the past due payments, including our expenses. To learn the exact amount you must pay, call us at (*telephone number*).

{5} If you want us to explain to you (in writing or in (*description of electronic record*)) how we have figured the amount that you owe us, you may

{6} call us at (*telephone number*) or write us at (*secured party's address*) (or contact us by (*description of electronic communication method*))

{7} and request a (written explanation) (a written explanation or an explanation in (description of electronic record)) (an explanation in (description of electronic record)).

{8} (We will charge you $ (*amount*) for the explanation if we sent you another written explanation of the amount you owe us within the last six months.)

{9} If you need more information about the sale call us at (*telephone number*) or write us at (*secured party's address*).

{10} We are sending this notice to the following other people who have an interest in (*describe collateral*) or who owe money under your agreement:

(*Names of all other debtors and obligors, if any*)

(4) A notification in the form of paragraph (3) is sufficient, even if additional information appears at the end of the form.

(5) A notification in the form of paragraph (3) is sufficient, even if it includes errors in information not required by paragraph (1), unless the error is misleading with respect to rights arising under this article.

(6) If a notification under this section is not in the form of paragraph (3), law other than this article determines the effect of including information not required by paragraph (1).

(b) [Instructions for form of notification.] The following instructions apply to the form of notification in subsection (a)(3):

(1) The instructions in this subsection refer to the numbers in braces before items in the form of notification in subsection (a)(3). Do not include the numbers or braces in the notification. The numbers and braces are used only for the purpose of these instructions.

(2) Include and complete either item {1}, if the notification relates to a public disposition of the collateral, or item {2}, if the notification relates to a private disposition of the collateral.

(3) Include and complete items {3}, {4}, {5}, {6}, and {7}.

(4) In item {5}, include and complete any one of the three alternative methods for the explanation — writing, writing or electronic record, or electronic record.

(5) In item {6}, include the telephone number. In addition, the sender may include and complete either or both of the two additional alternative methods of communication — writing or electronic communication — for the recipient of the notification to communicate with the sender. Neither of the two additional methods of communication is required to be included.

(6) In item {7}, include and complete the method or methods for the explanation — writing, writing or electronic record, or electronic record — included in item {5}.

(7) Include and complete item {8} only if a written explanation is included in item {5} as a method for communicating the explanation and the sender will charge the recipient for another written explanation.

(8) In item {9}, include either the telephone number or the address or both the telephone number and the address. In addition, the sender may include and complete the additional method of communication — electronic communication — for the recipient of the notification to communicate with the sender. The additional method of electronic communication is not required to be included.

(9) If item {10} does not apply, insert "None" after "agreement:".

Definitional Cross References:

Agreement	Section 1-201(b)(3)
Collateral	Section 9-102(a)(12)
Consumer-goods transaction	Section 9-102(a)(24)
Debtor	Section 9-102(a)(28)
Electronic	Section 1-201(b)(16A)
Lease	Section 2A-103(1)(j)
Money	Section 9-102(a)(54A)
Notice	Section 1-202(a)
Notification	Section 1-202(d)
Obligor	Section 9-102(a)(59)
Person	Section 1-201(b)(27)
Record	Section 9-102(a)(70)
Right	Section 1-201(b)(34)
Sale	Section 2-106(1)
Secured party	Section 9-102(a)(73)
Send	Section 1-201(b)(36)
Written or writing	Section 1-201(b)(43)

Official Comment

1. Source. New.

2. Notification in Consumer-Goods Transactions. Paragraph (a)(1) sets forth the information required for a reasonable notification in a consumer-goods transaction. A notification that lacks any of the information set forth in paragraph (a)(1) is insufficient as a matter of law. Compare Section 9-613(a)(2), under which the trier of fact may find a notification to be sufficient even if it lacks some information listed in paragraph (a)(1) of that section.

3. Safe-Harbor Form of Notification; Errors in Information. Although paragraph (a)(2) provides that a particular phrasing of a notification is not required, paragraph (a)(3) specifies a safe-harbor form that, when properly completed, satisfies paragraph (a)(1). Paragraphs (a)(4), (5), and (6) contain special rules applicable to erroneous and additional information. Under paragraph (a)(4), a notification in the safe-harbor form specified in paragraph (a)(3) is not rendered insufficient if it contains additional information at the end of the form. Paragraph (a)(5) provides that non-misleading errors in information contained in a notification are permitted if the safe-harbor form is used *and if the errors are in information not required by paragraph (a)(1)*. Finally, if a notification is in a form other than the paragraph (a)(3) safe-harbor form, other law determines the effect of including in the notification information other than that required by paragraph (a)(1).

4. Style Changes in Safe-harbor Form and medium Neutrality. No change in substance is intended by the changes in style to the form provided in paragraph (3) of the pre- 2022 text of this section, except that in furtherance of medium neutrality references to "electronic record" and "electronic communication method" have been added to the form. However, the presentation and explanation of how to use the form has been simplified and clarified.

Section 9-615. Application of Proceeds of Disposition; Liability for Deficiency and Rights to Surplus

(a) [Application of proceeds.] A secured party shall apply or pay over for application the cash proceeds of disposition under Section 9-610 in the following order to:

(1) the reasonable expenses of retaking, holding, preparing for disposition, processing, and disposing, and, to the extent provided for by agreement and not prohibited by law, reasonable attorney's fees and legal expenses incurred by the secured party;

(2) the satisfaction of obligations secured by the security interest or agricultural lien under which the disposition is made;

(3) the satisfaction of obligations secured by any subordinate security interest in or other subordinate lien on the collateral if:

(A) the secured party receives from the holder of the subordinate security interest or other lien a signed demand for proceeds before distribution of the proceeds is completed; and

(B) in a case in which a consignor has an interest in the collateral, the subordinate security interest or other lien is senior to the interest of the consignor; and

(4) a secured party that is a consignor of the collateral if the secured party receives from the consignor a signed demand for proceeds before distribution of the proceeds is completed.

(b) [Proof of subordinate interest.] If requested by a secured party, a holder of a subordinate security interest or other lien shall furnish reasonable proof of the interest or lien within a reasonable time. Unless the holder does so, the secured party need not comply with the holder's demand under subsection (a)(3).

(c) [Application of noncash proceeds.] A secured party need not apply or pay over for application noncash proceeds of disposition under Section 9-610 unless the failure to do so would be commercially unreasonable. A secured party that applies or pays over for application noncash proceeds shall do so in a commercially reasonable manner.

(d) [Surplus or deficiency if obligation secured.] If the security interest under which a disposition is made secures payment or performance of an obligation, after making the payments and applications required by subsection (a) and permitted by subsection (c):

(1) unless subsection (a)(4) requires the secured party to apply or pay over cash proceeds to a consignor, the secured party shall account to and pay a debtor for any surplus; and

(2) the obligor is liable for any deficiency.

(e) [No surplus or deficiency in sales of certain rights to payment.] If the underlying transaction is a sale of accounts, chattel paper, payment intangibles, or promissory notes:

(1) the debtor is not entitled to any surplus; and

(2) the obligor is not liable for any deficiency.

(f) [Calculation of surplus or deficiency in disposition to person related to secured party.] The surplus or deficiency following a disposition is calculated based on the amount of proceeds that would have been realized in a disposition complying with this part to a transferee other than the secured party, a person related to the secured party, or a secondary obligor if:

(1) the transferee in the disposition is the secured party, a person related to the secured party, or a secondary obligor; and

(2) the amount of proceeds of the disposition is significantly below the range of proceeds that a complying disposition to a person other than the secured party, a person related to the secured party, or a secondary obligor would have brought.

(g) [Cash proceeds received by junior secured party.] A secured party that receives cash proceeds of a disposition in good faith and without knowledge that the receipt violates the rights of the holder of a security interest or other lien that is not subordinate to the security interest or agricultural lien under which the disposition is made:

(1) takes the cash proceeds free of the security interest or other lien;

(2) is not obligated to apply the proceeds of the disposition to the satisfaction of obligations secured by the security interest or other lien; and

(3) is not obligated to account to or pay the holder of the security interest or other lien for any surplus.

Definitional Cross References:

Account	Section 9-102(a)(2)
Agreement	Section 1-201(b)(3)
Agricultural lien	Section 9-102(a)(5)
Cash proceeds	Section 9-102(a)(9)
Chattel paper	Section 9-102(a)(11)
Collateral	Section 9-102(a)(12)
Consignor	Section 9-102(a)(21)
Debtor	Section 9-102(a)(28)

Good faith	Section 1-201(b)(20)
Holder	Section 1-201(b)(21)
Noncash proceeds	Section 9-102(a)(58)
Obligor	Section 9-102(a)(59)
Payment intangible	Section 9-102(a)(61)
Person related to individual	Section 9-102(a)(62)
Person related to organization	Section 9-102(a)(63)
Proceeds	Section 9-102(a)(64)
Promissory note	Section 9-102(a)(65)
Right	Section 1-201(b)(34)
Sale	Section 2-106(1)
Secondary obligor	Section 9-102(a)(72)
Secured party	Section 9-102(a)(73)
Security interest	Section 1-201(b)(35)
Sign	Section 1-201(b)(37)

Comment Reference: 9-610 C5

Official Comment

1. Source. Former Section 9-504(1), (2).

2. Application of Proceeds. This section contains the rules governing application of proceeds and the debtor's liability for a deficiency following a disposition of collateral. Subsection (a) sets forth the basic order of application. The proceeds are applied first to the expenses of disposition, second to the obligation secured by the security interest that is being enforced, and third, in the specified circumstances, to interests that are subordinate to that security interest.

Subsections (a) and (d) also address the right of a consignor to receive proceeds of a disposition by a secured party whose interest is senior to that of the consignor. Subsection (a) requires the enforcing secured party to pay excess proceeds first to subordinate secured parties or lienholders whose interests are senior to that of a consignor and, finally, to a consignor. Inasmuch as a consignor is the owner of the collateral, secured parties and lienholders whose interests are junior to the consignor's interest will not be entitled to any proceeds. In like fashion, under subsection (d)(1) the debtor is not entitled to a surplus when the enforcing secured party is required to pay over proceeds to a consignor.

3. Noncash Proceeds. Subsection (c) addresses the application of noncash proceeds of a disposition, such as a note or lease. The explanation in Section 9-608, Comment 4, generally applies to this subsection.

> **Example:** A secured party in the business of selling or financing automobiles takes possession of collateral (an automobile) following its debtor's default. The secured party decides to sell the automobile in a private disposition under Section 9-610 and sends appropriate notification under Section 9-611. After undertaking its normal credit investigation and in accordance with its normal credit policies, the secured party sells the automobile on credit, on terms typical of the credit terms normally extended by the secured party in the ordinary course of its business. The automobile stands as collateral for the remaining balance of the price. The noncash proceeds received by the secured party are chattel paper. The secured party may wish to credit its debtor (the assignor) with the principal amount of the chattel paper or may wish to credit the debtor only as and when the payments are made on the chattel paper by the buyer.

Under subsection (c), the secured party is under no duty to apply the noncash proceeds (here, the chattel paper) or their value to the secured obligation unless its failure to do so would be commercially unreasonable. If a secured party elects to apply the chattel paper to the outstanding obligation, however, it must do so in a commercially reasonable manner. The facts in the example indicate that it would be commercially unreasonable for the secured party to fail to apply the value of the chattel paper to the original debtor's secured obligation. Unlike the example in Comment 4 to Section 9-608, the noncash proceeds received in this example are of the type that the secured party regularly generates in the ordinary course of its financing business in nonforeclosure transactions. The original debtor should not be exposed to delay or uncertainty in this situation. Of course, there will be many situations that fall between the examples presented in the Comment to Section 9-608 and in this Comment. This Article leaves their resolution to the court based on the facts of each case.

One would expect that where noncash proceeds are or may be material, the secured party and debtor would agree to more specific standards in an agreement entered into before or after default. The parties may agree to the method of application of noncash proceeds if the method is not manifestly unreasonable. See Section 9-603.

When the secured party is not required to "apply or pay over for application noncash proceeds," the proceeds nonetheless remain collateral subject to this Article. See Section 9-608, Comment 4.

4. Surplus and Deficiency. Subsection (d) deals with surplus and deficiency. It revises former Section 9-504(2) by imposing an explicit requirement that the secured party "pay" the debtor for any surplus, while retaining the secured party's duty to "account." Inasmuch as the debtor may not be an obligor, subsection (d) provides that the obligor (not the debtor) is liable for the deficiency. The special rule governing surplus and deficiency when receivables have been sold likewise takes into account the distinction between a debtor and an obligor. Subsection (d) also addresses the situation in which a consignor has an interest that is subordinate to the security interest being enforced.

5. Collateral Under New Ownership. When the debtor sells collateral subject to a security interest, the original debtor (creator of the security interest) is no longer a debtor inasmuch as it no longer has a property interest in the collateral; the buyer is the debtor. See Section 9-102. As between the debtor (buyer of the collateral) and the original debtor (seller of the collateral), the debtor (buyer) normally would be entitled to the surplus following a disposition. Subsection (d) therefore requires the secured party to pay the surplus to the debtor (buyer), not to the original debtor (seller) with which it has dealt. But, because this situation typically arises as a result of the debtor's wrongful act, this Article does not expose the secured party to the risk of determining ownership of the collateral. If the secured party does not know about the buyer and accordingly pays the surplus to the original debtor, the exculpatory provisions of this Article exonerate the secured party from liability to the buyer. See Sections 9-605, 9-628(a), (b). If a debtor sells collateral free of a security interest, as in a sale to a buyer in ordinary course of business (see Section 9-320(a)), the property is no longer collateral and the buyer is not a debtor.

6. Certain "Low-Price" Dispositions. Subsection (f) provides a special method for calculating a deficiency or surplus when the secured party, a person related to the secured party (defined in Section 9-102), or a secondary obligor acquires the collateral at a foreclosure disposition. It recognizes that when the foreclosing secured party or a related party is the transferee of the collateral, the secured party sometimes lacks the incentive to maximize the proceeds of disposition. As a consequence, the disposition may comply with the procedural requirements of this Article (e.g., it is conducted in a commercially reasonable manner following reasonable notice) but nevertheless fetch a low price.

Subsection (f) adjusts for this lack of incentive. If the proceeds of a disposition of collateral to a secured party, a person related to the secured party, or a secondary obligor are "significantly below the range of proceeds that a complying disposition to a person other than the secured party, a person related to the secured party, or a secondary obligor would have brought," then instead of calculating a deficiency (or surplus) based on the actual net proceeds, the calculation is based upon the amount that would have been received in a commercially reasonable disposition to a person other than the secured party, a person related to the secured party, or a secondary obligor. Subsection (f) thus rejects the view that the secured party's receipt of such a price necessarily constitutes noncompliance with Part 6. However, such a price may suggest the need for greater judicial scrutiny. See Section 9-610, Comment 10.

7. "Person Related To." Section 9-102 defines "person related to." That term is a key element of the system provided in subsection (f) for low-price dispositions. One part of the definition applies when the secured party is an individual, and the other applies when the secured party is an organization. The definition is patterned closely on the corresponding definition in Section 1.301(32) of the Uniform Consumer Credit Code.

8. "Signed" Replaces "Authenticated." Consistent with the revised definition of "sign" in Section 1-201(b)(37), the cognate term "signed" replaces the reference to "authenticated" in the pre-2022 text of this section.

Section 9-616. Explanation of Calculation of Surplus or Deficiency

(a) [Definitions.] In this section:

(1) "Explanation" means a record that:

(A) states the amount of the surplus or deficiency;

(B) provides an explanation in accordance with subsection (c) of how the secured party calculated the surplus or deficiency;

(C) states, if applicable, that future debits, credits, charges, including additional credit service charges or interest, rebates, and expenses may affect the amount of the surplus or deficiency; and

(D) provides a telephone number or mailing address from which additional information concerning the transaction is available.

(2) "Request" means a record:

(A) signed by a debtor or consumer obligor;

(B) requesting that the recipient provide an explanation; and

(C) sent after disposition of the collateral under Section 9-610.

(b) [Explanation of calculation.] In a consumer-goods transaction in which the debtor is entitled to a surplus or a consumer obligor is liable for a deficiency under Section 9-615, the secured party shall:

(1) send an explanation to the debtor or consumer obligor, as applicable, after the disposition and:

(A) before or when the secured party accounts to the debtor and pays any surplus or first makes demand in a record on the consumer obligor after the disposition for payment of the deficiency; and

(B) within 14 days after receipt of a request; or

(2) in the case of a consumer obligor who is liable for a deficiency, within 14 days after receipt of a request, send to the consumer obligor a record waiving the secured party's right to a deficiency.

(c) [Required information.] To comply with subsection (a)(1)(B), an explanation must provide the following information in the following order:

(1) the aggregate amount of obligations secured by the security interest under which the disposition was made, and, if the amount reflects a rebate of unearned interest or credit service charge, an indication of that fact, calculated as of a specified date:

(A) if the secured party takes or receives possession of the collateral after default, not more than 35 days before the secured party takes or receives possession; or

(B) if the secured party takes or receives possession of the collateral before default or does not take possession of the collateral, not more than 35 days before the disposition;

(2) the amount of proceeds of the disposition;

(3) the aggregate amount of the obligations after deducting the amount of proceeds;

(4) the amount, in the aggregate or by type, and types of expenses, including expenses of retaking, holding, preparing for disposition, processing, and disposing of the collateral, and attorney's fees secured by the collateral which are known to the secured party and relate to the current disposition;

(5) the amount, in the aggregate or by type, and types of credits, including rebates of interest or credit service charges, to which the obligor is known to be entitled and which are not reflected in the amount in paragraph (1); and

(6) the amount of the surplus or deficiency.

(d) [Substantial compliance.] A particular phrasing of the explanation is not required. An explanation complying substantially with the requirements of subsection (a) is sufficient, even if it includes minor errors that are not seriously misleading.

(e) [Charges for responses.] A debtor or consumer obligor is entitled without charge to one response to a request under this section during any six-month period in which the secured party did not send to the debtor or consumer obligor an explanation pursuant to subsection (b)(1). The secured party may require payment of a charge not exceeding $25 for each additional response.

Definitional Cross References:

Collateral	Section 9-102(a)(12)
Consumer-goods transaction	Section 9-102(a)(24)
Consumer obligor	Section 9-102(a)(25)
Debtor	Section 9-102(a)(28)
Obligor	Section 9-102(a)(59)
Proceeds	Section 9-102(a)(64)
Record	Section 9-102(a)(70)
Secured party	Section 9-102(a)(73)
Security interest	Section 1-201(b)(35)
Send	Section 1-201(b)(36)
Sign	Section 1-201(b)(37)

Official Comment

1. Source. New.

2. Duty to Send Information Concerning Surplus or Deficiency. This section reflects the view that, in every consumer-goods transaction, the debtor or obligor is entitled to know the amount of a surplus or deficiency and the basis upon which the surplus or deficiency was calculated. Under subsection (b)(1)(B), a secured party is obligated to provide this information (an "explanation," defined in subsection (a)(1)) no later than the time that it accounts for and pays a surplus or the time of its first demand in a record in an attempt to collect the deficiency. The obligor need not make a request for an accounting in order to receive an explanation. A secured party who does not attempt to collect a deficiency in a demand in a record or account for and pay a surplus has no obligation to send an explanation under subsection (b)(1) and, consequently, cannot be liable for noncompliance.

A debtor or secondary obligor need not wait until the secured party commences collection efforts in a demand in a record in order to receive an explanation of how a deficiency or surplus was calculated. Subsection (b)(1)(B) obliges the secured party to send an explanation within 14 days after it receives a "request" (defined in subsection (a)(2)).

3. Explanation of Calculation of Surplus or Deficiency. Subsection (c) contains the requirements for how a calculation of a surplus or deficiency must be explained in order to satisfy subsection (a)(1)(B). It gives a secured party some discretion concerning rebates of interest or credit service charges. The secured party may include these rebates in the aggregate amount of obligations secured, under subsection (c)(1), or may include them with other types of rebates and credits under subsection (c)(5). Rebates of interest or credit service charges are the only types of rebates for which this discretion is provided. If the secured party provides an explanation that includes rebates of pre-computed interest, its explanation must so indicate. The expenses and attorney's fees to be described pursuant to subsection (c)(4) are those relating to the most recent disposition, not those that may have been incurred in connection with earlier enforcement efforts and which have been resolved by the parties.

4. Liability for Noncompliance. A secured party who fails to comply with subsection (b)(2) is liable for any loss caused plus $500. See Section 9-625(b), (c), (e)(6). A secured party who fails to send an explanation under subsection (b)(1) is liable for any loss caused plus, if the noncompliance was "part of a pattern, or consistent with a practice of noncompliance," $500. See Section 9-625(b), (c), (e)(5). However, a secured party who fails to comply with this section is not liable for statutory minimum damages under Section 9-625(c)(2). See Section 9-628(d).

5. "Signed" Replaces "Authenticated"; Medium Neutrality. Consistent with the revised definition of "sign" in Section 1-201(b)(37), the cognate term "signed" replaces the reference to "authenticated" in the pre-2022 text of this section. In furtherance of medium neutrality, the reference in the pre-2022 text of this section to a "written demand" has been replaced by a reference to a "demand in a record" and the reference to a "writing" has been replaced by a reference to a "record."

Section 9-617. Rights of Transferee of Collateral

(a) [Effects of disposition.] A secured party's disposition of collateral after default:

(1) transfers to a transferee for value all of the debtor's rights in the collateral;

(2) discharges the security interest under which the disposition is made; and

(3) discharges any subordinate security interest or other subordinate lien [other than liens created

under [cite acts or statutes providing for liens, if any, that are not to be discharged]].

(b) [Rights of good-faith transferee.] A transferee that acts in good faith takes free of the rights and interests described in subsection (a), even if the secured party fails to comply with this article or the requirements of any judicial proceeding.

(c) [Rights of other transferee.] If a transferee does not take free of the rights and interests described in subsection (a), the transferee takes the collateral subject to:

(1) the debtor's rights in the collateral;

(2) the security interest or agricultural lien under which the disposition is made; and

(3) any other security interest or other lien.

Definitional Cross References:

Agricultural lien	Section 9-102(a)(5)
Collateral	Section 9-102(a)(12)
Debtor	Section 9-102(a)(28)
Good faith	Section 1-201(b)(20)
Right	Section 1-201(b)(34)
Secured party	Section 9-102(a)(73)
Security interest	Section 1-201(b)(35)
Value	Section 1-204

Official Comment

1. Source. Former Section 9-504(4).

2. Title Taken by Good-Faith Transferee. Subsection (a) sets forth the rights acquired by persons who qualify under subsection (b)—transferees who act in good faith. Such a person is a "transferee," inasmuch as a buyer at a foreclosure sale does not meet the definition of "purchaser" in Section 1-201(b)(29) and (30) (the transfer is not, vis-à-vis the debtor, "voluntary"). By virtue of the expanded definition of the term "debtor" in Section 9-102(a)(28), subsection (a) makes clear that the ownership interest of a person who bought the collateral subject to the security interest is terminated by a subsequent disposition under this Part. Such a person is a debtor under this Article. Under former Article 9, the result arguably was the same, but the statute was less clear. Under subsection (a), a disposition normally discharges the security interest being foreclosed and any subordinate security interests and other liens.

A disposition has the effect specified in subsection (a), even if the secured party fails to comply with this Article. An aggrieved person (e.g., the holder of a subordinate security interest to whom a notification required by Section 9-611 was not sent) has a right to recover any loss under Section 9-625(b).

3. Unitary Standard in Public and Private Dispositions. Subsection (b) now contains a unitary standard that applies to transferees in both private and public dispositions—acting in good faith. However, this change from former Section 9-504(4) should not be interpreted to mean that a transferee acts in good faith even though it has knowledge of defects or buys in collusion, standards applicable to public dispositions under the former section. Properly understood, those standards were specific examples of the absence of good faith.

4. Title Taken by Nonqualifying Transferee. Subsection (c) specifies the consequences for a transferee who does not qualify for protection under subsections (a) and (b) (i.e., a transferee who does not act in good faith). The transferee takes subject to the rights of the debtor, the enforcing secured party, and other security interests or other liens. In such a case the disposition is ineffective to the extent that it would otherwise have cut off the debtor's rights in the collateral, and the debtor retains those rights, including the debtor's right of redemption under Section 9-623, albeit subject to the security interest under which the disposition was made and any other security interests or liens. See PEB Commentary No. 22, dated August 24, 2020. The Commentary is available at https://www.ali.org/peb-ucc.

Section 9-618. Rights and Duties of Certain Secondary Obligors

(a) [Rights and duties of secondary obligor.] A secondary obligor acquires the rights and becomes obligated to perform the duties of the secured party after the secondary obligor:

(1) receives an assignment of a secured obligation from the secured party;

(2) receives a transfer of collateral from the secured party and agrees to accept the rights and assume the duties of the secured party; or

(3) is subrogated to the rights of a secured party with respect to collateral.

(b) [Effect of assignment, transfer, or subrogation.] An assignment, transfer, or subrogation described in subsection (a):

(1) is not a disposition of collateral under Section 9-610; and

(2) relieves the secured party of further duties under this article.

Definitional Cross References:

Collateral	Section 9-102(a)(12)
Right	Section 1-201(b)(34)
Secondary obligor	Section 9-102(a)(72)
Secured party	Section 9-102(a)(73)

Official Comment

1. Source. Former Section 9-504(5).

2. Scope of This Section. Under this section, assignments of secured obligations and other transactions (regardless of form) that function like assignments of secured obligations are not dispositions to which Part 6 applies. Rather, they constitute assignments of rights and (occasionally) delegations of duties. Application of this section may require an investigation into the agreement of the parties, which may not be reflected in the words of the repurchase agreement (e.g., when the agreement requires a recourse party to "purchase the collateral" but contemplates that the purchaser will then conduct an Article 9 foreclosure disposition).

This section, like former Section 9-504(5), does not constitute a general and comprehensive rule for allocating rights and duties upon assignment of a secured obligation. Rather, it applies only in situations involving a secondary obligor described in subsection (a). In other contexts, the agreement of the parties and applicable law other than Article 9 determine whether the assignment imposes upon the assignee any duty to the debtor and whether the assignor retains its duties to the debtor after the assignment.

Subsection (a)(1) applies when there has been an assignment of an obligation that is secured at the time it is assigned. Thus, if a secondary obligor acquires the collateral at a disposition under Section 9-610 and simultaneously or subsequently discharges the unsecured deficiency claim, subsection (a)(1) is not implicated. Similarly, subsection (a)(3) applies only when the secondary obligor is subrogated to the secured party's rights with respect to collateral. Thus, this subsection will not be implicated if a secondary obligor discharges the debtor's unsecured obligation for a post-disposition deficiency. Similarly, if the secured party disposes of some of the collateral and the secondary obligor thereafter discharges the remaining obligation, subsection (a) applies only with respect to rights and duties concerning the remaining collateral, and, under subsection (b), the subrogation is not a disposition of the remaining collateral.

As discussed more fully in Comment 3, a secondary obligor may receive a transfer of collateral in a disposition under Section 9-610 in exchange for a payment that is applied against the secured obligation. However, a secondary obligor who pays and receives a transfer of collateral does not necessarily become subrogated to the rights of the secured party as contemplated by subsection (a)(3). Only to the extent the secondary obligor makes a payment in satisfaction of its secondary obligation would it become subrogated. To the extent its payment constitutes the price of the collateral in a Section 9-610 disposition by the secured party, the secondary obligor would not be subrogated. Thus, if the amount paid by the secondary obligor for the collateral in a Section 9-610 disposition is itself insufficient to discharge the secured obligation, but the secondary obligor makes an additional payment that satisfies the remaining balance, the secondary obligor would be subrogated to the secured party's deficiency claim. However, the duties of the secured party as such would have come to an end with respect to that collateral. In some situations the capacity in which the payment is made may be unclear. Accordingly, the parties should in their relationship provide clear evidence of the nature and circumstances of the payment by the secondary obligor.

3. Transfer of Collateral to Secondary Obligor. It is possible for a secured party to transfer collateral to a secondary obligor in a transaction that is a disposition under Section 9-610 and that establishes a surplus or deficiency under Section 9-615. Indeed, this Article includes a special rule, in Section 9-615(f), for establishing a deficiency in the case of some dispositions to, *inter alia,* secondary obligors. This Article rejects the view, which some may have ascribed to former Section 9-504(5), that a transfer of collateral to a recourse party can never constitute a disposition of collateral which discharges a security interest. Inasmuch as a secured party could itself buy collateral at its own public sale, it makes no sense to prohibit a recourse party ever from buying at the sale.

4. Timing and Scope of Obligations. Under subsection (a), a recourse party acquires rights and incurs obligations only "after" one of the specified circumstances occurs. This makes clear that when a successor assignee, transferee, or subrogee becomes obligated it does not assume any liability for earlier actions or inactions of the secured party whom it has succeeded unless it agrees to do so. Once the successor becomes obligated, however, it is responsible for complying with the secured party's duties thereafter. For example, if the successor is in possession of collateral, then it has the duties specified in Section 9-207.

Under subsection (b), the same event (assignment, transfer, or subrogation) that gives rise to rights to, and imposes obligations on, a successor relieves its predecessor of any further duties under this Article. For example, if the security interest is enforced after the secured obligation is assigned, the assignee—but not the assignor—has the duty to comply with this Part. Similarly, the assignment does not excuse the assignor from liability for failure to comply with duties that arose before the event or impose liability on the assignee for the assignor's failure to comply.

Section 9-619. Transfer of Record or Legal Title

(a) ["Transfer statement."] In this section, "transfer statement" means a record signed by a secured party stating:

(1) that the debtor has defaulted in connection with an obligation secured by specified collateral;

(2) that the secured party has exercised its post-default remedies with respect to the collateral;

(3) that, by reason of the exercise, a transferee has acquired the rights of the debtor in the collateral; and

(4) the name and mailing address of the secured party, debtor, and transferee.

(b) [Effect of transfer statement.] A transfer statement entitles the transferee to the transfer of record of all rights of the debtor in the collateral specified in the statement in any official filing, recording, registration, or certificate-of-title system covering the collateral. If a transfer statement is presented with the applicable fee and request form to the official or office responsible for maintaining the system, the official or office shall:

(1) accept the transfer statement;

(2) promptly amend its records to reflect the transfer; and

(3) if applicable, issue a new appropriate certificate of title in the name of the transferee.

(c) [Transfer not a disposition; no relief of secured party's duties.] A transfer of the record or legal title to collateral to a secured party under subsection (b) or otherwise is not of itself a disposition of collateral under this article and does not of itself relieve the secured party of its duties under this article.

Definitional Cross References:

Certificate of title	Section 9-102(a)(10)
Collateral	Section 9-102(a)(12)
Debtor	Section 9-102(a)(28)
Record	Section 9-102(a)(70)
Remedy	Section 1-201(b)(32)
Right	Section 1-201(b)(34)
Secured party	Section 9-102(a)(73)
Sign	Section 1-201(b)(37)

Official Comment

1. Source. New.

2. Transfer of Record or Legal Title. Potential buyers of collateral that is covered by a certificate of title (e.g., an automobile) or is subject to a registration system (e.g., a copyright) typically require as a condition of their purchase that the certificate or registry reflect their ownership. In many cases, this condition can be met only with the consent of the record owner. If the record owner is the debtor and, as may be the case after the default, the debtor refuses to cooperate, the secured party may have great difficulty disposing of the collateral.

Subsection (b) provides a simple mechanism for obtaining record or legal title, for use primarily when other law does not provide one. Of course, use of this mechanism will not be effective to clear title to the extent that subsection (b) is preempted by federal law. Subsection (b) contemplates a transfer of record or legal title to a third party, following a secured party's exercise of its disposition or acceptance remedies under this Part, as well as a transfer by a debtor to a secured party prior to the secured party's exercise of those remedies. Under subsection (c), a transfer of record or legal title (under subsection (b) or under other law) to a secured party prior to the exercise of those remedies merely puts the secured party in a position to pass legal or record title to a transferee at foreclosure. A secured party who has obtained record or legal title retains its duties with respect to enforcement of its security interest, and the debtor retains its rights as well.

3. Title-Clearing Systems under Other Law. Applicable non-UCC law (e.g., a certificate-of-title statute, federal registry rules, or the like) may provide a means by which the secured party may obtain or transfer record or legal title for the purpose of a disposition of the property under this Article. The mechanism provided by this section is in addition to any title-clearing provision under law other than this Article.

4. "Signed" Replaced "Authenticated." Consistent with the revised definition of "sign" in Section 1-201, the cognate term "signed" replaces the reference to "authenticated" in the pre-2022 text of this section.

Section 9-620. Acceptance of Collateral in Full or Partial Satisfaction of Obligation; Compulsory Disposition of Collateral

(a) [Conditions to acceptance in satisfaction.] Except as otherwise provided in subsection (g), a secured party may accept collateral in full or partial satisfaction of the obligation it secures only if:

(1) the debtor consents to the acceptance under subsection (c);

(2) the secured party does not receive, within the time set forth in subsection (d), a notification of objection to the proposal signed by:

(A) a person to which the secured party was required to send a proposal under Section 9-621; or

(B) any other person, other than the debtor, holding an interest in the collateral subordinate to the security interest that is the subject of the proposal;

(3) if the collateral is consumer goods, the collateral is not in the possession of the debtor when the debtor consents to the acceptance; and

(4) subsection (e) does not require the secured party to dispose of the collateral or the debtor waives the requirement pursuant to Section 9-624.

(b) [Purported acceptance ineffective.] A purported or apparent acceptance of collateral under this section is ineffective unless:

(1) the secured party consents to the acceptance in a signed record or sends a proposal to the debtor; and

(2) the conditions of subsection (a) are met.

(c) [Debtor's consent.] For purposes of this section:

(1) a debtor consents to an acceptance of collateral in partial satisfaction of the obligation it secures only if the debtor agrees to the terms of the acceptance in a record signed after default; and

(2) a debtor consents to an acceptance of collateral in full satisfaction of the obligation it secures only if the debtor agrees to the terms of the acceptance in a record signed after default or the secured party:

(A) sends to the debtor after default a proposal that is unconditional or subject only to a condition that collateral not in the possession of the secured party be preserved or maintained;

(B) in the proposal, proposes to accept collateral in full satisfaction of the obligation it secures; and

(C) does not receive a notification of objection signed by the debtor within 20 days after the proposal is sent.

(d) [Effectiveness of notification.] To be effective under subsection (a)(2), a notification of objection must be received by the secured party:

(1) in the case of a person to which the proposal was sent pursuant to Section 9-621, within 20 days after notification was sent to that person; and

(2) in other cases:

(A) within 20 days after the last notification was sent pursuant to Section 9-621; or

(B) if a notification was not sent, before the debtor consents to the acceptance under subsection (c).

(e) [Mandatory disposition of consumer goods.] A secured party that has taken possession of collateral shall dispose of the collateral pursuant to Section 9-610 within the time specified in subsection (f) if:

(1) 60 percent of the cash price has been paid in the case of a purchase-money security interest in consumer goods; or

(2) 60 percent of the principal amount of the obligation secured has been paid in the case of a non-purchase-money security interest in consumer goods.

(f) [Compliance with mandatory disposition requirement.] To comply with subsection (e), the secured party shall dispose of the collateral:

(1) within 90 days after taking possession; or

(2) within any longer period to which the debtor and all secondary obligors have agreed in an agreement to that effect entered into and signed after default.

(g) [No partial satisfaction in consumer transaction.] In a consumer transaction, a secured party may not accept collateral in partial satisfaction of the obligation it secures.

Definitional Cross References:

Agreement	Section 1-201(b)(3)
Collateral	Section 9-102(a)(12)
Consumer goods	Section 9-102(a)(23)
Consumer transaction	Section 9-102(a)(26)
Debtor	Section 9-102(a)(28)
Proposal	Section 9-102(a)(66)
Person	Section 1-201(b)(27)
Record	Section 9-102(a)(70)
Secondary obligor	Section 9-102(a)(72)
Secured party	Section 9-102(a)(73)
Security interest	Section 1-201(b)(35)
Send	Section 1-201(b)(36)
Sign	Section 1-201(b)(37)
Term	Section 1-201(b)(40)

Official Comment

1. Source. Former Section 9-505.

2. Overview. This section and the two sections following deal with strict foreclosure, a procedure by which the secured party acquires the debtor's interest in the collateral without the need for a sale or other disposition under Section 9-610. Although these provisions derive from former Section 9-505, they have been entirely reorganized and substantially rewritten. The more straightforward approach taken in this Article eliminates the fiction that the secured party always will present a "proposal" for the retention of collateral and the debtor will have a fixed period to respond. By eliminating the need (but preserving the possibility) for proceeding in that fashion, this section eliminates much of the awkwardness of former Section 9-505. It reflects the belief that strict foreclosures should be encouraged and often will produce better results than a disposition for all concerned.

Subsection (a) sets forth the conditions necessary to an effective acceptance (formerly, retention) of collateral in full or partial satisfaction of the secured obligation. Section 9-621 requires in addition that a secured party who wishes to proceed under this section notify certain other persons who have or claim to have an interest in the collateral. Unlike the failure to meet the conditions in subsection (a), under Section 9-622(b) the failure to comply with the notification requirement of Section 9-621 does not render the acceptance of collateral ineffective. Rather, the acceptance can take effect notwithstanding the secured party's noncompliance. A person to whom the required notice was not sent has the right to recover damages under Section 9-625(b). Section 9-622(a) sets forth the effect of an acceptance of collateral.

3. Conditions to Effective Acceptance. Subsection (a) contains the conditions necessary to the effectiveness of an acceptance of collateral. Subsection (a)(1) requires the debtor's consent. Under subsections (c)(1) and (c)(2), the debtor may consent by agreeing to the acceptance in writing after default. Subsection (c)(2) contains an alternative method by which to satisfy the debtor's-consent condition in subsection (a)(1). It follows the proposal-and-objection model found in pre-1998 Section 9-505: The debtor consents if the secured party sends a proposal to the debtor and does not receive an objection within 20 days. Under subsection (c)(1), however, that silence is not deemed to be consent with respect to acceptances in partial satisfaction. Thus, a secured party who wishes to conduct a "partial strict foreclosure" must obtain the debtor's agreement in a record signed after default. In all other respects, the conditions necessary to an effective partial strict foreclosure are the same as those governing acceptance of collateral in full satisfaction. (But see subsection (g), prohibiting partial strict foreclosure of a security interest in consumer transactions.)

The time when a debtor consents to a strict foreclosure is significant in several circumstances under this section and the following one. See Sections 9-620(a)(1), (d)(2), 9-621(a)(1), (a)(2), (a)(3). For purposes of determining the time of consent, a debtor's conditional consent constitutes consent.

Subsection (a)(2) contains the second condition to the effectiveness of an acceptance under this section: the absence of a timely objection from a person holding a junior interest in the collateral or from a secondary obligor. Any junior party—secured party or lienholder—is entitled to lodge an objection to a proposal, even if that person was not entitled to notification under Section 9-621. Subsection (d), discussed below, indicates when an objection is timely.

Subsections (a)(3) and (a)(4) contain special rules for transactions in which consumers are involved. See Comment 12.

4. Proposals. Section 9-102 defines the term "proposal." It is necessary to send a "proposal" to the debtor only if the debtor does not agree to an acceptance in a signed record as described in subsection (c)(1) or (c)(2). Section 9-621(a) determines whether it is necessary to send a proposal to third parties. A proposal need not take any particular form as long as it sets forth the terms under which the secured party is willing to accept collateral in satisfaction. A proposal to accept collateral should specify the amount (or a means of calculating the amount, such as by including a per diem accrual figure) of the secured obligations to be satisfied, state the conditions (if any) under which the proposal may be revoked, and describe any other applicable conditions. Note, however, that a conditional proposal generally requires the debtor's agreement in order to take effect. See subsection (c).

5. Secured Party's Agreement; No "Constructive" Strict Foreclosure. The conditions of subsection (a) relate to actual or implied consent by the debtor and any secondary obligor or holder of a junior security interest or lien. To ensure that the debtor cannot unilaterally cause an acceptance of collateral, subsection (b) provides that compliance with these conditions is necessary but not sufficient to cause an acceptance of collateral. Rather, under subsection (b), acceptance does not occur unless, in addition, the secured party consents to the acceptance in a signed record or sends to the debtor a proposal. For this reason, a mere delay in collection or disposition of collateral does not constitute a "constructive" strict foreclosure. Instead, delay is a factor relating to whether the secured party acted in a commercially reasonable manner for purposes of Section 9-607 or 9-610. A debtor's voluntary surrender of collateral to a secured party and the secured party's acceptance of possession of the collateral does not, of itself, necessarily raise an implication that the secured party intends or is proposing to accept the collateral in satisfaction of the secured obligation under this section.

6. When Acceptance Occurs. This section does not impose any formalities or identify any steps that a secured party must take in order to accept collateral once the conditions of subsections (a) and (b) have been met. Absent facts or circumstances indicating a contrary intention, the fact that the conditions have been met provides a sufficient indication that the secured party has accepted the collateral on the terms to which the secured party has consented or proposed and the debtor has consented or failed to object. Following a proposal, acceptance of the collateral normally is automatic upon the secured party's becoming bound and the time for objection passing. As a matter of good business practice, an enforcing secured party may wish to memorialize its acceptance following a proposal, such as by notifying the debtor that the strict foreclosure is effective or by placing a written record to that effect in its files. The secured party's agreement to accept collateral is self-executing and cannot be breached. The secured party is bound by its agreement to accept collateral and by any proposal to which the debtor consents.

7. No Possession Requirement. This section eliminates the requirement in former Section 9-505 that the secured party be "in possession" of collateral. It clarifies that intangible collateral, which cannot be possessed, may be subject to a strict foreclosure under this section. However, under subsection (a)(3), if the collateral is consumer goods, acceptance does not occur unless the debtor is not in possession.

8. When Objection Timely. Subsection (d) explains when an objection is timely and thus prevents an acceptance of collateral from taking effect. An objection by a person to which notification was sent under Section 9-621 is effective if it is received by the secured party within 20 days from the date the notification was sent to that person. Other objecting parties (i.e., third parties who are not entitled to notification) may object at any time within 20 days after the last notification is sent under Section 9-621. If no such notification is sent, third parties must object before the debtor agrees to the acceptance in writing or is deemed to have consented by silence. The former may occur any time after default, and the latter requires a 20-day waiting period. See subsection (c).

9. Applicability of Other Law. This section does not purport to regulate all aspects of the transaction by which a secured party may become the owner of collateral previously owned by the debtor. For example, a secured party's acceptance of a motor vehicle in satisfaction of secured obligations may require compliance with the applicable motor vehicle certificate-of-title law. State legislatures should conform those laws so that they mesh well with this section and Section 9-610, and courts should construe those laws and this section harmoniously. A secured party's acceptance of collateral in the possession of the debtor also may implicate statutes dealing with a seller's retention of possession of goods sold.

10. Accounts, Chattel Paper, Payment Intangibles, and Promissory Notes. If the collateral is accounts, chattel paper, payment intangibles, or promissory notes, then a secured party's acceptance of the collateral in satisfaction of secured obligations would constitute a sale to the secured party. That sale normally would give rise to a new security interest (the ownership interest) under Sections 1-201(b)(35) and 9-109. In the case of accounts and chattel paper, the new security interest would remain perfected by a filing that was effective to perfect the secured party's original security interest. In the case of payment intangibles or promissory notes, the security interest would be perfected when it attaches. See Section 9-309. However, the procedures for acceptance of collateral under this section satisfy all necessary formalities and a new security agreement signed by the debtor would not be necessary.

11. Role of Good Faith. Section 1-304 imposes an obligation of good faith on a secured party's enforcement under this Article. This obligation may not be disclaimed by agreement. See Section 1-302(b). Thus, a proposal and acceptance made under this section in bad faith would not be effective. For example, a secured party's proposal to accept marketable securities worth $1,000 in full satisfaction of indebtedness in the amount of $100, made in the hopes that the debtor might inadvertently fail to object, would be made in bad faith. On the other hand, in the normal case proposals and acceptances should be not second-guessed on the basis of the "value" of the collateral involved. Disputes about valuation or even a clear excess of collateral value over the amount of obligations satisfied do not necessarily demonstrate the absence of good faith.

12. Special Rules in Consumer Cases. Subsection (e) imposes an obligation on the secured party to dispose of consumer goods under certain circumstances. Subsection (f) explains when a disposition that is required under subsection (e) is timely. An effective acceptance of collateral cannot occur if subsection (e) requires a disposition unless the debtor waives this requirement pursuant to Section 9-624(b). Moreover, a secured party who takes possession of collateral and unreasonably delays disposition violates subsection (e), if applicable, and may also violate Section 9-610 or other provisions of this Part. Subsection (e) eliminates as superfluous the express statutory reference to "conversion" found in former Section 9-505. Remedies available under other law, including conversion, remain available under this Article in appropriate cases. See Sections 1-103, 1-305.

Subsection (g) prohibits the secured party in consumer transactions from accepting collateral in partial satisfaction of the obligation it secures. If a secured party attempts an acceptance in partial satisfaction in a consumer transaction, the attempted acceptance is void.

13. "Signed" Replaces "Authenticated." Consistent with the revised definition of "sign" in Section 1-201(b)(37), the cognate term "signed" replaces the references to "authenticated" in the pre-2022 text of this section.

Section 9-621. Notification of Proposal to Accept Collateral

(a) [Persons to which proposal to be sent.] A secured party that desires to accept collateral in full or partial satisfaction of the obligation it secures shall send its proposal to:

(1) any person from which the secured party has received, before the debtor consented to the acceptance, a signed notification of a claim of an interest in the collateral;

(2) any other secured party or lienholder that, 10 days before the debtor consented to the acceptance, held a security interest in or other lien on the collateral perfected by the filing of a financing statement that:

(A) identified the collateral;

(B) was indexed under the debtor's name as of that date; and

(C) was filed in the office or offices in which to file a financing statement against the debtor covering the collateral as of that date; and

(3) any other secured party that, 10 days before the debtor consented to the acceptance, held a security interest in the collateral perfected by compliance with a statute, regulation, or treaty described in Section 9-311(a).

(b) [Proposal to be sent to secondary obligor in partial satisfaction.] A secured party that desires to accept collateral in partial satisfaction of the obligation it secures shall send its proposal to any secondary obligor in addition to the persons described in subsection (a).

Definitional Cross References:

Collateral	Section 9-102(a)(12)
Debtor	Section 9-102(a)(28)
Financing statement	Section 9-102(a)(39)
Person	Section 1-201(b)(27)
Proposal	Section 9-102(a)(66)
Secondary obligor	Section 9-102(a)(72)
Secured party	Section 9-102(a)(73)
Security interest	Section 1-201(b)(35)
Send	Section 1-201(b)(36)
Sign	Section 1-201(b)(37)

Official Comment

1. Source. Former Section 9-505.

2. Notification Requirement. Subsection (a) specifies three classes of competing claimants to whom the secured party must send notification of its proposal: (i) those who notify the secured party that they claim an interest in the collateral, (ii) holders of certain security interests and liens who have filed against the debtor, and (iii) holders of certain security interests who have perfected by compliance with a statute (including a certificate-of-title statute), regulation, or treaty described in Section 9-311(a). With regard to (ii), see Section 9-611, Comment 4. Subsection (b) also requires notification to any secondary obligor if the proposal is for acceptance in partial satisfaction.

Unlike Section 9-611, this section contains no "safe harbor," which excuses an enforcing secured party from notifying certain secured parties and other lienholders. This is because, unlike Section 9-610, which requires that a disposition of collateral be commercially reasonable, Section 9-620 permits the debtor and secured party to set the amount of credit the debtor will receive for the collateral subject only to the requirement of good faith. An effective acceptance discharges subordinate security interests and other subordinate liens. See Section 9-622. If collateral is subject to several liens securing debts much larger than the value of the collateral, the debtor may be disinclined to refrain from consenting to an acceptance by the holder of the senior security interest, even though, had the debtor objected and the senior disposed of the collateral under Section 9-610, the collateral may have yielded more than enough to satisfy the senior security interest (but not enough to satisfy all the liens). Accordingly, this section imposes upon the enforcing secured party the risk of the filing office's errors and delay. The holder of a security interest who is entitled to notification under this section but to whom the enforcing secured party does not send notification has the right to recover under Section 9-625(b) any loss resulting from the secured party's noncompliance with this section.

3. "Signed" Replaces "Authenticated." Consistent with the revised definition of "sign" in Section 1-201(b)(37), the cognate term "signed" replaces the reference to "authenticated" in the pre-2022 text of this section.

Section 9-622. Effect of Acceptance of Collateral

(a) [Effect of acceptance.] A secured party's acceptance of collateral in full or partial satisfaction of the obligation it secures:

(1) discharges the obligation to the extent consented to by the debtor;

(2) transfers to the secured party all of a debtor's rights in the collateral;

(3) discharges the security interest or agricultural lien that is the subject of the debtor's consent and any subordinate security interest or other subordinate lien; and

(4) terminates any other subordinate interest.

(b) [Discharge of subordinate interest notwithstanding noncompliance.] A subordinate interest is discharged or terminated under subsection (a), even if the secured party fails to comply with this article.

Definitional Cross References:

Agricultural lien	Section 9-102(a)(5)
Collateral	Section 9-102(a)(12)
Debtor	Section 9-102(a)(28)
Right	Section 1-201(b)(34)
Secured party	Section 9-102(a)(73)
Security interest	Section 1-201(b)(35)

Official Comment

1. Source. New.

2. Effect of Acceptance. Subsection (a) specifies the effect of an acceptance of collateral in full or partial satisfaction of the secured obligation. The acceptance to which it refers is an effective acceptance. If a purported acceptance is ineffective under Section 9-620, e.g., because the secured party receives a timely objection from a person entitled to notification, then neither this subsection nor subsection (b) applies. Paragraph (1) expresses the fundamental consequence of accepting collateral in full or partial satisfaction of the secured obligation—the obligation is discharged to the extent consented to by the debtor. Unless otherwise agreed, the obligor remains liable for any deficiency. Paragraphs (2) through (4) indicate the effects of an acceptance on various property rights and interests. Paragraph (2) follows Section 9-617(a) in providing that the secured party acquires "all of a debtor's rights in the collateral." Under paragraph (3), the effect of strict foreclosure on holders of junior security interests and other liens is the same regardless of whether the collateral is accepted in full or partial satisfaction of the secured obligation: all junior encumbrances are discharged. Paragraph (4) provides for the termination of other subordinate interests.

Subsection (b) makes clear that subordinate interests are discharged under subsection (a) regardless of whether the secured party complies with this Article. Thus, subordinate interests are discharged regardless of whether a proposal was required to be sent or, if required, was sent. However, a secured party's failure to send a proposal or otherwise to comply with this Article may subject the secured party to liability under Section 9-625.

Section 9-623. Right to Redeem Collateral

(a) [Persons that may redeem.] A debtor, any secondary obligor, or any other secured party or lienholder may redeem collateral.

(b) [Requirements for redemption.] To redeem collateral, a person shall tender:

(1) fulfillment of all obligations secured by the collateral; and

(2) the reasonable expenses and attorney's fees described in Section 9-615(a)(1).

(c) [When redemption may occur.] A redemption may occur at any time before a secured party:

(1) has collected collateral under Section 9-607;

(2) has disposed of collateral or entered into a contract for its disposition under Section 9-610; or

(3) has accepted collateral in full or partial satisfaction of the obligation it secures under Section 9-622.

Definitional Cross References:

Collateral	Section 9-102(a)(12)
Contract	Section 1-201(b)(12)
Debtor	Section 9-102(a)(28)

Person	Section 1-201(b)(27)
Right	Section 1-201(b)(34)
Secondary obligor	Section 9-102(a)(72)
Secured party	Section 9-102(a)(73)

Official Comment

1. Source. Former Section 9-506.

2. Redemption Right. Under this section, as under former Section 9-506, the debtor or another secured party may redeem collateral as long as the secured party has not collected (Section 9-607), disposed of or contracted for the disposition of (Section 9-610), or accepted (Section 9-620) the collateral. Although this section generally follows former Section 9-506, it extends the right of redemption to holders of nonconsensual liens. To redeem the collateral a person must tender fulfillment of all obligations secured, plus certain expenses. If the entire balance of a secured obligation has been accelerated, it would be necessary to tender the entire balance. A tender of fulfillment obviously means more than a new promise to perform an existing promise. It requires payment in full of all monetary obligations then due and performance in full of all other obligations then matured. If unmatured secured obligations remain, the security interest continues to secure them (i.e., as if there had been no default).

3. Redemption of Remaining Collateral Following Partial Enforcement. Under Section 9-610 a secured party may make successive dispositions of portions of its collateral. These dispositions would not affect the debtor's, another secured party's, or a lienholder's right to redeem the remaining collateral.

4. Effect of "Repledging." Section 9-207 generally permits a secured party having possession or control of collateral to create a security interest in the collateral. As explained in the Comments to that section, the debtor's right (as opposed to its practical ability) to redeem collateral is not affected by, and does not affect, the priority of a security interest created by the debtor's secured party.

Section 9-624. Waiver

(a) [Waiver of disposition notification.] A debtor or secondary obligor may waive the right to notification of disposition of collateral under Section 9-611 only by an agreement to that effect entered into and signed after default.

(b) [Waiver of mandatory disposition.] A debtor may waive the right to require disposition of collateral under Section 9-620(e) only by an agreement to that effect entered into and signed after default.

(c) [Waiver of redemption right.] Except in a consumer-goods transaction, a debtor or secondary obligor may waive the right to redeem collateral under Section 9-623 only by an agreement to that effect entered into and signed after default.

Definitional Cross References:

Agreement	Section 1-201(b)(3)
Collateral	Section 9-102(a)(12)
Consumer-goods transaction	Section 9-102(a)(24)
Debtor	Section 9-102(a)(28)
Secondary obligor	Section 9-102(a)(72)
Sign	Section 1-201(b)(37)

Official Comment

1. Source. Former Sections 9-504(3), 9-505, 9-506.

2. Waiver. This section is a limited exception to Section 9-602, which generally prohibits waiver by debtors and obligors. It makes no provision for waiver of the rule prohibiting a secured party from buying at its own private disposition. Transactions of this kind are equivalent to "strict foreclosures" and are governed by Sections 9-620, 9-621, and 9-622.

3. "Signed" Replaces "Authenticated." Consistent with the revised definition of "sign" in Section 1-201(b)(37), the cognate term "signed" replaces the references to "authenticated" in the pre-2022 text of this section.

[Subpart 2. Noncompliance with Article]

Section 9-625. Remedies for Secured Party's Failure to Comply with Article

(a) [Judicial orders concerning noncompliance.] If it is established that a secured party is not proceeding in accordance with this article, a court may order or restrain collection, enforcement, or disposition of collateral on appropriate terms and conditions.

(b) [Damages for noncompliance.] Subject to subsections (c), (d), and (f), a person is liable for damages in the amount of any loss caused by a failure to comply with this article. Loss caused by a failure to comply may include loss resulting from the debtor's inability to obtain, or increased costs of, alternative financing.

(c) [Persons entitled to recover damages; statutory damages if collateral is consumer goods.] Except as otherwise provided in Section 9-628:

(1) a person that, at the time of the failure, was a debtor, was an obligor, or held a security interest in or other lien on the collateral may recover damages under subsection (b) for its loss; and

(2) if the collateral is consumer goods, a person that was a debtor or a secondary obligor at the time a secured party failed to comply with this part may recover for that failure in any event an amount not less than the credit service charge plus 10 percent of the principal amount of the obligation or the time-price differential plus 10 percent of the cash price.

(d) [Recovery when deficiency eliminated or reduced.] A debtor whose deficiency is eliminated under Section 9-626 may recover damages for the loss of any surplus. However, a debtor or secondary obligor whose deficiency is eliminated or reduced under Section 9-626 may not otherwise recover under subsection (b) for noncompliance with the provisions of this part relating to collection, enforcement, disposition, or acceptance.

(e) [Statutory damages: noncompliance with specified provisions.] In addition to any damages recoverable under subsection (b), the debtor, consumer obligor, or person named as a debtor in a filed record, as applicable, may recover $500 in each case from a person that:

(1) fails to comply with Section 9-208;

(2) fails to comply with Section 9-209;

(3) files a record that the person is not entitled to file under Section 9-509(a);

(4) fails to cause the secured party of record to file or send a termination statement as required by Section 9-513(a) or (c);

(5) fails to comply with Section 9-616(b)(1) and whose failure is part of a pattern, or consistent with a practice, of noncompliance; or

(6) fails to comply with Section 9-616(b)(2).

(f) [Statutory damages: noncompliance with Section 9-210.] A debtor or consumer obligor may recover damages under subsection (b) and, in addition, $500 in each case from a person that, without reasonable cause, fails to comply with a request under Section 9-210. A recipient of a request under Section 9-210 which never claimed an interest in the collateral or obligations that are the subject of a request under that section has a reasonable excuse for failure to comply with the request within the meaning of this subsection.

(g) [Limitation of security interest: noncompliance with Section 9-210.] If a secured party fails to comply with a request regarding a list of collateral or a statement of account under Section 9-210, the secured party may claim a security interest only as shown in the list or statement included in the request as against a person that is reasonably misled by the failure.

Definitional Cross References:

Account	Section 9-102(a)(2)
Collateral	Section 9-102(a)(12)
Consumer goods	Section 9-102(a)(23)
Consumer-goods transaction	Section 9-102(a)(24)
Consumer obligor	Section 9-102(a)(25)
Debtor	Section 9-102(a)(28)
Obligor	Section 9-102(a)(59)
Person	Section 1-201(b)(27)
Record	Section 9-102(a)(70)
Remedy	Section 1-201(b)(32)
Secondary obligor	Section 9-102(a)(72)
Secured party	Section 9-102(a)(73)
Security interest	Section 1-201(b)(35)
Send	Section 1-201(b)(36)
Term	Section 1-201(b)(40)
Termination statement	Section 9-102(a)(80)

Official Comment

1. Source. Former Section 9-507.

2. Remedies for Noncompliance; Scope. Subsections (a) and (b) provide the basic remedies afforded to those aggrieved by a secured party's failure to comply with this Article. Like all provisions that create liability, they are subject to Section 9-628, which should be read in conjunction with Section 9-605. The principal limitations under this Part on a secured party's right to enforce its security interest against collateral are the requirements that it proceed in good faith (Section 1-304), in a commercially reasonable manner (Sections 9-607 and 9-610), and, in most cases, with reasonable notification (Sections 9-611 through 9-614). Following former Section 9-507, under subsection (a) an aggrieved person may seek injunctive relief, and under subsection (b) the person may recover damages for losses caused by noncompliance. Unlike former Section 9-507, however, subsections (a) and (b) are not limited to noncompliance with provisions of this Part of Article 9. Rather, they apply to noncompliance with any provision of this Article. The change makes this section applicable to noncompliance with Sections 9-207 (duties of secured party in possession of collateral), 9-208 (duties of secured party having control over deposit account), 9-209 (duties of secured party if account debtor has been notified of an assignment), 9-210 (duty to comply with request for accounting, etc.), 9-509(a) (duty to refrain from filing unauthorized financing statement), and 9-513(a) or (c) (duty to provide termination statement). Subsection (a) also modifies the first sentence of former Section 9-507(1) by adding the references to "collection" and "enforcement." Subsection (c)(2), which gives a minimum damage recovery in consumer-goods transactions, applies only to noncompliance with the provisions of this Part.

Subsection (a) displaces other state law governing availability of the types of relief addressed in that subsection to the extent that the other state law would preclude the availability of injunctive relief in an otherwise appropriate case solely because the aggrieved party would be able to obtain a collectible money judgment for noncompliance with the rules of this Article. Rather, under subsection (a), in an appropriate case the aggrieved party should be able to obtain relief of the sort described in that subsection even if it would be possible for the aggrieved party to obtain such a judgment. See PEB Commentary No. 27, dated December 16, 2022, discussing the issue in the context of a noncomplying disposition under Section 9-610. The Commentary is available at https://www.ali.org/peb-ucc.

3. Damages for Noncompliance with This Article. Subsection (b) sets forth the basic remedy for failure to comply with the requirements of this Article: a damage recovery in the amount of loss caused by the noncompliance. Subsection (c) identifies who may recover under subsection (b). It affords a remedy to any aggrieved person who is a debtor or obligor. However, a principal obligor who is not a debtor may recover damages only for noncompliance with Section 9-616, inasmuch as none of the other rights and duties in this Article run in favor of such a principal obligor. Such a principal obligor could not suffer any loss or damage on account of noncompliance with rights or duties of which it is not a beneficiary. Subsection (c) also affords a remedy to an aggrieved person who holds a competing security interest or other lien, regardless of whether the aggrieved person is entitled to notification under Part 6. The remedy is available even to holders of senior security interests and other liens. The exercise of this remedy is subject to the normal rules of pleading and proof. A person who has delegated the duties of a secured party but who remains obligated to perform them is liable under this subsection. The last sentence of subsection (d) eliminates the possibility of double recovery or other over-compensation arising out of a reduction or elimination of a deficiency under Section 9-626, based on noncompliance with the provisions of this Part relating to collection, enforcement, disposition, or acceptance. Assuming no double recovery, a debtor whose deficiency is eliminated under Section 9-626 may pursue a claim for a surplus. Because Section 9-626 does not apply to consumer transactions, the statute is silent as to whether a double recovery or other over-compensation is possible in a consumer transaction.

Damages for violation of the requirements of this Article, including Section 9-609, are those reasonably calculated to put an eligible claimant in the position that it would have occupied had no violation occurred. See Section 1-305(a). Subsection (b) supports the recovery of actual damages for committing a breach of the peace in violation of Section 9-609, and principles of tort law supplement this subsection. See Section 1-103(b). However, to the extent that damages in tort compensate the debtor for the same loss dealt with by this Article, the debtor should be entitled to only one recovery.

4. Minimum Damages in Consumer-Goods Transactions. Subsection (c)(2) provides a minimum, statutory, damage recovery for a debtor and secondary obligor in a consumer-goods transaction. It is patterned on former Section 9-507(1) and is designed to ensure that every noncompliance with the requirements of Part 6 in a consumer-goods transaction results in liability, regardless of any injury that may have resulted. Subsection (c)(2) leaves the treatment of statutory damages as it was under former Article 9. A secured party is not liable for statutory damages under this subsection more than once with respect to any one secured obligation (see Section 9-628(e)), nor is a secured party liable under this subsection for failure to comply with Section 9-616 (see Section 9-628(d)).

Following former Section 9-507(1), this Article does not include a definition or explanation of the terms "credit service charge," "principal amount," "time-price differential," or "cash price," as used in subsection (c)(2). It leaves their construction and application to the court, taking into account the subsection's purpose of providing a minimum recovery in consumer-goods transactions.

5. Supplemental Damages. Subsections (e) and (f) provide damages that supplement the recovery, if any, under subsection (b). Subsection (e) imposes an additional $500 liability upon a person who fails to comply with the provisions specified in that subsection, and subsection (f) imposes like damages on a person who, without reasonable excuse, fails to comply with a request for an accounting or a request regarding a list of collateral or statement of account under Section 9-210. However, under subsection (f), a person has a reasonable excuse for the failure if the person never claimed an interest in the collateral or obligations that were the subject of the request.

6. Estoppel. Subsection (g) limits the extent to which a secured party who fails to comply with a request regarding a list of collateral or statement of account may claim a security interest.

Section 9-626. Action in Which Deficiency or Surplus Is in Issue

(a) [Applicable rules if amount of deficiency or surplus in issue.] In an action arising from a transaction, other than a consumer transaction, in which the amount of a deficiency or surplus is in issue, the following rules apply:

(1) A secured party need not prove compliance with the provisions of this part relating to collection, enforcement, disposition, or acceptance unless the debtor or a secondary obligor places the secured party's compliance in issue.

(2) If the secured party's compliance is placed in issue, the secured party has the burden of establishing that the collection, enforcement, disposition, or acceptance was conducted in accordance with this part.

(3) Except as otherwise provided in Section 9-628, if a secured party fails to prove that the collection, enforcement, disposition, or acceptance was conducted in accordance with the provisions of this part relating to collection, enforcement, disposition, or acceptance, the liability of a debtor or a secondary obligor for a deficiency is limited to an amount by which the sum of the secured obligation, expenses, and attorney's fees exceeds the greater of:

(A) the proceeds of the collection, enforcement, disposition, or acceptance; or

(B) the amount of proceeds that would have been realized had the noncomplying secured party proceeded in accordance with the provisions of this part relating to collection, enforcement, disposition, or acceptance.

(4) For purposes of paragraph (3)(B), the amount of proceeds that would have been realized is equal to the sum of the secured obligation, expenses, and attorney's fees unless the secured party proves that the amount is less than that sum.

(5) If a deficiency or surplus is calculated under Section 9-615(f), the debtor or obligor has the burden of establishing that the amount of proceeds of the disposition is significantly below the range of prices that a complying disposition to a person other than the secured party, a person related to the secured party, or a secondary obligor would have brought.

(b) [Non-consumer transactions; no inference.] The limitation of the rules in subsection (a) to transactions other than consumer transactions is intended to leave to the court the determination of the proper rules in consumer transactions. The court may not infer from that limitation the nature of the proper rule in consumer transactions and may continue to apply established approaches.

Definitional Cross References:

Action	Section 1-201(b)(1)
Burden of establishing	Section 1-201(b)(8)
Consumer transaction	Section 9-102(a)(26)
Debtor	Section 9-102(a)(28)
Obligor	Section 9-102(a)(59)
Person	Section 1-201(b)(27)
Person related to individual	Section 9-102(a)(62)
Person related to organization	Section 9-102(a)(63)
Proceeds	Section 9-102(a)(64)
Prove	Section 3-103(a)(10)
Secondary obligor	Section 9-102(a)(72)
Secured party	Section 9-102(a)(73)

Official Comment

1. Source. New.

2. Scope. The basic damage remedy under Section 9-625(b) is subject to the special rules in this section for transactions other than consumer transactions. This section addresses situations in which the amount of a deficiency or surplus is in issue, i.e., situations in which the secured party has collected, enforced, disposed of, or accepted the collateral. It contains special rules applicable to a determination of the amount of a deficiency or surplus. Because this section affects a person's liability for a deficiency, it is subject to Section 9-628, which should be read in conjunction with Section 9-605. The rules in this section apply only to noncompliance in connection with the "collection, enforcement, disposition, or acceptance" under Part 6. For other types of noncompliance with Part 6, the general liability rule of Section 9-625(b)—recovery of actual damages—applies. Consider, for example, a repossession that does not comply with Section 9-609 for want of a default. The debtor's remedy is under Section 9-625(b). In a proper case, the secured party also may be liable for conversion under non-UCC law. If the secured party thereafter disposed of the collateral, however, it would violate Section 9-610 at that time, and this section would apply.

3. Rebuttable Presumption Rule. Subsection (a) establishes the rebuttable presumption rule for transactions other than consumer transactions. Under paragraph (a)(1), the secured party need not prove compliance with the relevant provisions of this Part as part of its prima facie case. If, however, the debtor or a secondary obligor raises the issue (in accordance with the forum's rules of pleading and practice), then the secured party bears the burden of proving that the collection, enforcement, disposition, or acceptance complied. In the event the secured party is unable to meet this burden, then paragraph (a)(3) explains how to calculate the deficiency. Under this rebuttable presumption rule, the debtor or obligor is to be credited with the greater of the actual proceeds of the disposition or the proceeds that would have been realized had the secured party complied with the relevant provisions. If a deficiency remains, then the secured party is entitled to recover it. The references to "the secured obligation, expenses, and attorney's fees" in paragraphs (a)(3) and (4) embrace the application rules in Sections 9-608(a) and 9-615(a).

Unless the secured party proves that compliance with the relevant provisions would have yielded a smaller amount, under paragraph (a)(4) the amount that a complying collection, enforcement, or disposition would have yielded is deemed to be equal to the amount of the secured obligation, together with expenses and attorney's fees. Thus, the secured party may not recover any deficiency unless it meets this burden.

4. Consumer Transactions. Although subsection (a) adopts a version of the rebuttable presumption rule for transactions other than consumer transactions, with certain exceptions Part 6 does not specify the effect of a secured party's noncompliance in consumer transactions. (The exceptions are the provisions for the recovery of damages in Section 9-625.) Subsection (b) provides that the limitation of subsection (a) to transactions other than consumer transactions is intended to leave to the court the determination of the proper rules in consumer transactions. It also instructs the court not to draw any inference from the limitation as to the proper rules for consumer transactions and leaves the court free to continue to apply established approaches to those transactions.

Courts construing former Section 9-507 disagreed about the consequences of a secured party's failure to comply with the requirements of former Part 5. Three general approaches emerged. Some courts have held that a noncomplying secured party may not recover a deficiency (the "absolute bar" rule). A few courts held that the debtor can offset against a claim to a deficiency all damages recoverable under former Section 9-507 resulting from the secured party's noncompliance (the "offset" rule). A plurality of courts considering the issue held that the noncomplying secured party is barred from recovering a deficiency unless it overcomes a rebuttable presumption that compliance with former Part 5 would have yielded an amount sufficient to satisfy the secured debt. In addition to the nonuniformity resulting from court decisions, some States enacted special rules governing the availability of deficiencies.

5. Burden of Proof When Section 9-615(f) Applies. In a non-consumer transaction, subsection (a)(5) imposes upon a debtor or obligor the burden of proving that the proceeds of a disposition are so low that, under Section 9-615(f), the actual proceeds should not serve as the basis upon which a deficiency or surplus is calculated. Were the burden placed on the secured party, then debtors might be encouraged to challenge the price received in every disposition to the secured party, a person related to the secured party, or a secondary obligor.

6. Delay in Applying This Section. There is an inevitable delay between the time a secured party engages in a noncomplying collection, enforcement, disposition, or acceptance and the time of a subsequent judicial determination that the secured party did not comply with Part 6. During the interim, the secured party, believing that the secured obligation is larger than it ultimately is determined to be, may continue to enforce its security interest in collateral. If some or all of the secured indebtedness ultimately is discharged under this section, a reasonable application of this section would impose liability on the secured party for the amount of any excess, unwarranted recoveries but would not make the enforcement efforts wrongful.

Section 9-627. Determination of Whether Conduct Was Commercially Reasonable

(a) [Greater amount obtainable under other circumstances; no preclusion of commercial reasonableness.] The fact that a greater amount could have been obtained by a collection, enforcement, disposition, or acceptance at a different time or in a different method from that selected by the secured party is not of itself sufficient to preclude the secured party from establishing that the collection, enforcement, disposition, or acceptance was made in a commercially reasonable manner.

(b) [Dispositions that are commercially reasonable.] A disposition of collateral is made in a commercially reasonable manner if the disposition is made:

(1) in the usual manner on any recognized market;

(2) at the price current in any recognized market at the time of the disposition; or

(3) otherwise in conformity with reasonable commercial practices among dealers in the type of property that was the subject of the disposition.

(c) [Approval by court or on behalf of creditors.] A collection, enforcement, disposition, or acceptance is commercially reasonable if it has been approved:

(1) in a judicial proceeding;

(2) by a bona fide creditors' committee;

(3) by a representative of creditors; or

(4) by an assignee for the benefit of creditors.

(d) [Approval under subsection (c) not necessary; absence of approval has no effect.] Approval under subsection (c) need not be obtained, and lack of approval does not mean that the collection, enforcement, disposition, or acceptance is not commercially reasonable.

Definitional Cross References:

Collateral	Section 9-102(a)(12)
Creditor	Section 1-201(b)(13)
Representative	Section 1-201(b)(33)
Secured party	Section 9-102(a)(73)

Official Comment

1. Source. Former Section 9-507(2).

2. Relationship of Price to Commercial Reasonableness. Some observers have found the notion contained in subsection (a) (derived from former Section 9-507(2)) (the fact that a better price could have been obtained does not establish lack of commercial reasonableness) to be inconsistent with that found in Section 9-610(b) (derived from former Section 9-504(3)) (every aspect of the disposition, including its terms, must be commercially reasonable). There is no such inconsistency. While not itself sufficient to establish a violation of this Part, a low price suggests that a court should scrutinize carefully all aspects of a disposition to ensure that each aspect was commercially reasonable.

The law long has grappled with the problem of dispositions of personal and real property which comply with applicable procedural requirements (e.g., advertising, notification to interested persons, etc.) but which yield a price that seems low. This Article addresses that issue in Section 9-615(f). That section applies only when the transferee is the secured party, a person related to the secured party, or a secondary obligor. It contains a special rule for calculating a deficiency or surplus in a complying disposition that yields a price that is "significantly below the range of proceeds that a complying disposition to a person other than the secured party, a person related to the secured party, or a secondary obligor would have brought."

3. Determination of Commercial Reasonableness; Advance Approval. It is important to make clear the conduct and procedures that are commercially reasonable and to provide a secured party with the means of obtaining, by court order or negotiation with a creditors' committee or a representative of creditors, advance approval of a proposed method of enforcement as commercially reasonable. This section contains rules that assist in that determination and provides for advance approval in appropriate situations. However, none of the specific methods of disposition specified in subsection (b) is required or exclusive.

4. "Recognized Market." As in Sections 9-610(c) and 9-611(d), the concept of a "recognized market" in subsections (b)(1) and (2) is quite limited; it applies only to markets in which there are standardized price quotations for property that is essentially fungible, such as (but not limited to) securities and commodities exchanges. See Section 9-610, Comment 9 (discussing standard for a "recognized market").

Section 9-628. Nonliability and Limitation on Liability of Secured Party; Liability of Secondary Obligor

(a) [Limitation of liability of secured party for noncompliance with article.] Subject to subsection (f), unless a secured party knows that a person is a debtor or obligor, knows the identity of the person, and knows how to communicate with the person:

(1) the secured party is not liable to the person, or to a secured party or lienholder that has filed a financing statement against the person, for failure to comply with this article; and

(2) the secured party's failure to comply with this article does not affect the liability of the person for a deficiency.

(b) [Limitation of liability based on status as secured party.] Subject to subsection (f), a secured party is not liable because of its status as secured party:

(1) to a person that is a debtor or obligor, unless the secured party knows:

(A) that the person is a debtor or obligor;

(B) the identity of the person; and

(C) how to communicate with the person; or

(2) to a secured party or lienholder that has filed a financing statement against a person, unless the secured party knows:

(A) that the person is a debtor; and

(B) the identity of the person.

(c) [Limitation of liability if reasonable belief that transaction not a consumer-goods transaction or consumer transaction.] A secured party is not liable to any person, and a person's liability for a deficiency is not affected, because of any act or omission arising out of the secured party's reasonable belief that a transaction is not a consumer-goods transaction or a consumer transaction or that goods are not consumer goods, if the secured party's belief is based on its reasonable reliance on:

(1) a debtor's representation concerning the purpose for which collateral was to be used, acquired, or held; or

(2) an obligor's representation concerning the purpose for which a secured obligation was incurred.

(d) [Limitation of liability for statutory damages.] A secured party is not liable to any person under Section 9-625(c)(2) for its failure to comply with Section 9-616.

(e) [Limitation of multiple liability for statutory damages.] A secured party is not liable under Section 9-625(c)(2) more than once with respect to any one secured obligation.

(f) [Exception: Limitation of liability under subsections (a) and (b) does not apply.] Subsections (a) and (b) do not apply to limit the liability of a secured party to a person if, at the time the secured party obtains control of collateral that is a controllable account, controllable electronic record, or controllable payment intangible or at the time the security interest attaches to the collateral, whichever is later:

(1) the person is a debtor or obligor; and

(2) the secured party knows that the information in subsection (b)(1)(A), (B), or (C) relating to the person is not provided by the collateral, a record attached to or logically associated with the collateral, or the system in which the collateral is recorded.

Definitional Cross References:

Collateral	Section 9-102(a)(12)
Communicate	Section 9-102(a)(18)
Consumer goods	Section 9-102(a)(23)
Consumer-goods transaction	Section 9-102(a)(24)
Consumer transaction	Section 9-102(a)(26)
Controllable account	Section 9-102(a)(27A)
Controllable electronic record	Section 12-102(a)(1)
Controllable payment intangible	Section 9-102(a)(27B)
Debtor	Section 9-102(a)(28)
Financing statement	Section 9-102(a)(39)
Goods	Section 9-102(a)(44)
Obligor	Section 9-102(a)(59)
Person	Section 1-201(b)(27)
Record	Section 9-102(a)(70)
Secondary obligor	Section 9-102(a)(72)
Secured party	Section 9-102(a)(73)
Security interest	Section 1-201(b)(35)

Official Comment

1. Source. New.

2. Exculpatory Provisions. With respect to subsection (f), see Section 9-605, Comments 2 and 3.

If a secured party reasonably, but mistakenly, believes that a consumer transaction or consumer-goods transaction is a non-consumer transaction or non-consumer-goods transaction, and if the secured party's belief is based on its reasonable reliance on a representation of the type specified in subsection (c)(1) or (c)(2), then this Article should be applied as if the facts reasonably believed and the representation reasonably relied upon were true. For example, if a secured party reasonably believed that a transaction was a non-consumer transaction and its belief was based on reasonable reliance on the debtor's representation that the collateral secured an obligation incurred for business purposes, the secured party is not liable to any person, and the debtor's liability for a deficiency is not affected, because of any act or omission of the secured party which arises out of the reasonable belief. Of course, if the secured party's belief is not reasonable or, even if reasonable, is not based on reasonable reliance on the debtor's representation, this limitation on liability is inapplicable.

3. Inapplicability of Statutory Damages to Section 9-616. Subsection (d) excludes noncompliance with Section 9-616 entirely from the scope of statutory damage liability under Section 9-625(c)(2).

4. Single Liability for Statutory Minimum Damages. Subsection (e) ensures that a secured party will incur statutory damages only once in connection with any one secured obligation.

PART 7. TRANSITION

Section 9-701. Effective Date

This [Act] takes effect on July 1, 2001.

Official Comment

A uniform law as complex as Article 9 necessarily gives rise to difficult problems and uncertainties during the transition to the new law. As is customary for uniform laws, this Article is based on the general assumption that all States will have enacted substantially identical versions. While always important, uniformity is essential to the success of this Article. If former Article 9 is in effect in some jurisdictions, and this Article is in effect in others, horrendous complications may arise. For example, the proper place in which to file to perfect a security interest (and thus the status of a particular security interest as perfected or unperfected) would depend on whether the matter was litigated in a State in which former Article 9 was in effect or a State in which this Article was in effect. Accordingly, this section contemplates that States will adopt a uniform effective date for this Article. Any one State's failure to adopt the uniform effective date will greatly increase the cost and uncertainty surrounding the transition.

Other problems arise from transactions and relationships that were entered into under former Article 9 or under non-UCC law and which remain outstanding on the effective date of this Article. The difficulties arise primarily because this Article expands the scope of former Article 9 to cover additional types of collateral and transactions and because it provides new methods of perfection for some types of collateral, different priority rules, and different choice-of-law rules governing perfection and priority. This Section and the other sections in this Part address primarily this second set of problems.

Section 9-702. Savings Clause

(a) [Pre-effective-date transactions or liens.] Except as otherwise provided in this part, this [Act] applies to a transaction or lien within its scope, even if the transaction or lien was entered into or created before this [Act] takes effect.

(b) [Continuing validity.] Except as otherwise provided in subsection (c) and Sections 9-703 through 9-709:

(1) transactions and liens that were not governed by [former Article 9], were validly entered into or created before this [Act] takes effect, and would be subject to this [Act] if they had been entered into or created after this [Act] takes effect, and the rights, duties, and interests flowing from those transactions and liens remain valid after this [Act] takes effect; and

(2) the transactions and liens may be terminated, completed, consummated, and enforced as required or permitted by this [Act] or by the law that otherwise would apply if this [Act] had not taken effect.

(c) [Pre-effective-date proceedings.] This [Act] does not affect an action, case, or proceeding commenced before this [Act] takes effect.

Definitional Cross References:

Action	Section 1-201(b)(1)
Right	Section 1-201(b)(34)

Official Comment

1. Pre-Effective-Date Transactions. Subsection (a) contains the general rule that this Article applies to transactions, security interests, and other liens within its scope (see Section 9-109), even if the transaction or lien was entered into or created before the effective date. Thus, secured transactions entered into under former Article 9 must be terminated, completed, consummated, and enforced under this Article. Subsection (b) is an exception to the general rule. It applies to valid, pre-effective-date transactions and liens that were not governed by former Article 9 but would be governed by this Article if they had been entered into or created after this Article takes effect. Under subsection (b), these valid transactions, such as the creation of agricultural liens and security interests in commercial tort claims, retain their validity under this Article and may be terminated, completed, consummated, and enforced under this Article. However, these transactions also may be terminated, completed, consummated, and enforced by the law that otherwise would apply had this Article not taken effect.

2. Judicial Proceedings Commenced Before Effective Date. As is usual in transition provisions, subsection (c) provides that this Article does not affect litigation pending on the effective date.

Section 9-703. Security Interest Perfected before Effective Date

(a) [Continuing priority over lien creditor: perfection requirements satisfied.] A security interest that is enforceable immediately before this [Act] takes effect and would have priority over the rights of a person that becomes a lien creditor at that time is a perfected security interest under this [Act] if, when this [Act] takes effect, the applicable requirements for enforceability and perfection under this [Act] are satisfied without further action.

(b) [Continuing priority over lien creditor: perfection requirements not satisfied.] Except as otherwise provided in Section 9-705, if, immediately before this [Act] takes effect, a security interest is enforceable and would have priority over the rights of a person that becomes a lien creditor at that time, but the applicable requirements for enforceability or perfection under this [Act] are not satisfied when this [Act] takes effect, the security interest:

(1) is a perfected security interest for one year after this [Act] takes effect;

(2) remains enforceable thereafter only if the security interest becomes enforceable under Section 9-203 before the year expires; and

(3) remains perfected thereafter only if the applicable requirements for perfection under this [Act] are satisfied before the year expires.

Definitional Cross References:

Action	Section 1-201(b)(1)
Lien creditor	Section 9-102(a)(52)
Person	Section 1-201(b)(27)
Right	Section 1-201(b)(34)
Security interest	Section 1-201(b)(35)

Official Comment

1. Perfected Security Interests Under Former Article 9 and This Article. This section deals with security interests that are perfected (i.e., that are enforceable and have priority over the rights of a lien creditor) under former Article 9 or other applicable law immediately before this Article takes effect. Subsection (a) provides, not surprisingly, that if the security interest would be a perfected security interest under this Article (i.e., if the transaction satisfies this Article's requirements for enforceability (attachment) and perfection), no further action need be taken for the security interest to be a perfected security interest.

2. Security Interests Enforceable and Perfected Under Former Article 9 but Unenforceable or Unperfected Under This Article. Subsection (b) deals with security interests that are enforceable and perfected under former Article 9 or other applicable law immediately before this Article takes effect but do not satisfy the requirements for enforceability (attachment) or perfection under this Article. Except as otherwise provided in Section 9-705, these security interests are perfected security interests for one year after the effective date. If the security interest satisfies the requirements for attachment and perfection within that period, the security interest remains perfected thereafter. If the security interest satisfies only the requirements for attachment within that period, the security interest becomes unperfected at the end of the one-year period.

Example 1: A pre-effective-date security agreement in a consumer transaction covers "all securities accounts." The security interest is properly perfected. The collateral description was adequate under former Article 9 (see former Section 9-115(3)) but is insufficient under this Article (see Section 9-108(e)(2)). Unless the debtor authenticates a new security agreement describing the collateral other than by "type" (or Section 9-203(b)(3) otherwise is satisfied) within the one-year period following the effective date, the security interest becomes unenforceable at the end of that period.

Other examples under former Article 9 or other applicable law that may be effective as attachment or enforceability steps but may be ineffective under this Article include an oral agreement to sell a payment intangible or possession by virtue of a notification to a bailee under former Section 9-305. Neither the oral agreement nor the notification would satisfy the revised Section 9-203 requirements for attachment.

Example 2: A pre-effective-date possessory security interest in instruments is perfected by a bailee's receipt of notification under former 9-305. The bailee has not, however, acknowledged that it holds for the secured party's benefit under revised Section 9-313. Unless the bailee authenticates a record acknowledging that it holds for the secured party (or another appropriate perfection step is taken) within the one-year period following the effective date, the security interest becomes unperfected at the end of that period.

3. Interpretation of Pre-Effective-Date Security Agreements. Section 9-102 defines "security agreement" as "an agreement that creates or provides for a security interest." Under Section 1-201(b)(3), an "agreement" is a "bargain of the parties in fact." If parties to a pre-effective-date security agreement describe the collateral by using a term defined in former Article 9 in one way and defined in this Article in another way, in most cases it should be presumed that the bargain of the parties contemplated the meaning of the term under former Article 9.

Example 3: A pre-effective-date security agreement covers "all accounts" of a debtor. As defined under former Article 9, an "account" did not include a right to payment for lottery winnings. These rights to payment are "accounts" under this Article, however. The agreement of the parties presumptively created a security interest in "accounts" as defined in former Article 9. A different result might be appropriate, for example, if the security agreement explicitly contemplated future changes in the Article 9 definitions of types of collateral—e.g., "'Accounts' means 'accounts' as defined in the UCC Article 9 of [State X], as that definition may be amended from time to time." Whether a different approach is appropriate in any given case depends on the bargain of the parties, as determined by applying ordinary principles of contract construction.

Section 9-704. Security Interest Unperfected before Effective Date

A security interest that is enforceable immediately before this [Act] takes effect but which would be subordinate to the rights of a person that becomes a lien creditor at that time:

(1) remains an enforceable security interest for one year after this [Act] takes effect;

(2) remains enforceable thereafter if the security interest becomes enforceable under Section 9-203 when this [Act] takes effect or within one year thereafter; and

(3) becomes perfected:

(A) without further action, when this [Act] takes effect if the applicable requirements for perfection under this [Act] are satisfied before or at that time; or

(B) when the applicable requirements for perfection are satisfied if the requirements are satisfied after that time.

Definitional Cross References:

Action	Section 1-201(b)(1)
Lien creditor	Section 9-102(a)(52)
Person	Section 1-201(b)(27)
Right	Section 1-201(b)(34)
Security interest	Section 1-201(b)(35)

Official Comment

This section deals with security interests that are enforceable but unperfected (i.e., subordinate to the rights of a person who becomes a lien creditor) under former Article 9 or other applicable law immediately before this Article takes effect. These security interests remain enforceable for one year after the effective date, and thereafter if the appropriate steps for attachment under this Article are taken before the one-year period expires. (This section's treatment of enforceability is the same as that of Section 9-703.) The security interest becomes a perfected security interest on the effective date if, at that time, the security interest satisfies the requirements for perfection under this Article. If the security interest does not satisfy the requirements for perfection until sometime thereafter, it becomes a perfected security interest at that later time.

Example: A security interest has attached under former Article 9 but is unperfected because the filed financing statement covers "all of debtor's personal property" and controlling case law in the applicable jurisdiction has determined that this identification of collateral in a financing statement is insufficient. Upon the effective date of this Article, the financing statement becomes sufficient under Section 9-504(2). On that date the security interest becomes perfected. (This assumes, of course, that the financing statement is filed in the proper filing office under this Article.)

Section 9-705. Effectiveness of Action Taken before Effective Date

(a) [Pre-effective-date action; one-year perfection period unless reperfected.] If action, other than the filing of a financing statement, is taken before this [Act] takes effect and the action would have resulted in priority of a security interest over the rights of a person that becomes a lien creditor had the security interest become enforceable before this [Act] takes effect, the action is effective to perfect a security interest that attaches under this [Act] within one year after this [Act] takes effect. An attached security interest becomes unperfected one year after this [Act] takes effect unless the security interest becomes a perfected security interest under this [Act] before the expiration of that period.

(b) [Pre-effective-date filing.] The filing of a financing statement before this [Act] takes effect is effective to perfect a security interest to the extent the filing would satisfy the applicable requirements for perfection under this [Act].

(c) [Pre-effective-date filing in jurisdiction formerly governing perfection.] This [Act] does not render ineffective an effective financing statement that, before this [Act] takes effect, is filed and satisfies the applicable requirements for perfection under the law of the jurisdiction governing perfection as provided in [former Section 9-103]. However, except as otherwise provided in subsections (d) and (e) and Section 9-706, the financing statement ceases to be effective at the earlier of:

(1) the time the financing statement would have ceased to be effective under the law of the jurisdiction in which it is filed; or

(2) June 30, 2006.

(d) [Continuation statement.] The filing of a continuation statement after this [Act] takes effect does not continue the effectiveness of the financing statement filed before this [Act] takes effect. However, upon the timely filing of a continuation statement after this [Act] takes effect and in accordance with the law of the jurisdiction governing perfection as provided in Part 3, the effectiveness of a financing statement filed in the same office in that jurisdiction before this [Act] takes effect continues for the period provided by the law of that jurisdiction.

(e) [Application of subsection (c)(2) to transmitting utility financing statement.] Subsection (c)(2) applies to a financing statement that, before this [Act] takes effect, is filed against a transmitting utility and satisfies the applicable requirements for perfection under the law of the jurisdiction governing perfection as provided in [former Section 9-103] only to the extent that Part 3 provides that the law of a jurisdiction other than the jurisdiction in which the financing statement is filed governs perfection of a security interest in collateral covered by the financing statement.

(f) [Application of Part 5.] A financing statement that includes a financing statement filed before this [Act] takes effect and a continuation statement filed after this [Act] takes effect is effective only to the extent that it satisfies the requirements of Part 5 for an initial financing statement.

Definitional Cross References:

Action	Section 1-201(b)(1)
Collateral	Section 9-102(a)(12)
Continuation statement	Section 9-102(a)(27)
Financing statement	Section 9-102(a)(39)
Lien creditor	Section 9-102(a)(52)
Person	Section 1-201(b)(27)
Right	Section 1-201(b)(34)
Security interest	Section 1-201(b)(35)
Transmitting utility	Section 9-102(a)(81)

Official Comment

1. General. This section addresses primarily the situation in which the perfection step is taken under former Article 9 or other applicable law before the effective date of this Article, but the security interest does not attach until after that date.

2. Perfection Other Than by Filing. Subsection (a) applies when the perfection step is a step other than the filing of a financing statement. If the step that would be a valid perfection step under former Article 9 or other law is taken before this Article takes effect, and if a security interest attaches within one year after this Article takes effect, then the security interest becomes a perfected security interest upon attachment. However, the security interest becomes unperfected one year after the effective date unless the requirements for attachment and perfection under this Article are satisfied within that period.

3. Perfection by Filing: Ineffective Filings Made Effective. Subsection (b) deals with financing statements that were filed under former Article 9 and which would not have perfected a security interest under the former Article (because, e.g., they did not accurately describe the collateral or were filed in the wrong place), but which would perfect a security interest under this Article. Under subsection (b), such a financing statement is effective to perfect a security interest to the extent it complies with this Article. Subsection (b) applies regardless of the reason for the filing. For example, a secured party need not wait until the effective date to respond to the change this Article makes with respect to the jurisdiction whose law governs perfection of certain security interests. Rather, a secured party may wish to prepare for this change by filing a financing statement before the effective date in the jurisdiction whose law governs perfection under this Article. When this Article takes effect, the filing becomes effective to perfect a security interest (assuming the filing satisfies the perfection requirements of this Article). Note, however, that Section 9-706 determines whether a financing statement filed before the effective date operates to continue the effectiveness of a financing statement filed in another office before the effective date.

4. Perfection by Filing: Change in Applicable Law or Filing Office. Subsection (c) provides that a financing statement filed in the proper jurisdiction under former Section 9-103 remains effective for all purposes, despite the fact that Part 3 of this Article would require filing of a financing statement in a different jurisdiction or in a different office in the same jurisdiction. This means that, during the early years of this Article's effectiveness, it may be necessary to search not only in the filing office of the jurisdiction whose law governs perfection under this Article but also (if different) in the jurisdiction(s) and filing office(s) designated by former Article 9. To limit this burden, subsection (c) provides that a financing statement filed in the jurisdiction determined by former Section 9-103 becomes ineffective at the earlier of the time it would become ineffective under the law of that jurisdiction or June 30, 2006. The June 30, 2006, limitation addresses some nonuniform versions of former Article 9 that extended the effectiveness of a financing statement beyond five years. Note that a financing statement filed before the effective date may remain effective beyond June 30, 2006, if subsection (d) (concerning continuation statements) or (e) (concerning transmitting utilities) or Section 9-706 (concerning initial financing statements that operate to continue pre-effective-date financing statements) so provides.

Subsection (c) is an exception to Section 9-703(b). Under the general rule in Section 9-703(b), a security interest that is enforceable and perfected on the effective date of this Article is a perfected security interest for one year after this Article takes effect, even if the security interest is not enforceable under this Article and the applicable requirements for perfection under this Article have not been met. However, in some cases subsection (c) may shorten the one-year period of perfection; in others, if the security interest is enforceable under Section 9-203, it may extend the period of perfection.

> **Example 1:** On July 3, 1996, D, a State X corporation, creates a security interest in certain manufacturing equipment located in State Y. On July 6, 1996, SP perfects a security interest in the equipment under former Article 9 by filing in the office of the State Y Secretary of State. See former Section 9-103(1)(b). This Article takes effect in States X and Y on July 1, 2001. Under Section 9-705(c), the financing statement remains effective until it lapses in July 2001. See former Section 9-403. Had SP continued the effectiveness of the financing statement by filing a continuation statement in State Y under former Article 9 before July 1, 2001, the financing statement would have remained effective to perfect the security interest through June 30, 2006. See subsection (c)(2). Alternatively, SP could have filed an initial financing statement in State X under subsection (b) or Section 9-706 before the State Y financing statement lapsed. Had SP done so, the security

interest would have remained perfected without interruption until the State X financing statement lapsed.

5. Continuing Effectiveness of Filed Financing Statement. A financing statement filed before the effective date of this Article may be continued only by filing in the State and office designated by this Article. This result is accomplished in the following manner: Subsection (d) indicates that, as a general matter, a continuation statement filed after the effective date of this Article does not continue the effectiveness of a financing statement filed under the law designated by former Section 9-103. Instead, an initial financing statement must be filed under Section 9-706. The second sentence of subsection (d) contains an exception to the general rule. It provides that a continuation statement is effective to continue the effectiveness of a financing statement filed before this Article takes effect if this Article prescribes not only the same jurisdiction but also the same filing office.

Example 2: On November 8, 2000, D, a State X corporation, creates a security interest in certain manufacturing equipment located in State Y. On November 15, 2000, SP perfects a security interest in the equipment under former Article 9 by filing in office of the State Y Secretary of State. See former Section 9-103(1)(b). This Article takes effect in States X and Y on July 1, 2001. Under Section 9-705(c), the financing statement ceases to be effective in November, 2005, when it lapses. See Section 9-515. Under this Article, the law of D's location (State X, see Section 9-307) governs perfection. See Section 9-301. Thus, the filing of a continuation statement in State Y after the effective date would not continue the effectiveness of the financing statement. See subsection (d). However, the effectiveness of the financing statement could be continued under Section 9-706.

Example 3: The facts are as in Example 2, except that D is a State Y corporation. Assume State Y adopted former Section 9-401(1) (second alternative). State Y law governs perfection under Part 3 of this Article. (See Sections 9-301, 9-307.) Under the second sentence of subsection (d), the timely filing of a continuation statement in accordance with the law of State Y continues the effectiveness of the financing statement.

Example 4: The facts are as in Example 3, except that the collateral is equipment used in farming operations and, in accordance with former Section 9-401(1) (second alternative) as enacted in State Y, the financing statement was filed in State Y, in the office of the Shelby County Recorder of Deeds. Under this Article, a continuation statement must be filed in the office of the State Y Secretary of State. See Section 9-501(a)(2). Under the second sentence of subsection (d), the timely filing of a continuation statement in accordance with the law of State Y operates to continue a pre-effective-date financing statement only if the continuation statement is filed in the same office as the financing statement. Accordingly, the continuation statement is not effective in this case, but the financing statement may be continued under Section 9-706.

Example 5: The facts are as in Example 3, except that State Y enacted former Section 9-401(1) (third alternative). As required by former Section 9-401(1), SP filed financing statements in both the office of the State Y Secretary of State and the office of the Shelby County Recorder of Deeds. Under this Article, a continuation statement must be filed in the office of the State Y Secretary of State. See Section 9-501(a)(2). The timely filing of a continuation statement in that office after this Article takes effect would be effective to continue the effectiveness of the financing statement (and thus continue the perfection of the security interest), even if the financing statement filed with the County Recorder lapses.

6. Continuation Statements. In some cases, this Article reclassifies collateral covered by a financing statement filed under former Article 9. For example, collateral consisting of the right to payment for real property sold would be a "general intangible" under the former Article but an "account" under this Article. To continue perfection under those circumstances, a continuation statement must comply with the normal requirements for a continuation statement. See Section 9-515. In addition, the pre-effective-date financing statement and continuation statement, taken together, must satisfy the requirements of this Article concerning the sufficiency of the debtor's name, secured party's name, and indication of collateral. See subsection (f).

Example 6: A pre-effective-date financing statement covers "all general intangibles" of a debtor. As defined under former Article 9, a "general intangible," would include rights to payment for lottery winnings. These rights to payment are "accounts" under this Article, however. A post-effective-date continuation statement will not continue the effectiveness of the pre-effective-date financing statement with respect to lottery winnings unless it amends the indication of collateral covered to include lottery winnings (e.g., by adding "accounts," "rights to payment for lottery winnings," or the like). If the continuation statement does not amend the indication of collateral, the continuation statement will be effective to continue the effectiveness of the financing statement only with respect to "general intangibles" as defined in this Article.

Example 7: The facts are as in Example 6, except that the pre-effective-date financing statement covers "all accounts and general intangibles." Even though rights to payment for lottery winnings are "general intangibles" under former Article 9 and "accounts" under this Article, a post-effective-date continuation statement would continue the effectiveness of the pre-effective-date financing statement with respect to lottery winnings. There would be no need to amend the indication of collateral covered, inasmuch as the indication ("accounts") satisfies the requirements of this Article.

Section 9-706. When Initial Financing Statement Suffices to Continue Effectiveness of Financing Statement

(a) [Initial financing statement in lieu of continuation statement.] The filing of an initial financing statement in the office specified in Section 9-501 continues the effectiveness of a financing statement filed before this [Act] takes effect if:

(1) the filing of an initial financing statement in that office would be effective to perfect a security interest under this [Act];

(2) the pre-effective-date financing statement was filed in an office in another State or another office in this State; and

(3) the initial financing statement satisfies subsection (c).

(b) [Period of continued effectiveness.] The filing of an initial financing statement under subsection (a) continues the effectiveness of the pre-effective-date financing statement:

(1) if the initial financing statement is filed before this [Act] takes effect, for the period provided in [former Section 9-403] with respect to a financing statement; and

(2) if the initial financing statement is filed after this [Act] takes effect, for the period provided in Section 9-515 with respect to an initial financing statement.

(c) [Requirements for initial financing statement under subsection (a).] To be effective for purposes of subsection (a), an initial financing statement must:

(1) satisfy the requirements of Part 5 for an initial financing statement;

(2) identify the pre-effective-date financing statement by indicating the office in which the financing statement was filed and providing the dates of filing and file numbers, if any, of the financing statement and of the most recent continuation statement filed with respect to the financing statement; and

(3) indicate that the pre-effective-date financing statement remains effective.

Definitional Cross References:

Continuation statement	Section 9-102(a)(27)
File number	Section 9-102(a)(36)
Financing statement	Section 9-102(a)(39)
Security interest	Section 1-201(b)(35)
State	Section 9-102(a)(77)

Official Comment

1. Continuation of Financing Statements Not Filed in Proper Filing Office Under This Article. This section deals with continuing the effectiveness of financing statements that are filed in the proper State and office under former Article 9, but which would be filed in the wrong State or in the wrong office of the proper State under this Article. Section 9-705(d) provides that, under these circumstances, filing a continuation statement after the effective date of this Article in the office designated by former Article 9 would not be effective. This section provides the means by which the effectiveness of such a financing statement can be continued if this Article governs perfection under the applicable choice-of-law rule: filing an initial financing statement in the office specified by Section 9-501.

Although it has the effect of continuing the effectiveness of a pre-effective-date financing statement, an initial financing statement described in this section is not a continuation statement. Rather, it is governed by the rules applicable to initial financing statements. (However, the debtor need not authorize the filing. See Section 9-708.) Unlike a continuation statement, the initial financing statement described in this section may be filed any time during the effectiveness of the pre-effective-date financing statement—even before this Article is enacted—and not only within the six months immediately prior to lapse. In contrast to a continuation statement, which extends the lapse date of a filed financing statement for five years, the initial financing statement has its own lapse date, which bears no relation to the lapse date of the pre-effective-date financing statement whose effectiveness the initial financing statement continues. See subsection (b).

As subsection (a) makes clear, the filing of an initial financing statement under this section continues the effectiveness of a pre-effective-date financing statement. If the effectiveness of a pre-effective-date financing statement lapses before the initial financing statement is filed, the effectiveness of the pre-effective-date financing statement cannot be continued. Rather, unless the security interest is perfected otherwise, there will be a period during which the security interest is unperfected before becoming perfected again by the filing of the initial financing statement under this section.

If an initial financing statement is filed under this section before the effective date of this Article, it takes effect when this Article takes effect (assuming that it is ineffective under former Article 9). Note, however, that former Article 9 determines whether the filing office is obligated to accept such an initial financing statement. For the reason given in the preceding paragraph, an initial financing statement filed before the effective date of this Article does not continue the effectiveness of a pre-effective-date financing statement unless the latter remains effective on the effective date of this Article. Thus, for example, if the effectiveness of the pre-effective-date financing statement lapses before this Article takes effect, the initial financing statement would not continue its effectiveness.

2. Requirements of Initial Financing Statement Filed in Lieu of Continuation Statement. Subsection (c) sets forth the requirements for the initial financing statement under subsection (a). These requirements are needed to inform searchers that the initial financing statement operates to continue a financing statement filed elsewhere and to enable searchers to locate and discover the attributes of the other financing statement. The notice-filing policy of this Article applies to the initial financing statements described in this section. Accordingly, an initial financing statement that substantially satisfies the requirements of subsection (c) is effective, even if it has minor errors or omissions, unless the errors or omissions make the financing statement seriously misleading. See Section 9-506.

A single initial financing statement may continue the effectiveness of more than one financing statement filed before this Article's effective date. See Section 1-106 (words in the singular include the plural). If a financing statement has been filed in more than one office in a given jurisdiction, as may be the case if the jurisdiction had adopted former Section 9-401(l), the third alternative, then an identification of the filing in the central filing office suffices for purposes of subsection (c)(2). If under this Article the collateral is of a type different from its type under former Article 9—as would be the case, e.g., with a right to payment of lottery winnings (a "general intangible" under former Article 9 and an "account" under this Article), then subsection (c) requires that the initial financing statement indicate the type under this Article.

Section 9-707. Amendment of Pre-Effective-Date Financing Statement

(a) ["Pre-effective-date financing statement".] In this section, "pre-effective-date financing statement" means a financing statement filed before this [Act] takes effect.

(b) [Applicable law.] After this [Act] takes effect, a person may add or delete collateral covered by, continue or terminate the effectiveness of, or otherwise amend the information provided in, a pre-effective-date financing statement only in accordance with the law of the jurisdiction governing perfection as provided in Part 3. However, the effectiveness of a pre-effective-date financing statement also may be terminated in accordance with the law of the jurisdiction in which the financing statement is filed.

(c) [Method of amending: general rule.] Except as otherwise provided in subsection (d), if the law of this State governs perfection of a security interest, the information in a pre-effective-date financing statement may be amended after this [Act] takes effect only if:

(1) the pre-effective-date financing statement and an amendment are filed in the office specified in Section 9-501;

(2) an amendment is filed in the office specified in Section 9-501 concurrently with, or after the filing in that office of, an initial financing statement that satisfies Section 9-706(c); or

(3) an initial financing statement that provides the information as amended and satisfies Section 9-706(c) is filed in the office specified in Section 9-501.

(d) [Method of amending: continuation.] If the law of this State governs perfection of a security interest, the effectiveness of a pre-effective-date financing statement may be continued only under Section 9-705(d) and (f) or 9-706.

(e) [Method of amending: additional termination rule.] Whether or not the law of this State governs perfection of a security interest, the effectiveness of a pre-effective-date financing statement filed in this State may be terminated after this [Act] takes effect by filing a termination statement in the office in which the pre-effective-date financing statement is filed, unless an initial financing statement that satisfies Section 9-706(c) has been filed in the office specified by the law of the jurisdiction governing perfection as provided in Part 3 as the office in which to file a financing statement.

Definitional Cross References:

Collateral	Section 9-102(a)(12)
Continuation statement	Section 9-102(a)(27)
Financing statement	Section 9-102(a)(39)
Person	Section 1-201(b)(27)
Secured party	Section 9-102(a)(73)
Security interest	Section 1-201(b)(35)

Official Comment

1. Scope of This Section. This section addresses post-effective-date amendments to pre-effective-date financing statements.

2. Applicable Law. Determining how to amend a pre-effective-date financing statement requires one first to determine the jurisdiction whose law applies. Subsection (b) provides that, as a general matter, post-effective-date amendments to pre-effective-date financing statements are effective only if they are accomplished in accordance with the substantive (or local) law of the jurisdiction governing perfection under Part 3 of this Article. However, under certain circumstances, the effectiveness of a financing statement may be terminated in accordance with the substantive law of the jurisdiction in which the financing statement is filed. See Comment 5, below.

Example 1: D is a corporation organized under the law of State Y. It owns equipment located in State X. Under former Article 9, SP properly perfected a security interest in the equipment by filing a financing statement in State X. Under this Article, the law of State Y governs perfection of the security interest. See Sections 9-301, 9-307. After this Article takes effect, SP wishes to amend the financing statement to reflect a change in D's name. Under subsection (b), the financing statement may be amended in accordance with the law of State Y, i.e., in accordance with subsection (c) as enacted in State Y.

Example 2: The facts are as in Example 1, except that SP wishes to terminate the effectiveness of the State X filing. The first sentence of subsection (b) provides that the financing statement may be terminated after the effective date of this Article in accordance with the law of State Y, i.e., in accordance with subsection (c) as enacted in State Y. However, the second sentence provides that the financing statement also may be terminated in accordance with the law of the jurisdiction in which it is filed, i.e., in accordance with subsection (e) as enacted in State X. If the pre-effective-date financing statement is filed in the jurisdiction whose law governs perfection (here, State Y), then both sentences would designate the law of State Y as applicable to the termination of the financing statement. That is, the financing statement could be terminated in accordance with subsection (c) or (e) as enacted in State Y.

3. Method of Amending. Subsection (c) provides three methods of effectuating a post-effective-date amendment to a pre-effective-date financing statement. Under subsection (c)(1), if the financing statement is filed in the jurisdiction and office determined by this Article, then an effective amendment may be filed in the same office.

Example 3: D is a corporation organized under the law of State Z. It owns equipment located in State Z. Before the effective date of this Article, SP perfected a security interest in the equipment by filing in two offices in State Z, a local filing office and the office of the Secretary of State. See former Section 9-401(1) (third alternative). State Z enacts this Article and specifies in Section 9-501 that a financing statement covering equipment is to be filed in the office of the Secretary of State. SP wishes to assign its power as secured party of record. Under subsection (b), the substantive law of State Z applies. Because the pre-effective-date financing statement is filed in the office specified in subsection (c)(1) as enacted by State Z, SP may effectuate the assignment by filing an amendment under Section 9-514 with the office of the Secretary of State. SP need not amend the local filing, and the priority of the security interest perfected by the filing of the financing statement would not be affected by the failure to amend the local filing.

If a pre-effective-date financing statement is filed in an office other than the one specified by Section 9-501 of the relevant jurisdiction, then ordinarily an amendment filed in that office is ineffective. (Subsection (e) provides an exception for termination statements.) Rather, the amendment must be effectuated by a filing in the jurisdiction and office determined by this Article. That filing may consist of an initial financing statement followed by an amendment, an initial financing statement together with an amendment, or an initial financing statement that indicates the information provided in the financing statement, as amended. Subsection (c)(2) encompasses the first two options; subsection (c)(3) contemplates the last. In each instance, the initial financing statement must satisfy Section 9-706(c).

4. Continuation. Subsection (d) refers to the two methods by which a secured party may continue the effectiveness of a pre-effective-date financing statement under this Part. The Comments to Sections 9-705 and 9-706 explain these methods.

5. Termination. The effectiveness of a pre-effective-date financing statement may be terminated pursuant to subsection (c). This section also provides an alternative method for accomplishing this result: filing a termination statement in the office in which the financing statement is filed. The alternative method becomes unavailable once an initial financing statement that relates to the pre-effective-date financing statement and satisfies Section 9-706(c) is filed in the jurisdiction and office determined by this Article.

Example 4: The facts are as in Example 1, except that SP wishes to terminate a financing statement filed in State X. As explained in Example 1, the financing statement may be amended in accordance with the law of the jurisdiction governing perfection under this Article, i.e., in accordance with the substantive law of State Y. As enacted in State Y, subsection (c)(1) is inapplicable because the financing statement was not filed in the State Y filing office specified in Section 9-501. Under subsection (c)(2), the financing statement may be amended by filing in the State Y filing office an initial financing statement followed by a termination statement. The filing of an initial financing statement together with a termination statement also would be legally sufficient under subsection (c)(2), but Section 9-512(a)(1) may render this method impractical. The financing statement also may be amended under subsection (c)(3), but the resulting initial financing statement is likely to be very confusing. In each instance, the initial financing statement must satisfy Section 9-706(c). Applying the law of State Y, subsection (e) is inapplicable, because the financing statement was not filed in "this State," i.e., State Y.

This section affords another option to SP. Subsection (b) provides that the effectiveness of a financing statement may be terminated either in accordance with the law of the jurisdiction governing perfection (here, State Y) or in accordance with the substantive law of the jurisdiction in which the financing statement is filed (here, State X). Applying the law of State X, the financing statement is filed in "this State," i.e., State X, and subsection (e) applies. Accordingly, the effectiveness of the financing statement can be terminated by filing a termination statement in the State X office in which the financing statement is filed, unless an initial financing statement that relates to the financing statement and satisfies Section 9-706(c) as enacted in State X has been filed in the jurisdiction and office determined by this Article (here, the State Y filing office).

Section 9-708. Persons Entitled to File Initial Financing Statement or Continuation Statement

A person may file an initial financing statement or a continuation statement under this part if:

(1) the secured party of record authorizes the filing; and

(2) the filing is necessary under this part:

(A) to continue the effectiveness of a financing statement filed before this [Act] takes effect; or

(B) to perfect or continue the perfection of a security interest.

Definitional Cross References:

Financing statement	Section 9-102(a)(39)
Person	Section 1-201(b)(27)
Security interest	Section 1-201(b)(35)
Secured party	Section 9-102(a)(73)

Official Comment

This section permits a secured party to file an initial financing statement or continuation statement necessary under this Part to continue the effectiveness of a financing statement filed before this Article takes effect or to perfect or otherwise continue the perfection of a security interest. Because a filing described in this section typically operates to continue the effectiveness of a financing statement whose filing the debtor already has authorized, this section does not require authorization from the debtor.

Section 9-709. Priority

(a) [Law governing priority.] This [Act] determines the priority of conflicting claims to collateral. However, if the relative priorities of the claims were established before this [Act] takes effect, [former Article 9] determines priority.

(b) [Priority if security interest becomes enforceable under Section 9-203.] For purposes of Section 9-322(a), the priority of a security interest that becomes enforceable under Section 9-203 of this [Act] dates from the time this [Act] takes effect if the security interest is perfected under this [Act] by the filing of a financing statement before this [Act] takes effect which would not have been effective to perfect the security interest under [former Article 9]. This subsection does not apply to conflicting security interests each of which is perfected by the filing of such a financing statement.

Definitional Cross References:

Collateral	Section 9-102(a)(12)
Financing statement	Section 9-102(a)(39)
Security interest	Section 1-201(b)(35)

Official Comment

1. Law Governing Priority. Ordinarily, this Article determines the priority of conflicting claims to collateral. However, when the relative priorities of the claims were established before this Article takes effect, former Article 9 governs.

Example 1: In 1999, SP-1 obtains a security interest in a right to payment for goods sold ("account"). SP-1 fails to file a financing statement. This Article takes effect on July 1, 2001. Thereafter, on August 1, 2001, D creates a security interest in the same account in favor of SP-2, who files a financing statement. This Article determines the relative priorities of the claims. SP-2's security interest has priority under Section 9-322(a)(1).

Example 2: In 1999, SP-1 obtains a security interest in a right to payment for goods sold ("account"). SP-1 fails to file a financing statement. In 2000, D creates a security interest in the same account in favor of SP-2, who likewise fails to file a financing statement. This Article takes effect on July 1, 2001. Because the relative priorities of the security interests were established before the effective date of this Article, former Article 9 governs priority, and SP-1's security interest has priority under former Section 9-312(5)(b).

Example 3: The facts are as in Example 2, except that, on August 1, 2001, SP-2 files a proper financing statement under this Article. Until August 1, 2001, the relative priorities of the security interests were established before the effective date of this Article, as in Example 2. However, by taking the affirmative step of filing a financing statement, SP-2 established anew the relative priority of the conflicting claims after the effective date. Thus, this Article determines priority. SP-2's security interest has priority under Section 9-322(a)(1).

As Example 3 illustrates, relative priorities that are "established" before the effective date do not necessarily remain unchanged following the effective date. Of course, unlike priority contests among unperfected security interests, some priorities are established permanently, e.g., the rights of a buyer of property who took free of a security interest under former Article 9.

One consequence of the rule in subsection (a) is that the mere taking effect of this Article does not of itself adversely affect the priority of conflicting claims to collateral.

Example 4: In 1999, SP-1 obtains a security interest in a right to payment for lottery winnings (a "general intangible" as defined in former Article 9 but an "account" as defined in this Article). SP-1's security interest is unperfected because its filed financing statement covers only "accounts." In 2000, D creates a security interest in the same right to payment in favor of SP-2, who files a financing statement covering "accounts and general intangibles." Before this Article takes effect on July 1, 2001, SP-2's perfected security interest has priority over SP-1's unperfected security interest under former Section 9-312(5). Because the relative priorities of the security interests were established before the effective date of this Article, former Article 9 continues to govern priority after this Article takes effect. Thus, SP-2's priority is not adversely affected by this Article's having taken effect.

Note that were this Article to govern priority, SP-2 would become subordinated to SP-1 under Section 9-322(a)(1), even though nothing changes other than this Article's having taken effect. Under Section 9-704, SP-1's security interest would become perfected; the financing statement covering "accounts" adequately covers the lottery winnings and complies with the other perfection requirements of this Article, e.g., it is filed in the proper office.

Example 5: In 1999, SP-1 obtains a security interest in a right to payment for lottery winnings—a "general intangible" (as defined under former Article 9). SP-1's security interest is unperfected because its filed financing statement covers only "accounts." In 2000, D creates a security interest in the same right to payment in favor of SP-2, who makes the same mistake and also files a financing statement covering only "accounts." Before this Article takes effect on July 1, 2001, SP-1's unperfected security interest has priority over SP-2's unperfected security interest, because SP-1's security interest was the first to attach. See former Section 9-312(5)(b). Because the relative priorities of the security interests were established before the effective date of this Article, former Article 9 continues to govern priority after this Article takes effect. Although Section 9-704 makes both security interests perfected for purposes of this Article, both are unperfected under former Article 9, which determines their relative priorities.

2. Financing Statements Ineffective Under Former Article 9 But Effective Under This Article. If this Article determines priority, subsection (b) may apply. It deals with the case in which a filing that occurs before the effective date of this Article would be ineffective to perfect a security interest under former Article 9 but effective under this Article. For purposes of Section 9-322(a), the priority of a security interest that attaches after this Article takes effect and is perfected in this manner dates from the time this Article takes effect.

Example 6: In 1999, SP-1 obtains a security interest in D's existing and after-acquired instruments and files a financing statement covering "instruments." In 2000, D grants a security interest in its existing and after-acquired accounts in favor of SP-2, who files a financing statement covering "accounts." After this Article takes effect on July 1, 2001, one of D's account debtors gives D a negotiable note to evidence its obligation to pay an overdue account. Under the first-to-file-or-perfect rule in Section 9-322(a), SP-1 would have priority in the instrument, which constitutes SP-2's proceeds. SP-1's filing in 1999 was earlier than SP-2's in 2000. However, subsection (b) provides that, for purposes of Section 9-322(a), SP-1's priority dates from the time this Article takes effect (July 1, 2001). Under Section 9-322(b), SP-2's priority with respect to the proceeds (instrument) dates from its filing as to the original collateral (accounts). Accordingly, SP-2's security interest would be senior.

Subsection (b) does not apply to conflicting security interests each of which is perfected by a pre-effective-date filing that was not effective under former Article 9 but is effective under this Article.

Example 7: In 1999, SP-1 obtains a security interest in D's existing and after-acquired instruments and files a financing statement covering "instruments." In 2000, D grants a security interest in its existing and after-acquired instruments in favor of SP-2, who files a financing statement covering "instruments." After this Article takes effect on July 1, 2001, one of D's account debtors gives D a negotiable note to evidence its obligation to pay an overdue account. Under the first-to-file-or-perfect rule in Section 9-322(a), SP-1 would have priority in the instrument. Both filings are effective under this Article, see Section 9-705(b), and SP-1's filing in 1999 was earlier than SP-2's in 2000. Subsection (b) does not change this result.

PART 8 TRANSITION PROVISIONS FOR 2010 AMENDMENTS

Section 9-801. Effective Date

This [Act] takes effect on July 1, 2013.

Legislative Note: *Because these amendments change the proper place in which to file to perfect certain security interests, it is particularly important that States adopt a uniform effective date. Otherwise, the status of a particular security interest as perfected or unperfected would depend on whether the matter was litigated in a State in which the amendments were in effect or a State in which the amendments were not in effect. Any one State's failure to adopt the uniform effective date will significantly increase the cost and uncertainty surrounding the affected transactions.*

Official Comment

These transition provisions largely track the provisions of Part 7, which govern the transition to the 1998 revision of this Article. The Comments to the sections of Part 7 generally are relevant to the corresponding sections of Part 8. The 2010 amendments are less far-reaching than the 1998 revision. Although Part 8 does not carry forward those Part 7 provisions that clearly would have no application to the transition to the amendments, as a matter of prudence Part 8 does carry forward all Part 7 provisions that are even arguably relevant to the transition.

The most significant transition problem raised by the 2010 amendments arises from changes to Section 9-503(a), concerning the name of the debtor that must be provided for a financing statement to be sufficient. Sections 9-805 and 9-806 address this problem.

Example: On November 8, 2012, Debtor, an individual whose "individual name" is "Lon Debtor" and whose principal residence is located in State A, creates a security interest in certain manufacturing equipment. On November 15, 2012, SP perfects a security interest in the equipment under Article 9 (as in effect prior to the 2010 amendments) by filing a financing statement against "Lon Debtor" in the State A filing office. On July 1, 2013, the 2010 amendments, including Alternative A to Section 9-503(a), take effect in State A. Debtor's unexpired State A driver's indicates that Debtor's name is "Polonius Debtor." Assuming that a search under "Polonius Debtor" using the filing office's standard search logic would not disclose the filed financing statement, the financing statement would be insufficient under amended Section 9-503(a)(4) (Alt. A). However, Section 9-805(b) provides that the 2010 amendments do not render the financing statement ineffective. Rather, the financing statement remains effective—even if it has become seriously misleading—until it would have ceased to be effective had the amendments not taken effect. See Section 9-805(b)(1). SP can continue the effectiveness of the financing statement by filing a continuation statement with the State A filing office. To do so, however, SP must amend Debtor's name on the financing statement to provide the name that is sufficient under Section 9-503(a)(4) (Alt. A) at the time the continuation statement is filed. See Section 9-805(c), (e).

The most significant transition problem addressed by the 1998 revision arose from the change in the choice-of-law rules governing where to file a financing statement. The 2010 amendments do not change the choice-of-law rules. Even so, the amendments will change the place to file in a few cases, because certain entities that were not previously classified as "registered organizations" would fall within that category under the amendments.

Section 9-802. Savings Clause

(a) [Pre-effective-date transactions or liens.] Except as otherwise provided in this part, this [Act] applies to a transaction or lien within its scope, even if the transaction or lien was entered into or created before this [Act] takes effect.

(b) [Pre-effective-date proceedings.] This [Act] does not affect an action, case, or proceeding commenced before this [Act] takes effect.

Section 9-803. Security Interest Perfected before Effective Date

(a) [Continuing perfection: perfection requirements satisfied.] A security interest that is a perfected security interest immediately before this [Act] takes effect is a perfected security interest under [Article 9 as amended by this [Act]] if, when this [Act] takes effect, the applicable requirements for attachment and perfection under [Article 9 as amended by this [Act]] are satisfied without further action.

(b) [Continuing perfection: perfection requirements not satisfied.] Except as otherwise provided in Section 9-805, if, immediately before this [Act] takes effect, a security interest is a perfected security interest, but the applicable requirements for perfection under [Article 9 as amended by this [Act]] are not satisfied when this [Act] takes effect, the security interest remains perfected thereafter only if the applicable requirements for perfection under [Article 9 as amended by this [Act]] are satisfied within one year after this [Act] takes effect.]

Section 9-804. Security Interest Unperfected before Effective Date

A security interest that is an unperfected security interest immediately before this [Act] takes effect becomes a perfected security interest:

(1) without further action, when this [Act] takes effect if the applicable requirements for perfection under [Article 9 as amended by this [Act]] are satisfied before or at that time; or

(2) when the applicable requirements for perfection are satisfied if the requirements are satisfied after that time.

Section 9-805. Effectiveness of Action Taken before Effective Date

(a) [Pre-effective-date filing effective.] The filing of a financing statement before this [Act] takes effect is effective to perfect a security interest to the extent the filing would satisfy the applicable requirements for perfection under [Article 9 as amended by this [Act]].

(b) [When pre-effective-date filing becomes ineffective.] This [Act] does not render ineffective an effective financing statement that, before this [Act] takes effect, is filed and satisfies the applicable requirements for perfection under the law of the jurisdiction governing perfection as provided in [Article 9 as it existed before amendment]. However, except as otherwise provided in subsections (c) and (d) and Section 9-806, the financing statement ceases to be effective:

(1) if the financing statement is filed in this State, at the time the financing statement would have ceased to be effective had this [Act] not taken effect; or

(2) if the financing statement is filed in another jurisdiction, at the earlier of:

(A) the time the financing statement would have ceased to be effective under the law of that jurisdiction; or

(B) June 30, 2018.

(c) [Continuation statement.] The filing of a continuation statement after this [Act] takes effect does not continue the effectiveness of a financing statement filed before this [Act] takes effect. However, upon the timely filing of a continuation statement after this [Act] takes effect and in accordance with the law of the jurisdiction governing perfection as provided in [Article 9 as amended by this [Act]], the effectiveness of a financing statement filed in the same office in that jurisdiction before this [Act] takes effect continues for the period provided by the law of that jurisdiction.

(d) [Application of subsection (b)(2)(B) to transmitting utility financing statement.] Subsection (b)(2)(B) applies to a financing statement that, before this [Act] takes effect, is filed against a transmitting utility and satisfies the applicable requirements for perfection under the law of the jurisdiction governing perfection as provided in [Article 9 as it existed before amendment], only to the extent that [Article 9 as amended by this [Act]] provides that the law of a jurisdiction other than the jurisdiction in which the financing statement is filed governs perfection of a security interest in collateral covered by the financing statement.

(e) [Application of Part 5.] A financing statement that includes a financing statement filed before this [Act] takes effect and a continuation statement filed after this [Act] takes effect is effective only to the extent that it satisfies the requirements of [Part 5 as amended by this [Act]] for an initial financing statement. A financing statement that indicates that the debtor is a decedent's estate indicates that the collateral is being administered by a personal representative within the meaning of Section 9-503(a)(2) as amended by this [Act]. A financing statement that indicates that the debtor is a trust or is a trustee acting with respect to property held in trust indicates that the collateral is held in a trust within the meaning of Section 9-503(a)(3) as amended by this [Act].

Section 9-806. When Initial Financing Statement Suffices to Continue Effectiveness of Financing Statement

(a) [Initial financing statement in lieu of continuation statement.] The filing of an initial financing statement in the office specified in Section 9-501 continues the effectiveness of a financing statement filed before this [Act] takes effect if:

(1) the filing of an initial financing statement in that office would be effective to perfect a security interest under [Article 9 as amended by this [Act]];

(2) the pre-effective-date financing statement was filed in an office in another State; and

(3) the initial financing statement satisfies subsection (c).

(b) [Period of continued effectiveness.] The filing of an initial financing statement under subsection (a) continues the effectiveness of the pre-effective-date financing statement:

(1) if the initial financing statement is filed before this [Act] takes effect, for the period provided in [unamended Section 9-515] with respect to an initial financing statement; and

(2) if the initial financing statement is filed after this [Act] takes effect, for the period provided in Section 9-515 as amended by this [Act] with respect to an initial financing statement.

(c) [Requirements for initial financing statement under subsection (a).] To be effective for purposes of subsection (a), an initial financing statement must:

(1) satisfy the requirements of [Part 5 as amended by this [Act]] for an initial financing statement;

(2) identify the pre-effective-date financing statement by indicating the office in which the financing statement was filed and providing the dates of filing and file numbers, if any, of the financing statement and of the most recent continuation statement filed with respect to the financing statement; and

(3) indicate that the pre-effective-date financing statement remains effective.

Section 9-807. Amendment of Pre-Effective-Date Financing Statement

(a) ["Pre-effective-date financing statement".] In this section, "pre-effective-date financing statement" means a financing statement filed before this [Act] takes effect.

(b) [Applicable law.] After this [Act] takes effect, a person may add or delete collateral covered by, continue or terminate the effectiveness of, or otherwise amend the information provided in, a pre-effective-date financing statement only in accordance with the law of the jurisdiction governing perfection as provided in [Article 9 as amended by this [Act]]. However, the effectiveness of a pre-effective-date financing statement also may be terminated in accordance with the law of the jurisdiction in which the financing statement is filed.

(c) [Method of amending: general rule.] Except as otherwise provided in subsection

(d) , if the law of this State governs perfection of a security interest, the information in a pre-effective-date financing statement may be amended after this [Act] takes effect only if:

(1) the pre-effective-date financing statement and an amendment are filed in the office specified in Section 9-501;

(2) an amendment is filed in the office specified in Section 9-501 concurrently with, or after the filing in that office of, an initial financing statement that satisfies Section 9-806(c); or

(3) an initial financing statement that provides the information as amended and satisfies Section 9-806(c) is filed in the office specified in Section 9-501.

(d) [Method of amending: continuation.] If the law of this State governs perfection of a security interest, the effectiveness of a pre-effective-date financing statement may be continued only under Section 9-805(c) and (e) or 9-806.

(e) [Method of amending: additional termination rule.] Whether or not the law of this State governs perfection of a security interest, the effectiveness of a pre-effective-date financing statement filed in this State may be terminated after this [Act] takes effect by filing a termination statement in the office in which the pre-effective-date financing statement is filed, unless an initial financing statement that satisfies Section 9-806(c) has been filed in the office specified by the law of the jurisdiction governing perfection as provided in [Article 9 as amended by this [Act]] as the office in which to file a financing statement.

Section 9-808. Person Entitled to File Initial Financing Statement or Continuation Statement

A person may file an initial financing statement or a continuation statement under this part if:

(1) the secured party of record authorizes the filing; and

(2) the filing is necessary under this part:

(A) to continue the effectiveness of a financing statement filed before this [Act] takes effect; or

(B) to perfect or continue the perfection of a security interest.Section 9-809. Priority

This [Act] determines the priority of conflicting claims to collateral. However, if the relative priorities of the claims were established before this [Act] takes effect, [Article 9 as it existed before amendment] determines priority.

Legislative Note: *The term "this [Act]" as used in this part refers to the legislation enacting these amendments to Article 9, not to the legislation that enacted Article 9. States should substitute appropriate references.*

APPENDICES

Appendix I. [Omitted]

Appendix Ii. Model Provisions for Production-Money Priority

Legislative Note: *States that enact these model provisions should add the following definitions to Section 9-102(a) following the definition of "proceeds," and preceding the definition of "promissory note", renumbering paragraphs in Section 9-102(a) accordingly:*

(xx) "Production-money crops" means crops that secure a production-money obligation incurred with respect to the production of those crops.

(xx) "Production-money obligation" means an obligation of an obligor incurred for new value given to enable the debtor to produce crops if the value is in fact used for the production of the crops.

(xx) "Production of crops" includes tilling and otherwise preparing land for growing, planting, cultivating, fertilizing, irrigating, harvesting, and gathering crops, and protecting them from damage or disease.[Model Section[9-103a]. "Production-Money Crops"; "Production-Money Obligation"; Production-Money Security Interest; Burden of Establishing

(a) A security interest in crops is a production-money security interest to the extent that the crops are production-money crops.

(b) If the extent to which a security interest is a production-money security interest depends on the application of a payment to a particular obligation, the payment must be applied:

(1) in accordance with any reasonable method of application to which the parties agree;

(2) in the absence of the parties' agreement to a reasonable method, in accordance with any intention of the obligor manifested at or before the time of payment; or

(3) in the absence of an agreement to a reasonable method and a timely manifestation of the obligor's intention, in the following order:

(A) to obligations that are not secured; and

(B) if more than one obligation is secured, to obligations secured by production-money security interests in the order in which those obligations were incurred.

(c) A production-money security interest does not lose its status as such, even if:

(1) the production-money crops also secure an obligation that is not a production-money obligation;

(2) collateral that is not production-money crops also secures the production-money obligation; or

(3) the production-money obligation has been renewed, refinanced, or restructured.

(d) A secured party claiming a production-money security interest has the burden of establishing the extent to which the security interest is a production-money security interest.]

Legislative Note: *This section is optional. States that enact this section should place it between Sections 9-103 and 9-104 and number it accordingly, e.g., as Section 9-103A or 9-103.1.*

Official Comment

1. Source. New.

2. Production-Money Priority; "Production-Money Security Interest." This section is patterned closely on Section 9-103, which defines "purchase-money security interest." Subsection (b) makes clear that a security interest can obtain production-money status only to the extent that it secures value that actually can be traced to the direct production of crops. To the extent that a security interest is not entitled to production-money treatment.

[Model Section[9-324a]. Priority of Production-Money Security Interests and Agricultural Liens

(a) Except as otherwise provided in subsections (c), (d), and (e), if the requirements of subsection (b) are met, a perfected production-money security interest in production-money crops has priority over a conflicting security interest in the same crops and, except as otherwise provided in Section 9-327, also has priority in their identifiable proceeds.

(b) A production-money security interest has priority under subsection (a) if:

(1) the production-money security interest is perfected by filing when the production-money secured party first gives new value to enable the debtor to produce the crops;

(2) the production-money secured party sends an authenticated notification to the holder of the conflicting security interest not less than 10 or more than 30 days before the production-money secured party first gives new value to enable the debtor to produce the crops if the holder had filed a financing statement covering the crops before the date of the filing made by the production-money secured party; and

(3) the notification states that the production-money secured party has or expects to acquire a production-money security interest in the debtor's crops and provides a description of the crops.

(c) Except as otherwise provided in subsection (d) or (e), if more than one security interest qualifies for priority in the same collateral under subsection (a), the security interests rank according to priority in time of filing under Section 9-322(a).

(d) To the extent that a person holding a perfected security interest in production-money crops that are the subject of a production-money security interest gives new value to enable the debtor to produce the production-money crops and the value is in fact used for the production of the production-money crops, the security interests rank according to priority in time of filing under Section 9-322(a).

(e) To the extent that a person holds both an agricultural lien and a production-money security interest in the same collateral securing the same obligations, the rules of priority applicable to agricultural liens govern priority.

Legislative Note: *This section is optional. States that enact this section should place it between Sections 9-324 and 9-325 and number it accordingly, e.g., as Section 9-324A or 9-324.1.*

Official Comment

1. Source. New; replaces former Section 9-312(2).

2. Priority of Production-Money Security Interests and Conflicting Security Interests. This section replaces the limited priority in crops afforded by former Section 9-312(2). That priority generally has been though to be of little value for its intended beneficiaries. This section attempts to balance the interests of the production-money secured party with those of a secured party who has previously filed a financing statement covering the crops that are to be produced. For example, to qualify for priority under this section, the production-money secured party must notify the earlier-filed secured party prior to extending the production-money credit. The notification affords the earlier secured party the opportunity to prevent subordination by extending the credit itself. Subsection (d) makes this explicit. If the holder of a security interest in production-money crops which conflicts with a production-money security interest gives new value for the production of the crops, the security interests rank according to priority in time of filing under Section 9-322(a).

3. Multiple Production-Money Security Interests. In the case of multiple production-money security interests that qualify for priority under subsection (a), the first to file has priority. See subsection (c). Note that only a security interest perfected by filing is entitled to production-money priority. See subsection (b)(1). Consequently, subsection (c) does not adopt the first-to-file-or-perfect formulation.

4. Holder of Agricultural Lien and Production-Money Security Interest. Subsection (e) deals with a creditor who holds both an agricultural lien and an Article 9 production-money security interest in the same collateral. In these cases, the priority rules applicable to agricultural liens govern. The creditor can avoid this result by waiving its agricultural lien.

TABLE OF DISPOSITION OF SECTIONS IN FORMER ARTICLE 9 AND OTHER CODE SECTIONS

Old Article 9	New Article 9
9-101	9-101
9-102	9-109
9-103(1)(a), (b); (c) omitted	9-301
9-103(1)(d)	9-316
9-103(2)(a), (b); (c) omitted	9-303, 9-316
9-103(2)(d)	9-337
9-103(3)(a), (b); (c) omitted	9-301
9-103(3)(d)	9-307
9-103(3)(e)	9-316
9-103(4)	9-301
9-103(5)	9-301
9-103(6)	9-304, 9-305, 9-306
9-104	9-109
9-105	9-102
9-106	9-102
9-107	9-103
9-108	Omitted as no longer needed
9-109	9-102
9-110	9-108
9-111	Deleted as unnecessary Omitted (see 9-102(a)(28))
9-113	9-110
9-114	Omitted (see 9-103 and 9-324)
9-115(1)	9-102, 9-106
9-115(2)	9-203, 9-308
9-115(3)	9-108
9-115(4)	9-309, 9-312, 9-314
9-115(5)	9-327, 9-328, 9-329
9-115(6)	9-203, 9-313
9-115(e)	9-106
9-116	9-206, 9-309
9-201	9-201
9-202	9-202
9-203(1)-(3)	9-203
9-203(4)	9-201
9-204	9-204
9-205	9-205
9-206	9-403
9-207	9-207
9-208	9-210
9-301(1)-(2)	9-317
9-301(3)	9-102
9-301(4)	9-323
9-302(1)	9-309, 9-310
9-302(2)	9-310
9-302(3), (4)	9-311
9-303	9-308
9-304	9-312
9-305	9-306, 9-313
9-306	9-315
9-307(1)-(2)	9-320
9-307(3)	9-323
9-308	9-330
9-309	9-331
9-310	9-333
9-311	9-401
9-312(1)	9-322
9-312(2) omitted	See Appendix II
9-312(3), (4)	9-324
9-312(5), (6)	9-322
9-312(7)	9-323
9-313(1)-(7)	9-334
9-313(8)	9-604
9-314	9-335
9-315	9-336
9-316	9-339
9-317	9-402
9-318(1)	9-404
9-318(2)	9-405
9-318(3), (4)	9-406
9-401	9-501
9-402(1)	9-504, 9-502
9-402(2)	Omitted as unnecessary
9-402(3)	9-521
9-402(4)	9-512
9-402(5), (6)	9-502
9-402(7)	9-503(a)(4), 9-507
9-402(8)	9-506
9-403(1)	9-516(a)
9-403(2)	9-515
9-403(3)	9-515, 9-522
9-403(4)	9-519
9-403(5)	9-525
9-403(6)	9-515
9-403(7)	9-519
9-404	9-513
9-405	9-514, 9-519
9-406	9-512
9-407	9-523
9-408	9-505
9-501(1), (2)	9-601
9-501(3)	9-602, 9-603
9-501(4)	9-604
9-501 (5)	9-601
9-502	9-607, 9-608
9-503	9-609

9-504(1)	9-610, 9-615
9-504(2)	9-615
9-504(3)	9-610, 9-611, 9-624
9-504(4)	9-617
9-504(5)	9-618
9-505	9-620, 9-621, 9-624
9-506	9-623, 9-624

TABLE INDICATING SOURCES OR DERIVATIONS OF NEW ARTICLE 9 SECTIONS AND CONFORMING AMENDMENTS

New Article 9 sections	Old Article 9, and other code sections (Note: Many sections contain some new coverage)
9-101	9-101
9-102	9-105, 9-106, 9-109,9-301(3), 9-306(1),
9-103	9-115, 2-326(3)
9-103	9-107
9-104 (New)	Derived from 8-106
9-105 (New)	Derived from 8-106
9-106	8-106 and 9-115(e)
9-107 (New)	Derived from 8-106
9-108	9-110, 9-115(3)
9-109	9-102, 9-104
9-110	9-113
9-201	9-201, 9-203(4)
9-202	9-202
9-203	9-203, 9-115(2), (6)
9-204	9-204
9-205	9-205
9-206	9-116
9-207	9-207
9-208 (New)	
9-209 (New)	
9-210	9-208
9-301	9-103(1)(a),(b), 9-103(3) (a), (b), 9-103(4),
9-302	9-103(5) substantially modified
9-302 (New)	
9-303	9-103(2)(a), (b), substantially revised
9-304 (New)	Derived from 8-110(e) and former 9-103(6)
9-305	9-103(6)
9-306 (New)	Derived in part from 8-110(e) and 9-305 and former 9-103(6)
9-307	9-103(3)(d), as substantially revised
9-308	9-303, 9-115(2)
9-309	9-302(1), 9-115(4)(c), (d), 9-116
9-310	9-302(1), (2)
9-311	9-302(3), (4)
9-312	9-115(4) and 9-304, with additions and some changes
9-313	9-305, 9-115(6)
9-314 (New in part)	9-115(4) and derived from 8-106
9-315	9-306
9-316	9-103(1)(d), (2)(b), (3)(e), as modified
9-317	9-301, 2A-307(2)
9-318 (New)	
9-319 (New)	
9-320	9-307
9-321	2A-103(1)(o), 2A-307(3)
9-322	9-312(5), (6)
9-323	9-312(7), 9-301(4), 9-307(3), 2A-307(4)
9-324	9-312(3), (4)
9-325 (New)	But see 9-402(7)
9-326 (New)	But see 9-402(7)
9-327	Derived from 9-115(5)
9-328	9-115(5)
9-329 (New)	Loosely modeled after former 9-115(5). See also 5-114 and 5-118
9-330	9-308
9-331	9-309
9-332 (New)	But see Comment 2(c) to 9-306
9-333	9-310
9-334	9-313
9-335 (New)	Section replaces former 9-314
9-336 (New)	Section replaces former 9-315
9-337	Derived from 9-103(2)(d)
9-338 (New)	
9-339	9-316
9-340 (New)	
9-341 (New)	
9-342 (New)	Derived from 8-106(g)
9-401	9-311
9-402	9-317
9-403	9-206
9-404	9-318(1)
9-405	9-318(2)
9-406	9-318(3), (4)
9-407	2A-303
9-408 (New)	
9-409 (New)	See also 5-114
9-501	Derived from former 9-401
9-502	9-402(1), (5), (6)
9-503 (New)	Subsection (a)(4), (b) and (c) derive from former 9-402(7); otherwise, new
9-504	9-402(1)
9-505	9-408
9-506	9-402(8)
9-507	9-402(7)
9-508 (New)	But see 9-402(7)
9-509 (New)	

9-510 (New)	
9-511 (New)	
9-512	9-402(4)
9-513	9-404
9-514	9-405
9-515	9-403(2), (3), (6)
9-516 (Basically New)	Subsection (a) is former 9-403(1); the remainder is new
9-517 (New)	
9-518 (New)	
9-519	9-403(4), (7); 9-405(2)
9-520 (New)	
9-521 (New)	
9-522	9-403(3), revised substantially
9-523	9-407; subsections (d) and (e) are new
9-524 (New)	Derived from 4-109
9-525	Various sections of former Part 4
9-526 (New)	Subsection (b) derives in part from the Uniform Consumer Credit Code (1974)
9-527 (New)	Derived in part from the Uniform Consumer Credit Code (1974)
9-601	9-501(1), (2), (5)
9-602	9-501(3)
9-603	9-501(3)
9-604	9-501(4), 9-313(8)
9-605 (New)	
9-606 (New)	
9-607	9-502, subsections (b), (d), and (e) are new
9-608	Subsection (a) is new. Subsection (b) derives from former 9-502(2)
9-609	9-503
9-610	9-504(1), (3)
9-611	9-504(3)
9-612 (New)	
9-613 (New)	
9-614 (New)	
9-615	9-504(1), (2)
9-616 (New)	
9-617	9-504(4)
9-618	9-504(5)
9-619 (New)	
9-620	9-505
9-621	9-505
9-622 (New)	
9-623	9-506
9-624	9-504(3), 9-505, 9-506
9-625	9-507
9-626 (New)	
9-627	9-507(2)
9-628 (New)	
9-701	No comparable provision in Article 9 (See Article 10)
9-702	No comparable provision in Article 9 (See Article 10)
9-703	No comparable provision in Article 9 (See Article 10)
9-704	No comparable provision in Article 9 (See Article 10)
9-705	No comparable provision in Article 9 (See Article 10)
9-706	No comparable provision in Article 9 (See Article 10)
9-707	No comparable provision in Article 9 (See Article 10)
9-708	No comparable provision in Article 9 (See Article 10)
9-709	No comparable provision in Article 9(See Article 10)

UNIFORM COMMERCIAL CODE
Article 12—Controllable Electronic Records

PREFATORY NOTE TO ARTICLE 12

Section

ARTICLE 12

CONTROLLABLE ELECTRONIC RECORDS

Prefatory Note to Article 12

1. Introduction to Controllable Electronic Records. Article 12, which deals with controllable electronic records, and the conforming amendments to Articles 1 and 9, in particular, are a major part of the effort to adapt the UCC to emerging technologies as they might affect electronic commerce.

Article 12 creates a legal regime that is meant to apply more broadly than to electronic (intangible) assets that are created using existing technologies such as distributed ledger technology (DLT), including blockchain technology, which records transactions in bitcoin and other digital assets. It also aspires to apply to electronic assets that may be created using technologies that have yet to be developed, or even imagined.

The adoption of DLT has underscored two important trends in electronic commerce. First, people have begun to assign economic value to some electronic records that bear no relationship to extrinsic rights and interests. For example, without any law or legally enforceable agreement, people around the world have agreed to treat virtual currencies such as bitcoin (or, more precisely "transaction outputs" generated by the Bitcoin protocol) as a medium of exchange and store of value. Second, people are using the creation or transfer of electronic records to transfer rights to receive payment, rights to receive performance of other obligations (e.g., services or delivery of goods), and other rights and interests in personal and real property.

These trends will inevitably result in disputes among claimants to electronic records and their related rights and other benefits. Uncertainty as to the criteria for resolving these claims creates commercial risk. The magnitude of these risks will grow as these trends continue.

As explained in more detail below, Article 12 is designed to reduce these risks by providing legal rules governing the transfer—both outright and for security—of interests in some, but not all, electronic records (controllable electronic records). These rules specify certain rights in a controllable electronic record that a purchaser would acquire. Many systems for transferring controllable electronic records are pseudonymous, so that the transferee of a controllable electronic record may be unable to verify the identity of the transferor or the source of the transferor's title. Accordingly, the Article 12 rules would make controllable electronic records negotiable, in the sense that a qualifying good faith purchaser for value could take a controllable electronic record free of third-party claims of a property interest in the controllable electronic record.

Experience with DLT and other records-management systems has established some general functions required for electronic records to serve as an effective and reliable means of transferring economic value.

- The electronic record must have some "use" or benefit that one person can enjoy and can exclude all others from enjoying, e.g., the power to "spend" a bitcoin (or, more precisely, the power to include an unspent transaction output (a UTXO) in a message that the Bitcoin protocol will record to its blockchain).
- A person must be able to transfer to another person this exclusive power to use and the exclusive power to transfer the electronic record. To remain exclusive, the transfer must divest the transferor of the power to use the electronic record.
- A person must be able to demonstrate to others that the person has the power to use and transfer control of the electronic record.

As discussed in the Comments to Section 12-105, these functions form the basis of the Article 12 concept of control. To receive the benefits of negotiability and take free of third-party claims of a property interest in a controllable electronic record, a person must have control of the controllable electronic record. In addition, control serves as a method of perfection of a security interest in a controllable electronic record and as a condition for achieving a non-temporal priority of a security interest. In this context, it may be useful to think of control as the functional analogue of possession of tangible personal property such as goods. Note that the concept of control allows for certain exceptions to the exclusivity of powers.

Article 12 governs certain rights (primarily property rights) of transacting parties and other persons that might be affected by the transactions. Article 12 does not govern assets other than controllable electronic records except, in coordination with Article 9, controllable accounts and controllable payment intangibles evidenced by controllable electronic records (discussed below). Like the UCC in general, Article 12 is not a regulatory statute. The fact that an asset is or is not a controllable electronic record under the UCC would not necessarily affect the application of laws regulating, for example, banking, securities, commodities, money transmission, and taxation.

2. Scope of Article 12. Article 12 applies to controllable electronic records. Controllable electronic records are a subset of what often are referred to as digital assets. Article 12 is designed to work for both technologies that are known and those that may be developed in the future. Whether an asset is a controllable electronic record (and therefore within the scope of Article 12) depends on whether the characteristics of the asset and the protocols of any system on which the asset is recorded make it suitable for the application of Article 12's substantive rules. The nature of electronic commerce is constantly changing. For this reason, the technology on which an asset depends, the type of asset, and the prevailing use of the asset should all be irrelevant to whether the asset is a controllable electronic record.

To determine whether Article 12 applies to a particular asset, for example, bitcoin, one must determine whether the asset falls within the definition of controllable electronic record. A controllable electronic record is a record, as the UCC defines the term. A record is information that is retrievable in perceivable form. Section 1-201(b)(31) (defining "record"). A controllable electronic record is a record that is stored in an electronic medium and that can be subjected to control, as defined in Section 12-105. Sections 1-201(b)(16A) (defining "electronic"); 12- 102(a)(1) (defining "controllable electronic record"). An electronic record that cannot be subjected to control under Section 12-105 is outside the scope of Article 12. As already mentioned, Article 12 addresses primarily certain property rights in controllable electronic records. Of course, that an electronic record is not subject to control does not imply that it does not have commercial utility. Businesses generate and sell or license large quantities of electronic records that do not require the attributes of negotiability that Article 12 affords to controllable electronic records.

The meaning of control in the UCC depends on the type of property involved. See Sections 7-106 (electronic documents of title); 8-106 (four different types of investment property, each with a different definition of "control"); 9-104 (deposit accounts); 9-105 (chattel paper); 9-105A (electronic money). The Comments to Section 12-105 explain the requirements for obtaining control of a controllable electronic record. For present purposes of exposition, it is sufficient to think of bitcoin and other virtual currencies as prototypical controllable electronic records. The provisions under other law that govern control and other matters for other types of electronic records (some of which are modified by these amendments) are not addressed by Article 12.

3. Substantive Provisions of Article 12. The principal function of Article 12 is to specify certain rights of a purchaser of a controllable electronic record. A purchaser is a person that acquires an interest in property by a voluntary transaction, such as a sale. Section 1-201(b)(29) (defining "purchase"), (30) (defining "purchaser"). Purchasers include both buyers and secured parties. Law other than Article 12 would determine whether a person acquires any rights in a controllable electronic record and so would be eligible to be a purchaser. Section 12-104(c).

Section 12-104 adopts the "shelter" principle, under which a purchaser of a controllable electronic record acquires whatever rights the transferor had or had power to transfer. Section 12-104(d). A similar rule appears in Articles 2, 3, 7, and 8. See Sections 2-403(1) (goods); 3- 203(b) (negotiable instruments); 7-504(a) (documents of title); 8-302(a) (certificated and uncertificated securities).

The ability to take a controllable electronic record free of third-party property claims appears to be necessary for a controllable electronic record to have commercial utility. As is the case with Articles 2, 3, 7, and 9, Article 12 would facilitate commerce by affording to certain good-faith purchasers for value (buyers as well as secured parties) greater rights than their transferors had or had power to transfer. (Article 8 also provides for certain purchasers for value to take greater rights than their transferors had, but does not contain an explicit good-faith requirement. See Section 8-303.) Article 12 refers to these purchasers as qualifying purchasers. Qualifying purchasers are purchasers that obtain control of a controllable electronic record for value, in good faith, and without notice of any claim of a property interest in the controllable electronic record. Section 12-102(a)(2). Like a holder in due course of a negotiable instrument, a qualifying purchaser of a controllable electronic record takes the controllable electronic record free of property claims. Section 12-104(e).

Consider an example in which B contracts to buy bitcoin from S.

- Law other than Article 12 generally would determine whether S is the owner of the bitcoin.
- Law other than Article 12 would resolve issues concerning the formation of the contract of sale between B and S and the obligations of the parties under the contract.
- Except to the extent provided by Article 12, law other than Article 12 would determine what steps are necessary for B to acquire rights in the bitcoin.
- By acquiring rights in the bitcoin by sale, B would become a purchaser of the bitcoin within the meaning of UCC Article 1.

- Article 12 provides that if B becomes a purchaser, B will acquire whatever rights S had or had power to transfer. As a general matter, law other than Article 12 would define these rights. B would acquire these rights regardless of whether B obtained control of the bitcoin.

In this example, law other than Article 12 includes UCC Article 9, which determines the steps necessary for a security interest to attach to a controllable electronic record. More generally, Article 9 governs any conflict between Article 9 and Article 12. Section 12-103(a).

Now assume that O is the owner of the bitcoin and that S is a hacker, who acquired control of the bitcoin illegally from O.

- Just as a buyer of goods can obtain possession from a seller that has no rights in the goods, B can obtain control of the bitcoin, even if S "stole" it from O.
- If B obtains control of the bitcoin for value, in good faith, and without notice of any claim of a property interest, B would be a qualifying purchaser.
- Even if B would not have acquired any rights in the bitcoin under non-Article 12 law (for example, because S, a "thief," had no rights to give), as an Article 12 qualifying purchaser, B would acquire the bitcoin free of all claims of a property interest in the bitcoin. S's control of the bitcoin gave S the power to transfer rights to a qualifying purchaser, such as B. Even if O could locate B, B would defeat O's claim of ownership and own the bitcoin free and clear. (The same result would obtain if B bought a negotiable instrument from a thief under circumstances where B became a holder in due course. This distinguishes "negotiable" property from property such as goods, as to which a buyer from a thief normally obtains no rights.)

4. Rights or Property Linked to a Controllable Electronic Record.

a. General Rules. Recall that a controllable electronic record is a record, i.e., information. Some records have what one might call "inherent value" solely because the market treats them as having value. Bitcoin would be an example of such a record. Bitcoin can be exchanged (sold) for cash or other valuable assets. Or, the owner of bitcoin can hold the bitcoin as an investment.

The value of many records, however, is as evidence of the rights of the parties to a transaction or of the rights of a party in other property. In these situations, it is essential to differentiate between the record and the rights that are evidenced by the record.

Suppose, for example, that S and B enter into a written contract for the sale of 100 air purifiers. The contract provides that at a specified time in the future, S is to deliver the goods and B is to pay for them. B may sell (assign) to P the right to receive delivery of the goods from S. P has acquired a valuable asset, i.e., the right to receive delivery.

In contrast, if B sells to P only the paper (record) on which the contract is written, P might or might not acquire the right to delivery of the goods, depending on whether applicable law treats the sale of the paper as an assignment of the right to delivery (as can be the case with a negotiable document of title under UCC Article 7). P would become the owner of the paper in any event, but the paper itself may be of little value.

If the contract for the sale of air purifiers were electronic rather than written, the same analysis would apply. The right evidenced by the electronic record (i.e., B's right to receive delivery from S) would be the valuable asset, not the record itself.

Suppose that the contract of sale between B and S is evidenced by a controllable electronic record that B sells to P. Under Section 12-104(d), P would acquire all rights in the controllable electronic record that the transferor (B) had or had power to transfer. If P obtains control of the controllable electronic record for value, in good faith, and without notice of any claim of a property right in the controllable electronic record, P will become a qualifying purchaser and, as such, would acquire its rights in the controllable electronic record free of any claim of a property right under Section 12-104.

But the controllable electronic record itself may or may not be a valuable asset. In this example, unlike bitcoin, the record would have value to P only if by virtue of acquiring rights in the controllable electronic record, P would also acquire the right to receive delivery of the goods from S.

Except to the extent provided by Article 12, that Article leaves to other law the question whether P's acquisition of rights in the controllable electronic record gives P the right to receive delivery of the goods. Section 12-104(f). We would typically expect that under other law P would not acquire the right to receive the goods merely by acquiring rights in the controllable electronic record, any more than P would have acquired the right to receive the goods if the record were in paper form, the paper were physically delivered to P, and P acquired rights in the paper.

Suppose, however, that other law does provide that, by acquiring the controllable electronic record, P would acquire the right to receive delivery of the goods from S. Suppose also that P becomes a qualifying purchaser of the controllable electronic record. As we have seen, as a qualifying purchaser, P would take its rights in the controllable electronic record free of property claims. But even though under non-Article 12 law P would (as posited) acquire the right to receive delivery of the goods, P would not acquire that right free of property claims unless non-Article 12 law also were to provide otherwise. Section 12-104(f).

b. Exceptions: Controllable Accounts and Controllable Payment Intangibles. As a general rule, Article 12 applies to records and not to rights evidenced by records (or to rights that records are purported to evidence). And, in general, law other than Article 12 would govern what steps must be taken or conditions must be satisfied for a person to acquire an interest in a controllable electronic record and the rights, if any, that the person acquires in other property (including a right to payment or performance of an obligation) as a result of acquiring an interest in the record. This "other" law includes UCC Article 9.

Article 12 provides an important exception to this general rule. The exception concerns rights to payment (specifically, accounts and payment intangibles) that are evidenced by a controllable electronic record and as to which the obligor (account debtor) undertakes to pay the person that has control of the controllable electronic record. These rights to payment are referred to as "controllable accounts" and "controllable payment intangibles." See Section 9-102(a)(27A) (defining "controllable account") and (27B) (defining "controllable payment intangible"). A qualifying purchaser of a controllable account or controllable payment intangible takes free of property claims and is protected from certain actions. See Section 12-104(a) through (e), (g), and (h), and Comments 6 through 10. As to the feasibility and rationale for this exception for controllable accounts and controllable payment intangibles, see Section 12-104, Comments 9 and 10.

The 2022 Article 9 Revisions amend several sections of Article 9 to deal with various aspects of security interests in controllable accounts, controllable electronic records, and controllable payment intangibles. See Sections 9-101, Comment 4.a.; 9-102, Comment 5.d.1.

5. Governing Law for Article 12. Section 12-107 provides rules on governing law. The general rule under subsection (a) is that the local law of a "controllable electronic record's jurisdiction" governs matters covered by Article 12. The controllable electronic record's jurisdiction is determined by an express provision in the record or in the system in which the record is recorded. If not so designated, it is determined based on the designation of the law governing the record or the system generally.

Absent any such designations, at the bottom of this "waterfall" of alternatives, the governing law will be that of the District of Columbia. Subsection (b) provides an exception for the rights and duties of account debtors under Section 12-106 if an agreement between the account debtor and an assignor of the record provides for the law of another jurisdiction to govern those rights and duties.

The law of the controllable electronic record's jurisdiction also governs perfection and priority of security interests in controllable electronic records, controllable accounts, and controllable payment intangibles. Perfection by filing, however, is governed by the law of the location of the debtor. See Section 9-306B.

Section 12-101. Title

This article may be cited as Uniform Commercial Code—Controllable Electronic Records.

Official Comment

Subsection headings. Subsection headings are not a part of the official text itself and have not been approved by the sponsors. See Section 1-107, Comment 1.

Section 12-102. Definitions

(a) [Article 12 definitions.] In this article:

(1) "Controllable electronic record" means a record stored in an electronic medium that can be subjected to control under Section 12-105. The term does not include a controllable account, a controllable payment intangible, a deposit account, an electronic copy of a record evidencing chattel paper, an electronic document of title, electronic money, investment property, or a transferable record.

(2) "Qualifying purchaser" means a purchaser of a controllable electronic record or an interest in a controllable electronic record that obtains control of the controllable electronic record for value, in good faith, and without notice of a claim of a property right in the controllable electronic record.

(3) "Transferable record" has the meaning provided for that term in:

(A) Section 201(a)(1) of the Electronic Signatures in Global and National Commerce Act, 15 U.S.C. Section 7021(a)(1)[, as amended]; or

(B) [cite to Uniform Electronic Transactions Act Section 16(a)].

(4) "Value" has the meaning provided in Section 3-303(a), as if references in that subsection to an "instrument" were references to a controllable account, controllable electronic record, or controllable payment intangible.

(b) [Definitions in Article 9.] The definitions in Article 9 of "account debtor", "controllable account", "controllable payment intangible", "chattel paper", "deposit account", "electronic money", and "investment property" apply to this article.

(c) [Article 1 definitions and principles.] Article 1 contains general definitions and principles of construction and interpretation applicable throughout this article.

Legislative Note: *It is the intent of this act to incorporate future amendments to the federal law cited in subsection (a)(3)(A). A state in which the constitution or other law does not permit incorporation of future amendments when a federal statute is incorporated into state law should omit the phrase "[as amended]". A state in which, in the absence of a legislative declaration, future amendments are incorporated into state law also should omit the phrase.*

In subsection (a)(3)(B), the state should cite to the state's version of the Uniform Electronic Transactions Act Section 16(a) or comparable state law.

Official Comment

1. Source. Subsection (a)(2), defining "qualifying purchaser," derives from Section 3-302(a)(2), which defines "holder in due course" of a negotiable instrument.

2. "Controllable electronic record." To be a "controllable electronic record" (CER) within the scope of Article 12, an electronic record must be susceptible of control under Section 12-105. Unlike "transferable records" under the Electronic Signatures in Global and National Commerce Act (E-SIGN) or a "transferable record" under the Uniform Electronic Transactions Act (UETA), a record can be a CER under Article 12 in the absence of an agreement to that effect.

This definition uses the term "record," defined in Section 1-201 to include "information ... that is stored in an electronic or other medium and is retrievable in perceivable form." The term "electronic" also is defined in Section 1-201. These broad definitions of "record" and "electronic" necessarily produce an expansive meaning of "electronic record." An electronic record would include, for example, music stored on compact disks, email messages, digital photos, personal and other information stored on a social media platform, and all types of databases stored on in an electronic medium. But most of these electronic records typically would not fall within the definition of a CER in subsection (a)(1), which includes only those electronic records "that can be subjected to control under Section 12-105." See generally Prefatory Note 2.

Consider, for example, a so-called "page" on a social media platform. Generalizations about social media/social networking platforms are difficult and these systems no doubt will continue to evolve. But these platforms typically involve licensing arrangements with users that do not permit the users (or anyone) to acquire the exclusive powers contemplated by the definition of "control" in Section 12-105. Consequently, these electronic records are not controllable electronic records as defined.

The provisions of Article 12 also do not apply to certain specified types of electronic records, and the definition has been limited accordingly. For example, the definition does not include a "transferable record" under E-SIGN or UETA. It also does not include "investment property," as defined in Section 9-102(a)(49). For this reason, the rights of an entitlement holder in a controllable electronic record that is a financial asset with respect to which the entitlement holder has a security entitlement are excluded from the definition (although the entitlement holder's securities intermediary may hold directly an interest in a controllable electronic record that it has credited to a securities account). See Sections 8-102(a)(9) (defining "financial asset"), (a)(14) (defining "securities intermediary"), (a)(17) (defining "security entitlement"), and Comment 9; 9-102(a)(49) (defining "investment property"). See also Section 8-103(h), clarifying that a controllable electronic record is not a "financial asset" except pursuant to Section 8- 102(a)(9)(iii).

A controllable electronic record is not itself a "security," defined in part in Section 8- 102(a)(15) as "an obligation of an issuer or a share, participation, or other interest in an issuer or in property or an enterprise of an issuer." It also is not "a share or similar equity interest," an "investment company security," or "an interest in a partnership or limited liability company." See Section 8-103(a), (b), and (c). For a discussion of the roles that controllable electronic records may play in transactions involving uncertificated securities, see Section 8-102, Comment 18.

3. "Qualifying purchaser." The conditions for becoming a qualifying purchaser were drawn from Article 3. More specifically, the conditions for becoming a qualifying purchaser were drawn from Section 3-302(a)(2), which defines "holder in due course" of a negotiable instrument. Among these conditions is that a person take the instrument "for value."

See subsection (a)(4) (defining "value") and Comment 5. To meet the requirements for a qualifying purchaser under subsection (a)(2) there must be a time at which all of the requirements are satisfied. For example, if a purchaser obtains notice of a claim of a property right before giving value or satisfying the requirements for control, the purchaser cannot be a qualifying purchaser.

Under Section 12-104(a), not only a purchaser of a controllable electronic record but also a purchaser of a controllable account or controllable payment intangible may be a qualifying purchaser. Moreover, a purchaser of a controllable account or a controllable payment intangible may be a qualifying purchaser even if the purchaser does not also purchase the controllable electronic record that evidences the account or payment intangible. For example, a secured party having a security interest in all of a debtor's accounts and payment intangibles would be a purchaser of those rights to payment, which would include the debtor's controllable accounts and payment intangibles. If the secured party were to obtain control of the debtor's controllable account or payment intangible, it would become a qualifying purchaser if it also met the other conditions for that status. However, to obtain control of the controllable account or controllable payment intangible, a requirement for qualifying purchaser status, the purchaser must obtain control of the controllable electronic record evidencing the controllable account or controllable payment intangible. Section 12-104(b); see also Section 9-107A. A person need not be a purchaser, however, to obtain control of a controllable electronic record.

4. "Transferable record." This definition facilitates the exclusion of transferable records from the definition of controllable electronic record.

5. "Value." This definition adopts the concept of value in Section 3-303, which is narrower than the generally applicable concept in Section 1-204. Comment 10 to Section 12-104 explains the difference between the two concepts.

Section 12-103. Relation to Article 9 and Consumer Laws

(a) [Article 9 governs in case of conflict.] If there is conflict between this article and Article 9, Article 9 governs.

(b) [Applicable consumer law and other laws.] A transaction subject to this article is subject to any applicable rule of law that establishes a different rule for consumers and [insert reference to (i) any other statute or regulation that regulates the rates, charges, agreements, and practices for loans, credit sales, or other extensions of credit and (ii) any consumer-protection statute or regulation].

Official Comment

Source. Subsection (a) follows Section 3-102(b). Notwithstanding subsection (a), as is the case with respect to Article 3, Article 9 explicitly defers to Article 12 in some instances. See, e.g., Section 9-331. Subsection (b) is copied from Section 9-201(b). To the extent that Article 9 contains provisions described in subsection (b), subsections (a) and (b) are not mutually exclusive.

Section 12-104. Rights in Controllable Account, Controllable Electronic Record, and Controllable Payment Intangible

(a) [Applicability of section to controllable account and controllable payment intangible.] This section applies to the acquisition and purchase of rights in a controllable account or controllable payment intangible, including the rights and benefits under subsections (c), (d), (e), (g), and (h) of a purchaser and qualifying purchaser, in the same manner this section applies to a controllable electronic record.

(b) [Control of controllable account and controllable payment intangible.] To determine whether a purchaser of a controllable account or a controllable payment intangible is a qualifying purchaser, the purchaser obtains control of the account or payment intangible if it obtains control of the controllable electronic record that evidences the account or payment intangible.

(c) [Applicability of other law to acquisition of rights.] Except as provided in this section, law other than this article determines whether a person acquires a right in a controllable electronic record and the right the person acquires.

(d) [Shelter principle and purchase of limited interest.] A purchaser of a controllable electronic record acquires all rights in the controllable electronic record that the transferor had or had power to transfer, except that a purchaser of a limited interest in a controllable electronic record acquires rights only to the extent of the interest purchased.

(e) [Rights of qualifying purchaser.] A qualifying purchaser acquires its rights in the controllable electronic record free of a claim of a property right in the controllable electronic record.

(f) [Limitation of rights of qualifying purchaser in other property.] Except as provided in subsections (a) and (e) for a controllable account and a controllable payment intangible or law other than this article, a qualifying purchaser takes a right to payment, right to performance, or other interest in property evidenced by the controllable electronic record subject to a claim of a property right in the right to payment, right to performance, or other interest in property.

(g) [No-action protection for qualifying purchaser.] An action may not be asserted against a qualifying purchaser based on both a purchase by the qualifying purchaser of a controllable electronic record and a claim of a property right in another controllable electronic record, whether the action is framed in conversion, replevin, constructive trust, equitable lien, or other theory.

(h) [Filing not notice.] Filing of a financing statement under Article 9 is not notice of a claim of a property right in a controllable electronic record.

Official Comment

1. Source. Subsection (d) derives from Section 2-403(1) (concerning the rights of a purchaser).

Subsection (e) derives from Sections 3-306 (concerning the rights of a holder in due course of an instrument) and 8-303 (concerning rights of a protected purchaser of a security).

Subsection (g) derives from Section 8-502 (protecting entitlement holders).

Subsection (h) derives from Section 9-331(c) (filing under Article 9 does not provide notice for purposes of protections of purchasers under other articles).

2. Applicability of section to controllable accounts and controllable payment intangibles. Under subsection (a), the provisions of this section apply to controllable accounts and controllable payment intangibles in the same manner that they apply to controllable electronic records. For example, a qualifying purchaser of a controllable account that obtains control of the controllable electronic record that evidences the account (and who thereby obtains control of the account under subsection (b) and Section 9-107A) would take the account free of conflicting claims of a property right in the account under subsection (e). Under subsection (b), for purposes of determining whether a purchaser of a controllable account or controllable payment intangible obtains control, the purchaser obtains control by obtaining control of the controllable electronic record that evidences the account or payment intangible. Unless otherwise specified or the context otherwise requires, references to a controllable electronic record in the official comments in this Article also refer to a controllable account or controllable payment intangible.

3. Applicability of other law. As a general matter, subsection (c) leaves to other law the resolution of questions concerning the transfer of rights in a controllable electronic record, such as the acts that must be taken to effectuate a transfer of rights and the scope of the rights that a transferee acquires. Subsections (d) through (h) contain important exceptions to subsection (c).

> **Example 1:** A creates a controllable electronic record. Although the system in which the electronic record is recorded may determine how the electronic record can be used and control may be transferred, other law would determine what rights A has in the controllable electronic record. If, for example, A created the electronic record in the scope of its employment, A's rights would be subject to the terms of A's employment contract.

A and B agree to the sale of the controllable electronic record to B. Other law would determine what steps need to be taken for B to acquire rights in the controllable electronic record. Once B acquires those rights under other law, B would be a purchaser (as defined in Section 1-201), whose rights also would be determined by subsection (d) (i.e., the shelter principle, discussed below in Comment 4). However, even if B did not acquire rights under other law, if B met the requirements for a qualifying purchaser, its rights would be determined by subsections (e) and (g). See Comments 7 and 8, below.

The "law other than this article" that may apply to the transfer of rights in a controllable electronic record under subsection (c) includes UCC Article 9. Section 9-203 would apply, for example, to determine whether a purported secured party acquired an enforceable security interest in a controllable electronic record.

4. Purchaser and transferor under subsection (d): shelter principle and resulting controllable electronic records. Subsection (d) sets forth the familiar "shelter" principle, under which a purchaser of a controllable electronic record acquires whatever rights the transferor had or had power to transfer. However, in some cases the controllable electronic record that is acquired by the purchaser will not be the "same" controllable electronic record that was transferred by the transferor. Such a transfer might involve the elimination of a "transferred" controllable electronic record and the resulting and corresponding derivative creation and acquisition of a new controllable electronic record. An example of such a resulting controllable electronic record is the unspent transaction output (UTXO) generated by a transaction in bitcoin.

The Bitcoin protocol operates by allowing users to "spend" their UTXOs to create one or more new UTXOs for the same amount of bitcoin, so each transfer produces new UTXOs controlled by the transferees (one of which may be the transferor—spender—of the bitcoin). Subsection (d) should be construed broadly to encompass such transfers and resulting derivative controllable electronic records acquired by a purchaser. Because subsection (d) addresses the rights of a purchaser in the "purchased" asset and not the "transferred" asset, this construction is wholly consistent with the statutory text.

Notwithstanding the broad subsection (d) shelter principle, which provides that a purchaser acquires "all rights" of the transferor, those rights are subject to the reach of Section 1- 304. Under that section a contract or duty under the UCC imposes an overarching "obligation of good faith in its performance and enforcement." Section 1-304. In this context, "performance and enforcement" include the exercise of rights under the UCC, such as the rights conferred on a purchaser by the subsection (d) shelter principle. See Section 1-304, Comment 2. For example, consider a qualifying purchaser of a controllable electronic record, controllable account, or controllable payment intangible who then sells that asset to a person who is not a qualifying purchaser. If the second purchaser had previously engaged in fraudulent or illegal activity in connection with the purchased asset or an asset to which the purchased asset is attributable, the purchaser's exercise of rights under subsection (d) as to the purchased asset may be in breach of its obligation of good faith. Section 3-203(b) states this result directly with respect to a transferee of a negotiable instrument if the transferee previously engaged in fraud or illegality with respect to the same instrument. Section 3-203(b). The same result would apply under subsection (d).

Subsection (d) relies on the application of the general obligation of good faith under Section 1- 304 to reach the appropriate result. However, unlike negotiable instruments, many controllable electronic records are fungible. For this reason, in some cases it might not be possible to establish that an acquired controllable electronic record has a sufficient nexus with a transferee's earlier fraud or illegality.

5. Nonpurchaser having control. Under Section 12-105, a person may have control of a controllable electronic record even if the person has no property interest in the controllable electronic record. A person that has control of, but no property interest in, a controllable electronic record would not be a purchaser of the controllable electronic record and so would not be eligible to be a qualifying purchaser under this section.

> **Example 2:** Debtor granted to Secured Party a security interest in all Debtor's existing and after-acquired accounts, chattel paper, and payment intangibles. Secured Party perfected its security interest in a specific controllable account by obtaining control of the controllable electronic record that evidences the controllable account. See Section 9- 107A.

Because Debtor's security agreement does not cover controllable electronic records, Secured Party would have no interest in the controllable electronic record. Accordingly, Secured Party would not be a purchaser of the controllable electronic record. However, as a purchaser of the controllable accounts and controllable payment intangibles, Secured Party could benefit from the take-free rule in subsection (e) (discussed in Comment 7).

6. Distinction between controllable electronic record and controllable account or controllable payment intangible evidenced by the controllable electronic record. Even though a controllable electronic record evidences a controllable account or controllable payment intangible, the controllable electronic record is distinct from the account or payment intangible that it evidences. The account or payment intangible is connected with (or "tethered" to) the electronic record by virtue of the relevant account debtor's obligation to pay the person in control of the controllable electronic record. Moreover, control of the controllable account or payment intangible is achieved only by obtaining control of the controllable electronic record that evidences the account or payment intangible. Example 2 explains that a purchaser may obtain a property interest in the controllable account or controllable payment intangible even if it does not acquire any interest in the controllable electronic record that evidences the account or payment intangible. (On the other hand, merely obtaining control of a controllable electronic record does not result in the acquisition of an interest in the record.) This approach is intended to avoid a trap for the unwary purchaser that obtains an interest in the account or payment intangible (which is the asset that has stand-alone value) but might fail to acquire an interest in the related controllable electronic record. However, good practice may encourage a purchaser to acquire an interest in the controllable electronic record as well, which would eliminate any potential confusion.

7. The take-free rule. Subsection (e) makes controllable electronic records and, under subsection (a), controllable accounts and controllable payment intangibles, highly negotiable. Subsection (e) derives from Section 3-306, under which a holder in due course takes a negotiable instrument free of a claim of a property right in the instrument. A qualifying purchaser of a controllable electronic record, controllable account, or controllable payment intangible takes free of all claims of a property right in the purchased controllable electronic record, account, or payment intangible.

> **Example 3:** Hacker, a thief, "steals" and obtains control of a controllable electronic record. Hacker then sells the controllable electronic record to Buyer, who obtains control and otherwise meets the requirements for a qualifying purchaser (by obtaining control and purchasing for value, in good faith, and without notice of a claim of a property right).

As a general matter, law other than Article 12 would determine whether any particular transaction creates a property interest in a controllable electronic record. Section 12- 104(c). However, even if under other applicable law Hacker has no rights in, and no right to transfer, the "stolen" controllable electronic record, subsection (e) enables Buyer, a qualifying purchaser, to take the controllable electronic record (or any purchased controllable account or controllable payment intangible evidenced by the controllable electronic record) free of claims of a property right—including that of the rightful owner.

As Example 3 illustrates, a person in control of a controllable electronic record, such as Hacker, has the power, even if not the right, to transfer rights in the record to a qualifying purchaser. Of course, if the qualifying purchaser is a secured party whose security interest secures an obligation, the purchaser would take free of the conflicting property right only to the extent of the obligation secured. See Section 12-104(d) (purchaser of a limited interest); cf. Section 3- 302(e). Moreover, even if a secured party were not a qualifying purchaser of a controllable electronic record, controllable account, or controllable payment intangible, its security interest in the collateral over which it obtained control would, however, have priority over a conflicting security interest that was perfected by a method other than control. Section 9-326A.

8. Subsection (g)—the "no-action" rule. Subsection (g) applies in the situation (explained in Comment 4) in which the "resulting" controllable electronic record (or controllable account or controllable payment intangible) purchased by a qualifying purchaser is not the "same" record, account, or payment intangible that was transferred. In such a situation, a person claiming a property right in the transferred asset may assert a claim against a purchaser of the "resulting" asset even though the claimant is not asserting a claim of a property right in the purchased asset. If the claim is based on both the purchaser's purchase of the acquired asset and the claimant's claim of a property right in the transferred asset, subsection (g) protects the qualifying purchaser from liability to the claimant based on any theory. The qualifying purchaser's protection from the assertion of such a claim does not depend on any proof that the purchased asset is somehow "traceable" to the transferred asset.

If instead, such a claimant were to assert a claim based on a property right in the purchased asset, then the qualifying purchaser would take free of that claim under subsection (e). Subsection (e) applies whether or not the acquired asset is the same asset that was transferred.

9. "Tethered" assets. Certain controllable electronic records may carry with them rights to other assets, for example, goods or rights to payment. By its terms, the take-free rule in subsection (e) applies to controllable electronic records (and, under subsection (a), controllable accounts and controllable payment intangibles evidenced by a controllable electronic record). One might argue that the inclusion of controllable accounts and controllable payment intangibles in the scope of subsection (e) is unnecessary. By taking a controllable electronic record free of property claims, the argument would be that a person takes not only the controllable electronic record itself but also all rights that are "carried" in the controllable electronic record free and clear.

Subsection (f) defeats that argument. It limits the application of the take-free rule in subsection (e) to controllable electronic records and, through the application of subsection (a), controllable accounts and controllable payment intangibles evidenced by a controllable electronic record. Under subsection (f), except as provided in subsections (a) and (e), a qualifying purchaser takes rights to payment (other than controllable accounts and controllable payment intangibles), rights to performance, and interests in property that are evidenced by a controllable electronic record subject to third-party property claims, unless law other than Article 12 provides to the contrary. The reference in subsection (f) to "law other than this article" contemplates that another article of the UCC might provide a contrary rule for some types of property that might be tethered to a controllable electronic record.

The treatment of controllable accounts and controllable payment intangibles in Articles 9 and 12 is feasible because Article 9 already provides the legal framework for assignments of accounts and payment intangibles. In addition, because accounts and payment intangibles are rights to payment of monetary obligations, tethering of an account or payment intangible to a controllable electronic record is straightforward. The account debtor is obligated to pay the person that has control of the relevant controllable electronic record (subject to the qualifications imposed by Section 12-106).

10. Creating the functional equivalent of a negotiable instrument. Two defining characteristics of an Article 3 negotiable instrument are that a holder in due course (i) takes free of claims of a property or possessory right to the instrument (Section 3-306) and (ii) takes free of most defenses and claims in recoupment (Section 3-305). Article 3 applies only to written instruments. Article 12 and the revisions to Article 9 provide a method for reaching a similar result with respect to controllable accounts and controllable payment intangibles.

As regards the first characteristic, a qualifying purchaser could acquire the controllable account or controllable payment intangible free of any claim of a property interest. As regards the second characteristic, the definition of "qualifying purchaser" omits some of the conditions for becoming a holder in due course. For example, to qualify as a holder in due course, a holder must take "without notice that any party has a defense or claim in recoupment " Section 3-302(a)(2)(vi). A controllable electronic record is information; there are no parties to a controllable electronic record. However, there are parties to a controllable account or controllable payment intangible. Accordingly, Sections 9-404 and 9-403 would determine whether a purchaser of the controllable account or controllable payment intangible takes free of a defense. Section 9-403 ordinarily would give effect to the account debtor's agreement not to assert claims or defenses.

Section 9-403 adopts the meaning of value in Section 3-303, as does Article 12. The concept of value in Section 3-303 is narrower than the concept in Section 1-204, which applies generally to UCC transactions. Under Section 1-204, a person gives value for rights if the person acquires them in return for a promise. However, under Section 3-303, if a negotiable instrument is issued or transferred for a promise of performance, the instrument is transferred for value only to the extent that the promise has been performed.

Section 12-105. Control of Controllable Electronic Record

(a) [General rule: control of controllable electronic record.] A person has control of a controllable electronic record if the electronic record, a record attached to or logically associated with the electronic record, or a system in which the electronic record is recorded:

(1) gives the person:

(A) power to avail itself of substantially all the benefit from the electronic record; and

(B) exclusive power, subject to subsection (b), to:

(i) prevent others from availing themselves of substantially all the benefit from the electronic record; and

(ii) transfer control of the electronic record to another person or cause another person to obtain control of another controllable electronic record as a result of the transfer of the electronic record; and

(2) enables the person readily to identify itself in any way, including by name, identifying number, cryptographic key, office, or account number, as having the powers specified in paragraph (1).

(b) [Meaning of exclusive.] Subject to subsection (c), a power is exclusive under subsection (a)(1)(B)(i) and (ii) even if:

(1) the controllable electronic record, a record attached to or logically associated with the electronic record, or a system in which the electronic record is recorded limits the use of the electronic record or has a protocol programmed to cause a change, including a transfer or loss of control or a modification of benefits afforded by the electronic record; or

(2) the power is shared with another person.

(c) [When power not shared with another person.] A power of a person is not shared with another person under subsection (b)(2) and the person's power is not exclusive if:

(1) the person can exercise the power only if the power also is exercised by the other person; and

(2) the other person:

(A) can exercise the power without exercise of the power by the person; or

(B) is the transferor to the person of an interest in the controllable electronic record or a controllable account or controllable payment intangible evidenced by the controllable electronic record.

(d) [Presumption of exclusivity of certain powers.] If a person has the powers specified in subsection (a)(1)(B)(i) and (ii), the powers are presumed to be exclusive.

(e) [Control through another person.] A person has control of a controllable electronic record if another person, other than the transferor to the person of an interest in the controllable electronic record or a controllable account or controllable payment intangible evidenced by the controllable electronic record:

(1) has control of the electronic record and acknowledges that it has control on behalf of the person; or

(2) obtains control of the electronic record after having acknowledged that it will obtain control of the electronic record on behalf of the person.

(f) [No requirement to acknowledge.] A person that has control under this section is not required to acknowledge that it has control on behalf of another person.

(g) [No duties or confirmation.] If a person acknowledges that it has or will obtain control on behalf of another person, unless the person otherwise agrees or law other than this article or Article 9 otherwise provides, the person does not owe any duty to the other person and is not required to confirm the acknowledgment to any other person.

Official Comment

1. Why "control" matters. Control serves two major functions in Article 12. An electronic record is a "controllable electronic record" and is subject to the provisions of this Article only if it can be subjected to control under this section. See Section 12-102(a)(1) (defining "controllable electronic record"). And only a person having control of a controllable electronic record is eligible to become a qualifying purchaser and so to take free of claims of a property interest in the controllable electronic record, or any controllable account or controllable payment intangible evidenced by the controllable electronic record, and to be protected by the "no-action" rule. See Section 12-104(e) and (g).

Article 9 provides that obtaining control of a controllable electronic record is one method by which to perfect a security interest in the controllable electronic record or in any controllable account or controllable payment intangible evidenced by the controllable electronic record. See Sections 9-107A; 9-314. Moreover, a security interest perfected by control has priority over a conflicting security interest that was perfected by a method other than control and "control ... pursuant to the debtor's agreement" may substitute for an authenticated a signed security agreement as an element of attachment. See Sections 9-326A; 9-203(b)(3)(D).

2. Powers and sources of powers; inability to exercise a power. This section conditions control on a person's having the three powers specified in subsection (a)(1). A person would have the powers described in that subsection if the controllable electronic record, a record attached to or logically associated with the controllable electronic record, or any system in which it is recorded gives the person those powers. This description of the source of the relevant powers should be construed broadly and functionally. For example, a person would have a power even if the characteristics of the particular purchaser disable the person from exercising the power. This would be the case, for example, when the purchaser holds the private key required to access the benefit of the controllable electronic record but lacks the hardware required to use it. In addition, a system in which the person in control is identified is a permissible source of a power even if it is related to but not precisely the "same" system in which the controllable electronic record is recorded. Moreover, this broad and functional construction is particularly important for references to "a record attached to or logically associated with the electronic record, or a system in which the electronic record is recorded," as used in Section 12-105(a) and (b) (and elsewhere). For example, overly literal or technical interpretations of the terminology "attached to" or "logically associated" are inappropriate. The statutory language must be adapted and applied in a functional manner to technology, systems, and infrastructure that may be developed and employed in the future. The goal is to embrace records and systems that are connected to a particular electronic record in such a manner that the information contained in or the functions performed by those "attached" or "associated" records are appropriately and reasonably attributable to and identifiable as connected with the electronic record itself. See also, e.g., Sections 7-106, 9-105, 9-105A, 9-306A, 9-605, 9-628, and 12-107.

3. "Benefit." Subsection (a)(1)(A) and (a)(1)(B)(i) condition control of a controllable electronic record on a person's relationship to the benefit of the controllable electronic record.

As used in this section, the "benefit" of a controllable electronic record refers to the rights that are afforded by the controllable electronic record and the uses to which the controllable electronic record can be put. These, in turn, depend on the characteristics of the controllable electronic record in question. For example, the benefit afforded by control of a bitcoin is that it can be held or disposed of (sold or spent). And control of a controllable electronic record evidencing a controllable account or controllable payment intangible affords the benefit of the right to collect from the account debtor (obligor).

The system in which a controllable electronic record is recorded may limit the benefit from the controllable electronic record that is available to those who interact with the system. In determining whether a person has the power to avail itself of substantially all the benefit from a controllable electronic record under subsection (a)(1)(A), or to prevent others from availing themselves of substantially all the benefit from a controllable electronic record under subsection (a)(1)(B)(i), only the benefit that the system makes available (subject to the system's inherent limitations) should be considered.

4. Power to retrieve information. By definition, the information constituting an electronic record must be "retrievable in perceivable form." Section 1-201(b)(31) (defining "record"). The power to retrieve the record in perceivable form is included in the benefit of a controllable electronic record. "Perceivable form" means that the contents of the record are intelligible; the ability to perceive the indecipherable jumble of an encrypted record does not give a person the power to retrieve the record in perceivable form.

To have control of a controllable electronic record under subsection (a)(1)(A), a person must have at least the nonexclusive power to avail itself of this benefit. If a person also has the exclusive power to decrypt the encrypted record, the person will have the exclusive power to prevent others from availing themselves of substantially all the benefit from the controllable electronic record and thereby will satisfy the condition in subsection (a)(1)(B)(i).

5. Exclusive powers. Unlike the power in subsection (a)(1)(A), the powers in subsection (a)(1)(B)(i) and (a)(1)(B)(ii) must be held exclusively by the person claiming control in order to establish control. However, once it is established that a person has received those powers, subsection (d) provides a presumption of exclusivity. Consequently, a person asserting control need not prove exclusivity in order to make out a prima facie case. Application of the presumption will be governed also by Section 1-206 (effects of a presumption under the UCC) and applicable non-UCC law (including rules of procedure and evidence). In addition, subsection (b) contains two qualifications of the term "exclusive" as used in subsection (a)(1)(B). A power can be "exclusive" under subsection (a)(1)(B) even if one or both of these qualifications apply.

Subsection (b)(1) takes account of the fact that the powers of a purchaser of a controllable electronic record necessarily are subject to the attributes of the controllable electronic record, records associated with the controllable electronic record, and the protocols of any system in which the controllable electronic record is recorded. For example, a transfer of control resulting from a program that is a part of a system's protocol is inherent in the controllable electronic record and does not impair the exclusivity of the power of the person in control of the record. Subsection (b)(1) also contemplates that the potential for the system to otherwise modify (or even destroy) controllable electronic records would not impair the exclusivity.

> **Example 1:** Pursuant to the governance apparatus of a system (Propofolium) for a cryptocurrency (propofol), an upgrade to the system was made that modified the consensus mechanism for determining the effectiveness of transfers of propofols within the system. Although this change did not divest any holder of propofols of its control, it prospectively modified the system for all propofols. The adoption of this change and the potential for such a change (or any other change) are functions of the attributes of the system and, consequently, of all propofols. Neither this change nor such potential impaired the exclusivity, for purposes of subsection (a)(1)(B), of the powers of a person in control of propofols.

Subsection (b)(2) allows for a power to be shared with another person without impairing the exclusivity of the power. One effect of subsection (b)(2) is that, under a multi-signature (multi-sig) agreement, any person that is readily identifiable under subsection (a)(2) and shares the relevant power would be eligible to have control, even if the action of another person is a condition for the exercise of the power. For example, a person in control may agree that another person's action on the relevant system would be required to effect a transfer of control without impairing the requisite exclusivity.

> **Example 2:** Pursuant to a multi-sig arrangement, control of propofols (in the system described in Example 1) is shared by Campbell, Elizabeth, Mia, and Natasha. Under the multi-sig arrangement, the exercise of powers over the propofols requires action by three of the four persons having control. None of the participants acting alone has the power to exercise the relevant powers. Subsection (b)(2) makes clear that all four participants have control over the propofols and exclusivity is not impaired by the shared control under the multi-sig arrangement.

Although all four persons in Example 2 have control, that may leave many questions as to the rights of the four as among themselves. For example, if more than one of the four were secured parties, it would be important for them to settle by agreement issues such as relative priorities and enforcement rights. Similar situations can arise in other contexts and with respect to other types of collateral.

A multi-sig arrangement for a controllable electronic record, such as that described in Example 2, may provide enhanced security. For example, if the power of one participant is compromised by a "hacker," the required actions by the other participants would prevent the hacker from exercising unauthorized power over the record. Although the hacker might possess the power along with the remaining multi-sig participants, those participants would continue to have control. A multi-sig structure also may protect against the misuse of a record by ensuring that actions by multiple persons are required for exercising power over the record.

Subsection (c) provides that in certain circumstances a power is not shared within the meaning of subsection (b)(2), the relaxation of the exclusivity requirement provided by subsection (b)(2) does not apply, and, consequently, a person's power is not exclusive.

Subsection (c) provides that a person does not share an exclusive power with another person if the person can exercise the power only with the other person's cooperation (subsection (c)(1)) but the other person either (i) can exercise the power without the person's cooperation (subsection (c)(2)(A)) or (ii) is the transferor to the person (transferee) of an interest in the controllable electronic record or a controllable account or controllable payment intangible evidenced by the controllable electronic record (subsection (c)(2)(B)). It follows that a person to which subsection (c) applies does not have control based on its exclusive powers (although it might have control through another person under subsection (e), discussed below, or if another person having control is acting as the person's agent).

Comment 9 addresses the rationale for disqualifying the transferee from a transferor under subsection (c)(2)(B) from the benefit of sharing a power under subsection (b)(2).

The following examples illustrate the application of subsection (c):

Example 3: Under a multi-sig arrangement, exercise by any two of Campbell, Elizabeth, and Mia is required to exercise a power with respect to a controllable electronic record (CER). None of the three can exercise a power without the cooperation of another, so all three have control because they share the power. Even if Campbell were the transferor of the CER to Elizabeth, Elizabeth's power is shared, and therefore treated as exclusive, because Campbell cannot block Elizabeth's exercise of the power if Mia acts with Elizabeth. It follows that subsection (c)(1) does not apply, subsection (b)(2) does apply, and Elizabeth shares the power with Campbell. (The same result would apply with respect to Mia's power if Campbell were the transferor of the CER to Mia.)

Example 4: Under a multi-sig arrangement, exercise by both Campbell and Elizabeth are required to exercise a power, so subsection (c)(1) applies with respect to each person. However, neither Campbell nor Elizabeth can exercise the power without cooperation of the other and neither is the transferor to the other, so subsection (c)(2)(A) and (2)(B) does not apply with respect to either person. It follows that Campbell and Elizabeth each share the power.

Example 5: The facts are the same as in Example 4, but Campbell is the transferor of an interest in the CER to Elizabeth. Elizabeth does not share the power with Campbell and Elizabeth's power is not exclusive because subsection (c)(1) and (2)(B) applies.

Example 6: Under a multi-sig arrangement, Mia or Natasha can exercise a power only with the exercise by Campbell, but Campbell can exercise the power unilaterally without the exercise by either Mia or Natasha. Neither Mia nor Natasha shares the power with Campbell because subsection (c)(1) and (2)(A) apply, so neither Mia's nor Natasha's power is treated as exclusive. Campbell's power is exclusive in fact and Campbell need not rely on subsection (b)(2) for shared power.

Example 7: Under a multi-sig arrangement, Mia can exercise a power only with exercise by Elizabeth or Natasha, but Elizabeth and Natasha each can exercise the power unilaterally without the exercise by the other or by Mia. Elizabeth and Natasha share the power, but Mia does not share the power with Elizabeth or Natasha. Mia's power is not exclusive because subsection (c)(1) and (2)(A) applies.

Although the presumption in subsection (d) is not expressly made subject to subsection (c), it is functionally so. Under Section 1-206, once evidence is introduced that subsection (c) applies and that, accordingly, a person relying on the presumption cannot rely on the relaxation of the exclusivity requirement provided by subsection (b)(2), the presumption would no longer apply.

6. Transfer of control. The power to transfer control of a controllable electronic record under subsection (a)(1)(B)(ii) includes the power to cause another person to obtain control of another derivative and resulting controllable electronic record that results from the transfer of the controllable electronic record. See Section 12-104, Comment 4.

7. Readily identify itself. Subsection (a)(2) provides that a person does not have control of a controllable electronic record unless the controllable electronic record, a record attached to or logically associated with the controllable electronic record, or any system in which the controllable electronic record is recorded enables the person readily to identify itself as the person having the requisite powers. The identification need not be by a "name," but also may be by "identifying number, cryptographic key, office, or account number"—language derived from Section 3-110(c). The reference to "office" means a public office. See Section 3-110, Comment 3. This subsection does not obligate a person to identify itself as having control. However, to prove that it has control, a person would need to prove that the relevant records or any system in which the controllable electronic record is recorded readily identifies the person as such.

Consistent with the subsection (d) presumption of exclusivity, proof that a person has the powers specified in section (a)(1) does not require proof of exclusivity—i.e., proof of a negative (that no one else has such powers). The means of identification mentioned in subsection (a)(2) derive from Section 3-110(c). Subsection (a)(2) adds "cryptographic key" as an example of a way in which a person may be identified.

8. Control through another person. Neither Article 12 nor any other provision of the UCC would restrict or render ineffective any agreement of a person in control of a controllable electronic record to hold control on behalf of another person. This result is implicit from subsection (b)(2) dealing with sharing of control. It also would follow under principles of agency. But such an arrangement should be effective regardless of any agency or fiduciary relationship.

This concept is expressly addressed in Section 8-106(d)(3), on control of a security entitlement, which achieves perfection of a security interest under Sections 9-106(a) and 9- 314(a). It also applies to perfection by possession under Section 9-313(c) if a person other than the debtor or the secured party (or the secured party's agent) is in possession of collateral. Under those provisions, however, effectiveness is conditioned in some circumstances on an "acknowledgment" by the person in control or possession. Under Section 9-313(c) the acknowledgment must be in a signed record. These provisions appear to derive from practices involving bailees of tangible property, such as goods, chattel paper, and certificated securities. See Section 9-313, Comment 4.

Subsection (e) likewise provides for control by a person through another person's acknowledgment that it has control on behalf of the person. Subsection (e) is patterned on Section 9-313(c), but like Section 8-106(d)(3), subsection (e) omits the requirement in Section 9- 313(c) that an acknowledgment be made in a signed record. Although best practices might suggest the wisdom of relying on a signed record to evidence such an acknowledgment, subsection (e) would permit proof by other means. Under subsection (e) for an acknowledgment by another person to be effective to confer control on a person, the other person making the acknowledgment must be one "other than the transferor of an interest in the electronic record" to the person. The rationale for this limitation is discussed in Comment 9. Control based on an acknowledgment under subsection (e) by another person having control continues only while the other person retains control. This result necessarily follows because such control derives solely from the other person's continued control.

The combined operation of subsections (b)(2) and (e) ensure that the continuance of various existing practices would not prevent or cause the loss of control. For example, a person in control may wish to grant another person the power to approve or disapprove a transfer of control on the system. Alternatively, a person in control may wish to permit a system administrator, the system itself, or a prearranged operation to transfer control to another person under specified conditions without participation by the person in control. And, of course, a person in control may wish to delegate the power to transfer control to an agent or fiduciary.

Provisions substantially similar to subsection (e) are included in Section 7-106 (control of electronic documents of title), Section 8-106(d)(3) (control of security entitlement), 9-104 (control of deposit accounts), 9-105 (control of authoritative electronic copies of records evidencing chattel paper), and 9-105A (control of electronic money).

9. Shared powers under subsection (b)(2) and control through another person under subsection (e). Limitations related to transferors and transferees of interests in controllable electronic records. Subsection (c)(2)(B) disqualifies a transferee (which includes a secured party in a secured transaction) of an interest in a controllable electronic record (or controllable account or controllable payment intangible) from the benefit of a shared power under subsection (b)(2) when the transferor retains a blocking power (i.e., when the transferee cannot exercise the power unless the transferor also exercises the power). In similar fashion, under subsection (e), an acknowledgment by a transferor of an interest in a controllable electronic record (or controllable account or controllable payment intangible) that the transferor has control for the benefit of a person is ineffective to confer control on the person. Each of these limitations is premised on the view that the transferor has not been divested sufficiently of its powers over the relevant controllable electronic record so as to warrant treating the transferee as a secured party having a security interest perfected by control or as having the requisite control to be a qualifying purchaser.

Subsection (c)(1) and (c)(2)(B) contemplates that the transferor has retained a blocking power over the transferee's exercise of a power. Subsection (e) contemplates that the transferor remains in control and has merely acknowledged that its control is for the transferee's benefit and that the acknowledgment is ineffective to confer control on the transferee. Although the concept of shared control is newly introduced in the UCC, holding possession or control for another is not. Section 9-313(c) expressly provides in this context that an acknowledging person having possession of goods must be a person "other than the debtor" for a secured party to take possession through the acknowledging person. The official comments to Section 8-106 are to the same effect in the context of control of a security entitlement. See Section 8-106(d)(3), Comment 4A and pre-2022 Comment 4. The same policy that underpins the inapplicability of this method of control to an acknowledgment by a debtor applies as well to a transferor that is not an Article 9 debtor. Control is intended to be a proxy for and a functional equivalent of the transfer of physical possession of goods. In general, a person can obtain control through control by an agent, but under subsection (e) an acknowledgment by a debtor or transferor (even "as agent") that acknowledges control on behalf of a secured party or other transferee would be ineffective. This corresponds to the policy underlying Section 9-313 that "the debtor cannot qualify as an agent for the secured party for purposes of the secured party's taking possession." Section 9-313, Comment 3.

Notwithstanding these limitations, they would not impair the continued perfection by control upon a secured party's assignment of a perfected-by-control security interest in a controllable electronic record to a successor secured party. The following example illustrates.

> **Example 8:** Debtor (D) buys a CER and obtains control. D then grants a security interest in the CER to Secured Party A (SPA) to secure D's obligation to SPA and transfers to SPA control of the CER (not pursuant to shared control with D or pursuant to subsection (e)). SPA then assigns to Secured Party B (SPB) the secured obligation owed by D to SPA.

As to perfection of the security interest granted by D, perfection by control is not affected even if SPA retains powers over the CER (as between SPA and SPB) following the assignment to SPB. The security interest remains perfected. This is consistent with the policy underlying 9-310(c)—an assignment of a security interest should not require the assignee to refile or take an assignment of record of a filed financing statement in favor of the assignor for protection against a debtor's creditors and transferees.

The economic interest being assigned by SPA to SPB in Example 8 is primarily the right to payment or performance of the obligation of D that is secured by the CER. If the transfer of the secured obligation by SPA to SPB itself creates a security interest securing an obligation (e.g., owed by SPA to SPB), then SPB should perfect the security interest granted by SPA (which is distinct from the security interest in the CER granted by D and assigned by SPA to SPB). The method of perfection will depend on the nature of the secured obligation—the type of collateral—being assigned. Is the right to payment an instrument, an account, or a payment intangible? Or is performance of the secured obligation pursuant to another type of general intangible? SPB should file a financing statement against SPA, as debtor, or take possession of the instrument, if applicable. However, as to the underlying collateral securing the assigned obligation—the CER—attachment and perfection of SPB's security interest in the obligation of D owed to SPA would also constitute attachment and perfection as to the security interest in the CER securing that obligation. Sections 9-203(g); 9-308(e); see also 1 Restatement (Second) of Contracts § 340, Comment b ("b. Security follows the debt. Where a secured claim is assigned, the collateral is ordinarily assigned as well.").

If the transfer by SPA to SPB is an outright transfer (a sale) of an account, a payment intangible, or a promissory note, the transfer creates a security interest and the analysis in the preceding paragraph applies (except that the security interest arising from the sale of a payment intangible or promissory note is automatically perfected under Section 9-309(a)(3) and (4)). If the transfer is a sale of another type of general intangible or instrument that is secured by the CER, then non-Article 9 law applies to the transfer. However, the same result may occur under the common-law rule that the collateral (the CER) follows a secured obligation that is transferred. See Sections 9-203, Comment 9; 9-308, Comment 6.

For obvious business reasons, SPB may not wish to allow SPA to remain in control of the CER and may require SPA to transfer control to it as a condition to the transaction. Alternatively, SPB may obtain control through sharing powers with SPA or through SPA's acknowledgment pursuant to subsection (e). It is true that SPA's assignment to SPB of D's secured obligation carried with it the collateral—the CER—securing the obligation. But such a derivative acquisition (through the operation of Sections 9-203(g) and 9-308(e)) by SPB would not be a transfer by SPA of "an interest in" the CER within the meaning of the limitations imposed in subsections (c)(2)(B) or (e). The operation of these rules, providing that collateral follows the transfer of a secured obligation, are based on the premise that any necessary public notice provided in connection with the assignment of the obligation provides, in turn, sufficient public notice with respect to the underlying collateral. It follows that the policy to be implemented by subsections (c)(2)(B) and (e) is not implicated by such an assignment.

10. No requirement to acknowledge, no duties, and no requirement to confirm acknowledgment. Subsections (f) and (g) derive from Section 9-313(f) and (g). Subsection (f) makes clear that a person that has control under this section has no duty to acknowledge that it has or will obtain control on behalf of another person. Arrangements for a person to acknowledge that it has or will obtain control on behalf of another person are not standardized. Accordingly, subsection (g) leaves to the agreement of the parties and to any other applicable law (other than this Article or Article 9) any duties of a person that does acknowledge that it has or will obtain control on behalf of another person and provides that a person making an acknowledgment is not required to confirm the acknowledgment to another person.

For example, subsection (e) would apply to give control to a person, Alpha, when another person, Beta, has control of a controllable electronic record and acknowledges that it has control on behalf of Alpha. However, under subsection (f), Beta is not required to so acknowledge. And under subsection (g), even if Beta does so acknowledge, Beta owes no duty to Alpha unless Beta agrees or other law so provides, and Beta is not required to confirm its acknowledgment to any other person.

Section 12-106. Discharge of Account Debtor on Controllable Account or Controllable Payment Intangible

(a) [Discharge of account debtor.] An account debtor on a controllable account or controllable payment intangible may discharge its obligation by paying:

(1) the person having control of the controllable electronic record that evidences the controllable account or controllable payment intangible; or

(2) except as provided in subsection (b), a person that formerly had control of the controllable electronic record.

(b) [Content and effect of notification.] Subject to subsection (d), the account debtor may not discharge its obligation by paying a person that formerly had control of the controllable electronic record if the account debtor receives a notification that:

(1) is signed by a person that formerly had control or the person to which control was transferred;

(2) reasonably identifies the controllable account or controllable payment intangible;

(3) notifies the account debtor that control of the controllable electronic record that evidences the controllable account or controllable payment intangible was transferred;

(4) identifies the transferee, in any reasonable way, including by name, identifying number, cryptographic key, office, or account number; and

(5) provides a commercially reasonable method by which the account debtor is to pay the transferee.

(c) [Discharge following effective notification.] After receipt of a notification that complies with subsection (b), the account debtor may discharge its obligation by paying in accordance with the notification and may not discharge the obligation by paying a person that formerly had control.

(d) [When notification ineffective.] Subject to subsection (h), notification is ineffective under subsection (b):

(1) unless, before the notification is sent, the account debtor and the person that, at that time, had control of the controllable electronic record that evidences the controllable account or controllable payment intangible agree in a signed record to a commercially reasonable method by which a person may furnish reasonable proof that control has been transferred;

(2) to the extent an agreement between the account debtor and seller of a payment intangible limits the account debtor's duty to pay a person other than the seller and the limitation is effective under law other than this article; or

(3) at the option of the account debtor, if the notification notifies the account debtor to:

(A) divide a payment;

(B) make less than the full amount of an installment or other periodic payment; or

(C) pay any part of a payment by more than one method or to more than one person.

(e) [Proof of transfer of control.] Subject to subsection (h), if requested by the account debtor, the person giving the notification under subsection (b) seasonably shall furnish reasonable proof, using the method in the agreement referred to in subsection (d)(1), that control of the controllable electronic record has been transferred. Unless the person complies with the request, the account debtor may discharge its obligation by paying a person that formerly had control, even if the account debtor has received a notification under subsection (b).

(f) [What constitutes reasonable proof.] A person furnishes reasonable proof under subsection (e) that control has been transferred if the person demonstrates, using the method in the agreement referred to in subsection (d)(1), that the transferee has the power to:

(1) avail itself of substantially all the benefit from the controllable electronic record;

(2) prevent others from availing themselves of substantially all the benefit from the controllable electronic record; and

(3) transfer the powers specified in paragraphs (1) and (2) to another person.

(g) [Rights not waivable.] Subject to subsection (h), an account debtor may not waive or vary its rights under subsections (d)(1) and (e) or its option under subsection (d)(3).

(h) [Rule for individual under other law.] This section is subject to law other than this article which establishes a different rule for an account debtor who is an individual and who incurred the obligation primarily for personal, family, or household purposes.

Official Comment

1. Source. These provisions derive from Section 3-602, which governs the discharge of a person obligated on a negotiable instrument, and Section 9-406(a), (b) and (c), which governs the discharge of an account debtor, including a person obligated on an account or payment intangible.

2. The basic rules. This section applies only to an account debtor that has undertaken to pay the person that has control of the controllable electronic record that evidences the obligation to pay. See Section 9-102 (defining "controllable account" and "controllable payment intangible"). Section 9-406 would continue to apply in other respects and to all other account debtors. As to the relationship between this section and Section 9-406, see Comment 5.

Under subsection (a)(1), an account debtor may discharge its obligation on the controllable account or controllable payment intangible by paying the person that has control of the related controllable electronic record at the time of payment. Subsections (a)(2) and (b) would remove from an account debtor the burden of determining who has control of the related controllable electronic record at any given time—a burden that, with respect to some controllable electronic records, an account debtor may be unable to satisfy. Under subsection (a)(2), subject to subsection (b), an account debtor may discharge its obligation by paying a person that formerly had control of the related controllable electronic record, which presumably would include the initial obligee.

Subsection (b) reflects the fact that a person to which control has been transferred may not wish to take the risk that the account debtor will discharge its obligation by paying the transferor. Subsection (b) protects the transferee by providing that, if the account debtor receives an effective notification that control has been transferred, the account debtor may discharge its obligation by paying in accordance with the notification and may not discharge its obligation by paying a person that formerly had control. The notification must be signed by a person formerly having control or by the transferee.

To be effective under subsection (b), a notification must reasonably identify the controllable account or controllable payment intangible, notify the account debtor that control of the controllable electronic record that evidences the controllable account or controllable payment intangible was transferred, identify the transferee in any reasonable way, and provide a commercially reasonable method by which the account debtor is to make payments to the transferee. A change in the identity of the person to which the account debtor must make payment should not, and typically will not, impose a significant burden on the account debtor.

However, one can imagine a method of making payment that would be burdensome, for example, making a payment through a trading platform or payment service with which the account debtor does not have an account. For this reason, the designated method of making payment must be "commercially reasonable."

3. "Reasonable proof." As noted above, this section derives in large part from Section 9-406, which provides for notification that an account or payment intangible has been assigned. Experience suggests that account debtors that have received notification of an assignment under Section 9-406 typically make payments in accordance with the notice. Recognizing that an account debtor may be uncertain whether a notification is legitimate, Section 9-406 affords to an account debtor the right to request proof that the account or payment intangible was assigned. See generally, Section 9-406, Comment 4.

Subsection (e) contains a similar provision. On the account debtor's request, the person giving the notification must seasonably furnish reasonable proof that control of the controllable electronic record has been transferred. If the person does not comply with the request, the account debtor may ignore the notification and discharge its obligation by paying a person formerly in control.

"Reasonable proof" requires evidence that would be understood by a typical account debtor to whom it is proffered as demonstrating to a reasonably high probability that control of the controllable electronic record has been transferred to the transferee. Subsection (f) provides a safe harbor for providing reasonable proof. It enables a person to satisfy the account debtor's request by demonstrating that the transferee has the power to avail itself of substantially all the benefit from the controllable electronic record, to prevent others from availing themselves of substantially all the benefit from the controllable electronic record, and to transfer these powers to another person. This demonstration would not necessarily prove that a person actually has control of a controllable electronic record because it need not show that the transferee held the last two powers exclusively. Nevertheless, such a demonstration would constitute "reasonable proof" under subsection (f). A person that has control should have little difficulty providing this proof, as a person cannot have control unless it can readily identify itself as having the requisite powers. See Section 12-105(a)(2). Reasonable proof that is seasonably furnished by a person other than the person that gave the notification would constitute compliance with the account debtor's request.

Subsection (e) requires that reasonable proof be provided "using the agreed method." Subsection (f) requires that a person use "the agreed method" to demonstrate that the transferee has the specified powers. "Agreed method" refers to the commercially reasonable method to which the parties agreed, in a signed record, before the notification was sent. If parties did not so agree, the notification is ineffective under subsection (d)(1).

An account debtor may agree to participate in a system providing for the control of controllable accounts or controllable payment intangibles. If the system is programmed to provide for notification to the account debtor upon the transfer of control, the account debtor's agreement and the operation of the system may satisfy the requirements of subsections (d)(1), (e), and (f).

4. Additional considerations for account debtors. The requirement in subsection (e) that reasonable proof be furnished using the "agreed method" provides considerable protection for account debtors upon receipt of a notification of assignment and making a request for proof. There are, however, other considerations that are of importance to account debtors but are beyond the scope of the frameworks provided by Articles 9 and 12. One such consideration is the potential involvement of pseudonymous payees, which may raise issues such as compliance with anti-money laundering regulations and sanctions compliance. These are examples of issues that a well-structured program for controllable accounts and controllable payment intangibles might address.

5. Relationship to Section 9-406. Section 9-406 governs the discharge of the obligation of an account debtor. Section 9-406 carves out of its scope transactions to the extent covered by this section. See Section 9-406(l).

Section 12-107. Governing Law

(a) [Governing law: general rule.] Except as provided in subsection (b), the local law of a controllable electronic record's jurisdiction governs a matter covered by this article.

(b) [Governing law: Section 12-106.] For a controllable electronic record that evidences a controllable account or controllable payment intangible, the local law of the controllable electronic record's jurisdiction governs a matter covered by Section 12-106 unless an effective agreement determines that the local law of another jurisdiction governs.

(c) [Controllable electronic record's jurisdiction.] The following rules determine a controllable electronic record's jurisdiction under this section:

(1) If the controllable electronic record, or a record attached to or logically associated with the controllable electronic record and readily available for review, expressly provides that a particular jurisdiction is the controllable electronic record's jurisdiction for purposes of this article or [the Uniform Commercial Code], that jurisdiction is the controllable electronic record's jurisdiction.

(2) If paragraph (1) does not apply and the rules of the system in which the controllable electronic record is recorded are readily available for review and expressly provide that a particular jurisdiction is the controllable electronic record's jurisdiction for purposes of this article or [the Uniform Commercial Code], that jurisdiction is the controllable electronic record's jurisdiction.

(3) If paragraphs (1) and (2) do not apply and the controllable electronic record, or a record attached to or logically associated with the controllable electronic record and readily available for review,

expressly provides that the controllable electronic record is governed by the law of a particular jurisdiction, that jurisdiction is the controllable electronic record's jurisdiction.

(4) If paragraphs (1), (2), and (3) do not apply and the rules of the system in which the controllable electronic record is recorded are readily available for review and expressly provide that the controllable electronic record or the system is governed by the law of a particular jurisdiction, that jurisdiction is the controllable electronic record's jurisdiction.

(5) If paragraphs (1) through (4) do not apply, the controllable electronic record's jurisdiction is the District of Columbia.

(d) [Applicability of Article 12.] If subsection (c)(5) applies and Article 12 is not in effect in the District of Columbia without material modification, the governing law for a matter covered by this article is the law of the District of Columbia as though Article 12 were in effect in the District of Columbia without material modification. In this subsection, "Article 12" means Article 12 of Uniform Commercial Code Amendments (2022).

(e) [Relation of matter or transaction to controllable electronic record's jurisdiction not necessary.] To the extent subsections (a) and (b) provide that the local law of the controllable electronic record's jurisdiction governs a matter covered by this article, that law governs even if the matter or a transaction to which the matter relates does not bear any relation to the controllable electronic record's jurisdiction.

(f) [Rights of purchasers determined at time of purchase.] The rights acquired under Section 12-104 by a purchaser or qualifying purchaser are governed by the law applicable under this section at the time of purchase.

Official Comment

1. Source. The provisions of Section 12-107 (as well as Sections 9-306A and 9- 306B) derive from Sections 8-110 and 9-305 on law governing perfection and priority of security interests in investment property and the relevance of a securities intermediary's jurisdiction and a commodity intermediary's jurisdiction.

2. The basic rule. Law governing matters covered by Article 12. Subsection (a) states the basic rule that the local law of the controllable electronic record's jurisdiction governs the matters covered by this Article. The "matters covered by" this Article are relatively narrow and discrete, albeit enormously important. If the choice-of-law rule provided by this section points to a jurisdiction that has adopted Article 12, those matters would include the interpretation and application of Article 12, including its definitions. In general, issues that would be determined by the provisions of this Article are to be determined under the law that is applicable as determined by this section. These include the rights of purchasers and property claimants more generally with respect to controllable electronic records, controllable accounts, and controllable payment intangibles to the extent dealt with by this Article—issues addressed by section 12-104. The rights and obligations of account debtors, to the extent dealt with by section 12-106, are also matters covered. Matters not covered by this Article, including matters as to which this Article expressly provides are covered by other law, are not within the scope of this section.

3. Practical considerations on determination of governing law. This section relating to the law governing the matters covered by this Article must confront substantial practical considerations. These considerations arise primarily from two factors. First, as described below, this section relies primarily on a "waterfall" of alternatives for determining a controllable electronic record's jurisdiction. The first four elements of the waterfall require for their applicability express provisions of a controllable electronic record, an attached or logically associated record, or the system in which a controllable electronic record is recorded. However, many controllable electronic records and systems existing at the time of the 2022 Amendments do not contain these provisions. As explained in Comment 6, the expectation is that over time electronic records and related systems will adopt these provisions in reliance on this section, thereby satisfying at least one of the first four elements of the waterfall. Second, in the absence of these provisions, at the bottom of the waterfall the controllable electronic record's jurisdiction is the District of Columbia. See Comment 6.

4. Governing law for Section 12-106. Subsection (b) provides an exception to the general rule of subsection (a) that "the local law of a controllable electronic record's jurisdiction governs the matters covered by this Article." The exception recognizes that an account debtor's rights and duties generally are governed by the law applicable to the underlying obligation of the account debtor, and not by the law applicable to the agreement between the assignor (debtor) and the assignee (secured party)—a security agreement. See Section 9-401, Comment 3. Subsection (b) recognizes that an effective agreement (i.e., one effective under Section 1-301(a)) between the account debtor and assignor may choose a different law to cover the matters covered by Section 12-106 (i.e., the account debtor's rights and duties addressed in that section). Such an agreement may, of course, address matters other than those covered by Section 12-106 (for example, an agreement that all obligations of the account debtor are governed by the laws of State X).

5. Determination of controllable electronic record's jurisdiction. The basic rule that the law of a controllable electronic record's jurisdiction governs the matters covered by Article 12 may be viewed as a rough proxy for the traditional role of the location of tangible asset (e.g., goods) in determining the applicable law (lex rei sitae). Drawing on the analogous provisions in Sections 8-110 and 9-305 in the context of a security entitlement or securities account or a commodity contract or commodity account, under subsection (c) it is the controllable electronic record itself, records attached thereto or associated therewith, or the system in which the controllable electronic record is recorded that determines the controllable electronic record's jurisdiction and, thereby, the governing law. Subsection (c) provides a "waterfall" of rules based on provisions that identify a particular jurisdiction as the controllable electronic record's jurisdiction or alternatively that provide the governing law for a controllable electronic record or the system in which the record is recorded. As to subsection (e), see Section 8-110, Comment 5A.

Paragraphs (1) through (4) of the subsection (c) waterfall each relies on information available from a controllable electronic record, an attached or logically associated record, or rules of a system in which the record is recorded. A controllable electronic record's jurisdiction is determined by one of these sources that "expressly provide[s]" that a jurisdiction is the controllable electronic record's jurisdiction or that a particular jurisdiction's law is the governing law. These paragraphs refer to attached or logically associated records or system rules that are "readily available." They also assume that the controllable electronic record is itself readily available to anyone choosing to deal with the record. These provisions are based on the assumption that the relevant express provision will be available to an interested person without the imposition of unreasonable burdens.

6. Bottom of the waterfall. District of Columbia. Many controllable electronic records, attached or logically associated records, and systems in which controllable electronic records are recorded that exist at the time of the 2022 Amendments do not identify the "controllable electronic record's jurisdiction" or the governing law (some permissioned systems being exceptions). (It is anticipated that, upon widespread adoption of Article 12 and accompanying amendments, systems will adapt and the first four elements of the waterfall will become more generally applicable for identifying a controllable electronic record's jurisdiction.) Consequently, subsection (c)(5) addresses an issue that does not normally exist in the context of Sections 8-110 and 9-305. It might be thought that the logical choice for the residual rule for designating the controllable electronic record's jurisdiction at bottom of the waterfall would be, the location of the debtor. That approach would follow the role of the location of a debtor under Sections 9-301 and 9-307. However, that location may not readily be determined by parties to a transaction, primarily because in many cases involving controllable electronic records the transferor is not known to or easily discoverable by a purchaser. See Prefatory Note 1 to Article 12. Consequently, Subsection (c)(5) resolves this issue by providing that the controllable electronic record's jurisdiction is the District of Columbia.

7. District of Columbia as controllable electronic record's jurisdiction. The designation of the District of Columbia as the controllable electronic record's jurisdiction follows Section 9-307(c), which designates the District of Columbia as the location of a debtor that otherwise would be located in a jurisdiction whose law does not provide for a generally applicable system of public notice (such a filing or registration) for nonpossessory security interests. This designation also assumes that the District of Columbia will have adopted Article 12 and the conforming amendments to Articles 1 and 9 in substantially the uniform version—i.e., without material modification of the official text. This is a plausible assumption based on the history of adoptions in that jurisdiction. Because the controllable electronic record's jurisdiction does not govern perfection of a security interest by filing, the designation of the District of Columbia at the bottom of the waterfall will not confer on that jurisdiction any economic benefits of fees for filing of financing statements. See Section 9-306B(b). Subsection (d) addresses the unlikely situation that the District of Columbia does not adopt Article 12 without material modification of the official text or later adopts materially non-uniform amendments. Subsection (d) is patterned loosely (but as closely as feasible) on the TRADES Regulations, 31 CFR § 357.11(e), for U.S. Treasury securities.

The term "Article 12" is defined in subsection (d) as the officially promulgated 2022 version of Article 12 and conforming amendments. In determining whether the District of Columbia has enacted Article 12 without material modification, a court or other tribunal should consider the materiality of any provision in the context of the issue or issues before it. A modification of a provision that would be material in another context should be disregarded if it has no bearing on the issue or issues before the tribunal. In connection with any future revision of the Article 12 official text, it will be important for transitional provisions to address the situations in which the District of Columbia may or may not have adopted the revised official text.

8. Relevant time for determination of governing law. Subsection (f) provides that the rights of purchasers are governed by the applicable law as of the time of purchase. Note that Sections 8-110 and 9-305 do not contain an analogous rule with respect to a securities intermediary's jurisdiction. However, Section 8-110(c) does provide a similar rule for the delivery of a security certificate and adverse claims. As to the timing of the determination of the governing law for other issues under Article 12, such as the rights and duties of account debtors under Section 12-106, the section does not specify a time. As with most statutory provisions relating to governing law, courts are free to determine the appropriate relevant time taking into account the relevant facts and the nature of the issues involved.

PART II

BANKRUPTCY

Title 11—Bankruptcy

Chapter

This title was enacted by Pub. L. 95–598, title I, §101, Nov. 6, 1978, 92 Stat. 2549.

CHAPTER 1—GENERAL PROVISIONS

Section

§ 101. Definitions

In this title the following definitions shall apply:

(1) The term "accountant" means accountant authorized under applicable law to practice public accounting, and includes professional accounting association, corporation, or partnership, if so authorized.

(2) The term "affiliate" means—

(A) entity that directly or indirectly owns, controls, or holds with power to vote, 20 percent or more of the outstanding voting securities of the debtor, other than an entity that holds such securities—

(i) in a fiduciary or agency capacity without sole discretionary power to vote such securities; or

(ii) solely to secure a debt, if such entity has not in fact exercised such power to vote;

(B) corporation 20 percent or more of whose outstanding voting securities are directly or indirectly owned, controlled, or held with power to vote, by the debtor, or by an entity that directly or indirectly owns, controls, or holds with power to vote, 20 percent or more of the outstanding voting securities of the debtor, other than an entity that holds such securities—

(i) in a fiduciary or agency capacity without sole discretionary power to vote such securities; or

(ii) solely to secure a debt, if such entity has not in fact exercised such power to vote;

(C) person whose business is operated under a lease or operating agreement by a debtor, or person substantially all of whose property is operated under an operating agreement with the debtor; or

(D) entity that operates the business or substantially all of the property of the debtor under a lease or operating agreement.

(3) The term "assisted person" means any person whose debts consist primarily of consumer debts and the value of whose nonexempt property is less than $256,800.

(4) The term "attorney" means attorney, professional law association, corporation, or partnership, authorized under applicable law to practice law.

(4A) The term "bankruptcy assistance" means any goods or services sold or otherwise provided to an assisted person with the express Uor implied purpose of providing information, advice, counsel, document preparation, or filing, or attendance at a creditors' meeting or appearing in a case or proceeding on behalf of another or providing legal representation with respect to a case or proceeding under this title.

(5) The term "claim" means—

(A) right to payment, whether or not such right is reduced to judgment, liquidated, unliquidated, fixed, contingent, matured, unmatured, disputed, undisputed, legal, equitable, secured, or unsecured; or

(B) right to an equitable remedy for breach of performance if such breach gives rise to a right to payment, whether or not such right to an equitable remedy is reduced to judgment, fixed, contingent, matured, unmatured, disputed, undisputed, secured, or unsecured.

(6) The term "commodity broker" means futures commission merchant, foreign futures commission merchant, clearing organization, leverage transaction merchant, or commodity options dealer, as defined in section 761 of this title, with respect to which there is a customer, as defined in section 761 of this title.

(7) The term "community claim" means claim that arose before the commencement of the case concerning the debtor for which property of the kind specified in section 541(a)(2) of this title is liable, whether or not there is any such property at the time of the commencement of the case.

(7A) The term "commercial fishing operation" means—

(A) the catching or harvesting of fish, shrimp, lobsters, urchins, seaweed, shellfish, or other aquatic species or products of such species; or

(B) for purposes of section 109 and chapter 12, aquaculture activities consisting of raising for market any species or product described in subparagraph (A).

(7B) The term "commercial fishing vessel" means a vessel used by a family fisherman to carry out a commercial fishing operation.

(8) The term "consumer debt" means debt incurred by an individual primarily for a personal, family, or household purpose.

(9) The term "corporation"—

(A) includes—

(i) association having a power or privilege that a private corporation, but not an individual or a partnership, possesses;

(ii) partnership association organized under a law that makes only the capital subscribed responsible for the debts of such association;

(iii) joint-stock company;

(iv) unincorporated company or association; or

(v) business trust; but

(B) does not include limited partnership.

(10) The term "creditor" means—

(A) entity that has a claim against the debtor that arose at the time of or before the order for relief concerning the debtor;

(B) entity that has a claim against the estate of a kind specified in section 348(d), 502(f), 502(g), 502(h) or 502(i) of this title; or

(C) entity that has a community claim.

(10A) The term "current monthly income"—

(A) means the average monthly income from all sources that the debtor receives (or in a joint case the debtor and the debtor's spouse receive) without regard to whether such income is taxable income, derived during the 6-month period ending on—

(i) the last day of the calendar month immediately preceding the date of the commencement of the case if the debtor files the schedule of current income required by section 521(a)(1)(B)(ii); or

(ii) the date on which current income is determined by the court for purposes of this title if the debtor does not file the schedule of current income required by section 521(a)(1)(B)(ii); and

(B)(i) includes any amount paid by any entity other than the debtor (or in a joint case the debtor and the debtor's spouse), on a regular basis for the household expenses of the debtor or the debtor's dependents (and, in a joint case, the debtor's spouse if not otherwise a dependent); and

(ii) excludes—

(I) benefits received under the Social Security Act (42 U.S.C. 301 et seq.);

(II) payments to victims of war crimes or crimes against humanity on account of their status as victims of such crimes;

(III) payments to victims of international terrorism or domestic terrorism, as those terms are defined in section 2331 of title 18, on account of their status as victims of such terrorism;

(IV) any monthly compensation, pension, pay, annuity, or allowance paid under title 10, 37, or 38 in connection with a disability, combat-related injury or disability, or death of a member of the uniformed services, except that any retired pay excluded under this subclause shall include retired pay paid under chapter 61 of title 10 only to the extent that such retired pay exceeds the amount of retired pay to which the debtor would otherwise be entitled if retired under any provision of title 10 other than chapter 61 of that title.

(11) The term "custodian" means—

(A) receiver or trustee of any of the property of the debtor, appointed in a case or proceeding not under this title;

(B) assignee under a general assignment for the benefit of the debtor's creditors; or

(C) trustee, receiver, or agent under applicable law, or under a contract, that is appointed or authorized to take charge of property of the debtor for the purpose of enforcing a lien against such property, or for the purpose of general administration of such property for the benefit of the debtor's creditors.

(12) The term "debt" means liability on a claim.

(12A) The term "debt relief agency" means any person who provides any bankruptcy assistance to an assisted person in return for the payment of money or other valuable consideration, or who is a bankruptcy petition preparer under section 110, but does not include—

(A) any person who is an officer, director, employee, or agent of a person who provides such assistance or of the bankruptcy petition preparer;

(B) a nonprofit organization that is exempt from taxation under section 501(c)(3) of the Internal Revenue Code of 1986;

(C) a creditor of such assisted person, to the extent that the creditor is assisting such assisted person to restructure any debt owed by such assisted person to the creditor;

(D) a depository institution (as defined in section 3 of the Federal Deposit Insurance Act) or any Federal credit union or State credit union (as those terms are defined in section 101 of the Federal Credit Union Act), or any affiliate or subsidiary of such depository institution or credit union; or

(E) an author, publisher, distributor, or seller of works subject to copyright protection under title 17, when acting in such capacity.

(13) The term "debtor" means person or municipality concerning which a case under this title has been commenced.

(13A) The term "debtor's principal residence"—

(A) means a residential structure if used as the principal residence by the debtor, including incidental property, without regard to whether that structure is attached to real property; and

(B) includes an individual condominium or cooperative unit, a mobile or manufactured home, or trailer if used as the principal residence by the debtor.

(14) The term "disinterested person" means a person that—

(A) is not a creditor, an equity security holder, or an insider;

(B) is not and was not, within 2 years before the date of the filing of the petition, a director, officer, or employee of the debtor; and

(C) does not have an interest materially adverse to the interest of the estate or of any class of creditors or equity security holders, by reason of any direct or indirect relationship to, connection with, or interest in, the debtor, or for any other reason.

(14A) The term "domestic support obligation" means a debt that accrues before, on, or after the date of the order for relief in a case under this title, including interest that accrues on that debt as provided under applicable nonbankruptcy law notwithstanding any other provision of this title, that is—

(A) owed to or recoverable by—

(i) a spouse, former spouse, or child of the debtor or such child's parent, legal guardian, or responsible relative; or

(ii) a governmental unit;

(B) in the nature of alimony, maintenance, or support (including assistance provided by a governmental unit) of such spouse, former spouse, or child of the debtor or such child's parent, without regard to whether such debt is expressly so designated;

(C) established or subject to establishment before, on, or after the date of the order for relief in a case under this title, by reason of applicable provisions of—

(i) a separation agreement, divorce decree, or property settlement agreement;

(ii) an order of a court of record; or

(iii) a determination made in accordance with applicable nonbankruptcy law by a governmental unit; and

(D) not assigned to a nongovernmental entity, unless that obligation is assigned voluntarily by the spouse, former spouse, child of the debtor, or such child's parent, legal guardian, or responsible relative for the purpose of collecting the debt.

(15) The term "entity" includes person, estate, trust, governmental unit, and United States trustee.

(16) The term "equity security" means—

(A) share in a corporation, whether or not transferable or denominated "stock", or similar security;

(B) interest of a limited partner in a limited partnership; or

(C) warrant or right, other than a right to convert, to purchase, sell, or subscribe to a share, security, or interest of a kind specified in subparagraph (A) or (B) of this paragraph.

(17) The term "equity security holder" means holder of an equity security of the debtor.

(18) The term "family farmer" means—

(A) individual or individual and spouse engaged in a farming operation whose aggregate debts do not exceed $12,562,250 and not less than 50 percent of whose aggregate noncontingent, liquidated debts (excluding a debt for the principal residence of such individual or such individual and spouse unless such debt arises out of a farming operation), on the date the case is filed, arise out of a farming operation owned or operated by such individual or such individual and spouse, and such individual or such individual and spouse receive from such farming operation more than 50 percent of such individual's or such individual and spouse's gross income for—

(i) the taxable year preceding; or

(ii) each of the 2d and 3d taxable years preceding; the taxable year in which the case concerning such individual or such individual and spouse was filed; or

(B) corporation or partnership in which more than 50 percent of the outstanding stock or equity is held by one family, or by one family and the relatives of the members of such family, and such family or such relatives conduct the farming operation, and

(i) more than 80 percent of the value of its assets consists of assets related to the farming operation;

(ii) its aggregate debts do not exceed $12,562,250 and not less than 50 percent of its aggregate noncontingent, liquidated debts (excluding a debt for one dwelling which is owned by such corporation or partnership and which a shareholder or partner maintains as a principal residence, unless such debt arises out of a farming operation), on the date the case is filed, arise out of the farming operation owned or operated by such corporation or such partnership; and

(iii) if such corporation issues stock, such stock is not publicly traded.

(19) The term "family farmer with regular annual income" means family farmer whose annual income is sufficiently stable and regular to enable such family farmer to make payments under a plan under chapter 12 of this title.

(19A) The term "family fisherman" means—

(A) an individual or individual and spouse engaged in a commercial fishing operation—

(i) whose aggregate debts do not exceed $2,568,000 and not less than 80 percent of whose aggregate noncontingent, liquidated debts (excluding a debt for the principal residence of such individual or such individual and spouse, unless such debt arises out of a commercial fishing operation), on the date the case is filed, arise out of a commercial fishing operation owned or operated by such individual or such individual and spouse; and

(ii) who receive from such commercial fishing operation more than 50 percent of such individual's or such individual's and spouse's gross income for the taxable year preceding the taxable year in which the case concerning such individual or such individual and spouse was filed; or

(B) a corporation or partnership—

(i) in which more than 50 percent of the outstanding stock or equity is held by—

(I) 1 family that conducts the commercial fishing operation; or

(II) 1 family and the relatives of the members of such family, and such family or such relatives conduct the commercial fishing operation; and (ii)(I) more than 80 percent of the value of its assets consists of assets related to the commercial fishing operation;

(II) its aggregate debts do not exceed $2,568,000 and not less than 80 percent of its aggregate noncontingent, liquidated debts (excluding a debt for 1 dwelling which is owned by such corporation or partnership and which a shareholder or partner maintains as a principal residence, unless such debt arises out of a commercial fishing operation), on the date the case is filed, arise out of a commercial fishing operation owned or operated by such corporation or such partnership; and

(III) if such corporation issues stock, such stock is not publicly traded.

(19B) The term "family fisherman with regular annual income" means a family fisherman whose annual income is sufficiently stable and regular to enable such family fisherman to make payments under a plan under chapter 12 of this title.

(20) The term "farmer" means (except when such term appears in the term "family farmer") person that received more than 80 percent of such person's gross income during the taxable year of such person immediately preceding the taxable year of such person during which the case under this title concerning such person was commenced from a farming operation owned or operated by such person.

(21) The term "farming operation" includes farming, tillage of the soil, dairy farming, ranching, production or raising of crops, poultry, or livestock, and production of poultry or livestock products in an unmanufactured state.

(21A) The term "farmout agreement" means a written agreement in which—

(A) the owner of a right to drill, produce, or operate liquid or gaseous hydrocarbons on property agrees or has agreed to transfer or assign all or a part of such right to another entity; and

(B) such other entity (either directly or through its agents or its assigns), as consideration, agrees to perform drilling, reworking, recompleting, testing, or similar or related operations, to develop or produce liquid or gaseous hydrocarbons on the property.

(21B) The term "Federal depository institutions regulatory agency" means—

(A) with respect to an insured depository institution (as defined in section 3(c)(2) of the Federal Deposit Insurance Act) for which no conservator or receiver has been appointed, the appropriate Federal banking agency (as defined in section 3(q) of such Act);

(B) with respect to an insured credit union (including an insured credit union for which the National Credit Union Administration has been appointed conservator or liquidating agent), the National Credit Union Administration;

(C) with respect to any insured depository institution for which the Resolution Trust Corporation has been appointed conservator or receiver, the Resolution Trust Corporation; and

(D) with respect to any insured depository institution for which the Federal Deposit Insurance Corporation has been appointed conservator or receiver, the Federal Deposit Insurance Corporation.

(22) The term "financial institution" means—

(A) a Federal reserve bank, or an entity that is a commercial or savings bank, industrial savings bank, savings and loan association, trust company, federally-insured credit union, or receiver, liquidating agent, or conservator for such entity and, when any such Federal reserve bank, receiver, liquidating agent, conservator or entity is acting as agent or custodian for a customer (whether or not a "customer", as defined in section 741) in connection with a securities contract (as defined in section 741) such customer; or

(B) in connection with a securities contract (as defined in section 741) an investment company registered under the Investment Company Act of 1940.

(22A) The term "financial participant" means—

(A) an entity that, at the time it enters into a securities contract, commodity contract, swap agreement, repurchase agreement, or forward contract, or at the time of the date of the filing of the petition, has one or more agreements or transactions described in paragraph (1), (2), (3), (4), (5), or (6) of section 561(a) with the debtor or any other entity (other than an affiliate) of a total gross dollar value of not less than $1,000,000,000 in notional or actual principal amount outstanding (aggregated across counterparties) at such time or on any day during the 15-month period preceding the date of the filing of the petition, or has gross mark-to-market positions of not less than $100,000,000 (aggregated across counterparties) in one or more such agreements or transactions with the debtor or any other entity (other than an affiliate) at such time or on any day during the 15-month period preceding the date of the filing of the petition; or

(B) a clearing organization (as defined in section 402 of the Federal Deposit Insurance Corporation Improvement Act of 1991).

(23) The term "foreign proceeding" means a collective judicial or administrative proceeding in a foreign country, including an interim proceeding, under a law relating to insolvency or adjustment of debt in which proceeding the assets and affairs of the debtor are subject to control or supervision by a foreign court, for the purpose of reorganization or liquidation.

(24) The term "foreign representative" means a person or body, including a person or body appointed on an interim basis, authorized in a foreign proceeding to administer the reorganization or the liquidation of the debtor's assets or affairs or to act as a representative of such foreign proceeding.

(25) The term "forward contract" means—

(A) a contract (other than a commodity contract, as defined in Section 761) for the purchase, sale, or transfer of a commodity, as defined in section 761(8) of this title, or any similar good, article, service, right, or interest which is presently or in the future becomes the subject of dealing in the forward contract trade, or product or byproduct thereof, with a maturity date more than two days after the date the contract is entered into, including, but not limited to, a repurchase or reverse repurchase transaction (whether or not such repurchase or reverse repurchase transaction is a "repurchase agreement", as defined in this section)[1] consignment, lease, swap, hedge transaction, deposit, loan, option, allocated transaction, unallocated transaction, or any other similar agreement;

(B) any combination of agreements or transactions referred to in subparagraphs (A) and (C);

(C) any option to enter into an agreement or transaction referred to in subparagraph (A) or (B);

(D) a master agreement that provides for an agreement or transaction referred to in subparagraph (A), (B), or (C), together with all supplements to any such master agreement, without regard to whether such master agreement provides for an agreement or transaction that is not a forward contract under this paragraph, except that such master agreement shall be considered to be a forward contract under this paragraph only with respect to each agreement or transaction under such master agreement that is referred to in subparagraph (A), (B), or (C); or

(E) any security agreement or arrangement, or other credit enhancement related to any agreement or transaction referred to in subparagraph (A), (B), (C), or (D), including any guarantee or reimbursement obligation by or to a forward contract merchant or financial participant in connection with any agreement or transaction referred to in any such subparagraph, but not to exceed the damages in connection with any such agreement or transaction, measured in accordance with section 562.

(26) The term "forward contract merchant" means a Federal reserve bank, or an entity the business of which consists in whole or in part of entering into forward contracts as or with merchants in a commodity (as defined in section 761) or any similar good, article, service, right, or interest which is presently or in the future becomes the subject of dealing in the forward contract trade.

(27) The term "governmental unit" means United States; State; Commonwealth; District; Territory; municipality; foreign state; department, agency, or instrumentality of the United States (but not a United States trustee while serving as a trustee in a case under this title), a State, a Commonwealth, a District, a Territory, a municipality, or a foreign state; or other foreign or domestic government.

(27A) The term "health care business"—

(A) means any public or private entity (without regard to whether that entity is organized for profit or not for profit) that is primarily engaged in offering to the general public facilities and services for—

(i) the diagnosis or treatment of injury, deformity, or disease; and

(ii) surgical, drug treatment, psychiatric, or obstetric care; and

(B) includes—

(i) any—

(I) general or specialized hospital;

(II) ancillary ambulatory, emergency, or surgical treatment facility;

(III) hospice;

(IV) home health agency; and

[1] So in original. Probably should be followed by a comma.

(V) other health care institution that is similar to an entity referred to in subclause (I), (II), (III), or (IV); and

(ii) any long-term care facility, including any—

(I) skilled nursing facility;

(II) intermediate care facility;

(III) assisted living facility;

(IV) home for the aged;

(V) domiciliary care facility; and

(VI) health care institution that is related to a facility referred to in subclause (I), (II), (III), (IV), or (V), if that institution is primarily engaged in offering room, board, laundry, or personal assistance with activities of daily living and incidentals to activities of daily living.

(27B) The term "incidental property" means, with respect to a debtor's principal residence—

(A) property commonly conveyed with a principal residence in the area where the real property is located;

(B) all easements, rights, appurtenances, fixtures, rents, royalties, mineral rights, oil or gas rights or profits, water rights, escrow funds, or insurance proceeds; and

(C) all replacements or additions.

(28) The term "indenture" means mortgage, deed of trust, or indenture, under which there is outstanding a security, other than a voting-trust certificate, constituting a claim against the debtor, a claim secured by a lien on any of the debtor's property, or an equity security of the debtor.

(29) The term "indenture trustee" means trustee under an indenture.

(30) The term "individual with regular income" means individual whose income is sufficiently stable and regular to enable such individual to make payments under a plan under chapter 13 of this title, other than a stockbroker or a commodity broker.

(31) The term "insider" includes—

(A) if the debtor is an individual—

(i) relative of the debtor or of a general partner of the debtor;

(ii) partnership in which the debtor is a general partner;

(iii) general partner of the debtor; or

(iv) corporation of which the debtor is a director, officer, or person in control;

(B) if the debtor is a corporation—

(i) director of the debtor;

(ii) officer of the debtor;

(iii) person in control of the debtor;

(iv) partnership in which the debtor is a general partner;

(v) general partner of the debtor; or

(vi) relative of a general partner, director, officer, or person in control of the debtor;

(C) if the debtor is a partnership—

(i) general partner in the debtor;

(ii) relative of a general partner in, general partner of, or person in control of the debtor;

(iii) partnership in which the debtor is a general partner;

(iv) general partner of the debtor; or

(v) person in control of the debtor;

(D) if the debtor is a municipality, elected official of the debtor or relative of an elected official of the debtor;

(E) affiliate, or insider of an affiliate as if such affiliate were the debtor; and

(F) managing agent of the debtor.

(32) The term "insolvent" means—

(A) with reference to an entity other than a partnership and a municipality, financial condition such that the sum of such entity's debts is greater than all of such entity's property, at a fair valuation, exclusive of—

(i) property transferred, concealed, or removed with intent to hinder, delay, or defraud such entity's creditors; and

(ii) property that may be exempted from property of the estate under section 522 of this title;

(B) with reference to a partnership, financial condition such that the sum of such partnership's debts is greater than the aggregate of, at a fair valuation—

(i) all of such partnership's property, exclusive of property of the kind specified in subparagraph (A)(i) of this paragraph; and

(ii) the sum of the excess of the value of each general partner's nonpartnership property, exclusive of property of the kind specified in subparagraph (A) of this paragraph, over such partner's nonpartnership debts; and

(C) with reference to a municipality, financial condition such that the municipality is—

(i) generally not paying its debts as they become due unless such debts are the subject of a bona fide dispute; or

(ii) unable to pay its debts as they become due.

(33) The term "institution-affiliated party"—

(A) with respect to an insured depository institution (as defined in section 3(c)(2) of the Federal Deposit Insurance Act), has the meaning given it in section 3(u) of the Federal Deposit Insurance Act; and

(B) with respect to an insured credit union, has the meaning given it in section 206(r) of the Federal Credit Union Act.

(34) The term "insured credit union" has the meaning given it in section 101(7) of the Federal Credit Union Act.

(35) The term "insured depository institution"—

(A) has the meaning given it in section 3(c)(2) of the Federal Deposit Insurance Act; and

(B) includes an insured credit union (except in the case of paragraphs (21B) and (33)(A) of this subsection).

(35A) The term "intellectual property" means—

(A) trade secret;

(B) invention, process, design, or plant protected under title 35;

(C) patent application;

(D) plant variety;

(E) work of authorship protected under title 17; or

(F) mask work protected under chapter 9 of title 17; to the extent protected by applicable nonbankruptcy law.

(36) The term "judicial lien" means lien obtained by judgment, levy, sequestration, or other legal or equitable process or proceeding.

(37) The term "lien" means charge against or interest in property to secure payment of a debt or performance of an obligation.

(38) The term "margin payment" means, for purposes of the forward contract provisions of this title, payment or deposit of cash, a security or other property, that is commonly known in the forward contract trade as original margin, initial margin, maintenance margin, or variation margin, including mark-to-market payments, or variation payments.

(38A) The term "master netting agreement"—

(A) means an agreement providing for the exercise of rights, including rights of netting, setoff, liquidation, termination, acceleration, or close out, under or in connection with one or more contracts that are described in any one or more of paragraphs (1) through (5) of section 561(a), or any security agreement or arrangement or other credit enhancement related to one or more of the foregoing, including any guarantee or reimbursement obligation related to 1 or more of the foregoing; and

(B) if the agreement contains provisions relating to agreements or transactions that are not contracts described in paragraphs (1) through (5) of section 561(a), shall be deemed to be a master netting agreement only with respect to those agreements or transactions that are described in any one or more of paragraphs (1) through (5) of section 561(a).

(38B) The term "master netting agreement participant" means an entity that, at any time before the date of the filing of the petition, is a party to an outstanding master netting agreement with the debtor.

(39) The term "mask work" has the meaning given it in section 901(a)(2) of title 17.

(39A) The term "median family income" means for any year—

(A) the median family income both calculated and reported by the Bureau of the Census in the then most recent year; and

(B) if not so calculated and reported in the then current year, adjusted annually after such most recent year until the next year in which median family income is both calculated and reported by the Bureau of the Census, to reflect the percentage change in the Consumer Price Index for All Urban Consumers during the period of years occurring after such most recent year and before such current year.

(40) The term "municipality" means political subdivision or public agency or instrumentality of a State.

(40A) The term "patient" means any individual who obtains or receives services from a health care business.

(40B) The term "patient records" means any record relating to a patient, including a written document or a record recorded in a magnetic, optical, or other form of electronic medium.

(40C) The terms "payment stablecoin" and "permitted payment stablecoin issuer" have the meanings given those terms in section 2 of the GENIUS Act.

(41) The term "person" includes individual, partnership, and corporation, but does not include governmental unit, except that a governmental unit that—

(A) acquires an asset from a person—

(i) as a result of the operation of a loan guarantee agreement; or

(ii) as receiver or liquidating agent of a person;

(B) is a guarantor of a pension benefit payable by or on behalf of the debtor or an affiliate of the debtor; or

(C) is the legal or beneficial owner of an asset of—

(i) an employee pension benefit plan that is a governmental plan, as defined in section 414(d) of the Internal Revenue Code of 1986; or

(ii) an eligible deferred compensation plan, as defined in section 457(b) of the Internal Revenue Code of 1986;

shall be considered, for purposes of section 1102 of this title, to be a person with respect to such asset or such benefit.

(41A) The term "personally identifiable information" means—

(A) if provided by an individual to the debtor in connection with obtaining a product or a service from the debtor primarily for personal, family, or household purposes—

(i) the first name (or initial) and last name of such individual, whether given at birth or time of adoption, or resulting from a lawful change of name;

(ii) the geographical address of a physical place of residence of such individual;

(iii) an electronic address (including an e-mail address) of such individual;

(iv) a telephone number dedicated to contacting such individual at such physical place of residence;

(v) a social security account number issued to such individual; or

(vi) the account number of a credit card issued to such individual; or

(B) if identified in connection with 1 or more of the items of information specified in subparagraph (A)—

(i) a birth date, the number of a certificate of birth or adoption, or a place of birth; or

(ii) any other information concerning an identified individual that, if disclosed, will result in contacting or identifying such individual physically or electronically.

(42) The term "petition" means petition filed under section 301, 302, 303 and[2] 1504 of this title, as the case may be, commencing a case under this title.

(42A) The term "production payment" means a term overriding royalty satisfiable in cash or in kind—

(A) contingent on the production of a liquid or gaseous hydrocarbon from particular real property; and

(B) from a specified volume, or a specified value, from the liquid or gaseous hydrocarbon produced from such property, and determined without regard to production costs.

(43) The term "purchaser" means transferee of a voluntary transfer, and includes immediate or mediate transferee of such a transferee.

(44) The term "railroad" means common carrier by railroad engaged in the transportation of individuals or property or owner of trackage facilities leased by such a common carrier.

(45) The term "relative" means individual related by affinity or consanguinity within the third degree as determined by the common law, or individual in a step or adoptive relationship within such third degree.

(46) The term "repo participant" means an entity that, at any time before the filing of the petition, has an outstanding repurchase agreement with the debtor.

(47) The term "repurchase agreement" (which definition also applies to a reverse repurchase agreement)—

(A) means—

(i) an agreement, including related terms, which provides for the transfer of one or more certificates of deposit, mortgage related securities (as defined in section 3 of the Securities Exchange Act of 1934), mortgage loans, interests in mortgage related securities or mortgage loans, eligible bankers' acceptances, qualified foreign government securities (defined as a security that is a direct obligation of, or that is fully guaranteed by, the central government of a member of the Organization for Economic Cooperation and Development), or securities that are direct obligations of, or that are fully guaranteed by, the United States

[2] So in original. Probably should be "or".

or any agency of the United States against the transfer of funds by the transferee of such certificates of deposit, eligible bankers' acceptances, securities, mortgage loans, or interests, with a simultaneous agreement by such transferee to transfer to the transferor thereof certificates of deposit, eligible bankers' acceptance, securities, mortgage loans, or interests of the kind described in this clause, at a date certain not later than 1 year after such transfer or on demand, against the transfer of funds;

(ii) any combination of agreements or transactions referred to in clauses (i) and (iii);

(iii) an option to enter into an agreement or transaction referred to in clause (i) or (ii);

(iv) a master agreement that provides for an agreement or transaction referred to in clause (i), (ii), or (iii), together with all supplements to any such master agreement, without regard to whether such master agreement provides for an agreement or transaction that is not a repurchase agreement under this paragraph, except that such master agreement shall be considered to be a repurchase agreement under this paragraph only with respect to each agreement or transaction under the master agreement that is referred to in clause (i), (ii), or (iii); or

(v) any security agreement or arrangement or other credit enhancement related to any agreement or transaction referred to in clause (i), (ii), (iii), or (iv), including any guarantee or reimbursement obligation by or to a repo participant or financial participant in connection with any agreement or transaction referred to in any such clause, but not to exceed the damages in connection with any such agreement or transaction, measured in accordance with section 562 of this title; and

(B) does not include a repurchase obligation under a participation in a commercial mortgage loan.

(48) The term "securities clearing agency" means person that is registered as a clearing agency under section 17A of the Securities Exchange Act of 1934, or exempt from such registration under such section pursuant to an order of the Securities and Exchange Commission, or whose business is confined to the performance of functions of a clearing agency with respect to exempted securities, as defined in section 3(a)(12) of such Act for the purposes of such section 17A.

(48A) The term "securities self regulatory organization" means either a securities association registered with the Securities and Exchange Commission under section 15A of the Securities Exchange Act of 1934 or a national securities exchange registered with the Securities and Exchange Commission under section 6 of the Securities Exchange Act of 1934.

(49) The term "security"—

(A) includes—

(i) note;

(ii) stock;

(iii) treasury stock;

(iv) bond;

(v) debenture;

(vi) collateral trust certificate;

(vii) pre-organization certificate or subscription;

(viii) transferable share;

(ix) voting-trust certificate;

(x) certificate of deposit;

(xi) certificate of deposit for security;

(xii) investment contract or certificate of interest or participation in a profit-sharing agreement or in an oil, gas, or mineral royalty or lease, if such contract or interest is required to be the subject of a registration statement filed with the Securities and Exchange Commission under the provisions of the Securities Act of 1933, or is exempt under section 3(b) of such Act from the requirement to file such a statement;

(xiii) interest of a limited partner in a limited partnership;

(xiv) other claim or interest commonly known as "security"; and

(xv) certificate of interest or participation in, temporary or interim certificate for, receipt for, or warrant or right to subscribe to or purchase or sell, a security; but

(B) does not include—

(i) currency, check, draft, bill of exchange, or bank letter of credit;

(ii) leverage transaction, as defined in section 761 of this title;

(iii) commodity futures contract or forward contract;

(iv) option, warrant, or right to subscribe to or purchase or sell a commodity futures contract;

(v) option to purchase or sell a commodity;

(vi) contract or certificate of a kind specified in subparagraph (A)(xii) of this paragraph that is not required to be the subject of a registration statement filed with the Securities and Exchange Commission and is not exempt under section 3(b) of the Securities Act of 1933 from the requirement to file such a statement; or

(vii) debt or evidence of indebtedness for goods sold and delivered or services rendered.

(50) The term "security agreement" means agreement that creates or provides for a security interest.

(51) The term "security interest" means lien created by an agreement.

(51A) The term "settlement payment" means, for purposes of the forward contract provisions of this title, a preliminary settlement payment, a partial settlement payment, an interim settlement payment, a settlement payment on account, a final settlement payment, a net settlement payment, or any other similar payment commonly used in the forward contract trade.

(51B) The term "single asset real estate" means real property constituting a single property or project, other than residential real property with fewer than 4 residential units, which generates substantially all of the gross income of a debtor who is not a family farmer and on which no substantial business is being conducted by a debtor other than the business of operating the real property and activities incidental thereto.

(51C) The term "small business case" means a case filed under chapter 11 of this title in which the debtor is a small business debtor and has not elected that subchapter V of chapter 11 of this title shall apply.

(51D) The term "small business debtor"—

(A) subject to subparagraph (B), means a person engaged in commercial or business activities (including any affiliate of such person that is also a debtor under this title and excluding a person whose primary activity is the business of owning single asset real estate) that has aggregate noncontingent liquidated secured and unsecured debts as of the date of the filing of the petition or the date of the order for relief in an amount not more than $3,424,000 (excluding debts owed to 1 or more affiliates or insiders) not less than 50 percent of which arose from the commercial or business activities of the debtor; and

(B) does not include—

(i) any member of a group of affiliated debtors under this title that has aggregate noncontingent liquidated secured and unsecured debts in an amount greater than $3,424,000 (excluding debt owed to 1 or more affiliates or insiders);

(ii) any debtor that is a corporation subject to the reporting requirements under section 13 or 15(d) of the Securities Exchange Act of 1934 (15 U.S.C. 78m, 78o(d)); or

(iii) any debtor that is an affiliate of a corporation described in clause (ii).

(52) The term "State" includes the District of Columbia and Puerto Rico, except for the purpose of defining who may be a debtor under chapter 9 of this title.

(53) The term "statutory lien" means lien arising solely by force of a statute on specified circumstances or conditions, or lien of distress for rent, whether or not statutory, but does not include security interest or judicial lien, whether or not such interest or lien is provided by or is dependent on a statute and whether or not such interest or lien is made fully effective by statute.

(53A) The term "stockbroker" means person—

(A) with respect to which there is a customer, as defined in section 741 of this title; and

(B) that is engaged in the business of effecting transactions in securities—

(i) for the account of others; or

(ii) with members of the general public, from or for such person's own account.

(53B) The term "swap agreement"—

(A) means—

(i) any agreement, including the terms and conditions incorporated by reference in such agreement, which is—

(I) an interest rate swap, option, future, or forward agreement, including a rate floor, rate cap, rate collar, cross-currency rate swap, and basis swap;

(II) a spot, same day-tomorrow, tomorrow-next, forward, or other foreign exchange, precious metals, or other commodity agreement;

(III) a currency swap, option, future, or forward agreement;

(IV) an equity index or equity swap, option, future, or forward agreement;

(V) a debt index or debt swap, option, future, or forward agreement;

(VI) a total return, credit spread or credit swap, option, future, or forward agreement;

(VII) a commodity index or a commodity swap, option, future, or forward agreement;

(VIII) a weather swap, option, future, or forward agreement;

(IX) an emissions swap, option, future, or forward agreement; or

(X) an inflation swap, option, future, or forward agreement;

(ii) any agreement or transaction that is similar to any other agreement or transaction referred to in this paragraph and that—

(I) is of a type that has been, is presently, or in the future becomes, the subject of recurrent dealings in the swap or other derivatives markets (including terms and conditions incorporated by reference therein); and

(II) is a forward, swap, future, option, or spot transaction on one or more rates, currencies, commodities, equity securities, or other equity instruments, debt securities or other debt instruments, quantitative measures associated with an occurrence, extent of an occurrence, or contingency associated with a financial, commercial, or economic consequence, or economic or financial indices or measures of economic or financial risk or value;

(iii) any combination of agreements or transactions referred to in this subparagraph;

(iv) any option to enter into an agreement or transaction referred to in this subparagraph;

(v) a master agreement that provides for an agreement or transaction referred to in clause (i), (ii), (iii), or (iv), together with all supplements to any such master agreement, and without regard to whether the master agreement contains an agreement or transaction that is not a swap agreement under this paragraph, except that the master agreement shall be considered to be a swap agreement under this paragraph only with respect to each agreement or transaction under the master agreement that is referred to in clause (i), (ii), (iii), or (iv); or

(vi) any security agreement or arrangement or other credit enhancement related to any agreements or transactions referred to in clause (i) through (v), including any guarantee or reimbursement obligation by or to a swap participant or financial participant in connection with any agreement or transaction referred to in any such clause, but not to exceed the damages in connection with any such agreement or transaction, measured in accordance with section 562; and

(B) is applicable for purposes of this title only, and shall not be construed or applied so as to challenge or affect the characterization, definition, or treatment of any swap agreement under any other statute, regulation, or rule, including the Gramm-Leach-Bliley Act, the Legal Certainty for Bank Products Act of 2000, the securities laws (as such term is defined in section 3(a)(47) of the Securities Exchange Act of 1934) and the Commodity Exchange Act.

(53C) The term "swap participant" means an entity that, at any time before the filing of the petition, has an outstanding swap agreement with the debtor.

(56A) [3]The term "term overriding royalty" means an interest in liquid or gaseous hydrocarbons in place or to be produced from particular real property that entitles the owner thereof to a share of production, or the value thereof, for a term limited by time, quantity, or value realized.

(53D) The term "timeshare plan" means and shall include that interest purchased in any arrangement, plan, scheme, or similar device, but not including exchange programs, whether by membership, agreement, tenancy in common, sale, lease, deed, rental agreement, license, right to use agreement, or by any other means, whereby a purchaser, in exchange for consideration, receives a right to use accommodations, facilities, or recreational sites, whether improved or unimproved, for a specific period of time less than a full year during any given year, but not necessarily for consecutive years, and

[3] So in original.

which extends for a period of more than three years. A "timeshare interest" is that interest purchased in a timeshare plan which grants the purchaser the right to use and occupy accommodations, facilities, or recreational sites, whether improved or unimproved, pursuant to a timeshare plan.

(54) The term "transfer" means—

(A) the creation of a lien;

(B) the retention of title as a security interest;

(C) the foreclosure of a debtor's equity of redemption; or

(D) each mode, direct or indirect, absolute or conditional, voluntary or involuntary, of disposing of or parting with—

(i) property; or

(ii) an interest in property.

(54A) The term "uninsured State member bank" means a State member bank (as defined in section 3 of the Federal Deposit Insurance Act) the deposits of which are not insured by the Federal Deposit Insurance Corporation.

(55) The term "United States", when used in a geographical sense, includes all locations where the judicial jurisdiction of the United States extends, including territories and possessions of the United States.

§ 102. Rules of Construction

In this title—

(1) "after notice and a hearing", or a similar phrase—

(A) means after such notice as is appropriate in the particular circumstances, and such opportunity for a hearing as is appropriate in the particular circumstances; but

(B) authorizes an act without an actual hearing if such notice is given properly and if—

(i) such a hearing is not requested timely by a party in interest; or

(ii) there is insufficient time for a hearing to be commenced before such act must be done, and the court authorizes such act;

(2) "claim against the debtor" includes claim against property of the debtor;

(3) "includes" and "including" are not limiting;

(4) "may not" is prohibitive, and not permissive;

(5) "or" is not exclusive;

(6) "order for relief" means entry of an order for relief;

(7) the singular includes the plural;

(8) a definition, contained in a section of this title that refers to another section of this title, does not, for the purpose of such reference, affect the meaning of a term used in such other section; and

(9) "United States trustee" includes a designee of the United States trustee.

§ 103. Applicability of Chapters

(a) Except as provided in section 1161 of this title, chapters 1, 3, and 5 of this title apply in a case under chapter 7, 11, 12, or 13 of this title, and this chapter, sections 307, 362(o), 555 through 557, and 559 through 562 apply in a case under chapter 15.

(b) Subchapters I and II of chapter 7 of this title apply only in a case under such chapter.

(c) Subchapter III of chapter 7 of this title applies only in a case under such chapter concerning a stockbroker.

(d) Subchapter IV of chapter 7 of this title applies only in a case under such chapter concerning a commodity broker.

(e) Scope of application.—Subchapter V of chapter 7 of this title shall apply only in a case under such chapter concerning the liquidation of an uninsured State member bank, or a corporation organized under section 25A of the Federal Reserve Act, which operates, or operates as, a multilateral clearing organization pursuant to section 409 of the Federal Deposit Insurance Corporation Improvement Act of 1991.

(f) Except as provided in section 901 of this title, only chapters 1 and 9 of this title apply in a case under such chapter 9.

(g) Except as provided in section 901 of this title, subchapters I, II, and III of chapter 11 of this title apply only in a case under such chapter.

(h) Subchapter IV of chapter 11 of this title applies only in a case under such chapter concerning a railroad.

(i) Subchapter V of chapter 11 of this title applies only in a case under chapter 11 in which a debtor (as defined in section 1182) elects that subchapter V of chapter 11 shall apply.

(j) Chapter 13 of this title applies only in a case under such chapter.

(k) Chapter 12 of this title applies only in a case under such chapter.

(l) Chapter 15 applies only in a case under such chapter, except that—

(1) sections 1505, 1513, and 1514 apply in all cases under this title; and

(2) section 1509 applies whether or not a case under this title is pending.

§ 104. Adjustment of Dollar Amounts

(a) On April 1, 1998, and at each 3-year interval ending on April 1 thereafter, each dollar amount in effect under sections 101(3), 101(18), 101(19A), 101(51D), 109(e), 303(b), 507(a), 522(d), 522(f)(3) and 522(f)(4), 522(n), 522(p), 522(q), 523(a)(2)(C), 541(b), 547(c)(9), 707(b), 1182(1), 1322(d), 1325(b), and 1326(b)(3) of this title and section 1409(b) of title 28 immediately before such April 1 shall be adjusted—

(1) to reflect the change in the Consumer Price Index for All Urban Consumers, published by the Department of Labor, for the most recent 3-year period ending immediately before January 1 preceding such April 1, and

(2) to round to the nearest $25 the dollar amount that represents such change.

(b) Not later than March 1, 1998, and at each 3-year interval ending on March 1 thereafter, the Judicial Conference of the United States shall publish in the Federal Register the dollar amounts that will become effective on such April 1 under sections 101(3), 101(18), 101(19A), 101(51D), 109(e), 303(b), 507(a), 522(d), 522(f)(3) and 522(f)(4), 522(n), 522(p), 522(q), 523(a)(2)(C), 541(b), 547(c)(9), 707(b), 1182(1), 1322(d), 1325(b), and 1326(b)(3) of this title and section 1409(b) of title 28.

(c) Adjustments made in accordance with subsection (a) shall not apply with respect to cases commenced before the date of such adjustments.

§ 105. Power of Court

(a) The court may issue any order, process, or judgment that is necessary or appropriate to carry out the provisions of this title. No provision of this title providing for the raising of an issue by a party in interest shall be construed to preclude the court from, sua sponte, taking any action or making any determination necessary or appropriate to enforce or implement court orders or rules, or to prevent an abuse of process.

(b) Notwithstanding subsection (a) of this section, a court may not appoint a receiver in a case under this title.

(c) The ability of any district judge or other officer or employee of a district court to exercise any of the authority or responsibilities conferred upon the court under this title shall be determined by reference to the provisions relating to such judge, officer, or employee set forth in title 28. This subsection shall not be interpreted to exclude bankruptcy judges and other officers or employees appointed pursuant to chapter 6 of title 28 from its operation.

(d) The court, on its own motion or on the request of a party in interest—

(1) shall hold such status conferences as are necessary to further the expeditious and economical resolution of the case; and

(2) unless inconsistent with another provision of this title or with applicable Federal Rules of Bankruptcy Procedure, may issue an order at any such conference prescribing such limitations and conditions as the court deems appropriate to ensure that the case is handled expeditiously and economically, including an order that—

(A) sets the date by which the trustee must assume or reject an executory contract or unexpired lease; or

(B) in a case under chapter 11 of this title—

(i) sets a date by which the debtor, or trustee if one has been appointed, shall file a disclosure statement and plan;

(ii) sets a date by which the debtor, or trustee if one has been appointed, shall solicit acceptances of a plan;

(iii) sets the date by which a party in interest other than a debtor may file a plan;

(iv) sets a date by which a proponent of a plan, other than the debtor, shall solicit acceptances of such plan;

(v) fixes the scope and format of the notice to be provided regarding the hearing on approval of the disclosure statement; or

(vi) provides that the hearing on approval of the disclosure statement may be combined with the hearing on confirmation of the plan.

§ 106. Waiver of Sovereign Immunity

(a) Notwithstanding an assertion of sovereign immunity, sovereign immunity is abrogated as to a governmental unit to the extent set forth in this section with respect to the following:

(1) Sections 105, 106, 107, 108, 303, 346, 362, 363, 364, 365, 366, 502, 503, 505, 506, 510, 522, 523, 524, 525, 542, 543, 544, 545, 546, 547, 548, 549, 550, 551, 552, 553, 722, 724, 726, 744, 749, 764, 901, 922, 926, 928, 929, 944, 1107, 1141, 1142, 1143, 1146, 1201, 1203, 1205, 1206, 1227, 1231, 1301, 1303, 1305, and 1327 of this title.

(2) The court may hear and determine any issue arising with respect to the application of such sections to governmental units.

(3) The court may issue against a governmental unit an order, process, or judgment under such sections or the Federal Rules of Bankruptcy Procedure, including an order or judgment awarding a money

recovery, but not including an award of punitive damages. Such order or judgment for costs or fees under this title or the Federal Rules of Bankruptcy Procedure against any governmental unit shall be consistent with the provisions and limitations of section 2412(d)(2)(A) of title 28.

(4) The enforcement of any such order, process, or judgment against any governmental unit shall be consistent with appropriate nonbankruptcy law applicable to such governmental unit and, in the case of a money judgment against the United States, shall be paid as if it is a judgment rendered by a district court of the United States.

(5) Nothing in this section shall create any substantive claim for relief or cause of action not otherwise existing under this title, the Federal Rules of Bankruptcy Procedure, or nonbankruptcy law.

(b) A governmental unit that has filed a proof of claim in the case is deemed to have waived sovereign immunity with respect to a claim against such governmental unit that is property of the estate and that arose out of the same transaction or occurrence out of which the claim of such governmental unit arose.

(c) Notwithstanding any assertion of sovereign immunity by a governmental unit, there shall be offset against a claim or interest of a governmental unit any claim against such governmental unit that is property of the estate.

§ 107. Public Access to Papers

(a) Except as provided in subsections (b) and (c) and subject to section 112, a paper filed in a case under this title and the dockets of a bankruptcy court are public records and open to examination by an entity at reasonable times without charge.

(b) On request of a party in interest, the bankruptcy court shall, and on the bankruptcy court's own motion, the bankruptcy court may—

(1) protect an entity with respect to a trade secret or confidential research, development, or commercial information; or

(2) protect a person with respect to scandalous or defamatory matter contained in a paper filed in a case under this title.

(c)(1) The bankruptcy court, for cause, may protect an individual, with respect to the following types of information to the extent the court finds that disclosure of such information would create undue risk of identity theft or other unlawful injury to the individual or the individual's property:

(A) Any means of identification (as defined in section 1028(d) of title 18) contained in a paper filed, or to be filed, in a case under this title.

(B) Other information contained in a paper described in subparagraph (A).

(2) Upon ex parte application demonstrating cause, the court shall provide access to information protected pursuant to paragraph (1) to an entity acting pursuant to the police or regulatory power of a domestic governmental unit.

(3) The United States trustee, bankruptcy administrator, trustee, and any auditor serving under section 586(f) of title 28—

(A) shall have full access to all information contained in any paper filed or submitted in a case under this title; and

(B) shall not disclose information specifically protected by the court under this title.

§ 108. Extension of Time

(a) If applicable nonbankruptcy law, an order entered in a nonbankruptcy proceeding, or an agreement fixes a period within which the debtor may commence an action, and such period has not expired before the date of the filing of the petition, the trustee may commence such action only before the later of—

(1) the end of such period, including any suspension of such period occurring on or after the commencement of the case; or

(2) two years after the order for relief.

(b) Except as provided in subsection (a) of this section, if applicable nonbankruptcy law, an order entered in a nonbankruptcy proceeding, or an agreement fixes a period within which the debtor or an individual protected under section 1201 or 1301 of this title may file any pleading, demand, notice, or proof of claim or loss, cure a default, or perform any other similar act, and such period has not expired before the date of the filing of the petition, the trustee may only file, cure, or perform, as the case may be, before the later of—

(1) the end of such period, including any suspension of such period occurring on or after the commencement of the case; or

(2) 60 days after the order for relief.

(c) Except as provided in section 524 of this title, if applicable nonbankruptcy law, an order entered in a nonbankruptcy proceeding, or an agreement fixes a period for commencing or continuing a civil action in a court other than a bankruptcy court on a claim against the debtor, or against an individual with respect to which such individual is protected under section 1201 or 1301 of this title, and such period has not expired before the date of the filing of the petition, then such period does not expire until the later of—

(1) the end of such period, including any suspension of such period occurring on or after the commencement of the case; or

(2) 30 days after notice of the termination or expiration of the stay under section 362, 922, 1201, or 1301 of this title, as the case may be, with respect to such claim.

§ 109. Who May Be a Debtor

(a) Notwithstanding any other provision of this section, only a person that resides or has a domicile, a place of business, or property in the United States, or a municipality, may be a debtor under this title.

(b) A person may be a debtor under chapter 7 of this title only if such person is not—

(1) a railroad;

(2) a domestic insurance company, bank, savings bank, cooperative bank, savings and loan association, building and loan association, homestead association, a New Markets Venture Capital company as defined in section 351 of the Small Business Investment Act of 1958, a small business investment company licensed by the Small Business Administration under section 301 of the Small Business Investment Act of 1958, credit union, or industrial bank or similar institution which is an insured bank as defined in section 3(h) of the Federal Deposit Insurance Act, except that an uninsured State member bank, or a corporation organized under section 25A of the Federal Reserve Act, which operates, or operates as, a multilateral clearing organization pursuant to section 409 of the Federal Deposit Insurance Corporation Improvement Act of 1991 may be a debtor if a petition is filed at the direction of the Board of Governors of the Federal Reserve System; or

(3)(A) a foreign insurance company, engaged in such business in the United States; or

(B) a foreign bank, savings bank, cooperative bank, savings and loan association, building and loan association, or credit union, that has a branch or agency (as defined in section 1(b) of the International Banking Act of 1978) in the United States.

(c) An entity may be a debtor under chapter 9 of this title if and only if such entity—

(1) is a municipality;

(2) is specifically authorized, in its capacity as a municipality or by name, to be a debtor under such chapter by State law, or by a governmental officer or organization empowered by State law to authorize such entity to be a debtor under such chapter;

(3) is insolvent;

(4) desires to effect a plan to adjust such debts; and

(5)(A) has obtained the agreement of creditors holding at least a majority in amount of the claims of each class that such entity intends to impair under a plan in a case under such chapter;

(B) has negotiated in good faith with creditors and has failed to obtain the agreement of creditors holding at least a majority in amount of the claims of each class that such entity intends to impair under a plan in a case under such chapter;

(C) is unable to negotiate with creditors because such negotiation is impracticable; or

(D) reasonably believes that a creditor may attempt to obtain a transfer that is avoidable under section 547 of this title.

(d) Only a railroad, a person that may be a debtor under chapter 7 of this title (except a stockbroker or a commodity broker), and an uninsured State member bank, or a corporation organized under section 25A of the Federal Reserve Act, which operates, or operates as, a multilateral clearing organization pursuant to section 409 of the Federal Deposit Insurance Corporation Improvement Act of 1991 may be a debtor under chapter 11 of this title.

(e) Only an individual with regular income that owes, on the date of the filing of the petition, noncontingent, liquidated, unsecured debts of less than $526,700 and noncontingent, liquidated, secured debts of less than $1,580,125, or an individual with regular income and such individual's spouse, except a stockbroker or a commodity broker, that owe, on the date of the filing of the petition, noncontingent, liquidated, unsecured debts that aggregate less than $526,700 and noncontingent, liquidated, secured debts of less than $1,580,125 may be a debtor under chapter 13 of this title.

(f) Only a family farmer or family fisherman with regular annual income may be a debtor under chapter 12 of this title.

(g) Notwithstanding any other provision of this section, no individual or family farmer may be a debtor under this title who has been a debtor in a case pending under this title at any time in the preceding 180 days if—

(1) the case was dismissed by the court for willful failure of the debtor to abide by orders of the court, or to appear before the court in proper prosecution of the case; or

(2) the debtor requested and obtained the voluntary dismissal of the case following the filing of a request for relief from the automatic stay provided by section 362 of this title.

(h)(1) Subject to paragraphs (2) and (3), and notwithstanding any other provision of this section other than paragraph (4) of this subsection, an individual may not be a debtor under this title unless such individual has, during the 180-day period ending on the date of filing of the petition by such individual, received from an approved nonprofit budget and credit counseling agency described in section 111(a) an individual or group briefing (including a briefing conducted by telephone or on the Internet) that outlined the opportunities for available credit counseling and assisted such individual in performing a related budget analysis.

(2)(A) Paragraph (1) shall not apply with respect to a debtor who resides in a district (for which the United States trustee or the bankruptcy administrator, if any) determines that the approved nonprofit budget and credit counseling agencies for such district are not reasonably able to provide adequate services to the additional individuals who would otherwise seek credit counseling from such agencies by reason of the requirements of paragraph (1).

(B) The United States trustee (or the bankruptcy administrator, if any) who makes a determination described in subparagraph (A) shall review such determination not later than 1 year after the date of such determination, and not less frequently than annually thereafter. Notwithstanding the preceding sentence, a nonprofit budget and credit counseling agency may be disapproved by the United States trustee (or the bankruptcy administrator, if any) at any time.

(3)(A) Subject to subparagraph (B), the requirements of paragraph (1) shall not apply with respect to a debtor who submits to the court a certification that—

(i) describes exigent circumstances that merit a waiver of the requirements of paragraph (1);

(ii) states that the debtor requested credit counseling services from an approved nonprofit budget and credit counseling agency, but was unable to obtain the services referred to in paragraph (1) during the 7-day period beginning on the date on which the debtor made that request; and

(iii) is satisfactory to the court.

(B) With respect to a debtor, an exemption under subparagraph (A) shall cease to apply to that debtor on the date on which the debtor meets the requirements of paragraph (1), but in no case may the exemption apply to that debtor after the date that is 30 days after the debtor files a petition, except that the court, for cause, may order an additional 15 days.

(4) The requirements of paragraph (1) shall not apply with respect to a debtor whom the court determines, after notice and hearing, is unable to complete those requirements because of incapacity, disability, or active military duty in a military combat zone. For the purposes of this paragraph, incapacity means that the debtor is impaired by reason of mental illness or mental deficiency so that he is incapable of realizing and making rational decisions with respect to his financial responsibilities; and "disability" means that the debtor is so physically impaired as to be unable, after reasonable effort, to participate in an in person, telephone, or Internet briefing required under paragraph (1).

§ 110. Penalty for Persons Who Negligently or Fraudulently Prepare Bankruptcy Petitions

(a) In this section—

(1) "bankruptcy petition preparer" means a person, other than an attorney for the debtor or an employee of such attorney under the direct supervision of such attorney, who prepares for compensation a document for filing; and

(2) "document for filing" means a petition or any other document prepared for filing by a debtor in a United States bankruptcy court or a United States district court in connection with a case under this title.

(b)(1) A bankruptcy petition preparer who prepares a document for filing shall sign the document and print on the document the preparer's name and address. If a bankruptcy petition preparer is not an individual, then an officer, principal, responsible person, or partner of the bankruptcy petition preparer shall be required to—

(A) sign the document for filing; and

(B) print on the document the name and address of that officer, principal, responsible person, or partner.

(2)(A) Before preparing any document for filing or accepting any fees from or on behalf of a debtor, the bankruptcy petition preparer shall provide to the debtor a written notice which shall be on an official form prescribed by the Judicial Conference of the United States in accordance with rule 9009 of the Federal Rules of Bankruptcy Procedure.

(B) The notice under subparagraph (A)—

(i) shall inform the debtor in simple language that a bankruptcy petition preparer is not an attorney and may not practice law or give legal advice;

(ii) may contain a description of examples of legal advice that a bankruptcy petition preparer is not authorized to give, in addition to any advice that the preparer may not give by reason of subsection (e)(2); and

(iii) shall—

(I) be signed by the debtor and, under penalty of perjury, by the bankruptcy petition preparer; and

(II) be filed with any document for filing.

(c)(1) A bankruptcy petition preparer who prepares a document for filing shall place on the document, after the preparer's signature, an identifying number that identifies individuals who prepared the document.

(2)(A) Subject to subparagraph (B), for purposes of this section, the identifying number of a bankruptcy petition preparer shall be the Social Security account number of each individual who prepared the document or assisted in its preparation.

(B) If a bankruptcy petition preparer is not an individual, the identifying number of the bankruptcy petition preparer shall be the Social Security account number of the officer, principal, responsible person, or partner of the bankruptcy petition preparer.

(d) A bankruptcy petition preparer shall, not later than the time at which a document for filing is presented for the debtor's signature, furnish to the debtor a copy of the document.

(e)(1) A bankruptcy petition preparer shall not execute any document on behalf of a debtor.

(2)(A) A bankruptcy petition preparer may not offer a potential bankruptcy debtor any legal advice, including any legal advice described in subparagraph (B).

(B) The legal advice referred to in subparagraph (A) includes advising the debtor—

(i) whether—

(I) to file a petition under this title; or

(II) commencing a case under chapter 7, 11, 12, or 13 is appropriate;

(ii) whether the debtor's debts will be discharged in a case under this title;

(iii) whether the debtor will be able to retain the debtor's home, car, or other property after commencing a case under this title;

(iv) concerning—

(I) the tax consequences of a case brought under this title; or

(II) the dischargeability of tax claims;

(v) whether the debtor may or should promise to repay debts to a creditor or enter into a reaffirmation agreement with a creditor to reaffirm a debt;

(vi) concerning how to characterize the nature of the debtor's interests in property or the debtor's debts; or

(vii) concerning bankruptcy procedures and rights.

(f) A bankruptcy petition preparer shall not use the word "legal" or any similar term in any advertisements, or advertise under any category that includes the word "legal" or any similar term.

(g) A bankruptcy petition preparer shall not collect or receive any payment from the debtor or on behalf of the debtor for the court fees in connection with filing the petition.

(h)(1) The Supreme Court may promulgate rules under section 2075 of title 28, or the Judicial Conference of the United States may prescribe guidelines, for setting a maximum allowable fee chargeable by a bankruptcy petition preparer. A bankruptcy petition preparer shall notify the debtor of any such maximum amount before preparing any document for filing for the debtor or accepting any fee from or on behalf of the debtor.

(2) A declaration under penalty of perjury by the bankruptcy petition preparer shall be filed together with the petition, disclosing any fee received from or on behalf of the debtor within 12 months immediately prior to the filing of the case, and any unpaid fee charged to the debtor. If rules or guidelines setting a maximum fee for services have been promulgated or prescribed under paragraph (1), the declaration under this paragraph shall include a certification that the bankruptcy petition preparer complied with the notification requirement under paragraph (1).

(3)(A) The court shall disallow and order the immediate turnover to the bankruptcy trustee any fee referred to in paragraph (2)—

(i) found to be in excess of the value of any services rendered by the bankruptcy petition preparer during the 12-month period immediately preceding the date of the filing of the petition; or

(ii) found to be in violation of any rule or guideline promulgated or prescribed under paragraph (1).

(B) All fees charged by a bankruptcy petition preparer may be forfeited in any case in which the bankruptcy petition preparer fails to comply with this subsection or subsection (b), (c), (d), (e), (f), or (g).

(C) An individual may exempt any funds recovered under this paragraph under section 522(b).

(4) The debtor, the trustee, a creditor, the United States trustee (or the bankruptcy administrator, if any) or the court, on the initiative of the court, may file a motion for an order under paragraph (3).

(5) A bankruptcy petition preparer shall be fined not more than $500 for each failure to comply with a court order to turn over funds within 30 days of service of such order.

(i)(1) If a bankruptcy petition preparer violates this section or commits any act that the court finds to be fraudulent, unfair, or deceptive, on the motion of the debtor, trustee, United States trustee (or the bankruptcy administrator, if any), and after notice and a hearing, the court shall order the bankruptcy petition preparer to pay to the debtor—

(A) the debtor's actual damages;

(B) the greater of—

(i) $2,000; or

(ii) twice the amount paid by the debtor to the bankruptcy petition preparer for the preparer's services; and

(C) reasonable attorneys' fees and costs in moving for damages under this subsection.

(2) If the trustee or creditor moves for damages on behalf of the debtor under this subsection, the bankruptcy petition preparer shall be ordered to pay the movant the additional amount of $1,000 plus reasonable attorneys' fees and costs incurred.

(j)(1) A debtor for whom a bankruptcy petition preparer has prepared a document for filing, the trustee, a creditor, or the United States trustee in the district in which the bankruptcy petition preparer resides, has conducted business, or the United States trustee in any other district in which the debtor resides may bring a civil action to enjoin a bankruptcy petition preparer from engaging in any conduct in violation of this section or from further acting as a bankruptcy petition preparer.

(2)(A) In an action under paragraph (1), if the court finds that—

(i) a bankruptcy petition preparer has—

(I) engaged in conduct in violation of this section or of any provision of this title;

(II) misrepresented the preparer's experience or education as a bankruptcy petition preparer; or

(III) engaged in any other fraudulent, unfair, or deceptive conduct; and

(ii) injunctive relief is appropriate to prevent the recurrence of such conduct,

the court may enjoin the bankruptcy petition preparer from engaging in such conduct.

(B) If the court finds that a bankruptcy petition preparer has continually engaged in conduct described in subclause (I), (II), or (III) of clause (i) and that an injunction prohibiting such conduct would not be sufficient to prevent such person's interference with the proper administration of this title, has not paid a penalty imposed under this section, or failed to disgorge all fees ordered by the court, the court may enjoin the person from acting as a bankruptcy petition preparer.

(3) The court, as part of its contempt power, may enjoin a bankruptcy petition preparer that has failed to comply with a previous order issued under this section. The injunction under this paragraph may be issued on the motion of the court, the trustee, or the United States trustee (or the bankruptcy administrator, if any).

(4) The court shall award to a debtor, trustee, or creditor that brings a successful action under this subsection reasonable attorneys' fees and costs of the action, to be paid by the bankruptcy petition preparer.

(k) Nothing in this section shall be construed to permit activities that are otherwise prohibited by law, including rules and laws that prohibit the unauthorized practice of law.

(l)(1) A bankruptcy petition preparer who fails to comply with any provision of subsection (b), (c), (d), (e), (f), (g), or (h) may be fined not more than $500 for each such failure.

(2) The court shall triple the amount of a fine assessed under paragraph (1) in any case in which the court finds that a bankruptcy petition preparer—

(A) advised the debtor to exclude assets or income that should have been included on applicable schedules;

(B) advised the debtor to use a false Social Security account number;

(C) failed to inform the debtor that the debtor was filing for relief under this title; or

(D) prepared a document for filing in a manner that failed to disclose the identity of the bankruptcy petition preparer.

(3) A debtor, trustee, creditor, or United States trustee (or the bankruptcy administrator, if any) may file a motion for an order imposing a fine on the bankruptcy petition preparer for any violation of this section.

(4)(A) Fines imposed under this subsection in judicial districts served by United States trustees shall be paid to the United States trustees, who shall deposit an amount equal to such fines in the United States Trustee Fund.

(B) Fines imposed under this subsection in judicial districts served by bankruptcy administrators shall be deposited as offsetting receipts to the fund established under section 1931 of title 28, and shall remain available until expended to reimburse any appropriation for the amount paid out of such appropriation for expenses of the operation and maintenance of the courts of the United States.

§ 111. Nonprofit Budget and Credit Counseling Agencies; Financial Management Instructional Courses

(a) The clerk shall maintain a publicly available list of—

(1) nonprofit budget and credit counseling agencies that provide 1 or more services described in section 109(h) currently approved by the United States trustee (or the bankruptcy administrator, if any); and

(2) instructional courses concerning personal financial management currently approved by the United States trustee (or the bankruptcy administrator, if any), as applicable.

(b) The United States trustee (or bankruptcy administrator, if any) shall only approve a nonprofit budget and credit counseling agency or an instructional course concerning personal financial management as follows:

(1) The United States trustee (or bankruptcy administrator, if any) shall have thoroughly reviewed the qualifications of the nonprofit budget and credit counseling agency or of the provider of the instructional course under the standards set forth in this section, and the services or instructional courses that will be offered by such agency or such provider, and may require such agency or such provider that has sought approval to provide information with respect to such review.

(2) The United States trustee (or bankruptcy administrator, if any) shall have determined that such agency or such instructional course fully satisfies the applicable standards set forth in this section.

(3) If a nonprofit budget and credit counseling agency or instructional course did not appear on the approved list for the district under subsection (a) immediately before approval under this section, approval under this subsection of such agency or such instructional course shall be for a probationary period not to exceed 6 months.

(4) At the conclusion of the applicable probationary period under paragraph (3), the United States trustee (or bankruptcy administrator, if any) may only approve for an additional 1-year period, and for successive 1-year periods thereafter, an agency or instructional course that has demonstrated during the probationary or applicable subsequent period of approval that such agency or instructional course—

(A) has met the standards set forth under this section during such period; and

(B) can satisfy such standards in the future.

(5) Not later than 30 days after any final decision under paragraph (4), an interested person may seek judicial review of such decision in the appropriate district court of the United States.

(c)(1) The United States trustee (or the bankruptcy administrator, if any) shall only approve a nonprofit budget and credit counseling agency that demonstrates that it will provide qualified counselors, maintain adequate provision for safekeeping and payment of client funds, provide adequate counseling with respect to client credit problems, and deal responsibly and effectively with other matters relating to the quality, effectiveness, and financial security of the services it provides.

(2) To be approved by the United States trustee (or the bankruptcy administrator, if any), a nonprofit budget and credit counseling agency shall, at a minimum—

(A) have a board of directors the majority of which—

(i) are not employed by such agency; and

(ii) will not directly or indirectly benefit financially from the outcome of the counseling services provided by such agency;

(B) if a fee is charged for counseling services, charge a reasonable fee, and provide services without regard to ability to pay the fee;

(C) provide for safekeeping and payment of client funds, including an annual audit of the trust accounts and appropriate employee bonding;

(D) provide full disclosures to a client, including funding sources, counselor qualifications, possible impact on credit reports, and any costs of such program that will be paid by such client and how such costs will be paid;

(E) provide adequate counseling with respect to a client's credit problems that includes an analysis of such client's current financial condition, factors that caused such financial condition, and how such client can develop a plan to respond to the problems without incurring negative amortization of debt;

(F) provide trained counselors who receive no commissions or bonuses based on the outcome of the counseling services provided by such agency, and who have adequate experience, and have been adequately trained to provide counseling services to individuals in financial difficulty, including the matters described in subparagraph (E);

(G) demonstrate adequate experience and background in providing credit counseling; and

(H) have adequate financial resources to provide continuing support services for budgeting plans over the life of any repayment plan.

(d) The United States trustee (or the bankruptcy administrator, if any) shall only approve an instructional course concerning personal financial management—

(1) for an initial probationary period under subsection (b)(3) if the course will provide at a minimum—

(A) trained personnel with adequate experience and training in providing effective instruction and services;

(B) learning materials and teaching methodologies designed to assist debtors in understanding personal financial management and that are consistent with stated objectives directly related to the goals of such instructional course;

(C) adequate facilities situated in reasonably convenient locations at which such instructional course is offered, except that such facilities may include the provision of such instructional course by telephone or through the Internet, if such instructional course is effective;

(D) the preparation and retention of reasonable records (which shall include the debtor's bankruptcy case number) to permit evaluation of the effectiveness of such instructional course, including any evaluation of satisfaction of instructional course requirements for each debtor attending such instructional course, which shall be available for inspection and evaluation by the Executive Office for United States Trustees, the United States trustee (or the bankruptcy administrator, if any), or the chief bankruptcy judge for the district in which such instructional course is offered; and

(E) if a fee is charged for the instructional course, charge a reasonable fee, and provide services without regard to ability to pay the fee; and

(2) for any 1-year period if the provider thereof has demonstrated that the course meets the standards of paragraph (1) and, in addition—

(A) has been effective in assisting a substantial number of debtors to understand personal financial management; and

(B) is otherwise likely to increase substantially the debtor's understanding of personal financial management.

(e) The district court may, at any time, investigate the qualifications of a nonprofit budget and credit counseling agency referred to in subsection (a), and request production of documents to ensure the integrity and effectiveness of such agency. The district court may, at any time, remove from the approved list under subsection (a) a nonprofit budget and credit counseling agency upon finding such agency does not meet the qualifications of subsection (b).

(f) The United States trustee (or the bankruptcy administrator, if any) shall notify the clerk that a nonprofit budget and credit counseling agency or an instructional course is no longer approved, in which case the clerk shall remove it from the list maintained under subsection (a).

(g)(1) No nonprofit budget and credit counseling agency may provide to a credit reporting agency information concerning whether a debtor has received or sought instruction concerning personal financial management from such agency.

(2) A nonprofit budget and credit counseling agency that willfully or negligently fails to comply with any requirement under this title with respect to a debtor shall be liable for damages in an amount equal to the sum of—

(A) any actual damages sustained by the debtor as a result of the violation; and

(B) any court costs or reasonable attorneys' fees (as determined by the court) incurred in an action to recover those damages.

§ 112. Prohibition on Disclosure of Name of Minor Children

The debtor may be required to provide information regarding a minor child involved in matters under this title but may not be required to disclose in the public records in the case the name of such minor child. The debtor may be required to disclose the name of such minor child in a nonpublic record that is maintained by the court and made available by the court for examination by the United States trustee, the trustee, and the auditor (if any) serving under section 586(f) of title 28, in the case. The court, the United States trustee, the trustee, and such auditor shall not disclose the name of such minor child maintained in such nonpublic record.

CHAPTER 3—CASE ADMINISTRATION

SUBCHAPTER I—COMMENCEMENT OF A CASE

SUBCHAPTER II—OFFICERS

SUBCHAPTER III—ADMINISTRATION

SUBCHAPTER IV—ADMINISTRATIVE POWERS

SUBCHAPTER I—COMMENCEMENT OF A CASE

§ 301. Voluntary Cases

(a) A voluntary case under a chapter of this title is commenced by the filing with the bankruptcy court of a petition under such chapter by an entity that may be a debtor under such chapter.

(b) The commencement of a voluntary case under a chapter of this title constitutes an order for relief under such chapter.

§ 302. Joint Cases

(a) A joint case under a chapter of this title is commenced by the filing with the bankruptcy court of a single petition under such chapter by an individual that may be a debtor under such chapter and such individual's spouse. The commencement of a joint case under a chapter of this title constitutes an order for relief under such chapter.

(b) After the commencement of a joint case, the court shall determine the extent, if any, to which the debtors' estates shall be consolidated.

§ 303. Involuntary Cases

(a) An involuntary case may be commenced only under chapter 7 or 11 of this title, and only against a person, except a farmer, family farmer, or a corporation that is not a moneyed, business, or commercial corporation, that may be a debtor under the chapter under which such case is commenced.

(b) An involuntary case against a person is commenced by the filing with the bankruptcy court of a petition under chapter 7 or 11 of this title—

(1) by three or more entities, each of which is either a holder of a claim against such person that is not contingent as to liability or the subject of a bona fide dispute as to liability or amount, or an indenture trustee representing such a holder, if such noncontingent, undisputed claims aggregate at least

$21,050 more than the value of any lien on property of the debtor securing such claims held by the holders of such claims;

(2) if there are fewer than 12 such holders, excluding any employee or insider of such person and any transferee of a transfer that is voidable under section 544, 545, 547, 548, 549, or 724(a) of this title, by one or more of such holders that hold in the aggregate at least $21,050 of such claims;

(3) if such person is a partnership—

(A) by fewer than all of the general partners in such partnership; or

(B) if relief has been ordered under this title with respect to all of the general partners in such partnership, by a general partner in such partnership, the trustee of such a general partner, or a holder of a claim against such partnership; or

(4) by a foreign representative of the estate in a foreign proceeding concerning such person.

(c) After the filing of a petition under this section but before the case is dismissed or relief is ordered, a creditor holding an unsecured claim that is not contingent, other than a creditor filing under subsection (b) of this section, may join in the petition with the same effect as if such joining creditor were a petitioning creditor under subsection (b) of this section.

(d) The debtor, or a general partner in a partnership debtor that did not join in the petition, may file an answer to a petition under this section.

(e) After notice and a hearing, and for cause, the court may require the petitioners under this section to file a bond to indemnify the debtor for such amounts as the court may later allow under subsection (i) of this section.

(f) Notwithstanding section 363 of this title, except to the extent that the court orders otherwise, and until an order for relief in the case, any business of the debtor may continue to operate, and the debtor may continue to use, acquire, or dispose of property as if an involuntary case concerning the debtor had not been commenced.

(g) At any time after the commencement of an involuntary case under chapter 7 of this title but before an order for relief in the case, the court, on request of a party in interest, after notice to the debtor and a hearing, and if necessary to preserve the property of the estate or to prevent loss to the estate, may order the United States trustee to appoint an interim trustee under section 701 of this title to take possession of the property of the estate and to operate any business of the debtor. Before an order for relief, the debtor may regain possession of property in the possession of a trustee ordered appointed under this subsection if the debtor files such bond as the court requires, conditioned on the debtor's accounting for and delivering to the trustee, if there is an order for relief in the case, such property, or the value, as of the date the debtor regains possession, of such property.

(h) If the petition is not timely controverted, the court shall order relief against the debtor in an involuntary case under the chapter under which the petition was filed. Otherwise, after trial, the court shall order relief against the debtor in an involuntary case under the chapter under which the petition was filed, only if—

(1) the debtor is generally not paying such debtor's debts as such debts become due unless such debts are the subject of a bona fide dispute as to liability or amount; or

(2) within 120 days before the date of the filing of the petition, a custodian, other than a trustee, receiver, or agent appointed or authorized to take charge of less than substantially all of the property of the debtor for the purpose of enforcing a lien against such property, was appointed or took possession.

(i) If the court dismisses a petition under this section other than on consent of all petitioners and the debtor, and if the debtor does not waive the right to judgment under this subsection, the court may grant judgment—

(1) against the petitioners and in favor of the debtor for—

(A) costs; or

(B) a reasonable attorney's fee; or

(2) against any petitioner that filed the petition in bad faith, for—

(A) any damages proximately caused by such filing; or

(B) punitive damages.

(j) Only after notice to all creditors and a hearing may the court dismiss a petition filed under this section—

(1) on the motion of a petitioner;

(2) on consent of all petitioners and the debtor; or

(3) for want of prosecution.

(k)(1) If—

(A) the petition under this section is false or contains any materially false, fictitious, or fraudulent statement;

(B) the debtor is an individual; and

(C) the court dismisses such petition, the court, upon the motion of the debtor, shall seal all the records of the court relating to such petition, and all references to such petition.

(2) If the debtor is an individual and the court dismisses a petition under this section, the court may enter an order prohibiting all consumer reporting agencies (as defined in section 603(f) of the Fair Credit Reporting Act (15 U.S.C. 1681a(f)) from making any consumer report (as defined in section 603(d) of that Act) that contains any information relating to such petition or to the case commenced by the filing of such petition.

(3) Upon the expiration of the statute of limitations described in section 3282 of title 18, for a violation of section 152 or 157 of such title, the court, upon the motion of the debtor and for good cause, may expunge any records relating to a petition filed under this section.

§ 305. Abstention

(a) The court, after notice and a hearing, may dismiss a case under this title, or may suspend all proceedings in a case under this title, at any time if—

(1) the interests of creditors and the debtor would be better served by such dismissal or suspension; or

(2)(A) a petition under section 1515 for recognition of a foreign proceeding has been granted; and

(B) the purposes of chapter 15 of this title would be best served by such dismissal or suspension.

(b) A foreign representative may seek dismissal or suspension under subsection (a)(2) of this section.

(c) An order under subsection (a) of this section dismissing a case or suspending all proceedings in a case, or a decision not so to dismiss or suspend, is not reviewable by appeal or otherwise by the court of appeals under section 158(d), 1291, or 1292 of title 28 or by the Supreme Court of the United States under section 1254 of title 28.

§ 306. Limited Appearance

An appearance in a bankruptcy court by a foreign representative in connection with a petition or request under section 303 or 305 of this title does not submit such foreign representative to the jurisdiction of any court in the United States for any other purpose, but the bankruptcy court may condition any order under section 303 or 305 of this title on compliance by such foreign representative with the orders of such bankruptcy court.

§ 307. United States Trustee

The United States trustee may raise and may appear and be heard on any issue in any case or proceeding under this title but may not file a plan pursuant to section 1121(c) of this title.

§ 308. Debtor Reporting Requirements

(a) For purposes of this section, the term "profitability" means, with respect to a debtor, the amount of money that the debtor has earned or lost during current and recent fiscal periods.

(b) A debtor in a small business case shall file periodic financial and other reports containing information including—

(1) the debtor's profitability;

(2) reasonable approximations of the debtor's projected cash receipts and cash disbursements over a reasonable period;

(3) comparisons of actual cash receipts and disbursements with projections in prior reports;

(4) whether the debtor is—

(A) in compliance in all material respects with postpetition requirements imposed by this title and the Federal Rules of Bankruptcy Procedure; and

(B) timely filing tax returns and other required government filings and paying taxes and other administrative expenses when due;

(5) if the debtor is not in compliance with the requirements referred to in paragraph (4)(A) or filing tax returns and other required government filings and making the payments referred to in paragraph (4)(B), what the failures are and how, at what cost, and when the debtor intends to remedy such failures; and

(6) such other matters as are in the best interests of the debtor and creditors, and in the public interest in fair and efficient procedures under chapter 11 of this title.

SUBCHAPTER II—OFFICERS

§ 321. Eligibility to Serve as Trustee

(a) A person may serve as trustee in a case under this title only if such person is—

(1) an individual that is competent to perform the duties of trustee and, in a case under chapter 7, 12, or 13 of this title, resides or has an office in the judicial district within which the case is pending, or in any judicial district adjacent to such district; or

(2) a corporation authorized by such corporation's charter or bylaws to act as trustee, and, in a case under chapter 7, 12, or 13 of this title, having an office in at least one of such districts.

(b) A person that has served as an examiner in the case may not serve as trustee in the case.

(c) The United States trustee for the judicial district in which the case is pending is eligible to serve as trustee in the case if necessary.

§ 322. Qualification of Trustee

(a) Except as provided in subsection (b)(1), a person selected under section 701, 702, 703, 1104, 1163, 1183, 1202, or 1302 of this title to serve as trustee in a case under this title qualifies if before seven days after such selection, and before beginning official duties, such person has filed with the court a bond in favor of the United States conditioned on the faithful performance of such official duties.

(b)(1) The United States trustee qualifies wherever such trustee serves as trustee in a case under this title.

(2) The United States trustee shall determine—

(A) the amount of a bond required to be filed under subsection (a) of this section; and

(B) the sufficiency of the surety on such bond.

(c) A trustee is not liable personally or on such trustee's bond in favor of the United States for any penalty or forfeiture incurred by the debtor.

(d) A proceeding on a trustee's bond may not be commenced after two years after the date on which such trustee was discharged.

§ 323. Role and Capacity of Trustee

(a) The trustee in a case under this title is the representative of the estate.

(b) The trustee in a case under this title has capacity to sue and be sued.

§ 324. Removal of Trustee or Examiner

(a) The court, after notice and a hearing, may remove a trustee, other than the United States trustee, or an examiner, for cause.

(b) Whenever the court removes a trustee or examiner under subsection (a) in a case under this title, such trustee or examiner shall thereby be removed in all other cases under this title in which such trustee or examiner is then serving unless the court orders otherwise.

§ 325. Effect of Vacancy

A vacancy in the office of trustee during a case does not abate any pending action or proceeding, and the successor trustee shall be substituted as a party in such action or proceeding.

§ 326. Limitation on Compensation of Trustee

(a) In a case under chapter 7 or 11, other than a case under subchapter V of chapter 11, the court may allow reasonable compensation under section 330 of this title of the trustee for the trustee's services, payable after the trustee renders such services, not to exceed 25 percent on the first $5,000 or less, 10 percent on any amount in excess of $5,000 but not in excess of $50,000, 5 percent on any amount in excess of $50,000 but not in excess of $1,000,000, and reasonable compensation not to exceed 3 percent of such moneys in excess of $1,000,000, upon all moneys disbursed or turned over in the case by the trustee to parties in interest, excluding the debtor, but including holders of secured claims.

(b) In a case under subchapter V of chapter 11 or chapter 12 or 13 of this title, the court may not allow compensation for services or reimbursement of expenses of the United States trustee or of a standing trustee appointed under section 586(b) of title 28, but may allow reasonable compensation under section 330 of this title of a trustee appointed under section 1202(a) or 1302(a) of this title for the trustee's services, payable after the trustee renders such services, not to exceed five percent upon all payments under the plan.

(c) If more than one person serves as trustee in the case, the aggregate compensation of such persons for such service may not exceed the maximum compensation prescribed for a single trustee by subsection (a) or (b) of this section, as the case may be.

(d) The court may deny allowance of compensation for services or reimbursement of expenses of the trustee if the trustee failed to make diligent inquiry into facts that would permit denial of allowance under section 328(c) of this title or, with knowledge of such facts, employed a professional person under section 327 of this title.

§ 327. Employment of Professional Persons

(a) Except as otherwise provided in this section, the trustee, with the court's approval, may employ one or more attorneys, accountants, appraisers, auctioneers, or other professional persons, that do not hold or represent an interest adverse to the estate, and that are disinterested persons, to represent or assist the trustee in carrying out the trustee's duties under this title.

(b) If the trustee is authorized to operate the business of the debtor under section 721, 1202, or 1108 of this title, and if the debtor has regularly employed attorneys, accountants, or other professional persons on salary, the trustee may retain or replace such professional persons if necessary in the operation of such business.

(c) In a case under chapter 7, 12, or 11 of this title, a person is not disqualified for employment under this section solely because of such person's employment by or representation of a creditor, unless there is objection by another creditor or the United States trustee, in which case the court shall disapprove such employment if there is an actual conflict of interest.

(d) The court may authorize the trustee to act as attorney or accountant for the estate if such authorization is in the best interest of the estate.

(e) The trustee, with the court's approval, may employ, for a specified special purpose, other than to represent the trustee in conducting the case, an attorney that has represented the debtor, if in the best interest of the estate, and if such attorney does not represent or hold any interest adverse to the debtor or to the estate with respect to the matter on which such attorney is to be employed.

(f) The trustee may not employ a person that has served as an examiner in the case.

§ 328. Limitation on Compensation of Professional Persons

(a) The trustee, or a committee appointed under section 1102 of this title, with the court's approval, may employ or authorize the employment of a professional person under section 327 or 1103 of this title, as the case may be, on any reasonable terms and conditions of employment, including on a retainer, on an hourly basis, on a fixed or percentage fee basis, or on a contingent fee basis. Notwithstanding such terms and conditions, the court may allow compensation different from the compensation provided under such terms and conditions after the conclusion of such employment, if such terms and conditions prove to have been improvident in light of developments not capable of being anticipated at the time of the fixing of such terms and conditions.

(b) If the court has authorized a trustee to serve as an attorney or accountant for the estate under section 327(d) of this title, the court may allow compensation for the trustee's services as such attorney or accountant only to the extent that the trustee performed services as attorney or accountant for the estate and not for performance of any of the trustee's duties that are generally performed by a trustee without the assistance of an attorney or accountant for the estate.

(c) Except as provided in section 327(c), 327(e), or 1107(b) of this title, the court may deny allowance of compensation for services and reimbursement of expenses of a professional person employed under section 327 or 1103 of this title if, at any time during such professional person's employment under section 327 or 1103 of this title, such professional person is not a disinterested person, or represents or holds an interest adverse to the interest of the estate with respect to the matter on which such professional person is employed.

§ 329. Debtor's Transactions with Attorneys

(a) Any attorney representing a debtor in a case under this title, or in connection with such a case, whether or not such attorney applies for compensation under this title, shall file with the court a statement of the compensation paid or agreed to be paid, if such payment or agreement was made after one year before the date of the filing of the petition, for services rendered or to be rendered in contemplation of or in connection with the case by such attorney, and the source of such compensation.

(b) If such compensation exceeds the reasonable value of any such services, the court may cancel any such agreement, or order the return of any such payment, to the extent excessive, to—

(1) the estate, if the property transferred—

(A) would have been property of the estate; or

(B) was to be paid by or on behalf of the debtor under a plan under chapter 11, 12, or 13 of this title; or

(2) the entity that made such payment.

§ 330. Compensation of Officers

(a)(1) After notice to the parties in interest and the United States Trustee and a hearing, and subject to sections 326, 328, and 329, the court may award to a trustee, a consumer privacy ombudsman appointed under section 332, an examiner, an ombudsman appointed under section 333, or a professional person employed under section 327 or 1103—

(A) reasonable compensation for actual, necessary services rendered by the trustee, examiner, ombudsman, professional person, or attorney and by any paraprofessional person employed by any such person; and

(B) reimbursement for actual, necessary expenses.

(2) The court may, on its own motion or on the motion of the United States Trustee, the United States Trustee for the District or Region, the trustee for the estate, or any other party in interest, award compensation that is less than the amount of compensation that is requested.

(3) In determining the amount of reasonable compensation to be awarded to an examiner, trustee under chapter 11, or professional person, the court shall consider the nature, the extent, and the value of such services, taking into account all relevant factors, including—

(A) the time spent on such services;

(B) the rates charged for such services;

(C) whether the services were necessary to the administration of, or beneficial at the time at which the service was rendered toward the completion of, a case under this title;

(D) whether the services were performed within a reasonable amount of time commensurate with the complexity, importance, and nature of the problem, issue, or task addressed;

(E) with respect to a professional person, whether the person is board certified or otherwise has demonstrated skill and experience in the bankruptcy field; and

(F) whether the compensation is reasonable based on the customary compensation charged by comparably skilled practitioners in cases other than cases under this title.

(4)(A) Except as provided in subparagraph (B), the court shall not allow compensation for—

(i) unnecessary duplication of services; or

(ii) services that were not—

(I) reasonably likely to benefit the debtor's estate; or

(II) necessary to the administration of the case.

(B) In a chapter 12 or chapter 13 case in which the debtor is an individual, the court may allow reasonable compensation to the debtor's attorney for representing the interests of the debtor in connection with the bankruptcy case based on a consideration of the benefit and necessity of such services to the debtor and the other factors set forth in this section.

(5) The court shall reduce the amount of compensation awarded under this section by the amount of any interim compensation awarded under section 331, and, if the amount of such interim compensation exceeds the amount of compensation awarded under this section, may order the return of the excess to the estate.

(6) Any compensation awarded for the preparation of a fee application shall be based on the level and skill reasonably required to prepare the application.

(7) In determining the amount of reasonable compensation to be awarded to a trustee, the court shall treat such compensation as a commission, based on section 326.

(b)(1) There shall be paid from the filing fee in a case under chapter 7 of this title $105 to the trustee serving in such case, after such trustee's services are rendered.

(2) The Judicial Conference of the United States—

(A) shall prescribe additional fees of the same kind as prescribed under section 1914(b) of title 28; and

(B) may prescribe notice of appearance fees and fees charged against distributions in cases under this title;

to pay $15 to trustees serving in cases after such trustees' services are rendered. Beginning 1 year after the date of the enactment of the Bankruptcy Reform Act of 1994, such $15 shall be paid in addition to the amount paid under paragraph (1).

(c) Unless the court orders otherwise, in a case under chapter 12 or 13 of this title the compensation paid to the trustee serving in the case shall not be less than $5 per month from any distribution under the plan during the administration of the plan.

(d) In a case in which the United States trustee serves as trustee, the compensation of the trustee under this section shall be paid to the clerk of the bankruptcy court and deposited by the clerk into the United States Trustee System Fund established by section 589a of title 28.

§ 331. Interim Compensation

A trustee, an examiner, a debtor's attorney, or any professional person employed under section 327 or 1103 of this title may apply to the court not more than once every 120 days after an order for relief in a case under this title, or more often if the court permits, for such compensation for services rendered before the date of such an application or reimbursement for expenses incurred before such date as is provided under section 330 of this title. After notice and a hearing, the court may allow and disburse to such applicant such compensation or reimbursement.

§ 332. Consumer Privacy Ombudsman

(a) If a hearing is required under section 363(b)(1)(B), the court shall order the United States trustee to appoint, not later than 7 days before the commencement of the hearing, 1 disinterested person (other than the United States trustee) to serve as the consumer privacy ombudsman in the case and shall require that notice of such hearing be timely given to such ombudsman.

(b) The consumer privacy ombudsman may appear and be heard at such hearing and shall provide to the court information to assist the court in its consideration of the facts, circumstances, and conditions of the proposed sale or lease of personally identifiable information under section 363(b)(1)(B). Such information may include presentation of—

(1) the debtor's privacy policy;

(2) the potential losses or gains of privacy to consumers if such sale or such lease is approved by the court;

(3) the potential costs or benefits to consumers if such sale or such lease is approved by the court; and

(4) the potential alternatives that would mitigate potential privacy losses or potential costs to consumers.

(c) A consumer privacy ombudsman shall not disclose any personally identifiable information obtained by the ombudsman under this title.

§ 333. Appointment of Patient Care Ombudsman

(a)(1) If the debtor in a case under chapter 7, 9, or 11 is a health care business, the court shall order, not later than 30 days after the commencement of the case, the appointment of an ombudsman to monitor the quality of patient care and to represent the interests of the patients of the health care business unless the court finds that the appointment of such ombudsman is not necessary for the protection of patients under the specific facts of the case.

(2)(A) If the court orders the appointment of an ombudsman under paragraph (1), the United States trustee shall appoint 1 disinterested person (other than the United States trustee) to serve as such ombudsman.

(B) If the debtor is a health care business that provides long-term care, then the United States trustee may appoint the State Long-Term Care Ombudsman appointed under the Older Americans Act of 1965 for the State in which the case is pending to serve as the ombudsman required by paragraph (1).

(C) If the United States trustee does not appoint a State Long-Term Care Ombudsman under subparagraph (B), the court shall notify the State Long-Term Care Ombudsman appointed under the Older Americans Act of 1965 for the State in which the case is pending, of the name and address of the person who is appointed under subparagraph (A).

(b) An ombudsman appointed under subsection (a) shall—

(1) monitor the quality of patient care provided to patients of the debtor, to the extent necessary under the circumstances, including interviewing patients and physicians;

(2) not later than 60 days after the date of appointment, and not less frequently than at 60-day intervals thereafter, report to the court after notice to the parties in interest, at a hearing or in writing, regarding the quality of patient care provided to patients of the debtor; and

(3) if such ombudsman determines that the quality of patient care provided to patients of the debtor is declining significantly or is otherwise being materially compromised, file with the court a motion or a written report, with notice to the parties in interest immediately upon making such determination.

(c)(1) An ombudsman appointed under subsection (a) shall maintain any information obtained by such ombudsman under this section that relates to patients (including information relating to patient records) as confidential information. Such ombudsman may not review confidential patient records unless the court approves such review in advance and imposes restrictions on such ombudsman to protect the confidentiality of such records.

(2) An ombudsman appointed under subsection (a)(2)(B) shall have access to patient records consistent with authority of such ombudsman under the Older Americans Act of 1965 and under non-Federal laws governing the State Long-Term Care Ombudsman program.

SUBCHAPTER III—ADMINISTRATION

§ 341. Meetings of Creditors and Equity Security Holders

(a) Within a reasonable time after the order for relief in a case under this title, the United States trustee shall convene and preside at a meeting of creditors.

(b) The United States trustee may convene a meeting of any equity security holders.

(c) The court may not preside at, and may not attend, any meeting under this section including any final meeting of creditors. Notwithstanding any local court rule, provision of a State constitution, any otherwise applicable nonbankruptcy law, or any other requirement that representation at the meeting of creditors under subsection (a) be by an attorney, a creditor holding a consumer debt or any representative of the creditor (which may include an entity or an employee of an entity and may be a representative for more than 1 creditor) shall be permitted to appear at and participate in the meeting of creditors in a case under chapter 7 or 13, either alone or in conjunction with an attorney for the creditor. Nothing in this subsection shall be construed to require any creditor to be represented by an attorney at any meeting of creditors.

(d) Prior to the conclusion of the meeting of creditors or equity security holders, the trustee shall orally examine the debtor to ensure that the debtor in a case under chapter 7 of this title is aware of—

(1) the potential consequences of seeking a discharge in bankruptcy, including the effects on credit history;

(2) the debtor's ability to file a petition under a different chapter of this title;

(3) the effect of receiving a discharge of debts under this title; and

(4) the effect of reaffirming a debt, including the debtor's knowledge of the provisions of section 524(d) of this title.

(e) Notwithstanding subsections (a) and (b), the court, on the request of a party in interest and after notice and a hearing, for cause may order that the United States trustee not convene a meeting of creditors or equity security holders if the debtor has filed a plan as to which the debtor solicited acceptances prior to the commencement of the case.

§ 342. Notice

(a) There shall be given such notice as is appropriate, including notice to any holder of a community claim, of an order for relief in a case under this title.

(b) Before the commencement of a case under this title by an individual whose debts are primarily consumer debts, the clerk shall give to such individual written notice containing—

(1) a brief description of—

(A) chapters 7, 11, 12, and 13 and the general purpose, benefits, and costs of proceeding under each of those chapters; and

(B) the types of services available from credit counseling agencies; and

(2) statements specifying that—

(A) a person who knowingly and fraudulently conceals assets or makes a false oath or statement under penalty of perjury in connection with a case under this title shall be subject to fine, imprisonment, or both; and

(B) all information supplied by a debtor in connection with a case under this title is subject to examination by the Attorney General.

(c)(1) If notice is required to be given by the debtor to a creditor under this title, any rule, any applicable law, or any order of the court, such notice shall contain the name, address, and last 4 digits of the taxpayer identification number of the debtor. If the notice concerns an amendment that adds a creditor to the schedules of assets and liabilities, the debtor shall include the full taxpayer identification number in the notice sent to that creditor, but the debtor shall include only the last 4 digits of the taxpayer identification number in the copy of the notice filed with the court.

(2)(A) If, within the 90 days before the commencement of a voluntary case, a creditor supplies the debtor in at least 2 communications sent to the debtor with the current account number of the debtor and the address at which such creditor requests to receive correspondence, then any notice required by this title to be sent by the debtor to such creditor shall be sent to such address and shall include such account number.

(B) If a creditor would be in violation of applicable nonbankruptcy law by sending any such communication within such 90-day period and if such creditor supplies the debtor in the last 2 communications with the current account number of the debtor and the address at which such creditor requests to receive correspondence, then any notice required by this title to be sent by the debtor to such creditor shall be sent to such address and shall include such account number.

(d) In a case under chapter 7 of this title in which the debtor is an individual and in which the presumption of abuse arises under section 707(b), the clerk shall give written notice to all creditors not later than 10 days after the date of the filing of the petition that the presumption of abuse has arisen.

(e)(1) In a case under chapter 7 or 13 of this title of a debtor who is an individual, a creditor at any time may both file with the court and serve on the debtor a notice of address to be used to provide notice in such case to such creditor.

(2) Any notice in such case required to be provided to such creditor by the debtor or the court later than 7 days after the court and the debtor receive such creditor's notice of address, shall be provided to such address.

(f)(1) An entity may file with any bankruptcy court a notice of address to be used by all the bankruptcy courts or by particular bankruptcy courts, as so specified by such entity at the time such notice is filed, to provide notice to such entity in all cases under chapters 7 and 13 pending in the courts with respect to which such notice is filed, in which such entity is a creditor.

(2) In any case filed under chapter 7 or 13, any notice required to be provided by a court with respect to which a notice is filed under paragraph (1), to such entity later than 30 days after the filing of such notice under paragraph (1) shall be provided to such address unless with respect to a particular case a different address is specified in a notice filed and served in accordance with subsection (e).

(3) A notice filed under paragraph (1) may be withdrawn by such entity.

(g)(1) Notice provided to a creditor by the debtor or the court other than in accordance with this section (excluding this subsection) shall not be effective notice until such notice is brought to the attention of such creditor. If such creditor designates a person or an organizational subdivision of such creditor to be responsible for receiving notices under this title and establishes reasonable procedures so that such notices receivable by such creditor are to be delivered to such person or such subdivision, then a notice provided to such creditor other than in accordance with this section (excluding this subsection) shall not be considered to have been brought to the attention of such creditor until such notice is received by such person or such subdivision.

(2) A monetary penalty may not be imposed on a creditor for a violation of a stay in effect under section 362(a) (including a monetary penalty imposed under section 362(k)) or for failure to comply with section 542 or 543 unless the conduct that is the basis of such violation or of such failure occurs after such creditor receives notice effective under this section of the order for relief.

§ 343. Examination of the Debtor

The debtor shall appear and submit to examination under oath at the meeting of creditors under section 341(a) of this title. Creditors, any indenture trustee, any trustee or examiner in the case, or the United States trustee may examine the debtor. The United States trustee may administer the oath required under this section.

§ 344. Self-Incrimination; Immunity

Immunity for persons required to submit to examination, to testify, or to provide information in a case under this title may be granted under part V of title 18.

§ 345. Money of Estates

(a) A trustee in a case under this title may make such deposit or investment of the money of the estate for which such trustee serves as will yield the maximum reasonable net return on such money, taking into account the safety of such deposit or investment.

(b) Except with respect to a deposit or investment that is insured or guaranteed by the United States or by a department, agency, or instrumentality of the United States or backed by the full faith and credit of the United States, the trustee shall require from an entity with which such money is deposited or invested—

(1) a bond—

(A) in favor of the United States;

(B) secured by the undertaking of a corporate surety approved by the United States trustee for the district in which the case is pending; and

(C) conditioned on—

(i) a proper accounting for all money so deposited or invested and for any return on such money;

(ii) prompt repayment of such money and return; and

(iii) faithful performance of duties as a depository; or

(2) the deposit of securities of the kind specified in section 9303 of title 31; unless the court for cause orders otherwise.

(c) An entity with which such moneys are deposited or invested is authorized to deposit or invest such moneys as may be required under this section.

§ 346. Special Provisions Related to the Treatment of State and Local Taxes

(a) Whenever the Internal Revenue Code of 1986 provides that a separate taxable estate or entity is created in a case concerning a debtor under this title, and the income, gain, loss, deductions, and credits of such estate shall be taxed to or claimed by the estate, a separate taxable estate is also created for purposes of any State and local law imposing a tax on or measured by income and such income, gain, loss, deductions, and credits shall be taxed to or claimed by the estate and may not be taxed to or claimed by the debtor. The preceding sentence shall not apply if the case is dismissed. The trustee shall make tax returns of income required under any such State or local law.

(b) Whenever the Internal Revenue Code of 1986 provides that no separate taxable estate shall be created in a case concerning a debtor under this title, and the income, gain, loss, deductions, and credits of an estate shall be taxed to or claimed by the debtor, such income, gain, loss, deductions, and credits shall be taxed to or claimed by the debtor under a State or local law imposing a tax on or measured by income and may not be taxed to or claimed by the estate. The trustee shall make such tax returns of income of corporations and of partnerships as are required under any State or local law, but with respect to partnerships, shall make such returns only to the extent such returns are also required to be made under such Code. The estate shall be liable for any tax imposed on such corporation or partnership, but not for any tax imposed on partners or members.

(c) With respect to a partnership or any entity treated as a partnership under a State or local law imposing a tax on or measured by income that is a debtor in a case under this title, any gain or loss resulting from a distribution of property from such partnership, or any distributive share of any income, gain, loss, deduction, or credit of a partner or member that is distributed, or considered distributed, from such partnership, after the commencement of the case, is gain, loss, income, deduction, or credit, as the case may be, of the partner or member, and if such partner or member is a debtor in a case under this title, shall be subject to tax in accordance with subsection (a) or (b).

(d) For purposes of any State or local law imposing a tax on or measured by income, the taxable period of a debtor in a case under this title shall terminate only if and to the extent that the taxable period of such debtor terminates under the Internal Revenue Code of 1986.

(e) The estate in any case described in subsection (a) shall use the same accounting method as the debtor used immediately before the commencement of the case, if such method of accounting complies with applicable nonbankruptcy tax law.

(f) For purposes of any State or local law imposing a tax on or measured by income, a transfer of property from the debtor to the estate or from the estate to the debtor shall not be treated as a disposition for purposes of any provision assigning tax consequences to a disposition, except to the extent that such transfer is treated as a disposition under the Internal Revenue Code of 1986.

(g) Whenever a tax is imposed pursuant to a State or local law imposing a tax on or measured by income pursuant to subsection (a) or (b), such tax shall be imposed at rates generally applicable to the same types of entities under such State or local law.

(h) The trustee shall withhold from any payment of claims for wages, salaries, commissions, dividends, interest, or other payments, or collect, any amount required to be withheld or collected under applicable State or local tax law, and shall pay such withheld or collected amount to the appropriate governmental unit at the time and in the manner required by such tax law, and with the same priority as the claim from which such amount was withheld or collected was paid.

(i)(1) To the extent that any State or local law imposing a tax on or measured by income provides for the carryover of any tax attribute from one taxable period to a subsequent taxable period, the estate shall succeed to such tax attribute in any case in which such estate is subject to tax under subsection (a).

(2) After such a case is closed or dismissed, the debtor shall succeed to any tax attribute to which the estate succeeded under paragraph (1) to the extent consistent with the Internal Revenue Code of 1986.

(3) The estate may carry back any loss or tax attribute to a taxable period of the debtor that ended before the date of the order for relief under this title to the extent that—

(A) applicable State or local tax law provides for a carryback in the case of the debtor; and

(B) the same or a similar tax attribute may be carried back by the estate to such a taxable period of the debtor under the Internal Revenue Code of 1986.

(j)(1) For purposes of any State or local law imposing a tax on or measured by income, income is not realized by the estate, the debtor, or a successor to the debtor by reason of discharge of indebtedness in a case under this title, except to the extent, if any, that such income is subject to tax under the Internal Revenue Code of 1986.

(2) Whenever the Internal Revenue Code of 1986 provides that the amount excluded from gross income in respect of the discharge of indebtedness in a case under this title shall be applied to reduce the tax attributes of the debtor or the estate, a similar reduction shall be made under any State or local law imposing a tax on or measured by income to the extent such State or local law recognizes such attributes. Such State or local law may also provide for the reduction of other attributes to the extent that the full amount of income from the discharge of indebtedness has not been applied.

(k)(1) Except as provided in this section and section 505, the time and manner of filing tax returns and the items of income, gain, loss, deduction, and credit of any taxpayer shall be determined under applicable nonbankruptcy law.

(2) For Federal tax purposes, the provisions of this section are subject to the Internal Revenue Code of 1986 and other applicable Federal nonbankruptcy law.

§ 347. Unclaimed Property

(a) Ninety days after the final distribution under section 726, 1194, 1226, or 1326 of this title in a case under chapter 7, subchapter V of chapter 11, 12, or 13 of this title, as the case may be, the trustee shall stop payment on any check remaining unpaid, and any remaining property of the estate shall be paid into the court and disposed of under chapter 129 of title 28.

(b) Any security, money, or other property remaining unclaimed at the expiration of the time allowed in a case under chapter 9, 11, or 12 of this title for the presentation of a security or the performance of any other act as a condition to participation in the distribution under any plan confirmed under section 943(b), 1129, 1173, 1191, or 1225 of this title, as the case may be, becomes the property of the debtor or of the entity acquiring the assets of the debtor under the plan, as the case may be.

§ 348. Effect of Conversion

(a) Conversion of a case from a case under one chapter of this title to a case under another chapter of this title constitutes an order for relief under the chapter to which the case is converted, but, except as provided in subsections (b) and (c) of this section, does not effect a change in the date of the filing of the petition, the commencement of the case, or the order for relief.

(b) Unless the court for cause orders otherwise, in sections 701(a), 727(a)(10), 727(b), 1102(a), 1110(a)(1), 1121(b), 1121(c), 1141(d)(4), 1201(a), 1221, 1228(a), 1301(a), and 1305(a) of this title, "the order for relief under this chapter" in a chapter to which a case has been converted under section 706, 1112, 1208, or 1307 of this title means the conversion of such case to such chapter.

(c) Sections 342 and 365(d) of this title apply in a case that has been converted under section 706, 1112, 1208, or 1307 of this title, as if the conversion order were the order for relief.

(d) A claim against the estate or the debtor that arises after the order for relief but before conversion in a case that is converted under section 1112, 1208, or 1307 of this title, other than a claim specified in section 503(b) of this title, shall be treated for all purposes as if such claim had arisen immediately before the date of the filing of the petition.

(e) Conversion of a case under section 706, 1112, 1208, or 1307 of this title terminates the service of any trustee or examiner that is serving in the case before such conversion.

(f)(1) Except as provided in paragraph (2), when a case under chapter 13 of this title is converted to a case under another chapter under this title—

(A) property of the estate in the converted case shall consist of property of the estate, as of the date of filing of the petition, that remains in the possession of or is under the control of the debtor on the date of conversion;

(B) valuations of property and of allowed secured claims in the chapter 13 case shall apply only in a case converted to a case under chapter 11 or 12, but not in a case converted to a case under chapter 7, with allowed secured claims in cases under chapters 11 and 12 reduced to the extent that they have been paid in accordance with the chapter 13 plan; and

(C) with respect to cases converted from chapter 13—

(i) the claim of any creditor holding security as of the date of the filing of the petition shall continue to be secured by that security unless the full amount of such claim determined under applicable nonbankruptcy law has been paid in full as of the date of conversion, notwithstanding any valuation or determination of the amount of an allowed secured claim made for the purposes of the case under chapter 13; and

(ii) unless a prebankruptcy default has been fully cured under the plan at the time of conversion, in any proceeding under this title or otherwise, the default shall have the effect given under applicable nonbankruptcy law.

(2) If the debtor converts a case under chapter 13 of this title to a case under another chapter under this title in bad faith, the property of the estate in the converted case shall consist of the property of the estate as of the date of conversion.

§ 349. Effect of Dismissal

(a) Unless the court, for cause, orders otherwise, the dismissal of a case under this title does not bar the discharge, in a later case under this title, of debts that were dischargeable in the case dismissed; nor does the dismissal of a case under this title prejudice the debtor with regard to the filing of a subsequent petition under this title, except as provided in section 109(g) of this title.

(b) Unless the court, for cause, orders otherwise, a dismissal of a case other than under section 742 of this title—

(1) reinstates—

(A) any proceeding or custodianship superseded under section 543 of this title;

(B) any transfer avoided under section 522, 544, 545, 547, 548, 549, or 724(a) of this title, or preserved under section 510(c)(2), 522(i)(2), or 551 of this title; and

(C) any lien voided under section 506(d) of this title;

(2) vacates any order, judgment, or transfer ordered, under section 522(i)(1), 542, 550, or 553 of this title; and

(3) revests the property of the estate in the entity in which such property was vested immediately before the commencement of the case under this title.

§ 350. Closing and Reopening Cases

(a) After an estate is fully administered and the court has discharged the trustee, the court shall close the case.

(b) A case may be reopened in the court in which such case was closed to administer assets, to accord relief to the debtor, or for other cause.

§ 351. Disposal of Patient Records

If a health care business commences a case under chapter 7, 9, or 11, and the trustee does not have a sufficient amount of funds to pay for the storage of patient records in the manner required under applicable Federal or State law, the following requirements shall apply:

(1) The trustee shall—

(A) promptly publish notice, in 1 or more appropriate newspapers, that if patient records are not claimed by the patient or an insurance provider (if applicable law permits the insurance provider to make that claim) by the date that is 365 days after the date of that notification, the trustee will destroy the patient records; and

(B) during the first 180 days of the 365-day period described in subparagraph (A), promptly attempt to notify directly each patient that is the subject of the patient records and appropriate insurance carrier concerning the patient records by mailing to the most recent known address of that patient, or a family member or contact person for that patient, and to the appropriate insurance carrier an appropriate notice regarding the claiming or disposing of patient records.

(2) If, after providing the notification under paragraph (1), patient records are not claimed during the 365-day period described under that paragraph, the trustee shall mail, by certified mail, at the end of such 365-day period a written request to each appropriate Federal agency to request permission from that agency to deposit the patient records with that agency, except that no Federal agency is required to accept patient records under this paragraph.

(3) If, following the 365-day period described in paragraph (2) and after providing the notification under paragraph (1), patient records are not claimed by a patient or insurance provider, or request is not granted by a Federal agency to deposit such records with that agency, the trustee shall destroy those records by—

(A) if the records are written, shredding or burning the records; or

(B) if the records are magnetic, optical, or other electronic records, by otherwise destroying those records so that those records cannot be retrieved.

SUBCHAPTER IV—ADMINISTRATIVE POWERS

§ 361. Adequate Protection

When adequate protection is required under section 362, 363, or 364 of this title of an interest of an entity in property, such adequate protection may be provided by—

(1) requiring the trustee to make a cash payment or periodic cash payments to such entity, to the extent that the stay under section 362 of this title, use, sale, or lease under section 363 of this title, or any grant of a lien under section 364 of this title results in a decrease in the value of such entity's interest in such property;

(2) providing to such entity an additional or replacement lien to the extent that such stay, use, sale, lease, or grant results in a decrease in the value of such entity's interest in such property; or

(3) granting such other relief, other than entitling such entity to compensation allowable under section 503(b)(1) of this title as an administrative expense, as will result in the realization by such entity of the indubitable equivalent of such entity's interest in such property.

§ 362. Automatic Stay

(a) Except as provided in subsection (b) of this section, a petition filed under section 301, 302, or 303 of this title, or an application filed under section 5(a)(3) of the Securities Investor Protection Act of 1970, operates as a stay, applicable to all entities, of—

(1) the commencement or continuation, including the issuance or employment of process, of a judicial, administrative, or other action or proceeding against the debtor that was or could have been commenced before the commencement of the case under this title, or to recover a claim against the debtor that arose before the commencement of the case under this title;

(2) the enforcement, against the debtor or against property of the estate, of a judgment obtained before the commencement of the case under this title;

(3) any act to obtain possession of property of the estate or of property from the estate or to exercise control over property of the estate;

(4) any act to create, perfect, or enforce any lien against property of the estate;

(5) any act to create, perfect, or enforce against property of the debtor any lien to the extent that such lien secures a claim that arose before the commencement of the case under this title;

(6) any act to collect, assess, or recover a claim against the debtor that arose before the commencement of the case under this title;

(7) the setoff of any debt owing to the debtor that arose before the commencement of the case under this title against any claim against the debtor;

(8) the commencement or continuation of a proceeding before the United States Tax Court concerning a tax liability of a debtor that is a corporation for a taxable period the bankruptcy court may determine or concerning the tax liability of a debtor who is an individual for a taxable period ending before the date of the order for relief under this title; and

(9) the redemption of payment stablecoins issued by the permitted payment stablecoin issuer, from payment stablecoin reserves required to be maintained under section 4 of the GENIUS Act.

(b) The filing of a petition under section 301, 302, or 303 of this title, or of an application under section 5(a)(3) of the Securities Investor Protection Act of 1970, does not operate as a stay—

(1) under subsection (a) of this section, of the commencement or continuation of a criminal action or proceeding against the debtor;

(2) under subsection (a)—

(A) of the commencement or continuation of a civil action or proceeding—

(i) for the establishment of paternity;

(ii) for the establishment or modification of an order for domestic support obligations;

(iii) concerning child custody or visitation;

(iv) for the dissolution of a marriage, except to the extent that such proceeding seeks to determine the division of property that is property of the estate; or

(v) regarding domestic violence;

(B) of the collection of a domestic support obligation from property that is not property of the estate;

(C) with respect to the withholding of income that is property of the estate or property of the debtor for payment of a domestic support obligation under a judicial or administrative order or a statute;

(D) of the withholding, suspension, or restriction of a driver's license, a professional or occupational license, or a recreational license, under State law, as specified in section 466(a)(16) of the Social Security Act;

(E) of the reporting of overdue support owed by a parent to any consumer reporting agency as specified in section 466(a)(7) of the Social Security Act;

(F) of the interception of a tax refund, as specified in sections 464 and 466(a)(3) of the Social Security Act or under an analogous State law; or

(G) of the enforcement of a medical obligation, as specified under title IV of the Social Security Act;

(3) under subsection (a) of this section, of any act to perfect, or to maintain or continue the perfection of, an interest in property to the extent that the trustee's rights and powers are subject to such perfection under section 546(b) of this title or to the extent that such act is accomplished within the period provided under section 547(e)(2)(A) of this title;

(4) under paragraph (1), (2), (3), or (6) of subsection (a) of this section, of the commencement or continuation of an action or proceeding by a governmental unit or any organization exercising authority under the Convention on the Prohibition of the Development, Production, stockpiling and Use of Chemical Weapons and on Their Destruction, opened for signature on January 13, 1993, to enforce such governmental unit's or organization's police and regulatory power, including the enforcement of a judgment other than a money judgment, obtained in an action or proceeding by the governmental unit to enforce such governmental unit's or organization's police or regulatory power;

[(5) Repealed. Pub. L. 105–277, div. I, title VI, § 603(1), Oct. 21, 1998, 112 Stat. 2681–866;]

(6) under subsection (a) of this section, of the exercise by a commodity broker, forward contract merchant, stockbroker, financial institution, financial participant, or securities clearing agency of any contractual right (as defined in section 555 or 556) under any security agreement or arrangement or other credit enhancement forming a part of or related to any commodity contract, forward contract or securities contract, or of any contractual right (as

defined in section 555 or 556) to offset or net out any termination value, payment amount, or other transfer obligation arising under or in connection with 1 or more such contracts, including any master agreement for such contracts;

(7) under subsection (a) of this section, of the exercise by a repo participant or financial participant of any contractual right (as defined in section 559) under any security agreement or arrangement or other credit enhancement forming a part of or related to any repurchase agreement, or of any contractual right (as defined in section 559) to offset or net out any termination value, payment amount, or other transfer obligation arising under or in connection with 1 or more such agreements, including any master agreement for such agreements;

(8) under subsection (a) of this section, of the commencement of any action by the Secretary of Housing and Urban Development to foreclose a mortgage or deed of trust in any case in which the mortgage or deed of trust held by the Secretary is insured or was formerly insured under the National Housing Act and covers property, or combinations of property, consisting of five or more living units;

(9) under subsection (a), of—

(A) an audit by a governmental unit to determine tax liability;

(B) the issuance to the debtor by a governmental unit of a notice of tax deficiency;

(C) a demand for tax returns; or

(D) the making of an assessment for any tax and issuance of a notice and demand for payment of such an assessment (but any tax lien that would otherwise attach to property of the estate by reason of such an assessment shall not take effect unless such tax is a debt of the debtor that will not be discharged in the case and such property or its proceeds are transferred out of the estate to, or otherwise revested in, the debtor).

(10) under subsection (a) of this section, of any act by a lessor to the debtor under a lease of nonresidential real property that has terminated by the expiration of the stated term of the lease before the commencement of or during a case under this title to obtain possession of such property;

(11) under subsection (a) of this section, of the presentment of a negotiable instrument and the giving of notice of and protesting dishonor of such an instrument;

(12) under subsection (a) of this section, after the date which is 90 days after the filing of such petition, of the commencement or continuation, and conclusion to the entry of final judgment, of an action which involves a debtor subject to reorganization pursuant to chapter 11 of this title and which was brought by the Secretary of Transportation under section 31325 of title 46 (including distribution of any proceeds of sale) to foreclose a preferred ship or fleet mortgage, or a security interest in or relating to a vessel or vessel under construction, held by the Secretary of Transportation under chapter 537 of title 46 or section 109(h) of title 49, or under applicable state law;

(13) under subsection (a) of this section, after the date which is 90 days after the filing of such petition, of the commencement or continuation, and conclusion to the entry of final judgment, of an action which involves a debtor subject to reorganization pursuant to chapter 11 of this title and which was brought by the Secretary of Commerce under section 31325 of title 46 (including distribution of any proceeds of sale) to foreclose a preferred ship or fleet mortgage in a vessel or a mortgage, deed of trust, or other security interest in a fishing facility held by the Secretary of Commerce under chapter 537 of title 46;

(14) under subsection (a) of this section, of any action by an accrediting agency regarding the accreditation status of the debtor as an educational institution;

(15) under subsection (a) of this section, of any action by a state licensing body regarding the licensure of the debtor as an educational institution;

(16) under subsection (a) of this section, of any action by a guaranty agency, as defined in section 435(j) of the Higher Education Act of 1965 or the Secretary of Education regarding the eligibility of the debtor to participate in programs authorized under such Act;

(17) under subsection (a) of this section, of the exercise by a swap participant or financial participant of any contractual right (as defined in section 560) under any security agreement or arrangement or other credit enhancement forming a part of or related to any swap agreement, or of any contractual right (as defined in section 560) to offset or net out any termination value, payment amount, or other transfer obligation arising under or in connection with 1 or more such agreements, including any master agreement for such agreements;

(18) under subsection (a) of the creation or perfection of a statutory lien for an ad valorem property

tax, or a special tax or special assessment on real property whether or not ad valorem, imposed by a governmental unit, if such tax or assessment comes due after the date of the filing of the petition;

(19) under subsection (a), of withholding of income from a debtor's wages and collection of amounts withheld, under the debtor's agreement authorizing that withholding and collection for the benefit of a pension, profit-sharing, stock bonus, or other plan established under section 401, 403, 408, 408A, 414, 457, or 501(c) of the Internal Revenue Code of 1986, that is sponsored by the employer of the debtor, or an affiliate, successor, or predecessor of such employer—

(A) to the extent that the amounts withheld and collected are used solely for payments relating to a loan from a plan under section 408(b)(1) of the Employee Retirement Income Security Act of 1974 or is subject to section 72(p) of the Internal Revenue Code of 1986; or

(B) a loan from a thrift savings plan permitted under subchapter III of chapter 84 of title 5, that satisfies the requirements of section 8433(g) of such title; but nothing in this paragraph may be construed to provide that any loan made under a governmental plan under section 414(d), or a contract or account under section 403(b), of the Internal Revenue Code of 1986 constitutes a claim or a debt under this title;

(20) under subsection (a), of any act to enforce any lien against or security interest in real property following entry of the order under subsection (d)(4) as to such real property in any prior case under this title, for a period of 2 years after the date of the entry of such an order, except that the debtor, in a subsequent case under this title, may move for relief from such order based upon changed circumstances or for other good cause shown, after notice and a hearing;

(21) under subsection (a), of any act to enforce any lien against or security interest in real property—

(A) if the debtor is ineligible under section 109(g) to be a debtor in a case under this title; or

(B) if the case under this title was filed in violation of a bankruptcy court order in a prior case under this title prohibiting the debtor from being a debtor in another case under this title;

(22) subject to subsection (l), under subsection (a)(3), of the continuation of any eviction, unlawful detainer action, or similar proceeding by a lessor against a debtor involving residential property in which the debtor resides as a tenant under a lease or rental agreement and with respect to which the lessor has obtained before the date of the filing of the bankruptcy petition, a judgment for possession of such property against the debtor;

(23) subject to subsection (m), under subsection (a)(3), of an eviction action that seeks possession of the residential property in which the debtor resides as a tenant under a lease or rental agreement based on endangerment of such property or the illegal use of controlled substances on such property, but only if the lessor files with the court, and serves upon the debtor, a certification under penalty of perjury that such an eviction action has been filed, or that the debtor, during the 30-day period preceding the date of the filing of the certification, has endangered property or illegally used or allowed to be used a controlled substance on the property;

(24) under subsection (a), of any transfer that is not avoidable under section 544 and that is not avoidable under section 549;

(25) under subsection (a), of—

(A) the commencement or continuation of an investigation or action by a securities self regulatory organization to enforce such organization's regulatory power;

(B) the enforcement of an order or decision, other than for monetary sanctions, obtained in an action by such securities self regulatory organization to enforce such organization's regulatory power; or

(C) any act taken by such securities self regulatory organization to delist, delete, or refuse to permit quotation of any stock that does not meet applicable regulatory requirements;

(26) under subsection (a), of the setoff under applicable nonbankruptcy law of an income tax refund, by a governmental unit, with respect to a taxable period that ended before the date of the order for relief against an income tax liability for a taxable period that also ended before the date of the order for relief, except that in any case in which the setoff of an income tax refund is not permitted under applicable nonbankruptcy law because of a pending action to determine the amount or legality of a tax liability, the governmental unit may hold the refund pending the resolution of the action, unless the court, on the motion of the trustee and after notice and a hearing, grants the taxing authority

adequate protection (within the meaning of section 361) for the secured claim of such authority in the setoff under section 506(a);

(27) under subsection (a) of this section, of the exercise by a master netting agreement participant of any contractual right (as defined in section 555, 556, 559, or 560) under any security agreement or arrangement or other credit enhancement forming a part of or related to any master netting agreement, or of any contractual right (as defined in section 555, 556, 559, or 560) to offset or net out any termination value, payment amount, or other transfer obligation arising under or in connection with 1 or more such master netting agreements to the extent that such participant is eligible to exercise such rights under paragraph (6), (7), or (17) for each individual contract covered by the master netting agreement in issue;

(28) under subsection (a), of the exclusion by the Secretary of Health and Human Services of the debtor from participation in the medicare program or any other Federal health care program (as defined in section 1128B(f) of the Social Security Act pursuant to title XI or XVIII of such Act); and

(29) under subsection (a)(1) of this section, of any action by—

(A) an amateur sports organization, as defined in section 220501(b) of title 36, to replace a national governing body, as defined in that section, under section 220528 of that title; or

(B) the corporation, as defined in section 220501(b) of title 36, to revoke the certification of a national governing body, as defined in that section, under section 220521 of that title.

The provisions of paragraphs (12) and (13) of this subsection shall apply with respect to any such petition filed on or before December 31, 1989.

(c) Except as provided in subsections (d), (e), (f), and (h) of this section—

(1) the stay of an act against property of the estate under subsection (a) of this section continues until such property is no longer property of the estate;

(2) the stay of any other act under subsection (a) of this section continues until the earliest of—

(A) the time the case is closed;

(B) the time the case is dismissed; or

(C) if the case is a case under chapter 7 of this title concerning an individual or a case under chapter 9, 11, 12, or 13 of this title, the time a discharge is granted or denied;

(3) if a single or joint case is filed by or against a debtor who is an individual in a case under chapter 7, 11, or 13, and if a single or joint case of the debtor was pending within the preceding 1-year period but was dismissed, other than a case refiled under a chapter other than chapter 7 after dismissal under section 707(b)—

(A) the stay under subsection (a) with respect to any action taken with respect to a debt or property securing such debt or with respect to any lease shall terminate with respect to the debtor on the 30th day after the filing of the later case;

(B) on the motion of a party in interest for continuation of the automatic stay and upon notice and a hearing, the court may extend the stay in particular cases as to any or all creditors (subject to such conditions or limitations as the court may then impose) after notice and a hearing completed before the expiration of the 30-day period only if the party in interest demonstrates that the filing of the later case is in good faith as to the creditors to be stayed; and

(C) for purposes of subparagraph (B), a case is presumptively filed not in good faith (but such presumption may be rebutted by clear and convincing evidence to the contrary)—

(i) as to all creditors, if—

(I) more than 1 previous case under any of chapters 7, 11, and 13 in which the individual was a debtor was pending within the preceding 1-year period;

(II) a previous case under any of chapters 7, 11, and 13 in which the individual was a debtor was dismissed within such 1-year period, after the debtor failed to—

(aa) file or amend the petition or other documents as required by this title or the court without substantial excuse (but mere inadvertence or negligence shall not be a substantial excuse unless the dismissal was caused by the negligence of the debtor's attorney);

(bb) provide adequate protection as ordered by the court; or

(cc) perform the terms of a plan confirmed by the court; or

(III) there has not been a substantial change in the financial or personal affairs of the debtor since the dismissal of the next most previous case under chapter 7, 11, or 13 or any other reason to conclude that the later case will be concluded—

(aa) if a case under chapter 7, with a discharge; or

(bb) if a case under chapter 11 or 13, with a confirmed plan that will be fully performed; and

(ii) as to any creditor that commenced an action under subsection (d) in a previous case in which the individual was a debtor if, as of the date of dismissal of such case, that action was still pending or had been resolved by terminating, conditioning, or limiting the stay as to actions of such creditor; and

(4)(A)(i) if a single or joint case is filed by or against a debtor who is an individual under this title, and if 2 or more single or joint cases of the debtor were pending within the previous year but were dismissed, other than a case refiled under a chapter other than chapter 7 after dismissal under section 707(b), the stay under subsection (a) shall not go into effect upon the filing of the later case; and

(ii) on request of a party in interest, the court shall promptly enter an order confirming that no stay is in effect;

(B) if, within 30 days after the filing of the later case, a party in interest requests the court may order the stay to take effect in the case as to any or all creditors (subject to such conditions or limitations as the court may impose), after notice and a hearing, only if the party in interest demonstrates that the filing of the later case is in good faith as to the creditors to be stayed;

(C) a stay imposed under subparagraph (B) shall be effective on the date of the entry of the order allowing the stay to go into effect; and

(D) for purposes of subparagraph (B), a case is presumptively filed not in good faith (but such presumption may be rebutted by clear and convincing evidence to the contrary)—

(i) as to all creditors if—

(I) 2 or more previous cases under this title in which the individual was a debtor were pending within the 1-year period;

(II) a previous case under this title in which the individual was a debtor was dismissed within the time period stated in this paragraph after the debtor failed to file or amend the petition or other documents as required by this title or the court without substantial excuse (but mere inadvertence or negligence shall not be substantial excuse unless the dismissal was caused by the negligence of the debtor's attorney), failed to provide adequate protection as ordered by the court, or failed to perform the terms of a plan confirmed by the court; or

(III) there has not been a substantial change in the financial or personal affairs of the debtor since the dismissal of the next most previous case under this title, or any other reason to conclude that the later case will not be concluded, if a case under chapter 7, with a discharge, and if a case under chapter 11 or 13, with a confirmed plan that will be fully performed; or

(ii) as to any creditor that commenced an action under subsection (d) in a previous case in which the individual was a debtor if, as of the date of dismissal of such case, such action was still pending or had been resolved by terminating, conditioning, or limiting the stay as to such action of such creditor.

(d) On request of a party in interest and after notice and a hearing, the court shall grant relief from the stay provided under subsection (a) of this section, such as by terminating, annulling, modifying, or conditioning such stay—

(1) for cause, including the lack of adequate protection of an interest in property of such party in interest;

(2) with respect to a stay of an act against property under subsection (a) of this section, if—

(A) the debtor does not have an equity in such property; and

(B) such property is not necessary to an effective reorganization;

(3) with respect to a stay of an act against single asset real estate under subsection (a), by a creditor whose claim is secured by an interest in such real estate, unless, not later than the date that is 90 days after the entry of the order for relief (or such later date as the court may determine for cause by order entered within that 90-day period) or 30 days after the court determines that the debtor is subject to this paragraph, whichever is later—

(A) the debtor has filed a plan of reorganization that has a reasonable possibility of being confirmed within a reasonable time; or

(B) the debtor has commenced monthly payments that—

(i) may, in the debtor's sole discretion, notwithstanding section 363(c)(2), be made from rents or other income generated before, on, or after the date of the commencement of the case by or from the property to each creditor whose claim is secured by such real estate (other than a claim secured by a judgment lien or by an unmatured statutory lien); and

(ii) are in an amount equal to interest at the then applicable nondefault contract rate of interest on the value of the creditor's interest in the real estate;

(4) with respect to a stay of an act against real property under subsection (a), by a creditor whose claim is secured by an interest in such real property, if the court finds that the filing of the petition was part of a scheme to delay, hinder, or defraud creditors that involved either—

(A) transfer of all or part ownership of, or other interest in, such real property without the consent of the secured creditor or court approval; or

(B) multiple bankruptcy filings affecting such real property. If recorded in compliance with applicable State laws governing notices of interests or liens in real property, an order entered under paragraph (4) shall be binding in any other case under this title purporting to affect such real property filed not later than 2 years after the date of the entry of such order by the court, except that a debtor in a subsequent case under this title may move for relief from such order based upon changed circumstances or for good cause shown, after notice and a hearing. Any Federal, State, or local governmental unit that accepts notices of interests or liens in real property shall accept any certified copy of an order described in this subsection for indexing and recording; or

(5) with respect to the redemption of payment stablecoins held by a person, if the court finds, subject to the motion and attestation of the permitted payment stablecoin issuer, which shall be filed on the petition date or as soon as practicable thereafter, there are payment stablecoin reserves available for distribution on a ratable basis to similarly situated payment stablecoin holders, provided that the court shall use best efforts to enter a final order to begin distributions under this paragraph not later than 14 days after the date of the required hearing.

(e)(1) Thirty days after a request under subsection (d) of this section for relief from the stay of any act against property of the estate under subsection (a) of this section, such stay is terminated with respect to the party in interest making such request, unless the court, after notice and a hearing, orders such stay continued in effect pending the conclusion of, or as a result of, a final hearing and determination under subsection (d) of this section. A hearing under this subsection may be a preliminary hearing, or may be consolidated with the final hearing under subsection (d) of this section. The court shall order such stay continued in effect pending the conclusion of the final hearing under subsection (d) of this section if there is a reasonable likelihood that the party opposing relief from such stay will prevail at the conclusion of such final hearing. If the hearing under this subsection is a preliminary hearing, then such final hearing shall be concluded not later than thirty days after the conclusion of such preliminary hearing, unless the 30-day period is extended with the consent of the parties in interest or for a specific time which the court finds is required by compelling circumstances.

(2) Notwithstanding paragraph (1), in a case under chapter 7, 11, or 13 in which the debtor is an individual, the stay under subsection (a) shall terminate on the date that is 60 days after a request is made by a party in interest under subsection (d), unless—

(A) a final decision is rendered by the court during the 60- day period beginning on the date of the request; or

(B) such 60-day period is extended—

(i) by agreement of all parties in interest; or

(ii) by the court for such specific period of time as the court finds is required for good cause, as described in findings made by the court.

(f) Upon request of a party in interest, the court, with or without a hearing, shall grant such relief from the stay provided under subsection (a) of this section as is necessary to prevent irreparable damage to the interest of an entity in property, if such interest will suffer such damage before there is an opportunity for notice and a hearing under subsection (d) or (e) of this section.

(g) In any hearing under subsection (d) or (e) of this section concerning relief from the stay of any act under subsection (a) of this section—

(1) the party requesting such relief has the burden of proof on the issue of the debtor's equity in property; and

(2) the party opposing such relief has the burden of proof on all other issues.

(h)(1) In a case in which the debtor is an individual, the stay provided by subsection (a) is terminated with respect to personal property of the estate or of the debtor securing in whole or in part a claim, or subject to an unexpired lease, and such personal property shall no longer be property of the estate if the debtor fails within the applicable time set by section 521(a)(2)—

(A) to file timely any statement of intention required under section 521(a)(2) with respect to such personal property or to indicate in such statement that the debtor will either surrender such personal property or retain it and, if retaining such personal property, either redeem such personal property pursuant to section 722, enter into an agreement of the kind specified in section 524(c) applicable to the debt secured by such personal property, or assume such unexpired lease pursuant to section 365(p) if the trustee does not do so, as applicable; and

(B) to take timely the action specified in such statement, as it may be amended before expiration of the period for taking action, unless such statement specifies the debtor's intention to reaffirm such debt on the original contract terms and the creditor refuses to agree to the reaffirmation on such terms.

(2) Paragraph (1) does not apply if the court determines, on the motion of the trustee filed before the expiration of the applicable time set by section 521(a)(2), after notice and a hearing, that such personal property is of consequential value or benefit to the estate, and orders appropriate adequate protection of the creditor's interest, and orders the debtor to deliver any collateral in the debtor's possession to the trustee. If the court does not so determine, the stay provided by subsection (a) shall terminate upon the conclusion of the hearing on the motion.

(i) If a case commenced under chapter 7, 11, or 13 is dismissed due to the creation of a debt repayment plan, for purposes of subsection (c)(3), any subsequent case commenced by the debtor under any such chapter shall not be presumed to be filed not in good faith.

(j) On request of a party in interest, the court shall issue an order under subsection (c) confirming that the automatic stay has been terminated.

(k)(1) Except as provided in paragraph (2), an individual injured by any willful violation of a stay provided by this section shall recover actual damages, including costs and attorneys' fees, and, in appropriate circumstances, may recover punitive damages.

(2) If such violation is based on an action taken by an entity in the good faith belief that subsection (h) applies to the debtor, the recovery under paragraph (1) of this subsection against such entity shall be limited to actual damages.

(l)(1) Except as otherwise provided in this subsection, subsection (b)(22) shall apply on the date that is 30 days after the date on which the bankruptcy petition is filed, if the debtor files with the petition and serves upon the lessor a certification under penalty of perjury that—

(A) under nonbankruptcy law applicable in the jurisdiction, there are circumstances under which the debtor would be permitted to cure the entire monetary default that gave rise to the judgment for possession, after that judgment for possession was entered; and

(B) the debtor (or an adult dependent of the debtor) has deposited with the clerk of the court, any rent that would become due during the 30-day period after the filing of the bankruptcy petition.

(2) If, within the 30-day period after the filing of the bankruptcy petition, the debtor (or an adult dependent of the debtor) complies with paragraph (1) and files with the court and serves upon the lessor a further certification under penalty of perjury that the debtor (or an adult dependent of the debtor) has cured, under nonbankruptcy law applicable in the jurisdiction, the entire monetary default that gave rise to the judgment under which possession is sought by the lessor, subsection (b)(22) shall not apply, unless ordered to apply by the court under paragraph (3).

(3)(A) If the lessor files an objection to any certification filed by the debtor under paragraph (1) or (2), and serves such objection upon the debtor, the court shall hold a hearing within 10 days after the filing and service of such objection to determine if the certification filed by the debtor under paragraph (1) or (2) is true.

(B) If the court upholds the objection of the lessor filed under subparagraph (A)—

(i) subsection (b)(22) shall apply immediately and relief from the stay provided under subsection (a)(3) shall not be required to enable the lessor to complete the process to recover full possession of the property; and

(ii) the clerk of the court shall immediately serve upon the lessor and the debtor a certified copy of the court's order upholding the lessor's objection.

(4) If a debtor, in accordance with paragraph (5), indicates on the petition that there was a judgment for possession of the residential rental property in which the debtor resides and does not file a certification under paragraph (1) or (2)—

(A) subsection (b)(22) shall apply immediately upon failure to file such certification, and relief from the stay provided under subsection (a)(3) shall not be required to enable the lessor to complete the process to recover full possession of the property; and

(B) the clerk of the court shall immediately serve upon the lessor and the debtor a certified copy of the docket indicating the absence of a filed certification and the applicability of the exception to the stay under subsection (b)(22).

(5)(A) Where a judgment for possession of residential property in which the debtor resides as a tenant under a lease or rental agreement has been obtained by the lessor, the debtor shall so indicate on the bankruptcy petition and shall provide the name and address of the lessor that obtained that pre-petition judgment on the petition and on any certification filed under this subsection.

(B) The form of certification filed with the petition, as specified in this subsection, shall provide for the debtor to certify, and the debtor shall certify—

(i) whether a judgment for possession of residential rental housing in which the debtor resides has been obtained against the debtor before the date of the filing of the petition; and

(ii) whether the debtor is claiming under paragraph (1) that under nonbankruptcy law applicable in the jurisdiction, there are circumstances under which the debtor would be permitted to cure the entire monetary default that gave rise to the judgment for possession, after that judgment of possession was entered, and has made the appropriate deposit with the court.

(C) The standard forms (electronic and otherwise) used in a bankruptcy proceeding shall be amended to reflect the requirements of this subsection.

(D) The clerk of the court shall arrange for the prompt transmittal of the rent deposited in accordance with paragraph (1)(B) to the lessor.

(m)(1) Except as otherwise provided in this subsection, subsection (b)(23) shall apply on the date that is 15 days after the date on which the lessor files and serves a certification described in subsection (b)(23).

(2)(A) If the debtor files with the court an objection to the truth or legal sufficiency of the certification described in subsection (b)(23) and serves such objection upon the lessor, subsection (b)(23) shall not apply, unless ordered to apply by the court under this subsection.

(B) If the debtor files and serves the objection under subparagraph (A), the court shall hold a hearing within 10 days after the filing and service of such objection to determine if the situation giving rise to the lessor's certification under paragraph (1) existed or has been remedied.

(C) If the debtor can demonstrate to the satisfaction of the court that the situation giving rise to the lessor's certification under paragraph (1) did not exist or has been remedied, the stay provided under subsection (a)(3) shall remain in effect until the termination of the stay under this section.

(D) If the debtor cannot demonstrate to the satisfaction of the court that the situation giving rise to the lessor's certification under paragraph (1) did not exist or has been remedied—

(i) relief from the stay provided under subsection (a)(3) shall not be required to enable the lessor to proceed with the eviction; and

(ii) the clerk of the court shall immediately serve upon the lessor and the debtor a certified copy of the court's order upholding the lessor's certification.

(3) If the debtor fails to file, within 15 days, an objection under paragraph (2)(A)—

(A) subsection (b)(23) shall apply immediately upon such failure and relief from the stay provided under subsection (a)(3) shall not be required to enable the lessor to complete the process to recover full possession of the property; and

(B) the clerk of the court shall immediately serve upon the lessor and the debtor a certified copy of the docket indicating such failure.

(n)(1) Except as provided in paragraph (2), subsection (a) does not apply in a case in which the debtor—

(A) is a debtor in a small business case pending at the time the petition is filed;

(B) was a debtor in a small business case that was dismissed for any reason by an order that became final in the 2-year period ending on the date of the order for relief entered with respect to the petition;

(C) was a debtor in a small business case in which a plan was confirmed in the 2-year period ending on the date of the order for relief entered with respect to the petition; or

(D) is an entity that has acquired substantially all of the assets or business of a small business debtor described in subparagraph (A), (B), or (C), unless such entity establishes by a preponderance of the evidence that such entity acquired substantially all of the assets or business of such small business debtor in good faith and not for the purpose of evading this paragraph.

(2) Paragraph (1) does not apply—

(A) to an involuntary case involving no collusion by the debtor with creditors; or

(B) to the filing of a petition if—

(i) the debtor proves by a preponderance of the evidence that the filing of the petition resulted from circumstances beyond the control of the debtor not foreseeable at the time the case then pending was filed; and

(ii) it is more likely than not that the court will confirm a feasible plan, but not a liquidating plan, within a reasonable period of time.

(o) The exercise of rights not subject to the stay arising under subsection (a) pursuant to paragraph (6), (7), (17), or (27) of subsection (b) shall not be stayed by any order of a court or administrative agency in any proceeding under this title.

§ 363. Use, Sale, or Lease of Property

(a) In this section, "cash collateral" means cash, negotiable instruments, documents of title, securities, deposit accounts, or other cash equivalents whenever acquired in which the estate and an entity other than the estate have an interest and includes the proceeds, products, offspring, rents, or profits of property and the fees, charges, accounts or other payments for the use or occupancy of rooms and other public facilities in hotels, motels, or other lodging properties subject to a security interest as provided in section 552(b) of this title, whether existing before or after the commencement of a case under this title.

(b)(1) The trustee, after notice and a hearing, may use, sell, or lease, other than in the ordinary course of business, property of the estate, except that if the debtor in connection with offering a product or a service discloses to an individual a policy prohibiting the transfer of personally identifiable information about individuals to persons that are not affiliated with the debtor and if such policy is in effect on the date of the commencement of the case, then the trustee may not sell or lease personally identifiable information to any person unless—

(A) such sale or such lease is consistent with such policy; or

(B) after appointment of a consumer privacy ombudsman in accordance with section 332, and after notice and a hearing, the court approves such sale or such lease—

(i) giving due consideration to the facts, circumstances, and conditions of such sale or such lease; and

(ii) finding that no showing was made that such sale or such lease would violate applicable nonbankruptcy law.

(2) If notification is required under subsection (a) of section 7A of the Clayton Act in the case of a transaction under this subsection, then—

(A) notwithstanding subsection (a) of such section, the notification required by such subsection to be given by the debtor shall be given by the trustee; and

(B) notwithstanding subsection (b) of such section, the required waiting period shall end on the 15th day after the date of the receipt, by the Federal Trade Commission and the Assistant Attorney General in charge of the Antitrust Division of the Department of Justice, of the notification required under such subsection (a), unless such waiting period is extended—

(i) pursuant to subsection (e)(2) of such section, in the same manner as such subsection (e)(2) applies to a cash tender offer;

(ii) pursuant to subsection (g)(2) of such section; or

(iii) by the court after notice and a hearing.

(c)(1) If the business of the debtor is authorized to be operated under section 721, 1108, 1183, 1184, 1203, 1204, or 1304 of this title and unless the court orders otherwise, the trustee may enter into transactions, including the sale or lease of property of the estate, in the ordinary course of business, without notice or a hearing, and may use property of the estate in the ordinary course of business without notice or a hearing.

(2) The trustee may not use, sell, or lease cash collateral under paragraph (1) of this subsection unless—

(A) each entity that has an interest in such cash collateral consents; or

(B) the court, after notice and a hearing, authorizes such use, sale, or lease in accordance with the provisions of this section.

(3) Any hearing under paragraph (2)(B) of this subsection may be a preliminary hearing or may be consolidated with a hearing under subsection (e) of this section, but shall be scheduled in accordance with the needs of the debtor. If the hearing under paragraph (2)(B) of this subsection is a preliminary hearing, the court may authorize such use, sale, or lease only if there is a reasonable likelihood that the trustee will prevail at the final hearing under subsection (e) of this section. The court shall act promptly on any request for authorization under paragraph (2)(B) of this subsection.

(4) Except as provided in paragraph (2) of this subsection, the trustee shall segregate and account for any cash collateral in the trustee's possession, custody, or control.

(d) The trustee may use, sell, or lease property under subsection (b) or (c) of this section—

(1) in the case of a debtor that is a corporation or trust that is not a moneyed business, commercial corporation, or trust, only in accordance with nonbankruptcy law applicable to the transfer of property by a debtor that is such a corporation or trust; and

(2) only to the extent not inconsistent with any relief granted under subsection (c), (d), (e), or (f) of section 362.

(e) Notwithstanding any other provision of this section, at any time, on request of an entity that has an interest in property used, sold, or leased, or proposed to be used, sold, or leased, by the trustee, the court, with or without a hearing, shall prohibit or condition such use, sale, or lease as is necessary to provide adequate protection of such interest. This subsection also applies to property that is subject to any unexpired lease of personal property (to the exclusion of such property being subject to an order to grant relief from the stay under section 362).

(f) The trustee may sell property under subsection (b) or (c) of this section free and clear of any interest in such property of an entity other than the estate, only if—

(1) applicable nonbankruptcy law permits sale of such property free and clear of such interest;

(2) such entity consents;

(3) such interest is a lien and the price at which such property is to be sold is greater than the aggregate value of all liens on such property;

(4) such interest is in bona fide dispute; or

(5) such entity could be compelled, in a legal or equitable proceeding, to accept a money satisfaction of such interest.

(g) Notwithstanding subsection (f) of this section, the trustee may sell property under subsection (b) or (c) of this section free and clear of any vested or contingent right in the nature of dower or curtesy.

(h) Notwithstanding subsection (f) of this section, the trustee may sell both the estate's interest, under subsection (b) or (c) of this section, and the interest of any co-owner in property in which the debtor had, at the time of the commencement of the case, an undivided interest as a tenant in common, joint tenant, or tenant by the entirety, only if—

(1) partition in kind of such property among the estate and such co-owners is impracticable;

(2) sale of the estate's undivided interest in such property would realize significantly less for the estate than sale of such property free of the interests of such co-owners;

(3) the benefit to the estate of a sale of such property free of the interests of co-owners outweighs the detriment, if any, to such co-owners; and

(4) such property is not used in the production, transmission, or distribution, for sale, of electric energy or of natural or synthetic gas for heat, light, or power.

(i) Before the consummation of a sale of property to which subsection (g) or (h) of this section applies, or of property of the estate that was community property of the debtor and the debtor's spouse immediately before the commencement of the case, the debtor's spouse, or a co-owner of such property, as the case may be, may purchase such property at the price at which such sale is to be consummated.

(j) After a sale of property to which subsection (g) or (h) of this section applies, the trustee shall distribute to the debtor's spouse or the co-owners of such property, as the case may be, and to the estate, the proceeds of such sale, less the costs and expenses, not including any compensation of the trustee, of such sale, according to the interests of such spouse or co-owners, and of the estate.

(k) At a sale under subsection (b) of this section of property that is subject to a lien that secures an allowed claim, unless the court for cause orders otherwise the holder of such claim may bid at such sale, and, if the holder of such claim purchases such property, such holder may offset such claim against the purchase price of such property.

(l) Subject to the provisions of section 365, the trustee may use, sell, or lease property under subsection (b) or (c) of this section, or a plan under chapter 11, 12, or 13 of this title may provide for the use, sale, or lease of property, notwithstanding any provision in a contract, a lease, or applicable law that is conditioned on the insolvency or financial condition of the debtor, on the commencement of a case under this title concerning the debtor, or on the appointment of or the taking possession by a trustee in a case under this title or a custodian, and that effects, or gives an option to effect, a forfeiture, modification, or termination of the debtor's interest in such property.

(m) The reversal or modification on appeal of an authorization under subsection (b) or (c) of this section of a sale or lease of property does not affect the validity of a sale or lease under such authorization to an entity that purchased or leased such property in good faith, whether or not such entity knew of the pendency of the appeal, unless such authorization and such sale or lease were stayed pending appeal.

(n) The trustee may avoid a sale under this section if the sale price was controlled by an agreement among potential bidders at such sale, or may recover from a party to such agreement any amount by which the value of the property sold exceeds the price at which such sale was consummated, and may recover any costs, attorneys' fees, or expenses incurred in avoiding such sale or recovering such amount. In addition to any recovery under the preceding sentence, the court may grant judgment for punitive damages in favor of the estate and against any such party that entered into such an agreement in willful disregard of this subsection.

(o) Notwithstanding subsection (f), if a person purchases any interest in a consumer credit transaction that is subject to the Truth in Lending Act or any interest in a consumer credit contract (as defined in section 433.1 of title 16 of the Code of Federal Regulations (January 1, 2004), as amended from time to time), and if such interest is purchased through a sale under this section, then such person shall remain subject to all claims and defenses that are related to such consumer credit transaction or such consumer credit contract, to the same extent as such person would be subject to such claims and defenses of the consumer had such interest been purchased at a sale not under this section.

(p) In any hearing under this section—

(1) the trustee has the burden of proof on the issue of adequate protection; and

(2) the entity asserting an interest in property has the burden of proof on the issue of the validity, priority, or extent of such interest.

§ 364. Obtaining Credit

(a) If the trustee is authorized to operate the business of the debtor under section 721, 1108, 1183, 1184, 1203, 1204, or 1304 of this title, unless the court orders otherwise, the trustee may obtain unsecured credit and incur unsecured debt in the ordinary course of business allowable under section 503(b)(1) of this title as an administrative expense.

(b) The court, after notice and a hearing, may authorize the trustee to obtain unsecured credit or to incur unsecured debt other than under subsection (a) of this section, allowable under section 503(b)(1) of this title as an administrative expense.

(c) If the trustee is unable to obtain unsecured credit allowable under section 503(b)(1) of this title as an administrative expense, the court, after notice and a hearing, may authorize the obtaining of credit or the incurring of debt—

(1) with priority over any or all administrative expenses of the kind specified in section 503(b) or 507(b) of this title;

(2) secured by a lien on property of the estate that is not otherwise subject to a lien; or

(3) secured by a junior lien on property of the estate that is subject to a lien.

(d)(1) The court, after notice and a hearing, may authorize the obtaining of credit or the incurring of debt secured by a senior or equal lien on property of the estate that is subject to a lien only if—

(A) the trustee is unable to obtain such credit otherwise; and

(B) there is adequate protection of the interest of the holder of the lien on the property of the estate on which such senior or equal lien is proposed to be granted.

(2) In any hearing under this subsection, the trustee has the burden of proof on the issue of adequate protection.

(e) The reversal or modification on appeal of an authorization under this section to obtain credit or incur debt, or of a grant under this section of a priority or a lien, does not affect the validity of any debt so incurred, or any priority or lien so granted, to an entity that extended such credit in good faith, whether or not such entity knew of the pendency of the appeal, unless such authorization and the incurring of such debt, or the granting of such priority or lien, were stayed pending appeal.

(f) Except with respect to an entity that is an underwriter as defined in section 1145(b) of this title, section 5 of the Securities Act of 1933, the Trust Indenture Act of 1939, and any state or local law requiring registration for offer or sale of a security or registration or licensing of an issuer of, underwriter of, or broker or dealer in, a security does not apply to the offer or sale under this section of a security that is not an equity security.

§ 365. Executory Contracts and Unexpired Leases

(a) Except as provided in sections 765 and 766 of this title and in subsections (b), (c), and (d) of this section, the trustee, subject to the court's approval, may assume or reject any executory contract or unexpired lease of the debtor.

(b)(1) If there has been a default in an executory contract or unexpired lease of the debtor, the trustee may not assume such contract or lease unless, at the time of assumption of such contract or lease, the trustee—

(A) cures, or provides adequate assurance that the trustee will promptly cure, such default other than a default that is a breach of a provision relating to the satisfaction of any provision (other than a penalty rate or penalty provision) relating to a default arising from any failure to perform nonmonetary obligations under an unexpired lease of real property, if it is impossible for the trustee to cure such default by performing nonmonetary acts at and after the time of assumption, except that if such default arises from a failure to operate in accordance with a nonresidential real property lease, then such default shall be cured by performance at and after the time of assumption in accordance with such lease, and pecuniary losses resulting from such default shall be compensated in accordance with the provisions of this paragraph;

(B) compensates, or provides adequate assurance that the trustee will promptly compensate, a party other than the debtor to such contract or lease, for any actual pecuniary loss to such party resulting from such default; and

(C) provides adequate assurance of future performance under such contract or lease.

(2) Paragraph (1) of this subsection does not apply to a default that is a breach of a provision relating to—

(A) the insolvency or financial condition of the debtor at any time before the closing of the case;

(B) the commencement of a case under this title;

(C) the appointment of or taking possession by a trustee in a case under this title or a custodian before such commencement; or

(D) the satisfaction of any penalty rate or penalty provision relating to a default arising from any failure by the debtor to perform nonmonetary obligations under the executory contract or unexpired lease.

(3)(A) For the purposes of paragraph (1) of this subsection and paragraph (2)(B) of subsection (f), adequate assurance of future performance of a lease of real property in a shopping center includes adequate assurance—

(A) of the source of rent and other consideration due under such lease, and in the case of an assignment, that the financial condition and operating performance of the proposed assignee and its guarantors, if any, shall be similar to the financial condition and operating performance of the debtor and its guarantors, if any, as of the time the debtor became the lessee under the lease;

(B) that any percentage rent due under such lease will not decline substantially;

(C) that assumption or assignment of such lease is subject to all the provisions thereof, including (but not limited to) provisions such as a radius, location, use, or exclusivity provision, and will not breach any such provision contained in any other lease, financing agreement, or master agreement relating to such shopping center; and

(D) that assumption or assignment of such lease will not disrupt any tenant mix or balance in such shopping center.

(4) Notwithstanding any other provision of this section, if there has been a default in an unexpired lease of the debtor, other than a default of a kind specified in paragraph (2) of this subsection, the trustee may not require a lessor to provide services or supplies incidental to such lease before assumption of such lease unless the lessor is compensated under the terms of such lease for any services and supplies provided under such lease before assumption of such lease.

(c) The trustee may not assume or assign any executory contract or unexpired lease of the debtor, whether or not such contract or lease prohibits or restricts assignment of rights or delegation of duties, if—

(1)(A) applicable law excuses a party, other than the debtor, to such contract or lease from accepting performance from or rendering performance to an entity other than the debtor or the debtor in possession, whether or not such contract or lease prohibits or restricts assignment of rights or delegation of duties; and

(B) such party does not consent to such assumption or assignment; or

(2) such contract is a contract to make a loan, or extend other debt financing or financial accommodations, to or for the benefit of the debtor, or to issue a security of the debtor; or

(3) such lease is of nonresidential real property and has been terminated under applicable nonbankruptcy law prior to the order for relief.

(d)(1) In a case under chapter 7 of this title, if the trustee does not assume or reject an executory contract or unexpired lease of residential real property or of personal property of the debtor within 60 days after the order for relief, or within such additional time as the court, for cause, within such 60-day period, fixes, then such contract or lease is deemed rejected.

(2) In a case under chapter 9, 11, 12, or 13 of this title, the trustee may assume or reject an executory contract or unexpired lease of residential real property or of personal property of the debtor at any time before the confirmation of a plan but the court, on the request of any party to such contract or lease, may order the trustee to determine within a specified period of time whether to assume or reject such contract or lease.

(3) The trustee shall timely perform all the obligations of the debtor, except those specified in section 365(b)(2), arising from and after the order for relief under any unexpired lease of nonresidential real property, until such lease is assumed or rejected, notwithstanding section 503(b)(1) of this title. The court may extend, for cause, the time for performance of any such obligation that arises within 60 days after the date of the order for relief, but the time for performance shall not be extended beyond such 60-day period, except as provided in subparagraph (B). This subsection shall not be deemed to affect the trustee's obligations under the provisions of subsection (b) or (f) of this section. Acceptance of any such performance does not constitute waiver or relinquishment of the lessor's rights under such lease or under this title.

(4)(A) Subject to subparagraph (B), an unexpired lease of nonresidential real property under which the debtor is the lessee shall be deemed rejected, and the trustee shall immediately surrender that nonresidential real property to the lessor, if the trustee does not assume or reject the unexpired lease by the earlier of—

(i) the date that is 120 days after the date of the order for relief; or

(ii) the date of the entry of an order confirming a plan.

(B)(i) The court may extend the period determined under subparagraph (A), prior to the expiration of the 120-day period, for 90 days on the motion of the trustee or lessor for cause.

(ii) If the court grants an extension under clause (i), the court may grant a subsequent extension only upon prior written consent of the lessor in each instance.

(5) The trustee shall timely perform all of the obligations of the debtor, except those specified in section 365(b)(2), first arising from or after 60 days after the order for relief in a case under chapter 11 of this title under an unexpired lease of personal property (other than personal property leased to an individual primarily for personal, family, or household purposes), until such lease is assumed or rejected notwithstanding section 503(b)(1) of this title, unless the court, after notice and a hearing and based on the equities of the case, orders otherwise with respect to the obligations or timely performance thereof. This subsection shall not be deemed to affect the trustee's obligations under the provisions of subsection (b) or (f). Acceptance of any such performance does not constitute waiver or relinquishment of the lessor's rights under such lease or under this title.

(e)(1) Notwithstanding a provision in an executory contract or unexpired lease, or in applicable law, an executory contract or unexpired lease of the debtor may not be terminated or modified, and any right or obligation under such contract or lease may not be terminated or modified, at any time after the commencement of the case solely because of a provision in such contract or lease that is conditioned on—

(A) the insolvency or financial condition of the debtor at any time before the closing of the case;

(B) the commencement of a case under this title; or

(C) the appointment of or taking possession by a trustee in a case under this title or a custodian before such commencement.

(2) Paragraph (1) of this subsection does not apply to an executory contract or unexpired lease of the debtor, whether or not such contract or lease prohibits or restricts assignment of rights or delegation of duties, if—

(A)(i) applicable law excuses a party, other than the debtor, to such contract or lease from accepting performance from or rendering performance to the trustee or to an assignee of such contract or lease, whether or not such contract or lease prohibits or restricts assignment of rights or delegation of duties; and

(ii) such party does not consent to such assumption or assignment; or

(B) such contract is a contract to make a loan, or extend other debt financing or financial accommodations, to or for the benefit of the debtor, or to issue a security of the debtor.

(f)(1) Except as provided in subsections (b) and (c) of this section, notwithstanding a provision in an executory contract or unexpired lease of the debtor, or in applicable law, that prohibits, restricts, or conditions the assignment of such contract or lease, the trustee may assign such contract or lease under paragraph (2) of this subsection.

(2) The trustee may assign an executory contract or unexpired lease of the debtor only if—

(A) the trustee assumes such contract or lease in accordance with the provisions of this section; and

(B) adequate assurance of future performance by the assignee of such contract or lease is provided, whether or not there has been a default in such contract or lease.

(3) Notwithstanding a provision in an executory contract or unexpired lease of the debtor, or in applicable law that terminates or modifies, or permits a party other than the debtor to terminate or modify, such contract or lease or a right or obligation under such contract or lease on account of an assignment of such contract or lease, such contract, lease, right, or obligation may not be terminated or modified under such provision because of the assumption or assignment of such contract or lease by the trustee.

(g) Except as provided in subsections (h)(2) and (i)(2) of this section, the rejection of an executory contract or unexpired lease of the debtor constitutes a breach of such contract or lease—

(1) if such contract or lease has not been assumed under this section or under a plan confirmed under chapter 9, 11, 12, or 13 of this title, immediately before the date of the filing of the petition; or

(2) if such contract or lease has been assumed under this section or under a plan confirmed under chapter 9, 11, 12, or 13 of this title—

(A) if before such rejection the case has not been converted under section 1112, 1208, or 1307 of this title, at the time of such rejection; or

(B) if before such rejection the case has been converted under section 1112, 1208, or 1307 of this title—

(i) immediately before the date of such conversion, if such contract or lease was assumed before such conversion; or

(ii) at the time of such rejection, if such contract or lease was assumed after such conversion.

(h)(1)(A) If the trustee rejects an unexpired lease of real property under which the debtor is the lessor and—

(i) if the rejection by the trustee amounts to such a breach as would entitle the lessee to treat such lease as terminated by virtue of its terms, applicable nonbankruptcy law, or any agreement made by the lessee, then the lessee under such lease may treat such lease as terminated by the rejection; or

(ii) if the term of such lease has commenced, the lessee may retain its rights under such lease (including rights such as those relating to the amount and timing of payment of rent and other amounts payable by the lessee and any right of use, possession, quiet enjoyment, subletting, assignment, or hypothecation) that are in or appurtenant to the real property for the balance of the term of such lease and for any renewal or extension of such rights to the extent that such rights are enforceable under applicable nonbankruptcy law.

(B) If the lessee retains its rights under subparagraph (A)(ii), the lessee may offset against the rent reserved under such lease for the balance of the term after the date of the rejection of such lease and for the term of any renewal or extension of such lease, the value of any damage caused by the nonperformance after the date of such rejection, of any obligation of the debtor under such lease, but the lessee shall not have any other right against the estate or the debtor on account of any damage occurring after such date caused by such nonperformance.

(C) The rejection of a lease of real property in a shopping center with respect to which the lessee elects to retain its rights under subparagraph (A)(ii) does not affect the enforceability under applicable nonbankruptcy law of any provision in the lease pertaining to radius, location, use, exclusivity, or tenant mix or balance.

(D) In this paragraph, "lessee" includes any successor, assign, or mortgagee permitted under the terms of such lease.

(2)(A) If the trustee rejects a timeshare interest under a timeshare plan under which the debtor is the timeshare interest seller and—

(i) if the rejection amounts to such a breach as would entitle the timeshare interest purchaser to treat the timeshare plan as terminated under its terms, applicable nonbankruptcy law, or any agreement made by timeshare interest purchaser, the timeshare interest purchaser under the timeshare plan may treat the timeshare plan as terminated by such rejection; or

(ii) if the term of such timeshare interest has commenced, then the timeshare interest purchaser may retain its rights in such timeshare interest for the balance of such term and for any term of renewal or extension of such timeshare interest to the extent that such rights are enforceable under applicable nonbankruptcy law.

(B) If the timeshare interest purchaser retains its rights under subparagraph (A), such timeshare interest purchaser may offset against the moneys due for such timeshare interest for the balance of the term after the date of the rejection of such timeshare interest, and the term of any renewal or extension of such timeshare interest, the value of any damage caused by the nonperformance after the date of such rejection, of any obligation of the debtor under such timeshare plan, but the timeshare interest purchaser shall not have any right against the estate or the debtor on account of any damage occurring after such date caused by such nonperformance.

(i)(1) If the trustee rejects an executory contract of the debtor for the sale of real property or for the sale of a timeshare interest under a timeshare plan, under which the purchaser is in possession, such purchaser may treat such contract as terminated, or, in the alternative, may remain in possession of such real property or timeshare interest.

(2) If such purchaser remains in possession—

(A) such purchaser shall continue to make all payments due under such contract, but may, offset against such payments any damages occurring after the date of the rejection of such contract caused by the nonperformance of any obligation of the debtor after such date, but such purchaser does not have any rights against the estate on account of any damages arising after such date from such rejection, other than such offset; and

(B) the trustee shall deliver title to such purchaser in accordance with the provisions of such contract, but is relieved of all other obligations to perform under such contract.

(j) A purchaser that treats an executory contract as terminated under subsection (i) of this section, or a party whose executory contract to purchase real property from the debtor is rejected and under which such party is not in possession, has a lien on the interest of the debtor in such property for the recovery of any portion of the purchase price that such purchaser or party has paid.

(k) Assignment by the trustee to an entity of a contract or lease assumed under this section relieves the trustee and the estate from any liability for any breach of such contract or lease occurring after such assignment.

(l) If an unexpired lease under which the debtor is the lessee is assigned pursuant to this section, the lessor of the property may require a deposit or other security for the performance of the debtor's obligations under the lease substantially the same as would have been required by the landlord upon the initial leasing to a similar tenant.

(m) For purposes of this section 365 and sections 541(b)(2) and 362(b)(10), leases of real property shall include any rental agreement to use real property.

(n)(1) If the trustee rejects an executory contract under which the debtor is a licensor of a right to intellectual property, the licensee under such contract may elect—

(A) to treat such contract as terminated by such rejection if such rejection by the trustee amounts to such a breach as would entitle the licensee to treat such contract as terminated by virtue of its own terms, applicable nonbankruptcy law, or an agreement made by the licensee with another entity; or

(B) to retain its rights (including a right to enforce any exclusivity provision of such contract, but excluding any other right under applicable nonbankruptcy law to specific performance of such contract) under such contract and under any agreement supplementary to such contract, to such intellectual property (including any embodiment of such intellectual property to the extent protected by applicable nonbankruptcy law), as such rights existed immediately before the case commenced, for—

(i) the duration of such contract; and

(ii) any period for which such contract may be extended by the licensee as of right under applicable nonbankruptcy law.

(2) If the licensee elects to retain its rights, as described in paragraph (1)(B) of this subsection, under such contract—

(A) the trustee shall allow the licensee to exercise such rights;

(B) the licensee shall make all royalty payments due under such contract for the duration of such contract and for any period described in paragraph (1)(B) of this subsection for which the licensee extends such contract; and

(C) the licensee shall be deemed to waive—

(i) any right of setoff it may have with respect to such contract under this title or applicable nonbankruptcy law; and

(ii) any claim allowable under section 503(b) of this title arising from the performance of such contract.

(3) If the licensee elects to retain its rights, as described in paragraph (1)(B) of this subsection, then on the written request of the licensee the trustee shall—

(A) to the extent provided in such contract, or any agreement supplementary to such contract, provide to the licensee any intellectual property (including such embodiment) held by the trustee; and

(B) not interfere with the rights of the licensee as provided in such contract, or any agreement supplementary to such contract, to such intellectual property (including such embodiment) including any right to obtain such intellectual property (or such embodiment) from another entity.

(4) Unless and until the trustee rejects such contract, on the written request of the licensee the trustee shall—

(A) to the extent provided in such contract or any agreement supplementary to such contract—

(i) perform such contract; or

(ii) provide to the licensee such intellectual property (including any embodiment of such intellectual property to the extent protected by applicable nonbankruptcy law) held by the trustee; and

(B) not interfere with the rights of the licensee as provided in such contract, or any agreement supplementary to such contract, to such intellectual property (including such embodiment), including any right to obtain such intellectual property (or such embodiment) from another entity.

(o) In a case under chapter 11 of this title, the trustee shall be deemed to have assumed (consistent with the debtor's other obligations under section 507), and shall immediately cure any deficit under, any commitment by the debtor to a Federal depository institutions regulatory agency (or predecessor to such agency) to maintain the capital of an insured depository institution, and any claim for a subsequent breach of the obligations thereunder shall be entitled to priority under section 507. This subsection shall not extend any commitment that would otherwise be terminated by any act of such an agency.

(p)(1) If a lease of personal property is rejected or not timely assumed by the trustee under subsection (d), the leased property is no longer property of the estate and the stay under section 362(a) is automatically terminated.

(2)(A) If the debtor in a case under chapter 7 is an individual, the debtor may notify the creditor in writing that the debtor desires to assume the lease. Upon being so notified, the creditor may, at its option, notify the debtor that it is willing to have the lease assumed by the debtor and may condition such assumption on cure of any outstanding default on terms set by the contract.

(B) If, not later than 30 days after notice is provided under subparagraph (A), the debtor notifies the lessor in writing that the lease is assumed, the liability under the lease will be assumed by the debtor and not by the estate.

(C) The stay under section 362 and the injunction under section 524(a)(2) shall not be violated by notification of the debtor and negotiation of cure under this subsection.

(3) In a case under chapter 11 in which the debtor is an individual and in a case under chapter 13, if the debtor is the lessee with respect to personal property and the lease is not assumed in the plan confirmed by the court, the lease is deemed rejected as of the conclusion of the hearing on confirmation. If the

lease is rejected, the stay under section 362 and any stay under section 1301 is automatically terminated with respect to the property subject to the lease.

§ 366. Utility Service

(a) Except as provided in subsections (b) and (c) of this section, a utility may not alter, refuse, or discontinue service to, or discriminate against, the trustee or the debtor solely on the basis of the commencement of a case under this title or that a debt owed by the debtor to such utility for service rendered before the order for relief was not paid when due.

(b) Such utility may alter, refuse, or discontinue service if neither the trustee nor the debtor, within 20 days after the date of the order for relief, furnishes adequate assurance of payment, in the form of a deposit or other security, for service after such date. On request of a party in interest and after notice and a hearing, the court may order reasonable modification of the amount of the deposit or other security necessary to provide adequate assurance of payment.

(c)(1)(A) For purposes of this subsection, the term "assurance of payment" means—

(i) a cash deposit;

(ii) a letter of credit;

(iii) a certificate of deposit;

(iv) a surety bond;

(v) a prepayment of utility consumption; or

(vi) another form of security that is mutually agreed on between the utility and the debtor or the trustee.

(B) For purposes of this subsection an administrative expense priority shall not constitute an assurance of payment.

(2) Subject to paragraphs (3) and (4), with respect to a case filed under chapter 11, a utility referred to in subsection (a) may alter, refuse, or discontinue utility service, if during the 30-day period beginning on the date of the filing of the petition, the utility does not receive from the debtor or the trustee adequate assurance of payment for utility service that is satisfactory to the utility.

(3)(A) On request of a party in interest and after notice and a hearing, the court may order modification of the amount of an assurance of payment under paragraph (2).

(B) In making a determination under this paragraph whether an assurance of payment is adequate, the court may not consider—

(i) the absence of security before the date of the filing of the petition;

(ii) the payment by the debtor of charges for utility service in a timely manner before the date of the filing of the petition; or

(iii) the availability of an administrative expense priority.

(4) Notwithstanding any other provision of law, with respect to a case subject to this subsection, a utility may recover or set off against a security deposit provided to the utility by the debtor before the date of the filing of the petition without notice or order of the court.

CHAPTER 5. CREDITORS, THE DEBTOR, AND THE ESTATE

SUBCHAPTER I—CREDITORS AND CLAIMS

Section

SUBCHAPTER II—DEBTOR'S DUTIES AND BENEFITS

Section

SUBCHAPTER III—THE ESTATE

Section

SUBCHAPTER I—CREDITORS AND CLAIMS

§ 501. Filing of Proofs of Claims or Interests

(a) A creditor or an indenture trustee may file a proof of claim. An equity security holder may file a proof of interest.

(b) If a creditor does not timely file a proof of such creditor's claim, an entity that is liable to such creditor with the debtor, or that has secured such creditor, may file a proof of such claim.

(c) If a creditor does not timely file a proof of such creditor's claim, the debtor or the trustee may file a proof of such claim.

(d) A claim of a kind specified in section 502(e)(2), 502(f), 502(g), 502(h) or 502(i) of this title may be filed under subsection (a), (b), or (c) of this section the same as if such claim were a claim against the debtor and had arisen before the date of the filing of the petition.

(e) A claim arising from the liability of a debtor for fuel use tax assessed consistent with the requirements of section 31705 of title 49 may be filed by the base jurisdiction designated pursuant to the International Fuel Tax Agreement (as defined in section 31701 of title 49) and, if so filed, shall be allowed as a single claim.

§ 502. Allowance of Claims or Interests

(a) A claim or interest, proof of which is filed under section 501 of this title, is deemed allowed, unless a party in interest, including a creditor of a general partner in a partnership that is a debtor in a case under chapter 7 of this title, objects.

(b) Except as provided in subsections (e)(2), (f), (g), (h) and (i) of this section, if such objection to a claim is made, the court, after notice and a hearing, shall determine the amount of such claim in lawful currency of the United States as of the date of the filing of the petition, and shall allow such claim in such amount, except to the extent that—

(1) such claim is unenforceable against the debtor and property of the debtor, under any agreement or applicable law for a reason other than because such claim is contingent or unmatured;

(2) such claim is for unmatured interest;

(3) if such claim is for a tax assessed against property of the estate, such claim exceeds the value of the interest of the estate in such property;

(4) if such claim is for services of an insider or attorney of the debtor, such claim exceeds the reasonable value of such services;

(5) such claim is for a debt that is unmatured on the date of the filing of the petition and that is excepted from discharge under section 523(a)(5) of this title;

(6) if such claim is the claim of a lessor for damages resulting from the termination of a lease of real property, such claim exceeds—

(A) the rent reserved by such lease, without acceleration, for the greater of one year, or 15 percent, not to exceed three years, of the remaining term of such lease, following the earlier of—

(i) the date of the filing of the petition; and

(ii) the date on which such lessor repossessed, or the lessee surrendered, the leased property; plus

(B) any unpaid rent due under such lease, without acceleration, on the earlier of such dates;

(7) if such claim is the claim of an employee for damages resulting from the termination of an employment contract, such claim exceeds—

(A) the compensation provided by such contract, without acceleration, for one year following the earlier of—

(i) the date of the filing of the petition; or

(ii) the date on which the employer directed the employee to terminate, or such employee terminated, performance under such contract; plus

(B) any unpaid compensation due under such contract, without acceleration, on the earlier of such dates;

(8) such claim results from a reduction, due to late payment, in the amount of an otherwise applicable credit available to the debtor in connection with an employment tax on wages, salaries, or commissions earned from the debtor; or

(9) proof of such claim is not timely filed, except to the extent tardily filed as permitted under paragraph (1), (2), or (3) of section 726(a) of this title or under the Federal Rules of Bankruptcy Procedure, except that—

(A) a claim of a governmental unit shall be timely filed if it is filed before 180 days after the date of the order for relief or such later time as the Federal Rules of Bankruptcy Procedure may provide; and

(B) in a case under chapter 13, a claim of a governmental unit for a tax with respect to a return filed under section 1308 shall be timely if the claim is filed on or before the date that is 60 days after the date on which such return was filed as required.

(c) There shall be estimated for purpose of allowance under this section—

(1) any contingent or unliquidated claim, the fixing or liquidation of which, as the case may be, would unduly delay the administration of the case; or

(2) any right to payment arising from a right to an equitable remedy for breach of performance.

(d) Notwithstanding subsections (a) and (b) of this section, the court shall disallow any claim of any entity from which property is recoverable under section 542, 543, 550, or 553 of this title or that is a transferee of a transfer avoidable under section 522(f), 522(h), 544, 545, 547, 548, 549, or 724(a) of this title, unless such entity or transferee has paid the amount, or turned over any such property, for which such entity or transferee is liable under section 522(i), 542, 543, 550, or 553 of this title.

(e)(1) Notwithstanding subsections (a), (b), and (c) of this section and paragraph (2) of this subsection, the court shall disallow any claim for reimbursement or contribution of an entity that is liable with the debtor on or has secured the claim of a creditor, to the extent that—

(A) such creditor's claim against the estate is disallowed;

(B) such claim for reimbursement or contribution is contingent as of the time of allowance or disallowance of such claim for reimbursement or contribution; or

(C) such entity asserts a right of subrogation to the rights of such creditor under section 509 of this title.

(2) A claim for reimbursement or contribution of such an entity that becomes fixed after the commencement of the case shall be determined, and shall be allowed under subsection (a), (b), or (c) of this section, or disallowed under subsection (d) of this section, the same as if such claim had become fixed before the date of the filing of the petition.

(f) In an involuntary case, a claim arising in the ordinary course of the debtor's business or financial affairs after the commencement of the case but before the earlier of the appointment of a trustee and the order for relief shall be determined as of the date such claim arises, and shall be allowed under subsection (a), (b), or (c) of this section or disallowed under subsection (d) or (e) of this section, the same as if such claim had arisen before the date of the filing of the petition.

(g)(1) A claim arising from the rejection, under section 365 of this title or under a plan under chapter 9, 11, 12, or 13 of this title, of an executory contract or unexpired lease of the debtor that has not been assumed shall be determined, and shall be allowed under subsection (a), (b), or (c) of this section or disallowed under subsection (d) or (e) of this section, the same as if such claim had arisen before the date of the filing of the petition.

(2) A claim for damages calculated in accordance with section 562 shall be allowed under subsection (a), (b), or (c), or disallowed under subsection (d) or (e), as if such claim had arisen before the date of the filing of the petition.

(h) A claim arising from the recovery of property under section 522, 550, or 553 of this title shall be determined, and shall be allowed under subsection (a), (b), or (c) of this section, or disallowed under subsection (d) or (e) of this section, the same as if such claim had arisen before the date of the filing of the petition.

(i) A claim that does not arise until after the commencement of the case for a tax entitled to priority under section 507(a)(8) of this title shall be determined, and shall be allowed under subsection (a), (b), or (c) of this section, or disallowed under subsection (d) or (e) of this section, the same as if such claim had arisen before the date of the filing of the petition.

(j) A claim that has been allowed or disallowed may be reconsidered for cause. A reconsidered claim may be allowed or disallowed according to the equities of the case. Reconsideration of a claim under this subsection does not affect the validity of any payment or transfer from the estate made to a holder of an allowed claim on account of such allowed claim that is not reconsidered, but if a reconsidered claim is allowed and is of the same class as such holder's claim, such holder may not receive any additional payment or transfer from the estate on account of such holder's allowed claim until the holder of such reconsidered and allowed claim receives payment on account of such claim proportionate in value to that already received by such other holder. This subsection does not alter or modify the trustee's right to recover from a creditor any excess payment or transfer made to such creditor.

(k)(1) The court, on the motion of the debtor and after a hearing, may reduce a claim filed under this section based in whole on an unsecured consumer debt by not more than 20 percent of the claim, if—

(A) the claim was filed by a creditor who unreasonably refused to negotiate a reasonable alternative repayment schedule proposed on behalf of the debtor by an approved nonprofit budget and credit counseling agency described in section 111;

(B) the offer of the debtor under subparagraph (A)—

(i) was made at least 60 days before the date of the filing of the petition; and

(ii) provided for payment of at least 60 percent of the amount of the debt over a period not to exceed the repayment period of the loan, or a reasonable extension thereof; and

(C) no part of the debt under the alternative repayment schedule is nondischargeable.

(2) The debtor shall have the burden of proving, by clear and convincing evidence, that—

(A) the creditor unreasonably refused to consider the debtor's proposal; and

(B) the proposed alternative repayment schedule was made prior to expiration of the 60-day period specified in paragraph (1)(B)(i).

§ 503. Allowance of Administrative Expenses

(a) An entity may timely file a request for payment of an administrative expense, or may tardily file such request if permitted by the court for cause.

(b) After notice and a hearing, there shall be allowed administrative expenses, other than claims allowed under section 502(f) of this title, including—

(1)(A) the actual, necessary costs and expenses of preserving the estate including—

(i) wages, salaries, and commissions for services rendered after the commencement of the case; and

(ii) wages and benefits awarded pursuant to a judicial proceeding or a proceeding of the National Labor Relations Board as back pay attributable to any period of time occurring after commencement of the case under this title, as a result of a violation of Federal or State law by the debtor, without regard to the time of the occurrence of unlawful conduct on which such award is based or to whether any services were rendered, if the court determines that payment of wages and benefits by reason of the operation of this clause will not substantially increase the probability of layoff or termination of current employees, or of nonpayment of domestic support obligations, during the case under this title;

(B) any tax—

(i) incurred by the estate, whether secured or unsecured, including property taxes for which liability is in rem, in personam, or both, except a tax of a kind specified in section 507(a)(8) of this title; or

(ii) attributable to an excessive allowance of a tentative carryback adjustment that the estate received, whether the taxable year to which such adjustment relates ended before or after the commencement of the case;

(C) any fine, penalty, or reduction in credit relating to a tax of a kind specified in subparagraph (B) of this paragraph; and

(D) notwithstanding the requirements of subsection (a), a governmental unit shall not be required to file a request for the payment of an expense described in subparagraph (B) or (C), as a condition of its being an allowed administrative expense;

(2) compensation and reimbursement awarded under section 330(a) of this title;

(3) the actual, necessary expenses, other than compensation and reimbursement specified in paragraph (4) of this subsection, incurred by—

(A) a creditor that files a petition under section 303 of this title;

(B) a creditor that recovers, after the court's approval, for the benefit of the estate any property transferred or concealed by the debtor;

(C) a creditor in connection with the prosecution of a criminal offense relating to the case or to the business or property of the debtor;

(D) a creditor, an indenture trustee, an equity security holder, or a committee representing creditors or equity security holders other than a committee appointed under section 1102 of this title, in making a substantial contribution in a case under chapter 9 or 11 of this title;

(E) a custodian superseded under section 543 of this title, and compensation for the services of such custodian; or

(F) a member of a committee appointed under section 1102 of this title, if such expenses are incurred in the performance of the duties of such committee;

(4) reasonable compensation for professional services rendered by an attorney or an accountant of an entity whose expense is allowable under subparagraph (A), (B), (C), (D), or (E) of paragraph (3) of this subsection, based on the time, the nature, the extent, and the value of such services, and the cost of comparable services other than in a case under this title, and reimbursement for actual, necessary expenses incurred by such attorney or accountant;

(5) reasonable compensation for services rendered by an indenture trustee in making a substantial contribution in a case under chapter 9 or 11 of this title, based on the time, the nature, the extent, and the value of such services, and the cost of comparable services other than in a case under this title;

(6) the fees and mileage payable under chapter 119 of title 28;

(7) with respect to a nonresidential real property lease previously assumed under section 365, and subsequently rejected, a sum equal to all monetary obligations due, excluding those arising from or relating to a failure to operate or a penalty provision, for the period of 2 years following the later of the rejection date or the date of actual turnover of the premises, without reduction or setoff for any reason whatsoever except for sums actually received or to be received from an entity other than the debtor, and the claim for remaining sums due for the balance of the term of the lease shall be a claim under section 502(b)(6);

(8) the actual, necessary costs and expenses of closing a health care business incurred by a trustee or by a Federal agency (as defined in section 551(1) of title 5) or a department or agency of a State or political subdivision thereof, including any cost or expense incurred—

(A) in disposing of patient records in accordance with section 351; or

(B) in connection with transferring patients from the health care business that is in the process of being closed to another health care business;

(9) the value of any goods received by the debtor within 20 days before the date of commencement of a case under this title in which the goods have been sold to the debtor in the ordinary course of such debtor's business.

(c) Notwithstanding subsection (b), there shall neither be allowed, nor paid—

(1) a transfer made to, or an obligation incurred for the benefit of, an insider of the debtor for the purpose of inducing such person to remain with the debtor's business, absent a finding by the court based on evidence in the record that—

(A) the transfer or obligation is essential to retention of the person because the individual has a bona fide job offer from another business at the same or greater rate of compensation;

(B) the services provided by the person are essential to the survival of the business; and

(C) either—

(i) the amount of the transfer made to, or obligation incurred for the benefit of, the person is not greater than an amount equal to 10 times the amount of the mean transfer or obligation of a similar kind given to nonmanagement employees for any purpose during the calendar year in which the transfer is made or the obligation is incurred; or

(ii) if no such similar transfers were made to, or obligations were incurred for the benefit of, such nonmanagement employees during such calendar year, the amount of the transfer or obligation is not greater than an amount equal to 25 percent of the amount of any similar transfer or obligation made to or incurred for the benefit of such insider for any purpose during the calendar year before the year in which such transfer is made or obligation is incurred;

(2) a severance payment to an insider of the debtor, unless—

(A) the payment is part of a program that is generally applicable to all full-time employees; and

(B) the amount of the payment is not greater than 10 times the amount of the mean severance pay given to nonmanagement employees during the calendar year in which the payment is made; or

(3) other transfers or obligations that are outside the ordinary course of business and not justified by the facts and circumstances of the case, including transfers made to, or obligations incurred for the benefit of, officers, managers, or consultants hired after the date of the filing of the petition.

§ 504. Sharing of Compensation

(a) Except as provided in subsection (b) of this section, a person receiving compensation or reimbursement under section 503(b)(2) or 503(b)(4) of this title may not share or agree to share—

(1) any such compensation or reimbursement with another person; or

(2) any compensation or reimbursement received by another person under such sections.

(b)(1) A member, partner, or regular associate in a professional association, corporation, or partnership may share compensation or reimbursement received under section 503(b)(2) or 503(b)(4) of this title with another member, partner, or regular associate in such association, corporation, or partnership, and may share in any compensation or reimbursement received under such sections by another member, partner, or regular associate in such association, corporation, or partnership.

(2) An attorney for a creditor that files a petition under section 303 of this title may share compensation and reimbursement received under section 503(b)(4) of this title with any other attorney contributing to the services rendered or expenses incurred by such creditor's attorney.

(c) This section shall not apply with respect to sharing, or agreeing to share, compensation with a bona fide public service attorney referral program that operates in accordance with non-Federal law regulating attorney referral services and with rules of professional responsibility applicable to attorney acceptance of referrals.

§ 505. Determination of Tax Liability

(a)(1) Except as provided in paragraph (2) of this subsection, the court may determine the amount or legality of any tax, any fine or penalty relating to a tax, or any addition to tax, whether or not previously assessed, whether or not paid, and whether or not contested before and adjudicated by a judicial or administrative tribunal of competent jurisdiction.

(2) The court may not so determine—

(A) the amount or legality of a tax, fine, penalty, or addition to tax if such amount or legality was contested before and adjudicated by a judicial or administrative tribunal of competent jurisdiction before the commencement of the case under this title;

(B) any right of the estate to a tax refund, before the earlier of—

(i) 120 days after the trustee properly requests such refund from the governmental unit from which such refund is claimed; or

(ii) a determination by such governmental unit of such request; or

(C) the amount or legality of any amount arising in connection with an ad valorem tax on real or personal property of the estate, if the applicable period for contesting or redetermining that amount under applicable nonbankruptcy law has expired.

(b)(1)(A) The clerk shall maintain a list under which a Federal, State, or local governmental unit responsible for the collection of taxes within the district may—

(i) designate an address for service of requests under this subsection; and

(ii) describe where further information concerning additional requirements for filing such requests may be found.

(B) If such governmental unit does not designate an address and provide such address to the clerk under subparagraph (A), any request made under this subsection may be served at the address for the filing of a tax return or protest with the appropriate taxing authority of such governmental unit.

(2) A trustee may request a determination of any unpaid liability of the estate for any tax incurred during the administration of the case by submitting a tax return for such tax and a request for such a determination to the governmental unit charged with responsibility for collection or determination of such tax at the address and in the manner designated in paragraph (1). Unless such return is fraudulent, or contains a material misrepresentation, the estate, the trustee, the debtor, and any successor to the debtor are discharged from any liability for such tax—

(A) upon payment of the tax shown on such return, if—

(i) such governmental unit does not notify the trustee, within 60 days after such request, that such return has been selected for examination; or

(ii) such governmental unit does not complete such an examination and notify the trustee of any tax due, within 180 days after such request or within such additional time as the court, for cause, permits;

(B) upon payment of the tax determined by the court, after notice and a hearing, after completion by such governmental unit of such examination; or

(C) upon payment of the tax determined by such governmental unit to be due.

(c) Notwithstanding section 362 of this title, after determination by the court of a tax under this section, the governmental unit charged with responsibility for collection of such tax may assess such tax against the estate, the debtor, or a successor to the debtor, as the case may be, subject to any otherwise applicable law.

§ 506. Determination of Secured Status

(a)(1) An allowed claim of a creditor secured by a lien on property in which the estate has an interest, or that is subject to setoff under section 553 of this title, is a secured claim to the extent of the value of such creditor's interest in the estate's interest in such property, or to the extent of the amount subject to setoff, as the case may be, and is an unsecured claim to the extent that the value of such creditor's interest or the amount so subject to setoff is less than the amount of such allowed claim. Such value shall be determined in light of the purpose of the valuation and of the proposed disposition or use of such property, and in conjunction with any hearing on such disposition or use or on a plan affecting such creditor's interest.

(2) If the debtor is an individual in a case under chapter 7 or 13, such value with respect to personal property securing an allowed claim shall be determined based on the replacement value of such property as of the date of the filing of the petition without deduction for costs of sale or marketing. With respect to property acquired for personal, family, or household purposes, replacement value shall mean the price a retail merchant would charge for property of that kind considering the age and condition of the property at the time value is determined.

(b) To the extent that an allowed secured claim is secured by property the value of which, after any recovery under subsection (c) of this section, is greater than the amount of such claim, there shall be allowed to the holder of such claim, interest on such claim, and any reasonable fees, costs, or charges provided for under the agreement or state statute under which such claim arose.

(c) The trustee may recover from property securing an allowed secured claim the reasonable, necessary costs and expenses of preserving, or disposing of, such property to the extent of any benefit to the holder of such claim, including the payment of all ad valorem property taxes with respect to the property.

(d) To the extent that a lien secures a claim against the debtor that is not an allowed secured claim, such lien is void, unless—

(1) such claim was disallowed only under section 502(b)(5) or 502(e) of this title; or

(2) such claim is not an allowed secured claim due only to the failure of any entity to file a proof of such claim under section 501 of this title.

§ 507. Priorities

(a) Subject to subsection (e), the following expenses and claims have priority in the following order:

(1) First:

(A) Allowed unsecured claims for domestic support obligations that, as of the date of the filing of the petition in a case under this title, are owed to or recoverable by a spouse, former spouse, or child of the debtor, or such child's parent, legal guardian, or responsible relative, without regard to whether the claim is filed by such person or is filed by a governmental unit on behalf of such person, on the condition that funds received under this paragraph by a governmental unit under this title after the date of the filing of the petition shall be applied and distributed in accordance with applicable nonbankruptcy law.

(B) Subject to claims under subparagraph (A), allowed unsecured claims for domestic support obligations that, as of the date of the filing of the petition, are assigned by a spouse, former spouse, child of the debtor, or such child's parent, legal guardian, or responsible relative to a governmental unit (unless such obligation is assigned voluntarily by the spouse, former spouse, child, parent, legal guardian, or responsible relative of the child for the purpose of collecting the debt) or are owed directly to or recoverable by a governmental unit under applicable nonbankruptcy law, on the condition that funds received under this paragraph by a governmental unit under this title after the date of the filing of the petition be applied and distributed in accordance with applicable nonbankruptcy law.

(C) If a trustee is appointed or elected under section 701, 702, 703, 1104, 1202, or 1302, the administrative expenses of the trustee allowed under paragraphs (1)(A), (2), and (6) of section 503(b) shall be paid before payment of claims under subparagraphs (A) and (B), to the extent that the trustee administers assets that are otherwise available for the payment of such claims.

(2) Second, administrative expenses allowed under section 503(b) of this title, unsecured claims of any Federal reserve bank related to loans made through programs or facilities authorized under section 13(3) of the Federal Reserve Act (12 U.S.C. 343), and any fees and charges assessed against the estate under chapter 123 of title 28.

(3) Third, unsecured claims allowed under section 502(f) of this title.

(4) Fourth, allowed unsecured claims, but only to the extent of $17,150 for each individual or corporation, as the case may be, earned within 180 days before the date of the filing of the petition or the date of the cessation of the debtor's business, whichever occurs first, for—

(A) wages, salaries, or commissions, including vacation, severance, and sick leave pay earned by an individual; or

(B) sales commissions earned by an individual or by a corporation with only 1 employee, acting as an independent contractor in the sale of goods or services for the debtor in the ordinary course of the debtor's business if, and only if, during the 12 months preceding that date, at least 75 percent of the amount that the individual or corporation earned by acting as an independent contractor in the sale of goods or services was earned from the debtor.

(5) Fifth, allowed unsecured claims for contributions to an employee benefit plan—

(A) arising from services rendered within 180 days before the date of the filing of the petition or the date of the cessation of the debtor's business, whichever occurs first; but only

(B) for each such plan, to the extent of—

(i) the number of employees covered by each such plan multiplied by $17,150; less

(ii) the aggregate amount paid to such employees under paragraph (4) of this subsection, plus the aggregate amount paid by the estate on behalf of such employees to any other employee benefit plan.

(6) Sixth, allowed unsecured claims of persons—

(A) engaged in the production or raising of grain, as defined in section 557(b) of this title, against a debtor who owns or operates a grain storage facility, as defined in section 557(b) of this title, for grain or the proceeds of grain, or

(B) engaged as a United States fisherman against a debtor who has acquired fish or fish produce from a fisherman through a sale or conversion, and who is engaged in operating a fish produce storage or processing facility—

but only to the extent of $8,450 for each such individual.

(7) Seventh, allowed unsecured claims of individuals, to the extent of $3,800 for each such individual, arising from the deposit, before the commencement of the case, of money in connection with the purchase, lease, or rental of property, or the purchase of services, for the personal, family, or household use of such individuals, that were not delivered or provided.

(8) Eighth, allowed unsecured claims of governmental units, only to the extent that such claims are for—

(A) a tax on or measured by income or gross receipts for a taxable year ending on or before the date of the filing of the petition—

(i) for which a return, if required, is last due, including extensions, after three years before the date of the filing of the petition;

(ii) assessed within 240 days before the date of the filing of the petition, exclusive of—

(I) any time during which an offer in compromise with respect to that tax was pending or in effect during that 240-day period, plus 30 days; and

(II) any time during which a stay of proceedings against collections was in effect in a prior case under this title during that 240-day period, plus 90 days; or

(iii) other than a tax of a kind specified in section 523(a)(1)(B) or 523(a)(1)(C) of this title, not assessed before, but assessable, under applicable law or by agreement, after, the commencement of the case;

(B) a property tax incurred before the commencement of the case and last payable without penalty after one year before the date of the filing of the petition;

(C) a tax required to be collected or withheld and for which the debtor is liable in whatever capacity;

(D) an employment tax on a wage, salary, or commission of a kind specified in paragraph

(4) of this subsection earned from the debtor before the date of the filing of the petition, whether or not actually paid before such date, for which a return is last due, under applicable law or under any extension, after three years before the date of the filing of the petition;

(E) an excise tax on—

(i) a transaction occurring before the date of the filing of the petition for which a return, if required, is last due, under applicable law or under any extension, after three years before the date of the filing of the petition; or

(ii) if a return is not required, a transaction occurring during the three years immediately preceding the date of the filing of the petition;

(F) a customs duty arising out of the importation of merchandise—

(i) entered for consumption within one year before the date of the filing of the petition;

(ii) covered by an entry liquidated or reliquidated within one year before the date of the filing of the petition; or

(iii) entered for consumption within four years before the date of the filing of the petition but unliquidated on such date, if the Secretary of the Treasury certifies that failure to liquidate such entry was due to an investigation pending on such date into assessment of antidumping or countervailing duties or fraud, or if information needed for the proper appraisement or classification of such merchandise was not available to the appropriate customs officer before such date; or

(G) a penalty related to a claim of a kind specified in this paragraph and in compensation for actual pecuniary loss. An otherwise applicable time period specified in this paragraph shall be suspended for any period during which a governmental unit is prohibited under applicable nonbankruptcy law from collecting a tax as a result of a request by the debtor for a hearing and an appeal of any collection action taken or proposed against the debtor, plus 90 days; plus any time during which the stay of proceedings was in effect in a prior case under this title or during which collection was precluded by the existence of 1 or more confirmed plans under this title, plus 90 days.

(9) Ninth, allowed unsecured claims based upon any commitment by the debtor to a Federal depository institutions regulatory agency (or predecessor to such agency) to maintain the capital of an insured depository institution.

(10) Tenth, allowed claims for death or personal injury resulting from the operation of a motor vehicle or vessel if such operation was unlawful because the debtor was intoxicated from using alcohol, a drug, or another substance.

(b) If the trustee, under section 362, 363, or 364 of this title, provides adequate protection of the interest of a holder of a claim secured by a lien on property of the debtor and if, notwithstanding such protection, such creditor has a claim allowable under subsection (a)(2) of this section arising from the stay of action against such property under section 362 of this title, from the use, sale, or lease of such property under section 363 of this title, or from the granting of a lien under section 364(d) of this title, then such creditor's claim under such subsection shall have priority over every other claim allowable under such subsection.

(c) For the purpose of subsection (a) of this section, a claim of a governmental unit arising from an erroneous refund or credit of a tax has the same priority as a claim for the tax to which such refund or credit relates.

(d) An entity that is subrogated to the rights of a holder of a claim of a kind specified in subsection (a)(1), (a)(4), (a)(5), (a)(6), (a)(7), (a)(8) excluding subparagraph (F), or (a)(9) of this section is not subrogated to the right of the holder of such claim to priority under such subsection.

(e) Notwithstanding subsection (a), if a payment stablecoin holder is not able to redeem all outstanding payment stablecoin claims from required payment stablecoin reserves maintained by the permitted payment stablecoin issuer, any such remaining claim arising from a person's holding of a payment stablecoin issued by the permitted payment stablecoin issuer shall be a claim against the estate and shall have first priority over any other claim, including over any expenses and claims that have priority under that subsection, to the extent compliance with section 4 of the GENIUS Act would have required additional reserves to be maintained by the permitted payment stablecoin issuer for payment stablecoin holders.

§ 508. Effect of Distribution Other Than Under This Title

If a creditor of a partnership debtor receives, from a general partner that is not a debtor in a case under chapter 7 of this title, payment of, or a transfer of property on account of, a claim that is allowed under this title and that is not secured by a lien on property of such partner, such creditor may not receive any payment under this title on account of such claim until each of the other holders of claims on account of which such holders are entitled to share equally with such creditor under this title has received payment under this title equal in value to the consideration received by such creditor from such general partner.

§ 509. Claims of Codebtors

(a) Except as provided in subsection (b) or (c) of this section, an entity that is liable with the debtor on, or that has secured, a claim of a creditor against the debtor, and that pays such claim, is subrogated to the rights of such creditor to the extent of such payment.

(b) such entity is not subrogated to the rights of such creditor to the extent that—

(1) a claim of such entity for reimbursement or contribution on account of such payment of such creditor's claim is—

(A) allowed under section 502 of this title;

(B) disallowed other than under section 502(e) of this title; or

(C) subordinated under section 510 of this title; or

(2) as between the debtor and such entity, such entity received the consideration for the claim held by such creditor.

(c) the court shall subordinate to the claim of a creditor and for the benefit of such creditor an allowed claim, by way of subrogation under this section, or for reimbursement or contribution, of an entity that is liable with the debtor on, or that has secured, such creditor's claim, until such creditor's claim is paid in full, either through payments under this title or otherwise.

§ 510. Subordination

(a) A subordination agreement is enforceable in a case under this title to the same extent that such agreement is enforceable under applicable nonbankruptcy law.

(b) For the purpose of distribution under this title, a claim arising from rescission of a purchase or sale of a security of the debtor or of an affiliate of the debtor, for damages arising from the purchase or sale of such a security, or for reimbursement or contribution allowed under section 502 on account of such a claim, shall be subordinated to all claims or interests that are senior to or equal the claim or interest represented by such security, except that if such security is common stock, such claim has the same priority as common stock.

(c) Notwithstanding subsections (a) and (b) of this section, after notice and a hearing, the court may—

(1) under principles of equitable subordination, subordinate for purposes of distribution all or part of an allowed claim to all or part of another allowed claim or all or part of an allowed interest to all or part of another allowed interest; or

(2) order that any lien securing such a subordinated claim be transferred to the estate.

§ 511. Rate of Interest on Tax Claims

(a) If any provision of this title requires the payment of interest on a tax claim or on an administrative expense tax, or the payment of interest to enable a creditor to receive the present value of the allowed amount of a tax claim, the rate of interest shall be the rate determined under applicable nonbankruptcy law.

(b) In the case of taxes paid under a confirmed plan under this title, the rate of interest shall be determined as of the calendar month in which the plan is confirmed.

SUBCHAPTER II—DEBTOR'S DUTIES AND BENEFITS

§ 521. Debtor's Duties

(a) The debtor shall—

(1) file—

(A) a list of creditors; and

(B) unless the court orders otherwise—

(i) a schedule of assets and liabilities;

(ii) a schedule of current income and current expenditures;

(iii) a statement of the debtor's financial affairs and, if section 342(b) applies, a certificate—

(I) of an attorney whose name is indicated on the petition as the attorney for the debtor, or a bankruptcy petition preparer signing the petition under section 110(b)(1), indicating that such attorney or the bankruptcy petition preparer delivered to the debtor the notice required by section 342(b); or

(II) if no attorney is so indicated, and no bankruptcy petition preparer signed the petition, of the debtor that such notice was received and read by the debtor;

(iv) copies of all payment advices or other evidence of payment received within 60 days before the date of the filing of the petition, by the debtor from any employer of the debtor;

(v) a statement of the amount of monthly net income, itemized to show how the amount is calculated; and

(vi) a statement disclosing any reasonably anticipated increase in income or expenditures over the 12-month period following the date of the filing of the petition;

(2) if an individual debtor's schedule of assets and liabilities includes debts which are secured by property of the estate—

(A) within thirty days after the date of the filing of a petition under chapter 7 of this title or on or before the date of the meeting of creditors, whichever is earlier, or within such additional time as the court, for cause, within such period fixes, file with the clerk a statement of his intention with respect to the retention or surrender of such property and, if applicable, specifying that such property is claimed as exempt, that the debtor intends to redeem such property, or that the debtor intends to reaffirm debts secured by such property; and

(B) within 30 days after the first date set for the meeting of creditors under section 341(a), or within such additional time as the court, for cause, within such 30-day period fixes, perform his intention with respect to such property, as specified by subparagraph (A) of this paragraph;

except that nothing in subparagraphs (A) and (B) of this paragraph shall alter the debtor's or the trustee's rights with regard to such property under this title, except as provided in section 362(h);

(3) if a trustee is serving in the case or an auditor is serving under section 586(f) of title 28, cooperate with the trustee as necessary to enable the trustee to perform the trustee's duties under this title;

(4) if a trustee is serving in the case or an auditor is serving under section 586(f) of title 28, surrender to the trustee all property of the estate and any recorded information, including books, documents, records, and papers, relating to property of the estate, whether or not immunity is granted under section 344 of this title;

(5) appear at the hearing required under section 524(d) of this title;

(6) in a case under chapter 7 of this title in which the debtor is an individual, not retain possession of personal property as to which a creditor has an allowed claim for the purchase price secured in whole or in part by an interest in such personal property unless the debtor, not later than 45 days after the first meeting of creditors under section 341(a), either—

(A) enters into an agreement with the creditor pursuant to section 524(c) with respect to the claim secured by such property; or

(B) redeems such property from the security interest pursuant to section 722; and

(7) unless a trustee is serving in the case, continue to perform the obligations required of the administrator (as defined in section 3 of the Employee Retirement Income Security Act of 1974) of an employee benefit plan if at the time of the commencement of the case the debtor (or any entity designated by the debtor) served as such administrator.

If the debtor fails to so act within the 45-day period referred to in paragraph (6), the stay under section 362(a) is terminated with respect to the personal property of the estate or of the debtor which is affected, such property shall no longer be property of the estate, and the creditor may take whatever action as to such property as is permitted by applicable nonbankruptcy law, unless the court determines on the motion of the trustee filed before the expiration of such 45-day period, and after notice and a hearing, that such property is of consequential value or benefit to the estate, orders appropriate adequate protection of the creditor's interest, and orders the debtor to deliver any collateral in the debtor's possession to the trustee.

(b) In addition to the requirements under subsection (a), a debtor who is an individual shall file with the court—

(1) a certificate from the approved nonprofit budget and credit counseling agency that provided the debtor services under section 109(h) describing the services provided to the debtor; and

(2) a copy of the debt repayment plan, if any, developed under section 109(h) through the approved nonprofit budget and credit counseling agency referred to in paragraph (1).

(c) In addition to meeting the requirements under subsection (a), a debtor shall file with the court a record of any interest that a debtor has in an education individual retirement account (as defined in section 530(b)(1) of the Internal Revenue Code of 1986), an interest in an account in a qualified ABLE program (as defined in section 529A(b) of such Code, or under a qualified State tuition program (as defined in section 529(b)(1) of such Code).

(d) If the debtor fails timely to take the action specified in subsection (a)(6) of this section, or in paragraphs (1) and (2) of section 362(h), with respect to property which a lessor or bailor owns and has leased, rented, or bailed to the debtor or as to which a creditor holds a security interest not otherwise voidable under section 522(f), 544, 545, 547, 548, or 549, nothing in this title shall prevent or limit the operation of a provision in the underlying lease or agreement that has the effect of placing the debtor in default under such lease or agreement by reason of the occurrence, pendency, or existence of a proceeding under this title or the insolvency of the debtor. Nothing in this subsection shall be deemed to justify limiting such a provision in any other circumstance.

(e)(1) If the debtor in a case under chapter 7 or 13 is an individual and if a creditor files with the court at any time a request to receive a copy of the petition, schedules, and statement of financial affairs filed by the debtor, then the court shall make such petition, such schedules, and such statement available to such creditor.

(2)(A) The debtor shall provide—

(i) not later than 7 days before the date first set for the first meeting of creditors, to the trustee a copy of the Federal income tax return required under applicable law (or at the election of the debtor, a transcript of such return) for the most recent tax year ending immediately before the commencement of the case and for which a Federal income tax return was filed; and

(ii) at the same time the debtor complies with clause (i), a copy of such return (or if elected under clause (i), such transcript) to any creditor that timely requests such copy.

(B) If the debtor fails to comply with clause (i) or (ii) of subparagraph (A), the court shall dismiss the case unless the debtor demonstrates that the failure to so comply is due to circumstances beyond the control of the debtor.

(C) If a creditor requests a copy of such tax return or such transcript and if the debtor fails to provide a copy of such tax return or such transcript to such creditor at the time the debtor provides such tax return or such transcript to the trustee, then the court shall dismiss the case unless the debtor demonstrates that the failure to provide a copy of such tax return or such transcript is due to circumstances beyond the control of the debtor.

(3) If a creditor in a case under chapter 13 files with the court at any time a request to receive a copy of the plan filed by the debtor, then the court shall make available to such creditor a copy of the plan—

(A) at a reasonable cost; and

(B) not later than 7 days after such request is filed.

(f) At the request of the court, the United States trustee, or any party in interest in a case under chapter 7, 11, or 13, a debtor who is an individual shall file with the court—

(1) at the same time filed with the taxing authority, a copy of each Federal income tax return required under applicable law (or at the election of the debtor, a transcript of such tax return) with respect to each tax year of the debtor ending while the case is pending under such chapter;

(2) at the same time filed with the taxing authority, each Federal income tax return required under applicable law (or at the election of the debtor, a transcript of such tax return) that had not been filed with such authority as of the date of the commencement of the case and that was subsequently filed for any tax year of the debtor ending in the 3-year period ending on the date of the commencement of the case;

(3) a copy of each amendment to any Federal income tax return or transcript filed with the court under paragraph (1) or (2); and

(4) in a case under chapter 13—

(A) on the date that is either 90 days after the end of such tax year or 1 year after the date of the commencement of the case, whichever is later, if a plan is not confirmed before such later date; and

(B) annually after the plan is confirmed and until the case is closed, not later than the date that is 45 days before the anniversary of the confirmation of the plan; a statement, under penalty of perjury, of the income and expenditures of the debtor during the tax year of the debtor most recently concluded before such statement is filed under this paragraph, and of the monthly income of the debtor, that shows how income, expenditures, and monthly income are calculated.

(g)(1) A statement referred to in subsection (f)(4) shall disclose—

(A) the amount and sources of the income of the debtor;

(B) the identity of any person responsible with the debtor for the support of any dependent of the debtor; and

(C) the identity of any person who contributed, and the amount contributed, to the household in which the debtor resides.

(2) The tax returns, amendments, and statement of income and expenditures described in subsections (e)(2)(A) and (f) shall be available to the United States trustee (or the bankruptcy administrator, if any), the trustee, and any party in interest for inspection and copying, subject to the requirements of section 315(c) of the Bankruptcy Abuse Prevention and Consumer Protection Act of 2005.

(h) If requested by the United States trustee or by the trustee, the debtor shall provide—

(1) a document that establishes the identity of the debtor, including a driver's license, passport, or other document that contains a photograph of the debtor; or

(2) such other personal identifying information relating to the debtor that establishes the identity of the debtor.

(i)(1) Subject to paragraphs (2) and (4) and notwithstanding section 707(a), if an individual debtor in a voluntary case under chapter 7 or 13 fails to file all of the information required under subsection (a)(1) within 45 days after the date of the filing of the petition, the case shall be automatically dismissed effective on the 46th day after the date of the filing of the petition.

(2) Subject to paragraph (4) and with respect to a case described in paragraph (1), any party in interest may request the court to enter an order dismissing the case. If requested, the court shall enter an order of dismissal not later than 7 days after such request.

(3) Subject to paragraph (4) and upon request of the debtor made within 45 days after the date of the filing of the petition described in paragraph (1), the court may allow the debtor an additional period of not to exceed 45 days to file the information required under subsection (a)(1) if the court finds justification for extending the period for the filing.

(4) Notwithstanding any other provision of this subsection, on the motion of the trustee filed before the expiration of the applicable period of time specified in paragraph (1), (2), or (3), and after notice and a hearing, the court may decline to dismiss the case if the court finds that the debtor attempted in good faith to file all the information required by subsection (a)(1)(B)(iv) and that the best interests of creditors would be served by administration of the case.

(j)(1) Notwithstanding any other provision of this title, if the debtor fails to file a tax return that becomes due after the commencement of the case or to properly obtain an extension of the due date for filing such return, the taxing authority may request that the court enter an order converting or dismissing the case.

(2) If the debtor does not file the required return or obtain the extension referred to in paragraph (1) within 90 days after a request is filed by the taxing authority under that paragraph, the court shall convert or dismiss the case, whichever is in the best interests of creditors and the estate.

§ 522. Exemptions

(a) In this section—

(1) "dependent" includes spouse, whether or not actually dependent; and

(2) "value" means fair market value as of the date of the filing of the petition or, with respect to property that becomes property of the estate after such date, as of the date such property becomes property of the estate.

(b)(1) Notwithstanding section 541 of this title, an individual debtor may exempt from property of the estate the property listed in either paragraph (2) or, in the alternative, paragraph (3) of this subsection. In joint cases filed under section 302 of this title and individual cases filed under section 301 or 303 of this title by or against debtors who are husband and wife, and whose estates are ordered to be jointly administered under Rule 1015(b) of the Federal Rules of Bankruptcy Procedure, one debtor may not elect to exempt property listed in paragraph (2) and the other debtor elect to exempt property listed in paragraph (3) of this subsection. If the parties cannot agree on the alternative to be elected, they shall be deemed to elect paragraph (2), where such election is permitted under the law of the jurisdiction where the case is filed.

(2) Property listed in this paragraph is property that is specified under subsection (d), unless the State law that is applicable to the debtor under paragraph (3)(A) specifically does not so authorize.

(3) Property listed in this paragraph is—

(A) subject to subsections (o) and (p), any property that is exempt under Federal law, other than subsection (d) of this section, or state or local law that is applicable on the date of the filing of the petition to the place in which the debtor's domicile has been located for the 730 days immediately preceding the date of the filing of the petition or if the debtor's domicile has not been located in a single State for such 730-day period, the place in which the debtor's domicile was located for 180 days immediately preceding the 730-day period or for a longer portion of such 180-day period than in any other place;

(B) any interest in property in which the debtor had, immediately before the commencement of the case, an interest as a tenant by the entirety or joint tenant to the extent that such interest as a tenant by the entirety or joint tenant is exempt from process under applicable nonbankruptcy law; and

(C) retirement funds to the extent that those funds are in a fund or account that is exempt from taxation under section 401, 403, 408, 408A, 414, 457, or 501(a) of the Internal Revenue Code of 1986.

If the effect of the domiciliary requirement under subparagraph (A) is to render the debtor ineligible for any exemption, the debtor may elect to exempt property that is specified under subsection (d).

(4) For purposes of paragraph (3)(C) and subsection (d)(12), the following shall apply:

(A) If the retirement funds are in a retirement fund that has received a favorable determination under section 7805 of the Internal Revenue Code of 1986, and that determination is in effect as of the date of the filing of the petition in a case under this title, those funds shall be presumed to be exempt from the estate.

(B) If the retirement funds are in a retirement fund that has not received a favorable determination under such section 7805, those funds are exempt from the estate if the debtor demonstrates that—

(i) no prior determination to the contrary has been made by a court or the Internal Revenue Service; and

(ii)(I) the retirement fund is in substantial compliance with the applicable requirements of the Internal Revenue Code of 1986; or

(II) the retirement fund fails to be in substantial compliance with the applicable requirements of the Internal Revenue Code of 1986 and the debtor is not materially responsible for that failure.

(C) A direct transfer of retirement funds from 1 fund or account that is exempt from taxation under section 401, 403, 408, 408A, 414, 457, or 501(a) of the Internal Revenue Code of 1986, under section 401(a)(31) of the Internal Revenue Code of 1986, or otherwise, shall not cease to qualify for exemption under paragraph (3)(C) or subsection (d)(12) by reason of such direct transfer.

(D)(i) Any distribution that qualifies as an eligible rollover distribution within the meaning of section 402(c) of the Internal Revenue Code of 1986 or that is described in clause (ii) shall not cease to qualify for exemption under paragraph (3)(C) or subsection (d)(12) by reason of such distribution.

(ii) A distribution described in this clause is an amount that—

(I) has been distributed from a fund or account that is exempt from taxation under section 401, 403, 408, 408A, 414, 457, or 501(a) of the Internal Revenue Code of 1986; and

(II) to the extent allowed by law, is deposited in such a fund or account not later than 60 days after the distribution of such amount.

(c) Unless the case is dismissed, property exempted under this section is not liable during or after the case for any debt of the debtor that arose, or that is determined under section 502 of this title as if such debt had arisen, before the commencement of the case, except—

(1) a debt of a kind specified in paragraph (1) or (5) of section 523(a) (in which case, notwithstanding any provision of applicable nonbankruptcy law to the contrary, such property shall be liable for a debt of a kind specified in such paragraph);

(2) a debt secured by a lien that is—

(A)(i) not avoided under subsection (f) or (g) of this section or under section 544, 545, 547, 548, 549, or 724(a) of this title; and

(ii) not void under section 506(d) of this title; or

(B) a tax lien, notice of which is properly filed;

(3) a debt of a kind specified in section 523(a)(4) or 523(a)(6) of this title owed by an institution-affiliated party of an insured depository institution to a Federal depository institutions regulatory agency acting in its capacity as conservator, receiver, or liquidating agent for such institution; or

(4) a debt in connection with fraud in the obtaining or providing of any scholarship, grant, loan, tuition, discount, award, or other financial assistance for purposes of financing an education at an institution of higher education (as that term is defined in section 101 of the Higher Education Act of 1965 (20 U.S.C. 1001)).

(d) The following property may be exempted under subsection (b)(2) of this section:

(1) The debtor's aggregate interest, not to exceed $31,575 in value, in real property or personal property that the debtor or a dependent of the debtor uses as a residence, in a cooperative that owns property that the debtor or a dependent of the debtor uses as a residence, or in a burial plot for the debtor or a dependent of the debtor.

(2) The debtor's interest, not to exceed $5,025 in value, in one motor vehicle.

(3) The debtor's interest, not to exceed $800 in value in any particular item or $16,850 in aggregate value, in household furnishings, household goods, wearing apparel, appliances, books, animals, crops, or musical instruments, that are held primarily for the personal, family, or household use of the debtor or a dependent of the debtor.

(4) The debtor's aggregate interest, not to exceed $2,125 in value, in jewelry held primarily for the personal, family, or household use of the debtor or a dependent of the debtor.

(5) The debtor's aggregate interest in any property, not to exceed in value $1,675 plus up to $15,800 of any unused amount of the exemption provided under paragraph (1) of this subsection.

(6) The debtor's aggregate interest, not to exceed $3,175 in value, in any implements, professional books, or tools, of the trade of the debtor or the trade of a dependent of the debtor.

(7) Any unmatured life insurance contract owned by the debtor, other than a credit life insurance contract.

(8) The debtor's aggregate interest, not to exceed in value $16,850 less any amount of property of the estate transferred in the manner specified in section 542(d) of this title, in any accrued dividend or interest under, or loan value of, any unmatured life insurance contract owned by the debtor under which the insured is the debtor or an individual of whom the debtor is a dependent.

(9) Professionally prescribed health aids for the debtor or a dependent of the debtor.

(10) The debtor's right to receive—

(A) a social security benefit, unemployment compensation, or a local public assistance benefit;

(B) a veterans' benefit;

(C) a disability, illness, or unemployment benefit;

(D) alimony, support, or separate maintenance, to the extent reasonably necessary for the support of the debtor and any dependent of the debtor;

(E) a payment under a stock bonus, pension, profitsharing, annuity, or similar plan or contract on account of illness, disability, death, age, or length of service, to the extent reasonably necessary for the support of the debtor and any dependent of the debtor, unless—

(i) such plan or contract was established by or under the auspices of an insider that employed the debtor at the time the debtor's rights under such plan or contract arose;

(ii) such payment is on account of age or length of service; and

(iii) such plan or contract does not qualify under section 401(a), 403(a), 403(b), or 408 of the Internal Revenue Code of 1986.

(11) The debtor's right to receive, or property that is traceable to—

(A) an award under a crime victim's reparation law;

(B) a payment on account of the wrongful death of an individual of whom the debtor was a dependent, to the extent reasonably necessary for the support of the debtor and any dependent of the debtor;

(C) a payment under a life insurance contract that insured the life of an individual of whom the debtor was a dependent on the date of such individual's death, to the extent reasonably necessary for the support of the debtor and any dependent of the debtor;

(D) a payment, not to exceed $31,575, on account of personal bodily injury, not including pain and suffering or compensation for actual pecuniary loss, of the debtor or an individual of whom the debtor is a dependent; or

(E) a payment in compensation of loss of future earnings of the debtor or an individual of whom the debtor is or was a dependent, to the extent reasonably necessary for the support of the debtor and any dependent of the debtor.

(12) Retirement funds to the extent that those funds are in a fund or account that is exempt from taxation under section 401, 403, 408, 408A, 414, 457, or 501(a) of the Internal Revenue Code of 1986.

(e) A waiver of an exemption executed in favor of a creditor that holds an unsecured claim against the debtor is unenforceable in a case under this title with respect to such claim against property that the debtor may exempt under subsection (b) of this section. A waiver by the debtor of a power under subsection (f) or (h) of this section to avoid a transfer, under subsection (g) or (i) of this section to exempt property, or under subsection (i) of this section to recover property or to preserve a transfer, is unenforceable in a case under this title.

(f)(1) Notwithstanding any waiver of exemptions but subject to paragraph (3), the debtor may avoid the fixing of a lien on an interest of the debtor in property to the extent that such lien impairs an exemption to which the debtor would have been entitled under subsection (b) of this section, if such lien is—

(A) a judicial lien, other than a judicial lien that secures a debt of a kind that is specified in section 523(a)(5); or

(B) a nonpossessory, nonpurchase-money security interest in any—

(i) household furnishings, household goods, wearing apparel, appliances, books, animals, crops, musical instruments, or jewelry that are held primarily for the personal, family, or household use of the debtor or a dependent of the debtor;

(ii) implements, professional books, or tools, of the trade of the debtor or the trade of a dependent of the debtor; or

(iii) professionally prescribed health aids for the debtor or a dependent of the debtor.

(2)(A) For the purposes of this subsection, a lien shall be considered to impair an exemption to the extent that the sum of—

(i) the lien;

(ii) all other liens on the property; and

(iii) the amount of the exemption that the debtor could claim if there were no liens on the property;

exceeds the value that the debtor's interest in the property would have in the absence of any liens.

(B) In the case of a property subject to more than 1 lien, a lien that has been avoided shall not be considered in making the calculation under subparagraph (A) with respect to other liens.

(C) This paragraph shall not apply with respect to a judgment arising out of a mortgage foreclosure.

(3) In a case in which state law that is applicable to the debtor—

(A) permits a person to voluntarily waive a right to claim exemptions under subsection (d) or prohibits a debtor from claiming exemptions under subsection (d); and

(B) either permits the debtor to claim exemptions under state law without limitation in amount, except to the extent that the debtor has permitted the fixing of a consensual lien on any property or prohibits avoidance of a consensual lien on property otherwise eligible to be claimed as exempt property;

the debtor may not avoid the fixing of a lien on an interest of the debtor or a dependent of the debtor in property if the lien is a nonpossessory, nonpurchase-money security interest in implements, professional books, or tools of the trade of the debtor or a dependent of the debtor or farm animals or crops of the debtor or a dependent of the debtor to the extent the value of such implements, professional books, tools of the trade, animals, and crops exceeds $8,575.

(4)(A) Subject to subparagraph (B), for purposes of paragraph (1)(B), the term "household goods" means—

(i) clothing;

(ii) furniture;

(iii) appliances;

(iv) 1 radio;

(v) 1 television;

(vi) 1 VCR;

(vii) linens;

(viii) china;

(ix) crockery;

(x) kitchenware;

(xi) educational materials and educational equipment primarily for the use of minor dependent children of the debtor;

(xii) medical equipment and supplies;

(xiii) furniture exclusively for the use of minor children, or elderly or disabled dependents of the debtor;

(xiv) personal effects (including the toys and hobby equipment of minor dependent children and wedding rings) of the debtor and the dependents of the debtor; and

(xv) 1 personal computer and related equipment.

(B) The term "household goods" does not include—

(i) works of art (unless by or of the debtor, or any relative of the debtor);

(ii) electronic entertainment equipment with a fair market value of more than $900 in the aggregate (except 1 television, 1 radio, and 1 VCR);

(iii) items acquired as antiques with a fair market value of more than $900 in the aggregate;

(iv) jewelry with a fair market value of more than $900 in the aggregate (except wedding rings); and

(v) a computer (except as otherwise provided for in this section), motor vehicle (including a tractor or lawn tractor), boat, or a motorized recreational device, conveyance, vehicle, watercraft, or aircraft.

(g) Notwithstanding sections 550 and 551 of this title, the debtor may exempt under subsection (b) of this section property that the trustee recovers under section 510(c)(2), 542, 543, 550, 551, or 553 of this title, to the extent that the debtor could have exempted such property under subsection (b) of this section if such property had not been transferred, if—

(1)(A) such transfer was not a voluntary transfer of such property by the debtor; and

(B) the debtor did not conceal such property; or

(2) the debtor could have avoided such transfer under subsection (f)(1)(B) of this section.

(h) The debtor may avoid a transfer of property of the debtor or recover a setoff to the extent that the debtor could have exempted such property under subsection (g)(1) of this section if the trustee had avoided such transfer, if—

(1) such transfer is avoidable by the trustee under section 544, 545, 547, 548, 549, or 724(a) of this title or recoverable by the trustee under section 553 of this title; and

(2) the trustee does not attempt to avoid such transfer.

(i)(1) If the debtor avoids a transfer or recovers a setoff under subsection (f) or (h) of this section, the debtor may recover in the manner prescribed by, and subject to the limitations of, section 550 of this title, the same as if the trustee had avoided such transfer, and may exempt any property so recovered under subsection (b) of this section.

(2) Notwithstanding section 551 of this title, a transfer avoided under section 544, 545, 547, 548, 549, or 724(a) of this title, under subsection (f) or (h) of this section, or property recovered under section 553 of this title, may be preserved for the benefit of the debtor to the extent that the debtor may exempt such property under subsection (g) of this section or paragraph (1) of this subsection.

(j) Notwithstanding subsections (g) and (i) of this section, the debtor may exempt a particular kind of property under subsections (g) and (i) of this section only to the extent that the debtor has exempted less property in value of such kind than that to which the debtor is entitled under subsection (b) of this section.

(k) Property that the debtor exempts under this section is not liable for payment of any administrative expense except—

(1) the aliquot share of the costs and expenses of avoiding a transfer of property that the debtor exempts under subsection (g) of this section, or of recovery of such property, that is attributable to the value of the portion of such property exempted in relation to the value of the property recovered; and

(2) any costs and expenses of avoiding a transfer under subsection (f) or (h) of this section, or of recovery of property under subsection (i)(1) of this section, that the debtor has not paid.

(l) The debtor shall file a list of property that the debtor claims as exempt under subsection (b) of this section. If the debtor does not file such a list, a dependent of the debtor may file such a list, or may claim property as exempt from property of the estate on behalf of the debtor. Unless a party in interest objects, the property claimed as exempt on such list is exempt.

(m) Subject to the limitation in subsection (b), this section shall apply separately with respect to each debtor in a joint case.

(n) For assets in individual retirement accounts described in section 408 or 408A of the Internal Revenue Code of 1986, other than a simplified employee pension under section 408(k) of such Code or a simple retirement account under section 408(p) of such Code, the aggregate value of such assets exempted under this section, without regard to amounts attributable to rollover contributions under section 402(c), 402(e)(6), 403(a)(4), 403(a)(5), and 403(b)(8) of the Internal Revenue Code of 1986, and earnings thereon, shall not exceed $1,711,975 in a case filed by a debtor who is an individual, except that such amount may be increased if the interests of justice so require.

(o) For purposes of subsection (b)(3)(A), and notwithstanding subsection (a), the value of an interest in—

(1) real or personal property that the debtor or a dependent of the debtor uses as a residence;

(2) a cooperative that owns property that the debtor or a dependent of the debtor uses as a residence;

(3) a burial plot for the debtor or a dependent of the debtor; or

(4) real or personal property that the debtor or a dependent of the debtor claims as a homestead; shall be reduced to the extent that such value is attributable to any portion of any property that the debtor

disposed of in the 10-year period ending on the date of the filing of the petition with the intent to hinder, delay, or defraud a creditor and that the debtor could not exempt, or that portion that the debtor could not exempt, under subsection (b), if on such date the debtor had held the property so disposed of.

(p)(1) Except as provided in paragraph (2) of this subsection and sections 544 and 548, as a result of electing under subsection (b)(3)(A) to exempt property under State or local law, a debtor may not exempt any amount of interest that was acquired by the debtor during the 1215-day period preceding the date of the filing of the petition that exceeds in the aggregate $214,000 in value in—

(A) real or personal property that the debtor or a dependent of the debtor uses as a residence;

(B) a cooperative that owns property that the debtor or a dependent of the debtor uses as a residence;

(C) a burial plot for the debtor or a dependent of the debtor; or

(D) real or personal property that the debtor or dependent of the debtor claims as a homestead.

(2)(A) The limitation under paragraph (1) shall not apply to an exemption claimed under subsection (b)(3)(A) by a family farmer for the principal residence of such farmer.

(B) For purposes of paragraph (1), any amount of such interest does not include any interest transferred from a debtor's previous principal residence (which was acquired prior to the beginning of such 1215-day period) into the debtor's current principal residence, if the debtor's previous and current residences are located in the same State.

(q)(1) As a result of electing under subsection (b)(3)(A) to exempt property under State or local law, a debtor may not exempt any amount of an interest in property described in subparagraphs (A), (B), (C), and (D) of subsection (p)(1) which exceeds in the aggregate $214,000 if—

(A) the court determines, after notice and a hearing, that the debtor has been convicted of a felony (as defined in section 3156 of title 18), which under the circumstances, demonstrates that the filing of the case was an abuse of the provisions of this title; or

(B) the debtor owes a debt arising from—

(i) any violation of the Federal securities laws (as defined in section 3(a)(47) of the Securities Exchange Act of 1934), any State securities laws, or any regulation or order issued under Federal securities laws or State securities laws;

(ii) fraud, deceit, or manipulation in a fiduciary capacity or in connection with the purchase or sale of any security registered under section 12 or 15(d) of the Securities Exchange Act of 1934 or under section 6 of the Securities Act of 1933;

(iii) any civil remedy under section 1964 of title 18; or

(iv) any criminal act, intentional tort, or willful or reckless misconduct that caused serious physical injury or death to another individual in the preceding 5 years.

(2) Paragraph (1) shall not apply to the extent the amount of an interest in property described in subparagraphs (A), (B), (C), and (D) of subsection (p)(1) is reasonably necessary for the support of the debtor and any dependent of the debtor.

§ 523. Exceptions to Discharge

(a) A discharge under section 727, 1141, 1192, 1228(a), 1228(b), or 1328(b) of this title does not discharge an individual debtor from any debt—

(1) for a tax or a customs duty—

(A) of the kind and for the periods specified in section 507(a)(3) or 507(a)(8) of this title, whether or not a claim for such tax was filed or allowed;

(B) with respect to which a return, or equivalent report or notice, if required—

(i) was not filed or given; or

(ii) was filed or given after the date on which such return, report, or notice was last due, under applicable law or under any extension, and after two years before the date of the filing of the petition; or

(C) with respect to which the debtor made a fraudulent return or willfully attempted in any manner to evade or defeat such tax;

(2) for money, property, services, or an extension, renewal, or refinancing of credit, to the extent obtained by—

(A) false pretenses, a false representation, or actual fraud, other than a statement respecting the debtor's or an insider's financial condition;

(B) use of a statement in writing—

(i) that is materially false;

(ii) respecting the debtor's or an insider's financial condition;

(iii) on which the creditor to whom the debtor is liable for such money, property, services, or credit reasonably relied; and

(iv) that the debtor caused to be made or published with intent to deceive; or

(C)(i) for purposes of subparagraph (A)—

(I) consumer debts owed to a single creditor and aggregating more than $900 for luxury goods or services incurred by an individual debtor on or within 90 days before the order for relief under this title are presumed to be nondischargeable; and

(II) cash advances aggregating more than $1,250 that are extensions of consumer credit under an open end credit plan obtained by an individual debtor on or within 70 days before the order for relief under this title, are presumed to be nondischargeable; and

(ii) for purposes of this subparagraph—

(I) the terms "consumer", "credit", and "open end credit plan" have the same meanings as in section 103 of the Truth in Lending Act; and

(II) the term "luxury goods or services" does not include goods or services reasonably necessary for the support or maintenance of the debtor or a dependent of the debtor;

(3) neither listed nor scheduled under section 521(a)(1) of this title, with the name, if known to the debtor, of the creditor to whom such debt is owed, in time to permit—

(A) if such debt is not of a kind specified in paragraph (2), (4), or (6) of this subsection, timely filing of a proof of claim, unless such creditor had notice or actual knowledge of the case in time for such timely filing; or

(B) if such debt is of a kind specified in paragraph (2), (4), or (6) of this subsection, timely filing of a proof of claim and timely request for a determination of dischargeability of such debt under one of such paragraphs, unless such creditor had notice or actual knowledge of the case in time for such timely filing and request;

(4) for fraud or defalcation while acting in a fiduciary capacity, embezzlement, or larceny;

(5) for a domestic support obligation;

(6) for willful and malicious injury by the debtor to another entity or to the property of another entity;

(7) to the extent such debt is for a fine, penalty, or forfeiture payable to and for the benefit of a governmental unit, and is not compensation for actual pecuniary loss, other than a tax penalty—

(A) relating to a tax of a kind not specified in paragraph (1) of this subsection; or

(B) imposed with respect to a transaction or event that occurred before three years before the date of the filing of the petition;

(8) unless excepting such debt from discharge under this paragraph would impose an undue hardship on the debtor and the debtor's dependents, for—

(A)(i) an educational benefit overpayment or loan made, insured, or guaranteed by a governmental unit, or made under any program funded in whole or in part by a governmental unit or nonprofit institution; or

(ii) an obligation to repay funds received as an educational benefit, scholarship, or stipend; or

(B) any other educational loan that is a qualified education loan, as defined in section 221(d)(1) of the Internal Revenue Code of 1986, incurred by a debtor who is an individual;

(9) for death or personal injury caused by the debtor's operation of a motor vehicle, vessel, or aircraft if such operation was unlawful because the debtor was intoxicated from using alcohol, a drug, or another substance;

(10) that was or could have been listed or scheduled by the debtor in a prior case concerning the debtor under this title or under the Bankruptcy Act in which the debtor waived discharge, or was denied a discharge under section 727(a)(2), (3), (4), (5), (6), or (7) of this title, or under section 14c(1), (2), (3), (4), (6), or (7) of such Act;

(11) provided in any final judgment, unreviewable order, or consent order or decree entered in any court of the United States or of any state, issued by a Federal depository institutions regulatory agency, or contained in any settlement agreement entered into by the debtor, arising from any act of fraud or defalcation while acting in a fiduciary capacity committed with respect to any depository institution or insured credit union;

(12) for malicious or reckless failure to fulfill any commitment by the debtor to a Federal depository institutions regulatory agency to maintain the capital of an insured depository institution, except that this paragraph shall not extend any such

commitment which would otherwise be terminated due to any act of such agency;

(13) for any payment of an order of restitution issued under title 18, United States Code;

(14) incurred to pay a tax to the United States that would be nondischargeable pursuant to paragraph (1);

(14A) incurred to pay a tax to a governmental unit, other than the United States, that would be nondischargeable under paragraph (1);

(14B) incurred to pay fines or penalties imposed under Federal election law;

(15) to a spouse, former spouse, or child of the debtor and not of the kind described in paragraph (5) that is incurred by the debtor in the course of a divorce or separation or in connection with a separation agreement, divorce decree or other order of a court of record, or a determination made in accordance with state or territorial law by a governmental unit;

(16) for a fee or assessment that becomes due and payable after the order for relief to a membership association with respect to the debtor's interest in a unit that has condominium ownership, in a share of a cooperative corporation, or a lot in a homeowners association, for as long as the debtor or the trustee has a legal, equitable, or possessory ownership interest in such unit, such corporation, or such lot, but nothing in this paragraph shall except from discharge the debt of a debtor for a membership association fee or assessment for a period arising before entry of the order for relief in a pending or subsequent bankruptcy case.

(17) for a fee imposed on a prisoner by any court for the filing of a case, motion, complaint, or appeal, or for other costs and expenses assessed with respect to such filing, regardless of an assertion of poverty by the debtor under subsection (b) or (f)(2) of section 1915 of title 28 (or a similar non-Federal law), or the debtor's status as a prisoner, as defined in section 1915(h) of title 28 (or a similar non-Federal law);

(18) owed to a pension, profit-sharing, stock bonus, or other plan established under section 401, 403, 408, 408A, 414, 457, or 501(c) of the Internal Revenue Code of 1986, under—

(A) a loan permitted under section 408(b)(1) of the Employee Retirement Income Security Act of 1974, or subject to section 72(p) of the Internal Revenue Code of 1986; or

(B) a loan from a thrift savings plan permitted under subchapter III of chapter 84 of title 5, that satisfies the requirements of section 8433(g) of such title; but nothing in this paragraph may be construed to provide that any loan made under a governmental plan under section 414(d), or a contract or account under section 403(b), of the Internal Revenue Code of 1986 constitutes a claim or a debt under this title; or

(19) that—

(A) is for—

(i) the violation of any of the Federal securities laws (as that term is defined in section 3(a)(47) of the Securities Exchange Act of 1934), any of the State securities laws, or any regulation or order issued under such Federal or State securities laws; or

(ii) common law fraud, deceit, or manipulation in connection with the purchase or sale of any security; and

(B) results, before, on, or after the date on which the petition was filed, from—

(i) any judgment, order, consent order, or decree entered in any Federal or State judicial or administrative proceeding;

(ii) any settlement agreement entered into by the debtor;

(iii) any court or administrative order for any damages, fine, penalty, citation, restitutionary payment, disgorgement payment, attorney fee, cost, or other payment owed by the debtor; or

(20) for injury to an individual by the debtor relating to a violation of chapter 77 of title 18, including injury caused by an instance in which the debtor knowingly benefitted financially, or by receiving anything of value, from participation in a venture that the debtor knew or should have known engaged in an act in violation of chapter 77 of title 18.

For purposes of this subsection, the term "return" means a return that satisfies the requirements of applicable nonbankruptcy law (including applicable filing requirements). Such term includes a return prepared pursuant to section 6020(a) of the Internal Revenue Code of 1986, or similar State or local law, or a written stipulation to a judgment or a final order entered by a nonbankruptcy tribunal, but does not include a return made pursuant to section 6020(b) of the Internal Revenue Code of 1986, or a similar State or local law.

(b) Notwithstanding subsection (a) of this section, a debt that was excepted from discharge under subsection (a)(1), (a)(3), or (a)(8) of this section, under section

17a(1), 17a(3), or 17a(5) of the Bankruptcy Act, under section 439A of the Higher Education Act of 1965, or under section 733(g) of the Public Health Service Act in a prior case concerning the debtor under this title, or under the Bankruptcy Act, is dischargeable in a case under this title unless, by the terms of subsection (a) of this section, such debt is not dischargeable in the case under this title.

(c)(1) Except as provided in subsection (a)(3)(B) of this section, the debtor shall be discharged from a debt of a kind specified in paragraph (2), (4), or (6) of subsection (a) of this section, unless, on request of the creditor to whom such debt is owed, and after notice and a hearing, the court determines such debt to be excepted from discharge under paragraph (2), (4), or (6), as the case may be, of subsection (a) of this section.

(2) Paragraph (1) shall not apply in the case of a Federal depository institutions regulatory agency seeking, in its capacity as conservator, receiver, or liquidating agent for an insured depository institution, to recover a debt described in subsection (a)(2), (a)(4), (a)(6), or (a)(11) owed to such institution by an institution-affiliated party unless the receiver, conservator, or liquidating agent was appointed in time to reasonably comply, or for a Federal depository institutions regulatory agency acting in its corporate capacity as a successor to such receiver, conservator, or liquidating agent to reasonably comply, with subsection (a)(3)(B) as a creditor of such institution-affiliated party with respect to such debt.

(d) If a creditor requests a determination of dischargeability of a consumer debt under subsection (a)(2) of this section, and such debt is discharged, the court shall grant judgment in favor of the debtor for the costs of, and a reasonable attorney's fee for, the proceeding if the court finds that the position of the creditor was not substantially justified, except that the court shall not award such costs and fees if special circumstances would make the award unjust.

(e) Any institution-affiliated party of an insured depository institution shall be considered to be acting in a fiduciary capacity with respect to the purposes of subsection (a)(4) or (11).

§ 524. Effect of Discharge

(a) A discharge in a case under this title—

(1) voids any judgment at any time obtained, to the extent that such judgment is a determination of the personal liability of the debtor with respect to any debt discharged under section 727, 944, 1141, 1192, 1228, or 1328 of this title, whether or not discharge of such debt is waived;

(2) operates as an injunction against the commencement or continuation of an action, the employment of process, or an act, to collect, recover or offset any such debt as a personal liability of the debtor, whether or not discharge of such debt is waived; and

(3) operates as an injunction against the commencement or continuation of an action, the employment of process, or an act, to collect or recover from, or offset against, property of the debtor of the kind specified in section 541(a)(2) of this title that is acquired after the commencement of the case, on account of any allowable community claim, except a community claim that is excepted from discharge under section 523, 1192, 1228(a)(1), or 1328(a)(1), or that would be so excepted, determined in accordance with the provisions of sections 523(c) and 523(d) of this title, in a case concerning the debtor's spouse commenced on the date of the filing of the petition in the case concerning the debtor, whether or not discharge of the debt based on such community claim is waived.

(b) Subsection (a)(3) of this section does not apply if—

(1)(A) the debtor's spouse is a debtor in a case under this title, or a bankrupt or a debtor in a case under the Bankruptcy Act, commenced within six years of the date of the filing of the petition in the case concerning the debtor; and

(B) the court does not grant the debtor's spouse a discharge in such case concerning the debtor's spouse; or

(2)(A) the court would not grant the debtor's spouse a discharge in a case under chapter 7 of this title concerning such spouse commenced on the date of the filing of the petition in the case concerning the debtor; and

(B) a determination that the court would not so grant such discharge is made by the bankruptcy court within the time and in the manner provided for a determination under section 727 of this title of whether a debtor is granted a discharge.

(c) An agreement between a holder of a claim and the debtor, the consideration for which, in whole or in part, is based on a debt that is dischargeable in a case under this title is enforceable only to any extent enforceable under applicable nonbankruptcy law, whether or not discharge of such debt is waived, only if—

(1) such agreement was made before the granting of the discharge under section 727, 1192, 1141, 1228, or 1328 of this title;

(2) the debtor received the disclosures described in subsection (k) at or before the time at which the debtor signed the agreement;

(3) such agreement has been filed with the court and, if applicable, accompanied by a declaration or an affidavit of the attorney that represented the debtor during the course of negotiating an agreement under this subsection, which states that—

(A) such agreement represents a fully informed and voluntary agreement by the debtor;

(B) such agreement does not impose an undue hardship on the debtor or a dependent of the debtor; and

(C) the attorney fully advised the debtor of the legal effect and consequences of—

(i) an agreement of the kind specified in this subsection; and

(ii) any default under such an agreement;

(4) the debtor has not rescinded such agreement at any time prior to discharge or within sixty days after such agreement is filed with the court, whichever occurs later, by giving notice of rescission to the holder of such claim;

(5) the provisions of subsection (d) of this section have been complied with; and

(6)(A) in a case concerning an individual who was not represented by an attorney during the course of negotiating an agreement under this subsection, the court approves such agreement as—

(i) not imposing an undue hardship on the debtor or a dependent of the debtor; and

(ii) in the best interest of the debtor.

(B) Subparagraph (A) shall not apply to the extent that such debt is a consumer debt secured by real property.

(d) In a case concerning an individual, when the court has determined whether to grant or not to grant a discharge under section 727, 1141, 1192, 1228, or 1328 of this title, the court may hold a hearing at which the debtor shall appear in person. At any such hearing, the court shall inform the debtor that a discharge has been granted or the reason why a discharge has not been granted. If a discharge has been granted and if the debtor desires to make an agreement of the kind specified in subsection (c) of this section and was not represented by an attorney during the course of negotiating such agreement, then the court shall hold a hearing at which the debtor shall appear in person and at such hearing the court shall—

(1) inform the debtor—

(A) that such an agreement is not required under this title, under nonbankruptcy law, or under any agreement not made in accordance with the provisions of subsection (c) of this section; and

(B) of the legal effect and consequences of—

(i) an agreement of the kind specified in subsection (c) of this section; and

(ii) a default under such an agreement; and

(2) determine whether the agreement that the debtor desires to make complies with the requirements of subsection (c)(6) of this section, if the consideration for such agreement is based in whole or in part on a consumer debt that is not secured by real property of the debtor.

(e) Except as provided in subsection (a)(3) of this section, discharge of a debt of the debtor does not affect the liability of any other entity on, or the property of any other entity for, such debt.

(f) Nothing contained in subsection (c) or (d) of this section prevents a debtor from voluntarily repaying any debt.

(g)(1)(A) After notice and hearing, a court that enters an order confirming a plan of reorganization under chapter 11 may issue, in connection with such order, an injunction in accordance with this subsection to supplement the injunctive effect of a discharge under this section.

(B) An injunction may be issued under subparagraph (A) to enjoin entities from taking legal action for the purpose of directly or indirectly collecting, recovering, or receiving payment or recovery with respect to any claim or demand that, under a plan of reorganization, is to be paid in whole or in part by a trust described in paragraph (2)(B)(i), except such legal actions as are expressly allowed by the injunction, the confirmation order, or the plan of reorganization.

(2)(A) Subject to subsection (h), if the requirements of subparagraph (B) are met at the time an injunction described in paragraph (1) is entered, then after entry of such injunction, any proceeding that involves the validity, application, construction, or modification of such injunction, or of this subsection with respect to such injunction, may be commenced only in the district court in which such injunction was entered, and such court shall have exclusive jurisdiction over any such proceeding without regard to the amount in controversy.

(B) The requirements of this subparagraph are that—

(i) the injunction is to be implemented in connection with a trust that, pursuant to the plan of reorganization—

(I) is to assume the liabilities of a debtor which at the time of entry of the order for relief has been named as a defendant in personal injury, wrongful death, or property-damage actions seeking recovery for damages allegedly caused by the presence of, or exposure to, asbestos or asbestos-containing products;

(II) is to be funded in whole or in part by the securities of 1 or more debtors involved in such plan and by the obligation of such debtor or debtors to make future payments, including dividends;

(III) is to own, or by the exercise of rights granted under such plan would be entitled to own if specified contingencies occur, a majority of the voting shares of—

(aa) each such debtor;

(bb) the parent corporation of each such debtor; or

(cc) a subsidiary of each such debtor that is also a debtor; and

(IV) is to use its assets or income to pay claims and demands; and

(ii) subject to subsection (h), the court determines that—

(I) the debtor is likely to be subject to substantial future demands for payment arising out of the same or similar conduct or events that gave rise to the claims that are addressed by the injunction;

(II) the actual amounts, numbers, and timing of such future demands cannot be determined;

(III) pursuit of such demands outside the procedures prescribed by such plan is likely to threaten the plan's purpose to deal equitably with claims and future demands;

(IV) as part of the process of seeking confirmation of such plan—

(aa) the terms of the injunction proposed to be issued under paragraph (1)(A), including any provisions barring actions against third parties pursuant to paragraph (4)(A), are set out in such plan and in any disclosure statement supporting the plan; and

(bb) a separate class or classes of the claimants whose claims are to be addressed by a trust described in clause (i) is established and votes, by at least 75 percent of those voting, in favor of the plan; and

(V) subject to subsection (h), pursuant to court orders or otherwise, the trust will operate through mechanisms such as structured, periodic, or supplemental payments, pro rata distributions, matrices, or periodic review of estimates of the numbers and values of present claims and future demands, or other comparable mechanisms, that provide reasonable assurance that the trust will value, and be in a financial position to pay, present claims and future demands that involve similar claims in substantially the same manner.

(3)(A) If the requirements of paragraph (2)(B) are met and the order confirming the plan of reorganization was issued or affirmed by the district court that has jurisdiction over the reorganization case, then after the time for appeal of the order that issues or affirms the plan—

(i) the injunction shall be valid and enforceable and may not be revoked or modified by any court except through appeal in accordance with paragraph (6);

(ii) no entity that pursuant to such plan or thereafter becomes a direct or indirect transferee of, or successor to any assets of, a debtor or trust that is the subject of the injunction shall be liable with respect to any claim or demand made against such entity by reason of its becoming such a transferee or successor; and

(iii) no entity that pursuant to such plan or thereafter makes a loan to such a debtor or trust or to such a successor or transferee shall, by reason of making the loan, be liable with respect to any claim or demand made against such entity, nor shall any pledge of assets made in connection with such a loan be upset or impaired for that reason;

(B) Subparagraph (A) shall not be construed to—

(i) imply that an entity described in subparagraph (A)(ii) or (iii) would, if this paragraph were not applicable, necessarily be liable to any entity by reason of any of the acts described in subparagraph (A);

(ii) relieve any such entity of the duty to comply with, or of liability under, any Federal or state law regarding the making of a fraudulent conveyance in a transaction described in subparagraph (A)(ii) or (iii); or

(iii) relieve a debtor of the debtor's obligation to comply with the terms of the plan of reorganization, or affect the power of the court to exercise its authority under sections 1141 and 1142 to compel the debtor to do so.

(4)(A)(i) Subject to subparagraph (B), an injunction described in paragraph (1) shall be valid and enforceable against all entities that it addresses.

(ii) Notwithstanding the provisions of section 524(e), such an injunction may bar any action directed against a third party who is identifiable from the terms of such injunction (by name or as part of an identifiable group) and is alleged to be directly or indirectly liable for the conduct of, claims against, or demands on the debtor to the extent such alleged liability of such third party arises by reason of—

(I) the third party's ownership of a financial interest in the debtor, a past or present affiliate of the debtor, or a predecessor in interest of the debtor;

(II) the third party's involvement in the management of the debtor or a predecessor in interest of the debtor, or service as an officer, director or employee of the debtor or a related party;

(III) the third party's provision of insurance to the debtor or a related party; or

(IV) the third party's involvement in a transaction changing the corporate structure, or in a loan or other financial transaction affecting the financial condition, of the debtor or a related party, including but not limited to—

(aa) involvement in providing financing (debt or equity), or advice to an entity involved in such a transaction; or

(bb) acquiring or selling a financial interest in an entity as part of such a transaction.

(iii) As used in this subparagraph, the term "related party" means—

(I) a past or present affiliate of the debtor;

(II) a predecessor in interest of the debtor; or

(III) any entity that owned a financial interest in—

(aa) the debtor;

(bb) a past or present affiliate of the debtor; or

(cc) a predecessor in interest of the debtor.

(B) Subject to subsection (h), if, under a plan of reorganization, a kind of demand described in such plan is to be paid in whole or in part by a trust described in paragraph (2)(B)(i) in connection with which an injunction described in paragraph (1) is to be implemented, then such injunction shall be valid and enforceable with respect to a demand of such kind made, after such plan is confirmed, against the debtor or debtors involved, or against a third party described in subparagraph (A)(ii), if—

(i) as part of the proceedings leading to issuance of such injunction, the court appoints a legal representative for the purpose of protecting the rights of persons that might subsequently assert demands of such kind, and

(ii) the court determines, before entering the order confirming such plan, that identifying such debtor or debtors, or such third party (by name or as part of an identifiable group), in such injunction with respect to such demands for purposes of this subparagraph is fair and equitable with respect to the persons that might subsequently assert such demands, in light of the benefits provided, or to be provided, to such trust on behalf of such debtor or debtors or such third party.

(5) In this subsection, the term "demand" means a demand for payment, present or future, that—

(A) was not a claim during the proceedings leading to the confirmation of a plan of reorganization;

(B) arises out of the same or similar conduct or events that gave rise to the claims addressed by the injunction issued under paragraph (1); and

(C) pursuant to the plan, is to be paid by a trust described in paragraph (2)(B)(i).

(6) Paragraph (3)(A)(i) does not bar an action taken by or at the direction of an appellate court on appeal of an injunction issued under paragraph (1) or of the order of confirmation that relates to the injunction.

(7) This subsection does not affect the operation of section 1144 or the power of the district court to refer a proceeding under section 157 of title 28 or any reference of a proceeding made prior to the date of the enactment of this subsection.

(h) Application to existing injunctions.—For purposes of subsection (g)—

(1) subject to paragraph (2), if an injunction of the kind described in subsection (g)(1)(B) was issued before the date of the enactment of this Act, as part of a plan of reorganization confirmed by an order entered before such date, then the injunction shall be considered to meet the requirements of subsection (g)(2)(B) for purposes of subsection (g)(2)(A), and to satisfy subsection (g)(4)(A)(ii), if—

(A) the court determined at the time the plan was confirmed that the plan was fair and equitable in accordance with the requirements of section 1129(b);

(B) as part of the proceedings leading to issuance of such injunction and confirmation of such plan, the court had appointed a legal representative for the purpose of protecting the rights of persons that might subsequently assert demands described in subsection (g)(4)(B) with respect to such plan; and

(C) such legal representative did not object to confirmation of such plan or issuance of such injunction; and

(2) for purposes of paragraph (1), if a trust described in subsection (g)(2)(B)(i) is subject to a court order on the date of the enactment of this Act staying such trust from settling or paying further claims—

(A) the requirements of subsection (g)(2)(B)(ii)(V) shall not apply with respect to such trust until such stay is lifted or dissolved; and

(B) if such trust meets such requirements on the date such stay is lifted or dissolved, such trust shall be considered to have met such requirements continuously from the date of the enactment of this Act.

(i) The willful failure of a creditor to credit payments received under a plan confirmed under this title, unless the order confirming the plan is revoked, the plan is in default, or the creditor has not received payments required to be made under the plan in the manner required by the plan (including crediting the amounts required under the plan), shall constitute a violation of an injunction under subsection (a)(2) if the act of the creditor to collect and failure to credit payments in the manner required by the plan caused material injury to the debtor.

(j) Subsection (a)(2) does not operate as an injunction against an act by a creditor that is the holder of a secured claim, if—

(1) such creditor retains a security interest in real property that is the principal residence of the debtor;

(2) such act is in the ordinary course of business between the creditor and the debtor; and

(3) such act is limited to seeking or obtaining periodic payments associated with a valid security interest in lieu of pursuit of in rem relief to enforce the lien.

(k)(1) The disclosures required under subsection (c)(2) shall consist of the disclosure statement described in paragraph (3), completed as required in that paragraph, together with the agreement specified in subsection (c), statement, declaration, motion and order described, respectively, in paragraphs (4) through (8), and shall be the only disclosures required in connection with entering into such agreement.

(2) Disclosures made under paragraph (1) shall be made clearly and conspicuously and in writing. The terms "Amount Reaffirmed" and "Annual Percentage Rate" shall be disclosed more conspicuously than other terms, data or information provided in connection with this disclosure, except that the phrases "Before agreeing to reaffirm a debt, review these important disclosures" and "Summary of Reaffirmation Agreement" may be equally conspicuous. Disclosures may be made in a different order and may use terminology different from that set forth in paragraphs (2) through (8), except that the terms "Amount Reaffirmed" and "Annual Percentage Rate" must be used where indicated.

(3) The disclosure statement required under this paragraph shall consist of the following:

(A) The statement: "Part A: Before agreeing to reaffirm a debt, review these important disclosures:";

(B) Under the heading "Summary of Reaffirmation Agreement", the statement: "This Summary is made pursuant to the requirements of the Bankruptcy Code";

(C) The "Amount Reaffirmed", using that term, which shall be—

(i) the total amount of debt that the debtor agrees to reaffirm by entering into an agreement of the kind specified in subsection (c), and

(ii) the total of any fees and costs accrued as of the date of the disclosure statement, related to such total amount.

(D) In conjunction with the disclosure of the "Amount Reaffirmed", the statements—

(i) "The amount of debt you have agreed to reaffirm"; and

(ii) "Your credit agreement may obligate you to pay additional amounts which may come due after the date of this disclosure. Consult your credit agreement.".

(E) The "Annual Percentage Rate", using that term, which shall be disclosed as—

(i) if, at the time the petition is filed, the debt is an extension of credit under an open end credit plan, as the terms "credit" and "open end credit plan" are defined in section 103 of the Truth in Lending Act, then—

(I) the annual percentage rate determined under paragraphs (5) and (6) of section 127(b) of the Truth in Lending Act, as applicable, as disclosed to the debtor in the most recent periodic statement prior to entering into an agreement of the kind specified in subsection (c) or, if no such periodic statement has been given to the debtor during the prior 6 months, the annual percentage rate as it would have been so disclosed at the time the disclosure statement is given to the debtor, or to the extent this annual percentage rate is not readily available or not applicable, then

(II) the simple interest rate applicable to the amount reaffirmed as of the date the disclosure statement is given to the debtor, or if different simple interest rates apply to different balances, the simple interest rate applicable to each such balance, identifying the amount of each such balance included in the amount reaffirmed, or

(III) if the entity making the disclosure elects, to disclose the annual percentage rate under subclause (I) and the simple interest rate under subclause (II); or

(ii) if, at the time the petition is filed, the debt is an extension of credit other than under an open end credit plan, as the terms "credit" and "open end credit plan" are defined in section 103 of the Truth in Lending Act, then—

(I) the annual percentage rate under section 128(a)(4) of the Truth in Lending Act, as disclosed to the debtor in the most recent disclosure statement given to the debtor prior to the entering into an agreement of the kind specified in subsection (c) with respect to the debt, or, if no such disclosure statement was given to the debtor, the annual percentage rate as it would have been so disclosed at the time the disclosure statement is given to the debtor, or to the extent this annual percentage rate is not readily available or not applicable, then

(II) the simple interest rate applicable to the amount reaffirmed as of the date the disclosure statement is given to the debtor, or if different simple interest rates apply to different balances, the simple interest rate applicable to each such balance, identifying the amount of such balance included in the amount reaffirmed, or

(III) if the entity making the disclosure elects, to disclose the annual percentage rate under (I) and the simple interest rate under (II).

(F) If the underlying debt transaction was disclosed as a variable rate transaction on the most recent disclosure given under the Truth in Lending Act, by stating "The interest rate on your loan may be a variable interest rate which changes from time to time, so that the annual percentage rate disclosed here may be higher or lower.".

(G) If the debt is secured by a security interest which has not been waived in whole or in part or determined to be void by a final order of the court at the time of the disclosure, by disclosing that a security interest or lien in goods or property is asserted over some or all of the debts the debtor is reaffirming and listing the items and their original purchase price that are subject to the asserted security interest, or if not a purchase-money security interest then listing by items or types and the original amount of the loan.

(H) At the election of the creditor, a statement of the repayment schedule using 1 or a combination of the following—

(i) by making the statement: "Your first payment in the amount of $______ is due on ______ but the future payment amount may be different. Consult your reaffirmation agreement or credit agreement, as applicable.", and stating the amount of the first payment and the due date of that payment in the places provided;

(ii) by making the statement: "Your payment schedule will be:", and describing the repayment schedule with the number, amount, and due dates or period of payments scheduled to repay the debts reaffirmed to the extent then known by the disclosing party; or

(iii) by describing the debtor's repayment obligations with reasonable specificity to the extent then known by the disclosing party.

(I) The following statement:"Note: When this disclosure refers to what a creditor 'may' do, it does not use the word 'may' to give the creditor specific permission. The word 'may' is used to tell you what might occur if the law permits the creditor to take the action. If you have questions about your reaffirming a debt or what the law requires, consult with the attorney who helped you negotiate this agreement reaffirming a debt. If you don't have an attorney helping you, the judge will explain the effect of your reaffirming a debt when the hearing on the reaffirmation agreement is held.".

(J)(i) The following additional statements:

"Reaffirming a debt is a serious financial decision. The law requires you to take certain steps to make sure the decision is in your best interest. If these steps are not completed, the reaffirmation agreement is not effective, even though you have signed it.

"1. Read the disclosures in this Part A carefully. Consider the decision to reaffirm carefully. Then, if you want to reaffirm, sign the reaffirmation agreement in Part B (or you may use a separate agreement you and your creditor agree on).

"2. Complete and sign Part D and be sure you can afford to make the payments you are agreeing to make and have received a copy of the disclosure statement and a completed and signed reaffirmation agreement.

"3. If you were represented by an attorney during the negotiation of your reaffirmation agreement, the attorney must have signed the certification in Part C.

"4. If you were not represented by an attorney during the negotiation of your reaffirmation agreement, you must have completed and signed Part E.

"5. The original of this disclosure must be filed with the court by you or your creditor. If a separate reaffirmation agreement (other than the one in Part B) has been signed, it must be attached.

"6. If you were represented by an attorney during the negotiation of your reaffirmation agreement, your reaffirmation agreement becomes effective upon filing with the court unless the reaffirmation is presumed to be an undue hardship as explained in Part D.

"7. If you were not represented by an attorney during the negotiation of your reaffirmation agreement, it will not be effective unless the court approves it. The court will notify you of the hearing on your reaffirmation agreement. You must attend this hearing in bankruptcy court where the judge will review your reaffirmation agreement. The bankruptcy court must approve your reaffirmation agreement as consistent with your best interests, except that no court approval is required if your reaffirmation agreement is for a consumer debt secured by a mortgage, deed of trust, security deed, or other lien on your real property, like your home.

"Your right to rescind (cancel) your reaffirmation agreement. You may rescind (cancel) your reaffirmation agreement at any time before the bankruptcy court enters a discharge order, or before the expiration of the 60-day period that begins on the date your reaffirmation agreement is filed with the court, whichever occurs later. To rescind (cancel) your reaffirmation agreement, you must notify the creditor that your reaffirmation agreement is rescinded (or canceled).

"What are your obligations if you reaffirm the debt? A reaffirmed debt remains your personal legal obligation. It is not discharged in your bankruptcy case. That means that if you default on your reaffirmed debt after your bankruptcy case is over, your creditor may be able to take your property or your wages. Otherwise, your obligations will be determined by the reaffirmation agreement which may have changed the terms of the original agreement. For example, if you are reaffirming an open end credit agreement, the creditor may be permitted by that agreement or applicable law to change the terms of that agreement in the future under certain conditions.

"Are you required to enter into a reaffirmation agreement by any law? No, you are not required to reaffirm a debt by any law. Only agree to reaffirm a debt if it is in your best interest. Be sure you can afford the payments you agree to make.

"What if your creditor has a security interest or lien? Your bankruptcy discharge does not eliminate any lien on your property. A 'lien' is often referred to as a security interest, deed of trust, mortgage or security deed. Even if you do not reaffirm and your personal liability on the debt is discharged, because of the lien your creditor may still have the right to take the property securing the lien if you do not pay the debt or default on it. If the lien is on an item of personal property that is exempt under your State's law or that the trustee has abandoned, you may be able to redeem the item rather than reaffirm the debt. To redeem, you must make a single payment to the creditor equal to the amount of the allowed secured claim, as agreed by the parties or determined by the court.".

(ii) In the case of a reaffirmation under subsection (m)(2), numbered paragraph 6 in the disclosures required by clause (i) of this subparagraph shall read as follows:"6. If you were represented by an attorney during the negotiation of your reaffirmation agreement, your reaffirmation agreement becomes effective upon filing with the court.".

(4) The form of such agreement required under this paragraph shall consist of the following:

"**Part B:** Reaffirmation Agreement. I (we) agree to reaffirm the debts arising under the credit agreement described below.

"Brief description of credit agreement:

"Description of any changes to the credit agreement made as part of this reaffirmation agreement:

"Signature:

Date:

"Borrower:

"Co-borrower, if also reaffirming these debts:

"Accepted by creditor:

"Date of creditor acceptance:".

(5) The declaration shall consist of the following:

(A) The following certification:

"**Part C:** Certification by Debtor's Attorney (If Any).

"I hereby certify that (1) this agreement represents a fully informed and voluntary agreement by the debtor;

(2) this agreement does not impose an undue hardship on the debtor or any dependent of the debtor; and

(3) I have fully advised the debtor of the legal effect and consequences of this agreement and any default under this agreement.

"Signature of Debtor's Attorney:

Date:".

(B) If a presumption of undue hardship has been established with respect to such agreement, such certification shall state that, in the opinion of the attorney, the debtor is able to make the payment.

(C) In the case of a reaffirmation agreement under subsection (m)(2), subparagraph (B) is not applicable.

(6)(A) The statement in support of such agreement, which the debtor shall sign and date prior to filing with the court, shall consist of the following:

"Part D: Debtor's Statement in Support of Reaffirmation Agreement.

"1. I believe this reaffirmation agreement will not impose an undue hardship on my dependents or me. I can afford to make the payments on the reaffirmed debt because my monthly income (take home pay plus any other income received) is $______, and my actual current monthly expenses including monthly payments on postbankruptcy debt and other reaffirmation agreements total $______, leaving $______ to make the required payments on this reaffirmed debt. I understand that if my income less my monthly expenses does not leave enough to make the payments, this reaffirmation agreement is presumed to be an undue hardship on me and must be reviewed by the court. However, this presumption may be overcome if I explain to the satisfaction of the court how I can afford to make the payments here: ______.

"2. I received a copy of the Reaffirmation Disclosure Statement in Part A and a completed and signed reaffirmation agreement.".

(B) Where the debtor is represented by an attorney and is reaffirming a debt owed to a creditor defined in section 19(b)(1)(A)(iv) of the Federal Reserve Act, the statement of support of the reaffirmation agreement, which the debtor shall sign and date prior to filing with the court, shall consist of the following:"I believe this reaffirmation agreement is in my financial interest. I can afford to make the payments on the reaffirmed debt. I received a copy of the Reaffirmation Disclosure Statement in Part A and a completed and signed reaffirmation agreement.".

(7) The motion that may be used if approval of such agreement by the court is required in order for it to be effective, shall be signed and dated by the movant and shall consist of the following:"Part E: Motion for Court Approval (To be completed only if the debtor is not represented by an attorney.). I (we), the debtor(s), affirm the following to be true and correct:

"I am not represented by an attorney in connection with this reaffirmation agreement.

"I believe this reaffirmation agreement is in my best interest based on the income and expenses I have disclosed in my Statement in Support of this reaffirmation agreement, and because (provide any additional relevant reasons the court should consider):

"Therefore, I ask the court for an order approving this reaffirmation agreement.".

(8) The court order, which may be used to approve such agreement, shall consist of the following:"Court Order: The court grants the debtor's motion and approves the reaffirmation agreement described above.".

(l) Notwithstanding any other provision of this title the following shall apply:

(1) A creditor may accept payments from a debtor before and after the filing of an agreement of the kind specified in subsection (c) with the court.

(2) A creditor may accept payments from a debtor under such agreement that the creditor believes in good faith to be effective.

(3) The requirements of subsections (c)(2) and (k) shall be satisfied if disclosures required under those subsections are given in good faith.

(m)(1) Until 60 days after an agreement of the kind specified in subsection (c) is filed with the court (or such additional period as the court, after notice and a hearing and for cause, orders before the expiration of such period), it shall be presumed that such agreement is an undue hardship on the debtor if the debtor's monthly income less the debtor's monthly expenses as shown on the debtor's completed and signed statement in support of such agreement required under subsection (k)(6)(A) is less than the scheduled payments on the reaffirmed debt. This presumption shall be reviewed by the court. The presumption may be rebutted in writing by the debtor if the statement includes an explanation that identifies additional sources of funds to make the payments as agreed upon under the terms of such agreement. If the presumption is not rebutted to the satisfaction of the court, the court may disapprove such agreement. No agreement shall be disapproved without notice and a hearing to the debtor and creditor, and such hearing shall be concluded before the entry of the debtor's discharge.

(2) This subsection does not apply to reaffirmation agreements where the creditor is a credit union, as defined in section 19(b)(1)(A)(iv) of the Federal Reserve Act.

§ 525. Protection Against Discriminatory Treatment

(a) Except as provided in the Perishable Agricultural Commodities Act, 1930, the Packers and Stockyards Act, 1921, and section 1 of the Act entitled "An Act making appropriations for the Department of Agriculture for the fiscal year ending June 30, 1944, and for other purposes," approved July 12, 1943, a governmental unit may not deny, revoke, suspend, or refuse to renew a license, permit, charter, franchise, or other similar grant to, condition such a grant to, discriminate with respect to such a grant against, deny employment to, terminate the employment of, or discriminate with respect to employment against, a person that is or has been a debtor under this title or a bankrupt or a debtor under the Bankruptcy Act, or another person with whom such bankrupt or debtor has been associated, solely because such bankrupt or debtor is or has been a debtor under this title or a bankrupt or debtor under the Bankruptcy Act, has been insolvent before the commencement of the case under this title, or during the case but before the debtor is granted or denied a discharge, or has not paid a debt that is dischargeable in the case under this title or that was discharged under the Bankruptcy Act.

(b) No private employer may terminate the employment of, or discriminate with respect to employment against, an individual who is or has been a debtor under this title, a debtor or bankrupt under the Bankruptcy Act, or an individual associated with such debtor or bankrupt, solely because such debtor or bankrupt—

(1) is or has been a debtor under this title or a debtor or bankrupt under the Bankruptcy Act;

(2) has been insolvent before the commencement of a case under this title or during the case but before the grant or denial of a discharge; or

(3) has not paid a debt that is dischargeable in a case under this title or that was discharged under the Bankruptcy Act.

(c)(1) A governmental unit that operates a student grant or loan program and a person engaged in a business that includes the making of loans guaranteed or insured under a student loan program may not deny a student grant, loan, loan guarantee, or loan insurance to a person that is or has been a debtor under this title or a bankrupt or debtor under the Bankruptcy Act, or another person with whom the debtor or bankrupt has been associated, because the debtor or bankrupt is or has been a debtor under this title or a bankrupt or debtor under the Bankruptcy Act, has been insolvent before the commencement of a case under this title or during the pendency of the case but before the debtor is granted or denied a discharge, or has not paid a debt that is dischargeable in the case under this title or that was discharged under the Bankruptcy Act.

(2) In this section, "student loan program" means any program operated under title IV of the Higher Education Act of 1965 or a similar program operated under state or local law.

§ 526. Restrictions on Debt Relief Agencies

(a) A debt relief agency shall not—

(1) fail to perform any service that such agency informed an assisted person or prospective assisted person it would provide in connection with a case or proceeding under this title;

(2) make any statement, or counsel or advise any assisted person or prospective assisted person to make a statement in a document filed in a case or proceeding under this title, that is untrue or misleading, or that upon the exercise of reasonable

care, should have been known by such agency to be untrue or misleading;

(3) misrepresent to any assisted person or prospective assisted person, directly or indirectly, affirmatively or by material omission, with respect to—

(A) the services that such agency will provide to such person; or

(B) the benefits and risks that may result if such person becomes a debtor in a case under this title; or

(4) advise an assisted person or prospective assisted person to incur more debt in contemplation of such person filing a case under this title or to pay an attorney or bankruptcy petition preparer a fee or charge for services performed as part of preparing for or representing a debtor in a case under this title.

(b) Any waiver by any assisted person of any protection or right provided under this section shall not be enforceable against the debtor by any Federal or State court or any other person, but may be enforced against a debt relief agency.

(c)(1) Any contract for bankruptcy assistance between a debt relief agency and an assisted person that does not comply with the material requirements of this section, section 527, or section 528 shall be void and may not be enforced by any Federal or State court or by any other person, other than such assisted person.

(2) Any debt relief agency shall be liable to an assisted person in the amount of any fees or charges in connection with providing bankruptcy assistance to such person that such debt relief agency has received, for actual damages, and for reasonable attorneys' fees and costs if such agency is found, after notice and a hearing, to have—

(A) intentionally or negligently failed to comply with any provision of this section, section 527, or section 528 with respect to a case or proceeding under this title for such assisted person;

(B) provided bankruptcy assistance to an assisted person in a case or proceeding under this title that is dismissed or converted to a case under another chapter of this title because of such agency's intentional or negligent failure to file any required document including those specified in section 521; or

(C) intentionally or negligently disregarded the material requirements of this title or the Federal Rules of Bankruptcy Procedure applicable to such agency.

(3) In addition to such other remedies as are provided under State law, whenever the chief law enforcement officer of a State, or an official or agency designated by a State, has reason to believe that any person has violated or is violating this section, the State—

(A) may bring an action to enjoin such violation;

(B) may bring an action on behalf of its residents to recover the actual damages of assisted persons arising from such violation, including any liability under paragraph (2); and

(C) in the case of any successful action under subparagraph (A) or (B), shall be awarded the costs of the action and reasonable attorneys' fees as determined by the court.

(4) The district courts of the United States for districts located in the State shall have concurrent jurisdiction of any action under subparagraph (A) or (B) of paragraph (3).

(5) Notwithstanding any other provision of Federal law and in addition to any other remedy provided under Federal or State law, if the court, on its own motion or on the motion of the United States trustee or the debtor, finds that a person intentionally violated this section, or engaged in a clear and consistent pattern or practice of violating this section, the court may—

(A) enjoin the violation of such section; or

(B) impose an appropriate civil penalty against such person.

(d) No provision of this section, section 527, or section 528 shall—

(1) annul, alter, affect, or exempt any person subject to such sections from complying with any law of any State except to the extent that such law is inconsistent with those sections, and then only to the extent of the inconsistency; or

(2) be deemed to limit or curtail the authority or ability—

(A) of a State or subdivision or instrumentality thereof, to determine and enforce qualifications for the practice of law under the laws of that State; or

(B) of a Federal court to determine and enforce the qualifications for the practice of law before that court.

§ 527. Disclosures

(a) A debt relief agency providing bankruptcy assistance to an assisted person shall provide—

(1) the written notice required under section 342(b)(1); and

(2) to the extent not covered in the written notice described in paragraph (1), and not later than 3 business days after the first date on which a debt relief agency first offers to provide any bankruptcy assistance services to an assisted person, a clear and conspicuous written notice advising assisted persons that—

(A) all information that the assisted person is required to provide with a petition and thereafter during a case under this title is required to be complete, accurate, and truthful;

(B) all assets and all liabilities are required to be completely and accurately disclosed in the documents filed to commence the case, and the replacement value of each asset as defined in section 506 must be stated in those documents where requested after reasonable inquiry to establish such value;

(C) current monthly income, the amounts specified in section 707(b)(2), and, in a case under chapter 13 of this title, disposable income (determined in accordance with section 707(b)(2)), are required to be stated after reasonable inquiry; and

(D) information that an assisted person provides during their case may be audited pursuant to this title, and that failure to provide such information may result in dismissal of the case under this title or other sanction, including a criminal sanction.

(b) A debt relief agency providing bankruptcy assistance to an assisted person shall provide each assisted person at the same time as the notices required under subsection (a)(1) the following statement, to the extent applicable, or one substantially similar. The statement shall be clear and conspicuous and shall be in a single document separate from other documents or notices provided to the assisted person:

"IMPORTANT INFORMATION ABOUT BANKRUPTCY ASSISTANCE SERVICES FROM AN ATTORNEY OR BANKRUPTCY PETITION PREPARER.

"If you decide to seek bankruptcy relief, you can represent yourself, you can hire an attorney to represent you, or you can get help in some localities from a bankruptcy petition preparer who is not an attorney. THE LAW REQUIRES AN ATTORNEY OR BANKRUPTCY PETITION PREPARER TO GIVE YOU A WRITTEN CONTRACT SPECIFYING WHAT THE ATTORNEY OR BANKRUPTCY PETITION PREPARER WILL DO FOR YOU AND HOW MUCH IT WILL COST. Ask to see the contract before you hire anyone.

"The following information helps you understand what must be done in a routine bankruptcy case to help you evaluate how much service you need. Although bankruptcy can be complex, many cases are routine.

"Before filing a bankruptcy case, either you or your attorney should analyze your eligibility for different forms of debt relief available under the Bankruptcy Code and which form of relief is most likely to be beneficial for you. Be sure you understand the relief you can obtain and its limitations. To file a bankruptcy case, documents called a Petition, Schedules, and Statement of Financial Affairs, and in some cases a Statement of Intention, need to be prepared correctly and filed with the bankruptcy court. You will have to pay a filing fee to the bankruptcy court. Once your case starts, you will have to attend the required first meeting of creditors where you may be questioned by a court official called a 'trustee' and by creditors.

"If you choose to file a chapter 7 case, you may be asked by a creditor to reaffirm a debt. You may want help deciding whether to do so. A creditor is not permitted to coerce you into reaffirming your debts.

"If you choose to file a chapter 13 case in which you repay your creditors what you can afford over 3 to 5 years, you may also want help with preparing your chapter 13 plan and with the confirmation hearing on your plan which will be before a bankruptcy judge.

"If you select another type of relief under the Bankruptcy Code other than chapter 7 or chapter 13, you will want to find out what should be done from someone familiar with that type of relief.

"Your bankruptcy case may also involve litigation. You are generally permitted to represent yourself in litigation in bankruptcy court, but only attorneys, not bankruptcy petition preparers, can give you legal advice."

(c) Except to the extent the debt relief agency provides the required information itself after reasonably diligent inquiry of the assisted person or others so as to obtain such information reasonably accurately for inclusion on the petition, schedules or statement of financial affairs, a debt relief agency providing bankruptcy assistance to an assisted person, to the extent permitted by nonbankruptcy law, shall provide each assisted person at the time required for the notice required under subsection (a)(1) reasonably sufficient information (which shall be provided in a clear and conspicuous writing) to the assisted person on how to provide all the information the assisted person is required to provide under this title pursuant to section 521, including—

(1) how to value assets at replacement value, determine current monthly income, the amounts specified in section 707(b)(2) and, in a chapter 13 case, how to determine disposable income in accordance with section 707(b)(2) and related calculations;

(2) how to complete the list of creditors, including how to determine what amount is owed and what address for the creditor should be shown; and

(3) how to determine what property is exempt and how to value exempt property at replacement value as defined in section 506.

(d) A debt relief agency shall maintain a copy of the notices required under subsection (a) of this section for 2 years after the date on which the notice is given the assisted person.

§ 528. Requirements for Debt Relief Agencies

(a) A debt relief agency shall—

(1) not later than 5 business days after the first date on which such agency provides any bankruptcy assistance services to an assisted person, but prior to such assisted person's petition under this title being filed, execute a written contract with such assisted person that explains clearly and conspicuously—

(A) the services such agency will provide to such assisted person; and

(B) the fees or charges for such services, and the terms of payment;

(2) provide the assisted person with a copy of the fully executed and completed contract;

(3) clearly and conspicuously disclose in any advertisement of bankruptcy assistance services or of the benefits of bankruptcy directed to the general public (whether in general media, seminars or specific mailings, telephonic or electronic messages, or otherwise) that the services or benefits are with respect to bankruptcy relief under this title; and

(4) clearly and conspicuously use the following statement in such advertisement: "We are a debt relief agency. We help people file for bankruptcy relief under the Bankruptcy Code." or a substantially similar statement.

(b)(1) An advertisement of bankruptcy assistance services or of the benefits of bankruptcy directed to the general public includes—

(A) descriptions of bankruptcy assistance in connection with a chapter 13 plan whether or not chapter 13 is specifically mentioned in such advertisement; and

(B) statements such as "federally supervised repayment plan" or "Federal debt restructuring help" or other similar statements that could lead a reasonable consumer to believe that debt counseling was being offered when in fact the services were directed to providing bankruptcy assistance with a chapter 13 plan or other form of bankruptcy relief under this title.

(2) An advertisement, directed to the general public, indicating that the debt relief agency provides assistance with respect to credit defaults, mortgage foreclosures, eviction proceedings, excessive debt, debt collection pressure, or inability to pay any consumer debt shall—

(A) disclose clearly and conspicuously in such advertisement that the assistance may involve bankruptcy relief under this title; and

(B) include the following statement: "We are a debt relief agency. We help people file for bankruptcy relief under the Bankruptcy Code." or a substantially similar statement.

SUBCHAPTER III—THE ESTATE

§ 541. Property of the Estate

(a) The commencement of a case under section 301, 302, or 303 of this title creates an estate. Such estate is comprised of all the following property, wherever located and by whomever held:

(1) Except as provided in subsections (b) and (c)(2) of this section, all legal or equitable interests of the debtor in property as of the commencement of the case.

(2) All interests of the debtor and the debtor's spouse in community property as of the commencement of the case that is—

(A) under the sole, equal, or joint management and control of the debtor; or

(B) liable for an allowable claim against the debtor, or for both an allowable claim against the debtor and an allowable claim against the debtor's spouse, to the extent that such interest is so liable.

(3) Any interest in property that the trustee recovers under section 329(b), 363(n), 543, 550, 553, or 723 of this title.

(4) Any interest in property preserved for the benefit of or ordered transferred to the estate under section 510(c) or 551 of this title.

(5) Any interest in property that would have been property of the estate if such interest had been an

interest of the debtor on the date of the filing of the petition, and that the debtor acquires or becomes entitled to acquire within 180 days after such date—

(A) by bequest, devise, or inheritance;

(B) as a result of a property settlement agreement with the debtor's spouse, or of an interlocutory or final divorce decree; or

(C) as a beneficiary of a life insurance policy or of a death benefit plan.

(6) Proceeds, product, offspring, rents, or profits of or from property of the estate, except such as are earnings from services performed by an individual debtor after the commencement of the case.

(7) Any interest in property that the estate acquires after the commencement of the case.

(b) Property of the estate does not include—

(1) any power that the debtor may exercise solely for the benefit of an entity other than the debtor;

(2) any interest of the debtor as a lessee under a lease of nonresidential real property that has terminated at the expiration of the stated term of such lease before the commencement of the case under this title, and ceases to include any interest of the debtor as a lessee under a lease of nonresidential real property that has terminated at the expiration of the stated term of such lease during the case;

(3) any eligibility of the debtor to participate in programs authorized under the Higher Education Act of 1965 (20 U.S.C. 1001 et seq.; 42 U.S.C. 2751 et seq.), or any accreditation status or state licensure of the debtor as an educational institution;

(4) any interest of the debtor in liquid or gaseous hydrocarbons to the extent that—

(A)(i) the debtor has transferred or has agreed to transfer such interest pursuant to a farmout agreement or any written agreement directly related to a farmout agreement; and

(ii) but for the operation of this paragraph, the estate could include the interest referred to in clause (i) only by virtue of section 365 or 544(a)(3) of this title; or

(B)(i) the debtor has transferred such interest pursuant to a written conveyance of a production payment to an entity that does not participate in the operation of the property from which such production payment is transferred; and

(ii) but for the operation of this paragraph, the estate could include the interest referred to in clause (i) only by virtue of section 365 or 542 of this title;

(5) funds placed in an education individual retirement account (as defined in section 530(b)(1) of the Internal Revenue Code of 1986) not later than 365 days before the date of the filing of the petition in a case under this title, but—

(A) only if the designated beneficiary of such account was a child, stepchild, grandchild, or stepgrandchild of the debtor for the taxable year for which funds were placed in such account;

(B) only to the extent that such funds—

(i) are not pledged or promised to any entity in connection with any extension of credit; and

(ii) are not excess contributions (as described in section 4973(e) of the Internal Revenue Code of 1986); and

(C) in the case of funds placed in all such accounts having the same designated beneficiary not earlier than 720 days nor later than 365 days before such date, only so much of such funds as does not exceed $8,575;

(6) funds used to purchase a tuition credit or certificate or contributed to an account in accordance with section 529(b)(1)(A) of the Internal Revenue Code of 1986 under a qualified State tuition program (as defined in section 529(b)(1) of such Code) not later than 365 days before the date of the filing of the petition in a case under this title, but—

(A) only if the designated beneficiary of the amounts paid or contributed to such tuition program was a child, stepchild, grandchild, or stepgrandchild of the debtor for the taxable year for which funds were paid or contributed;

(B) with respect to the aggregate amount paid or contributed to such program having the same designated beneficiary, only so much of such amount as does not exceed the total contributions permitted under section 529(b)(6) of such Code with respect to such beneficiary, as adjusted beginning on the date of the filing of the petition in a case under this title by the annual increase or decrease (rounded to the nearest tenth of 1 percent) in the education expenditure category of the Consumer Price Index prepared by the Department of Labor; and

(C) in the case of funds paid or contributed to such program having the same designated beneficiary not earlier than 720 days nor later than 365 days before such date, only so much of such funds as does not exceed $8,575;

(7) any amount—

(A) withheld by an employer from the wages of employees for payment as contributions—

(i) to—

(I) an employee benefit plan that is subject to title I of the Employee Retirement Income Security Act of 1974 or under an employee benefit plan which is a governmental plan under section 414(d) of the Internal Revenue Code of 1986;

(II) a deferred compensation plan under section 457 of the Internal Revenue Code of 1986; or

(III) a tax-deferred annuity under section 403(b) of the Internal Revenue Code of 1986; except that such amount under this subparagraph shall not constitute disposable income as defined in section 1325(b)(2); or

(ii) to a health insurance plan regulated by State law whether or not subject to such title; or

(B) received by an employer from employees for payment as contributions—

(i) to—

(I) an employee benefit plan that is subject to title I of the Employee Retirement Income Security Act of 1974 or under an employee benefit plan which is a governmental plan under section 414(d) of the Internal Revenue Code of 1986;

(II) a deferred compensation plan under section 457 of the Internal Revenue Code of 1986; or

(III) a tax-deferred annuity under section 403(b) of the Internal Revenue Code of 1986; except that such amount under this subparagraph shall not constitute disposable income, as defined in section 1325(b)(2); or

(ii) to a health insurance plan regulated by State law whether or not subject to such title;

(8) subject to subchapter III of chapter 5, any interest of the debtor in property where the debtor pledged or sold tangible personal property (other than securities or written or printed evidences of indebtedness or title) as collateral for a loan or advance of money given by a person licensed under law to make such loans or advances, where—

(A) the tangible personal property is in the possession of the pledgee or transferee;

(B) the debtor has no obligation to repay the money, redeem the collateral, or buy back the property at a stipulated price; and

(C) neither the debtor nor the trustee have exercised any right to redeem provided under the contract or State law, in a timely manner as provided under State law and section 108(b);

(9) any interest in cash or cash equivalents that constitute proceeds of a sale by the debtor of a money order that is made—

(A) on or after the date that is 14 days prior to the date on which the petition is filed; and

(B) under an agreement with a money order issuer that prohibits the commingling of such proceeds with property of the debtor (notwithstanding that, contrary to the agreement, the proceeds may have been commingled with property of the debtor),

unless the money order issuer had not taken action, prior to the filing of the petition, to require compliance with the prohibition,

(10) funds placed in an account of a qualified ABLE program (as defined in section 529A(b) of the Internal Revenue Code of 1986) not later than 365 days before the date of the filing of the petition in a case under this title, but—

(A) only if the designated beneficiary of such account was a child, stepchild, grandchild, or stepgrandchild of the debtor for the taxable year for which funds were placed in such account;

(B) only to the extent that such funds—

(i) are not pledged or promised to any entity in connection with any extension of credit; and

(ii) are not excess contributions (as described in section 4973(h) of the Internal Revenue Code of 1986); and

(C) in the case of funds placed in all such accounts having the same designated beneficiary not earlier than 720 days nor later than 365 days before such date, only so much of such funds as does not exceed $8,575; or

(11) required payment stablecoin reserves under section 4 of the GENIUS Act, provided that notwithstanding the exclusion of such reserves from the property of the estate, section 362 of this title shall apply to such reserves.

(c)(1) Except as provided in paragraph (2) of this subsection, an interest of the debtor in property becomes property of the estate under subsection (a)(1), (a)(2), or (a)(5) of this section notwithstanding any provision in an agreement, transfer instrument, or applicable nonbankruptcy law—

(A) that restricts or conditions transfer of such interest by the debtor; or

(B) that is conditioned on the insolvency or financial condition of the debtor, on the commencement of a case under this title, or on the appointment of or taking possession by a trustee in a case under this title or a custodian before such commencement, and that effects or gives an option to effect a forfeiture, modification, or termination of the debtor's interest in property.

(2) A restriction on the transfer of a beneficial interest of the debtor in a trust that is enforceable under applicable nonbankruptcy law is enforceable in a case under this title.

(d) Property in which the debtor holds, as of the commencement of the case, only legal title and not an equitable interest, such as a mortgage secured by real property, or an interest in such a mortgage, sold by the debtor but as to which the debtor retains legal title to service or supervise the servicing of such mortgage or interest, becomes property of the estate under subsection (a)(1) or (2) of this section only to the extent of the debtor's legal title to such property, but not to the extent of any equitable interest in such property that the debtor does not hold.

(e) In determining whether any of the relationships specified in paragraph (5)(A) or (6)(A) of subsection (b) exists, a legally adopted child of an individual (and a child who is a member of an individual's household, if placed with such individual by an authorized placement agency for legal adoption by such individual), or a foster child of an individual (if such child has as the child's principal place of abode the home of the debtor and is a member of the debtor's household) shall be treated as a child of such individual by blood.

(f) Notwithstanding any other provision of this title, property that is held by a debtor that is a corporation described in section 501(c)(3) of the Internal Revenue Code of 1986 and exempt from tax under section 501(a) of such Code may be transferred to an entity that is not such a corporation, but only under the same conditions as would apply if the debtor had not filed a case under this title.

§ 542. Turnover of Property to the Estate

(a) Except as provided in subsection (c) or (d) of this section, an entity, other than a custodian, in possession, custody, or control, during the case, of property that the trustee may use, sell, or lease under section 363 of this title, or that the debtor may exempt under section 522 of this title, shall deliver to the trustee, and account for, such property or the value of such property, unless such property is of inconsequential value or benefit to the estate.

(b) Except as provided in subsection (c) or (d) of this section, an entity that owes a debt that is property of the estate and that is matured, payable on demand, or payable on order, shall pay such debt to, or on the order of, the trustee, except to the extent that such debt may be offset under section 553 of this title against a claim against the debtor.

(c) Except as provided in section 362(a)(7) of this title, an entity that has neither actual notice nor actual knowledge of the commencement of the case concerning the debtor may transfer property of the estate, or pay a debt owing to the debtor, in good faith and other than in the manner specified in subsection (d) of this section, to an entity other than the trustee, with the same effect as to the entity making such transfer or payment as if the case under this title concerning the debtor had not been commenced.

(d) A life insurance company may transfer property of the estate or property of the debtor to such company in good faith, with the same effect with respect to such company as if the case under this title concerning the debtor had not been commenced, if such transfer is to pay a premium or to carry out a nonforfeiture insurance option, and is required to be made automatically, under a life insurance contract with such company that was entered into before the date of the filing of the petition and that is property of the estate.

(e) Subject to any applicable privilege, after notice and a hearing, the court may order an attorney, accountant, or other person that holds recorded information, including books, documents, records, and papers, relating to the debtor's property or financial affairs, to turn over or disclose such recorded information to the trustee.

§ 543. Turnover of Property by a Custodian

(a) A custodian with knowledge of the commencement of a case under this title concerning the debtor may not make any disbursement from, or take any action in the administration of, property of the debtor, proceeds, product, offspring, rents, or profits of such property, or property of the estate, in the possession, custody, or control of such custodian, except such action as is necessary to preserve such property.

(b) A custodian shall—

(1) deliver to the trustee any property of the debtor held by or transferred to such custodian, or proceeds, product, offspring, rents, or profits of

such property, that is in such custodian's possession, custody, or control on the date that such custodian acquires knowledge of the commencement of the case; and

(2) file an accounting of any property of the debtor, or proceeds, product, offspring, rents, or profits of such property, that, at any time, came into the possession, custody, or control of such custodian.

(c) The court, after notice and a hearing, shall—

(1) protect all entities to which a custodian has become obligated with respect to such property or proceeds, product, offspring, rents, or profits of such property;

(2) provide for the payment of reasonable compensation for services rendered and costs and expenses incurred by such custodian; and

(3) surcharge such custodian, other than an assignee for the benefit of the debtor's creditors that was appointed or took possession more than 120 days before the date of the filing of the petition, for any improper or excessive disbursement, other than a disbursement that has been made in accordance with applicable law or that has been approved, after notice and a hearing, by a court of competent jurisdiction before the commencement of the case under this title.

(d) After notice and hearing, the bankruptcy court—

(1) may excuse compliance with subsection (a), (b), or (c) of this section if the interests of creditors and, if the debtor is not insolvent, of equity security holders would be better served by permitting a custodian to continue in possession, custody, or control of such property, and

(2) shall excuse compliance with subsections (a) and (b)(1) of this section if the custodian is an assignee for the benefit of the debtor's creditors that was appointed or took possession more than 120 days before the date of the filing of the petition, unless compliance with such subsections is necessary to prevent fraud or injustice.

§ 544. Trustee as Lien Creditor and as Successor to Certain Creditors and Purchasers

(a) The trustee shall have, as of the commencement of the case, and without regard to any knowledge of the trustee or of any creditor, the rights and powers of, or may avoid any transfer of property of the debtor or any obligation incurred by the debtor that is voidable by—

(1) a creditor that extends credit to the debtor at the time of the commencement of the case, and that obtains, at such time and with respect to such credit, a judicial lien on all property on which a creditor on a simple contract could have obtained such a judicial lien, whether or not such a creditor exists;

(2) a creditor that extends credit to the debtor at the time of the commencement of the case, and obtains, at such time and with respect to such credit, an execution against the debtor that is returned unsatisfied at such time, whether or not such a creditor exists; or

(3) a bona fide purchaser of real property, other than fixtures, from the debtor, against whom applicable law permits such transfer to be perfected, that obtains the status of a bona fide purchaser and has perfected such transfer at the time of the commencement of the case, whether or not such a purchaser exists.

(b)(1) Except as provided in paragraph (2), the trustee may avoid any transfer of an interest of the debtor in property or any obligation incurred by the debtor that is voidable under applicable law by a creditor holding an unsecured claim that is allowable under section 502 of this title or that is not allowable only under section 502(e) of this title.

(2) Paragraph (1) shall not apply to a transfer of a charitable contribution (as that term is defined in section 548(d)(3)) that is not covered under section 548(a)(1)(B), by reason of section 548(a)(2). Any claim by any person to recover a transferred contribution described in the preceding sentence under Federal or state law in a Federal or state court shall be preempted by the commencement of the case.

§ 545. Statutory Liens

The trustee may avoid the fixing of a statutory lien on property of the debtor to the extent that such lien—

(1) first becomes effective against the debtor—

(A) when a case under this title concerning the debtor is commenced;

(B) when an insolvency proceeding other than under this title concerning the debtor is commenced;

(C) when a custodian is appointed or authorized to take or takes possession;

(D) when the debtor becomes insolvent;

(E) when the debtor's financial condition fails to meet a specified standard; or

(F) at the time of an execution against property of the debtor levied at the instance of an entity other than the holder of such statutory lien;

(2) is not perfected or enforceable at the time of the commencement of the case against a bona fide purchaser that purchases such property at the time of the commencement of the case, whether or not

such a purchaser exists, except in any case in which a purchaser is a purchaser described in section 6323 of the Internal Revenue Code of 1986, or in any other similar provision of State or local law;

(3) is for rent; or

(4) is a lien of distress for rent.

§ 546. Limitations on Avoiding Powers

(a) An action or proceeding under section 544, 545, 547, 548, or 553 of this title may not be commenced after the earlier of—

(1) the later of—

(A) 2 years after the entry of the order for relief; or

(B) 1 year after the appointment or election of the first trustee under section 702, 1104, 1163, 1202, or 1302 of this title if such appointment or such election occurs before the expiration of the period specified in subparagraph (A); or

(2) the time the case is closed or dismissed.

(b)(1) The rights and powers of a trustee under sections 544, 545, and 549 of this title are subject to any generally applicable law that—

(A) permits perfection of an interest in property to be effective against an entity that acquires rights in such property before the date of perfection; or

(B) provides for the maintenance or continuation of perfection of an interest in property to be effective against an entity that acquires rights in such property before the date on which action is taken to effect such maintenance or continuation.

(2) If—

(A) a law described in paragraph (1) requires seizure of such property or commencement of an action to accomplish such perfection, or maintenance or continuation of perfection of an interest in property; and

(B) such property has not been seized or such an action has not been commenced before the date of the filing of the petition;

such interest in such property shall be perfected, or perfection of such interest shall be maintained or continued, by giving notice within the time fixed by such law for such seizure or such commencement.

(c)(1) Except as provided in subsection (d) of this section and in section 507(c), and subject to the prior rights of a holder of a security interest in such goods or the proceeds thereof, the rights and powers of the trustee under sections 544(a), 545, 547, and 549 are subject to the right of a seller of goods that has sold goods to the debtor, in the ordinary course of such seller's business, to reclaim such goods if the debtor has received such goods while insolvent, within 45 days before the date of the commencement of a case under this title, but such seller may not reclaim such goods unless such seller demands in writing reclamation of such goods—

(A) not later than 45 days after the date of receipt of such goods by the debtor; or

(B) not later than 20 days after the date of commencement of the case, if the 45-day period expires after the commencement of the case.

(2) If a seller of goods fails to provide notice in the manner described in paragraph (1), the seller still may assert the rights contained in section 503(b)(9).

(d) In the case of a seller who is a producer of grain sold to a grain storage facility, owned or operated by the debtor, in the ordinary course of such seller's business (as such terms are defined in section 557 of this title) or in the case of a United States fisherman who has caught fish sold to a fish processing facility owned or operated by the debtor in the ordinary course of such fisherman's business, the rights and powers of the trustee under sections 544(a), 545, 547, and 549 of this title are subject to any statutory or common law right of such producer or fisherman to reclaim such grain or fish if the debtor has received such grain or fish while insolvent, but—

(1) such producer or fisherman may not reclaim any grain or fish unless such producer or fisherman demands, in writing, reclamation of such grain or fish before ten days after receipt thereof by the debtor; and

(2) the court may deny reclamation to such a producer or fisherman with a right of reclamation that has made such a demand only if the court secures such claim by a lien.

(e) Notwithstanding sections 544, 545, 547, 548(a)(1)(B), and 548(b) of this title, the trustee may not avoid a transfer that is a margin payment, as defined in section 101, 741, or 761 of this title, or settlement payment, as defined in section 101 or 741 of this title, made by or to (or for the benefit of) a commodity broker, forward contract merchant, stockbroker, financial institution, financial participant, or securities clearing agency, or that is a transfer made by or to (or for the benefit of) a commodity broker, forward contract merchant, stockbroker, financial institution, financial participant, or securities clearing agency, in connection with a securities contract, as defined in section 741(7), commodity contract, as defined in section 761(4), or forward contract, that is made before the commencement of the case, except under section 548(a)(1)(A) of this title.

(f) Notwithstanding sections 544, 545, 547, 548(a)(1)(B), and 548(b) of this title, the trustee may not avoid a transfer made by or to (or for the benefit of) a repo participant or financial participant, in connection with a repurchase agreement and that is made before the commencement of the case, except under section 548(a)(1)(A) of this title.

(g) Notwithstanding sections 544, 545, 547, 548(a)(1)(B) and 548(b) of this title, the trustee may not avoid a transfer, made by or to (or for the benefit of) a swap participant or financial participant, under or in connection with any swap agreement and that is made before the commencement of the case, except under section 548(a)(1)(A) of this title.

(h) Notwithstanding the rights and powers of a trustee under sections 544(a), 545, 547, 549, and 553, if the court determines on a motion by the trustee made not later than 120 days after the date of the order for relief in a case under chapter 11 of this title and after notice and a hearing, that a return is in the best interests of the estate, the debtor, with the consent of a creditor and subject to the prior rights of holders of security interests in such goods or the proceeds of such goods, may return goods shipped to the debtor by the creditor before the commencement of the case, and the creditor may offset the purchase price of such goods against any claim of the creditor against the debtor that arose before the commencement of the case.

(i)(1) Notwithstanding paragraphs (2) and (3) of section 545, the trustee may not avoid a warehouseman's lien for storage, transportation, or other costs incidental to the storage and handling of goods.

(2) The prohibition under paragraph (1) shall be applied in a manner consistent with any State statute applicable to such lien that is similar to section 7–209 of the Uniform Commercial Code, as in effect on the date of enactment of the Bankruptcy Abuse Prevention and Consumer Protection Act of 2005, or any successor to such section 7–209.

(j) Notwithstanding sections 544, 545, 547, 548(a)(1)(B), and 548(b) the trustee may not avoid a transfer made by or to (or for the benefit of) a master netting agreement participant under or in connection with any master netting agreement or any individual contract covered thereby that is made before the commencement of the case, except under section 548(a)(1)(A) and except to the extent that the trustee could otherwise avoid such a transfer made under an individual contract covered by such master netting agreement.

§ 547. Preferences

(a) In this section—

(1) "inventory" means personal property leased or furnished, held for sale or lease, or to be furnished under a contract for service, raw materials, work in process, or materials used or consumed in a business, including farm products such as crops or livestock, held for sale or lease;

(2) "new value" means money or money's worth in goods, services, or new credit, or release by a transferee of property previously transferred to such transferee in a transaction that is neither void nor voidable by the debtor or the trustee under any applicable law, including proceeds of such property, but does not include an obligation substituted for an existing obligation;

(3) "receivable" means right to payment, whether or not such right has been earned by performance; and

(4) a debt for a tax is incurred on the day when such tax is last payable without penalty, including any extension.

(b) Except as provided in subsections (c), (i), and (j) of this section, the trustee may, based on reasonable due diligence in the circumstances of the case and taking into account a party's known or reasonably knowable affirmative defenses under subsection (c), avoid any transfer of an interest of the debtor in property—

(1) to or for the benefit of a creditor;

(2) for or on account of an antecedent debt owed by the debtor before such transfer was made;

(3) made while the debtor was insolvent;

(4) made—

(A) on or within 90 days before the date of the filing of the petition; or

(B) between ninety days and one year before the date of the filing of the petition, if such creditor at the time of such transfer was an insider; and

(5) that enables such creditor to receive more than such creditor would receive if—

(A) the case were a case under chapter 7 of this title;

(B) the transfer had not been made; and

(C) such creditor received payment of such debt to the extent provided by the provisions of this title.

(c) The trustee may not avoid under this section a transfer—

(1) to the extent that such transfer was—

(A) intended by the debtor and the creditor to or for whose benefit such transfer was made to be a contemporaneous exchange for new value given to the debtor; and

(B) in fact a substantially contemporaneous exchange;

(2) to the extent that such transfer was in payment of a debt incurred by the debtor in the ordinary course of business or financial affairs of the debtor and the transferee, and such transfer was—

(A) made in the ordinary course of business or financial affairs of the debtor and the transferee; or

(B) made according to ordinary business terms;

(3) that creates a security interest in property acquired by the debtor—

(A) to the extent such security interest secures new value that was—

(i) given at or after the signing of a security agreement that contains a description of such property as collateral;

(ii) given by or on behalf of the secured party under such agreement;

(iii) given to enable the debtor to acquire such property; and

(iv) in fact used by the debtor to acquire such property; and

(B) that is perfected on or before 30 days after the debtor receives possession of such property;

(4) to or for the benefit of a creditor, to the extent that, after such transfer, such creditor gave new value to or for the benefit of the debtor—

(A) not secured by an otherwise unavoidable security interest; and

(B) on account of which new value the debtor did not make an otherwise unavoidable transfer to or for the benefit of such creditor;

(5) that creates a perfected security interest in inventory or a receivable or the proceeds of either, except to the extent that the aggregate of all such transfers to the transferee caused a reduction, as of the date of the filing of the petition and to the prejudice of other creditors holding unsecured claims, of any amount by which the debt secured by such security interest exceeded the value of all security interests for such debt on the later of—

(A)(i) with respect to a transfer to which subsection (b)(4)(A) of this section applies, 90 days before the date of the filing of the petition; or

(ii) with respect to a transfer to which subsection (b)(4)(B) of this section applies, one year before the date of the filing of the petition; or

(B) the date on which new value was first given under the security agreement creating such security interest;

(6) that is the fixing of a statutory lien that is not avoidable under section 545 of this title;

(7) to the extent such transfer was a bona fide payment of a debt for a domestic support obligation;

(8) if, in a case filed by an individual debtor whose debts are primarily consumer debts, the aggregate value of all property that constitutes or is affected by such transfer is less than $600; or

(9) if, in a case filed by a debtor whose debts are not primarily consumer debts, the aggregate value of all property that constitutes or is affected by such transfer is less than $8,575.

(d) The trustee may avoid a transfer of an interest in property of the debtor transferred to or for the benefit of a surety to secure reimbursement of such a surety that furnished a bond or other obligation to dissolve a judicial lien that would have been avoidable by the trustee under subsection (b) of this section. The liability of such surety under such bond or obligation shall be discharged to the extent of the value of such property recovered by the trustee or the amount paid to the trustee.

(e)(1) For the purposes of this section—

(A) a transfer of real property other than fixtures, but including the interest of a seller or purchaser under a contract for the sale of real property, is perfected when a bona fide purchaser of such property from the debtor against whom applicable law permits such transfer to be perfected cannot acquire an interest that is superior to the interest of the transferee; and

(B) a transfer of a fixture or property other than real property is perfected when a creditor on a simple contract cannot acquire a judicial lien that is superior to the interest of the transferee.

(2) For the purposes of this section, except as provided in paragraph (3) of this subsection, a transfer is made—

(A) at the time such transfer takes effect between the transferor and the transferee, if such transfer is perfected at, or within 30 days after, such time, except as provided in subsection (c)(3)(B);

(B) at the time such transfer is perfected, if such transfer is perfected after such 30 days; or

(C) immediately before the date of the filing of the petition, if such transfer is not perfected at the later of—

(i) the commencement of the case; or

(ii) 30 days after such transfer takes effect between the transferor and the transferee.

(3) For the purposes of this section, a transfer is not made until the debtor has acquired rights in the property transferred.

(f) For the purposes of this section, the debtor is presumed to have been insolvent on and during the 90 days immediately preceding the date of the filing of the petition.

(g) For the purposes of this section, the trustee has the burden of proving the avoidability of a transfer under subsection (b) of this section, and the creditor or party in interest against whom recovery or avoidance is sought has the burden of proving the nonavoidability of a transfer under subsection (c) of this section.

(h) The trustee may not avoid a transfer if such transfer was made as a part of an alternative repayment schedule between the debtor and any creditor of the debtor created by an approved nonprofit budget and credit counseling agency.

(i) If the trustee avoids under subsection (b) a transfer made between 90 days and 1 year before the date of the filing of the petition, by the debtor to an entity that is not an insider for the benefit of a creditor that is an insider, such transfer shall be considered to be avoided under this section only with respect to the creditor that is an insider.

§ 548. Fraudulent Transfers and Obligations

(a)(1) The trustee may avoid any transfer (including any transfer to or for the benefit of an insider under an employment contract) of an interest of the debtor in property, or any obligation (including any obligation to or for the benefit of an insider under an employment contract) incurred by the debtor, that was made or incurred on or within 2 years before the date of the filing of the petition, if the debtor voluntarily or involuntarily—

(A) made such transfer or incurred such obligation with actual intent to hinder, delay, or defraud any entity to which the debtor was or became, on or after the date that such transfer was made or such obligation was incurred, indebted; or

(B)(i) received less than a reasonably equivalent value in exchange for such transfer or obligation; and

(ii)(I) was insolvent on the date that such transfer was made or such obligation was incurred, or became insolvent as a result of such transfer or obligation;

(II) was engaged in business or a transaction, or was about to engage in business or a transaction, for which any property remaining with the debtor was an unreasonably small capital;

(III) intended to incur, or believed that the debtor would incur, debts that would be beyond the debtor's ability to pay as such debts matured; or

(IV) made such transfer to or for the benefit of an insider, or incurred such obligation to or for the benefit of an insider, under an employment contract and not in the ordinary course of business.

(2) A transfer of a charitable contribution to a qualified religious or charitable entity or organization shall not be considered to be a transfer covered under paragraph (1)(B) in any case in which—

(A) the amount of that contribution does not exceed 15 percent of the gross annual income of the debtor for the year in which the transfer of the contribution is made; or

(B) the contribution made by a debtor exceeded the percentage amount of gross annual income specified in subparagraph (A), if the transfer was consistent with the practices of the debtor in making charitable contributions.

(b) The trustee of a partnership debtor may avoid any transfer of an interest of the debtor in property, or any obligation incurred by the debtor, that was made or incurred on or within 2 years before the date of the filing of the petition, to a general partner in the debtor, if the debtor was insolvent on the date such transfer was made or such obligation was incurred, or became insolvent as a result of such transfer or obligation.

(c) Except to the extent that a transfer or obligation voidable under this section is voidable under section 544, 545, or 547 of this title, a transferee or obligee of such a transfer or obligation that takes for value and in good faith has a lien on or may retain any interest transferred or may enforce any obligation incurred, as the case may be, to the extent that such transferee or obligee gave value to the debtor in exchange for such transfer or obligation.

(d)(1) For the purposes of this section, a transfer is made when such transfer is so perfected that a bona fide purchaser from the debtor against whom applicable law permits such transfer to be perfected cannot acquire an interest in the property transferred that is superior to the interest in such property of the transferee, but if such transfer is not so perfected before the commencement of the case, such transfer is made immediately before the date of the filing of the petition.

(2) In this section—

(A) "value" means property, or satisfaction or securing of a present or antecedent debt of the debtor, but does not include an unperformed promise to furnish support to the debtor or to a relative of the debtor;

(B) a commodity broker, forward contract merchant, stockbroker, financial institution, financial participant, or securities clearing agency that receives a margin payment, as defined in section 101, 741, or 761 of this title, or settlement payment, as defined in section 101 or 741 of this title, takes for value to the extent of such payment;

(C) a repo participant or financial participant that receives a margin payment, as defined in section 741 or 761 of this title, or settlement payment, as defined in section 741 of this title, in connection with a repurchase agreement, takes for value to the extent of such payment;

(D) a swap participant or financial participant that receives a transfer in connection with a swap agreement takes for value to the extent of such transfer; and

(E) a master netting agreement participant that receives a transfer in connection with a master netting agreement or any individual contract covered thereby takes for value to the extent of such transfer, except that, with respect to a transfer under any individual contract covered thereby, to the extent that such master netting agreement participant otherwise did not take (or is otherwise not deemed to have taken) such transfer for value.

(3) In this section, the term "charitable contribution" means a charitable contribution, as that term is defined in section 170(c) of the Internal Revenue Code of 1986, if that contribution—

(A) is made by a natural person; and

(B) consists of—

(i) a financial instrument (as that term is defined in section 731(c)(2)(C) of the Internal Revenue Code of 1986); or

(ii) cash.

(4) In this section, the term "qualified religious or charitable entity or organization" means—

(A) an entity described in section 170(c)(1) of the Internal Revenue Code of 1986; or

(B) an entity or organization described in section 170(c)(2) of the Internal Revenue Code of 1986.

(e)(1) In addition to any transfer that the trustee may otherwise avoid, the trustee may avoid any transfer of an interest of the debtor in property that was made on or within 10 years before the date of the filing of the petition, if—

(A) such transfer was made to a self-settled trust or similar device;

(B) such transfer was by the debtor;

(C) the debtor is a beneficiary of such trust or similar device; and

(D) the debtor made such transfer with actual intent to hinder, delay, or defraud any entity to which the debtor was or became, on or after the date that such transfer was made, indebted.

(2) For the purposes of this subsection, a transfer includes a transfer made in anticipation of any money judgment, settlement, civil penalty, equitable order, or criminal fine incurred by, or which the debtor believed would be incurred by—

(A) any violation of the securities laws (as defined in section 3(a)(47) of the Securities Exchange Act of 1934 (15 U.S.C. 78c(a)(47))), any State securities laws, or any regulation or order issued under Federal securities laws or State securities laws; or

(B) fraud, deceit, or manipulation in a fiduciary capacity or in connection with the purchase or sale of any security registered under section 12 or 15(d) of the Securities Exchange Act of 1934 (15 U.S.C. 78l and 78o(d)) or under section 6 of the Securities Act of 1933 (15 U.S.C. 77f).

§ 549. Postpetition Transactions

(a) Except as provided in subsection (b) or (c) of this section, the trustee may avoid a transfer of property of the estate—

(1) that occurs after the commencement of the case; and

(2)(A) that is authorized only under section 303(f) or 542(c) of this title; or

(B) that is not authorized under this title or by the court.

(b) In an involuntary case, the trustee may not avoid under subsection (a) of this section a transfer made after the commencement of such case but before the order for relief to the extent any value, including services, but not including satisfaction or securing of a debt that arose before the commencement of the case, is given after the commencement of the case in exchange for such transfer, notwithstanding any notice or knowledge of the case that the transferee has.

(c) The trustee may not avoid under subsection (a) of this section a transfer of an interest in real property to a good faith purchaser without knowledge of the commencement of the case and for present fair equivalent value unless a copy or notice of the petition was filed, where a transfer of an interest in such real property may be recorded to perfect such transfer, before such transfer is so perfected that a bona fide purchaser of such real property, against whom applicable law permits such transfer to be perfected, could not acquire an interest that is superior to such interest of such good faith purchaser. A good faith purchaser without knowledge of the commencement of the case and for less than present fair equivalent value has a lien on the property transferred to the extent of any present value given, unless a copy or notice of the petition was so filed before such transfer was so perfected.

(d) An action or proceeding under this section may not be commenced after the earlier of—

(1) two years after the date of the transfer sought to be avoided; or

(2) the time the case is closed or dismissed.

§ 550. Liability of Transferee of Avoided Transfer

(a) Except as otherwise provided in this section, to the extent that a transfer is avoided under section 544, 545, 547, 548, 549, 553(b), or 724(a) of this title, the trustee may recover, for the benefit of the estate, the property transferred, or, if the court so orders, the value of such property, from—

(1) the initial transferee of such transfer or the entity for whose benefit such transfer was made; or

(2) any immediate or mediate transferee of such initial transferee.

(b) The trustee may not recover under section (a)(2) of this section from—

(1) a transferee that takes for value, including satisfaction or securing of a present or antecedent debt, in good faith, and without knowledge of the voidability of the transfer avoided; or

(2) any immediate or mediate good faith transferee of such transferee.

(c) If a transfer made between 90 days and one year before the filing of the petition—

(1) is avoided under section 547(b) of this title; and

(2) was made for the benefit of a creditor that at the time of such transfer was an insider;

the trustee may not recover under subsection (a) from a transferee that is not an insider.

(d) The trustee is entitled to only a single satisfaction under subsection (a) of this section.

(e)(1) A good faith transferee from whom the trustee may recover under subsection (a) of this section has a lien on the property recovered to secure the lesser of—

(A) the cost, to such transferee, of any improvement made after the transfer, less the amount of any profit realized by or accruing to such transferee from such property; and

(B) any increase in the value of such property as a result of such improvement, of the property transferred.

(2) In this subsection, "improvement" includes—

(A) physical additions or changes to the property transferred;

(B) repairs to such property;

(C) payment of any tax on such property;

(D) payment of any debt secured by a lien on such property that is superior or equal to the rights of the trustee; and

(E) preservation of such property.

(f) An action or proceeding under this section may not be commenced after the earlier of—

(1) one year after the avoidance of the transfer on account of which recovery under this section is sought; or

(2) the time the case is closed or dismissed.

§ 551. Automatic Preservation of Avoided Transfer

Any transfer avoided under section 522, 544, 545, 547, 548, 549, or 724(a) of this title, or any lien void under section 506(d) of this title, is preserved for the benefit of the estate but only with respect to property of the estate.

§ 552. Postpetition Effect of Security Interest

(a) Except as provided in subsection (b) of this section, property acquired by the estate or by the debtor after the commencement of the case is not subject to any lien resulting from any security agreement entered into by the debtor before the commencement of the case.

(b)(1) Except as provided in sections 363, 506(c), 522, 544, 545, 547, and 548 of this title, if the debtor and an entity entered into a security agreement before the commencement of the case and if the security interest created by such security agreement extends to property of the debtor acquired before the commencement of the case and to proceeds, products, offspring, or profits of such property, then such security interest extends to such proceeds, products, offspring, or profits acquired by the estate after the commencement of the case to the extent provided by such security agreement and by applicable nonbankruptcy law, except to any extent that the court, after notice and a hearing and based on the equities of the case, orders otherwise.

(2) Except as provided in sections 363, 506(c), 522, 544, 545, 547, and 548 of this title, and notwithstanding section 546(b) of this title, if the debtor and an entity entered into a security agreement before the commencement of the case and if the security interest created by such security agreement extends to property of the debtor acquired before the commencement of the case and to amounts paid as rents of such property or the fees, charges, accounts, or other payments for the use or occupancy of rooms and other public facilities in hotels, motels, or other lodging properties, then such security interest extends to such rents and such fees, charges, accounts, or other payments acquired by the estate after the commencement of the case to the extent provided in such security agreement, except to any extent that the court, after notice and a hearing and based on the equities of the case, orders otherwise.

§ 553. Setoff

(a) Except as otherwise provided in this section and in sections 362 and 363 of this title, this title does not affect any right of a creditor to offset a mutual debt owing by such creditor to the debtor that arose before the commencement of the case under this title against a claim of such creditor against the debtor that arose before the commencement of the case, except to the extent that—

(1) the claim of such creditor against the debtor is disallowed;

(2) such claim was transferred, by an entity other than the debtor, to such creditor—

(A) after the commencement of the case; or

(B)(i) after 90 days before the date of the filing of the petition; and

(ii) while the debtor was insolvent (except for a setoff of a kind described in section 362(b)(6), 362(b)(7), 362(b)(17), 362(b)(27), 555, 556, 559, 560, or 561); or

(3) the debt owed to the debtor by such creditor was incurred by such creditor—

(A) after 90 days before the date of the filing of the petition;

(B) while the debtor was insolvent; and

(C) for the purpose of obtaining a right of setoff against the debtor (except for a setoff of a kind described in section 362(b)(6), 362(b)(7), 362(b)(17), 362(b)(27), 555, 556, 559, 560, or 561).

(b)(1) Except with respect to a setoff of a kind described in section 362(b)(6), 362(b)(7), 362(b)(17), 362(b)(27), 555, 556, 559, 560, 561, 365(h), 546(h), or 365(i)(2) of this title, if a creditor offsets a mutual debt owing to the debtor against a claim against the debtor on or within 90 days before the date of the filing of the petition, then the trustee may recover from such creditor the amount so offset to the extent that any insufficiency on the date of such setoff is less than the insufficiency on the later of—

(A) 90 days before the date of the filing of the petition; and

(B) the first date during the 90 days immediately preceding the date of the filing of the petition on which there is an insufficiency.

(2) In this subsection, "insufficiency" means amount, if any, by which a claim against the debtor exceeds a mutual debt owing to the debtor by the holder of such claim.

(c) For the purposes of this section, the debtor is presumed to have been insolvent on and during the 90 days immediately preceding the date of the filing of the petition.

§ 554. Abandonment of Property of the Estate

(a) After notice and a hearing, the trustee may abandon any property of the estate that is burdensome to the estate or that is of inconsequential value and benefit to the estate.

(b) On request of a party in interest and after notice and a hearing, the court may order the trustee to abandon any property of the estate that is burdensome to the estate or that is of inconsequential value and benefit to the estate.

(c) Unless the court orders otherwise, any property scheduled under section 521(a)(1) of this title not otherwise administered at the time of the closing of a case is abandoned to the debtor and administered for purposes of section 350 of this title.

(d) Unless the court orders otherwise, property of the estate that is not abandoned under this section and that is not administered in the case remains property of the estate.

§ 555. Contractual Right to Liquidate, Terminate, or Accelerate a Securities Contract

The exercise of a contractual right of a stockbroker, financial institution, financial participant, or securities clearing agency to cause the liquidation, termination, or acceleration of a securities contract, as defined in section 741 of this title, because of a condition of the kind specified in section 365(e)(1) of this title shall not be stayed, avoided, or otherwise limited by operation of any provision of this title or by order of a court or administrative agency in any proceeding under this title unless such order is authorized under the provisions of the Securities Investor Protection Act of 1970 or any statute administered by the Securities and Exchange Commission. As used in this section, the term "contractual right" includes a right set forth in a rule or bylaw of a derivatives clearing organization (as defined in the Commodity Exchange Act), a multilateral clearing organization (as defined in the Federal Deposit Insurance Corporation Improvement Act of 1991), a national securities exchange, a national securities association, a securities clearing agency, a contract market designated under the Commodity Exchange Act, a derivatives transaction execution facility registered under the Commodity Exchange Act, or a board of trade (as defined in the Commodity Exchange Act), or in a resolution of the governing board thereof, and a right, whether or not in writing, arising under common law, under law merchant, or by reason of normal business practice.

§ 556. Contractual Right to Liquidate, Terminate, or Accelerate a Commodities Contract or Forward Contract

The contractual right of a commodity broker, financial participant, or forward contract merchant to cause the liquidation, termination, or acceleration of a commodity contract, as defined in section 761 of this title, or forward contract because of a condition of the kind specified in section 365(e)(1) of this title, and the right to a variation or maintenance margin payment received from a trustee with respect to open commodity contracts or forward contracts, shall not be stayed, avoided, or otherwise limited by operation of any provision of this title or by the order of a court in any proceeding under this title. As used in this section, the term "contractual right" includes a right set forth in a rule or bylaw of a derivatives clearing organization (as defined in the Commodity Exchange Act), a multilateral clearing organization (as defined in the Federal Deposit Insurance Corporation Improvement Act of 1991), a national securities exchange, a national securities association, a securities clearing agency, a contract market designated under the Commodity Exchange Act, a derivatives transaction execution facility registered under the Commodity Exchange Act, or a board of trade (as defined in the Commodity Exchange Act) or in a resolution of the governing board thereof and a right, whether or not evidenced in writing, arising under common law, under law merchant or by reason of normal business practice.

§ 557. Expedited Determination of Interests in, and Abandonment or Other Disposition of Grain Assets

(a) This section applies only in a case concerning a debtor that owns or operates a grain storage facility and only with respect to grain and the proceeds of grain. This section does not affect the application of any other section of this title to property other than grain and proceeds of grain.

(b) In this section—

(1) "grain" means wheat, corn, flaxseed, grain sorghum, barley, oats, rye, soybeans, other dry edible beans, or rice;

(2) "grain storage facility" means a site or physical structure regularly used to store grain for producers, or to store grain acquired from producers for resale; and

(3) "producer" means an entity which engages in the growing of grain.

(c)(1) Notwithstanding sections 362, 363, 365, and 554 of this title, on the court's own motion the court may, and on the request of the trustee or an entity that claims an interest in grain or the proceeds of grain the court shall, expedite the procedures for the determination of interests in and the disposition of grain and the proceeds of grain, by shortening to the greatest extent feasible such time periods as are otherwise applicable for such procedures and by establishing, by order, a timetable having a duration of not to exceed 120 days for the completion of the applicable procedure specified in subsection (d) of this section. Such time periods and such timetable may be modified by the court, for cause, in accordance with subsection (f) of this s ection.

(2) The court shall determine the extent to which such time periods shall be shortened, based upon—

(A) any need of an entity claiming an interest in such grain or the proceeds of grain for a prompt determination of such interest;

(B) any need of such entity for a prompt disposition of such grain;

(C) the market for such grain;

(D) the conditions under which such grain is stored;

(E) the costs of continued storage or disposition of such grain;

(F) the orderly administration of the estate;

(G) the appropriate opportunity for an entity to assert an interest in such grain; and

(H) such other considerations as are relevant to the need to expedite such procedures in the case.

(d) The procedures that may be expedited under subsection (c) of this section include—

(1) the filing of and response to—

(A) a claim of ownership;

(B) a proof of claim;

(C) a request for abandonment;

(D) a request for relief from the stay of action against property under section 362(a) of this title;

(E) a request for determination of secured status;

(F) a request for determination of whether such grain or the proceeds of grain—

(i) is property of the estate;

(ii) must be turned over to the estate; or

(iii) may be used, sold, or leased; and

(G) any other request for determination of an interest in such grain or the proceeds of grain;

(2) the disposition of such grain or the proceeds of grain, before or after determination of interests in such grain or the proceeds of grain, by way of—

(A) sale of such grain;

(B) abandonment;

(C) distribution; or

(D) such other method as is equitable in the case;

(3) subject to sections 701, 702, 703, 1104, 1183, 1202, and 1302 of this title, the appointment of a trustee or examiner and the retention and compensation of any professional person required to assist with respect to matters relevant to the determination of interests in or disposition of such grain or the proceeds of grain; and

(4) the determination of any dispute concerning a matter specified in paragraph (1), (2), or (3) of this subsection.

(e)(1) Any governmental unit that has regulatory jurisdiction over the operation or liquidation of the debtor or the debtor's business shall be given notice of any request made or order entered under subsection (c) of this section.

(2) Any such governmental unit may raise, and may appear and be heard on, any issue relating to grain or the proceeds of grain in a case in which a request is made, or an order is entered, under subsection (c) of this section.

(3) The trustee shall consult with such governmental unit before taking any action relating to the disposition of grain in the possession, custody, or control of the debtor or the estate.

(f) The court may extend the period for final disposition of grain or the proceeds of grain under this section beyond 120 days if the court finds that—

(1) the interests of justice so require in light of the complexity of the case; and

(2) the interests of those claimants entitled to distribution of grain or the proceeds of grain will not be materially injured by such additional delay.

(g) Unless an order establishing an expedited procedure under subsection (c) of this section, or determining any interest in or approving any disposition of grain or the proceeds of grain, is stayed pending appeal—

(1) the reversal or modification of such order on appeal does not affect the validity of any procedure, determination, or disposition that occurs before such reversal or modification, whether or not any entity knew of the pendency of the appeal; and

(2) neither the court nor the trustee may delay, due to the appeal of such order, any proceeding in the case in which such order is issued.

(h)(1) The trustee may recover from grain and the proceeds of grain the reasonable and necessary costs and expenses allowable under section 503(b) of this title attributable to preserving or disposing of grain or the proceeds of grain, but may not recover from such grain or the proceeds of grain any other costs or expenses.

(2) Notwithstanding section 326(a) of this title, the dollar amounts of money specified in such section include the value, as of the date of disposition, of any grain that the trustee distributes in kind.

(i) In all cases where the quantity of a specific type of grain held by a debtor operating a grain storage facility exceeds ten thousand bushels, such grain shall be sold by the trustee and the assets thereof distributed in accordance with the provisions of this section.

§ 558. Defenses of the Estate

The estate shall have the benefit of any defense available to the debtor as against any entity other than the estate, including statutes of limitation, statutes of frauds, usury, and other personal defenses. A waiver of any such defense by the debtor after the commencement of the case does not bind the estate.

§ 559. Contractual Right to Liquidate, Terminate, or Accelerate a Repurchase Agreement

The exercise of a contractual right of a repo participant or financial participant to cause the liquidation, termination, or acceleration of a repurchase agreement because of a condition of the kind specified in section 365(e)(1) of this title shall not be stayed, avoided, or otherwise limited by operation of any provision of this title or by order of a court or administrative agency in any proceeding under this title, unless, where the debtor is a stockbroker or securities clearing agency, such order is authorized under the provisions of the Securities Investor Protection Act of 1970 or any statute administered by the Securities and Exchange Commission. In the event that a repo participant or financial participant liquidates one or more repurchase agreements with a debtor and under the terms of one or more such agreements has agreed to deliver assets subject to repurchase agreements to the debtor, any excess of the market prices received on liquidation of such assets (or if any such assets are not disposed of on the date of liquidation of such repurchase agreements, at the prices available at the time of liquidation of such repurchase agreements from a generally recognized source or the most recent closing bid quotation from such a source) over the sum of the stated repurchase prices and all expenses in connection with the liquidation of such repurchase agreements shall be deemed property of the estate, subject to the available rights of setoff. As used in this section, the term "contractual right" includes a right set forth in a rule or bylaw of a derivatives clearing organization (as defined in the Commodity Exchange Act), a multilateral clearing organization (as defined in the Federal Deposit Insurance Corporation Improvement Act of 1991), a national securities exchange, a national securities association, a securities clearing agency, a contract market designated under the Commodity Exchange Act, a derivatives transaction execution facility registered under the Commodity Exchange Act, or a board of trade (as defined in the Commodity Exchange Act) or in a resolution of the governing board thereof and a right, whether or not evidenced in writing, arising under common law, under law merchant or by reason of normal business practice.

§ 560. Contractual Right to Liquidate, Terminate, or Accelerate a Swap Agreement

The exercise of any contractual right of any swap participant or financial participant to cause the liquidation, termination, or acceleration of one or more swap agreements because of a condition of the kind specified in section 365(e)(1) of this title or to offset or net out any termination values or payment amounts arising under or in connection with the termination, liquidation, or acceleration of one or more swap agreements shall not be stayed, avoided, or otherwise limited by operation of any provision of this title or by order of a court or administrative agency in any proceeding under this title. As used in this section, the term "contractual right" includes a right set forth in a rule or bylaw of a derivatives clearing organization (as defined in the Commodity Exchange Act), a multilateral clearing organization (as defined in the Federal Deposit Insurance Corporation Improvement Act of 1991), a national securities exchange, a national securities association, a securities clearing agency, a contract market designated under the Commodity Exchange Act, a derivatives transaction execution facility registered under the Commodity Exchange Act, or a board of trade (as defined in the Commodity Exchange Act) or in a resolution of the governing board thereof and a right, whether or not evidenced in writing, arising under common law, under law merchant, or by reason of normal business practice.

§ 561. Contractual Right to Terminate, Liquidate, Accelerate, or Offset Under a Master Netting Agreement and Across Contracts; Proceedings Under Chapter 15

(a) Subject to subsection (b), the exercise of any contractual right, because of a condition of the kind specified in section 365(e)(1), to cause the termination, liquidation, or acceleration of or to offset or net termination values, payment amounts, or other transfer obligations arising under or in connection with one or more (or the termination, liquidation, or acceleration of one or more)—

(1) securities contracts, as defined in section 741(7);

(2) commodity contracts, as defined in section 761(4);

(3) forward contracts;

(4) repurchase agreements;

(5) swap agreements; or

(6) master netting agreements,

shall not be stayed, avoided, or otherwise limited by operation of any provision of this title or by any order of a court or administrative agency in any proceeding under this title.

(b)(1) A party may exercise a contractual right described in subsection (a) to terminate, liquidate, or accelerate only to the extent that such party could exercise such a right under section 555, 556, 559, or 560 for each individual contract covered by the master netting agreement in issue.

(2) If a debtor is a commodity broker subject to subchapter IV of chapter 7—

(A) a party may not net or offset an obligation to the debtor arising under, or in connection with, a commodity contract traded on or subject to the rules of a contract market designated under the Commodity Exchange Act or a derivatives transaction execution facility registered under the Commodity Exchange Act against any claim arising under, or in connection with, other instruments, contracts, or agreements listed in subsection (a) except to the extent that the party has positive net equity in the commodity accounts at the debtor, as calculated under such subchapter; and

(B) another commodity broker may not net or offset an obligation to the debtor arising under, or in connection with, a commodity contract entered into or held on behalf of a customer of the debtor and traded on or subject to the rules of a contract market designated under the Commodity Exchange Act or a derivatives transaction execution facility registered under the Commodity Exchange Act against any claim arising under, or in connection with, other instruments, contracts, or agreements listed in subsection (a).

(3) No provision of subparagraph (A) or (B) of paragraph (2) shall prohibit the offset of claims and obligations that arise under—

(A) a cross-margining agreement or similar arrangement that has been approved by the Commodity Futures Trading Commission or submitted to the Commodity Futures Trading Commission under paragraph (1) or (2) of section 5c(c) of the Commodity Exchange Act and has not been abrogated or rendered ineffective by the Commodity Futures Trading Commission; or

(B) any other netting agreement between a clearing organization (as defined in section 761) and another entity that has been approved by the Commodity Futures Trading Commission.

(c) As used in this section, the term "contractual right" includes a right set forth in a rule or bylaw of a derivatives clearing organization (as defined in the Commodity Exchange Act), a multilateral clearing organization (as defined in the Federal Deposit Insurance Corporation Improvement Act of 1991), a national securities exchange, a national securities association, a securities clearing agency, a contract market designated under the Commodity Exchange Act, a derivatives transaction execution facility registered under the Commodity Exchange Act, or a board of trade (as defined in the Commodity Exchange Act) or in a resolution of the governing board thereof, and a right, whether or not evidenced in writing, arising under common law, under law merchant, or by reason of normal business practice.

(d) Any provisions of this title relating to securities contracts, commodity contracts, forward contracts, repurchase agreements, swap agreements, or master netting agreements shall apply in a case under chapter 15, so that enforcement of contractual provisions of such contracts and agreements in accordance with their terms will not be stayed or otherwise limited by operation of any provision of this title or by order of a court in any case under this title, and to limit avoidance powers to the same extent as in a proceeding under chapter 7 or 11 of this title (such enforcement not to be limited based on the presence or absence of assets of the debtor in the United States).

§ 562. Timing of Damage Measurement in Connection with Swap Agreements, Securities Contracts, Forward Contracts, Commodity Contracts, Repurchase Agreements, and Master Netting Agreements

(a) If the trustee rejects a swap agreement, securities contract (as defined in section 741), forward contract, commodity contract (as defined in section 761), repurchase agreement, or master netting agreement pursuant to section 365(a), or if a forward contract merchant, stockbroker, financial institution, securities clearing agency, repo participant, financial participant, master netting agreement participant, or swap participant liquidates, terminates, or accelerates such contract or agreement, damages shall be measured as of the earlier of—

(1) the date of such rejection; or

(2) the date or dates of such liquidation, termination, or acceleration.

(b) If there are not any commercially reasonable determinants of value as of any date referred to in paragraph (1) or (2) of subsection (a), damages shall be measured as of the earliest subsequent date or dates on which there are commercially reasonable determinants of value.

(c) For the purposes of subsection (b), if damages are not measured as of the date or dates of rejection, liquidation, termination, or acceleration, and the forward contract merchant, stockbroker, financial institution, securities clearing agency, repo participant, financial participant, master netting agreement participant, or swap participant or the trustee objects to the timing of the measurement of damages—

(1) the trustee, in the case of an objection by a forward contract merchant, stockbroker, financial institution, securities clearing agency, repo participant, financial participant, master netting agreement participant, or swap participant; or

(2) the forward contract merchant, stockbroker, financial institution, securities clearing agency, repo participant, financial participant, master netting agreement participant, or swap participant, in the case of an objection by the trustee, has the burden of proving that there were no commercially reasonable determinants of value as of such date or dates.

CHAPTER 7. LIQUIDATION

SUBCHAPTER I—OFFICERS AND ADMINISTRATION

Section

SUBCHAPTER II—COLLECTION, LIQUIDATION, AND DISTRIBUTION OF THE ESTATE

Section

SUBCHAPTER I—OFFICERS AND ADMINISTRATION

§ 701. Interim Trustee

(a)(1) Promptly after the order for relief under this chapter, the United States trustee shall appoint one disinterested person that is a member of the panel of private trustees established under section 586(a)(1) of title 28 or that is serving as trustee in the case immediately before the order for relief under this chapter to serve as interim trustee in the case.

(2) If none of the members of such panel is willing to serve as interim trustee in the case, then the United States trustee may serve as interim trustee in the case.

(b) The service of an interim trustee under this section terminates when a trustee elected or designated under section 702 of this title to serve as trustee in the case qualifies under section 322 of this title.

(c) An interim trustee serving under this section is a trustee in a case under this title.

§ 702. Election of Trustee

(a) A creditor may vote for a candidate for trustee only if such creditor—

(1) holds an allowable, undisputed, fixed, liquidated, unsecured claim of a kind entitled to distribution under section 726(a)(2), 726(a)(3), 726(a)(4), 752(a), 766(h), or 766(i) of this title;

(2) does not have an interest materially adverse, other than an equity interest that is not substantial in relation to such creditor's interest as a creditor, to the interest of creditors entitled to such distribution; and

(3) is not an insider.

(b) At the meeting of creditors held under section 341 of this title, creditors may elect one person to serve as trustee in the case if election of a trustee is requested by creditors that may vote under subsection (a) of this section, and that hold at least 20 percent in amount of the claims specified in subsection (a)(1) of this section that are held by creditors that may vote under subsection (a) of this section.

(c) A candidate for trustee is elected trustee if—

(1) creditors holding at least 20 percent in amount of the claims of a kind specified in subsection (a)(1) of this section that are held by creditors that may vote under subsection (a) of this section vote; and

(2) such candidate receives the votes of creditors holding a majority in amount of claims specified in subsection (a)(1) of this section that are held by creditors that vote for a trustee.

(d) If a trustee is not elected under this section, then the interim trustee shall serve as trustee in the case.

§ 703. Successor Trustee

(a) If a trustee dies or resigns during a case, fails to qualify under section 322 of this title, or is removed under section 324 of this title, creditors may elect, in the manner specified in section 702 of this title, a person to fill the vacancy in the office of trustee.

(b) Pending election of a trustee under subsection (a) of this section, if necessary to preserve or prevent loss to the estate, the United States trustee may appoint an interim trustee in the manner specified in section 701(a).

(c) If creditors do not elect a successor trustee under subsection (a) of this section or if a trustee is needed in a case reopened under section 350 of this title, then the United States trustee—

(1) shall appoint one disinterested person that is a member of the panel of private trustees established under section 586(a)(1) of title 28 to serve as trustee in the case; or

(2) may, if none of the disinterested members of such panel is willing to serve as trustee, serve as trustee in the case.

§ 704. Duties of Trustee

(a) The trustee shall—

(1) collect and reduce to money the property of the estate for which such trustee serves, and close such estate as expeditiously as is compatible with the best interests of parties in interest;

(2) be accountable for all property received;

(3) ensure that the debtor shall perform his intention as specified in section 521(a)(2)(B) of this title;

(4) investigate the financial affairs of the debtor;

(5) if a purpose would be served, examine proofs of claims and object to the allowance of any claim that is improper;

(6) if advisable, oppose the discharge of the debtor;

(7) unless the court orders otherwise, furnish such information concerning the estate and the estate's administration as is requested by a party in interest;

(8) if the business of the debtor is authorized to be operated, file with the court, with the United States trustee, and with any governmental unit charged with responsibility for collection or determination of any tax arising out of such operation, periodic reports and summaries of the operation of such business, including a statement of receipts and disbursements, and such other information as the United States trustee or the court requires;

(9) make a final report and file a final account of the administration of the estate with the court and with the United States trustee;

(10) if with respect to the debtor there is a claim for a domestic support obligation, provide the applicable notice specified in subsection (c);

(11) if, at the time of the commencement of the case, the debtor (or any entity designated by the debtor) served as the administrator (as defined in section 3 of the Employee Retirement Income Security Act of 1974) of an employee benefit plan, continue to perform the obligations required of the administrator; and

(12) use all reasonable and best efforts to transfer patients from a health care business that is in the process of being closed to an appropriate health care business that—

(A) is in the vicinity of the health care business that is closing;

(B) provides the patient with services that are substantially similar to those provided by the health care business that is in the process of being closed; and

(C) maintains a reasonable quality of care.

(b)(1) With respect to a debtor who is an individual in a case under this chapter—

(A) the United States trustee (or the bankruptcy administrator, if any) shall review all materials filed by the debtor and, not later than 10 days after the date of the first meeting of creditors, file with the court a statement as to whether the debtor's case would be presumed to be an abuse under section 707(b); and

(B) not later than 7 days after receiving a statement under subparagraph (A), the court shall provide a copy of the statement to all creditors.

(2) The United States trustee (or bankruptcy administrator, if any) shall, not later than 30 days after the date of filing a statement under paragraph (1), either file a motion to dismiss or convert under section 707(b) or file a statement setting forth the reasons the United States trustee (or the bankruptcy administrator, if any) does not consider such a motion to be appropriate, if the United States trustee (or the bankruptcy administrator, if any) determines that the debtor's case should be presumed to be an abuse under section 707(b) and the product of the debtor's current monthly income, multiplied by 12 is not less than—

(A) in the case of a debtor in a household of 1 person, the median family income of the applicable State for 1 earner; or

(B) in the case of a debtor in a household of 2 or more individuals, the highest median family income of the applicable State for a family of the same number or fewer individuals.

(c)(1) In a case described in subsection (a)(10) to which subsection (a)(10) applies, the trustee shall—

(A)(i) provide written notice to the holder of the claim described in subsection (a)(10) of such claim and of the right of such holder to use the services of the State child support enforcement agency established under sections 464 and 466 of the Social Security Act for the State in which such holder resides, for assistance in collecting child support during and after the case under this title;

(ii) include in the notice provided under clause (i) the address and telephone number of such State child support enforcement agency; and

(iii) include in the notice provided under clause (i) an explanation of the rights of such holder to payment of such claim under this chapter;

(B)(i) provide written notice to such State child support enforcement agency of such claim; and

(ii) include in the notice provided under clause (i) the name, address, and telephone number of such holder; and

(C) at such time as the debtor is granted a discharge under section 727, provide written notice to such holder and to such State child support enforcement agency of—

(i) the granting of the discharge;

(ii) the last recent known address of the debtor;

(iii) the last recent known name and address of the debtor's employer; and

(iv) the name of each creditor that holds a claim that—

(I) is not discharged under paragraph (2), (4), or (14A) of section 523(a); or

(II) was reaffirmed by the debtor under section 524(c).

(2)(A) The holder of a claim described in subsection (a)(10) or the State child support enforcement agency of the State in which such holder resides may request from a creditor described in paragraph (1)(C)(iv) the last known address of the debtor.

(B) Notwithstanding any other provision of law, a creditor that makes a disclosure of a last known address of a debtor in connection with a request made under subparagraph (A) shall not be liable by reason of making such disclosure.

§ 705. Creditors' Committee

(a) At the meeting under section 341(a) of this title, creditors that may vote for a trustee under section 702(a) of this title may elect a committee of not fewer than three, and not more than eleven, creditors, each of whom holds an allowable unsecured claim of a kind entitled to distribution under section 726(a)(2) of this title.

(b) A committee elected under subsection (a) of this section may consult with the trustee or the United States trustee in connection with the administration of the estate, make recommendations to the trustee or the United States trustee respecting the performance of the trustee's duties, and submit to the court or the United States trustee any question affecting the administration of the estate.

§ 706. Conversion

(a) The debtor may convert a case under this chapter to a case under chapter 11, 12, or 13 of this title at any time, if the case has not been converted under section 1112, 1208, or 1307 of this title. Any waiver of the right to convert a case under this subsection is unenforceable.

(b) On request of a party in interest and after notice and a hearing, the court may convert a case under this chapter to a case under chapter 11 of this title at any time.

(c) The court may not convert a case under this chapter to a case under chapter 12 or 13 of this title unless the debtor requests or consents to such conversion.

(d) Notwithstanding any other provision of this section, a case may not be converted to a case under another chapter of this title unless the debtor may be a debtor under such chapter.

§ 707. Dismissal of a Case or Conversion to a Case under Chapter 11 or 13

(a) The court may dismiss a case under this chapter only after notice and a hearing and only for cause, including—

(1) unreasonable delay by the debtor that is prejudicial to creditors;

(2) nonpayment of any fees or charges required under chapter 123 of title 28; and

(3) failure of the debtor in a voluntary case to file, within fifteen days or such additional time as the court may allow after the filing of the petition commencing such case, the information required by paragraph (1) of section 521(a), but only on a motion by the United States trustee.

(b)(1) After notice and a hearing, the court, on its own motion or on a motion by the United States trustee, trustee (or bankruptcy administrator, if any), or any party in interest, may dismiss a case filed by an individual debtor under this chapter whose debts are primarily consumer debts, or, with the debtor's consent, convert such a case to a case under chapter 11 or 13 of this title, if it finds that the granting of relief would be an abuse of the provisions of this chapter. In making a determination whether to dismiss a case under this section, the court may not take into consideration whether a debtor has made, or continues to make, charitable contributions (that meet the definition of "charitable contribution" under section 548(d)(3)) to any qualified religious or charitable entity or organization (as that term is defined in section 548(d)(4)).

(2)(A)(i) In considering under paragraph (1) whether the granting of relief would be an abuse of the provisions of this chapter, the court shall presume abuse exists if the debtor's current monthly income reduced by the amounts determined under clauses (ii), (iii), and (iv), and multiplied by 60 is not less than the lesser of—

(I) 25 percent of the debtor's nonpriority unsecured claims in the case, or $10,275, whichever is greater; or

(II) $17,150.

(ii)(I) The debtor's monthly expenses shall be the debtor's applicable monthly expense amounts specified under the National Standards and Local Standards, and the debtor's actual monthly expenses for the categories specified as Other Necessary Expenses issued by the Internal Revenue Service for the area in which the debtor resides, as in effect on the date of the order for relief, for the debtor, the dependents of the debtor, and the spouse of the debtor in a joint case, if the spouse is not otherwise a dependent. Such expenses shall include reasonably necessary health insurance, disability insurance, and health savings account expenses for the debtor, the spouse of the debtor, or the dependents of the debtor. Notwithstanding any other provision of this clause, the monthly expenses of the debtor shall not include any payments for debts. In addition, the debtor's monthly expenses shall include the debtor's reasonably necessary expenses incurred to maintain the safety of the debtor and the family of the debtor from family violence as identified under section 302 of the Family Violence Prevention and Services Act, or other applicable Federal law. The expenses included in the debtor's monthly expenses described in the preceding sentence shall be kept confidential by the court. In addition, if it is demonstrated that it is reasonable and necessary, the debtor's monthly expenses may also include an additional allowance for food and clothing of up to 5 percent of the food and clothing categories as specified by the National Standards issued by the Internal Revenue Service.

(II) In addition, the debtor's monthly expenses may include, if applicable, the continuation of actual expenses paid by the debtor that are reasonable and necessary for care and support of an elderly, chronically ill, or disabled household member or member of the debtor's immediate family (including parents, grandparents, siblings, children, and grandchildren of the debtor, the dependents of the debtor, and the spouse of the debtor in a joint case who is not a dependent) and who is unable to pay for such reasonable and necessary expenses. Such monthly expenses may include, if applicable, contributions to an account of a qualified ABLE program to the extent such contributions are not excess contributions (as described in section 4973(h) of the Internal Revenue Code of 1986) and if the designated beneficiary of such account is a child, stepchild, grandchild, or stepgrandchild of the debtor.

(III) In addition, for a debtor eligible for chapter 13, the debtor's monthly expenses may include the actual administrative expenses of administering a chapter 13 plan for the district in which the debtor resides, up to an amount of 10 percent of the projected plan payments, as determined under schedules issued by the Executive Office for United States Trustees.

(IV) In addition, the debtor's monthly expenses may include the actual expenses for each dependent child less than 18 years of age, not to exceed $2,575 per year per child, to attend a private or public elementary or secondary school if the debtor provides documentation of such expenses and a detailed explanation of why such expenses are reasonable and necessary, and why such expenses are not already accounted for in the National Standards,

Local Standards, or Other Necessary Expenses referred to in subclause (I).

(V) In addition, the debtor's monthly expenses may include an allowance for housing and utilities, in excess of the allowance specified by the Local Standards for housing and utilities issued by the Internal Revenue Service, based on the actual expenses for home energy costs if the debtor provides documentation of such actual expenses and demonstrates that such actual expenses are reasonable and necessary.

(iii) The debtor's average monthly payments on account of secured debts shall be calculated as the sum of—

(I) the total of all amounts scheduled as contractually due to secured creditors in each month of the 60 months following the date of the filing of the petition; and

(II) any additional payments to secured creditors necessary for the debtor, in filing a plan under chapter 13 of this title, to maintain possession of the debtor's primary residence, motor vehicle, or other property necessary for the support of the debtor and the debtor's dependents, that serves as collateral for secured debts; divided by 60.

(iv) The debtor's expenses for payment of all priority claims (including priority child support and alimony claims) shall be calculated as the total amount of debts entitled to priority, divided by 60.

(B)(i) In any proceeding brought under this subsection, the presumption of abuse may only be rebutted by demonstrating special circumstances, such as a serious medical condition or a call or order to active duty in the Armed Forces, to the extent such special circumstances that justify additional expenses or adjustments of current monthly income for which there is no reasonable alternative.

(ii) In order to establish special circumstances, the debtor shall be required to itemize each additional expense or adjustment of income and to provide—

(I) documentation for such expense or adjustment to income; and

(II) a detailed explanation of the special circumstances that make such expenses or adjustment to income necessary and reasonable.

(iii) The debtor shall attest under oath to the accuracy of any information provided to demonstrate that additional expenses or adjustments to income are required.

(iv) The presumption of abuse may only be rebutted if the additional expenses or adjustments to income referred to in clause (i) cause the product of the debtor's current monthly income reduced by the amounts determined under clauses (ii), (iii), and (iv) of subparagraph (A) when multiplied by 60 to be less than the lesser of—

(I) 25 percent of the debtor's nonpriority unsecured claims, or $10,275, whichever is greater; or

(II) $17,150.

(C) As part of the schedule of current income and expenditures required under section 521, the debtor shall include a statement of the debtor's current monthly income, and the calculations that determine whether a presumption arises under subparagraph (A)(i), that show how each such amount is calculated.

(D) Subparagraphs (A) through (C) shall not apply, and the court may not dismiss or convert a case based on any form of means testing—

(i) if the debtor is a disabled veteran (as defined in section 3741(1) of title 38), and the indebtedness occurred primarily during a period during which he or she was—

(I) on active duty (as defined in section 101(d)(1) of title 10); or

(II) performing a homeland defense activity (as defined in section 901(1) of title 32); or

(ii) with respect to the debtor, while the debtor is—

(I) on, and during the 540-day period beginning immediately after the debtor is released from, a period of active duty (as defined in section 101(d)(1) of title 10) of not less than 90 days; or

(II) performing, and during the 540-day period beginning immediately after the debtor is no longer performing, a homeland defense activity (as defined in section 901(1) of title 32) performed for a period of not less than 90 days; if after September 11, 2001, the debtor while a member of a reserve component of the Armed Forces or a member of the National Guard, was called to such active duty or performed such homeland defense activity.

(3) In considering under paragraph (1) whether the granting of relief would be an abuse of the provisions of this chapter in a case in which the presumption in paragraph (2)(A)(i) does not arise or is rebutted, the court shall consider—

(A) whether the debtor filed the petition in bad faith; or

(B) the totality of the circumstances (including whether the debtor seeks to reject a personal services contract and the financial need for such rejection as sought by the debtor) of the debtor's financial situation demonstrates abuse.

(4)(A) The court, on its own initiative or on the motion of a party in interest, in accordance with the procedures described in rule 9011 of the Federal Rules of Bankruptcy Procedure, may order the attorney for the debtor to reimburse the trustee for all reasonable costs in prosecuting a motion filed under section 707(b), including reasonable attorneys' fees, if—

(i) a trustee files a motion for dismissal or conversion under this subsection; and

(ii) the court—

(I) grants such motion; and

(II) finds that the action of the attorney for the debtor in filing a case under this chapter violated rule 9011 of the Federal Rules of Bankruptcy Procedure.

(B) If the court finds that the attorney for the debtor violated rule 9011 of the Federal Rules of Bankruptcy Procedure, the court, on its own initiative or on the motion of a party in interest, in accordance with such procedures, may order—

(i) the assessment of an appropriate civil penalty against the attorney for the debtor; and

(ii) the payment of such civil penalty to the trustee, the United States trustee (or the bankruptcy administrator, if any).

(C) The signature of an attorney on a petition, pleading, or written motion shall constitute a certification that the attorney has—

(i) performed a reasonable investigation into the circumstances that gave rise to the petition, pleading, or written motion; and

(ii) determined that the petition, pleading, or written motion—

(I) is well grounded in fact; and

(II) is warranted by existing law or a good faith argument for the extension, modification, or reversal of existing law and does not constitute an abuse under paragraph (1).

(D) The signature of an attorney on the petition shall constitute a certification that the attorney has no knowledge after an inquiry that the information in the schedules filed with such petition is incorrect.

(5)(A) Except as provided in subparagraph (B) and subject to paragraph (6), the court, on its own initiative or on the motion of a party in interest, in accordance with the procedures described in rule 9011 of the Federal Rules of Bankruptcy Procedure, may award a debtor all reasonable costs (including reasonable attorneys' fees) in contesting a motion filed by a party in interest (other than a trustee or United States trustee (or bankruptcy administrator, if any)) under this subsection if—

(i) the court does not grant the motion; and

(ii) the court finds that—

(I) the position of the party that filed the motion violated rule 9011 of the Federal Rules of Bankruptcy Procedure; or

(II) the attorney (if any) who filed the motion did not comply with the requirements of clauses (i) and (ii) of paragraph (4)(C), and the motion was made solely for the purpose of coercing a debtor into waiving a right guaranteed to the debtor under this title.

(B) A small business that has a claim of an aggregate amount less than $1,725 shall not be subject to subparagraph (A)(ii)(I).

(C) For purposes of this paragraph—

(i) the term "small business" means an unincorporated business, partnership, corporation, association, or organization that—

(I) has fewer than 25 full-time employees as determined on the date on which the motion is filed; and

(II) is engaged in commercial or business activity; and

(ii) the number of employees of a wholly owned subsidiary of a corporation includes the employees of—

(I) a parent corporation; and

(II) any other subsidiary corporation of the parent corporation.

(6) Only the judge or United States trustee (or bankruptcy administrator, if any) may file a motion under section 707(b), if the current monthly income of the debtor, or in a joint case, the debtor and the debtor's spouse, as of the date of the order for relief, when multiplied by 12, is equal to or less than—

(A) in the case of a debtor in a household of 1 person, the median family income of the applicable State for 1 earner;

(B) in the case of a debtor in a household of 2, 3, or 4 individuals, the highest median family income of the applicable State for a family of the same number or fewer individuals; or

(C) in the case of a debtor in a household exceeding 4 individuals, the highest median family income of the applicable State for a family of 4 or fewer individuals, plus $925 per month for each individual in excess of 4.

(7)(A) No judge, United States trustee (or bankruptcy administrator, if any), trustee, or other party in interest may file a motion under paragraph (2) if the current monthly income of the debtor, including a veteran (as that term is defined in section 101 of title 38), and the debtor's spouse combined, as of the date of the order for relief when multiplied by 12, is equal to or less than—

(i) in the case of a debtor in a household of 1 person, the median family income of the applicable State for 1 earner;

(ii) in the case of a debtor in a household of 2, 3, or 4 individuals, the highest median family income of the applicable State for a family of the same number or fewer individuals; or

(iii) in the case of a debtor in a household exceeding 4 individuals, the highest median family income of the applicable State for a family of 4 or fewer individuals, plus $925 per month for each individual in excess of 4.

(B) In a case that is not a joint case, current monthly income of the debtor's spouse shall not be considered for purposes of subparagraph (A) if—

(i)(I) the debtor and the debtor's spouse are separated under applicable nonbankruptcy law; or

(II) the debtor and the debtor's spouse are living separate and apart, other than for the purpose of evading subparagraph (A); and

(ii) the debtor files a statement under penalty of perjury—

(I) specifying that the debtor meets the requirement of subclause (I) or (II) of clause (i); and

(II) disclosing the aggregate, or best estimate of the aggregate, amount of any cash or money payments received from the debtor's spouse attributed to the debtor's current monthly income.

(c)(1) In this subsection—

(A) the term "crime of violence" has the meaning given such term in section 16 of title 18; and

(B) the term "drug trafficking crime" has the meaning given such term in section 924(c)(2) of title 18.

(2) Except as provided in paragraph (3), after notice and a hearing, the court, on a motion by the victim of a crime of violence or a drug trafficking crime, may when it is in the best interest of the victim dismiss a voluntary case filed under this chapter by a debtor who is an individual if such individual was convicted of such crime.

(3) The court may not dismiss a case under paragraph (2) if the debtor establishes by a preponderance of the evidence that the filing of a case under this chapter is necessary to satisfy a claim for a domestic support obligation.

SUBCHAPTER II—COLLECTION, LIQUIDATION, AND DISTRIBUTION OF THE ESTATE

§ 721. Authorization to Operate Business

The court may authorize the trustee to operate the business of the debtor for a limited period, if such operation is in the best interest of the estate and consistent with the orderly liquidation of the estate.

§ 722. Redemption

An individual debtor may, whether or not the debtor has waived the right to redeem under this section, redeem tangible personal property intended primarily for personal, family, or household use, from a lien securing a dischargeable consumer debt, if such property is exempted under section 522 of this title or has been abandoned under section 554 of this title, by paying the holder of such lien the amount of the allowed secured claim of such holder that is secured by such lien in full at the time of redemption.

§ 723. Rights of Partnership Trustee Against General Partners

(a) If there is a deficiency of property of the estate to pay in full all claims which are allowed in a case under this chapter concerning a partnership and with respect to which a general partner of the partnership is personally liable, the trustee shall have a claim against such general partner to the extent that under applicable nonbankruptcy law such general partner is personally liable for such deficiency.

(b) To the extent practicable, the trustee shall first seek recovery of such deficiency from any general partner in such partnership that is not a debtor in a case under this title. Pending determination of such deficiency, the court may order any such partner to provide the estate with indemnity for, or assurance of payment of, any deficiency recoverable from such partner, or not to dispose of property.

(c) The trustee has a claim against the estate of each general partner in such partnership that is a debtor in a case under this title for the full amount of all claims of creditors allowed in the case concerning such partnership. Notwithstanding section 502 of this title, there shall not be allowed in such partner's case a claim against such partner on which both such partner and such partnership are liable, except to any extent that such claim is secured only by property of such partner and not by property of such partnership. The claim of the trustee under this subsection is entitled to distribution in such partner's case under section 726(a) of this title the same as any other claim of a kind specified in such section.

(d) If the aggregate that the trustee recovers from the estates of general partners under subsection (c) of this section is greater than any deficiency not recovered under subsection (b) of this section, the court, after notice and a hearing, shall determine an equitable distribution of the surplus so recovered, and the trustee shall distribute such surplus to the estates of the general partners in such partnership according to such determination.

§ 724. Treatment of Certain Liens

(a) The trustee may avoid a lien that secures a claim of a kind specified in section 726(a)(4) of this title.

(b) Property in which the estate has an interest and that is subject to a lien that is not avoidable under this title (other than to the extent that there is a properly perfected unavoidable tax lien arising in connection with an ad valorem tax on real or personal property of the estate) and that secures an allowed claim for a tax, or proceeds of such property, shall be distributed—

(1) first, to any holder of an allowed claim secured by a lien on such property that is not avoidable under this title and that is senior to such tax lien;

(2) second, to any holder of a claim of a kind specified in section 507(a)(1)(c) or 507(a)(2) (except that such expenses under each such section, other than claims for wages, salaries, or commissions that arise after the date of the filing of the petition, shall be limited to expenses incurred under this chapter and shall not include expenses incurred under chapter 11 of this title), 507(a)(1)(A), 507(a)(1)(B), 507(a)(3), 507(a)(4), 507(a)(5), 507(a)(6), or 507(a)(7) of this title, to the extent of the amount of such allowed tax claim that is secured by such tax lien;

(3) third, to the holder of such tax lien, to any extent that such holder's allowed tax claim that is secured by such tax lien exceeds any amount distributed under paragraph (2) of this subsection;

(4) fourth, to any holder of an allowed claim secured by a lien on such property that is not avoidable under this title and that is junior to such tax lien;

(5) fifth, to the holder of such tax lien, to the extent that such holder's allowed claim secured by such tax lien is not paid under paragraph (3) of this subsection; and

(6) sixth, to the estate.

(c) If more than one holder of a claim is entitled to distribution under a particular paragraph of subsection (b) of this section, distribution to such holders under such paragraph shall be in the same order as distribution to such holders would have been other than under this section.

(d) A statutory lien the priority of which is determined in the same manner as the priority of a tax lien under section 6323 of the Internal Revenue Code of 1986 shall be treated under subsection (b) of this section the same as if such lien were a tax lien.

(e) Before subordinating a tax lien on real or personal property of the estate, the trustee shall—

(1) exhaust the unencumbered assets of the estate; and

(2) in a manner consistent with section 506(c), recover from property securing an allowed secured claim the reasonable, necessary costs and expenses of preserving or disposing of such property.

(f) Notwithstanding the exclusion of ad valorem tax liens under this section and subject to the requirements of subsection (e), the following may be paid from property of the estate which secures a tax lien, or the proceeds of such property:

(1) Claims for wages, salaries, and commissions that are entitled to priority under section 507(a)(4).

(2) Claims for contributions to an employee benefit plan entitled to priority under section 507(a)(5).

§ 725. Disposition of Certain Property

After the commencement of a case under this chapter, but before final distribution of property of the estate under section 726 of this title, the trustee, after notice and a hearing, shall dispose of any property in which an entity other than the estate has an interest, such as a lien, and that has not been disposed of under another section of this title.

§ 726. Distribution of Property of the Estate

(a) Except as provided in section 510 of this title, property of the estate shall be distributed—

(1) first, in payment of claims of the kind specified in, and in the order specified in, section 507 of this title, proof of which is timely filed under section 501 of this title or tardily filed on or before the earlier of—

(A) the date that is 10 days after the mailing to creditors of the summary of the trustee's final report; or

(B) the date on which the trustee commences final distribution under this section;

(2) second, in payment of any allowed unsecured claim, other than a claim of a kind specified in paragraph (1), (3), or (4) of this subsection, proof of which is—

(A) timely filed under section 501(a) of this title;

(B) timely filed under section 501(b) or 501(c) of this title; or

(C) tardily filed under section 501(a) of this title, if—

(i) the creditor that holds such claim did not have notice or actual knowledge of the case in time for timely filing of a proof of such claim under section 501(a) of this title; and

(ii) proof of such claim is filed in time to permit payment of such claim;

(3) third, in payment of any allowed unsecured claim proof of which is tardily filed under section 501(a) of this title, other than a claim of the kind specified in paragraph (2)(C) of this subsection;

(4) fourth, in payment of any allowed claim, whether secured or unsecured, for any fine, penalty, or forfeiture, or for multiple, exemplary, or punitive damages, arising before the earlier of the order for relief or the appointment of a trustee, to the extent that such fine, penalty, forfeiture, or damages are not compensation for actual pecuniary loss suffered by the holder of such claim;

(5) fifth, in payment of interest at the legal rate from the date of the filing of the petition, on any claim paid under paragraph (1), (2), (3), or (4) of this subsection; and

(6) sixth, to the debtor.

(b) Payment on claims of a kind specified in paragraph (1), (2), (3), (4), (5), (6), (7), (8), (9), or (10) of section 507(a) of this title, or in paragraph (2), (3), (4), or (5) of subsection (a) of this section, shall be made pro rata among claims of the kind specified in each such particular paragraph, except that in a case that has been converted to this chapter under section 1112, 1208, or 1307 of this title, a claim allowed under section 503(b) of this title incurred under this chapter after such conversion has priority over a claim allowed under section 503(b) of this title incurred under any other chapter of this title or under this chapter before such conversion and over any expenses of a custodian superseded under section 543 of this title.

(c) Notwithstanding subsections (a) and (b) of this section, if there is property of the kind specified in section 541(a)(2) of this title, or proceeds of such property, in the estate, such property or proceeds shall be segregated from other property of the estate, and such property or proceeds and other property of the estate shall be distributed as follows:

(1) Claims allowed under section 503 of this title shall be paid either from property of the kind specified in section 541(a)(2) of this title, or from other property of the estate, as the interest of justice requires.

(2) Allowed claims, other than claims allowed under section 503 of this title, shall be paid in the order specified in subsection (a) of this section, and, with respect to claims of a kind specified in a particular paragraph of section 507 of this title or subsection (a) of this section, in the following order and manner:

(A) First, community claims against the debtor or the debtor's spouse shall be paid from property of the kind specified in section 541(a)

(2) of this title, except to the extent that such property is solely liable for debts of the debtor.

(B) Second, to the extent that community claims against the debtor are not paid under subparagraph (A) of this paragraph, such community claims shall be paid from property of the kind specified in section 541(a)(2) of this title that is solely liable for debts of the debtor.

(C) Third, to the extent that all claims against the debtor including community claims against the debtor are not paid under subparagraph (A) or (B) of this paragraph such claims shall be paid from property of the estate other than property of the kind specified in section 541(a)(2) of this title.

(D) Fourth, to the extent that community claims against the debtor or the debtor's spouse are not paid under subparagraph (A), (B), or (C) of this paragraph, such claims shall be paid from all remaining property of the estate.

§ 727. Discharge

(a) The court shall grant the debtor a discharge, unless—

(1) the debtor is not an individual;

(2) the debtor, with intent to hinder, delay, or defraud a creditor or an officer of the estate charged with custody of property under this title, has transferred, removed, destroyed, mutilated, or concealed, or has permitted to be transferred, removed, destroyed, mutilated, or concealed—

(A) property of the debtor, within one year before the date of the filing of the petition; or

(B) property of the estate, after the date of the filing of the petition;

(3) the debtor has concealed, destroyed, mutilated, falsified, or failed to keep or preserve any recorded information, including books, documents, records, and papers, from which the debtor's financial condition or business transactions might be ascertained, unless such act or failure to act was justified under all of the circumstances of the case;

(4) the debtor knowingly and fraudulently, in or in connection with the case—

(A) made a false oath or account;

(B) presented or used a false claim;

(C) gave, offered, received, or attempted to obtain money, property, or advantage, or a promise of money, property, or advantage, for acting or forbearing to act; or

(D) withheld from an officer of the estate entitled to possession under this title, any recorded information, including books, documents, records, and papers, relating to the debtor's property or financial affairs;

(5) the debtor has failed to explain satisfactorily, before determination of denial of discharge under this paragraph, any loss of assets or deficiency of assets to meet the debtor's liabilities;

(6) the debtor has refused, in the case—

(A) to obey any lawful order of the court, other than an order to respond to a material question or to testify;

(B) on the ground of privilege against self-incrimination, to respond to a material question approved by the court or to testify, after the debtor has been granted immunity with respect to the matter concerning which such privilege was invoked; or

(C) on a ground other than the properly invoked privilege against self-incrimination, to respond to a material question approved by the court or to testify;

(7) the debtor has committed any act specified in paragraph (2), (3), (4), (5), or (6) of this subsection, on or within one year before the date of the filing of the petition, or during the case, in connection with another case, under this title or under the Bankruptcy Act, concerning an insider;

(8) the debtor has been granted a discharge under this section, under section 1141 of this title, or under section 14, 371, or 476 of the Bankruptcy Act, in a case commenced within 8 years before the date of the filing of the petition;

(9) the debtor has been granted a discharge under section 1228 or 1328 of this title, or under section 660 or 661 of the Bankruptcy Act, in a case commenced within six years before the date of the filing of the petition, unless payments under the plan in such case totaled at least—

(A) 100 percent of the allowed unsecured claims in such case; or

(B)(i) 70 percent of such claims; and

(ii) the plan was proposed by the debtor in good faith, and was the debtor's best effort;

(10) the court approves a written waiver of discharge executed by the debtor after the order for relief under this chapter;

(11) after filing the petition, the debtor failed to complete an instructional course concerning personal financial management described in section 111, except that this paragraph shall not apply

with respect to a debtor who is a person described in section 109(h)(4) or who resides in a district for which the United States trustee (or the bankruptcy administrator, if any) determines that the approved instructional courses are not adequate to service the additional individuals who would otherwise be required to complete such instructional courses under this section (The United States trustee (or the bankruptcy administrator, if any) who makes a determination described in this paragraph shall review such determination not later than 1 year after the date of such determination, and not less frequently than annually thereafter.); or

(12) the court after notice and a hearing held not more than 10 days before the date of the entry of the order granting the discharge finds that there is reasonable cause to believe that—

(A) section 522(q)(1) may be applicable to the debtor; and

(B) there is pending any proceeding in which the debtor may be found guilty of a felony of the kind described in section 522(q)(1)(A) or liable for a debt of the kind described in section 522(q)(1)(B).

(b) Except as provided in section 523 of this title, a discharge under subsection (a) of this section discharges the debtor from all debts that arose before the date of the order for relief under this chapter, and any liability on a claim that is determined under section 502 of this title as if such claim had arisen before the commencement of the case, whether or not a proof of claim based on any such debt or liability is filed under section 501 of this title, and whether or not a claim based on any such debt or liability is allowed under section 502 of this title.

(c)(1) The trustee, a creditor, or the United States trustee may object to the granting of a discharge under subsection (a) of this section.

(2) On request of a party in interest, the court may order the trustee to examine the acts and conduct of the debtor to determine whether a ground exists for denial of discharge.

(d) On request of the trustee, a creditor, or the United States trustee, and after notice and a hearing, the court shall revoke a discharge granted under subsection (a) of this section if—

(1) such discharge was obtained through the fraud of the debtor, and the requesting party did not know of such fraud until after the granting of such discharge;

(2) the debtor acquired property that is property of the estate, or became entitled to acquire property that would be property of the estate, and knowingly and fraudulently failed to report the acquisition of or entitlement to such property, or to deliver or surrender such property to the trustee;

(3) the debtor committed an act specified in subsection (a)(6) of this section; or

(4) the debtor has failed to explain satisfactorily—

(A) a material misstatement in an audit referred to in section 586(f) of title 28; or

(B) a failure to make available for inspection all necessary accounts, papers, documents, financial records, files, and all other papers, things, or property belonging to the debtor that are requested for an audit referred to in section 586(f) of title 28.

(e) The trustee, a creditor, or the United States trustee may request a revocation of a discharge—

(1) under subsection (d)(1) of this section within one year after such discharge is granted; or

(2) under subsection (d)(2) or (d)(3) of this section before the later of—

(A) one year after the granting of such discharge; and

(B) the date the case is closed.

CHAPTER 9. ADJUSTMENT OF DEBTS OF A MUNICIPALITY

SUBCHAPTER I—GENERAL PROVISIONS

Section

SUBCHAPTER II—ADMINISTRATION

Section

SUBCHAPTER III—THE PLAN

SUBCHAPTER I—GENERAL PROVISIONS

§ 901. Applicability of Other Sections of This Title

(a) Sections 301, 333, 344, 347(b), 349, 350(b), 351, 361, 362, 364(c), 364(d), 364(e), 364(f), 365, 366, 501, 502, 503, 504, 506, 507(a)(2), 509, 510, 524(a)(1), 524(a)(2), 544, 545, 546, 547, 548, 549(a), 549(c), 549(d), 550, 551, 552, 553, 555, 556, 557, 559, 560, 561, 562, 1102, 1103, 1109, 1111(b), 1122, 1123(a)(1), 1123(a)(2), 1123(a)(3), 1123(a)(4), 1123(a)(5), 1123(b), 1123(d), 1124, 1125, 1126(a), 1126(b), 1126(c), 1126(e), 1126(f), 1126(g), 1127(d), 1128, 1129(a)(2), 1129(a)(3), 1129(a)(6), 1129(a)(8), 1129(a)(10), 1129(b)(1), 1129(b)(2)(A), 1129(b)(2)(B), 1142(b), 1143, 1144, and 1145 of this title apply in a case under this chapter.

(b) A term used in a section of this title made applicable in a case under this chapter by subsection (a) of this section or section 103(e) of this title has the meaning defined for such term for the purpose of such applicable section, unless such term is otherwise defined in section 902 of this title.

(c) A section made applicable in a case under this chapter by subsection (a) of this section that is operative if the business of the debtor is authorized to be operated is operative in a case under this chapter.

§ 902. Definitions for This Chapter

In this chapter—

(1) "property of the estate", when used in a section that is made applicable in a case under this chapter by section 103(e) or 901 of this title, means property of the debtor;

(2) "special revenues" means—

(A) receipts derived from the ownership, operation, or disposition of projects or systems of the debtor that are primarily used or intended to be used primarily to provide transportation, utility, or other services, including the proceeds of borrowings to finance the projects or systems;

(B) special excise taxes imposed on particular activities or transactions;

(C) incremental tax receipts from the benefited area in the case of tax-increment financing;

(D) other revenues or receipts derived from particular functions of the debtor, whether or not the debtor has other functions; or

(E) taxes specifically levied to finance one or more projects or systems, excluding receipts from general property, sales, or income taxes (other than tax-increment financing) levied to finance the general purposes of the debtor;

(3) "special tax payer" means record owner or holder of legal or equitable title to real property against which a special assessment or special tax has been levied the proceeds of which are the sole source of payment of an obligation issued by the debtor to defray the cost of an improvement relating to such real property;

(4) "special tax payer affected by the plan" means special tax payer with respect to whose real property the plan proposes to increase the proportion of special assessments or special taxes referred to in paragraph (2) of this section assessed against such real property; and

(5) "trustee", when used in a section that is made applicable in a case under this chapter by section 103(e) or 901 of this title, means debtor, except as provided in section 926 of this title.

§ 903. Reservation of State Power to Control Municipalities

This chapter does not limit or impair the power of a state to control, by legislation or otherwise, a municipality of or in such state in the exercise of the political or governmental powers of such municipality, including expenditures for such exercise, but—

(1) a state law prescribing a method of composition of indebtedness of such municipality may not bind any creditor that does not consent to such composition; and

(2) a judgment entered under such a law may not bind a creditor that does not consent to such composition.

§ 904. Limitation on Jurisdiction and Powers of Court

Notwithstanding any power of the court, unless the debtor consents or the plan so provides, the court may not, by any stay, order, or decree, in the case or otherwise, interfere with—

(1) any of the political or governmental powers of the debtor;

(2) any of the property or revenues of the debtor; or

(3) the debtor's use or enjoyment of any income-producing property.

SUBCHAPTER II—ADMINISTRATION

§ 921. Petition and Proceedings Relating to Petition

(a) Notwithstanding sections 109(d) and 301 of this title, a case under this chapter concerning an unincorporated tax or special assessment district that does not have such district's own officials is commenced by the filing under section 301 of this title of a petition under this chapter by such district's governing authority or the board or body having authority to levy taxes or assessments to meet the obligations of such district.

(b) The chief judge of the court of appeals for the circuit embracing the district in which the case is commenced shall designate the bankruptcy judge to conduct the case.

(c) After any objection to the petition, the court, after notice and a hearing, may dismiss the petition if the debtor did not file the petition in good faith or if the petition does not meet the requirements of this title.

(d) If the petition is not dismissed under subsection (c) of this section, the court shall order relief under this chapter notwithstanding section 301(b).

(e) The court may not, on account of an appeal from an order for relief, delay any proceeding under this chapter in the case in which the appeal is being taken; nor shall any court order a stay of such proceeding pending such appeal. The reversal on appeal of a finding of jurisdiction does not affect the validity of any debt incurred that is authorized by the court under section 364(c) or 364(d) of this title.

§ 922. Automatic Stay of Enforcement of Claims Against the Debtor

(a) A petition filed under this chapter operates as a stay, in addition to the stay provided by section 362 of this title, applicable to all entities, of—

(1) the commencement or continuation, including the issuance or employment of process, of a judicial, administrative, or other action or proceeding against an officer or inhabitant of the debtor that seeks to enforce a claim against the debtor; and

(2) the enforcement of a lien on or arising out of taxes or assessments owed to the debtor.

(b) Subsections (c), (d), (e), (f), and (g) of section 362 of this title apply to a stay under subsection (a) of this section the same as such subsections apply to a stay under section 362(a) of this title.

(c) If the debtor provides, under section 362, 364, or 922 of this title, adequate protection of the interest of the holder of a claim secured by a lien on property of the debtor and if, notwithstanding such protection such creditor has a claim arising from the stay of action against such property under section 362 or 922 of this title or from the granting of a lien under section 364(d) of this title, then such claim shall be allowable as an administrative expense under section 503(b) of this title.

(d) Notwithstanding section 362 of this title and subsection (a) of this section, a petition filed under this chapter does not operate as a stay of application of pledged special revenues in a manner consistent with section 927 of this title to payment of indebtedness secured by such revenues.

§ 923. Notice

There shall be given notice of the commencement of a case under this chapter, notice of an order for relief under this chapter, and notice of the dismissal of a case under this chapter. Such notice shall also be published at least once a week for three successive weeks in at least one newspaper of general circulation published within the district in which the case is commenced, and in such other newspaper having a general circulation among bond dealers and bondholders as the court designates.

§ 924. List of Creditors

The debtor shall file a list of creditors.

§ 925. Effect of List of Claims

A proof of claim is deemed filed under section 501 of this title for any claim that appears in the list filed under section 924 of this title, except a claim that is listed as disputed, contingent, or unliquidated.

§ 926. Avoiding Powers

(a) If the debtor refuses to pursue a cause of action under section 544, 545, 547, 548, 549(a), or 550 of this title, then on request of a creditor, the court may appoint a trustee to pursue such cause of action.

(b) A transfer of property of the debtor to or for the benefit of any holder of a bond or note, on account of such bond or note, may not be avoided under section 547 of this title.

§ 927. Limitation on Recourse

The holder of a claim payable solely from special revenues of the debtor under applicable nonbankruptcy law shall not be treated as having recourse against the debtor on account of such claim pursuant to section 1111(b) of this title.

§ 928. Post Petition Effect of Security Interest

(a) Notwithstanding section 552(a) of this title and subject to subsection (b) of this section, special revenues acquired by the debtor after the commencement of the case shall remain subject to any lien resulting from any security agreement entered into by the debtor before the commencement of the case.

(b) Any such lien on special revenues, other than municipal betterment assessments, derived from a project or system shall be subject to the necessary operating expenses of such project or system, as the case may be.

§ 929. Municipal Leases

A lease to a municipality shall not be treated as an executory contract or unexpired lease for the purposes of section 365 or 502(b)(6) of this title solely by reason of its being subject to termination in the event the debtor fails to appropriate rent.

§ 930. Dismissal

(a) After notice and a hearing, the court may dismiss a case under this chapter for cause, including—

(1) want of prosecution;

(2) unreasonable delay by the debtor that is prejudicial to creditors;

(3) failure to propose a plan within the time fixed under section 941 of this title;

(4) if a plan is not accepted within any time fixed by the court;

(5) denial of confirmation of a plan under section 943(b) of this title and denial of additional time for filing another plan or a modification of a plan; or

(6) if the court has retained jurisdiction after confirmation of a plan—

(A) material default by the debtor with respect to a term of such plan; or

(B) termination of such plan by reason of the occurrence of a condition specified in such plan.

(b) The court shall dismiss a case under this chapter if confirmation of a plan under this chapter is refused.

SUBCHAPTER III—THE PLAN

§ 941. Filing of Plan

The debtor shall file a plan for the adjustment of the debtor's debts. If such a plan is not filed with the petition, the debtor shall file such a plan at such later time as the court fixes.

§ 942. Modification of Plan

The debtor may modify the plan at any time before confirmation, but may not modify the plan so that the plan as modified fails to meet the requirements of this chapter. After the debtor files a modification, the plan as modified becomes the plan.

§ 943. Confirmation

(a) A special tax payer may object to confirmation of a plan.

(b) The court shall confirm the plan if—

(1) the plan complies with the provisions of this title made applicable by sections 103(e) and 901 of this title;

(2) the plan complies with the provisions of this chapter;

(3) all amounts to be paid by the debtor or by any person for services or expenses in the case or incident to the plan have been fully disclosed and are reasonable;

(4) the debtor is not prohibited by law from taking any action necessary to carry out the plan;

(5) except to the extent that the holder of a particular claim has agreed to a different treatment of such claim, the plan provides that on the effective date of the plan each holder of a claim of a kind specified in section 507(a)(2) of this title will receive on account of such claim cash equal to the allowed amount of such claim;

(6) any regulatory or electoral approval necessary under applicable nonbankruptcy law in order to carry out any provision of the plan has been obtained, or such provision is expressly conditioned on such approval; and

(7) the plan is in the best interests of creditors and is feasible.

§ 944. Effect of Confirmation

(a) The provisions of a confirmed plan bind the debtor and any creditor, whether or not—

(1) a proof of such creditor's claim is filed or deemed filed under section 501 of this title;

(2) such claim is allowed under section 502 of this title; or

(3) such creditor has accepted the plan.

(b) Except as provided in subsection (c) of this section, the debtor is discharged from all debts as of the time when—

(1) the plan is confirmed;

(2) the debtor deposits any consideration to be distributed under the plan with a disbursing agent appointed by the court; and

(3) the court has determined—

(A) that any security so deposited will constitute, after distribution, a valid legal obligation of the debtor; and

(B) that any provision made to pay or secure payment of such obligation is valid.

(c) The debtor is not discharged under subsection (b) of this section from any debt—

(1) excepted from discharge by the plan or order confirming the plan; or

(2) owed to an entity that, before confirmation of the plan, had neither notice nor actual knowledge of the case.

§ 945. Continuing Jurisdiction and Closing of the Case

(a) The court may retain jurisdiction over the case for such period of time as is necessary for the successful implementation of the plan.

(b) Except as provided in subsection (a) of this section, the court shall close the case when administration of the case has been completed.

§ 946. Effect of Exchange of Securities Before the Date of the Filing of the Petition.

The exchange of a new security under the plan for a claim covered by the plan, whether such exchange occurred before or after the date of the filing of the petition, does not limit or impair the effectiveness of the plan or of any provision of this chapter. The amount and number specified in section 1126(c) of this title include the amount and number of claims formerly held by a creditor that has participated in any such exchange.

CHAPTER 11. REORGANIZATION

SUBCHAPTER I—OFFICERS AND ADMINISTRATION

Section

SUBCHAPTER II—THE PLAN

Section

SUBCHAPTER III—POSTCONFIRMATION MATTERS

Section

SUBCHAPTER IV—RAILROAD REORGANIZATION

Section

SUBCHAPTER V—SMALL BUSINESS DEBTOR REORGANIZATION

Section

SUBCHAPTER I—OFFICERS AND ADMINISTRATION

§ 1101. Definitions for This Chapter

In this chapter—

(1) "debtor in possession" means debtor except when a person that has qualified under section 322 of this title is serving as trustee in the case;

(2) "substantial consummation" means—

(A) transfer of all or substantially all of the property proposed by the plan to be transferred;

(B) assumption by the debtor or by the successor to the debtor under the plan of the business or of the management of all or substantially all of the property dealt with by the plan; and

(C) commencement of distribution under the plan.

§ 1102. Creditors' and Equity Security Holders' Committees

(a)(1) Except as provided in paragraph (3), as soon as practicable after the order for relief under chapter 11 of this title, the United States trustee shall appoint a committee of creditors holding unsecured claims and may appoint additional committees of creditors or of equity security holders as the United States trustee deems appropriate.

(2) On request of a party in interest, the court may order the appointment of additional committees of creditors or of equity security holders if necessary to assure adequate representation of creditors or of equity security holders. The United States trustee shall appoint any such committee.

(3) Unless the court for cause orders otherwise, a committee of creditors may not be appointed in a small business case or a case under subchapter V of this chapter.

(4) On request of a party in interest and after notice and a hearing, the court may order the United States trustee to change the membership of a committee appointed under this subsection, if the court determines that the change is necessary to ensure adequate representation of creditors or equity security holders. The court may order the United States trustee to increase the number of members of a committee to include a creditor that is a small business concern (as described in section 3(a)(1) of the Small Business Act), if the court determines that the creditor holds claims (of the kind represented by the committee) the aggregate amount of which, in comparison to the annual gross revenue of that creditor, is disproportionately large.

(b)(1) A committee of creditors appointed under subsection (a) of this section shall ordinarily consist of the persons, willing to serve, that hold the seven largest claims against the debtor of the kinds represented on such committee, or of the members of a committee organized by creditors before the commencement of the case under this chapter, if such committee was fairly chosen and is representative of the different kinds of claims to be represented.

(2) A committee of equity security holders appointed under subsection (a)(2) of this section shall ordinarily consist of the persons, willing to serve, that hold the seven largest amounts of equity securities of the debtor of the kinds represented on such committee.

(3) A committee appointed under subsection (a) shall—

(A) provide access to information for creditors who—

(i) hold claims of the kind represented by that committee; and

(ii) are not appointed to the committee;

(B) solicit and receive comments from the creditors described in subparagraph (A); and

(C) be subject to a court order that compels any additional report or disclosure to be made to the creditors described in subparagraph (A).

§ 1103. Powers and Duties of Committees

(a) At a scheduled meeting of a committee appointed under section 1102 of this title, at which a majority of the members of such committee are present, and with the court's approval, such committee may select and authorize the employment by such committee of one or more attorneys, accountants, or other agents, to represent or perform services for such committee.

(b) An attorney or accountant employed to represent a committee appointed under section 1102 of this title may not, while employed by such committee, represent any other entity having an adverse interest in connection with the case. Representation of one or more creditors of the same class as represented by the committee shall not per se constitute the representation of an adverse interest.

(c) A committee appointed under section 1102 of this title may—

(1) consult with the trustee or debtor in possession concerning the administration of the case;

(2) investigate the acts, conduct, assets, liabilities, and financial condition of the debtor, the operation of the debtor's business and the desirability of the continuance of such business, and any other matter relevant to the case or to the formulation of a plan;

(3) participate in the formulation of a plan, advise those represented by such committee of such committee's determinations as to any plan formulated, and collect and file with the court acceptances or rejections of a plan;

(4) request the appointment of a trustee or examiner under section 1104 of this title; and

(5) perform such other services as are in the interest of those represented.

(d) As soon as practicable after the appointment of a committee under section 1102 of this title, the trustee shall meet with such committee to transact such business as may be necessary and proper.

§ 1104. Appointment of Trustee or Examiner

(a) At any time after the commencement of the case but before confirmation of a plan, on request of a party in interest or the United States trustee, and after notice and a hearing, the court shall order the appointment of a trustee—

(1) for cause, including fraud, dishonesty, incompetence, or gross mismanagement of the affairs of the debtor by current management, either before or after the commencement of the case, or similar cause, but not including the number of holders of securities of the debtor or the amount of assets or liabilities of the debtor; or

(2) if such appointment is in the interests of creditors, any equity security holders, and other interests of the estate, without regard to the number of holders of securities of the debtor or the amount of assets or liabilities of the debtor.

(b)(1) Except as provided in section 1163 of this title, on the request of a party in interest made not later than 30 days after the court orders the appointment of a trustee under subsection (a), the United States trustee shall convene a meeting of creditors for the purpose of electing one disinterested person to serve as trustee in the case. The election of a trustee shall be conducted in the manner provided in subsections (a), (b), and (c) of section 702 of this title.

(2)(A) If an eligible, disinterested trustee is elected at a meeting of creditors under paragraph (1), the United States trustee shall file a report certifying that election.

(B) Upon the filing of a report under subparagraph (A)—

(i) the trustee elected under paragraph (1) shall be considered to have been selected and appointed for purposes of this section; and

(ii) the service of any trustee appointed under subsection (a) shall terminate.

(C) The court shall resolve any dispute arising out of an election described in subparagraph (A).

(c) If the court does not order the appointment of a trustee under this section, then at any time before the confirmation of a plan, on request of a party in interest or the United States trustee, and after notice and a hearing, the court shall order the appointment of an examiner to conduct such an investigation of the debtor as is appropriate, including an investigation of any allegations of fraud, dishonesty, incompetence, misconduct, mismanagement, or irregularity in the management of the affairs of the debtor of or by current or former management of the debtor, if—

(1) such appointment is in the interests of creditors, any equity security holders, and other interests of the estate; or

(2) the debtor's fixed, liquidated, unsecured debts, other than debts for goods, services, or taxes, or owing to an insider, exceed $5,000,000.

(d) If the court orders the appointment of a trustee or an examiner, if a trustee or an examiner dies or resigns during the case or is removed under section 324 of this title, or if a trustee fails to qualify under section 322 of this title, then the United States trustee, after consultation with parties in interest, shall appoint, subject to the court's approval, one disinterested person other than the United States trustee to serve as trustee or examiner, as the case may be, in the case.

(e) The United States trustee shall move for the appointment of a trustee under subsection (a) if there are reasonable grounds to suspect that current members of the governing body of the debtor, the debtor's chief executive or chief financial officer, or members of the governing body who selected the debtor's chief executive or chief financial officer, participated in actual fraud, dishonesty, or criminal conduct in the management of the debtor or the debtor's public financial reporting.

§ 1105. Termination of Trustee's Appointment

At any time before confirmation of a plan, on request of a party in interest or the United States trustee, and after notice and a hearing, the court may terminate the trustee's appointment and restore the debtor to possession and management of the property of the estate and of the operation of the debtor's business.

§ 1106. Duties of Trustee and Examiner

(a) A trustee shall—

(1) perform the duties of the trustee, as specified in paragraphs (2), (5), (7), (8), (9), (10), (11), and (12) of section 704(a);

(2) if the debtor has not done so, file the list, schedule, and statement required under section 521(a)(1) of this title;

(3) except to the extent that the court orders otherwise, investigate the acts, conduct, assets, liabilities, and financial condition of the debtor, the operation of the debtor's business and the desirability of the continuance of such business, and any other matter relevant to the case or to the formulation of a plan;

(4) as soon as practicable—

(A) file a statement of any investigation conducted under paragraph (3) of this subsection, including any fact ascertained pertaining to fraud, dishonesty, incompetence, misconduct, mismanagement, or irregularity in the management of the affairs of the debtor, or to a cause of action available to the estate; and

(B) transmit a copy or a summary of any such statement to any creditors' committee or equity security holders' committee, to any indenture trustee, and to such other entity as the court designates;

(5) as soon as practicable, file a plan under section 1121 of this title, file a report of why the trustee will not file a plan, or recommend conversion of the case to a case under chapter 7, 12, or 13 of this title or dismissal of the case;

(6) for any year for which the debtor has not filed a tax return required by law, furnish, without personal liability, such information as may be required by the governmental unit with which such tax return was to be filed, in light of the condition of the debtor's books and records and the availability of such information;

(7) after confirmation of a plan, file such reports as are necessary or as the court orders; and

(8) if with respect to the debtor there is a claim for a domestic support obligation, provide the applicable notice specified in subsection (c).

(b) An examiner appointed under section 1104(d) of this title shall perform the duties specified in paragraphs (3) and (4) of subsection (a) of this section, and, except to the extent that the court orders otherwise, any other duties of the trustee that the court orders the debtor in possession not to perform.

(c)(1) In a case described in subsection (a)(8) to which subsection (a)(8) applies, the trustee shall—

(A)(i) provide written notice to the holder of the claim described in subsection (a)(8) of such claim and of the right of such holder to use the services of the State child support enforcement agency established under sections 464 and 466 of the Social Security Act for the State in which such holder resides, for assistance in collecting child support during and after the case under this title; and

(ii) include in the notice required by clause (i) the address and telephone number of such State child support enforcement agency;

(B)(i) provide written notice to such State child support enforcement agency of such claim; and

(ii) include in the notice required by clause (i) the name, address, and telephone number of such holder; and

(C) at such time as the debtor is granted a discharge under section 1141, provide written notice to such holder and to such State child support enforcement agency of—

(i) the granting of the discharge;

(ii) the last recent known address of the debtor;

(iii) the last recent known name and address of the debtor's employer; and

(iv) the name of each creditor that holds a claim that—

(I) is not discharged under paragraph (2), (4), or (14A) of section 523(a); or

(II) was reaffirmed by the debtor under section 524(c).

(2)(A) The holder of a claim described in subsection (a)(8) or the State child enforcement support agency of the State in which such holder resides may request from a creditor described in paragraph (1)(C)(iv) the last known address of the debtor.

(B) Notwithstanding any other provision of law, a creditor that makes a disclosure of a last known address of a debtor in connection with a request made under subparagraph (A) shall not be liable by reason of making such disclosure.

§ 1107. Rights, Powers, and Duties of Debtor in Possession

(a) Subject to any limitations on a trustee serving in a case under this chapter, and to such limitations or conditions as the court prescribes, a debtor in possession shall have all the rights, other than the right to compensation under section 330 of this title, and powers, and shall perform all the functions and duties, except the duties specified in sections 1106(a)(2), (3), and (4) of this title, of a trustee serving in a case under this chapter.

(b) Notwithstanding section 327(a) of this title, a person is not disqualified for employment under section 327 of this title by a debtor in possession solely because of such person's employment by or representation of the debtor before the commencement of the case.

§ 1108. Authorization to Operate Business

Unless the court, on request of a party in interest and after notice and a hearing, orders otherwise, the trustee may operate the debtor's business.

§ 1109. Right to Be Heard

(a) The Securities and Exchange Commission may raise and may appear and be heard on any issue in a case under this chapter, but the Securities and Exchange Commission may not appeal from any judgment, order, or decree entered in the case.

(b) A party in interest, including the debtor, the trustee, a creditors' committee, an equity security holders' committee, a creditor, an equity security holder, or any indenture trustee, may raise and may appear and be heard on any issue in a case under this chapter.

(c) The Comptroller of the Currency or State payment stablecoin regulator (as defined in section 2 of the GENIUS Act) shall raise, and shall appear and be heard on, any issue, including the protection of customers, in a case under this chapter in which the debtor is a permitted payment stablecoin issuer.

§ 1110. Aircraft Equipment and Vessels

(a)(1) Except as provided in paragraph (2) and subject to subsection (b), the right of a secured party with a security interest in equipment described in paragraph (3), or of a lessor or conditional vendor of such equipment, to take possession of such equipment in compliance with a security agreement, lease, or conditional sale contract, and to enforce any of its other rights or remedies, under such security agreement, lease, or conditional sale contract, to sell, lease, or otherwise retain or dispose of such equipment, is not limited or otherwise affected by any other provision of this title or by any power of the court.

(2) The right to take possession and to enforce the other rights and remedies described in paragraph (1) shall be subject to section 362 if—

(A) before the date that is 60 days after the date of the order for relief under this chapter, the trustee, subject to the approval of the court, agrees to perform all obligations of the debtor under such security agreement, lease, or conditional sale contract; and

(B) any default, other than a default of a kind specified in section 365(b)(2), under such security agreement, lease, or conditional sale contract—

(i) that occurs before the date of the order is cured before the expiration of such 60-day period;

(ii) that occurs after the date of the order and before the expiration of such 60-day period is cured before the later of—

(I) the date that is 30 days after the date of the default; or

(II) the expiration of such 60-day period; and

(iii) that occurs on or after the expiration of such 60-day period is cured in compliance with the terms of such security agreement, lease, or conditional sale contract, if a cure is permitted under that agreement, lease, or contract.

(3) The equipment described in this paragraph—

(A) is—

(i) an aircraft, aircraft engine, propeller, appliance, or spare part (as defined in section 40102 of title 49) that is subject to a security interest granted by, leased to, or conditionally sold to a debtor that, at the time such transaction is entered into, holds an air carrier operating certificate issued pursuant to chapter 447 of title 49 for aircraft capable of carrying 10 or more individuals or 6,000 pounds or more of cargo; or

(ii) a vessel documented under chapter 121 of title 46 that is subject to a security interest granted by, leased to, or conditionally sold to a debtor that is a water carrier that, at the time such transaction is entered into, holds a certificate of public convenience and necessity or permit issued by the Department of Transportation; and

(B) includes all records and documents relating to such equipment that are required, under the terms of the security agreement, lease, or conditional sale contract, to be surrendered or returned by the debtor in connection with the surrender or return of such equipment.

(4) Paragraph (1) applies to a secured party, lessor, or conditional vendor acting in its own behalf or acting as trustee or otherwise in behalf of another party.

(b) The trustee and the secured party, lessor, or conditional vendor whose right to take possession is protected under subsection (a) may agree, subject to the approval of the court, to extend the 60-day period specified in subsection (a)(1).

(c)(1) In any case under this chapter, the trustee shall immediately surrender and return to a secured party, lessor, or conditional vendor, described in subsection (a)(1), equipment described in subsection (a)(3), if at any time after the date of the order for relief under this chapter such secured party, lessor, or conditional vendor is entitled pursuant to subsection (a)(1) to take possession of such equipment and makes a written demand for such possession to the trustee.

(2) At such time as the trustee is required under paragraph (1) to surrender and return equipment described in subsection (a)(3), any lease of such equipment, and any security agreement or conditional sale contract relating to such equipment, if such security agreement or conditional sale contract is an executory contract, shall be deemed rejected.

(d) With respect to equipment first placed in service on or before October 22, 1994, for purposes of this section—

(1) the term "lease" includes any written agreement with respect to which the lessor and the debtor, as lessee, have expressed in the agreement or in a substantially contemporaneous writing that the agreement is to be treated as a lease for Federal income tax purposes; and

(2) the term "security interest" means a purchase-money equipment security interest.

§ 1111. Claims and Interests

(a) A proof of claim or interest is deemed filed under section 501 of this title for any claim or interest that appears in the schedules filed under section 521(a)(1) or 1106(a)(2) of this title, except a claim or interest that is scheduled as disputed, contingent, or unliquidated.

(b)(1)(A) A claim secured by a lien on property of the estate shall be allowed or disallowed under section 502 of this title the same as if the holder of such claim had recourse against the debtor on account of such claim, whether or not such holder has such recourse, unless—

(i) the class of which such claim is a part elects, by at least two-thirds in amount and more than half in number of allowed claims of such class, application of paragraph (2) of this subsection; or

(ii) such holder does not have such recourse and such property is sold under section 363 of this title or is to be sold under the plan.

(B) A class of claims may not elect application of paragraph (2) of this subsection if—

(i) the interest on account of such claims of the holders of such claims in such property is of inconsequential value; or

(ii) the holder of a claim of such class has recourse against the debtor on account of such claim and such property is sold under section 363 of this title or is to be sold under the plan.

(2) If such an election is made, then notwithstanding section 506(a) of this title, such claim is a secured claim to the extent that such claim is allowed.

§ 1112. Conversion or Dismissal

(a) The debtor may convert a case under this chapter to a case under chapter 7 of this title unless—

(1) the debtor is not a debtor in possession;

(2) the case originally was commenced as an involuntary case under this chapter; or

(3) the case was converted to a case under this chapter other than on the debtor's request.

(b)(1) Except as provided in paragraph (2) and subsection (c), on request of a party in interest, and after notice and a hearing, the court shall convert a case under this chapter to a case under chapter 7 or dismiss a case under this chapter, whichever is in the best interests of creditors and the estate, for cause unless the court determines that the appointment under section 1104(a) of a trustee or an examiner is in the best interests of creditors and the estate.

(2) The court may not convert a case under this chapter to a case under chapter 7 or dismiss a case under this chapter if the court finds and specifically identifies unusual circumstances establishing that converting or dismissing the case is not in the best interests of creditors and the estate, and the debtor or any other party in interest establishes that—

(A) there is a reasonable likelihood that a plan will be confirmed within the timeframes established in sections 1121(e) and 1129(e) of this title, or if such sections do not apply, within a reasonable period of time; and

(B) the grounds for converting or dismissing the case include an act or omission of the debtor other than under paragraph (4)(A)—

(i) for which there exists a reasonable justification for the act or omission; and

(ii) that will be cured within a reasonable period of time fixed by the court.

(3) The court shall commence the hearing on a motion under this subsection not later than 30 days after filing of the motion, and shall decide the motion not later than 15 days after commencement of such hearing, unless the movant expressly consents to a continuance for a specific period of time or compelling circumstances prevent the court from meeting the time limits established by this paragraph.

(4) For purposes of this subsection, the term "cause" includes—

(A) substantial or continuing loss to or diminution of the estate and the absence of a reasonable likelihood of rehabilitation;

(B) gross mismanagement of the estate;

(C) failure to maintain appropriate insurance that poses a risk to the estate or to the public;

(D) unauthorized use of cash collateral substantially harmful to 1 or more creditors;

(E) failure to comply with an order of the court;

(F) unexcused failure to satisfy timely any filing or reporting requirement established by this title or by any rule applicable to a case under this chapter;

(G) failure to attend the meeting of creditors convened under section 341(a) or an examination ordered under rule 2004 of the Federal Rules of Bankruptcy Procedure without good cause shown by the debtor;

(H) failure timely to provide information or attend meetings reasonably requested by the United States trustee (or the bankruptcy administrator, if any);

(I) failure timely to pay taxes owed after the date of the order for relief or to file tax returns due after the date of the order for relief;

(J) failure to file a disclosure statement, or to file or confirm a plan, within the time fixed by this title or by order of the court;

(K) failure to pay any fees or charges required under chapter 123 of title 28;

(L) revocation of an order of confirmation under section 1144;

(M) inability to effectuate substantial consummation of a confirmed plan;

(N) material default by the debtor with respect to a confirmed plan;

(O) termination of a confirmed plan by reason of the occurrence of a condition specified in the plan; and

(P) failure of the debtor to pay any domestic support obligation that first becomes payable after the date of the filing of the petition.

(c) The court may not convert a case under this chapter to a case under chapter 7 of this title if the debtor is a farmer or a corporation that is not a moneyed, business, or commercial corporation, unless the debtor requests such conversion.

(d) The court may convert a case under this chapter to a case under chapter 12 or 13 of this title only if—

(1) the debtor requests such conversion;

(2) the debtor has not been discharged under section 1141(d) of this title; and

(3) if the debtor requests conversion to chapter 12 of this title, such conversion is equitable.

(e) Except as provided in subsections (c) and (f), the court, on request of the United States trustee, may convert a case under this chapter to a case under chapter 7 of this title or may dismiss a case under this chapter, whichever is in the best interest of creditors and the estate if the debtor in a voluntary case fails to file, within fifteen days after the filing of the petition commencing such case or such additional time as the court may allow, the information required by paragraph (1) of section 521(a), including a list containing the names and addresses of the holders of the twenty largest unsecured claims (or of all unsecured claims if there are fewer than twenty unsecured claims), and the approximate dollar amounts of each of such claims.

(f) Notwithstanding any other provision of this section, a case may not be converted to a case under another chapter of this title unless the debtor may be a debtor under such chapter.

§ 1113. Rejection of Collective Bargaining Agreements

(a) The debtor in possession, or the trustee if one has been appointed under the provisions of this chapter, other than a trustee in a case covered by subchapter IV of this chapter and by title I of the Railway Labor Act, may assume or reject a collective bargaining agreement only in accordance with the provisions of this section.

(b)(1) Subsequent to filing a petition and prior to filing an application seeking rejection of a collective bargaining agreement, the debtor in possession or trustee (hereinafter in this section "trustee" shall include a debtor in possession), shall—

(A) make a proposal to the authorized representative of the employees covered by such agreement, based on the most complete and reliable information available at the time of such proposal, which provides for those necessary modifications in the employees benefits and protections that are necessary to permit the reorganization of the debtor and assures that all creditors, the debtor and all of the affected parties are treated fairly and equitably; and

(B) provide, subject to subsection (d)(3), the representative of the employees with such relevant information as is necessary to evaluate the proposal.

(2) During the period beginning on the date of the making of a proposal provided for in paragraph (1) and ending on the date of the hearing provided for in subsection (d)(1), the trustee shall meet, at reasonable times, with the authorized representative to confer in good faith in attempting to reach mutually satisfactory modifications of such agreement.

(c) The court shall approve an application for rejection of a collective bargaining agreement only if the court finds that—

(1) the trustee has, prior to the hearing, made a proposal that fulfills the requirements of subsection (b)(1);

(2) the authorized representative of the employees has refused to accept such proposal without good cause; and

(3) the balance of the equities clearly favors rejection of such agreement.

(d)(1) Upon the filing of an application for rejection the court shall schedule a hearing to be held not later than fourteen days after the date of the filing of such application. All interested parties may appear and be heard at such hearing. Adequate notice shall be provided to such parties at least ten days before the date of such hearing. The court may extend the time for the commencement of such hearing for a period not exceeding seven days where the circumstances of the case, and the interests of justice require such extension, or for additional periods of time to which the trustee and representative agree.

(2) The court shall rule on such application for rejection within thirty days after the date of the commencement of the hearing. In the interests of justice, the court may extend such time for ruling for such additional period as the trustee and the employees' representative may agree to. If the court does not rule on such application within thirty days after the date of the commencement of the hearing, or within such additional time as the trustee and the employees' representative may agree to, the trustee may terminate or alter any provisions of the collective bargaining agreement pending the ruling of the court on such application.

(3) The court may enter such protective orders, consistent with the need of the authorized representative of the employee to evaluate the trustee's proposal and the application for rejection, as may be necessary to prevent disclosure of information provided to such representative where such disclosure could compromise the position of the debtor with respect to its competitors in the industry in which it is engaged.

(e) If during a period when the collective bargaining agreement continues in effect, and if essential to the continuation of the debtor's business, or in order to avoid irreparable damage to the estate, the court, after notice and a hearing, may authorize the trustee to implement interim changes in the terms, conditions, wages, benefits, or work rules provided by a collective bargaining agreement. Any hearing under this paragraph shall be scheduled in accordance with the needs of the trustee. The implementation of such interim changes shall not render the application for rejection moot.

(f) No provision of this title shall be construed to permit a trustee to unilaterally terminate or alter any provisions of a collective bargaining agreement prior to compliance with the provisions of this section.

§ 1114. Payment of Insurance Benefits to Retired Employees

(a) For purposes of this section, the term "retiree benefits" means payments to any entity or person for the purpose of providing or reimbursing payments for retired employees and their spouses and dependents, for medical, surgical, or hospital care benefits, or benefits in the event of sickness, accident, disability, or death under any plan, fund, or program (through the purchase of insurance or otherwise) maintained or established in whole or in part by the debtor prior to filing a petition commencing a case under this title.

(b)(1) For purposes of this section, the term "authorized representative" means the authorized representative designated pursuant to subsection (c) for persons receiving any retiree benefits covered by a collective bargaining agreement or subsection (d) in the case of persons receiving retiree benefits not covered by such an agreement.

(2) Committees of retired employees appointed by the court pursuant to this section shall have the same rights, powers, and duties as committees appointed under sections 1102 and 1103 of this title for the purpose of carrying out the purposes of sections 1114 and 1129(a)(13) and, as permitted by the court, shall have the power to enforce the rights of persons under this title as they relate to retiree benefits.

(c)(1) A labor organization shall be, for purposes of this section, the authorized representative of those persons receiving any retiree benefits covered by any collective bargaining agreement to which that labor organization is signatory, unless (A) such labor organization elects not to serve as the authorized representative of such persons, or (B) the court, upon a motion by any party in interest, after notice and hearing, determines that different representation of such persons is appropriate.

(2) In cases where the labor organization referred to in paragraph (1) elects not to serve as the authorized representative of those persons receiving any retiree benefits covered by any collective bargaining agreement to which that labor organization is signatory, or in cases where the court, pursuant to paragraph (1) finds different representation of such persons appropriate, the court, upon a motion by any party in interest, and after notice and a hearing, shall appoint a committee of retired employees if the debtor seeks to modify or not pay the retiree benefits or if the court otherwise determines that it is appropriate, from among such persons, to serve as the authorized representative of such persons under this section.

(d) The court, upon a motion by any party in interest, and after notice and a hearing, shall order the appointment of a committee of retired employees if the debtor seeks to modify or not pay the retiree benefits or if the court otherwise determines that it is appropriate, to serve as the authorized representative, under this section, of those persons receiving any retiree benefits not covered by a collective bargaining agreement. The United States trustee shall appoint any such committee.

(e)(1) Notwithstanding any other provision of this title, the debtor in possession, or the trustee if one has been appointed under the provisions of this chapter (hereinafter in this section "trustee" shall include a debtor in possession), shall timely pay and shall not modify any retiree benefits, except that—

(A) the court, on motion of the trustee or authorized representative, and after notice and a hearing, may order modification of such payments, pursuant to the provisions of subsections (g) and (h) of this section, or

(B) the trustee and the authorized representative of the recipients of those benefits may agree to modification of such payments, after which such benefits as modified shall continue to be paid by the trustee.

(2) Any payment for retiree benefits required to be made before a plan confirmed under section 1129 of this title is effective has the status of an allowed administrative expense as provided in section 503 of this title.

(f)(1) Subsequent to filing a petition and prior to filing an application seeking modification of the retiree benefits, the trustee shall—

(A) make a proposal to the authorized representative of the retirees, based on the most complete and reliable information available at the time of such proposal, which provides for those necessary modifications in the retiree benefits that are necessary to permit the reorganization of the debtor and assures that all creditors, the debtor and all of the affected parties are treated fairly and equitably; and

(B) provide, subject to subsection (k)(3), the representative of the retirees with such relevant information as is necessary to evaluate the proposal.

(2) During the period beginning on the date of the making of a proposal provided for in paragraph (1), and ending on the date of the hearing provided for in subsection (k)(1), the trustee shall meet, at reasonable times, with the authorized representative to confer in good faith in attempting to reach mutually satisfactory modifications of such retiree benefits.

(g) The court shall enter an order providing for modification in the payment of retiree benefits if the court finds that—

(1) the trustee has, prior to the hearing, made a proposal that fulfills the requirements of subsection (f);

(2) the authorized representative of the retirees has refused to accept such proposal without good cause; and

(3) such modification is necessary to permit the reorganization of the debtor and assures that all creditors, the debtor, and all of the affected parties are treated fairly and equitably, and is clearly favored by the balance of the equities;

except that in no case shall the court enter an order providing for such modification which provides for a modification to a level lower than that proposed by the trustee in the proposal found by the court to have complied with the requirements of this subsection and subsection (f): *Provided, however,* That at any time after an order is entered providing for modification in the payment of retiree benefits, or at any time after an agreement modifying such benefits is made between the trustee and the authorized representative of the recipients of such benefits, the authorized representative may apply to the court for an order increasing those benefits which order shall be granted if the increase in retiree benefits sought is consistent with the standard set forth in paragraph (3): *Provided further,* That neither the trustee nor the authorized representative is precluded from making more than one motion for a modification order governed by this subsection.

(h)(1) Prior to a court issuing a final order under subsection (g) of this section, if essential to the continuation of the debtor's business, or in order to avoid irreparable damage to the estate, the court, after notice and a hearing, may authorize the trustee to implement interim modifications in retiree benefits.

(2) Any hearing under this subsection shall be scheduled in accordance with the needs of the trustee.

(3) The implementation of such interim changes does not render the motion for modification moot.

(i) No retiree benefits paid between the filing of the petition and the time a plan confirmed under section 1129 of this title becomes effective shall be deducted or offset from the amounts allowed as claims for any benefits which remain unpaid, or from the amounts to be paid under the plan with respect to such claims for unpaid benefits, whether such claims for unpaid benefits are based upon or arise from a right to future unpaid benefits or from any benefits not paid as a result of modifications allowed pursuant to this section.

(j) No claim for retiree benefits shall be limited by section 502(b)(7) of this title.

(k)(1) Upon the filing of an application for modifying retiree benefits, the court shall schedule a hearing to be held not later than fourteen days after the date of the filing of such application. All interested parties may appear and be heard at such hearing. Adequate notice shall be provided to such parties at least ten days before the date of such hearing. The court may extend the time for the commencement of such hearing for a period not exceeding seven days where the circumstances of the case, and the interests of justice require such extension, or for additional periods of time to which the trustee and the authorized representative agree.

(2) The court shall rule on such application for modification within ninety days after the date of the commencement of the hearing. In the interests of justice, the court may extend such time for ruling for such additional period as the trustee and the authorized representative may agree to. If the court does not rule on such application within ninety days after the date of the commencement of the hearing, or within such additional time as the trustee and the authorized representative may agree to, the trustee may implement the proposed modifications pending the ruling of the court on such application.

(3) The court may enter such protective orders, consistent with the need of the authorized representative of the retirees to evaluate the trustee's proposal and the application for modification, as may be necessary to prevent disclosure of information provided to such representative where such disclosure could compromise the position of the debtor with respect to its competitors in the industry in which it is engaged.

(l) If the debtor, during the 180-day period ending on the date of the filing of the petition—

(1) modified retiree benefits; and

(2) was insolvent on the date such benefits were modified; the court, on motion of a party in interest, and after notice and a hearing, shall issue an order reinstating as of the date the modification was made, such benefits as in effect immediately before such date unless the court finds that the balance of the equities clearly favors such modification.

(m) This section shall not apply to any retiree, or the spouse or dependents of such retiree, if such retiree's gross income for the twelve months preceding the filing of the bankruptcy petition equals or exceeds $250,000, unless such retiree can demonstrate to the satisfaction of the court that he is unable to obtain health, medical, life, and disability coverage for himself, his spouse, and his dependents who would otherwise be covered by the employer's insurance plan, comparable to the coverage provided by the employer on the day before the filing of a petition under this title.

§ 1115. Property of the Estate

(a) In a case in which the debtor is an individual, property of the estate includes, in addition to the property specified in section 541—

(1) all property of the kind specified in section 541 that the debtor acquires after the commencement of the case but before the case is closed, dismissed, or converted to a case under chapter 7, 12, or 13, whichever occurs first; and

(2) earnings from services performed by the debtor after the commencement of the case but before the case is closed, dismissed, or converted to a case under chapter 7, 12, or 13, whichever occurs first.

(b) Except as provided in section 1104 or a confirmed plan or order confirming a plan, the debtor shall remain in possession of all property of the estate.

§ 1116. Duties of Trustee or Debtor in Possession in Small Business Cases

In a small business case, a trustee or the debtor in possession, in addition to the duties provided in this title and as otherwise required by law, shall—

(1) append to the voluntary petition or, in an involuntary case, file not later than 7 days after the date of the order for relief—

(A) its most recent balance sheet, statement of operations, cash-flow statement, and Federal income tax return; or

(B) a statement made under penalty of perjury that no balance sheet, statement of operations, or cash-flow statement has been prepared and no Federal tax return has been filed;

(2) attend, through its senior management personnel and counsel, meetings scheduled by the court or the United States trustee, including initial debtor interviews, scheduling conferences, and meetings of creditors convened under section 341 unless the court, after notice and a hearing, waives that requirement upon a finding of extraordinary and compelling circumstances;

(3) timely file all schedules and statements of financial affairs, unless the court, after notice and a hearing, grants an extension, which shall not extend such time period to a date later than 30 days after the date of the order for relief, absent extraordinary and compelling circumstances;

(4) file all postpetition financial and other reports required by the Federal Rules of Bankruptcy Procedure or by local rule of the district court;

(5) subject to section 363(c)(2), maintain insurance customary and appropriate to the industry;

(6)(A) timely file tax returns and other required government filings; and

(B) subject to section 363(c)(2), timely pay all taxes entitled to administrative expense priority except those being contested by appropriate proceedings being diligently prosecuted; and

(7) allow the United States trustee, or a designated representative of the United States trustee, to inspect the debtor's business premises, books, and records at reasonable times, after reasonable prior written notice, unless notice is waived by the debtor.

SUBCHAPTER II—THE PLAN

§ 1121. Who May File a Plan

(a) The debtor may file a plan with a petition commencing a voluntary case, or at any time in a voluntary case or an involuntary case.

(b) Except as otherwise provided in this section, only the debtor may file a plan until after 120 days after the date of the order for relief under this chapter.

(c) Any party in interest, including the debtor, the trustee, a creditors' committee, an equity security holders' committee, a creditor, an equity security holder, or any indenture trustee, may file a plan if and only if—

(1) a trustee has been appointed under this chapter;

(2) the debtor has not filed a plan before 120 days after the date of the order for relief under this chapter; or

(3) the debtor has not filed a plan that has been accepted, before 180 days after the date of the order for relief under this chapter, by each class of claims or interests that is impaired under the plan.

(d)(1) Subject to paragraph (2), on request of a party in interest made within the respective periods specified in subsections (b) and (c) of this section and after notice and a hearing, the court may for cause reduce or increase the 120-day period or the 180-day period referred to in this section.

(2)(A) The 120-day period specified in paragraph (1) may not be extended beyond a date that is 18 months after the date of the order for relief under this chapter.

(B) The 180-day period specified in paragraph (1) may not be extended beyond a date that is 20 months after the date of the order for relief under this chapter.

(e) In a small business case—

(1) only the debtor may file a plan until after 180 days after the date of the order for relief, unless that period is—

(A) extended as provided by this subsection, after notice and a hearing; or

(B) the court, for cause, orders otherwise;

(2) the plan and a disclosure statement (if any) shall be filed not later than 300 days after the date of the order for relief; and

(3) the time periods specified in paragraphs (1) and (2), and the time fixed in section 1129(e) within which the plan shall be confirmed, may be extended only if—

(A) the debtor, after providing notice to parties in interest (including the United States trustee), demonstrates by a preponderance of the evidence that it is more likely than not that the court will confirm a plan within a reasonable period of time;

(B) a new deadline is imposed at the time the extension is granted; and

(C) the order extending time is signed before the existing deadline has expired.

§ 1122. Classification of Claims or Interests

(a) Except as provided in subsection (b) of this section, a plan may place a claim or an interest in a particular class only if such claim or interest is substantially similar to the other claims or interests of such class.

(b) A plan may designate a separate class of claims consisting only of every unsecured claim that is less than or reduced to an amount that the court approves as reasonable and necessary for administrative convenience.

§ 1123. Contents of Plan

(a) Notwithstanding any otherwise applicable nonbankruptcy law, a plan shall—

(1) designate, subject to section 1122 of this title, classes of claims, other than claims of a kind specified in section 507(a)(2), 507(a)(3), or 507(a)(8) of this title, and classes of interests;

(2) specify any class of claims or interests that is not impaired under the plan;

(3) specify the treatment of any class of claims or interests that is impaired under the plan;

(4) provide the same treatment for each claim or interest of a particular class, unless the holder of a particular claim or interest agrees to a less favorable treatment of such particular claim or interest;

(5) provide adequate means for the plan's implementation, such as—

(A) retention by the debtor of all or any part of the property of the estate;

(B) transfer of all or any part of the property of the estate to one or more entities, whether organized before or after the confirmation of such plan;

(C) merger or consolidation of the debtor with one or more persons;

(D) sale of all or any part of the property of the estate, either subject to or free of any lien, or the distribution of all or any part of the property of the estate among those having an interest in such property of the estate;

(E) satisfaction or modification of any lien;

(F) cancellation or modification of any indenture or similar instrument;

(G) curing or waiving of any default;

(H) extension of a maturity date or a change in an interest rate or other term of outstanding securities;

(I) amendment of the debtor's charter; or

(J) issuance of securities of the debtor, or of any entity referred to in subparagraph (B) or (C) of this paragraph, for cash, for property, for existing securities, or in exchange for claims or interests, or for any other appropriate purpose;

(6) provide for the inclusion in the charter of the debtor, if the debtor is a corporation, or of any corporation referred to in paragraph (5)(B) or (5)(C) of this subsection, of a provision prohibiting the issuance of nonvoting equity securities, and providing, as to the several classes of securities possessing voting power, an appropriate distribution of such power among such classes, including, in the case of any class of equity securities having a preference over another class of equity securities with respect to dividends, adequate provisions for the election of directors representing such preferred class in the event of default in the payment of such dividends;

(7) contain only provisions that are consistent with the interests of creditors and equity security holders and with public policy with respect to the manner of selection of any officer, director, or trustee under the plan and any successor to such officer, director, or trustee; and

(8) in a case in which the debtor is an individual, provide for the payment to creditors under the plan

of all or such portion of earnings from personal services performed by the debtor after the commencement of the case or other future income of the debtor as is necessary for the execution of the plan.

(b) Subject to subsection (a) of this section, a plan may—

(1) impair or leave unimpaired any class of claims, secured or unsecured, or of interests;

(2) subject to section 365 of this title, provide for the assumption, rejection, or assignment of any executory contract or unexpired lease of the debtor not previously rejected under such section;

(3) provide for—

(A) the settlement or adjustment of any claim or interest belonging to the debtor or to the estate; or

(B) the retention and enforcement by the debtor, by the trustee, or by a representative of the estate appointed for such purpose, of any such claim or interest;

(4) provide for the sale of all or substantially all of the property of the estate, and the distribution of the proceeds of such sale among holders of claims or interests;

(5) modify the rights of holders of secured claims, other than a claim secured only by a security interest in real property that is the debtor's principal residence, or of holders of unsecured claims, or leave unaffected the rights of holders of any class of claims; and

(6) include any other appropriate provision not inconsistent with the applicable provisions of this title.

(c) In a case concerning an individual, a plan proposed by an entity other than the debtor may not provide for the use, sale, or lease of property exempted under section 522 of this title, unless the debtor consents to such use, sale, or lease.

(d) Notwithstanding subsection (a) of this section and sections 506(b), 1129(a)(7), and 1129(b) of this title, if it is proposed in a plan to cure a default the amount necessary to cure the default shall be determined in accordance with the underlying agreement and applicable nonbankruptcy law.

§ 1124. Impairment of Claims or Interests

Except as provided in section 1123(a)(4) of this title, a class of claims or interests is impaired under a plan unless, with respect to each claim or interest of such class, the plan—

(1) leaves unaltered the legal, equitable, and contractual rights to which such claim or interest entitles the holder of such claim or interest; or

(2) notwithstanding any contractual provision or applicable law that entitles the holder of such claim or interest to demand or receive accelerated payment of such claim or interest after the occurrence of a default—

(A) cures any such default that occurred before or after the commencement of the case under this title, other than a default of a kind specified in section 365(b)(2) of this title or of a kind that section 365(b)(2) expressly does not require to be cured;

(B) reinstates the maturity of such claim or interest as such maturity existed before such default;

(C) compensates the holder of such claim or interest for any damages incurred as a result of any reasonable reliance by such holder on such contractual provision or such applicable law;

(D) if such claim or such interest arises from any failure to perform a nonmonetary obligation, other than a default arising from failure to operate a nonresidential real property lease subject to section 365(b)(1)(A), compensates the holder of such claim or such interest (other than the debtor or an insider) for any actual pecuniary loss incurred by such holder as a result of such failure; and

(E) does not otherwise alter the legal, equitable, or contractual rights to which such claim or interest entitles the holder of such claim or interest.

§ 1125. Postpetition Disclosure and Solicitation

(a) In this section—

(1) "adequate information" means information of a kind, and in sufficient detail, as far as is reasonably practicable in light of the nature and history of the debtor and the condition of the debtor's books and records, including a discussion of the potential material Federal tax consequences of the plan to the debtor, any successor to the debtor, and a hypothetical investor typical of the holders of claims or interests in the case, that would enable such a hypothetical investor of the relevant class to make an informed judgment about the plan, but adequate information need not include such information about any other possible or proposed plan and in determining whether a disclosure statement provides adequate information, the court shall consider the complexity of the case, the benefit of additional information to creditors and other parties in interest, and the cost of providing additional information; and

(2) "investor typical of holders of claims or interests of the relevant class" means investor having—

(A) a claim or interest of the relevant class;

(B) such a relationship with the debtor as the holders of other claims or interests of such class generally have; and

(C) such ability to obtain such information from sources other than the disclosure required by this section as holders of claims or interests in such class generally have.

(b) An acceptance or rejection of a plan may not be solicited after the commencement of the case under this title from a holder of a claim or interest with respect to such claim or interest, unless, at the time of or before such solicitation, there is transmitted to such holder the plan or a summary of the plan, and a written disclosure statement approved, after notice and a hearing, by the court as containing adequate information. The court may approve a disclosure statement without a valuation of the debtor or an appraisal of the debtor's assets.

(c) The same disclosure statement shall be transmitted to each holder of a claim or interest of a particular class, but there may be transmitted different disclosure statements, differing in amount, detail, or kind of information, as between classes.

(d) Whether a disclosure statement required under subsection (b) of this section contains adequate information is not governed by any otherwise applicable nonbankruptcy law, rule, or regulation, but an agency or official whose duty is to administer or enforce such a law, rule, or regulation may be heard on the issue of whether a disclosure statement contains adequate information. Such an agency or official may not appeal from, or otherwise seek review of, an order approving a disclosure statement.

(e) A person that solicits acceptance or rejection of a plan, in good faith and in compliance with the applicable provisions of this title, or that participates, in good faith and in compliance with the applicable provisions of this title, in the offer, issuance, sale, or purchase of a security, offered or sold under the plan, of the debtor, of an affiliate participating in a joint plan with the debtor, or of a newly organized successor to the debtor under the plan, is not liable, on account of such solicitation or participation, for violation of any applicable law, rule, or regulation governing solicitation of acceptance or rejection of a plan or the offer, issuance, sale, or purchase of securities.

(f) Notwithstanding subsection (b), in a small business case—

(1) the court may determine that the plan itself provides adequate information and that a separate disclosure statement is not necessary;

(2) the court may approve a disclosure statement submitted on standard forms approved by the court or adopted under section 2075 of title 28; and

(3)(A) the court may conditionally approve a disclosure statement subject to final approval after notice and a hearing;

(B) acceptances and rejections of a plan may be solicited based on a conditionally approved disclosure statement if the debtor provides adequate information to each holder of a claim or interest that is solicited, but a conditionally approved disclosure statement shall be mailed not later than 25 days before the date of the hearing on confirmation of the plan; and

(C) the hearing on the disclosure statement may be combined with the hearing on confirmation of a plan.

(g) Notwithstanding subsection (b), an acceptance or rejection of the plan may be solicited from a holder of a claim or interest if such solicitation complies with applicable nonbankruptcy law and if such holder was solicited before the commencement of the case in a manner complying with applicable nonbankruptcy law.

§ 1126. Acceptance of Plan

(a) The holder of a claim or interest allowed under section 502 of this title may accept or reject a plan. If the United States is a creditor or equity security holder, the Secretary of the Treasury may accept or reject the plan on behalf of the United States.

(b) For the purposes of subsections (c) and (d) of this section, a holder of a claim or interest that has accepted or rejected the plan before the commencement of the case under this title is deemed to have accepted or rejected such plan, as the case may be, if—

(1) the solicitation of such acceptance or rejection was in compliance with any applicable nonbankruptcy law, rule, or regulation governing the adequacy of disclosure in connection with such solicitation; or

(2) if there is not any such law, rule, or regulation, such acceptance or rejection was solicited after disclosure to such holder of adequate information, as defined in section 1125(a) of this title.

(c) A class of claims has accepted a plan if such plan has been accepted by creditors, other than any entity designated under subsection (e) of this section, that hold at least two-thirds in amount and more than one-half in number of the allowed claims of such class held by creditors, other than any entity designated under subsection (e) of this section, that have accepted or rejected such plan.

(d) A class of interests has accepted a plan if such plan has been accepted by holders of such interests, other than any entity designated under subsection (e) of this section, that hold at least two-thirds in amount of the allowed interests of such class held by holders of such interests, other than any entity designated under subsection (e) of this section, that have accepted or rejected such plan.

(e) On request of a party in interest, and after notice and a hearing, the court may designate any entity whose acceptance or rejection of such plan was not in good faith, or was not solicited or procured in good faith or in accordance with the provisions of this title.

(f) Notwithstanding any other provision of this section, a class that is not impaired under a plan, and each holder of a claim or interest of such class, are conclusively presumed to have accepted the plan, and solicitation of acceptances with respect to such class from the holders of claims or interests of such class is not required.

(g) Notwithstanding any other provision of this section, a class is deemed not to have accepted a plan if such plan provides that the claims or interests of such class do not entitle the holders of such claims or interests to receive or retain any property under the plan on account of such claims or interests.

§ 1127. Modification of Plan

(a) The proponent of a plan may modify such plan at any time before confirmation, but may not modify such plan so that such plan as modified fails to meet the requirements of sections 1122 and 1123 of this title. After the proponent of a plan files a modification of such plan with the court, the plan as modified becomes the plan.

(b) The proponent of a plan or the reorganized debtor may modify such plan at any time after confirmation of such plan and before substantial consummation of such plan, but may not modify such plan so that such plan as modified fails to meet the requirements of sections 1122 and 1123 of this title. Such plan as modified under this subsection becomes the plan only if circumstances warrant such modification and the court, after notice and a hearing, confirms such plan as modified, under section 1129 of this title.

(c) The proponent of a modification shall comply with section 1125 of this title with respect to the plan as modified.

(d) Any holder of a claim or interest that has accepted or rejected a plan is deemed to have accepted or rejected, as the case may be, such plan as modified, unless, within the time fixed by the court, such holder changes such holder's previous acceptance or rejection.

(e) If the debtor is an individual, the plan may be modified at any time after confirmation of the plan but before the completion of payments under the plan, whether or not the plan has been substantially consummated, upon request of the debtor, the trustee, the United States trustee, or the holder of an allowed unsecured claim, to—

(1) increase or reduce the amount of payments on claims of a particular class provided for by the plan;

(2) extend or reduce the time period for such payments; or

(3) alter the amount of the distribution to a creditor whose claim is provided for by the plan to the extent necessary to take account of any payment of such claim made other than under the plan.

(f)(1) Sections 1121 through 1128 and the requirements of section 1129 apply to any modification under subsection (e).

(2) The plan, as modified, shall become the plan only after there has been disclosure under section 1125 as the court may direct, notice and a hearing, and such modification is approved.

§ 1128. Confirmation Hearing

(a) After notice, the court shall hold a hearing on confirmation of a plan.

(b) A party in interest may object to confirmation of a plan.

§ 1129. Confirmation of Plan

(a) The court shall confirm a plan only if all of the following requirements are met:

(1) The plan complies with the applicable provisions of this title.

(2) The proponent of the plan complies with the applicable provisions of this title.

(3) The plan has been proposed in good faith and not by any means forbidden by law.

(4) Any payment made or to be made by the proponent, by the debtor, or by a person issuing securities or acquiring property under the plan, for services or for costs and expenses in or in connection with the case, or in connection with the plan and incident to the case, has been approved by, or is subject to the approval of, the court as reasonable.

(5)(A)(i) The proponent of the plan has disclosed the identity and affiliations of any individual proposed to serve, after confirmation of the plan, as a director, officer, or voting trustee of the debtor, an affiliate of the debtor participating in a joint plan with the debtor, or a successor to the debtor under the plan; and

(ii) the appointment to, or continuance in, such office of such individual, is consistent with the interests of creditors and equity security holders and with public policy; and

(B) the proponent of the plan has disclosed the identity of any insider that will be employed or retained by the reorganized debtor, and the nature of any compensation for such insider.

(6) Any governmental regulatory commission with jurisdiction, after confirmation of the plan, over the rates of the debtor has approved any rate change provided for in the plan, or such rate change is expressly conditioned on such approval.

(7) With respect to each impaired class of claims or interests—

(A) each holder of a claim or interest of such class—

(i) has accepted the plan; or

(ii) will receive or retain under the plan on account of such claim or interest property of a value, as of the effective date of the plan, that is not less than the amount that such holder would so receive or retain if the debtor were liquidated under chapter 7 of this title on such date; or

(B) if section 1111(b)(2) of this title applies to the claims of such class, each holder of a claim of such class will receive or retain under the plan on account of such claim property of a value, as of the effective date of the plan, that is not less than the value of such holder's interest in the estate's interest in the property that secures such claims.

(8) With respect to each class of claims or interests—

(A) such class has accepted the plan; or

(B) such class is not impaired under the plan.

(9) Except to the extent that the holder of a particular claim has agreed to a different treatment of such claim, the plan provides that—

(A) with respect to a claim of a kind specified in section 507(a)(2) or 507(a)(3) of this title, on the effective date of the plan, the holder of such claim will receive on account of such claim cash equal to the allowed amount of such claim;

(B) with respect to a class of claims of a kind specified in section 507(a)(1), 507(a)(4), 507(a)(5), 507(a)(6), or 507(a)(7) of this title, each holder of a claim of such class will receive—

(i) if such class has accepted the plan, deferred cash payments of a value, as of the effective date of the plan, equal to the allowed amount of such claim; or

(ii) if such class has not accepted the plan, cash on the effective date of the plan equal to the allowed amount of such claim;

(C) with respect to a claim of a kind specified in section 507(a)(8) of this title, the holder of such claim will receive on account of such claim regular installment payments in cash—

(i) of a total value, as of the effective date of the plan, equal to the allowed amount of such claim;

(ii) over a period ending not later than 5 years after the date of the order for relief under section 301, 302, or 303; and

(iii) in a manner not less favorable than the most favored nonpriority unsecured claim provided for by the plan (other than cash payments made to a class of creditors under section 1122(b)); and

(D) with respect to a secured claim which would otherwise meet the description of an unsecured claim of a governmental unit under section 507(a)(8), but for the secured status of that claim, the holder of that claim will receive on account of that claim, cash payments, in the same manner and over the same period, as prescribed in subparagraph (C).

(10) If a class of claims is impaired under the plan, at least one class of claims that is impaired under the plan has accepted the plan, determined without including any acceptance of the plan by any insider.

(11) Confirmation of the plan is not likely to be followed by the liquidation, or the need for further financial reorganization, of the debtor or any successor to the debtor under the plan, unless such liquidation or reorganization is proposed in the plan.

(12) All fees payable under section 1930 of title 28, as determined by the court at the hearing on confirmation of the plan, have been paid or the plan provides for the payment of all such fees on the effective date of the plan.

(13) The plan provides for the continuation after its effective date of payment of all retiree benefits, as that term is defined in section 1114 of this title, at the level established pursuant to subsection (e)(1)(B) or (g) of section 1114 of this title, at any time prior to confirmation of the plan, for the duration of the period the debtor has obligated itself to provide such benefits.

(14) If the debtor is required by a judicial or administrative order, or by statute, to pay a domestic support obligation, the debtor has paid all amounts payable under such order or such statute for such obligation that first become payable after the date of the filing of the petition.

(15) In a case in which the debtor is an individual and in which the holder of an allowed unsecured claim objects to the confirmation of the plan—

(A) the value, as of the effective date of the plan, of the property to be distributed under the plan on account of such claim is not less than the amount of such claim; or

(B) the value of the property to be distributed under the plan is not less than the projected disposable income of the debtor (as defined in section 1325(b)(2)) to be received during the 5-year period beginning on the date that the first payment is due under the plan, or during the period for which the plan provides payments, whichever is longer.

(16) All transfers of property under the plan shall be made in accordance with any applicable provisions of nonbankruptcy law that govern the transfer of property by a corporation or trust that is not a moneyed, business, or commercial corporation or trust.

(b)(1) Notwithstanding section 510(a) of this title, if all of the applicable requirements of subsection (a) of this section other than paragraph (8) are met with respect to a plan, the court, on request of the proponent of the plan, shall confirm the plan notwithstanding the requirements of such paragraph if the plan does not discriminate unfairly, and is fair and equitable, with respect to each class of claims or interests that is impaired under, and has not accepted, the plan.

(2) For the purpose of this subsection, the condition that a plan be fair and equitable with respect to a class includes the following requirements:

(A) With respect to a class of secured claims, the plan provides—

(i)(I) that the holders of such claims retain the liens securing such claims, whether the property subject to such liens is retained by the debtor or transferred to another entity, to the extent of the allowed amount of such claims; and

(II) that each holder of a claim of such class receive on account of such claim deferred cash payments totaling at least the allowed amount of such claim, of a value, as of the effective date of the plan, of at least the value of such holder's interest in the estate's interest in such property;

(ii) for the sale, subject to section 363(k) of this title, of any property that is subject to the liens securing such claims, free and clear of such liens, with such liens to attach to the proceeds of such sale, and the treatment of such liens on proceeds under clause (i) or (iii) of this subparagraph; or

(iii) for the realization by such holders of the indubitable equivalent of such claims.

(B) With respect to a class of unsecured claims—

(i) the plan provides that each holder of a claim of such class receive or retain on account of such claim property of a value, as of the effective date of the plan, equal to the allowed amount of such claim; or

(ii) the holder of any claim or interest that is junior to the claims of such class will not receive or retain under the plan on account of such junior claim or interest any property, except that in a case in which the debtor is an individual, the debtor may retain property included in the estate under section 1115, subject to the requirements of subsection (a)(14) of this section.

(C) With respect to a class of interests—

(i) the plan provides that each holder of an interest of such class receive or retain on account of such interest property of a value, as of the effective date of the plan, equal to the greatest of the allowed amount of any fixed liquidation preference to which such holder is entitled, any fixed redemption price to which such holder is entitled, or the value of such interest; or

(ii) the holder of any interest that is junior to the interests of such class will not receive or retain under the plan on account of such junior interest any property.

(c) Notwithstanding subsections (a) and (b) of this section and except as provided in section 1127(b) of this title, the court may confirm only one plan, unless the order of confirmation in the case has been revoked under section 1144 of this title. If the requirements of subsections (a) and (b) of this section are met with respect to more than one plan, the court shall consider the preferences of creditors and equity security holders in determining which plan to confirm.

(d) Notwithstanding any other provision of this section, on request of a party in interest that is a governmental unit, the court may not confirm a plan if the principal purpose of the plan is the avoidance of taxes or the avoidance of the application of section 5 of the Securities Act of 1933. In any hearing under this subsection, the governmental unit has the burden of proof on the issue of avoidance.

(e) In a small business case, the court shall confirm a plan that complies with the applicable provisions of this title and that is filed in accordance with section 1121(e) not later than 45 days after the plan is filed unless the time for confirmation is extended in accordance with section 1121(e)(3).

SUBCHAPTER III—POSTCONFIRMATION MATTERS

§ 1141. Effect of Confirmation

(a) Except as provided in subsections (d)(2) and (d)(3) of this section, the provisions of a confirmed plan bind the debtor, any entity issuing securities under the plan, any entity acquiring property under the plan, and any creditor, equity security holder, or general partner in the debtor, whether or not the claim or interest of such creditor, equity security holder, or general partner is impaired under the plan and whether or not such creditor, equity security holder, or general partner has accepted the plan.

(b) Except as otherwise provided in the plan or the order confirming the plan, the confirmation of a plan vests all of the property of the estate in the debtor.

(c) Except as provided in subsections (d)(2) and (d)(3) of this section and except as otherwise provided in the plan or in the order confirming the plan, after confirmation of a plan, the property dealt with by the plan is free and clear of all claims and interests of creditors, equity security holders, and of general partners in the debtor.

(d)(1) Except as otherwise provided in this subsection, in the plan, or in the order confirming the plan, the confirmation of a plan—

(A) discharges the debtor from any debt that arose before the date of such confirmation, and any debt of a kind specified in section 502(g), 502(h), or 502(i) of this title, whether or not—

(i) a proof of the claim based on such debt is filed or deemed filed under section 501 of this title;

(ii) such claim is allowed under section 502 of this title; or

(iii) the holder of such claim has accepted the plan; and

(B) terminates all rights and interests of equity security holders and general partners provided for by the plan.

(2) A discharge under this chapter does not discharge a debtor who is an individual from any debt excepted from discharge under section 523 of this title.

(3) The confirmation of a plan does not discharge a debtor if—

(A) the plan provides for the liquidation of all or substantially all of the property of the estate;

(B) the debtor does not engage in business after consummation of the plan; and

(C) the debtor would be denied a discharge under section 727(a) of this title if the case were a case under chapter 7 of this title.

(4) The court may approve a written waiver of discharge executed by the debtor after the order for relief under this chapter.

(5) In a case in which the debtor is an individual—

(A) unless after notice and a hearing the court orders otherwise for cause, confirmation of the plan does not discharge any debt provided for in the plan until the court grants a discharge on completion of all payments under the plan;

(B) at any time after the confirmation of the plan, and after notice and a hearing, the court may grant a discharge to the debtor who has not completed payments under the plan if—

(i) the value, as of the effective date of the plan, of property actually distributed under the plan on account of each allowed unsecured claim is not less than the amount that would have been paid on such claim if the estate of the debtor had been liquidated under chapter 7 on such date;

(ii) modification of the plan under section 1127 is not practicable; and

(iii) subparagraph (c) permits the court to grant a discharge; and

(C) the court may grant a discharge if, after notice and a hearing held not more than 10 days before the date of the entry of the order granting the discharge, the court finds that there is no reasonable cause to believe that—

(i) section 522(q)(1) may be applicable to the debtor; and

(ii) there is pending any proceeding in which the debtor may be found guilty of a felony of the kind described in section 522(q)(1)(A) or liable for a debt of the kind described in section 522(q)(1)(B); and if the requirements of subparagraph (A) or (B) are met.

(6) Notwithstanding paragraph (1), the confirmation of a plan does not discharge a debtor that is a corporation from any debt—

(A) of a kind specified in paragraph (2)(A) or (2)(B) of section 523(a) that is owed to a domestic governmental unit, or owed to a person as the result of an action filed under subchapter III of chapter 37 of title 31 or any similar State statute; or

(B) for a tax or customs duty with respect to which the debtor—

(i) made a fraudulent return; or

(ii) willfully attempted in any manner to evade or to defeat such tax or such customs duty.

§ 1142. Implementation of Plan

(a) Notwithstanding any otherwise applicable nonbankruptcy law, rule, or regulation relating to financial condition, the debtor and any entity organized or to be organized for the purpose of carrying out the plan shall carry out the plan and shall comply with any orders of the court.

(b) The court may direct the debtor and any other necessary party to execute or deliver or to join in the execution or delivery of any instrument required to effect a transfer of property dealt with by a confirmed plan, and to perform any other act, including the satisfaction of any lien, that is necessary for the consummation of the plan.

§ 1143. Distribution

If a plan requires presentment or surrender of a security or the performance of any other act as a condition to participation in distribution under the plan, such action shall be taken not later than five years after the date of the entry of the order of confirmation. Any entity that has not within such time presented or surrendered such entity's security or taken any such other action that the plan requires may not participate in distribution under the plan.

§ 1144. Revocation of an Order of Confirmation

On request of a party in interest at any time before 180 days after the date of the entry of the order of confirmation, and after notice and a hearing, the court may revoke such order if and only if such order was procured by fraud. An order under this section revoking an order of confirmation shall—

(1) contain such provisions as are necessary to protect any entity acquiring rights in good faith reliance on the order of confirmation; and

(2) revoke the discharge of the debtor.

§ 1145. Exemption from Securities Laws

(a) Except with respect to an entity that is an underwriter as defined in subsection (b) of this section, section 5 of the Securities Act of 1933 and any state or local law requiring registration for offer or sale of a security or registration or licensing of an issuer of, underwriter of, or broker or dealer in, a security do not apply to—

(1) the offer or sale under a plan of a security of the debtor, of an affiliate participating in a joint plan with the debtor, or of a successor to the debtor under the plan—

(A) in exchange for a claim against, an interest in, or a claim for an administrative expense in the case concerning, the debtor or such affiliate; or

(B) principally in such exchange and partly for cash or property;

(2) the offer of a security through any warrant, option, right to subscribe, or conversion privilege that was sold in the manner specified in paragraph (1) of this subsection, or the sale of a security upon the exercise of such a warrant, option, right, or privilege;

(3) the offer or sale, other than under a plan, of a security of an issuer other than the debtor or an affiliate, if—

(A) such security was owned by the debtor on the date of the filing of the petition;

(B) the issuer of such security is—

(i) required to file reports under section 13 or 15(d) of the Securities Exchange Act of 1934; and

(ii) in compliance with the disclosure and reporting provision of such applicable section; and

(C) such offer or sale is of securities that do not exceed—

(i) during the two-year period immediately following the date of the filing of the petition, four percent of the securities of such class outstanding on such date; and

(ii) during any 180-day period following such two-year period, one percent of the securities outstanding at the beginning of such 180-day period; or

(4) a transaction by a stockbroker in a security that is executed after a transaction of a kind specified in paragraph (1) or (2) of this subsection in such security and before the expiration of 40 days after the first date on which such security was bona fide offered to the public by the issuer or by or through an underwriter, if such stockbroker provides, at the time of or before such transaction by such stockbroker, a disclosure statement approved under section 1125 of this title, and, if the court orders, information supplementing such disclosure statement.

(b)(1) Except as provided in paragraph (2) of this subsection and except with respect to ordinary trading transactions of an entity that is not an issuer, an entity is an underwriter under section 2(a)(11) of the Securities Act of 1933, if such entity—

(A) purchases a claim against, interest in, or claim for an administrative expense in the case concerning, the debtor, if such purchase is with a view to distribution of any security received or to be received in exchange for such a claim or interest;

(B) offers to sell securities offered or sold under the plan for the holders of such securities;

(C) offers to buy securities offered or sold under the plan from the holders of such securities, if such offer to buy is—

(i) with a view to distribution of such securities; and

(ii) under an agreement made in connection with the plan, with the consummation of the plan, or with the offer or sale of securities under the plan; or

(D) is an issuer, as used in such section 2(a)(11), with respect to such securities.

(2) An entity is not an underwriter under section 2(a)(11) of the Securities Act of 1933 or under paragraph (1) of this subsection with respect to an agreement that provides only for—

(A)(i) the matching or combining of fractional interests in securities offered or sold under the plan into whole interests; or

(ii) the purchase or sale of such fractional interests from or to entities receiving such fractional interests under the plan; or

(B) the purchase or sale for such entities of such fractional or whole interests as are necessary to adjust for any remaining fractional interests after such matching.

(3) An entity other than an entity of the kind specified in paragraph (1) of this subsection is not an underwriter under section 2(a)(11) of the Securities Act of 1933 with respect to any securities offered or sold to such entity in the manner specified in subsection (a)(1) of this section.

(c) An offer or sale of securities of the kind and in the manner specified under subsection (a)(1) of this section is deemed to be a public offering.

(d) The Trust Indenture Act of 1939 does not apply to a note issued under the plan that matures not later than one year after the effective date of the plan.

§ 1146. Special Tax Provisions

(a) The issuance, transfer, or exchange of a security, or the making or delivery of an instrument of transfer under a plan confirmed under section 1129 or 1191 of this title, may not be taxed under any law imposing a stamp tax or similar tax.

(b) The court may authorize the proponent of a plan to request a determination, limited to questions of law, by a state or local governmental unit charged with responsibility for collection or determination of a tax on or measured by income, of the tax effects, under section 346 of this title and under the law imposing such tax, of the plan. In the event of an actual controversy, the court may declare such effects after the earlier of—

(1) the date on which such governmental unit responds to the request under this subsection; or

(2) 270 days after such request.

SUBCHAPTER IV—RAILROAD REORGANIZATION

§ 1161. Inapplicability of Other Sections

Sections 341, 343, 1102(a)(1), 1104, 1105, 1107, 1129(a)(7), and 1129(c) of this title do not apply in a case concerning a railroad.

§ 1162. Definition

In this subchapter, "Board" means the "Surface Transportation Board".

§ 1163. Appointment of Trustee

As soon as practicable after the order for relief the Secretary of Transportation shall submit a list of five disinterested persons that are qualified and willing to serve as trustees in the case. The United States trustee shall appoint one of such persons to serve as trustee in the case.

§ 1164. Right to Be Heard

The Board, the Department of Transportation, and any State or local commission having regulatory jurisdiction over the debtor may raise and may appear and be heard on any issue in a case under this chapter, but may not appeal from any judgment, order, or decree entered in the case.

§ 1165. Protection of the Public Interest

In applying sections 1166, 1167, 1169, 1170, 1171, 1172, 1173, and 1174 of this title, the court and the trustee shall consider the public interest in addition to the interests of the debtor, creditors, and equity security holders.

§ 1166. Effect of Subtitle IV of Title 49 and of Federal, State, or Local Regulations

Except with respect to abandonment under section 1170 of this title, or merger, modification of the financial structure of the debtor, or issuance or sale of securities under a plan, the trustee and the debtor are subject to the provisions of subtitle IV of title 49 that are applicable to railroads, and the trustee is subject to orders of any Federal, state, or local regulatory body to the same extent as the debtor would be if a petition commencing the case under this chapter had not been filed, but—

(1) any such order that would require the expenditure, or the incurring of an obligation for the expenditure, of money from the estate is not effective unless approved by the court; and

(2) the provisions of this chapter are subject to section 601(b) of the Regional Rail Reorganization Act of 1973.

§ 1167. Collective Bargaining Agreements

Notwithstanding section 365 of this title, neither the court nor the trustee may change the wages or working conditions of employees of the debtor established by a collective bargaining agreement that is subject to the Railway Labor Act except in accordance with section 6 of such Act.

§ 1168. Rolling Stock Equipment

(a)(1) The right of a secured party with a security interest in or of a lessor or conditional vendor of equipment described in paragraph (2) to take possession of such equipment in compliance with an equipment security agreement, lease, or conditional sale contract, and to enforce any of its other rights or remedies under such security agreement, lease, or conditional sale contract, to sell, lease, or otherwise retain or dispose of such equipment, is not limited or otherwise affected by any other provision of this title or by any power of the court, except that right to take possession and enforce those other rights and remedies shall be subject to section 362, if—

(A) before the date that is 60 days after the date of commencement of a case under this chapter, the trustee, subject to the court's approval, agrees to perform all obligations of the debtor under such security agreement, lease, or conditional sale contract; and

(B) any default, other than a default of a kind described in section 365(b)(2), under such security agreement, lease, or conditional sale contract—

(i) that occurs before the date of commencement of the case and is an event of default therewith is cured before the expiration of such 60-day period;

(ii) that occurs or becomes an event of default after the date of commencement of the case and before the expiration of such 60-day period is cured before the later of—

(I) the date that is 30 days after the date of the default or event of the default; or

(II) the expiration of such 60-day period; and

(iii) that occurs on or after the expiration of such 60-day period is cured in accordance with the terms of such security agreement, lease, or conditional sale contract, if cure is permitted under that agreement, lease, or conditional sale contract.

(2) The equipment described in this paragraph—

(A) is rolling stock equipment or accessories used on rolling stock equipment, including superstructures or racks, that is subject to a security interest granted by, leased to, or conditionally sold to a debtor; and

(B) includes all records and documents relating to such equipment that are required, under the terms of the security agreement, lease, or conditional sale contract, that is to be surrendered or returned by the debtor in connection with the surrender or return of such equipment.

(3) Paragraph (1) applies to a secured party, lessor, or conditional vendor acting in its own behalf or acting as trustee or otherwise in behalf of another party.

(b) The trustee and the secured party, lessor, or conditional vendor whose right to take possession is protected under subsection (a) may agree, subject to the court's approval, to extend the 60-day period specified in subsection (a)(1).

(c)(1) In any case under this chapter, the trustee shall immediately surrender and return to a secured party, lessor, or conditional vendor, described in subsection (a)(1), equipment described in subsection (a)(2), if at any time after the date of commencement of the case under this chapter such secured party, lessor, or conditional vendor is entitled pursuant to subsection (a)(1) to take possession of such equipment and makes a written demand for such possession of the trustee.

(2) At such time as the trustee is required under paragraph (1) to surrender and return equipment described in subsection (a)(2), any lease of such equipment, and any security agreement or conditional sale contract relating to such equipment, if such security agreement or conditional sale contract is an executory contract, shall be deemed rejected.

(d) With respect to equipment first placed in service on or prior to October 22, 1994, for purposes of this section—

(1) the term "lease" includes any written agreement with respect to which the lessor and the debtor, as lessee, have expressed in the agreement or in a substantially contemporaneous writing that the agreement is to be treated as a lease for Federal income tax purposes; and

(2) the term "security interest" means a purchase-money equipment security interest.

(e) With respect to equipment first placed in service after October 22, 1994, for purposes of this section, the term "rolling stock equipment" includes rolling stock equipment that is substantially rebuilt and accessories used on such equipment.

§ 1169. Effect of Rejection of Lease of Railroad Line

(a) Except as provided in subsection (b) of this section, if a lease of a line of railroad under which the debtor is the lessee is rejected under section 365 of this title, and if the trustee, within such time as the court fixes, and with the court's approval, elects not to operate the leased line, the lessor under such lease, after such approval, shall operate the line.

(b) If operation of such line by such lessor is impracticable or contrary to the public interest, the court, on request of such lessor, and after notice and a hearing, shall order the trustee to continue operation of such line for the account of such lessor until abandonment is ordered under section 1170 of this title, or until such operation is otherwise lawfully terminated, whichever occurs first.

(c) During any such operation, such lessor is deemed a carrier subject to the provisions of subtitle IV of title 49 that are applicable to railroads.

§ 1170. Abandonment of Railroad Line

(a) The court, after notice and a hearing, may authorize the abandonment of all or a portion of a railroad line if such abandonment is—

(1)(A) in the best interest of the estate; or

(B) essential to the formulation of a plan; and

(2) consistent with the public interest.

(b) If, except for the pendency of the case under this chapter, such abandonment would require approval by the Board under a law of the United States, the trustee shall initiate an appropriate application for such abandonment with the Board. The court may fix a time within which the Board shall report to the court on such application.

(c) After the court receives the report of the Board, or the expiration of the time fixed under subsection (b) of this section, whichever occurs first, the court may authorize such abandonment, after notice to the Board, the Secretary of Transportation, the trustee, any party in interest that has requested notice, any affected shipper or community, and any other entity prescribed by the court, and a hearing.

(d)(1) Enforcement of an order authorizing such abandonment shall be stayed until the time for taking an appeal has expired, or, if an appeal is timely taken, until such order has become final.

(2) If an order authorizing such abandonment is appealed, the court, on request of a party in interest, may authorize suspension of service on a line or a portion of a line pending the determination of such appeal, after notice to the Board, the Secretary of Transportation, the trustee, any party in interest that has requested notice, any affected shipper or community, and any other entity prescribed by the court, and a hearing. An appellant may not obtain a stay of the enforcement of an order authorizing such suspension by the giving of a supersedeas bond or otherwise, during the pendency of such appeal.

(e)(1) In authorizing any abandonment of a railroad line under this section, the court shall require the rail carrier to provide a fair arrangement at least as protective of the interests of employees as that established under section 11326(a) of title 49.

(2) Nothing in this subsection shall be deemed to affect the priorities or timing of payment of

employee protection which might have existed in the absence of this subsection.

§ 1171. Priority Claims

(a) There shall be paid as an administrative expense any claim of an individual or of the personal representative of a deceased individual against the debtor or the estate, for personal injury to or death of such individual arising out of the operation of the debtor or the estate, whether such claim arose before or after the commencement of the case.

(b) Any unsecured claim against the debtor that would have been entitled to priority if a receiver in equity of the property of the debtor had been appointed by a Federal court on the date of the order for relief under this title shall be entitled to the same priority in the case under this chapter.

§ 1172. Contents of Plan

(a) In addition to the provisions required or permitted under section 1123 of this title, a plan—

(1) shall specify the extent to and the means by which the debtor's rail service is proposed to be continued, and the extent to which any of the debtor's rail service is proposed to be terminated; and

(2) may include a provision for—

(A) the transfer of any or all of the operating railroad lines of the debtor to another operating railroad; or

(B) abandonment of any railroad line in accordance with section 1170 of this title.

(b) If, except for the pendency of the case under this chapter, transfer of, or operation of or over, any of the debtor's rail lines by an entity other than the debtor or a successor to the debtor under the plan would require approval by the Board under a law of the United States, then a plan may not propose such a transfer or such operation unless the proponent of the plan initiates an appropriate application for such a transfer or such operation with the Board and, within such time as the court may fix, not exceeding 180 days, the Board, with or without a hearing, as the Board may determine, and with or without modification or condition, approves such application, or does not act on such application. Any action or order of the Board approving, modifying, conditioning, or disapproving such application is subject to review by the court only under sections 706(2)(A), 706(2)(B), 706(2)(C), and 706(2)(D) of title 5.

(c)(1) In approving an application under subsection (b) of this section, the Board shall require the rail carrier to provide a fair arrangement at least as protective of the interests of employees as that established under section 11326(a) of title 49.

(2) Nothing in this subsection shall be deemed to affect the priorities or timing of payment of employee protection which might have existed in the absence of this subsection.

§ 1173. Confirmation of Plan

(a) The court shall confirm a plan if—

(1) the applicable requirements of section 1129 of this title have been met;

(2) each creditor or equity security holder will receive or retain under the plan property of a value, as of the effective date of the plan, that is not less than the value of property that each such creditor or equity security holder would so receive or retain if all of the operating railroad lines of the debtor were sold, and the proceeds of such sale, and the other property of the estate, were distributed under chapter 7 of this title on such date;

(3) in light of the debtor's past earnings and the probable prospective earnings of the reorganized debtor, there will be adequate coverage by such prospective earnings of any fixed charges, such as interest on debt, amortization of funded debt, and rent for leased railroads, provided for by the plan; and

(4) the plan is consistent with the public interest.

(b) If the requirements of subsection (a) of this section are met with respect to more than one plan, the court shall confirm the plan that is most likely to maintain adequate rail service in the public interest.

§ 1174. Liquidation

On request of a party in interest and after notice and a hearing, the court may, or, if a plan has not been confirmed under section 1173 of this title before five years after the date of the order for relief, the court shall, order the trustee to cease the debtor's operation and to collect and reduce to money all of the property of the estate in the same manner as if the case were a case under chapter 7 of this title.

SUBCHAPTER V—SMALL BUSINESS DEBTOR REORGANIZATION

§ 1181. Inapplicability of Other Sections

(a) In general.—Sections 105(d), 1101(1), 1104, 1105, 1106, 1107, 1108, 1115, 1116, 1121, 1123(a)(8), 1123(c), 1127, 1129(a)(15), 1129(b), 1129(c), 1129(e), and 1141(d)(5) of this title do not apply in a case under this subchapter.

(b) Court authority.—Unless the court for cause orders otherwise, paragraphs (1), (2), and (4) of section 1102(a) and sections 1102(b), 1103, and 1125 of this title do not apply in a case under this subchapter

(c) Special rule for discharge.—If a plan is confirmed under section 1191(b) of this title, section 1141(d) of this title shall not apply, except as provided in section 1192 of this title.

§ 1182. Definitions

In this subchapter:

(1) Debtor.—The term "debtor" means a small business debtor.

(2) Debtor in possession.—The term "debtor in possession" means the debtor, unless removed as debtor in possession under section 1185(a) of this title.

§ 1183. Trustee

(a) In general.—If the United States trustee has appointed an individual under section 586(b) of title 28 to serve as standing trustee in cases under this subchapter, and if such individual qualifies as a trustee under section 322 of this title, then that individual shall serve as trustee in any case under this subchapter. Otherwise, the United States trustee shall appoint one disinterested person to serve as trustee in the case or the United States trustee may serve as trustee in the case, as necessary.

(b) Duties.—The trustee shall—

(1) perform the duties specified in paragraphs (2), (5), (6), (7), and (9) of section 704(a) of this title;

(2) perform the duties specified in paragraphs (3), (4), and (7) of section 1106(a) of this title, if the court, for cause and on request of a party in interest, the trustee, or the United States trustee, so orders;

(3) appear and be heard at the status conference under section 1188 of this title and any hearing that concerns—

(A) the value of property subject to a lien;

(B) confirmation of a plan filed under this subchapter;

(C) modification of the plan after confirmation; or

(D) the sale of property of the estate;

(4) ensure that the debtor commences making timely payments required by a plan confirmed under this subchapter;

(5) if the debtor ceases to be a debtor in possession—

(A) perform the duties specified in section 704(a)(8) and paragraphs (1), (2), and (6) of section 1106(a) of this title; and

(B) be authorized to operate the business of the debtor;

(6) if there is a claim for a domestic support obligation with respect to the debtor, perform the duties specified in section 704(c) of this title; and

(7) facilitate the development of a consensual plan of reorganization.

(c) Termination of trustee service.—

(1) In general.—If the plan of the debtor is confirmed under section 1191(a) of this title, the service of the trustee in the case shall terminate when the plan has been substantially consummated, except that the United States trustee may reappoint a trustee as needed for performance of duties under subsection (b)(3)(C) of this section and section 1185(a) of this title.

(2) Service of notice of substantial consummation.—Not later than 14 days after the plan of the debtor is substantially consummated, the debtor shall file with the court and serve on the trustee, the United States trustee, and all parties in interest notice of such substantial consummation.

§ 1184. Rights and Powers of a Debtor in Possession

Subject to such limitations or conditions as the court may prescribe, a debtor in possession shall have all the rights, other than the right to compensation under section 330 of this title, and powers, and shall perform all functions and duties, except the duties specified in paragraphs (2), (3), and (4) of section 1106(a) of this title, of a trustee serving in a case under this chapter, including operating the business of the debtor.

§ 1185. Removal of Debtor in Possession

(a) In general.—On request of a party in interest, and after notice and a hearing, the court shall order that the debtor shall not be a debtor in possession for cause, including fraud, dishonesty, incompetence, or gross mismanagement of the affairs of the debtor, either before or after the date of commencement of the case, or for failure to perform the obligations of the debtor under a plan confirmed under this subchapter.

(b) Reinstatement.—On request of a party in interest, and after notice and a hearing, the court may reinstate the debtor in possession.

§ 1186. Property of the Estate

(a) Inclusions.—If a plan is confirmed under section 1191(b) of this title, property of the estate includes, in addition to the property specified in section 541 of this title—

(1) all property of the kind specified in that section that the debtor acquires after the date of commencement of the case but before the case is closed, dismissed, or converted to a case under chapter 7, 12, or 13 of this title, whichever occurs first; and

(2) earnings from services performed by the debtor after the date of commencement of the case but before the case is closed, dismissed, or converted to a case under chapter 7, 12, or 13 of this title, whichever occurs first.

(b) Debtor remaining in possession.—Except as provided in section 1185 of this title, a plan confirmed under this subchapter, or an order confirming a plan under this subchapter, the debtor shall remain in possession of all property of the estate.

§ 1187. Duties and Reporting Requirements of Debtors

(a) Filing requirements.—Upon electing to be a debtor under this subchapter, the debtor shall file the documents required by subparagraphs (A) and (B) of section 1116(1) of this title.

(b) Other applicable provisions.—A debtor, in addition to the duties provided in this title and as otherwise required by law, shall comply with the requirements of section 308 and paragraphs (2), (3), (4), (5), (6), and (7) of section 1116 of this title.

(c) Separate disclosure statement exemption.—If the court orders under section 1181(b) of this title that section 1125 of this title applies, section 1125(f) of this title shall apply.

§ 1188. Status Conference

(a) In general.—Except as provided in subsection (b), not later than 60 days after the entry of the order for relief under this chapter, the court shall hold a status conference to further the expeditious and economical resolution of a case under this subchapter.

(b) Exception.—The court may extend the period of time for holding a status conference under subsection (a) if the need for an extension is attributable to circumstances for which the debtor should not justly be held accountable.

(c) Report.—Not later than 14 days before the date of the status conference under subsection (a), the debtor shall file with the court and serve on the trustee and all parties in interest a report that details the efforts the debtor has undertaken and will undertake to attain a consensual plan of reorganization.

§ 1189. Filing of the Plan

(a) Who may file a plan.—Only the debtor may file a plan under this subchapter.

(b) Deadline.—The debtor shall file a plan not later than 90 days after the order for relief under this chapter, except that the court may extend the period if the need for the extension is attributable to circumstances for which the debtor should not justly be held accountable.

§ 1190. Contents of Plan

A plan filed under this subchapter—

(1) shall include—

(A) a brief history of the business operations of the debtor;

(B) a liquidation analysis; and

(C) projections with respect to the ability of the debtor to make payments under the proposed plan of reorganization;

(2) shall provide for the submission of all or such portion of the future earnings or other future income of the debtor to the supervision and control of the trustee as is necessary for the execution of the plan; and

(3) notwithstanding section 1123(b)(5) of this title, may modify the rights of the holder of a claim secured only by a security interest in real property that is the principal residence of the debtor if the new value received in connection with the granting of the security interest was—

(A) not used primarily to acquire the real property; and

(B) used primarily in connection with the small business of the debtor.

§ 1191. Confirmation of Plan

(a) Terms.—The court shall confirm a plan under this subchapter only if all of the requirements of section 1129(a), other than paragraph (15) of that section, of this title are met.

(b) Exception.—Notwithstanding section 510(a) of this title, if all of the applicable requirements of section 1129(a) of this title, other than paragraphs (8), (10), and (15) of that section, are met with respect to a plan, the court, on request of the debtor, shall confirm the plan notwithstanding the requirements of such paragraphs if the plan does not discriminate unfairly, and is fair and equitable, with respect to each class of claims or interests that is impaired under, and has not accepted, the plan.

(c) Rule of construction.—For purposes of this section, the condition that a plan be fair and equitable with respect to each class of claims or interests includes the following requirements:

(1) With respect to a class of secured claims, the plan meets the requirements of section 1129(b)(2)(A) of this title.

(2) As of the effective date of the plan—

(A) the plan provides that all of the projected disposable income of the debtor to be received in the 3-year period, or such longer period not to exceed 5 years as the court may fix, beginning on the date that the first payment is due under the plan will be applied to make payments under the plan; or

(B) the value of the property to be distributed under the plan in the 3-year period, or such longer period not to exceed 5 years as the court may fix, beginning on the date on which the first distribution is due under the plan is not less than the projected disposable income of the debtor.

(3)(A)The debtor will be able to make all payments under the plan; or

(B)(i) there is a reasonable likelihood that the debtor will be able to make all payments under the plan; and

(ii) the plan provides appropriate remedies, which may include the liquidation of nonexempt assets, to protect the holders of claims or interests in the event that the payments are not made.

(d) Disposable income.—For purposes of this section, the term "disposable income" means the income that is received by the debtor and that is not reasonably necessary to be expended—

(1) for—

(A) the maintenance or support of the debtor or a dependent of the debtor; or

(B) a domestic support obligation that first becomes payable after the date of the filing of the petition; or

(2) for the payment of expenditures necessary for the continuation, preservation, or operation of the business of the debtor.

(e) Special rule.—Notwithstanding section 1129(a)(9)(A) of this title, a plan that provides for the payment through the plan of a claim of a kind specified in paragraph (2) or (3) of section 507(a) of this title may be confirmed under subsection (b) of this section.

§ 1192. Discharge

If the plan of the debtor is confirmed under section 1191(b) of this title, as soon as practicable after completion by the debtor of all payments due within the first 3 years of the plan, or such longer period not to exceed 5 years as the court may fix, unless the court approves a written waiver of discharge executed by the debtor after the order for relief under this chapter, the court shall grant the debtor a discharge of all debts provided in section 1141(d)(1)(A) of this title, and all other debts allowed under section 503 of this title and provided for in the plan, except any debt—

(1) on which the last payment is due after the first 3 years of the plan, or such other time not to exceed 5 years fixed by the court; or

(2) of the kind specified in section 523(a) of this title.

§ 1193. Modification of Plan

(a) Modification before confirmation.—The debtor may modify a plan at any time before confirmation, but may not modify the plan so that the plan as modified fails to meet the requirements of sections 1122 and 1123 of this title, with the exception of subsection (a)(8) of such section 1123. After the modification is filed with the court, the plan as modified becomes the plan.

(b) Modification after confirmation.—If a plan has been confirmed under section 1191(a) of this title, the debtor may modify the plan at any time after confirmation of the plan and before substantial consummation of the plan, but may not modify the plan so that the plan as modified fails to meet the requirements of sections 1122 and 1123 of this title, with the exception of subsection (a)(8) of such section 1123. The plan, as modified under this subsection, becomes the plan only if circumstances warrant the modification and the court, after notice and a hearing, confirms the plan as modified under section 1191(a) of this title.

(c) Certain other modifications.—If a plan has been confirmed under section 1191(b) of this title, the debtor may modify the plan at any time within 3 years, or such longer time not to exceed 5 years, as fixed by the court, but may not modify the plan so that the plan as modified fails to meet the requirements of section 1191(b) of this title. The plan as modified under this subsection becomes the plan only if circumstances warrant such modification and the court, after notice and a hearing, confirms such plan, as modified, under section 1191(b) of this title.

(d) Holders of a claim or interest.—If a plan has been confirmed under section 1191(a) of this title, any holder of a claim or interest that has accepted or rejected the plan is deemed to have accepted or rejected, as the case may be, the plan as modified, unless, within the time fixed by the court, such holder changes the previous acceptance or rejection of the holder.

§ 1194. Payments

(a) Retention and distribution by trustee.—Payments and funds received by the trustee shall be retained by the trustee until confirmation or denial of confirmation of a plan. If a plan is confirmed, the trustee shall distribute any such payment in accordance with the plan. If a plan is not confirmed, the trustee shall return any such payments to the debtor after deducting—

(1) any unpaid claim allowed under section 503(b) of this title;

(2) any payment made for the purpose of providing adequate protection of an interest in property due to the holder of a secured claim; and

(3) any fee owing to the trustee.

(b) Other plans.—If a plan is confirmed under section 1191(b) of this title, except as otherwise provided in the plan or in the order confirming the plan, the trustee shall make payments to creditors under the plan.

(c) Payments prior to confirmation.—Prior to confirmation of a plan, the court, after notice and a hearing, may authorize the trustee to make payments to the holder of a secured claim for the purpose of providing adequate protection of an interest in property.

§ 1195. Transactions with Professionals

Notwithstanding section 327(a) of this title, a person is not disqualified for employment under section 327 of this title, by a debtor solely because that person holds a claim of less than $10,000 that arose prior to commencement of the case.

CHAPTER 12. ADJUSTMENT OF DEBTS OF A FAMILY FARMER OR FISHERMAN WITH REGULAR INCOME

SUBCHAPTER I—OFFICERS, ADMINISTRATION, AND THE ESTATE

Section

SUBCHAPTER II—THE PLAN

Section

SUBCHAPTER I—OFFICERS, ADMINISTRATION, AND THE ESTATE

§ 1201. Stay of Action Against Codebtor

(a) Except as provided in subsections (b) and (c) of this section, after the order for relief under this chapter, a creditor may not act, or commence or continue any civil action, to collect all or any part of a consumer debt of the debtor from any individual that is liable on such debt with the debtor, or that secured such debt, unless—

(1) such individual became liable on or secured such debt in the ordinary course of such individual's business; or

(2) the case is closed, dismissed, or converted to a case under chapter 7 of this title.

(b) A creditor may present a negotiable instrument, and may give notice of dishonor of such an instrument.

(c) On request of a party in interest and after notice and a hearing, the court shall grant relief from the stay provided by subsection (a) of this section with respect to a creditor, to the extent that—

(1) as between the debtor and the individual protected under subsection (a) of this section, such individual received the consideration for the claim held by such creditor;

(2) the plan filed by the debtor proposes not to pay such claim; or

(3) such creditor's interest would be irreparably harmed by continuation of such stay.

(d) Twenty days after the filing of a request under subsection (c)(2) of this section for relief from the stay provided by subsection (a) of this section, such stay is terminated with respect to the party in interest making such request, unless the debtor or any individual that is liable on such debt with the debtor files and serves upon such party in interest a written objection to the taking of the proposed action.

§ 1202. Trustee

(a) If the United States trustee has appointed an individual under section 586(b) of title 28 to serve as standing trustee in cases under this chapter and if such individual qualifies as a trustee under section 322 of this title, then such individual shall serve as trustee in any case filed under this chapter. Otherwise, the United States trustee shall appoint one disinterested person to serve as trustee in the case or the United States trustee may serve as trustee in the case if necessary.

(b) The trustee shall—

(1) perform the duties specified in sections 704(a)(2), 704(a)(3), 704(a)(5), 704(a)(6), 704(a)(7), and 704(a)(9) of this title;

(2) perform the duties specified in section 1106(a)(3) and 1106(a)(4) of this title if the court, for cause and on request of a party in interest, the trustee, or the United States trustee, so orders;

(3) appear and be heard at any hearing that concerns—

(A) the value of property subject to a lien;

(B) confirmation of a plan;

(C) modification of the plan after confirmation; or

(D) the sale of property of the estate;

(4) ensure that the debtor commences making timely payments required by a confirmed plan;

(5) if the debtor ceases to be a debtor in possession, perform the duties specified in sections 704(a)(8), 1106(a)(1), 1106(a)(2), 1106(a)(6), 1106(a)(7), and 1203; and

(6) if with respect to the debtor there is a claim for a domestic support obligation, provide the applicable notice specified in subsection (c).

(c)(1) In a case described in subsection (b)(6) to which subsection (b)(6) applies, the trustee shall—

(A)(i) provide written notice to the holder of the claim described in subsection (b)(6) of such claim and of the right of such holder to use the services of the State child support enforcement agency established under sections 464 and 466 of the Social Security Act for the State in which such holder resides, for assistance in collecting child support during and after the case under this title; and

(ii) include in the notice provided under clause (i) the address and telephone number of such State child support enforcement agency;

(B)(i) provide written notice to such State child support enforcement agency of such claim; and

(ii) include in the notice provided under clause (i) the name, address, and telephone number of such holder; and

(C) at such time as the debtor is granted a discharge under section 1228, provide written notice to such holder and to such State child support enforcement agency of—

(i) the granting of the discharge;

(ii) the last recent known address of the debtor;

(iii) the last recent known name and address of the debtor's employer; and

(iv) the name of each creditor that holds a claim that—

(I) is not discharged under paragraph (2), (4), or (14A) of section 523(a); or

(II) was reaffirmed by the debtor under section 524(c).

(2)(A) The holder of a claim described in subsection (b)(6) or the State child support enforcement agency of the State in which such holder resides may request from a creditor described in paragraph (1)(C)(iv) the last known address of the debtor.

(B) Notwithstanding any other provision of law, a creditor that makes a disclosure of a last known address of a debtor in connection with a request made under subparagraph (A) shall not be liable by reason of making that disclosure.

§ 1203. Rights and Powers of Debtor

Subject to such limitations as the court may prescribe, a debtor in possession shall have all the rights, other than the right to compensation under section 330, and powers, and shall perform all the functions and duties, except the duties specified in paragraphs (3) and (4) of section 1106(a), of a trustee serving in a case under chapter 11, including operating the debtor's farm or commercial fishing operation.

§ 1204. Removal of Debtor as Debtor in Possession

(a) On request of a party in interest, and after notice and a hearing, the court shall order that the debtor shall not be a debtor in possession for cause, including fraud, dishonesty, incompetence, or gross mismanagement of the affairs of the debtor, either before or after the commencement of the case.

(b) On request of a party in interest, and after notice and a hearing, the court may reinstate the debtor in possession.

§ 1205. Adequate Protection

(a) Section 361 does not apply in a case under this chapter.

(b) In a case under this chapter, when adequate protection is required under section 362, 363, or 364 of this title of an interest of an entity in property, such adequate protection may be provided by—

(1) requiring the trustee to make a cash payment or periodic cash payments to such entity, to the extent that the stay under section 362 of this title, use, sale, or lease under section 363 of this title, or any grant of a lien under section 364 of this title results in a decrease in the value of property securing a claim or of an entity's ownership interest in property;

(2) providing to such entity an additional or replacement lien to the extent that such stay, use, sale, lease, or grant results in a decrease in the value of property securing a claim or of an entity's ownership interest in property;

(3) paying to such entity for the use of farmland the reasonable rent customary in the community where the property is located, based upon the rental value, net income, and earning capacity of the property; or

(4) granting such other relief, other than entitling such entity to compensation allowable under section 503(b)(1) of this title as an administrative expense, as will adequately protect the value of property securing a claim or of such entity's ownership interest in property.

§ 1206. Sales Free of Interests

After notice and a hearing, in addition to the authorization contained in section 363(f), the trustee in a case under this chapter may sell property under section 363(b) and (c) free and clear of any interest in such property of an entity other than the estate if the property is farmland, farm equipment, or property used to carry out a commercial fishing operation (including a commercial fishing vessel), except that the proceeds of such sale shall be subject to such interest.

§ 1207. Property of the Estate

(a) Property of the estate includes, in addition to the property specified in section 541 of this title—

(1) all property of the kind specified in such section that the debtor acquires after the commencement of the case but before the case is closed, dismissed, or converted to a case under chapter 7 of this title, whichever occurs first; and

(2) earnings from services performed by the debtor after the commencement of the case but before the case is closed, dismissed, or converted to a case under chapter 7 of this title, whichever occurs first.

(b) Except as provided in section 1204, a confirmed plan, or an order confirming a plan, the debtor shall remain in possession of all property of the estate.

§ 1208. Conversion or Dismissal

(a) The debtor may convert a case under this chapter to a case under chapter 7 of this title at any time. Any waiver of the right to convert under this subsection is unenforceable.

(b) On request of the debtor at any time, if the case has not been converted under section 706 or 1112 of this title, the court shall dismiss a case under this chapter. Any waiver of the right to dismiss under this subsection is unenforceable.

(c) On request of a party in interest, and after notice and a hearing, the court may dismiss a case under this chapter for cause, including—

(1) unreasonable delay, or gross mismanagement, by the debtor that is prejudicial to creditors;

(2) nonpayment of any fees and charges required under chapter 123 of title 28;

(3) failure to file a plan timely under section 1221 of this title;

(4) failure to commence making timely payments required by a confirmed plan;

(5) denial of confirmation of a plan under section 1225 of this title and denial of a request made for additional time for filing another plan or a modification of a plan;

(6) material default by the debtor with respect to a term of a confirmed plan;

(7) revocation of the order of confirmation under section 1230 of this title, and denial of confirmation of a modified plan under section 1229 of this title;

(8) termination of a confirmed plan by reason of the occurrence of a condition specified in the plan;

(9) continuing loss to or diminution of the estate and absence of a reasonable likelihood of rehabilitation; and

(10) failure of the debtor to pay any domestic support obligation that first becomes payable after the date of the filing of the petition.

(d) On request of a party in interest, and after notice and a hearing, the court may dismiss a case under this chapter or convert a case under this chapter to a case under chapter 7 of this title upon a showing that the debtor has committed fraud in connection with the case.

(e) Notwithstanding any other provision of this section, a case may not be converted to a case under another chapter of this title unless the debtor may be a debtor under such chapter.

SUBCHAPTER II—THE PLAN

§ 1221. Filing of Plan

The debtor shall file a plan not later than 90 days after the order for relief under this chapter, except that the court may extend such period if the need for an extension is attributable to circumstances for which the debtor should not justly be held accountable.

§ 1222. Contents of Plan

(a) The plan shall—

(1) provide for the submission of all or such portion of future earnings or other future income of the debtor to the supervision and control of the trustee as is necessary for the execution of the plan;

(2) provide for the full payment, in deferred cash payments, of all claims entitled to priority under section 507, unless—

(A) the claim is a claim owed to a governmental unit that arises as a result of the sale, transfer, exchange, or other disposition of any farm asset used in the debtor's farming operation, in which case the claim shall be treated as an unsecured claim that is not entitled to priority under section 507, but the debt shall be treated in such manner only if the debtor receives a discharge; or

(B) the holder of a particular claim agrees to a different treatment of that claim;

(3) if the plan classifies claims and interests, provide the same treatment for each claim or interest within a particular class unless the holder of a particular claim or interest agrees to less favorable treatment; and

(4) notwithstanding any other provision of this section, a plan may provide for less than full payment of all amounts owed for a claim entitled to priority under section 507(a)(1)(B) only if the plan provides that all of the debtor's projected disposable income for a 5-year period beginning on the date that the first payment is due under the plan will be applied to make payments under the plan; and

(5) subject to section 1232, provide for the treatment of any claim by a governmental unit of a kind described in section 1232(a).

(b) Subject to subsections (a) and (c) of this section, the plan may—

(1) designate a class or classes of unsecured claims, as provided in section 1122 of this title, but may not discriminate unfairly against any class so designated; however, such plan may treat claims for a consumer debt of the debtor if an individual is liable on such consumer debt with the debtor differently than other unsecured claims;

(2) modify the rights of holders of secured claims, or of holders of unsecured claims, or leave unaffected the rights of holders of any class of claims;

(3) provide for the curing or waiving of any default;

(4) provide for payments on any unsecured claim to be made concurrently with payments on any secured claim or any other unsecured claim;

(5) provide for the curing of any default within a reasonable time and maintenance of payments while the case is pending on any unsecured claim or secured claim on which the last payment is due after the date on which the final payment under the plan is due;

(6) subject to section 365 of this title, provide for the assumption, rejection, or assignment of any executory contract or unexpired lease of the debtor not previously rejected under such section;

(7) provide for the payment of all or part of a claim against the debtor from property of the estate or property of the debtor;

(8) provide for the sale of all or any part of the property of the estate or the distribution of all or any part of the property of the estate among those having an interest in such property;

(9) provide for payment of allowed secured claims consistent with section 1225(a)(5) of this title, over a period exceeding the period permitted under section 1222(c);

(10) provide for the vesting of property of the estate, on confirmation of the plan or at a later time, in the debtor or in any other entity;

(11) provide for the payment of interest accruing after the date of the filing of the petition on unsecured claims that are nondischargeable under section 1228(a), except that such interest may be paid only to the extent that the debtor has disposable income available to pay such interest after making provision for full payment of all allowed claims; and

(12) include any other appropriate provision not inconsistent with this title.

(c) Except as provided in subsections (b)(5) and (b)(9), the plan may not provide for payments over a period that is longer than three years unless the court for cause approves a longer period, but the court may not approve a period that is longer than five years.

(d) Notwithstanding subsection (b)(2) of this section and sections 506(b) and 1225(a)(5) of this title, if it is proposed in a plan to cure a default, the amount necessary to cure the default, shall be determined in accordance with the underlying agreement and applicable nonbankruptcy law.

§ 1223. Modification of Plan Before Confirmation

(a) The debtor may modify the plan at any time before confirmation, but may not modify the plan so that the plan as modified fails to meet the requirements of section 1222 of this title.

(b) After the debtor files a modification under this section, the plan as modified becomes the plan.

(c) Any holder of a secured claim that has accepted or rejected the plan is deemed to have accepted or rejected, as the case may be, the plan as modified, unless the modification provides for a change in the rights of such holder from what such rights were under the plan before modification, and such holder changes such holder's previous acceptance or rejection.

§ 1224. Confirmation Hearing

After expedited notice, the court shall hold a hearing on confirmation of the plan. A party in interest, the trustee, or the United States trustee may object to the confirmation of the plan. Except for cause, the hearing shall be concluded not later than 45 days after the filing of the plan.

§ 1225. Confirmation of Plan

(a) Except as provided in subsection (b), the court shall confirm a plan if—

(1) the plan complies with the provisions of this chapter and with the other applicable provisions of this title;

(2) any fee, charge, or amount required under chapter 123 of title 28, or by the plan, to be paid before confirmation, has been paid;

(3) the plan has been proposed in good faith and not by any means forbidden by law;

(4) the value, as of the effective date of the plan, of property to be distributed under the plan on account of each allowed unsecured claim is not less than the amount that would be paid on such claim if the estate of the debtor were liquidated under chapter 7 of this title on such date;

(5) with respect to each allowed secured claim provided for by the plan—

(A) the holder of such claim has accepted the plan;

(B)(i) the plan provides that the holder of such claim retain the lien securing such claim; and

(ii) the value, as of the effective date of the plan, of property to be distributed by the trustee or the debtor under the plan on account of such claim is not less than the allowed amount of such claim; or

(C) the debtor surrenders the property securing such claim to such holder;

(6) the debtor will be able to make all payments under the plan and to comply with the plan; and

(7) the debtor has paid all amounts that are required to be paid under a domestic support obligation and that first become payable after the date of the filing of the petition if the debtor is required by a judicial or administrative order, or by statute, to pay such domestic support obligation.

(b)(1) If the trustee or the holder of an allowed unsecured claim objects to the confirmation of the plan, then the court may not approve the plan unless, as of the effective date of the plan—

(A) the value of the property to be distributed under the plan on account of such claim is not less than the amount of such claim;

(B) the plan provides that all of the debtor's projected disposable income to be received in the three-year period, or such longer period as the court may approve under section 1222(c), beginning on the date that the first payment is due under the plan will be applied to make payments under the plan; or

(C) the value of the property to be distributed under the plan in the 3-year period, or such longer period as the court may approve under section 1222(c), beginning on the date that the first distribution is due under the plan is not less than the debtor's projected disposable income for such period.

(2) For purposes of this subsection, "disposable income" means income which is received by the debtor and which is not reasonably necessary to be expended—

(A) for the maintenance or support of the debtor or a dependent of the debtor or for a domestic support obligation that first becomes payable after the date of the filing of the petition; or

(B) for the payment of expenditures necessary for the continuation, preservation, and operation of the debtor's business.

(c) After confirmation of a plan, the court may order any entity from whom the debtor receives income to pay all or any part of such income to the trustee.

§ 1226. Payments

(a) Payments and funds received by the trustee shall be retained by the trustee until confirmation or denial of confirmation of a plan. If a plan is confirmed, the trustee shall distribute any such payment in accordance with the plan. If a plan is not confirmed, the trustee shall return any such payments to the debtor, after deducting—

(1) any unpaid claim allowed under section 503(b) of this title; and

(2) if a standing trustee is serving in the case, the percentage fee fixed for such standing trustee.

(b) Before or at the time of each payment to creditors under the plan, there shall be paid—

(1) any unpaid claim of the kind specified in section 507(a)(2) of this title; and

(2) if a standing trustee appointed under section 1202(c) of this title is serving in the case, the percentage fee fixed for such standing trustee under section 1202(d) of this title.

(c) Except as otherwise provided in the plan or in the order confirming the plan, the trustee shall make payments to creditors under the plan.

§ 1227. Effect of Confirmation

(a) Except as provided in section 1228(a) of this title, the provisions of a confirmed plan bind the debtor, each creditor, each equity security holder, and each general partner in the debtor, whether or not the claim of such creditor, such equity security holder, or such general partner in the debtor is provided for by the plan, and whether or not such creditor, such equity security holder, or such general partner in the debtor has objected to, has accepted, or has rejected the plan.

(b) Except as otherwise provided in the plan or the order confirming the plan, the confirmation of a plan vests all of the property of the estate in the debtor.

(c) Except as provided in section 1228(a) of this title and except as otherwise provided in the plan or in the order confirming the plan, the property vesting in the debtor under subsection (b) of this section is free and clear of any claim or interest of any creditor provided for by the plan.

§ 1228. Discharge

(a) Subject to subsection (d), as soon as practicable after completion by the debtor of all payments under the plan, and in the case of a debtor who is required by a judicial or administrative order, or by statute, to pay a domestic support obligation, after such debtor certifies that all amounts payable under such order or such statute that are due on or before the date of the certification (including amounts due before the petition was filed, but only to the extent provided for by the plan) have been paid, other than payments to holders of allowed claims provided for under section 1222(b)(5) or 1222(b)(9) of this title, unless the court approves a written waiver of discharge executed by the debtor after the order for relief under this chapter, the court shall grant the debtor a discharge of all debts provided for by the plan allowed under section 503 of this title or disallowed under section 502 of this title, except any debt—

(1) provided for under section 1222(b)(5) or 1222(b)(9) of this title; or

(2) of the kind specified in section 523(a) of this title.

(b) Subject to subsection (d), at any time after the confirmation of the plan and after notice and a hearing, the court may grant a discharge to a debtor that has not completed payments under the plan only if—

(1) the debtor's failure to complete such payments is due to circumstances for which the debtor should not justly be held accountable;

(2) the value, as of the effective date of the plan, of property actually distributed under the plan on account of each allowed unsecured claim is not less than the amount that would have been paid on such claim if the estate of the debtor had been liquidated under chapter 7 of this title on such date; and

(3) modification of the plan under section 1229 of this title is not practicable.

(c) A discharge granted under subsection (b) of this section discharges the debtor from all unsecured debts provided for by the plan or disallowed under section 502 of this title, except any debt—

(1) provided for under section 1222(b)(5) or 1222(b)(9) of this title; or

(2) of a kind specified in section 523(a) of this title.

(d) On request of a party in interest before one year after a discharge under this section is granted, and after notice and a hearing, the court may revoke such discharge only if—

(1) such discharge was obtained by the debtor through fraud; and

(2) the requesting party did not know of such fraud until after such discharge was granted.

(e) After the debtor is granted a discharge, the court shall terminate the services of any trustee serving in the case.

(f) The court may not grant a discharge under this chapter unless the court after notice and a hearing held not more than 10 days before the date of the entry of the order granting the discharge finds that there is no reasonable cause to believe that—

(1) section 522(q)(1) may be applicable to the debtor; and

(2) there is pending any proceeding in which the debtor may be found guilty of a felony of the kind described in section 522(q)(1)(A) or liable for a debt of the kind described in section 522(q)(1)(B).

§ 1229. Modification of Plan After Confirmation

(a) At any time after confirmation of the plan but before the completion of payments under such plan, the plan may be modified, on request of the debtor, the trustee, or the holder of an allowed unsecured claim, to—

(1) increase or reduce the amount of payments on claims of a particular class provided for by the plan;

(2) extend or reduce the time for such payments; or

(3) alter the amount of the distribution to a creditor whose claim is provided for by the plan to the extent necessary to take account of any payment of such claim other than under the plan.

(b)(1) Sections 1222(a), 1222(b), and 1223(c) of this title and the requirements of section 1225(a) of this title apply to any modification under subsection (a) of this section.

(2) The plan as modified becomes the plan unless, after notice and a hearing, such modification is disapproved.

(c) A plan modified under this section may not provide for payments over a period that expires after three years after the time that the first payment under the original confirmed plan was due, unless the court, for cause, approves a longer period, but the court may not approve a period that expires after five years after such time.

(d) A plan may not be modified under this section—

(1) to increase the amount of any payment due before the plan as modified becomes the plan;

(2) by anyone except the debtor, based on an increase in the debtor's disposable income, to increase the amount of payments to unsecured creditors required for a particular month so that the aggregate of such payments exceeds the debtor's disposable income for such month; or

(3) in the last year of the plan by anyone except the debtor, to require payments that would leave the debtor with insufficient funds to carry on the farming operation after the plan is completed.

§ 1230. Revocation of an Order of Confirmation

(a) On request of a party in interest at any time within 180 days after the date of the entry of an order of confirmation under section 1225 of this title, and after notice and a hearing, the court may revoke such order if such order was procured by fraud.

(b) If the court revokes an order of confirmation under subsection (a) of this section, the court shall dispose of the case under section 1207 of this title, unless, within the time fixed by the court, the debtor proposes and the court confirms a modification of the plan under section 1229 of this title.

§ 1231. Special Tax Provisions

(a) The issuance, transfer, or exchange of a security, or the making or delivery of an instrument of transfer under a plan confirmed under section 1225 of this title, may not be taxed under any law imposing a stamp tax or similar tax.

(b) The court may authorize the proponent of a plan to request a determination, limited to questions of law, by any governmental unit charged with responsibility for collection or determination of a tax on or measured by income, of the tax effects, under section 346 of this title and under the law imposing such tax, of the plan. In the event of an actual controversy, the court may declare such effects after the earlier of—

(1) the date on which such governmental unit responds to the request under this subsection; or

(2) 270 days after such request.

CHAPTER 13. ADJUSTMENT OF DEBTS OF AN INDIVIDUAL WITH REGULAR INCOME

SUBCHAPTER I—OFFICERS, ADMINISTRATION, AND THE ESTATE

Section

SUBCHAPTER II—THE PLAN

Section

SUBCHAPTER I—OFFICERS, ADMINISTRATION, AND THE ESTATE

§ 1301. Stay of Action Against Codebtor

(a) Except as provided in subsections (b) and (c) of this section, after the order for relief under this chapter, a creditor may not act, or commence or continue any civil action, to collect all or any part of a consumer debt of the debtor from any individual that is liable on such debt with the debtor, or that secured such debt, unless—

(1) such individual became liable on or secured such debt in the ordinary course of such individual's business; or

(2) the case is closed, dismissed, or converted to a case under chapter 7 or 11 of this title.

(b) A creditor may present a negotiable instrument, and may give notice of dishonor of such an instrument.

(c) On request of a party in interest and after notice and a hearing, the court shall grant relief from the stay provided by subsection (a) of this section with respect to a creditor, to the extent that—

(1) as between the debtor and the individual protected under subsection (a) of this section, such individual received the consideration for the claim held by such creditor;

(2) the plan filed by the debtor proposes not to pay such claim; or

(3) such creditor's interest would be irreparably harmed by continuation of such stay.

(d) Twenty days after the filing of a request under subsection (c)(2) of this section for relief from the stay provided by subsection (a) of this section, such stay is terminated with respect to the party in interest making such request, unless the debtor or any individual that is liable on such debt with the debtor files and serves upon such party in interest a written objection to the taking of the proposed action.

§ 1302. Trustee

(a) If the United States trustee appoints an individual under section 586(b) of title 28 to serve as standing trustee in cases under this chapter and if such individual qualifies under section 322 of this title, then such individual shall serve as trustee in the case. Otherwise, the United States trustee shall appoint one disinterested person to serve as trustee in the case or the United States trustee may serve as a trustee in the case.

(b) The trustee shall—

(1) perform the duties specified in sections 704(a)(2), 704(a)(3), 704(a)(4), 704(a)(5), 704(a)(6), 704(a)(7), and 704(a)(9) of this title;

(2) appear and be heard at any hearing that concerns—

(A) the value of property subject to a lien;

(B) confirmation of a plan; or

(C) modification of the plan after confirmation;

(3) dispose of, under regulations issued by the Director of the Administrative Office of the United States Courts, moneys received or to be received in a case under chapter XIII of the Bankruptcy Act;

(4) advise, other than on legal matters, and assist the debtor in performance under the plan;

(5) ensure that the debtor commences making timely payments under section 1326 of this title; and

(6) if with respect to the debtor there is a claim for a domestic support obligation, provide the applicable notice specified in subsection (d).

(c) If the debtor is engaged in business, then in addition to the duties specified in subsection (b) of this section, the trustee shall perform the duties specified in sections 1106(a)(3) and 1106(a)(4) of this title.

(d)(1) In a case described in subsection (b)(6) to which subsection (b)(6) applies, the trustee shall—

(A)(i) provide written notice to the holder of the claim described in subsection (b)(6) of such claim and of the right of such holder to use the services of the State child support enforcement agency established under sections 464 and 466 of the Social Security Act for the State in which such holder resides, for assistance in collecting child support during and after the case under this title; and

(ii) include in the notice provided under clause (i) the address and telephone number of such State child support enforcement agency;

(B)(i) provide written notice to such State child support enforcement agency of such claim; and

(ii) include in the notice provided under clause (i) the name, address, and telephone number of such holder; and

(C) at such time as the debtor is granted a discharge under section 1328, provide written notice to such holder and to such State child support enforcement agency of—

(i) the granting of the discharge;

(ii) the last recent known address of the debtor;

(iii) the last recent known name and address of the debtor's employer; and

(iv) the name of each creditor that holds a claim that—

(I) is not discharged under paragraph (2) or (4) of section 523(a); or

(II) was reaffirmed by the debtor under section 524(c).

(2)(A) The holder of a claim described in subsection (b)(6) or the State child support enforcement agency of the State in which such holder resides may request from a creditor described in paragraph (1)(C)(iv) the last known address of the debtor.

(B) Notwithstanding any other provision of law, a creditor that makes a disclosure of a last known address of a debtor in connection with a request made under subparagraph (A) shall not be liable by reason of making that disclosure.

§ 1303. Rights and Powers of Debtor

Subject to any limitations on a trustee under this chapter, the debtor shall have, exclusive of the trustee, the rights and powers of a trustee under sections 363(b), 363(d), 363(e), 363(f), and 363(l), of this title.

§ 1304. Debtor Engaged in Business

(a) A debtor that is self-employed and incurs trade credit in the production of income from such employment is engaged in business.

(b) Unless the court orders otherwise, a debtor engaged in business may operate the business of the debtor and, subject to any limitations on a trustee under sections 363(c) and 364 of this title and to such limitations or conditions as the court prescribes, shall have, exclusive of the trustee, the rights and powers of the trustee under such sections.

(c) A debtor engaged in business shall perform the duties of the trustee specified in section 704(a)(8) of this title.

§ 1305. Filing and Allowance of Postpetition Claims

(a) A proof of claim may be filed by any entity that holds a claim against the debtor—

(1) for taxes that become payable to a governmental unit while the case is pending; or

(2) that is a consumer debt, that arises after the date of the order for relief under this chapter, and that is for property or services necessary for the debtor's performance under the plan.

(b) Except as provided in subsection (c) of this section, a claim filed under subsection (a) of this section shall be allowed or disallowed under section 502 of this title, but shall be determined as of the date such claim arises, and shall be allowed under section 502(a), 502(b), or 502(c) of this title, or disallowed under section 502(d) or 502(e) of this title, the same as if such claim had arisen before the date of the filing of the petition.

(c) A claim filed under subsection (a)(2) of this section shall be disallowed if the holder of such claim knew or should have known that prior approval by the trustee of the debtor's incurring the obligation was practicable and was not obtained.

§ 1306. Property of the Estate

(a) Property of the estate includes, in addition to the property specified in section 541 of this title—

(1) all property of the kind specified in such section that the debtor acquires after the commencement of the case but before the case is closed, dismissed, or converted to a case under chapter 7, 11, or 12 of this title, whichever occurs first; and

(2) earnings from services performed by the debtor after the commencement of the case but before the case is closed, dismissed, or converted to a case under chapter 7, 11, or 12 of this title, whichever occurs first.

(b) Except as provided in a confirmed plan or order confirming a plan, the debtor shall remain in possession of all property of the estate.

§ 1307. Conversion or Dismissal

(a) The debtor may convert a case under this chapter to a case under chapter 7 of this title at any time. Any waiver of the right to convert under this subsection is unenforceable.

(b) On request of the debtor at any time, if the case has not been converted under section 706, 1112, or 1208 of this title, the court shall dismiss a case under this chapter. Any waiver of the right to dismiss under this subsection is unenforceable.

(c) Except as provided in subsection (f) of this section, on request of a party in interest or the United States trustee and after notice and a hearing, the court may convert a case under this chapter to a case under chapter 7 of this title, or may dismiss a case under this chapter, whichever is in the best interests of creditors and the estate, for cause, including—

(1) unreasonable delay by the debtor that is prejudicial to creditors;

(2) nonpayment of any fees and charges required under chapter 123 of title 28;

(3) failure to file a plan timely under section 1321 of this title;

(4) failure to commence making timely payments under section 1326 of this title;

(5) denial of confirmation of a plan under section 1325 of this title and denial of a request made for additional time for filing another plan or a modification of a plan;

(6) material default by the debtor with respect to a term of a confirmed plan;

(7) revocation of the order of confirmation under section 1330 of this title, and denial of confirmation of a modified plan under section 1329 of this title;

(8) termination of a confirmed plan by reason of the occurrence of a condition specified in the plan other than completion of payments under the plan;

(9) only on request of the United States trustee, failure of the debtor to file, within fifteen days, or such additional time as the court may allow, after the filing of the petition commencing such case, the information required by paragraph (1) of section 521(a);

(10) only on request of the United States trustee, failure to timely file the information required by paragraph (2) of section 521(a); or

(11) failure of the debtor to pay any domestic support obligation that first becomes payable after the date of the filing of the petition.

(d) Except as provided in subsection (f) of this section, at any time before the confirmation of a plan under section 1325 of this title, on request of a party in interest or the United States trustee and after notice and a hearing, the court may convert a case under this chapter to a case under chapter 11 or 12 of this title.

(e) Upon the failure of the debtor to file a tax return under section 1308, on request of a party in interest or the United States trustee and after notice and a hearing, the court shall dismiss a case or convert a case under this chapter to a case under chapter 7 of this title, whichever is in the best interest of the creditors and the estate.

(f) The court may not convert a case under this chapter to a case under chapter 7, 11, or 12 of this title if the debtor is a farmer, unless the debtor requests such conversion.

(g) Notwithstanding any other provision of this section, a case may not be converted to a case under another chapter of this title unless the debtor may be a debtor under such chapter.

§ 1308. Filing of Prepetition Tax Returns

(a) Not later than the day before the date on which the meeting of the creditors is first scheduled to be held under section 341(a), if the debtor was required to file a tax return under applicable nonbankruptcy law, the debtor shall file with appropriate tax authorities all tax returns for all taxable periods ending during the 4-year period ending on the date of the filing of the petition.

(b)(1) Subject to paragraph (2), if the tax returns required by subsection (a) have not been filed by the date on which the meeting of creditors is first scheduled to be held under section 341(a), the trustee may hold open that meeting for a reasonable period of time to allow the debtor an additional period of time to file any unfiled returns, but such additional period of time shall not extend beyond—

(A) for any return that is past due as of the date of the filing of the petition, the date that is 120 days after the date of that meeting; or

(B) for any return that is not past due as of the date of the filing of the petition, the later of—

(i) the date that is 120 days after the date of that meeting; or

(ii) the date on which the return is due under the last automatic extension of time for filing that return to which the debtor is entitled, and for which request is timely made, in accordance with applicable nonbankruptcy law.

(2) After notice and a hearing, and order entered before the tolling of any applicable filing period determined under paragraph (1), if the debtor demonstrates by a preponderance of the evidence that the failure to file a return as required under paragraph (1) is attributable to circumstances beyond the control of the debtor, the court may extend the filing period established by the trustee under paragraph (1) for—

(A) a period of not more than 30 days for returns described in paragraph (1)(a); and

(B) a period not to extend after the applicable extended due date for a return described in paragraph (1)(b).

(c) For purposes of this section, the term "return" includes a return prepared pursuant to subsection (a) or (b) of section 6020 of the Internal Revenue Code of 1986, or a similar State or local law, or a written stipulation to a judgment or a final order entered by a nonbankruptcy tribunal.

SUBCHAPTER II—THE PLAN

§ 1321. Filing of Plan

The debtor shall file a plan.

§ 1322. Contents of Plan

(a) The plan—

(1) shall provide for the submission of all or such portion of future earnings or other future income of the debtor to the supervision and control of the trustee as is necessary for the execution of the plan;

(2) shall provide for the full payment, in deferred cash payments, of all claims entitled to priority under section 507 of this title, unless the holder of a particular claim agrees to a different treatment of such claim;

(3) if the plan classifies claims, shall provide the same treatment for each claim within a particular class; and

(4) notwithstanding any other provision of this section, may provide for less than full payment of all amounts owed for a claim entitled to priority under section 507(a)(1)(B) only if the plan provides that all of the debtor's projected disposable income for a 5-year period beginning on the date that the first payment is due under the plan will be applied to make payments under the plan.

(b) Subject to subsections (a) and (c) of this section, the plan may—

(1) designate a class or classes of unsecured claims, as provided in section 1122 of this title, but may not discriminate unfairly against any class so designated; however, such plan may treat claims for a consumer debt of the debtor if an individual is liable on such consumer debt with the debtor differently than other unsecured claims;

(2) modify the rights of holders of secured claims, other than a claim secured only by a security interest in real property that is the debtor's principal residence, or of holders of unsecured claims, or leave unaffected the rights of holders of any class of claims;

(3) provide for the curing or waiving of any default;

(4) provide for payments on any unsecured claim to be made concurrently with payments on any secured claim or any other unsecured claim;

(5) notwithstanding paragraph (2) of this subsection, provide for the curing of any default within a reasonable time and maintenance of payments while the case is pending on any unsecured claim or secured claim on which the last payment is due after the date on which the final payment under the plan is due;

(6) provide for the payment of all or any part of any claim allowed under section 1305 of this title;

(7) subject to section 365 of this title, provide for the assumption, rejection, or assignment of any executory contract or unexpired lease of the debtor not previously rejected under such section;

(8) provide for the payment of all or part of a claim against the debtor from property of the estate or property of the debtor;

(9) provide for the vesting of property of the estate, on confirmation of the plan or at a later time, in the debtor or in any other entity;

(10) provide for the payment of interest accruing after the date of the filing of the petition on unsecured claims that are nondischargeable under section 1328(a), except that such interest may be paid only to the extent that the debtor has disposable income available to pay such interest after making provision for full payment of all allowed claims; and

(11) include any other appropriate provision not inconsistent with this title.

(c) Notwithstanding subsection (b)(2) and applicable nonbankruptcy law—

(1) a default with respect to, or that gave rise to, a lien on the debtor's principal residence may be cured under paragraph (3) or (5) of subsection (b) until such residence is sold at a foreclosure sale that is conducted in accordance with applicable nonbankruptcy law; and

(2) in a case in which the last payment on the original payment schedule for a claim secured only by a security interest in real property that is the debtor's principal residence is due before the date on which the final payment under the plan is due, the plan may provide for the payment of the claim as modified pursuant to section 1325(a)(5) of this title.

(d)(1) If the current monthly income of the debtor and the debtor's spouse combined, when multiplied by 12, is not less than—

(A) in the case of a debtor in a household of 1 person, the median family income of the applicable State for 1 earner;

(B) in the case of a debtor in a household of 2, 3, or 4 individuals, the highest median family income of the applicable State for a family of the same number or fewer individuals; or

(C) in the case of a debtor in a household exceeding 4 individuals, the highest median family income of the applicable State for a family of 4 or fewer individuals, plus $925 per month for each individual in excess of 4, the plan may not provide for payments over a period that is longer than 5 years.

(2) If the current monthly income of the debtor and the debtor's spouse combined, when multiplied by 12, is less than—

(A) in the case of a debtor in a household of 1 person, the median family income of the applicable State for 1 earner;

(B) in the case of a debtor in a household of 2, 3, or 4 individuals, the highest median family income of the applicable State for a family of the same number or fewer individuals; or

(C) in the case of a debtor in a household exceeding 4 individuals, the highest median family income of the applicable State for a family of 4 or fewer individuals, plus $925 per month for each individual in excess of 4, the plan may not provide for payments over a period that is longer than 3 years, unless the court, for cause, approves a longer period, but the court may not approve a period that is longer than 5 years.

(e) Notwithstanding subsection (b)(2) of this section and sections 506(b) and 1325(a)(5) of this title, if it is proposed in a plan to cure a default, the amount necessary to cure the default, shall be determined in accordance with the underlying agreement and applicable nonbankruptcy law.

(f) A plan may not materially alter the terms of a loan described in section 362(b)(19) and any amounts required to repay such loan shall not constitute "disposable income" under section 1325.

§ 1323. Modification of Plan Before Confirmation

(a) The debtor may modify the plan at any time before confirmation, but may not modify the plan so that the plan as modified fails to meet the requirements of section 1322 of this title.

(b) After the debtor files a modification under this section, the plan as modified becomes the plan.

(c) Any holder of a secured claim that has accepted or rejected the plan is deemed to have accepted or rejected, as the case may be, the plan as modified, unless the modification provides for a change in the rights of such holder from what such rights were under the plan before modification, and such holder changes such holder's previous acceptance or rejection.

§ 1324. Confirmation Hearing

(a) Except as provided in subsection (b) and after notice, the court shall hold a hearing on confirmation of the plan. A party in interest may object to confirmation of the plan.

(b) The hearing on confirmation of the plan may be held not earlier than 20 days and not later than 45 days after the date of the meeting of creditors under section 341(a), unless the court determines that it would be in the best interests of the creditors and the estate to hold such hearing at an earlier date and there is no objection to such earlier date.

§ 1325. Confirmation of Plan

(a) Except as provided in subsection (b), the court shall confirm a plan if—

(1) The plan complies with the provisions of this chapter and with the other applicable provisions of this title;

(2) any fee, charge, or amount required under chapter 123 of title 28, or by the plan, to be paid before confirmation, has been paid;

(3) the plan has been proposed in good faith and not by any means forbidden by law;

(4) the value, as of the effective date of the plan, of property to be distributed under the plan on account of each allowed unsecured claim is not less than the amount that would be paid on such claim if the estate of the debtor were liquidated under chapter 7 of this title on such date;

(5) with respect to each allowed secured claim provided for by the plan—

(A) the holder of such claim has accepted the plan;

(B)(i) the plan provides that—

(I) the holder of such claim retain the lien securing such claim until the earlier of—

(aa) the payment of the underlying debt determined under nonbankruptcy law; or

(bb) discharge under section 1328; and

(II) if the case under this chapter is dismissed or converted without completion of the plan, such lien shall also be retained by such holder to the extent recognized by applicable nonbankruptcy law;

(ii) the value, as of the effective date of the plan, of property to be distributed under the plan on account of such claim is not less than the allowed amount of such claim; and

(iii) if—

(I) property to be distributed pursuant to this subsection is in the form of periodic payments, such payments shall be in equal monthly amounts; and

(II) the holder of the claim is secured by personal property, the amount of such payments shall not be less than an amount sufficient to provide to the holder of such claim adequate protection during the period of the plan; or

(C) the debtor surrenders the property securing such claim to such holder;

(6) the debtor will be able to make all payments under the plan and to comply with the plan;

(7) the action of the debtor in filing the petition was in good faith;

(8) the debtor has paid all amounts that are required to be paid under a domestic support obligation and that first become payable after the date of the filing of the petition if the debtor is required by a judicial or administrative order, or by statute, to pay such domestic support obligation; and

(9) the debtor has filed all applicable Federal, State, and local tax returns as required by section 1308.

For purposes of paragraph (5), section 506 shall not apply to a claim described in that paragraph if the creditor has a purchase money security interest securing the debt that is the subject of the claim, the debt was incurred within the 910-day period preceding the date of the filing of the petition, and the collateral for that debt consists of a motor vehicle (as defined in section 30102 of title 49) acquired for the personal use of the debtor, or if collateral for that debt consists of any other thing of value, if the debt was incurred during the 1-year period preceding that filing.

(b)(1) If the trustee or the holder of an allowed unsecured claim objects to the confirmation of the plan, then the court may not approve the plan unless, as of the effective date of the plan—

(A) the value of the property to be distributed under the plan on account of such claim is not less than the amount of such claim; or

(B) the plan provides that all of the debtor's projected disposable income to be received in the applicable commitment period beginning on the date that the first payment is due under the plan will be applied to make payments to unsecured creditors under the plan.

(2) For purposes of this subsection, the term "disposable income" means current monthly income received by the debtor (other than child support payments, foster care payments, or disability payments for a dependent child made in accordance with applicable nonbankruptcy law to the extent reasonably necessary to be expended for such child) less amounts reasonably necessary to be expended—

(A)(i) for the maintenance or support of the debtor or a dependent of the debtor, or for a domestic support obligation, that first becomes payable after the date the petition is filed; and

(ii) for charitable contributions (that meet the definition of "charitable contribution" under section 548(d)(3)) to a qualified religious or charitable entity or organization (as defined in section 548(d)(4)) in an amount not to exceed 15 percent of gross income of the debtor for the year in which the contributions are made; and

(B) if the debtor is engaged in business, for the payment of expenditures necessary for the continuation, preservation, and operation of such business.

(3) Amounts reasonably necessary to be expended under paragraph (2), other than subparagraph (A)(ii) of paragraph (2), shall be determined in accordance with subparagraphs (A) and (B) of section 707(b)(2), if the debtor has current monthly income, when multiplied by 12, greater than—

(A) in the case of a debtor in a household of 1 person, the median family income of the applicable State for 1 earner;

(B) in the case of a debtor in a household of 2, 3, or 4 individuals, the highest median family income of the applicable State for a family of the same number or fewer individuals; or

(C) in the case of a debtor in a household exceeding 4 individuals, the highest median family income of the applicable State for a family of

4 or fewer individuals, plus $925 per month for each individual in excess of 4.

(4) For purposes of this subsection, the "applicable commitment period"—

(A) subject to subparagraph (B), shall be—

(i) 3 years; or

(ii) not less than 5 years, if the current monthly income of the debtor and the debtor's spouse combined, when multiplied by 12, is not less than—

(I) in the case of a debtor in a household of 1 person, the median family income of the applicable State for 1 earner;

(II) in the case of a debtor in a household of 2, 3, or 4 individuals, the highest median family income of the applicable State for a family of the same number or fewer individuals; or

(III) in the case of a debtor in a household exceeding 4 individuals, the highest median family income of the applicable State for a family of 4 or fewer individuals, plus $925 per month for each individual in excess of 4; and

(B) may be less than 3 or 5 years, whichever is applicable under subparagraph (A), but only if the plan provides for payment in full of all allowed unsecured claims over a shorter period.

(c) After confirmation of a plan, the court may order any entity from whom the debtor receives income to pay all or any part of such income to the trustee.

§ 1326. Payments

(a)(1) Unless the court orders otherwise, the debtor shall commence making payments not later than 30 days after the date of the filing of the plan or the order for relief, whichever is earlier, in the amount—

(A) proposed by the plan to the trustee;

(B) scheduled in a lease of personal property directly to the lessor for that portion of the obligation that becomes due after the order for relief, reducing the payments under subparagraph (A) by the amount so paid and providing the trustee with evidence of such payment, including the amount and date of payment; and

(C) that provides adequate protection directly to a creditor holding an allowed claim secured by personal property to the extent the claim is attributable to the purchase of such property by the debtor for that portion of the obligation that becomes due after the order for relief, reducing the payments under subparagraph (A) by the amount so paid and providing the trustee with evidence of such payment, including the amount and date of payment.

(2) A payment made under paragraph (1)(A) shall be retained by the trustee until confirmation or denial of confirmation. If a plan is confirmed, the trustee shall distribute any such payment in accordance with the plan as soon as is practicable. If a plan is not confirmed, the trustee shall return any such payments not previously paid and not yet due and owing to creditors pursuant to paragraph (3) to the debtor, after deducting any unpaid claim allowed under section 503(b).

(3) Subject to section 363, the court may, upon notice and a hearing, modify, increase, or reduce the payments required under this subsection pending confirmation of a plan.

(4) Not later than 60 days after the date of filing of a case under this chapter, a debtor retaining possession of personal property subject to a lease or securing a claim attributable in whole or in part to the purchase price of such property shall provide the lessor or secured creditor reasonable evidence of the maintenance of any required insurance coverage with respect to the use or ownership of such property and continue to do so for so long as the debtor retains possession of such property.

(b) Before or at the time of each payment to creditors under the plan, there shall be paid—

(1) any unpaid claim of the kind specified in section 507(a)(2) of this title;

(2) if a standing trustee appointed under section 586(b) of title 28 is serving in the case, the percentage fee fixed for such standing trustee under section 586(e)(1)(B) of title 28; and

(3) if a chapter 7 trustee has been allowed compensation due to the conversion or dismissal of the debtor's prior case pursuant to section 707(b), and some portion of that compensation remains unpaid in a case converted to this chapter or in the case dismissed under section 707(b) and refiled under this chapter, the amount of any such unpaid compensation, which shall be paid monthly—

(A) by prorating such amount over the remaining duration of the plan; and

(B) by monthly payments not to exceed the greater of—

(i) $25; or

(ii) the amount payable to unsecured nonpriority creditors, as provided by the plan, multiplied by 5 percent, and the result divided by the number of months in the plan.

(c) Except as otherwise provided in the plan or in the order confirming the plan, the trustee shall make payments to creditors under the plan.

(d) Notwithstanding any other provision of this title—

(1) compensation referred to in subsection (b)(3) is payable and may be collected by the trustee under that paragraph, even if such amount has been discharged in a prior case under this title; and

(2) such compensation is payable in a case under this chapter only to the extent permitted by subsection (b)(3).

§ 1327. Effect of Confirmation

(a) The provisions of a confirmed plan bind the debtor and each creditor, whether or not the claim of such creditor is provided for by the plan, and whether or not such creditor has objected to, has accepted, or has rejected the plan.

(b) Except as otherwise provided in the plan or the order confirming the plan, the confirmation of a plan vests all of the property of the estate in the debtor.

(c) Except as otherwise provided in the plan or in the order confirming the plan, the property vesting in the debtor under subsection (b) of this section is free and clear of any claim or interest of any creditor provided for by the plan.

§ 1328. Discharge

(a) Subject to subsection (d), as soon as practicable after completion by the debtor of all payments under the plan, and in the case of a debtor who is required by a judicial or administrative order, or by statute, to pay a domestic support obligation, after such debtor certifies that all amounts payable under such order or such statute that are due on or before the date of the certification (including amounts due before the petition was filed, but only to the extent provided for by the plan) have been paid, unless the court approves a written waiver of discharge executed by the debtor after the order for relief under this chapter, the court shall grant the debtor a discharge of all debts provided for by the plan or disallowed under section 502 of this title, except any debt—

(1) provided for under section 1322(b)(5);

(2) of the kind specified in section 507(a)(8)(C) or in paragraph (1)(B), (1)(C), (2), (3), (4), (5), (8), or (9) of section 523(a);

(3) for restitution, or a criminal fine, included in a sentence on the debtor's conviction of a crime; or

(4) for restitution, or damages, awarded in a civil action against the debtor as a result of willful or malicious injury by the debtor that caused personal injury to an individual or the death of an individual.

(b) Subject to subsection (d), at any time after the confirmation of the plan and after notice and a hearing, the court may grant a discharge to a debtor that has not completed payments under the plan only if—

(1) the debtor's failure to complete such payments is due to circumstances for which the debtor should not justly be held accountable;

(2) the value, as of the effective date of the plan, of property actually distributed under the plan on account of each allowed unsecured claim is not less than the amount that would have been paid on such claim if the estate of the debtor had been liquidated under chapter 7 of this title on such date; and

(3) modification of the plan under section 1329 of this title is not practicable.

(c) A discharge granted under subsection (b) of this section discharges the debtor from all unsecured debts provided for by the plan or disallowed under section 502 of this title, except any debt—

(1) provided for under section 1322(b)(5) of this title; or

(2) of a kind specified in section 523(a) of this title.

(d) Notwithstanding any other provision of this section, a discharge granted under this section does not discharge the debtor from any debt based on an allowed claim filed under section 1305(a)(2) of this title if prior approval by the trustee of the debtor's incurring such debt was practicable and was not obtained.

(e) On request of a party in interest before one year after a discharge under this section is granted, and after notice and a hearing, the court may revoke such discharge only if—

(1) such discharge was obtained by the debtor through fraud; and

(2) the requesting party did not know of such fraud until after such discharge was granted.

(f) Notwithstanding subsections (a) and (b), the court shall not grant a discharge of all debts provided for in the plan or disallowed under section 502, if the debtor has received a discharge—

(1) in a case filed under chapter 7, 11, or 12 of this title during the 4-year period preceding the date of the order for relief under this chapter, or

(2) in a case filed under chapter 13 of this title during the 2-year period preceding the date of such order.

(g)(1) The court shall not grant a discharge under this section to a debtor unless after filing a petition the debtor has completed an instructional course concerning personal financial management described in section 111.

(2) Paragraph (1) shall not apply with respect to a debtor who is a person described in section 109(h)(4) or who resides in a district for which the United States trustee (or the bankruptcy administrator, if any) determines that the approved instructional courses are not adequate to service the additional individuals who would otherwise be required to complete such instructional course by reason of the requirements of paragraph (1).

(3) The United States trustee (or the bankruptcy administrator, if any) who makes a determination described in paragraph (2) shall review such determination not later than 1 year after the date of such determination, and not less frequently than annually thereafter.

(h) The court may not grant a discharge under this chapter unless the court after notice and a hearing held not more than 10 days before the date of the entry of the order granting the discharge finds that there is no reasonable cause to believe that—

(1) section 522(q)(1) may be applicable to the debtor; and

(2) there is pending any proceeding in which the debtor may be found guilty of a felony of the kind described in section 522(q)(1)(A) or liable for a debt of the kind described in section 522(q)(1)(B).

§ 1329. Modification of Plan After Confirmation

(a) At any time after confirmation of the plan but before the completion of payments under such plan, the plan may be modified, upon request of the debtor, the trustee, or the holder of an allowed unsecured claim, to—

(1) increase or reduce the amount of payments on claims of a particular class provided for by the plan;

(2) extend or reduce the time for such payments;

(3) alter the amount of the distribution to a creditor whose claim is provided for by the plan to the extent necessary to take account of any payment of such claim other than under the plan; or

(4) reduce amounts to be paid under the plan by the actual amount expended by the debtor to purchase health insurance for the debtor (and for any dependent of the debtor if such dependent does not otherwise have health insurance coverage) if the debtor documents the cost of such insurance and demonstrates that—

(A) such expenses are reasonable and necessary;

(B)(i) if the debtor previously paid for health insurance, the amount is not materially larger than the cost the debtor previously paid or the cost necessary to maintain the lapsed policy; or

(ii) if the debtor did not have health insurance, the amount is not materially larger than the reasonable cost that would be incurred by a debtor who purchases health insurance, who has similar income, expenses, age, and health status, and who lives in the same geographical location with the same number of dependents who do not otherwise have health insurance coverage; and

(C) the amount is not otherwise allowed for purposes of determining disposable income under section 1325(b) of this title;

and upon request of any party in interest, files proof that a health insurance policy was purchased.

(b)(1) Sections 1322(a), 1322(b), and 1323(c) of this title and the requirements of section 1325(a) of this title apply to any modification under subsection (a) of this section.

(2) The plan as modified becomes the plan unless, after notice and a hearing, such modification is disapproved.

(c) A plan modified under this section may not provide for payments over a period that expires after the applicable commitment period under section 1325(b)(1)(B) after the time that the first payment under the original confirmed plan was due, unless the court, for cause, approves a longer period, but the court may not approve a period that expires after five years after such time.

§ 1330. Revocation of an Order of Confirmation

(a) On request of a party in interest at any time within 180 days after the date of the entry of an order of confirmation under section 1325 of this title, and after notice and a hearing, the court may revoke such order if such order was procured by fraud.

(b) If the court revokes an order of confirmation under subsection (a) of this section, the court shall dispose of the case under section 1307 of this title, unless, within the time fixed by the court, the debtor proposes and the court confirms a modification of the plan under section 1329 of this title.

CHAPTER 15. ANCILLARY AND OTHER CROSS-BORDER CASES

SUBCHAPTER I—GENERAL PROVISIONS

Section.

SUBCHAPTER II—ACCESS OF FOREIGN REPRESENTATIVES AND CREDITORS TO THE COURT

Section

SUBCHAPTER III—RECOGNITION OF A FOREIGN PROCEEDING AND RELIEF

Section

SUBCHAPTER IV—COOPERATION WITH FOREIGN COURTS AND FOREIGN REPRESENTATIVES

Section

SUBCHAPTER V—CONCURRENT PROCEEDINGS

Section

§ 1501. Purpose and Scope of Application

(a) The purpose of this chapter is to incorporate the Model Law on Cross-Border Insolvency so as to provide effective mechanisms for dealing with cases of cross-border insolvency with the objectives of—

(1) cooperation between—

(A) courts of the United States, United States trustees, trustees, examiners, debtors, and debtors in possession; and

(B) the courts and other competent authorities of foreign countries involved in cross-border insolvency cases;

(2) greater legal certainty for trade and investment;

(3) fair and efficient administration of cross-border insolvencies that protects the interests of all creditors, and other interested entities, including the debtor;

(4) protection and maximization of the value of the debtor's assets; and

(5) facilitation of the rescue of financially troubled businesses, thereby protecting investment and preserving employment.

(b) This chapter applies where—

(1) assistance is sought in the United States by a foreign court or a foreign representative in connection with a foreign proceeding;

(2) assistance is sought in a foreign country in connection with a case under this title;

(3) a foreign proceeding and a case under this title with respect to the same debtor are pending concurrently; or

(4) creditors or other interested persons in a foreign country have an interest in requesting the commencement of, or participating in, a case or proceeding under this title.

(c) This chapter does not apply to—

(1) a proceeding concerning an entity, other than a foreign insurance company, identified by exclusion in section 109(b);

(2) an individual, or to an individual and such individual's spouse, who have debts within the limits specified in section 109(e) and who are citizens of the United States or aliens lawfully admitted for permanent residence in the United States; or

(3) an entity subject to a proceeding under the Securities Investor Protection Act of 1970, a stockbroker subject to subchapter III of chapter 7 of this title, or a commodity broker subject to subchapter IV of chapter 7 of this title.

(d) The court may not grant relief under this chapter with respect to any deposit, escrow, trust fund, or other security required or permitted under any applicable State insurance law or regulation for the benefit of claim holders in the United States.

SUBCHAPTER I—GENERAL PROVISIONS

§ 1502. Definitions

For the purposes of this chapter, the term—

(1) "debtor" means an entity that is the subject of a foreign proceeding;

(2) "establishment" means any place of operations where the debtor carries out a nontransitory economic activity;

(3) "foreign court" means a judicial or other authority competent to control or supervise a foreign proceeding;

(4) "foreign main proceeding" means a foreign proceeding pending in the country where the debtor has the center of its main interests;

(5) "foreign nonmain proceeding" means a foreign proceeding, other than a foreign main proceeding, pending in a country where the debtor has an establishment;

(6) "trustee" includes a trustee, a debtor in possession in a case under any chapter of this title, or a debtor under chapter 9 of this title;

(7) "recognition" means the entry of an order granting recognition of a foreign main proceeding or foreign nonmain proceeding under this chapter; and

(8) "within the territorial jurisdiction of the United States", when used with reference to property of a debtor, refers to tangible property located within the territory of the United States and intangible property deemed under applicable nonbankruptcy law to be located within that territory, including any property subject to attachment or garnishment that may properly be seized or garnished by an action in a Federal or State court in the United States.

§ 1503. International Obligations of the United States

To the extent that this chapter conflicts with an obligation of the United States arising out of any treaty or other form of agreement to which it is a party with one or more other countries, the requirements of the treaty or agreement prevail.

§ 1504. Commencement of Ancillary Case

A case under this chapter is commenced by the filing of a petition for recognition of a foreign proceeding under section 1515.

§ 1505. Authorization to Act in a Foreign Country

A trustee or another entity (including an examiner) may be authorized by the court to act in a foreign country on behalf of an estate created under section 541. An entity authorized to act under this section may act in any way permitted by the applicable foreign law.

§ 1506. Public Policy Exception

Nothing in this chapter prevents the court from refusing to take an action governed by this chapter if the action would be manifestly contrary to the public policy of the United States.

§ 1507. Additional Assistance

(a) Subject to the specific limitations stated elsewhere in this chapter the court, if recognition is granted, may provide additional assistance to a foreign representative under this title or under other laws of the United States.

(b) In determining whether to provide additional assistance under this title or under other laws of the United States, the court shall consider whether such additional assistance, consistent with the principles of comity, will reasonably assure—

(1) just treatment of all holders of claims against or interests in the debtor's property;

(2) protection of claim holders in the United States against prejudice and inconvenience in the processing of claims in such foreign proceeding;

(3) prevention of preferential or fraudulent dispositions of property of the debtor;

(4) distribution of proceeds of the debtor's property substantially in accordance with the order prescribed by this title; and

(5) if appropriate, the provision of an opportunity for a fresh start for the individual that such foreign proceeding concerns.

§ 1508. Interpretation

In interpreting this chapter, the court shall consider its international origin, and the need to promote an application of this chapter that is consistent with the application of similar statutes adopted by foreign jurisdictions.

SUBCHAPTER II—ACCESS OF FOREIGN REPRESENTATIVES AND CREDITORS TO THE COURT

§ 1509. Right of Direct Access

(a) A foreign representative may commence a case under section 1504 by filing directly with the court a petition for recognition of a foreign proceeding under section 1515.

(b) If the court grants recognition under section 1517, and subject to any limitations that the court may impose consistent with the policy of this chapter—

(1) the foreign representative has the capacity to sue and be sued in a court in the United States;

(2) the foreign representative may apply directly to a court in the United States for appropriate relief in that court; and

(3) a court in the United States shall grant comity or cooperation to the foreign representative.

(c) A request for comity or cooperation by a foreign representative in a court in the United States other than the court which granted recognition shall be accompanied by a certified copy of an order granting recognition under section 1517.

(d) If the court denies recognition under this chapter, the court may issue any appropriate order necessary to prevent the foreign representative from obtaining comity or cooperation from courts in the United States.

(e) Whether or not the court grants recognition, and subject to sections 306 and 1510, a foreign representative is subject to applicable nonbankruptcy law.

(f) Notwithstanding any other provision of this section, the failure of a foreign representative to commence a case or to obtain recognition under this chapter does not affect any right the foreign representative may have to sue in a court in the United States to collect or recover a claim which is the property of the debtor.

§ 1510. Limited Jurisdiction

The sole fact that a foreign representative files a petition under section 1515 does not subject the foreign representative to the jurisdiction of any court in the United States for any other purpose.

§ 1511. Commencement of Case Under Section 301, 302, or 303

(a) Upon recognition, a foreign representative may commence—

(1) an involuntary case under section 303; or

(2) a voluntary case under section 301 or 302, if the foreign proceeding is a foreign main proceeding.

(b) The petition commencing a case under subsection (a) must be accompanied by a certified copy of an order granting recognition. The court where the petition for recognition has been filed must be advised of the foreign representative's intent to commence a case under subsection (a) prior to such commencement.

§ 1512. Participation of a Foreign Representative in a Case Under This Title

Upon recognition of a foreign proceeding, the foreign representative in the recognized proceeding is entitled to participate as a party in interest in a case regarding the debtor under this title.

§ 1513. Access of Foreign Creditors to a Case Under This Title

(a) Foreign creditors have the same rights regarding the commencement of, and participation in, a case under this title as domestic creditors.

(b)(1) Subsection (a) does not change or codify present law as to the priority of claims under section 507 or 726, except that the claim of a foreign creditor under those sections shall not be given a lower priority than that of general unsecured claims without priority solely because the holder of such claim is a foreign creditor.

(2)(A) Subsection (a) and paragraph (1) do not change or codify present law as to the allowability of foreign revenue claims or other foreign public law claims in a proceeding under this title.

(B) Allowance and priority as to a foreign tax claim or other foreign public law claim shall be governed by any applicable tax treaty of the United States, under the conditions and circumstances specified therein.

§ 1514. Notification to Foreign Creditors Concerning a Case Under This Title

(a) Whenever in a case under this title notice is to be given to creditors generally or to any class or category of creditors, such notice shall also be given to the known creditors generally, or to creditors in the notified class or category, that do not have addresses in the United States. The court may order that appropriate steps be taken with a view to notifying any creditor whose address is not yet known.

(b) Such notification to creditors with foreign addresses described in subsection (a) shall be given individually, unless the court considers that, under the circumstances, some other form of notification would be more appropriate. No letter or other formality is required.

(c) When a notification of commencement of a case is to be given to foreign creditors, such notification shall—

(1) indicate the time period for filing proofs of claim and specify the place for filing such proofs of claim;

(2) indicate whether secured creditors need to file proofs of claim; and

(3) contain any other information required to be included in such notification to creditors under this title and the orders of the court.

(d) Any rule of procedure or order of the court as to notice or the filing of a proof of claim shall provide such additional time to creditors with foreign addresses as is reasonable under the circumstances.

SUBCHAPTER III—RECOGNITION OF A FOREIGN PROCEEDING AND RELIEF

§ 1515. Application for Recognition

(a) A foreign representative applies to the court for recognition of a foreign proceeding in which the foreign representative has been appointed by filing a petition for recognition.

(b) A petition for recognition shall be accompanied by—

(1) a certified copy of the decision commencing such foreign proceeding and appointing the foreign representative;

(2) a certificate from the foreign court affirming the existence of such foreign proceeding and of the appointment of the foreign representative; or

(3) in the absence of evidence referred to in paragraphs (1) and (2), any other evidence acceptable to the court of the existence of such foreign proceeding and of the appointment of the foreign representative.

(c) A petition for recognition shall also be accompanied by a statement identifying all foreign proceedings with respect to the debtor that are known to the foreign representative.

(d) The documents referred to in paragraphs (1) and (2) of subsection (b) shall be translated into English. The court may require a translation into English of additional documents.

§ 1516. Presumptions Concerning Recognition

(a) If the decision or certificate referred to in section 1515(b) indicates that the foreign proceeding is a foreign proceeding and that the person or body is a foreign representative, the court is entitled to so presume.

(b) The court is entitled to presume that documents submitted in support of the petition for recognition are authentic, whether or not they have been legalized.

(c) In the absence of evidence to the contrary, the debtor's registered office, or habitual residence in the case of an individual, is presumed to be the center of the debtor's main interests.

§ 1517. Order Granting Recognition

(a) Subject to section 1506, after notice and a hearing, an order recognizing a foreign proceeding shall be entered if—

(1) such foreign proceeding for which recognition is sought is a foreign main proceeding or foreign nonmain proceeding within the meaning of section 1502;

(2) the foreign representative applying for recognition is a person or body; and

(3) the petition meets the requirements of section 1515.

(b) Such foreign proceeding shall be recognized—

(1) as a foreign main proceeding if it is pending in the country where the debtor has the center of its main interests; or

(2) as a foreign nonmain proceeding if the debtor has an establishment within the meaning of section 1502 in the foreign country where the proceeding is pending.

(c) A petition for recognition of a foreign proceeding shall be decided upon at the earliest possible time. Entry of an order recognizing a foreign proceeding constitutes recognition under this chapter.

(d) The provisions of this subchapter do not prevent modification or termination of recognition if it is shown that the grounds for granting it were fully or partially lacking or have ceased to exist, but in considering such action the court shall give due weight to possible prejudice to parties that have relied upon the order granting recognition. A case under this chapter may be closed in the manner prescribed under section 350.

§ 1518. Subsequent Information

From the time of filing the petition for recognition of a foreign proceeding, the foreign representative shall file with the court promptly a notice of change of status concerning—

(1) any substantial change in the status of such foreign proceeding or the status of the foreign representative's appointment; and

(2) any other foreign proceeding regarding the debtor that becomes known to the foreign representative.

§ 1519. Relief That May Be Granted upon Filing Petition for Recognition

(a) From the time of filing a petition for recognition until the court rules on the petition, the court may, at the request of the foreign representative, where relief is urgently needed to protect the assets of the debtor or the interests of the creditors, grant relief of a provisional nature, including—

(1) staying execution against the debtor's assets;

(2) entrusting the administration or realization of all or part of the debtor's assets located in the United States to the foreign representative or another person authorized by the court, including an examiner, in order to protect and preserve the value of assets that, by their nature or because of other circumstances, are perishable, susceptible to devaluation or otherwise in jeopardy; and

(3) any relief referred to in paragraph (3), (4), or (7) of section 1521(a).

(b) Unless extended under section 1521(a)(6), the relief granted under this section terminates when the petition for recognition is granted.

(c) It is a ground for denial of relief under this section that such relief would interfere with the administration of a foreign main proceeding.

(d) The court may not enjoin a police or regulatory act of a governmental unit, including a criminal action or proceeding, under this section.

(e) The standards, procedures, and limitations applicable to an injunction shall apply to relief under this section.

(f) The exercise of rights not subject to the stay arising under section 362(a) pursuant to paragraph (6), (7), (17), or (27) of section 362(b) or pursuant to section 362(o) shall not be stayed by any order of a court or administrative agency in any proceeding under this chapter.

§ 1520. Effects of Recognition of a Foreign Main Proceeding

(a) Upon recognition of a foreign proceeding that is a foreign main proceeding—

(1) sections 361 and 362 apply with respect to the debtor and the property of the debtor that is within the territorial jurisdiction of the United States;

(2) sections 363, 549, and 552 apply to a transfer of an interest of the debtor in property that is within the territorial jurisdiction of the United States to the same extent that the sections would apply to property of an estate;

(3) unless the court orders otherwise, the foreign representative may operate the debtor's business and may exercise the rights and powers of a trustee under and to the extent provided by sections 363 and 552; and

(4) section 552 applies to property of the debtor that is within the territorial jurisdiction of the United States.

(b) Subsection (a) does not affect the right to commence an individual action or proceeding in a foreign country to the extent necessary to preserve a claim against the debtor.

(c) Subsection (a) does not affect the right of a foreign representative or an entity to file a petition commencing a case under this title or the right of any party to file claims or take other proper actions in such a case.

§ 1521. Relief That May Be Granted upon Recognition

(a) Upon recognition of a foreign proceeding, whether main or nonmain, where necessary to effectuate the purpose of this chapter and to protect the assets of the debtor or the interests of the creditors, the court may, at the request of the foreign representative, grant any appropriate relief, including—

(1) staying the commencement or continuation of an individual action or proceeding concerning the debtor's assets, rights, obligations or liabilities

to the extent they have not been stayed under section 1520(a);

(2) staying execution against the debtor's assets to the extent it has not been stayed under section 1520(a);

(3) suspending the right to transfer, encumber or otherwise dispose of any assets of the debtor to the extent this right has not been suspended under section 1520(a);

(4) providing for the examination of witnesses, the taking of evidence or the delivery of information concerning the debtor's assets, affairs, rights, obligations or liabilities;

(5) entrusting the administration or realization of all or part of the debtor's assets within the territorial jurisdiction of the United States to the foreign representative or another person, including an examiner, authorized by the court;

(6) extending relief granted under section 1519(a); and

(7) granting any additional relief that may be available to a trustee, except for relief available under sections 522, 544, 545, 547, 548, 550, and 724(a).

(b) Upon recognition of a foreign proceeding, whether main or nonmain, the court may, at the request of the foreign representative, entrust the distribution of all or part of the debtor's assets located in the United States to the foreign representative or another person, including an examiner, authorized by the court, provided that the court is satisfied that the interests of creditors in the United States are sufficiently protected.

(c) In granting relief under this section to a representative of a foreign nonmain proceeding, the court must be satisfied that the relief relates to assets that, under the law of the United States, should be administered in the foreign nonmain proceeding or concerns information required in that proceeding.

(d) The court may not enjoin a police or regulatory act of a governmental unit, including a criminal action or proceeding, under this section.

(e) The standards, procedures, and limitations applicable to an injunction shall apply to relief under paragraphs (1), (2), (3), and (6) of subsection (a).

(f) The exercise of rights not subject to the stay arising under section 362(a) pursuant to paragraph (6), (7), (17), or (27) of section 362(b) or pursuant to section 362(o) shall not be stayed by any order of a court or administrative agency in any proceeding under this chapter.

§ 1522. Protection of Creditors and Other Interested Persons

(a) The court may grant relief under section 1519 or 1521, or may modify or terminate relief under subsection (c), only if the interests of the creditors and other interested entities, including the debtor, are sufficiently protected.

(b) The court may subject relief granted under section 1519 or 1521, or the operation of the debtor's business under section 1520(a)(3), to conditions it considers appropriate, including the giving of security or the filing of a bond.

(c) The court may, at the request of the foreign representative or an entity affected by relief granted under section 1519 or 1521, or at its own motion, modify or terminate such relief.

(d) Section 1104(d) shall apply to the appointment of an examiner under this chapter. Any examiner shall comply with the qualification requirements imposed on a trustee by section 322.

§ 1523. Actions to Avoid Acts Detrimental to Creditors

(a) Upon recognition of a foreign proceeding, the foreign representative has standing in a case concerning the debtor pending under another chapter of this title to initiate actions under sections 522, 544, 545, 547, 548, 550, 553, and 724(a).

(b) When a foreign proceeding is a foreign nonmain proceeding, the court must be satisfied that an action under subsection (a) relates to assets that, under United States law, should be administered in the foreign nonmain proceeding.

§ 1524. Intervention by a Foreign Representative

Upon recognition of a foreign proceeding, the foreign representative may intervene in any proceedings in a State or Federal court in the United States in which the debtor is a party.

SUBCHAPTER IV—COOPERATION WITH FOREIGN COURTS AND FOREIGN REPRESENTATIVES

§ 1525. Cooperation and Direct Communication Between the Court and Foreign Courts or Foreign Representatives

(a) Consistent with section 1501, the court shall cooperate to the maximum extent possible with a foreign court or a foreign representative, either directly or through the trustee.

(b) The court is entitled to communicate directly with, or to request information or assistance directly from, a foreign court or a foreign representative, subject to the rights of a party in interest to notice and participation.

§ 1526. Cooperation and Direct Communication Between the Trustee and Foreign Courts or Foreign Representatives

(a) Consistent with section 1501, the trustee or other person, including an examiner, authorized by the court, shall, subject to the supervision of the court, cooperate to the maximum extent possible with a foreign court or a foreign representative.

(b) The trustee or other person, including an examiner, authorized by the court is entitled, subject to the supervision of the court, to communicate directly with a foreign court or a foreign representative.

§ 1527. Forms of Cooperation

Cooperation referred to in sections 1525 and 1526 may be implemented by any appropriate means, including—

(1) appointment of a person or body, including an examiner, to act at the direction of the court;

(2) communication of information by any means considered appropriate by the court;

(3) coordination of the administration and supervision of the debtor's assets and affairs;

(4) approval or implementation of agreements concerning the coordination of proceedings; and

(5) coordination of concurrent proceedings regarding the same debtor.

SUBCHAPTER V—CONCURRENT PROCEEDINGS

§ 1528. Commencement of a Case Under This Title After Recognition of a Foreign Main Proceeding

After recognition of a foreign main proceeding, a case under another chapter of this title may be commenced only if the debtor has assets in the United States. The effects of such case shall be restricted to the assets of the debtor that are within the territorial jurisdiction of the United States and, to the extent necessary to implement cooperation and coordination under sections 1525, 1526, and 1527, to other assets of the debtor that are within the jurisdiction of the court under sections 541(a) of this title, and 1334(e) of title 28, to the extent that such other assets are not subject to the jurisdiction and control of a foreign proceeding that has been recognized under this chapter.

§ 1529. Coordination of a Case Under This Title and a Foreign Proceeding

If a foreign proceeding and a case under another chapter of this title are pending concurrently regarding the same debtor, the court shall seek cooperation and coordination under sections 1525, 1526, and 1527, and the following shall apply:

(1) If the case in the United States is pending at the time the petition for recognition of such foreign proceeding is filed—

(A) any relief granted under section 1519 or 1521 must be consistent with the relief granted in the case in the United States; and

(B) section 1520 does not apply even if such foreign proceeding is recognized as a foreign main proceeding.

(2) If a case in the United States under this title commences after recognition, or after the date of the filing of the petition for recognition, of such foreign proceeding—

(A) any relief in effect under section 1519 or 1521 shall be reviewed by the court and shall be modified or terminated if inconsistent with the case in the United States; and

(B) if such foreign proceeding is a foreign main proceeding, the stay and suspension referred to in section 1520(a) shall be modified or terminated if inconsistent with the relief granted in the case in the United States.

(3) In granting, extending, or modifying relief granted to a representative of a foreign nonmain proceeding, the court must be satisfied that the relief relates to assets that, under the laws of the United States, should be administered in the foreign nonmain proceeding or concerns information required in that proceeding.

(4) In achieving cooperation and coordination under sections 1528 and 1529, the court may grant any of the relief authorized under section 305.

§ 1530. Coordination of More Than 1 Foreign Proceeding

In matters referred to in section 1501, with respect to more than 1 foreign proceeding regarding the debtor, the court shall seek cooperation and coordination under sections 1525, 1526, and 1527, and the following shall apply:

(1) Any relief granted under section 1519 or 1521 to a representative of a foreign nonmain proceeding after recognition of a foreign main proceeding must be consistent with the foreign main proceeding.

(2) If a foreign main proceeding is recognized after recognition, or after the filing of a petition for recognition, of a foreign nonmain proceeding, any relief in effect under section 1519 or 1521 shall be reviewed by the court and shall be modified or terminated if inconsistent with the foreign main proceeding.

(3) If, after recognition of a foreign nonmain proceeding, another foreign nonmain proceeding is recognized, the court shall grant, modify, or terminate relief for the purpose of facilitating coordination of the proceedings.

§ 1531. Presumption of Insolvency Based on Recognition of a Foreign Main Proceeding

In the absence of evidence to the contrary, recognition of a foreign main proceeding is, for the purpose of commencing a proceeding under section 303, proof that the debtor is generally not paying its debts as such debts become due.

§ 1532. Rule of Payment in Concurrent Proceedings

Without prejudice to secured claims or rights in rem, a creditor who has received payment with respect to its claim in a foreign proceeding pursuant to a law relating to insolvency may not receive a payment for the same claim in a case under any other chapter of this title regarding the debtor, so long as the payment to other creditors of the same class is proportionately less than the payment the creditor has already received.

FEDERAL RULES OF BANKRUPTCY PROCEDURE

Rule 1015. Consolidating or Jointly Administering Cases Pending in the Same District

(a) Consolidating Cases Involving the Same Debtor. The court may consolidate two or more cases that are regarding or brought by or against the same debtor and that are pending in its district.

(b) Jointly Administering Cases Involving Related Debtors; Exemptions of Spouses; Protective Orders to Avoid Conflicts of Interest.

(1) *In General.* The court may order joint administration of the estates in a joint case or in two or more cases pending in the court if they are brought by or against:

(A) spouses;

(B) a partnership and one or more of its general partners;

(C) two or more general partners; or

(D) a debtor and an affiliate.

(2) *Potential Conflicts of Interest.* Before issuing a joint-administration order, the court must consider how to protect the creditors of different estates against potential conflicts of interest.

(3) *Exemptions in Cases Involving Spouses.* If spouses have filed separate petitions—with one electing exemptions under § 522(b)(2) and the other under § 522(b)(3)—and the court orders joint administration, that order must:

(A) set a reasonable time for the debtors to elect the same exemptions; and

(B) advise the debtors that if they fail to do so, they will be considered to have elected exemptions under § 522(b)(2).

(c) Protective Orders to Avoid Unnecessary Costs and Delay. When cases are consolidated or jointly administered, the court may issue orders to avoid unnecessary costs and delay while still protecting the parties' rights under the Code.

Rule 2002. Notices

(a) 21-Day Notices to the Debtor, Trustee, Creditors, and Indenture Trustees. Except as (h), (i), (l), (p), and (q) provide otherwise, the clerk or the court's designee must give the debtor, the trustee, all creditors, and all indenture trustees at least 21 days' notice by mail of:

(1) the meeting of creditors under § 341 or § 1104(b), which notice—unless the court orders otherwise—must include the debtor's:

(A) employer-identification number;

(B) social-security number; and

(C) any other federal taxpayer- identification number;

(2) a proposal to use, sell, or lease property of the estate other than in the ordinary course of business—unless the court, for cause, shortens the time or orders another method of giving notice;

(3) a hearing to approve a compromise or settlement other than an agreement under Rule 4001(d)—unless the court, for cause, orders that notice not be given;

(4) a hearing on a motion to dismiss a chapter 7, 11, or 12 case or to convert it to another chapter—

unless the hearing is under § 707(a)(3) or § 707(b) or is on a motion to dismiss the case for failure to pay the filing fee;

(5) the time to accept or reject a proposed modification to a plan;

(6) a hearing on a request for compensation or for reimbursement of expenses, if the request exceeds $1,000;

(7) the time to file a proof of claim under Rule 3003(c);

(8) the time to file an objection to—and the time of the hearing to consider whether to confirm—a chapter 12 plan; and (9) the time to object to confirming a chapter 13 plan.

(b) 28-Day Notices to the Debtor, Trustee, Creditors, and Indenture Trustees. Except as (l) provides otherwise, the clerk or the court's designee must give the debtor, trustee, all creditors, and all indenture trustees at least 28 days' notice by mail of:

(1) the time to file an objection and the time of the hearing to:

(A) consider approving a disclosure statement; or

(B) determine under § 1125(f) whether a plan includes adequate information to make a separate disclosure statement unnecessary;

(2) the time to file an objection to—and the time of the hearing to consider whether to confirm—a chapter 9 or 11 plan; and

(3) the time of the hearing to consider whether to confirm a chapter 13 plan.

(c) Content of a Notice.

(1) *Proposed Use, Sale, or Lease of Property.* Subject to Rule 6004, a notice of a proposed use, sale, or lease of property under (a)(2) must include:

(A) a general description of the property;

(B) the time and place of any public sale;

(C) the terms and conditions of any private sale;

(D) the time to file objections; and

(E) for a proposed sale or lease of personally identifiable information under § 363(b)(1), a statement whether the sale is consistent with any policy that prohibits transferring the information.

(2) *Hearing on an Application for Compensation or Reimbursement.* A notice under (a)(6) of a hearing on a request for compensation or for reimbursement of expenses must identify the applicant and the amounts requested.

(3) *Hearing on Confirming a Plan That Proposes an Injunction.* If a plan proposes an injunction against conduct not otherwise enjoined under the Code, the notice under (b)(2) must:

(A) state in conspicuous language (bold, italic, or underlined text) that the plan proposes an injunction;

(B) describe briefly the nature of the injunction; and

(C) identify the entities that would be subject to it.

(d) Notice to Equity Security Holders in a Chapter 11 Case. Unless the court orders otherwise, in a chapter 11 case the clerk or the court's designee must give notice as the court orders to the equity security holders of:

(1) the order for relief;

(2) a meeting of equity security holders under § 341;

(3) a hearing on a proposed sale of all, or substantially all, the debtor's assets;

(4) a hearing on a motion to dismiss a case or convert it to another chapter;

(5) the time to file an objection to—and the time of the hearing to consider whether to approve—a disclosure statement;

(6) the time to file an objection to—and the time of the hearing to consider whether to confirm—a chapter 11 plan; and

(7) the time to accept or reject a proposal to modify a plan.

(e) Giving Notice of No Dividend in a Chapter 7 Case. In a chapter 7 case, if it appears from the schedules that there are no assets from which to pay a dividend, the notice of the meeting of creditors may state:

(1) that fact;

(2) that filing proofs of claim is unnecessary; and

(3) that further notice of the time to file proofs of claim will be given if enough assets become available to pay a dividend.

(f) Other Notices.

(1) *Various Notices to the Debtor, Creditors, and Indenture Trustees.* Except as (l) provides otherwise, the clerk, or some other person as the court may direct, must give the debtor, creditors, and indenture trustees notice by mail of:

(A) the order for relief;

(B) a case's dismissal or conversion to another chapter;

(C) a suspension of proceedings under § 305;

(D) the time to file a proof of claim under Rule 3002;

(E) the time to file a complaint to object to the debtor's discharge under § 727, as Rule 4004 provides;

(F) the time to file a complaint to determine whether a debt is dischargeable under § 523, as Rule 4007 provides;

(G) a waiver, denial, or revocation of a discharge, as Rule 4006 provides;

(H) entry of an order confirming a plan in a chapter 9, 11, 12 or 13 case;

(I) a summary of the trustee's final report in a chapter 7 case if the net proceeds realized exceed $1,500;

(J) a notice under Rule 5008 regarding the presumption of abuse;

(K) a statement under § 704(b)(1) about whether the debtor's case would be presumed to be an abuse under § 707(b); and

(L) the time to request a delay in granting the discharge under § 1141(d)(5)(C), 1228(f), or 1328(h).

(2) *Notice of the Time to Accept or Reject a Plan.* Notice of the time to accept or reject a plan under Rule 3017(c) must be given in accordance with Rule 3017(d).

(g) Addressing Notices.

(1) *In General.* A notice mailed to a creditor, indenture trustee, or equity security holder must be addressed as the entity or its authorized agent provided in its last request filed in the case. The request may be:

(A) a proof of claim filed by a creditor or an indenture trustee designating a mailing address (unless a notice of no dividend has been given under (e) and a later notice of a possible dividend under Rule 3002(c)(5) has not been given); or

(B) a proof of interest filed by an equity security holder designating a mailing address.

(2) *When No Request Has Been Filed.* Except as § 342(f) provides otherwise, if a creditor or indenture trustee has not filed a request under (1) or Rule 5003(e), the notice must be mailed to the address shown on the list of creditors or schedule of liabilities, whichever is filed later. If an equity security holder has not filed a request, the notice must be mailed to the address shown on the list of equity security holders.

(3) *Notices to Representatives of an Infant or Incompetent Person.* This paragraph (3) applies if a list or schedule filed under Rule 1007 includes a name and address of an infant's or an incompetent person's representative, and a person other than that representative files a request or proof of claim designating a different name and mailing address. Unless the court orders otherwise, the notice must be mailed to the designated address of:

(A) the representative; and

(B) the person filing the request or proof of claim.

(4) *Using an Address Agreed to Between an Entity and a Notice Provider.* Notwithstanding (g)(1)–(3), when the court orders that notice be given, the notice provider may do so in the manner agreed to between the provider and an entity, and at the address or addresses the entity supplies. An address supplied by the entity is conclusively presumed to be a proper address. But a failure to use a supplied address does not invalidate a notice that is otherwise effective under applicable law.

(5) *When a Notice Is Not Brought to a Creditor's Attention.* A creditor may treat a notice as not having been brought to the creditor's attention under § 342(g)(1) only if, before the notice was issued, the creditor has filed a statement:

(A) designating the name and address of the person or organizational subdivision responsible for receiving notices; and

(B) describing the creditor's procedures for delivering notices to the designated person or organizational subdivision.

(h) Notice to Creditors Who Filed Proofs of Claim in a Chapter 7, 12, or 13 Case.

(1) *Voluntary Case.* This paragraph (1) applies in a voluntary chapter 7 case, or in a chapter 12 or 13 case. After 70 days following the order for relief under that chapter or the date of the order converting the case to chapter 12 or 13, the court may direct that all notices required by (a) be mailed only to:

- the debtor;
- the trustee;
- indenture trustees;
- creditors with claims for which proofs of claim have been filed; and
- creditors that are still permitted to file proofs of claim because they have received an extension of time under Rule 3002(c)(1) or (2).

(2) *Involuntary Case.* In an involuntary chapter 7 case, after 90 days following the order for relief, the court may order that all notices required by (a) be mailed only to those entities listed in (1).

(3) *When Notice of Insufficient Assets Has Been Given.* If notice of insufficient assets to pay a dividend has been given to creditors under (e), after 90 days following the mailing of a notice of the time to file proofs of claim under Rule 3002(c)(5), the court may order that notices be mailed only to those entities listed in (1).

(i) Notice to a Committee.

(1) *In General.* Any notice required to be mailed under this Rule 2002 must also be mailed to a committee elected under § 705 or appointed under § 1102, or to its authorized agent.

(2) *Limiting Notices.* The court may order that a notice required by (a)(2), (3), or (6) be:

(A) sent to the United States trustee; and

(B) mailed only to:

(i) the committees elected under § 705 or appointed under § 1102, or to their authorized agents; and

(ii) those creditors and equity security holders who file—and serve on the trustee or debtor in possession—a request that all notices be mailed to them.

(3) *Copy to a Committee.* A notice required under (a)(1), (a)(5), (b), (f)(1)(B)–(C), or (f)(1)(H)—and any other notice as the court orders—must be sent to a committee appointed under § 1114.

(j) Notice to the United States. A notice required to be mailed to all creditors under this Rule 2002 must also be mailed:

(1) in a chapter 11 case in which the Securities and Exchange Commission has filed either a notice of appearance or a request to receive notices, to the SEC at any place it designates;

(2) in a commodity-broker case, to the Commodity Futures Trading Commission at Washington, D.C.;

(3) in a chapter 11 case, to the Internal Revenue Service at the address in the register maintained under Rule 5003(e) for the district where the case is pending;

(4) in a case in which the documents disclose that a debt (other than for taxes) is owed to the United States, to the United States attorney for the district where the case is pending and to the United States department, agency, or instrumentality through which the debtor became indebted; or

(5) in a case in which the filed documents disclose a stock interest of the United States, to the Secretary of the Treasury at Washington, D.C.

(k) Notice to the United States Trustee.

(1) *In General.* Except in a chapter 9 case or unless the United States trustee requests otherwise, the clerk or the court's designee must send to the United States trustee notice of:

(A) all matters described in (a)(2)–(4), (a)(8)–(9), (b),(f)(1)(A)–(C), (f)(1)(E), (f)(1)(G)–(I), and (q);

(B) all hearings on applications for compensation or for reimbursement of expenses; and

(C) any other matter if the United States trustee requests it or the court orders it.

(2) *Time to Send.* The notice must be sent within the time that (a) or (b) prescribes.

(3) *Exception Under the Securities Investor Protection Act.* In a case under the Securities Investor Protection Act, 15 U.S.C. § 78aaa et seq., these rules do not require any document to be sent to the United States trustee.

(l) Notice by Publication. The court may order notice by publication if notice by mail is impracticable or if it is desirable to supplement the notice.

(m) Orders Concerning Notices. Except as these rules provide otherwise, the court may designate the matters about which, the entity to whom, and the form and manner in which a notice must be sent.

(n) Notice of an Order for Relief in a Consumer Case. In a voluntary case commenced under the Code by an individual debtor whose debts are primarily consumer debts, the clerk, or some other person as the court may direct, shall give the trustee and all creditors notice by mail of the order for relief not more than 20 days after the entry of such order.

(o) Caption. The caption of a notice given under this Rule 2002 must conform to Rule 1005. The caption of a debtor's notice to a creditor must also include the information that § 342(c) requires.

(p) Notice to a Creditor with a Foreign Address.

(1) *When Notice by Mail Does Not Suffice.* At the request of the United States trustee or a party in interest, or on its own, the court may find that a notice mailed to a creditor with a foreign address within the time these rules prescribe would not give the creditor reasonable notice. The court may then order that the notice be supplemented with notice by other means or that the time prescribed for the notice by mail be extended.

(2) *Notice of the Time to File a Proof of Claim.* Unless the court, for cause, orders otherwise, a creditor with a foreign address must be given at least 30 days' notice of the time to file a proof of claim under Rule 3002(c) or Rule 3003(c).

(3) *Determining a Foreign Address.* Unless the court, for cause, orders otherwise, the mailing address of a creditor with a foreign address must be determined under (g).

(q) Notice of a Petition for Recognition of a Foreign Proceeding; Notice of an Intent to Communicate with a Foreign Court or Foreign Representative.

(1) *Timing of the Notice; Who Must Receive It.* After a petition for recognition of a foreign

proceeding is filed, the court must promptly hold a hearing on it. The clerk or the court's designee must promptly give at least 21 days' notice by mail of the hearing to:

- the debtor;
- all persons or bodies authorized to administer the debtor's foreign proceedings;
- all entities against whom provisional relief is being sought under § 1519;
- all parties to litigation pending in the United States in which the debtor was a party when the petition was filed; and
- any other entities as the court orders.

If the court consolidates the hearing on the petition with a hearing on a request for provisional relief, the court may set a shorter notice period.

(2) Content of the Notice. The notice must:

(A) state whether the petition seeks recognition as a foreign main proceeding or a foreign nonmain proceeding; and

(B) include a copy of the petition and any other document the court specifies.

(3) *Communicating with a Foreign Court or Foreign Representative.* If the court intends to communicate with a foreign court or foreign representative, the clerk or the court's designee must give notice by mail of the court's intention to all those listed in (q)(1).

Rule 2003. Meeting of Creditors or Equity Security Holders

(a) Date and Place of the Meeting.

(1) *Date.* Except as provided in § 341(e), the United States trustee must call a meeting of creditors to be held:

(A) in a chapter 7 or 11 case, no fewer than 21 days and no more than 40 days after the order for relief;

(B) in a chapter 12 case, no fewer than 21 days and no more than 35 days after the order for relief; or

(C) in a chapter 13 case, no fewer than 21 days and no more than 50 days after the order for relief.

(2) *Effect of a Motion or an Appeal.* The United States trustee may set a later date for the meeting if there is a motion to vacate the order for relief, an appeal from such an order, or a motion to dismiss the case.

(3) *Place; Possible Change in the Meeting Date.* The meeting may be held at a regular place for holding court. Or the United States trustee may designate any other place in the district that is convenient for the parties in interest. If the designated meeting place is not regularly staffed by the United States trustee or an assistant who may preside, the meeting may be held no more than 60 days after the order for relief.

(b) Conducting the Meeting; Agenda; Who May Vote.

(1) *At a Meeting of Creditors.*

(A) *Generally.* The United States trustee must preside at the meeting of creditors. The meeting must include an examination of the debtor under oath. The presiding officer has the authority to administer oaths.

(B) *Chapter 7 Cases.* In a chapter 7 case, the meeting may include the election of a creditors' committee; and if the case is not under subchapter V, the meeting may include electing a trustee.

(2) *At a Meeting of Equity Security Holders.* If the United States trustee convenes a meeting of equity security holders under § 341(b), the United States trustee must set a date for the meeting and preside over it.

(3) *Who Has a Right to Vote; Objecting to the Right to Vote.*

(A) *In a Chapter 7 Case.* A creditor in a chapter 7 case may vote if, at or before the meeting:

(i) the creditor has filed a proof of claim or a writing setting forth facts evidencing a right to vote under § 702(a);

(ii) the proof of claim is not insufficient on its face; and

(iii) no objection is made to the claim.

(B) *In a Partnership Case.* A creditor in a partnership case may file a proof of claim or a writing evidencing a right to vote for a trustee for the general partner's estate even if a trustee for the partnership's estate has previously qualified.

(C) *Objecting to the Amount or Allowability of a Claim for Voting Purposes.* Unless the court orders otherwise, if there is an objection to the amount or allowability of a claim for voting purposes, the United States trustee must tabulate the votes for each alternative presented by the dispute. If resolving the dispute is necessary to determine the election's result, the United States trustee must report to the court the tabulations for each alternative.

(c) Recording the Proceedings. At the meeting of creditors under § 341(a), the United States trustee must:

(1) record verbatim—using electronic sound-recording equipment or other means of recording—all examinations under oath;

(2) preserve the recording and make it available for public access for 2 years after the meeting concludes; and

(3) upon request, certify and provide a copy or transcript of the recording to any entity at that entity's expense.

(d) Reporting Election Results in a Chapter 7 Case.

(1) *Undisputed Election.* In a chapter 7 case, if the election of a trustee or a member of a creditors' committee is undisputed, the United States trustee must promptly file a report of the election. The report must include the name and address of the person or entity elected and a statement that the election was undisputed.

(2) *Disputed Election.*

(A) *United States Trustee's Report.* If the election is disputed, the United States trustee must:

(i) promptly file a report informing the court of the nature of the dispute and listing the name and address of any candidate elected under any alternative presented by the dispute; and

(ii) no later than the date on which the report is filed, mail a copy to any party in interest that has requested one.

(B) *Interim Trustee.* Until the court resolves the dispute, the interim trustee continues in office. Unless a motion to resolve the dispute is filed within 14 days after the report is filed, the interim trustee serves as trustee in the case.

(e) Adjournment. The presiding official may adjourn the meeting from time to time by announcing at the meeting the date and time to reconvene. The presiding official must promptly file a statement showing the adjournment and the date and time to reconvene.

(f) Special Meetings of Creditors. The United States trustee may call a special meeting of creditors or may do so on request of a party in interest.

(g) Final Meeting of Creditors. If the United States trustee calls a final meeting of creditors in a case in which the net proceeds realized exceed $1,500, the clerk must give notice of the meeting to the creditors. The notice must include a summary of the trustee's final account and a statement of the amount of the claims allowed. The trustee must attend the meeting and, if requested, report on the estate's administration.

Rule 2004. Examinations

(a) In General. On a party in interest's motion, the court may order the examination of any entity.

(b) Scope of the Examination.

(1) *In General.* The examination of an entity under this Rule 2004, or of a debtor under § 343, may relate only to:

(A) the debtor's acts, conduct, or property;

(B) the debtor's liabilities and financial condition;

(C) any matter that may affect the administration of the debtor's estate; or

(D) the debtor's right to a discharge.

(2) *Other Topics in Certain Cases.* In a chapter 12 or 13 case, or in a chapter 11 case that is not a railroad reorganization, the examination may also relate to:

(A) the operation of any business and the desirability of its continuing;

(B) the source of any money or property the debtor acquired or will acquire for the purpose of consummating a plan and the consideration given or offered; and

(C) any other matter relevant to the case or to formulating a plan.

(c) Compelling Attendance and the Production of Documents or Electronically Stored Information. Regardless of the district where the examination will be conducted, an entity may be compelled under Rule 9016 to attend and produce documents or electronically stored information. An attorney may issue and sign a subpoena on behalf of the court where the case is pending if the attorney is admitted to practice in that court.

(d) Time and Place to Examine the Debtor. The court may, for cause and on terms it may impose, order the debtor to be examined under this Rule 2004 at any designated time and place, in or outside the district.

(e) Witness Fees and Mileage.

(1) *For a Nondebtor Witness.* An entity, except the debtor, may be required to attend as a witness only if the lawful mileage and witness fee for 1 day's attendance are first tendered.

(2) *For a Debtor Witness.* A debtor who is required to appear for examination more than 100 miles from the debtor's residence must be tendered a mileage fee. The fee need cover only the distance exceeding 100 miles from the nearer of where the debtor resides:

(A) when the first petition was filed; or

(B) when the examination takes place.

Rule 2014. Employing Professionals

(a) Order Approving Employment; Application for Employment.

(1) *Order Approving Employment.* The court may approve the employment of an attorney,

accountant, appraiser, auctioneer, agent, or other professional under § 327, § 1103, or § 1114 only on the trustee's or committee's application.

(2) *Application for Employment.* The applicant must file the application and, except in a chapter 9 case, must send a copy to the United States trustee. The application must state specific facts showing:

(A) the need for the employment;

(B) the name of the person to be employed;

(C) the reasons for the selection;

(D) the professional services to be rendered;

(E) any proposed arrangement for compensation; and

(F) to the best of the applicant's knowledge, all the person's connections with:

- the debtor;
- creditors;
- any other party in interest;
- their respective attorneys and accountants;
- the United States trustee; and
- any person employed in the United States trustee's office.

(3) *Verified Statement of the Person to Be Employed.* The application must be accompanied by a verified statement of the person to be employed, setting forth that person's connections with any entity listed in (2)(F).

(b) Services Rendered by a Member or Associate of a Law or Accounting Firm. If a law partnership or corporation is employed as an attorney, or an accounting partnership or corporation is employed as an accountant—or if a named attorney or accountant is employed—then any partner, member, or regular associate may act as so employed, without further court order.

Rule 2016. Compensation for Services Rendered; Reimbursing Expenses

(a) In General.

(1) *Application.* If an entity seeks from the estate interim or final compensation for services or reimbursement of necessary expenses, the entity must file an application showing:

(A) in detail the amounts requested and the services rendered, time spent, and expenses incurred;

(B) all payments previously made or promised for services rendered or to be rendered in connection with the case;

(C) the source of the paid or promised compensation;

(D) whether any previous compensation has been shared;

(E) whether an agreement or understanding exists between the applicant and any other entity for sharing compensation for services rendered or to be rendered in connection with the case; and

(F) the particulars of any compensation sharing or agreement or understanding to share, except with a member or regular associate of a law or accounting firm.

(2) *Application for Services Rendered or to be Rendered by an Attorney or Accountant.* The requirements of (a) apply to an application for compensation for services rendered by an attorney or accountant, even though a creditor or other entity files the application.

(3) *Copy to the United States Trustee.* Except in a chapter 9 case, the applicant must send a copy of the application to the United States trustee.

(b) Disclosing Compensation Paid or Promised to the Debtor's Attorney.

(1) *Basic Requirements.* Within 14 days after the order for relief—or at another time as the court orders—every debtor's attorney (whether or not applying for compensation) must file and send to the United States trustee the statement required by § 329. The statement must:

(A) show whether the attorney has shared or agreed to share compensation with any other entity; and

(B) if so, the particulars of any sharing or agreement to share, except with a member or regular associate of the attorney's law firm.

(2) *Supplemental Statement.* Within 14 days after any payment or agreement to pay not previously disclosed, the attorney must file and send to the United States trustee a supplemental statement.

(c) Disclosing Compensation Paid or Promised to a Bankruptcy-Petition Preparer.

(1) *Basic Requirements.* Before a petition is filed, every bankruptcy-petition preparer for a debtor must deliver to the debtor the declaration under penalty of perjury required by § 110(h)(2). The declaration must:

(A) disclose any fee, and its source, received from or on behalf of the debtor within 12 months before the petition's filing, together with all unpaid fees charged to the debtor;

(B) describe the services performed and the documents prepared or caused to be prepared by the bankruptcy-petition preparer; and

(C) be filed with the petition.

(2) *Supplemental Statement.* Within 14 days after any later payment or agreement to pay not previously disclosed, the bankruptcy-petition preparer must file a supplemental statement.

Rule 2017. Examining Transactions Between a Debtor and the Debtor's Attorney

(a) Payments or Transfers to an Attorney Made in Contemplation of Filing a Petition or Before the Order for Relief. On a party in interest's motion, or on its own, the court may, after notice and a hearing, determine whether a debtor's direct or indirect payment of money or transfer of property to an attorney for services rendered or to be rendered was excessive if it was made:

(1) in contemplation of the filing of a bankruptcy petition by or against the debtor; or

(2) before the order for relief is entered in an involuntary case.

(b) Payments or Transfers to an Attorney Made After the Order for Relief Is Entered. On motion of the debtor or the United States trustee, or on its own, the court may, after notice and a hearing, determine whether a debtor's payment of money or transfer of property—or agreement to pay money or transfer property—to an attorney after an order for relief is entered is excessive. It does not matter whether the payment or transfer is made, or to be made, directly or indirectly, if the payment, transfer, or agreement is for services related to the case.

Rule 2019. Disclosures by Groups, Committees, and Other Entities in a Chapter 9 or 11 Case

(a) Definitions. In this Rule 2019:

(1) "disclosable economic interest" means any claim, interest, pledge, lien, option, participation, derivative instrument, or other right or derivative right granting the holder an economic interest that is affected by the value, acquisition, or disposition of a claim or interest; and

(2) "represent" or "represents" means to take a position before the court or to solicit votes regarding a plan's confirmation on another's behalf.

(b) Who Must Disclose.

(1) *In General.* In a chapter 9 or 11 case, a verified statement containing the information listed in (c) must be filed by every group or committee consisting of or representing—and every entity representing—multiple creditors or equity security holders that are:

(A) acting in concert to advance their common interests; and

(B) not composed entirely of affiliates or insiders of one another.

(2) *When a Disclosure Statement Is Not Required.* Unless the court orders otherwise, an entity need not file the statement described in (1) solely because it is:

(A) an indenture trustee;

(B) an agent for one or more other entities under an agreement to extend credit;

(C) a class-action representative; or

(D) a governmental unit that is not a person.

(c) Required Information. The verified statement must include:

(1) the pertinent facts and circumstances concerning:

(A) for a group or committee (except a committee appointed under § 1102 or § 1114), its formation, including the name of each entity at whose instance it was formed or for whom it has agreed to act; or

(B) for an entity, the entity's employment, including the name of each creditor or equity security holder at whose instance the employment was arranged;

(2) if not disclosed under (1), for each member of a group or committee and for an entity:

(A) name and address;

(B) the nature and amount of each disclosable economic interest held in relation to the debtor when the group or committee was formed or the entity was employed; and (C) for each member of a group or committee claiming to represent any entity in addition to its own members (except a committee appointed under § 1102 or § 1114), the quarter and year in which each disclosable economic interest was acquired—unless it was acquired more than 1 year before the petition was filed;

(3) if not disclosed under (1) or (2), for each creditor or equity security holder represented by an entity, group, or committee (except a committee appointed under § 1102 or § 1114):

(A) name and address; and

(B) the nature and amount of each disclosable economic interest held in relation to the debtor on the statement's date; and

(4) a copy of any instrument authorizing the group, committee, or entity to act on behalf of creditors or equity security holders.

(d) Supplemental Statement. If a fact disclosed in its most recent statement has changed materially, a group, committee, or entity must file a verified supplemental statement whenever it takes a position before the court or solicits votes on a plan's confirmation. The supplemental statement must set forth any material changes in the information specified in (c).

(e) Failure to Comply; Sanctions.

(1) *Failure to Comply.* On a party in interest's motion, or on its own, the court may determine whether there has been a failure to comply with this Rule 2019.

(2) *Sanctions.* If the court finds a failure to comply, it may:

(A) refuse to permit the group, committee, or entity to be heard or to intervene in the case;

(B) hold invalid any authority, acceptance, rejection, or objection that the group, committee, or entity has given, procured, or received; or

(C) grant other appropriate relief.

Rule 3014. Chapter 9 or 11—Secured Creditors' Election to Apply § 1111(b)

(a) Time for an Election.

(1) *Chapter 9 or 11.* In a chapter 9 or 11 case, before a hearing on the disclosure statement concludes, a class of secured creditors may elect to apply § 1111(b)(2). If the disclosure statement is conditionally approved under Rule 3017.1 and a final hearing on it is not held, the election must be made within the time provided in Rule 3017.1(a)(2). In either situation, the court may set another time for the election.

(2) *Subchapter V of Chapter 11.* In a case under subchapter V of chapter 11 in which § 1125 does not apply, the election may be made no later than a date the court sets.

(b) Signed Writing; Binding Effect. The election must be made in writing and signed, unless made at the hearing on the disclosure statement. An election made by the majorities required by § 1111(b)(1)(A)(i) is binding on all members of the class.

Rule 4001. Relief from the Automatic Stay; Prohibiting or Conditioning the Use, Sale, or Lease of Property; Using Cash Collateral; Obtaining Credit; Various Agreements

(a) Relief from the Automatic Stay; Prohibiting or Conditioning the Use, Sale, or Lease of Property.

(1) *Motion.* A motion under § 362(d) for relief from the automatic stay—or a motion under § 363(e) to prohibit or condition the use, sale, or lease of property—must comply with Rule 9014. The motion must be served on:

(A) the following, as applicable:

- a committee elected under § 705 or appointed under § 1102;
- the committee's authorized agent; or
- the creditors included on the list filed under Rule 1007(d) if the case is a chapter 9 or chapter 11 case and no committee of unsecured creditors has been appointed under § 1102; and

(B) any other entity the court designates.

(2) *Relief Without Notice.* Relief from a stay under § 362(a)—or a request under § 363(e) to prohibit or condition the use, sale, or lease of property—may be granted without prior notice only if:

(A) specific facts—shown by either an affidavit or a verified motion—clearly demonstrate that the movant will suffer immediate and irreparable injury, loss, or damage before the adverse party or its attorney can be heard in opposition; and

(B) the movant's attorney certifies to the court in writing what efforts, if any, have been made to give notice and why it should not be required.

(3) *Notice of Relief; Motion for Reinstatement or Reconsideration.*

(A) *Notice of Relief.* A party who obtains relief under (2) and under § 362(f) or § 363(e) must:

(i) immediately give oral notice both to the debtor and to the trustee or the debtor in possession; and

(ii) promptly send them a copy of the order granting relief.

(B) *Motion for Reinstatement or Reconsideration.* On 2 days' notice to the party who obtained relief under (2)—or on shorter notice as the court may order—the adverse party may move to reinstate the stay or reconsider the order prohibiting or conditioning the use, sale, or lease of property. The court must proceed expeditiously to hear and decide the motion.

(4) *Stay of an Order Granting Relief from the Automatic Stay.* Unless the court orders otherwise, an order granting a motion for relief from the automatic stay under (1) is stayed for 14 days after it is entered.

(b) Using Cash Collateral.

(1) *Motion; Content; Service.*

(A) *Motion.* A motion for authorization to use cash collateral must comply with Rule 9014 and must be accompanied by a proposed form of order.

(B) *Content.* The motion must consist of—or if the motion exceeds five pages, begin with—a concise statement of the relief requested, no longer than five pages. The statement must list or summarize all material provisions (citing their locations in the relevant documents), including:

- the name of each entity with an interest in the cash collateral;
- how it will be used;
- the material terms of its use, including duration; and
- all liens, cash payments, or other adequate protection that will be provided to each entity with an interest in the cash collateral—or if no such protection is proposed, an explanation of how each entity's interest is adequately protected.

(C) *Service.* The motion must be served on:

- each entity with an interest in the cash collateral;
- all those who must be served under (a)(1)(A); and
- any other entity the court designates.

(2) *Hearings; Notice.*

(A) *Preliminary and Final Hearings.* The court may begin a final hearing on the motion no earlier than 14 days after it has been served. If the motion so requests, the court may conduct a preliminary hearing before that 14-day period ends. After a preliminary hearing, the court may authorize using only the cash collateral necessary to avoid immediate and irreparable harm to the estate pending a final hearing.

(B) *Notice.* Notice of a hearing must be given to the parties who must be served with the motion under (1)(C) and to any other entity the court designates.

(c) Obtaining Credit.

(1) *Motion; Content; Service.*

(A) *Motion.* A motion for authorization to obtain credit must comply with Rule 9014 and must be accompanied by a copy of the credit agreement and a proposed form of order.

(B) *Content.* The motion must consist of—or if the motion exceeds five pages, begin with—a concise statement of the relief requested, no longer than five pages. The statement must list or summarize all material provisions of the credit agreement and form of order (citing their locations in the relevant documents), including interest rates, maturity dates, default provisions, liens, and borrowing limits and conditions. If the credit agreement or form of order includes any of the provisions listed below in (i)–(xi), the concise statement must also list or summarize each one, describe its nature and extent, cite its location in the proposed agreement and form of order, and identify any that would remain effective if interim approval were to be granted but final relief denied under (2). The provisions are:

(i) a grant of priority or a lien on property of the estate under § 364(c) or (d);

(ii) the providing of adequate protection or priority for a claim that arose before the case commenced—including a lien on property of the estate, or its use, or of credit obtained under § 364 to make cash payments on the claim;

(iii) a determination of the validity, enforceability, priority, or amount of a claim that arose before the case commenced, or of any lien securing the claim;

(iv) a waiver or modification of Code provisions or applicable rules regarding the automatic stay;

(v) a waiver or modification of an entity's right to file a plan, seek to extend the time in which the debtor has the exclusive right to file a plan, request the use of cash collateral under § 363(c), or request authorization to obtain credit under § 364;

(vi) the establishment of deadlines for filing a plan of reorganization, approving a disclosure statement, holding a hearing on confirmation, or entering a confirmation order;

(vii) a waiver or modification of applicable nonbankruptcy law regarding perfecting or enforcing a lien on property of the estate;

(viii) a release, waiver, or limitation on a claim or other cause of action belonging to the estate or the trustee, including any modification of the statute of limitations or other deadline to commence an action;

(ix) the indemnification of any entity;

(x) a release, waiver, or limitation of any right under § 506(c); or

(xi) the granting of a lien on a claim or cause of action arising under § 544, 545, 547, 548, 549, 553(b), 723(a), or 724(a).

(C) *Service.* The motion must be served on all those who must be served under (a)(1)(A) and any other entity the court designates.

(2) *Hearings; Notice.*

(A) *Preliminary and Final Hearings.* The court may begin a final hearing on the motion no earlier than 14 days after it has been served. If the motion so requests, the court may conduct a preliminary hearing before that 14-day period ends. After a preliminary hearing, the court may authorize obtaining credit only to the extent necessary to avoid immediate and irreparable harm to the estate pending a final hearing.

(B) *Notice.* Notice of a hearing must be given to the parties who must be served with the motion under (1)(C) and to any other entity the court designates.

(3) *Inapplicability in a Chapter 13 Case.* This subdivision (c) does not apply in a chapter 13 case.

(d) Various Agreements: Relief from the Automatic Stay; Prohibiting or Conditioning the Use, Sale, or Lease of Property; Providing Adequate Protection; Using Cash Collateral; or Obtaining Credit.

(1) *Motion; Content; Service.*

(A) *Motion.* A motion to approve any of the following must be accompanied by a copy of the agreement and a proposed form of order:

(i) an agreement to provide adequate protection;

(ii) an agreement to prohibit or condition the use, sale, or lease of property;

(iii) an agreement to modify or terminate the stay provided for in § 362;

(iv) an agreement to use cash collateral; or

(v) an agreement between the debtor and an entity that has a lien or interest in property of the estate under which the entity consents to creating a lien that is senior or equal to the entity's lien or interest.

(B) *Content.* The motion must consist of—or if the motion exceeds five pages, begin with—a concise statement of the relief requested, no longer than five pages. The statement must:

(i) list or summarize all the agreement's material provisions (citing their locations in the relevant documents); and

(ii) briefly list or summarize, cite the location of, and describe the nature and extent of each provision in the proposed form of order, agreement, or other document of the type listed in (c)(1)(B).

(C) *Service.* The motion must be served on all those who must be served under (a)(1)(A) and any other entity the court designates.

(2) *Objection.* Notice of the motion must be mailed to the parties on whom service of the motion is required and any other entity the court designates. The notice must include the time within which objections may be filed and served on the debtor in possession or trustee. Unless the court sets a different time, any objections must be filed within 14 days after the notice is mailed.

(3) *Disposition Without a Hearing.* If no objection is filed, the court may enter an order approving or disapproving the agreement without holding a hearing.

(4) *Hearing.* If an objection is filed or if the court decides that a hearing is appropriate, the court must hold one after giving at least 7 days' notice to:

- the objector;
- the movant;
- the parties who must be served with the motion under (1)(C); and
- any other entity the court designates.

(5) *Agreement to Settle a Motion.* The court may decide that a motion made under (a), (b), or (c) was sufficient to give reasonable notice of the agreement's material provisions and an opportunity for a hearing. If so, the court may order that the procedures prescribed in (1)–(4) do not apply and may approve the agreement without further notice.

Rule 4005. Burden of Proof in Objecting to a Discharge

At a trial on a complaint objecting to a discharge, the plaintiff has the burden of proof.

Rule 4007. Determining Whether a Debt Is Dischargeable

(a) Who May File a Complaint. A debtor or any creditor may file a complaint to determine whether a debt is dischargeable.

(b) Time to File; No Fee for a Reopened Case. A complaint, except one under § 523(c), may be filed at any time. If a case is reopened to permit filing the complaint, no fee for reopening is required.

(c) Chapter 7, 11, 12, or 13—Time to File a Complaint Under § 523(c); Notice of Time; Extension. Except as (d) provides, a complaint to determine whether a debt is dischargeable under § 523(c) must be filed within 60 days after the first date set for the § 341(a) meeting of creditors. The clerk must give all creditors at least 30 days' notice of the time to file in the manner provided by Rule 2002. On a party in interest's motion filed before the time expires, the court may, after notice and a hearing and for cause, extend the time to file.

(d) Chapter 13—Time to File a Complaint Under § 523(a)(6); Notice of Time; Extension. When a debtor files a motion for a discharge under § 1328(b), the court must set the time to file a complaint under § 523(a)(6) to determine whether a debt is dischargeable. The clerk must give all creditors at least 30 days' notice of the time to file in the manner provided by Rule 2002. On a party in interest's motion filed before the time expires, the court may, after notice and a hearing and for cause, extend the time to file.

(e) Applying Part VII Rules. The Part VII rules govern a proceeding on a complaint filed under this Rule 4007.

Rule 7001. Types of Adversary Proceedings

An adversary proceeding is governed by the rules in this Part VII. The following are adversary proceedings:

(a) a proceeding to recover money or property—except a proceeding to compel the debtor to deliver property to the trustee, or a proceeding under § 554(b), § 725, Rule 2017, or Rule 6002;

(b) a proceeding to determine the validity, priority, or extent of a lien or other interest in property—except a proceeding under Rule 3012 or Rule 4003(d);

(c) a proceeding to obtain authority under § 363(h) to sell both the estate's interest in property and that of a co-owner;

(d) a proceeding to revoke or object to a discharge—except an objection under § 727(a)(8) or (a)(9), or § 1328(f);

(e) a proceeding to revoke an order confirming a plan in a chapter 11, 12, or 13 case;

(f) a proceeding to determine whether a debt is dischargeable;

(g) a proceeding to obtain an injunction or other equitable relief—except when the relief is provided in a chapter 9, 11, 12, or 13 plan;

(h) a proceeding to subordinate an allowed claim or interest—except when subordination is provided in a chapter 9, 11, 12, or 13 plan;

(i) a proceeding to obtain a declaratory judgment related to any proceeding described in (a)–(h); and

(j) a proceeding to determine a claim or cause of action removed under 28 U.S.C. § 1452.

Rule 8002. Time to File a Notice of Appeal

(a) In General.

(1) *Time to File.* Except as (b) and (c) provide otherwise, a notice of appeal must be filed with the bankruptcy clerk within 14 days after the judgment, order, or decree to be appealed is entered.

(2) *Filing Before the Entry of Judgment.* A notice of appeal filed after the bankruptcy court announces a decision or order—but before entry of the judgment, order, or decree—is treated as filed on the date of and after the entry.

(3) *Multiple Appeals.* If one party timely files a notice of appeal, any other party may file a notice of appeal within 14 days after the date when the first notice was filed, or within the time otherwise allowed by this rule—whichever is later.

(4) *Mistaken Filing in Another Court.* If a notice of appeal is mistakenly filed in a district court, BAP, or court of appeals, that court's clerk must note on it the date when it was received and send it to the bankruptcy clerk. The notice is then considered filed in the bankruptcy court on the date noted.

(5) *Entry Defined.*

(A) *In General.* A judgment, order, or decree is entered for purposes of this subdivision (a):

(i) when it is entered in the docket under Rule 5003(a); or

(ii) if Rule 7058 applies and Fed. R. Civ. P. 58(a) requires a separate document, when the judgment, order, or decree is entered in the docket under Rule 5003(a) and when the earlier of these events occurs:

• the judgment, order, or decree is set out in a separate document; or

• 150 days have run from entry of the judgment, order, or decree in the docket under Rule 5003(a).

(B) *Failure to Use a Separate Document.* A failure to set out a judgment, order, or decree in a separate document when required by Fed. R. Civ. P. 58(a) does not affect the validity of an appeal from that judgment, order, or decree.

(b) Effect of a Motion on the Time to Appeal.

(1) *In General.* If a party files in the bankruptcy court any of the following motions—and does so within the time allowed by these rules—the time to file an appeal runs for all parties from the entry of the order disposing of the last such remaining motion:

(A) to amend or make additional findings under Rule 7052, whether or not granting the motion would alter the judgment;

(B) to alter or amend the judgment under Rule 9023;

(C) for a new trial under Rule 9023; or

(D) for relief under Rule 9024 if the motion is filed within 14 days after the judgment is entered.

(2) *Notice of Appeal Filed Before a Motion Is Decided.* If a party files a notice of appeal after

the court announces or enters a judgment, order, or decree—but before it disposes of any motion listed in (1)—the notice becomes effective when the order disposing of the last such remaining motion is entered.

(3) *Appealing a Ruling on a Motion.* A party intending to challenge an order disposing of a motion listed in (1)—or an alteration or amendment of a judgment, order, or decree made by a decision on the motion—must file a notice of appeal or an amended notice of appeal. It must:

(A) comply with Rule 8003 or 8004; and

(B) be filed within the time allowed by this rule, measured from the entry of the order disposing of the last such remaining motion.

(4) *No Additional Fee for an Amended Notice.* No additional fee is required to file an amended notice of appeal.

(c) Appeal by an Inmate Confined in an Institution.

(1) *In General.* If an institution has a system designed for legal mail, an inmate confined there must use that system to receive the benefit of this paragraph (1). If an inmate files a notice of appeal from a bankruptcy court's judgment, order, or decree, the notice is timely if it is deposited in the institution's internal mail system on or before the last day for filing and:

(A) it is accompanied by:

(i) a declaration in compliance with 28 U.S.C. § 1746—or a notarized statement—setting out the date of deposit and stating that first-class postage is being prepaid; or

(ii) evidence (such as a postmark or date stamp) showing that the notice was so deposited and that postage was prepaid; or

(B) the appellate court exercises its discretion to permit the later filing of a declaration or notarized statement that satisfies (A)(i).

(2) *Multiple Appeals.* If an inmate files under this subdivision (c) the first notice of appeal, the 14-day period provided in (a)(3) for another party to file a notice of appeal runs from the date when the bankruptcy clerk dockets the first notice.

(d) Extending the Time to File a Notice of Appeal.

(1) *When the Time May Be Extended.* Except as (2) provides otherwise, the bankruptcy court may, on motion, extend the time to file a notice of appeal if the motion is filed:

(A) within the time allowed by this rule; or

(B) within 21 days after that time expires if the party shows excusable neglect.

(2) *When the Time Must Not Be Extended.* The bankruptcy court must not extend the time to file the notice if the judgment, order, or decree being appealed:

(A) grants relief from an automatic stay under § 362, 922, 1201, or 1301;

(B) authorizes the sale or lease of property or the use of cash collateral under § 363

(C) authorizes obtaining credit under § 364;

(D) authorizes assuming or assigning an executory contract or unexpired lease under § 365;

(E) approves a disclosure statement under § 1125; or

(F) confirms a plan under § 943, 1129, 1225, or 1325.

(3) *Limit on Extending Time.* An extension of time must not exceed 21 days after the time allowed by this rule, or 14 days after the order granting the motion to extend time is entered—whichever is later.

Rule 8007. Stay Pending Appeal; Bond; Suspending Proceedings

(a) Initial Motion in the Bankruptcy Court.

(1) *In General.* Ordinarily, a party must move first in the bankruptcy court for the following relief:

(A) a stay of the bankruptcy court's judgment, order, or decree pending appeal;

(B) the approval of a bond or other security provided to obtain a stay of judgment;

(C) an order suspending, modifying, restoring, or granting an injunction while an appeal is pending; or

(D) an order suspending or continuing proceedings or granting other relief permitted by (e).

(2) *Time to File.* The motion may be filed either before or after the notice of appeal is filed.

(b) Motion in the District Court, BAP, or Court of Appeals on Direct Appeal.

(1) *In General.* A motion for the relief specified in (a)(1)—or to vacate or modify a bankruptcy court's order granting such relief—may be filed in the court where the appeal is pending.

(2) *Required Showing.* The motion must:

(A) show that moving first in the bankruptcy court would be impracticable; or

(B) if a motion has already been made in the bankruptcy court, state whether the court has ruled on it, and if so, state any reasons given for the ruling.

(3) *Additional Requirements.* The motion must also include:

(A) the reasons for granting the relief requested and the facts relied on;

(B) affidavits or other sworn statements supporting facts subject to dispute; and

(C) relevant parts of the record.

(4) *Serving Notice.* The movant must give reasonable notice of the motion to all parties.

(c) Filing a Bond or Other Security as a Condition of Relief. The district court, BAP, or court of appeals may condition relief on filing a bond or other security with the bankruptcy court.

(d) Bond or Other Security for a Trustee; Not for the United States. The court may require a trustee who appeals to file a bond or other security. No bond or security is required when:

(1) the United States, its officer, or its agency appeals; or

(2) an appeal is taken by direction of any federal governmental department.

(e) Continuing Proceedings in the Bankruptcy Court. Despite Rule 7062—but subject to the authority of the district court, BAP, or court of appeals—while the appeal is pending, the bankruptcy court may:

(1) suspend or order the continuation of other proceedings in the case, or

(2) issue any appropriate order to protect the rights of all parties in interest.

Rule 9014. Contested Matters

(a) Motion Required. In a contested matter not otherwise governed by these rules, relief must be requested by motion. Reasonable notice and an opportunity to be heard must be given to the party against whom relief is sought. No response is required unless the court orders otherwise.

(b) Service.

(1) *Motion.* The motion must be served within the time prescribed by Rule 9006(d) and in the manner for serving a summons and complaint provided by Rule 7004.

(2) *Response.* Any written response must be served within the time prescribed by Rule 9006(d).

(3) *Later Filings.* After a motion is served, any other document must be served in the manner prescribed by Fed. R. Civ. P. 5(b).

(c) Applying Part VII Rules.

• *In General.* Unless this rule or a court order provides otherwise, the following rules apply in a contested matter: 7009, 7017, 7021, 7025–7026, 7028–7037, 7041–7042, 7052, 7054–7056, 7064, 7069, and 7071. At any stage of a contested matter, the court may order that one or more other Part VII rules apply.

• *Exception.* Unless the court orders otherwise, the following subdivisions of Fed. R. Civ. P. 26, as incorporated by Rule 7026, do not apply in a contested matter:

• (a)(1), mandatory disclosure;

• (a)(2), disclosures about expert testimony;

• (a)(3), other pretrial disclosures; and

• (f), mandatory meeting before a scheduling conference.

• *Procedural Order.* In issuing any procedural order under this subdivision (c), the court must give the parties notice and a reasonable opportunity to comply.

• *Perpetuating Testimony.* An entity desiring to perpetuate testimony may do so in the manner provided by Rule 7027 for taking a deposition before an adversary proceeding.

(d) Taking Testimony; Interpreter.

(1) *In Open Court.* A witness's testimony on a disputed material factual issue must be taken in open court unless a federal statute, the Federal Rules of Evidence, these rules, or other rules adopted by the Supreme Court provide otherwise. For cause and with appropriate safeguards, the court may permit testimony in open court by contemporaneous transmission from a different location.

(2) *Evidence.* When resolution of a contested matter relies on facts outside the record, the court may hear the matter on affidavits or may hear it wholly or partly on oral testimony or on depositions.

(3) *Interpreter.* Fed. R. Civ. P. 43(d) applies in a contested matter.

(e) Determining Whether a Hearing Will Be an Evidentiary Hearing. The court must provide procedures that allow parties—at a reasonable time before a scheduled hearing—to determine whether it will be an evidentiary hearing at which witnesses may testify.

Rule 9029. Adopting Local Rules; Limit on Enforcing a Local Rule; Absence of Controlling Law

(a) Adopting Local Rules.

(1) *By District Courts.* Each district court, acting by a majority of its judges, may make and amend rules governing practice and procedure in all cases and proceedings within its bankruptcy jurisdiction.

Fed. R. Civ. P. 83 governs the procedure for adopting local rules. The rules must:

(A) be consistent with — but not duplicate — Acts of Congress and these rules;

(B) not prohibit or limit using Official Forms; and

(C) conform to any uniform numbering system prescribed by the Judicial Conference of the United States.

(2) *Delegating Authority to the Bankruptcy Judges.* A district court may — subject to any limitation or condition it may prescribe and Fed. R. Civ. P. 83 — authorize the district's bankruptcy judges to make and amend local bankruptcy rules.

(b) Limit on Enforcing a Local Rule Regarding Form. A local rule imposing a requirement of form must not be enforced in a way that causes a party to lose any right because of a nonwillful failure to comply.

(c) Procedure When There Is No Controlling Law. A judge may regulate practice in any manner consistent with federal law, these rules, the Official Forms, and the district's local rules. For any requirement set out elsewhere, a sanction or other disadvantage may be imposed for noncompliance only if the alleged violator was given actual notice of the requirement in the particular case.

TITLE 18—CRIMES AND CRIMINAL PROCEDURE

CHAPTER 9—BANKRUPTCY

§ 151. Definition.

As used in this chapter, the term "debtor" means a debtor concerning whom a petition has been filed under title 11.

§ 152. Concealment of Assets; False Oaths and Claims; Bribery.

A person who—

(1) knowingly and fraudulently conceals from a custodian, trustee, marshal, or other officer of the court charged with the control or custody of property, or, in connection with a case under title 11, from creditors or the United States Trustee, any property belonging to the estate of a debtor;

(2) knowingly and fraudulently makes a false oath or account in or in relation to any case under title 11;

(3) knowingly and fraudulently makes a false declaration, certificate, verification, or statement under penalty of perjury as permitted under section 1746 of title 28, in or in relation to any case under title 11;

(4) knowingly and fraudulently presents any false claim for proof against the estate of a debtor, or uses any such claim in any case under title 11, in a personal capacity or as or through an agent, proxy, or attorney;

(5) knowingly and fraudulently receives any material amount of property from a debtor after the filing of a case under title 11, with intent to defeat the provisions of title 11;

(6) knowingly and fraudulently gives, offers, receives, or attempts to obtain any money or property, remuneration, compensation, reward, advantage, or promise thereof for acting or forbearing to act in any case under title 11;

(7) in a personal capacity or as an agent or officer of any person or corporation, in contemplation of a case under title 11 by or against the person or any other person or corporation, or with intent to defeat the provisions of title 11, knowingly and fraudulently transfers or conceals any of his property or the property of such other person or corporation;

(8) after the filing of a case under title 11 or in contemplation thereof, knowingly and fraudulently conceals, destroys, mutilates, falsifies, or makes a false entry in any recorded information (including books, documents, records, and papers) relating to the property ors financial affairs of a debtor; or

(9) after the filing of a case under title 11, knowingly and fraudulently withholds from a custodian, trustee, marshal, or other officer of the court or a United States Trustee entitled to its possession, any recorded information (including books, documents, records, and papers) relating to the property or financial affairs of a debtor,

shall be fined under this title, imprisoned not more than 5 years, or both.

§ 156. Knowing Disregard of Bankruptcy Law or Rule.

(a) Definitions.—In this section—

(1) the term "bankruptcy petition preparer" means a person, other than the debtor's attorney or an employee of such an attorney, who prepares for compensation a document for filing; and

(2) the term "document for filing" means a petition or any other document prepared for filing by a debtor

in a United States bankruptcy court or a United States district court in connection with a case under title 11.

(b) Offense.—If a bankruptcy case or related proceeding is dismissed because of a knowing attempt by a bankruptcy petition preparer in any manner to disregard the requirements of title 11, United States Code, or the Federal Rules of Bankruptcy Procedure, the bankruptcy petition preparer shall be fined under this title, imprisoned not more than 1 year, or both.

§ 157. Bankruptcy Fraud.

A person who, having devised or intending to devise a scheme or artifice to defraud and for the purpose of executing or concealing such a scheme or artifice or attempting to do so —

(1) files a petition under title 11, including a fraudulent involuntary petition under section 303 of such title;

(2) files a document in a proceeding under title 11; or

(3) makes a false or fraudulent representation, claim, or promise concerning or in relation to a proceeding under title 11, at any time before or after the filing of the petition, or in relation to a proceeding falsely asserted to be pending under such title,

shall be fined under this title, imprisoned not more than 5 years, or both.

§ 158. Designation of United States Attorneys and Agents of the Federal Bureau of Investigation to Address Abusive Reaffirmations of Debt and Materially Fraudulent Statements in Bankruptcy Schedules.

(a) IN GENERAL.—The Attorney General of the United States shall designate the individuals described in subsection (b) to have primary responsibility in carrying out enforcement activities in addressing violations of section 152 or 157 relating to abusive reaffirmations of debt. In addition to addressing the violations referred to in the preceding sentence, the individuals described under subsection (b) shall address violations of section 152 or 157 relating to materially fraudulent statements in bankruptcy schedules that are intentionally false or intentionally misleading.

(b) UNITED STATES ATTORNEYS AND AGENTS OF THE FEDERAL BUREAU OF INVESTIGATION.—The individuals referred to in subsection (a) are—

(1) the United States attorney for each judicial district of the United States; and

(2) an agent of the Federal Bureau of Investigation for each field office of the Federal Bureau of Investigation.

(c) BANKRUPTCY INVESTIGATIONS.—Each United States attorney designated under this section shall, in addition to any other responsibilities, have primary responsibility for carrying out the duties of a United States attorney under section 3057.

(d) BANKRUPTCY PROCEDURES.—The bankruptcy courts shall establish procedures for referring any case that may contain a materially fraudulent statement in a bankruptcy schedule to the individuals designated under this section.

CHAPTER 203—ARREST AND COMMITMENT

§ 3057. Bankruptcy Investigations.

(a) Any judge, receiver, or trustee having reasonable grounds for believing that any violation under chapter 9 of this title or other laws of the United States relating to insolvent debtors, receiverships or reorganization plans has been committed, or that an investigation should be had in connection therewith, shall report to the appropriate United States attorney all the facts and circumstances of the case, the names of the witnesses and the offense or offenses believed to have been committed. Where one of such officers has made such report, the others need not do so.

(b) The United States attorney thereupon shall inquire into the facts and report thereon to the referee, and if it appears probable that any such offense has been committed, shall without delay, present the matter to the grand jury, unless upon inquiry and examination he decides that the ends of public justice do not require investigation or prosecution, in which case he shall report the facts to the Attorney General for his direction.

CHAPTER 213—LIMITATIONS

§ 3284. Concealment of Bankrupt's Assets.

The concealment of assets of a debtor in a case under title 11 shall be deemed to be a continuing offense until the debtor shall have been finally discharged or a discharge denied, and the period of limitations shall not begin to run until such final discharge or denial of discharge.

TITLE 28—JUDICIARY AND JUDICIAL PROCEDURE

Chapter 6—Bankruptcy Judges

§ 151. Designation of Bankruptcy Courts.

In each judicial district, the bankruptcy judges in regular active service shall constitute a unit of the district court to be known as the bankruptcy court for that district. Each bankruptcy judge, as a judicial officer of the district court, may exercise the authority conferred under this chapter with respect to any action, suit, or proceeding and may preside alone and hold a regular or special session of the court, except as otherwise provided by law or by rule or order of the district court.

§ 152. Appointment of Bankruptcy Judges.

(a)(1) Each bankruptcy judge to be appointed for a judicial district, as provided in paragraph (2), shall be appointed by the court of appeals of the United States for the circuit in which such district is located. Such appointments shall be made after considering the recommendations of the Judicial Conference submitted pursuant to subsection (b). Each bankruptcy judge shall be appointed for a term of fourteen years, subject to the provisions of subsection (e). However, upon the expiration of the term, a bankruptcy judge may, with the approval of the judicial council of the circuit, continue to perform the duties of the office until the earlier of the date which is 180 days after the expiration of the term or the date of the appointment of a successor. Bankruptcy judges shall serve as judicial officers of the United States district court established under Article III of the Constitution.

§ 157. Procedures.

(a) Each district court may provide that any or all cases under title 11 and any or all proceedings arising under title 11 or arising in or related to a case under title 11 shall be referred to the bankruptcy judges for the district.

(b) (1) Bankruptcy judges may hear and determine all cases under title 11 and all core proceedings arising under title 11, or arising in a case under title 11, referred under subsection (a) of this section, and may enter appropriate orders and judgments, subject to review under section 158 of this title.

(2) Core proceedings include, but are not limited to—

(A) matters concerning the administration of the estate;

(B) allowance or disallowance of claims against the estate or exemptions from property of the estate, and estimation of claims or interests for the purposes of confirming a plan under chapter 11, 12, or 13 of title 11 but not the liquidation or estimation of contingent or unliquidated personal injury tort or wrongful death claims against the estate for purposes of distribution in a case under title 11;

(C) counterclaims by the estate against persons filing claims against the estate;

(D) orders in respect to obtaining credit;

(E) orders to turn over property of the estate;

(F) proceedings to determine, avoid, or recover preferences;

(G) motions to terminate, annul, or modify the automatic stay;

(H) proceedings to determine, avoid, or recover fraudulent conveyances;

(I) determinations as to the dischargeability of particular debts;

(J) objections to discharges;

(K) determinations of the validity, extent, or priority of liens;

(L) confirmations of plans;

(M) orders approving the use or lease of property, including the use of cash collateral;

(N) orders approving the sale of property other than property resulting from claims brought by the estate against persons who have not filed claims against the estate;

(O) other proceedings affecting the liquidation of the assets of the estate or the adjustment of the debtor-creditor or the equity security holder relationship, except personal injury tort or wrongful death claims; and

(P) recognition of foreign proceedings and other matters under chapter 15 of title 11.

(3) The bankruptcy judge shall determine, on the judge's own motion or on timely motion of a party, whether a proceeding is a core proceeding under this subsection or is a proceeding that is otherwise related to a case under title 11. A determination that a proceeding is not a core proceeding shall not be made solely on the basis that its resolution may be affected by State law.

(4) Non-core proceedings under section 157(b)(2)(B) of title 28, United States Code, shall not be subject to the mandatory abstention provisions of section 1334(c)(2).

(5) The district court shall order that personal injury tort and wrongful death claims shall be tried in the district court in which the bankruptcy case is pending, or in the district court in the district in which the claim arose, as determined by the district court in which the bankruptcy case is pending.

(c)(1) A bankruptcy judge may hear a proceeding that is not a core proceeding but that is otherwise related to a case under title 11. In such proceeding, the bankruptcy judge shall submit proposed findings of fact and conclusions of law to the district court, and any final order or judgment shall be entered by the district judge after considering the bankruptcy judge's proposed findings and conclusions and after reviewing de novo those matters to which any party has timely and specifically objected.

(2) Notwithstanding the provisions of paragraph (1) of this subsection, the district court, with the consent of all the parties to the proceeding, may refer a proceeding related to a case under title 11 to a bankruptcy judge to hear and determine and to enter appropriate orders and judgments, subject to review under section 158 of this title.

(d) The district court may withdraw, in whole or in part, any case or proceeding referred under this section, on its own motion or on timely motion of any party, for cause shown. The district court shall, on timely motion of a party, so withdraw a proceeding if the court determines that resolution of the proceeding requires consideration of both title 11 and other laws of the United States regulating organizations or activities affecting interstate commerce.

(e) If the right to a jury trial applies in a proceeding that may be heard under this section by a bankruptcy judge, the bankruptcy judge may conduct the jury trial if specially designated to exercise such jurisdiction by the district court and with the express consent of all the parties.

§ 158. Appeals.

(a) The district courts of the United States shall have jurisdiction to hear appeals[1]

(1) from final judgments, orders, and decrees;

---

[1] So in original. Probably should be followed by a dash.

(2) from interlocutory orders and decrees issued under section 1121(d) of title 11 increasing or reducing the time periods referred to in section 1121 of such title; and

(3) with leave of the court, from other interlocutory orders and decrees;

and, with leave of the court, from interlocutory orders and decrees, of bankruptcy judges entered in cases and proceedings referred to the bankruptcy judges under section 157 of this title. An appeal under this subsection shall be taken only to the district court for the judicial district in which the bankruptcy judge is serving.

(b)(1) The judicial council of a circuit shall establish a bankruptcy appellate panel service composed of bankruptcy judges of the districts in the circuit who are appointed by the judicial council in accordance with paragraph (3), to hear and determine, with the consent of all the parties, appeals under subsection (a) unless the judicial council finds that—

(A) there are insufficient judicial resources available in the circuit; or

(B) establishment of such service would result in undue delay or increased cost to parties in cases under title 11.

Not later than 90 days after making the finding, the judicial council shall submit to the Judicial Conference of the United States a report containing the factual basis of such finding.

(2) (A) A judicial council may reconsider, at any time, the finding described in paragraph (1).

(B) On the request of a majority of the district judges in a circuit for which a bankruptcy appellate panel service is established under paragraph (1), made after the expiration of the 1-year period beginning on the date such service is established, the judicial council of the circuit shall determine whether a circumstance specified in subparagraph (A) or (B) of such paragraph exists.

(C) On its own motion, after the expiration of the 3-year period beginning on the date a bankruptcy appellate panel service is established under paragraph (1), the judicial council of the circuit may determine whether a circumstance specified in subparagraph (A) or (B) of such paragraph exists.

(D) If the judicial council finds that either of such circumstances exists, the judicial council may provide for the completion of the appeals then pending before such service and the orderly termination of such service.

(3) Bankruptcy judges appointed under paragraph (1) shall be appointed and may be reappointed under such paragraph.

(4) If authorized by the Judicial Conference of the United States, the judicial councils of 2 or more circuits may establish a joint bankruptcy appellate panel comprised of bankruptcy judges from the districts within the circuits for which such panel is established, to hear and determine, upon the consent of all the parties, appeals under subsection (a) of this section.

(5) An appeal to be heard under this subsection shall be heard by a panel of 3 members of the bankruptcy appellate panel service, except that a member of such service may not hear an appeal originating in the district for which such member is appointed or designated under section 152 of this title.

(6) Appeals may not be heard under this subsection by a panel of the bankruptcy appellate panel service unless the district judges for the district in which the appeals occur, by majority vote, have authorized such service to hear and determine appeals originating in such district.

(c)(1) Subject to subsections (b) and (d)(2), each appeal under subsection (a) shall be heard by a 3-judge panel of the bankruptcy appellate panel service established under subsection (b)(1) unless—

(A) the appellant elects at the time of filing the appeal; or

(B) any other party elects, not later than 30 days after service of notice of the appeal;

to have such appeal heard by the district court.

(2) An appeal under subsections (a) and (b) of this section shall be taken in the same manner as appeals in civil proceedings generally are taken to the courts of appeals from the district courts and in the time provided by Rule 8002 of the Bankruptcy Rules.

(d)(1) The courts of appeals shall have jurisdiction of appeals from all final decisions, judgments, orders, and decrees entered under subsections (a) and (b) of this section.

(2)(A) The appropriate court of appeals shall have jurisdiction of appeals described in the first sentence of subsection (a) if the bankruptcy court, the district court, or the bankruptcy appellate panel involved, acting on its own motion or on the request of a party to the judgment, order, or decree described in such first sentence, or all the appellants and appellees (if any) acting jointly, certify that—

(i) the judgment, order, or decree involves a question of law as to which there is no controlling decision of the court of appeals for the circuit or of the Supreme Court of the United States, or involves a matter of public importance;

(ii) the judgment, order, or decree involves a question of law requiring resolution of conflicting decisions; or

(iii) an immediate appeal from the judgment, order, or decree may materially advance the progress of the case or proceeding in which the appeal is taken;

and if the court of appeals authorizes the direct appeal of the judgment, order, or decree.

(B) If the bankruptcy court, the district court, or the bankruptcy appellate panel—

(i) on its own motion or on the request of a party, determines that a circumstance specified in clause (i), (ii), or (iii) of subparagraph (A) exists; or

(ii) receives a request made by a majority of the appellants and a majority of appellees (if any) to make the certification described in subparagraph (A);

then the bankruptcy court, the district court, or the bankruptcy appellate panel shall make the certification described in subparagraph (A).

(C) The parties may supplement the certification with a short statement of the basis for the certification.

(D) An appeal under this paragraph does not stay any proceeding of the bankruptcy court, the district court, or the bankruptcy appellate panel from which the appeal is taken, unless the respective bankruptcy court, district court, or bankruptcy appellate panel, or the court of appeals in which the appeal in pending, issues a stay of such proceeding pending the appeal.

(E) Any request under subparagraph (B) for certification shall be made not later than 60 days after the entry of the judgment, order, or decree.

§ 159. Bankruptcy Statistics.

(a) The clerk of the district court, or the clerk of the bankruptcy court if one is certified pursuant to section 156(b) of this title, shall collect statistics regarding debtors who are individuals with primarily consumer debts seeking relief under chapters 7, 11, and 13 of title 11. Those statistics shall be in a standardized format prescribed by the Director of the Administrative Office of the United States Courts (referred to in this section as the "Director").

(b) The Director shall—

(1) compile the statistics referred to in subsection (a);

(2) make the statistics available to the public; and

(3) not later than July 1, 2008, and annually thereafter, prepare, and submit to Congress a report concerning the information collected under subsection (a) that contains an analysis of the information.

(c) The compilation required under subsection (b) shall—

(1) be itemized, by chapter, with respect to title 11;

(2) be presented in the aggregate and for each district; and

(3) include information concerning—

(A) the total assets and total liabilities of the debtors described in subsection (a), and in each category of assets and liabilities, as reported in the schedules prescribed pursuant to section 2075 of this title and filed by debtors;

(B) the current monthly income, average income, and average expenses of debtors as reported on the schedules and statements that each such debtor files under sections 521 and 1322 of title 11;

(C) the aggregate amount of debt discharged in cases filed during the reporting period, determined as the difference between the total amount of debt and obligations of a debtor reported on the schedules and the amount of such debt reported in categories which are predominantly nondischargeable;

(D) the average period of time between the date of the filing of the petition and the closing of the case for cases closed during the reporting period;

(E) for cases closed during the reporting period—

(i) the number of cases in which a reaffirmation agreement was filed; and

(ii) (I) the total number of reaffirmation agreements filed;

(II) of those cases in which a reaffirmation agreement was filed, the number of cases in which the debtor was not represented by an attorney; and

(III) of those cases in which a reaffirmation agreement was filed, the number of cases in which the reaffirmation agreement was approved by the court;

(F) with respect to cases filed under chapter 13 of title 11, for the reporting period—

(i) (I) the number of cases in which a final order was entered determining the value of property securing a claim in an amount less than the amount of the claim; and

(II) the number of final orders entered determining the value of property securing a claim;

(ii) the number of cases dismissed, the number of cases dismissed for failure to make payments under the plan, the number of cases refiled after dismissal, and the number of cases in which the plan was completed, separately itemized with respect to the number of modifications made before completion of the plan, if any; and

(iii) the number of cases in which the debtor filed another case during the 6-year period preceding the filing;

(G) the number of cases in which creditors were fined for misconduct and any amount of punitive damages awarded by the court for creditor misconduct; and

(H) the number of cases in which sanctions under rule 9011 of the Federal Rules of Bankruptcy Procedure were imposed against debtor's attorney or damages awarded under such Rule.

CHAPTER 39—UNITED STATES TRUSTEES

§ 581. United States Trustees.

(a) The Attorney General shall appoint one United States trustee for each of the following regions composed of Federal judicial districts (without regard to section 451):

(1) The judicial districts established for the States of Maine, Massachusetts, New Hampshire, and Rhode Island.

(2) The judicial districts established for the States of Connecticut, New York, and Vermont.

(3) The judicial districts established for the States of Delaware, New Jersey, and Pennsylvania.

(4) The judicial districts established for the States of Maryland, North Carolina, South Carolina, Virginia, and West Virginia and for the District of Columbia.

(5) The judicial districts established for the States of Louisiana and Mississippi.

(6) The Northern District of Texas and the Eastern District of Texas.

(7) The Southern District of Texas and the Western District of Texas.

(8) The judicial districts established for the States of Kentucky and Tennessee.

(9) The judicial districts established for the States of Michigan and Ohio.

(10) The Central District of Illinois and the Southern District of Illinois; and the judicial districts established for the State of Indiana.

(11) The Northern District of Illinois; and the judicial districts established for the State of Wisconsin.

(12) The judicial districts established for the States of Minnesota, Iowa, North Dakota, and South Dakota.

(13) The judicial districts established for the States of Arkansas, Nebraska, and Missouri.

(14) The District of Arizona.

(15) The Southern District of California; and the judicial districts established for the State of Hawaii, and for Guam and the Commonwealth of the Northern Mariana Islands.

(16) The Central District of California.

(17) The Eastern District of California and the Northern District of California; and the judicial district established for the State of Nevada.

(18) The judicial districts established for the States of Alaska, Idaho (exclusive of Yellowstone National Park), Montana (exclusive of Yellowstone National Park), Oregon, and Washington.

(19) The judicial districts established for the States of Colorado, Utah, and Wyoming (including those portions of Yellowstone National Park situated in the States of Montana and Idaho).

(20) The judicial districts established for the States of Kansas, New Mexico, and Oklahoma.

(21) The judicial districts established for the States of Alabama, Florida, and Georgia and for the Commonwealth of Puerto Rico and the Virgin Islands of the United States.

(b) Each United States trustee shall be appointed for a term of five years. On the expiration of his term, a United States trustee shall continue to perform the duties of his office until his successor is appointed and qualifies.

(c) Each United States trustee is subject to removal by the Attorney General.

§ 586. Duties; Supervision by Attorney General.

(a) Each United States trustee, within the region for which such United States trustee is appointed, shall—

(1) establish, maintain, and supervise a panel of private trustees that are eligible and available to serve as trustees in cases under chapter 7 of title 11;

(2) serve as and perform the duties of a trustee in a case under title 11 when required under title 11 to serve as trustee in such a case;

(3) supervise the administration of cases and trustees in cases under chapter 7, 11 (including subchapter V of chapter 11), 12, 13, or 15 of title 11 by, whenever the United States trustee considers it to be appropriate—

(A) (i) reviewing, in accordance with procedural guidelines adopted by the Executive Office of the United States Trustee (which guidelines shall be applied uniformly by the United States trustee except when circumstances warrant different treatment), applications filed for compensation and reimbursement under section 330 of title 11; and

(ii) filing with the court comments with respect to such application and, if the United States Trustee considers it to be appropriate, objections to such application;

(B) monitoring plans and disclosure statements filed in cases under chapter 11 of title 11 and filing with the court, in connection with hearings under sections 1125 and 1128 of such title, comments with respect to such plans and disclosure statements;

(C) monitoring plans filed under chapters 12 and 13 of title 11 and filing with the court, in connection with hearings under sections 1224, 1229, 1324, and 1329 of such title, comments with respect to such plans;

(D) taking such action as the United States trustee deems to be appropriate to ensure that all reports, schedules, and fees required to be filed under title 11 and this title by the debtor are properly and timely filed;

(E) monitoring creditors' committees appointed under title 11;

(F) notifying the appropriate United States attorney of matters which relate to the occurrence of any action which may constitute a crime under the laws of the United States and, on the request of the United States attorney, assisting the United States attorney in carrying out prosecutions based on such action;

(G) monitoring the progress of cases under title 11 and taking such actions as the United States trustee deems to be appropriate to prevent undue delay in such progress;

(H) in small business cases (as defined in section 101 of title 11), performing the additional duties specified in title 11 pertaining to such cases; and

(I) monitoring applications filed under section 327 of title 11 and, whenever the United States trustee deems it to be appropriate, filing with the court comments with respect to the approval of such applications;

(4) deposit or invest under section 345 of title 11 money received as trustee in cases under title 11;

(5) perform the duties prescribed for the United States trustee under title 11 and this title, and such duties consistent with title 11 and this title as the Attorney General may prescribe;

(6) make such reports as the Attorney General directs, including the results of audits performed under section 603(a) of the Bankruptcy Abuse Prevention and Consumer Protection Act of 2005;

(7) in each of such small business cases—

(A) conduct an initial debtor interview as soon as practicable after the date of the order for relief but before the first meeting scheduled under section 341(a) of title 11, at which time the United States trustee shall—

(i) begin to investigate the debtor's viability;

(ii) inquire about the debtor's business plan;

(iii) explain the debtor's obligations to file monthly operating reports and other required reports;

(iv) attempt to develop an agreed scheduling order; and

(v) inform the debtor of other obligations;

(B) if determined to be appropriate and advisable, visit the appropriate business premises of the debtor, ascertain the state of the debtor's books and records, and verify that the debtor has filed its tax returns; and

(C) review and monitor diligently the debtor's activities, to determine as promptly as possible whether the debtor will be unable to confirm a plan; and

(8) in any case in which the United States trustee finds material grounds for any relief under section

1112 of title 11, apply promptly after making that finding to the court for relief.

(b) If the number of cases under subchapter V of chapter 11 or chapter 12 or 13 of title 11 commenced in a particular region so warrants, the United States trustee for such region may, subject to the approval of the Attorney General, appoint one or more individuals to serve as standing trustee, or designate one or more assistant United States trustees to serve in cases under such chapter. The United States trustee for such region shall supervise any such individual appointed as standing trustee in the performance of the duties of standing trustee.

(c) Each United States trustee shall be under the general supervision of the Attorney General, who shall provide general coordination and assistance to the United States trustees.

(d) (1) The Attorney General shall prescribe by rule qualifications for membership on the panels established by United States trustees under paragraph (a)(1) of this section, and qualifications for appointment under subsection (b) of this section to serve as standing trustee in cases under subchapter V of chapter 11 or chapter 12 or 13 of title 11. The Attorney General may not require that an individual be an attorney in order to qualify for appointment under subsection (b) of this section to serve as standing trustee in cases under subchapter V of chapter 11 or chapter 12 or 13 of title 11.

(2) A trustee whose appointment under subsection (a)(1) or under subsection (b) is terminated or who ceases to be assigned to cases filed under title 11, United States Code, may obtain judicial review of the final agency decision by commencing an action in the district court of the United States for the district for which the panel to which the trustee is appointed under subsection (a)(1), or in the district court of the United States for the district in which the trustee is appointed under subsection (b) resides, after first exhausting all available administrative remedies, which if the trustee so elects, shall also include an administrative hearing on the record. Unless the trustee elects to have an administrative hearing on the record, the trustee shall be deemed to have exhausted all administrative remedies for purposes of this paragraph if the agency fails to make a final agency decision within 90 days after the trustee requests administrative remedies. The Attorney General shall prescribe procedures to implement this paragraph. The decision of the agency shall be affirmed by the district court unless it is unreasonable and without cause based on the administrative record before the agency.

(e) (1) The Attorney General, after consultation with a United States trustee that has appointed an individual under subsection (b) of this section to serve as standing trustee in cases under subchapter V of chapter 11 or chapter 12 or 13 of title 11, shall fix—

(A) a maximum annual compensation for such individual consisting of—

(i) an amount not to exceed the highest annual rate of basic pay in effect for level V of the Executive Schedule; and

(ii) the cash value of employment benefits comparable to the employment benefits provided by the United States to individuals who are employed by the United States at the same rate of basic pay to perform similar services during the same period of time; and

(B) a percentage fee not to exceed—

(i) in the case of a debtor who is not a family farmer, ten percent; or

(ii) in the case of a debtor who is a family farmer, the sum of—

(I) not to exceed ten percent of the payments made under the plan of such debtor, with respect to payments in an aggregate amount not to exceed $450,000; and

(II) three percent of payments made under the plan of such debtor, with respect to payments made after the aggregate amount of payments made under the plan exceeds $450,000;

based on such maximum annual compensation and the actual, necessary expenses incurred by such individual as standing trustee.

(2) Such individual shall collect such percentage fee from all payments received by such individual under plans in the cases under subchapter V of chapter 11 or chapter 12 or 13 of title 11 for which such individual serves as standing trustee. Such individual shall pay to the United States trustee, and the United States trustee shall deposit in the United States Trustee System Fund—

(A) any amount by which the actual compensation of such individual exceeds 5 per centum upon all payments received under plans in cases under chapter 12 or 13 of title 11 for which such individual serves as standing trustee; and

(B) any amount by which the percentage for all such cases exceeds—

(i) such individual's actual compensation for such cases, as adjusted under subparagraph (A) of paragraph (1); plus

(ii) the actual, necessary expenses incurred by such individual as standing trustee in such cases. Subject to the approval of the Attorney General, any or all of the interest earned from the deposit of payments under plans by such individual may be utilized to pay actual, necessary expenses without regard to the percentage limitation contained in subparagraph (d)(1)(B) of this section.

(3) After first exhausting all available administrative remedies, an individual appointed under subsection (b) may obtain judicial review of final agency action to deny a claim of actual, necessary expenses under this subsection by commencing an action in the district court of the United States for the district where the individual resides. The decision of the agency shall be affirmed by the district court unless it is unreasonable and without cause based upon the administrative record before the agency.

(4) The Attorney General shall prescribe procedures to implement this subsection.

(5) In the event that the services of the trustee in a case under subchapter V of chapter 11 of title 11 are terminated by dismissal or conversion of the case, or upon substantial consummation of a plan under section 1183(c)(1) of that title, the court shall award compensation to the trustee consistent with services performed by the trustee and the limits on the compensation of the trustee established pursuant to paragraph (1) of this subsection.

(f) (1) The United States trustee for each district is authorized to contract with auditors to perform audits in cases designated by the United States trustee, in accordance with the procedures established under section 603(a) of the Bankruptcy Abuse Prevention and Consumer Protection Act of 2005.

(2) (A) The report of each audit referred to in paragraph (1) shall be filed with the court and transmitted to the United States trustee. Each report shall clearly and conspicuously specify any material misstatement of income or expenditures or of assets identified by the person performing the audit. In any case in which a material misstatement of income or expenditures or of assets has been reported, the clerk of the district court (or the clerk of the bankruptcy court if one is certified under section 156(b) of this title) shall give notice of the misstatement to the creditors in the case.

(B) If a material misstatement of income or expenditures or of assets is reported, the United States trustee shall—

(i) report the material misstatement, if appropriate, to the United States Attorney pursuant to section 3057 of title 18; and

(ii) if advisable, take appropriate action, including but not limited to commencing an adversary proceeding to revoke the debtor's discharge pursuant to section 727(d) of title 11.

§ 589b. Bankruptcy Data.

(a) RULES.—The Attorney General shall, within a reasonable time after the effective date of this section, issue rules requiring uniform forms for (and from time to time thereafter to appropriately modify and approve)—

(1) final reports by trustees in cases under subchapter V of chapter 11 and chapters 7, 12, and 13 of title 11; and

(2) periodic reports by debtors in possession or trustees in cases under chapter 11 of title 11.

(b) REPORTS.—Each report referred to in subsection (a) shall be designed (and the requirements as to place and manner of filing shall be established) so as to facilitate compilation of data and maximum possible access of the public, both by physical inspection at one or more central filing locations, and by electronic access through the Internet or other appropriate media.

(c) REQUIRED INFORMATION.—The information required to be filed in the reports referred to in subsection (b) shall be that which is in the best interests of debtors and creditors, and in the public interest in reasonable and adequate information to evaluate the efficiency and practicality of the Federal bankruptcy system. In issuing rules proposing the forms referred to in subsection (a), the Attorney General shall strike the best achievable practical balance between—

(1) the reasonable needs of the public for information about the operational results of the Federal bankruptcy system;

(2) economy, simplicity, and lack of undue burden on persons with a duty to file reports; and

(3) appropriate privacy concerns and safeguards.

(d) FINAL REPORTS.—The uniform forms for final reports required under subsection (a) for use by trustees under subchapter V of chapter 11 and chapters 7, 12, and 13 of title 11 shall, in addition to such other matters as are required by law or as the Attorney General in the discretion of the Attorney General shall propose, include with respect to a case under such title—

(1) information about the length of time the case was pending;

(2) assets abandoned;

(3) assets exempted;

(4) receipts and disbursements of the estate;

(5) expenses of administration, including for use under section 707(b), actual costs of administering cases under chapter 13 of title 11;

(6) claims asserted;

(7) claims allowed; and

(8) distributions to claimants and claims discharged without payment,

in each case by appropriate category and, in cases under subchapter V of chapter 11 and chapters 12 and 13 of title 11, date of confirmation of the plan, each modification thereto, and defaults by the debtor in performance under the plan.

(e) PERIODIC REPORTS.—The uniform forms for periodic reports required under subsection (a) for use by trustees or debtors in possession under chapter 11 of title 11 shall, in addition to such other matters as are required by law or as the Attorney General in the discretion of the Attorney General shall propose, include—

(1) information about the industry classification, published by the Department of Commerce, for the businesses conducted by the debtor;

(2) length of time the case has been pending;

(3) number of full-time employees as of the date of the order for relief and at the end of each reporting period since the case was filed;

(4) cash receipts, cash disbursements and profitability of the debtor for the most recent period and cumulatively since the date of the order for relief;

(5) compliance with title 11, whether or not tax returns and tax payments since the date of the order for relief have been timely filed and made;

(6) all professional fees approved by the court in the case for the most recent period and cumulatively since the date of the order for relief (separately reported, for the professional fees incurred by or on behalf of the debtor, between those that would have been incurred absent a bankruptcy case and those not); and

(7) plans of reorganization filed and confirmed and, with respect thereto, by class, the recoveries of the holders, expressed in aggregate dollar values and, in the case of claims, as a percentage of total claims of the class allowed.

CHAPTER 57—GENERAL PROVISIONS APPLICABLE TO COURT OFFICERS AND EMPLOYEES

§ 959. Trustees and Receivers Suable; Management; State Laws.

(a) Trustees, receivers or managers of any property, including debtors in possession, may be sued, without leave of the court appointing them, with respect to any of their acts or transactions in carrying on business connected with such property. Such actions shall be subject to the general equity power of such court so far as the same may be necessary to the ends of justice, but this shall not deprive a litigant of his right to trial by jury.

(b) Except as provided in section 1166 of title 11, a trustee, receiver or manager appointed in any cause pending in any court of the United States, including a debtor in possession, shall manage and operate the property in his possession as such trustee, receiver or manager according to the requirements of the valid laws of the State in which such property is situated, in the same manner that the owner or possessor thereof would be bound to do if in possession thereof.

CHAPTER 85—DISTRICT COURTS; JURISDICTION

§ 1334. Bankruptcy Cases and Proceedings.

(a) Except as provided in subsection (b) of this section, the district courts shall have original and exclusive jurisdiction of all cases under title 11.

(b) Except as provided in subsection (e)(2), and notwithstanding any Act of Congress that confers exclusive jurisdiction on a court or courts other than the district courts, the district courts shall have original but not exclusive jurisdiction of all civil proceedings arising under title 11, or arising in or related to cases under title 11.

(c) (1) Except with respect to a case under chapter 15 of title 11, nothing in this section prevents a district court in the interest of justice, or in the interest of comity with State courts or respect for State law, from abstaining from hearing a particular proceeding arising under title 11 or arising in or related to a case under title 11.

(2) Upon timely motion of a party in a proceeding based upon a State law claim or State law cause of action, related to a case under title 11 but not arising under title 11 or arising in a case under title 11, with respect to which an action could not have been commenced in a court of the United States absent jurisdiction under this section, the district court shall abstain from hearing such proceeding if an action

is commenced, and can be timely adjudicated, in a State forum of appropriate jurisdiction.

(d) Any decision to abstain or not to abstain made under subsection (c) (other than a decision not to abstain in a proceeding described in subsection (c)(2)) is not reviewable by appeal or otherwise by the court of appeals under section 158(d), 1291, or 1292 of this title or by the Supreme Court of the United States under section 1254 of this title. Subsection (c) and this subsection shall not be construed to limit the applicability of the stay provided for by section 362 of title 11, United States Code, as such section applies to an action affecting the property of the estate in bankruptcy.

(e) The district court in which a case under title 11 is commenced or is pending shall have exclusive jurisdiction—

(1) of all the property, wherever located, of the debtor as of the commencement of such case, and of property of the estate; and

(2) over all claims or causes of action that involve construction of section 327 of title 11, United States Code, or rules relating to disclosure requirements under section 327.

CHAPTER 87—DISTRICT COURTS; VENUE

§ 1408. Venue of Cases under Title 11.

Except as provided in section 1410 of this title, a case under title 11 may be commenced in the district court for the district—

(1) in which the domicile, residence, principal place of business in the United States, or principal assets in the United States, of the person or entity that is the subject of such case have been located for the one hundred and eighty days immediately preceding such commencement, or for a longer portion of such one-hundred-and-eighty-day period than the domicile, residence, or principal place of business, in the United States, or principal assets in the United States, of such person were located in any other district; or

(2) in which there is pending a case under title 11 concerning such person's affiliate, general partner, or partnership.

§ 1409. Venue of Proceedings Arising under Title 11 or Arising in or Related to Cases under Title 11.

(a) Except as otherwise provided in subsections (b) and (d), a proceeding arising under title 11 or arising in or related to a case under title 11 may be commenced in the district court in which such case is pending.

(b) Except as provided in subsection (d) of this section, a trustee in a case under title 11 may commence a proceeding arising in or related to such case to recover a money judgment of or property worth less than $1,725 or a consumer debt of less than $27,750, or a debt (excluding a consumer debt) against a noninsider of less than $31,425, only in the district court for the district in which the defendant resides.

(c) Except as provided in subsection (b) of this section, a trustee in a case under title 11 may commence a proceeding arising in or related to such case as statutory successor to the debtor or creditors under section 541 or 544(b) of title 11 in the district court for the district where the State or Federal court sits in which, under applicable nonbankruptcy venue provisions, the debtor or creditors, as the case may be, may have commenced an action on which such proceeding is based if the case under title 11 had not been commenced.

(d) A trustee may commence a proceeding arising under title 11 or arising in or related to a case under title 11 based on a claim arising after the commencement of such case from the operation of the business of the debtor only in the district court for the district where a State or Federal court sits in which, under applicable nonbankruptcy venue provisions, an action on such claim may have been brought.

(e) A proceeding arising under title 11 or arising in or related to a case under title 11, based on a claim arising after the commencement of such case from the operation of the business of the debtor, may be commenced against the representative of the estate in such case in the district court for the district where the State or Federal court sits in which the party commencing such proceeding may, under applicable nonbankruptcy venue provisions, have brought an action on such claim, or in the district court in which such case is pending.

§ 1410. Venue of Cases Ancillary to Foreign Proceedings.

A case under chapter 15 of title 11 may be commenced in the district court of the United States for the district—

(1) in which the debtor has its principal place of business or principal assets in the United States;

(2) if the debtor does not have a place of business or assets in the United States, in which there is

pending against the debtor an action or proceeding in a Federal or State court; or

(3) in a case other than those specified in paragraph (1) or (2), in which venue will be consistent with the interests of justice and the convenience of the parties, having regard to the relief sought by the foreign representative.

§ 1411. Jury Trials.

(a) Except as provided in subsection (b) of this section, this chapter and title 11 do not affect any right to trial by jury that an individual has under applicable nonbankruptcy law with regard to a personal injury or wrongful death tort claim.

(b) The district court may order the issues arising under section 303 of title 11 to be tried without a jury.

§ 1412. Change of Venue.

A district court may transfer a case or proceeding under title 11 to a district court for another district, in the interest of justice or for the convenience of the parties.

CHAPTER 89—DISTRICT COURTS; REMOVAL OF CASES FROM STATE COURTS

§ 1452. Removal of Claims Related to Bankruptcy Cases.

(a) A party may remove any claim or cause of action in a civil action other than a proceeding before the United States Tax Court or a civil action by a governmental unit to enforce such governmental unit's police or regulatory power, to the district court for the district where such civil action is pending, if such district court has jurisdiction of such claim or cause of action under section 1334 of this title.

(b) The court to which such claim or cause of action is removed may remand such claim or cause of action on any equitable ground. An order entered under this subsection remanding a claim or cause of action, or a decision to not remand, is not reviewable by appeal or otherwise by the court of appeals under section 158(d), 1291, or 1292 of this title or by the Supreme Court of the United States under section 1254 of this title.

PART III

OTHER FEDERAL STATUTES AND RELATED REGULATIONS

Magnuson-Moss Warranty Act

15 U.S.C. §§ 2301–2312

§ 2301. Definitions

For the purposes of this chapter:

(1) The term "consumer product" means any tangible personal property which is distributed in commerce and which is normally used for personal, family, or household purposes (including any such property intended to be attached to or installed in any real property without regard to whether it is so attached or installed).

(2) The term "Commission" means the Federal Trade Commission.

(3) The term "consumer" means a buyer (other than for purposes of resale) of any consumer product, any person to whom such product is transferred during the duration of an implied or written warranty (or service contract) applicable to the product, and any other person who is entitled by the terms of such warranty (or service contract) or under applicable State law to enforce against the warrantor (or service contractor) the obligations of the warranty (or service contract).

(4) The term "supplier" means any person engaged in the business of making a consumer product directly or indirectly available to consumers.

(5) The term "warrantor" means any supplier or other person who gives or offers to give a written warranty or who is or may be obligated under an implied warranty.

(6) The term "written warranty" means—

(A) any written affirmation of fact or written promise made in connection with the sale of a consumer product by a supplier to a buyer which relates to the nature of the material or workmanship and affirms or promises that such material or workmanship is defect free or will meet a specified level of performance over a specified period of time, or

(B) any undertaking in writing in connection with the sale by a supplier of a consumer product to refund, repair, replace, or take other remedial action with respect to such product in the event that such product fails to meet the specifications set forth in the undertaking, which written affirmation, promise, or undertaking becomes part of the basis of the bargain between a supplier and a buyer for purposes other than resale of such product.

(7) The term "implied warranty" means an implied warranty arising under State law (as modified by sections 2308 and 2304(a) of this title) in connection with the sale by a supplier of a consumer product.

(8) The term "service contract" means a contract in writing to perform, over a fixed period of time or for a specified duration, services relating to the maintenance or repair (or both) of a consumer product.

(9) The term "reasonable and necessary maintenance" consists of those operations

(A) which the consumer reasonably can be expected to perform or have performed and

(B) which are necessary to keep any consumer product performing its intended function and operating at a reasonable level of performance.

(10) The term "remedy" means whichever of the following actions the warrantor elects:

(A) repair,

(B) replacement, or

(C) refund; except that the warrantor may not elect refund unless

(i) the warrantor is unable to provide replacement and repair is not commercially practicable or cannot be timely made, or

(ii) the consumer is willing to accept such refund.

(11) The term "replacement" means furnishing a new consumer product which is identical or reasonably equivalent to the warranted consumer product.

(12) The term "refund" means refunding the actual purchase price (less reasonable depreciation based on actual use where permitted by rules of the Commission).

(13) The term "distributed in commerce" means sold in commerce, introduced or delivered for introduction into commerce, or held for sale or distribution after introduction into commerce.

(14) The term "commerce" means trade, traffic, commerce, or transportation—

(A) between a place in a State and any place outside thereof, or

(B) which affects trade, traffic, commerce, or transportation described in subparagraph (A).

(15) The term "State" means a State, the District of Columbia, the Commonwealth of Puerto Rico, the Virgin Islands, Guam, the Canal Zone, or American Samoa. The term "State law" includes a law of the United States applicable only to the District of Columbia or only to a territory or possession of the United States; and the term "Federal law" excludes any State law.

§ 2302. Rules Governing Contents of Warranties

(a) Full and conspicuous disclosure of terms and conditions; additional requirements for contents. In order to improve the adequacy of information available to consumers, prevent deception, and improve competition in the marketing of consumer products, any warrantor warranting a consumer product to a consumer by means of a written warranty shall, to the extent required by rules of the Commission, fully and conspicuously disclose in simple and readily understood language the terms and conditions of such warranty. Such rules may require inclusion in the written warranty of any of the following items among others:

(1) The clear identification of the names and addresses of the warrantors.

(2) The identity of the party or parties to whom the warranty is extended.

(3) The products or parts covered.

(4) A statement of what the warrantor will do in the event of a defect, malfunction, or failure to conform with such written warranty— at whose expense— and for what period of time.

(5) A statement of what the consumer must do and expenses he must bear.

(6) Exceptions and exclusions from the terms of the warranty.

(7) The step-by-step procedure which the consumer should take in order to obtain performance of any obligation under the warranty, including the identification of any person or class of persons authorized to perform the obligations set forth in the warranty.

(8) Information respecting the availability of any informal dispute settlement procedure offered by the warrantor and a recital, where the warranty so provides, that the purchaser may be required to resort to such procedure before pursuing any legal remedies in the courts.

(9) A brief, general description of the legal remedies available to the consumer.

(10) The time at which the warrantor will perform any obligations under the warranty.

(11) The period of time within which, after notice of a defect, malfunction, or failure to conform with the warranty, the warrantor will perform any obligations under the warranty.

(12) The characteristics or properties of the products, or parts thereof, that are not covered by the warranty.

(13) The elements of the warranty in words or phrases which would not mislead a reasonable, average consumer as to the nature or scope of the warranty.

(b) Availability of terms to consumer; manner and form for presentation and display of information; duration; extension of period for written warranty or service contract

(1) (A) The Commission shall prescribe rules requiring that the terms of any written warranty on

a consumer product be made available to the consumer (or prospective consumer) prior to the sale of the product to him.

(B) The Commission may prescribe rules for determining the manner and form in which information with respect to any written warranty of a consumer product shall be clearly and conspicuously presented or displayed so as not to mislead the reasonable, average consumer, when such information is contained in advertising, labeling, point-of-sale material, or other representations in writing.

(2) Nothing in this chapter (other than paragraph (3) of this subsection) shall be deemed to authorize the Commission to prescribe the duration of written warranties given or to require that a consumer product or any of its components be warranted.

(3) The Commission may prescribe rules for extending the period of time a written warranty or service contract is in effect to correspond with any period of time in excess of a reasonable period (not less than 10 days) during which the consumer is deprived of the use of such consumer product by reason of failure of the product to conform with the written warranty or by reason of the failure of the warrantor (or service contractor) to carry out such warranty (or service contract) within the period specified in the warranty (or service contract).

(c) Prohibition on conditions for written or implied warranty; waiver by Commission. No warrantor of a consumer product may condition his written or implied warranty of such product on the consumer's using, in connection with such product, any article or service (other than article or service provided without charge under the terms of the warranty) which is identified by brand, trade, or corporate name; except that the prohibition of this subsection may be waived by the Commission if—

(1) the warrantor satisfies the Commission that the warranted product will function properly only if the article or service so identified is used in connection with the warranted product, and

(2) the Commission finds that such a waiver is in the public interest. The Commission shall identify in the Federal Register, and permit public comment on, all applications for waiver of the prohibition of this subsection, and shall publish in the Federal Register its disposition of any such application, including the reasons therefor.

(d) Incorporation by reference of detailed substantive warranty provisions. The Commission may by rule devise detailed substantive warranty provisions which warrantors may incorporate by reference in their warranties.

(e) Applicability to consumer products costing more than $5. The provisions of this section apply only to warranties which pertain to consumer products actually costing the consumer more than $5.

§ 2303. Designation of Written Warranties

(a) Full (statement of duration) or limited warranty. Any warrantor warranting a consumer product by means of a written warranty shall clearly and conspicuously designate such warranty in the following manner, unless exempted from doing so by the Commission pursuant to subsection (c) of this section:

(1) If the written warranty meets the Federal minimum standards for warranty set forth in section 2304 of this title, then it shall be conspicuously designated a "full (statement of duration) warranty."

(2) If the written warranty does not meet the Federal minimum standards for warranty set forth in section 2304 of this title, then it shall be conspicuously designated a "limited warranty."

(b) Applicability of requirements, standards, etc., to representations or statements of customer satisfaction. This section and sections 2302 and 2304 of this title shall not apply to statements or representations which are similar to expressions of general policy concerning customer satisfaction and which are not subject to any specific limitations.

(c) Exemptions by Commission. In addition to exercising the authority pertaining to disclosure granted in section 2302 of this title, the Commission may by rule determine when a written warranty does not have to be designated either "full (statement of duration)" or "limited" in accordance with this section.

(d) Applicability to consumer products costing more than $10 and not designated as full warranties. The provisions of subsections (a) and (c) of this section apply only to warranties which pertain to consumer products actually costing the consumer more than $10 and which are not designated "full (statement of duration) warranties."

§ 2304. Federal Minimum Standards for Warranties

(a) Remedies under written warranty; duration of implied warranty; exclusion or limitation on consequential damages for breach of written or implied warranty; election of refund or replacement. In order for a warrantor warranting a consumer product by means of a written warranty to meet the Federal minimum standards for warranty—

(1) such warrantor must as a minimum remedy such consumer product within a reasonable time and without charge, in the case of a defect, malfunction, or failure to conform with such written warranty;

(2) notwithstanding section 2308(b) of this title, such warrantor may not impose any limitation on the duration of any implied warranty on the product;

(3) such warrantor may not exclude or limit consequential damages for breach of any written or implied warranty on such product, unless such exclusion or limitation conspicuously appears on the face of the warranty; and

(4) if the product (or a component part thereof) contains a defect or malfunction after a reasonable number of attempts by the warrantor to remedy defects or malfunctions in such product, such warrantor must permit the consumer to elect either a refund for, or replacement without charge of, such product or part (as the case may be). The Commission may by rule specify for purposes of this paragraph, what constitutes a reasonable number of attempts to remedy particular kinds of defects or malfunctions under different circumstances. If the warrantor replaces a component part of a consumer product, such replacement shall include installing the part in the product without charge.

(b) Duties and conditions imposed on consumer by warrantor

(1) In fulfilling the duties under subsection (a) of this section respecting a written warranty, the warrantor shall not impose any duty other than notification upon any consumer as a condition of securing remedy of any consumer product which malfunctions, is defective, or does not conform to the written warranty, unless the warrantor has demonstrated in a rulemaking proceeding, or can demonstrate in an administrative or judicial enforcement proceeding including private enforcement), or in an informal dispute settlement proceeding, that such a duty is reasonable.

(2) Notwithstanding paragraph (1), a warrantor may require, as a condition to replacement of, or refund for, any consumer product under subsection (a) of this section, that such consumer product shall be made available to the warrantor free and clear of liens and other encumbrances, except as otherwise provided by rule or order of the Commission in cases in which such a requirement would not be practicable.

(3) The Commission may, by rule define in detail the duties set forth in subsection (a) of this section and the applicability of such duties to warrantors of different categories of consumer products with "full (statement of duration)" warranties.

(4) The duties under subsection (a) of this section extend from the warrantor to each person who is a consumer with respect to the consumer product.

(c) Waiver of standards. The performance of the duties under subsection (a) of this section shall not be required of the warrantor if he can show that the defect, malfunction, or failure of any warranted consumer product to conform with a written warranty, was caused by damage (not resulting from defect or malfunction) while in the possession of the consumer, or unreasonable use (including failure to provide reasonable and necessary maintenance).

(d) Remedy without charge. For purposes of this section and of section 2302(c) of this title, the term "without charge" means that the warrantor may not assess the consumer for any costs the warrantor or his representatives incur in connection with the required remedy of a warranted consumer product. An obligation under subsection (a)(1)(A) of this section to remedy without charge does not necessarily require the warrantor to compensate the consumer for incidental expenses; however, if any incidental expenses are incurred because the remedy is not made within a reasonable time or because the warrantor imposed an unreasonable duty upon the consumer as a condition of securing remedy, then the consumer shall be entitled to recover reasonable incidental expenses which are so incurred in any action against the warrantor.

(e) Incorporation of standards to products designated with full warranty for purposes of judicial actions. If a supplier designates a warranty applicable to a consumer product as a "full (statement of duration)" warranty, then the warranty on such product shall, for purposes of any action under section 2310(d) of this title or under any State law, be deemed to incorporate at least the minimum requirements of this section and rules prescribed under this section.

§ 2305. Full and Limited Warranting of a Consumer Product

Nothing in this chapter shall prohibit the selling of a consumer product which has both full and limited warranties if such warranties are clearly and conspicuously differentiated.

§ 2306. Service Contracts; Rules for Full, Clear and Conspicuous Disclosure of Terms and Conditions; Addition to or in Lieu of Written Warranty

(a) The Commission may prescribe by rule the manner and form in which the terms and conditions of service contracts shall be fully, clearly, and conspicuously disclosed.

(b) Nothing in this chapter shall be construed to prevent a supplier or warrantor from entering into a service contract with the consumer in addition to or in lieu of a written warranty if such contract fully, clearly, and conspicuously discloses its terms and conditions in simple and readily understood language.

§ 2307. Designation of Representatives by Warrantor to Perform Duties Under Written or Implied Warranty

Nothing in this chapter shall be construed to prevent any warrantor from designating representatives to perform duties under the written or implied warranty: Provided, That such warrantor shall make reasonable arrangements for compensation of such designated representatives, but no such designation shall relieve the warrantor of his direct responsibilities to the consumer or make the representative a cowarrantor.

§ 2308. Implied Warranties

(a) Restrictions on disclaimers or modifications. No supplier may disclaim or modify (except as provided in subsection (b) of this section) any implied warranty to a consumer with respect to such consumer product if

(1) such supplier makes any written warranty to the consumer with respect to such consumer Product, or

(2) at the time of sale, or within 90 days thereafter, such supplier enters into a service contract with the consumer which applies to such consumer product.

(b) Limitation on duration. For purposes of this chapter (other than section 2304(a)(2) of this title), implied warranties may be limited in duration to the duration of a written warranty of reasonable duration, if such limitation is conscionable and is set forth in clear and unmistakable language and prominently displayed on the face of the warranty.

(c) Effectiveness of disclaimers, modifications, or limitations. A disclaimer, modification, or limitation made in violation of this section shall be ineffective for purposes of this chapter and State law.

§ 2309. Procedures Applicable to Promulgation of Rules by Commission

(a) Oral presentation. Any rule prescribed under this chapter shall be prescribed in accordance with section 553 of title 5; except that the Commission shall give interested persons an opportunity for oral presentations of data, views, and arguments, in addition to written submissions. A transcript shall be kept of any oral presentation. Any such rule shall be subject to judicial review under section 57a(e) of this title in the same manner as rules prescribed under section 57a(a)(1)(B) of this title, except that section 57a(e)(3)(B) of this title shall not apply.

(b) Warranties and warranty practices involved in sale of used motor vehicles. The Commission shall initiate within one year after January 4, 1975, a rulemaking proceeding dealing with warranties and warranty practices in connection with the sale of used motor vehicles; and, to the extent necessary to supplement the protections offered the consumer by this chapter, shall prescribe rules dealing with such warranties and practices. In prescribing rules under this subsection, the Commission may exercise any authority it may have under this chapter, or other law, and in addition it may require disclosure that a used motor vehicle is sold without any warranty and specify the form and content of such disclosure.

§ 2310. Remedies in Consumer Disputes

(a) Informal dispute settlement procedures; establishment; rules setting forth minimum requirements; effect of compliance by warrantor; review of informal procedures or implementation by Commission; application to existing informal procedures

(1) Congress hereby declares it to be its policy to encourage warrantors to establish procedures whereby consumer disputes are fairly and expeditiously settled through informal dispute settlement mechanisms.

(2) The Commission shall prescribe rules setting forth minimum requirements for any informal dispute settlement procedure which is incorporated into the terms of a written warranty to which any provision of this chapter applies. Such rules shall provide for participation in such procedure by independent or governmental entities.

(3) One or more warrantors may establish an informal dispute settlement procedure which meets the requirements of the Commission's rules under paragraph (2). If—

(A) a warrantor establishes such a procedure,

(B) such procedure, and its implementation, meets the requirements of such rules, and

(C) he incorporates in a written warranty a requirement that the consumer resort to such procedure before pursuing any legal remedy under this section respecting such warranty, then

(i) the consumer may not commence a civil action (other than a class action) under subsection (d) of this section unless he initially resorts to such procedure; and

(ii) a class of consumers may not proceed in a class action under subsection (d) of this section except to the extent the court determines necessary to establish the representative capacity of the named plaintiffs, unless the named plaintiffs (upon notifying the defendant that they are named plaintiffs in a class action with respect to a warranty obligation) initially resort to such procedure. In the case of such a class action which is brought in a district court of the United States, the representative capacity of the named plaintiffs shall be established in the application of rule 23 of the Federal Rules of Civil Procedure. In any civil action arising out of a warranty obligation and relating to a matter considered in such a procedure, any decision in such procedure shall be admissible in evidence.

(4) The Commission on its own initiative may, or upon written complaint filed by any interested person shall, review the bona fide operation of any dispute settlement procedure resort to which is stated in a written warranty to be a prerequisite to pursuing a legal remedy under this section. If the Commission finds that such procedure or its implementation fails to comply with the requirements of the rules under paragraph (2), the Commission may take appropriate remedial action under any authority it may have under this chapter or any other provision of law.

(5) Until rules under paragraph (2) take effect, this subsection shall not affect the validity of any informal dispute settlement procedure respecting consumer warranties, but in any action under subsection (d) of this section, the court may invalidate any such procedure if it finds that such procedure is unfair.

(b) Prohibited acts. It shall be a violation of section 45(a)(1) of this title for any person to fail to comply with any requirement imposed on such person by this chapter (or a rule thereunder) or to violate any prohibition contained in this chapter (or a rule thereunder).

(c) Injunction proceedings by Attorney General or Commission for deceptive warranty, noncompliance with requirements, or violating prohibitions; procedures; definitions

(1) The district courts of the United States shall have jurisdiction of any action brought by the Attorney General (in his capacity as such), or by the Commission by any of its attorneys designated by it for such purpose, to restrain

(A) any warrantor from making a deceptive warranty with respect to a consumer product, or

(B) any person from failing to comply with any requirement imposed on such person by or pursuant to this chapter or from violating any prohibition contained in this chapter. Upon proper showing that, weighing the equities and considering the Commission's or Attorney General's likelihood of ultimate success, such action would be in the public interest and after notice to the defendant, a temporary restraining order or preliminary injunction may be granted without bond. In the case of an action brought by the Commission, if a complaint under section 45 of this title is not filed within such period (not exceeding 10 days) as may be specified by the court after the issuance of the temporary restraining order or preliminary injunction, the order or injunction shall be dissolved by the court and be of no further force and effect. Any suit shall be brought in the district in which such person resides or transacts business. Whenever it appears to the court that the ends of justice require that other persons should be parties in the action, the court may cause them to be summoned whether or not they reside in the district in which the court is held, and to that end process may be served in any district.

(2) For the purposes of this subsection, the term "deceptive warranty" means

(A) a written warranty which

(i) contains an affirmation, promise, description, or representation which is either false or fraudulent, or which, in light of all of the circumstances, would mislead a reasonable individual exercising due care; or

(ii) fails to contain information which is necessary in light of all of the circumstances, to make the warranty not misleading to a reasonable individual exercising due care; or

(B) a written warranty created by the use of such terms as "guaranty" or "warranty," if the terms and conditions of such warranty so limit its scope and application as to deceive a reasonable individual.

(d) Civil action by consumer for damages, etc.; jurisdiction; recovery of costs and expenses; cognizable claims

(1) Subject to subsections (a)(3) and (e) of this section, a consumer who is damaged by the failure of a supplier, warrantor, or service contractor to comply with any obligation under this chapter, or under a written warranty, implied warranty, or service contract, may bring suit for damages and other legal and equitable relief—

(A) in any court of competent jurisdiction in any State or the District of Columbia; or

(B) in an appropriate district court of the United States, subject to paragraph (3) of this subsection.

(2) If a consumer finally prevails in any action brought under paragraph (1) of this subsection, he may be allowed by the court to recover as part of the judgment a sum equal to the aggregate amount of cost and expenses (including attorneys' fees based on actual time expended) determined by the court to have been reasonably incurred by the plaintiff for or in connection with the commencement and prosecution of such action, unless the court in its discretion shall determine that such an award of attorneys' fees would be inappropriate.

(3) No claim shall be cognizable in a suit brought under paragraph (1)(B) of this subsection—

(A) if the amount in controversy of any individual claim is less than the sum or value of $25;

(B) if the amount in controversy is less than the sum or value of $50,000 (exclusive of interests and costs) computed on the basis of all claims to be determined in this suit; or

(C) if the action is brought as a class action, and the number of named plaintiffs is less than one hundred.

(e) Class actions; conditions; procedures applicable. No action (other than a class action or an action respecting a warranty to which subsection (a)(3) of this section applies) may be brought under subsection (d) of this section for failure to comply with any obligation under any written or implied warranty or service contract, and a class of consumers may not proceed in a class action under such subsection with respect to such a failure except to the extent the court determines necessary to establish the representative capacity of the named plaintiffs, unless the person obligated under the warranty or service contract is afforded a reasonable opportunity to cure such failure to comply. In the case of such a class action (other than a class action respecting a warranty to which subsection (a)(3) of this section applies) brought under subsection (d) of this section for breach of any written or implied warranty or service contract, such reasonable opportunity will be afforded by the named plaintiffs and they shall at that time notify the defendant that they are acting on behalf of the class. In the case of such a class action which is brought in a district court of the United States, the representative capacity of the named plaintiffs shall be established in the application of rule 23 of the Federal Rules of Civil Procedure.

(f) Warrantors subject to enforcement of remedies. For purposes of this section, only the warrantor actually making a written affirmation of fact, promise, or undertaking shall be deemed to have created a written warranty, and any rights arising thereunder may be enforced under this section only against such warrantor and no other person.

§ 2311. Applicability to Other Laws

(a) Federal Trade Commission Act and Federal Seed Act

(1) Nothing contained in this chapter shall be construed to repeal, invalidate, or supersede the Federal Trade Commission Act (15 U.S.C. 41 et seq.) or any statute defined therein as an Antitrust Act.

(2) Nothing in this chapter shall be construed to repeal, invalidate, or supersede the Federal Seed Act (7 U.S.C. 1551 et seq.) and nothing in this chapter shall apply to seed for planting.

(b) Rights, remedies, and liabilities

(1) Nothing in this chapter shall invalidate or restrict any right or remedy of any consumer under State law or any other Federal law.

(2) Nothing in this chapter (other than sections 2308 and 2304(a)(2) and (4) of this title) shall

(A) affect the liability of, or impose liability on, any person for personal injury, or

(B) supersede any provision of State law regarding consequential damages for injury to the person or other injury.

(c) State warranty laws

(1) Except as provided in subsection (b) of this section and in paragraph (2) of this subsection, a State requirement—

(A) which relates to labeling or disclosure with respect to written warranties or performance thereunder;

(B) which is within the scope of an applicable requirement of sections 2302, 2303, and 2304 of this title (and rules implementing such sections), and

(C) which is not identical to a requirement of section 2302, 2303, or 2304 of this title (or a rule thereunder), shall not be applicable to written warranties complying with such sections (or rules thereunder).

(2) If, upon application of an appropriate State agency, the Commission determines (pursuant to rules issued in accordance with section 2309 of this title) that any requirement of such State covering any transaction to which this chapter applies

(A) affords protection to consumers greater than the requirements of this chapter and

(B) does not unduly burden interstate commerce, then such State requirement shall be applicable (notwithstanding the provisions of paragraph (1) of this subsection) to the extent specified in such determination for so long as the State administers and enforces effectively any such greater requirement.

(d) Other Federal warranty laws. This chapter (other than section 2302(c) of this title) shall be inapplicable to any written warranty the making or content of which is otherwise governed by Federal law. If only a portion of a written warranty is so governed by Federal law, the remaining portion shall be subject to this chapter.

§ 2312. Effective Dates

(a) Effective date of chapter. Except as provided in subsection (b) of this section, this chapter shall take effect 6 months after January 4, 1975, but shall not apply to consumer products manufactured prior to such date.

(b) Effective date of section 2302(a). Section 2302(a) of this title shall take effect 6 months after the final publication of rules respecting such section; except that the Commission, for good cause shown, may postpone the applicability of such sections until one year after such final publication in order to permit any designated classes of suppliers to bring their written warranties into compliance with rules promulgated pursuant to this chapter.

(c) Promulgation of rules. The Commission shall promulgate rules for initial implementation of this chapter as soon as possible after January 4, 1975, but in no event later than one year after such date.

Regulation J

12 C.F.R. Part 210

SUBPART A. COLLECTION OF CHECKS AND OTHER ITEMS BY FEDERAL RESERVE BANKS

SUBPART B. FUNDS TRANSFERS THROUGH FEDWIRE FUNDS SERVICE

SUBPART A. COLLECTION OF CHECKS AND OTHER ITEMS BY FEDERAL RESERVE BANKS

§ 210.1 Authority, Purpose, and Scope

The Board of Governors of the Federal Reserve System (Board) has issued this subpart pursuant to the Federal Reserve Act, sections 11 (i) and (j) (12 U.S.C. 248 (i) and (j)), section 13 (12 U.S.C. 342), section 16 (12 U.S.C. 248(o) and 360), and section 19(f) (12 U.S.C. 464); the Expedited Funds Availability Act (12 U.S.C. 4001 et seq.); the Check Clearing for the 21st Century Act (12 U.S.C. 5001-5018); and other laws. This subpart governs the collection of checks and other cash and noncash items and the handling of returned checks by Federal Reserve Banks. Its purpose is to provide rules for collecting and returning items and settling balances.

§ 210.2 Definitions

As used in this subpart, unless the context otherwise requires:

Account means an account on the books of a Federal Reserve Bank. A subaccount is an informational record of a subset of transactions that affect an account and is not a separate account.

Actually and finally collected funds means cash or any other form of payment that is, or has become, final and irrevocable.

Administrative Reserve Bank with respect to an entity means the Reserve Bank in whose District the entity is located, as determined under the procedure described in § 204.3(g) of this chapter (Regulation D), even if the entity is not otherwise subject to that section.

Bank means any person engaged in the business of banking. A branch or separate office of a bank is a separate bank to the extent provided in the Uniform Commercial Code.

Bank draft means a check drawn by one bank on another bank.

Banking day means the part of a day on which a bank is open to the public for carrying on substantially all of its banking functions.

Cash item means—

(1) A check other than one classified as a noncash item under this section; or

(2) Any other item payable on demand and collectible at par that the Reserve Bank that receives the item is willing to accept as a cash item. Cash item does not include a returned check.

Check means a check or an electronic check, as those terms are defined in § 229.2 of this chapter (Regulation CC).

Clock hour and *clock half-hour.*

(1) Clock hour means a time that is on the hour, such as 1:00, 2:00, etc.

(2) Clock half-hour means a time that is on the half-hour, such as 1:30, 2:30, etc.

Fedwire Funds Service and *Fedwire* have the same meaning as that set forth in § 210.26.

Item.

(1) Means—

(i) An instrument or a promise or order to pay money, whether negotiable or not, that is—

(A) Payable in a Federal Reserve District[1] (District);

(B) Sent by a sender to a Reserve Bank for handling under this subpart; and

(C) Collectible in funds acceptable to the Reserve Bank of the District in which the instrument is payable; or

(ii) A check.

(2) Unless otherwise indicated, item includes both a cash and a noncash item, and includes a returned check sent by a paying or returning bank. Item does not include a check that cannot be collected at par, or a payment order as defined in § 210.26(i) and handled under subpart B of this part. The term also does not include an electronically-created item as defined in § 229.2 of this chapter (Regulation CC).

Nonbank payor means a payor of an item, other than a bank.

Noncash item means an item that a receiving Reserve Bank classifies in its operating circulars as requiring special handling. The term also means an item normally received as a cash item if a Reserve Bank decides that special conditions require that it handle the item as a noncash item.

Paying bank means—

(1) The bank by which an item is payable unless the item is payable or collectible at or through another bank and is sent to the other bank for payment or collection;

(2) The bank at or through which an item is payable or collectible and to which it is sent for payment or collection; or

(3) The bank whose routing number appears on a check in the MICR line or in fractional form (or in the MICR-line information that accompanies an electronic item) and to which the check is sent for payment or collection.

Returned check means a cash item returned by a paying bank, including an electronic returned check as defined in § 229.2 of this chapter (Regulation CC) and a notice of nonpayment in lieu of a returned check, whether or not a Reserve Bank handled the check for collection.

Sender means any of the following entities that sends an item to a Reserve Bank for forward collection—

(1) A depository institution, as defined in section 19(b) of the Federal Reserve Act (12 U.S.C. 461(b));

(2) A member bank, as defined in section 1 of the Federal Reserve Act (12 U.S.C. 221)

(3) A clearing institution, defined as—

(i) An institution that is not a depository institution but that maintains with a Reserve Bank the balance referred to in the first paragraph of section 13 of the Federal Reserve Act (12 U.S.C. 342); or

(ii) A corporation that maintains an account with a Reserve Bank in conformity with § 211.4 of this chapter (Regulation K);

(4) Another Reserve Bank;

(5) An international organization for which a Reserve Bank is empowered to act as depositary or fiscal agent and maintains an account;

(6) A foreign correspondent, defined as any of the following entities for which a Reserve Bank maintains an account: a foreign bank or banker, a foreign state as defined in section 25(b) of the Federal Reserve Act (12 U.S.C. 632), or a foreign correspondent or agency referred to in section 14(e) of that act (12 U.S.C. 358); or

(7) A branch or agency of a foreign bank maintaining reserves under section 7 of the International Banking Act of 1978 (12 U.S.C. 347d, 3105).

State means a State of the United States, the District of Columbia, Puerto Rico, or a territory, possession, or dependency of the United States.

Uniform Commercial Code and *U.C.C.* mean the Uniform Commercial Code as adopted in a state.

Terms not defined in this section. Unless the context otherwise requires—

(1) The terms not defined herein have the meanings set forth in § 229.2 of this chapter applicable to subpart C or subpart D of part 229 of this chapter (Regulation CC), as appropriate; and

(2) The terms not defined herein or in § 229.2 of this chapter have the meanings set forth in the Uniform Commercial Code.

§ 210.3 General Provisions

(a) *General.* Each Reserve Bank shall receive and handle items in accordance with this subpart, and shall issue operating circulars governing the details of its

[1] For purposes of this subpart, the Virgin Islands and Puerto Rico are deemed to be in the Second District, and Guam, American Samoa, and the Northern Mariana Islands in the Twelfth District.

handling of items and other matters deemed appropriate by the Reserve Bank. The circulars may, among other things, classify cash items and noncash items, require separate sorts and letters, provide different closing times for the receipt of different classes or types of items, provide for instructions by an Administrative Reserve Bank to other Reserve Banks, set forth terms of services, and establish procedures for adjustments on a Reserve Bank's books, including amounts, waiver of expenses, and payment of compensation. As deemed appropriate by the Reserve Bank, the circulars may also require the sender to provide warranties and indemnities that only items and any noncash items the Reserve Banks have agreed to handle will be sent to the Reserve Banks. The Reserve Banks may provide to a subsequent collecting bank and to the paying bank any warranties and indemnities provided by the sender pursuant to this paragraph (a).

(b) *Binding effect.* This subpart, together with subparts C and D of part 229 and the operating circulars of the Reserve Banks, are binding on all parties interested in an item handled by any Reserve Bank.

(c) *Government items.* As depositaries and fiscal agents of the United States, Reserve Banks handle certain items payable by the United States or certain Federal agencies as cash or noncash items. To the extent provided by regulations issued by, and arrangements made with, the United States Treasury Department and other Government departments and agencies, the handling of such items is governed by this subpart. The Reserve Banks shall include in their operating circulars such information regarding these regulations and arrangements as the Reserve Banks deem appropriate.

(d) *Government senders.* Except as otherwise provided by statutes of the United States, or regulations issued or arrangements made thereunder, this subpart and the operating circulars of the Reserve Banks apply to the following when acting as a sender: a department, agency, instrumentality, independent establishment, or office of the United States, or a wholly owned or controlled Government corporation, that maintains or uses an account with a Reserve Bank.

(e) *Foreign items.* A Reserve Bank also may receive and handle certain items payable outside a Federal Reserve District, as provided in its operating circulars. The handling of such items in a state is governed by this subpart, and the handling of such items outside a state is governed by the local law.

(f) *Relation to other law.* The provisions of this subpart supersede any inconsistent provisions of the Uniform Commercial Code, of any other state law, or of part 229 of this title, but only to the extent of the inconsistency.

§ 210.4 Sending Items to Reserve Banks

(a) *Sending of items.* A sender's Administrative Reserve Bank may direct a sender other than a Reserve Bank to send any item to a specified Reserve Bank, whether or not the item is payable within the Reserve Bank's District.

(b) *Handling of items.*

(1) The following parties, in the following order, are deemed to have handled an item that is sent to a Reserve Bank for collection—

(i) The initial sender;

(ii) The initial sender's Administrative Reserve Bank (which is deemed to have accepted deposit of the item from the initial sender);

(iii) The Reserve Bank that receives the item from the initial sender (if different from the initial sender's Administrative Reserve Bank); and

(iv) Another Reserve Bank, if any, that receives the item from a Reserve Bank.

(2) A Reserve Bank that is not described in paragraph (b)(1) of this section is not a person that handles an item and is not a collecting bank with respect to an item.

(3) The identity and order of the parties under paragraph (b)(1) of this section determine the relationships and the rights and liabilities of the parties under this subpart, part 229 of this chapter (Regulation CC), section 13(1) and section 16(13) of the Federal Reserve Act, and the Uniform Commercial Code. An initial sender's Administrative Reserve Bank that is deemed to accept an item for deposit or handle an item is also deemed to be a sender with respect to that item. The Reserve Banks that are deemed to handle an item are deemed to be agents or subagents of the owner of the item, as provided in § 210.6(a).

(c) *Checks received at par.* The Reserve Banks shall receive cash items and other checks at par.

§ 210.5 Sender's Agreement: Recovery by Reserve Bank

(a) *Sender's agreement.* The warranties, indemnities, authorizations, and agreements made pursuant to this paragraph (a) may not be disclaimed and are made whether or not the item bears an indorsement of the sender. By sending an item to a Reserve Bank, the sender does all of the following.

(1) *Authorization to handle item.* The sender authorizes the sender's Administrative Reserve Bank and any other Reserve Bank or collecting bank to which the item is sent to handle the item (and authorizes any Reserve Bank that handles settlement for the item to make accounting entries), subject to this subpart and to the Reserve Banks' operating circulars, and warrants its authority to give this authorization.

(2) *Warranties for all items.* The sender warrants to each Reserve Bank handling the item that—

(i) The sender is a person entitled to enforce the item or authorized to obtain payment of the item on behalf of a person entitled to enforce the item;

(ii) The item has not been altered; and

(iii) The item bears all indorsements applied by parties that previously handled the item for forward collection or return.

(3) *Warranties and indemnities as set forth in Regulation CC and U.C.C.* As applicable and unless otherwise provided, the sender of an item makes to each Reserve Bank that handles the item all the warranties and indemnities set forth in and subject to the terms of subparts C and D of part 229 of this chapter (Regulation CC) and Article 4 of the U.C.C. The sender makes all the warranties set forth in and subject to the terms of 4-207 of the U.C.C. for an electronic item as if it were an item subject to the U.C.C.

(4) *Warranties and indemnities as set forth in Reserve Bank operating circulars.* The sender makes any warranties and indemnities regarding the sending of items as set forth in an operating circular issued in accordance with § 210.3(a).

(5) *Sender's liability to Reserve Bank.*

(i) Except as provided in paragraphs (a)(5)(ii) and (iii) of this section, the sender agrees to indemnify each Reserve Bank for any loss or expense sustained (including attorneys' fees and expenses of litigation) resulting from—

(A) The sender's lack of authority to make the warranty in paragraph (a)(1) of this section;

(B) Any action taken by the Reserve Bank within the scope of its authority in handling the item; or

(C) Any warranty or indemnity made by the Reserve Bank under § 210.6(b), part 229 of this chapter, the U.C.C., or, regarding the sending of items, an operating circular issued in accordance with § 210.3(a).

(ii) A sender's liability for warranties and indemnities that the Reserve Bank makes for a substitute check, a paper or electronic representation thereof, or for an electronic check is subject to the following conditions and limitations—

(A) A sender of an original check shall not be liable under paragraph (a)(5)(i) of this section for any amount that the Reserve Bank pays under subpart D of part 229 of this chapter or under § 2229.34 of this chapter with respect to an electronic check, absent the sender's agreement to the contrary; and

(B) Nothing in this subpart alters the liability of a sender of a substitute check or paper or electronic representation of a substitute check under subpart D of part 229 of this chapter, or a sender of an electronic check under § 229.34 of this chapter.

(iii) A sender shall not be liable for any amount that the Reserve Bank pays under this subpart or part 229 of this chapter that is attributable to the Reserve Bank's own lack of good faith or failure to exercise ordinary care.

(b) *Sender's liability under other law.* Nothing in paragraph (a) of this section limits any warranty or indemnity by a sender (or a person that handled an item prior to the sender) arising under state law or regulation (such as the U.C.C.), other federal law or regulation (such as part 229 of this chapter), or an agreement with a Reserve Bank.

(c) *Recovery by Reserve Bank.*

(1) A Reserve Bank that has handled an item may recover as provided in paragraph (c)(2) of this section if an action or proceeding is brought against (or if defense is tendered to) the Reserve Bank based on—

(i) The alleged failure of the sender to have the authority to make the warranty and agreement in paragraph (a)(1) of this section;

(ii) Any action by the Reserve Bank within the scope of its authority in handling the item; or

(iii) Any warranty or indemnity made by the Reserve Bank under section 210.6(b) of this subpart, part 229 of this chapter, or the U.C.C.

(2) Upon entry of a final judgment or decree in an action or proceeding described in paragraph (c)(1) of this section, a Reserve Bank may recover from the sender the amount of attorneys' fees and other expenses of litigation incurred, as well as any

amount the Reserve Bank is required to pay because of the judgment or decree or the tender of defense, together with interest thereon.

(d) *Methods of recovery.*

(1) The Reserve Bank may recover the amount stated in paragraph (c) of this section by charging any account on its books that is maintained or used by the sender (or by charging a Reserve Bank sender), if—

(i) The Reserve Bank made seasonable written demand on the sender to assume defense of the action or proceeding; and

(ii) The sender has not made any other arrangement for payment that is acceptable to the Reserve Bank.

(2) The Reserve Bank is not responsible for defending the action or proceeding before using this method of recovery. A Reserve Bank that has been charged under this paragraph (d) may recover from its sender in the manner and under the circumstances set forth in this paragraph (d).

(3) A Reserve Bank's failure to avail itself of the remedy provided in this paragraph (d) does not prejudice its enforcement in any other manner of the indemnity agreement referred to in paragraph (a)(5) of this section.

(e) *Security interest.* When a sender sends an item to a Reserve Bank, the sender and any prior collecting bank grant to the sender's Administrative Reserve Bank a security interest in all of their respective assets in the possession of, or held for the account of, any Reserve Bank to secure their respective obligations due or to become due to the Administrative Reserve Bank under this subpart or subpart C or D of part 229 of this chapter (Regulation CC). The security interest attaches when a warranty is breached or any other obligation to the Reserve Bank is incurred. If the Reserve Bank, in its sole discretion, deems itself insecure and gives notice thereof to the sender or prior collecting bank, or if the sender or prior collecting bank suspends payments or is closed, the Reserve Bank may take any action authorized by law to recover the amount of an obligation, including, but not limited to, the exercise of rights of set off, the realization on any available collateral, and any other rights it may have as a creditor under applicable law.

§ 210.6 Status, Warranties, and Liability of Reserve Bank

(a) (1) *Status.* A Reserve Bank that handles an item shall act as agent or subagent of the owner with respect to the item. This agency terminates when a Reserve Bank receives final payment for the item in actually and finally collected funds, a Reserve Bank makes the proceeds available for use by the sender, and the time for commencing all actions against the Reserve Bank has expired.

(2) *Limitations on Reserve Bank liability.* A Reserve Bank shall not have or assume any liability with respect to an item or its proceeds except—

(i) For the Reserve Bank's own lack of good faith or failure to exercise ordinary care;

(ii) As provided in paragraph (b) of this section;

(iii) As provided in an operating circular issued in accordance with § 210.3(a) regarding the sending of items; and

(iv) As provided in subparts C and D of part 299 of this chapter (Regulation CC).

(3) *Reliance on routing designation appearing on item.* A Reserve Bank may present or send an item based on the routing number or other designation of a paying bank or nonbank payor appearing in any form on the item when the Reserve Bank receives it. A Reserve Bank shall not be responsible for any delay resulting from its acting on any designation, whether inscribed by magnetic ink or by other means, and whether or not the designation acted on is consistent with any other designation appearing on the item.

(b) *Warranties and liability.* The following provisions apply when a Reserve Bank presents or sends an item.

(1) *Warranties for all items.* The Reserve Bank warrants to a subsequent collecting bank and to the paying bank and any other payor that—

(i) The Reserve Bank is a person entitled to enforce the item (or is authorized to obtain payment of the item on behalf of a person that is either entitled to enforce the item or authorized to obtain payment on behalf of a person entitled to enforce the item);

(ii) The item has not been altered; and

(iii) The item bears all indorsements applied by parties that previously handled the item for forward collection or return.

(2) *Warranties and indemnities as set forth in Reserve Bank operating circulars.* The Reserve Bank makes any warranties and indemnities regarding the sending of items as set forth in an operating circular issued in accordance with § 210.3(a).

(3) *Warranties and indemnities as set forth in Regulation CC and U.C.C.* As applicable and unless otherwise provided, the Reserve Bank makes all the warranties and indemnities set forth in and subject

to the terms of subparts C and D of part 229 of this chapter (Regulation CC) and Article 4 of the U.C.C. The Reserve Bank makes all the warranties set forth in and subject to the terms of 4-207 of the U.C.C. for an electronic check as if it were an item subject to the U.C.C.

(4) *Indemnity for substitute check created from an electronic check.* (i) Except as provided in paragraph (b)(4)(ii) of this section, the Reserve Bank shall indemnify the bank to which it transfers or presents an electronic check (the recipient bank) for the amount of any losses that the recipient bank incurs under subpart D of part 229 of this chapter (Regulation CC) for an indemnity that the recipient bank was required to make under subpart D of this chapter in connection with a substitute check later created from the electronic check.

(5) The Reserve Bank shall not be liable under paragraph (b)(3) of this section for any amount that the recipient bank pays under subpart D of part 229 of this chapter that is attributable to the lack of good faith or failure to exercise ordinary care of the recipient bank or a person that handled the item, in any form, after the recipient bank.

(c) *Time for commencing action against Reserve Bank.* (1) A claim against a Reserve Bank for lack of good faith or failure to exercise ordinary care shall be barred unless the action on the claim is commenced within two years after the claim accrues. Such a claim accrues on the date when a Reserve Bank's alleged failure to exercise ordinary care or to act in good faith first results in damages to the claimant.

(2) A claim that arises under paragraph (b)(3) of this section shall be barred unless the action on the claim is commenced within one year after the claim accrues. Such a claim accrues as of the date on which the claimant first learns, or by which the claimant reasonably should have learned, of the facts and circumstances giving rise to the claim.

(3) This paragraph (c) does not alter the time limit for claims under section 229.38(g) of this chapter (which include claims for breach of warranty under § 229.34 of this chapter) or subpart D of part 229 of this chapter.

§ 210.7 Presenting Items for Payment

(a) *Presenting or sending.* As provided under State law or as otherwise permitted by this section:

(1) A Reserve Bank or a subsequent collecting bank may present an item for payment or send the item for presentment and payment; and

(2) A Reserve Bank may send an item to a subsequent collecting bank with authority to present it for payment or to send it for presentment and payment.

(b) *Place of presentment.* A Reserve Bank or subsequent collecting bank may present an item—

(1) At a place requested by the paying bank;

(2) In accordance with § 229.36 of this chapter (Regulation CC);

(3) At a place requested by the nonbank payor, if the item is payable by a nonbank payor other than through or at a paying bank;

(4) Under a special collection agreement consistent with this subpart; or

(5) Through a clearinghouse and subject to its rules and practices.

(c) *Presenting or sending direct.* A Reserve Bank or subsequent collecting bank may, with respect to an item that may be sent to the paying bank or nonbank payor in the Reserve Bank's District—

(1) Present or send the item direct to the paying bank, or to a place requested by the paying bank; or

(2) If the item is payable by a nonbank payor other than through a paying bank, present it direct to the nonbank payor. Documents, securities, or other papers accompanying a noncash item shall not be delivered to the nonbank payor before the item is paid unless the sender specifically authorizes delivery.

(d) *Item sent to another district.* A Reserve Bank receiving an item that may be sent to a paying bank or nonbank payor in another District ordinarily sends the item to the Reserve Bank of the other District, but with the agreement of the other Reserve Bank, may present or send the item as if it were sent to a paying bank or nonbank payor in its own District.

§ 210.8 Presenting Noncash Items for Acceptance

(a) A Reserve Bank or a subsequent collecting bank may, if instructed by the sender, present a noncash item for acceptance in any manner authorized by law if—

(1) The item provides that it must be presented for acceptance;

(2) The item may be presented elsewhere than at the residence or place of business of the payor; or

(3) The date of payment of the item depends on presentment for acceptance.

(b) Documents accompanying a noncash item shall not be delivered to the payor upon acceptance of the item unless the sender specifically authorizes delivery. A Reserve Bank shall not have or assume any other obligation to present or to send for presentment for acceptance any noncash item.

§ 210.9 Settlement and Payment

(a) *Settlement through Administrative Reserve Bank.* A paying bank shall settle for an item under this subpart with its Administrative Reserve Bank, whether or not the paying bank received the item from that Reserve Bank. A paying bank's settlement with its Administrative Reserve Bank is deemed to be settlement with the Reserve Bank from which the paying bank received the item. A paying bank may settle for an item using any account on a Reserve Bank's books by agreement with its Administrative Reserve Bank, any other Reserve Bank holding the settlement account, and the account-holder. The paying bank remains responsible for settlement if the Reserve Bank holding the settlement account does not, for any reason, obtain settlement in that account.

(b) *Cash items*— (1) *Settlement obligation.* On the day a paying bank receives[2] a cash item from a Reserve Bank, it shall settle for the item such that the proceeds of the settlement are available to its Administrative Reserve Bank by the close of Fedwire on that day, or it shall return the item by the later of the close of its banking day or the close of Fedwire. If the paying bank fails to settle for or return a cash item in accordance with this paragraph (b)(1), it is accountable for the amount of the item as of the close of its banking day or the close of Fedwire on the day it receives the item, whichever is earlier.

(2) *Time of settlement.*

(i) On the day a paying bank receives a cash item from a Reserve Bank, it shall settle for the item so that the proceeds of the settlement are available to its Administrative Reserve Bank, or return the item, by the latest of—

(A) The next clock hour or clock half-hour that is at least one half-hour after the paying bank receives the item;

(B) 8:30 a.m. eastern time; or

(C) Such later time as provided in the Reserve Banks' operating circulars.

(ii) If the paying bank fails to settle for or return a cash item in accordance with paragraph (b)(2)(i) of this section, it shall be subject to any applicable overdraft charges. Settlement under paragraph (b)(2)(i) of this section satisfies the settlement requirements of paragraph (b)(1) of this section.

(3) *Paying bank closes voluntarily.*

(i) If a paying bank closes voluntarily so that it does not receive a cash item on a day that is a banking day for a Reserve Bank, and the Reserve Bank makes the cash item available to the paying bank on that day, the paying bank shall either—

(A) On that day, settle for the item so that the proceeds of the settlement are available to its Administrative Reserve Bank, or return the item, by the latest of the next clock hour or clock half-hour that is at least one half-hour after it ordinarily would have received the item, 8:30 a.m. eastern time, or such later time as provided in the Reserve Banks' operating circulars; or

(B) On the next day that is a banking day for both the paying bank and the Reserve Bank, settle for the item so that the proceeds of the settlement are available to its Administrative Reserve Bank by 8:30 a.m. eastern time on that day or such later time as provided in the Reserve Banks' operating circulars; and compensate the Reserve Bank for the value of the float associated with the item in accordance with procedures provided in the Reserve Bank's operating circular.

(ii) If a paying bank closes voluntarily so that it does not receive a cash item on a day that is a banking day for a Reserve Bank, and the Reserve Bank makes the cash item available to the paying bank on that day, the paying bank is not considered to have received the item until its next banking day, but it shall be subject to any applicable overdraft charges if it fails to settle for or return the item in accordance with paragraph (b)(3)(i) of this section. The settlement requirements of paragraphs (b)(1) and (b)(2) of this section do not apply to a paying bank that settles in accordance with paragraph (b)(3)(i) of this section.

(4) *Reserve Bank closed.* If a paying bank receives a cash item from a Reserve Bank on a banking day that is not a banking day for the Reserve Bank, the paying bank shall—

(i) Settle for the item so that the proceeds of the settlement are available to its Administrative Reserve Bank by the close of the Fedwire Funds Service on the Reserve Bank's next banking day, or return the item by midnight of the day it receives

---

[2] A paying bank is deemed to receive a cash item on its next banking day if it receives the item—

(1) On a day other than a banking day for it; or

(2) On a banking day for it, but after a "cut-off hour" established by it in accordance with state law.

the item (if the paying bank fails to settle for or return a cash item in accordance with this paragraph (b)(4)(i)(A), it shall become accountable for the amount of the item as of the close of its banking day on the day it receives the item); and

(ii) Settle for the item so that the proceeds of the settlement are available to its Administrative Reserve Bank by 8:30 a.m. eastern time on the Reserve Bank's next banking day or such later time as provided in the Reserve Bank's operating circular, or return the item by midnight of the day it receives the item. If the paying bank fails to settle for or return a cash item in accordance with this paragraph (b)(4)(ii), it shall be subject to any applicable overdraft charges. Settlement under this paragraph (b)(4)(ii) satisfies the settlement requirements of paragraph (b)(4)(i)(A) of this section.

(iii) The settlement requirements of paragraphs (b)(1) and (b)(2) of this section do not apply to a paying bank that settles in accordance with paragraph (b)(4)(i) of this section.

(5) *Manner of settlement.* Settlement with a Reserve Bank under paragraphs (b)(1) through (4) of this section shall be made by debit to an account on the Reserve Bank's books or other form of settlement to which the Reserve Bank agrees, except that the Reserve Bank may, in its discretion, obtain settlement by charging the paying bank's account. A paying bank may not set off against the amount of a settlement under this section the amount of a claim with respect to another cash item, cash letter, or other claim under § 229.34 of this chapter (Regulation CC) or other law.

(6) *Notice in lieu of return.* If a cash item is unavailable for return, the paying bank may send a notice in lieu of return as provided in § 229.31(f) of this chapter (Regulation CC).

(c) *Noncash items.* A Reserve Bank may require the paying or collecting bank to which it has presented or sent a noncash item to pay for the item by a debit to an account maintained or used by the paying or collecting bank on the Reserve Bank's books or by any other form of settlement acceptable to the Reserve Bank.

(d) *Nonbank payor.* A Reserve Bank may require a nonbank payor to which it has presented an item to pay for it by debit to an account on the Reserve Bank's books or other form of settlement acceptable to the Reserve Bank.

(e) *Liability of Reserve Bank.* Except as set forth in § 229.35(b) of this chapter (Regulation CC), a Reserve Bank shall not be liable for the failure of a collecting bank, paying bank, or nonbank payor to pay for an item, or for any loss resulting from the Reserve Bank's acceptance of any form of payment other than cash authorized in paragraphs (b), (c), and (d) of this section. A Reserve Bank that acts in good faith and exercises ordinary care shall not be liable for the nonpayment of, or failure to realize upon, any non-cash form of payment that it accepts under paragraphs (b), (c), and (d) of this section.

§ 210.10 Time Schedule and Availability of Credits for Cash Items and Returned Checks

(a) Each Reserve Bank shall publish a time schedule indicating when the amount of any cash item or returned check received by it is counted toward the balance maintained to satisfy a reserve balance requirement for purposes of part 204 of this chapter (Regulation D) and becomes available for use by the sender or paying or returning bank. The Reserve Bank that holds the settlement account shall give either immediate or deferred credit to a sender, a paying bank, or a returning bank (other than a foreign correspondent) in accordance with the time schedule of the receiving Reserve Bank. A Reserve Bank ordinarily gives credit to a foreign correspondent only when the Reserve Bank receives payment of the item in actually and finally collected funds, but, in its discretion, a Reserve Bank may give immediate or deferred credit in accordance with its time schedule.

(b) Notwithstanding its time schedule, a Reserve Bank may refuse at any time to permit the use of credit given by it for any cash item or returned check, and may defer availability after credit is received by the Reserve Bank for a period of time that is reasonable under the circumstances.

§ 210.11 Availability of Proceeds of Noncash Items; Time Schedule

(a) *Availability of credit.* A Reserve Bank shall give credit to the sender for the proceeds of a noncash item when it receives payment in actually and finally collected funds (or advice from another Reserve Bank of such payment to it). The amount of the item is counted toward the balance maintained to satisfy a reserve balance requirement for purposes of part 204 of this chapter (Regulation D) and becomes available for use by the sender when the Reserve Bank receives the payment or advice, except as provided in paragraph (b) of this section.

(b) *Time schedule.* A Reserve Bank may give credit for the proceeds of a noncash item subject to payment in actually and finally collected funds in accordance with a published time schedule. The time schedule shall indicate when the proceeds of the noncash item will be counted toward the balance maintained to satisfy a reserve balance requirement for purposes of part 204 of this chapter (Regulation D) and become available for use by the sender. A Reserve Bank may, however, refuse at any time to permit the use of credit given by it for a noncash item for which the Reserve Bank has not yet received payment in actually and finally collected funds.

§ 210.12 Return of Cash Items and Handling of Returned Checks

(a) *Return of items*— (1) *Return of cash items handled by Reserve Banks.* A paying bank that receives a cash item from a Reserve Bank, other than for immediate payment over the counter, and that settles for the item as provided in § 210.9(b), may, before it has finally paid the item, return the item to any Reserve Bank (unless its Administrative Reserve Bank directs it to return the item to a specific Reserve Bank) in accordance with subpart C of part 229 of this chapter (Regulation CC), the Uniform Commercial Code, and the Reserve Banks' operating circulars. A paying bank that receives a cash item from a Reserve Bank also may return the item prior to settlement, in accordance with § 210.9(b) and the Reserve Banks' operating circulars. The rules or practices of a clearinghouse through which the item was presented, or a special collection agreement under which the item was presented, may not extend these return times, but may provide for a shorter return time.

(2) *Return of checks not handled by Reserve Banks.* A paying bank that receives a check, other than from a Reserve Bank, and that determines not to pay the check, may send the returned check to any Reserve Bank (unless its Administrative Reserve Bank directs it to send the returned check to a specific Reserve Bank) in accordance with subpart C of part 229 of this chapter (Regulation CC), the Uniform Commercial Code, and the Reserve Banks' operating circulars. A returning bank may send a returned check to any Reserve Bank (unless its Administrative Reserve Bank directs it to send the returned check to a specific Reserve Bank) in accordance with subpart C of part 229 of this chapter (Regulation CC), the Uniform Commercial Code, and the Reserve Banks' operating circulars.

(b) *Handling of returned checks.*

(1) The following parties, in the following order, are deemed to have handled a returned check sent to a Reserve Bank under paragraph (a) of this section—

(i) The paying or returning bank;

(ii) The paying bank's or returning bank's Administrative Reserve Bank;

(iii) The Reserve Bank that receives the returned check from the paying or returning bank (if different from the paying bank's or returning bank's Administrative Reserve Bank); and

(iv) Another Reserve Bank, if any, that receives the returned check from a Reserve Bank.

(2) A Reserve Bank that is not described in paragraph (b)(1) of this section is not a person that handles a returned check and is not a returning bank with respect to a returned check.

(3) The identity and order of the parties under paragraph (b)(1) of this section determine the relationships and the rights and liabilities of the parties under this subpart, part 229 of this chapter (Regulation CC), and the Uniform Commercial Code.

(c) *Paying bank's and returning bank's agreement.* The warranties, indemnities, authorizations, and agreements made pursuant to this paragraph (c) may not be disclaimed and are made whether or not the returned check bears an indorsement of the paying bank or returning bank. By sending a returned check to a Reserve Bank, the paying bank or returning bank does all of the following.

(1) *Authorization to handled returned check.* The paying bank or returning bank authorizes the paying bank's or returning bank's Administrative Reserve Bank, and any other Reserve Bank or returning bank to which the returned check is sent, to handle the returned check (and authorizes any Reserve Bank that handles settlement for the returned check to make accounting entries) subject to this subpart and to the Reserve Banks' operating circulars.

(2) *Warranties for all returned checks.* The paying bank or returning bank warrants to each Reserve Bank handling a returned check that the returned check bears all indorsements applied by parties that previously handled the returned check, in paper or electronic form, for forward collection or return.

(3) *Warranties and indemnities as set forth in Regulation CC.* As applicable and unless otherwise provided, a paying bank or returning bank makes to each Reserve Bank that handles the returned

check all the warranties and indemnities set forth in and subject to the terms of part 229 of this chapter (Regulation CC).

(4) *Paying bank or returning bank's liability to Reserve Bank.*

(i) Except as provided in paragraph (c)(4)(ii) and (iii) of this section, a paying bank or returning bank agrees to indemnify each Reserve Bank for any loss or expense (including attorneys' fees and expenses of litigation) resulting from—

(A) The paying or returning bank's lack of authority to give the authorization in paragraph (c)(1) of this section;

(B) Any action taken by a Reserve Bank within the scope of its authority in handling the returned check; or

(C) Any warranty or indemnity made by the Reserve Bank under paragraph (e) of this section or part 229 of this chapter.

(ii) A paying bank's or returning bank's liability for warranties and indemnities that a Reserve Bank makes for a returned check that is a substitute check, a paper or electronic representation thereof, or an electronic returned check is subject to the following conditions and limitations—

(A) A paying bank or returning bank that sent an original returned check shall not be liable for any amount that a Reserve Bank pays under subpart D of part 229 of this chapter or under § 229.34 of this chapter with respect to an electronic returned check, absent the paying bank's or returning bank's agreement to the contrary; and

(B) Nothing in this subpart alters the liability under subpart D of part 229 of this chapter of a paying bank or returning bank that sent a substitute check or under § 229.34 of this chapter of a paying bank or returning bank that sent an electronic returned check; and

(C) A paying bank or returning bank shall not be liable for any amount that the Reserve Bank pays under this subpart or part 229 of this chapter that is attributable to the Reserve Bank's own lack of good faith or failure to exercise ordinary care.

(d) *Paying bank or returning bank's liability under other law.* Nothing in paragraph (c) of this section limits any warranty or indemnity by a returning bank or paying bank (or a person that handled an item prior to that bank) arising under state law or regulation (such as the U.C.C.), other federal law or regulation (such as part 229 of this chapter), or an agreement with a Reserve Bank.

(e) *Warranties by and liability of Reserve Bank*—(1) *Warranties and indemnities.* The following provisions apply when a Reserve Bank handles a returned check under this subpart.

(i) *Warranties for all items.* The Reserve Bank warrants to the bank to which it sends the returned check that the returned check bears all indorsements applied by parties that previously handled the returned check for forward collection or return.

(ii) *Warranties and indemnities as set forth in Regulation CC.* As applicable and unless otherwise provided, the Reserve Bank makes all the warranties and indemnities set forth in and subject to the terms of subparts C and D of part 229 of this chapter (Regulation CC).

(2) *Indemnity for substitute check created from electronic returned check.* (i) Except as provided in paragraph (e)(2)(i) of this section, the Reserve Bank shall indemnify the bank to which it transfers or presents an electronic returned check (the recipient bank) for the amount of any losses that the bank incurs under subpart D of part 229 of this chapter (Regulation CC) for an indemnity that the bank was required to make under subpart D of part 229 of this chapter in connection with a substitute check later created from the electronic returned check.

(ii) The Reserve Bank shall not be liable under paragraph (e)(2)(i) of this section for any amount that the recipient bank pays under subpart D of part 229 of this chapter that is attributable to the lack of good faith or failure to exercise ordinary care of the recipient bank or a person that handled the item, in any form, after the recipient bank.

(3) *Liability of Reserve Bank.* A Reserve Bank shall not have or assume any other liability to any person except—

(i) For the Reserve Bank's own lack of good faith or failure to exercise ordinary care;

(ii) As provided in this paragraph (e); and

(iii) As provided in subparts C and D of part 229 of this chapter (Regulation CC).

(f) *Recovery by Reserve Bank.* (1) A Reserve Bank that has handled a returned Check may recover as provided in paragraph (f)(2) of this section if an action or proceeding is brought against (or if defense is tendered to) the Reserve Bank based on—

(i) The alleged failure of the paying or returning bank to have the authority to give the authorization in paragraph (c)(1) of this section;

(ii) Any action by the Reserve Bank within the scope of its authority in handling the returned check; or

(iii) Any warranty or indemnity made by the Reserve Bank under paragraph (e) of this section or part 229 of this chapter; and

(2) Upon entry of a final judgment or decree in an action or proceeding described in paragraph (f)(1) of this section, a Reserve Bank may recover from the paying bank or returning bank the amount of attorneys' fees and other expenses of litigation incurred, as well as any amount the Reserve Bank is required to pay because of the judgment or decree or the tender of defense, together with interest thereon.

(g) *Methods of recovery.*

(1) The Reserve Bank may recover the amount stated in paragraph (f) of this section by charging any account on its books that is maintained or used by the paying or returning bank (or by charging another returning Reserve Bank), if—

(i) The Reserve Bank made seasonable written demand on the paying or returning bank to assume defense of the action or proceeding; and

(ii) The paying or returning bank has not made any other arrangement for payment that is acceptable to the Reserve Bank.

(2) The Reserve Bank is not responsible for defending the action or proceeding before using this method of recovery. A Reserve Bank that has been charged under this paragraph (g) may recover from the paying or returning bank in the manner and under the circumstances set forth in this paragraph (g).

(3) A Reserve Bank's failure to avail itself of the remedy provided in this paragraph (g) does not prejudice its enforcement in any other manner of the indemnity agreement referred to in paragraph (c)(4) of this section.

(h) *Reserve Bank's responsibility.* A Reserve Bank shall handle a returned check, or a notice of nonpayment, in accordance with subpart C of part 229 and its operating circular.

(i) *Settlement.* A subsequent returning bank or depositary bank shall settle with its Administrative Reserve Bank for returned checks in the same manner and by the same time as for cash items presented for payment under this subpart. Settlement with its Administrative Reserve Bank is deemed to be settlement with the Reserve Bank from which the returning bank or depositary bank received the item.

(j) *Security interest.* When a paying or returning bank sends a returned check to a Reserve Bank, the paying bank, returning bank, and any prior returning bank grant to the paying bank's or returning bank's Administrative Reserve Bank a security interest in all of their respective assets in the possession of, or held for the account of, any Reserve Bank, to secure their respective obligations due or to become due to the Administrative Reserve Bank under this subpart or subpart C of part 229 of this chapter (Regulation CC). The security interest attaches when a warranty is breached or any other obligation to the Reserve Bank is incurred. If the Reserve Bank, in its sole discretion, deems itself insecure and gives notice thereof to the paying bank, returning bank, or prior returning bank, or if the paying bank, returning bank, or prior returning bank suspends payments or is closed, the Reserve Bank may take any action authorized by law to recover the amount of an obligation, including, but not limited to, the exercise of rights of set off, the realization on any available collateral, and any other rights it may have as a creditor under applicable law.

§ 210.13 Unpaid Items

(a) *Right of recovery.* If a Reserve Bank does not receive payment in actually and finally collected funds for an item, the Reserve Bank shall recover by chargeback or otherwise the amount of the item from the sender, prior collecting bank, paying bank, or returning bank from or through which it was received, whether or not the item itself can be sent back. In the event of recovery from such a person, no person, including the owner or holder of the item, shall, for the purpose of obtaining payment of the amount of the item, have any interest in any reserve balance or other funds or property in the Reserve Bank's possession of the bank that failed to make payment in actually and finally collected funds.

(b) *Suspension or closing of bank.* A Reserve Bank shall not pay or act on a draft, authorization to charge (including a charge authorized by § 210.9(b)(5)), or other order on a reserve balance or other funds in its possession for the purpose of settling for items under § 210.9 or § 210.12 after it receives notice of suspension or closing of the bank making the settlement for that bank's own or another's account.

§ 210.14 Extension of Time Limits

If a bank (including a Reserve Bank) or nonbank payor is delayed in acting on an item beyond applicable time limits because of interruption of communication or computer facilities, suspension of payments by a bank or nonbank payor, war, emergency conditions, failure of equipment, or other circumstances beyond its control, its time for acting is extended for the time necessary to complete the action, if it exercises such diligence as the circumstances require.

§ 210.15 Direct Presentment of Certain Warrants

If a Reserve Bank elects to present direct to the payor a bill, note, or warrant that is issued and payable by a State or a political subdivision and that is a cash item not payable or collectible through a bank: (a) Sections 210.9, 210.12, and 210.13 and the operating circulars of the Reserve Banks apply to the payor as if it were a paying bank; (b) § 210.14 applies to the payor as if it were a bank; and (c) under § 210.9 each day on which the payor is open for the regular conduct of its affairs or the accommodation of the public is considered a banking day.

SUBPART B. FUNDS TRANSFERS THROUGH FEDWIRE FUNDS SERVICE

§ 210.25 Authority, Purpose, and Scope

(a) *Authority and purpose.* This subpart provides rules to govern funds transfers through the Fedwire Funds Service, and has been issued pursuant to the Federal Reserve Act— section 13 (12 U.S.C. 342), paragraph (f) of section 19 (12 U.S.C. 464), paragraph 14 of section 16 (12 U.S.C. 248(o)), and paragraphs (i) and (j) of section 11 (12 U.S.C. 248(i) and (j))— and other laws and has the force and effect of federal law. This subpart is not a funds-transfer system rule as defined in Section 4A-501(b) of Article 4A.

(b) *Scope.* (1) This subpart incorporates the provisions of Article 4A set forth in appendix B to this subpart. In the event of an inconsistency between the provisions of the sections of this subpart and appendix B, to this subpart, the provisions of the sections of this subpart shall prevail. In the event of an inconsistency between the provision of this subpart and section 919 of the Electronic Fund Transfer Act, section 919 of the Electronic Fund Transfer Act shall prevail.

(2) Except as otherwise provided in paragraphs (b)(3) and (4) of this section, including Article 4A as set forth in appendix B to this subpart, and operating circulars of the Reserve Banks issued in accordance with paragraph (c) of this section, this subpart governs the rights and obligations of:

(i) Federal Reserve Banks sending or receiving payment orders;

(ii) Senders that send payment orders directly to a Federal Reserve Bank;

(iii) Receiving banks that receive payment orders directly from a Federal Reserve Bank;

(iv) Beneficiaries that receive payment for payment orders sent to a Federal Reserve Bank by means of credit to an account maintained or used at a Federal Reserve Bank; and

(v) Other parties to a funds transfer any part of which is carried out through Fedwire to the same extent as if this subpart were considered a funds-transfer system rule under Article 4A.

(3) This subpart governs a funds transfer that is sent through the Fedwire Funds Service, as provided in paragraph (b)(2) of this section, even though a portion of the funds transfer is governed by the Electronic Fund Transfer Act, but the portion of such funds transfer that is governed by the Electronic Fund Transfer Act (other than section 919 governing remittance transfers) is not governed by this subpart.

(4) In the event that any portion of this Subpart establishes rights or obligations with respect to the availability of funds that are also governed by the Expedited Funds Availability Act or the Board's Regulation CC, Availability of Funds and Collection of Checks, those provisions of the Expedited Funds Availability Act or Regulation CC shall apply and the portion of this Subpart, including Article 4A as incorporated herein, shall not apply.

(c) *Operating Circulars.* Each Federal Reserve Bank shall issue an Operating Circular consistent with this Subpart that governs the details of its funds-transfer operations and other matters it deems appropriate. Among other things, the Operating Circular may: set cut-off hours and funds-transfer business days; address available security procedures; specify format and media requirements for payment orders; identify messages that are not payment orders; and impose charges for funds-transfer services.

(d) *Government senders, receiving banks, and beneficiaries.* Except as otherwise expressly provided by the statutes of the United States, the parties specified in paragraphs (b)(2)(ii) through (v) of this section include:

(1) A department, agency, instrumentality, independent establishment, or office of the United States, or a wholly-owned or controlled Government corporation;

(2) An international organization;

(3) A foreign central bank; and

(4) A department, agency, instrumentality, independent establishment, or office of a foreign

government, or a wholly-owned or controlled corporation of a foreign government.

(e) *Financial messaging standards.* Financial messaging standards (e.g., ISO 20022), including the financial messaging components, elements, technical documentation, tags, and terminology used to implement those standards, do not confer or connote legal status or responsibilities. This subpart, including Article 4A as set forth in appendix B to this subpart, and operating circulars of the Reserve Banks issued in accordance with paragraph (c) of this section govern the rights and obligations of parties to funds transfers sent through the Fedwire Funds Service as provided in paragraph (b) of this section. To the extent there is any inconsistency between a financial messaging standard adopted by the Fedwire Funds Service and this subpart, this subpart shall prevail.

§ 210.26 Definitions

As used in this subpart, the following definitions apply:

Article 4A means Article 4A of the Uniform Commercial Code as set forth in appendix A of this part, which is incorporated into this subpart in accordance with § 210.25(b).

Automated clearing house transfer means any transfer designated as an automated clearing house transfer in an operating circular issued by the Federal Reserve Banks.

Beneficiary has the same meaning as in Article 4A except that the term is limited to a beneficiary in a funds transfer any portion of which is sent through the Fedwire Funds Service.

Beneficiary's bank has the same meaning as in Article 4A, except that:

(1) The term is limited to a beneficiary's bank in a funds transfer any portion of which is sent through the Fedwire Funds Service;

(2) A Federal Reserve Bank need not be identified in the payment order in order to be the beneficiary's bank; and

(3) The term includes a Federal Reserve Bank when that Federal Reserve Bank is the beneficiary of a payment order.

Fedwire Funds Service means the funds-transfer system owned and operated by the Federal Reserve Banks that is used primarily for the transmission and settlement of payment orders governed by this subpart. The Fedwire Funds Service does not include the FedNow Service or the system for making automated clearing house transfers.

Interdistrict transfer means a funds transfer involving entries to accounts maintained at two Federal Reserve Banks.

Intradistrict transfer means a funds transfer involving entries to accounts maintained at one Federal Reserve Bank.

Off-line bank means a bank that sends payment orders to and receives payment orders from a Federal Reserve Bank by telephone orally or by other means other than electronic data transmission.

Payment order has the same meaning as in Article 4A except that the term includes only instructions sent or received through the Fedwire Funds Service and does not include automated clearing house transfers or any communication designated in an operating circular issued by a Federal Reserve Bank under this subpart as not being a payment order.

Receiving bank has the same meaning as in Article 4A except that the term is limited to a receiving bank in a funds transfer any portion of which is sent through the Fedwire Funds Service.

Sender has the same meaning as in Article 4A except that the term is limited to a sender in a funds transfer any portion of which is sent through the Fedwire Funds Service.

Sender's account, receiving bank's account, and *beneficiary's account* mean the reserve, clearing, or other funds deposit account at a Federal Reserve Bank maintained or used by the sender, receiving bank, or beneficiary, respectively.

Sender's Federal Reserve Bank and *receiving bank's Federal Reserve Bank* mean the Federal Reserve Bank at which the sender or receiving bank, respectively, maintains or uses an account.

§ 210.27 Reliance on Identifying Number

(a) *Reliance by a Federal Reserve Bank on number to identify an intermediary bank or beneficiary's bank.* A Federal Reserve Bank may rely on the number in a payment order that identifies the intermediary bank or beneficiary's bank, even if it identifies a bank different from the bank identified by name in the payment order, if the Federal Reserve Bank does not know of such an inconsistency in identification. A Federal Reserve Bank has no duty to detect any such inconsistency in identification.

(b) *Reliance by a Federal Reserve Bank on number to identify beneficiary.* A Federal Reserve Bank, acting as a beneficiary's bank, may rely on the number in a payment order that identifies the beneficiary, even if it identifies a person different from the person identified by name in the payment order, if the Federal Reserve Bank does not know of such an inconsistency in identification. A Federal Reserve Bank has no duty to detect any such inconsistency in identification.

§ 210.28 Agreement of Sender

(a) *Payment of sender's obligation to a Federal Reserve Bank.* A sender (other than a Federal Reserve Bank), by maintaining or using an account with a Federal Reserve Bank, authorizes the sender's Federal Reserve Bank to obtain payment for the sender's payment orders by debiting the amount of the payment order from the sender's account.

(b) *Overdrafts.*

(1) A sender does not have the right to an overdraft in the sender's account. In the event an overdraft is created, the overdraft shall be due and payable immediately without the need for a demand by the Federal Reserve Bank, at the earliest of the following times:

(i) At the end of the funds-transfer business day;

(ii) At the time the Federal Reserve Bank, in its sole discretion, deems itself insecure and gives notice thereof to the sender; or

(iii) At the time the sender suspends payments or is closed.

(2) The sender shall have in its account, at the time the overdraft is due and payable, a balance of actually and finally collected funds sufficient to cover the aggregate amount of all its obligations to the Federal Reserve Bank, whether the obligations result from the execution of a payment order or otherwise.

(3) To secure any overdraft, as well as any other obligation due or to become due to its Federal Reserve Bank, each sender, by sending a payment order to a Federal Reserve Bank that is accepted by the Federal Reserve Bank, grants to the Federal Reserve Bank a security interest in all of the sender's assets in the possession of, or held for the account of, the Federal Reserve Bank. The security interest attaches when an overdraft, or any other obligation to the Federal Reserve Bank, becomes due and payable.

(4) A Federal Reserve Bank may take any action authorized by law to recover the amount of an overdraft that is due and payable, including, but not limited to, the exercise of rights of set off, the realization on any available collateral, and any other rights it may have as a creditor under applicable law.

(5) If a sender, other than a government sender described in § 210.25(d), incurs an overdraft in its account as a result of a debit to the account by a Federal Reserve Bank under paragraph (a) of this section, the account will be subject to any applicable overdraft charges, regardless of whether the overdraft has become due and payable. A Federal Reserve Bank may debit a sender's account under paragraph (a) of this section immediately on acceptance of the payment order.

(c) *Review of payment orders.* A sender, by sending a payment order to a Federal Reserve Bank, agrees that for the purposes of sections 4A-204(a) and 4A-304 of Article 4A, a reasonable time to notify a Federal Reserve Bank of the relevant facts concerning an unauthorized or erroneously executed payment order is within 30 calendar days after the sender receives notice that the payment order was accepted or executed, or that the sender's account was debited with respect to the payment order.

§ 210.29 Agreement of Receiving Bank

(a) *Payment.* A receiving bank (other than a Federal Reserve Bank) that receives a payment order from its Federal Reserve Bank authorizes that Federal Reserve Bank to pay for the payment order by crediting the amount of the payment order to the receiving bank's account.

(b) *Off-line banks.* An off-line bank that does not expressly notify its Federal Reserve Bank in writing that it maintains an account for another bank warrants to that Federal Reserve Bank that the off-line bank does not act as an intermediary bank or a beneficiary's bank with respect to payment orders received through the Fedwire Funds Service for a beneficiary that is a bank.

§ 210.30 Payment Orders

(a) *Rejection.* A sender shall not send a payment order to a Federal Reserve Bank unless authorized to do so by the Federal Reserve Bank. A Federal Reserve Bank may reject, or impose conditions that must be satisfied before it will accept, a payment order for any reason.

(b) *Selection of an intermediary bank.* For an interdistrict transfer through the Fedwire Funds Service, a Federal Reserve Bank is authorized and directed to execute a payment order through another Federal Reserve Bank. A sender shall not send a payment order to a Federal Reserve Bank that requires the Federal Reserve Bank to issue a payment order to an intermediary bank (other than a Federal Reserve Bank) unless that intermediary bank is designated in the sender's payment order. A sender shall not send to a Federal Reserve Bank a payment order through the Fedwire Funds Service that instructs use by a Federal Reserve Bank of a funds-transfer system or means of transmission other than the Fedwire Funds Service unless the

Federal Reserve Bank agrees with the sender in writing to follow such instructions.

(c) *Execution date and payment date.* A sender shall not send a payment order through the Fedwire Funds Service that instructs a Federal Reserve Bank to execute the payment order or to pay the beneficiary on a funds-transfer business day that is later than the Fedwire Funds Service funds-transfer business day on which the order is received by the Federal Reserve Bank, unless the Federal Reserve Bank agrees with the sender in writing to follow such instructions.

§ 210.31 Payment by a Federal Reserve Bank to a Receiving Bank or Beneficiary

(a) *Payment to a receiving bank.* Payment of a Federal Reserve Bank's obligation to pay a receiving bank (other than a Federal Reserve Bank) occurs at the earlier of the time when the amount of the payment order is credited to the receiving bank's account or when the payment order is sent to the receiving bank.

(b) *Payment to a beneficiary.* Payment by a Federal Reserve Bank to a beneficiary of a payment order, where the Federal Reserve Bank is the beneficiary's bank, occurs at the earlier of the time when the amount of the payment order is credited to the beneficiary's account or when notice of the credit is sent to the beneficiary.

§ 210.32 Federal Reserve Bank Liability; Payment of Compensation

(a) *Damages.* In connection with its handling of a payment order under this subpart, a Federal Reserve Bank shall not be liable to a sender, receiving bank, beneficiary, or other Federal Reserve Bank, governed by this subpart, for any damages other than those payable under Article 4A. A Federal Reserve Bank shall not agree to be liable to a sender, receiving bank, beneficiary, or other Federal Reserve Bank for consequential damages under section 4A-305(d) of Article 4A.

(b) *Payment of compensation.* (1) A Federal Reserve Bank shall satisfy its obligation, or that of another Federal Reserve Bank, to pay compensation in the form of interest under Article 4A by paying such compensation in the form of interest to a sender, receiving bank, beneficiary, or another party to the funds transfer that is entitled to such payment in an amount that is calculated in accordance with section 4A–506 of Article 4A.

(2) If the sender or receiving bank that is the recipient of the payment of compensation is not the party entitled to compensation under Article 4A, the sender or receiving bank shall pass through the benefit of the compensation by making an interest payment, as of the day the compensation was paid by the Federal Reserve Bank, to the party entitled to compensation. The interest payment that is made to the party entitled to compensation shall not be less than the value of the compensation that was paid by the Federal Reserve Bank to the sender or receiving bank. The party entitled to compensation may agree to accept compensation in a form other than a direct interest payment, provided that such an alternative form of compensation is not less than the value of the interest payment that otherwise would be made.

(c) *Nonwaiver of right of recovery.* Nothing in this subpart or any Operating Circular issued hereunder shall constitute, or be construed as constituting, a waiver by a Federal Reserve Bank of a cause of action for recovery under any applicable law of mistake and restitution.

The Expedited Funds Availability Act

12 U.S.C. §§ 4001–4010

Section

§ 4001. Definitions

For purposes of this chapter—

(1) Account—The term "account" means a demand deposit account or other similar transaction account at a depository institution.

(2) Board—The term "Board" means the Board of Governors of the Federal Reserve System.

(3) Business day—The term "business day" means any day other than a Saturday, Sunday, or legal holiday.

(4) Cash—The term "cash" means United States coins and currency, including Federal Reserve notes.

(5) Cashier's check—The term "cashier's check" means any check which—

(A) is drawn on a depository institution;

(B) is signed by an officer or employee of such depository institution; and

(C) is a direct obligation of such depository institution.

(6) Certified check—The term "certified check" means any check with respect to which a depository institution certifies that—

(A) the signature on the check is genuine; and

(B) such depository institution has set aside funds which

(i) are equal to the amount of the check; and

(ii) will be used only to pay such check.

(7) Check—The term "check" means any negotiable demand draft drawn on or payable through an office of a depository institution located in the United States. Such term does not include noncash items.

(8) Check clearinghouse association—The term "check clearinghouse association" means any arrangement by which participant depository institutions exchange deposited checks on a local basis, including an entire metropolitan area, without using the check processing facilities of the Federal Reserve System.

(9) Check processing region—The term "check processing region" means the geographical area served by a Federal Reserve bank check processing center or such larger area as the Board may prescribe by regulations.

(10) Consumer account—The term "consumer account" means any account used primarily for personal, family, or household purposes.

(11) Depository check—The term "depository check" means any cashier's check, certified check, teller's check, and any other functionally equivalent instrument as determined by the Board.

(12) Depository institution—The term "depository institution" has the meaning given such term in clauses (i) through (vi) of section 461(b)(1)(A) of this title. Such term also includes an office, branch, or agency of a foreign bank located in the United States.

(13) Local originating depository institution—The term "local originating depository institution" means any originating depository institution which is located in the same check processing region as the receiving depository institution.

(14) Noncash item—The term "noncash item" means—

(A) a check or other demand item to which a passbook, certificate, or other document is attached;

(B) a check or other demand item which is accompanied by special instructions, such as a request for special advise of payment or dishonor; or

(C) any similar item which is otherwise classified as a noncash item in regulations of the Board.

(15) Nonlocal originating depository institution—The term "nonlocal originating depository institution" means any originating depository institution which is not a local depository institution.

(16) Proprietary ATM—The term "proprietary ATM" means an automated teller machine which is—

(A) located—

(i) at or adjacent to a branch of the receiving depository institution; or

(ii) in close proximity, as defined by the Board, to a branch of the receiving depository institution; or

(B) owned by, operated exclusively for, or operated by the receiving depository institution.

(17) Originating depository institution—The term "originating depository institution" means the branch of a depository institution on which a check is drawn.

(18) Nonproprietary ATM—The term "nonproprietary ATM" means an automated teller machine which is not a proprietary ATM.

(19) Participant—The term "participant" means a depository institution which—

(A) is located in the same geographic area as that served by a check clearinghouse association; and

(B) exchanges checks through the check clearinghouse association, either directly or through an intermediary.

(20) Receiving depository institution—The term "receiving depository institution" means the branch of a depository institution or the proprietary ATM in which a check is first deposited.

(21) State—The term "State" means any State, the District of Columbia, the commonwealth of Puerto Rico, or the Virgin Islands.

(22) Teller's check—The term "teller's check" means any check issued by a depository institution and drawn on another depository institution.

(23) United States—The term "United States" means the several States, the District of Columbia, the Commonwealth of Puerto Rico, and the Virgin Islands.

(24) Unit of general local government—The term "unit of general local government" means any city, county, town, township, parish, village, or other general purpose political subdivision of a State.

(25) Wire transfer—The term "wire transfer" has such meaning as the Board shall prescribe by regulations.

§ 4002. Expedited Funds Availability Schedules

(a) Next business day availability for certain deposits

(1) Cash deposits; wire transfers. Except as provided in subsection (e) of this section and in section 4003 of this title, in any case in which—

(A) any cash is deposited in an account at a receiving depository institution staffed by individuals employed by such institution, or

(B) funds are received by a depository institution by wire transfer for deposit in an account at such institution, such cash or funds shall be available for withdrawal not later than the business day after the business day on which such cash is deposited or such funds are received for deposit.

(2) Government checks; certain other checks. Funds deposited in an account at a depository institution by check shall be available for withdrawal not later than the business day after the business day on which such funds are deposited in the case of—

(A) a check which—

(i) is drawn on the Treasury of the United States; and

(ii) is endorsed only by the person to whom it was issued;

(B) a check which—

(i) is drawn by a State;

(ii) is deposited in a receiving depository institution which is located in such State and is staffed by individuals employed by such institution;

(iii) is deposited with a special deposit slip which indicates it is a check drawn by a State; and

(iv) is endorsed only by the person to whom it was issued;

(C) a check which—

(i) is drawn by a unit of general local government;

(ii) is deposited in a receiving depository institution which is located in the same State as such unit of general local government and is staffed by individuals employed by such institution;

(iii) is deposited with a special deposit slip which indicates it is a check drawn by a unit of general local government; and

(iv) is endorsed only by the person to whom it was issued;

(D) the first $200 deposited by check or checks on any one business day;

(E) a check deposited in a branch of a depository institution and drawn on the same or another branch of the same depository institution if both such branches are located in the same State or the same check processing region;

(F) a cashier's check, certified check, teller's check, or depository check which—

(i) is deposited in a receiving depository institution which is staffed by individuals employed by such institution;

(ii) is deposited with a special deposit slip which indicates it is a cashier's check, certified check, teller's check, or depository check, as the case may be; and

(iii) is endorsed only by the person to whom it was issued.

(b) Permanent schedule

(1) Availability of funds deposited by local checks. Subject to paragraph (3) of this subsection, subsections (a)(2), (d), and (e) of this section, and section 4003 of this title, not more than 1 business day shall intervene between the business day on which funds are deposited in an account at a depository institution by a check drawn on a local originating depository institution and the business day on which the funds involved are available for withdrawal.

(2) Availability of funds deposited by nonlocal checks. Subject to paragraph (3) of this subsection, subsections (a)(2), (d), and (e) of this section, and section 4003 of this title, not more than 4 business days shall intervene between the business day on which funds are deposited in an account at a depository institution by a check drawn on a nonlocal originating depository institution and the business day on which such funds are available for withdrawal.

(3) Time period adjustments for cash withdrawal of certain checks

(A) In general. Except as provided in subparagraph (B), funds deposited in an account in a depository institution by check (other than a check described in subsection (a)(2)) shall be available for cash withdrawal not later than the business day after the business day on which such funds otherwise are available under paragraph (1) or (2).

(B) 5 p.m. cash availability. Not more than $400 (or the maximum amount allowable in the case of a withdrawal from an automated teller machine but not more than $400) of funds deposited by one or more checks to which this paragraph applies shall be available for cash withdrawal not later than 5 o'clock post meridian of the business day on which such funds are available under paragraph (1) or (2). If funds deposited by checks described in both paragraph (1) and paragraph (2) become available for cash withdrawal under this paragraph on the same business day, the limitation contained in this subparagraph shall apply to the aggregate amount of such funds.

(C) $200 availability. Any amount available for withdrawal under this paragraph shall be in addition to the amount available under subsection (a)(2)(D).

(4) Applicability. This subsection shall apply with respect to funds deposited by check in an account at a depository institution on or after September 1, 1990, except that the Board may, by regulation, make this subsection or any part of this subsection applicable earlier than September 1, 1990.

(c) Temporary schedule

(1) Availability of local checks

(A) In general. Subject to subparagraph (B) of this paragraph, subsections (a)(2), (d), and (e) of this section, and section 4003 of this title, not more than 2 business days shall intervene between the business day on which funds are deposited in an account at a depository institution by a check drawn on a local originating depository institution and the business day on which such funds are available for withdrawal.

(B) Time period adjustment for cash withdrawal of certain checks

(i) In general. Except as provided in clause (ii), funds deposited in an account in a depository institution by check drawn on a local depository institution that is not a participant in the same check clearinghouse association as the receiving depository institution (other than a check described in subsection (a)(2)) shall be available for cash withdrawal not later than the business day after the business day on which such funds otherwise are available under subparagraph (A).

(ii) 5 p.m. cash availability. Not more than $400 (or the maximum amount allowable in the case of a withdrawal from an automated teller machine but not more than $400) of funds deposited by one or more checks to which this subparagraph applies shall be available for cash withdrawal not later than 5 o'clock post meridian of the business day on which such funds are available under subparagraph (A).

(iii) $200 availability. Any amount available for withdrawal under this subparagraph shall be in addition to the amount available under subsection (a)(2)(D) of this section.

(2) Availability of nonlocal checks. Subject to subsections (a)(2), (d), and (e) of this section and section 4003 of this title, not more than 6 business days shall intervene between the business day on which funds are deposited in an account at a depository institution by a check drawn on a nonlocal originating depository institution and the business day on which such funds are available for withdrawal.

(3) Applicability. This subsection shall apply with respect to funds deposited by check in an account at a depository institution after August 31, 1988, and before September 1, 1990, except as may be otherwise provided under subsection (b)(4).

(d) Time period adjustments

(1) Reduction generally. Notwithstanding any other provision of law, the Board, jointly with the Director of the Bureau of Consumer Financial Protection, shall, by regulation, reduce the time periods established under subsections (b), (c), and (e) of this section to as short a time as possible and equal to the period of time achievable under the improved check clearing system for a receiving depository institution to reasonably expect to learn of the nonpayment of most items for each category of checks.

(2) Extension for certain deposits in noncontiguous States or territories. Notwithstanding any other provision of law, any time period established under subsection (b), (c), or (e) of this section shall be extended by 1 business day in the case of any deposit which is both—

(A) deposited in an account at a depository institution which is located in Alaska, Hawaii, Puerto Rico, or the Virgin Islands; and

(B) deposited by a check drawn on an originating depository institution which is not located in the same State, commonwealth, or territory as the receiving depository institution.

(e) Deposits at ATM

(1) Nonproprietary ATM

(A) In general. Not more than 4 business days shall intervene between the business day a deposit described in subparagraph (B) is made at a nonproprietary automated teller machine (for deposit in an account at a depository institution) and the business day on which funds from such deposit are available for withdrawal.

(B) Deposits described in this [sub]paragraph. A deposit is described in this subparagraph if it is—

(i) a cash deposit;

(ii) a deposit made by a check described in subsection (a)(2);

(iii) a deposit made by a check drawn on a local originating depository institution (other than a check described in subsection (a)(2)); or

(iv) a deposit made by a check drawn on a nonlocal originating depository institution (other than a check described in subsection (a)(2)).

(2) Proprietary ATM—temporary and permanent schedules. The provisions of subsections (a), (b), and (c) of this section shall apply with respect to any funds deposited at a proprietary automated teller machine for deposit in an account at a depository institution.

(3) Study and report on ATM's. The Board shall, either directly or through the Consumer Advisory Council, establish and maintain a dialogue with depository institutions and their suppliers on the computer software and hardware available for use by automated teller machines, and shall, not later than September 1 of each of the first 3 calendar years beginning after August 10, 1987, report to the Congress regarding such software and hardware and regarding the potential for improving the processing of automated teller machine deposits.

(f) Check return; notice of nonpayment. No provision of this section shall be construed as requiring that, with respect to all checks deposited in a receiving depository institution—

(1) such checks be physically returned to such depository institution; or

(2) any notice of nonpayment of any such check be given to such depository institution within the times set forth in subsection (a), (b), (c), or (e) or in the regulations issued under any such subsection.

§ 4003. Safeguard Exceptions

(a) New accounts. Notwithstanding section 4002 of this title, in the case of any account established at a depository institution by a new depositor, the following provisions shall apply with respect to any deposit in such account during the 30-day period (or such shorter period as the Board, jointly with the Director of the Bureau of Consumer Financial Protection, may establish) beginning on the date such account is established—

(1) Next business day availability of cash and certain items. Except as provided in paragraph (3), in the case of—

(A) any cash deposited in such account;

(B) any funds received by such depository institution by wire transfer for deposit in such account;

(C) any funds deposited in such account by cashier's check, certified check, teller's check, depository check, or traveler's check; and

(D) any funds deposited by a government check which is described in subparagraph (A), (B), or (C) of section 4002(a)(2) of this title, such cash or funds shall be available for withdrawal on the business day after the business day on which such cash or funds are deposited or, in the case of a wire transfer, on the business day after the business day on which such funds are received for deposit.

(2) Availability of other items. In the case of any funds deposited in such account by a check (other than a check described in subparagraph (C) or (D) of paragraph (1)), the availability for withdrawal of such funds shall not be subject to the provisions of section 4002(b), 4002(c), or paragraphs (1) [sic] of section 4002(e) of this title.

(3) Limitation relating to certain checks in excess of $5,000. In the case of funds deposited in such account during such period by checks described in subparagraph (C) or (D) of paragraph (1) the aggregate amount of which exceeds $5,000—

(A) paragraph (1) shall apply only with respect to the first $5,000 of such aggregate amount; and

(B) not more than 8 business days shall intervene between the business day on which any such funds are deposited and the business day on which such excess amount shall be available for withdrawal.

(b) Large or redeposited checks; repeated overdrafts. The Board, jointly with the Director of the Bureau of Consumer Financial Protection, may, by regulation, establish reasonable exceptions to any time limitation established under subsection (a)(2), (b), (c), or (e) of section 4002 of this title for—

(1) the amount of deposits by one or more checks that exceeds the amount of $5,000 in any one day;

(2) checks that have been returned unpaid and redeposited; and

(3) deposit accounts which have been overdrawn repeatedly.

(c) Reasonable cause exception

(1) In general. In accordance with regulations which the Board, jointly with the Director of the Bureau of Consumer Financial Protection, shall prescribe, subsections (a)(2), (b), (c), and (e) of section 4002 of this title shall not apply with respect to any check deposited in an account at a depository institution if the receiving depository institution has reasonable cause to believe that the check is uncollectible from the originating depository institution. For purposes of the preceding sentence, reasonable cause to believe requires the existence of facts which would cause a well-grounded belief in the mind of a reasonable person. Such reasons shall be included in the notice required under subsection (f) of this section.

(2) Basis for determination. No determination under this subsection may be based on any class of checks or persons.

(3) Overdraft fees. If the receiving depository institution determines that a check deposited in an account is a check described in paragraph (1), the receiving depository institution shall not assess any fee for any subsequent overdraft with respect to such account, if—

(A) the depositor was not provided with the written notice required under subsection (f) (with respect to such determination) at the time the deposit was made;

(B) the overdraft would not have occurred but for the fact that the funds so deposited are not available; and

(C) the amount of the check is collected from the originating depository institution.

(4) Compliance. Each agency referred to in section 4009(a) of this title shall monitor compliance with the requirements of this subsection in each regular examination of a depository institution and shall describe in each report to the Congress the extent to which this subsection is being complied with. For the purpose of this paragraph, each depository institution shall retain a record of each notice provided under subsection (f) of this section as a result of the application of this subsection.

(d) Emergency conditions. Subject to such regulations as the Board, jointly with the Director of the Bureau of Consumer Financial Protection, may prescribe, subsections (a)(2), (b), (c), and (e) of section 4002 of this title shall not apply to funds deposited by check in any receiving depository institution in the case of—

(1) any interruption of communication facilities;

(2) suspension of payments by another depository institution;

(3) any war; or

(4) any emergency condition beyond the control of the receiving depository institution, if the receiving depository institution exercises such diligence as the circumstances require.

(e) Prevention of fraud losses

(1) In general. The Board, jointly with the Director of the Bureau of Consumer Financial Protection, may, by regulation or order, suspend the applicability of this chapter, or any portion thereof, to any classification of checks if the Board, jointly with the Director of the Bureau of Consumer Financial Protection, determines that—

(A) depository institutions are experiencing an unacceptable level of losses due to check-related fraud, and

(B) suspension of this chapter, or such portion of this chapter, with regard to the classification of checks involved in such fraud is necessary to diminish the volume of such fraud.

(2) Sunset provision. No regulation prescribed or order issued under paragraph (1) shall remain in effect for more than 45 days (excluding Saturdays, Sundays, legal holidays, or any day either House of Congress is not in session).

(3) Report to Congress

(A) Notice of each suspension. Within 10 days of prescribing any regulation or issuing any order under paragraph (1), the Board, jointly with the Director of the Bureau of Consumer Financial Protection, shall transmit a report of such action to the Committee on Banking, Finance and Urban Affairs of the House of Representatives and the Committee on Banking, Housing, and Urban Affairs of the Senate.

(B) Contents of report. Each report under subparagraph (A) shall contain—

(i) the specific reason for prescribing the regulation or issuing the order;

(ii) evidence considered by the Board, jointly with the Director of the Bureau of Consumer Financial Protection, in making the determination under paragraph (1) with respect to such regulation or order; and

(iii) specific examples of the check-related fraud giving rise to such regulation or order.

(f) Notice of exception; availability within reasonable time

(1) In general. If any exception contained in this section (other than subsection (a)) applies with respect to funds deposited in an account at a depository institution—

(A) the depository institution shall provide notice in the manner provided in paragraph (2) of—

(i) the time period within which the funds shall be made available for withdrawal; and

(ii) the reason the exception was invoked; and

(B) except where other time periods are specifically provided in this chapter, the availability of the funds deposited shall be governed by the policy of the receiving depository institution, but shall not exceed a reasonable period of time as determined by the Board, jointly with the Director of the Bureau of Consumer Financial Protection.

(2) Time for notice. The notice required under paragraph (1)(A) with respect to a deposit to which an exception contained in this section applies shall be made by the time provided in the following subparagraphs:

(A) In the case of a deposit made in person by the depositor at the receiving depository institution, the depository institution shall immediately provide such notice in writing to the depositor.

(B) In the case of any other deposit (other than a deposit described in subparagraph (C)), the receiving depository institution shall mail the notice to the depositor not later than the close of the next business day following the business day on which the deposit is received.

(C) In the case of a deposit to which subsection (d) or (e) of this section applies, notice shall be provided by the depository institution in accordance with regulations of the Board, jointly with the Director of the Bureau of Consumer Financial Protection.

(D) In the case of a deposit to which subsection (b)(1) or (b)(2) of this section applies, the depository institution may, for nonconsumer accounts and other classes of accounts, as defined by the Board, that generally have a large number of such deposits, provide notice at or before the time it first determines that the subsection applies.

(E) In the case of a deposit to which subsection (b)(3) of this section applies, the depository institution may, subject to regulations of the Board, provide notice at the beginning of each time period it determines that the subsection applies. In addition to the requirements contained in paragraph (1)(A), the notice shall specify the time period for which the exception will apply.

(3) Subsequent determinations. If the facts upon which the determination of the applicability of an exception contained in subsection (b) or (c) of this section to any deposit only become known to the receiving depository institution after the time notice is required under paragraph (2) with respect to such deposit, the depository institution shall mail such notice to the depositor as soon as practicable, but not later than the first business day following the day such facts become known to the depository institution.

§ 4004. Disclosure of Funds Availability Policies

(a) Notice for new accounts. Before an account is opened at a depository institution, the depository institution shall provide written notice to the potential customer of the specific policy of such depository institution with respect to when a customer may withdraw funds deposited into the customer's account.

(b) Preprinted deposit slips. All preprinted deposit slips that a depository institution furnishes to its customers shall contain a summary notice, as prescribed by the Board, jointly with the Director of the Bureau of Consumer Financial Protection, in regulations, that deposited items may not be available for immediate withdrawal.

(c) Mailing of notice

(1) First mailing after enactment. In the first regularly scheduled mailing to customers occurring after September 1, 1988, but not more than 60 days after September 1, 1988, each depository institution shall send a written notice containing the specific policy of such depository institution with respect to when a customer may withdraw funds deposited into such customer's account, unless the depository has provided a disclosure which meets the requirements of this section before September 1, 1988.

(2) Subsequent changes. A depository institution shall send a written notice to customers at least 30 days before implementing any change to the depository institution's policy with respect to when customers may withdraw funds deposited into consumer accounts, except that any change which expedites the availability of such funds shall be disclosed not later than 30 days after implementation.

(3) Upon request. Upon the request of any person, a depository institution shall provide or send such person a written notice containing the specific policy of such depository institution with respect to when a customer may withdraw funds deposited into a customer's account.

(d) Posting of notice

(1) Specific notice at manned teller stations. Each depository institution shall post, in a conspicuous place in each location where deposits are accepted by individuals employed by such depository institution, a specific notice which describes the time periods applicable to the availability of funds deposited in a consumer account.

(2) General notice at automated teller machines. In the case of any automated teller machine at which any funds are received for deposit in an account at any depository institution, the Board, jointly with the Director of the Bureau of Consumer Financial Protection, shall prescribe, by regulations, that the owner or operator of such automated teller machine shall post or provide a general notice that funds deposited in such machine may not be immediately available for withdrawal.

(e) Notice of interest payment policy. If a depository institution described in section 4005(b) of this title begins the accrual of interest or dividends at a later date than the date described in section 4005(a) of this title with respect to all funds, including cash, deposited in an interest-bearing account at such depository institution, any notice required to be provided under subsections (a) and (c) of this section shall contain a written description of the time at which such depository institution begins to accrue interest or dividends on such funds.

(f) Model disclosure forms

(1) Prepared by Board and Bureau. The Board, jointly with the Director of the Bureau of Consumer Financial Protection, shall publish model disclosure forms and clauses for common transactions to facilitate compliance with the disclosure requirements of this section and to aid customers by utilizing readily understandable language.

(2) Use of forms to achieve compliance. A depository institution shall be deemed to be in compliance with the requirements of this section if such institution—

(A) uses any appropriate model form or clause as published by the Board, jointly with the Director of the Bureau of Consumer Financial Protection, or

(B) uses any such model form or clause and changes such form or clause by—

(i) deleting any information which is not required by this chapter; or

(ii) rearranging the format.

(3) Voluntary use. Nothing in this chapter requires the use of any such model form or clause prescribed by the Board, jointly with the Director of the Bureau of Consumer Financial Protection, under this subsection.

(4) Notice and comment. Model disclosure forms and clauses shall be adopted by the Board, jointly with the Director of the Bureau of Consumer Financial Protection, only after notice duly given in the Federal Register and an opportunity for public comment in accordance with section 553 of title 5.

§ 4005. Payment of Interest

(a) In general. Except as provided in subsection (b) or (c) of this section and notwithstanding any other provision of law, interest shall accrue on funds deposited in an interest-bearing account at a depository institution beginning not later than the business day on which the depository institution receives provisional credit for such funds.

(b) Special rule for credit unions. Subsection (a) of this section shall not apply to an account at a depository institution described in section 461(b)(1)(A)(iv) of this title if the depository institution—

(1) begins the accrual of interest or dividends at a later date than the date described in subsection (a) of this section with respect to all funds, including cash, deposited in such account; and

(2) provides notice of the interest payment policy in the manner required under section 4004(e) of this title.

(c) Exception for checks returned unpaid. No provision of this chapter shall be construed as requiring the payment of interest or dividends on funds deposited by a check which is returned unpaid.

§ 4006. Miscellaneous Provisions

(a) After-hours deposits. For purposes of this chapter, any deposit which is made on a Saturday, Sunday, legal holiday, or after the close of business on any business day shall be deemed to have been made on the next business day.

(b) Availability at start of business day. Except as provided in subsections (b)(3) and (c)(1)(B) of section 4002 of this title, if any provision of this chapter requires that funds be available for withdrawal on any business day, such funds shall be available for withdrawal at the start of such business day.

(c) Effect on policies of depository institutions. No provision of this chapter shall be construed as—

(1) prohibiting a depository institution from making funds available for withdrawal in a shorter period of time than the period of time required by this chapter; or

(2) affecting a depository institution's right—

(A) to accept or reject a check for deposit;

(B) to revoke any provisional settlement made by the depository institution with respect to a check accepted by such institution for deposit;

(C) to charge back the depositor's account for the amount of such check; or

(D) to claim a refund of such provisional credit.

(d) Prohibition on freezing certain funds in an account. In any case in which a check is deposited in an account at a depository institution and the funds represented by such check are not yet available for withdrawal pursuant to this chapter, the depository institution may not freeze any other funds in such account (which are otherwise available for withdrawal pursuant to this chapter) solely because the funds so deposited are not yet available for withdrawal.

(e) Employee training on and compliance with requirements of this chapter. Each depository institution shall—

(1) take such actions as may be necessary fully to inform each employee (who performs duties subject to the requirements of this chapter) of the requirements of this chapter; and

(2) establish and maintain procedures reasonably designed to assure and monitor employee compliance with such requirements.

(f) Adjustments to dollar amounts for inflation. The dollar amounts under this title shall be adjusted every 5 years after December 31, 2011 by the annual percentage increase in the Consumer Price Index for Urban Wage Earners and Clerical Workers, as published by the Bureau of Labor Statistics, rounded to the nearest multiple of $25.

§ 4007. Effect on State Law

(a) In general. Any law or regulation of any State in effect on September 1, 1989, which requires that funds deposited or received for deposit in an account at a depository institution chartered by such State be made available for withdrawal in a shorter period of time than the period of time provided in this chapter or in regulations prescribed by the Board under this chapter (as in effect on September 1, 1989) shall—

(1) supersede the provisions of this chapter and any regulations by the Board to the extent such provisions relate to the time by which funds deposited or received for deposit in an account shall be available for withdrawal; and

(2) apply to all federally insured depository institutions located within such State.

(b) Override of certain State laws. Except as provided in subsection (a) of this section, this chapter and regulations prescribed under this chapter shall supersede any provision of the law of any State, including the Uniform Commercial Code as in effect in such State, which is inconsistent with this chapter or such regulations.

§ 4008. Regulations and Reports by Board

(a) In general. After notice and opportunity to submit comment in accordance with section 553(c) of title 5, the Board, jointly with the Director of the Bureau of Consumer Financial Protection, shall prescribe regulations—

(1) to carry out the provisions of this chapter;

(2) to prevent the circumvention or evasion of such provisions; and

(3) to facilitate compliance with such provisions.

(b) Regulations relating to improvement of check processing system. In order to improve the check processing system, the Board shall consider (among other proposals) requiring, by regulation, that—

(1) depository institutions be charged based upon notification that a check or similar instrument will be presented for payment;

(2) the Federal Reserve banks and depository institutions provide for check truncation;

(3) depository institutions be provided incentives to return items promptly to the depository institution of first deposit;

(4) the Federal Reserve banks and depository institutions take such actions as are necessary to automate the process of returning unpaid checks,

(5) each depository institution and Federal Reserve bank—

(A) place its endorsement, and other notations specified in regulations of the Board, on checks in the positions specified in such regulations; and

(B) take such actions as are necessary to—

(i) automate the process of reading endorsements; and

(ii) eliminate unnecessary endorsements;

(6) within one business day after an originating depository institution is presented a check (for more than such minimum amount as the Board may prescribe)—

(A) such originating depository institution determines whether it will pay such check; and

(B) if such originating depository institution determines that it will not pay such check, such originating depository institution directly notify the receiving depository institution of such determination;

(7) regardless of where a check is cleared initially, all returned checks be eligible to be returned through the Federal Reserve System;

(8) Federal Reserve banks and depository institutions participate in the development and implementation of an electronic clearinghouse process to the extent the Board determines, pursuant to the study under subsection (f), that such a process is feasible; and

(9) originating depository institutions be permitted to return unpaid checks directly to, and obtain reimbursement for such checks directly from, the receiving depository institution.

(c) Regulatory responsibility of Board for payment system

(1) Responsibility for payment system. In order to carry out the provisions of this chapter, the Board of Governors of the Federal Reserve System shall have the responsibility to regulate—

(A) any aspect of the payment system, including the receipt, payment, collection, or clearing of checks; and

(B) any related function of the payment system with respect to checks.

(2) Regulations. The Board shall prescribe such regulations as it may determine to be appropriate to carry out its responsibility under paragraph (1).

(d) Reports

(1) Implementation progress reports

(A) Required reports. The Board shall transmit a report to both Houses of the Congress not later than 18, 30, and 48 months after August 10, 1987.

(B) Contents of report. Each such report shall describe—

(i) the actions taken and progress made by the Board to implement the schedules established in section 4002 of this title, and

(ii) the impact of this chapter on consumers and depository institutions.

(2) Evaluation of temporary schedule report

(A) Report required. The Board shall transmit a report to both Houses of the Congress not later than 2 years after August 10, 1987, regarding the effects the temporary schedule established under section 4002(c) of this title have had on depository institutions and the public.

(B) Contents of report. Such report shall also assess the potential impact the implementation of the schedule established in section 4002(b) of this title will have on depository institutions and the public, including an estimate of the risks to and losses of depository institutions and the benefits to consumers. Such report shall also contain such recommendations for legislative or administrative action as the Board may determine to be necessary.

(3) Comptroller General evaluation report. Not later than 6 months after September 1, 1988, the Comptroller General of the United States shall transmit a report to the Congress evaluating the implementation and administration of this chapter.

(e) Consultations.—In prescribing regulations under subsections (a) and (b), the Board and the Director of the Bureau of Consumer Financial Protection, in the case of subsection (a), and the Board, in the case of subsection (b), shall consult with the Comptroller of the Currency, the Board of Directors of the Federal Deposit Insurance Corporation, and the National Credit Union Administration Board.

(f) Electronic clearinghouse study

(1) Study required. The Board shall study the feasibility of modernizing and accelerating the check payment system through the development of an electronic clearinghouse process utilizing existing telecommunications technology to avoid the necessity of actual presentment of the paper instrument to a payor institution before such institution is charged for the item.

(2) Consultation; factors to be studied. In connection with the study required under paragraph (1), the Board shall—

(A) consult with appropriate experts in telecommunications technology; and

(B) consider all practical and legal impediments to the development of an electronic clearinghouse process.

(3) Report required. The Board shall report its conclusions to the Congress within 9 months of August 10, 1987.

§ 4009. Administrative Enforcement

(a) Administrative enforcement. Compliance with the requirements imposed under this chapter, including regulations prescribed by and orders issued by the Board of Governors of the Federal Reserve System under this chapter, shall be enforced under—

(1) section 8 of the Federal Deposit Insurance Act (12 U.S.C. 1818) in the case of—

(A) national banks, and Federal branches and Federal agencies of foreign banks, by the Office of the Comptroller of the Currency;

(B) member banks of the Federal Reserve System (other than national banks), and offices, branches, and agencies of foreign banks located in the United States (other than Federal branches, Federal agencies, and insured State branches of foreign banks), by the Board of Governors of the Federal Reserve System; and

(C) banks insured by the Federal Deposit Insurance Corporation (other than members of the Federal Reserve System) and insured State branches of foreign banks, by the Board of Directors of the Federal Deposit Insurance Corporation;

(2) section 8 of the Federal Deposit Insurance Act (12 U.S.C. 1818), by the Director of the Office of Thrift Supervision in the case of savings associations the deposits of which are insured by the Federal Deposit Insurance Corporation; and

(3) the Federal Credit Union Act (12 U.S.C. 1751 et seq.), by the National Credit Union Administration Board with respect to any Federal credit union or insured credit union.

The terms used in paragraph (1) that are not defined in this chapter or otherwise defined in section 3(s) of the Federal Deposit Insurance Act (12 U.S.C. 1813(s)) shall have the meaning given to them in section 1(b) of the International Banking Act of 1978 (12 U.S.C. 3101).

(b) Additional powers

(1) Violation of this chapter treated as violation of other Acts. For purposes of the exercise by any agency referred to in subsection (a) of this section of its powers under any Act referred to in that subsection, a violation of any requirement imposed under this chapter shall be deemed to be a violation of a requirement imposed under that Act.

(2) Enforcement authority under other Acts. In addition to its powers under any provision of law specifically referred to in subsection (a) of this section, each of the agencies referred to in such subsection may exercise, for purposes of enforcing compliance

with any requirement imposed under this chapter, any other authority conferred on it by law.

(c) Enforcement by Board

(1) In general. Except to the extent that enforcement of the requirements imposed under this chapter is specifically committed to some other Government agency under subsection (a) of this section, the Board of Governors of the Federal Reserve System shall enforce such requirements.

(2) Additional remedy. If the Board determines that—

(A) any depository institution which is not a depository institution described in subsection (a), or

(B) any other person subject to the authority of the Board under this chapter, including any person subject to the authority of the Board under section 4004(d)(2) or 4008(c) of this title, has failed to comply with any requirement imposed by this chapter or by the Board under this chapter, the Board may issue an order prohibiting any depository institution, any Federal Reserve bank, or any other person subject to the authority of the Board from engaging in any activity or transaction which directly or indirectly involves such noncomplying depository institution or person (including any activity or transaction involving the receipt, payment, collection, and clearing of checks and any related function of the payment system with respect to checks).

(d) Procedural rules. The authority of the Board to prescribe regulations under this chapter does not impair the authority of any other agency designated in this section to make rules regarding its own procedures in enforcing compliance with requirements imposed under this chapter.

§ 4010. Civil Liability

(a) Civil liability. Except as otherwise provided in this section, any depository institution which fails to comply with any requirement imposed under this chapter or any regulation prescribed under this chapter with respect to any person other than another depository institution is liable to such person in an amount equal to the sum of—

(1) any actual damage sustained by such person as a result of the failure;

(2) (A) in the case of an individual action, such additional amount as the court may allow, except that the liability under this subparagraph shall not be less than $100 nor greater than $1,000; or

(B) in the case of a class action, such amount as the court may allow, except that—

(i) as to each member of the class, no minimum recovery shall be applicable; and

(ii) the total recovery under this subparagraph in any class action or series of class actions arising out of the same failure to comply by the same depository institution shall not be more than the lesser of $500,000 or 1 percent of the net worth of the depository institution involved; and

(3) in the case of any successful action to enforce the foregoing liability, the costs of the action, together with a reasonable attorney's fee as determined by the court.

(b) Class action awards. In determining the amount of any award in any class action, the court shall consider, among other relevant factors—

(1) the amount of any actual damages awarded;

(2) the frequency and persistence of failures of compliance;

(3) the resources of the depository institution;

(4) the number of persons adversely affected; and

(5) the extent to which the failure of compliance was intentional.

(c) Bona fide errors

(1) General rule. A depository institution may not be held liable in any action brought under this section for a violation of this chapter if the depository institution demonstrates by a preponderance of the evidence that the violation was not intentional and resulted from a bona fide error, notwithstanding the maintenance of procedures reasonably adapted to avoid any such error.

(2) Examples. Examples of a bona fide error include clerical, calculation, computer malfunction and programming, and printing errors, except that an error of legal judgment with respect to a depository institution's obligation under this chapter is not a bona fide error.

(d) Jurisdiction. Any action under this section may be brought in any United States district court, or in any other court of competent jurisdiction, within one year after the date of the occurrence of the violation involved.

(e) Reliance on Board rulings. No provision of this section imposing any liability shall apply to any act done or omitted in good faith in conformity with any rule, regulation, or interpretation thereof by the Board of Governors of the Federal Reserve System, notwithstanding the fact that after such act or omission has occurred, such rule, regulation, or interpretation is amended, rescinded, or determined by judicial or other authority to be invalid for any reason.

(f) Authority to establish rules regarding losses and liability among depository institutions. The Board is authorized to impose on or allocate among depository institutions the risks of loss and liability in connection with any aspect of the payment system, including the receipt, payment, collection, or clearing of checks, and any related function of the payment system with respect to checks. Liability under this subsection shall not exceed the amount of the check giving rise to the loss or liability, and, where there is bad faith, other damages, if any, suffered as a proximate consequence of any act or omission giving rise to the loss or liability.

Check 21 Act

12 U.S.C. §§ 5001–5018

§ 2 [12 U.S.C. § 5001]. Findings; Purposes

(a) Findings. The Congress finds as follows:

(1) In the Expedited Funds Availability Act, enacted on August 10, 1987, the Congress directed the Board of Governors of the Federal Reserve System to consider establishing regulations requiring Federal reserve banks and depository institutions to provide for check truncation, in order to improve the check processing system.

(2) In that same Act, the Congress—

(A) provided the Board of Governors of the Federal Reserve System with full authority to regulate all aspects of the payment system, including the receipt, payment, collection, and clearing of checks, and related functions of the payment system pertaining to checks; and

(B) directed that the exercise of such authority by the Board superseded any State law, including the Uniform Commercial Code, as in effect in any State.

(3) Check truncation is no less desirable in 2003 for both financial service customers and the financial services industry, to reduce costs, improve efficiency in check collections, and expedite funds availability for customers than it was over 15 years ago when Congress first directed the Board to consider establishing such a process.

(b) Purposes. The purposes of this chapter are as follows:

(1) To facilitate check truncation by authorizing substitute checks.

(2) To foster innovation in the check collection system without mandating receipt of checks in electronic form.

(3) To improve the overall efficiency of the Nation's payments system.

§ 3 [12 U.S.C. § 5002]. Definitions

For purposes of this chapter, the following definitions shall apply:

(1) Account—The term "account" means a deposit account at a bank.

(2) Bank—The term "bank" means any person that is located in a State and engaged in the business of banking and includes—

(A) any depository institution (as defined in section 461 (b)(1)(A) of this title);

(B) any Federal reserve bank;

(C) any Federal home loan bank; or

(D) to the extent it acts as a payor—

(i) the Treasury of the United States;

(ii) the United States Postal Service;

(iii) a State government; or

(iv) a unit of general local government (as defined in section 4001(24) of this title).

(3) Banking terms—

(A) Collecting bank—The term "collecting bank" means any bank handling a check for collection except the paying bank.

(B) Depositary bank—The term "depositary bank" means—

(i) the first bank to which a check is transferred, even if such bank is also the paying bank or the payee; or

(ii) a bank to which a check is transferred for deposit in an account at such bank, even if the check is physically received and indorsed first by another bank.

(C) Paying bank—The term "paying bank" means—

(i) the bank by which a check is payable, unless the check is payable at or through another bank and is sent to the other bank for payment or collection; or

(ii) the bank at or through which a check is payable and to which the check is sent for payment or collection.

(D) Returning bank—

(i) In general—The term "returning bank" means a bank (other than the paying or depositary bank) handling a returned check or notice in lieu of return.

(ii) Treatment as collecting bank – No provision of this chapter shall be construed as affecting the treatment of a returning bank as a collecting bank for purposes of section 4-202(b) of the Uniform Commercial Code.

(4) Board—The term "Board" means the Board of Governors of the Federal Reserve System.

(5) Business day—The term "business day" has the same meaning as in section 4001(3) of this title.

(6) Check—The term "check"—

(A) means a draft, payable on demand and drawn on or payable through or at an office of a bank, whether or not negotiable, that is handled for forward collection or return, including a substitute check and a travelers check; and

(B) does not include a noncash item or an item payable in a medium other than United States dollars.

(7) Consumer—The term "consumer" means an individual who—

(A) with respect to a check handled for forward collection, draws the check on a consumer account; or

(B) with respect to a check handled for return, deposits the check into, or cashes the check against, a consumer account.

(8) Consumer account

The term "consumer account" has the same meaning as in section 4001(10) of this title.

(9) Customer—The term "customer" means a person having an account with a bank.

(10) Forward collection—The term "forward collection" means the transfer by a bank of a check to a collecting bank for settlement or the paying bank for payment.

(11) Indemnifying bank—The term "indemnifying bank" means a bank that is providing an indemnity under section 5005 of this title with respect to a substitute check.

(12) MICR line—The terms "MICR line" and "magnetic ink character recognition line" mean the numbers, which may include the bank routing number, account number, check number, check amount, and other information, that are printed near the bottom of a check in magnetic ink in accordance with generally applicable industry standards.

(13) Noncash item—The term "noncash item" has the same meaning as in section 4001(14) of this title.

(14) Person—The term "person" means a natural person, corporation, unincorporated company, partnership, government unit or instrumentality, trust, or any other entity or organization.

(15) Reconverting bank—The term "reconverting bank" means—

(A) the bank that creates a substitute check; or

(B) if a substitute check is created by a person other than a bank, the first bank that transfers or presents such substitute check.

(16) Substitute check—The term "substitute check" means a paper reproduction of the original check that—

(A) contains an image of the front and back of the original check;

(B) bears a MICR line containing all the information appearing on the MICR line of the original check, except as provided under generally applicable industry standards for substitute checks to facilitate the processing of substitute checks;

(C) conforms, in paper stock, dimension, and otherwise, with generally applicable industry standards for substitute checks; and

(D) is suitable for automated processing in the same manner as the original check.

(17) State—The term "State" has the same meaning as in 1813(a) of this title.

(18) Truncate—The term "truncate" means to remove an original paper check from the check

collection or return process and send to a recipient, in lieu of such original paper check, a substitute check or, by agreement, information relating to the original check (including data taken from the MICR line of the original check or an electronic image of the original check), whether with or without subsequent delivery of the original paper check.

(19) Uniform Commercial Code—The term "Uniform Commercial Code" means the Uniform Commercial Code in effect in a State.

(20) Other terms—Unless the context requires otherwise, the terms not defined in this section shall have the same meanings as in the Uniform Commercial Code.

§ 4 [12 U.S.C. § 5003]. General Provisions Governing Substitute Checks

(a) No agreement required. A person may deposit, present, or send for collection or return a substitute check without an agreement with the recipient, so long as a bank has made the warranties in section 5004 of this title with respect to such substitute check.

(b) Legal equivalence. A substitute check shall be the legal equivalent of the original check for all purposes, including any provision of any Federal or State law, and for all persons if the substitute check—

(1) accurately represents all of the information on the front and back of the original check as of the time the original check was truncated; and

(2) bears the legend: "This is a legal copy of your check. You can use it the same way you would use the original check."

(c) Endorsements. A bank shall ensure that the substitute check for which the bank is the reconverting bank bears all endorsements applied by parties that previously handled the check (whether in electronic form or in the form of the original paper check or a substitute check) for forward collection or return.

(d) Identification of reconverting bank. A bank shall identify itself as a reconverting bank on any substitute check for which the bank is a reconverting bank so as to preserve any previous reconverting bank identifications in conformance with generally applicable industry standards.

(e) Applicable law. A substitute check that is the legal equivalent of the original check under subsection (b) of this section shall be subject to any provision, including any provision relating to the protection of customers, of part 229 of title 12 of the Code of Federal Regulations, the Uniform Commercial Code, and any other applicable Federal or State law as if such substitute check were the original check, to the extent such provision of law is not inconsistent with this chapter.

§ 5 [12 U.S.C. § 5004]. Substitute Check Warranties

A bank that transfers, presents, or returns a substitute check and receives consideration for the check warrants, as a matter of law, to the transferee, any subsequent collecting or returning bank, the depositary bank, the drawee, the drawer, the payee, the depositor, and any endorser (regardless of whether the warrantee receives the substitute check or another paper or electronic form of the substitute check or original check) that—

(1) the substitute check meets all the requirements for legal equivalence under section 5003(b) of this title; and

(2) no depositary bank, drawee, drawer, or endorser will receive presentment or return of the substitute check, the original check, or a copy or other paper or electronic version of the substitute check or original check such that the bank, drawee, drawer, or endorser will be asked to make a payment based on a check that the bank, drawee, drawer, or endorser has already paid.

§ 6 [12 U.S.C. § 5005]. Indemnity

(a) Indemnity. A reconverting bank and each bank that subsequently transfers, presents, or returns a substitute check in any electronic or paper form, and receives consideration for such transfer, presentment, or return shall indemnify the transferee, any subsequent collecting or returning bank, the depositary bank, the drawee, the drawer, the payee, the depositor, and any endorser, up to the amount described in subsections (b) and (c) of this section, as applicable, to the extent of any loss incurred by any recipient of a substitute check if that loss occurred due to the receipt of a substitute check instead of the original check.

(b) Indemnity amount.

(1) Amount in event of breach of warranty. The amount of the indemnity under subsection (a) of this section shall be the amount of any loss (including costs and reasonable attorney's fees and other expenses of representation) proximately caused by a breach of a warranty provided under section 5004 of this title.

(2) Amount in absence of breach of warranty. In the absence of a breach of a warranty provided under section 5004 of this title, the amount of the indemnity under subsection (a) of this section shall be the sum of—

(A) the amount of any loss, up to the amount of the substitute check; and

(B) interest and expenses (including costs and reasonable attorney's fees and other expenses of representation).

(c) Comparative negligence

(1) In general. If a loss described in subsection (a) of this section results in whole or in part from the negligence or failure to act in good faith on the part of an indemnified party, then that party's indemnification under this section shall be reduced in proportion to the amount of negligence or bad faith attributable to that party.

(2) Rule of construction. Nothing in this subsection reduces the rights of a consumer or any other person under the Uniform Commercial Code or other applicable provision of Federal or State law.

(d) Effect of producing original check or copy

(1) In general. If the indemnifying bank produces the original check or a copy of the original check (including an image or a substitute check) that accurately represents all of the information on the front and back of the original check (as of the time the original check was truncated) or is otherwise sufficient to determine whether or not a claim is valid, the indemnifying bank shall—

(A) be liable under this section only for losses covered by the indemnity that are incurred up to the time that the original check or copy is provided to the indemnified party; and

(B) have a right to the return of any funds it has paid under the indemnity in excess of those losses.

(2) Coordination of indemnity with implied warranty. The production of the original check, a substitute check, or a copy under paragraph (1) by an indemnifying bank shall not absolve the bank from any liability on a warranty established under this chapter or any other provision of law.

(e) Subrogation of rights

(1) In general. Each indemnifying bank shall be subrogated to the rights of any indemnified party to the extent of the indemnity.

(2) Recovery under warranty. A bank that indemnifies a party under this section may attempt to recover from another party based on a warranty or other claim.

(3) Duty of indemnified party. Each indemnified party shall have a duty to comply with all reasonable requests for assistance from an indemnifying bank in connection with any claim the indemnifying bank brings against a warrantor or other party related to a check that forms the basis for the indemnification.

§ 7 [12 U.S.C. § 5006]. Expedited Recredit for Consumers

(a) Recredit claims

(1) In general. A consumer may make a claim for expedited recredit from the bank that holds the account of the consumer with respect to a substitute check, if the consumer asserts in good faith that—

(A) the bank charged the consumer's account for a substitute check that was provided to the consumer;

(B) either—

(i) the check was not properly charged to the consumer's account; or

(ii) the consumer has a warranty claim with respect to such substitute check;

(C) the consumer suffered a resulting loss; and

(D) the production of the original check or a better copy of the original check is necessary to determine the validity of any claim described in subparagraph (B).

(2) 40-day period. Any claim under paragraph (1) with respect to a consumer account may be submitted by a consumer before the end of the 40-day period beginning on the later of—

(A) the date on which the financial institution mails or delivers, by a means agreed to by the consumer, the periodic statement of account for such account which contains information concerning the transaction giving rise to the claim; or

(B) the date on which the substitute check is made available to the consumer.

(3) Extension under extenuating circumstances. If the ability of the consumer to submit the claim within the 40-day period under paragraph (2) is delayed due to extenuating circumstances, including extended travel or the illness of the consumer, the 40-day period shall be extended by a reasonable amount of time.

(b) Procedures for claims

(1) In general. To make a claim for an expedited recredit under subsection (a) of this section with respect to a substitute check, the consumer shall provide to the bank that holds the account of such consumer—

(A) a description of the claim, including an explanation of—

(i) why the substitute check was not properly charged to the consumer's account; or

(ii) the warranty claim with respect to such check;

(B) a statement that the consumer suffered a loss and an estimate of the amount of the loss;

(C) the reason why production of the original check or a better copy of the original check is necessary to determine the validity of the charge to the consumer's account or the warranty claim; and

(D) sufficient information to identify the substitute check and to investigate the claim.

(2) Claim in writing

(A) In general. The bank holding the consumer account that is the subject of a claim by the consumer under subsection (a) of this section may, in the discretion of the bank, require the consumer to submit the information required under paragraph (1) in writing.

(B) Means of submission. A bank that requires a submission of information under subparagraph (A) may permit the consumer to make the submission electronically, if the consumer has agreed to communicate with the bank in that manner.

(c) Recredit to consumer

(1) Conditions for recredit. The bank shall recredit a consumer account in accordance with paragraph (2) for the amount of a substitute check that was charged against the consumer account if—

(A) a consumer submits a claim to the bank with respect to that substitute check that meets the requirement of subsection (b) of this section; and

(B) the bank has not—

(i) provided to the consumer—

(I) the original check; or

(II) a copy of the original check (including an image or a substitute check) that accurately represents all of the information on the front and back of the original check, as of the time at which the original check was truncated; and

(ii) demonstrated to the consumer that the substitute check was properly charged to the consumer account.

(2) Timing of recredit

(A) In general. The bank shall recredit the consumer's account for the amount described in paragraph (1) no later than the end of the business day following the business day on which the bank determines the consumer's claim is valid.

(B) Recredit pending investigation. If the bank has not yet determined that the consumer's claim is valid before the end of the 10th business day after the business day on which the consumer submitted the claim, the bank shall recredit the consumer's account for—

(i) the lesser of the amount of the substitute check that was charged against the consumer account, or $2,500, together with interest if the account is an interest-bearing account, no later than the end of such 10th business day; and

(ii) the remaining amount of the substitute check that was charged against the consumer account, if any, together with interest if the account is an interest-bearing account, not later than the 45th calendar day following the business day on which the consumer submits the claim.

(d) Availability of recredit

(1) Next business day availability. Except as provided in paragraph (2), a bank that provides a recredit to a consumer account under subsection (c) of this section shall make the recredited funds available for withdrawal by the consumer by the start of the next business day after the business day on which the bank recredits the consumer's account under subsection (c).

(2) Safeguard exceptions. A bank may delay availability to a consumer of a recredit provided under subsection (c)(2)(B)(i) of this section until the start of either the business day following the business day on which the bank determines that the consumer's claim is valid or the 45th calendar day following the business day on which the consumer submits a claim for such recredit in accordance with subsection (b) of this section, whichever is earlier, in any of the following circumstances:

(A) New accounts. The claim is made during the 30-day period beginning on the business day the consumer account was established.

(B) Repeated overdrafts. Without regard to the charge that is the subject of the claim for which the recredit was made—

(i) on 6 or more business days during the 6-month period ending on the date on which the consumer submits the claim, the balance in the consumer account was negative or would have become negative if checks or other charges to the account had been paid; or

(ii) on 2 or more business days during such 6-month period, the balance in the consumer account was negative or would have become negative in the amount of $5,000 or more if checks or other charges to the account had been paid.

(C) Prevention of fraud losses. The bank has reasonable cause to believe that the claim is fraudulent, based on facts (other than the fact that the check in question or the consumer is of a particular class) that would cause a well-grounded belief in the mind of a reasonable person that the claim is fraudulent.

(3) Overdraft fees. No bank that, in accordance with paragraph (2), delays the availability of a recredit under subsection (c) of this section to any consumer account may impose any overdraft fees with respect to drafts drawn by the consumer on such recredited amount before the end of the 5-day period beginning on the date notice of the delay in the availability of such amount is sent by the bank to the consumer.

(e) Reversal of recredit. A bank may reverse a recredit to a consumer account if the bank—

(1) determines that a substitute check for which the bank recredited a consumer account under subsection (c) of this section was in fact properly charged to the consumer account; and

(2) notifies the consumer in accordance with subsection (f)(3).

(f) Notice to consumer

(1) Notice if consumer claim not valid. If a bank determines that a substitute check subject to the consumer's claim was in fact properly charged to the consumer's account, the bank shall send to the consumer, no later than the business day following the business day on which the bank makes a determination—

(A) the original check or a copy of the original check (including an image or a substitute check) that—

(i) accurately represents all of the information on the front and back of the original check (as of the time the original check was truncated); or

(ii) is otherwise sufficient to determine whether or not the consumer's claim is valid; and

(B) an explanation of the basis for the determination by the bank that the substitute check was properly charged, including a statement that the consumer may request copies of any information or documents on which the bank relied in making the determination.

(2) Notice of recredit. If a bank recredits a consumer account under subsection (c) of this section, the bank shall send to the consumer, no later than the business day following the business day on which the bank makes the recredit, a notice of—

(A) the amount of the recredit; and

(B) the date the recredited funds will be available for withdrawal.

(3) Notice of reversal of recredit. In addition to the notice required under paragraph (1), if a bank reverses a recredited amount under subsection (e), the bank shall send to the consumer, no later than the business day following the business day on which the bank reverses the recredit, a notice of—

(A) the amount of the reversal; and

(B) the date the recredit was reversed.

(4) Mode of delivery. A notice described in this subsection shall be delivered by United States mail or by any other means through which the consumer has agreed to receive account information.

(g) Other claims not affected. Providing a recredit in accordance with this section shall not absolve the bank from liability for a claim made under any other law, such as a claim for wrongful dishonor under the Uniform Commercial Code, or from liability for additional damages under section 5005 or 5009 of this title.

(h) Clarification concerning consumer possession. A consumer who was provided a substitute check may make a claim for an expedited recredit under this section with regard to a transaction involving the substitute check whether or not the consumer is in possession of the substitute check.

(i) Scope of application. This section shall only apply to customers who are consumers.

§ 8 [12 U.S.C. § 5007]. Expedited Recredit Procedures for Banks

(a) Recredit claims

(1) In general. A bank may make a claim against an indemnifying bank for expedited recredit for which that bank is indemnified if—

(A) the claimant bank (or a bank that the claimant bank has indemnified) has received a claim for expedited recredit from a consumer under section 5006 of this title with respect to a substitute check or would have been subject to such a claim had the consumer's account been charged;

(B) the claimant bank has suffered a resulting loss or is obligated to recredit a consumer account under section 5006 of this title with respect to such substitute check; and

(C) production of the original check, another substitute check, or a better copy of the original check is necessary to determine the validity of the charge to the customer account or any warranty claim connected with such substitute check.

(2) 120-day period. Any claim under paragraph (1) may be submitted by the claimant bank to an indemnifying bank before the end of the 120-day period beginning on the date of the transaction that gave rise to the claim.

(b) Procedures for claims

(1) In general. To make a claim under subsection (a) of this section for an expedited recredit relating to a substitute check, the claimant bank shall send to the indemnifying bank—

(A) a description of—

(i) the claim, including an explanation of why the substitute check cannot be properly charged to the consumer account; or

(ii) the warranty claim;

(B) a statement that the claimant bank has suffered a loss or is obligated to recredit the consumer's account under section 5006 of this title, together with an estimate of the amount of the loss or recredit;

(C) the reason why production of the original check, another substitute check, or a better copy of the original check is necessary to determine the validity of the charge to the consumer account or the warranty claim; and

(D) information sufficient for the indemnifying bank to identify the substitute check and to investigate the claim.

(2) Requirements relating to copies of substitute checks. If the information submitted by a claimant bank pursuant to paragraph (1) in connection with a claim for an expedited recredit includes a copy of any substitute check for which any such claim is made, the claimant bank shall take reasonable steps to ensure that any such copy cannot be—

(A) mistaken for the legal equivalent of the check under section 5003(b) of this title; or

(B) sent or handled by any bank, including the indemnifying bank, as a forward collection or returned check.

(3) Claim in writing

(A) In general. An indemnifying bank may, in the discretion of the bank, require the claimant bank to submit the information required by paragraph (1) in writing, including a copy of the written or electronically submitted claim, if any, that the consumer provided in accordance with section 5006(b) of this title.

(B) Means of submission. An indemnifying bank that requires a submission of information under subparagraph (A) may permit the claimant bank to make the submission electronically, if the claimant bank has agreed to communicate with the indemnifying bank in that manner.

(c) Recredit by indemnifying bank

(1) Prompt action required. No later than 10 business days after the business day on which an indemnifying bank receives a claim under subsection (a) of this section from a claimant bank with respect to a substitute check, the indemnifying bank shall—

(A) provide, to the claimant bank, the original check (with respect to such substitute check) or a copy of the original check (including an image or a substitute check) that—

(i) accurately represents all of the information on the front and back of the original check (as of the time the original check was truncated); or

(ii) is otherwise sufficient to determine the bank's claim is not valid; and

(B) recredit the claimant bank for the amount of the claim up to the amount of the substitute check, plus interest if applicable; or

(C) provide information to the claimant bank as to why the indemnifying bank is not obligated to comply with subparagraph (A) or (B).

(2) Recredit does not abrogate other liabilities. Providing a recredit under this subsection to a claimant bank with respect to a substitute check shall not absolve the indemnifying bank from liability for claims brought under any other law or from additional damages under section 5005 or 5009 of this title with respect to such check.

(3) Refund to indemnifying bank. If a claimant bank reverses, in accordance with section 5006(e) of

this title, a recredit previously made to a consumer account under 5006(c) of this title, or otherwise receives a credit or recredit with regard to such substitute check, the claimant bank shall promptly refund to any indemnifying bank any amount previously advanced by the indemnifying bank in connection with such substitute check.

(d) Production of original check or a sufficient copy governed by 5005(d) of this title.

If the indemnifying bank provides the claimant bank with the original check or a copy of the original check (including an image or a substitute check) under subsection (c)(1)(A) of this section, section 5005(d) of this title shall govern any right of the indemnifying bank to any repayment of any funds the indemnifying bank has recredited to the claimant bank pursuant to subsection (c).

§ 9 [12 U.S.C. § 5008]. Delays in an Emergency

A delay by a bank beyond the time limits prescribed or permitted by this chapter shall be excused if the delay is caused by interruption of communication or computer facilities, suspension of payments by another bank, war, emergency conditions, failure of equipment, or other circumstances beyond the control of a bank and if the bank uses such diligence as the circumstances require.

§ 10 [12 U.S.C. § 5009]. Measure of Damages

(a) Liability

(1) In general. Except as provided in section 5005 of this title, any person who, in connection with a substitute check, breaches any warranty under this chapter or fails to comply with any requirement imposed by, or regulation prescribed pursuant to, this chapter with respect to any other person shall be liable to such person in an amount equal to the sum of—

(A) the lesser of—

(i) the amount of the loss suffered by the other person as a result of the breach or failure; or

(ii) the amount of the substitute check; and

(B) interest and expenses (including costs and reasonable attorney's fees and other expenses of representation) related to the substitute check.

(2) Offset of recredits. The amount of damages any person receives under paragraph (1), if any, shall be reduced by the amount, if any, that the claimant receives and retains as a recredit under section 5006 or 5007 of this title.

(b) Comparative negligence

(1) In general. If a person incurs damages that resulted in whole or in part from the negligence or failure of that person to act in good faith, then the amount of any liability due to that person under subsection (a) of this section shall be reduced in proportion to the amount of negligence or bad faith attributable to that person.

(2) Rule of construction. Nothing in this subsection reduces the rights of a consumer or any other person under the Uniform Commercial Code or other applicable provision of Federal or State law.

§ 11 [12 U.S.C. § 5010]. Statute of Limitations and Notice of Claim

(a) Actions under this chapter

(1) In general. An action to enforce a claim under this chapter may be brought in any United States district court, or in any other court of competent jurisdiction, before the end of the 1-year period beginning on the date the cause of action accrues.

(2) Accrual. A cause of action accrues as of the date the injured party first learns, or by which such person reasonably should have learned, of the facts and circumstances giving rise to the cause of action.

(b) Discharge of claims. Except as provided in subsection (c) of this section, unless a person gives notice of a claim to the indemnifying or warranting bank within 30 days after the person has reason to know of the claim and the identity of the indemnifying or warranting bank, the indemnifying or warranting bank is discharged from liability in an action to enforce a claim under this chapter to the extent of any loss caused by the delay in giving notice of the claim.

(c) Notice of claim by consumer. A timely claim by a consumer under section 5006 of this title for expedited recredit constitutes timely notice of a claim by the consumer for purposes of subsection (b).

§ 12 [12 U.S.C. § 5011]. Consumer Awareness

(a) In general. Each bank shall provide, in accordance with subsection (b), a brief notice about substitute checks that describes—

(1) how a substitute check is the legal equivalent of an original check for all purposes, including any provision of any Federal or State law, and for all persons, if the substitute check—

(A) accurately represents all of the information on the front and back of the original check as of the time at which the original check was truncated; and

(B) bears the legend: "This is a legal copy of your check. You can use it in the same way you would use the original check."; and

(2) the consumer recredit rights established under section 5006 of this title when a consumer believes in good faith that a substitute check was not properly charged to the account of the consumer.

(b) Distribution

(1) Existing customers. With respect to consumers who are customers of a bank on the effective date of this chapter and who receive original checks or substitute checks, a bank shall provide the notice described in subsection (a) to each such consumer no later than the first regularly scheduled communication with the consumer after the effective date of this chapter.

(2) New account holders. A bank shall provide the notice described in subsection (a) to each consumer who will receive original checks or substitute checks, other than existing customers referred to in paragraph (1), at the time at which the customer relationship is initiated.

(3) Mode of delivery. A bank may send the notices required by this subsection by United States mail or by any other means through which the consumer has agreed to receive account information.

(4) Consumers who request copies of checks. Notice shall be provided to each consumer of the bank that requests a copy of a check and receives a substitute check, at the time of the request.

(c) Model language

(1) In general. Before the end of the 9-month period beginning on October 28, 2003, the Board shall publish model forms and clauses that a bank may use to describe each of the elements required by subsection (a).

(2) Safe harbor

(A) In general. A bank shall be treated as being in compliance with the requirements of subsection (a) if the bank's substitute check notice uses a model form or clause published by the Board and such model form or clause accurately describes the bank's policies and practices.

(B) Deletion or rearrangement. A bank may delete any information in the model form or clause that is not required by this chapter or rearrange the format.

(3) Use of model language not required. This section shall not be construed as requiring any bank to use a model form or clause that the Board prepares under this subsection.

§ 13 [12 U.S.C. § 5012]. Effect on Other Law

This chapter shall supersede any provision of Federal or State law, including the Uniform Commercial Code, that is inconsistent with this chapter, but only to the extent of the inconsistency.

§ 14 [12 U.S.C. § 5013]. Variation by Agreement

(a) Section 5007 of this title. Any provision of section 5007 of this title may be varied by agreement of the banks involved.

(b) No other provisions may be varied. Except as provided in subsection (a), no provision of this chapter may be varied by agreement of any person or persons.

§ 15 [12 U.S.C. § 5014]. Regulations

The Board may prescribe such regulations as the Board determines to be necessary to implement, prevent circumvention or evasion of, or facilitate compliance with the provisions of this chapter.

§ 16 [12 U.S.C. § 5015]. Study and Report on Funds Availability

(a) Study. In order to evaluate the implementation and the impact of this chapter, the Board shall conduct a study of—

(1) the percentage of total checks cleared in which the paper check is not returned to the paying bank;

(2) the extent to which banks make funds available to consumers for local and nonlocal checks prior to the expiration of maximum hold periods;

(3) the length of time within which depositary banks learn of the nonpayment of local and nonlocal checks;

(4) the increase or decrease in check-related losses over the study period; and

(5) the appropriateness of the time periods and amount limits applicable under sections 4002 and 4003 of this title, as in effect on October 28, 2003.

(b) Report to Congress. Before the end of the 30-month period beginning on the effective date of this chapter, the Board shall submit a report to the Congress containing the results of the study conducted under this section, together with recommendations for legislative action.

§ 17 [12 U.S.C. § 5016]. Statistical Reporting of Costs and Revenues for Transporting Checks Between Reserve Banks

In the annual report prepared by the Board for the first full calendar year after October 28, 2003 and in each of the 9 subsequent annual reports by the Board, the Board shall include the amount of operating costs attributable to, and an estimate of the Federal Reserve banks' imputed revenues derived from, the transportation of commercial checks between Federal Reserve bank check processing centers.

§ 18 [12 U.S.C. § 5017]. Evaluation and Report by the Comptroller General

(a) Study. During the 5-year period beginning on October 28, 2003, the Comptroller General of the United States shall evaluate the implementation and administration of this chapter, including—

(1) an estimate of the gains in economic efficiency made possible from check truncation;

(2) an evaluation of the benefits accruing to consumers and financial institutions from reduced transportation costs, longer hours for accepting deposits for credit within 1 business day, the impact of fraud losses, and an estimate of consumers' share of the total benefits derived from this chapter; and

(3) an assessment of consumer acceptance of the check truncation process resulting from this chapter, as well as any new costs incurred by consumers who had their original checks returned with their regular monthly statements prior to October 28, 2003.

(b) Report to Congress. Before the end of the 5-year period referred to in subsection (a) of this section, the Comptroller General shall submit a report to the Congress containing the findings and conclusions of the Comptroller General in connection with the evaluation conducted pursuant to subsection (a), together with such recommendations for legislative and administrative action as the Comptroller General may determine to be appropriate.

§ 19 [12 U.S.C. § 5018]. Depositary Services Efficiency and Cost Reduction

(a) Findings. The Congress finds as follows:

(1) The Secretary of the Treasury has long compensated financial institutions for various critical depositary and financial agency services provided for or on behalf of the United States by—

(A) placing large balances, commonly referred to as "compensating balances", on deposit at such institutions; and

(B) using imputed interest on such funds to offset charges for the various depositary and financial agency services provided to or on behalf of the Government.

(2) As a result of sharp declines in interest rates over the last few years to record low levels, or the public debt outstanding reaching the statutory debt limit, the Department of the Treasury often has had to dramatically increase or decrease the size of the compensating balances on deposit at these financial institutions.

(3) The fluctuation of the compensating balances, and the necessary pledging of collateral by financial institutions to secure the value of compensating balances placed with those institutions, have created unintended financial uncertainty for the Secretary of the Treasury and for the management by financial institutions of their cash and securities.

(4) It is imperative that the process for providing financial services to the Government be transparent, and provide the information necessary for the Congress to effectively exercise its appropriation and oversight responsibilities.

(5) The use of direct payment for services rendered would strengthen cash and debt management responsibilities of the Secretary of the Treasury because the Secretary would no longer need to dramatically increase or decrease the level of such balances when interest rates fluctuate sharply or when the public debt outstanding reaches the statutory debt limit.

(6) An alternative to the use of compensating balances, such as direct payments to financial institutions, would ensure that payments to financial institutions for the services they provide would be made in a more predictable manner and could result in cost savings.

(7) Limiting the use of compensating balances could result in a more direct and cost-efficient method of obtaining those services currently provided under compensating balance arrangements.

(8) A transition from the use of compensating balances to another compensation method must be carefully managed to prevent higher-than-necessary transitional costs and enable participating financial institutions to modify their planned investment of cash and securities.

(b) Authorization of appropriations for services rendered by depositaries and financial agencies of the United States. There are authorized to be appropriated for fiscal years beginning after fiscal year 2003 to the Secretary of the Treasury such sums as may be necessary for reimbursing financial institutions in their capacity as depositaries and financial agents of the United States for all services required or directed by the Secretary of the Treasury, or a designee of the Secretary, to be performed by such financial institutions on behalf of the Secretary of the Treasury or another Federal agency, including services rendered before fiscal year 2004.

(c) Orderly transition

(1) In general. As appropriations authorized in subsection (b) become available, the Secretary of the Treasury shall promptly begin the process of phasing in the use of the appropriations to pay financial institutions serving as depositaries and financial agents of the United States, and transitioning from the use of compensating balances to fund these services.

(2) Post-transition use limited to extraordinary circumstances

(A) In general. Following the transition to the use of the appropriations authorized in subsection (b) of this section, the Secretary of the Treasury may use the compensating balances to pay financial institutions serving as depositaries and financial agents of the United States only in extraordinary situations where the Secretary determines that they are needed to ensure the fiscal operations of the Government continue to function in an efficient and effective manner.

(B) Report. Any use of compensating balances pursuant to subparagraph (A) shall promptly be reported by the Secretary of the Treasury to the Committee on Financial Services of the House of Representatives and the Committee on Banking, Housing, and Urban Affairs of the Senate.

(3) Requirements for orderly transition. In transitioning to the use of the appropriations authorized in subsection (b), the Secretary of the Treasury shall take such steps as may be appropriate to—

(A) prevent abrupt financial disruption to the functions of the Department of the Treasury or to the participating financial institutions; and

(B) maintain adequate accounting and management controls to ensure that payments to financial institutions for their banking services provided to the Government as depositaries and financial agents are accurate and that the arrangements last no longer than is necessary.

(4) Reports required

(A) Annual report

(i) In general. For each fiscal year, the Secretary of the Treasury shall submit a report to the Congress on the use of compensating balances and on the use of appropriations authorized in subsection (b) during that fiscal year.

(ii) Inclusion in budget. The report required under clause (i) may be submitted as part of the budget submitted by the President under section 1105 of Title 31 for the following fiscal year and if so, the report shall be submitted concurrently to the Committee on Financial Services of the House of Representatives and the Committee on Banking, Housing, and Urban Affairs of the Senate.

(B) Final report following transition

(i) In general. Following completion of the transition from the use of compensating balances to the use of the appropriations authorized in subsection (b) to pay financial institutions for their services as depositaries and financial agents of the United States, the Secretary of the Treasury shall submit a report on the transition to the Committee on Financial Services of the House of Representatives and the Committee on Banking, Housing, and Urban Affairs of the Senate.

(ii) Contents of report. The report submitted under clause (i) shall include a detailed analysis of—

(I) the cost of transition;

(II) the direct costs of the services being paid from the appropriations authorized in subsection (b); and

(III) the benefits realized from the use of direct payment for such services, rather than the use of compensating balance arrangements.

(d) Omitted

(e) Effective date. Notwithstanding section 20, this section shall take effect on October 28, 2003.

Regulation CC

12 C.F.R. Part 229—Availability of Funds and Collection of Checks

PART 229—AVAILABILITY OF FUNDS AND COLLECTION OF CHECKS (REGULATION CC)

SUBPART A. GENERAL

§ 229.1 Authority and Purpose; Organization.

(a) Authority and purpose

(1) In general. This part is issued by the Board of Governors of the Federal Reserve System (Board) to implement the Expedited Funds Availability Act (12 U.S.C. 4001-4010) (the EFA Act) and the Check Clearing for the 21st Century Act (12 U.S.C. 5001-5018) (the Check 21 Act).

(2) Joint authority of the Bureau. The Board issues regulations under Sections 603(d)(1), 604, 605, and 609(a) of the EFA Act (12 U.S.C. 4002(d)(1), 4003, 4004, 4008(a)) jointly with the Director of the Bureau of Consumer Financial Protection (Bureau).

(b) Organization. This part is divided into subparts and appendices as follows—

(1) Subpart A contains general information. It sets forth—

(i) The authority, purpose, and organization;

(ii) Definition of terms; and

(iii) Authority for administrative enforcement of this part's provisions.

(2) Subpart B of this part contains rules regarding the duty of banks to make funds deposited into accounts available for withdrawal, including availability schedules. Subpart B of this part also contains rules regarding exceptions to the schedules, disclosure of funds availability policies, payment of interest, liability of banks for failure to comply with Subpart B of this part, and other matters.

(3) Subpart C of this part contains rules to expedite the collection and return of electronic checks by banks. These rules cover the direct return of checks and electronic checks, the manner in which the paying bank and returning banks must return checks and electronic checks to the depositary bank, notification of nonpayment by the paying bank, indorsement and presentment of checks and electronic checks, same-day settlement for certain checks, the liability of banks for failure to comply with subpart C of this part, and other matters.

(4) Subpart D of this part contains rules relating to substitute checks. These rules address the creation and legal status of substitute checks; the substitute check warranties and indemnity; expedited recredit procedures for resolving improper charges and warranty claims associated with substitute checks provided to consumers; and the disclosure and notices that banks must provide.

§ 229.2. Definitions.

As used in this part, and unless the context requires otherwise, the following terms have the meanings set forth in this section, and the terms not defined in this section have the meanings set forth in the Uniform Commercial Code:

(a) Account

(1) Except as provided in paragraphs (a)(2) and (a)(3) of this section, account means a deposit as defined in 12 CFR 204.2(a)(1)(i) that is a transaction account as described in 12 CFR 204.2(e). As defined in these sections, account generally includes accounts at a bank from which the account holder is permitted to make transfers or withdrawals by negotiable or transferable instrument, payment order of withdrawal, telephone transfer, electronic payment, or other similar means for the purpose of making payments or transfers to third persons or others. Account also includes accounts at a bank from which the account holder may make third party payments at an ATM, remote service unit, or other electronic device, including by debit card, but the term does not include savings deposits or accounts described in 12 CFR 204.2(d)(2) even though such accounts permit third party transfers. An account may be in the form of—

(i) A demand deposit account,

(ii) A negotiable order of withdrawal account,

(iii) A share draft account,

(iv) An automatic transfer account, or

(v) Any other transaction account described in 12 CFR 204.2(e).

(2) For purposes of subpart B of this part and, in connection therewith, this subpart A, account does not include an account where the account holder is a bank, where the account holder is an office of an institution described in paragraphs (e)(1) through (e)(6) of this section or an office of a "foreign bank" as defined in section 1(b) of the International Banking Act (12 U.S.C. 3101) that is located outside the United States, or where the direct or indirect account holder is the Treasury of the United States.

(3) For purposes of subpart D of this part and, in connection therewith, this subpart A, account means any deposit, as defined in 12 CFR 204.2(a)(1)(i), at a bank, including a demand deposit or other transaction account and a savings deposit or other time deposit, as those terms are defined in 12 CFR 204.2.

(b) Automated clearinghouse or ACH means a facility that processes debit and credit transfers under rules established by a Federal Reserve Bank operating circular on automated clearinghouse items or under rules of an automated clearinghouse association.

(c) Automated teller machine or ATM means an electronic device located in the United States at which a natural person may make deposits to an account by cash or check and perform other account transactions.

(d) Available for withdrawal with respect to funds deposited means available for all uses generally permitted to the customer for actually and finally collected funds under the bank's account agreement or policies, such as for payment of checks drawn on the account, certification of checks drawn on the account, electronic payments, withdrawals by cash, and transfers between accounts.

(e) Bank means—

(1) An insured bank as defined in section 3 of the Federal Deposit Insurance Act (12 U.S.C. 1813) or a bank that is eligible to apply to become an insured bank under section 5 of that Act (12 U.S.C. 1815);

(2) A mutual savings bank as defined in section 3 of the Federal Deposit Insurance Act (12 U.S.C. 1813);

(3) A savings bank as defined in section 3 of the Federal Deposit Insurance Act (12 U.S.C. 1813);

(4) An insured credit union as defined in section 101 of the Federal Credit Union Act (12 U.S.C. 1752) or a credit union that is eligible to make application to become an insured credit union under section 201 of that Act (12 U.S.C. 1781);

(5) A member as defined in section 2 of the Federal Home Loan Bank Act (12 U.S.C. 1422);

(6) A savings association as defined in section 3 of the Federal Deposit Insurance Act (12 U.S.C. 1813) that is an insured depository institution as defined in section 3 of that Act (12 U.S.C. 1813(c)(2)) or that is eligible to apply to become an insured depository institution under section 5 of that Act (12 U.S.C. 1815); or

(7) An agency or a branch of a foreign bank as defined in section l(b) of the International Banking Act (12 U.S.C. 3101).

For purposes of subparts C and D of this part and, in connection therewith, this subpart A, the term bank also includes any person engaged in the business of banking, as well as a Federal Reserve Bank, a Federal Home Loan Bank, and a state or unit of general local government to the extent that the state or unit of general local government acts as a paying bank. Unless otherwise specified, the term bank includes all of a bank's offices in the United States, but not offices located outside the United States.

Note: For purposes of subpart D of this part and, in connection therewith, this subpart A, bank also includes the Treasury of the United States or the United States Postal Service to the extent that the Treasury or the Postal Service acts as a paying bank.

(f) Banking day means that part of any business day on which an office of a bank is open to the public for carrying on substantially all of its banking functions.

(g) Business day means a calendar day other than a Saturday or a Sunday, January 1, the third Monday in January, the third Monday in February, the last Monday in May, July 4, the first Monday in September, the second Monday in October, November 11, the fourth Thursday in November, or December 25. If January 1, July 4, November 11, or December 25 fall on a Sunday, the next Monday is not a business day.

(h) Cash means United States coins and currency.

(i) Cashier's check means a check that is—

(1) Drawn on a bank;

(2) Signed by an officer or employee of the bank on behalf of the bank as drawer;

(3) A direct obligation of the bank; and

(4) Provided to a customer of the bank or acquired from the bank for remittance purposes.

(j) Certified check means a check with respect to which the drawee bank certifies by signature on the check of an officer or other authorized employee of the bank that—

(1) (i) The signature of the drawer on the check is genuine; and

(ii) The bank has set aside funds that—

(A) Are equal to the amount of the check, and

(B) Will be used to pay the check; or

(2) The bank will pay the check upon presentment.

(k) Check means—

(1) A negotiable demand draft drawn on or payable through or at an office of a bank;

(2) A negotiable demand draft drawn on a Federal Reserve Bank or a Federal Home Loan Bank;

(3) A negotiable demand draft drawn on the Treasury of the United States;

(4) A demand draft drawn on a state government or unit of general local government that is not payable through or at a bank;

(5) A United States Postal Service money order; or

(6) A traveler's check drawn on or payable through or at a bank.

(7) The term check includes an original check and a substitute check.

Note: The term check does not include a noncash item or an item payable in a medium other than United States money. A draft may be a check even though it is described on its face by another term, such as money order. For purposes of subparts C and D, and in connection therewith, subpart A, of this part, the term check also includes a demand draft of the type described above that is nonnegotiable.

(l) [Reserved]

(m) Check processing region means the geographical area served by an office of a Federal Reserve Bank for purposes of its check processing activities.

(n) Consumer account means any account used primarily for personal, family, or household purposes.

(o) Depositary bank means the first bank to which a check is transferred even though it is also the paying bank or the payee. A check deposited in an account is deemed to be transferred to the bank holding the account into which the check is deposited, even though the check is physically received and indorsed first by another bank.

(p) Electronic payment means a wire transfer or an ACH credit transfer.

(q) Forward collection means the process by which a bank sends a check on a cash basis to a collecting bank for settlement or to the paying bank for payment.

(r) Local check means a check payable by or at a local paying bank, or a check payable by a nonbank payor and payable through a local paying bank.

(s) Local paying bank means a paying bank that is located in the same check-processing region as the physical location of the branch, contractual branch, or proprietary ATM of the depositary bank in which that check was deposited.

(t) Merger transaction means—

(1) A merger or consolidation of two or more banks; or

(2) The transfer of substantially all of the assets of one or more banks or branches to another bank in consideration of the assumption by the acquiring bank of substantially all of the liabilities of the transferring banks, including the deposit liabilities.

(u) Noncash item means an item that would otherwise be a check, except that—

(1) A passbook, certificate, or other document is attached;

(2) It is accompanied by special instructions, such as a request for special advice of payment or dishonor;

(3) It consists of more than a single thickness of paper, except a check that qualifies for handling by automated check processing equipment; or

(4) It has not been preprinted or post-encoded in magnetic ink with the routing number of the paying bank.

(v) Nonlocal check means a check payable by, through, or at a nonlocal paying bank.

(w) Nonlocal paying bank means a paying bank that is not a local paying bank with respect to the depositary bank.

(x) Nonproprietary ATM means an ATM that is not a proprietary ATM.

(y) [Reserved]

(z) Paying bank means—

(1) The bank by which a check is payable, unless the check is payable at another bank and is sent to the other bank for payment or collection;

(2) The bank at which a check is payable and to which it is sent for payment or collection;

(3) The Federal Reserve Bank or Federal Home Loan Bank by which a check is payable;

(4) The bank through which a check is payable and to which it is sent for payment or collection, if the check is not payable by a bank; or

(5) The state or unit of general local government on which a check is drawn and to which it is sent for payment or collection.

For purposes of subparts C and D, and in connection therewith, subpart A, paying bank includes the bank through which a check is payable and to which the check is sent for payment or collection, regardless of whether the check is payable by another bank, and the bank whose routing number appears on a check in fractional or magnetic form and to which the check is sent for payment or collection.

Note: For purposes of subpart D of this part and, in connection therewith, this subpart A, paying bank also includes the Treasury of the United States or the United States Postal Service for a check that is payable by that entity and that is sent to that entity for payment or collection.

(aa) Proprietary ATM means an ATM that is—

(1) Owned or operated by, or operated exclusively for, the depositary bank;

(2) Located on the premises (including the outside wall) of the depositary bank; or

(3) Located within 50 feet of the premises of the depositary bank, and not identified as being owned or operated by another entity. If more than one bank meets the owned or operated criterion of paragraph (aa)(1) of this section, the ATM is considered proprietary to the bank that operates it.

(bb) Qualified returned check means a returned check that is prepared for automated return to the depositary bank by placing the check in a carrier envelope or placing a strip on the check and encoding the strip or envelope in magnetic ink. A qualified returned check need not contain other elements of a check drawn on the depositary bank, such as the name of the depositary bank.

(cc) Returning bank means a bank (other than the paying or depositary bank) handling a returned check or notice in lieu of return. A returning bank is also a collecting bank for purposes of UCC 4-202(b).

(dd) Routing number means—

(1) The number printed on the face of a check in fractional form or in nine-digit form;

(2) The number in a bank's indorsement in fractional or nine-digit form; or

(3) For purposes of subpart C and subpart D, the bank-identification number contained in an electronic check or electronic returned check.

(ee) Similarly situated bank means a bank of similar size, located in the same community, and with similar check handling activities as the paying bank or returning bank.

(ff) State means a state, the District of Columbia, Puerto Rico, American Samoa, the Commonwealth of the Northern Mariana Islands, Guam, or the U.S. Virgin Islands. For purposes of subpart D of this part and, in connection therewith, this subpart A, state also means the Trust Territory of the Pacific Islands and any other territory of the United States.

(gg) Teller's check means a check provided to a customer of a bank or acquired from a bank for remittance purposes, that is drawn by the bank, and drawn on another bank or payable through or at a bank.

(hh) Traveler's check means an instrument for the payment of money that—

(1) Is drawn on or payable through or at a bank;

(2) Is designated on its face by the term traveler's check or by any substantially similar term or is commonly known and marketed as a traveler's check by a corporation or bank that is an issuer of traveler's checks;

(3) Provides for a specimen signature of the purchaser to be completed at the time of purchase; and

(4) Provides for a countersignature of the purchaser to be completed at the time of negotiation.

(ii) Uniform Commercial Code, Code, or U.C.C. means the Uniform Commercial Code as adopted in a state.

(jj) United States means the states, including the District of Columbia, the U.S. Virgin Islands, American Samoa, the Commonwealth of the Northern Mariana Islands, Guam, and Puerto Rico.

(kk) Unit of general local government means any city, county, parish, town, township, village, or other general purpose political subdivision of a state. The term does not include special purpose units of government, such as school districts or water districts.

(ll) Wire transfer means an unconditional order to a bank to pay a fixed or determinable amount of money to a beneficiary upon receipt or on a day stated in the order, that is transmitted by electronic or other means through Fedwire, the Clearing House Interbank Payments System, other similar network, between banks, or on the books of a bank. Wire transfer does not include an electronic fund transfer as defined in section 903(6) of the Electronic Fund Transfer Act (15 U.S.C. 1693a(6)).

(mm) Fedwire has the same meaning as that set forth in § 210.26(e) of this chapter.

(nn) Good faith means honesty in fact and observance of reasonable commercial standards of fair dealing.

(oo) Interest compensation means an amount of money calculated at the average of the Federal Funds rate published by the Federal Reserve Bank of New York for each of the days for which interest compensation is payable, divided by 360. The Federal Funds rate for any day on which a published rate is not available is the same as the published rate for the last preceding day for which there is a published rate.

(pp) Contractual branch, with respect to a bank, means a branch of another bank that accepts a deposit on behalf of the first bank.

(qq) Claimant bank means a bank that submits a claim for a recredit for a substitute check to an indemnifying bank under § 229.55.

(rr) Collecting bank means any bank handling a check for forward collection, except the paying bank.

(ss) Consumer means a natural person who—

(1) With respect to a check handled for forward collection, draws the check on a consumer account; or

(2) With respect to a check handled for return, deposits the check into or cashes the check against a consumer account.

(tt) Customer means a person having an account with a bank.

(uu) Indemnifying bank. Indemnifying bank means—

(1) For the purposes of § 229.34, a bank that provides an indemnity under § 229.34 with respect to remote deposit capture or an electronically-created item, or

(2) For the purposes of § 229.53, a bank that provides an indemnity under § 229.53 with respect to a substitute check.

(vv) Magnetic ink character recognition line and MICR line mean the numbers, which may include the routing number, account number, check number, check amount, and other information, that are (unless the Board by rule or order determines that different standards apply)—

(1) Printed near the bottom of a check in magnetic ink in accordance with American National Standard Specifications for Placement and Location of MICR Printing, X9.13 (hereinafter ANS X9.13) for an original check and American National Standard Specifications for an Image Replacement Document—IRD, X9.100-140 (hereinafter ANS X9.100-140) for a substitute check, or

(2) For purposes of subpart C and subpart D, contained in a record specified for MICR line data in an electronic check or electronic returned check in accordance with American National Standard Specifications for Electronic Exchange of Check Image Data—Domestic, X9.100-187 (hereinafter ANS X9.100-187).

(ww) Original check means the first paper check issued with respect to a particular payment transaction.

(xx) Paper or electronic representation of a substitute check means any copy of or information related to a substitute check that a bank handles for forward collection or return, charges to a customer's account, or provides to a person as a record of a check payment made by the person.

(yy) Person means a natural person, corporation, unincorporated company, partnership, government unit or instrumentality, trust, or any other entity or organization.

(zz) Reconverting bank means—

(1) The bank that creates a substitute check; or

(2) With respect to a substitute check that was created by a person that is not a bank, the first bank that transfers, presents, or returns that substitute check or, in lieu thereof, the first paper or electronic representation of that substitute check.

(aaa) Substitute check means a paper reproduction of an original check that—

(1) Contains an image of the front and back of the original check;

(2) Bears a MICR line that, except as provided under ANS X9.100-140 (unless the Board by rule or order determines that a different standard applies), contains all the information appearing on the MICR line of the original check at the time that the original check was issued and any additional information that was encoded on the original check's MICR line before an image of the original check was captured;

(3) Conforms in paper stock, dimension, and otherwise with ANS X9.100-140 (unless the Board by rule or order determines that a different standard applies); and

(4) Is suitable for automated processing in the same manner as the original check.

(bbb) Copy and sufficient copy.

(1) A copy of an original check means—

(i) Any paper reproduction of an original check, including a paper printout of an electronic image of the check, a photocopy of the original check, or a substitute check; or

(ii) Any electronic reproduction of a check that a recipient has agreed to receive from the sender instead of a paper reproduction.

(2) A sufficient copy is a copy of an original check that accurately represents all of the information on the front and back of the original check as of the time the original check was truncated or is otherwise sufficient to determine whether or not a claim is valid.

(ccc) Transfer and consideration. The terms transfer and consideration have the meanings set forth in the Uniform Commercial Code and in addition, for purposes of subpart D—

(1) The term transfer with respect to a substitute check or a paper or electronic representation of a substitute check means delivery of the substitute check or other representation of the substitute check by a bank to a person other than a bank; and

(2) A bank that transfers a substitute check or a paper or electronic representation of a substitute check directly to a person other than a bank has received consideration for the substitute check or other paper or electronic representation of the substitute check if it has charged, or has the right to charge, the person's account or otherwise has received value for the original check, a substitute check, or a representation of the original check or substitute check.

(ddd) Truncate means to remove an original check from the forward collection or return process and send to a recipient, in lieu of such original check, a substitute check or, by agreement, information relating to the original check (including data taken from the MICR line of the original check or an electronic image of the original check), whether with or without the subsequent delivery of the original check.

(eee) Truncating bank means—

(1) The bank that truncates the original check; or

(2) If a person other than a bank truncates the original check, the first bank that transfers, presents, or returns, in lieu of such original check, a substitute check or, by agreement with the recipient, information relating to the original check (including data taken from the MICR line of the original check or an electronic image of the original check), whether with or without the subsequent delivery of the original check.

(fff) Remotely created check means a check that is not created by the paying bank and that does not bear a signature applied, or purported to be applied, by the person on whose account the check is drawn. For purposes of this definition, "account" means an account as defined in paragraph (a) of this section as well as a credit or other arrangement that allows a person to draw checks that are payable by, through, or at a bank.

(ggg) Electronic check and electronic returned check mean an electronic image of, and electronic information derived from, a paper check or paper returned check, respectively, that—

(1) Is sent to a receiving bank pursuant to an agreement between the sender and the receiving bank; and

(2) Conforms with ANS X9.100-187, unless the Board by rule or order determines that a different standard applies or the parties otherwise agree.

(hhh) Electronically-created item means an electronic image that has all the attributes of an electronic check or electronic returned check but was created electronically and not derived from a paper check.

§ 229.3 Administrative Enforcement.

(a) Enforcement agencies. Compliance with this part is enforced under—

(1) Section 8 of the Federal Deposit Insurance Act (12 U.S.C. 1818 et seq.) in the case of—

(i) National banks, and Federal branches and Federal agencies of foreign banks, by the Office of the Comptroller of the Currency;

(ii) Member banks of the Federal Reserve System (other than national banks), and offices, branches, and agencies of foreign banks located in the United States (other than Federal branches, Federal agencies, and insured State branches of foreign banks), by the Board; and

(iii) Banks insured by the Federal Deposit Insurance Corporation (other than members of the Federal Reserve System) and insured State branches of foreign banks, by the Board of Directors of the Federal Deposit Insurance Corporation;

(2) Section 8 of the Federal Deposit Insurance Act, by the Director of the Office of Thrift Supervision in the case of savings associations the deposits of which are insured by the Federal Deposit Insurance Corporation; and

(3) The Federal Credit Union Act (12 U.S.C. 1751 et seq.) by the National Credit Union Administration Board with respect to any federal credit union or credit union insured by the National Credit Union Share Insurance Fund.

The terms used in paragraph (a)(1) of this section that are not defined in this part or otherwise defined in section 3(s) of the Federal Deposit Insurance Act (12 U.S.C. 1813(s)) shall have the meaning given to them in section 1(b) of the International Banking Act of 1978 (12 U.S.C. 3101).

(b) Additional powers.

(1) For the purposes of the exercise by any agency referred to in paragraph (a) of this section of its powers under any statute referred to in that paragraph, a violation of any requirement imposed under the EFA Act is deemed to be a violation of a requirement imposed under that statute.

(2) In addition to its powers under any provision of law specifically referred to in paragraph (a) of this section, each of the agencies referred to in that paragraph may exercise, for purposes of enforcing compliance with any requirement imposed under this part, any other authority conferred on it by law.

(c) Enforcement by the Board.

(1) Except to the extent that enforcement of the requirements imposed under this part is specifically committed to some other government agency, the Board shall enforce such requirements.

(2) If the Board determines that—

(i) Any bank that is not a bank described in paragraph (a) of this section; or

(ii) Any other person subject to the authority of the Board under the EFA Act and this part, has failed to comply with any requirement imposed by this part, the Board may issue an order prohibiting any bank, any Federal Reserve Bank, or any other person subject to the authority of the Board from engaging in any activity or transaction that directly or indirectly involves such noncomplying bank or person (including any activity or transaction involving the receipt, payment, collection, and clearing of checks, and any related function of the payment system with respect to checks).

SUBPART B. AVAILABILITY OF FUNDS AND DISCLOSURE OF FUNDS AVAILABILITY POLICIES

§ 229.10 Next-Day Availability.

(a) Cash deposits.

(1) A bank shall make funds deposited in an account by cash available for withdrawal not later than the business day after the banking day on which the cash is deposited, if the deposit is made in person to an employee of the depositary bank.

(2) A bank shall make funds deposited in an account by cash available for withdrawal not later than the second business day after the banking day on which the cash is deposited, if the deposit is not made in person to an employee of the depositary bank.

(b) Electronic payments—

(1) In general. A bank shall make funds received for deposit in an account by an electronic payment available for withdrawal not later than the business day after the banking day on which the bank received the electronic payment.

(2) When an electronic payment is received. An electronic payment is received when the bank receiving the payment has received both—

(i) Payment in actually and finally collected funds; and

(ii) Information on the account and amount to be credited. A bank receives an electronic payment only to the extent that the bank has received payment in actually and finally collected funds.

(c) Certain check deposits—

(1) General rule. A depositary bank shall make funds deposited in an account by check available for withdrawal not later than the business day after the banking day on which the funds are deposited, in the case of—

(i) A check drawn on the Treasury of the United States and deposited in an account held by a payee of the check;

(ii) A U.S. Postal Service money order deposited—

(A) In an account held by a payee of the money order; and

(B) In person to an employee of the depositary bank.

(iii) A check drawn on a Federal Reserve Bank or Federal Home Loan Bank and deposited—

(A) In an account held by a payee of the check; and

(B) In person to an employee of the depositary bank;

(iv) A check drawn by a state or a unit of general local government and deposited—

(A) In an account held by a payee of the check;

(B) In a depositary bank located in the state that issued the check, or the same state as the unit of general local government that issued the check;

(C) In person to an employee of the depositary bank; and

(D) With a special deposit slip or deposit envelope, if such slip or envelope is required by the depositary bank under paragraph (c)(3) of this section.

(v) A cashier's, certified, or teller's check deposited—

(A) In an account held by a payee of the check;

(B) In person to an employee of the depositary bank; and

(C) With a special deposit slip or deposit envelope, if such slip or envelope is required by the depositary bank under paragraph (c)(3) of this section.

(vi) A check deposited in a branch of the depositary bank and drawn on the same or another branch of the same bank if both branches are located in the same state or the same check processing region; and,

(vii) The lesser of—

(A) $275, or

(B) The aggregate amount deposited on any one banking day to all accounts of the customer by check or checks not subject to next-day availability under paragraphs (c)(1) (i) through (vi) of this section.

(2) Checks not deposited in person. A depositary bank shall make funds deposited in an account by check or checks available for withdrawal not later than the second business day after the banking day on which funds are deposited, in the case of a check deposit described in and that meets the requirements of paragraphs (c)(1) (ii), (iii), (iv), and (v), of this section, except that it is not deposited in person to an employee of the depositary bank.

(3) Special deposit slip.

(i) As a condition to making the funds available for withdrawal in accordance with this section, a depositary bank may require that a state or local government check or a cashier's, certified, or teller's check be deposited with a special deposit slip or deposit envelope that identifies the type of check.

(ii) If a depositary bank requires the use of a special deposit slip or deposit envelope, the bank must either provide the special deposit slip or deposit envelope to its customers or inform its customers how the slip or envelope may be prepared or obtained and make the slip or envelope reasonably available.

§ 229.12. Availability Schedule.

(a) Effective date. The availability schedule contained in this section is effective September 1, 1990.

(b) Local checks and certain other checks. Except as provided in paragraphs (d), (e), and (f) of this section, a depository bank shall make funds deposited in an account by a check available for withdrawal not later than the second business day following the banking day on which funds are deposited, in the case of—

(1) A local check;

(2) A check drawn on the Treasury of the United States that is not governed by the availability requirements of § 229.10(c);

(3) A U.S. Postal Service money order that is not governed by the availability requirements of § 229.10(c); and

(4) A check drawn on a Federal Reserve Bank or Federal Home Loan Bank; a check drawn by a state or unit of general local government; or a cashier's, certified, or teller's check; if any check referred to in this paragraph (b)(4) is a local check that is not governed by the availability requirements of § 229.10(c).

(c) Nonlocal checks—

(1) In general. Except as provided in paragraphs (d), (e), and (f) of this section, a depositary bank shall make funds deposited in an account by a check available for withdrawal not later than the fifth business day following the banking day on which funds are deposited, in the case of—

(i) A nonlocal check; and

(ii) A check drawn on a Federal Reserve Bank or Federal Home Loan Bank; a check drawn by a state or unit of general local government; a cashier's, certified, or teller's check; or a check deposited in a branch of the depositary bank and drawn on the same or another branch of the same bank, if any check referred to in this paragraph (c)(1)(ii) is a nonlocal check that is not governed by the availability requirements of § 229.10(c).

(2) Nonlocal checks specified in appendix B-2 to this part must be made available for withdrawal not later than the times prescribed in that appendix.

(d) Time period adjustment for withdrawal by cash or similar means. A depositary bank may extend by one business day the time that funds deposited in an account by one or more checks subject to paragraphs (b), (c), or (f) of this section are available for withdrawal by cash or similar means. Similar means include electronic payment, issuance of a cashier's or teller's check, or certification of a check, or other irrevocable commitment to pay, but do not include the granting of credit to a bank, a Federal Reserve Bank, or a Federal Home Loan Bank that presents a check to the depositary bank for payment. A depositary bank shall, however, make $550 of these funds available for withdrawal by cash or similar means not later than 5:00 p.m. on the business day on which the funds are available under paragraphs (b), (c), or (f) of this section. This $550 is in addition to the $275 available under § 229.10(c)(1)(vii).

(e) Extension of schedule for certain deposits in Alaska, Hawaii, Puerto Rico, American Samoa, the Commonwealth of the Northern Mariana Islands, Guam, and the U.S. Virgin Islands. The depositary bank may extend the time periods set forth in this section by one business day in the case of any deposit, other than a deposit described in § 229.10, that is—

(1) Deposited in an account at a branch of a depositary bank if the branch is located in Alaska, Hawaii, Puerto Rico, American Samoa, the Commonwealth of the Northern Mariana Islands, Guam, or the U.S. Virgin Islands; and

(2) Deposited by a check drawn on or payable at or through a paying bank not located in the same state as the depositary bank.

(f) Deposits at nonproprietary ATMs. A depositary bank shall make funds deposited in an account at a nonproprietary ATM by cash or check available for withdrawal not later than the fifth business day following the banking day on which the funds are deposited.

§ 229.13. Exceptions.

(a) New accounts. For purposes of this paragraph, checks subject to § 229.10(c)(1)(v) include traveler's checks.

(1) A deposit in a new account—

(i) Is subject to the requirements of § 229.10 (a) and (b) to make funds from deposits by cash and electronic payments available for withdrawal on the business day following the banking day of deposit or receipt;

(ii) Is subject to the requirements of § 229.10(c)(1)(i) through (v) and § 229.10(c)(2) only with respect to the first $6,725 of funds deposited on any one banking day; but the amount of the deposit in excess of $6,725 shall be available for withdrawal not later than the ninth business day following the banking day on which funds are deposited; and

(iii) Is not subject to the availability requirements of §§ 229.10(c)(1)(vi) and (vii) and 229.12.

(2) An account is considered a new account during the first 30 calendar days after the account is established. An account is not considered a new account if each customer on the account has had, within 30 calendar days before the account is established, another account at the depositary bank for at least 30 calendar days.

(b) Large deposits. Sections 229.10(c) and 229.12 do not apply to the aggregate amount of deposits by one or more checks to the extent that the aggregate amount is in excess of $6,725 on any one banking day. For customers that have multiple accounts at a depositary bank, the bank may apply this exception to the aggregate deposits to all accounts held by the customer, even if the customer is not the sole holder of the accounts and not all of the holders of the accounts are the same.

(c) Redeposited checks. Sections 229.10(c) and 229.12 do not apply to a check that has been returned unpaid and redeposited by the customer or the depositary bank. This exception does not apply—

(1) To a check that has been returned due to a missing indorsement and redeposited after the missing indorsement has been obtained, if the reason for return indication on the check states that it was returned due to a missing indorsement; or

(2) To a check that has been returned because it was postdated, if the reason for return indicated on the check states that it was returned because it was postdated, and if the check is no longer postdated when redeposited.

(d) Repeated overdrafts. If any account or combination of accounts of a depositary bank's customer has been repeatedly overdrawn, then for a period of six months after the last such overdraft, §§ 229.10(c) and 229.12 do not apply to any of the accounts. A depositary bank may consider a customer's account to be repeatedly overdrawn if—

(1) On six or more banking days within the preceding six months, the account balance is negative, or the account balance would have become negative if checks or other charges to the account had been paid; or

(2) On two or more banking days within the preceding six months, the account balance is negative, or the account balance would have become negative, in the amount of $6,725 or more, if checks or other charges to the account had been paid.

(e) Reasonable cause to doubt collectibility—

(1) In general. Sections 229.10(c) and 229.12 do not apply to a check deposited in an account at a depositary bank if the depositary bank has reasonable cause to believe that the check is uncollectible from the paying bank. Reasonable cause to believe a check is uncollectible requires the existence of facts that would cause a well-grounded belief in the mind of a reasonable person. Such belief shall not be based on the fact that the check is of a particular class or is deposited by a particular class of persons. The reason for the bank's belief that the check is uncollectible shall be included in the notice required under paragraph (g) of this section.

(2) Overdraft and returned check fees. A depositary bank that extends the time when funds will be available for withdrawal as described in paragraph (e)(1) of this section, and does not furnish the depositor with written notice at the time of deposit shall not assess any fees for any subsequent overdrafts (including use of a line of credit) or return of checks of other debits to the account, if—

(i) The overdraft or return of the check would not have occurred except for the fact that the deposited funds were delayed under paragraph (e)(1) of this section; and

(ii) The deposited check was paid by the paying bank.

Notwithstanding the foregoing, the depositary bank may assess an overdraft or returned check fee if it includes a notice concerning overdraft and returned check fees with the notice of exception required in paragraph (g) of this section and, when required, refunds any such fees upon the request of the customer. The notice must state that the customer may be entitled to a refund of overdraft or returned check fees that are assessed if the check subject to the exception is paid and how to obtain a refund.

(f) Emergency conditions. Sections 229.10(c) and 229.12 do not apply to funds deposited by check in a depositary bank in the case of—

(1) An interruption of communications or computer or other equipment facilities;

(2) A suspension of payments by another bank;

(3) A war; or

(4) An emergency condition beyond the control of the depositary bank, if the depositary bank exercises such diligence as the circumstances require.

(g) Notice of exception—

(1) In general. Subject to paragraphs (g)(2) and (g)(3) of this section, when a depositary bank extends the time when funds will be available for withdrawal based on the application of an exception contained in paragraphs (b) through (e) of this section, it must provide the depositor with a written notice.

(i) The notice shall include the following information—

(A) A number or code, which need not exceed four digits, that identifies the customer's account;

(B) The date of the deposit;

(C) The amount of the deposit that is being delayed;

(D) The reason the exception was invoked; and

(E) The time period within which the funds will be available for withdrawal.

(ii) Timing of notice. The notice shall be provided to the depositor at the time of the deposit, unless the deposit is not made in person to an employee of the depositary bank, or, if the facts upon which a determination to invoke one of the exceptions in paragraphs (b) through (e) of this section to delay a deposit only become known to the depositary bank after the time of the deposit. If the notice is not given at the time of the deposit, the depositary bank shall mail or deliver the notice to the customer as soon as practicable, but no later than the first business day following the day the facts become known to the depositary bank, or the deposit is made, whichever is later.

(2) One-time exception notice. In lieu of providing notice pursuant to paragraph (g)(1) of this section, a depositary bank that extends the time when the funds deposited in a nonconsumer account will be available for withdrawal based on an exception contained in paragraph (b) or (c) of this section may provide a single notice to the customer that includes the following information—

(i) The reason(s) the exception may be invoked; and

(ii) The time period within which deposits subject to the exception generally will be available for withdrawal.

This one-time notice shall be provided only if each type of exception cited in the notice will be invoked for most check deposits in the account to which the exception could apply. This notice shall be provided at or prior to the time notice must be provided under paragraph (g)(1)(ii) of this section.

(3) Notice of repeated overdrafts exception. In lieu of providing notice pursuant to paragraph (g)(1) of this section, a depositary bank that extends the time when funds deposited in an account will be available for withdrawal based on the exception contained in paragraph (d) of this section may provide a notice to the customer for each time period during which the exception will be in effect. The notice shall include the following information—

(i) The account number of the customer;

(ii) The fact that the availability of funds deposited in the customer's account will be delayed because the repeated overdrafts exception will be invoked;

(iii) The time period within which deposits subject to the exception generally will be available for withdrawal; and

(iv) The time period during which the exception will apply.

This notice shall be provided at or prior to the time notice must be provided under paragraph (g)(1)(ii) of this section and only if the exception cited in the notice will be invoked for most check deposits in the account.

(4) Emergency conditions exception notice. When a depositary bank extends the time when funds will be available for withdrawal based on the application of the emergency conditions exception contained in paragraph (f) of this section, it must provide the depositor with notice in a reasonable form and within a reasonable time given the circumstances. The notice shall include the reason the exception was invoked and the time period within which funds shall be made available for withdrawal, unless the depositary bank, in good faith, does not know at the time the notice is given the duration of the emergency and, consequently, when the funds must be made available. The depositary bank is not required to provide a notice if the funds subject to the exception become available before the notice must be sent.

(5) Record retention. A depositary bank shall retain a record, in accordance with § 229.21(g), of each notice provided pursuant to its application of the reasonable cause exception under paragraph (e) of this section, together with a brief statement of the facts giving rise to the bank's reason to doubt the collectibility of the check.

(h) Availability of deposits subject to exceptions.

(1) If an exception contained in paragraphs (b) through (f) of this section applies, the depositary bank may extend the time periods established under §§ 229.10(c) and 229.12 by a reasonable period of time.

(2) If a depositary bank invokes an exception contained in paragraphs (b) through (e) of this section with respect to a check described in § 229.10(c)(1) (i) through (v) or § 229.10(c)(2), it shall make the funds available for withdrawal not later than a reasonable period after the day the funds would have been required to be made available had the check been subject to 229.12.

(3) If a depositary bank invokes an exception under paragraph (f) of this section based on an emergency condition, the depositary bank shall make the funds available for withdrawal not later than a reasonable period after the emergency has ceased or the period established in §§ 229.10(c) and 229.12, whichever is later.

(4) For the purposes of this section, a "reasonable period" is an extension of up to one business day for checks described in § 229.10(c)(1)(vi), five business days for checks described in § 229.12(b)(1) through (4), and six business days for checks described in § 229.12(c) (1) and (2) or § 229.12(f). A longer extension may be reasonable, but the bank has the burden of so establishing.

§ 229.14. Payment of Interest.

(a) In general. A depositary bank shall begin to accrue interest or dividends on funds deposited in an interest-bearing account not later than the business day on which the depositary bank receives credit for the funds. For the purposes of this section, the depositary bank may—

(1) Rely on the availability schedule of its Federal Reserve Bank, Federal Home Loan Bank, or correspondent bank to determine the time credit is actually received; and

(2) Accrue interest or dividends on funds deposited in interest-bearing accounts by checks that the depositary bank sends to paying banks or subsequent collecting banks for payment or collection based on the availability of funds the depositary bank receives from the paying or collecting banks.

(b) Special rule for credit unions. Paragraph (a) of this section does not apply to any account at a bank described in § 229.2(e)(4), if the bank—

(1) Begins the accrual of interest or dividends at a later date than the date described in paragraph (a) of this section with respect to all funds, including cash, deposited in the account; and

(2) Provides notice of its interest or dividend payment policy in the manner required under § 229.16(d).

(c) Exception for checks returned unpaid. This subpart does not require a bank to pay interest or dividends on funds deposited by a check that is returned unpaid.

§ 229.15. General Disclosure Requirements.

(a) Form of disclosures. A bank shall make the disclosures required by this subpart clearly and conspicuously in writing. Disclosures, other than those posted at locations where employees accept consumer deposits and ATMs and the notice on preprinted deposit slips, must be in a form that the customer may keep. The disclosures shall be grouped together and shall not contain any information not related to the disclosures required by this subpart. If contained in a document that sets forth other account terms, the disclosures shall be highlighted within the document by, for example, use of a separate heading.

(b) Uniform reference to day of availability. In its disclosure, a bank shall describe funds as being available for withdrawal on "the ___________ business day after" the day of deposit. In this calculation, the first business day is the business day following the banking day the deposit was received, and the last business day is the day on which the funds are made available.

(c) Multiple accounts and multiple account holders. A bank need not give multiple disclosures to a customer that holds multiple accounts if the accounts are subject to the same availability policies. Similarly, a bank need not give separate disclosures to each customer on a jointly held account.

(d) Dormant or inactive accounts. A bank need not give availability disclosures to a customer that holds a dormant or inactive account.

§ 229.16. Specific Availability Policy Disclosure.

(a) General. To meet the requirements of a specific availability policy disclosure under §§ 229.17 and 229.18(d), a bank shall provide a disclosure describing the bank's policy as to when funds deposited in an account are available for withdrawal. The disclosure must reflect the policy followed by the bank in most cases. A bank may impose longer delays on a case-by-case basis or by invoking one of the exceptions in § 229.13, provided this is reflected in the disclosure.

(b) Content of specific availability policy disclosure. The specific availability policy disclosure shall contain the following, as applicable—

(1) A summary of the bank's availability policy;

(2) A description of any categories of deposits or checks used by the bank when it delays availability (such as local or nonlocal checks); how to determine the category to which a particular deposit or check belongs; and when each category will be available for withdrawal (including a description of the bank's business days and when a deposit is considered received);[1]

---

[1] A bank that distinguishes in its disclosure between local and nonlocal checks based on the routing number on the check must disclose that certain checks, such as some credit union share drafts that are payable by one bank but payable through another bank, will be treated as local or nonlocal checks based upon the location of the bank by which they are payable and not on the basis of the location of the bank whose routing number appears on the check. A bank that makes funds from nonlocal checks available for withdrawal within the time periods required for local checks under §§ 229.12 and 229.13 is not required to provide this disclosure on payable-through checks to its customers. The statement concerning payable-through checks must describe how the customer can determine whether these checks will be treated as local or nonlocal, or state that special rules apply to such checks and that the customer may ask about the availability of these checks.

(3) A description of any of the exceptions in § 229.13 that may be invoked by the bank, including the time following a deposit that funds generally will be available for withdrawal and a statement that the bank will notify the customer if the bank invokes one of the exceptions;

(4) A description, as specified in paragraph (c)(1) of this section, of any case-by-case policy of delaying availability that may result in deposited funds being available for withdrawal later than the time periods stated in the bank's availability policy; and

(5) A description of how the customer can differentiate between a proprietary and a nonproprietary ATM, if the bank makes funds from deposits at nonproprietary ATMs available for withdrawal later than funds from deposits at proprietary ATMs.

(c) Longer delays on a case-by-case basis—

(1) Notice in specific policy disclosure. A bank that has a policy of making deposited funds available for withdrawal sooner than required by this subpart may extend the time when funds are available up to the time periods allowed under this subpart on a case-by-case basis, provided the bank includes the following in its specific policy disclosure—

(i) A statement that the time when deposited funds are available for withdrawal may be extended in some cases, and the latest time following a deposit that funds will be available for withdrawal;

(ii) A statement that the bank will notify the customer if funds deposited in the customer's account will not be available for withdrawal until later than the time periods stated in the bank's availability policy; and

(iii) A statement that customers should ask if they need to be sure about when a particular deposit will be available for withdrawal.

(2) Notice at time of case-by-case delay—

(i) In general. When a depositary bank extends the time when funds will be available for withdrawal on a case-by-case basis, it must provide the depositor with a written notice. The notice shall include the following information—

(A) A number or code, which need not exceed four digits, that identifies the customer's account;

(B) The date of the deposit;

(C) The amount of the deposit that is being delayed; and

(D) The day the funds will be available for withdrawal.

(ii) Timing of notice. The notice shall be provided to the depositor at the time of the deposit, unless the deposit is not made in person to an employee of the depositary bank or the decision to extend the time when the deposited funds will be available is made after the time of the deposit. If notice is not given at the time of the deposit, the depositary bank shall mail or deliver the notice to the customer not later than the first business day following the banking day the deposit is made.

(3) Overdraft and returned check fees. A depositary bank that extends the time when funds will be available for withdrawal on a case-by-case basis and does not furnish the depositor with written notice at the time of deposit shall not assess any fees for any subsequent overdrafts (including use of a line of credit) or return of checks or other debits to the account, if—

(i) The overdraft or return of the check or other debit would not have occurred except for the fact that the deposited funds were delayed under paragraph (c)(1) of this section; and

(ii) The deposited check was paid by the paying bank.

Notwithstanding the foregoing, the depositary bank may assess an overdraft or returned check fee if it includes a notice concerning overdraft and returned check fees with the notice required in paragraph (c)(2) of this section and, when required, refunds any such fees upon the request of the customer. The notice must state that the customer may be entitled to a refund of overdraft or returned check fees that are assessed if the check subject to the delay is paid and how to obtain a refund.

(d) Credit union notice of interest payment policy. If a bank described in § 229.2(e)(4) begins to accrue interest or dividends on all deposits made in an interest-bearing account, including cash deposits, at a later time than the day specified in § 229.14(a), the bank's specific policy disclosures shall contain an explanation of when interest or dividends on deposited funds begin to accrue.

§ 229.17. Initial Disclosures.

Before opening a new account, a bank shall provide a potential customer with the applicable specific availability policy disclosure described in § 229.16.

§ 229.18. Additional Disclosure Requirements.

(a) Deposit slips. A bank shall include on all preprinted deposit slips furnished to its customers a notice that deposits may not be available for immediate withdrawal.

(b) Locations where employees accept consumer deposits. A bank shall post in a conspicuous place in each location where its employees receive deposits to consumer accounts a notice that sets forth the time periods applicable to the availability of funds deposited in a consumer account.

(c) Automated teller machines.

(1) A depositary bank shall post or provide a notice at each ATM location that funds deposited in the ATM may not be available for immediate withdrawal.

(2) A depositary bank that operates an off-premises ATM from which deposits are removed not more than two times each week, as described in § 229.19(a)(4), shall disclose at or on the ATM the days on which deposits made at the ATM will be considered received.

(d) Upon request. A bank shall provide to any person, upon oral or written request, a notice containing the applicable specific availability policy disclosure described in § 229.16.

(e) Changes in policy. A bank shall send a notice to holders of consumer accounts at least 30 days before implementing a change to the bank's availability policy regarding such accounts, except that a change that expedites the availability of funds may be disclosed not later than 30 days after implementation.

§ 229.19. Miscellaneous.

(a) When funds are considered deposited. For the purposes of this subpart—

(1) Funds deposited at a staffed facility, ATM, or contractual branch are considered deposited when they are received at the staffed facility, ATM, or contractual branch;

(2) Funds mailed to the depositary bank are considered deposited on the day they are received by the depositary bank;

(3) Funds deposited to a night depository, lock box, or similar facility are considered deposited on the day on which the deposit is removed from such facility and is available for processing by the depositary bank;

(4) Funds deposited at an ATM that is not on, or within 50 feet of, the premises of the depositary bank are considered deposited on the day the funds are removed from the ATM, if funds normally are removed from the ATM not more than two times each week; and

(5) Funds may be considered deposited on the next banking day, in the case of funds that are deposited—

(i) On a day that is not a banking day for the depositary bank; or

(ii) After a cut-off hour set by the depositary bank for the receipt of deposits of 2:00 p.m. or later, or, for the receipt of deposits at ATMs, contractual branches, or off-premise facilities, of 12:00 noon or later. Different cut-off hours later than these times may be established for receipt of different types of deposits, or receipt of deposits at different locations.

(b) Availability at start of business day. Except as otherwise provided in § 229.12(d), if any provision of this subpart requires that funds be made available for withdrawal on any business day, the funds shall be available for withdrawal by the later of:

(1) 9:00 a.m. (local time of the depositary bank); or

(2) The time the depositary bank's teller facilities (including ATMs) are available for customer account withdrawals.

(c) Effect on policies of depositary bank. This part does not—

(1) Prohibit a depositary bank from making funds available to a customer for withdrawal in a shorter period of time than the time required by this subpart;

(2) Affect a depositary bank's right—

(i) To accept or reject a check for deposit;

(ii) To revoke any settlement made by the depositary bank with respect to a check accepted by the bank for deposit, to charge back the customer's account for the amount of a check based on the return of the check or receipt of a notice of nonpayment of the check, or to claim a refund of such credit; and

(iii) To charge back funds made available to its customer for an electronic payment for which the bank has not received payment in actually and finally collected funds;

(3) Require a depositary bank to open or otherwise to make its facilities available for customer transactions on a given business day; or

(4) Supersede any policy of a depositary bank that limits the amount of cash a customer may withdraw from its account on any one day, if that policy—

(i) Is not dependent on the time the funds have been deposited in the account, as long as the funds have been on deposit for the time period specified in §§ 229.10, 229.12, or 229.13; and

(ii) In the case of withdrawals made in person to an employee of the depositary bank—

(A) Is applied without discrimination to all customers of the bank; and

(B) Is related to security, operating, or bonding requirements of the depositary bank.

(d) Use of calculated availability. A depositary bank may provide availability to its nonconsumer accounts based on a sample of checks that represents the average composition of the customer's deposits, if the terms for availability based on the sample are equivalent to or more prompt than the availability requirements of this subpart.

(e) Holds on other funds.

(1) A depositary bank that receives a check for deposit in an account may not place a hold on any funds of the customer at the bank, where—

(i) The amount of funds that are held exceeds the amount of the check; or

(ii) The funds are not made available for withdrawal within the times specified in §§ 229.10, 229.12, and 229.13.

(2) A depositary bank that cashes a check for a customer over the counter, other than a check drawn on the depositary bank, may not place a hold on funds in an account of the customer at the bank, if—

(i) The amount of funds that are held exceeds the amount of the check; or

(ii) The funds are not made available for withdrawal within the times specified in §§ 229.10, 229.12, and 229.13.

(f) Employee training and compliance. Each bank shall establish procedures to ensure that the bank complies with the requirements of this subpart, and shall provide each employee who performs duties subject to the requirements of this subpart with a statement of the procedures applicable to that employee.

(g) Effect of merger transaction.

(1) In general. For purposes of this subpart, except for the purposes of the new accounts exception of § 229.13(a), and when funds are considered deposited under § 229.19(a), two or more banks that have engaged in a merger transaction may be considered to be separate banks for a period of one year following the consummation of the merger transaction.

(2) Merger transactions on or after July 1, 1998, and before March 1, 2000. If banks have consummated a merger transaction on or after July 1, 1998, and before March 1, 2000, the merged banks may be considered separate banks until March 1, 2001.

§ 229.20. Relation to State Law.

(a) In general. Any provision of a law or regulation of any state in effect on or before September 1, 1989, that requires funds deposited in an account at a bank chartered by the state to be made available for withdrawal in a shorter time than the time provided in subpart B, and, in connection therewith, subpart A, shall—

(1) Supersede the provisions of the EFA Act and subpart B, and, in connection therewith, subpart A, to the extent the provisions relate to the time by which funds deposited or received for deposit in an account are available for withdrawal; and

(2) Apply to all federally insured banks located within the state.

No amendment to a state law or regulation governing the availability of funds that becomes effective after September 1, 1989, shall supersede the EFA Act and subpart B, and, in connection therewith, subpart A, but unamended provisions of state law shall remain in effect.

(b) Preemption of inconsistent law. Except as provided in paragraph (a), the EFA Act and subpart B, and, in connection therewith, subpart A, supersede any provision of inconsistent state law.

(c) Standards for preemption. A provision of a state law in effect on or before September 2, 1989, is not inconsistent with the EFA Act, or subpart B, or in connection therewith, subpart A, if it requires that funds shall be available in a shorter period of time than the time provided in this subpart. Inconsistency with the EFA Act and subpart B, and in connection therewith, subpart A, may exist when state law—

(1) Permits a depositary bank to make funds deposited in an account by cash, electronic payment, or check available for withdrawal in a longer period of time than the maximum period of time permitted under subpart B, and, in connection therewith, subpart A; or

(2) Provides for disclosures or notices concerning funds availability relating to accounts.

(d) Preemption determinations. The Board may determine, upon the request of any state, bank, or other interested party, whether the EFA Act and subpart B, and, in connection therewith, subpart A, preempt provisions of state laws relating to the availability of funds.

(e) Procedures for preemption determinations. A request for a preemption determination shall include the following—

(1) A copy of the full text of the state law in question, including any implementing regulations or judicial interpretations of that law; and

(2) A comparison of the provisions of state law with the corresponding provisions in the EFA Act and subparts A and B of this part, together with a discussion of the reasons why specific provisions of state law are either consistent or inconsistent with

corresponding sections of the EFA Act and subparts A and B of this part.

A request for a preemption determination shall be addressed to the Secretary, Board of Governors of the Federal Reserve System.

§ 229.21. Civil Liability.

(a) Civil liability. A bank that fails to comply with any requirement imposed under subpart B, and in connection therewith, subpart A, of this part or any provision of state law that supersedes any provision of subpart B, and in connection therewith, subpart A, with respect to any person is liable to that person in an amount equal to the sum of—

(1) Any actual damage sustained by that person as a result of the failure;

(2) Such additional amount as the court may allow, except that—

(i) In the case of an individual action, liability under this paragraph shall not be less than $125 nor greater than $1,350; and

(ii) In the case of a class action—

(A) No minimum recovery shall be applicable to each member of the class; and

(B) The total recovery under this paragraph in any class action or series of class actions arising out of the same failure to comply by the same depositary bank shall not be more than the lesser of $672,950 or 1 percent of the net worth of the bank involved; and

(3) In the case of a successful action to enforce the foregoing liability, the costs of the action, together with a reasonable attorney's fee as determined by the court.

(b) Class action awards. In determining the amount of any award in any class action, the court shall consider, among other relevant factors—

(1) The amount of any damages awarded;

(2) The frequency and persistence of failures of compliance;

(3) The resources of the bank;

(4) The number of persons adversely affected; and

(5) The extent to which the failure of compliance was intentional.

(c) Bona fide errors—

(1) General rule. A bank is not liable in any action brought under this section for a violation of this subpart if the bank demonstrates by a preponderance of the evidence that the violation was not intentional and resulted from a bona fide error, notwithstanding the maintenance of procedures reasonably adapted to avoid any such error.

(2) Examples. Examples of a bona fide error include clerical, calculation, computer malfunction and programming, and printing errors, except that an error of legal judgment with respect to the bank's obligation under this subpart is not a bona fide error.

(d) Jurisdiction. Any action under this section may be brought in any United States district court or in any other court of competent jurisdiction, and shall be brought within one year after the date of the occurrence of the violation involved.

(e) Reliance on Board rulings. No provision of this subpart imposing any liability shall apply to any act done or omitted in good faith in conformity with any rule, regulation, or interpretation thereof by the Board, regardless of whether such rule, regulation, or interpretation is amended, rescinded, or determined by judicial or other authority to be invalid for any reason after the act or omission has occurred.

(f) Exclusions. This section does not apply to claims that arise under subpart C of this part or to actions for wrongful dishonor.

(g) Record retention.

(1) A bank shall retain evidence of compliance with the requirements imposed by this subpart for not less than two years. Records may be stored by use of microfiche, microfilm, magnetic tape, or other methods capable of accurately retaining and reproducing information.

(2) If a bank has actual notice that it is being investigated, or is subject to an enforcement proceeding by an agency charged with monitoring that bank's compliance with the EFA Act and this subpart, or has been served with notice of an action filed under this section, it shall retain the records pertaining to the action or proceeding pending final disposition of the matter, unless an earlier time is allowed by order of the agency or court.

SUBPART C. COLLECTION OF CHECKS

§ 229.30. Electronic checks and electronic information.

(a) Checks under this subpart. Electronic checks and electronic returned checks are subject to this subpart as if they were checks or returned checks, except where "paper check" or "paper returned check" is specified. For the purposes of this subpart, the term "check" or "returned check" as used in Subpart A includes "electronic check" or "electronic returned check," except where "paper check" or "paper returned check" is specified.

(b) Writings. If a bank is required to provide information in writing under this subpart, the bank may satisfy that requirement by providing the information electronically if the receiving bank agrees to receive that information electronically.

§ 229.31. Paying bank's responsibility for return of checks and notices of nonpayment.

(a) Return of checks.

(1) Subject to the requirement of expeditious return under paragraph (b) of this section, a paying bank may send a returned check to the depositary bank, to any other bank agreeing to handle the returned check, or as provided in paragraph (a)(2) of this section.

(2) A paying bank that is unable to identify the depositary bank with respect to a check may send the returned check to any bank that handled the check for forward collection and must advise the bank to which the check is sent that the paying bank is unable to identify the depositary bank.

(3) A paying bank may convert a check to a qualified returned check. A qualified returned check shall be encoded in magnetic ink with the routing number of the depositary bank, the amount of the returned check, and a "2" in the case of an original check (or a "5" in the case of a substitute check) in position 44 of the qualified return MICR line as a return identifier. A qualified returned original check shall be encoded in accordance with ANS X9.13, and a qualified returned substitute check shall be encoded in accordance with ANS X9.100-140.

(4) Except as provided in paragraph (g) of this section, this section does not affect a paying bank's responsibility to return a check within the deadlines required by the UCC or Regulation J (12 CFR part 210).

(b) Expeditious return of checks.

(1) Except as provided in paragraph (d) of this section, if a paying bank determines not to pay a check, it shall return the check in an expeditious manner such that the check would normally be received by the depositary bank not later than 2 p.m. (local time of the depositary bank) on the second business day following the banking day on which the check was presented to the paying bank.

(2) If the second business day following the banking day on which the check was presented to the paying bank is not a banking day for the depositary bank, the paying bank satisfies the expeditious return requirement if it sends the returned check in a manner such that the depositary bank would normally receive the returned check not later than 2 p.m. (local time of the depositary bank) on the depositary bank's next banking day.

(c) Notice of nonpayment.

(1) If a paying bank determines not to pay a check in the amount of $5,000 or more, it shall provide notice of nonpayment such that the notice would normally be received by the depositary bank not later than 2 p.m. (local time of the depositary bank) on the second business day following the banking day on which the check was presented to the paying bank. If the day the paying bank is required to provide notice is not a banking day for the depositary bank, receipt of notice not later than 2 p.m. (local time of the depositary bank) on the depositary bank's next banking day constitutes timely notice. Notice may be provided by any reasonable means, including the returned check, a writing (including a copy of the check), or telephone.

(2)

(i) To the extent available to the paying bank, notice must include the information contained in the check's MICR line when the check is received by the paying bank, as well as—

(A) Name of the payee(s);

(B) Amount;

(C) Date of the indorsement of the depositary bank;

(D) The bank name, routing number, and trace or sequence number associated with the indorsement of the depositary bank; and

(E) Reason for nonpayment.

(ii) If the paying bank is not sure of the accuracy of an item of information, it shall include the information required by this paragraph to the extent possible, and identify any item of information for which the bank is not sure of the accuracy.

(iii) The notice may include other information from the check that may be useful in identifying the check being returned and the customer.

(d) Exceptions to the expeditious return of checks and notice of nonpayment requirements. The expeditious return and notice of nonpayment requirements of paragraphs (b) and (c) of this section do not apply if—

(1) The check is deposited in a depositary bank that is not subject to subpart B of this part; or

(2) A paying bank is unable to identify the depositary bank with respect to the check.

(e) Identification of returned check. A paying bank returning a check shall clearly indicate on the front of the check that it is a returned check and the reason for return. If the paying bank is returning a substitute check or an electronic returned check, the paying bank shall include this information such that the information would be retained on any subsequent substitute check.

(f) Notice in Lieu of Return. If a check is unavailable for return, the paying bank may send in its place a copy of the front and back of the returned check, or, if no such copy is available, a written notice of nonpayment containing the information specified in paragraph (c)(2) of this section. The copy or written notice shall clearly state that it constitutes a notice in lieu of return. A notice in lieu of return is considered a returned check subject to the requirements of this subpart.

(g) Extension of deadline. The deadline for return or notice of dishonor or nonpayment under the UCC or Regulation J (12 CFR part 210), or § 229.36(d)(3) and (4) is extended to the time of dispatch of such return or notice if the depositary bank (or the receiving bank, if the depositary bank is unidentifiable) receives the returned check or notice—

(1) On or before the depositary bank's (or receiving bank's) next banking day following the otherwise applicable deadline by the earlier of the close of that banking day or a cutoff hour of 2 p.m. (local time of the depositary bank or receiving bank) or later set by the depositary bank (or receiving bank) under UCC 4-108, for all deadlines other than those described in paragraph (g)(2) of this section; or

(2) Prior to the cut-off hour for the next processing cycle (if sent to a returning bank), or on the next banking day (if sent to the depositary bank), for a deadline falling on a Saturday that is a banking day (as defined in the UCC) for the paying bank.

(h) Payable-through and payable-at checks. A check payable at or through a paying bank is considered to be drawn on that bank for purposes of the expeditious return and notice of nonpayment requirements of this subpart.

(i) Reliance on routing number. A paying bank may return a returned check based on any routing number designating the depositary bank appearing on the returned check in the depositary bank's indorsement.

§ 229.32. Returning bank's responsibility for return of checks.

(a) Return of checks.

(1) Subject to the requirement of expeditious return under paragraph (b) of this section, a returning bank may send a returned check to the depositary bank, to any other bank agreeing to handle the returned check, or as provided in paragraph (a)(2) of this section.

(2) A returning bank that is unable to identify the depositary bank with respect to a check may send the returned check to any collecting bank that handled the returned check for forward collection if the returning bank was not a collecting bank with respect to the returned check, or to a prior collecting bank, if the returning bank was a collecting bank with respect to the returned check. A returning bank sending a returned check under this paragraph to a bank must advise the bank to which the returned check is sent that the returning bank is unable to identify the depositary bank.

(3) A returning bank may convert a check to a qualified returned check. A qualified returned check shall be encoded in magnetic ink with the routing number of the depositary bank, the amount of the returned check, and a "2" in the case of an original check (or a "5" in the case of a substitute check) in position 44 of the qualified return MICR line as a return identifier. A qualified returned original check shall be encoded in accordance with ANS X9.13, and a qualified returned substitute check shall be encoded in accordance with ANS X9.100-140.

(b) Expeditious return of checks.

(1) Except as provided in paragraph (c) of this section, a returning bank shall return a returned check in an expeditious manner such that the check would normally be received by the depositary bank not later than 2 p.m. (local time of the depositary bank) on the second business day following the banking day on which the check was presented to the paying bank.

(2) If the second business day following the banking day on which the check was presented to the paying bank is not a banking day for the depositary bank, the returning bank satisfies the expeditious return requirement if it sends the returned check in a manner such that the depositary bank would normally receive the returned check not later than 2 p.m. (local time of the depositary bank) on the depositary bank's next banking day.

(c) Exceptions to the expeditious return of checks. The expeditious return requirement of paragraph (b) of this section does not apply if—

(1) The check is deposited in a depositary bank that is not subject to subpart B of this part;

(2) A paying bank is unable to identify the depositary bank with respect to the check; or

(3) The bank handles a misrouted returned check pursuant to § 229.33(f).

(d) Notice in Lieu of Return. If a check is unavailable for return, the returning bank may send in its place a copy of the front and back of the returned check, or, if no such copy is available, a written notice of nonpayment containing the information specified in § 229.31(c). The copy or written notice shall clearly state that it constitutes a notice in lieu of return. A notice in lieu of return is considered a returned check subject to the requirements of this section and the other requirements of this subpart.

(e) Settlement. A returning bank shall settle with a bank sending a returned check to it for return by the same means that it settles or would settle with the sending bank for a check received for forward collection drawn on the depositary bank. This settlement is final when made.

(f) Charges. A returning bank may impose a charge on a bank sending a returned check for handling the returned check.

(g) Reliance on routing number. A returning bank may return a returned check based on any routing number designating the depositary bank appearing on the returned check in the depositary bank's indorsement or in magnetic ink on a qualified returned check.

§ 229.33. Depositary bank's responsibility for returned checks and notices of nonpayment.

(a) Right to assert claim.

(1) A paying bank or returning bank may be liable to a depositary bank under § 229.38 for failing to return a check in an expeditious manner only if the depositary bank has arrangements in place such that the paying bank or returning bank could return a returned check to the depositary bank electronically, directly or indirectly, by commercially reasonable means.

(2) For purposes of paragraph (a)(1) of this section, the depositary bank that has asserted a claim has the burden of proof for demonstrating that the depositary bank's arrangements meet the standard of paragraph (a)(1).

(b) Acceptance of electronic returned checks and electronic notices of nonpayment. A depositary bank's agreement with the transferor bank governs the terms under which the depositary bank will accept electronic returned checks and electronic written notices of nonpayment.

(c) Acceptance of paper returned checks and paper notices of nonpayment.

(1) A depositary bank shall accept paper returned checks and paper notices of nonpayment during its banking day—

(i) At a location, if any, at which presentment of paper checks for forward collection is requested by the depositary bank; and

(ii)

(A) At a branch, head office, or other location consistent with the name and address of the bank in its indorsement on the check;

(B) If no address appears in the indorsement, at a branch or head office associated with the routing number of the bank in its indorsement on the check; or

(C) If no routing number or address appears in its indorsement on the check, at any branch or head office of the bank.

(2) A depositary bank may require that paper returned checks be separated from paper forward collection checks.

(d) Acceptance of oral notices of nonpayment. A depositary bank shall accept oral notices of nonpayment during its banking day—

(1) At the telephone number indicated in the indorsement; and

(2) At any other number held out by the bank for receipt of notice of nonpayment.

(e) Payment.

(1) A depositary bank shall pay the returning bank or paying bank returning the check to it for the amount of the check prior to the close of business on the depositary bank's banking day on which it received the check ("payment date") by—

(i) Debit to an account of the depositary bank on the books of the returning bank or paying bank;

(ii) Cash;

(iii) Wire transfer; or

(iv) Any other form of payment acceptable to the returning bank or paying bank.

(2) The proceeds of the payment must be available to the returning bank or paying bank in cash or by credit to an account of the returning bank or paying bank on or as of the payment date. If the payment date is not a banking day for the returning bank or paying bank or the depositary bank is unable to make the payment on the payment date, payment shall be made by the next day that is a banking day for the returning bank or paying bank. These payments are final when made.

(f) Misrouted returned checks and written notices of nonpayment. If a bank receives a returned check or written notice of nonpayment on the basis that it is the depositary bank, and the bank determines that it is not the depositary bank with respect to the check or notice, it shall either promptly send the returned check or notice to the depositary bank directly or by means of a returning bank agreeing to handle the returned check or notice, or send the check or notice back to the bank from which it was received.

(g) Charges. A depositary bank may not impose a charge for accepting and paying checks being returned to it.

(h) Notification to customer. If the depositary bank receives a returned check, notice of nonpayment, or notice of recovery under § 229.35(b), it shall send or give notice to its customer of the facts by midnight of the banking day following the banking day on which it received the returned check, notice of nonpayment, or notice of recovery, or within a longer reasonable time.

(i) Depositary bank without accounts. The requirements of this section with respect to notices of nonpayment do not apply to checks deposited in a depositary bank that does not maintain accounts.

§ 229.34. Warranties and indemnities.

(a) Warranties with respect to electronic checks and electronic returned checks.

(1) Each bank that transfers or presents an electronic check or electronic returned check and receives a settlement or other consideration for it warrants that—

(i) The electronic image accurately represents all of the information on the front and back of the original check as of the time that the original check was truncated and the electronic information includes an accurate record of all MICR line information required for a substitute check under § 229.2(aaa) and the amount of the check, and

(ii) No person will receive a transfer, presentment, or return of, or otherwise be charged for an electronic check or electronic returned check, the original check, a substitute check, or a paper or electronic representation of a substitute check such that the person will be asked to make payment based on a check it has already paid.

(2) Each bank that makes the warranties under paragraph (a)(1) of this section makes the warranties to—

(i) In the case of transfers for collection or presentment, the transferee bank, any subsequent collecting bank, the paying bank, and the drawer; and

(ii) In the case of transfers for return, the transferee returning bank, any subsequent returning bank, the depositary bank, and the owner.

(b) Transfer and presentment warranties with respect to a remotely created check.

(1) A bank that transfers or presents a remotely created check and receives a settlement or other consideration warrants to the transferee bank, any subsequent collecting bank, and the paying bank that the person on whose account the remotely created check is drawn authorized the issuance of the check in the amount stated on the check and to the payee stated on the check. For purposes of this paragraph (b)(1), "account" includes an account as defined in § 229.2(a) as well as a credit or other arrangement that allows a person to draw checks that are payable by, through, or at a bank.

(2) If a paying bank asserts a claim for breach of warranty under paragraph (b)(1) of this section, the warranting bank may defend by proving that the customer of the paying bank is precluded under UCC 4-406, as applicable, from asserting against the paying bank the unauthorized issuance of the check.

(c) Settlement amount, encoding, and offset warranties.

(1) Each bank that presents one or more checks to a paying bank and in return receives a settlement or other consideration warrants to the paying bank that the total amount of the checks presented is equal to the total amount of the settlement demanded by the presenting bank from the paying bank.

(2) Each bank that transfers one or more checks or returned checks to a collecting bank, returning bank, or depositary bank and in return receives a settlement or other consideration warrants to the transferee bank that the accompanying information, if any, accurately indicates the total amount of the checks or returned checks transferred.

(3) Each bank that presents or transfers a check or returned check warrants to any bank that subsequently handles it that, at the time of presentment or transfer, the information encoded after issue regarding the check or returned check is accurate. For purposes of this paragraph, the information encoded after issue regarding the check or returned check means any information that could be encoded in the MICR line of a paper check.

(4) If a bank settles with another bank for checks presented, or for returned checks for which it is the depositary bank, in an amount exceeding the total amount of the checks, the settling bank may set off the excess settlement amount against subsequent settlements for checks presented, or for returned checks for which it is the depositary bank, that it receives from the other bank.

(d) Returned check warranties.

(1) Each paying bank or returning bank that transfers a returned check and receives a settlement or other consideration for it warrants to the

transferee returning bank, to any subsequent returning bank, to the depositary bank, and to the owner of the check, that—

(i) The paying bank, or in the case of a check payable by a bank and payable through another bank, the bank by which the check is payable, returned the check within its deadline under the UCC or § 229.31(g) of this part;

(ii) It is authorized to return the check;

(iii) The check has not been materially altered; and

(iv) In the case of a notice in lieu of return, the check has not and will not be returned.

(2) These warranties are not made with respect to checks drawn on the Treasury of the United States, U.S. Postal Service money orders, or checks drawn on a state or a unit of general local government that are not payable through or at a bank.

(e) Notice of nonpayment warranties.

(1) Each paying bank that gives a notice of nonpayment warrants to the transferee bank, to any subsequent transferee bank, to the depositary bank, and to the owner of the check that—

(i) The paying bank, or in the case of a check payable by a bank and payable through another bank, the bank by which the check is payable, returned or will return the check within its deadline under the UCC or § 229.31(g) of this part;

(ii) It is authorized to send the notice; and

(iii) The check has not been materially altered.

(2) These warranties are not made with respect to checks drawn on the Treasury of the United States, U.S. Postal Service money orders, or check drawn on a state or a unit of general local government that are not payable through or at a bank.

(f) Remote deposit capture indemnity.

(1) The indemnity described in paragraph (f)(2) of this section is provided by a depositary bank that—

(i) Is a truncating bank under § 229.2(eee)(2) because it accepts deposit of an electronic image or other electronic information related to an original check;

(ii) Does not receive the original check;

(iii) Receives settlement or other consideration for an electronic check or substitute check related to the original check; and

(iv) Does not receive a return of the check unpaid.

(2) A bank described in paragraph (f)(1) of this section shall indemnify, as set forth in § 229.34(i), a depositary bank that accepts the original check for deposit for losses incurred by that depositary bank if the loss is due to the check having already been paid.

(3) A depositary bank may not make an indemnity claim under paragraph (f)(2) of this section if the original check it accepted for deposit bore a restrictive indorsement inconsistent with the means of deposit.

(g) Indemnities with respect to electronically-created items. Each bank that transfers or presents an electronically-created item and receives a settlement or other consideration for it shall indemnify, as set forth in § 229.34(i), each transferee bank, any subsequent collecting bank, the paying bank, and any subsequent returning bank against losses that result from the fact that—

(1) The electronic image or electronic information is not derived from a paper check;

(2) The person on whose account the electronically-created item is drawn did not authorize the issuance of the item in the amount stated on the item or to the payee stated on the item (for purposes of this paragraph (g)(2), "account" includes an account as defined in section 229.2(a) as well as a credit or other arrangement that allows a person to draw checks that are payable by, through, or at a bank); or

(3) A person receives a transfer, presentment, or return of, or otherwise is charged for an electronically-created item such that the person is asked to make payment based on an item or check it has already paid.

(h) Damages. Damages for breach of the warranties in this section shall not exceed the consideration received by the bank that presents or transfers a check or returned check, plus interest compensation and expenses related to the check or returned check, if any.

(i) Indemnity amounts.

(1) The amount of the indemnity in paragraphs (f)(2) and (g) of this section shall not exceed the sum of—

(i) The amount of the loss of the indemnified bank, up to the amount of the settlement or other consideration received by the indemnifying bank; and

(ii) Interest and expenses of the indemnified bank (including costs and reasonable attorney's fees and other expenses of representation).

(2) (i) If a loss described in paragraph (f)(2) or (g) of this section results in whole or in part from the indemnified bank's negligence or failure to act in good faith, then the indemnity amount described

in paragraph (i)(1) of this section shall be reduced in proportion to the amount of negligence or bad faith attributable to the indemnified bank.

(ii) Nothing in this paragraph (i)(2) affects the rights of a person under the UCC or other applicable provision of state or federal law.

(j) Tender of defense. If a bank is sued for breach of a warranty or for indemnity under this section, it may give a prior bank in the collection or return chain written notice of the litigation, and the bank notified may then give similar notice to any other prior bank. If the notice states that the bank notified may come in and defend and that failure to do so will bind the bank notified in an action later brought by the bank giving the notice as to any determination of fact common to the two litigations, the bank notified is so bound unless after seasonable receipt of the notice the bank notified does come in and defend.

(k) Notice of claim. Unless a claimant gives notice of a claim for breach of warranty or for indemnity under this section to the bank that made the warranty or indemnification within 30 days after the claimant has reason to know of the breach or facts and circumstances giving rise to the indemnity and the identity of the warranting or indemnifying bank, the warranting or indemnifying bank is discharged to the extent of any loss caused by the delay in giving notice of the claim.

§ 229.35. Indorsements.

(a) Indorsement standards. A bank (other than a paying bank) that handles a check during forward collection or a returned check shall indorse the check in a manner that permits person to interpret the indorsement, in accordance with American National Standard (ANS) Specifications for Physical Check Endorsements, X9.100-111 (ANS X9.100-111), for a paper check other than a substitute check; ANS Specifications for an Image Replacement Document, X9.100-140 (ANS X9.100-140), for a substitute check; and ANS Specifications for Electronic Exchange of Check and Image Data—Domestic, X9.100-187 (ANS X9.100-187), for an electronic check; unless the Board by rule or order determines that different standards apply or the parties otherwise agree.

(b) Liability of bank handling check. A bank that handles a check for forward collection or return is liable to any bank that subsequently handles the check to the extent that the subsequent bank does not receive payment for the check because of suspension of payments by another bank or otherwise. This paragraph applies whether or not a bank has placed its indorsement on the check. This liability is not affected by the failure of any bank to exercise ordinary care, but any bank failing to do so remains liable. A bank seeking recovery against a prior bank shall send notice to that prior bank reasonably promptly after it learns the facts entitling it to recover. A bank may recover from the bank with which it settled for the check by revoking the settlement, charging back any credit given to an account, or obtaining a refund. A bank may have the rights of a holder with respect to each check it handles.

(c) Indorsement by a bank. After a check has been indorsed by a bank, only a bank may acquire the rights of a holder—

(1) Until the check has been returned to the person initiating collection; or

(2) Until the check has been specially indorsed by a bank to a person who is not a bank.

(d) Indorsement for depositary bank. A depositary bank may arrange with another bank to apply the other bank's indorsement as the depositary bank indorsement, provided that any indorsement of the depositary bank on the check avoids the area reserved for the depositary bank indorsement as specified in the indorsement standard applicable to the check under paragraph (a) of this section. The other bank indorsing as depositary bank is considered the depositary bank for purposes of subpart C of this part.

§ 229.36. Presentment and Issuance of Checks.

(a) Receipt of electronic checks. The terms under which a paying bank will accept presentment of an electronic check is governed by the paying bank's agreement with the presenting bank.

(b) Receipt of paper checks.

(1) A paper check is considered received by the paying bank when it is received—

(i) At a location to which delivery is requested by the paying bank;

(ii) At an address of the bank associated with the routing number on the check, whether contained in the MICR line or in fractional form;

(iii) At a branch, head office, or other location consistent with the name and address of the bank on the check if the bank is identified on the check by name and address; or

(iv) At any branch or head office, if the bank is identified on the check by name without address.

(2) A bank may require that checks presented to it as a paying bank be separated from returned checks.

(c) Liability of bank during forward collection. Settlements between banks for the forward collection of a check are final when made; however, a collecting bank handling a check for forward collection may be liable to a prior collecting bank, including the depositary bank, and the depositary bank's customer.

(d) Same-day settlement.

(1) A paper check is considered presented, and a paying bank must settle for or return the check pursuant to paragraph (d)(2) of this section, if a presenting bank delivers the check in accordance with reasonable delivery requirements established by the paying bank and demands payment under this paragraph (d)—

(i) At a location designated by the paying bank for receipt of paper checks under this paragraph (d) at which the paying bank would be considered to have received the paper check under paragraph (b) of this section or, if no location is designated, at any location described in paragraph (b) of this section; and

(ii) By 8 a.m. on a business day (local time of the location described in paragraph (d)(1)(i) of this section).

(2) A paying bank may require that paper checks presented for settlement pursuant to paragraph (d)(1) of this section be separated from other forward-collection checks or returned checks.

(3) If presentment of a paper check meets the requirements of paragraph (d)(1) of this section, the paying bank is accountable to the presenting bank for the amount of the check unless, by the close of Fedwire on the business day it receives the check, it either—

(i) Settles with the presenting bank for the amount of the check by credit to an account at a Federal Reserve Bank designated by the presenting bank; or

(ii) Returns the check.

(4) Notwithstanding paragraph (d)(3) of this section, if a paying bank closes on a business day and receives presentment of a paper check on that day in accordance with paragraph (d)(1) of this section—

(i) The paying bank is accountable to the presenting bank for the amount of the check unless, by the close of Fedwire on its next banking day, it either—

(A) Settles with the presenting bank for the amount of the check by credit to an account at a Federal Reserve Bank designated by the presenting bank; or

(B) Returns the check.

(ii) If the closing is voluntary, unless the paying bank settles for or returns the check in accordance with paragraph (d)(3) of this section, it shall pay interest compensation to the presenting bank for each day after the business day on which the check was presented until the paying bank settles for the check, including the day of settlement.

§ 229.37. Variation by Agreement.

The effect of the provisions of subpart C may be varied by agreement, except that no agreement can disclaim the responsibility of a bank for its own lack of good faith or failure to exercise ordinary care, or can limit the measure of damages for such lack or failure; but the parties may determine by agreement the standards by which such responsibility is to be measured if such standards are not manifestly unreasonable.

§ 229.38. Liability.

(a) Standard of care; liability; measure of damages. A bank shall exercise ordinary care and act in good faith in complying with the requirements of this subpart. A bank that fails to exercise ordinary care or act in good faith under this subpart may be liable to the depositary bank, the depositary bank's customer, the owner of a check, or another party to the check. The measure of damages for failure to exercise ordinary care is the amount of the loss incurred, up to the amount of the check, reduced by the amount of the loss that party would have incurred even if the bank had exercised ordinary care. A bank that fails to act in good faith under this subpart may be liable for other damages, if any, suffered by the party as a proximate consequence. Subject to a bank's duty to exercise ordinary care or act in good faith in choosing the means of return or notice of nonpayment, the bank is not liable for the insolvency, neglect, misconduct, mistake, or default of another bank or person, or for loss or destruction of a check or notice of nonpayment in transit or in the possession of others. This section does not affect a paying bank's liability to its customer under the U.C.C. or other law.

(b) Paying bank's failure to make timely return. If a paying bank fails both to comply with its expeditious return requirements under § 229.31(b) and with the deadline for return under the UCC, Regulation J (12 CFR part 210), or the extension of deadline under § 229.31(g) in connection with a single nonpayment of a check, the paying bank shall be liable under either § 229.31(b) or such other provision, but not both.

(c) Comparative negligence. If a person, including a bank, fails to exercise ordinary care or act in good faith under this subpart in indorsing a check (§ 229.35), accepting a returned check or notice of nonpayment (§ 229.33(b), (c), and (d)), or otherwise, the damages incurred by that person under § 229.38(a) shall be diminished in proportion to the amount of negligence or bad faith attributable to that person.

(d) Responsibility for certain aspects of checks.

(1) A paying bank, or in the case of a check payable through the paying bank and payable by another bank, the bank by which the check is payable, is responsible for damages under paragraph (a) of this section to the extent that the condition of the check when issued by it or its customer adversely affects the ability of a bank to indorse the check legibly in accordance with § 229.35. A depositary bank is responsible for damages under paragraph (a) of this section to the extent that the condition of the back of a check arising after the issuance of the check and prior to acceptance of the check by it adversely affects the ability of a bank to indorse the check legibly in accordance with § 229.35. A reconverting bank is responsible for damages under paragraph (a) of this section to the extent that the condition of the back of a substitute check transferred, presented, or returned by it—

(i) Adversely affects the ability of a subsequent bank to indorse the check legibly in accordance with § 229.35; or

(ii) Causes an indorsement that previously was applied in accordance with § 229.35 to become illegible.

(2) Responsibility under this paragraph (d) shall be treated as negligence of the paying bank, depositary bank, or reconverting bank for purposes of paragraph (c) of this section.

(e) Timeliness of action. If a bank is delayed in acting beyond the time limits set forth in this subpart because of interruption of communication or computer facilities, suspension of payments by a bank, war, emergency conditions, failure of equipment, or other circumstances beyond its control, its time for acting is extended for the time necessary to complete the action, if it exercises such diligence as the circumstances require.

(f) Exclusion. Section 229.21 of this part and section 611 (a), (b), and (c) of the EFA Act (12 U.S.C. 4010 (a), (b), and (c)) do not apply to this subpart.

(g) Jurisdiction. Any action under this subpart may be brought in any United States district court, or in any other court of competent jurisdiction, and shall be brought within one year after the date of the occurrence of the violation involved.

(h) Reliance on Board rulings. No provision of this subpart imposing any liability shall apply to any act done or omitted in good faith in conformity with any rule, regulation, or interpretation thereof by the Board, regardless of whether the rule, regulation, or interpretation is amended, rescinded, or determined by judicial or other authority to be invalid for any reason after the act or omission has occurred.

(i) Presumption of Alteration—

(1) Presumption. Subject to paragraphs (i)(2) and (3) of this section and in the absence of a Federal statute or regulation to the contrary, the presumption in this paragraph applies with respect to any banks arising under Federal or State law as to whether a substitute check or electronic check transferred between these banks contains an alteration or is derived from an original check that was issued with an unauthorized signature of the drawer. When such a dispute arises, there is a rebuttable presumption that the substitute check or electronic check contains an alteration.

(2) Rebuttal of presumption. The presumption of alteration may be overcome by proving by a preponderance of evidence that either the substitute check or electronic check does not contain an alteration, or that the substitute check or electronic check is derived from an original check that was issued with an unauthorized signature of the drawer.

(3) Effect of producing original check. If the original check is made available for examination by all banks involved in the dispute, the presumption in paragraph (i)(1) of this section shall no longer apply.

§ 229.39. Insolvency of Bank.

(a) Duty of receiver to return unpaid checks. A check or returned check in, or coming into, the possession of a paying bank, collecting bank, depositary bank, or returning bank that suspends payment, and which is not paid, shall be returned by the receiver, trustee, or agent in charge of the closed bank to the bank or customer that transferred the check to the closed bank.

(b) Claims against banks for checks not returned by receiver. If a check or returned check is not returned by the receiver, trustee, or agent in charge of the closed bank under paragraph (a) of this section, a bank shall have claims with respect to the check or returned check as follows:

(1) If the paying bank has finally paid the check, or if a depositary bank is obligated to pay the returned check, and suspends payment without making a settlement for the check or returned check with the prior bank that is or becomes final, the prior bank has a claim against the paying bank or the depositary bank.

(2) If a collecting bank, paying bank, or returning bank receives settlement from a subsequent

bank for a check or returned check, which settlement is or becomes final, and suspends payments without making a settlement for the check with the prior bank, which is or becomes final, the prior bank has a claim against the collecting bank or returning bank.

(c) Preferred claim against presenting bank for breach of warranty. If a paying bank settles with a presenting bank for one or more checks, and if the presenting bank breaches a warranty specified in § 229.34(c)(1) or (3) with respect to those checks and suspends payments before satisfying the paying bank's warranty claim, the paying bank has a preferred claim against the presenting bank for the amount of the warranty claim.

(d) Finality of settlement. If a paying bank or depositary bank gives, or a collecting bank, paying bank, or returning bank gives or receives, a settlement for a check or returned check and thereafter suspends payment, the suspension does not prevent or interfere with the settlement becoming final if such finality occurs automatically upon the lapse of a certain time or the happening of certain events.

§ 229.40. Effect of Merger Transaction.

For purposes of this subpart, two or more banks that have engaged in a merger transaction may be considered to be separate banks for a period of one year following the consummation of the merger transaction.

§ 229.41. Relation to State Law.

The provisions of this subpart supersede any inconsistent provisions of the U.C.C. as adopted in any state, or of any other state law, but only to the extent of the inconsistency.

§ 229.42. Exclusions.

The expeditious return (§§ 229.31(b) and 229.32(b)), notice of nonpayment (§ 229.31(c)), and same-day settlement (§ 229.36(d)) requirements of this subpart do not apply to a check drawn upon the United States Treasury, to a U.S. Postal Service money order, or to a check drawn on a state or a unit of general local government that is not payable through or at a bank.

SUBPART D. SUBSTITUTE CHECKS

§ 229.51. General Provisions Governing Substitute Checks.

(a) Legal equivalence. A substitute check for which a bank has provided the warranties described in § 229.52 is the legal equivalent of an original check for all persons and all purposes, including any provision of federal or state law, if the substitute check—

(1) Accurately represents all of the information on the front and back of the original check as of the time the original check was truncated; and

(2) Bears the legend, "This is a legal copy of your check. You can use it the same way you would use the original check."

(b) Reconverting bank duties. A bank shall ensure that a substitute check for which it is the reconverting bank—

(1) Bears all indorsements applied by parties that previously handled the check in any form (including the original check, a substitute check, or another paper or electronic representation of such original check or substitute check) for forward collection or return;

(2) Identifies the reconverting bank in a manner that preserves any previous reconverting-bank identifications, in accordance with ANS X9.100-140; and

(3) Identifies the bank that truncated the original check, in accordance with ANS X9.100-140.

(c) Applicable law. A substitute check that is the legal equivalent of an original check under paragraph (a) of this section shall be subject to any provision, including any provision relating to the protection of customers, of this part, the U.C.C., and any other applicable federal or state law as if such substitute check were the original check, to the extent such provision of law is not inconsistent with the Check 21 Act or this subpart.

§ 229.52. Substitute Check Warranties.

(a) Content and provision of substitute-check warranties.

(1) A bank that transfers, presents, or returns a substitute check (or a paper or electronic representation of a substitute check) for which it receives consideration warrants to the parties listed in paragraph (b) of this section that—

(i) The substitute check meets the requirements for legal equivalence described in § 229.51(a)(1) and (2); and

(ii) No depositary bank, drawee, drawer, or indorser will receive presentment or return of, or otherwise be charged for, the substitute check, the original check, or a paper or electronic representation of the substitute check or original check such that that person will be asked to make a payment based on a check that it already has paid.

(2) A bank that rejects a check submitted for deposit and returns to its customer a substitute

check (or a paper or electronic representation of a substitute check) makes the warranties in paragraph (a)(1) of this section regardless of whether the bank received consideration.

(b) Warranty recipients. A bank makes the warranties described in paragraph (a) of this section to the person to which the bank transfers, presents, or returns the substitute check or a paper or electronic representation of such substitute check and to any subsequent recipient, which could include a collecting or returning bank, the depositary bank, the drawer, the drawee, the payee, the depositor, and any indorser. These parties receive the warranties regardless of whether they received the substitute check or a paper or electronic representation of a substitute check.

§ 229.53. Substitute Check Indemnity.

(a) Scope of indemnity.

(1) A bank that transfers, presents, or returns a substitute check or a paper or electronic representation of a substitute check for which it receives consideration shall indemnify the recipient and any subsequent recipient (including a collecting or returning bank, the depositary bank, the drawer, the drawee, the payee, the depositor, and any indorser) for any loss incurred by any recipient of a substitute check if that loss occurred due to the receipt of a substitute check instead of the original check.

(2) A bank that rejects a check submitted for deposit and returns to its customer a substitute check (or a paper or electronic representation of a substitute check) shall indemnify the recipient as described in paragraph (a)(1) of this section regardless of whether the bank received consideration.

(b) Indemnity amount—

(1) In general. Unless otherwise indicated by paragraph (b)(2) or (b)(3) of this section, the amount of the indemnity under paragraph (a) of this section is as follows:

(i) If the loss resulted from a breach of a substitute check warranty provided under § 229.52, the amount of the indemnity shall be the amount of any loss (including interest, costs, reasonable attorney's fees, and other expenses of representation) proximately caused by the warranty breach.

(ii) If the loss did not result from a breach of a substitute check warranty provided under § 229.52, the amount of the indemnity shall be the sum of—

(A) The amount of the loss, up to the amount of the substitute check; and

(B) Interest and expenses (including costs and reasonable attorney's fees and other expenses of representation) related to the substitute check.

(2) Comparative negligence.

(i) If a loss described in paragraph (a) of this section results in whole or in part from the indemnified person's negligence or failure to act in good faith, then the indemnity amount described in paragraph (b)(1) of this section shall be reduced in proportion to the amount of negligence or bad faith attributable to the indemnified person.

(ii) Nothing in this paragraph (b)(2) reduces the rights of a consumer or any other person under the U.C.C. or other applicable provision of state or federal law.

(3) Effect of producing the original check or a sufficient copy—

(i) If an indemnifying bank produces the original check or a sufficient copy, the indemnifying bank shall—

(A) Be liable under this section only for losses that are incurred up to the time that the bank provides that original check or sufficient copy to the indemnified person; and

(B) Have a right to the return of any funds it has paid under this section in excess of those losses.

(ii) The production by the indemnifying bank of the original check or a sufficient copy under paragraph (b)(3)(i) of this section shall not absolve the indemnifying bank from any liability under any warranty that the bank has provided under § 229.52 or other applicable law.

(c) Subrogation of rights—

(1) In general. An indemnifying bank shall be subrogated to the rights of the person that it indemnifies to the extent of the indemnity it has provided and may attempt to recover from another person based on a warranty or other claim.

(2) Duty of indemnified person for subrogated claims. Each indemnified person shall have a duty to comply with all reasonable requests for assistance from an indemnifying bank in connection with any claim the indemnifying bank brings against a warrantor or other person related to a check that forms the basis for the indemnification.

§ 229.54. Expedited Recredit for Consumers.

(a) Circumstances giving rise to a claim. A consumer may make a claim under this section for a recredit with respect to a substitute check if the consumer asserts in good faith that—

(1) The bank holding the consumer's account charged that account for a substitute check that was provided to the consumer (although the consumer need not be in possession of that substitute check at the time he or she submits a claim);

(2) The substitute check was not properly charged to the consumer account or the consumer has a warranty claim with respect to the substitute check;

(3) The consumer suffered a resulting loss; and

(4) Production of the original check or a sufficient copy is necessary to determine whether or not the substitute check in fact was improperly charged or whether the consumer's warranty claim is valid.

(b) Procedures for making claims. A consumer shall make his or her claim for a recredit under this section with the bank that holds the consumer's account in accordance with the timing, content, and form requirements of this section.

(1) Timing of claim.

(i) The consumer shall submit his or her claim such that the bank receives the claim by the end of the 40th calendar day after the later of the calendar day on which the bank mailed or delivered, by a means agreed to by the consumer—

(A) The periodic account statement that contains information concerning the transaction giving rise to the claim; or

(B) The substitute check giving rise to the claim.

(ii) If the consumer cannot submit his or her claim by the time specified in paragraph (b)(1)(i) of this section because of extenuating circumstances, the bank shall extend the 40-calendar-day period by an additional reasonable amount of time.

(iii) If a consumer makes a claim orally and the bank requires the claim to be in writing, the consumer's claim is timely if the oral claim was received within the time described in paragraphs (b)(1)(i)-(ii) of this section and the written claim was received within the time described in paragraph (b)(3)(ii) of this section.

(2) Content of claim.

(i) The consumer's claim shall include the following information:

(A) A description of the consumer's claim, including the reason why the consumer believes his or her account was improperly charged for the substitute check or the nature of his or her warranty claim with respect to such check;

(B) A statement that the consumer suffered a loss and an estimate of the amount of that loss;

(C) The reason why production of the original check or a sufficient copy is necessary to determine whether or not the charge to the consumer's account was proper or the consumer's warranty claim is valid; and

(D) Sufficient information to allow the bank to identify the substitute check and investigate the claim.

(ii) If a consumer attempts to make a claim but fails to provide all the information in paragraph (b)(2)(i) of this section that is required to constitute a claim, the bank shall inform the consumer that the claim is not complete and identify the information that is missing.

(3) Form and submission of claim; computation of time for bank action. The bank holding the account that is the subject of the consumer's claim may, in its discretion, require the consumer to submit the information required by this section in writing. A bank that requires a written submission—

(i) May permit the consumer to submit the written claim electronically;

(ii) Shall inform a consumer who submits a claim orally of the written claim requirement at the time of the oral claim and may require such consumer to submit the written claim such that the bank receives the written claim by the 10th business day after the banking day on which the bank received the oral claim; and

(iii) Shall compute the time periods for acting on the consumer's claim described in paragraph (c) of this section from the date on which the bank received the written claim.

(c) Action on claims. A bank that receives a claim that meets the requirements of paragraph (b) of this section shall act as follows:

(1) Valid consumer claim. If the bank determines that the consumer's claim is valid, the bank shall—

(i) Recredit the consumer's account for the amount of the consumer's loss, up to the amount of the substitute check, plus interest if the account is an interest-bearing account, no later than the end of the business day after the banking day on which the bank makes that determination; and

(ii) Send to the consumer the notice required by paragraph (e)(1) of this section.

(2) Invalid consumer claim. If a bank determines that the consumer's claim is not valid, the bank shall send to the consumer the notice described in paragraph (e)(2) of this section.

(3) Recredit pending investigation. If the bank has not taken an action described in paragraph (c)(1) or (c)(2) of this section before the end of the 10th business day after the banking day on which the bank received the claim, the bank shall—

(i) By the end of that business day—

(A) Recredit the consumer's account for the amount of the consumer's loss, up to the lesser of the amount of the substitute check or $ 2,500, plus interest on that amount if the account is an interest-bearing account; and

(B) Send to the consumer the notice required by paragraph (e)(1) of this section; and

(ii) Recredit the consumer's account for the remaining amount of the consumer's loss, if any, up to the amount of the substitute check, plus interest if the account is an interest-bearing account, no later than the end of the 45th calendar day after the banking day on which the bank received the claim and send to the consumer the notice required by paragraph (e)(1) of this section, unless the bank prior to that time has determined that the consumer's claim is or is not valid in accordance with paragraph (c)(1) or (c)(2) of this section.

(4) Reversal of recredit. A bank may reverse a recredit that it has made to a consumer account under paragraph (c)(1) or (c)(3) of this section, plus interest that the bank has paid, if any, on that amount, if the bank—

(i) Determines that the consumer's claim was not valid; and

(ii) Notifies the consumer in accordance with paragraph (e)(3) of this section.

(d) Availability of recredit—

(1) Next-day availability. Except as provided in paragraph (d)(2) of this section, a bank shall make any amount that it recredits to a consumer account under this section available for withdrawal no later than the start of the business day after the banking day on which the bank provides the recredit.

(2) Safeguard exceptions. A bank may delay availability to a consumer of a recredit provided under paragraph (c)(3)(i) of this section until the start of the earlier of the business day after the banking day on which the bank determines the consumer's claim is valid or the 45th calendar day after the banking day on which the bank received the oral or written claim, as required by paragraph (b) of this section, if—

(i) The consumer submits the claim during the 30-calendar-day period beginning on the banking day on which the consumer account was established;

(ii) Without regard to the charge that gave rise to the recredit claim—

(A) On six or more business days during the six-month period ending on the calendar day on which the consumer submitted the claim, the balance in the consumer account was negative or would have become negative if checks or other charges to the account had been paid; or

(B) On two or more business days during such six-month period, the balance in the consumer account was negative or would have become negative in the amount of $5,000 or more if checks or other charges to the account had been paid; or

(iii) The bank has reasonable cause to believe that the claim is fraudulent, based on facts that would cause a well-grounded belief in the mind of a reasonable person that the claim is fraudulent. The fact that the check in question or the consumer is of a particular class may not be the basis for invoking this exception.

(3) Overdraft fees. A bank that delays availability as permitted in paragraph (d)(2) of this section may not impose an overdraft fee with respect to drafts drawn by the consumer on such recredited funds until the fifth calendar day after the calendar day on which the bank sent the notice required by paragraph (e)(1) of this section.

(e) Notices relating to consumer expedited recredit claims—

(1) Notice of recredit. A bank that recredits a consumer account under paragraph (c) of this section shall send notice to the consumer of the recredit no later than the business day after the banking day on which the bank recredits the consumer account. This notice shall describe—

(i) The amount of the recredit; and

(ii) The date on which the recredited funds will be available for withdrawal.

(2) Notice that the consumer's claim is not valid. If a bank determines that a substitute check for which a consumer made a claim under this

section was in fact properly charged to the consumer account or that the consumer's warranty claim for that substitute check was not valid, the bank shall send notice to the consumer no later than the business day after the banking day on which the bank makes that determination. This notice shall—

(i) Include the original check or a sufficient copy, except as provided in § 229.58;

(ii) Demonstrate to the consumer that the substitute check was properly charged or the consumer's warranty claim is not valid; and

(iii) Include the information or documents (in addition to the original check or sufficient copy), if any, on which the bank relied in making its determination or a statement that the consumer may request copies of such information or documents.

(3) Notice of a reversal of recredit. A bank that reverses an amount it previously recredited to a consumer account shall send notice to the consumer no later than the business day after the banking day on which the bank made the reversal. This notice shall include the information listed in paragraph (e)(2) of this section and also describe—

(i) The amount of the reversal, including both the amount of the recredit (including the interest component, if any) and the amount of interest paid on the recredited amount, if any, being reversed; and

(ii) The date on which the bank made the reversal.

(f) Other claims not affected. Providing a recredit in accordance with this section shall not absolve the bank from liability for a claim made under any other provision of law, such as a claim for wrongful dishonor of a check under the U.C.C., or from liability for additional damages, such as damages under § 229.53 or § 229.56 of this subpart or U.C.C. 4-402.

§ 229.55. Expedited Recredit for Banks.

(a) Circumstances giving rise to a claim. A bank that has an indemnity claim under § 229.53 with respect to a substitute check may make an expedited recredit claim against an indemnifying bank if—

(1) The claimant bank or a bank that the claimant bank has indemnified—

(i) Has received a claim for expedited recredit from a consumer under § 229.54; or

(ii) Would have been subject to such a claim if the consumer account had been charged for the substitute check;

(2) The claimant bank is obligated to provide an expedited recredit with respect to such substitute check under § 229.54 or otherwise has suffered a resulting loss; and

(3) The production of the original check or a sufficient copy is necessary to determine the validity of the charge to the consumer account or the validity of any warranty claim connected with such substitute check.

(b) Procedures for making claims. A claimant bank shall send its claim to the indemnifying bank, subject to the timing, content, and form requirements of this section.

(1) Timing of claim. The claimant bank shall submit its claim such that the indemnifying bank receives the claim by the end of the 120th calendar day after the date of the transaction that gave rise to the claim.

(2) Content of claim. The claimant bank's claim shall include the following information—

(i) A description of the consumer's claim or the warranty claim related to the substitute check, including why the bank believes that the substitute check may not be properly charged to the consumer account;

(ii) A statement that the claimant bank is obligated to recredit a consumer account under § 229.54 or otherwise has suffered a loss and an estimate of the amount of that recredit or loss, including interest if applicable;

(iii) The reason why production of the original check or a sufficient copy is necessary to determine the validity of the charge to the consumer account or the warranty claim; and

(iv) Sufficient information to allow the indemnifying bank to identify the substitute check and investigate the claim.

(3) Requirements relating to copies of substitute checks. If the information submitted by a claimant bank under paragraph (b)(2) of this section includes a copy of any substitute check, the claimant bank shall take reasonable steps to ensure that the copy cannot be mistaken for the legal equivalent of the check under § 229.51(a) or sent or handled by any bank, including the indemnifying bank, for forward collection or return.

(4) Form and submission of claim; computation of time. The indemnifying bank may, in its discretion, require the claimant bank to submit the information required by this section in writing, including a copy of the paper or electronic claim submitted

by the consumer, if any. An indemnifying bank that requires a written submission—

(i) May permit the claimant bank to submit the written claim electronically;

(ii) Shall inform a claimant bank that submits a claim orally of the written claim requirement at the time of the oral claim; and

(iii) Shall compute the 10-day time period for acting on the claim described in paragraph (c) of this section from the date on which the bank received the written claim.

(c) Action on claims. No later than the 10th business day after the banking day on which the indemnifying bank receives a claim that meets the requirements of paragraph (b) of this section, the indemnifying bank shall—

(1) Recredit the claimant bank for the amount of the claim, up to the amount of the substitute check, plus interest if applicable;

(2) Provide to the claimant bank the original check or a sufficient copy; or

(3) Provide information to the claimant bank regarding why the indemnifying bank is not obligated to comply with paragraph (c)(1) or (c)(2) of this section.

(d) Recredit does not abrogate other liabilities. Providing a recredit to a claimant bank under this section does not absolve the indemnifying bank from liability for claims brought under any other law or from additional damages under § 229.53 or § 229.56.

(e) Indemnifying bank's right to a refund.

(1) If a claimant bank reverses a recredit it previously made to a consumer account under § 229.54 or otherwise receives reimbursement for a substitute check that formed the basis of its claim under this section, the claimant bank shall provide a refund promptly to any indemnifying bank that previously advanced funds to the claimant bank. The amount of the refund to the indemnifying bank shall be the amount of the reversal or reimbursement obtained by the claimant bank, up to the amount previously advanced by the indemnifying bank.

(2) If the indemnifying bank provides the claimant bank with the original check or a sufficient copy under paragraph (c)(2) of this section, § 229.53(b)(3) governs the indemnifying bank's entitlement to repayment of any amount provided to the claimant bank that exceeds the amount of losses the claimant bank incurred up to that time.

§ 229.56. Liability.

(a) Measure of damages—

(1) In general. Except as provided in paragraph (a)(2) or (a)(3) of this section or § 229.53, any person that breaches a warranty described in § 229.52 or fails to comply with any requirement of this subpart with respect to any other person shall be liable to that person for an amount equal to the sum of—

(i) The amount of the loss suffered by the person as a result of the breach or failure, up to the amount of the substitute check; and

(ii) Interest and expenses (including costs and reasonable attorney's fees and other expenses of representation) related to the substitute check.

(2) Offset of recredits. The amount of damages a person receives under paragraph (a)(1) of this section shall be reduced by any amount that the person receives and retains as a recredit under § 229.54 or § 229.55.

(3) Comparative negligence.

(i) If a person incurs damages that resulted in whole or in part from that person's negligence or failure to act in good faith, then the amount of any damages due to that person under paragraph (a)(1) of this section shall be reduced in proportion to the amount of negligence or bad faith attributable to that person.

(ii) Nothing in this paragraph (a)(3) reduces the rights of a consumer or any other person under the U.C.C. or other applicable provision of federal or state law.

(b) Timeliness of action. Delay by a bank beyond any time limits prescribed or permitted by this subpart is excused if the delay is caused by interruption of communication or computer facilities, suspension of payments by another bank, war, emergency conditions, failure of equipment, or other circumstances beyond the control of the bank and if the bank uses such diligence as the circumstances require.

(c) Jurisdiction. A person may bring an action to enforce a claim under this subpart in any United States district court or in any other court of competent jurisdiction. Such claim shall be brought within one year of the date on which the person's cause of action accrues. For purposes of this paragraph, a cause of action accrues as of the date on which the injured person first learns, or by which such person reasonably should have learned, of the facts and circumstances giving rise to the cause of action, including the identity of the warranting or indemnifying bank against which the action is brought.

(d) Notice of claims. Except as otherwise provided in this paragraph (d), unless a person gives notice of a claim under this section to the warranting or indemnifying bank within 30 calendar days after the person has reason to know of both the claim and the identity of the warranting or indemnifying bank, the warranting or indemnifying bank is discharged from liability in an action to enforce a claim under this subpart to the extent of any loss caused by the delay in giving notice of the claim. A timely recredit claim by a consumer under § 229.54 constitutes timely notice under this paragraph.

§ 229.57. Consumer Awareness.

(a) General disclosure requirement and content. Each bank shall provide, in accordance with paragraph (b) of this section, a brief disclosure to each of its consumer customers that describes—

(1) That a substitute check is the legal equivalent of an original check; and

(2) The consumer recredit rights that apply when a consumer in good faith believes that a substitute check was not properly charged to his or her account.

(b) Distribution—

(1) Disclosure to consumers who receive paid checks with periodic account statements. A bank shall provide the disclosure described in paragraph (a) of this section to a consumer customer who receives paid original checks or paid substitute checks with his or her periodic account statement—

(i) No later than the first regularly scheduled communication with the consumer after October 28, 2004, for each consumer who is a customer of the bank on that date; and

(ii) At the time the customer relationship is initiated, for each customer relationship established after October 28, 2004.

(2) Disclosure to consumers who receive substitute checks on an occasional basis—

(i) The bank shall provide the disclosure described in paragraph (a) of this section to a consumer customer of the bank who requests an original check or a copy of a check and receives a substitute check. If feasible, the bank shall provide this disclosure at the time of the consumer's request; otherwise, the bank shall provide this disclosure no later than the time at which the bank provides a substitute check in response to the consumer's request.

(ii) The bank shall provide the disclosure described in paragraph (a) of this section to a consumer customer of the bank who receives a returned substitute check, at the time the bank provides such substitute check.

(3) Multiple account holders. A bank need not give separate disclosures to each customer on a jointly held account.

§ 229.58. Mode of Delivery of Information.

A bank may deliver any notice or other information that it is required to provide under this subpart by United States mail or by any other means through which the recipient has agreed to receive account information. If a bank is required to provide an original check or a sufficient copy, the bank instead may provide an electronic image of the original check or sufficient copy if the recipient has agreed to receive that information electronically.

§ 229.59. Relation to Other Law.

The Check 21 Act and this subpart supersede any provision of federal or state law, including the Uniform Commercial Code, that is inconsistent with the Check 21 Act or this subpart, but only to the extent of the inconsistency.

§ 229.60. Variation by Agreement.

Any provision of § 229.55 may be varied by agreement of the banks involved. No other provision of this subpart may be varied by agreement by any person or persons.

Truth-in-Lending Act

15 U.S.C. §§ 1601 et seq. (Selected Provisions)

§ 1601. Congressional Findings and Declaration of Purpose

(a) Informed use of credit. The Congress finds that economic stabilization would be enhanced and the competition among the various financial institutions and other firms engaged in the extension of consumer credit would be strengthened by the informed use of credit. The informed use of credit results from an awareness of the cost thereof by consumers. It is the purpose of this subchapter to assure a meaningful disclosure of credit terms so that the consumer will be able to compare more readily the various credit terms available to him and avoid the uninformed use of credit, and to protect the consumer against inaccurate and unfair credit billing and credit card practices.

(b) Terms of personal property leases. The Congress also finds that there has been a recent trend toward leasing automobiles and other durable goods for consumer use as an alternative to installment credit sales and that these leases have been offered without adequate cost disclosures. It is the purpose of this subchapter to assure a meaningful disclosure of the terms of leases of personal property for personal, family, or household purposes so as to enable the lessee to compare more readily the various lease terms available to him, limit balloon payments in consumer leasing, enable comparison of lease terms with credit terms where appropriate, and to assure meaningful and accurate disclosures of lease terms in advertisements.

§ 1602. Definitions and Rules of Construction

(a) The definitions and rules of construction set forth in this section are applicable for the purposes of this subchapter.

(b) Bureau.—The term "Bureau" means the Bureau of Consumer Financial Protection.

(c) The term "Board" refers to the Board of Governors of the Federal Reserve System.

(d) The term "organization" means a corporation, government or governmental subdivision or agency, trust, estate, partnership, cooperative, or association.

(e) The term "person" means a natural person or an organization.

(f) The term "credit" means the right granted by a creditor to a debtor to defer payment of debt or to incur debt and defer its payment.

(g) The term "creditor" refers only to a person who both

(1) regularly extends, whether in connection with loans, sales of property or services, or otherwise, consumer credit which is payable by agreement in more than four installments or for which the payment of a finance charge is or may be required, and

(2) is the person to whom the debt arising from the consumer credit transaction is initially payable on the face of the evidence of indebtedness or, if there is no such evidence of indebtedness, by agreement. Notwithstanding the preceding sentence, in the case of an open-end credit plan involving a credit card, the card issuer and any person who honors the credit card and offers a discount which is a finance charge are creditors. For the purpose of the requirements imposed under part D of this subchapter and sections 1637(a)(5), 1637(a)(6), 1637(a)(7), 1637(b)(1), 1637(b)(2), 1637(b)(3), 1637(b)(8), and 1637(b)(10) of this title, the term "creditor" shall also include card issuers whether or not the amount due is payable by agreement in more than four installments or the payment of a finance charge is or may be required, and the Bureau shall, by regulation, apply these requirements to such card issuers, to the extent appropriate, even though the requirements are by their terms applicable only to creditors offering open-end credit plans. Any person who originates 2 or more mortgages referred to in subsection (aa) of this section in any 12-month period or any person who originates 1 or more such mortgages through a mortgage broker shall be considered to be a creditor for purposes of this subchapter.

(h) The term "credit sale" refers to any sale in which the seller is a creditor. The term includes any contract in the form of a bailment or lease if the bailee or lessee contracts to pay as compensation for use a sum substantially equivalent to or in excess of the aggregate value of the property and services involved and it is agreed that the bailee or lessee will become, or for no other or a nominal consideration has the option to become, the owner of the property upon full compliance with his obligations under the contract.

(i) The adjective "consumer", used with reference to a credit transaction, characterizes the transaction as one in which the party to whom credit is offered or extended is a natural person, and the money, property, or services which are the subject of the transaction are primarily for personal, family, or household purposes.

(j) The terms "open end credit plan" and "open end consumer credit plan" mean a plan under which the creditor reasonably contemplates repeated transactions, which prescribes the terms of such transactions, and which provides for a finance charge which may be computed from time to time on the outstanding unpaid balance. A credit plan or open end consumer credit plan which is an open end credit plan or open end consumer credit plan within the meaning of the preceding sentence is an open end credit plan or open end consumer credit plan even if credit information is verified from time to time.

(k) The term "adequate notice," as used in section 1643 of this title, means a printed notice to a cardholder which sets forth the pertinent facts clearly and conspicuously so that a person against whom it is to operate could reasonably be expected to have noticed it and understood its meaning. Such notice may be given to a cardholder by printing the notice on any credit card, or on each periodic statement of account, issued to the cardholder, or by any other means reasonably assuring the receipt thereof by the cardholder.

(l) The term "credit card" means any card, plate, coupon book or other credit device existing for the purpose of obtaining money, property, labor, or services on credit.

(m) The term "accepted credit card" means any credit card which the cardholder has requested and received or has signed or has used, or authorized another to use, for the purpose of obtaining money, property, labor, or services on credit.

(n) The term "cardholder" means any person to whom a credit card is issued or any person who has agreed with the card issuer to pay obligations arising from the issuance of a credit card to another person.

(o) The term "card issuer" means any person who issues a credit card, or the agent of such person with respect to such card.

(p) The term "unauthorized use," as used in section 1643 of this title, means a use of a credit card by a person other than the cardholder who does not have actual, implied, or apparent authority for such use and from which the cardholder receives no benefit.

(q) The term "discount" as used in section 1666f of this title means a reduction made from the regular price. The term "discount" as used in section 1666f of this title shall not mean a surcharge.

(r) The term "surcharge" as used in this section and section 1666f of this title means any means of increasing the regular price to a cardholder which is not imposed upon customers paying by cash, check, or similar means.

(s) The term "State" refers to any State, the Commonwealth of Puerto Rico, the District of Columbia, and any territory or possession of the United States.

(t) The term "agricultural purposes" includes the production, harvest, exhibition, marketing, transportation, processing, or manufacture of agricultural products by a natural person who cultivates, plants, propagates, or nurtures those agricultural products, including but not limited to the acquisition of farmland, real property with a farm residence, and personal property and services used primarily in farming.

(u) The term "agricultural products" includes agricultural, horticultural, viticultural, and dairy products, livestock, wildlife, poultry, bees, forest products, fish and shellfish, and any products thereof, including processed and manufactured products, and any and all products raised or produced on farms and any processed or manufactured products thereof.

(v) The term "material disclosures" means the disclosure, as required by this subchapter, of the annual percentage rate, the method of determining the finance charge and the balance upon which a finance charge will be imposed, the amount of the finance charge, the amount to be financed, the total of payments, the number and amount of payments, the due dates or periods of payments scheduled to repay the indebtedness, and the disclosures required by section 1639(a) of this title.

(w) The term "dwelling" means a residential structure or mobile home which contains one to four family housing units, or individual units of condominiums or cooperatives.

(x) The term "residential mortgage transaction" means a transaction in which a mortgage, deed of trust, purchase money security interest arising under an installment sales contract, or equivalent consensual security interest is created or retained against the consumer's dwelling to finance the acquisition or initial construction of such dwelling.

(y) As used in this section and section 1666f of this title, the term "regular price" means the tag or posted price charged for the property or service if a single price is tagged or posted, or the price charged for the property or service when payment is made by use of an open-end credit plan or a credit card if either

(1) no price is tagged or posted, or

(2) two prices are tagged or posted, one of which is charged when payment is made by use of an open-end credit plan or a credit card and the other when payment is made by use of cash, check, or similar means. For purposes of this definition, payment by check, draft, or other negotiable instrument which may result in the debiting of an open-end credit plan or a credit cardholder's open-end account shall not be considered payment made by use of the plan or the account.

(z) Any reference to any requirement imposed under this subchapter or any provision thereof includes reference to the regulations of the Bureau under this subchapter or the provision thereof in question.

(aa) The disclosure of an amount or percentage which is greater than the amount or percentage required to be disclosed under this subchapter does not in itself constitute a violation of this subchapter.

(bb) High-cost Mortgage.—

(1) Definition.—

(A) In general. The term "high-cost mortgage", and a mortgage referred to in this subsection, means a consumer credit transaction that is secured by the consumer's principal dwelling, other than a reverse mortgage transaction, if—

(i) in the case of a credit transaction secured—

(I) by a first mortgage on the consumer's principal dwelling, the annual percentage rate at consummation of the transaction will exceed by more than

6.5 percentage points (8.5 percentage points, if the dwelling is personal property and the transaction is for less than $50,000) the average prime offer rate, as defined in section 1639c(b)(2)(B) of this title, for a comparable transaction; or

(II) by a subordinate or junior mortgage on the consumer's principal dwelling, the annual percentage rate at consummation of the transaction will exceed by more than 8.5 percentage points the average prime offer rate, as defined in section 1639c(b)(2)(B) of this title, for a comparable transaction;

(ii) the total points and fees payable in connection with the transaction, other than bona fide third party charges not retained by the mortgage originator, creditor, or an affiliate of the creditor or mortgage originator, exceed—

(I) in the case of a transaction for $20,000 or more, 5 percent of the total transaction amount; or

(II) in the case of a transaction for less than $20,000, the lesser of 8 percent of the total transaction amount or $1,000 (or such other dollar amount as the Board shall prescribe by regulation); or

(iii) the credit transaction documents permit the creditor to charge or collect prepayment fees or penalties more than 36 months after the transaction closing or such fees or penalties exceed, in the aggregate, more than 2 percent of the amount prepaid.

(B) Introductory rates taken into account.—For purposes of subparagraph (A)(i), the annual percentage rate of interest shall be determined based on the following interest rate:

(i) In the case of a fixed-rate transaction in which the annual percentage rate will not vary during the term of the loan, the interest rate in effect on the date of consummation of the transaction.

(ii) In the case of a transaction in which the rate of interest varies solely in accordance with an index, the interest rate determined by adding the index rate in effect on the date of consummation of the transaction to the maximum margin permitted at any time during the loan agreement.

(iii) In the case of any other transaction in which the rate may vary at any time during the term of the loan for any reason, the interest charged on the transaction at the maximum rate that may be charged during the term of the loan.

(C) Mortgage Insurance.—For the purposes of computing the total points and fees under paragraph (4), the total points and fees shall exclude—

(i) any premium provided by an agency of the Federal Government or an agency of a State;

(ii) any amount that is not in excess of the amount payable under policies in effect at the time of origination under section 203(c)(2)(A) of the National Housing Act (12 U.S.C. 1709(c)(2)(A)), provided that the premium, charge, or fee is required to be refundable on a pro-rated basis and the refund is automatically issued upon notification of the satisfaction of the underlying mortgage loan; and

(iii) any premium paid by the consumer after closing.

(2)(A) After the 2-year period beginning on the effective date of the regulations promulgated under section 155 of the Riegle Community Development and Regulatory Improvement Act of 1994, and no more frequently than biennially after the first increase or decrease under this subparagraph, the Bureau may by regulation increase or decrease the number of percentage points specified in paragraph (1)(A), if the Bureau determines that the increase or decrease is—

(i) consistent with the consumer protections against abusive lending provided by the amendments made by subtitle B of title I of the Riegle Community Development and Regulatory Improvement Act of 1994; and

(ii) warranted by the need for credit.

(B) An increase or decrease under subparagraph (A)—

(i) may not result in the number of percentage points referred to in paragraph (1)(A)(i)(I) being less than 6 percentage points or greater than 10 percentage points; and

(ii) may not result in the number of percentage points referred to in paragraph

(1)(A)(i)(II) being less than 8 percentage points or greater than 12 percentage points.

(C) In determining whether to increase or decrease the number of percentage points referred to in subparagraph (A), the Bureau shall consult with representatives of consumers, including low-income consumers, and lenders.

(3) The amount specified in paragraph (1)(B)(ii) shall be adjusted annually on January 1 by the annual percentage change in the Consumer Price Index, as reported on June 1 of the year preceding such adjustment.

(4) For purposes of paragraph (1)(B), points and fees shall include—

(A) all items included in the finance charge, except interest or the time-price differential;

(B) all compensation paid directly or indirectly by a consumer or creditor to a mortgage originator from any source, including a mortgage originator that is also the creditor in a table-funded transaction;

(C) each of the charges listed in section 1605(e) of this title (except an escrow for future payment of taxes), unless—

(i) the charge is reasonable;

(ii) the creditor receives no direct or indirect compensation; and

(iii) the charge is paid to a third party unaffiliated with the creditor; and

(D) premiums or other charges payable at or before closing for any credit life, credit disability, credit unemployment, or credit property insurance, or any other accident, loss-of-income, life or health insurance, or any payments directly or indirectly for any debt cancellation or suspension agreement or contract, except that insurance premiums or debt cancellation or suspension fees calculated and paid in full on a monthly basis shall not be considered financed by the creditor;

(E) the maximum prepayment fees and penalties which may be charged or collected under the terms of the credit transaction;

(F) all prepayment fees or penalties that are incurred by the consumer if the loan refinances a previous loan made or currently held by the same creditor or an affiliate of the creditor; and

(G) such other charges as the Bureau determines to be appropriate.

(5) Calculation of points and fees for open-end consumer credit plans.—In the case of open-end consumer credit plans, points and fees shall be calculated, for purposes of this section and section 1639 of this title, by adding the total points and fees known at or before closing, including the maximum prepayment penalties which may be charged or collected under the terms of the credit transaction, plus the minimum additional fees the consumer would be required to pay to draw down an amount equal to the total credit line.

(6) This subsection shall not be construed to limit the rate of interest or the finance charge that a person may charge a consumer for any extension of credit.

(cc) The term "reverse mortgage transaction" means a nonrecourse transaction in which a mortgage, deed of trust, or equivalent consensual security interest is created against the consumer's principal dwelling—

(1) securing one or more advances; and

(2) with respect to which the payment of any principal, interest, and shared appreciation or equity is due and payable (other than in the case of default) only after—

(A) the transfer of the dwelling;

(B) the consumer ceases to occupy the dwelling as a principal dwelling; or

(C) the death of the consumer.

(dd) Definitions Relating to Mortgage Origination and Residential Mortgage Loans.—

(1) Commission.—Unless otherwise specified, the term "Commission" means the Federal Trade Commission.

(2) Mortgage originator.—The term "mortgage originator"—

(A) means any person who, for direct or indirect compensation or gain, or in the expectation of direct or indirect compensation or gain—

(i) takes a residential mortgage loan application;

(ii) assists a consumer in obtaining or applying to obtain a residential mortgage loan; or

(iii) offers or negotiates terms of a residential mortgage loan;

(B) includes any person who represents to the public, through advertising or other means of communicating or providing information (including the use of business cards, stationery, brochures, signs, rate lists, or other promotional items), that such person can or will provide any of the services or perform any of the activities described in subparagraph (A);

(C) does not include any person who is—

(i) not otherwise described in subparagraph (A) or (B) and who performs purely administrative or clerical tasks on behalf of a person who is described in any such subparagraph; or

(ii) a retailer of manufactured or modular homes or an employee of the retailer if the retailer or employee, as applicable—

(I) does not receive compensation or gain for engaging in activities described in subparagraph (A) that is in excess of any compensation or gain received in a comparable cash transaction;

(II) discloses to the consumer—

(aa) in writing any corporate affiliation with any creditor; and

(bb) if the retailer has a corporate affiliation with any creditor, at least 1 unaffiliated creditor; and

(III) does not directly negotiate with the consumer or lender on loan terms (including rates, fees, and other costs).

(D) does not include a person or entity that only performs real estate brokerage activities and is licensed or registered in accordance with applicable State law, unless such person or entity is compensated by a lender, a mortgage broker, or other mortgage originator or by any agent of such lender, mortgage broker, or other mortgage originator;

(E) does not include, with respect to a residential mortgage loan, a person, estate, or trust that provides mortgage financing for the sale of 3 properties in any 12-month period to purchasers of such properties, each of which is owned by such person, estate, or trust and serves as security for the loan, provided that such loan—

(i) is not made by a person, estate, or trust that has constructed, or acted as a contractor for the construction of, a residence on the property in the ordinary course of business of such person, estate, or trust;

(ii) is fully amortizing;

(iii) is with respect to a sale for which the seller determines in good faith and documents that the buyer has a reasonable ability to repay the loan;

(iv) has a fixed rate or an adjustable rate that is adjustable after 5 or more years, subject to reasonable annual and lifetime limitations on interest rate increases; and

(v) meets any other criteria the Board may prescribe;

(F) does not include the creditor (except the creditor in a table-funded transaction) under paragraph (1), (2), or (4) of section 1639b(c) of this title; and

(G) does not include a servicer or servicer employees, agents and contractors, including but not limited to those who offer or negotiate terms of a residential mortgage loan for purposes of renegotiating, modifying, replacing and subordinating principal of existing mortgages where borrowers are behind in their payments, in default or have a reasonable likelihood of being in default or falling behind.

(3) Nationwide mortgage licensing system and registry.—The term "Nationwide Mortgage Licensing System and Registry" has the same meaning as in the Secure and Fair Enforcement for Mortgage Licensing Act of 2008 [12 U.S.C. 5101 et seq.].

(4) Other definitions relating to mortgage originator.—For purposes of this subsection, a person "assists a consumer in obtaining or applying to obtain a residential mortgage loan" by, among other things, advising on residential mortgage loan terms (including rates, fees, and other costs), preparing residential mortgage loan packages, or collecting information on behalf of the consumer with regard to a residential mortgage loan.

(5) Residential mortgage loan.—The term "residential mortgage loan" means any consumer credit transaction that is secured by a mortgage, deed of trust, or other equivalent consensual security interest on a dwelling or on residential real property that includes a dwelling, other than a consumer credit transaction under an open end credit plan or, for purposes of sections 1639b and 1639c of this title and section 1638(a) (16), (17), (18), and (19) of this title, and sections 1638(f) and 1640(k) of this title, and any regulations promulgated thereunder, an extension of credit relating to a plan described in section 101(53D) of title 11.

(6) Secretary.—The term "Secretary", when used in connection with any transaction or person involved with a residential mortgage loan, means the Secretary of Housing and Urban Development.

(7) Servicer.—The term "servicer" has the same meaning as in section 2605(i)(2) of title 12.

(ee) Bona Fide Discount Points and Prepayment Penalties.—For the purposes of determining the amount of points and fees for purposes of subsection (aa), either the amounts described in paragraph (1) or (2) of the following paragraphs, but not both, shall be excluded:

(1) Up to and including 2 bona fide discount points payable by the consumer in connection with the mortgage, but only if the interest rate from which the mortgage's interest rate will be discounted does not exceed by more than 1 percentage point—

(A) the average prime offer rate, as defined in section 1639c of this title; or

(B) if secured by a personal property loan, the average rate on a loan in connection with which insurance is provided under title I of the National Housing Act (12 U.S.C. 1702 et seq.).

(2) Unless 2 bona fide discount points have been excluded under paragraph (1), up to and including 1 bona fide discount point payable by the consumer in connection with the mortgage, but only if the interest rate from which the mortgage's interest rate will be discounted does not exceed by more than 2 percentage points—

(A) the average prime offer rate, as defined in section 1639c of this title; or

(B) if secured by a personal property loan, the average rate on a loan in connection with which insurance is provided under title I of the National Housing Act (12 U.S.C. 1702 et seq.).

(3) For purposes of paragraph (1), the term "bona fide discount points" means loan discount points which are knowingly paid by the consumer for the purpose of reducing, and which in fact result in a bona fide reduction of, the interest rate or time-price differential applicable to the mortgage.

(4) Paragraphs (1) and (2) shall not apply to discount points used to purchase an interest rate reduction unless the amount of the interest rate reduction purchased is reasonably consistent with established industry norms and practices for secondary mortgage market transactions.

§ 1603. Exempted Transactions

This subchapter does not apply to the following:

(1) Credit transactions involving extensions of credit primarily for business, commercial, or agricultural purposes, or to government or governmental agencies or instrumentalities, or to organizations.

(2) Transactions in securities or commodities accounts by a broker-dealer registered with the Securities and Exchange Commission.

(3) Credit transactions, other than those in which a security interest is or will be acquired in real property, or in personal property used or expected to be used as the principal dwelling of the consumer, in which the total amount financed exceeds $50,000.

(4) Transactions under public utility tariffs, if the Bureau determines that a State regulatory body regulates the charges for the public utility services involved, the charges for delayed payment, and any discount allowed for early payment.

(5) Transactions for which the Bureau, by rule, determines that coverage under this subchapter is not necessary to carry out the purposes of this subchapter.

(6) Repealed. Pub.L. 96221, title VI, Sec. 603(c)(3), Mar. 31, 1980, 94 Stat. 169.

(7) Loans made, insured, or guaranteed pursuant to a program authorized by title IV of the Higher Education Act of 1965 (20 U.S.C. 1070 et seq., 42 U.S.C. 2751 et seq.)

§ 1632. Form of Disclosure; Additional Information

(a) Information clearly and conspicuously disclosed; "annual percentage rate" and "finance charge"; order of disclosures and use of different terminology. Information required by this title shall be disclosed clearly and conspicuously, in accordance with regulations of the Bureau. The terms "annual percentage rate" and "finance charge" shall be disclosed more conspicuously than other terms, data, or information provided in connection with a transaction, except information relating to the identity of the creditor. Except as provided in subsection (c), regulations of the Bureau need not require that disclosures pursuant to this title be made in the order set forth in this title and, except as otherwise provided, may permit the use of terminology different from that employed in this title if it conveys substantially the same meaning.

(b) Optional information by creditor or lessor. Any creditor or lessor may supply additional information or explanation with any disclosures required under parts D and E and, except as provided in sections 1637a(b)(3) and 1638(b)(1) of this title, under this part.

(c) Tabular format required for certain disclosures under section § 1637(c).

(1) In general. The information described in paragraphs (1)(A), (3)(B)(i)(I), (4)(A), and (4)(C)(i)(I) of section 1637(c) shall be—

(A) disclosed in the form and manner which the Bureau shall prescribe by regulations; and

(B) placed in a conspicuous and prominent location on or with any written application, solicitation, or other document or paper with respect to which such disclosure is required.

(2) Tabular format.

(A) Form of table to be prescribed. In the regulations prescribed under paragraph (1)(A) of this subsection, the Bureau shall require that the disclosure of such information shall, to the extent the Bureau determines to be practicable and appropriate, be in the form of a table which—

(i) contains clear and concise headings for each item of such information; and

(ii) provides a clear and concise form for stating each item of information required to be disclosed under each such heading.

(B) Bureau discretion in prescribing order and wording of table. In prescribing the form of the table under subparagraph (A), the Bureau may—

(i) list the items required to be included in the table in a different order than the order in which such items are set forth in paragraph (1)(A) or (4)(A) of section 1637(c); and

(ii) subject to subparagraph (C), employ terminology which is different than the terminology which is employed in section 1637(c) if such terminology conveys substantially the same meaning.

(C) Grace period. Either the heading or the statement under the heading which relates to the time period referred to in section 1637(c)(1)(A)(iii) shall contain the term "grace period".

(d) Additional electronic disclosures.

(1) Posting agreements. Each creditor shall establish and maintain an Internet site on which the creditor shall post the written agreement between the creditor and the consumer for each credit card account under an open-end consumer credit plan.

(2) Creditor to provide contracts to the Bureau. Each creditor shall provide to the Bureau, in electronic format, the consumer credit card agreements that it publishes on its Internet site.

(3) Record repository. The Bureau shall establish and maintain on its publicly available Internet site a central repository of the consumer credit card agreements received from creditors pursuant to this subsection, and such agreements shall be easily accessible and retrievable by the public.

(4) Exception. This subsection shall not apply to individually negotiated changes to contractual terms, such as individually modified workouts or renegotiations of amounts owed by a consumer under an open end consumer credit plan.

(5) Regulations. The Bureau, in consultation with the other Federal banking agencies (as that term is defined in section 1681a of this title) and the Bureauf[1], may promulgate regulations to implement this subsection, including specifying the format for posting the agreements on the Internet sites of creditors and establishing exceptions to paragraphs (1) and (2), in any case in which the administrative burden outweighs the benefit of increased transparency, such as where a credit card plan has a de minimis number of consumer account holders.

§ 1637. Open End Consumer Credit Plans

(a) Required disclosures by creditor. Before opening any account under an open end consumer credit plan, the creditor shall disclose to the person to whom credit is to be extended each of the following items, to the extent applicable:

(1) The conditions under which a finance charge may be imposed, including the time period (if any) within which any credit extended may be repaid without incurring a finance charge, except that the creditor may, at his election and without disclosure, impose no such finance charge if payment is received after the termination of such time period. If no such time period is provided, the creditor shall disclose such fact.

(2) The method of determining the balance upon which a finance charge will be imposed.

(3) The method of determining the amount of the finance charge, including any minimum or fixed amount imposed as a finance charge.

(4) Where one or more periodic rates may be used to compute the finance charge, each such rate, the range of balances to which it is applicable, and the corresponding nominal annual percentage rate determined by multiplying the periodic rate by the number of periods in a year.

(5) Identification of other charges which may be imposed as part of the plan, and their method of computation, in accordance with regulations of the Bureau.

(6) In cases where the credit is or will be secured, a statement that a security interest has been or will be taken in (A) the property purchased as part of the credit transaction, or (B) property not

[1] Thus in statute. Apparently a revision error.

purchased as part of the credit transaction identified by item or type.

(7) A statement, in a form prescribed by regulations of the Bureau of the protection provided by sections 1666 and 1666i of this title to an obligor and the creditor's responsibilities under sections 1666a and 1666i of this title. With respect to one billing cycle per calendar year, at intervals of not less than six months or more than eighteen months, the creditor shall transmit such statement to each obligor to whom the creditor is required to transmit a statement pursuant to subsection (b) for such billing cycle.

(8) In the case of any account under an open end consumer credit plan which provides for any extension of credit which is secured by the consumer's principal dwelling, any information which—

(A) is required to be disclosed under section 1637a(a) of this title; and

(B) the Bureau determines is not described in any other paragraph of this subsection.

(b) Statement required with each billing cycle. The creditor of any account under an open end consumer credit plan shall transmit to the obligor, for each billing cycle at the end of which there is an outstanding balance in that account or with respect to which a finance charge is imposed, a statement setting forth each of the following items to the extent applicable:

(1) The outstanding balance in the account at the beginning of the statement period.

(2) The amount and date of each extension of credit during the period, and a brief identification, on or accompanying the statement of each extension of credit in a form prescribed by the Bureau sufficient to enable the obligor either to identify the transaction or to relate it to copies of sales vouchers or similar instruments previously furnished, except that a creditor's failure to disclose such information in accordance with this paragraph shall not be deemed a failure to comply with this chapter or this title if

(A) the creditor maintains procedures reasonably adapted to procure and provide such information, and

(B) the creditor responds to and treats any inquiry for clarification or documentation as a billing error and an erroneously billed amount under section 161. In lieu of complying with the requirements of the previous sentence, in the case of any transaction in which the creditor and seller are the same person, as defined by the Bureau, and such person's open end credit plan has fewer than 15,000 accounts, the creditor may elect to provide only the amount and date of each extension of credit during the period and the seller's name and location where the transaction took place if (A) a brief identification of the transaction has been previously furnished, and (B) the creditor responds to and treats any inquiry for clarification or documentation as a billing error and an erroneously billed amount under section 1666 of this title.

(3) The total amount credited to the account during the period.

(4) The amount of any finance charge added to the account during the period, itemized to show the amounts, if any, due to the application of percentage rates and the amount, if any, imposed as a minimum or fixed charge.

(5) Where one or more periodic rates may be used to compute the finance charge, each such rate, the range of balances to which it is applicable, and, unless the annual percentage rate (determined under section 1606(a)(2) of this title) is required to be disclosed pursuant to paragraph (6), the corresponding nominal annual percentage rate determined by multiplying the periodic rate by the number of periods in a year.

(6) Where the total finance charge exceeds 50 cents for a monthly or longer billing cycle, or the pro rata part of 50 cents for a billing cycle shorter than monthly, the total finance charge expressed as an annual percentage rate (determined under section 1606(a)(2) of this title), except that if the finance charge is the sum of two or more products of a rate times a portion of the balance, the creditor may, in lieu of disclosing a single rate for the total charge, disclose each such rate expressed as an annual percentage rate, and the part of the balance to which it is applicable.

(7) The balance on which the finance charge was computed and a statement of how the balance was determined. If the balance is determined without first deducting all credits during the period, that fact and the amount of such payments shall also be disclosed.

(8) The outstanding balance in the account at the end of the period.

(9) The date by which or the period (if any) within which, payment must be made to avoid additional finance charges, except that the creditor may, at his election and without disclosure, impose no such additional finance charge if payment is received after such date or the termination of such period.

(10) The address to be used by the creditor for the purpose of receiving billing inquiries from the obligor.

(11)(A) A written statement in the following form: "Minimum Payment Warning: Making only the minimum payment will increase the amount of interest you pay and the time it takes to repay your balance.", or such similar statement as is established by the Bureau pursuant to consumer testing.

(B) Repayment information that would apply to the outstanding balance of the consumer under the credit plan, including—

(i) the number of months (rounded to the nearest month) that it would take to pay the entire amount of that balance, if the consumer pays only the required minimum monthly payments and if no further advances are made;

(ii) the total cost to the consumer, including interest and principal payments, of paying that balance in full, if the consumer pays only the required minimum monthly payments and if no further advances are made;

(iii) the monthly payment amount that would be required for the consumer to eliminate the outstanding balance in 36 months, if no further advances are made, and the total cost to the consumer, including interest and principal payments, of paying that balance in full if the consumer pays the balance over 36 months; and

(iv) a toll-free telephone number at which the consumer may receive information about accessing credit counseling and debt management services.

(C)(i) Subject to clause (ii), in making the disclosures under subparagraph (B), the creditor shall apply the interest rate or rates in effect on the date on which the disclosure is made until the date on which the balance would be paid in full.

(ii) If the interest rate in effect on the date on which the disclosure is made is a temporary rate that will change under a contractual provision applying an index or formula for subsequent interest rate adjustment, the creditor shall apply the interest rate in effect on the date on which the disclosure is made for as long as that interest rate will apply under that contractual provision, and then apply an interest rate based on the index or formula in effect on the applicable billing date.

(D) All of the information described in subparagraph (B) shall—

(i) be disclosed in the form and manner which the Bureau shall prescribe, by regulation, and in a manner that avoids duplication; and

(ii) be placed in a conspicuous and prominent location on the billing statement.

(E) In the regulations prescribed under subparagraph (D), the Bureau shall require that the disclosure of such information shall be in the form of a table that—

(i) contains clear and concise headings for each item of such information; and

(ii) provides a clear and concise form stating each item of information required to be disclosed under each such heading.

(F) In prescribing the form of the table under subparagraph (E), the Bureau shall require that—

(i) all of the information in the table, and not just a reference to the table, be placed on the billing statement, as required by this paragraph; and

(ii) the items required to be included in the table shall be listed in the order in which such items are set forth in subparagraph (B).

(G) In prescribing the form of the table under subparagraph (D), the Bureau shall employ terminology which is different than the terminology which is employed in subparagraph (B), if such terminology is more easily understood and conveys substantially the same meaning.

(12) Requirements relating to late payment deadlines and penalties.

(A) Late payment deadline required to be disclosed. In the case of a credit card account under an open end consumer credit plan under which a late fee or charge may be imposed due to the failure of the obligor to make payment on or before the due date for such payment, the periodic statement required under subsection (b) with respect to the account shall include, in a conspicuous location on the billing statement, the date on which the payment is due or, if different, the date on which a late payment fee will be charged, together with the amount of the fee or charge to be imposed if payment is made after that date.

(B) Disclosure of increase in interest rates for late payments. If 1 or more late payments under an open end consumer credit plan may result in an increase in the annual percentage rate applicable to the account, the statement required under subsection (b) with respect to the account shall include conspicuous notice of such fact, together with the applicable penalty annual percentage rate, in close proximity to the disclosure required under subparagraph (A) of the date on which payment is due under the terms of the account.

(C) Payments at local branches. If the creditor, in the case of a credit card account referred to in subparagraph (A), is a financial institution which maintains branches or offices at which payments on any such account are accepted from the obligor in person, the date on which the obligor makes a payment on the account at such branch or office shall be considered to be the date on which the payment is made for purposes of determining whether a late fee or charge may be imposed due to the failure of the obligor to make payment on or before the due date for such payment.

(c) Disclosure in credit and charge card applications and solicitations.

(1) Direct mail applications and solicitations.

(A) Information in tabular format. Any application to open a credit card account for any person under an open end consumer credit plan, or a solicitation to open such an account without requiring an application, that is mailed to consumers shall disclose the following information, subject to subsection (e) and section 1632(c) of this title:

(i) Annual percentage rates.

(I) Each annual percentage rate applicable to extensions of credit under such credit plan.

(II) Where an extension of credit is subject to a variable rate, the fact that the rate is variable, the annual percentage rate in effect at the time of the mailing, and how the rate is determined.

(III) Where more than one rate applies, the range of balances to which each rate applies.

(ii) Annual and other fees.

(I) Any annual fee, other periodic fee, or membership fee imposed for the issuance or availability of a credit card, including any account maintenance fee or other charge imposed based on activity or inactivity for the account during the billing cycle.

(II) Any minimum finance charge imposed for each period during which any extension of credit which is subject to a finance charge is outstanding.

(III) Any transaction charge imposed in connection with use of the card to purchase goods or services.

(iii) Grace period.

(I) The date by which or the period within which any credit extended under such credit plan for purchases of goods or services must be repaid to avoid incurring a finance charge, and, if no such period is offered, such fact shall be clearly stated.

(II) If the length of such "grace period" varies, the card issuer may disclose the range of days in the grace period, the minimum number of days in the grace period, or the average number of days in the grace period, if the disclosure is identified as such.

(iv) Balance calculation method.

(I) The name of the balance calculation method used in determining the balance on which the finance charge is computed if the method used has been defined by the Bureau, or a detailed explanation of the balance calculation method used if the method has not been so defined.

(II) In prescribing regulations to carry out this clause, the Bureau shall define and name not more than the 5 balance calculation methods determined by the Bureau to be the most commonly used methods.

(B) Other information. In addition to the information required to be disclosed under subparagraph (A), each application or solicitation to which such subparagraph applies shall disclose clearly and conspicuously the following information, subject to subsections (e) and (f):

(i) Cash advance fee. Any fee imposed for an extension of credit in the form of cash.

(ii) Late fee. Any fee imposed for a late payment.

(iii) Over-the-limit fee. Any fee imposed in connection with an extension of credit in excess of the amount of credit authorized to be extended with respect to such account.

(2) Telephone solicitations.

(A) In general. In any telephone solicitation to open a credit card account for any person under an open end consumer credit plan, the person making the solicitation shall orally disclose the information described in paragraph (1)(A).

(B) Exception. Subparagraph (A) shall not apply to any telephone solicitation if—

(i) the credit card issuer—

(I) does not impose any fee described in paragraph (1)(A)(ii)(I); or

(II) does not impose any fee in connection with telephone solicitations unless the consumer signifies acceptance by using the card;

(ii) the card issuer discloses clearly and conspicuously in writing the information described in paragraph (1) within 30 days after the consumer requests the card, but in no event later than the date of delivery of the card; and

(iii) the card issuer discloses clearly and conspicuously that the consumer is not obligated to accept the card or account and the consumer will not be obligated to pay any of the fees or charges disclosed unless the consumer elects to accept the card or account by using the card.

(3) Applications and solicitations by other means.

(A) In general. Any application to open a credit card account for any person under an open end consumer credit plan, and any solicitation to open such an account without requiring an application, that is made available to the public or contained in catalogs, magazines, or other publications shall meet the disclosure requirements of subparagraph (B), (C), or (D).

(B) Specific information. An application or solicitation described in subparagraph (A) meets the requirement of this subparagraph if such application or solicitation contains—

(i) the information—

(I) described in paragraph (1)(A) in the form required under section 1632(c) of this title, subject to subsection (e), and

(II) described in paragraph (1)(B) in a clear and conspicuous form, subject to subsections (e) and (f);

(ii) a statement, in a conspicuous and prominent location on the application or solicitation, that—

(I) the information is accurate as of the date the application or solicitation was printed;

(II) the information contained in the application or solicitation is subject to change after such date; and

(III) the applicant should contact the creditor for information on any change in the information contained in the application or solicitation since it was printed;

(iii) a clear and conspicuous disclosure of the date the application or solicitation was printed; and

(iv) a disclosure, in a conspicuous and prominent location on the application or solicitation, of a toll-free telephone number or a mailing address at which the applicant may contact the creditor to obtain any change in the information provided in the application or solicitation since it was printed.

(C) General information without any specific term. An application or solicitation described in subparagraph (A) meets the requirement of this subparagraph if such application or solicitation—

(i) contains a statement, in a conspicuous and prominent location on the application or solicitation, that—

(I) there are costs associated with the use of credit cards; and

(II) the applicant may contact the creditor to request disclosure of specific information of such costs by calling a toll-free telephone number or by writing to an address, specified in the application;

(ii) contains a disclosure, in a conspicuous and prominent location on the application or solicitation, of a toll-free telephone number and a mailing address at which the applicant may contact the creditor to obtain such information; and

(iii) does not contain any of the items described in paragraph (1).

(D) Applications or solicitations containing subsection (a) disclosures. An application or solicitation meets the requirement of this subparagraph if it contains, or is accompanied by—

(i) the disclosures required by paragraphs (1) through (6) of subsection (a);

(ii) the disclosures required by subparagraphs (A) and (B) of paragraph (1) of this subsection included clearly and conspiciously (except that the provisions of section 1632(c) of this title shall not apply); and

(iii) a toll-free telephone number or a mailing address at which the applicant may contact the creditor to obtain any change in the information provided.

(E) Prompt response to information requests. Upon receipt of a request for any of the information referred to in subparagraph (B), (C), or (D), the card issuer or the agent of such issuer shall promptly disclose all of the information described in paragraph (1).

(4) Charge card applications and solicitations.

(A) In general. Any application or solicitation to open a charge card account shall disclose clearly and conspicuously the following information in the form required by section 1632(c) of this title, subject to subsection (e):

(i) Any annual fee, other periodic fee, or membership fee imposed for the issuance or availability of the charge card, including any account maintenance fee or other charge imposed based on activity or inactivity for the account during the billing cycle.

(ii) Any transaction charge imposed in connection with use of the card to purchase goods or services.

(iii) A statement that charges incurred by use of the charge card are due and payable upon receipt of a periodic statement rendered for such charge card account.

(B) Other information. In addition to the information required to be disclosed under subparagraph (A), each written application or solicitation to which such subparagraph applies shall disclose clearly and conspicuously the following information, subject to subsections (e) and (f):

(i) Cash advance fee. Any fee imposed for an extension of credit in the form of cash.

(ii) Late fee. Any fee imposed for a late payment.

(iii) Over-the-limit fee. Any fee imposed in connection with an extension of credit in excess of the amount of credit authorized to be extended with respect to such account.

(C) Applications and solicitations by other means. Any application to open a charge card account, and any solicitation to open such an account without requiring an application, that is made available to the public or contained in catalogs, magazines, or other publications shall contain—

(i) the information—

(I) described in subparagraph (A) in the form required under section 1632(c) of this title, subject to subsection (e), and

(II) described in subparagraph (B) in a clear and conspicuous form, subject to subsections (e) and (f);

(ii) a statement, in a conspicuous and prominent location on the application or solicitation, that—

(I) the information is accurate as of the date the application or solicitation was printed;

(II) the information contained in the application or solicitation is subject to change after such date; and

(III) the applicant should contact the creditor for information on any change in the information contained in the application or solicitation since it was printed;

(iii) a clear and conspicuous disclosure of the date the application or solicitation was printed; and

(iv) a disclosure, in a conspicuous and prominent location on the application or solicitation, of a toll-free telephone number or a mailing address at which the applicant may contact the creditor to obtain any change in the information provided in the application or solicitation since it was printed.

(D) Issuers of charge cards which provide access to open end consumer credit plans. If a charge card permits the card holder to receive an extension of credit under an open end consumer credit plan, which is not maintained by the charge card issuer, the charge card issuer may provide the information described in subparagraphs (A) and (B) in the form required by such subparagraphs in lieu of the information required to be provided under paragraph (1), (2), or (3) with respect to any credit extended under such plan, if the charge card issuer discloses clearly and conspicuously to the consumer in the application or solicitation that—

(i) the charge card issuer will make an independent decision as to whether to issue the card;

(ii) the charge card may arrive before the decision is made with respect to an extension of credit under an open end consumer credit plan; and

(iii) approval by the charge card issuer does not constitute approval by the issuer of the extension of credit.

The information required to be disclosed under paragraph (1) shall be provided to the charge card holder by the creditor which maintains such open end consumer credit plan before the first extension of credit under such plan.

(E) Charge card defined. For the purposes of this subsection, the term "charge card" means a card, plate, or other single credit device that may be used from time to time to obtain credit which is not subject to a finance charge.

(5) Regulatory authority of the Bureau. The Bureau may, by regulation, require the disclosure of information in addition to that otherwise required by this subsection or subsection (d), and modify any disclosure of information required by this subsection or subsection (d), in any application to open a credit card account for any person under an open end consumer credit plan or any application to open a charge card account for any person, or a solicitation to open any such account without requiring an application, if the Bureau determines that such action is necessary to carry out the purposes of, or prevent evasions of, any paragraph of this subsection.

(6) Additional notice concerning "introductory rates".

(A) In general. Except as provided in subparagraph (B), an application or solicitation to open a credit card account and all promotional materials accompanying such application or solicitation for which a disclosure is required under paragraph (1), and that offers a temporary annual percentage rate of interest, shall—

(i) use the term "introductory" in immediate proximity to each listing of the temporary annual percentage rate applicable to such account, which term shall appear clearly and conspicuously;

(ii) if the annual percentage rate of interest that will apply after the end of the temporary rate period will be a fixed rate, state in a clear and conspicuous manner in a prominent location closely proximate to the first listing of the temporary annual percentage rate (other than a listing of the temporary annual percentage rate in the tabular format described in section 1632(c) of this title), the time period in which the introductory period will end and the annual percentage rate that will apply after the end of the introductory period; and

(iii) if the annual percentage rate that will apply after the end of the temporary rate period will vary in accordance with an index, state in a clear and conspicuous manner in a prominent location closely proximate to the first listing of the temporary annual percentage rate (other than a listing in the tabular format prescribed by section 1632(c) of this title), the time period in which the introductory period will end and the rate that will apply after that, based on an annual percentage rate that was in effect within 60 days before the date of mailing the application or solicitation.

(B) Exception. Clauses (ii) and (iii) of subparagraph (A) do not apply with respect to any listing of a temporary annual percentage rate on an envelope or other enclosure in which an application or solicitation to open a credit card account is mailed.

(C) Conditions for introductory rates. An application or solicitation to open a credit card account for which a disclosure is required under paragraph (1), and that offers a temporary annual percentage rate of interest shall, if that rate of interest is revocable under any circumstance or upon any event, clearly and conspicuously disclose, in a prominent manner on or with such application or solicitation—

(i) a general description of the circumstances that may result in the revocation of the temporary annual percentage rate; and

(ii) if the annual percentage rate that will apply upon the revocation of the temporary annual percentage rate—

(I) will be a fixed rate, the annual percentage rate that will apply upon the revocation of the temporary annual percentage rate; or

(II) will vary in accordance with an index, the rate that will apply after the temporary rate, based on an annual percentage rate that was in effect within 60 days before the date of mailing the application or solicitation.

(D) Definitions. In this paragraph—

(i) the terms "temporary annual percentage rate of interest" and "temporary annual percentage rate" mean any rate of interest applicable to a credit card account for an introductory period of less than 1 year, if that rate is less than an annual percentage rate that was in effect within 60 days before the date of mailing the application or solicitation; and

(ii) the term "introductory period" means the maximum time period for which the temporary annual percentage rate may be applicable.

(E) Relation to other disclosure requirements. Nothing in this paragraph may be construed to supersede subsection (a) of section 1632 of this title, or any disclosure required by paragraph (1) or any other provision of this subsection.

(7) Internet-based solicitations.

(A) In general. In any solicitation to open a credit card account for any person under an open end consumer credit plan using the Internet or other interactive computer service, the person making the solicitation shall clearly and conspicuously disclose—

(i) the information described in subparagraphs (A) and (B) of paragraph (1); and

(ii) the information described in paragraph (6).

(B) Form of disclosure. The disclosures required by subparagraph (A) shall be—

(i) readily accessible to consumers in close proximity to the solicitation to open a credit card account; and

(ii) updated regularly to reflect the current policies, terms, and fee amounts applicable to the credit card account.

(C) Definitions. For purposes of this paragraph—

(i) the term "Internet" means the international computer network of both Federal and non-Federal interoperable packet switched data networks; and

(ii) the term "interactive computer service" means any information service, system, or access software provider that provides or enables computer access by multiple users to a computer server, including specifically a service or system that provides access to the Internet and such systems operated or services offered by libraries or educational institutions.

(8) Applications from underage consumers.

(A) Prohibition on issuance. No credit card may be issued to, or open end consumer credit plan established by or on behalf of, a consumer who has not attained the age of 21, unless the consumer has submitted a written application to the card issuer that meets the requirements of subparagraph (B).

(B) Application requirements. An application to open a credit card account by a consumer who has not attained the age of 21 as of the date of submission of the application shall require—

(i) the signature of a cosigner, including the parent, legal guardian, spouse, or any other individual who has attained the age of 21 having a means to repay debts incurred by the consumer in connection with the account, indicating joint liability for debts incurred by the consumer in connection with the account before the consumer has attained the age of 21; or

(ii) submission by the consumer of financial information, including through an application, indicating an independent means of repaying any obligation arising from the proposed extension of credit in connection with the account.

(C) Safe harbor. The Bureau shall promulgate regulations providing standards that, if met, would satisfy the requirements of subparagraph (B)(ii).

(d) Disclosure prior to renewal.

(1) In general. A card issuer that has changed or amended any term of the account since the last renewal that has not been previously disclosed or that imposes any fee described in subsection (c)(1)(A)(ii)(I) or (c)(4)(A)(i) shall transmit to a consumer at least 30 days prior to the scheduled renewal date of the consumer's credit or charge card account a clear and conspicuous disclosure of—

(A) the date by which, the month by which, or the billing period at the close of which, the account will expire if not renewed;

(B) the information described in subsection (c)(1)(A) or (c)(4)(A) that would apply if the account were renewed, subject to subsection (e); and

(C) the method by which the consumer may terminate continued credit availability under the account.

(2) Short-term renewals. The Bureau may by regulation provide for fewer disclosures than are required by paragraph (1) in the case of an account which is renewable for a period of less than 6 months.

(e) Other rules for disclosures under subsections (c) and (d).

(1) Fees determined on the basis of a percentage. If the amount of any fee required to be disclosed under subsection (c) or (d) is determined on the basis of a percentage of another amount, the percentage used in making such determination and the identification of the amount against which such percentage is applied shall be disclosed in lieu of the amount of such fee.

(2) Disclosure only of fees actually imposed. If a credit or charge card issuer does not impose any fee required to be disclosed under any provision of subsection (c) or (d), such provision shall not apply with respect to such issuer.

(f) Disclosure of range of certain fees which vary by State allowed. If the amount of any fee required to be disclosed by a credit or charge card issuer under paragraph (1)(B), (3)(B)(i)(II), (4)(B), or (4)(C)(i)(II) of subsection (c) varies from State to State, the card issuer may disclose the range of such fees for purposes of subsection (c) in lieu of the amount for each applicable State, if such disclosure includes a statement that the amount of such fee varies from State to State.

(g) Insurance in connection with certain open end credit card plans.

(1) Change in insurance carrier. Whenever a card issuer that offers any guarantee or insurance for repayment of all or part of the outstanding balance of an open end credit card plan proposes to change the person providing that guarantee or insurance, the card issuer shall send each insured consumer written notice of the proposed change not less than 30 days prior to the change, including notice of any increase in the rate or substantial decrease in coverage or service which will result from such change. Such notice may be included on or with the monthly statement provided to the consumer prior to the month in which the proposed change would take effect.

(2) Notice of new insurance coverage. In any case in which a proposed change described in paragraph (1) occurs, the insured consumer shall be given the name and address of the new guarantor or insurer and a copy of the policy or group certificate containing the basic terms and conditions, including the premium rate to be charged.

(3) Right to discontinue guarantee or insurance. The notices required under paragraphs (1) and (2) shall each include a statement that the consumer has the option to discontinue the insurance or guarantee.

(4) No preemption of State law. No provision of this subsection shall be construed as superseding any provision of State law which is applicable to the regulation of insurance.

(5) Bureau definition of substantial decrease in coverage or service. The Bureau shall define, in regulations, what constitutes a "substantial decrease in coverage or service" for purposes of paragraph (1).

(h) Prohibition on certain actions for failure to incur finance charges. A creditor of an account under an open end consumer credit plan may not terminate an account prior to its expiration date solely because the consumer has not incurred finance charges on the account. Nothing in this subsection shall prohibit a creditor from terminating an account for inactivity in 3 or more consecutive months.

(i) Advance notice of rate increase and other changes required.

(1) Advance notice of increase in interest rate required. In the case of any credit card account under an open end consumer credit plan, a creditor shall provide a written notice of an increase in an annual percentage rate (except in the case of an increase described in paragraph (1), (2), or (3) of section 1666i–1(b) of this title) not later than 45 days prior to the effective date of the increase.

(2) Advance notice of other significant changes required. In the case of any credit card account under an open end consumer credit plan, a creditor shall provide a written notice of any significant change, as determined by rule of the Bureau, in the terms (including an increase in any fee or finance charge, other than as provided in paragraph (1)) of the cardholder agreement between the creditor and the obligor, not later than 45 days prior to the effective date of the change.

(3) Notice of right to cancel. Each notice required by paragraph (1) or (2) shall be made in a clear and conspicuous manner, and shall contain a brief statement of the right of the obligor to cancel the account pursuant to rules established by the Bureau before the effective date of the subject rate increase or other change.

(4) Rule of construction. Closure or cancellation of an account by the obligor shall not constitute a default under an existing cardholder agreement, and shall not trigger an obligation to immediately repay the obligation in full or through a method that is less beneficial to the obligor than one of the methods described in section 1666i–1(c)(2) of this title, or the imposition of any other penalty or fee.

(j) Prohibition on penalties for on-time payments.

(1) Prohibition on double-cycle billing and penalties for on-time payments. Except as provided in paragraph (2), a creditor may not impose any finance charge on a credit card account under an open end consumer credit plan as a result of the loss of any time period provided by the creditor within which the obligor may repay any portion of the credit extended without incurring a finance charge, with respect to—

(A) any balances for days in billing cycles that precede the most recent billing cycle; or

(B) any balances or portions thereof in the current billing cycle that were repaid within such time period.

(2) Exceptions. Paragraph (1) does not apply to—

(A) any adjustment to a finance charge as a result of the resolution of a dispute; or

(B) any adjustment to a finance charge as a result of the return of a payment for insufficient funds.

(k) Opt-in required for over-the-limit transactions if fees are imposed.

(1) In general. In the case of any credit card account under an open end consumer credit plan under which an over-the-limit fee may be imposed by the creditor for any extension of credit in excess of the amount of credit authorized to be extended under such account, no such fee shall be charged, unless the consumer has expressly elected to permit the creditor, with respect to such account, to complete transactions involving the extension of credit under such account in excess of the amount of credit authorized.

(2) Disclosure by creditor. No election by a consumer under paragraph (1) shall take effect unless the consumer, before making such election, received a notice from the creditor of any over-the-limit fee in the form and manner, and at the time, determined by the Bureau. If the consumer makes the election referred to in paragraph (1), the creditor shall provide notice to the consumer of the right to revoke the election, in the form prescribed by the Bureau, in any periodic statement that includes notice of the imposition of an over-the-limit fee during the period covered by the statement.

(3) Form of election. A consumer may make or revoke the election referred to in paragraph (1) orally, electronically, or in writing, pursuant to regulations prescribed by the Bureau. The Bureau shall prescribe regulations to ensure that the same options are available for both making and revoking such election.

(4) Time of election. A consumer may make the election referred to in paragraph (1) at any time, and such election shall be effective until the election is revoked in the manner prescribed under paragraph (3).

(5) Regulations. The Bureau shall prescribe regulations—

(A) governing disclosures under this subsection; and

(B) that prevent unfair or deceptive acts or practices in connection with the manipulation of credit limits designed to increase over-the-limit fees or other penalty fees.

(6) Rule of construction. Nothing in this subsection shall be construed to prohibit a creditor from completing an over-the-limit transaction, provided that a consumer who has not made a valid election under paragraph (1) is not charged an over-the-limit fee for such transaction.

(7) Restriction on fees charged for an over-the-limit transaction. With respect to a credit card account under an open end consumer credit plan, an over-the-limit fee may be imposed only once during a billing cycle if the credit limit on the account is exceeded, and an over-the-limit fee, with respect to such excess credit, may be imposed only once in each of the 2 subsequent billing cycles, unless the consumer has obtained an additional extension of credit in excess of such credit limit during any such subsequent cycle or the consumer reduces the outstanding balance below the credit limit as of the end of such billing cycle.

(l) Limit on fees related to method of payment. With respect to a credit card account under an open end consumer credit plan, the creditor may not impose a separate fee to allow the obligor to repay an extension of credit or finance charge, whether such repayment is made by mail, electronic transfer, telephone authorization, or other means, unless such payment involves an expedited service by a service representative of the creditor.

(m) Use of term "fixed rate". With respect to the terms of any credit card account under an open end consumer credit plan, the term "fixed", when appearing in conjunction with a reference to the annual percentage rate or interest rate applicable with respect to such account, may only be used to refer to an annual percentage rate or interest rate that will not change or vary for any reason over the period specified clearly and conspicuously in the terms of the account.

(n) Standards applicable to initial issuance of subprime or "fee harvester" cards.

(1) In general. If the terms of a credit card account under an open end consumer credit plan require the payment of any fees (other than any late fee, over-the-limit fee, or fee for a payment returned for insufficient funds) by the consumer in the first year during which the account is opened in an aggregate amount in excess of 25 percent of the total amount of credit authorized under the account when the account is opened, no payment of any fees (other than any late fee, over-the-limit fee, or fee for a payment returned for insufficient funds) may be made from the credit made available under the terms of the account.

(2) Rule of construction. No provision of this subsection may be construed as authorizing any imposition or payment of advance fees otherwise prohibited by any provision of law.

(o) Due dates for credit card accounts.

(1) In general. The payment due date for a credit card account under an open end consumer credit plan shall be the same day each month.

(2) Weekend or holiday due dates. If the payment due date for a credit card account under an open end consumer credit plan is a day on which the creditor does not receive or accept payments by mail (including weekends and holidays), the creditor may not treat a payment received on the next business day as late for any purpose.

(p) Parental approval required to increase credit lines for accounts for which parent is jointly liable. No increase may be made in the amount of credit authorized to be extended under a credit card account for which a parent, legal guardian, or spouse of the consumer, or any other individual has assumed joint liability for debts incurred by the consumer in connection with the account before the consumer attains the age of 21, unless that parent, guardian, or spouse approves in writing, and assumes joint liability for, such increase.

(q) [reserved]

(r) College card agreements.

(1) Definitions. For purposes of this subsection, the following definitions shall apply:

(A) College affinity card. The term "college affinity card" means a credit card issued by a credit card issuer under an open end consumer credit plan in conjunction with an agreement between the issuer and an institution of higher education, or an alumni organization or foundation affiliated with or related to such institution, under which such cards are issued to college students who have an affinity with such institution, organization and—

(i) the creditor has agreed to donate a portion of the proceeds of the credit card to the institution, organization, or foundation (including a lump sum or 1-time payment of money for access);

(ii) the creditor has agreed to offer discounted terms to the consumer; or

(iii) the credit card bears the name, emblem, mascot, or logo of such institution, organization, or foundation, or other words, pictures, or symbols readily identified with such institution, organization, or foundation.

(B) College student credit card account. The term "college student credit card account" means a credit card account under an open end consumer credit plan established or maintained for or on behalf of any college student.

(C) College student. The term "college student" means an individual who is a full-time or a part-time student attending an institution of higher education.

(D) Institution of higher education. The term "institution of higher education" has the same meaning as in section 101 and 102 of the Higher Education Act of 1965 (20 U.S.C. 1001 and 1002).

(2) Reports by creditors.

(A) In general. Each creditor shall submit an annual report to the Bureau containing the terms and conditions of all business, marketing, and promotional agreements and college affinity card agreements with an institution of higher education, or an alumni organization or foundation affiliated with or related to such institution, with respect to any college student credit card issued to a college student at such institution.

(B) Details of report. The information required to be reported under subparagraph (A) includes—

(i) any memorandum of understanding between or among a creditor, an institution of higher education, an alumni association, or foundation that directly or indirectly relates to any aspect of any agreement referred to in such subparagraph or controls or directs any obligations or distribution of benefits between or among any such entities;

(ii) the amount of any payments from the creditor to the institution, organization, or foundation during the period covered by the report, and the precise terms of any agreement under which such amounts are determined; and

(iii) the number of credit card accounts covered by any such agreement that were opened during the period covered by the report, and the total number of credit card accounts covered by the agreement that were outstanding at the end of such period.

(C) Aggregation by institution. The information required to be reported under subparagraph (A) shall be aggregated with respect to each institution of higher education or alumni organization or foundation affiliated with or related to such institution.

(D) Initial report. The initial report required under subparagraph (A) shall be submitted to the Bureau before the end of the 9-month period beginning on the date of enactment of this subsection [enacted May 22, 2009].

(3) Reports by Bureau. The Bureau shall submit to the Congress, and make available to the public, an annual report that lists the information concerning credit card agreements submitted to the Bureau under paragraph (2) by each institution of higher education, alumni organization, or foundation.

§ 1640. Civil Liability

(a) Individual or class action for damages; amount of award; factors determining amount of award. Except as otherwise provided in this section, any creditor who fails to comply with any requirement imposed under this part, including any requirement under section 1635 of this title, subsection (f) or (g) of section 1641 of this title, or part D or E of this subchapter with respect to any person is liable to such person in an amount equal to the sum of—

(1) any actual damage sustained by such person as a result of the failure;

(2)(A)(i) in the case of an individual action twice the amount of any finance charge in connection with the transaction,

(ii) in the case of an individual action relating to a consumer lease under part E of this subchapter, 25 per centum of the total amount of monthly payments under the lease, except that the liability under this subparagraph shall not be less than $200 nor greater than $2,000,

(iii) in the case of an individual action relating to an open end consumer credit plan that is not secured by real property or a dwelling, twice the amount of any finance charge in connection with the transaction, with a minimum of $500 and a maximum of $5,000, or such higher amount as may be appropriate in the case of an established pattern or practice of such failures; or

(iv) in the case of an individual action relating to a credit transaction not under an open end credit plan that is secured by real property or a dwelling, not less than $400 or greater than $4,000; or

(B) in the case of a class action, such amount as the court may allow, except that as to each member of the class no minimum recovery shall be applicable, and the total recovery under this subparagraph in any class action or series of class actions arising out of the same failure to comply by the same creditor shall not be more than the lesser of $1,000,000 or 1 per centum of the net worth of the creditor;

(3) in the case of any successful action to enforce the foregoing liability or in any action in which a person is determined to have a right of rescission under section 1635 or 1638(e)(7) of this title, the costs of the action, together with a reasonable attorney's fee as determined by the court; and

(4) in the case of a failure to comply with any requirement under section 1639 of this title, paragraph (1) or (2) of section 1639b(c) of this title, or section 1639c(a) of this title, an amount equal to the sum of all finance charges and fees paid by the consumer, unless the creditor demonstrates that the failure to comply is not material.

In determining the amount of award in any class action, the court shall consider, among other relevant factors, the amount of any actual damages awarded, the frequency and persistence of failures of compliance by the creditor, the resources of the creditor, the number of persons adversely affected, and the extent to which the creditor's failure of compliance was intentional. In connection with the disclosures referred to in subsections (a) and (b) of section 1637 of this title, a creditor shall have a liability determined under paragraph (2) only for failing to comply with the requirements of section 1635 of this title, 1637(a) of this title, or any of paragraphs (4) through (13) of section 1637(b) of this title, or for failing to comply with disclosure requirements under State law for any term or item that the Bureau has determined to be substantially the same in meaning under section 1610(a)(2) of this title as any of the terms or items referred to in section 1637(a) of this title, or any of paragraphs (4) through (13) of section 1637(b) of this title. In connection with the disclosures referred to in subsection (c) or (d) of section 1637 of this title, a card issuer shall have a liability under this section only to a cardholder who pays a fee described in section 1637(c)(1)(A)(ii)(I) or section 1637(c)(4)(A)(i) of this title or who uses the credit card or charge card. In connection with the disclosures referred to in section 1638 of this title, a creditor shall have a liability determined under paragraph (2) only for failing to comply with the requirements of section 1635 of this title, of paragraph (2) (insofar as it requires a disclosure of the "amount financed"), (3), (4), (5), (6), or (9) of section 1638(a) of this title, or section 1638(b)(2)(C)(ii) of this title, of subparagraphs (A), (B), (D), (F), or (J) of section 1638(e)(2) of this title (for purposes of paragraph (2) or (4) of section 1638(e) of this title), or paragraph (4)(C), (6), (7), or (8) of section 1638(e) of this title, or for failing to comply with disclosure requirements under State law for any term which the Bureau has determined to be substantially the same in meaning under section 1610(a)(2) of this title as any of the terms referred to in any of those paragraphs of section 1638(a) of this title or section 1638(b)(2)(C)(ii) of this title. With respect to any failure to make disclosures required under this part or part D or E of this subchapter, liability shall be imposed only upon the creditor required to make disclosure, except as provided in section 1641 of this title.

(b) Correction of errors. A creditor or assignee has no liability under this section or section 1607 of this title or section 1611 of this title for any failure to comply with any requirement imposed under this part or part E of this subchapter, if within sixty days after discovering an error, whether pursuant to a final written examination report or notice issued under section 1607(e)(1) of this title or through the creditor's or assignee's own procedures, and prior to the institution of an action under this section or the receipt of written notice of the error from the obligor, the creditor or assignee notifies the person concerned of the error and makes whatever adjustments in the appropriate account are necessary to assure that the person will not be required to pay an amount in excess of the charge actually disclosed, or the dollar equivalent of the annual percentage rate actually disclosed, whichever is lower.

(c) Unintentional violations; bona fide errors. A creditor or assignee may not be held liable in any action brought under this section or section 1635 of this title for a violation of this subchapter if the creditor or assignee shows by a preponderance of evidence that the violation was not intentional and resulted from a bona fide error notwithstanding the maintenance of procedures reasonably adapted to avoid any such error. Examples of a bona fide error include, but are not limited to, clerical, calculation, computer malfunction and programing, and printing errors, except that an error of legal judgment with respect to a person's obligations under this subchapter is not a bona fide error.

(d) Liability in transaction or lease involving multiple obligors. When there are multiple obligors in a consumer credit transaction or consumer lease, there shall be no more than one recovery of damages under subsection (a)(2) of this section for a violation of this subchapter.

(e) Jurisdiction of courts; limitations on actions; State attorney general enforcement. Except as provided in the subsequent sentence, any action under this section may be brought in any United States district court, or in any other court of competent jurisdiction, within one year from the date of the occurrence of the violation involving a private education loan (as that term is defined in section 1650(a) of this title), 1 year from the date on which the first regular payment of principal is due under the loan. Any action under this section with respect to any violation of section 1639, 1639b, or 1639c of this title may be brought in any United States district court, or in any other court of competent jurisdiction, before the end of the 3-year period beginning on the date of the occurrence of the violation. This subsection does not bar a person from asserting a violation of this subchapter in an action to collect the debt which was brought more than one year from the date of the occurrence of the violation as a matter of defense by recoupment or set-off in such action, except as otherwise provided by State law. An action to enforce a violation of section 1639, 1639b, 1639c, 1639d, 1639e, 1639f, 1639g, or 1639h of this title may also be brought by the appropriate State attorney general in any appropriate United States district court, or any other court of competent jurisdiction, not later than 3 years after the date on which the violation occurs. The State attorney general shall provide prior written notice of any such civil action to the Federal agency responsible for enforcement under section 1607 of this title and shall provide the agency with a copy of the complaint. If prior notice is not feasible, the State attorney general shall provide notice to such agency immediately upon instituting the action. The Federal agency may—

(1) intervene in the action;

(2) upon intervening—

(A) remove the action to the appropriate United States district court, if it was not originally brought there; and

(B) be heard on all matters arising in the action; and

(3) file a petition for appeal.

(f) Good faith compliance with rule, regulation, or interpretation of Bureau or with interpretation or approval of duly authorized official or employee of Federal Reserve System. No provision of this section, section 1607(b) of this title, section 1607(c) of this title, section 1607(e) of this title, or section 1611 of this title imposing any liability shall apply to any act done or omitted in good faith in conformity with any rule, regulation, or interpretation thereof by the Bureau or in conformity with any interpretation or approval by an official or employee of the Federal Reserve System duly authorized by the Bureau to issue such interpretations or approvals under such procedures as the Bureau may prescribe therefor, notwithstanding that after such act or omission has occurred, such rule, regulation, interpretation, or approval is amended, rescinded, or determined by judicial or other authority to be invalid for any reason.

(g) Recovery for multiple failures to disclose. The multiple failure to disclose to any person any information required under this part or part D or E of this subchapter to be disclosed in connection with a single account under an open end consumer credit plan, other single consumer credit sale, consumer loan, consumer lease, or other extension of consumer credit, shall entitle the person to a single recovery under this section but continued failure to disclose after a recovery has been granted shall give rise to rights to additional recoveries. This subsection does not bar any remedy permitted by section 1635 of this title.

(h) Offset from amount owed to creditor or assignee; rights of defaulting consumer. A person may not take any action to offset any amount for which a creditor or assignee is potentially liable to such person under subsection (a)(2) of this section against any amount owed by such person, unless the amount of the creditor's or assignee's liability under this subchapter has been determined by judgment of a court of competent jurisdiction in an action of which such person was a party. This subsection does not bar a consumer then in default on the obligation from asserting a violation of this subchapter as an original action, or as a defense or counterclaim to an action to collect amounts owed by the consumer brought by a person liable under this subchapter.

(i) Class action moratorium

(1) In general. During the period beginning on May 18, 1995, and ending on October 1, 1995, no court may enter any order certifying any class in any action under this subchapter—

(A) which is brought in connection with any credit transaction not under an open end credit plan which is secured by a first lien on real property or a dwelling and constitutes a refinancing or consolidation of an existing extension of credit; and

(B) which is based on the alleged failure of a creditor—

(i) to include a charge actually incurred (in connection with the transaction) in the finance charge disclosed pursuant to section 1638 of this title;

(ii) to properly make any other disclosure required under section 1638 of this title as a result of the failure described in clause (i); or

(iii) to provide proper notice of rescission rights under section 1635(a) of this title due to the selection by the creditor of the incorrect form from among the model forms prescribed by the Bureau or from among forms based on such model forms.

(2) Exceptions for certain alleged violations. Paragraph (1) shall not apply with respect to any action—

(A) described in clause (i) or (ii) of paragraph (1)(B), if the amount disclosed as the finance charge results in an annual percentage rate that exceeds the tolerance provided in section 1606(c) of this title; or

(B) described in paragraph (1)(B)(iii), if—

(i) no notice relating to rescission rights under section 1635(a) of this title was provided in any form; or

(ii) proper notice was not provided for any reason other than the reason described in such paragraph.

(j) Private educational lender. A private educational lender (as that term is defined in section 1650(a) of this title) has no liability under this section for failure to comply with section 1638(e)(3) of this title).

(k) Defenses to foreclosure.

(1) In general. Notwithstanding any other provision of law, when a creditor, assignee, or other holder of a residential mortgage loan or anyone acting on behalf of such creditor, assignee, or holder, initiates a judicial or nonjudicial foreclosure of the residential mortgage loan, or any other action to collect the debt in connection with such loan, a consumer may assert a violation by a creditor of paragraph (1) or (2) of section 1639b(c) of this title, or of section 1639c(a) of this title, as a matter of defense by recoupment or set off without regard for the time limit on a private action for damages under subsection (e).

(2) Amount of recoupment or setoff.

(A) In general. The amount of recoupment or set-off under paragraph (1) shall equal the amount to which the consumer would be entitled under subsection (a) for damages for a valid claim brought in an original action against the creditor, plus the costs to the consumer of the action, including a reasonable attorney's fee.

(B) Special rule. Where such judgment is rendered after the expiration of the applicable time limit on a private action for damages under subsection (e), the amount of recoupment or set-off under paragraph (1) derived from damages under subsection (a)(4) shall not exceed the amount to which the consumer would have been entitled under subsection (a)(4) for damages computed up to the day preceding the expiration of the applicable time limit.

(l) Exemption from liability and rescission in case of borrower fraud or deception. In addition to any other remedy available by law or contract, no creditor or assignee shall be liable to an obligor under this section, if such obligor, or co-obligor has been convicted of obtaining by actual fraud such residential mortgage loan.

§ 1641. Liability of Assignees

(a) Prerequisites. Except as otherwise specifically provided in this subchapter, any civil action for a violation of this subchapter or proceeding under section 1607 of this title which may be brought against a creditor may be maintained against any assignee of such creditor only if the violation for which such action or proceeding is brought is apparent on the face of the disclosure statement, except where the assignment was involuntary. For the purpose of this section, a violation apparent on the face of the disclosure statement includes, but is not limited to (1) a disclosure which can be determined to be incomplete or inaccurate from the face of the disclosure statement or other documents assigned, or (2) a disclosure which does not use the terms required to be used by this subchapter.

(b) Proof of compliance with statutory provisions. Except as provided in section 1635(c) of this title, in any action or proceeding by or against any subsequent assignee of the original creditor without knowledge to the contrary by the assignee when he acquires the obligation, written acknowledgement of receipt by a person to whom a statement is required to be given pursuant to this subchapter shall be conclusive proof of the delivery thereof and, except as provided in subsection (a) of this section, of compliance with this part. This section does not affect the rights of the obligor in any action against the original creditor.

(c) Right of rescission by consumer unaffected. Any consumer who has the right to rescind a transaction under section 1635 of this title may rescind the transaction as against any assignee of the obligation.

(d) Rights upon assignment of certain mortgages

(1) In general. Any person who purchases or is otherwise assigned a mortgage referred to in section 1602(aa) of this title shall be subject to all claims and defenses with respect to that mortgage that the consumer could assert against the creditor of the mortgage, unless the purchaser or assignee demonstrates, by a preponderance of the evidence, that a reasonable person exercising ordinary due diligence, could not determine, based on the documentation required by this subchapter, the itemization of the amount financed, and other disclosure of disbursements that the mortgage was a mortgage referred to in section 1602(aa) of this title. The preceding sentence does not affect rights of a consumer under subsection (a), (b), or (c) of this section or any other provision of this subchapter.

(2) Limitation on damages. Notwithstanding any other provision of law, relief provided as a result of any action made permissible by paragraph (1) may not exceed—

(A) with respect to actions based upon a violation of this subchapter, the amount specified in section 1640 of this title; and

(B) with respect to all other causes of action, the sum of—

(i) the amount of all remaining indebtedness; and

(ii) the total amount paid by the consumer in connection with the transaction.

(3) Offset. The amount of damages that may be awarded under paragraph (2)(B) shall be reduced by the amount of any damages awarded under paragraph (2)(A).

(4) Notice. Any person who sells or otherwise assigns a mortgage referred to in section 1602(aa) of this title shall include a prominent notice of the potential liability under this subsection as determined by the Bureau.

(e) Liability of assignee for consumer credit transactions secured by real property

(1) In general. Except as otherwise specifically provided in this subchapter, any civil action against a creditor for a violation of this subchapter, and any proceeding under section 1607 of this title against a creditor, with respect to a consumer credit transaction secured by real property may be maintained against any assignee of such creditor only if—

(A) the violation for which such action or proceeding is brought is apparent on the face of the disclosure statement provided in connection with such transaction pursuant to this subchapter; and

(B) the assignment to the assignee was voluntary.

(2) Violation apparent on the face of the disclosure described. For the purpose of this section, a violation is apparent on the face of the disclosure statement if—

(A) the disclosure can be determined to be incomplete or inaccurate by a comparison among the disclosure statement, any itemization of the amount financed, the note, or any other disclosure of disbursement; or

(B) the disclosure statement does not use the terms or format required to be used by this subchapter.

(f) Treatment of servicer

(1) In general. A servicer of a consumer obligation arising from a consumer credit transaction shall not be treated as an assignee of such obligation for purposes of this section unless the servicer is or was the owner of the obligation.

(2) Servicer not treated as owner on basis of assignment for administrative convenience. A servicer of a consumer obligation arising from a consumer credit transaction shall not be treated as the owner of the obligation for purposes of this section on the basis of an assignment of the obligation from the creditor or another assignee to the servicer solely for the administrative convenience of the servicer in servicing the obligation. Upon written request by the obligor, the servicer shall provide the obligor, to the best knowledge of the servicer, with the name, address, and telephone number of the owner of the obligation or the master servicer of the obligation.

(3) "Servicer" defined. For purposes of this subsection, the term "servicer" has the same meaning as in section 2605(i)(2) of Title 12.

(4) Applicability. This subsection shall apply to all consumer credit transactions in existence or consummated on or after September 30, 1995.

(g) Notice of new creditor

(1) In general. In addition to other disclosures required by this subchapter, not later than 30 days after the date on which a mortgage loan is sold or otherwise transferred or assigned to a third party, the creditor that is the new owner or assignee of the debt shall notify the borrower in writing of such transfer, including—

(A) the identity, address, telephone number of the new creditor;

(B) the date of transfer;

(C) how to reach an agent or party having authority to act on behalf of the new creditor;

(D) the location of the place where transfer of ownership of the debt is recorded; and

(E) any other relevant information regarding the new creditor.

(2) Definition. As used in this subsection, the term "mortgage loan" means any consumer credit transaction that is secured by the principal dwelling of a consumer.

§ 1642. Issuance of Credit Cards

No credit card shall be issued except in response to a request or application therefor. This prohibition does not apply to the issuance of a credit card in renewal of, or in substitution for, an accepted credit card.

§ 1643. Liability of Holder of Credit Card

(a) Limits on liability

(1) A cardholder shall be liable for the unauthorized use of a credit card only if—

(A) the card is an accepted credit card;

(B) the liability is not in excess of $50;

(C) the card issuer gives adequate notice to the cardholder of the potential liability;

(D) the card issuer has provided the cardholder with a description of a means by which the card issuer may be notified of loss or theft of the card, which description may be provided on the face or reverse side of the statement required by section 1637(b) of this title or on a separate notice accompanying such statement;

(E) the unauthorized use occurs before the card issuer has been notified that an unauthorized use of the credit card has occurred or may occur as the result of loss, theft, or otherwise; and

(F) the card issuer has provided a method whereby the user of such card can be identified as the person authorized to use it.

(2) For purposes of this section, a card issuer has been notified when such steps as may be reasonably required in the ordinary course of business to provide the card issuer with the pertinent information have been taken, whether or not any particular officer, employee, or agent of the card issuer does in fact receive such information.

(b) Burden of proof. In any action by a card issuer to enforce liability for the use of a credit card, the burden of proof is upon the card issuer to show that the use was authorized or, if the use was unauthorized, then the burden of proof is upon the card issuer to show that the conditions of liability for the unauthorized use of a credit card, as set forth in subsection (a) of this section, have been met.

(c) Liability imposed by other laws or by agreement with issuer. Nothing in this section imposes liability upon a cardholder for the unauthorized use of a credit card in excess of his liability for such use under other applicable law or under any agreement with the card issuer.

(d) Exclusiveness of liability. Except as provided in this section, a cardholder incurs no liability from the unauthorized use of a credit card.

§ 1644. Fraudulent Use of Credit Cards; Penalties

(a) Use, attempt or conspiracy to use card in transaction affecting interstate or foreign commerce. Whoever knowingly in a transaction affecting interstate or foreign commerce, uses or attempts or conspires to use any counterfeit, fictitious, altered, forged, lost, stolen, or fraudulently obtained credit card to obtain money, goods, services, or anything else of value which within any one-year period has a value aggregating $1,000 or more; or

(b) Transporting, attempting or conspiring to transport card in interstate commerce. Whoever, with unlawful or fraudulent intent, transports or attempts or conspires to transport in interstate or foreign commerce a counterfeit, fictitious, altered, forged, lost, stolen, or fraudulently obtained credit card knowing the same to be counterfeit, fictitious, altered, forged, lost, stolen, or fraudulently obtained; or

(c) Use of interstate commerce to sell or transport card. Whoever, with unlawful or fraudulent intent, uses any instrumentality of interstate or foreign commerce to sell or transport a counterfeit, fictitious, altered, forged, lost, stolen, or fraudulently obtained credit card knowing the same to be counterfeit, fictitious, altered, forged, lost, stolen, or fraudulently obtained; or

(d) Receipt, concealment, etc., of goods obtained by use of card. Whoever knowingly receives, conceals, uses, or transports money, goods, services, or anything else of value (except tickets for interstate or foreign transportation) which

(1) within any one-year period has a value aggregating $1,000 or more,

(2) has moved in or is part of, or which constitutes interstate or foreign commerce, and

(3) has been obtained with a counterfeit, fictitious, altered, forged, lost, stolen, or fraudulently obtained credit card; or

(e) Receipt, concealment, etc., of tickets for interstate or foreign transportation obtained by use of card. Whoever knowingly receives, conceals, uses, sells, or transports in interstate or foreign commerce one or more tickets for interstate or foreign transportation, which

(1) within any one-year period have a value aggregating $500 or more, and

(2) have been purchased or obtained with one or more counterfeit, fictitious, altered, forged, lost, stolen, or fraudulently obtained credit cards; or

(f) Furnishing of money, etc., through use of card. Whoever in a transaction affecting interstate or foreign commerce furnishes money, property, services, or anything else of value, which within any one-year period has a value aggregating $1,000 or more, through the use of any counterfeit, fictitious, altered, forged, lost, stolen, or fraudulently obtained credit card knowing the same to be counterfeit, fictitious, altered, forged, lost, stolen, or fraudulently obtained—shall be fined not more than $10,000 or imprisoned not more than ten years, or both.

§ 1645. Business Credit Cards; Limits on Liability of Employees

The exemption provided by section 1603(1) of this title does not apply to the provisions of sections 1642, 1643, and 1644 of this title, except that a card issuer and a business or other organization which provides credit cards issued by the same card issuer to ten or more of its employees may by contract agree as to liability of the business or other organization with respect to unauthorized use of such credit cards without regard to the provisions of section 1643 of this title, but in no case may such business or other organization or card issuer impose liability upon any employee with respect to unauthorized use of such a credit card except in accordance with and subject to the limitations of section 1643 of this title.

§ 1650. Preventing Unfair and Deceptive Private Educational Practices and Eliminating Conflicts of Interest

(a) Definitions. As used in this section—

(1) the term "cosigner"—

(A) means any individual who is liable for the obligation of another without compensation, regardless of how designated in the contract or instrument with respect to that obligation, other than an obligation under a private education loan extended to consolidate a consumer's preexisting private education loans;

(B) includes any person the signature of which is requested as condition to grant credit or to forbear on collection; and

(C) does not include a spouse of an individual described in subparagraph (A), the signature of whom is needed to perfect the security interest in a loan.

(2) the term "covered educational institution"—

(A) means any educational institution that offers a postsecondary educational degree, certificate, or program of study (including any institution of higher education); and

(B) includes an agent, officer, or employee of the educational institution;

(3) the term "gift"—

(A)(i) means any gratuity, favor, discount, entertainment, hospitality, loan, or other item having more than a de minimis monetary value, including services, transportation, lodging, or meals, whether provided in kind, by purchase of a ticket, payment in advance, or reimbursement after the expense has been incurred; and

(ii) includes an item described in clause (i) provided to a family member of an officer, employee, or agent of a covered educational institution, or to any other individual based on that individual's relationship with the officer, employee, or agent, if—

(I) the item is provided with the knowledge and acquiescence of the officer, employee, or agent; and

(II) the officer, employee, or agent has reason to believe the item was provided because of the official position of the officer, employee, or agent; and

(B) does not include—

(i) standard informational material related to a loan, default aversion, default prevention, or financial literacy;

(ii) food, refreshments, training, or informational material furnished to an officer, employee, or agent of a covered educational institution, as an integral part of a training session or through participation in an advisory council that is designed to improve the service of the private educational lender to the covered educational institution, if such training or participation contributes to the professional development of the officer, employee, or agent of the covered educational institution;

(iii) favorable terms, conditions, and borrower benefits on a private education loan provided to a student employed by the covered educational institution, if such terms, conditions, or benefits are not provided because of the student's employment with the covered educational institution;

(iv) the provision of financial literacy counseling or services, including counseling or services provided in coordination with a covered educational institution, to the extent that such counseling or services are not undertaken to secure—

(I) applications for private education loans or private education loan volume;

(II) applications or loan volume for any loan made, insured, or guaranteed under title IV of the Higher Education Act of 1965 (20 U.S.C. 1070 et seq.); or

(III) the purchase of a product or service of a specific private educational lender;

(v) philanthropic contributions to a covered educational institution from a private educational lender that are unrelated to private education loans and are not made in exchange for any advantage related to private education loans; or

(vi) State education grants, scholarships, or financial aid funds administered by or on behalf of a State;

(4) the term "institution of higher education" has the same meaning as in section 102 of the Higher Education Act of 1965 (20 U.S.C. 1002);

(5) the term "postsecondary educational expenses" means any of the expenses that are included as part of the cost of attendance of a student, as defined under section 472 of the Higher Education Act of 1965 (20 U.S.C. 1087);

(6) the term "preferred lender arrangement" has the same meaning as in section 151 of the Higher Education Act of 1965 (20 U.S.C. § 1019);

(7) the term "private educational lender" means—

(A) a financial institution, as defined in section 3 of the Federal Deposit Insurance Act (12 U.S.C. 1813) that solicits, makes, or extends private education loans;

(B) a Federal credit union, as defined in section 101 of the Federal Credit Union Act (12 U.S.C. 1752) that solicits, makes, or extends private education loans; and

(C) any other person engaged in the business of soliciting, making, or extending private education loans;

(8) the term "private education loan"—

(A) means a loan provided by a private educational lender that—

(i) is not made, insured, or guaranteed under title IV of the Higher Education Act of 1965 (20 U.S.C. 1070 et seq.); and

(ii) is issued expressly for postsecondary educational expenses to a borrower, regardless of whether the loan is provided through the educational institution that the subject student attends or directly to the borrower from the private educational lender; and

(B) does not include an extension of credit under an open end consumer credit plan, a reverse mortgage transaction, a residential mortgage transaction, or any other loan that is secured by real property or a dwelling; and

(9) the term "revenue sharing" means an arrangement between a covered educational institution and a private educational lender under which—

(A) a private educational lender provides or issues private education loans with respect to students attending the covered educational institution;

(B) the covered educational institution recommends to students or others the private educational lender or the private education loans of the private educational lender; and

(C) the private educational lender pays a fee or provides other material benefits, including profit sharing, to the covered educational institution in connection with the private education loans provided to students attending the covered educational institution or a borrower acting on behalf of a student.

(b) Prohibition on certain gifts and arrangements. A private educational lender may not, directly or indirectly—

(1) offer or provide any gift to a covered educational institution in exchange for any advantage or consideration provided to such private educational lender related to its private education loan activities; or

(2) engage in revenue sharing with a covered educational institution.

(c) Prohibition on co-branding. A private educational lender may not use the name, emblem, mascot, or logo of the covered educational institution, or other words, pictures, or symbols readily identified with the covered educational institution, in the marketing of private education loans in any way that implies that the covered educational institution endorses the private education loans offered by the private educational lender.

(d) Advisory board compensation. Any person who is employed in the financial aid office of a covered educational institution, or who otherwise has responsibilities with respect to private education loans or other financial aid of the institution, and who serves on an advisory board, commission, or group established by a private educational lender or group of such lenders shall be prohibited from receiving anything of value from the private educational lender or group of lenders. Nothing in this subsection prohibits the reimbursement of reasonable expenses incurred by an employee of a covered educational institution as part of their service on an advisory board, commission, or group described in this subsection.

(e) Prohibition on prepayment or repayment fees or penalty. It shall be unlawful for any private educational lender to impose a fee or penalty on a borrower for early repayment or prepayment of any private education loan.

(f) Credit card protections for college students.

(1) Disclosure required. An institution of higher education shall publicly disclose any contract or other agreement made with a card issuer or creditor for the purpose of marketing a credit card.

(2) Inducements prohibited. No card issuer or creditor may offer to a student at an institution of higher education any tangible item to induce such student to apply for or participate in an open end consumer credit plan offered by such card issuer or creditor, if such offer is made—

(A) on the campus of an institution of higher education;

(B) near the campus of an institution of higher education, as determined by rule of the Bureau; or

(C) at an event sponsored by or related to an institution of higher education.

(3) Sense of the Congress. It is the sense of the Congress that each institution of higher education should consider adopting the following policies relating to credit cards:

(A) That any card issuer that markets a credit card on the campus of such institution notify the institution of the location at which such marketing will take place.

(B) That the number of locations on the campus of such institution at which the marketing of credit cards takes place be limited.

(C) That credit card and debt education and counseling sessions be offered as a regular part of any orientation program for new students of such institution.

(g) Additional protections relating to borrower or cosigner of a private education loan.

(1) Prohibition on automatic default in case of death or bankruptcy of non-student obligor. With respect to a private education loan involving a student obligor and 1 or more cosigners, the creditor shall not declare a default or accelerate the debt against the student obligor on the sole basis of a bankruptcy or death of a cosigner.

(2) Cosigner release in case of death of borrower.

(A) Release of cosigner. The holder of a private education loan, when notified of the death of a student obligor, shall release within a reasonable timeframe any cosigner from the obligations of the cosigner under the private education loan.

(B) Notification of release. A holder or servicer of a private education loan, as applicable, shall within a reasonable time-frame notify any cosigners for the private education loan if a cosigner is released from the obligations of the cosigner for the private education loan under this paragraph.

(C) Designation of individual to act on behalf of the borrower. Any lender that extends a private education loan shall provide the student obligor an option to designate an individual to have the legal authority to act on behalf of the student obligor with respect to the private education loan in the event of the death of the student obligor.

§ 1665c. Interest Rate Reduction on Open End Consumer Credit Plans

(a) In general. If a creditor increases the annual percentage rate applicable to a credit card account under an open end consumer credit plan, based on factors including the credit risk of the obligor, market conditions, or other factors, the creditor shall consider changes in such factors in subsequently determining whether to reduce the annual percentage rate for such obligor.

(b) Requirements. With respect to any credit card account under an open end consumer credit plan, the creditor shall—

(1) maintain reasonable methodologies for assessing the factors described in subsection (a);

(2) not less frequently than once every 6 months, review accounts as to which the annual percentage rate has been increased since January 1, 2009, to assess whether such factors have changed (including whether any risk has declined);

(3) reduce the annual percentage rate previously increased when a reduction is indicated by the review; and

(4) in the event of an increase in the annual percentage rate, provide in the written notice required under section 1637(i) of this title a statement of the reasons for the increase.

(c) Rule of construction. This section shall not be construed to require a reduction in any specific amount.

(d) Rulemaking. The Bureau shall issue final rules not later than 9 months after May 22, 2009, to implement the requirements of and evaluate compliance with this section, and subsections (a), (b), and (c) shall become effective 15 months after May 22, 2009.

§ 1665d. Reasonable Penalty Fees on Open End Consumer Credit Plans

(a) In general. The amount of any penalty fee or charge that a card issuer may impose with respect to a credit card account under an open end consumer credit plan in connection with any omission with respect to, or violation of, the cardholder agreement, including any late payment fee, over-the-limit fee, or any other penalty fee or charge, shall be reasonable and proportional to such omission or violation.

(b) Rulemaking required. The Bureau, in consultation with the Comptroller of the Currency, the Board of Directors of the Federal Deposit Insurance Corporation, the Director of the Office of Thrift Supervision, and the National Credit Union Administration Board, shall issue final rules not later than 9 months after May 22, 2009, to establish standards for assessing whether the amount of any penalty fee or charge described under subsection (a) is reasonable and proportional to the omission or violation to which the fee or charge relates. Subsection (a) shall become effective 15 months after May 22, 2009.

(c) Considerations. In issuing rules required by this section, the Bureau shall consider—

(1) the cost incurred by the creditor from such omission or violation;

(2) the deterrence of such omission or violation by the cardholder;

(3) the conduct of the cardholder; and

(4) such other factors as the Bureau may deem necessary or appropriate.

(d) Differentiation permitted. In issuing rules required by this subsection, the Bureau may establish different standards for different types of fees and charges, as appropriate.

(e) Safe Harbor Rule authorized. The Bureau, in consultation with the Comptroller of the Currency, the Board of Directors of the Federal Deposit Insurance Corporation, the Director of the Office of Thrift Supervision, and the National Credit Union Administration Board, may issue rules to provide an amount for any penalty fee or charge described under subsection (a) that is presumed to be reasonable and proportional to the omission or violation to which the fee or charge relates.

§ 1665e. Consideration of Ability to Repay

A card issuer may not open any credit card account for any consumer under an open end consumer credit plan, or increase any credit limit applicable to such account, unless the card issuer considers the ability of the consumer to make the required payments under the terms of such account.

§ 1666. Correction of Billing Errors

(a) Written notice by obligor to creditor; time for and contents of notice; procedure upon receipt of notice by creditor. If a creditor, within sixty days after having transmitted to an obligor a statement of the obligor's account in connection with an extension of consumer credit, receives at the address disclosed under section 1637(b)(10) of this title a written notice (other than notice on a payment stub or other payment medium supplied by the creditor if the creditor so stipulates with the disclosure required under section 1637(a)(7) of this title) from the obligor in which the obligor—

(1) sets forth or otherwise enables the creditor to identify the name and account number (if any) of the obligor,

(2) indicates the obligor's belief that the statement contains a billing error and the amount of such billing error, and

(3) sets forth the reasons for the obligor's belief (to the extent applicable) that the statement contains a billing error, the creditor shall, unless the obligor has, after giving such written notice and before the expiration of the time limits herein specified, agreed that the statement was correct—

(A) not later than thirty days after the receipt of the notice, send a written acknowledgment thereof to the obligor, unless the action required in subparagraph (B) is taken within such thirty-day period, and

(B) not later than two complete billing cycles of the creditor (in no event later than ninety days) after the receipt of the notice and prior to taking any action to collect the amount, or any part thereof, indicated by the obligor under paragraph (2) either—

(i) make appropriate corrections in the account of the obligor, including the crediting of any finance charges on amounts erroneously billed, and transmit to the obligor a notification of such corrections and the creditor's explanation of any change in the amount indicated by the obligor under paragraph (2) and, if any such change is made and the obligor so requests, copies of documentary evidence of the obligor's indebtedness; or

(ii) send a written explanation or clarification to the obligor, after having conducted an investigation, setting forth to the extent applicable the reasons why the creditor believes the account of the obligor was correctly shown in the statement and, upon request of the obligor, provide copies of documentary evidence of the obligor's indebtedness. In the case of a billing error where the obligor alleges that the creditor's billing statement reflects goods not delivered to the obligor or his designee in accordance with the agreement made at the time of the transaction, a creditor may not construe such amount to be correctly shown unless he determines that such goods were actually delivered, mailed, or otherwise sent to the obligor and provides the obligor with a statement of such determination.

After complying with the provisions of this subsection with respect to an alleged billing error, a creditor has no further responsibility under this section if the obligor continues to make substantially the same allegation with respect to such error.

(b) Billing error. For the purpose of this section, a "billing error" consists of any of the following:

(1) A reflection on a statement of an extension of credit which was not made to the obligor or, if made, was not in the amount reflected on such statement.

(2) A reflection on a statement of an extension of credit for which the obligor requests additional clarification including documentary evidence thereof.

(3) A reflection on a statement of goods or services not accepted by the obligor or his designee or not delivered to the obligor or his designee in accordance with the agreement made at the time of a transaction.

(4) The creditor's failure to reflect properly on a statement a payment made by the obligor or a credit issued to the obligor.

(5) A computation error or similar error of an accounting nature of the creditor on a statement.

(6) Failure to transmit the statement required under section 1637(b) of this title to the last address of the obligor which has been disclosed to the creditor, unless that address was furnished less than twenty days before the end of the billing cycle for which the statement is required.

(7) Any other error described in regulations of the Bureau.

(c) Action by creditor to collect amount or any part thereof regarded by obligor to be a billing error. For the purposes of this section, "action to collect the amount, or any part thereof, indicated by an obligor under paragraph (2)" does not include the sending of statements of account, which may include finance charges on amounts in dispute, to the obligor following written notice from the obligor as specified under subsection (a) of this section, if—

(1) the obligor's account is not restricted or closed because of the failure of the obligor to pay the amount indicated under paragraph (2) of subsection (a) of this section, and

(2) the creditor indicates the payment of such amount is not required pending the creditor's compliance with this section.

Nothing in this section shall be construed to prohibit any action by a creditor to collect any amount which has not been indicated by the obligor to contain a billing error.

(d) Restricting or closing by creditor of account regarded by obligor to contain a billing error. Pursuant to regulations of the Bureau, a creditor operating an open end consumer credit plan may not, prior to the sending of the written explanation or clarification required under paragraph (B)(ii), restrict or close an account with respect to which the obligor has indicated pursuant to subsection (a) of this section that he believes such account to contain a billing error solely because of the obligor's failure to pay the amount indicated to be in error. Nothing in this subsection shall be deemed to prohibit a creditor from applying against the credit limit on the obligor's account the amount indicated to be in error.

(e) Effect of noncompliance with requirements by creditor. Any creditor who fails to comply with the requirements of this section or section 1666a of this title forfeits any right to collect from the obligor the amount indicated by the obligor under paragraph (2) of subsection (a) of this section, and any finance charges thereon, except that the amount required to be forfeited under this subsection may not exceed $50.

§ 1666a. Regulation of Credit Reports

(a) Reports by creditor on obligor's failure to pay amount regarded as billing error. After receiving a notice from an obligor as provided in section 1666(a) of this title, a creditor or his agent may not directly or indirectly threaten to report to any person adversely on the obligor's credit rating or credit standing because of the obligor's failure to pay the amount indicated by the obligor under section 1666(a)(2) of this title, and such amount may not be reported as delinquent to any third party until the creditor has met the requirements of section 1666 of this title and has allowed the obligor the same number of days (not less than ten) thereafter to make payment as is provided under the credit agreement with the obligor for the payment of undisputed amounts.

(b) Reports by creditor on delinquent amounts in dispute; notification of obligor of parties notified of delinquency. If a creditor receives a further written notice from an obligor that an amount is still in dispute within the time allowed for payment under subsection (a) of this section, a creditor may not report to any third party that the amount of the obligor is delinquent because the obligor has failed to pay an amount which he has indicated under section 1666(a)(2) of this title, unless the creditor also reports that the amount is in dispute and, at the same time, notifies the obligor of the name and address of each party to whom the creditor is reporting information concerning the delinquency.

(c) Reports by creditor of subsequent resolution of delinquent amounts. A creditor shall report any subsequent resolution of any delinquencies reported pursuant to subsection (b) of this section to the parties to whom such delinquencies were initially reported.

§ 1666b. Timing of Payments

(a) Time to make payments. A creditor may not treat a payment on an open end consumer credit plan as late for any purpose, unless the creditor has adopted reasonable procedures designed to ensure that each periodic statement including the information required by section 127(b) is mailed or delivered to the consumer not later than 21 days before the payment due date.

(b) Grace period. If an open end consumer credit plan provides a time period within which an obligor may repay any portion of the credit extended without incurring an additional finance charge, such additional finance charge may not be imposed with respect to such portion of the credit extended for the billing cycle of which such period is a part, unless a statement which includes the amount upon which the finance charge for the period is based was mailed or delivered to the consumer not later than 21 days before the date specified in the statement by which payment must be made in order to avoid imposition of that finance charge.

§ 1666c. Prompt and Fair Crediting of Payments

(a) In general. Payments received from an obligor under an open end consumer credit plan by the creditor shall be posted promptly to the obligor's account as specified in regulations of the Bureau. Such regulations shall prevent a finance charge from being imposed on any obligor if the creditor has received the obligor's payment in readily identifiable form, by 5:00 p.m. on the date on which such payment is due, in the amount, manner, and location indicated by the creditor to avoid the imposition thereof.

(b) Application of payments.

(1) In general. Upon receipt of a payment from a cardholder, the card issuer shall apply amounts in excess of the minimum payment amount first to the card balance bearing the highest rate of interest, and then to each successive balance bearing the next highest rate of interest, until the payment is exhausted.

(2) Clarification relating to certain deferred interest arrangements. A creditor shall allocate the entire amount paid by the consumer in excess of the minimum payment amount to a balance on which interest is deferred during the last 2 billing cycles immediately preceding the expiration of the period during which interest is deferred.

(c) Changes by card issuer. If a card issuer makes a material change in the mailing address, office, or procedures for handling cardholder payments, and such change causes a material delay in the crediting of a cardholder payment made during the 60-day period following the date on which such change took effect, the card issuer may not impose any late fee or finance charge for a late payment on the credit card account to which such payment was credited.

§ 1666d. Treatment of Credit Balances

Whenever a credit balance in excess of $1 is created in connection with a consumer credit transaction through

(1) transmittal of funds to a creditor in excess of the total balance due on an account,

(2) rebates of unearned finance charges or insurance premiums, or

(3) amounts otherwise owed to or held for the benefit of an obligor, the creditor shall—

(A) credit the amount of the credit balance to the consumer's account;

(B) refund any part of the amount of the remaining credit balance, upon request of the consumer; and

(C) make a good faith effort to refund to the consumer by cash, check, or money order any part of the amount of the credit balance remaining in the account for more than six months, except that no further action is required in any case in which the consumer's current location is not known by the creditor and cannot be traced through the consumer's last known address or telephone number.

§ 1666e. Notification of Credit Card Issuer by Seller of Return of Goods, Etc., by Obligor; Credit for Account of Obligor

With respect to any sales transaction where a credit card has been used to obtain credit, where the seller is a person other than the card issuer, and where the seller accepts or allows a return of the goods or forgiveness of a debit for services which were the subject of such sale, the seller shall promptly transmit to the credit card issuer, a credit statement with respect thereto and the credit card issuer shall credit the account of the obligor for the amount of the transaction.

§ 1666f. Inducements to Cardholders by Sellers of Cash Discounts for Payments by Cash, Check or Similar Means; Finance Charge for Sales Transactions Involving Cash Discounts

(a) Cash discounts. With respect to credit card which may be used for extensions of credit in sales transactions in which the seller is a person other than the card issuer, the card issuer may not, by contract, or otherwise, prohibit any such seller from offering a discount to a cardholder to induce the cardholder to pay by cash, check, or similar means rather than use a credit card.

(b) Finance charge. With respect to any sales transaction, any discount from the regular price offered by the seller for the purpose of inducing payment by cash, checks, or other means not involving the use of an open-end credit plan or a credit card shall not constitute a finance charge as determined under section 1605 of this title if such discount is offered to all prospective buyers and its availability is disclosed clearly and conspicuously.

§ 1666g. Tie-in Services Prohibited for Issuance of Credit Card

Notwithstanding any agreement to the contrary, a card issuer may not require a seller, as a condition to participating in a credit card plan, to open an account with or procure any other service from the card issuer or its subsidiary or agent.

§ 1666h. Offset of Cardholder's Indebtedness by Issuer of Credit Card with Funds Deposited with Issuer by Cardholder; Remedies of Creditors Under State Law Not Affected

(a) Offset against consumer's funds. A card issuer may not take any action to offset a cardholder's indebtedness arising in connection with a consumer credit transaction under the relevant credit card plan against funds of the cardholder held on deposit with the card issuer unless—

(1) such action was previously authorized in writing by the cardholder in accordance with a credit plan whereby the cardholder agrees periodically to pay debts incurred in his open end credit account by permitting the card issuer periodically to deduct all or a portion of such debt from the cardholder's deposit account, and

(2) such action with respect to any outstanding disputed amount not be taken by the card issuer upon request of the cardholder.

In the case of any credit card account in existence on the effective date of this section, the previous written authorization referred to in clause (1) shall not be required until the date (after such effective date) when such account is renewed, but in no case later than one year after such effective date. Such written authorization shall be deemed to exist if the card issuer has previously notified the cardholder that the use of his credit card account will subject any funds which the card issuer holds in deposit accounts of such cardholder to offset against any amounts due and payable on his credit card account which have not been paid in accordance with the terms of the agreement between the card issuer and the cardholder.

(b) Attachments and levies. This section does not alter or affect the right under State law of a card issuer to attach or otherwise levy upon funds of a cardholder held on deposit with the card issuer if that remedy is constitutionally available to creditors generally.

§ 1666i. Assertion by Cardholder Against Card Issuer of Claims and Defenses Arising Out of Credit Card Transaction; Prerequisites; Limitation on Amount of Claims or Defenses

(a) Claims and defenses assertible. Subject to the limitation contained in subsection (b) of this section, a card issuer who has issued a credit card to a cardholder pursuant to an open end consumer credit plan shall be subject to all claims (other than tort claims) and defenses arising out of any transaction in which the credit card is used as a method of payment or extension of credit if

(1) the obligor has made a good faith attempt to obtain satisfactory resolution of a disagreement or problem relative to the transaction from the person honoring the credit card;

(2) the amount of the initial transaction exceeds \$50; and

(3) the place where the initial transaction occurred was in the same State as the mailing address previously provided by the cardholder or was within 100 miles from such address, except that the limitations set forth in clauses (2) and (3) with respect to an obligor's right to assert claims and defenses against a card issuer shall not be applicable to any transaction in which the person honoring the credit card

(A) is the same person as the card issuer,

(B) is controlled by the card issuer,

(C) is under direct or indirect common control with the card issuer,

(D) is a franchised dealer in the card issuer's products or services, or

(E) has obtained the order for such transaction through a mail solicitation made by or participated in by the card issuer in which the cardholder is solicited to enter into such transaction by using the credit card issued by the card issuer.

(b) Amount of claims and defenses assertible. The amount of claims or defenses asserted by the cardholder may not exceed the amount of credit outstanding with respect to such transaction at the time the cardholder first notifies the card issuer or the person honoring the credit card of such claim or defense. For the purpose of determining the amount of credit outstanding in the preceding sentence, payments and credits to the cardholder's account are deemed to have been applied, in the order indicated, to the payment of:

(1) late charges in the order of their entry to the account;

(2) finance charges in order of their entry to the account; and

(3) debits to the account other than those set forth above, in the order in which each debit entry to the account was made.

§ 1666i-1. Limits on Interest Rate, Fee, and Finance Charge Increases Applicable to Outstanding Balances

(a) In general. In the case of any credit card account under an open end consumer credit plan, no creditor may increase any annual percentage rate, fee, or finance charge applicable to any outstanding balance, except as permitted under subsection (b).

(b) Exceptions. The prohibition under subsection (a) shall not apply to—

(1) an increase in an annual percentage rate upon the expiration of a specified period of time, provided that—

(A) prior to commencement of that period, the creditor disclosed to the consumer, in a clear and conspicuous manner, the length of the period and the annual percentage rate that would apply after expiration of the period;

(B) the increased annual percentage rate does not exceed the rate disclosed pursuant to subparagraph (A); and

(C) the increased annual percentage rate is not applied to transactions that occurred prior to commencement of the period;

(2) an increase in a variable annual percentage rate in accordance with a credit card agreement that provides for changes in the rate according to operation of an index that is not under the control of the creditor and is available to the general public;

(3) an increase due to the completion of a workout or temporary hardship arrangement by the obligor or the failure of the obligor to comply with the terms of a workout or temporary hardship arrangement, provided that—

(A) the annual percentage rate, fee, or finance charge applicable to a category of transactions following any such increase does not exceed the rate, fee, or finance charge that applied to that category of transactions prior to commencement of the arrangement; and

(B) the creditor has provided the obligor, prior to the commencement of such arrangement, with clear and conspicuous disclosure of the terms of the arrangement (including any increases due to such completion or failure); or

(4) an increase due solely to the fact that a minimum payment by the obligor has not been received by the creditor within 60 days after the due date for such payment, provided that the creditor shall—

(A) include, together with the notice of such increase required under section 127(i), a clear and conspicuous written statement of the reason for the increase and that the increase will terminate not later than 6 months after the date on which it is imposed, if the creditor receives the required minimum payments on time from the obligor during that period; and

(B) terminate such increase not later than 6 months after the date on which it is imposed, if the creditor receives the required minimum payments on time during that period.

(c) Repayment of outstanding balance.

(1) In general. The creditor shall not change the terms governing the repayment of any outstanding balance, except that the creditor may provide the obligor with one of the methods described in paragraph (2) of repaying any outstanding balance, or a method that is no less beneficial to the obligor than one of those methods.

(2) Methods. The methods described in this paragraph are—

(A) an amortization period of not less than 5 years, beginning on the effective date of the increase set forth in the notice required under section 127(i); or

(B) a required minimum periodic payment that includes a percentage of the outstanding balance that is equal to not more than twice the percentage required before the effective date of the increase set forth in the notice required under section 127(i).

(d) Outstanding balance defined. For purposes of this section, the term "outstanding balance" means the amount owed on a credit card account under an open end consumer credit plan as of the end of the 14th day after the date on which the creditor provides notice of an increase in the annual percentage rate, fee, or finance charge in accordance with section 127(i).

§ 1666i-2. Additional Limits on Interest Rate Increases

(a) Limitation on increases within first year. Except in the case of an increase described in paragraph (1), (2), (3), or (4) of section 171(b), no increase in any annual percentage rate, fee, or finance charge on any credit card account under an open end consumer credit plan shall be effective before the end of the 1-year period beginning on the date on which the account is opened.

(b) Promotional rate minimum term. No increase in any annual percentage rate applicable to a credit card account under an open end consumer credit plan that is a promotional rate (as that term is defined by the Bureau) shall be effective before the end of the 6-month period beginning on the date on which the promotional rate takes effect, subject to such reasonable exceptions as the Bureau may establish, by rule.

§ 1666j. Applicability of State Laws

(a) Consistency of provisions. This part does not annul, alter, or affect, or exempt any person subject to the provisions of this part from complying with, the laws of any State with respect to credit billing practices, except to the extent that those laws are inconsistent with any provision of this part, and then only to the extent of the inconsistency. The Bureau is authorized to determine whether such inconsistencies exist. The Bureau may not determine that any State law is inconsistent with any provision of this part if the Bureau determines that such law gives greater protection to the consumer.

(b) Exemptions by Bureau from credit billing requirements. The Bureau shall by regulation exempt from the requirements of this part any class of credit transactions within any State if it determines that under the law of that State that class of transactions is subject to requirements substantially similar to those imposed under this part or that such law gives greater protection to the consumer, and that there is adequate provision for enforcement.

(c) Finance charge or other charge for credit for sales transactions involving cash discounts. Notwithstanding any other provisions of this subchapter, any discount offered under section 1666f(b) of this title shall not be considered a finance charge or other charge for credit under the usury laws of any State or under the laws of any State relating to disclosure of information in connection with credit transactions, or relating to the types, amounts or rates of charges, or to any element or elements of charges permissible under such laws in connection with the extension or use of credit.

Regulation Z (Selected Sections)
12 C.F.R. Part 1026

SUBPART A. GENERAL

§ 1026.1 Authority, Purpose, Coverage, Organization, Enforcement and Liability.

(a) Authority. This part, known as Regulation Z, is issued by the Bureau of Consumer Financial Protection to implement the Federal Truth in Lending Act, which is contained in title I of the Consumer Credit Protection Act, as amended (15 U.S.C. 1601 et seq.). This part also implements title XII, section 1204 of the Competitive Equality Banking Act of 1987 (Pub. L. 100–86, 101 Stat. 552). Furthermore, this part implements certain provisions of the Real Estate Settlement Procedures Act of 1974, as amended (12 U.S.C. 2601 et seq.). The Bureau's information-collection requirements contained in this part have been approved by the Office of Management and Budget under the provisions of 44 U.S.C. 3501 et seq. and have been assigned OMB No. 3170–0015 (Truth in Lending).

(b) Purpose. The purpose of this part is to promote the informed use of consumer credit by requiring disclosures about its terms and cost, to ensure that consumers are provided with greater and more timely information on the nature and costs of the residential real estate settlement process, and to effect certain changes in the settlement process for residential real estate that will result in more effective advance disclosure to home buyers and sellers of settlement costs. The regulation also includes substantive protections. It gives consumers the right to cancel certain credit transactions that involve a lien on a consumer's principal dwelling, regulates certain credit card practices, and provides a means for fair and timely resolution of credit billing disputes. The regulation does not generally govern charges for consumer credit, except that several provisions in subpart G set forth special rules addressing certain charges applicable to credit card accounts under an open-end (not home-secured) consumer credit plan. The regulation requires a maximum interest rate to be stated in variable-rate contracts secured by the consumer's dwelling. It also imposes limitations on home-equity plans that are subject to the requirements of § 1026.40 and mortgages that are subject to the requirements of § 1026.32. The regulation prohibits certain acts or practices in connection with credit secured by a dwelling in § 1026.36, and credit secured by a consumer's principal dwelling in § 1026.35. The regulation also regulates certain practices of creditors who extend private education loans as defined in § 1026.46(b)(5). In addition, it imposes certain limitations on increases in costs for mortgage transactions subject to § 1026.19(e) and (f).

(c) Coverage.

(1) In general, this part applies to each individual or business that offers or extends credit, other than a person excluded from coverage of this part by section 1029 of the Consumer Financial Protection Act of 2010, title X of the Dodd–Frank Wall Street Reform and Consumer Protection Act, Public Law 111–203, 124 Stat. 1376, when four conditions are met:

(i) The credit is offered or extended to consumers;

(ii) The offering or extension of credit is done regularly;

(iii) The credit is subject to a finance charge or is payable by a written agreement in more than four installments; and;

(iv) The credit is primarily for personal, family, or household purposes.

(2) If a credit card is involved, however, certain provisions apply even if the credit is not subject to a finance charge, or is not payable by a written agreement in more than four installments, or if the credit card is to be used for business purposes.

(3) In addition, certain requirements of § 1026.40 apply to persons who are not creditors but who provide applications for home-equity plans to consumers.

(4) Furthermore, certain requirements of § 1026.57 apply to institutions of higher education.

(5) Except in transactions subject to § 1026.19(e) and (f), no person is required to provide the disclosures required by sections 128(a)(16) through (19), 128(b)(4), 129C(f)(1), 129C(g)(2) and (3), 129D(h), or 129D(j)(1)(A) of the Truth in Lending Act, section 4(c) of the Real Estate Settlement Procedures Act, or the disclosure required prior to settlement by section 129C(h) of the Truth in Lending Act. Except in transactions subject to § 1026.20(e), no person is required to provide the disclosure required by section 129D(j)(1)(B) of the Truth in Lending Act. Except in transactions subject to § 1026.39(d)(5), no person becoming a creditor with respect to an existing residential mortgage loan is required to provide the disclosure required by section 129C(h) of the Truth in Lending Act.

(6) The requirements of § 1026.42(i) apply to certain persons regardless of whether they are creditors and even if the mortgage, as defined in § 1026.42(i)(2)(v), is primarily for business, commercial, agricultural, or organizational purposes.

(d) Organization. The regulation is divided into subparts and appendices as follows:

(1) Subpart A contains general information. It sets forth:

(i) The authority, purpose, coverage, and organization of the regulation;

(ii) The definitions of basic terms;

(iii) The transactions that are exempt from coverage; and

(iv) The method of determining the finance charge.

(2) Subpart B contains the rules for open-end credit. It requires that account-opening disclosures and periodic statements be provided, as well as additional disclosures for credit and charge card applications and solicitations and for home-equity plans subject to the requirements of § 1026.60 and § 1026.40, respectively. It also describes special rules that apply to credit card transactions, treatment of payments and credit balances, procedures for resolving credit billing errors, annual percentage rate calculations, rescission requirements, and advertising.

(3) Subpart C relates to closed-end credit. It contains rules on disclosures, treatment of credit balances, annual percentage rate calculations, rescission requirements, and advertising.

(4) Subpart D contains rules on oral disclosures, disclosures in languages other than English, record retention, effect on state laws, state exemptions, and rate limitations.

(5) Subpart E contains special rules for mortgage transactions. Section 1026.32 requires certain disclosures and provides limitations for closed-end credit transactions and open-end credit plans that have rates or fees above specified amounts or certain prepayment penalties. Section 1026.33 requires special disclosures, including the total annual loan cost rate, for reverse mortgage transactions. Section 1026.34 prohibits specific acts and practices in connection with high-cost mortgages, as defined in § 1026.32(a). Section 1026.35 prohibits specific acts and practices in connection with closed-end higher-priced mortgage loans, as defined in § 1026.35(a). Section 1026.36 prohibits specific acts and practices in connection with an extension of credit secured by a dwelling. Sections 1026.37 and 1026.38 set forth special disclosure requirements for certain closed-end transactions secured by real property, as required by § 1026.19(e) and (f).

(6) Subpart F relates to private education loans. It contains rules on disclosures, limitations on changes in terms after approval, the right to cancel the loan, and limitations on co-branding in the marketing of private education loans.

(7) Subpart G relates to credit card accounts under an open-end (not home-secured) consumer credit plan (except for § 1026.57(c), which applies to all open-end credit plans). Section 1026.51 contains rules on evaluation of a consumer's ability to make the required payments under the terms of an account. Section 1026.52 limits the fees that a consumer can be required to pay with respect to an open-end (not home-secured) consumer credit plan during the first year after account opening. Section 1026.53 contains rules on allocation of payments in excess of the minimum payment. Section 1026.54 sets forth certain limitations on the imposition of finance charges as the result of a loss of a grace period. Section 1026.55 contains

limitations on increases in annual percentage rates, fees, and charges for credit card accounts. Section 1026.56 prohibits the assessment of fees or charges for over-the-limit transactions unless the consumer affirmatively consents to the creditor's payment of over-the-limit transactions. Section 1026.57 sets forth rules for reporting and marketing of college student open-end credit. Section 1026.58 sets forth requirements for the Internet posting of credit card accounts under an open-end (not home-secured) consumer credit plan.

(8) Several appendices contain information such as the procedures for determinations about state laws, state exemptions and issuance of official interpretations, special rules for certain kinds of credit plans, and the rules for computing annual percentage rates in closed-end credit transactions and total-annual-loan-cost rates for reverse mortgage transactions.

(e) Enforcement and liability. Section 108 of the Truth in Lending Act contains the administrative enforcement provisions for that Act. Sections 112, 113, 130, 131, and 134 contain provisions relating to liability for failure to comply with the requirements of the Truth in Lending Act and the regulation. Section 1204(c) of title XII of the Competitive Equality Banking Act of 1987, Public Law 100–86, 101 Stat. 552, incorporates by reference administrative enforcement and civil liability provisions of sections 108 and 130 of the Truth in Lending Act. Section 19 of the Real Estate Settlement Procedures Act contains the administrative enforcement provisions for that Act.

§ 1026.2 Definitions and Rules of Construction.

(a) Definitions. For purposes of this part, the following definitions apply:

(1) Act means the Truth in Lending Act (15 U.S.C. 1601 et seq.).

(2) Advertisement means a commercial message in any medium that promotes, directly or indirectly, a credit transaction.

(3)(i) Application means the submission of a consumer's financial information for the purposes of obtaining an extension of credit.

(ii) For transactions subject to § 1026.19(e), (f), or (g) of this part, an application consists of the submission of the consumer's name, the consumer's income, the consumer's social security number to obtain a credit report, the property address, an estimate of the value of the property, and the mortgage loan amount sought.

(4) Billing cycle or cycle means the interval between the days or dates of regular periodic statements. These intervals shall be equal and no longer than a quarter of a year. An interval will be considered equal if the number of days in the cycle does not vary more than four days from the regular day or date of the periodic statement.

(5) Bureau means the Bureau of Consumer Financial Protection.

(6) Business day means a day on which the creditor's offices are open to the public for carrying on substantially all of its business functions. However, for purposes of rescission under §§ 1026.15 and 1026.23, and for purposes of §§ 1026.19(a)(1)(ii), 1026.19(a)(2), 1026.19(e)(1)(iii)(B), 1026.19(e)(1)(iv), 1026.19(e)(2)(i)(A), 1026.19(e)(4)(ii), 1026.19(f)(1)(ii), 1026.19(f)(1)(iii), 1026.20(e)(5), 1026.31, and 1026.46(d)(4), the term means all calendar days except Sundays and the legal public holidays specified in 5 U.S.C. 6103(a), such as New Year's Day, the Birthday of Martin Luther King, Jr., Washington's Birthday, Memorial Day, Independence Day, Labor Day, Columbus Day, Veterans Day, Thanksgiving Day, and Christmas Day.

(7) Card issuer means a person that issues a credit card or that person's agent with respect to the card.

(8) Cardholder means a natural person to whom a credit card is issued for consumer credit purposes, or a natural person who has agreed with the card issuer to pay consumer credit obligations arising from the issuance of a credit card to another natural person. For purposes of § 1026.12(a) and (b), the term includes any person to whom a credit card is issued for any purpose, including business, commercial or agricultural use, or a person who has agreed with the card issuer to pay obligations arising from the issuance of such a credit card to another person.

(9) Cash price means the price at which a creditor, in the ordinary course of business, offers to sell for cash property or service that is the subject of the transaction. At the creditor's option, the term may include the price of accessories, services related to the sale, service contracts and taxes and fees for license, title, and registration. The term does not include any finance charge.

(10) Closed-end credit means consumer credit other than "open-end credit" as defined in this section.

(11) Consumer means a cardholder or natural person to whom consumer credit is offered or extended. However, for purposes of rescission under §§ 1026.15 and 1026.23, the term also includes a natural person in whose principal dwelling a security interest is or will be retained or acquired, if that person's ownership interest in the dwelling is or will be subject to the security interest. For purposes of § 1026.42(i), the term means a natural person to whom credit is offered or extended, even if the credit is primarily for business, commercial, agricultural, or organizational purposes. For purposes of §§ 1026.20(c) through (e), 1026.36(c), 1026.39, and 1026.41, the term includes a confirmed successor in interest.

(12) Consumer credit means credit offered or extended to a consumer primarily for personal, family, or household purposes.

(13) Consummation means the time that a consumer becomes contractually obligated on a credit transaction.

(14) Credit means the right to defer payment of debt or to incur debt and defer its payment.

(15)(i) Credit card means any card, plate, or other single credit device that may be used from time to time to obtain credit. The term credit card includes a hybrid prepaid-credit card as defined in § 1026.61 and a hybrid debit-credit card as defined in § 1026.62.

(ii) Credit card account under an open-end (not home-secured) consumer credit plan means any open-end credit account that is accessed by a credit card, except:

(A) A home-equity plan subject to the requirements of § 1026.40 that is accessed by a credit card; or

(B) A covered overdraft credit account as defined in § 1026.62 offered by a creditor other than a very large financial institution as defined in § 1026.62 that is accessed by a debit card or account number.

(iii) Charge card means a credit card on an account for which no periodic rate is used to compute a finance charge. The term does not include a hybrid debit-credit card as defined in § 1026.62.

(iv) Debit card means any card, plate, or other single device that may be used from time to time to access an asset account other than a prepaid account as defined in § 1026.61. The term *debit card* does not include a prepaid card as defined in § 1026.61.

(16) Credit sale means a sale in which the seller is a creditor. The term includes a bailment or lease (unless terminable without penalty at any time by the consumer) under which the consumer:

(i) Agrees to pay as compensation for use a sum substantially equivalent to, or in excess of, the total value of the property and service involved; and

(ii) Will become (or has the option to become), for no additional consideration or for nominal consideration, the owner of the property upon compliance with the agreement.

(17) Creditor means:

(i) A person who regularly extends consumer credit that is subject to a finance charge or is payable by written agreement in more than four installments (not including a down payment), and to whom the obligation is initially payable, either on the face of the note or contract, or by agreement when there is no note or contract.

(ii) For purposes of §§ 1026.4(c)(8) (Discounts), 1026.9(d) (Finance charge imposed at time of transaction), and 1026.12(e) (Prompt notification of returns and crediting of refunds), a person that honors a credit card.

(iii) For purposes of subpart B, any card issuer that extends either open-end credit or credit that is not subject to a finance charge and is not payable by written agreement in more than four installments.

(iv) For purposes of subpart B (except for the credit and charge card disclosures contained in §§ 1026.60 and 1026.9(e) and (f), the finance charge disclosures contained in § 1026.6(a)(1) and (b)(3)(i) and § 1026.7(a)(4) through (7) and (b)(4) through (6) and the right of rescission set forth in § 1026.15) and subpart C, any card issuer that extends closed-end credit that is subject to a finance charge or is payable by written agreement in more than four installments.

(v) A person regularly extends consumer credit only if it extended credit (other than credit subject to the requirements of § 1026.32) more than 25 times (or more than 5 times for transactions secured by a dwelling) in the preceding calendar year. If a person did not meet these numerical standards in the preceding calendar year, the numerical standards shall be applied to the current calendar year. A person regularly extends consumer credit if, in any 12–month period, the person originates more than one credit extension that is subject to the requirements of § 1026.32 or one or more such credit extensions through a mortgage broker.

(18) Downpayment means an amount, including the value of property used as a trade-in, paid to a seller to reduce the cash price of goods or services purchased in a credit sale transaction. A deferred portion of a downpayment may be treated as part of the downpayment if it is payable not later than the due date of the second otherwise regularly scheduled payment and is not subject to a finance charge.

(19) Dwelling means a residential structure that contains one to four units, whether or not that structure is attached to real property. The term includes an individual condominium unit, cooperative unit, mobile home, and trailer, if it is used as a residence.

(20) Open-end credit means consumer credit extended by a creditor under a plan in which:

(i) The creditor reasonably contemplates repeated transactions;

(ii) The creditor may impose a finance charge from time to time on an outstanding unpaid balance; and

(iii) The amount of credit that may be extended to the consumer during the term of the plan (up to any limit set by the creditor) is generally made available to the extent that any outstanding balance is repaid.

(21) Periodic rate means a rate of finance charge that is or may be imposed by a creditor on a balance for a day, week, month, or other subdivision of a year.

(22) Person means a natural person or an organization, including a corporation, partnership, proprietorship, association, cooperative, estate, trust, or government unit.

(23) Prepaid finance charge means any finance charge paid separately in cash or by check before or at consummation of a transaction, or withheld from the proceeds of the credit at any time.

(24) Residential mortgage transaction means a transaction in which a mortgage, deed of trust, purchase money security interest arising under an installment sales contract, or equivalent consensual security interest is created or retained in the consumer's principal dwelling to finance the acquisition or initial construction of that dwelling.

(25) Security interest means an interest in property that secures performance of a consumer credit obligation and that is recognized by State or Federal law. It does not include incidental interests such as interests in proceeds, accessions, additions, fixtures, insurance proceeds (whether or not the creditor is a loss payee or beneficiary), premium rebates, or interests in after-acquired property. For purposes of disclosures under §§ 1026.6, 1026.18, 1026.19(e) and (f), and 1026.38(l)(6), the term does not include an interest that arises solely by operation of law. However, for purposes of the right of rescission under §§ 1026.15 and 1026.23, the term does include interests that arise solely by operation of law.

(26) State means any state, the District of Columbia, the Commonwealth of Puerto Rico, and any territory or possession of the United States.

(27)(i) Successor in interest means a person to whom an ownership interest in a dwelling securing a closed-end consumer credit transaction is transferred from a consumer, provided that the transfer is:

(A) A transfer by devise, descent, or operation of law on the death of a joint tenant or tenant by the entirety;

(B) A transfer to a relative resulting from the death of the consumer;

(C) A transfer where the spouse or children of the consumer become an owner of the property;

(D) A transfer resulting from a decree of a dissolution of marriage, legal separation agreement, or from an incidental property settlement agreement, by which the spouse of the consumer becomes an owner of the property; or

(E) A transfer into an *inter vivos* trust in which the consumer is and remains a beneficiary and which does not relate to a transfer of rights of occupancy in the property.

(ii) Confirmed successor in interest means a successor in interest once a servicer has confirmed the successor in interest's identity and ownership interest in the dwelling.

(28) The Board-selected benchmark replacement for consumer loans means the SOFR-based index selected by the Board of Governors of the Federal Reserve System to replace, as applicable, the 1-month, 3-month, 6-month, or 12-month tenor of U.S. Dollar LIBOR, as set forth in the Board of Governors of the Federal Reserve System's regulation at 12 CFR part 253, which implements the Adjustable Interest Rate (LIBOR) Act, Public Law 117-103, division U.

(b) Rules of construction. For purposes of this part, the following rules of construction apply:

(1) Where appropriate, the singular form of a word includes the plural form and plural includes singular.

(2) Where the words obligation and transaction are used in the regulation, they refer to a consumer credit obligation or transaction, depending upon the context. Where the word *credit* is used in the regulation, it means *consumer credit* unless the context clearly indicates otherwise.

(3) Unless defined in this part, the words used have the meanings given to them by state law or contract.

(4) Where the word *amount* is used in this part to describe disclosure requirements, it refers to a numerical amount.

§ 1026.8 Identifying Transactions on Periodic Statements.

The creditor shall identify credit transactions on or with the first periodic statement that reflects the transaction by furnishing the following information, as applicable:

(a) Sale credit.

(1) Except as provided in paragraph (a)(2) of this section, for each credit transaction involving the sale of property or services, the creditor must disclose the amount and date of the transaction, and either:

(i) A brief identification of the property or services purchased, for creditors and sellers that are the same or related; or

(ii) The seller's name; and the city and state or foreign country where the transaction took place. The creditor may omit the address or provide any suitable designation that helps the consumer to identify the transaction when the transaction took place at a location that is not fixed; took place in the consumer's home; or was a mail, Internet, or telephone order.

(2) Creditors need not comply with paragraph (a)(1) of this section if an actual copy of the receipt or other credit document is provided with the first periodic statement reflecting the transaction, and the amount of the transaction and either the date of the transaction to the consumer's account or the date of debiting the transaction are disclosed on the copy or on the periodic statement.

(b) Nonsale credit. For each credit transaction not involving the sale of property or services, the creditor must disclose a brief identification of the transaction; the amount of the transaction; and at least one of the following dates: The date of the transaction, the date the transaction was debited to the consumer's account, or, if the consumer signed the credit document, the date appearing on the document. If an actual copy of the receipt or other credit document is provided and that copy shows the amount and at least one of the specified dates, the brief identification may be omitted.

(c) Alternative creditor procedures; consumer inquiries for clarification or documentation. The following procedures apply to creditors that treat an inquiry for clarification or documentation as a notice of a billing error, including correcting the account in accordance with § 1026.13(e):

(1) Failure to disclose the information required by paragraphs (a) and (b) of this section is not a failure to comply with the regulation, provided that the creditor also maintains procedures reasonably designed to obtain and provide the information. This applies to transactions that take place outside a state, as defined in § 1026.2(a)(26), whether or not the creditor maintains procedures reasonably adapted to obtain the required information.

(2) As an alternative to the brief identification for sale or nonsale credit, the creditor may disclose a number or symbol that also appears on the receipt or other credit document given to the consumer, if the number or symbol reasonably identifies that transaction with that creditor.

§ 1026.10 Payments.

(a) General rule. A creditor shall credit a payment to the consumer's account as of the date of receipt, except when a delay in crediting does not result in a finance or other charge or except as provided in paragraph (b) of this section.

(b) Specific requirements for payments.

(1) General rule. A creditor may specify reasonable requirements for payments that enable most consumers to make conforming payments.

(2) Examples of reasonable requirements for payments. Reasonable requirements for making payment may include:

(i) Requiring that payments be accompanied by the account number or payment stub;

(ii) Setting reasonable cut-off times for payments to be received by mail, by electronic means, by telephone, and in person (except as provided in paragraph (b)(3) of this section), provided that such cut-off times shall be no earlier than 5 p.m. on the payment due date at the location specified by the creditor for the receipt of such payments;

(iii) Specifying that only checks or money orders should be sent by mail;

(iv) Specifying that payment is to be made in U.S. dollars; or

(v) Specifying one particular address for receiving payments, such as a post office box.

(3) In-person payments on credit card accounts.

(i) General. Notwithstanding § 1026.10(b), payments on a credit card account under an open-end (not home-secured) consumer credit plan made in person at a branch or office of a card issuer that is a financial institution prior to the close of business of that branch or office shall be considered received on the date on which the consumer makes the payment. A card issuer that is a financial institution shall not impose a cut-off time earlier than the close of business for any such payments made in person at any branch or office of the card issuer at which such payments are accepted. Notwithstanding § 1026.10(b)(2)(ii), a card issuer may impose a cut-off time earlier than 5 p.m. for such payments, if the close of business of the branch or office is earlier than 5 p.m.

(ii) Financial institution. For purposes of paragraph (b)(3) of this section, "financial institution" shall mean a bank, savings association, or credit union.

(4) Nonconforming payments.

(i) In general. Except as provided in paragraph (b)(4)(ii) of this section, if a creditor specifies, on or with the periodic statement, requirements for the consumer to follow in making payments as permitted under this § 1026.10, but accepts a payment that does not conform to the requirements, the creditor shall credit the payment within five days of receipt.

(ii) Payment methods promoted by creditor. If a creditor promotes a method for making payments, such payments shall be considered conforming payments in accordance with this paragraph (b) and shall be credited to the consumer's account as of the date of receipt, except when a delay in crediting does not result in a finance or other charge.

(c) Adjustment of account. If a creditor fails to credit a payment, as required by paragraphs (a) or (b) of this section, in time to avoid the imposition of finance or other charges, the creditor shall adjust the consumer's account so that the charges imposed are credited to the consumer's account during the next billing cycle.

(d) Crediting of payments when creditor does not receive or accept payments on due date.

(1) General. Except as provided in paragraph (d)(2) of this section, if a creditor does not receive or accept payments by mail on the due date for payments, the creditor may generally not treat a payment received the next business day as late for any purpose. For purposes of this paragraph (d), the "next business day" means the next day on which the creditor accepts or receives payments by mail.

(2) Payments accepted or received other than by mail. If a creditor accepts or receives payments made on the due date by a method other than mail, such as electronic or telephone payments, the creditor is not required to treat a payment made by that method on the next business day as timely, even if it does not accept mailed payments on the due date.

(e) Limitations on fees related to method of payment. For credit card accounts under an open-end (not home-secured) consumer credit plan, a creditor may not impose a separate fee to allow consumers to make a payment by any method, such as mail, electronic, or telephone payments, unless such payment method involves an expedited service by a customer service representative of the creditor. For purposes of paragraph (e) of this section, the term "creditor" includes a third party that collects, receives, or processes payments on behalf of a creditor.

(f) Changes by card issuer. If a card issuer makes a material change in the address for receiving payments or procedures for handling payments, and such change causes a material delay in the crediting of a payment to the consumer's account during the 60-day period following the date on which such change took effect, the card issuer may not impose any late fee or finance charge for a late payment on the credit card account during the 60-day period following the date on which the change took effect.

§ 1026.12 Special Credit Card Provisions.

(a) Issuance of credit cards. Regardless of the purpose for which a credit card is to be used, including business, commercial, or agricultural use, no credit card shall be issued to any person except:

(1) In response to an oral or written request or application for the card; or

(2) As a renewal of, or substitute for, an accepted credit card.

(b) Liability of cardholder for unauthorized use.

(1)(i) Definition of unauthorized use. For purposes of this section, the term "unauthorized use" means the use of a credit card by a person, other than the cardholder, who does not have actual, implied, or apparent authority for such use, and from which the cardholder receives no benefit.

(ii) Limitation on amount. The liability of a cardholder for unauthorized use of a credit card shall not exceed the lesser of $50 or the amount of money, property, labor, or services obtained by the unauthorized use before notification to the card issuer under paragraph (b)(3) of this section.

(2) Conditions of liability. A cardholder shall be liable for unauthorized use of a credit card only if:

(i) The credit card is an accepted credit card;

(ii) The card issuer has provided adequate notice of the cardholder's maximum potential liability and of means by which the card issuer may be notified of loss or theft of the card. The notice shall state that the cardholder's liability shall not exceed $50 (or any lesser amount) and that the cardholder may give oral or written notification, and shall describe a means of notification (for example, a telephone number, an address, or both); and

(iii) The card issuer has provided a means to identify the cardholder on the account or the authorized user of the card.

(3) Notification to card issuer. Notification to a card issuer is given when steps have been taken as may be reasonably required in the ordinary course of business to provide the card issuer with the pertinent information about the loss, theft, or possible unauthorized use of a credit card, regardless of whether any particular officer, employee, or agent of the card issuer does, in fact, receive the information. Notification may be given, at the option of the person giving it, in person, by telephone, or in writing. Notification in writing is considered given at the time of receipt or, whether or not received, at the expiration of the time ordinarily required for transmission, whichever is earlier.

(4) Effect of other applicable law or agreement. If state law or an agreement between a cardholder and the card issuer imposes lesser liability than that provided in this paragraph, the lesser liability shall govern.

(5) Business use of credit cards. If 10 or more credit cards are issued by one card issuer for use by the employees of an organization, this section does not prohibit the card issuer and the organization from agreeing to liability for unauthorized use without regard to this section. However, liability for unauthorized use may be imposed on an employee of the organization, by either the card issuer or the organization, only in accordance with this section.

(c) Right of cardholder to assert claims or defenses against card issuer.

(1) General rule. When a person who honors a credit card fails to resolve satisfactorily a dispute as to property or services purchased with the credit card in a consumer credit transaction, the cardholder may assert against the card issuer all claims (other than tort claims) and defenses arising out of the transaction and relating to the failure to resolve the dispute. The cardholder may withhold payment up to the amount of credit outstanding for the property or services that gave rise to the dispute and any finance or other charges imposed on that amount.

(2) Adverse credit reports prohibited. If, in accordance with paragraph (c)(1) of this section, the cardholder withholds payment of the amount of credit outstanding for the disputed transaction, the card issuer shall not report that amount as delinquent until the dispute is settled or judgment is rendered.

(3) Limitations.

(i) General. The rights stated in paragraphs (c)(1) and (c)(2) of this section apply only if:

(A) The cardholder has made a good faith attempt to resolve the dispute with the person honoring the credit card; and

(B) The amount of credit extended to obtain the property or services that result in the assertion of the claim or defense by the cardholder exceeds $50, and the disputed transaction occurred in the same state as the cardholder's current designated address or, if not within the same state, within 100 miles from that address.

(ii) Exclusion. The limitations stated in paragraph (c)(3)(i)(B) of this section shall not apply when the person honoring the credit card:

(A) Is the same person as the card issuer;

(B) Is controlled by the card issuer directly or indirectly;

(C) Is under the direct or indirect control of a third person that also directly or indirectly controls the card issuer;

(D) Controls the card issuer directly or indirectly;

(E) Is a franchised dealer in the card issuer's products or services; or

(F) Has obtained the order for the disputed transaction through a mail solicitation made or participated in by the card issuer.

(d) Offsets by card issuer prohibited.

(1) General rule. A card issuer may not take any action, either before or after termination of credit

card privileges, to offset a cardholder's indebtedness arising from a consumer credit transaction under the relevant credit card plan against funds of the cardholder held on deposit with the card issuer.

(2) Rights of the card issuer. This paragraph does not alter or affect the right of a card issuer acting under state or Federal law to do any of the following with regard to funds of a cardholder held on deposit with the card issuer if the same procedure is constitutionally available to creditors generally: Obtain or enforce a consensual security interest in the funds; attach or otherwise levy upon the funds; or obtain or enforce a court order relating to the funds.

(3) Periodic deductions.

(i) This paragraph (d) does not prohibit a plan, if authorized in writing by the cardholder, under which the card issuer may periodically deduct all or part of the cardholder's credit card debt from a deposit account held with the card issuer (subject to the limitations in § 1026.13(d)(1)).

(ii) With respect to a covered separate credit feature accessible by a hybrid prepaid-credit card as defined in § 1026.61, for purposes of this paragraph (d)(3), "periodically" means no more frequently than once per calendar month, such as on a monthly due date disclosed on the applicable periodic statement in accordance with the requirements of § 1026.7(b)(11)(i)(A) or on an earlier date in each calendar month in accordance with a written authorization signed by the consumer.

(e) Prompt notification of returns and crediting of refunds.

(1) When a creditor other than the card issuer accepts the return of property or forgives a debt for services that is to be reflected as a credit to the consumer's credit card account, that creditor shall, within 7 business days from accepting the return or forgiving the debt, transmit a credit statement to the card issuer through the card issuer's normal channels for credit statements.

(2) The card issuer shall, within 3 business days from receipt of a credit statement, credit the consumer's account with the amount of the refund.

(3) If a creditor other than a card issuer routinely gives cash refunds to consumers paying in cash, the creditor shall also give credit or cash refunds to consumers using credit cards, unless it discloses at the time the transaction is consummated that credit or cash refunds for returns are not given. This section does not require refunds for returns nor does it prohibit refunds in kind.

(f) Discounts; tie-in arrangements. No card issuer may, by contract or otherwise:

(1) Prohibit any person who honors a credit card from offering a discount to a consumer to induce the consumer to pay by cash, check, or similar means rather than by use of a credit card or its underlying account for the purchase of property or services; or

(2) Require any person who honors the card issuer's credit card to open or maintain any account or obtain any other service not essential to the operation of the credit card plan from the card issuer or any other person, as a condition of participation in a credit card plan. If maintenance of an account for clearing purposes is determined to be essential to the operation of the credit card plan, it may be required only if no service charges or minimum balance requirements are imposed.

(g) Relation to Electronic Fund Transfer Act and Regulation E. For guidance on whether Regulation Z (12 CFR part 1026) or Regulation E (12 CFR part 1005) applies in instances involving both credit and electronic fund transfer aspects, refer to Regulation E, 12 CFR 1005.12(a) regarding issuance and liability for unauthorized use. On matters other than issuance and liability, this section applies to the credit aspects of combined credit/electronic fund transfer transactions, as applicable.

§ 1026.13 Billing Error Resolution.

(a) Definition of billing error. For purposes of this section, the term billing error means:

(1) A reflection on or with a periodic statement of an extension of credit that is not made to the consumer or to a person who has actual, implied, or apparent authority to use the consumer's credit card or open-end credit plan.

(2) A reflection on or with a periodic statement of an extension of credit that is not identified in accordance with the requirements of §§ 1026.7(a)(2) or (b)(2), as applicable, and 1026.8.

(3) A reflection on or with a periodic statement of an extension of credit for property or services not accepted by the consumer or the consumer's designee, or not delivered to the consumer or the consumer's designee as agreed.

(4) A reflection on a periodic statement of the creditor's failure to credit properly a payment or other credit issued to the consumer's account.

(5) A reflection on a periodic statement of a computational or similar error of an accounting nature that is made by the creditor.

(6) A reflection on a periodic statement of an extension of credit for which the consumer requests

additional clarification, including documentary evidence.

(7) The creditor's failure to mail or deliver a periodic statement to the consumer's last known address if that address was received by the creditor, in writing, at least 20 days before the end of the billing cycle for which the statement was required.

(b) Billing error notice. A billing error notice is a written notice from a consumer that:

(1) Is received by a creditor at the address disclosed under § 1026.7(a)(9) or (b)(9), as applicable, no later than 60 days after the creditor transmitted the first periodic statement that reflects the alleged billing error;

(2) Enables the creditor to identify the consumer's name and account number; and

(3) To the extent possible, indicates the consumer's belief and the reasons for the belief that a billing error exists, and the type, date, and amount of the error.

(c) Time for resolution; general procedures.

(1) The creditor shall mail or deliver written acknowledgment to the consumer within 30 days of receiving a billing error notice, unless the creditor has complied with the appropriate resolution procedures of paragraphs (e) and (f) of this section, as applicable, within the 30-day period; and

(2) The creditor shall comply with the appropriate resolution procedures of paragraphs (e) and (f) of this section, as applicable, within 2 complete billing cycles (but in no event later than 90 days) after receiving a billing error notice.

(d) Rules pending resolution. Until a billing error is resolved under paragraph (e) or (f) of this section, the following rules apply:

(1) Consumer's right to withhold disputed amount; collection action prohibited. The consumer need not pay (and the creditor may not try to collect) any portion of any required payment that the consumer believes is related to the disputed amount (including related finance or other charges). If the cardholder has enrolled in an automatic payment plan offered by the card issuer and has agreed to pay the credit card indebtedness by periodic deductions from the cardholder's deposit account, the card issuer shall not deduct any part of the disputed amount or related finance or other charges if a billing error notice is received any time up to 3 business days before the scheduled payment date.

(2) Adverse credit reports prohibited. The creditor or its agent shall not (directly or indirectly) make or threaten to make an adverse report to any person about the consumer's credit standing, or report that an amount or account is delinquent, because the consumer failed to pay the disputed amount or related finance or other charges.

(3) Acceleration of debt and restriction of account prohibited. A creditor shall not accelerate any part of the consumer's indebtedness or restrict or close a consumer's account solely because the consumer has exercised in good faith rights provided by this section. A creditor may be subject to the forfeiture penalty under 15 U.S.C. 1666(e) for failure to comply with any of the requirements of this section.

(4) Permitted creditor actions. A creditor is not prohibited from taking action to collect any undisputed portion of the item or bill; from deducting any disputed amount and related finance or other charges from the consumer's credit limit on the account; or from reflecting a disputed amount and related finance or other charges on a periodic statement, provided that the creditor indicates on or with the periodic statement that payment of any disputed amount and related finance or other charges is not required pending the creditor's compliance with this section.

(e) Procedures if billing error occurred as asserted. If a creditor determines that a billing error occurred as asserted, it shall within the time limits in paragraph (c)(2) of this section:

(1) Correct the billing error and credit the consumer's account with any disputed amount and related finance or other charges, as applicable; and

(2) Mail or deliver a correction notice to the consumer.

(f) Procedures if different billing error or no billing error occurred. If, after conducting a reasonable investigation, a creditor determines that no billing error occurred or that a different billing error occurred from that asserted, the creditor shall within the time limits in paragraph (c)(2) of this section:

(1) Mail or deliver to the consumer an explanation that sets forth the reasons for the creditor's belief that the billing error alleged by the consumer is incorrect in whole or in part;

(2) Furnish copies of documentary evidence of the consumer's indebtedness, if the consumer so requests; and

(3) If a different billing error occurred, correct the billing error and credit the consumer's account with any disputed amount and related finance or other charges, as applicable.

(g) Creditor's rights and duties after resolution. If a creditor, after complying with all of the requirements of this section, determines that a consumer owes all or part of the disputed amount and related finance or other charges, the creditor:

(1) Shall promptly notify the consumer in writing of the time when payment is due and the portion of the disputed amount and related finance or other charges that the consumer still owes;

(2) Shall allow any time period disclosed under § 1026.6(a)(1) or (b)(2)(v), as applicable, and § 1026.7(a)(8) or (b)(8), as applicable, during which the consumer can pay the amount due under paragraph (g)(1) of this section without incurring additional finance or other charges;

(3) May report an account or amount as delinquent because the amount due under paragraph (g)(1) of this section remains unpaid after the creditor has allowed any time period disclosed under § 1026.6(a)(1) or (b)(2)(v), as applicable, and § 1026.7(a)(8) or (b)(8), as applicable or 10 days (whichever is longer) during which the consumer can pay the amount; but

(4) May not report that an amount or account is delinquent because the amount due under paragraph (g)(1) of the section remains unpaid, if the creditor receives (within the time allowed for payment in paragraph (g)(3) of this section) further written notice from the consumer that any portion of the billing error is still in dispute, unless the creditor also:

(i) Promptly reports that the amount or account is in dispute;

(ii) Mails or delivers to the consumer (at the same time the report is made) a written notice of the name and address of each person to whom the creditor makes a report; and

(iii) Promptly reports any subsequent resolution of the reported delinquency to all persons to whom the creditor has made a report.

(h) Reassertion of billing error. A creditor that has fully complied with the requirements of this section has no further responsibilities under this section (other than as provided in paragraph (g)(4) of this section) if a consumer reasserts substantially the same billing error.

(i) Relation to Electronic Fund Transfer Act and Regulation E. A creditor shall comply with the requirements of Regulation E, 12 CFR 1005.11, and 1005.18(e) as applicable, governing error resolution rather than those of paragraphs (a), (b), (c), (e), (f), and (h) of this section if:

(1) Except with respect to a prepaid account as defined in § 1026.61, an extension of credit that is incident to an electronic fund transfer occurs under an agreement between the consumer and a financial institution to extend credit when the consumer's account is overdrawn or to maintain a specified minimum balance in the consumer's account; or

(2) With regard to a covered separate credit feature and an asset feature of a prepaid account where both are accessible by a hybrid prepaid-credit card as defined in § 1026.61, an extension of credit that is incident to an electronic fund transfer occurs when the hybrid prepaid-credit card accesses both funds in the asset feature of the prepaid account and a credit extension from the credit feature with respect to a particular transaction.

§ 1026.51 Ability to Pay.

(a) General rule.

(1)(i) Consideration of ability to pay. A card issuer must not open a credit card account for a consumer under an open-end (not home-secured) consumer credit plan, or increase any credit limit applicable to such account, unless the card issuer considers the consumer's ability to make the required minimum periodic payments under the terms of the account based on the consumer's income or assets and the consumer's current obligations.

(ii) Reasonable policies and procedures. Card issuers must establish and maintain reasonable written policies and procedures to consider the consumer's ability to make the required minimum payments under the terms of the account based on a consumer's income or assets and a consumer's current obligations. Reasonable policies and procedures include treating any income and assets to which the consumer has a reasonable expectation of access as the consumer's income or assets, or limiting consideration of the consumer's income or assets to the consumer's independent income and assets. Reasonable policies and procedures also include consideration of at least one of the following: The ratio of debt obligations to income; the ratio of debt obligations to assets; or the income the consumer will have after paying debt obligations. It would be unreasonable for a card issuer not to review any information about a consumer's income or assets and current obligations, or to issue a credit card to a consumer who does not have any income or assets.

(2) Minimum periodic payments.

(i) Reasonable method. For purposes of paragraph (a)(1) of this section, a card issuer must use a reasonable method for estimating the minimum periodic payments the consumer would be required to pay under the terms of the account.

(ii) Safe harbor. A card issuer complies with paragraph (a)(2)(i) of this section if it estimates required minimum periodic payments using the following method:

(A) The card issuer assumes utilization, from the first day of the billing cycle, of the full credit line that the issuer is considering offering to the consumer; and

(B) The card issuer uses a minimum payment formula employed by the issuer for the product the issuer is considering offering to the consumer or, in the case of an existing account, the minimum payment formula that currently applies to that account, provided that:

(1) If the applicable minimum payment formula includes interest charges, the card issuer estimates those charges using an interest rate that the issuer is considering offering to the consumer for purchases or, in the case of an existing account, the interest rate that currently applies to purchases; and

(2) If the applicable minimum payment formula includes mandatory fees, the card issuer must assume that such fees have been charged to the account.

(b) Rules affecting young consumers.

(1) Applications from young consumers. A card issuer may not open a credit card account under an open-end (not home-secured) consumer credit plan for a consumer less than 21 years old, unless the consumer has submitted a written application and the card issuer has:

(i) Financial information indicating the consumer has an independent ability to make the required minimum periodic payments on the proposed extension of credit in connection with the account, consistent with paragraph (a) of this section; or

(ii)(A) A signed agreement of a cosigner, guarantor, or joint applicant who is at least 21 years old to be either secondarily liable for any debt on the account incurred by the consumer before the consumer has attained the age of 21 or jointly liable with the consumer for any debt on the account, and

(B) Financial information indicating such cosigner, guarantor, or joint applicant has the ability to make the required minimum periodic payments on such debts, consistent with paragraph (a) of this section.

(2) Credit line increases for young consumers.

(i) If a credit card account has been opened pursuant to paragraph (b)(1)(i) of this section, no increase in the credit limit may be made on such account before the consumer attains the age of 21 unless:

(A) At the time of the contemplated increase, the consumer has an independent ability to make the required minimum periodic payments on the increased limit consistent with paragraph (b)(1)(i) of this section; or

(B) A cosigner, guarantor, or joint applicant who is at least 21 years old agrees in writing to assume liability for any debt incurred on the account, consistent with paragraph (b)(1)(ii) of this section.

(ii) If a credit card account has been opened pursuant to paragraph (b)(1)(ii) of this section, no increase in the credit limit may be made on such account before the consumer attains the age of 21 unless the cosigner, guarantor, or joint accountholder who assumed liability at account opening agrees in writing to assume liability on the increase.

§ 1026.52 Limitations on Fees.

(a) Limitations during first year after account opening—

(1) General rule. Except as provided in paragraph (a)(2) of this section, the total amount of fees a consumer is required to pay with respect to a credit card account under an open-end (not home-secured) consumer credit plan during the first year after account opening must not exceed 25 percent of the credit limit in effect when the account is opened. For purposes of this paragraph, an account is considered open no earlier than the date on which the account may first be used by the consumer to engage in transactions.

(2) Fees not subject to limitations. Paragraph (a) of this section does not apply to:

(i) Late payment fees, over-the-limit fees, and returned-payment fees; or

(ii) Fees that the consumer is not required to pay with respect to the account.

(3) Rule of construction. Paragraph (a) of this section does not authorize the imposition or payment of fees or charges otherwise prohibited by law.

(b) Limitations on penalty fees. A card issuer must not impose a fee for violating the terms or other requirements of a credit card account under an open-end (not home-secured) consumer credit plan unless the dollar amount of the fee is consistent with paragraphs (b)(1) and (b)(2) of this section.

(1) General rule. Except as provided in paragraph (b)(2) of this section, a card issuer may impose a fee for violating the terms or other requirements of a credit card account under an open-end (not home-secured) consumer credit plan if the dollar amount of the fee is consistent with either paragraph (b)(1)(i) or (b)(1)(ii) of this section.

(i) Fees based on costs. A card issuer may impose a fee for violating the terms or other requirements of an account if the card issuer has determined that the dollar amount of the fee represents a reasonable proportion of the total costs incurred by the card issuer as a result of that type of violation. A card issuer must reevaluate this determination at least once every twelve months. If as a result of the reevaluation the card issuer determines that a lower fee represents a reasonable proportion of the total costs incurred by the card issuer as a result of that type of violation, the card issuer must begin imposing the lower fee within 45 days after completing the reevaluation. If as a result of the reevaluation the card issuer determines that a higher fee represents a reasonable proportion of the total costs incurred by the card issuer as a result of that type of violation, the card issuer may begin imposing the higher fee after complying with the notice requirements in § 1026.9.

(ii) Safe harbors. Except as provided in paragraph (b)(1)(ii)(E) of this section, a card issuer may impose a fee for a late payment on an account if the dollar amount of the fee does not exceed $8. A card issuer may impose a fee for other types of violations of the terms or other requirements of an account if the dollar amount of the fee does not exceed, as applicable:

(A) $32

(B) $43 if the card issuer previously imposed a fee pursuant to paragraph (b)(1)(ii)(A) of this section for a violation of the same type that occurred during the same billing cycle or one of the next six billing cycles; or

(C) Three percent of the delinquent balance on a charge card account that requires payment of outstanding balances in full at the end of each billing cycle if the card issuer has not received the required payment for two or more consecutive billing cycles, notwithstanding the limitation on the amount of a late payment fee in paragraph (b)(1)(ii) of this section.

(D) The amounts in paragraphs (b)(1)(ii)(A) and (b)(1)(ii)(B) of this section will be adjusted annually by the Bureau to reflect changes in the Consumer Price Index.

(E) A smaller card issuer, as defined in paragraph (b)(3) of this section, may impose a fee for a late payment on an account if the dollar amount of the fee does not exceed the amount in paragraph (b)(1)(ii)(A) or (B) of this section, as applicable, notwithstanding the limitation on the amount of a late payment fee in this paragraph (b)(1)(ii).

(2) Prohibited fees.

(i) Fees that exceed dollar amount associated with violation—

(A) Generally. A card issuer must not impose a fee for violating the terms or other requirements of a credit card account under an open-end (not home-secured) consumer credit plan that exceeds the dollar amount associated with the violation.

(B) No dollar amount associated with violation. A card issuer must not impose a fee for violating the terms or other requirements of a credit card account under an open-end (not home-secured) consumer credit plan when there is no dollar amount associated with the violation. For purposes of paragraph (b)(2)(i) of this section, there is no dollar amount associated with the following violations:

(1) Transactions that the card issuer declines to authorize;

(2) Account inactivity; and

(3) The closure or termination of an account.

(ii) Multiple fees based on a single event or transaction. A card issuer must not impose more than one fee for violating the terms or other requirements of a credit card account under an open-end (not home-secured) consumer credit plan based on a single event or transaction. A card issuer may, at its option, comply with this prohibition by imposing no more than one fee for violating the terms or other requirements of an account during a billing cycle.

(3) Smaller card issuer.

(i) Except as provided in paragraph (b)(3)(ii) of this section, a card issuer is a smaller card issuer for purposes of paragraph (b)(1)(ii)(E) of this section if the card issuer together with its affiliates had fewer than one million open credit card accounts, as defined in § 1026.58(b)(6), for the entire preceding calendar year. For purposes of this paragraph (b)(3), *affiliate* means any company that controls, is controlled by, or is under common control with another company, as set forth in the Bank Holding Company Act of 1956 (12 U.S.C. 1841 et seq.).

(ii) If a card issuer together with its affiliates had fewer than one million open credit card accounts for the entire preceding calendar year but meets or exceeds that number of open credit card accounts in the current calendar year, the card issuer will no longer be a smaller card issuer for purposes of paragraph (b)(1)(ii)(E) of this section as of 60 days after meeting or exceeding that number of open credit card accounts.

§ 1026.53 Allocation of Payments.

(a) General rule. Except as provided in paragraph (b) of this section, when a consumer makes a payment in excess of the required minimum periodic payment for a credit card account under an open-end (not home-secured) consumer credit plan, the card issuer must allocate the excess amount first to the balance with the highest annual percentage rate and any remaining portion to the other balances in descending order based on the applicable annual percentage rate.

(b) Special rules—

(1) Accounts with balances subject to deferred interest or similar program. When a balance on a credit card account under an open-end (not home-secured) consumer credit plan is subject to a deferred interest or similar program that provides that a consumer will not be obligated to pay interest that accrues on the balance if the balance is paid in full prior to the expiration of a specified period of time:

(i) Last two billing cycles. The card issuer must allocate any amount paid by the consumer in excess of the required minimum periodic payment consistent with paragraph (a) of this section, except that, during the two billing cycles immediately preceding expiration of the specified period, the excess amount must be allocated first to the balance subject to the deferred interest or similar program and any remaining portion allocated to any other balances consistent with paragraph (a) of this section; or

(ii) Consumer request. The card issuer may at its option allocate any amount paid by the consumer in excess of the required minimum periodic payment among the balances on the account in the manner requested by the consumer.

(2) Accounts with secured balances. When a balance on a credit card account under an open-end (not home-secured) consumer credit plan is secured, the card issuer may at its option allocate any amount paid by the consumer in excess of the required minimum periodic payment to that balance if requested by the consumer.

§ 1026.54 Limitations on the Imposition of Finance Charges.

(a) Limitations on imposing finance charges as a result of the loss of a grace period—

(1) General rule. Except as provided in paragraph (b) of this section, a card issuer must not impose finance charges as a result of the loss of a grace period on a credit card account under an open-end (not home-secured) consumer credit plan if those finance charges are based on:

(i) Balances for days in billing cycles that precede the most recent billing cycle; or

(ii) Any portion of a balance subject to a grace period that was repaid prior to the expiration of the grace period.

(2) Definition of grace period. For purposes of paragraph (a)(1) of this section, "grace period" has the same meaning as in § 1026.5(b)(2)(ii)(B)(3).

(b) Exceptions. Paragraph (a) of this section does not apply to:

(1) Adjustments to finance charges as a result of the resolution of a dispute under § 1026.12 or § 1026.13; or

(2) Adjustments to finance charges as a result of the return of a payment.

§ 1026.55 Limitations on Increasing Annual Percentage Rates, Fees, and Charges.

(a) General rule. Except as provided in paragraph (b) of this section, a card issuer must not increase an annual percentage rate or a fee or charge required to be disclosed under § 1026.6(b)(2)(ii), (b)(2)(iii), or (b)(2)(xii) on a credit card account under an open-end (not home-secured) consumer credit plan.

(b) Exceptions. A card issuer may increase an annual percentage rate or a fee or charge required to be disclosed under § 1026.6(b)(2)(ii), (b)(2)(iii), or (b)(2)(xii) pursuant to an exception set forth in this paragraph even if that increase would not be permitted under a different exception.

(1) Temporary rate, fee, or charge exception. A card issuer may increase an annual percentage rate or a fee or charge required to be disclosed under § 1026.6(b)(2)(ii), (b)(2)(iii), or (b)(2)(xii) upon the expiration of a specified period of six months or longer, provided that:

(i) Prior to the commencement of that period, the card issuer disclosed in writing to the consumer, in a clear and conspicuous manner, the length of the period and the annual percentage rate, fee, or charge that would apply after expiration of the period; and

(ii) Upon expiration of the specified period:

(A) The card issuer must not apply an annual percentage rate, fee, or charge to transactions that occurred prior to the period that exceeds the annual percentage rate, fee, or charge that applied to those transactions prior to the period;

(B) If the disclosures required by paragraph (b)(1)(i) of this section are provided pursuant to § 1026.9(c), the card issuer must not apply an annual percentage rate, fee, or charge to transactions that occurred within 14 days after provision of the notice that exceeds the annual percentage rate, fee or charge that applied to that category of transactions prior to provision of the notice; and

(C) The card issuer must not apply an annual percentage rate, fee, or charge to transactions that occurred during the period that exceeds the increased annual percentage rate, fee, or charge disclosed pursuant to paragraph (b)(1)(i) of this section.

(2) Variable rate exception. A card issuer may increase an annual percentage rate when:

(i) The annual percentage rate varies according to an index that is not under the card issuer's control and is available to the general public; and

(ii) The increase in the annual percentage rate is due to an increase in the index.

(3) Advance notice exception. A card issuer may increase an annual percentage rate or a fee or charge required to be disclosed under § 1026.6(b)(2)(ii), (b)(2)(iii), or (b)(2)(xii) after complying with the applicable notice requirements in § 1026.9(b), (c), or (g), provided that:

(i) If a card issuer discloses an increased annual percentage rate, fee, or charge pursuant to § 1026.9(b), the card issuer must not apply that rate, fee, or charge to transactions that occurred prior to provision of the notice;

(ii) If a card issuer discloses an increased annual percentage rate, fee, or charge pursuant to § 1026.9(c) or (g), the card issuer must not apply that rate, fee, or charge to transactions that occurred prior to or within 14 days after provision of the notice; and

(iii) This exception does not permit a card issuer to increase an annual percentage rate or a fee or charge required to be disclosed under § 1026.6(b)(2)(ii), (iii), or (xii) during the first year after the account is opened, while the account is closed, or while the card issuer does not permit the consumer to use the account for new transactions. For purposes of this paragraph, an account is considered open no earlier than the date on which the account may first be used by the consumer to engage in transactions.

(4) Delinquency exception. A card issuer may increase an annual percentage rate or a fee or charge required to be disclosed under § 1026.6(b)(2)(ii), (b)(2)(iii), or (b)(2)(xii) due to the card issuer not receiving the consumer's required minimum periodic payment within 60 days after the due date for that payment, provided that:

(i) The card issuer must disclose in a clear and conspicuous manner in the notice of the increase pursuant to § 1026.9(c) or (g):

(A) A statement of the reason for the increase; and

(B) That the increased annual percentage rate, fee, or charge will cease to apply if the card issuer receives six consecutive required minimum periodic payments on or before the payment due date beginning with the first payment due following the effective date of the increase; and

(ii) If the card issuer receives six consecutive required minimum periodic payments on or before the payment due date beginning with the first payment due following the effective date of the increase, the card issuer must reduce any annual percentage rate, fee, or charge increased pursuant to this exception to the annual percentage rate, fee, or charge that applied prior to the increase with respect to transactions that occurred prior to or within 14 days after provision of the § 1026.9(c) or (g) notice.

(5) Workout and temporary hardship arrangement exception. A card issuer may increase an annual percentage rate or a fee or charge required to be disclosed under § 1026.6(b)(2)(ii), (b)(2)(iii), or (b)(2)(xii) due to the consumer's completion of a workout or temporary hardship arrangement or the consumer's failure to comply with the terms of such an arrangement, provided that:

(i) Prior to commencement of the arrangement (except as provided in § 1026.9(c)(2)(v)(D)), the card issuer has provided the consumer with a clear and conspicuous written disclosure of the terms of the arrangement (including any increases due to the completion or failure of the arrangement); and

(ii) Upon the completion or failure of the arrangement, the card issuer must not apply to any transactions that occurred prior to commencement of the arrangement an annual percentage rate, fee, or charge that exceeds the annual percentage rate, fee, or charge that applied to those transactions prior to commencement of the arrangement.

(6) Servicemembers Civil Relief Act exception. If an annual percentage rate or a fee or charge required to be disclosed under § 1026.6(b)(2)(ii), (iii), or (xii) has been decreased pursuant to 50 U.S.C. app. 527 or a similar Federal or state statute or regulation, a card issuer may increase that annual percentage rate, fee, or charge once 50 U.S.C. app. 527 or the similar statute or regulation no longer applies, provided that the card issuer must not apply to any transactions that occurred prior to the decrease an annual percentage rate, fee, or charge that exceeds the annual percentage rate, fee, or charge that applied to those transactions prior to the decrease.

(7) Index replacement and margin change exception. A card issuer may increase an annual percentage rate when:

(i) The card issuer changes the index and margin used to determine the annual percentage rate if the original index becomes unavailable, as long as historical fluctuations in the original and replacement indices were substantially similar, and as long as the replacement index and replacement margin will produce a rate substantially similar to the rate that was in effect at the time the original index became unavailable. If the replacement index is newly established and therefore does not have any rate history, it may be used if it and the replacement margin will produce a rate substantially similar to the rate in effect when the original index became unavailable; or

(ii) If a variable rate on the plan is calculated using a LIBOR index, the card issuer changes the LIBOR index and the margin for calculating the variable rate on or after April 1, 2022, to a replacement index and a replacement margin, as long as historical fluctuations in the LIBOR index and replacement index were substantially similar, and as long as the replacement index value in effect on October 18, 2021, and replacement margin will produce an annual percentage rate substantially similar to the rate calculated using the LIBOR index value in effect on October 18, 2021, and the margin that applied to the variable rate immediately prior to the replacement of the LIBOR index used under the plan. If the replacement index is newly established and therefore does not have any rate history, it may be used if the replacement index value in effect on October 18, 2021, and the replacement margin will produce an annual percentage rate substantially similar to the rate calculated using the LIBOR index value in effect on October 18, 2021, and the margin that applied to the variable rate immediately prior to the replacement of the LIBOR index used under the plan. If the replacement index is not published on October 18, 2021, the card issuer generally must use the next calendar day for which both the LIBOR index and the replacement index are published as the date for selecting indices values in determining whether the annual percentage rate based on the replacement index is substantially similar to the rate based on the LIBOR index. The one exception is that if the replacement index is the Board-selected benchmark replacement for consumer loans to replace the 1-month, 3-month, 6-month, or 12-month U.S. Dollar LIBOR index, the card issuer must use the index value on June 30, 2023, for the LIBOR index and, for the Board-selected benchmark replacement for consumer loans, must use the index value on the first date that index is published, in determining whether the annual percentage rate based on the replacement index is substantially similar to the rate based on the LIBOR index.

(c) Treatment of protected balances—

(1) Definition of protected balance. For purposes of this paragraph, "protected balance" means the amount owed for a category of transactions to which an increased annual percentage rate or an increased fee or charge required to be disclosed under § 1026.6(b)(2)(ii), (b)(2)(iii), or (b)(2)(xii) cannot be applied after the annual percentage rate, fee, or charge for that category of transactions has been increased pursuant to paragraph (b)(3) of this section.

(2) Repayment of protected balance. The card issuer must not require repayment of the protected balance using a method that is less beneficial to the consumer than one of the following methods:

(i) The method of repayment for the account before the effective date of the increase;

(ii) An amortization period of not less than five years, beginning no earlier than the effective date of the increase; or

(iii) A required minimum periodic payment that includes a percentage of the balance that is equal to no more than twice the percentage required before the effective date of the increase.

(d) Continuing application. This section continues to apply to a balance on a credit card account under an open-end (not home-secured) consumer credit plan after:

(1) The account is closed or acquired by another creditor; or

(2) The balance is transferred from a credit card account under an open-end (not home-secured) consumer credit plan issued by a creditor to another credit account issued by the same creditor or its affiliate or subsidiary (unless the account to which the balance is transferred is subject to § 1026.40).

(e) Promotional waivers or rebates of interest, fees, and other charges. If a card issuer promotes the waiver or rebate of finance charges due to a periodic interest rate or fees or charges required to be disclosed under § 1026.6(b)(2)(ii), (iii), or (xii) and applies the waiver or rebate to a credit card account under an open-end (not home-secured) consumer credit plan, any cessation of the waiver or rebate on that account constitutes an increase in an annual percentage rate, fee, or charge for purposes of this section.

§ 1026.56 Requirements for Over-the-Limit Transactions.

(a) Definition. For purposes of this section, the term "over-the-limit transaction" means any extension of credit by a card issuer to complete a transaction that causes a consumer's credit card account balance to exceed the credit limit.

(b) Opt-in requirement—

(1) General. A card issuer shall not assess a fee or charge on a consumer's credit card account under an open-end (not home-secured) consumer credit plan for an over-the-limit transaction unless the card issuer:

(i) Provides the consumer with an oral, written or electronic notice, segregated from all other information, describing the consumer's right to affirmatively consent, or opt in, to the card issuer's payment of an over-the-limit transaction;

(ii) Provides a reasonable opportunity for the consumer to affirmatively consent, or opt in, to the card issuer's payment of over-the-limit transactions;

(iii) Obtains the consumer's affirmative consent, or opt-in, to the card issuer's payment of such transactions;

(iv) Provides the consumer with confirmation of the consumer's consent in writing, or if the consumer agrees, electronically; and

(v) Provides the consumer notice in writing of the right to revoke that consent following the assessment of an over-the-limit fee or charge.

(2) Completion of over-the-limit transactions without consumer consent. Notwithstanding the absence of a consumer's affirmative consent under paragraph (b)(1)(iii) of this section, a card issuer may pay any over-the-limit transaction on a consumer's account provided that the card issuer does not impose any fee or charge on the account for paying that over-the-limit transaction.

(c) Method of election. A card issuer may permit a consumer to consent to the card issuer's payment of any over-the-limit transaction in writing, orally, or electronically, at the card issuer's option. The card issuer must also permit the consumer to revoke his or her consent using the same methods available to the consumer for providing consent.

(d) Timing and placement of notices—

(1) Initial notice—

(i) General. The notice required by paragraph (b)(1)(i) of this section shall be provided prior to the assessment of any over-the-limit fee or charge on a consumer's account.

(ii) Oral or electronic consent. If a consumer consents to the card issuer's payment of any over-the-limit transaction by oral or electronic means, the card issuer must provide the notice required by paragraph (b)(1)(i) of this section immediately prior to obtaining that consent.

(2) Confirmation of opt-in. The notice required by paragraph (b)(1)(iv) of this section may be provided no later than the first periodic statement sent after the consumer has consented to the card issuer's payment of over-the-limit transactions.

(3) Notice of right of revocation. The notice required by paragraph (b)(1)(v) of this section shall be provided on the front of any page of each periodic statement that reflects the assessment of an over-the-limit fee or charge on a consumer's account.

(e) Content—

(1) Initial notice. The notice required by paragraph (b)(1)(i) of this section shall include all applicable items in this paragraph (e)(1) and may not contain any information not specified in or otherwise permitted by this paragraph.

(i) Fees. The dollar amount of any fees or charges assessed by the card issuer on a consumer's account for an over-the-limit transaction;

(ii) APRs. Any increased periodic rate(s) (expressed as an annual percentage rate(s)) that may be imposed on the account as a result of an over-the-limit transaction; and

(iii) Disclosure of opt-in right. An explanation of the consumer's right to affirmatively consent to the card issuer's payment of over-the-limit transactions, including the method(s) by which the consumer may consent.

(2) Subsequent notice. The notice required by paragraph (b)(1)(v) of this section shall describe the consumer's right to revoke any consent provided under paragraph (b)(1)(iii) of this section, including the method(s) by which the consumer may revoke.

(3) Safe harbor. Use of Model Forms G-25(A) or G-25(B) of Appendix G to this part, or substantially similar notices, constitutes compliance with the notice content requirements of paragraph (e) of this section.

(f) Joint relationships. If two or more consumers are jointly liable on a credit card account under an open-end (not home-secured) consumer credit plan, the card issuer shall treat the affirmative consent of any of the joint consumers as affirmative consent for that account. Similarly, the card issuer shall treat a revocation of consent by any of the joint consumers as revocation of consent for that account.

(g) Continuing right to opt in or revoke opt-in. A consumer may affirmatively consent to the card issuer's payment of over-the-limit transactions at any time in the manner described in the notice required by paragraph (b)(1)(i) of this section. Similarly, the consumer may revoke the consent at any time in the manner described in the notice required by paragraph (b)(1)(v) of this section.

(h) Duration of opt-in. A consumer's affirmative consent to the card issuer's payment of over-the-limit transactions is effective until revoked by the consumer, or until the card issuer decides for any reason to cease paying over-the-limit transactions for the consumer.

(i) Time to comply with revocation request. A card issuer must comply with a consumer's revocation request as soon as reasonably practicable after the card issuer receives it.

(j) Prohibited practices. Notwithstanding a consumer's affirmative consent to a card issuer's payment of over-the-limit transactions, a card issuer is prohibited from engaging in the following practices:

(1) Fees or charges imposed per cycle—

(i) General rule. A card issuer may not impose more than one over-the-limit fee or charge on a consumer's credit card account per billing cycle, and, in any event, only if the credit limit was exceeded during the billing cycle. In addition, except as provided in paragraph (j)(1)(ii) of this section, a card issuer may not impose an over-the-limit fee or charge on the consumer's credit card account for more than three billing cycles for the same over-the-limit transaction where the consumer has not reduced the account balance below the credit limit by the payment due date for either of the last two billing cycles.

(ii) Exception. The prohibition in paragraph (j)(1)(i) of this section on imposing an over-the-limit fee or charge in more than three billing cycles for the same over-the-limit transaction(s) does not apply if another over-the-limit transaction occurs during either of the last two billing cycles.

(2) Failure to promptly replenish. A card issuer may not impose an over-the-limit fee or charge solely because of the card issuer's failure to promptly replenish the consumer's available credit following the crediting of the consumer's payment under § 1026.10.

(3) Conditioning. A card issuer may not condition the amount of a consumer's credit limit on the consumer affirmatively consenting to the card issuer's payment of over-the-limit transactions if the card issuer assesses a fee or charge for such service.

(4) Over-the-limit fees attributed to fees or interest. A card issuer may not impose an over-the-limit fee or charge for a billing cycle if a consumer exceeds a credit limit solely because of fees or interest charged by the card issuer to the consumer's account during that billing cycle. For purposes of this paragraph (j)(4), the relevant fees or interest charges are charges imposed as part of the plan under § 1026.6(b)(3).

§ 1026.57 Reporting and Marketing Rules for College Student Open-end Credit.

(a) Definitions—

(1) College student credit card. The term "college student credit card" as used in this section means a credit card issued under a credit card account under an open-end (not home-secured) consumer credit plan to any college student.

(2) College student. The term "college student" as used in this section means a consumer who is a full-time or part-time student of an institution of higher education.

(3) Institution of higher education. The term "institution of higher education" as used in this section has the same meaning as in sections 101 and 102 of the Higher Education Act of 1965 (20 U.S.C. 1001 and 1002).

(4) Affiliated organization. The term "affiliated organization" as used in this section means an alumni organization or foundation affiliated with or related to an institution of higher education.

(5) College credit card agreement. The term "college credit card agreement" as used in this section means any business, marketing or promotional agreement between a card issuer and an institution of higher education or an affiliated organization in connection with which college student credit cards are issued to college students currently enrolled at that institution.

(b) Public disclosure of agreements. An institution of higher education shall publicly disclose any contract or other agreement made with a card issuer or creditor for the purpose of marketing a credit card.

(c) Prohibited inducements. No card issuer or creditor may offer a college student any tangible item to induce such student to apply for or open an open-end consumer credit plan offered by such card issuer or creditor, if such offer is made:

(1) On the campus of an institution of higher education;

(2) Near the campus of an institution of higher education; or

(3) At an event sponsored by or related to an institution of higher education.

(d) Annual report to the Bureau—

(1) Requirement to report. Any card issuer that was a party to one or more college credit card agreements in effect at any time during a calendar year must submit to the Bureau an annual report regarding those agreements in the form and manner prescribed by the Bureau.

(2) Contents of report. The annual report to the Bureau must include the following:

(i) Identifying information about the card issuer and the agreements submitted, including the issuer's name, address, and identifying number (such as an RSSD ID number or tax identification number);

(ii) A copy of any college credit card agreement to which the card issuer was a party that was in effect at any time during the period covered by the report;

(iii) A copy of any memorandum of understanding in effect at any time during the period covered by the report between the card issuer and an institution of higher education or affiliated organization that directly or indirectly relates to the college credit card agreement or that controls or directs any obligations or distribution of benefits between any such entities;

(iv) The total dollar amount of any payments pursuant to a college credit card agreement from the card issuer to an institution of higher education or affiliated organization during the period covered by the report, and the method or formula used to determine such amounts;

(v) The total number of credit card accounts opened pursuant to any college credit card agreement during the period covered by the report; and

(vi) The total number of credit card accounts opened pursuant to any such agreement that were open at the end of the period covered by the report.

(3) Timing of reports. Except for the initial report described in this paragraph (d)(3), a card issuer must submit its annual report for each

calendar year to the Bureau by the first business day on or after March 31 of the following calendar year.

§ 1026.58 Internet Posting of Credit Card Agreements.

(a) Applicability. The requirements of this section apply to any card issuer that issues credit cards under a credit card account under an open-end (not home-secured) consumer credit plan.

(b) Definitions—

(1) Agreement. For purposes of this section, "agreement" or "credit card agreement" means the written document or documents evidencing the terms of the legal obligation, or the prospective legal obligation, between a card issuer and a consumer for a credit card account under an open-end (not home-secured) consumer credit plan. "Agreement" or "credit card agreement" also includes the pricing information, as defined in § 1026.58(b)(7).

(2) Amends. For purposes of this section, an issuer "amends" an agreement if it makes a substantive change (an "amendment") to the agreement. A change is substantive if it alters the rights or obligations of the card issuer or the consumer under the agreement. Any change in the pricing information, as defined in § 1026.58(b)(7), is deemed to be substantive.

(3) Business day. For purposes of this section, "business day" means a day on which the creditor's offices are open to the public for carrying on substantially all of its business functions.

(4) Card issuer. For purposes of this section, "card issuer" or "issuer" means the entity to which a consumer is legally obligated, or would be legally obligated, under the terms of a credit card agreement.

(5) Offers. For purposes of this section, an issuer "offers" or "offers to the public" an agreement if the issuer is soliciting or accepting applications for accounts that would be subject to that agreement:

(6) Open account. For purposes of this section, an account is an "open account" or "open credit card account" if it is a credit card account under an open-end (not home-secured) consumer credit plan and either:

(i) The cardholder can obtain extensions of credit on the account; or

(ii) There is an outstanding balance on the account that has not been charged off. An account that has been suspended temporarily (for example, due to a report by the cardholder of unauthorized use of the card) is considered an "open account" or "open credit card account."

(7) Pricing information. For purposes of this section, "pricing information" means the information listed in § 1026.6(b)(2)(i) through (b)(2)(xii). Pricing information does not include temporary or promotional rates and terms or rates and terms that apply only to protected balances.

(8) Private label credit card account and private label credit card plan. For purposes of this section:

(i) "private label credit card account" means a credit card account under an open-end (not home-secured) consumer credit plan with a credit card that can be used to make purchases only at a single merchant or an affiliated group of merchants; and

(ii) "private label credit card plan" means all of the private label credit card accounts issued by a particular issuer with credit cards usable at the same single merchant or affiliated group of merchants.

(c) Submission of agreements to Bureau—

(1) Quarterly submissions. A card issuer must make quarterly submissions to the Bureau, in the form and manner specified by the Bureau. Quarterly submissions must be sent to the Bureau no later than the first business day on or after January 31, April 30, July 31, and October 31 of each year. Each submission must contain:

(i) Identifying information about the card issuer and the agreements submitted, including the issuer's name, address, and identifying number (such as an RSSD ID number or tax identification number);

(ii) The credit card agreements that the card issuer offered to the public as of the last business day of the preceding calendar quarter that the card issuer has not previously submitted to the Bureau;

(iii) Any credit card agreement previously submitted to the Bureau that was amended during the preceding calendar quarter and that the card issuer offered to the public as of the last business day of the preceding calendar quarter, as described in § 1026.58(c)(3); and

(iv) Notification regarding any credit card agreement previously submitted to the Board that the issuer is withdrawing, as described in § 1026.58(c)(4) and (c)(5), (c)(6), and (c)(7).

(2) [Reserved]

(3) Amended agreements. If a credit card agreement has been submitted to the Bureau, the agreement has not been amended and the card issuer continues to offer the agreement to the public, no additional submission regarding that agreement is required. If a credit card agreement that previously has been submitted to the Bureau is amended and the card issuer offered the amended agreement to the public as of the last business day of the calendar quarter in which the change became effective, the card issuer must submit the entire amended agreement to the Bureau, in the form and manner specified by the Bureau, by the first quarterly submission deadline after the last day of the calendar quarter in which the change became effective.

(4) Withdrawal of agreements. If a card issuer no longer offers to the public a credit card agreement that previously has been submitted to the Bureau, the card issuer must notify the Bureau, in the form and manner specified by the Bureau, by the first quarterly submission deadline after the last day of the calendar quarter in which the issuer ceased to offer the agreement.

(5) De minimis exception.

(i) A card issuer is not required to submit any credit card agreements to the Bureau if the card issuer had fewer than 10,000 open credit card accounts as of the last business day of the calendar quarter.

(ii) If an issuer that previously qualified for the de minimis exception ceases to qualify, the card issuer must begin making quarterly submissions to the Bureau no later than the first quarterly submission deadline after the date as of which the issuer ceased to qualify.

(iii) If a card issuer that did not previously qualify for the de minimis exception qualifies for the de minimis exception, the card issuer must continue to make quarterly submissions to the Board until the issuer notifies the Bureau that the card issuer is withdrawing all agreements it previously submitted to the Bureau.

(6) Private label credit card exception.

(i) A card issuer is not required to submit to the Bureau a credit card agreement if, as of the last business day of the calendar quarter, the agreement:

(A) is offered for accounts under one or more private label credit card plans each of which has fewer than 10,000 open accounts; and

(B) is not offered to the public other than for accounts under such a plan.

(ii) If an agreement that previously qualified for the private label credit card exception ceases to qualify, the card issuer must submit the agreement to the Bureau no later than the first quarterly submission deadline after the date as of which the agreement ceased to qualify.

(iii) If an agreement that did not previously qualify for the private label credit card exception qualifies for the exception, the card issuer must continue to make quarterly submissions to the Bureau with respect to that agreement until the issuer notifies the Bureau that the agreement is being withdrawn.

(7) Product testing exception.

(i) A card issuer is not required to submit to the Bureau a credit card agreement if, as of the last business day of the calendar quarter, the agreement:

(A) Is offered as part of a product test offered to only a limited group of consumers for a limited period of time;

(B) Is used for fewer than 10,000 open accounts; and

(C) Is not offered to the public other than in connection with such a product test.

(ii) If an agreement that previously qualified for the product testing exception ceases to qualify, the card issuer must submit the agreement to the Bureau no later than the first quarterly submission deadline after the date as of which the agreement ceased to qualify.

(iii) If an agreement that did not previously qualify for the product testing exception qualifies for the exception, the card issuer must continue to make quarterly submissions to the Bureau with respect to that agreement until the issuer notifies the Bureau that the agreement is being withdrawn.

(8) Form and content of agreements submitted to the Bureau—

(i) Form and content generally.

(A) Each agreement must contain the provisions of the agreement and the pricing information in effect as of the last business day of the preceding calendar quarter.

(B) Agreements must not include any personally identifiable information relating to any cardholder, such as name, address, telephone number, or account number.

(C) The following are not deemed to be part of the agreement for purposes of § 1026.58, and therefore are not required to be included in submissions to the Bureau:

(1) Disclosures required by state or federal law, such as affiliate marketing notices, privacy policies, billing right notices, or disclosures under the E-Sign Act;

(2) Solicitation materials;

(3) Periodic statements;

(4) Ancillary agreements between the issuer and the consumer, such as debt cancellation contracts or debt suspension agreements;

(5) Offers for credit insurance or other optional products and other similar advertisements; and

(6) Documents that may be sent to the consumer along with the credit card or credit card agreement such as a cover letter, a validation sticker on the card, or other information about card security.

(D) Agreements must be presented in a clear and legible font.

(ii) Pricing information.

(A) Pricing information must be set forth in a single addendum to the agreement. The addendum must contain all of the pricing information, as defined by § 1026.58(b)(7). The addendum may, but is not required to, contain any other information listed in § 1026.6(b), provided that information is complete and accurate as of the applicable date under § 1026.58. The addendum may not contain any other information.

(B) Pricing information that may vary from one cardholder to another depending on the cardholder's creditworthiness or state of residence or other factors must be disclosed either by setting forth all the possible variations (such as purchase APRs of 13 percent, 15 percent, 17 percent, and 19 percent) or by providing a range of possible variations (such as purchase APRs ranging from 13 percent to 19 percent).

(C) If a rate included in the pricing information is a variable rate, the issuer must identify the index or formula used in setting the rate and the margin. Rates that may vary from one cardholder to another must be disclosed by providing the index and the possible margins (such as the prime rate plus 5 percent, 8 percent, 10 percent, or 12 percent) or range of margins (such as the prime rate plus from 5 to 12 percent). The value of the rate and the value of the index are not required to be disclosed.

(iii) Optional variable terms addendum. Provisions of the agreement other than the pricing information that may vary from one cardholder to another depending on the cardholder's creditworthiness or state of residence or other factors may be set forth in a single addendum to the agreement separate from the pricing information addendum.

(iv) Integrated agreement. Issuers may not provide provisions of the agreement or pricing information in the form of change-in-terms notices or riders (other than the pricing information addendum and the optional variable terms addendum). Changes in provisions or pricing information must be integrated into the text of the agreement, the pricing information addendum or the optional variable terms addendum, as appropriate.

(d) Posting of agreements offered to the public.

(1) Except as provided below, a card issuer must post and maintain on its publicly available Web site the credit card agreements that the issuer is required to submit to the Bureau under § 1026.58(c). With respect to an agreement offered solely for accounts under one or more private label credit card plans, an issuer may fulfill this requirement by posting and maintaining the agreement in accordance with the requirements of this section on the publicly available Web site of at least one of the merchants at which credit cards issued under each private label credit card plan with 10,000 or more open accounts may be used.

(2) Except as provided in § 1026.58(d), agreements posted pursuant to § 1026.58(d) must conform to the form and content requirements for agreements submitted to the Bureau specified in § 1026.58(c)(8).

(3) Agreements posted pursuant to § 1026.58(d) may be posted in any electronic format that is readily usable by the general public. Agreements must be placed in a location that is prominent and readily accessible by the public and must be accessible without submission of personally identifiable information.

(4) The card issuer must update the agreements posted on its Web site pursuant to § 1026.58(d) at least as frequently as the quarterly schedule required for submission of agreements to the Bureau under § 1026.58(c). If the issuer chooses to update the agreements on its Web site more frequently, the agreements posted on the issuer's Web site may contain the provisions of the agreement and the pricing information in effect as of a date other than the last business day of the preceding calendar quarter.

(e) Agreements for all open accounts—

(1) Availability of individual cardholder's agreement. With respect to any open credit card account, a card issuer must either:

(i) Post and maintain the cardholder's agreement on its Web site; or

(ii) Promptly provide a copy of the cardholder's agreement to the cardholder upon the cardholder's request. If the card issuer makes an agreement available upon request, the issuer must provide the cardholder with the ability to request a copy of the agreement both by using the issuer's Web site (such as by clicking on a clearly identified box to make the request) and by calling a readily available telephone line the number for which is displayed on the issuer's Web site and clearly identified as to purpose. The card issuer must send to the cardholder or otherwise make available to the cardholder a copy of the cardholder's agreement in electronic or paper form no later than 30 days after the issuer receives the cardholder's request.

(2) Special rule for issuers without interactive Web sites. An issuer that does not maintain a Web site from which cardholders can access specific information about their individual accounts, instead of complying with § 1026.58(e)(1), may make agreements available upon request by providing the cardholder with the ability to request a copy of the agreement by calling a readily available telephone line, the number for which is displayed on the issuer's Web site and clearly identified as to purpose or included on each periodic statement sent to the cardholder and clearly identified as to purpose. The issuer must send to the cardholder or otherwise make available to the cardholder a copy of the cardholder's agreement in electronic or paper form no later than 30 days after the issuer receives the cardholder's request.

(3) Form and content of agreements.

(i) Except as provided in § 1026.58(e), agreements posted on the card issuer's Web site pursuant to § 1026.58(e)(1)(i) or made available upon the cardholder's request pursuant to § 1026.58(e)(1)(ii) or (e)(2) must conform to the form and content requirements for agreements submitted to the Bureau specified in § 1026.58(c)(8).

(ii) If the card issuer posts an agreement on its Web site or otherwise provides an agreement to a cardholder electronically under § 1026.58(e), the agreement may be posted or provided in any electronic format that is readily usable by the general public and must be placed in a location that is prominent and readily accessible to the cardholder.

(iii) Agreements posted or otherwise provided pursuant to § 1026.58(e) may contain personally identifiable information relating to the cardholder, such as name, address, telephone number, or account number, provided that the issuer takes appropriate measures to make the agreement accessible only to the cardholder or other authorized persons.

(iv) Agreements posted or otherwise provided pursuant to § 1026.58(e) must set forth the specific provisions and pricing information applicable to the particular cardholder. Provisions and pricing information must be complete and accurate as of a date no more than 60 days prior to.

(A) The date on which the agreement is posted on the card issuer's Web site under § 1026.58(e)(1)(i); or

(B) The date the cardholder's request is received under § 1026.58(e)(1)(ii) or (e)(2).

(v) Agreements provided upon cardholder request pursuant to § 1026.58(e)(1)(ii) or (e)(2) may be provided by the issuer in either electronic or paper form, regardless of the form of the cardholder's request.

(f) E-Sign Act requirements. Card issuers may provide credit card agreements in electronic form under § 1026.58(d) and (e) without regard to the consumer notice and consent requirements of section 101(c) of the Electronic Signatures in Global and National Commerce Act (E-Sign Act) (15 U.S.C. 7001 et seq.).

(g) Temporary suspension of agreement submission requirement—

(1) Quarterly submissions. The quarterly submission requirement in paragraph (c) of this section is suspended for the submissions that would otherwise be due to the Bureau by the first business day on

or after April 30, 2015; July 31, 2015; October 31, 2015; and January 31, 2016.

(2) Posting of agreements offered to the public. Nothing in paragraph (g)(1) of this section shall affect the agreement posting requirements in paragraph (d) of this section.

§ 1026.61 Hybrid prepaid-credit cards.

(a) Hybrid prepaid-credit card—

(1) In general.

(i) Credit offered in connection with a prepaid account is subject to this section and this regulation as specified below.

(ii) For purposes of this regulation, except as provided in paragraph (a)(4) of this section, a prepaid card is a hybrid prepaid-credit card with respect to a separate credit feature as described in paragraph (a)(2)(i) of this section when it can access credit from that credit feature, or with respect to a credit feature structured as a negative balance on the asset feature of the prepaid account as described in paragraph (a)(3) of this section when it can access credit from that credit feature. A hybrid prepaid-credit card is a credit card for purposes of this regulation with respect to those credit features.

(iii) With respect to a credit feature structured as a negative balance on the asset feature of the prepaid account as described in paragraph (a)(3) of this section, a prepaid card is not a hybrid prepaid-credit card or a credit card for purposes of this regulation if the conditions set forth in paragraph (a)(4) of this section are met.

(2) Prepaid card can access credit from a covered separate credit feature—

(i) Covered separate credit feature.

(A) A separate credit feature that can be accessed by a hybrid prepaid-credit card as described in this paragraph (a)(2)(i) is defined as a covered separate credit feature. A prepaid card is a hybrid prepaid-credit card with respect to a separate credit feature when it is a single device that can be used from time to time to access the separate credit feature where the following two conditions are both satisfied:

(1) The card can be used to draw, transfer, or authorize the draw or transfer of credit from the separate credit feature in the course of authorizing, settling, or otherwise completing transactions conducted with the card to obtain goods or services, obtain cash, or conduct person-to-person transfers; and

(2) The separate credit feature is offered by the prepaid account issuer, its affiliate, or its business partner.

(B) A separate credit feature that meets the conditions set forth in paragraph (a)(2)(i)(A) of this section is a covered separate credit feature accessible by a hybrid prepaid-credit card even with respect to credit that is drawn or transferred, or authorized to be drawn or transferred, from the credit feature outside the course of a transaction conducted with the card to obtain goods or services, obtain cash, or conduct person-to-person transfers.

(ii) Non-covered separate credit feature. A separate credit feature that does not meet the two conditions set forth in paragraph (a)(2)(i) of this section is defined as a non-covered separate credit feature. A prepaid card is not a hybrid prepaid-credit card with respect to a non-covered separate credit feature, even if the prepaid card is a hybrid prepaid-credit card with respect to a covered separate credit feature as described in paragraph (a)(2)(i) of this section. A non-covered separate credit feature is not subject to the rules applicable to hybrid prepaid-credit cards; however, it may be subject to this regulation depending on its own terms and conditions, independent of the connection to the prepaid account.

(3) Prepaid card can access credit extended through a negative balance on the asset feature of the prepaid account—

(i) In general. Except as provided in paragraph (a)(4) of this section, a prepaid card is a hybrid prepaid-credit card when it is a single device that can be used from time to time to access credit extended through a negative balance on the asset feature of the prepaid account.

(ii) Negative asset balances. Notwithstanding paragraph (a)(3)(i) of this section with regard to coverage under this regulation, structuring a hybrid prepaid-credit card to access credit through a negative balance on the asset feature violates paragraph (b) of this section. A prepaid account issuer can use a negative asset balance structure to extend credit on an asset feature of a prepaid account only if the prepaid card is not a hybrid prepaid-credit card with respect to that credit as described in paragraph (a)(4) of this section.

(4) Exception for credit extended through a negative balance. A prepaid card is not a hybrid prepaid-credit card with respect to credit extended through a negative balance on the asset feature and is not a credit card for purposes of this regulation where:

(i) The prepaid card cannot access credit from a covered separate credit feature as described in paragraph (a)(2)(i) of this section that is offered by a prepaid account issuer or its affiliate; and

(ii) The prepaid card only can access credit extended through a negative balance on the asset feature of the prepaid account where both paragraphs (a)(4)(ii)(A) and (B) of this section are satisfied.

(A) The prepaid account issuer has an established policy and practice of either declining to authorize any transaction for which it reasonably believes the consumer has insufficient or unavailable funds in the asset feature of the prepaid account at the time the transaction is authorized to cover the amount of the transaction, or declining to authorize any such transactions except in one or more of the following circumstances:

(1) The amount of the transaction will not cause the asset feature balance to become negative by more than $10 at the time of the authorization; or

(2) In cases where the prepaid account issuer has received an instruction or confirmation for an incoming electronic fund transfer originated from a separate asset account to load funds to the prepaid account or where the prepaid account issuer has received a request from the consumer to load funds to the prepaid account from a separate asset account but in either case the funds from the separate asset account have not yet settled, the amount of the transaction will not cause the asset feature balance to become negative at the time of the authorization by more than the incoming or requested load amount, as applicable.

(B) The following fees or charges are not imposed on the asset feature of the prepaid account:

(1) Any fees or charges for opening, issuing, or holding a negative balance on the asset feature, or for the availability of credit, whether imposed on a one-time or periodic basis. This paragraph does not include fees or charges to open, issue, or hold the prepaid account where the amount of the fee or charge imposed on the asset feature is not higher based on whether credit might be offered or has been accepted, whether or how much credit the consumer has accessed, or the amount of credit available;

(2) Any fees or charges that will be imposed only when credit is extended on the asset feature or when there is a negative balance on the asset feature, except that a prepaid account issuer may impose fees or charges for the actual costs of collecting the credit extended if otherwise permitted by law; or

(3) Any fees or charges where the amount of the fee or charge is higher when credit isextended on the asset feature or when there is a negative balance on the asset feature.

(C) A prepaid account issuer may still satisfy the exception in paragraph (a)(4) of this section even if it debits fees or charges from the asset feature when there are insufficient or unavailable funds in the asset feature to cover those fees or charges at the time they are imposed, so long as those fees or charges are not the type of fees or charges enumerated in paragraph (a)(4)(ii)(B) of this section.

(5) Definitions. For purposes of this section and other provisions in the regulation that relate to hybrid prepaid-credit cards:

(i) Affiliate means any company that controls, is controlled by, or is under common control with another company, as set forth in the Bank Holding Company Act of 1956 (12 U.S.C. 1841 *et seq.).*

(ii) Asset feature means an asset account that is a prepaid account, or an asset subaccount of a prepaid account.

(iii) Business partner means a person (other than the prepaid account issuer or its affiliates) that can extend credit through a separate credit feature where the person or its affiliate has an arrangement with a prepaid account issuer or its affiliate except as provided in paragraph (a)(5)(iii)(D) of this section.

(A) Arrangement defined. For purposes of paragraph (a)(5)(iii) of this section, a person that can extend credit through a separate credit feature or the person's affiliate has an arrangement with a prepaid account issuer or its affiliate if the circumstances in either paragraph (a)(5)(iii)(B) or (C) of this section are met.

(B) Arrangement by agreement. A person that can extend credit through a separate credit feature or its affiliate has an arrangement with a prepaid account issuer or its affiliate if the parties have an agreement that allows the prepaid card from time to time to draw, transfer, or authorize a draw or transfer of credit in the course of authorizing, settling, or otherwise completing transactions conducted with the card to obtain goods or services, obtain cash, or conduct person-to-person transfers.

(C) Marketing arrangement. A person that can extend credit through a separate credit feature or its affiliate has an arrangement with a prepaid account issuer or its affiliate if:

(1) The parties have a business, marketing, or promotional agreement or other arrangement which provides that prepaid accounts offered by the prepaid account issuer will be marketed to the customers of the person that can extend credit; or the separate credit feature offered by the person who can extend credit will be marketed to the holders of prepaid accounts offered by the prepaid account issuer (including any marketing to customers to encourage them to authorize the prepaid card to access the separate credit feature as described in paragraph (a)(5)(iii)(C)(2) of this section); and

(2) At the time of the marketing agreement or arrangement described in paragraph (a)(5)(iii)(C)(1) of this section, or at any time afterwards, the prepaid card from time to time can draw, transfer, or authorize the draw or transfer of credit from the separate credit feature offered by the person that can extend credit in the course of authorizing, settling, or otherwise completing transactions conducted with the card to obtain goods or services, obtain cash, or conduct person-to-person transfers. This requirement is satisfied even if there is no specific agreement between the parties that the card can access the credit feature, as described in paragraph (a)(5)(iii)(B) of this section.

(D) Exception for certain credit card account arrangements. For purposes of paragraph (a)(5)(iii) of this section, a person that can extend credit through a credit card account is not a business partner of a prepaid account issuer with which it has an arrangement as defined in paragraphs (a)(5)(iii)(A) through (C) of this section with regard to such credit card account if all of the following conditions are met:

(1) The credit card account is a credit card account under an open-end (not home-secured) consumer credit plan that a consumer can access through a traditional credit card.

(2) The prepaid account issuer and the card issuer do not allow the prepaid card to draw, transfer, or authorize the draw or transfer of credit from the credit card account from time to time in the course of authorizing, settling, or otherwise completing transactions conducted with the card to obtain goods or services, obtain cash, or conduct person-to-person transfers, except where the prepaid account issuer or the card issuer has received from the consumer a written request that is separately signed or initialized to authorize the prepaid card to access the credit card account as described above. If the credit card account is linked to the prepaid account prior to April 1, 2019, or prior to the arrangement between the prepaid account issuer and the card issuer as described in paragraphs (a)(5)(iii)(A) through (C) of this section, the prepaid account issuer and the card issuer will be deemed to have satisfied this condition even if they have not received

from the consumer a written request that is separately signed or initialized to authorize the prepaid card to access the credit card account as described in this paragraph.

(3) The prepaid account issuer and the card issuer do not condition the acquisition or retention of the prepaid account or the credit card account on whether a consumer authorizes the prepaid card to access the credit card account as described in paragraph (a)(5)(iii)(D)(2) of this section. If the credit card account is linked to the prepaid account prior to April 1, 2019, this condition only applies to the retention of the prepaid account and the credit card account on or after April 1, 2019.

(4) The prepaid account issuer applies the same terms, conditions, or features to the prepaid account when a consumer authorizes linking the prepaid card to the credit card account as described in paragraph (a)(5)(iii)(D)(2) of this section as it applies to the consumer's prepaid account when the consumer does not authorize such a linkage. In addition, the prepaid account issuer applies the same fees to load funds from the credit card account that is linked to the prepaid account as described above as it charges for a comparable load on the consumer's prepaid account to access a credit feature offered by a person that is not the prepaid account issuer, its affiliate, or a person with which the prepaid account issuer has an arrangement as described in paragraphs (a)(5)(iii)(A) through (C) of this section.

(5) The card issuer applies the same specified terms and conditions to the credit card account when a consumer authorizes linking the prepaid card to the credit card account as described in paragraph (a)(5)(iii)(D)(2) of this section as it applies to the consumer's credit card account when the consumer does not authorize such a linkage. In addition, the card issuer applies the same specified terms and conditions to extensions of credit accessed by the prepaid card from the credit card account as it applies to extensions of credit accessed by the traditional credit card. For purposes of this paragraph, "specified terms and conditions" means the terms and conditions required to be disclosed under § 1026.6(b), any repayment terms and conditions, and the limits on liability for unauthorized credit transactions.

(iv) Credit feature means a separate credit account or a credit subaccount of a prepaid account through which credit can be extended in connection with a prepaid card, or a negative balance on an asset feature of a prepaid account through which credit can be extended in connection with a prepaid card.

(v) Prepaid account means a prepaid account as defined in Regulation E, 12 CFR 1005.2(b)(3).

(vi) Prepaid account issuer means a financial institution as defined in Regulation E, 12 CFR 1005.2(i), with respect to a prepaid account.

(vii) Prepaid card means any card, code, or other device that can be used to access a prepaid account.

(viii) Separate credit feature means credit account or a credit subaccount of a prepaid account through which credit can be extended in connection with a prepaid card that is separate from the asset feature of the prepaid account. This term does not include a negative balance on an asset feature of a prepaid account.

(b) Structure of credit features accessible by hybrid prepaid-credit cards. With respect to a credit feature that is accessible by a hybrid prepaid-credit card, a card issuer shall not structure the credit feature as a negative balance on the asset feature of a prepaid account. A card issuer shall structure the credit feature as a separate credit feature, either as a separate credit account, or as a credit subaccount of a prepaid account that is separate from the asset feature of the prepaid account. The separate credit feature is a covered separate credit feature accessible by a hybrid prepaid-credit card under § 1026.61(a)(2)(i).

(c) Timing requirement for credit card solicitation or application with respect to hybrid prepaid-credit cards.

(1) With respect to a covered separate credit feature that could be accessible by a hybrid prepaid-credit card at any point, a card issuer must not do

any of the following until **30** days after the prepaid account has been registered:

(i) Open a covered separate credit feature that could be accessible by the hybrid prepaid-credit card;

(ii) Make a solicitation or provide an application to open a covered separate credit feature that could be accessible by the hybrid prepaid-credit card; or

(iii) Allow an existing credit feature that was opened prior to the consumer obtaining the prepaid account to become a covered separate credit feature accessible by the hybrid prepaid-credit card.

(2) For purposes of paragraph (c) of this section, the term *solicitation* has the meaning set forth in § 1026.60(a)(1).

Official Interpretation to Regulation Z

Supplement I to Part 1026—Official Staff Interpretations (Excerpts)

Paragraph 2(a)(15) Credit Card.

1. *Usable from time to time.* A credit card must be usable from time to time. Since this involves the possibility of repeated use of a single device, checks and similar instruments that can be used only once to obtain a single credit extension are not credit cards.

2. *Examples.*

i. Examples of credit cards include:

A. A card that guarantees checks or similar instruments, if the asset account is also tied to an overdraft line or if the instrument directly accesses a line of credit.

B. A debit card (other than a debit card that is solely an account number) that also accesses a credit account (that is, a debit-credit card or hybrid debit-credit card as defined in § 1026.62). See comment 2(a)(15)-2.ii.C for guidance on whether a debit card that is solely an account number is a credit card.

C. An identification card that permits the consumer to defer payment on a purchase.

D. An identification card indicating loan approval that is presented to a merchant or to a lender, whether or not the consumer signs a separate promissory note for each credit extension.

E. A card or device that can be activated upon receipt to access credit, even if the card has a substantive use other than credit, such as a purchase-price discount card. Such a card or device is a credit card notwithstanding the fact that the recipient must first contact the card issuer to access or activate the credit feature.

F. A prepaid card that is a hybrid prepaid-credit card as defined in § 1026.61.

ii. In contrast, credit card does not include, for example:

A. A check-guarantee or debit card with no credit feature or agreement.

B. Any card, key, plate, or other device that is used in order to obtain petroleum products for business purposes from a wholesale distribution facility or to gain access to that facility, and that is required to be used without regard to payment terms.

C. An account number that accesses a credit account, unless the account number can access an open-end line of credit to purchase goods or services or as provided in § 1026.61 with respect to a hybrid prepaid-credit card. An account number that can access an open-end line of credit to purchase goods or services includes an account number that can access a covered overdraft credit account offered by a very large financial institution. For example, if a creditor provides a consumer with an open-end line of credit that can be accessed by an account number in order to transfer funds into another account (such as an asset account with the same creditor), the account number is not a credit card for purposes of § 1026.2(a)(15)(i). However, if the account number can also access the line of credit to purchase goods or services (such as an account number that can be used to purchase goods or services on the internet), the account number is a credit card for purposes of § 1026.2(a)(15)(i), regardless of whether the creditor treats such transactions as purchases, cash advances, or some other type of transaction. Furthermore, if the line of credit can also be accessed by a card (such as a debit card), that card is a credit card for purposes of § 1026.2(a)(15)(i).

D. A prepaid card that is not a hybrid prepaid-credit card as defined in § 1026.61.

E. A check-guarantee or debit card that can access non-covered overdraft credit as defined in § 1026.62 and cannot access any other form of credit.

3. Charge card.

i. Charge cards are credit cards where no periodic rate is used to compute the finance charge. The term *charge card* does not include a hybrid debit-credit card as defined in § 1026.62. Thus, covered overdraft credit extended by a very large financial institution through a hybrid debit-credit card is not subject to special charge card rules.

A. Under the regulation, a reference to credit cards generally includes charge cards. In particular, references to credit card accounts under an open-end (not home-secured) consumer credit plan in subparts B and G generally include charge cards.

B. The term *charge card* is, however, distinguished from credit card or credit card account under an open-end (not home-secured) consumer credit plan in §§ 1026.6(b)(2)(xiv), 1026.7(b)(11) (except as described in comment 2(a)(15)-3.ii below), 1026.7(b)(12), 1026.9(e), 1026.9(f), 1026.28(d), 1026.52(b)(1)(ii)(C), 1026.60, and appendices G-10 through G-13.

ii. A hybrid prepaid-credit card as defined in § 1026.61 is a charge card with respect to a covered separate credit feature if no periodic rate is used to compute the finance charge in connection with the covered separate credit feature. Unlike other charge card accounts, the requirements in § 1026.7(b)(11) apply to a covered separate credit feature accessible by a hybrid prepaid-credit card that is a charge card when that covered separate credit feature is a credit card account under an open-end (not home-secured) consumer credit plan. Thus, under § 1026.5(b)(2)(ii)(A), with respect to a covered separate credit feature that is a credit card account under an openend (not home-secured) consumer credit plan, a card issuer of a hybrid prepaid-credit card that meets the definition of a charge card because no periodic rate is used to compute a finance charge in connection with the covered separate credit feature must adopt reasonable procedures for the covered separate credit feature designed to ensure that

(1) periodic statements are mailed or delivered at least 21 days prior to the payment due date disclosed on the statement pursuant to § 1026.7(b)(11)(i)(A); and

(2) the card issuer does not treat as late for any purposes a required minimum periodic payment received by the card issuer within 21 days after mailing or delivery of the periodic statement disclosing the due date for that payment.

*****

Section 1026.8—Identifying Transactions on Periodic Statements.

*****

8. Location of Transaction.

i. If the seller has multiple stores or branches within a city, the creditor need not identify the specific branch at which the sale occurred.

ii. When no meaningful address is available because the consumer did not make the purchase at any fixed location of the seller, the creditor may omit the address, or may provide some other identifying designation, such as "aboard plane," "ABC Airways Flight," "customer's home," "telephone order," "Internet order" or "mail order."

Section 1026.12—Special Credit Card Provisions.

*****

Paragraph 12(b)(2)(iii).

1. Means of identifying cardholder or user. To fulfill the condition set forth in § 1026.12(b)(2)(iii), the issuer must provide some method whereby the cardholder or the authorized user can be identified. This could include, for example, a signature, photograph, or fingerprint on the card or other biometric means, or electronic or mechanical confirmation.

2. *Identification by magnetic strip.* Unless a magnetic strip (or similar device not readable without physical aids) must be used in conjunction with a secret code or the like, it would not constitute sufficient means of identification. Sufficient identification also does not exist if a "pool" or group card, issued to a corporation and signed by a corporate agent who will not be a user of the card, is intended to be used by another employee for whom no means of identification is provided.

3. Transactions not involving card. The cardholder may not be held liable under § 1026.12(b) when the card itself (or some other sufficient means of identification of the cardholder) is not presented. Since the issuer has not provided a means to identify the user under these circumstances, the issuer has not fulfilled one of the conditions for imposing liability. For example, when merchandise is ordered by telephone or the Internet by a person without authority to do so, using a credit card account number by itself or with other information that appears on the card (for example, the card expiration date and a 3- or 4-digit cardholder identification number), no liability may be imposed on the cardholder.

Section 1026.13—Billing Error Resolution.

*****

13(f). Procedures If Different Billing Error or No Billing Error Occurred.

1. Different billing error. Examples of a different billing error include:

i. Differences in the amount of an error (for example, the customer asserts a $55.00 error but the error was only $53.00).

ii. Differences in other particulars asserted by the consumer (such as when a consumer asserts that a particular transaction never occurred, but the creditor determines that only the seller's name was disclosed incorrectly).

2. Form of creditor's explanation. The written explanation (which also may notify the consumer of corrections to the account) may take a variety of forms. It may be sent separately, or it may be included on or with a periodic statement that is mailed within the time for resolution. If the creditor uses the periodic statement for the explanation and correction(s), the corrections must be specifically identified. If a separate explanation, including the correction notice, is provided, the enclosed or subsequent periodic statement reflecting the corrected amount may simply identify it as a credit. The explanation may be combined with the creditor's notice to the consumer of amounts still owing, which is required under § 1026.13(g)(1), provided it is sent within the time limit for resolution. (See commentary to § 1026.13(e).)

3. Reasonable investigation. A creditor must conduct a reasonable investigation before it determines that no billing error occurred or that a different billing error occurred from that asserted. In conducting its investigation of an allegation of a billing error, the creditor may reasonably request the consumer's cooperation. The creditor may not automatically deny a claim based solely on the consumer's failure or refusal to comply with a particular request, including providing an affidavit or filing a police report. However, if the creditor otherwise has no knowledge of facts confirming the billing error, the lack of information resulting from the consumer's failure or refusal to comply with a particular request may lead the creditor reasonably to terminate the investigation. The procedures involved in investigating alleged billing errors may differ depending on the billing error type.

i. Unauthorized transaction. In conducting an investigation of a notice of billing error alleging an unauthorized transaction under § 1026.13(a)(1), actions such as the following represent steps that a creditor may take, as appropriate, in conducting a reasonable investigation:

A. Reviewing the types or amounts of purchases made in relation to the consumer's previous purchasing pattern.

B. Reviewing where the purchases were delivered in relation to the consumer's residence or place of business.

C. Reviewing where the purchases were made in relation to where the consumer resides or has normally shopped.

D. Comparing any signature on credit slips for the purchases to the signature of the consumer (or an authorized user in the case of a credit card account) in the creditor's records, including other credit slips.

E. Requesting documentation to assist in the verification of the claim.

F. Requiring a written, signed statement from the consumer (or authorized user, in the case of a credit card account). For example, the creditor may include a signature line on a billing rights form that the consumer may send in to provide notice of the claim. However, a creditor may not require the consumer to provide an affidavit or signed statement under penalty of perjury as a part of a reasonable investigation.

G. Requesting a copy of a police report, if one was filed.

H. Requesting information regarding the consumer's knowledge of the person who allegedly obtained an extension of credit on the account or of that person's authority to do so.

ii. Nondelivery of property or services. In conducting an investigation of a billing error notice alleging the nondelivery of property or services under § 1026.13(a)(3), the creditor shall not deny the assertion unless it conducts a reasonable investigation and determines that the property or services were actually delivered, mailed, or sent as agreed.

iii. Incorrect information. In conducting an investigation of a billing error notice alleging that information appearing on a periodic statement is incorrect because a person honoring the consumer's credit card or otherwise accepting an access device for an open-end plan has made an incorrect report to the creditor, the creditor shall not deny the assertion unless it conducts a reasonable investigation and determines that the information was correct.

Fair Credit Reporting Act

15 U.S.C. §§ 1681 et seq. (Selected Provisions)

§ 602. Congressional Findings and Statement of Purpose [15 U.S.C. § 1681].

(a) Accuracy and fairness of credit reporting. The Congress makes the following findings:

(1) The banking system is dependent upon fair and accurate credit reporting. Inaccurate credit reports directly impair the efficiency of the banking system, and unfair credit reporting methods undermine the public confidence which is essential to the continued functioning of the banking system.

(2) An elaborate mechanism has been developed for investigating and evaluating the credit worthiness, credit standing, credit capacity, character, and general reputation of consumers.

(3) Consumer reporting agencies have assumed a vital role in assembling and evaluating consumer credit and other information on consumers.

(4) There is a need to insure that consumer reporting agencies exercise their grave responsibilities with fairness, impartiality, and a respect for the consumer's right to privacy.

(b) Reasonable procedures. It is the purpose of this subchapter to require that consumer reporting agencies adopt reasonable procedures for meeting the needs of commerce for consumer credit, personnel, insurance, and other information in a manner which is fair and equitable to the consumer, with regard to the confidentiality, accuracy, relevancy, and proper utilization of such information in accordance with the requirements of this subchapter.

§ 603. Definitions; Rules of Construction [15 U.S.C. § 1681a].

(a) Definitions and rules of construction set forth in this section are applicable for the purposes of this subchapter.

(b) The term "person" means any individual, partnership, corporation, trust, estate, cooperative, association, government or governmental subdivision or agency, or other entity.

(c) The term "consumer" means an individual.

(d) Consumer Report.—

(1) In general.—The term "consumer report" means any written, oral, or other communication of any information by a consumer reporting agency bearing on a consumer's credit worthiness, credit standing, credit capacity, character, general reputation, personal characteristics, or mode of living which is used or expected to be used or collected in whole or in part for the purpose of serving as a factor in establishing the consumer's eligibility for—

(A) credit or insurance to be used primarily for personal, family, or household purposes;

(B) employment purposes; or

(C) any other purpose authorized under section 1681b of this title.

(2) Exclusions.—Except as provided in paragraph (3), the term "consumer report" does not include—

(A) subject to section 624 [15 U.S.C. 1681s-3] any—

(i) report containing information solely as to transactions or experiences between the consumer and the person making the report;

(ii) communication of that information among persons related by common ownership or affiliated by corporate control; or

(iii) communication of other information among persons related by common ownership or affiliated by corporate control, if it is clearly and conspicuously disclosed to the consumer that the information may be communicated among such persons and the consumer is given the opportunity, before the time that the information is initially communicated, to direct that such information not be communicated among such persons;

(B) any authorization or approval of a specific extension of credit directly or indirectly by the issuer of a credit card or similar device;

(C) any report in which a person who has been requested by a third party to make a specific extension of credit directly or indirectly to a consumer conveys his or her decision with respect to such request, if the third party advises the consumer of the name and address of the person to whom the request was made, and such person makes the disclosures to the consumer required under section 1681m of this title; or

(D) a communication described in subsection (o) or (y).

(3) Restriction on sharing of medical information.—Except for information or any communication of information disclosed as provided in section 1681b (g)(3) of this title, the exclusions in paragraph (2) shall not apply with respect to information disclosed to any person related by common ownership or affiliated by corporate control, if the information is—

(A) medical information;

(B) an individualized list or description based on the payment transactions of the consumer for medical products or services; or

(C) an aggregate list of identified consumers based on payment transactions for medical products or services.

(e) The term "investigative consumer report" means a consumer report or portion thereof in which information on a consumer's character, general reputation, personal characteristics, or mode of living is obtained through personal interviews with neighbors, friends, or associates of the consumer reported on or with others with whom he is acquainted or who may have knowledge concerning any such items of information. However, such information shall not include specific factual information on a consumer's credit record obtained directly from a creditor of the consumer or from a consumer reporting agency when such information was obtained directly from a creditor of the consumer or from the consumer.

(f) The term "consumer reporting agency" means any person which, for monetary fees, dues, or on a cooperative nonprofit basis, regularly engages in whole or in part in the practice of assembling or evaluating consumer credit information or other information on consumers for the purpose of furnishing consumer reports to third parties, and which uses any means or facility of interstate commerce for the purpose of preparing or furnishing consumer reports.

(g) The term "file", when used in connection with information on any consumer, means all of the information on that consumer recorded and retained by a consumer reporting agency regardless of how the information is stored.

(h) The term "employment purposes" when used in connection with a consumer report means a report used for the purpose of evaluating a consumer for employment, promotion, reassignment or retention as an employee.

(i) Medical Information.—The term "medical information"—

(1) means information or data, whether oral or recorded, in any form or medium, created by or

derived from a health care provider or the consumer, that relates to—

(A) the past, present, or future physical, mental, or behavioral health or condition of an individual;

(B) the provision of health care to an individual; or

(C) the payment for the provision of health care to an individual[; and]

(2) does not include the age or gender of a consumer, demographic information about the consumer, including a consumer's residence address or e-mail address, or any other information about a consumer that does not relate to the physical, mental, or behavioral health or condition of a consumer, including the existence or value of any insurance policy.

(j) Definitions Relating to Child Support Obligations.—

(1) Overdue support.—The term "overdue support" has the meaning given to such term in section 666(e) of title 42.

(2) State or local child support enforcement agency.—The term "State or local child support enforcement agency" means a State or local agency which administers a State or local program for establishing and enforcing child support obligations.

(k) Adverse Action.—

(1) Actions included.—The term "adverse action"—

(A) has the same meaning as in section 1691(d)(6) of this title; and

(B) means—

(i) a denial or cancellation of, an increase in any charge for, or a reduction or other adverse or unfavorable change in the terms of coverage or amount of, any insurance, existing or applied for, in connection with the underwriting of insurance;

(ii) a denial of employment or any other decision for employment purposes that adversely affects any current or prospective employee;

(iii) a denial or cancellation of, an increase in any charge for, or any other adverse or unfavorable change in the terms of, any license or benefit described in section 1681b(a)(3)(D) of this title; and

(iv) an action taken or determination that is—

(I) made in connection with an application that was made by, or a transaction that was initiated by, any consumer, or in connection with a review of an account under section 1681b(a)(3)(F)(ii) of this title; and

(II) adverse to the interests of the consumer.

(2) Applicable findings, decisions, commentary, and orders.—For purposes of any determination of whether an action is an adverse action under paragraph (1)(A), all appropriate final findings, decisions, commentary, and orders issued under section 1691(d)(6) of this title by the Bureau or any court shall apply.

(l) Firm Offer of Credit or Insurance.—The term "firm offer of credit or insurance" means any offer of credit or insurance to a consumer that will be honored if the consumer is determined, based on information in a consumer report on the consumer, to meet the specific criteria used to select the consumer for the offer, except that the offer may be further conditioned on one or more of the following:

(1) The consumer being determined, based on information in the consumer's application for the credit or insurance, to meet specific criteria bearing on credit worthiness or insurability, as applicable, that are established—

(A) before selection of the consumer for the offer; and

(B) for the purpose of determining whether to extend credit or insurance pursuant to the offer.

(2) Verification—

(A) that the consumer continues to meet the specific criteria used to select the consumer for the offer, by using information in a consumer report on the consumer, information in the consumer's application for the credit or insurance, or other information bearing on the credit worthiness or insurability of the consumer; or

(B) of the information in the consumer's application for the credit or insurance, to determine that the consumer meets the specific criteria bearing on credit worthiness or insurability.

(3) The consumer furnishing any collateral that is a requirement for the extension of the credit or insurance that was—

(A) established before selection of the consumer for the offer of credit or insurance; and

(B) disclosed to the consumer in the offer of credit or insurance.

(m) Credit or Insurance Transaction That Is Not Initiated by the Consumer.—The term "credit or insurance transaction that is not initiated by the consumer" does not include the use of a consumer report by a person with which the consumer has an account or insurance policy, for purposes of—

(1) reviewing the account or insurance policy; or

(2) collecting the account.

(n) State.—The term "State" means any State, the Commonwealth of Puerto Rico, the District of Columbia, and any territory or possession of the United States.

(o) Excluded Communications.—A communication is described in this subsection if it is a communication—

(1) that, but for subsection (d)(2)(D), would be an investigative consumer report;

(2) that is made to a prospective employer for the purpose of—

(A) procuring an employee for the employer; or

(B) procuring an opportunity for a natural person to work for the employer;

(3) that is made by a person who regularly performs such procurement;

(4) that is not used by any person for any purpose other than a purpose described in subparagraph (A) or (B) of paragraph (2); and

(5) with respect to which—

(A) the consumer who is the subject of the communication—

(i) consents orally or in writing to the nature and scope of the communication, before the collection of any information for the purpose of making the communication;

(ii) consents orally or in writing to the making of the communication to a prospective employer, before the making of the communication; and

(iii) in the case of consent under clause (i) or (ii) given orally, is provided written confirmation of that consent by the person making the communication, not later than 3 business days after the receipt of the consent by that person;

(B) the person who makes the communication does not, for the purpose of making the communication, make any inquiry that if made by a prospective employer of the consumer who is the subject of the communication would violate any applicable Federal or State equal employment opportunity law or regulation; and

(C) the person who makes the communication—

(i) discloses in writing to the consumer who is the subject of the communication, not later than 5 business days after receiving any request from the consumer for such disclosure, the nature and substance of all information in the consumer's file at the time of the request, except that the sources of any information that is acquired solely for use in making the communication and is actually used for no other purpose, need not be disclosed other than under appropriate discovery procedures in any court of competent jurisdiction in which an action is brought; and

(ii) notifies the consumer who is the subject of the communication, in writing, of the consumer's right to request the information described in clause (i).

(p) Consumer Reporting Agency That Compiles and Maintains Files on Consumers on a Nationwide Basis.—The term "consumer reporting agency that compiles and maintains files on consumers on a nationwide basis" means a consumer reporting agency that regularly engages in the practice of assembling or evaluating, and maintaining, for the purpose of furnishing consumer reports to third parties bearing on a consumer's credit worthiness, credit standing, or credit capacity, each of the following regarding consumers residing nationwide:

(1) Public record information.

(2) Credit account information from persons who furnish that information regularly and in the ordinary course of business.

(q) Definitions Relating to Fraud Alerts.—

(1) Active duty military consumer.—The term "active duty military consumer" means a consumer in military service who—

(A) is on active duty (as defined in section 101(d)(1) of title 10) or is a reservist performing duty under a call or order to active duty under a provision of law referred to in section 101(a)(13) of title 10; and

(B) is assigned to service away from the usual duty station of the consumer.

(2) Fraud alert; active duty alert.—The terms "fraud alert" and "active duty alert" mean a statement in the file of a consumer that—

(A) notifies all prospective users of a consumer report relating to the consumer that the consumer may be a victim of fraud, including identity theft, or is an active duty military consumer, as applicable; and

(B) is presented in a manner that facilitates a clear and conspicuous view of the statement described in subparagraph (A) by any person requesting such consumer report.

(3) Identity theft.—The term "identity theft" means a fraud committed using the identifying information of another person, subject to such further definition as the Bureau may prescribe, by regulation.

(4) Identity theft report.—The term "identity theft report" has the meaning given that term by rule of the Bureau, and means, at a minimum, a report—

(A) that alleges an identity theft;

(B) that is a copy of an official, valid report filed by a consumer with an appropriate Federal, State, or local law enforcement agency, including the United States Postal Inspection Service, or such other government agency deemed appropriate by the Bureau; and

(C) the filing of which subjects the person filing the report to criminal penalties relating to the filing of false information if, in fact, the information in the report is false.

(5) New credit plan.—The term "new credit plan" means a new account under an open end credit plan (as defined in section 103(j) of the Truth in Lending Act [15 U.S.C. 1602(j)]) or a new credit transaction not under an open end credit plan.

(r) Credit and Debit Related Terms—

(1) Card issuer.—The term "card issuer" means—

(A) a credit card issuer, in the case of a credit card; and

(B) a debit card issuer, in the case of a debit card.

(2) Credit card.—The term "credit card" has the same meaning as in section 103 of the Truth in Lending Act [15 U.S.C. 1602].

(3) Debit card.—The term "debit card" means any card issued by a financial institution to a consumer for use in initiating an electronic fund transfer from the account of the consumer at such financial institution, for the purpose of transferring money between accounts or obtaining money, property, labor, or services.

(4) Account and electronic fund transfer.—The terms "account" and "electronic fund transfer" have the same meanings as in section 903 of the Electronic Fund Transfer Act.

(5) Credit and creditor.—The terms "credit" and "creditor" have the same meanings as in section 1691a of this title.

(s) Federal Banking Agency.—The term "Federal banking agency" has the same meaning as in section 3 of the Federal Deposit Insurance Act [12 U.S.C. 1813].

(t) Financial Institution.—The term "financial institution" means a State or National bank, a State or Federal savings and loan association, a mutual savings bank, a State or Federal credit union, or any other person that, directly or indirectly, holds a transaction account (as defined in section 19(b) of the Federal Reserve Act [12 U.S.C. 461(b)]) belonging to a consumer.

(u) Reseller.—The term "reseller" means a consumer reporting agency that—

(1) assembles and merges information contained in the database of another consumer reporting agency or multiple consumer reporting agencies concerning any consumer for purposes of furnishing such information to any third party, to the extent of such activities; and

(2) does not maintain a database of the assembled or merged information from which new consumer reports are produced.

(v) Commission.—The term "Commission" means the Bureau.

(w) The term "Bureau" means the Bureau of Consumer Financial Protection.

(x) Nationwide Specialty Consumer Reporting Agency.—The term "nationwide specialty consumer reporting agency" means a consumer reporting agency that compiles and maintains files on consumers on a nationwide basis relating to—

(1) medical records or payments;

(2) residential or tenant history;

(3) check writing history;

(4) employment history; or

(5) insurance claims.

(y) Exclusion of Certain Communications for Employee Investigations.—

(1) Communications described in this subsection.—A communication is described in this subsection if—

(A) but for subsection (d)(2)(D), the communication would be a consumer report;

(B) the communication is made to an employer in connection with an investigation of—

(i) suspected misconduct relating to employment; or

(ii) compliance with Federal, State, or local laws and regulations, the rules of a self-regulatory organization, or any preexisting written policies of the employer;

(C) the communication is not made for the purpose of investigating a consumer's credit worthiness, credit standing, or credit capacity; and

(D) the communication is not provided to any person except—

(i) to the employer or an agent of the employer;

(ii) to any Federal or State officer, agency, or department, or any officer, agency, or department of a unit of general local government;

(iii) to any self-regulatory organization with regulatory authority over the activities of the employer or employee;

(iv) as otherwise required by law; or

(v) pursuant to section 1681f of this title.

(2) Subsequent disclosure. After taking any adverse action based in whole or in part on a communication described in paragraph (1), the employer shall disclose to the consumer a summary containing the nature and substance of the communication upon which the adverse action is based, except that the sources of information acquired solely for use in preparing what would be but for subsection (d)(2)(D) an investigative consumer report need not be disclosed.

(3) Self-regulatory organization defined.—For purposes of this subsection, the term "self-regulatory organization" includes any self-regulatory organization (as defined in section 3(a)(26) of the Securities Exchange Act of 1934 [15 U.S.C. 78c(a)(26)]), any entity established under title I of the Sarbanes-Oxley Act of 2002 [15 U.S.C. 7211 et seq.], any board of trade designated by the Commodity Futures Trading Commission, and any futures association registered with such Commission. . . .

§ 604. Permissible Purposes of Consumer Reports [15 U.S.C. § 1681b].

(a) In general. Subject to subsection (c), any consumer reporting agency may furnish a consumer report under the following circumstances and no other:

(1) In response to the order of a court having jurisdiction to issue such an order, a subpoena issued in connection with proceedings before a Federal grand jury, or a subpoena issued in accordance with section 5318 of title 31 or section 3486 of title 18.

(2) In accordance with the written instructions of the consumer to whom it relates.

(3) To a person which it has reason to believe—

(A) intends to use the information in connection with a credit transaction involving the consumer on whom the information is to be furnished and involving the extension of credit to, or review or collection of an account of, the consumer; or

(B) intends to use the information for employment purposes; or

(C) intends to use the information in connection with the underwriting of insurance involving the consumer; or

(D) intends to use the information in connection with a determination of the consumer's eligibility for a license or other benefit granted by a governmental instrumentality required by law to consider an applicant's financial responsibility or status; or

(E) intends to use the information, as a potential investor or servicer, or current insurer, in connection with a valuation of, or an assessment of the credit or prepayment risks associated with, an existing credit obligation; or

(F) otherwise has a legitimate business need for the information—

(i) in connection with a business transaction that is initiated by the consumer; or

(ii) to review an account to determine whether the consumer continues to meet the terms of the account. . . .

(4) In response to a request by the head of a State or local child support enforcement agency (or a State or local government official authorized by the head of such an agency), if the person making the request certifies to the consumer reporting agency that—

(A) the consumer report is needed for the purpose of establishing an individual's capacity to make child support payments, determining the appropriate level of such payments, or enforcing a child support order, award, agreement, or judgment;

(B) the parentage of the consumer for the child to which the obligation relates has been established or acknowledged by the consumer in accordance with State laws under which the obligation arises (if required by those laws); and

(C) the consumer report will be kept confidential, will be used solely for a purpose described in subparagraph (A), and will not be used in connection with any other civil, administrative, or criminal proceeding, or for any other purpose.

(5) To an agency administering a State plan under section 654 of title 42 for use to set an initial or modified child support award. . . .

(b) Conditions for furnishing and using consumer reports for employment purposes

(1) Certification from user. A consumer reporting agency may furnish a consumer report for employment purposes only if—

(A) the person who obtains such report from the agency certifies to the agency that—

(i) the person has complied with paragraph (2) with respect to the consumer report, and the person will comply with paragraph (3) with respect to the consumer report if paragraph (3) becomes applicable; and

(ii) information from the consumer report will not be used in violation of any applicable Federal or State equal employment opportunity law or regulation; and

(B) the consumer reporting agency provides with the report, or has previously provided, a summary of the consumer's rights under this subchapter, as prescribed by the Bureau under section 1681g(c)(1) of this title.

(2) Disclosure to consumer

(A) In general. Except as provided in subparagraph (B), a person may not procure a consumer report, or cause a consumer report to be procured, for employment purposes with respect to any consumer, unless—

(i) a clear and conspicuous disclosure has been made in writing to the consumer at any time before the report is procured or caused to be procured, in a document that consists solely of the disclosure, that a consumer report may be obtained for employment purposes; and

(ii) the consumer has authorized in writing (which authorization may be made on the document referred to in clause (i)) the procurement of the report by that person.

(B) Application by mail, telephone, computer, or other similar means. If a consumer described in subparagraph (C) applies for employment by mail, telephone, computer, or other similar means, at any time before a consumer report is procured or caused to be procured in connection with that application—

(i) the person who procures the consumer report on the consumer for employment purposes shall provide to the consumer, by oral, written, or electronic means, notice that a consumer report may be obtained for employment purposes, and a summary of the consumer's rights under section 1681m(a)(4) of this title; and

(ii) the consumer shall have consented, orally, in writing, or electronically to the procurement of the report by that person.

(C) Scope. Subparagraph (B) shall apply to a person procuring a consumer report on a consumer in connection with the consumer's application for employment only if—

(i) the consumer is applying for a position over which the Secretary of Transportation has the power to establish qualifications and maximum hours of service pursuant to the provisions of section 31502 of title 49, or a position subject to safety regulation by a State transportation agency; and

(ii) as of the time at which the person procures the report or causes the report to be procured the only interaction between the consumer and the person in connection with that employment application has been by mail, telephone, computer, or other similar means.

(3) Conditions on use for adverse actions

(A) In general. Except as provided in subparagraph (B), in using a consumer report for employment purposes, before taking any adverse action based in whole or in part on the report, the person intending to take such adverse action shall provide to the consumer to whom the report relates—

(i) a copy of the report; and

(ii) a description in writing of the rights of the consumer under this subchapter, as prescribed by the Bureau under section 1681g(c)(1) of this title.

(B) Application by mail, telephone, computer, or other similar means

(i) If a consumer described in subparagraph (C) applies for employment by mail, telephone, computer, or other similar means, and if a person who has procured a consumer report on the consumer for employment purposes takes adverse action on the employment application based in whole or in part on the report, then the person must provide to the consumer to whom the report relates, in lieu of the notices required under subparagraph (A) of this section and under section 1681m(a) of this title, within 3 business days of taking such action, an oral, written or electronic notification—

(I) that adverse action has been taken based in whole or in part on a consumer report received from a consumer reporting agency;

(II) of the name, address and telephone number of the consumer reporting agency that furnished the consumer report (including a toll-free telephone number established by the agency if the agency compiles and maintains files on consumers on a nationwide basis);

(III) that the consumer reporting agency did not make the decision to take the adverse action and is unable to provide to the consumer the specific reasons why the adverse action was taken; and

(IV) that the consumer may, upon providing proper identification, request a free copy of a report and may dispute with the consumer reporting agency the accuracy or completeness of any information in a report.

(ii) If, under clause (B)(i)(IV), the consumer requests a copy of a consumer report from the person who procured the report, then, within 3 business days of receiving the consumer's request, together with proper identification, the person must send or provide to the consumer a copy of a report and a copy of the consumer's rights as prescribed by the Bureau under section 1681g(c)(1) of this title.

(C) Scope. Subparagraph (B) shall apply to a person procuring a consumer report on a consumer in connection with the consumer's application for employment only if—

(i) the consumer is applying for a position over which the Secretary of Transportation has the power to establish qualifications and maximum hours of service pursuant to the provisions of section 31502 of title 49, or a position subject to safety regulation by a State transportation agency; and

(ii) as of the time at which the person procures the report or causes the report to be procured the only interaction between the consumer and the person in connection with that employment application has been by mail, telephone, computer, or other similar means. . . .

(c) Furnishing reports in connection with credit or insurance transactions that are not initiated by consumer

(1) In general. A consumer reporting agency may furnish a consumer report relating to any consumer pursuant to subparagraph (A) or (C) of subsection (a)(3) in connection with any credit or insurance transaction that is not initiated by the consumer only if—

(A) the consumer authorizes the agency to provide such report to such person; or

(B) (i) the transaction consists of a firm offer of credit or insurance;

(ii) the consumer reporting agency has complied with subsection (e);

(iii) there is not in effect an election by the consumer, made in accordance with subsection (e), to have the consumer's name and address excluded from lists of names provided by the agency pursuant to this paragraph; and

(iv) the consumer report does not contain a date of birth that shows that the consumer has not attained the age of 21, or, if the date of birth on the consumer report shows that the consumer has not attained the age of 21, such consumer consents to the consumer reporting agency to such furnishing.

(2) Limits on information received under paragraph (1)(B). A person may receive pursuant to paragraph (1)(B) only—

(A) the name and address of a consumer;

(B) an identifier that is not unique to the consumer and that is used by the person solely for the purpose of verifying the identity of the consumer; and

(C) other information pertaining to a consumer that does not identify the relationship or experience of the consumer with respect to a particular creditor or other entity.

(3) Information regarding inquiries. Except as provided in section 1681g(a)(5) of this title, a consumer

reporting agency shall not furnish to any person a record of inquiries in connection with a credit or insurance transaction that is not initiated by a consumer.

(4) Treatment of prescreening report requests

(A) Definitions. In this paragraph:

(i) Credit union. The term "credit union" means a Federal credit union or a State credit union, as those terms are defined, respectively, in section 101 of the Federal Credit Union Act (12 U.S.C. 1752).

(ii) Insured depository institution. The term "insured depository institution" has the meaning given the term in section 3 of the Federal Deposit Insurance Act (12 U.S.C. 1813(c)).

(iii) Residential mortgage loan. The term "residential mortgage loan" has the meaning given the term in section 5102 of title 12.

(iv) Servicer. The term "servicer" has the meaning given the term in section 2605(i) of title 12.

(B) Limitation. If a person requests a consumer report from a consumer reporting agency in connection with a credit transaction involving a residential mortgage loan, that agency may not, based in whole or in part on that request, furnish a consumer report to another person under this subsection unless—

(i) the transaction consists of a firm offer of credit or insurance; and

(ii) that other person—

(I) has submitted documentation to that agency certifying that such other person has, pursuant to paragraph (1)(A), the authorization of the consumer to whom the consumer report relates; or

(II) (aa) has originated a current residential mortgage loan of the consumer to whom the consumer report relates;

(bb) is the servicer of a current residential mortgage loan of the consumer to whom the consumer report relates;

(cc) (AA) is an insured depository institution or credit union; and

(BB) holds a current account for the consumer to whom the consumer report relates.

(d) Reserved

(e) Election of consumer to be excluded from lists

(1) In general. A consumer may elect to have the consumer's name and address excluded from any list provided by a consumer reporting agency under subsection (c)(1)(B) in connection with a credit or insurance transaction that is not initiated by the consumer, by notifying the agency in accordance with paragraph (2) that the consumer does not consent to any use of a consumer report relating to the consumer in connection with any credit or insurance transaction that is not initiated by the consumer.

(2) Manner of notification. A consumer shall notify a consumer reporting agency under paragraph (1)—

(A) through the notification system maintained by the agency under paragraph (5); or

(B) by submitting to the agency a signed notice of election form issued by the agency for purposes of this subparagraph.

(3) Response of agency after notification through system. Upon receipt of notification of the election of a consumer under paragraph (1) through the notification system maintained by the agency under paragraph (5), a consumer reporting agency shall—

(A) inform the consumer that the election is effective only for the 5-year period following the election if the consumer does not submit to the agency a signed notice of election form issued by the agency for purposes of paragraph (2)(B); and

(B) provide to the consumer a notice of election form, if requested by the consumer, not later than 5 business days after receipt of the notification of the election through the system established under paragraph (5), in the case of a request made at the time the consumer provides notification through the system.

(4) Effectiveness of election. An election of a consumer under paragraph (1)—

(A) shall be effective with respect to a consumer reporting agency beginning 5 business days after the date on which the consumer notifies the agency in accordance with paragraph (2);

(B) shall be effective with respect to a consumer reporting agency—

(i) subject to subparagraph (C), during the 5-year period beginning 5 business days after the date on which the consumer notifies the agency of the election, in the case of an election for which a consumer notifies the agency only in accordance with paragraph (2)(A); or

(ii) until the consumer notifies the agency under subparagraph (C), in the case of an election for which a consumer notifies the agency in accordance with paragraph (2)(B);

(C) shall not be effective after the date on which the consumer notifies the agency, through the notification system established by the agency under paragraph (5), that the election is no longer effective; and

(D) shall be effective with respect to each affiliate of the agency.

(5) Notification system

(A) In general. Each consumer reporting agency that, under subsection (c)(1)(B), furnishes a consumer report in connection with a credit or insurance transaction that is not initiated by a consumer, shall—

(i) establish and maintain a notification system, including a toll-free telephone number, which permits any consumer whose consumer report is maintained by the agency to notify the agency, with appropriate identification, of the consumer's election to have the consumer's name and address excluded from any such list of names and addresses provided by the agency for such a transaction; and

(ii) publish by not later than 365 days after September 30, 1996, and not less than annually thereafter, in a publication of general circulation in the area served by the agency—

(I) a notification that information in consumer files maintained by the agency may be used in connection with such transactions; and

(II) the address and toll-free telephone number for consumers to use to notify the agency of the consumer's election under clause (i).

(B) Establishment and maintenance as compliance. Establishment and maintenance of a notification system (including a toll-free telephone number) and publication by a consumer reporting agency on the agency's own behalf and on behalf of any of its affiliates in accordance with this paragraph is deemed to be compliance with this paragraph by each of those affiliates.

(6) Notification system by agencies that operate nationwide. Each consumer reporting agency that compiles and maintains files on consumers on a nationwide basis shall establish and maintain a notification system for purposes of paragraph (5) jointly with other such consumer reporting agencies.

(f) Certain use or obtaining of information prohibited. A person shall not use or obtain a consumer report for any purpose unless—

(1) the consumer report is obtained for a purpose for which the consumer report is authorized to be furnished under this section; and

(2) the purpose is certified in accordance with section 1681e of this title by a prospective user of the report through a general or specific certification.

(g) Protection of medical information

(1) Limitation on consumer reporting agencies. A consumer reporting agency shall not furnish for employment purposes, or in connection with a credit or insurance transaction, a consumer report that contains medical information (other than medical contact information treated in the manner required under section 1681c(a)(6) of this title) about a consumer, unless—

(A) if furnished in connection with an insurance transaction, the consumer affirmatively consents to the furnishing of the report;

(B) if furnished for employment purposes or in connection with a credit transaction—

(i) the information to be furnished is relevant to process or effect the employment or credit transaction; and

(ii) the consumer provides specific written consent for the furnishing of the report that describes in clear and conspicuous language the use for which the information will be furnished; or

(C) the information to be furnished pertains solely to transactions, accounts, or balances relating to debts arising from the receipt of medical services, products, or devises [sic], where such information, other than account status or amounts, is restricted or reported using codes that do not identify, or do not provide information sufficient to infer, the specific provider or the nature of such services, products, or devices, as provided in section 1681c(a)(6) of this title.

(2) Limitation on creditors. Except as permitted pursuant to paragraph (3)(C) or regulations prescribed under paragraph (5)(A), a creditor shall not obtain or use medical information (other than medical information treated in the manner required under section 1681c(a)(6) of this title) pertaining to a consumer in connection with any determination of the consumer's eligibility, or continued eligibility, for credit.

(3) Actions authorized by Federal law, insurance activities and regulatory determinations. Section 1681a(d)(3) of this title shall not be construed so as to treat information or any communication of information as a consumer report if the information or communication is disclosed—

(A) in connection with the business of insurance or annuities, including the activities described in section 18B of the model Privacy of Consumer Financial and Health Information Regulation issued by the National Association of Insurance Commissioners (as in effect on January 1, 2003);

(B) for any purpose permitted without authorization under the Standards for Individually Identifiable Health Information promulgated by the Department of Health and Human Services pursuant to the Health Insurance Portability and Accountability Act of 1996, or referred to under section 1179 of such Act, or described in section 6802(e) of this title; or

(C) as otherwise determined to be necessary and appropriate, by regulation or order, by the Bureau or the applicable State insurance authority (with respect to any person engaged in providing insurance or annuities).

(4) Limitation on redisclosure of medical information. Any person that receives medical information pursuant to paragraph (1) or (3) shall not disclose such information to any other person, except as necessary to carry out the purpose for which the information was initially disclosed, or as otherwise permitted by statute, regulation, or order.

(5) Regulations and effective date for paragraph (2)

(A) Regulations required. The Bureau may, after notice and opportunity for comment, prescribe regulations that permit transactions under paragraph (2) that are determined to be necessary and appropriate to protect legitimate operational, transactional, risk, consumer, and other needs (and which shall include permitting actions necessary for administrative verification purposes), consistent with the intent of paragraph (2) to restrict the use of medical information for inappropriate purposes.

(6) Coordination with other laws. No provision of this subsection shall be construed as altering, affecting, or superseding the applicability of any other provision of Federal law relating to medical confidentiality.

§ 605. Requirements Relating to Information Contained in Consumer Reports [15 U.S.C. § 1681c].

(a) Information excluded from consumer reports. Except as authorized under subsection (b), no consumer reporting agency may make any consumer report containing any of the following items of information:

(1) Cases under title 11 or under the Bankruptcy Act that, from the date of entry of the order for relief or the date of adjudication, as the case may be, antedate the report by more than 10 years.

(2) Civil suits, civil judgments, and records of arrest that, from date of entry, antedate the report by more than seven years or until the governing statute of limitations has expired, whichever is the longer period.

(3) Paid tax liens which, from date of payment, antedate the report by more than seven years.

(4) Accounts placed for collection or charged to profit and loss which antedate the report by more than seven years.

(5) Any other adverse item of information, other than records of convictions of crimes which antedates the report by more than seven years.

(6) The name, address, and telephone number of any medical information furnisher that has notified the agency of its status, unless—

(A) such name, address, and telephone number are restricted or reported using codes that do not identify, or provide information sufficient to infer, the specific provider or the nature of such services, products, or devices to a person other than the consumer; or

(B) the report is being provided to an insurance company for a purpose relating to engaging in the business of insurance other than property and casualty insurance. . . .

(b) Exempted cases. The provisions of paragraphs (1) through (5) of subsection (a) are not applicable in the case of any consumer credit report to be used in connection with—

(1) a credit transaction involving, or which may reasonably be expected to involve, a principal amount of $150,000 or more;

(2) the underwriting of life insurance involving, or which may reasonably be expected to involve, a face amount of $150,000 or more; or

(3) the employment of any individual at an annual salary which equals, or which may reasonably be expected to equal $75,000, or more.

(c) Running of reporting period

(1) In general. The 7-year period referred to in paragraphs (4) and (6) of subsection (a) shall begin, with respect to any delinquent account that is placed for collection (internally or by referral to a third party, whichever is earlier), charged to profit and loss, or subjected to any similar action, upon the expiration of the 180-day period beginning on the date of the commencement of the delinquency which immediately preceded the collection activity, charge to profit and loss, or similar action.

(2) Effective date. Paragraph (1) shall apply only to items of information added to the file of a consumer on or after the date that is 455 days after September 30, 1996.

(d) Information required to be disclosed

(1) Title 11 information. Any consumer reporting agency that furnishes a consumer report that contains information regarding any case involving the consumer that arises under title 11 shall include in the report an identification of the chapter of such title 11 under which such case arises if provided by the source of the information. If any case arising or filed under title 11 is withdrawn by the consumer before a final judgment, the consumer reporting agency shall include in the report that such case or filing was withdrawn upon receipt of documentation certifying such withdrawal.

(2) Key factor in credit score information. Any consumer reporting agency that furnishes a consumer report that contains any credit score or any other risk score or predictor on any consumer shall include in the report a clear and conspicuous statement that a key factor (as defined in section 1681g(f)(2)(B) of this title) that adversely affected such score or predictor was the number of enquiries, if such a predictor was in fact a key factor that adversely affected such score. This paragraph shall not apply to a check services company, acting as such, which issues authorizations for the purpose of approving or processing negotiable instruments, electronic fund transfers, or similar methods of payments, but only to the extent that such company is engaged in such activities.

(e) Indication of closure of account by consumer. If a consumer reporting agency is notified pursuant to section 1681s-2(a)(4) of this title that a credit account of a consumer was voluntarily closed by the consumer, the agency shall indicate that fact in any consumer report that includes information related to the account.

(f) Indication of dispute by consumer. If a consumer reporting agency is notified pursuant to section 1681s-2(a)(3) of this title that information regarding a consumer wh[ich]* was furnished to the agency is disputed by the consumer, the agency shall indicate that fact in each consumer report that includes the disputed information.

(g) Truncation of credit card and debit card numbers

(1) In general. Except as otherwise provided in this subsection, no person that accepts credit cards or debit cards for the transaction of business shall print more than the last 5 digits of the card number or the expiration date upon any receipt provided to the cardholder at the point of the sale or transaction.

(2) Limitation. This subsection shall apply only to receipts that are electronically printed, and shall not apply to transactions in which the sole means of recording a credit card or debit card account number is by handwriting or by an imprint or copy of the card.

(3) Effective date. This subsection shall become effective—

(A) 3 years after December 4, 2003, with respect to any cash register or other machine or device that electronically prints receipts for credit card or debit card transactions that is in use before January 1, 2005; and

(B) 1 year after December 4, 2003, with respect to any cash register or other machine or device that electronically prints receipts for credit card or debit card transactions that is first put into use on or after January 1, 2005.

(h) Notice of discrepancy in address

(1) In general. If a person has requested a consumer report relating to a consumer from a consumer reporting agency described in section 1681a(p) of this title, the request includes an address for the consumer that substantially differs from the addresses

---

* Correction by editor

in the file of the consumer, and the agency provides a consumer report in response to the request, the consumer reporting agency shall notify the requester of the existence of the discrepancy.

(2) Regulations

(A) Regulations required. The Bureau shall, in consultation with the Federal banking agencies, the National Credit Union Administration, and the Federal Trade Commission, prescribe regulations providing guidance regarding reasonable policies and procedures that a user of a consumer report should employ when such user has received a notice of discrepancy under paragraph (1).

(B) Policies and procedures to be included. The regulations prescribed under subparagraph (A) shall describe reasonable policies and procedures for use by a user of a consumer report—

(i) to form a reasonable belief that the user knows the identity of the person to whom the consumer report pertains; and

(ii) if the user establishes a continuing relationship with the consumer, and the user regularly and in the ordinary course of business furnishes information to the consumer reporting agency from which the notice of discrepancy pertaining to the consumer was obtained, to reconcile the address of the consumer with the consumer reporting agency by furnishing such address to such consumer reporting agency as part of information regularly furnished by the user for the period in which the relationship is established.

§ 605A. Identity Theft Prevention; Fraud Alerts and Active Duty Alerts [15 U.S.C. § 1681c-1].

(a) One-call fraud alerts

(1) Initial alerts. Upon the direct request of a consumer, or an individual acting on behalf of or as a personal representative of a consumer, who asserts in good faith a suspicion that the consumer has been or is about to become a victim of fraud or related crime, including identity theft, a consumer reporting agency described in section 1681a(p) of this title that maintains a file on the consumer and has received appropriate proof of the identity of the requester shall—

(A) include a fraud alert in the file of that consumer, and also provide that alert along with any credit score generated in using that file, for a period of not less than 1 year, beginning on the date of such request, unless the consumer or such representative requests that such fraud alert be removed before the end of such period, and the agency has received appropriate proof of the identity of the requester for such purpose; and

(B) refer the information regarding the fraud alert under this paragraph to each of the other consumer reporting agencies described in section 1681a(p) of this title, in accordance with procedures developed under section 1681s(f) of this title.

(2) Access to free reports. In any case in which a consumer reporting agency includes a fraud alert in the file of a consumer pursuant to this subsection, the consumer reporting agency shall—

(A) disclose to the consumer that the consumer may request a free copy of the file of the consumer pursuant to section 1681j(d) of this title; and

(B) provide to the consumer all disclosures required to be made under section 1681g of this title, without charge to the consumer, not later than 3 business days after any request described in subparagraph (A).

(b) Extended alerts

(1) In general. Upon the direct request of a consumer, or an individual acting on behalf of or as a personal representative of a consumer, who submits an identity theft report to a consumer reporting agency described in section 1681a(p) of this title that maintains a file on the consumer, if the agency has received appropriate proof of the identity of the requester, the agency shall—

(A) include a fraud alert in the file of that consumer, and also provide that alert along with any credit score generated in using that file, during the 7-year period beginning on the date of such request, unless the consumer or such representative requests that such fraud alert be removed before the end of such period and the agency has received appropriate proof of the identity of the requester for such purpose;

(B) during the 5-year period beginning on the date of such request, exclude the consumer from any list of consumers prepared by the consumer reporting agency and provided to any third party to offer credit or insurance to the consumer as part of a transaction that was not initiated by the consumer, unless the consumer or such representative requests that such exclusion be rescinded before the end of such period; and

(C) refer the information regarding the extended fraud alert under this paragraph to each of the other consumer reporting agencies described in section 1681a(p) of this title, in accordance with procedures developed under section 1681s(f) of this title.

(2) Access to free reports. In any case in which a consumer reporting agency includes a fraud alert in the file of a consumer pursuant to this subsection, the consumer reporting agency shall—

(A) disclose to the consumer that the consumer may request 2 free copies of the file of the consumer pursuant to section 1681j(d) of this title during the 12-month period beginning on the date on which the fraud alert was included in the file; and

(B) provide to the consumer all disclosures required to be made under section 1681g of this title, without charge to the consumer, not later than 3 business days after any request described in subparagraph (A).

(c) Active duty alerts. Upon the direct request of an active duty military consumer, or an individual acting on behalf of or as a personal representative of an active duty military consumer, a consumer reporting agency described in section 1681a(p) of this title that maintains a file on the active duty military consumer and has received appropriate proof of the identity of the requester shall—

(1) include an active duty alert in the file of that active duty military consumer, and also provide that alert along with any credit score generated in using that file, during a period of not less than 12 months, or such longer period as the Bureau shall determine, by regulation, beginning on the date of the request, unless the active duty military consumer or such representative requests that such fraud alert be removed before the end of such period, and the agency has received appropriate proof of the identity of the requester for such purpose;

(2) during the 2-year period beginning on the date of such request, exclude the active duty military consumer from any list of consumers prepared by the consumer reporting agency and provided to any third party to offer credit or insurance to the consumer as part of a transaction that was not initiated by the consumer, unless the consumer requests that such exclusion be rescinded before the end of such period; and

(3) refer the information regarding the active duty alert to each of the other consumer reporting agencies described in section 1681a(p) of this title, in accordance with procedures developed under section 1681s(f) of this title.

(d) Procedures. Each consumer reporting agency described in section 1681a(p) of this title shall establish policies and procedures to comply with this section, including procedures that inform consumers of the availability of initial, extended, and active duty alerts and procedures that allow consumers and active duty military consumers to request initial, extended, or active duty alerts (as applicable) in a simple and easy manner, including by telephone.

(e) Referrals of alerts. Each consumer reporting agency described in section 1681a(p) of this title that receives a referral of a fraud alert or active duty alert from another consumer reporting agency pursuant to this section shall, as though the agency received the request from the consumer directly, follow the procedures required under—

(1) paragraphs (1)(A) and (2) of subsection (a), in the case of a referral under subsection (a)(1)(B);

(2) paragraphs (1)(A), (1)(B), and (2) of subsection (b), in the case of a referral under subsection (b)(1)(C); and

(3) paragraphs (1) and (2) of subsection (c), in the case of a referral under subsection (c)(3).

(f) Duty of reseller to reconvey alert. A reseller shall include in its report any fraud alert or active duty alert placed in the file of a consumer pursuant to this section by another consumer reporting agency.

(g) Duty of other consumer reporting agencies to provide contact information. If a consumer contacts any consumer reporting agency that is not described in section 1681a(p) of this title to communicate a suspicion that the consumer has been or is about to become a victim of fraud or related crime, including identity theft, the agency shall provide information to the consumer on how to contact the Bureau and the consumer reporting agencies described in section 1681a(p) of this title to obtain more detailed information and request alerts under this section.

(h) Limitations on use of information for credit extensions

(1) Requirements for initial and active duty alerts

(A) Notification. Each initial fraud alert and active duty alert under this section shall include information that notifies all prospective users of a consumer report on the consumer to which the alert relates that the consumer does not authorize the establishment of any new credit plan or extension of credit, other than under an open-end credit plan (as defined in section 1602(j) of this title), in the name of the consumer, or issuance of an additional card on an existing credit account requested by a consumer, or any increase in credit limit on an existing credit account requested by a consumer, except in accordance with subparagraph (B).

(B) Limitation on users

(i) In general. No prospective user of a consumer report that includes an initial fraud alert or an active duty alert in accordance with this section may establish a new credit plan or extension of credit, other than under an open-end credit plan (as defined in section 1602(j) of this title), in the name of the consumer, or issue an additional card on an existing credit account requested by a consumer, or grant any increase in credit limit on an existing credit account requested by a consumer, unless the user utilizes reasonable policies and procedures to form a reasonable belief that the user knows the identity of the person making the request.

(ii) Verification. If a consumer requesting the alert has specified a telephone number to be used for identity verification purposes, before authorizing any new credit plan or extension described in clause (i) in the name of such consumer, a user of such consumer report shall contact the consumer using that telephone number or take reasonable steps to verify the consumer's identity and confirm that the application for a new credit plan is not the result of identity theft.

(2) Requirements for extended alerts

(A) Notification. Each extended alert under this section shall include information that provides all prospective users of a consumer report relating to a consumer with—

(i) notification that the consumer does not authorize the establishment of any new credit plan or extension of credit described in clause (i), other than under an open-end credit plan (as defined in section 1602(i) of this title), in the name of the consumer, or issuance of an additional card on an existing credit account requested by a consumer, or any increase in credit limit on an existing credit account requested by a consumer, except in accordance with subparagraph (B); and

(ii) a telephone number or other reasonable contact method designated by the consumer.

(B) Limitation on users. No prospective user of a consumer report or of a credit score generated using the information in the file of a consumer that includes an extended fraud alert in accordance with this section may establish a new credit plan or extension of credit, other than under an open-end credit plan (as defined in section 1602(i) of this title), in the name of the consumer, or issue an additional card on an existing credit account requested by a consumer, or any increase in credit limit on an existing credit account requested by a consumer, unless the user contacts the consumer in person or using the contact method described in subparagraph (A)(ii) to confirm that the application for a new credit plan or increase in credit limit, or request for an additional card is not the result of identity theft.

(i) National security freeze

(1) Definitions. For purposes of this subsection:

(A) The term "consumer reporting agency" means a consumer reporting agency described in section 1681a(p) of this title.

(B) The term "proper identification" has the meaning of such term as used under section 1681h of this title.

(C) The term "security freeze" means a restriction that prohibits a consumer reporting agency from disclosing the contents of a consumer report that is subject to such security freeze to any person requesting the consumer report.

(2) Placement of security freeze

(A) In general. Upon receiving a direct request from a consumer that a consumer reporting agency place a security freeze, and upon receiving proper identification from the consumer, the consumer reporting agency shall, free of charge, place the security freeze not later than—

(i) in the case of a request that is by toll-free telephone or secure electronic means, 1 business day after receiving the request directly from the consumer; or

(ii) in the case of a request that is by mail, 3 business days after receiving the request directly from the consumer.

(B) Confirmation and additional information. Not later than 5 business days after placing a security freeze under subparagraph (A), a consumer reporting agency shall—

(i) send confirmation of the placement to the consumer; and

(ii) inform the consumer of—

(I) the process by which the consumer may remove the security freeze, including a mechanism to authenticate the consumer; and

(II) the consumer's right described in section 1681m(d)(1)(D) of this title.

(C) Notice to third parties. A consumer reporting agency may advise a third party that a security freeze has been placed with respect to a consumer under subparagraph (A).

(3) Removal of security freeze

(A) In general. A consumer reporting agency shall remove a security freeze placed on the consumer report of a consumer only in the following cases:

(i) Upon the direct request of the consumer.

(ii) The security freeze was placed due to a material misrepresentation of fact by the consumer.

(B) Notice if removal not by request. If a consumer reporting agency removes a security freeze under subparagraph (A)(ii), the consumer reporting agency shall notify the consumer in writing prior to removing the security freeze.

(C) Removal of security freeze by consumer request. Except as provided in subparagraph (A)(ii), a security freeze shall remain in place until the consumer directly requests that the security freeze be removed. Upon receiving a direct request from a consumer that a consumer reporting agency remove a security freeze, and upon receiving proper identification from the consumer, the consumer reporting agency shall, free of charge, remove the security freeze not later than—

(i) in the case of a request that is by toll-free telephone or secure electronic means, 1 hour after receiving the request for removal; or

(ii) in the case of a request that is by mail, 3 business days after receiving the request for removal.

(D) Third-party requests. If a third party requests access to a consumer report of a consumer with respect to which a security freeze is in effect, where such request is in connection with an application for credit, and the consumer does not allow such consumer report to be accessed, the third party may treat the application as incomplete.

(E) Temporary removal of security freeze. Upon receiving a direct request from a consumer under subparagraph (A)(i), if the consumer requests a temporary removal of a security freeze, the consumer reporting agency shall, in accordance with subparagraph (C), remove the security freeze for the period of time specified by the consumer.

(4) Exceptions. A security freeze shall not apply to the making of a consumer report for use of the following:

(A) A person or entity, or a subsidiary, affiliate, or agent of that person or entity, or an assignee of a financial obligation owed by the consumer to that person or entity, or a prospective assignee of a financial obligation owed by the consumer to that person or entity in conjunction with the proposed purchase of the financial obligation, with which the consumer has or had prior to assignment an account or contract including a demand deposit account, or to whom the consumer issued a negotiable instrument, for the purposes of reviewing the account or collecting the financial obligation owed for the account, contract, or negotiable instrument. For purposes of this subparagraph, "reviewing the account" includes activities related to account maintenance, monitoring, credit line increases, and account upgrades and enhancements.

(B) Any Federal, State, or local agency, law enforcement agency, trial court, or private collection agency acting pursuant to a court order, warrant, or subpoena.

(C) A child support agency acting pursuant to part D of title IV of the Social Security Act (42 U.S.C. 651 et seq.).

(D) A Federal agency or a State or its agents or assigns acting to investigate fraud or acting to investigate or collect delinquent taxes or unpaid court orders or to fulfill any of its other statutory responsibilities, provided such responsibilities are consistent with a permissible purpose under section 1681b of this title.

(E) By a person using credit information for the purposes described under section 1681b(c) of this title.

(F) Any person or entity administering a credit file monitoring subscription or similar service to which the consumer has subscribed.

(G) Any person or entity for the purpose of providing a consumer with a copy of the consumer's consumer report or credit score, upon the request of the consumer.

(H) Any person using the information in connection with the underwriting of insurance.

(I) Any person using the information for employment, tenant, or background screening purposes.

(J) Any person using the information for assessing, verifying, or authenticating a consumer's identity for purposes other than the granting of credit, or for investigating or preventing actual or potential fraud.

(5) Notice of rights. At any time a consumer is required to receive a summary of rights required under section 1681g of this title, the following notice shall be included:

"Consumers Have the Right To Obtain a Security Freeze

"You have a right to place a 'security freeze' on your credit report, which will prohibit a consumer reporting agency from releasing information in your credit report without your express authorization. The security freeze is designed to prevent credit, loans, and services from being approved in your name without your consent. However, you should be aware that using a security freeze to take control over who gets access to the personal and financial information in your credit report may delay, interfere with, or prohibit the timely approval of any subsequent request or application you make regarding a new loan, credit, mortgage, or any other account involving the extension of credit.

"As an alternative to a security freeze, you have the right to place an initial or extended fraud alert on your credit file at no cost. An initial fraud alert is a 1-year alert that is placed on a consumer's credit file. Upon seeing a fraud alert display on a consumer's credit file, a business is required to take steps to verify the consumer's identity before extending new credit. If you are a victim of identity theft, you are entitled to an extended fraud alert, which is a fraud alert lasting 7 years.

"A security freeze does not apply to a person or entity, or its affiliates, or collection agencies acting on behalf of the person or entity, with which you have an existing account that requests information in your credit report for the purposes of reviewing or collecting the account. Reviewing the account includes activities related to account maintenance, monitoring, credit line increases, and account upgrades and enhancements.".

(6) Webpage.

(A) Consumer reporting agencies. A consumer reporting agency shall establish a webpage that—

(i) allows a consumer to request a security freeze;

(ii) allows a consumer to request an initial fraud alert;

(iii) allows a consumer to request an extended fraud alert;

(iv) allows a consumer to request an active duty fraud alert;

(v) allows a consumer to opt-out of the use of information in a consumer report to send the consumer a solicitation of credit or insurance, in accordance with section 1681m(d) of this title; and

(vi) shall not be the only mechanism by which a consumer may request a security freeze.

(B) FTC. The Federal Trade Commission shall establish a single webpage that includes a link to each webpage established under subparagraph (A) within the Federal Trade Commission's website www.Identitytheft.gov, or a successor website.

(j) National protection for files and credit records of protected consumers

(1) Definitions. As used in this subsection:

(A) The term "consumer reporting agency" means a consumer reporting agency described in section 1681a(p) of this title.

(B) The term "protected consumer" means an individual who is—

(i) under the age of 16 years at the time a request for the placement of a security freeze is made; or

(ii) an incapacitated person or a protected person for whom a guardian or conservator has been appointed.

(C) The term "protected consumer's representative" means a person who provides to a consumer reporting agency sufficient proof of authority to act on behalf of a protected consumer.

(D) The term "record" means a compilation of information that—

(i) identifies a protected consumer;

(ii) is created by a consumer reporting agency solely for the purpose of complying with this subsection; and

(iii) may not be created or used to consider the protected consumer's credit worthiness, credit standing, credit capacity, character, general reputation, personal characteristics, or mode of living.

(E) The term "security freeze" means a restriction that prohibits a consumer reporting agency from disclosing the contents of a consumer report that is the subject of such security freeze or, in the case of a protected consumer for whom the consumer reporting agency does not have a file, a record that is subject to such security freeze to any person requesting the consumer report for the purpose of opening a new account involving the extension of credit.

(F) The term "sufficient proof of authority" means documentation that shows a protected consumer's representative has authority to act on behalf of a protected consumer and includes—

(i) an order issued by a court of law;

(ii) a lawfully executed and valid power of attorney;

(iii) a document issued by a Federal, State, or local government agency in the United States showing proof of parentage, including a birth certificate; or

(iv) with respect to a protected consumer who has been placed in a foster care setting, a written communication from a county welfare department or its agent or designee, or a county probation department or its agent or designee, certifying that the protected consumer is in a foster care setting under its jurisdiction.

(G) The term "sufficient proof of identification" means information or documentation that identifies a protected consumer and a protected consumer's representative and includes—

(i) a social security number or a copy of a social security card issued by the Social Security Administration;

(ii) a certified or official copy of a birth certificate issued by the entity authorized to issue the birth certificate; or

(iii) a copy of a driver's license, an identification card issued by the motor vehicle administration, or any other government issued identification.

(2) Placement of security freeze for a protected consumer

(A) In general. Upon receiving a direct request from a protected consumer's representative that a consumer reporting agency place a security freeze, and upon receiving sufficient proof of identification and sufficient proof of authority, the consumer reporting agency shall, free of charge, place the security freeze not later than—

(i) in the case of a request that is by toll-free telephone or secure electronic means, 1 business day after receiving the request directly from the protected consumer's representative; or

(ii) in the case of a request that is by mail, 3 business days after receiving the request directly from the protected consumer's representative.

(B) Confirmation and additional information. Not later than 5 business days after placing a security freeze under subparagraph (A), a consumer reporting agency shall—

(i) send confirmation of the placement to the protected consumer's representative; and

(ii) inform the protected consumer's representative of the process by which the protected consumer may remove the security freeze, including a mechanism to authenticate the protected consumer's representative.

(C) Creation of file. If a consumer reporting agency does not have a file pertaining to a protected consumer when the consumer reporting agency receives a direct request under subparagraph (A), the consumer reporting agency shall create a record for the protected consumer.

(3) Prohibition on release of record or file of protected consumer. After a security freeze has been placed under paragraph (2)(A), and unless the security freeze is removed in accordance with this subsection, a consumer reporting agency may not release the protected consumer's consumer report, any information derived from the protected consumer's consumer report, or any record created for the protected consumer.

(4) Removal of a protected consumer security freeze

(A) In general. A consumer reporting agency shall remove a security freeze placed on the consumer report of a protected consumer only in the following cases:

(i) Upon the direct request of the protected consumer's representative.

(ii) Upon the direct request of the protected consumer, if the protected consumer is not under the age of 16 years at the time of the request.

(iii) The security freeze was placed due to a material misrepresentation of fact by the protected consumer's representative.

(B) Notice if removal not by request. If a consumer reporting agency removes a security freeze under subparagraph (A)(iii), the consumer reporting agency shall notify the protected consumer's representative in writing prior to removing the security freeze.

(C) Removal of freeze by request. Except as provided in subparagraph (A)(iii), a security freeze shall remain in place until a protected consumer's representative or protected consumer described in subparagraph (A)(ii) directly requests that the security freeze be removed. Upon receiving a direct request from the protected consumer's representative or protected consumer described in subparagraph (A)(ii) that a consumer reporting agency remove a security freeze, and upon receiving sufficient proof of identification and sufficient proof of authority, the consumer reporting agency shall, free of charge, remove the security freeze not later than—

(i) in the case of a request that is by toll-free telephone or secure electronic means, 1 hour after receiving the request for removal; or

(ii) in the case of a request that is by mail, 3 business days after receiving the request for removal.

(B) Temporary removal of security freeze. Upon receiving a direct request from a protected consumer or a protected consumer's representative under subparagraph (A)(i), if the protected consumer or protected consumer's representative requests a temporary removal of a security freeze, the consumer reporting agency shall, in accordance with subparagraph (C), remove the security freeze for the period of time specified by the protected consumer or protected consumer's representative.

(k) Credit monitoring

(1) Definitions. In this subsection:

(A) The term "active duty military consumer" includes a member of the National Guard.

(B) The term "National Guard" has the meaning given the term in section 101(c) of title 10.

(2) Credit monitoring. A consumer reporting agency described in section 1681a(p) of this title shall provide a free electronic credit monitoring service that, at a minimum, notifies a consumer of material additions or modifications to the file of the consumer at the consumer reporting agency to any consumer who provides to the consumer reporting agency—

(A) appropriate proof that the consumer is an active duty military consumer; and

(B) contact information of the consumer.

(3) Rulemaking. Not later than 1 year after May 24, 2018, the Federal Trade Commission shall promulgate regulations regarding the requirements of this subsection, which shall at a minimum include—

(A) a definition of an electronic credit monitoring service and material additions or modifications to the file of a consumer; and

(B) what constitutes appropriate proof.

(4) Applicability

(A) Sections 1681n and 1681o of this title shall not apply to any violation of this subsection.

(B) This subsection shall be enforced exclusively under section 1681s of this title by the Federal agencies and Federal and State officials identified in that section.

§ 605B. Block of Information Resulting from Identity Theft [15 U.S.C. § 1681c-2].

(a) Block. Except as otherwise provided in this section, a consumer reporting agency shall block the reporting of any information in the file of a consumer that the consumer identifies as information that resulted from an alleged identity theft, not later than 4 business days after the date of receipt by such agency of—

(1) appropriate proof of the identity of the consumer;

(2) a copy of an identity theft report;

(3) the identification of such information by the consumer; and

(4) a statement by the consumer that the information is not information relating to any transaction by the consumer.

(b) Notification. A consumer reporting agency shall promptly notify the furnisher of information identified by the consumer under subsection (a)—

(1) that the information may be a result of identity theft;

(2) that an identity theft report has been filed;

(3) that a block has been requested under this section; and

(4) of the effective dates of the block.

(c) Authority to decline or rescind

(1) In general. A consumer reporting agency may decline to block, or may rescind any block, of information relating to a consumer under this section, if the consumer reporting agency reasonably determines that—

(A) the information was blocked in error or a block was requested by the consumer in error;

(B) the information was blocked, or a block was requested by the consumer, on the basis of a material misrepresentation of fact by the consumer relevant to the request to block; or

(C) the consumer obtained possession of goods, services, or money as a result of the blocked transaction or transactions.

(2) Notification to consumer. If a block of information is declined or rescinded under this subsection, the affected consumer shall be notified promptly, in the same manner as consumers are notified of the reinsertion of information under section 1681i(a)(5)(B) of this title.

(3) Significance of block. For purposes of this subsection, if a consumer reporting agency rescinds a block, the presence of information in the file of a consumer prior to the blocking of such information is not evidence of whether the consumer knew or should have known that the consumer obtained possession of any goods, services, or money as a result of the block.

(d) Exception for resellers

(1) No reseller file. This section shall not apply to a consumer reporting agency, if the consumer reporting agency—

(A) is a reseller;

(B) is not, at the time of the request of the consumer under subsection (a), otherwise furnishing or reselling a consumer report concerning the information identified by the consumer; and

(C) informs the consumer, by any means, that the consumer may report the identity theft to the Bureau to obtain consumer information regarding identity theft.

(2) Reseller with file. The sole obligation of the consumer reporting agency under this section, with regard to any request of a consumer under this section, shall be to block the consumer report maintained by the consumer reporting agency from any subsequent use, if—

(A) the consumer, in accordance with the provisions of subsection (a), identifies, to a consumer reporting agency, information in the file of the consumer that resulted from identity theft; and

(B) the consumer reporting agency is a reseller of the identified information.

(3) Notice. In carrying out its obligation under paragraph (2), the reseller shall promptly provide a notice to the consumer of the decision to block the file. Such notice shall contain the name, address, and telephone number of each consumer reporting agency from which the consumer information was obtained for resale.

(e) Exception for verification companies. The provisions of this section do not apply to a check services company, acting as such, which issues authorizations for the purpose of approving or processing negotiable instruments, electronic fund transfers, or similar methods of payments, except that, beginning 4 business days after receipt of information described in paragraphs (1) through (3) of subsection (a), a check services company shall not report to a national consumer reporting agency described in section 1681a(p) of this title, any information identified in the subject identity theft report as resulting from identity theft.

(f) Access to blocked information by law enforcement agencies. No provision of this section shall be construed as requiring a consumer reporting agency to prevent a Federal, State, or local law enforcement agency from accessing blocked information in a consumer file to which the agency could otherwise obtain access under this subchapter.

§ 606. Disclosure of Investigative Consumer Reports [15 U.S.C. § 1681d].

(a) Disclosure of fact of preparation. A person may not procure or cause to be prepared an investigative consumer report on any consumer unless—

(1) it is clearly and accurately disclosed to the consumer that an investigative consumer report including information as to his character, general reputation, personal characteristics, and mode of living, whichever are applicable, may be made, and such disclosure (A) is made in a writing mailed, or

otherwise delivered, to the consumer, not later than three days after the date on which the report was first requested, and (B) includes a statement informing the consumer of his right to request the additional disclosures provided for under subsection (b) of this section and the written summary of the rights of the consumer prepared pursuant to section 1681g(c) of this title; and

(2) the person certifies or has certified to the consumer reporting agency that—

(A) the person has made the disclosures to the consumer required by paragraph (1); and

(B) the person will comply with subsection (b).

(b) Disclosure on request of nature and scope of investigation. Any person who procures or causes to be prepared an investigative consumer report on any consumer shall, upon written request made by the consumer within a reasonable period of time after the receipt by him of the disclosure required by subsection (a)(1), make a complete and accurate disclosure of the nature and scope of the investigation requested. This disclosure shall be made in a writing mailed, or otherwise delivered, to the consumer not later than five days after the date on which the request for such disclosure was received from the consumer or such report was first requested, whichever is the later.

(c) Limitation on liability upon showing of reasonable procedures for compliance with provisions. No person may be held liable for any violation of subsection (a) or (b) of this section if he shows by a preponderance of the evidence that at the time of the violation he maintained reasonable procedures to assure compliance with subsection (a) or (b).

(d) Prohibitions

(1) Certification. A consumer reporting agency shall not prepare or furnish an investigative consumer report unless the agency has received a certification under subsection (a)(2) from the person who requested the report.

(2) Inquiries. A consumer reporting agency shall not make an inquiry for the purpose of preparing an investigative consumer report on a consumer for employment purposes if the making of the inquiry by an employer or prospective employer of the consumer would violate any applicable Federal or State equal employment opportunity law or regulation.

(3) Certain public record information. Except as otherwise provided in section 1681k of this title, a consumer reporting agency shall not furnish an investigative consumer report that includes information that is a matter of public record and that relates to an arrest, indictment, conviction, civil judicial action, tax lien, or outstanding judgment, unless the agency has verified the accuracy of the information during the 30-day period ending on the date on which the report is furnished.

(4) Certain adverse information. A consumer reporting agency shall not prepare or furnish an investigative consumer report on a consumer that contains information that is adverse to the interest of the consumer and that is obtained through a personal interview with a neighbor, friend, or associate of the consumer or with another person with whom the consumer is acquainted or who has knowledge of such item of information, unless—

(A) the agency has followed reasonable procedures to obtain confirmation of the information, from an additional source that has independent and direct knowledge of the information; or

(B) the person interviewed is the best possible source of the information.

§ 607. Compliance Procedures [15 U.S.C. § 1681e].

(a) Identity and purposes of credit users. Every consumer reporting agency shall maintain reasonable procedures designed to avoid violations of section 1681c of this title and to limit the furnishing of consumer reports to the purposes listed under section 1681b of this title. These procedures shall require that prospective users of the information identify themselves, certify the purposes for which the information is sought, and certify that the information will be used for no other purpose. Every consumer reporting agency shall make a reasonable effort to verify the identity of a new prospective user and the uses certified by such prospective user prior to furnishing such user a consumer report. No consumer reporting agency may furnish a consumer report to any person if it has reasonable grounds for believing that the consumer report will not be used for a purpose listed in section 1681b of this title.

(b) Accuracy of report. Whenever a consumer reporting agency prepares a consumer report it shall follow reasonable procedures to assure maximum possible accuracy of the information concerning the individual about whom the report relates.

(c) Disclosure of consumer reports by users allowed. A consumer reporting agency may not prohibit a user of a consumer report furnished by the agency on a consumer from disclosing the contents of the report to the consumer, if adverse action against the consumer has been taken by the user based in whole or in part on the report.

(d) Notice to users and furnishers of information

(1) Notice requirement. A consumer reporting agency shall provide to any person—

(A) who regularly and in the ordinary course of business furnishes information to the agency with respect to any consumer; or

(B) to whom a consumer report is provided by the agency; a notice of such person's responsibilities under this subchapter.

(2) Content of notice. The Bureau shall prescribe the content of notices under paragraph (1), and a consumer reporting agency shall be in compliance with this subsection if it provides a notice under paragraph (1) that is substantially similar to the Bureau prescription under this paragraph.

(e) Procurement of consumer report for resale

(1) Disclosure. A person may not procure a consumer report for purposes of reselling the report (or any information in the report) unless the person discloses to the consumer reporting agency that originally furnishes the report—

(A) the identity of the end-user of the report (or information); and

(B) each permissible purpose under section 1681b of this title for which the report is furnished to the end-user of the report (or information).

(2) Responsibilities of procurers for resale. A person who procures a consumer report for purposes of reselling the report (or any information in the report) shall—

(A) establish and comply with reasonable procedures designed to ensure that the report (or information) is resold by the person only for a purpose for which the report may be furnished under section 1681b of this title, including by requiring that each person to which the report (or information) is resold and that resells or provides the report (or information) to any other person—

(i) identifies each end user of the resold report (or information);

(ii) certifies each purpose for which the report (or information) will be used; and

(iii) certifies that the report (or information) will be used for no other purpose; and

(B) before reselling the report, make reasonable efforts to verify the identifications and certifications made under subparagraph (A).

(3) Resale of consumer report to a Federal agency or department. Notwithstanding paragraph (1) or (2), a person who procures a consumer report for purposes of reselling the report (or any information in the report) shall not disclose the identity of the end-user of the report under paragraph (1) or (2) if—

(A) the end user is an agency or department of the United States Government which procures the report from the person for purposes of determining the eligibility of the consumer concerned to receive access or continued access to classified information (as defined in section 1681b(b)(4)(D)(i) of this title); and

(B) the agency or department certifies in writing to the person reselling the report that nondisclosure is necessary to protect classified information or the safety of persons employed by or contracting with, or undergoing investigation for work or contracting with the agency or department.

§ 609. Disclosures to Consumers [15 U.S.C. § 1681g].

(a) Information on file; sources; report recipients. Every consumer reporting agency shall, upon request, and subject to section 1681h(a)(1) of this title, clearly and accurately disclose to the consumer:

(1) All information in the consumer's file at the time of the request,

(A) if the consumer to whom the file relates requests that the first 5 digits of the social security number (or similar identification number) of the consumer not be included in the disclosure and the consumer reporting agency has received appropriate proof of the identity of the requester, the consumer reporting agency shall so truncate such number in such disclosure; and

(B) nothing in this paragraph shall be construed to require a consumer reporting agency to disclose to a consumer any information concerning credit scores or any other risk scores or predictors relating to the consumer.

(2) The sources of the information; except that the sources of information acquired solely for use in preparing an investigative consumer report and actually used for no other purpose need not be disclosed: Provided, That in the event an action is brought under this subchapter, such sources shall be available to the plaintiff under appropriate discovery procedures in the court in which the action is brought.

(3) (A) Identification of each person (including each end-user identified under section 1681e(e)(1) of this title) that procured a consumer report—

(i) for employment purposes, during the 2-year period preceding the date on which the request is made; or

(ii) for any other purpose, during the 1-year period preceding the date on which the request is made.

(B) An identification of a person under subparagraph (A) shall include—

(i) the name of the person or, if applicable, the trade name (written in full) under which such person conducts business; and

(ii) upon request of the consumer, the address and telephone number of the person.

(C) Subparagraph (A) does not apply if—

(i) the end user is an agency or department of the United States Government that procures the report from the person for purposes of determining the eligibility of the consumer to whom the report relates to receive access or continued access to classified information (as defined in section 1681b(b)(4)(D)(i) of this title); and

(ii) the head of the agency or department makes a written finding as prescribed under section 1681b(b)(4)(A) of this title.

(4) The dates, original payees, and amounts of any checks upon which is based any adverse characterization of the consumer, included in the file at the time of the disclosure.

(5) A record of all inquiries received by the agency during the 1-year period preceding the request that identified the consumer in connection with a credit or insurance transaction that was not initiated by the consumer.

(6) If the consumer requests the credit file and not the credit score, a statement that the consumer may request and obtain a credit score.

(b) Exempt information. The requirements of subsection (a) of this section respecting the disclosure of sources of information and the recipients of consumer reports do not apply to information received or consumer reports furnished prior to the effective date of this subchapter except to the extent that the matter involved is contained in the files of the consumer reporting agency on that date.

(c) Summary of rights to obtain and dispute information in consumer reports and to obtain credit scores

(1) Bureau summary of rights required

(A) In general. The Bureau shall prepare a model summary of the rights of consumers under this subchapter.

(B) Content of summary. The summary of rights prepared under subparagraph (A) shall include a description of—

(i) the right of a consumer to obtain a copy of a consumer report under subsection (a) from each consumer reporting agency;

(ii) the frequency and circumstances under which a consumer is entitled to receive a consumer report without charge under section 1681j of this title;

(iii) the right of a consumer to dispute information in the file of the consumer under section 1681i of this title;

(iv) the right of a consumer to obtain a credit score from a consumer reporting agency, and a description of how to obtain a credit score;

(v) the method by which a consumer can contact, and obtain a consumer report from, a consumer reporting agency without charge, as provided in the regulations of the Bureau prescribed under section 211(d) of Pub. L. 108-159; and

(vi) the method by which a consumer can contact, and obtain a consumer report from, a consumer reporting agency described in section 1681a(x) of this title, as provided in the regulations of the Bureau prescribed under section 1681j(a)(1)(C) of this title.

(C) Availability of summary of rights. The Bureau shall—

(i) actively publicize the availability of the summary of rights prepared under this paragraph;

(ii) conspicuously post on its Internet website the availability of such summary of rights; and

(iii) promptly make such summary of rights available to consumers, on request.

(2) Summary of rights required to be included with agency disclosures. A consumer reporting agency shall provide to a consumer, with each written disclosure by the agency to the consumer under this section—

(A) the summary of rights prepared by the Bureau under paragraph (1);

(B) in the case of a consumer reporting agency described in section 1681a(p) of this title, a toll-free telephone number established by the agency, at which personnel are accessible to consumers during normal business hours;

(C) a list of all Federal agencies responsible for enforcing any provision of this subchapter, and the address and any appropriate phone number of each such agency, in a form that will assist the consumer in selecting the appropriate agency;

(D) a statement that the consumer may have additional rights under State law, and that the consumer may wish to contact a State or local consumer protection agency or a State attorney general (or the equivalent thereof) to learn of those rights; and

(E) a statement that a consumer reporting agency is not required to remove accurate derogatory information from the file of a consumer, unless the information is outdated under section 1681c of this title or cannot be verified.

(d) Summary of rights of identity theft victims

(1) In general. The Bureau, in consultation with the Federal banking agencies and the National Credit Union Administration, shall prepare a model summary of the rights of consumers under this subchapter with respect to the procedures for remedying the effects of fraud or identity theft involving credit, an electronic fund transfer, or an account or transaction at or with a financial institution or other creditor.

(2) Summary of rights and contact information. Beginning 60 days after the date on which the model summary of rights is prescribed in final form by the Bureau pursuant to paragraph (1), if any consumer contacts a consumer reporting agency and expresses a belief that the consumer is a victim of fraud or identity theft involving credit, an electronic fund transfer, or an account or transaction at or with a financial institution or other creditor, the consumer reporting agency shall, in addition to any other action that the agency may take, provide the consumer with a summary of rights that contains all of the information required by the Bureau under paragraph (1), and information on how to contact the Bureau to obtain more detailed information.

(e) Information available to victims

(1) In general. For the purpose of documenting fraudulent transactions resulting from identity theft, not later than 30 days after the date of receipt of a request from a victim in accordance with paragraph (3), and subject to verification of the identity of the victim and the claim of identity theft in accordance with paragraph (2), a business entity that has provided credit to, provided for consideration products, goods, or services to, accepted payment from, or otherwise entered into a commercial transaction for consideration with, a person who has allegedly made unauthorized use of the means of identification of the victim, shall provide a copy of application and business transaction records in the control of the business entity, whether maintained by the business entity or by another person on behalf of the business entity, evidencing any transaction alleged to be a result of identity theft to—

(A) the victim;

(B) any Federal, State, or local government law enforcement agency or officer specified by the victim in such a request; or

(C) any law enforcement agency investigating the identity theft and authorized by the victim to take receipt of records provided under this subsection.

(2) Verification of identity and claim. Before a business entity provides any information under paragraph (1), unless the business entity, at its discretion, otherwise has a high degree of confidence that it knows the identity of the victim making a request under paragraph (1), the victim shall provide to the business entity—

(A) as proof of positive identification of the victim, at the election of the business entity—

(i) the presentation of a government-issued identification card;

(ii) personally identifying information of the same type as was provided to the business entity by the unauthorized person; or

(iii) personally identifying information that the business entity typically requests from new applicants or for new transactions, at the time of the victim's request for information, including any documentation described in clauses (i) and (ii); and

(B) as proof of a claim of identity theft, at the election of the business entity—

(i) a copy of a police report evidencing the claim of the victim of identity theft; and

(ii) a properly completed—

(I) copy of a standardized affidavit of identity theft developed and made available by the Bureau; or

(II) affidavit of fact that is acceptable to the business entity for that purpose.

(3) Procedures. The request of a victim under paragraph (1) shall—

(A) be in writing;

(B) be mailed to an address specified by the business entity, if any; and

(C) if asked by the business entity, include relevant information about any transaction alleged to be a result of identity theft to facilitate compliance with this section including—

(i) if known by the victim (or if readily obtainable by the victim), the date of the application or transaction; and

(ii) if known by the victim (or if readily obtainable by the victim), any other identifying information such as an account or transaction number.

(4) No charge to victim. Information required to be provided under paragraph (1) shall be so provided without charge.

(5) Authority to decline to provide information. A business entity may decline to provide information under paragraph (1) if, in the exercise of good faith, the business entity determines that—

(A) this subsection does not require disclosure of the information;

(B) after reviewing the information provided pursuant to paragraph (2), the business entity does not have a high degree of confidence in knowing the true identity of the individual requesting the information;

(C) the request for the information is based on a misrepresentation of fact by the individual requesting the information relevant to the request for information; or

(D) the information requested is Internet navigational data or similar information about a person's visit to a website or online service.

(6) Limitation on liability. Except as provided in section 1681s of this title, sections 1681n and 1681o of this title do not apply to any violation of this subsection.

(7) Limitation on civil liability. No business entity may be held civilly liable under any provision of Federal, State, or other law for disclosure, made in good faith pursuant to this subsection.

(8) No new recordkeeping obligation. Nothing in this subsection creates an obligation on the part of a business entity to obtain, retain, or maintain information or records that are not otherwise required to be obtained, retained, or maintained in the ordinary course of its business or under other applicable law.

(9) Rule of construction

(A) In general. No provision of subtitle A of title V of Public Law 106-102 [15 U.S.C. 6801 et seq.], prohibiting the disclosure of financial information by a business entity to third parties shall be used to deny disclosure of information to the victim under this subsection.

(B) Limitation. Except as provided in subparagraph (A), nothing in this subsection permits a business entity to disclose information, including information to law enforcement under subparagraphs (B) and (C) of paragraph (1), that the business entity is otherwise prohibited from disclosing under any other applicable provision of Federal or State law.

(10) Affirmative defense. In any civil action brought to enforce this subsection, it is an affirmative defense (which the defendant must establish by a preponderance of the evidence) for a business entity to file an affidavit or answer stating that—

(A) the business entity has made a reasonably diligent search of its available business records; and

(B) the records requested under this subsection do not exist or are not reasonably available.

(11) Definition of victim. For purposes of this subsection, the term "victim" means a consumer whose means of identification or financial information has been used or transferred (or has been alleged to have been used or transferred) without the authority of that consumer, with the intent to commit, or to aid or abet, an identity theft or a similar crime.

(12) Effective date. This subsection shall become effective 180 days after December 4, 2003.

(13) Effectiveness study. Not later than 18 months after December 4, 2003, the Comptroller General of the United States shall submit a report to Congress assessing the effectiveness of this provision.

(f) Disclosure of credit scores

(1) In general. Upon the request of a consumer for a credit score, a consumer reporting agency shall supply to the consumer a statement indicating that the information and credit scoring model may be different than the credit score that may be used by the lender, and a notice which shall include—

(A) the current credit score of the consumer or the most recent credit score of the consumer that was previously calculated by the credit reporting agency for a purpose related to the extension of credit;

(B) the range of possible credit scores under the model used;

(C) all of the key factors that adversely affected the credit score of the consumer in the model used, the total number of which shall not exceed 4, subject to paragraph (9);

(D) the date on which the credit score was created; and

(E) the name of the person or entity that provided the credit score or credit file upon which the credit score was created.

(2) Definitions. For purposes of this subsection, the following definitions shall apply:

(A) Credit score. The term "credit score"—

(i) means a numerical value or a categorization derived from a statistical tool or modeling system used by a person who makes or arranges a loan to predict the likelihood of certain credit behaviors, including default (and the numerical value or the categorization derived from such analysis may also be referred to as a "risk predictor" or "risk score"); and

(ii) does not include—

(I) any mortgage score or rating of an automated underwriting system that considers one or more factors in addition to credit information, including the loan to value ratio, the amount of down payment, or the financial assets of a consumer; or

(II) any other elements of the underwriting process or underwriting decision.

(B) Key factors. The term "key factors" means all relevant elements or reasons adversely affecting the credit score for the particular individual, listed in the order of their importance based on their effect on the credit score.

(3) Timeframe and manner of disclosure. The information required by this subsection shall be provided in the same timeframe and manner as the information described in subsection (a).

(4) Applicability to certain uses. This subsection shall not be construed so as to compel a consumer reporting agency to develop or disclose a score if the agency does not—

(A) distribute scores that are used in connection with residential real property loans; or

(B) develop scores that assist credit providers in understanding the general credit behavior of a consumer and predicting the future credit behavior of the consumer.

(5) Applicability to credit scores developed by another person

(A) In general. This subsection shall not be construed to require a consumer reporting agency that distributes credit scores developed by another person or entity to provide a further explanation of them, or to process a dispute arising pursuant to section 1681i of this title, except that the consumer reporting agency shall provide the consumer with the name and address and website for contacting the person or entity who developed the score or developed the methodology of the score.

(B) Exception. This paragraph shall not apply to a consumer reporting agency that develops or modifies scores that are developed by another person or entity.

(6) Maintenance of credit scores not required. This subsection shall not be construed to require a consumer reporting agency to maintain credit scores in its files.

(7) Compliance in certain cases. In complying with this subsection, a consumer reporting agency shall—

(A) supply the consumer with a credit score that is derived from a credit scoring model that is widely distributed to users by that consumer reporting agency in connection with residential real property loans or with a credit score that assists the consumer in understanding the credit scoring assessment of the credit behavior of the consumer and predictions about the future credit behavior of the consumer; and

(B) a statement indicating that the information and credit scoring model may be different than that used by the lender.

(8) Fair and reasonable fee. A consumer reporting agency may charge a fair and reasonable fee, as determined by the Bureau, for providing the information required under this subsection.

(9) Use of enquiries as a key factor. If a key factor that adversely affects the credit score of a consumer consists of the number of enquiries made with respect to a consumer report, that factor shall be included in the disclosure pursuant to paragraph (1)(C) without regard to the numerical limitation in such paragraph.

(g) Disclosure of credit scores by certain mortgage lenders

(1) In general. Any person who makes or arranges loans and who uses a consumer credit score, as defined in subsection (f), in connection with an application initiated or sought by a consumer for a closed end loan or the establishment of an open end loan for a consumer purpose that is secured by 1 to 4 units of residential real property (hereafter in this subsection referred to as the "lender") shall provide the following to the consumer as soon as reasonably practicable:

(A) Information required under subsection (f)

(i) In general. A copy of the information identified in subsection (f) that was obtained from a consumer reporting agency or was developed and used by the user of the information.

(ii) Notice under subparagraph (d). In addition to the information provided to it by a third party that provided the credit score or scores, a lender, is only required to provide the notice contained in subparagraph (D).

(B) Disclosures in case of automated underwriting system

(i) In general. If a person that is subject to this subsection uses an automated underwriting system to underwrite a loan, that person may satisfy the obligation to provide a credit score by disclosing a credit score and associated key factors supplied by a consumer reporting agency.

(ii) Numerical credit score. However, if a numerical credit score is generated by an automated underwriting system used by an enterprise, and that score is disclosed to the person, the score shall be disclosed to the consumer consistent with subparagraph (C).

(iii) Enterprise defined. For purposes of this subparagraph, the term "enterprise" has the same meaning as in paragraph (6) of section 4502 of title 12.

(C) Disclosures of credit scores not obtained from a consumer reporting agency. A person that is subject to the provisions of this subsection and that uses a credit score, other than a credit score provided by a consumer reporting agency, may satisfy the obligation to provide a credit score by disclosing a credit score and associated key factors supplied by a consumer reporting agency.

(D) Notice to home loan applicants. A copy of the following notice, which shall include the name, address, and telephone number of each consumer reporting agency providing a credit score that was used:

"Notice to the Home Loan Applicant

"In connection with your application for a home loan, the lender must disclose to you the score that a consumer reporting agency distributed to users and the lender used in connection with your home loan, and the key factors affecting your credit scores.

"The credit score is a computer generated summary calculated at the time of the request and based on information that a consumer reporting agency or lender has on file. The scores are based on data about your credit history and payment patterns. Credit scores are important because they are used to assist the lender in determining whether you will obtain a loan. They may also be used to determine what interest rate you may be offered on the mortgage. Credit scores can change over time, depending on your conduct, how your credit history and payment patterns change, and how credit scoring technologies change.

"Because the score is based on information in your credit history, it is very important that you review the credit-related information that is being furnished to make sure it is accurate. Credit records may vary from one company to another.

"If you have questions about your credit score or the credit information that is furnished to you, contact the consumer reporting agency at the address and telephone number provided with this notice, or contact the lender, if the lender developed or generated the credit score. The consumer reporting agency plays no part in the decision to take any action on the loan application and is unable to provide you with specific reasons for the decision on a loan application.

"If you have questions concerning the terms of the loan, contact the lender.".

(E) Actions not required under this subsection. This subsection shall not require any person to—

(i) explain the information provided pursuant to subsection (f);

(ii) disclose any information other than a credit score or key factors, as defined in subsection (f);

(iii) disclose any credit score or related information obtained by the user after a loan has closed;

(iv) provide more than 1 disclosure per loan transaction; or

(v) provide the disclosure required by this subsection when another person has made the disclosure to the consumer for that loan transaction.

(F) No obligation for content

(i) In general. The obligation of any person pursuant to this subsection shall be limited solely to providing a copy of the information that was received from the consumer reporting agency.

(ii) Limit on liability. No person has liability under this subsection for the content of that information or for the omission of any information within the report provided by the consumer reporting agency.

(G) Person defined as excluding enterprise. As used in this subsection, the term "person" does not include an enterprise (as defined in paragraph (6) of section 4502 of title 12.

(2) Prohibition on disclosure clauses null and void

(A) In general. Any provision in a contract that prohibits the disclosure of a credit score by a person who makes or arranges loans or a consumer reporting agency is void.

(B) No liability for disclosure under this subsection. A lender shall not have liability under any contractual provision for disclosure of a credit score pursuant to this subsection.

§ 610. Conditions and Form of Disclosure to Consumers [15 U.S.C. § 1681h].

(a) In general

(1) Proper identification. A consumer reporting agency shall require, as a condition of making the disclosures required under section 1681g of this title, that the consumer furnish proper identification.

(2) Disclosure in writing. Except as provided in subsection (b), the disclosures required to be made under section 1681g of this title shall be provided under that section in writing.

(b) Other forms of disclosure

(1) In general. If authorized by a consumer, a consumer reporting agency may make the disclosures required under [section] 1681g of this title—

(A) other than in writing; and

(B) in such form as may be—

(i) specified by the consumer in accordance with paragraph (2); and

(ii) available from the agency.

(2) Form. A consumer may specify pursuant to paragraph (1) that disclosures under section 1681g of this title shall be made—

(A) in person, upon the appearance of the consumer at the place of business of the consumer reporting agency where disclosures are regularly provided, during normal business hours, and on reasonable notice;

(B) by telephone, if the consumer has made a written request for disclosure by telephone;

(C) by electronic means, if available from the agency; or

(D) by any other reasonable means that is available from the agency.

(c) Trained personnel. Any consumer reporting agency shall provide trained personnel to explain to the consumer any information furnished to him pursuant to section 1681g of this title.

(d) Persons accompanying consumer. The consumer shall be permitted to be accompanied by one other person of his choosing, who shall furnish reasonable identification. A consumer reporting agency may require the consumer to furnish a written statement granting permission to the consumer reporting agency to discuss the consumer's file in such person's presence.

(e) Limitation of liability. Except as provided in sections 1681n and 1681o of this title, no consumer may bring any action or proceeding in the nature of defamation, invasion of privacy, or negligence with respect to the reporting of information against any consumer reporting agency, any user of information, or any person who furnishes information to a consumer reporting agency, based on information disclosed pursuant to section 1681g, 1681h, or 1681m of this title, or based on information disclosed by a user of a consumer report to or for a consumer against whom the user has taken adverse action, based in whole or in part on the report, except as to false information furnished with malice or willful intent to injure such consumer.

§ 611. Procedure in Case of Disputed Accuracy [15 U.S.C. § 1681i].

(a) Reinvestigations of disputed information

(1) Reinvestigation required

(A) In general. Subject to subsection (f) and except as provided in subsection (g), if the completeness or accuracy of any item of information contained in a consumer's file at a consumer reporting agency is disputed by the consumer and the consumer notifies the agency directly, or indirectly through a reseller, of such dispute, the agency shall, free of charge, conduct a reasonable reinvestigation to determine whether the disputed information is inaccurate and record the current status of the disputed information, or delete the item from the file in accordance with paragraph (5), before the end of the 30-day period beginning on the date on which the agency receives the notice of the dispute from the consumer or reseller.

(B) Extension of period to reinvestigate. Except as provided in subparagraph (C), the 30-day period described in subparagraph (A) may be extended for not more than 15 additional days if the consumer reporting agency receives information from the consumer during that 30-day period that is relevant to the reinvestigation.

(C) Limitations on extension of period to reinvestigate. Subparagraph (B) shall not apply to any reinvestigation in which, during the 30-day period described in subparagraph (A), the information that is the subject of the reinvestigation is found to be inaccurate or incomplete or the consumer reporting agency determines that the information cannot be verified.

(2) Prompt notice of dispute to furnisher of information

(A) In general. Before the expiration of the 5-business-day period beginning on the date on which a consumer reporting agency receives notice of a dispute from any consumer or a reseller in accordance with paragraph (1), the agency shall provide notification of the dispute to any person who provided any item of information in dispute, at the address and in the manner established with the person. The notice shall include all relevant information regarding the dispute that the agency has received from the consumer or reseller.

(B) Provision of other information. The consumer reporting agency shall promptly provide to the person who provided the information in dispute all relevant information regarding the dispute that is received by the agency from the consumer or the reseller after the period referred to in subparagraph (A) and before the end of the period referred to in paragraph (1)(A).

(3) Determination that dispute is frivolous or irrelevant

(A) In general. Notwithstanding paragraph (1), a consumer reporting agency may terminate a reinvestigation of information disputed by a consumer under that paragraph if the agency reasonably determines that the dispute by the consumer is frivolous or irrelevant, including by reason of a failure by a consumer to provide sufficient information to investigate the disputed information.

(B) Notice of determination. Upon making any determination in accordance with subparagraph (A) that a dispute is frivolous or irrelevant, a consumer reporting agency shall notify the consumer of such determination not later than 5 business days after making such determination, by mail or, if authorized by the consumer for that purpose, by any other means available to the agency.

(C) Contents of notice. A notice under subparagraph (B) shall include—

(i) the reasons for the determination under subparagraph (A); and

(ii) identification of any information required to investigate the disputed information, which may consist of a standardized form describing the general nature of such information.

(4) Consideration of consumer information. In conducting any reinvestigation under paragraph (1) with respect to disputed information in the file of any consumer, the consumer reporting agency shall review and consider all relevant information submitted by the consumer in the period described in paragraph (1)(A) with respect to such disputed information.

(5) Treatment of inaccurate or unverifiable information

(A) In general. If, after any reinvestigation under paragraph (1) of any information disputed by a consumer, an item of the information is found to be inaccurate or incomplete or cannot be verified, the consumer reporting agency shall—

(i) promptly delete that item of information from the file of the consumer, or modify that item of information, as appropriate, based on the results of the reinvestigation; and

(ii) promptly notify the furnisher of that information that the information has been modified or deleted from the file of the consumer.

(B) Requirements relating to reinsertion of previously deleted material

(i) Certification of accuracy of information. If any information is deleted from a consumer's file pursuant to subparagraph (A), the information may not be reinserted in the file by the consumer reporting agency unless the person who furnishes the information certifies that the information is complete and accurate.

(ii) Notice to consumer. If any information that has been deleted from a consumer's file pursuant to subparagraph (A) is reinserted in the file, the consumer reporting agency shall notify the consumer of the reinsertion in writing not later than 5 business days after the reinsertion or, if authorized by the consumer for that purpose, by any other means available to the agency.

(iii) Additional information. As part of, or in addition to, the notice under clause (ii), a consumer reporting agency shall provide to a consumer in writing not later than 5 business days after the date of the reinsertion—

(I) a statement that the disputed information has been reinserted;

(II) the business name and address of any furnisher of information contacted and the telephone number of such furnisher, if reasonably available, or of any furnisher of information that contacted the consumer reporting agency, in connection with the reinsertion of such information; and

(III) a notice that the consumer has the right to add a statement to the consumer's file disputing the accuracy or completeness of the disputed information.

(C) Procedures to prevent reappearance. A consumer reporting agency shall maintain reasonable procedures designed to prevent the reappearance in a consumer's file, and in consumer reports on the consumer, of information that is deleted pursuant to this paragraph (other than information that is reinserted in accordance with subparagraph (B)(i)).

(D) Automated reinvestigation system. Any consumer reporting agency that compiles and maintains files on consumers on a nationwide basis shall implement an automated system through which furnishers of information to that consumer reporting agency may report the results of a reinvestigation that finds incomplete or inaccurate information in a consumer's file to other such consumer reporting agencies.

(6) Notice of results of reinvestigation

(A) In general. A consumer reporting agency shall provide written notice to a consumer of the results of a reinvestigation under this subsection not later than 5 business days after the completion of the reinvestigation, by mail or, if authorized by the consumer for that purpose, by other means available to the agency.

(B) Contents. As part of, or in addition to, the notice under subparagraph (A), a consumer reporting agency shall provide to a consumer in writing before the expiration of the 5-day period referred to in subparagraph (A)—

(i) a statement that the reinvestigation is completed;

(ii) a consumer report that is based upon the consumer's file as that file is revised as a result of the reinvestigation;

(iii) a notice that, if requested by the consumer, a description of the procedure used to determine the accuracy and completeness of the information shall be provided to the consumer by the agency, including the business name and address of any furnisher of information contacted in connection with such information and the telephone number of such furnisher, if reasonably available;

(iv) a notice that the consumer has the right to add a statement to the consumer's file disputing the accuracy or completeness of the information; and

(v) a notice that the consumer has the right to request under subsection (d) that the consumer reporting agency furnish notifications under that subsection.

(7) Description of reinvestigation procedure. A consumer reporting agency shall provide to a consumer a description referred to in paragraph (6)(B)(iii) by not later than 15 days after receiving a request from the consumer for that description.

(8) Expedited dispute resolution. If a dispute regarding an item of information in a consumer's file at a consumer reporting agency is resolved in accordance with paragraph (5)(A) by the deletion of the disputed information by not later than 3 business days after the date on which the agency receives notice of the dispute from the consumer in accordance with paragraph (1)(A), then the agency shall not be required to comply with paragraphs (2), (6), and (7) with respect to that dispute if the agency—

(A) provides prompt notice of the deletion to the consumer by telephone;

(B) includes in that notice, or in a written notice that accompanies a confirmation and consumer report provided in accordance with subparagraph (C), a statement of the consumer's right to request under subsection (d) that the agency furnish notifications under that subsection; and

(C) provides written confirmation of the deletion and a copy of a consumer report on the consumer that is based on the consumer's file after the deletion, not later than 5 business days after making the deletion.

(b) Statement of dispute. If the reinvestigation does not resolve the dispute, the consumer may file a brief statement setting forth the nature of the dispute. The consumer reporting agency may limit such statements to not more than one hundred words if it provides the consumer with assistance in writing a clear summary of the dispute.

(c) Notification of consumer dispute in subsequent consumer reports. Whenever a statement of a dispute is filed, unless there is reasonable grounds to believe that it is frivolous or irrelevant, the consumer reporting agency shall, in any subsequent consumer report containing the information in question, clearly note that it is disputed by the consumer and provide either the consumer's statement or a clear and accurate codification or summary thereof.

(d) Notification of deletion of disputed information. Following any deletion of information which is found to be inaccurate or whose accuracy can no longer be verified or any notation as to disputed information, the consumer reporting agency shall, at the request of the consumer, furnish notification that the item has been deleted or the statement, codification or summary pursuant to subsection (b) or (c) to any person specifically designated by the consumer who has within two years prior thereto received a consumer report for employment purposes, or within six months prior thereto received a consumer report for any other purpose, which contained the deleted or disputed information.

(e) Treatment of complaints and report to Congress.

(1) In general. The Bureau shall—

(A) compile all complaints that it receives that a file of a consumer that is maintained by a consumer reporting agency described in section 1681a(p) of this title contains incomplete or inaccurate information, with respect to which, the consumer appears to have disputed the completeness or accuracy with the consumer reporting agency or otherwise utilized the procedures provided by subsection (a); and

(B) transmit each such complaint to each consumer reporting agency involved.

(2) Exclusion. Complaints received or obtained by the Bureau pursuant to its investigative authority under the Consumer Financial Protection Act of 2010 shall not be subject to paragraph (1).

(3) Agency responsibilities. Each consumer reporting agency described in section 1681a(p) of this title that receives a complaint transmitted by the Bureau pursuant to paragraph (1) shall—

(A) review each such complaint to determine whether all legal obligations imposed on the consumer reporting agency under this subchapter (including any obligation imposed by an applicable court or administrative order) have been met with respect to the subject matter of the complaint;

(B) provide reports on a regular basis to the Bureau regarding the determinations of and actions taken by the consumer reporting agency, if any, in connection with its review of such complaints; and

(C) maintain, for a reasonable time period, records regarding the disposition of each such complaint that is sufficient to demonstrate compliance with this subsection.

(4) Rulemaking authority. The Bureau may prescribe regulations, as appropriate to implement this subsection.

(5) Annual report. The Bureau shall submit to the Committee on Banking, Housing, and Urban Affairs of the Senate and the Committee on Financial Services of the House of Representatives an annual report regarding information gathered by the Bureau under this subsection.

(f) Reinvestigation requirement applicable to resellers

(1) Exemption from general reinvestigation requirement. Except as provided in paragraph (2), a reseller shall be exempt from the requirements of this section.

(2) Action required upon receiving notice of a dispute. If a reseller receives a notice from a consumer of a dispute concerning the completeness or accuracy of any item of information contained in a consumer report on such consumer produced by the reseller, the reseller shall, within 5 business days of receiving the notice, and free of charge—

(A) determine whether the item of information is incomplete or inaccurate as a result of an act or omission of the reseller; and

(B) if—

(i) the reseller determines that the item of information is incomplete or inaccurate as a result of an act or omission of the reseller, not later than 20 days after receiving the notice, correct the information in the consumer report or delete it; or

(ii) if the reseller determines that the item of information is not incomplete or inaccurate as a result of an act or omission of the reseller, convey the notice of the dispute, together with all relevant information provided by the consumer, to each consumer reporting agency that provided the reseller with the information that is the subject of the dispute, using an address or a notification mechanism specified by the consumer reporting agency for such notices.

(3) Responsibility of consumer reporting agency to notify consumer through reseller. Upon the completion of a reinvestigation under this section of a dispute concerning the completeness or accuracy of any information in the file of a consumer by a consumer reporting agency that received notice of the dispute from a reseller under paragraph (2)—

(A) the notice by the consumer reporting agency under paragraph (6), (7), or (8) of subsection (a) shall be provided to the reseller in lieu of the consumer; and

(B) the reseller shall immediately reconvey such notice to the consumer, including any notice of a deletion by telephone in the manner required under paragraph (8)(A).

(4) Reseller reinvestigations. No provision of this subsection shall be construed as prohibiting a reseller from conducting a reinvestigation of a consumer dispute directly.

§ 612. Charges for Certain Disclosures [15 U.S.C. § 1681j].

(a) Free annual disclosure

(1) Nationwide consumer reporting agencies

(A) In general. All consumer reporting agencies described in subsections (p) and (x) of section 1681a of this title shall make all disclosures pursuant to section 609 [15 U.S.C. 1681g] once during any 12-month period upon request of the consumer and without charge to the consumer.

(B) Centralized source. Subparagraph (A) shall apply with respect to a consumer reporting agency described in section 1681a(p) of this title only if the request from the consumer is made using the centralized source established for such purpose in accordance with section 211(d) of Pub. L. 108-159.

(C) Nationwide specialty consumer reporting agency

(i) In general. The Bureau shall prescribe regulations applicable to each consumer reporting agency described in section 1681a(x) of this title to require the establishment of a streamlined process for consumers to request consumer reports under subparagraph (A), which shall include, at a minimum, the establishment by each such agency of a toll-free telephone number for such requests.

(ii) Considerations. In prescribing regulations under clause (i), the Bureau shall consider—

(I) the significant demands that may be placed on consumer reporting agencies in providing such consumer reports;

(II) appropriate means to ensure that consumer reporting agencies can satisfactorily meet those demands, including the efficacy of a system of staggering the availability to consumers of such consumer reports; and

(III) the ease by which consumers should be able to contact consumer reporting agencies with respect to access to such consumer reports.

(iii) Date of issuance. The Bureau shall issue the regulations required by this subparagraph in final form not later than 6 months after December 4, 2003.

(iv) Consideration of ability to comply. The regulations of the Bureau under this subparagraph shall establish an effective date by which each nationwide specialty consumer reporting agency (as defined in section 1681a(x) of this title) shall be required to comply with subsection (a), which effective date—

(I) shall be established after consideration of the ability of each nationwide specialty consumer reporting agency to comply with subsection (a); and

(II) shall be not later than 6 months after the date on which such regulations are issued in final form (or such additional period not to exceed 3 months, as the Bureau determines appropriate).

(2) Timing. A consumer reporting agency shall provide a consumer report under paragraph (1) not later than 15 days after the date on which the request is received under paragraph (1).

(3) Reinvestigations. Notwithstanding the time periods specified in section 1681i(a)(1) of this title, a reinvestigation under that section by a consumer reporting agency upon a request of a consumer that is made after receiving a consumer report under this subsection shall be completed not later than 45 days after the date on which the request is received.

(4) Exception for first 12 months of operation. This subsection shall not apply to a consumer reporting agency that has not been furnishing consumer reports to third parties on a continuing basis during the 12-month period preceding a request under paragraph (1), with respect to consumers residing nationwide.

(b) Free disclosure after adverse notice to consumer. Each consumer reporting agency that maintains a file on a consumer shall make all disclosures pursuant to section 1681g of this title without charge to the consumer if, not later than 60 days after receipt by such consumer of a notification pursuant to section 1681m of this title, or of a notification from a debt collection agency affiliated with that consumer reporting agency stating that the consumer's credit rating may be or has been adversely affected, the consumer makes a request under section 1681g of this title.

(c) Free disclosure under certain other circumstances. Upon the request of the consumer, a consumer reporting agency shall make all disclosures pursuant to section 1681g of this title once during any 12-month period without charge to that consumer if the consumer certifies in writing that the consumer—

(1) is unemployed and intends to apply for employment in the 60-day period beginning on the date on which the certification is made;

(2) is a recipient of public welfare assistance; or

(3) has reason to believe that the file on the consumer at the agency contains inaccurate information due to fraud.

(d) Free disclosures in connection with fraud alerts. Upon the request of a consumer, a consumer reporting agency described in section 1681g of this title shall make all disclosures pursuant to section 609 without charge to the consumer, as provided in subsections (a)(2) and (b)(2) of section 1681c-1 of this title, as applicable.

(e) Other charges prohibited. A consumer reporting agency shall not impose any charge on a consumer for providing any notification required by this subchapter or making any disclosure required by this subchapter, except as authorized by subsection (f).

(f) Reasonable charges allowed for certain disclosures

(1) In general. In the case of a request from a consumer other than a request that is covered by any of subsections (a) through (d), a consumer reporting agency may impose a reasonable charge on a consumer—

(A) for making a disclosure to the consumer pursuant to section 1681g of this title, which charge—

(i) shall not exceed $8; and

(ii) shall be indicated to the consumer before making the disclosure; and

(B) for furnishing, pursuant to section 1681i(d) of this title, following a reinvestigation under section 1681i(a) of this title, a statement, codification, or summary to a person designated by the consumer under that section after the 30-day period beginning on the date of notification of the consumer under paragraph (6) or (8) of section 1681i(a) of this title with respect to the reinvestigation, which charge—

(i) shall not exceed the charge that the agency would impose on each designated recipient for a consumer report; and

(ii) shall be indicated to the consumer before furnishing such information.

(2) Modification of amount. The Bureau shall increase the amount referred to in paragraph (1)(A)(i) on January 1 of each year, based proportionally on changes in the Consumer Price Index, with fractional changes rounded to the nearest fifty cents.

(g) Prevention of deceptive marketing of credit reports.

(1) In general. Subject to rulemaking pursuant to section 205(b) of the Credit CARD Act of 2009, any advertisement for a free credit report in any medium shall prominently disclose in such advertisement that free credit reports are available under Federal law at: "AnnualCreditReport.com" (or such other source as may be authorized under Federal law).

(2) Television and radio advertisement. In the case of an advertisement broadcast by television, the disclosures required under paragraph (1) shall be included in the audio and visual part of such advertisement. In the case of an advertisement broadcast by televis[i]on or radio, the disclosure required under paragraph (1) shall consist only of the following: "This is not the free credit report provided for by Federal law".

§ 615. Requirements on Users of Consumer Reports [15 U.S.C. § 1681m].

(a) Duties of users taking adverse actions on basis of information contained in consumer reports. If any person takes any adverse action with respect to any consumer that is based in whole or in part on any information contained in a consumer report, the person shall—

(1) provide oral, written, or electronic notice of the adverse action to the consumer;

(2) provide to the consumer written or electronic disclosure—

(A) of a numerical credit score as defined in section 609(f)(2)(A) [15 U.S.C. 1681g(f)(2)(A)] used by such person in taking any adverse action based in whole or in part on any information in a consumer report; and

(B) of the information set forth in subparagraphs (B) through (E) of section 609(f)(1) [15 U.S.C. 1681g(f)(1)];

(3) provide to the consumer orally, in writing, or electronically—

(A) the name, address, and telephone number of the consumer reporting agency (including a toll-free telephone number established by the agency if the agency compiles and maintains files on consumers on a nationwide basis) that furnished the report to the person; and

(B) a statement that the consumer reporting agency did not make the decision to take the adverse action and is unable to provide the consumer the specific reasons why the adverse action was taken; and

(4) provide to the consumer an oral, written, or electronic notice of the consumer's right—

(A) to obtain, under section 1681j of this title, a free copy of a consumer report on the consumer from the consumer reporting agency referred to in paragraph (3), which notice shall include an indication of the 60-day period under that section for obtaining such a copy; and

(B) to dispute, under section 1681i of this title, with a consumer reporting agency the accuracy or completeness of any information in a consumer report furnished by the agency.

(b) Adverse action based on information obtained from third parties other than consumer reporting agencies

(1) In general. Whenever credit for personal, family, or household purposes involving a consumer is denied or the charge for such credit is increased either wholly or partly because of information obtained from a person other than a consumer reporting agency bearing upon the consumer's credit worthiness, credit standing, credit capacity, character, general reputation, personal characteristics, or mode of living, the user of such information shall, within a reasonable period of time, upon the consumer's written request for the reasons for such adverse action received within sixty days after learning of such adverse action, disclose the nature of the information to the consumer. The user of such information shall clearly and accurately disclose to the consumer his right to make such written request at the time such adverse action is communicated to the consumer.

(2) Duties of person taking certain actions based on information provided by affiliate

(A) Duties, generally. If a person takes an action described in subparagraph (B) with respect to a consumer, based in whole or in part on information described in subparagraph (C), the person shall—

(i) notify the consumer of the action, including a statement that the consumer may obtain the information in accordance with clause (ii); and

(ii) upon a written request from the consumer received within 60 days after transmittal of the notice required by clause (i), disclose to the consumer the nature of the information upon which the action is based by not later than 30 days after receipt of the request.

(B) Action described. An action referred to in subparagraph (A) is an adverse action described in section 1681a(k)(1)(A) of this title, taken in connection with a transaction initiated by the consumer, or any adverse action described in clause (i) or (ii) of section 1681a(k)(1)(B) of this title.

(C) Information described. Information referred to in subparagraph (A)—

(i) except as provided in clause (ii), is information that—

(I) is furnished to the person taking the action by a person related by common ownership or affiliated by common corporate control to the person taking the action; and

(II) bears on the credit worthiness, credit standing, credit capacity, character, general reputation, personal characteristics, or mode of living of the consumer; and

(ii) does not include—

(I) information solely as to transactions or experiences between the consumer and the person furnishing the information; or

(II) information in a consumer report.

(c) Reasonable procedures to assure compliance. No person shall be held liable for any violation of this section if he shows by a preponderance of the evidence that at the time of the alleged violation he maintained reasonable procedures to assure compliance with the provisions of this section.

(d) Duties of users making written credit or insurance solicitations on basis of information contained in consumer files

(1) In general. Any person who uses a consumer report on any consumer in connection with any credit or insurance transaction that is not initiated by the consumer, that is provided to that person under section 1681b(c)(1)(B) of this title, shall provide with each written solicitation made to the consumer regarding the transaction a clear and conspicuous statement that—

(A) information contained in the consumer's consumer report was used in connection with the transaction;

(B) the consumer received the offer of credit or insurance because the consumer satisfied the criteria for credit worthiness or insurability under which the consumer was selected for the offer;

(C) if applicable, the credit or insurance may not be extended if, after the consumer responds to the offer, the consumer does not meet the criteria used to select the consumer for the offer or any applicable criteria bearing on credit worthiness or insurability or does not furnish any required collateral;

(D) the consumer has a right to prohibit information contained in the consumer's file with any consumer reporting agency from being used in connection with any credit or insurance transaction that is not initiated by the consumer; and

(E) the consumer may exercise the right referred to in subparagraph (D) by notifying a notification system established under section 1681b(e) of this title.

(2) Disclosure of address and telephone number; format. A statement under paragraph (1) shall—

(A) include the address and toll-free telephone number of the appropriate notification system established under section 1681b(e) of this title; and

(B) be presented in such format and in such type size and manner as to be simple and easy to understand, as established by the Bureau, by rule, in consultation with the Federal Trade Commission, the Federal banking agencies and the National Credit Union Administration.

(3) Maintaining criteria on file. A person who makes an offer of credit or insurance to a consumer under a credit or insurance transaction described in paragraph (1) shall maintain on file the criteria used to select the consumer to receive the offer, all criteria bearing on credit worthiness or insurability, as applicable, that are the basis for determining whether or not to extend credit or insurance pursuant to the offer, and any requirement for the furnishing of collateral as a condition of the extension of credit or insurance, until the expiration of the 3-year period beginning on the date on which the offer is made to the consumer.

(4) Authority of Federal agencies regarding unfair or deceptive acts or practices not affected. This section is not intended to affect the authority of any Federal or State agency to enforce a prohibition against unfair or deceptive acts or practices, including the making of false or misleading statements in connection with a credit or insurance transaction that is not initiated by the consumer.

(e) Red flag guidelines and regulations required

(1) Guidelines. The Federal banking agencies, the National Credit Union Administration, the Federal Trade Commission, the Commodity Futures Trading Commission, and the Securities and Exchange Commission shall jointly, with respect to the entities

that are subject to their respective enforcement authority under section 1681s of this title—

(A) establish and maintain guidelines for use by each financial institution and each creditor regarding identity theft with respect to account holders at, or customers of, such entities, and update such guidelines as often as necessary;

(B) prescribe regulations requiring each financial institution and each creditor to establish reasonable policies and procedures for implementing the guidelines established pursuant to subparagraph (A), to identify possible risks to account holders or customers or to the safety and soundness of the institution or customers; and

(C) prescribe regulations applicable to card issuers to ensure that, if a card issuer receives notification of a change of address for an existing account, and within a short period of time (during at least the first 30 days after such notification is received) receives a request for an additional or replacement card for the same account, the card issuer may not issue the additional or replacement card, unless the card issuer, in accordance with reasonable policies and procedures—

(i) notifies the cardholder of the request at the former address of the cardholder and provides to the cardholder a means of promptly reporting incorrect address changes;

(ii) notifies the cardholder of the request by such other means of communication as the cardholder and the card issuer previously agreed to; or

(iii) uses other means of assessing the validity of the change of address, in accordance with reasonable policies and procedures established by the card issuer in accordance with the regulations prescribed under subparagraph (B).

(2) Criteria

(A) In general. In developing the guidelines required by paragraph (1)(A), the agencies described in paragraph (1) shall identify patterns, practices, and specific forms of activity that indicate the possible existence of identity theft.

(B) Inactive accounts. In developing the guidelines required by paragraph (1)(A), the agencies described in paragraph (1) shall consider including reasonable guidelines providing that when a transaction occurs with respect to a credit or deposit account that has been inactive for more than 2 years, the creditor or financial institution shall follow reasonable policies and procedures that provide for notice to be given to a consumer in a manner reasonably designed to reduce the likelihood of identity theft with respect to such account.

(3) Consistency with verification requirements. Guidelines established pursuant to paragraph (1) shall not be inconsistent with the policies and procedures required under section 5318(l) of title 31.

(4) Definitions. As used in this subsection, the term "creditor"—

(A) means a creditor, as defined in section 1691a of this title, that regularly and in the ordinary course of business—

(i) obtains or uses consumer reports, directly or indirectly, in connection with a credit transaction;

(ii) furnishes information to consumer reporting agencies, as described in section 1681s-2 of this title, in connection with a credit transaction; or

(iii) advances funds to or on behalf of a person, based on an obligation of the person to repay the funds or repayable from specific property pledged by or on behalf of the person;

(B) does not include a creditor described in subparagraph (A)(iii) that advances funds on behalf of a person for expenses incidental to a service provided by the creditor to that person; and

(C) includes any other type of creditor, as defined in that section 1691a of this title, as the agency described in paragraph (1) having authority over that creditor may determine appropriate by rule promulgated by that agency, based on a determination that such creditor offers or maintains accounts that are subject to a reasonably foreseeable risk of identity theft.

(f) Prohibition on sale or transfer of debt caused by identity theft

(1) In general. No person shall sell, transfer for consideration, or place for collection a debt that such person has been notified under section 1681c-2 of this title has resulted from identity theft.

(2) Applicability. The prohibitions of this subsection shall apply to all persons collecting a debt described in paragraph (1) after the date of a notification under paragraph (1).

(3) Rule of construction. Nothing in this subsection shall be construed to prohibit—

(A) the repurchase of a debt in any case in which the assignee of the debt requires such repurchase because the debt has resulted from identity theft;

(B) the securitization of a debt or the pledging of a portfolio of debt as collateral in connection with a borrowing; or

(C) the transfer of debt as a result of a merger, acquisition, purchase and assumption transaction, or transfer of substantially all of the assets of an entity.

(g) Debt collector communications concerning identity theft. If a person acting as a debt collector (as that term is defined in title VIII) on behalf of a third party that is a creditor or other user of a consumer report is notified that any information relating to a debt that the person is attempting to collect may be fraudulent or may be the result of identity theft, that person shall—

(1) notify the third party that the information may be fraudulent or may be the result of identity theft; and

(2) upon request of the consumer to whom the debt purportedly relates, provide to the consumer all information to which the consumer would otherwise be entitled if the consumer were not a victim of identity theft, but wished to dispute the debt under provisions of law applicable to that person.

(h) Duties of users in certain credit transactions

(1) In general. Subject to rules prescribed as provided in paragraph (6), if any person uses a consumer report in connection with an application for, or a grant, extension, or other provision of, credit on material terms that are materially less favorable than the most favorable terms available to a substantial proportion of consumers from or through that person, based in whole or in part on a consumer report, the person shall provide an oral, written, or electronic notice to the consumer in the form and manner required by regulations prescribed in accordance with this subsection.

(2) Timing. The notice required under paragraph (1) may be provided at the time of an application for, or a grant, extension, or other provision of, credit or the time of communication of an approval of an application for, or grant, extension, or other provision of, credit, except as provided in the regulations prescribed under paragraph (6).

(3) Exceptions. No notice shall be required from a person under this subsection if—

(A) the consumer applied for specific material terms and was granted those terms, unless those terms were initially specified by the person after the transaction was initiated by the consumer and after the person obtained a consumer report; or

(B) the person has provided or will provide a notice to the consumer under subsection (a) in connection with the transaction.

(4) Other notice not sufficient. A person that is required to provide a notice under subsection (a) cannot meet that requirement by providing a notice under this subsection.

(5) Content and delivery of notice. A notice under this subsection shall, at a minimum—

(A) include a statement informing the consumer that the terms offered to the consumer are set based on information from a consumer report;

(B) identify the consumer reporting agency furnishing the report;

(C) include a statement informing the consumer that the consumer may obtain a copy of a consumer report from that consumer reporting agency without charge;

(D) include the contact information specified by that consumer reporting agency for obtaining such consumer reports (including a toll-free telephone number established by the agency in the case of a consumer reporting agency described in section 1681a(p) of this title); and

(E) include a statement informing the consumer of—

(i) a numerical credit score as defined in section 609(f)(2)(A) [15 U.S.C. 1681g(f)(2)(A)], used by such person in making the credit decision described in paragraph (1) based in whole or in part on any information in a consumer report; and

(ii) the information set forth in subparagraphs (B) through (E) of section 609(f)(1) [15 U.S.C. 1681g(f)(1)].

(6) Rulemaking

(A) Rules required. The Bureau shall prescribe rules to carry out this subsection.

(B) Content. Rules required by subparagraph (A) shall address, but are not limited to—

(i) the form, content, time, and manner of delivery of any notice under this subsection;

(ii) clarification of the meaning of terms used in this subsection, including what credit terms are material, and when credit terms are materially less favorable;

(iii) exceptions to the notice requirement under this subsection for classes of persons or transactions regarding which the agencies determine that notice would not significantly benefit consumers;

(iv) a model notice that may be used to comply with this subsection; and

(v) the timing of the notice required under paragraph (1), including the circumstances under which the notice must be provided after the terms offered to the consumer were set based on information from a consumer report.

(7) Compliance. A person shall not be liable for failure to perform the duties required by this section if, at the time of the failure, the person maintained reasonable policies and procedures to comply with this section.

(8) Enforcement

(A) No civil actions. Sections 1681n and 1681o of this title shall not apply to any failure by any person to comply with this section.

(B) Administrative enforcement. This section shall be enforced exclusively under section 1681s of this title by the Federal agencies and officials identified in that section.

§ 616. Civil Liability for Willful Noncompliance [15 U.S.C. § 1681n].

(a) In general. Any person who willfully fails to comply with any requirement imposed under this subchapter with respect to any consumer is liable to that consumer in an amount equal to the sum of—

(1)(A) any actual damages sustained by the consumer as a result of the failure or damages of not less than $100 and not more than $1,000; or

(B) in the case of liability of a natural person for obtaining a consumer report under false pretenses or knowingly without a permissible purpose, actual damages sustained by the consumer as a result of the failure or $1,000, whichever is greater;

(2) such amount of punitive damages as the court may allow; and

(3) in the case of any successful action to enforce any liability under this section, the costs of the action together with reasonable attorney's fees as determined by the court.

(b) Civil liability for knowing noncompliance. Any person who obtains a consumer report from a consumer reporting agency under false pretenses or knowingly without a permissible purpose shall be liable to the consumer reporting agency for actual damages sustained by the consumer reporting agency or $1,000, whichever is greater.

(c) Attorney's fees. Upon a finding by the court that an unsuccessful pleading, motion, or other paper filed in connection with an action under this section was filed in bad faith or for purposes of harassment, the court shall award to the prevailing party attorney's fees reasonable in relation to the work expended in responding to the pleading, motion, or other paper.

§ 617. Civil Liability for Negligent Noncompliance [15 U.S.C. § 1681o].

(a) In general. Any person who is negligent in failing to comply with any requirement imposed under this subchapter with respect to any consumer is liable to that consumer in an amount equal to the sum of—

(1) any actual damages sustained by the consumer as a result of the failure; and

(2) in the case of any successful action to enforce any liability under this section, the costs of the action together with reasonable attorney's fees as determined by the court.

(b) Attorney's fees. On a finding by the court that an unsuccessful pleading, motion, or other paper filed in connection with an action under this section was filed in bad faith or for purposes of harassment, the court shall award to the prevailing party attorney's fees reasonable in relation to the work expended in responding to the pleading, motion, or other paper.

§ 618. Jurisdiction of Courts; Limitation of Actions [15 U.S.C. § 1681p].

An action to enforce any liability created under this subchapter may be brought in any appropriate United States district court, without regard to the amount in controversy, or in any other court of competent jurisdiction, not later than the earlier of—

(1) 2 years after the date of discovery by the plaintiff of the violation that is the basis for such liability; or

(2) 5 years after the date on which the violation that is the basis for such liability occurs.

§ 621. Administrative Enforcement [15 U.S.C. § 1681s].

(a) Enforcement by Federal Trade Commission

(1) In general. The Federal Trade Commission shall be authorized to enforce compliance with the requirements imposed by this subchapter under the Federal Trade Commission Act (15 U.S.C. 41 et seq.), with respect to consumer reporting agencies and all

other persons subject thereto, except to the extent that enforcement of the requirements imposed under this subchapter is specifically committed to some other Government agency under any of subparagraphs (A) through (G) of subsection (b)(1), and subject to subtitle B of the Consumer Financial Protection Act of 2010 [12 U.S.C. 5511 et seq.], subsection (b). For the purpose of the exercise by the Federal Trade Commission of its functions and powers under the Federal Trade Commission Act, a violation of any requirement or prohibition imposed under this subchapter shall constitute an unfair or deceptive act or practice in commerce, in violation of section 5(a) of the Federal Trade Commission Act (15 U.S.C. 45(a)), and shall be subject to enforcement by the Federal Trade Commission under section 5(b) of that Act [15 U.S.C. 45(b)] with respect to any consumer reporting agency or person that is subject to enforcement by the Federal Trade Commission pursuant to this subsection, irrespective of whether that person is engaged in commerce or meets any other jurisdictional tests under the Federal Trade Commission Act. The Federal Trade Commission shall have such procedural, investigative, and enforcement powers, including the power to issue procedural rules in enforcing compliance with the requirements imposed under this subchapter and to require the filing of reports, the production of documents, and the appearance of witnesses, as though the applicable terms and conditions of the Federal Trade Commission Act were part of this subchapter. Any person violating any of the provisions of this subchapter shall be subject to the penalties and entitled to the privileges and immunities provided in the Federal Trade Commission Act as though the applicable terms and provisions of such Act are part of this subchapter.

(2) Penalties

(A) Knowing violations. Except as otherwise provided by subtitle B of the Consumer Financial Protection Act of 2010, in the event of a knowing violation, which constitutes a pattern or practice of violations of this subchapter, the Federal Trade Commission may commence a civil action to recover a civil penalty in a district court of the United States against any person that violates this subchapter. In such action, such person shall be liable for a civil penalty of not more than $2,500 per violation.

(B) Determining penalty amount. In determining the amount of a civil penalty under subparagraph (A), the court shall take into account the degree of culpability, any history of such prior conduct, ability to pay, effect on ability to continue to do business, and such other matters as justice may require.

(C) Limitation. Notwithstanding paragraph (2), a court may not impose any civil penalty on a person for a violation of section 623(a)(1) [15 U.S.C. 1681s-2(a)(1)], unless the person has been enjoined from committing the violation, or ordered not to commit the violation, in an action or proceeding brought by or on behalf of the Federal Trade Commission, and has violated the injunction or order, and the court may not impose any civil penalty for any violation occurring before the date of the violation of the injunction or order.

(b) Enforcement by other agencies

(1) In general. Subject to subtitle B of the Consumer Financial Protection Act of 2010, compliance with the requirements imposed under this subchapter with respect to consumer reporting agencies, persons who use consumer reports from such agencies, persons who furnish information to such agencies, and users of information that are subject to section 615(d) [15 U.S.C. 1681m(d)] shall be enforced under—

(A) section 8 of the Federal Deposit Insurance Act (12 U.S.C. 1818), by the appropriate Federal banking agency, as defined in section 3(q) of the Federal Deposit Insurance Act (12 U.S.C. 1813(q)), with respect to—

(i) any national bank or State savings association, and any Federal branch or Federal agency of a foreign bank;

(ii) any member bank of the Federal Reserve System (other than a national bank), a branch or agency of a foreign bank (other than a Federal branch, Federal agency, or insured State branch of a foreign bank), a commercial lending company owned or controlled by a foreign bank, and any organization operating under section 25 or 25A of the Federal Reserve Act [12 U.S.C. 601 et seq., 611 et seq.]; and

(iii) any bank or Federal savings association insured by the Federal Deposit Insurance Corporation (other than a member of the Federal Reserve System) and any insured State branch of a foreign bank;

(B) the Federal Credit Union Act (12 U.S.C. 1751 et seq.), by the Administrator of the National Credit Union Administration with respect to any Federal credit union;

(C) subtitle IV of title 49, by the Secretary of Transportation, with respect to all carriers subject to the jurisdiction of the Surface Transportation Board;

(D) part A of subtitle VII of title 49, by the Secretary of Transportation, with respect to any air carrier or foreign air carrier subject to that part;

(E) the Packers and Stockyards Act, 1921 (7 U.S.C. 181 et seq.) (except as provided in section 406 of that Act [7 U.S.C. 226, 227]), by the Secretary of Agriculture, with respect to any activities subject to that Act;

(F) the Commodity Exchange Act [7 U.S.C. 1 et seq.], with respect to a person subject to the jurisdiction of the Commodity Futures Trading Commission;

(G) the Federal securities laws, and any other laws that are subject to the jurisdiction of the Securities and Exchange Commission, with respect to a person that is subject to the jurisdiction of the Securities and Exchange Commission; and

(H) subtitle E of the Consumer Financial Protection Act of 2010 [12 U.S.C. 5561 et seq.], by the Bureau, with respect to any person subject to this subchapter.

(2) Incorporated definitions. The terms used in paragraph (1) that are not defined in this subchapter or otherwise defined in section 3(s) of the Federal Deposit Insurance Act (12 U.S.C. 1813(s)) have the same meanings as in section 1(b) of the International Banking Act of 1978 (12 U.S.C. 3101).

(c) State action for violations

(1) Authority of States. In addition to such other remedies as are provided under State law, if the chief law enforcement officer of a State, or an official or agency designated by a State, has reason to believe that any person has violated or is violating this subchapter, the State—

(A) may bring an action to enjoin such violation in any appropriate United States district court or in any other court of competent jurisdiction;

(B) subject to paragraph (5), may bring an action on behalf of the residents of the State to recover—

(i) damages for which the person is liable to such residents under sections 1681n and 1681o of this title as a result of the violation;

(ii) in the case of a violation described in any of paragraphs (1) through (3) of section 1681s-2(c) of this title, damages for which the person would, but for section 1681s-2(c) of this title, be liable to such residents as a result of the violation; or

(iii) damages of not more than $1,000 for each willful or negligent violation; and

(C) in the case of any successful action under subparagraph (A) or (B), shall be awarded the costs of the action and reasonable attorney fees as determined by the court.

(2) Rights of Federal regulators. The State shall serve prior written notice of any action under paragraph (1) upon the Bureau and the Federal Trade Commission or the appropriate Federal regulator determined under subsection (b) and provide the Bureau and the Federal Trade Commission or appropriate Federal regulator with a copy of its complaint, except in any case in which such prior notice is not feasible, in which case the State shall serve such notice immediately upon instituting such action. The Bureau and the Federal Trade Commission or appropriate Federal regulator shall have the right—

(A) to intervene in the action;

(B) upon so intervening, to be heard on all matters arising therein;

(C) to remove the action to the appropriate United States district court; and

(D) to file petitions for appeal.

(3) Investigatory powers. For purposes of bringing any action under this subsection, nothing in this subsection shall prevent the chief law enforcement officer, or an official or agency designated by a State, from exercising the powers conferred on the chief law enforcement officer or such official by the laws of such State to conduct investigations or to administer oaths or affirmations or to compel the attendance of witnesses or the production of documentary and other evidence.

(4) Limitation on State action while Federal action pending. If the Bureau, the Federal Trade Commission, or the appropriate Federal regulator has instituted a civil action or an administrative action under section 8 of the Federal Deposit Insurance Act [12 U.S.C. 1818] for a violation of this subchapter, no State may, during the pendency of such action, bring an action under this section

against any defendant named in the complaint of the Bureau, the Federal Trade Commission or the appropriate Federal regulator for any violation of this subchapter that is alleged in that complaint.

(5) Limitations on State actions for certain violations

(A) Violation of injunction required. A State may not bring an action against a person under paragraph (1)(B) for a violation described in any of paragraphs (1) through (3) of section 1681s-2(c) of this title, unless—

(i) the person has been enjoined from committing the violation, in an action brought by the State under paragraph (1)(A); and

(ii) the person has violated the injunction.

(B) Limitation on damages recoverable. In an action against a person under paragraph (1)(B) for a violation described in any of paragraphs (1) through (3) of section 1681s-2(c) of this title, a State may not recover any damages incurred before the date of the violation of an injunction on which the action is based.

(d) Enforcement under other authority. For the purpose of the exercise by any agency referred to in subsection (b) of its powers under any Act referred to in that subsection, a violation of any requirement imposed under this subchapter shall be deemed to be a violation of a requirement imposed under that Act. In addition to its powers under any provision of law specifically referred to in subsection (b), each of the agencies referred to in that subsection may exercise, for the purpose of enforcing compliance with any requirement imposed under this subchapter any other authority conferred on it by law.

(e) Regulatory authority

(1) In general. The Bureau shall prescribe such regulations as are necessary to carry out the purposes of this subchapter, except with respect to sections 615(e) and 628 [15 U.S.C. 1681m(e) and 1681w]. The Bureau may prescribe regulations as may be necessary or appropriate to administer and carry out the purposes and objectives of this subchapter, and to prevent evasions thereof or to facilitate compliance therewith. Except as provided in section 1029(a) of the Consumer Financial Protection Act of 2010 [12 U.S.C. 5519(a)], the regulations prescribed by the Bureau under this title shall apply to any person that is subject to this subchapter, notwithstanding the enforcement authorities granted to other agencies under this section.

(2) Deference. Notwithstanding any power granted to any Federal agency under this subchapter, the deference that a court affords to a Federal agency with respect to a determination made by such agency relating to the meaning or interpretation of any provision of this subchapter that is subject to the jurisdiction of such agency shall be applied as if that agency were the only agency authorized to apply, enforce, interpret, or administer the provisions of this subchapter. The regulations prescribed by the Bureau under this subchapter shall apply to any person that is subject to this subchapter, notwithstanding the enforcement authorities granted to other agencies under this section.

(f) Coordination of consumer complaint investigations

(1) In general. Each consumer reporting agency described in section 1681a(p) of this title shall develop and maintain procedures for the referral to each other such agency of any consumer complaint received by the agency alleging identity theft, or requesting a fraud alert under section 1681c-l of this title or a block under section 1681c-2 of this title.

(2) Model form and procedure for reporting identity theft. The Bureau, in consultation with the Federal Trade Commission, the Federal banking agencies, and the National Credit Union Administration, shall develop a model form and model procedures to be used by consumers who are victims of identity theft for contacting and informing creditors and consumer reporting agencies of the fraud.

(3) Annual summary reports. Each consumer reporting agency described in section 1681a(p) of this title shall submit an annual summary report to the Bureau on consumer complaints received by the agency on identity theft or fraud alerts.

(g) Bureau regulation of coding of trade names. If the Bureau determines that a person described in paragraph (9) of section 1681s-2(a) of this title has not met the requirements of such paragraph, the Bureau shall take action to ensure the person's compliance with such paragraph, which may include issuing model guidance or prescribing reasonable policies and procedures, as necessary to ensure that such person complies with such paragraph.

§ 623. Responsibilities of Furnishers of Information to Consumer Reporting Agencies [15 U.S.C. § 1681s-2].

(a) Duty of furnishers of information to provide accurate information

(1) Prohibition

(A) Reporting information with actual knowledge of errors. A person shall not furnish any information relating to a consumer to any consumer reporting agency if the person knows or has reasonable cause to believe that the information is inaccurate.

(B) Reporting information after notice and confirmation of errors. A person shall not furnish information relating to a consumer to any consumer reporting agency if—

(i) the person has been notified by the consumer, at the address specified by the person for such notices, that specific information is inaccurate; and

(ii) the information is, in fact, inaccurate.

(C) No address requirement. A person who clearly and conspicuously specifies to the consumer an address for notices referred to in subparagraph (B) shall not be subject to subparagraph (A); however, nothing in subparagraph (B) shall require a person to specify such an address.

(D) Definition. For purposes of subparagraph (A), the term "reasonable cause to believe that the information is inaccurate" means having specific knowledge, other than solely allegations by the consumer, that would cause a reasonable person to have substantial doubts about the accuracy of the information.

(E) Rehabilitation of private education loans

(i) In general. Notwithstanding any other provision of this section, a consumer may request a financial institution to remove from a consumer report a reported default regarding a private education loan, and such information shall not be considered inaccurate, if—

(I) the financial institution chooses to offer a loan rehabilitation program which includes, without limitation, a requirement of the consumer to make consecutive on-time monthly payments in a number that demonstrates, in the assessment of the financial institution offering the loan rehabilitation program, a renewed ability and willingness to repay the loan; and

(II) the requirements of the loan rehabilitation program described in subclause (I) are successfully met.

(ii) Banking agencies.

(I) In general. If a financial institution is supervised by a Federal banking agency, the financial institution shall seek written approval concerning the terms and conditions of the loan rehabilitation program described in clause (i) from the appropriate Federal banking agency.

(II) Feedback. An appropriate Federal banking agency shall provide feedback to a financial institution within 120 days of a request for approval under subclause (I).

(iii) Limitation.

(I) In general. A consumer may obtain the benefits available under this subsection with respect to rehabilitating a loan only 1 time per loan.

(II) Rule of construction. Nothing in this subparagraph may be construed to require a financial institution to offer a loan rehabilitation program or to remove any reported default from a consumer report as a consideration of a loan rehabilitation program, except as described in clause (i).

(iv) Definitions. For purpose of this subparagraph—

(I) the term "appropriate Federal banking agency" has the meaning given the term in section 1813 of title 12; and

(II) the term "private education loan" has the meaning given the term in section 1650(a) of this title.

(F) Reporting information during COVID–19 pandemic.

(i) Definitions. In this subsection:

(I) Accommodation. The term "accommodation" includes an agreement to defer 1 or more payments, make a partial payment, forbear any delinquent amounts, modify a loan or contract, or any other assistance or relief granted to a consumer who is affected by the coronavirus disease

2019 (COVID–19) pandemic during the covered period.

(II) Covered period. The term "covered period" means the period beginning on January 31, 2020 and ending on the later of—

(aa) 120 days after March 27, 2020; or

(bb) 120 days after the date on which the national emergency concerning the novel coronavirus disease (COVID–19) outbreak declared by the President on March 13, 2020 under the National Emergencies Act (50 U.S.C. 1601 et seq.) terminates.

(ii) Reporting. Except as provided in clause (iii), if a furnisher makes an accommodation with respect to 1 or more payments on a credit obligation or account of a consumer, and the consumer makes the payments or is not required to make 1 or more payments pursuant to the accommodation, the furnisher shall—

(I) report the credit obligation or account as current; or

(II) if the credit obligation or account was delinquent before the accommodation—

(aa) maintain the delinquent status during the period in which the accommodation is in effect; and

(bb) if the consumer brings the credit obligation or account current during the period described in item (aa), report the credit obligation or account as current.

(iii) Exception. Clause (ii) shall not apply with respect to a credit obligation or account of a consumer that has been charged-off.

(2) Duty to correct and update information. A person who—

(A) regularly and in the ordinary course of business furnishes information to one or more consumer reporting agencies about the person's transactions or experiences with any consumer; and

(B) has furnished to a consumer reporting agency information that the person determines is not complete or accurate, shall promptly notify the consumer reporting agency of that determination and provide to the agency any corrections to that information, or any additional information, that is necessary to make the information provided by the person to the agency complete and accurate, and shall not thereafter furnish to the agency any of the information that remains not complete or accurate.

(3) Duty to provide notice of dispute. If the completeness or accuracy of any information furnished by any person to any consumer reporting agency is disputed to such person by a consumer, the person may not furnish the information to any consumer reporting agency without notice that such information is disputed by the consumer.

(4) Duty to provide notice of closed accounts. A person who regularly and in the ordinary course of business furnishes information to a consumer reporting agency regarding a consumer who has a credit account with that person shall notify the agency of the voluntary closure of the account by the consumer, in information regularly furnished for the period in which the account is closed.

(5) Duty to provide notice of delinquency of accounts.

(A) In general. A person who furnishes information to a consumer reporting agency regarding a delinquent account being placed for collection, charged to profit or loss, or subjected to any similar action shall, not later than 90 days after furnishing the information, notify the agency of the date of delinquency on the account, which shall be the month and year of the commencement of the delinquency on the account that immediately preceded the action.

(B) Rule of construction. For purposes of this paragraph only, and provided that the consumer does not dispute the information, a person that furnishes information on a delinquent account that is placed for collection, charged for profit or loss, or subjected to any similar action, complies with this paragraph, if—

(i) the person reports the same date of delinquency as that provided by the creditor to which the account was owed at the time at which the commencement of the delinquency occurred, if the creditor previously reported that date of delinquency to a consumer reporting agency;

(ii) the creditor did not previously report the date of delinquency to a consumer reporting agency, and the person establishes and follows reasonable procedures to obtain the date of delinquency from the creditor or another reliable source and reports that date to a consumer reporting agency as the date of delinquency; or

(iii) the creditor did not previously report the date of delinquency to a consumer reporting agency and the date of delinquency cannot be reasonably obtained as provided in clause (ii), the person establishes and follows reasonable procedures to ensure the date reported as the date of delinquency precedes the date on which the account is placed for collection, charged to profit or loss, or subjected to any similar action, and reports such date to the credit reporting agency.

(6) Duties of furnishers upon notice of identity theft-related information

(A) Reasonable procedures. A person that furnishes information to any consumer reporting agency shall have in place reasonable procedures to respond to any notification that it receives from a consumer reporting agency under section 1681c-2 of this title relating to information resulting from identity theft, to prevent that person from refurnishing such blocked information.

(B) Information alleged to result from identity theft. If a consumer submits an identity theft report to a person who furnishes information to a consumer reporting agency at the address specified by that person for receiving such reports stating that information maintained by such person that purports to relate to the consumer resulted from identity theft, the person may not furnish such information that purports to relate to the consumer to any consumer reporting agency, unless the person subsequently knows or is informed by the consumer that the information is correct.

(7) Negative information

(A) Notice to consumer required

(i) In general. If any financial institution that extends credit and regularly and in the ordinary course of business furnishes information to a consumer reporting agency described in section 1681a(p) of this title furnishes negative information to such an agency regarding credit extended to a customer, the financial institution shall provide a notice of such furnishing of negative information, in writing, to the customer.

(ii) Notice effective for subsequent submissions. After providing such notice, the financial institution may submit additional negative information to a consumer reporting agency described in section 1681a(p) of this title with respect to the same transaction, extension of credit, account, or customer without providing additional notice to the customer.

(B) Time of notice

(i) In general. The notice required under subparagraph (A) shall be provided to the customer prior to, or no later than 30 days after, furnishing the negative information to a consumer reporting agency described in section 1681a(p) of this title.

(ii) Coordination with new account disclosures. If the notice is provided to the customer prior to furnishing the negative information to a consumer reporting agency, the notice may not be included in the initial disclosures provided under section 127(a) of the Truth in Lending Act [15 U.S.C. 1637(a)].

(C) Coordination with other disclosures. The notice required under subparagraph (A)—

(i) may be included on or with any notice of default, any billing statement, or any other materials provided to the customer; and

(ii) must be clear and conspicuous.

(D) Model disclosure

(i) Duty of Bureau. The Bureau shall prescribe a brief model disclosure that a financial institution may use to comply with subparagraph (A), which shall not exceed 30 words.

(ii) Use of model not required. No provision of this paragraph may be construed to require a financial institution to use any such model form prescribed by the Bureau.

(iii) Compliance using model. A financial institution shall be deemed to be in compliance with subparagraph (A) if the financial institution uses any model form prescribed by the Bureau under this subparagraph, or the financial institution uses any such model form and rearranges its format.

(E) Use of notice without submitting negative information. No provision of this paragraph shall be construed as requiring a financial institution that has provided a customer with a notice described in subparagraph (A) to furnish negative information about the customer to a consumer reporting agency.

(F) Safe harbor. A financial institution shall not be liable for failure to perform the duties required by this paragraph if, at the time of the failure, the financial institution maintained reasonable policies and procedures to comply with this paragraph or the financial institution reasonably believed that the institution is prohibited, by law, from contacting the consumer.

(G) Definitions. For purposes of this paragraph, the following definitions shall apply:

(i) Negative information. The term "negative information" means information concerning a customer's delinquencies, late payments, insolvency, or any form of default.

(ii) Customer; financial institution. The terms "customer" and "financial institution" have the same meanings as in section 6809 of this title.

(8) Ability of consumer to dispute information directly with furnisher

(A) In general. The Bureau, in consultation with the Federal Trade Commission, the Federal banking agencies, and the National Credit Union Administration, shall prescribe regulations that shall identify the circumstances under which a furnisher shall be required to reinvestigate a dispute concerning the accuracy of information contained in a consumer report on the consumer, based on a direct request of a consumer.

(B) Considerations. In prescribing regulations under subparagraph (A), the agencies shall weigh—

(i) the benefits to consumers with the costs on furnishers and the credit reporting system;

(ii) the impact on the overall accuracy and integrity of consumer reports of any such requirements;

(iii) whether direct contact by the consumer with the furnisher would likely result in the most expeditious resolution of any such dispute; and

(iv) the potential impact on the credit reporting process if credit repair organizations, as defined in section 403(3) [15 U.S.C. 1679a(3)], including entities that would be a credit repair organization, but for section 403(3)(B)(i) [15 U.S.C. 1678a(3)(B)(i)], are able to circumvent the prohibition in subparagraph (G).

(C) Applicability. Subparagraphs (D) through (G) shall apply in any circumstance identified under the regulations promulgated under subparagraph (A).

(D) Submitting a notice of dispute. A consumer who seeks to dispute the accuracy of information shall provide a dispute notice directly to such person at the address specified by the person for such notices that—

(i) identifies the specific information that is being disputed;

(ii) explains the basis for the dispute; and

(iii) includes all supporting documentation required by the furnisher to substantiate the basis of the dispute.

(E) Duty of person after receiving notice of dispute. After receiving a notice of dispute from a consumer pursuant to subparagraph (D), the person that provided the information in dispute to a consumer reporting agency shall—

(i) conduct an investigation with respect to the disputed information;

(ii) review all relevant information provided by the consumer with the notice;

(iii) complete such person's investigation of the dispute and report the results of the investigation to the consumer before the expiration of the period under section 611(a)(1) [15 U.S.C. 1681i(a)(1)] within which a consumer reporting agency would be required to complete its action if the consumer had elected to dispute the information under that section; and

(iv) if the investigation finds that the information reported was inaccurate, promptly notify each consumer reporting agency to which the person furnished the inaccurate information of that determination and provide to the agency any correction to that information that is necessary to make the information provided by the person accurate.

(F) Frivolous or irrelevant dispute

(i) In general. This paragraph shall not apply if the person receiving a notice of a dispute from a consumer reasonably determines that the dispute is frivolous or irrelevant, including—

(I) by reason of the failure of a consumer to provide sufficient information to investigate the disputed information; or

(II) the submission by a consumer of a dispute that is substantially the same as a dispute previously submitted by or for the consumer, either directly to the person or through a consumer reporting agency under subsection (b), with respect to which the person has already performed the person's duties under this paragraph or subsection (b), as applicable.

(ii) Notice of determination. Upon making any determination under clause (i) that a dispute is frivolous or irrelevant, the person shall notify the consumer of such determination not later than 5 business days after making such determination, by mail or, if authorized by the consumer for that purpose, by any other means available to the person.

(iii) Contents of notice. A notice under clause (ii) shall include—

(I) the reasons for the determination under clause (i); and

(II) identification of any information required to investigate the disputed information, which may consist of a standardized form describing the general nature of such information.

(G) Exclusion of credit repair organizations. This paragraph shall not apply if the notice of the dispute is submitted by, is prepared on behalf of the consumer by, or is submitted on a form supplied to the consumer by, a credit repair organization, as defined in section 403(3) [15 U.S.C. 1679a(3)], or an entity that would be a credit repair organization, but for section 403(3)(B)(i) [15 U.S.C. 1679a(3)(B)(i)].

(9) Duty to provide notice of status as medical information furnisher. A person whose primary business is providing medical services, products, or devices, or the person's agent or assignee, who furnishes information to a consumer reporting agency on a consumer shall be considered a medical information furnisher for purposes of this subchapter, and shall notify the agency of such status.

(b) Duties of furnishers of information upon notice of dispute

(1) In general. After receiving notice pursuant to section 1681i(a)(2) of this title of a dispute with regard to the completeness or accuracy of any information provided by a person to a consumer reporting agency, the person shall—

(A) conduct an investigation with respect to the disputed information;

(B) review all relevant information provided by the consumer reporting agency pursuant to section 1681i(a)(2) of this title;

(C) report the results of the investigation to the consumer reporting agency;

(D) if the investigation finds that the information is incomplete or inaccurate, report those results to all other consumer reporting agencies to which the person furnished the information and that compile and maintain files on consumers on a nationwide basis; and

(E) if an item of information disputed by a consumer is found to be inaccurate or incomplete or cannot be verified after any reinvestigation under paragraph (1), for purposes of reporting to a consumer reporting agency only, as appropriate, based on the results of the reinvestigation promptly—

(i) modify that item of information;

(ii) delete that item of information; or

(iii) permanently block the reporting of that item of information.

(2) Deadline. A person shall complete all investigations, reviews, and reports required under paragraph (1) regarding information provided by the person to a consumer reporting agency, before the expiration of the period under section 1681i(a)(1) of this title within which the consumer reporting agency is required to complete actions required by that section regarding that information.

(c) Limitation on liability. Except as provided in section 1681s(c)(1)(B) of this title, sections 1681n and 1681o of this title do not apply to any violation of—

(1) subsection (a) of this section, including any regulations issued thereunder;

(2) subsection (e) of this section, except that nothing in this paragraph shall limit, expand, or otherwise affect liability under section 1681n or 1681o of this title, as applicable, for violations of subsection (b) of this section; or

(3) subsection (e) of section 1681m of this title.

(d) Limitation on enforcement. The provisions of law described in paragraphs (1) through (3) of subsection (c) (other than with respect to the exception described in paragraph (2) of subsection (c)) shall be enforced exclusively as provided under section 1681s of this title by the Federal agencies and officials and the State officials identified in section 1681s of this title.

(e) Accuracy guidelines and regulations required

(1) Guidelines. The Bureau shall, with respect to persons or entities that are subject to the enforcement authority of the Bureau under section 621[15 U.S.C. 1681s]—

(A) establish and maintain guidelines for use by each person that furnishes information to a consumer reporting agency regarding the accuracy and integrity of the information relating to consumers that such entities furnish to consumer reporting agencies, and update such guidelines as often as necessary; and

(B) prescribe regulations requiring each person that furnishes information to a consumer reporting agency to establish reasonable policies and procedures for implementing the guidelines established pursuant to subparagraph (A).

(2) Criteria. In developing the guidelines required by paragraph (1)(A), the Bureau shall—

(A) identify patterns, practices, and specific forms of activity that can compromise the accuracy and integrity of information furnished to consumer reporting agencies;

(B) review the methods (including technological means) used to furnish information relating to consumers to consumer reporting agencies;

(C) determine whether persons that furnish information to consumer reporting agencies maintain and enforce policies to ensure the accuracy and integrity of information furnished to consumer reporting agencies; and

(D) examine the policies and processes that persons that furnish information to consumer reporting agencies employ to conduct reinvestigations and correct inaccurate information relating to consumers that has been furnished to consumer reporting agencies.

§ 624. Affiliate Sharing [15 U.S.C. § 1681s-3].

(a) Special rule for solicitation for purposes of marketing

(1) Notice. Any person that receives from another person related to it by common ownership or affiliated by corporate control a communication of information that would be a consumer report, but for clauses (i), (ii), and (iii) of section 1681a(d)(2)(A) of this title, may not use the information to make a solicitation for marketing purposes to a consumer about its products or services, unless—

(A) it is clearly and conspicuously disclosed to the consumer that the information may be communicated among such persons for purposes of making such solicitations to the consumer; and

(B) the consumer is provided an opportunity and a simple method to prohibit the making of such solicitations to the consumer by such person.

(2) Consumer choice

(A) In general. The notice required under paragraph (1) shall allow the consumer the opportunity to prohibit all solicitations referred to in such paragraph, and may allow the consumer to choose from different options when electing to prohibit the sending of such solicitations, including options regarding the types of entities and information covered, and which methods of delivering solicitations the consumer elects to prohibit.

(B) Format. Notwithstanding subparagraph (A), the notice required under paragraph (1) shall be clear, conspicuous, and concise, and any method provided under paragraph (1)(B) shall be simple. The regulations prescribed to implement this section shall provide specific guidance regarding how to comply with such standards.

(3) Duration

(A) In general. The election of a consumer pursuant to paragraph (1)(B) to prohibit the making of solicitations shall be effective for at least 5 years, beginning on the date on which the person receives the election of the consumer, unless the consumer requests that such election be revoked.

(B) Notice upon expiration of effective period

At such time as the election of a consumer pursuant to paragraph (1)(B) is no longer effective, a person may not use information that the person receives in the manner described in paragraph (1) to make any solicitation for marketing purposes to the consumer, unless the consumer receives a notice and an opportunity, using a simple method, to extend the opt-out for another period of at least 5 years, pursuant to the procedures described in paragraph (1).

(4) Scope. This section shall not apply to a person—

(A) using information to make a solicitation for marketing purposes to a consumer with whom the person has a pre-existing business relationship;

(B) using information to facilitate communications to an individual for whose benefit the person provides employee benefit or other services pursuant to a contract with an employer related to and arising out of the current employment relationship or status of the individual as a participant or beneficiary of an employee benefit plan;

(C) using information to perform services on behalf of another person related by common ownership or affiliated by corporate control, except that this subparagraph shall not be construed as permitting a person to send solicitations on behalf of another person, if such other person would not be permitted to send the solicitation on its own behalf as a result of the election of the consumer to prohibit solicitations under paragraph (1)(B);

(D) using information in response to a communication initiated by the consumer;

(E) using information in response to solicitations authorized or requested by the consumer; or

(F) if compliance with this section by that person would prevent compliance by that person with any provision of State insurance laws pertaining to unfair discrimination in any State in which the person is lawfully doing business.

(5) No retroactivity. This subsection shall not prohibit the use of information to send a solicitation to a consumer if such information was received prior to the date on which persons are required to comply with regulations implementing this subsection.

(b) Notice for other purposes permissible. A notice or other disclosure under this section may be coordinated and consolidated with any other notice required to be issued under any other provision of law by a person that is subject to this section, and a notice or other disclosure that is equivalent to the notice required by subsection (a), and that is provided by a person described in subsection (a) to a consumer together with disclosures required by any other provision of law, shall satisfy the requirements of subsection (a).

(c) User requirements. Requirements with respect to the use by a person of information received from another person related to it by common ownership or affiliated by corporate control, such as the requirements of this section, constitute requirements with respect to the exchange of information among persons affiliated by common ownership or common corporate control, within the meaning of section 1681t(b)(2) of this title.

(d) Definitions. For purposes of this section, the following definitions shall apply:

(1) Pre-existing business relationship. The term "pre-existing business relationship" means a relationship between a person, or a person's licensed agent, and a consumer, based on—

(A) a financial contract between a person and a consumer which is in force;

(B) the purchase, rental, or lease by the consumer of that person's goods or services, or a financial transaction (including holding an active account or a policy in force or having another continuing relationship) between the consumer and that person during the 18-month period immediately preceding the date on which the consumer is sent a solicitation covered by this section;

(C) an inquiry or application by the consumer regarding a product or service offered by that person, during the 3-month period immediately preceding the date on which the consumer is sent a solicitation covered by this section; or

(D) any other pre-existing customer relationship defined in the regulations implementing this section.

(2) Solicitation. The term "solicitation" means the marketing of a product or service initiated by a person to a particular consumer that is based on an exchange of information described in subsection (a), and is intended to encourage the consumer to purchase such product or service, but does not include communications that are directed at the general public or determined not to be a solicitation by the regulations prescribed under this section.

§ 628. Disposal of Records [15 U.S.C. § 1681w].

(a) Regulations

(1) In general. The Federal Trade Commission, the Securities and Exchange Commission, the Commodity Futures Trading Commission, the Federal banking agencies, and the National Credit Union Administration, with respect to the entities that are subject to their respective enforcement authority under section 621 [15 U.S.C. 1681s], and in coordination as described in paragraph (2), shall issue final regulations requiring any person that maintains or otherwise possesses consumer information, or any compilation of consumer information, derived from consumer reports for a business purpose to properly dispose of any such information or compilation.

(2) Coordination. Each agency required to prescribe regulations under paragraph (1) shall—

(A) consult and coordinate with each other such agency so that, to the extent possible, the regulations prescribed by each such agency are consistent and comparable with the regulations by each such other agency; and

(B) ensure that such regulations are consistent with the requirements and regulations issued pursuant to Public Law 106-102 and other provisions of Federal law.

(3) Exemption authority. In issuing regulations under this section, the agencies identified in paragraph (1) may exempt any person or class of persons from application of those regulations, as such agency deems appropriate to carry out the purpose of this section.

(b) Rule of construction. Nothing in this section shall be construed—

(1) to require a person to maintain or destroy any record pertaining to a consumer that is not imposed under other law; or

(2) to alter or affect any requirement imposed under any other provision of law to maintain or destroy such a record.

§ 629. Corporate and Technological Circumvention Prohibited [15 U.S.C. § 1681x].

The Bureau shall prescribe regulations, to become effective not later than 90 days after December 4, 2003, to prevent a consumer reporting agency from circumventing or evading treatment as a consumer reporting agency described in section 1681a(p) of this title for purposes of this subchapter, including—

(1) by means of a corporate reorganization or restructuring, including a merger, acquisition, dissolution, divestiture, or asset sale of a consumer reporting agency; or

(2) by maintaining or merging public record and credit account information in a manner that is substantially equivalent to that described in paragraphs (1) and (2) of section 1681a(p) of this title, in the manner described in section 1681a(p) of this title.

FAIR DEBT COLLECTION PRACTICES ACT

Section

As amended by Pub. L. 109-351, §§ 801-02, 120 Stat. 1966 (2006)

§ 801. Short Title (15 U.S.C. 1601 note)

This title may be cited as the "Fair Debt Collection Practices Act."

§ 802. Congressional Findings and Declaration of Purpose (15 U.S.C. 1692)

(a) There is abundant evidence of the use of abusive, deceptive, and unfair debt collection practices by many debt collectors. Abusive debt collection practices contribute to the number of personal bankruptcies, to marital instability, to the loss of jobs, and to invasions of individual privacy.

(b) Existing laws and procedures for redressing these injuries are inadequate to protect consumers.

(c) Means other than misrepresentation or other abusive debt collection practices are available for the effective collection of debts.

(d) Abusive debt collection practices are carried on to a substantial extent in interstate commerce and through means and instrumentalities of such commerce. Even where abusive debt collection practices are purely intrastate in character, they nevertheless directly affect interstate commerce.

(e) It is the purpose of this title to eliminate abusive debt collection practices by debt collectors, to insure that those debt collectors who refrain from using abusive debt collection practices are not competitively disadvantaged, and to promote consistent State action to protect consumers against debt collection abuses.

§ 803. Definitions (15 U.S.C. 1692a)

As used in this subchapter—

(1) The term "Bureau" means the Bureau of Consumer Financial Protection.

(2) The term "communication" means the conveying of information regarding a debt directly or indirectly to any person through any medium.

(3) The term "consumer" means any natural person obligated or allegedly obligated to pay any debt.

(4) The term "creditor" means any person who offers or extends credit creating a debt or to whom a debt is owed, but such term does not include any person to the extent that he receives an assignment or transfer of a debt in default solely for the purpose of facilitating collection of such debt for another.

(5) The term "debt" means any obligation or alleged obligation of a consumer to pay money arising out of a transaction in which the money, property, insurance, or services which are the subject of the transaction are primarily for personal, family, or household purposes, whether or not such obligation has been reduced to judgment.

(6) The term "debt collector" means any person who uses any instrumentality of interstate commerce or the mails in any business the principal purpose of which is the collection of any debts, or who regularly collects or attempts to collect, directly or indirectly, debts owed or due or asserted to be owed or due another. Notwithstanding the exclusion provided by clause (F) of the last sentence of this paragraph, the term includes any creditor who, in the process of collecting his own debts, uses any name other than his own which would indicate that a third person is collecting or attempting to collect such debts. For the purpose of section 1692f(6) of this title, such term also includes any person who uses any instrumentality of interstate commerce or the mails in any business the principal purpose of which is the enforcement of security interests. The term does not include—

(A) any officer or employee of a creditor while, in the name of the creditor, collecting debts for such creditor;

(B) any person while acting as a debt collector for another person, both of whom are related by common ownership or affiliated by corporate control, if the person acting as a debt collector does so only for persons to whom it is so related or affiliated and if the principal business of such person is not the collection of debts;

(C) any officer or employee of the United States or any State to the extent that collecting or attempting to collect any debt is in the performance of his official duties;

(D) any person while serving or attempting to serve legal process on any other person in connection with the judicial enforcement of any debt;

(E) any nonprofit organization which, at the request of consumers, performs bona fide consumer credit counseling and assists consumers in the liquidation of their debts by receiving payments from such consumers and distributing such amounts to creditors; and

(F) any person collecting or attempting to collect any debt owed or due or asserted to be owed or due another to the extent such activity (i) is incidental to a bona fide fiduciary obligation or a bona fide escrow arrangement; (ii) concerns a debt which was originated by such person; (iii) concerns a debt which was not in default at the time it was obtained by such person; or (iv) concerns a debt obtained by such person as a secured party in a commercial credit transaction involving the creditor.

(7) The term "location information" means a consumer's place of abode and his telephone number at such place, or his place of employment.

(8) The term "State" means any State, territory, or possession of the United States, the District of Columbia, the Commonwealth of Puerto Rico, or any political subdivision of any of the foregoing.

§ 804. Acquisition of Location Information (15 U.S.C. 1692b)

Any debt collector communicating with any person other than the consumer for the purpose of acquiring location information about the consumer shall—

(1) identify himself, state that he is confirming or correcting location information concerning the consumer, and, only if expressly requested, identify his employer;

(2) not state that such consumer owes any debt;

(3) not communicate with any such person more than once unless requested to do so by such person or unless the debt collector reasonably believes that the earlier response of such person is erroneous or incomplete and that such person now has correct or complete location information;

(4) not communicate by post card;

(5) not use any language or symbol on any envelope or in the contents of any communication effected by the mails or telegram that indicates that the debt collector is in the debt collection business or that the communication relates to the collection of a debt; and

(6) after the debt collector knows the consumer is represented by an attorney with regard to the subject debt and has knowledge of, or can readily ascertain, such attorney's name and address, not communicate with any person other than that attorney, unless the attorney fails to respond within a reasonable period of time to communication from the debt collector.

§ 805. Communication in Connection with Debt Collection (15 U.S.C. 1692c)

(a) Communication with the Consumer Generally. Without the prior consent of the consumer given directly to the debt collector or the express permission of a court of competent jurisdiction, a debt collector may not communicate with a consumer in connection with the collection of any debt—

(1) at any unusual time or place or a time or place known or which should be known to be inconvenient to the consumer. In the absence of knowledge of circumstances to the contrary, a debt collector shall assume that the convenient time for communicating with a consumer is after 8 o'clock antemeridian and before 9 o'clock postmeridian, local time at the consumer's location;

(2) if the debt collector knows the consumer is represented by an attorney with respect to such debt and has knowledge of, or can readily ascertain, such attorney's name and address, unless the attorney fails to respond within a reasonable period of time to a communication from the debt collector or unless the attorney consents to direct communication with the consumer; or

(3) at the consumer's place of employment if the debt collector knows or has reason to know that the consumer's employer prohibits the consumer from receiving such communication.

(b) Communication with Third Parties. Except as provided in section 1692b of this title, without the prior consent of the consumer given directly to the debt collector, or the express permission of a court of competent jurisdiction, or as reasonably necessary to effectuate a post-judgment judicial remedy, a debt collector may not communicate, in connection with the collection of any debt, with any person other than the consumer, his attorney, a consumer reporting agency if otherwise permitted by law, the creditor, the attorney of the creditor, or the attorney of the debt collector.

(c) Ceasing Communication. If a consumer notifies a debt collector in writing that the consumer refuses to pay a debt or that the consumer wishes the debt collector to cease further communication with the consumer, the debt collector shall not communicate further with the consumer with respect to such debt, except—

(1) to advise the consumer that the debt collector's further efforts are being terminated;

(2) to notify the consumer that the debt collector or creditor may invoke specified remedies which are ordinarily invoked by such debt collector or creditor; or

(3) where applicable, to notify the consumer that the debt collector or creditor intends to invoke a specified remedy.

If such notice from the consumer is made by mail, notification shall be complete upon receipt.

(d) "Consumer" Defined. For the purpose of this section, the term "consumer" includes the consumer's spouse, parent (if the consumer is a minor), guardian, executor, or administrator.

§ 806. Harassment or Abuse (15 U.S.C. 1692d)

A debt collector may not engage in any conduct the natural consequence of which is to harass, oppress, or abuse any person in connection with the collection of a debt. Without limiting the general application of the foregoing, the following conduct is a violation of this section:

(1) The use or threat of use of violence or other criminal means to harm the physical person, reputation, or property of any person.

(2) The use of obscene or profane language or language the natural consequence of which is to abuse the hearer or reader.

(3) The publication of a list of consumers who allegedly refuse to pay debts, except to a consumer reporting agency or to persons meeting the requirements of section 1681a(f) or 1681b(3) of this title.

(4) The advertisement for sale of any debt to coerce payment of the debt.

(5) Causing a telephone to ring or engaging any person in telephone conversation repeatedly or continuously with intent to annoy, abuse, or harass any person at the called number.

(6) Except as provided in section 1692b of this title, the placement of telephone calls without meaningful disclosure of the caller's identity.

§ 807. False or Misleading Representations (15 U.S.C. 1692e)

A debt collector may not use any false, deceptive, or misleading representation or means in connection with the collection of any debt. Without limiting the general application of the foregoing, the following conduct is a violation of this section:

(1) The false representation or implication that the debt collector is vouched for, bonded by, or affiliated with the United States or any State, including the use of any badge, uniform, or facsimile thereof.

(2) The false representation of—

(A) the character, amount, or legal status of any debt; or

(B) any services rendered or compensation which may be lawfully received by any debt collector for the collection of a debt.

(3) The false representation or implication that any individual is an attorney or that any communication is from an attorney.

(4) The representation or implication that nonpayment of any debt will result in the arrest or imprisonment of any person or the seizure, garnishment, attachment, or sale of any property or wages of any person unless such action is lawful and the debt collector or creditor intends to take such action.

(5) The threat to take any action that cannot legally be taken or that is not intended to be taken.

(6) The false representation or implication that a sale, referral, or other transfer of any interest in a debt shall cause the consumer to—

(A) lose any claim or defense to payment of the debt; or

(B) become subject to any practice prohibited by this subchapter.

(7) The false representation or implication that the consumer committed any crime or other conduct in order to disgrace the consumer.

(8) Communicating or threatening to communicate to any person credit information which is known or which should be known to be false, including the failure to communicate that a disputed debt is disputed.

(9) The use or distribution of any written communication which simulates or is falsely represented to be a document authorized, issued, or approved by

any court, official, or agency of the United States or any State, or which creates a false impression as to its source, authorization, or approval.

(10) The use of any false representation or deceptive means to collect or attempt to collect any debt or to obtain information concerning a consumer.

(11) The failure to disclose in the initial written communication with the consumer and, in addition, if the initial communication with the consumer is oral, in that initial oral communication, that the debt collector is attempting to collect a debt and that any information obtained will be used for that purpose, and the failure to disclose in subsequent communications that the communication is from a debt collector, except that this paragraph shall not apply to a formal pleading made in connection with a legal action.

(12) The false representation or implication that accounts have been turned over to innocent purchasers for value.

(13) The false representation or implication that documents are legal process.

(14) The use of any business, company, or organization name other than the true name of the debt collector's business, company, or organization.

(15) The false representation or implication that documents are not legal process forms or do not require action by the consumer.

(16) The false representation or implication that a debt collector operates or is employed by a consumer reporting agency as defined by section 1681a(f) of this title.

§ 808. Unfair Practices (15 U.S.C. 1692f)

A debt collector may not use unfair or unconscionable means to collect or attempt to collect any debt. Without limiting the general application of the foregoing, the following conduct is a violation of this section:

(1) The collection of any amount (including any interest, fee, charge, or expense incidental to the principal obligation) unless such amount is expressly authorized by the agreement creating the debt or permitted by law.

(2) The acceptance by a debt collector from any person of a check or other payment instrument postdated by more than five days unless such person is notified in writing of the debt collector's intent to deposit such check or instrument not more than ten nor less than three business days prior to such deposit.

(3) The solicitation by a debt collector of any postdated check or other postdated payment instrument for the purpose of threatening or instituting criminal prosecution.

(4) Depositing or threatening to deposit any postdated check or other postdated payment instrument prior to the date on such check or instrument.

(5) Causing charges to be made to any person for communications by concealment of the true purpose of the communication. Such charges include, but are not limited to, collect telephone calls and telegram fees.

(6) Taking or threatening to take any nonjudicial action to effect dispossession or disablement of property if—

(A) there is no present right to possession of the property claimed as collateral through an enforceable security interest;

(B) there is no present intention to take possession of the property; or

(C) the property is exempt by law from such dispossession or disablement.

(7) Communicating with a consumer regarding a debt by post card.

(8) Using any language or symbol, other than the debt collector's address, on any envelope when communicating with a consumer by use of the mails or by telegram, except that a debt collector may use his business name if such name does not indicate that he is in the debt collection business.

§ 809. Validation of Debts (15 U.S.C. 1692g)

(a) Within five days after the initial communication with a consumer in connection with the collection of any debt, a debt collector shall, unless the following information is contained in the initial communication or the consumer has paid the debt, send the consumer a written notice containing—

(1) the amount of the debt;

(2) the name of the creditor to whom the debt is owed;

(3) a statement that unless the consumer, within thirty days after receipt of the notice, disputes the validity of the debt, or any portion thereof, the debt will be assumed to be valid by the debt collector;

(4) a statement that if the consumer notifies the debt collector in writing within the thirty-day period that the debt, or any portion thereof, is disputed, the debt collector will obtain verification of the debt or a copy of a judgment against the consumer and a copy of such verification or judgment will be mailed to the consumer by the debt collector; and

(5) a statement that, upon the consumer's written request within the thirty-day period, the debt

collector will provide the consumer with the name and address of the original creditor, if different from the current creditor.

(b) If the consumer notifies the debt collector in writing within the thirty-day period described in subsection (a) of this section that the debt, or any portion thereof, is disputed, or that the consumer requests the name and address of the original creditor, the debt collector shall cease collection of the debt, or any disputed portion thereof, until the debt collector obtains verification of the debt or a copy of a judgment, or the name and address of the original creditor, and a copy of such verification or judgment, or name and address of the original creditor, is mailed to the consumer by the debt collector. Collection activities and communications that do not otherwise violate this subchapter may continue during the 30-day period referred to in subsection (a) of this section unless the consumer has notified the debt collector in writing that the debt, or any portion of the debt, is disputed or that the consumer requests the name and address of the original creditor. Any collection activities and communication during the 30-day period may not overshadow or be inconsistent with the disclosure of the consumer's right to dispute the debt or request the name and address of the original creditor.

(c) The failure of a consumer to dispute the validity of a debt under this section may not be construed by any court as an admission of liability by the consumer.

(d) A communication in the form of a formal pleading in a civil action shall not be treated as an initial communication for purposes of subsection (a).

(e) The sending or delivery of any form or notice which does not relate to the collection of a debt and is expressly required by the Internal Revenue Code of 1986, chapter 94 of this title [15 U.S.C.A. § 6801 et seq.], or any provision of Federal or State law relating to notice of data security breach or privacy, or any regulation prescribed under any such provision of law, shall not be treated as an initial communication in connection with debt collection for purposes of this section.

§ 810. Multiple Debts (15 U.S.C. 1692h)

If any consumer owes multiple debts and makes any single payment to any debt collector with respect to such debts, such debt collector may not apply such payment to any debt which is disputed by the consumer and, where applicable, shall apply such payment in accordance with the consumer's directions.

§ 811. Legal Actions by Debt Collectors (15 U.S.C. 1692i)

(a) Any debt collector who brings any legal action on a debt against any consumer shall—

(1) in the case of an action to enforce an interest in real property securing the consumer's obligation, bring such action only in a judicial district or similar legal entity in which such real property is located; or

(2) in the case of an action not described in paragraph (1), bring such action only in the judicial district or similar legal entity—

(A) in which such consumer signed the contract sued upon; or

(B) in which such consumer resides at the commencement of the action.

(b) Nothing in this subchapter shall be construed to authorize the bringing of legal actions by debt collectors.

§ 812. Furnishing Certain Deceptive Forms (15 U.S.C. 1692j)

(a) It is unlawful to design, compile, and furnish any form knowing that such form would be used to create the false belief in a consumer that a person other than the creditor of such consumer is participating in the collection of or in an attempt to collect a debt such consumer allegedly owes such creditor, when in fact such person is not so participating.

(b) Any person who violates this section shall be liable to the same extent and in the same manner as a debt collector is liable under section 1692k of this title for failure to comply with a provision of this subchapter.

§ 813. Civil Liability (15 U.S.C. 1692k)

(a) Except as otherwise provided by this section, any debt collector who fails to comply with any provision of this subchapter with respect to any person is liable to such person in an amount equal to the sum of—

(1) any actual damage sustained by such person as a result of such failure;

(2) (A) in the case of any action by an individual, such additional damages as the court may allow, but not exceeding $1,000; or

(B) in the case of a class action, (i) such amount for each named plaintiff as could be recovered under subparagraph (A), and (ii) such amount as the court may allow for all other class members, without regard to a minimum individual recovery, not to exceed the lesser of $500,000 or 1 per centum of the net worth of the debt collector; and

(3) in the case of any successful action to enforce the foregoing liability, the costs of the action, together with a reasonable attorney's fee as determined by the court. On a finding by the court that an action under this section was brought in bad faith and for the purpose of harassment, the court may

award to the defendant attorney's fees reasonable in relation to the work expended and costs.

(b) In determining the amount of liability in any action under subsection (a) of this section, the court shall consider, among other relevant factors—

(1) in any individual action under subsection (a)(2)(A) of this section, the frequency and persistence of noncompliance by the debt collector, the nature of such noncompliance, and the extent to which such noncompliance was intentional; or

(2) in any class action under subsection (a)(2)(B) of this section, the frequency and persistence of noncompliance by the debt collector, the nature of such noncompliance, the resources of the debt collector, the number of persons adversely affected, and the extent to which the debt collector's noncompliance was intentional.

(c) A debt collector may not be held liable in any action brought under this subchapter if the debt collector shows by a preponderance of evidence that the violation was not intentional and resulted from a bona fide error notwithstanding the maintenance of procedures reasonably adapted to avoid any such error.

(d) An action to enforce any liability created by this subchapter may be brought in any appropriate United States district court without regard to the amount in controversy, or in any other court of competent jurisdiction, within one year from the date on which the violation occurs.

(e) No provision of this section imposing any liability shall apply to any act done or omitted in good faith in conformity with any advisory opinion of the Bureau, notwithstanding that after such act or omission has occurred, such opinion is amended, rescinded, or determined by judicial or other authority to be invalid for any reason.

§ 814. Administrative Enforcement (15 U.S.C. 1692l)

(a) Federal Trade Commission

The Federal Trade Commission shall be authorized to enforce compliance with this subchapter, except to the extent that enforcement of the requirements imposed under this subchapter is specifically committed to another Government agency under any of paragraphs (1) through (5) of subsection (b), subject to subtitle B of the Consumer Financial Protection Act of 2010. For purpose of the exercise by the Federal Trade Commission of its functions and powers under the Federal Trade Commission Act (15 U.S.C. 41 et seq.), a violation of this subchapter shall be deemed an unfair or deceptive act or practice in violation of that Act. All of the functions and powers of the Federal Trade Commission under the Federal Trade Commission Act are available to the Federal Trade Commission to enforce compliance by any person with this subchapter, irrespective of whether that person is engaged in commerce or meets any other jurisdictional tests under the Federal Trade Commission Act, including the power to enforce the provisions of this subchapter, in the same manner as if the violation had been a violation of a Federal Trade Commission trade regulation rule.

(b) Applicable provisions of law

Subject to subtitle B of the Consumer Financial Protection Act of 2010, compliance with any requirements imposed under this subchapter shall be enforced under—

(1) section 8 of the Federal Deposit Insurance Act, by the appropriate Federal banking agency, as defined in section 3(q) of the Federal Deposit Insurance Act (12 U.S.C. § 1813(q)), with respect to—

(A) national banks, Federal savings associations, and Federal branches and Federal agencies of foreign banks;

(B) member banks of the Federal Reserve System (other than national banks), branches and agencies of foreign banks (other than Federal branches, Federal agencies, and insured State branches of foreign banks), commercial lending companies owned or controlled by foreign banks, and organizations operating under section 25 or 25A of the Federal Reserve Act; and

(C) banks and State savings associations insured by the Federal Deposit Insurance Corporation (other than members of the Federal Reserve System), and insured State branches of foreign banks;

(2) the Federal Credit Union Act, by the Administrator of the National Credit Union Administration with respect to any Federal credit union;

(3) subtitle IV of Title 49, by the Secretary of Transportation, with respect to all carriers subject to the jurisdiction of the Surface Transportation Board;

(4) part A of subtitle VII of Title 49, by the Secretary of Transportation with respect to any air carrier or any foreign air carrier subject to that part;

(5) the Packers and Stockyards Act, 1921 (except as provided in section 406 of that Act), by the Secretary of Agriculture with respect to any activities subject to that Act; and

(6) subtitle E of the Consumer Financial Protection Act of 2010, by the Bureau, with respect to any person subject to this subchapter.

The terms used in paragraph (1) that are not defined in this subchapter or otherwise defined in section 3(s) of the Federal Deposit Insurance Act (12 U.S.C. 1813(s)) shall have the meaning given to them in section 1(b) of the International Banking Act of 1978 (12 U.S.C. 3101).

(c) For the purpose of the exercise by any agency referred to in subsection (b) of this section of its powers under any Act referred to in that subsection, a violation of any requirement imposed under this subchapter shall be deemed to be a violation of a requirement imposed under that Act. In addition to its powers under any provision of law specifically referred to in subsection (b) of this section, each of the agencies referred to in that subsection may exercise, for the purpose of enforcing compliance with any requirement imposed under this subchapter any other authority conferred on it by law, except as provided in subsection (d).

(d) Except as provided in section 1029(a) of the Consumer Financial Protection Act of 2010, the Bureau may prescribe rules with respect to the collection of debts by debt collectors, as defined in this subchapter.

§ 815. Reports to Congress by the Bureau; Views of Other Federal Agencies (15 U.S.C. 1692m)

(a) Not later than one year after the effective date of this subchapter and at one-year intervals thereafter, the Bureau shall make reports to the Congress concerning the administration of its functions under this subchapter, including such recommendations as the Bureau deems necessary or appropriate. In addition, each report of the Bureau shall include its assessment of the extent to which compliance with this subchapter is being achieved and a summary of the enforcement actions taken by the Bureau under section 1692l of this title.

(b) In the exercise of its functions under this subchapter, the Bureau may obtain upon request the views of any other Federal agency which exercises enforcement functions under section 1692l of this title.

§ 816. Relation to State Laws (15 U.S.C. 1692n)

This subchapter does not annul, alter, or affect, or exempt any person subject to the provisions of this subchapter from complying with the laws of any State with respect to debt collection practices, except to the extent that those laws are inconsistent with any provision of this subchapter, and then only to the extent of the inconsistency. For purposes of this section, a State law is not inconsistent with this subchapter if the protection such law affords any consumer is greater than the protection provided by this subchapter.

§ 817. Exemption for State Regulation (15 U.S.C. 1692o)

The Bureau shall by regulation exempt from the requirements of this subchapter any class of debt collection practices within any State if the Bureau determines that under the law of that State that class of debt collection practices is subject to requirements substantially similar to those imposed by this subchapter, and that there is adequate provision for enforcement.

§ 818. Exception for Certain Bad Check Enforcement Programs Operated by Private Entities (15 U.S.C. 1692p)

(a) In general—

(1) Treatment of Certain Private Entities. Subject to paragraph (2), a private entity shall be excluded from the definition of a debt collector, pursuant to the exception provided in section 1692a(6) of this title, with respect to the operation by the entity of a program described in paragraph (2)(A) under a contract described in paragraph (2)(B).

(2) Conditions of Applicability. Paragraph (1) shall apply if—

(A) a State or district attorney establishes, within the jurisdiction of such State or district attorney and with respect to alleged bad check violations that do not involve a check described in subsection (b) of this section, a pretrial diversion program for alleged bad check offenders who agree to participate voluntarily in such program to avoid criminal prosecution;

(B) a private entity, that is subject to an administrative support services contract with a State or district attorney and operates under the direction, supervision, and control of such State or district attorney, operates the pretrial diversion program described in subparagraph (A); and

(C) in the course of performing duties delegated to it by a State or district attorney under the contract, the private entity referred to in subparagraph (B)—

(i) complies with the penal laws of the State;

(ii) conforms with the terms of the contract and directives of the State or district attorney;

(iii) does not exercise independent prosecutorial discretion;

(iv) contacts any alleged offender referred to in subparagraph (A) for purposes of participating in a program referred to in such paragraph—

(I) only as a result of any determination by the State or district attorney that probable cause of a bad check violation under State penal law exists, and that contact with the alleged offender for purposes of participation in the program is appropriate; and

(II) the alleged offender has failed to pay the bad check after demand for payment, pursuant to State law, is made for payment of the check amount;

(v) includes as part of an initial written communication with an alleged offender a clear and conspicuous statement that—

(I) the alleged offender may dispute the validity of any alleged bad check violation;

(II) where the alleged offender knows, or has reasonable cause to believe, that the alleged bad check violation is the result of theft or forgery of the check, identity theft, or other fraud that is not the result of the conduct of the alleged offender, the alleged offender may file a crime report with the appropriate law enforcement agency; and

(III) if the alleged offender notifies the private entity or the district attorney in writing, not later than 30 days after being contacted for the first time pursuant to clause (iv), that there is a dispute pursuant to this subsection, before further restitution efforts are pursued, the district attorney or an employee of the district attorney authorized to make such a determination makes a determination that there is probable cause to believe that a crime has been committed; and

(vi) charges only fees in connection with services under the contract that have been authorized by the contract with the State or district attorney.

(b) Certain checks excluded.—A check is described in this subsection if the check involves, or is subsequently found to involve—

(1) a postdated check presented in connection with a payday loan, or other similar transaction, where the payee of the check knew that the issuer had insufficient funds at the time the check was made, drawn, or delivered;

(2) a stop payment order where the issuer acted in good faith and with reasonable cause in stopping payment on the check;

(3) a check dishonored because of an adjustment to the issuer's account by the financial institution holding such account without providing notice to the person at the time the check was made, drawn, or delivered;

(4) a check for partial payment of a debt where the payee had previously accepted partial payment for such debt;

(5) a check issued by a person who was not competent, or was not of legal age, to enter into a legal contractual obligation at the time the check was made, drawn, or delivered; or

(6) a check issued to pay an obligation arising from a transaction that was illegal in the jurisdiction of the State or district attorney at the time the check was made, drawn, or delivered.

(c) Definitions.—For purposes of this section, the following definitions shall apply:

(1) State or District Attorney.—The term "State or district attorney" means the chief elected or appointed prosecuting attorney in a district, county (as defined in section 2 of title 1, United States Code), municipality, or comparable jurisdiction, including State attorneys general who act as chief elected or appointed prosecuting attorneys in a district, county (as so defined), municipality or comparable jurisdiction, who may be referred to by a variety of titles such as district attorneys, prosecuting attorneys, commonwealth's attorneys, solicitors, county attorneys, and state's attorneys, and who are responsible for the prosecution of State crimes and violations of jurisdiction-specific local ordinances.

(2) Check.—The term "check" has the same meaning as in section 5002(6) of Title 12.

(3) Bad Check Violation.—The term "bad check violation" means a violation of the applicable State criminal law relating to the writing of dishonored checks.

§ 819. Effective Date (15 U.S.C. 1692 note)

This title takes effect upon the expiration of six months after the date of its enactment, but section 809 shall apply only with respect to debts for which the initial attempt to collect occurs after such effective date.

Electronic Fund Transfers Act

15 U.S.C. §§ 1693 et seq.

Section

§ 902 [15 U.S.C. § 1693]. Congressional Findings and Declaration of Purpose

(a) Rights and liabilities undefined. The Congress finds that the use of electronic systems to transfer funds provides the potential for substantial benefits to consumers. However, due to the unique characteristics of such systems, the application of existing consumer protection legislation is unclear, leaving the rights and liabilities of consumers, financial institutions, and intermediaries in electronic fund transfers undefined.

(b) Purposes. It is the purpose of this subchapter to provide a basic framework establishing the rights, liabilities, and responsibilities of participants in electronic fund and remittance transfer systems. The primary objective of this subchapter, however, is the provision of individual consumer rights.

§ 903 [15 U.S.C. § 1693a]. Definitions

As used in this subchapter—

(1) the term "accepted card or other means of access" means a card, code, or other means of access to a consumer's account for the purpose of initiating electronic fund transfers when the person to whom such card or other means of access was issued has requested and received or has signed or has used, or authorized another to use, such card or other means of access for the purpose of transferring money between accounts or obtaining money, property, labor, or services;

(2) the term "account" means a demand deposit, savings deposit, or other asset account (other than an occasional or incidental credit balance in an open end credit plan as defined in section 1602(i) of this title), as described in regulations of the Bureau, established primarily for personal, family, or household purposes, but such term does not include an account held by a financial institution pursuant to a bona fide trust agreement;

[(3)] the term "Board" means the Board of Governors of the Federal Reserve System;

(4) the term 'Bureau' means the Bureau of Consumer Financial Protection;

(5) the term "business day" means any day on which the offices of the consumer's financial institution involved in an electronic fund transfer are open to the public for carrying on substantially all of its business functions;

(6) the term "consumer" means a natural person;

(7) the term "electronic fund transfer" means any transfer of funds, other than a transaction originated by check, draft, or similar paper instrument, which is initiated through an electronic terminal,

telephonic instrument, or computer or magnetic tape so as to order, instruct, or authorize a financial institution to debit or credit an account. Such term includes, but is not limited to, point-of-sale transfers, automated teller machine transactions, direct deposits or withdrawals of funds, and transfers initiated by telephone. Such term does not include—

(A) any check guarantee or authorization service which does not directly result in a debit or credit to a consumer's account[;]

(B) any transfer of funds, other than those processed by automated clearinghouse, made by a financial institution on behalf of a consumer by means of a service that transfers funds held at either Federal Reserve banks or other depository institutions and which is not designed primarily to transfer funds on behalf of a consumer;

(C) any transaction the primary purpose of which is the purchase or sale of securities or commodities through a broker-dealer registered with or regulated by the Securities and Exchange Commission.

(D) any automatic transfer from a savings account to a demand deposit account pursuant to an agreement between a consumer and a financial institution for the purpose of covering an overdraft or maintaining an agreed upon minimum balance in the consumer's demand deposit account; or

(E) any transfer of funds which is initiated by a telephone conversation between a consumer and an officer or employee of a financial institution which is not pursuant to a prearranged plan and under which periodic or recurring transfers are not contemplated;

as determined under regulations of the Bureau;

(8) the term "electronic terminal" means an electronic device, other than a telephone operated by a consumer, through which a consumer may initiate an electronic fund transfer. Such term includes, but is not limited to, point-of-sale terminals, automated teller machines, and cash dispensing machines;

(9) the term "financial institution" means a State or National bank, a State or Federal savings and loan association, a mutual savings bank, a State or Federal credit union, or any other person who, directly or indirectly, holds an account belonging to a consumer;

(10) the term "preauthorized electronic fund transfer" means an electronic fund transfer authorized in advance to recur at substantially regular intervals;

(11) the term "State" means any State, territory, or possession of the United States, the District of Columbia, the Commonwealth of Puerto Rico, or any political subdivision of any of the foregoing; and

(12) the term "unauthorized electronic fund transfer" means an electronic fund transfer from a consumer's account initiated by a person other than the consumer without actual authority to initiate such transfer and from which the consumer receives no benefit, but the term does not include any electronic fund transfer.

(A) initiated by a person other than the consumer who was furnished with the card, code, or other means of access to such consumer's account by such consumer, unless the consumer has notified the financial institution involved that transfers by such other person are no longer authorized,

(B) initiated with fraudulent intent by the consumer or any person acting in concert with the consumer, or

(C) which constitutes an error committed by a financial institution.

§ 904 [15 U.S.C. § 1693b]. Regulations

(a) Prescription by the Bureau and the Board.

(1) In General.—Except as provided in paragraph (2), the Bureau shall prescribe rules to carry out the purposes of this subchapter.

(2) Authority of the Board.—The Board shall have sole authority to prescribe rules—

(A) to carry out the purposes of this subchapter with respect to a person described in section 5519(a) of title 12; and

(B) to carry out the purposes of section 1693o–2 of this title.

In prescribing such regulations, the Board shall:

(1) consult with the other agencies referred to in section 1693o of this title and take into account, and allow for, the continuing evolution of electronic banking services and the technology utilized in such services,

(2) prepare an analysis of economic impact which considers the costs and benefits to financial institutions, consumers, and other users of electronic fund transfers, including the extent to which additional documentation, reports, records, or other paper work would be required, and the effects upon competition in the provision of electronic banking services among large and small financial institutions and the availability of such services to different

classes of consumers, particularly low income consumers,

(3) to the extent practicable, the Board shall demonstrate that the consumer protections of the proposed regulations outweigh the compliance costs imposed upon consumers and financial institutions, and

(4) any proposed regulations and accompanying analyses shall be sent promptly to Congress by the Board.

(b) Issuance of model clauses. The Bureau shall issue model clauses for optional use by financial institutions to facilitate compliance with the disclosure requirements of section 1693c of this title and to aid consumers in understanding the rights and responsibilities of participants in electronic fund transfers by utilizing readily understandable language. Such model clauses shall be adopted after notice duly given in the Federal Register and opportunity for public comment in accordance with section 553 of title 5. With respect to the disclosures required by section 1693c(a)(3) and (4) of this title, the Bureau shall take account of variations in the services and charges under different electronic fund transfer systems and, as appropriate, shall issue alternative model clauses for disclosure of these differing account terms.

(c) Criteria; modification of requirements. Regulations prescribed hereunder may contain such classifications, differentiations, or other provisions, and may provide for such adjustments and exceptions for any class of electronic fund transfers or remittance transfers, as in the judgment of the Bureau are necessary or proper to effectuate the purposes of this subchapter, to prevent circumvention or evasion thereof, or to facilitate compliance therewith. The Bureau shall by regulation modify the requirements imposed by this subchapter on small financial institutions if the Bureau determines that such modifications are necessary to alleviate any undue compliance burden on small financial institutions and such modifications are consistent with the purpose and objective of this subchapter.

(d) Applicability to service providers other than certain financial institutions

(1) In general. If electronic fund transfer services are made available to consumers by a person other than a financial institution holding a consumer's account, the Bureau shall by regulation assure that the disclosures, protections, responsibilities, and remedies created by this subchapter are made applicable to such persons and services.

(2) State and local government electronic benefit transfer systems

(A) "Electronic benefit transfer system" defined. In this paragraph, the term "electronic benefit transfer system"—

(i) means a system under which a government agency distributes needs-tested benefits by establishing accounts that may be accessed by recipients electronically, such as through automated teller machines or point-of-sale terminals; and

(ii) does not include employment-related payments, including salaries and pension, retirement, or unemployment benefits established by a Federal, State, or local government agency.

(B) Exemption generally. The disclosures, protections, responsibilities, and remedies established under this subchapter, and any regulation prescribed or order issued by the Bureau in accordance with this subchapter, shall not apply to any electronic benefit transfer system established under State or local law or administered by a State or local government.

(C) Exception for direct deposit into recipient's account. Subparagraph (B) shall not apply with respect to any electronic funds transfer under an electronic benefit transfer system for a deposit directly into a consumer account held by the recipient of the benefit.

(D) Rule of construction. No provision of this paragraph—

(i) affects or alters the protections otherwise applicable with respect to benefits established by any other provision [of] Federal, State, or local law; or

(ii) otherwise supersedes the application of any State or local law.

(3) Fee disclosures at automated teller machines

(A) In general. The regulations prescribed under paragraph (1) shall require any automated teller machine operator who imposes a fee on any consumer for providing host transfer services to such consumer to provide notice in accordance with subparagraph (B) to the consumer (at the time the service is provided) of—

(i) the fact that a fee is imposed by such operator for providing the service; and

(ii) the amount of any such fee.

(B) Notice requirement. The notice required under clauses (i) and (ii) of subparagraph (A) with respect to any fee described in such subparagraph shall appear on the screen of the automated teller machine, or on a paper notice issued from such machine, after the transaction is initiated and before the consumer is irrevocably committed to completing the transaction.

(C) Prohibition on fees not properly disclosed and explicitly assumed by consumer. No fee may be imposed by any automated teller machine operator in connection with any electronic fund transfer initiated by a consumer for which a notice is required under subparagraph (A), unless—

(i) the consumer receives such notice in accordance with subparagraph (B); and

(ii) the consumer elects to continue in the manner necessary to effect the transaction after receiving such notice.

(D) Definitions. For purposes of this paragraph, the following definitions shall apply:

(i) Automated teller machine operator. The term "automated teller machine operator" means any person who—

(I) operates an automated teller machine at which consumers initiate electronic fund transfers; and

(II) is not the financial institution that holds the account of such consumer from which the transfer is made.

(ii) Electronic fund transfer. The term "electronic fund transfer" includes a transaction that involves a balance inquiry initiated by a consumer in the same manner as an electronic fund transfer, whether or not the consumer initiates a transfer of funds in the course of the transaction.

(iii) Host transfer services. The term "host transfer services" means any electronic fund transfer made by an automated teller machine operator in connection with a transaction initiated by a consumer at an automated teller machine operated by such operator.

(e) Deference.—No provision of this subchapter may be construed as altering, limiting, or otherwise affecting the deference that a court affords to—

(1) the Bureau in making determinations regarding the meaning or interpretation of any provision of this subchapter for which the Bureau has the authority to prescribe regulations; or

(2) the Board in making determinations regarding the meaning or interpretation of section 1693o–2 of this title.

§ 905 [15 U.S.C. § 1693c]. Terms and Conditions of Transfers

(a) Disclosures; time; form; contents. The terms and conditions of electronic fund transfers involving a consumer's account shall be disclosed at the time the consumer contracts for an electronic fund transfer service, in accordance with regulations of the Bureau. Such disclosures shall be in readily understandable language and shall include, to the extent applicable—

(1) the consumer's liability for unauthorized electronic fund transfers and, at the financial institution's option, notice of the advisability of prompt reporting of any loss, theft, or unauthorized use of a card, code, or other means of access;

(2) the telephone number and address of the person or office to be notified in the event the consumer believes tha[t] an unauthorized electronic fund transfer has been or may be effected;

(3) the type and nature of electronic fund transfers which the consumer may initiate, including any limitations on the frequency or dollar amount of such transfers, except that the details of such limitations need not be disclosed if their confidentiality is necessary to maintain the security of an electronic fund transfer system, as determined by the Bureau;

(4) any charges for electronic fund transfers or for the right to make such transfers;

(5) the consumer's right to stop payment of a preauthorized electronic fund transfer and the procedure to initiate such a stop payment order;

(6) the consumer's right to receive documentation of electronic fund transfers under section 1693d of this title;

(7) a summary, in a form prescribed by regulations of the Bureau, of the error resolution provisions of section 1693f of this title and the consumer's rights thereunder. The financial institution shall thereafter transmit such summary at least once per calendar year;

(8) the financial institution's liability to the consumer under section 1693h of this title;

(9) under what circumstances the financial institution will in the ordinary course of business disclose information concerning the consumer's account to third persons; and

(10) a notice to the consumer that a fee may be imposed by—

(A) an automated teller machine operator (as defined in section 1693b(d)(3)(D)(i) of this title) if the consumer initiates a transfer from an automated teller machine that is not operated by the person issuing the card or other means of access; and

(B) any national, regional, or local network utilized to effect the transaction.

(b) Notification of changes to consumer. A financial institution shall notify a consumer in writing at least twenty-one days prior to the effective date of any change in any term or condition of the consumer's account required to be disclosed under subsection (a) if such change would result in greater cost or liability for such consumer or decreased access to the consumer's account. A financial institution may, however, implement a change in the terms or conditions of an account without prior notice when such change is immediately necessary to maintain or restore the security of an electronic fund transfer system or a consumer's account. Subject to subsection (a)(3), the Bureau shall require subsequent notification if such a change is made permanent.

(c) Time for disclosures respecting accounts accessible prior to effective date of this subchapter. For any account of a consumer made accessible to electronic fund transfers prior to the effective date of this subchapter, the information required to be disclosed to the consumer under subsection (a) shall be disclosed not later than the earlier of—

(1) the first periodic statement required by section 1693d(c) of this title after the effective date of this subchapter; or

(2) thirty days after the effective date of this subchapter.

§ 906 [15 U.S.C. § 1693d]. Documentation of Transfers

(a) Availability of written documentation to consumer; contents. For each electronic fund transfer initiated by a consumer from an electronic terminal, the financial institution holding such consumer's account shall, directly or indirectly, at the time the transfer is initiated, make available to the consumer written documentation of such transfer. The documentation shall clearly set forth to the extent applicable—

(1) the amount involved and date the transfer is initiated;

(2) the type of transfer;

(3) the identity of the consumer's account with the financial institution from which or to which funds are transferred;

(4) the identity of any third party to whom or from whom funds are transferred; and

(5) the location or identification of the electronic terminal involved.

(b) Notice of credit to consumer. For a consumer's account which is scheduled to be credited by a preauthorized electronic fund transfer from the same payor at least once in each successive sixty-day period, except where the payor provides positive notice of the transfer to the consumer, the financial institution shall elect to provide promptly either positive notice to the consumer when the credit is made as scheduled, or negative notice to the consumer when the credit is not made as scheduled, in accordance with regulations of the Board. The means of notice elected shall be disclosed to the consumer in accordance with section 1693c of this title.

(c) Periodic statement; contents. A financial institution shall provide each consumer with a periodic statement for each account of such consumer that may be accessed by means of an electronic fund transfer. Except as provided in subsections (d) and (e), such statement shall be provided at least monthly for each monthly or shorter cycle in which an electronic fund transfer affecting the account has occurred, or every three months, whichever is more frequent. The statement, which may include information regarding transactions other than electronic fund transfers, shall clearly set forth—

(1) with regard to each electronic fund transfer during the period, the information described in subsection (a), which may be provided on an accompanying document;

(2) the amount of any fee or charge assessed by the financial institution during the period for electronic fund transfers or for account maintenance;

(3) the balances in the consumer's account at the beginning of the period and at the close of the period; and

(4) the address and telephone number to be used by the financial institution for the purpose of receiving any statement inquiry or notice of account error from the consumer. Such address and telephone number shall be preceded by the caption "Direct Inquiries To:" or other similar language indicating that the address and number are to be used for such inquiries or notices.

(d) Consumer passbook accounts. In the case of a consumer's passbook account which may not be accessed by electronic fund transfers other than preauthorized electronic fund transfers crediting the account, a financial institution may, in lieu of complying with the requirements of subsection (c), upon presentation of the passbook provide the consumer in writing with the amount and date of each such transfer involving the account since the passbook was last presented.

(e) Accounts other than passbook accounts. In the case of a consumer's account, other than a passbook account, which may not be accessed by electronic fund transfers other than preauthorized electronic fund transfers crediting the account, the financial institution may provide a periodic statement on a quarterly basis which otherwise complies with the requirements of subsection (c).

(f) Documentation as evidence. In any action involving a consumer, any documentation required by this section to be given to the consumer which indicates that an electronic fund transfer was made to another person shall be admissible as evidence of such transfer and shall constitute prima facie proof that such transfer was made.

§ 907 [15 U.S.C. § 1693e]. Preauthorized Transfers

(a) A preauthorized electronic fund transfer from a consumer's account may be authorized by the consumer only in writing, and a copy of such authorization shall be provided to the consumer when made. A consumer may stop payment of a preauthorized electronic fund transfer by notifying the financial institution orally or in writing at any time up to three business days preceding the scheduled date of such transfer. The financial institution may require written confirmation to be provided to it within fourteen days of an oral notification if, when the oral notification is made, the consumer is advised of such requirement and the address to which such confirmation should be sent.

(b) In the case of preauthorized transfers from a consumer's account to the same person which may vary in amount, the financial institution or designated payee shall, prior to each transfer, provide reasonable advance notice to the consumer, in accordance with regulations of the Bureau, of the amount to be transferred and the scheduled date of the transfer.

§ 908 [15 U.S.C. § 1693f]. Error Resolution

(a) Notification to financial institution of error. If a financial institution, within sixty days after having transmitted to a consumer documentation pursuant to section 1693d(a), (c), or (d) of this title or notification pursuant to section 1693d(b) of this title, receives oral or written notice in which the consumer—

(1) sets forth or otherwise enables the financial institution to identify the name and account number of the consumer;

(2) indicates the consumer's belief that the documentation, or, in the case of notification pursuant to section 1693d(b) of this title, the consumer's account, contains an error and the amount of such error; and

(3) sets forth the reasons for the consumer's belief (where applicable) that an error has occurred,

the financial institution shall investigate the alleged error, determine whether an error has occurred, and report or mail the results of such investigation and determination to the consumer within ten business days. The financial institution may require written confirmation to be provided to it within ten business days of an oral notification of error if, when the oral notification is made, the consumer is advised of such requirement and the address to which such confirmation should be sent. A financial institution which requires written confirmation in accordance with the previous sentence need not provisionally recredit a consumer's account in accordance with subsection (c), nor shall the financial institution be liable under subsection (e) if the written confirmation is not received within the ten-day period referred to in the previous sentence.

(b) Correction of error; interest. If the financial institution determines that an error did occur, it shall promptly, but in no event more than one business day after such determination, correct the error, subject to section 1693g of this title, including the crediting of interest where applicable.

(c) Provisional recredit of consumer's account. If a financial institution receives notice of an error in the manner and within the time period specified in subsection (a), it may, in lieu of the requirements of subsections (a) and (b), within ten business days after receiving such notice provisionally recredit the consumer's account for the amount alleged to be in error, subject to section 1693g of this title, including interest where applicable, pending the conclusion of its investigation and its determination of whether an error has occurred.

Such investigation shall be concluded not later than forty-five days after receipt of notice of the error. During the pendency of the investigation, the consumer shall have full use of the funds provisionally recredited.

(d) Absence of error; finding; explanation. If the financial institution determines after its investigation pursuant to subsection (a) or (c) that an error did not occur, it shall deliver or mail to the consumer an explanation of its findings within 3 business days after the conclusion of its investigation, and upon request of the consumer promptly deliver or mail to the consumer reproductions of all documents which the financial institution relied on to conclude that such error did not occur. The financial institution shall include notice of the right to request reproductions with the explanation of its findings.

(e) Treble damages. If in any action under section 1693m of this title, the court finds that—

(1) the financial institution did not provisionally recredit a consumer's account within the ten-day period specified in subsection (c), and the financial institution

(A) did not make a good faith investigation of the alleged error, or

(B) did not have a reasonable basis for believing that the consumer's account was not in error; or

(2) the financial institution knowingly and willfully concluded that the consumer's account was not in error when such conclusion could not reasonably have been drawn from the evidence available to the financial institution at the time of its investigation, then the consumer shall be entitled to treble damages determined under section 1693m(a)(1) of this title.

(f) Acts constituting error. For the purpose of this section, an error consists of—

(1) an unauthorized electronic fund transfer;

(2) an incorrect electronic fund transfer from or to the consumer's account;

(3) the omission from a periodic statement of an electronic fund transfer affecting the consumer's account which should have been included;

(4) a computational error by the financial institution;

(5) the consumer's receipt of an incorrect amount of money from an electronic terminal;

(6) a consumer's request for additional information or clarification concerning an electronic fund transfer or any documentation required by this subchapter; or

(7) any other error described in regulations of the Bureau.

§ 909 [15 U.S.C. § 1693g]. Consumer Liability

(a) Unauthorized electronic fund transfers; limit. A consumer shall be liable for any unauthorized electronic fund transfer involving the account of such consumer only if the card or other means of access utilized for such transfer was an accepted card or other means of access and if the issuer of such card, code, or other means of access has provided a means whereby the user of such card, code, or other means of access can be identified as the person authorized to use it, such as by signature, photograph, or fingerprint or by electronic or mechanical confirmation. In no event, however, shall a consumer's liability for an unauthorized transfer exceed the lesser of—

(1) $50; or

(2) the amount of money or value of property or services obtained in such unauthorized electronic fund transfer prior to the time the financial institution is notified of, or otherwise becomes aware of, circumstances which lead to the reasonable belief that an unauthorized electronic fund transfer involving the consumer's account has been or may be effected. Notice under this paragraph is sufficient when such steps have been taken as may be reasonably required in the ordinary course of business to provide the financial institution with the pertinent information, whether or not any particular officer, employee, or agent of the financial institution does in fact receive such information.

Notwithstanding the foregoing, reimbursement need not be made to the consumer for losses the financial institution establishes would not have occurred but for the failure of the consumer to report within sixty days of transmittal of the statement (or in extenuating circumstances such as extended travel or hospitalization, within a reasonable time under the circumstances) any unauthorized electronic fund transfer or account error which appears on the periodic statement provided to the consumer under section 1693d of this title. In addition, reimbursement need not be made to the consumer for losses which the financial institution establishes would not have occurred but for the failure of the consumer to report any loss or theft of a card or other means of access within two business days after the consumer learns of the loss or theft (or in extenuating circumstances such as extended travel or hospitalization, within a longer period which is reasonable under the circumstances), but the consumer's liability under this subsection in any such case may not exceed a total of $500, or the amount of unauthorized electronic fund transfers which occur following the close of two business days (or such longer period) after the consumer learns of the loss or theft but prior to notice to the financial institution under this subsection, whichever is less.

(b) Burden of proof. In any action which involves a consumer's liability for an unauthorized electronic fund transfer, the burden of proof is upon the financial institution to show that the electronic fund transfer was authorized or, if the electronic fund transfer was unauthorized, then the burden of proof is upon the financial institution to establish that the conditions of liability set forth in subsection (a) have been met, and, if the transfer was initiated after the effective date of section 1693c of this title, that the disclosures required to be made to the consumer under section 1693c(a)(1) and (2) of this title were in fact made in accordance with such section.

(c) Determination of limitation on liability. In the event of a transaction which involves both an unauthorized electronic fund transfer and an extension of credit as defined in section 1602(e) of this title pursuant to an agreement between the consumer and the financial institution to extend such credit to the consumer in the event the consumer's account is overdrawn, the limitation on the consumer's liability for such transaction shall be determined solely in accordance with this section.

(d) Restriction on liability. Nothing in this section imposes liability upon a consumer for an unauthorized electronic fund transfer in excess of his liability for such a transfer under other applicable law or under any agreement with the consumer's financial institution.

(e) Scope of liability. Except as provided in this section, a consumer incurs no liability from an unauthorized electronic fund transfer.

§ 910 [15 U.S.C. § 1693h]. Liability of Financial Institutions

(a) Action or failure to act proximately causing damages. Subject to subsections (b) and (c), a financial institution shall be liable to a consumer for all damages proximately caused by—

(1) the financial institution's failure to make an electronic fund transfer, in accordance with the terms and conditions of an account, in the correct amount or in a timely manner when properly instructed to do so by the consumer, except where—

(A) the consumer's account has insufficient funds;

(B) the funds are subject to legal process or other encumbrance restricting such transfer;

(C) such transfer would exceed an established credit limit;

(D) an electronic terminal has insufficient cash to complete the transaction; or

(E) as otherwise provided in regulations of the Bureau;

(2) the financial institution's failure to make an electronic fund transfer due to insufficient funds when the financial institution failed to credit, in accordance with the terms and conditions of an account, a deposit of funds to the consumer's account which would have provided sufficient funds to make the transfer, and

(3) the financial institution's failure to stop payment of a preauthorized transfer from a consumer's account when instructed to do so in accordance with the terms and conditions of the account.

(b) Acts of God and technical malfunctions. A financial institution shall not be liable under subsection (a)(1) or (2) if the financial institution shows by a preponderance of the evidence that its action or failure to act resulted from—

(1) an act of God or other circumstance beyond its control, that it exercised reasonable care to prevent such an occurrence, and that it exercised such diligence as the circumstances required; or

(2) a technical malfunction which was known to the consumer at the time he attempted to initiate an electronic fund transfer or, in the case of a preauthorized transfer, at the time such transfer should have occurred.

(c) Intent. In the case of a failure described in subsection (a) which was not intentional and which resulted from a bona fide error, notwithstanding the maintenance of procedures reasonably adapted to avoid any such error, the financial institution shall be liable for actual damages proved.

(d) Exception for damaged notices. If the notice required to be posted pursuant to section 1693b(d)(3)(B)(i) of this title by an automated teller machine operator has been posted by such operator in compliance with such section and the notice is subsequently removed, damaged, or altered by any person other than the operator of the automated teller machine, the operator shall have no liability under this section for failure to comply with section 1693b(d)(3)(B)(i) of this title.

§ 911 [15 U.S.C. § 1693i]. Issuance of Cards or Other Means of Access

(a) Prohibition; proper issuance. No person may issue to a consumer any card, code, or other means of access to such consumer's account for the purpose of initiating an electronic fund transfer other than—

(1) in response to a request or application therefor; or

(2) as a renewal of, or in substitution for, an accepted card, code, or other means of access, whether issued by the initial issuer or a successor.

(b) Exceptions. Notwithstanding the provisions of subsection (a), a person may distribute to a consumer on an unsolicited basis a card, code, or other means of access for use in initiating an electronic fund transfer from such consumer's account, if—

(1) such card, code, or other means of access is not validated;

(2) such distribution is accompanied by a complete disclosure, in accordance with section 1693c of this title, of the consumer's rights and liabilities which will apply if such card, code, or other means of access is validated;

(3) such distribution is accompanied by a clear explanation, in accordance with regulations of the

Bureau, that such card, code, or other means of access is not validated and how the consumer may dispose of such code, card, or other means of access if validation is not desired; and

(4) such card, code, or other means of access is validated only in response to a request or application from the consumer, upon verification of the consumer's identity.

(c) Validation. For the purpose of subsection (b), a card, code, or other means of access is validated when it may be used to initiate an electronic fund transfer.

§ 912 [15 U.S.C. § 1693j]. Suspension of Obligations

If a system malfunction prevents the effectuation of an electronic fund transfer initiated by a consumer to another person, and such other person has agreed to accept payment by such means, the consumer's obligation to the other person shall be suspended until the malfunction is corrected and the electronic fund transfer may be completed, unless such other person has subsequently, by written request, demanded payment by means other than an electronic fund transfer.

§ 913 [15 U.S.C. § 1693k]. Compulsory Use of Electronic Fund Transfers

No person may—

(1) condition the extension of credit to a consumer on such consumer's repayment by means of preauthorized electronic fund transfers; or

(2) require a consumer to establish an account for receipt of electronic fund transfers with a particular financial institution as a condition of employment or receipt of a government benefit.

§ 914 [15 U.S.C. § 1693l]. Waiver of Rights

No writing or other agreement between a consumer and any other person may contain any provision which constitutes a waiver of any right conferred or cause of action created by this subchapter. Nothing in this section prohibits, however, any writing or other agreement which grants to a consumer a more extensive right or remedy or greater protection than contained in this subchapter or a waiver given in settlement of a dispute or action.

§ 915 [15 U.S.C. § 1693l-1]. General-Use Prepaid Cards, Gift Certificates, and Store Gift Cards

(a) Definitions.—In this section, the following definitions shall apply:

(1) Dormancy fee; inactivity charge or fee.—The terms "dormancy fee" and "inactivity charge or fee" mean a fee, charge, or penalty for non-use or inactivity of a gift certificate, store gift card, or general-use prepaid card.

(2) General use prepaid card, gift certificate, and store gift card.—

(A) General-use prepaid card.—The term "general-use prepaid card" means a card or other payment code or device issued by any person that is—

(i) redeemable at multiple, unaffiliated merchants or service providers, or automated teller machines;

(ii) issued in a requested amount, whether or not that amount may, at the option of the issuer, be increased in value or reloaded if requested by the holder;

(iii) purchased or loaded on a prepaid basis; and

(iv) honored, upon presentation, by merchants for goods or services, or at automated teller machines.

(B) Gift certificate.—The term "gift certificate" means an electronic promise that is—

(i) redeemable at a single merchant or an affiliated group of merchants that share the same name, mark, or logo;

(ii) issued in a specified amount that may not be increased or reloaded;

(iii) purchased on a prepaid basis in exchange for payment; and

(iv) honored upon presentation by such single merchant or affiliated group of merchants for goods or services.

(C) Store gift card.—The term "store gift card" means an electronic promise, plastic card, or other payment code or device that is—

(i) redeemable at a single merchant or an affiliated group of merchants that share the same name, mark, or logo;

(ii) issued in a specified amount, whether or not that amount may be increased in value or reloaded at the request of the holder;

(iii) purchased on a prepaid basis in exchange for payment; and

(iv) honored upon presentation by such single merchant or affiliated group of merchants for goods or services.

(D) Exclusions.—The terms "general-use prepaid card", "gift certificate", and "store gift card" do not include an electronic promise, plastic card, or payment code or device that is—

(i) used solely for telephone services;

(ii) reloadable and not marketed or labeled as a gift card or gift certificate;

(iii) a loyalty, award, or promotional gift card, as defined by the Bureau;

(iv) not marketed to the general public;

(v) issued in paper form only (including for tickets and events); or

(vi) redeemable solely for admission to events or venues at a particular location or group of affiliated locations, which may also include services or goods obtainable—

(I) at the event or venue after admission; or

(II) in conjunction with admission to such events or venues, at specific locations affiliated with and in geographic proximity to the event or venue.

(3) Service fee.—

(A) In general.—The term "service fee" means a periodic fee, charge, or penalty for holding or use of a gift certificate, store gift card, or general-use prepaid card.

(B) Exclusion.—With respect to a general-use prepaid card, the term "service fee" does not include a one-time initial issuance fee.

(b) Prohibition on imposition of fees or charges.—

(1) In general.—Except as provided under paragraphs (2) through (4), it shall be unlawful for any person to impose a dormancy fee, an inactivity charge or fee, or a service fee with respect to a gift certificate, store gift card, or general-use prepaid card.

(2) Exceptions.—A dormancy fee, inactivity charge or fee, or service fee may be charged with respect to a gift certificate, store gift card, or general-use prepaid card, if—

(A) there has been no activity with respect to the certificate or card in the 12-month period ending on the date on which the charge or fee is imposed;

(B) the disclosure requirements of paragraph (3) have been met;

(C) not more than one fee may be charged in any given month; and

(D) any additional requirements that the Bureau may establish through rulemaking under subsection (d) have been met.

(3) Disclosure requirements.—The disclosure requirements of this paragraph are met if—

(A) the gift certificate, store gift card, or general-use prepaid card clearly and conspicuously states—

(i) that a dormancy fee, inactivity charge or fee, or service fee may be charged;

(ii) the amount of such fee or charge;

(iii) how often such fee or charge may be assessed; and

(iv) that such fee or charge may be assessed for inactivity; and

(B) the issuer or vendor of such certificate or card informs the purchaser of such charge or fee before such certificate or card is purchased, regardless of whether the certificate or card is purchased in person, over the Internet, or by telephone.

(4) Exclusion.—The prohibition under paragraph (1) shall not apply to any gift certificate—

(A) that is distributed pursuant to an award, loyalty, or promotional program, as defined by the Bureau; and

(B) with respect to which, there is no money or other value exchanged.

(c) Prohibition on sale of gift cards with expiration dates.—

(1) In general.—Except as provided under paragraph (2), it shall be unlawful for any person to sell or issue a gift certificate, store gift card, or general-use prepaid card that is subject to an expiration date.

(2) Exceptions.—A gift certificate, store gift card, or general-use prepaid card may contain an expiration date if—

(A) the expiration date is not earlier than 5 years after the date on which the gift certificate was issued, or the date on which card funds were last loaded to a store gift card or general-use prepaid card; and (B) the terms of expiration are clearly and conspicuously stated.

(d) Additional rulemaking.—

(1) In general.—The Bureau shall—

(A) prescribe regulations to carry out this section, in addition to any other rules or regulations required by this subchapter, including such additional requirements as appropriate relating to the amount of dormancy fees, inactivity charges or fees, or service fees that may be assessed and the amount of remaining value of a gift certificate, store gift card, or general-use prepaid card below which such charges or fees may be assessed; and

(B) shall determine the extent to which the individual definitions and provisions of this subchapter or Regulation E should apply to general-use prepaid cards, gift certificates, and store gift cards.

(2) Consultation.—In prescribing regulations under this subsection, the Bureau shall consult with the Federal Trade Commission.

(3) Timing; effective date.—The regulations required by this subsection shall be issued in final form not later than 9 months after May 22, 2009.

§ 916 [15 U.S.C. § 1693m]. Civil Liability

(a) Individual or class action for damages; amount of award. Except as otherwise provided by this section and section 1693h of this title, any person who fails to comply with any provision of this subchapter with respect to any consumer, except for an error resolved in accordance with section 1693f of this title, is liable to such consumer in an amount equal to the sum of—

(1) any actual damage sustained by such consumer as a result of such failure;

(2) (A) in the case of an individual action, an amount not less than $100 nor greater than $1,000; or

(B) in the case of a class action, such amount as the court may allow, except that

(i) as to each member of the class no minimum recovery shall be applicable, and

(ii) the total recovery under this subparagraph in any class action or series of class actions arising out of the same failure to comply by the same person shall not be more than the lesser of $500,000 or 1 per centum of the net worth of the defendant; and

(3) in the case of any successful action to enforce the foregoing liability, the costs of the action, together with a reasonable attorney's fee as determined by the court.

(b) Factors determining amount of award. In determining the amount of liability in any action under subsection (a), the court shall consider, among other relevant factors—

(1) in any individual action under subsection (a)(2)(A), the frequency and persistence of noncompliance, the nature of such noncompliance, and the extent to which the noncompliance was intentional; or

(2) in any class action under subsection (a)(2)(B), the frequency and persistence of noncompliance, the nature of such noncompliance, the resources of the defendant, the number of persons adversely affected, and the extent to which the noncompliance was intentional.

(c) Unintentional violations; bona fide error. Except as provided in section 1693h of this title, a person may not be held liable in any action brought under this section for a violation of this subchapter if the person shows by a preponderance of evidence that the violation was not intentional and resulted from a bona fide error notwithstanding the maintenance of procedures reasonably adapted to avoid any such error.

(d) Good faith compliance with rule, regulation, or interpretation. No provision of this section or section 1693n of this title imposing any liability shall apply to—

(1) any act done or omitted in good faith in conformity with any rule, regulation, or interpretation thereof by the Bureau or the Board or in conformity with any interpretation or approval by an official or employee of the Bureau of Consumer Financial Protection or the Federal Reserve System duly authorized by the Bureau or the Board to issue such interpretations or approvals under such procedures as the Bureau or the Board may prescribe therefor; or

(2) any failure to make disclosure in proper form if a financial institution utilized an appropriate model clause issued by the Bureau or the Board,

notwithstanding that after such act, omission, or failure has occurred, such rule, regulation, approval, or model clause is amended, rescinded, or determined by judicial or other authority to be invalid for any reason.

(e) Notification to consumer prior to action; adjustment of consumer's account. A person has no liability under this section for any failure to comply with any requirement under this subchapter if, prior to the institution of an action under this section, the person notifies the consumer concerned of the failure, complies with the requirements of this subchapter, and makes an appropriate adjustment to the consumer's account and pays actual damages or, where applicable, damages in accordance with section 1693h of this title.

(f) Action in bad faith or for harassment; attorney's fees. On a finding by the court that an unsuccessful action under this section was brought in bad faith or for purposes of harassment, the court shall award to the defendant attorney's fees reasonable in relation to the work expended and costs.

(g) Jurisdiction of courts; time for maintenance of action. Without regard to the amount in controversy, any action under this section may be brought in any United States district court, or in any other court of competent jurisdiction, within one year from the date of the occurrence of the violation.

§ 917 [15 U.S.C. § 1693n]. Criminal Liability

(a) Violations respecting giving of false or inaccurate information, failure to provide information, and failure to comply with provisions of this subchapter. Whoever knowingly and willfully—

(1) gives false or inaccurate information or fails to provide information which he is required to disclose by this subchapter or any regulation issued thereunder; or

(2) otherwise fails to comply with any provision of this subchapter; shall be fined not more than $5,000 or imprisoned not more than one year, or both.

(b) Violations affecting interstate or foreign commerce. Whoever—

(1) knowingly, in a transaction affecting interstate or foreign commerce, uses or attempts or conspires to use any counterfeit, fictitious, altered, forged, lost, stolen, or fraudulently obtained debit instrument to obtain money, goods, services, or anything else of value which within any one-year period has a value aggregating $1,000 or more; or

(2) with unlawful or fraudulent intent, transports or attempts or conspires to transport in interstate or foreign commerce a counterfeit, fictitious, altered, forged, lost, stolen, or fraudulently obtained debit instrument knowing the same to be counterfeit, fictitious, altered, forged, lost, stolen, or fraudulently obtained; or

(3) with unlawful or fraudulent intent, uses any instrumentality of interstate or foreign commerce to sell or transport a counterfeit, fictitious, altered, forged, lost, stolen, or fraudulently obtained debit instrument knowing the same to be counterfeit, fictitious, altered, forged, lost, stolen, or fraudulently obtained; or

(4) knowingly receives, conceals, uses, or transports money, goods, services, or anything else of value (except tickets for interstate or foreign transportation) which

(A) within any one-year period has a value aggregating $1,000 or more,

(B) has moved in or is part of, or which constitutes interstate or foreign commerce, and

(C) has been obtained with a counterfeit, fictitious, altered, forged, lost, stolen, or fraudulently obtained debit instrument; or

(5) knowingly receives, conceals, uses, sells, or transports in interstate or foreign commerce one or more tickets for interstate or foreign transportation, which

(A) within any one-year period have a value aggregating $500 or more, and

(B) have been purchased or obtained with one or more counterfeit, fictitious, altered, forged, lost, stolen, or fraudulently obtained debit instrument; or

(6) in a transaction affecting interstate or foreign commerce, furnishes money, property, services, or anything else of value, which within any one-year period has a value aggregating $1,000 or more, through the use of any counterfeit, fictitious, altered, forged, lost, stolen, or fraudulently obtained debit instrument knowing the same to be counterfeit, fictitious, altered, forged, lost, stolen, or fraudulently obtained—shall be fined not more than $10,000 or imprisoned not more than ten years, or both.

(c) "Debit instrument" defined. As used in this section, the term "debit instrument" means a card, code, or other device, other than a check, draft, or similar paper instrument, by the use of which a person may initiate an electronic fund transfer.

§ 918 [15 U.S.C. § 1693o]. Administrative Enforcement

(a) Enforcing agencies. Subject to subtitle B of the Consumer Financial Protection Act of 2010, compliance with the requirements imposed under this subchapter shall be enforced under—

(1) section 8 of the Federal Deposit Insurance Act (12 U.S.C. 1818), by the appropriate Federal banking agency, as defined in section 3(q) of the Federal Deposit Insurance Act (12 U.S.C. 1813(q)), with respect to—

(A) national banks, Federal savings associations, and Federal branches and Federal agencies of foreign banks;

(B) member banks of the Federal Reserve System (other than national banks), branches and agencies of foreign banks (other than Federal branches, Federal agencies, and insured State branches of foreign banks), commercial lending companies owned or controlled by foreign banks, and organizations operating under section 25 or 25A of the Federal Reserve Act (12 U.S.C. 601 et seq., 611 et seq.); and

(C) banks and State savings associations insured by the Federal Deposit Insurance Corporation (other than members of the Federal Reserve System) and insured State branches of foreign banks;

(2) the Federal Credit Union Act (12 U.S.C. 1751 et seq.), by the Administrator of the National Credit Union Administration with respect to any Federal credit union;

(3) part A of subtitle VII of title 49, by the Secretary of Transportation, with respect to any air carrier or foreign air carrier subject to that part;

(4) the Securities Exchange Act of 1934 (15 U.S.C. 78a et seq.), by the Sureties and Exchange Commission, with respect to any broker or dealer subject to that Act; and

(5) subtitle E of the Consumer Financial Protection Act of 2010 (12 U.S.C. 5561 et seq.), by the Bureau, with respect to any person subject to this title, except that the Bureau shall not have authority to enforce the requirements of section 920 or any regulations prescribed by the Board under section 920.

The terms used in paragraph (1) that are not defined in this subchapter or otherwise defined in section 3(s) of the Federal Deposit Insurance Act (12 U.S.C. 1813(s)) shall have the meaning given to them in section 1(b) of the International Banking Act of 1978 (12 U.S.C. 3101).

(b) Violations of subchapter deemed violations of pre-existing statutory requirements; additional powers. For the purpose of the exercise by any agency referred to in any of paragraphs (1) through (4) of subsection (a) of its powers under any Act referred to in that subsection, a violation of any requirement imposed under this subchapter shall be deemed to be a violation of a requirement imposed under that Act. In addition to its powers under any provision of law specifically referred to in any of paragraphs (1) through (4) of subsection (a), each of the agencies referred to in that subsection may exercise, for the purpose of enforcing compliance with any requirement imposed under this subchapter, any other authority conferred on it by law.

(c) Overall enforcement authority of the Federal Trade Commission. Except to the extent that enforcement of the requirements imposed under this subchapter is specifically committed to some other Government agency under any of paragraphs (1) through (4) of subsection (a), subject to subtitle B of the Consumer Financial Protection Act of 2010, the Federal Trade Commission shall be authorized to enforce such requirements. For the purpose of the exercise by the Federal Trade Commission of its functions and powers under the Federal Trade Commission Act (15 U.S.C. 41 et seq.), a violation of any requirement imposed under this subchapter shall be deemed a violation of a requirement imposed under that Act. All of the functions and powers of the Federal Trade Commission under the Federal Trade Commission Act are available to the Commission to enforce compliance by any person subject to the jurisdiction of the Commission with the requirements imposed under this subchapter, irrespective of whether that person is engaged in commerce or meets any other jurisdictional tests in the Federal Trade Commission Act.

§ 919 [15 U.S.C. § 1693o-1]. Remittance transfers

(a) Disclosures required for remittance transfers.

(1) In general. Each remittance transfer provider shall make disclosures as required under this section and in accordance with rules prescribed by the Bureau. Disclosures required under this section shall be in addition to any other disclosures applicable under this title.

(2) Disclosures. Subject to rules prescribed by the Bureau, a remittance transfer provider shall provide, in writing and in a form that the sender may keep, to each sender requesting a remittance transfer, as applicable to the transaction—

(A) at the time at which the sender requests a remittance transfer to be initiated, and prior to the sender making any payment in connection with the remittance transfer, a disclosure describing—

(i) the amount of currency that will be received by the designated recipient, using the values of the currency into which the funds will be exchanged;

(ii) the amount of transfer and any other fees charged by the remittance transfer provider for the remittance transfer; and

(iii) any exchange rate to be used by the remittance transfer provider for the remittance transfer, to the nearest 1/100th of a point; and

(B) at the time at which the sender makes payment in connection with the remittance transfer—

(i) a receipt showing—

(I) the information described in subparagraph (A);

(II) the promised date of delivery to the designated recipient; and

(III) the name and either the telephone number or the address of the designated recipient, if either the telephone number or the address of the designated recipient is provided by the sender; and

(ii) a statement containing—

(I) information about the rights of the sender under this section regarding the resolution of errors; and

(II) appropriate contact information for—

(aa) the remittance transfer provider; and

(bb) the State agency that regulates the remittance transfer provider and the Bureau, including the toll-free telephone number established under section 1013 of the Consumer Financial Protection Act of 2010 (12 U.S.C. 5493).

(3) Requirements relating to disclosures. With respect to each disclosure required to be provided under paragraph (2) a remittance transfer provider shall—

(A) provide an initial notice and receipt, as required by subparagraphs (A) and (B) of paragraph (2), and an error resolution statement, as required by subsection (d), that clearly and conspicuously describe the information required to be disclosed therein; and

(B) with respect to any transaction that a sender conducts electronically, comply with the Electronic Signatures in Global and National Commerce Act (15 U.S.C. 7001 et seq.).

(4) Exception for disclosures of amount received.

(A) In general. Subject to the rules prescribed by the Bureau, and except as provided under subparagraph (B), the disclosures required regarding the amount of currency that will be received by the designated recipient shall be deemed to be accurate, so long as the disclosures provide a reasonably accurate estimate of the foreign currency to be received. This paragraph shall apply only to a remittance transfer provider who is an insured depository institution, as defined in section 3 of the Federal Deposit Insurance Act (12 U.S.C. 1813), or an insured credit union, as defined in section 101 of the Federal Credit Union Act (12 U.S.C. 1752), and if—

(i) a remittance transfer is conducted through a demand deposit, savings deposit, or other asset account that the sender holds with such remittance transfer provider; and

(ii) at the time at which the sender requests the transaction, the remittance transfer provider is unable to know, for reasons beyond its control, the amount of currency that will be made available to the designated recipient.

(B) Deadline. The application of subparagraph (A) shall terminate 5 years after July 21, 2010, unless the Bureau determines that termination of such provision would negatively affect the ability of remittance transfer providers described in subparagraph (A) to send remittances to locations in foreign countries, in which case, the Bureau may, by rule, extend the application of subparagraph (A) to not longer than 10 years after July 21, 2010.

(5) Exemption authority. The Bureau may, by rule, permit a remittance transfer provider to satisfy the requirements of—

(A) paragraph (2)(A) orally, if the transaction is conducted entirely by telephone;

(B) paragraph (2)(B), in the case of a transaction conducted entirely by telephone, by mailing the disclosures required under such subparagraph to the sender, not later than 1 business day after the date on which the transaction is conducted, or by including such documents in the next periodic statement, if the telephone transaction is conducted through a demand deposit, savings deposit, or other asset account that the sender holds with the remittance transfer provider;

(C) subparagraphs (A) and (B) of paragraph (2) together in one written disclosure, but only to the extent that the information provided in accordance with paragraph (3)(A) is accurate at the time at which payment is made in connection with the subject remittance transfer; and

(D) paragraph (2)(A), without compliance with section 101(c) of the Electronic Signatures in Global Commerce Act (15 U.S.C. 7001(c)), if a sender initiates the transaction electronically and the information is displayed electronically in a manner that the sender can keep.

(6) Storefront and internet notices.

(A) In general.

(i) Prominent posting. Subject to subparagraph (B), the Bureau may prescribe rules to require a remittance transfer provider to prominently post, and timely update, a notice describing a model remittance transfer for one or more amounts, as the Bureau may determine, which notice shall show the amount of currency that will be received by the designated recipient, using the values of the currency into which the funds will be exchanged.

(ii) Onsite displays. The Bureau may require the notice prescribed under this subparagraph to be displayed in every physical storefront location owned or controlled by the remittance transfer provider.

(iii) Internet notices. Subject to paragraph (3), the Bureau shall prescribe rules to require a remittance transfer provider that provides remittance transfers via the Internet to provide a notice, comparable to a storefront notice described in this subparagraph, located on the home page or landing page (with respect to such remittance transfer services) owned or controlled by the remittance transfer provider.

(iv) Rulemaking authority. In prescribing rules under this subparagraph, the Bureau may impose standards or requirements regarding the provision of the storefront and Internet notices required under this subparagraph and the provision of the disclosures required under paragraphs (2) and (3).

(B) Study and analysis. Prior to proposing rules under subparagraph (A), the Bureau shall undertake appropriate studies and analyses, which shall be consistent with section 1693b(a)(2) of this title, and may include an advanced notice of proposed rulemaking, to determine whether a storefront notice or Internet notice facilitates the ability of a consumer—

(i) to compare prices for remittance transfers; and

(ii) to understand the types and amounts of any fees or costs imposed on remittance transfers.

(b) Foreign language disclosures. The disclosures required under this section shall be made in English and in each of the foreign languages principally used by the remittance transfer provider, or any of its agents, to advertise, solicit, or market, either orally or in writing, at that office.

(c) Regulations regarding transfers to certain nations. If the Bureau determines that a recipient nation does not legally allow, or the method by which transactions are made in the recipient country do not allow, a remittance transfer provider to know the amount of currency that will be received by the designated recipient, the Bureau may prescribe rules (not later than 18 months after Julu 21, 2010) addressing the issue, which rules shall include standards for a remittance transfer provider to provide—

(1) a receipt that is consistent with subsections (a) and (b); and

(2) a reasonably accurate estimate of the foreign currency to be received, based on the rate provided to the sender by the remittance transfer provider at the time at which the transaction was initiated by the sender.

(d) Remittance transfer errors.

(1) Error resolution.

(A) In general. If a remittance transfer provider receives oral or written notice from the sender within 180 days of the promised date of delivery that an error occurred with respect to a remittance transfer, including the amount of currency designated in subsection (a)(3)(A) that was to be sent to the designated recipient of the remittance transfer, using the values of the currency into which the funds should have been exchanged, but was not made available to the designated recipient in the foreign country, the remittance transfer provider shall resolve the error pursuant to this subsection and investigate the reason for the error.

(B) Remedies. Not later than 90 days after the date of receipt of a notice from the sender pursuant to subparagraph (A), the remittance transfer provider shall, as applicable to the error and as designated by the sender—

(i) refund to the sender the total amount of funds tendered by the sender in connection with the remittance transfer which was not properly transmitted;

(ii) make available to the designated recipient, without additional cost to the designated recipient or to the sender, the amount appropriate to resolve the error;

(iii) provide such other remedy, as determined appropriate by rule of the Bureau for the protection of senders; or

(iv) provide written notice to the sender that there was no error with an explanation responding to the specific complaint of the sender.

(2) Rules. The Bureau shall establish, by rule issued not later than 18 months after July 21, 2010, clear and appropriate standards for remittance transfer providers with respect to error resolution relating to remittance transfers, to protect senders from such errors. Standards prescribed under this paragraph shall include appropriate standards regarding record keeping, as required, including documentation—

(A) of the complaint of the sender;

(B) that the sender provides the remittance transfer provider with respect to the alleged error; and

(C) of the findings of the remittance transfer provider regarding the investigation of the alleged error that the sender brought to their attention.

(3) Cancellation and refund policy rules. Not later than 18 months after Julu 21, 2010, the Bureau shall issue final rules regarding appropriate remittance transfer cancellation and refund policies for consumers.

(e) Applicability of this subchapter.

(1) In general. A remittance transfer that is not an electronic fund transfer, as defined in section 1693a of this title, shall not be subject to any of the provisions of sections 1693c through 1695k of this title. A remittance transfer that is an electronic fund transfer, as defined in section 1693a of this title, shall be subject to all provisions of this, except for section 1693f of this title, that are otherwise applicable to electronic fund transfers under this title.

(2) Rule of construction. Nothing in this section shall be construed—

(A) to affect the application to any transaction, to any remittance provider, or to any other person of any of the provisions of subchapter II of chapter 53 of title 31, section 1829b of title 12, or chapter 2 of title I of Public Law 91-508 (12 U.S.C. 1951-1959), or any regulations promulgated thereunder; or

(B) to cause any fund transfer that would not otherwise be treated as such under paragraph (1) to be treated as an electronic fund transfer, or as otherwise subject to this subchapter, for the purposes of any of the provisions referred to in subparagraph (A) or any regulations promulgated thereunder.

(f) Acts of agents.

(1) In general. A remittance transfer provider shall be liable for any violation of this section by any agent, authorized delegate, or person affiliated with such provider, when such agent, authorized delegate, or affiliate acts for that remittance transfer provider.

(2) Obligations of remittance transfer providers. The Bureau shall prescribe rules to implement appropriate standards or conditions of, liability of a remittance transfer provider, including a provider who acts through an agent or authorized delegate. An agency charged with enforcing the requirements of this section, or rules prescribed by the Bureau under this section, may consider, in any action or other proceeding against a remittance transfer provider, the extent to which the provider had established and maintained policies or procedures for compliance, including policies, procedures, or other appropriate oversight measures designed to assure compliance by an agent or authorized delegate acting for such provider.

(g) Definitions. As used in this section—

(1) the term "designated recipient" means any person located in a foreign country and identified by the sender as the authorized recipient of a remittance transfer to be made by a remittance transfer provider, except that a designated recipient shall not be deemed to be a consumer for purposes of this chapter;

(2) the term "remittance transfer"—

(A) means the electronic (as defined in section 106(2) of the Electronic Signatures in Global and National Commerce Act (15 U.S.C. 7006(2))) transfer of funds requested by a sender located in any State to a designated recipient that is initiated by a remittance transfer provider, whether or not the sender holds an account with the remittance transfer provider or whether or not the remittance transfer is also an electronic fund transfer, as defined in section 1693a of this title; and

(B) does not include a transfer described in subparagraph (A) in an amount that is equal to or lesser than the amount of a small-value transaction determined, by rule, to be excluded from the requirements under section 1693d(a) of this title;

(3) the term "remittance transfer provider" means any person or financial institution that provides remittance transfers for a consumer in the normal course of its business, whether or not the consumer holds an account with such person or financial institution; and

(4) the term "sender" means a consumer who requests a remittance provider to send a remittance transfer for the consumer to a designated recipient.

§ 920 [15 U.S.C. § 1693o-2]. Reasonable fees and rules for payment card transactions

(a) Reasonable interchange transaction fees for electronic debit transactions.

(1) Regulatory authority over interchange transaction fees. The Board may prescribe regulations, pursuant to section 553 of title 5, regarding any interchange transaction fee that an issuer may receive or charge with respect to an electronic debit

transaction, to implement this subsection (including related definitions), and to prevent circumvention or evasion of this subsection.

(2) Reasonable interchange transaction fees. The amount of any interchange transaction fee that an issuer may receive or charge with respect to an electronic debit transaction shall be reasonable and proportional to the cost incurred by the issuer with respect to the transaction.

(3) Rulemaking required.

(A) In general. The Board shall prescribe regulations in final form not later than 9 months after July 10, 2010, to establish standards for assessing whether the amount of any interchange transaction fee described in paragraph (2) is reasonable and proportional to the cost incurred by the issuer with respect to the transaction.

(B) Information collection. The Board may require any issuer (or agent of an issuer) or payment card network to provide the Board with such information as may be necessary to carry out the provisions of this subsection and the Board, in issuing rules under subparagraph (A) and on at least a bi-annual basis thereafter, shall disclose such aggregate or summary information concerning the costs incurred, and interchange transaction fees charged or received, by issuers or payment card networks in connection with the authorization, clearance or settlement of electronic debit transactions as the Board considers appropriate and in the public interest.

(4) Considerations; consultation. In prescribing regulations under paragraph (3)(A), the Board shall—

(A) consider the functional similarity between—

(i) electronic debit transactions; and

(ii) checking transactions that are required within the Federal Reserve bank system to clear at par;

(B) distinguish between—

(i) the incremental cost incurred by an issuer for the role of the issuer in the authorization, clearance, or settlement of a particular electronic debit transaction, which cost shall be considered under paragraph (2); and

(ii) other costs incurred by an issuer which are not specific to a particular electronic debit transaction, which costs shall not be considered under paragraph (2); and

(C) consult, as appropriate, with the Comptroller of the Currency, the Board of Directors of the Federal Deposit Insurance Corporation, the Director of the Office of Thrift Supervision, the National Credit Union Administration Board, the Administrator of the Small Business Administration, and the Director of the Bureau of Consumer Financial Protection.

(5) Adjustments to interchange transaction fees for fraud prevention costs.

(A) Adjustments. The Board may allow for an adjustment to the fee amount received or charged by an issuer under paragraph (2), if—

(i) such adjustment is reasonably necessary to make allowance for costs incurred by the issuer in preventing fraud in relation to electronic debit transactions involving that issuer; and

(ii) the issuer complies with the fraud-related standards established by the Board under subparagraph (B), which standards shall—

(I) be designed to ensure that any fraud-related adjustment of the issuer is limited to the amount described in clause (i) and takes into account any fraud-related reimbursements (including amounts from charge-backs) received from consumers, merchants, or payment card networks in relation to electronic debit transactions involving the issuer; and

(II) require issuers to take effective steps to reduce the occurrence of, and costs from, fraud in relation to electronic debit transactions, including through the development and implementation of cost-effective fraud prevention technology.

(B) Rulemaking required.

(i) In general. The Board shall prescribe regulations in final form not later than 9 months after July 21, 2010, to establish standards for making adjustments under this paragraph.

(ii) Factors for consideration. In issuing the standards and prescribing regulations under this paragraph, the Board shall consider—

(I) the nature, type, and occurrence of fraud in electronic debit transactions;

(II) the extent to which the occurrence of fraud depends on whether authorization in an electronic debit transaction is based on signature, PIN, or other means;

(III) the available and economical means by which fraud on electronic debit transactions may be reduced;

(IV) the fraud prevention and data security costs expended by each party involved in electronic debit transactions (including consumers, persons who accept debit cards as a form of payment, financial institutions, retailers and payment card networks);

(V) the costs of fraudulent transactions absorbed by each party involved in such transactions (including consumers, persons who accept debit cards as a form of payment, financial institutions, retailers and payment card networks);

(VI) the extent to which interchange transaction fees have in the past reduced or increased incentives for parties involved in electronic debit transactions to reduce fraud on such transactions; and

(VII) such other factors as the Board considers appropriate.

(6) Exemption for small issuers.

(A) In general. This subsection shall not apply to any issuer that, together with its affiliates, has assets of less than $ 10,000,000,000, and the Board shall exempt such issuers from regulations prescribed under paragraph (3)(A).

(B) Definition. For purposes of this paragraph, the term "issuer" shall be limited to the person holding the asset account that is debited through an electronic debit transaction.

(7) Exemption for government-administered payment programs and reloadable prepaid cards.

(A) In general. This subsection shall not apply to an interchange transaction fee charged or received with respect to an electronic debit transaction in which a person uses—

(i) a debit card or general-use prepaid card that has been provided to a person pursuant to a Federal, State or local government-administered payment program, in which the person may only use the debit card or general-use prepaid card to transfer or debit funds, monetary value, or other assets that have been provided pursuant to such program; or

(ii) a plastic card, payment code, or device that is—

(I) linked to funds, monetary value, or assets which are purchased or loaded on a prepaid basis;

(II) not issued or approved for use to access or debit any account held by or for the benefit of the card holder (other than a subaccount or other method of recording or tracking funds purchased or loaded on the card on a prepaid basis);

(III) redeemable at multiple, unaffiliated merchants or service providers, or automated teller machines;

(IV) used to transfer or debit funds, monetary value, or other assets; and

(V) reloadable and not marketed or labeled as a gift card or gift certificate.

(B) Exception. Notwithstanding subparagraph (A), after the end of the 1-year period beginning on the effective date provided in paragraph (9), this subsection shall apply to an interchange transaction fee charged or received with respect to an electronic debit transaction described in subparagraph (A)(i) in which a person uses a general-use prepaid card, or an electronic debit transaction described in subparagraph (A)(ii), if any of the following fees may be charged to a person with respect to the card:

(i) A fee for an overdraft, including a shortage of funds or a transaction processed for an amount exceeding the account balance.

(ii) A fee imposed by the issuer for the first withdrawal per month from an automated teller machine that is part of the issuer's designated automated teller machine network.

(C) Definition. For purposes of subparagraph (B), the term "designated automated teller machine network" means either—

(i) all automated teller machines identified in the name of the issuer; or

(ii) any network of automated teller machines identified by the issuer that provides reasonable and convenient access to the issuer's customers.

(D) Reporting. Beginning 12 months after July 21, 2010, the Board shall annually provide a report to the Congress regarding—

(i) the prevalence of the use of general-use prepaid cards in Federal, State or local government-administered payment programs; and

(ii) the interchange transaction fees and cardholder fees charged with respect to the use of such general-use prepaid cards.

(8) Regulatory authority over network fees.

(A) In general. The Board may prescribe regulations, pursuant to section 553 of title 5, regarding any network fee.

(B) Limitation. The authority under subparagraph (A) to prescribe regulations shall be limited to regulations to ensure that—

(i) a network fee is not used to directly or indirectly compensate an issuer with respect to an electronic debit transaction; and

(ii) a network fee is not used to circumvent or evade the restrictions of this subsection and regulations prescribed under such subsection.

(C) Rulemaking required. The Board shall prescribe regulations in final form before the end of the 9-month period beginning on July 21, 2010, to carry out the authorities provided under subparagraph (A).

(9) Effective date. This subsection shall take effect at the end of the 12-month period beginning on July 21, 2010.

(b) Limitation on payment card network restrictions.

(1) Prohibitions against exclusivity arrangements.

(A) No exclusive network. The Board shall, before the end of the 1-year period beginning on July 21, 2010, prescribe regulations providing that an issuer or payment card network shall not directly or through any agent, processor, or licensed member of a payment card network, by contract, requirement, condition, penalty, or otherwise, restrict the number of payment card networks on which an electronic debit transaction may be processed to—

(i) 1 such network; or

(ii) 2 or more such networks which are owned, controlled, or otherwise operated by—

(I) affiliated persons; or

(II) networks affiliated with such issuer.

(B) No routing restrictions. The Board shall, before the end of the 1-year period beginning on July 21, 2010, prescribe regulations providing that an issuer or payment card network shall not, directly or through any agent, processor, or licensed member of the network, by contract, requirement, condition, penalty, or otherwise, inhibit the ability of any person who accepts debit cards for payments to direct the routing of electronic debit transactions for processing over any payment card network that may process such transactions.

(2) Limitation on restrictions on offering discounts for use of a form of payment.

(A) In general. A payment card network shall not, directly or through any agent, processor, or licensed member of the network, by contract, requirement, condition, penalty, or otherwise, inhibit the ability of any person to provide a discount or in-kind incentive for payment by the use of cash, checks, debit cards, or credit cards to the extent that—

(i) in the case of a discount or in-kind incentive for payment by the use of debit cards, the discount or in-kind incentive does not differentiate on the basis of the issuer or the payment card network;

(ii) in the case of a discount or in-kind incentive for payment by the use of credit cards, the discount or in-kind incentive does not differentiate on the basis of the issuer or the payment card network; and

(iii) to the extent required by Federal law and applicable State law, such discount or in-kind incentive is offered to all prospective buyers and disclosed clearly and conspicuously.

(B) Lawful discounts. For purposes of this paragraph, the network may not penalize any person for the providing of a discount that is in compliance with Federal law and applicable State law.

(3) Limitation on restrictions on setting transaction minimums or maximums.

(A) In general. A payment card network shall not, directly or through any agent, processor, or licensed member of the network, by contract, requirement, condition, penalty, or otherwise, inhibit the ability—

(i) of any person to set a minimum dollar value for the acceptance by that person of credit cards, to the extent that—

(I) such minimum dollar value does not differentiate between issuers or between payment card networks; and

(II) such minimum dollar value does not exceed $ 10.00; or

(ii) of any Federal agency or institution of higher education to set a maximum dollar value for the acceptance by that Federal agency or institution of higher education of credit cards, to the extent that such maximum dollar value does not differentiate between issuers or between payment card networks.

(B) Increase in minimum dollar amount. The Board may, by regulation prescribed pursuant to section 553 of title 5, increase the amount of the dollar value listed in subparagraph (A)(i)(II).

(4) Rule of construction:. No provision of this subsection shall be construed to authorize any person—

(A) to discriminate between debit cards within a payment card network on the basis of the issuer that issued the debit card; or

(B) to discriminate between credit cards within a payment card network on the basis of the issuer that issued the credit card.

(c) Definitions. For purposes of this section, the following definitions shall apply:

(1) Affiliate. The term "affiliate" means any company that controls, is controlled by, or is under common control with another company.

(2) Debit card. The term "debit card"—

(A) means any card, or other payment code or device, issued or approved for use through a payment card network to debit an asset account (regardless of the purpose for which the account is established), whether authorization is based on signature, PIN, or other means;

(B) includes a general-use prepaid card, as that term is defined in section 1693l-1(a)(2)(A) of this title; and

(C) does not include paper checks.

(3) Credit card. The term "credit card" has the same meaning as in section 1602 of this title.

(4) Discount. The term "discount"—

(A) means a reduction made from the price that customers are informed is the regular price; and

(B) does not include any means of increasing the price that customers are informed is the regular price.

(5) Electronic debit transaction. The term "electronic debit transaction" means a transaction in which a person uses a debit card.

(6) Federal agency. The term "Federal agency" means—

(A) an agency (as defined in section 101 of title 31); and

(B) a Government corporation (as defined in section 103 of title 5).

(7) Institution of higher education. The term "institution of higher education" has the same meaning as in [sections] 1001 and 1002 of title 20.

(8) Interchange transaction fee. The term "interchange transaction fee" means any fee established, charged or received by a payment card network for the purpose of compensating an issuer for its involvement in an electronic debit transaction.

(9) Issuer. The term "issuer" means any person who issues a debit card, or credit card, or the agent of such person with respect to such card.

(10) Network fee. The term "network fee" means any fee charged and received by a payment card network with respect to an electronic debit transaction, other than an interchange transaction fee.

(11) Payment card network. The term "payment card network" means an entity that directly, or through licensed members, processors, or agents, provides the proprietary services, infrastructure, and software that route information and data to conduct debit card or credit card transaction authorization, clearance, and settlement, and that a person uses in order to accept as a form of payment a brand of debit card, credit card or other device that may be used to carry out debit or credit transactions.

(d) Enforcement.

(1) In general. Compliance with the requirements imposed under this section shall be enforced under section 1693o of this title.

(2) Exception. Sections 1693m and 1693n of this title shall not apply with respect to this section or the requirements imposed pursuant to this section.

§ 921 [15 U.S.C. § 1693p]. Reports to Congress

(a) Not later than twelve months after the effective date of this subchapter and at one-year intervals thereafter, the Bureau shall make reports to the Congress concerning the administration of its functions under this subchapter, including such recommendations as the Bureau deems necessary and appropriate. In addition, each report of the Bureau shall include its assessment of the extent to which compliance with this subchapter is being achieved, and a summary of the enforcement actions taken under section 1693o of this title. In such report, the Bureau shall particularly address the effects of this subchapter on the costs and benefits to financial institutions and consumers, on competition, on the introduction of new technology, on the operations of financial institutions, and on the adequacy of consumer protection.

(b) In the exercise of its functions under this subchapter, the Bureau may obtain upon request the views of any other Federal agency which, in the judgment of the Bureau, exercises regulatory or supervisory functions with respect to any class of persons subject to this subchapter.

§ 922 [15 U.S.C. § 1693q]. Relation to State Laws

This subchapter does not annul, alter, or affect the laws of any State relating to electronic fund transfers, dormancy fees, inactivity charges or fees, service fees, or expiration dates of gift certificates, store gift cards, or general-use prepaid cards, except to the extent that those laws are inconsistent with the provisions of this subchapter, and then only to the extent of the inconsistency. A State law is not inconsistent with this subchapter if the protection such law affords any consumer is greater than the protection afforded by this subchapter. The Bureau shall, upon its own motion or upon the request of any financial institution, State, or other interested party, submitted in accordance with procedures prescribed in regulations of the Bureau, determine whether a State requirement is inconsistent or affords greater protection. If the Bureau determines that a State requirement is inconsistent, financial institutions shall incur no liability under the law of that State for a good faith failure to comply with that law, notwithstanding that such determination is subsequently amended, rescinded, or determined by judicial or other authority to be invalid for any reason. This subchapter does not extend the applicability of any such law to any class of persons or transactions to which it would not otherwise apply.

§ 923 [15 U.S.C. § 1693r]. Exemption for State Regulation

The Bureau shall by regulation exempt from the requirements of this subchapter any class of electronic fund transfers within any State if the Bureau determines that under the law of that State that class of electronic fund transfers is subject to requirements substantially similar to those imposed by this subchapter, and that there is adequate provision for enforcement.

Regulation E — Electronic Funds Transfer
12 C.F.R. Part 1005

Section

§ 1005.1 Authority and Purpose

(a) Authority. The regulation in this part, known as Regulation E, is issued by the Bureau of Consumer Financial Protection (Bureau) pursuant to the Electronic Fund Transfer Act (15 U.S.C. 1693 et seq.). The information-collection requirements have been approved by the Office of Management and Budget under 44 U.S.C. 3501 et seq. and have been assigned OMB No. 3170-0014.

(b) Purpose. This part carries out the purposes of the Electronic Fund Transfer Act, which establishes the basic rights, liabilities, and responsibilities of consumers who use electronic fund transfer and remittance transfer services and of financial institutions or other persons that offer these services. The primary objective of the act and this part is the protection of individual consumers engaging in electronic fund transfers and remittance transfers.

§ 1005.2 Definitions

For purposes of this part, the following definitions apply:

(a) (1) "Access device" means a card, code, or other means of access to a consumer's account, or any combination thereof, that may be used by the consumer to initiate electronic fund transfers.

(2) An access device becomes an "accepted access device" when the consumer:

(i) Requests and receives, or signs, or uses (or authorizes another to use) the access device to transfer money between accounts or to obtain money, property, or services;

(ii) Requests validation of an access device issued on an unsolicited basis; or

(iii) Receives an access device in renewal of, or in substitution for, an accepted access device from either the financial institution that initially issued the device or a successor.

(b) (1) "Account" means a demand deposit (checking), savings, or other consumer asset account (other than an occasional or incidental credit balance in a credit plan) held directly or indirectly by a financial institution and established primarily for personal, family, or household purposes.

(2) The term does not include an account held by a financial institution under a bona fide trust agreement.

(3) The term includes a prepaid account.

(i) "Prepaid account" means:

(A) A "payroll card account," which is an account that is directly or indirectly established through an employer and to which electronic fund transfers of the consumer's wages, salary, or other employee compensation (such as commissions) are made on a recurring basis, whether the account is operated or managed by the employer, a third-party payroll processor, a depository institution, or any other person; or

(B) A "government benefit account," as defined in § 1005.15(a)(2); or

(C) An account that is marketed or labeled as "prepaid" and that is redeemable upon presentation at multiple, unaffiliated merchants for goods or services or usable at automated teller machines; or

(D) An account:

(1) That is issued on a prepaid basis in a specified amount or not issued on a prepaid basis but capable of being loaded with funds thereafter,

(2) Whose primary function is to conduct transactions with multiple, unaffiliated merchants for goods or services, or at automated teller machines, or to conduct person-to-person transfers, and

(3) That is not a checking account, share draft account, or negotiable order of withdrawal account.

(ii) For purposes of paragraphs (b)(3)(i)(C) and (D) of this section, the term "prepaid account" does not include:

(A) An account that is loaded only with funds from a health savings account, flexible spending arrangement, medical savings account, health reimbursement arrangement, dependent care assistance program, or transit or parking reimbursement arrangement;

(B) An account that is directly or indirectly established through a third party and loaded only with qualified disaster relief payments;

(C) The person-to-person functionality of an account established by or through the United States government whose primary function is to conduct closed-loop transactions on U.S. military installations or vessels, or similar government facilities;

(D) (1) A gift certificate as defined in § 1005.20(a)(1) and (b);

(2) A store gift card as defined in § 1005.20(a)(2) and (b);

(3) A loyalty, award, or promotional gift card as defined in § 1005.20(a)(4), or that satisfies the criteria in § 1005.20(a)(4)(i) and (ii) and is excluded from § 1005.20 pursuant to § 1005.20(b)(4); or

(4) A general-use prepaid card as defined in § 1005.20(a)(3) and (b) that is both marketed and labeled as a gift card or gift certificate; or

(E) An account established for distributing needs-tested benefits in a program established under state or local law or administered by a state or local agency, as set forth in § 1005.15(a)(2).

(c) "Act" means the Electronic Fund Transfer Act (Title IX of the Consumer Credit Protection Act, 15 U.S.C. 1693 et seq.).

(d) "Business day" means any day on which the offices of the consumer's financial institution are open to the public for carrying on substantially all business functions.

(e) "Consumer" means a natural person.

(f) "Credit" means the right granted by a financial institution to a consumer to defer payment of debt, incur debt and defer its payment, or purchase property or services and defer payment therefor.

(g) "Electronic fund transfer" is defined in § 1005.3.

(h) "Electronic terminal" means an electronic device, other than a telephone operated by a consumer, through which a consumer may initiate an electronic fund transfer. The term includes, but is not limited to, point-of-sale terminals, automated teller machines (ATMs), and cash dispensing machines.

(i) "Financial institution" means a bank, savings association, credit union, or any other person that directly or indirectly holds an account belonging to a consumer, or that issues an access device and agrees with a consumer to provide electronic fund transfer services, other than a person excluded from coverage of this part by section 1029 of the Consumer Financial Protection Act of 2010, title X of the Dodd-Frank Wall Street Reform and Consumer Protection Act, Public Law 111-203, 124 Stat. 1376.

(j) "Person" means a natural person or an organization, including a corporation, government agency, estate, trust, partnership, proprietorship, cooperative, or association.

(k) "Preauthorized electronic fund transfer" means an electronic fund transfer authorized in advance to recur at substantially regular intervals.

(l) "State" means any state, territory, or possession of the United States; the District of Columbia; the Commonwealth of Puerto Rico; or any political subdivision of the thereof in this paragraph (l).

(m) "Unauthorized electronic fund transfer" means an electronic fund transfer from a consumer's account initiated by a person other than the consumer without actual authority to initiate the transfer and from which the consumer receives no benefit. The term does not include an electronic fund transfer initiated:

(1) By a person who was furnished the access device to the consumer's account by the consumer, unless the consumer has notified the financial

institution that transfers by that person are no longer authorized;

(2) With fraudulent intent by the consumer or any person acting in concert with the consumer; or

(3) By the financial institution or its employee.

§ 1005.3 Coverage

(a) General. This part applies to any electronic fund transfer that authorizes a financial institution to debit or credit a consumer's account. Generally, this part applies to financial institutions. For purposes of §§ 1005.3(b)(2) and (3), 1005.10(b), (d), and (e), 1005.13, and 1005.20, this part applies to any person, other than a person excluded from coverage of this part by section 1029 of the Consumer Financial Protection Act of 2010, Title X of the Dodd-Frank Wall Street Reform and Consumer Protection Act, Pub. L. 111-203, 124 Stat. 1376. The requirements of subpart B apply to remittance transfer providers.

(b) Electronic fund transfer—

(1) Definition. The term "electronic fund transfer" means any transfer of funds that is initiated through an electronic terminal, telephone, computer, or magnetic tape for the purpose of ordering, instructing, or authorizing a financial institution to debit or credit a consumer's account. The term includes, but is not limited to:

(i) Point-of-sale transfers;

(ii) Automated teller machine transfers;

(iii) Direct deposits or withdrawals of funds;

(iv) Transfers initiated by telephone; and

(v) Transfers resulting from debit card transactions, whether or not initiated through an electronic terminal.

(2) Electronic fund transfer using information from a check.

(i) This part applies where a check, draft, or similar paper instrument is used as a source of information to initiate a one-time electronic fund transfer from a consumer's account. The consumer must authorize the transfer.

(ii) The person initiating an electronic fund transfer using the consumer's check as a source of information for the transfer must provide a notice that the transaction will or may be processed as an electronic fund transfer, and obtain a consumer's authorization for each transfer. A consumer authorizes a one-time electronic fund transfer (in providing a check to a merchant or other payee for the MICR encoding, that is, the routing number of the financial institution, the consumer's account number and the serial number) when the consumer receives notice and goes forward with the underlying transaction. For point-of-sale transfers, the notice must be posted in a prominent and conspicuous location, and a copy thereof, or a substantially similar notice, must be provided to the consumer at the time of the transaction.

(iii) A person may provide notices that are substantially similar to those set forth in appendix A-6 to comply with the requirements of this paragraph (b)(2).

(3) Collection of returned-item fees via electronic fund transfer—

(i) General. The person initiating an electronic fund transfer to collect a fee for the return of an electronic fund transfer or a check that is unpaid, including due to insufficient or uncollected funds in the consumer's account, must obtain the consumer's authorization for each transfer. A consumer authorizes a one-time electronic fund transfer from his or her account to pay the fee for the returned item or transfer if the person collecting the fee provides notice to the consumer stating that the person may electronically collect the fee, and the consumer goes forward with the underlying transaction. The notice must state that the fee will be collected by means of an electronic fund transfer from the consumer's account if the payment is returned unpaid and must disclose the dollar amount of the fee. If the fee may vary due to the amount of the transaction or due to other factors, then, except as otherwise provided in paragraph (b)(3)(ii) of this section, the person collecting the fee may disclose, in place of the dollar amount of the fee, an explanation of how the fee will be determined.

(ii) Point-of-sale transactions. If a fee for an electronic fund transfer or check returned unpaid may be collected electronically in connection with a point-of-sale transaction, the person initiating an electronic fund transfer to collect the fee must post the notice described in paragraph (b)(3)(i) of this section in a prominent and conspicuous location. The person also must either provide the consumer with a copy of the posted notice (or a substantially similar notice) at the time of the transaction, or mail the copy (or a substantially similar notice) to the consumer's address as soon as reasonably practicable after the person initiates the electronic fund transfer to collect the fee. If the amount of the fee may vary due to the amount of the transaction or due to other factors, the posted notice may explain how the fee will be determined, but the notice provided to the consumer must state the dollar amount of the fee if the amount can be calculated at the time the notice is provided or mailed to the consumer.

(c) Exclusions from coverage. The term "electronic fund transfer" does not include:

(1) Checks. Any transfer of funds originated by check, draft, or similar paper instrument; or any payment made by check, draft, or similar paper instrument at an electronic terminal.

(2) Check guarantee or authorization. Any transfer of funds that guarantees payment or authorizes acceptance of a check, draft, or similar paper instrument but that does not directly result in a debit or credit to a consumer's account.

(3) Wire or other similar transfers. Any transfer of funds through Fedwire or through a similar wire transfer system that is used primarily for transfers between financial institutions or between businesses.

(4) Securities and commodities transfers. Any transfer of funds the primary purpose of which is the purchase or sale of a security or commodity, if the security or commodity is:

(i) Regulated by the Securities and Exchange Commission or the Commodity Futures Trading Commission;

(ii) Purchased or sold through a broker-dealer regulated by the Securities and Exchange Commission or through a futures commission merchant regulated by the Commodity Futures Trading Commission; or

(iii) Held in book-entry form by a Federal Reserve Bank or Federal agency.

(5) Automatic transfers by account-holding institution. Any transfer of funds under an agreement between a consumer and a financial institution which provides that the institution will initiate individual transfers without a specific request from the consumer:

(i) Between a consumer's accounts within the financial institution;

(ii) From a consumer's account to an account of a member of the consumer's family held in the same financial institution; or

(iii) Between a consumer's account and an account of the financial institution, except that these transfers remain subject to § 1005.10(e) regarding compulsory use and sections 916 and 917 of the Act regarding civil and criminal liability.

(6) Telephone-initiated transfers. Any transfer of funds that:

(i) Is initiated by a telephone communication between a consumer and a financial institution making the transfer; and

(ii) Does not take place under a telephone bill-payment or other written plan in which periodic or recurring transfers are contemplated.

(7) Small institutions. Any preauthorized transfer to or from an account if the assets of the account-holding financial institution were $100 million or less on the preceding December 31. If assets of the account-holding institution subsequently exceed $100 million, the institution's exemption for preauthorized transfers terminates one year from the end of the calendar year in which the assets exceed $100 million. Preauthorized transfers exempt under this paragraph (c)(7) remain subject to § 1005.10(e) regarding compulsory use and sections 916 and 917 of the Act regarding civil and criminal liability.

§ 1005.4 General Disclosure Requirements; Jointly Offered Services

(a) (1) Form of disclosures. Disclosures required under this part shall be clear and readily understandable, in writing, and in a form the consumer may keep, except as otherwise provided in this part. The disclosures required by this part may be provided to the consumer in electronic form, subject to compliance with the consumer-consent and other applicable provisions of the Electronic Signatures in Global and National Commerce Act (E-Sign Act) (15 U.S.C. 7001 et seq.). A financial institution may use commonly accepted or readily understandable abbreviations in complying with the disclosure requirements of this part.

(2) Foreign language disclosures. Disclosures required under this part may be made in a language other than English, provided that the disclosures are made available in English upon the consumer's request.

(b) Additional information; disclosures required by other laws. A financial institution may include additional information and may combine disclosures required by other laws (such as the Truth in Lending Act (15 U.S.C. 1601 et seq.) or the Truth in Savings Act (12 U.S.C. 4301 et seq.) with the disclosures required by this part.

(c) Multiple accounts and account holders—

(1) Multiple accounts. A financial institution may combine the required disclosures into a single statement for a consumer who holds more than one account at the institution.

(2) Multiple account holders. For joint accounts held by two or more consumers, a financial institution need provide only one set of the required disclosures and may provide them to any of the account holders.

(d) Services offered jointly. Financial institutions that provide electronic fund transfer services jointly may contract among themselves to comply with the requirements that this part imposes on any or all of them. An institution need make only the disclosures required by §§ 1005.7 and 1005.8 that are within its knowledge and within the purview of its relationship with the consumer for whom it holds an account.

§ 1005.5 Issuance of Access Devices

(a) Solicited issuance. Except as provided in paragraph (b) of this section, a financial institution may issue an access device to a consumer only:

(1) In response to an oral or written request for the device; or

(2) As a renewal of, or in substitution for, an accepted access device whether issued by the institution or a successor.

(b) Unsolicited issuance. A financial institution may distribute an access device to a consumer on an unsolicited basis if the access device is:

(1) Not validated, meaning that the institution has not yet performed all the procedures that would enable a consumer to initiate an electronic fund transfer using the access device;

(2) Accompanied by a clear explanation that the access device is not validated and how the consumer may dispose of it if validation is not desired;

(3) Accompanied by the disclosures required by § 1005.7, of the consumer's rights and liabilities that will apply if the access device is validated; and

(4) Validated only in response to the consumer's oral or written request for validation, after the institution has verified the consumer's identity by a reasonable means.

§ 1005.6 Liability of Consumer for Unauthorized Transfers

(a) Conditions for liability. A consumer may be held liable, within the limitations described in paragraph (b) of this section, for an unauthorized electronic fund transfer involving the consumer's account only if the financial institution has provided the disclosures required by § 1005.7(b)(1), (2), and (3). If the unauthorized transfer involved an access device, it must be an accepted access device and the financial institution must have provided a means to identify the consumer to whom it was issued.

(b) Limitations on amount of liability. A consumer's liability for an unauthorized electronic fund transfer or a series of related unauthorized transfers shall be determined as follows:

(1) Timely notice given. If the consumer notifies the financial institution within two business days after learning of the loss or theft of the access device, the consumer's liability shall not exceed the lesser of $50 or the amount of unauthorized transfers that occur before notice to the financial institution.

(2) Timely notice not given. If the consumer fails to notify the financial institution within two business days after learning of the loss or theft of the access device, the consumer's liability shall not exceed the lesser of $500 or the sum of:

(i) $50 or the amount of unauthorized transfers that occur within the two business days, whichever is less; and

(ii) The amount of unauthorized transfers that occur after the close of two business days and before notice to the institution, provided the institution establishes that these transfers would not have occurred had the consumer notified the institution within that two-day period.

(3) Periodic statement; timely notice not given. A consumer must report an unauthorized electronic fund transfer that appears on a periodic statement within 60 days of the financial institution's transmittal of the statement to avoid liability for subsequent transfers. If the consumer fails to do so, the consumer's liability shall not exceed the amount of the unauthorized transfers that occur after the close of the 60 days and before notice to the institution, and that the institution establishes would not have occurred had the consumer notified the institution within the 60-day period. When an access device is involved in the unauthorized transfer, the consumer may be liable for other amounts set forth in paragraphs (b)(1) or (b)(2) of this section, as applicable.

(4) Extension of time limits. If the consumer's delay in notifying the financial institution was due to extenuating circumstances, the institution shall extend the times specified above to a reasonable period.

(5) Notice to financial institution.

(i) Notice to a financial institution is given when a consumer takes steps reasonably necessary to provide the institution with the pertinent information, whether or not a particular employee or agent of the institution actually receives the information.

(ii) The consumer may notify the institution in person, by telephone, or in writing.

(iii) Written notice is considered given at the time the consumer mails the notice or delivers it for transmission to the institution by any other usual means. Notice may be considered constructively given when the institution becomes aware of circumstances leading to the reasonable belief that an unauthorized transfer to or from the consumer's account has been or may be made.

(6)) Liability under state law or agreement. If state law or an agreement between the consumer and the financial institution imposes less liability than is provided by this section, the consumer's liability shall not exceed the amount imposed under the state law or agreement.

§ 1005.7 Initial Disclosures

(a) Timing of disclosures. A financial institution shall make the disclosures required by this section at the time a consumer contracts for an electronic fund transfer service or before the first electronic fund transfer is made involving the consumer's account.

(b) Content of disclosures. A financial institution shall provide the following disclosures, as applicable:

(1) Liability of consumer. A summary of the consumer's liability, under § 1005.6 or under state or other applicable law or agreement, for unauthorized electronic fund transfers.

(2) Telephone number and address. The telephone number and address of the person or office to be notified when the consumer believes that an unauthorized electronic fund transfer has been or may be made.

(3) Business days. The financial institution's business days.

(4) Types of transfers; limitations. The type of electronic fund transfers that the consumer may make and any limitations on the frequency and dollar amount of transfers. Details of the limitations need not be disclosed if confidentiality is essential to maintain the security of the electronic fund transfer system.

(5) Fees. Any fees imposed by the financial institution for electronic fund transfers or for the right to make transfers.

(6) Documentation. A summary of the consumer's right to receipts and periodic statements, as provided in § 1005.9 of this part, and notices regarding preauthorized transfers as provided in § 1005.10(a) and (d).

(7) Stop payment. A summary of the consumer's right to stop payment of a preauthorized electronic fund transfer and the procedure for placing a stop-payment order, as provided in § 1005.10(c).

(8) Liability of institution. A summary of the financial institution's liability to the consumer under section 910 of the Act for failure to make or to stop certain transfers.

(9) Confidentiality. The circumstances under which, in the ordinary course of business, the financial institution may provide information concerning the consumer's account to third parties.

(10) Error resolution. A notice that is substantially similar to Model Form A-3 as set out in appendix A of this part concerning error resolution.

(11) ATM fees. A notice that a fee may be imposed by an automated teller machine operator as defined in § 1005.16(a)(1), when the consumer initiates an electronic fund transfer or makes a balance inquiry, and by any network used to complete the transaction.

(c) Addition of electronic fund transfer services. If an electronic fund transfer service is added to a consumer's account and is subject to terms and conditions different from those described in the initial disclosures, disclosures for the new service are required.

§ 1005.8 Change in Terms Notice; Error Resolution Notice

(a) Change in terms notice—

(1) Prior notice required. A financial institution shall mail or deliver a written notice to the consumer, at least 21 days before the effective date, of any change in a term or condition required to be disclosed under § 1005.7(b) of this part if the change would result in:

(i) Increased fees for the consumer;

(ii) Increased liability for the consumer;

(iii) Fewer types of available electronic fund transfers; or

(iv) Stricter limitations on the frequency or dollar amount of transfers.

(2) Prior notice exception. A financial institution need not give prior notice if an immediate change in terms or conditions is necessary to maintain or restore the security of an account or an electronic fund transfer system. If the institution makes such

a change permanent and disclosure would not jeopardize the security of the account or system, the institution shall notify the consumer in writing on or with the next regularly scheduled periodic statement or within 30 days of making the change permanent.

(b) Error resolution notice. For accounts to or from which electronic fund transfers can be made, a financial institution shall mail or deliver to the consumer, at least once each calendar year, an error resolution notice substantially similar to the model form set forth in appendix A of this part (Model Form A-3). Alternatively, an institution may include an abbreviated notice substantially similar to the model form error resolution notice set forth in appendix A of this part (Model Form A-3), on or with each periodic statement required by § 1005.9(b).

§ 1005.9 Receipts at Electronic Terminals; Periodic Statements

(a) Receipts at electronic terminals— General. Except as provided in paragraph (e) of this section, a financial institution shall make a receipt available to a consumer at the time the consumer initiates an electronic fund transfer at an electronic terminal. The receipt shall set forth the following information, as applicable:

(1) Amount. The amount of the transfer. A transaction fee may be included in this amount, provided the amount of the fee is disclosed on the receipt and displayed on or at the terminal.

(2) Date. The date the consumer initiates the transfer.

(3) Type. The type of transfer and the type of the consumer's account(s) to or from which funds are transferred. The type of account may be omitted if the access device used is able to access only one account at that terminal.

(4)) Identification. A number or code that identifies the consumer's account or accounts, or the access device used to initiate the transfer. The number or code need not exceed four digits or letters to comply with the requirements of this paragraph (a)(4).

(5) Terminal location. The location of the terminal where the transfer is initiated, or an identification such as a code or terminal number. Except in limited circumstances where all terminals are located in the same city or state, if the location is disclosed, it shall include the city and state or foreign country and one of the following:

(i) The street address; or

(ii) A generally accepted name for the specific location; or

(iii) The name of the owner or operator of the terminal if other than the account-holding institution.

(6) Third party transfer. The name of any third party to or from whom funds are transferred.

(b) Periodic statements. For an account to or from which electronic fund transfers can be made, a financial institution shall send a periodic statement for each monthly cycle in which an electronic fund transfer has occurred; and shall send a periodic statement at least quarterly if no transfer has occurred. The statement shall set forth the following information, as applicable:

(1) Transaction information. For each electronic fund transfer occurring during the cycle:

(i) The amount of the transfer;

(ii) The date the transfer was credited or debited to the consumer's account;

(iii) The type of transfer and type of account to or from which funds were transferred;

(iv) For a transfer initiated by the consumer at an electronic terminal (except for a deposit of cash or a check, draft, or similar paper instrument), the terminal location described in paragraph (a)(5) of this section; and

(v) The name of any third party to or from whom funds were transferred.

(2) Account number. The number of the account.

(3) Fees. The amount of any fees assessed against the account during the statement period for electronic fund transfers, the right to make transfers, or account maintenance.

(4) Account balances. The balance in the account at the beginning and at the close of the statement period.

(5) Address and telephone number for inquiries. The address and telephone number to be used for inquiries or notice of errors, preceded by "Direct inquiries to" or similar language. The address and telephone number provided on an error resolution notice under § 1005.8(b) given on or with the statement satisfies this requirement.

(6) Telephone number for preauthorized transfers. A telephone number the consumer may call to ascertain whether preauthorized transfers to the consumer's account have occurred, if the financial institution uses the telephone-notice option under § 1005.10(a)(1)(iii).

(c) Exceptions to the periodic statement requirement for certain accounts—

(1) Preauthorized transfers to accounts. For accounts that may be accessed only by

preauthorized transfers to the account the following rules apply:

(i) Passbook accounts. For passbook accounts, the financial institution need not provide a periodic statement if the institution updates the passbook upon presentation or enters on a separate document the amount and date of each electronic fund transfer since the passbook was last presented.

(ii) Other accounts. For accounts other than passbook accounts, the financial institution must send a periodic statement at least quarterly.

(2) Intra-institutional transfers. For an electronic fund transfer initiated by the consumer between two accounts of the consumer in the same institution, documenting the transfer on a periodic statement for one of the two accounts satisfies the periodic statement requirement.

(3) Relationship between paragraphs (c)(1) and (2) of this section. An account that is accessed by preauthorized transfers to the account described in paragraph (c)(1) of this section and by intra-institutional transfers described in paragraph (c)(2) of this section, but by no other type of electronic fund transfers, qualifies for the exceptions provided by paragraph (c)(1) of this section.

(d) Documentation for foreign-initiated transfers. The failure by a financial institution to provide a terminal receipt for an electronic fund transfer or to document the transfer on a periodic statement does not violate this part if:

(1) The transfer is not initiated within a state; and

(2) The financial institution treats an inquiry for clarification or documentation as a notice of error in accordance with § 1005.11.

(e) Exception for receipts in small-value transfers. A financial institution is not subject to the requirement to make available a receipt under paragraph (a) of this section if the amount of the transfer is $15 or less.

§ 1005.10 Preauthorized Transfers

(a) Preauthorized transfers to consumer's account—

(1) Notice by financial institution. When a person initiates preauthorized electronic fund transfers to a consumer's account at least once every 60 days, the account-holding financial institution shall provide notice to the consumer by:

(i) Positive notice. Providing oral or written notice of the transfer within two business days after the transfer occurs; or

(ii) Negative notice. Providing oral or written notice, within two business days after the date on which the transfer was scheduled to occur, that the transfer did not occur; or

(iii) Readily-available telephone line. Providing a readily available telephone line that the consumer may call to determine whether the transfer occurred and disclosing the telephone number on the initial disclosure of account terms and on each periodic statement.

(2) Notice by payor. A financial institution need not provide notice of a transfer if the payor gives the consumer positive notice that the transfer has been initiated.

(3) Crediting. A financial institution that receives a preauthorized transfer of the type described in paragraph (a)(1) of this section shall credit the amount of the transfer as of the date the funds for the transfer are received.

(b) Written authorization for preauthorized transfers from consumer's account. Preauthorized electronic fund transfers from a consumer's account may be authorized only by a writing signed or similarly authenticated by the consumer. The person that obtains the authorization shall provide a copy to the consumer.

(c) Consumer's right to stop payment—

(1) Notice. A consumer may stop payment of a preauthorized electronic fund transfer from the consumer's account by notifying the financial institution orally or in writing at least three business days before the scheduled date of the transfer.

(2) Written confirmation. The financial institution may require the consumer to give written confirmation of a stop-payment order within 14 days of an oral notification. An institution that requires written confirmation shall inform the consumer of the requirement and provide the address where confirmation must be sent when the consumer gives the oral notification. An oral stop-payment order ceases to be binding after 14 days if the consumer fails to provide the required written confirmation.

(d) Notice of transfers varying in amount—

(1) Notice. When a preauthorized electronic fund transfer from the consumer's account will vary in amount from the previous transfer under the same authorization or from the preauthorized amount, the designated payee or the financial institution shall send the consumer written notice of the amount and date of the transfer at least 10 days before the scheduled date of transfer.

(2) Range. The designated payee or the institution shall inform the consumer of the right to receive notice of all varying transfers, but may give the consumer the option of receiving notice only when

a transfer falls outside a specified range of amounts or only when a transfer differs from the most recent transfer by more than an agreed-upon amount.

(e) Compulsory use—

(1) Credit. No financial institution or other person may condition an extension of credit to a consumer on the consumer's repayment by preauthorized electronic fund transfers, except for credit extended under an overdraft credit plan or extended to maintain a specified minimum balance in the consumer's account. This exception does not apply to a covered separate credit feature accessible by a hybrid prepaid-credit card as defined in Regulation Z, 12 CFR 1026.61. This exception also does not apply to covered overdraft credit extended by very large financial institutions as those terms are defined in Regulation Z, 12 CFR 1026.62.

(2) Employment or government benefit. No financial institution or other person may require a consumer to establish an account for receipt of electronic fund transfers with a particular institution as a condition of employment or receipt of a government benefit.

§ 1005.11 Procedures for Resolving Errors

(a) Definition of error—

(1) Types of transfers or inquiries covered. The term "error" means:

(i) An unauthorized electronic fund transfer;

(ii) An incorrect electronic fund transfer to or from the consumer's account;

(iii) The omission of an electronic fund transfer from a periodic statement;

(iv) A computational or bookkeeping error made by the financial institution relating to an electronic fund transfer;

(v) The consumer's receipt of an incorrect amount of money from an electronic terminal;

(vi) An electronic fund transfer not identified in accordance with § 1005.9 or § 1005.10(a); or

(vii) The consumer's request for documentation required by § 1005.9 or § 1005.10(a) or for additional information or clarification concerning an electronic fund transfer, including a request the consumer makes to determine whether an error exists under paragraphs (a)(1)(i) through (vi) of this section.

(2) Types of inquiries not covered. The term "error" does not include:

(i) A routine inquiry about the consumer's account balance;

(ii) A request for information for tax or other recordkeeping purposes; or

(iii) A request for duplicate copies of documentation.

(b) Notice of error from consumer—

(1) Timing; contents. A financial institution shall comply with the requirements of this section with respect to any oral or written notice of error from the consumer that:

(i) Is received by the institution no later than 60 days after the institution sends the periodic statement or provides the passbook documentation, required by § 1005.9, on which the alleged error is first reflected;

(ii) Enables the institution to identify the consumer's name and account number; and

(iii) Indicates why the consumer believes an error exists and includes to the extent possible the type, date, and amount of the error, except for requests described in paragraph (a)(1)(vii) of this section.

(2) Written confirmation. A financial institution may require the consumer to give written confirmation of an error within 10 business days of an oral notice. An institution that requires written confirmation shall inform the consumer of the requirement and provide the address where confirmation must be sent when the consumer gives the oral notification.

(3) Request for documentation or clarifications. When a notice of error is based on documentation or clarification that the consumer requested under paragraph (a)(1)(vii) of this section, the consumer's notice of error is timely if received by the financial institution no later than 60 days after the institution sends the information requested.

(c) Time limits and extent of investigation—

(1) Ten-day period. A financial institution shall investigate promptly and, except as otherwise provided in this paragraph (c), shall determine whether an error occurred within 10 business days of receiving a notice of error. The institution shall report the results to the consumer within three business days after completing its investigation. The institution shall correct the error within one business day after determining that an error occurred.

(2) Forty-five day period. If the financial institution is unable to complete its investigation within 10 business days, the institution may take up to 45 days from receipt of a notice of error to investigate and determine whether an error occurred, provided the institution does the following:

(i) Provisionally credits the consumer's account in the amount of the alleged error (including interest where applicable) within 10 business days of receiving the error notice. If the financial institution has a reasonable basis for believing that an unauthorized electronic fund transfer has occurred and the institution has satisfied the requirements of § 1005.6(a), the institution may withhold a maximum of $50 from the amount credited. An institution need not provisionally credit the consumer's account if:

(A) The institution requires but does not receive written confirmation within 10 business days of an oral notice of error; or

(B) The alleged error involves an account that is subject to Regulation T of the Board of Governors of the Federal Reserve System (Securities Credit by Brokers and Dealers, 12 CFR part 220);

(ii) Informs the consumer, within two business days after the provisional crediting, of the amount and date of the provisional crediting and gives the consumer full use of the funds during the investigation;

(iii) Corrects the error, if any, within one business day after determining that an error occurred; and

(iv) Reports the results to the consumer within three business days after completing its investigation (including, if applicable, notice that a provisional credit has been made final).

(3) Extension of time periods. The time periods in paragraphs (c)(1) and (c)(2) of this section are extended as follows:

(i) The applicable time is 20 business days in place of 10 business days under paragraphs (c)(1) and (2) of this section if the notice of error involves an electronic fund transfer to or from the account within 30 days after the first deposit to the account was made.

(ii) The applicable time is 90 days in place of 45 days under paragraph (c)(2) of this section, for completing an investigation, if a notice of error involves an electronic fund transfer that:

(A) Was not initiated within a state;

(B) Resulted from a point-of-sale debit card transaction; or

(C) Occurred within 30 days after the first deposit to the account was made.

(4) Investigation. With the exception of transfers covered by § 1005.14 of this part, a financial institution's review of its own records regarding an alleged error satisfies the requirements of this section if:

(i) The alleged error concerns a transfer to or from a third party; and

(ii) There is no agreement between the institution and the third party for the type of electronic fund transfer involved.

(d) Procedures if financial institution determines no error or different error occurred. In addition to following the procedures specified in paragraph (c) of this section, the financial institution shall follow the procedures set forth in this paragraph (d) if it determines that no error occurred or that an error occurred in a manner or amount different from that described by the consumer:

(1) Written explanation. The institution's report of the results of its investigation shall include a written explanation of the institution's findings and shall note the consumer's right to request the documents that the institution relied on in making its determination. Upon request, the institution shall promptly provide copies of the documents.

(2) Debiting provisional credit. Upon debiting a provisionally credited amount, the financial institution shall:

(i) Notify the consumer of the date and amount of the debiting;

(ii) Notify the consumer that the institution will honor checks, drafts, or similar instruments payable to third parties and preauthorized transfers from the consumer's account (without charge to the consumer as a result of an overdraft) for five business days after the notification. The institution shall honor items as specified in the notice, but need honor only items that it would have paid if the provisionally credited funds had not been debited.

(e) Reassertion of error. A financial institution that has fully complied with the error resolution requirements has no further responsibilities under this section should the consumer later reassert the same error, except in the case of an error asserted by the consumer following receipt of information provided under paragraph (a)(1)(vii) of this section.

§ 1005.12 Relation to Other Laws

(a) Relation to Truth in Lending.

(1) The Electronic Fund Transfer Act and this part govern:

(i) The addition to an accepted credit card, as defined in Regulation Z (12 CFR 1026.12, comment 12-2), of the capability to initiate electronic fund transfers;

(ii) The issuance of an access device (other than an access device for a prepaid account) that permits credit extensions (under a preexisting agreement between a consumer and a financial institution) only when the consumer's account is overdrawn or to maintain a specified minimum balance in the consumer's account, or under an overdraft service, as defined in § 1005.17(a) of this part;

(iii) The addition of an overdraft service, as defined in § 1005.17(a), to an accepted access device; and

(iv) A consumer's liability for an unauthorized electronic fund transfer and the investigation of errors involving:

(A) Except with respect to a prepaid account, an extension of credit that is incident to an electronic fund transfer that occurs under an agreement between the consumer and a financial institution to extend credit when the consumer's account is overdrawn or to maintain a specified minimum balance in the consumer's account, or under an overdraft service, as defined in § 1005.17(a);

(B) With respect to transactions that involve a covered separate credit feature and an asset feature on a prepaid account that are both accessible by a hybrid prepaid-credit card as those terms are defined in Regulation Z, 12 CFR 1026.61, an extension of credit that is incident to an electronic fund transfer that occurs when the hybrid prepaid-credit card accesses both funds in the asset feature of the prepaid account and a credit extension from the credit feature with respect to a particular transaction;

(C) Transactions that involves credit extended through a negative balance to the asset feature of a prepaid account that meets the conditions set forth in Regulation Z, 12 CFR 1026.61(a)(4); and

(D) With respect to transactions involving a prepaid account and a non-covered separate credit feature as defined in Regulation Z, 12 CFR 1026.61, transactions that access the prepaid account, as applicable.

(2) The Truth in Lending Act and Regulation Z (12 CFR part 1026), which prohibit the unsolicited issuance of credit cards, govern:

(i) The addition of a credit feature or plan to an accepted access device, including an access device for a prepaid account, that would make the access device into a credit card under Regulation Z (12 CFR part 1026);

(ii) Except as provided in paragraph (a)(1)(ii) of this section, the issuance of a credit card that is also an access device; and

(iii) With respect to transactions involving a prepaid account and a non-covered separate credit feature as defined in Regulation Z, 12 CFR 1026.61, a consumer's liability for unauthorized use and the investigation of errors involving transactions that access the non-covered separate credit feature, as applicable.

(b) Preemption of inconsistent state laws—

(1) Inconsistent requirements. The Bureau shall determine, upon its own motion or upon the request of a state, financial institution, or other interested party, whether the Act and this part preempt state law relating to electronic fund transfers, or dormancy, inactivity, or service fees, or expiration dates in the case of gift certificates, store gift cards, or general-use prepaid cards.

(2) Standards for determination. State law is inconsistent with the requirements of the Act and this part if state law:

(i) Requires or permits a practice or act prohibited by the federal law;

(ii) Provides for consumer liability for unauthorized electronic fund transfers that exceeds the limits imposed by the Federal law;

(iii) Allows longer time periods than the Federal law for investigating and correcting alleged errors, or does not require the financial institution to credit the consumer's account during an error investigation in accordance with § 1005.11(c)(2)(i) of this part; or

(iv) Requires initial disclosures, periodic statements, or receipts that are different in content from those required by the Federal law except to the extent that the disclosures relate to consumer rights granted by the state law and not by the Federal law.

(c) State exemptions—

(1) General rule. General rule. Any state may apply for an exemption from the requirements of the Act or this part for any class of electronic fund transfers within the state. The Bureau shall grant an exemption if it determines that:

(i) Under state law the class of electronic fund transfers is subject to requirements substantially similar to those imposed by the Federal law; and

(ii) There is adequate provision for state enforcement.

(2) Exception. To assure that the Federal and state courts continue to have concurrent jurisdiction, and to aid in implementing the Act:

(i) No exemption shall extend to the civil liability provisions of section 916 of the Act; and

(ii) When the Bureau grants an exemption, the state law requirements shall constitute the requirements of the Federal law for purposes of section 916 of the Act, except for state law requirements not imposed by the Federal law.

§ 1005.13 Administrative Enforcement; Record Retention

(a) Enforcement by Federal agencies. Compliance with this part is enforced in accordance with section 918 of the Act.

(b) Record retention—

(1) Any person subject to the Act and this part shall retain evidence of compliance with the requirements imposed by the Act and this part for a period of not less than two years from the date disclosures are required to be made or action is required to be taken.

(2) Any person subject to the Act and this part having actual notice that it is the subject of an investigation or an enforcement proceeding by its enforcement agency, or having been served with notice of an action filed under sections 910, 916, or 917(a) of the Act, shall retain the records that pertain to the investigation, action, or proceeding until final disposition of the matter unless an earlier time is allowed by court or agency order.

§ 1005.14 Electronic Fund Transfer Service Provider Not Holding Consumer's Accoun

(a) Provider of electronic fund transfer service. A person that provides an electronic fund transfer service to a consumer but that does not hold the consumer's account is subject to all requirements of this part if the person:

(1) Issues a debit card (or other access device) that the consumer can use to access the consumer's account held by a financial institution; and

(2) Has no agreement with the account-holding institution regarding such access.

(b) Compliance by service provider. In addition to the requirements generally applicable under this part, the service provider shall comply with the following special rules:

(1) Disclosures and documentation. The service provider shall give the disclosures and documentation required by §§ 1005.7, 1005.8, and 1005.9 of this part that are within the purview of its relationship with the consumer. The service provider need not furnish the periodic statement required by § 1005.9(b) if the following conditions are met:

(i) The debit card (or other access device) issued to the consumer bears the service provider's name and an address or telephone number for making inquiries or giving notice of error;

(ii) The consumer receives a notice concerning use of the debit card that is substantially similar to the notice contained in appendix A of this part;

(iii) The consumer receives, on or with the receipts required by § 1005.9(a), the address and telephone number to be used for an inquiry, to give notice of an error, or to report the loss or theft of the debit card;

(iv) The service provider transmits to the account-holding institution the information specified in § 1005.9(b)(1), in the format prescribed by the automated clearinghouse (ACH) system used to clear the fund transfers;

(v) The service provider extends the time period for notice of loss or theft of a debit card, set forth in § 1005.6(b)(1) and (2), from two business days to four business days after the consumer learns of the loss or theft; and extends the time periods for reporting unauthorized transfers or errors, set forth in §§ 1005.6(b)(3) and 1005.11(b)(1)(i), from 60 days to 90 days following the transmittal of a periodic statement by the account-holding institution.

(2) Error resolution.

(i) The service provider shall extend by a reasonable time the period in which notice of an error must be received, specified in § 1005.11(b)(1)(i), if a delay resulted from an initial attempt by the consumer to notify the account-holding institution.

(ii) The service provider shall disclose to the consumer the date on which it initiates a transfer to effect a provisional credit in accordance with § 1005.11(c)(2)(ii).

(iii) If the service provider determines an error occurred, it shall transfer funds to or from the consumer's account, in the appropriate amount and within the applicable time period, in accordance with § 1005.11(c)(2)(i).

(iv) If funds were provisionally credited and the service provider determines no error occurred, it may reverse the credit. The service provider shall notify the account-holding institution of the period during which the account-holding institution must honor debits to the account in accordance with § 1005.11(d)(2)(ii). If an overdraft results, the service provider shall promptly reimburse the account-holding institution in the amount of the overdraft.

(c) Compliance by account-holding institution. The account-holding institution need not comply with the requirements of the Act and this part with respect to electronic fund transfers initiated through the service provider except as follows:

(1) Documentation. The account-holding institution shall provide a periodic statement that describes each electronic fund transfer initiated by the consumer with the access device issued by the service provider. The account-holding institution has no liability for the failure to comply with this requirement if the service provider did not provide the necessary information; and

(2) Error resolution. Upon request, the account-holding institution shall provide information or copies of documents needed by the service provider to investigate errors or to furnish copies of documents to the consumer. The account-holding institution shall also honor debits to the account in accordance with § 1005.11(d)(2)(ii).

§ 1005.15 Electronic Fund Transfer of Government Benefits

(a) Government agency subject to regulation.

(1) A government agency is deemed to be a financial institution for purposes of the Act and this part if directly or indirectly it issues an access device to a consumer for use in initiating an electronic fund transfer of government benefits from an account, other than needs-tested benefits in a program established under state or local law or administered by a state or local agency. The agency shall comply with all applicable requirements of the Act and this part except as modified by this section.

(2) For purposes of this section, the term "account" or "government benefit account" means an account established by a government agency for distributing government benefits to a consumer electronically, such as through automated teller machines or point-of-sale terminals, but does not include an account for distributing needs-tested benefits in a program established under state or local law or administered by a state or local agency.

(b) Issuance of access devices. For purposes of this section, a consumer is deemed to request an access device when the consumer applies for government benefits that the agency disburses or will disburse by means of an electronic fund transfer. The agency shall verify the identity of the consumer receiving the device by reasonable means before the device is activated.

(c) Pre-acquisition disclosure requirements.

(1) Before a consumer acquires a government benefit account, a government agency shall comply with the pre-acquisition disclosure requirements applicable to prepaid accounts as set forth in § 1005.18(b).

(2) Additional content for government benefit accounts—

(i) Statement regarding consumer's payment options. As part of its short form pre-acquisition disclosures, the agency must provide a statement that the consumer does not have to accept the government benefit account and directing the consumer to ask about other ways to receive their benefit payments from the agency instead of receiving them via the account, using the following clause or a substantially similar clause: "You do not have to accept this benefits card. Ask about other ways to receive your benefits." Alternatively, an agency may provide a statement that the consumer has several options to receive benefit payments, followed by a list of the options available to the consumer, and directing the consumer to indicate which option the consumer chooses using the following clause or a substantially similar clause: "You have several options to receive your payments: [list of options available to the consumer]; or this benefits card. Tell the benefits office which option you choose." This statement must be located above the information required by § 1005.18(b)(2)(i) through (iv). This statement must appear in a minimum type size of eight points (or 11 pixels) and appear in no larger a type size than what is used for the fee headings required by § 1005.18(b)(2)(i) through (iv).

(ii) Statement regarding state-required information or other fee discounts and waivers. An agency may, but is not required to, include a statement in one additional line of text in the short form disclosure directing the consumer to a particular location outside the short form disclosure for information on ways the consumer may access government benefit account funds and balance information for free or for a reduced fee. This statement must be located directly below any statements disclosed pursuant to § 1005.18(b)(3)(i) and (ii), or, if no such statements are disclosed, above the statement required by § 1005.18(b)(2)(x). This statement must appear in the same type size used to disclose variable fee information pursuant to § 1005.18(b)(3)(i) and (ii), or, if none, the same type size used for the information required by § 1005.18(b)(2)(x) through (xiii).

(3) Form of disclosures. When a short form disclosure required by paragraph (c) of this section is provided in writing or electronically, the information required by § 1005.18(b)(2)(i) through (ix) shall be provided in the form of a table. Except as provided in § 1005.18(b)(6)(iii)(B), the short form disclosure required by § 1005.18(b)(2) shall be provided in a form substantially similar to Model Form A-10(a) of appendix A of this part. Sample Form A-10(f) in appendix A of this part provides an example of the long form disclosure required by § 1005.18(b)(4) when the agency does not offer multiple service plans.

(d) Access to account information—

(1) Periodic statement alternative. A government agency need not furnish periodic statements required by § 1005.9(b) if the agency makes available to the consumer:

(i) The consumer's account balance, through a readily available telephone line and at a terminal (such as by providing balance information at a balance-inquiry terminal or providing it, routinely or upon request, on a terminal receipt at the time of an electronic fund transfer);

(ii) An electronic history of the consumer's account transactions, such as through a Web site, that covers at least 12 months preceding the date the consumer electronically accesses the account; and

(iii) A written history of the consumer's account transactions that is provided promptly in response to an oral or written request and that covers at least 24 months preceding the date the agency receives the consumer's request.

(2) Additional access to account information requirements. For government benefit accounts, a government agency shall comply with the account information requirements applicable to prepaid accounts as set forth in § 1005.18(c)(3) through (5).

(e) Modified disclosure, limitations on liability, and error resolution requirements. A government agency that provides information under paragraph (d)(1) of this section shall comply with the following:

(1) Initial disclosures. The agency shall modify the disclosures under § 1005.7(b) by disclosing:

(i) Access to account information. A telephone number that the consumer may call to obtain the account balance, the means by which the consumer can obtain an electronic account history, such as the address of a Web site, and a summary of the consumer's right to receive a written account history upon request (in place of the summary of the right to receive a periodic statement required by § 1005.7(b)(6)), including a telephone number to call to request a history. The disclosure required by this paragraph (e)(1)(i) may be made by providing a notice substantially similar to the notice contained in paragraph (a) of appendix A-5 of this part.

(ii) Error resolution. A notice concerning error resolution that is substantially similar to the notice contained in paragraph (b) of appendix A-5 of this part, in place of the notice required by § 1005.7(b)(10).

(2) Annual error resolution notice. The agency shall provide an annual notice concerning error resolution that is substantially similar to the notice contained in paragraph (b) of appendix A-5 of this part, in place of the notice required by § 1005.8(b). Alternatively, the agency may include on or with each electronic or written history provided in accordance with paragraph (d)(1) of this section, a notice substantially similar to the abbreviated notice for periodic statements contained in paragraph (b) in appendix A-3 of this part, modified as necessary to reflect the error resolution provisions set forth in this section.

(3) Modified limitations on liability requirements.

(i) For purposes of § 1005.6(b)(3), the 60-day period for reporting any unauthorized transfer shall begin on the earlier of:

(A) The date the consumer electronically accesses the consumer's account under paragraph (d)(1)(ii) of this section, provided that the electronic history made available to the consumer reflects the unauthorized transfer; or

(B) The date the agency sends a written history of the consumer's account transactions requested by the consumer under paragraph (d)(1)(iii) of this section in which the unauthorized transfer is first reflected.

(ii) An agency may comply with paragraph (e)(3)(i) of this section by limiting the consumer's liability for an unauthorized transfer as provided under § 1005.6(b)(3) for any transfer reported by the consumer within 120 days after the transfer was credited or debited to the consumer's account.

(4) Modified error resolution requirements.

(i) The agency shall comply with the requirements of § 1005.11 in response to an oral or written notice of an error from the consumer that is received by the earlier of:

(A) Sixty days after the date the consumer electronically accesses the consumer's account under paragraph (d)(1)(ii) of this section, provided that the electronic history made available to the consumer reflects the alleged error; or

(B) Sixty days after the date the agency sends a written history of the consumer's account transactions requested by the consumer under paragraph (d)(1)(iii) of this section in which the alleged error is first reflected.

(ii) In lieu of following the procedures in paragraph (e)(4)(i) of this section, an agency complies with the requirements for resolving errors in § 1005.11 if it investigates any oral or written notice of an error from the consumer that is received by the agency within 120 days after the transfer allegedly in error was credited or debited to the consumer's account.

(f) Disclosure of fees and other information. For government benefit accounts, a government agency shall comply with the disclosure and change-in-terms requirements applicable to prepaid accounts as set forth in § 1005.18(f).

(g) Government benefit accounts accessible by hybrid prepaid-credit cards. For government benefit accounts accessible by hybrid prepaid-credit cards as defined in Regulation Z, 12 CFR 1026.61, a government agency shall comply with prohibitions and requirements applicable to prepaid accounts as set forth in § 1005.18(g).

§ 1005.17 Requirements for Overdraft Services

(a) Definition. For purposes of this section, the term "overdraft service" means a service under which a financial institution assesses a fee or charge on a consumer's account held by the institution for paying a transaction (including a check or other item) when the consumer has insufficient or unavailable funds in the account. The term "overdraft service" does not include any payment of overdrafts pursuant to:

(1) A line of credit subject to Regulation Z (12 CFR part 1026), including transfers from a credit card account, home equity line of credit, or overdraft line of credit;

(2) A service that transfers funds from another account held individually or jointly by a consumer, such as a savings account;

(3) A line of credit or other transaction exempt from Regulation Z (12 CFR part 1026) pursuant to 12 CFR 1026.3(d); or

(4) A covered separate credit feature accessible by a hybrid prepaid-credit card as defined in Regulation Z, 12 CFR 1026.61; or credit extended through a negative balance on the asset feature of the prepaid account that meets the conditions of 12 CFR 1026.61(a)(4).

(b) Opt-in requirement—

(1) General. Except as provided under paragraph (c) of this section, a financial institution holding a consumer's account shall not assess a fee or charge on a consumer's account for paying an ATM or one-time debit card transaction pursuant to the institution's overdraft service, unless the institution:

(i) Provides the consumer with a notice in writing, or if the consumer agrees, electronically, segregated from all other information, describing the institution's overdraft service;

(ii) Provides a reasonable opportunity for the consumer to affirmatively consent, or opt in, to the service for ATM and one-time debit card transactions;

(iii) Obtains the consumer's affirmative consent, or opt-in, to the institution's payment of ATM or one-time debit card transactions; and

(iv) Provides the consumer with confirmation of the consumer's consent in writing, or if the consumer agrees, electronically, which includes a statement informing the consumer of the right to revoke such consent.

(2) Conditioning payment of other overdrafts on consumer's affirmative consent. A financial institution shall not:

(i) Condition the payment of any overdrafts for checks, ACH transactions, and other types of transactions on the consumer affirmatively consenting to the institution's payment of ATM and one-time debit card transactions pursuant to the institution's overdraft service; or

(ii) Decline to pay checks, ACH transactions, and other types of transactions that overdraw the consumer's account because the consumer has not affirmatively consented to the institution's overdraft service for ATM and one-time debit card transactions.

(3) Same account terms, conditions, and features. A financial institution shall provide to consumers who do not affirmatively consent to the institution's overdraft service for ATM and one-time debit card transactions the same account terms, conditions, and features that it provides to consumers who affirmatively consent, except for the overdraft service for ATM and one-time debit card transactions.

(c) Timing.

(1) Existing account holders. For accounts opened prior to July 1, 2010, the financial institution must not assess any fees or charges on a consumer's account on or after August 15, 2010, for paying an ATM or one-time debit card transaction pursuant to the overdraft service, unless the institution has complied with § 1005.17(b)(1) and obtained the consumer's affirmative consent.

(2) New account holders. For accounts opened on or after July 1, 2010, the financial institution must comply with § 1005.17(b)(1) and obtain the consumer's affirmative consent before the institution assesses any fee or charge on the consumer's account for paying an ATM or one-time debit card transaction pursuant to the institution's overdraft service.

(d) Content and format. The notice required by paragraph (b)(1)(i) of this section shall be substantially similar to Model Form A-9 set forth in appendix A of this part, include all applicable items in this paragraph, and may not contain any information not specified in or otherwise permitted by this paragraph.

(1) Overdraft service. A brief description of the financial institution's overdraft service and the types of transactions for which a fee or charge for paying an overdraft may be imposed, including ATM and one-time debit card transactions.

(2) Fees imposed. The dollar amount of any fees or charges assessed by the financial institution for paying an ATM or one-time debit card transaction pursuant to the institution's overdraft service, including any daily or other overdraft fees. If the amount of the fee is determined on the basis of the number of times the consumer has overdrawn the account, the amount of the overdraft, or other factors, the institution must disclose the maximum fee that may be imposed.

(3) Limits on fees charged. The maximum number of overdraft fees or charges that may be assessed per day, or, if applicable, that there is no limit.

(4) Disclosure of opt-in right. An explanation of the consumer's right to affirmatively consent to the financial institution's payment of overdrafts for ATM and one-time debit card transactions pursuant to the institution's overdraft service, including the methods by which the consumer may consent to the service; and

(5) Alternative plans for covering overdrafts. If the institution offers a line of credit subject to Regulation Z (12 CFR part 1026) or a service that transfers funds from another account of the consumer held at the institution to cover overdrafts, the institution must state that fact. An institution may, but is not required to, list additional alternatives for the payment of overdrafts.

(6) Permitted modifications and additional content. If applicable, the institution may modify the content required by § 1005.17(d) to indicate that the consumer has the right to opt into, or opt out of, the payment of overdrafts under the institution's overdraft service for other types of transactions, such as checks, ACH transactions, or automatic bill payments; to provide a means for the consumer to exercise this choice; and to disclose the associated returned item fee and that additional merchant fees may apply. The institution may also disclose the consumer's right to revoke consent. For notices provided to consumers who have opened accounts prior to July 1, 2010, the financial institution may describe the institution's overdraft service with respect to ATM and one-time debit card transactions with a statement such as "After August 15, 2010, we will not authorize and pay overdrafts for the following types of transactions unless you ask us to (see below)."

(e) Joint relationships. If two or more consumers jointly hold an account, the financial institution shall treat the affirmative consent of any of the joint consumers as affirmative consent for that account. Similarly, the financial institution shall treat a revocation of affirmative consent by any of the joint consumers as revocation of consent for that account.

(f) Continuing right to opt in or to revoke the opt-in. A consumer may affirmatively consent to the financial institution's overdraft service at any time in the manner described in the notice required by paragraph (b)(1)(i) of this section. A consumer may also revoke consent at any time in the manner made available to the consumer for providing consent. A financial institution must implement a consumer's revocation of consent as soon as reasonably practicable.

(g) Duration and revocation of opt-in. A consumer's affirmative consent to the institution's overdraft service is effective until revoked by the consumer, or unless the financial institution terminates the service.

§ 1005.18 Requirements for Financial Institutions Offering Prepaid Accounts

(a) Coverage. A financial institution shall comply with all applicable requirements of the Act and this part with respect to prepaid accounts except as modified by this section. For rules governing government benefit accounts, see § 1005.15.

(b) Pre-acquisition disclosure requirements—

(1) Timing of disclosures—

(i) General. Except as provided in paragraph (b)(1)(ii) or (iii) of this section, a financial institution shall provide the disclosures required by paragraph (b) of this section before a consumer acquires a prepaid account. When a prepaid account is used for disbursing funds to a consumer, and the financial institution or third party making the disbursement does not offer any alternative means for the consumer to receive those funds in lieu of accepting the prepaid account, for purposes of this paragraph, the disclosures required by paragraph (b) of this section may be provided at the time the consumer receives the prepaid account.

(ii) Disclosures for prepaid accounts acquired in retail locations. A financial institution is not required to provide the long form disclosure required by paragraph (b)(4) of this section before a consumer acquires a prepaid account in person at a retail location if the following conditions are met:

(A) The prepaid account access device is contained inside the packaging material.

(B) The disclosure required by paragraph (b)(2) of this section is provided on or are visible through an outward-facing, external surface of a prepaid account access device's packaging material.

(C) The disclosure required by paragraph (b)(2) of this section includes the information set forth in paragraph (b)(2)(xiii) of this section that allows a consumer to access the information required to be disclosed by paragraph (b)(4) of this section by telephone and via a website.

(D) The long form disclosure required by paragraph (b)(4) of this section is provided after the consumer acquires the prepaid account. If a financial institution does not provide the long form disclosure inside the prepaid account packaging material, and it is not otherwise already mailing or delivering to the consumer written account-related communications within 30 days of obtaining the consumer's contact information, it may provide the long form disclosure pursuant to this paragraph in electronic form without regard to the consumer notice and consent requirements of section 101(c) of the Electronic Signatures in Global and National Commerce Act (E-Sign Act) (15 U.S.C. 7001 et seq.).

(iii) Disclosures for prepaid accounts acquired orally by telephone. A financial institution is not required to provide the long form disclosure required by paragraph (b)(4) of this section before a consumer acquires a prepaid account orally by telephone if the following conditions are met:

(A) The financial institution communicates to the consumer orally, before the consumer acquires the prepaid account, that the information required to be disclosed by paragraph (b)(4) of this section is available both by telephone and on a Web site.

(B) The financial institution makes the information required to be disclosed by paragraph (b)(4) of this section available both by telephone and on a Web site.

(C) The long form disclosure required by paragraph (b)(4) of this section is provided after the consumer acquires the prepaid account.

(2) Short form disclosure content. In accordance with paragraph (b)(1) of this section, a financial institution shall provide a disclosure setting forth the following fees and information for a prepaid account, as applicable:

(i) Periodic fee. The periodic fee charged for holding the prepaid account, assessed on a monthly or other periodic basis, using the term "Monthly fee," "Annual fee," or a substantially similar term.

(ii) Per purchase fee. The fee for making a purchase using the prepaid account, using the term "Per purchase" or a substantially similar term.

(iii) ATM withdrawal fees. Two fees for using an automated teller machine to initiate a withdrawal of cash in the United States from the prepaid account, both within and outside of the financial institution's network or a network affiliated with the financial institution, using the term "ATM withdrawal" or a substantially similar term, and "in-network" or "out-of-network," respectively, or substantially similar terms.

(iv) Cash reload fee. The fee for reloading cash into the prepaid account using the term "Cash reload" or a substantially similar term. The fee disclosed must be the total of all charges from the financial institution and any third parties for a cash reload.

(v) ATM balance inquiry fees. Two fees for using an automated teller machine to check the balance of the prepaid account in the United States, both within and outside of the financial institution's network or a network affiliated with the financial institution, using the term "ATM balance inquiry" or a substantially similar term, and "in-network" or "out-of-network," respectively, or substantially similar terms.

(vi) Customer service fees. Two fees for calling the financial institution about the prepaid account, both for calling an interactive voice response system and a live customer service agent, using the term "Customer service" or a substantially similar term, and "automated" or "live agent," or substantially similar terms, respectively, and "per call" or a substantially similar term. When providing a short form disclosure for multiple service plans pursuant to paragraph (b)(6)(iii)(B)(*2*) of this section, disclose only the fee for calling the live agent customer service about the prepaid account, using the term "Live customer service" or a substantially similar term and "per call" or a substantially similar term.

(vii) Inactivity fee. The fee for non-use, dormancy, or inactivity of the prepaid account, using the term "Inactivity" or a substantially similar term, as well as the conditions that trigger the financial institution to impose that fee.

(viii) Statements regarding additional fee types—

(A) Statement regarding number of additional fee types charged. A statement disclosing the number of additional fee types the financial institution may charge consumers with respect to the prepaid account, using the following clause or a substantially similar clause: "We charge [x] other types of fees." The number of additional fee types disclosed must reflect the total number of fee types under which the financial institution may charge fees, excluding:

(*1*) Fees required to be disclosed pursuant to paragraphs (b)(2)(i) through (vii) and (b)(5) of this section; and

(*2*) Any finance charges as described in Regulation Z, 12 CFR 1026.4(b)(11), imposed in connection with a covered separate credit feature accessible by a hybrid prepaid-credit card as defined in 12 CFR 1026.61.

(B) Statement directing consumers to disclosure of additional fee types. If a financial institution makes a disclosure pursuant to paragraph (b)(2)(ix) of this section, a statement directing consumers to that disclosure, located after but on the same line of text as the statement regarding the number of additional fee types required by paragraph (b)(2)(viii)(A) of this section, using the following clause or a substantially similar clause: "Here are some of them:".

(ix) Disclosure of additional fee types—

(A) Determination of which additional fee types to disclose. The two fee types that generate the highest revenue from consumers for the prepaid account program or across prepaid account programs that share the same fee schedule during the time period provided in paragraphs (b)(2)(ix)(D) and (E) of this section, excluding:

(*1*) Fees required to be disclosed pursuant to paragraphs (b)(2)(i) through (vii) and (b)(5) of this section;

(*2*) Any fee types that generated less than 5 percent of the total revenue from consumers for the prepaid account program or across prepaid account programs that share the same fee schedule during the time period provided in paragraphs (b)(2)(ix)(D) and (E) of this section; and

(3) Any finance charges as described in Regulation Z, 12 CFR 1026.4(b)(11), imposed in connection with a covered separate credit feature accessible by a hybrid prepaid-credit card as defined in 12 CFR 1026.61.

(B) Disclosure of fewer than two additional fee types. A financial institution that has only one additional fee type that satisfies the criteria in paragraph (b)(2)(ix)(A) of this section must disclose that one additional fee type; it may, but is not required to, also disclose another additional fee type of its choice. A financial institution that has no additional fee types that satisfy the criteria in paragraph (b)(2)(ix)(A) of this section is not required to make a disclosure under this paragraph (b)(2)(ix); it may, but is not required to, disclose one or two fee types of its choice.

(C) Fee variations in additional fee types. If an additional fee type required to be disclosed pursuant to paragraph (b)(2)(ix)(A) of this section has more than two fee variations, or when providing a short form disclosure for multiple service plans pursuant to paragraph (b)(6)(iii)(B)(*2*) of this section, the financial institution must disclose the name of the additional fee type and the highest fee amount in accordance with paragraph (b)(3)(i) of this section; for disclosures other than for multiple service plans, it may, but is not required to, consolidate the fee variations into two categories and disclose the names of those two fee variation categories and the fee amounts in a format substantially similar to that used to disclose the two-tier fees required by paragraphs (b)(2)(v) and (vi) of this section and in accordance with paragraphs (b)(3)(i) and (b)(7)(ii)(B)(*1*) of this section. Except when providing a short form disclosure for multiple service plans pursuant to paragraph (b)(6)(iii)(B)(*2*) of this section, if an additional fee type has two fee variations, the financial institution must disclose the name of the additional fee type together with the names of the two fee variations and the fee amounts in a format substantially similar to that used to disclose the two-tier fees required by paragraphs (b)(2)(v) and (vi) of this section and in accordance with paragraph (b)(7)(ii)(B)(*1*) of this section. If a financial institution only charges one fee under a particular fee type, the financial institution must disclose the name of the additional fee type and the fee amount; it may, but is not required to, disclose also the name of the one fee variation for which the fee amount is charged, in a format substantially similar to that used to disclose the two-tier fees required by paragraphs (b)(2)(v) and (vi) of this section, except that the financial institution would disclose only the one fee variation name and fee amount instead of two.

(D) Timing of initial assessment of additional fee types disclosure—

(1) Existing prepaid account programs as of April 1, 2019. For a prepaid account program in effect as of April 1, 2019, the financial institution must disclose the additional fee types based on revenue for a 24-month period that begins no earlier than October 1, 2014.

(2) Existing prepaid account programs as of April 1, 2019 with unavailable data. If a financial institution does not have 24 months of fee revenue data for a particular prepaid account program from which to calculate the additional fee types disclosure in advance of April 1, 2019, the financial institution must disclose the additional fee types based on revenue it reasonably anticipates the prepaid account program will generate over the 24-month period that begins on April 1, 2019.

(3) New prepaid account programs created on or after April 1, 2019. For a prepaid account program created on or after October 1, 2017, the financial institution must disclose the additional fee types based on revenue it reasonably anticipates the prepaid account program will generate over the first 24 months of the program.

(E) Timing of periodic reassessment and update of additional fee types disclosure—

(*1*) General. A financial institution must reassess its additional fee types disclosure periodically as described in paragraph (b)(2)(ix)(E)(*2*) of this section and upon a fee schedule change as described in paragraph (b)(2)(ix)(E)(*3*) of this section. The financial institution must update its additional fee types disclosure if the previous disclosure no longer complies with the requirements of this paragraph (b)(2)(ix).

(*2*) Periodic reassessment. A financial institution must reassess whether its previously disclosed additional fee types continue to comply with the requirements of this paragraph (b)(2)(ix) every 24 months based on revenue for the previous 24-month period. The financial institution must complete this reassessment and update its disclosure, if applicable, within three months of the end of the 24-month period, except as provided in the update printing exception in paragraph (b)(2)(ix)(E)(*4*) of this section. A financial institution may, but is not required to, carry out this reassessment and update, if applicable, more frequently than every 24 months, at which time a new 24-month period commences.

(*3*) Fee schedule change. If a financial institution revises the fee schedule for a prepaid account program, it must determine whether it reasonably anticipates that the previously disclosed additional fee types will continue to comply with the requirements of this paragraph (b)(2)(ix) for the 24 months following implementation of the fee schedule change. If the financial institution reasonably anticipates that the previously disclosed additional fee types will not comply with the requirements of this paragraph (b)(2)(ix), it must update the disclosure based on its reasonable anticipation of what those additional fee types will be at the time the fee schedule change goes into effect, except as provided in the update printing exception in paragraph (b)(2)(ix)(E)(*4*) of this section. If an immediate change in terms and conditions is necessary to maintain or restore the security of an account or an electronic fund transfer system as described in § 1005.8(a)(2) and that change affects the prepaid account program's fee schedule, the financial institution must complete its reassessment and update its disclosure, if applicable, within three months of the date it makes the change permanent, except as provided in the update printing exception in paragraph (b)(2)(ix)(E)(*4*) of this section.

(*4*) Update printing exception. Notwithstanding the requirements to update an additional fee types disclosure in paragraph (b)(2)(ix)(E) of this section, a financial institution is not required to update the listing of additional fee types that are provided on, in, or with prepaid account packaging materials that were manufactured, printed, or otherwise produced prior to a periodic reassessment and update pursuant to paragraph (b)(2)(ix)(E)(*2*) of this section or prior to a fee schedule change pursuant to paragraph (b)(2)(ix)(E)(*3*) of this section.

(x) Statement regarding overdraft credit features. If a covered separate credit feature accessible by a hybrid prepaid-credit card as defined in Regulation Z, 12 CFR 1026.61, may be offered at any point to a consumer in connection with the prepaid account, a statement that overdraft/credit may be offered, the time period after which it may be offered, and that fees would apply, using the following clause or a substantially similar clause: "You may be offered overdraft/credit after [x] days. Fees would apply." If no such credit feature will be offered at any point to a consumer in connection with the prepaid account, a statement that no overdraft credit feature is offered, using the following clause or a substantially similar clause: "No overdraft/credit feature."

(xi) Statement regarding registration and FDIC or NCUA insurance. A statement regarding the prepaid account program's eligibility for FDIC deposit insurance or NCUA share insurance, as appropriate, and directing the consumer to register the prepaid account for insurance and other account protections, where applicable, as follows:

(A) Account is insurance eligible and does not have pre-acquisition consumer identification/verification. If a prepaid account program is set up to be eligible for FDIC deposit or NCUA share insurance, and consumer identification and verification does not occur before the account is opened, using the following clause or a substantially similar clause: "Register your card for [FDIC insurance eligibility] [NCUA insurance, if eligible,] and other protections."

(B) Account is not insurance eligible and does not have pre-acquisition consumer identification/verification. If a prepaid account program is not set up to be eligible for FDIC deposit or NCUA share insurance, and consumer identification and verification does not occur before the account is opened, using the following clause or a substantially similar clause: "Not [FDIC] [NCUA] insured. Register your card for other protections."

(C) Account is insurance eligible and has pre-acquisition consumer identification/verification. If a prepaid account program is set up to be eligible for FDIC deposit or NCUA share insurance, and consumer identification and verification occurs for all prepaid accounts within the prepaid program before the account is opened, using the following clause or a substantially similar clause: "Your funds are [eligible for FDIC insurance] [NCUA insured, if eligible]."

(D) Account is not insurance eligible and has pre-acquisition consumer identification/verification. If a prepaid account program is not set up to be eligible for FDIC deposit or NCUA share insurance, and consumer identification and verification occurs for all prepaid accounts within the prepaid account program before the account is opened, using the following clause or a substantially similar clause: "Your funds are not [FDIC] [NCUA] insured."

(E) No consumer identification/verification. If a prepaid account program is set up such that there is no consumer identification and verification process for any prepaid accounts within the prepaid account program, using the following clause or a substantially similar clause: "Treat this card like cash. Not [FDIC] [NCUA] insured."

(xii) Statement regarding CFPB Web site. A statement directing the consumer to a Web site URL of the Consumer Financial Protection Bureau (cfpb.gov/prepaid) for general information about prepaid accounts, using the following clause or a substantially similar clause: "For general information about prepaid accounts, visit cfpb.gov/prepaid."

(xiii) Statement regarding information on all fees and services. A statement directing the consumer to the location of the long form disclosure required by paragraph (b)(4) of this section to find details and conditions for all fees and services. For a financial institution offering prepaid accounts at a retail location pursuant to the retail location exception in paragraph (b)(1)(ii) of this section, this statement must also include a telephone number and a Web site URL that a consumer may use to directly access, respectively, an oral and an electronic version of the long form disclosure required under paragraph (b)(4) of this section. The disclosure required by this paragraph must be made using the following clause or a substantially similar clause: "Find details and conditions for all fees and services in [location]" or, for prepaid accounts offered at retail locations pursuant to paragraph (b)(1)(ii) of this section, made using the following clause or a substantially similar clause: "Find details and conditions for all fees and services inside the package, or call [telephone number] or visit [Web site]." The Web site URL may not exceed 22 characters and must be meaningfully named. A financial institution may, but is not required to, disclose an SMS code at the end of the statement disclosing the telephone number and Web site URL, if the SMS code can be accommodated on the same line of text as the statement required by this paragraph.

(xiv) Additional content for payroll card accounts—

(A) Statement regarding wage or salary payment options. For payroll card accounts, a statement that the consumer does not have to accept the payroll card account and directing the consumer to ask about other ways to receive wages or salary from the employer instead of receiving them via the payroll card account using the following clause or a substantially similar clause: "You do not have to accept this payroll card. Ask your employer about other ways to receive your wages." Alternatively, a financial institution may provide a statement that the consumer has several options to receive wages or salary, followed by a list of the options available to the consumer, and directing the consumer to tell the employer which option the consumer chooses using the following clause or a substantially similar clause: "You have several options to receive your wages: [list of options available to the consumer]; or this payroll card. Tell your employer which option you choose." This statement must be located above the information required by paragraphs (b)(2)(i) through (iv).

(B) Statement regarding state-required information or other fee discounts and waivers. For payroll card accounts, a financial institution may, but is not required to, include a statement in one additional line of text directing the consumer to a particular location outside the short form disclosure for information on ways the consumer may access payroll card account funds and balance information for free or for a reduced fee. This statement must be located directly below any statements disclosed pursuant to paragraphs (b)(3)(i) and (ii) of this section, or, if no such statements are disclosed, above the statement required by paragraph (b)(2)(x) of this section.

(3) Short form disclosure of variable fees and third-party fees and prohibition on disclosure of finance charges—

(i) General disclosure of variable fees. If the amount of any fee that is required to be disclosed in the short form disclosure pursuant to paragraphs (b)(2)(i) through (vii) and (ix) of this section could vary, a financial institution shall disclose the highest amount it may impose for that fee, followed by a symbol, such as an asterisk, linked to a statement explaining that the fee could be lower depending on how and where the prepaid account is used, using the following clause or a substantially similar clause: "This fee can be lower depending on how and where this card is used." Except as provided in paragraph (b)(3)(ii) of this section, a financial institution must use the same symbol and statement for all fees that could vary. The linked statement must be located above the statement required by paragraph (b)(2)(x) of this section.

(ii) Disclosure of variable periodic fee. If the amount of the periodic fee disclosed in the short form disclosure pursuant to paragraph (b)(2)(i) of this section could vary, as an alternative to the disclosure required by paragraph (b)(3)(i) of this section, the financial institution may disclose the highest amount it may impose for the periodic fee, followed by a symbol, such as a dagger, that is different from the symbol the financial institution uses pursuant to paragraph (b)(3)(i) of this section, to indicate that a waiver of the fee or a lower fee might apply, linked to a statement in one additional line of text disclosing the waiver or reduced fee amount and explaining the circumstances under which the fee waiver or reduction may occur. The linked statement must be located directly above or in place of the linked statement required by paragraph (b)(3)(i) of this section, as applicable.

(iii) Single disclosure for like fees. As an alternative to the two-tier fee disclosure required by paragraphs (b)(2)(iii), (v), and (vi) of this section and any two-tier fee required by paragraph (b)(2)(ix) of this section, a financial institution may disclose a single fee amount when the amount is the same for both fees.

(iv) Third-party fees in general. Except as provided in paragraph (b)(3)(v) of this section, a financial institution may not include any third-party fees in a disclosure made pursuant to paragraph (b)(2) of this section.

(v) Third-party cash reload fees. Any third-party fee included in the cash reload fee disclosed in the short form pursuant to paragraph (b)(2)(iv) of this section must be the highest fee known by the financial institution at the time it prints, or otherwise prepares, the short form disclosure required by paragraph (b)(2) of this section. A financial institution is not required to revise its short form disclosure to reflect a cash reload fee change by a third party until such time that the financial institution manufactures, prints, or otherwise produces new prepaid account packaging materials or otherwise updates the short form disclosure.

(vi) Prohibition on disclosure of finance charges. A financial institution may not include in a disclosure made pursuant to paragraphs (b)(2)(i) through (ix) of this section any finance charges as described in Regulation Z, 12 CFR 1026.4(b)(11), imposed in connection with a covered separate credit feature accessible by a hybrid prepaid-credit card as defined in 12 CFR 1026.61.

(4) Long form disclosure content. In accordance with paragraph (b)(1) of this section, a financial institution shall provide a disclosure setting forth the following fees and information for a prepaid account, as applicable:

(i) Title for long form disclosure. A heading stating the name of the prepaid account program and that the long form disclosure contains a list of all fees for that particular prepaid account program.

(ii) Fees. All fees that may be imposed in connection with a prepaid account. For each fee, the financial institution must disclose the amount of the fee and the conditions, if any, under which the fee may be imposed, waived, or reduced. A financial institution may not use any symbols, such as an asterisk, to explain conditions under which any fee may be imposed. A financial institution may, but is not required to, include in the long form disclosure any service or feature it provides or offers at no charge to the consumer. The financial institution must also disclose any third-party fee amounts known to the financial institution that may apply. For any such third-party fee disclosed, the financial institution may, but is not required to, include either or both a statement that the fee is accurate as of or through a specific date or that the third-party fee is subject to change. If a third-party fee may apply but the amount of that fee is not known by the financial institution, it must include a statement indicating that the third-party fee may apply without specifying the fee amount. A financial institution is not required to revise the long form disclosure required by paragraph (b)(4) of this section to reflect a fee change by a third party until such time that the financial institution manufactures, prints, or otherwise produces new prepaid account packaging materials or otherwise updates the long form disclosure.

(iii) Statement regarding registration and FDIC or NCUA insurance. The statement required by paragraph (b)(2)(xi) of this section, together with an explanation of FDIC or NCUA insurance coverage and the benefit of such coverage or the consequence of the lack of such coverage, as applicable.

(iv) Statement regarding overdraft credit features. The statement required by paragraph (b)(2)(x) of this section.

(v) Statement regarding financial institution contact information. A statement directing the consumer to a telephone number, mailing address, and Web site URL of the person or office that a consumer may contact to learn about the terms and conditions of the prepaid account, to obtain prepaid account balance information, to request a copy of transaction history pursuant to paragraph (c)(1)(iii) of this section if the financial institution does not provide periodic statements pursuant to § 1005.9(b), or to notify the financial institution when the consumer believes that an unauthorized electronic fund transfer occurred as required by § 1005.7(b)(2) and paragraph (d)(1)(ii) of this section.

(vi) Statement regarding CFPB Web site and telephone number. A statement directing the consumer to a Web site URL of the Consumer Financial Protection Bureau (cfpb.gov/prepaid) for general information about prepaid accounts, and a statement directing the consumer to a Consumer Financial Protection Bureau telephone number (1-855-411-2372) and Web site URL (cfpb.gov/complaint) to submit a complaint about a prepaid account, using the following clause or a substantially similar clause: "For general information about prepaid accounts, visit cfpb.gov/prepaid. If you have a complaint about a prepaid account, call the Consumer Financial Protection Bureau at 1-855-411-2372 or visit cfpb.gov/complaint."

(vii) Regulation Z disclosures for overdraft credit features. The disclosures described in Regulation Z, 12 CFR 1026.60(e)(1), in accordance with the requirements for such disclosures in 12 CFR 1026.60, if, at any point, a covered separate credit feature accessible by a hybrid prepaid-credit card as defined in 12 CFR 1026.61, may be offered in connection with the prepaid account. A financial institution may, but is not required to, include above the Regulation Z disclosures required by this paragraph a heading and other explanatory information introducing the overdraft credit feature. A financial institution is not required to revise the disclosure required by this paragraph to reflect a change in the fees or other terms disclosed therein until such time as the financial institution manufactures, prints, or otherwise produces new prepaid account packaging materials or otherwise updates the long form disclosure.

(5) Disclosure requirements outside the short form disclosure. At the time a financial institution provides the short form disclosure, it must also disclose the following information: the name of the financial institution; the name of the prepaid account program; the purchase price for the prepaid account, if any; and the fee for activating the prepaid account, if any. In a setting other than in a retail location, this information must be disclosed in close proximity to the short form. In a retail location, this information, other than the purchase price, must be disclosed on the exterior of the access device's packaging material. In a retail location, the purchase price must be disclosed either on the exterior of or in close proximity to the prepaid account access device's packaging material.

(6) Form of pre-acquisition disclosures—

(i) General—

(A) Written disclosures. Except as provided in paragraphs (b)(6)(i)(B) and (C) of this section, disclosures required by paragraph (b) of this section must be in writing.

(B) Electronic disclosures. Unless provided in written form prior to acquisition pursuant to paragraph (b)(1)(i) of this section, the disclosures required by paragraph (b) of this section must be provided in electronic form when a consumer acquires a prepaid account through electronic means, including via a website or mobile application, and must be viewable across all screen sizes. The long form disclosure must be provided electronically through a website when a financial institution is offering prepaid accounts at a retail location pursuant to the retail location exception in paragraph (b)(1)(ii) of this section. Electronic disclosures must be provided in a manner which is reasonably expected to be accessible in light of how a consumer is acquiring the prepaid account, in a responsive form, and using machine-readable text that is accessible via Web browsers or mobile applications, as applicable, and via screen readers. Electronic disclosures provided pursuant to paragraph (b) of this section need not meet the consumer consent and other applicable provisions of the Electronic Signatures in Global and National Commerce Act (E-Sign Act) (15 U.S.C. 7001 et seq.).

(C) Oral disclosures. Unless provided in written form prior to acquisition pursuant to paragraph (b)(1)(i) of this section, disclosures required by paragraphs (b)(2) and (5) of this section must be provided orally when a consumer acquires a prepaid account orally by telephone pursuant to the exception in paragraph (b)(1)(iii) of this section. For prepaid accounts acquired in retail locations or orally by telephone, the disclosure required by paragraph (b)(4) of this section provided by telephone pursuant to paragraph (b)(1)(ii)(C) or (b)(1)(iii)(B) of this section also must be made orally.

(ii) Retainable form. Pursuant to § 1005.4(a)(1), disclosures required by paragraph (b) of this section must be made in a form that a consumer may keep, except for disclosures provided orally pursuant to paragraphs (b)(1)(ii) or (iii) of this section, long form disclosure provided via SMS as permitted by paragraph (b)(2)(xiii) of this section for a prepaid account sold at retail locations pursuant to the retail location exception in paragraph (b)(1)(ii) of this section, and the disclosure of a purchase price pursuant to paragraph (b)(5) of this section that is not disclosed on the exterior of the packaging material for a prepaid account sold at a retail location pursuant to the retail location exception in paragraph (b)(1)(ii) of this section.

(iii) Tabular format—

(A) General. When a short form disclosure is provided in writing or electronically, the information required by paragraphs (b)(2)(i) through (ix) of this section shall be provided in the form of a table. Except as provided in paragraph (b)(6)(iii)(B) of this section, the short form disclosure required by paragraph (b)(2) of this section shall be provided in a form substantially similar to Model Forms A-10(a) through (d) in appendix A of this part, as applicable. When a long form disclosure is provided in writing or electronically, the information required by paragraph (b)(4)(ii) of this section shall be provided in the form of a table. Sample Form A-10(f) in appendix A of this part provides an example of the long form disclosure required by paragraph (b)(4) of this section when the financial institution does not offer multiple service plans.

(B) Multiple service plans—

(*1*) Short form disclosure for default service plan. When a financial institution offers multiple service plans within a particular prepaid account program and each plan has a different fee schedule, the information required by paragraphs (b)(2)(i) through (ix) of this section may be provided in the tabular format described in paragraph (b)(6)(iii)(A) of this section for the service plan in which a consumer is initially enrolled by default upon acquiring the prepaid account.

(*2*) Short form disclosure for multiple service plans. As an alternative to disclosing the default service plan pursuant to paragraph (b)(6)(iii)(B)(*1*) of this section, when a financial institution offers multiple service plans within a particular prepaid account program and each plan has a different fee schedule, fee disclosures required by paragraphs (b)(2)(i) through (vii) and (ix) of this section may be provided in the form of a table with separate columns for each service plan, in a form substantially similar to Model Form A-10(e) in appendix A of this part. Column headings must describe each service plan included in the table, using the terms "Pay-as-you-go plan," "Monthly plan," "Annual plan," or substantially similar terms; or, for multiple service plans offering preferred rates or fees for the prepaid accounts of consumers who also use another non-prepaid service, column headings must describe each service plan included in the table for the preferred and non-preferred service plans, as applicable.

(*3*) Long form disclosure. The information in the long form disclosure required by paragraph (b)(4)(ii) of this section must be presented in the form of a table for all service plans.

(7) Specific formatting requirements for pre-acquisition disclosures—

(i) Grouping—

(A) Short form disclosure. The information required in the short form disclosure by paragraphs (b)(2)(i) through (iv) of this section must be grouped together and provided in that order. The information required by paragraphs (b)(2)(v) through (ix) of this section must be generally grouped together and provided in that order. The information required by paragraphs (b)(3)(i) and (ii) of this section, as applicable, must be generally grouped together and in the location described by paragraphs (b)(3)(i) and (ii) of this section. The information required by paragraphs (b)(2)(x) through (xiii) of this section must be generally grouped together and provided in that order. The statement regarding wage or salary payment options for payroll card accounts required by paragraph (b)(2)(xiv)(A) of this section must be located above the information required by paragraphs (b)(2)(i) through (iv) of this section, as described in paragraph (b)(2)(xiv)(A) of this section. The statement regarding state-required information or other fee discounts or waivers permitted by paragraph (b)(2)(xiv)(B) of this section, when applicable, must appear in the location described by paragraph (b)(2)(xiv)(B) of this section.

(B) Long form disclosure. The information required by paragraph (b)(4)(i) of this section must be located in the first line of the long form disclosure. The information required by paragraph (b)(4)(ii) of this section must be generally grouped together and organized under subheadings by the categories of function for which a financial institution may impose the fee. Text describing the conditions under which a fee may be imposed must appear in the table required by paragraph (b)(6)(iii)(A) of this section in close proximity to the fee amount. The statements in the long form disclosure required by paragraphs (b)(4)(iii) through (vi) of this section must be generally grouped together, provided in that order, and appear below the information required by paragraph (b)(4)(ii) of this section. If, pursuant to paragraph (b)(4)(vii) of this section, the financial institution includes the disclosures described in Regulation Z, 12 CFR 1026.60(e)(1), such disclosures must appear below the statements required by paragraph (b)(4)(vi) of this section.

(C) Multiple service plan disclosure. When providing a short form disclosure for multiple service plans pursuant to paragraph (b)(6)(iii)(B)(*2*) of this section, in lieu of the requirements in paragraph (b)(7)(i)(A) of this section for grouping of the disclosures required by paragraphs (b)(2)(i) through (iv) and (v) through (ix) of this section, the information required by paragraphs (b)(2)(i) through (ix) of this section must be grouped together and provided in that order.

(ii) Prominence and size—

(A) General. All text used to disclose information in the short form or in the long form disclosure pursuant to paragraphs (b)(2), (b)(3)(i) and (ii), and (b)(4) of this section must be in a single, easy-to-read type that is all black or one color and printed on a background that provides a clear contrast.

(B) Short form disclosure—

(1) Fees and other information. The information required in the short form disclosure by paragraphs (b)(2)(i) through (iv) of this section must appear as follows: Fee amounts in bold-faced type; single fee amounts in a minimum type size of 15 points (or 21 pixels); two-tier fee amounts for ATM withdrawal in a minimum type size of 11 points (or 16 pixels) and in no larger a type size than what is used for the single fee amounts; and fee headings in a minimum type size of eight points (or 11 pixels) and in no larger a type size than what is used for the single fee amounts. The information required by paragraphs (b)(2)(v) through (ix) of this section must appear in a minimum type size of eight points (or 11 pixels) and appear in the same or a smaller type size than what is used for the fee headings required by paragraphs (b)(2)(i) through (iv) of this section. The information required by paragraphs (b)(2)(x) through (xiii) of this section must appear in a minimum type size of seven points (or nine pixels) and appear in no larger a type size than what is used for the information required to be disclosed by paragraphs (b)(2)(v) through (ix) of this section. Additionally, the statements disclosed pursuant to paragraphs (b)(2)(viii)(A) and (b)(2)(x) of this section and the telephone number and URL disclosed pursuant to paragraph (b)(2)(xiii) of this section, where applicable, must appear in bold-faced type. The following information must appear in a minimum type size of six points (or eight pixels) and appear in no larger a type size that what is used for the information required by paragraphs (b)(2)(x) through (xiii) of this section: text used to distinguish each of the two-tier fees pursuant to paragraphs (b)(2)(iii), (v), (vi), and (ix) of this section; text used to explain that the fee required by paragraph (b)(2)(vi) of this section applies "per call," where applicable; and text used to explain the conditions that trigger an inactivity fee and that the fee applies monthly or for the applicable time period, pursuant to paragraph (b)(2)(vii) of this section.

(2) Variable fees. The symbols and corresponding statements regarding variable fees disclosed in the short form pursuant to paragraphs (b)(3)(i) and (ii) of this section, when applicable, must appear in a minimum type size of seven points (or nine pixels) and appear in no larger a type size than what is used for the information required by paragraphs (b)(2)(x) through (xiii) of this section. A symbol required next to the fee amount pursuant to paragraphs (b)(3)(i) and (ii) of this section must appear in the same type size or pixel size as what is used for the corresponding fee amount.

(3) Payroll card account additional content. The statement regarding wage or salary payment options for payroll card accounts required by paragraph (b)(2)(xiv)(A) of this section, when

applicable, must appear in a minimum type size of eight points (or 11 pixels) and appear in no larger a type size than what is used for the fee headings required by paragraphs (b)(2)(i) through (iv) of this section. The statement regarding state-required information and other fee discounts or waivers permitted by paragraph (b)(2)(xiv)(B) of this section must appear in the same type size used to disclose variable fee information pursuant to paragraph (b)(3)(i) and (ii) of this section, or, if none, the same type size used for the information required by paragraphs (b)(2)(x) through (xiii) of this section.

(C) Long form disclosure. The long form disclosure required by paragraph (b)(4) of this section must appear in a minimum type size of eight points (or 11 pixels).

(D) Multiple service plan short form disclosure. When providing a short form disclosure for multiple service plans pursuant to paragraph (b)(6)(iii)(B)(2) of this section, the fee headings required by paragraphs (b)(2)(i) through (iv) of this section must appear in bold-faced type. The information required by paragraphs (b)(2)(i) through (xiii) of this section must appear in a minimum type size of seven points (or nine pixels), except the following must appear in a minimum type size of six points (or eight pixels) and appear in no larger a type size than what is used for the information required by paragraphs (b)(2)(i) through (xiii) of this section: Text used to distinguish each of the two-tier fees required by paragraphs (b)(2)(iii) and (v) of this section; text used to explain that the fee required by paragraph (b)(2)(vi) of this section applies "per call," where applicable; text used to explain the conditions that trigger an inactivity fee pursuant to paragraph (b)(2)(vii) of this section; and text used to distinguish that fees required by paragraphs (b)(2)(i) and (vii) of this section apply monthly or for the applicable time period.

(iii) Segregation. Short form and long form disclosures required by paragraphs (b)(2) and (4) of this section must be segregated from other information and must contain only information that is required or permitted for those disclosures by paragraph (b) of this section.

(8) Terminology of pre-acquisition disclosures. Fee names and other terms must be used consistently within and across the disclosures required by paragraph (b) of this section.

(9) Prepaid accounts acquired in foreign languages—

(i) General. A financial institution must provide the pre-acquisition disclosures required by paragraph (b) of this section in a foreign language, if the financial institution uses that same foreign language in connection with the acquisition of a prepaid account in the following circumstances:

(A) The financial institution principally uses a foreign language on the prepaid account packaging material;

(B) The financial institution principally uses a foreign language to advertise, solicit, or market a prepaid account and provides a means in the advertisement, solicitation, or marketing material that the consumer uses to acquire the prepaid account by telephone or electronically; or

(C) The financial institution provides a means for the consumer to acquire a prepaid account by telephone or electronically principally in a foreign language. However, foreign language pre-acquisition disclosures are not required for payroll card accounts and government benefit accounts where the foreign language is offered by telephone via a real-time language interpretation service provided by a third party or by the employer or government agency on an informal or ad hoc basis as an accommodation to prospective payroll card account or government benefit account holders.

(ii) Long form disclosures in English upon request. A financial institution required to provide pre-acquisition disclosures in a foreign language pursuant to paragraph (b)(9)(i) of this section must also provide the information required to be disclosed in its pre-acquisition long form disclosure pursuant to paragraph (b)(4) of this section in English upon a consumer's request and on any part of the Web site where it discloses this information in a foreign language.

(c) Access to prepaid account information—

(1) Periodic statement alternative. A financial institution need not furnish periodic statements required by § 1005.9(b) if the financial institution makes available to the consumer:

(i) The consumer's account balance, through a readily available telephone line;

(ii) An electronic history of the consumer's account transactions, such as through a Web site, that covers at least 12 months preceding the date the consumer electronically accesses the account; and

(iii) A written history of the consumer's account transactions that is provided promptly in response to an oral or written request and that covers at least 24 months preceding the date the financial institution receives the consumer's request.

(2) Periodic statement alternative for unverified prepaid accounts. For prepaid accounts that are not payroll card accounts or government benefit accounts, a financial institution is not required to provide a written history of the consumer's account transactions pursuant to paragraph (c)(1)(iii) of this section for any prepaid account for which the financial institution has not completed its consumer identification and verification process as described in paragraph (e)(3)(i)(A) through (C) of this section.

(3) Information included on electronic or written histories. The history of account transactions provided under paragraphs (c)(1)(ii) and (iii) of this section must include the information set forth in § 1005.9(b).

(4) Inclusion of all fees charged. A financial institution must disclose the amount of any fees assessed against the account, whether for electronic fund transfers or otherwise, on any periodic statement provided pursuant to § 1005.9(b) and on any history of account transactions provided or made available by the financial institution.

(5) Summary totals of fees. A financial institution must display a summary total of the amount of all fees assessed by the financial institution against the consumer's prepaid account for the prior calendar month and for the calendar year to date on any periodic statement provided pursuant to § 1005.9(b) and on any history of account transactions provided or made available by the financial institution.

(d) Modified disclosure requirements. A financial institution that provides information under paragraph (c)(1) of this section shall comply with the following:

(1) Initial disclosures. The financial institution shall modify the disclosures under § 1005.7(b) by disclosing:

(i) Access to account information. A telephone number that the consumer may call to obtain the account balance, the means by which the consumer can obtain an electronic account transaction history, such as the address of a Web site, and a summary of the consumer's right to receive a written account transaction history upon request (in place of the summary of the right to receive a periodic statement required by § 1005.7(b)(6)), including a telephone number to call to request a history. The disclosure required by this paragraph may be made by providing a notice substantially similar to the notice contained in paragraph (a) of appendix A-7 of this part.

(ii) Error resolution. A notice concerning error resolution that is substantially similar to the notice contained in paragraph (b) of appendix A-7 of this part, in place of the notice required by § 1005.7(b)(10). Alternatively, for prepaid account programs for which the financial institution does not have a consumer identification and verification process, the financial institution must describe its error resolution process and limitations on consumers' liability for unauthorized transfers or, if none, state that there are no such protections.

(2) Annual error resolution notice. The financial institution shall provide an annual notice concerning error resolution that is substantially similar to the notice contained in paragraph (b) of appendix A-7 of this part, in place of the notice required by § 1005.8(b). Alternatively, a financial institution may include on or with each electronic and written account transaction history provided in accordance with paragraph (c)(1) of this section, a notice substantially similar to the abbreviated notice for periodic statements contained in paragraph (b) of appendix A-3 of this part, modified as necessary to reflect the error resolution provisions set forth in paragraph (e) of this section.

(e) Modified limitations on liability and error resolution requirements—

(1) Modified limitations on liability requirements. A financial institution that provides information under paragraph (c)(1) of this section shall comply with the following:

(i) For purposes of § 1005.6(b)(3), the 60-day period for reporting any unauthorized transfer shall begin on the earlier of:

(A) The date the consumer electronically accesses the consumer's account under paragraph (c)(1)(ii) of this section, provided that the electronic account transaction history made available to the consumer reflects the unauthorized transfer; or

(B) The date the financial institution sends a written history of the consumer's account transactions requested by the consumer under paragraph (c)(1)(iii) of this section in which the unauthorized transfer is first reflected.

(ii) A financial institution may comply with paragraph (e)(1)(i) of this section by limiting the consumer's liability for an unauthorized transfer as provided under § 1005.6(b)(3) for any transfer reported by the consumer within 120 days after the transfer was credited or debited to the consumer's account.

(2) Modified error resolution requirements. A financial institution that provides information under paragraph (c)(1) of this section shall comply with the following:

(i) The financial institution shall comply with the requirements of § 1005.11 in response to an oral or written notice of an error from the consumer that is received by the earlier of:

(A) Sixty days after the date the consumer electronically accesses the consumer's account under paragraph (c)(1)(ii) of this section, provided that the electronic account transaction history made available to the consumer reflects the alleged error; or

(B) Sixty days after the date the financial institution sends a written history of the consumer's account transactions requested by the consumer under paragraph (c)(1)(iii) of this section in which the alleged error is first reflected.

(ii) In lieu of following the procedures in paragraph (e)(2)(i) of this section, a financial institution complies with the requirements for resolving errors in § 1005.11 if it investigates any oral or written notice of an error from the consumer that is received by the institution within 120 days after the transfer allegedly in error was credited or debited to the consumer's account.

(3) Limitations on liability and error resolution for unverified accounts.

(i) For prepaid accounts that are not payroll card accounts or government benefit accounts, a financial institution is not required to comply with the liability limits and error resolution requirements in §§ 1005.6 and 1005.11 for any prepaid account for which it has not successfully completed its consumer identification and verification process.

(ii) For purposes of paragraph (e)(3)(i) of this section, a financial institution has not successfully completed its consumer identification and verification process where:

(A) The financial institution has not concluded its consumer identification and verification process with respect to a particular prepaid account, provided that it has disclosed to the consumer the risks of not registering and verifying the account using a notice that is substantially similar to the model notice contained in paragraph (c) of appendix A-7 of this part.

(B) The financial institution has concluded its consumer identification and verification process with respect to a particular prepaid account, but could not verify the identity of the consumer, provided that it has disclosed to the consumer the risks of not registering and verifying the account using a notice that is substantially similar to the model notice contained in paragraph (c) of appendix A-7 of this part; or

(C) The financial institution does not have a consumer identification and verification process for the prepaid account program, provided that it has made the alternative disclosure described in paragraph (d)(1)(ii) of this section and complies with the process it has disclosed.

(iii) Resolution of errors following successful verification. Once a financial institution successfully completes its consumer identification and verification process with respect to a prepaid account, the financial institution must limit the consumer's liability for unauthorized transfers and resolve errors that occur following verification in accordance with § 1005.6 or § 1005.11, or the modified timing requirements in this paragraph (e), as applicable.

(f) Disclosure of fees and other information—

(1) Initial disclosure of fees and other information. A financial institution must include, as part of the initial disclosures given pursuant to § 1005.7, all of the information required to be disclosed in its pre-acquisition long form disclosure pursuant to paragraph (b)(4) of this section.

(2) Change-in-terms notice. The change-in-terms notice provisions in § 1005.8(a) apply to any change in a term or condition that is required to be disclosed under § 1005.7 or paragraph (f)(1) of this section. If a financial institution discloses the amount of a third-party fee in its pre-acquisition long form disclosure pursuant to paragraph (b)(4)(ii) of this section and initial disclosures pursuant to paragraph (f)(1) of this section, the financial institution is not required to provide a change-in-terms notice solely to reflect a change in that fee amount imposed by the third party. If a financial institution provides pursuant to paragraph (f)(1) of this section the Regulation Z disclosures required by paragraph (b)(4)(vii) of this section for an overdraft credit feature, the financial institution is not required to provide a change-in-terms notice solely to reflect a change in the fees or other terms disclosed therein.

(3) Disclosures on prepaid account access devices. The name of the financial institution and the Web site URL and a telephone number a consumer can use to contact the financial institution about the prepaid account must be disclosed on the prepaid account access device. If a financial institution does not provide a physical access device in connection with a prepaid account, the disclosure must appear on the Web site, mobile application, or other entry point a consumer must visit to access the prepaid account electronically.

(g) Prepaid accounts accessible by hybrid prepaid-credit cards—

(1) In general. Except as provided in paragraph (g)(2) of this section, with respect to a prepaid account program where consumers may be offered a covered separate credit feature accessible by a hybrid prepaid-credit card as defined by Regulation Z, 12 CFR 1026.61, a financial institution must provide to any prepaid account without a covered separate credit feature the same account terms, conditions, and features that it provides on prepaid accounts in the same prepaid account program that have such a credit feature.

(2) Exception for higher fees or charges. A financial institution is not prohibited under paragraph (g)(1) of this section from imposing a higher fee or charge on the asset feature of a prepaid account with a covered separate credit feature accessible by a hybrid prepaid-credit card than the amount of a comparable fee or charge that it imposes on any prepaid account in the same prepaid account program that does not have such a credit feature.

(h) Effective date and special transition rules for disclosure provisions—

(1) Effective date generally. Except as provided in paragraphs (h)(2) and (3) of this section, the requirements of this subpart, as modified by this section, apply to prepaid accounts as defined in § 1005.2(b)(3), including government benefit accounts subject to § 1005.15, beginning April 1, 2019.

(2) Early disclosures—

(i) Exception for disclosures on existing prepaid account access devices and prepaid account packaging materials. The disclosure requirements of this subpart, as modified by this section, shall not apply to any disclosures that are provided, or that would otherwise be required to be provided, on prepaid account access devices, or on, in, or with prepaid account packaging materials that were manufactured, printed, or otherwise produced in the normal course of business prior to April 1, 2019.

(ii) Disclosures for prepaid accounts acquired on or after April 1, 2019. This paragraph applies to prepaid accounts acquired by consumers on or after April 1, 2019 via packaging materials that were manufactured, printed, or otherwise produced prior to April 1, 2019.

(A) Notices of certain changes. If a financial institution has changed a prepaid account's terms and conditions as a result of paragraph (h)(1) of this section taking effect such that a change-in-terms notice would have been required under § 1005.8(a) or paragraph (f)(2) of this section for existing customers, the financial institution must provide to the consumer a notice of the change within 30 days of obtaining the consumer's contact information.

(B) Initial disclosures. The financial institution must mail or deliver to the consumer initial disclosures pursuant to § 1005.7 and paragraph (f)(1) of this section that have been updated as a result of paragraph (h)(1) of this section taking effect, within 30 days of obtaining the consumer's contact information.

(iii) Disclosures for prepaid accounts acquired before April 1, 2019. This paragraph applies to prepaid accounts acquired by consumers before April 1, 2019. If a financial institution has changed a prepaid account's terms and conditions as a result of paragraph (h)(1) of this section taking effect such that a change-in-terms notice would have been required under § 1005.8(a) or paragraph (f)(2) of this section for existing customers, the financial institution must provide to the consumer a notice of the change at least 21 days in advance of the change becoming effective, provided the financial institution has the consumer's contact information. If the financial institution obtains the consumer's contact information less than 30 days in advance of the change becoming effective or after it has become effective, the financial institution is permitted instead to notify the consumer of the change in accordance with the timing requirements set forth in paragraph (h)(2)(ii)(A) of this section.

(iv) Method of providing notice to consumers. With respect to prepaid accounts governed by paragraph (h)(2)(ii) or (iii) of this section, if a financial institution has not obtained a consumer's consent to provide disclosures in electronic form pursuant to the Electronic Signatures in Global and National Commerce Act (E-Sign Act) (15 U.S.C. 7001 et seq.), or is not otherwise already mailing or delivering to the consumer written account-related communications within the respective time periods specified in paragraphs (h)(2)(ii) or (iii) of this section, the financial institution may provide to the consumer a notice of a change in terms and conditions pursuant to paragraph (h)(2)(ii) or (iii) of this section or required or voluntary updated initial disclosures as a result of paragraph (h)(1) of this section taking effect in electronic form without regard to the consumer notice and consent requirements of section 101(c) of the E-Sign Act.

(3) Account information not available on April 1, 2019—

(i) Electronic and written account transaction history. If, on April 1, 2019, a financial institution does not have readily accessible the data necessary to make available 12 months of electronic account transaction history pursuant to paragraph (c)(1)(ii) of this section or to provide 24 months of written account transaction history upon request pursuant to paragraph (c)(1)(iii) of this section, the financial institution may make available or provide such histories using the data for the time period it has until the financial institution has accumulated the data necessary to comply in full with the requirements set forth in paragraphs (c)(1)(ii) and (iii) of this section.

(ii) Summary totals of fees. If, on April 1, 2019, the financial institution does not have readily accessible the data necessary to calculate the summary totals of the amount of all fees assessed by the financial institution on the consumer's prepaid account for the prior calendar month and for the calendar year to date pursuant to paragraph (c)(5) of this section, the financial institution may display the summary totals using the data it has until the financial institution has accumulated the data necessary to display the summary totals as required by paragraph (c)(5) of this section.

§ 1005.19 Internet posting of prepaid account agreements

(a) Definitions—

(1) Agreement. For purposes of this section, "agreement" or "prepaid account agreement" means the written document or documents evidencing the terms of the legal obligation, or the prospective legal obligation, between a prepaid account issuer and a consumer for a prepaid account. "Agreement" or "prepaid account agreement" also includes fee information, as defined in paragraph (a)(3) of this section.

(2) Amends. For purposes of this section, an issuer "amends" an agreement if it makes a substantive change (an "amendment") to the agreement. A change is substantive if it alters the rights or obligations of the issuer or the consumer under the agreement. Any change in the fee information, as defined in paragraph (a)(3) of this section, is deemed to be substantive.

(3) Fee information. For purposes of this section, "fee information" means the short form disclosure for the prepaid account pursuant to § 1005.18(b)(2) and the fee information and statements required to be disclosed in the pre-acquisition long form disclosure for the prepaid account pursuant to § 1005.18(b)(4).

(4) Issuer. For purposes of this section, "issuer" or "prepaid account issuer" means the entity to which a consumer is legally obligated, or would be legally obligated, under the terms of a prepaid account agreement.

(5) Offers. For purposes of this section, an issuer "offers" an agreement if the issuer markets, solicits applications for, or otherwise makes available a prepaid account that would be subject to that agreement, regardless of whether the issuer offers the prepaid account to the general public.

(6) Offers to the general public. For purposes of this section, an issuer "offers to the general public" an agreement if the issuer markets, solicits applications for, or otherwise makes available to the general public a prepaid account that would be subject to that agreement.

(7) Open account. For purposes of this section, a prepaid account is an "open account" or "open prepaid account" if: There is an outstanding balance in the account; the consumer can load funds to the account even if the account does not currently hold a balance; or the consumer can access credit from a covered separate credit feature accessible by a hybrid prepaid-credit card as defined in Regulation Z, 12 CFR 1026.61, in connection with the account. A prepaid account that has been suspended temporarily (for example, due to a report by the consumer of unauthorized use of the card) is considered an "open account" or "open prepaid account."

(8) Prepaid account. For purposes of this section, "prepaid account" means a prepaid account as defined in § 1005.2(b)(3).

(b) Submission of agreements to the Bureau—

(1) Submissions on a rolling basis. An issuer must make submissions of prepaid account agreements to the Bureau on a rolling basis, in the form and manner specified by the Bureau. Rolling submissions must be sent to the Bureau no later than 30 days after an issuer offers, amends, or ceases to offer any prepaid account agreement as described in paragraphs (b)(1)(ii) through (iv) of this section. Each submission must contain:

(i) Identifying information about the issuer and the agreements submitted, including the issuer's name, address, and identifying number (such as an RSSD ID number or tax identification number), the effective date of the prepaid account agreement, the name of the program manager, if any, and the list of names of other relevant parties, if applicable (such as the employer for a payroll card program or the agency for a government benefit program);

(ii) Any prepaid account agreement offered by the issuer that has not been previously submitted to the Bureau;

(iii) Any prepaid account agreement previously submitted to the Bureau that has been amended, as described in paragraph (b)(2)(i) of this section; and

(iv) Notification regarding any prepaid account agreement previously submitted to the Bureau that the issuer is withdrawing, as described in paragraphs (b)(3), (b)(4)(ii), and (b)(5)(ii) of this section.

(2) Amended agreements—

(i) Submission of amended agreements generally. If a prepaid account agreement previously submitted to the Bureau is amended, the issuer must submit the entire amended agreement to the Bureau, in the form and manner specified by the Bureau, no later than 30 days after the change becomes effective. If other identifying information about the issuer and its submitted agreements pursuant to paragraph (b)(1)(i) of this section previously submitted to the Bureau is amended, the issuer must submit updated information to the Bureau, in the form and manner specified by the Bureau, no later than 30 days after the change becomes effective.

(ii) Submission of updated list of names of other relevant parties. Notwithstanding paragraph (b)(2)(i) of this section, an issuer may delay submitting a change to the list of names of other relevant parties to a particular agreement until the earlier of:

(A) Such time as the issuer is otherwise submitting an amended agreement or changes to other identifying information about the issuer and its submitted agreements pursuant to paragraph (b)(1)(i) of this section; or

(B) May 1 of each year, for any updates to the list of names of other relevant parties for that agreement that occurred between the issuer's last submission of relevant party information and April 1 of that year.

(3) Withdrawal of agreements no longer offered. If an issuer no longer offers a prepaid account agreement that was previously submitted to the Bureau, the issuer must notify the Bureau, in the form and manner specified by the Bureau, no later than 30 days after the issuer ceases to offer the agreement, that it is withdrawing the agreement.

(4) De minimis exception.

(i) An issuer is not required to submit any prepaid account agreements to the Bureau if the issuer has fewer than 3,000 open prepaid accounts. If the issuer has 3,000 or more open prepaid accounts as of the last day of the calendar quarter, the issuer must submit to the Bureau its prepaid account agreements no later than 30 days after the last day of that calendar quarter.

(ii) If an issuer that did not previously qualify for the de minimis exception newly qualifies for the de minimis exception, the issuer must continue to make submissions to the Bureau on a rolling basis until the issuer notifies the Bureau that the issuer is withdrawing all agreements it previously submitted to the Bureau.

(5) Product testing exception.

(i) An issuer is not required to submit a prepaid account agreement to the Bureau if the agreement meets the criteria set forth in paragraphs (b)(5)(i)(A) through (C) of this section. If the agreement fails to meet the criteria set forth in paragraphs (b)(5)(i)(A) through (C) of this section as of the last day of the calendar quarter, the issuer must submit to the Bureau that prepaid account agreement no later than 30 days after the last day of that calendar quarter. An agreement qualifies for the product testing exception if the agreement:

(A) Is offered as part of a product test offered to only a limited group of consumers for a limited period of time;

(B) Is used for fewer than 3,000 open prepaid accounts; and

(C) Is not offered other than in connection with such a product test.

(ii) If an agreement that did not previously qualify for the product testing exception newly qualifies for the exception, the issuer must continue to make submissions to the Bureau on a rolling basis with respect to that agreement until the issuer notifies the Bureau that the issuer is withdrawing the agreement.

(6) Form and content of agreements submitted to the Bureau—

(i) Form and content generally.

(A) Each agreement must contain the provisions of the agreement and the fee information currently in effect.

(B) Agreements must not include any personally identifiable information relating to any consumer, such as name, address, telephone number, or account number.

(C) The following are not deemed to be part of the agreement for purposes of this section, and therefore are not required to be included in submissions to the Bureau:

(1) Ancillary disclosures required by state or Federal law, such as affiliate marketing notices, privacy policies, or disclosures under the E-Sign Act;

(2) Solicitation or marketing materials;

(3) Periodic statements; and

(4) Documents that may be sent to the consumer along with the prepaid account or prepaid account agreement such as a cover letter, a validation sticker on the card, or other information about card security.

(D) Agreements must be presented in a clear and legible font.

(ii) Fee information. Fee information must be set forth either in the prepaid account agreement or in addenda to that agreement that attach either or both the short form disclosure for the prepaid account pursuant to § 1005.18(b)(2) and the fee information and statements required to be disclosed in the long form disclosure for the prepaid account pursuant to § 1005.18(b)(4). The agreement or addenda thereto must contain all of the fee information, as defined by paragraph (a)(3) of this section.

(iii) Integrated agreement. An issuer may not provide provisions of the agreement or fee information to the Bureau in the form of change-in-terms notices or riders (other than the optional fee information addenda described in paragraph (b)(6)(ii) of this section). Changes in provisions or fee information must be integrated into the text of the agreement, or the optional fee information addenda, as appropriate.

(c) Posting of agreements offered to the general public.

(1) An issuer must post and maintain on its publicly available Web site any prepaid account agreements offered to the general public that the issuer is required to submit to the Bureau under paragraph (b) of this section.

(2) Agreements posted pursuant to this paragraph (c) must conform to the form and content requirements for agreements submitted to the Bureau set forth in paragraph (b)(6) of this section.

(3) The issuer must post and update the agreements posted on its Web site pursuant to this paragraph (c) as frequently as the issuer is required to submit new or amended agreements to the Bureau pursuant to paragraph (b)(2)(i) of this section.

(4) Agreements posted pursuant to this paragraph (c) may be posted in any electronic format that is readily usable by the general public. Agreements must be placed in a location that is prominent and readily accessible to the public and must be accessible without submission of personally identifiable information.

(d) Agreements for all open accounts—

(1) Availability of an individual consumer's prepaid account agreement. With respect to any open prepaid account, an issuer must either:

(i) Post and maintain the consumer's agreement on its Web site; or

(ii) Promptly provide a copy of the consumer's agreement to the consumer upon the consumer's request. If the issuer makes an agreement available upon request, the issuer must provide the consumer with the ability to request a copy of the agreement by telephone. The issuer must send to the consumer a copy of the consumer's prepaid account agreement no later than five business days after the issuer receives the consumer's request.

(2) Form and content of agreements.

(i) Except as provided in this paragraph (d), agreements posted on the issuer's Web site pursuant to paragraph (d)(1)(i) of this section or sent to the consumer upon the consumer's request pursuant to paragraph (d)(1)(ii) of this section must conform to the form and content requirements for agreements submitted to the Bureau as set forth in paragraph (b)(6) of this section.

(ii) If the issuer posts an agreement on its Web site under paragraph (d)(1)(i) of this section, the agreement may be posted in any electronic format that is readily usable by the general public and must be placed in a location that is prominent and readily accessible to the consumer.

(iii) Agreements posted or otherwise provided pursuant to this paragraph (d) may contain personally identifiable information relating to the consumer, such as name, address, telephone number, or account number, provided that the issuer takes appropriate measures to make the agreement accessible only to the consumer or other authorized persons.

(iv) Agreements posted or otherwise provided pursuant to this paragraph (d) must set forth the specific provisions and fee information applicable to the particular consumer.

(v) Agreements posted pursuant to paragraph (d)(1)(i) of this section must be updated as frequently as the issuer is required to submit amended agreements to the Bureau pursuant to paragraph (b)(2)(i) of this section. Agreements provided upon consumer request pursuant to paragraph (d)(1)(ii) of this section must be accurate as of the date the agreement is sent to the consumer.

(vi) Agreements provided upon consumer request pursuant to paragraph (d)(1)(ii) of this section must be provided by the issuer in paper form, unless the consumer agrees to receive the agreement electronically.

(e) E-Sign Act requirements. Except as otherwise provided in this section, issuers may provide prepaid account agreements in electronic form under paragraphs (c) and (d) of this section without regard to the consumer notice and consent requirements of section 101(c) of the Electronic Signatures in Global and National Commerce Act(E-Sign Act) (15 U.S.C. 7001 et seq.).

(f) Initial submission date. The requirements of this section apply to prepaid accounts beginning on April 1, 2019. An issuer must submit to the Bureau no later than May 1, 2019 all prepaid account agreements it offers as of April 1, 2019.

§ 1005.20 Requirements for gift cards and gift certificates

(a) Definitions. For purposes of this section, except as excluded under paragraph (b), the following definitions apply:

(1) "Gift certificate" means a card, code, or other device that is:

(i) Issued on a prepaid basis primarily for personal, family, or household purposes to a consumer in a specified amount that may not be increased or reloaded in exchange for payment; and

(ii) Redeemable upon presentation at a single merchant or an affiliated group of merchants for goods or services.

(2) "Store gift card" means a card, code, or other device that is:

(i) Issued on a prepaid basis primarily for personal, family, or household purposes to a consumer in a specified amount, whether or not that amount may be increased or reloaded, in exchange for payment; and

(ii) Redeemable upon presentation at a single merchant or an affiliated group of merchants for goods or services.

(3) "General-use prepaid card" means a card, code, or other device that is:

(i) Issued on a prepaid basis primarily for personal, family, or household purposes to a consumer in a specified amount, whether or not that amount may be increased or reloaded, in exchange for payment; and

(ii) Redeemable upon presentation at multiple, unaffiliated merchants for goods or services, or usable at automated teller machines.

(4) "Loyalty, award, or promotional gift card" means a card, code, or other device that:

(i) Is issued on a prepaid basis primarily for personal, family, or household purposes to a consumer in connection with a loyalty, award, or promotional program;

(ii) Is redeemable upon presentation at one or more merchants for goods or services, or usable at automated teller machines; and

(iii) Sets forth the following disclosures, as applicable:

(A) A statement indicating that the card, code, or other device is issued for loyalty, award, or promotional purposes, which must be included on the front of the card, code, or other device;

(B) The expiration date for the underlying funds, which must be included on the front of the card, code, or other device;

(C) The amount of any fees that may be imposed in connection with the card, code, or other device, and the conditions under which they may be imposed, which must be provided on or with the card, code, or other device; and

(D) A toll-free telephone number and, if one is maintained, a Web site, that a consumer may use to obtain fee information, which must be included on the card, code, or other device.

(5) Dormancy or inactivity fee. The terms "dormancy fee" and "inactivity fee" mean a fee for non-use of or inactivity on a gift certificate, store gift card, or general-use prepaid card.

(6) Service fee. The term "service fee" means a periodic fee for holding or use of a gift certificate, store gift card, or general-use prepaid card. A periodic fee includes any fee that may be imposed on a gift certificate, store gift card, or general-use prepaid card from time to time for holding or using the certificate or card.

(7) Activity. The term "activity" means any action that results in an increase or decrease of the funds underlying a certificate or card, other than the imposition of a fee, or an adjustment due to an error or a reversal of a prior transaction.

(b) Exclusions. The terms "gift certificate," "store gift card," and "general-use prepaid card", as defined in paragraph (a) of this section, do not include any card, code, or other device that is:

(1) Useable solely for telephone services;

(2) Reloadable and not marketed or labeled as a gift card or gift certificate. For purposes of this paragraph (b)(2), the term "reloadable" includes a temporary non-reloadable card issued solely in connection with a reloadable card, code, or other device;

(3) A loyalty, award, or promotional gift card;

(4) Not marketed to the general public;

(5) Issued in paper form only; or

(6) Redeemable solely for admission to events or venues at a particular location or group of affiliated locations, or to obtain goods or services in conjunction with admission to such events or venues, either at the event or venue or at specific locations affiliated with and in geographic proximity to the event or venue.

(c) Form of disclosures—

(1) Clear and conspicuous. Disclosures made under this section must be clear and conspicuous. The disclosures may contain commonly accepted or readily understandable abbreviations or symbols.

(2) Format. Disclosures made under this section generally must be provided to the consumer in written or electronic form. Except for the disclosures in paragraphs (c)(3) and (h)(2) of this section, written and electronic disclosures made under this section must be in a retainable form. Only disclosures provided under paragraphs (c)(3) and (h)(2) may be given orally.

(3) Disclosures prior to purchase. Before a gift certificate, store gift card, or general-use prepaid card is purchased, a person that issues or sells such certificate or card must disclose to the consumer the information required by paragraphs (d)(2), (e)(3), and (f)(1) of this section. The fees and terms and conditions of expiration that are required to be

disclosed prior to purchase may not be changed after purchase.

(4) Disclosures on the certificate or card. Disclosures required by paragraphs (a)(4)(iii), (d)(2), (e)(3), and (f)(2) of this section must be made on the certificate or card, or in the case of a loyalty, award, or promotional gift card, on the card, code, or other device. A disclosure made in an accompanying terms and conditions document, on packaging surrounding a certificate or card, or on a sticker or other label affixed to the certificate or card does not constitute a disclosure on the certificate or card. For an electronic certificate or card, disclosures must be provided electronically on the certificate or card provided to the consumer. An issuer that provides a code or confirmation to a consumer orally must provide to the consumer a written or electronic copy of the code or confirmation promptly, and the applicable disclosures must be provided on the written copy of the code or confirmation.

(d) Prohibition on imposition of fees or charges. No person may impose a dormancy, inactivity, or service fee with respect to a gift certificate, store gift card, or general-use prepaid card, unless:

(1) There has been no activity with respect to the certificate or card, in the one-year period ending on the date on which the fee is imposed;

(2) The following are stated, as applicable, clearly and conspicuously on the gift certificate, store gift card, or general-use prepaid card:

(i) The amount of any dormancy, inactivity, or service fee that may be charged;

(ii) How often such fee may be assessed; and

(iii) That such fee may be assessed for inactivity; and

(3) Not more than one dormancy, inactivity, or service fee is imposed in any given calendar month.

(e) Prohibition on sale of gift certificates or cards with expiration dates. No person may sell or issue a gift certificate, store gift card, or general-use prepaid card with an expiration date, unless:

(1) The person has established policies and procedures to provide consumers with a reasonable opportunity to purchase a certificate or card with at least five years remaining until the certificate or card expiration date;

(2) The expiration date for the underlying funds is at least the later of:

(i) Five years after the date the gift certificate was initially issued, or the date on which funds were last loaded to a store gift card or general-use prepaid card; or

(ii) The certificate or card expiration date, if any;

(3) The following disclosures are provided on the certificate or card, as applicable:

(i) The expiration date for the underlying funds or, if the underlying funds do not expire, that fact;

(ii) A toll-free telephone number and, if one is maintained, a Web site that a consumer may use to obtain a replacement certificate or card after the certificate or card expires if the underlying funds may be available; and

(iii) Except where a non-reloadable certificate or card bears an expiration date that is at least seven years from the date of manufacture, a statement, disclosed with equal prominence and in close proximity to the certificate or card expiration date, that:

(A) The certificate or card expires, but the underlying funds either do not expire or expire later than the certificate or card, and;

(B) The consumer may contact the issuer for a replacement card; and

(4) No fee or charge is imposed on the cardholder for replacing the gift certificate, store gift card, or general-use prepaid card or for providing the certificate or card holder with the remaining balance in some other manner prior to the funds expiration date, unless such certificate or card has been lost or stolen.

(f) Additional disclosure requirements for gift certificates or cards. The following disclosures must be provided in connection with a gift certificate, store gift card, or general-use prepaid card, as applicable:

(1) Fee disclosures. For each type of fee that may be imposed in connection with the certificate or card (other than a dormancy, inactivity, or service fee subject to the disclosure requirements under paragraph (d)(2) of this section), the following information must be provided on or with the certificate or card:

(i) The type of fee;

(ii) The amount of the fee (or an explanation of how the fee will be determined); and

(iii) The conditions under which the fee may be imposed.

(2) Telephone number for fee information. A toll-free telephone number and, if one is maintained, a Web site, that a consumer may use to obtain information about fees described in paragraphs (d)

(2) and (f)(1) of this section must be disclosed on the certificate or card.

(g) Compliance dates—

(1) Effective date for gift certificates, store gift cards, and general-use prepaid cards. Except as provided in paragraph (h) of this section, the requirements of this section apply to any gift certificate, store gift card, or general-use prepaid card sold to a consumer on or after August 22, 2010, or provided to a consumer as a replacement for such certificate or card.

(2) Effective date for loyalty, award, or promotional gift cards. The requirements in paragraph (a)(4)(iii) of this section apply to any card, code, or other device provided to a consumer in connection with a loyalty, award, or promotional program if the period of eligibility for such program began on or after August 22, 2010.

(h) Temporary exemption—

(1) Delayed mandatory compliance date. For any gift certificate, store gift card, or general-use prepaid card produced prior to April 1, 2010, the mandatory compliance date of the requirements of paragraphs (c)(3), (d)(2), (e)(1), (e)(3), and (f) of this section is January 31, 2011, provided that an issuer of such certificate or card:

(i) Complies with all other provisions of this section;

(ii) Does not impose an expiration date with respect to the funds underlying such certificate or card;

(iii) At the consumer's request, replaces such certificate or card if it has funds remaining at no cost to the consumer; and

(iv) Satisfies the requirements of paragraph (h)(2) of this section.

(2) Additional disclosures. Issuers relying on the delayed effective date in § 1005.20(h)(1) must disclose through in-store signage, messages during customer service calls, Web sites, and general advertising, that:

(i) The underlying funds of such certificate or card do not expire;

(ii) Consumers holding such certificate or card have a right to a free replacement certificate or card, which must be accompanied by the packaging and materials typically associated with such certificate or card; and

(iii) Any dormancy, inactivity, or service fee for such certificate or card that might otherwise be charged will not be charged if such fees do not comply with section 916 of the Act.

(3) Expiration of additional disclosure requirements. The disclosures in paragraph (h)(2) of this section:

(i) Are not required to be provided on or after January 31, 2011, with respect to in-store signage and general advertising.

(ii) Are not required to be provided on or after January 31, 2013, with respect to messages during customer service calls and Web sites.

Official Interpretation to Regulation E

Supplement I to Part 1005— Official Staff Interpretations (Excerpts)

Part 1005—Electronic Fund Transfers (Regulation E) Official Staff Commentary (Selected Provisions)

§ 1005.2 Definitions

2(a) Access Device

1. Examples. The term "access device" includes debit cards, personal identification numbers (PINs), telephone transfer and telephone bill payment codes, and other means that may be used by a consumer to initiate an electronic fund transfer (EFT) to or from a consumer account. The term does not include magnetic tape or other devices used internally by a financial institution to initiate electronic transfers.

2. Checks used to capture information. The term "access device" does not include a check or draft used to capture the Magnetic Ink Character Recognition (MICR) encoding to initiate a one-time automated clearinghouse (ACH) debit. For example, if a consumer authorizes a one-time ACH debit from the consumer's account using a blank, partially completed, or fully completed and signed check for the merchant to capture the routing, account, and serial numbers to initiate the debit, the check is not an access device. (Although the check is not an access device under Regulation E, the transaction is nonetheless covered by the regulation. See comment 3(b)(1)-1.v.). …

2(h) Electronic Terminal

1. Point-of-sale (POS) payments initiated by telephone. Because the term "electronic terminal" excludes a telephone operated by a consumer, a financial institution need not provide a terminal receipt when:

i. A consumer uses a debit card at a public telephone to pay for the call.

ii. A consumer initiates a transfer by a means analogous in function to a telephone, such as by home banking equipment or a facsimile machine.

2. POS terminals. A POS terminal that captures data electronically, for debiting or crediting to a consumer's asset account, is an electronic terminal for purposes of Regulation E even if no access device is used to initiate the transaction. See § 1005.9 for receipt requirements.

3. Teller-operated terminals. A terminal or other computer equipment operated by an employee of a financial institution is not an electronic terminal for purposes of the regulation. However, transfers initiated at such terminals by means of a consumer's access device (using the consumer's PIN, for example) are EFTs and are subject to other requirements of the regulation. If an access device is used only for identification purposes or for determining the account balance, the transfers are not EFTs for purposes of the regulation. …

2(m) Unauthorized Electronic Fund Transfer

1. Transfer by institution's employee. A consumer has no liability for erroneous or fraudulent transfers initiated by an employee of a financial institution.

2. Authority. If a consumer furnishes an access device and grants authority to make transfers to a person (such as a family member or co-worker) who exceeds the authority given, the consumer is fully liable for the transfers unless the consumer has notified the financial institution that transfers by that person are no longer authorized.

3. Access device obtained through robbery or fraud. An unauthorized EFT includes a transfer initiated by a person who obtained the access device from the consumer through fraud or robbery.

4. Forced initiation. An EFT at an ATM is an unauthorized transfer if the consumer has been induced by force to initiate the transfer.

5. Reversal of direct deposits. The reversal of a direct deposit made in error is not an unauthorized EFT when it involves:

i. A credit made to the wrong consumer's account;

ii. A duplicate credit made to a consumer's account; or

iii. A credit in the wrong amount (for example, when the amount credited to the consumer's account differs from the amount in the transmittal instructions). …

§ 1005.3 Coverage

3(b) Electronic Fund Transfer

Paragraph 3(b)(1)— Definition

1. Fund transfers covered. The term "electronic fund transfer" includes:

i. A deposit made at an ATM or other electronic terminal (including a deposit in cash or by check) provided a specific agreement exists between the financial institution and the consumer for EFTs to or from the account to which the deposit is made.

ii. A transfer sent via ACH. For example, social security benefits under the U.S. Treasury's direct-deposit program are covered, even if the listing of payees and payment amounts reaches the account-holding institution by means of a computer printout from a correspondent bank.

iii. A preauthorized transfer credited or debited to an account in accordance with instructions contained on magnetic tape, even if the financial institution holding the account sends or receives a composite check.

iv. A transfer from the consumer's account resulting from a debit-card transaction at a merchant location, even if no electronic terminal is involved at the time of the transaction, if the consumer's asset account is subsequently debited for the amount of the transfer.

v. A transfer via ACH where a consumer has provided a check to enable the merchant or other payee to capture the routing, account, and serial numbers to initiate the transfer, whether the check is blank, partially completed, or fully completed and signed; whether the check is presented at POS or is mailed to a merchant or other payee or lockbox and later converted to an EFT; or whether the check is retained by the consumer, the merchant or other payee, or the payee's financial institution.

vi. A payment made by a bill payer under a bill-payment service available to a consumer via computer or other electronic means, unless the terms of the bill-payment service explicitly state that all payments, or all payments to a particular payee or payees, will be solely by check, draft, or similar paper instrument drawn on the consumer's account, and the payee or payees that will be paid in this manner are identified to the consumer.

2. Fund transfers not covered. The term "electronic fund transfer" does not include:

i. A payment that does not debit or credit a consumer asset account, such as a payroll allotment to a creditor to repay a credit extension (which is deducted from salary).

ii. A payment made in currency by a consumer to another person at an electronic terminal.

iii. A preauthorized check drawn by the financial institution on the consumer's account (such as an interest or other recurring payment to the consumer or another party), even if the check is computer-generated.

iv. Transactions arising from the electronic collection, presentment, or return of checks through the check collection system, such as through transmission of electronic check images.

Paragraph 3(b)(2)— Electronic Fund Transfer Using Information from a Check

1. Notice at POS not furnished due to inadvertent error. Notice at POS not furnished due to inadvertent error. If the copy of the notice under section 1005.3(b)(2)(ii) for electronic check conversion (ECK) transactions is not provided to the consumer at POS because of a bona fide unintentional error, such as when a terminal printing mechanism jams, no violation results if the payee maintains procedures reasonably adapted to avoid such occurrences.

2. Authorization to process a transaction as an EFT or as a check. In order to process a transaction as an EFT, or alternatively as a check, the payee must obtain the consumer's authorization to do so. A payee may, at its option, specify the circumstances under which a check may not be converted to an EFT. See model clauses in appendix A-6.

3. Notice for each transfer. Generally, a notice to authorize an electronic check conversion transaction must be provided for each transaction. For example, a consumer must receive a notice that the transaction will be processed as an EFT for each transaction at POS or each time a consumer mails a check in an accounts receivable (ARC) transaction to pay a bill, such as a utility bill, if the payee intends to convert a check received as payment. Similarly, the consumer must receive notice if the payee intends to collect a service fee for insufficient or uncollected funds via an EFT for each transaction whether at POS or if the consumer mails a check to pay a bill. The notice about when funds may be debited from a consumer's account and the non-return of consumer checks by the consumer's financial institution must also be provided for each transaction. However, if in an ARC transaction, a payee provides a coupon book to a consumer, for example, for mortgage loan payments, and the payment dates and amounts are

set out in the coupon book, the payee may provide a single notice on the coupon book stating all of the required disclosures under paragraph (b)(2) of this section in order to obtain authorization for each conversion of a check and any debits via EFT to the consumer's account to collect any service fees imposed by the payee for insufficient or uncollected funds in the consumer's account. The notice must be placed on a conspicuous location of the coupon book that a consumer can retain— for example, on the first page, or inside the front cover.

4. Multiple payments/multiple consumers. If a merchant or other payee will use information from a consumer's check to initiate an EFT from the consumer's account, notice to a consumer listed on the billing account that a check provided as payment during a single billing cycle or after receiving an invoice or statement will be processed as a one-time EFT or as a check transaction constitutes notice for all checks provided in payment for the billing cycle or the invoice for which notice has been provided, whether the check(s) is submitted by the consumer or someone else. The notice applies to all checks provided in payment for the billing cycle or invoice until the provision of notice on or with the next invoice or statement. Thus, if a merchant or other payee receives a check as payment for the consumer listed on the billing account after providing notice that the check will be processed as a one-time EFT, the authorization from that consumer constitutes authorization to convert any other checks provided for that invoice or statement. Other notices required under this paragraph (b)(2) (for example, to collect a service fee for insufficient or uncollected funds via an EFT) provided to the consumer listed on the billing account also constitutes notice to any other consumer who may provide a check for the billing cycle or invoice.

5. Additional disclosures about ECK transactions at POS. When a payee initiates an EFT at POS using information from the consumer's check, and returns the check to the consumer at POS, the payee need not provide a notice to the consumer that the check will not be returned by the consumer's financial institution.

Paragraph 3(b)(3)— Collection of Returned-Item Fees via Electronic Fund Transfer

1. Fees imposed by account-holding institution. The requirement to obtain a consumer's authorization to collect a fee via EFT for the return of an EFT or check unpaid applies only to the person that intends to initiate an EFT to collect the returned item fee from the consumer's account. The authorization requirement does not apply to any fees assessed by the consumer's account-holding financial institution when it returns the unpaid underlying EFT or check or pays the amount of an overdraft.

2. Accounts receivable transactions. In an accounts receivable (ARC) transaction where a consumer sends in a payment for amounts owed (or makes an in-person payment at a biller's physical location, such as when a consumer makes a loan payment at a bank branch or places a payment in a drop box), a person seeking to electronically collect a fee for items returned unpaid must obtain the consumer's authorization to collect the fee in this manner. A consumer authorizes a person to electronically collect a returned item fee when the consumer receives notice, typically on an invoice or statement, that the person may collect the fee through an EFT to the consumer's account, and the consumer goes forward with the underlying transaction by providing payment. The notice must also state the dollar amount of the fee. However, an explanation of how that fee will be determined may be provided in place of the dollar amount of the fee if the fee may vary due to the amount of the transaction or due to other factors, such as the number of days the underlying transaction is left outstanding. For example, if a state law permits a maximum fee of $30 or 10% of the underlying transaction, whichever is greater, the person collecting the fee may explain how the fee is determined, rather than state a specific dollar amount for the fee.

3. Disclosure of dollar amount of fee for POS transactions. The notice provided to the consumer in connection with a POS transaction under § 1005.3(b)(3)(ii) must state the amount of the fee for a returned item if the dollar amount of the fee can be calculated at the time the notice is provided or mailed. For example, if notice is provided to the consumer at the time of the transaction, if the applicable state law sets a maximum fee that may be collected for a returned item based on the amount of the underlying transaction (such as where the amount of the fee is expressed as a percentage of the underlying transaction), the person collecting the fee must state the actual dollar amount of the fee on the notice provided to the consumer. Alternatively, if the amount of the fee to be collected cannot be calculated at the time of the transaction (for example, where the amount of the fee will depend

on the number of days a debt continues to be owed), the person collecting the fee may provide a description of how the fee will be determined on both the posted notice as well as on the notice provided at the time of the transaction. However, if the person collecting the fee elects to send the consumer notice after the person has initiated an EFT to collect the fee, that notice must state the amount of the fee to be collected.

4. Third party providing notice. The person initiating an EFT to a consumer's account to electronically collect a fee for an item returned unpaid may obtain the authorization and provide the notices required under § 1005.3(b)(3) through third parties, such as merchants.

3(c) Exclusions From Coverage.

Paragraph 3(c)(1)— Checks

1. Re-presented checks. The electronic re-presentment of a returned check is not covered by Regulation E because the transaction originated by check. Regulation E does apply, however, to any fee debited via an EFT from a consumer's account by the payee because the check was returned for insufficient or uncollected funds. The person debiting the fee electronically must obtain the consumer's authorization.

2. Check used to capture information for a one-time EFT. See comment 3(b)(1)-1.v.

Paragraph 3(c)(2)— Check Guarantee or Authorization

1. Memo posting. Under a check guarantee or check authorization service, debiting of the consumer's account occurs when the check or draft is presented for payment. These services are exempt from coverage, even when a temporary hold on the account is memo-posted electronically at the time of authorization.

Paragraph 3(c)(3)— Wire or Other Similar Transfers

1. Fedwire and ACH. If a financial institution makes a fund transfer to a consumer's account after receiving funds through Fedwire or a similar network, the transfer by ACH is covered by the regulation even though the Fedwire or network transfer is exempt.

2. Article 4A. Financial institutions that offer telephone-initiated Fedwire payments are subject to the requirements of UCC section 4A-202, which encourages verification of Fedwire payment orders pursuant to a security procedure established by agreement between the consumer and the receiving bank. These transfers are not subject to Regulation E and the agreement is not considered a telephone plan if the service is offered separately from a telephone bill-payment or other prearranged plan subject to Regulation E. Regulation J of the Board of Governors of the Federal Reserve System (12 CFR part 210) specifies the rules applicable to funds handled by Federal Reserve Banks. To ensure that the rules for all fund transfers through Fedwire are consistent, the Board of Governors used its preemptive authority under UCC section 4A-107 to determine that subpart B of the Board's Regulation J, including the provisions of Article 4A, applies to all fund transfers through Fedwire, even if a portion of the fund transfer is governed by the EFTA. The portion of the fund transfer that is governed by the EFTA is not governed by subpart B of the Board's Regulation J.

3. Similar fund transfer systems. Fund transfer systems that are similar to Fedwire include the Clearing House Interbank Payments System (CHIPS), Society for Worldwide Interbank Financial Telecommunication (SWIFT), Telex, and transfers made on the books of correspondent banks.

Paragraph 3(c)(4)— Securities and Commodities Transfers

1. Coverage. The securities exemption applies to securities and commodities that may be sold by a registered broker-dealer or futures commission merchant, even when the security or commodity itself is not regulated by the Securities and Exchange Commission or the Commodity Futures Trading Commission.

2. Example of exempt transfer. The exemption applies to a transfer involving a transfer initiated by a telephone order to a stockbroker to buy or sell securities or to exercise a margin call.

3. Examples of nonexempt transfers. The exemption does not apply to a transfer involving:

i. A debit card or other access device that accesses a securities or commodities account such as a money market mutual fund and that the consumer uses for purchasing goods or services or for obtaining cash.

ii. A payment of interest or dividends into the consumer's account (for example, from a brokerage firm or from a Federal Reserve Bank for government securities).

Paragraph 3(c)(5)— Automatic Transfers by Account-Holding Institution

1. Automatic transfers exempted. The exemption applies to:

i. Electronic debits or credits to consumer accounts for check charges, stop-payment charges, non-sufficient funds (NSF) charges, overdraft charges, provisional credits, error adjustments, and similar items that are initiated automatically on the occurrence of certain events.

ii. Debits to consumer accounts for group insurance available only through the financial institution and payable only by means of an aggregate payment from the institution to the insurer.

iii. EFTs between a thrift institution and its paired commercial bank in the state of Rhode Island, which are deemed under state law to be intra-institutional.

iv. Automatic transfers between a consumer's accounts within the same financial institution, even if the account holders on the two accounts are not identical.

2. Automatic transfers not exempted. Transfers between accounts of the consumer at affiliated institutions (such as between a bank and its subsidiary or within a holding company) are not intra-institutional transfers, and thus do not qualify for the exemption.

Paragraph 3(c)(6)— Telephone-Initiated Transfers

1. Written plan or agreement. A transfer that the consumer initiates by telephone is covered by Regulation E if the transfer is made under a written plan or agreement between the consumer and the financial institution making the transfer. A written statement available to the public or to account holders that describes a service allowing a consumer to initiate transfers by telephone constitutes a plan; for example, a brochure, or material included with periodic statements. The following, however, do not by themselves constitute a written plan or agreement:

i. A hold-harmless agreement on a signature card that protects the institution if the consumer requests a transfer.

ii. A legend on a signature card, periodic statement, or passbook that limits the number of telephone-initiated transfers the consumer can make from a savings account because of reserve requirements under Regulation D of the Board of Governors of the Federal Reserve System (12 CFR part 204).

iii. An agreement permitting the consumer to approve by telephone the rollover of funds at the maturity of an instrument.

2. Examples of covered transfers. When a written plan or agreement has been entered into, a transfer initiated by a telephone call from a consumer is covered even though:

i. An employee of the financial institution completes the transfer manually (for example, by means of a debit memo or deposit slip).

ii. The consumer is required to make a separate request for each transfer.

iii. The consumer uses the plan infrequently.

iv. The consumer initiates the transfer via a facsimile machine.

v. The consumer initiates the transfer using a financial institution's audio-response or voice-response telephone system.

Paragraph 3(c)(7)— Small Institutions

1. Coverage. This exemption is limited to preauthorized transfers; institutions that offer other EFTs must comply with the applicable sections of the regulation as to such services. The preauthorized transfers remain subject to sections 913, 916, and 917 of the Act and § 1005.10(e), and are therefore exempt from UCC Article 4A. …

§ 1005.6 Liability of Consumer for Unauthorized Transfers

6(a) Conditions for Liability

1. Means of identification. A financial institution may use various means for identifying the consumer to whom the access device is issued, including but not limited to:

i. Electronic or mechanical confirmation (such as a PIN).

ii. Comparison of the consumer's signature, fingerprint, or photograph.

2. Multiple users. When more than one access device is issued for an account, the financial institution may, but need not, provide a separate means to identify each user of the account.

6(b) Limitations on Amount of Liability

1. Application of liability provisions. There are three possible tiers of consumer liability for unauthorized EFTs depending on the situation. A consumer may be liable for: (1) up to $50; (2) up to $500; or (3) an unlimited amount depending on when the unauthorized EFT occurs. More than one tier may apply to a given situation because each corresponds to a different (sometimes overlapping) time period or set of conditions.

2. Consumer negligence. Negligence by the consumer cannot be used as the basis for imposing greater liability than is permissible under Regulation E. Thus, consumer behavior that may constitute

negligence under state law, such as writing the PIN on a debit card or on a piece of paper kept with the card, does not affect the consumer's liability for unauthorized transfers. (However, refer to comment 2(m)-2 regarding termination of the authority of given by the consumer to another person.)

3. Limits on liability. The extent of the consumer's liability is determined solely by the consumer's promptness in reporting the loss or theft of an access device. Similarly, no agreement between the consumer and an institution may impose greater liability on the consumer for an unauthorized transfer than the limits provided in Regulation E.

Paragraph 6(b)(1)— Timely Notice Given

1. $50 limit applies. The basic liability limit is $50. For example, the consumer's card is lost or stolen on Monday and the consumer learns of the loss or theft on Wednesday. If the consumer notifies the financial institution within two business days of learning of the loss or theft (by midnight Friday), the consumer's liability is limited to $50 or the amount of the unauthorized transfers that occurred before notification, whichever is less.

2. Knowledge of loss or theft of access device. The fact that a consumer has received a periodic statement that reflects unauthorized transfers may be a factor in determining whether the consumer had knowledge of the loss or theft, but cannot be deemed to represent conclusive evidence that the consumer had such knowledge.

3. Two business day rule. The two business day period does not include the day the consumer learns of the loss or theft or any day that is not a business day. The rule is calculated based on two 24-hour periods, without regard to the financial institution's business hours or the time of day that the consumer learns of the loss or theft. For example, a consumer learns of the loss or theft at 6 p.m. on Friday. Assuming that Saturday is a business day and Sunday is not, the two business day period begins on Saturday and expires at 11:59 p.m. on Monday, not at the end of the financial institution's business day on Monday.

Paragraph 6(b)(2)— Timely Notice Not Given

1. $500 limit applies. The second tier of liability is $500. For example, the consumer's card is stolen on Monday and the consumer learns of the theft that same day. The consumer reports the theft on Friday. The $500 limit applies because the consumer failed to notify the financial institution within two business days of learning of the theft (which would have been by midnight Wednesday). How much the consumer is actually liable for, however, depends on when the unauthorized transfers take place. In this example, assume a $100 unauthorized transfer was made on Tuesday and a $600 unauthorized transfer on Thursday. Because the consumer is liable for the amount of the loss that occurs within the first two business days (but no more than $50), plus the amount of the unauthorized transfers that occurs after the first two business days and before the consumer gives notice, the consumer's total liability is $500 ($50 of the $100 transfer plus $450 of the $600 transfer, in this example). But if $600 was taken on Tuesday and $100 on Thursday, the consumer's maximum liability would be $150 ($50 of the $600 plus $100).

Paragraph 6(b)(3)— Periodic Statement; Timely Notice Not Given

1. Unlimited liability applies. The standard of unlimited liability applies if unauthorized transfers appear on a periodic statement, and may apply in conjunction with the first two tiers of liability. If a periodic statement shows an unauthorized transfer made with a lost or stolen debit card, the consumer must notify the financial institution within 60 calendar days after the periodic statement was sent; otherwise, the consumer faces unlimited liability for all unauthorized transfers made after the 60-day period. The consumer's liability for unauthorized transfers before the statement is sent, and up to 60 days following, is determined based on the first two tiers of liability: up to $50 if the consumer notifies the financial institution within two business days of learning of the loss or theft of the card and up to $500 if the consumer notifies the institution after two business days of learning of the loss or theft.

2. Transfers not involving access device. The first two tiers of liability do not apply to unauthorized transfers from a consumer's account made without an access device. If, however, the consumer fails to report such unauthorized transfers within 60 calendar days of the financial institution's transmittal of the periodic statement, the consumer may be liable for any transfers occurring after the close of the 60 days and before notice is given to the institution. For example, a consumer's account is electronically debited for $200 without the consumer's authorization and by means other than the consumer's access device. If the consumer notifies the institution within 60 days of the transmittal of the periodic statement that shows the unauthorized

transfer, the consumer has no liability. However, if in addition to the $200, the consumer's account is debited for a $400 unauthorized transfer on the 61st day and the consumer fails to notify the institution of the first unauthorized transfer until the 62nd day, the consumer may be liable for the full $400.

Paragraph 6(b)(4)— Extension of Time Limits

1. Extenuating circumstances. Examples of circumstances that require extension of the notification periods under this section include the consumer's extended travel or hospitalization.

Paragraph 6(b)(5)— Notice to Financial Institution

1. Receipt of notice. A financial institution is considered to have received notice for purposes of limiting the consumer's liability if notice is given in a reasonable manner, even if the consumer notifies the institution but uses an address or telephone number other than the one specified by the institution.

2. Notice by third party. Notice to a financial institution by a person acting on the consumer's behalf is considered valid under this section. For example, if a consumer is hospitalized and unable to report the loss or theft of an access device, notice is considered given when someone acting on the consumer's behalf notifies the bank of the loss or theft. A financial institution may require appropriate documentation from the person representing the consumer to establish that the person is acting on the consumer's behalf.

3. Content of notice. Notice to a financial institution is considered given when a consumer takes reasonable steps to provide the institution with the pertinent account information. Even when the consumer is unable to provide the account number or the card number in reporting a lost or stolen access device or an unauthorized transfer, the notice effectively limits the consumer's liability if the consumer otherwise identifies sufficiently the account in question. For example, the consumer may identify the account by the name on the account and the type of account in question. . . .

§ 1005.11 Procedures for Resolving Errors

11(a) Definition of Error

1. Terminal location. With regard to deposits at an ATM, a consumer's request for the terminal location or other information triggers the error-resolution procedures, but the financial institution need only provide the ATM location if it has captured that information.

2. Verifying an account debit or credit. If the consumer contacts the financial institution to ascertain whether a payment (for example, in a home-banking or bill-payment program) or any other type of EFT was debited to the account, or whether a deposit made via ATM, preauthorized transfer, or any other type of EFT was credited to the account, without asserting an error, the error-resolution procedures do not apply.

3. Loss or theft of access device. A financial institution is required to comply with the error-resolution procedures when a consumer reports the loss or theft of an access device if the consumer also alleges possible unauthorized use as a consequence of the loss or theft.

4. Error asserted after account closed. The financial institution must comply with the error-resolution procedures when a consumer properly asserts an error, even if the account has been closed.

5. Request for documentation or information. A request for documentation or other information must be treated as an error unless it is clear that the consumer is requesting a duplicate copy for tax or other record-keeping purposes.

6. Terminal receipts for transfers of $15 or less. The fact that an institution does not make a terminal receipt available for a transfer of $15 or less in accordance with § 1005.9(e) is not an error for purposes of § 1005.11(a)(1)(vi) or (vii).

11(b) Notice of Error From Consumer

Paragraph 11(b)(1)— Timing; Contents

1. Content of error notice. The notice of error is effective even if it does not contain the consumer's account number, so long as the financial institution is able to identify the account in question. For example, the consumer could provide a Social Security number or other unique means of identification.

2. Investigation pending receipt of information. While a financial institution may request a written, signed statement from the consumer relating to a notice of error, it may not delay initiating or completing an investigation pending receipt of the statement.

3. Statement held for consumer. When a consumer has arranged for periodic statements to be held until picked up, the statement for a particular cycle is deemed to have been transmitted on the date the financial institution first makes the statement available to the consumer.

4. Failure to provide statement. When a financial institution fails to provide the consumer with a periodic statement, a request for a copy is governed by this section if the consumer gives notice within 60 days from the date on which the statement should have been transmitted.

5. Discovery of error by institution. The error-resolution procedures of this section apply when a notice of error is received from the consumer, and not when the financial institution itself discovers and corrects an error.

6. Notice at particular phone number or address. A financial institution may require the consumer to give notice only at the telephone number or address disclosed by the institution, provided the institution maintains reasonable procedures to refer the consumer to the specified telephone number or address if the consumer attempts to give notice to the institution in a different manner.

7. Effect of late notice. An institution is not required to comply with the requirements of this section for any notice of error from the consumer that is received by the institution later than 60 days from the date on which the periodic statement first reflecting the error is sent. Where the consumer's assertion of error involves an unauthorized EFT, however, the institution must comply with § 1005.6 before it may impose any liability on the consumer.

Paragraph 11(b)(2)— Written Confirmation

1. Written confirmation-of-error notice. If the consumer sends a written confirmation of error to the wrong address, the financial institution must process the confirmation through normal procedures. But the institution need not provisionally credit the consumer's account if the written confirmation is delayed beyond 10 business days in getting to the right place because it was sent to the wrong address.

11(c) Time Limits and Extent of Investigation

1. Notice to consumer. Unless otherwise indicated in this section, the financial institution may provide the required notices to the consumer either orally or in writing.

2. Written confirmation of oral notice. A financial institution must begin its investigation promptly upon receipt of an oral notice. It may not delay until it has received a written confirmation.

3. Charges for error resolution. If a billing error occurred, whether as alleged or in a different amount or manner, the financial institution may not impose a charge related to any aspect of the error-resolution process (including charges for documentation or investigation). Since the Act grants the consumer error-resolution rights, the institution should avoid any chilling effect on the good-faith assertion of errors that might result if charges are assessed when no billing error has occurred.

4. Correction without investigation. A financial institution may make, without investigation, a final correction to a consumer's account in the amount or manner alleged by the consumer to be in error, but must comply with all other applicable requirements of § 1005.11.

5. Correction notice. A financial institution may include the notice of correction on a periodic statement that is mailed or delivered within the 10-business-day or 45-calendar-day time limits and that clearly identifies the correction to the consumer's account. The institution must determine whether such a mailing will be prompt enough to satisfy the requirements of this section, taking into account the specific facts involved.

6. Correction of an error. If the financial institution determines an error occurred, within either the 10-day or 45-day period, it must correct the error (subject to the liability provisions of §§ 1005.6(a) and (b)) including, where applicable, the crediting of interest and the refunding of any fees imposed by the institution. In a combined credit/EFT transaction, for example, the institution must refund any finance charges incurred as a result of the error. The institution need not refund fees that would have been imposed whether or not the error occurred.

7. Extent of required investigation. A financial institution complies with its duty to investigate, correct, and report its determination regarding an error described in § 1005.11(a)(1)(vii) by transmitting the requested information, clarification, or documentation within the time limits set forth in § 1005.11(c). If the institution has provisionally credited the consumer's account in accordance with § 1005.11(c)(2), it may debit the amount upon transmitting the requested information, clarification, or documentation.

Paragraph 11(c)(2)(i)

1. Compliance with all requirements. Financial institutions exempted from provisionally crediting a consumer's account under §§ 1005.11(c)(2)(i)(A) and (B) must still comply with all other requirements of § 1005.11.

Paragraph 11(c)(3)— Extension of Time Periods

1. POS debit card transactions. The extended deadlines for investigating errors resulting from POS debit card transactions apply to all debit card transactions, including those for cash only, at merchants' POS terminals, and also including mail and telephone orders. The deadlines do not apply to

transactions at an ATM, however, even though the ATM may be in a merchant location.

Paragraph 11(c)(4)—Investigation

1. Third parties. When information or documentation requested by the consumer is in the possession of a third party with whom the financial institution does not have an agreement, the institution satisfies the error-resolution requirement by so advising the consumer within the specified time period.

2. Scope of investigation. When an alleged error involves a payment to a third party under the financial institution's telephone bill-payment plan, a review of the institution's own records is sufficient, assuming no agreement exists between the institution and the third party concerning the bill-payment service.

3. POS transfers. When a consumer alleges an error involving a transfer to a merchant via a POS terminal, the institution must verify the information previously transmitted when executing the transfer. For example, the financial institution may request a copy of the sales receipt to verify that the amount of the transfer correctly corresponds to the amount of the consumer's purchase.

4. Agreement. An agreement that a third party will honor an access device is an agreement for purposes of this paragraph. A financial institution does not have an agreement for purposes of § 1005.11(c)(4)(ii) solely because it participates in transactions that occur under the Federal recurring payments programs, or that are cleared through an ACH or similar arrangement for the clearing and settlement of fund transfers generally, or because the institution agrees to be bound by the rules of such an arrangement.

5. No EFT agreement. When there is no agreement between the institution and the third party for the type of EFT involved, the financial institution must review any relevant information within the institution's own records for the particular account to resolve the consumer's claim. The extent of the investigation required may vary depending on the facts and circumstances. However, a financial institution may not limit its investigation solely to the payment instructions where additional information within its own records pertaining to the particular account in question could help to resolve a consumer's claim. Information that may be reviewed as part of an investigation might include:

i. The ACH transaction records for the transfer;

ii. The transaction history of the particular account for a reasonable period of time immediately preceding the allegation of error;

iii. Whether the check number of the transaction in question is notably out-of-sequence;

iv. The location of either the transaction or the payee in question relative to the consumer's place of residence and habitual transaction area;

v. Information relative to the account in question within the control of the institution's third-party service providers if the financial institution reasonably believes that it may have records or other information that could be dispositive; or

vi. Any other information appropriate to resolve the claim.

11(d) Procedures if Financial Institution Determines No Error or Different Error Occurred

1. Error different from that alleged. When a financial institution determines that an error occurred in a manner or amount different from that described by the consumer, it must comply with the requirements of both §§ 1005.11(c) and (d), as relevant. The institution may give the notice of correction and the explanation separately or in a combined form.

Paragraph 11(d)(1)—Written Explanation

1. Request for documentation. When a consumer requests copies of documents, the financial institution must provide the copies in an understandable form. If an institution relied on magnetic tape, it must convert the applicable data into readable form, for example, by printing it and explaining any codes.

Paragraph 11(d)(2)—Debiting Provisional Credit

1. Alternative procedure for debiting of credited funds. The financial institution may comply with the requirements of this section by notifying the consumer that the consumer's account will be debited five business days from the transmittal of the notification, specifying the calendar date on which the debiting will occur.

2. Fees for overdrafts. The financial institution may not impose fees for items it is required to honor under § 1005.11. It may, however, impose any normal transaction or item fee that is unrelated to an overdraft resulting from the debiting. If the account is still overdrawn after five business days, the institution may impose the fees or finance charges to which it is entitled, if any, under an overdraft credit plan.

11(e) Reassertion of Error

1. Withdrawal of error; right to reassert. The financial institution has no further error-resolution

responsibilities if the consumer voluntarily withdraws the notice alleging an error. A consumer who has withdrawn an allegation of error has the right to reassert the allegation unless the financial institution had already complied with all of the error-resolution requirements before the allegation was withdrawn. The consumer must do so, however, within the original 60-day period.

§ 1005.12 Relation to Other Laws

1. Determining applicable regulation.

i. For transactions involving access devices that also function as credit cards, whether Regulation E or Regulation Z (12 CFR 226) applies depends on the nature of the transaction. For example, if the transaction solely involves an extension of credit, and does not include a debit to a checking account (or other consumer asset account), the liability limitations and error-resolution requirements of Regulation Z apply. If the transaction debits a checking account only (with no credit extended), the provisions of Regulation E apply. If the transaction debits a checking account but also draws on an overdraft line of credit attached to the account, Regulation E's liability limitations apply, in addition to section 226.13(d) and (g) of Regulation Z (which apply because of the extension of credit associated with the overdraft feature on the checking account). If a consumer's access device is also a credit card and the device is used to make unauthorized withdrawals from a checking account, but also is used to obtain unauthorized cash advances directly from a line of credit that is separate from the checking account, both Regulation E and Regulation Z apply.

ii. The following examples illustrate these principles:

A. A consumer has a card that can be used either as a credit card or a debit card. When used as a debit card, the card draws on the consumer's checking account. When used as a credit card, the card draws only on a separate line of credit. If the card is stolen and used as a credit card to make purchases or to get cash advances at an ATM from the line of credit, the liability limits and error-resolution provisions of Regulation Z apply; Regulation E does not apply.

B. In the same situation, if the card is stolen and is used as a debit card to make purchases or to get cash withdrawals at an ATM from the checking account, the liability limits and error-resolution provisions of Regulation E apply; Regulation Z does not apply.

C. In the same situation, assume the card is stolen and used both as a debit card and as a credit card; for example, the thief makes some purchases using the card as a debit card, and other purchases using the card as a credit card. Here, the liability limits and error-resolution provisions of Regulation E apply to the unauthorized transactions in which the card was used as a debit card, and the corresponding provisions of Regulation Z apply to the unauthorized transactions in which the card was used as a credit card.

D. Assume a somewhat different type of card, one that draws on the consumer's checking account and can also draw on an overdraft line of credit attached to the checking account. There is no separate line of credit, only the overdraft line, associated with the card. In this situation, if the card is stolen and used, the liability limits and the error-resolution provisions of Regulation E apply. In addition, if the use of the card has resulted in accessing the overdraft line of credit, the error-resolution provisions of section 226.13(d) and (g) of Regulation Z also apply, but not the other error-resolution provisions of Regulation Z.

2. Issuance rules. For access devices that also constitute credit cards, the issuance rules of Regulation E apply if the only credit feature is a preexisting credit line attached to the asset account to cover overdrafts (or to maintain a specified minimum balance) or an overdraft service, as defined in section 205.17(a). Regulation Z (12 CFR part 226) rules apply if there is another type of credit feature; for example, one permitting direct extensions of credit that do not involve the asset account.

3. Overdraft service. The addition of an overdraft service, as that term is defined in section 205.17(a), to an accepted access device does not constitute the addition of a credit feature subject to Regulation Z. Instead, the provisions of Regulation E apply, including the liability limitations (section 205.6) and the requirement to obtain consumer consent to the service before any fees or charges for paying an overdraft may be assessed on the account (section 205.17).

§ 1005.14 Electronic Fund Transfer Service Provider Not Holding Consumer's Account

14(a) Electronic Fund Transfer Service Providers Subject to Regulation

1. Applicability. This section applies only when a service provider issues an access device to a consumer for initiating transfers to or from the consumer's account at a financial institution and the two entities have no agreement regarding this EFT service. If the service provider does not issue an access device to the consumer for accessing an account held by another institution, it does not qualify for the treatment accorded by § 1005.14. For example, this section does not apply to an institution that initiates preauthorized payroll deposits to consumer accounts on behalf of an employer. By contrast, § 1005.14 can apply to an institution that issues a code for initiating telephone transfers to be carried out through the ACH from a consumer's account at another institution. This is the case even if the consumer has accounts at both institutions.

2. ACH agreements. The ACH rules generally do not constitute an agreement for purposes of this section. However, an ACH agreement under which members specifically agree to honor each other's debit cards is an "agreement," and thus this section does not apply.

14(b) Compliance by Electronic Fund Transfer Service Provider

1. Liability. The service provider is liable for unauthorized EFTs that exceed limits on the consumer's liability under § 1005.6.

Paragraph 14(b)(1)— Disclosures and Documentation

1. Periodic statements from electronic fund transfer service provider. A service provider that meets the conditions set forth in this paragraph does not have to issue periodic statements. A service provider that does not meet the conditions need only include on periodic statements information about transfers initiated with the access device it has issued.

Paragraph 14(b)(2)— Error Resolution

1. Error resolution. When a consumer notifies the service provider of an error, the EFT service provider must investigate and resolve the error in compliance with § 1005.11 as modified by § 1005.14(b)(2). If an error occurred, any fees or charges imposed as a result of the error, either by the service provider or by the account-holding institution (for example, overdraft or dishonor fees) must be reimbursed to the consumer by the service provider.

14(c) Compliance by Account-Holding Institution

Paragraph 14(c)(1)

1. Periodic statements from account-holding institution. The periodic statement provided by the account-holding institution need only contain the information required by § 1005.9(b)(1). ...

Electronic Signatures in Global and National Commerce Act

15 U.S.C. §§ 7001–7031

Section

§ 7001. General Rule of Validity

(a) In General.—Notwithstanding any statute, regulation, or other rule of law (other than this title and title II), with respect to any transaction in or affecting interstate or foreign commerce—

(1) a signature, contract, or other record relating to such transaction may not be denied legal effect, validity, or enforceability solely because it is in electronic form; and

(2) a contract relating to such transaction may not be denied legal effect, validity, or enforceability solely because an electronic signature or electronic record was used in its formation.

(b) Preservation of rights and obligations.—This title does not—

(1) limit, alter, or otherwise affect any requirement imposed by a statute, regulation, or rule of law relating to the rights and obligations of persons under such statute, regulation, or rule of law other than a requirement that contracts or other records be written, signed, or in nonelectronic form; or

(2) require any person to agree to use or accept electronic records or electronic signatures, other than a governmental agency with respect to a record other than a contract to which it is a party.

(c) Consumer disclosures.—

(1) Consent to electronic records.—Notwithstanding subsection (a), if a statute, regulation, or other rule of law requires that information relating to a transaction or transactions in or affecting interstate or foreign commerce be provided or made available to a consumer in writing, the use of an electronic record to provide or make available (whichever is required) such information satisfies the requirement that such information be in writing if—

(A) the consumer has affirmatively consented to such use and has not withdrawn such consent;

(B) the consumer, prior to consenting, is provided with a clear and conspicuous statement—

(i) informing the consumer of

(I) any right or option of the consumer to have the record provided or made available on paper or in nonelectronic form, and

(II) the right of the consumer to withdraw the consent to have the record provided or made available in an electronic form and of any conditions, consequences (which may include termination of the parties' relationship), or fees in the event of such withdrawal;

(ii) informing the consumer of whether the consent applies

(I) only to the particular transaction which gave rise to the obligation to provide the record, or

(II) to identified categories of records that may be provided or made available during the course of the parties' relationship;

(iii) describing the procedures the consumer must use to withdraw consent as provided in clause (i) and to update information needed to contact the consumer electronically; and

(iv) informing the consumer

(I) how, after the consent, the consumer may, upon request, obtain a paper copy of an electronic record, and

(II) whether any fee will be charged for such copy;

(C) the consumer—

(i) prior to consenting, is provided with a statement of the hardware and software requirements for access to and retention of the electronic records; and

(ii) consents electronically, or confirms his or her consent electronically, in a manner that reasonably demonstrates that the consumer can access information in the electronic form that will be used to provide the information that is the subject of the consent; and

(D) after the consent of a consumer in accordance with subparagraph (A), if a change in the hardware or software requirements needed to access or retain electronic records creates a material risk that the consumer will not be able to access or retain a subsequent electronic record that was the subject of the consent, the person providing the electronic record—

(i) provides the consumer with a statement of

(I) the revised hardware and software requirements for access to and retention of the electronic records, and

(II) the right to withdraw consent without the imposition of any fees for such withdrawal and without the imposition of any condition or consequence that was not disclosed under subparagraph (B)(i); and

(ii) again complies with subparagraph (C).

(2) Other rights.—

(A) Preservation of consumer protections.—Nothing in this title affects the content or timing of any disclosure or other record required to be provided or made available to any consumer under any statute, regulation, or other rule of law.

(B) Verification or acknowledgment.—If a law that was enacted prior to this Act expressly requires a record to be provided or made available by a specified method that requires verification or acknowledgment of receipt, the record may be provided or made available electronically only if the method used provides verification or acknowledgment of receipt (whichever is required).

(3) Effect of failure to obtain electronic consent or confirmation of consent.—The legal effectiveness, validity, or enforceability of any contract executed by a consumer shall not be denied solely because of the failure to obtain electronic consent or confirmation of consent by that consumer in accordance with paragraph (1)(C)(ii).

(4) Prospective effect.—Withdrawal of consent by a consumer shall not affect the legal effectiveness, validity, or enforceability of electronic records provided or made available to that consumer in accordance with paragraph (1) prior to implementation of the consumer's withdrawal of consent. A consumer's withdrawal of consent shall be effective within a reasonable period of time after receipt of the withdrawal by the provider of the record. Failure to comply with paragraph (1)(D) may, at the election of the consumer, be treated as a withdrawal of consent for purposes of this paragraph.

(5) Prior consent.—This subsection does not apply to any records that are provided or made available to a consumer who has consented prior to the effective date of this title to receive such records in electronic form as permitted by any statute, regulation, or other rule of law.

(6) Oral communications.—An oral communication or a recording of an oral communication shall not qualify as an electronic record for purposes of this subsection except as otherwise provided under applicable law.

(d) Retention of contracts and records.—

(1) Accuracy and accessibility.—if a statute, regulation, or other rule of law requires that a contract or other record relating to a transaction in or affecting interstate or foreign commerce be retained, that requirement is met by retaining an electronic record of the information in the contract or other record that—

(A) accurately reflects the information set forth in the contract or other record; and

(B) remains accessible to all persons who are entitled to access by statute, regulation, or rule of law, for the period required by such statute, regulation, or rule of law, in a form that is capable of being accurately reproduced for later reference, whether by transmission, printing, or otherwise.

(2) Exception.—a requirement to retain a contract or other record in accordance with paragraph (1) does not apply to any information whose sole purpose is to enable the contract or other record to be sent, communicated, or received.

(3) Originals.—if a statute, regulation, or other rule of law requires a contract or other record relating to a transaction in or affecting interstate or foreign commerce to be provided, available, or retained in its original form, or provides consequences if the

contract or other record is not provided, available, or retained in its original form, that statute, regulation, or rule of law is satisfied by an electronic record that complies with paragraph (1).

(4) checks.—if a statute, regulation, or other rule of law requires the retention of a check, that requirement is satisfied by retention of an electronic record of the information on the front and back of the check in accordance with paragraph (1).

(e) Accuracy and ability to retain contracts and other records.—Notwithstanding subsection (a), if a statute, regulation, or other rule of law requires that a contract or other record relating to a transaction in or affecting interstate or foreign commerce be in writing, the legal effect, validity, or enforceability of an electronic record of such contract or other record may be denied if such electronic record is not in a form that is capable of being retained and accurately reproduced for later reference by all parties or persons who are entitled to retain the contract or other record.

(f) Proximity.—nothing in this title affects the proximity required by any statute, regulation, or other rule of law with respect to any warning, notice, disclosure, or other record required to be posted, displayed, or publicly affixed.

(g) Notarization and acknowledgment.—if a statute, regulation, or other rule of law requires a signature or record relating to a transaction in or affecting interstate or foreign commerce to be notarized, acknowledged, verified, or made under oath, that requirement is satisfied if the electronic signature of the person authorized to perform those acts, together with all other information required to be included by other applicable statute, regulation, or rule of law, is attached to or logically associated with the signature or record.

(h) Electronic agents.—a contract or other record relating to a transaction in or affecting interstate or foreign commerce may not be denied legal effect, validity, or enforceability solely because its formation, creation, or delivery involved the action of one or more electronic agents so long as the action of any such electronic agent is legally attributable to the person to be bound.

(i) Insurance.—it is the specific intent of the congress that this title and title ii apply to the business of insurance.

(j) Insurance agents and brokers.—an insurance agent or broker acting under the direction of a party that enters into a contract by means of an electronic record or electronic signature may not be held liable for any deficiency in the electronic procedures agreed to by the parties under that contract if—

(1) the agent or broker has not engaged in negligent, reckless, or intentional tortious conduct;

(2) the agent or broker was not involved in the development or establishment of such electronic procedures; and

(3) the agent or broker did not deviate from such procedures.

§ 7002. Exemption to Preemption

(a) In general.—a state statute, regulation, or other rule of law may modify, limit, or supersede the provisions of section 101 with respect to state law only if such statute, regulation, or rule of law—

(1) constitutes an enactment or adoption of the uniform electronic transactions act as approved and recommended for enactment in all the states by the national conference of commissioners on uniform state laws in 1999, except that any exception to the scope of such act enacted by a state under section 3(b)(4) of such act shall be preempted to the extent such exception is inconsistent with this title or title ii, or would not be permitted under paragraph (2)(A)(ii) of this subsection; or

(2)(A) specifies the alternative procedures or requirements for the use or acceptance (or both) of electronic records or electronic signatures to establish the legal effect, validity, or enforceability of contracts or other records, if—

(i) such alternative procedures or requirements are consistent with this title and title ii; and

(ii) such alternative procedures or requirements do not require, or accord greater legal status or effect to, the implementation or application of a specific technology or technical specification for performing the functions of creating, storing, generating, receiving, communicating, or authenticating electronic records or electronic signatures; and

(B) if enacted or adopted after the date of the enactment of this act, makes specific reference to this act.

(b) Exceptions for actions by states as market participants.—subsection (a)(2)(a)(ii) shall not apply to the statutes, regulations, or other rules of law governing procurement by any state, or any agency or instrumentality thereof.

(c) Prevention of circumvention.— subsection (a) does not permit a state to circumvent this title or title ii through the imposition of nonelectronic delivery methods under section 8(b)(2) of the uniform electronic transactions act.

§ 7003. Specific Exceptions

(a) Excepted requirements.—the provisions of section 101 shall not apply to a contract or other record to the extent it is governed by—

(1) a statute, regulation, or other rule of law governing the creation and execution of wills, codicils, or testamentary trusts;

(2) a state statute, regulation, or other rule of law governing adoption, divorce, or other matters of family law; or

(3) the uniform commercial code, as in effect in any state, other than sections 1107 and 1206 and articles 2 and 2a.

(b) Additional exceptions.—the provisions of section 101 shall not apply to—

(1) court orders or notices, or official court documents (including briefs, pleadings, and other writings) required to be executed in connection with court proceedings;

(2) any notice of—

(A) the cancellation or termination of utility services (including water, heat, and power);

(B) default, acceleration, repossession, foreclosure, or eviction, or the right to cure, under a credit agreement secured by, or a rental agreement for, a primary residence of an individual;

(C) the cancellation or termination of health insurance or benefits or life insurance benefits (excluding annuities); or

(D) recall of a product, or material failure of a product, that risks endangering health or safety; or

(3) any document required to accompany any transportation or handling of hazardous materials, pesticides, or other toxic or dangerous materials.

(c) Review of exceptions.—

(1) evaluation required.—the secretary of commerce, acting through the assistant secretary for communications and information, shall review the operation of the exceptions in subsections (a) and (b) to evaluate, over a period of 3 years, whether such exceptions continue to be necessary for the protection of consumers. Within 3 years after the date of enactment of this act, the assistant secretary shall submit a report to the congress on the results of such evaluation.

(2) determinations.—if a federal regulatory agency, with respect to matter within its jurisdiction, determines after notice and an opportunity for public comment, and publishes a finding, that one or more such exceptions are no longer necessary for the protection of consumers and eliminating such exceptions will not increase the material risk of harm to consumers, such agency may extend the application of section 101 to the exceptions identified in such finding.

§ 7004. Applicability to Federal and State Governments

(a) Filing and access requirements.—subject to subsection (c)(2), nothing in this title limits or supersedes any requirement by a federal regulatory agency, self-regulatory organization, or state regulatory agency that records be filed with such agency or organization in accordance with specified standards or formats.

(b) Preservation of existing rulemaking authority.—

(1) use of authority to interpret.—Subject to paragraph (2) and subsection (c), a Federal regulatory agency or State regulatory agency that is responsible for rulemaking under any other statute may interpret section 101 with respect to such statute through—

(A) the issuance of regulations pursuant to a statute; or

(B) to the extent such agency is authorized by statute to issue orders or guidance, the issuance of orders or guidance of general applicability that are publicly available and published (in the Federal Register in the case of an order or guidance issued by a Federal regulatory agency).

This paragraph does not grant any Federal regulatory agency or State regulatory agency authority to issue regulations, orders, or guidance pursuant to any statute that does not authorize such issuance.

(2) Limitations on interpretation authority.—Notwithstanding paragraph (1), a Federal regulatory agency shall not adopt any regulation, order, or guidance described in paragraph (1), and a State regulatory agency is preempted by section 101 from adopting any regulation, order, or guidance described in paragraph (1), unless—

(A) such regulation, order, or guidance is consistent with section 101;

(B) such regulation, order, or guidance does not add to the requirements of such section; and

(C) such agency finds, in connection with the issuance of such regulation, order, or guidance, that—

(i) there is a substantial justification for the regulation, order, or guidance;

(ii) the methods selected to carry out that purpose—

(I) are substantially equivalent to the requirements imposed on records that are not electronic records; and

(II) will not impose unreasonable costs on the acceptance and use of electronic records; and

(iii) the methods selected to carry out that purpose do not require, or accord greater legal status or effect to, the implementation or application of a specific technology or technical specification for performing the functions of creating, storing, generating, receiving, communicating, or authenticating electronic records or electronic signatures.

(3) Performance standards.—

(A) accuracy, record integrity, accessibility.—notwithstanding paragraph (2)(c)(iii), a federal regulatory agency or state regulatory agency may interpret section 101(d) to specify performance standards to assure accuracy, record integrity, and accessibility of records that are required to be retained. Such performance standards may be specified in a manner that imposes a requirement in violation of paragraph (2)(c)(iii) if the requirement

(i) serves an important governmental objective; and

(ii) is substantially related to the achievement of that objective. Nothing in this paragraph shall be construed to grant any federal regulatory agency or state regulatory agency authority to require use of a particular type of software or hardware in order to comply with section 101(d).

(B) paper or printed form.—Notwithstanding subsection (c)(1), a Federal regulatory agency or State regulatory agency may interpret section 101(d) to require retention of a record in a tangible printed or paper form if—

(i) there is a compelling governmental interest relating to law enforcement or national security for imposing such requirement; and

(ii) imposing such requirement is essential to attaining such interest.

(4) exceptions for actions by government as market participant.—paragraph (2)(c)(iii) shall not apply to the statutes, regulations, or other rules of law governing procurement by the federal or any state government, or any agency or instrumentality thereof.

(c) Additional limitations.—

(1) reimposing paper prohibited.—nothing in subsection (b) (other than paragraph (3)(b) thereof) shall be construed to grant any federal regulatory agency or state regulatory agency authority to impose or reimpose any requirement that a record be in a tangible printed or paper form.

(2) continuing obligation under government paperwork elimination act.—nothing in subsection (a) or (b) relieves any federal regulatory agency of its obligations under the government paperwork elimination act (title xvii of public law 105277).

(d) Authority to exempt from consent provision.—

(1) in general.—a federal regulatory agency may, with respect to matter within its jurisdiction, by regulation or order issued after notice and an opportunity for public comment, exempt without condition a specified category or type of record from the requirements relating to consent in section 101(c) if such exemption is necessary to eliminate a substantial burden on electronic commerce and will not increase the material risk of harm to consumers.

(2) prospectuses.—within 30 days after the date of enactment of this act, the securities and exchange commission shall issue a regulation or order pursuant to paragraph (1) exempting from section 101(c) any records that are required to be provided in order to allow advertising, sales literature, or other information concerning a security issued by an investment company that is registered under the investment company act of 1940, or concerning the issuer thereof, to be excluded from the definition of a prospectus under section 2(a)(10)(a) of the securities act of 1933.

(e) Electronic letters of agency.—the federal communications commission shall not hold any contract for telecommunications service or letter of agency for a preferred carrier change, that otherwise complies with the commission's rules, to be legally ineffective, invalid, or unenforceable solely because an electronic record or electronic signature was used in its formation or authorization.

§ 7005. Studies

(a) Delivery.—Within 12 months after the date of the enactment of this Act, the Secretary of Commerce shall conduct an inquiry regarding the effectiveness of the delivery of electronic records to consumers using electronic mail as compared with delivery of written records via the United States Postal Service and private express mail services. The Secretary shall submit a report to the Congress regarding the results of such inquiry by the conclusion of such 12-month period.

(b) Study of electronic consent.—Within 12 months after the date of the enactment of this Act, the Secretary of Commerce and the Federal Trade Commission shall submit a report to the Congress evaluating any benefits provided to consumers by the procedure required by section 101(c)(1)(C)(ii); any burdens imposed on electronic commerce by that provision; whether the benefits outweigh the burdens; whether the absence of the procedure required by section 101(c)(1)(C)(ii) would increase the incidence of fraud directed against consumers; and suggesting any revisions to the provision deemed appropriate by the Secretary and the Commission. In conducting this evaluation, the Secretary and the Commission shall solicit comment from the general public, consumer representatives, and electronic commerce businesses.

§ 7006. Definitions

For purposes of this title:

(1) consumer.—the term "consumer" means an individual who obtains, through a transaction, products or services which are used primarily for personal, family, or household purposes, and also means the legal representative of such an individual.

(2) electronic.—the term "electronic" means relating to technology having electrical, digital, magnetic, wireless, optical, electromagnetic, or similar capabilities.

(3) electronic agent.—the term "electronic agent" means a computer program or an electronic or other automated means used independently to initiate an action or respond to electronic rec- ords or performances in whole or in part without review or action by an individual at the time of the action or response.

(4) electronic record.—the term "electronic record" means a contract or other record created, generated, sent, communicated, received, or stored by electronic means.

(5) electronic signature.—the term "electronic signature" means an electronic sound, symbol, or process, attached to or logically associated with a contract or other record and executed or adopted by a person with the intent to sign the record.

(6) federal regulatory agency.—the term "federal regulatory agency" means an agency, as that term is defined in section 552(f) of title 5, United States Code.

(7) information.—the term "information" means data, text, images, sounds, codes, computer programs, software, databases, or the like.

(8) person.—the term "person" means an individual, corporation, business trust, estate, trust, partnership, limited liability company, association, joint venture, governmental agency, public corporation, or any other legal or commercial entity.

(9) record.—the term "record" means information that is inscribed on a tangible medium or that is stored in an electronic or other medium and is retrievable in perceivable form.

(10) requirement.—the term "requirement" includes a prohibition.

(11) self-regulatory organization.—the term "self-regulatory organization" means an organization or entity that is not a federal regulatory agency or a state, but that is under the supervision of a federal regulatory agency and is authorized under federal law to adopt and administer rules applicable to its members that are enforced by such organization or entity, by a federal regulatory agency, or by another self-regulatory organization.

(12) state.—the term "state" includes the district of Columbia and the territories and possessions of the united states.

(13) transaction.—the term "transaction" means an action or set of actions relating to the conduct of business, consumer, or commercial affairs between two or more persons, including any of the following types of conduct—

(A) the sale, lease, exchange, licensing, or other disposition of

(i) personal property, including goods and intangibles,

(ii) services, and

(iii) any combination thereof; and

(B) the sale, lease, exchange, or other disposition of any interest in real property, or any combination thereof.

§ 7007. Effective Date

(a) In general.—except as provided in subsection (b), this title shall be effective on October 1, 2000.

(b) Exceptions.—

(1) record retention.—

(A) in general.—Subject to subparagraph (B), this title shall be effective on March 1, 2001, with respect to a requirement that a record be retained imposed by—

(i) a Federal statute, regulation, or other rule of law, or

(ii) a State statute, regulation, or other rule of law administered or promulgated by a State regulatory agency.

(B) delayed effect for pending rulemakings.—if on March 1, 2001, a federal regulatory agency or state regulatory agency has announced, proposed, or initiated, but not completed, a rulemaking proceeding to prescribe a regulation under section 104(b)(3) with respect to a requirement described in subparagraph (a), this title shall be effective on June 1, 2001, with respect to such requirement.

(2) certain guaranteed and insured loans.—With regard to any transaction involving a loan guarantee or loan guarantee commitment (as those terms are defined in section 502 of the federal credit reform act of 1990), or involving a program listed in the federal credit supplement, budget of the United States, FY 2001, this title applies only to such transactions entered into, and to any loan or mortgage made, insured, or guaranteed by the united states government thereunder, on and after one year after the date of enactment of this act.

(3) student loans.—With respect to any records that are provided or made available to a consumer pursuant to an application for a loan, or a loan made, pursuant to title IV of the Higher Education Act of 1965, section 101(c) of this Act shall not apply until the earlier of—

(A) such time as the Secretary of Education publishes revised promissory notes under section 432(m) of the Higher Education Act of 1965; or

(B) one year after the date of enactment of this Act.

§ 7021. Transferable Records

(a) Definitions.—For purposes of this section:

(1) Transferable Record.—The term "transferable record" means an electronic record that—

(A) would be a note under Article 3 of the Uniform Commercial Code if the electronic record were in writing;

(B) the issuer of the electronic record expressly has agreed is a transferable record; and

(C) relates to a loan secured by real property.

A transferable record may be executed using an electronic signature.

(2) Other Definitions.—The terms "electronic record", "electronic signature", and "person" have the same meanings provided in section 106 of this Act.

(b) Control.—A person has control of a transferable record if a system employed for evidencing the transfer of interests in the transferable record reliably establishes that person as the person to which the transferable record was issued or transferred.

(c) Conditions.—A system satisfies subsection (b), and a person is deemed to have control of a transferable record, if the transferable record is created, stored, and assigned in such a manner that—

(1) a single authoritative copy of the transferable record exists which is unique, identifiable, and, except as otherwise provided in paragraphs (4), (5), and (6), unalterable;

(2) the authoritative copy identifies the person asserting control as—

(A) the person to which the transferable record was issued; or

(B) if the authoritative copy indicates that the transferable record has been transferred, the person to which the transferable record was most recently transferred;

(3) the authoritative copy is communicated to and maintained by the person asserting control or its designated custodian;

(4) copies or revisions that add or change an identified assignee of the authoritative copy can be made only with the consent of the person asserting control;

(5) each copy of the authoritative copy and any copy of a copy is readily identifiable as a copy that is not the authoritative copy; and

(6) any revision of the authoritative copy is readily identifiable as authorized or unauthorized.

(d) Status as Holder.—Except as otherwise agreed, a person having control of a transferable record is the holder, as defined in section 1201(20) of the Uniform Commercial Code, of the transferable record and has the same rights and defenses as a holder of an equivalent record or writing under the Uniform Commercial Code, including, if the applicable statutory requirements under section 3302(a), 9308, or revised section 9330 of the Uniform Commercial Code are satisfied, the rights and defenses of a holder in due course or a purchaser, respectively. Delivery, possession, and endorsement are not required to obtain or exercise any of the rights under this subsection.

(e) Obligor Rights.—Except as otherwise agreed, an obligor under a transferable record has the same rights and defenses as an equivalent obligor under equivalent records or writings under the Uniform Commercial Code.

(f) Proof of Control.—If requested by a person against which enforcement is sought, the person seeking to enforce the transferable record shall provide reasonable proof that the person is in control of the transferable record. Proof may include access to the authoritative copy of the transferable record and related business records sufficient to review the terms of the transferable record and to establish the identity of the person having control of the transferable record.

(g) UCC References.—For purposes of this subsection, all references to the Uniform Commercial Code are to the Uniform Commercial Code as in effect in the jurisdiction the law of which governs the transferable record.

§ 7022. Effective Date

This title shall be effective 90 days after the date of enactment of this Act.

§ 7031. Principles Governing the Use of Electronic Signatures in International Transactions

(a) Promotion of Electronic Signatures.—

(1) Required Actions.—The Secretary of Commerce shall promote the acceptance and use, on an international basis, of electronic signatures in accordance with the principles specified in paragraph (2) and in a manner consistent with section 101 of this Act. The Secretary of Commerce shall take all actions necessary in a manner consistent with such principles to eliminate or reduce, to the maximum extent possible, the impediments to commerce in electronic signatures, for the purpose of facilitating the development of interstate and foreign commerce.

(2) Principles.—The principles specified in this paragraph are the following:

(A) Remove paper-based obstacles to electronic transactions by adopting relevant principles from the Model Law on Electronic Commerce adopted in 1996 by the United Nations Commission on International Trade Law.

(B) Permit parties to a transaction to determine the appropriate authentication technologies and implementation models for their transactions, with assurance that those technologies and implementation models will be recognized and enforced.

(C) Permit parties to a transaction to have the opportunity to prove in court or other proceedings that their authentication approaches and their transactions are valid.

(D) Take a nondiscriminatory approach to electronic signatures and authentication methods from other jurisdictions.

(b) Consultation.—In conducting the activities required by this section, the Secretary shall consult with users and providers of electronic signature products and services and other interested persons.

(c) Definitions.—As used in this section, the terms "electronic record" and "electronic signature" have the same meanings provided in section 106 of this Act.

Depository Institutions Deregulation and Monetary Control Act of 1980

12 U.S.C. § 1735f-7a

12 U.S.C. § 1735f-7a. State Constitution or Laws Limiting Mortgage Interest, Discount Points, and Finance or Other Charges; Exemption For Obligations Made After March 31, 1980

(a) Applicability to loan, mortgage, credit sale, or advance; applicability to deposit, account, or obligation

(1) The provisions of the constitution or the laws of any State expressly limiting the rate or amount of interest, discount points, finance charges, or other charges which may be charged, taken, received, or reserved shall not apply to any loan, mortgage, credit sale, or advance which is—

(A) secured by a first lien on residential real property, by a first lien on all stock allocated to a dwelling unit in a residential cooperative housing corporation, or by a first lien on a residential manufactured home;

(B) made after March 31, 1980; and

(C) described in section 527(b) of the National Housing Act (12 U.S.C. 1735f5(b)), except that for the purpose of this section—

(i) the limitation described in section 527(b)(1) of such Act [12 U.S.C.A. § 1735f5(b)(1)] that the property must be designed principally for the occupancy of from one to four families shall not apply;

(ii) the requirement contained in section 527(b)(1) of such Act [12 U.S.C.A. § 1735f5(b)(1)] that the loan be secured by residential real property shall not apply to a loan secured by stock in a residential cooperative housing corporation or to a loan or credit sale secured by a first lien on a residential manufactured home;

(iii) the term "federally related mortgage loan" in section 527(b) of such Act [12 U.S.C.A. § 1735f5(b)] shall include a credit sale which is secured by a first lien on a residential manufactured home and which otherwise meets the definitional requirements of section 527(b) of such Act [12 U.S.C.A. § 1735f5(b)], as those requirements are modified by this section;

(iv) the term "residential loans" in section 527(b)(2)(D) of such Act [12 U.S.C.A. § 1735f5(b)(2)(D)] shall also include loans or credit sales secured by a first lien on a residential manufactured home;

(v) the requirement contained in section 527(b)(2)(D) of such Act [12 U.S.C.A. § 1735f5(b)(2)(D)] that a creditor make or invest in loans aggregating more than $1,000,000 per year shall not apply to a creditor selling residential manufactured homes financed by loans or credit sales secured by first liens on residential manufactured homes if the creditor has an arrangement to sell such loans or credit sales in whole or in part, or if such loans or credit sales are sold in whole or in part to a lender, institution, or creditor described in section 527(b) of such Act [12 U.S.C.A. § 1735f5(b)] or in this section or a creditor, as defined in section 103(f) of the Truth in Lending Act [15 U.S.C.A. § 1602(f)], as such section was in effect on the day preceding March 31, 1980, if such creditor makes or invests in residential real estate loans or loans or credit sales secured by first liens on residential manufactured homes aggregating more than $1,000,000 per year; and

(vi) the term "lender" in section 527(b)(2)(A) of such Act [12 U.S.C.A. § 1735f 5(b)(2)(A)] shall also be deemed to include any lender approved by the Secretary of Housing and Urban Development for participation in any mortgage insurance program under the National Housing Act [12 U.S.C.A. § 1701 et seq.], and any individual who finances the sale or exchange of residential real property or a residential manufactured home which such individual owns and which such individual occupies or has occupied as his principal residence.

(2) The provisions of the constitution or law of any State expressly limiting the rate or amount of interest which may be charged, taken, received, or reserved shall not apply to any deposit or account held by, or other obligation of a depository

institution. For purposes of this paragraph, the term "depository institution" means—

(i) any insured bank as defined in section 3 of the Federal Deposit Insurance Act (12 U.S.C. 1813);

(ii) any mutual savings bank as defined in section 3 of the Federal Deposit Insurance Act (12 U.S.C. 1813);

(iii) any savings bank as defined in section 3 of the Federal Deposit Insurance Act (12 U.S.C. 1813);

(iv) any insured credit union as defined in section 101 of the Federal Credit Union Act (12 U.S.C. 1752);

(v) any member as defined in section 2 of the Federal Home Loan Bank Act (12 U.S.C. 1422); and

(vi) any insured institution as defined in section 408 of the National Housing Act (12 U.S.C. 1730a).

(b) Applicability to loan, mortgage, credit sale, or advance made in any State after April 1, 1980

(1) Except as provided in paragraphs (2) and (3), the provisions of subsection (a)(1) of this section shall apply to any loan, mortgage, credit sale, or advance made in any State on or after April 1, 1980.

(2) Except as provided in paragraph (3), the provisions of subsection (a)(1) of this section shall not apply to any loan, mortgage, credit sale, or advance made in any State after the date (on or after April 1, 1980, and before April 1, 1983) on which such State adopts a law or certifies that the voters of such State have voted in favor of any provision, constitutional or otherwise, which states explicitly and by its terms that such State does not want the provisions of subsection (a)(1) of this section to apply with respect to loans, mortgages, credit sales, and advances made in such State.

(3) In any case in which a State takes an action described in paragraph (2), the provisions of subsection (a)(1) of this section shall continue to apply to—

(A) any loan, mortgage, credit sale, or advance which is made after the date such action was taken pursuant to a commitment therefor which was entered during the period beginning on April 1, 1980, and ending on the date on which such State takes such action; and

(B) any loan, mortgage, or advance which is a rollover of a loan, mortgage, or advance, as described in regulations of the Federal Home Loan Bank Board, which was made or committed to be made during the period beginning on April 1, 1980, and ending on the date on which such State takes any action described in paragraph (2).

(4) At any time after March 31, 1980, any State may adopt a provision of law placing limitations on discount points or such other charges on any loan, mortgage, credit sale, or advance described in subsection (a)(1) of this section.

(c) Applicability to loan, mortgage, credit sale, or advance secured by first lien on residential manufactured home. The provisions of subsection (a)(1) of this section shall not apply to a loan, mortgage, credit sale, or advance which is secured by a first lien on a residential manufactured home unless the terms and conditions relating to such loan, mortgage, credit sale, or advance comply with consumer protection provisions specified in regulations prescribed by the Federal Home Loan Bank Board. Such regulations shall—

(1) include consumer protection provisions with respect to balloon payments, prepayment penalties, late charges, and deferral fees;

(2) require a 30-day notice prior to instituting any action leading to repossession or foreclosure (except in the case of abandonment or other extreme circumstances);

(3) require that upon prepayment in full, the debtor shall be entitled to a refund of the unearned portion of the precomputed finance charge in an amount not less than the amount which would be calculated by the actuarial method, except that the debtor shall not be entitled to a refund which is less than $1; and

(4) include such other provisions as the Federal Home Loan Bank Board may prescribe after a finding that additional protections are required.

(d) Implementation of provisions applicable to residential manufactured home. The provisions of subsection (c) of this section shall not apply to a loan, mortgage, credit sale, or advance secured by a first lien on a residential manufactured home until regulations required to be issued pursuant to paragraphs (1), (2), and (3) of subsection (c) of this section take effect, except that the provisions of subsection (c) of this section shall apply in the case of such a loan, mortgage, credit sale, or advance made prior to the date on which such regulations take effect if the loan, mortgage, credit sale, or advance includes a precomputed finance charge and does not provide that, upon prepayment in full, the refund of the unearned portion of the precomputed finance charge is in an amount not less the amount which would be calculated by the actuarial method, except that the debtor shall not be entitled to a refund which is less than $1. The Federal Home Loan Bank Board shall issue regulations pursuant to the provisions of paragraphs (1), (2), and (3) of subsection (c) of this section that shall take effect prospectively not less than 30 days after publication in the Federal Register and not later than 120 days from March 31, 1980.

(e) Definitions. For the purpose of this section—

(1) a "prepayment" occurs upon—

(A) the refinancing or consolidation of the indebtedness;

(B) the actual prepayment of the indebtedness by the consumer whether voluntarily or following acceleration of the payment obligation by the creditor; or

(C) the entry of a judgment for the indebtedness in favor of the creditor;

(2) the term "actuarial method" means the method of allocating payments made on a debt between the outstanding balance of the obligation and the precomputed finance charge pursuant to which a payment is applied first to the accrued precomputed finance charge and any remainder is subtracted from, or any deficiency is added to, the outstanding balance of the obligation;

(3) the term "precomputed finance charge" means interest or a time price differential within the meaning of sections 106(a)(1) and (2) of the Truth in Lending Act (15 U.S.C. 1605(a)(1) and (2)) as computed by an add-on or discount method; and

(4) the term "residential manufactured home" means a manufactured home as defined in section 603(6) of the National Mobile Home Construction and Safety Standards Act of 1974 [42 U.S.C.A. § 5402(6)] which is used as a residence.

(f) Rules, regulations, and interpretations. The Federal Home Loan Bank Board is authorized to issue rules and regulations and to publish interpretations governing the implementation of this section.

(g) Effective date. This section takes effect on April 1, 1980.

Federal Bill of Lading Act

49 U.S.C. §§ 80101–80116

Section

§ 80101. Definitions

In this chapter—

(1) "consignee" means the person named in a bill of lading as the person to whom the goods are to be delivered.

(2) "consignor" means the person named in a bill of lading as the person from whom the goods have been received for shipment.

(3) "goods" means merchandise or personal property that has been, is being, or will be transported.

(4) "holder" means a person having possession of, and a property right in, a bill of lading.

(5) "order" means an order by indorsement on a bill of lading.

(6) "purchase" includes taking by mortgage or pledge.

(7) "State" means a State of the United States, the District of Columbia, and a territory or possession of the United States.

§ 80102. Application

This chapter applies to a bill of lading when the bill is issued by a common carrier for the transportation of goods—

(1) between a place in the District of Columbia and another place in the District of Columbia;

(2) between a place in a territory or possession of the United States and another place in the same territory or possession;

(3) between a place in a State and a place in another State;

(4) between a place in a State and a place in the same State through another State or a foreign country; or

(5) from a place in a State to a place in a foreign country.

§ 80103. Negotiable and Nonnegotiable Bills

(a) Negotiable bills.—

(1) A bill of lading is negotiable if the bill—

(A) states that the goods are to be delivered to the order of a consignee; and

(B) does not contain on its face an agreement with the shipper that the bill is not negotiable.

(2) Inserting in a negotiable bill of lading the name of a person to be notified of the arrival of the goods—

(A) does not limit its negotiability; and

(B) is not notice to the purchaser of the goods of a right the named person has to the goods.

(b) Nonnegotiable bills.—

(1) A bill of lading is nonnegotiable if the bill states that the goods are to be delivered to a consignee. The indorsement of a nonnegotiable bill does not—

(A) make the bill negotiable; or

(B) give the transferee any additional right.

(2) A common carrier issuing a nonnegotiable bill of lading must put "nonnegotiable" or "not negotiable" on the bill. This paragraph does not apply to an informal memorandum or acknowledgment.

§ 80104. Form and Requirements for Negotiation

(a) General rules.—

(1) A negotiable bill of lading may be negotiated by indorsement. An indorsement may be made in blank or to a specified person. If the goods are deliverable to the order of a specified person, then the bill must be indorsed by that person.

(2) A negotiable bill of lading may be negotiated by delivery when the common carrier, under the terms of the bill, undertakes to deliver the goods to the order of a specified person and that person or a subsequent indorsee has indorsed the bill in blank.

(3) A negotiable bill of lading may be negotiated by a person possessing the bill, regardless of the way in which the person got possession, if—

(A) a common carrier, under the terms of the bill, undertakes to deliver the goods to that person; or

(B) when the bill is negotiated, it is in a form that allows it to be negotiated by delivery.

(b) Validity not affected.—The validity of a negotiation of a bill of lading is not affected by the negotiation having been a breach of duty by the person making the negotiation, or by the owner of the bill having been deprived of possession by fraud, accident, mistake, duress, loss, theft, or conversion, if the person to whom the bill is negotiated, or a person to whom the bill is subsequently negotiated, gives value for the bill in good faith and without notice of the breach of duty, fraud, accident, mistake, duress, loss, theft, or conversion.

(c) Negotiation by seller, mortgagor, or pledgor to person without notice.—When goods for which a negotiable bill of lading has been issued are in a common carrier's possession, and the person to whom the bill has been issued retains possession of the bill after selling, mortgaging, or pledging the goods or bill, the subsequent negotiation of the bill by that person to another person receiving the bill for value, in good faith, and without notice of the prior sale, mortgage, or pledge has the same effect as if the first purchaser of the goods or bill had expressly authorized the subsequent negotiation.

§ 80105. Title and Rights Affected by Negotiation

(a) Title.—When a negotiable bill of lading is negotiated—

(1) the person to whom it is negotiated acquires the title to the goods that—

(A) the person negotiating the bill had the ability to convey to a purchaser in good faith for value; and

(B) the consignor and consignee had the ability to convey to such a purchaser; and

(2) the common carrier issuing the bill becomes obligated directly to the person to whom the bill is negotiated to hold possession of the goods under the terms of the bill the same as if the carrier had issued the bill to that person.

(b) Superiority of rights.—When a negotiable bill of lading is negotiated to a person for value in good faith, that person's right to the goods for which the bill was issued is superior to a seller's lien or to a right to stop the transportation of the goods. This subsection applies whether the negotiation is made before or after the common carrier issuing the bill receives notice of the seller's claim. The carrier may deliver the goods to an unpaid seller only if the bill first is surrendered for cancellation.

(c) Mortgagee and lien holder rights not affected.—Except as provided in subsection (b) of this section, this chapter does not limit a right of a mortgagee or lien holder having a mortgage or lien on goods against a person that purchased for value in good faith from the owner, and got possession of the goods immediately before delivery to the common carrier.

§ 80106. Transfer Without Negotiation

(a) Delivery and agreement.—The holder of a bill of lading may transfer the bill without negotiating it by delivery and agreement to transfer title to the bill or to the goods represented by it. Subject to the agreement, the person to whom the bill is transferred has title to the goods against the transferor.

(b) Compelling indorsement.—When a negotiable bill of lading is transferred for value by delivery without being negotiated and indorsement of the transferor is essential for negotiation, the transferee may compel the transferor to indorse the bill unless a contrary intention appears. The negotiation is effective when the indorsement is made.

(c) Effect of notification.—

(1) When a transferee notifies the common carrier that a nonnegotiable bill of lading has been transferred under subsection (a) of this section, the carrier is obligated directly to the transferee for any obligations the carrier owed to the transferor immediately before the notification. However, before the carrier is notified, the transferee's title to the goods and right to acquire the obligations of the carrier may be defeated by—

(A) garnishment, attachment, or execution on the goods by a creditor of the transferor; or

(B) notice to the carrier by the transferor or a purchaser from the transferor of a later purchase of the goods from the transferor.

(2) A common carrier has been notified under this subsection only if—

(A) an officer or agent of the carrier, whose actual or apparent authority includes acting on the notification, has been notified; and

(B) the officer or agent has had time, exercising reasonable diligence, to communicate with the agent having possession or control of the goods.

§ 80107. Warranties and Liability

(a) General rule.—Unless a contrary intention appears, a person negotiating or transferring a bill of lading for value warrants that—

(1) the bill is genuine;

(2) the person has the right to transfer the bill and the title to the goods described in the bill;

(3) the person does not know of a fact that would affect the validity or worth of the bill; and

(4) the goods are merchantable or fit for a particular purpose when merchantability or fitness would have been implied if the agreement of the parties had been to transfer the goods without a bill of lading.

(b) Security for debt.—A person holding a bill of lading as security for a debt and in good faith demanding or receiving payment of the debt from another person does not warrant by the demand or receipt—

(1) the genuineness of the bill; or

(2) the quantity or quality of the goods described in the bill.

(c) Duplicates.—A common carrier issuing a bill of lading, on the face of which is the word "duplicate" or another word indicating that the bill is not an original bill, is liable the same as a person that represents and warrants that the bill is an accurate copy of an original bill properly issued. The carrier is not otherwise liable under the bill.

(d) Indorser liability.—Indorsement of a bill of lading does not make the indorser liable for failure of the common carrier or a previous indorser to fulfill its obligations.

§ 80108. Alterations and Additions

An alteration or addition to a bill of lading after its issuance by a common carrier, without authorization from the carrier in writing or noted on the bill, is void. However, the original terms of the bill are enforceable.

§ 80109. Liens under Negotiable Bills

A common carrier issuing a negotiable bill of lading has a lien on the goods covered by the bill for—

(1) charges for storage, transportation, and delivery (including demurrage and terminal charges), and expenses necessary to preserve the goods or incidental to transporting the goods after the date of the bill; and

(2) other charges for which the bill expressly specifies a lien is claimed to the extent the charges are allowed by law and the agreement between the consignor and carrier.

§ 80110. Duty to Deliver Goods

(a) General rules.—Except to the extent a common carrier establishes an excuse provided by law, the carrier must deliver goods covered by a bill of lading on demand of the consignee named in a nonnegotiable bill or the holder of a negotiable bill for the goods when the consignee or holder—

(1) offers in good faith to satisfy the lien of the carrier on the goods;

(2) has possession of the bill and, if a negotiable bill, offers to indorse and give the bill to the carrier; and

(3) agrees to sign, on delivery of the goods, a receipt for delivery if requested by the carrier.

(b) Persons to whom goods may be delivered.—Subject to section 80111 of this title, a common carrier may deliver the goods covered by a bill of lading to—

(1) a person entitled to their possession;

(2) the consignee named in a nonnegotiable bill; or

(3) a person in possession of a negotiable bill if—

(A) the goods are deliverable to the order of that person; or

(B) the bill has been indorsed to that person or in blank by the consignee or another indorsee.

(c) Common carrier claims of title and possession.—A claim by a common carrier that the carrier has title to goods or right to their possession is an excuse for nondelivery of the goods only if the title or right is derived from—

(1) a transfer made by the consignor or consignee after the shipment; or

(2) the carrier's lien.

(d) Adverse claims.—If a person other than the consignee or the person in possession of a bill of lading claims title to or possession of goods and the common carrier knows of the claim, the carrier is not required to deliver the goods to any claimant until the carrier has had a reasonable time to decide the validity of the adverse claim or to bring a civil action to require all claimants to interplead.

(e) Interpleader.—If at least 2 persons claim title to or possession of the goods, the common carrier may—

(1) bring a civil action to interplead all known claimants to the goods; or

(2) require those claimants to interplead as a defense in an action brought against the carrier for nondelivery.

(f) Third person claims not a defense.—Except as provided in subsections (b), (d), and (e) of this section, title or a right of a third person is not a defense to an action brought by the consignee of a nonnegotiable bill of lading or by the holder of a negotiable bill against the common carrier for failure to deliver the goods on demand unless enforced by legal process.

§ 80111. Liability for Delivery of Goods

(a) General rules.—A common carrier is liable for damages to a person having title to, or right to possession of, goods when—

(1) the carrier delivers the goods to a person not entitled to their possession unless the delivery is authorized under section 80110(b)(2) or (3) of this title;

(2) the carrier makes a delivery under section 80110(b)(2) or (3) of this title after being requested by or for a person having title to, or right to possession of, the goods not to make the delivery; or

(3) at the time of delivery under section 80110(b)(2) or (3) of this title, the carrier has information it is delivering the goods to a person not entitled to their possession.

(b) Effectiveness of request or information.—A request or information is effective under subsection (a)(2) or (3) of this section only if—

(1) an officer or agent of the carrier, whose actual or apparent authority includes acting on the request or information, has been given the request or information; and

(2) the officer or agent has had time, exercising reasonable diligence, to stop delivery of the goods.

(c) Failure to take and cancel bills.—Except as provided in subsection (d) of this section, if a common carrier delivers goods for which a negotiable bill of lading has been issued without taking and canceling the bill, the carrier is liable for damages for failure to deliver the goods to a person purchasing the bill for value in good faith whether the purchase was before or after delivery and even when delivery was made to the person entitled to the goods. The carrier also is liable under this paragraph if part of the goods are delivered without taking and canceling the bill or plainly noting on the bill that a partial delivery was made and generally describing the goods or the remaining goods kept by the carrier.

(d) Exceptions to liability.—A common carrier is not liable for failure to deliver goods to the consignee or owner of the goods or a holder of the bill if—

(1) a delivery described in subsection (c) of this section was compelled by legal process;

(2) the goods have been sold lawfully to satisfy the carrier's lien;

(3) the goods have not been claimed; or

(4) the goods are perishable or hazardous.

§ 80112. Liability under Negotiable Bills Issued in Parts, Sets, or Duplicates

(a) Parts and sets.—A negotiable bill of lading issued in a State for the transportation of goods to a place in the 48 contiguous States or the District of Columbia may not be issued in parts or sets. A common carrier issuing a bill in violation of this subsection is liable for damages for failure to deliver the goods to a purchaser of one part for value in good faith even though the purchase occurred after the carrier delivered the goods to a holder of one of the other parts.

(b) Duplicates.—When at least 2 negotiable bills of lading are issued in a State for the same goods to be transported to a place in the 48 contiguous States or the District of Columbia, the word "duplicate" or another word indicating that the bill is not an original must be put plainly on the face of each bill except the original. A common carrier violating this subsection is liable for damages caused by the violation to a purchaser of the bill for value in good faith as an original bill even though the purchase occurred after the carrier delivered the goods to the holder of the original bill.

§ 80113. Liability for Nonreceipt, Misdescription, and Improper Loading

(a) Liability for nonreceipt and misdescription.—Except as provided in this section, a common carrier issuing a bill of lading is liable for damages caused by nonreceipt by the carrier of any part of the goods by the date shown in the bill or by failure of the goods to correspond with the description contained in the bill. The carrier is liable to the owner of goods transported under a nonnegotiable bill (subject to the right of stoppage in transit) or to the holder of a negotiable bill if the owner or holder gave value in good faith relying on the description of the goods in the bill or on the shipment being made on the date shown in the bill.

(b) Nonliability of carriers.—A common carrier issuing a bill of lading is not liable under subsection (a) of this section—

(1) when the goods are loaded by the shipper;

(2) when the bill—

(A) describes the goods in terms of marks or labels, or in a statement about kind, quantity, or condition; or

(B) is qualified by "contents or condition of contents of packages unknown", "said to contain", "shipper's weight, load, and count", or words of the same meaning; and

(3) to the extent the carrier does not know whether any part of the goods were received or conform to the description.

(c) Liability for improper loading.—A common carrier issuing a bill of lading is not liable for damages caused by improper loading if—

(1) the shipper loads the goods; and

(2) the bill contains the words "shipper's weight, load, and count", or words of the same meaning indicating the shipper loaded the goods.

(d) Carrier's duty to determine kind, quantity, and number.—

(1) When bulk freight is loaded by a shipper that makes available to the common carrier adequate facilities for weighing the freight, the carrier must determine the kind and quantity of the freight within a reasonable time after receiving the written request of the shipper to make the determination. In that situation, inserting the words "shipper's weight" or words of the same meaning in the bill of lading has no effect.

(2) When goods are loaded by a common carrier, the carrier must count the packages of goods, if package freight, and determine the kind and quantity, if bulk freight. In that situation, inserting in the bill of lading or in a notice, receipt, contract, rule, or tariff, the words "shipper's weight, load, and count" or words indicating that the shipper described and loaded the goods, has no effect except for freight concealed by packages.

§ 80114. Lost, Stolen, and Destroyed Negotiable Bills

(a) Delivery on court order and surety bond.—If a negotiable bill of lading is lost, stolen, or destroyed, a court of competent jurisdiction may order the common carrier to deliver the goods if the person claiming the goods gives a surety bond, in an amount approved by the court, to indemnify the carrier or a person injured by delivery against liability under the outstanding original bill. The court also may order payment of reasonable costs and attorney's fees to the carrier. A voluntary surety bond, without court order, is binding on the parties to the bond.

(b) Liability to holder.—Delivery of goods under a court order under subsection (a) of this section does not relieve a common carrier from liability to a person to whom the negotiable bill has been or is negotiated for value without notice of the court proceeding or of the delivery of the goods.

§ 80115. Limitation on Use of Judicial Process to Obtain Possession of Goods from Common Carriers

(a) Attachment and levy.—Except when a negotiable bill of lading was issued originally on delivery of goods by a person that did not have the power to dispose of the goods, goods in the possession of a common carrier for which a negotiable bill has been issued may be attached through judicial process or levied on in execution of a judgment only if the bill is surrendered to the carrier or its negotiation is enjoined.

(b) Delivery.—A common carrier may be compelled by judicial process to deliver goods under subsection (a) of this section only when the bill is surrendered to the carrier or impounded by the court.

§ 80116. Criminal Penalty

A person shall be fined under title 18, imprisoned for not more than 5 years, or both, if the person—

(1) violates this chapter with intent to defraud; or

(2) knowingly or with intent to defraud—

(A) falsely makes, alters, or copies a bill of lading subject to this chapter;

(B) utters, publishes, or issues a falsely made, altered, or copied bill subject to this chapter; or

(C) negotiates or transfers for value a bill containing a false statement.

TITLE 26—FEDERAL TAX LIEN ACT

Section

§ 6321. Lien for Taxes

If any person liable to pay any tax neglects or refuses to pay the same after demand, the amount (including any interest, additional amount, addition to tax, or assessable penalty, together with any costs that may accrue in addition thereto) shall be a lien in favor of the United States upon all property and rights to property, whether real or personal, belonging to such person.

§ 6322. Period of Lien

Unless another date is specifically fixed by law, the lien imposed by section 6321 shall arise at the time the assessment is made and shall continue until the liability for the amount so assessed (or a judgment against the taxpayer arising out of such liability) is satisfied or becomes unenforceable by reason of lapse of time.

§ 6323. Validity and Priority Against Certain Persons

(a) Purchasers, holders of security interests, mechanic's lienors, and judgment lien creditors. The lien imposed by section 6321 shall not be valid as against any purchaser, holder of a security interest, mechanic's lienor, or judgment lien creditor until notice thereof which meets the requirements of subsection (f) has been filed by the Secretary.

(b) Protection for certain interests even though notice filed. Even though notice of a lien imposed by section 6321 has been filed, such lien shall not be valid—

(1) Securities. With respect to a security (as defined in subsection (h)(4))—

(A) as against a purchaser of such security who at the time of purchase did not have actual notice or knowledge of the existence of such lien; and

(B) as against a holder of a security interest in such security who, at the time such interest came into existence, did not have actual notice or knowledge of the existence of such lien.

(2) Motor vehicles. With respect to a motor vehicle (as defined in subsection (h)(3)), as against a purchaser of such motor vehicle, if—

(A) at the time of the purchase such purchaser did not have actual notice or knowledge of the existence of such lien, and

(B) before the purchaser obtains such notice or knowledge, he has acquired possession of such motor vehicle and has not thereafter relinquished possession of such motor vehicle to the seller or his agent.

(3) Personal property purchased at retail. With respect to tangible personal property purchased at retail, as against a purchaser in the ordinary course of the seller's trade or business, unless at the time of such purchase such purchaser intends such purchase to (or knows such purchase will) hinder, evade, or defeat the collection of any tax under this title.

(4) Personal property purchased in casual sale [See § 3.32 of *Rev. Proc. 2004-71 (26 USCS § 1* note) for provision that, for calendar year 2005, a federal tax lien is not valid against certain purchasers under this paragraph that purchased personal property in a casual sale for less than $1,200.]. With respect to household goods, personal effects, or other tangible personal property described in section 6334(a) purchased (not for resale) in a casual sale for less than $1,000, as against the purchaser, but only if such purchaser does not have actual notice or knowledge (A) of the existence of such lien, or (B) that this sale is one of a series of sales.

(5) Personal property subject to possessory lien. With respect to tangible personal property subject to a lien under local law securing the reasonable price of the repair or improvement of such property, as against a holder of such a lien, if such holder is, and has been, continuously in possession of such property from the time such lien arose.

(6) Real property tax and special assessment liens. With respect to real property, as against a holder of a lien upon such property, if such lien is entitled under local law to priority over security interests in such property which are prior in time, and such lien secures payment of—

(A) a tax of general application levied by any taxing authority based upon the value of such property;

(B) a special assessment imposed directly upon such property by any taxing authority, if such assessment is imposed for the purpose of defraying the cost of any public improvement; or

(C) charges for utilities or public services furnished to such property by the United States, a State or political subdivision thereof, or an instrumentality of any one or more of the foregoing.

(7) Residential property subject to a mechanic's lien for certain repairs and improvements [Caution: See § 3.32 of *Rev. Proc. 2004-71 (26 USCS § 1* note) for provision that, for calendar year 2005, a federal tax lien is not valid against a mechanic's lienor under this paragraph that repaired or improved certain residential property if the contract price with the owner is not more than $6,020.]. With respect to real property subject to a lien for repair or improvement of a personal residence (containing not more than four dwelling units) occupied by the owner of such residence, as against a mechanic's lienor, but only if the contract price on the contract with the owner is not more than $5,000.

(8) Attorneys' liens. With respect to a judgment or other amount in settlement of a claim or of a cause of action, as against an attorney who, under local law, holds a lien upon or a contract enforcible against such judgment or amount, to the extent of his reasonable compensation for obtaining such judgment or procuring such settlement, except that this paragraph shall not apply to any judgment or amount in settlement of a claim or of a cause of action against the United States to the extent that the United States offsets such judgment or amount against any liability of the taxpayer to the United States.

(9) Certain insurance contracts. With respect to a life insurance, endowment, or annuity contract, as against the organization which is the insurer under such contract, at any time—

(A) before such organization had actual notice or knowledge of the existence of such lien;

(B) after such organization had such notice or knowledge, with respect to advances required to be made automatically to maintain such contract in force under an agreement entered into before such organization had such notice or knowledge; or

(C) after satisfaction of a levy pursuant to section 6332 (b), unless and until the Secretary delivers to such organization a notice, executed after the date of such satisfaction, of the existence of such lien.

(10) Deposit-secured loans. With respect to a savings deposit, share, or other account with an institution described in section 581 or 591, to the extent of any loan made by such institution without actual notice or knowledge of the existence of such lien, as against such institution, if such loan is secured by such account.

(c) Protection for certain commercial transactions financing agreements, etc.

(1) In general. To the extent provided in this subsection, even though notice of a lien imposed by section 6321 has been filed, such lien shall not be valid with respect to a security interest which came into existence after tax lien filing but which—

(A) is in qualified property covered by the terms of a written agreement entered into before tax lien filing and constituting—

(i) a commercial transactions financing agreement,

(ii) a real property construction or improvement financing agreement, or

(iii) an obligatory disbursement agreement, and

(B) is protected under local law against a judgment lien arising, as of the time of tax lien filing, out of an unsecured obligation.

(2) Commercial transactions financing agreement. For purposes of this subsection—

(A) Definition. The term "commercial transactions financing agreement" means an agreement (entered into by a person in the course of his trade or business)—

(i) to make loans to the taxpayer to be secured by commercial financing security acquired by the taxpayer in the ordinary course of his trade or business, or

(ii) to purchase commercial financing security (other than inventory) acquired by the taxpayer in the ordinary course of his trade or business;

but such an agreement shall be treated as coming within the term only to the extent that such loan or purchase is made before the 46th day after the date of tax lien filing or (if earlier) before the lender or purchaser had actual notice or knowledge of such tax lien filing.

(B) Limitation on qualified property. The term "qualified property", when used with respect to a commercial transactions financing agreement, includes only commercial financing security acquired by the taxpayer before the 46th day after the date of tax lien filing.

(C) Commercial financing security defined. The term "commercial financing security" means (i) paper of a kind ordinarily arising in commercial transactions, (ii) accounts receivable, (iii) mortgages on real property, and (iv) inventory.

(D) Purchaser treated as acquiring security interest. A person who satisfies subparagraph (A) by reason of clause (ii) thereof shall be treated as having acquired a security interest in commercial financing security

(3) Real property construction or improvement financing agreement. For purposes of this subsection—

(A) Definition. The term "real property construction or improvement financing agreement" means an agreement to make cash disbursements to finance—

(i) the construction or improvement of real property,

(ii) a contract to construct or improve real property, or

(iii) the raising or harvesting of a farm crop or the raising of livestock or other animals.

For purposes of clause (iii), the furnishing of goods and services shall be treated as the disbursement of cash.

(B) Limitation on qualified property. The term "qualified property", when used with respect to a real property construction or improvement financing agreement, includes only—

(i) in the case of subparagraph (A)(i), the real property with respect to which the construction or improvement has been or is to be made,

(ii) in the case of subparagraph (A)(ii), the proceeds of the contract described therein, and

(iii) in the case of subparagraph (A)(iii), property subject to the lien imposed by section 6321 at the time of tax lien filing and the crop or the livestock or other animals referred to in subparagraph (A)(iii).

(4) Obligatory disbursement agreement. For purposes of this subsection—

(A) Definition. The term "obligatory disbursement agreement" means an agreement (entered into by a person in the course of his trade or business) to make disbursements, but such an agreement shall be treated as coming within the term only to the extent of disbursements which are required to be made by reason of the intervention of the rights of a person other than the taxpayer.

(B) Limitation on qualified property. The term "qualified property", when used with respect to an obligatory disbursement agreement, means property subject to the lien imposed by section 6321 at the time of tax lien filing and (to the extent that the acquisition is directly traceable to the disbursements referred to in subparagraph (A)) property acquired by the taxpayer after tax lien filing.

(C) Special rules for surety agreements. Where the obligatory disbursement agreement is an agreement ensuring the performance of a contract between the taxpayer and another person—

(i) the term "qualified property" shall be treated as also including the proceeds of the contract the performance of which was ensured, and

(ii) if the contract the performance of which was ensured was a contract to construct or improve real property, to produce goods, or to furnish services, the term "qualified property" shall be treated as also including any tangible personal property used by the taxpayer in the performance of such ensured contract.

(d) 45-day period for making disbursements. Even though notice of a lien imposed by section 6321 has been filed, such lien shall not be valid with respect to a security interest which came into existence after tax lien filing by reason of disbursements made before the 46th day after the date of tax lien filing, or (if earlier) before the person making such disbursements had actual notice or knowledge of tax lien filing, but only if such security interest—

(1) is in property (A) subject, at the time of tax lien filing, to the lien imposed by section 6321, and (B) covered by the terms of a written agreement entered into before tax lien filing, and

(2) is protected under local law against a judgment lien arising, as of the time of tax lien filing, out of an unsecured obligation.

(e) Priority of interest and expenses. If the lien imposed by section 6321 is not valid as against a lien or security interest, the priority of such lien or security interest shall extend to—

(1) any interest or carrying charges upon the obligation secured,

(2) the reasonable charges and expenses of an indenture trustee or agent holding the security

interest for the benefit of the holder of the security interest,

(3) the reasonable expenses, including reasonable compensation for attorneys, actually incurred in collecting or enforcing the obligation secured,

(4) the reasonable costs of insuring, preserving, or repairing the property to which the lien or security interest relates,

(5) the reasonable costs of insuring payment of the obligation secured, and

(6) amounts paid to satisfy any lien on the property to which the lien or security interest relates, but only if the lien so satisfied is entitled to priority over the lien imposed by section 6321, to the extent that, under local law, any such item has the same priority as the lien or security interest to which it relates.

(f) Place for filing notice; form.

(1) Place for filing. The notice referred to in subsection (a) shall be filed—

(A) Under State laws.

(i) Real property. In the case of real property, in one office within the State (or the county, or other governmental subdivision), as designated by the laws of such State, in which the property subject to the lien is situated; and

(ii) Personal property. In the case of personal property, whether tangible or intangible, in one office within the State (or the county, or other governmental subdivision), as designated by the laws of such State, in which the property subject to the lien is situated, except that State law merely conforming to or reenacting Federal law establishing a national filing system does not constitute a second office for filing as designated by the laws of such State; or

(B) With clerk of district court. In the office of the clerk of the United States district court for the judicial district in which the property subject to the lien is situated, whenever the State has not by law designated one office which meets the requirements of subparagraph (A); or

(C) With Recorder of Deeds of the District of Columbia. In the office of the Recorder of Deeds of the District of Columbia, if the property subject to the lien is situated in the District of Columbia.

(2) Situs of property subject to lien. For purposes of paragraphs (1) and (4), property shall be deemed to be situated—

(A) Real property. In the case of real property, at its physical location; or

(B) Personal property. In the case of personal property, whether tangible or intangible, at the residence of the taxpayer at the time the notice of lien is filed.

For purposes of paragraph (2)(B), the residence of a corporation or partnership shall be deemed to be the place at which the principal executive office of the business is located, and the residence of a taxpayer whose residence is without the United States shall be deemed to be in the District of Columbia.

(3) Form. The form and content of the notice referred to in subsection (a) shall be prescribed by the Secretary. Such notice shall be valid notwithstanding any other provision of law regarding the form or content of a notice of lien.

(4) Indexing required with respect to certain real property. In the case of real property, if—

(A) under the laws of the State in which the real property is located, a deed is not valid as against a purchaser of the property who (at the time of purchase) does not have actual notice or knowledge of the existence of such deed unless the fact of filing of such deed has been entered and recorded in a public index at the place of filing in such a manner that a reasonable inspection of the index will reveal the existence of the deed, and

(B) there is maintained (at the applicable office under paragraph (1)) an adequate system for the public indexing of Federal tax liens,

then the notice of lien referred to in subsection (a) shall not be treated as meeting the filing requirements under paragraph (1) unless the fact of filing is entered and recorded in the index referred to in subparagraph (B) in such a manner that a reasonable inspection of the index will reveal the existence of the lien.

(5) National filing systems. The filing of a notice of lien shall be governed solely by this title and shall not be subject to any other Federal law establishing a place or places for the filing of liens or encumbrances under a national filing system.

(g) Refiling of notice. For purposes of this section—

(1) General rule. Unless notice of lien is refiled in the manner prescribed in paragraph (2) during the required refiling period, such notice of lien shall be treated as filed on the date on which it is filed (in accordance with subsection (f)) after the expiration of such refiling period.

(2) Place for filing. A notice of lien refiled during the required refiling period shall be effective only—

(A) if—

(i) such notice of lien is refiled in the office in which the prior notice of lien was filed, and

(ii) in the case of real property, the fact of refiling is entered and recorded in an index to the extent required by subsection (f)(4); and

(B) in any case in which, 90 days or more prior to the date of a refiling of notice of lien under subparagraph (A), the Secretary received written information (in the manner prescribed in regulations issued by the Secretary) concerning a change in the taxpayer's residence, if a notice of such lien is also filed in accordance with subsection (f) in the State in which such residence is located.

(3) Required refiling period. In the case of any notice of lien, the term "required refiling period" means—

(A) the one-year period ending 30 days after the expiration of 10 years after the date of the assessment of the tax, and

(B) the one-year period ending with the expiration of 10 years after the close of the preceding required refiling period for such notice of lien.

(4) Transitional rule. Notwithstanding paragraph (3), if the assessment of the tax was made before January 1, 1962, the first required refiling period shall be the calendar year 1967.

(h) Definitions. For purposes of this section and section 6324—

(1) Security interest. The term "security interest" means any interest in property acquired by contract for the purpose of securing payment or performance of an obligation or indemnifying against loss or liability. A security interest exists at any time

(A) if, at such time, the property is in existence and the interest has become protected under local law against a subsequent judgment lien arising out of an unsecured obligation, and

(B) to the extent that, at such time, the holder has parted with money or money's worth.

(2) Mechanic's lienor. The term "mechanic's lienor" means any person who under local law has a lien on real property (or on the proceeds of a contract relating to real property) for services, labor, or materials furnished in connection with the construction or improvement of such property. For purposes of the preceding sentence, a person has a lien on the earliest date such lien becomes valid under local law against subsequent purchasers without actual notice, but not before he begins to furnish the services, labor, or materials.

(3) Motor vehicle. The term "motor vehicle" means a self-propelled vehicle which is registered for highway use under the laws of any State or foreign country.

(4) Security. The term "security" means any bond, debenture, note, or certificate or other evidence of indebtedness, issued by a corporation or a government or political subdivision thereof, with interest coupons or in registered form, share of stock, voting trust certificate, or any certificate of interest or participation in, certificate of deposit or receipt for, temporary or interim certificate for, or warrant or right to subscribe to or purchase, any of the foregoing; negotiable instrument; or money.

(5) Tax lien filing. The term "tax lien filing" means the filing of notice (referred to in subsection (a)) of the lien imposed by section 6321.

(6) Purchaser. The term "purchaser" means a person who, for adequate and full consideration in money or money's worth, acquires an interest (other than a lien or security interest) in property which is valid under local law against subsequent purchasers without actual notice. In applying the preceding sentence for purposes of subsection (a) of this section, and for purposes of section 6324—

(A) a lease of property,

(B) a written executory contract to purchase or lease property,

(C) an option to purchase or lease property or any interest therein, or

(D) an option to renew or extend a lease of property,

which is not a lien or security interest shall be treated as an interest in property.

(i) Special rules.

(1) Actual notice or knowledge. For purposes of this subchapter, an organization shall be deemed for purposes of a particular transaction to have actual notice or knowledge of any fact from the time such fact is brought to the attention of the individual conducting such transaction, and in any event from the time such fact would have been brought to such individual's attention if the organization had exercised due diligence. An organization exercises due diligence if it maintains reasonable routines

for communicating significant information to the person conducting the transaction and there is reasonable compliance with the routine. Due diligence does not require an individual acting for the organization to communicate information unless such communication is part of his regular duties or unless he has reason to know of the transaction and that the transaction would be materially affected by the information.

(2) Subrogation. Where, under local law, one person is subrogated to the rights of another with respect to a lien or interest, such person shall be subrogated to such rights for purposes of any lien imposed by section 6321 or 6324.

(3) Forfeitures. For purposes of this subchapter, a forfeiture under local law of property seized by a law enforcement agency of a State, county, or other local governmental subdivision shall relate back to the time of seizure, except that this paragraph shall not apply to the extent that under local law the holder of an intervening claim or interest would have priority over the interest of the State, county, or other local governmental subdivision in the property.

(4) Cost-of-living adjustment. In the case of notices of liens imposed by section 6321 which are filed in any calendar year after 1998, each of the dollar amounts under paragraph (4) or (7) of subsection (b) shall be increased by an amount equal to—

(A) such dollar amount, multiplied by

(B) the cost-of-living adjustment determined under section 1(f)(3) for the calendar year, determined by substituting "calendar year 1996" for "calendar year 2016" in subparagraph (A)(ii) thereof.

If any amount as adjusted under the preceding sentence is not a multiple of $10, such amount shall be rounded to the nearest multiple of $10.

(j) Withdrawal of notice in certain circumstances.

(1) In general. The Secretary may withdraw a notice of a lien filed under this section and this chapter shall be applied as if the withdrawn notice had not been filed, if the Secretary determines that—

(A) the filing of such notice was premature or otherwise not in accordance with administrative procedures of the Secretary,

(B) the taxpayer has entered into an agreement under section 6159 to satisfy the tax liability for which the lien was imposed by means of installment payments, unless such agreement provides otherwise,

(C) the withdrawal of such notice will facilitate the collection of the tax liability, or

(D) with the consent of the taxpayer or the National Taxpayer Advocate, the withdrawal of such notice would be in the best interests of the taxpayer (as determined by the National Taxpayer Advocate) and the United States.

Any such withdrawal shall be made by filing notice at the same office as the withdrawn notice. A copy of such notice of withdrawal shall be provided to the taxpayer.

(2) Notice to credit agencies, etc. Upon written request by the taxpayer with respect to whom a notice of a lien was withdrawn under paragraph (1), the Secretary shall promptly make reasonable efforts to notify credit reporting agencies, and any financial institution or creditor whose name and address is specified in such request, of the withdrawal of such notice. Any such request shall be in such form as the Secretary may prescribe.

Federal Exemption Regulation
26 C.F.R. § 301.6334-1

§ 301.6334-1. Property Exempt from Levy

(a) Enumeration. In addition to exemptions allowed as a matter of Internal Revenue Service policy, there shall be exempt from levy—

(1) Wearing apparel and school books. Such items of wearing apparel and such school books as are necessary for the taxpayer or for members of his family. Expensive items of wearing apparel, such as furs, which are luxuries and are not necessary for the taxpayer or for members of his family, are not exempt from levy.

(2) Fuel, provisions, furniture, and personal effects. So much of the fuel, provisions, furniture, and personal effects in the taxpayer's household, and of the arms for personal use, livestock, and poultry of the taxpayer, that does not exceed $6,250 in value.

(3) Books and tools of a trade, business or profession. So many of the books and tools necessary for the trade, business, or profession of an individual taxpayer as do not exceed in the aggregate $3,125 in value.

(4) Unemployment benefits. . . .

(5) Undelivered mail. Mail, addressed to any person, which has not been delivered to the addressee.

(6) Certain annuity and pension payments. . . .

(7) Workmen's compensation. Any amount payable to an individual as workmen's compensation (including any portion thereof payable with respect to dependents) under a workmen's compensation law. . . .

(8) Judgments for support of minor children. If the taxpayer is required under any type of order or decree (including an interlocutory decree or a decree of support pendente lite) of a court of competent jurisdiction, entered prior to the date of levy, to contribute to the support of his minor children, so much of his salary, wages, or other income as is necessary to comply with such order or decree. The taxpayer must establish the amount necessary to comply with the order or decree. . . .

(9) Minimum exemption for wages, salary, and other income. Amounts payable to or received by the taxpayer as wages or salary for personal services, or as other income, to the extent provided in Sec. 301.6334-2 through Sec. 301.6334-4. [For taxpayers paid weekly, the amount would be a minimum of about $303 a week for a single person and $606 for a married couple filing jointly.]

(10) Certain service-connected disability payments. Any amount payable to an individual as a service-connected (within the meaning of section 101(16) of title 38, United States Code (U.S.C.)) disability benefit under [federal military disabilities].

(11) Certain public assistance payments. Any amount payable to an individual as a recipient of public assistance under—

(i) Title IV or title XVI (relating to supplemental security income for the aged, blind, and disabled) of the Social Security Act (42 U.S.C. 301 et seq.); or

(ii) State or local government public assistance or public welfare programs for which eligibility is determined by a needs or income test.

(12) Assistance under Job Training Partnership Act. Any amount payable to a participant under the Job Training Partnership Act (29 U.S.C. 1501 et. seq.) from funds appropriated pursuant to such Act.

(13) Residences exempt in small deficiency cases and principal residences and certain business assets exempt in absence of certain approval or jeopardy—

(i) Residences in small deficiency cases. If the amount of the levy does not exceed $5,000, any real property used as a residence of the taxpayer or any real property of the taxpayer (other than real property which is rented) used by any other individual as a residence.

(ii) Principal residences and certain business assets. Except to the extent provided in section 6334(e), the principal residence (within the meaning of section 121) of the taxpayer and tangible personal property or real property (other than real property which is rented) used in the trade or business of an individual taxpayer. . . .

(c) Other property. No other property or rights to property are exempt from levy except the property specifically exempted by section 6334(a). No provision of a State law may exempt property or rights to property from levy for the collection of any Federal tax. Thus, property exempt from execution under State personal or homestead exemption laws is, nevertheless, subject to levy by the United States for collection of its taxes.

(d) Levy allowed on principal residence. The Service will seek approval, in writing, by a judge or magistrate of a district court of the United States prior to levy of property that is owned by the taxpayer and used as the principal residence of the taxpayer, the taxpayer's spouse, the taxpayer's former spouse, or the taxpayer's minor child.

(1) Nature of judicial proceeding. The Government will initiate a proceeding for judicial approval of levy on a principal residence by filing a petition with the appropriate United States District Court demonstrating that the underlying liability has not been satisfied, the requirements of any applicable law or administrative procedure relevant to the levy have been met, and no reasonable alternative for collection of the taxpayer's debt exists. The petition will ask the court to issue to the taxpayer an order to show cause why the principal residence property should not be levied and will also ask the court to issue a notice of hearing.

(2) The taxpayer will be granted a hearing to rebut the Government's prima facie case if the taxpayer files an objection within the time period required by the court raising a genuine issue of material fact demonstrating that the underlying tax liability has been satisfied, that the taxpayer has other assets from which the liability can be satisfied, or that the Service did not follow the applicable laws or procedures pertaining to the levy. The taxpayer is not permitted to challenge the merits underlying the tax liability in the proceeding. Unless the taxpayer files a timely and appropriate objection, the court would be expected to enter an order approving the levy of the principal residence property.

(3) Notice letter to be issued to certain family members. If the property to be levied is owned by the taxpayer but is used as the principal residence of the taxpayer's spouse, the taxpayer's former spouse, or the taxpayer's minor child, the Government will send a letter to each such person providing notice of the commencement of the proceeding. The letter will be addressed in the name of the taxpayer's spouse or ex-spouse, individually or on behalf of any minor children. If it is unclear who is living in the principal residence property and/or what such person's relationship is to the taxpayer, a letter will be addressed to "Occupant". The purpose of the letter is to provide notice to the family members that the property may be levied. The family members may not be joined as parties to the judicial proceeding because the levy attaches only to the taxpayer's legal interest in the subject property and the family members have no legal standing to contest the proposed levy. . . .

(g) Inflation adjustment. For any calendar year beginning after 1999, each dollar amount referred to in paragraphs (a)(2) and (3) of this section will be increased by an amount equal to the dollar amount multiplied by the cost-of-living adjustment determined under section 1(f)(3) for the calendar year (using the language "calendar year 1998" instead of "calendar year 1992" in section 1(f)(3)(B)). If any dollar amount as adjusted is not a multiple of $10, the dollar amount will be rounded to the nearest multiple of $10 (rounding up if the amount is a multiple of $5). . . .

16 CFR Part 433

Consumer-Credit Regulations (Excerpts)

Section

§ 433.1. Definitions

(a) Person. An individual, corporation, or any other business organization.

(b) Consumer. A natural person who seeks or acquires goods or services for personal, family, or household use.

(c) Creditor. A person who, in the ordinary course of business, lends purchase money or finances the sale of goods or services to consumers on a deferred payment basis; Provided, such person is not acting, for the purposes of a particular transaction, in the capacity of a credit card issuer.

(d) Purchase money loan. A cash advance which is received by a consumer in return for a "Finance Charge" within the meaning of the Truth in Lending Act and Regulation Z, which is applied, in whole or substantial part, to a purchase of goods or services from a seller who

(1) refers consumers to the creditor or

(2) is affiliated with the creditor by common control, contract, or business arrangement.

(e) Financing a sale. Extending credit to a consumer in connection with a "Credit Sale" within the meaning of the Truth in Lending Act and Regulation Z.

(f) Contract. Any oral or written agreement, formal or informal, between a creditor and a seller, which contemplates or provides for cooperative or concerted activity in connection with the sale of goods or services to consumers or the financing thereof.

(g) Business arrangement. Any understanding, procedure, course of dealing, or arrangement, formal or informal, between a creditor and a seller, in connection with the sale of goods or services to consumers or the financing thereof.

(h) Credit card issuer. A person who extends to cardholders the right to use a credit card in connection with purchases of goods or services.

(i) Consumer credit contract. Any instrument which evidences or embodies a debt arising from a "Purchase Money Loan" transaction or a "financed sale" as defined in paragraphs (d) and (e) of this section.

(j) Seller. A person who, in the ordinary course of business, sells or leases goods or services to consumers.

§ 433.2. Preservation of Consumers' Claims and Defenses, Unfair or Deceptive Acts or Practices

In connection with any sale or lease of goods or services to consumers, in or affecting commerce as "commerce" is defined in the Federal Trade Commission Act, it is an unfair or deceptive act or practice within the meaning of section 5 of that Act for a seller, directly or indirectly, to:

(a) Take or receive a consumer credit contract which fails to contain the following provision in at least ten point, bold face, type:

NOTICE

ANY HOLDER OF THIS CONSUMER CREDIT CONTRACT IS SUBJECT TO ALL CLAIMS AND DEFENSES WHICH THE DEBTOR COULD ASSERT AGAINST THE SELLER OF GOODS OR SERVICES OBTAINED PURSUANT HERETO OR WITH THE PROCEEDS HEREOF. RECOVERY HEREUNDER BY THE DEBTOR SHALL NOT EXCEED AMOUNTS PAID BY THE DEBTOR HEREUNDER. or,

(b) Accept, as full or partial payment for such sale or lease, the proceeds of any purchase money loan (as purchase money loan is defined herein), unless any consumer credit contract made in connection with such purchase money loan contains the following provision in at least ten point, bold face, type:

NOTICE

ANY HOLDER OF THIS CONSUMER CREDIT CONTRACT IS SUBJECT TO ALL CLAIMS AND DEFENSES WHICH THE DEBTOR COULD ASSERT AGAINST THE SELLER OF GOODS OR SERVICES OBTAINED WITH THE PROCEEDS HEREOF. RECOVERY HEREUNDER BY THE DEBTOR SHALL NOT EXCEED AMOUNTS PAID BY THE DEBTOR HEREUNDER.

16 CFR Part 444

Consumer Lending Regulations (Excerpts)

§ 444.1 Definitions

(a) Lender. A person who engages in the business of lending money to consumers within the jurisdiction of the Federal Trade Commission.

(b) Retail installment seller. A person who sells goods or services to consumers on a deferred payment basis or pursuant to a lease-purchase arrangement within the jurisdiction of the Federal Trade Commission.

(c) Person. An individual, corporation, or other business organization.

(d) Consumer. A natural person who seeks or acquires goods, services, or money for personal, family, or household use.

(e) Obligation. An agreement between a consumer and a lender or retail installment seller.

(f) Creditor. A lender or a retail installment seller.

(g) Debt. Money that is due or alleged to be due from one to another.

(h) Earnings. Compensation paid or payable to an individual or for his or her account for personal services rendered or to be rendered by him or her, whether denominated as wages, salary, commission, bonus, or otherwise, including periodic payments pursuant to a pension, retirement, or disability program.

(i) Household goods. Clothing, furniture, appliances, one radio and one television, linens, china, crockery, kitchenware, and personal effects (including wedding rings) of the consumer and his or her dependents, provided that the following are not included within the scope of the term household goods:

(1) Works of art;

(2) Electronic entertainment equipment (except one television and one radio);

(3) Items acquired as antiques; and

(4) Jewelry (except wedding rings).

(j) Antique. Any item over one hundred years of age, including such items that have been repaired or renovated without changing their original form or character.

(k) Cosigner. A natural person who renders himself or herself liable for the obligation of another person without compensation. The term shall include any person whose signature is requested as a condition to granting credit to another person, or as a condition for forbearance on collection of another person's obligation that is in default. The term shall not include a spouse whose signature is required on a credit obligation to perfect a security interest pursuant to state law. A person who does not receive goods, services, or money in return for a credit obligation does not receive compensation within the meaning of this definition. A person is a cosigner within the meaning of this definition whether or not he or she is designated as such on a credit obligation.

§ 444.2 Unfair Credit Practices

(a) In connection with the extension of credit to consumers in or affecting commerce, as commerce is defined in the Federal Trade Commission Act, it is an unfair act or practice within the meaning of Section 5 of that Act for a lender or retail installment seller directly or indirectly to take or receive from a consumer an obligation that:

(1) Constitutes or contains a cognovit or confession of judgment (for purposes other than executory process in the State of Louisiana), warrant of attorney, or other waiver of the right to notice and the opportunity to be heard in the event of suit or process thereon.

(2) Constitutes or contains an executory waiver or a limitation of exemption from attachment, execution, or other process on real or personal property held, owned by, or due to the consumer, unless the waiver applies solely to property subject to a security interest executed in connection with the obligation.

(3) Constitutes or contains an assignment of wages or other earnings unless:

(i) The assignment by its terms is revocable at the will of the debtor, or

(ii) The assignment is a payroll deduction plan or preauthorized payment plan, commencing at the time of the transaction, in which the consumer authorizes a series of wage deductions as a method of making each payment, or

(iii) The assignment applies only to wages or other earnings already earned at the time of the assignment.

(4) Constitutes or contains a nonpossessory security interest in household goods other than a purchase money security interest.

National Bank Act

12 U.S.C. § 85

§ 85. Rate of Interest on Loans, Discounts and Purchases

Any association may take, receive, reserve, and charge on any loan or discount made, or upon any notes, bills of exchange, or other evidences of debt, interest at the rate allowed by the laws of the State, Territory, or District where the bank is located, or at a rate of 1 per centum in excess of the discount rate on ninety-day commercial paper in effect at the Federal reserve bank in the Federal reserve district where the bank is located, whichever may be the greater, and no more, except that where by the laws of any State a different rate is limited for banks organized under State laws, the rate so limited shall be allowed for associations organized or existing in any such State under title 62 of the Revised Statutes. When no rate is fixed by the laws of the State, or Territory, or District, the bank may take, receive, reserve, or charge a rate not exceeding 7 per centum, or 1 per centum in excess of the discount rate on ninety day commercial paper in effect at the Federal reserve bank in the Federal reserve district where the bank is located, whichever may be the greater, and such interest may be taken in advance, reckoning the days for which the note, bill, or other evidence of debt has to run. The maximum amount of interest or discount to be charged at a branch of an association located outside of the States of the United States and the District of Columbia shall be at the rate allowed by the laws of the country, territory, dependency, province, dominion, insular possession, or other political subdivision where the branch is located. And the purchase, discount, or sale of a bona fide bill of exchange, payable at another place than the place of such purchase, discount, or sale, at not more than the current rate of exchange for sight drafts in addition to the interest, shall not be considered as taking or receiving a greater rate of interest.

PART IV

UNIFORM STATE LAWS AND RESTATEMENTS

Uniform Electronic Transactions Act (1999)

§ 1. Short Title

This [Act] may be cited as the Uniform Electronic Transactions Act.

§ 2. Definitions

In this [Act]:

(1) "Agreement" means the bargain of the parties in fact, as found in their language or inferred from other circumstances and from rules, regulations, and procedures given the effect of agreements under laws otherwise applicable to a particular transaction.

(2) "Automated transaction" means a transaction conducted or performed, in whole or in part, by electronic means or electronic records, in which the acts or records of one or both parties are not reviewed by an individual in the ordinary course in forming a contract, performing under an existing contract, or fulfilling an obligation required by the transaction.

(3) "Computer program" means a set of statements or instructions to be used directly or indirectly in an information processing system in order to bring about a certain result.

(4) "Contract" means the total legal obligation resulting from the parties' agreement as affected by this [Act] and other applicable law.

(5) "Electronic" means relating to technology having electrical, digital, magnetic, wireless, optical, electromagnetic, or similar capabilities.

(6) "Electronic agent" means a computer program or an electronic or other automated means used independently to initiate an action or respond to electronic records or performances in whole or in part, without review or action by an individual.

(7) "Electronic record" means a record created, generated, sent, communicated, received, or stored by electronic means.

(8) "Electronic signature" means an electronic sound, symbol, or process attached to or logically associated with a record and executed or adopted by a person with the intent to sign the record.

(9) "Governmental agency" means an executive, legislative, or judicial agency, department, board, commission, authority, institution, or instrumentality of the federal government or of a State or of a county, municipality, or other political subdivision of a State.

(10) "Information" means data, text, images, sounds, codes, computer programs, software, databases, or the like.

(11) "Information processing system" means an electronic system for creating, generating, sending, receiving, storing, displaying, or processing information.

(12) "Person" means an individual, corporation, business trust, estate, trust, partnership, limited liability company, association, joint venture, governmental agency, public corporation, or any other legal or commercial entity.

(13) "Record" means information that is inscribed on a tangible medium or that is stored in an electronic or other medium and is retrievable in perceivable form.

(14) "Security procedure" means a procedure employed for the purpose of verifying that an electronic signature, record, or performance is that of a specific person or for detecting changes or errors in the information in an electronic record. The term includes a procedure that requires the use of algorithms or other codes, identifying words or numbers, encryption, or callback or other acknowledgment procedures.

(15) "State" means a State of the United States, the District of Columbia, Puerto Rico, the United States Virgin Islands, or any territory or insular possession subject to the jurisdiction of the United States. The term includes an Indian tribe or band, or Alaskan native village, which is recognized by federal law or formally acknowledged by a State.

(16) "Transaction" means an action or set of actions occurring between two or more persons relating to the conduct of business, commercial, or governmental affairs.

Sources: UNCITRAL Model Law on Electronic Commerce; Uniform Commercial Code; Uniform Computer Information Transactions Act; Restatement 2d Contracts.

Comment

1. "Agreement." Whether the parties have reached an agreement is determined by their express language and all surrounding circumstances. The Restatement 2d Contracts § 3 provides that, "An agreement is a manifestation of mutual assent on the part of two or more persons." See also Restatement 2d Contracts, Section 2, Comment b. The Uniform Commercial Code specifically includes in the circumstances from which an agreement may be inferred "course of performance, course of dealing and usage of trade . . ." as defined in the UCC. Although the definition of agreement in this Act does not make specific reference to usage of trade and other party conduct, this definition is not intended to affect the construction of the parties' agreement under the substantive law applicable to a particular transaction. Where that law takes account of usage and conduct in informing the terms of the parties' agreement, the usage or conduct would be relevant as "other circumstances" included in the definition under this Act.

Where the law applicable to a given transaction provides that system rules and the like constitute part of the agreement of the parties, such rules will have the same effect in determining the parties agreement under this Act. For example, UCC Article 4 (Section 4103(b)) provides that Federal Reserve regulations and operating circulars and clearinghouse rules have the effect of agreements. Such agreements by law properly would be included in the definition of agreement in this Act.The parties' agreement is relevant in determining whether the provisions of this Act have been varied by agreement. In addition, the parties' agreement may establish the parameters of the parties' use of electronic records and signatures, security procedures and similar aspects of the transaction. See Model Trading Partner Agreement, 45 Business Lawyer Supp. Issue (June 1990). See Section 5(b) and Comments thereto.

2. "Automated transaction." An automated transaction is a transaction performed or conducted by electronic means in which machines are used without human intervention to form contracts and perform obligations under existing contracts. Such broad coverage is necessary because of the diversity of transactions to which this Act may apply.

As with electronic agents, this definition addresses the circumstance where electronic records may result in action or performance by a party although no human review of the electronic records is anticipated. Section 14 provides specific rules to assure that where one or both parties do not review the electronic records, the resulting agreement will be effective.The critical element in this definition is the lack of a human actor on one or both sides of a transaction. For example, if one orders books from Bookseller.com through Bookseller's website, the transaction would be an automated transaction because Bookseller took and confirmed the order via its machine. Similarly, if Automaker and supplier do business through Electronic Data Interchange, Automaker's computer, upon receiving information within certain pre-programmed parameters, will send an electronic order to Supplier's computer. If Supplier's computer confirms the order and processes the shipment because the order falls within pre-programmed parameters in Supplier's computer, this would be a fully automated transaction. If, instead, the Supplier relies on a human employee to review, accept, and process the Buyer's order, then only the Automaker's side of the transaction would be automated. In either case, the entire transaction falls within this definition.

3. "Computer program." This definition refers to the functional and operating aspects of an electronic, digital system. It relates to operating instructions used in an electronic system such as an electronic agent. (See definition of "Electronic Agent.")

4. "Electronic." The basic nature of most current technologies and the need for a recognized, single term warrants the use of "electronic" as the defined term. The definition is intended to assure that the Act will be applied broadly as new technologies develop. The term must be construed broadly in light of developing technologies in order to fulfill the purpose of this Act to validate commercial transactions regardless of the medium used by the parties. Current legal requirements for "writings" can be satisfied by almost any tangible media, whether paper, other fibers, or even stone. The purpose and applicability of this Act covers intangible media which are technologically capable of storing, transmitting and reproducing information in human perceivable form, but which lack the tangible aspect of paper, papyrus or stone.

While not all technologies listed are technically "electronic" in nature (e.g., optical fiber technology), the term "electronic" is the most descriptive term available to describe the majority of current technologies. For example, the development of biological and chemical processes for communication and storage of data, while not specifically mentioned in the definition, are included within the technical definition because such processes operate on electromagnetic impulses. However, whether a particular technology may be characterized as technically "electronic," i.e., operates on electromagnetic impulses, should not be determinative of whether records and signatures created, used and stored by means of a particular technology are covered by this Act. This Act is intended to apply to all records and signatures created, used and stored by any medium which permits the information to be retrieved in perceivable form.

5. "Electronic agent." This definition establishes that an electronic agent is a machine. As the term "electronic agent" has come to be recognized, it is limited to a tool function. The effect on the party using the agent is addressed in the operative provisions of the Act (e.g., Section 14).

An electronic agent, such as a computer program or other automated means employed by a person, is a tool of that person. As a general rule, the employer of a tool is responsible for the results obtained by the use of that tool since the tool has no independent volition of its own. However, an electronic agent, by definition, is capable within the parameters of its programming, of initiating, responding or interacting with other parties or their electronic agents once it has been activated by a party, without further attention of that party.While this Act proceeds on the paradigm that an electronic agent is capable of performing only within the technical strictures of its preset programming, it is conceivable that, within the useful life of this Act, electronic agents may be created with the ability to act autonomously, and not just automatically. That is, through developments in artificial intelligence, a computer may be able to "learn through experience, modify the instructions in their own programs, and even devise new instructions." Allen and Widdison, "Can Computers Make Contracts?" *9 Harv. J.L. & Tech 25* (Winter, 1996). If such developments occur, courts may construe the definition of electronic agent accordingly, in order to recognize such new capabilities.The examples involving Bookseller.com and Automaker in the Comment to the definition of Automated Transaction are equally applicable here. Bookseller acts through an electronic agent in processing an order for books. Automaker and the supplier each act through electronic agents in facilitating and effectuating the just-in-time inventory process through EDI.

6. "Electronic record." An electronic record is a subset of the broader defined term "record." It is any record created, used or stored in a medium other than paper (see definition of electronic). The defined term is also used in this Act as a limiting definition in those provisions in which it is used.

Information processing systems, computer equipment and programs, electronic data interchange, electronic mail, voice mail, facsimile, telex, telecopying, scanning, and similar technologies all qualify as electronic under this Act. Accordingly information stored on a computer hard drive or floppy disc, facsimiles, voice mail messages, messages on a telephone answering machine, audio and video tape recordings, among other records, all would be electronic records under this Act.

7. "Electronic signature." The idea of a signature is broad and not specifically defined. Whether any particular record is "signed" is a question of fact. Proof of that fact must be made under other applicable law. This Act simply assures that the signature may be accomplished through electronic means. No specific technology need be used in order to create a valid signature. One's voice on an answering machine may suffice if the requisite intention is present. Similarly, including one's name as part of an electronic mail communication also may suffice, as may the firm name on a facsimile. It also may be shown that the requisite intent was not present and accordingly the symbol, sound or process did not amount to a signature. One may use a digital signature with the requisite intention, or one may use the private key solely as an access device with no intention to sign, or otherwise accomplish a legally binding act. In any case the critical element is the intention to execute or adopt the sound or symbol or process for the purpose of signing the related record.

The definition requires that the signer execute or adopt the sound, symbol, or process with the intent to sign the record. The act of applying a sound, symbol or process to an electronic record could have differing meanings and effects. The consequence of the act and the effect of the act as a signature are determined under other applicable law. However, the essential attribute of a signature involves applying a sound, symbol or process with an intent to do a legally significant act. It is that intention that is understood in the law as a part of the word "sign," without the need for a definition.

This Act establishes, to the greatest extent possible, the equivalency of electronic signatures and manual signatures. Therefore the term "signature" has been used to connote and convey that equivalency. The purpose is to overcome unwarranted biases against electronic methods of signing and authenticating records. The term "authentication," used in other laws, often has a narrower meaning and purpose than an electronic signature as used in this Act. However, an authentication under any of those other laws constitutes an electronic signature under this Act.

The precise effect of an electronic signature will be determined based on the surrounding circumstances under Section 9(b).

This definition includes as an electronic signature the standard webpage click through process. For example, when a person orders goods or services through a vendor's website, the person will be required to provide information as part of a process which will result in receipt of the goods or services. When the customer ultimately gets to the last step and clicks "I agree," the person has adopted the process and has done so with the intent to associate the person with the record of that process. The actual effect of the electronic signature will be determined from all the surrounding circumstances, however, the person adopted a process which the circumstances indicate s/he intended to have the effect of getting the goods/services and being bound to pay for them. The adoption of the process carried the intent to do a legally significant act, the hallmark of a signature.

Another important aspect of this definition lies in the necessity that the electronic signature be linked or logically associated with the record. In the paper world, it is assumed that the symbol adopted by a party is attached to or located somewhere in the same paper that is intended to be authenticated, e.g., an allonge firmly attached to a promissory note, or the classic signature at the end of a long contract. These tangible manifestations do not exist in the electronic environment, and accordingly, this definition expressly provides that the symbol must in some way be linked to, or connected with, the electronic record being signed. This linkage is consistent with the regulations promulgated by the Food and Drug Administration. 21 CFR Part 11 (March 20, 1997).

A digital signature using public key encryption technology would qualify as an electronic signature, as would the mere inclusion of one's name as a part of an email message—so long as in each case the signer executed or adopted the symbol with the intent to sign.

8. "Governmental agency." This definition is important in the context of optional Sections 1719.

9. "Information processing system." This definition is consistent with the UNCITRAL Model Law on Electronic Commerce. The term includes computers and other information systems. It is principally used in Section 15 in connection with the sending and receiving of information. In that context, the key aspect is that the information enter a system from which a person can access it.

10. "Record." This is a standard definition designed to embrace all means of communicating or storing information except human memory. It includes any method for storing or communicating information, including "writings." A record need not be indestructible or permanent, but the term does not include oral or other communications which are not stored or preserved by some means. Information that has not been retained other than through human memory does not qualify as a record. As in the case of the terms "writing" or "written," the term "record" does not establish the purposes, permitted uses or legal effect which a record may have under any particular provision of substantive law. ABA Report on Use of the Term "Record," October 1, 1996.

11. "Security procedure." A security procedure may be applied to verify an electronic signature, verify the identity of the sender, or assure the informational integrity of an electronic record. The definition does not identify any particular technology. This permits the use of procedures which the parties select or which are established by law. It permits the greatest flexibility among the parties and allows for future technological development.

The definition in this Act is broad and is used to illustrate one way of establishing attribution or content integrity of an electronic record or signature. The use of a security procedure is not accorded operative legal effect, through the use of presumptions or otherwise, by this Act. In this Act, the use of security procedures is simply one method for proving the source or content of an electronic record or signature.

A security procedure may be technologically very sophisticated, such as an asymetric cryptographic system. At the other extreme the security procedure may be as simple as a telephone call to confirm the identity of the sender through another channel of communication. It may include the use of a mother's maiden name or a personal identification number (PIN). Each of these examples is a method for confirming the identity of a person or accuracy of a message.

12. "Transaction." The definition has been limited to actions between people taken in the context of business, commercial or governmental activities. The term includes all interactions between people for business, commercial, including specifically consumer, or governmental purposes. However, the term does not include unilateral or non-transactional actions. As such it provides a structural limitation on the scope of the Act as stated in the next section.

It is essential that the term commerce and business be understood and construed broadly to include commercial and business transactions involving individuals who may qualify as "consumers" under other applicable law. If Alice and Bob agree to the sale of Alice's car to Bob for $2000 using an internet auction site, that transaction is fully covered by this Act. Even if Alice and Bob each qualify as typical "consumers" under other applicable law, their interaction is a transaction in commerce. Accordingly their actions would be related to commercial affairs, and fully qualify as a transaction governed by this Act.

Other transaction types include:

1. A single purchase by an individual from a retail merchant, which may be accomplished by an order from a printed catalog sent by facsimile, or by exchange of electronic mail.

2. Recurring orders on a weekly or monthly basis between large companies which have entered into a master trading partner agreement to govern the methods and manner of their transaction parameters.

3. A purchase by an individual from an online internet retail vendor. Such an arrangement may develop into an ongoing series of individual purchases, with security procedures and the like, as a part of doing ongoing business.

4. The closing of a business purchase transaction via facsimile transmission of documents or even electronic mail. In such a transaction, all parties may participate through electronic conferencing technologies. At the appointed time all electronic records are executed electronically and transmitted to the other party. In such a case, the electronic records and electronic signatures are validated under this Act, obviating the need for "in person" closings.

A transaction must include interaction between two or more persons. Consequently, to the extent that the execution of a will, trust, or a health care power of attorney or similar health care designation does not involve another person and is a unilateral act, it would not be covered by this Act because not occurring as a part of a transaction as defined in this Act. However, this Act *does* apply to all electronic records and signatures *related* to a transaction, and so does cover, for example, internal auditing and accounting records related to a transaction.

§ 3. Scope

(a) Except as otherwise provided in subsection (b), this [Act] applies to electronic records and electronic signatures relating to a transaction.

(b) This [Act] does not apply to a transaction to the extent it is governed by:

(1) a law governing the creation and execution of wills, codicils, or testamentary trusts;

(2) [The Uniform Commercial Code other than Sections 1107 and 1206, Article 2, and Article 2A];

(3) [the Uniform Computer Information Transactions Act]; and

(4) [other laws, if any, identified by State].

(c) This [Act] applies to an electronic record or electronic signature otherwise excluded from the application of this [Act] under subsection (b) to the extent it is governed by a law other than those specified in subsection (b).

(d) A transaction subject to this [Act] is also subject to other applicable substantive law.

See Legislative Note below — Following Comments.

Comment

1. The scope of this Act is inherently limited by the fact that it only applies to transactions related to business, commercial (including consumer) and governmental matters. Consequently, transactions with no relation to business, commercial or governmental transactions would not be subject to this Act. Unilaterally generated electronic records and signatures which are not part of a transaction also are not covered by this Act. See Section 2, Comment 12.

2. This Act affects the medium in which information, records and signatures may be presented and retained under current legal requirements. While this Act covers all electronic records and signatures which are used in a business, commercial (including consumer) or governmental transaction, the operative provisions of the Act relate to requirements for writings and signatures under other laws. Accordingly, the exclusions in subsection (b) focus on those legal rules imposing certain writing and signature requirements which will *not* be affected by this Act.

3. The exclusions listed in subsection (b) provide clarity and certainty regarding the laws which are and are not affected by this Act. This section provides that transactions subject to specific laws are unaffected by this Act and leaves the balance subject to this Act.

4. Paragraph (1) excludes wills, codicils and testamentary trusts. This exclusion is largely salutary given the unilateral context in which such records are generally created and the unlikely use of such records in a transaction as defined in this Act (i.e., actions taken by two or more persons in the context of business, commercial or governmental affairs). Paragraph (2) excludes all of the Uniform Commercial Code other than UCC Sections 1107 and 1206, and Articles 2 and 2A. This Act does not apply to the excluded UCC articles, whether in "current" or "revised" form. The Act does apply to UCC Articles 2 and 2A and to UCC Sections 1107 and 1206.

5. Articles 3, 4 and 4A of the UCC impact payment systems and have specifically been removed from the coverage of this Act. The check collection and electronic fund transfer systems governed by Articles 3, 4 and 4A involve systems and relationships involving numerous parties beyond the parties to the underlying contract. The impact of validating electronic media in such systems involves considerations beyond the scope of this Act. Articles 5, 8 and 9 have been excluded because the revision process relating to those Articles included significant consideration of electronic practices. Paragraph 4 provides for exclusion from this Act of the Uniform Computer Information Transactions Act (UCITA) because the drafting process of that Act also included significant consideration of electronic contracting provisions.

6. The very limited application of this Act to Transferable Records in Section 16 does not affect payment systems, and the section is designed to apply to a transaction only through express agreement of the parties. The exclusion of Articles 3 and 4 will not affect the Act's coverage of Transferable Records. Section 16 is designed to allow for the development of systems which will provide "control" as defined in Section 16. Such control is necessary as a substitute for the idea of possession which undergirds negotiable instrument law. The technology has yet to be developed which will allow for the possession of a unique electronic token embodying the rights associated with a negotiable promissory note. Section 16's concept of control is intended as a substitute for possession.

The provisions in Section 16 operate as free standing rules, establishing the rights of parties using Transferable Records *under this Act*. The references in Section 16 to UCC Sections 3302, 7501, and 9308 (R9330(d)) are designed to incorporate the substance of those provisions into this Act for the limited purposes noted in Section 16(c). Accordingly, an electronic record which is also a Transferable Record, would not be used for purposes of a transaction governed by Articles 3, 4, or 9, but would be an electronic record used for purposes of a transaction governed by Section 16. However, it is important to remember that those UCC Articles will still apply to the transferable record in their own right. Accordingly any other substantive requirements, e.g., method and manner of perfection under Article 9, must be complied with under those other laws. See Comments to Section 16.

7. This Act does apply, *in toto*, to transactions under unrevised Articles 2 and 2A. There is every reason to validate electronic contracting in these situations. Sale and lease transactions do not implicate broad systems beyond the parties to the underlying transaction, such as are present in check collection and electronic funds transfers. Further sales and leases generally do not have as far reaching effect on the rights of third parties beyond the contracting parties, such as exists in the secured transactions system. Finally, it is in the area of sales, licenses and leases that electronic commerce is occurring to its greatest extent today. To exclude these transactions would largely gut the purpose of this Act.

In the event that Articles 2 and 2A are revised and adopted in the future, UETA will only apply to the extent provided in those Acts.

8. An electronic record/signature may be used for purposes of more than one legal requirement, or may be covered by more than one law. Consequently, it is important to make clear, despite any apparent redundancy, in subsection (c) that an electronic record used for purposes of a law which is *not* affected by this Act under subsection (b) may nonetheless be used and validated for purposes of other laws not excluded by subsection (b). For example, this Act does not apply to an electronic record of a check when used for purposes of a transaction governed by Article 4 of the Uniform Commercial Code, i.e., the Act does not validate so-called electronic checks. However, for purposes of check retention statutes, the same electronic record of the check is covered by this Act, so that retention of an electronic image/record of a check will satisfy such retention statutes, so long as the requirements of Section 12 are fulfilled.

In another context, subsection (c) would operate to allow this Act to apply to what would appear to be an excluded transaction under subsection (b). For example, Article 9 of the Uniform Commercial Code applies generally to any transaction that creates a security interest in personal property. However, Article 9 excludes landlord's liens. Accordingly, although this Act excludes from its application transactions subject to Article 9, this Act would apply to the creation of a landlord lien if the law otherwise applicable to landlord's liens did not provide otherwise, because the landlord's lien transaction is excluded from Article 9.

9. Additional exclusions under subparagraph (b)(4) should be limited to laws which govern electronic records and signatures which may be used in transactions as defined in Section 2(16). Records used unilaterally, or which do not relate to business, commercial (including consumer), or governmental affairs are not governed by this Act in any event, and exclusion of laws relating to such records may create unintended inferences about whether other records and signatures are covered by this Act.

It is also important that additional exclusions, if any, be incorporated under subsection (b)(4). As noted in Comment 8 above, an electronic record used in a transaction excluded under subsection (b), e.g., a check used to pay one's taxes, will nonetheless be validated for purposes of other, non-excluded laws under subsection (c), e.g., the check when used as proof of payment. It is critical that additional exclusions, if any, be incorporated into subsection (b) so that the salutary effect of subsection (c) apply to validate those records in other, non-excluded transactions. While a legislature may determine that a particular notice, such as a utility shutoff notice, be provided to a person in writing on paper, it is difficult to see why the utility should not be entitled to use electronic media for storage and evidentiary purposes.

Legislative Note Regarding Possible Additional Exclusions under Section 3(b)(4).

The following discussion is derived from the Report dated September 21, 1998 of The Task Force on State Law Exclusions (the "Task Force") presented to the Drafting Committee. After consideration of the Report, the Drafting Committee determined that exclusions other than those specified in the Act were not warranted. In addition, other inherent limitations on the applicability of the Act (the definition of transaction, the requirement that the parties acquiesce in the use of an electronic format) also militate against additional exclusions. Nonetheless, the Drafting Committee recognized that some legislatures may wish to exclude additional transactions from the Act, and determined that guidance in some major areas would be helpful to those legislatures considering additional areas for exclusion.Because of the overwhelming number of references in state law to writings and signatures, the following list of possible transactions is not exhaustive. However, they do represent those areas most commonly raised during the course of the drafting process as areas that might be inappropriate for an electronic medium. It is important to keep in mind however, that the Drafting Committee determined that exclusion of these additional areas was not warranted.

1. Trusts (other than testamentary trusts). Trusts can be used for both business and personal purposes. By virtue of the definition of transaction, trusts used outside the area of business and commerce would not be governed by this Act. With respect to business or commercial trusts, the laws governing their formation contain few or no requirements for paper or signatures. Indeed, in most jurisdictions trusts of any kind may be created orally. Consequently, the Drafting Committee believed that the Act should apply to any transaction where the law leaves to the parties the decision of whether to use a writing. Thus, in the absence of legal requirements for writings, there is no sound reason to exclude laws governing trusts from the application of this Act.

2. Powers of Attorney. A power of attorney is simply a formalized type of agency agreement. In general, no formal requirements for paper or execution were found to be applicable to the validity of powers of attorney.

Special health powers of attorney have been established by statute in some States. These powers may have special requirements under state law regarding execution, acknowledgment and possibly notarization. In the normal case such powers will not arise in a transactional context and so would not be covered by this Act. However, even if such a record were to arise in a transactional context, this Act operates simply to remove the barrier to the use of an electronic medium, and preserves other requirements of applicable substantive law, avoiding any necessity to exclude such laws from the operation of this Act. Especially in light of the provisions of Sections 8 and 11, the substantive requirements under such laws will be preserved and may be satisfied in an electronic format.

3. Real Estate Transactions. It is important to distinguish between the efficacy of paper documents involving real estate between the parties, as opposed to their effect on third parties. As between the parties it is unnecessary to maintain existing barriers to electronic contracting. There are no unique characteristics to contracts relating to real property as opposed to other business and commercial (including consumer) contracts. Consequently, the decision whether to use an electronic medium for their agreements should be a matter for the parties to determine. Of course, to be effective against third parties state law generally requires filing with a governmental office. Pending adoption of electronic filing systems by States, the need for a piece of paper to file to perfect rights against third parties, will be a consideration for the parties. In the event notarization and acknowledgment are required under other laws, Section 11 provides a means for such actions to be accomplished electronically.

With respect to the requirements of government filing, those are left to the individual States in the decision of whether to adopt and implement electronic filing systems. (See optional Sections 1719.) However, government recording systems currently require paper deeds including notarized, manual signatures. Although California and Illinois are experimenting with electronic filing systems, until such systems become widespread, the parties likely will choose to use, at the least, a paper deed for filing purposes. Nothing in this Act precludes the parties from selecting the medium best suited to the needs of the particular transaction. Parties may wish to consummate the transaction using electronic media in order to avoid expensive travel. Yet the actual deed may be in paper form to assure compliance with existing recording systems and requirements. The critical point is that nothing in this Act prevents the parties from selecting paper or electronic media for all or part of their transaction.

4. Consumer Protection Statutes. Consumer protection provisions in state law often require that information be disclosed or provided to a consumer in writing. Because this Act does apply to such transactions, the question of whether such laws should be specifically excluded was considered. Exclusion of consumer transactions would eliminate a huge group of commercial transactions which benefit consumers by enabling the efficiency of the electronic medium. Commerce over the internet is driven by consumer demands and concerns and must be included.

At the same time, it is important to recognize the protective effects of many consumer statutes. Consumer statutes often require that information be provided in writing, or may require that the consumer separately sign or initial a particular provision to evidence that the consumer's attention was brought to the provision. Subsection (1) requires electronic records to be retainable by a person whenever the law requires information to be delivered in writing. The section imposes a significant burden on the sender of information. The sender must assure that the information system of the recipient is compatible with, and capable of retaining the information sent by, the sender's system. Furthermore, nothing in this Act permits the avoidance of legal requirements of separate signatures or initialing. The Act simply permits the signature or initialing to be done electronically.

Other consumer protection statutes require (expressly or implicitly) that certain information be presented in a certain manner or format. Laws requiring information to be presented in particular fonts, formats or in similar fashion, as well as laws requiring conspicuous displays of information are preserved. Section 8(b)(3) specifically preserves the applicability of such requirements in an electronic environment. In the case of legal requirements that information be presented or appear conspicuous, the determination of what is conspicuous will be left to other law. Section 8 was included to specifically preserve the protective functions of such disclosure statutes, while at the same time allowing the use of electronic media if the substantive requirements of the other laws could be satisfied in the electronic medium.

Formatting and separate signing requirements serve a critical purpose in much consumer protection legislation, to assure that information is not slipped past the unsuspecting consumer. Not only does this Act not disturb those requirements, it preserves those requirements. In addition, other bodies of substantive law continue to operate to allow the courts to police any such bad conduct or overreaching, e.g., unconscionability, fraud, duress, mistake and the like. These bodies of law remain applicable regardless of the medium in which a record appears.

The requirement that both parties agree to conduct a transaction electronically also prevents the imposition of an electronic medium on unwilling parties See Section 5(b). In addition, where the law requires inclusion of specific terms or language, those requirements are preserved broadly by Section 5(e).

Requirements that information be sent to, or received by, someone have been preserved in Section 15. As in the paper world, obligations to send do not impose any duties on the sender to assure receipt, other than reasonable methods of dispatch. In those cases where receipt is required legally, Sections 5, 8, and 15 impose the burden on the sender to assure delivery to the recipient if satisfaction of the legal requirement is to be fulfilled.

The preservation of existing safeguards, together with the ability to opt out of the electronic medium entirely, demonstrate the lack of any need generally to exclude consumer protection laws from the operation of this Act. Legislatures may wish to focus any review on those statutes which provide for post-contract formation and post-breach notices to be in paper. However, any such consideration must also balance the needed protections against the potential burdens which may be imposed. Consumers and others will not be well served by restrictions which preclude the employment of electronic technologies sought and desired by consumers.

§ 4. Prospective Application

This [Act] applies to any electronic record or electronic signature created, generated, sent, communicated, received, or stored on or after the effective date of this [Act].

Comment

This section makes clear that the Act only applies to validate electronic records and signatures which arise subsequent to the effective date of the Act. Whether electronic records and electronic signatures arising before the effective date of this Act are valid is left to other law.

§ 5. Use of Electronic Records and Electronic Signatures; Variation by Agreement

(a) This [Act] does not require a record or signature to be created, generated, sent, communicated, received, stored, or otherwise processed or used by electronic means or in electronic form.

(b) This [Act] applies only to transactions between parties each of which has agreed to conduct transactions by electronic means. Whether the parties agree to conduct a transaction by electronic means is determined from the context and surrounding circumstances, including the parties' conduct.

(c) A party that agrees to conduct a transaction by electronic means may refuse to conduct other transactions by electronic means. The right granted by this subsection may not be waived by agreement.

(d) Except as otherwise provided in this [Act], the effect of any of its provisions may be varied by agreement. The presence in certain provisions of this [Act] of the words "unless otherwise agreed," or words of similar import, does not imply that the effect of other provisions may not be varied by agreement.

(e) Whether an electronic record or electronic signature has legal consequences is determined by this [Act] and other applicable law.

Comment

This section limits the applicability of this Act to transactions which parties have agreed to conduct electronically. Broad interpretation of the term agreement is necessary to assure that this Act has the widest possible application consistent with its purpose of removing barriers to electronic commerce.

1. This section makes clear that this Act is intended to facilitate the use of electronic means, but does not require the use of electronic records and signatures. This fundamental principle is set forth in subsection (a) and elaborated by subsections (b) and (c), which require an intention to conduct transactions electronically and preserve the right of a party to refuse to use electronics in any subsequent transaction.

2. The paradigm of this Act is two willing parties doing transactions electronically. It is therefore appropriate that the Act is voluntary and preserves the greatest possible party autonomy to refuse electronic transactions. The requirement that party agreement be found from all the surrounding circumstances is a limitation on the scope of this Act.

3. If this Act is to serve to facilitate electronic transactions, it must be applicable under circumstances not rising to a full fledged contract to use electronics. While absolute certainty can be accomplished by obtaining an explicit contract before relying on electronic transactions, such an explicit contract should not be necessary before one may feel safe in conducting transactions electronically. Indeed, such a requirement would itself be an unreasonable barrier to electronic commerce, at odds with the fundamental purpose of this Act. Accordingly, the requisite agreement, express or implied, must be determined from all available circumstances and evidence.

4. Subsection (b) provides that the Act applies to transactions in which the parties have agreed to conduct the transaction electronically. In this context it is essential that the parties' actions and words be broadly construed in determining whether the requisite agreement exists. Accordingly, the Act expressly provides that the party's agreement is to be found from all circumstances, including the parties' conduct. The critical element is the intent of a party to conduct a transaction electronically. Once that intent is established, this Act applies. See Restatement 2d Contracts, Sections 2, 3, and 19.

Examples of circumstances from which it may be found that parties have reached an agreement to conduct transactions electronically include the following:

A. Automaker and supplier enter into a Trading Partner Agreement setting forth the terms, conditions and methods for the conduct of business between them electronically.

B. Joe gives out his business card with his business email address. It may be reasonable, under the circumstances, for a recipient of the card to infer that Joe has agreed to communicate electronically for business purposes. However, in the absence of additional facts, it would not necessarily be reasonable to infer Joe's agreement to communicate electronically for purposes outside the scope of the business indicated by use of the business card.

C. Sally may have several email addresses—home, main office, office of a non-profit organization on whose board Sally sits. In each case, it may be reasonable to infer that Sally is willing to communicate electronically with respect to business related to the business/purpose associated with the respective email addresses. However, depending on the circumstances, it may not be reasonable to communicate with Sally for purposes other than those related to the purpose for which she maintained a particular email account.

D. Among the circumstances to be considered in finding an agreement would be the time when the assent occurred relative to the timing of the use of electronic communications. If one orders books from an on-line vendor, such as Bookseller.com, the intention to conduct that transaction and to receive any correspondence related to the transaction electronically can be inferred from the conduct. Accordingly, as to information related to that transaction it is reasonable for Bookseller to deal with the individual electronically.

The examples noted above are intended to focus the inquiry on the party's agreement to conduct a transaction electronically. Similarly, if two people are at a meeting and one tells the other to send an email to confirm a transaction—the requisite agreement under subsection (b) would exist. In each case, the use of a business card, statement at a meeting, or other evidence of willingness to conduct a transaction electronically must be viewed in light of all the surrounding circumstances with a view toward broad validation of electronic transactions.

5. Just as circumstances may indicate the existence of agreement, express or implied from surrounding circumstances, circumstances may also demonstrate the absence of true agreement. For example:

A. If Automaker, Inc. were to issue a recall of automobiles via its Internet website, it would not be able to rely on this Act to validate that notice in the case of a person who never logged on to the website, or indeed, had no ability to do so, notwithstanding a clause in a paper purchase contract by which the buyer agreed to receive such notices in such a manner.

B. Buyer executes a standard form contract in which an agreement to receive all notices electronically in set forth on page 3 in the midst of other fine print. Buyer has never communicated with Seller electronically, and has not provided any other information in the contract to suggest a willingness to deal electronically. Not only is it unlikely that any but the most formalistic of agreements may be found, but nothing in this Act prevents courts from policing such form contracts under common law doctrines relating to contract formation, unconscionability and the like.

6. Subsection (c) has been added to make clear the ability of a party to refuse to conduct a transaction electronically, even if the person has conducted transactions electronically in the past. The effectiveness of a party's refusal to conduct a transaction electronically will be determined under other applicable law in light of all surrounding circumstances. Such circumstances must include an assessment of the transaction involved.

A party's right to decline to act electronically under a specific contract, on the ground that each action under that contract amounts to a separate "transaction," must be considered in light of the purpose of the contract and the action to be taken electronically. For example, under a contract for the purchase of goods, the giving and receipt of notices electronically, as provided in the contract, should not be viewed as discreet transactions. Rather such notices amount to separate actions which are part of the "transaction" of purchase evidenced by the contract. Allowing one party to require a change of medium in the middle of the transaction evidenced by that contract is not the purpose of this subsection. Rather this subsection is intended to preserve the party's right to conduct the next purchase in a non-electronic medium.

7. Subsection (e) is an essential provision in the overall scheme of this Act. While this Act validates and effectuates electronic records and electronic signatures, the legal effect of such records and signatures is left to existing substantive law outside this Act except in very narrow circumstances. See, e.g., Section 16. Even when this Act operates to validate records and signatures in an electronic medium, it expressly preserves the substantive rules of other law applicable to such records. See, e.g., Section 11.

For example, beyond validation of records, signatures and contracts based on the medium used, Section 7 (a) and (b) should not be interpreted as establishing the legal effectiveness of any given record, signature or contract. Where a rule of law requires that the record contain minimum substantive content, the legal effect of such a record will depend on whether the record meets the substantive requirements of other applicable law.Section 8 expressly preserves a number of legal requirements in currently existing law relating to the presentation of information in writing. Although this Act now would allow such information to be presented in an electronic record, Section 8 provides that the other substantive requirements of law must be satisfied in the electronic medium as well.

§ 6. Construction and Application

This [Act] must be construed and applied:

(1) to facilitate electronic transactions consistent with other applicable law;

(2) to be consistent with reasonable practices concerning electronic transactions and with the continued expansion of those practices; and

(3) to effectuate its general purpose to make uniform the law with respect to the subject of this [Act] among States enacting it.

Comment

1. The purposes and policies of this Act are

(a) to facilitate and promote commerce and governmental transactions by validating and authorizing the use of electronic records and electronic signatures;

(b) to eliminate barriers to electronic commerce and governmental transactions resulting from uncertainties relating to writing and signature requirements;

(c) to simplify, clarify and modernize the law governing commerce and governmental transactions through the use of electronic means;

(d) to permit the continued expansion of commercial and governmental electronic practices through custom, usage and agreement of the parties;

(e) to promote uniformity of the law among the States (and worldwide) relating to the use of electronic and similar technological means of effecting and performing commercial and governmental transactions;

(f) to promote public confidence in the validity, integrity and reliability of electronic commerce and governmental transactions; and

(g) to promote the development of the legal and business infrastructure necessary to implement electronic commerce and governmental transactions.

2. This Act has been drafted to permit flexible application consistent with its purpose to validate electronic transactions. The provisions of this Act validating and effectuating the employ of electronic media allow the courts to apply them to new and unforeseen technologies and practices. As time progresses, it is anticipated that what is new and unforeseen today will be commonplace tomorrow. Accordingly, this legislation is intended to set a framework for the validation of media which may be developed in the future and which demonstrate the same qualities as the electronic media contemplated and validated under this Act.

§ 7. Legal Recognition of Electronic Records, Electronic Signatures, and Electronic Contracts

(a) A record or signature may not be denied legal effect or enforceability solely because it is in electronic form.

(b) A contract may not be denied legal effect or enforceability solely because an electronic record was used in its formation.

(c) If a law requires a record to be in writing, an electronic record satisfies the law.

(d) If a law requires a signature, an electronic signature satisfies the law.

Source: UNCITRAL Model Law on Electronic Commerce, Articles 5, 6, and 7.

Comment

1. This section sets forth the fundamental premise of this Act: namely, that the medium in which a record, signature, or contract is created, presented or retained does not affect it's legal significance. Subsections (a) and (b) are designed to eliminate the single element of medium as a reason to deny effect or enforceability to a record, signature, or contract. The fact that the information is set forth in an electronic, as opposed to paper, record is irrelevant.

2. Under Restatement 2d Contracts Section 8, a contract may have legal effect and yet be unenforceable. Indeed, one circumstance where a record or contract may have effect but be unenforceable is in the context of the Statute of Frauds. Though a contract may be unenforceable, the records may have collateral effects, as in the case of a buyer that insures goods purchased under a contract unenforceable under the Statute of Frauds. The insurance company may not deny a claim on the ground that the buyer is not the owner, though the buyer may have no direct remedy against seller for failure to deliver. See Restatement 2d Contracts, Section 8, Illustration 4.

While this section would validate an electronic record for purposes of a statute of frauds, if an agreement to conduct the transaction electronically cannot reasonably be found (See Section 5(b)) then a necessary predicate to the applicability of this Act would be absent and this Act would not validate the electronic record. Whether the electronic record might be valid under other law is not addressed by this Act.

3. Subsections (c) and (d) provide the positive assertion that electronic records and signatures satisfy legal requirements for writings and signatures. The provisions are limited to requirements in laws that a record be in writing or be signed. This section does not address requirements imposed by other law in addition to requirements for writings and signatures See, e.g., Section 8.

Subsections (c) and (d) are particularized applications of subsection (a). The purpose is to validate and effectuate electronic records and signatures as the equivalent of writings, subject to all of the rules applicable to the efficacy of a writing, except as such other rules are modified by the more specific provisions of this Act.

Illustration 1: A sends the following email to B: "I hereby offer to buy widgets from you, delivery next Tuesday./s/ A." B responds with the following email: "I accept your offer to buy widgets for delivery next Tuesday./s/ B." The emails may not be denied effect solely because they are electronic. In addition, the emails do qualify as records under the Statute of Frauds. However, because there is no quantity stated in either record, the parties' agreement would be unenforceable under existing UCC Section 2201(1).

Illustration 2: A sends the following email to B: "I hereby offer to buy 100 widgets for $1000, delivery next Tuesday./s/ A." B responds with the following email: "I accept your offer to purchase 100 widgets for $1000, delivery next Tuesday./ s/ B." In this case the analysis is the same as in Illustration 1 except that here the records otherwise satisfy the requirements of UCC Section 2-201(1). The transaction may not be denied legal effect solely because there is not a pen and ink "writing" or "signature."

4. Section 8 addresses additional requirements imposed by other law which may affect the legal effect or enforceability of an electronic record in a particular case. For example, in Section 8(a) the legal requirement addressed is *the provision of information* in writing. The section then sets forth the standards to be applied in determining whether the provision of information by an electronic record is the equivalent of the provision of information in writing. The requirements in Section 8 are in addition to the bare validation that occurs under this section.

5. Under the substantive law applicable to a particular transaction within this Act, the legal effect of an electronic record may be separate from the issue of whether the record contains a signature. For example, where notice must be given as part of a contractual obligation, the effectiveness of the notice will turn on whether the party provided the notice regardless of whether the notice was signed (See Section 15). An electronic record attributed to a party under Section 9 and complying with the requirements of Section 15 would suffice in that case, notwithstanding that it may not contain an electronic signature.

§ 8. Provision of Information in Writing; Presentation of Records

(a) If parties have agreed to conduct a transaction by electronic means and a law requires a person to provide, send, or deliver information in writing to another person, the requirement is satisfied if the information is provided, sent, or delivered, as the case may be, in an electronic record capable of retention by the recipient at the time of receipt. An electronic record is not capable of retention by the recipient if the sender or its information processing system inhibits the ability of the recipient to print or store the electronic record.

(b) If a law other than this [Act] requires a record (i) to be posted or displayed in a certain manner, (ii) to be sent, communicated, or transmitted by a specified method, or (iii) to contain information that is formatted in a certain manner, the following rules apply:

(1) The record must be posted or displayed in the manner specified in the other law.

(2) Except as otherwise provided in subsection (d)(2), the record must be sent, communicated, or transmitted by the method specified in the other law.

(3) The record must contain the information formatted in the manner specified in the other law.

(c) If a sender inhibits the ability of a recipient to store or print an electronic record, the electronic record is not enforceable against the recipient.

(d) The requirements of this section may not be varied by agreement, but:

(1) to the extent a law other than this [Act] requires information to be provided, sent, or delivered in writing but permits that requirement to be varied by agreement, the requirement under subsection (a) that the information be in the form of an electronic record capable of retention may also be varied by agreement; and

(2) a requirement under a law other than this [Act] to send, communicate, or transmit a record by [first-class mail, postage prepaid] [regular United States mail], may be varied by agreement to the extent permitted by the other law.

Source: Canadian-Uniform Electronic Commerce Act

Comment

1. This section is a savings provision, designed to assure, consistent with the fundamental purpose of this Act, that otherwise applicable substantive law will not be overridden by this Act. The section makes clear that while the pen and ink provisions of such other law may be satisfied electronically, nothing in this Act vitiates the other requirements of such laws. The section addresses a number of issues related to disclosures and notice provisions in other laws.

2. This section is independent of the prior section. Section 7 refers to legal requirements for a writing. This section refers to legal requirements for the provision of information in writing or relating to the method or manner of presentation or delivery of information. The section addresses more specific legal requirements of other laws, provides standards for satisfying the more particular legal requirements, and defers to other law for satisfaction of requirements under those laws.

3. Under subsection (a), to meet a requirement of other law that information be provided in writing, the recipient of an electronic record of the information must be able to get to the electronic record and read it, and must have the ability to get back to the information in some way at a later date. Accordingly, the section requires that the electronic record be capable of retention for later review.

The section specifically provides that any inhibition on retention imposed by the sender or the sender's system will preclude satisfaction of this section. Use of technological means now existing or later developed which prevents the recipient from retaining a copy the information would result in a determination that information has not been provided under subsection (a). The policies underlying laws requiring the provision of information in writing warrant the imposition of an additional burden on the sender to make the information available in a manner which will permit subsequent reference. A difficulty does exist for senders of information because of the disparate systems of their recipients and the capabilities of those systems. However, in order to satisfy the *legal requirement* of other law to make information available, the sender must assure that the recipient receives and can retain the information. However, it is left for the courts to determine whether the sender has complied with this subsection if evidence demonstrates that it is something peculiar to the recipient's system which precludes subsequent reference to the information.

4. Subsection (b) is a savings provision for laws which provide for the means of delivering or displaying information and which are not affected by the Act. For example, if a law requires delivery of notice by first class US mail, that means of delivery would not be affected by this Act. The information to be delivered may be provided on a disc, i.e., in electronic form, but the particular means of delivery must still be via the US postal service. Display, delivery and formatting requirements will continue to be applicable to electronic records and signatures. If those legal requirements can be satisfied in an electronic medium, e.g., the information can be presented in the equivalent of 20 point bold type as required by other law, this Act will validate the use of the medium, leaving to the other applicable law the question of whether the particular electronic record meets the other legal requirements. If a law requires that particular records be delivered together, or attached to other records, this Act does not preclude the delivery of the records together in an electronic communication, so long as the records are connected or associated with each other in a way determined to satisfy the other law.

5. Subsection (c) provides incentives for senders of information to use systems which will not inhibit the other party from retaining the information. However, there are circumstances where a party providing certain information may wish to inhibit retention in order to protect intellectual property rights or prevent the other party from retaining confidential information about the sender. In such cases inhibition is understandable, but if the sender wishes to enforce the record in which the information is contained, the sender may not inhibit its retention by the recipient. Unlike subsection (a), subsection (c) applies in all transactions and simply provides for unenforceability against the recipient. Subsection (a) applies only where another law imposes the writing requirement, and subsection (a) imposes a broader responsibility on the sender to assure retention capability by the recipient.

6. The protective purposes of this section justify the non-waivability provided by subsection (d). However, since the requirements for sending and formatting and the like are imposed by other law, to the extent other law permits waiver of such protections, there is no justification for imposing a more severe burden in an electronic environment.

§ 9. Attribution and Effect of Electronic Record and Electronic Signature

(a) An electronic record or electronic signature is attributable to a person if it was the act of the person. The act of the person may be shown in any manner, including a showing of the efficacy of any security procedure applied to determine the person to which the electronic record or electronic signature was attributable.

(b) The effect of an electronic record or electronic signature attributed to a person under subsection (a) is determined from the context and surrounding circumstances at the time of its creation, execution, or adoption, including the parties' agreement, if any, and otherwise as provided by law.

Comment

1. Under subsection (a), so long as the electronic record or electronic signature resulted from a person's action it will be attributed to that person B the legal effect of that attribution is addressed in subsection (b). This section does not alter existing rules of law regarding attribution. The section assures that such rules will be applied in the electronic environment. A person's actions include actions taken by human agents of the person, as well as actions taken by an electronic agent, i.e., the tool, of the person. Although the rule may appear to state the obvious, it assures that the record or signature is not ascribed to a machine, as opposed to the person operating or programming the machine.

In each of the following cases, both the electronic record and electronic signature would be attributable to a person under subsection (a):

A. The person types his/her name as part of an email purchase order;
B. The person's employee, pursuant to authority, types the person's name as part of an email purchase order;
C. The person's computer, programmed to order goods upon receipt of inventory information within particular parameters, issues a purchase order which includes the person's name, or other identifying information, as part of the order.

In each of the above cases, law other than this Act would ascribe both the signature and the action to the person if done in a paper medium. Subsection (a) expressly provides that the same result will occur when an electronic medium is used.

2. Nothing in this section affects the use of a signature as a device for attributing a record to a person. Indeed, a signature is often the primary method for attributing a record to a person. In the foregoing examples, once the electronic signature is attributed to the person, the electronic record would also be attributed to the person, unless the person established fraud, forgery, or other invalidating cause. However, a signature is not the only method for attribution.

3. The use of facsimile transmissions provides a number of examples of attribution using information other than a signature. A facsimile may be attributed to a person because of the information printed across the top of the page that indicates the machine from which it was sent. Similarly, the transmission may contain a letterhead which identifies the sender. Some cases have held that the letterhead actually constituted a signature because it was a symbol adopted by the sender with intent to authenticate the facsimile. However, the signature determination resulted from the necessary finding of intention in that case. Other cases have found facsimile letterheads NOT to be signatures because the requisite intention was not present. The critical point is that with or without a signature, information within the electronic record may well suffice to provide the facts resulting in attribution of an electronic record to a particular party.

In the context of attribution of records, normally the content of the record will provide the necessary information for a finding of attribution. It is also possible that an established course of dealing between parties may result in a finding of attribution Just as with a paper record, evidence of forgery or counterfeiting may be introduced to rebut the evidence of attribution.

4. Certain information may be present in an electronic environment that does not appear to attribute but which clearly links a person to a particular record. Numerical codes, personal identification numbers, public and private key combinations all serve to establish the party to whom an electronic record should be attributed. Of course security procedures will be another piece of evidence available to establish attribution.

The inclusion of a specific reference to security procedures as a means of proving attribution is salutary because of the unique importance of security procedures in the electronic environment. In certain processes, a technical and technological security procedure may be the best way to convince a trier of fact that a particular electronic record or signature was that of a particular person. In certain circumstances, the use of a security procedure to establish that the record and related signature came from the person's business might be necessary to overcome a claim that a hacker intervened. The reference to security procedures is not intended to suggest that other forms of proof of attribution should be accorded less persuasive effect. It is also important to recall that the particular strength of a given procedure does not affect the procedure's status as a security procedure, but only affects the weight to be accorded the evidence of the security procedure as tending to establish attribution.

5. This section does apply in determining the effect of a "click-through" transaction. A "click-through" transaction involves a process which, if executed with an intent to "sign," will be an electronic signature. See definition of Electronic Signature. In the context of an anonymous "click-through," issues of proof will be paramount. This section will be relevant to establish that the resulting electronic record is attributable to a particular person upon the requisite proof, including security procedures which may track the source of the click-through.

6. Once it is established that a record or signature is attributable to a particular party, the effect of a record or signature must be determined in light of the context and surrounding circumstances, including the parties' agreement, if any. Also informing the effect of any attribution will be other legal requirements considered in light of the context. Subsection (b) addresses the effect of the record or signature once attributed to a person.

§ 10. Effect of Change or Error

If a change or error in an electronic record occurs in a transmission between parties to a transaction, the following rules apply:

(1) If the parties have agreed to use a security procedure to detect changes or errors and one party has conformed to the procedure, but the other party has not, and the nonconforming party would have detected the change or error had that party also conformed, the conforming party may avoid the effect of the changed or erroneous electronic record.

(2) In an automated transaction involving an individual, the individual may avoid the effect of an electronic record that resulted from an error made by the individual in dealing with the electronic agent of another person if the electronic agent did not provide an opportunity for the prevention or correction of the error and, at the time the individual learns of the error, the individual:

(A) promptly notifies the other person of the error and that the individual did not intend to be bound by the electronic record received by the other person;

(B) takes reasonable steps, including steps that conform to the other person's reasonable instructions, to return to the other person or, if instructed by the other person, to destroy the consideration received, if any, as a result of the erroneous electronic record; and

(C) has not used or received any benefit or value from the consideration, if any, received from the other person.

(3) If neither paragraph (1) nor paragraph (2) applies, the change or error has the effect provided by other law, including the law of mistake, and the parties' contract, if any.

(4) Paragraphs (2) and (3) may not be varied by agreement.

Source: Restatement 2d Contracts, Sections 152–155.

Comment

1. This section is limited to changes and errors occurring in transmissions between parties—whether person-person (paragraph 1) or in an automated transaction involving an individual and a machine (paragraphs 1 and 2). The section focuses on the effect of changes and errors occurring when records are exchanged between parties. In cases where changes and errors occur in contexts other than transmission, the law of mistake is expressly made applicable to resolve the conflict.

The section covers both changes and errors. For example, if Buyer sends a message to Seller ordering 100 widgets, but Buyer's information processing system changes the order to 1000 widgets, a "change" has occurred between what Buyer transmitted and what Seller received. If on the other hand, Buyer typed in 1000 intending to order only 100, but sent the message before noting the mistake, an error would have occurred which would also be covered by this section.

2. Paragraph (1) deals with any transmission where the parties have agreed to use a security procedure to detect changes and errors. It operates against the non-conforming party, i.e., the party in the best position to have avoided the change or error, regardless of whether that person is the sender or recipient. The source of the error/change is not indicated, and so both human and machine errors/changes would be covered. With respect to errors or changes that would not be detected by the security procedure even if applied, the parties are left to the general law of mistake to resolve the dispute.

3. Paragraph (1) applies only in the situation where a security procedure would detect the error/change but one party fails to use the procedure and does not detect the error/change. In such a case, consistent with the law of mistake generally, the record is made avoidable at the instance of the party who took all available steps to avoid the mistake. See Restatement 2d Contracts Sections 152–154.

Making the erroneous record avoidable by the conforming party is consistent with Sections 153 and 154 of the Restatement 2d Contracts because the non-conforming party was in the best position to avoid the problem, and would bear the risk of mistake. Such a case would constitute mistake by one party. The mistaken party (the conforming party) would be entitled to avoid any resulting contract under Section 153 because s/he does not have the risk of mistake and the non-conforming party had reason to know of the mistake.

4. As with paragraph (1), paragraph (2), when applicable, allows the mistaken party to avoid the effect of the erroneous electronic record. However, the subsection is limited to human error on the part of an individual when dealing with the electronic agent of the other party. In a transaction between individuals there is a greater ability to correct the error before parties have acted on it. However, when an individual makes an error while dealing with the electronic agent of the other party, it may not be possible to correct the error before the other party has shipped or taken other action in reliance on the erroneous record.

Paragraph (2) applies only to errors made by individuals. If the error results from the electronic agent, it would constitute a system error. In such a case the effect of that error would be resolved under paragraph (1) if applicable, otherwise under paragraph (3) and the general law of mistake.

5. The party acting through the electronic agent/ machine is given incentives by this section to build in safeguards which enable the individual to prevent the sending of an erroneous record, or correct the error once sent. For example, the electronic agent may be programed to provide a "confirmation screen" to the individual setting forth all the information the individual initially approved. This would provide the individual with the ability to prevent the erroneous record from ever being sent. Similarly, the electronic agent might receive the record sent by the individual and then send back a confirmation which the individual must again accept before the transaction is completed. This would allow for correction of an erroneous record. In either case, the electronic agent would "provide an opportunity for prevention or correction of the error," *and the subsection would not apply*. Rather, the affect of any error is governed by other law.

6. Paragraph (2) also places additional requirements on the mistaken individual before the paragraph may be invoked to avoid an erroneous electronic record. The individual must take prompt action to advise the other party of the error and the fact that the individual did not intend the electronic record. Whether the action is prompt must be determined from all the circumstances including the individual's ability to contact the other party. The individual should advise the other party both of the error and of the lack of intention to be bound (i.e., avoidance) by the electronic record received. Since this provision allows avoidance by the mistaken party, that party should also be required to expressly note that it is seeking to avoid the electronic record, i.e., lacked the intention to be bound.

Second, restitution is normally required in order to undo a mistaken transaction. Accordingly, the individual must also return or destroy any consideration received, adhering to instructions from the other party in any case. This is to assure that the other party retains control over the consideration sent in error.

Finally, and most importantly in regard to transactions involving intermediaries which may be harmed because transactions cannot be unwound, the individual cannot have received any benefit from the transaction. This section prevents a party from unwinding a transaction after the delivery of value and consideration which cannot be returned or destroyed. For example, if the consideration received is information, it may not be possible to avoid the benefit conferred. While the information itself could be returned, mere access to the information, or the ability to redistribute the information would constitute a benefit precluding the mistaken party from unwinding the transaction. It may also occur that the mistaken party receives consideration which changes in value between the time of receipt and the first opportunity to return. In such a case restitution cannot be made adequately, and the transaction would not be avoidable. In each of the foregoing cases, under subparagraph (2)(c), the individual would have received the benefit of the consideration and would NOT be able to avoid the erroneous electronic record under this section.

7. In all cases not covered by paragraphs (1) or (2), where error or change to a record occur, the parties contract, or other law, specifically including the law of mistake, applies to resolve any dispute. In the event that the parties' contract and other law would achieve different results, the construction of the parties' contract is left to the other law. If the error occurs in the context of record retention, Section 12 will apply. In that case the standard is one of accuracy and retrievability of the information.

8. Paragraph (4) makes the error correction provision in paragraph (2) and the application of the law of mistake in paragraph (3) non-variable. Paragraph (2) provides incentives for parties using electronic agents to establish safeguards for individuals dealing with them. It also avoids unjustified windfalls to the individual by erecting stringent requirements before the individual may exercise the right of avoidance under the paragraph. Therefore, there is no reason to permit parties to avoid the paragraph by agreement. Rather, parties should satisfy the paragraph's requirements.

§ 11. Notarization and Acknowledgment

If a law requires a signature or record to be notarized, acknowledged, verified, or made under oath, the requirement is satisfied if the electronic signature of the person authorized to perform those acts, together with all other information required to be included by other applicable law, is attached to or logically associated with the signature or record.

Comment

This section permits a notary public and other authorized officers to act electronically, effectively removing the stamp/ seal requirements. However, the section does not eliminate any of the other requirements of notarial laws, and consistent with the entire thrust of this Act, simply allows the signing and information to be accomplished in an electronic medium.

For example, Buyer wishes to send a notarized Real Estate Purchase Agreement to Seller via email. The notary must appear in the room with the Buyer, satisfy him/herself as to the identity of the Buyer, and swear to that identification. All that activity must be reflected as part of the electronic Purchase Agreement and the notary's electronic signature must appear as a part of the electronic real estate purchase contract.

As another example, Buyer seeks to send Seller an affidavit averring defects in the products received. A court clerk, authorized under state law to administer oaths, is present with Buyer in a room. The Clerk administers the oath and includes the statement of the oath, together with any other requisite information, in the electronic record to be sent to the Seller. Upon administering the oath and witnessing the application of Buyer's electronic signature to the electronic record, the Clerk also applies his electronic signature to the electronic record. So long as all substantive requirements of other applicable law have been fulfilled and are reflected in the electronic record, the sworn electronic record of Buyer is as effective as if it had been transcribed on paper.

§ 12. Retention of Electronic Records; Originals

(a) If a law requires that a record be retained, the requirement is satisfied by retaining an electronic record of the information in the record which:

(1) accurately reflects the information set forth in the record after it was first generated in its final form as an electronic record or otherwise; and

(2) remains accessible for later reference.

(b) A requirement to retain a record in accordance with subsection (a) does not apply to any information the sole purpose of which is to enable the record to be sent, communicated, or received.

(c) A person may satisfy subsection (a) by using the services of another person if the requirements of that subsection are satisfied.

(d) If a law requires a record to be presented or retained in its original form, or provides consequences if the record is not presented or retained in its original form, that law is satisfied by an electronic record retained in accordance with subsection (a).

(e) If a law requires retention of a check, that requirement is satisfied by retention of an electronic record of the information on the front and back of the check in accordance with subsection (a).

(f) A record retained as an electronic record in accordance with subsection (a) satisfies a law requiring a person to retain a record for evidentiary, audit, or like purposes, unless a law enacted after the effective date of this [Act] specifically prohibits the use of an electronic record for the specified purpose.

(g) This section does not preclude a governmental agency of this State from specifying additional requirements for the retention of a record subject to the agency's jurisdiction.

Source: UNCITRAL Model Law On Electronic Commerce Articles 8 and 10.

Comment

1. This section deals with the serviceability of electronic records as retained records and originals. So long as there exists reliable assurance that the electronic record accurately reproduces the information, this section continues the theme of establishing the functional equivalence of electronic and paper-based records. This is consistent with Fed. R. Evid. 1001(3) and Unif. R. Evid. 1001(3) (1974). This section assures that information stored electronically will remain effective for all audit, evidentiary, archival and similar purposes.

2. In an electronic medium, the concept of an original document is problematic. For example, as one drafts a document on a computer the "original" is either on a disc or the hard drive to which the document has been initially saved. If one periodically saves the draft, the fact is that at times a document may be first saved to disc then to hard drive, and at others vice versa. In such a case the "original" may change from the information on the disc to the information on the hard drive. Indeed, it may be argued that the "original" exists solely in RAM and, in a sense, the original is destroyed when a "copy" is saved to a disc or to the hard drive. In any event, in the context of record retention, the concern focuses on the integrity of the information, and not with its "originality."

3. Subsection (a) requires accuracy and the ability to access at a later time. The requirement of accuracy is derived from the Uniform and Federal Rules of Evidence. The requirement of continuing accessibility addresses the issue of technology obsolescence and the need to update and migrate information to developing systems. It is not unlikely that within the span of 510 years (a period during which retention of much information is required) a corporation may evolve through one or more generations of technology. More to the point, this technology may be incompatible with each other necessitating the reconversion of information from one system to the other.

For example, certain operating systems from the early 1980's, e.g., memory typewriters, became obsolete with the development of personal computers. The information originally stored on the memory typewriter would need to be converted to the personal computer system in a way meeting the standards for accuracy contemplated by this section. It is also possible that the medium on which the information is stored is less stable. For example, information stored on floppy discs is generally less stable, and subject to a greater threat of disintegration, than information stored on a computer hard drive. In either case, the continuing accessibility issue must be satisfied to validate information stored by electronic means under this section.

This section permits parties to convert original written records to electronic records for retention so long as the requirements of subsection (a) are satisfied. Accordingly, in the absence of specific requirements to retain written records, written records may be destroyed once saved as electronic records satisfying the requirements of this section.

The subsection refers to the information contained in an electronic record, rather than relying on the term electronic record, as a matter of clarity that the critical aspect in retention is the information itself. What information must be retained is determined by the purpose for which the information is needed. If the addressing and pathway information regarding an email is relevant, then that information should also be retained. However if it is the substance of the email that is relevant, only that information need be retained. Of course, wise record retention would include all such information since what information will be relevant at a later time will not be known.

4. Subsections (b) and (c) simply make clear that certain ancillary information or the use of third parties, does not affect the serviceability of records and information retained electronically. Again, the relevance of particular information will not be known until that information is required at a subsequent time.

5. Subsection (d) continues the theme of the Act as validating electronic records as originals where the law requires retention of an original. The validation of electronic records and electronic information as originals is consistent with the Uniform Rules of Evidence. See Uniform Rules of Evidence 1001(3), 1002, 1003 and 1004.

6. Subsection (e) specifically addresses particular concerns regarding check retention statutes in many jurisdictions. A Report compiled by the Federal Reserve Bank of Boston identifies hundreds of state laws which require the retention or production of original canceled checks. Such requirements preclude banks and their customers from realizing the benefits and efficiencies related to truncation processes otherwise validated under current law. The benefits to banks and their customers from electronic check retention are effectuated by this provision.

7. Subsections (f) and (g) generally address other record retention statutes. As with check retention, all businesses and individuals may realize significant savings from electronic record retention. So long as the standards in Section 12 are satisfied, this section permits all parties to obtain those benefits. As always the government may require records in any medium, however, these subsections require a governmental agency to specifically identify the types of records and requirements that will be imposed.

§ 13. Admissibility in Evidence

In a proceeding, evidence of a record or signature may not be excluded solely because it is in electronic form.

Source: UNCITRAL Model Law on Electronic Commerce Article 9.

Comment

Like Section 7, this section prevents the nonrecognition of electronic records and signatures solely on the ground of the media in which information is presented.

Nothing in this section relieves a party from establishing the necessary foundation for the admission of an electronic record. See Uniform Rules of Evidence 1001(3), 1002,1003 and 1004.

§ 14. Automated Transaction

In an automated transaction, the following rules apply:

(1) A contract may be formed by the interaction of electronic agents of the parties, even if no individual was aware of or reviewed the electronic agents' actions or the resulting terms and agreements.

(2) A contract may be formed by the interaction of an electronic agent and an individual, acting on the individual's own behalf or for another person, including by an interaction in which the individual performs actions that the individual is free to refuse to perform and which the individual knows or has reason to know will cause the electronic agent to complete the transaction or performance.

(3) The terms of the contract are determined by the substantive law applicable to it.

Source: UNCITRAL Model Law on Electronic Commerce Article 11.

Comment

1. This section confirms that contracts can be formed by machines functioning as electronic agents for parties to a transaction. It negates any claim that lack of human intent, at the time of contract formation, prevents contract formation. When machines are involved, the requisite intention flows from the programing and use of the machine. As in other cases, these are salutary provisions consistent with the fundamental purpose of the Act to remove barriers to electronic transactions while leaving the substantive law, e.g., law of mistake, law of contract formation, unaffected to the greatest extent possible.

2. The process in paragraph (2) validates an anonymous click-through transaction. It is possible that an anonymous click-through process may simply result in no recognizable legal relationship, e.g., A goes to a person's website and acquires access without in any way identifying herself, or otherwise indicating agreement or assent to any limitation or obligation, and the owner's site grants A access. In such a case no legal relationship has been created.

On the other hand it may be possible that A's actions indicate agreement to a particular term. For example, A goes to a website and is confronted by an initial screen which advises her that the information at this site is proprietary, that A may use the information for her own personal purposes, but that, by clicking below, A agrees that any other use without the site owner's permission is prohibited. If A clicks "agree" and downloads the information and then uses the information for other, prohibited purposes, should not A be bound by the click? It seems the answer properly should be, and would be, yes.

If the owner can show that the only way A could have obtained the information was from his website, and that the process to access the subject information required that A must have clicked the "I agree" button after having the ability to see the conditions on use, A has performed actions which A was free to refuse, which A knew would cause the site to grant her access, i.e., "complete the transaction." The terms of the resulting contract will be determined under general contract principles, but will include the limitation on A's use of the information, as a condition precedent to granting her access to the information.

3. In the transaction set forth in Comment 2, the record of the transaction also will include an electronic signature. By clicking "I agree" A adopted a process with the intent to "sign," i.e., bind herself to a legal obligation, the resulting record of the transaction. If a "signed writing" were required under otherwise applicable law, this transaction would be enforceable. If a "signed writing" were not required, it may be sufficient to establish that the electronic record is attributable to A under Section 9. Attribution may be shown in any manner reasonable including showing that, of necessity, A could only have gotten the information through the process at the website.

§ 15. Time and Place of Sending and Receipt

(a) Unless otherwise agreed between the sender and the recipient, an electronic record is sent when it:

(1) is addressed properly or otherwise directed properly to an information processing system that the recipient has designated or uses for the purpose of receiving electronic records or information of the type sent and from which the recipient is able to retrieve the electronic record;

(2) is in a form capable of being processed by that system; and

(3) enters an information processing system outside the control of the sender or of a person that sent the electronic record on behalf of the sender or enters a region of the information processing system designated or used by the recipient which is under the control of the recipient.

(b) Unless otherwise agreed between a sender and the recipient, an electronic record is received when:

(1) it enters an information processing system that the recipient has designated or uses for the purpose of receiving electronic records or information of the type sent and from which the recipient is able to retrieve the electronic record; and

(2) it is in a form capable of being processed by that system.

(c) Subsection (b) applies even if the place the information processing system is located is different from the place the electronic record is deemed to be received under subsection (d).

(d) Unless otherwise expressly provided in the electronic record or agreed between the sender and the recipient, an electronic record is deemed to be sent from the sender's place of business and to be received at the recipient's place of business. For purposes of this subsection, the following rules apply:

(1) If the sender or recipient has more than one place of business, the place of business of that person is the place having the closest relationship to the underlying transaction.

(2) If the sender or the recipient does not have a place of business, the place of business is the sender's or recipient's residence, as the case may be.

(e) An electronic record is received under subsection (b) even if no individual is aware of its receipt.

(f) Receipt of an electronic acknowledgment from an information processing system described in subsection (b) establishes that a record was received but, by itself, does not establish that the content sent corresponds to the content received.

(g) If a person is aware that an electronic record purportedly sent under subsection (a), or purportedly received under subsection (b), was not actually sent or received, the legal effect of the sending or receipt is determined by other applicable law. Except to the extent permitted by the other law, the requirements of this subsection may not be varied by agreement.

Source: UNCITRAL Model Law on Electronic Commerce Article 15.

Comment

1. This section provides default rules regarding when and from where an electronic record is sent and when and where an electronic record is received. This section does not address the efficacy of the record that is sent or received. That is, whether a record is unintelligible or unusable by a recipient is a separate issue from whether that record was sent or received. The effectiveness of an illegible record, whether it binds any party, are questions left to other law.

2. Subsection (a) furnishes rules for determining when an electronic record is sent. The effect of the sending and its import are determined by other law once it is determined that a sending has occurred.

In order to have a proper sending, the subsection requires that information be properly addressed or otherwise directed to the recipient. In order to send within the meaning of this section, there must be specific information which will direct the record to the intended recipient. Although mass electronic sending is not precluded, a general broadcast message, sent to systems rather than individuals, would not suffice as a sending.

The record will be considered sent once it leaves the control of the sender, or comes under the control of the recipient. Records sent through email or the internet will pass through many different server systems. Accordingly, the critical element when more than one system is involved is the loss of control by the sender.

However, the structure of many message delivery systems is such that electronic records may actually never leave the control of the sender. For example, within a university or corporate setting, email sent within the system to another faculty member is technically not out of the sender's control since it never leaves the organization's server. Accordingly, to qualify as a sending, the email must arrive at a point where the recipient has control. This section does not address the effect of an electronic record that is thereafter "pulled back," e.g., removed from a mailbox. The analog in the paper world would be removing a letter from a person's mailbox. As in the case of providing information electronically under Section 8, the recipient's ability to receive a message should be judged from the perspective of whether the sender has done any action which would preclude retrieval. This is especially the case in regard to sending, since the sender must direct the record to a system designated or used by the recipient.

3. Subsection (b) provides simply that when a record enters the system which the recipient has designated or uses and to which it has access, in a form capable of being processed by that system, it is received. Keying receipt to a system accessible by the recipient removes the potential for a recipient leaving messages with a server or other service in order to avoid receipt. However, the section does not resolve the issue of how the sender proves the time of receipt.

To assure that the recipient retains control of the place of receipt, subsection (b) requires that the system be specified or used by the recipient, and that the system be used or designated for the type of record being sent. Many people have multiple email addresses for different purposes. Subsection (b) assures that recipients can designate the email address or system to be used in a particular transaction. For example, the recipient retains the ability to designate a home email for personal matters, work email for official business, or a separate organizational email solely for the business purposes of that organization. If A sends B a notice at his home which relates to business, it may not be deemed received if B designated his business address as the sole address for business purposes. Whether actual knowledge upon seeing it at home would qualify as receipt is determined under the otherwise applicable substantive law.

4. Subsections (c) and (d) provide default rules for determining where a record will be considered to have been sent or received. The focus is on the place of business of the recipient and not the physical location of the information processing system, which may bear absolutely no relation to the transaction between the parties. It is not uncommon for users of electronic commerce to communicate from one State to another without knowing the location of information systems through which communication is operated. In addition, the location of certain communication systems may change without either of the parties being aware of the change. Accordingly, where the place of sending or receipt is an issue under other applicable law, e.g., conflict of laws issues, tax issues, the relevant location should be the location of the sender or recipient and not the location of the information processing system.

Subsection (d) assures individual flexibility in designating the place from which a record will be considered sent or at which a record will be considered received. Under subsection (d) a person may designate the place of sending or receipt unilaterally in an electronic record. This ability, as with the ability to designate by agreement, may be limited by otherwise applicable law to places having a reasonable relationship to the transaction.

5. Subsection (e) makes clear that receipt is not dependent on a person having notice that the record is in the person's system. Receipt occurs when the record reaches the designated system whether or not the recipient ever retrieves the record. The paper analog is the recipient who never reads a mail notice.

6. Subsection (f) provides legal certainty regarding the effect of an electronic acknowledgment. It only addresses the fact of receipt, not the quality of the content, nor whether the electronic record was read or "opened."

7. Subsection (g) limits the parties' ability to vary the method for sending and receipt provided in subsections (a) and (b), when there is a legal requirement for the sending or receipt. As in other circumstances where legal requirements derive from other substantive law, to the extent that the other law permits variation by agreement, this Act does not impose any additional requirements, and provisions of this Act may be varied to the extent provided in the other law.

§ 16. Transferable Records

(a) In this section, "transferable record" means an electronic record that:

(1) would be a note under [Article 3 of the Uniform Commercial Code] or a document under [Article 7 of the Uniform Commercial Code] if the electronic record were in writing; and

(2) the issuer of the electronic record expressly has agreed is a transferable record.

(b) A person has control of a transferable record if a system employed for evidencing the transfer of interests in the transferable record reliably establishes that person as the person to which the transferable record was issued or transferred.

(c) A system satisfies subsection (b), and a person is deemed to have control of a transferable record, if the transferable record is created, stored, and assigned in such a manner that:

(1) a single authoritative copy of the transferable record exists which is unique, identifiable, and, except as otherwise provided in paragraphs (4), (5), and (6), unalterable;

(2) the authoritative copy identifies the person asserting control as:

(A) the person to which the transferable record was issued; or

(B) if the authoritative copy indicates that the transferable record has been transferred, the person to which the transferable record was most recently transferred;

(3) the authoritative copy is communicated to and maintained by the person asserting control or its designated custodian;

(4) copies or revisions that add or change an identified assignee of the authoritative copy can be made only with the consent of the person asserting control;

(5) each copy of the authoritative copy and any copy of a copy is readily identifiable as a copy that is not the authoritative copy; and

(6) any revision of the authoritative copy is readily identifiable as authorized or unauthorized.

(d) Except as otherwise agreed, a person having control of a transferable record is the holder, as defined in [Section 1-201(20) of the Uniform Commercial Code], of the transferable record and has the same rights and defenses as a holder of an equivalent record or writing under [the Uniform Commercial Code], including, if the applicable statutory requirements under [Section 3-302(a), 7-501, or 9-308 of the Uniform Commercial Code] are satisfied, the rights and defenses of a holder in due course, a holder to which a negotiable document of title has been duly negotiated, or a purchaser, respectively. Delivery, possession, and indorsement are not required to obtain or exercise any of the rights under this subsection.

(e) Except as otherwise agreed, an obligor under a transferable record has the same rights and defenses as an equivalent obligor under equivalent records or writings under [the Uniform Commercial Code].

(f) If requested by a person against which enforcement is sought, the person seeking to enforce the transferable record shall provide reasonable proof that the person is in control of the transferable record. Proof may include access to the authoritative copy of the transferable record and related business records sufficient to review the terms of the transferable record and to establish the identity of the person having control of the transferable record.

Source: Revised Article 9, Section 9-105.

Comment

1. Paper negotiable instruments and documents are unique in the fact that a tangible token—a piece of paper—actually embodies intangible rights and obligations. The extreme difficulty of creating a unique electronic token which embodies the singular attributes of a paper negotiable document or instrument dictates that the rules relating to negotiable documents and instruments not be simply amended to allow the use of an electronic record for the requisite paper writing. However, the desirability of establishing rules by which business parties might be able to acquire some of the benefits of negotiability in an electronic environment is recognized by the inclusion of this section on Transferable Records.

This section provides legal support for the creation, transferability and enforceability of electronic note and document equivalents, as against the issuer/obligor. The certainty created by the section provides the requisite incentive for industry to develop the systems and processes, which involve significant expenditures of time and resources, to enable the use of such electronic documents.

The importance of facilitating the development of systems which will permit electronic equivalents is a function of cost, efficiency and safety for the records. The storage cost and space needed for the billions of paper notes and documents is phenomenal. Further, natural disasters can wreak havoc on the ability to meet legal requirements for retaining, retrieving and delivering paper instruments. The development of electronic systems meeting the rigorous standards of this section will permit retention of copies which reflect the same integrity as the original. As a result storage, transmission and other costs will be reduced, while security and the ability to satisfy legal requirements governing such paper records will be enhanced.

Section 16 provides for the creation of an electronic record which may be controlled by the holder, who in turn may obtain the benefits of holder in due course and good faith purchaser status. If the benefits and efficiencies of electronic media are to be realized in this industry it is essential to establish a means by which transactions involving paper promissory notes may be accomplished completely electronically. Particularly as other aspects of such transactions are accomplished electronically, the drag on the transaction of requiring a paper note becomes evident. In addition to alleviating the logistical problems of generating, storing and retrieving paper, the mailing and transmission costs associated with such transactions will also be reduced.

2. The definition of transferable record is limited in two significant ways. First, only the equivalent of paper promissory notes and paper documents of title can be created as transferable records. Notes and Documents of Title do not impact the broad systems that relate to the broader payments mechanisms related, for example, to checks. Impacting the check collection system by allowing for "electronic checks" has ramifications well beyond the ability of this Act to address. Accordingly, this Act excludes from its scope transactions governed by UCC Articles 3 and 4. The limitation to promissory note equivalents in Section 16 is quite important in that regard because of the ability to deal with many enforcement issues by contract without affecting such systemic concerns.

Second, not only is Section 16 limited to electronic records which would qualify as negotiable promissory notes or documents if they were in writing, but the issuer of the electronic record must expressly agree that the electronic record is to be considered a transferable record. The definition of transferable record as "an electronic record that . . . the issuer of the electronic record expressly has agreed is a transferable record" indicates that the electronic record itself will likely set forth the issuer's agreement, though it may be argued that a contemporaneous electronic or written record might set forth the issuer's agreement. However, conversion of a paper note issued as such would not be possible because the issuer would not be the issuer, in such a case, of an electronic record. The purpose of such a restriction is to assure that transferable records can only be created at the time of issuance by the obligor. The possibility that a paper note might be converted to an electronic record and then intentionally destroyed, and the effect of such action, was not intended to be covered by Section 16.

The requirement that the obligor expressly agree in the electronic record to its treatment as a transferable record does not otherwise affect the characterization of a transferable record (i.e., does not affect what would be a paper note) because it is a statutory condition. Further, it does not obligate the issuer to undertake to do any other act than the payment of the obligation evidenced by the transferable record. Therefore, it does not make the transferable record "conditional" within the meaning of Section 3-104(a)(3) of the Uniform Commercial Code.

3. Under Section 16 acquisition of "control" over an electronic record serves as a substitute for "possession" in the paper analog. More precisely, "control" under Section 16 serves as the substitute for delivery, indorsement and possession of a negotiable promissory note or negotiable document of title. Section 16(b) allows control to be found so long as "a system employed for evidencing the transfer of interests in the transferable record reliably establishes [the person claiming control] as the person to which the transferable record was issued or transferred." The key point is that a system, whether involving third party registry or technological safeguards, must be shown to reliably establish the identity of *the* person entitled to payment. Section 16(c) then sets forth a safe harbor list of very strict requirements for such a system. The specific provisions listed in Section 16(c) are derived from Section 105 of Revised Article 9 of the Uniform Commercial Code. Generally, the transferable record must be unique, identifiable, and except as specifically permitted, unalterable. That "authoritative copy" must (i) identify the person claiming control as the person to whom the record was issued or most recently transferred, (ii) be maintained by the person claiming control or its designee, and (iii) be unalterable except with the permission of the person claiming control. In addition any copy of the authoritative copy must be readily identifiable as a copy and all revisions must be readily identifiable as authorized or unauthorized.

The control requirements may be satisfied through the use of a trusted third party registry system. Such systems are currently in place with regard to the transfer of securities entitlements under Article 8 of the Uniform Commercial Code, and in the transfer of cotton warehouse receipts under the program sponsored by the United States Department of Agriculture. This Act would recognize the use of such a system so long as the standards of subsection (c) were satisfied. In addition, a technological system which met such exacting standards would also be permitted under Section 16.

For example, a borrower signs an electronic record which would be a promissory note or document if it were paper. The borrower specifically agrees in the electronic record that it will qualify as a transferable record under this section. The lender implements a newly developed technological system which dates, encrypts, and stores all the electronic information in the transferable record in a manner which lender can demonstrate reliably establishes lender as the person to which the transferable record was issued. In the alternative, the lender may contract with a third party to act as a registry for all such transferable records, retaining records establishing the party to whom the record was issued and all subsequent transfers of the record. An example of this latter method for assuring control is the system established for the issuance and transfer of electronic cotton warehouse receipts under 7 C.F.R. section 735 et seq.

Of greatest importance in the system used is the ability to securely and demonstrably be able to transfer the record to others in a manner which assures that only one "holder" exists. The need for such certainty and security resulted in the very stringent standards for a system outlined in subsection (c). A system relying on a third party registry is likely the most effective way to satisfy the requirements of subsection (c) that the transferable record remain unique, identifiable and unalterable, while also providing the means to assure that the transferee is clearly noted and identified.

It must be remembered that Section 16 was drafted in order to provide sufficient legal certainty regarding the rights of those in control of such electronic records, that legal incentives would exist to warrant the development of systems which would establish the requisite control. During the drafting of Section 16, representatives from the Federal Reserve carefully scrutinized the impact of any electronicization of any aspect of the national payment system. Section 16 represents a compromise position which, as noted, serves as a bridge pending more detailed study and consideration of what legal changes, if any, are necessary or appropriate in the context of the payment systems impacted. Accordingly, Section 16 provides limited scope for the attainment of important rights derived from the concept of negotiability, in order to permit the development of systems which will satisfy its strict requirements for control.

4. It is important to note what the section does not provide. Issues related to enforceability against intermediate transferees and transferors (i.e., indorser liability under a paper note), warranty liability that would attach in a paper note, and issues of the effect of taking a transferable record on the underlying obligation, are NOT addressed by this section. Such matters must be addressed, if at all, by contract between and among the parties in the chain of transmission and transfer of the transferable record. In the event that such matters are not addressed by the contract, the issues would need to be resolved under otherwise applicable law. Other law may include general contract principles of assignment and assumption, or may include rules from Article 3 of the Uniform Commercial Code applied by analogy.

For example, Issuer agrees to pay a debt by means of a transferable record issued to A. Unless there is agreement between issuer and A that the transferable record "suspends" the underlying obligation (see Section 3-310 of the Uniform Commercial Code), A would not be prevented from enforcing the underlying obligation without the transferable record. Similarly, if A transfers the transferable record to B by means granting B control, B may obtain holder in due course rights against the obligor/issuer, but B's recourse against A would not be clear unless A agreed to remain liable under the transferable record. Although the rules of Article 3 may be applied by analogy in an appropriate context, in the absence of an express agreement in the transferable record or included by applicable system rules, the liability of the transferor would not be clear.

5. Current business models exist which rely for their efficacy on the benefits of negotiability. A principal example, and one which informed much of the development of Section 16, involves the mortgage backed securities industry. Aggregators of commercial paper acquire mortgage secured promissory notes following a chain of transfers beginning with the origination of the mortgage loan by a mortgage broker. In the course of the transfers of this paper, buyers of the notes and lenders/secured parties for these buyers will intervene. For the ultimate purchaser of the paper, the ability to rely on holder in due course and good faith purchaser status creates the legal security necessary to issue its own investment securities which are backed by the obligations evidenced by the notes purchased. Only through their HIDC status can these purchasers be assured that third party claims will be barred. Only through their HIDC status can the end purchaser avoid the incredible burden of requiring and assuring that each person in the chain of transfer has waived any and all defenses to performance which may be created during the chain of transfer.

6. This section is a stand-alone provision. Although references are made to specific provisions in Article 3, Article 7, and Article 9 of the Uniform Commercial Code, these provisions are incorporated into this Act and made the applicable rules for purposes of this Act. The rights of parties to transferable records are established under subsections (d) and (e). Subsection (d) provides rules for determining the rights of a party in control of a transferable record. The subsection makes clear that the rights are determined under this section, and not under other law, by incorporating the rules on the manner of acquisition into this statute. The last sentence of subsection (d) is intended to assure that requirements related to notions of possession, which are inherently inconsistent with the idea of an electronic record, are not incorporated into this statute.

If a person establishes control, Section 16(d) provides that that person is the "holder" of the transferable record which is equivalent to a holder of an analogous paper negotiable instrument. More importantly, if the person acquired control in a manner which would make it a holder in due course of an equivalent paper record, the person acquires the rights of a HIDC. The person in control would therefore be able to enforce the transferable record against the obligor regardless of intervening claims and defenses. However, by pulling these rights into Section 16, this Act does NOT validate the wholesale electrification of promissory notes under Article 3 of the Uniform Commercial Code.

Further, it is important to understand that a transferable record under Section 16, while having no counterpart under Article 3 of the Uniform Commercial Code, would be an "account," "general intangible," or "payment intangible" under Article 9 of the Uniform Commercial Code. Accordingly, two separate bodies of law would apply to that asset of the obligee. A taker of the transferable record under Section 16 may acquire purchaser rights under Article 9 of the Uniform Commercial Code, however, those rights may be defeated by a trustee in bankruptcy of a prior person in control unless perfection under Article 9 of the Uniform Commercial Code by filing is achieved. If the person in control also takes control in a manner granting it holder in due course status, of course that person would take free of any claim by a bankruptcy trustee or lien creditor.

7. Subsection (e) accords to the obligor of the transferable record rights equal to those of an obligor under an equivalent paper record. Accordingly, unless a waiver of defense clause is obtained in the electronic record, or the transferee obtains HDC rights under subsection (d), the obligor has all the rights and defenses available to it under a contract assignment. Additionally, the obligor has the right to have the payment noted or otherwise included as part of the electronic record.

8. Subsection (f) grants the obligor the right to have the transferable record and other information made available for purposes of assuring the correct person to pay. This will allow the obligor to protect its interest and obtain the defense of discharge by payment or performance. This is particularly important because a person receiving subsequent control under the appropriate circumstances may well qualify as a holder in course who can enforce payment of the transferable record.

9. Section 16 is a singular exception to the thrust of this Act to simply validate electronic media used in commercial transactions. Section 16 actually provides a means for expanding electronic commerce. It provides certainty to lenders and investors regarding the enforceability of a new class of financial services. It is hoped that the legal protections afforded by Section 16 will engender the development of technological and business models which will permit realization of the significant cost savings and efficiencies available through electronic transacting in the financial services industry. Although only a bridge to more detailed consideration of the broad issues related to negotiability in an electronic context, Section 16 provides the impetus for that broader consideration while allowing continuation of developing technological and business models.

§ 17. Creation and Retention of Electronic Records and Conversion of Written Records by Governmental Agencies

[Each governmental agency] [The [designated state officer]] of this State shall determine whether, and the extent to which, [it] [a governmental agency] will create and retain electronic records and convert written records to electronic records.

Comment

See Comments following Section 19.

§ 18. Acceptance and Distribution of Electronic Records by Governmental Agencies

(a) Except as otherwise provided in Section 12(f), [each governmental agency] [the [designated state officer]] of this State shall determine whether, and the extent to which, [it] [a governmental agency] will send and accept electronic records and electronic signatures to and from other persons and otherwise create, generate, communicate, store, process, use, and rely upon electronic records and electronic signatures.

(b) To the extent that a governmental agency uses electronic records and electronic signatures under subsection (a), the [governmental agency] [designated state officer], giving due consideration to security, may specify:

(1) the manner and format in which the electronic records must be created, generated, sent, communicated, received, and stored and the systems established for those purposes;

(2) if electronic records must be signed by electronic means, the type of electronic signature required, the manner and format in which the electronic signature must be affixed to the electronic record, and the identity of, or criteria that must be met by, any third party used by a person filing a document to facilitate the process;

(3) control processes and procedures as appropriate to ensure adequate preservation, disposition, integrity, security, confidentiality, and auditability of electronic records; and

(4) any other required attributes for electronic records which are specified for corresponding non-electronic records or reasonably necessary under the circumstances.

(c) Except as otherwise provided in Section 12(f), this [Act] does not require a governmental agency of this State to use or permit the use of electronic records or electronic signatures.

Source: Illinois Act Section 25-101; Florida Electronic Signature Act, Chapter 96-324, Section 7 (1996).

Comment

See Comments following Section 19.

§ 19. Interoperability

The [governmental agency] [designated officer] of this State which adopts standards pursuant to Section 18 may encourage and promote consistency and interoperability with similar requirements adopted by other governmental agencies of this and other States and the federal government and nongovernmental persons interacting with governmental agencies of this State. If appropriate, those standards may specify differing levels of standards from which governmental agencies of this State may choose in implementing the most appropriate standard for a particular application.

Source: Illinois Act Section 25-115.

See Legislative Note below—Following Comments.

Comment

1. Sections 17–19 have been bracketed as optional provisions to be considered for adoption by each State. Among the barriers to electronic commerce are barriers which exist in the use of electronic media by state governmental agencies—whether among themselves or in external dealing with the private sector. In those circumstances where the government acts as a commercial party, e.g., in areas of procurement, the general validation provisions of this Act will apply. That is to say, the government must agree to conduct transactions electronically with vendors and customers of government services.

However, there are other circumstances when government ought to establish the ability to proceed in transactions electronically. Whether in regard to records and communications within and between governmental agencies, or with respect to information and filings which must be made with governmental agencies, these sections allow a State to establish the ground work for such electronicization.

2. The provisions in Sections 17–19 are broad and very general. In many States they will be unnecessary because enacted legislation designed to facilitate governmental use of electronic records and communications is in place. However, in many States broad validating rules are needed and desired. Accordingly, this Act provides these sections as a baseline.

Of paramount importance in all States however, is the need for States to assure that whatever systems and rules are adopted, the systems established are compatible with the systems of other governmental agencies and with common systems in the private sector. A very real risk exists that implementation of systems by myriad governmental agencies and offices may create barriers because of a failure to consider compatibility, than would be the case otherwise.

3. The provisions in Sections 17–19 are broad and general to provide the greatest flexibility and adaptation to the specific needs of the individual States. The differences and variations in the organization and structure of governmental agencies mandates this approach. However, it is imperative that each State always keep in mind the need to prevent the erection of barriers through appropriate coordination of systems and rules within the parameters set by the State.

4. Section 17 authorizes state agencies to use electronic records and electronic signatures generally for intra-governmental purposes, and to convert written records and manual signatures to electronic records and electronic signatures. By its terms the section gives enacting legislatures the option to leave the decision to use electronic records or convert written records and signatures to the governmental agency or assign that duty to a designated state officer. It also authorizes the destruction of written records after conversion to electronic form.

5. Section 18 broadly authorizes state agencies to send and receive electronic records and signatures in dealing with non-governmental persons. Again, the provision is permissive and not obligatory (see subsection (c)). However, it does provide specifically that with respect to electronic records used for evidentiary purposes, Section 12 will apply unless a particular agency expressly opts out.

6. Section 19 is the most important section of the three. It requires governmental agencies or state officers to take account of consistency in applications and interoperability to the extent practicable when promulgating standards. This section is critical in addressing the concern that inconsistent applications may promote barriers greater than currently exist. Without such direction the myriad systems that could develop independently would be new barriers to electronic commerce, not a removal of barriers. The key to interoperability is flexibility and adaptability. The requirement of a single system may be as big a barrier as the proliferation of many disparate systems.

Legislative Note Regarding Adoption of Sections 17–19

1. Sections 17–19 are optional sections for consideration by individual legislatures for adoption, and have been bracketed to make this clear. The inclusion or exclusion of Sections 17–19 will not have a detrimental impact on the uniformity of adoption of this Act, so long as Sections 1–16 are adopted uniformly as presented. In some States Sections 17–19 will be unnecessary because legislation is already in place to authorize and implement government use of electronic media. However, the general authorization provided by Sections 17–19 may be critical in some States which desire to move forward in this area.

2. In the event that a state legislature chooses to adopt Sections 17–19, a number of issues must be addressed:

A. Is the general authorization to adopt electronic media, provided by Sections 17–19 sufficient for the needs of the particular jurisdiction, or is more detailed and specific authorization necessary? This determination may be affected by the decision regarding the appropriate entity or person to oversee implementation of the use of electronic media (See next paragraph). Sections 17–19 are broad and general in the authorization granted. Certainly greater specificity can be added subsequent to adoption of these sections. The question for the legislature is whether greater direction and specificity is needed at this time. If so, the legislature should not enact Sections 17–19 at this time.

B. Assuming a legislature decides to enact Sections 17–19, what entity or person should oversee implementation of the government's use of electronic media? As noted in each of Sections 17–19, again by brackets, a choice must be made regarding the entity to make critical decisions regarding the systems and rules which will govern the use of electronic media by the State. Each State will need to consider its particular structure and administration in making this determination. However, legislatures are strongly encouraged to make compatibility and interoperability considerations paramount in making this determination.

C. Finally, a decision will have to be made regarding the process by which coordination of electronic systems will occur between the various branches of state government and among the various levels of government within the State. Again this will require consideration of the unique situation in each State.

3. If a State chooses not to enact Sections 17–19, UETA Sections 1–16 will still apply to governmental entities when acting as a "person" engaging in "transactions" within its scope. The definition of transaction includes "governmental affairs." Of course, like any other party, the circumstances surrounding a transaction must indicate that the governmental actor has agreed to act electronically (See Section 5(b)), but otherwise all the provisions of Sections 1–16 will apply to validate the use of electronic records and signatures in transactions involving governmental entities.

If a State does choose to enact Sections 17–19, Sections 1–16 will continue to apply as above. In addition, Sections 17–19 will provide authorization for intra-governmental uses of electronic media. Finally, Sections 17–19 provide a broader authorization for the State to develop systems and procedures for the use of electronic media in its relations with non-governmental entities and persons.

§ 20. Severability Clause

If any provision of this [Act] or its application to any person or circumstance is held invalid, the invalidity does not affect other provisions or applications of this [Act] which can be given effect without the invalid provision or application, and to this end the provisions of this [Act] are severable.

§ 21. Effective Date

This [Act] takes effect____.

UNIFORM MOTOR VEHICLE CERTIFICATE OF TITLE AND ANTI-THEFT ACT

PART 1. DEFINITIONS AND EXCLUSIONS

Section

PART 2. CERTIFICATES OF TITLE

PART 1. DEFINITIONS AND EXCLUSIONS

§ 1. [Definitions]

Except when the context otherwise requires, as used in this act:

(a) "Dealer" means a person engaged in the business of buying, selling, or exchanging vehicles who has an established place of business in this state [and to whom current dealer registration plates have been issued by the Department].

(b) "Department" means the [Department of Motor Vehicles] of this state. [The term includes a [County Clerk] when authorized by the Department to receive a document [or article] on its behalf.]

(c) "Identifying number" means the numbers, and letters if any, on a vehicle designated by the Department for the purpose of identifying the vehicle.

(d) "Implement of husbandry" means a vehicle designed and adapted exclusively for agricultural, horticultural or livestock raising operations or for lifting or carrying an implement of husbandry and in either case not subject to registration if used upon the highways.

(e) "Lienholder" means a person holding a security interest in a vehicle.

(f) To "mail" means to deposit in the United States mail properly addressed and with postage prepaid.

(g) "Owner" means a person, other than a lienholder, having the property in or title to a vehicle. The term includes a person entitled to the use and possession of a vehicle subject to a security interest in another person, but excludes a lessee under a lease not intended as security.

(h) "Person" means a natural person, firm, copartnership, association or corporation.

[(i) "Pole trailer" means a vehicle without motive power designed to be drawn by another vehicle and attached to the towing vehicle by means of a reach, or pole, or by being boomed or otherwise secured to the towing vehicle, and ordinarily used for transporting long or irregularly shaped loads such as logs, poles, pipes, or structural members capable, generally, of sustaining themselves as beams between the supporting connections.]

(j) "Security agreement" means a written agreement which reserves or creates a security interest.

(k) "Security interest" means an interest in a vehicle reserved or created by agreement and which secures payment or performance of an obligation. The term includes the interest of a lessor under a lease intended as security. A security interest is "perfected" when it is valid against third parties generally, subject only to specific statutory exceptions.

(l) "Special mobile equipment" means a vehicle not designed for the transportation of persons or property upon a highway and only incidentally operated or moved over a highway, including but not limited to: ditch digging apparatus, well boring apparatus and road construction and maintenance machinery such as asphalt spreaders, bituminous mixers, bucket loaders, tractors other than truck tractors, ditchers, levelling graders, finishing machines, motor graders, road rollers, scarifiers, earth moving carry-alls and scrapers, power shovels and drag lines, and self-propelled cranes and earth moving equipment. The term does not include house trailers, dump trucks, truck mounted transit mixers, cranes or shovels, or other vehicles designed for the transportation of persons or property to which machinery has been attached.

(m) "State" means a state, territory or possession of the United States, the District of Columbia, the Commonwealth of Puerto Rico, or a province of the Dominion of Canada.

(n) "Vehicle" means a device in, upon, or by which a person or property is or may be transported or drawn upon a highway, except a device moved by human power or used exclusively upon stationary rails or tracks.

§ 2. [Exclusions]

(a) No certificate of title need be obtained for:

(1) A vehicle owned by the United States unless it is registered in this state;

(2) A vehicle owned by a manufacturer or dealer and held for sale, even though incidentally moved on the highway or used for purposes of testing or demonstration; or a vehicle used by a manufacturer solely for testing;

(3) A vehicle owned by a non-resident of this state and not required by law to be registered in this state;

(4) A vehicle regularly engaged in the interstate transportation of persons or property for which a currently effective certificate of title has been issued in another state;

(5) A vehicle moved solely by animal power;

(6) An implement of husbandry;

(7) Special mobile equipment;

[(8) A self-propelled wheel chair or invalid tricycle;]

[(9) A pole trailer.]

(b) Part 3 of this act does not apply to:

(1) A vehicle moved solely by animal power;

(2) An implement of husbandry;

(3) Special mobile equipment;

(4) A self-propelled wheel chair or invalid tricycle.

§ 3. [Excepted Liens and Security Interests[; Buyer from Manufacturer or Dealer]]

This act does not apply to or affect:

(a) A lien given by statute or rule of law to a supplier of services or materials for the vehicle;

(b) A lien given by statute to the United States, this state, or any political subdivision of this state;

(c) A security interest in a vehicle created by a manufacturer or dealer who holds the vehicle for sale [but a buyer in the ordinary course of trade from the manufacturer or dealer takes free of the security interest].

PART 2. CERTIFICATES OF TITLE

§ 4. [Certificate of Title Required]

(a) Except as provided in Section 2, every owner of a vehicle which is in this state and for which no certificate of title has been issued by the Department shall make application to the Department for a certificate of title of the vehicle.

(b) The Department shall not register or renew the registration of a vehicle unless an application for a certificate of title has been delivered to the Department.

§ 5. [Optional Certificates of Title]

The owner of an implement of husbandry or special mobile equipment may apply for and obtain a certificate of title on it. All of the provisions of this Part are applicable to a certificate of title so issued, except that a person who receives a transfer of an interest in the vehicle without knowledge of the certificate of title is not prejudiced by reason of the existence of the certificate, and the perfection of a security interest under this act is not effective until the lienholder has complied with the provisions of applicable law which otherwise relate to the perfection of security interests in personal property.

§ 6. [Application for First Certificate of Title]

(a) The application for the first certificate of title of a vehicle in this state shall be made by the owner to the Department on the form it prescribes and shall contain:

(1) The name, residence and mail address of the owner;

(2) A description of the vehicle including, so far as the following data exists: its make, model, identifying number, type of body, the number of cylinders, and whether new or used;

(3) The date of purchase by applicant, the name and address of the person from whom the vehicle was acquired and the names and addresses of any lienholders in the order of their priority and the dates of their security agreements; and

(4) Any further information the Department reasonably requires to identify the vehicle and to enable it to determine whether the owner is entitled to a certificate of title and the existence or non-existence of security interests in the vehicle.

(b) If the application refers to a vehicle purchased from a dealer, it shall contain the name and address of any lienholder holding a security interest created or reserved at the time of the sale and the date of his security agreement and be signed by the dealer as well as the owner, and the dealer shall promptly mail or deliver the application to the Department.

(c) If the application refers to a vehicle last previously registered in another state or country, the application shall contain or be accompanied by:

(1) Any certificate of title issued by the other state or country;

(2) Any other information and documents the Department reasonably requires to establish the ownership of the vehicle and the existence or non-existence of security interests in it; and

(3) The certificate of a person authorized by the Department that the identifying number of the vehicle has been inspected and found to conform to the description given in the application, or any other proof of the identity of the vehicle the Department reasonably requires.

§ 7. [Examination of Records]

The Department, upon receiving application for a first certificate of title, shall check the identifying number of the vehicle shown in the application against the records of vehicles required to be maintained by Section 8 and against the record of stolen and converted vehicles required to be maintained by Section 35.

§ 8. [Issuance and Records]

(a) The Department shall file each application received and, when satisfied as to its genuineness and regularity and that the applicant is entitled to the issuance of a certificate of title, shall issue a certificate of title of the vehicle.

(b) The Department shall maintain a record of all certificates of title issued by it:

(1) Under a distinctive title number assigned to the vehicle;

(2) Under the identifying number of the vehicle;

[(3) Alphabetically, under the name of the owner;]

and, in the discretion of the Department, in any other method it determines.

§ 9. [Contents and Effect]

(a) Each certificate of title issued by the Department shall contain:

(1) The date issued;

(2) The name and address of the owner;

(3) The names and addresses of any lienholders, in the order of priority as shown on the application or, if the application is based on a certificate of title, as shown on the certificate;

(4) The title number assigned to the vehicle;

(5) A description of the vehicle including, so far as the following data exists: its make, model, identifying number, type of body, number of cylinders, whether new or used, and, if a new vehicle, the date of the first sale of the vehicle for use; and

(6) Any other data the Department prescribes.

(b) Unless a bond is filed as provided in Section 11(b), a distinctive certificate of title shall be issued for a vehicle last previously registered in another state or country the laws of which do not require that lienholders be named on a certificate of title to perfect their security interests. The certificate shall contain the legend "This vehicle may be subject to an undisclosed lien" and may contain any other information the Department prescribes. If no notice of a security interest in the vehicle is received by the Department within four (4) months from the issuance of the distinctive certificate of title, it shall, upon application and surrender of the distinctive certificate, issue a certificate of title in ordinary form.

(c) The certificate of title shall contain forms for assignment and warranty of title by the owner, and for assignment and warranty of title by a dealer, and may contain forms for applications for a certificate of title by a transferee, the naming of a lienholder and the assignment or release of the security interest of a lienholder;

(d) A certificate of title issued by the Department is prima facie evidence of the facts appearing on it.

(e) A certificate of title for a vehicle is not subject to garnishment, attachment, execution or other judicial process, but this Subsection does not prevent a lawful levy upon the vehicle.

§ 10. [Delivery]

The certificate of title shall be mailed to the first lienholder named in it or, if none, to the owner.

§ 11. [Registration Without Certificate of Title; Bond]

If the Department is not satisfied as to the ownership of the vehicle or that there are no undisclosed security interests in it, the Department may register the vehicle but shall either:

(a) Withhold issuance of a certificate of title until the applicant presents documents reasonably sufficient to satisfy the Department as to the applicant's ownership of the vehicle and that there are no undisclosed security interests in it; or

(b) As a condition of issuing a certificate of title, require the applicant to file with the Department a bond in the form prescribed by the Department and executed by the application, and either accompanied by the deposit of cash with the Department or also executed by a person authorized to conduct a surety business in this state. The bond shall be in an amount equal to one and one-half times the value of the vehicle as determined by the Department and conditioned to indemnify any prior owner and lienholder and any subsequent purchaser of the vehicle or person acquiring any security interest in it, and their respective successors in interest, against any expense, loss or damage, including reasonable attorney's fees, by reason of the issuance of the certificate of title of the vehicle or on account of any defect in or undisclosed security interest upon the right, title and interest of the applicant in and to the vehicle. Any such interested person has a right of action to recover on the bond for any breach of its conditions, but the aggregate liability of the surety to all persons shall not exceed the amount of the bond. The bond, and any deposit accompanying it, shall be returned at the end of three (3) years or prior thereto if the vehicle is no longer registered in this state and the currently valid certificate of title is surrendered to the Department, unless the Department has been notified of the pendency of an action to recover on the bond.

§ 12. [Refusing Certificate of Title]

The Department shall refuse issuance of a certificate of title if any required fee is not paid or if it has reasonable grounds to believe that:

(a) The applicant is not the owner of the vehicle;

(b) The application contains a false or fraudulent statement; or

(c) The applicant fails to furnish required information or documents or any additional information the Department reasonably requires.

§ 13. [Lost, Stolen, or Mutilated Certificates]

(a) If a certificate of title is lost, stolen, mutilated or destroyed or becomes illegible, the first lienholder or, if none, the owner or legal representative of the owner named in the certificate, as shown by the records of the Department, shall promptly make application for and may obtain a duplicate upon furnishing information satisfactory, to the Department. The duplicate certificate of title shall contain the legend "This is a duplicate certificate and may be subject to the rights of a person under the original certificate." It shall be mailed to the first lienholder named in it or, if none, to the owner.

(b) The Department shall not issue a new certificate of title to a transferee upon application made on a duplicate until fifteen (15) days after receipt of the application.

(c) A person recovering an original certificate of title for which a duplicate has been issued shall promptly surrender the original certificate to the Department.

§ 14. [Transfer]

(a) If an owner transfers his interest in a vehicle, other than by the creation of a security interest, he shall, at the time of the delivery of the vehicle, execute an assignment and warranty of title to the transferee in the space provided therefore on the certificate or as the Department prescribes, and cause the certificate and assignment to be mailed or delivered to the transferee or to the Department.

(b) Except as provided in Section 15, the transferee shall, promptly after delivery to him of the vehicle, execute the application for a new certificate of title in the space provided therefore on the certificate or as the Department prescribes, and cause the certificate and application to be mailed or delivered to the Department.

(c) Upon request of the owner or transferee, a lienholder in possession of the certificate of title shall, unless the transfer was a breach of his security agreement, either deliver the certificate to the transferee for delivery to the Department or, upon receipt from the transferee of the owner's assignment, the transferee's application for a new certificate[, the registration card] [, license plates] and the required fee, mail or deliver them to the Department. The delivery of the certificate does not affect the rights of the lienholder under his security agreement.

(d) If a security interest is reserved or created at the time of the transfer, the certificate of title shall be retained by or delivered to the person who becomes the lienholder, and the parties shall comply with the provisions of Section 21.

(e) Except as provided in Section 15 and as between the parties, a transfer by an owner is not effective until the provisions of this Section [and Section 17] have been complied with [; however, an owner who has delivered possession of the vehicle of the transferee and has complied with the provisions of this Section [and Section 17] requiring action by him is not liable as owner for any damages thereafter resulting from operation of the vehicle].

§ 15. [Transfer to or from Dealer; Records]

(a) If a dealer buys a vehicle and holds it for resale and procures the certificate of title from the owner or the lienholder within ten (10) days after delivery to him of the vehicle, he need not send the certificate to the Department but, upon transferring the vehicle to another person other than by the creation of a security interest, shall promptly execute the assignment and warranty of title by a dealer, showing the names and addresses of the transferee and of any lienholder holding a security interest created or reserved at the time of the resale and the date of his security agreement, in the spaces provided therefore on the certificate or as the Department prescribes, and mail or deliver the certificate to the Department with the transferee's application for a new certificate.

(b) Every dealer shall maintain for five (5) years a record in the form the Department prescribes of every vehicle bought, sold or exchanged by him, or received by him for sale or exchange, which shall be open to inspection by a representative of the Department or peace officer during reasonable business hours.

§ 16. [Transfer by Operation of Law]

(a) If the interest of an owner in a vehicle passes to another other than by voluntary transfer, the transferee shall, except as provided in Subsection (b), promptly mail or deliver to the Department the last certificate of title, if available, proof of the transfer, and his application for a new certificate in the form the Department prescribes.

(b) If the interest of the owner is terminated or the vehicle is sold under a security agreement by a lienholder named in the certificate of title, the transferee shall promptly mail or deliver to the Department the last certificate of title, his application for a new certificate in the form the Department prescribes, and an affidavit made by or on behalf of the lienholder that the vehicle was repossessed and that the interest of the owner was lawfully terminated or sold pursuant to the terms of the security agreement. If the lienholder succeeds to the interest of the owner and holds the vehicle for resale, he need not secure a new certificate of title but, upon transfer to another person, shall promptly mail or deliver to the transferee or to the Department the certificate, affidavit and other documents [and articles] required to be sent to the Department by the transferee.

(c) A person holding a certificate of title whose interest in the vehicle has been extinguished or transferred other than by voluntary transfer shall mail or deliver the certificate to the Department upon request of the Department. The delivery of the certificate pursuant to the request of the Department does not affect the rights of the person surrendering the certificate, and the action of the Department in issuing a new certificate of title as provided herein is not conclusive upon the rights of an owner or lienholder named the old certificate.

§ 17. [Fees[; Registration Cards][; License Plates]]

(a) An application for a certificate of title shall be accompanied by [the registration card][,] [license plates] [and] the required fee when mailed or delivered to the Department.

(b) An application for the naming of a lienholder or his assignee on a certificate of title shall be accompanied by [the registration card and] the required fee when mailed or delivered to the Department.

[(c) A transferor of a vehicle, other than a dealer transferring a new vehicle, shall deliver to the transferee at the time of the delivery of possessi on of the vehicle [the registration card] [and] [license plates] for the vehicle.]

§ 18. [When Department to Issue New Certificate]

(a) The Department, upon receipt of a properly assigned certificate of title, with an application for a new certificate of title, the required fee and any other documents [and articles] required by law, shall issue a new certificate of title in the name of the transferee as owner and mail it to the first lienholder named in it or, if none, to the owner.

(b) The Department, upon receipt of an application for a new certificate of title by a transferee other than by voluntary transfer, with proof of the transfer, the required fee and any other documents [and articles] required by law, shall issue a new certificate of title in the name of the transferee as owner. If the outstanding certificate of title is not delivered to it, the Department shall make demand therefore from the holder thereof.

(c) The Department shall file and retain for [five (5)] years every surrendered I certificate of title, the file to be maintained so as to permit the tracing of title of the vehicle designated therein.

§ 19. [Scrapping, Dismantling, or Destroying Vehicle]

An owner who scraps, dismantles or destroys a vehicle and a person who purchases a vehicle as scrap or to be dismantled or destroyed shall immediately cause the certificate of title to be mailed or delivered to the Department for cancellation. A certificate of title of the vehicle shall not again be issued except upon application containing the information the Department requires accompanied by a certificate of inspection in the form and content specified in Section 6(c)(3).

§ 20. [Perfection of Security Interests]

(a) Unless excepted by Section 3, a security interest in a vehicle of a type for which a certificate of title is required is not valid against creditors of the owner or subsequent transferees or lienholders of the vehicle unless perfected as provided in this act.

(b) A security interest is perfected by the delivery to the Department of the existing certificate of title, if any, an application for a certificate of title containing the name and address of the lienholder and the date of his security agreement and the required fee [and registration card]. It is perfected as of the time of its creation if the delivery is completed within ten (10) days thereafter, otherwise, as of the time of the delivery.

(c) If a vehicle is subject to a security interest when brought into this state, the validity of the security interest is determined by the law of the jurisdiction where the vehicle was when the security interest attached, subject to the following:

(1) If the parties understood at the time the security interest attached that the vehicle would be kept in this state and it was brought into this state within thirty (30) days thereafter for purposes other than transportation through this state, the validity of the security interest in this state is determined by the law of this state.

(2) If the security interest was perfected under the law of the jurisdiction where the vehicle was when the security interest attached, the following rules apply:

(A) If the name of the lienholder is shown on an existing certificate of title issued by that jurisdiction, his security interest continues perfected in this state.

(B) If the name of the lienholder is not shown on an existing certificate of title issued by that jurisdiction, the security interest continues perfected in this state for four (4) months after a first certificate of title of the vehicle is issued in this state, and also, thereafter if, within the four (4) month period, it is perfected in this state. This security interest may also be perfected in this state after the expiration of the four (4) month period; in that case perfection dates from the time of perfection in this state.

(3) If the security interest was not perfected under the law of the jurisdiction where the vehicle was when the security interest attached, it may be perfected in this state; in that case, perfection dates from the time of perfection in this state.

(4) A security interest may be perfected under paragraph (2)(B) or paragraph (3) of this Subsection either as provided in Subsection (b) or by the lienholder delivering to the Department a notice of security interest in the form the Department prescribes and the required fee.

§ 21. [Security Interest]

If an owner creates a security interest in a vehicle:

(a) The owner shall immediately execute the application, in the space provided lienholder on the certificate of title or on a separate form the Department prescribes, to name the lienholder on the certificate, showing the name and address of the lienholder and the date of his security agreement, and cause the certificate, application and the required fee [and registration card] to be delivered to the lienholder.

(b) The lienholder shall immediately cause the certificate, application and the required fee [and registration card] to be mailed or delivered to the Department.

(c) Upon request of the owner or subordinate lienholder, a lienholder in possession of the certificate of title shall either mail or deliver the certificate to the subordinate lienholder for delivery to the Department or, upon receipt from the subordinate lienholder of the owner's application and the required fee [and registration card], mail or deliver them to the Department with the certificate. The delivery of the certificate does not affect the rights of the first lienholder under his security agreement.

(d) Upon receipt of the certificate of title, application and the required fee [and registration card], the Department shall either endorse on the certificate or issue a new certificate containing the name and address of the new lienholder, and mail the certificate to the first lienholder named in it.

§ 22. [Assignment by Lienholder]

(a) A lienholder may assign, absolutely or otherwise, his security interest in the vehicle to a person other than the owner without affecting the interest of the owner or the validity of the security interest, but any person without notice of the assignment is protected in dealing with the lienholder as the holder of the security interest and the lienholder remains liable for any obligations as lienholder until the assignee is named as lienholder on the certificate.

(b) The assignee may, but need not to perfect the assignment, have the certificate of title endorsed or issued with the assignee named as lienholder, upon delivering to the Department the certificate and an assignment by the lienholder named in the certificate in the form the Department prescribes.

§ 23. [Release of Security Interest]

(a) Upon the satisfaction of a security interest in a vehicle for which the certificate of title is in the possession of the lienholder, he shall, within ten (10) days after demand and, in any event, within thirty (30) days, execute a release of his security interest, in the space provided therefore on the certificate or as the Department prescribes, and mail or deliver the certificate and release to the next lienholder named therein, or, if none, to the owner or any person who delivers to the lienholder an authorization from the owner to receive the certificate. The owner, other than a dealer holding the vehicle for resale, shall promptly cause the certificate and release to be mailed or delivered to the Department, which shall release the lienholder's rights on the certificate or issue a new certificate.

(b) Upon the satisfaction of a security interest in a vehicle for which the certificate of title is in the possession of a prior lienholder, the lienholder whose security interest is satisfied shall within ten (10) days after demand and, in any event, within thirty (30) days execute a release in the form the Department prescribes and deliver the release to the owner or any person who delivers to the lienholder an authorization from the owner to receive it. The lienholder in possession of the certificate of title shall either deliver the certificate to the owner, or the person authorized by him, for delivery to the Department, or, upon receipt of the release [and registration card], mail or deliver it [them] with the certificate to the Department, which shall release the subordinate lienholder's rights on the certificate or issue a new certificate.

§ 24. [Duty of Lienholder]

A lienholder named in a certificate of title shall, upon written request of the owner or of another lienholder named on the certificate, disclose any pertinent information as to his security agreement and the indebtedness secured by it.

§ 25. [Exclusiveness of Procedure]

The method provided in this act of perfecting and giving notice of security interests subject to this act is exclusive. Security interests subject to this act are hereby exempted from the provisions of law which otherwise require or relate to the [[recording] [filing] of instruments creating or evidencing security interests ...].

§ 26. [Suspension or Revocation of Certificates]

(a) The Department shall suspend or revoke a certificate of title, upon notice and reasonable opportunity to be heard in accordance with Section 29, when authorized by any other provision of law or if it finds:

(1) The certificate of title was fraudulently procured or erroneously issued, or

(2) The vehicle has been scrapped, dismantled or destroyed.

(b) Suspension or revocation of a certificate of title does not, in itself, affect the validity of a security interest noted on it.

(c) When the Department suspends or revokes a certificate of title, the owner or person in possession of it shall, immediately upon receiving notice of the suspension or revocation, mail or deliver the certificate to the Department.

(d) The Department may seize and impound any certificate of title which has been suspended or revoked.

§ 27. [Fees]

(a) The Department shall be paid the following fees:

(1) For filing an application for a first certificate of title, $________;

(2) For each security interest noted upon a certificate of title, $________;

(3) For a certificate of title after a transfer, $________;

(4) For each assignment of a security interest noted upon a certificate of title, $________;

(5) For a duplicate certificate of title, $________;

(6) For an ordinary certificate of title issued upon surrender of a distinctive certificate, $________;

(7) For filing a notice of security interest, $________; and

(8) For a certificate of search of its records for each name or identifying number searched against, $________.

(b) If an application, certificate of title or other document [or article] required to be mailed or delivered to the Department under any provision of this act is not delivered to the Department within ten (10) days from the time it is required to be mailed or delivered, the Department shall collect, as a penalty, an amount equal to the fee required for the transaction.

§ 28. [Powers of Department]

(a) The Department shall prescribe and provide suitable forms of applications, certificates of title, notices of security interests, and all other notices and forms necessary to carry out the provisions of this act.

(b) The Department may:

(1) Make necessary investigations to procure information required to carry out the provisions of this act;

(2) Adopt and enforce reasonable rules and regulations to carry out the provisions of this act;

(3) Assign a new identifying number to a vehicle if it has none, or its identifying number is destroyed or obliterated, or its motor is changed, and shall either issue a new certificate of title showing the new identifying number or make an appropriate indorsement on the original certificate.

§ 29. [Hearings]

A person aggrieved by an act or omission to act of the Department under this act is entitled, upon request, to a hearing in accordance with [the Administrative Procedure Act of this state] [law].

§ 30. [Court Review]

A person aggrieved by an act or omission to act of the Department under this act is also entitled to a review thereof by the [] Court in accordance with [the Administrative Procedure Act of this state] [law].

UNIFORM VOIDABLE TRANSACTIONS ACT

(Formerly Uniform Fraudulent Transfer Act)
(As Amended in 2014)

§ 1. Definitions

As used in this [Act]:

(1) "Affiliate" means:

(i) a person that directly or indirectly owns, controls, or holds with power to vote, 20 percent or more of the outstanding voting securities of the debtor, other than a person that holds the securities:

(A) as a fiduciary or agent without sole discretionary power to vote the securities; or

(B) solely to secure a debt, if the person has not in fact exercised the power to vote;

(ii) a corporation 20 percent or more of whose outstanding voting securities are directly or indirectly owned, controlled, or held with power to vote, by the debtor or a person that directly or indirectly owns, controls, or holds, with power to vote, 20 percent or more of the outstanding voting securities of the debtor, other than a person that holds the securities:

(A) as a fiduciary or agent without sole discretionary power to vote the securities; or

(B) solely to secure a debt, if the person has not in fact exercised the power to vote;

(iii) a person whose business is operated by the debtor under a lease or other agreement, or a person substantially all of whose assets are controlled by the debtor; or

(iv) a person that operates the debtor's business under a lease or other agreement or controls substantially all of the debtor's assets.

(2) "Asset" means property of a debtor, but the term does not include:

(i) property to the extent it is encumbered by a valid lien;

(ii) property to the extent it is generally exempt under nonbankruptcy law; or

(iii) an interest in property held in tenancy by the entireties to the extent it is not subject to process by a creditor holding a claim against only one tenant.

(3) "Claim", except as used in "claim for relief", means a right to payment, whether or not the right is reduced to judgment, liquidated, unliquidated, fixed, contingent, matured, unmatured, disputed, undisputed, legal, equitable, secured, or unsecured.

(4) "Creditor" means a person that has a claim.

(5) "Debt" means liability on a claim.

(6) "Debtor" means a person that is liable on a claim.

(7) "Electronic" means relating to technology having electrical, digital, magnetic, wireless, optical, electromagnetic, or similar capabilities.

(8) "Insider" includes:

(i) if the debtor is an individual:

(A) a relative of the debtor or of a general partner of the debtor;

(B) a partnership in which the debtor is a general partner;

(C) a general partner in a partnership described in clause (B); or

(D) a corporation of which the debtor is a director, officer, or person in control;

(ii) if the debtor is a corporation:

(A) a director of the debtor;

(B) an officer of the debtor;

(C) a person in control of the debtor;

(D) a partnership in which the debtor is a general partner;

(E) a general partner in a partnership described in clause (D); or

(F) a relative of a general partner, director, officer, or person in control of the debtor;

(iii) if the debtor is a partnership:

(A) a general partner in the debtor;

(B) a relative of a general partner in, a general partner of, or a person in control of the debtor;

(C) another partnership in which the debtor is a general partner;

(D) a general partner in a partnership described in clause (C); or

(E) a person in control of the debtor;

(iv) an affiliate, or an insider of an affiliate as if the affiliate were the debtor; and

(v) a managing agent of the debtor.

(9) "Lien" means a charge against or an interest in property to secure payment of a debt or performance of an obligation, and includes a security interest created by agreement, a judicial lien obtained by legal or equitable process or proceedings, a common-law lien, or a statutory lien.

(10) "Organization" means a person other than an individual.

(11) "Person" means an individual, estate, partnership, association, trust, business or nonprofit entity, public corporation, government or governmental subdivision, agency, or instrumentality, or other legal entity.

(12) "Property" means anything that may be the subject of ownership.

(13) "Record" means information that is inscribed on a tangible medium or that is stored in an electronic or other medium and is retrievable in perceivable form.

(14) "Relative" means an individual related by consanguinity within the third degree as determined by the common law, a spouse, or an individual related to a spouse within the third degree as so determined, and includes an individual in an adoptive relationship within the third degree.

(15) "Sign" means, with present intent to authenticate or adopt a record:

(i) to execute or adopt a tangible symbol; or

(ii) to attach to or logically associate with the record an electronic symbol, sound, or process.

(16) "Transfer" means every mode, direct or indirect, absolute or conditional, voluntary or involuntary, of disposing of or parting with an asset or an interest in an asset, and includes payment of money, release, lease, license, and creation of a lien or other encumbrance.

(17) "Valid lien" means a lien that is effective against the holder of a judicial lien subsequently obtained by legal or equitable process or proceedings.

§ 2. Insolvency

(a) A debtor is insolvent if, at a fair valuation, the sum of the debtor's debts is greater than the sum of the debtor's assets.

(b) A debtor that is generally not paying the debtor's debts as they become due other than as a result of a bona fide dispute is presumed to be insolvent. The presumption imposes on the party against which the presumption is directed the burden of proving that the nonexistence of insolvency is more probable than its existence.

(c) Assets under this section do not include property that has been transferred, concealed, or removed with intent to hinder, delay, or defraud creditors or that has been transferred in a manner making the transfer voidable under this [Act].

(d) Debts under this section do not include an obligation to the extent it is secured by a valid lien on property of the debtor not included as an asset.

§ 3. Value

(a) Value is given for a transfer or an obligation if, in exchange for the transfer or obligation, property is transferred or an antecedent debt is secured or satisfied, but value does not include an unperformed promise made otherwise than in the ordinary course of the promisor's business to furnish support to the debtor or another person.

(b) For the purposes of Section 4(a)(2) and Section 5, a person gives a reasonably equivalent value if the person acquires an interest of the debtor in an asset pursuant to a regularly conducted, noncollusive foreclosure sale or execution of a power of sale for the acquisition or disposition of the interest of the debtor upon default under a mortgage, deed of trust, or security agreement.

(c) A transfer is made for present value if the exchange between the debtor and the transferee is intended by them to be contemporaneous and is in fact substantially contemporaneous.

§ 4. Transfer or Obligation Voidable as to Present or Future Creditor

(a) A transfer made or obligation incurred by a debtor is voidable as to a creditor, whether the creditor's claim arose before or after the transfer was made or the obligation was incurred, if the debtor made the transfer or incurred the obligation:

(1) with actual intent to hinder, delay, or defraud any creditor of the debtor; or

(2) without receiving a reasonably equivalent value in exchange for the transfer or obligation, and the debtor:

(i) was engaged or was about to engage in a business or a transaction for which the remaining assets of the debtor were unreasonably small in relation to the business or transaction; or

(ii) intended to incur, or believed or reasonably should have believed that the debtor would incur, debts beyond the debtor's ability to pay as they became due.

(b) In determining actual intent under subsection (a)(1), consideration may be given, among other factors, to whether:

(1) the transfer or obligation was to an insider;

(2) the debtor retained possession or control of the property transferred after the transfer;

(3) the transfer or obligation was disclosed or concealed;

(4) before the transfer was made or obligation was incurred, the debtor had been sued or threatened with suit;

(5) the transfer was of substantially all the debtor's assets;

(6) the debtor absconded;

(7) the debtor removed or concealed assets;

(8) the value of the consideration received by the debtor was reasonably equivalent to the value of the asset transferred or the amount of the obligation incurred;

(9) the debtor was insolvent or became insolvent shortly after the transfer was made or the obligation was incurred;

(10) the transfer occurred shortly before or shortly after a substantial debt was incurred; and

(11) the debtor transferred the essential assets of the business to a lienor that transferred the assets to an insider of the debtor.

(c) A creditor making a claim for relief under subsection (a) has the burden of proving the elements of the claim for relief by a preponderance of the evidence.

§ 5. Transfer or Obligation Voidable as to Present Creditor

(a) A transfer made or obligation incurred by a debtor is voidable as to a creditor whose claim arose before the transfer was made or the obligation was incurred if the debtor made the transfer or incurred the obligation without receiving a reasonably equivalent value in exchange for the transfer or obligation and the debtor was insolvent at that time or the debtor became insolvent as a result of the transfer or obligation.

(b) A transfer made by a debtor is voidable as to a creditor whose claim arose before the transfer was made if the transfer was made to an insider for an antecedent debt, the debtor was insolvent at that time, and the insider had reasonable cause to believe that the debtor was insolvent.

(c) Subject to Section 2(b), a creditor making a claim for relief under subsection (a) or (b) has the burden of proving the elements of the claim for relief by a preponderance of the evidence.

§ 6. When Transfer Is Made or Obligation Is Incurred

For the purposes of this [Act]:

(1) a transfer is made:

(i) with respect to an asset that is real property other than a fixture, but including the interest of a seller or purchaser under a contract for the sale of the asset, when the transfer is so far perfected that a good-faith purchaser of the asset from the debtor against which applicable law permits the transfer to be perfected cannot acquire an interest in the asset that is superior to the interest of the transferee; and

(ii) with respect to an asset that is not real property or that is a fixture, when the transfer is so far perfected that a creditor on a simple contract cannot acquire a judicial lien otherwise than under this [Act] that is superior to the interest of the transferee;

(2) if applicable law permits the transfer to be perfected as provided in paragraph (1) and the transfer is not so perfected before the commencement of an action for relief under this [Act], the transfer is deemed made immediately before the commencement of the action;

(3) if applicable law does not permit the transfer to be perfected as provided in paragraph (1), the transfer is made when it becomes effective between the debtor and the transferee;

(4) a transfer is not made until the debtor has acquired rights in the asset transferred; and

(5) an obligation is incurred:

(i) if oral, when it becomes effective between the parties; or

(ii) if evidenced by a record, when the record signed by the obligor is delivered to or for the benefit of the obligee.

§ 7. Remedies of Creditor

(a) In an action for relief against a transfer or obligation under this [Act], a creditor, subject to the limitations in Section 8, may obtain:

(1) avoidance of the transfer or obligation to the extent necessary to satisfy the creditor's claim;

(2) an attachment or other provisional remedy against the asset transferred or other property of the transferee if available under applicable law; and

(3) subject to applicable principles of equity and in accordance with applicable rules of civil procedure:

(i) an injunction against further disposition by the debtor or a transferee, or both, of the asset transferred or of other property;

(ii) appointment of a receiver to take charge of the asset transferred or of other property of the transferee; or

(iii) any other relief the circumstances may require.

(b) If a creditor has obtained a judgment on a claim against the debtor, the creditor, if the court so orders, may levy execution on the asset transferred or its proceeds.

§ 8. Defenses, Liability, and Protection of Transferee or Obligee

(a) A transfer or obligation is not voidable under Section 4(a)(1) against a person that took in good faith and for a reasonably equivalent value given the debtor or against any subsequent transferee or obligee.

(b) To the extent a transfer is avoidable in an action by a creditor under Section 7(a)(1), the following rules apply:

(1) Except as otherwise provided in this section, the creditor may recover judgment for the value of the asset transferred, as adjusted under subsection (c), or the amount necessary to satisfy the creditor's claim, whichever is less. The judgment may be entered against:

(i) the first transferee of the asset or the person for whose benefit the transfer was made; or

(ii) an immediate or mediate transferee of the first transferee, other than:

(A) a good-faith transferee that took for value; or

(B) an immediate or mediate good-faith transferee of a person described in clause (A).

(2) Recovery pursuant to Section 7(a)(1) or (b) of or from the asset transferred or its proceeds, by levy or otherwise, is available only against a person described in paragraph (1)(i) or (ii).

(c) If the judgment under subsection (b) is based upon the value of the asset transferred, the judgment must be for an amount equal to the value of the asset at the time of the transfer, subject to adjustment as the equities may require.

(d) Notwithstanding voidability of a transfer or an obligation under this [Act], a good-faith transferee or obligee is entitled, to the extent of the value given the debtor for the transfer or obligation, to:

(1) a lien on or a right to retain an interest in the asset transferred;

(2) enforcement of an obligation incurred; or

(3) a reduction in the amount of the liability on the judgment.

(e) A transfer is not voidable under Section 4(a)(2) or Section 5 if the transfer results from:

(1) termination of a lease upon default by the debtor when the termination is pursuant to the lease and applicable law; or

(2) enforcement of a security interest in compliance with Article 9 of the Uniform Commercial Code, other than acceptance of collateral in full or partial satisfaction of the obligation it secures.

(f) A transfer is not voidable under Section 5(b):

(1) to the extent the insider gave new value to or for the benefit of the debtor after the transfer was made, except to the extent the new value was secured by a valid lien;

(2) if made in the ordinary course of business or financial affairs of the debtor and the insider; or

(3) if made pursuant to a good-faith effort to rehabilitate the debtor and the transfer secured present value given for that purpose as well as an antecedent debt of the debtor.

(g) The following rules determine the burden of proving matters referred to in this section:

(1) A party that seeks to invoke subsection (a), (d), (e), or (f) has the burden of proving the applicability of that subsection.

(2) Except as otherwise provided in paragraphs (3) and (4), the creditor has the burden of proving each applicable element of subsection (b) or (c).

(3) The transferee has the burden of proving the applicability to the transferee of subsection (b)(1)(ii)(A) or (B).

(4) A party that seeks adjustment under subsection (c) has the burden of proving the adjustment.

(h) The standard of proof required to establish matters referred to in this section is preponderance of the evidence.

§ 9. Extinguishment of Claim for Relief

A claim for relief with respect to a transfer or obligation under this [Act] is extinguished unless action is brought:

(a) under Section 4(a)(1), not later than four years after the transfer was made or the obligation was incurred or, if later, not later than one year after the transfer or obligation was or could reasonably have been discovered by the claimant;

(b) under Section 4(a)(2) or 5(a), not later than four years after the transfer was made or the obligation was incurred; or

(c) under Section 5(b), not later than one year after the transfer was made.

§ 10. Governing Law

(a) In this section, the following rules determine a debtor's location:

(1) A debtor who is an individual is located at the individual's principal residence.

(2) A debtor that is an organization and has only one place of business is located at its place of business.

(3) A debtor that is an organization and has more than one place of business is located at its chief executive office.

(b) A claim for relief in the nature of a claim for relief under this [Act] is governed by the local law of the jurisdiction in which the debtor is located when the transfer is made or the obligation is incurred.

§ 11. Application to Series Organization

(a) In this section:

(1) "Protected series" means an arrangement, however denominated, created by a series organization that, pursuant to the law under which the series organization is organized, has the characteristics set forth in paragraph (2).

(2) "Series organization" means an organization that, pursuant to the law under which it is organized, has the following characteristics:

(i) The organic record of the organization provides for creation by the organization of one or more protected series, however denominated, with respect to specified property of the organization, and for records to be maintained for each protected series that identify the property of or associated with the protected series.

(ii) Debt incurred or existing with respect to the activities of, or property of or associated with, a particular protected series is enforceable against the property of or associated with the protected series only, and not against the property of or associated with the organization or other protected series of the organization.

(iii) Debt incurred or existing with respect to the activities or property of the organization is enforceable against the property of the organization only, and not against the property of or associated with a protected series of the organization.

(b) A series organization and each protected series of the organization is a separate person for purposes of this [Act], even if for other purposes a protected series is not a person separate from the organization or other protected series of the organization.

Legislative Note: *This section should be enacted even if the enacting jurisdiction does not itself have legislation enabling the creation of protected series. For example, in such an enacting jurisdiction this section will apply if a protected series of a series organization organized under the law of a different jurisdiction makes a transfer to another protected series of that organization and, under applicable choice of law rules, the voidability of the transfer is governed by the law of the enacting jurisdiction.*

§ 12. Supplementary Provisions

Unless displaced by the provisions of this [Act], the principles of law and equity, including the law merchant and the law relating to principal and agent, estoppel, laches, fraud, misrepresentation, duress, coercion, mistake, insolvency, or other validating or invalidating cause, supplement its provisions.

§ 13. Uniformity of Application and Construction

This [Act] shall be applied and construed to effectuate its general purpose to make uniform the law with respect to the subject of this [Act] among states enacting it.

§ 14. Relation to Electronic Signature in Global and National Commerce Act

This [Act] modifies, limits, or supersedes the Electronic Signatures in Global and National Commerce Act, 15 U.S.C. Section 7001 et seq., but does not modify, limit, or supersede Section 101(c) of that act, 15 U.S.C. Section 7001(c), or authorize electronic delivery of any of the notices described in Section 103(b) of that act, 15 U.S.C. Section 7003(b).

§ 15. Short Title

This [Act], which was formerly cited as the Uniform Fraudulent Transfer Act, may be cited as the Uniform Voidable Transactions Act.

§ 16. Repeals; Conforming Amendments

(a) . . . .

(b) . . . .

(c) . . . .

Legislative Note: *The legislation enacting the 2014 amendments in a jurisdiction in which the act is already in force should provide as follows: (i) the amendments apply to a transfer made or obligation incurred on or after the effective date of the enacting legislation, (ii) the amendments do not apply to a transfer made or obligation incurred before the effective date of the enacting legislation, (iii) the amendments do not apply to a right of action that has accrued before the effective date of the enacting legislation, and (iv) for the foregoing purposes a transfer is made and an obligation is incurred at the time provided in Section 6 of the act. In addition, the enacting legislation should revise any reference to the act by its former title in other permanent legislation of the enacting jurisdiction.*

Restatement of Suretyship

Selected Provisions

§ 15. Interpretation of the Secondary Obligation— Use of Particular Terms

Unless indicated to the contrary by applicable law, the language employed by the parties, agreement of the parties, or the context:

(a) If the parties to a contract identify one party as a "guarantor" or the contract as a "guaranty," the party so identified is a secondary obligor and the secondary obligation is, upon default of the principal obligor on the underlying obligation, to satisfy the obligee's claim with respect to the underlying obligation;

(b) If the parties to a contract identify one party as a "guarantor of collection" or the contract as a "guaranty of collection," the party so identified is a secondary obligor and the secondary obligation is, upon default of the principal obligor, to satisfy the obligee's claim with respect to the underlying obligation, if:

(1) execution of judgment against the principal obligor has been returned unsatisfied; or

(2) the principal obligor is insolvent or in an insolvency proceeding; or

(3) the principal obligor cannot be served with process; or

(4) it is otherwise apparent that payment cannot be obtained from the principal obligor;

(c) if the parties to a contract to which the principal obligor and secondary obligor are both parties identify one party as a "surety," or the contract as a "suretyship" contract, the party so identified is a secondary obligor who is subject to a secondary obligation pursuant to which the secondary obligor is jointly and severally liable with the principal obligor to perform the obligation set forth in that contract;

(d) if the parties to a contract identify one party as a "cosigner," the party so identified is a secondary obligor who is subject to a secondary obligation pursuant to which the secondary obligor is jointly and severally liable with the principal obligor to perform the obligation set forth in that contract;

(e) a contract denominated as a "continuing guaranty" is a contract governed by § 16 pursuant to which a person agrees to be a secondary obligor with respect to subsequent obligations of another person.

§ 21. Principal Obligor's Duty of Performance

(1) If the principal obligor is charged with notice of the secondary obligation (§ 20), the principal obligor has the duty to the secondary obligor

(a) to perform the underlying obligation to the extent that failure to do so would leave the secondary obligor liable for performance that would entitle the secondary obligor to reimbursement by the principal obligor, and

(b) to refrain from conduct that impairs the expectation of the secondary obligor that the principal obligor will honor its duty of performance.

(2) Upon breach by the principal obligor of a duty set forth in subsection (1), the secondary obligor is entitled to relief that will properly protect its rights with respect to the principal obligor's duty of performance.

(3) In cases in which the principal obligor is not charged with notice of the secondary obligation, upon the principal obligor's failure to perform its duties pursuant to the underlying obligation, the secondary obligor is entitled to relief that will properly protect its interest in the principal obligor's performance of that obligation if:

(a) the obligee seeks performance of the secondary obligation; or

(b) continued failure of the principal obligor to perform is likely to increase the cost of performance for which the principal obligor may be liable to the secondary obligor pursuant to §§ 26–28; or

(c) continued failure of the principal obligor to perform will otherwise cause the secondary obligor irreparable harm.

§ 22. Duty of Principal Obligor to Reimburse Secondary Obligor

(1) Except as provided in § 24, when the principal obligor is charged with notice of the secondary obligation it is the duty of the principal obligor to reimburse the secondary obligor to the extent that the secondary obligor:

(a) performs the secondary obligation; or

(b) makes a settlement with the obligee that discharges the principal obligor, in whole or part, with respect to the underlying obligation.

(2) The duty of the principal obligor to reimburse the secondary obligor does not arise until the time for performance, pursuant to the underlying obligation, of the duty satisfied by the secondary obligor's performance or settlement.

§ 27. When Secondary Obligor Has a Right of Subrogation

(1) Upon total satisfaction of the underlying obligation, the secondary obligor is subrogated to all rights of the obligee with respect to the underlying obligation to the extent that performance of the secondary obligation contributed to the satisfaction.

(2) For purposes of subsection (1), an underlying obligation that has been totally satisfied except to the extent of discharge of the secondary obligor from the secondary obligation pursuant to §§ 39–46 is treated as totally satisfied.

§ 28. Rights Obtained Through Subrogation

(1) To the extent that the secondary obligor is subrogated to the rights of the obligee, the secondary obligor may enforce, for its benefit, the rights of the obligee as though the underlying obligation had not been satisfied:

(a) against the principal obligor pursuant to the underlying obligation;

(b) against any other secondary obligor for the same underlying obligation, unless the other secondary obligor is a subsurety for the subrogated secondary obligor;

(c) against any interest in property securing either the obligation of the principal obligor or that of any other secondary obligor against whom the rights of the obligee may be enforced: and

(d) against any other persons whose conduct has made them liable to the obligee with respect to the default on the underlying obligation.

(2) Recovery under this section is limited as follows:

(a) the total recovery of the secondary obligor pursuant to subsection (1) may not exceed the secondary obligor's cost of performance of the secondary obligation;

(b) the enforcement of the obligee's rights against a cosurety, and against any interest in property securing performance of the obligation of a cosurety, is limited to the amount that will satisfy the cosurety's duty of contribution (§ 55).

§ 32. Effect of Suretyship Status on Duties of Secondary Obligor and Obligee; Undisclosed Suretyship Status and Change in Relationship of Parties

(1) The duties of the secondary obligor to the obligee are determined by the contract creating the secondary obligation, subject to defenses resulting from suretyship status (§§ 37–49). The duties of the obligee to the secondary obligor are determined by the contract creating the secondary obligation and by suretyship status (§ 37).

(2) Except as provided in subsection (3), when a person whom the obligee reasonably believes to be a principal obligor is a secondary obligor, the obligee is not affected by the incidents of the secondary obligor's suretyship status until the obligee has notice that the person is a secondary obligor.

(3) To the extent that a person originally obligated to an obligee as a principal obligor becomes a secondary obligor with respect to that obligation:

(a) the obligee is not affected by the incidents of such obligor's suretyship status until the obligee has knowledge that the original obligor has become a secondary obligor; and

(b) if (i) the original obligor furnishes collateral for its obligation before that obligor becomes a secondary obligor, and (ii) the original obligor's interest in that collateral is transferred to a person who becomes a principal obligor, then, until the obligee manifests assent to the original obligor's change of status, the obligee's failure to do any act does not discharge the secondary obligation pursuant to § 42 (impairment of collateral) except to the extent that such failure would have discharged the original obligor if the original obligor had remained a principal obligor.

§ 36. Right of Secondary Obligor to Set Off Claims Against Obligee Against Secondary Obligation

A secondary obligor who has a claim against the obligee that is unrelated to the transaction giving rise to the secondary obligation may set off that claim against the secondary obligation. In such case, the secondary obligor's rights against the principal obligor are those that would exist if the secondary obligor had performed the secondary obligation to the extent of such set-off.

§ 37. Impairment of Suretyship Status

(1) If the obligee acts to increase the secondary obligor's risk of loss by increasing its potential cost of potential cost of performance or decreasing its potential ability to cause the principal obligor to bear the cost of performance, the secondary obligor is discharged as described in subsections (2) and (3), and the secondary obligor has a claim against the obligee as described in subsection (4). An act that increases the secondary obligor's risk of loss by increasing its potential cost of performance or decreasing its potential ability to cause the principal obligor to bear the cost of performance is an "impairment of suretyship status."

(2) If the obligee fundamentally alters the risks imposed on the secondary obligor by:

(a) releasing the principal obligor from a duty other than the payment of money (§ 39(c)(iii)); or

(b) agreeing to a modification of the duties of the principal obligor that either amounts to a substituted contract or imposes risks on the secondary obligor fundamentally different from those imposed on the secondary obligor prior to modification (§ 41(b)(i));

the secondary obligor is discharged from any unperformed portion of the secondary obligation as more fully set forth in those sections.

(3) If the obligee impairs the secondary obligor's recourse against the principal obligor by:

(a) releasing the principal obligor from a duty to pay money (§ 39(c)(ii));

(b) granting the principal obligor an extension of time for performance of its duties pursuant to the underlying obligation (§ 40(b));

(c) agreeing to a modification of the duties of the principal obligor, other than a release or an extension of time, that does not amount to a substituted contract or impose risks on the secondary obligor fundamentally different from those imposed on the secondary obligor prior to modification (§ 41(b)(ii));

(d) impairing the value of an interest in collateral securing the underlying obligation (§ 42);

(e) failing to institute an action before expiration of the statute of limitation s governing the underlying obligation (§ 43); or

(f) any other act or omission that impair the principal obligor's duty of performance, the principal obligor's duty to reimburse, or the secondary obligor's right of restitution or subrogation (§ 44);

the secondary obligor is discharged from its duties pursuant to the secondary obligation to the extent set forth in those sections in order to prevent the impairment of recourse from causing the secondary obligor a loss.

(4) If the obligee impairs the secondary obligor's suretyship status

(a) after the secondary obligor performs any portion of the secondary obligation; or

(b) before the secondary obligor performs a portion of the secondary obligation, if the secondary obligor then performs:

(i) without knowledge of such impairment;

(ii) for the benefit of an intended beneficiary who can enforce the secondary obligation notwithstanding such impairment; or

(iii) under business compulsion;

the secondary obligor has a claim against the obligee with respect to such performance to the extent that such impairment would have discharged the secondary obligor with respect to that performance.

§ 38. Preservation of Secondary Obligor's Recourse

(1) When an obligee releases the principal obligor from, or agrees to extend the time for performance of, a duty to pay money pursuant to the underlying obligation, the release or extension effects a "preservation of the secondary obligor's recourse" with respect to that duty if the express terms of the release or extension provide that:

(a) the obligee retains the right to seek performance of the secondary obligation by the secondary obligor; and

(b) the rights of the secondary obligor to recourse against the principal obligor (§§ 21–28) continue as though the release or extension had not been granted.

(2) When the obligee effects a preservation of the secondary obligor's recourse in conjunction with a release or extension, the principal obligor's duties of performance and reimbursement and the secondary obligor's rights of restitution and subrogation continue as though the release or extension did not occur.

§ 39. Release of Underlying Obligation

To the extent that the obligee releases the principal obligor from its duties pursuant to the underlying obligation:

(a) the principal obligor is also discharged from any corresponding duties of performance and reimbursement owed to the secondary obligor unless the terms of the release effect a preservation of the secondary obligor's recourse (§ 38);

(b) the secondary obligor is discharged from any unperformed duties pursuant to the secondary obligation unless:

(i) the terms of the release effect a preservation of the secondary obligor's recourse (§ 38); or

(ii) the language or circumstances of the release otherwise show the obligee's intent to retain its claim against the secondary obligor;

(c) if the secondary obligor is not discharged from its unperformed duties pursuant to the secondary obligation by operation of paragraph (b), the secondary obligor is discharged from those duties to the extent:

(i) of the value of the consideration for the release;

(ii) that the release of a duty to pay money pursuant to the underlying obligation would otherwise cause the secondary obligor a loss; and

(iii) that the release discharges a duty of the principal obligor other than the payment of money;

(d) the secondary obligor has a claim against the obligee to the extent provided in § 37(4).

§ 40. Extension of Time

If the obligee grants the principal obligor an extension of the time for performance of its duties pursuant to the underlying obligation:

(a) the extension also extends the time for performance of any corresponding duties of performance and reimbursement owed by the principal obligor to the secondary obligor, unless the extension effects a preservation of the secondary obligor's recourse (§ 38);

(b) to the extent that the secondary obligor has not performed its duties pursuant to the secondary obligation, it is discharged from those duties to the extent that the extension would otherwise cause the secondary obligor a loss;

(c) to the extent that the secondary obligor is not discharged from its duties pursuant to the secondary obligation by operation of paragraph (b), the secondary obligor may perform the secondary obligation as though the time for performance had not been extended or, unless the extension effected a preservation of the secondary obligor's recourse, treat the time for performance of the secondary obligation as having been extended correspondingly; and

(d) the secondary obligor has a claim against the obligee to the extent provided in § 37(4).

§ 41. Modification of Underlying Obligation

If the principal obligor and the obligee agree to a modification, other than an extension of time or a complete or partial release, of the principal obligor's duties pursuant to the underlying obligation;

(a) any duty of the principal obligor to the secondary obligor of performance or reimbursement is correspondingly modified;

(b) the secondary obligor is discharged from any unperformed duties pursuant to the secondary obligation:

(i) if the modification creates a substituted contract or imposes risks on the secondary obligor fundamentally different from those imposed pursuant to the transaction prior to modification;

(ii) in other cases, to the extent that the modification would otherwise cause the secondary obligor a loss;

(c) to the extent that the secondary obligor is not discharged by operation of paragraph (b) from its duties:

(i) the secondary obligation is correspondingly modified; but

(ii) if the modification of the underlying obligation changes the amount of money payable thereunder, or the timing of such payment, the secondary obligor may perform the secondary obligation as though there had been no modification;

(d) the secondary obligor has a claim against the obligee to the extent provided in § 37(4).

§ 42. Impairment of Collateral

(1) If the underlying obligation is secured by a security interest in collateral and the obligee impairs the value of that interest, the secondary obligation is discharged to the extent that such impairment would otherwise increase the difference between the maximum amount recoverable by the secondary obligor pursuant to its subrogation rights (§§ 27–31) and the value of the secondary obligor's interest in the collateral.

(2) Impairing the value of a security interest in collateral includes:

(a) failure to obtain or maintain perfection or recordation of the interest in collateral;

(b) release of collateral without substitution of collateral of equal value or equivalent reduction of the underlying obligation;

(c) failure to perform a duty to preserve the value of collateral owed to the principal obligor or the secondary obligor; and

(d) failure to comply with applicable law in disposing of collateral.

§ 48. Waiver of Suretyship Defenses; Consent

(1) The secondary obligation is not discharged pursuant to § 39(c)(ii)–(iii), § 40(b), § 41(b)(ii), § 42(1), § 43, or § 44 to the extent that, in the contract creating the secondary obligation or otherwise, the secondary obligor consents to acts that would otherwise be the basis of the discharge, agrees that such discharges are unavailable to the secondary obligor, or waives such discharges. Consent may be express or implied from the circumstances. Such consent, agreement, or waiver, if express, may be effectuated by specific language or by general language indicating that the secondary obligor waives defenses based on suretyship.

(2) Unless the circumstances indicate otherwise, when the secondary obligor either controls the principal obligor or deals with the obligee on behalf of the principal obligor, consent by the principal obligor to an act that would lead to discharge pursuant to § 37 constitutes consent to that act by the secondary obligor.

PART V

STATE LAWS AND PRIVATE RULES

New York Debtor & Creditor Law

§§ 282–284

§ 282. Permissible Exemptions in Bankruptcy

Under section five hundred twenty-two of title eleven of the United States Code, entitled "Bankruptcy", an individual debtor domiciled in this state may exempt from the property of the estate, to the extent permitted by subsection (b) thereof, only (i) personal and real property exempt from application to the satisfaction of money judgments under sections fifty-two hundred five and fifty-two hundred six of the civil practice law and rules, (ii) insurance policies and annuity contrts and the proceeds and avails thereof as provided in section three thousand two hundred twelve of the insurance law and (iii) the following property:

1. Bankruptcy exemption of a motor vehicle. One motor vehicle not exceeding four thousand dollars in value above liens and encumbrances of the debtor; provided, however, if such vehicle has been equipped for use by a disabled debtor, then ten thousand dollars in value above liens and encumbrances of the debtor.

2. Bankruptcy exemption for right to receive benefits. The debtor's right to receive or the debtor's interest in: (a) a social security benefit, unemployment compensation or a local public assistance benefit; (b) a veterans' benefit; (c) a disability, illness, or unemployment benefit; (d) alimony, support, or separate maintenance, to the extent reasonably necessary for the support of the debtor and any dependent of the debtor; and (e) the debtor's interest in his or her rent-stabilized lease; and (f) all payments under a stock bonus, pension, profit sharing, or similar plan or contract on account of illness, disability, death, age, or length of service unless (i) such plan or contract, except those qualified under section 401, 408 or 408A of the United States Internal Revenue Code of 1986, as amended, was established by the debtor or under the auspices of an insider that employed the debtor at the time the debtor's rights under such plan or contract arose, (ii) such plan is on account of age or length of service, and (iii) such plan or contract does not qualify under section four hundred one (a), four hundred three (a), four hundred three (b), four hundred eight, four hundred eight A, four hundred nine or four hundred fifty-seven of the Internal Revenue Code of nineteen hundred eighty-six, as amended.

3. Bankruptcy exemption for right to receive certain property. The debtor's right to receive, or property that is traceable to: (i) an award under a crime victim's reparation law; (ii) a payment on account of the wrongful death of an individual of whom the debtor was a dependent to the extent reasonably necessary for the support of the debtor and any dependent of the debtor; (iii) a payment, not to exceed seventy-five hundred dollars on account of personal bodily injury, not including pain and suffering or compensation for actual pecuniary loss, of the debtor or an individual of whom the debtor is a dependent; and (iv) a payment in compensation of loss of future earnings of the debtor or an individual of whom the debtor is or was a dependent, to the extent reasonably necessary for the support of the debtor and any dependent of the debtor.

§ 283. Aggregate Individual Bankruptcy Exemption for Certain Annuities and Personal Property

1. General application. The aggregate amount the debtor may exempt from the property of the estate for personal property exempt from application to the satisfaction of a money judgment under subdivision (a) of section fifty-two hundred five of the civil practice law and rules and for benefits, rights, privileges, and options of annuity contracts described in the following sentence shall not exceed ten thousand dollars. Annuity contracts subject to the foregoing limitation are those that are: (a) initially purchased by the debtor within six months of the debtor's filing a petition in bankruptcy, (b) not described in any paragraph of section eight hundred five (d) of the Internal Revenue Code of nineteen hundred fifty-four, and (c) not purchased by application of proceeds under settlement options of annuity contracts purchased more than six months before the debtor's filing a petition in

bankruptcy or under settlement options of life insurance policies.

2. Contingent alternative bankruptcy exemption. Notwithstanding section two hundred eighty-two of this article, a debtor, who (a) does not elect, claim, or otherwise avail himself of an exemption described in section fifty-two hundred six of the civil practice law and rules; (b) utilizes to the fullest extent permitted by law as applied to said debtor's property, the exemptions referred to in subdivision one of this section which are subject to the ten thousand dollar aggregate limit; and (c) does not reach such aggregate limit, may exempt cash in the amount by which ten thousand dollars exceeds the aggregate of his exemptions referred to in subdivision one of this section or in the amount of two thousand five hundred dollars, whichever amount is less. For purposes of this subdivision, cash means currency of the United States at face value, savings bonds of the United States at face value, the right to receive a refund of federal, state and local income taxes, and deposit accounts in any state or federally chartered depository institution.

§ 284. Exclusivity of Exemptions

In accordance with the provisions of section five hundred twenty-two (b) of title eleven of the United States Code, debtors domiciled in this state are not authorized to exempt from the estate property that is specified under subsection (d) of such section.

§ 285. Alternative Federal Exemptions

Notwithstanding any inconsistent provision of law, an individual debtor may opt to exempt from property of the estate such property as is permitted to be exempted pursuant to section five hundred twenty-two of title eleven of the United States Code in lieu of such property as is permitted to be exempted pursuant to the applicable provisions of this article.

PART VI

UNIFORM INTERNATIONAL LAWS AND RULES

UNCITRAL Convention on Contracts for the International Sale of Goods

Preamble

The States Parties to this Convention,

Bearing in mind the broad objectives in the resolutions adopted by the sixth special session of the General Assembly of the United Nations on the establishment of a New International Economic Order,

Considering that the development of international trade on the basis of equality and mutual benefit is an important element in promoting friendly relations among States,

Being of the opinion that the adoption of uniform rules which govern contracts for the international sale of goods and take into account the different social, economic and legal systems would contribute to the removal of legal barriers in international trade and promote the development of international trade,

Have agreed as follows:

PART I. SPHERE OF APPLICATION AND GENERAL PROVISIONS

Chapter I. Sphere of Application

Article 1.

(1) This Convention applies to contracts of sale of goods between parties whose places of business are in different States:

(a) when the States are Contracting States; or

(b) when the rules of private international law lead to the application of the law of a Contracting State.

(2) The fact that the parties have their places of business in different States is to be disregarded whenever this fact does not appear either from the contract or from any dealings between, or from information disclosed by, the parties at any time before or at the conclusion of the contract.

(3) Neither the nationality of the parties nor the civil or commercial character of the parties or of the contract is to be taken into consideration in determining the application of this Convention.

Article 2.

This Convention does not apply to sales:

(a) of goods bought for personal, family or household use, unless the seller, at any time before or at the conclusion of the contract, neither knew nor ought to have known that the goods were bought for any such use;

(b) by auction;

(c) on execution or otherwise by authority of law;

(d) of stocks, shares, investment securities, negotiable instruments or money;

(e) of ships, vessels, hovercraft or aircraft;

(f) of electricity.

Article 3.

(1) Contracts for the supply of goods to be manufactured or produced are to be considered sales unless the party who orders the goods undertakes to supply a substantial part of the materials necessary for such manufacture or production.

(2) This Convention does not apply to contracts in which the preponderant part of the obligations of the party who furnishes the goods consists in the supply of labour or other services.

Article 4.

This Convention governs only the formation of the contract of sale and the rights and obligations of the seller and the buyer arising from such a contract. In particular, except as otherwise expressly provided in this Convention, it is not concerned with:

(a) the validity of the contract or of any of its provisions or of any usage;

(b) the effect which the contract may have on the property in the goods sold.

Article 5.

This Convention does not apply to the liability of the seller for death or personal injury caused by the goods to any person.

Article 6.

The parties may exclude the application of this Convention or, subject to article 12, derogate from or vary the effect of any of its provisions.

Chapter II. General Provisions

Article 7.

(1) In the interpretation of this Convention, regard is to be had to its international character and to the need to promote uniformity in its application and the observance of good faith in international trade.

(2) Questions concerning matters governed by this Convention which are not expressly settled in it are to be settled in conformity with the general principles on which it is based or, in the absence of such principles, in conformity with the law applicable by virtue of the rules of private international law.

Article 8.

(1) For the purposes of this Convention statements made by and other conduct of a party are to be interpreted according to his intent where the other party knew or could not have been unaware what that intent was.

(2) If the preceding paragraph is not applicable, statements made by and other conduct of a party are to be interpreted according to the understanding that a reasonable person of the same kind as the other party would have had in the same circumstances.

(3) In determining the intent of a party or the understanding a reasonable person would have had, due consideration is to be given to all relevant circumstances of the case including the negotiations, any practices which the parties have established between themselves, usages and any subsequent conduct of the parties.

Article 9.

(1) The parties are bound by any usage to which they have agreed and by any practices which they have established between themselves.

(2) The parties are considered, unless otherwise agreed, to have impliedly made applicable to their contract or its formation a usage of which the parties knew or ought to have known and which in international trade is widely known to, and regularly observed by, parties to contracts of the type involved in the particular trade concerned.

Article 10.

For the purposes of this Convention:

(a) if a party has more than one place of business, the place of business is that which has the closest relationship to the contract and its performance, having regard to the circumstances known to or contemplated by the parties at any time before or at the conclusion of the contract;

(b) if a party does not have a place of business, reference is to be made to his habitual residence.

Article 11.

A contract of sale need not be concluded in or evidenced by writing and is not subject to any other requirement as to form. It may be proved by any means, including witnesses.

Article 12.

Any provision of article 11, article 29 or Part II of this Convention that allows a contract of sale or its modification or termination by agreement or any offer, acceptance or other indication of intention to be made in any form other than in writing does not apply where any party has his place of business in a Contracting State which has made a declaration under article 96 of this Convention. The parties may not derogate from or vary the effect of this article.

Article 13.

For the purposes of this Convention "writing" includes telegram and telex.

PART II. FORMATION OF THE CONTRACT

Article 14.

(1) A proposal for concluding a contract addressed to one or more specific persons constitutes an offer if it is sufficiently definite and indicates the intention of the offeror to be bound in case of acceptance. A proposal is sufficiently definite if it indicates the goods and expressly or implicitly fixes or makes provision for determining the quantity and the price.

(2) A proposal other than one addressed to one or more specific persons is to be considered merely as an invitation to make offers, unless the contrary is clearly indicated by the person making the proposal.

Article 15.

(1) An offer becomes effective when it reaches the offeree.

(2) An offer, even if it is irrevocable, may be withdrawn if the withdrawal reaches the offeree before or at the same time as the offer.

Article 16.

(1) Until a contract is concluded an offer may be revoked if the revocation reaches the offeree before he has dispatched an acceptance.

(2) However, an offer cannot be revoked:

(a) if it indicates, whether by stating a fixed time for acceptance or otherwise, that it is irrevocable; or

(b) if it was reasonable for the offeree to rely on the offer as being irrevocable and the offeree has acted in reliance on the offer.

Article 17.

An offer, even if it is irrevocable, is terminated when a rejection reaches the offeror.

Article 18.

(1) A statement made by or other conduct of the offeree indicating assent to an offer is an acceptance. Silence or inactivity does not in itself amount to acceptance.

(2) An acceptance of an offer becomes effective at the moment the indication of assent reaches the offeror. An acceptance is not effective if the indication of assent does not reach the offeror within the time he has fixed or, if no time is fixed, within a reasonable time, due account being taken of the circumstances of the transaction, including the rapidity of the means of communication employed by the offeror. An oral offer must be accepted immediately unless the circumstances indicate otherwise.

(3) However, if, by virtue of the offer or as a result of practices which the parties have established between themselves or of usage, the offeree may indicate assent by performing an act, such as one relating to the dispatch of the goods or payment of the price, without notice to the offeror, the acceptance is effective at the moment the act is performed, provided that the act is performed within the period of time laid down in the preceding paragraph.

Article 19.

(1) A reply to an offer which purports to be an acceptance but contains additions, limitations or other modifications is a rejection of the offer and constitutes a counteroffer.

(2) However, a reply to an offer which purports to be an acceptance but contains additional or different terms which do not materially alter the terms of the offer constitutes an acceptance, unless the offeror, without undue delay, objects orally to the discrepancy or dispatches a notice to that effect. If he does not so object, the terms of the contract are the terms of the offer with the modifications contained in the acceptance.

(3) Additional or different terms relating, among other things, to the price, payment, quality and quantity of the goods, place and time of delivery, extent of one party's liability to the other or the settlement of disputes are considered to alter the terms of the offer materially.

Article 20.

(1) A period of time of acceptance fixed by the offeror in a telegram or a letter begins to run from the moment the telegram is handed in for dispatch or from the date shown on the letter or, if no such date is shown, from the date shown on the envelope. A period of time for acceptance fixed by the offeror by telephone, telex or other means of instantaneous communication, begins to run from the moment that the offer reaches the offeree.

(2) Official holidays or non-business days occurring during the period for acceptance are included in calculating the period. However, if a notice of acceptance cannot be delivered at the address of the offeror on the last day of the period because that day falls on an official holiday or a non-business day at the place of business of the offeror, the period is extended until the first business day which follows.

Article 21.

(1) A late acceptance is nevertheless effective as an acceptance if without delay the offeror orally so informs the offeree or dispatches a notice to that effect.

(2) If a letter or other writing containing a late acceptance shows that it has been sent in such circumstances that if its transmission had been normal it would have reached the offeror in due time, the late acceptance is effective as an acceptance unless, without delay, the offeror orally informs the offeree that he considers his offer as having lapsed or dispatches a notice to that effect.

Article 22.

An acceptance may be withdrawn if the withdrawal reaches the offeror before or at the same time as the acceptance would have become effective.

Article 23.

A contract is concluded at the moment when an acceptance of an offer becomes effective in accordance with the provisions of this Convention.

Article 24.

For the purposes of this Part of the Convention, an offer, declaration of acceptance or any other indication of intention "reaches" the addressee when it is made orally to him or delivered by any other means to him personally, to his place of business or mailing address or, if he does not have a place of business or mailing address, to his habitual residence.

PART III. SALE OF GOODS

Chapter I. General Provisions

Article 25.

A breach of contract committed by one of the parties is fundamental if it results in such detriment to the other party as substantially to deprive him of what he is entitled to expect under the contract, unless the party in breach did not foresee and a reasonable person of the same kind in the same circumstances would not have foreseen such a result.

Article 26.

A declaration of avoidance of the contract is effective only if made by notice to the other party.

Article 27.

Unless otherwise expressly provided in this Part of the Convention, if any notice, request or other communication is given or made by a party in accordance with this Part and by means appropriate in the circumstances, a delay or error in the transmission of the communication or its failure to arrive does not deprive that party of the right to rely on the communication.

Article 28.

If, in accordance with the provisions of this Convention, one party is entitled to require performance of any obligation by the other party, a court is not bound to enter a judgement for specific performance unless the court would do so under its own law in respect of similar contracts of sale not governed by this Convention.

Article 29.

(1) A contract may be modified or terminated by the mere agreement of the parties.

(2) A contract in writing which contains a provision requiring any modification or termination by agreement to be in writing may not be otherwise modified or terminated by agreement. However, a party may be precluded by his conduct from asserting such a provision to the extent that the other party has relied on that conduct.

Chapter II. Obligations of the Seller

Article 30.

The seller must deliver the goods, hand over any documents relating to them and transfer the property in the goods, as required by the contract and this Convention.

SECTION I. DELIVERY OF THE GOODS AND HANDING OVER OF DOCUMENTS

Article 31.

If the seller is not bound to deliver the goods at any other particular place, his obligation to deliver consists:

(a) if the contract of sale involves carriage of the goods— in handing the goods over to the first carrier for transmission to the buyer;

(b) if, in cases not within the preceding subparagraph, the contract relates to specific goods, or unidentified goods to be drawn from a specific stock or to be manufactured or produced, and at the time of the conclusion of the contract the parties knew that the goods were at, or were to be manufactured or produced at, a particular place— in placing the goods at the buyer's disposal at that place;

(c) in other cases— in placing the goods at the buyer's disposal at the place where the seller had his place of business at the time of the conclusion of the contract.

Article 32.

(1) If the seller, in accordance with the contract or this Convention, hands the goods over to a carrier and if the goods are not dearly identified to the contract by markings on the goods, by shipping documents or otherwise, the seller must give the buyer notice of the consignment specifying the goods.

(2) If the seller is bound to arrange for carriage of the goods, he must make such contracts as are necessary for carriage to the place fixed by means of transportation appropriate in the circumstances and according to the usual terms for such transportation.

(3) If the seller is not bound to effect insurance in respect of the carriage of the goods, he must, at the buyer's request, provide him with all available information necessary to enable him to effect such insurance.

Article 33.

The seller must deliver the goods:

(a) if a date is fixed by or determinable from the contract, on that date;

(b) if a period of time is fixed by or determinable from the contract, at any time within that period unless circumstances indicate that the buyer is to choose a date; or

(c) in any other case, within a reasonable time after the conclusion of the contract.

Article 34.

If the seller is bound to hand over documents relating to the goods, he must hand them over at the time and place and in the form required by the contract. If the seller has handed over documents before that time, he may, up to that time, cure any lack of conformity in the documents, if the exercise of this right does not cause the buyer unreasonable inconvenience or unreasonable expense. However, the buyer retains any right to claim damages as provided for in this Convention.

SECTION II. CONFORMITY OF THE GOODS AND THIRD PARTY CLAIMS

Article 35.

(1) The seller must deliver goods which are of the quantity, quality and description required by the contract and which are contained or packaged in the manner required by the contract.

(2) Except where the parties have agreed otherwise, the goods do not conform with the contract unless they:

(a) are fit for the purposes for which goods of the same description would ordinarily be used;

(b) are fit for any particular purpose expressly or impliedly made known to the seller at the time of the conclusion of the contract, except where the circumstances show that the buyer did not rely, or that it was unreasonable for him to rely, on the seller's skill and judgement;

(c) possess the qualities of goods which the seller has held out to the buyer as a sample or model;

(d) are contained or packaged in the manner usual for such goods or, where there is no such manner, in a manner adequate to preserve and protect the goods.

(3) The seller is not liable under subparagraphs (a) to (d) of the preceding paragraph for any lack of conformity of the goods if at the time of the conclusion of the contract the buyer knew or could not have been unaware of such lack of conformity.

Article 36.

(1) The seller is liable in accordance with the contract and this Convention for any lack of conformity which exists at the time when the risk passes to the buyer, even though the lack of conformity becomes apparent only after that time.

(2) The seller is also liable for any lack of conformity which occurs after the time indicated in the preceding paragraph and which is due to a breach of any of his obligations, including a breach of any guarantee that for a period of time the goods will remain fit for their ordinary purpose or for some particular purpose or will retain specified qualities or characteristics.

Article 37.

If the seller has delivered goods before the date for delivery, he may, up to that date, deliver any missing part or make up any deficiency in the quantity of the goods delivered, or deliver goods in replacement of any non-conforming goods delivered or remedy any lack of conformity in the goods delivered, provided that the exercise of this right does not cause the buyer unreasonable inconvenience or unreasonable expense. However, the buyer retains any right to claim damages as provided for in this Convention.

Article 38.

(1) The buyer must examine the goods, or cause them to be examined, within as short a period as is practicable in the circumstances.

(2) If the contract involves carriage of the goods, examination may be deferred until after the goods have arrived at their destination.

(3) If the goods are redirected in transit or redispatched by the buyer without a reasonable opportunity for examination by him and at the time of the conclusion of the contract the seller knew or ought to have known of the possibility of such redirection or redispatch, examination may be deferred until after the goods have arrived at the new destination.

Article 39.

(1) The buyer loses the right to rely on a lack of conformity of the goods if he does not give notice to the seller specifying the nature of the lack of conformity within a reasonable time after he has discovered it or ought to have discovered it.

(2) In any event, the buyer loses the right to rely on a lack of conformity of the goods if he does not give the seller notice thereof at the latest within a period of two years from the date on which the goods were actually handed over to the buyer, unless this time-limit is inconsistent with a contractual period of guarantee.

Article 40.

The seller is not entitled to rely on the provisions of articles 38 and 39 if the lack of conformity relates to facts of which he knew or could not have been unaware and which he did not disclose to the buyer.

Article 41.

The seller must deliver goods which are free from any right or claim of a third party, unless the buyer agreed to take the goods subject to that right or claim. However, if such right or claim is based on industrial property or other intellectual property, the seller's obligation is governed by article 42.

Article 42.

(1) The seller must deliver goods which are free from any right or claim of a third party based on industrial property or other intellectual property, of which at the time of the conclusion of the contract the seller knew or could not have been unaware, provided that the right or claim is based on industrial property or other intellectual property:

(a) under the law of the State where the goods will be resold or otherwise used, if it was contemplated by the parties at the time of the conclusion of the contract that the goods would be resold or otherwise used in that State; or

(b) in any other case, under the law of the State where the buyer has his place of business.

(2) The obligation of the seller under the preceding paragraph does not extend to cases where:

(a) at the time of the conclusion of the contract the buyer knew or could not have been unaware of the right or claim; or

(b) the right or claim results from the seller's compliance with technical drawings, designs, formulae or other such specifications furnished by the buyer.

Article 43.

(1) The buyer loses the right to rely on the provisions of article 41 or article 42 if he does not give notice to the seller specifying the nature of the right or claim of the third party within a reasonable time after he has become aware or ought to have become aware of the right or claim.

(2) The seller is not entitled to rely on the provisions of the preceding paragraph if he knew of the right or claim of the third party and the nature of it.

Article 44.

Notwithstanding the provisions of paragraph (1) of article 39 and paragraph (1) of article 43, the buyer may reduce the price in accordance with article 50 or claim damages, except for loss of profit, if he has a reasonable excuse for his failure to give the required notice.

SECTION III. REMEDIES FOR BREACH OF CONTRACT BY THE SELLER

Article 45.

(1) If the seller fails to perform any of his obligations under the contract or this Convention, the buyer may:

(a) exercise the rights provided in articles 46 to 52;

(b) claim damages as provided in articles 74 to 77.

(2) The buyer is not deprived of any right he may have to claim damages by exercising his right to other remedies.

(3) No period of grace may be granted to the seller by a court or arbitral tribunal when the buyer resorts to a remedy for breach of contract.

Article 46.

(1) The buyer may require performance by the seller of his obligations unless the buyer has resorted to a remedy which is inconsistent with this requirement.

(2) If the goods do not conform with the contract, the buyer may require delivery of substitute goods only if the lack of conformity constitutes a fundamental breach of contract and a request for substitute goods is made either in conjunction with notice given under article 39 or within a reasonable time thereafter.

(3) If the goods do not conform with the contract, the buyer may require the seller to remedy the lack of conformity by repair, unless this is unreasonable having regard to all the circumstances. A request for repair must be made either in conjunction with notice given under article 39 or within a reasonable time thereafter.

Article 47.

(1) The buyer may fix an additional period of time of reasonable length for performance by the seller of his obligations.

(2) Unless the buyer has received notice from the seller that he will not perform within the period so fixed, the buyer may not, during that period, resort to any remedy for breach of contract. However, the buyer is not deprived thereby of any right he may have to claim damages for delay in performance.

Article 48.

(1) Subject to article 49, the seller may, even after the date for delivery, remedy at his own expense any failure to perform his obligations, if he can do so without unreasonable delay and without causing the buyer unreasonable inconvenience or uncertainty of reimbursement by the seller of expenses advanced by the buyer. However, the buyer retains any right to claim damages as provided for in this Convention.

(2) If the seller requests the buyer to make known whether he will accept performance and the buyer does not comply with the request within a reasonable time, the seller may perform within the time indicated in his request. The buyer may not, during that period of time, resort to any remedy which is inconsistent with performance by the seller.

(3) A notice by the seller that he will perform within a specified period of time is assumed to include a request, under the preceding paragraph, that the buyer make known his decision.

(4) A request or notice by the seller under paragraph (2) or (3) of this article is not effective unless received by the buyer.

Article 49.

(1) The buyer may declare the contract avoided:

(a) if the failure by the seller to perform any of his obligations under the contract or this Convention amounts to a fundamental breach of contract; or

(b) in case of non-delivery, if the seller does not deliver the goods within the additional period of time fixed by the buyer in accordance with paragraph (1) of article 47 or declares that he will not deliver within the period so fixed.

(2) However, in cases where the seller has delivered the goods, the buyer loses the right to declare the contract avoided unless he does so:

(a) in respect of late delivery, within a reasonable time after he has become aware that delivery has been made;

(b) in respect of any breach other than late delivery, within a reasonable time:

(i) after he knew or ought to have known of the breach;

(ii) after the expiration of any additional period of time fixed by the buyer in accordance with paragraph (1) of article 47, or after the seller has declared that he will not perform his obligations within such an additional period; or

(iii) after the expiration of any additional period of time indicated by the seller in accordance with paragraph (2) of article 48, or after the buyer has declared that he will not accept performances.

Article 50.

If the goods do not conform with the contract and whether or not the price has already been paid, the buyer may reduce the price in the same proportion as the value that the goods actually delivered had at the time of the delivery bears to the value that conforming goods would have had at that time. However, if the seller remedies any failure to perform his obligations in accordance with article 37 or article 48 or if the buyer refuses to accept performance by the seller in accordance with those articles, the buyer may not reduce the price.

Article 51.

(1) If the seller delivers only a part of the goods or if only a part of the goods delivered is in conformity with the contract, articles 46 to 50 apply in respect of the part which is missing or which does not conform.

(2) The buyer may declare the contract avoided in its entirety only if the failure to make delivery completely or in conformity with the contract amounts to a fundamental breach of the contract.

Article 52.

(1) If the seller delivers the goods before the date fixed, the buyer may take delivery or refuse to take delivery.

(2) If the seller delivers a quantity of goods greater than that provided for in the contract, the buyer may take delivery or refuse to take delivery of the excess quantity. If the buyer takes delivery of all or part of the excess quantity, he must pay for it at the contract rate.

Chapter III. Obligations of the Buyer

Article 53.

The buyer must pay the price for the goods and take delivery of them as required by the contract and this Convention.

SECTION I. PAYMENT OF THE PRICE

Article 54.

The buyer's obligation to pay the price includes taking such steps and complying with such formalities as may be required under the contract or any laws and regulations to enable payment to be made.

Article 55.

Where a contract has been validly concluded but does not expressly or implicitly fix or make provision for determining the price, the parties are considered, in the absence of any indication to the contrary, to have impliedly made reference to the price generally charged at the time of the conclusion of the contract for such goods sold under comparable circumstances in the trade concerned.

Article 56.

If the price is fixed according to the weight of the goods, in case of doubt it is to be determined by the net weight.

Article 57.

(1) If the buyer is not bound to pay the price at any other particular place, he must pay it to the seller:

(a) at the seller's place of business; or

(b) if the payment is to be made against the handing over of the goods or of documents, at the place where the handing over takes place.

(2) The seller must bear any increase in the expenses incidental to payment which is caused by a change in his place of business subsequent to the conclusion of the contract.

Article 58.

(1) If the buyer is not bound to pay the price at any other specific time he must pay it when the seller places either the goods or documents controlling their disposition at the buyer's disposal in accordance with the contract and this Convention. The seller may make such payment a condition for handing over the goods or documents.

(2) If the contract involves carriage of the goods, the seller may dispatch the goods on terms whereby the goods, or documents controlling their disposition, will not be handed over to the buyer except against payment of the price.

(3) The buyer is not bound to pay the price until he has had an opportunity to examine the goods, unless the procedures for delivery or payment agreed upon by the parties are inconsistent with his having such an opportunity.

Article 59.

The buyer must pay the price on the date fixed by or determinable from the contract and this Convention without the need for any request or compliance with any formality on the part of the seller.

SECTION II. TAKING DELIVERY

Article 60.

The buyer's obligation to take delivery consists:

(a) in doing all the acts which could reasonably be expected of him in order to enable the seller to make delivery; and

(b) in taking over the goods.

SECTION III. REMEDIES FOR BREACH OF CONTRACT BY THE BUYER

Article 61.

(1) If the buyer fails to perform any of his obligations under the contract or this Convention, the seller may:

(a) exercise the rights provided in articles 62 to 65;

(b) claim damages as provided in articles 74 to 77.

(2) The seller is not deprived of any right he may have to claim damages by exercising his right to other remedies.

(3) No period of grace may be granted to the buyer by a court or arbitral tribunal when the seller resorts to a remedy for breach of contract.

Article 62.

The seller may require the buyer to pay the price, take delivery or perform his other obligations, unless the seller has resorted to a remedy which is inconsistent with this requirement.

Article 63.

(1) The seller may fix an additional period of time of reasonable length for performance by the buyer of his obligations.

(2) Unless the seller has received notice from the buyer that he will not perform within the period so fixed, the seller may not, during that period, resort to any remedy for breach of contract. However, the seller is not deprived thereby of any right he may have to claim damages for delay in performance.

Article 64.

(1) The seller may declare the contract avoided:

(a) if the failure by the buyer to perform any of his obligations under the contract or this Convention amounts to a fundamental breach of contract; or

(b) if the buyer does not, within the additional period of time fixed by the seller in accordance with paragraph (1) of article 63, perform his obligation to pay the price or take delivery of the goods, or if he declares that he will not do so within the period so fixed;

(2) However, in cases where the buyer has paid the price, the seller loses the right to declare the contract avoided unless he does so:

(a) in respect of late performance by the buyer, before the seller has become aware that performance has been rendered; or

(b) in respect of any breach other than late performance by the buyer, within a reasonable time:

(i) after the seller knew or ought to have known of the breach; or

(ii) after the expiration of any additional period of time fixed by the seller in accordance with paragraph (1) of article 63, or after the buyer has declared that he will not perform his obligations within such an additional period.

Article 65.

(1) If under the contract the buyer is to specify the form, measurement or other features of the goods and he fails to make such specification either on the date agreed upon or within a reasonable time after receipt of a request from the seller, the seller may, without prejudice to any other rights he may have, make the specification himself in accordance with the requirements of the buyer that may be known to him.

(2) If the seller makes the specification himself, he must inform the buyer of the details thereof and must fix a reasonable time within which the buyer may make a different specification. If, after receipt of such a communication, the buyer fails to do so within the time so fixed, the specification made by the seller is binding.

Chapter IV. Passing of Risk

Article 66.

Loss of or damage to the goods after the risk has passed to the buyer does not discharge him from his obligation to pay the price, unless the loss or damage is due to an act or omission of the seller.

Article 67.

(1) If the contract of sale involves carriage of the goods and the seller is not bound to hand them over at a particular place, the risk passes to the buyer when the goods are handed over to the first carrier for transmission to the buyer in accordance with the contract of sale. If the seller is bound to hand the goods over to a carrier at a particular place, the risk does not pass to the buyer until the goods are handed over to the carrier at that place. The fact that the seller is authorized to retain documents controlling the disposition of the goods does not affect the passage of the risk.

(2) Nevertheless, the risk does not pass to the buyer until the goods are clearly identified to the contract, whether by markings on the goods, by shipping documents, by notice given to the buyer or otherwise.

Article 68.

The risk in respect of goods sold in transit passes to the buyer from the time of the conclusion of the contract. However, if the circumstances so indicate, the risk is assumed by the buyer from the time the goods were handed over to the carrier who issued the documents embodying the contract of carriage. Nevertheless, if at the time of the conclusion of the contract of sale the seller knew or ought to have known that the goods had been lost or damaged and did not disclose this to the buyer, the loss or damage is at the risk of the seller.

Article 69.

(1) In cases not within articles 67 and 68, the risk passes to the buyer when he takes over the goods or, if he does not do so in due time, from the time when the goods are placed at his disposal and he commits a breach of contract by failing to take delivery.

(2) However, if the buyer is bound to take over the goods at a place other than a place of business of the seller, the risk passes when delivery is due and the buyer is aware of the fact that the goods are placed at his disposal at that place.

(3) If the contract relates to goods not then identified, the goods are considered not to be placed at the disposal of the buyer until they are clearly identified to the contract.

Article 70.

If the seller has committed a fundamental breach of contract, articles 67, 68 and 69 do not impair the remedies available to the buyer on account of the breach.

Chapter V. Provisions Common to the Obligations of the Seller and of the Buyer

SECTION I. ANTICIPATORY BREACH AND INSTALMENT CONTRACTS

Article 71.

(1) A party may suspend the performance of his obligations if, after the conclusion of the contract, it becomes apparent that the other party will not perform a substantial part of his obligations as a result of:

(a) a serious deficiency in his ability of perform or in his creditworthiness; or

(b) his conduct in preparing to perform or in performing the contract.

(2) If the seller has already dispatched the goods before the grounds described in the preceding paragraph become evident, he may prevent the handing over of the goods to the buyer even though the buyer holds a document which entitles him to obtain them. The present paragraph relates only to the rights in the goods as between the buyer and the seller.

(3) A party suspending performance, whether before or after dispatch of the goods, must immediately give notice of the suspension to the other party and must continue with performance if the other party provides adequate assurance of his performance.

Article 72.

(1) If prior to the date for performance of the contract it is clear that one of the parties will commit a fundamental breach of contract, the other party may declare the contract avoided.

(2) If time allows, the party intending to declare the contract avoided must give reasonable notice to the other party in order to permit him to provide adequate assurance of his performance.

(3) The requirements of the preceding paragraph do not apply if the other party has declared that he will not perform his obligations.

Article 73.

(1) In the case of a contract for delivery of goods by instalments, if the failure of one party to perform any of his obligations in respect of any instalment constitutes a fundamental breach of contract with respect to that instalment, the other party may declare the contract avoided with respect to that instalment.

(2) If one party's failure to perform any of his obligations in respect of any instalment gives the other party good grounds to conclude that a fundamental breach of contract will occur with respect to future installments, he may declare the contract avoided for the future, provided that he does so within a reasonable time.

(3) A buyer who declares the contract avoided in respect of any delivery may, at the same time, declare it avoided in respect of deliveries already made or of future deliveries if, by reason of their interdependence, those deliveries could not be used for the purpose contemplated by the parties at the time of the conclusion of the contract.

SECTION II. DAMAGES

Article 74.

Damages for breach of contract by one party consist of a sum equal to the loss, including loss of profit, suffered by the other party as a consequence of the breach. Such damages may not exceed the loss which the party in breach foresaw or ought to have foreseen at the time of the conclusion of the contract, in the light of the facts and matters of which he then knew or ought to have known, as a possible consequence of the breach of contract.

Article 75.

If the contract is avoided and if, in a reasonable manner and within a reasonable time after avoidance, the buyer has bought goods in replacement or the seller has resold the goods, the party claiming damages may recover the difference between the contract price and the price in the substitute transaction as well as any further damages recoverable under article 74.

Article 76.

(1) If the contract is avoided and there is a current price for the goods, the party claiming damages may, if he has not made a purchase or resale under article 75, recover the difference between the price fixed by the contract and the current price at the time of avoidance as well as any further damages recoverable under article 74.

If, however, the party claiming damages has avoided the contract after taking over the goods, the current price at the time of such taking over shall be applied instead of the current price at the time of avoidance.

(2) For the purposes of the preceding paragraph, the current price is the price prevailing at the place where delivery of the goods should have been made or, if there is no current price at that place, the price at such other place as serves as a reasonable substitute, making due allowance for differences in the cost of transporting the goods.

Article 77.

A party who relies on a breach of contract must take such measures as are reasonable in the circumstances to mitigate the loss, including loss of profit, resulting from the breach. If he fails to take such measures, the party in breach may claim a reduction in the damages in the amount by which the loss should have been mitigated.

SECTION III. INTEREST

Article 78.

If a party fails to pay the price or any other sum that is in arrears, the other party is entitled to interest on it, without prejudice to any claim for damages recoverable under article 74.

SECTION IV. EXEMPTION

Article 79.

(1) A party is not liable for a failure to perform any of his obligations if he proves that the failure was due to an impediment beyond his control and that he could not reasonably be expected to have taken the impediment into account at the time of the conclusion of the contract or to have avoided or overcome it or its consequences.

(2) If the party's failure is due to the failure by a third person whom he has engaged to perform the whole or a part of the contract, that party is exempt from liability only if:

(a) he is exempt under the preceding paragraph; and

(b) the person whom he has so engaged would be so exempt if the provisions of that paragraph were applied to him.

(3) The exemption provided by this article has effect for the period during which the impediment exists.

(4) The party who fails to perform must give notice to the other party of the impediment and its effect on his ability to perform. If the notice is not received by the other party within a reasonable time after the party who fails to perform knew or ought to have known of the impediment, he is liable for damages resulting from such nonreceipt.

(5) Nothing in this article prevents either party from exercising any right other than to claim damages under this Convention.

Article 80.

A party may not rely on a failure of the other party to perform, to the extent that such failure was caused by the first party's act or omission.

SECTION V. EFFECTS OF AVOIDANCE

Article 81.

(1) Avoidance of the contract releases both parties from their obligations under it, subject to any damages which may be due. Avoidance does not affect any provision of the contract for the settlement of disputes or any other provision of the contract governing the rights and obligations of the parties consequent upon the avoidance of the contract.

(2) A party who has performed the contract either wholly or in part may claim restitution from the other party of whatever the first party has supplied or paid under the contract. If both parties are bound to make restitution, they must do so concurrently.

Article 82.

(1) The buyer loses the right to declare the contract avoided or to require the seller to deliver substitute goods if it is impossible for him to make restitution of the goods substantially in the condition in which he received them.

(2) The preceding paragraph does not apply:

(a) if the impossibility of making restitution of the goods or of making restitution of the goods substantially in the condition in which the buyer received them is not due to his act or omission;

(b) the goods or part of the goods have perished or deteriorated as a result of the examination provided for in article 38; or

(c) if the goods or part of the goods have been sold in the normal course of business or have been consumed or transformed by the buyer in the course of normal use before he discovered or ought to have discovered the lack of conformity.

Article 83.

A buyer who has lost the right to declare the contract avoided or to require the seller to deliver substitute goods in accordance with article 82 retains all other remedies under the contract and this Convention.

Article 84.

(1) If the seller is bound to refund the price, he must also pay interest on it, from the date on which the price was paid.

(2) The buyer must account to the seller for all benefits which he has derived from the goods or part of them:

(a) if he must make restitution of the goods or part of them; or

(b) if it is impossible for him to make restitution of all or part of the goods or to make restitution of all or part of the goods substantially in the condition in which he received them, but he has nevertheless declared the contract avoided or required the seller to deliver substitute goods.

SECTION VI. PRESERVATION OF THE GOODS

Article 85.

If the buyer is in delay in taking delivery of the goods or, where payment of the price and delivery of the goods are to be made concurrently, if he fails to pay the price, and the seller is either in possession of the goods or otherwise able to control their disposition, the seller must take such steps as are reasonable in the circumstances to preserve them. He is entitled to retain them until he has been reimbursed his reasonable expenses by the buyer.

Article 86.

(1) If the buyer has received the goods and intends to exercise any right under the contract or this Convention to reject them, he must take such steps to preserve them as are reasonable in the circumstances. He is entitled to retain them until he has been reimbursed his reasonable expenses by the seller.

(2) If goods dispatched to the buyer have been placed at his disposal at their destination and he exercises the right to reject them, he must take possession of them on behalf of the seller, provided that this can be done without payment of the price and without unreasonable inconvenience or unreasonable expense. This provision does not apply if the seller or a person authorized to take charge of the goods on his behalf is present at the destination. If the buyer takes possession of the goods under this paragraph, his rights and obligations are governed by the preceding paragraph.

Article 87.

A party who is bound to take steps to preserve the goods may deposit them in a warehouse of a third person at the expense of the other party provided that the expense incurred is not unreasonable.

Article 88.

(1) A party who is bound to preserve the goods in accordance with article 85 or 86 may sell them by any appropriate means if there has been an unreasonable delay by the other party in taking possession of the goods or in taking them back or in paying the price or the cost of preservation, provided that reasonable notice of the intention to sell has been given to the other party.

(2) If the goods are subject to rapid deterioration or their preservation would involve unreasonable expense, a party who is bound to preserve the goods in accordance with article 85 or 86 must take reasonable measures to sell them. To the extent possible he must give notice to the other party of his intention to sell.

(3) A party selling the goods has the right to retain out of the proceeds of sale an amount equal to the reasonable expenses of preserving the goods and of selling them. He must account to the other party for the balance.

PART IV. FINAL PROVISIONS

Article 89.

The Secretary-General of the United Nations is hereby designated as the depositary for this Convention.

Article 90.

This Convention does not prevail over any international agreement which has already been or may be entered into and which contains provisions concerning the matters governed by this Convention, provided that the parties have their places of business in States parties, to such agreement.

Article 91.

(1) This Convention is open for signature at the concluding meeting of the United Nations Conference on Contracts for the International Sale of Goods and will remain open for signature by all States at the Headquarters of the United Nations, New York until 30 September 1981.

(2) This Convention is subject to ratification, acceptance or approval by the signatory States.

(3) This Convention is open for accession by all States which are not signatory States as from the date it is open for signature.

(4) Instruments of ratification, acceptance, approval and accession are to be deposited with the Secretary-General of the United Nations.

Article 92.

(1) A Contracting State may declare at the time of signature, ratification, acceptance, approval or accession

that it will not be bound by Part II of this Convention or that it will not be bound by Part III of this Convention.

(2) A Contracting State which makes a declaration in accordance with the preceding paragraph in respect of Part II or Part III of this Convention is not to be considered a Contracting State within paragraph (1) of article 1 of this Convention in respect of matters governed by the Part to which the declaration applies.

Article 93.

(1) If a Contracting State has two or more territorial units in which, according to its constitution, different systems of law are applicable in relation to the matters dealt with in this Convention, it may, at the time of signature, ratification, acceptance, approval or accession, declare that this Convention is to extend to all its territorial units or only to one or more of them, and may amend its declaration by submitting another declaration at any time.

(2) These declarations are to be notified to the depositary and are to state expressly the territorial units to which the Convention extends.

(3) If, by virtue of a declaration under this article, this Convention extends to one or more but not all of the territorial units of a Contracting State, and if the place of business of a party is located in that State, this place of business, for the purposes of this Convention, is considered not to be in a Contracting State, unless it is in a territorial unit to which the Convention extends.

(4) If a Contracting State makes no declaration under paragraph (1) of this article, the Convention is to extend to all territorial units of that State.

Article 94.

(1) Two or more Contracting States which have the same or closely related legal rules on matters governed by this Convention may at any time declare that the Convention is not to apply to contracts of sale or to their formation where the parties have their places of business in those States. Such declarations may be made jointly or by reciprocal unilateral declarations.

(2) A Contracting State which has the same or closely related legal rules on matters governed by this Convention as one or more non-Contracting States may at any time declare that the Convention is not to apply to contracts of sale or to their formation where the parties have their places of business in those States.

(3) If a State which is the object of a declaration under the preceding paragraph subsequently becomes a Contracting State, the declaration made will, as from the date on which the Convention enters into force in respect of the new Contracting State, have the effect of a declaration made under paragraph (1), provided that the new Contracting State joins in such declaration or makes a reciprocal unilateral declaration.

Article 95.

Any State may declare at the time of the deposit of its instrument of ratification, acceptance, approval or accession that it will not be bound by subparagraph (1) (b) of article 1 of this Convention.

Article 96.

A Contracting State whose legislation requires contracts of sale to be concluded in or evidenced by writing may at any time make a declaration in accordance with article 12 that any provision of article 11, article 29, or Part II of this Convention, that allows a contract of sale or its modification or termination by agreement or any offer, acceptance, or other indication of intention to be made in any form other than in writing, does not apply where any party has his place of business in that State.

Article 97.

(1) Declarations made under this Convention at the time of signature are subject to confirmation upon ratification, acceptance or approval.

(2) Declarations and confirmations of declarations are to be in writing and be formally notified to the depositary.

(3) A declaration takes effect simultaneously with the entry into force of this Convention in respect of the State concerned. However, a declaration of which the depositary receives formal notification after such entry into force takes effect on the first day of the month following the expiration of six months after the date of its receipt by the depositary. Reciprocal unilateral declarations under article 94 take effect on the first day of the month following the expiration of six months after the receipt of the latest declaration by the depositary.

(4) Any State which makes a declaration under this Convention may withdraw it at any time by a formal notification in writing addressed to the depositary. Such withdrawal is to take effect on the first day of the month following the expiration of six months after the date of the receipt of the notification by the depositary.

(5) A withdrawal of a declaration made under article 94 renders inoperative, as from the date on which the withdrawal takes effect, any reciprocal declaration made by another State under that article.

Article 98.

No reservations are permitted except those expressly authorized in this Convention.

Article 99.

(1) This Convention enters into force, subject to the provisions of paragraph (6) of this article, on the first day of the month following the expiration of twelve months after the date of deposit of the tenth instrument of ratification, acceptance, approval or accession, including an instrument which contains a declaration made under article 92.

(2) When a State ratifies, accepts, approves or accedes to this Convention after the deposit of the tenth instrument of ratification, acceptance, approval or accession, this Convention, with the exception of the Part excluded, enters into force in respect of that State, subject to the provisions of paragraph (6) of this article, on the first day of the month following the expiration of twelve months after the date of the deposit of its instrument of ratification, acceptance, approval or accession.

(3) A State which ratifies, accepts, approves or accedes to this Convention and is a party to either or both the Convention relating to a Uniform Law on the Formation of Contracts for the International Sale of Goods done at The Hague on 1 July 1964 (1964 Hague Formation Convention) and the Convention relating to a Uniform Law on the International Sale of Goods done at The Hague on 1 July 1964 (1964 Hague Sales Convention) shall at the same time denounce, as the case may be, either or both the 1964 Hague Sales Convention and the 1964 Hague Formation Convention by notifying the Government of the Netherlands to that effect.

(4) A State party to the 1964 Hague Sales Convention which ratifies, accepts, approves or accedes to the present Convention and declares or has declared under article 92 that it will not be bound by Part II of this Convention shall at the time of ratification, acceptance, approval or accession denounce the 1964 Hague Sales Convention by notifying the Government of the Netherlands to that effect.

(5) A State party to the 1964 Hague Formation Convention which ratifies, accepts, approves or accedes to the present Convention and declares or has declared under article 92 that it will not be bound by Part III of this Convention shall at the time of ratification, acceptance, approval or accession denounce the 1964 Hague Formation Convention by notifying the Government of the Netherlands to that effect.

(6) For the purpose of this article, ratifications, acceptances, approvals and accessions in respect of this Convention by States parties to the 1964 Hague Formation Convention or to the 1964 Hague Sales Convention shall not be effective until such denunciations as may be required on the part of those States in respect of the latter two Conventions have themselves become effective. The depositary of this Convention shall consult with the Government of the Netherlands, as the depositary of the 1964 Conventions, so as to ensure necessary co-ordination in this respect.

Article 100.

(1) This Convention applies to the formation of a contract only when the proposal for concluding the contract is made on or after the date when the Convention enters into force in respect of the Contracting States referred to in subparagraph (1) (a) or the Contracting State referred to in subparagraph (1) (b) of article 1.

(2) This Convention applies only to contracts concluded on or after the date when the Convention enters into force in respect of the Contracting States referred to in subparagraph (1)(a) or the Contracting State referred to in subparagraph (1)(b) of article 1.

Article 101.

(1) A Contracting State may denounce this Convention, or Part II or Part III of the Convention, by a formal notification in writing addressed to the depositary.

(2) The denunciation takes effect on the first day of the month following the expiration of twelve months after the notification is received by the depositary. Where a longer period for the denunciation to take effect is specified in the notification, the denunciation takes effect upon the expiration of such longer period after the notification is received by the depositary.

DONE at Vienna, this day of eleventh day of April, one thousand nine hundred and eighty, in a single original, of which the Arabic, Chinese, English, French, Russian and Spanish texts are equally authentic.

IN WITNESS WHEREOF the undersigned plenipotentiaries, being duly authorized by their respective Governments, have signed this Convention.

International Standby Practices (ISP98)

Selected Provisions*

PREFACE

RULE 6: TRANSFER, ASSIGNMENT, AND TRANSFER BY OPERATION OF LAW

RULE 7: CANCELLATION

RULE 8: REIMBURSEMENT OBLIGATIONS

RULE 9: TIMING

RULE 10: SYNDICATION/ PARTICIPATION

PREFACE

The International Standby Practices (ISP98) reflects generally accepted practice, custom, and usage of standby letters of credit. It provides separate rules for standby letters of credit in the same sense that the Uniform Customs and Practice for Documentary Credits (UCP) and the Uniform Rules for Demand Guarantees (URDG) do for commercial letters of credit and independent bank guarantees.

The formulation of standby letter of credit practices in separate rules evidences the maturity and importance of this financial product. The amounts outstanding of standbys greatly exceed the outstanding amounts of commercial letters of credit. While the standby is associated with the United States where it originated and where it is most widely used, it is truly an international product. Non-U.S. bank outstandings have exceeded those of U.S. banks in the United States alone. Moreover, the standby is used increasingly throughout the world.

Standbys are issued to support payment, when due or after default, of obligations based on money loaned or advanced, or upon the occurrence or non-occurrence of another contingency.

For convenience, standbys are commonly classified descriptively (and without operative significance in the application of these Rules) based on their function in the underlying transaction or other factors not necessarily related to the terms and conditions of the standby itself. For example:

A "Performance Standby" supports an obligation to perform other than to pay money, including for the purpose of covering losses arising from a default of the applicant in completion of the underlying transactions.

An "Advance Payment Standby" supports an obligation to account for an advance payment made by the beneficiary to the applicant.

A "Bid Bond/Tender Bond Standby" supports an obligation of the applicant to execute a contract if the applicant is awarded a bid.

A "Counter Standby" supports the issuance of a separate standby or other undertaking by the beneficiary of the counter standby.

A "Financial Standby" supports an obligation to pay money, including any instrument evidencing an obligation to repay borrowed money.

A "Direct Pay" Standby supports payment when due of an underlying payment obligation typically in connection with a financial standby without regard to a default.

An "Insurance Standby" supports an insurance or reinsurance obligation of the applicant.

A "Commercial Standby" supports the obligations of an applicant to pay for goods or services in the event of non-payment by other methods.

In the past, many standbys have been issued subject to the UCP even though it was intended for commercial letters of credit. The UCP reinforced the independence and documentary character of the standby. It also provided standards for examination and notice of dishonor and a basis to resist market pressures to embrace troublesome practices such as the issuance of standbys without expiration dates.

Despite these important contributions, it has long been apparent that the UCP was not fully applicable nor appropriate for standbys, as is recognized in UCP 500 Article 1 which provides that it applies "to the extent to which they may be applicable." Even the least complex standbys (those calling for presentation of a draft only) pose problems not addressed by the UCP. More complex standbys (those involving longer terms or automatic extensions, transfer on demand, requests that the beneficiary issue its own undertaking to another, and the like) require more specialized rules of practice. The ISP fills these needs.

The ISP differs from the UCP in style and approach because it must receive acceptance not only from bankers and merchants, but also from a broader range of those actively involved in standby law and practice—corporate treasurers and credit managers, rating agencies, government agencies and regulators, and indenture trustees as well as their counsel. Because standbys are often intended to be available in the event of disputes or applicant insolvency, their texts are subject to a degree of scrutiny not encountered in the commercial letter of credit context. As a result, the ISP is also written to provide guidance to lawyers and judges in the interpretation of standby practice.

Differences in substance result either from different practices, different problems, or the need for more precision. In addition, the ISP proposes basic definitions should the standby permit or require presentation of documents by electronic means. Since standbys infrequently require presentation of negotiable documents, standby practice is currently more conducive to electronic presentations, and the ISP provides definitions and rules encouraging such presentations. The development of S.W.I.F.T. message types for the ISP is anticipated.

The ISP, like the UCP for commercial letters of credit, simplifies, standardizes, and streamlines the drafting of standbys, and provides clear and widely accepted answers to common problems. There are basic similarities with the UCP because standby and commercial practices are fundamentally the same. Even where the rules overlap, however, the ISP is more precise, stating the intent implied in the UCP rule, in order to make the standby more dependable when a drawing or honor is questioned.

Like the UCP and the URDG, the ISP will apply to any independent undertaking issued subject to it. This approach avoids the impractical and often impossible task of identifying and distinguishing standbys from independent guarantees and, in many cases, commercial letters of credit. The choice of which set of rules to select is, therefore, left to the parties—as it should be. One may well choose to use the ISP for certain types of standbys, the UCP for others, and the URDG for still others. While the ISP is not intended to be used for dependent undertakings such as accessory guarantees and insurance contracts, it may be useful in some situations in indicating that a particular undertaking which might otherwise be treated as dependent under local law is intended to be independent.

For the ISP to apply to a standby, an undertaking should be made subject to these Rules by including language such as (but not limited to):

> This undertaking is issued subject to the International Standby Practices 1998.
>
> or
>
> Subject to ISP98.

Although the ISP can be varied by the text of a standby, it provides neutral rules acceptable in the majority of situations and a useful starting point for negotiations in other situations. It will save parties (including banks that issue, confirm, or are beneficiaries of standbys) considerable time and expense in negotiating and drafting standby terms.

The ISP is designed to be compatible with the United Nations Convention on Independent Guarantees and Stand-by Letters of Credit (which represents a useful and practical formulation of basic standby and independent guarantee law) and also with local law, whether statutory or judicial, and to embody standby letter of credit practice under that law. If these rules conflict with mandatory law on issues such as assignment of proceeds or transfer by operation of law, applicable law will, of course, control. Nonetheless, most of these issues are rarely addressed by local law and progressive commercial law will often look to the practice as recorded in the ISP for guidance in such situations, especially with respect to cross border undertakings. As a result, it is expected that the ISP will complement local law rather than conflict with it.

The ISP is intended to be used also in arbitration as well as judicial proceedings (such as the expert based letter of credit arbitration system developed by the International Center for Letter of Credit Arbitration (ICLOCA) Rules or general commercial ICC arbitration) or with alternative methods of dispute resolution. Such a choice should be made expressly and with appropriate detail. At a minimum, it can be made in connection with the clause relating to ISP98—e.g., This undertaking is issued subject to ISP98, and all disputes arising out of it or related to it are subject to arbitration under ICLOCA Rules (1996).

Although translations of the ISP into other languages are envisioned and will be monitored for integrity, the English text is the official text of the ISP in the event of disputes.

The ISP is the product of the work of the ISP Working Group under the auspices of the Institute of International Banking Law & Practice, Inc. which interacted with hundreds of persons over a five year period, and has benefitted from comments received from individuals, banks, and national and international associations. In particular, the participation of the International Financial Services Association (formerly the USCIB) and the Ad Hoc Working Group under the chairmanship of Gary Collyer (which led to its endorsement by the ICC Banking Commission) is gratefully recognized. In addition, the sponsorship and support of Citibank N.A., The Chase Manhattan Bank, ABN AMRO, Baker & McKenzie, and the National Law Center for Inter-American Free Trade is acknowledged. Perhaps the greatest significance of the ISP is that its creation marks a new chapter in the collaboration between the international banking operations community and the legal community at an international level. In this respect, the active role played in this process by the Secretariat of the United Nations Commission on International Trade Law has been invaluable.

The ISP is drafted as a set of rules intended for use in daily practice. It is not intended to provide introductory information on standbys and their uses. While it is recognized that specific rules would benefit from explanatory comments, such comments are not appended to the ISP because the resulting work would be too cumbersome for daily use. Instead, introductory materials and Official Comments are available in the *Official Commentary on the International Standby Practices (ISP98)*. For further information on support materials and developments on the ISP and to pose queries, consult the ISP98 website: www. ISP98.com.

To address inevitable questions, to provide for official interpretation of the rules, and to assure their proper evolution, the Institute of International Banking Law & Practice, Inc. has created a Council on International Standby Practices which is representative of the several constituencies which have contributed to the ISP and has charged it with the task of maintaining the integrity of the ISP in cooperation with the Institute, the ICC Banking Commission, the IFSA, and various supporting organizations.

RULE 1: GENERAL PROVISIONS

Scope, Application, Definitions, and Interpretation of These Rules

§ 1.01. Scope and Application

a. These Rules are intended to be applied to standby letters of credit (including performance, financial, and direct pay standby letters of credit).

b. A standby letter of credit or other similar undertaking, however named or described, whether for domestic or international use, may be made subject to these Rules by express reference to them.

c. An undertaking subject to these Rules may expressly modify or exclude their application.

d. An undertaking subject to these Rules is hereinafter referred to as a **"standby"**.

§ 1.02. Relationship to Law and Other Rules

a. These Rules supplement the applicable law to the extent not prohibited by that law.

b. These Rules supersede conflicting provisions in any other rules of practice to which a standby letter of credit is also made subject.

§ 1.03. Interpretative Principles

These Rules shall be interpreted as mercantile usage with regard for:

a. integrity of standbys as reliable and efficient undertakings to pay;

b. practice and terminology of banks and businesses in day-to-day transactions;

c. consistency within the worldwide system of banking operations and commerce; and

d. worldwide uniformity in their interpretation and application.

§ 1.04. Effect of the Rules

Unless the context otherwise requires, or unless expressly modified or excluded, these Rules apply as terms and conditions incorporated into a standby, confirmation, advice, nomination, amendment, transfer, request for issuance, or other agreement of:

i. the issuer;

ii. the beneficiary to the extent it uses the standby;

iii. any advisor;

iv. any confirmer;

v. any person nominated in the standby who acts or agrees to act; and

vi. the applicant who authorises issuance of the standby or otherwise agrees to the application of these Rules.

§ 1.05. Exclusion of Matters Related to Due Issuance and Fraudulent or Abusive Drawing

These Rules do not define or otherwise provide for:

a. power or authority to issue a standby;

b. formal requirements for execution of a standby (e.g. a signed writing); or

c. defenses to honour based on fraud, abuse, or similar matters.

These matters are left to applicable law.

General Principles

§ 1.06. Nature of Standbys

a. A standby is an irrevocable, independent, documentary, and binding undertaking when issued and need not so state.

b. Because a standby is irrevocable, an issuer's obligations under a standby cannot be amended or cancelled by the issuer except as provided in the standby or as consented to by the person against whom the amendment or cancellation is asserted.

c. Because a standby is independent, the enforceability of an issuer's obligations under a standby does not depend on:

i. the issuer's right or ability to obtain reimbursement from the applicant;

ii. the beneficiary's right to obtain payment from the applicant;

iii. a reference in the standby to any reimbursement agreement or underlying transaction; or

iv. the issuer's knowledge of performance or breach of any reimbursement agreement or underlying transaction.

d. Because a standby is documentary, an issuer's obligations depend on the presentation of documents and an examination of required documents on their face.

e. Because a standby or amendment is binding when issued, it is enforceable against an issuer whether or not the applicant authorised its issuance, the issuer received a fee, or the beneficiary received or relied on the standby or the amendment.

§ 1.07. Independence of the Issuer-Beneficiary Relationship

An issuer's obligations toward the beneficiary are not affected by the issuer's rights and obligations toward the applicant under any applicable agreement, practice, or law.

§ 1.08. Limits to Responsibilities

An issuer is not responsible for:

a. performance or breach of any underlying transaction;

b. accuracy, genuineness, or effect of any document presented under the standby;

c. action or omission of others even if the other person is chosen by the issuer or nominated person; or

d. observance of law or practice other than that chosen in the standby or applicable at the place of issuance.

Terminology

§ 1.09. Defined Terms

In addition to the meanings given in standard banking practice and applicable law, the following terms have or include the meanings indicated below:

a. Definitions

"**Applicant**" is a person who applies for issuance of a standby or for whose account it is issued, and includes (i) a person applying in its own name but for the account of another person or (ii) an issuer acting for its own account.

"**Beneficiary**" is a named person who is entitled to draw under a standby. See Rule 1.11(c)(ii).

"**Business Day**" means a day on which the place of business at which the relevant act is to be performed is regularly open; and "**Banking Day**" means a day on which the relevant bank is regularly open at the place at which the relevant act is to be performed.

"**Confirmer**" is a person who, upon an issuer's nomination to do so, adds to the issuer's undertaking its own undertaking to honour a standby. See Rule 1.11(c)(i).

"**Demand**" means, depending on the context, either a request to honour a standby or a document that makes such request.

"**Document**" means a draft, demand, document of title, investment security, invoice, certificate of default, or any other representation of fact, law, right, or opinion, that upon presentation (whether in a paper or electronic medium), is capable of being examined for compliance with the terms and conditions of a standby.

"**Drawing**" means, depending on the context, either a demand presented or a demand honoured.

"**Expiration Date**" means the latest day for a complying presentation provided in a standby.

"**Person**" includes a natural person, partnership, corporation, limited liability company, government agency, bank, trustee, and any other legal or commercial association or entity.

"**Presentation**" means, depending on the context, either the act of delivering documents for examination under a standby or the documents so delivered.

"**Presenter**" is a person who makes a presentation as or on behalf of a beneficiary or nominated person.

"**Signature**" includes any symbol executed or adopted by a person with a present intent to authenticate a document.

b. Cross References

"**Amendment**"—Rule 2.06

"**Advice**"—Rule 2.05

"**Approximately**" ("About" or "Circa")—Rule 3.08(f)

"**Assignment of Proceeds**"—Rule 6.06

"**Automatic Amendment**"—Rule 2.06(a)

"**Copy**"—Rule 4.15(d)

"**Cover Instructions**"—Rule 5.08

"**Honour**"—Rule 2.01

"**Issuer**"—Rule 2.01

"**Multiple Presentations**"—Rule 3.08(b)

"**Nominated Person**"—Rule 2.04

"**Non-documentary Conditions**"—Rule 4.11

"**Original**"—Rule 4.15(b) & (c)

"**Partial Drawing**"—Rule 3.08(a)

"**Standby**"—Rule 1.01(d)

"**Transfer**"—Rule 6.01

"**Transferee Beneficiary**"—Rule 1.11(c)(ii)

"**Transfer by Operation of Law**"—Rule 6.11

c. Electronic Presentations. The following terms in a standby providing for or permitting electronic presentation shall have the following meanings unless the context otherwise requires:

"Electronic Record" means:

i. a record (information that is inscribed on a tangible medium or that is stored in an electronic or other medium and is retrievable in perceivable form);

ii. communicated by electronic means to a system for receiving, storing, re-transmitting, or otherwise processing information (data, text, images, sounds, codes, computer programs, software, databases, and the like); and

iii. capable of being authenticated and then examined for compliance with the terms and conditions of the standby.

"Authenticate" means to verify an electronic record by generally accepted procedure or methodology in commercial practice:

i. the identity of a sender or source, and

ii. the integrity of or errors in the transmission of information content.

The criteria for assessing the integrity of information in an electronic record is whether the information has remained complete and unaltered, apart from the addition of any endorsement and any change which arises in the normal course of communication, storage, and display.

"Electronic signature" means letters, characters, numbers, or other symbols in electronic form, attached to or logically associated with an electronic record that are executed or adopted by a party with present intent to authenticate an electronic record.

"Receipt" occurs when:

i. an electronic record enters in a form capable of being processed by the information system designated in the standby, or

ii. an issuer retrieves an electronic record sent to an information system other than that designated by the issuer.

§ 1.10. Redundant or Otherwise Undesirable Terms

a. A standby should not or need not state that it is:

i. **unconditional** or **abstract** (if it does, it signifies merely that payment under it is conditioned solely on presentation of specified documents);

ii. **absolute** (if it does, it signifies merely that it is irrevocable);

iii. **primary** (if it does, it signifies merely that it is the independent obligation of the issuer);

iv. **payable from the issuer's own funds** (if it does, it signifies merely that payment under it does not depend on the availability of applicant funds and is made to satisfy the issuer's own independent obligation);

v. **clean** or **payable on demand** (if it does, it signifies merely that it is payable upon presentation of a written demand or other documents specified in the standby).

b. A standby should not use the term **"and/or"** (if it does it means either or both).

c. The following terms have no single accepted meaning:

i. and shall be disregarded:
"callable",
"divisible",
"fractionable",
"indivisible", and
"transmissible".

ii. and shall be disregarded unless their context gives them meaning:
"assignable",
"evergreen",
"reinstate", and
"revolving".

§ 1.11. Interpretation of These Rules

a. These Rules are to be interpreted in the context of applicable standard practice.

b. In these Rules, **"standby letter of credit"** refers to the type of independent undertaking for which these Rules were intended, whereas **"standby"** refers to an undertaking subjected to these Rules.

c. Unless the context otherwise requires:

i. **"Issuer"** includes a **"confirmer"** as if the confirmer were a separate issuer and its confirmation were a separate standby issued for the account of the issuer;

ii. **"Beneficiary"** includes a person to whom the named beneficiary has effectively transferred drawing rights (**"transferee beneficiary"**);

iii. **"Including"** means "including but not limited to";

iv. "A **or** B" means "A or B or both"; "**either** A **or** B" means "A or B, but not both"; and "A **and** B" means "both A and B";

v. Words in the singular number include the plural, and in the plural include the singular; and

vi. Words of the neuter gender include any gender.

d. i. Use of the phrase **"unless a standby otherwise states"** or the like in a rule emphasizes that the text of the standby controls over the rule;

ii. Absence of such a phrase in other rules does not imply that other rules have priority over the text of the standby;

iii. Addition of the term **"expressly"** or **"clearly"** to the phrase "unless a standby otherwise states" or the like emphasizes that the rule should be excluded or modified only by wording in the standby that is specific and unambiguous; and

iv. While the effect of all of these Rules may be varied by the text of the standby, variations of the effect of some of these Rules may disqualify the standby as an independent undertaking under applicable law.

e. The phrase **"stated in the standby"** or the like refers to the actual text of a standby (whether as issued or effectively amended) whereas the phrase **"provided in the standby"** or the like refers to both the text of the standby and these Rules as incorporated.

RULE 2: OBLIGATIONS

§ 2.01. Undertaking to Honour by Issuer and Any Confirmer to Beneficiary

a. An issuer undertakes to the beneficiary to honour a presentation that appears on its face to comply with the terms and conditions of the standby in accordance with these Rules supplemented by standard standby practice.

b. An issuer honours a complying presentation made to it by paying the amount demanded of it at sight, unless the standby provides for honour:

i. by acceptance of a draft drawn by the beneficiary on the issuer, in which case the issuer honours by:

(a) timely accepting the draft; and

(b) thereafter paying the holder of the draft on presentation of the accepted draft on or after its maturity.

ii. by deferred payment of a demand made by the beneficiary on the issuer, in which case the issuer honours by:

(a) timely incurring a deferred payment obligation; and

(b) thereafter paying at maturity.

iii. by negotiation, in which case the issuer honours by paying the amount demanded at sight without recourse.

c. An issuer acts in a timely manner if it pays at sight, accepts a draft, or undertakes a deferred payment obligation (or if it gives notice of dishonour) within the time permitted for examining the presentation and giving notice of dishonour.

d. i. A confirmer undertakes to honour a complying presentation made to it by paying the amount demanded of it at sight or, if the standby so states, by another method of honour consistent with the issuer's undertaking.

ii. If the confirmation permits presentation to the issuer, then the confirmer undertakes also to honour upon the issuer's wrongful dishonour by performing as if the presentation had been made to the confirmer.

iii. If the standby permits presentation to the confirmer, then the issuer undertakes also to honour upon the confirmer's wrongful dishonour by performing as if the presentation had been made to the issuer.

e. An issuer honours by paying in immediately available funds in the currency designated in the standby unless the standby states it is payable by:

i. payment of a monetary unit of account, in which case the undertaking is to pay in that unit of account; or

ii. delivery of other items of value, in which case the undertaking is to deliver those items.

§ 2.02. Obligation of Different Branches, Agencies, or Other Offices

For the purposes of these Rules, an issuer's branch, agency, or other office acting or undertaking to act under a standby in a capacity other than as issuer is obligated in that capacity only and shall be treated as a different person.

§ 2.03. Conditions to Issuance

A standby is issued when it leaves an issuer's control unless it clearly specifies that it is not then "issued" or "enforceable". Statements that a standby is not "available", "operative", "effective", or the like do not affect its irrevocable and binding nature at the time it leaves the issuer's control.

§ 2.04. Nomination

a. A standby may nominate a person to advise, receive a presentation, effect a transfer, confirm, pay, negotiate, incur a deferred payment obligation, or accept a draft.

b. Nomination does not obligate the nominated person to act except to the extent that the nominated person undertakes to act.

c. A nominated person is not authorised to bind the person making the nomination.

§ 2.05. Advice of Standby or Amendment

a. Unless an advice states otherwise, it signifies that:

i. the advisor has checked the apparent authenticity of the advised message in accordance with standard letter of credit practice; and

ii. the advice accurately reflects what has been received.

b. A person who is requested to advise a standby and decides not to do so should notify the requesting party.

§ 2.06. When an Amendment Is Authorised and Binding

a. If a standby expressly states that it is subject to **"automatic amendment"** by an increase or decrease in the amount available, an extension of the expiration date, or the like, the amendment is effective automatically without any further notification or consent beyond that expressly provided for in the standby. (Such an amendment may also be referred to as becoming effective **"without amendment".**)

b. If there is no provision for automatic amendment, an amendment binds:

i. the issuer when it leaves the issuer's control; and

ii. the confirmer when it leaves the confirmer's control, unless the confirmer indicates that it does not confirm the amendment.

c. If there is no provision for automatic amendment:

i. the beneficiary must consent to the amendment for it to be binding;

ii. the beneficiary's consent must be made by an express communication to the person advising the amendment unless the beneficiary presents documents which comply with the standby as amended and which would not comply with the standby prior to such amendment; and

iii. an amendment does not require the applicant's consent to be binding on the issuer, the confirmer, or the beneficiary.

d. Consent to only part of an amendment is a rejection of the entire amendment.

§ 2.07. Routing of Amendments

a. An issuer using another person to advise a standby must advise all amendments to that person.

b. An amendment or cancellation of a standby does not affect the issuer's obligation to a nominated person that has acted within the scope of its nomination before receipt of notice of the amendment or cancellation.

c. Non-extension of an automatically extendable (renewable) standby does not affect an issuer's obligation to a nominated person who has acted within the scope of its nomination before receipt of a notice of non-extension.

RULE 3: PRESENTATION

§ 3.01. Complying Presentation Under a Standby

A standby should indicate the time, place and location within that place, person to whom, and medium in which presentation should be made. If so, presentation must be so made in order to comply. To the extent that a standby does not so indicate, presentation must be made in accordance with these Rules in order to be complying.

§ 3.02. What Constitutes a Presentation

The receipt of a document required by and presented under a standby constitutes a presentation requiring examination for compliance with the terms and conditions of the standby even if not all of the required documents have been presented.

§ 3.03. Identification of Standby

a. A presentation must identify the standby under which the presentation is made.

b. A presentation may identify the standby by stating the complete reference number of the standby and the name and location of the issuer or by attaching the original or a copy of the standby.

c. If the issuer cannot determine from the face of a document received that it should be processed under a standby or cannot identify the standby to which it relates, presentation is deemed to have been made on the date of identification.

§ 3.04. Where and to Whom Complying Presentation Made

a. To comply, a presentation must be made at the place and any location at that place indicated in the standby or provided in these Rules.

b. If no place of presentation to the issuer is indicated in the standby, presentation to the issuer must be made at the place of business from which the standby was issued.

c. If a standby is confirmed, but no place for presentation is indicated in the confirmation, presentation for the purpose of obligating the confirmer (and the issuer) must be made at the place of business of the confirmer from which the confirmation was issued or to the issuer.

d. If no location at a place of presentation is indicated (such as department, floor, room, station, mail stop, post office box, or other location), presentation may be made to:

i. the general postal address indicated in the standby;

ii. any location at the place designated to receive deliveries of mail or documents; or

iii. any person at the place of presentation actually or apparently authorised to receive it.

§ 3.05. When Timely Presentation Made

a. A presentation is timely if made at any time after issuance and before expiry on the expiration date.

b. A presentation made after the close of business at the place of presentation is deemed to have been made on the next business day.

§ 3.06. Complying Medium of Presentation

a. To comply, a document must be presented in the medium indicated in the standby.

b. Where no medium is indicated, to comply a document must be presented as a paper document, unless only a demand is required, in which case:

i. a demand that is presented via S.W.I.F.T., tested telex, or other similar authenticated means by a beneficiary that is a S.W.I.F.T. participant or a bank complies; otherwise

ii. a demand that is not presented as a paper document does not comply unless the issuer permits, in its sole discretion, the use of that medium.

c. A document is not presented as a paper document if it is communicated by electronic means even if the issuer or nominated person receiving it generates a paper document from it.

d. Where presentation in an electronic medium is indicated, to comply a document must be presented as an electronic record capable of being authenticated by the issuer or nominated person to whom it is presented.

§ 3.07. Separateness of Each Presentation

a. Making a non-complying presentation, withdrawing a presentation, or failing to make any one of a number of scheduled or permitted presentations does not waive or otherwise prejudice the right to make another timely presentation or a timely re-presentation whether or not the standby prohibits partial or multiple drawings or presentations.

b. Wrongful dishonour of a complying presentation does not constitute dishonour of any other presentation under a standby or repudiation of the standby.

c. Honour of a non-complying presentation, with or without notice of its non-compliance, does not waive requirements of a standby for other presentations.

§ 3.08. Partial Drawing and Multiple Presentations; Amount of Drawings

a. A presentation may be made for less than the full amount available (**"partial drawing"**).

b. More than one presentation (**"multiple presentations"**) may be made.

c. The statement "partial drawings prohibited" or a similar expression means that a presentation must be for the full amount available.

d. The statement "multiple drawings prohibited" or a similar expression means that only one presentation may be made and honoured but that it may be for less than the full amount available.

e. If a demand exceeds the amount available under the standby, the drawing is discrepant. Any document other than the demand stating an amount in excess of the amount demanded is not discrepant for that reason.

f. Use of **"approximately"**, **"about"**, **"circa"**, or a similar word permits a tolerance not to exceed 10% more or 10% less of the amount to which such word refers.

§ 3.09. Extend or Pay

A beneficiary's request to extend the expiration date of the standby or, alternatively, to pay the amount available under it:

a. is a presentation demanding payment under the standby, to be examined as such in accordance with these Rules; and

b. implies that the beneficiary:

i. consents to the amendment to extend the expiry date to the date requested;

ii. requests the issuer to exercise its discretion to seek the approval of the applicant and to issue that amendment;

iii. upon issuance of that amendment, retracts its demand for payment; and

iv. consents to the maximum time available under these Rules for examination and notice of dishonour.

§ 3.10. No Notice of Receipt of Presentation

An issuer is not required to notify the applicant of receipt of a presentation under the standby.

§ 3.11. Issuer Waiver and Applicant Consent to Waiver of Presentation Rules

In addition to other discretionary provisions in a standby or these Rules, an issuer may, in its sole discretion, without notice to or consent of the applicant and without effect on the applicant's obligations to the issuer, waive

a. the following Rules and any similar terms stated in the standby which are primarily for the issuer's benefit or operational convenience:

i. treatment of documents received, at the request of the presenter, as having been presented at a later date (Rule 3.02);

ii. identification of a presentation to the standby under which it is presented (Rule 3.03(a));

iii. where and to whom presentation is made (Rule 3.04(b), (c), and (d)), except the country of presentation stated in the standby; or

iv. treatment of a presentation made after the close of business as if it were made on the next business day (Rule 3.05(b)).

b. the following Rule but not similar terms stated in the standby:

i. a required document dated after the date of its stated presentation (Rule 4.06); or

ii. the requirement that a document issued by the beneficiary be in the language of the standby (Rule 4.04).

c. the following Rule relating to the operational integrity of the standby only in so far as the bank is in fact dealing with the true beneficiary:

acceptance of a demand in an electronic medium (Rule 3.06(b)).

Waiver by the confirmer requires the consent of the issuer with respect to paragraphs (b) and (c) of this Rule.

§ 3.12. Original Standby Lost, Stolen, Mutilated, or Destroyed

a. If an original standby is lost, stolen, mutilated, or destroyed, the issuer need not replace it or waive any requirement that the original be presented under the standby.

b. If the issuer agrees to replace an original standby or to waive a requirement for its presentation, it may provide a replacement or copy to the beneficiary without affecting the applicant's obligations to the issuer to reimburse, but, if it does so, the issuer must mark the replacement or copy as such. The issuer may, in its sole discretion, require indemnities satisfactory to it from the beneficiary and assurances from nominated persons that no payment has been made.

Closure On Expiry Date

§ 3.13. Expiration Date on a Non-Business Day

a. If the last day for presentation stated in a standby (whether stated to be the expiration date or the date by which documents must be received) is not a business day of the issuer or nominated person where presentation is to be made, then presentation made there on the first following business day shall be deemed timely.

b. A nominated person to whom such a presentation is made must so notify the issuer.

§ 3.14. Closure on a Business Day and Authorization of Another Reasonable Place for Presentation

a. If on the last business day for presentation the place for presentation stated in a standby is for any reason closed and presentation is not timely made because of the closure, then the last day for presentation is automatically extended to the day occurring thirty calendar days after the place for presentation re-opens for business, unless the standby otherwise provides.

b. Upon or in anticipation of closure of the place of presentation, an issuer may authorise another reasonable place for presentation in the standby or in a communication received by the beneficiary. If it does so, then

i. presentation must be made at that reasonable place; and

ii. if the communication is received fewer than thirty calendar days before the last day for presentation and for that reason presentation is not timely made, the last day for presentation is automatically extended to the day occurring thirty calendar days after the last day for presentation.

RULE 4: EXAMINATION

§ 4.01. Examination for Compliance

a. Demands for honour of a standby must comply with the terms and conditions of the standby.

b. Whether a presentation appears to comply is determined by examining the presentation on its face against the terms and conditions stated in the standby as interpreted and supplemented by these Rules which are to be read in the context of standard standby practice.

§ 4.02. Non-Examination of Extraneous Documents

Documents presented which are not required by the standby need not be examined and, in any event, shall be disregarded for purposes of determining compliance of the presentation. They may without responsibility be returned to the presenter or passed on with the other documents presented.

§ 4.03. Examination for Inconsistency

An issuer or nominated person is required to examine documents for inconsistency with each other only to the extent provided in the standby.

§ 4.04. Language of Documents

The language of all documents issued by the beneficiary is to be that of the standby.

§ 4.05. Issuer of Documents

Any required document must be issued by the beneficiary unless the standby indicates that the document is to be issued by a third person or the document is of a type that standard standby practice requires to be issued by a third person.

§ 4.06. Date of Documents

The issuance date of a required document may be earlier but not later than the date of its presentation.

§ 4.07. Required Signature on a Document

a. A required document need not be signed unless the standby indicates that the document must be signed or the document is of a type that standard standby practice requires be signed.

b. A required signature may be made in any manner that corresponds to the medium in which the signed document is presented.

c. Unless a standby specifies:

i. the name of a person who must sign a document, any signature or authentication will be regarded as a complying signature.

ii. the status of a person who must sign, no indication of status is necessary.

d. If a standby specifies that a signature must be made by:

i. a named natural person without requiring that the signer's status be identified, a signature complies that appears to be that of the named person;

ii. a named legal person or government agency without identifying who is to sign on its behalf or its status, any signature complies that appears to have been made on behalf of the named legal person or government agency; or

iii. a named natural person, legal person, or government agency requiring the status of the signer be indicated, a signature complies which appears to be that of the named natural person, legal person, or government agency and indicates its status.

§ 4.08. Demand Document Implied

If a standby does not specify any required document, it will still be deemed to require a documentary demand for payment.

§ 4.09. Identical Wording and Quotation Marks

If a standby requires:

a. a statement without specifying precise wording, then the wording in the document presented must appear to convey the same meaning as that required by the standby;

b. specified wording by the use of quotation marks, blocked wording, or an attached exhibit or form, then typographical errors in spelling, punctuation, spacing, or the like that are apparent when read in context are not required to be duplicated and blank lines or spaces for data may be completed in any manner not inconsistent with the standby; or

c. specified wording by the use of quotation marks, blocked wording, or an attached exhibit or form, and also provides that the specified wording be "exact" or "identical", then the wording in the documents presented must duplicate the specified wording, including typographical errors in spelling, punctuation, spacing and the like, as well as blank lines and spaces for data must be exactly reproduced.

§ 4.10. Applicant Approval

A standby should not specify that a required document be issued, signed, or counter-signed by the applicant. However, if the standby includes such a requirement, the issuer may not waive the requirement and is not responsible for the applicant's withholding of the document or signature.

§ 4.11. Non-Documentary Terms or Conditions

a. A standby term or condition which is non-documentary must be disregarded whether or not it affects the issuer's obligation to treat a presentation as complying or to treat the standby as issued, amended, or terminated.

b. Terms or conditions are non-documentary if the standby does not require presentation of a document in which they are to be evidenced and if their fulfillment cannot be determined by the issuer from the issuer's own records or within the issuer's normal operations.

c. Determinations from the issuer's own records or within the issuer's normal operations include determinations of:

i. when, where, and how documents are presented or otherwise delivered to the issuer;

ii. when, where, and how communications affecting the standby are sent or received by the issuer, beneficiary, or any nominated person;

iii. amounts transferred into or out of accounts with the issuer; and

iv. amounts determinable from a published index (e.g., if a standby provides for determining amounts of interest accruing according to published interest rates).

d. An issuer need not re-compute a beneficiary's computations under a formula stated or referenced in a standby except to the extent that the standby so provides.

§ 4.12. Formality of Statements in Documents

a. A required statement need not be accompanied by a solemnity, officialization, or any other formality.

b. If a standby provides for the addition of a formality to a required statement by the person making it without specifying form or content, the statement complies if it indicates that it was declared, averred, warranted, attested, sworn under oath, affirmed, certified, or the like.

c. If a standby provides for a statement to be witnessed by another person without specifying form or content, the witnessed statement complies if it appears to contain a signature of a person other than the beneficiary with an indication that the person is acting as a witness.

d. If a standby provides for a statement to be countersigned, legalized, visaed, or the like by a person other than the beneficiary acting in a governmental, judicial, corporate, or other representative capacity without specifying form or content, the statement complies if it contains the signature of a person other than the beneficiary and includes an indication of that person's representative capacity and the organization on whose behalf the person has acted.

§ 4.13. No Responsibility to Identify Beneficiary

Except to the extent that a standby requires presentation of an electronic record:

a. a person honouring a presentation has no obligation to the applicant to ascertain the identity of any person making a presentation or any assignee of proceeds;

b. payment to a named beneficiary, transferee, an acknowledged assignee, successor by operation of law, to an account or account number stated in the standby or in a cover instruction from the beneficiary or nominated person fulfills the obligation under the standby to effect payment.

§ 4.14. Name of Acquired or Merged Issuer or Confirmer

If the issuer or confirmer is reorganized, merged, or changes its name, any required reference by name to the issuer or confirmer in the documents presented may be to it or its successor.

§ 4.15. Original, Copy, and Multiple Documents

a. A presented document must be an original.

b. Presentation of an electronic record, where an electronic presentation is permitted or required, is deemed to be an **"original"**.

c. i. A presented document is deemed to be an original unless it appears on its face to have been reproduced from an original.

ii. A document which appears to have been reproduced from an original is deemed to be an original if the signature or authentication appears to be original.

d. A standby that requires presentation of a **"copy"** permits presentation of either an original or copy unless the standby states that only a copy be presented or otherwise addresses the disposition of all originals.

e. If multiples of the same document are requested, only one must be an original unless:

i. "duplicate originals" or "multiple originals" are requested in which case all must be originals; or

ii. "two copies", "two-fold", or the like are requested in which case either originals or copies may be presented.

Standby Document Types

§ 4.16. Demand for Payment

a. A demand for payment need not be separate from the beneficiary's statement or other required document.

b. If a separate demand is required, it must contain:

i. a demand for payment from the beneficiary directed to the issuer or nominated person;

ii. a date indicating when the demand was issued;

iii. the amount demanded; and

iv. the beneficiary's signature.

c. A demand may be in the form of a draft or other instruction, order, or request to pay. If a standby requires presentation of a "draft" or "bill of exchange", that draft or bill of exchange need not be in negotiable form unless the standby so states.

§ 4.17. Statement of Default or Other Drawing Event

If a standby requires a statement, certificate, or other recital of a default or other drawing event and does not specify content, the document complies if it contains:

a. a representation to the effect that payment is due because a drawing event described in the standby has occurred;

b. a date indicating when it was issued; and

c. the beneficiary's signature.

§ 4.18. Negotiable Documents

If a standby requires presentation of a document that is transferable by endorsement and delivery without stating whether, how, or to whom endorsement must be made, then the document may be presented without endorsement, or, if endorsed, the endorsement may be in blank and, in any event, the document may be issued or negotiated with or without recourse.

§ 4.19. Legal or Judicial Documents

If a standby requires presentation of a government-issued document, a court order, an arbitration award, or the like, a document or a copy is deemed to comply if it appears to be:

i. issued by a government agency, court, tribunal, or the like;

ii. suitably titled or named;

iii. signed;

iv. dated; and

v. originally certified or authenticated by an official of a government agency, court, tribunal, or the like.

§ 4.20. Other Documents

a. If a standby requires a document other than one whose content is specified in these Rules without specifying the issuer, data content, or wording, a document complies if it appears to be appropriately titled or to serve the function of that type of document under standard standby practice.

b. A document presented under a standby is to be examined in the context of standby practice under these Rules even if the document is of a type (such as a commercial invoice, transport documents, insurance documents or the like) for which the Uniform Customs and Practice for Documentary Credits contains detailed rules.

§ 4.21. Request to Issue Separate Undertaking

If a standby requests that the beneficiary of the standby issue its own separate undertaking to another (whether or not the standby recites the text of that undertaking):

a. the beneficiary receives no rights other than its rights to draw under the standby even if the issuer pays a fee to the beneficiary for issuing the separate undertaking;

b. neither the separate undertaking nor any documents presented under it need be presented to the issuer; and

c. if originals or copies of the separate undertaking or documents presented under it are received by the issuer although not required to be presented as a condition to honour of the standby:

i. the issuer need not examine, and, in any event, shall disregard their compliance or consistency with the standby, with the beneficiary's demand under the standby, or with the beneficiary's separate undertaking; and

ii. the issuer may without responsibility return them to the presenter or forward them to the applicant with the presentation.

RULE 5: NOTICE, PRECLUSION, AND DISPOSITION OF DOCUMENTS

§ 5.01. Timely Notice of Dishonour

a. Notice of dishonour must be given within a time after presentation of documents which is not unreasonable.

i. Notice given within three business days is deemed to be not unreasonable and beyond seven business days is deemed to be unreasonable.

ii. Whether the time within which notice is given is unreasonable does not depend upon an imminent deadline for presentation.

iii. The time for calculating when notice of dishonour must be given begins on the business day following the business day of presentation.

iv. Unless a standby otherwise expressly states a shortened time within which notice of dishonour must be given, the issuer has no obligation to accelerate its examination of a presentation.

b. i. The means by which a notice of dishonour is to be given is by telecommunication, if available, and, if not, by another available means which allows for prompt notice.

ii. If notice of dishonour is received within the time permitted for giving the notice, then it is deemed to have been given by prompt means.

c. Notice of dishonour must be given to the person from whom the documents were received (whether the beneficiary, nominated person, or person other than a delivery person) except as otherwise requested by the presenter.

§ 5.02. Statement of Grounds for Dishonour

A notice of dishonour shall state all discrepancies upon which dishonour is based.

§ 5.03. Failure to Give Timely Notice of Dishonour

a. Failure to give notice of a discrepancy in a notice of dishonour within the time and by the means specified in the standby or these rules precludes assertion of that discrepancy in any document containing the discrepancy that is retained or re-presented, but does not preclude assertion of that discrepancy in any different presentation under the same or a separate standby.

b. Failure to give notice of dishonour or acceptance or acknowledgment that a deferred payment undertaking has been incurred obligates the issuer to pay at maturity.

§ 5.04. Notice of Expiry

Failure to give notice that a presentation was made after the expiration date does not preclude dishonour for that reason.

§ 5.05. Issuer Request for Applicant Waiver Without Request by Presenter

If the issuer decides that a presentation does not comply and if the presenter does not otherwise instruct, the issuer may, in its sole discretion, request the applicant to waive non-compliance or otherwise to authorise honour within the time available for giving notice of dishonour but without extending it. Obtaining the applicant's waiver does not obligate the issuer to waive non-compliance.

§ 5.06. Issuer Request for Applicant Waiver upon Request of Presenter

If, after receipt of notice of dishonour, a presenter requests that the presented documents be forwarded to the issuer or that the issuer seek the applicant's waiver:

a. no person is obligated to forward the discrepant documents or seek the applicant's waiver;

b. the presentation to the issuer remains subject to these Rules unless departure from them is expressly consented to by the presenter; and

c. if the documents are forwarded or if a waiver is sought:

i. the presenter is precluded from objecting to the discrepancies notified to it by the issuer;

ii. the issuer is not relieved from examining the presentation under these Rules;

iii. the issuer is not obligated to waive the discrepancy even if the applicant waives it; and

iv. the issuer must hold the documents until it receives a response from the applicant or is requested by the presenter to return the documents, and if the issuer receives no such response or request within ten business days of its notice of dishonour, it may return the documents to the presenter.

§ 5.07. Disposition of Documents

Dishonoured documents must be returned, held, or disposed of as reasonably instructed by the presenter. Failure to give notice of the disposition of documents in the notice of dishonour does not preclude the issuer from asserting any defense otherwise available to it against honour.

§ 5.08. Cover Instructions/Transmittal Letter

a. Instructions accompanying a presentation made under a standby may be relied on to the extent that they are not contrary to the terms or conditions of the standby, the demand, or these Rules.

b. Representations made by a nominated person accompanying a presentation may be relied upon to the extent that they are not contrary to the terms or conditions of a standby or these Rules.

c. Notwithstanding receipt of instructions, an issuer or nominated person may pay, give notice, return the documents, or otherwise deal directly with the presenter.

d. A statement in the cover letter that the documents are discrepant does not relieve the issuer from examining the presentation for compliance.

§ 5.09. Applicant Notice of Objection

a. An applicant must timely object to an issuer's honour of a noncomplying presentation by giving timely notice by prompt means.

b. An applicant acts timely if it objects to discrepancies by sending a notice to the issuer stating the discrepancies on which the objection is based within a time after the applicant's receipt of the documents which is not unreasonable.

c. Failure to give a timely notice of objection by prompt means precludes assertion by the applicant against the issuer of any discrepancy or other matter apparent on the face of the documents received by the applicant, but does not preclude assertion of that objection to any different presentation under the same or a different standby.

RULE 6: TRANSFER, ASSIGNMENT, AND TRANSFER BY OPERATION OF LAW

Transfer of Drawing Rights

§ 6.01. Request to Transfer Drawing Rights

Where a beneficiary requests that an issuer or nominated person honour a drawing from another person as if that person were the beneficiary, these Rules on transfer of drawing rights (**"transfer"**) apply.

§ 6.02. When Drawing Rights Are Transferable

a. A standby is not transferable unless it so states.

b. A standby that states that it is transferable without further provision means that drawing rights:

i. may be transferred in their entirety more than once;

ii. may not be partially transferred; and

iii. may not be transferred unless the issuer (including the confirmer) or another person specifically nominated in the standby agrees to and effects the transfer requested by the beneficiary.

§ 6.03. Conditions to Transfer

An issuer of a transferable standby or a nominated person need not effect a transfer unless:

a. it is satisfied as to the existence and authenticity of the original standby; and

b. the beneficiary submits or fulfills:

i. a request in a form acceptable to the issuer or nominated person including the effective date of the transfer and the name and address of the transferee;

ii. the original standby;

iii. verification of the signature of the person signing for the beneficiary;

iv. verification of the authority of the person signing for the beneficiary;

v. payment of the transfer fee; and

vi. any other reasonable requirements.

§ 6.04. Effect of Transfer on Required Documents

Where there has been a transfer of drawing rights in their entirety:

a. a draft or demand must be signed by the transferee beneficiary; and

b. the name of the transferee beneficiary may be used in place of the name of the transferor beneficiary in any other required document.

§ 6.05. Reimbursement for Payment Based on a Transfer

An issuer or nominated person paying under a transfer pursuant to Rule 6.03(a), (b)(i), and (b)(ii) is entitled to reimbursement as if it had made payment to the beneficiary.

Acknowledgment of Assignment of Proceeds

§ 6.06. Assignment of Proceeds

Where an issuer or nominated person is asked to acknowledge a beneficiary's request to pay an assignee all or part of any proceeds of the beneficiary's drawing under the standby, these Rules on acknowledgment of an assignment of proceeds apply except where applicable law otherwise requires.

§ 6.07. Request for Acknowledgment

a. Unless applicable law otherwise requires, an issuer or nominated person

i. is not obligated to give effect to an assignment of proceeds which it has not acknowledged; and

ii. is not obligated to acknowledge the assignment.

b. If an assignment is acknowledged:

i. the acknowledgment confers no rights with respect to the standby to the assignee who is only entitled to the proceeds assigned, if any, and whose rights may be affected by amendment or cancellation; and

ii. the rights of the assignee are subject to:

(a) the existence of any net proceeds payable to the beneficiary by the person making the acknowledgment;

(b) rights of nominated persons and transferee beneficiaries;

(c) rights of other acknowledged assignees; and

(d) any other rights or interests that may have priority under applicable law.

§ 6.08. Conditions to Acknowledgment of Assignment of Proceeds

An issuer or nominated person may condition its acknowledgment on receipt of:

a. the original standby for examination or notation;

b. verification of the signature of the person signing for the beneficiary;

c. verification of the authority of the person signing for the beneficiary;

d. an irrevocable request signed by the beneficiary for acknowledgment of the assignment that includes statements, covenants, indemnities, and other provisions which may be contained in the issuer's or nominated person's required form requesting acknowledgment of assignment, such as:

i. the identity of the affected drawings if the standby permits multiple drawings;

ii. the full name, legal form, location, and mailing address of the beneficiary and the assignee;

iii. details of any request affecting the method of payment or delivery of the standby proceeds;

iv. limitation on partial assignments and prohibition of successive assignments;

v. statements regarding the legality and relative priority of the assignment; or

vi. right of recovery by the issuer or nominated person of any proceeds received by the assignee that are recoverable from the beneficiary;

e. payment of a fee for the acknowledgment; and

f. fulfillment of other reasonable requirements.

§ 6.09. Conflicting Claims to Proceeds

If there are conflicting claims to proceeds, then payment to an acknowledged assignee may be suspended pending resolution of the conflict.

§ 6.10. Reimbursement for Payment Based on an Assignment

An issuer or nominated person paying under an acknowledged assignment pursuant to Rule 6.08(a) and (b) is entitled to reimbursement as if it had made payment to the beneficiary. If the beneficiary is a bank, the acknowledgment may be based solely upon an authenticated communication.

Transfer by Operation of Law

§ 6.11. Transferee by Operation of Law

Where an heir, personal representative, liquidator, trustee, receiver, successor corporation, or similar person who claims to be designated by law to succeed to the interests of a beneficiary presents documents in its own name as if it were the authorised transferee of the beneficiary, these Rules on transfer by operation of law apply.

§ 6.12. Additional Document in Event of Drawing in Successor's Name

A claimed successor may be treated as if it were an authorised transferee of a beneficiary's drawing rights in their entirety if it presents an additional document or documents which appear to be issued by a public official or representative (including a judicial officer) and indicate:

a. that the claimed successor is the survivor of a merger, consolidation, or similar action of a corporation, limited liability company, or other similar organization;

b. that the claimed successor is authorised or appointed to act on behalf of the named beneficiary or its estate because of an insolvency proceeding;

c. that the claimed successor is authorised or appointed to act on behalf of the named beneficiary because of death or incapacity; or

d. that the name of the named beneficiary has been changed to that of the claimed successor.

§ 6.13. Suspension of Obligations upon Presentation by Successor

An issuer or nominated person which receives a presentation from a claimed successor which complies in all respects except for the name of the beneficiary:

a. may request in a manner satisfactory as to form and substance:

i. a legal opinion;

ii. an additional document referred to in Rule 6.12 (Additional Document in Event of Drawing in Successor's Name) from a public official;

iii. statements, covenants, and indemnities regarding the status of the claimed successor as successor by operation of law;

iv. payment of fees reasonably related to these determinations; and

v. anything which may be required for a transfer under Rule 6.03 (Conditions to Transfer) or an acknowledgment of assignment of proceeds under Rule 6.08 (Conditions to Acknowledgment of Assignment of Proceeds);

but such documentation shall not constitute a required document for purposes of expiry of the standby.

b. Until the issuer or nominated person receives the requested documentation, its obligation to honour or give notice of dishonour is suspended, but any deadline for presentation of required documents is not thereby extended.

§ 6.14. Reimbursement for Payment Based on a Transfer by Operation of Law

An issuer or nominated person paying under a transfer by operation of law pursuant to Rule 6.12 (Additional Document in Event of Drawing in Successor's Name) is entitled to reimbursement as if it had made payment to the beneficiary.

RULE 7: CANCELLATION

§ 7.01. When an Irrevocable Standby Is Cancelled or Terminated

A beneficiary's rights under a standby may not be cancelled without its consent. Consent may be evidenced in writing or by an action such as return of the original standby in a manner which implies that the beneficiary consents to cancellation. A beneficiary's consent to cancellation is irrevocable when communicated to the issuer.

§ 7.02. Issuer's Discretion Regarding a Decision to Cancel

Before acceding to a beneficiary's authorization to cancel and treating the standby as cancelled for all purposes, an issuer may require in a manner satisfactory as to form and substance:

a. the original standby;

b. verification of the signature of the person signing for the beneficiary;

c. verification of the authorization of the person signing for the beneficiary;

d. a legal opinion;

e. an irrevocable authority signed by the beneficiary for cancellation that includes statements, covenants, indemnities, and similar provisions contained in a required form;

f. satisfaction that the obligation of any confirmer has been cancelled;

g. satisfaction that there has not been a transfer or payment by any nominated person; and

h. any other reasonable measure.

RULE 8: REIMBURSEMENT OBLIGATIONS

§ 8.01. Right to Reimbursement

a. Where payment is made against a complying presentation in accordance with these Rules, reimbursement must be made by:

i. an applicant to an issuer requested to issue a standby; and

ii. an issuer to a person nominated to honour or otherwise give value.

b. An applicant must indemnify the issuer against all claims, obligations, and responsibilities (including attorney's fees) arising out of:

i. the imposition of law or practice other than that chosen in the standby or applicable at the place of issuance;

ii. the fraud, forgery, or illegal action of others; or

iii. the issuer's performance of the obligations of a confirmer that wrongfully dishonours a confirmation.

c. This Rule supplements any applicable agreement, course of dealing, practice, custom or usage providing for reimbursement or indemnification on lesser or other grounds.

§ 8.02. Charges for Fees and Costs

a. An applicant must pay the issuer's charges and reimburse the issuer for any charges that the issuer is obligated to pay to persons nominated with the applicant's consent to advise, confirm, honour, negotiate, transfer, or to issue a separate undertaking.

b. An issuer is obligated to pay the charges of other persons:

i. if they are payable in accordance with the terms of the standby; or

ii. if they are the reasonable and customary fees and expenses of a person requested by the issuer to advise, honour, negotiate, transfer, or to issue a separate undertaking, and they are unrecovered and unrecoverable from the beneficiary or other presenter because no demand is made under the standby.

§ 8.03. Refund of Reimbursement

A nominated person that obtains reimbursement before the issuer timely dishonours the presentation must refund the reimbursement with interest if the issuer dishonours. The refund does not preclude the nominated person's wrongful dishonour claims.

§ 8.04. Bank-to-Bank Reimbursement

Any instruction or authorization to obtain reimbursement from another bank is subject to the International Chamber of Commerce standard rules for bank-to-bank reimbursements.

RULE 9: TIMING

§ 9.01. Duration of Standby

A standby must:

a. contain an expiry date; or

b. permit the issuer to terminate the standby upon reasonable prior notice or payment.

§ 9.02. Effect of Expiration on Nominated Person

The rights of a nominated person that acts within the scope of its nomination are not affected by the subsequent expiry of the standby.

§ 9.03. Calculation of Time

a. A period of time within which an action must be taken under these Rules begins to run on the first business day following the business day when the action could have been undertaken at the place where the action should have been undertaken.

b. An extension period starts on the calendar day following the stated expiry date even if either day falls on a day when the issuer is closed.

§ 9.04. Time of Day of Expiration

If no time of day is stated for expiration, it occurs at the close of business at the place of presentation.

§ 9.05. Retention of Standby

Retention of the original standby does not preserve any rights under the standby after the right to demand payment ceases.

RULE 10: SYNDICATION/ PARTICIPATION

§ 10.01. Syndication

If a standby with more than one issuer does not state to whom presentation may be made, presentation may be made to any issuer with binding effect on all issuers.

§ 10.02. Participation

a. Unless otherwise agreed between an applicant and an issuer, the issuer may sell participations in the issuer's rights against the applicant and any presenter and may disclose relevant applicant information in confidence to potential participants.

b. An issuer's sale of participations does not affect the obligations of the issuer under the standby or create any rights or obligations between the beneficiary and any participant.

UNCITRAL Convention on International Bills of Exchange and Promissory Notes, 1988

CHAPTER I. SPHERE OF APPLICATION AND FORM OF THE INSTRUMENT

Article 1.

1. This Convention applies to an international bill of exchange when it contains the heading "International bill of exchange (UNCITRAL Convention)" and also contains in its text the words "International bill of exchange (UNCITRAL Convention)".

2. This Convention applies to an international promissory note when it contains the heading "International promissory note (UNCITRAL Convention)" and also contains in its text the words "International promissory note (UNCITRAL Convention)".

3. This Convention does not apply to cheques.

Article 2.

1. An international bill of exchange is a bill of exchange which specifies at least two of the following places and indicates that any two so specified are situated in different States:

(a) The place where the bill is drawn;

(b) The place indicated next to the signature of the drawer;

(c) The place indicated next to the name of the drawee;

(d) The place indicated next to the name of the payee;

(e) The place of payment, provided that either the place where the bill is drawn or the place of payment is specified on the bill and that such place is situated in a Contracting State.

2. An international promissory note is a promissory note which specifies at least two of the following places and indicates that any two so specified are situated in different States:

(a) The place where the note is made;

(b) The place indicated next to the signature of the maker;

(c) The place indicated next to the name of the payee;

(d) The place of payment, provided that the place of payment is specified on the note and that such place is situated in a Contracting State.

3. This Convention does not deal with the question of sanctions that may be imposed under national law in cases where an incorrect or false statement has been made on an instrument in respect of a place referred to in paragraph 1 or 2 of this article. However, any such sanctions shall not affect the validity of the instrument or the application of this Convention.

Article 3.

1. A bill of exchange is a written instrument which:

(a) Contains an unconditional order whereby the drawer directs the drawee to pay a definite sum of money to the payee or to his order;

(b) Is payable on demand or at a definite time;

(c) Is dated;

(d) Is signed by the drawer.

2. A promissory note is a written instrument which:

(a) Contains an unconditional promise whereby the maker undertakes to pay a definite sum of money to the payee or to his order;

(b) Is payable on demand or at a definite time;

(c) Is dated;

(d) Is signed by the maker.

CHAPTER II. INTERPRETATION

Section 1. General Provisions

Article 4.

In the interpretation of this Convention, regard is to be had to its international character and to the need to promote uniformity in its application and the observance of good faith in international transactions.

Article 5.

In this Convention:

(a) "Bill" means an international bill of exchange governed by this Convention;

(b) "Note" means an international promissory note governed by this Convention;

(c) "Instrument" means a bill or a note;

(d) "Drawee" means a person on whom a bill is drawn and who has not accepted it;

(e) "Payee" means a person in whose favour the drawer directs payment to be made or to whom the maker promises to pay;

(f) "Holder" means a person in possession of an instrument in accordance with article 15;

(g) "Protected holder" means a holder who meets the requirements of article 29;

(h) "Guarantor" means any person who undertakes an obligation of guarantee under article 46, whether governed by paragraph 4 (b) ("guaranteed") or paragraph 4 (c) ("*aval*") of article 47;

(i) "Party" means a person who has signed an instrument as drawer, maker, acceptor, endorser or guarantor;

(j) "Maturity" means the time of payment referred to in paragraphs 4, 5, 6 and 7 of article 9;

(k) "Signature" means a handwritten signature, its facsimile or an equivalent authentication effected by any other means; "forged signature" includes a signature by the wrongful use of such means;

(l) "Money" or "currency" includes a monetary unit of account which is established by an intergovernmental institution or by agreement between two or more States, provided that this Convention shall apply without prejudice to the rules of the intergovernmental institution or to the stipulations of the agreement.

Article 6.

For the purposes of this Convention, a person is considered to have knowledge of a fact if he has actual knowledge of that fact or could not have been unaware of its existence.

Section 2. Interpretation of Formal Requirements

Article 7.

The sum payable by an instrument is deemed to be a definite sum although the instrument states that it is to be paid:

(a) With interest;

(b) By instalments at successive dates;

(c) By instalments at successive dates with a stipulation in the instrument that upon default in payment of any instalment the unpaid balance becomes due;

(d) According to a rate of exchange indicated in the instrument or to be determined as directed by the instrument; or

(e) In a currency other than the currency in which the sum is expressed in the instrument.

Article 8.

1. If there is a discrepancy between the sum expressed in words and the sum expressed in figures, the sum payable by the instrument is the sum expressed in words.

2. If the sum is expressed more than once in words, and there is a discrepancy, the sum payable is the smaller sum. The same rule applies if the sum is expressed more than once in figures only, and there is a discrepancy.

3. If the sum is expressed in a currency having the same description as that of at least one other State than the State where payment is to be made, as indicated in

the instrument, and the specified currency is not identified as the currency of any particular State, the currency is to be considered as the currency of the State where payment is to be made.

4. If an instrument states that the sum is to be paid with interest, without specifying the date from which interest is to run, interest runs from the date of the instrument.

5. A stipulation stating that the sum is to be paid with interest is deemed not to have been written on the instrument unless it indicates the rate at which interest is to be paid.

6. A rate at which interest is to be paid may be expressed either as a definite rate or as a variable rate. For a variable rate to qualify for this purpose, it must vary in relation to one or more reference rates of interest in accordance with provisions stipulated in the instrument and each such reference rate must be published or otherwise available to the public and not be subject, directly or indirectly, to unilateral determination by a person who is named in the instrument at the time the bill is drawn or the note is made, unless the person is named only in the reference rate provisions.

7. If the rate at which interest is to be paid is expressed as a variable rate, it may be stipulated expressly in the instrument that such rate shall not be less than or exceed a specified rate of interest, or that the variations are otherwise limited.

8. If a variable rate does not qualify under paragraph 6 of this article or for any reason it is not possible to determine the numerical value of the variable rate for any period, interest shall be payable for the relevant period at the rate calculated in accordance with paragraph 2 of article 70.

Article 9.

1. An instrument is deemed to be payable on demand:

(a) If it states that it is payable at sight or on demand or on presentment or if it contains words of similar import; or

(b) If no time of payment is expressed.

2. An instrument payable at a definite time which is accepted or endorsed or guaranteed after maturity is an instrument payable on demand as regards the acceptor, the endorser or the guarantor.

3. An instrument is deemed to be payable at a definite time if it states that it is payable:

(a) On a stated date or at a fixed period after a stated date or at a fixed period after the date of the instrument;

(b) At a fixed period after sight;

(c) By instalments at successive dates; or

(d) By instalments at successive dates with the stipulation in the instrument that upon default in payment of any instalment the unpaid balance becomes due.

4. The time of payment of an instrument payable at a fixed period after date is determined by reference to the date of the instrument.

5. The time of payment of a bill payable at a fixed period after sight is determined by the date of acceptance or, if the bill is dishonoured by non-acceptance, by the date of protest or, if protest is dispensed with, by the date of dishonour.

6. The time of payment of an instrument payable on demand is the date on which the instrument is presented for payment.

7. The time of payment of a note payable at a fixed period after sight is determined by the date of the visa signed by the maker on the note or, if his visa is refused, by the date of presentment.

8. If an instrument is drawn, or made, payable one or more months after a stated date or after the date of the instrument or after sight, the instrument is payable on the corresponding date of the month when payment must be made. If there is no corresponding date, the instrument is payable on the last day of that month.

Article 10.

1. A bill may be drawn:

(a) By two or more drawers;

(b) Payable to two or more payees.

2. A note may be made:

(a) By two or more makers;

(b) Payable to two or more payees.

3. If an instrument is payable to two or more payees in the alternative, it is payable to any one of them and any one of them in possession of the instrument may exercise the rights of a holder. In any other case the instrument is payable to all of them and the rights of a holder may be exercised only by all of them.

Article 11.

A bill may be drawn by the drawer:

(a) On himself;

(b) Payable to his order.

Section 3. Completion of an Incomplete Instrument

Article 12.

1. An incomplete instrument which satisfies the requirements set out in paragraph 1 of article 1 and

bears the signature of the drawer or the acceptance of the drawee, or which satisfies the requirements set out in paragraph 2 of article 1 and paragraph 2 (d) of article , but which lacks other elements pertaining to one or more of the requirements set out in articles 2 and 3, may be completed, and the instrument so completed is effective as a bill or a note.

2. If such an instrument is completed without authority or otherwise than in accordance with the authority given:

(a) A party who signed the instrument before the completion may invoke such lack of authority as a defence against a holder who had knowledge of such lack of authority when he became a holder;

(b) A party who signed the instrument after the completion is liable according to the terms of the instrument so completed.

CHAPTER III. TRANSFER

Article 13.

An instrument is transferred:

(a) By endorsement and delivery of the instrument by the endorser to the endorsee; or

(b) By mere delivery of the instrument if the last endorsement is in blank.

Article 14.

1. An endorsement must be written on the instrument or on a slip affixed thereto ("*allonge*"). It must be signed.

2. An endorsement may be:

(a) In blank, that is, by a signature alone or by a signature accompanied by a statement to the effect that the instrument is payable to a person in possession of it;

(b) Special, that is, by a signature accompanied by an indication of the person to whom the instrument is payable.

3. A signature alone, other than that of the drawee, is an endorsement only if placed on the back of the instrument.

Article 15.

1. A person is a holder if he is:

(a) The payee in possession of the instrument; or

(b) In possession of an instrument which has been endorsed to him, or on which the last endorsement is in blank, and on which there appears an uninterrupted series of endorsements, even if any endorsement was forged or was signed by an agent without authority.

2. If an endorsement in blank is followed by another endorsement, the person who signed this last endorsement is deemed to be an endorsee by the endorsement in blank.

3. A person is not prevented from being a holder by the fact that the instrument was obtained by him or any previous holder under circumstances, including incapacity or fraud, duress or mistake of any kind, that would give rise to a claim to, or a defence against liability on, the instrument.

Article 16.

The holder of an instrument on which the last endorsement is in blank may:

(a) Further endorse it either by an endorsement in blank or by a special endorsement;

(b) Convert the blank endorsement into a special endorsement by indicating in the endorsement that the instrument is payable to himself or to some other specified person; or

(c) Transfer the instrument in accordance with subparagraph (b) of article 13.

Article 17.

1. If the drawer or the maker has inserted in the instrument such words as "not negotiable", "not transferable", "not to order", "pay (X) only", or words of similar import, the instrument may not be transferred except for purposes of collection, and any endorsement, even if it does not contain words authorizing the endorsee to collect the instrument, is deemed to be an endorsement for collection.

2. If an endorsement contains the words "not negotiable", "not transferable", "not to order", "pay (X) only", or words of similar import, the instrument may not be transferred further except for purposes of collection, and any subsequent endorsement, even if it does not contain words authorizing the endorsee to collect the instrument, is deemed to be an endorsement for collection.

Article 18.

1. An endorsement must be unconditional.

2. A conditional endorsement transfers the instrument whether or not the condition is fulfilled. The condition is ineffective as to those parties and transferees who are subsequent to the endorsee.

Article 19.

An endorsement in respect of a part of the sum due under the instrument is ineffective as an endorsement.

Article 20.

If there are two or more endorsements, it is presumed, unless the contrary is proved, that each endorsement was made in the order in which it appears on the instrument.

Article 21.

1. If an endorsement contains the words "for collection", "for deposit", "value in collection", "by procuration", "pay any bank", or words of similar import authorizing the endorsee to collect the instrument, the endorsee is a holder who:

(a) May exercise all rights arising out of the instrument;

(b) May endorse the instrument only for purposes of collection;

(c) Is subject only to the claims and defences which may be set up against the endorser.

2. The endorser for collection is not liable on the instrument to any subsequent holder.

Article 22.

1. If an endorsement contains the words "value in security", "value in pledge", or any other words indicating a pledge, the endorsee is a holder who:

(a) May exercise all rights arising out of the instrument;

(b) May endorse the instrument only for purposes of collection;

(c) Is subject only to the claims and defences specified in article 28 or article 30.

2. If such an endorsee endorses for collection, he is not liable on the instrument to any subsequent holder.

Article 23.

The holder of an instrument may transfer it to a prior party or to the drawee in accordance with article 13; however, if the transferee has previously been a holder of the instrument, no endorsement is required, and any endorsement which would prevent him from qualifying as a holder may be struck out.

Article 24.

An instrument may be transferred in accordance with article 13 after maturity, except by the drawee, the acceptor or the maker.

Article 25.

1. If an endorsement is forged, the person whose endorsement is forged, or a party who signed the instrument before the forgery, has the right to recover compensation for any damage that he may have suffered because of the forgery against:

(a) The forger;

(b) The person to whom the instrument was directly transferred by the forger;

(c) A party or the drawee who paid the instrument to the forger directly or through one or more endorsees for collection.

2. However, an endorsee for collection is not liable under paragraph 1 of this article if he is without knowledge of the forgery:

(a) At the time he pays the principal or advises him of the receipt of payment; or

(b) At the time he receives payment, if this is later,

unless his lack of knowledge is due to his failure to act in good faith or to exercise reasonable care.

3. Furthermore, a party or the drawee who pays an instrument is not liable under paragraph 1 of this article if, at the time he pays the instrument, he is without knowledge of the forgery, unless his lack of knowledge is due to his failure to act in good faith or to exercise reasonable care.

4. Except as against the forger, the damages recoverable under paragraph 1 of this article may not exceed the amount referred to in article 70 or article 71.

Article 26.

1. If an endorsement is made by an agent without authority or power to bind his principal in the matter, the principal, or a party who signed the instrument before such endorsement, has the right to recover compensation for any damage that he may have suffered because of such endorsement against:

(a) The agent;

(b) The person to whom the instrument was directly transferred by the agent;

(c) A party or the drawee who paid the instrument to the agent directly or through one or more endorsees for collection.

2. However, an endorsee for collection is not liable under paragraph 1 of this article if he is without knowledge that the endorsement does not bind the principal:

(a) At the time he pays the principal or advises him of the receipt of payment; or

(b) At the time he receives payment, if this is later, unless his lack of knowledge is due to his failure to act in good faith or to exercise reasonable care.

3. Furthermore, a party or the drawee who pays an instrument is not liable under paragraph 1 of this article if, at the time he pays the instrument, he is without knowledge that the endorsement does not bind the principal, unless his lack of knowledge is due to his failure to act in good faith or to exercise reasonable care.

4. Except as against the agent, the damages recoverable under paragraph 1 of this article may not exceed the amount referred to in article 70 or article 71.

CHAPTER IV. RIGHTS AND LIABILITIES

Section 1. The Rights of a Holder and of a Protected Holder

Article 27.

1. The holder of an instrument has all the rights conferred on him by this Convention against the parties to the instrument.

2. The holder may transfer the instrument in accordance with article 13.

Article 28.

1. A party may set up against a holder who is not a protected holder:

(a) Any defence that may be set up against a protected holder in accordance with paragraph 1 of article 30;

(b) Any defence based on the underlying transaction between himself and the drawer or between himself and his transferee, but only if the holder took the instrument with knowledge of such defence or if he obtained the instrument by fraud or theft or participated at any time in a fraud or theft concerning it;

(c) Any defence arising from the circumstances as a result of which he became a party, but only if the holder took the instrument with knowledge of such defence or if he obtained the instrument by fraud or theft or participated at any time in a fraud or theft concerning it;

(d) Any defence which may be raised against an action in contract between himself and the holder;

(e) Any other defence available under this Convention.

2. The rights to an instrument of a holder who is not a protected holder are subject to any valid claim to the instrument on the part of any person, but only if he took the instrument with knowledge of such claim or if he obtained the instrument by fraud or theft or participated at any time in a fraud or theft concerning it.

3. A holder who takes an instrument after the expiration of the time-limit for presentment for payment is subject to any claim to, or defence against liability on, the instrument to which his transferor is subject.

4. A party may not raise as a defence against a holder who is not a protected holder the fact that a third person has a claim to the instrument unless:

(a) The third person asserted a valid claim to the instrument; or

(b) The holder acquired the instrument by theft or forged the signature of the payee or an endorsee, or participated in the theft or the forgery.

Article 29.

"Protected holder" means the holder of an instrument which was complete when he took it or which was incomplete within the meaning of paragraph 1 of article 12 and was completed in accordance with authority given, provided that when he became a holder:

(a) He was without knowledge of a defence against liability on the instrument referred to in paragraphs 1(a), (b), (c) and (e) of article 28;

(b) He was without knowledge of a valid claim to the instrument of any person;

(c) He was without knowledge of the fact that it had been dishonoured by non-acceptance or by non-payment;

(d) The time-limit provided by article 55 for presentment of that instrument for payment had not expired;

(e) He did not obtain the instrument by fraud or theft or participate in a fraud or theft concerning it.

Article 30.

1. A party may not set up against a protected holder any defence except:

(a) Defences under paragraph 1 of article 33, article 34, paragraph 1 of article 35, paragraph 3 of article 36, paragraph 1 of article 53, paragraph 1 of article 57, paragraph 1 of article 63 and article 84 of this Convention;

(b) Defences based on the underlying transaction between himself and such holder or arising from any fraudulent act on the part of such holder in obtaining the signature on the instrument of that party;

(c) Defences based on his incapacity to incur liability on the instrument or on the fact that he signed without knowledge that his signature made him a party to the instrument, provided that his lack of knowledge was not due to his negligence and provided that he was fraudulently induced so to sign.

2. The rights to an instrument of a protected holder are not subject to any claim to the instrument on the part of any person, except a valid claim arising from the underlying transaction between himself and the person by whom the claim is raised.

Article 31.

1. The transfer of an instrument by a protected holder vests in any subsequent holder the rights to and on the instrument which the protected holder had.

2. Those rights are not vested in a subsequent holder if:

(a) He participated in a transaction which gives rise to a claim to, or a defence against liability on, the instrument;

(b) He has previously been a holder, but not a protected holder.

Article 32.

Every holder is presumed to be a protected holder unless the contrary is proved.

Section 2. Liabilities of the Parties

A. GENERAL PROVISIONS

Article 33.

1. Subject to the provisions of articles 34 and 36, a person is not liable on an instrument unless he signs it.

2. A person who signs an instrument in a name which is not his own is liable as if he had signed it in his own name.

Article 34.

A forged signature on an instrument does not impose any liability on the person whose signature was forged. However, if he consents to be bound by the forged signature or represents that it is his own, he is liable as if he had signed the instrument himself.

Article 35.

1. If an instrument is materially altered:

(a) A party who signs it after the material alteration is liable according to the terms of the altered text;

(b) A party who signs it before the material alteration is liable according to the terms of the original text. However, if a party makes, authorizes or assents to a material alteration, he is liable according to the terms of the altered text.

2. A signature is presumed to have been placed on the instrument after the material alteration unless the contrary is proved.

3. Any alteration is material which modifies the written undertaking on the instrument of any party in any respect.

Article 36.

1. An instrument may be signed by an agent.

2. The signature of an agent placed by him on an instrument with the authority of his principal and showing on the instrument that he is signing in a representative capacity for that named principal, or the signature of a principal placed on the instrument by an agent with his authority, imposes liability on the principal and not on the agent.

3. A signature placed on an instrument by a person as agent but who lacks authority to sign or exceeds his authority, or by an agent who has authority to sign but who does not show on the instrument that he is signing in a representative capacity for a named person, or who shows on the instrument that he is signing in a representative capacity but does not name the person whom he represents, imposes liability on the person signing and not on the person whom he purports to represent.

4. The question whether a signature was placed on the instrument in a representative capacity may be determined only by reference to what appears on the instrument.

5. A person who is liable pursuant to paragraph 3 of this article and who pays the instrument has the same rights as the person for whom he purported to act would have had if that person had paid the instrument.

Article 37.

The order to pay contained in a bill does not of itself operate as an assignment to the payee of funds made available for payment by the drawer with the drawee.

B. THE DRAWER

Article 38.

1. The drawer engages that upon dishonour of the bill by non-acceptance or by non-payment, and upon any necessary protest, he will pay the bill to the holder, or to any endorser or any endorser's guarantor who takes up and pays the bill.

2. The drawer may exclude or limit his own liability for acceptance or for payment by an express stipulation in the bill. Such a stipulation is effective only with respect to the drawer. A stipulation excluding or limiting liability for payment is effective only if another party is or becomes liable on the bill.

C. THE MAKER

Article 39.

1. The maker engages that he will pay the note in accordance with its terms to the holder, or to any party who takes up and pays the note.

2. The maker may not exclude or limit his own liability by a stipulation in the note. Any such stipulation is ineffective.

D. THE DRAWEE AND THE ACCEPTOR

Article 40.

1. The drawee is not liable on a bill until he accepts it.

2. The acceptor engages that he will pay the bill in accordance with the terms of his acceptance to the holder, or to any party who takes up and pays the bill.

Article 41.

1. An acceptance must be written on the bill and may be effected:

(a) By the signature of the drawee accompanied by the word "accepted" or by words of similar import; or

(b) By the signature alone of the drawee.

2. An acceptance may be written on the front or on the back of the bill.

Article 42.

1. An incomplete bill which satisfies the requirements set out in paragraph 1 of article 1 may be accepted by the drawee before it has been signed by the drawer, or while otherwise incomplete.

2. A bill may be accepted before, at or after maturity, or after it has been dishonoured by non-acceptance or by non-payment.

3. If a bill drawn payable at a fixed period after sight, or a bill which must be presented for acceptance before a specified date, is accepted, the acceptor must indicate the date of his acceptance; failing such indication by the acceptor, the drawer or the holder may insert the date of acceptance.

4. If a bill drawn payable at a fixed period after sight is dishonoured by non-acceptance and the drawee subsequently accepts it, the holder is entitled to have the acceptance dated as of the date on which the bill was dishonoured.

Article 43.

1. An acceptance must be unqualified. An acceptance is qualified if it is conditional or varies the terms of the bill.

2. If the drawee stipulates in the bill that his acceptance is subject to qualification:

(a) He is nevertheless bound according to the terms of his qualified acceptance;

(b) The bill is dishonoured by non-acceptance.

3. An acceptance relating to only a part of the sum payable is a qualified acceptance. If the holder takes such an acceptance, the bill is dishonoured by non-acceptance only as to the remaining part.

4. An acceptance indicating that payment will be made at a particular address or by a particular agent is not a qualified acceptance, provided that:

(a) The place in which payment is to be made is not changed;

(b) The bill is not drawn payable by another agent.

E. THE ENDORSER

Article 44.

1. The endorser engages that upon dishonour of the instrument by non-acceptance or by non-payment, and upon any necessary protest, he will pay the instrument to the holder, or to any subsequent endorser or any endorser's guarantor who takes up and pays the instrument.

2. An endorser may exclude or limit his own liability by an express stipulation in the instrument. Such a stipulation is effective only with respect to that endorser.

F. THE TRANSFEROR BY ENDORSEMENT OR BY MERE DELIVERY

Article 45.

1. Unless otherwise agreed, a person who transfers an instrument, by endorsement and delivery or by mere

delivery, represents to the holder to whom he transfers the instrument that:

(a) The instrument does not bear any forged or unauthorized signature;

(b) The instrument has not been materially altered;

(c) At the time of transfer, he has no knowledge of any fact which would impair the right of the transferee to payment of the instrument against the acceptor of a bill or, in the case of an unaccepted bill, the drawer, or against the maker of a note.

2. Liability of the transferor under paragraph 1 of this article is incurred only if the transferee took the instrument without knowledge of the matter giving rise to such liability.

3. If the transferor is liable under paragraph 1 of this article, the transferee may recover, even before maturity, the amount paid by him to the transferor, with interest calculated in accordance with article 70, against return of the instrument.

G. THE GUARANTOR

Article 46.

1. Payment of an instrument, whether or not it has been accepted, may be guaranteed, as to the whole or part of its amount, for the account of a party or the drawee. A guarantee may be given by any person, who may or may not already be a party.

2. A guarantee must be written on the instrument or on a slip affixed thereto ("*allonge*").

3. A guarantee is expressed by the words "guaranteed", "*aval*", "good as *aval*" or words of similar import, accompanied by the signature of the guarantor. For the purposes of this Convention, the words "prior endorsements guaranteed" or words of similar import do not constitute a guarantee.

4. A guarantee may be effected by a signature alone on the front of the instrument. A signature alone on the front of the instrument, other than that of the maker, the drawer or the drawee, is a guarantee.

5. A guarantor may specify the person for whom he has become guarantor. In the absence of such specification, the person for whom he has become guarantor is the acceptor or the drawee in the case of a bill, and the maker in the case of a note.

6. A guarantor may not raise as a defence to his liability the fact that he signed the instrument before it was signed by the person for whom he is a guarantor, or while the instrument was incomplete.

Article 47.

1. The liability of a guarantor on the instrument is of the same nature as that of the party for whom he has become guarantor.

2. If the person for whom he has become guarantor is the drawee, the guarantor engages:

(a) To pay the bill at maturity to the holder, or to any party who takes up and pays the bill;

(b) If the bill is payable at a definite time, upon dishonour by non-acceptance and upon any necessary protest, to pay it to the holder, or to any party who takes up and pays the bill.

3. In respect of defences that are personal to himself, a guarantor may set up:

(a) Against a holder who is not a protected holder only those defences which he may set up under paragraphs 1, 3 and 4 of article 28;

(b) Against a protected holder only those defences which he may set up under paragraph 1 of article 30.

4. In respect of defences that may be raised by the person for whom he has become a guarantor:

(a) A guarantor may set up against a holder who is not a protected holder only those defences which the person for whom he has become a guarantor may set up against such holder under paragraphs 1, 3 and 4 of article 28;

(b) A guarantor who expresses his guarantee by the words "guaranteed", "payment guaranteed" or "collection guaranteed", or words of similar import, may set up against a protected holder only those defences which the person for whom he has become a guarantor may set up against a protected holder under paragraph 1 of article 30;

(c) A guarantor who expresses his guarantee by the words "*aval*" or "good as *aval*" may set up against a protected holder only:

(i) The defence, under paragraph 1 (b) of article 30, that the protected holder obtained the signature on the instrument of the person for whom he has become a guarantor by a fraudulent act;

(ii) The defence, under article 53 or article 57, that the instrument was not presented for acceptance or for payment;

(iii) The defence, under article 63, that the instrument was not duly protested for non-acceptance or for non-payment;

(iv) The defence, under article 84, that a right of action may no longer be exercised against the person for whom he has become guarantor;

(d) A guarantor who is not a bank or other financial institution and who expresses his guarantee by a signature alone may set up against a protected holder only the defences referred to in subparagraph (b) of this paragraph;

(e) A guarantor which is a bank or other financial institution and which expresses its guarantee by a signature alone may set up against a protected holder only the defences referred to in subparagraph (c) of this paragraph.

Article 48.

1. Payment of an instrument by the guarantor in accordance with article 72 discharges the party for whom he became guarantor of his liability on the instrument to the extent of the amount paid.

2. The guarantor who pays the instrument may recover from the party for whom he has become guarantor and from the parties who are liable on it to that party the amount paid and any interest.

CHAPTER V. PRESENTMENT, DISHONOUR BY NON-ACCEPTANCE OR NON-PAYMENT, AND RECOURSE

Section 1. Presentment for Acceptance and Dishonour by Non-Acceptance

Article 49.

1. A bill may be presented for acceptance.

2. A bill must be presented for acceptance:

(a) If the drawer has stipulated in the bill that it must be presented for acceptance;

(b) If the bill is payable at a fixed period after sight; or

(c) If the bill is payable elsewhere than at the residence or place of business of the drawee, unless it is payable on demand.

Article 50.

1. The drawer may stipulate in the bill that it must not be presented for acceptance before a specified date or before the occurrence of a specified event. Except where a bill must be presented for acceptance under paragraph 2 (b) or (c) of article 49, the drawer may stipulate that it must not be presented for acceptance.

2. If a bill is presented for acceptance notwithstanding a stipulation permitted under paragraph 1 of this article and acceptance is refused, the bill is not thereby dishonoured.

3. If the drawee accepts a bill notwithstanding a stipulation that it must not be presented for acceptance, the acceptance is effective.

Article 51.

A bill is duly presented for acceptance if it is presented in accordance with the following rules:

(a) The holder must present the bill to the drawee on a business day at a reasonable hour;

(b) Presentment for acceptance may be made to a person or authority other than the drawee if that person or authority is entitled under the applicable law to accept the bill;

(c) If a bill is payable on a fixed date, presentment for acceptance must be made before or on that date;

(d) A bill payable on demand or at a fixed period after sight must be presented for acceptance within one year of its date;

(e) A bill in which the drawer has stated a date or time-limit for presentment for acceptance must be presented on the stated date or within the stated time-limit.

Article 52.

1. A necessary or optional presentment for acceptance is dispensed with if:

(a) The drawee is dead, or no longer has the power freely to deal with his assets by reason of his insolvency, or is a fictitious person, or is a person not having capacity to incur liability on the instrument as an acceptor; or

(b) The drawee is a corporation, partnership, association or other legal entity which has ceased to exist.

2. A necessary presentment for acceptance is dispensed with if:

(a) A bill is payable on a fixed date, and presentment for acceptance cannot be effected before or on that date due to circumstances which are beyond the control of the holder and which he could neither avoid nor overcome; or

(b) A bill is payable at a fixed period after sight, and presentment for acceptance cannot be effected within one year of its date due to circumstances which are beyond the control of the holder and which he could neither avoid nor overcome.

3. Subject to paragraphs 1 and 2 of this article, delay in a necessary presentment for acceptance is excused, but presentment for acceptance is not dispensed with, if the bill is drawn with a stipulation that it must be presented for acceptance within a stated time-limit, and the delay in presentment for acceptance is caused by circumstances

which are beyond the control of the holder and which he could neither avoid nor overcome. When the cause of the delay ceases to operate, presentment must be made with reasonable diligence.

Article 53.

1. If a bill which must be presented for acceptance is not so presented, the drawer, the endorsers and their guarantors are not liable on the bill.

2. Failure to present a bill for acceptance does not discharge the guarantor of the drawee of liability on the bill.

Article 54.

1. A bill is considered to be dishonoured by non-acceptance:

(a) If the drawee, upon due presentment, expressly refuses to accept the bill or acceptance cannot be obtained with reasonable diligence or if the holder cannot obtain the acceptance to which he is entitled under this Convention;

(b) If presentment for acceptance is dispensed with pursuant to article 52, unless the bill is in fact accepted.

2. (a) If a bill is dishonoured by non-acceptance in accordance with paragraph 1 (a) of this article, the holder may exercise an immediate right of recourse against the drawer, the endorsers and their guarantors, subject to the provisions of article 59.

(b) If a bill is dishonoured by non-acceptance in accordance with paragraph 1 (b) of this article, the holder may exercise an immediate right of recourse against the drawer, the endorsers and their guarantors.

(c) If a bill is dishonoured by non-acceptance in accordance with paragraph 1 of this article, the holder may claim payment from the guarantor of the drawee upon any necessary protest.

3. If a bill payable on demand is presented for acceptance, but acceptance is refused, it is not considered to be dishonoured by non-acceptance.

Section 2. Presentment for Payment and Dishonour by Non-Payment

Article 55.

An instrument is duly presented for payment if it is presented in accordance with the following rules:

(a) The holder must present the instrument to the drawee or to the acceptor or to the maker on a business day at a reasonable hour;

(b) A note signed by two or more makers may be presented to any one of them, unless the note clearly indicates otherwise;

(c) If the drawee or the acceptor or the maker is dead, presentment must be made to the persons who under the applicable law are his heirs or the persons entitled to administer his estate;

(d) Presentment for payment may be made to a person or authority other than the drawee, the acceptor or the maker if that person or authority is entitled under the applicable law to pay the instrument;

(e) An instrument which is not payable on demand must be presented for payment on the date of maturity or on one of the two business days which follow;

(f) An instrument which is payable on demand must be presented for payment within one year of its date;

(g) An instrument must be presented for payment:

(i) At the place of payment specified on the instrument;

(ii) If no place of payment is specified, at the address of the drawee or the acceptor or the maker indicated in the instrument; or

(iii) If no place of payment is specified and the address of the drawee or the acceptor or the maker is not indicated, at the principal place of business or habitual residence of the drawee or the acceptor or the maker;

(h) An instrument which is presented at a clearing-house is duly presented for payment if the law of the place where the clearing-house is located or the rules or customs of that clearing-house so provide.

Article 56.

1. Delay in making presentment for payment is excused if the delay is caused by circumstances which are beyond the control of the holder and which he could neither avoid nor overcome. When the cause of the delay ceases to operate, presentment must be made with reasonable diligence.

2. Presentment for payment is dispensed with:

(a) If the drawer, an endorser or a guarantor has expressly waived presentment; such waiver:

(i) If made on the instrument by the drawer, binds any subsequent party and benefits any holder;

(ii) If made on the instrument by a party other than the drawer, binds only that party but benefits any holder;

(iii) If made outside the instrument, binds only the party making it and benefits only a holder in whose favour it was made;

(b) If an instrument is not payable on demand, and the cause of delay in making presentment referred to in paragraph 1 of this article continues to operate beyond thirty days after maturity;

(c) If an instrument is payable on demand, and the cause of delay in making presentment referred to in paragraph 1 of this article continues to operate beyond thirty days after the expiration of the time-limit for presentment for payment;

(d) If the drawee, the maker or the acceptor has no longer the power freely to deal with his assets by reason of his insolvency, or is a fictitious person or a person not having capacity to make payment, or if the drawee, the maker or the acceptor is a corporation, partnership, association or other legal entity which has ceased to exist;

(e) If there is no place at which the instrument must be presented in accordance with subparagraph (g) of article 55.

3. Presentment for payment is also dispensed with as regards a bill, if the bill has been protested for dishonour by non-acceptance.

Article 57.

1. If an instrument is not duly presented for payment, the drawer, the endorsers and their guarantors are not liable on it.

2. Failure to present an instrument for payment does not discharge the acceptor, the maker and their guarantors or the guarantor of the drawee of liability on it.

Article 58.

1. An instrument is considered to be dishonoured by non-payment:

(a) If payment is refused upon due presentment or if the holder cannot obtain the payment to which he is entitled under this Convention;

(b) If presentment for payment is dispensed with pursuant to paragraph 2 of article 56 and the instrument is unpaid at maturity.

2. If a bill is dishonoured by non-payment, the holder may, subject to the provisions of article 59, exercise a right of recourse against the drawer, the endorsers and their guarantors.

3. If a note is dishonoured by non-payment, the holder may, subject to the provisions of article 59, exercise a right of recourse against the endorsers and their guarantors.

Section 3. Recourse

Article 59.

If an instrument is dishonoured by non-acceptance or by non-payment, the holder may exercise a right of recourse only after the instrument has been duly protested for dishonour in accordance with the provisions of articles 60 to 62.

A. PROTEST

Article 60.

1. A protest is a statement of dishonour drawn up at the place where the instrument has been dishonoured and signed and dated by a person authorized in that respect by the law of that place. The statement must specify:

(a) The person at whose request the instrument is protested;

(b) The place of protest;

(c) The demand made and the answer given, if any, or the fact that the drawee or the acceptor or the maker could not be found.

2. A protest may be made:

(a) On the instrument or on a slip affixed thereto ("*allonge*"); or

(b) As a separate document, in which case it must clearly identify the instrument that has been dishonoured.

3. Unless the instrument stipulates that protest must be made, a protest may be replaced by a declaration written on the instrument and signed and dated by the drawee or the acceptor or the maker, or, in the case of an instrument domiciled with a named person for payment, by that named person; the declaration must be to the effect that acceptance or payment is refused.

4. A declaration made in accordance with paragraph 3 of this article is a protest for the purpose of this Convention.

Article 61.

Protest for dishonour of an instrument by non-acceptance or by non-payment must be made on the day on which the instrument is dishonoured or on one of the four business days which follow.

Article 62.

1. Delay in protesting an instrument for dishonour is excused if the delay is caused by circumstances which are beyond the control of the holder and which he could neither avoid nor overcome. When the cause of the delay ceases to operate, protest must be made with reasonable diligence.

2. Protest for dishonour by non-acceptance or by non-payment is dispensed with:

(a) If the drawer, an endorser or a guarantor has expressly waived protest; such waiver:

(i) If made on the instrument by the drawer, binds any subsequent party and benefits any holder;

(ii) If made on the instrument by a party other than the drawer, binds only that party but benefits any holder;

(iii) If made outside the instrument, binds only the party making it and benefits only a holder in whose favour it was made;

(b) If the cause of the delay in making protest referred to in paragraph 1 of this article continues to operate beyond thirty days after the date of dishonour;

(c) As regards the drawer of a bill, if the drawer and the drawee or the acceptor are the same person;

(d) If presentment for acceptance or for payment is dispensed with in accordance with article 52 or paragraph 2 of article 56.

Article 63.

1. If an instrument which must be protested for non-acceptance or for non-payment is not duly protested, the drawer, the endorsers and their guarantors are not liable on it.

2. Failure to protest an instrument does not discharge the acceptor, the maker and their guarantors or the guarantor of the drawee of liability on it.

B. NOTICE OF DISHONOUR

Article 64.

1. The holder, upon dishonour of an instrument by non-acceptance or by non-payment, must give notice of such dishonour:

(a) To the drawer and the last endorser;

(b) To all other endorsers and guarantors whose addresses the holder can ascertain on the basis of information contained in the instrument.

2. An endorser or a guarantor who receives notice must give notice of dishonour to the last party preceding him and liable on the instrument.

3. Notice of dishonour operates for the benefit of any party who has a right of recourse on the instrument against the party notified.

Article 65.

1. Notice of dishonour may be given in any form whatever and in any terms which identify the instrument and state that it has been dishonoured. The return of the dishonoured instrument is sufficient notice, provided it is accompanied by a statement indicating that it has been dishonoured.

2. Notice of dishonour is duly given if it is communicated or sent to the party to be notified by means appropriate in the circumstances, whether or not it is received by that party.

3. The burden of proving that notice has been duly given rests upon the person who is required to give such notice.

Article 66.

Notice of dishonour must be given within the two business days which follow:

(a) The day of protest or, if protest is dispensed with, the day of dishonour; or

(b) The day of receipt of notice of dishonour.

Article 67.

1. Delay in giving notice of dishonour is excused if the delay is caused by circumstances which are beyond the control of the person required to give notice, and which he could neither avoid nor overcome. When the cause of the delay ceases to operate, notice must be given with reasonable diligence.

2. Notice of dishonour is dispensed with:

(a) If, after the exercise of reasonable diligence, notice cannot be given;

(b) If the drawer, an endorser or a guarantor has expressly waived notice of dishonour; such waiver:

(i) If made on the instrument by the drawer, binds any subsequent party and benefits any holder;

(ii) If made on the instrument by a party other than the drawer, binds only that party but benefits any holder;

(iii) If made outside the instrument, binds only the party making it and benefits only a holder in whose favour it was made;

(c) As regards the drawer of the bill, if the drawer and the drawee or the acceptor are the same person.

Article 68.

If a person who is required to give notice of dishonour fails to give it to a party who is entitled to receive it, he is liable for any damages which that party may suffer from such failure, provided that such damages do not exceed the amount referred to in article 70 or article 71.

Section 4. Amount Payable

Article 69.

1. The holder may exercise his rights on the instrument against any one party, or several or all parties, liable on it and is not obliged to observe the order in which the parties have become bound. Any party who takes up and pays the instrument may exercise his rights in the same manner against parties liable to him.

2. Proceedings against a party do not preclude proceedings against any other party, whether or not subsequent to the party originally proceeded against.

Article 70.

1. The holder may recover from any party liable:

(a) At maturity: the amount of the instrument with interest, if interest has been stipulated for;

(b) After maturity:

(i) The amount of the instrument with interest, if interest has been stipulated for, to the date of maturity;

(ii) If interest has been stipulated to be paid after maturity, interest at the rate stipulated, or, in the absence of such stipulation, interest at the rate specified in paragraph 2 of this article, calculated from the date of presentment on the sum specified in subparagraph (b) (i) of this paragraph;

(iii) Any expenses of protest and of the notices given by him;

(c) Before maturity:

(i) The amount of the instrument with interest, if interest has been stipulated for, to the date of payment; or, if no interest has been stipulated for, subject to a discount from the date of payment to the date of maturity, calculated in accordance with paragraph 4 of this article;

(ii) Any expenses of protest and of the notices given by him.

2. The rate of interest shall be the rate that would be recoverable in legal proceedings taken in the jurisdiction where the instrument is payable.

3. Nothing in paragraph 2 of this article prevents a court from awarding damages or compensation for additional loss caused to the holder by reason of delay in payment.

4. The discount shall be at the official rate (discount rate) or other similar appropriate rate effective on the date when recourse is exercised at the place where the holder has his principal place of business, or, if he does not have a place of business, his habitual residence, or, if there is no such rate, then at such rate as is reasonable in the circumstances.

Article 71.

A party who pays an instrument and is thereby discharged in whole or in part of his liability on the instrument may recover from the parties liable to him:

(a) The entire sum which he has paid;

(b) Interest on that sum at the rate specified in paragraph 2 of article 70, from the date on which he made payment;

(c) Any expenses of the notices given by him.

CHAPTER VI. DISCHARGE

Section 1. Discharge by Payment

Article 72.

1. A party is discharged of liability on the instrument when he pays the holder, or a party subsequent to himself who has paid the instrument and is in possession of it, the amount due pursuant to article 70 or article 71:

(a) At or after maturity; or

(b) Before maturity, upon dishonour by non-acceptance.

2. Payment before maturity other than under paragraph 1(b) of this article does not discharge the party making the payment of his liability on the instrument except in respect of the person to whom payment was made.

3. A party is not discharged of liability if he pays a holder who is not a protected holder, or a party who has taken up and paid the instrument, and knows at the time of payment that the holder or that party acquired the instrument by theft or forged the signature of the payee or an endorsee, or participated in the theft or the forgery.

4. (a) A person receiving payment of an instrument must, unless agreed otherwise, deliver:

(i) To the drawee making such payment, the instrument;

(ii) To any other person making such payment, the instrument, a receipted account, and any protest.

(b) In the case of an instrument payable by instalments at successive dates, the drawee or a party making a payment, other than payment of the last instalment, may require that mention of such payment be made on the instrument or on a slip affixed thereto ("*allonge*") and that a receipt therefor be given to him.

(c) If an instrument payable by instalments at successive dates is dishonoured by non-acceptance or by non-payment as to any of its instalments and a party, upon dishonour, pays the instalment, the holder who receives such payment must give the party a certified copy of the instrument and any necessary authenticated protest in order to enable such party to exercise a right on the instrument.

(d) The person from whom payment is demanded may withhold payment if the person demanding payment does not deliver the instrument to him. Withholding payment in these circumstances does not constitute dishonour by non-payment under article 58.

(e) If payment is made but the person paying, other than the drawee, fails to obtain the instrument, such person is discharged but the discharge cannot be set up as a defence against a protected holder to whom the instrument has been subsequently transferred.

Article 73.

1. The holder is not obliged to take partial payment.

2. If the holder who is offered partial payment does not take it, the instrument is dishonoured by non-payment.

3. If the holder takes partial payment from the drawee, the guarantor of the drawee, or the acceptor or the maker:

(a) The guarantor of the drawee, or the acceptor or the maker is discharged of his liability on the instrument to the extent of the amount paid;

(b) The instrument is to be considered as dishonoured by non-payment as to the amount unpaid.

4. If the holder takes partial payment from a party to the instrument other than the acceptor, the maker or the guarantor of the drawee:

(a) The party making payment is discharged of his liability on the instrument to the extent of the amount paid;

(b) The holder must give such party a certified copy of the instrument and any necessary authenticated protest in order to enable such party to exercise a right on the instrument.

5. The drawee or a party making partial payment may require that mention of such payment be made on the instrument and that a receipt therefor be given to him.

6. If the balance is paid, the person who receives it and who is in possession of the instrument must deliver to the payor the receipted instrument and any authenticated protest.

Article 74.

1. The holder may refuse to take payment at a place other than the place where the instrument was presented for payment in accordance with article 55.

2. In such case if payment is not made at the place where the instrument was presented for payment in accordance with article 55, the instrument is considered to be dishonoured by non-payment.

Article 75.

1. An instrument must be paid in the currency in which the sum payable is expressed.

2. If the sum payable is expressed in a monetary unit of account within the meaning of subparagraph (l) of article 5 and the monetary unit of account is transferable between the person making payment and the person receiving it, then, unless the instrument specifies a currency of payment, payment shall be made by transfer of monetary units of account. If the monetary unit of account is not transferable between those persons, payment shall be made in the currency specified in the instrument or, if no such currency is specified, in the currency of the place of payment.

3. The drawer or the maker may indicate in the instrument that it must be paid in a specified currency other than the currency in which the sum payable is expressed. In that case:

(a) The instrument must be paid in the currency so specified;

(b) The amount payable is to be calculated according to the rate of exchange indicated in the instrument. Failing such indication, the amount payable is to be calculated according to the rate of exchange for sight drafts (or, if there is no such rate, according to the appropriate established rate of exchange) on the date of maturity:

(i) Ruling at the place where the instrument must be presented for payment in accordance with subparagraph (g) of article 55, if the specified currency is that of that place (local currency); or

(ii) If the specified currency is not that of that place, according to the usages of the place where the instrument must be presented for payment in accordance with subparagraph (g) of article 55;

(c) If such an instrument is dishonoured by non-acceptance, the amount payable is to be calculated:

(i) If the rate of exchange is indicated in the instrument, according to that rate;

(ii) If no rate of exchange is indicated in the instrument, at the option of the holder, according to the rate of exchange ruling on the date of dishonour or on the date of actual payment;

(d) If such an instrument is dishonoured by non-payment, the amount payable is to be calculated:

(i) If the rate of exchange is indicated in the instrument, according to that rate;

(ii) If no rate of exchange is indicated in the instrument, at the option of the holder, according to the rate of exchange ruling on the date of maturity or on the date of actual payment.

4. Nothing in this article prevents a court from awarding damages for loss caused to the holder by reason of fluctuations in rates of exchange if such loss is caused by dishonour for non-acceptance or by non-payment.

5. The rate of exchange ruling at a certain date is the rate of exchange ruling, at the option of the holder, at the place where the instrument must be presented for payment in accordance with subparagraph (g) of article 55 or at the place of actual payment.

Article 76.

1. Nothing in this Convention prevents a Contracting State from enforcing exchange control regulations applicable in its territory and its provisions relating to the protection of its currency, including regulations which it is bound to apply by virtue of international agreements to which it is a party.

2. (a) If, by virtue of the application of paragraph 1 of this article, an instrument drawn in a currency which is not that of the place of payment must be paid in local currency, the amount payable is to be calculated according to the rate of exchange for sight drafts (or, if there is no such rate, according to the appropriate established rate of exchange) on the date of presentment ruling at the place where the instrument must be presented for payment in accordance with subparagraph (g) of article 55.

(b) (i) If such an instrument is dishonoured by non-acceptance, the amount payable is to be calculated, at the option of the holder, at the rate of exchange ruling on the date of dishonour or on the date of actual payment.

(ii) If such an instrument is dishonoured by non-payment, the amount is to be calculated, at the option of the holder, according to the rate of exchange ruling on the date of presentment or on the date of actual payment.

(iii) Paragraphs 4 and 5 of article 75 are applicable where appropriate.

Section 2. Discharge of Other Parties

Article 77.

1. If a party is discharged in whole or in part of his liability on the instrument, any party who has a right on the instrument against him is discharged to the same extent.

2. Payment by the drawee of the whole or a part of the amount of a bill to the holder, or to any party who takes up and pays the bill, discharges all parties of their liability to the same extent, except where the drawee pays a holder who is not a protected holder, or a party who has taken up and paid the bill, and knows at the time of payment that the holder or that party acquired the bill by theft or forged the signature of the payee or an endorsee, or participated in the theft or the forgery.

CHAPTER VII. LOST INSTRUMENTS

Article 78.

1. If an instrument is lost, whether by destruction, theft or otherwise, the person who lost the instrument has, subject to the provisions of paragraph 2 of this article, the same right to payment which he would have had if he had been in possession of the instrument. The party from whom payment is claimed cannot set up as a defence against liability on the instrument the fact that the person claiming payment is not in possession of the instrument.

2. (a) The person claiming payment of a lost instrument must state in writing to the party from whom he claims payment:

(i) The elements of the lost instrument pertaining to the requirements set forth in paragraph 1 or paragraph 2 of articles 1, 2 and 3; for this purpose the person claiming payment of the lost instrument may present to that party a copy of that instrument;

(ii) The facts showing that, if he had been in possession of the instrument, he would have had a right to payment from the party from whom payment is claimed;

(iii) The facts which prevent production of the instrument.

(b) The party from whom payment of a lost instrument is claimed may require the person claiming payment to give security in order to indemnify him for any loss which he may suffer by reason of the subsequent payment of the lost instrument.

(c) The nature of the security and its terms are to be determined by agreement between the person claiming payment and the party from whom payment is claimed. Failing such an agreement, the court may determine whether security is called for and, if so, the nature of the security and its terms.

(d) If the security cannot be given, the court may order the party from whom payment is claimed to deposit the sum of the lost instrument, and any interest and expenses which may be claimed under article 70 or article 71, with the court or any other competent authority or institution, and may determine the duration of such deposit. Such deposit is to be considered as payment to the person claiming payment.

Article 79.

1. A party who has paid a lost instrument and to whom the instrument is subsequently presented for payment by another person must give notice of such presentment to the person whom he paid.

2. Such notice must be given on the day the instrument is presented or on one of the two business days which follow and must state the name of the person presenting the instrument and the date and place of presentment.

3. Failure to give notice renders the party who has paid the lost instrument liable for any damages which the person whom he paid may suffer from such failure, provided that the damages do not exceed the amount referred to in article 70 or article 71.

4. Delay in giving notice is excused when the delay is caused by circumstances which are beyond the control of the person who has paid the lost instrument and which he could neither avoid nor overcome. When the cause of the delay ceases to operate, notice must be given with reasonable diligence.

5. Notice is dispensed with when the cause of delay in giving notice continues to operate beyond thirty days after the last day on which it should have been given.

Article 80.

1. A party who has paid a lost instrument in accordance with the provisions of article 78 and who is subsequently required to, and does, pay the instrument, or who, by reason of the loss of the instrument, then loses his right to recover from any party liable to him, has the right:

(a) If security was given, to realize the security; or

(b) If an amount was deposited with the court or other competent authority or institution, to reclaim the amount so deposited.

2. The person who has given security in accordance with the provisions of paragraph 2 (b) of article 78 is entitled to obtain release of the security when the party for whose benefit the security was given is no longer at risk to suffer loss because of the fact that the instrument is lost.

Article 81.

For the purpose of making protest for dishonour by non-payment, a person claiming payment of a lost instrument may use a written statement that satisfies the requirements of paragraph 2 (a) of article 78.

Article 82.

A person receiving payment of a lost instrument in accordance with article 78 must deliver to the party paying the written statement required under paragraph 2 (a) of article 78, receipted by him, and any protest and a receipted account.

Article 83.

1. A party who pays a lost instrument in accordance with article 78 has the same rights which he would have had if he had been in possession of the instrument.

2. Such party may exercise his rights only if he is in possession of the receipted written statement referred to in article 82.

CHAPTER VIII. LIMITATION (PRESCRIPTION)

Article 84.

1. A right of action arising on an instrument may no longer be exercised after four years have elapsed:

(a) Against the maker, or his guarantor, of a note payable on demand, from the date of the note;

(b) Against the acceptor or the maker or their guarantor of an instrument payable at a definite time, from the date of maturity;

(c) Against the guarantor of the drawee of a bill payable at a definite time, from the date of maturity or, if the bill is dishonoured by non-acceptance, from the date of protest for dishonour or, where protest is dispensed with, from the date of dishonour;

(d) Against the acceptor of a bill payable on demand or his guarantor, from the date on which it was accepted or, if no such date is shown, from the date of the bill;

(e) Against the guarantor of the drawee of a bill payable on demand, from the date on which he signed the bill or, if no such date is shown, from the date of the bill;

(f) Against the drawer or an endorser or their guarantor, from the date of protest for dishonour by non-acceptance or by non-payment or, where protest is dispensed with, from the date of dishonour.

2. A party who pays the instrument in accordance with article 70 or article 71 may exercise his right of action against a party liable to him within one year from the date on which he paid the instrument.

CHAPTER IX. FINAL PROVISIONS

Article 85.

The Secretary-General of the United Nations is hereby designated as the Depositary for this Convention.

Article 86.

1. This Convention is open for signature by all States at the Headquarters of the United Nations, New York, until 30 June 1990.

2. This Convention is subject to ratification, acceptance or approval by the signatory States.

3. This Convention is open for accession by all States which are not signatory States as from the date it is open for signature.

4. Instruments of ratification, acceptance, approval and accession are to be deposited with the Secretary-General of the United Nations.

Article 87.

1. If a Contracting State has two or more territorial units in which, according to its constitution, different systems of law are applicable in relation to the matters dealt with in this Convention, it may, at the time of signature, ratification, acceptance, approval or accession, declare that this Convention is to extend to all its territorial units or only to one or more of them, and may amend its declaration by submitting another declaration at any time.

2. These declarations are to be notified to the Depositary and are to state expressly the territorial units to which the Convention extends.

3. If a Contracting State makes no declaration under paragraph 1 of this article, the Convention is to extend to all territorial units of that State.

Article 88.

1. Any State may declare at the time of signature, ratification, acceptance, approval or accession that its courts will apply the Convention only if both the place indicated in the instrument where the bill is drawn, or the note is made, and the place of payment indicated in the instrument are situated in Contracting States.

2. No other reservations are permitted.

Article 89.

1. This Convention enters into force on the first day of the month following the expiration of twelve months after the date of deposit of the tenth instrument of ratification, acceptance, approval or accession.

2. When a State ratifies, accepts, approves or accedes to this Convention after the deposit of the tenth instrument of ratification, acceptance, approval or accession, this Convention enters into force in respect of that State on the first day of the month following the expiration of twelve months after the date of deposit of its instrument of ratification, acceptance, approval or accession.

Article 90.

1. A Contracting State may denounce this Convention by a formal notification in writing addressed to the Depositary.

2. The denunciation takes effect on the first day of the month following the expiration of six months after the notification is received by the Depositary. Where a longer period for the denunciation to take effect is specified in the notification, the denunciation takes effect upon the expiration of such longer period after the notification is received by the Depositary. The Convention remains applicable to instruments drawn or made before the date at which the denunciation takes effect.

DONE at New York, this ninth day of December, one thousand nine hundred and eighty-eight in a single original, of which the Arabic, Chinese, English, French, Russian and Spanish texts are equally authentic.

IN WITNESS WHEREOF the undersigned plenipotentiaries, being duly authorized by their respective Governments, have signed this Convention.